D0145902

INSTITUTE
OF
TRANSPORTATION ENGINEERS

TRANSPORTATION AND TRAFFIC ENGINEERING HANDBOOK

SECOND EDITION

Wolfgang S. Homburger
Editor

Louis E. Keefer and William R. McGrath
Associate Editors

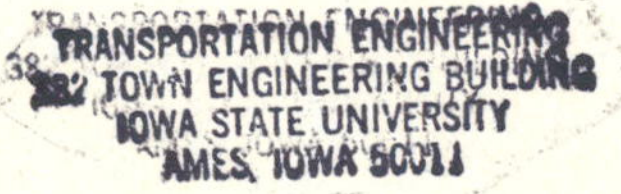

PRENTICE-HALL, INC., *Englewood Cliffs, New Jersey 07632*

Library of Congress Cataloging in Publication Data

Main entry under title:

Transportation and traffic engineering handbook.

At head of title: INSTITUTE OF TRANSPORTATION ENGINEERS.

Includes bibliographies and index.

1. Traffic engineering. 2. Transportation.
I. Homburger, Wolfgang S. II. Keefer, Louis E.
III. McGrath, William R. (William Restore),
date. IV. Institute of Transportation
Engineers.
HE333.T68 1982 388.3'1 82-340
ISBN 0-13-930362-6 AACR2

Editorial/production supervision
and interior design by Virginia Huebner
Page layout by Gail Collis
Manufacturing buyer: Joyce Levatino
Cover design by Edsal Enterprise

Printed in the United States of America

10 9 8 7 6 5 4 3 2 1

ISBN 0-13-930362-6

PRENTICE-HALL INTERNATIONAL, INC., *London*
PRENTICE-HALL OF AUSTRALIA PTY. LIMITED, *Sydney*
PRENTICE-HALL OF CANADA, LTD., *Toronto*
PRENTICE-HALL OF INDIA PRIVATE LIMITED, *New Delhi*
PRENTICE-HALL OF JAPAN, INC., *Tokyo*
PRENTICE-HALL OF SOUTHEAST ASIA PTE. LTD., *Singapore*
WHITEHALL BOOKS LIMITED, WELLINGTON, *New Zealand*

A TRIBUTE TO DEAN QUINBY

Upon the death of H. D. Quinby on December 16, 1978, at the age of 53, the transportation engineering profession lost an outstanding practitioner, and this handbook lost an outstanding contributor.

Dean Quinby joined the consulting firm of Parsons, Brinckerhoff in New York soon after graduation from Yale University in 1949. When Parsons undertook the preliminary planning of the San Francisco Bay Area Rapid Transit System in the early fifties, Mr. Quinby moved to the West Coast and played a leading role in developing traffic analyses and patronage forecasts. He gained both national and international recognition through his work and his publications on a wide range of urban transportation problems. In 1974, he became Deputy General Manager of the San Francisco Municipal Railway; in 1977, he established a practice as an independent consultant.

Mr. Quinby was an active member of the Institute of Transportation Engineers and headed Department 6, Transportation Planning, of the Technical Council for a number of years. He chaired the special committee charged with setting the guidelines for this edition of the handbook. He was the author of the chapter on Mass Transportation Characteristics in the previous edition of the Handbook, and had begun work on a similar contribution for this edition.

Dean Quinby was a professional in the highest sense of the word. He had complete command of his specialty, namely, the transportation of persons in urban centers, and he wrote and spoke from wide knowledge, with a global perspective and a sense of history. He was concerned with more than a set of technical problems and a way to earn a livelihood; he felt a sense of social responsibility and viewed professional work not as an end in itself but as a contribution to a decent and humane way of life in the city.

Dean's interests and expertise ranged wide, and included music, the study of history, and the protection of the environment. He was as familiar with the hiking trails of the Bay Area as he was with its transit routes.

Dean Quinby's dedication to his goals and to the excellence of his professional work assure him of a permanent place in the profession of Transportation Engineering.

ERIC MOHR

The Institute of Transportation Engineers is an international, individual member, scientific, and educational association. The purpose of the Institute is twofold: to enable engineers and other professionals with knowledge and competence in transportation and traffic engineering to contribute individually and collectively toward meeting human needs for mobility and safety; and to promote professional development of members, by the support and encouragement of education, stimulation of research, development of public awareness, exchange of professional information, and maintenance of a central point of reference and action.

The Institute's programs include publications, technical committees, professional development seminars, training, local, regional and international meetings, and standards. For current information on the Institute's programs, please contact:

INSTITUTE OF TRANSPORTATION ENGINEERS

525 School Street, S.W., Suite 410
Washington, D.C. 20024
(202) 554-8050

CONTENTS

PREFACE

The short span of six years, by which this edition of the *Transportation and Traffic Engineering Handbook* follows its predecessor, is indicative of the multiplication of challenges facing the transportation engineering profession, and of the rapid rate at which information must be updated and augmented. When the First Edition went to press, the first "oil crisis" was in full swing, but its implications had not yet been absorbed within the practice of transportation engineering—the term "energy" was missing from the index of that book. As Professor Baerwald pointed out in his Preface to the 1976 edition, the major concern at that time was the preservation of the environment. Today, high-priced fuels and the prospect of rapid depletion of fossil fuel resources have become another omnipresent environment within which transportation specialists must plan, design, and operate.

There has been a continuing shift in emphasis away from the construction of new transportation facilities, especially highways, toward optimizing their operations; this has been mandated by inflation and resistance to higher taxes, as well as by energy and environmental concerns. At the same time, the long-accepted concept that an attempt must be made to satisfy what Baerwald called "the insatiable desire of motorists for individual freedom" has been modified. It has become policy as well as practice to develop methods of influencing the demand for mobility toward a more efficient utilization of transportation networks—promoting the attractiveness of public transportation and of travel during off-peak hours, establishing priorities for the use of certain highways, and, in some cases, working toward reducing tripmaking itself.

This inevitably leads to the need for transportation planners and engineers to consider the interrelationships of different modes. Not only is this necessary because one cannot find the optimum solutions to transportation problems without understanding the performance characteristics and capabilities of all systems, but it is also appropriate because many tools and techniques used in planning, designing, and operating one kind of transportation system have at least some degree of applicability to other systems.

The Institute of Transportation Engineers, having changed its name in recognition of the multimodal nature of transportation work, has also expanded its horizons. The Handbook follows this trend without claiming to be the complete compendium of all transportation knowledge. Such a work would be encyclopedic in scope and would take so long to produce that it would be obsolete by the time it appeared in print. Even this less ambitious work will be found to contain some material which has been overtaken by the rush of events on the day of its publication, the unavoidable result of the length of the publication process.

Comparison of the contents of this edition of the Handbook with those of the 1976 edition illustrates the broadening scope of transportation engineering. To a very modest extent, the contents of this book have become more international. While the highway system and traffic engineering methods of operating and controlling it still represent a major part of the coverage, other modes are surveyed in four new chapters (2–5), and are involved in at least six of the other chapters.

The practice of transportation engineering involves familiarity with, and often application of, other disciplines. Two of these are the subjects of new chapters. Some basic concepts of economic analysis of transportation projects are introduced in one of these. The legal implications of transportation engineering, particularly the problems of public liability, are the subject of another. Although space limitations restricted the coverage of these topics to basic aspects, their inclusion reflects the growing concern in these issues.

The sheer bulk of this book is the most obvious illustration of the expansion of the field of transportation engineering. The book is about as large as can be bound in a single volume and perused without the aid of a dictionary stand. Even so, there are gaps and half-told tales. The editors had to impose constraints on both themselves and the authors, and were forced to omit almost as much subject matter as they were able to include. The reader is therefore urged to look beyond it into many of the items listed as "Suggestions for Further Reading" at the ends of many of the chapters. It is hoped that this Handbook will serve as a starting point rather than as an end in the search for information and increased knowledge in the practice of transportation engineering.

WOLFGANG S. HOMBURGER

LOUIS E. KEEFER

WILLIAM R. MCGRATH

ACKNOWLEDGMENTS

The completion of this book has involved the unstinting dedication of many persons. The chapter authors, selected for their eminent expertise, are recognized within this volume. Many others worked behind the scenes; just a few can be singled out in this space for grateful acknowledgment:

- The International Board of Directors of the Institute of Transportation Engineers (ITE) and Thomas W. Brahms, its Executive Director, who authorized and then generously supported the writing of this volume.
- The members of the ITE Technical Council and others designated by them—too numerous to list—who reviewed chapters in draft form and made many valuable suggestions.
- Jonathan Upchurch, Director of Technical Affairs for ITE until September 1980, who ably controlled and expedited the traffic of manuscripts and reviews between about one hundred origins and destinations.
- Charles Iossi, Engineering Editor of Prentice-Hall, Inc., who has encouraged this book from the day he assumed that post.
- Virginia Huebner, Senior Production Editor at Prentice-Hall, Inc. who once again undertook the huge task of converting snowstorms of manuscript pages into a coherent book.

1

TRANSPORTATION AND SOCIETY

HANS J. PETERS

The World Bank
Washington, D.C.

The evolution of transport

The evolution of transport has been closely linked to the development of humankind throughout the earth's history. Transport's early function was to meet the basic need of hauling food supplies and building materials. But with the formation of tribes, then peoples, and finally nations, the societal and economic functions of transport became more and more complex. At first there was mobility required for individuals, clans, households, and animals to protect them against, and to escape from, the dangers of natural disasters and tribal aggressions, and in the search for the best places to settle. As tribal groups formed and gradually established their geographical identity, transport was increasingly needed to open up regions for development, to provide access to natural resources, to promote intercommunal trade, and to mobilize territorial defense. When the first nations came into being, transport played a major role in establishing national integrity.

After basic societal needs had generally been attended to, local communities could increasingly devote their efforts to enhancing their economic, cultural, and technological development through trade links with other peoples and regions. Again, transport provided the mobility required for such intertribal, international, and finally intercontinental cultural exchange and trade. During all of this gradual development toward an organized human society, represented today through the international family of nations, transport as a physical process of moving people and goods, thus promoting such development, continuously underwent technological and organizational changes. Such changes were induced by several factors and circumstances. In fact, today's transport in its various forms and organizational arrangements remains highly subject to changes in response to societal requirements and preferences.

Clearly, the first and foremost criterion to be satisfied by transport was efficiency. For centuries, and particularly during the takeoff stages of local economies, society required reliable, fast, and low-cost transport. The search for appropriate technologies was relatively unconstrained. There were times in human history when the demand for reliable and fast transport was especially pronounced, and quick solutions were required for national self-defense. During such periods of local and international conflict, human ingenuity devised new transport technologies which often proved to be the decisive element for survival, and sometimes victory. Subsequently refined and developed, such new technologies made it possible to better meet increasing transport demand, thus improving both economic progress and human welfare.

The need for better strategic mobility induced efforts to improve sea and land transport. This resulted in bigger and faster ships and more reliable and sturdy land vehicles. Eventually, self-propulsion was introduced, exemplified by steamboats, the railways, and then the automobile. Research and development in the transport field finally became an organized undertaking with specific goals and objectives. As the result of the consequent concentration of talent and expertise, more and more sophisticated transport technologies evolved, such as the aircraft and, most recently, rocket propulsion.

The gradual evolution of increasingly sophisticated means of transport is manifested by today's transport systems, which include air, surface, and water transport. Special industry needs have led to the development of transport modes that have rather limited applications, such as pipelines, cables, and belts. Within current societal needs and preferences, as well as the economic requirements of cost effectiveness, the various existing transport modes generally fulfill rather specific functions. These functions are schematically outlined in Table 1-1. Each mode, with its technical, operational, and organizational characteristics, is described in detail in Chapters 2 to 7.

Although transport's potential to meet effectively nu-

TABLE 1–1
Functions of Various Transport Modes

Major System	Mode	Passenger Service	Freight Service
Highways	Trucks	None	Intercity and local; all commodities; generally small shipments; containers
	Buses	Intercity and local	Packages on intercity service
	Automobiles	Intercity and local	Personal items only
	Bicycles	Local; recreational	None
Rail transport	Railroads	Intercity—mostly < 500 km; commuter	Intercity; generally bulk and oversize shipments; containers
	Rail transit	Regional and intracity	None
Air transport	Air carriers	Intercity—mostly > 500 km; transocean	Shipments of high-value freight on long hauls only; containers
	General aviation	Intercity; recreational; business	Minor
Water transport	Transocean	Cruise traffic only	Bulk cargos, containers
	Coastal and inland	Ferry service	Mostly bulk cargos on ships and barges
Continuous-flow transport	Pipelines	None	Oil and natural gas; long and short hauls
	Belts	Escalators and horizontal belts for short distances	Materials handling—mostly < 15 km
	Cables	Lifts and tows for short distances in rough terrain	Materials handling in rough terrain

SOURCE: E. C. CARTER, and W. S. HOMBURGER, *Introduction to Transportation Engineering* (Reston, Va.: Reston, 1978), Table 2–1. Copyright by Institute of Transportation Engineers.

merous societal mobility needs improved continuously, it became evident that such effectiveness had its price. A number of transport technologies implied high energy consumption and required substantial capital inputs in production and operation. As a result, several transport modes became expensive to the user. This caused equity problems because charges required to cover operating costs were not affordable by all population groups, thus limiting their mobility and welfare. Many governments chose to subsidize transport, but quickly realized that the budget implications often caused serious distortions in their national economies.

Pollution caused by various transport modes gradually became another serious problem as world transport demand increased in the face of rapidly growing populations in most countries and the need to cope with rising volumes of commodity flows and person travel. In several regions of the world having high population and industry concentrations, such detrimental impacts on the environment have reached high levels. This has caused irreparable damage in many instances. The effects of such damage are yet to be fully explored.

Finally, problems caused by dwindling world energy resources, particularly petroleum, have increasingly impeded transport services and operations. Most existing transport modes are critically dependent on petroleum derivatives for proper functioning. With unabated growth of demand for transport and a progressively limited supply of energy, the costs of providing transport have increased steadily. In particular, the disproportion of petroleum requirements and petroleum supply has caused serious inflationary problems to arise in many countries. Especially hard hit are countries with a partial or total dependence on an external petroleum supply, which have experienced growing deficits in their current accounts.

The transport sector's increasing inability to satisfy demand efficiently and equitably is a problem with which all nations have to cope in trying to advance economic and social progress. Energy-supply constraints, high capital and operating costs, often with excessive foreign-exchange components, and the seriousness of transport-related environmental pollution account in large part for this problem. But transport is and will continue to be an essential requirement for world development and human welfare. There is no other choice but to look for alternatives to present transport systems or to modify the technical and operational characteristics of related modes so that energy consumption and costs will be reduced and environmental impacts can be kept at a minimum. Obviously, at the same time, the development of transport demand will have to be controlled.

World transport in the 1970s

Transportation in the world in the 1970s involved about 300×10^6 cars and 80×10^6 commercial vehicles in circulation. There was an average of 70 passenger cars for every 1,000 people living all over the world. The highway network comprised some 22×10^6 km of roads of different categories and with different functions. Distributed evenly, there would have been 14 cars and 4 commercial vehicles on each kilometer of road worldwide; and each 1 km^2 of land area of the globe would have had 0.16 km of road. Transportation in the 1970s also involved 1.41×10^6 km of railroad track, with an average density of 0.01 km of track per square kilometer of the world's land area. Rolling stock included some 8.5 $\times$ 10^6 units, an average density of 6 units/km of track. Common-carrier domestic and international air transport linked the communities of the world through a network of almost 4000 airports served by an estimated fleet of about 10,000 commercial aircraft of different categories. This fleet flew in 1976 about 300 $\times$ 10^9 revenue-km. The world merchant fleet comprised some 65,000 vessels, with a combined capacity of almost 375 $\times$ 10^6 gross tons. Pipelines had assumed an important role in goods transport in many countries, providing up to 20% of the modal share.

In terms of performance, road transport produced about 7800 $\times$ 10^9 passenger-km annually, the railway system about 1300 $\times$ 10^9, and commercial air transport about 775 $\times$ 10^9 passenger-km. Looking at goods movements, road transport accounted for an estimated average annual 3400 $\times$ 10^9 ton-km; rail and air transport for 6200 $\times$ 10^9 and 26 $\times$ 10^9 ton-km, respectively; and maritime transport more than 17,000 $\times$ 10^9 ton-km. About 6700 $\times$ 10^6 tons of cargo were loaded and unloaded in some 800 major ports all over the world during the year 1976. In the same year about 29 $\times$ 10^6 cars and 10 $\times$ 10^6 commercial road vehicles were manufactured. About 350 new commercial aircraft made their maiden flights and were introduced into regular service. Merchant vessels with a total capacity of 31.2 $\times$ 10^6 gross tons were launched. Typically, between 4 and 6% of the economically active population in a country was directly employed in the transport sector, regardless of the country's economic development stage, type of society, or political system.

During the 1970s, transportation in all its forms and arrangements experienced a distinct growth as the world's population increased and as production and trade developed. With improvement in society's economic conditions, all segments of human activity required more transport to satisfy travel demand and the need for goods movements.

Transportation and world growth

In the mid-1970s, the world's population had reached a level of about 4 $\times$ 10^9. During the preceding 25 years, global population growth had averaged 1.9% annually. The societies of the developing countries grew about twice as fast as those of the industrialized countries. These trends are illustrated in Table 1-2. In both groups the urban population increased remarkably faster than the proportion of the population living in rural areas. In the industrialized nations of Europe and North America, rural population declined in absolute terms. Population growth projections to the end of this century suggest that the world's population will continue to grow at about the same rate as it did between 1950 and 1975. But population growth in developing countries will accelerate to reach about 2.3%, almost three times the rate predicted for the industrialized economies. Table 1-3 gives an overview of past and projected population growth trends in the 30 most populous countries of the world.

The global phenomenon of rapid urbanization of society is expected to become even more pronounced. By the year 2000 it is estimated that more than half of the world's population will be living in urban areas, up from 38% in 1975. In the mid-1970s the world had approximately 170 metropolitan areas with populations of more than 1 million; by the end of this century more than 400 such urban agglomerations are expected to exist. It has been observed that the higher the standard of living of a society, regardless of its political organization, the larger is the percentage of its members living in urban areas (see Figure 1.1). Consequently, there is presently a higher proportion of people living in urban areas in the industrialized nations than in the developing countries. But the rate of urbanization growth will continue to be higher in the developing countries than in the industrialized part of the world. Between 1950 and 1975 the pace of urbanization in developing countries was twice that of the industrialized nations as a whole. During the next 20 years this difference is expected to become even more impressive: the rate of urbanization in developing countries will be almost three times that of the industrialized nations. In some developing countries there will be real urban population explosions—a tripling and even quadrupling of the population of major urban centers in less than one generation. By the year 2000, some 40 cities in developing countries are projected to exceed 5 million people in size, and 18 of them may be larger than 10 million.

TABLE 1-2
World Population Growth

Group of Countries	Population ($\times$ 10^6)			Population Growth (%)	
	1950	1975	2000	1950–1975	1975–2000
Developing countries					
Rural	1382	2075	2939	1.65	1.40
Urban	273	819	2134	4.50	3.95
Total	1655	2894	5073	2.25	2.30
Industrial countries					
Rural	402	362	267	−0.55	−1.55
Urban	429	731	1048	2.15	1.45
Total	831	1093	1315	1.10	0.75
World	2485	3988	6388	1.90	1.90

SOURCE: *U.N. Selected World Demographic Indicators by Countries, 1950–2000*, United Nations, 1975.

Although still far from being a static situation, it may be said that the population distribution in most industrialized countries appears largely to reflect an increasingly complete adjustment to the needs of national economies and societal preferences. In most of these countries the urban proportion of their population varies between 70 and 80%. There will be some continuing migration from rural to urban areas, but the rate will be marginal. Most cities will grow at less than 1.5% per year. The economic activities of these countries are generally well established and spatially distributed. Production processes, especially in the agricultural sector, will not undergo drastic changes which might lead to serious distortions in employment and which might induce massive spatial redistributions of people in search for income opportunities. In short, substantial structural changes in these economies with consequences for population distribution are unlikely to take place.

By contrast, almost all developing countries go through

TABLE 1-3
Demographic Trends in the 30 Most Populous Countries of the World

Country	1976 Population (× 10^6)	Projected Population in Year 2000 (× 10^6)	1975 Urban Population (% of total population)	1960–1975 Growth (average annual rate, %)	
				Total Population	Urban Population
1. China	836	1093	24	1.65	3.25
2. India	620	958	22	2.20	3.65
3. USSR	257	320	61	1.05	2.60
4. United States	215	254	76	1.05	1.70
5. Indonesia	135	198	19	2.30	4.50
6. Japan	113	133	75	1.20	2.35
7. Brazil	110	205	60	2.90	4.80
8. Bangladesh	80	146	9	2.50	4.40
9. Germany*	79	80	80	0.45	1.10
10. Nigeria	77	154	29	2.50	5.80
11. Pakistan	71	135	27	2.90	4.00
12. Mexico	62	126	63	3.45	4.85
13. United Kingdom	56	61	78	0.45	0.45
14. Italy	56	63	67	0.75	1.40
15. France	53	60	76	0.90	2.30
16. Korea†	52	79	45	2.60	5.50
17. Philippines	43	75	36	2.90	4.50
18. Thailand	43	76	17	3.00	5.00
19. Turkey	41	63	43	2.50	4.80
20. Egypt	38	59	48	2.45	4.15
21. Spain	36	45	70	1.05	2.30
22. Poland	34	41	57	0.95	2.15
23. Iran	34	60	44	2.85	4.90
24. Burma	31	50	22	2.20	4.20
25. Ethiopia	29	54	11	2.25	4.45
26. South Africa	26	46	50	2.85	3.45
27. Argentina	26	33	80	1.35	2.20
28. Zaïre	25	47	26	2.70	5.00
29. Colombia	24	37	62	2.85	5.20
30. Canada	23	28	78	1.65	2.50

*Federal Republic of Germany and German Democratic Republic.
†Republic of Korea (South) and Democratic Republic of Korea (North).

SOURCE: WORLD BANK, *World Development Report*, 1978.

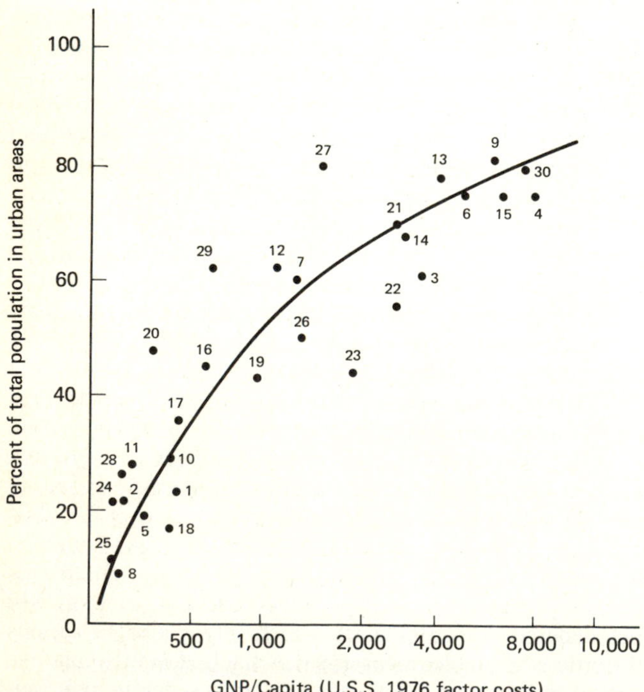

Figure 1.1. Degree of urbanization in relation to gross national product per capita. SOURCE: Data in Table 1-3 (numbers in chart refer to countries in that table); GNP/capita from *1978 World Bank Atlas*.

the traumatic experience of having to cope with the need to improve economic performance and to enhance social welfare under extreme resource constraints. Planned or, more frequently, spontaneous adjustments of population to production processes and the use of land resources are unavoidable. In the majority of developed countries, today's population distribution is not conducive to optimal resource utilization and makes the provision of social services unaffordably costly and difficult. The task with which they are confronted is to encourage a pattern of industrial development that will rapidly expand productive employment and strengthen the mutually beneficial links between industry and agriculture. What takes place in these countries is an enormous adjustment of population distribution to available income sources and services. This trend is likely to continue well into the twenty-first century. To sum up, whereas in the industrialized countries, population growth and population redistribution trends appear to be relatively low and stable, the developing nations experience extremely volatile trends, both in absolute population growth and in population redistribution.

The implied growth of demand for transport is consequently different in the industrialized and the developing worlds. In the industrialized countries, this growth of demand is largely determined by production and trade expansion, and increasing standards of living, with higher proportions of family income becoming available for leisure travel. In other words, the basic societal transport needs are by and large already satisfied. The developing countries are in a totally different situation. Basic transport needs remain largely unsatisfied. The task of alleviating this problem is aggravated tremendously by the rapid population growth and continuously changing population distribution. Overall, further development of transport demand in the industrialized countries will follow a generally stable trend, presumably with a diminishing rate of growth. On the other hand, the developing countries will experience a very steep growth of transport demand as their economies and populations are being restructured or are self-adjusting in response to production and trade development and social welfare improvement.

An important factor in the development of transport demand in the industrialized as well as the developing countries is the travel behavior exhibited by households, mainly in the form of car travel. Although there is still ongoing growth of car travel in the industrialized countries, this growth is generally marginal. Growth of car travel in the developing nations is likely to be tremendous. In these countries there is considerable latent travel demand, a fact that will contribute to quick increases in car ownership and car travel. These basic tendencies become clear when looking at the worldwide development of car registrations between 1950 and 1977 (Table 1-4) and corresponding levels of motorization (Table 1-5). As can be seen, the United States shows the lowest rate of increase, and Europe and Asia—mainly because of Japan—the highest. The rest of the world, by and large the developing nations, shows moderate increases.

In the case of the United States, the economy was already relatively well established during this period, the social welfare level was high, and the society had generally adjusted to the spatial distribution of the economy. Because of the concomitant high standard of living, the level of motorization was comparatively high. Most European countries and Japan came out of the World War II era with enormous reconstruction and development needs. Standards of living in these societies were low. But recovery was quick in most cases; economic activities and population adjusted to each other and to space. The standard of living rose, in many cases to levels close to that of the United States.

TABLE 1-4
World Car Registrations

Continent	Car Registrations (× 10⁶)					
	1950	1955	1960	1965	1970	1978
North and Central America	42,610	55,780	66,860	81,770	97,870	131,073
South America	760	1,150	1,650	3,010	4,590	12,355
Europe	5,440	12,980	23,560	45,940	69,930	113,888
Africa	800	1,250	1,890	2,500	3,440	5,260
Asia	500	920	1,730	4,350	12,250	27,926
Oceania	1,010	1,890	2,470	3,670	4,880	6,858
World total	51,120	73,970	98,160	141,240	192,960	297,361
United States	40,339	52,145	61,684	75,261	89,280	116,575

Note: Data for the entire USSR are included in Europe.

SOURCE: MOTOR VEHICLE MANUFACTURERS ASSOCIATION OF THE UNITED STATES, INC., *Motor Vehicle Facts and Figures* (annual reports).

TABLE 1-5
World Motorization

Continent	Motorization Trends (cars/1000 population)					
	1950	1955	1960	1965	1970	1978
North and Central America	197.0	235.0	250.0	281.0	306.0	365.0
South America	7.1	9.6	12.3	20.1	27.3	55.0
Europe	9.3	21.3	37.0	68.9	100.0	154.0
Africa	3.8	5.2	7.0	8.1	9.8	12.7
Asia	0.4	0.7	1.2	2.6	6.3	11.8
Oceania	82.4	134.0	164.0	210.0	254.0	320.0
World average	19.5	26.1	32.0	42.5	53.6	71.0
United States	255.0	312.0	350.0	404.0	454.0	534.0

Note: Data for the entire USSR are included in Europe.

SOURCE: *1978 World Bank Atlas;* MOTOR VEHICLE MANUFACTURERS ASSOCIATION OF THE UNITED STATES, INC., *Motor Vehicle Facts and Figures* (annual reports).

Travel demand surged, and accordingly the level of motorization increased steeply.

Most of the developing countries obtained their independence during this period. Their economies had to be started up; lack of financial and skilled human resources hampered this process. In many cases this initial startup has not yet been accomplished. There are just too many other problems to be dealt with at the same time which seriously overstretches the national economies and available scarce resources. As a result, the rate of motorization is very low. This not only implies latent travel demand, but actually impedes economic growth for lack of mobility. Figure 1.2 indicates motorization trends in 25 selected countries of the developing and the industrialized countries for the period 1970–1977. The data in the figure suggest an interesting phenomenon. There seems to be a clear relation between the level of car ownership, defined as motorization, and its growth rate. At low levels of car ownership there is little increase in motorization. From about 20 cars per 1000 population, motorization growth picks up rapidly to culminate at about 20% per year at a car ownership level of about 40 to 50. Then it declines steadily to approach zero at a level of 550 to 600 cars per 1000 population, which appears to be the saturation level of car ownership.

Straightforward as this conclusion appears to be, it should be considered that the rate of change of car ownership is influenced in any country by economic growth, disposable household income, costs of motoring, with fuel cost as the most important component, and population density. Obviously, government policies with respect to traffic control and transport pricing also have their impact on people's propensity to buy cars. It seems that these criteria have their influence on the saturation level of car ownership. An interesting aspect is the effect of population density on car ownership. Figure 1.3 depicts the results of a recent survey carried out in U.S. and U.K. counties and cities with the objective of determining the relationship between population density and car ownership. It becomes apparent that car ownership tends to decline as population density increases. Population density also influences the saturation level of car ownership. Thirteen densely populated metropolitan areas worldwide were studied over a 10-year period to assess the

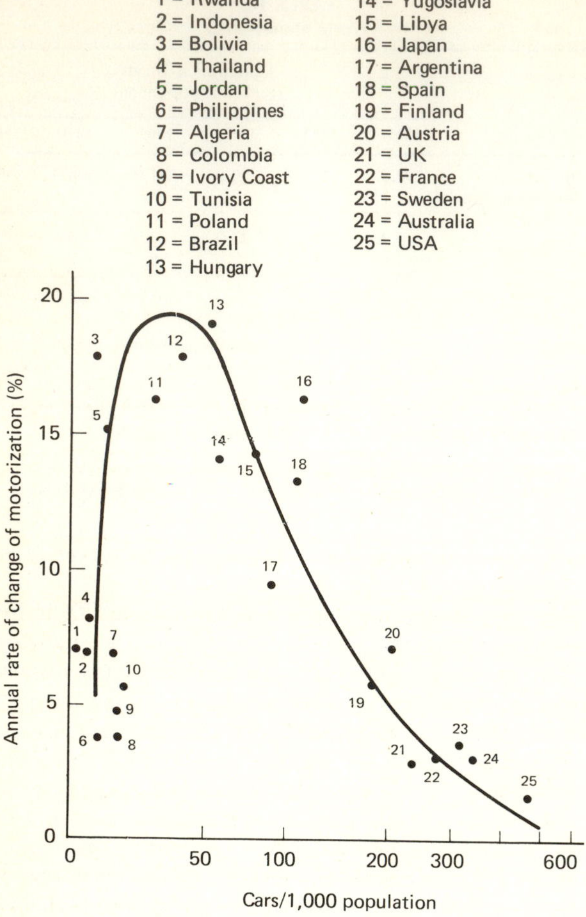

Figure 1.2. Relation of national level of motorization and annual rate of motorization (1970–1977 data and trends). SOURCE: Motor Vehicle Manufacturers' Association of the United States, Inc., *Motor Vehicle Facts and Figures,* 1979; International Road Transport Union, *World Transport Data,* 1976.

development of car ownership. The results are shown in Figure 1.4. The saturation level of car ownership in urban areas appears to be of the order of 400 cars per 1000 population. As a further case in point, Figure 1.5 illustrates the results of surveys in four densely populated European countries and four countries in North America and Oceania which represent sparsely populated huge land masses. Based on the outcome of these surveys, the countries with high population densities have lower saturation levels of car ownership than do the non-European countries with low population densities.

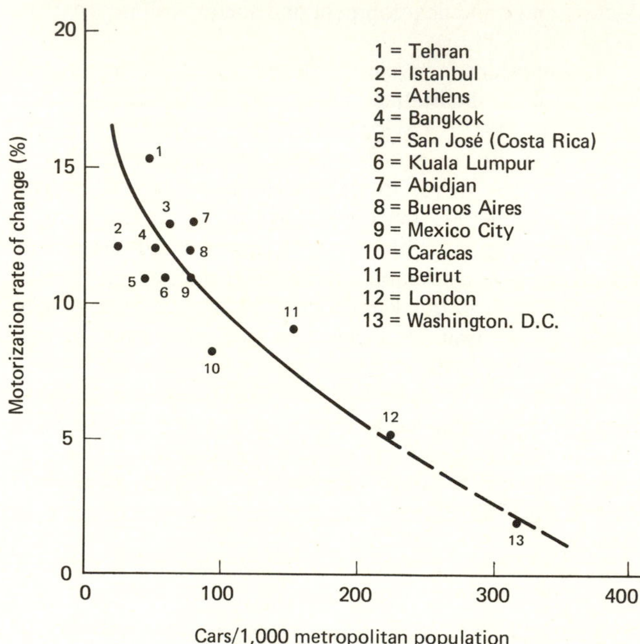

Figure 1.4. Development of motorization in urban areas (1960–1970 data and trends). SOURCE: World Bank, *Urban Transport Sector Policy Paper,* 1975.

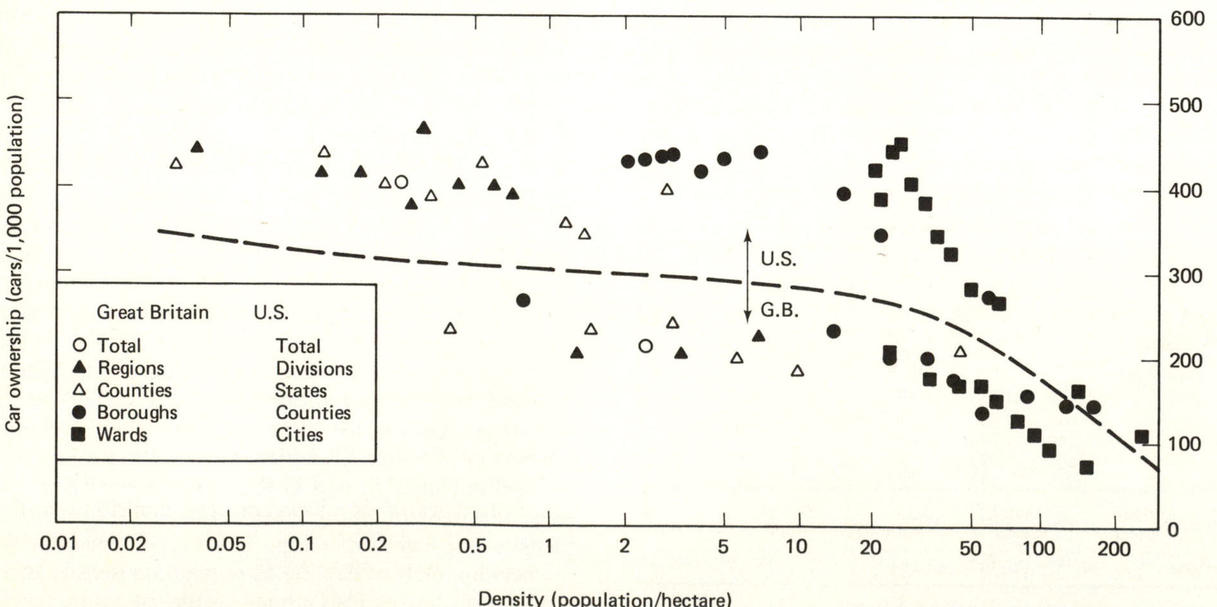

Figure 1.3. Relation between car ownership and population density. SOURCE: U.K. Department of the Environment, *TRRL Laboratory Report 799,* 1977.

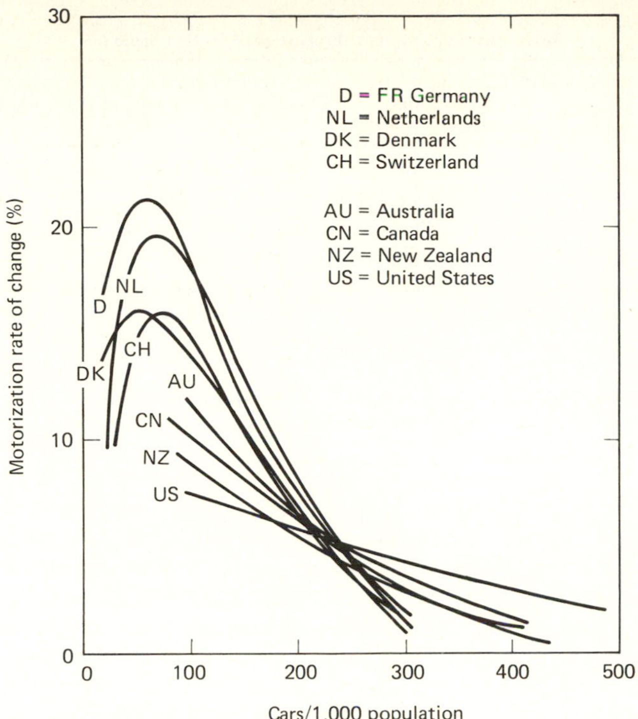

Figure 1.5. Growth of motorization in selected countries during the period 1950–1976. SOURCE: Motor Vehicle Manufacturers' Association of the United States, Inc., *Motor Vehicle Facts and Figures* (annual reports).

Looking ahead to the end of this century, it is expected that the developing economies of this world will show steep increases in travel demand, as indicated by the world car projections of the Organization for Economic Cooperation and Development (Table 1-6). Travel demand in the United States will increase at about the same rate as population growth, (i.e., almost no further demand growth in absolute terms). Industrialized Europe will experience some further increases in travel demand, which will ultimately level off before the end of the century to attain the same stable trend as that of the United States.

But any projection of travel demand by mode, particularly future car ownership, is critically dependent on the future economic performance of a country and on developments in the energy field. Transport's dependence on energy is illustrated by statistics on the sector's share of final energy consumption in five selected countries (Table 1-7). Petroleum is the most important energy source for transport. The transport sector's share in national petroleum consumption ranges between 50 and 55% in the United States and 30%, on average, in the Western European countries. A breakdown of petroleum consumption by mode of transport in the United Kingdom is given in Table 1-8. This heavy dependence on petroleum makes the transport sector very susceptible to petroleum price changes. Statistics on first registrations of motor vehicles in most countries exhibit extremely volatile trends in the post-1973 period, when petroleum prices were periodically adjusted upward by the Organization of Petroleum Exporting Countries. The possible effects of different scenarios of economic growth and future petroleum prices on the development of car ownership in the United Kingdom until the year 2010 are shown in Table 1-9.

TABLE 1–6
World Car Projections ($\times$ 10[6])

	Western Europe	United States	Japan	Rest of World	World Total
1980	108	111	33	45	297
1990	142	131	60	98	431
2000	169	154	66	135	524

SOURCE: OECD projections.

TABLE 1–7
Transport-Sector Share of Final Energy Consumption (%)

	1965*	1970	1976
Germany, West	14.3	14.9	16.0
France	16.0	16.5	19.4
United Kingdom	n.a.	14.4	17.4
Ireland	n.a.	20.7	24.1
United States	27.8	29.4	32.4

*n.a., not available.

SOURCE: *1978 Statistical Yearbook* (Transport, Communications, Tourism), Statistical Office of the European Communities; *1977 National Transportation Statistics*, U.S. Department of Transportation, Transportation Systems Center.

TABLE 1–8
Petroleum Consumption by Transport in the United Kingdom (%)

Mode of Transport	Share of Transport Petroleum Consumption	Share of All National Petroleum Consumption
Rail	4.3	1.1
Private cars and motorcycles	47.5	12.4
Goods vehicles	28.5	6.8
Buses and taxis	4.1	1.1
Other road vehicles	1.5	0.4
Domestic air	1.2	0.3
International air	13.7	3.6
Domestic water	1.9	0.5
All transport	100.0	26.2

SOURCE: *Digest of U.K. Energy Statistics.*

Transportation and the economy

Transportation is an essential requirement for the development of any economy, regardless of its political setting, anywhere in the world. From the embryonic beginnings to the most advanced and sophisticated form, an economy needs transportation to function properly and to spur its growth. As an economy evolves and expands, its backward and forward linkages become increasingly complex, which implies growing demand for transport. Consequently, the share of transport in the *gross domestic product* (GDP) will vary from economy to economy and in relation to the respective stages of development. The contribution of transport to the domestic production effort is usually understated by national accounting methods; many transport activities are not included under transport headings.

Looking at the GDP breakdowns in the national statistics of various countries, it appears that the transport share varies

TABLE 1–9
Forecast of Car Ownership in the United Kingdom through the Year 2000

Assumed Car Ownership Saturation Level (per 1000 population)	Year	Car Ownership per 1000 Population for Indicated Scenario* EG: Low FPI: High	EG: Middle FPI: Middle	EG: High FPI: Low
400 cars	1975	253	253	253
	1980	286	292	298
	1985	316	328	338
	1990	339	353	364
	1995	356	370	379
	2000	369	382	389
500 cars	1975	253	253	253
	1980	290	297	304
	1985	327	343	357
	1990	359	380	398
	1995	386	410	429
	2000	408	433	451
600 cars	1975	253	253	253
	1980	292	299	307
	1985	331	349	365
	1990	367	393	425
	1995	399	431	457
	2000	428	464	490

*EG, economic growth; FPI, fuel price increases.

SOURCE: U.K. DEPARTMENT OF THE ENVIRONMENT, *TRRL Laboratory Report 799*, 1977.

TABLE 1–10
Transport Share of GDP, 1976

Country	Proportion of GDP (%)	Country	Proportion of GDP (%)
Algeria	8	India	4
Egypt	4	Iraq	4
South Africa	9	Japan	7
Tanzania	7	Mongolia	6
Tunisia	5	Thailand	6
Argentina	8	Belgium	8
Brazil	4	Denmark	9
Canada	7	Greece	7
Mexico	3	Poland	8
United States	6	United Kingdom	8

SOURCE: THE ECONOMIST, *The World in Figures*, 1978.

between 3 and 9% (see Table 1-10). A typical breakdown of the transport share in GDP into modal contributions is given in Table 1-11. However, these percentages do not reflect the relative importance of transport in a national economy, in that private and other costs are not included. Allowing, for instance, for the running cost of cars and the economic costs of accidents, as well as for the costs of traffic police, street cleaning and lighting, garages attached to houses and business premises, and so on, the true share of transport in GDP might range anywhere between 10 and 20% in the various economies, depending on their stage of development. As an economy grows and diversifies and as the per capita income of its population increases, the transport share in GDP will normally become more pronounced. For example, transport expenditures as a percentage of GDP grew in the United Kingdom from 10.3% in 1958 to an estimated 16% in 1978. The transport share in the 1976 GDP of the United States was 18.1%.

Apart from its important role in the internal functioning and development of each economy, transportation also has

TABLE 1–11
Modal Share in Transport Proportion of GDP in Spain (%)

Year	Rail Transport	Road Transport	Maritime Transport	Other Transport*	Transport Proportion of GDP
1965	17.4	51.1	13.4	18.1	5.5
1966	15.9	52.6	12.6	18.9	5.6
1967	14.6	53.1	12.6	19.7	5.8
1968	12.9	53.5	13.4	20.2	5.9
1969	13.3	52.3	13.4	21.1	5.9
1970	13.5	55.5	19.8	11.2	5.4
1971	12.5	54.5	20.3	12.7	5.6
1972	12.7	54.2	19.7	13.4	5.7
1973	12.5	52.7	20.5	14.3	5.8
1974	12.6	52.2	20.2	15.0	5.9
1975	12.0	51.0	21.6	15.4	5.9

*Includes air transport, pipelines, and urban transport.

SOURCE: Instituto Nacional de Estadística, Spain.

a major share in the trade relations among economies. In 1976, world trade totaled about US\$1040 $\times$ 10^9 in imports and about US\$1013 $\times$ 10^9 in exports. Almost one-fourth of world exports were "invisible"; that is, it was made up of services such as transport and banking, and transfers of investment income. The share of transport in invisible trade was about US\$64 $\times$ 10^9, or 26%. Invisible trade has grown roughly as fast as visible trade and is dominated by the industrialized countries. Usually, these countries run a large surplus on their invisible account whereas the developing countries show big deficits.

The reason developing countries have done less well in world trade generally is their greater dependence on exporting primary goods. Roughly a third of world primary goods exports originate in developing countries but only a tenth of all exports of manufactured commodities. To generate the same income considerably more primary goods will have to be exported than manufactured commodities. The transport share in exporting such primary goods, such as agricultural products, crude oil and ore, is high. Consequently, the developing countries usually run deficits in their invisible accounts as a result of the steady rise in the payments made to foreign transport–related services, such as to shipowners and port installations and for freight insurance.

Commensurate with its role in production and trade, transport absorbs a significant part of total investment in each economy. The less developed an economy, the larger will be the proportion of annual gross fixed investment allocated to transport. In relatively advanced economies this proportion will have as a major component investment in automotive equipment, as the basic infrastructure usually is already well established. By contrast, in developing countries, with their limited resource base, transport infrastructure generally remains to be completed to meet even basic transport demand. As a result, the share in total annual investment will be relatively high. In countries where the local economy is still at the early formation stage, the share of transport investment in annual gross fixed investment will typically vary between 30 and 50%. In the industrialized countries this share usually ranges between 15 and 20%.

Employment in the transport sector as a proportion of total employment in any economy varies with its level of development. Less developed economies will have rela-

TABLE 1–12
Employment in the Transport Sector

Country	Proportion of Economically Active Population Employed in Transport Sector (%)	GDP Growth, 1970–1976	Employment Growth in Transport Sector, 1970–1976
New Zealand	7.4	1.13	1.18
Hungary	6.7	1.21	1.09
Finland	6.0	1.31	1.10
Belgium	5.6	1.27	1.13
Japan	5.4	1.39	1.05
United Kingdom	5.4	1.15	< 1.00
Poland	4.9	1.46	1.14
Italy	4.7	1.19	1.14
France	4.6	1.26	1.06
Spain	4.4	1.37	1.62
United States	4.1	1.16	< 1.00
India	2.4	1.17	1.10

SOURCE: INTERNATIONAL LABOR OFFICE, *1977 Yearbook of Labor Statistics;* WORLD BANK, *World Development Report,* 1978.

tively smaller proportions of their economically active population employed in the provision of transport services than will more advanced economies. Table 1-12 indicates such proportions for 12 countries with economies at different stages of development. It should be noted that these proportions relate to the services sector and do not include the

TABLE 1–13
Typical Breakdown of Employment in the Transport Sector, Spain, 1977

	Proportion (%)
Urban transport (except taxis)	5.1
Taxi services	9.6
Regulated intercity road passenger transport	3.4
Unregulated intercity road passenger transport	2.7
Goods transport on roads	61.4
Rail transport	11.5
Maritime transport	3.2
Air transport	3.1
Total	100.0

SOURCE: Instituto Nacional de Estadística, Spain.

labor force involved in transport infrastructure design, construction and maintenance, automotive equipment development and manufacturing, and transport management and administration. Allowing for employment in these sectors, the combined share of direct and indirect employment in transportation as part of total employment in an economy will vary between 15 and 25%, depending on its stage of development. Generally, the labor force will grow proportionally with GDP (see Table 1-12). A typical breakdown of employment in the provision of transport services is given in Table 1-13. In interpreting the data, the public sector's share in providing transport services in different countries has to be taken into account. Economies with a largely publicly managed transport sector, particularly railways, are usually characterized by high employment in transport.

The development stage and the nature of a local economy can generally be inferred from the transportation characteristics it exhibits. Table 1-14 gives the goods transport volumes and GDPs in the year 1976 of 18 economies. These economies have different political orientations, are located in different parts of the world, and reflect different development stages. It becomes evident that in some of these economies the total annual goods transport volume is relatively high in relation to GDP; in others the annual volume is comparatively low for the size of GDP. Further analysis reveals that those economies with a high incidence of goods transport in relation to GDP usually have agriculture as the predominant sector and typically find themselves in the preindustrial or early industrialization phase, a phenomenon that can generally be considered as characterizing a developing economy. The less developed an economy, the more pronounced is its agricultural orientation. This implies predominance of production of primary goods, which usually takes place all over the country and which generates substantial transport demand. Such economies will have relatively small GDPs, which explains the high incidence of goods transport in relation to GDP. As the economy grows and diversifies, primary goods will be increasingly processed, which usually means that there will be increases in

TABLE 1–14
Annual Goods Transport Volume in Relation to GDP

Country	1976 Goods Transport (ton-km × 10⁶)	1976 GDP (US$ × 10⁶)	Ratio of Goods Transport to GDP	GDP Share (%) of:	
				Agriculture	Manufacturing
USSR	3,875,598	700,000	5.54	17	18*
United States	2,726,890	1,702,000	1.60	3	33
India	220,606	85,000	2.60	43	14
Japan	177,746	555,157	0.32	7	28
France	174,598	346,740	0.50	5	20*
Poland	169,699	95,000	1.79	15	22
United Kingdom	113,988	220,295	0.52	3	25
Czechoslovakia	89,624	55,000	1.63	9	20*
Spain	88,857	104,619	0.85	8	20*
Italy	80,815	170,765	0.47	8	23
Netherlands	48,718	89,523	0.54	5	28
Hungary	32,682	24,000	1.36	16	22
Finland	27,736	28,145	0.99	10	27
Belgium	21,778	67,640	0.32	3	28
Colombia	17,015	13,429	1.27	27	22
Norway	8,048	31,307	0.25	5	22
Taiwan	8,033	17,258	0.49	14	29
Mongolia	3,765	1,200	3.14	22	20

*Estimate.

SOURCE: *U.N. 1977 Annual Statistical Yearbook,* United Nations.

transport demand but possibly even more substantial growth of the GDP. Hence, the ratio of annual goods transport volume to the size of GDP will become smaller. Finally, when the economy transforms and becomes progressively industrial in nature, production activities will tend to concentrate spatially. Transport demand will increase but distances will decrease. The size of GDP will grow rapidly, and the ratio of goods transport volume to GDP will reduce further.

As the ratio of goods transport volume to GDP gives some general information about the basic orientation and the development stage of an economy, the ratio of total annual person travel to GDP can serve as an indicator for the spatial organization of its population. The higher the incidence of total annual person travel in relation to the size of GDP in a national economy, the higher will be the percentage of its population living in urban areas. This observation is illustrated in Figure 1.6.

Growth of GDP in any economy implies increases in goods transport and travel demand (see Tables 1-15 and 1-16). These relations appear to be linear. The response of travel demand to increases in GDP is more pronounced than that of goods transport demand. Figure 1.7 depicts these relationships. As can be seen, at low levels of GDP growth the magnitude of goods transport demand increases is relatively more important than that of travel demand. Except for the lowest-income countries, which had an average annual GDP growth of 2.9% during the period 1970–1976, most developing countries showed a quite dramatic increase in economic performance. Their GDPs rose by 5.5% on average during the period 1970–1978. The industrialized countries averaged a more modest 4.2% during the same period. According to World Bank estimates, these trends appear to continue. Consequently, the developing countries will experience rapid and substantial increases in goods transport demand in the years ahead. The same can be said about travel demand. The relationship of the level of urbanization and the incidence of travel in a society has been demonstrated. Information was given earlier about the observed and expected annual increase of urbanization in the different economies of the world (Table 1-2). The developing countries will have to cope with the enormous task

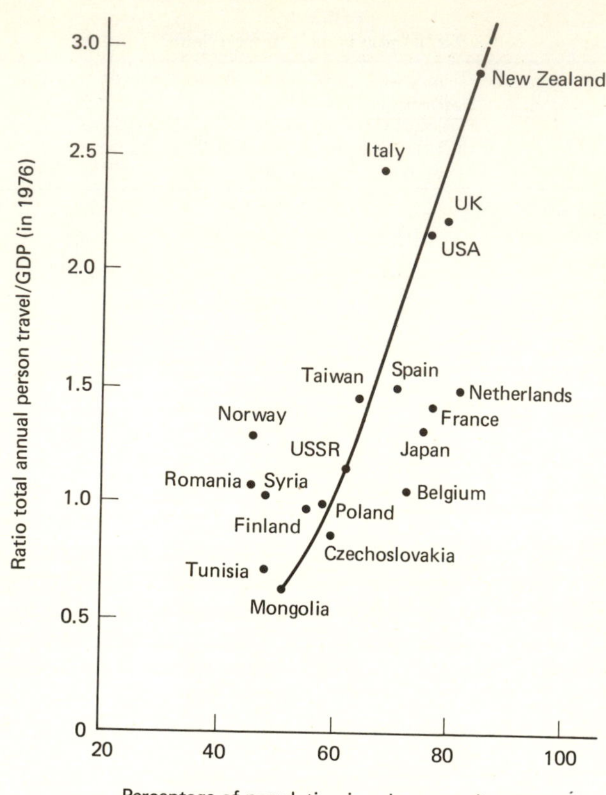

Figure 1.6. Total annual person travel in relation to GDP and level of urbanization. SOURCE: The Economist, *The World in Figures*, 1978; World Bank, *World Development Report*, 1978.

TABLE 1–15
Development of Goods Transport* in Relation to Growth of GDP

Country	Total Annual Goods Transport (ton-km × 10^6) 1970	1976	Average Annual Growth (%), 1970–1976 Goods Transport	GDP
USSR	2,891,416	3,875,598	5.0	3.9
United States	2,522,031	2,726,890	1.3	2.5
India	173,719	220,606	4.1	2.7
France	151,028	174,598	2.4	3.9
Poland	117,326	169,699	6.4	6.5
Italy	77,022	80,815	0.8	2.9
Czechoslovakia	71,104	89,624	3.9	3.2
Spain	61,148	88,857	6.4	5.4
Romania	54,708	79,238	6.4	11.2
Netherlands	47,064	48,718	0.4	3.4
Hungary	26,290	32,682	3.7	3.2
Finland	24,094	27,736	2.5	4.6
Colombia	11,565	17,015	6.6	6.5
New Zealand	8,316	10,670	4.2	2.0
Norway	5,944	8,048	5.2	4.5
Taiwan	4,020	8,033	12.1	7.8
Syria	3,429	4,063	2.9	7.0
Mongolia	2,157	3,765	9.7	4.6
Tunisia	1,830	2,021	1.7	9.4

*Excluding pipelines and maritime transport.

SOURCE: *U.N. Annual Statistical Yearbooks.*

TABLE 1–16
Development of Travel Demand (All Modes)

Country	Total Annual Person Travel (passenger-km × 10⁶)		Average Annual Growth (%), 1970–1976	
	1970	1976	Person Travel	GDP
United States	3,169,941	3,713,832	2.7	2.5
Japan	587,287	732,018	3.7	5.6
USSR	546,114	782,427	6.2	3.9
United Kingdom	415,140	489,695	2.8	2.3
France	347,667	491,362	5.9	3.9
Italy	307,252	418,229	5.3	2.9
India	222,443	286,365	4.3	2.7
Spain	103,424	156,520	7.2	5.4
Netherlands	101,680	134,719	4.8	3.4
Poland	66,581	92,499	5.6	6.5
Belgium	56,796	71,005	3.8	4.0
Colombia	49,668	68,452	5.5	6.5
Hungary	47,950	74,957	7.7	3.2
Czechoslovakia	42,800	48,371	2.1	3.2
New Zealand	26,592	36,980	5.7	2.0
Norway	26,104	40,230	7.5	4.5
Romania	26,005	42,514	8.5	11.2
Finland	21,629	27,526	4.1	4.6
Taiwan	14,170	25,030	10.0	7.8
Syria	4,397	6,185	5.9	7.0
Tunisia	1,828	3,248	10.3	9.4
Mongolia	447	769	9.5	4.6

SOURCE: THE ECONOMIST, *The World in Figures*, 1978; UN ECONOMIC COMMISSION FOR EUROPE, *Annual Bulletin of Transport Statistics*, 1976.

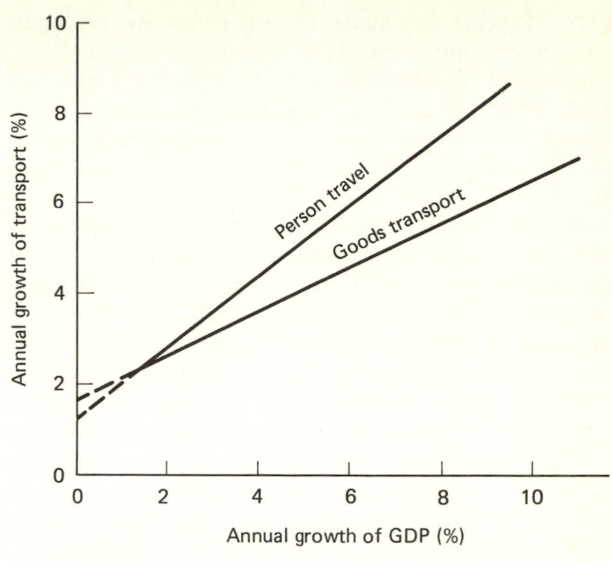

Annual growth of person travel = 1.23 + 0.78 (annual growth of GDP)
Annual growth of goods transport = 1.62 + 0.49 (annual growth of GDP)

Figure 1.7. Relation between annual growth of GDP and annual growth of person travel and goods transport (during period 1970–1976, all modes in 22 selected countries). SOURCE: Tables 1-15 and 1-16.

of meeting steeply increasing travel demand in an efficient and equitable manner.

Transportation and the society

The population of any economy displays a distinct behavior with respect to travel demand and modal use. With increasing personal income, travel demand tends to grow. Figure 1.8 demonstrates the observed relationship in 1976 between the rate of travel per capita in 22 selected countries and the respective levels of *gross national product* (GNP) per capita. Average annual travel per capita ranges between 500 and 2000 km in most developing countries. In the industrialized economies of Western Europe and in Japan, the incidence of annual person travel is typically of the order 7000 to 10,000 km. The United States, with over 17,000 km average annual per capita travel in 1976, stands out at the extreme end of the societies included in this figure. As

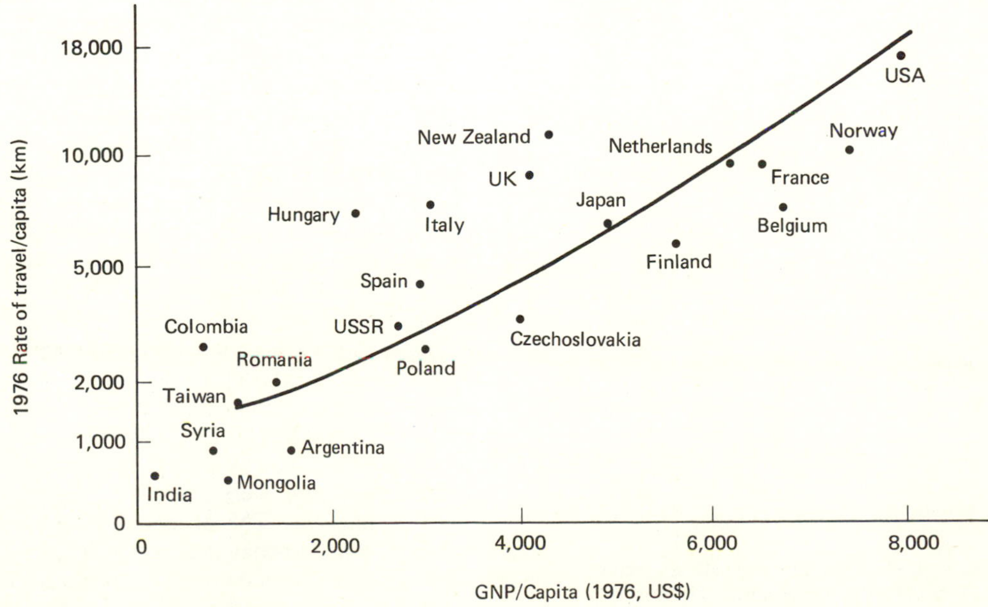

Figure 1.8. GNP/capita and its relation to annual person travel (all modes). SOURCE: Table 1-16; *1978 World Bank Atlas*.

was shown earlier, the higher the annual income per capita in a society, the more people will be living in urban areas, and the more people there are in urban areas, the higher will be the incidence of total annual person travel. As a general rule, then, it can be said that the more urbanized a society, the more pronounced will be the per capita travel demand it displays.

Annual per capita income is also a clear determinant for modal preference in any society. The higher the annual per capita income in a society, the more cars will be owned. Figure 1.9 shows the relationship of GNP per capita and the number of cars per 1000 population in 20 different societies of the world during the year 1976. These societies include some of the developing, the industrialized, and the centrally planned economies. Notwithstanding the political orientation or the development stage of these societies, they all exhibit the same relationship between income and car ownership. It is interesting to note that the level of motorization of a society as a function of GNP per capita results in a curve that appears to become asymptotic at a car ownership level of about 550 to 600 per thousand population. This can be considered as a confirmation of the earlier observation that car ownership tends to reach saturation at that level (Figure 1.2). A similar relationship has been observed

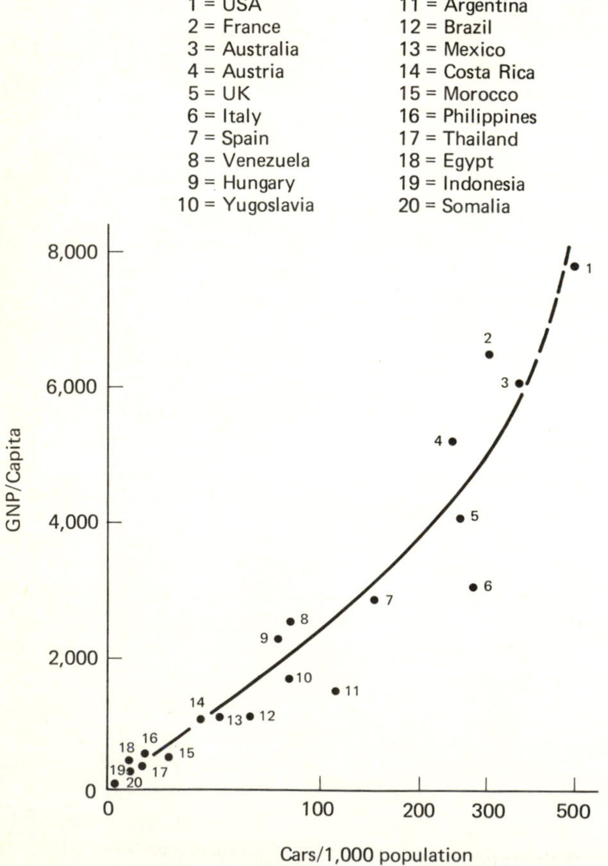

Figure 1.9. Relation of GNP/capita and national car ownership (1976 data, GNP in US dollars at factor costs). SOURCE: World Bank, *World Development Report*, 1978; Motor Vehicle Manufacturers' Association of the United States, Inc., *Motor Vehicle Facts and Figures*, 1978.

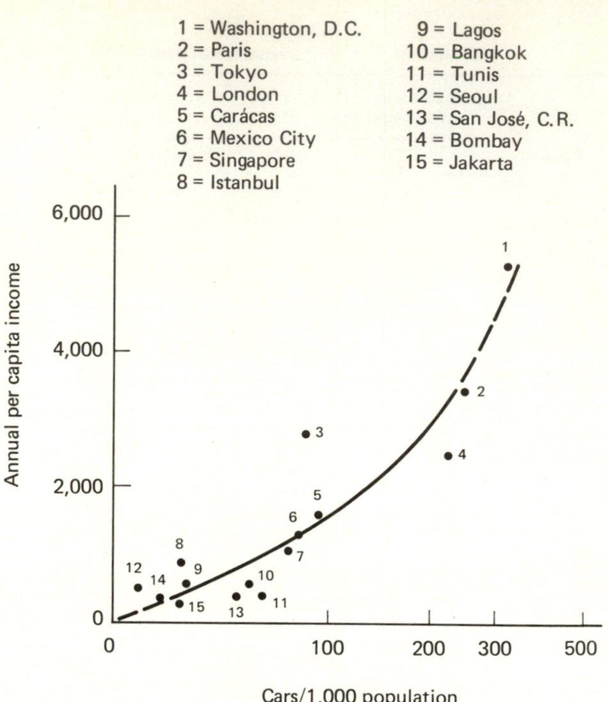

Figure 1.10. Effect of per capita income on car ownership in selected urban areas (1975 data, income in US dollars). SOURCE: World Bank, *Urban Transport Sector Policy Paper*, 1975.

in large metropolitan areas in different parts of the world: the higher the average annual per capita income, the more cars will be owned. The functional form of urban income versus urban car ownership is given in Figure 1.10. Again, one can infer a confirmation of the urban car ownership saturation level identified earlier (see Figure 1.4).

In summary, and as another general observation, it can be stated that most developing countries that still exhibit low to moderate GNP per capita levels will experience rapid and steep increases in car ownership, particularly in urban areas. The industrialized countries have reached a high motorization level, so that growth of the respective car populations depends largely on the custom of motorists replacing their existing vehicles or purchasing second cars rather than on first-time buyers.

Personal income and the related degree of motorization in a society have a clear influence on modal use for different trip purposes by the members of that society. For instance, the 1972 family income surveys in the United Kingdom revealed that with growing income, households used the private car increasingly for daily trips and correspondingly used less public transport (see Table 1-17). Observations made in 22 metropolitan areas in different parts of the world confirm this tendency. The higher the average per capita income was and, consequently, the more cars were owned, the less daily trips were made by public transport. Figure 1.11 illustrates this. This observed relationship can be stated as a third general behavioral pattern of society with respect to transport. As a final note, it appears from statistical evidence that the percentage of daily trips made by public transport will not drop below 20, regardless of per capita income and degree of motorization.

TABLE 1–17
Household Expenditure for Travel and Modal Use Related to Income (United Kingdom Data)

Weekly Income (£)	Weekly Expenditures for Private Car (£)	Weekly Expenditures for Public Transport (£)	Total Weekly Expenditures for Daily Travel (% of income)	Public Transport Use (% of all daily trips)
0–10	0.06	0.15	3.3	60.0
10–20	0.48	0.37	6.0	41.6
20–30	2.07	0.55	11.0	20.0
30–40	3.11	0.64	11.2	16.4
40–50	4.19	0.75	11.5	14.6
50–80	7.00	1.07	12.3	12.4
80+	10.23	1.49	12.8	11.7

SOURCE: U.K. Family Income Surveys, 1972.

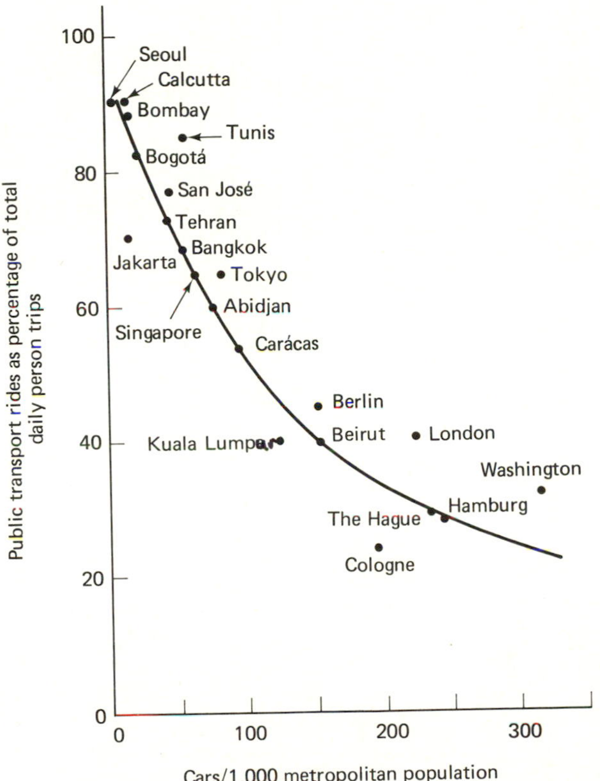

Figure 1.11. Public transport use in relation to levels of motorization in urban areas (1970–1972 data). SOURCE: World Bank, *Urban Transport Sector Policy Paper*, 1975.

TABLE 1–18
Development of World Passenger Transport

Mode	Volume (passenger-km × 10⁶)* 1965	1970	1976
Road transport	n.a.	n.a.	7,740,000†
Railways	995,000	1,130,000	1,280,000
Air transport	290,500	460,000	763,000

*n.a., not available.
†Estimate.

SOURCE: INTERNATIONAL ROAD FEDERATION, *World Road Statistics;* INTERNATIONAL ROAD TRANSPORT UNION, *World Transport Data.*

TABLE 1–19
Development of World Goods Transport

Mode	Volume (ton-km × 10^6)* 1965	1970	1976
Road transport	n.a.	n.a.	3,250,000†
Railways	4,179,000	5,020,000	6,101,000
Air transport	9,290	15,230	24,470
Maritime transport	5,849,000	10,654,000	17,053,000

*n.a., not available.
†Estimate.

SOURCE: UNCTAD, *Review of Maritime Transport,.* 1977; INTERNATIONAL ROAD TRANSPORT UNION, *World Transport Data.*

Current trends in the development of transport modes

In general terms it can be asserted that over the past 15 to 20 years the individual transport modes have experienced quite different growth trends. Road transport has shown tremendous increases. Today, it accounts for about 80% of all person travel worldwide and for about 35% of domestic goods transport. Air transport has had an even steeper growth in relative terms. Its share in passenger and goods transport grew by more than 9% annually since 1965. However, in absolute terms its share in passenger and goods transport remains limited with 8% and less than 2% of the respective total world volumes. These trends are illustrated in Tables 1-18 and 1-19. Maritime goods transport has grown at an average annual rate of more than 10% since 1965. By and large this reflects the enormous increase of petroleum shipments in response to rapid increases of world travel and transport demand, particularly the steep growth of world motorization. Railways are the only mode that, on a worldwide basis, has shown only modest increases in passenger and goods transport over the past 20 years. It should be noted that in several countries the contribution of railways to meeting national passenger and goods transport demand has declined, both in absolute and in relative terms. Table 1-20 indicates the modal shares in total annual transport volume in five selected countries during the period 1960–1976. As can be seen, the relative importance of railways in passenger and goods transport has diminished in all five countries. Pipelines have assumed an increasingly important role in goods transport. Their growing share is illustrated in Table 1-21 for six selected countries during the period 1970–1976.

Modal contribution with respect to domestic passenger and goods transport in the 1970s in 22 representative countries of the industrialized and of the developing world is

TABLE 1–20
Modal Share Development in Passenger and Goods* Transport in Five Selected Countries, 1960–1976

		Share as Percentage of Total Volume†					
		1960		1970		1976	
Country	Mode	Passengers	Goods	Passengers	Goods	Passengers	Goods
United States	Road	95.33	23.80	92.82	24.50	92.52	24.94
	Rail	1.66	46.24	0.55	44.27	0.42	42.05
	Air	3.01	0.08	6.63	0.30	7.06	0.33
	Water	n.a.	29.88	n.a.	30.93	n.a.	30.68
USSR	Road	25.00	5.31	37.08	7.64	42.06	9.15
	Rail	70.03	88.78	48.60	86.28	41.26	85.03
	Air	4.97	0.03	14.32	0.06	16.68	0.07
	Water	n.a.	5.88	n.a.	6.02	n.a.	5.75
Italy	Road	69.61	73.16	86.70	76.16	87.93	78.79
	Rail	29.12	26.80	10.56	23.46	9.49	20.63
	Air	1.27	0.04	2.74	0.38	2.58	0.11
Mongolia	Road	59.90	6.29	46.09	29.10	49.42	28.04
	Rail	28.43	93.67	30.20	70.81	30.35	71.85
	Air	11.67	0.04	23.71	0.09	20.73	0.11
United Kingdom	Road	83.97	62.89	87.20	76.21	86.11	81.26
	Rail	13.54	36.89	8.60	23.27	7.57	17.94
	Air	2.49	0.22	4.20	0.52	6.32	0.80

*Excluding pipelines.
†n.a., not available.

SOURCE: UN ECONOMIC COMMISSION FOR EUROPE, *Annual Bulletin of Transport Statistics for Europe*, 1976; INTERNATIONAL ROAD TRANSPORT UNION, *World Transport Data,* 1976.

TABLE 1–21
Development of Pipeline Transport in Relation to Total Goods Transport

	Total Goods Transport (ton-km × 10^6)		Pipeline Transport* (ton-km × 10^6)		Pipeline Share (%)	
Country	1970	1976	1970	1976	1970	1976
USSR	3,173,116	4,669,798	281,700	794,600	8.9	17.0
United States	3,152,466	3,491,890	630,435	765,000	20.0	21.9
France	168,272	194,040	17,244	19,442	10.2	10.0
United Kingdom	117,876	119,310	2,665	5,322	2.3	4.5
Czechoslovakia	78,837	98,088	7,733	8,464	9.8	8.6
Spain	61,810	91,594	662	2,737	1.1	3.0

*Not including goods in transit.

SOURCE: U.S. DEPARTMENT OF TRANSPORTATION, Transportation Systems Center, *National Transportation Statistics,* 1977; UN ECONOMIC COMMISSION FOR EUROPE, *Annual Bulletin of Transport Statistics for Europe,* 1976.

demonstrated in Tables 1-22 and 1-23. As regards goods transport, the industrialized economies of Europe and North America haul most of their commodities on roads. In the centrally planned economies rail transport of goods is still the prevailing arrangement. There is no uniform trend discernible in the developing countries. Modal use in these countries still largely reflects the respective policies and resulting arrangements of the colonial age. The transport systems inherited by these countries do not always provide the infrastructure required for efficient and equitable transport services. The adjustment to more efficient procedures and arrangements for meeting today's and tomorrow's transport and travel demand will be a slow process given existing resource constraints.

TABLE 1–22
Goods Transport Volumes and Modal Shares in 22 Selected Countries, 1976

Country	Total 1976 Goods Transport Volume (ton-km × 10^6)	Modal Share (%) Road	Rail	Air	Water
USSR	3,875,598	9	85	6	<1
United States	2,726,890	27	42	<1	31
India	220,606	35	65	<1	<1
Japan	177,746	73	27	<1	<1
France	174,598	53	39	<1	7
Poland	169,699	22	77	<1	<1
United Kingdom	113,988	81	18	<1	<1
Czechoslovakia	89,624	18	79	<1	3
Spain	88,857	88	12	<1	<1
Italy	80,815	79	21	<1	<1
Romania	79,238	12	85	<1	3
Netherlands	48,718	33	6	<1	60
Hungary	32,682	27	69	<1	4
Finland	27,736	59	24	<1	17
Belgium	21,788	46	30	2	22
Colombia	17,015	92	7	1	<1
New Zealand	10,670	64	34	2	<1
Norway	8,048	64	34	2	<1
Taiwan	8,033	62	36	2	<1
Syria	4,063	92	7	<1	<1
Mongolia	3,765	28	72	<1	<1
Tunisia	2,021	36	63	<1	<1

SOURCE: THE ECONOMIST, *The World in Figures,* 1978.

TABLE 1–23
Average Person Travel Rates and Modal Shares in 22 Selected Countries, 1976

Country	Average Travel Rate (km)	GNP/Capita (US$)	Modal Share (%) Road	Rail	Air
United States	17,264	7,890	93	1	7
New Zealand	11,814	4,250	85	2	13
Norway	9,983	7,420	85	6	9
Netherlands	9,784	6,200	86	6	8
France	9,285	6,550	85	10	5
United Kingdom	8,761	4,020	86	8	6
Italy	7,445	3,050	87	10	3
Belgium	7,231	6,780	85	12	3
Hungary	7,071	2,280	81	18	1
Japan	6,491	4,910	51	45	4
Finland	5,819	5,620	84	11	4
Spain	4,374	2,920	82	11	7
Czechoslovakia	3,242	3,840	60	37	3
USSR	3,048	2,760	42	41	17
Colombia	2,808	630	95	1	4
Poland	2,692	2,860	52	46	2
Romania	1,982	1,450	44	54	2
Taiwan	1,533	1,070	54	34	12
Syria	814	780	86	3	11
Tunisia	566	840	49	20	31
Mongolia	516	860	49	30	21
India	496	150	48	50	2

SOURCE: THE ECONOMIST, *The World in Figures,* 1978.

Future aspects of transport

As has been demonstrated above, world transport has grown at progressively increasing rates over the last quarter-century in response to an unprecedented pace of world population growth and a rapid development of world production and trade. But in many regions of the world, goods transport and person travel demand remain largely unsatisfied. This applies particularly to the developing nations, and impedes their economic and social progress. Yet most of the industrialized countries also continue to have their generally public sector problems of equitably providing transport to all segments of their population. In many countries, including the United States, the travel requirements of low-income households remain to some extent quite unsatisfied. Efforts to meet such unsatisfied demand through the introduction of new or additional transport services at affordable costs to the user often provoke serious financial problems.

In most countries worldwide public transport does not recover its operating costs from the users; there are also numerous countries in which car owners and truckers do not fully pay for the facilities they use and for the repair of the wear they cause to such facilities. This implies sizable annual budgetary deficits, which could be matched only by increases in public transport tariffs and road-user charges. Both possibilities are frequently not feasible from an equity or efficiency point of view. But most of the industrialized countries have a substantial tax base, which generates sufficient revenues to allow some form of cross-subsidization to offset deficits in their transport-sector budgets. In case of the developing countries, this possibility usually does not exist without seriously distorting the allocation of resources to different sectors of the local economy.

With a limit to increasing revenues, the only avenue for many national and local governments is to cut costs without curtailing services in order to reduce deficits. This policy has already been adopted by many governments; others follow successively. In general terms this policy calls for better utilization of existing transport facilities and resources through improved management, regulation, and administration. Thereby cost increases in existing services can be controlled, and the introduction of costly new facilities and services can be kept at a minimum. This trend will dominate the transport scene for years to come. One of the principal aspects of this approach is the planned and regulated interrelationship between land use and transport. All these efforts require considerable skilled manpower resources. Unfortunately, the developing countries, whose need for such measures is much larger than that of the industrialized countries, also are faced with the problem of their still limited pool of professionals.

Better management of existing transport facilities and resources will also control energy consumption by consolidating trips, reducing driving time, and so on. Design, construction or manufacturing, and management of transport facilities will be considerably influenced by the objective to control energy consumption for many future years. In vehicle design much effort will go into the utilization of nonpetroleum energy sources. In addition to cost reduction and control of energy consumption, a third principal objective in the future development of the transport sector will be control of the environmental impact by different modes and forms of transport. In several regions, particularly in urban areas, pollution caused by transport has reached intolerable levels. Several countries have already introduced legislation aimed at controlling pollution through transportation systems management.

For many governments the equitable provision of transport facilities and services at affordable cost to all segments of their population remains an important transport sector policy objective. At the same time the efficiency objective of transport has to be satisfied, calling for optimal resource allocation to meet the country's transport and travel demands so that the economy can function efficiently and develop to meet rising societal needs. Striving for the highest possible achievement of these objectives under the constraints of cost recovery, energy conservation and environmental impact control will be the challenge for transport professionals, the politicians and the administrators for many future years.

2

AIR TRANSPORTATION

LOUIS E. KEEFER

Louis E. Keefer Associates
Washington, D.C.

The development of a safe and efficient civil air transportation system is essential to the continuing economic growth of most regions, states, and nations. Air transportation, like ground transportation, serves a dual purpose: it provides for the movement of persons and goods, and makes possible the creation and expansion of various businesses and industries, often opening up vast opportunities for exploiting raw materials and markets in otherwise inaccessible areas. The most progressive nations of the world all have successful air transportation systems, and many of the newly developing nations are following suit.

Many traffic and transportation engineers are actively engaged in all facets of civil aviation. They are involved in airport systems planning; airport master planning; in the design, construction, and maintenance of airports, including airport parking and internal circulation systems; and hold important positions in various aviation industry organizations. New challenges are ahead. The continued growth of air passenger traffic will, in particular, place ever greater demands on terminal building facilities and the ground access system. Traffic and transportation engineers and planners will be making major contributions to provide the facilities to meet this growth.

This chapter provides a broad look at what the civil air transportation system is all about (military aviation is excluded). The key elements of that system are airports, aircraft, and the air traffic control system. The principal products are the necessary linkages among the nations and communities served. The basic objectives are the safe, convenient, and economical transportation of persons and goods. After presenting a statistical overview, the chapter then deals with airport planning and design as well as with airport-user traffic characteristics and their implications to traffic and transportation engineers charged with providing effective ground access to airports.

General history and development

Following the Wright brothers' historic flight at Kitty Hawk in 1903, and further stimulated by trophies and prize money, flying enthusiasts throughout the world began to demonstrate the feasibility of air travel. World War I brought fast technological gains. Postwar barnstorming in surplus military aircraft popularized flying in the United States, but Europe remained the leader in commercial aviation (Germany had had regularly scheduled passenger service by "zeppelins" even before World War I). Domestic U.S. airmail service started in 1925. Transpacific airmail service began in 1934. Transoceanic passenger service was inaugurated in 1937 with the Pan-American Airways *China Clipper* flights to Hong Kong. Transatlantic passenger service by flying boat began in 1939. Again, during World War II, advances were made in aircraft design and construction, including the development of the jet engine. Regular commercial jet service was started by the British Overseas Airways Company with its *Comet* in 1952. Full-scale commercial jet service was offered in the late 1950s by a number of airlines using the Boeing 707. By the late 1970s, thanks to the development of the supersonic *Concorde,* whole oceans and continents could be spanned in a matter of hours.

Air carriers

In the United States, the Federal Aviation Administration of the U.S. Department of Transportation (FAA) defines an air carrier as any operator of large aircraft that transports passengers or cargo for hire. In 1979, there were 82 U.S. carriers of various classes operating 2623 aircraft.[1] Some

[1]*FAA Aviation Forecasts, Fiscal Years 1980–1991*, U.S. Department of Transportation, Federal Aviation Administration, Office of Aviation Policy, Washington, D.C., Sept. 1979, p. 38.

TABLE 2–1
Passenger Operations in Scheduled Domestic Service of Certificated Route Air Carriers, 1968, 1973, and 1978*

Year	Revenue Passenger Enplanements† (× 10³)	Revenue Passenger Miles (× 10³)	Available Seat-Miles (× 10³)	Revenue Passenger Load Factor‡	Average On-Line Passenger Trip Length (mi)	Average Passenger Revenue per Passenger-Mile (Cents)
1968	134,423	87,507,677	166,870,750	52.4	651	5.61
1973	183,272	126,317,334	244,699,119	51.6	689	6.63
1978	253,960	182,669,424	299,541,652	61.0	719	8.49

*1 mi = 1.609 km.
†1968 data are revenue passenger originations.
‡Percent revenue passenger-miles of available seat-miles.

SOURCE: U.S. DEPARTMENT OF TRANSPORTATION, Federal Aviation Administration, Office of Management Systems, *FAA Statistical Handbook of Aviation, Calendar Year 1978,* Washington, D.C., Dec. 31, 1978, p. 76.

87% were operated by the 31 airlines providing trunk and local service under Civil Aeronautics Board (CAB) certificates. During the 11 years 1968–1978, the number of revenue passenger enplanements in scheduled domestic air carrier service increased from 134 million per year to 254 million per year, an average of over 8% annually (see Table 2-1). Over the same period, the number of revenue passenger enplanements in scheduled international air carrier service by U.S. carriers increased from about 15 million to 21 million per year. Through 1977, revenue passenger load factors (percent revenue passenger-miles of available seat-miles) ranged between 48 and 56% every year for both domestic and international travel. In 1978, discount fares and the competitive environment fostered by CAB as a result of the Airline Deregulation Act of 1978 produced an annual average load factor of 61% on domestic flights and 64% on international flights, and resulted in a 14% gain in passenger enplanements over the previous year.

FAA expects the future demand for air transportation to continue to grow faster than the gross national product and disposable personal income, but not as fast as in the past. Total revenue passenger enplanements of U.S. air carriers are expected to reach 541 million by 1991, up about 71% over the preliminary estimate for 1979, or an average of about 6% annually. Domestic travel is expected to increase by 70%, while international travel increases by nearly 76%.[2]

The outlook for commuter air carriers is particularly bright. Enplanements have been climbing steadily, reaching a preliminary estimate of 9.9 million in 1979, up more than 12% from the previous year.[3] FAA forecasts a doubling by 1990. This is largely because trunk and local service carriers will probably continue to withdraw service to smaller communities where demand is more limited, with substitute service provided by air commuter and air taxi operators (the difference between commuter and taxi service is basically that the latter fly smaller aircraft and are subject to slightly different regulations).

Air carrier passenger traffic throughout the world is increasing almost as fast as in the United States. In 1978, the 103 airline members of the International Air Transport Association (IATA) and nonmember airlines in other countries, including the USSR, carried in scheduled service about 685 million revenue passengers, up from 515 million in 1974, or an average annual increase of just under 8%.[4] Excluding traffic carried by the U.S. airlines which were then IATA members, the annual growth rate for those 5 years was about two-thirds the U.S. rate. A relatively higher proportion of non-U.S. airline travel is international, because of the smaller size and proximity of some other nations.

According to the International Civil Aviation Organization (ICAO) three-fourths of the world's passenger traffic originated in North America and Europe. Asia (excluding the USSR and China) and the Pacific nations accounted for the next largest share, about 13%. Latin America and the Caribbean nations accounted for about 6%, and the Middle East and Africa about equally for the remainder. Passenger load factors for 1977 varied from a low of 56% in North America to a high of 66% in Europe (see Table 2-2).

TABLE 2–2
Scheduled Air Carrier Passenger Traffic by World Region, 1977

World Region	Scheduled Airline Traffic: Total Passengers Carried (× 10³)	Scheduled Airline Traffic: Passenger Load Factor (%)
Europe	204,887	66
Middle East	14,163	58
Asia and the Pacific*	79,537	65
Africa	14,689	58
North America	258,771	56
Latin America and the Caribbean	37,973	59
Total	610,020	61

*Excludes USSR and China.

SOURCE: INTERNATIONAL CIVIL AVIATION ORGANIZATION, *Civil Aviation Statistics of the World, 1977,* 3rd ed., 1978, Montreal, Canada, p. 38.

Like passenger traffic, cargo traffic is also on the rise. In the United States during the 11 years 1968–1978, domestic air cargo ton-miles flown by U.S. carriers increased from about 2.3 billion to about 3.8 billion, a 62% increase (see Table 2-3). In 1978, about 22% of the annual ton-miles flown was handled by all-cargo carriers, compared to 30% in 1968. About one-fourth of the total tonnage flown is mail. International air cargo flown by U.S. carriers represents about one-third of their total cargo business. FAA expects this share to grow markedly: domestic air cargo enplaned

[2]Ibid., p. 40.
[3]Ibid., p. 42.

[4]*World Air Transport Statistics, 1978,* International Air Transport Association, Montreal, Canada, June 1979, p. 7.

TABLE 2–3

Domestic Air Cargo Revenue Ton-Miles Flown, by Type of Carrier, 1968, 1973, and 1978 (Ton-Miles × 10^3)*

Year	Total All Carriers†	Scheduled Passenger/Cargo Carriers			Scheduled All-Cargo Carriers			Supplemental Carriers
		Total†	Scheduled	Non scheduled	Total†	Scheduled	Non scheduled	
1968	2,325,358	1,643,748	1,579,091	64,657	376,559	195,581	180,978	305,057
1973	3,267,003	2,470,232	2,453,517	16,717	505,187	468,076	37,111	291,584
1978	3,768,897	2,666,723	2,636,203	30,520	840,542	813,561	26,561	261,632

*1 ton-mile = 1.46 tonne-km.
†Categories may not add to totals due to rounding.

SOURCE: U.S. DEPARTMENT OF TRANSPORTATION, Federal Aviation Administration, Office of Management Systems, *FAA Statistical Handbook of Aviation, Calendar Year 1978*, Washington, D.C., Dec. 31, 1978, p. 74.

tons are forecast to increase 106% from 1979 to 1991, while international enplaned tons are estimated to grow by 114%.

According to forecasts by the Aerospace Industries Association of America, an increasing share of air cargo will be shipped in special or intermodal containers. Almost all air cargo was manually loaded until the mid-1960s (see Figure 2.1). Pallets and special containers were developed mainly to reduce aircraft ground time and air cargo handling costs, and about 80% of all air cargo is now shipped in that manner. The Association expects that "as very large jet cargo transports enter service in the future, it will be possible for air cargo operators to offer shippers door-to-door movement of large quantities of air freight in standard containers."[5] Speed is essential. Air cargo is a selective service, generally used where an emergency, the perishability of goods, or a high value/weight ratio dictates fast movement.

Air cargo transportation in the rest of the world is not yet as significant as in the United States, in part because of the relatively high quality of other transportation modes, particularly railroads and waterways. The trend is upward, nevertheless: IATA reports that its members and other airlines carried 10.8 million tons of air cargo in 1978, up from 8.7 million tons 5 years earlier. As all the other nations continue to improve their air transportation systems and become increasingly industrialized, the total tonnage of air cargo flown seems certain to increase.

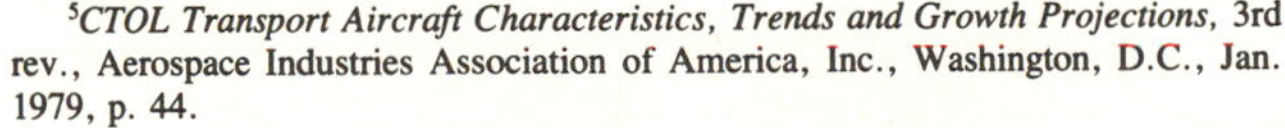

[5]*CTOL Transport Aircraft Characteristics, Trends and Growth Projections*, 3rd rev., Aerospace Industries Association of America, Inc., Washington, D.C., Jan. 1979, p. 44.

General aviation

General aviation embraces all air activity other than that by air carriers and the military. In numbers of operations (takeoffs or landings) general aviation greatly overshadows all other air activity. At airports with FAA control towers, general aviation accounts for about three-fourths of all operations, and the proportion is expected to grow (see Figure 2.2). During the years 1968–1976, the estimated miles flown for all purposes by general aviation aircraft increased from 3.7 billion to 4.5 billion, an annual average gain of about 2.3% (see Table 2-4). The proportions of that travel devoted to business, commercial, instructional, and personal flying remained virtually constant.

The outlook for general aviation in the United States is for slightly slower growth. FAA expects hours flown to increase to about 64.0 million by 1991, 64% more than the 39.0 million flown in 1979. This 4.2% average annual growth rate compares to a 5.1% gain between 1978 and 1979. FAA attributes the growth slowdown to rising fuel costs.

Figure 2.1. Air cargo unitization trend. SOURCE: Aerospace Industries Association of America, Inc., *CTOL Transport Aircraft Characteristics, Trends and Growth Projections*, 3rd rev., Jan. 1979, Washington, D.C., p. 45.

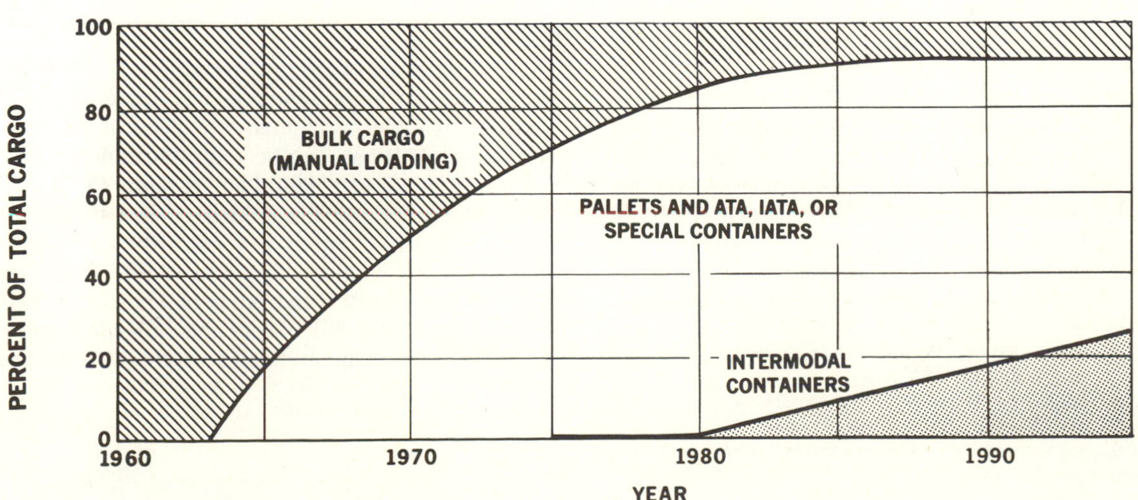

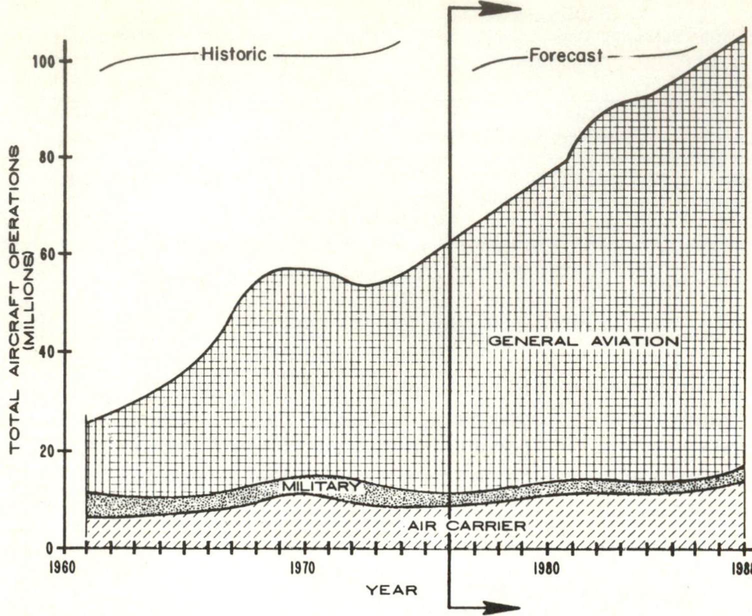

Figure 2.2. Total aircraft operations in the United States, 1960–1976, and forecasted to 1988. SOURCE: U.S. Department of Transportation, Federal Aviation Administration, Office of Airports Programs, *Final Environmental Impact Statement for the National Airport System (NASP),* Washington, D.C., Dec. 1977, p. III-14.

TABLE 2–4
Estimated Miles Flown in Active General Aviation by Type of Flying, 1968, 1973, and 1976—Actual Use*,† (Miles × 10³)

Year	Estimated Total Miles Flown	Business		Commercial		Instructional		Personal		Other	
		Miles	Percent	Miles	Percent	Miles	Percent	Miles	Percent	Miles	Percent
1968‡	3,700,864	1,406,328	38	666,156	18	814,190	22	777,181	21	37,009	1
1973§	3,728,534	1,343,723	36	688,402	18	777,868	21	825,099	22	93,442	3
1976§	4,476,014	1,562,939	35	885,021	20	873,025	20	1,068,114	24	86,915	2

*1 mi = 1.609 km.
†Business includes business and executive; commercial includes air taxi, aerial application, and industrial/special; instructional includes training and rental.
‡Estimated from FAA Form 8320-3.
§Estimated from AC Form 8050-73.

SOURCE: U.S. DEPARTMENT OF TRANSPORTATION, Federal Aviation Administration, Office of Management Systems, *FAA Statistical Handbook of Aviation, Calendar Year 1977,* Washington, D.C., Dec. 31, 1977, p. 117.

In numbers, general aviation is far more advanced in the United States than elsewhere. Whereas in 1977 the United States accounted for about 3.7 billion miles flown, all remaining nations together (excluding the USSR and China) accounted for only 0.9 billion miles flown.[6] The disparity has nothing to do with the quality of aircraft or airports available, but with the greater economic resources available in the United States for general aviation flying.

The fastest growing component of general aviation in the United States is corporate flying: large companies owning and operating their own aircraft. Of the estimated 245,000 civil aircraft used throughout the world, some 60,000 are operated by companies for business purposes, the bulk of that fleet based in the United States, Canada, the United Kingdom, and Europe.[7] In 1977, more than half of the 1000 largest U.S. industrial companies listed by *Fortune* owned and operated their own aircraft. Many companies had sizable fleets: 34 companies owned at least 10 aircraft, and 5 owned at least 25 aircraft.[8]

Aircraft

The evolution of aircraft from flimsy contraptions straining to sustain flight at all, to ultrasophisticated machines capable of flight faster than the speed of sound is a fascinating story. What may be more intriguing is that the evolution continues. It should not be supposed that the American Boeing 747, or the British–French *Concorde,* are the ultimate designs. There will certainly be both larger and faster aircraft within a few years. The following section reviews the numbers and types of aircraft in current operation, and considers some of their physical and operating characteristics as they relate to airport planning and design.

[6]*Civil Aviation Statistics of the World, 1977,* International Civil Aviation Organization, 3rd ed., Montreal, Canada, 1978, p. 10.

[7]JOHN H. WINANT, "The Scope of the Business Aircraft," remarks at the Eagle Aircraft Services Limited Symposium, London, England, May 16, 1978, National Business Aircraft Association, Inc., Washington, D.C., p. 2.

[8]"Business Aircraft Productivity: 1977 Update," *Business Flying, 1979,* Sec. I, National Business Aircraft Association, Inc., Washington, D.C., n.d., n.p.

TABLE 2–5
Active* U.S. Civil Aircraft and Airports on Record with FAA, 1968, 1973, and 1976

	Active Civil Aircraft									
			General Aviation Aircraft							
			Fixed-Wing Aircraft							
					Single-Engine					
Year	Total	Total Air Carrier†	Total	Multiengine	Four-Place and Over	Three-Place and Less	Rotorcraft‡	Other§	Airports on Record with FAA
1968	127,164	2,927	124,237	16,760	60,977	42,830	2,350	1,320	10,470
1973	156,207	2,667	153,540	21,929	74,831	51,386	3,143	2,251	12,700
1976	180,854	2,550	178,304	25,684	88,211	56,730	4,505	3,174	13,770

*Prior to 1970 this category was defined as eligible aircraft.
†Includes helicopters.
‡Includes autogyros; excludes air carrier helicopters.
§Includes gliders, blimps, balloons, and dirigibles.

SOURCE: U.S. DEPARTMENT OF TRANSPORTATION, Federal Aviation Administration, Office of Management Systems, *FAA Statistical Handbook of Aviation, Calendar Year 1977*, Washington, D.C., Dec. 31, 1977, p. 118.

Numbers and types of aircraft

The world's fleet of civil aircraft continues to grow: from about 200,000 in 1968 to an estimated 305,000 ten years later, an average annual increase of just over 5%.[9] In 1977, the United States was home base for over 187,000 civilian aircraft, nearly two-thirds of the world total (see Table 2-5 for the 1976 distribution by type of aircraft).

The U.S. air carrier fleet, however, has actually been decreasing. This has been made possible by the use of larger aircraft and by slightly rising passenger load factors. Nevertheless, FAA expects that fleet to grow from its 2623 aircraft in 1979 to 3164 aircraft in 1991, a 21% gain. The world's air carrier fleet (excluding the USSR and China) has also been decreasing. IATA's member airlines owned 4225 aircraft in 1973, but only 3801 in 1978. The trend has been to higher seating capacity two- and three-engine wide-body jets to replace older, uneconomical, and more noisy four-engine jets and propeller-driven aircraft.[10]

By contrast to the air carriers, the general aviation fleet has experienced remarkable growth. In the United States, the number of fixed-wing aircraft in 1977 reached about 178,000 compared to about 124,000 in 1968, a 47% gain. The number of single-engine aircraft increased less than the number of multi-engine aircraft, a clear reflection of the sharp gain in corporate flying. Rotocraft posted a 101% gain during the same years. The great majority of the world's aircraft (air carrier plus general aviation) is based in North America and Europe: 87%. Almost nine-tenths of all general aviation aircraft are based on those two continents, as are four-fifths of all air carrier aircraft (see Table 2-6). Both in the United States and abroad, most of the general aviation fleet consists of smaller aircraft. In the United States, some 88% of all fixed-wing, piston-powered aircraft are single-engine. Of those, about 70% are powered by engines of 200 hp or less. Some 43% have only one to three seats, and 49% have 4–5 seats. Aircraft have a relatively long life: a third of the general aviation fleet in the United States is over 10 years old.[11]

TABLE 2–6
Aircraft Ownership by World Region, 1977

World Region	Aircraft Ownership: Air Carrier	Aircraft Ownership: General Aviation	Total
Europe	2,740	31,170	33,910
Middle East	690	370	1,060
Asia and the Pacific*	2,280	8,820	11,100
Africa	3,050	3,210	6,260
North America	38,990	192,540	231,530
Latin America and the Caribbean	4,650	16,520	21,170
Total	52,400	252,630	305,030

*Excludes USSR and China.

SOURCE: INTERNATIONAL CIVIL AVIATION ORGANIZATION, *Civil Aviation Statistics of the World, 1977*, 3rd ed., 1978, Montreal, Canada, p. 34.

In the United States, the utility of general aviation apart from sports flying is suggested by the geographic distribution of ownership. As shown by Figure 2.3, the number of active aircraft per 10,000 population is highest in the larger states west of the Mississippi River, especially the northern plains states, where because of the distances involved some professional and business persons, ranchers, public officials, and others use small airplanes very much as their counterparts elsewhere might use cars. Indeed, many small airplanes provide better fuel economy than do some cars.

FAA expects the active general aviation fleet in the United States to continue to grow: from an estimated 193,000 in 1979 to 303,800 in 1991, an average annual increase of 3.9% (by comparison, the 1973–1978 growth rate averaged 5.2%). Private flying for pleasure is not expected to increase as rapidly as business flying, and this

[9]*Civil Aviation Statistics of the World*, p. 44.

[10]*World Air Transport Statistics*, p. 19.

[11]*Census of U.S. Civil Aircraft Calendar Year 1977*, U.S. Department of Transportation, Federal Aviation Administration, Office of Management Systems, Washington, D.C., Dec. 31, 1977, various pages.

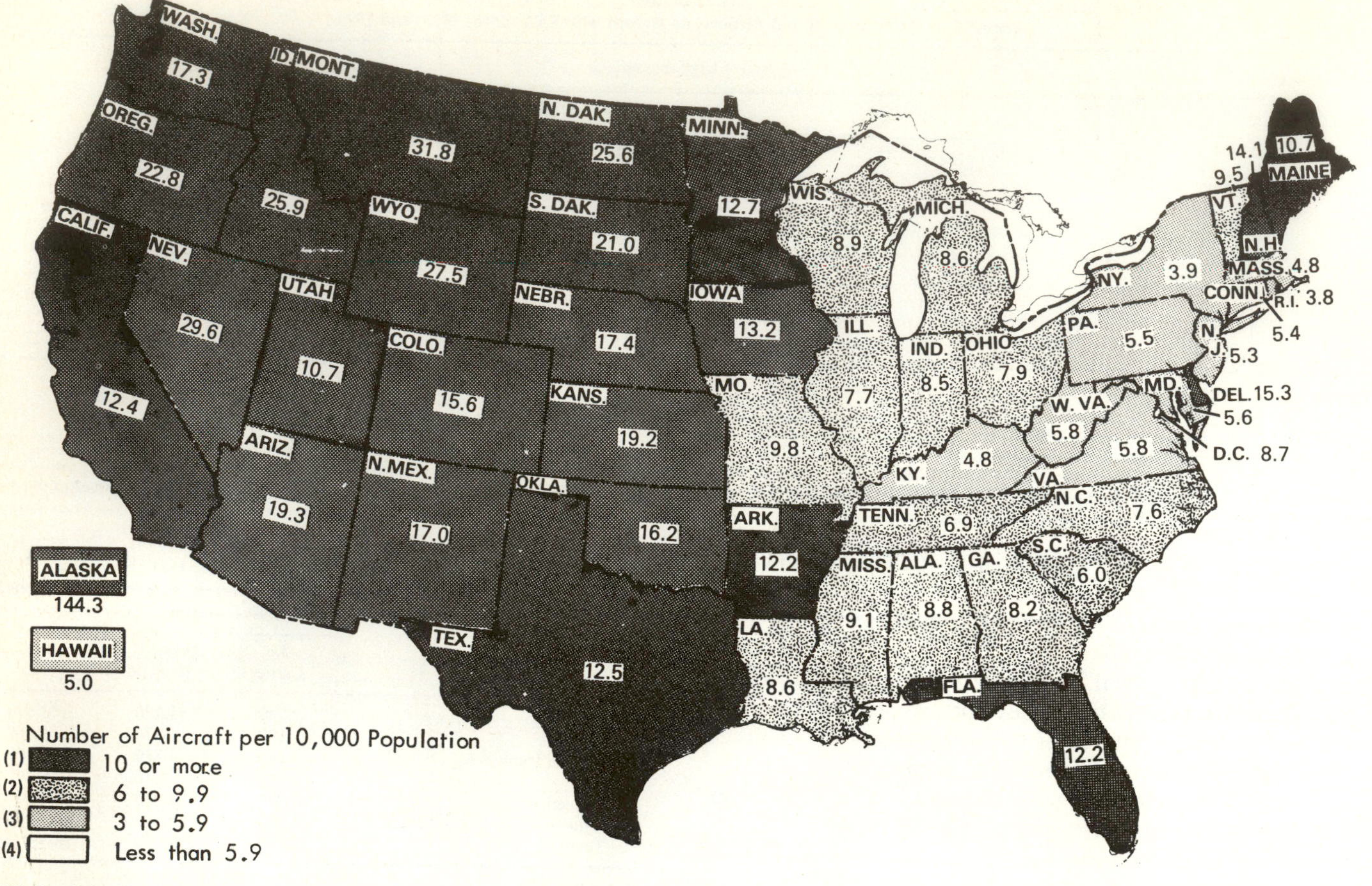

Figure 2.3. Average active aircraft per 10,000 population by state (U.S. average = 9.8), December 31, 1977. SOURCE: U.S. Department of Transportation, Federal Aviation Administration, Office of Management Systems, *Census of U.S. Civil Aircraft, Calendar Year 1977,* Washington, D.C., Dec. 31, 1977, p. 20.

will be reflected in fleet composition: there will be relatively more multi-engine piston and turbine aircraft and fewer single-engine piston aircraft.

Aircraft size and performance characteristics

Aircraft sizes and weights are crucial determinants in the design and construction of runways, taxiways, aprons, and terminal loading arrangements. In the early days of flight, aircraft size was often simply expressed in terms of wingspan. Thus, it might be said that the "largest" aircraft ever built was Howard Hughes' *Spruce Goose,* an all-plywood flying boat with a 300-ft (91-m) wingspan. With today's high-lift air foils and superpowerful jet engines, however, huge wingspans are no longer a good measure of either size or payload capability. An all-economy configuration of the Boeing 747 can carry up to 550 passengers with only two-thirds the wingspan of the *Spruce Goose*. Although wingspan remains important in the design of airport facilities, it is now equally necessary to consider such other characteristics as aircraft length, height, wheelbase, and gross weight.

The best single measure of an aircraft's size is probably its payload, and the trend has been sharply upward since the introduction of the Boeing 707 in the late 1950s. The Douglas aircraft of the 1930s and 1940s all had fewer than 100 seats. Not until 1970, with the introduction of the Boeing 747, were more than 200 seats available on a single aircraft. As shown by Figure 2.4, conceptual studies are under way for aircraft that can seat 700 to 1000 passengers by the early 1990s. Most cargo is still carried by aircraft designed primarily to accommodate passengers. Payloads have nevertheless increased significantly: from about 20 tons (18.1 tonnes) in the 1952 Douglas DC-6B to more than 130 tons (118 tonnes) in the 1972 Boeing 747-200F. Future all-cargo freighters may be designed specifically to carry payloads approaching 200 tons (181 tonnes).[12]

As aircraft payloads have increased, so have aircraft gross weights (the aircraft itself, plus its fuel and payload) and other dimensions. As shown in Figure 2.5, a fully loaded Boeing 747-200 weighs just over 750,000 lb or about 375 tons (340 tonnes). Even with that weight distributed among 16 main-gear tires, each tire carries more than 40,000 lb (18,100 kg). Although aircraft manufacturers have, through the use of multiple landing gear, wide lateral and longitudinal wheel spacings, and large tires, attempted to

[12] *CTOL Transport Aircraft Characteristics,* p. 7.

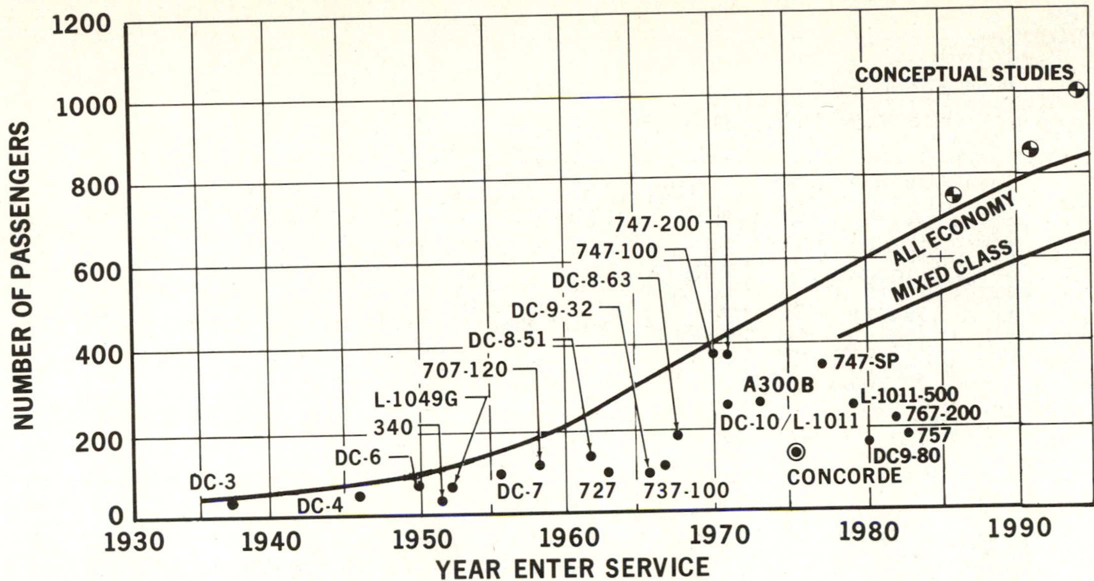

Figure 2.4. Passenger aircraft capacity growth trend. SOURCE: Aerospace Industries of America, Inc., *CTOL Transport Aircraft Characteristics, Trends and Growth Projections,* Washington, D.C., 3rd rev., Jan. 1977, p. 5.

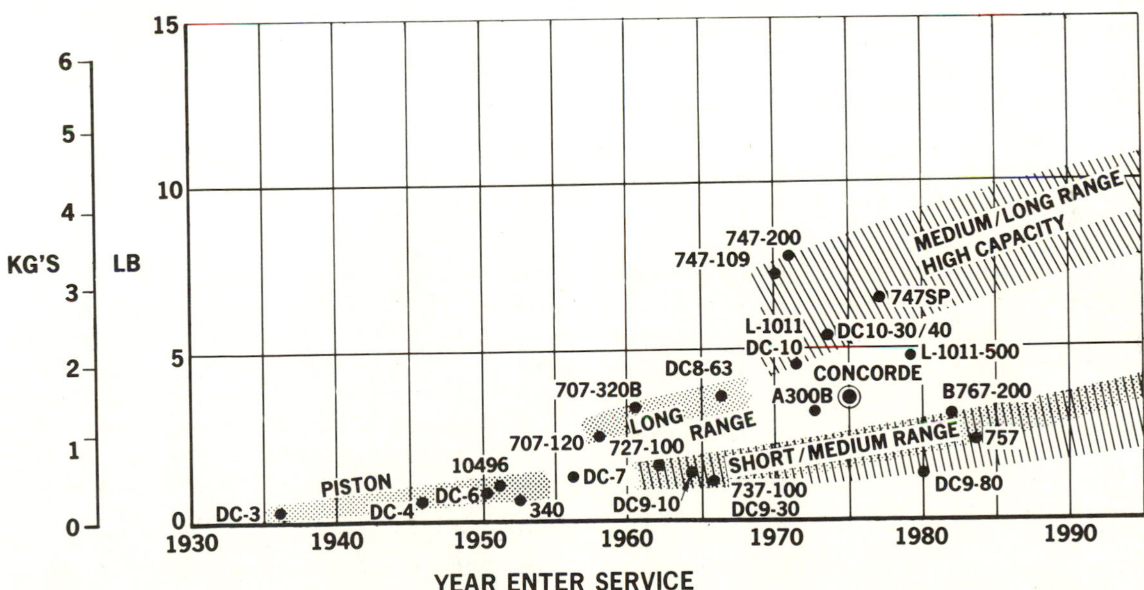

Figure 2.5. Gross weight growth. SOURCE: Aerospace Industries Association of America, Inc., *CTOL Transport Aircraft Characteristics, Trends and Growth Projections,* Washington, D.C., 3rd rev., Jan. 1979, p. 9.

stay within existing pavement strengths, there will probably be some airports where increased pavement thickness will be required in the future.[13] With higher gross weights have come increased wingspans (Figure 2.6), higher and longer fuselages (Figure 2.7), and wider landing-gear treads (Figure 2.8). It should be noted for reference that the general dimensions, minimum turning radii, ground clearances, and ground servicing arrangements for most large aircraft operating in the United States are provided in FAA's *Apron and Terminal Planning Report*[14] and supplementary material.

[13]Ibid., p. 26.

[14]*The Apron and Terminal Building Planning Report,* prepared for the U.S. Department of Transportation, Federal Aviation Administration, Systems Research and Development Service, by the Ralph M. Parsons Company, Washington, D.C., July 1975.

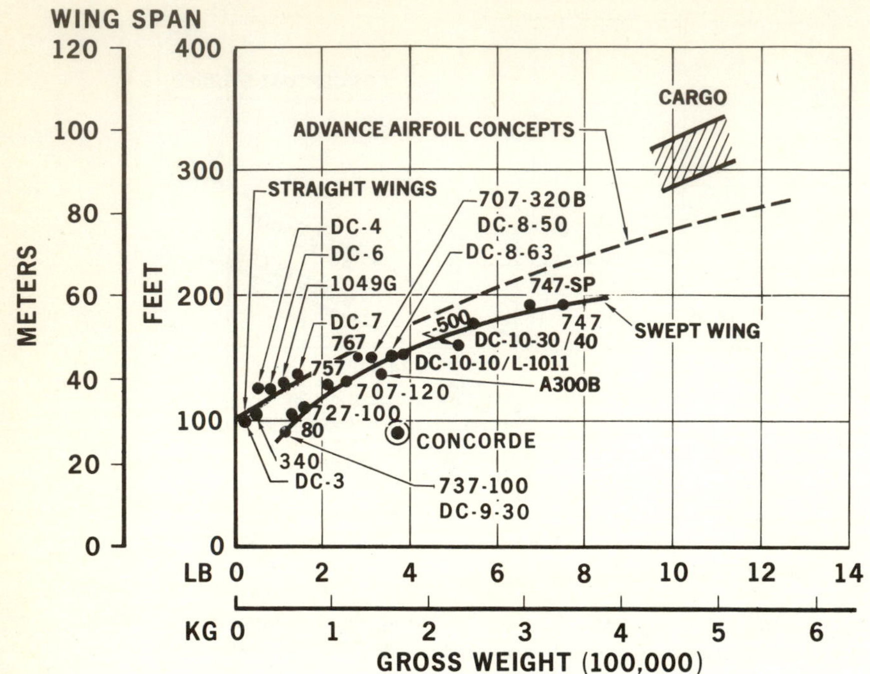

Figure 2.6. Wing span growth versus gross weight. SOURCE: Aerospace Industries Association of America, Inc., *CTOL Transport Aircraft Characteristics, Trends and Growth Projections,* Washington, D.C., 3rd rev., Jan. 1979, p. 13.

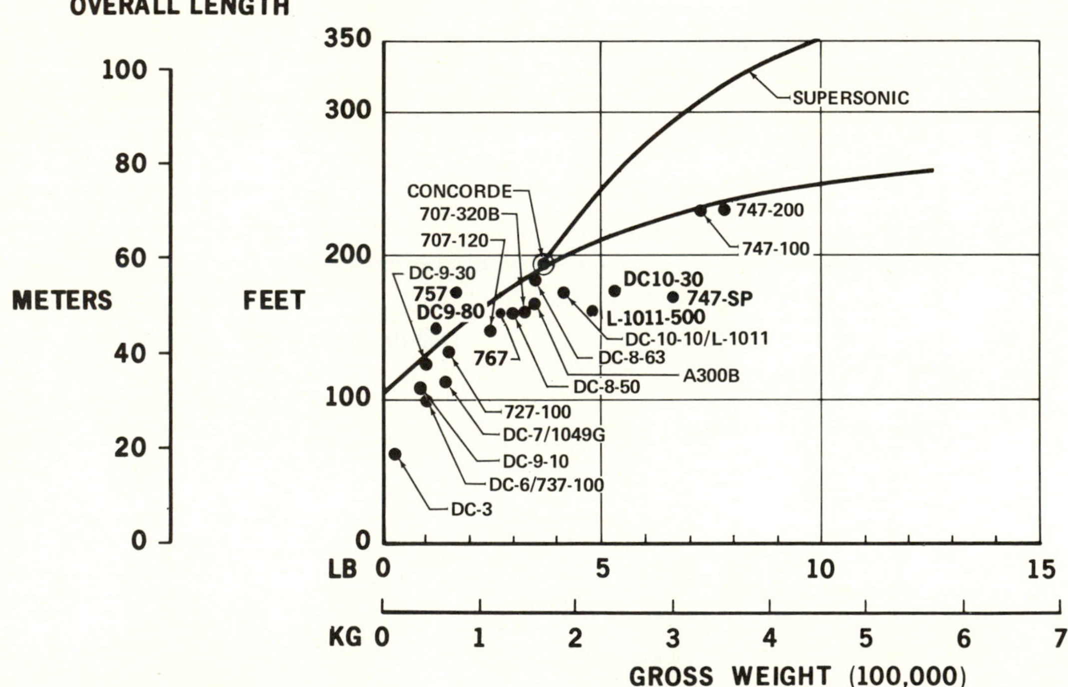

Figure 2.7. Overall length growth versus gross weight. SOURCE: Aerospace Industries Association of America, Inc., *CTOL Transport Aircraft Characteristics, Trends and Growth Projections,* Washington, D.C., 3rd rev., Jan. 1979, p. 17.

Such larger aircraft obviously require greater ramp and apron space for maneuvering. Thus, ramp requirements per aircraft, based on the area encompassed by the wingspan plus 25 ft (7.6 m) and the overall aircraft length plus 25 ft (7.6 m), have also increased. As shown in Figure 2.9, most midsize jets require between 20,000 ft^2 (1860 m^2) and 40,000 ft^2 (3720 m^2). By contrast, the Boeing 747 requires about 60,000 ft^2 (5570 m^2). In calculating the amount of ramp area per aircraft, consideration should also be given to the considerable ground traffic that may crowd around the aircraft for servicing purposes.

In addition to the characteristics of larger, long-haul aircraft, airport designers must also reckon increasingly with the characteristics of smaller turbojet, turboprop, and piston-powered short-haul aircraft which may be used to serve somewhat smaller communities. During the 1970s, a num-

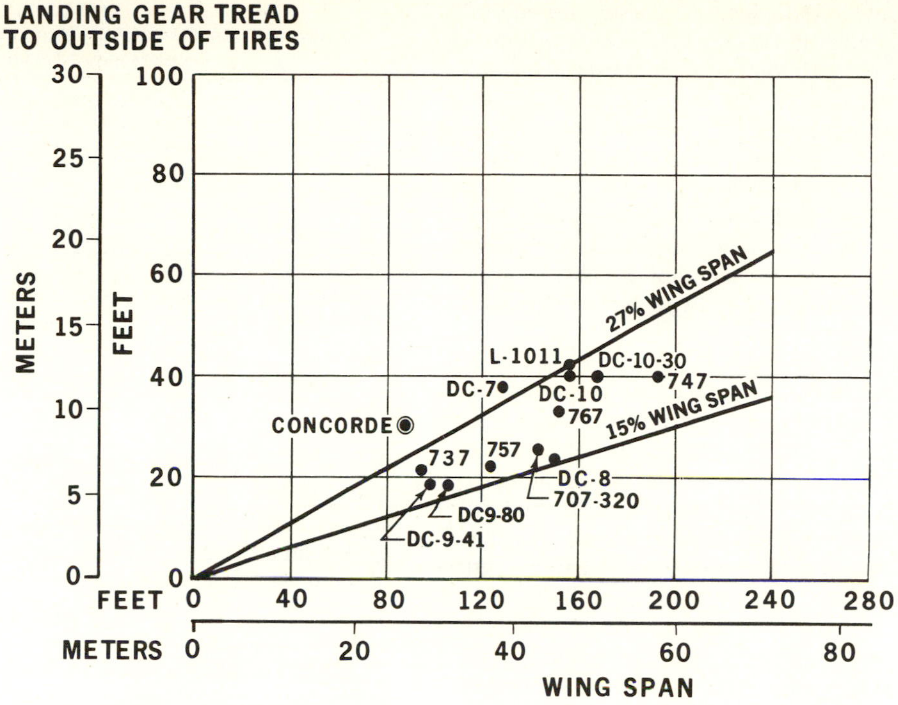

Figure 2.8. Landing gear trend versus wing span trend. SOURCE: Aerospace Industries of America, Inc., *CTOL Transport Aircraft Characteristics, Trends and Growth Projections,* Washington, D.C., 3rd rev., Jan. 1979, p. 21.

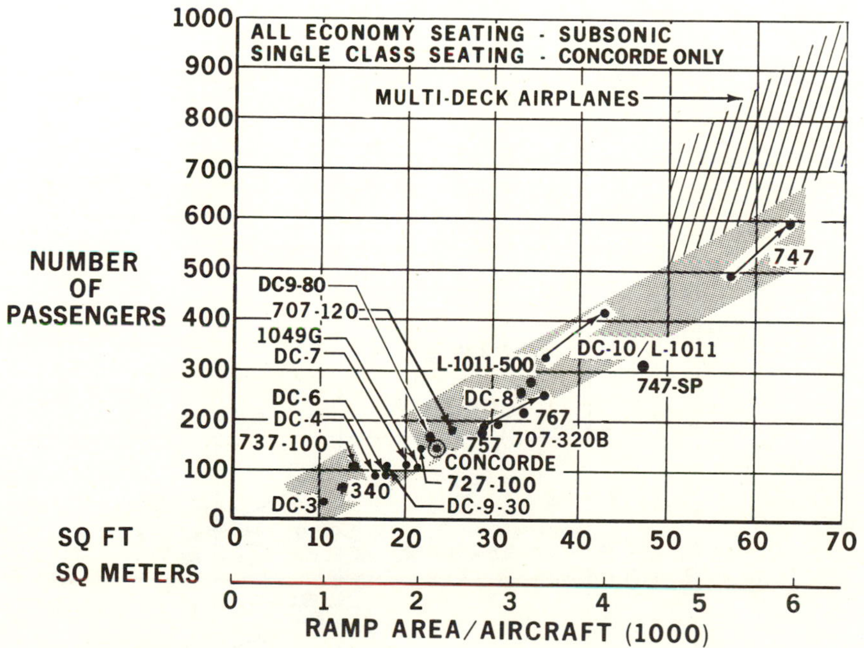

Figure 2.9. Ramp area trend. SOURCE: Aerospace Industries Association of America, Inc., *CTOL Transport Aircraft Characteristics, Trends and Growth Projections,* Washington, D.C., 3rd rev., Jan. 1979, p. 37.

ber of smaller aircraft of about 40 to 80 seats were introduced. During the 1980s, new short-haul aircraft with up to 200-seat capacity are expected. The pertinent characteristics of existing short-haul aircraft are available in the Aerospace Industries Association publication, "Short-Haul Transport Aircraft Future Trends," a companion document to its "CTOL [Conventional Takeoff and Landing] Transport Aircraft Characteristics, Trends, and Growth Projections" report from which Figures 2.4 to 2.10 are taken.

Designers of airports that will never have to accommodate either long-haul or short-haul air carrier aircraft still must consider the gradually increasing size and weight of general aviation aircraft. Although light aircraft used mainly for pleasure have remained about the same size for many years and will probably continue so, general aviation aircraft used for business have grown heavier (if not physically larger) as speeds and payloads have increased. As larger airports become overcrowded, some business aircraft owners tend to shift their bases of operation to smaller reliever airports. This may produce a need for longer runways, stronger pavements, and other improvements in airport facilities.

Fortunately for the neighbors of both large and small airports, most newer aircraft produce less noise and air pollution than their predecessors. Air pollution associated with airports and aircraft actually stems from several sources in addition to aircraft engine exhausts: aircraft fueling operations, ground service equipment, heating plants, highway traffic, and so on. On a national basis, exhaust emissions from all types of aircraft engines contribute relatively little to total air pollution in the United States (see Table 2-7). Locally, of course, a major airport can be a significant polluter. Of greatest concern are hydrocarbons (HC) and carbon monoxide (CO), which are highest at idle power settings, and oxides of nitrogen (NO_x), which are highest at high powers.[15] Programs are continuing, sponsored by both the federal government and industry, to reduce these emissions both through retrofit of existing engines and the design of still more efficient jet engines. Figure 2.10 suggests the success of these programs between the late 1950s and the late 1970s. FAA expects that the construction or expansion of reliever airports, and the consequent reduction of delays at larger airports, will also contribute to the reduction of the HC and CO concentrations at those larger airports.

Aircraft noise may be a more persistent problem. It is a significant annoyance for some 6 to 7 million Americans living near major airports.[16] As air travel increases, such noise may become a serious problem for still others. It is

[15] *CTOL Transport Aircraft Characteristics*, p. 56.

[16] *FAR, Part 36, Compliance Regulation, Final Environmental Impact Statement*, U.S. Department of Transportation, Federal Aviation Administration, Washington, D.C., 1976, p. 3.

TABLE 2–7
Total Aircraft Engine Exhaust Emissions as a Percentage of Total National Emissions from All Sources, 1975

Emission	All Aircraft Operations* (Transport, Military, and General Aviation)	General Aviation Operations Only†
Particulates	1.00	0.07
Carbon monoxide	0.86	0.27
Hydrocarbons	2.04	0.20
Nitrogen oxides	0.72	0.04

*National Emissions Data System, Research Triangle Park, North Carolina, 1975.
†"An Assessment of the Potential Air Quality Impact of General Aviation Aircraft Emissions," U.S. EPA Office of Air Quality Planning and Standards, June 1977.

SOURCE: U.S. DEPARTMENT OF TRANSPORTATION, Federal Aviation Administration, Office of Airports Programs, *Final Environmental Impact Statement for the National Airport System Plan* (NASP), Dec. 1977, Washington, D.C., p. V-21.

Figure 2.10. Exhaust emission trend. SOURCE: Aerospace Industries Association of America, Inc., *CTOL Transport Aircraft Characteristics, Trends and Growth Projections*, Washington, D.C., 3rd rev., Jan. 1979, p. 57.

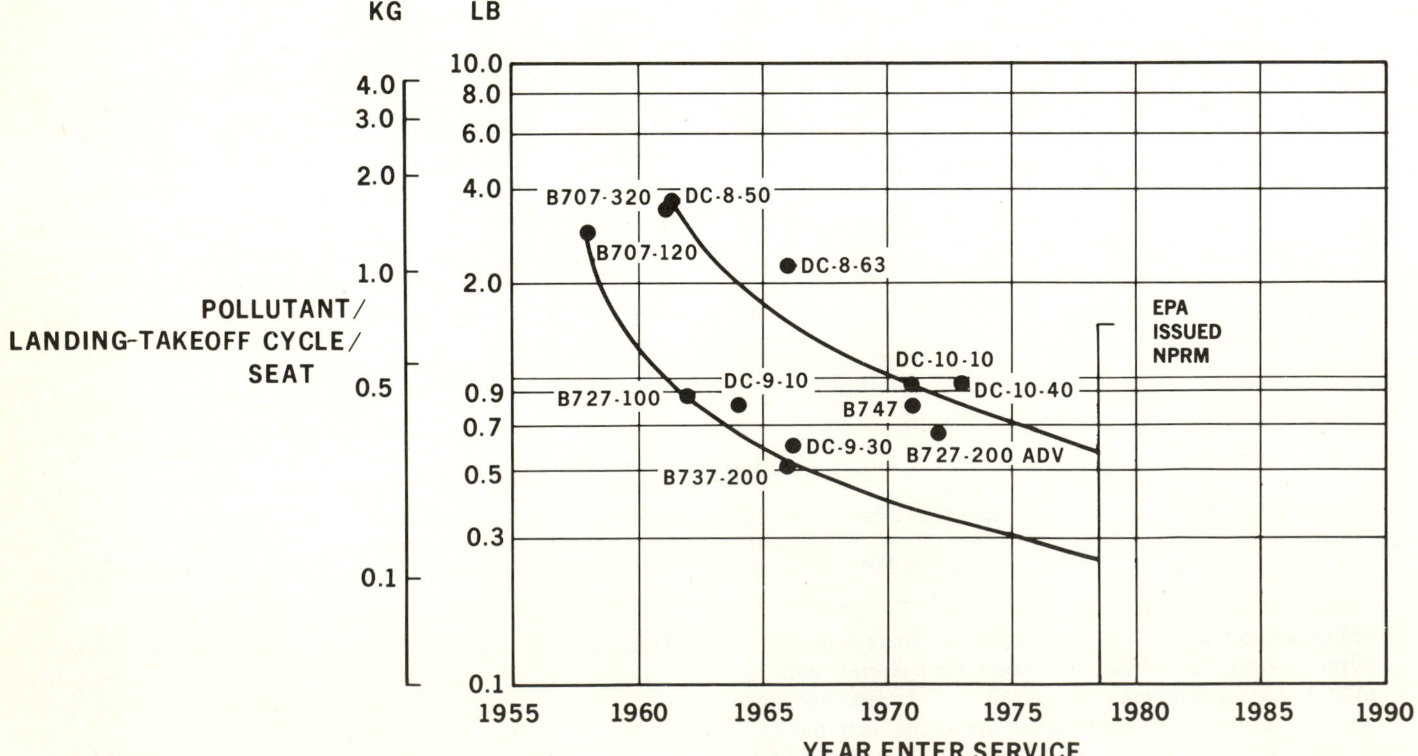

TABLE 2–8
Vehicle Efficiency Statistics*,†

(1) Vehicle	(2) Miles per Gallon‡	(3) Average Available Seats per Vehicle-Mile	(4) Average Load Factor (%)	(5) = (3) × (4) Average Number of Seats Filled	(6) = (2) × (3) Average Available Seat-Miles per Gallon	(7) = (2) × (5) Average Actual Passenger-Miles per Gallon
Domestic trunks						
747	0.13	342.4	51.3	175.7	46.2	23.7
DC-8/707	0.23	141.4	56.1	79.3	33.0	18.5
DC-10/L1011	0.18	233.9	48.1	112.5	42.1	20.2
727	0.29	110.4	58.4	64.5	31.9	18.7
DC-9/737	0.34	89.5	63.6	56.9	30.6	19.4
General aviation						
Single-engine piston	10.47	5	60.0	3.0	52.4	31.4
Multi-engine piston	6.65	6	60.0	3.6	39.9	23.9
Turboprop	1.54	20	70.0	14.0	30.8	21.6
Turbojet	1.22	15	75.0	11.3	18.3	13.8
Other modes						
Auto	13.10	4.0	32.5	1.3	52.4	17.0
Bus	4.90	38.0	60.0	22.8	186.2	111.7
Train (Metroliner)	0.83	382.0	60.0	229.2	317.1	190.2

*Compare Tables 6–57 and 6–58.
†1 mi = 1.609 km; 1 mpg = 0.425 km/liter.
‡Rounded to two decimal places (original table showed five decimal places).

SOURCE: U.S. DEPARTMENT OF TRANSPORTATION, Federal Aviation Administration, Office of Airports Programs, *Final Environmental Impact Statement for the National Airport System Plan (NASP)*, Washington, D.C., December 1977, p. V-37. Domestic trunk data are from *Aircraft Operating Cost and Performance Report* (1974 data). General aviation data are from *General Aviation Cost Impact Study*, Vol. 4 (1974 data). Automobile and bus data are from *Highway Statistics* (1973 data). Train data are from *Transportation Vehicle Energy Intensities* (1974 data). Table taken from Office of Aviation *Policy Bull.*, Jan. 1976.

noteworthy that the U.S. Congress in the Airport and Airway Development Act Amendments of 1976 provided federal funding assistance for the purchase of noise-suppressing equipment, development of barriers and screening to reduce noise, and the acquisition of land for compatible land-use control. Despite all this, as well as extensive research into quieting jet engines and the introduction of revised noise-abatement aircraft operating procedures, however, the aircraft noise problem has yet to be completely solved.

Perhaps partially offsetting their environmental disadvantages is that fact that aircraft are a highly energy efficient means of passenger transportation. As shown by Table 2-8, even the mammoth Boeing 747, with its 0.13-mpg (0.055-km/liter) fuel consumption rate, and only 51% loaded, can average 23.7 passenger-mpg (10 passenger-km/liter), equal to many cars. Single-engine, piston-powered general aviation aircraft can average 31.4 passenger mpg (13.3 passenger-km/liter). Aircraft are not, of course, an energy-efficient means of moving freight; on the basis of ton-miles per gallon of fuel consumed, they are among the least effective of all major transportation modes (compare Table 6-58). Overall, aircraft operations represent about 15% of the total U.S. transportation energy consumption, or about 3.4% of all U.S. energy consumption.

Air traffic control, pilots, and safety records

Somewhere in the world, there is an airplane taking off or landing every fifth of a second. At the 430 FAA-towered airports in the United States, there were in 1979 some 71 million operations, an average of more than 8000 takeoffs or landings an hour. Given the projected increases in air carrier passenger enplanements, and business and pleasure flying, FAA expects that total aircraft operations at 490 towered airports in 1991 will increase by 40% over 1979. Some fundamentals of how this traffic is handled, with steadily increasing safety, is discussed in the following sections.

Air traffic control activity

In most of the world, there are two basic flight conditions; visual flight rules (VFR) and instrument flight rules (IFR). The great majority of pleasure flying, and at least half of all business flying by general aviation aircraft, is under VFR conditions. Although highly recommended for any cross-country flight, a VFR flight plan need not be filed with FAA, and less than half of all cross-country VFR pilots do so. By contrast, all IFR flights must have a flight plan approved by FAA as to route and altitude, and those flights are then constantly monitored both by radio and radar. Most air carrier flights are conducted IFR even under VFR conditions. The continuous ground contact provided by flying IFR is an added safety measure.

Needless to say, the safe operation of all types of aircraft, flying under a variety of rules far too complex to describe here, makes the air traffic control system exceedingly complicated. Much highly sophisticated equipment and many highly skilled technicians are required. One indication of this is the growing workload at various FAA control facilities. Total itinerant and local aircraft operations at airports with FAA traffic control service increased from about 54 million in 1973 to about 71 million only 6 years later.[17] By 1991, the number is expected to reach 100 million. The number of FAA control towers has grown, and will grow,

[17]*FAA Aviation Forecasts*, p. 62.

accordingly: from 362 in 1973, to 430 in 1979, and estimated to reach 490 by 1991. As might be expected, the proportion of instrument operations has also grown steadily: from 42% in 1973, to 49% in 1979, and estimated to reach 55% by 1991.

Looking ahead, aircraft navigational instruments will be improved, in both quality and functions performed, as a result of miniaturization and new technology. Navigational accuracy is expected to improve, and airborne collision-avoidance systems may become almost standard by the 1990s. Obviously by then, as FAA puts it, "air carriers and other users of the aviation system will compete for air traffic control services in air spaces that will become increasingly congested,"[18] so that such improvements will be greatly needed.

Pilots

In the United States, everybody who flies, maintains, or controls aircraft operations is licensed by FAA. This includes pilots and flight crews (excepting cabin attendants), ground instructors, mechanics, dispatchers, and control tower operators. Such licensing is an important factor in maintaining safety standards. In the United States, between 1968 and 1977, the number of active pilots of all classes increased from about 692,000 to 799,000 (see Table 2-9). While the number of private pilots increased only 20% during that time, the number of commercial and airline transport pilots increased 25%. Airline transport pilots alone increased 95%. The largest gain was in the number of glider pilots: 198% (excluding hang-glider operators, who are not licensed).

The outlook is for a continuation of these increases. By 1990, FAA expects there will be about 1,110,700 active pilots of all classes, a 39% gain over the estimated number in 1979. Most pilots continue to take advanced instruction to improve their competency and upgrade their certificates. This is illustrated by the growing proportion of pilots with instrument ratings: 20% in 1968, 30% in 1979, and a projected 50% in 1991. All commercial and airline transport pilots must, of course, have instrument ratings, and those private pilots who own their own aircraft find that the economics of ownership dictate that they must be able to fly them even in IFR weather.

Throughout the world, there were in 1977 about 975,000 licensed pilots (see Table 2-10). Some 63% were private pilots, 26% were commercial pilots, and 11% were senior commercial and airline transport pilots. About four-fifths of all pilots were based in North America and Europe. Although pilots are not generally considered part of the air transportation system, their competency and skill is certainly needed to maintain and improve its safety record.

Safety

Air transportation is extremely safe. As shown by Table 2-11, the estimated 1978 passenger fatality rate per 100 million passenger miles on U.S. certified route air carriers, including both domestic and international service, was 0.006 and has trended sharply downward since 1968. The

[18]Ibid., p. 28.

TABLE 2–9
Active Pilot Certificates Held, 1968 and 1978

Category	1968	1978
Pilot—total	*691,695*	*798,833*
Student	209,406	204,874
Private	281,728	337,644
Commercial	164,458	185,833
Airline transport	28,607	55,881
Helicopter (only)	3,166	4,874
Glider (only)†*	2,193	6,541
Lighter-than-air†*	2,137	3,186
Nonpilot—total	*250,151*	*362,350*
Mechanic†	158,211	228,743
Parachute rigger†	5,700	9,200
Ground instructor†	37,889	57,738
Dispatcher†	4,766	6,061
Control tower operator	18,610	25,388
Flight navigator	2,966	2,092
Flight engineer	22,009	33,028
Flight instructor certificates	30,361	52,201
Instrument ratings‡	139,346	236,312

*Glider and lighter-than-air pilots are not required to have a medical examination; however, the totals above are the pilots who received a medical.
†Numbers represent all certificates on record. No medical examination required.
‡Special ratings shown on pilot certificates (i.e., do not indicate additional certificates).

SOURCE: U.S. Department of Transportation, Federal Aviation Administration, Office of Management Systems, *FAA Statistical Handbook of Aviation, Calendar Year 1978*, Washington, D.C., Dec. 31, 1978, p. 88.

TABLE 2–10
Licensed Pilots by World Region, 1977

World Region	Pilot Category: Private	Commercial	Senior Commercial and Airline Transport	Total
Europe	129,270	18,300	23,050	170,620
Middle East	610	3,080	2,340	6,030
Asia and the Pacific*	46,250	13,100	9,890	69,240
Africa	8,870	7,350	7,350	23,570
North America	366,790	196,420	55,190	618,400
Latin America and the Caribbean	60,850	16,050	10,000	86,900
Total	612,640	254,300	107,820	974,760

*Excludes USSR and China.

SOURCE: INTERNATIONAL CIVIL AVIATION ORGANIZATION, *Civil Aviation Statistics of the World, 1977*, 3rd ed., Montreal, Canada, 1978, p. 44.

TABLE 2–11

Aircraft Accidents, Fatalities, and Fatality Rate: U.S. Certificated Route Air Carrier Scheduled Domestic and International Passenger Service, 1968–1978

	Aircraft Accidents		Fatalities					
Year	Total	Fatal	Total	Passenger	Crew and Other	Passengers Carried	Passenger-Miles* Flown (× 10³)	Passenger Fatality Rate per 100 Million Passenger-Miles*·†
1968	53	13†	345	305	40	150,162,701	119,612,578	0.255
1969	48	7	152	132	20	159,213,414	132,161,593	0.100
1970	39	2	3	2	1	171,697,097	139,157,806	0.001
1971	41	6‡	194	174	20	173,664,737	145,678,876	0.119
1972	43	7	186	160	26	188,938,932	159,722,015	0.100
1973	32	6	217	197	20	202,207,000	171,436,549	0.115
1974	42	7	460	420	40	207,449,006	173,349,894	0.197
1975	28	2	122	113	9	205,059,571	174,173,138	0.065
1976	21	2	38	36	2	223,313,131	190,915,721	0.019
1977	17	2	75	64	11	240,326,516	206,205,410	0.031
1978§	20	4	16	13	3	268,000,000	232,900,000	0.006

*1 mi = 1.609 km.
†Passenger deaths occurring in sabotage accidents are included in the passenger fatality column, but are excluded in the computation of fatality rates for the years 1974–1977.
‡Includes two midair collisions that were nonfatal to air carrier occupants.
§Preliminary.

SOURCE: U.S. DEPARTMENT OF TRANSPORTATION, Federal Aviation Administration, Office of Management Systems, *FAA Statistical Handbook of Aviation, Calendar Year 1978*, Washington, D.C., Dec. 31, 1978, p. 125.

total number of aircraft accidents, and the number that included fatalities, also trended downward. For general aviation, Table 2-12 shows that 4609 accidents occurred in 1978, 795 of which involved fatalities. Over the 1968–1978 period, the total number of accidents decreased, while the number of fatal accidents increased. The accident rates per 100,000 aircraft hours flown, however, showed a steady improvement.

Comparable safety records have been compiled the world over. IATA reports that its member carriers in 1978 experienced only 0.08 passenger fatality per 100 million passenger-miles flown, down sharply from 1968. Over the same period, fatal accidents per 100 million miles flown decreased steadily from 0.45 to 0.23.[19] ICAO reports that general aviation in its member nations counted an estimated 1940 fatalities.[20]

Airport and aircraft security have become an important aspect of air safety. The statistics on attempted hijacking are incomplete, but it is clearly a worldwide problem. The success of FAA's civil aviation security program can be judged from the results of a single 6-month period: "2,840 firearms were detected and prevented from being taken aboard; 1,833 persons were referred to law enforcement officials for violations of the law; and more than 20 attempts at what were clearly intended to be hijackings were disrupted before the weapons with which they were to be accomplished could be brought aboard."[21] Provisions for security

[19]*World Air Transport Statistics*, p. 21.

[20]*Civil Aviation Statistics*, p. 11.

[21]*U.S. Department of Transportation: 10th Annual Report, Fiscal Year 1976*, U.S. Department of Transportation, Washington, D.C., n.d., p. 24.

TABLE 2–12

Aircraft Accidents, Fatalities, and Accident Rates: U.S. General Aviation Flying, 1968–1978.

	Accidents					Accident Rates			
						per 100,000 Aircraft-Hours		per Million Aircraft-Miles†	
Year	Total	Fatal	Fatalities	Aircraft-Hours Flown (× 10³)*	Aircraft-Miles† Flown (× 10³)*	Total	Fatal	Total	Fatal
1968	4968‡	692‡	1399	24,053	3,700,864	20.6	2.86	1.34	0.186
1969	4767	647	1495§	25,351	3,926,461	18.8	2.55	1.21	0.164
1970	4712‡	641‡	1310	26,030	3,207,127**	18.1	2.46	1.47	0.200
1971	4648	661	1355	25,512	3,143,181	18.2	2.59	1.48	0.211
1972	4256‡	695‡	1426§	26,974	3,317,100	15.8	2.57	1.28	0.209
1973	4255‡	723‡	1412	30,048	3,728,500	14.2	2.40	1.14	0.193
1974	4425‡	729‡	1438	32,475	4,042,700	13.6	2.24	1.04	0.180
1975	4237‡	675‡	1345	34,165	4,238,400	12.4	1.97	1.00	0.159
1976	4193	695	1320	36,128	4,476,014	11.6	1.92	0.94	0.155
1977	4286	702	1436	n.a.	n.a.	n.a.	n.a.	n.a.	n.a.
1978	4609	795	1690§	36,600	n.a.	12.6	2.17	n.a.	n.a.

*Statistics compiled by FAA.
†1 mi = 1.609 km.
‡Suicide/sabotage accidents are included in all computations except for rates (1968, 3; 1970, 1; 1972, 3; 1973, 2; 1974, 2; 1975, 2; 1976, 4; 1977, 1).
§Includes air carrier fatalities (1967, 104; 1969, 82; 1972, 5; 1978, 142) when in collision with general aviation aircraft.
**Beginning in 1970, the decrease in aircraft-miles flown is the result of a change in the FAA standard for estimating miles flown.

SOURCE: U.S. DEPARTMENT OF TRANSPORTATION, Federal Aviation Administration, Office of Management Systems, *FAA Statistical Handbook of Aviation, Calendar Year 1978*, Dec. 31, 1978, Washington, D.C., p. 147.

checks have become an important factor in airport terminal design.

Airports

The world's first airports were no more than cow pastures, often surrounded by trees and farm buildings, from which flight was achieved off grass runways no more than a few hundred feet long. Today, paved runways over 10,000 ft (3050 m) are relatively common in the United States, and large airports may occupy a space of several square miles. The following section describes the world's airport system in the late 1970s and discusses some of the major elements in airport planning and design.

Kinds and numbers of airports

One definition of an airport is "an area of land or water that is used or intended to be used for the landing and takeoff of aircraft, and includes its buildings and facilities, if any."[22] Within this broad definition, airports can be further classed by type (seaplane bases, heliports, stolports—short takeoff and landing—and conventional), by ownership (public or private), by usage (public or private), by annual activity (enplanements or operations), and by facilities available (number and kind of runways, navigational aides, hangars, etc.).

There are more than 30,000 civil and joint-use (used by both civil and military aviation) airports in active use throughout the world. Of this total, the United States, including Puerto Rico, the Virgin Islands, and the U.S. protectorates in the South Pacific, in 1978 accounted for 14,574 airports. This included 1986 heliports, 46 stolports, and 536 seaplane bases. As shown in Table 2-13, about 31% were equipped with runway lights, and about 38% had paved runways, with those percentages increasing through the 10-year period. The number of "airports of entry" (international airports designated by the U.S. Bureau of Customs for the landing of aircraft from a foreign country) remained about the same.

Although 200 to 300 airports are abandoned every year, most of them privately owned grass strips, the U.S. total continues to climb: up 39% from 1968 to 1978. About one-third of all U.S. airports are publicly owned; the rest privately owned. Most privately owned airports are, however, open to public use. Those which are not are termed "restricted-use" airports, where access by the general flying public is prohibited except in case of forced landing or by previous arrangement with the owner.

Airports are also sometimes classed by the type of aircraft they are designed to serve. The Basic Utility (BU) airport accommodates most single-engine and light twin-engine aircraft, which comprise 95% of the U.S. fleet. The General Utility (GU) airport additionally accommodates medium twin-engine aircraft under 12,500 lb (5670 kg). The Basic Transport (BT) airport can handle business jets under 60,000 lb (27,200 kg), and the General Transport (GT) airport can accommodate almost everything that flies.

TABLE 2–13
Airports on Record with FAA, 1968–1978*

Year	Total	With Runway Lights	With Paved Runways	Airports of Entry
1968	10,470	3,312	3,353	64
1969	11,050	3,430	3,650	63
1970	11,261	3,554	3,805	61
1971	12,070	3,759	4,176	64
1972	12,405	3,827	4,390	63
1973	12,700	3,880	4,527	60
1974	13,062	3,999	4,716	61
1975	13,251	4,171	4,865	62
1976	13,770	4,362	5,106	76
1977	14,117	4,483	5,313	70
1978	14,574	4,567	5,484	70

*Includes seaplane bases, heliports, stolports, and military fields having joint civil–military use.

SOURCE: U.S. DEPARTMENT OF TRANSPORTATION, Federal Aviation Administration, Office of Management Systems, *FAA Statistical Handbook of Aviation, Calendar Year 1978,* Washington, D.C., Dec. 31, 1978, p. 17.

TABLE 2–14
1978–1987 National Airport System Plan:
Number of Locations by Service Level

Service Level	Existing Airports	New Airports 0–5 yr	New Airports 6–10 yr	Total NASP Locations 0–5 yr	Total NASP Locations 6–10 yr
Air carrier	620	23	6	648	635
Commuter service	133	4	0	167	193
Reliever	147	48	5	200	204
General aviation	2237	397	0	2594	2571
Total	3137	472	11	3609	3603

SOURCE: U.S. DEPARTMENT OF TRANSPORTATION, Federal Aviation Administration, Office of Airports Programs, *Final Environmental Impact Statement for the National System Plan (NASP),* Washington, D.C., Dec. 1977, p. III-8.

According to the National Airport System Plan (NASP), another 483 U.S. airports may be opened by 1987. As shown in Table 2-14, while the great majority (397) will accommodate only small general-aviation aircraft, a significant number (82) will serve as air carrier and reliever airports. "Typically, these airports will be located at the edge of urban areas and many will serve as reliever airports, thus reducing traffic at the major hubs. . . . In some communities, however, the need for land for airports may be deemed less important than other needs, and airports may be closed or moved to locations where land is cheaper. Regional shifts of population may also contribute to changes."[23]

Most U.S. airports are rather small. The average size of all airports is about 1.5 mi^2 (3.9 km^2). Small hub airports average 2.3 mi^2 (6.0 km^2), and large hubs average 5.9 mi^2 (15.3 km^2). Such airports as Dallas–Ft. Worth at 27.4 mi^2 (71.0 km^2), and Dulles International at 15.6 mi^2 (40.4 km^2) are the exception. Smallness is also reflected in the distribution of runway lengths. In the United States in 1977, 88% of all airports had longest runways of less than 5000 ft (1524 m), and 63% had longest runways under 3000 ft (915 m). Many small airports are simply grass strips and blend into

[22]*FAA Statistical Handbook,* p. 150.

[23]*FAA Aviation Forecasts,* p. 17.

the adjoining landscape almost invisibly, both from the ground and from the air.

In the United States, air traffic "hubs" are not airports; they are the cities and Standard Metropolitan Statistical Areas (SMSAs) requiring aviation services, and they may have several airports. By CAB definition, individual communities or SMSAs fall into one of four classifications: large, medium, and small hubs, and nonhubs. Classification is determined by each community's percentage of total enplaned revenue passengers in all services and operations of U.S. certified route air carriers within the United States. In 1977, any community or SMSA with 1% or more was classed a large hub; with between 0.25 and 0.99%, a medium hub; and with between 0.05 and 0.24%, a small hub. Although there were but 159 hubs altogether, they accounted for almost 97% of all revenue passenger enplanements. Large hubs alone accounted for 68%. This intense concentration of air passenger traffic in a few SMSAs helps explain the challenging airspace control problems in these regions and the ground traffic problems at the major airports serving them.

Activity at the world's busiest airports is truly intense. As shown in Table 2-15, 44 million passengers embarked or disembarked at Chicago's O'Hare in 1978, an average of well over 100,000 per day. The United States had no monopoly on busy airports, however. ICAO's ranking of the world's 25 busiest airports includes 10 in other nations. Ranked in terms of international passenger traffic only, London's Heathrow was first, followed next by New York's John F. Kennedy, and then by airports in Frankfurt, Amsterdam, Paris, and Copenhagen. In many cases, if not most, there were serious ground transportation problems at these top-ranking airports.

TABLE 2–15
World's Busiest Airports: Ranking by Passengers Embarked Plus Disembarked—Commercial Air Transport, 1977

	Total		
Airport	Rank-Order Number	Number (× 10³)	International Only* (× 10³)
Chicago—O'Hare	1	44,030	2,240
Atlanta—Intl.	2	29,977	n.r.
Los Angeles Intl.	3	28,362	3,293
London—Heathrow	4	23,390	20,568
Tokyo Intl.	5	22,576	6,156
New York—John F. Kennedy	6	22,546	11,490
San Francisco Intl.	7	18,747	n.r.
Dallas—Fort Worth	8	17,301	n.r.
Denver—Stapleton Intl.	9	15,282	n.r.
New York—La Guardia	10	15,088	n.r.
Frankfurt—Main	11	13,963	9,634
Miami Intl.	12	13,736	5,009
Osaka Intl.	13	13,371	1,584
Washington—National	14	12,612	n.r.
Paris—Orly	15	12,560	7,543
Boston—Logan	16	12,120	1,634
Honolulu Intl.	17	12,061	1,603
Toronto Intl.	18	11,654	5,516
Rome—Fiumicino	19	9,568	6,027
Madrid—Barajas	20	9,379	3,499
Pittsburgh Greater Intl.	21	8,752	n.r.
Detroit Metropolitan	22	8,604	350
Amsterdam—Schiphol	23	8,591	8,444
Philadelphia Intl.	24	8,569	646
Copenhagen—Kastrup	25	8,475	6,795

*n.r., not reported.

SOURCE: INTERNATIONAL CIVIL AVIATION ORGANIZATION, *Civil Aviation Statistics of the World, 1978,* 4th ed., Montreal, Canada, 1979, p. 138.

Airport planning

The air transportation system, like the ground transportation system, is planned at several levels of detail: the national, state, regional, and local. In the United States, the National Airport System Plan (NASP) is prepared by FAA. Officially, it describes "for a ten-year period, the type and estimated cost of airport development considered to be necessary to provide a system of public airports adequate to anticipate and meet the needs of civil aeronautics, to meet requirements in support of the national defense, and to meet the special needs of the U.S. Postal Service."[24] Many observers regard the NASP as simply a composite of airport systems plans prepared by state and regional agencies, and master plans for individual airports prepared by local agencies.

Until recently, most state plans were also simply composites of master plans (or more correctly, Airport Layout Plans) for individual airports. Pennsylvania, through the efforts of its Department of Transportation (PennDOT), was one of the first states to prepare and test alternative future statewide airport plans using an adaptation of the urban transportation planning process, complete with trip generation, trip distribution, and trip assignment computer models.[25] For this purpose, PennDOT received a $1 million grant from FAA out of funds established by the Airport and Airway Development Act of 1970. Many states have now followed suit, and are using the systems planning approach (see Chapter 11).

Because statewide aviation systems plans are necessarily general in many respects, regional plans, as for southeastern Wisconsin, have more specific focus: "The primary objective of the regional airport system planning program is the development of a sound and workable plan to guide the staged improvement of public airport facilities to serve the developing Region, providing not only for the full coordination of airport facility development within the Region but also for the coordination of airport development with areawide land use, surface transportation facility, and community facility development."[26] Such regional plans can be prepared as part of the statewide planning effort (as was Wisconsin's) or as a follow-up to state plans.

The final, most detailed level of airport planning occurs at the master-planning stage, which in the United States produces official Airport Layout Plans (ALPs) for individual airports according to FAA guidelines. An ALP shows the

[24]*Final Environmental Impact Statement for the National Airport System Plan (NASP),* U.S. Department of Transportation, Federal Aviation Administration, Office of Airports Programs, Washington, D.C., Dec. 1977, p. 1.

[25]*Pennsylvania Statewide Airport System Plan, Summary Report,* Pennsylvania Department of Transportation, Bureau of Advance Planning, Harrisburg, Pa., Jan. 1978.

[26]SOUTHEASTERN WISCONSIN REGIONAL PLANNING COMMISSION, *A Regional Airport System Plan for Southeastern Wisconsin,* Waukesha, Wis., Dec. 1975, p. 19.

boundaries of all areas owned or controlled for airport purposes, together with proposed additions thereto, the location and nature of existing and proposed airport facilities and structures, and the location of existing and proposed nonaviation areas and improvements. An ALP is FAA's controlling document for the review and approval of federal grants in partial support of proposed airport improvements.

Master planning cannot be described here in any detail, but it may be illustrative briefly to review the general approach taken by the Port Authority of New York and New Jersey.[27] A 3-year concurrent study of La Guardia, Kennedy International, and Newark International Airports, costing about $2.4 million, had three principal phases. First, existing data were assembled and capacity problems analyzed to identify a program of immediately needed improvements; at the same time, new data were collected on passengers, employees, and air cargo, for forecasting purposes. Second, the detailed capacities of runways, terminal areas, roadways, and other facilities were determined, and by comparisons with forecast demands for 5-, 10- and 20-year periods, the need and timing for new facilities determined; a concurrent environmental study, particularly concerning aircraft noise, was conducted. In the final phase, after considering all alternatives, airport layout, terminal area, and airport access plans were prepared for the 5-, 10- and 20-year development for each airport.

Airport master planning involves many economic analyses (see Chapter 14). The question of determining what airport expansion improvements are warranted, and when to make them, is particularly complex. The natural demand for passenger service tends to have certain pronounced peaks, so the need for expanding the capacity of airport facilities is often related to long delays at peak hours rather than to insufficient total capacity throughout the day. A report[28] has suggested that airport officials more vigorously consider various policies to smooth out that demand rather than to attempt to meet it fully, for example, by setting higher peak-period landing fees. This approach may not be practical. In scheduling flight times, both departure *and* arrival times are important to the traveler, and the basic utility of air travel could be seriously affected by attempting to restrict that freedom of scheduling.

A further complication is the fact that predicting future passenger demand appears still to be somewhat inexact:[29] "Despite extensive work to date on forecasting traffic on individual airports, the problem of the manner in which this volume develops is constantly full of surprises. Experts in the area are not even agreed on the simple question of whether fare raises produce more revenue for the airlines or not. Nor are the precise effects of fare structure, frequency of service, or demographic characteristics of airport traffic well understood." The implications of the Airline Deregulation Act of 1978 and the phaseout of the Civil Aeronautics Board by 1985 add still more uncertainties to the forecasting process.

This is not meant to embarrass aviation forecasters—their work is certainly comparable in accuracy to that done by most traffic and transportation engineers engaged in forecasting future usage of highways and public transit—but to highlight a basic problem that makes airport master planning extremely challenging. The future demand for aviation services is dependent on so many variables that FAA makes not only a series of "baseline forecasts" (from which the forecast figures in this chapter have been taken), but also a "high-prosperity" and a "slow-growth" series. Traffic and transportation engineers and planners involved in providing ground access and parking for airports should be aware of those variations on the baseline forecasts.

Airport design

Excellent texts by Horonjeff,[30] de Neufville,[31] and Ashford and Wright,[32] as well as manuals published by FAA[33] and IATA,[34] provide virtually every detail that anyone would need to design an airport, its terminal facilities, and its ground access requirements. An excellent, partially annotated bibliography of airport planning and design references is also available from the Air Transport Association.[35] This section only summarizes some of the major factors involved.

The first and often most difficult step in airport design is locating a desirable and available site. The essential considerations are: sufficient, reasonably level space; firm ground, easily drained; potential runway approaches free of hills, tall buildings, or other glide slope obstructions; freedom from perpetual smoke or fog; freedom from adjoining incompatible land uses; and, of course, reasonable proximity to the demand to be served. More and more, such sites for major airports can be found only at the distant periphery of metropolitan areas.

Given an appropriate site, the actual design and construction of the airport involves three major areas of examination: (1) the runways, taxiways, and aprons; (2) the terminal; and (3) the circulation roads and parking. First consideration must be given to airport "configuration," because that determines the number and orientation of runways and their location relative to the terminal area. Basically, configuration is a function of the types and volumes of aircraft to be accommodated in relation to prevailing wind conditions. The capacity of a single runway under VFR conditions generally ranges from 45 to 100 operations per hour, and under IFR conditions, from 40 to 50 operations per hour.[36] At

[27] *Master Planning Studies for La Guardia, John F. Kennedy International and Newark International Airports,* The Port Authority of New York and New Jersey, New York, Apr. 1977.

[28] David G. Smith, Daniel P. Maxfield, and Stan Fromovitz, *The Airport Investment Model: A Methodology for Airport Investment Planning,* U.S. Department of Transportation, Office of the Secretary, Office of Systems Analysis and Information, Washington, D.C., Feb. 1977.

[29] Ibid., p. 1.

[30] Robert Horonjeff, *Planning and Design of Airports,* 2nd ed., McGraw-Hill, New York, 1975.

[31] Richard de Neufville, *Airport Systems Planning,* MIT Press, Cambridge, Mass., 1976.

[32] Norman Ashford and Paul H. Wright, *Airport Engineering,* Wiley, New York, 1979.

[33] *Apron and Terminal Building Planning Report.*

[34] *Airport Terminals Reference Manual,* 6th ed., International Air Transport Association, Montreal, Canada, 1978.

[35] *Airport Planning and Design Reference Handbook,* Airports and Materials Department, Air Transport Association of America, Washington, D.C., Jan. 1979.

[36] Horonjeff, *Planning and Design of Airports,* p. 194.

most airports, wind direction determines which of several runways will be "active" at any given time (some airports are large enough to accommodate different types of aircraft on different runways at the same time, while at less busy airports, with no wind, pilots may sometimes be allowed to use the runway of their choice). Generally speaking, this means that "runway capacity" can be increased significantly only by installing parallel runways sufficiently far apart to permit simultaneous operations. This has become a common arrangement at newer, larger airports. Many runway configurations are possible, however, and total capacity becomes a function of runway lengths and spacing, how runways intersect, the frequency and location of turnoffs to taxiways, and what navigation aids are available.

Taxiways and holding aprons provide the means of getting aircraft to and from runways, and storing them preparatory to takeoff. Because two aircraft may not use an active runway at the same time, the faster a landing aircraft can turn off the runway, the sooner another may land or take off. Exit taxiways, or turnoffs, should be spaced to expedite the maneuvering of aircraft from an active runway. Taxiways should be arranged to avoid crossing any runways. At busy airports, parallel taxiways for each runway may be needed. Holding aprons, or "warmup pads," near the ends of each runway should be large enough to allow aircraft to pass one another if necessary.

According to Horonjeff,[37] "the key to a desirable airport layout is to provide the shortest taxiing distances from the terminal area to the takeoff ends of runways and to shorten the taxiing distances for landing aircraft as much as practicable." This suggests a central position for the terminal area, much as shown in Figure 2.11 for airports in Los Angeles, Wichita, Washington, and Hamburg. Unnecessary time on the ground is time wasted for the air traveler and additional operating cost for the air carrier. A central terminal location should, at the same time, not be subjected to aircraft landing or taking off directly overhead.

The terminal is the interface between "landside" and "airside" (see Figure 2.12). Here there must be adequate facilities for handling passengers and cargo and for housing various airport administrative functions. Although there are several classification systems, Horonjeff identifies five basic passenger-processing concepts: gate arrival, pier finger, pier satellite, remote satellite, and mobile conveyance.[38] The gate arrival concept brings the ground transportation mode as close as possible to the waiting aircraft. The pier finger involves passenger processing in a central building from which passengers walk along a corridor to aircraft parked on either side. The pier satellite ends in a circular rotunda

[37]Ibid., p. 199.

[38]Ibid., p. 247 ff.

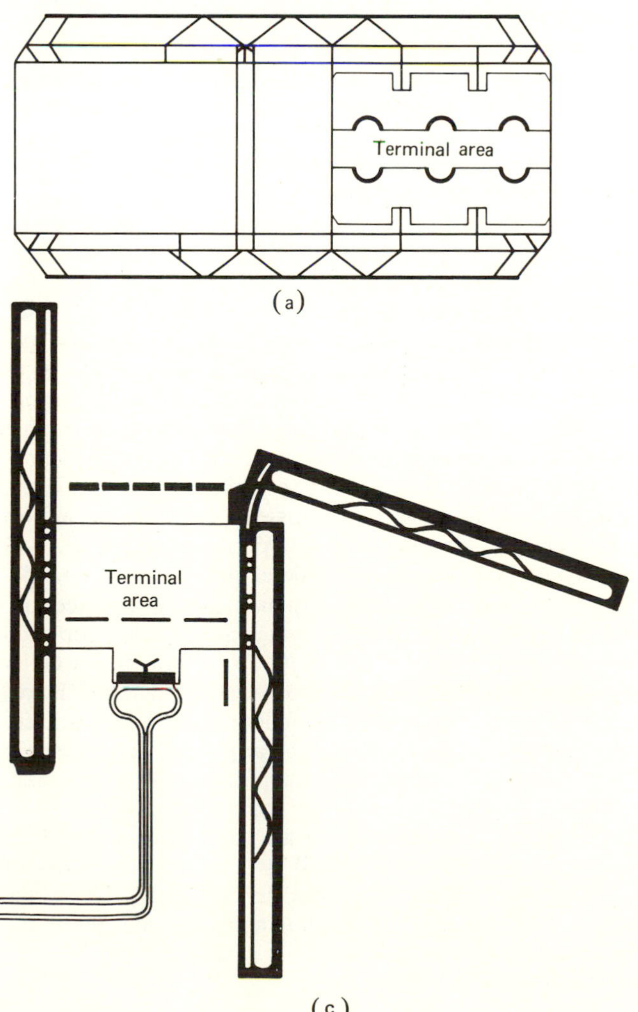

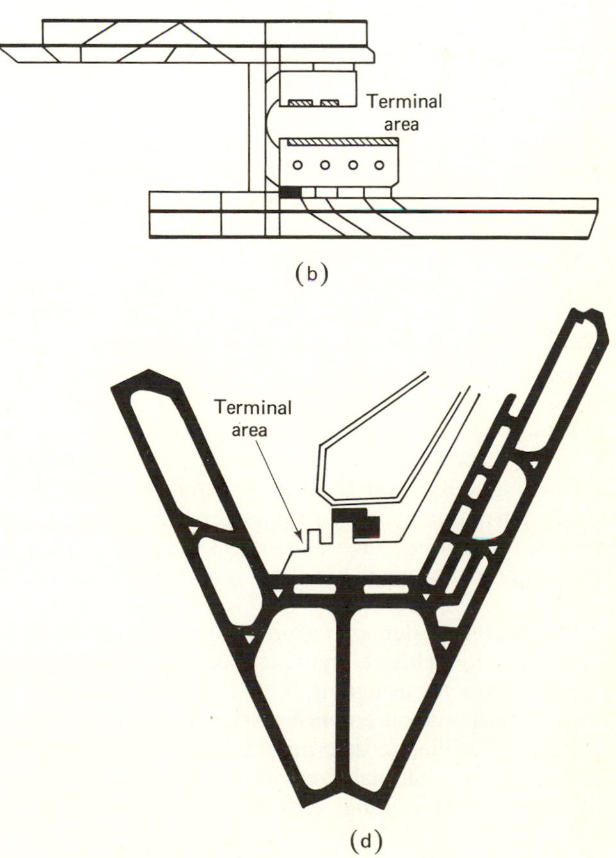

Figure 2.11. Selected airport configurations showing centralized terminal area locations: (a) Hamburg Kaltenkirchen Airport; (b) Los Angeles International Airport; (c) Dulles International Airport, Washington, D.C.; (d) airport at Wichita, Kansas. SOURCE: Robert Horonjeff, *Planning and Design of Airports,* 2nd ed., McGraw-Hill, New York, 1975, pp. 202–204.

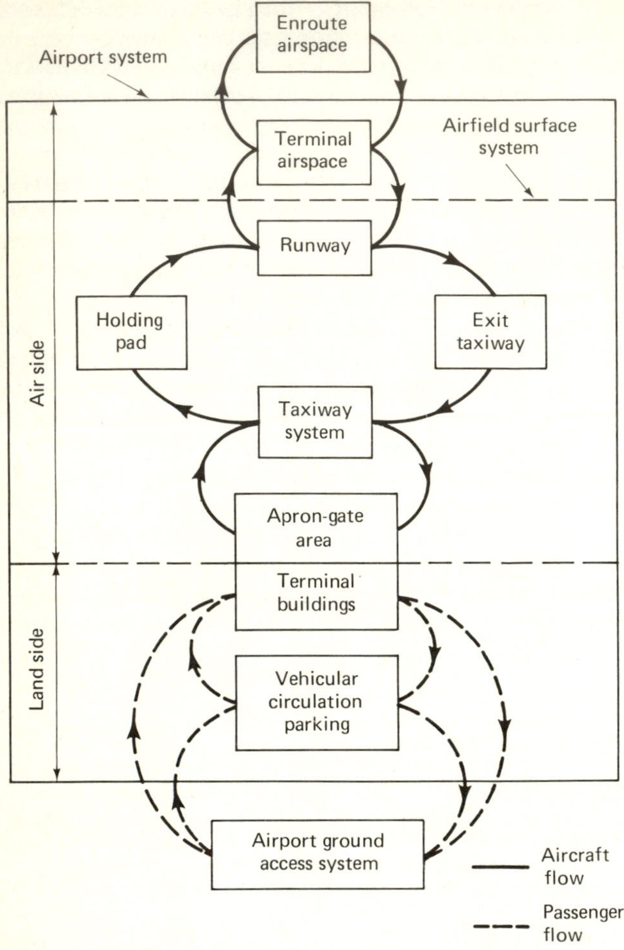

Figure 2.12. Airport landside and airside systems. SOURCE: Robert Horonjeff, *Planning and Design of Airports,* 2nd ed., McGraw-Hill, New York, 1975, p. 156.

providing relatively more space for passengers and ticketing activities, and about which waiting aircraft can park circularly. The remote satellite involves boarding from units separate from the terminal building proper, reached through tunnels under the parked aircraft. The mobile conveyance system (such as used at Washington's Dulles Airport) involves moving the fully processed passenger from terminal building to waiting aircraft by bus or mobile lounge. Each concept has advantages and disadvantages in terms of cost, speed of processing, perceived delay to passengers, and flexibility of accommodating to changes in aircraft size and maneuvering ability. For further information about the interior design of terminals after the basic concept of passenger processing is chosen, such as systems analyses applicable to passenger and baggage handling systems, see References 30–34.

Whereas the design of terminal buildings is often the province of the architect, transportation engineers are usually responsible for designing both airside and landside facilities. Transportation engineers specializing in traffic are particularly qualified to determine the layout and operation of ground access, internal circulation, and parking. Internal circulation systems should be designed to accomplish several principal objectives, among them the safe and convenient ingress and egress to the external highway system; the safe and convenient circulation of traffic among the various areas within the airport, segregating inbound and outbound passenger, visitor, employee, and air cargo traffic; and the expeditious movement of emergency vehicles and other special traffic. The design of roadways, intersections, and parking areas, as well as the installation and operation of necessary signing, marking, and other traffic control devices, should follow standard traffic engineering practices.

The total design of a modern airport is a complex undertaking, and many facets have been totally omitted here. Among them are the lighting, marking, and signing of airside facilities such as runways and taxiways, and the geometric and structural design of airport pavement and drainage facilities. Information on these and other factors of particular interest to traffic and transportation engineers can be found in various FAA Advisory Circulars, Regulations, and orders, and in the abundant technical literature on the subject.

Airport and aviation system financing

The primary benefits conferred by an effective air transportation system stem from its ability to move people and goods swiftly and safely from one place to another. The broad-ranging benefits include employment in the aviation industry itself, additional employment in the communities served by aviation because of their better access to the national and international transportation system, and the opportunities provided for opening up otherwise undevelopable areas to new growth.

In many nations such benefits have been deemed important enough to warrant a high level of central government funding assistance. Indeed, in most nations other than the United States, major airports are owned and operated by the central governments (rather than by cities, counties, or special authorities), which also own and operate the major airlines. Although the U.S. government is totally responsible for the national air traffic control system, it neither owns nor operates airlines or airports (excepting Washington's Dulles and National). The U.S. government does, however, provide considerable assistance for making airport improvements. The Federal-Aid Airport Program (FAAP) authorized FAA to provide federal grants for airport development and for advanced planning and engineering. Under FAAP, about $1.2 billion was awarded for such purposes from 1947 through 1970. FAAP was followed by the Airport Development Aid Program (ADAP), which provided an even higher level of federal funding assistance. FAA appropriations available for airport development for fiscal years 1976–1979, for example, totaled almost $2.2 billion.[39]

Only publicly owned airports are eligible for such federal funding assistance, and not all owners and operators of eligible airports apply for grants. In fact, only 3137 of the U.S. total of some 14,000 landing areas are included in the

[39] *FAA Statistical Handbook,* p. 4.

present NASP—as previously mentioned, a precondition for federal aid. As FAA puts it: "Federal and local interests in air transportation are not necessarily identical in all cases. The NASP contains those airports which . . . have been determined to have significant national interest. Not included in the system are airports which are considered to meet only local requirements."[40] In short, about three-fourths of all U.S. airport owners and operators must find nonfederal sources of funding.

ADAP provides federal participation in the amount of 75% of eligible project costs at large- and medium-size air carrier airports, and 90% for small air carrier airports and all publicly owned general aviation airports. Many states share with local governments or other sponsors the nonfederal matching share. Despite the relatively high level of federal aid, therefore, the overall cost of airport development in the United States is borne largely by state and local government. Of the $269 million reported as needed to implement the Pennsylvania Statewide Airport System Plan through 1995, for example, 45% is expected to come from local government, 8% from state government, and 18% from the private sector. Only 29% will come from the federal government.[41]

The need to find nonfederal funding sources is not an unfamiliar situation. In the United States, the ownership of airports in the early years of aviation was almost entirely in private hands. The depression of the 1920s and early 1930s caused widespread bankruptcies and fostered public ownership. Now, while about half of all U.S. airports are still privately owned, most airports with paved runways are publicly owned, the majority by municipalities. The next most common ownership is by counties, with the remainder owned and operated by special districts and authorities. These public owners raise necessary funds for airport operation and expansion in many ways, including general taxation, general obligation bonds, revenue bonds, landing fees, rentals, parking lot revenues, and leases to concessionnaires.

Airport user traffic characteristics

Relatively few traffic and transportation engineers have much concern for the planning, design, construction, and operation of the air transportation system per se. Many are very much concerned, however, with parking, internal circulation, and airport accessibility. The Institute of Transportation Engineers in 1976 published "Airport User Traffic Characteristics for Ground Transportation Planning" to provide information on the latter subjects.[42] Although some references are now somewhat dated, this report remains an excellent single-source summary, and has provided much of the material for the following part of this chapter.

[40]*Final Environmental Impact Statement,* p. III-20.

[41]*Pennsylvania Statewide Airport System Plan,* p. 15.

[42]*Airport User Traffic Characteristics for Ground Transportation Planning,* Institute of Transportation Engineers, Washington, D.C., 1976 (prepared by ITE Technical Committee 6F-Y, Richard I. Strickland, chairman).

Airport users

There are three basic groups of airport users: air travelers, visitors (including greeters and Godspeeders), and employees. The mix of these groups can vary considerably at individual airports, as shown by Table 2-16, and it is possible for visitors and employees to outnumber air passengers by a considerable margin. Ashford and Wright[43] have noted the dramatic dimensions of total activity at major airports: "In the early 1970s London's Heathrow and Chicago's O'Hare Airport employed more than 50,000 and 25,000 people, respectively. This is equivalent to the entire population of a substantial town and generates a number of work trips equivalent to a city of close to a quarter of a million persons. A study carried out by Los Angeles Airport planning department showed that the airport generated about 129,000 daily vehicular trips (in and out) on an average day in 1972, and a rise to 178,000 by 1980 was forecast. Clearly the design of a system of movement of this magnitude is a major consideration in the selection of a suitable airport site and in the overall planning and design of any facility on the chosen location."

TABLE 2–16
Estimated Airport Population—Average Day

	Air Passengers*	Employees†	Visitors‡	Total‡
Los Angeles Intl., 1972	49,000	37,000	43,000	129,000
Atlanta Intl., 1966–67	29,600	12,000	36,700	78,300
Chicago—O'Hare Intl., 1966–67	50,000	16,000	25,000	91,000
New York				
JFK Intl., 1973	58,600	27,500	n.a.	n.a.
La Guardia, 1973	38,400	5,200	n.a.	n.a.
Newark Intl., 1973	18,700	3,300	n.a.	n.a.
Washington—National, 1966–67	26,000	13,100	26,000	65,100

*Total enplaning and deplaning passengers.
†Data indicate employee counts on typical day. Total airport employee population may be considerably higher due to flight crew rotations, shifts, etc.
‡n.a., not available.

SOURCE: "Survey of Ground Access Problems at Airports," Transp. Eng. J., Proc. Am. Soc. Civ. Eng., Feb. 1969, and various airport reports.

Although relatively little information is available on visitors and employees, because they are seldom the focus of specific surveys, a great deal is known about air passengers. In addition to various on-board surveys of air passengers enplaning or deplaning at many different airports, Gallup surveys conducted for the Air Transport Association each year from 1971 through 1974, and again in 1977, provide excellent trend data.[44] Based on personal interviews conducted with a national sample of about 3000 adults 18 years and older, they show the propensity for air travel by different demographic groups. For example, more men (67%) than women (59%) had by 1977 flown commercially, and more whites (65%) than nonwhites (45%). The participation rate was greater for people in the middle years (age 25 to 49) than either the younger or older groups; greater in upper-

[43]ASHFORD AND WRIGHT, *Airport Engineering,* p. 346.

[44]"The Frequency of Flying among the General Public," results of a survey conducted by The Gallup Organization, Inc., for the Air Transport Association of America, Washington, D.C., Sept. 1977.

income than in lower-income groups; greater for people from cities than from small towns and rural areas; greater for people from the western states than from elsewhere in the country; and so on. The 1977 survey also showed that 63% of the noninstitutional population 18 and over had flown commercially at some time in their lives, the proportion increasing steadily since the 49% found in 1971. More than half who had flown during the last year made only one trip during that year; those who had made more than 12 trips during the last year numbered only 3% but made more than 28% of all trips. Business trips as a proportion of all trips increased from 46% in 1973 to 52% in 1977. The trip purposes and demographic characteristics of air travelers are significant considerations for planning, because they affect the traveler's choice of ground travel mode, parking requirements, and other factors relating to ground transportation.

Temporal variations in air travel

Air travel varies by month, day, and hour; by domestic and international operations; and by airport. August is normally the high month for domestic operations and February the low month. July is more often the high month for international operations; February and November are the low months. Figure 2.13 shows the monthly patterns of total passenger enplanements (both domestic and international) at four major U.S. airports during 1978. Figure 2.14 shows very much the same pattern for domestic enplanements at New York City's three major airports, but a much different, more peaked pattern for international enplanements. Particular note should be made that both domestic and international *aircraft* movements are far less peaked.

Daily variation in air passenger activity is relatively more dynamic:[45] "Friday is usually the peak activity day for domestic travel. At airports where international travel is significant, Saturday or Sunday often becomes the day of highest air passenger movement. . . . Peak day of the week may change during heaviest travel seasons, and the peak day may be moderated by economy travel rates available for travel only on certain days. High-day activity was found to exceed low-day activity by 20 to 70 percent, usually by less than 50 percent. The spreading of peak activity to two and three days of the week is notable at several airports during peak travel periods of the year."

Hourly variation in air passenger traffic also depends on a number of factors.[46] "Peak-hour enplaning and deplaning movements generally occur in the afternoon and are 9 to 14 percent of the day's activity. Hour of occurrence varies and can be influenced by such factors as airport location in the metropolitan area and its air travel time location with respect to other airports, especially overseas travel gateways. . . . In translating air travel peaks to ground transportation peaks, it is necessary to recognize lead-time and lag-time of ground transportation movements related to air travel movements." Figure 2.15 illustrates the common situation of both enplaning and deplaning passenger peaks occurring together in the late afternoon.

Ground transportation demands vary drastically with the proportions of "through" air passengers (those continuing on the same plane) and "transfer" air passengers (those continuing their trip on another plane). Obviously, these two groups need no ground transportation. Surveys from various years show that the proportions of such travelers at major airports can be very high: 73% at Atlanta International, 53% at Chicago O'Hare, and 46% at Greater Pittsburgh.[47]

In considering temporal variations in air passenger activity, mention should also be made of those major airports, such as Washington National, Chicago O'Hare, and New

[45]*Airport User Traffic Characteristics*, p. 5.

[46]Ibid., p. 5.

[47]Ibid., p. 9.

Figure 2.13. Monthly variation in total passenger emplanement at four U.S. airports, 1978. SOURCE: Air Transport Association.

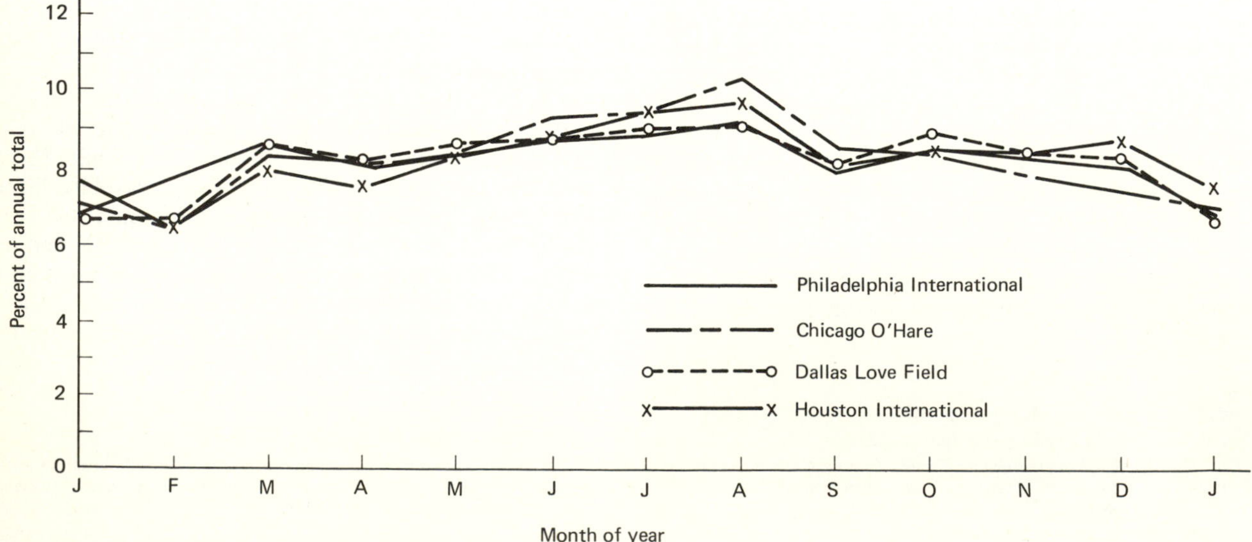

Transportation and Traffic Engineering Handbook 2nd Edition

Second Errata List*

PAGE	CORRECTION
168	Formula 6.5 should read: $$S = \frac{V^2}{30\,(f \pm g)} \text{ (U.S. units)} = \frac{V^2}{255\,(f \pm g)} \text{ (metric units)}$$
255	The author's correct title is **Consultant and Professor of Civil Engineering.**
262	The source for Table 10-10 should read: **Comprehensive urban area transportation planning studies.**
272	The small table at the end of the page should read:

Entering:	daily (avg)	18,000
	P.M. peak hour	1,600
	peak shopping hour	2,700
Exiting:	P.M. peak hour	1,800
	peak exit hour	3,200

PAGE	CORRECTION
299	The complete citation of the source for Fig. 10.24 is: **Abdus-Samad, U.R., and W.L. Grecco.** *Predicting Park 'n Ride Demand.* **Lafayette, IN: Purdue University Joint Highway Research Project Report 1972:50, 1972.**
350	In the source listing for Fig. 12.3, the author is **Richard M. Soberman**.
354	In footnote 16, the second author is **Anthony Kane**.
359	In the caption to Fig. 12.10, delete **Woonerf** after **SOURCE:**
364	In the source listing for Fig. 12.12, the second author is **Keith Gilbert**.
387	In the second line from the end of the page, **37 grams** should read **28 grams**.
388	In Fig. 13.4, the lowest curve should be labelled **1977** instead of **1979**.
	The last line on the page should read: **pre-1968 conditions.**
389	In Figures 13.5 and 13.6, the curves marked **1979** should be replaced by curves for **1977** to correspond to the text. The correct curves are shown below. The right-hand scale for Fig. 13.6 should show decimal numbers throughout.

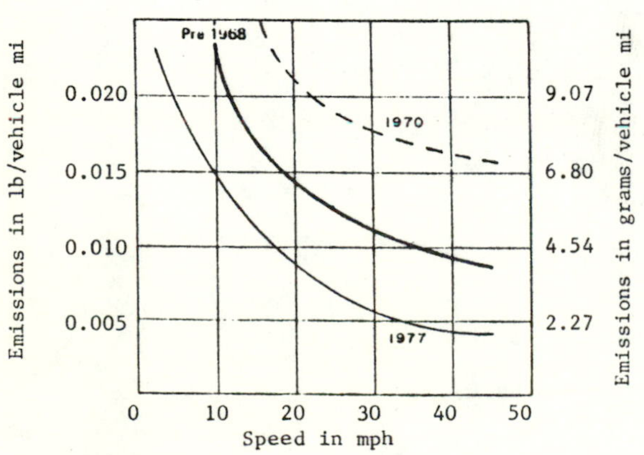

Figure 13.5

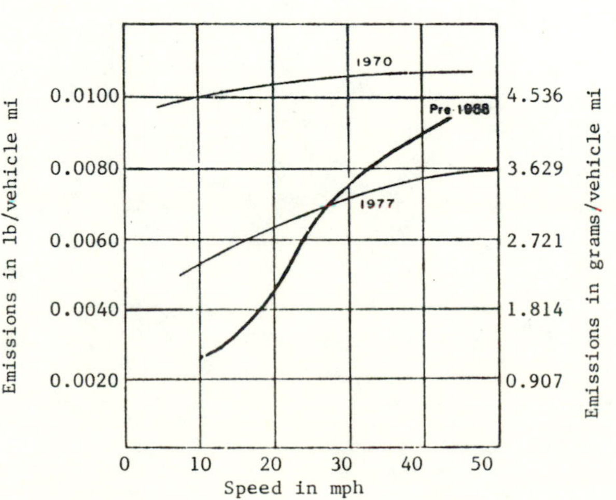

Figure 13.6

* For the first list, see **ITE Journal**, December 1982, page 7.

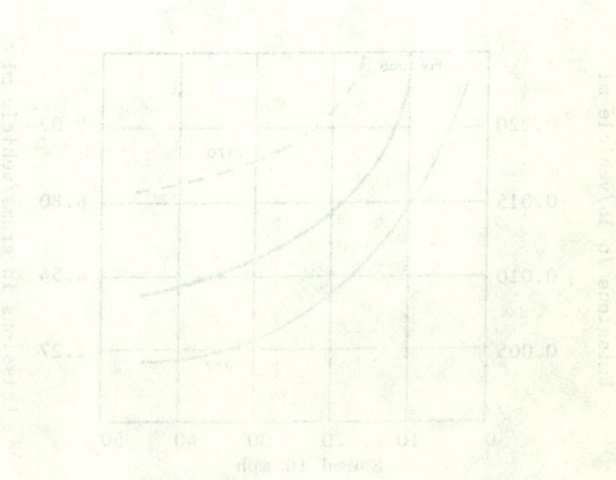

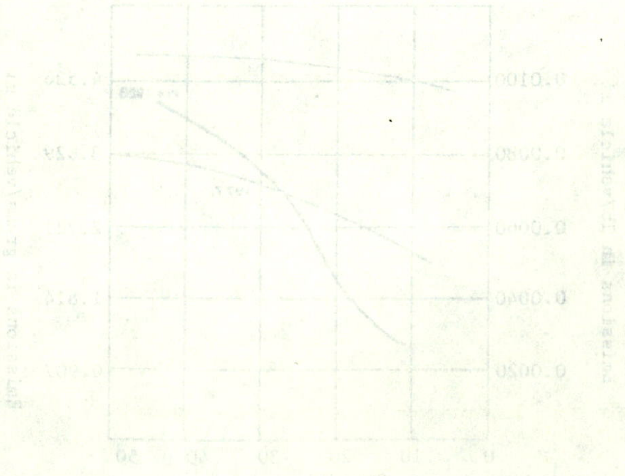

Transportation and Traffic Engineering Handbook 2nd Edition

The following is the errata to the first printing of the handbook.

PAGE	CORRECTION
13	In Fig. 1.11, the correct spelling is **Kuala Lumpur**.
96/7	In Table 4-30, entry for **China, Republic of,** change superscript *g* to *e*. In entry for **United Kingdom,** change superscripts *n,p* after both data items to *g,p*. In entry for **United States,** change superscript *c* after both data items to *q*.
99	In Table 4-32, first column, change **Dc** and **Ac** to **DC** and **AC** respectively.
162/3	In Formulae 6.1 through 6.4, each last term (after the second = sign) must be multiplied by 10. These terms therefore are $0.011AV^2$, $100\,Wg$, $280\,WA$, and $0.036RV$ respectively. — In the first definition below each of these formulae, the metric unit for resistance change **kg** to **Newton.**
168	In Table 6-47, columns 3 and 5, the subheadings should read **mph/s.**
174	In Table 6-59, change title to read: **Minimum Parking Dimensions by Vehicle Type.** — Change fourth entry in column 1 to read **Compact cars.** — Change fifth entry in column 1 to read **Vans, pickups.** — Insert a new line of data between the changed fourth and fifth lines, to read: **Standard cars 18 5.5 8 2.7 5 1.7.** — At the end of the footnote, add: **All heights of less than 8 ft are applicable only in special situations (lockers, split-level overhangs); otherwise normal ceiling heights designed for walking persons apply. See also pp. 649-650.**
203	In Fig. 7.9, change superscript after "Industrial employees' earnings" from **2** to **3.**
209	Change title of Table 8-1 to read: **Accidental Deaths in the United States, by Cause***
232/3	In Figs. 8.18 and 8.19, after the column headings **Dimensions** add **(m).** Delete the entries in parentheses in the first two entries of Fig. 8.18 and the first entry of Fig. 8.19.
268	In the caption to Fig. 10.3, change **drive** to **driver.**
270	The top curve in *all* four graphs of Fig. 10.4 should be labelled **3+.** — Delete the superscript 6 after SOURCE: in the caption to this figure.
293	In the legend for Fig. 10.19, change item 7 to read: **Edmonton, Alberta** and item 8 to read: **Manhattan (residential).**
296	In Fig. 10.20, the label for the curve should read: **Spaces per 1000 pop.**
467	Formula 15.150 should read: $d = \dfrac{\left(r - \dfrac{1}{2s}\right)^2}{2c(1-y)}$
506	In Fig.16.27 the line above the figure should read: **One-way—No Parking.**
510	In Fig. 16.31 the line above the figure should read: **Two-way—Parking.**
527	All entries in the last two columns of Table 17-1 should be raised one-half line.
538	In Fig. 17.12 the handwritten entry in the "Total" column on the line for the 32-second gap should be **4** instead of **5.**
551	The caption to Fig. 17.21 should start: **Seven of the most common types...**
559	In Fig. 18.3 the label for the 1979 point on the lower graph is **51.9.**
560	In Fig. 18.5, delete "Ref. data in table on page 59".
569	In Fig. 18.10, middle graph (Accidents) the 1979 point should have been plotted higher than the two adjacent points.
570	In Fig. 18.11 delete † and * where they appear on the horizontal scale.
606	In Table 19-17, column 3, the lowest line of the heading should read $\mathbf{R_1{-}R_2{-}R_3}$.
631	In Table 20-2, column 5 (Wattage Range), change the entry for high-pressure sodium to read **70-1000** from **175-1000.**
637	At the right of Fig. 20.7, in the first paragraph of the legend, insert a comma after "rural areas". In the fourth paragraph, the second and third sentences should read: **Greater than average cars and trucks. Expressways, freeways.**
650	In the table below Fig. 21.1, in the 75° column, change the fifth entry to **19.0** from **18.5**; in the 60° column, change the eighth entry to **52.5** from **53.2.**
654	In Fig. 21.4, Area/car for the lower diagram is **323** ft^2 instead of **365** ft^2.
659	The SOURCE for Table 21-9 is *Traffic Considerations for Special Events* (op. cit. as source for Table 21-8).
683	The SOURCE for Fig. 22.2 should read: Lindqvist, S. "The Traffic Zone System in the City Core of Gothenburg, Sweden," *Highway Research Record 474.* Washington, DC: Highway Research Board, 1973, p. 33,34.
754	In formula 24.6, the last term in the numerator should be an exponent of *e*; the *x* in the denominator should be lower case. The correct formula therefore reads: $P(N) = \sum_{x=0}^{N} \dfrac{(VC/3600)^x e^{\frac{-VC}{3600}}}{x!}$
756	At the end of the first paragraph in the second column add: **See Table 24-7.**
757	In the column heads of Table 24-7 the numbers in parentheses refer to the formulae on page 756.
777	The lower half of this page is Fig. 24.23. The missing caption reads: **Fig. 24.23 Sample output of CYCLES program.**

ITE Journal 52, No. 12 (Dec. 1982), p. 7

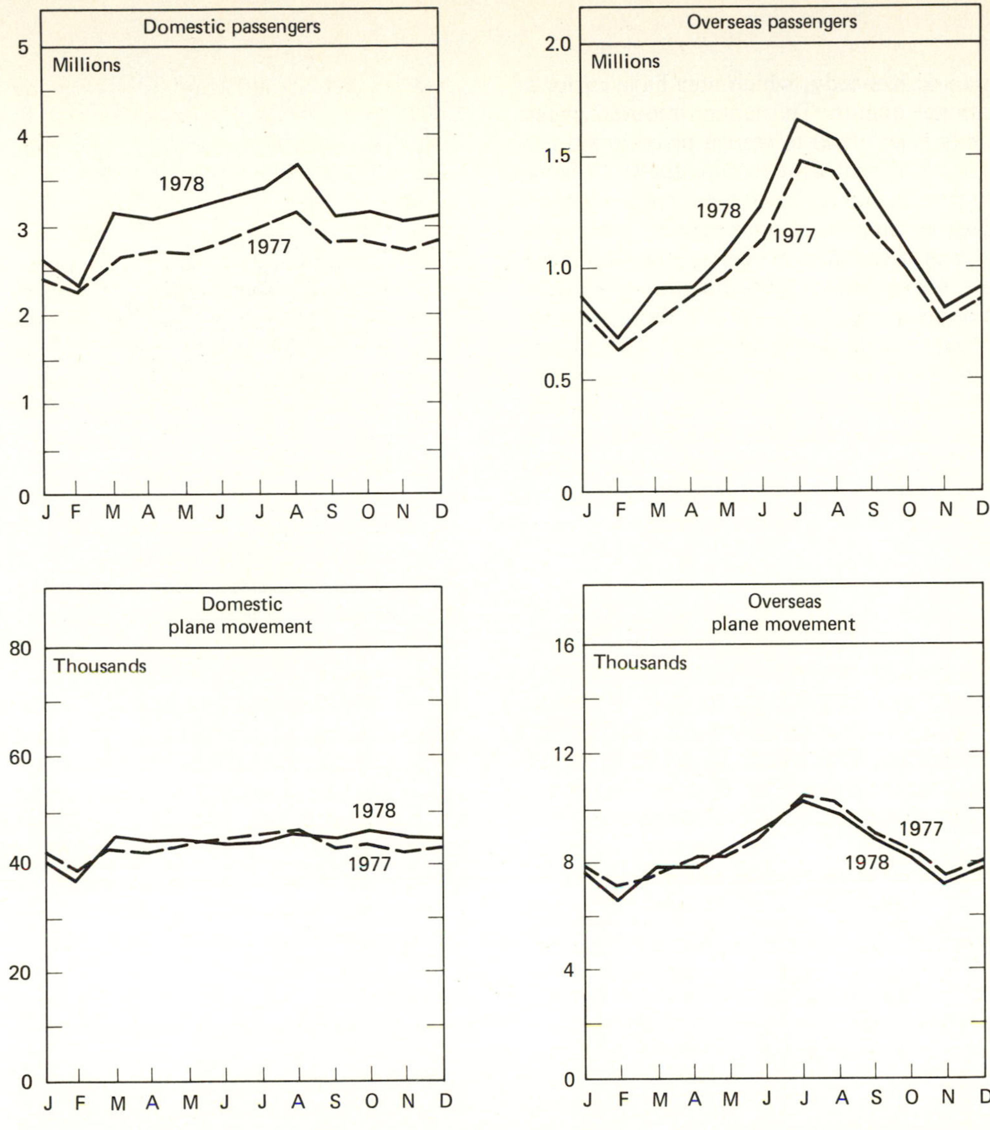

Figure 2.14. Monthly variations in passenger emplanements and plane movements at Newark, La Guardia, and Kennedy Airports (combined), 1978. SOURCE: *Monthly Airport Traffic,* Dec. 1978, prepared by The Aviation Economics Division, The Port Authority of New York and New Jersey.

Figure 2.15. Hourly air passenger activity at La Guardia Airport, August 1974 (Friday).

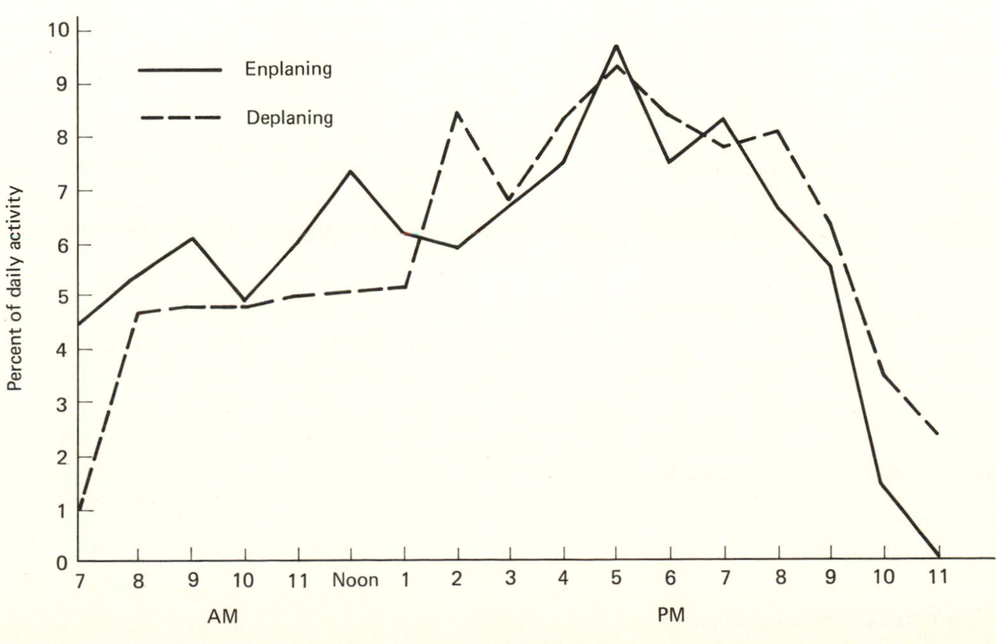

York's La Guardia and Kennedy, which may have curfews and hourly operational quotas. The latter, imposed under FAA's "high-density rule," tend to spread peak period activity. At Washington National, for example, the 1979 quota under IFR conditions was 40 scheduled air carriers, 12 general aviation, and 8 commuter operations per hour (the number of operations was sometimes higher under VFR conditions). Under such rules, Washington National experienced little or no peaking in aircraft operations during a typical day (see Figures 2.16 and 2.17). Since Washington National has relatively few through and transfer passengers, any peaking of air passenger activity was largely a function of variable load factors experienced during the day. FAA expects that over 20 airports are likely to increase their levels of activity to the point of requiring such restrictions within the next decade.

Ground transportation modes

A number of factors influence the air passenger's choice of ground transportation mode. Among them is when and where the airport trip is made. Air passengers come from all parts of a metropolitan area. The factors for allocating their origins or destinations within the area vary so much from city to city that no simple rule of thumb seems trust-

Figure 2.16. Scheduled aircraft operations by hour of arrival and departure, Washington National Airport, Friday, August 4, 1978. SOURCE: *Profiles of Scheduled Air Carrier Departure and Arrival Operations for Top 100 U.S. Airports,* U.S. Department of Transportation, Federal Aviation Administration, Office of Aviation Policy, Washington, D.C., Nov. 1978, p. 290.

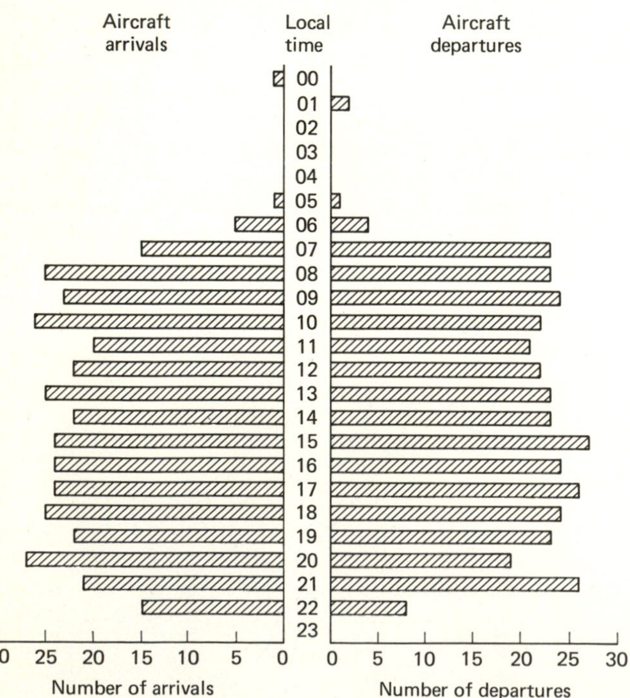

Source: Profiles of Scheduled Air Carrier Departure and Arrival Operations for Top 100 U.S. Airports, U.S. Department of Transportation, Federal Aviation Administration, Office of Aviation Policy, Washington D.C. November 1978, P. 290

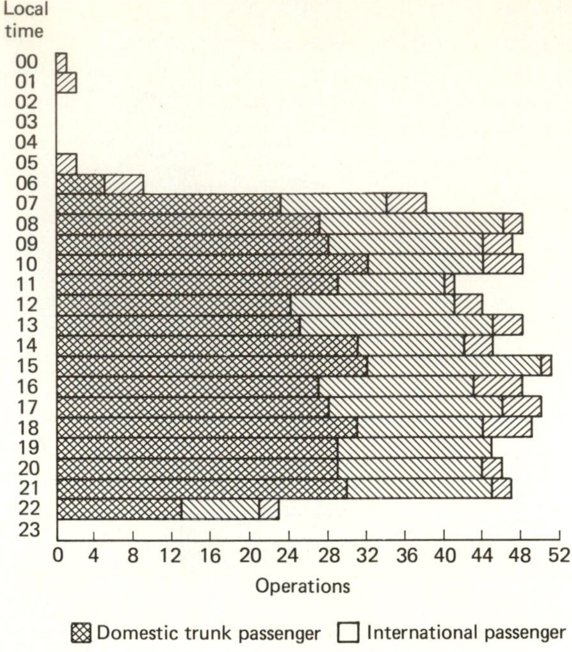

Source: Profiles of Scheduled Air Carrier Departure and Arrival Operations for Top 100 U.S. Airports, U.S. Department of Transportation, Federal Aviation Administration, Office of Aviation Policy, Washington D.C. November 1978, P. 291.

Figure 2.17. Scheduled operations by hour, by type of operation, Washington National Airport, Friday, August 4, 1978. SOURCE: *Profiles of Scheduled Air Carrier Departure and Arrival Operations for Top 100 U.S. Airports,* U.S. Department of Transportation, Federal Aviation Administration, Office of Aviation Policy, Washington, D.C., Nov. 1978, p. 291.

worthy. Various surveys have shown that the proportion of air passengers with central-business-district origins can vary from under 10% (Los Angeles) to as high as 45% (recorded at New York's La Guardia).[48] The proportion of origins within the remainder of the metropolitan area can range up to 80% (Los Angeles), and from beyond the metropolitan area, up to 64% (San Francisco) and higher. Such distributions have led many observers to the conclusion that highways will continue to be by far the dominant delivery system by which air passengers reach the airport. Although rapid transit has its proponents, especially for major metropolitan areas, de Neufville et al.[49] have commented that "An airport rapid-transit link would have to be part of a large network conveniently [located] to serve an appreciable portion of air passengers. Conversely, there are not enough air passengers to warrant a separate rapid transit link, much less a separate system."

Depending on the size and density of development of the urban area served, however, a significant number of air passengers may arrive by airport limousine, airport coach, public bus, or hotel courtesy van. Data needs for planning

[48]Ibid., p. 14.

[49]RICHARD DE NEUFVILLE, NIGEL M. WILSON, HARLEY L. MOORE III, VZI LANDAU, AND JOHN YANCY, "Airport and Air Service Access," Massachusetts Institute of Technology, School of Engineering, Cambridge, Mass. June 1972, p. 10.

airport access by such modes may be fairly extensive.[50] Although surveys at various airports for various years indicate that ground transport is still predominantly by automobile or taxi (observed range 73 to 95%), the public transport modes may accommodate nearly a fourth of all air passengers in some areas (observed range 5 to 27%).[51] There is considerable variation by airport, as well as by day and hour, but trend data suggest a continuing preference for private means of transportation. Typically, 90% of all airport employees commute by automobile. Accordingly, provisions for parking, rental car storage, and taxi loading areas are a major element of airport design (see Chapter 21).

This highly variable mix of ground traffic at any given airport calls for the utmost consideration in planning for internal circulation, designated loading areas, and short-term and long-term parking areas. In general, circulation is eased by a two-level approach: usually an upper-level roadway for departing passengers, and a lower-level roadway for arriving passengers, with parking at the lower, or ground level. Short-term parking near the terminal building may be kept fairly limited by providing much cheaper long-term parking some distance away and served by feeder bus or shuttle service. IATA's "Airport Terminals Reference Manual" stresses the need for survey data and offers various suggestions for planning the airport's public-use roads, among them:[52]

1. Roads should be designed to accommodate peak traffic volumes and have adequate expansion capability.
2. The link between the external public road system and the nonpublic or service road system must be planned carefully to avoid congestion or lack of future expansion capability in either system.
3. Main through roads should bypass the road running along the face of the terminal building.
4. Roads running along the terminal building face should be wide enough to permit the passing of stopped vehicles and have a minimum of three lanes.
5. There must be no uncontrolled access to runways or taxiways from public roads.
6. The public road system accommodating service vehicles should connect with the terminals only for delivery of goods at designated locations.
7. Roads connecting to cargo areas must have sufficient height clearances to accommodate existing and projected cargo-carrying vehicles.
8. On large airports, special lanes may be reserved for privileged traffic (e.g., public buses, taxis, etc.) and provision should be made for future transit systems.

Highway impact

Although airports may be among the largest single-site travel generators in major metropolitan areas, they account for only a fraction (usually less than 2%) of the total travel within those areas, so their measurable traffic impacts are usually limited to those parts of the highway network within a radius of a few miles.[53] The localized impact on roads providing direct airport access can, however, be quite severe, especially where total airport traffic discharges into an already busy urban expressway as at Chicago's O'Hare or New York's La Guardia and Kennedy Airports.

Fortunately, peak-period airport and peak-period non-airport related traffic on access roads do not necessarily coincide. Because of the peaking characteristics of employee trips, the afternoon airport traffic peak at many airports precedes that of the principal airport access road. But again, there are sharp variations from airport to airport:[54] "Generally, the greatest peaks are experienced in the afternoon outbound from the airport. This peak is determined by employee traffic and is therefore usually earlier (4 to 5 P.M.) than the city traffic peak. The inbound to the airport weekday peak is also employee determined and usually is an early (7 to 8 A.M.) hour, but may be an early afternoon hour as well. Atlanta and Los Angeles International Airport data show a late evening peak outbound movement, but it appears that sharply peaked employee traffic exited the airports via other access routes."

Summary

This chapter has attempted to provide the traffic and transportation engineer with the larger dimensions of what the civil air transportation system is all about. Certainly, it is a complex system, and difficult to summarize evenhandedly in a single chapter. Readers desiring more information will find it readily available, however, in the abundant aviation literature published by various levels of government and by aviation industry organizations. In the United States, immediate answers to many questions can be obtained simply by telephoning the nearest office of the Federal Aviation Administration, the state aeronautics commission or aviation section of the state department of transportation, city or county aviation department, or appropriate aviation industry organization. Counterpart sources are available in other countries. References for Further Reading list the more important publications that traffic and transportation engineers may wish to acquire for their personal bookshelves.

Acknowledgments

The writer takes this opportunity to express special appreciation to Gordon Y. Watada (AM. ITE) and Philip H. Agee (AM. ITE) of the Air Transport Association of America. They are directly and importantly involved in the aviation industry, and gave unstinting support to the preparation of this chapter.

[50] "Data Needs for Planning Airport Access by Public Transportation," Information Report by ITE Technical Council Committee 6A19, ITE *Journal*, Vol. 50., No. 10, Washington, D.C., October, 1980.

[51] de Neufville, et al, p. 10.

[52] *Airport Terminals Reference Manual*, p. 6.4.1.

[53] LOUIS E. KEEFER, *Urban Travel Patterns for Airports, Shopping Centers, and Industrial Plants*, National Cooperative Highway Research Program Report No. 24, Highway Research Board, Washington, D.C., 1966, p. 30.

[54] *Airport User Traffic Characteristics*, p. 45.

REFERENCES FOR FURTHER READING

Airport Planning and Design Reference Handbook, Air Transport Association of America, Airports and Materials Department, Washington, D.C., Jan. 1979. 47 pp., with appendices.

Airport Terminals Reference Manual, 6th ed., International Air Transport Association, Montreal, Canada, 1978.

Airport User Traffic Characteristics for Ground Transportation Planning, Institute of Transportation Engineers, Washington, D.C., 1976, 56 pp.

The Apron and Terminal Building Planning Report, prepared for the U.S. Department of Transportation, Federal Aviation Administration, Systems Research and Development Service by the Ralph M. Parsons Company, Washington, D.C., July 1975.

ASHFORD, NORMAN, AND PAUL H. WRIGHT, *Airport Engineering,* Wiley, New York, 1979. 530 pp.

HORONJEFF, ROBERT, *Planning and Design of Airports,* 2nd ed., McGraw-Hill, New York, 1975. 460 pp.

U.S. DEPARTMENT OF TRANSPORTATION, Federal Aviation Administration, *Advisory Circular Series* (on various topics, in several publications per year, many of which are available from the U.S. Government Printing Office, Washington, D.C.). See also *Guide to Federal Aviation Administration Publications,* published periodically by FAA.

3

WATER TRANSPORTATION

HAROLD KATZ,* *Professor of Economics and Assistant Head*
Department of Maritime Law and Economics
United States Merchant Marine Academy
Kings Point, New York

Waterborne transportation is one of the oldest forms of transportation in existence. The original settlement of the United States as well as its early commerce owes more to this form of transportation than any other. Ocean travel was of course the only mode of transportation available for colonization originally, and during colonial times, coastal and natural inland waterways provided the principal means for the movement of people and goods. Water transportation continued to play an important part in the development of the country into the nineteenth century as canals and other man-made waterways supplemented the natural ones. Although ultimately overshadowed by railroads for domestic commerce in the latter part of the nineteenth century and by air and other forms of surface transportation in the twentieth century, water transportation has continued to play an important role in the movement of certain types of commodities. And water is still the dominant form of transportation in international trade.

Water transportation has certain unique characteristics that make it suitable for some types of cargo. Most important, it is one of the most energy-efficient and therefore lowest-cost forms of transportation (Table 3-1). The amount of energy required to overcome friction and propel a vehicle in water is significantly less than is required on land and far less than is needed to keep a vehicle airborne. This advantage in efficiency is most pronounced for large vehicles designed to transport great quantities of materials. The disadvantage of water transportation is that it is slow. It is therefore most suitable for movement of low-value commodities in bulk such as ore and grain, and liquids such as petroleum. For commodities with a high value per unit of weight, such as manufactured goods, where speed of shipment is very important, other modes of transportation are more suitable. In domestic transportation, where surface methods are available without too much cost differential, the use of water is almost entirely limited to low-value bulk commodities. In international trade, where air is often the only alternative, water is the mode for all but the highest-value commodities.

Although there is some passenger traffic that moves by water, mainly in the ocean trade, by far the greatest importance of water is as a mover of cargo.

International and domestic water transportation are very different in more than one respect. First, the nature of the cargo carried is different in each case. Also, the fact that the waterways utilized have different characteristics leads to different types of vehicles as well. Next, the waterways themselves and their characteristics are described. Then the following sections cover the types of cargo and the vessels used for their transport. Descriptions of technology also include systems, terminal facilities, and interface with other modes. Finally, some economic characteristics and regulations of water transport are discussed.

Water transportation systems

International waterways

About 70% of international trade travels by water with the remainder moving either by air or by land between contiguous nations. The United States is a major shipper and receiver, but for economic reasons U.S. flag ships only carry a minority of the cargo moving between the United States and other countries and even less between other nations.

Total cargo can be divided into three main categories, each moving under a different type of service. Manufactured goods, metals, and other high-value commodities are generally transported by regularly scheduled liner service. Low-

*The views expressed in this chapter are solely those of the author and should not be taken to represent in any way those of the U.S. Maritime Administration.

TABLE 3-1
Comparative Costs of Transportation

Mode	Cents per Ton-Mile
Air	22.0
Truck	6.0 –8.0
Rail	0.5 –1.5
Pipeline	0.2 –0.5
Tug and barge	0.2 –0.3
Liner vessel	0.1 –0.4
Bulk carrier	0.03–0.06

SOURCE: DAVID BESS, *Marine Transportation* (Danville, Ill.: Interstate, 1976), p. 8.

TABLE 3-2
United States, Oceanborne International Trade* (long ton × 10^3)

	Total Trade	Liner	Nonliner	Tanker
By weight				
Total U.S. tonnage	775,332	47,754	289,024	438,554
U.S. flag tonnage	34,759	14,418	5,722	14,619
U.S. flag % of total	4.5	30.2	2.0	3.3
By value ($ × 10^6)				
Total dollars	171,178	82,261	42,714	46,203
U.S. flag share	28,046	25,245	1,190	1,611
U.S. flag % of total	16.4	30.7	2.8	3.5

*Data for 1977.

SOURCE: U.S. Oceanborne Foreign Trade Routes, U.S. Department of Commerce, Maritime Administration, Oct. 1979, pp. 3, 5, 7.

value bulk commodities are usually carried on individually chartered bulk carriers (referred to as nonliner service). Liquid products, primarily petroleum, are carried by tankers.

Table 3-2 shows the importance of each of these three categories of cargo by weight and by value for total U.S. trade and the percentage of this cargo carried on U.S. flag ships.

Cargo movements take place along specific trade routes. Some of these routes have been designated as essential to U.S. commerce by the government (Figure 3.1). Table 3-3 shows the amount of U.S. international trade with each of the major trading areas by type of service.

Domestic waterways

The term "domestic water transportation" covers three distinct transportation systems, each with its own characteristics and technology. Coastwise transportation in the United States refers to the movement of cargo along the Atlantic, Gulf, or Pacific coasts, and intercoastal is shipment between these coasts. Coastwise and intercoastal transportation is "deepwater" in the sense that it utilizes oceans and ocean ports. The vessels and terminals are very similar to those used in international shipping, the only major difference being that the terminals on both ends of the voyage are in the United States rather than only one as in international shipping. This distinction does lead to differences in the economic and regulatory environment applying to each type of shipping. For example, coastwise and intercoastal shipping is protected from foreign competition by law but international trade is not so protected.

TABLE 3-3
U.S. Oceanborne International Trade by Trading Area* (Tons × 10^3)

	Total	Liner	Nonliner	Tanker
U.S./Continental Europe	91,078	12,697	60,176	18,207
U.S./Far East	98,848	13,560	78,210	3,078
U.S./Mediterranean	103,911	4,880	33,654	65,377
U.S./Indian Ocean	79,768	4,864	6,255	68,648

*Data for 1977.

SOURCE: U.S. Oceanborne Foreign Trade Routes, U.S. Department of Commerce, Maritime Administration, Oct. 1979, pp. 11–14.

The second major domestic water transportation system in the United States is the Great Lakes together with certain connecting waterways such as the St. Lawrence Seaway. While shipping on the Great Lakes utilizes large vessels, they differ in important characteristics from ocean-going vessels due to the environment within which they operate. Fresh water has different effects on buoyancy, maintenance requirements, and even seasonal limitations on operations than does salt water.

The third domestic water transportation system consists of various inland and intracoastal waterways, rivers, canals, channels, and other natural and man-made mediums. This transportation system employs a technology and mode of conveyance vastly different from the others already described. Commodities are loaded onto barges and moved in groups by tugs or towboats. In the United States, the Mississippi River and its tributaries form the largest single part of this system.

A map showing the principal waterways of the United States is presented in Figure 3.2.

Vessel types and technology

International water transportation

Ocean transportation of general cargo by regularly scheduled liner service is provided by a number of different types of ships. Originally, such transportation was provided by "break-bulk" ships, with the cargo being loaded and unloaded in individual units or packages by cranes located on the decks of the ships.

During the last few decades most break-bulk vessels have been replaced by container ships. Cargo is loaded into large boxes, usually 20 or 40 ft long, sometimes at the origin or point of manufacture of the cargo and sometimes at the port. These containers may be transported over land by truck or railroad flatcar. At the port the containers are loaded onto the ship by special cranes and other equipment located on the dock. Container ships can be loaded and unloaded much faster than break-bulk ships because the cargo is moved in much larger units. There are also some partial containerships which carry break-bulk cargo as well as containers.

Another type of general cargo vessel is the barge carrier. In this case, individual barges will be loaded with cargo, perhaps at remote locations. The barges will then be taken aboard the mother ship for the ocean voyage. One advantage of this system is that the mother ship need not put in at all locations where there is cargo to be loaded.

Figure 3.1. U.S. essential international trade routes. SOURCE: *United States Oceanborne Foreign Trade Routes,* U.S. Department of Commerce, Maritime Administration, Washington, D.C., Mar. 1978, p. 361.

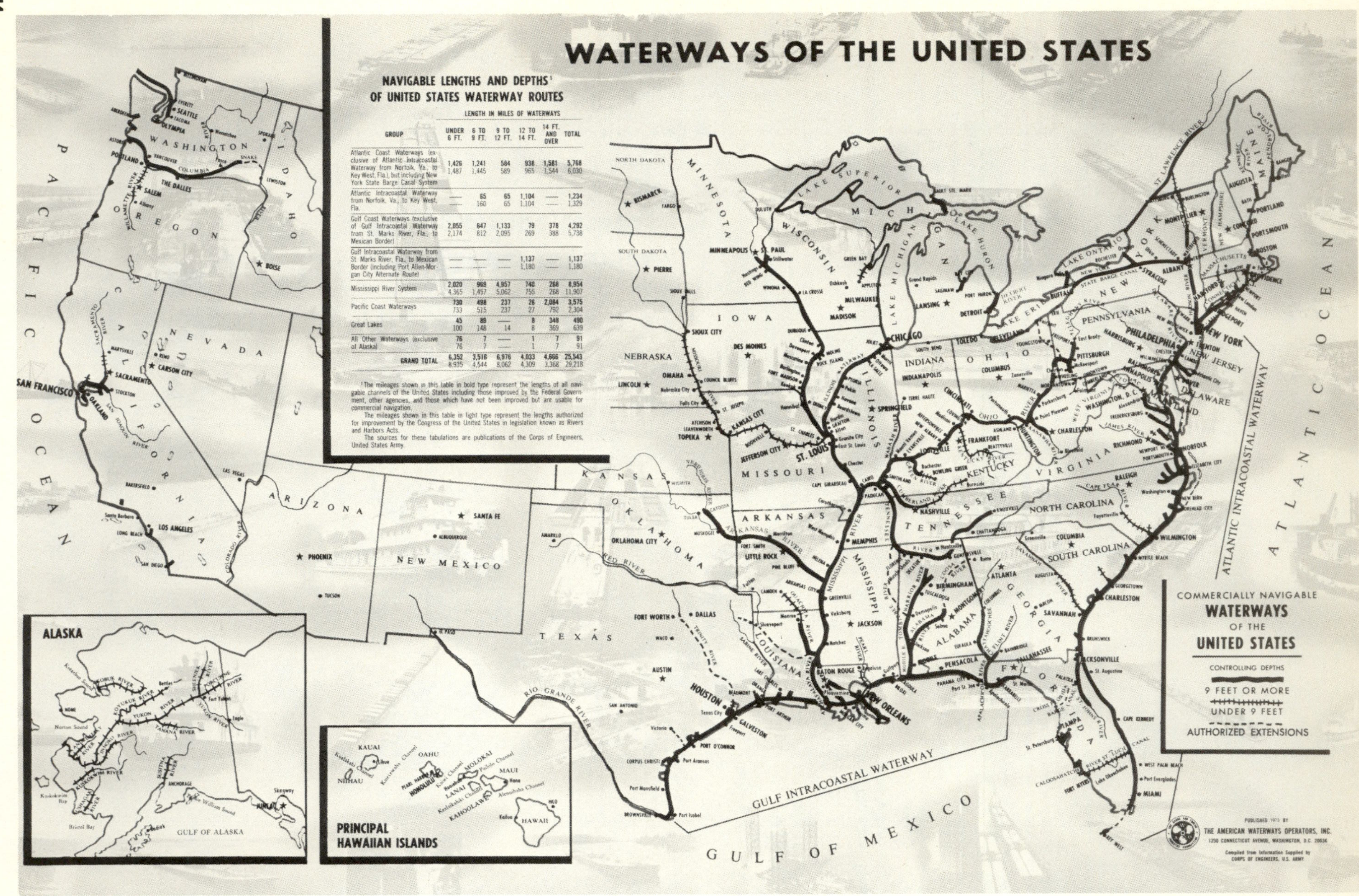

NAVIGABLE LENGTHS AND DEPTHS[1]
OF UNITED STATES WATERWAY ROUTES

GROUP	LENGTH IN MILES OF WATERWAYS					
	UNDER 6 FT.	6 TO 9 FT.	9 TO 12 FT.	12 TO 14 FT.	14 FT. AND OVER	TOTAL
Atlantic Coast Waterways (exclusive of Atlantic Intracoastal Waterway from Norfolk, Va., to Key West, Fla.), but including New York State Barge Canal System	**1,426** 1,487	**1,241** 1,445	**584** 589	**938** 965	**1,581** 1,544	**5,768** 6,030
Atlantic Intracoastal Waterway from Norfolk, Va., to Key West, Fla.	— —	**65** 160	**65** 65	**1,104** 1,104	— —	**1,234** 1,329
Gulf Coast Waterways (exclusive of Gulf Intracoastal Waterway from St. Marks River, Fla., to Mexican Border)	**2,055** 2,174	**647** 812	**1,133** 2,095	**79** 269	**378** 388	**4,292** 5,738
Gulf Intracoastal Waterway from St. Marks River, Fla., to Mexican Border (including Port Allen-Morgan City Alternate Route)	— —	— —	— —	**1,137** 1,180	— —	**1,137** 1,180
Mississippi River System	**2,020** 4,365	**969** 1,457	**4,957** 5,062	**740** 755	**268** 268	**8,954** 11,907
Pacific Coast Waterways	**730** 733	**498** 515	**237** 237	**26** 27	**2,084** 792	**3,575** 2,304
Great Lakes	**45** 100	**89** 148	— 14	**8** 8	**348** 369	**490** 639
All Other Waterways (exclusive of Alaska)	**76** 76	**7** 7	— —	**1** 1	**7** 7	**91** 91
GRAND TOTAL	**6,352** 8,935	**3,516** 4,544	**6,976** 8,062	**4,033** 4,309	**4,666** 3,368	**25,543** 29,218

[1] The mileages shown in this table in bold type represent the lengths of all navigable channels of the United States including those improved by the Federal Government, other agencies, and those which have not been improved but are usable for commercial navigation.

The mileages shown in this table in light type represent the lengths authorized for improvement by the Congress of the United States in legislation known as Rivers and Harbors Acts.

The sources for these tabulations are publications of the Corps of Engineers, United States Army.

Figure 3.2. Waterways of the United States. SOURCE: *Big Load Afloat: U.S. Domestic Water Transportation Resources,* American Waterways Operators, Inc., 1973, p. 159.

An additional type of general carrier is the roll on/roll off ship. This ship is designed so that bulky products such as vehicles or farm machinery can be driven directly onto the ship.

Some of the types of ships just described also carry passengers. If a ship carries 13 or more passengers, it will be known as a combination passenger and cargo ship.

Nonliner cargo is carried on bulk carriers. There are some designed to carry only dry bulk cargo, such as ore or grain. There are also combination carriers, which can carry bulk commodities and oil, ore and oil, as well as ore/bulk/oil carriers. The final category of ocean vessel is the tanker, designed to carry liquid in bulk, primarily oil.

In domestic water transportation large bulk carriers are also used to carry grain and ore on the Great Lakes. Ocean-going general cargo-type vessels are used in intercoastal transportation, while inland waterways generally make use of tugs and barges.

More detailed descriptions and examples of each of these types of vessels follows.

General cargo ships. The two main parts of a ship are the hull and the machinery. The hull is divided into holds, where the cargo is stored, sealed by hatch covers, and separated by decks. The machinery is contained in the engine room and includes engines that propel the ship and generators for lighting, refrigeration, and other electrical systems. Situated near the machinery will be the bridge for navigation and accommodations for the crew. Above deck will be the derricks for loading and unloading cargo. These derricks may be capable of lifting up to 50 tons each.

Diagrams of a typical break-bulk cargo ship are shown in Figure 3.3.

Container ships differ from break-bulk cargo ships in the arrangement of their cargo-carrying space. The holds are in the form of a series of specially designed cells where the containers are placed. There will also be provision for storage of some containers on deck. Rather than derricks aboard ship to load and unload cargo, container ships will generally rely on more elaborate shoreside equipment for this purpose. Large container ships may have a capacity of 2200 containers and a top speed of 16 to 22 knots.

In the past, most general cargo ships were propelled by steam engines fueled by oil. In recent years, however, the diesel engine has come into increasing use in spite of its slower speeds because of its lower fuel consumption. Today, more than half of the world fleet uses diesel engines. A typical container ship is pictured in Figure 3.4.

There are also a number of specialized types of ships operating in the liner trade. One is the barge-carrying vessel. Two examples of barge-carrying vessels are Lash and Seabee. Lash or lighter-aboard-ship vessels were first developed in the 1960s. A lash ship of 44,000 dead-weight tons (DWT) will carry 73 barges with a capacity of 27,000 tons of cargo. Traveling cranes located aboard the ship are used to load the barges. The barges can travel along inland waterways and obtain cargo at places too small to be serviced by ocean-going vessels. The mother ship can then be loaded in a minimum amount of time for its ocean voyage. Barge-carrying ships are shown in Figures 3.5 and 3.6.

A roll on/roll off type of vessel is designed so that passenger cars and commercial vehicles can be driven directly on or off the ship. One of its main advantages is fast turnaround time. It is capable of having 250 to 350 truck trailers driven on or off its huge deck in a few hours and moving them at 24 knots. Such vessels are very popular along short-haul routes such as to Puerto Rico and Hawaii, and in military service as fast logistics ships. Figure 3.7 shows a roll on/roll off type of ship.

Bulk carriers. The most prominent type of bulk carrier is the tanker, a very specialized type of ship designed to carry a liquid cargo, primarily petroleum, in bulk. Its hull is divided into numerous tanks each with a watertight hatch

Figure 3.3. Break-bulk cargo ship (23-knot). SOURCE: *Ship Design and Construction,* A.M. D'Arcangelo, ed., The Society of Naval Architects and Marine Engineers, New York, 1969.

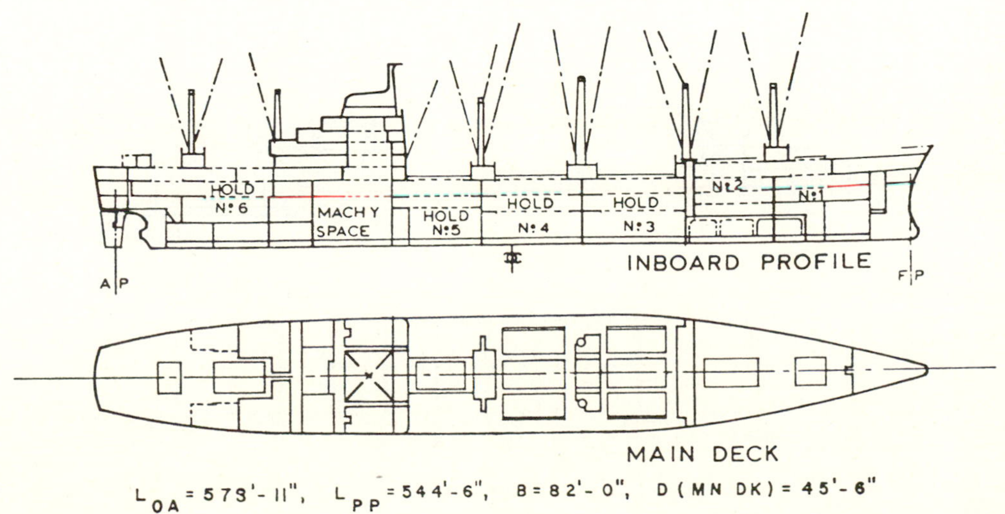

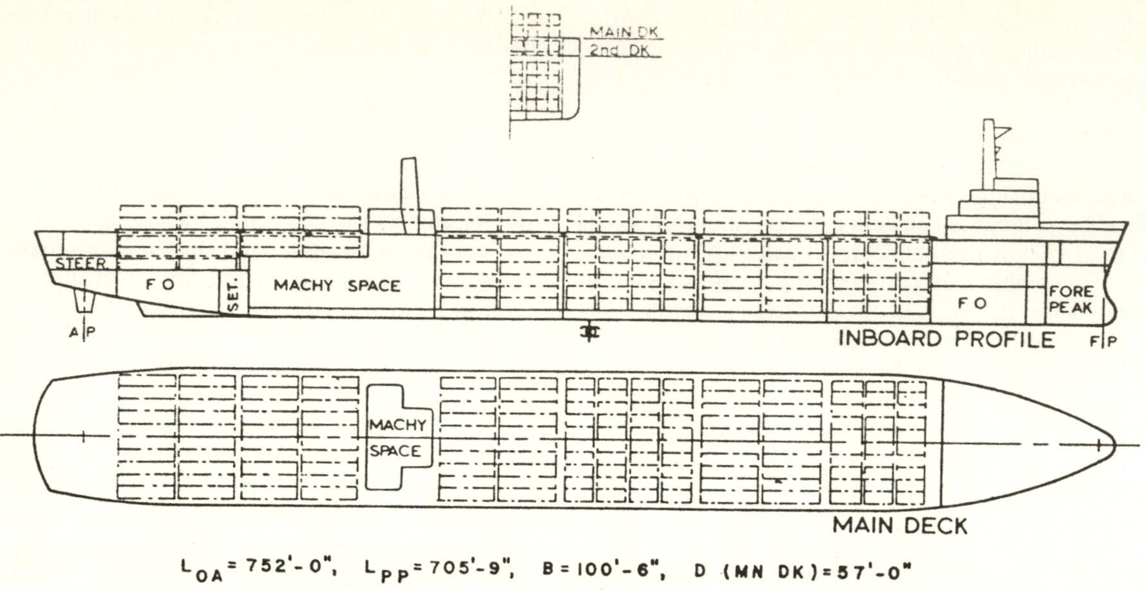

Figure 3.4. Container ship. SOURCE: *Ship Design and Construction,* A.M. D'Arcangelo, ed., The Society of Naval Architects and Marine Engineers, New York, 1969.

and ventilator. Pumping machinery and pipes for each tank are designed for quick loading and unloading of the liquid cargo.

The trend in recent years has been toward larger and larger tankers because of the economics of large-scale operation. In the 1960s the average tanker size was about 30,000 DWT. By 1974 there were more than 30 tankers in operation classified as Very Large Crude Carriers (VLCCs) with a size greater than 150,000 DWT. Some more recent vessels are classified as Ultra Large Crude Carriers (ULCCs) with a size greater than 500,000 DWT.

Although large tankers may be more economical movers of liquid cargo, they also create a series of problems that are difficult to solve. The drafts of these ships are too deep

Figure 3.5. Barge-carrying ship (gantry crane type). SOURCE: *Ship Design and Construction,* A.M. D'Arcangelo, ed., The Society of Naval Architects and Marine Engineers, New York, 1969.

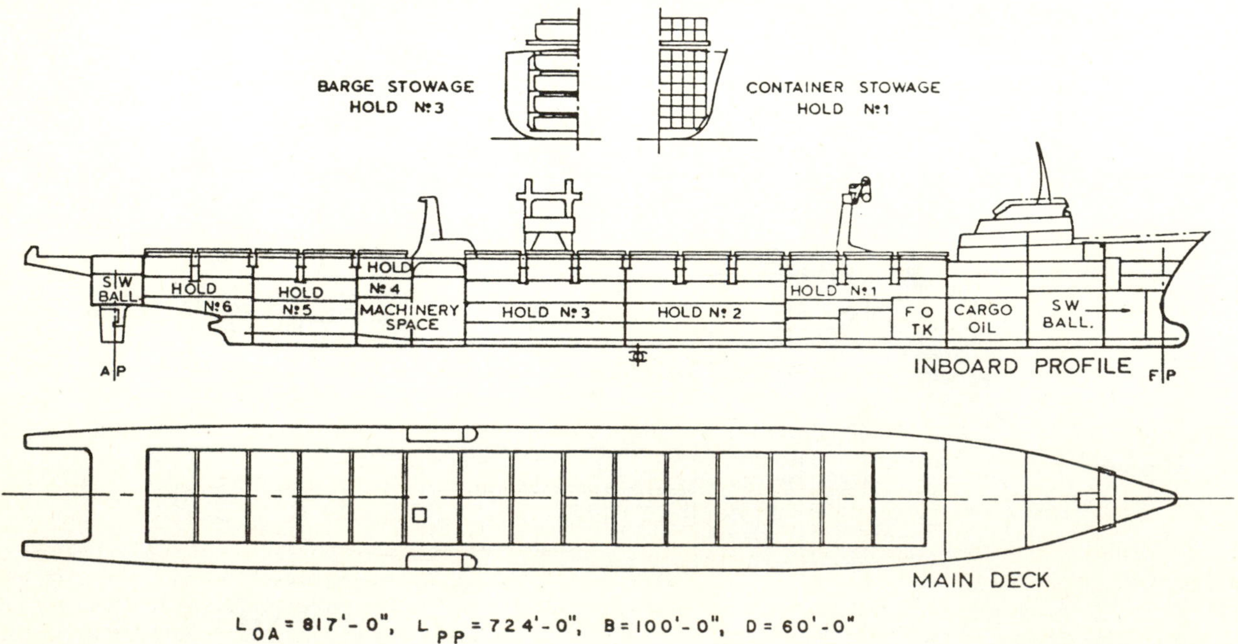

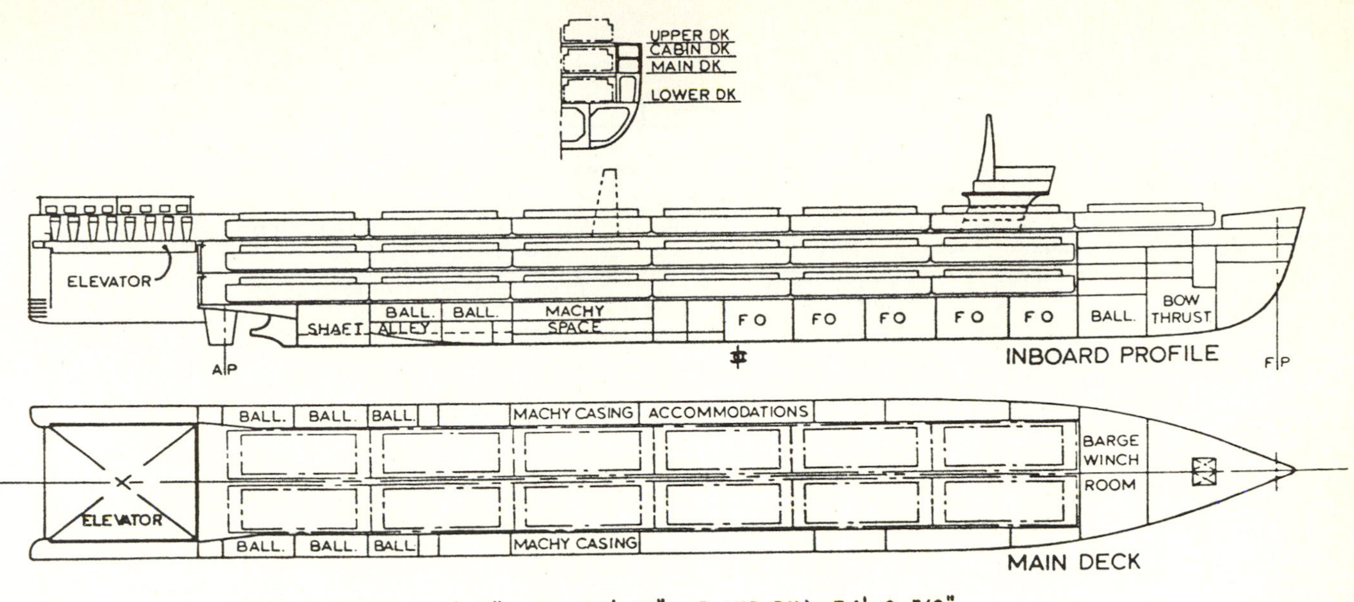

Figure 3.6. Barge-carrying ship (platform elevator type). SOURCE: *Ship Design and Construction,* A.M. D'Arcangelo, ed., The Society of Naval Architects and Marine Engineers, New York, 1969.

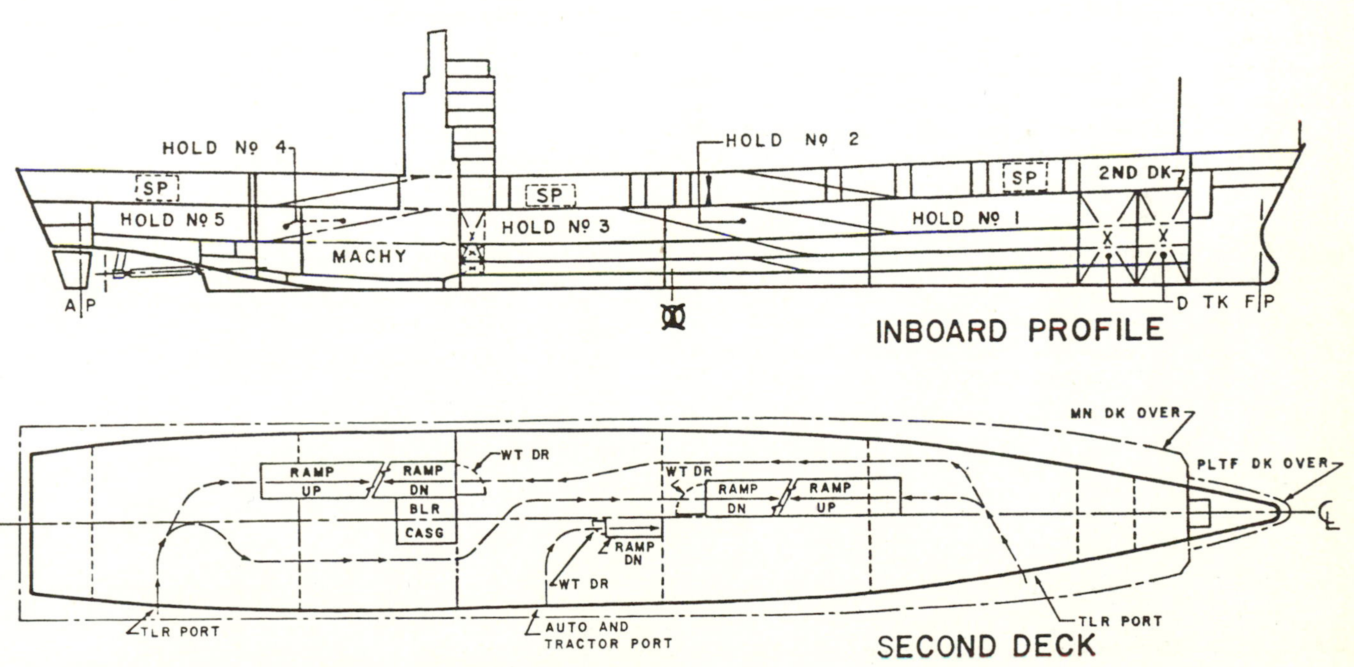

Figure 3.7. Roll-on/roll-off ship. SOURCE: *Ship Design and Construction,* A.M. D'Arcangelo, ed., The Society of Naval Architects and Marine Engineers, New York, 1969.

to allow them to pass through some canals, and they must therefore take longer routes to their destinations. Many world ports have harbors that are not deep enough to accommodate these vessels, so they must be unloaded at special offshore facilities and their contents must be brought ashore via pipelines or smaller vessels. Also, the weight of the cargo creates special demands in the construction of these ships to ensure their strength and prevent damage that

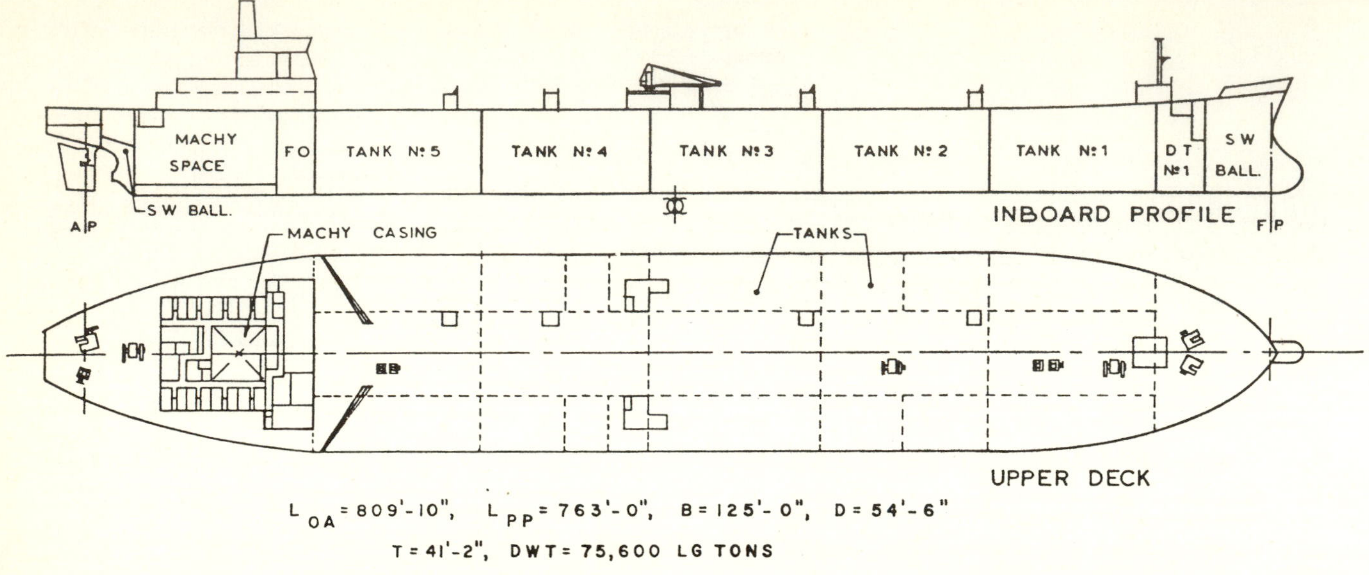

Figure 3.8. Tanker. SOURCE: *Ship Design and Construction,* A.M. D'Arcangelo, ed., The Society of Naval Architects and Marine Engineers, New York, 1969.

would result in oil spills. When such vessels are involved in accidents causing oil spills, the environmental and political repercussions are very severe. A typical tanker is illustrated in Figure 3.8.

Ships designed to carry dry cargoes in bulk have had a development parallel to that of tankers. Although a dry carrier "tramp"-type vessel may have averaged a 7000-ton capacity in 1957, average size was up to 18,000 tons by 1966 and ships are now being built with a capacity of 250,000 tons.

The ore carrier is one type of bulk carrier whose number has increased substantially in recent years. Cargo handling is generally by shoreside gear: conveyer belts (self-unloaders), magnetic loaders, or grabs. Some of these ships today may exceed 100,000 DWT in size. An ore carrier is shown in Figure 3.9.

The ore/bulk/oil ship is a multipurpose vessel designed to switch back and forth between the various types of cargo to take advantage of the cargo available. Although not as economical as a carrier dedicated solely to oil or dry bulk cargo, their versatility does make them advantageous in some trades.

A very specialized bulk carrier is that designed to carry liquefied natural gas. To keep the gas in liquid form, its temperature must be kept down to minus 161°C or minus 258°F. To do this, the gas is kept in internally insulated aluminum tanks and the holds that contain the tanks are insulated with panels of balsawood lined with plywood.

Figure 3.9. Ore carrier. SOURCE: *Ship Design and Construction,* A.M. D'Arcangelo, ed., The Society of Naval Architects and Marine Engineers, New York, 1969.

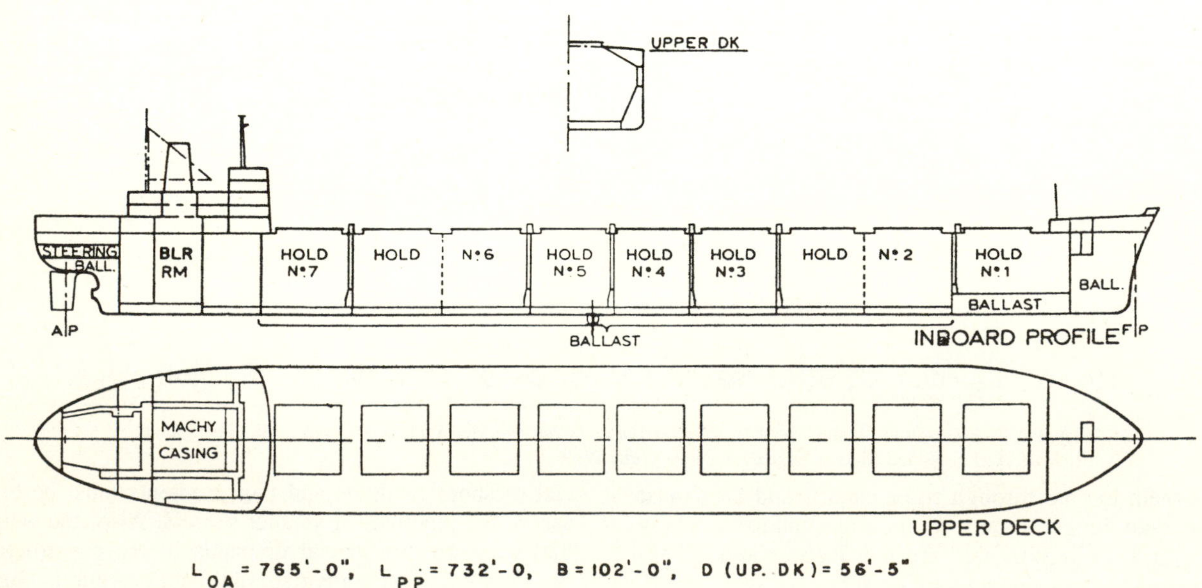

Table 3-4 shows comparable specifications for most of the ship types discussed.

Table 3-5 shows the composition of the U.S. ocean-going fleet by major ship type.

Domestic water transportation

Domestic water transportation can be divided into three distinct areas: coastwise, Great Lakes, and inland waterways. As far as technology is concerned, coastwise transportation involves the same conditions and utilizes the same vessels as deepwater ocean-going vessels, so no more need be said about this type in this section. Technology of the other two types of transportation are described next.

Great Lakes. Most of the cargo carried on the Great Lakes is low-value, bulk commodities such as coal, ores, and grain. This means that most of the vessels utilized will be bulk carriers. There are also some tankers and general cargo vessels as well.

The Great Lakes are a freshwater system and differ from saltwater ocean shipping in a number of respects. First, fresh water is lighter and therefore less buoyant than salt water. As a result, a ship carrying a given weight will sink lower into the water, therefore, Great Lakes ships have a smaller tonnage capacity than equivalent ocean-going vessels. One way that Great Lakes vessels partially compensate for this is to have flatter hulls that can carry more cargo with the same draft.

Another difference is that fresh water freezes in very cold weather, so that the Great Lakes are usually navigable only about 9 months out of the year. Fresh water also produces less barnacle formation and less rusting, so equipment tends to last longer. Tides are lower and more regular, and waves are smaller, so ships can be lower and shallower.

Some ocean-going vessels enter the Great Lakes through the St. Lawrence Seaway, but the size of the locks limit the dimension of the ships that can traverse this channel. When it was originally opened in 1959, the St. Lawrence Seaway provided openings 800 ft long, 80 ft wide, with 27 ft minimum depth and 120 ft overhead clearance. This limited ships to 730 ft in length, 75 ft in beam, 25.5 ft in draft, and under 120 ft in mast height. This means that some ships which exceed these dimensions cannot utilize the seaway.

The Great Lakes border on Canada as well as the United States, of course, and are therefore not serviced exclusively by American flag vessels as is the case on inland waterways. In addition to Canadian carriers, some European companies also provide service through the seaway to Great Lakes ports. Table 3-6 shows the composition of U.S. flag ships on the Great Lakes.

Inland waterways. The mode of transportation for freight moving on inland waterways is vastly different from that previously described for ocean and Great Lakes transport. Since the standard depth for an inland channel is 9 ft, most freight is carried on unmanned shallow-draft barges moved in groups by towing vessels.

There are two main types of towing systems. Towboats are designed to push barges ahead of them while a tug will generally pull the barges on a hawser. Generally, the type of water determines which method is used. On most inland waterways that are relatively calm and protected by sur-

TABLE 3–4
General Characteristics of Merchant Ships

	Ship Type					
	Comb. Passenger–Reefer–Container Ship	Container Ship	Barge-Carrying Ship (Gantry)	Barge-Carrying Ship (Platform Elevator)	Tanker	Ore Carrier
Length overall (L_{OA}) (ft-in.)	546′8″	752′0″	820′0″	873′9″	809′10″	765′0″
Length between perpendiculars (L_{PP}) (ft-in.)	508′6″	705′9″	724′0″	719′11″	763′0″	732′0″
Beam (B) (ft-in.)	79′0″	100′6″	100′0″	105′10″	125′0″	102′0″
Depth to strength deck (D_3) (ft-in.)	48′1″	57′0″	60′0″	74′9″	54′6″	56′5″
Draft (maximum), molded (T) (ft-in.)	29′1″	29′0″	28′0″	32′9″	41′2″	38′3″
Displacement, total (tons)	19,799	33,924	32,800	44,500	90,400	66,200
Deadweight, total (tons)	9,234	19,524	18,760	26,600	75,600	51,050
Deadweight/displacement	0.466	0.575	0.572	0.598	0.836	0.771
Capacities						
Number of passengers	119	0	4	4	0	0
Number of crew	121	40	39	40	28	47
Cargo (bale) (ft^3)						
Dry	625,000	1200 20-ft centers	1,208,235	1,421,000	641,000 bbl	2,150,000
Refrigerated	19,355	—	—	—	—	—
Stores, etc. (net) (ft^3)						
Dry	5,194	—	—	—	—	—
Refrigerated	5,955	—	3125.4	—	—	—
Machinery particulars						
Type of machinery	Steam turbine	Steam turbine	Steam turbine	Steam turbine	Steam turbine	Steam turbine
Shp, maximum and rpm, ABS	19,800, 119	60,000, 135	32,000, 105	36,000, 90	19,000, 80	22,000, 112
Number of boilers	Two	Two	Two	Two	One	Two
Steam conditions (psi)/(gauge) temp. (°F)	600/900	850/950	850/950	850/950	600/860	825/950
Speed						
On trial at 80% of normal shp at max draft (knots)	20	27	22.5	20.2	16.8	16.5

SOURCE: AMELIO M. D'ARCANGELO, Ed, *Ship Design and Construction,* Society of Naval Architects and Marine Engineers, 1969, p. 30.

TABLE 3–5
U.S. Oceangoing Merchant Marine, January 1, 1980* (Tons × 10³)†

	Privately Owned			Government Owned			Total		
	Number of Ships	Gross Tons	Dead-Weight Tons	Number of Ships	Gross Tons	Dead-Weight Tons	Number of Ships	Gross Tons	Dead-Weight Tons
Active fleet									
Combination pass./cargo	4	45	37	5	56	38	9	101	75
Freighters	106	1,181	1,471	18	158	198	124	1,339	1,669
Bulk carriers	16	284	508	0	0	0	16	284	508
Tankers	256	7,220	13,898	2	14	21	258	7,234	13,919
Intermodal	133	2,629	2,680	2	36	39	135	2,664	2,719
Tug/barge	8	126	242	0	0	0	8	126	242
LNG	10	792	699	0	0	0	10	792	699
Total	533	12,276	19,534	27	264	296	560	12,541	19,830
Inactive fleet									
Combination pass./cargo	2	30	13	57	612	373	59	641	386
Freighters	11	126	140	190	1,516	2,057	201	1,642	2,197
Bulk carriers	2	25	40	0	0	0	2	25	40
Tankers	13	324	626	20	190	301	33	514	927
Intermodal	7	103	116	2	15	22	9	117	138
Tug/barge	0	0	0	0	0	0	0	0	0
LNG	1	83	72	0	0	0	1	83	72
Total	36	691	1,006	269‡	2,332	2,754	305	3,023	3,760
Total American Flag									
Combination pass./cargo	6	74	50	62	668	411	68	743	461
Freighters	117	1,307	1,611	208	1,674	2,255	325	2,982	3,866
Bulk carriers	18	309	548	0	0	0	18	309	548
Tankers	269	7,544	14,523	22	204	322	291	7,748	14,845
Intermodal	140	2,731	2,796	4	50	61	144	2,782	2,857
Tug/barge	8	126	242	0	0	0	8	126	242
LNG	11	876	770	0	0	0	11	876	770
Total	569	12,967	20,540	296§	2,596	3,049	865	15,564	23,589

*Tonnage figures are preliminary and may not be additive due to rounding.
†Data supplied by Division of Trade Studies and Statistics.
‡Includes 21 vessels in bareboat charter and 10 vessels in custody of other agencies.
§National Defense Reserve Fleet consists of 262 ships, of which 22 are scrap candidates.

SOURCE: U.S. Department of Commerce, Maritime Administration, *U.S. Merchant Marine Data Sheet,* February 5, 1980, p. 2.

TABLE 3–6
U.S. Great Lakes Fleet as of January 1, 1980* (Self-Propelled Vessels of 1000 Gross Registered Tons and Over)†

	Vessels	Gross Registered Tons	Estimated Dead Weight
Total	158	1,675,963	2,969,918
Bulk carriers	142	1,603,720	2,929,275
Tankers	6	29,326	40,643
Others	10‡	42,917	n.a.§

*All tonnage figures are preliminary and may not be additive due to rounding.
†Does not include vessels in the Russian grain trade.
‡Includes railroad car ferries and auto ferries.
§n.a., not available.

SOURCE: U.S. Department of Commerce, Maritime Administration, *U.S. Merchant Marine Data Sheet* February 5, 1980, p. 3.

rounding land masses, the towboat is used for push-towing operations. For this mode of transport the barges are tied rigidly together by steel cables or ropes to form a single unit which is lashed solidly against the boat's towing knees. The bow is square, to fit right up against the barges.

Towboats may have very powerful engines, sometimes as much as 6000 hp, and may push as many as 40 barges lashed together containing 40,000 to 50,000 tons of cargo. Average speed will be about 6 mph with some high-speed integrated tows making as much as 15 mph. Towboats are the main form of transport on major rivers and their tributaries, such as the lower Mississippi and the Missouri.

On waterways where wind, wave, and tidal actions would break up a tow of vessels lashed rigidly together, the pull-towing method is used instead. This is true on the open water of the intra-coastal canals, in the Gulf of Mexico, and off the Atlantic and Pacific coasts. The tug differs greatly from the towboat. It has a shaped bow, sits higher in the water, and in general is designed to operate as an ocean-going vessel rather than to operate in calm, protected water, as does the tow. A tugboat can only transport a severely limited number of barges and will not have the same control over their movement as the towboat because of the more flexible attachment between the tug and its barges. Figure 3.10 indicates the shape and characteristics of some typical sizes of towboats and tugboats.

Barges can vary in size and shape depending on the type of cargo they are meant to carry or their mode of use. Barges designed for single tow with a rake at both ends would create a great deal of drag and therefore loss of efficiency

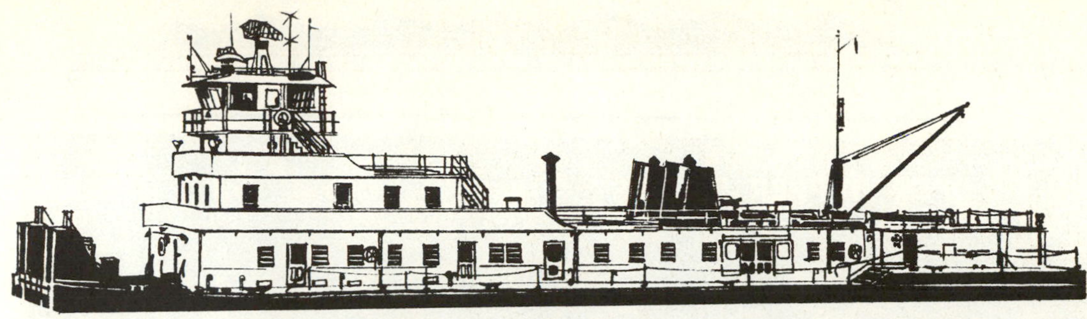

TOWBOATS	Length Feet	Breadth Feet	Draft Feet	Horsepower
	117	30	7.6	1000 to 2000
	142	34	8	2000 to 4000
	160	40	8.6	4000 to 6000

TUGBOATS	Length Feet	Breadth Feet	Draft Feet	Horsepower
	65 to 80	21 to 23	8	350 to 650
	90	24	10 to 11	800 to 1200
	95 to 105	25 to 30	12 to 14	1200 to 3500
	125 to 150	30 to 34	14 to 15	2000 to 4500

Figure 3.10. Tugs and towboats. SOURCE: *Big Load Afloat: U.S. Domestic Water Transportation Resources,* American Waterways Operators, Inc., 1973, p. 12.

when towed in multiple units. Barges with both ends square designed for joining with other barges can reduce water resistance to almost that of an equivalent single vessel but are very unwieldy to handle when separate. Many barges, therefore, represent a compromise, with a rake on one end and square on the other. These barges create about 18% less resistance at ordinary towing speeds when assembled into towing units and can also be handled singly without difficulty.

The most versatile, least costly, and most numerous type is the hopper barge which is basically a double-skinned open-top box capable of carrying any solid commodity in bulk or package. Hopper barges may be either open or covered. Open hopper barges are for carrying commodities such as coal or ore, whereas covered barges will carry grain, coffee, soybeans, paper, and other commodities that must be kept dry.

Tank barges are used for the transportation of liquid commodities. They are of three types: single-skinned for ordinary liquids, double-skinned for poisonous or other hazardous liquids, and barges with independent cylindrical tanks for liquids under pressure. Other types of barges are deck barges for transporting machinery, vehicles, and heavy equipment; carfloats for railroad cars; and dump scows. Illustrations and characteristics of the types of barges described are shown in Figures 3.11 and 3.12.

The size and composition of the inland waterway fleet and its distribution by area is shown in Table 3-7.

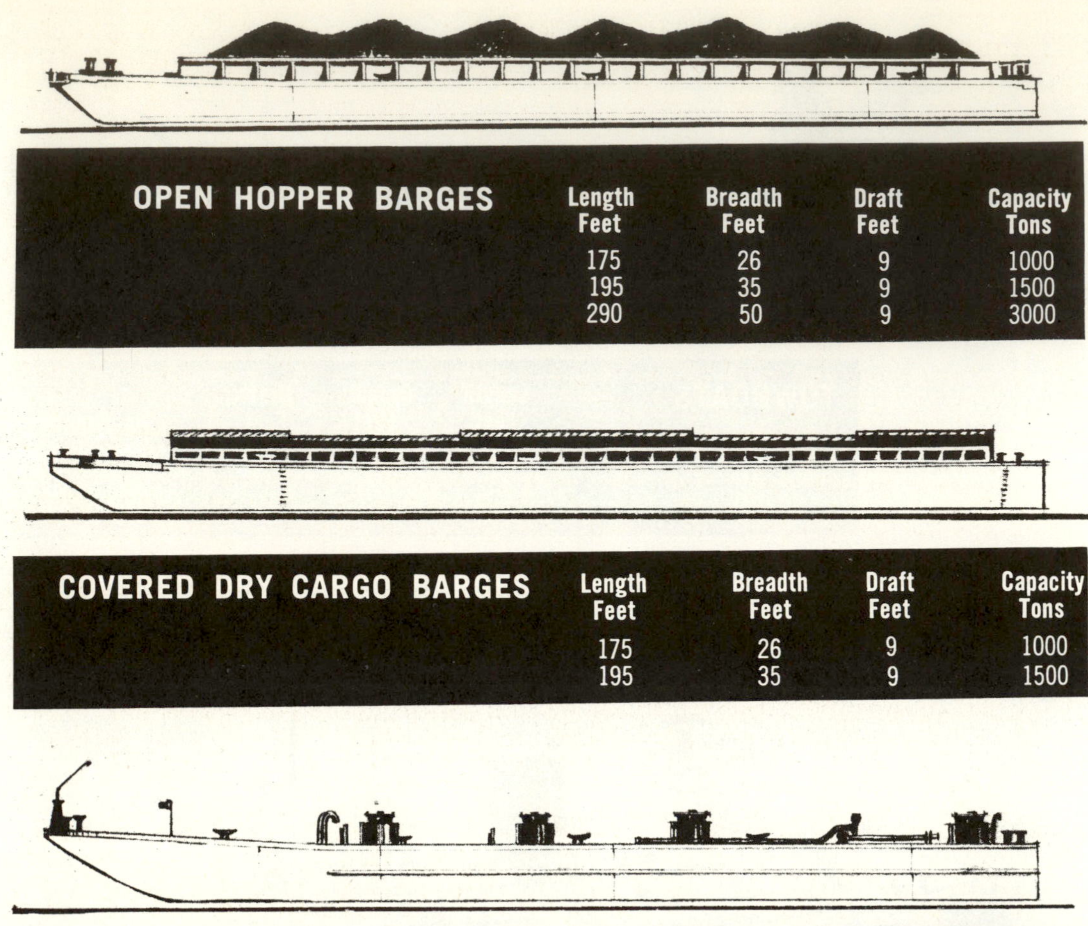

OPEN HOPPER BARGES	Length Feet	Breadth Feet	Draft Feet	Capacity Tons
	175	26	9	1000
	195	35	9	1500
	290	50	9	3000

COVERED DRY CARGO BARGES	Length Feet	Breadth Feet	Draft Feet	Capacity Tons
	175	26	9	1000
	195	35	9	1500

LIQUID CARGO (TANK) BARGES	Length Feet	Breadth Feet	Draft Feet	Capacity Tons	Capacity Gallons*
	175	26	9	1000	302,000
	195	35	9	1500	454,000
	290	50	9	3000	907,200

* Based on an average of 7.2 barrels per ton and 42 gallons per barrel.

Figure 3.11. Barges. SOURCE: *Big Load Afloat: U.S. Domestic Water Transportation Resources,* American Waterways Operators, Inc., 1973, p. 27.

Cargo patterns and characteristics

In general, many of the same commodities move in ocean transportation as in domestic water transportation although in different proportions. Petroleum products make up the bulk of cargo in both areas. Low-grade bulk commodities such as coal, sand, and gravel move to a greater extent on low-cost barges in domestic trade, while higher-value commodities that may move overland domestically by surface transportation are more likely to be shipped by boat in intercontinental trade. Table 3-8 lists the principal commodities involved in waterborne commerce in both cases.

International trade

The three types of service in international trade—liner, nonliner, and tanker—have already been described. The different nature of the commodities carried on each service can be seen from the following figures. When measured by weight, liners account for only 4% of U.S. oceanborne imports and 11.5% of oceanborne exports. By dollar value, however, liner service accounts for 42% of our oceanborne imports and 57.7% of our oceanborne exports. This can be seen in Table 3-9.

The explanation for the difference between weight and dollar value is that liners generally transport higher-value manufactured goods, while nonliner and tanker services are involved with lower-valued dry and liquid bulk commodities. Table 3-10 shows the composition of liner cargo as well as the percent accounted for by U.S. flag ships.

Table 3-11 shows the same data for nonliner cargo. In value terms, this category represents the least significant part of U.S. waterborne commerce, consisting mainly of raw material imports such as ore and wood and grain or cereal exports.

DECK BARGES	Length Feet	Breadth Feet	Draft Feet	Capacity Tons
	110	26	6	350
	130	30	7	900
	195	35	8	1200

CARFLOATS				Capacity Railroad Cars
	257	40	10	10
	366	36	10	19

SCOWS	Length Feet	Breadth Feet	Draft Feet	Capacity Tons
	90	30	9	350
	120	38	11	1000
	130	40	12	1350

Figure 3.12. Specialized barges. SOURCE: *Big Load Afloat: U.S. Domestic Water Transportation Resources,* American Waterways Operators, Inc., 1973, p. 31.

TABLE 3–7

Number of Towing Vessels and Barges of the United States Operated for the Transportation of Freight as of January 1, 1976

Types of Vessels	Mississippi River System and the Gulf Intracoastal Waterway	Atlantic, Gulf, and Pacific Coasts	Great Lakes System	Total
Self-propelled				
Towboats and tugs				
Number of vessels	2,541	1,554	145	4,240*
Horsepower	3,574,850	1,860,026	151,015	5,585,891
Non-self-propelled				
Dry cargo barges and scows				
Number of vessels	18,049	4,917	198	23,164
Cargo capacity (net tons)	22,255,050	4,565,839	314,447	27,135,336
Tank barges				
Number of vessels	2,979	577	67	3,623
Cargo capacity (net tons)	6,295,236	2,056,813	157,967	8,510,016
Total non-self-propelled				
Number of vessels	21,028	5,494	265	26,787
Cargo capacity (net tons)	28,550,286	6,622,652	472,414	35,645,352

*U.S. Coast Guard reports; as of January 1, 1976, 6548 documented vessels of the United States having a towing service. The vessels reported by the Corps of Engineers are those used only in the performance of transportation services.

SOURCE: Corps of Engineers, U.S. Army. Reproduced in: 1976 Inland Waterborne Commerce Statistics p 2, American Waterways Operators Inc.

TABLE 3-8
Principal Commodities in U.S. Waterborne Commerce, 1976 and 1977 (%)

Commodity	Total Commerce 1976	Total Commerce 1977	International Commerce 1976	International Commerce 1977	Domestic Commerce 1976	Domestic Commerce 1977
Petroleum and products	45.9	49.1	48.8	52.6	43.5	46.0
Coal and coke	12.5	12.3	8.5	8.0	15.9	16.3
Iron ore and iron and steel	8.5	6.6	8.6	7.2	8.4	6.0
Sand, gravel, and stone	5.7	5.4	1.6	1.6	9.3	9.0
Grains	6.9	6.2	10.2	8.7	4.0	3.8
Logs and lumber	2.9	2.8	3.4	3.2	2.5	2.4
Chemicals	5.0	5.3	4.6	4.9	5.4	5.7
Seashells	0.7	0.6	0.0	0.0	1.2	1.2
All other commodities	11.9	11.7	14.3	13.8	9.8	9.6
Total	100.0	100.0	100.0	100.0	100.0	100.0

SOURCE: Department of the Army, Corps of Engineers, *Waterborne Commerce of the United States*. Calendar Year 1977. Part 5 (National Summaries), p. 3.

TABLE 3-9
Percent of U.S. Oceanborne Trade

	Imports By Weight	Imports By Value	Exports By Weight	Exports By Value
Liner	4.0	42.0	11.5	57.7
Nonliner	19.7	17.8	80.3	36.3
Tanker	76.3	40.2	8.1	6.0

SOURCE: Compiled From Data in: U.S. Department of Commerce, Maritime Administration, *United States Oceanborne Foreign Trade Routes,* October 1979.

Table 3-12 shows the data for tanker imports dominated by petroleum and exports dominated by chemicals.

Another way to examine U.S. oceanborne foreign trade is by region. The map of essential foreign trade routes (Figure 3.1) indicates that U.S. trade can be broken down into trade with a few major geographical areas. Tables 3-13 to 3-16 show U.S. trade broken down this way, with the volume indicated for each type of service.

Domestic trade

More than half of the domestic waterborne commerce of the United States, 54%, moves on internal waterways. Twenty-five percent is coastwise traffic and 11% is on the Great Lakes. The remainder is local traffic. Of the internal water traffic, the largest part is carried on the Mississippi River system. Freight on inland waterways breaks down as shown in Table 3-17.

The principal commodities carried on inland waterways are shown in Table 3-18.

Container systems

In international water transportation, the most noteworthy development of the last few decades has been the development and progressive dominance of this mode of transportation by what has come to be known as containerization. This development has affected not only ocean carriers but port and terminal technology and the interface with other modes and systems of domestic transportation as well. This

TABLE 3-10
Liner Imports and Exports, Top 10 Commodity Groups in Descending Tonnage Order, 1977

Commodity Code	Commodity	Tons (long tons × 10^3) U.S. Flag	Tons Total	Tons U.S. %	Value ($ × 10^6) U.S. Flag	Value Total	Value U.S. %
Imports							
67	Iron and steel	644	2,712	24	303	1,296	23
71	Machinery—nonelectric	329	1,410	23	1,147	4,664	25
69	Manufactures of metal	387	1,323	29	473	1,663	28
07	Coffee, cocoa, tea, and spices	445	1,261	35	1,687	4,839	35
11	Alcoholic and nonalcoholic beverages	530	1,224	43	428	983	44
05	Fruit and vegetables	482	1,193	40	362	797	45
73	Transport equipment	249	1,103	23	579	3,391	17
66	Nonmetallic mineral manufacturing	281	865	32	265	822	32
89	Misc. manufactured articles	295	850	35	1,122	3,508	32
68	Nonferrous metals	207	832	25	324	1,642	20
	All Other	2,994	9,101	33	7,232	20,533	35
	Total	6,846	21,874	31	13,922	44,138	32
Exports							
04	Cereals and cereal preparations	1,354	2,753	49	303	641	47
25	Pulp and wastepaper	514	2,182	24	154	602	26
71	Machinery—nonelectric	523	1,790	29	2,766	9,363	30
64	Paper, paperboard, and manufactures	367	1,477	25	230	809	28
51	Chemical elements and compounds	441	1,399	32	602	2,116	28
26	Textile fibers and waste	292	1,280	23	367	1,605	23
05	Fruit and vegetables	441	1,274	35	238	841	28
27	Crude fertilizer and mineral	218	1,182	18	34	154	22
24	Wood, lumber, and cork	178	947	19	46	251	18
58	Synthetic resins and plastic materials	346	916	38	399	1,053	38
	All Other	2,898	10,680	27	6,184	20,688	30
	Total	7,572	25,880	29	11,323	38,123	30

SOURCE: *Ibid.* (Same reference as table 3-9), p. 4.

TABLE 3–11
Nonliner Imports and Exports, Top 10 Commodity Groups in Descending Tonnage Order, 1977

Commodity Code	Commodity	Tons (long tons × 10^3)			Value ($ × 10^6)		
		U.S. Flag	Total	U.S. %	U.S. Flag	Total	U.S. %
Imports							
28	Metalliferous ore and scraps	972	49,644	2	34	1,560	2
27	Crude fertilizer and mineral	145	15,777	1	7	147	5
67	Iron and steel	46	13,979	*	22	4,095	1
06	Sugar, molasses, and honey	10	5,063	*	1	994	*
51	Chemical elements and compounds	155	3,779	4	25	547	5
24	Wood, lumber, and cork	508	3,153	16	99	468	21
32	Coal, coke, and briquets	0	3,136	0	0	170	0
05	Fruit and vegetables	39	2,316	2	12	373	3
73	Transport equipment	3	1,869	*	8	6,133	*
66	Nonmetallic mineral manufacturing	72	1,836	4	5	69	7
	All Other	491	7,674	6	261	4,145	6
	Total	2,441	108,226	2	474	18,701	2
Exports							
04	Cereals and cereal preparations	2,307	67,647	3	285	7,540	4
32	Coal, coke, and briquets	334	33,605	1	18	1,947	1
22	Oilseeds, oilnuts, and kernels	88	15,633	1	21	4,294	*
27	Crude fertilizer and mineral	95	15,356	1	2	467	*
24	Wood, lumber, and cork	67	11,858	1	10	1,065	1
63	Wood and cork manufactures	5	7,401	*	4	281	1
08	Feedstuffs for animals	6	6,808	*	2	1,225	*
56	Manuf. fertilizers and materials	65	5,990	1	9	612	1
33	Petroleum and petroleum products	8	5,234	*	3	358	1
28	Metalliferous ores and scraps	1	4,830	*	†	407	*
	All Other	305	6,436	5	362	5,817	6
	Total	3,281	180,798	2	716	24,013	3

*Less than 0.5%.
†Less than $500,000.

SOURCE: *Ibid.*, p. 6.

TABLE 3–12
Tanker Imports and Exports, Top 10 Commodity Groups in Descending Tonnage Order, 1977

Commodity Code	Commodity	Tons (long tons × 10^3)			Value ($ × 10^6)		
		U.S. Flag	Total	U.S. %	U.S. Flag	Total	U.S. %
Imports							
33	Petroleum and petroleum products	12,017	411,716	3	1,190	40,926	3
51	Chemical elements and compounds	14	2,174	1	3	441	1
34	Gas—natural and manufactured	6	2,039	*	1	206	*
06	Sugar, molasses, and honey	86	1,824	5	4	89	4
42	Vegetable oils and fats	5	765	1	†	402	*
56	Manuf. fertilizer and materials	7	761	1	1	64	1
27	Crude fertilizer and minerals	83	708	12	4	36	12
32	Coal, coke, and briquets	0	66	0	0	3	0
52	Mineral tar, tar oils, and chemicals	0	65	0	0	10	0
28	Metalliferous ore and scraps	0	48	0	0	6	0
	All Other	1	127	1	3	79	4
	Total	12,219	420,293	3	1,206	42,262	3
Exports							
51	Chemical elements and compounds	35	5,874	1	7	1,339	1
04	Cereals and cereal preparations	2,145	3,381	63	270	411	66
33	Petroleum and petroleum products	142	3,358	4	14	334	4
42	Vegetable oils and fats	60	1,046	6	43	615	7
41	Animal oils and fats	‡	955	*	†	400	*
34	Gas—natural and manufactured	0	856	0	0	84	0
27	Crude fertilizers and minerals	‡	838	*	†	34	*
22	Oilseeds, oilnuts, and kernels	0	572	0	0	167	0
52	Mineral tar, tar oils, and chemicals	0	365	0	0	61	0
59	Chemical products, and materials	‡	330	*	1	208	*
	All Other	18	686	3	70	288	24
	Total	2,400	18,261	13	405	3,941	10

*Less than 0.5%.
†Less than $500,000.
‡Less than 500 tons.

SOURCE: *Ibid.*, p. 8.

TABLE 3–13
U.S. Oceanborne International Trade between the United States and Continental Europe, Scandinavia, and the Baltic, 1976–1977 (Tons × 10^3)

	Imports		Exports		Total	
	1977	1976	1977	1976	1977	1976
Liner	6,336	6,099	6,359	7,263	12,695	13,362
Nonliner	10,777	6,798	49,399	57,023	60,176	63,821
Tanker	12,254	8,018	5,953	6,308	18,207	14,326
Total	29,317	20,901	61,711	70,586	91,078	91,487

SOURCE: *Ibid.*, p. 11.

TABLE 3–14
U.S. Oceanborne International Trade between the United States and the Far East, 1976–1977 (Tons × 10^3)

	Imports		Exports		Total	
	1977	1976	1977	1976	1977	1976
Liner	7,362	6,737	6,198	6,352	13,560	13,089
Nonliner	12,175	10,150	66,035	65,586	78,210	75,736
Tanker	756	703	2,322	3,045	3,078	3,748
Total	20,293	18,566	74,555	74,948	94,848	93,514

SOURCE: *Ibid.*, p. 12.

TABLE 3–15
U.S. Oceanborne International Trade between the United States and the Mediterranean, 1976–1977 (Tons × 10^3)

	Imports		Exports		Total	
	1977	1976	1977	1976	1977	1976
Liner	2,010	2,032	2,870	3,103	4,880	5,135
Nonliner	2,742	3,117	30,912	30,158	33,654	33,275
Tanker	61,967	44,408	3,410	4,032	65,377	48,440
Total	66,719	51,699	37,192	36,976	103,911	88,675

SOURCE: *Ibid.*, p. 13.

TABLE 3–16
U.S. Oceanborne International Trade between the United States and Indonesia, Malaysia, Singapore, and Indian Ocean, 1976–1977 (Tons × 10^3)

	Imports		Exports		Total	
	1977	1976	1977	1976	1977	1976
Liner	1,673	1,696	3,191	3,304	4,864	5,000
Nonliner	396	990	5,859	7,827	6,255	8,817
Tanker	67,231	60,583	1,417	1,744	68,648	62,327
Total	69,301	64,411	10,467	12,616	79,768	77,027

SOURCE: *Ibid.*, p. 14.

TABLE 3–17
Ton-Mileage of Freight (× 10^3) Carried on the Inland Waterways of the United States, by System, 1976–1977

System	1976	1977
Atlantic Coast waterways	32,105,144	30,381,926
Gulf Coast waterways	34,296,250	37,571,386
Pacific Coast waterways	11,304,678	12,774,038
Mississippi River system	189,510,779	196,853,367
Great Lakes system*	105,647,789	90,694,592
Total	372,864,648	368,275,389

*Does not include traffic between international ports.

SOURCE: Department of the Army Corps of Engineers, *Waterborne Commerce of the United States*, Calendar Year 1977, p. 26.

TABLE 3–18
Principal Commodities Transported on the Inland Waterways of the United States (Exclusive of the Great Lakes), 1975–1976 (Net Tons)

Commodity	1975	1976
Grain and grain products	34,302,575	42,707,659
Soybeans	9,429,582	11,205,843
Fresh fish and shellfish	1,989,015	1,817,304
Marine shells, unmanufactured	15,334,659	12,124,215
Iron ore and concentrates	3,526,102	5,968,223
Bituminous coal and lignite	127,567,743	129,822,299
Crude petroleum	51,848,423	52,743,679
Limestone	2,488,134	2,138,340
Sand, gravel, and crushed rock	63,177,608	58,085,741
Clay and structural clay products	1,521,102	1,923,657
Sulfur, dry and liquid	4,766,372	4,250,260
Nonmetallic minerals, n.e.c.*	5,067,946	5,436,254
Vegetable oils, margarine, shortening	772,289	1,115,177
Rafted logs	18,152,096	16,948,511
Pulpwood, logs	1,375,284	1,589,018
Lumber and lumber products	2,245,073	2,575,394
Paper and paper products	1,670,519	1,967,643
Sodium hydroxide	3,135,305	3,681,031
Crude tar, oil, gas products	2,288,531	2,749,241
Alcohols	2,060,550	2,306,468
Benzene and toluene	2,977,767	3,664,542
Sulfuric acid	2,253,219	2,354,479
Basic chemicals and products, n.e.c.	12,079,233	12,267,298
Fertilizer and fertilizer materials	6,510,494	6,557,423
Gasoline	39,233,564	37,981,831
Jet fuel	5,262,600	5,109,397
Kerosene	1,572,942	1,981,404
Distillate fuel oil	38,986,678	41,294,094
Residual fuel oil	62,283,142	74,738,421
Lubricating oils and greases	1,946,499	2,429,528
Naphtha petroleum solvents	1,569,761	2,058,210
Asphalt tar and pitches	4,677,920	4,373,084
Coke, petroleum coke	2,198,061	1,850,740
Liquefied gases	1,171,950	1,332,465
Other petroleum and coal products	1,879,420	2,233,208
Building cement	3,714,435	3,812,558
Iron and steel products	6,437,754	6,331,019
Miscellaneous manufactured products	1,361,811	1,894,973
Iron and steel scrap	1,378,857	1,855,714
Waste and scrap, n.e.c.	16,908,724	14,895,619
Water	2,434,743	2,893,196
Total—principal commodities	545,869,943	593,166,161
All other commodities	35,341,539	14,537,504
Grand total	582,211,482	607,703,665

SOURCE: American Waterway Operators, Inc., 1976, *Inland Waterborne Commerce Statistics*, June 1978, p. 7.

*n.e.c.—not elsewhere classified.

section describes the technology and economics of containerization and then explores its implications for other modes of transportation.

Containerization refers to the movement of goods by the use of large reusable boxes called containers. After loading into these containers, the goods will move from origin to destination using a number of different modes of transport without the need for the individual units of cargo to be handled.

A container is rectangular in shape with a waterproof outer shell over a strong inner structure. The inner structure is usually a steel frame, and the outer shell may be steel, aluminum, or fiber-reinforced plywood. There are a number of different types of containers, each differing in accordance with the type of cargo it is designed to carry. The types of cargo are:

1. Dry cargoes
2. Liquid cargoes and bulk commodities

3. Special cargoes requiring protection from the environment

The construction of the containers varies accordingly. Usually, containers will be fully enclosed with a door at the rear for loading cargo. Those for handling large objects or bulk commodities may have a removable top or an open or canvas-covered top, called "ragtops." There are also refrigerated containers; "reefers," tank containers for handling liquids; and containers which consist of a flat-bottom deck and front wall. The latter are known as "tilts" and constitute the minimum unitized equipment.

The most common sizes of containers are 20 × 8 × 8 ft (6.10 × 2.43 × 2.43 m) and 40 × 8 × 8.5 ft (12.20 × 2.43 × 2.58 m). Recently some 40-ft containers 9 ft 6 in. high have been introduced. Some companies still use nonstandard containers 24 or 35 ft in length, but these are decreasing.

Containers may be loaded and unloaded at dockside either by shipboard cranes or by dockside gantries; however, most modern containerships do not carry container equipment but rely on dockside facilities instead. This makes for simplicity and economy of ship construction but requires that vessels utilize only those ports with container-handling facilities. The system has led to standardization of container sizes, strengths, and lifting facilities. This standardization has meant that containers have developed not just as a convenient means of packaging, but as the basis for a worldwide system of intermodal transportation which through standardization of boxes, vessels, handling facilities, and inland transportation equipment expedites the rapid and efficient movement of a significant proportion of the world's general cargo trade.

The construction of a typical dry freight container can be seen in Figure 3.13. Dimensions and capacities of some of the standardized sizes and types of containers are shown in Table 3-19. The composition of the U.S. container inventory by size and type is shown in Table 3-20.

Containerization has greatly affected not only oceanborne trade but domestic trade as well. Tables 3-21 and 3-22 show

Figure 3.13. Dry freight container. SOURCE: Lawrence J. Rinaldi, *Containerization: The New Method of Intermodal Transport,* Sterling Publishing Co., 1972, p. 23.

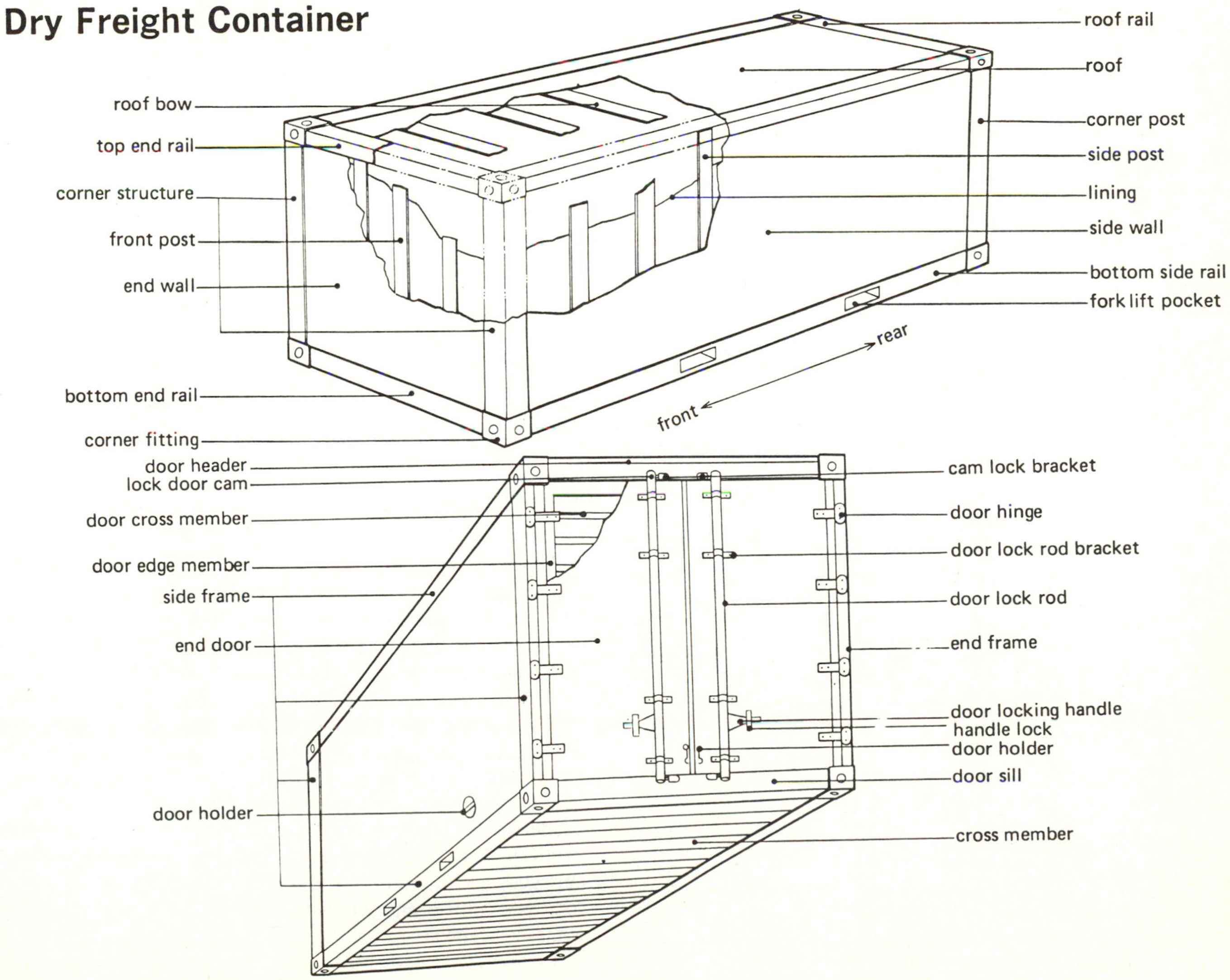

TABLE 3–19
Typical Long-Line Steamship Company Container Equipment*

	40-ft Dry Cargo	40-ft Dry Cargo Hi-Cube	40-ft Reefer	40-ft Tank	40-ft Open Top	40-ft Half-High Open Top	(AL) 20-ft Dry Cargo	(FRP) 20-ft Dry Cargo
Outside dimensions								
Length	40′	40′	40′	40′	40′	40′	20′	20′
Width	8′	8′	8′	8′	8′	8′	8′	8′
Height	8′	8′6″	8′6″	4′3″	8′6″	4′3″	8′	8′
Inside dimensions								
Length	39′7″	39′6″	37′10″		39′6″	39′6″	19′6″	19′7″
Width	7′9″	7′9″	7′4″		6′8″	7′9″	7′8″	7′10″
Height	7′4″	7′10″	7′1/2″		7′6″	3′4″	7′4″	7′6″
Door opening								
Width	7′5-3/4″	7′6″	7′6″		7′6″	7′6″	7′5-3/4″	7′5-3/4″
Height	6′11-3/4″	7′5-1/2″	7′5-3/4″		6′11″	3′4″	6′11-3/4″	6′11-3/4″
Construction	Aluminum	Aluminum	Aluminum	Stainless steel AISI 304	Aluminum	Aluminum	Aluminum	Plastic plywood
Internal cubic capacity	2,250 ft³	2,398 ft³	1,988 ft³	6,020 gal	2,296 ft³	1,020 ft³	1,096 ft³	1,151 ft³
Max. load capacity	60,260 lb	60,950 lb	50,000 lb	51,600 lb	59,280 lb	45,000 lb	44,800 lb	40,650 lb
Tare weight	6,400 lb	6,940 lb	10,700 lb	9,260 lb	7,750 lb	6,660 lb	4,500 lb	4,500 lb
Special features	End door opening	End door opening	Temp. control; meat rails	Bulk liq.; loading equip.; supplied	End door opening; open top loading; swinging roof bows	End door opening; open top loading; swinging roof bows	End door opening	End door opening

*Dimensioned worldwide in English units. Use standard conversion factors for approximate metric sizes.

SOURCE: ERIC RATH, *Container Systems*, John Wiley & Sons, 1973, p. 52.

TABLE 3–20
U.S. Container Inventory Comparison, 1974 and 1977

Container Type	Quantity by Type 1977	Quantity by Type 1974	Type as Percent of Total Fleet 1977	Type as Percent of Total Fleet 1974
40-ft containers	*179,016*	*145,049*	*31.44*	*32.83*
Dry van	169,468	137,666	29.75	31.16
Refrigerated	6,476	3,345	1.14	0.76
Insulated	208	227	0.04	0.05
Tank	145	109	0.03	0.02
Open top	2,086	2,205	0.37	0.50
Open top, ½-ht.	259	203	0.05	0.05
Platform	165	65	0.03	0.01
Misc. types	209	1,229	0.02	0.28
35-ft containers	*60,221*	*59,932*	*10.56*	*13.56*
Dry van	46,026	48,892	8.08	11.06
Refrigerated	7,575	6,222	1.33	1.41
Insulated	1,364	1,098	0.24	0.25
Tank	993	883	0.17	0.20
Open top	3,330	2,194	0.58	0.50
Platform	256	158	0.04	0.04
Platform, ½-ht.	390	287	0.07	0.06
Car carrier	224	198	0.04	0.04
Misc. types	63	0	0.01	0
30-ft containers	*535*	*1,250*	*0.09*	*0.29*
Dry van	525	1,040	0.09	0.24
Misc. types	10	210	*	0.05
27-ft containers	*3,528*	*3,528*	*0.62*	*0.80*
Dry van	2,878	2,878	0.51	0.65
Refrigerated	400	400	0.07	0.09
Platform	250	250	0.04	0.06
24-ft containers	*11,615*	*10,810*	*2.04*	*2.45*
Dry van	8,319	7,754	1.47	1.77
Refrigerated	1,657	1,417	0.29	0.32
Dry bulk	129	129	0.02	0.03
Platform	1,165	1,165	0.20	0.26
Ventilated	231	231	0.04	0.05
Misc. types	114	114	0.02	0.02
20-ft containers	*314,767*	*221,185*	*55.25*	*50.05*
Dry van	301,632	211,575	52.95	47.87
Refrigerated	2,621	1,625	0.46	0.37
Insulated	5,161	2,540	0.91	0.57
Tank	322	347	0.06	0.08
Open top	2,169	2,037	0.38	0.46
Side door—van	288	350	0.05	0.08

TABLE 3–20 Continued

Container Type	Quantity by Type 1977	Quantity by Type 1974	Type as Percent of Total Fleet 1977	Type as Percent of Total Fleet 1974
Open side	127	110	0.02	0.02
Dry bulk	170	220	0.03	0.05
Platform	1,616	1,496	0.28	0.34
Platform, ½-ht.	234	200	0.04	0.05
Hide	300	165	0.05	0.04
Misc. types	127	520	0.1	0.12
10-ft containers	0	*100*	0	*0.02*
Dry van	0	100	0	0.02
TOTAL	569,682	441,854	100.00	100.00

*Negligible percent.

SOURCE: U.S. Department of Commerce Maritime Administration *Inventory of American Intermodal Equipment 1978*, March 1978, p. 41.

the capacity of containerized equipment and other types of specialized ship types for both of these trades respectively. Figures are expressed in 20-ft equivalent units (TEU) with the capacities based on the estimated number of voyages each vessel completed in 1978.

In U.S. international trade, Trade Route 29 (U.S. Pacific/Far East) and Trades Routes 5-7-8-9, 6, and 11 (U.S. North and South Atlantic/United States, Continental Europe, Scandinavia, and Baltic areas) led all others in TEU capacity by a wide margin. Total container vessel capacity servicing Trade Route 29 under all flags amounted to 853,508 TEU in 1978. This was 31% of all container vessel capacity engaged in U.S. foreign trade. Total container capacity on routes 5-7-8-9-6 and 11 was 771,880 TEU or 28% of all container capacity.

In U.S. domestic trade, the U.S. Atlantic/Puerto Rico

TABLE 3–21

U.S. Flag Container Vessel Capacity in the Oceanborne U.S. International Trade by Trade Route and Vessel Type, 1978 (TEU)

No.	Trade Route	Full Containership	Partial Containership	RO/RO*	LASH†	Container Barge	Total
1	U.S. Atl./east coast S. America	—	11,710	—	—	—	11,710
2	U.S. Atl./west coast S. America	—	5,070	—	—	—	5,070
4	U.S. Atl./Carib., east coast Mexico	36,105	828	1,033	6,762	8,286	53,014
5-7-8-9, 6 and 11	U.S. Atl./U.K., contl. Europe, Scand., Baltic	272,514	—	—	—	—	272,514
10 and 13	U.S. Atl. and Gulf/Med., Black Sea, Portugal	40,060	13,238	—	5,796	—	59,094‡
12	U.S. Atl./Far East	29,300	2,268	—	—	—	31,568
14-1 and 14-2	U.S. Atl. and Gulf/West Africa	—	5,246	—	—	—	5,246
15-A and 15-B	U.S. Atl. and Gulf/south and east coast Africa	—	5,657	—	—	—	5,657
16	U.S. Atl. and Gulf/Australasia	22,495	—	—	—	—	22,495
17	U.S. Atl., Gulf, Pac./Indo., Malaysia, Singapore		Linked to either T.R. 12, T.R. 29, or both				
18	U.S. Atl. and Gulf/Red Sea to Burma	—	4,327	1,640	2,304	—	8,271‡
19	U.S. Gulf/Carib., east coast Mexico	7,026	—	—	—	570	7,596
20	U.S. Gulf/east coast S. America	—	292	—	7,056	—	7,348
21	U.S. Gulf/U.K., contl. Europe	43,160	1,000	—	12,000	—	56,160
22	U.S. Gulf/Far East	—	4,712	—	—	—	4,712
23-24-25	U.S. Pacific/west coast Mex., Cen. America, Carib., east and west S. America	3,200	3,715	—	—	—	6,915
26	U.S. Pac., Haw., Alas./U.K., contl. Europe	—	—	—	—	—	—
27	U.S. Pac., Hawaii/Australasia	—	—	—	5,772	—	5,772
28	U.S. Pacific/Red Sea to Burma		Linked to T.R. 29, T.R. 18, T.R. 5-7-8-9, T.R. 10 and 13				
29	U.S. Pac., Haw., Alas./Far East	262,062	9,860	23,184	7,180	—	302,286
31	U.S. Gulf/west coast S. America	—	2,632	—	—	—	2,632
Total		715,922	70,555	25,857	46,870	8,856	868,060

*RO/RO, roll on/roll off ship.
†LASH, lighter aboard ship.
‡Does not include transshipments via other trade routes.

SOURCE: U.S. Department of Commerce Maritime Administration, *Container Vessel Capacity in the U.S. Oceanborne Trade Foreign and Domestic, 1978 and Forecast*, June 1979, p. 13.

TABLE 3–22

1978 Container Vessel Capacity in the Oceanborne U.S. Domestic Trade by Trade Route and Operator (TEU)

Trade Route Operator	1978 Container Vessel Capacity* Full Containership	RO/RO	Container Barge	Total	Percent
U.S. Atl./Puerto Rico and V.I.					76
Navieras De P.R. (PRMSA)	202,383	90,068	—	292,451	5
Sea-Land Service	19,911	—	—	19,911	7
Seatrain Lines	19,200	—	5,160	24,360†	12
Trailer Marine Transport	—	—	46,954	46,954	
Total	241,494	90,068	52,114	383,676	100
U.S. Gulf/Puerto Rico and V.I.					
Navieras De P.R. (PRMSA)	45,275	—	—	45,275	62
Sea-Land Service	24,505	—	—	24,505	34
Trailer Marine Transport	—	—	3,210	3,210	4
Total	69,780	—	3,210	72,990	100
California/Hawaii					
Hawaiian Marine Lines	—	—	3,240	3,240‡	2
Matson Lines	153,098	—	—	153,098	92
U.S. Lines	9,180	—	—	9,180‡	6
Total	162,278	—	3,240	165,518	100
California/Guam					
Matson Lines	10,548	—	—	10,548	66
U.S. Lines	5,500	—	—	5,500‡	34
Total	16,048	—	—	16,048	100
Pacific Northwest/Hawaii					
Hawaiian Marine Lines	—	—	7,560	7,560‡	25
Matson Lines	22,481	—	—	22,481	75
Total	22,481	—	7,560	30,041	100
Pacific Northwest/Alaska					
Alaskan Hydrotrain	—	—	9,000	9,000	5
Foss Alaska	—	—	19,120	19,120	11
Pacific Alaska	—	—	2,525	2,525	1
Pacific Western	—	—	1,600	1,600	1
Sea-Land Service	73,620	—	—	73,620	40
Totem Ocean Trailer	—	76,500	—	76,500	42
Total	73,620	76,500	32,245	182,365	100
Total domestic trade capacity	585,701	166,568	98,369	850,638	

*There are no partial container ships on LASH in U.S. domestic trade.
†Includes capacity provided the GITMO service.
‡Allocated capacity.

SOURCE: *Ibid.*, p. 35.

and Virgin Islands route had the biggest concentration of container capacity, at 383,676 TEU. This was equivalent to 45% of all types of capacity. It also ranked first in full containership service, with 241,494 TEU, 41% of the total full containership capacity.

Terminal technology and interface with other modes

Ports or terminals in a narrow sense are places where vessels receive or discharge their cargoes. In addition, they have traditionally served as vessel "shelters," as a home base or home away from home for ships and their crews, and as a place where provisioning, crewing, and various administrative tasks connected with shipping are performed. Because of their various activities, they are often centers of commerce, trade, and population, and many major cities have developed around natural harbors and seaports. With the development of intermodalism, they have become the hubs of multimodal transportation systems.

The advent of containerization and intermodalism has created a need for more elaborate terminal equipment and facilities. The cargo-handling equipment, while involving greater capital costs, also provides much greater capacity. The result is lower terminal costs provided that the equipment is adequately utilized. The consequence of this has been a tendency toward concentration of cargo handled by fewer but larger ports.

Table 3-23 compares cargo-handling rates and costs for four representative types of vessels. The greater capacity and lower cost for newer technologies compared to conventional break-bulk operation can be seen.

TABLE 3–23
Comparison of Cargo-Handling Methods

	Barge Carrier	Containers Carrier	Pallet Carrier	Conventional Cargo Vessel
Bale capacity (ft^3 × 10^6)	1.2	1.2	1.2	0.8
Number of barges or containers	62	1,130	0	0
Cargo annually (tons × 10^6)	1.04	1.09	1.0	0.8
Handling rate/hr:	4 barges	40 conts.	250 tons	110 tons
R.C.H.R. (bale capacity)*	7.0	3.9	2.7	1.0
Time per round trip (days)	~21	~21	~28	~42
Ships for weekly service	3	3	4	6
Building price per ship ($ × 10^6)	8.4	10.5	9.2	5.3
Total investment ($ × 10^6)	42.46	38.3	37.15	31.8
Total yearly ship-related costs ($ × 10^6)	9.21	10.42	10.06	9.57
Ship cost per ton ($)	8.85	9.60	10.05	12.00
Handling cost per ton ($)	14.00	11.50	8.60	20.00
Total cost per ton ($)	22.85	21.10	18.65	32.00
Comparative Costs	(108%)	(100%)	(82%)	(152%)

*R.C.H.R.—ratio of cargo handling rates.

SOURCE: ERIC RATH, *Container Systems*. (John Wiley & Sons, 1973), p. 486.

Intermodal systems are total transportation systems designed to provide "door-to-door" shipping service for cargo from origin to destination. As an example, containers by themselves or loaded onto highway trailers may be carried "piggyback" on railroad flatcars and loaded onto ships at terminals for ocean movement. A typical container port showing the facilities needed for intermodal transfers is illustrated in Figure 3.14.

Examples of the major types of container-lifting equipment are shown in Figure 3.15, and alternative containerport handling systems are shown in Figure 3.16.

Other aspects of water transportation

Economics

When most ocean transportation was by break-bulk general cargo vessels, labor was by far the largest cost item. Capital costs both for the vessels and for the terminal facilities were relatively low compared to other modes of

Figure 3.14. Transfer center traffic flow. SOURCE: Schwimmer and Amundsen, *Management of a Seaport*, National Maritime Research Center, 1973, p. 385.

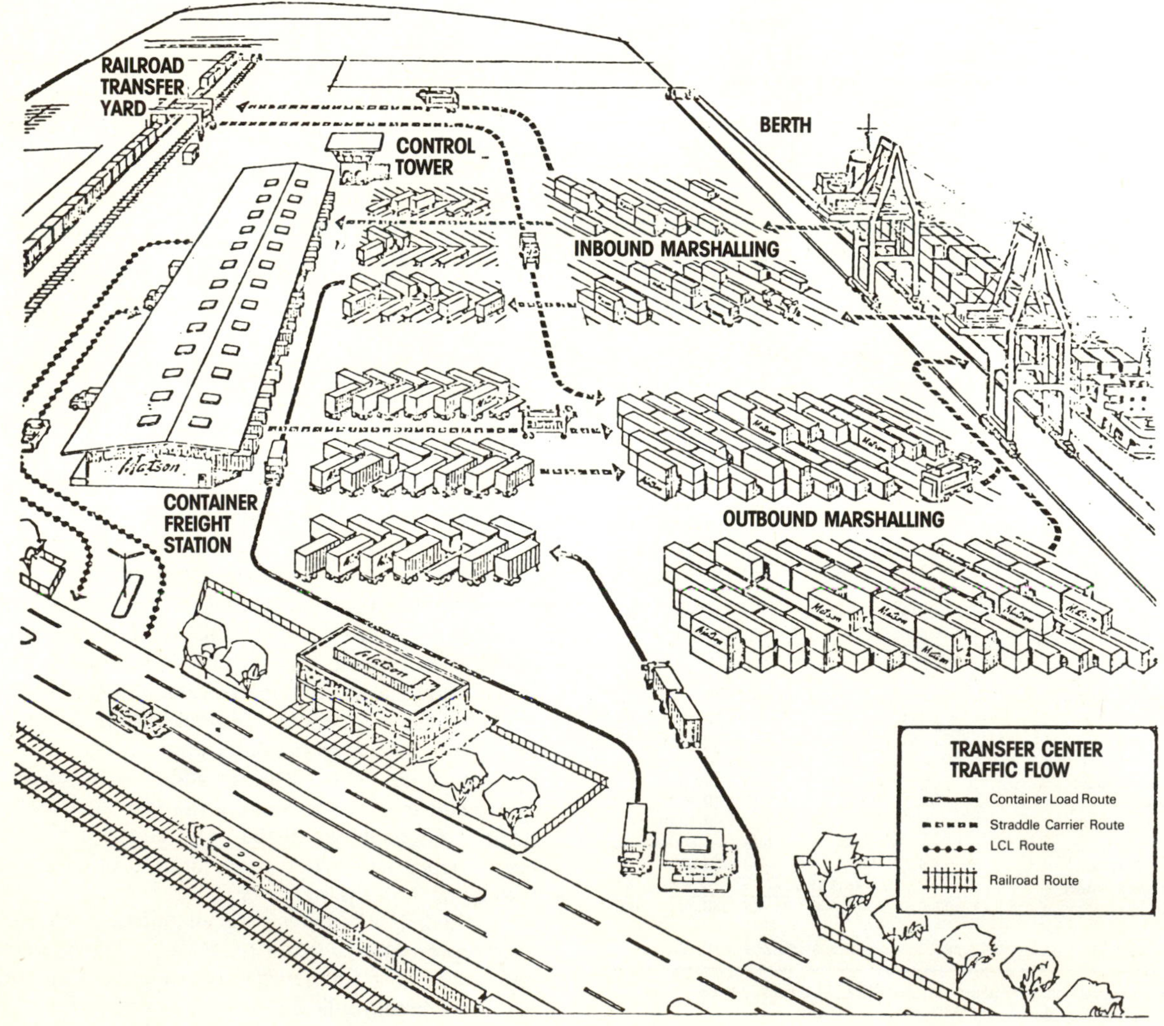

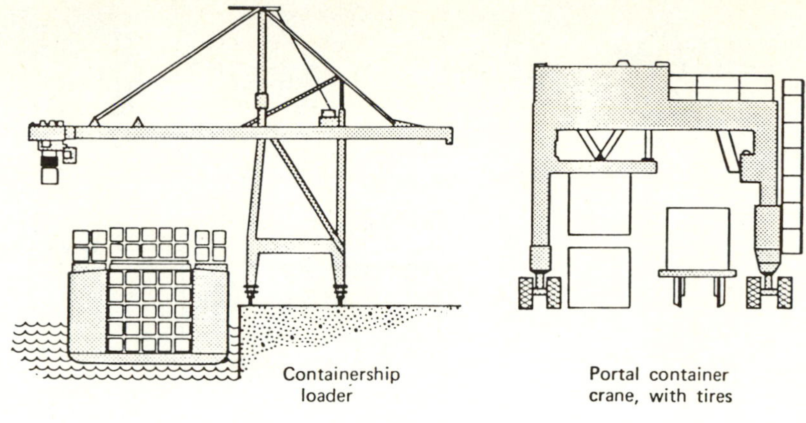

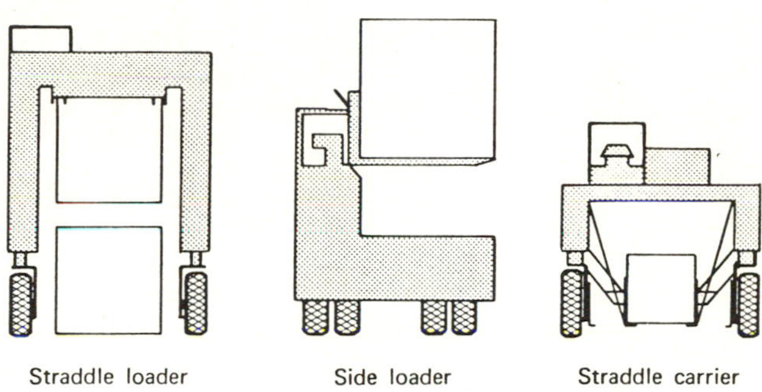

Figure 3.15. Containerport lifting equipment. SOURCE: Eric Rath, *Container Systems,* John Wiley & Sons, 1973, p. 320.

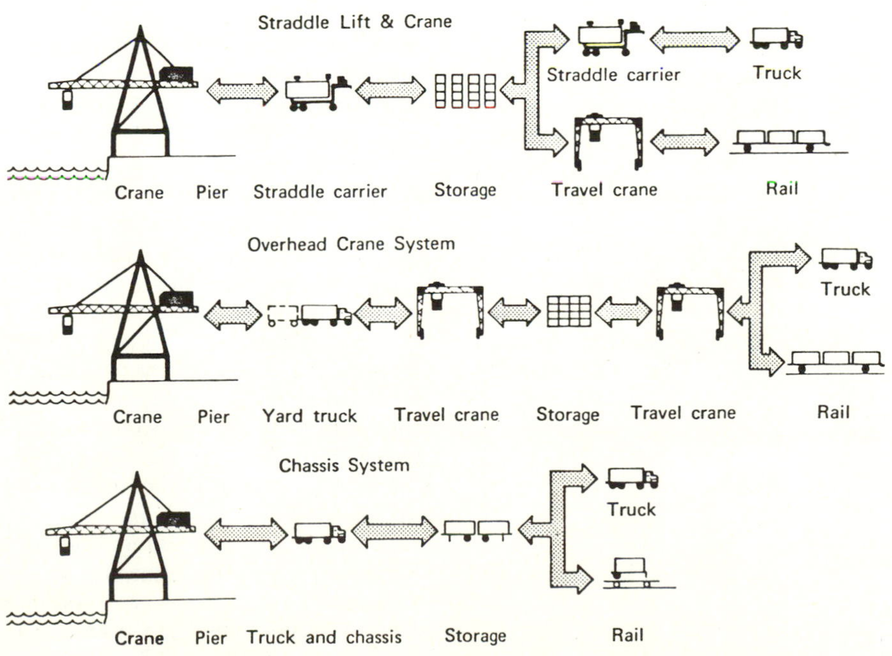

Figure 3.16. Major containerport handling alternatives. SOURCE: Eric Rath, *Container Systems,* John Wiley & Sons, 1973, p. 322.

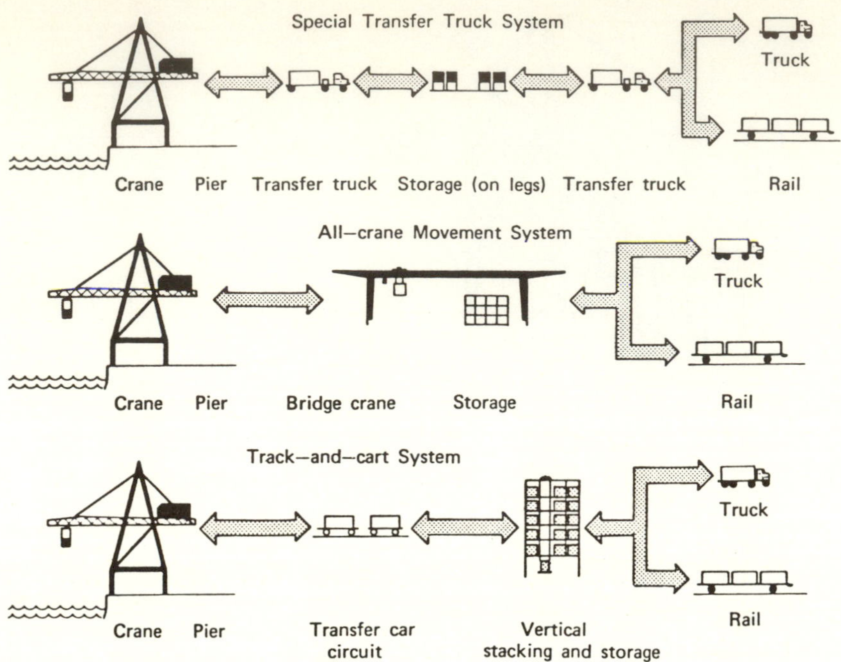

Figure 3.16. Continued.

transportation. The advent of containerization has changed this picture a great deal. In the 1960s a general cargo ship may have required an investment of about $12 million and cost about $3500 per day to operate. A containership may require an investment of $25 million and cost $10,000 per day to operate. It will handle three times as much cargo, however, resulting in a lower cost per ton-mile of cargo carried.

A company in a containerized trade must have about three times as many containers as will be aboard ship at any given time, because some will always be in transit on land, being loaded or unloaded or being shipped to a manufacturer for loading. When the capital investment in elaborate terminal equipment required is also considered, it should become clear that water transportation has become a much more capital-intensive industry. The new technology makes possible lower unit costs of moving cargo because of greater capacity and faster turnaround time, but only if the equipment is fully utilized.

Another economic factor that affects water transportation, especially of liquid and bulk commodities, is that significant economies of scale exist. A rule of thumb holds that resistance increases with the square of hull dimensions while capacity increases with its cube. Table 3-24 shows how cargo capacities increase rapidly with proportionately much smaller increases in hull resistance. A 15-fold increase in hull resistance results in an 80-fold increase in capacity in the example given. Since the engine horsepower required is in proportion to resistance to be overcome, larger ships will require less fuel per unit of cargo.

TABLE 3–24
Increases in Ship Resistance and Capacity

	Submerged Hull Square (ft^2)	Resistance Index	Cargo Carrying Capacity (tons)	Capacity Index
Small liner	528	1	2,500	1
Large liner	1,404	2.7	10,000	4
Dry bulk	3,995	7.6	60,000	24
Large tanker	7,824	14.8	200,000	80

SOURCE: JOHN L. HAZARD, *Transportation Management, Economics, Policy,* (Cornell Maritime Press, 1977), p. 300.

Government policy

Public policy toward the U.S. maritime industries falls into two main categories: subsidy and regulation. There are subsidies of various kinds, both direct and indirect. The two types of direct subsidies are the operating differential and the construction differential subsidy. The operating differential subsidy is paid to U.S. flag carriers in the foreign trade to enable them to compete with foreign flag carriers, who have lower costs, primarily for labor. The construction differential subsidy is in effect a subsidy to American shipyards stemming from the same rationale.

By law, coastwise and intercoastal shipping is restricted to U.S. flag ships. Many foreign aid programs also carry provisions restricting a certain proportion of the cargo to American ships. Since some of this cargo could undoubtedly be carried at lower cost by foreign vessels, both programs amount to concealed subsidies paid by customers. Other subsidy programs involve tax concessions and mortgage insurance for ship construction. An estimate of the amount expended in these subsidy programs is given in Table 3-25.

Ocean transportation is regulated by the Federal Maritime Commission; part of domestic water transportation, like other modes of domestic transportation, comes under the authority of the Interstate Commerce Commission.

The Federal Maritime Commission is concerned primarily with regulation of rates for the shipping of various commodities. The schedule of tariffs for cargo shipped by ocean

TABLE 3–25
Maritime Subsidies

		Estimated Total, to (× 10^6)	Recent Annual Amount, (× 10^6)
Operating differential	1936–77	$4000	$230
Construction differential	1936–77	2000	300
U.S. flag shipping rules (cabotage laws)	1950–77	3000	150
Tax subsidies	1936–77	500	40
Cargo preference	1950–77	6000	200

SOURCE: WILLIAM SHEPHERS and CLAIR WILCOX, *Public Policies Toward Business*, (Richard D. Irwin, Inc. 1979), p. 580.

vessel is extremely complex and detailed, with commodities broken down into very narrow classifications. The commission does not have the power to set rates or disapprove rates set by carriers unless they are clearly unreasonable. Rather, the commission is concerned that carriers use proper procedures and give sufficient notification when rate schedules are changed. The Interstate Commerce Commission has greater authority with respect to the rates under its control and as a general policy tries to ensure that rates affecting competing modes of transportation maintain the viability of each mode involved. A more detailed description of policy in this area is beyond the scope of this book.

In general, government policy toward ocean shipping has been to preserve the American flag fleet as a significant factor in the industry. This policy has not been too effective in the past as the share of the market accounted for by U.S. carriers has declined over the last few decades. The last major law in this area, the Merchant Marine Act of 1970, has had only mixed results. Congress has been debating new legislation in this area for several years. A major bill resulted from these deliberations in 1980 but could not be agreed upon by all constituencies—the various government agencies, the shipowners, the labor unions, and the shippers—so no legislation passed Congress. Although technology in the maritime industry has shown great progress in recent years, economic and political problems still remain.

REFERENCES FOR FURTHER READING

ABRAHAMSSON, B. J., *International Ocean Shipping: Current Concepts and Principles,* Westview Press, Boulder, Colo., 1980.

BESS, D., *Marine Transportation,* The Interstate Printers & Publishers, Inc., Danville, Ill., 1976.

BRANCH, A. E., *The Elements of Shipping,* Chapman and Hall, London, 1975.

CLARK, E. W. and H. S. HADDOCK, *The U.S. Merchant Marine Today: Sunrise or Sunset?,* Washington, D.C., Labor-Management Maritime Committee, 1970.

H. P. DREWRY, LTD., *The Advance of Deep-Sea, Fully Cellular Container Shipping,* H. P. Drewry, London, 1978.

HEINE, I. M., *The United States Merchant Marine A National Asset,* National Maritime Council, Washington, D.C., 1976.

KENDALL, L. C., *The Business of Shipping,* Cornell Maritime Press, Inc., Cambridge, Md., Third Edition, 1979.

LAWRENCE, S. A., *United States Merchant Shipping Policies and Politics,* The Brooking Institution, Washington, D.C., 1966.

RINMAN, T. and R. LENDEN, *Shipping - How it Works,* Rinman & Lenden, AB, Gothenberg, Sweden, 1978.

TABAK, H. D., *Cargo Containers: Their Stowage Handling and Movement,* Cornell Maritime Press, Cambridge, Md., 1970.

U.S. Department of Commerce, Maritime Administration, *Inventory of American Intermodal Equipment,* 1978.

U.S. Department of Commerce and Federal Maritime Commission, *Ocean Freight Rate Guidelines For Shippers,* 1974.

U.S. Department of Commerce, Maritime Administration, *U.S. Flag Bulk Shipping,* 1976.

4

RAILROAD TRANSPORTATION

ROBERT H. LEILICH, *President*

Corporate Strategies, Inc., Springfield, Virginia

In most countries of the world—the United States, Canada, and a few European countries being the major exceptions—railroads handle more intercity passengers and freight than all other modes combined. These exceptions notwithstanding, railroads are absolutely essential to the commerce and economy of most industrialized nations. The concept of a steel wheel rolling on a steel rail, with multiple vehicles in tow, is virtually unmatched for efficiency and economy. Yet the paradox is that in the United States the industry is not a healthy one, although it has done as much as or more than almost any major industry to modernize and improve productivity. In the United States, as in much of the world, railroads are heavily capital-intensive and are subject to political and regulatory influences and the upsetting effect of unequal subsidies among competing modes.

This chapter cannot provide a complete understanding of the railroad industry and the issues it faces. It can, however, describe the basic characteristics and economies of railroads, compare these to other modes, and provide references for more detailed information and statistics. To highlight the railroad industry, this chapter discusses the railroads' role in intercity transportation and its economic and energy-consumption characteristics; most referenced terms, definitions, and nomenclature; fundamental physical and engineering relationships; technology and new developments; some financial and statistical highlights; some future trends in the industry; and some international comparisons.

Overview

Although its share of the U.S. freight transportation market has declined by 48% since World War II, railroads remain a bulwark of the nation's transportation system. In 1979, they produced 1.5 times the ton-miles of their most significant competitor, trucks, and 2.3 times the ton-miles of waterways. Although petroleum pipelines produce slightly less ton-miles than trucks, their services are confined to a limited, narrowly defined segment of the transportation market. Table 4-1 summarizes the general modal shares of the U.S. freight transport system, as measured in ton-miles.

The railroad's decline of market share has been princi-

TABLE 4–1
Volume of U.S. Intercity Freight Traffic, Including Mail and Express (Millions of Revenue Freight Ton-Miles and Percentage of Total)

Year	Railroads	Percent	Trucks	Percent	Great Lakes	Percent	Rivers and Canals	Percent	Oil Pipelines	Percent	Air	Percent	Total
1939	338,850	62.4	52,821	9.7	76,312	14.0	19,937	3.7	55,602	10.2	12	—	543,534
1944	746,912	68.6	58,264	5.4	118,769	10.9	31,386	2.9	132,864	12.2	71	—	1,088,266
1950	596,940	56.2	172,860	16.3	111,687	10.5	51,657	4.9	129,175	12.1	318	—	1,062,637
1960	579,130	44.1	285,483	21.7	99,468	7.6	120,785	9.2	228,626	17.4	778	—	1,314,270
1970	771,168	39.8	412,000	21.3	114,475	5.9	204,085	10.5	431,000	22.3	3,295	0.2	1,936,023
1974	855,582	38.6	495,000	22.3	107,451	4.9	247,431	11.2	506,000	22.8	3,580	0.2	2,215,044
1976	799,000	36.2	510,000	23.1	105,648	4.8	267,217	12.1	523,000	23.6	3,900	0.2	2,208,765
1978	870,000	35.8	602,000	24.8	94,000	3.9	288,000	11.9	568,000	23.4	5,000	0.2	2,427,000
1979	927,000	36.6	614,000	24.2	100,000	3.9	302,000	11.9	588,000	23.2	5,000	0.2	2,536,000

SOURCE: ASSOCIATION OF AMERICAN RAILROADS, *Yearbook of Railroad Facts*, 1980.

TABLE 4-2
Volume of U.S. Intercity Passenger Traffic* (Millions of Revenue Passenger-Miles and Percentage of Total)

Year	Railroads*	Percent	Buses	Percent	Air Carriers	Percent	Inland Waterways	Percent	Total (Except Private)	Private Automobiles	Private Airplanes	Total (Including Private)
1929	33,965	77.1	6,800	15.4	—	—	3,300	7.5	44,065	175,000	—	219,065
1939	23,669	67.7	9,100	26.0	683	2.0	1,486	4.3	34,938	275,000	—	309,938
1944	97,705	75.7	26,920	20.9	2,177	1.7	2,187	1.7	128,989	181,000	1	309,990
1950	32,481	47.2	26,436	38.4	8,773	12.7	1,190	1.7	68,880	438,293	1,299	508,472
1960	21,574	28.6	19,327	25.7	31,730	42.1	2,688	3.6	75,319	706,079	2,228	738,626
1970	10,903	5.7	25,300	14.3	109,499	77.7	4,000	2.3	149,702	1,026,000	9,101	1,184,803
1974	10,475	5.9	26,700	15.1	135,469	76.7	4,000	2.3	176,644	1,143,440	11,000	1,331,044
1977†	10,400	5.1	25,900	12.7	164,200	80.3	4,000	1.9	204,500	1,234,500	12,100	1,451,100
1978†	10,500	4.6	25,000	10.9	190,000	82.8	4,000	1.7	229,500	1,298,000	15,000	1,542,500
1979†	11,600	4.6	26,600	10.5	210,300	83.3	4,000	1.6	252,500	1,289,200	13,300	1,555,000

*Railroads of all classes, including electric railways, Amtrak, and Auto-Train.
†Preliminary estimates subject to frequent subsequent adjustments.

SOURCE: ASSOCIATION OF AMERICAN RAILROADS, *Yearbook of Railroad Facts*, 1980. Air carrier data from reports of CAB and TAA; Great Lakes and rivers and canals from Corps of Engineers and TAA; some figures for 1977–1979 are partially estimated by AAR and TAA.

pally in areas most susceptible to motor carrier competition, that is, high-value or service-sensitive freight moving short distances in low volume. The inherent slower service and high origin–destination costs have made railroads highly vulnerable to loss of traffic in the high-volume, short-haul market.

In specific situations, railroads have also become vulnerable to motor carriers in the long-haul market. Although long-distance trucking is common, it tends to be concentrated on specific commodities (such as perishables and very high value freight) or special situations.

Except for petroleum pipelines, and waterway operators in limited markets, railroads still handle most regulated commodities moving long distances in high volume. New technology, however, may challenge this market in the form of coal slurry pipelines.

To most people, the apparent decline of U.S. railroads is measured by passenger service. From over 1300 pages of name passenger trains and lesser known schedules on over 150 railroads in the 1920s, the "Official Railway Guide"[1] can now be printed in a single coat-pocket-size Amtrak timetable of about 30 pages. In 1981, the Denver and Rio Grande Western had the distinction of being the last railroad to operate its own passenger service. Table 4-2 summarizes statistically the relative decline of the rail intercity passenger market. The jet plane and Interstate highways have superseded rail as prime modes of intercity passenger travel in the United States.

Although passenger trains are disappearing, it is not appropriate to judge the railroad industry through passenger service—even at its peak, it never generated more than 25% of revenues, and most railroads made little or no profit on the service. Local freight trains on light-density branch lines are also disappearing, as economics and service favor trucking and the expense to rehabilitate poor track cannot be justified. The U.S. rail plant is slowly shrinking to a hard core of high-density lines between major commerce centers. Even shortline railroads (a general term for small railroads) are having problems similar to those of the major roads, except for the few roads serving primarily as vehicles or conduits for daily renting of cars to other roads at high, very profitable rates.

Although certain rail services are no longer economical or in demand, railroads are still very much alive and, as some statistics indicate, growing. Railroads are producing more ton-miles of transportation than at the peak of World War II—and this with 35% of the number of employees, 63% of the locomotives, and 81% of the cars.

Coal presents one of the brightest futures for railroads. Hundreds of miles of new railroad lines are being built to reach these resources, with a level of construction activity that has not been seen since the early 1900s. TOFC/COFC (trailer or container on flat car) has been enjoying remarkable growth, and new or improved technologies in this area promise an even brighter future.

The inherent energy efficiency of the steel wheel, opportunity for substantial productivity improvements through changes in restrictive labor agreements, and a continuing bright future for technological innovation virtually ensure a need and place for railroads in the future. Even in the passenger market, there is an encouraging potential for short-haul (under 300 mi or 500 km), high-density intercity corridor traffic.

Central to a brighter future for railroads is an improvement in earnings from an abysmal 1.6% return on investment during 1976–1978,[2] the lowest earnings since the Great Depression. Chronically low earnings since the end of World War II (with a few years of singular exceptions) have resulted in railroads' spending far more for capital plant and equipment than they could support with retained funds. In the period 1963–1979, capital expenditures exceeded retained funds in every single year—a cumulative total of more than $13.7 billion.[3] The gap between the two has been steadily increasing—from $0.3 billion in 1972 to $2 billion in 1978 and 1979.

[1]*The Official Railway Guide*, National Railway Publishing Co., New York, published bimonthly.

[2]*Yearbook of Railroad Facts*, 1980 ed., Association of American Railroads, Washington, D.C., p. 21.

[3]Ibid.

Trends in plant and rolling stock

Table 4-3 summarizes statistics of railroad roadway and track. Table 4-4 summarizes the number of revenue cars owned and leased, aggregate carrying capacity, and average capacity per car for Class I U.S. roads.[4] Table 4-5 includes a selected summary of revenue freight cars owned and leased for railroads other than Class I and private owners, and the total fleet of all railroads and private owners.

The decline in car ownership by Class I railroads is partially offset by increases in average capacity, slight improvements in productivity, and increased private ownership of freight cars, particularly open-top hoppers, covered hoppers, and special service boxcars. Table 4-6 summarizes new and rebuilt cars placed in service on Class I roads, the number retired, and the net gain or loss.

Investment in freight equipment is rising at a much faster rate than revenue. During the 20-year period 1958–1978, net investment in freight cars by Class I railroads increased

TABLE 4–3
Mileage of Class I* Line-Haul Carriers

Year	Number of Roads	Miles of Road Owned	Miles of Road Operated	Total Mileage Owned (All Tracks)	Total Mileage Operated (All Tracks)
1970	71	176,745	209,836	281,948	346,592
1979	42	157,905	181,870	256,340	302,754†

*See footnote 4 in the text for a definition of Class I.
†Although the ICC no longer summarizes mileage statistics for switching and terminal companies and other than Class I roads, there are roughly 500 operating railroads, 330,000 miles of owned track, and 350,000 miles of track operated.

SOURCE: ICC, *Transport Statistics for the Year 1979.*

TABLE 4–4
Ownership, Aggregate Carrying Capacity, and Average Capacity per Car, Class I U.S. Roads as of January 1

Car Type	Ownership			Aggregate Capacity (tons × 10^3)			Average Carrying Capacity (tons)		
	1960	1970	1979	1960	1970	1979	1960	1970	1979
Plain box	655,418	386,499	217,301	32,365	20,720	13,740	49.4	53.6	63.2
Equipped box	50,320	159,574	166,719	2,479	10,169	11,564	49.3	63.7	69.4
Total box	705,738	546,073	384,020	34,843	30,890	25,311	49.4	56.6	65.9
Covered hoppers	61,407	125,867	161,885	4,267	10,641	14,982	69.5	84.5	92.6
Gondolas	271,626	192,238	157,587	16,765	13,423	12,694	61.7	69.8	80.6
Hoppers	490,020	394,204	327,044	29,421	28,207	27,275	60.0	71.6	83.4
Stock	31,470	11,797	*	1,238	487	*	39.4	41.3	*
Flat	51,257	71,498	97,746	2,881	4,732	6,828	56.2	66.2	69.9
Refrigerators	20,173	55,068	68,059	850	3,493	4,779	42.1	63.4	70.2
Tank	*	4,541	2,542	*	262	175	*	57.8	68.9
Others	46,274	36,904	26,491	2,347	2,242	1,698	50.7	60.8	64.1
Total, all types	1,677,965	1,438,190	1,225,374	92,607	94,378	93,962	55.2	65.2	76.7

*Included in others.

SOURCE: Association of American Railroads, Car Service Division.

TABLE 4–5
Revenue Freight Cars Owned and Leased as of January 1

	Railroads Other Than Class I			Private Owners			Total Fleet, All Railroads and Private Owners*		
	1960	1970	1979	1960	1970	1979	1960	1970	1979
Plain box	6,401	7,393	32,335	3,301	113	13,344	665,120	394,005	262,986
Equipped box	2,650	1,576	5,733	—	1,004	233	52,970	162,154	172,685
Total box	9,051	9,969	38,068	3,301	1,117	13,577	718,090	556,159	435,671
Covered hoppers	802	703	3,409	5,703	34,452	80,775	67,912	161,022	246,087
Gondolas	7,331	4,185	5,240	278	2,025	11,857	279,235	198,448	175,777
Hoppers	9,616	7,011	11,296	4,798	2,386	15,743	504,434	403,603	354,086
Stock	321	—	—	483	372	†	32,274	12,169	†
Flat	40,024‡	545	3,799	3,685	50,198	44,851	94,966	122,241	146,402
Refrigerators	432	1,458	3,648	92,068	59,318	15,894	112,673	115,844	87,601
Tank	6,163‡	106	37	160,511	176,114	171,591	166,674	180,761	174,170
Others	−43,589‡	922	3,384	1,415	1,555	3,105	4,100	39,381	32,980
Total, all types	30,151	23,899	68,881	272,242	327,539	357,393	1,980,358	1,789,628	1,652,774

†Included in others.
*Totals may not equal sum of Tables 4–4 and 4–5 because of reporting differences.
‡Error due to inconsistency in AAR collected reporting. Total for flat, tank, and others is 2598 cars.

SOURCE: Association of American Railroads.

[4] Railroad operating companies are classified for statistical purposes on the basis of average operating revenues for a 3-year period. The classification schedules used by the Interstate Commerce Commission are as follows:

Effective Date	Class I	Class II	Class III
Jan. 1, 1978	$50 million or more	$5–50 million	Less than $5 million
Jan. 1, 1965	$5 million or more	Less than $5 million	—
Jan. 1, 1956	$3 million or more	Less than $3 million	—
Prior to 1956	$1 million or more	$100,000 but less than $1 million	Less than $100,000

TABLE 4–6
New and Rebuilt Cars Placed in Service and Cars Retired, Class I U.S. Railroads

Period	Box	Covered Hoppers	Gondolas	Hoppers	Other	Total	Cars Retired	Net Gain (Loss)
1950–1954	114,962	17,764	65,553	62,001	23,511	283,791	297,974	(14,183)
1955–1959	109,254	23,510	34,960	74,945	22,010	264,679	316,111	(51,432)
1960–1964	61,965	21,366	12,496	75,651	30,182	201,660	384,922	(183,262)
1965–1969	121,681	50,581	33,380	79,529	43,832	329,003	377,340	(48,337)
1970–1974	77,300	37,154	23,057	45,517	22,406	205,434	268,359	(62,925)
1975–1978	57,953	43,003	19,027	65,725	59,417	245,125	395,016	(149,891)
Total 29 years	543,115	193,378	188,473	403,368	201,358	1,529,692	2,039,722	(510,030)

SOURCE: Association of American Railroads.

TABLE 4–7
Net Investment per Ton of Capacity (Current Dollars)*

Year	$/Ton	Year	$/Ton
1960	49.81	1972	83.83
1965	66.23	1973	84.95
1970	82.90	1974	88.06
1971	83.54	1978	106.37

*Investment less accumulated depreciation plus capitalized leases divided by total cars owned or leased. Statistics for 1975 through 1978 are no longer published by the Interstate Commerce Commission. 1978 Statistics were developed from a special study of ICC annual reports of 40 Class I railroads.

SOURCE: ICC, *Transport Statistics* (through 1974) and Form R-1 annual reports.

from $3.8 billion to $9.7 billion, whereas freight revenue increased from $8.0 billion to $20.0 billion. Average investment per car increased from $2302 to $7876. To eliminate the effects of increased size, the average net investment per ton of capacity was about $42 in 1958 versus $106 in 1978—an increase of 242% (4.7%, compounded annually). Dividing the Association of American Railroads (AAR) reported net investment average by average capacity per car yields the change in capacity costs shown in Table 4-7. (In 1980, new-car costs were about $440 per ton.)

The AAR reported the average freight car age to be about 14.4 years for all car types. The age distribution of the car fleet in 1979 was as shown in Table 4-8.

Age distribution by car type varies greatly. Because of additions to the fleet, the age distribution of bulk commodity cars of covered hoppers and open-top hopper cars is, on the average, skewed more toward the younger ages. Other car types, such as plain boxcars, gondolas, stock, and flat (except multilevel and TOFC/COFC) are skewed toward the older ages.

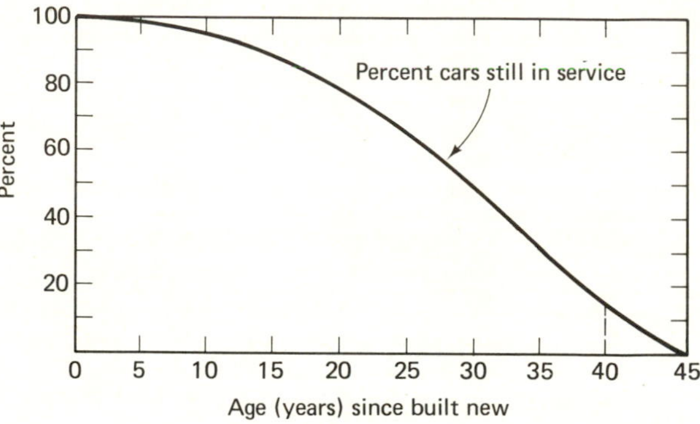

Figure 4.1. Estimated freight car survival curve (average railroad freight car). SOURCE: American Railway Car Institute.

Although the data base exists, complete information concerning the average life of freight cars is not available. The only known study that attempted to determine average car life for the U.S. rail fleet was one performed by the American Freight Car Institute in 1966. This study developed the freight car survival curve shown in Figure 4.1; it shows, for a group of new cars, the percentage still in service as of the *n*th year. Cars older than 40 years (50 years, if rebuilt between the tenth and twenty-fifth years) cannot be used in interchange service among railroads; they are usually scrapped or confined to local service.

Table 4-9 summarizes selected locomotive statistics. Although the number of locomotive units has decreased, the aggregate horsepower has increased. In 1968, the average horsepower per unit was 1791. In 1979, it was 2188. New road (line-haul) power installed typically ranges from 3000 to 3600 hp per unit. Unit reliability and maintainability

TABLE 4–8
Freight Car Age Distribution, 1979

Years	Number of Cars (× 10^3) (Including Rebuilt): Class I RR	Private Line	Total*	Percent of Fleet Total: Class I RR	Private Line	Total*
0–10	464.1	239.5	777.2	35.6	53.9	39.2
11–20	495.3	136.9	677.9	38.0	30.8	34.2
21–30	269.2	53.3	396.1	20.7	12.0	20.0
31–40	60.0	11.9	105.9	4.6	2.7	5.3
Over 40	13.5	2.8	23.3	1.0	0.6	1.2
Total	1302.1	444.4	1980.4	100.0	100.0	100.0

*Includes Canada and Mexico.

SOURCE: Association of American Railroads, Car Service Division.

TABLE 4–9
Locomotives U.S. Class I Railroads

	1970	1979
Number of Locomotives at end of year		
Diesel locomotive units	26,796	26,928
Electric locomotive units	268	103
Aggregate horsepower		
Diesel locomotive units	51,601,362	58,923,744
Electric locomotive units	1,007,930	428,130
Average horsepower		
Diesel locomotive units	1,926	2,188
Electric locomotive units	3,761	4,157

SOURCE: ICC, *Transport Statistics*.

TABLE 4–10
Relative Dependency on Rail Freight Service of the Nation's Various Economic Sectors, 1975

Category	Rank	Ton-Miles ($\times 10^9$)	Cumulative Ton-Miles*	Percent Cumulative Ton-Miles	Percent Cumulative Revenues
Coal mining	1	170	170	20.48	13.39
Food and drugs	2	93	263	31.69	18.80
Lumber and products	3	82	345	41.57	22.27
Agriculture	4	73	418	50.36	37.46
Miscellaneous mining	5	60	478	57.59	44.41
Chemicals	6	56	534	64.34	49.12
Paper and products	7	49	583	70.24	52.73
Stone, clay, glass products	8	35	618	74.40	56.55
Iron and steel	9	29	647	77.95	59.91
Government enterprises	10	24	671	80.84	61.46
Iron ore mining	11	20	691	83.25	62.53
Nonferrous metal	12	19	710	85.54	64.11
Petroleum products	13	13	723	87.11	76.00
Scrap sales	14	13	736	88.67	76.72
Plastic, paint, rubber	15	12	748	90.12	80.19
Motor vehicles	16	12	760	91.57	82.45
Nonferrous mining	17	11	771	92.89	82.92
Railroads	18	9	780	93.98	83.37
Gross imports	19	8	788	94.94	83.63
Fabricated metal products	20	8	796	95.90	85.54
Miscellaneous manufacturing	21	5	801	96.51	87.17
Furniture	22	5	806	97.11	87.98
Farm construction machines	23	4	810	97.59	88.59
Industrial machines	24	4	814	98.07	90.21
Ordnance	25	4	818	98.55	90.73
Electrical machines	26	4	822	99.04	92.98
Business travel, gifts	27	3	825	99.40	93.50
Other transportation equipment	28	2	827	99.64	93.94
Textiles and apparel	29	2	829	99.88	97.47
Scientific, optical instruments	30	.2	829	99.88	99.24
Printing	31	.2	830	100	99.93
Aircraft	32	.04	830	100	100

*1 ton-mile = 1.46 tonne-km.

SOURCE: *National Transportation Trends and Choices* (to the year 2000), U.S. Department of Transportation, Jan. 12, 1977.

have also been improved. Unit availability and utilization have improved correspondingly, requiring fewer units and less horsepower to produce more ton-miles.

General traffic trends

Table 4-10, from a 1977 U.S. DOT study, shows the relative dependency of the nation's various economic sectors on rail freight service. According to this study, the products of nine industries comprise 78% of railroad ton-miles and 60% of total freight revenues. Coal is by far the leading commodity in terms of ton-miles, and it is also the fastest growing in terms of percentage of ton-miles. Coal represents 26% of tonnage shipped but only 20% of total ton-miles and 13% of revenues.[5] This is because coal is shipped over distances less than the average haul for all commodities and, to a very large extent, in efficient and economical unit trains at relatively low rates compared to other commodities. It is significant that these top nine industries ship mostly bulk commodities by rail. Specialized services are the fastest-growing areas of rail service—most notably intermodal TOFC/COFC and coal unit train.

[5]*National Transportation Trends and Choices* (to the year 2000), U.S. Department of Transportation, Washington, D.C., Jan. 12, 1977.

Intermodal traffic

The railroad industry offers intermodal (TOFC/COFC) rail service in five basic tariff plans, as follows:

- Plan I—The railroad provides line-haul (ramp-to-ramp) service under a contract with a motor carrier, handling its traffic and trailers.
- Plan II—The railroad provides line-haul service and pickup and delivery service, and furnishes trailers/containers. (In Plan II 1/4, the railroad provides either pickup or delivery service; in Plan II 1/2, the shipper arranges for local pickup and delivery service.)
- Plan III—The railroad provides line-haul service and intermodal flatcar; the shipper furnishes trailers/containers and provides for pickup and delivery service.
- Plan IV—The railroad provides line-haul service and the shipper furnishes intermodal flatcars and trailers/containers and provides for loading and unloading.
- Plan V—The railroad provides line-haul service and furnishes trailers/containers under a revenue division agreement [rather than a subcontract on a joint (through) rate]. The motor carriers provide pickup and delivery service and prior or subsequent line-haul (if any).

Plan II 1/2 is a popular and fast growing segment of rail intermodal traffic, although Plan III is rapidly increasing in favor as many railroads prefer shippers to furnish trailers

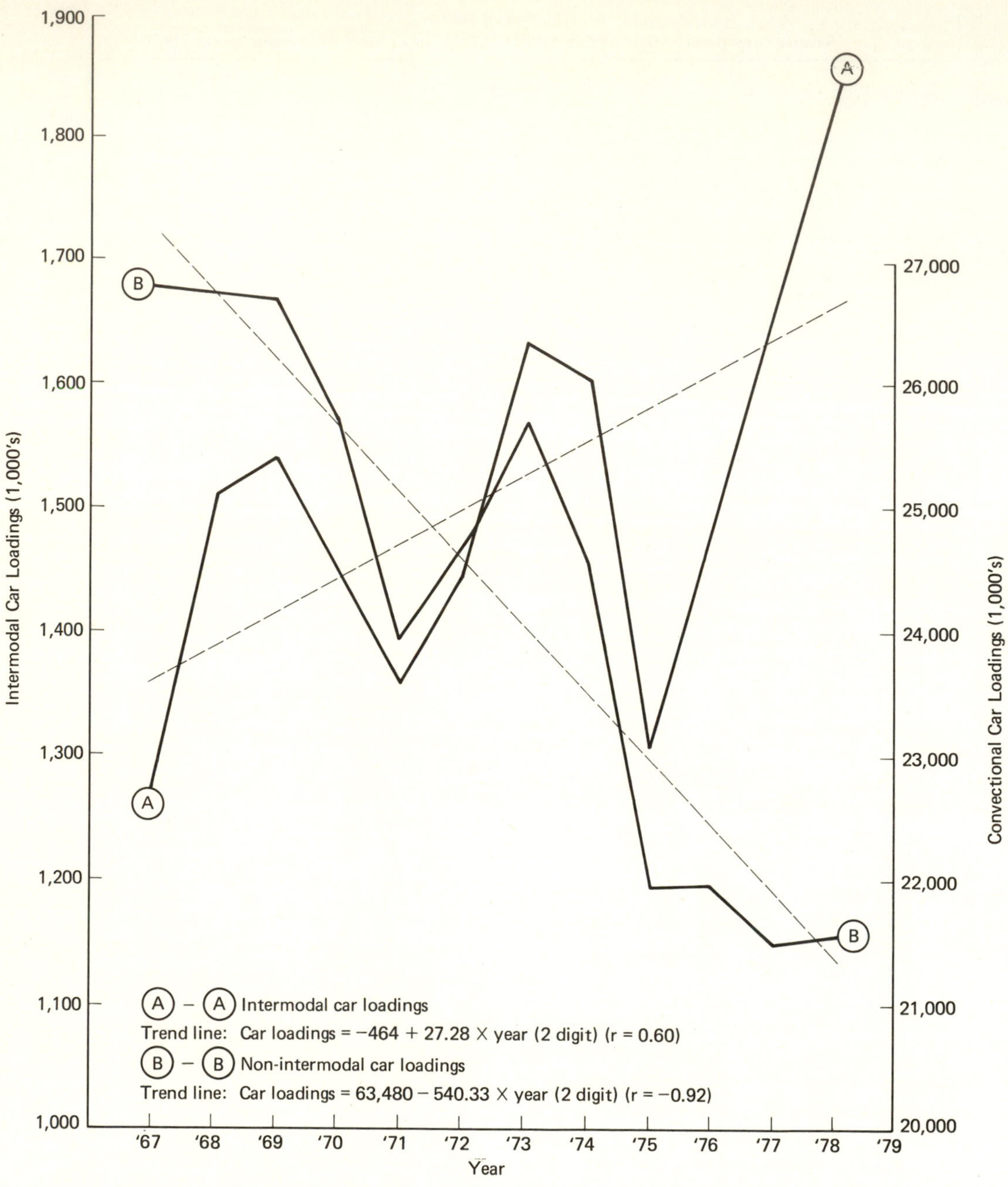

Figure 4.2. Number of revenue carloadings in intermodal service and conventional freight service, 1967–1978. SOURCE: Association of American Railroads, *Yearbook of Railroad Facts*, and Bureau of Labor Statistics.

or containers. "Land bridge" service (movement of containers between Europe and the Orient via rail across the United States) and "minibridge" service (container traffic between the U.S. east coast and the Orient) are two growing areas of intermodalism.

Figure 4.2 compares carloadings of conventional and intermodal freight, including trend lines for the 11-year period 1967–1978. Rail-based intermodal freight service is offered by all Class I roads from 1400 facilities.[6] Twenty-three railroads, operating 131 terminals with mechanized facilities to load and unload trailers, handle approximately 75% of rail intermodal traffic.[7]

The average length of haul for intermodal traffic is over 1000 mi (1600 km), as compared with 587 mi (945 km) for carload traffic.[8] Excluding the high concentration of traffic moving over 2000 mi (3200 km), the average haul per ton is about 790 mi (1270 km).

The cost structure of rail intermodal service prevents it

[6]*Systems Engineering for Intermodal Freight Systems*, Peat, Marwick, Mitchell & Co. for the Federal Railroad Administration, Mar. 1978 Contract DOT-FR-4273, p. III.6.

[7]Ibid., p. III.9.

[8]Ibid., p. III.24; Association of American Railroads, *Yearbook of Railroad Facts, 1978*.

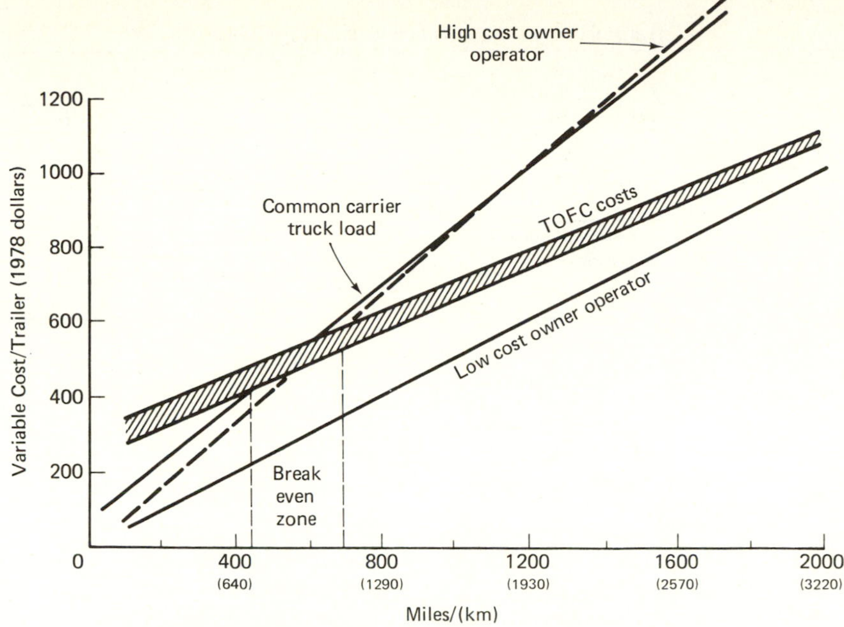

Figure 4.3. Truck versus TOFC costs. SOURCE: *Systems Engineering for Intermodal Freight Systems,* Peat, Marwick, Mitchell & Co., Mar. 1978.

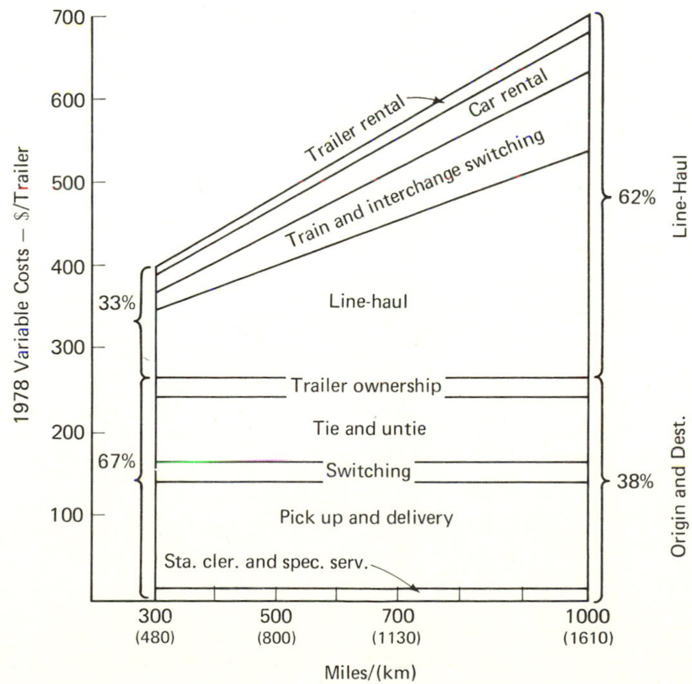

Figure 4.4. Typical TOFC costs, 20-ton load. SOURCE: Peat, Marwick, Mitchell & Co.

from competing profitably with motor carriers in the short-haul market (under 300 mi or 500 km). Figures 4.3 and 4.4 summarize the cost characteristics of rail intermodal service versus truck and the components of rail costs.

The economic deregulation of certain agricultural commodities in 1979, and the reversal of the ICC's position to now allow contract rates, may be a harbinger of renewed intermodal growth to help railroads recapture a significant share of agricultural traffic lost to highways. Some roads, one under economic sponsorship of the Federal Railroad Administration, are experimenting with short, fast TOFC/COFC trains on a point-to-point, quick-turnaround basis. Highway fuel costs may be another factor favoring intermodal rail traffic.

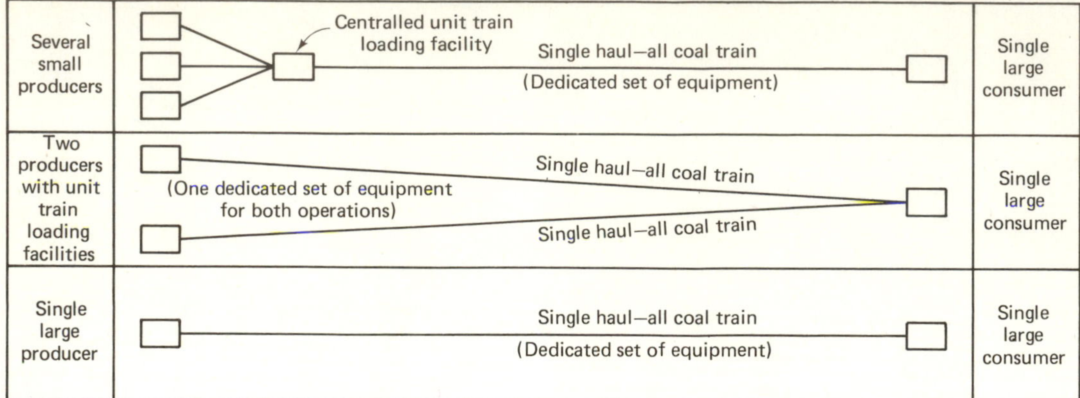

Figure 4.5. Types of unit train movement. SOURCE: U.S. Bureau of Mines.

Unit trains

Of the 800 million tons (730 million tonnes) of coal produced in 1978, 13% were consumed at mine mouth, with the balance transported by rail, highway, and water.[9] Railroads transported about 75% of the total coal shipped, with 12% and 13% having moved via water and highway, respectively. Highway moves are usually less than 50 mi (80 km) versus lengths of haul ranging from 200 to 1500 mi (320 to 2400 km) for rail or water. Eight railroads accounted for over 80% of originated coal tonnage.[10]

Most coal moves in solid trainload lots. Forms of coal train service are shown in Figure 4.5. The last movement shown (single origin, single destination) is, in the strictest sense, a true unit train move. The proportion of coal moving in unit trains is increasing. In 1968, 27% of originated tons moved by unit trains; now it is over 50%,[11] and by 1990, it may rise to as much as 75%. Typical unit trains range from 84 to 110 cars, totaling 11,000 to 14,300 gross trailing (behind the locomotive) tons (10,000 to 13,000 tonnes), with each car carrying about 100 net tons (91 tonnes) of coal. Four or five locomotives typically pull such trains, with power averaging from 0.75 to 1.5 hp per trailing ton. Helper engines are frequently used on grades over 1%.

Coal is not the only commodity moving in unit trains. Movement of grain from large inland elevators to ports is increasing in popularity. Unit train movements of oil, fertilizer, rock, and other bulk commodities exist and may be expected to increase as a result of the November 1978 order by the ICC permitting railroads to enter into contract rates. Contract rates are specifically encouraged by the Staggers Rail Act of 1980.

Passenger services

Three types of passenger services are operated on U.S. railroads: intercity, commuter, and auto/passenger. Intercity passenger service is provided exclusively by Amtrak (with the one remaining exception, in 1981, of the Denver and Rio Grande Western). Commuter services are performed by 11 railroads in seven cities, often under contract to a commuter operating authority. Auto-Train, a private company, operates the only U.S. service, between Lorton, Virginia, and Sanford, Florida, where both passengers and their cars are transported.

Virtually all intercity and commuter passenger service operates at a deficit. Although service is but a fraction of what railroads used to offer, Amtrak's operating subsidies run over $500 million per year, not including capital grants such as the $1.7 billion Northeast Corridor project for higher-speed track up to 125 mph (200 km/h) and additional electrification from New Haven to Boston. Fares cover less than half of operating expenses.[12]

Revenues and operating statistics

Table 4-11 summarizes passenger traffic statistics for the years 1970 and 1978. Table 4-12 summarizes passenger train car ownership and average capacity.

Table 4-13 summarizes the gross financial and operating statistics of U.S. railroads for 1978. Table 4-14 shows the distribution of operating revenues. Table 4-15 summarizes employment and average wages.

Competition

Shipper modal choice is governed primarily by the following factors:

- Tariff rates and provisions
- Service (reliability, transit time)
- Historical loss and damage experience
- Freight car loading and unloading costs
- Shipper/receiver facilities (absence of a rail siding is a major deterrent to use of rail)

[9] "National Policy Study Commission Draft Report," *Railw. Age,* May 9, 1977.

[10] Conrail, Norfolk & Western, Chesapeake and Ohio, Baltimore and Ohio, Louisville and Nashville, Southern, Illinois Central Gulf, and Burlington Northern.

[11] *Railw. Age,* July 31, 1978, p. 23.

[12] *National Transportation Trends and Choices* (to year 2000), p. 191.

TABLE 4-11
Passenger Traffic, Class I Railroads (× 10³)

	1970	1978
Revenue		
Commutation	$172,301	$240,196
Intercity	248,151	367,692
Total	$420,452	$607,888
Passengers carried		
Commutation	206,090	199,824
Intercity	77,804	81,137
Total	283,894	280,961
Passenger miles		
Commutation	4,591,668	4,666,235
Intercity	6,147,950	5,555,718
Total	10,739,618	10,221,953
Averages		
Revenue per passenger		
Commutation	$0.84	$1.20
Intercity	3.19	4.53
Revenue per passenger-mile		
Commutation	$0.0375	$0.0515
Intercity	0.0416	0.0612
Average trip length (mi)		
Commutation	22.3	23.4
Intercity	79.3	68.5

SOURCE: ASSOCIATION OF AMERICAN RAILROADS, *Statistics of Railroads of Class I.*

TABLE 4-12
Passenger Train Cars, Class I Railroads

	1970	1978*
Passenger train cars at end of year		
Coaches	6,472	3,067
Parlor	219	161
Sleeping	677	331
Dining	495	244†
Baggage, express, mail, or combination	3,010	—‡
All other nonpassenger	304	523
Total	11,177	4,326
Average seating capacity		
Coaches	80	105
Parlor	48	40
Sleeping	23	20

*Includes Amtrak and Auto-Train.
†Also includes grill and tavern cars.
‡Included under all other nonpassenger.

SOURCE: ASSOCIATION OF AMERICAN RAILROADS, *Statistics of Railroads of Class I.*

Many shippers consider transportation as just one part of the cost of physical distribution. Besides transportation, physical distribution costs include material handling, inventory (in warehouses and in transit), loss and damage, paperwork, shipment tracing, and interest costs. Inherent service and cost characteristics generally give railroads the cost and service advantage in long-haul service for most commodities. In short-haul markets, railroads are generally competitive only for high-volume bulk commodities of high density. This accounts for the railroad average length of haul of about 590 mi (950 km), as compared with 251 mi (418 km) for trucks.[13]

Trucks handle 85% of shipments under 30,000 lb (13,600 kg), 21% of the U.S. total.[14] Railroads handle 55% of traffic

TABLE 4-13
1979 Statistical Highlights of U.S. Class I Line-Haul Railroads*

Plant and equipment	
Net Investment	$29,692,000,000
Locomotives	28,402
Freight cars*	1,700,310
Capital expenditures	$3,324,840,000
Locomotives added	1,931
Freight cars added†	90,903
Traffic	
Revenue carloadings	23,876,447
Revenue ton-miles	913,669,000,000
Revenue per ton-mile (units)	2.617
Miles hauled per ton	595
Financial results	
Operating revenues	$25,714,136,000
Operating expenses	24,517,860,000
Taxes	
Current incomes taxes	209,419,000
Deferred taxes	213,874,000
Net railway operating income	794,423,000
Rate of return (%)	2.68
Net income (ordinary)	$813,888,000
Cash dividends	533,701,000
Net working capital	508,200,000
Employment and wages	
Average number of employees	502,975
Total wage compensation	$10,907,500,000
Average hourly wages	9.25
Average yearly wages	22,585
Operations	
Cars per freight train	66.4
Tons per carload	64.0
Net ton-miles per train-hour	35,960
Car-miles per car-day	59.2
Net ton-miles per car-day	1,869

*Data include Amtrak locomotive statistics and average number of employees.
†Freight car data are for all railroads and private car companies.

SOURCE: ASSOCIATION OF AMERICAN RAILROADS, *Yearbook of Railroad Facts*, 1980, p. 9.

in the over 30,000-lb shipment category (excluding pipelines), about 42% of originated tonnage. Principal commodities originated by mode are roughly summarized in Table 4-16.

About 47% of originated freight tons moves less than 200 mi. Railroads handle less than an estimated 20% of this market, trucks an estimated 75%.[15] Trucks have gained in market share because of their flexible, dependable, and tailored service, their favorable short-haul economics, and the convenience of handling smaller shipment sizes (as compared with carload lots). Improved highways also contributed greatly to the growth of the motor carrier industry.

The private motor carrier is the main competitor of both the railroads and the regulated motor common carrier. For-hire common carriers exhibited an average compound growth rate of 7.1% in ton-miles between 1947 and 1970, as compared with a rate of 0.7% for railroads and 8.7% for private carriers. The latter's growth rate was also heaviest in the 1970s: for 1970–1980, the average estimated compound growth rate was 4.9%, compared with 4.0% for for-hire trucks and 2.3% for railroads.[16]

In a rail versus truck modal advantage study, the American Trucking Association (ATA)[17] determined that one

[13]*1972 Census of Transportation,* Bureau of Labor Statistics, Washington, D.C.

[14]*Industrial Energy Studies in Ground Freight Transportation,* Peat, Marwick, Mitchell & Co., Washington, D.C., July 1974, p. III-1. Based on 1967 Census of Transportation Data analysis. Since 1967, railroad share of ton-miles has dropped from 44% to about 36%.

[15]According to the Peat, Marwick, Mitchell & Co. study, *Systems Engineering,* it was 29% for rail and 69% for truck in 1967 (p. III-4).

[16]*Transportation Projections: 1970 and 1980,* U.S. Department of Transportation, Washington, D.C., 1972.

[17]R. D. ROTH, "An Approach to Measurement of Modal Advantage," Department of Economics, American Trucking Association, Washington, D.C., Jan. 1977.

TABLE 4-14
Distribution of Operating Revenues (Dollar Amounts in Millions)

	1979 (Est.)	1978	Increase
Total operating revenues	$25,714	$21,721	$3,993
Wages charged to expenses*	10,362	9,216	1,146
Health and welfare and pensions	758	722	36
Payroll taxes	1,618	1,458	160
Total labor costs*	12,738	11,396	1,342
Income taxes on ordinary income†	209	183	26
Provision for deferred taxes	214	93	121
Fuel and power locomotives	2,414	1,556	858
Loss and damage, injuries, and insurance	945	822	123
Depreciation	1,058	975	83
All other expenses‡§	7,342	6,269	1,073
Total expenses and taxes§	24,920	21,294	3,626
Net railway operating income	794	427	367

The Revenue Dollar—1979

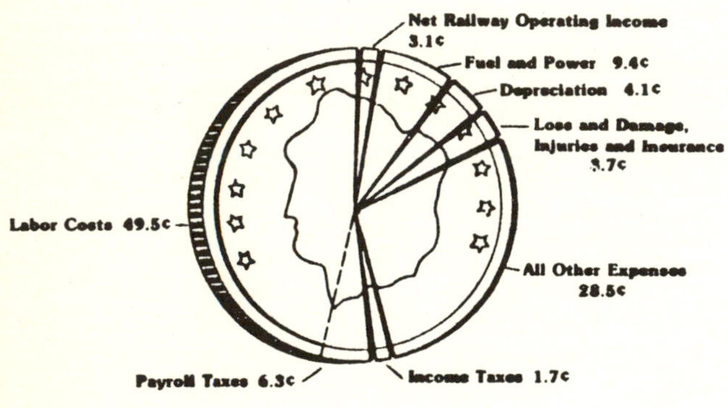

*Does not include wages charged to investment accounts. Total wages, health and welfare benefits, pensions, and payroll taxes applicable to 1978 amounted to 53.8 cents of each revenue dollar.

†Includes state income taxes in 1978 only. In 1977, state taxes are included in other expenses.

‡Includes other materials and supplies and miscellaneous, equipment and joint facility rents, current taxes (other than payroll taxes and income taxes), and retirement charges.

§Excludes rent for leased roads and equipment (minus income from lease of road and equipment).

SOURCE: ASSOCIATION OF AMERICAN RAILROADS, *Yearbook of Railroad Facts*, 1980, p. 11.

carrier was modal-dominant if the other transported less than 10% of the total goods shipped. According to this definition, 45% of total tons of manufactured goods transported are truck-dominated, 29% are rail-dominated, and the balance is competitive—that is, both rail and truck handled more than 10% of goods transported. Table 4-17 shows the distribution of modal domination, rail versus truck, by distance and shipment size.

TABLE 4-15
Employment and Annual Wages by Classes, 1979*

Employee Group	Average Number of Employees	Total Payroll ($\times 10^3$)	Average Annual Earnings
Executive, officials, and staff	17,295	$ 554,166	$32,042
Professional, clerical, and general	95,606	1,897,836	19,851
Maintenance of way and structures	89,152	1,730,585	19,412
Maintenance of equipment and stores	106,716	2,169,144	20,326
Transportation, other than train, engine, and yard	22,009	473,617	21,519
Yardmasters, switch-tenders, and hostlers	8,567	203,442	23,747
Train and engine service	143,617	3,875,098	26,982
Total	482,962	10,903,888	22,577

*Preliminary figures.

SOURCE: ASSOCIATION OF AMERICAN RAILROADS, *Yearbook of Railroad Facts*, 1980, p. 58.

Water competition for railroads occurs on the Great Lakes, inland waterways, coastal waterways (barge), and by intercoastal (ship) operations. Great Lakes competition has been declining slowly for many years in absolute and relative terms. Great Lakes traffic now amounts to about 4% of revenue freight ton-miles (95 billion), compared with 10.5% in 1950 (112 billion). Revenue freight ton-miles via rivers and canals had edged erratically upward from 9.2% (121 billion) in 1960 to about 12% (275 billion) of the U.S. total in 1978 (Table 4-1).

Labor and capital productivity

Railroad labor and capital productivity can be measured in several ways, including the following:

1. *Labor*—per employee-hour or employee:
   a. Ton-miles
   b. Tons originated
   c. Carloads
   d. Car-miles
   e. Train-miles
   f. Revenue
2. *Capital*
   a. Turnover (revenue divided by net assets employed)
   b. After-tax return on investment, owners' equity, or net assets employed

TABLE 4-16
Percent of Total Freight Originated

Truck		Rail		Water	
Products of agriculture	6.2	Coal	16.7	Petroleum products	35.0
General for-hire freight	55.7	Other bulk commodities	24.0	Coal	11.0
Retail and wholesale trade	16.0	Agriculture and agricultural products	16.7	Iron ore, iron, and steel	21.0
Private carriage	15.5	Wood and lumber	11.4	Chemicals	10.0
All others	6.6	All others	31.2	Grain	6.0
				All others	17.0
Total	100.0		100.0		100.0

SOURCE: "Impact of Middle East Embargo on U.S. Domestic Freight Transportation," U.S. Department of Transportation Discussion Paper, 1974.

TABLE 4–17
Distribution of Shipment Size and Distance of Modally Dominated and Intermodally Competitive Freight for All Manufactured Products, 1972*

	Under 1000 lb	1000–9999 lb	10,000–29,999 lb	30,000–59,999 lb	60,000–89,999 lb	90,000 lb or More
Less than 100 mi	0.51	2.28	6.05	11.84	1.29	6.93
100–199 mi	0.27	1.24	2.51	7.22	1.02	4.57
200–299 mi	0.20	0.93	1.60	4.88	1.05	4.09
300–499 mi	0.30	1.22	1.90	4.84	1.37	5.46
500–999 mi	0.44	1.34	1.85	4.55	2.12	6.63
1000–1499 mi	0.11	0.29	0.38	1.12	0.80	2.27
1500 mi or more	0.12	0.37	0.33	0.77	1.17	1.76

*Solid box, truck-dominant; dashed box, rail-dominant; others, competitive.

SOURCE: R.D. ROTH, "An Approach to Measurement of Modal Advantage," Department of Economics, American Trucking Associations, Jan. 1977.

TABLE 4–18
Indices of Change in Railroad Labor and Capital Productivity Line-Haul, U.S. Class I Railroads

	Per Employee-Day (8 h) 1970	Per Employee-Day (8 h) 1978	Average Annual Change (Compounded) (%)	Per Employee 1970	Per Employee 1978	Averge Annual Change (Compounded) (%)
Labor						
Ton-miles	4,435	6,020	3.9	1,350,579	1,819,885	3.8
Tons originated	8.61	9.75	1.6	2,622	2,946	1.5
Carloads	0.158	0.164	0.5	48.0	49.6	0.4
Car-miles	173.3	203.8	2.1	52,783	61,614	2.0
Train-miles	2.48	3.04	2.6	754	918	2.5
Freight revenue	$63.34	$142.65	10.7	$19,287	43,122	10.6

Capital	1970	1978
Turnover (revenue ÷ net assets)	0.358	0.550
After-tax return* on:		
Net investment (%)	0.83	1.53
Owner's equity	1.40	2.47
Net assets (%)	0.58	1.28

*Ordinary income or net railway operating income.

SOURCE: ASSOCIATION OF AMERICAN RAILROADS, *Yearbook of Railroad Facts*, 1978; ICC, *Transport Statistics of the United States*.

No single measure for either labor or capital tells the full story of productivity improvement. Table 4-18 summarizes changes in labor and capital productivity of the factors enumerated above. Problems in freight car utilization underscore the need for productivity improvement. This is examined in some detail in a separate section on freight cars.

Since there are trade-offs between labor and capital, considering only one dimension of measuring railroad productivity can be misleading. A 1973 federal government–commissioned task force on railroad productivity stated:[18]

> Conventional and widely-used measures of railroad productivity, such as "ton-miles per man-hour," indicate that rail productivity has grown at a rate of 5–6% a year during recent decades, considerably above the average growth of labor productivity in the private economy (3.0%) during these same decades. However, using alternative assumptions and measures (e.g., allowing for changes in the composition of rail traffic), it can be argued that growth in rail labor productivity has been only about 3.7%. Capital inputs to the railroad industry have not declined nearly so rapidly as labor inputs, and the indicated growth of rail capital productivity is near zero. When labor, capital and other inputs are weighted together, total rail productivity may have grown only about 1–2% per year during recent decades. This low level of total productivity growth, considerably below the level of total productivity growth in the private economy (2.5% per year), is consistent with the railroads' loss of traffic to other modes and with the low rate of return on investment in railroad property.

The railroad industry has greatly outperformed motor carrier competition in labor productivity improvements since World War II; but in terms of ton-miles per employee-hour,[19] the motor carrier industry has made great inroads into gaining market share and in narrowing the price difference between the two modes. The task force reported that the capital/labor ratio for the rail industry had been growing at an annual rate of 4.7% during the 1948–1966 period, compared with 2.6% for the private domestic economy as a whole[20] (more recent comparison studies have not been made).

Other factors make it difficult to measure rail productivity and, in general, contribute to lowering the overall gains. These factors include:

- Increased reliance on purchased services and materials instead of company resources

[18]*Improving Railroad Productivity*, Final Report of the Task Force on Railroad Productivity to the National Commission on Productivity and the Council of Economic Advisors, Washington, D.C., Nov. 1973.

[19]Ibid., p. 54.

[20]JOHN W. KENDRICK, *Postwar Productivity Trends in the United States, 1948–1969*, National Bureau of Economic Research, New York, 1971, pp. 5–8.

- ○ Change in traffic characteristics
- ○ Additions of nonrailroad capital in the form of privately owned cars
- ○ Deferral of maintenance expenses
- ○ Reduction of fixed plant
- ○ Shedding of capital/labor-intensive services

The use of ton-miles per employee-hour as a measure of labor productivity growth is misleading. The rail industry has experienced a significant change in composition of traffic, toward that which is less costly to produce (such as unit train) and less valuable in the marketplace (such as lower-rated bulk commodities moving over longer lengths of haul). The task force was quite negative on railroad productivity improvements, after all factors had been considered, and attributed the poor condition of the railroad industry to an insufficient true growth rate in productivity.

Industry blames high labor costs and severely restrictive work rules as the principal cause of low-productivity improvements because they have:

- ○ Forced substitution of capital for labor as a partial solution
- ○ Deprived industry of the cash needed to capitalize on available opportunities
- ○ Held down traffic volume and economies of utilizing excess fixed plant capacity

Union labor restrictions have been a major factor in the decline of the industry, and removal of these restrictions offers promise of substantial traffic and profitability gains. The Florida East Coast (FEC) cut its transportation employment by 70% (from 880 employees to 264) in the 11-year span 1960–1971, as compared with the U.S. average of about 27%, when it successfully eliminated restrictive labor work-rule practices. In 1978, the FEC produced 2.99 million revenue ton-miles (4.37 million tonne-km) annually per employee (total), as compared with the U.S. average of 1.86 million revenue ton-miles (2.72 million tonne-km) per employee. The flexibility regained by management enabled the FEC to reduce its net investment in transportation property and perform increased levels of service. Its return on investment tripled in the 11-year period. In 1978, it averaged 17%, as compared with the industry average of 1.62%.

In 1979, the Norfolk and Western demonstrated, during an 82-day strike by the Brotherhood of Railway and Airline Clerks, that 3000 supervisory employees—out of a total of 33,000 employees—could handle 30% of the prestrike traffic, and the percentage was still growing at the time the strike was settled.

A major midwestern railroad analyzed the impact that better labor utilization could have on operations of a major division in terms of cost, profits, and market share. The road concluded that traffic could increase by 20% (chiefly modal diversion from trucks), costs would increase by less than half the projected revenue increase, and a marginal division of the railroad would be made solidly profitable. Furthermore, net employment would not drop because projected traffic increases would more than offset productivity increases.[21]

There is hope that labor is accepting the need for change. Labor–management task forces in Chicago and St. Louis have achieved substantial service and productivity gains. Several railroads now have crewing arrangements that are much more flexible and efficient, although expensive.

Developments in other areas include the following:

1. Improved freight car control systems are being developed by railroads, the Federal Railroad Administration, and the Association of American Railroads.
2. Freight car service orders are being changed to improve car utilization.
3. A clearinghouse experiment to reduce empty car-miles has been successful and offers promise of better car utilization.
4. Tariff incentives are encouraging improved rail/shipper cooperation to clean cars and improve utilization (loading to capacity, multiple-car shipments, reducing free time, reloading empty cars, etc.).
5. A national freight car pool of boxcars and flatcars for trailers or containers has greatly increased car utilization.
6. Unit trains and some special labor-agreement trains without cabooses have been extremely successful.
7. Improved technology in cars, locomotives, track, and other equipment is paying off.
8. Under new regulatory freedoms, many railroads are offering rate incentives to fill cars that would otherwise move empty.

Mergers, consolidations, and abandonments

The railroad industry has a long history of mergers and consolidations—trends that began with the birth of the industry itself. As small railroads were built by local entrepreneurs in the middle and late 1800s, other entrepreneurs were buying the more successful and promising of the small roads, combining them into even larger companies. Some of the eastern roads, such as Chessie (now a part of CSX Corporation) and Conrail, were assembled from over 100 lesser companies. Indeed, the nation's 42 Class I roads in 1979 were built from nearly 6000 independent predecessors.[22] Most mergers occurred in distinct periods:[23]

- ○ The unregulated period (prior to 1904)
- ○ The planned merger period (1920–1940)
- ○ The regulated but unplanned period (1955 to present)

As large as many roads are today [e.g., Burlington Northern has 25,000 mi (40,000 km) of railroad, roughly 10%

[21] *The Iowa Experiment: Short, High Frequency Train Operations through Labor–Management Cooperation*, Illinois Central Gulf Railroad, Sept. 1972.

[22] *A Prospectus for Change in the Freight Railroad Industry*, a preliminary report by the Secretary of Transportation (known as the "504/901 Report" after sections of the 1976 Railroad Revitalizaton and Regulatory Reform Act—"4R Act"), Washington, D.C., Oct. 1978, p. 90.

[23] Ibid.

of the U.S. total, and Conrail grosses $3.3 billion in revenue, 14.5% of the U.S. total], roughly 70% of rail traffic terminates on a railroad other than the one on which it originated.[24]

Experience has shown that parallel mergers (where railroads compete with each other) in the 1950s and 1960s, which were supposed to eliminate duplicate facilities and costs, have not achieved the expectations of the merging parties.[25] The costs of merger, labor settlements, and difficulties in combining managements of historically competing companies have proved to be major offsets to supposed economies. Where too few railroads compete, parallel mergers invoke fears of monopoly. A more recent trend is end-to-end mergers where railroads do not compete. Past such mergers have not always produced the benefits that were claimed for them. However, they offer promise of continued regional competition in most instances. While some cost saving may result from combining corporate overheads, the principal benefits of single-carrier operations are improved service, higher traffic, and better utilization of plant and facilities.[26]

Although reducing duplicate facilities through mergers takes many years, elimination of light density and duplicate rail lines is taking place at a rapid rate. From a low of less than 1000 mi (1600 km) per year in the early 1950s, in the late 1970s railroads were abandoning 3000 mi (5000 km) or more of line each year.[27] Eight percent of main tracks and 10% of yard tracks are now shared (trackage rights) or operated for the common benefit of two or more railroads.[28] As an alternative to mergers, cooperative arrangements between both competing and noncompeting railroads are occurring, driven by common economic forces of survival. Consolidations are taking place through trackage-rights agreement, joint ownership, contract arrangements, or joint agency (tenancy) agreements.

Of 230,000 mi (370,000 km) of main track and 55,000 mi (89,000 km) of yard switching tracks, 8.4% and 10.4% of the respective totals were operated under trackage-rights agreements in 1977.[29] This represents a 50% increase since 1949. Furthermore, it does not count the duplicate track mileages eliminated through mergers.

Mergers, consolidations, trackage rights, and so on, are not panaceas to industry problems. Their benefits are often overestimated and underrealized. None of these focus on the fundamental issues of railroad unprofitability: too-low rates on traffic that naturally moves by rail; problems and delays in shedding uneconomical plants and unneeded workers; competition that is subsidized to a much greater extent (directly or indirectly); and economic regulation that creates a price umbrella for competition.

Role of government

The role of government in railroading has been increasing at a dramatic rate. In 1957, only the ICC exercised any significant control over railroads. In early 1980, the Federal Railroad Administration alone (not counting other agencies of the Department of Transportation) had approximately 1400 persons. Staffing in the five broad areas, each headed by an associate administrator, is as follows:

- Administration, 100
- Federal assistance, 70
- Safety, 410
- Policy and program development, 60
- Research and development, 50

Each of these functional areas sponsors and administers a number of programs, functions, and operations from Washington, D.C., and regional offices in major U.S. cities. The staff total also includes about 500 persons employed on the Alaska Railway, 40 at the FRA's Pueblo, Colorado, Test Center, and 40 in the General Counsel's office. The remainder are included in other smaller staff categories.

State governments, as well as the federal government, have, to varying degrees, taken active roles in railroad matters. Approximately 20 states now have departments of transportation with railroad sections. The rest (except Hawaii) include railroad activities as part of their highway departments, commissions, or authorities. Several states now own and operate railroads or subsidize shortline railroad operators. Approximately 31 states monitor and inspect railroad track and/or equipment for safety.

Table 4-19 summarizes agencies having jurisdiction over economic and noneconomic areas of railroad transportation. It includes the area of responsibility for each agency.

The two most important railroad regulatory areas focus on economics and safety. The Interstate Commerce Act of 1886 created the ICC and charged it with protecting the public interest against railroad monopolies and abuses of the late 1800s. It also served to prevent the destructive competition that frequently existed between railroads. Although the Interstate Commerce Act has been changed and updated many times since 1886, it has lagged behind changes in the transportation industry.

Railroads experienced the first movements toward deregulation when they were granted authority to enter into contract rates (November 1978), after innumerable litigated precedents found such rates illegal, discriminatory, and in restraint of competition. In March 1979, railroads won the agricultural exemption that with certain exceptions—most notably grain and grain products—motor carriers have long enjoyed. In October 1980, Congress passed its most sweeping change in rail deregulation under the title of the "Staggers Rail Act of 1980." This Act:

---

[24] *Improving Railroad Productivity*, p. 232.

[25] Ibid., Chap. 7. Also, according to *Forbes* magazine (Mar. 5, 1979, p. 43), only 3 out of 17 mergers during the 1960s rank as a success—Southern's acquisition of the Central of Georgia; the Missouri Pacific/Louisville and Nashville acquisition of the Chicago and Eastern Illinois; and the Norfolk and Western's acquisition of the Virginian.

[26] Kent T. Healy, in his study *The Effects of Scale in the Railroad Industry* (Yale University Press, New Haven, 1961), determined that railroad economics of scale were maximized at a size of about 10,000 employees and that diseconomies of scale occur at significantly larger sizes.

[27] *Analysis and Evaluation of Past Experience in Rationalizing Railroad Networks*, U.S. Department of Transportation, Washington, D.C., Oct. 1974.

[28] *A Prospectus for Change in the Freight Railroad Industry*, p. 88.

[29] Ibid.

○ Encourages greater pricing flexibility, unless a shipper can prove "captive" harm.
○ Encourages greater use of negotiated transportation contracts.
○ Reduces restrictions on abandoning unprofitable lines.
○ Encourages the formation of intermodal transportation companies.
○ Limits the activities of rate bureaus (where railroads collectively set rates under the antitrust immunity of the 1948 Reed-Bulwinkle Act), and opens them to the public.
○ Eliminates general (industry-wide) rate increases (although allowing for the ICC to permit increases tied to industry inflation factors).

Deregulation of both motor carriers and railroads is supposed to do two things: raise the return on investment of railroads (from 1.6% in 1978) and reduce the return on investment of motor carriers (19.7% in 1977).[30] The theory is that railroads will shed their losses and improve their strengths, while fewer restrictions on motor carrier entry will increase competition and drive rates down. Motor carrier operating certificates—once a highly prized and expensive commodity—are now next to worthless (the write-down of this asset alone will have a significant short-term effect on motor carrier profitability).

The second area of government regulation that is of great concern to the railroads is safety regulation. Some statistical evidence suggests that railroads are becoming less safe than they were in the past—that accidents are increasing in number (per unit of related operating statistics) and severity.

A study by the Office of Technology Assessment[31] found the following:

○ Railroad accident costs accounted for 3.5% of total industry operating revenue (in 1975). Of this amount, 45% was for property and lading damage, and 10% for clearing wrecks and damage to livestock.
○ In constant dollars, accident costs increased by 38% between 1966 and 1975, whereas ton-miles rose by only 1%.
○ Track-caused accidents accounted for nearly 50% of derailments in 1974—up from about 30% from 1966.[32]
○ Equipment failures accounted for about 23% of derailments in 1974—down from 35% in 1966.
○ Bankrupt carriers have twice as many track-caused accidents as do nonbankrupt carriers.

Table 4-20 summarizes train accidents by class for the period 1966–1978, unnormalized for inflation-induced changes in reporting thresholds. Casualties and rail–highway grade-crossing accidents are summarized in Tables 4-21 and 4-22.

[30]"Ready or Not—Here Comes Transportation Deregulation," *ICC Practitioners J.*, *46*(3), 352 (Mar.–Apr. 1979).

[31]"An Evaluation of Railroad Safety," Office of Technology Assessment, U.S. Congress, May 1978. Although more recent data are available, they are not strictly comparable to pre-1975 statistics; hence, OTA did not use more recent data when making comparisons.

[32]Changes in reporting requirements in 1975 make comparison with pre-1975 data not entirely appropriate.

TABLE 4–19
Agencies Having Regulatory Authority over Rail Transportation

Agency	Nature of Authority
Federal	
Interstate Commerce Commission	Economic regulation of railroads engaged in interstate commerce
	Economic regulation of interstate motor carriers (including rail trucking subsidiaries)
U.S. Department of Transportation	
Federal Railroad Administration	Safety regulation of railroad operations, track, and equipment
	Enforcement of railroad noise standards
Federal Highway Administration	Rail/highway crossing safety regulation
	Enforcement of motor carrier noise standards
Materials Transportation Board	Safety regulations for hazardous materials
U.S. Coast Guard	Safety regulation of waterway operations (railroad bridges over navigable waterways and rail marine equipment, such as tugboats, ferries, and car floats)
National Highway Traffic Safety Administration	Design standards for motor carriers (rail intermodes equipment)
U.S. Environmental Protection Agency	Establish noise standards for railroads and motor carriers
	Establish and enforce air emission standards for motor carriers
National Transportation Safety Board	Accident investigation and safety recommendations
U.S. Department of Labor	
Occupational Safety and Health Administration	Regulations concerning safety conditions for those engaged in operating transportation modes
U.S. Department of Interior	Regulations concerning use of federal and Indian lands (e.g., right-of-way acquisition)
U.S. Corps of Engineers	Regulation of use waterway facilities (railroad marine equipment and facilities)
State and local	
Department of transportation	Establishment and enforcement of weight limitations for motor carriers
	State rail planning and safety inspection
	Establishment and enforcement of speed limits for motor carriers and railroads
Regulatory commissions	Economic regulation of intrastate common carriers
Environmental and planning agencies	Regulation of water use for pipelines
	Permits for new construction, acquisition of right-of-way

TABLE 4–20
Train Accidents by Class (Unnormalized)

Year	Derailments	Collisions	Other	Total Train Accidents
1966	4,447	1,552	794	6,793
1967	4,960	1,522	812	7,294
1968	5,487	1,727	814	8,028
1969	5,960	1,810	773	8,543
1970	5,602	1,756	737	8,095
1971	5,131	1,529	644	7,304
1972	5,509	1,348	675	7,532
1973	7,389	1,657	652	9,698
1974	8,513	1,551	630	10,694
1975*	6,328	1,002	711	8,041
1976*	7,934	1,370	944	10,248
1977*	8,073	1,363	926	10,362
1978*	8,763	1,476	1,038	11,277

*A direct comparison of data for 1975 and later with earlier years is not feasible because of major revisions in reporting requirements.

SOURCE: Federal Railroad Administration.

TABLE 4–21
Casualties Resulting from Class I and II Railroad Accidents (Unnormalized)

	Employees		Passengers		Trespassers		Other*		Total	
Year	Fatalities	Injuries	Fatalities	Injuries	Fatalities	Injuries	Fatalities	Injuries	Fatalities	Injuries
1966	168	18,651	23	1,244	678	702	1,815	4,955	2,684	25,552
1968	150	18,116	11	1,329	628	663	1,570	4,500	2,359	24,608
1970	172	16,285	8	489	593	646	1,452	3,907	2,225	21,327
1972	133	12,973	47	680	537	586	1,228	3,691	1,945	17,930
1974	144	16,002	7	574	565	674	1,192	3,568	1,908	20,818
1975†	113	47,855	8	1,307	524	703	915	4,441	1,560	54,306
1976†	109	58,477	5	998	457	766	1,059	5,090	1,630	65,331
1977†	116	61,643	4	503	458	689	952	5,032	1,530	67,867
1978†	131	65,794	13	1,252	492	746	1,010	4,732	1,646	72,545

*This group is made up primarily of casualties resulting from grade-crossing accidents.
†A direct comparison of data for 1975 and later with earlier years is not feasible because of major revisions in reporting requirements.

SOURCE: Federal Railroad Administration data.

TABLE 4–22
Rail–Highway Grade-Crossing Accidents

Year	Number of Accidents	Accidents per Billion Vehicle-Miles*	Killed	Injured	Total Casualties	Casualties per Accident
1966	4,097	4.4	1,780	4,043	5,823	1.42
1968	3,816	3.8	1,546	3,774	5,320	1.39
1970	3,559	3.2	1,440	3,336	4,776	1.34
1972	3,379	2.7	1,260	3,285	4,545	1.34
1974	3,268	2.5	1,220	3,249	4,469	1.36
1975†	11,354	n.a.	978	4,168	5,146	0.45
1976†	12,114	n.a.	1,114	4,831	5,945	0.49
1977†	12,299	n.a.	944	4,649	5,593	0.45
1978†	12,435	n.a.	1,021	4,256	5,277	0.42

*n.a., not available.
†A direct comparison of data for 1975 and later with earlier years is not feasible because of major revisions in reporting requirements. Number of accidents has been redesignated as rail–highway accidents/incidents, which include both vehicles and pedestrians and accidents involving and not involving casualties.

SOURCE: Compiled by OTA from Federal Railroad Administration and Association of American Railroads data.

The government solution to railroad safety is to legislate, rule, regulate, or inspect. Authority to promulgate railroad safety began in 1893, with the passage of the Safety Appliance Act. Since that time, major safety legislation has included coverage of:

- Air brakes and related equipment on freight cars
- Locomotive inspections
- Equipment inspections and standards
- Accident reporting
- Hours of service
- Hazardous materials transportation
- Signal inspection
- Track standards and inspection

Today, the government is searching for new alternatives to promote railroad safety, as engineering and new technology push both track and equipment to the limits of design. Train speed is being regulated based on federal track standards. Freight cars and locomotives are subject to periodic federal inspections and standards. Safety appliances (brake gear, grab irons, ladders, etc.) must be in compliance with federal laws or equipment cannot be moved. Hazardous materials must move in accordance with federal rules, and certain cars (principally tank) must meet new construction standards. Trains must be completely inspected at least once every 500 mi. Locomotive and caboose windows must be shatterproof. Employees working on equipment must protect the track in accordance with federal "Blue Flag" rules.

The Office of Technology Assessment, U.S. Congress, observed that experience with federal safety regulation has been, at best, marginally effective. Since railroad accidents are often very costly, economic benefits have generally provided more incentive than regulations to reduce accidents. The biggest handicap to achieving gains in operating safety is a lack of understanding of the complex physical relationships and interrelationships which create an environment for accidents to happen. More and better research to identify accident-contributing engineering relationships which could be designed out of or avoided in train, track, or equipment operation appears to offer far more to improve safety than increased legislation, which, of necessity, focuses more on symptoms than causes. The Department of Transportation's test track facility and research center at Pueblo, Colorado, is beginning to tackle more of these little-understood relationships.

Physical characteristics and technology

The economic and service characteristics of railroading are attributable to its physical characteristics and the present state of technology. By their very nature, railroads are efficient movers of large volumes of freight in high-density traffic corridors. Freight of many descriptions, from many sources, and to many destinations is assembled to form a train for all or a part of a journey that is common to each car in that train. Unlike their principal competition, trucks, railroads are wholesale, bulk producers of transportation.

Terminals

Terminals form the heart of railroad operations. With the exception of just a few train operations (such as coal unit trains), all trains originate and terminate at terminals. There are three basic kinds of railroad terminals: main, intermediate, and industry or satellite.

Main terminals. A main terminal is a complex of main lines, secondary lines, one or more classification yards, and one or more industry or satellite yards. The classification yard is where trains are made and broken up. It consists of three parts: a receiving yard, a classification yard, and a departure yard. These are often laid out in sequential order, or they may be side by side. Very large terminals have two such facilities, one for traffic moving in each direction.

Trains terminate in a receiving yard, on a track designated by the yardmaster. A receiving yard may be 3 to 12 tracks wide (sometimes more) on centers of 12 to 16 ft (3.7 to 4.9 m), and 2500 to 7000 ft (760 to 2130 m) long. Where tracks are insufficient to hold an entire train, trains may be "doubled" over to a second track. In the receiving yard, air is bled from the train to release the brakes for switching. Cars are inspected by carmen ("car knockers" or "car toads"), and necessary minor repairs, such as replacing brake shoes, are made. After each car is assigned a classification track corresponding to its destination, it is switched into the classification yard. There are two types of classification yards: flat-switch and hump.

Flat-Switch Classification Yard. In a flat-switch yard, cars are "kicked" by a locomotive into designated classification tracks. It is a push-pull type of operation taking place on the yard "lead" track, and it is performed by a crew consisting of an engineer (sometimes plus a fireman), a foreman, and one to three helpers (often known as switchmen). Working from a switch list, they align lead switches, uncouple the designated cars, and signal the engineer for movement. A typical crew can classify 200 to 250 cars per day in this fashion.

Hump Yard. Most modern, high-capacity yards have a hump, or crest, over which cars are pushed, uncoupled, and moved by gravity through a complex of switches into a designated track. The hump is usually 12 to 20 ft (3.7 to 6.1 m) high, and can accelerate a car up to 15 to 18 mph (24 to 29 km/h). Hump activity is governed by a yardmaster in a tower adjacent to the crest. In some cases, the yardmaster even governs the locomotive directly by radio control, although the use of signals is more common. The "pin puller" on the advance side of the crest uncouples one or more cars in the "cut." Once they are free, gravity accelerates the cut and automatic technology takes over. Controlled by a process computer, switches are aligned to the designated track stored in computer memory. Cars are automatically weighed on an in-motion scale (often for freight billing as well as yard operation), and their "rollability" is measured by radar. With weight, initial speed, wind, temperature, and how far to go in the designated "bowl" (class) track (the computer keeps track of each car in the "bowl" yard), the computer actuates an air-operated master retarder to control the speed into a "group" lead. Under between-the-track radar surveillance, the car(s) is(are) given a second "squeeze" by a "group" retarder before being released to roll into the designated group track, to a safe coupling at 4 mph (6.4 km/h) or less.

A "group" may consist of six to eight tracks; a hump yard may have anywhere from five to eight groups. The "hump engine" consists of one or more locomotives designed for (or converted to) low-speed, high-tractive operation. Often, one locomotive will be coupled to a "slug" (a weighted non-self-propelled unit that draws its power from an adjacent, coupled unit). Assisting the hump engine is the "trimmer," whose principal role is to make up the long "cuts" (a second definition of the term) which the hump engine shoves over "the hill." (Years ago, the trimmer's key role was to keep the bowl clear, correct misclassifications, and perform other chores.) Cuts of 100 to up to 250 cars may be shoved, depending on the length of the hump lead. Humping speeds are from 2 to 4 mph (3.2 to 6.4 km/h). In a modern hump yard, it is possible to classify 3000 cars in a 24-h period.

From the bowl or class yard (for both hump and flat-switch yards), cars are pulled from several tracks, each track constituting a "block" in the train. The assembled cars are then pulled to the departure yard, where air hoses are coupled, a caboose is added, and the air brake system is charged. The train may again be inspected, and a "standing" air brake test is made and observed by carmen according to prescribed federal rules. A locomotive is then added to the head end, and the crew climbs aboard. Once given the authority to proceed, the engineer "snakes" the train out of the yard onto the "main." Once on the main, the engineer advances the throttle to "Run 8" (full power) to begin the "100-mile day." A trip may take as little as 2 h between terminals (excluding initial or final terminal time), for which additional pay, usually after an allowance of 20 or 30 min at either end, is earned.

Intermediate terminals. Intermediate terminals are usually smaller yards between major terminals. They provide for crew changes on through trains, basing points for local trains, and handle local traffic which may be set out or picked up. Intermediate terminals may or may not have regularly assigned switch engines.

Industry or satellite terminals. In large metropolitan areas, many railroads have industry, or satellite terminals that receive and deliver cars to main terminals. These smaller facilities serve local industrial areas and, in some cases, one single rail customer. Switch engines and industry runs may operate out of these yards. Movements between main terminals and industry or satellite terminals are typically performed by "transfer runs."

In addition to their primary purpose, all terminals are used to hold empty cars for prospective loadings and loaded cars for billing and disposition. Repairs that cannot be performed in the train yard are made on "rip" tracks. Heavy repairs are made in the car shop.

Locomotives and cabooses are also serviced and then placed on the "ready" track. Heavy locomotive repairs are made in the "back" shop. "Roundhouses," with "turntables" for turning locomotives, are disappearing. For infrequent occasions when locomotives must be "turned," they are run around a wye or a "loop" track.

Track

Railroad track gauge is nominally 4 ft 8½ in. (1.44 m) between the "gauge" sides of the rail head (inside distance). Rail sections weigh from 100 to 140 lb/yd (50 to 69 kg/m) on mainline track, with rail of 112, 115, 132, and 136 lb (56, 57, 65 and 67 kg) being most common. Old branchline rail may range as low as 65 lb/yd (32 kg/m). Rail comes in 39-ft (12-m) and 80-ft (24-m) lengths and is bolted together with "four-hole" or "six-hole" joint bars. Most new mainline rail is welded into ¼-mi ribbons at fixed or portable rail welding plants. These sections are, in turn, field-welded, virtually eliminating rail joints.

Rail is made from high-quality steel, with 0.7 to 0.8% carbon to regulate hardness. In a special application to resist wear, rail may be of special silicone ("hi-si") alloy or be flame (surface)-hardened. New rail will typically be "work-hardened" by traffic. Heavy (high-axle-load) traffic on new rail will not give the rail adequate time to work-harden and may shorten its life. Next to wear, "creeping" (cold metal flow) and "shelling" (metal peeling) are the two most common rail problems. Rail detector cars are used to search for defects—fissures, inclusions, and fractures—which may cause rail failure. Under favorable conditions, rail may carry 600 million gross tons (544 million metric tons) of traffic in its lifetime.[33]

A four-unit 12,000-hp locomotive consist weighs about 1000 tons (900 metric tons) and spans about 260 ft (80 m). Under the locomotive, approximately 12 tons (11 tonnes) of steel rail is held in place by 600 lb (272 kg) of spikes and rail anchors resting on 3.1 tons (2.8 tonnes) of tie plates, 17 tons (15 tonnes) of treated cross-ties, and 130 tons (118 tonnes) of ballast.[34]

Rail is laid on tie plates anchored to wooden ties using spikes. Where concrete or other ties are used, various other forms of fasteners (or "clips") may be used. Rail anchors on either side of the tie keep the rail from moving due to temperature change or train forces. Ties may be 8 to 9 ft (2.4 to 2.7 m) long, 7 × 8 in. (17.8 × 20.3 cm) to 8 × 9 in. (20.3 × 22.9 cm) in cross section, and laid on centers 18 to 30 in. (46 to 76 cm). Wooden ties are usually creosote-impregnated and last 10 to 50 years, depending on traffic and climate.

On mainline track, a ballast of crushed granite, basalt, trap rock slag, gravel, or other coarse material is used. Particle sizes of ¾ to 1½ in. (1.9 to 3.8 cm) are most common. Pressure distribution is increased by a subgrade whose size is influenced by the load-bearing capacity of the soil. The average pressure at depths of 4 to 30 in. (10 to 76 cm) below the center of the tie may be calculated from the empirical relationship[35]

$$P_c = \frac{16.8P_a}{h^{1.25}} \tag{4.1}$$

where P_c = pounds per square inch at depth h

h = depth below center of the ties, in.

P_a = average unit load over the area of the tie face in compacted contact with the ballast (usually one-third of tie length)

For pressures at X inches to the right or left of the center of the tie under the rail,

$$P_x = \frac{16.8P_a}{h^{1.25}} \times 10^m \tag{4.2}$$

where

$$m = -6.05 \times \frac{X^2}{h^{2.5}} \tag{4.3}$$

Track needs to be maintained in gauge, alignment, profile, and cross-level. "Alignment" refers to straightness or uniform smoothness of curvature, "profile" to elimination of humps and depressions, and "cross-level" to the difference in elevation between the two rails of a track. Track is maintained in regular cycles, or programs, with spot work performed as needed between programs. Track safety standards are administered by the Federal Railroad Administration and classified as shown in Table 4-23.

Curves are measured in degrees, or the angle (degrees of a circle) subtended by 100 ft (30.5 m) of track (chord distance).

$$\text{Degrees} = \frac{5729}{\text{radius in ft}} \quad \text{or} \quad \frac{1746}{\text{radius in m}} \tag{4.4}$$

Straight track is known as tangent track. Curves often begin gradually with a "spiral" and may be "superelevated" (the elevation of the outside rail on a curve above the inside rail) up to 6 in. (15.2 cm) to neutralize some of the centrifugal force of a moving train. Superelevation for tracks having only freight trains rarely exceeds 4 in. (10.2 cm). Six inches of superelevation compensates for the centrifugal force of a 95-mph (150-km/h) train on a 1° curve, or a 45-mph (70-km/h) train on a 5° curve.

Switches or turnouts consist of the components shown in Figure 4.6. The switch number (or frog number) indicates the sharpness of the turnout, a measure of safe operating speed through the turnout. Switches may be "left hand," "right hand," or "equilateral" (wye). A switch is considered a facing (or leading) point switch if it faces the direction

TABLE 4–23
FRA Track Class Standards

Track Class	Maximum Allowable Operating Speed for Freight Trains [mph (km/h)]	Maximum Allowable Operating Speed for Passenger Trains [mph (km/h)]
1	10 (16)	15 (24)
2	25 (40)	30 (48)
3	40 (64)	60 (97)
4	60 (97)	80 (129)
5	80 (129)	90 (145)
6	110 (177)	110 (177)

SOURCE: Code of Federal Regulations.

[33] *The Railroad—What It Is, What It Does,* Simmons Boardman, New York, 1978, p. 31.

[34] Ibid., p. 25.

[35] Reported in WILLIAM W. HAY, *An Introduction to Transportation Engineering,* 2nd ed., Wiley, New York, 1977.

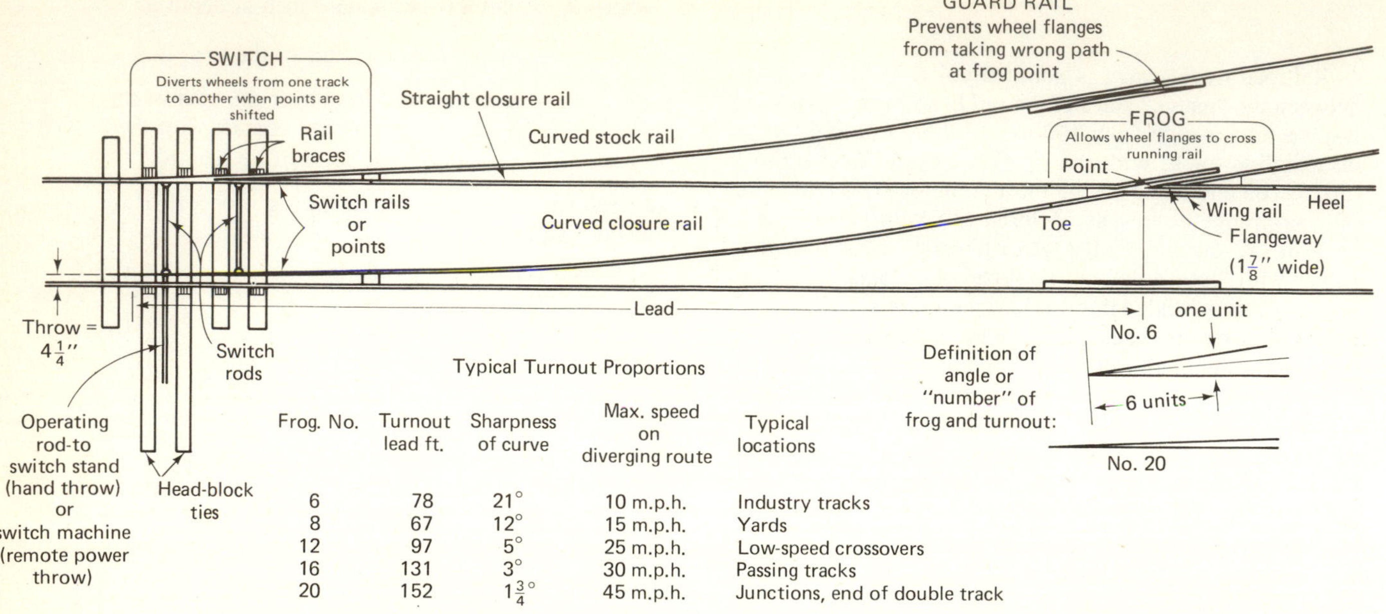

Typical Turnout Proportions

Frog. No.	Turnout lead ft.	Sharpness of curve	Max. speed on diverging route	Typical locations
6	78	21°	10 m.p.h.	Industry tracks
8	67	12°	15 m.p.h.	Yards
12	97	5°	25 m.p.h.	Low-speed crossovers
16	131	3°	30 m.p.h.	Passing tracks
20	152	$1\frac{3}{4}$°	45 m.p.h.	Junctions, end of double track

Figure 4.6. Turnout (left-hand no. 6 shown). (Courtesy: Simmons-Boardman.)

of movement and presents a train with a choice of two tracks. A switch is a trailing point switch if it faces the opposite direction. Complex switches used in dense terminal networks are called "slip" or "puzzle" switches and offer various selections of routes between adjacent tracks.

A crossover is a complex of switches allowing a train to change from one track to another. A crossing allows a train to cross another track "at grade," without the possibility of switching.

Freight cars

Freight cars are designed to haul general commodities or, increasingly, to handle specific commodities; in some cases, they are even used for shipments by specific shippers. They range in length from 40 to 90 ft (12 to 27 m) and weigh (empty) 20 to 40 tons (18 to 36 tonnes) with special exceptions. Width and height are designed to fit the contours of "plates," or an outline of maximum permissable dimensions. Plate A and B cars allow unrestricted operation. Other "plates" may impose operating (clearance) restrictions. Each car must meet AAR design requirements for pull and compression [up to 1.25 million lb (0.57 million kg) sill compression without distress].

Car capacities range from 50 to 100 tons (45.4 to 90.8 tonnes) and in some cases more. Net carrying capacity is limited by cube or the gross weight on rails, which, in turn, is a function of wheel diameter and journal (bearing) size. Each four-wheel (two-axle) truck of a typical car may weigh 9000 lb (4080 kg) or 9 tons (8.1 tonnes) for both trucks—roughly one-third the weight of a car. In most cases, running gear (including brake systems) requires the greatest attention and cost. Wheels last for 150,000 to 250,000 mi (240,000 to 400,000 km) in most cases. Some roads use multiple-wear wheels, whose treads and wheel flanges may be restored once or twice by machining for additional life.

The components of a freight car truck are illustrated in Figure 4.7. Suspension and shock control are provided by springs. Friction dampers, snubbers, or shock absorbers reduce harmonic oscillations. Rock-and-roll, a phenomenon of harmonic motion on inadequately maintained jointed track at speeds of 12 to 22 mph (19 to 35 km/h), is also reduced by these devices. Side bearings also keep car bodies from excessive swaying. Constant-contact side bearings also keep car trucks from "hunting" (severe high-speed lateral oscillations of empty cars) but may increase flange wear.

All new and rebuilt freight cars must be equipped with roller bearings. New roller-bearing designs eliminate bearing lubrication for the life of the wheel tread. Although these are much more reliable than friction bearings (which are being phased out), when failure does occur, it does so more quickly and with less visible warning and is usually more catastrophic. Only wayside heat detectors are normally capable of detecting incipient roller-bearing failure. Historically, because of the smoke and odor generated by a hot friction bearing, the train crew—particularly crew in the caboose and wayside employees—were relied upon to perform this function.

Principal inspections for car safety and running gear are made before every train terminal departure, or at 500-mi (800-km) intervals. COT&S (clean, oil, test, and stencil) inspections are made of the air brake equipment every 4 years, and an IDT (in-date test) inspection of the brake system must be performed every 6 months and if the car is on a "rip" track for any reason.

Couplings are made up of draft gear to absorb shock, a coupler yoke, draft gear housing, a yoke key, springs, dampers, a coupler head, and a coupler knuckle. The coupler knuckle is designed to fail before other system components [350,000 lb (159,000 kg) pull in general service, 650,000 lb (295,000 kg) pull in special captive service] and may easily be replaced in the field by the train crew in case of a break-in-two. Some cars have cushioned underframes that

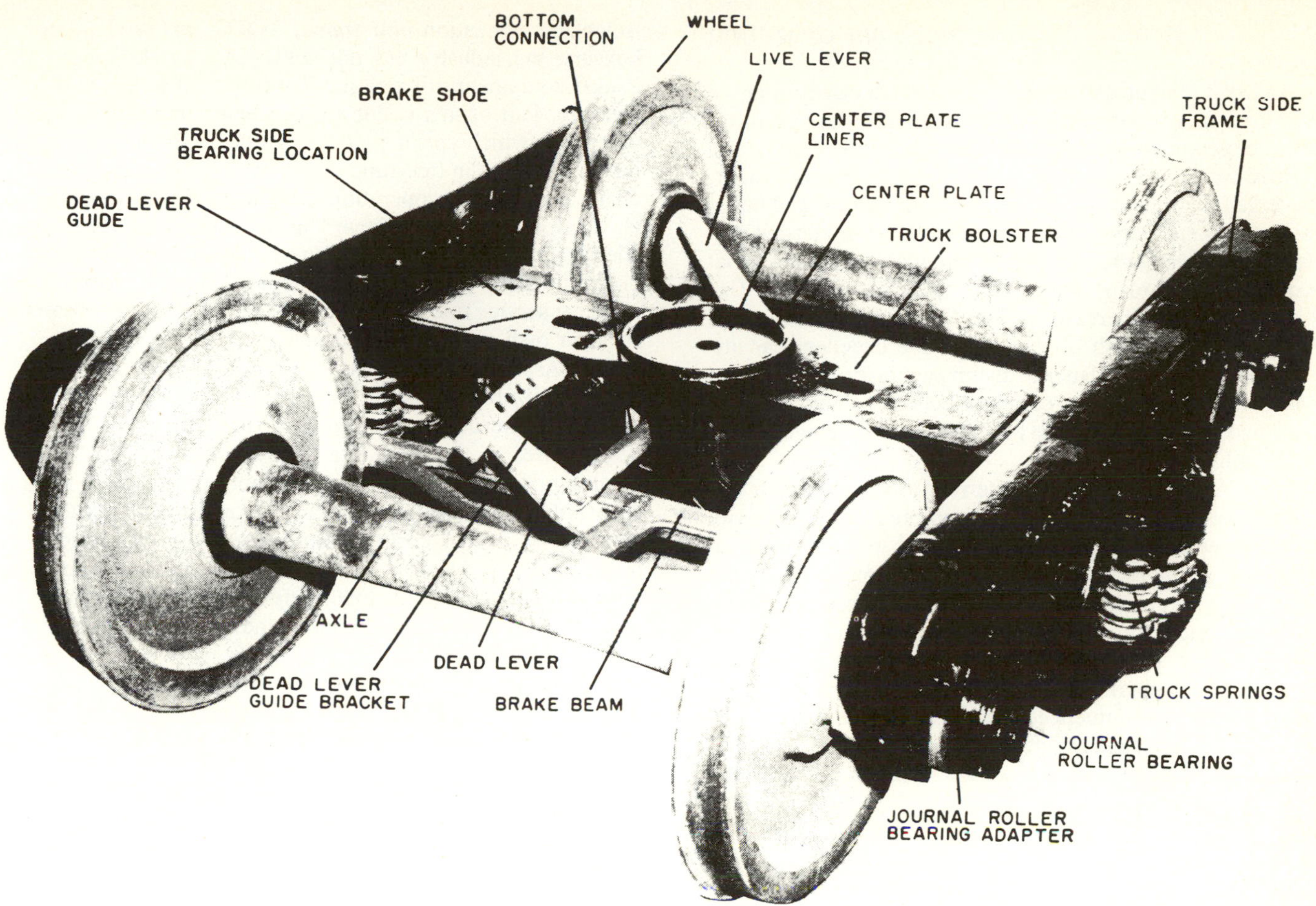

Figure 4.7. Freight car truck-component nomenclature. (Courtesy: Simmons-Boardman.)

provide additional shock control. On others, the car body slides on a rigid centersill to provide the same protection.

Couplers contain "slack," chiefly for the historic reason that high initial journal resistance and low starting tractive efforts of steam engines required that the engine start one car at a time by "bunching" slack and then moving ahead. With today's roller bearings (which start easily) and high initial locomotive tractive efforts, "taking slack" to start a train is rarely needed and may even be undesirable. Newer coupler types reduce coupler slack.

Freight cars are depreciated for tax purposes in 11 years; and for the ICC, in 33 years or less.[36] The average life of a freight car is about 30 years, although many live up to the statutory 40-year limit, after which they can no longer be used in interchange service. Freight cars are expensive. Table 4-24 summarizes the average cost of new freight train cars installed for selected years between 1960 and 1978.

[36] The ICC basis of depreciation is generally used for costing, ratemaking, and determining industry financial performance.

TABLE 4–24
Average Cost of New Freight Train Cars Installed for Selected Years between 1960 and 1978($)*

Year	Boxcars: General Service	Boxcars: Special Service	Flatcars: General Service	Flatcars: Special Service	Rack Cars	Gondola Cars	Hopper Cars: Open Top	Hopper Cars: Covered	Refrigerator cars	Tank Cars	All Freight-Carrying Cars	Caboose Cars	All Freight Train Cars
1960	10,629	12,767	12,254	†	13,712	13,521	8,866	13,892	16,529		11,100	16,497	11,115
1965	14,610	19,821	15,682	17,371	13,311	12,451	11,085	14,582	22,359	18,150	15,448	19,752	15,466
1970	13,355	20,912	15,534	22,275	‡	14,203	12,726	16,221	31,592		17,163	19,390	17,199
1975§	31,168	37,005	32,815	40,201	‡	27,076	25,834	26,480	42,553	22,300	27,777	41,023	27,921
1978§	40,065	50,794	34,320	37,954	‡	29,301	30,520	31,086	55,734		33,817	53,239	33,883

*The variations in the average cost of freight cars from year to year can relate, in part, to changes in the mix of car subtypes within each category and to differences in the capacities of cars installed.
†Included with general service flat cars.
‡Included with special service flat cars.
§Preliminary.

Source: ICC and AAR; Abstracted from *Railw. Age*, Nov. 27, 1978, p. 28.

Freight car utilization

Railroad freight car utilization, or productivity, can be measured in various ways. In terms of physical performance, most yardsticks indicate improved utilization of the railroad car fleet—partly because of changing mix of freight, longer length of hauls, new operating procedures, and better car controls and car distribution practices. The clearest picture of improvement in freight car productivity requires that comparisons be made under very similar conditions. Unfortunately, rapid increases in TOFC (trailer-on-flatcar) and unit train traffic, both of which provide excellent car utilization by any yardstick, distort average performance among flatcar and hopper car types compared with 10 to 15 years ago. Indeed, they also help distort the average for the entire rail fleet.

Excess fleet capacity is a deterrent to improved car utilization because idle cars automatically reduce productivity for the fleet as a whole. Without any change in operating or control practices, car utilization can be improved simply by reducing or eliminating excess capacity—operating with a car shortage. An examination of real gains in freight car productivity resulting from expensive, computerized car control and distribution programs requires adjusting for factors that are not influenced by these programs, such as reductions in fleet excess capacity. Selective physical and economic measurements of productivity are discussed in the following sections.

Car-miles

Loaded car-miles per car-day remained constant, and empty car-miles increased at an average compound rate of 1.8% between 1950 and 1978 (Figure 4.8). In spite of high-freight-car-utilization unit trains, TOFC cars, and pooled boxcars, the industry has not achieved a breakthrough in loaded equipment utilization according to this standard of measure. Part of this is due to the higher empty mileages, older cars which spend more time out of service, no significant changes in free-time allowances, greater use of specialized cars, and operating practices which have not changed enough to improve this measure of utilization. Clearly, increased empty mileage reflects the trend to specialized, often "one-way," cars demanded by shippers and more car service rules forcing cars to return empty to owners for their own originating traffic.

The Association of American Railroads typically calculates utilization based on the serviceable car fleet, which excludes bad-order cars awaiting repair. Utilization should be measured in terms of total cars owned or leased (excluding private line cars which are not entirely carrier responsibility) because bad-order cars represent an unutilized asset whose capital costs continue regardless of serviceability. Unless otherwise specified, subsequent utilization discussions are based on total freight cars owned or operated, including other than Class I railroad and excluding private line cars.

Selected loaded and empty car-miles per car-day for the year 1978 show that the average car traveled less than 60 mi/day, and loaded for just a little less than 60% of the total.

Ton-miles

Ton-miles per car-day have increased as shown in Figure 4.9. This is largely a result of longer hauls and higher loadings per car, not just because of specific measures to

Figure 4.8. Car-mile trends. SOURCE: ICC, *Transport Statistics*.

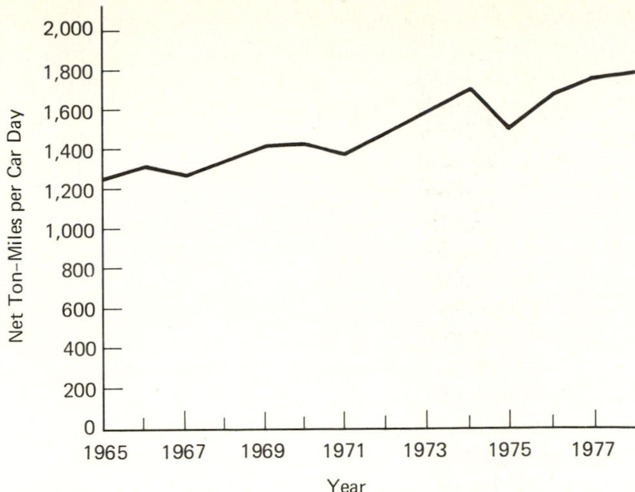

Figure 4.9. Revenue ton-miles per freight car-day. SOURCE: Association of American Railroads, *Yearbook of Railroad Facts.*

improve car utilization. Data for revenue ton-miles by car type are not available.

Turnaround

Turnaround can be expressed in terms of either loads per year or days per load, and in terms of serviceable cars or total cars. In terms of serviceable cars, turnaround is an indicator of performance relative to cars in active service, and only cars that are available for use. The second term indicates performance relative to total investment in freight cars. Each has its place, depending on what objective performance is being measured against. Table 4-25 summarizes turnaround for various car types for serviceable cars.

Unequipped boxcars have good utilization in terms of loaded to total car-miles but have the poorest utilization in terms of loaded trips per year. This apparent anomaly is caused by plain boxcars spending more time empty than other types of equipment waiting for loads, and in line-haul because of longer average length of haul; and car-delaying tariff privileges of diversion and reconsignment accorded certain commodities that move in these cars. Specialized open-top hopper cars typically generate one empty car-mile for every loaded car-mile; but because so many of them are in dedicated quick-turnaround unit train coal service, they generate a large number of loaded trips per year.

TABLE 4–25
Turnaround Times for Selected Car Types, 1972 and 1978

	Per Serviceable Car*,†			
	Trips per Year		Days per Trip	
Car Type	1972	1978	1972	1978
Box (unequipped)	15.5	12.0	23.6	30.5
Box (equipped)	16.2	13.8	22.6	26.5
Gondola	18.8	16.5	19.4	22.1
Open-top hoppers				
General service	23.5	18.3	15.5	19.9
Special service	37.6	53.3	9.7	6.9
Total	24.8	22.0	14.7	16.4
Covered hoppers	17.6	15.1	20.7	24.1
All cars	n.a.	16.5	n.a.	22.2

*Class I loads originated, divided into average number of serviceable cars on line between January 1 and December 31, times 365.
†n.a., not available.

SOURCE: Association of American Railroads.

Revenue per load

Physical measurements of utilization are important from an operating viewpoint, to deal with the ability of equipment to satisfy demand and meet the nation's transportation requirements. The economic utilization of capital in the railroad industry is also important, as well as the ability of railroads and private carriers to finance new equipment to replace retirements and accommodate growth and new demands for service. In this area, railroads are clearly experiencing problems.

Between 1960 and 1978, revenue per carload increased by a factor of 3.2, as shown in Figure 4.10. This significant gain is primarily the result of rate increases, but also larger loads per car and longer hauls per load. Revenue per car per year has increased at a slightly lower rate because longer hauls and cycle times have reduced the number of loaded trips per year.

Economic utilization in terms of revenue per loaded car-mile minimizes the effect of the length of haul factor in comparing revenue earnings from year to year and among car types. Revenue per total car-mile indicates the overall per car-mile earning power of a car, reflecting the fact that cars are increasingly traveling more empty miles per loaded car-mile. Figure 4.11 shows that on a per total car-mile basis, earnings since 1969 have not increased in terms of constant dollars. The earnings benefit of heavier loads per carload is offset by an increase in empty car-miles to produce one loaded car-mile, and lower per ton-mile rates for longer lengths of haul.

Figure 4.10. Historical changes in revenue per carload and per car per year. SOURCE: Association of American Railroads, *Yearbook of Railroad Facts.*

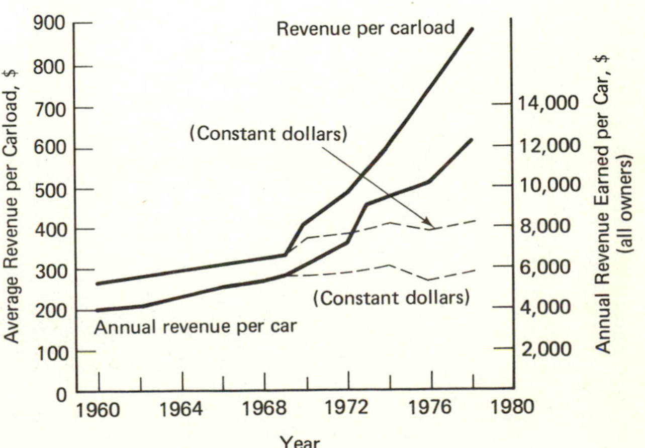

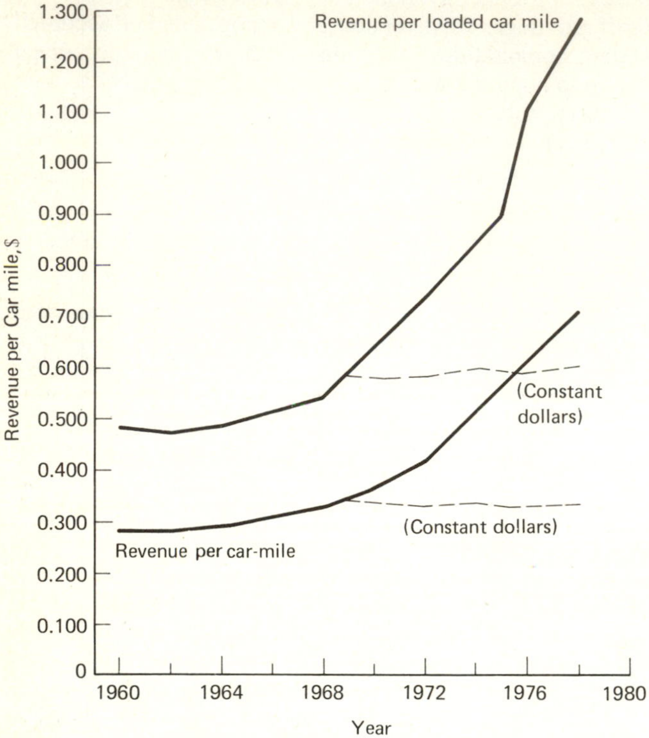

Figure 4.11. Historical changes in revenue per car-mile. SOURCE: Association of American Railroads, *Yearbook of Railroad Facts;* Bureau of Labor Statistics, Department of Economics, *Price Indexes for Railroad Freight.*

Freight revenue/freight car investment

The preceding discussion of economic utilization helps to suggest trends and the changing nature of railroad transportation. From a different perspective, yet another indicator of freight car capital utilization is illustrated in Figure 4.12—the ratio of annual freight revenues to net freight car investment, using the ICC basis of calculating net investment.

Figure 4.12. Historical changes in ratio of freight revenues to net freight car investment. SOURCE: ICC, *Transport Statistics;* Association of American Railroads, *Yearbook of Railroad Facts;* estimates of non-class 1 railroad freight car investment.

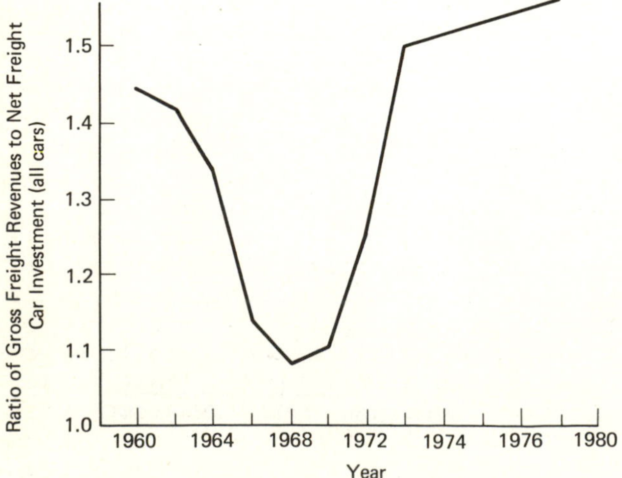

Up to 1968, this curve shows the decline in earning power of railroad freight cars which was caused by increases in cost of equipment that were not being offset by increases in car utilization (productivity) or in freight rates. Since 1968 (especially since 1972), rapid inflationary increases in current costs, with corresponding impact on rates and revenues, have worked favorably (perhaps artificially) to improve (increase) this ratio. The very high current cost of new equipment to replace retired cars may cause this ratio to decline in the 1980s unless high inflation rates continue to increase revenue faster than net freight car investment increases. The earning capabilities of various car types vary greatly and have changed significantly over the years. Data are not readily available but can be developed from the Department of Transportation's "Carload Waybill Statistics" 1% waybill sample.

Some constraints on car utilization

Origin–destination tariff provisions. The general freight car fleet is subject to a complex set of tariff provisions governing loading and unloading. Shippers and receivers are allowed specified time limits—known as "free time"—within which to load or unload shipments, after which a detention charge known as "demurrage" is assessed. Demurrage rules vary widely to reflect many special service considerations. Cars in general service most often utilize provisions of either a demurrage "straight plan" or an "averaging agreement."

Under the standard straight demurrage plan, shippers are generally allowed 48 h of "free time," exclusive of weekends and holidays, to load cars placed for such purposes. Receivers are allowed a similar 48 h of "free time" to unload cars. With very few exceptions, detention after the free time results in the assessment of demurrage charges. Computation of free time and demurrage begins at the first 7:00 A.M. (working day) following (1) car placement at the loading dock, (2) notification of placement on public team track, or (3) "constructive" placement (notification that a car is at a rail yard available for delivery when physical delivery is prevented by a full loading dock, team track, etc.). At the request of a shipper, relief from demurrage may be granted for days when loading/unloading is prevented by adverse weather, strikes, "acts of God," and so forth.

As an alternative to the "straight plan," shippers may enter into "averaging agreements" with railroads, whereby demurrage is computed on the basis of average car detention time over a month. Under this agreement, in the majority of states, shippers are allowed one credit for release of the car within 24 h. After 24 h, one debit is assessed for each day of detention up to 2 days after free time. Cars held over 2 days are assessed the normal demurrage rates. At the end of the month, credits are subtracted from debits and a charge is assessed on each net debit. With both regular demurrage and averaging agreements, Saturdays, Sundays, and holidays after the second "non-free-time" day are subject to demurrage. Thus, shippers usually have considerably more free time than 48 h. Private shipper cars, or cars leased to shippers, may be subject to demurrage charges under conditions defined in the tariff.

Car service rules. To help protect an owning railroad's investment in its own freight cars, the AAR establishes rules to govern the movement of empty freight cars. Generally, unequipped boxcars, gondolas, open-top hopper cars, and flat cars may be loaded by a foreign carrier for movement back toward the owning road, or returned empty via a prescribed "home" route. Specialized cars must be returned via "reverse" routes (the same route as followed by the load), no matter how circuitous, unless the owner gives permission to load the car otherwise or secures an off-line load for a return move. Private line cars are almost always returned empty.

To improve car utilization for some car types the railroads are experimenting with various alternatives such as a "clearinghouse" where, under a prescribed arrangement, cooperating roads may use each other's cars without regard to car service rules. The Trailer Train Corporation was established by the industry to provide an industry pool of TOFC/COFC and multilevel (auto) flat cars to improve utilization. Another company—Rail Box (managed by Trailer Train)—was established to do the same thing with unequipped boxcars. Both organizations have been very successful in achieving large increases in car productivity. The concept was expanded to gondolas in 1980.

Locomotives

In contrast to many other modern, high-capacity railroads in the world, electric propulsion trains in the United States produce an insignificant proportion of freight transportation. The diesel-electric locomotive is the standard workhorse of the U.S., Canadian, and Mexican railroads. In the United States, electric locomotives are used principally in the northeast corridor between Washington, Harrisburg, New York, and New Haven to handle passenger and freight trains. Self-propelled electric cars are also used in this corridor for intercity and commuter service. Outside this area, the Illinois Central Gulf out of Chicago and the Long Island Railroad use catenary and third-rail to power commuter trains. The discouraging factor in electric propulsion is the high capital cost for adding catenary to lines not originally designed for such systems. The costs are formidable—roughly $250,000 per mile for a single-track line (1980 dollars) and $400,000 per mile for a double-track line, excluding costs of locomotives and power source. Additional large costs may be incurred if overhead clearance under bridges and in tunnels must be provided.

Most diesel-electric locomotives used by U.S. Class I railroads are built by Electro Motive Division (EMD) of General Motors at La Grange, Illinois, or General Electric (GE) at Erie, Pennsylvania. Several other smaller manufacturers also produce diesel-electric or diesel-hydraulic locomotives. EMD locomotives utilize two-cycle diesel engines, with or without supercharging. GE locomotives and those of other manufacturers are typically four-cycle units, usually supercharged.

In modern locomotives, the diesel engine drives an electrical alternator whose ac current is rectified to 600 V dc by thyristors. Engine output is controlled by the throttle, which regulates engine rpm and horsepower. Alternator output is controlled by varying alternator-field excitation. Current is fed to traction motors, which in turn provide tractive effort to the locomotive.

Figure 4.13 illustrates the variety of locomotive configurations built since 1936. The dual-purpose unit of the 1950s and 1960s has given way to more specialized units. Today's high horsepower units (3000 hp or more) are not well suited to way train or switching service because of their very high costs to own and operate. Some roads have taken older high-horsepower units and added "slugs" (concrete weighted old locomotives with only traction motors thatdraw power from the connected locomotive) for use in low-speed switching service such as in hump yards. Figure 4.14 illustrates a modern SD45-2 (read "dash 2") locomotive built by EMD.

Locomotive brakes may be applied or released independent of train brakes to keep the train "bunched" or "stretched," to prevent dangerous "run-ins" or "run-outs" of train slack.

On most modern U.S. locomotives, each axle is driven by one traction motor. Most road locomotives are equipped with dynamic brakes, where traction motors turn into dc generators. The electrical current generated provides resistance to forward motion. This energy is dissipated as heat through resistor grids in the locomotive roof or body.

Traction motors must be cooled to avoid windings being damaged by heat from resistance and hysteresis (polarization) energy losses. Traction motor temperature and cooling requirements limit the minimum speed at which a locomotive may be operated at full throttle. In certain conditions, or on some locomotives, rail adhesion is lost (wheel slippage occurs) before traction motors can heat up to the point of damage.

Locomotive driving wheels must be kept from excessive slipping because they will damage or "burn" the rail and possibly cause traction motor damage by excessive voltage differentials in a motor. Excessive voltage differentials may cause a "flashover" and thus short out a motor. Wheel-slip correction is generally automatic: power may be temporarily reduced until adhesion is recovered, sand may be applied to the rail, or brakes on the slipping wheel may be temporarily applied (or some combination of the above).

Four-axle locomotives are generally preferable in high-speed service, where power is more important than low-speed tractive effort. Six-axle locomotives are generally preferable where high-tractive efforts at low speeds are needed, such as in handling unit trains over grades.

One 3000-hp unit can handle 5000 tons on level track, depending on required operating speed. Power on most trains generally ranges from 0.75 hp/ton in slow-speed service on relatively level track to 3 hp/gross trailing ton (weight behind the locomotive) in high-speed merchandise or piggyback train service. Heavy-grade territory may require even more power in the form of helpers.

The power on the head of a train is limited to an amount that does not exceed the safe drawbar pulling limits of the cars behind the locomotive. In heavy drag service, this is generally 8000 to 10,000 hp. Heavy unit trains, however, have stronger draft gears that permit head-end power up to 15,000 hp. Where speed is important, head-end power of up to 15,000 hp may also be used. Where more power at low speeds is needed, "helper engines" or "slave" units may be added to the train. A slave unit is a locomotive consist

	DIAGRAM (DIESEL ENGINE & GENERATOR / POWERED AXLE / IDLER AXLE / STEAM BOILER)	TYPE OF LOCOMOTIVE UNIT	AAR STD. AXLE-TRUCK DESIGNATION (SEE NOTE)	TYPICAL HORSEPOWER (PER UNIT) AND DATES BUILT
1	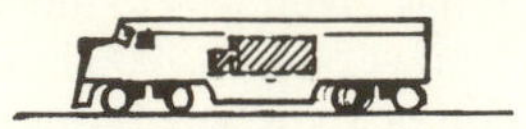	ROAD FREIGHT CAB ("A" UNIT)	B-B	1,350 (1941) ↓ 1,750 (1950)
2		ROAD FREIGHT BOOSTER ("B" UNIT) HOSTLER CONTROLS ONLY	B-B	1,350 (1941) ↓ 1,750 (1950)
3		PASSENGER CAB UNIT ("B" UNITS ALSO USED)	A1A-A1A	1,800 (1937) ↓ 2,400 (1950)
4		LIGHT-DUTY 44-TON SWITCHER	B-B	380 (1937-1950)
5		MEDIUM / HEAVY DUTY SWITCHERS (100 & 125 TON UNITS)	B-B	600 (1936) ↓ 1000 (DATE); 1,000 (1936) ↓ 1,500 (DATE)
6		"COW AND CALF" TRANSFER UNIT (PERMANENTLY COUPLED)	B-B × B-B	1800 (1941) TO 2400 (1955)
7	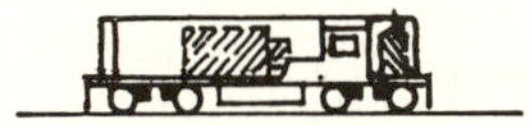	GENERAL-PURPOSE ROAD-SWITCHER (HOOD-TYPE CARBODY; STEAM BOILER OPTIONAL)	B-B	1,000 (1940) TO 2,000 (1960)
8		LOW-AXLE-LOAD ROAD SWITCHER	A1A-A1A	1,600 (1946) ↓ 1,800 (1950)
9		SPECIAL-DUTY SIX-AXLE ROAD SWITCHER (LATER MODELS LOW-NOSE)	C-C	2,400 (1953) ↓ 3,600 (1965)
10		HIGH-HORSEPOWER ROAD-SWITCHER (LOW NOSE)	B-B	2,500 (1961) ↓ 3,600 (1970)
11		DUAL-ENGINE "UNIT REDUCTION" LOCOMOTIVE (WIDE-CAB HOOD CARBODY)	D-D (ALSO BUILT AS B-B + B-B)	5,000 (1964) ↓ 6,600 (1969)
12	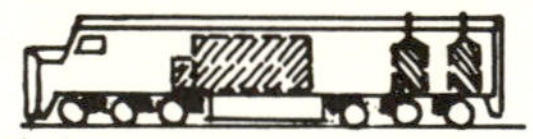	COWL-CARBODY PASSENGER (STEAM BOILERS OR DIESEL ELECTRIC CAR HEATING SYSTEM)	C-C (ALSO B-B)	3,000-3,600 1968 ↓ DATE

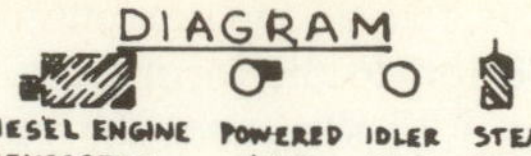

NOTE: IN EUROPEAN PRACTICE, WOULD BE DESIGNATED "B_o-B_o" OR "C_o-C_o", "B-B" OR "C-C" BEING USED TO INDICATE TRUCKS WITH CONNECTED DRIVE BETWEEN AXLES.
A = SINGLE DRIVING AXLE, B = TWO DRIVING AXLES, ETC. 1 = SINGLE IDLER AXLE, ETC.

Figure 4.13. Representative diesel-electric locomotive types.

Figure 4.14. SD45-2 locomotive. (Courtesy of ElectroMotive Division, General Motors.)

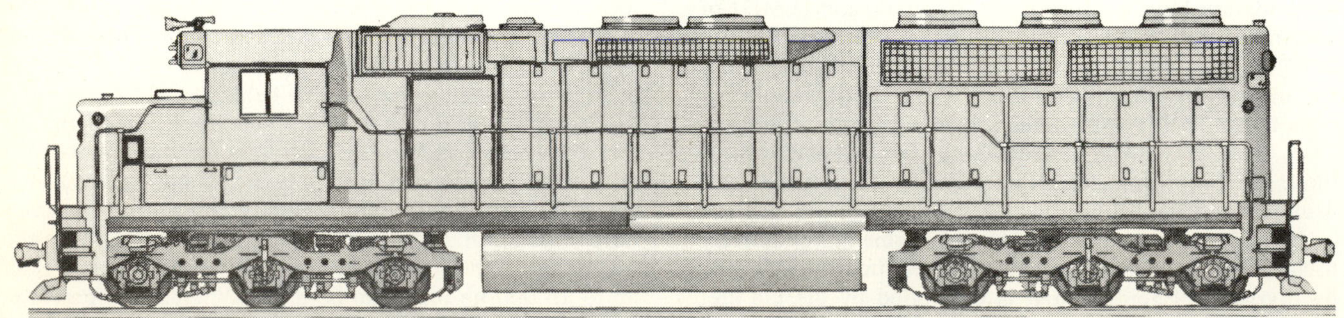

17629

(one or more units) remotely controlled by radio by the engineer. It is usually strategically placed in the middle or rear third of the train. Slave units help distribute drawbar forces throughout the train and provide the distinct advantage of applying and releasing train air brakes at two additional points within a train (ahead of and behind the point where the power is "cut in"). Helpers or slave units are generally used only in heavy-grade territory.

Road locomotives last 15 to 25 years (and sometimes longer with "heavy" rebuilding) and log 100,000 to 300,000 mi (160,000 to 480,000 km) per year, depending on the service. Two to four million miles (3.3 to 6.4 million km) of useful service before retirement is common. Lifetime availability usually exceeds 90%.

Locomotive costs (in 1980 dollars) range from $260 to about $300 per hp, depending on the variety of options chosen. Fuel capacities range up to 4000 gal (15,100 liters). Fuel consumption may be roughly estimated at 0.35 lb (0.054 gal, or 0.16 kg, or 0.20 liters) per nominal hp-hour. Maintenance costs vary from $0.40 to $1.25 per unit mile ($0.25 to $0.78 per km), depending on the unit size, model, and age.

Locomotive tractive effort (T.E.) can be approximated according to the following formula:

$$\text{T.E.} = (\text{hp}_r - \text{hp}_a) \times 375 \times \frac{e}{V} \qquad (4.5)$$

where T.E. = tractive effort, lb

hp_r = rated output of the diesel engine

hp_a = horsepower used by auxiliaries

e = efficiency factor, mechanical–electrical

V = mph

When an overall mechanical–electrical efficiency factor of about 82% is used, the equation reduces to

$$\text{T.E.} = 308 \times \frac{\text{hp}_r}{V} \qquad (4.6)$$

Tractive effort is limited by the horsepower, speed, and locomotive weight. T.E. can rarely exceed 25% of weight on drivers, and in most cases is a more nominal 18 to 20%. Tractive effort is not a function of gearing, as different gearing is compensated for by varying motor amperages. Gearing, however, does govern minimum speed at maximum horsepower (the heat-removal rate of power losses in a traction motor, which is a function of the square of the current) and maximum locomotive speed (traction motor rpm). Gear ratios of 74:18 (axle gear/traction motor pinion) and 65:18 are common in freight service; these ratios correspond to maximum speeds of roughly 65 and 75 mph. Gear ratios of 64:19 are used more in passenger service, corresponding to roughly 80 mph (129 km/h).

Figure 4.15 illustrates the T.E. curves for various locomotives, and the corresponding fuel consumption for various speed, tonnage, and locomotive horsepower. Use of this novel nomograph enables the user to find, for any specified locomotive, the corresponding unit tonnage rating and fuel-consumption rate on grades of varying percentages.

Train resistance and energy

Transportation energy amounted to about 10% of railroad operating expenses in 1979.[37] In 1980, this expense is estimated to be about 11%. While as much as 20% of energy may be used nonproductively (waste, idling, etc.), the remaining 80% or so is used to overcome train, inertial, and gravitational resistance for both loaded and empty cars.

Railroads are often touted as very energy-efficient as compared with trucks, by an order of magnitude of 4:1. Although this is perhaps true on a net ton-mile basis, the nature of the freight between the two modes is so different that it in itself is a major factor in energy usage. For comparable situations, the energy advantage of rail is less than 4:1. For trailers of COFC, evidence suggests that rail does not have a significant energy-intensity advantage over truck, although this is likely to change as a result of new technology. For example, the Santa Fe Railway reports 15 to 17% fuel savings with its "Ten-Pack" (now called the "fuel foiler") lightweight, streamlined intermodal car. The Bimodal Roadrailer—a highway trailer capable of being coupled together in a train to run on railroads—shows great promise of energy efficiency because of streamlining and a greatly reduced net-to-tare weight ratio.

Calculating train resistance and thus power and fuel needs is, at best, an inaccurate science. Total train resistance is a function of so many combinations of factors that actual power needs and fuel usage rates can vary by as much as 30% from predicted values.

Of the many U.S. and foreign independently developed formulas for calculating train resistance, the modified Davis formula is most often used:[38]

$$R = 0.6 + \frac{20}{W} + 0.01V + \frac{0.07V^2}{WN} \qquad (4.7)$$

where R = resistance, lb/gross ton

W = gross weight of a car, tons/axle

N = number of axles per car

V = velocity, mph

The original Davis formula contained a cross-sectional area component and an aerodynamic drag coefficient, which are averaged in the modified Davis formula.

In addition to resistance on straight track, other components of train resistance include grade resistance, curve resistance, and acceleration resistance. Other important factors are wheel-bearing temperatures, track condition, and particularly ambient wind speed and direction relative to the train.

Grade resistance is equal to 20 lb/ton (10 kg/tonne) for each 1% of grade. Curve resistance is greatly influenced by many factors, but railroads typically allow 0.8 lb of resistance per ton (0.4 kg/tonne) per 1° of curvature. On grades,

[37]Association of American Railroads, *Yearbook of Railroad Facts*.

[38]For a more exhaustive analysis of various approaches to determine train resistance, see *Resistance of a Freight Train to Forward Motion*, a study conducted by Mitre Corporation (MT-7664) for the U.S. Department of Transportation, November 1977, Contract DOT-FR-54090.

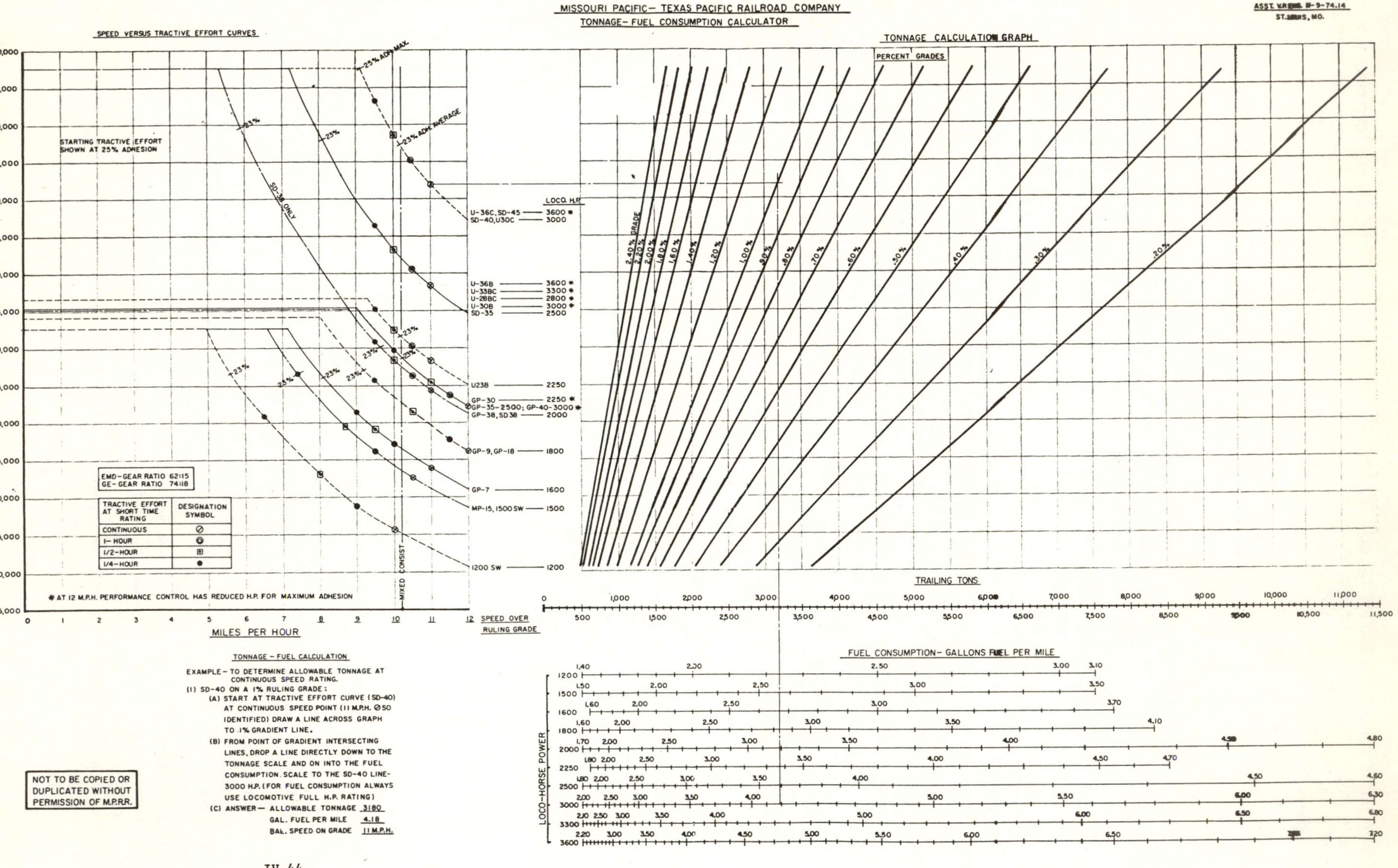

Figure 4.15. Missouri Pacific Railroad Company tonnage—fuel consumption calculator.

railroads typically reduce gradient by 0.04% for each degree of curvature to compensate for curve resistance.[39]

Acceleration resistance is the sum of linear acceleration of the train and angular acceleration of the wheels and axles of the train:

$$R = \frac{70}{S}(V_2^2 - V_1^2) + \frac{95.6}{T}(V_2 - V_1) \tag{4.8}$$

where R = acceleration resistance, lb/ton

S = distance, ft

T = time, s

V_2 = final velocity, mph

V_1 = initial velocity, mph

Figure 4.16 illustrates various resistances for an average train at various speeds. Above about 40 mph, air resistance exceeds mechanical resistance by a rapidly increasing marginal rate.

On a "steady-state" basis, fuel consumption is calculated from the equation[40]

$$G = 0.048965 \times \frac{R_T}{E} \tag{4.9}$$

where G = gallons of diesel fuel (138,690 Btu/gal) per 1000 net ton-miles

R_T = total resistance per 1000 net tons

E = engine thermal efficiency ratio, usually about 0.22

Thus, assuming that $E = 0.22$, the equation simplifies to $G = 0.2226R_T$. To account for non-steady-state conditions, formula (4.9) may be multiplied by the factor

$$1 + \frac{K_1}{e^{V/K_2}} \tag{4.10}$$

where K_1 and K_2 = constants

V = speed, mph

e = base of natural logarithms, 2.71828

Observed values of $K_1 = 1$ and $K_2 = 20$ seem to relate adequately to observed experience,[41] making the modified equation

$$G = 0.2226R_T\left(1 + \frac{1}{e^{V/20}}\right) \tag{4.11}$$

An allowance for empty return and circuity should be included in energy-consumption estimates. Typical car tare weights, average revenue-tons, empty return ratios, and circuities are shown in Table 4-26. Thus, R_T should be the sum of the resistance for 1000 net tons in the loaded direction, plus the resistance for the tare moving in the opposite direction times the appropriate empty return ratio. Gallons per 1000 net ton-miles should then be increased by the

[39] *Kent's Mechanical Engineers' Handbook*, 12th ed. Wiley, New York, 1950.

[40] *Industrial Energy Studies of Ground Freight Transportation*, p. IX-8.

[41] Ibid.

Figure 4.16. Various resistances for average train, high speeds. SOURCE: Resistance of a Freight Train to Forward Motion, Mitre Corporation, McLean, Va.; DOT Contract FR-54090, 1977.

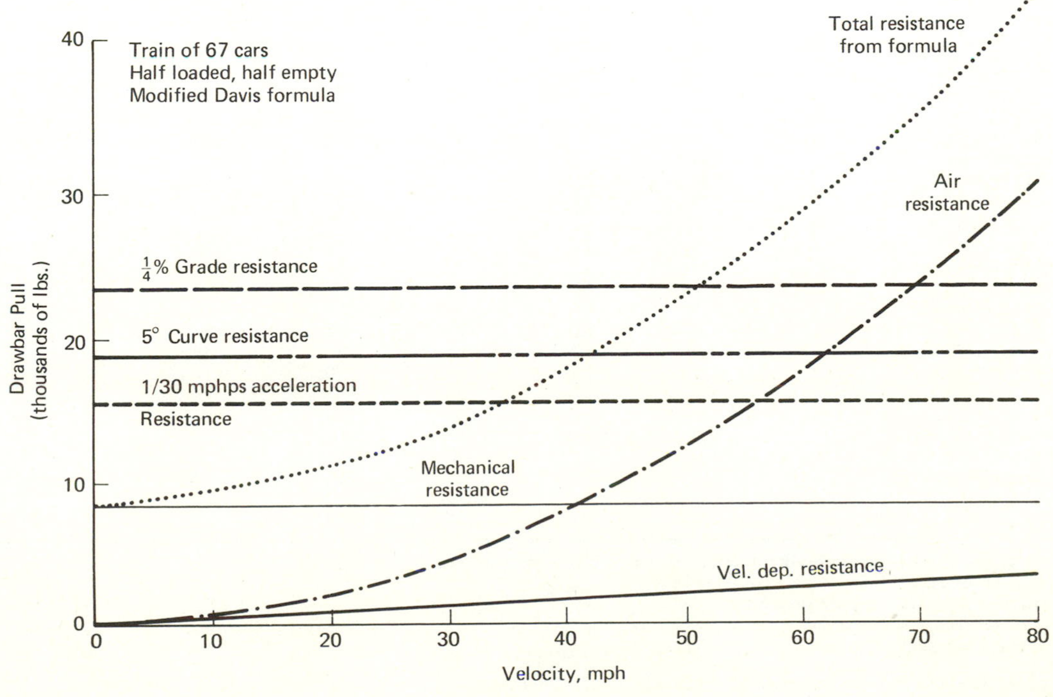

TABLE 4–26
Typical Car Tare Weights, Empty Return Ratios, and Circuity

Car Type	Typical Tare (tons)	Typical Load (net tons)	Typical Empty Return Ratio*	Typical Circuity†
Boxcar	27–36	36	0.70	1.16
Gondola	29–31	61	0.88	1.16
Open hopper	27–30	75	0.91	1.13
Covered hopper	32	75	1.02	1.18
TOFC flat	33	25‡	0.40	1.09
Truck average	17	11	0.15	1.08§

*Empty miles per loaded mile, reported by the Interstate Commerce Commission, *Ratios of Empty to Loaded Freight Car Miles by Type of Car and Performance Functions for Way Through, and All Trains Combined, 1972*.
†Ratio of actual miles to shortest tariff rate mileage, ICC Rail Carload Cost Scales publication.
‡Tons per trailer × 1.8 trailers per car.
§Estimated.

SOURCE: *Industrial Energy Studies of Ground Freight Transportation*, Peat, Marwick, Mitchell & Co., Washington, D.C., 1974.

circuity factor. Energy-consumption estimates for loaded and related empty movements for specific commodities and car types are shown in Table 4-27.

The resistance comparisons for TOFC, truck, and boxcar freight shown in Figure 4.17 were calculated using the formulas shown in this section. Light loads and grades discriminate heavily against TOFC, whereas speed and light loads discriminate against truck. A more specific comparison of TOFC and truck is shown in Figure 4.18. No allowance for empty return, which reduces modal energy (as well as economic) efficiency, is made in Figure 4.18. For a known empty return ratio, approximate fuel use per ton-mile or trailer-mile can be calculated by dividing the net load per trailer by 1 plus the empty return ratio and reading the fuel-use rate corresponding to the calculated number. The observed gallons per loaded trailer-mile should then be multiplied by the same ratio to estimate the effective fuel-use rate. The resultant energy consumption may then be

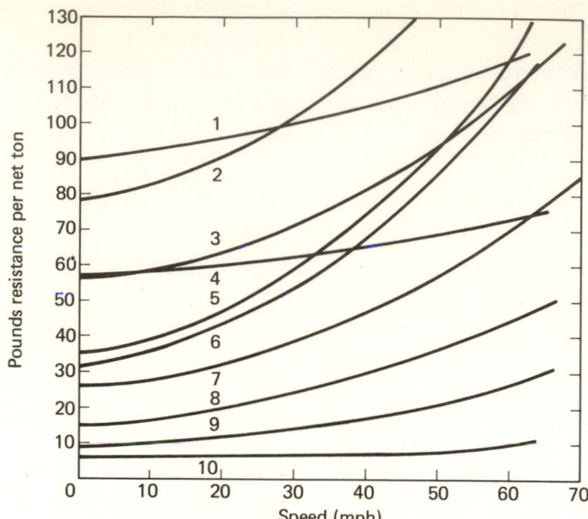

1. TOFC 10 ton load per trailer 1% grade
2. Truck 10 ton load 1% grade
3. Truck 20 ton load 1% grade
4. TOFC 20 ton load per trailer 1% grade
5. Truck 10 ton load 0% grade
6. Truck 11 ton average load 0% grade
7. Truck 20 ton load 0% grade
8. TOFC 10 ton load per trailer 0% grade
9. TOFC 20 ton load per trailer 0% grade
10. Box car 20 ton load 0% grade

Figure 4.17. Resistance per net ton—TOFC, truck and boxcar. SOURCE: *Industrial Energy Studies in Ground Freight Transportation*, Peat, Marwick, Mitchell & Co., Washington, D.C., 1974.

TABLE 4–27
BTU per Ton-Mile Estimates for Loaded Movements*

	Car Type						
Commodity	Boxcar	Covered Hopper	Flat Car†	Gondola	Open-Top Hopper	Tank Car	Misc. Cars‡
Agricultural products	335	235	725	290	380		715
Metallic ores	265	225		195	180		
Coal, coke produced from coal				195	210		
Crude oil, petroleum	440		725			275	415
Nonmetallic minerals	310	225		280	180	195	315
Food, kindred products, tobacco	420	310	750			266	410
Textiles, apparel, leather	775		725				
Lumber, wood products, furniture	475	300	600	340	360		380
Pulp, paper, allied products	395		700			270	410
Chemicals, allied products	390	240	725			257	380
Rubber, plastic products	875		730				610
Clay, concrete, glass, stone	350	225	600	295	225		380
Primary metal products	290	175	295	285	185		320
Fabricated metal products	820		725	370			530
Nonelectrical machinery	675		730	425			
Electrical machinery	1,050		750	340			725
Transportation equipment	650	480	846	400		570	
Instruments, photo goods	1,020		770				
Waste, scrap materials	420	300	725	300	190	252	400
Empty movement—all commodities	390§	420	796	420	320	399	390‖

*Total transportation energy = (loaded Btu + empty movement Btu) × net ton-miles.
†Includes TOFC/COFC.
‡Includes auto rack, refrigerator, and stock cars.
§596 Btu for transportation equipment.
‖450 Btu for agricultural products.

SOURCE: *Energy and Economic Impacts of Freight Transportation Improvements*, Peat, Marwick, Mitchell & Co., Washington, D.C., 1976.

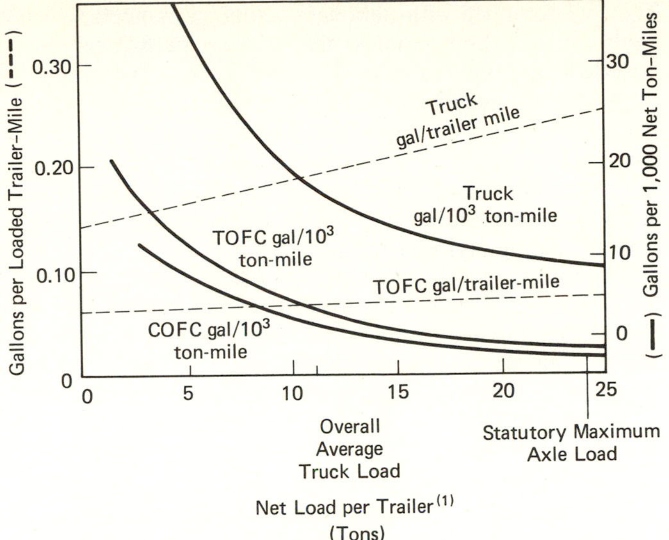

Figure 4.18. Average fuel consumption for hauling a trailer by truck and rail at 50 mph. SOURCE: *Industrial Energy Studies in Ground Freight Transportation,* Peat, Marwick, Mitchell & Co., Washington, D.C., 1974.

further increased by the circuity factor to estimate point-to-point fuel consumption. Energy consumption for loading and unloading trailers or containers and pickup or delivery is not included.

Comparisons of energy consumption by transportation modes are given in Chapter 6.

Communication and signals

The first recorded form of instant long-distance communication in the railroad industry began with the application of the Morse telegraph in 1851. In its time, the telegraph represented a significant technological improvement to railroad transportation as its use gained acceptance in the period to 1865.

Today, not only is the telegraph gone, but many of the wires once used in communication of data and information have also vanished. Railroad communication needs—especially data transmission—have grown to such an extent that many railroads have adopted the use of microwave. The industry now has the second largest privately owned communication system in the United States, with miles of line and capacity second only to American Telephone and Telegraph.

Many railroads are also transmitting documents electronically. Some railroads have centralized the preparation of freight waybills, where either the document or document information is transmitted to central points for preparation of billing and other computer file data. As part of the communication system, railroads have large data processing systems, many with message switching and direct computer-to-computer communication.

Many roads have installed direct-dial internal communications systems that are as modern as those commercially available. Indeed, some railroads are currently marketing their communication systems capability in competition with AT&T.

In addition to high-density microwave communications systems, almost every road locomotive, caboose, and yard locomotive today is equipped with radio transmission. Radio communication is also used by engineering forces to keep in constant communication with train movements during track maintenance operations. Some railroads also operate station agencies using mobile vans which are in constant radio communication with a base center. Using increased communication system capabilities, many roads—particularly those involving centralized traffic control systems—are consolidating train dispatching.

Railroads today are also in the forefront of experimentation with new technology, such as the use of optical fibers. In such a system, a single-fiber optic cable no more than 1 in. in diameter is capable of transmitting simultaneously over 100,000 messages in a stream of 8 million light pulses per second.[42]

Communication systems provide the backbone of train operation. Although outward appearances suggest that wayside track signals have changed little, behind-the-scenes technology has changed immensely. Train control systems can be described at three levels:

- Timetable/train order
- Automatic block system (ABS)
- Centralized traffic control (CTC) or traffic control systems (TCS)

Timetable/train order

On many lightly traveled lines today, as in the early days of railroading, trains operate according to a timetable or by authority of a train order prepared by the dispatcher. The train order prescribes the time, track, and points between which a train has exclusive operating authority. With the disappearance of many passenger trains in the United States, very few trains today operate on timetable authority. Operating rights can be changed or amended by the issuance of train orders, which supersede or cancel previous orders. Train orders or timetable rights do not relieve crews of stopped trains from protecting their trains against following or opposing movements.

Automatic block system

Where ABS systems are installed, tracks are divided into "blocks." The minimum size of a block is determined by the longest distance required by a train to stop under normal braking conditions (usually 1 to 3 mi, longer on down grades). The old "semaphore" signal has been replaced with a "three-aspect" signal, which displays the following:

[42]"Union Pacific First to Use Optical Fibers," *Prog. Railroading* (Chicago), 93 (Jan. 1979).

○ Green (clear)—proceed at authorized speed to the next signal.
○ Yellow (approach)—proceed to the next signal, and be prepared to stop short of that signal. Do not exceed specified (usually medium) speed.
○ Red (stop)—do not enter the next block; stop and proceed (at restricted speed) prepared to stop short of train, switch, or obstruction; or proceed at restricted speed, prepared to stop short of train, switch, or obstruction.

For red (stop) signals, the choice depends on whether the signal is absolute, permissive (a signal with a numbered mast plate), or a grade signal (denoted by a "G" on the signal mast). The latter is used to minimize the stopping and restarting of trains on upgrades.

Some automatic block and centralized traffic control systems may have five or more aspects to permit shorter block length and increase line capacity.

ABS systems are "fail-safe": they are "dark" or display red at all times except when it is safe for an approaching train to proceed. A "dark" signal is always an indication to stop immediately. ABS systems are almost always bidirectional on single-track lines. Generally (but not always), double-track ABS systems are signaled with the current of traffic. Trains operating in ABS territory must have either timetable authority, a clearance card issued by the dispatcher, or a train order permitting movement on signal indication. Meets and passings are arranged by timetable or train order.

Centralized traffic control or traffic control systems

CTC or TCS systems place the dispatcher in complete operational control of a designated section of the railroad. The dispatcher can control wayside signals (except when overridden by train occupancy) and operate electric switches on command (except when the block is occupied). Train movements are indicated on a computerized CRT (cathode ray tube) device or on a large console display. By observing movements, the dispatcher arranges meeting points and passing—often without ever causing a train to come to a complete stop. Dispatchers are generally in constant radio communication with every train under their control, and pass or receive trains from dispatchers controlling adjacent territories. No clearance cards or train orders are used in CTC or TCS systems. Trains operate by authority of signal indication.

Other devices

Some railroads utilize cab signals (where signal indication is continuously displayed in the locomotive cab), or automatic train stop (ATS) device. Unless speed is below the permitted signal speed, these devices cause the application of brakes to stop the train unless the engineer manually applies the brakes within a predetermined time—usually 7 to 20 s after passing a reduced-speed indication. ATS devices are trackside units connected to the signal system. They are equipped with stationary actuating magnets which apply the train brakes unless the engineer deliberately acknowledges a signal display that is other than "proceed."

Modern electronic technology has also improved grade-crossing warning devices. State-of-the-art devices detect train speed and initiate timely actuation of grade-crossing warning to minimize traffic delay. Some devices also "time-out" to permit a train to stop within a grade-crossing circuit without fouling highway traffic.

One of the most important improvements in railroad safety has been the development of trackside detectors to monitor bearing temperatures and sense dragging equipment which could cause a potential derailment. Other detectors have been developed which check wheels for flange breaks or other defects.

Optimally, "hot-box" detectors are located every 10 to 30 mi (15 to 50 km) along railroad main tracks, depending on train speeds in the territory and other factors. At this interval, these systems are almost always capable of detecting incipient bearing failure before visual or odor indications are given (usually too late to prevent complete failure).

Management and information systems

Railroads are among the largest industrial users of computers and related on-line and off-line communication devices. It is estimated that as much as 3% of total railway operating expenses is associated with computer services and related support. In 1977, this would have amounted to roughly $500 million.

In addition to customary uses of computers for routine jobs such as payroll, accounts payable, accounts receivable, general ledger accounting, and inventory control, railroads—like airlines—utilize sophisticated, specialized procedures for equipment control and monitoring. Managing and controlling car-hire expenses and the location of 1.8 million cars requires some of the most sophisticated MIS techniques available today. Integrated with these management and control systems is the use of sophisticated operating systems by local management and supervisors in everyday operations.

No modern classification yard can operate effectively without the computer. Computers are used literally to control yard classifications, maintain a perpetual inventory of car location (PICL), and prepare information lists of many kinds. Advance information on inbound trains consists (known as "wheel reports") help operating personnel plan switching operations and schedule departing trains and connections. As outbound trains are made up, the computer is used to prepare outbound wheel reports for information to the next terminal down the railroad or to connecting lines to which traffic is interchanged. Arriving cars are automatically entered into inventory, and departing cars are automatically removed. Many systems note the total detention time for statistical reports on terminal performance and the assignment of car-hire costs to a particular terminal under profit-center cost accounting concepts. Car distribution, bad-order cars, and cars awaiting billing are often computer-monitored.

TABLE 4–28
Data Processing Equipment Summary (AAR Member Railroads)

	Manufacturer								
	IBM								
	360	370	Other	RCA/Univac	Honeywell	NCR	Burroughs	Minis	Other
Total machines	29	57	13	15	5	2	6	143	28

SOURCE: Association of American Railroads, Feb. 1979.

The extent to which computers are used is indicated in Table 4-28, which summarizes the hardware in place on AAR member roads in early 1979. Of interest is the growing use of "minis"; the concept of centralized data processing is losing favor to distributed processing as the power of small machines increases and their costs decrease.

In an effort to help manage the national car fleet, the AAR has developed reporting requirements for a complex communication–data processing system known as TRAIN (Tele-Rail Automated Information Network). This system automatically keeps track of every railroad car (1.8 million) rolling on Class I U.S. railroads. Between 80 and 90% of the information on this file is less than 4 h old. Railroads are required to report on a 4 h basis to the AAR, via a combined linkage of railroad and public communication systems, computerized information on the movements of cars across defined boundaries, and key railroad interchange points. At lesser interchange points, some reported information may be up to 24 h old; but in no case are changes in car status or car movement to be more than 48 h old.

TRAIN II, which became operational in 1978, is a computer-controlled communication network linking railroads and private car lines with a central computer operated by the AAR in Washington, D.C. Whereas TRAIN I consisted solely of interchange data, TRAIN II includes the following inputs:

- Reports of crossing of car service regional boundaries
- Waybill data
- Loadings
- Unloadings
- Arrivals
- Placements
- Reports to and from bad order, storage, and hold

The universal machine language equipment register (UMLER) is integrated into the TRAIN II system to provide additional information concerning equipment type and car characteristics.

An important derivative of the TRAIN II system is that shippers can directly query a railroad's car service data base for current status and location of equipment assigned to that shipper. Over 400 shippers with assigned cars or private fleets now utilize the capabilities of the TRAIN II-based system to query individual railroads. Some railroads have computer-to-computer systems that automatically facilitate this transfer of information. The possibility of central inquiry into the TRAIN II system to provide the same information exists as well and is under study by the AAR. This could relieve shippers of the need to contact every railroad over which its equipment operates by providing, instead, a single one-source center of information for car location messages (CLM).

The CLM capabilities of TRAIN II are used by the AAR to collect continuous data on changes in status and location of a randomly selected fleet sample of 8500 railroad and private freight cars. This study, which began in March 1976, is designed to give much more definitive information on car time spent in various elements of the load-to-load cycle and to identify problem terminal areas where cars are excessively delayed. This information will be extremely useful to the industry for making tariff changes and modifying industry operating practices.

Every Class I railroad operating today in the United States uses management information systems. Since communication between railroads is so important to the efficient movement of freight cars and billing information, many systems are compatible among roads. An example of an advanced system is the Southern Pacific's "TOPS" (Total Operations Processing System), which cost $23 million and 800 person-years to develop.[43] This system controls and monitors movements of all cars on the Southern Pacific and provides on-line operating information to local supervisors. It is used to distribute cars for loading and to move empty cars to various points on the railroad to meet anticipated equipment needs. The system provides service accountability, monitors freight train performance, and gives top management daily summaries of activities and measurements of service effectiveness. This and systems like it are being used by many Class I railroads in the United States and abroad.

The Missouri Pacific reportedly has the biggest commercial application of computer technology in the United States.[44] The computer information systems used to support this program are said to be bigger than those used to put men on the moon. The return on investment—some $45 million annually—is in better car utilization. Every car movement is under tight computer monitoring and control, including scheduling in specific train movements. The system is even used to predict for the shipper the approximate time of arrival and placement of cars.

Besides typical business applications, railroads are using the computer to make engineering decisions and determinations. Mechanical departments are mechanizing the preparation of unit maintenance records for freight cars and locomotives, cost control, evaluation of engineering improvements, and scheduling and control of equipment preventive maintenance.

There is computer utilization for simulation and evaluation of train performance, train-track dynamics, operations in proposed terminals, and line changes. Many roads also use train dispatching models that simulate operations of the railroads to identify line-capacity bottlenecks and the effect that modification of the signal system or track structure would have on reducing or eliminating those bottlenecks.

[43] *Computers Are Working on the Railroads*, Chilton, Radnor, Pa., Apr. 1979, p. 30.

[44] Ibid., p. 32.

International developments

Railway Gazette International estimates that as much as 70% of the ton-kilometers carried in the world by land go by rail; this is twice the proportion reported for the United States. Foreign railroads utilize more the combination of rail and highway whereby freight is transloaded between rail and highway at origin and destination for pickup and delivery. Most non-U.S. railroads place heavy emphasis on intercity passenger and commuter transportation where public highways are less developed.

While railroads in the United States are fighting for economic survival, pruning away excess capacity and abandoning unprofitable lines, most railroads elsewhere are experiencing continued or resurgent growth. First, almost all major non-U.S. railroads (the Canadian Pacific is a major exception) are government-owned. Second, with few exceptions (such as the Canadian National), government-owned railroads operate at heavily subsidized deficits. While a large part of the deficit of non-U.S. railroads is attributable to passenger service, many countries maintain unprofitably low freight rates for political reasons (although comparative rates may still be much higher than in the United States). Third, productivity rates on most railroads throughout the world are substantially lower than in the United States and Canada. Some governments, such as Italy, use railroads as a way to absorb significant unemployment.

One of the principal reasons for continued interest in railroad transportation throughout the world is that it is the least expensive mode to construct per ton of transport capability; it is also the least expensive in terms of adding incremental capacity. Railway Gazette International estimates that some 14,500 route-kilometers of new railway were constructed in 1977, and plans for starting the construction of another 70,000 km were being actively pursued.

In 1979, U.S. railroads spent about $5 billion (1978 dollars) for capital improvements. For the rest of the noncommunist world, estimated capital expenses for 1 year were approximately $19 billion. The divisions of capital expenditure are quite different in the United States from the rest of the world. In the United States, primary emphasis is on locomotives—roughly 2200 bought in 1979—and freight cars—about 80,000 purchased. In the rest of the noncommunist world there were only about new 1200 locomotives and 35,000 freight cars;[45] more emphasis is on new construction and passenger cars.

Table 4-29 summarizes national railway income of selected railway systems, excluding national income taxes (the Canadian Pacific and U.S. railroads are the only ones that pay such taxes).[46]

Although dollar-converted statistics are hard to develop and more difficult to compare on a meaningful basis, Tables 4-30 and 4-31 summarize selected traffic and system statistics.

[45]"World Poll of Railway Capital Expenditures," *Int. Railw. J.*, 42 (Jan. 1979).

[46]A survey of selected railroads of selected industrial countries prepared by Union Pacific Railroad Company, New York, Sept. 1977.

TABLE 4–29
International Rail Systems 1975 Income (Loss) (× 10^6)

	Income as Reported	Subsidies Included in Income	Income Excluding Subsidies
U.S. Class I railroads			
Excluding Amtrak	$ 317	$ 152	$ 165
Including Amtrak	(36)	157	(193)
Canadian Pacific Limited	333	70	263
South African Railways	(141)	30	(171)
Canadian National Railways	(168)	269	(437)
British Railways	11	829	(818)
Italian State Railways	(1188)	1252	(2440)
French National Railways	(265)	3111	(3376)
Japanese National Railways	(3027)	649	(3676)
West German Railways	(1665)	2386	(4051)

SOURCE: Union Pacific Railway.

TABLE 4–30
Selected International Railroad Traffic Statistics, 1976

Country	Rail Traffic[a]	
	Passenger-Kilometers[b] (× 10^6)	Freight (net-ton kilometers) (× 10^6)
Algeria	1,369	1,727
Angola	418[c]	5,461[c]
Argentina	14,480	11,038
Australia	n.a.	30,816
Austria	6,712	10,685
Belgium	7,565	6,626
Brazil	11,638	63,246
Bulgaria	7,499	17,055
Canada	2,942	202,223
Chile	2,464	2,165
China, People's Republic of	n.a.	301,000[d]
China, Republic of	8,412	2,700
Colombia	511	1,157
Cuba	767	1,848
Czechoslovakia	17,910	70,748
Denmark	3,415[f]	1,805[f]
Ecuador	65[g]	46[g]
Egypt	8,748	2,201
Finland	2,985	6,547
France	51,168	68,508
Germany, East	21,955	58,181
Germany, West	36,451	59,219
Ghana	431[h]	305[h]
Greece	1,583	844[i]
Hong Kong	251	47
Hungary	13,365	22,552
India	163,836[j]	144,030[j]
Indonesia	3,258	717
Iran	3,511	4,627
Iraq	797[j]	2,254[j]
Ireland	788	585
Israel	280	449
Italy	39,118	16,376
Ivory Coast	1,040	559
Jamaica	69	159
Japan	322,911	47,550
Korea, Republic of	14,305	9,728
Lebanon	2[c]	42[c]
Malaysia	1,139[k]	1,008[k]
Mexico	4,058	34,821
Morocco	828	3,143
Netherlands	8,218	2,700
New Zealand	589[f]	3,649[f]
Nigeria	785[l]	972[l]
Norway	1,997	2,709
Pakistan	12,957[m]	8,677[m]
Peru	528	635
Philippines	780	40
Poland	42,799	130,857
Portugal	5,235	854
Romania	23,077[i]	67,560
Saudi Arabia	72[c]	66[c]

TABLE 4–30 (Continued)

Country	Rail Traffic[a]	
	Passenger-Kilometers[b] ($\times 10^6$)	Freight (net-ton kilometers) ($\times 10^6$)
South Africa	n.a.	69,336[j,n]
Spain	16,686	9,842
Sri Lanka	3,004[o]	273[o]
Sweden	5,617	16,238
Switzerland	9,357	6,044
Syria	166	305
Thailand	5,628	2,505
Tunisia	641[i]	1,277
Turkey	4,615	7,278
USSR	315,061	3,295,399
United Kingdom	28,608[g,p,q]	23,050[g,p,q]
United States	15,688[q]	1,112,689[q]
Uruguay	372	372
Venezuela	42[f]	15[f]
Yugoslavia	9,941	21,017
Zaïre	467	2,203

[a]Relates to domestic and international traffic on all railway lines within each country shown, excluding railways entirely within an urban unit and plantation, industrial mining, funicular, and cable railways. In general, passenger-kilometers include all passengers except military, government, and railway personnel when carried without revenue; ton-kilometers relate to freight net ton-kilometers and include all goods whether carried by fast or ordinary trains except service traffic, mail, baggage, and nonrevenue governmental stores.
[b]n.a., not available.
[c]For 1974.
[d]For 1971.
[e]Source: U.S. Bureau of the Census. Data from Republic of China publications. Includes vehicles no longer in circulation.
[f]Year ending March 31, 1976.
[g]For 1975.
[h]For 1972.
[i]Includes military traffic.
[j]Year beginning Apr. 1, 1976.
[k]West Malasia only.
[l]Year ending Mar. 31, 1974.
[m]Year beginning July 1.
[n]Includes Namibia.
[o]Year ending Sept. 30.
[p]Excludes Northern Ireland.
[q]Class I railways only.

SOURCE: Except as noted, Statistical Office of the United Nations, New York, *Statistical Yearbook* 1978 (copyrighted).

Growth and new construction

USSR. For sheer size, the railways of the Soviet Union hold top honors. With approximately 84,000 mi (135,200 km) of route, the Soviet railways constitute the largest individual rail system in the world, roughly 10% of the world's route length. However, they handle almost 50% of the world's rail freight ton-miles.

The USSR railways operate in a unique environment where train size and car size are more comparable to those in the United States than anywhere else in the world. The Russian gauge is 5 ft (1.525 m) compared to 4 ft 8½ in. (1.435 m) in the United States. Car sizes are nearly comparable to those found in the United States, except that net loading is generally limited to around 80 tons (73 tonnes) per car; the Soviets believe that U.S. axle loadings are too heavy and thereby overstress system components to a point inconsistent with long-run economics.

Like many European countries, the USSR operates trains on a preselected schedule, that is, trains can only depart at origin at certain times and must operate on a fixed schedule based on the starting time at point of origin. For the most part, passenger and freight trains operate at the same average speed, although passenger trains may operate at slightly higher top speeds to allow for more frequent stopping and starting. By operating all trains at the same average speed, the Soviets claim they are able to operate traffic at higher densities and with less interference.

Shippers in the USSR must schedule their freight car requirements as long as 30 days in advance and must utilize the equipment or face penalties. Furthermore, they are given only a matter of hours to load and unload equipment, again facing severe economic penalties if these times are exceeded. Although such noncompetitive behavior could not be tolerated in the United States, it is very effective in maximizing equipment utilization—twice or more that of the United States.

One of the most notable differences between the United States and foreign railroads is in the construction of new lines. The USSR, for instance, is currently completing the new 1800-mi (2900-km) Baikal–Amur line in Siberia to help tap the wealth of mineral and other resources in the vast desolate territory. This line is being built under some of the most adverse railroad construction conditions anywhere in the world. Soil conditions, permafrost, and surface thawing in the warm months have challenged most contemporary civil engineering approaches to railroad right-of-way construction. Temperatures above 100°F (38°C) during the summer, and as low as −60°F (−51°C) in the winter require careful selection of rail metallurgy and methods of instal-

TABLE 4–31
World Railway Track Mileage by Gauge*

	Narrow: 381–800 mm	Meter: 950–1050 mm	1065–1067 mm	Standard: 1432–1440 mm	1498–1524 mm	1600 mm	1665–1676 mm
Africa	2,134	15,682	50,414	11,342	—	—	—
America, Central	3,949	96	2,639	25,540	76	—	—
America, North	531	—	1,148	402,471	167	—	—
America, South	3,919	42,281	1,171	9,438	—	4,137	26,375
Australasia	657	—	22,036	17,479	—	9,820	—
Europe	6,690	7,741	115	235,210	145,977†	2,369	16,534
Far East	6,446	39,127	31,398	47,732	1,425	—	41,272
Middle East	—	2,493	—	16,569	92	—	—
Total	24,326	107,420	108,921	765,781	147,737	16,326	84,181

*Grand total world railway route 1,254,692 km.
†Including railways in Siberia.

SOURCE: *Railway Directory and Yearbook*, 1979, IPC Transport Press, London.

lation to avoid sun-kinks and distortion in the summer and brittle, fragile rail in the winter.

Like many other railroads in the world, the Soviets also place great emphasis on electrification as a most desirable source of locomotive power. In the late 1960s and 1970s, electrification progressed at an average rate of nearly 1250 route-miles (2000 km) per year, and now totals over 25,000 mi (40,300 km).

China. In 1980, the People's Republic of China had approximately 32,300 mi (52,000 km) of mainline routes, employing about 2.4 million persons to operate 260,000 freight wagons and 15,000 passenger coaches. Of 10,000 locomotives, approximately 80% were steam (with the steam engines being built as recently as 1980) and the remainder diesel hydraulic, diesel electric, or straight electric. The railroads produced approximately 365 billion ton-miles (533.3 billion tonne-km) of transportation, compared to about 18.7 billion ton-miles (27.4 billion tonne-km) for highway and 258.7 billion ton-miles (377.9 billion tonne-km) for waterways.[47]

China is very active in new railway construction, in an effort to improve logistics and the transportation of people and goods. Between 1949 and 1979, China built 18,000 mi (29,000 km) of new lines, doubled the number of single-track lines, and built many new spurs and branch lines into industrial complexes and areas of forest and mineral resources. The new lines built since 1949 are 1¼ times greater than all Chinese railroad lines built between 1876 and 1949. Recently, the pace of railroad construction has accelerated to meet objectives of modernization and greater self-sufficiency.

In 1970, the Chinese completed the 675-mi (1085-km) Chengdu–Kuming Railroad, which passes through territory so rugged that the line averages one bridge for 1 mi (1.6 km) of track and one tunnel for every 1.6 mi (2.5 km). The combined length of bridges and tunnels on this line exceeds 250 mi (400 km). Nearly 33% of the line is either on bridges or in tunnels. This line, like others in China, crosses numerous mountain ranges, rivers, and passes through several areas with geological faults.

China, like most countries with railroads, is adopting the latest technology in railway construction and operation. The use of welded rail and concrete "sleepers" (ties) is the near universal standard of new railway construction. China is also considering building a "junior Shinkansen" line between Beijing and Tientsin with the assistance of the Japanese. Top speed would be 100 mph (160 km/h) versus the Japanese 130 mph (210 km/h).

Japan. Although the deficit of the Japanese railways approaches $2 billion per year, the Japanese are noted for having some of the most modern railroad operations in the world. Most famous was the construction and operation of the "Shinkansen" or "New Tokaido" line between Tokyo and Kobe. The original Tokaido line, a 372-mi (600-km) meter gauge line, was opened in 1889. The new standard gauge, passenger-only line has now been extended to cover the 665 mi (1070 km) between Tokyo and Hakata. Trains run at a maximum speed of 130 mph (210 km/h). The total number of trains operated in both directions is now approximately 300 per day, many being on headway only a few minutes apart.

Three new Shinkansen lines are under construction between Tokyo and Sapporo, Omiya, and Niigata, and a line between Tokyo and Naraita Airport. This construction includes connecting the islands of Honshu and Hokkaido by undersea railway tunnel and connecting the islands of Honshu and Shikoku with suspension bridges. Construction of the tunnel began in 1972, and it is earmarked for completion in 1982. Work on the first of the two suspension bridges was begun in 1976 and will take at least 15 years to complete. Five more Shinkansen lines are currently in the planning stages, and the Japanese government is contemplating construction of yet another 12 Shinkansen lines.

Central and South America. Great emphasis is being placed on improving and expanding railway operations in Central and South America. *Venezuela,* for instance, has established long-range goals of increasing its present rail lines from a token 107 route-miles (173 km) to 2300 mi (3700 km) by the year 1991—although as time passes this is likely to be scaled down considerably. The plan is to link the interior of the country to numerous ocean and seaports, providing outlets for petrochemical plants and enabling the country to supply fertilizer and handle agricultural products from interior areas under development.

Brazil is planning to spend over $4 billion in new railway construction to nearly triple the volume of traffic handled, from 80 million tons (73 million tonnes) in 1973 to 2650 million tons (236 million tonnes) by 1980. Concurrent with the expansion of the railroads, Brazil has embarked on a modernization program to replace old and obsolete equipment and modernize motive power. To do this, Brazil and other Central and South American countries are turning to European technology.

In the early 1970s, *Argentina* was faced with a railroad system so decrepit and obsolete that commerce and passenger transportation was greatly imperiled. Recognizing the importance of its railroads, Argentina has embarked on an ambitious program to rehabilitate lines, rebuild thousands of out-of-service freight and passenger cars and locomotives, and buy new equipment on the world market. The country's traffic demands simply cannot be fully met by other modes of transportation.

Freight traffic growth in *Mexico* increased 3.4 times between 1950 and 1974, and since 1974 it has continued to increase at a rate approaching 10% per year. Four new railway lines are currently near completion or under construction. The government has given railway modernization and expansion top priority in its national objective to achieve industrial growth and higher living standards.

Other. Perhaps more than in the United States, railroads throughout the world (particularly in Europe) are greatly concerned about energy conservation and uses of other than petroleum energy. The higher cost of oil and its scarcity greatly encourages electrification—more so than in the

[47] "Rail Freight Grows Fast in China," *Int. Railw. J.*, 10, (Sept. 1979).

TABLE 4–32
World Total Electrified Rail Route Mileage, by Type of Power

Source	Kilometers	Miles
DC		
Low voltage	7,899	4,908
Medium voltage	17,709	11,003
High voltage	57,249	35,572
AC—single phase		
16⅔ No. 2	28,484	17,699
20 No. 2	124	77
25 No. 2	1,743	1,083
50 No. 2	38,494	23,919
60 No. 2	2,791	1,734
Ac—three phase	81	50
Total	154,574	96,047

SOURCE: *Railway Directory and Yearbook*, 1978, IPC Transport Press, London.

United States. Also, traffic density on most European railroads is significantly greater than in the United States in terms of the number of trains operating per mile of track; this makes the investment in capital to support an electric catenary economically more justifiable. France and the Federal Republic of Germany each have electrified about 6200 route-miles (about 10,000 km) of line, compared to only about 500 mi (800 km) in the United States. Even Britain, with its investment in North Sea oil, is exploring mainline and electrification over the next 20 years that could embrace up to 3000 mi (4800 km) of intercity routes. In 1977, the world total of electrified lines was approximately 96,000 mi (155,000 km), as shown in Table 4-32.

High-speed transport developments

Increased energy consumption is usually associated with higher speeds. The British Rail's new high-speed advanced passenger train (APT) has proved that increasing speed need not increase energy consumption. This train is designed to run at 125 mph (200 km/h) and faster, and consumes approximately the same amount of energy as a conventional 100-mph (160-km/h) locomotive-hauled train.

The world leader in passenger train speed is, of course, the Shinkansen service in Japan. Seven southbound and six northbound trains cover the 664 mi (1069 km) between Tokyo and Hakata with six intermediate stops in just under 7 h at an average speed of 95.8 mph (154.2 km/h). The 213 mi (342 km) between Tokyo and Nagoya are covered by three to four trains per hour in each direction in 121 min at a start-to-stop speed of 105.4 mph (169.6 km/h).

As in Japan, railroads in Europe are focusing on increasing passenger-train speeds. The diesel-hauled high-speed trains (HST) of Britain are scheduled at start-to-stop speeds of 103 mph (166 km/h) between London and Bristol Parkway (112 mi; 180 km). In France, several trains exceed 100 mph (160 km/h), with the Paris–Bordeaux line now certified for 124 mph (200 km/h) operating speed throughout.

The United States is in fourth place with respect to timetable running speed; Amtrak Metroliner schedules show an average of 93 mph (150 km/h) over the 68.5-mi (110 km) Baltimore to Wilmington section of the Northeast Corridor; this is scheduled to increase to over 100 mph (160 km/h) by 1981.

Whereas the FRA's Pueblo, Colorado, research and test facility was originally intended to explore new technologies, including high-speed rail transport, lack of U.S. railroad industry support has caused the FRA to change its focus toward solving more contemporary railroad engineering problems. Much of its high-speed facilities and equipment is idle and little used. Meanwhile, Japan has nearly completed (in 1979) a 25-mi (40-km) test track, costing about $54 million, to test JNR's "maglev" vehicle propelled by a linear induction motor. Earlier tests of a linear motor railway vehicle (LMRV) on a 3-mi (4.7-km) test track have already resulted in achieved speeds of 210 mph (337 km/h). The Ministry of Transport would like to start maglev (where trains are magnetically suspended above the guideway) service between Tokyo and Osaka (348 mi; 560 km) in the late 1980s.[48] Nonstop running speed is expected to average close to 310 mph (500 km/h), requiring a little more than 1 h for the run. In 1979, the experimental test train established a world record speed, exceeding 300 mph (480 km/h).

Conclusions

Financially troubled as many railroads in the United States and the rest of the world appear to be, it is evident from growth and new technological developments that they remain the backbone of commerce in most countries. The energy efficiency of railroads is more important than ever in a scarce and expensive petroleum environment.

This chapter has only begun to cover the technical, operational, and financial aspects of railroading. Much more detailed information can be obtained from the U.S. Department of Transportation, the Interstate Commerce Commission, various railroad associations and organizations, technical libraries, the United Nations, and railroad themselves. The following section includes a small selected sample source of additional railroad technical information.

REFERENCES FOR FURTHER READING

Periodicals

International Railway Journal (Simmons Boardman)—monthly.

Modern Railroads (Cahners)—monthly.

Progressive Railroading (Murphy-Richter)—monthly.

Railway Age (Simmons Boardman)—biweekly.

Railway Gazette International (IPC Transport Press)—monthly.

Railway Track and Structures (Simmons Boardman)—monthly.

Traffic World (Traffic Services Corp.)—weekly.

Publications

The following are abstracted from *A Bibliography of Literature*, Association of American Railroads, Washington, D.C., Dec. 1976, with updating.

All about Signals, by John Armstrong. Kalmbach Publishing Co., 1967. 28 p. Illustrated. $2.00. The various signal systems are explained and illustrated. Reprinted from the pages of *Trains* magazine.

Car and Locomotive Cyclopedia of American Practices, compiled and edited for the Mechanical Division of the Association of American

[48] *Int. Railw. J.*, 6 (Nov. 1978).

Railroads by Kenneth G. Ellsworth, Simmons Boardman Publishing Co., 1980. p. 1047 Definitions and illustrations of railroad cars and their components built for domestic and export service. Includes shop practices and electrical fundamentals, photographs, and scale drawings.

The Compendium of Signals, by R. F. Karl, Boynton & Associates, 1976. 85 p. Diagrams and sketches. $3.00. A reference work on day and night signals from early North American ball-and-semaphore days to modern operations. It includes turn-of-the-century coverage of locomotive and train signals. British practice is also discussed.

Handy Railroad Atlas of the United States. Rand McNally & Company, 1980. 64 p. $6.95. These are specialized, state-by-state maps, with supplemental information about the railroads and the states they serve. Two-color maps identify all rail lines and distances between points. (ISBN 528-21065-3)

Herb's Hot Box of Railroad Slang, by J. Herbert Lund, Jay Herbert Publishing Co., 1975. 225 p. Illustrated. $7.95. Poems and cartoons explain various railroad slang terms or expressions. Book also features a special illustrated section on 12 heroes of the American railroads, dating from 1906 through 1943. (ISBN 0-916-214-01-X; LC AA-642744)

The Railroad—What It Is, What It Does, by John H. Armstrong, Simmons Boardman Publishing Co., 1977. 240 p. Illustrated. An introduction to railroading with descriptions and illustrations of important aspects of railroad engineering, operations, and rolling stock.

Railway Passenger Car Annual, by W. D. Randall and L. R. Hansen, RPC Publications, issued approximately annually. 150–200 p. Illustrated. An updated list of all passenger cars in active service in the United States and Canada. Also includes transit and light rail cars. Shows accommodations, names and/or numbers, prior owners, builder, and date built. Other interesting facts on the cars are given. Vol. 4, 1978/79. $6.75. (Vol. 5 planned for late 1980.)

The Track Cyclopedia, compiled and edited in cooperation with the Association of American Railroads, Simmons Boardman Publishing Co., 9th Ed., 1978. v.p. Illustrations and scale drawings.

Who's Who in Railroading and Rail Transit, edited by Russell F. Moore. Simmons Boardman Publishing Co , 1977. 439 p. $50.00. In its 18th edition, this is the oldest "Who's Who" book published in the United States. Biographical sketches of more than 6000 persons of importance in the railroad field are presented.

Publisher's Addresses

Boynton & Associates, Clifton House, Clifton, VA 22024.

Cahners Publishing Co., 5 South Wabash, Chicago, IL 60603.

IPC Transport Press International, Dorset House, Stamford Street, London SE1 9LU, United Kingdom.

Jay Herbert Publishing Co., 2236 West Lunt Avenue, Chicago, IL 60645.

Kalmbach Publishing Co., 1027 North 7th Street, Milwaukee, WI 53233.

Murphy-Richter Publishing Co., 20 North Wacker Drive, Chicago, IL 60606.

Rand McNally & Company, P.O. Box 7600, Chicago, IL 60680.

RPC Publications, P.O. Box 296, Godfrey, IL 62002.

Simmons Boardman Publishing Co., 8109 Capitol Avenue, Omaha, NE 68102.

Traffic Services Corp., 815 Washington Building, Washington, DC 20005.

5

CONTINUOUS-FLOW SYSTEMS

Preceding and paralleling the development of special continuous-flow, fixed-guideway devices for passenger transport (Chapter 22), a significant proportion of goods movement is made via this class of transportation technology. These systems have in common the capability for continuous throughput of goods, relatively high capacities and low speeds, and the absence of discrete vehicles. Liquids such as petroleum and gases and high-volume bulk products such as grain or coal are particularly well suited to this form of transportation. Some solids can be converted to slurries by mixing with liquids and there are systems for that as well.

This chapter describes some of the characteristics of systems in use as petroleum pipelines, slurry conveyors, and solid material conveyors. The details of design and operation can be found in handbooks for each specific type as identified in the references.

Part A

PETROLEUM PIPELINES

V. K. LEONARD, *Transportation Director*
American Petroleum Institute, Washington, D.C.

The term *pipeline* has many meanings. In its narrowest sense, it means the pipe and fittings used for transporting fluids or gases. In its broadest sense, it means all the facilities that are needed to transport a commodity from its source to a delivery point.

A modern pipeline system comprises storage tanks, pump stations, communications facilities, and control centers in addition to pipes and fittings. The system includes the means for measuring, monitoring, controlling, and accounting for commodities transported. These facilities require a company organization to plan, finance, design, construct, acquire, manage, operate, and maintain them. The term "pipeline" therefore encompasses an entire company, with all its properties and personnel.

Pipelining has long been regarded as an efficient way to transport large volumes of liquids and gases. In ancient times, fired clay pipes carried water for irrigation. Almost a thousand years ago, the Chinese transported fuel gas through bamboo tubes. The Greeks devised piping of hollowed stone, lead, and bronze to move water and wine. Roman aqueducts still stand, testimony to the centuries-old art of pipelining, and extensive sewage lines mark the historical growth of many European cities.

Pipelines still transport almost all water and sewage. The widespread use of natural gas and crude oil has spurred unprecedented expansion and development of pipeline systems throughout the world. The basic characteristics and advantages of pipelines make them uniquely suitable for transporting many kinds of commodities, and efforts are constantly underway to increase the number and variety of materials carried.

This section of the chapter is limited to petroleum pipelines which carry crude oil and petroleum products, such as gasoline, jet fuel, kerosene, liquefied gas, and heating oil. Heavier products such as residual fuel oil, wax, and asphalt are transported by pipeline but require special handling procedures. Natural gas is carried in pipelines of substantially different character.

There are over 200,000 miles (320,000 km) of petroleum pipelines in the United States alone, enough to circle the earth nine times. This vast system crisscrosses the lower 48 states and 800 miles (1300 km) of Alaska. Virtually all crude oil and petroleum products used in the United States are transported by pipeline at one or more points on the way from extraction to processing and distribution.

Petroleum pipeline development in the United States

There are three basic types of petroleum pipeline systems:

1. Gathering systems
2. Crude oil trunk line systems
3. Refined-products systems

Taken together, these systems provide a continuous link among extraction, processing, distribution, and consumption.

Gathering systems

As crude oil comes out of production fields, gathering systems collect and move it to central locations by means of a maze of small-diameter low-pressure lines, usually feeding many streams into storage tanks for eventual transfer to trunk lines. Gathering systems usually include pumping stations and meters and samplers to measure the quantity and quality of the oil received.

Generally, a gathering system serves a single oil field or area where hundreds of wells may produce the same kind or grade of oil. For different kinds of oil that cannot be mixed, separate gathering systems are necessary.

Almost 90% of all gathering lines are 6 in. (15 cm) or smaller in diameter. The gathering systems in the United States add up to 70,000 mi (110,000 km), or about 30% of the total pipeline mileage.

Crude oil trunk line systems

Crude oil transportation is carried out in trunk lines which receive crude oil from storage tanks, gathering systems, ships, barges, or other trunk lines.

Trunk lines comprise about one-third (34.3%) of the pipeline mileage in the United States. They cover great distances, mostly underground, from major oil-field regions to major refining areas. Trunk lines also carry offshore or imported crude oil from terminals and ports to inland refining centers. The Trans-Alaska pipeline is unusual for the United States because it is a crude oil trunk line which extends from a production field to a port terminal. In this regard, it is like the pipelines of Saudi Arabia and other great producing and exporting areas.

U.S. crude oil trunk lines usually range from 8 to 48 in. (20 to 120 cm) in diameter and can transport from 30,000 barrels to over 1 million barrels of oil a day. Large-diameter trunk pipelines are an important factor in making it economically feasible to extract oil in remote areas and transport it to refining areas, because the unit cost of transporting commodities by pipeline decreases as the size of the pipe increases. This economy requires that the total volume, the "throughput," be sufficient to keep the pipeline as full as possible. As a rule, the key to a successful pipeline is proper sizing for the amount of oil that will be transported.

Refined products systems

Products pipelines are delivery systems that transport finished petroleum products from refineries and seaports to market area terminals, from which they are usually moved by trucks to their final destinations. Delivery systems are an inverted image of gathering systems. Instead of small streams flowing into high volume trunk lines via storage tanks, products pipelines start out as large capacity systems emanating from storage tanks and branch into smaller capacity units to service widespread delivery points.

The products pipeline segment of the industry is much younger than the gathering and trunk line systems, but it has stimulated many technological changes because of the products' relatively high unit value and rigid quality requirements. For example, separation of different kinds and grades of products has generated many advances in pipeline equipment and in switching, quality control, monitoring, and measuring.

Refined products are generally lighter and less viscous than crude oil; therefore, they require smaller diameter pipe or less pumping pressure to move equal volumes. Like crude oil systems, however, successful products pipelines depend on large volume to reduce the cost of moving each unit or barrel.

Development of pipelines in the United States

The modern oil industry began on August 28, 1859, with Colonel Edwin Drake's well near Titusville, Pennsylvania. Initially, oil at the wellhead was put into barrels which teamsters hauled from the field to the nearest river or railroad loading point. From there, it was either floated downstream or put in wooden tanks on flat railway cars and moved to the refinery. The total transportation cost for a barrel of oil from Titusville to New York was $8.35, 54% of the total selling price; profit on the same barrel was only 1.0%.

The hazards, limited capacity, and high costs associated with this procedure stimulated construction of the first crude oil pipeline in 1865—a 6 mi, 2-in. gathering line, built between a production field and a railroad station. It cost about $3000 per mile to lay.

By the early 1900's with the opening of Texas and Oklahoma oil fields, railroads were no longer considered the primary means of transporting crude oil. As oil exploration and production moved west, more crude oil trunk lines were constructed to connect existing lines to eastern refineries.

Intense competition for farflung new marketing areas also

fostered a demand for product pipelines between refineries and distribution centers. By World War II, about 10,000 mi (16,000 km) of petroleum pipelines were in operation.

World War II generated a hugh demand for petroleum supplies. To meet the need, industry and government added some 11,000 mi (18,000 km) of trunk lines in 2 years, and made system changes in more than 6000 mi (10,000 km) of older lines. From prewar deliveries of less than 200,000 bbl/day, U.S. pipeline shipments soared to 754,000 bbl.

Perhaps the most significant cooperative pipeline projects during World War II were the $170 million "Big Inch" and "Little Inch" lines. These 24-in. (60-cm) crude and 20-in. (50-cm) products lines—then the largest in existence—quickly demonstrated the important economies of scale made possible by large diameter trunk lines. They were to have a profound and lasting influence on subsequent pipeline design and construction.

The wartime experience marked a turning point in petroleum pipelining. Between 1948 and 1974, total pipeline mileage rose 28% while the total number of barrel-miles delivered increased almost 500%—a significant measure of the effect of large diameter systems.

By the beginning of 1977, there were 227,066 mi (365,350 km) of petroleum pipelines in the United States—and this network moved 8.4 million bbl of crude oil and 10 million bbl of products per day.

Crude petroleum carried in domestic transportation by the various modes of transport in 1977, as shown in Table 5-1, totaled 636.8 million U.S. tons, of which 72.26% was transported by pipelines, 13.32% by water carriers, 14.09% by motor carriers, and 0.33% by railroads. The consistent high percentage of crude petroleum carried by pipeline over the past 40 years, while total production more than tripled, is quite evident.

In the movement in 1977 of petroleum products, as shown in Table 5-2, pipelines, which carry only light prod-

TABLE 5–1
Crude Petroleum Carried in U.S. Domestic Transportation by Mode of Transportation (U.S. Tons × 10^6)*

Year	Total Petroleum Carried (U.S. tons)	Pipelines		Water Carriers		Motor Carriers†		Railroads	
		U.S. Tons Carried	Percent of Total	U.S. Tons Carried	Percent of Total	U.S. Tons Carried	Percent of Total	U.S. Tons Carried	Percent of Total
1938	180.5	128.2	71.01	46.2	25.58	2.1	1.17	4.0	2.24
1943	240.7	176.8	73.46	31.1	12.93	7.9	3.27	24.9	10.34
1948	332.0	221.2	68.48	75.1	23.26	12.4	3.86	14.2	4.40
1953	376.9	283.4	75.19	70.6	18.73	19.0	5.05	3.9	1.03
1958	402.2	307.1	76.35	8.0	16.90	26.0	6.45	1.2	0.30
1963	468.1	351.9	75.17	83.2	17.78	32.2	6.88	0.8	0.17
1968	574.8	425.8	74.08	107.0	18.62	40.9	7.11	1.1	0.19
1973	640.4	492.4	76.89	90.5	14.13	55.6	8.68	1.9	0.30
1974	620.6	464.3	74.81	83.6	13.47	70.0	11.29	2.7	0.43
1975	611.6	454.7	74.34	77.9	12.74	76.2	12.46	2.8	0.46
1976	608.6	458.5	75.33	75.2	12.36	72.6	11.93	2.3	0.38
1977	636.8	460.1	72.26	84.8	13.32	89.7	14.09	2.1	0.33

*1 U.S. ton (2000 lb) = 0.907 metric tons. Multiply by 6.65 to convert tons to barrels at an average crude oil density of 7.16 lb/U.S. Standard gallon.
†The amounts carried by motor carriers are estimates.

SOURCE: Oil pipelines: *Crude Petroleum, Petroleum Products and Natural Liquids,* U.S. Department of Energy, Energy Information Service, Tables 14 and 30, annual. Water carriers: *Waterborne Commerce of the United States,* U.S. Department of the Army, Corps of Engineers, P. 5, Table 2, annual. Motor carriers: *Motor Carrier Statistical Summary,* American Trucking Associations, Inc., Table VII-A, annual; *Crude Petroleum, Petroleum Products and Natural Liquids,* U.S. Department of Energy, Energy Information Service, Table 14, annual. Railroads: *Freight Commodity Statistics,* Class I Railroads, Interstate Commerce Commission, Commodity Codes 13 and 291, annual.

TABLE 5–2
Petroleum Products Carried in Domestic Transportation by Mode of Transportation (U.S. Tons × 10^6)*

Year	Total Petroleum Products Carried (U.S. tons)	Pipelines†		Water Carriers		Motor Carriers‡		Railroads	
		U.S. Tons Carried	Percent of Total	U.S. Tons Carried	Percent of Total	U.S. Tons Carried	Percent of Total	U.S. Tons Carried	Percent of Total
1938	173.9	11.0	6.35	91.6	52.65	18.4	10.59	52.9	30.41
1943	233.0	19.6	8.39	84.9	36.42	68.6	29.44	60.0	25.75
1948	363.3	41.3	11.36	162.4	44.70	108.4	29.85	51.2	14.09
1953	485.8	75.8	15.59	202.9	41.76	165.6	34.09	41.6	8.56
1958	615.0	126.0	20.48	230.7	37.51	226.1	36.76	32.3	5.25
1963	727.9	169.3	23.25	252.4	34.67	280.4	38.52	25.9	3.56
1968	988.6	300.6	30.41	254.0	25.69	408.8	41.35	25.2	2.55
1973	1282.5	419.8	32.74	330.7	25.78	504.2	39.31	27.8	2.17
1974	1253.5	420.4	33.54	323.9	25.89	482.0	38.45	27.2	2.17
1975	1219.9	424.8	34.82	326.1	26.73	444.4	36.43	24.7	2.02
1976	1336.6	475.6	35.58	349.9	26.18	486.6	36.41	24.4	1.83
1977	1438.7	526.0	36.56	361.7	25.14	524.6	36.46	26.4	1.84

*1 U.S. ton (2000 lb) = 0.907 metric ton. Typical petroleum product densities are as follows (lb/gal): aviation gasoline, 5.90 regular gasoline, 6.18; kerosene, 6.77; lubricating oil, 7.50; asphalt, 8.66.
†Products pipelines move only light petroleum products: gasoline, heating and fuel oils, liquid petroleum gas, kerosene, and jet fuel.
‡The amounts carried by motor carriers are estimates.

TABLE 5–3
Crude Petroleum Carried in Domestic Transportation by Mode of Transportation (U.S. Ton-Miles × 10⁹)*

Year	Total Crude U.S. Ton-Miles	Pipelines† U.S. Ton-Miles	Pipelines† Percent of Total	Water Carriers U.S. Ton-Miles	Water Carriers Percent of Total	Motor Carriers† U.S. Ton-Miles	Motor Carriers† Percent of Total	Railroads U.S. Ton-Miles	Railroads Percent of Total
1973	363.2	302	83.1	58.8	16.1	1.3	0.3	1.1	0.4
1974	358.9	303	84.4	53	14.3	1.3	0.4	1.6	0.4
1975	331.5	288	86.9	40.6	12.2	1.4	0.4	1.5	0.5
1976	343.8	303	88.1	37.8	11.0	2.1	0.6	0.9	0.3
1977	392.5§	326.6§	83.2§	63.1	16.1	2.0§	0.5§	0.8§	0.2§

*1 U.S. ton-mile = 1.46 metric ton-km. Multiply by 6.65 to convert ton-miles to barrel-miles at an average crude oil density of 7.16 lb/U.S. Standard gallon.
†The amounts carried by pipeline are based on ton-miles of crude and petroleum products for federally regulated pipelines (84%) plus an estimated breakdown of crude and petroleum products for the ton-miles for pipelines not federally regulated (16%).
‡The amounts carried by motor carriers are estimates.
§Preliminary.

SOURCE: Oil pipelines· Annual Report to Congress, Interstate Commerce Commission, App. E, Table 3. Water carriers: *Waterborne Commerce of the United States*, U.S. Department of the Army, Corps of Engineers, P. 5, Table 4, annual. Motor carriers: Federal Highway Administration estimate based on state highway department truck weight surveys. Railroads: U.S. Department of Transportation, Federal Railroad Administration, Statement TD-1, *Carload Way Bill Statistics*, annual.

TABLE 5–4
Petroleum Products Carried in Domestic Transportation by Mode of Transportation (U.S. Ton-Miles × 10⁹)*

Year	Total Petroleum Products Carried (U.S. Ton-Miles)	Pipelines† U.S. Ton-Miles	Pipelines† Percent of Total	Water Carriers U.S. Ton-Miles	Water Carriers Percent of Total	Motor Carriers‡ U.S. Ton-Miles	Motor Carriers‡ Percent of Total	Railroads U.S. Ton-Miles	Railroads Percent of Total
1973	480.4	205	42.7	238	49.5	23.7	4.9	13.7	2.9
1974	488.8	203[R]	41.5	244	49.9	27.7	5.7	14.1	2.9
1975	515.2	219	42.5	257.4	50.0	26.2	5.1	12.6	2.4
1976	523.9	212[R]	40.5	269.1	51.4	30.4	5.8	12.4	2.3
1977	532[R]	219.4[R]	41.2[R]	270.2	50.8	28.7[P]	5.4[P]	13.7[P]	2.6[P]

*1 U.S. ton-mile = 1.46 metric ton-km. Typical petroleum product densities are as follows (lb/gal): aviation gasoline, 5.90; regular gasoline, 6.18; kerosene, 6.77; lubricating oil, 7.50; asphalt, 8.66. P, preliminary; R, revised.
†The amounts carried by pipeline are based on ton-miles of crude and petroleum products for federally regulated pipelines (84%) plus an estimated breakdown of crude and petroleum products for the ton-miles for pipelines not federally regulated (16%).
‡The amounts carried by motor carriers are estimates.

SOURCE: Oil pipelines: Annual Report to Congress, Interstate Commerce Commission, App. E, Table 3. Water carriers: *Waterborne Commerce of the United States*, U.S. Department of the Army, Corps of Engineers, P. 5, Table 4, annual. Motor carriers: Federal Highway Administration estimate based on state highway department truck weight surveys. Railroads: U.S. Department of Transportation, Federal Railroad Administration, Statement TD-1, *Carload Way Bill Statistics*, annual.

ucts (gasoline, heating and fuel oils, liquid petroleum gas, kerosene), carried 36.56% of the 1438.7 million U.S. tons transported. Table 5-2 shows that the quantity of these specialized products carried has increased almost tenfold in the past 40 years and the share carried by pipeline increased sixfold.

As shown in Table 5-3, the total ton-mileage of crude petroleum for 1977 was 392.5 billion, of which 83.2% was transported by pipelines, 16.1% by water carriers, 0.5% by motor carriers, and 0.2% by railroads. Table 5-4 indicates that pipelines accounted for 41.2% of the 532 billion ton-miles of petroleum products transported in 1977.

The petroleum pipeline industry

The structure of the pipeline industry has been influenced by three key economic factors:

1. Pipelines are capital intensive.
2. Pipelines are high risk investments.
3. Pipelines benefit from economies of scale.

By the end of 1977, interstate petroleum pipelines, including the Trans-Alaska pipeline, represented a $15 billion investment. Of that total, the Trans-Alaska pipeline, amounted to approximately $9 billion.

Pipelines are relatively inflexible. They are built to move their commodities over a fixed route in one direction. If market conditions or contractual arrangements change after a pipeline is built, it is not practical for the pipe to be moved, and in most cases it has no resale value. Excess capacity is not readily divertible to other uses. It is possible to reverse the flow or carry other commodities by making alterations to the line, but such alterations depend on economic feasibility.

A significant factor is the economy of scale. Essentially, the larger the pipe diameter, the more economical it is to move commodities through the system given sufficient volume. For example, at equal operating pressure a 36-in. (90-cm)-diameter pipeline can carry 17 times as much petroleum as a 12-in. (30-cm) pipeline. The initial cost of a 36-in. line, however, is less than three times as much as a 12-in. line. For a given volume, then, the large installation would cost only about one-sixth as much for equal capacity as the required number of small installations.

Another element in pipeline economy of scale is operating cost. While energy needs increase with volume, other operating costs, such as labor and maintenance, do not increase proportionately. Thus, when cost is divided by volume, the operating cost per barrel is substantially lower in a larger pipeline than in a smaller one.

Pipeline ownership patterns

Successful pipelines depend on maximum volume over a long term. As a result, they are considered feasible only when major shippers guarantee their use. These guarantees usually take the form of "throughput" agreements, assurances by the shippers of specified minimum usage over a given period, which are used in turn as security to obtain financing for the pipeline. Conversely, the shippers at any given location are the ones most interested in pipeline service from the location.

Until the late 1920s, individual refineries usually built their own pipelines with capacities about equal to their own needs. With the development of large diameter pipe, some built larger lines and transported other shippers' oil in order to benefit from the economies of scale. Soon prospective pipeline shipper–owners formed joint venture pipeline companies to build large diameter systems to transport their combined volumes of crude oil and refined products at the lowest possible cost.

In the United States there are about 61,000 mi (98,000 km) of private single owner pipelines moving crude oil or products relatively short distances, usually within one state. It is rare, however, for one shipper to have enough volume to benefit fully from the economies of scale of a large diameter line. Therefore, most major interstate systems are joint venture common carriers, financed with long term commercial loans, secured with throughput agreements from several shipper–owners. Over 100 U.S. oil pipeline companies serve as common carriers in interstate petroleum transportation.

No one company or group of companies dominates the industry. In 1976, the largest interstate pipeline company moved about 10% of the industry's total barrel-miles; the top four companies transported about 32%, and the top eight about 54%. Concentration has declined since 1950, and indications are that this trend will continue.

Regulation of common carrier pipelines

The Hepburn Act of 1906 required that petroleum pipelines engaged in interstate transportation serve as common carriers, that is, available to all shippers and subject to regulation by the Interstate Commerce Commission (ICC). To prevent discrimination among shippers, all common carriers must publish reasonable use conditions and charges (tariffs) and must accommodate any shipper who complies.

The Pipeline Cases of 1914 tested the applicability of the Hepburn Act to all pipelines. The U.S. Supreme Court confirmed ICC jurisdiction over crude oil pipelines except where a company engages solely in transporting its own oil from its own wells through its own lines to its own refineries.

In 1940 and 1941, the ICC established guidelines for setting tariffs which limited earnings to not more than 8% of a crude oil carrier's property valuation and 10% of a products carrier's property valuation. In 1941, a Consent Decree between the U.S. Department of Justice and 59 pipeline companies and 20 major oil companies limited the payment to each of the affected shipper-owners to 7% of the valuation of the carriers property.

When the U.S. Department of Energy (DOE) was created in 1977, ICC jurisdiction over common carriers was transferred. DOE requires pipelines to submit weekly reports of inventories, both in tankage and in the pipeline, and may mandate specific routings or facilities. Valuation, tariffs, and tariff investigations are now the province of the Federal Energy Regulatory Commission (FERC).

In addition to economic regulation, oil pipelines come under the jurisdiction of federal and state regulatory agencies in several other areas, of which the most important is safety.

Under the Explosives and Combustibles Act of 1909, amended in 1921 to include flammable liquids and solids, the ICC was given jurisdiction over pipeline safety. The ICC decided in 1942 that the petroleum industry had set sufficiently high standards for its operations and that there was no need to establish new regulations. About 20 years later the ICC began to formulate a single federal safety code for the pipeline industry, primarily to protect interstate carriers from multiple and conflicting state regulations.

In 1967, safety jurisdiction over oil pipelines was transferred to the newly established U.S. Department of Transportation (DOT). The DOT adopted regulations which require that any accident on any petroleum pipeline must be reported if it involved injury, death, a spill of 50 bbl or more, or damage to another's property of $1000 or more. Three years later, DOT adopted a uniform safety code based substantially on the pipeline industry's voluntary standards. Statistics gathered under these requirements confirm a satisfactory safety record for the industry. The DOT gained new authority over the regulation of intrastate and interstate pipelines with the passage of the Pipeline Safety Act of 1979 which replaced all previous federal legislation.

Profile of a pipeline

Building a new crude oil pipeline was relatively simple at one time. Discovery of an oil field brought with it the need for a pipeline to move the oil to a refinery. The shortest practical route was chosen between the field and a trunk line, port, or refinery. Only a few standard-size pipes were available; selection of the optimum size was imprecise, and frequently a small line was built with the intention of laying additional parallel lines, or loops, later. Some systems ended up with stations pumping oil through as many as six parallel lines.

Today, the whole process of planning, constructing, and operating a petroleum pipeline has become more complex. This section describes the life cycle of a crude oil pipeline through the years of planning, financing, design, construction, and startup.

Planning

The need for a new crude oil pipeline arises when:

1. A new oil producing area is discovered.
2. Production in an existing area exceeds current capacity.
3. Shipments through a port increase.
4. A new point of entry is established.
5. A refining center needs additional supplies.

First, the project's economic feasibility is established. Geologists confirm the significance of the oil find and calculate the reserves and production capacity. These are the basis for estimating expected throughput.

Economists study potential markets and the value of future production. They forecast conditions that might affect the pipeline, directly or indirectly, over the next 15 to 20 years, such as the state of the economy, shifts in population, product demand growth; refinery construction, expansions, and shutdowns, domestic and foreign crude production, prospects for competitive pipelines, industry changes, and government actions.

If studies indicate that a pipeline is economically justifiable, engineers proceed to plan and design the project in detail.

Another phase of the planning process focuses on the organization and financial specifics of the project. If the pipeline is a joint venture, those involved form a company, secure throughput agreements, and arrange for financing.

In the meantime, the precise characteristics of the crude oils are analyzed. The viscosity, specific gravity (density), vapor pressure, corrosiveness, composition, and grade are some of the chemical and physical properties critical to the ultimate design of the pipeline system.

Pinpointing the exact route is no less important. Engineers might prefer the shortest, most direct line between origin and destination, but deviations may be necessary because of natural features such as mountains, difficulty in obtaining rights-of-way, the need to pass near some supply or delivery point or to skirt heavily populated areas, and other environmental considerations.

After selection of the best possible route, the pipeline company obtains the necessary rights-of-way from landowners or local governments to build and operate the pipeline. They must acquire permits for crossing railroads, highways, streets, rivers, drainage ditches, and other public facilities. Before any construction can begin, they must file environmental impact statements for federal and state agencies with jurisdiction over areas through which the pipeline will run.

Basic design

Once economic, geographic, and environmental studies confirm that a pipeline is possible, planning gives way to design. Throughout this phase, engineers ensure that construction features comply with industry and governmental standards for safety and structural integrity.

The major feature in the system's design is the pipe, even though it is usually almost entirely buried. The aboveground features are an occasional pump station, marking sign, road crossing vent, tank farm, or radio tower along the route. Selecting the specific pipe for a given project is affected by economic factors, as noted above, as well as by the nature of the oil, expected throughput, terrain, and construction conditions.

Pipes vary in diameter, wall thickness, length, and protective coatings. Most pipe today is made of high-strength steel, although other materials may be used for special applications. Suitable casings, valves, and other pipe fittings are also chosen to satisfy requirements established in the planning stage.

Viscosity, specific gravity, and pipe walls friction, throughput, and elevation affect oil flow. Pumps must be placed at intervals along the line to keep the oil moving at the desired rate. Uphill terrain requires closer pump spacing. On a modern pipeline, pump stations are typically spaced at intervals of 25 to 100 mi (40 to 60 km).

Tank farms are another element of the basic design of a pipeline system. At originating points they receive oil from gathering systems and feed it into the trunk line. Along the trunk line, they are used to sidetrack oil in transit temporarily for batching, measuring, rerouting, or holding during repairs. At the pipeline terminal, the various oil shipments are again segregated into tanks for delivery to other pipelines, refineries, or marine terminals.

In addition to the physical features—pipe, pumps, and tanks—the pipeline's basic design includes control centers utilizing modern computer systems, communications equipment, and other electronic control mechanisms. Linking the system together through telephone and radio, these controls maintain a high degree of automation, cost and time savings, and built-in safeguards. They permit a few people in a central location to keep the entire system running safely and efficiently around the clock. They permit rapid and accurate pipeline accounting.

Construction

The construction of an oil pipeline is fast-moving. Construction units are organized and equipped to move across country covering up to 3 mi (5 km) per day, clearing right-of-way, ditching, welding, x-raying welds, lowering the pipe, testing the line, backfilling, and restoring the ground surface. Advance units may be several miles ahead of finishing units. It usually takes between a week and a month at each point along the way to complete the entire operation from start to restoration—a relatively short time for a construction job of this magnitude.

In preparation for laying the pipe, the crew brings individual pipe sections to the site and places them end to end along the right-of-way. This stringing operation, accomplished before or after ditching, aligns the pipe's sections for welding, joining valves, and other fittings. At this point, individual pipe lengths are bent to conform to the direction of the ditch.

To limit external corrosion the pipe is coated at the mill with material or the crew applies it on the job. Additional long-term protection from external corrosion is provided by introducing low-voltage currents into the ground around the line, which mitigate natural corrosive forces in the soil. This is called cathodic protection.

Inspection is conducted throughout the materials acquisition and construction process. The pipe is checked for obstructions, proper placement of the seams is confirmed, the welds are inspected and tested, and the coatings are examined. Every part of the line must meet the safety standards set forth by the industry as well as local, state, and federal regulations.

When it passes inspection, the pipe is lowered into the ditch with special roller cradles, cranes, and hoists mounted on tractors, called sidebooms. At water crossings or other wetland areas, the pipe is pulled or pushed into place by section. To counteract the empty pipe's natural buoyancy, weights or screw anchors may be placed on these sections or a concrete coating applied to the pipe.

Once the line is laid, the crew backfills the ditch, covering it completely with earth, and prepares for the final cleaning and regrading of the entire right-of-way. At intervals along the right-of-way, aerial markers and valves to shut off the flow of oil in case of leaks are installed for later monitoring and control of the line.

Testing

The final step before starting operations is testing the pipeline and equipment of the completed system. Testing begins when a plug or "pig" is inserted in the line, and water is injected behind it to push it through the line. Named for the characteristic noise it makes as it moves along, the pig fits snugly inside the pipe, with discs, bristles, or blades positioned to clean and scrape off any foreign matter. When the plug or pig has completed its job and water fills the entire line, the engineers slowly increase pressure to a predetermined maximum. Any drop in the pressure over the next 24 h which is not temperature related could indicate a leak that must be repaired.

Pumps, valves, tanks, and all communications facilities are also run through final check routines and approved for operations.

Startup

After all systems are approved, the pumps are started and a stream of oil flows through the pipeline. The pumping rate is gradually increased until the line is filled and daily throughput reaches the expected operating level. Depending on the length of the line and the rate of the flow, it takes from a week to a month for the first barrel of oil to move through the entire line. When the 800-mi (1,300 km) Trans-Alaska pipeline was opened, it took first oil 38 days to go from Prudhoe Bay to the terminal in Valdez.

Throughout the initial run, monitors track the oil's progress; sometimes a special team follows it along the line, alerted for any unusual situation. When the line is completely full and oil emerges at the terminal station, the system is operational, and the normal routine of the pipeline begins.

Pipeline operations

Optimum throughput is essential for maximum efficiency, and pipelines are, by nature, high-volume operations. There is always a significant in-transit inventory in the pipeline.

A typical shipment of crude oil through a pipeline goes as follows: It is pumped out of the ground into separator tanks, where natural gas is diverted to another system. The crude oil then flows into heat treaters, where water and sediments are removed, and then into "lease tanks," where it is held until the required volume is ready for delivery to the pipeline gathering system.

For custody transfer of crude from the producer's lease tanks to the pipeline, the crude must be accurately measured and tested to determine volume, API gravity, temperature, and water and sediment content. Measuring and testing may be done manually by gauging the lease tank and sampling the crude or automatically through the use of Lease Automatic Custody Transfer (LACT) equipment. The LACT equipment meters the crude as it flows into the pipeline and automatically collects a small sample of the entire volume in a sample container. The collected sample is then manually tested for API gravity and water and sediment content.

After the entire volume of crude has moved into the pipeline, a custody transfer ticket is written showing the volume and quality of the crude which entered the pipeline. A copy of the ticket is issued to the lease operator.

When the shipper's crude oil enters the trunk line, it joins other shippers' crude oil. The various crudes are batched according to grade. The pipeline company delivers approximately the same quantity of comparable oil at the destination as was received from the producer. Equal grades of crude oil are "fungible"; a given volume for one shipment may be substituted for the same volume from any other shipment.

When the oil is delivered, it is again tested for quantity and quality, and another custody transfer ticket is written with a copy furnished to everyone involved in the transaction. The delivery ticket for the batch of oil delivered to the pipeline company by the producers is the basic document used in buying and selling the crude oil leaving U.S. fields through pipeline systems every year.

The key to efficient pipeline operations is scheduling. This requires programming each shipment from origin to destination within the trunk line so that the entire stream moves smoothly and at an optimum rate all the time. Schedulers canvass all potential shippers for their supplies, sales, purchases, and requirements. They then develop the monthly barrel-per-day line pumping rates, apportioning capacity between shippers if more crude is tendered than the line can move.

Even if several grades of oil are to be batched, a continuous flow is maintained with very little mixing. Depending on the material, the interface oil is put in a tank of the less valued grade. Batches with unusual qualities that cannot be mixed are sometimes separated by inflated rubber spheres or plugs.

Scheduling becomes very complicated when several shippers are involved, when diverse shipments move in and out of the main stream, and when pumping rates vary. Automation has revolutionized these operations. Today, almost all major pipeline systems use sophisticated computers and communications to develop and implement complicated schedules.

From a single control room, dispatchers have the operations of the entire trunkline system at their fingertips. Using microwave, telephone, and even satellite communications as well as control computers, they are in constant touch with all points on the pipeline. They start and stop pump stations hundreds of miles away, monitor pressures, flow rates, and specific gravity, and are able to switch streams from one delivery point to another.

Speed and accuracy are vital. In the around-the-clock operations, the dispatcher on duty tracks every batch, computes volumes received and delivered, maintains the proper balances and sequences throughout the system, and handles emergencies if they arise. The status of all equipment, the number of barrels pumped from or into a location, and the amount of unused capacity in every tank at every delivery point are continually monitored. Data from remote sources are telemetered back to the operator and displayed regularly and frequently.

Pipeline maintenance

In the past, pipeline maintenance was almost synonymous with repair. Crews were dispersed throughout the system on call to make emergency repairs when leaks occurred. Common causes of leaks were failures or ruptures of welds, seams, and above all, corrosion and third party damage.

Recently, pipeline maintenance has undergone many changes. Emphasis is on preventing deterioration that was formerly considered to be normal wear and tear. Improvements in materials, design, construction methods, and operating procedures have eliminated or greatly reduced many of the previous causes of failure.

Better techniques are now used for gathering timely information on the condition of the line. For decades linewalkers regularly inspected the entire pipeline on foot. They have been largely replaced by aerial patrols. Flying small planes at low speeds and low altitudes, patrol pilots spot minor leaks which are too small to affect operating pressures from oil stains on the ground, vegetation, or water near a pipeline. They also report on construction activities and utility changes that could endanger the pipeline. The major cause of pipeline breaks and leaks today is mechanical damage from heavy equipment belonging to outside parties that operate around the pipeline right-of-way.

Internal coatings and scraper runs or inhibitors injected into the oil can effectively control internal corrosion. Since the 1940s, special external coatings and cathodic protection with low-voltage currents have steadily reduced the incidence of external corrosion.

The "pig," which is used to clean the line before startup, is also used for preventive maintenance. In this case, the pig is inserted into the pipeline through a special launching assembly called a pig trap or scraper trap. Propelled along with the stream of oil, it scrapes off wax, sediment and other foreign matter, which is removed through another scraper trap down the line.

Major leaks or breaks in the line are usually detected by station operators, who spot a drop in pressure on the control console indicators. In addition, controls at automatic pump stations are usually set to shut down and signal an alarm at the control center when unprogrammed pressure changes occur.

When an alarm goes off to indicate a leak, the line is usually shut down until repaired. Methods have now been developed for making small repairs without having to shut down the entire line. The overriding consideration is to prevent or minimize spills.

Refined products pipelining

In many respects, products pipelines are similar to crude oil pipelines. The key to economy is again the low unit cost achieved by proper sizing and optimum throughput. Construction, operating procedures, and maintenance of products pipelines are also very similar.

Nevertheless, the service provided by the two systems is essentially different; crude oil pipelines basically perform a gathering service. Products pipelines provide a distribution service. Beginning at refineries, they branch out into smaller lines and terminate in marketing centers.

In addition to the fundamental service difference, products movement requires greater quality control and care in handling. There are many different grades of gasoline, blending stock, turbine fuel, kerosene, and diesel fuels. Depending on their particular specifications, some grades must be segregated, whereas some grades may be shipped on a fungible basis.

The last leg in a products pipeline is often through a lateral line feeding into a series of tanks near a large city. For volatile products such as gasoline, these tanks usually have floating roofs to control vapor emissions and to reduce product loss through evaporation. Tank trucks make the final distribution to service stations.

The largest and most complete products pipeline in the United States today is the Colonial system, completed in 1965 at a cost of $360 million. Through its pipes stretching over 3700 mi (5920 km) of right-of-way, Colonial carries over 1.7 million barrels of products daily. This includes 120 separate grades from 10 different source points being distributed to more than 265 terminals. The complex scheduling and dispatching task is accomplished on a 10-day cycle by an automatic supervisory control system. Colonial is a joint venture owned by 10 shippers and marketers, but its services are available on equal terms to all shippers.

Marine pipeline systems

In 1951, the first U.S. offshore pipeline, 10 mi in length, was laid to carry natural gas from the Gulf of Mexico to an inland point in Louisiana. There are now more than 7000 mi (11,000 km) of marine pipelines in the United States, carrying almost 10% of the daily flow.

Marine line costs vary with size, depth, underwater terrain, and geological conditions. They can easily exceed $1 million per mile; in parts of the North Sea, they have cost more than $3 million per mile. Twice the expenditure for onshore lines is common.

Despite their high cost, marine pipelines are the safest, most dependable, and most environmentally sound method for bringing offshore oil to land. In some cases, they are the only practical means of transporting large quantities.

As with overland systems, design and engineering of a pipeline's specific characteristics depend on several key factors, such as total reserves, producing capacity, type of oil in the field, location of production platforms, delivery points on land, and geological and environmental features.

A marine pipeline is similar to overland pipelines in its major physical elements. It includes a pressure source, usually located on the offshore production platform gathering lines, the main trunk line to shore, and sometimes, intermediate pressure-booster stations. In addition, it requires a landfall site where it comes ashore and onshore terminal facilities.

Laying a marine pipeline

Pipelaying offshore is similar to underwater river crossings of an overland pipeline route, except that the depths are generally greater, the underwater segment longer, and construction must be carried out in the open waters of gulfs and seas.

Marine pipe and all related submarine equipment is designed to withstand the extreme stresses of the laying procedures, as well as many years of exposure to salt water, seabeds, and unpredictable weather encountered during "normal" operations.

The pipelaying operation requires a well equipped and well coordinated "work spread": pipe supply vessels, tugboats, a pipe-laying barge, and a trenching barge. Rental fees for such a spread could be $200,000 a day in the Gulf of Mexico and $500,000 a day in the North Sea.

The most common method of laying offshore pipeline is the "lay barge," using the "stovepipe" technique. Sections of pipe are delivered to the lay barge which is positioned over the chosen route. Crane operators and other crew members move one section at a time into position in large clamps and line them up with the previous section. Welders then join the two ends together, x-ray the welds, and coat them.

As the team adds each section to the string, the lay barge inches forward, finished pipeline slide down a ramp called a "stinger," and the team brings another section forward to repeat the cycle. The barge resembles a floating mill that moves while its handiwork steadily comes to rest on the seabed. In good weather a rate of 1 mi/day is normal.

Another method used to lay marine pipelines is the "reel barge" technique, which involves welding, testing, and coating the pipe ashore, winding it onto a larger diameter reel on a barge, and then towing it to the site. At the site, the pipe is welded to the previously laid section, and the barge is towed forward, spooling the pipe off the reel. This method permits fast installation with minimum exposure to weather. It is not practical with concrete-weight coating and is usually limited to 12-in. (30-cm) diameter pipe or smaller.

The "pull" technique is a third method, and it has several variations. It entails assembly of the pipe sections in one location either on land or on a barge and then pulling or towing them to the pipeline location.

There are special procedures for special tasks, such as connecting pipeline to the production platform with prefabricated risers.

Trenching

Government regulations require that pipelines must be trenched for stability and protection from currents, waves, anchors, and fishing activity in water depths of less than 200 ft (60 m). Underwater trenches average about 3 feet (1 m) in depth in the Gulf of Mexico.

In trenching operations, the pipeline is first lowered onto the seafloor. Then a specially designed dredge or "trenching barge" is used. A "jetting sled" straddles the pipe and slowly moves along the line. As it moves, built-in pressure jets flush out the bottom mud and sand, leaving a trench into which the pipeline naturally settles. With the help of currents and waves, the sediments gradually sink down and cover the line—often in a matter of hours. Before long, the water's turbidity has dissipated entirely.

Shore approach and landfall

The preferred location of a landfall site is usually determined by the shortest possible route between the production platform and land. The physical characteristics of the shoreline, ecological factors, population patterns, and existing uses of the area must also be taken into consideration.

If the oil is to be retransported by tanker, the landfall must be at a suitable tanker terminal site with sufficient land nearby for a tank farm. If the oil is to be retransported further inland, only a pumping station is needed at the landfall site, with the pipeline continuing beyond.

Generally, the environmental impact of a marine pipeline is minimal. Local disruption of sediments and underwater contours is temporary; in shallow waters and even in deeper water, local contours are quickly rebuilt naturally. Onshore construction activities may cause some disruption at the landfall and near shore areas. Offshore pipeline companies have available construction and restoration techniques that are sensitive to the ecologies of marshes, estuaries, beaches, and barrier islands.

Potentially, oil spills are the most serious environmental impact of a marine pipeline system. In the past, external corrosion was the major cause of failure and leaks. Technological progress in recent years has dramatically reduced the number of oil spills caused by corrosion from U.S. offshore pipelines. Most offshore pipeline accidents that involved spills of 50 barrels or more were caused by damage from external sources.

Spills from any failure are more quickly detected than in the past because of technological advances in underwater inspection and maintenance equipment. There is closer monitoring of pipeline operations and widespread use of special valves and control systems which automatically shut down the line if a leak occurs or pressure drops.

There are several options for dealing with oil from spills. These include burning, sinking, containing and removing, dispersing, and leaving it to be dispersed naturally. Recently, an oil-consuming bacteria has been developed through genetic research and development. The type and amount of oil as well as sea and weather conditions determine which method or methods are used. Spills in rough seas are usually dispersed naturally by the turbulent water and pose little threat to shoreline or marine life. Skimming, absorbing, and subsequently removing the oil are the most widely used mechanical treatments. Oil spills can also be broken up with chemical dispersants and sinking agents.

The need for offshore pipelines has greatly increased worldwide in the past decade, involving greater water depths and harsher environments. In the early 1970s, the world's depth record for an offshore pipeline installation was in 480 ft (145 m) of water. Test lines lie at 1850 ft (565 m).

The demand for energy continues, and forecasters look to offshore areas as an important source of future oil and natural gas reserves. Inevitably, successful development is linked to hundreds of more miles of pipelines—larger pipe, farther out to sea, and deeper below the surface of the water and the ocean floor. Feasibility studies have shown that a semisubmersible vessel may be capable of laying lines in 2000 ft (600 m) of water. Techniques and equipment for construction and maintenance of pipelines at 3000 ft (900 m) are being explored. These include new concepts for remote repair capabilities.

Petroleum pipelines compared to other transportation modes

Pipelines are unique among transportation modes in that they alone use the commodity to move itself. Unlike other transportation systems, most pipelines lie buried beneath the surface, almost totally invisible, silent, without harmful emissions, and once built, with virtually no adverse impact on the environment. They provide continuous service 24 hours/day, 7 days/week, and are practically immune to the effects of weather and traffic congestion. In addition, the pipelines' safety record is the best in the transportation industry.

Pipelines are a noncontainerized form of transportation for liquid commodities, thus eliminating costs for packaging and returning empties. They provide a direct and continuous link between production, processing, and consumption, virtually eliminating product handling, losses, and damage en route.

All of these features add up to major advantages in efficiency for shipper, consumer, and operator in transporting energy by land and, in some cases, by water.

There are several factors that place pipelines at a disadvantage among transportation modes. As has been noted, they are extremely capital-intensive, requiring large initial investments with limited returns on capital. They also are inflexible; typically, they can carry only relatively low viscosity liquids on a single route in one direction.

It is possible to reverse the flow of a pipeline with modifications to piping, pumps, and other station equipment. This was done successfully during World War II and there are recent examples in which accommodation was made to major shifts in markets or opening of new crude oil fields. However, the fixed route of a pipeline makes it largely inflexible, particularly when compared with other modes of transportation.

The economic disadvantages of pipelines, therefore, are high risk, minimum investment interest aside from that of potential users, and minimum salvage value once the pipeline is no longer economical.

Tariff rates for domestic transportation

The first shipments of oil from Titusville to New York cost $8.35 per barrel ($0.20 per U.S. gallon) for transportation cost on a trip of about 350 mi. In 1977, a barrel of oil moved more than 1600 mi (2600 km) from Houston, Texas, to New York in a modern pipeline for about $0.60 per gallon. Overall, typical 1977 costs were $0.03 to $0.12 per 100 bbl-mi.

Long-haul petroleum pipeline rates usually are 75 to 80% lower than the next-lowest-cost overland carrier, rail. Within the past few years, pipeline tariffs have even become competitive with traditionally lower barge and coastal tanker rates.

Only coastal tankers are cost-competitive for relatively long hauls between domestic seaports or on major rivers. However, they are subject to weather conditions and river congestion.

Rail tariff rates range from $0.11 to $0.60/100 bbl-mi. They compete for long-haul traffic where volumes are not too large or where special segregation in tankcars is required. Transportation by truck is clearly the most costly, at $0.52 to $0.75/100 bbl-mi; trucks are used primarily for small volume, short-haul movement of products from terminals to bulk plants or local outlets.

Comparative rates per mile do not reflect all the important cost advantages of petroleum pipelines. Direct pipeline routing eliminates circuitous travel, minimizing the total distance between two points and therefore the total cost per trip. In addition, pipelines' relative immunity to external factors permits continuous travel and eliminates costs incurred by delays.

Additional aspects of pipeline operations

In comparing petroleum pipelines with other transportation modes, it is useful to look briefly at two additional aspects of their operations: safety and energy consumption.

Safety. Petroleum pipelines are by far the safest mode of transportation. In its official reports on liquid pipeline safety statistics, the Department of Transportation has consistently shown that there are an extraordinarily small number of deaths and injuries associated with pipeline operations.

It should be noted in this context that the safety of human lives is directly related to the safety of property and to environmental protection, and that all three are ultimately contingent upon the physical integrity of the system.

The built-in control and the fail-safe features of modern petroleum pipelines have been highlighted because human error is the principal cause of most transportation accidents. The high degree of automation throughout pipeline systems accounts to a large extent for their excellent safety record. A voluntary industry safety code with very high standards of design, construction, testing, preventive maintenance, and monitoring techniques has been another significant safety factor for many years. Increased use of computers for scheduling, monitoring, and control promises to make petroleum pipeline operations even safer in the future.

Energy consumption. All transportation modes together use about one-fourth of the total energy and more than half of all the petroleum consumed in the United States. A significant proportion of this energy is actually consumed in the process of transporting energy, particularly petroleum and coal, the nation's largest fuel sources.

Among the energy-transportation modes, petroleum pipelines use the least energy per unit of energy moved. Fuel consumption by tank trucks, for example, is several hundred times as great as that by pipeline to deliver the same commodity. A truck may use 3 to 4% of its payload, whereas a pipeline can accomplish the job using only 0.01% of the material delivered.

The Trans-Alaska pipeline system

One of the most difficult engineering feats of modern times, the construction of the Trans-Alaska pipeline system, is a unique and significant achievement—a tribute to the pipelining industry.

From its inception, the Alaska pipeline project posed extraordinary physical and environmental challenges. In economic terms, it was the largest privately funded construction effort ever undertaken. When it was completed in June 1977, just 3 years after it was started, the project had increased total pipeline miles in the United States by less than one-half of 1%, but it had doubled total industry investment in pipeline facilities from less than $7 billion to almost $15 billion.

In 1968, the largest petroleum field in the western hemisphere to date was found at Prudhoe Bay on Alaska's North Slope. After considerable study, it was decided that the most desirable way to bring the field's 9.6 billion bbl of oil to the lower 48 states was by pipeline, 800 mi (1300 km) across Alaska from the frozen North Slope to a south Alaskan port from which the oil could be transshipped by tanker.

Eight companies formed an undivided-interest consortium, the Alyeska Pipeline Service Company, to undertake the effort. Planning for the pipeline began shortly after discovery of the oil, but legislative and regulatory challenges, many based on environmental issues, delayed the actual start of construction for over 4 years.

It finally took a special act of Congress, The Trans-Alaska Pipeline Authorization Act, signed into law in November 1973, to give the pipeline the go-ahead. Shortly thereafter, federal and state permits were issued and the project began.

Planning and design

From the initial concept, throughout the project, and continuing during the pipeline's operation, a singular effort has been made to safeguard as well as to accommodate the harsh, yet delicate, Alaskan environment. Teams of ecologists, archaeologists, biologists, botanists, and oceanographers from industry, government, and academia researched and monitored geological and seismic conditions, fish and wildlife populations, vegetation, revegetation, and soil, air, and water quality. Detailed comparative analyses were prepared on resource values and potential risks, and many unique safety features were incorporated in the final design.

More than 100 of the most stringent construction and operation stipulations ever imposed on any project were set forth and met. Permits were obtained from some 56 government agencies, and the Department of the Interior's environmental impact statement alone exceeded 10,000 pages.

The pipeline's final route as well as sites for pump stations and terminals were based on detailed studies of eight possible routes from the North Slope oil fields to four alternative terminal locations. The ice-free port of Valdez was finally chosen for the southern terminus; the general route was further defined by major mountain and river crossings, soil conditions, environmental factors, and overall route length.

The pipeline leaves the Arctic plains of Prudhoe Bay, climbs 4800 ft (1460 m) over the Brooks Mountain Range, crosses the Yukon River, climbs 3300 ft (1000 m) over the Alaska Range, and then winds over the Chugach Mountains before descending to Valdez. On its way, it crosses more than 800 streams and occupies, in all, only 12 mi^2 (31 km^2) of Alaska's total 586,000 mi^2 (1.5 million km^2).

A unique 48-in. (120-cm) diameter steel pipe was developed to meet the stringent requirements of the system. Special alloys, thicknesses, coatings, and insulation were used to permit the pipe to withstand extreme pressures, stresses, and temperature variations. In normal operation, the oil enters the pipe at about 140°F (60°C) and arrives at Valdez at between 35 and 55°F (2 to 13°C), while outside temperatures might range from the 90°F (35°C) in summer to −80°F (−60°C) in Alaska's sunless winter.

To allow for the unusual soil and seismic conditions along the route, unique construction and pipelaying techniques were developed. Every aspect of the pipeline system—pipe, pump stations, and terminal—was designed to withstand the most extreme earthquake likely all along the line.

Equal attention was devoted to ensuring that the pipeline would be as leakpoof as possible. However, in case of an accident, detailed contingency plans are ready for every element of the system to respond immediately to prevent spills or to minimize them when they occur, and then to restore affected areas promptly.

GLOSSARY OF PIPELINE TERMS

Barrel of Oil — A unit of petroleum liquid measurement equal to 42 U.S. standard gallons. On the average, 7.33 bbl of crude oil weigh one metric ton.

Barrel-Mile — A unit of measurement used in pipelines to signify one barrel of oil moved one mile.

Batch — A discrete volume of one grade of crude or one grade of product.

BS & W — Basic sediment and water. Foreign matter, such as wax, asphalt and brine, which settles to the bottom of storage tanks as crude oil solutions are cooled. Pipeline regulations generally limit BS & W to 1% of the volume of oil.

Capacity of a Pipeline — The maximum volume of crude oil or product that can be moved through a pipeline over a unit of time, usually measured in barrels per hour (BPH) or barrels per day (BPD).

Dispatcher — The person responsible for scheduling movement of crude oil or product through pipelines.

Fungible — Interchangeable, permitting the substitution of a given volume of one product, such as kerosene, for the same volume of another shipment of the product.

Fungible Common Stream — Products of comparable quality commingled and moved in a single batch through a pipeline.

Gauging — Measuring the volume of oil in a tank by determining the level and temperature of the oil, calculating the number of barrels, and adjusting it for 60°F.

Grade of Oil — The quality of oil as determined by its BS & W (purity) and specific gravity (density). In general, the lighter the oil, the higher the grade.

Interface — The point or area where two dissimilar products or grades of crude oil meet as they are pumped, one behind another through a pipeline.

Lease — A contract giving an operator the right to drill for oil or gas in a particular location in exchange for a stipulated sum.

Lease Automatic Custody Transfer (LACT) — An automated system for handling crude oil produced on a lease; receiving it into tankage; measuring, testing and transferring it from a gathering system into a pipeline.

Linewalker — A person who patrols a pipeline route on foot checking for leaks or other problems. "Line-riders" patrol by car or truck; patrol planes can also perform the same function.

Maximum Operating Pressure — The maximum pressure allowed at any point in a pipeline during the normal operations, as determined by the pipe's thickness, grade of steel, diameter and strength of line fittings, valves, etc.

Petroleum Products — Commodities which result from refining crude oil; mainly common fuels, including gasolines of different grades, kerosenes, turbine fuels, and heating oils.

Pig — A plastic or metal cylindrical device which fits flush with the inside perimeter of the pipe and is regularly moved through the line to clean and scrape off foreign matter. Also called "Go-devil."

Plug — A rubber or metal sphere used to separate batches of products in a stream and keep them from intermixing. Also called a "batch separator."

Run Ticket — A record of the quality and quantity of oil run from a lease tank into a connecting pipeline.

Scheduling — Planning future movement of separate batches through a pipeline system.

Scraper Trap — A type of loading tube for inserting and retrieving a "pig."

Specific Gravity — The density of any liquid compared with that of water. In the case of oil and petroleum products, it is expressed in "Degrees API," as the ratio of the weight of a given volume of the material at 60° F to the weight of an equal volume of distilled water at the same temperature, with both weights corrected for buoyancy of air.

Stream — The continuous supply of oil or product flowing from a specific source or through a pipeline. "On stream" means in production or in operation.

Stringing — Placing individual lengths of pipe end to end along a pipeline right-of-way in preparation for laying.

Tanks — Large cylindrical vessels for storage of crude oil or products. A "tank battery" receives crude oil from producing wells. "Tank farms" along a pipeline hold oil in transit. A "lease tank" temporarily stores oil produced and gathered from leases until it can be gauged and moved to a trunk line. A "separator tank" is a tall, cylindrical tank in which gas is separated from crude oil and water.

Tender A shipment of oil or product presented by a shipper to a pipeline for movement.

Throughput The volume of material moved through a pipeline during a specified time period, usually measured in barrels per hour (BPH) or barrels per day (BPD).

Throughput Agreement A long-term commitment to ship a minimum quantity of petroleum products or crude oil through a pipeline.

Viscosity A measure of the resistance of oil to flow. The more viscous the oil, the less readily it will flow; the viscosity of oil increases as its temperature decreases.

Part B

SLURRY PIPELINES

R. H. DERAMMELAERE

Project Engineer, Bechtel, Inc.

E. J. WASP

Manager of Special Projects, Bechtel, Inc.

Slurry pipeline systems are an efficient and reliable transportation mode. They originated in the mining industry, where wet grinding of minerals made slurry transportation an inherent part of the process. In those early applications, distance seldom exceeded several hundred feet except in tailings lines. The latter could transport *gangue* material from the concentrator to a tailings pond no more than 5 to 10 km away.

Innovative slurry system design now permits cross-country transportation over hundreds of kilometers. Particle-size consist, which is an important slurry transport parameter, can be made compatible with other process requirements. The pipeline can be buried using conventional cross-country construction techniques.

These systems had their modern beginnings in the 1950s with the 175-km, 0.254-m-diameter Consolidation Coal pipeline and the 116-km, 0.152-m-diameter American Gilsonite pipeline. Considerable technical and operating knowledge has been gained which, coupled with broad experience with short-distance slurry pipelines and slurry handling, has advanced the design and building of long-distance systems from an art to a maturing technology.

The slurry transportation concept remained relatively obscure to the general public until the oil embargo and rising oil prices forced attention to the critical energy situation in the latter half of the 1970s. Coal is being recognized as one of the United States' major short-term solutions to the energy crisis.

The economics of coal is heavily dependent on transportation costs. Until recently, the railroads have had a virtual monopoly on coal transportation, but being labor-intensive and using diesel-powered locomotives, they suffer from heavily escalating operating costs. Long-distance coal slurry pipelines are emerging as a strongly competitive transportation mode with many environmental advantages.

On August 14, 1970, coal began flowing in an underground slurry pipeline 440 km across the state of Arizona to a 1500-MW power plant near Davis Dam in Nevada. This installation is the 0.457-m-diameter Black Mesa coal slurry pipeline, which is equivalent in capacity to two 100-car railroad trains per day and is the longest slurry pipeline in the world to date.[1] The relative length and geographic relationship of this system to others now in the planning stage is shown in Figure 5.1. The magnitude of anticipated expansion is quite evident. The most advanced of the planned facilities is the ETSI (Energy Transportation Systems, Inc.). This is a multi-billion-dollar pipeline system intended to transport coal from the Powder River Basin in Wyoming to utilities in Oklahoma, Arkansas, and Louisiana. ETSI's pipeline capacity would be 23 million metric tons of subbituminous coal, enough to generate approximately 7000 MW. It is shown in Figure 5.2.

[1]H. D. LEVENE, "The Longest, Largest Coal Slurry Pipeline Ever Built," *Coal Min. Process.*, Feb. 1971.

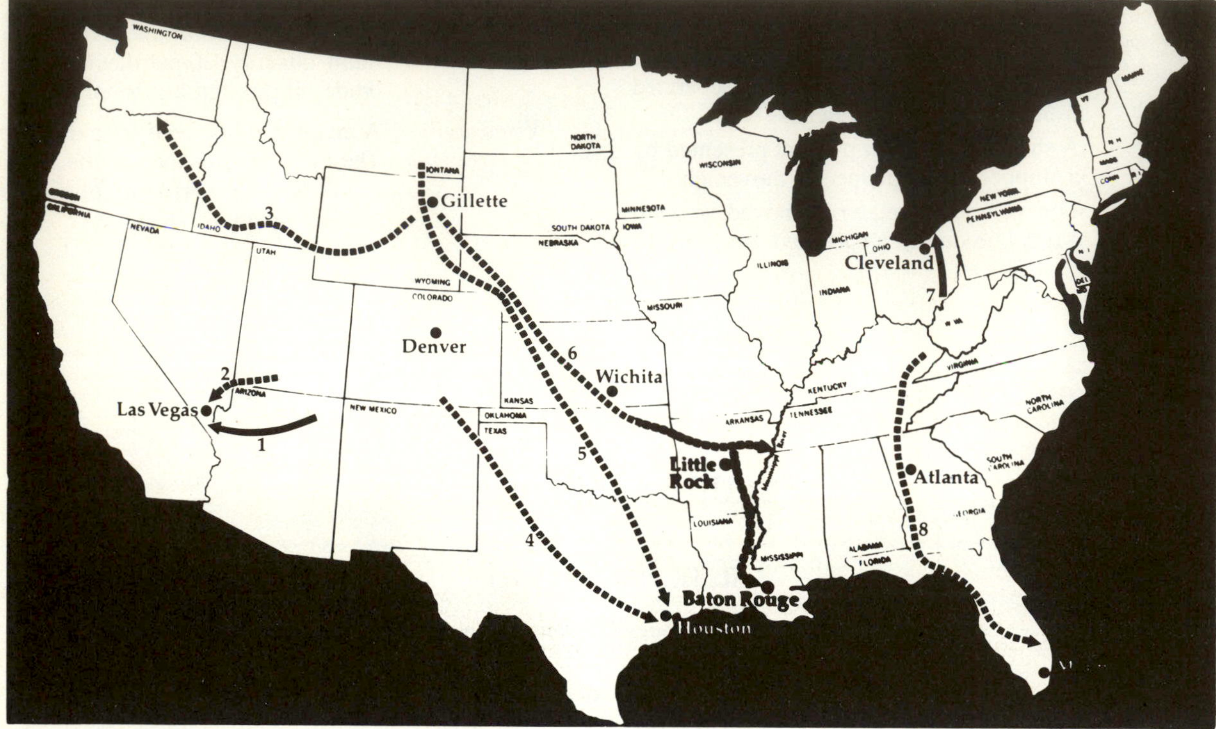

Pipeline System	Length	Annual Capacity
1. *Black Mesa Pipeline*	*273 miles*	*4,800,000 tons*
2. *Alton Pipeline*	*183 miles*	*11,600,000 tons*
3. *Gulf Interstate-Northwest Pipeline*	*1,100 miles*	*10,000,000 tons*
4. *San Marco Pipeline*	*900 miles*	*15,000,000 tons*
5. *Wytex Pipeline*	*1,260 miles*	*22,000,000 tons*
6. *ETSI Pipeline*	*1,378 miles*	*25,000,000 tons*
7. *Ohio Pipeline*	*108 miles*	*1,300,000 tons*
8. *Florida Pipeline*	*1,500 miles*	*15-45,000,000 tons*

Figure 5.1. Coal slurry pipeline systems. Coal has steadily grown in importance as a fuel for generating electricity, particularly in states formerly dependent on natural gas. Several slurry pipelines are under development to help transport increased coal production. SOURCE: Energy Transportation Systems, Inc., San Francisco, Calif.

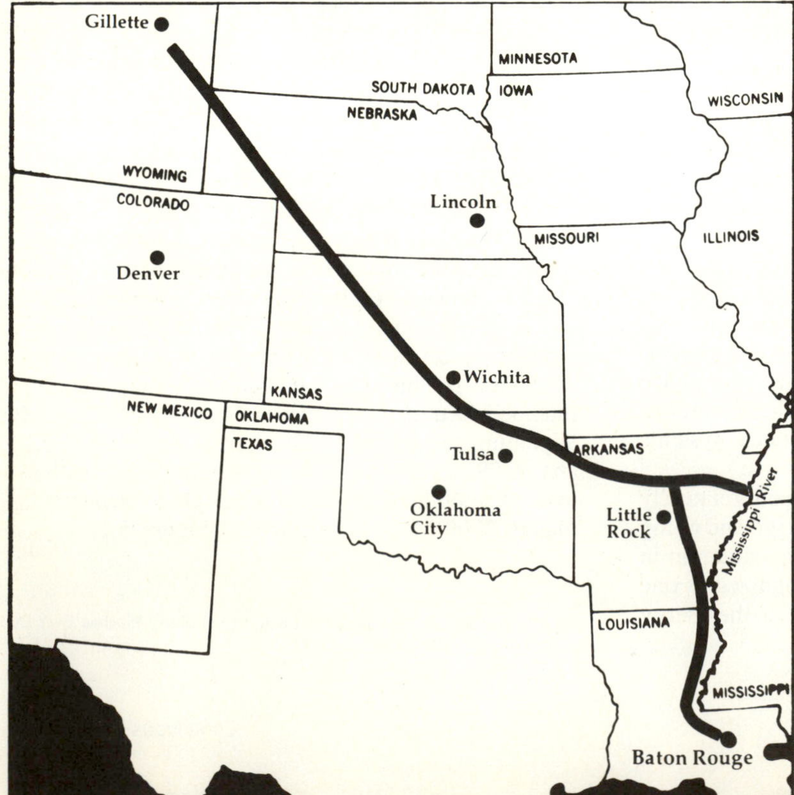

Figure 5.2. The ETSI pipeline route. Originating in the coal fields of the Powder River Basin, the ETSI line will run underground 1378 mi past major power plant sites along its route to the Mississippi River. Coal can be delivered en route or transferred to barges for further shipment on the waterway system.

Slurry pipeline design

Slurry pipeline design is a complex procedure that cannot be adequately covered here. The methods of hydraulic analysis, adapted to materials that are neither solid nor liquid but something in between, are essential to the design process. Two reference textbooks deserve special attention from those interested in in-depth study of slurry characteristics and flow. *The Flow Complex Mixtures in Pipes* by Govier and Azia[2] provides an excellent theoretical background for behavior and flow of non-Newtonian fluids and other complex mixtures. *Slurry Pipeline Transportation* by Wasp, Kenny, and Gandhi[3] is a current practical design manual for the slurry engineer.

For a given material to be moved, the design process aims at the selection of an appropriate pipe type and size and pumping pressure. Abrasion, corrosion, usable velocities, friction losses, amount and gradient of rise and fall, and ambient and generated temperatures are but some of the more important parameters to be considered.

Seven basic design-calculation steps are required:

1. Classify the slurry as being either homogeneous or heterogeneous.
2. Establish the slurry concentration.
3. Select a pipe size, based on the system's throughput requirement.
4. Calculate the critical velocity.
5. Check that the design velocity is at least 1 ft/s above, but not excessively above, the critical velocity. It may be necessary to select another trial pipe size and repeat the calculations until an acceptable relationship between critical velocity and design velocity is achieved.
6. Calculate the design friction losses (distinguishing between horizontal and vertical pipe for heterogeneous slurries).
7. Calculate the system pressure gradient and pump discharge pressure.

Slurry processing

Processing may be broadly classified into slurry preparation and/or slurry utilization. Figure 5.3 indicates the various processing steps that may be required. The purpose of this section is to indicate the processing steps that are associated with the emerging slurry-transport systems, to discuss types of equipment presently used, and to note various key design parameters that will be useful to the design engineer.

Slurry preparation

This is the physical and chemical processing necessary to give the slurry characteristics required for hydraulic transport and utilization. Preparation normally involves both size

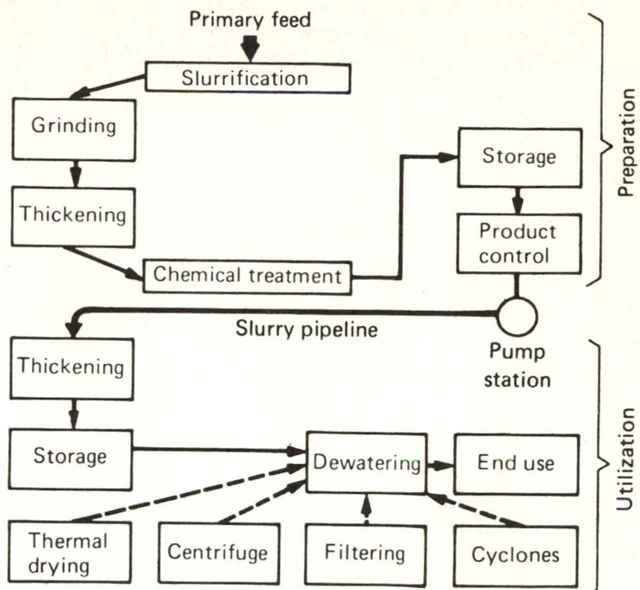

Figure 5.3. Typical processing for slurry system.

reduction (crushing and grinding) and slurrification or addition of the liquid phase. Chemical treatment may also be part of slurry preparation for corrosion inhibition, thinning, and improving the characteristics of the final product.

Before utilization, there is virtually always a storage step involved, because it is rarely practical to close-couple the pipeline transport system with the processing plant. Various storage facilities, such as tanks and ponds and associated agitators, and recovery dredges, must be included in the system. The utilization process may include facilities to change the concentration of the slurry—normally to increase the solids content via thickening, decanting, cycloning, and screening. More expensive dewatering methods may be needed, depending on the slurry and its ultimate use, such as vacuum filtration, centrifugation, or thermal drying. Further, the filtrate or effluent might need treatment before it returns to the environment. Additional processing steps can be used to enhance final product characteristics (e.g., heating to improve centrifugation or chemical additions to enhance thickening).

Some systems require special slurry-preparation facilities (see Table 5-5). Coal preparation for slurry pipeline trans-

TABLE 5–5
Commercial Slurries for Pipelines

Material	Specific Gravity	Maximum Particle Diameter (mesh)	Special Preparation Required?	Size Reduction Equipment Commonly Used
Gilsonite	1.05	4	Yes	High-pressure water jets, crushers
Coal	1.40	8	Yes	Impactors, cage mills, rod mills
Limestone	2.70	48	No	Impactors, ball mills
Copper	4.30	65	No	Crushers, autogenous mills, ball mills
Magnetite	4.90	150	No	Autogenous mills, ball mills

[2] G. W. Govier and K. Azia, *The Flow of Complex Mixtures in Pipe*, Van Nostrand Reinhold, New York, 1972.

[3] E. J. Wasp, J. P. Kenny, and R. L. Gandhi, *Slurry Pipeline Transportation*, TransTech Publications, 1977.

portation is an example. In this case, a particle size specifically suited for slurry transportation must be produced.

In all slurry systems, a balance has to be made between pumpability and dewatering characteristics. If sizing is too fine, pumpability may be good but the slurry may be difficult to dewater at the pipeline terminal. If the size is too coarse, the slurry is heterogeneous and must be pumped at higher flow rates to maintain suspension. The cost of pumping then goes up. The choice of particle size for a slurry depends on (1) overall cost of preparation, pumping, and use of the slurry; and (2) operability of the slurry, including shutdown/startup characteristics and critical velocity.

Grinding solids. Mineral extraction generally requires very fine grinding of ore; 70 to 80% of particles passing 325 mesh [44 microns (micrometers)] is common. Size reduction of the ore normally involves a wet process and the resulting slurries are readily handled hydraulically. As a result, the minerals industry is ideally suited for hydraulic transportation of solids.

Where grinding is done specifically to prepare a material for pipelining, the step will normally involve conventional milling equipment. In some cases, the equipment may be a new application to grinding the specific material.[4] In the Black Mesa coal-preparation plant, shown in Figure 5.4, rod mills (typical of those found in ore-dressing plants) are used for the final coal-grinding stage. It was necessary to apply the known milling technology of metal-ore dressing to the grinding of coal.[5] Preparing coal for slurry transport involves screening, crushing, grinding, and storage in mixing tanks, as depicted in Figure 5.4.

In slurry preparation, two variables are quite important which may have only minor significance in other crushing processes. These are the slurry density and product top size.

Control of slurry density is necessary to produce a consistent material that fits the hydraulic design of the pipeline.

[4]F. C. Bond, "Crushing and Grinding Calculations, Parts I and II," Allis-Chalmers (rev. Jan 1961), reprint from *Br. Chem. Eng.*

[5]F. C. Bond, "Metal Wear in Crushing and Grinding," 56th Ann. Meet. AIChE, Houston, Tex., Dec. 1–5, 1963.

Figure 5.4. Preparing coal for slurry transport involves screening, crushing, grinding, and storage in mixing tanks.

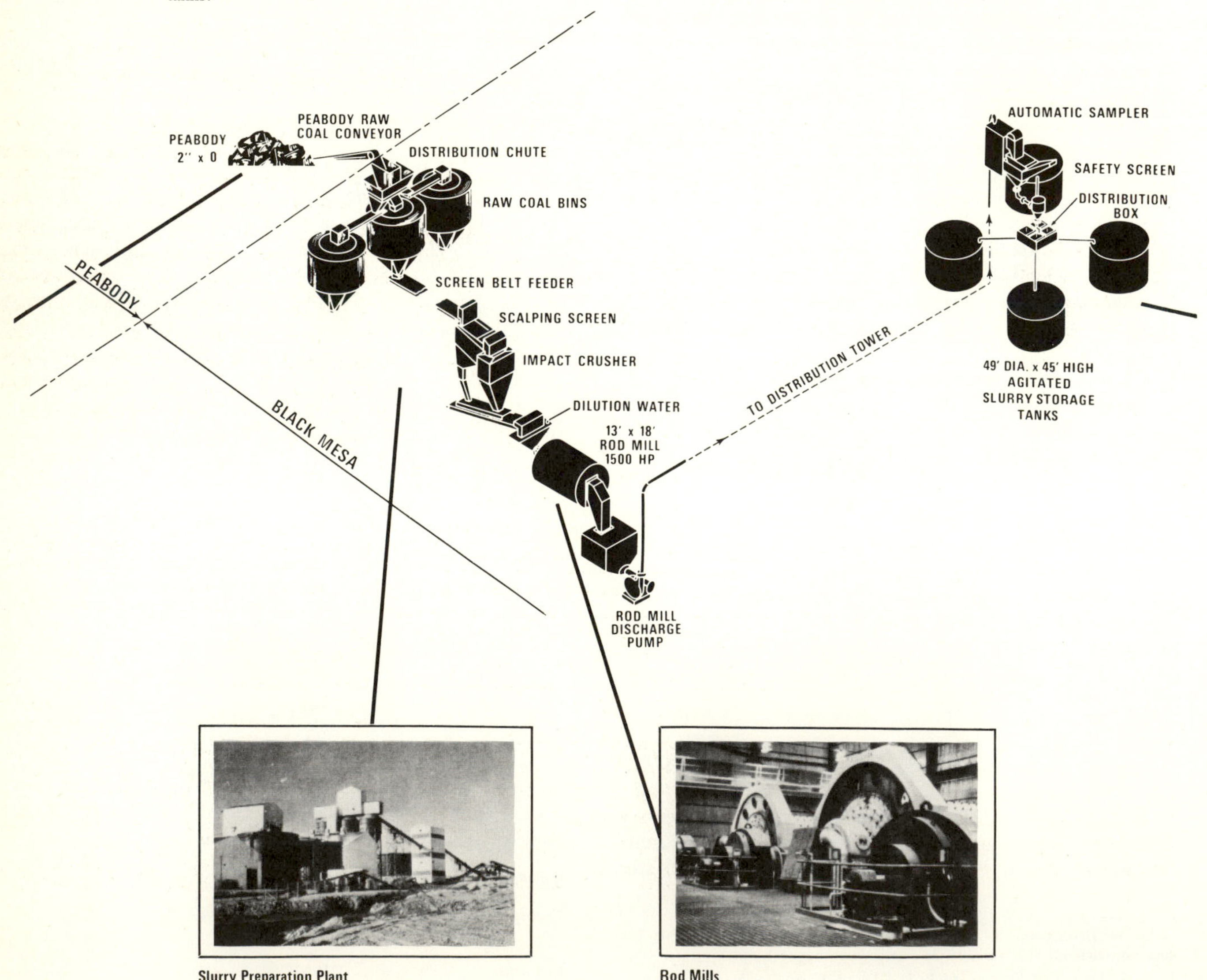

Slurry concentration plays an important role in both the friction loss in the pipeline and the critical velocity of the slurry. The preparation step is usually performed at a solids concentration slightly higher than that required for the pipeline, with dilution control instrumentation provided downstream in the line.

Top-size control is extremely important for any slurry transported over a long distance. Large quantities of coarse, fast-settling particles can cause pipeline plugs. To prevent this, safety screens are installed to prevent coarse particles from entering the pipeline. In systems where a minimum amount of crushing is done and where the slurry is relatively high in density and slow settling, conventional classification devices such as cyclones and screen are not satisfactory for top-size control unless the slurry can be diluted and later thickened prior to transportation.

Available equipment. There are many types of mills available for grinding ores. The most common include autogenous, impact cage, rod, and ball mills. Selection of the most suitable mill depends on the characteristics of the ore, particularly hardness, and the required fineness of the final product.

Slurrification: mixing water and solids. Slurrification normally takes the form of mixing water and solids together in a gravity-feed chute, where the water assists the travel of solids through the chute. This is common practice in a wet-grinding process. The water and coarse solids feed directly into the grinding mill, which discharges a uniform slurry. A notable exception to this is the cutter-head suction dredge. A rotating cutter head provides the shearing action to break down the bed of sand or gravel into particles that can be transported hydraulically in slurry form. The solids in the sand are sheared downward, thus are dragged down toward the dredge suction, where they are picked up in the suction flow. The maximum suction lift of a slurry pump limits the density of a slurry that can be recovered by a dredge.

Slurrification is also often achieved by using hopper-shaped sumps (Figure 5.5). Solids disperse over the surface of the liquid in the sump, usually by gravity flow through a screen. Water is sprayed onto the surface of the screen to assist in screening, to break up conglomerates, and to distribute the particles. Liquid in the sump is maintained at a constant level independent of solids addition. In the sump, the particles settle at their terminal settling velocity. As the cross-sectional area of the sump narrows (an inverted cone or pyramid shape), slurry concentration increases.

Another slurrification method requires using energy of a high-velocity stream of water to break up the solids and form a slurry. The high-velocity water stream is formed by a high-pressure nozzle. Hydraulic mining and the Marconaflo jet system, slowly rotating jets at about 300 psi, decompact and reslurry caked concentrate.[6] The reslurried concentrate then flows by gravity through grates to sumps and sump pumps (Figure 5.6).

[6] "Macronaflo—The System and the Concept," *Eng. Min. J.*, May 1970.

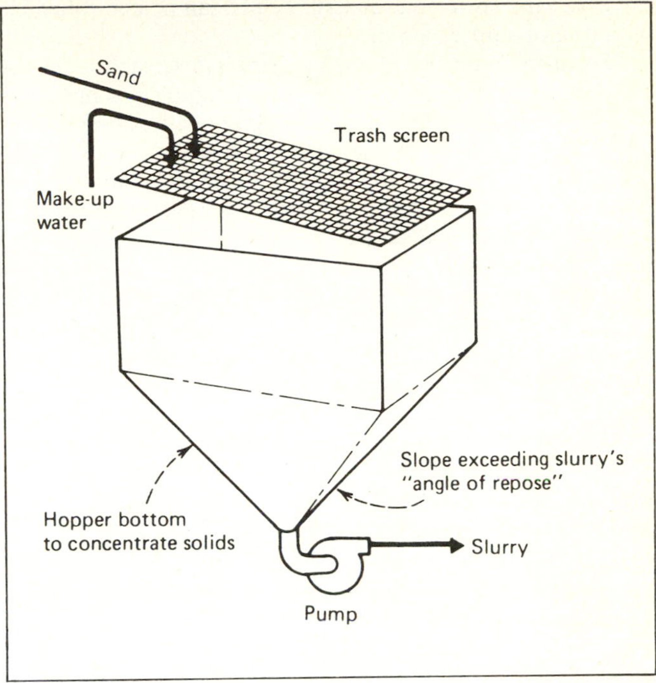

Figure 5.5. Screen system for reslurrying coarse sand.

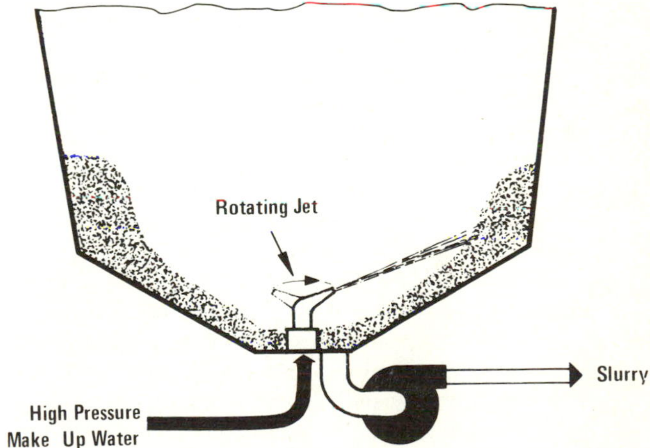

Figure 5.6. High-pressure jet can reslurry caked solids.

Chemical treatments. Corrosion in a pipeline transporting a water–solids slurry is controlled by adding corrosion inhibitors.[7] Laboratory-scale tests determine the most suitable type and dosage of inhibitor to be added to a slurry. Various inhibitors may be used, depending on the corrosion mechanism taking place. For example, sodium dichromate will form a film on the pipe wall and protect the pipe; severe attack by dissolved oxygen can be controlled by adding an oxygen scavenger such as sodium sulfite.[8] In other systems, a high-slurry pH controls corrosion.

Normally, a solution containing inhibitor is added to the slurry by a metering pump. A corrosion meter monitors

[7] J. P. Swan, et al., "Corrosion Control Achieved in Coal Slurry Pipeline," *Mater. Prot.*, Sept. 1963.

[8] D. R. Bomberger, "Hexavalent Chromium Reduces Corrosion in Coal-Water Slurry Pipeline," *Mater. Prot.*, Jan. 1965.

internal pipe corrosion, and slurry pH can be controlled by addition of slurried lime.

Shear-thinning materials, or dispersants, such as lignin compounds and polyphosphates, are examples of materials that are effective in breaking up agglomerates. Such chemicals are used in the cement industry. These materials reduce the electric charges on the edge of the particles so that they are dispersed in the fluid trapped in the agglomerates. This fluid is released and becomes part of the free fluid. The effect is to increase the dilution of the slurry. A surprising reduction in pressure losses is possible with low dosage additions.[9]

Drag reducers suppress turbulence in the pipe. These materials are usually macromolecules of very large molecular weight (large-chain polymers). The exact mechanics of how they reduce turbulence is not understood. They are quite effective in astonishingly small quantities in nonslurry systems; but they are less effective in slurry systems because considerable suppression of turbulent energy dissipation already has taken place. In addition, most slurry systems operate near the laminar-turbulent transition point, where turbulent dissipation is not very high.

Controlling product quality. As a final control step to ensure that only specification slurry is committed to the main pipeline, a "test loop" should be included in the system. This test loop, made of the same-size-diameter pipe as used in the main slurry pipeline, should have a length 400 to 500 times the pipe diameter. All slurry must pass through this section before going into the main pipeline. The test loop on the Savage River system (iron concentrates transportation in Tasmania, Australia) is located between the feed tank and the mainline pumps.

Since the test loop is simply a short in-line version of the main pipeline, it is useful in monitoring changes in slurry hydraulics. Pressure drop (usually by differential pressure cell) is measured in the loop together with flow, temperature, and density. Any increase in the test-loop pressure drop above specified limits signifies a deleterious change in slurry properties and probably indicates that coarse, fast-settling particles are forming a bed in the loop. In such an event, the off-specification slurry is either recycled or sent to the dump pond.

Slurry piping

The designer of slurry systems is always faced with the selection of the most economical pipe that will have an expected life consistent with the particular application. Pipe choice depends on pressure, temperature limitations, corrosiveness, and abrasiveness of the slurry. Available pipe includes:

- Conventional unlined carbon steel
- Rubber-lined carbon steel
- Concrete-lined carbon steel
- Special abrasion-resistant steel
- Aluminum

The last four types are more expensive than conventional unlined carbon steel and would only be used with a very abrasive or corrosive slurry. As noted, general pipe abrasion becomes a consideration at velocities of 4 m/s. Also, pipe wear increases exponentially with velocity[10] above a certain threshold velocity. This exponential value has been reported to range from 2.1 to 2.9.

The amount of annual wear on a pipe is a function not only of the velocity but, of course, the abrasive character of the slurry. This must be evaluated on a case-by-case basis. However, some general relative values of abrasivity as measured by the Miller Number[11] on a scale of 0 to 1000 are as follows:

Material	Miller Number
Detergent	0
Coal A	11
Coal B	28
Fine magnetite	64
Hematite	260
Carborundum	1000

Corrosiveness must also be evaluated on a case-by-case basis. If conventional unlined pipe is used, extra wall thickness must be added to compensate for the metal that will corrode away during the life of the system. As discussed earlier, it may also be desirable to add corrosion inhibitors.

After selecting the pipe, the designer must specify the pipe minimum yield strength and the wall thickness required to contain the expected pressures. This is done using standard formulas.

In areas subjected to prolonged subfreezing temperatures, slurry pipelines require the same degree of protection as any water-supply piping. Although a flowing solids–water slurry will usually generate sufficient heat from wall friction to prevent freezing, a prolonged system shutdown in subzero temperatures may produce frozen pipes. To minimize this risk, exposed piping in the immediate area of the plant can be protected by external insulation or heat tracing. For long-distance slurry pipelines, burying the pipe below the frost line is the accepted method of protecting against water–solids slurry freezing.

Slurry utilization

Storage. Size and type of storage depend on the throughput of the preparation plant and slurry pipeline, the operating factor of the preparation plant, and the type of slurry. The storage facilities provide a buffer capacity between the preparation plant and pipeline and between the pipeline and terminal facilities.

For most long-distance slurry pipelines, it is good practice, as a rule of thumb, to have a minimum storage capacity equivalent to 6 h of plant throughput. The time between

[9] I. Zandi, "Decreased Head Losses in Raw Water Conducts," *J. Am. Water Works Assoc.*, Feb. 1967.

[10] J. M. Link, and C. E. Tuason, "Pipe Wear in Hydraulic Transport of Solids," Am. Min. Congr., Las Vegas, Nev., Oct. 14, 1971.

[11] Ibid.

receiving the slurry into storage and committing it to the pipeline is necessary for laboratory analyses, such as slurry percent solids and size distribution. If the slurry is outside the specification for pumping, the retention time in storage can be used to carry out corrective measures without shutting down the system.

Agitated Storage. Slurries may be stored under agitation to maintain desired characteristics. The engineer must specify carefully what is needed in the way of performance. Two comments on this:

1. The variation of concentration of the slurry upon withdrawal from the tank must be held within specified limits. However, there is usually little interest in the actual concentration gradient in the tank. Situations have been observed where a water layer was present at the top of the tank when full, and upon emptying, the concentration remained relatively uniform.

2. The design should avoid large quantities of solids being deposited at the edge of the bank due to insufficient turbulence.

The Mohave coal tanks, with 22.7 m^3 in useful capacity per tank, are the largest agitated slurry tanks in existence, being 38 m in diameter by 26 m high. The agitator-drive horsepower is 500, the upper larger agitator blade is 10 m in diameter, and the lower agitator blade is 9 m in diameter. These blades rotate at a speed of 7 rpm.

The calculation of mixing power requirements is explained by Holland and Chapman.[12]

Static Storage. For the bulk storing of large quantities of slurry, either nonagitated tanks or ponds are usually the most economical method. Usually, large-volume storage is necessary only in processes that operate very intermittently or in industries that require large, on-site feed stockpiles. The bulk storing of iron-ore concentrate at marine terminals for shipment using the Marconaflo concept is an example of nonagitated storage. Another example is the storing of a coal slurry in nonagitated, emergency storage ponds for use in the event of long-term stoppage of the pipeline process.

In operation, the slurry is discharged directly into the tank or pond, and the solids settle to their terminal concentrations. Depending on particle size of the solids, in-flow slurry concentration, and specific gravity of the solids, the settled slurry will remain semifluid for extended periods (provided that it is not compacted by induced vibration). It is possible to reclaim this settled slurry via suitably located drawoff points. Fast-settling, high-specific-gravity slurries settle into a compact bed, and shearing action is required for reslurrification. One method now being adopted is to use water jets to reslurry the solids to a pumpable consistency. Another method involves dredge recovery.

Thickening. The thickening of a slurry prior to pipeline pumping is necessary with some slurry pipelines. This is done for two reasons: (1) to raise the slurry density to a controllable level for pumping, and (2) to limit the amount of unnecessary water pumped into the slurry. But if the density is too high, the slurry will be too thick for economic pumping. Therefore, the economic trade-off must be analyzed. At the terminal end of the pipeline, the slurry is often thickened as the first step in the dewatering process, to reduce the size of the more expensive filtering equipment.

A *thickener* is a tank or basin, usually circular, in which solids settle by gravity. The primary objective of a thickener is to recover settled solids as a concentration slurry (clarifiers produce a clear liquor from a dilute suspension). Sedimentation in a thickener is by zone or line settling. The particles in the feed slurry cohere in a floc structure, and the solids settle as a consolidated mass, leaving a sharp boundary between the settling suspension and the supernatant liquor. Thickeners usually have a raking mechanism to convey the settled solids to the center-cone discharge points.

The degree to which a slurry can be thickened depends on the settling characteristics of the solids, the physical size of the thickener (area and depth), the feed rate, and the underflow concentration.

Bench-scale batch testing of the settling characteristics of various concentrations of slurry as measured in graduates are useful for sizing thickeners as large as 300 ft (90 m) in diameter. In these tests, the subsidence of the slurry supernatant interface is measured as a function of time.[13]

Decanters. Thickening by decanting is helpful in dewatering a slow-settling, low-specific-gravity slurry such as coal. The procedure is simply to fill a nonagitated tank or pond with slurry through a distribution pipe with evenly spaced spigots to ensure an even, uniform deposit of slurry and allow time for the solids to settle. If necessary, coagulating chemicals that are not harmful to the final process can be added to assist in clarification of the excess liquors. The clear liquid above the settled solids is then decanted.

Cyclones. Cyclones have been very successfully used in dewatering of heavy beach-sand minerals, such as rutile, which is a uniformly graded, round-shaped material. For very little expenditure of energy (only 10 to 15 psi of head loss), a 25% slurry can be dewatered to a moist sand of 80 to 90% solids by weight.

Screens. Dewatering screens also thicken certain selected slurries. Solids, retained in the slurry, form the screen oversize and water is the screen undersize. This is especially effective on slurries that have a gapped size distribution.

Dewatering. The principal aim in dewatering a slurry is to recover the solids with a minimum moisture content. Clarification of the liquid phase of the slurry is usually of subsidiary importance. Table 5-6 shows a cross section of available dewatering equipment for solids recovery. In most cases, a centrifuge or a filter is necessary.

Vacuum Filters. Continuous vacuum filters are popular devices for dewatering slurries. In most of these situations, primary thickening precedes the filter.

---

[12]F. Holland and F. Chapman, *Liquid Mixing and Processing in Stirred Tanks*, Reinhold, New York, 1966.

[13]B. Fitch, "Batch Tests Predict Thickener Performance," *Chem. Eng.*, Aug. 23, 1971.

TABLE 5-6
Classifying Dewatering Equipment

Major Function	Operation	General Equipment Classification	Equipment Subclassification
		Solid-bowl centrifuge	Cylinder-conical bowl (vertical, horizontal); solid/screen bowl combination
	Continuous	Centrifugal filter	Conical screen (helix conveyor, oscillator); cylinder screen (pusher, conveyor)
		Vacuum filter	Rotary belt/drum, horizontal belt, horizontal pan
		Other	Various wet screens, cyclones, special filters and centrifuges, settling tanks
		Centrifugal filter	Vertical perforated basket, constant speed; horizontal basket, variable speed
Recover solids	Batch automatic	Screen-basket centrifuge	Vertical basket; constant speed; horizontal basket, variable speed
	Batch	Pressure leaf filter	Plate and frame; pressure leaf, vertical/horizontal leaf
		Settling tank	

A typical vacuum filter incorporates a filtering cloth or surface attached to a moving frame. The frame moves through the thickened slurry, and the solids are caked onto the filter through the action of a vacuum. The frame continues its journey to a point where the cake is removed by mechanical and pneumatic methods. This cake goes onto a conveyor and the filtrate flows to a clariflocculator. The filter frame then moves back into the thickened slurry to repeat the cycle.

Flood et al. provide a practical guide on equipment selection and a good explanation of the filtration.[14]

Centrifuges. Continuous centrifuges are often used for dewatering slurries. The solid-bowl centrifuge consists of a rotating bowl and a rotating-screw-conveyor section that revolves concentrically within the bowl. The bowl "conveyor" conforms to the inside of the bowl. Slurry enters via a stationary feedpipe concentrically located within the hollow conveyor shaft. This feedpipe extends inward to a rotating chamber located within the screw conveyor. Here the slurry is accelerated and moves radially outward to the bowl. The liquid portion of the feed tends to form a cylinder of revolution within the bowl. Liquid depth is controlled by adjustable weir plates at the outboard end of the cylindrical section of the bowl. A rotating-screw conveyor keeps the solids moving up the conical slope. At the discharge ports, the solids fall into a discharge hopper.

Tests have shown that screen-bowl centrifuges (Figure 5.7) can remove more moisture than solid-bowl centrifuges for pipeline slurry. Surface moistures can be as low as 12% to 15% with screen bowls. The effluent of the screen bowl after being treated in a clariflocculator can be burned directly in the furnace, as was done at Mohave, or can be further treated in filter presses or solid-bowl centrifuges before being blended with the screen-bowl product. This product can be further dried in fluid bed dryers, rotary drum dryers, flash dryers or other devices. Figure 5.8 represents a typical dewatering flow sheet. Heating of the slurry prior to centrifuging has been found to improve moisture removal.

[14]J. E. Flood, H. F. Porter, and F. W. Rennie, "Filtration Practice Today, Centrifugation Equipment," *Chem. Eng.* June 20, 1966.

Figure 5.7. Principles of screen-bowl centrifuge.

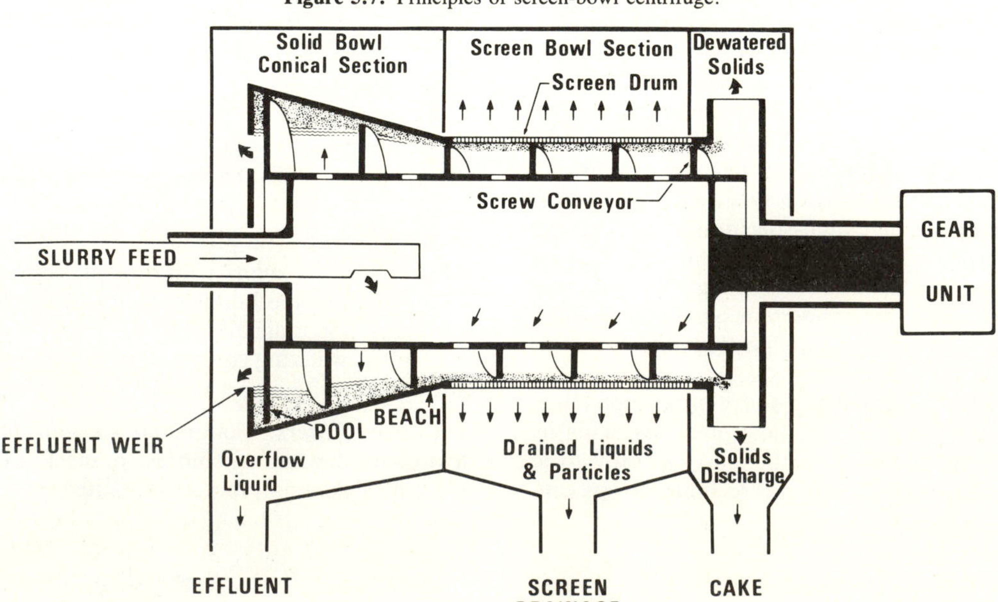

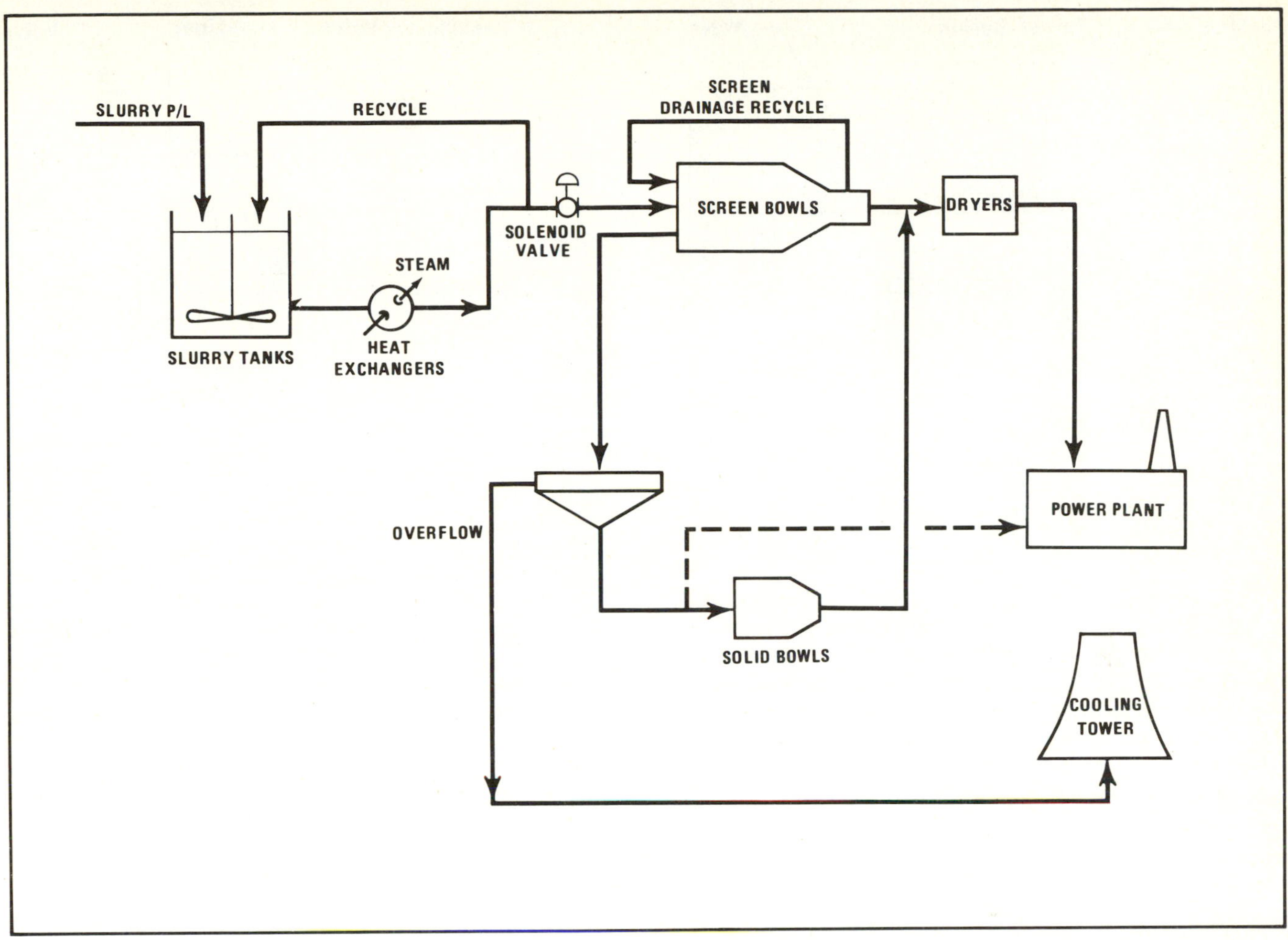

Figure 5.8. Typical system for dewatering coal slurry.

Mechanical considerations

Slurries are abrasive by their very nature. They "sand-blast" on impingement at high velocity; they are a "grinding compound" between moving mechanical parts; they are a "cutting tool" when throttled through a restriction; and they are "sandpaper" when dragged along the bottom of a pipe. The abrasive nature of slurries is a major consideration in design and selection of equipment for the slurry system. Selection of major mechanical components of the system—pipe, valves and fittings, and instrumentation—is discussed below.

Slurry pumps

Slurry pumping is roughly split between centrifugal and positive-displacement pumps, depending on the system pressure requirements. Various lockhopper and surge-leg pumping systems have been constructed to isolate the primary pump from the slurry.

Centrifugal pumps. These are limited in casing pressure and efficiency, owing to the nature of the material they are designed to handle. Their casing-pressure capacity is limited by the vertical-split-casing design necessary for easy replacement of the impeller and of the wear linings of the casing. Impeller tip speed is generally limited to 1350 m/s to minimize wear of the volute. Multiple pumps in series can develop final-stage discharge pressures up to about 600 psi.

Positive-displacement pumps. These are used where pumping pressures above 600 psi are required. For very abrasive slurries, the plunger-type pump is used, with a flushing arrangement injecting clear liquid to keep solids away from the plunger packing. This is illustrated in the fluid-end schematic diagram of Figure 5.9.

Figure 5.10 shows a schematic diagram for a double-acting piston pump. Piston pumps have application in less-abrasive service, such as for coal slurry; they have the advantage of displacing slurry on both the in and out strokes, but depend on sealing the full differential pressure across the piston. Positive-displacement pumps up to 1700 hp are now in service at flows about 2000 gal/min. Units in excess of 3000 hp are being considered, but large-volume and high-pressure systems will require multiple units in parallel.

A pulsation-dampening system is required when positive-

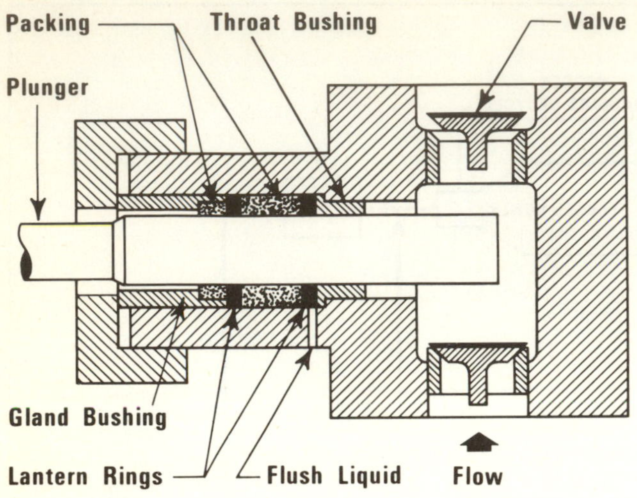
Packing
Throat Bushing
Valve
Plunger
Gland Bushing
Lantern Rings
Flush Liquid
Flow

Figure 5.9. Plunger pumps flushing arrangements are useful for very abrasive slurries.

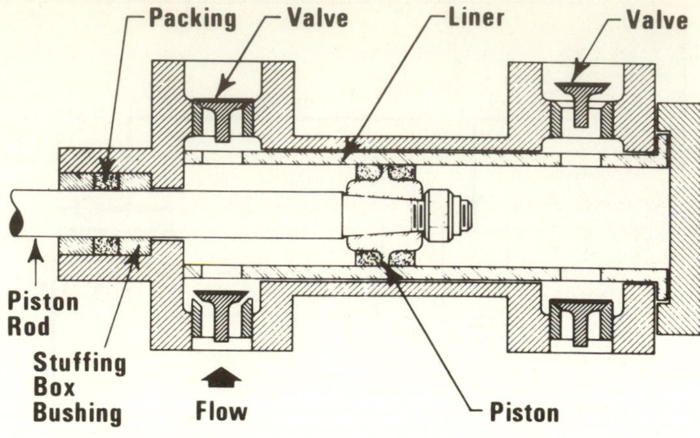
Packing
Valve
Liner
Valve
Piston Rod
Stuffing Box Bushing
Flow
Piston

Figure 5.10. Piston pumps are useful for moderately abrasive slurries such as coal.

displacement pumps are used. The primary elements of this system should be proper piping configuration and restraint, and gas-filled pulsation dampeners. Short, straight, suction lines are preferable; longer ones call for a centrifugal pump to charge the positive-displacement pumps. Pulsation dampeners should be fitted as close to the pump as possible on both the suction and discharge side.

Multiple-pump installations will require detailed vibration analysis of the piping system. Instrument connections to positive-displacement-pump piping, such as pressure gauges, are quite susceptible to vibration damage to the instrument, or failure at the line connection.

Other pumps. Various pump designs have been developed to isolate the abrasive slurry from the pumping equipment.

Figure 5.11. Lockhopper system is designed to allow use of centrifugal water pumps by isolating the abrasive slurry.

LOCKHOPPER CONCEPTUAL OPERATION

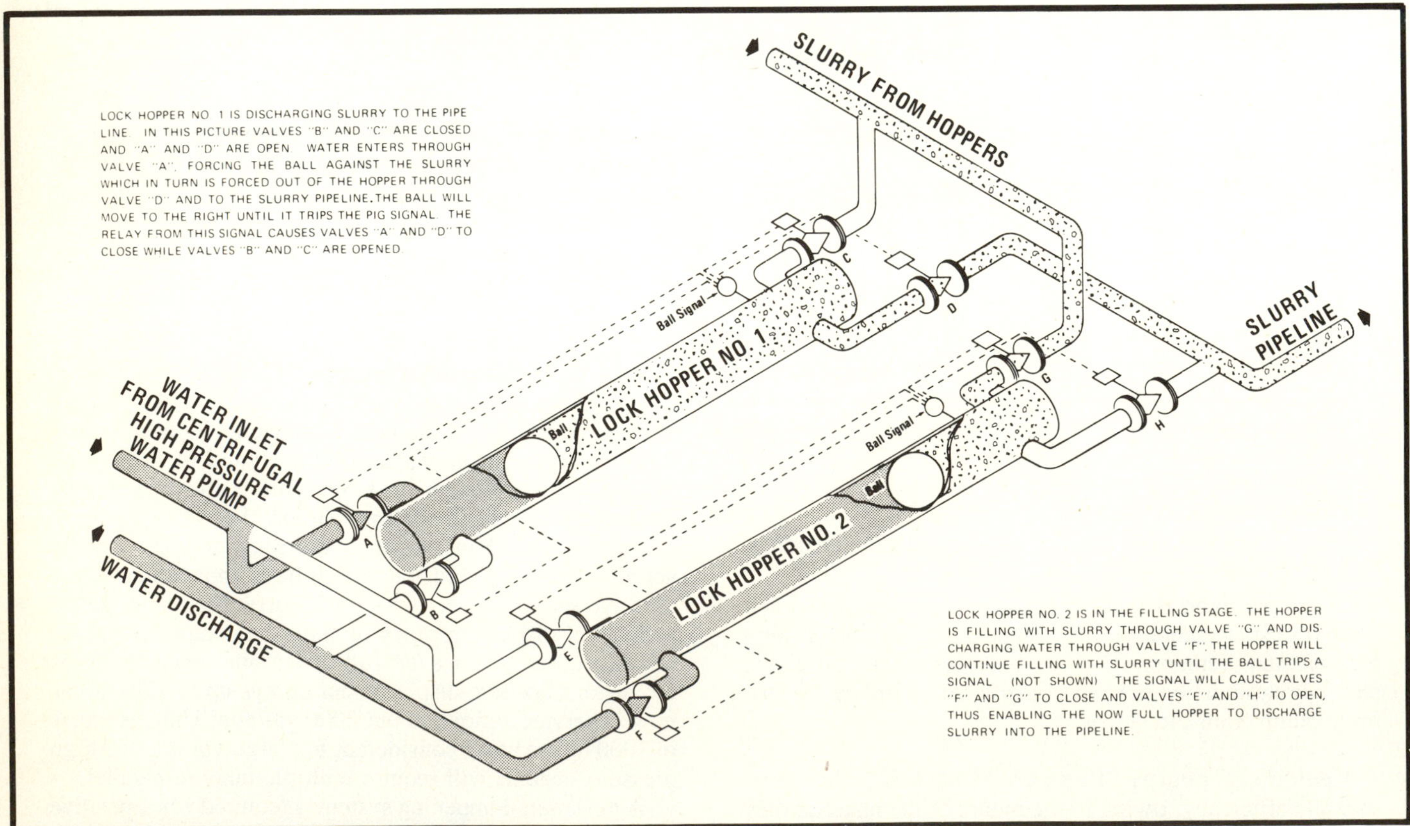
LOCK HOPPER NO 1 IS DISCHARGING SLURRY TO THE PIPE LINE. IN THIS PICTURE VALVES "B" AND "C" ARE CLOSED AND "A" AND "D" ARE OPEN. WATER ENTERS THROUGH VALVE "A", FORCING THE BALL AGAINST THE SLURRY WHICH IN TURN IS FORCED OUT OF THE HOPPER THROUGH VALVE "D" AND TO THE SLURRY PIPELINE.THE BALL WILL MOVE TO THE RIGHT UNTIL IT TRIPS THE PIG SIGNAL. THE RELAY FROM THIS SIGNAL CAUSES VALVES "A" AND "D" TO CLOSE WHILE VALVES "B" AND "C" ARE OPENED.
SLURRY FROM HOPPERS
SLURRY PIPELINE
WATER INLET FROM CENTRIFUGAL HIGH PRESSURE WATER PUMP
WATER DISCHARGE
LOCK HOPPER NO. 1
LOCK HOPPER NO. 2
Ball Signal
Ball Signal
Ball
Ball
A
B
C
D
E
F
G
H
LOCK HOPPER NO. 2 IS IN THE FILLING STAGE. THE HOPPER IS FILLING WITH SLURRY THROUGH VALVE "G" AND DISCHARGING WATER THROUGH VALVE "F". THE HOPPER WILL CONTINUE FILLING WITH SLURRY UNTIL THE BALL TRIPS A SIGNAL (NOT SHOWN) THE SIGNAL WILL CAUSE VALVES "F" AND "G" TO CLOSE AND VALVES "E" AND "H" TO OPEN, THUS ENABLING THE NOW FULL HOPPER TO DISCHARGE SLURRY INTO THE PIPELINE.

1. The "lockhopper" system shown in Figure 5.11 is designed to allow the use of conventional, multistage water pumps, and to let them develop high heads while the slurry is switched in and out of the lockhopper by sequenced valves. This system is now used in hydraulic hoisting from underground mines, where the pump is mounted on the surface and the lockhopper at the working level.
2. The "surge leg" pump is a special case of the lockhopper concept, where a positive-displacement pump is fitted with a chamber (surge leg) full of clear liquid between the piston and pump valves. The isolating fluid may be oil or water, and makeup fluid must be periodically added. This type of pump has been installed in some very abrasive services.
3. Diaphragm pumps have been used in low-volume, low-head systems; however, they are emerging as competition to the plungers pumps. They can now deliver high volumes at high discharge heads and have superior expendable parts life.
4. The "advancing cavity," Moyno pump is ideal for slurries at moderate flow and pressures where steady delivery is required. It is well suited to very thick slurries.

Piping system

When laying out the slurry piping system, the designer must consider:

- ○Flushing or draining the piping on normal or emergency shutdown.
- ○Replacement of wear points: near pump discharge, sharp bends, at and downstream of restrictions.
- ○Rotation of straight horizontal sections (very coarse slurries).
- ○Access for unplugging.
- ○Elimination of dead spaces at tees and tappings.

These considerations apply much more strongly to heterogeneous slurries.

Corrosion may be a consideration in pipe-schedule selection, but this must be evaluated case by case. The designer should realize that the internal pipe-wall protection often gained from corrosion products may be eroded away in a slurry system, resulting in a much higher metal loss than would be expected in a liquid pumping system having the same chemical properties.

The abrasive slurry effects discussed under slurry pumps above are also operating in the pipeline system, although to a lesser degree (Figure 5.12). General pipe abrasion becomes a consideration above about 2 m/s and is a major consideration at velocities about 4 m/s. Rubber or concrete lining may be desirable for these high velocities. Extra-long-radius elbows are often used to minimize wear at changes of direction.

Another consideration in piping design is the slope limitation. Upon shutdown with slurry in the pipeline, solids will settle and where slopes are too steep will slough to the valleys, thereby plugging the pipeline (Figure 5.13).

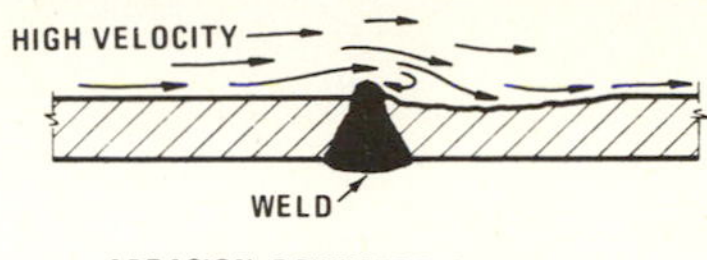

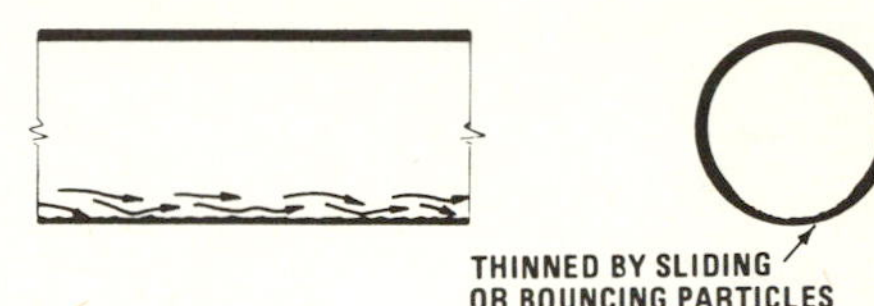

Figure 5.12. Abrasive wear can have various causes.

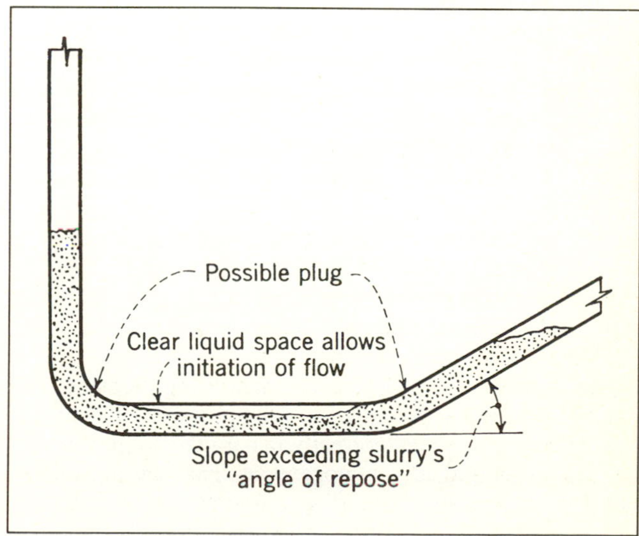

Figure 5.13. Vertical or inclined sections may undergo plugging when shutting down the system.

Valves, like pumps, must be designed for abrasive service and with consideration to sedimentation and plugging. They preferably provide a full opening, should not depend on machined-metal surfaces for closure, and do not have dead pockets that can fill with solids and restrict operation.

VALVES

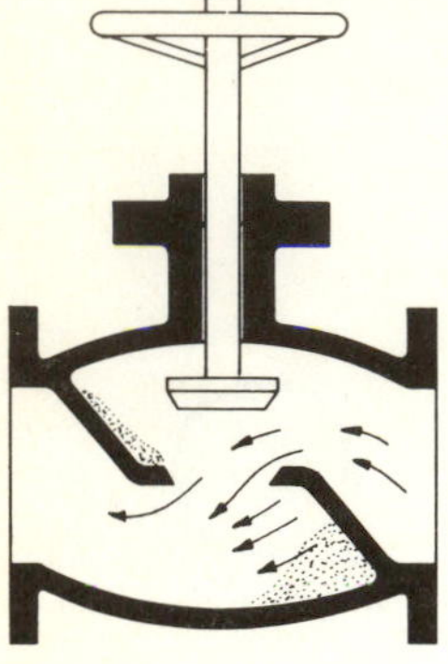

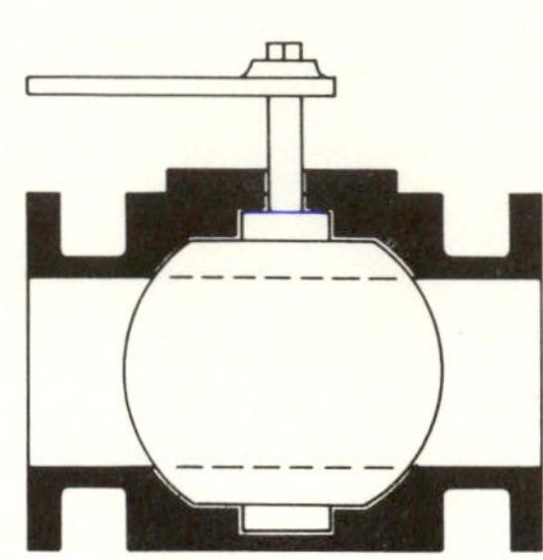

Figure 5.14. Valves: impingement on seat and walls will cause excessive wear (left); the full-opening flow arrangement (right) minimizes wear.

Valves with restricted or circuitous openings create abrasion downstream (Figure 5.14). Many suitable low-pressure valves are available, often with rubber-to-rubber or metal-to-rubber sealing. To date, high-pressure/large-diameter applications have used lubricated plug or ball valves, neither of which is ideally suited for slurry service.

In some cases plug valves are specified with Stellite facing on the plug and internal body to reduce wear. Most ball valves must be fitted with flush and drain connections so that solids can be removed from the body after operation.

Instrumentation

The presence of solids in a slurry system complicates measurement of the system variables, because many conventional primary measuring elements will be worn or plugged by the solids. Wear may affect the measuring elements themselves (such as orifices or turbine blades), or the system (i.e., due to turbulence created by the measuring element).

The need to avoid plugging of the sensing element or impulse lines is a major consideration in selecting measuring elements for slurry systems. It is a particularly troublesome problem at pressure tappings, and can disable any element with small clearances or static zones.

Segregation of a slurry in the measuring element must also be considered. A radiation density meter or magnetic flow meter will not read correctly in a horizontal pipe unless the suspension is ideally homogeneous. Fast-settling slurries will foil instruments, requiring a side stream if flows are not maintained above critical velocity.

An excellent review of instrumentation for slurry systems is given by Liptak.[15] The major sensing elements are discussed briefly below:

1. Magnetic flow meters have proved to be adequate, although expensive, primary flow-measuring elements; their chief advantage is that they create no flow restriction.
2. Where positive-displacement pumps are used, their speed provides an accurate flow-rate indication.
3. Radiation-density meters provide a slurry-concentration indication, again without flow restriction; but they require frequent calibration. Continuous weighing devices such as the Halliburton densometer have been used, although they present the problem of taking a side stream and returning it to the main stream.
4. The difficulty in pressure measurement is in keeping the pressure taps from plugging. This is best overcome by using a diaphragm close-mounted to the pipe to separate the slurry from the pressure sensor. In some cases, a continuous backflow of pressure-sensing lines may be required.
5. Transmitters or gauges should not be mounted on the piping around positive-displacement pumps, because they will often quickly fail from the vibration.
6. Pressure devices can be supported separately with a capillary connecting element and diaphragm.

[15]B. G. Liptak, "Instrumentation for Slurries and Viscous Materials," *Chem. Eng.*, 133 (Jan. 30, 1967); 151 (Feb. 13, 1967).

Economic aspects

Having followed the general design procedures, the design engineer is usually faced with several choices that can only be decided on the basis of economics. Often, after considering critical velocity limitations, it will be found that more than one pipe diameter is technically feasible. To select the correct diameter, the alternatives must be compared both on the basis of first cost and annual operating costs. Because operating costs are incurred over the life of the project, they must be discounted in order to realistically weigh them against capital costs. For very short distance lines, however, operating costs (power and supplies) may be quite low, which would allow the diameter decision to be made on the basis of capital costs alone.

Short-distance, in-plant pipelines

For quick evaluations of alternatives, some very simple procedures can be used. These should be considered as initial screening techniques only. If the economic impact of the decision is large, such as would be the case in longer-distance pipelines, more sophisticated techniques must be employed.

The concept of capital charges is necessary for the analysis. Capital charges are simply the average annual payments necessary to support a capital investment. They include depreciation, interest, property taxes, profit, and income taxes. As a percent of initial investment, they usually range from 15% for a utility to 25% or more for more speculative ventures. A good percentage for preliminary evaluations is 20%.

The significant operating costs are usually power (e.g., electricity or fuel) and supplies such as pump parts. Normally, the operating labor for the various alternatives would be the same and therefore could be neglected. Capital expenses are largely comprised of pipeline-steel and pump costs (including installation labor). For preliminary analysis of alternatives, these two cost components will suffice; instrumentation costs usually do not have to be estimated until later.

In addition to the pipe-diameter decision, the type of pump selected often must also be based on economics. For example, in a particular application, either a series of centrifugal pumps or positive-displacement pumps in parallel might be technically feasible. The fact that positive-displacement pumps have a higher efficiency than centrifugal pumps should not be overlooked (85% versus 60% is typical). In this case, the higher initial cost of positive-displacement pumps should be weighed against higher power costs for centrifugal ones. Maintenance costs should also be included in the evaluation.

In certain very abrasive slurries, there may be a choice of installing a more expensive, abrasion-resistant or lined pipe versus a lower-cost conventional pipe that would have to be replaced during the life of the project. Assuming that replacement is tolerable, the familiar "present-worth" analysis must be made at several appropriate interest rates to select the economic alternative.

Long-distance pipelines

A more detailed analysis is required for evaluation of long-distance slurry pipelines, since the economic impact of conservative design, as well as pipe-diameter and pump-type decisions, can be quite significant.[16] However, Figures 5.15 and 5.16 can help the engineer compare a slurry system (coal and copper slurry) with alternative modes of transportation, to make a preliminary determination as to whether the slurry alternative merits a more complete investigation.

Operating costs. Direct operating costs include electrical power, operating and maintenance labor, corrosion inhibitors, expendable pump parts, and other maintenance supplies—plus administrative costs and a contingency allowance. Operating labor is assumed to include a system operator for each shift and a day employee at each of the automated pump stations to perform routine maintenance jobs and inspection.

Capital costs. The capital costs provide for a complete pipeline transportation system—including pipe, positive-displacement pump stations, communications and supervisory-control facilities, maintenance bases, as well as installation of all these. An indirect cost allowance must be made for contingencies, interest during construction, working capital, engineering, and management.

Slurry pipeline applications

Pipeline applications may be considered in two distinct classifications: short-distance in-plant transport and long-distance transport. The latter, for purposes of this discussion, will involve systems whose major purpose is to move the slurry to another geographical area that is closer to the point of end use, usually distances from 20 to several hundred kilometers.

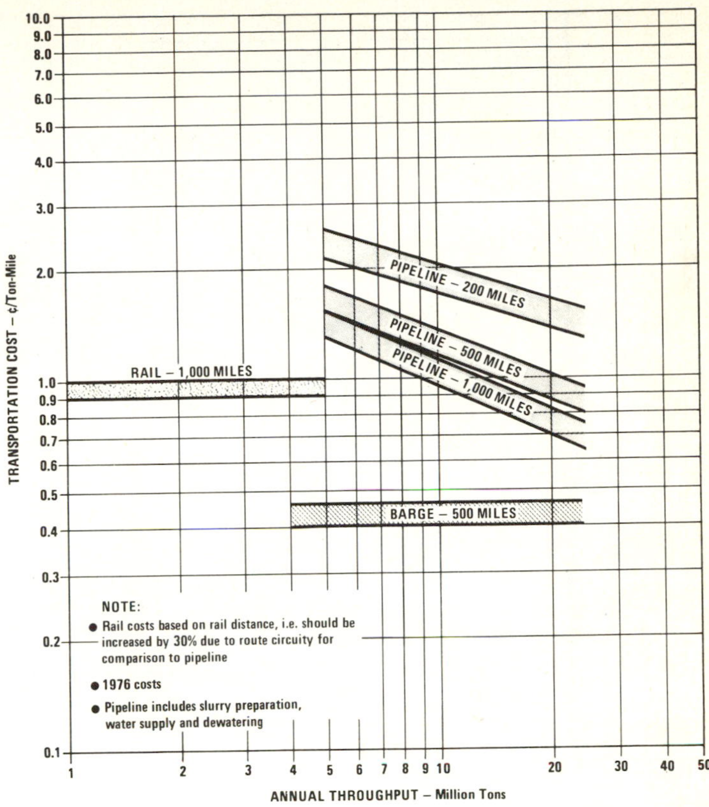

Figure 5.15. Slurry pipeline—coal transportation costs.

Short-distance in-plant or intraplant systems, on the other hand, are primarily associated with moving slurry from one point in a process to another, and usually are in the range of a few meters to several hundred meters. Pipelines for tailing and dredging materials will also be considered as short-distance, although in certain cases they can be many miles in length.

Short-distance, in-plant applications

Short-distance applications are as varied and numerous as types of chemical processes. The types of slurry pumped number in the hundreds[17] and include various foodstuffs, chemicals, chemical wastes, industrial wastes, sewage, and mine and quarry products.

One of the most interesting specialized applications is the transport of a thorium–uranium slurry for nuclear power generation; a great deal of basic theoretical work in slurry transport was done at Oak Ridge for this application.

Virtually every mineral-processing installation has a tailings pipeline to transport gangue and waste from the mineral-disposal site. On the Mesabi range in Minnesota, for example, 40,000 tons of tailings are carried daily through

[16] R. J. Prudhomme, M. L. Rizzone, T. H. Schieman, and J. E. Miller, "Reciprocating Pumps for Long Distance Slurry Pipelines," First Int. Conf. on Hydraulic Transport of Solids in Pipes, Coventry, England, Sept. 1–4, 1970.

[17] G. W. Maurer, "Pipelining Can Transport Your Bulk Solids," *Mater. Handl. Eng.*, 56 (Mar. 1966).

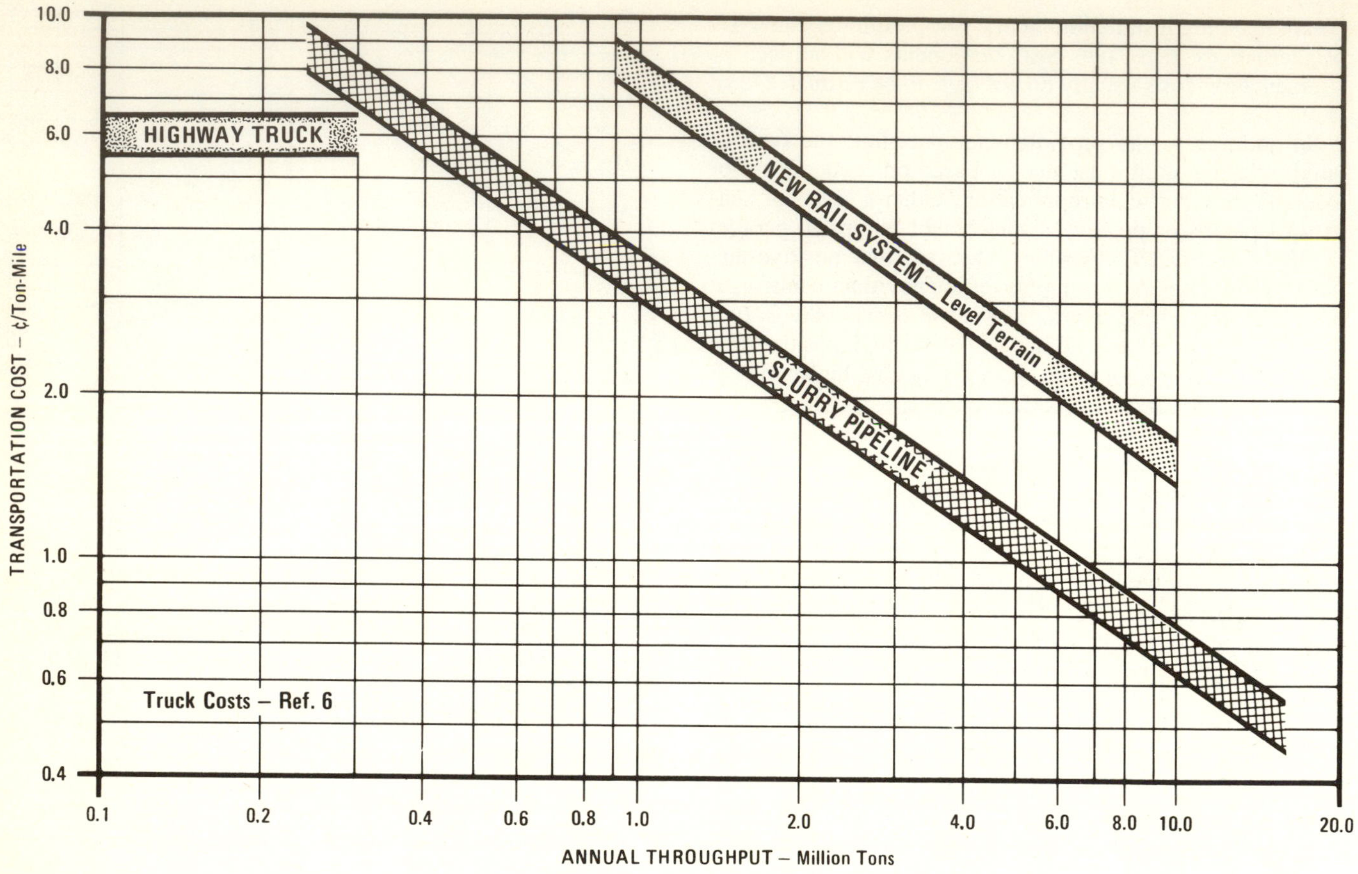

Figure 5.16. Slurry pipeline transportation cost—iron concentrate, copper concentrate, and limestone.

nine 305-mm-diameter pipelines for distances up to 12,200 m. On the island of Bougainville in the Solomons, Bougainville Copper Pty. Ltd.'s new copper facilities will include an extendable 1.22 to 4.57-m-diameter tailing pipeline to move more than 6800 m³/h.

Design of tailing pipelines involves nearly all the considerations of longer pipelines, and is further complicated by the variability in screen analysis, concentration, and tonnage throughput. The tailings line must be able to handle all these variables. Since the processing plants are usually modular with several lines, consideration must be given to the operating mode when one or more process lines are interrupted. Owing to critical velocity considerations, the answer in many instances is a multiple-line system.

Dredging pipelines are normally associated with the deepening of harbor channels, but could also involve mining. Probably the best known hydraulic mining operation is in the Florida phosphate fields, where phosphate-rock systems pumping up to 5700 m³/h are in use. Pipelines with diameters up to 508 mm and lengths up to 10 km exist.

TABLE 5–7
Selected Commercial Slurry Pipelines

	Length (mi)	Pipe Size (in.)	Capacity (tons/yr × 10⁶)	Operation (year)
Coal				
Consolidation	108	10	1.3	1957
Black Mesa	273	18	4.8	1970
ETSI	1378	38	25	198-
Alton	180	24	10	198-
Iron concentrate				
Savage River	53	9	2.25	1967
Waipipi (iron sands)	6	8 and 12	1.0	1971
Peña Colorada	28	8	1.8	1974
Las Truchas	17	10	1.5	1976
Sierra Grande	20	8	2.1	1978
Samarco	253	20	12	1977
Copper concentrate				
Bougainville	17	6	1.0	1972
West Irian	69	4	0.3	1972
Pinto Valley	11	4	0.4	1974
Limestone				
Rugby	57	10	1.7	1964
Calaveras	17	7	1.5	1971
Phosphate concentrate				
Valep	80	8	2.0	1979

Long-distance applications

Although materials amenable to long-distance slurry pipeline transport are fewer than for short-distance in-plant applications, the list is still quite large. Materials presently transported by long-distance slurry pipelines include limestone and other cement raw materials, iron concentrate, coal, gilsonite, salt in brine, phosphate rock, kaolin, copper concentrate, sewage sludge, uranium-bearing slimes, sugar cane, and wood pulp. Other materials for which the technical feasibility of long-distance slurry transport has been established include potash, lead–zinc concentrates, sulfur, laterite (nickel ore), pyrite, coke wood chips, and solid wastes. Table 5-7 summarizes some selected commercial slurries

Figure 5.17. Savage River pipeline.

in operation or planned. Several of these are described briefly below.

Black Mesa coal pipeline. The longest slurry pipeline in operation to date is the 440-km Black Mesa coal pipeline, which traverses the state of Arizona and was commissioned in the fall of 1970. This 457-mm-diameter pipeline can transport over 5½ million tons of coal annually from the mine site in the Navajo–Hopi Indian reservation to the Mohave power plant site on the Nevada side of the Colorado River, south of Davis Dam. The coal will supply all the fuel requirements for the two 750-MW generating units at Mohave.

The >50-mm coal provided at the mine site by Peabody Coal Co. is reduced to 19 mm by impactors and then ground to pass 14 mesh in three parallel rod-mill lines. From the rod mills, the slurry is stored in three agitated slurry tanks that feed the initial pump station. Three additional pump stations are required along the route. Pumps are electric-powered 1700-hp Wilson–Snyder double-acting duplex piston pumps, the largest of this type in existence. Each station has three of these pumps in parallel, except Station Two, which has four. The pipeline system is owned and operated by Black Mesa Pipeline Inc., a subsidiary of the Southern Pacific Transportation Company.

At the power plant, the coal discharges into one of three 24-h holding tanks and is then pumped to centrifuges for dewatering. There are 20 centrifuges for each 750-MW generating unit. The dewatered coal, at about 25% total moisture, then goes through a mill and is blown into the boiler with heated air.[18] Coffey et al. provide a more extensive description of the system.[19]

Savage River pipeline: mountains and valleys. The first long-distance iron-concentrate pipeline in the world is the 85-km 244-mm-diameter slurry pipeline operated by Pickands Mather & Co. This line is in the island state of Tasmania, Australia, and traverses some exceedingly rugged terrain (Figure 5.17) over its route from the mine-site concentrator at Savage River to the pelletizing and shipping facilities at Port Latta. In fact, the ore deposit was known for more than 100 years but was considered inaccessible even though it was only 85 km from tidewater. The slurry-pipeline concept made development of that ore body economical. The pipeline, which has been in operation since November 1967, is designed to transport 2 million tons of iron concentrate per year.

A single pump station consisting of four electric-motor-driven 600-hp plunger pumps is used for the slurry, which is transported as it is produced from the concentrator (i.e., no special processing is required). Design concentration is 60% solids by weight. The material is 100% minus 100 mesh. A detailed description is provided in the report by McDermott et al.[20]

---

[18] D. M. Taylor, "Liquefied Coal Piped Directly into Boiler," *Pipe Line Ind.*, Dec. 1961.

[19] R. C. Coffey, H. G. Lyons, and A. C. Oakes, "Mohave Generating Station, Design Features," Am. Power Conf., Chicago, Apr. 1969.

[20] W. F. McDermott et al., "Savage River Mines—The World's First Long Distance Iron Ore Slurry Pipeline," Soc. Min. Eng. Fall Meet. Prepr. 68-b-364, Sept. 1968.

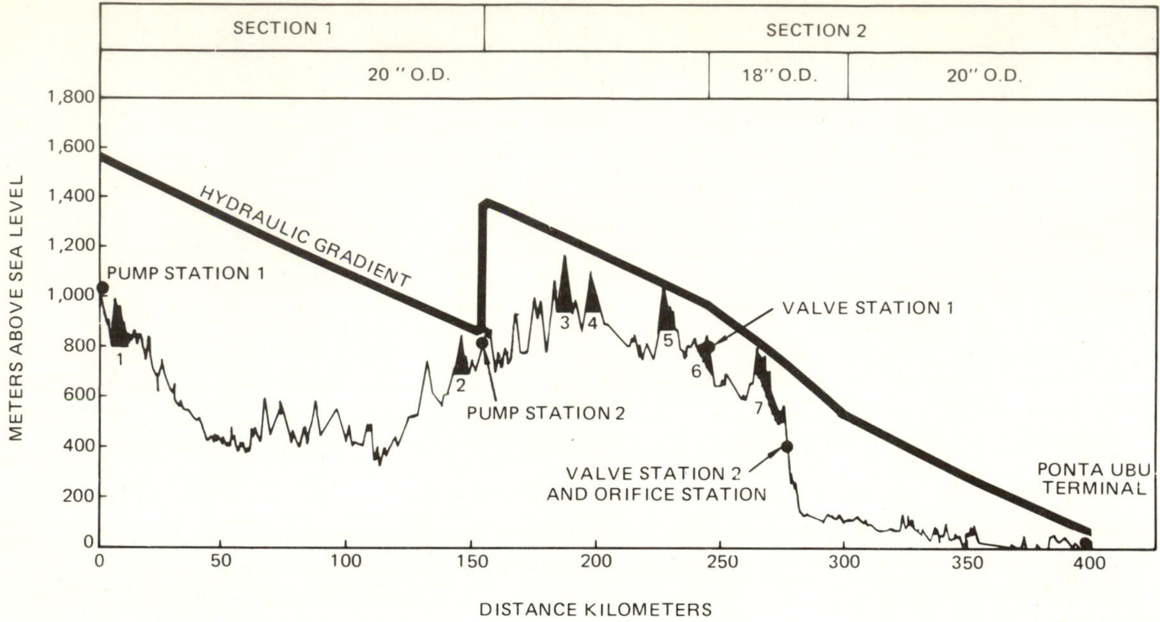

Figure 5.18. SAMARCO profile and gradient.

Consolidation coal pipeline: a pioneer. No discussion of slurry pipelines would be complete without acknowledging the significant contribution made by the landmark 174-km, 254-mm coal slurry pipeline put into operation in 1957 by Consolidation Coal Company. The line extends from Cadiz, Ohio, to Eastlake, Ohio, and uses three pumping stations, each containing three 450-hp, positive-displacement, double-acting, duplex piston pumps. The flow rate is 250 m^3/h, about one-fourth that of the Black Mesa line.

This pipeline has operated very successfully, has experienced a 98% availability factor, and has had considerable economic impact. As a result of the pipeline, the railroads have made radical reductions not only on the 1.3 million tons/yr of pipeline coal but on all 5 million tons/yr of coal that is being transported from that region in Ohio.

SAMARCO hematite slurry pipeline: an engineering challenge. The SAMARCO pipeline, which began operation on May 21, 1977, became the largest and second longest concentrate slurry pipeline in the world at that time. It begins at the Germano mine site in the state of Minas Gerais, Brazil, and ends near the coastal resort town of Guarapari in the state of Espirito Santo. Its rugged 400-km route passes through farmland, cane fields, and coffee and eucalyptus plantations. The high point of the line, at about 1200 m, lies in the Caparao Mountains, about halfway between the mine site and the coast; from there, the line descends rapidly to sea level.[21]

The iron slurry pipeline system is part of the US$600 million SAMARCO project, consisting of:

- A mine and concentrator with a 7 million tons/yr product capacity located at Germano.
- A slurry pipeline rated for the ultimate production of 12 million tons/yr.
- A terminal facility on the Atlantic Ocean at Ponta Ubu with a 5 million tons/yr pelletizing plant and filtering equipment for an additional 2 million tons/yr of pellet feed fines.
- An ocean terminal at Ponta Ubu with a loading capacity of 8000 tons/h of pellets or filter cake into 150,000-DWT ships.
- Housing developments and support facilities.

The pipeline system itself consists of:

- 400 km of 508-mm and 457-mm-diameter pipeline
- Centralized control system
- Pumpstation (P.S.) No. 1 and feed tankage at Germano
- P.S. No. 2 located approximately 151 km east of Germano
- Two valve stations, an orifice station, and pipeline terminal facilities, all in section 2 of the pipeline between P.S. No. 2 and Ponta Ubu

The pipeline is designed to transport its yearly throughput with a system availability of 93%. The design availability is low because of possible power outages, especially at P.S. No. 2. The design is based on a slurry with a concentration of 66% by weight at P.S. No. 1, with a size consist of 85% minus 325 mesh and not more than 4% plus 200 mesh pumped at 1045 m^3/h, which corresponds to a velocity of 1.65 m/s in the 0.508-m line. Some dilution takes place at P.S. No. 2; therefore, these values change. The pipeline is

[21] R. A. Hill, M. E. Jennings, and R. H. Derammelaere, "SAMARCO Iron Ore Slurry Pipeline," Proc. 3rd Int. Tech. Conf. on Slurry Transportation.

designed to operate by batching for the immediate future, as it has more capacity than the concentrator. The profile shown in Figure 5.18 reflects the rugged terrain the pipeline had to cross.

The pipeline was designed in conformance with ANSI Code B31.4. The pipe is API 5L × 60 with wall thicknesses of 8.7 to 21 mm and averaging over 13 mm. Most of the pipeline is 508 mm in diameter; however, a 40-km sector of 457 mm was installed on the downslope leading to the terminal to help dissipate some of the potential energy.

The most challenging of the many engineering feats on the SAMARCO slurry pipeline was resolution of the slack flow problem.[22] As with many other concentrate slurry pipelines, the product must be transported from the mine to a terminal on the coast for export; the difference in elevation between the mine site and the terminal causes release of energies exceeding those required to overcome friction losses in normal "packed-line" conditions. With no restriction in the line, the excess energy dissipates itself through the formation of slack or open-channel flow in which velocities are an order of magnitude higher than normal packed-line flow velocities. If slack flow conditions were allowed to continue with an abrasive slurry, the pipeline would rapidly wear out, because wear is in an exponential relation with flow velocity. An orifice station is used to apply variable back pressure, required to eliminate slack flow.

[22]R. H. Derammelaere and J. P. Chapman, "Slack Flow in the World's Largest Iron Concentrate Slurry Pipeline," Proc. 4th Int. Tech. Conf. on Slurry Transportation.

REFERENCES FOR FURTHER READING

Ellis, J. L., and P. Bacchetti, "Pipeline Transport of Liquid Coal," Lignite Symposium, Bismarck, N.D., May 1971.

Hanks, R. W., and D. R. Pratt, "On the Flow of Bingham Plastic Slurries in Pipes and between Parallel Plates," *Soc. Petrol. Eng. J.*, 342–345 (Dec. 1967).

Hedstrom, B. O. A., "Flow of Plastic Materials in Pipes," *Ind. Eng. Chem.*, *44*, p. 651 (1952).

Job, A. L., "Transport of Solids in Pipeline, with Special Reference to Mineral Ores, Concentrates, and Unconsolidated Deposits," literature survey, Dept. of Energy, Mines and Resources of Canada, Inf. Circ. 230, Oct. 1969.

Kenny, J. P., et al., *FWPCA Waste Management Study*, Vol. 3, *Technical Aspects of Pipelining of Waste Materials*, Bechtel Corp., Sept. 1969.

Perry, J. H., *Chemical Engineers' Handbook*, 4th ed., McGraw-Hill, New York, 1963, pp. 5–59.

Rotary Grinding Mills—Selection and Capacity Determination, Allis-Chalmers, PM3.2, Aug. 30, 1963.

Thomas, D. G., "Non-Newtonian Suspension, Part I," *Ind. Eng. Chem.* 55(11), 18–29 (Nov. 1963).

Thomas, D. G., "Transport Characteristics of Suspension: VIII. A Note on the Viscosity of Newtonian Suspensions of Uniform Spherical Particles," *J. Colloid Sci.*, 20(3), 267–277 (1965).

Walker, G. H., and E. J. Wasp, "Experience and Prospects in Economic Transportation of Coal in Pipelines," 6th World Power Conf., Melbourne, Australia, Oct. 1962.

Wasp, E. J., et al., "Depositions Velocities, Transition Velocities and Spatial Distribution of Solids in Slurry Pipelines," First Int. Conf. on Hydraulic Transport of Solids in Pipe, Coventry, England, Sept. 1970.

Wasp, E. J., et al., Hetero-homogeneous Solids—Liquid Flow in the Turbulent Regime," ASCE, Int. Symp. on Solid-Liquid Flow, Univ. of Pennsylvania, Philadelphia, Mar. 1968.

Wasp, E. J., T. L. Thompson, and T. C. Aude, "Slurry Pipeline Economics and Application," First Int. Conf. on Hydraulic Transport of Solids in Pipes, Coventry, England, Sept. 1970.

*Part C**

BELT CONVEYORS

R. W. Suman

Conveyor Equipment Manufacturers Association

Belt conveyors are of interest to engineers, managers, and others who are responsible for selecting equipment for handling bulk materials. This section is intended to acquaint the reader with the many uses of belt conveyors and their advantages under widely varying conditions of operation.

Belt conveyors have attained a dominant position in transporting bulk materials, owing to such inherent advantages as their economy and safety of operation, reliability, versatility, and a practically unlimited range of capacities. In addition, they are suitable for performing numerous processing functions in connection with their normal purpose of providing a continuous flow of material between operations. Recently, their conformity to environmental requirements has provided a further incentive for selection of belt conveyors over other means of transportation.

*The presentation, both text and photographs, in Part C of Chapter 5, is substantially a copy of Chapter 1 of *Belt Conveyors for Bulk Materials*, Second Edition, CBI Publications, Boston, Mass., 1979.

Low labor and low energy requirements are fundamental with belt conveyors. Dramatic increase in general operating costs has placed conveyors in an extremely favorable position for applications that were not considered a few years ago.

Illustrated and described here are some of the advantages of belt conveyors, which are performing a wide variety of intraplant functions. Included are examples of relatively long distance belt conveyor systems which are being used because they combine important benefits such as reliability, safety, and low cost per ton of material transported.

Variety of materials to be conveyed

The size of materials that can be conveyed can range from very fine, dusty chemicals to large, lumpy ore, stone, coal, or pulpwood logs (Figure 5.19). Closely sized or friable materials can be carried with minimum degradation.

Figure 5.19. Fifty-four-inch conveyor.

Because rubber belts are highly resistant to corrosion and abrasion, maintenance costs are comparatively low when handling highly corrosive materials or those that are extremely abrasive, such as alumina and sinter.

Materials that might cause sticking or packing if transported by other means are often handled successfully on belt conveyors. Hot materials such as foundry shakeout sand, coke, sinter, and iron ore pellets can be conveyed successfully.

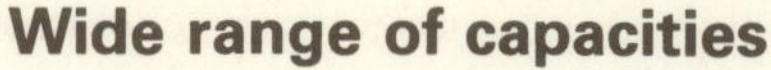

Wide range of capacities

Currently available belt conveyors are capable of handling hourly capacities in excess of any practical requirement (Figure 5.20). Yet they are also used economically in plants for transporting materials between process units at a wide range of rates—sometimes as little as a mere dribble.

Belt conveyors can operate continuously—around the clock and around the calendar when required—without loss of time for loading and unloading. Material is loaded to and unloaded from the belt conveyor automatically. Operating labor costs differ little, regardless of capacity ratings. Costs per ton decrease as annual tonnage handled increases.

For these reasons, belt conveyors are capable of handling tonnages of bulk materials that would be more costly and often impractical to transport by other means.

Adaptability of the path of travel

Belt conveyor systems provide the means of transporting materials via the shortest distance between the required loading and unloading points. They can follow existing terrain on grades of 30 to 35% (Figure 5.21). They can be provided with structures that prevent the escape of dust to the surrounding atmosphere and are weather-protected (Figures 5.22 and 5.23). Belt conveyors provide a continuous flow of material and avoid confusion, delays, and safety hazards in plants and other congested areas.

Paths of travel can be flexible, and the length of the routes can be extended as required. In some open-pit mining operations, conveyors thousands of feet long are shifted

Figure 5.20. Ninety-six-inch conveyor.

Figure 5.21. Regenerative conveyor.

Figure 5.22. Corrugated metal cover over belt.

Figure 5.23. Cable-suspended support across river.

laterally on the bench to follow the progress of excavation at the face.

Loading, discharging, and stockpiling capabilities

Belt conveyors can receive material from one or more locations and deliver it to several points or areas. They can be the main transportation artery and also be loaded at several points (Figure 5.24) along their length by equipment which provides a uniform feed to the belt (Figure 5.25).

They are particularly useful in tunnels beneath stockpiles, from which they can reclaim and, where required, blend materials from various piles (Figure 5.26). Material can simply be discharged over the head end of each conveyor (Figure 5.27) or anywhere along its length by means of plows or traveling trippers (Figure 5.28).

Belt conveyors, with stackers and reclaimers, are practical for large-scale stockpiling and reclaiming of such bulk materials as coal, ore, and taconite pellets. The combination stacker-reclaimer in Figure 5.29 illustrates the trend in modern rail to ship terminals.

Self-unloading ships (Figure 5.30) equipped with belt conveyors can be unloaded in all ports, even those which do not have dockside unloading equipment (Figure 5.31). Unloading capacities of such systems are usually greater than those of several grab-bucket unloaders, requiring less turnaround time and lower labor and other operating costs.

Figure 5.24. Multiple loading stations.

Figure 5.25. Rail-mounted hopper.

Figure 5.26. Multiple feeders in tunnel.

Figure 5.27. Discharging over conveyor head pulley.

Figure 5.28. Power-driven tripper.

Figure 5.29. Combination stacker-reclaimer.

Figure 5.30. Self-unloading ship.

Figure 5.31. Rail-mounted ship unloaders.

Figure 5.32. V-type plow.

Certain materials, such as foundry sand, can be plowed from the belts (Figure 5.32) at specific locations in quantities controlled by the requirements of the application.

Although belt conveyors are generally used to transport and distribute materials, they are also used with auxiliary equipment for performing numerous functions during various stages of processing. A high degree of blending is accomplished as materials are bedded into and reclaimed from stockpiles (Figure 5.33). Several dissimilar materials can be proportioned continuously onto a common collecting belt.

Samples of the material conveyed can be taken by devices which cut through the stream of material as it flows from one conveyor to the next. Magnetic objects can be removed from the material. While being transported on the conveyor, materials can also be weighed or they can be sorted, picked, or sprayed.

Reliability and availability

The reliability of belt conveyors has been proved over decades and in practically every industry. Many serve vital process units whose success depends on continuous operation, such as handling coal in power plants and transporting raw bulk materials in steel plants, in cement plants, and to and from ships in ports, where downtime is very costly. Belt conveyors can be operated from central control boards (Figure 5.34). They can and do operate continuously, shift after shift. They can be housed so that both they and the material being transported are protected from elements that would impede other means of transportation.

Environmental advantages

Belt conveyors can transport bulk materials without polluting the air or deafening the ears. They can operate quietly, often in their own enclosures, which, when desirable, can be located above the confusion and safety hazards of surface traffic or in small tunnels, out of sight and hearing (Figure 5.35). They do not contaminate the air with hydrocarbons. At transfers, dust can be contained within transfer chutes or collected. Overland belt conveyor systems can be designed to blend into the landscape, resulting in an unscarred, quiet, and pollution-free operation (Figure 5.36).

Safety

Belt conveyors operate with a high degree of safety. Few personnel are required for operation and they are exposed to few hazards. Personnel are not endangered by the malfunctions or accidents of large transport vehicles. They do not operate over highways or in other areas accessible to the public. They offer fewer hazards to careless personnel than is inherent in other means of transporting bulk materials. The conveyor equipment itself can be protected from overload and malfunction by built-in mechanical and electrical safety devices.

Figure 5.33. Bridge-mounted bucket wheel reclaimer.

Figure 5.34. Conveyor system control center.

Figure 5.35. Conveyor in enclosed gallery.

Figure 5.36. Overland conveyor system.

Economic advantages

Labor costs

The labor hours per ton required to operate belt conveyor systems are usually the lowest of any method of transporting bulk materials. Like other minimum-labor, highly automated operations, belt conveyors have low operating costs and can provide a high net return on investment. Most functions of the system can be monitored from a central control panel, allowing a minimum number of operating personnel to inspect the equipment and report conditions that may require attention by the maintenance department.

Maintenance is also minimal. Repairs and replacements of relatively small parts can be made quickly at the site. Most belts can be replaced in one shift, and some belts have conveyed well over 100,000,000 tons before wearing out.

Power costs

The increasing cost of energy increases the importance of power costs for transporting bulk materials. Belt conveyors consume power only when they are being used. There are no empty return trips or idling in line for the next load. On long systems the decline section often assists in propelling an inclined or horizontal portion. Conveyor systems that carry downgrade over all or most of their route can be completely regenerative (Figure 5.37).

Maintenance costs

Maintenance costs for belt conveyors are extremely low compared with most other means of transporting bulk materials. Extensive external support systems, such as those associated with rail or truck haulage, are not required. Component parts are usually housed and have very long life compared with that of motor vehicles. Usually, they need only scheduled inspection and lubrication. Most repairs or replacements can be anticipated and unscheduled downtime avoided. Parts are small and accessible, so replacements can be made on the site quickly and with minimal service equipment. Inventories of spare parts can be maintained at a low cost with relatively little storage space.

Long-distance transportation

The economic benefits of low labor and energy operating costs, as well as some of their other advantages, have led to adoption of belt conveyor systems as a means of transporting bulk materials over increasingly long distances. Recent dramatic increases in the costs of labor and fuel have greatly enhanced their value. A few of these systems are described below.

Seattle, Washington

The system shown in Figure 5.38 established a landmark in the use of belt conveyors for long-distance transportation of bulk materials. In the late 1920's a contractor pioneered the use of belt conveyors for relatively long distance haulage by transporting 5,000,000 yards of excavated material from Denny Hill in downtown Seattle to scows waiting in the harbor. It was so highly profitable and dependable that such systems were later adopted by other contractors. Now they are commonplace in the construction industry in cases where large tonnages must be transported economically.

Lost Creek Dam[23]

A recent example of belt conveyor haulage on a construction project is the 1974 installation at Lost Creek Dam on the Rogue River near Bedford, Oregon (Figure 5.37).

[23] "Conveyors the Key to $6,000,000 Savings," *Constr. Equip. Mag.*, Aug. 1974; and "Conveyor Generates Power While Delivering Rock to Dam," *Contractors Eng. Mag.*, Nov. 1974.

Figure 5.37. Fifty-four-inch conveyor, 3000 ft long, and a 17° decline.

Figure 5.38. Denny Hill conveyor system.

Army Corps of Engineers plans had indicated a 10,000-ft, 8% haul road down a steep mountainside for handling 7,000,000 tons of shot rock from the quarry to the dam site. However, the contractor used one 54-in. (1.35-m) wide by 3,000-ft (900-m) centers belt conveyor down a 17° decline. The following benefits were revealed by his economic study:

1. An initial saving of $1,800,000 investment in trucks was realized, and an estimated 1,375,000 gal of diesel fuel over the life of the project were not required.
2. The cost of constructing the haul road was avoided, as well as the much greater cost of restoring the terrain as required by the Corps of Engineers specifications.
3. The conveyor was regenerative and its motor generators supplied enough electrical energy for the project and returned the excess to the local public utility.
4. A substantial saving in labor enabled the contractor to bid a price $3,200,000 below the next competitor.
5. The project was completed ahead of time because the conveyor handled 2000 tons/h, whereas the schedule was based on 1200 tons/h.
6. The safety hazards and maintenance cost for trucks operating down an 8% winding road were eliminated.

One worker monitored all critical points of the system on closed-circuit TV from a station on the loadout hopper. The system was protected by numerous safety devices, including magnetic brakes that stopped the loaded conveyor within 23 ft (7 m) from 450 ft/min (137 m/min).

Oklahoma cement plant[24]

Another example of the economy and adaptability to terrain of the belt conveyor is its use in a 5½-mi (8.8-km) system from quarry to mill at an Oklahoma cement plant (Figure 5.39). The estimated total direct and indirect costs

[24]Thomas B. Douglas, "Economics of 5½-Mile Transport Conveyor Belt at Ideal Cement Company's Ada, Oklahoma Plant," paper presented to Am. Inst. Min., Metall. Petrol. Eng., St. Louis, Mo., Mar. 2, 1961.

Figure 5.39. Five-and-one-half-mile overland conveyor.

(cents per ton) for railroad, truck, and conveyor haulage were as follows:

Estimated Cost (cents per ton)

	Belt Conveyors	Truck	Railroad
Half production	34.5	—	44.4
Full production	21.6	32.1	35.1

Trucks were ruled out not only because of their higher costs, but because of hilly terrain and the necessity for crossing two railroads and two highways. The disadvantage of rail transportation was the need for extensive trackage, switchers, loading and unloading, and storage. Also, scheduling and dispatching would pose problems for full production.

After the first year of operation it was found that the cost per ton for conveyors for full production was only 13.3 cents/ton, compared with an estimated 21.6 cents/ton. For half production it was 23.6 cents/ton. This was due to an extended depreciation period and the fact that the entire system was operated and maintained by only two workers and a supervisor.

Texas iron ore mine to steel mill[25]

A Texas steel plant was faced with mounting costs for transporting sticky, abrasive iron ore from the nearby mine to an ore-washing plant adjacent to the mill. When operation began in 1946, the mine was about 1 mi (1.6 km) from the plant, but by 1964 the haul had increased to 5.5 mi (8.8 km). At that distance the haul alone was costing 6 cents/ton-mile, which represented 55% of the total cost per ton for mining and delivering the ore to the washer. It was then that an exhaustive feasibility study was made of all operations, from excavating and loading in the pit through transportation to the washer.

The elimination of trucks as a shuttle between loading machines and mainline haulage was not considered, because of the rapid progress of the mining machines in the shallow ore bodies and the need to mix ores from several locations. The problem was to determine the best method of transporting the ore from a truck dumping station at the mine to the washer. A railroad was ruled out because of the large capital investment in equipment and terminal facilities, as well as anticipated difficulties in handling the sticky, lumpy ore.

A pipeline for the main transport appeared promising according to preliminary estimates, but further consideration was abandoned because of:

1. The difficulties of crushing the sticky ore to minus 2 or 3 in. at the mine.
2. Unavailability of water and reservoir sites.
3. The problem of designing a pump suitable for such coarse, abrasive ore, as well as wear and maintenance costs of pipe and pumps.

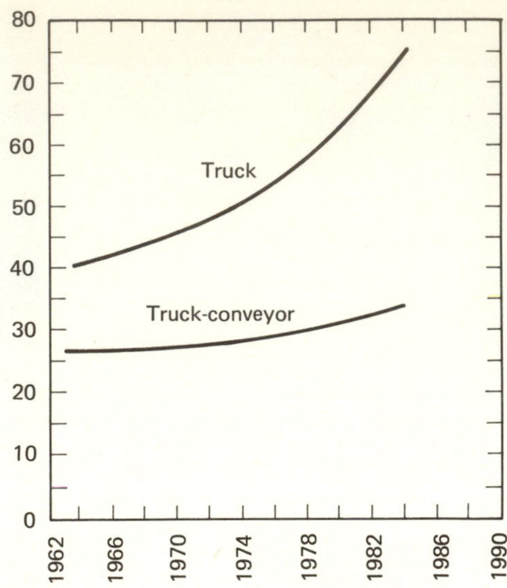

Figure 5.40. Economic advantage of the truck-conveyor system.

4. Undesirability of creating excess fines and the need for their subsequent agglomeration.
5. Dewatering and storage of ore at the mill.
6. Clearing the pipeline in case of mill stoppages.

An all-truck haulage operation, with an investment in new, larger trucks, was estimated to be much more costly than belt conveyor haulage. Also, the difference would increase as the shallow ore bodies were mined out and the length of haul increased (Figure 5.40).

Jamaican bauxite mine to seaport[26]

The adaptability and economy of belt conveyors for transporting bulk materials over rugged terrain despite adverse weather conditions is illustrated by a system designed to deliver 1300 tons/h of bauxite from ore dryers at the mine to a port facility in Jamaica (Figure 5.41).

The investment decision for this system was based on an intensive economic study when it was decided to increase production at the mine. The existing tramline was inadequate for the increase, so the economics of truck, railroad, tramline, pipeline, and conveyor haulage were analyzed, and such other factors as availability, reliability, and the effects of weather were considered. The results of the study can be summarized as follows:

	Economic Comparison*			
	Conveyor†	Railroad†	Tramline	Truck
Distance from mine to port (mi)	6.5	14.0	6.5	10.8
Relative transportation cost per ton-mile	1.00	0.58	2.29	1.30
Relative transportation cost per ton	1.00	1.26	2.29	2.16
Relative capital cost	1.00	1.30	0.81	0.97

*Based on an annual production rate of 3 million net tons.
†The truck, conveyor, and railroad systems are readily expandable to 5 million tons/yr. The cost of the tramline would increase substantially at this rate.

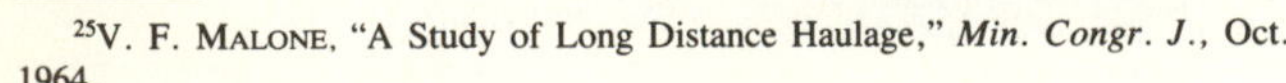

[25] V. F. Malone, "A Study of Long Distance Haulage," *Min. Congr. J.*, Oct. 1964.

[26] Robert C. Temps, "Bulk Transportation of Jamaican Bauxite," *Min. Congr. J.*, *52*(10) (1966).

Figure 5.41. Six-and-one-half-mile conveyor system.

The pipeline method was rejected because of the serious problem of dewatering the slurried bauxite. Truck costs per ton were not only higher than conveyor costs, but operating problems were anticipated due to tropical weather (e.g., rainfall of 6 in. (15 cm) per month and frequent dense fogs). A railroad would also entail high operating costs because of the circuitous route down long grades and over deep gullies subject to flooding. The profile of the conveyor route (Figure 5.42) suggests the considerably longer distances that would have been required for both trucks and railroad because of their inability to negotiate steep grades. The resulting higher costs are shown above. Actual power consumption by the belt conveyors is low because the fully loaded system is virtually in balance. The power generated by the overall descent of the material is about equivalent to the power demands to propel the belts. Spare parts are minimal because all belts are identical, and there are only two sizes of speed reducers and three sizes or types of motors. The belts are covered to protect the dried bauxite from the weather, and the return belts are of the "turnover" type, to prevent buildup of ore on the return idlers.

Ore and waste haulage from an Arizona copper mine[27]

Characteristic of the open-pit copper mines in Arizona and other parts of the Southwest is their great depth. Often it is necessary to remove several hundred feet of waste rock and alluvial gravel to reach the uppermost ore in the pit. Early operations employed railroads to haul the ore and waste over a circuitous route to the surface. Then trucks became more economical for the haul from loading shovels, up 8% grades to the crest of the pit, and on to the primary crushers.

In 1968 a new mine was opened in Arizona, where the ore was overlaid with 700 ft (215 m) of waste rock and alluvial gravel. Based on exhaustive economic feasibility studies, belt conveyors were installed to transport minus 10-in. (25-cm) waste and ore from primary crushers in the pit to the surface and then to waste dump and mill (Figure 5.43). The system successfully justifies preinvestment calculations. A fringe benefit of the belt conveyor system is its environmental desirability—there is practically no dust discharged to the air, and noise pollution is almost non-

[27]J. J. Coile, "In-Pit Crushing and Conveying vs. Truck Haulage," *Min. Congr. J.*, Jan. 1974.

Figure 5.42. Conveyor route profile.

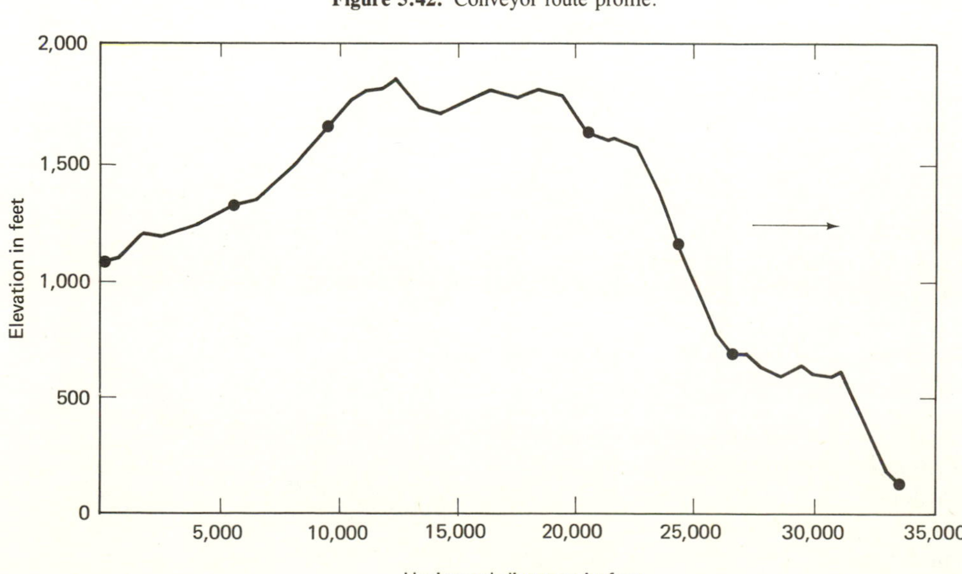

Figure 5.43. High-capacity conveyor system.

existent. This is particularly important because of a nearby retirement community.

In light of the experience at this mine, a study was conducted in 1973 to compare conveyor and truck haulage for a similar but hypothetical operation. The study was based on recovering in 20 years 200 million tons of ore overlaid with 400 ft (120 m) of waste rock and gravel, where the waste rock/ore ratio was 2:1. Individual studies were made for ore and waste, as well as for conveyor and truck systems. The combined results are summarized in Table 5-8. The figures for each system include a 400-ft (120-m) haul from pit crest to waste dump and a 1000-ft (300-m) haul for ore to mill. The adverse grade to pit crest for trucks was figured at 8% and for conveyors 25%.

Obviously, for these tonnages the conveyor was the best investment for a lift of more than 200 ft (60 m) and would become more profitable as the depth of the pit increased.

TABLE 5–8
Comparison of Truck versus Conveyor Haulage Pit with Annual Tonnage of 30 Million (20 Million Waste and 10 Million Ore Tons)

	Trucking Costs		Conveying Costs		Advantage (Disadvantage) Conveyor to Trucking	
Lift in Pit (ft)	Annual Cost	Cost per Ton Handled	Annual Cost	Cost per Ton	Annual	Per Ton
100	$1,889,000	$0.0630	$2,252,000	$0.0751	($ 363,000)	($0.0121)
200	2,477,000	0.0826	2,489,000	0.0830	(12,000)	(0.0004)
300	3,128,000	0.1043	2,726,000	0.0909	402,000	0.0134
400	3,846,000	0.1282	2,963,000	0.0988	883,000	0.0294
500	4,619,000	0.1540	3,203,000	0.1068	1,416,000	0.0472
600	5,458,000	0.1819	3,440,000	0.1147	2,018,000	0.0672

Moving a mountain to a cement plant[28]

In contrast with the foregoing examples of conveyor systems operating over rugged terrain and from deep-pit mines, this 4-mi (6.4-km) system operates over relatively level Arizona desert (Figure 5.44). The system hauls stone, shale, and silica at a substantially lower cost per ton than trucks, even though there are excellent roads between mine and plant.

In addition to its economic advantage over trucks, the conveyor system has interesting design features:

1. The system consists of only two conveyors; one conveyor spans 18,500 ft (5.6 km) with a single belt and the other is 2600 ft (800 m) long.

Figure 5.44. Belt conveyor in concrete support housing.

[28]"Belt Conveyor Beats Trucks for Moving Bulk Materials," *Mater. Handl. Eng.*, Sept. 1973.

2. A special precision accelerating drive accurately controls belt tensions and optimizes load sharing between the two drive pulleys of the longer conveyor. This feature allows the use of a lower-cost belt and safeguards against belt abuse.
3. Among other safety features is the prestressed concrete housing that supports the conveyor and devices that provide for automatic shutdown in case of excessive belt tensions or unusual side-tracking of the belt.

Investment decision: belt conveyors versus trucks

Numerous factors contributed to the selection of each long-distance belt conveyor system described above. However, final investment decisions were based primarily on economics—the lowest cost per ton for the tonnage to be handled during the life of the operation. In cases where the initial cost of a belt conveyor system is higher than that for trucks, the difference can be overcome by its lower operating costs.

Outlined below are some of the factors that must be considered by those who wish to decide whether to invest in a belt conveyor system or a truck operation. The applicable items can be used to suit specific requirements and circumstances and costs estimated to obtain the financial information desired. Such information could vary from a brief estimate of owning and operating costs and the anticipated salvage value for a temporary system to highly sophisticated accounting procedures applied to an extensive permanent installation.

An excellent example of the use of sophisticated accounting methods for an investment decision was presented by F. W. Schweitzer and L. G. Dykers.[29] It is based on appropriate cost estimates for a specific set of operating conditions and develops comparisons on present worth, discounted cash flow on investment, and wealth growth rate over a period of 10 years.

To make a true cost comparison between two or more haulage systems, all costs chargeable to each system must be considered, including ancillary facilities required for each system. For example, crushing facilities might be required to reduce lump size for handling on the belt conveyor but would not be necessary for truck haulage. Conversely, a very large shop with extensive special equipment would be required for a fleet of trucks, whereas only relatively inexpensive equipment is necessary for servicing the small components of a belt conveyor. Also, the effect of inflation and added investment for additional or replacement equipment and facilities must be considered.

Owning and operating costs

Tables 5-9 and 5-10 present suggested formats for determining the capital investment and annual owning and operating costs for truck and conveyor hauls. These forms

[29]F. W. Schweitzer and L. G. Dykers, "Belt Conveyors vs. Truck Haulage: Capital vs. Expense," paper presented to Soc. Min. Eng./AIME, Denver, Colo., Sept. 1976.

TABLE 5-9
Owning and Operating Costs—Conveyor Haul (Annual Expenditures in Current Dollars)

	Year									
	1	2	3	4	5	6	7	8	9	N*
Capital investment										
Loading arrangement										
Conveyor equipment and structures										
Belting										
Erection of equipment and structures										
Foundations										
Electrical equipment and installation										
Site preparation										
Access road construction										
Lighting										
Repair shop and equipment										
Repair parts storage										
Unloading arrangement										
Maintenance equipment for access road, conveyor movement, cleanup, etc.										
Owning costs per year										
Depreciation										
Interest, taxes, and insurance (% of book value)										
Operating costs per year										
Power										
Maintenance and repair of conveyor installation (labor and material)										
Maintenance of haul road										
Maintenance and repair of auxiliary equipment										
Labor										
Total cost										

*Extend to Nth year—expected life

TABLE 5-10
Owning and Operating Costs—Truck Haul (Annual Expenditures in Current Dollars)

	Year									
	1	2	3	4	5	6	7	8	9	N*
Capital investment										
Trucks less tires										
Haul road construction										
Haul road maintenance equipment										
Lighting										
Repair shop and equipment										
Repair parts storage building										
Loading arrangement										
Unloading arrangement										
Engineering										
Owning costs per year										
Depreciation										
Interest, taxes, and insurance (% of book value)										
Operating costs per year										
Haul road maintenance										
Maintenance and repair of trucks										
Tires										
Fuel/oil/grease										
Labor										
Operators										
Mechanics (usually included in truck repair)										
Power for lighting										
Total cost										

*Extend to Nth year—expected life

show the major factors contributing to the costs of each of the two systems. However, for an actual comparison, factors will be added or deducted to suit the particular project. The purpose of this discussion is to point out items other than actual truck or conveyor costs that must be considered in making a valid comparison.

To account for inflation and additional investments, the format allows for annual entries over the life of the project and therefore gives annual costs. These annual figures are important in analyzing present worth.

As mentioned above, one of the considerations in the investment decision is the owning and operating cost per ton. The annual owning and operating cost is determined for each over the life of the project. The cost per ton is then determined by dividing the annual owning and operating cost by the tonnage expected to be handled during that year. It is important to note that the annual operating hours have a significant effect on the results of the cost analysis, because the frequency of replacement and annual depreciation are directly affected.

Even though the owning and operating costs analysis indicates an advantage of one system over another, the more economical plan may require an initial investment that is higher than the alternate plan. The worth of this investment may be the determining factor in the investment decision. The following example illustrates one common method of measuring the worth.

Present worth: required rate of return

Tables 5-11 to 5-13 demonstrate the procedure for evaluating the present worth of an investment. The cost figures used in Tables 5-11 and 5-12 are arbitrary and do not represent comparative figures for a specific truck and conveyor haul. They *do not* apply to specific conditions, nor are they intended as an accurate comparison of the two haulage methods. To simplify the example, investment tax credit and other tax considerations (mainly depreciation), which would be advisable in an actual analysis, have been ignored. The example assumes 5% annual inflation.

Tables 5-11 and 5-12 show how the annual expenditures are determined for each system. The present worth of a system is the value of an investment (made today at the rate of return required by the investor) that will produce the annual owning and operating costs for the system over the

TABLE 5–11
Cash Flow—Conveyor System (Dollars × 10³)

	Year									
	1	2	3	4	5	6	7	8	9	10
Capital investment										
Conveyor system	$1900	0	0	0	0	0	0	0	0	0
Loading system	260	0	0	0	0	330*	0	0	0	0
Belting	700	0	0	0	0	890*	0	0	0	0
Access road	50	0	0	0	0	0	0	0	0	0
Operating costs										
Taxes and insurance	116	101	85	70	54	88	70	53	35	18
Power, Maintenance and repair†, Labor	287	301	316	332	349	366	385	404	424	445
Access road maintenance	3	3	3	3	4		4	4	4	5
Total cash flow	$3316	405	404	405	407	1678	459	461	463	468

*For the purpose of this example, these items are replaced at the end of year 5. Anticipated hours of operation and life expectancy of equipment determine the proper entry.
†Includes repair shop and parts storage.

TABLE 5–12
Cash Flow—Truck System (Dollars × 10³)

	Year									
	1	2	3	4	5	6	7	8	9	10
Capital investment										
Trucks	$1400	0	0	0	0	1787*	0	0	0	0
Repair shop and parts storage	50	0	0	0	0	0	0	0	0	0
Haul road	100	0	0	0	0	0	0	0	0	0
Loading system	460	0	0	0	0	588*	0	0	0	0
Operating costs										
Taxes and insurance	80	65	49	34	18	98	78	59	39	20
Maintenance of trucks, Maintenance of loaders, Labor, Fuel, Tires	704	739	776	815	856	899	944	991	1040	1092
Haul road maintenance	10	10	11	12	12	13	13	14	15	15
Total cash flow	$2804	814	836	861	886	3385	1035	1064	1094	1127

*For the purpose of this example, these items are replaced at the end of year 5. Anticipated hours of operation and life expectancy of equipment determine the proper entry.

life of the project. Since each system performs the same function, the system representing the lower investment is more attractive to the investor.

Table 5-13 shows the result using 20% as the required rate of return. In this example, the conveyor system requires a $4,599,000 investment, and the truck system, a $6,222,000 investment. Since the conveyor system's present worth is lower than that of the truck system, the conveyor is considered to be a more attractive investment. In fact, it could justify an additional capital expenditure of $1,623,000 ($6,222,000 less $4,599,000).

SUGGESTED FURTHER READING

"Belt Conveyors for Bulk Materials" 2nd Ed. 1979, Conveyor Equipment Manufacturers Assoc., CBI Publications, Boston, Mass.

TABLE 5–13
Present Value Annual Costs Discounted at 20% (Dollars × 10³)

	Belt System			Truck System		
Year	Cash Flow	Factor	Present Value	Cash Flow	Factor	Present Value
1	$3316	0.833	$2762	$2804	0.833	$2336
2	405	0.694	281	814	0.694	565
3	404	0.579	234	836	0.579	484
4	405	0.482	195	861	0.482	415
5	407	0.402	164	886	0.402	356
6	1678	0.335	562	3385	0.335	1134
7	459	0.279	128	1035	0.279	289
8	461	0.233	107	1064	0.233	248
9	463	0.194	90	1094	0.194	212
10	468	0.162	76	1127	0.162	183
Total*			$4599			$6222

*Difference in present value = $6,222,000 − $4,599,000 = $1,623,000.

6

HIGHWAY TRANSPORTATION

Part A

VEHICLE AND HIGHWAY CHARACTERISTICS

EARL R. KREHER, *Senior Staff Associate*
Motor Vehicle Manufacturers Association of the United States
Detroit, Michigan

Population

The growth, spatial distribution and standard of living of a population are contributing factors of demand for transportation and for the modes and facilities that are provided to fulfill that demand. This is illustrated for the United States in Figure 6.1. During the period 1950–1978, the population of the United States grew 43% and the standard of living, as measured by the U.S. gross national product in constant dollars, grew 160%. During the same period, highway vehicle registrations rose 203% and vehicular travel on U.S. highways grew 238%.

During the 1950s, the population of the United States increased at a modern-day high rate of 1.7% per year: from 152,271,000 in 1950 to 180,671,000 in 1960. The annual growth rate during the 1960s declined to about 1.0% in the late 1960s and continued to decline through the mid-1970s to 0.8% in 1977. The overall growth resulted in a 1977 population of 216,745,000. Population change is the sum of net migration plus births minus deaths. A downward change in the U.S. fertility rate (and, by extension, the annual number of births) has been the key factor in slower population growth. From 1973 through 1976, the annual number of births in the United States was between 3.1 and 3.2 million. This is the lowest annual figure since 1945, and it is well below the 4.3 million births recorded annually during the 1957–1961 period.

U.S. Bureau of the Census Series II projections suggest that the U.S. population will grow to 260 million by the year 2000 and to 315 million by 2050. If there is a static standard of living and population density, demand for travel will change as population size changes. With the U.S. population projected to grow at a decreasing rate, travel demand and consequent highway travel (98% of all person trips being by highway) also will grow at a decreasing rate.

Changes in population distribution and density are significant to transportation demand. The lower the density, the more likely that the populace will rely on the private motor vehicle for transportation. Conversely, the greater the density, the more able public transit is to fulfill demand. Movement of population from larger urban areas to smaller, or from central city to suburbs, will probably result in increased demand for highway transportation.

As Table 6-1 indicates, the proportion of the United States population residing in urban areas increased from 70% to 74% from 1960 to 1970. The extent of the total urban area during this period increased by almost 35% from 40,238 mi^2 (104,000 km^2) in 1960 to 54,103 mi^2 (140,000 km^2) in 1970. The density of the urban population decreased from 3113 persons per mi^2 (1200 per km^2) in 1960 to 2760 persons per mi^2 (1065 per km^2) in 1970. The massive movements of population during the earlier part of the century from farm to city has shifted from city to suburb, starting nearly three decades ago.

Growth and increased urbanization are characteristics of the population changes in many countries. Data on changes in urbanization and population growth for selected countries that have a high level of motor vehicle use are shown in Table 6-2.

Currently, there is some evidence of a trend from larger

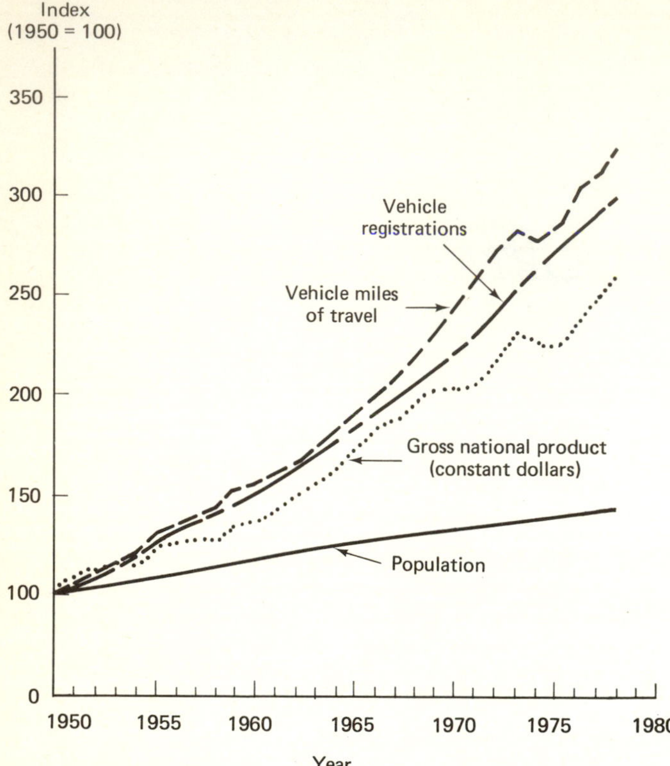

Figure 6.1. Population, motor vehicle registration, travel, and gross national product—U.S. (1950–1978). SOURCE: Compiled by MOTOR VEHICLE MANUFACTURERS ASSOCIATION OF THE UNITED STATES, Inc., from U.S. Bureau of the Census, U.S. Bureau of Economic Analysis and U.S. Federal Highway Administration data.

urbanized areas toward the smaller places. Energy considerations may alter these patterns in the near future.

Motor vehicle statistics

World registration of motor vehicles in 1978 totaled 380 million, more than five times the number registered in 1950. Not included in these figures are millions of mopeds and motorcycles (nearly 5 million motorcycles registered in the United States alone). Passenger cars represented 78% of the registered vehicles in 1978 while trucks and buses accounted for 22%, slightly less than the nearly 25% portion held in 1950. Figure 6.2 portrays the growth in worldwide registrations for 1950–1978. Table 6-3 provides the distribution of the 1978 worldwide registrations by continental area and selected countries.

In 1978, U.S. registrations of passenger cars totaled 116,574,999, a 189% increase over 1950. Bus registrations in that year were 500,000, more than double the number registered in 1950. Truck registrations totaled 31,703,000, more than triple the 8,599,000 in 1950. Motorcycle registrations, which totaled 454,000 in 1950, were 5,138,000 in 1978. Included with the 1978 truck registration figures were 1.7 million motor homes and 2 million truck campers. In addition, there were about 2.8 million travel trailers and 1.4 million camping trailers being pulled by motor vehicles in the United States. Table 6-4 provides the pattern of growth of motor vehicles in the United States. The ratios of persons per car and persons per vehicle indicate the level of reliance on the passenger car for personal mobility and measures potential demand for highway travel. Worldwide

TABLE 6–1
Population Trends, United States, 1950–2050

Year	Total Population (× 10³)	Growth*: Percent Urban	Growth*: Percent Rural
Recorded			
1950	152,271	64	36
1960	180,671	70	30
1970	204,878	74	26
Projected			
1980	222,159	n.a.	n.a.
1990	243,518	n.a.	n.a.
2000	260,378	n.a.	n.a.
2010	275,335	n.a.	n.a.
2020	290,115	n.a.	n.a.
2030	300,349	n.a.	n.a.
2040	308,400	n.a.	n.a.
2050	315,622	n.a.	n.a.

*n.a., not available.

SOURCE: U.S. BUREAU OF THE CENSUS, *Current Population Reports*, Ser. P.25, No. 704, Table D.

Urban Changes

	Population (× 10³) 1950*	1960	1970
Urbanized areas	69,249	95,848	118,325
Other urban	27,219	29,420	30,878
Total urban	96,468	125,269	149,325
	Land Area (Square Miles)		
Urbanized areas	12,733	25,544	35,081
Other urban	n.a.	14,694	19,022
Total urban	n.a.	40,238	54,103
	Density (Persons per Square Mile)		
Urbanized areas	5,439	3,752	3,376
Other urban	n.a.	2,002	1,623
Total urban	n.a.	3,113	2,760

*n.a., not available.

SOURCE: U.S. BUREAU OF THE CENSUS, *Statistical Abstract of the United States, 1977.*

TABLE 6–2
Population Trends, Selected Countries

Country	Year	Urban Population (%)	Annual Growth (%)	Projected Population (× 10⁶) 1980	1990	2000
Australia	1971	85.6	2.5	15.1	17.8	20.2
Brazil	1976	60.4	4.2	126.4	165.8	212.5
Canada	1971	76.1	2.2	24.6	28.4	31.6
France	1968	70.0	2.7*	55.1	58.8	62.1
Germany, West	1969	83.4	0.8	62.0	64.2	66.2
Netherlands	1975	76.3	0.7	14.1	15.1	16.0
Sweden	1975	82.7	0.8	8.5	9.0	9.4
United Kingdom	1973	77.7	0.2	57.5	60.0	62.8
United States	1970	74.0	0.3	222.2	243.5	260.4
Total World	1975	39.3	0.3	4373.0	5279.0	6253.0

*Rate of growth during 1970s has been less than 1%.

SOURCE: UNITED NATIONS, *Demographics Yearbooks*, 1970, 1973, 1976; U.S. BUREAU OF THE CENSUS, *Statistical Abstract of the United States*, 1977.

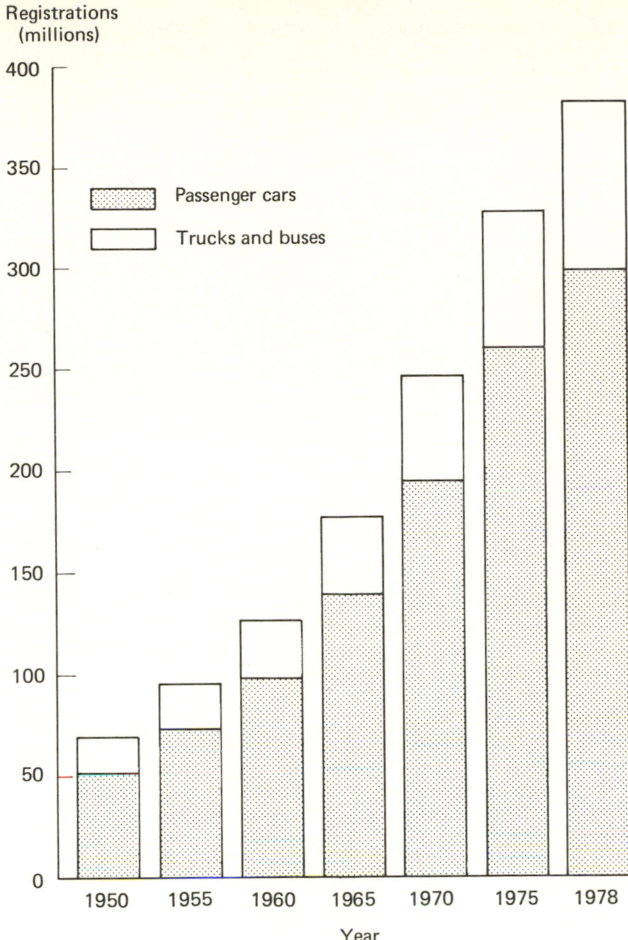

Figure 6.2. World motor vehicle registrations (1950–1978). SOURCE: MOTOR VEHICLE MANUFACTURERS ASSOCIATION OF THE UNITED STATES, Inc., *Automobile Facts and Figures,* 1952, 1957, and *Motor Vehicle Facts and Figures,* 1980.

TABLE 6–3
World Motor Vehicle Registration, Continents and Selected Countries, 1978

Location	Passenger Cars	Trucks and Buses	Total Vehicles*	Percent
Africa	5,260,366	2,387,020	7,647,386	2.01
Asia	27,926,365	18,121,454	46,047,819	12.12
Europe	113,887,877	19,405,981	133,293,858	35.07
North and Central America	131,073,066	36,737,846	167,810,912	44.16
Oceania	6,858,424	1,670,975	8,529,399	2.24
South America	12,354,897	4,335,987	16,690,884	4.39
World total	297,360,995	82,659,263	380,020,258	100.00
Australia	5,462,200	1,359,900	6,822,100	1.79
Brazil	6,926,866	1,875,000	8,801,866	2.11
Canada	9,744,994	2,770,798	12,515,792	3.29
France	17,780,000	2,478,500	20,258,500	5.33
Germany, West	21,619,697	1,423,618	23,043,315	6.06
Italy	16,985,980	1,326,000	18,311,980	4.82
Japan	21,279,689	12,841,045	34,120,734	8.97
Spain	6,598,885	1,227,767	7,826,652	2.06
USSR	6,600,000	6,200,000	12,800,000	3.37
United Kingdom	14,416,989	2,116,552	16,533,541	4.35
United States	116,574,999	32,202,966	148,777,965	39.13

*Passenger cars, trucks and buses.

SOURCE: MOTOR VEHICLE MANUFACTURERS ASSOCIATION OF THE UNITED STATES, INC., *MVMA Motor Vehicle Facts and Figures, 1980.*

TABLE 6–4
Motor Vehicle Registration, United States, 1900–1978
(× 10³)

Year	Automobiles	Buses	Trucks	All Motor Vehicles Public and Private*
1900	8	—	—	8
1910	458	—	10	469
1920	8,132	—	1,108	9,239
1930	23,035	41	3,675	26,750
1940	27,466	101	4,886	32,453
1950	40,339	224	8,599	49,162
1960†	61,671	272	11,914	73,858
1970	89,244	377	18,797	108,418
1971	92,718	397	19,871	112,986
1972	97,082	407	21,308	118,797
1973	101,985	425	23,244	125,654
1974	104,856	447	24,630	129,934
1975	106,706	462	25,781	132,949
1976	110,188	478	27,875	138,546
1977	112,288	492	29,602	142,381
1978	116,575	500	31,703	148,778

*Excludes motorcycles.
†Includes Alaska and Hawaii for 1960 and subsequent years.

SOURCE: U.S. FEDERAL HIGHWAY ADMINISTRATION, *Highway Statistics Summary to 1975,* and *Highway Statistics,* annual.

in 1978, there were 14 persons per car and 11 persons per vehicle compared to 44 persons per car and 33 persons per vehicle in 1950. Table 6-5 provides data for 1950 and 1978 by continental area and for selected countries. It should be noted that the number of persons per vehicle throughout the world varied from 2.1 in North and Central America to 54 in Africa in 1978. Also, an extraordinary increase in vehicles from 1950 to 1978 is noted for Asia.

In the United States in 1978 there was an average of 1.5 persons per vehicle and 1.1 persons of driving age (15 years old and over) per vehicle. On an individual state basis, persons per vehicle ranged from 2.6 in the District of Columbia to 1.1 persons per vehicle in North Dakota and Wyoming. Except for the period during World War II, the

TABLE 6–5
Vehicle Ownership Ratios, Continents and Selected Countries

Location	Persons/Passenger Car		Persons/Vehicle	
	1950	1978	1950	1978
Africa	217.0	79.0	148.0	54.0
Asia	2593.0	85.0	1023.0	51.0
Europe	78.0	6.5	45.0	5.5
North and Central America	5.1	2.7	4.1	2.1
Oceania	10.0	3.1	6.7	2.5
South America	147.0	18.0	84.0	14.0
World average	44.0	14.0	33.0	11.0
Australia	9.1	2.6	5.9	2.1
Brazil	206.0	16.0	111.0	13.0
Canada	7.2	2.4	5.4	1.9
France	26.0	3.0	17.0	2.6
Germany, West	76.0	2.8	45.0	2.7
Italy	104.0	3.3	61.0	3.1
Japan	1918.0	5.4	245.0	3.4
Spain	467.0	5.6	239.0	4.7
USSR	312.0	40.0	75.0	20.0
United Kingdom	21.0	3.9	14.0	3.4
United States	3.7	1.9	3.1	1.5

SOURCE: AUTOMOBILE MANUFACTURERS ASSOCIATION, *Automobile Facts and Figures 1951;* MOTOR VEHICLE MANUFACTURERS ASSOCIATION OF THE UNITED STATES, INC., *MVMA Motor Vehicle Facts and Figures, 1980.*

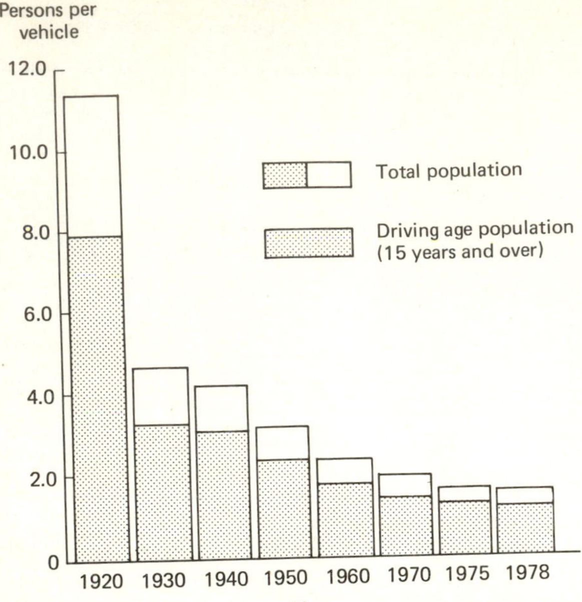

Figure 6.3. Persons per registered vehicle, U.S. (1920–1978). SOURCE: U.S. FEDERAL HIGHWAY ADMINISTRATION, *Highway Statistics Summary to 1975* and *Highway Statistics*, annual.

population/vehicle ratio in the United States has been declining. Even the temporary slowdown in World War II did not alter the trend, as shown in Figure 6.3.

Household ownership of automobiles is an indication of the significance of the automobile in personal transportation. Cross-tabulated with household income, it can become a measure of potential automobile usage. Table 6-6 indicates the relationship in the United States between household income, annual trip rate, and annual vehicle-miles per household. In 1975, 83% of U.S. households owned at least one automobile and 35% owned two or more cars. In Canada, 79% of households owned an automobile in 1975, with 23% owning two or more cars. The growth in household ownership of automobiles in the United States and Canada is shown in Table 6-7.

Automobile availability to U.S. households varied in 1976 from a low of 78% having at least one car in the Northeast, to a high of nearly 87% in the North Central region. Central cities of metropolitan areas had the lowest rate, with 73% of households having cars. Automobiles were available to nearly 91% of households in suburban rings of metropolitan areas. Light trucks were available to 28% of the households in the West in 1976 and to 10% in the Northeast. Table 6-8 shows households with vehicles

TABLE 6–6
Income and Passenger-Car-Trip Generation, United States

Annual Household Income	Annual Trip Rate/ Household	Annual Vehicle-Miles/ Household	Average Trip Length (mi)
Under $4,000	580	4,708	8.1
$4000–$9999	1433	12,262	8.6
$10,000–$14,999	1949	17,497	9.0
$15,000 and over	2526	24,410	9.7

SOURCE: U.S. FEDERAL HIGHWAY ADMINISTRATION, *Nationwide Personal Transportation Study*, 1970, as shown in *Highway Travel Forecasts*, Nov. 1974.

TABLE 6–7
Automobile Ownership Trends, United States and Canada, 1965–1975

	Percent of Households Owning Cars					
	United States			Canada		
Year	None	One	Two or More	None	One	Two or More
1965	23	53	24	25	63	12
1966	22	53	25	23	61	14
1967	21	53	27	24	61	15
1968	22	51	27	24	61	15
1969	20	51	29	23	61	16
1970	20	50	29	23	60	17
1971	20	50	30	23	59	18
1972	21	49	30	23	59	18
1973	19	48	34	22	57	21
1974	19	49	33	22	56	22
1975	17	48	35	21	56	23

SOURCE: U.S. BUREAU OF THE CENSUS, Consumer Buying Indicators, *Current Population Reports*, Ser. P.65, annual, and Current Housing Reports, *Annual Housing Survey;* Statistics for Canada, *Household Facilities and Equipment*, annual.

by region and residence for 1970 and 1976. Household ownership of automobiles varies substantially throughout the world. Recent data for selected countries is provided in Table 6-9.

In 1977, there were 26,213,000 privately owned trucks in the United States: 22,395,000 light [10,000 lb or less gross vehicle weight (GVW)], 1,583,000 medium (10,001 to 19,500 lb GVW), 803,000 light-heavy (19,501 to 26,000 lb GVW) and 1,432,000 heavy (26,001 lb GVW or more). Table 6-10 indicates the major uses of each group, their body type, and the distribution of their annual mileage.

TABLE 6–8
Vehicle Availability by Geographical Area, United States*

	Percent of Households						
	Automobiles				Light Trucks†		
	None	One	Two	Three or More	None	One	Two or More
1976							
Region							
Northeast	22.0	44.8	26.4	6.9	89.7	9.5	0.8
North Central	13.4	47.8	31.1	7.7	78.7	19.3	2.0
South	16.0	49.1	27.8	7.1	73.3	24.3	2.3
West	13.7	50.2	28.3	7.7	72.0	24.7	3.3
Residence							
Metropolitan area	17.1	45.5	29.6	7.8	84.2	14.5	1.3
Central cities	26.7	45.4	22.5	5.4	88.9	10.2	0.8
Suburban rings	9.1	45.6	35.5	9.7	80.2	18.1	1.7
Outside metropolitan area	14.3	53.3	26.0	6.4	65.3	31.0	3.8
Total U.S.	16.2	48.0	28.4	7.3	78.2	19.7	2.1
1970							
Region							
Northeast	24.7	46.6	24.5	4.2	n.a.	n.a.	n.a.
North Central	14.7	50.4	29.7	5.1	n.a.	n.a.	n.a.
South	17.1	47.0	30.4	5.6	n.a.	n.a.	n.a.
West	12.5	46.2	33.6	7.8	n.a.	n.a.	n.a.
Residence							
Metropolitan area	18.6	45.8	30.0	5.7	n.a.	n.a.	n.a.
Central cities	28.4	45.4	22.1	4.1	n.a.	n.a.	n.a.
Suburban rings	9.2	46.1	37.4	7.2	n.a.	n.a.	n.a.
Outside metropolitan area	15.0	52.1	27.9	5.1	n.a.	n.a.	n.a.
Total U.S.	17.5	47.7	29.3	5.5	n.a.	n.a.	n.a.

*Vehicle availability should not be construed as ownership.
†n.a., not available.

SOURCE: U.S. BUREAU OF THE CENSUS, *Annual Housing Survey: 1976 United States and Regions.*

TABLE 6–9
Automobile Ownership, Selected Countries

Country	Year	Percent of Households*: No Car	One Car	Two or More
Germany, West	1972	50.0	44.4	5.6
Japan	1976	54.9	n.a.	n.a.
United Kingdom	1973	46.0	44.0	10.0
Netherlands	1976	35.8	56.4	7.8
France	1972	70.0	n.a.	n.a.
Canada	1975	21.0	56.0	23.0
United States	1975	17.0	48.0	35.0

*n.a., not available.

SOURCE: Compiled from various sources by the MOTOR VEHICLE MANUFACTURERS ASSOCIATION OF THE UNITED STATES, INC.

There were 2,293,629 publicly owned vehicles in the United States in 1978. The federal government operated a fleet of 280,483 vehicles—78,275 automobiles, 199,791 trucks, and 2417 buses. State, county, and local governments owned 670,228 automobiles, 1,091,707 trucks, and 251,211 buses.

In the United States during the period 1950–1978, the average age of registered passenger cars ranged from 7.8 years in 1950 to 5.5 years in 1970. The average age of trucks during this period ranged from 8.1 to 6.6 years. The average age of passenger cars in 1978 was 6.3 years, while the average age of a truck in operation was 6.9 years. Table 6-11 shows the average age of registered passenger cars and trucks for selected years 1950–1978.

TABLE 6–10
Use of Privately Owned Trucks, United States, 1977

Characteristic	Numbers/by GVW* (× 10³): 10,000 or Less	10,001–19,500	19,501–26,000	26,001 or More	(× 10³) Total	Percent
Major use						
Agriculture	3,269.8	477.2	288.8	212.9	4,248.8	16.2
Forestry	111.8	29.8	17.7	58.2	217.5	0.8
Mining	70.2	17.9	10.6	40.3	139.0	0.5
Construction	1,237.9	169.9	103.3	253.7	1,764.9	6.7
Manufacturing	174.4	53.4	30.1	110.5	368.5	1.4
Wholesale and retail trade	1,252.2	291.6	188.2	275.7	2,007.9	7.7
For hire†	104.0	124.4	60.4	364.9	653.8	2.5
Personal transportation	14,108.1	150.3	1.9	.2	14,260.6	54.4
Utilities	361.8	57.9	34.1	27.3	481.2	1.8
Services	1,371.4	155.2	49.0	65.7	1,641.3	6.3
All other‡	333.3	55.3	18.1	22.8	429.6	1.6
Body type						
Pickup, panel, multistop, or walk-in	21,714.9	429.4	5.8	.7	22,151.0	84.5
Platform§	269.4	415.6	273.6	319.5	1,278.2	4.9
Platform with added device	66.3	120.8	77.4	68.6	333.1	1.3
Cattlerack	50.6	58.1	32.9	26.2	168.0	0.6
Insulated nonrefrigerated van	2.9	13.4	9.8	31.9	58.0	0.2
Insulated refrigerated van	6.1	37.7	26.8	79.7	150.5	0.6
Furniture van	16.8	45.1	20.5	35.1	117.6	0.5
Open top van	2.2	8.2	2.9	16.6	30.0	0.1
All other vans	15.7	143.7	81.5	290.3	531.3	2.0
Beverage truck	.6	12.7	26.2	28.3	67.9	0.3
Utility truck	106.6	55.9	24.4	13.7	200.7	0.8
Garbage and refuse collector	1.2	7.7	11.7	29.9	50.7	0.2
Winch or crane	23.3	38.3	12.5	18.8	92.9	0.4
Wrecker	68.6	23.3	5.4	3.8	101.2	0.4
Pole and logging	2.0	9.5	8.3	40.2	60.0	0.2
Auto transport	.9	1.2	.6	12.4	15.1	0.1
Dump truck	31.8	107.0	101.5	211.7	452.0	1.7
Tank truck for liquids	7.0	48.5	63.4	117.9	236.9	0.9
Tank truck for dry bulk	—	3.1	7.6	24.1	34.8	0.1
Concrete mixer	—	—	2.7	53.3	56.0	0.2
All other‖	8.0	3.5	6.7	8.8	27.1	0.1
Annual miles						
Less than 5,000	5,083.7	613.6	332.3	250.0	6,279.7	24.0
5,000–9,999	5,616.6	332.5	168.9	179.8	6,297.9	24.00
10,000–19,999	8,851.2	395.8	175.5	268.0	9,690.6	37.0
20,000–29,999	2,045.4	138.6	66.7	157.0	2,407.7	9.2
30,000–49,999	677.1	75.4	42.5	185.0	980.1	3.7
50,000–74,999	92.8	20.4	12.4	165.9	291.5	1.1
75,000 or More	28.1	6.7	4.2	226.6	265.7	1.0
Total trucks	22,395.1	1,583.2	802.5	1,432.5	26,213.4	—
Total percent	85.4	6.0	3.1	5.5	—	100.0

*GVW, gross vehicle weight (lbs).
†For-hire includes for hire and daily rental.
‡All other includes other not in use and not reported.
§Platform includes low boy with depressed center and other platform.
‖Other includes other and not reported boat transport and mobile home puller.

SOURCE: U.S. BUREAU OF THE CENSUS, *1977 Census of Transportation, Truck Inventory and Use Survey.*

TABLE 6-11
Motor Vehicle Age Trends, United States, 1950–1978*

Year	Average Age (yr) Passenger Cars	Trucks
1950	7.8	7.0
1952	6.8	6.6
1954	6.2	6.6
1956	5.6	6.8
1958	5.6	7.2
1960	5.9	7.7
1962	6.0	8.0
1964	6.0	8.1
1966	5.7	7.8
1968	5.6	7.6
1970	5.5	7.4
1972	5.7	7.2
1974	5.7	7.0
1976	6.2	7.0
1977	6.2	7.0
1978	6.3	6.9

*Weighted average of vehicles by model year.

SOURCE: MOTOR VEHICLE MANUFACTURERS ASSOCIATION OF THE UNITED STATES, INC., *MVMA Motor Vehicle Facts and Figures, 1978.*

These data provide an indication of the model-year mix in use on U.S. highways. In 1978, 18% of U.S. passenger cars and 25% of trucks were 10 or more years old. Figure 6.4 portrays the age grouping of registered vehicles in the United States between 1950 and 1978. The phaseout of pre–World War II automobiles after 1950 is evident.

Availability and cost of highway fuel may provide a limiting factor on highway transportation, while fuel efficiency of vehicles may be a counterfactor. The Arab oil embargo which began in October 1973 and the OPEC cartel focused world attention on petroleum supply, demand, and price. Elasticity of the demand for gasoline, although highly controversial, is generally thought in the short run to be −0.1 to −0.2, with no agreement on long-term elasticity. The relationship between price and purchasing rate, which is known as the elasticity of demand, expresses the percentage change in the buying rate divided by the percentage change in price. When the number is less than 1, demand is said to be inelastic. Thus, attempting to decrease demand for highway transportation through pricing to conserve petroleum has been viewed by some as having a limited effect.

Figure 6.4. Age of registered vehicles, U.S. (1950–1978). SOURCE: Compiled by the MOTOR VEHICLE MANUFACTURERS ASSOCIATION OF THE UNITED STATES, INC., from R.L. Polk & Co. data.

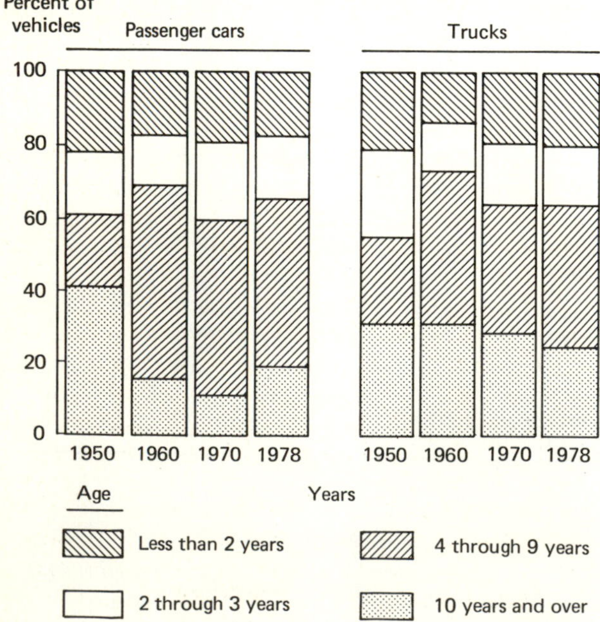

Consumption of highway motor fuel in the United States has risen consistently since 1919, with a few notable exceptions: 1932 and 1933, during the trough of the Great Depression; 1942 and 1943, during World War II and U.S. gas rationing; and in 1974, following the Arab oil embargo. Table 6-12 shows U.S. highway motor fuel consumption by type of fuel and also by type of vehicle in use for 1936–1977.

Average fuel consumption per vehicle for the years 1936–1978 is shown in Table 6-13. Noteworthy in this table is that the average fuel consumption trends follow the total fuel consumption trends by type of vehicle shown in Table 6-12 through 1975. Average fuel consumption of passenger cars decreased slightly in 1976 and continued downward in 1977, rising in 1978. Truck and bus average fuel consumption joined the downward movement in 1977, but bus fuel consumption then rose in 1978.

The downtrend in average fuel consumption per vehicle contrasts with the continued increase in average miles of travel by type of vehicle. It is the result of motor vehicle manufacturers throughout the world producing more-fuel-efficient vehicles starting with the 1975 model year and following the 1973 Arab oil embargo. Table 6-14 depicts the change in manufacturers' U.S. passenger car sales weighted miles per gallon data for model years 1974–1979. Significant passenger car fuel economy improvements, as

TABLE 6-12
Fuel Consumption Trends, United States, 1936–1978* (Gallons × 10⁶)

Year	Total‖	Fuel Type† Gasoline	Special‡	Vehicle Type Passenger Cars§	Trucks	Buses
1936	18,099	n.a.	n.a.	13,648	4,003	378
1940	22,001	n.a.	n.a.	16,323	5,156	436
1945	19,149	n.a.	n.a.	13,323	5,055	700
1950	35,622	35,125	537	24,305	10,566	732
1955	47,732	46,527	1,205	33,548	13,308	771
1960	57,880**	55,429	2,451	41,169	15,882	827
1965	71,104	66,978	4,126	50,275	19,935	894
1970	92,329	85,598	6,731	65,784	25,600	944
1973	110,473	100,636	9,837	78,011	31,615	847
1974	106,301	96,505	9,796	74,217	31,226	858
1975	108,984	99,353	9,631	76,457	31,632	895
1976	115,700	104,978	10,722	78,740	35,996	964
1977	119,625	107,978	11,647	80,677	37,964	984
1978	124,982	112,438	12,544	83,775	40,271	1021

*1 gal = 3.7854 liters.
†n.a., not available.
‖Highway fuel consumed by vehicle type do not add to total for 1936–1955.
‡Special fuels include diesel fuel, liquefied petroleum gases and those fuels known by such names as "tractor fuel" and "power fuel" when they are used to operate vehicles on the highway.
§Includes motorcycles.
**Includes Alaska and Hawaii beginning 1960.

SOURCE: U.S. FEDERAL HIGHWAY ADMINISTRATION, *Highway Statistics Summary to 1975*, and *Highway Statistics*, annual.

TABLE 6–13
Fuel Consumption per Vehicle, United States, 1936–1978
(Gallons/Year)*

Year	Passenger Cars	Buses	Trucks	All Motor Vehicles
1936	564	3048	983	635
1940	594	3049	1097	678
1945	517	4294	1020	617
1950	603	3752	1257	728
1955	644	3021	1278	759
1960	661†	3040	1330	777
1965	667	2844	1347	775
1970	735	2491	1365	830
1973	763	1991	1361	851
1974	704	1919	1268	788
1975	712	1937	1227	790
1976	711	2015	1292	807
1977	706	2002	1284	804
1978	715	2041	1270	813

*1 gal = 3.7854 liters.
†The 1960 data include Alaska and Hawaii for the first time.

SOURCE: U.S. FEDERAL HIGHWAY ADMINISTRATION, *Highway Statistics Summary to 1975*, and *Highway Statistics*, annual.

TABLE 6–14
Fuel Consumption Ratings by Manufacturer

Manufacturer	Fuel Consumption (mpg)*						Percent Change, 1974–1979
	1974	1975	1976	1977	1978	1979	
American Motors	16.4	19.0	18.3	19.2	19.1	20.0	22
Chrysler	13.7	15.5	16.4	16.6	18.4	20.6	50
Ford	14.2	13.6	17.3	17.1	18.3	19.0	34
Fuji (Subaru)	25.7	26.5	29.7	30.2	31.6	29.3	14
General Motors	12.0	15.4	16.6	18.4	18.8	19.2	60
Nissan (Datsun)	24.0	24.9	25.9	27.1	26.3	26.4	10
Toyota	22.5	22.2	25.0	28.1	27.1	24.1	7
Volkswagen–Porsche–Audi	25.9	26.5	27.5	28.8	29.0	30.6	18
Volvo	19.4	19.2	19.4	19.9	21.1	20.7	7
Fleet	14.2	15.8	17.5	18.3	19.6	20.1	42

*U.S. sales weighted miles per gallon.

SOURCE: Compiled by the MOTOR VEHICLE MANUFACTURERS ASSOCIATION OF THE UNITED STATES, INC., from Society of Automotive Engineers, Inc., paper nos. 740970, 760795, 780036, 790225 and unpublished data of the U.S. Environmental Protection Agency.

measured by U.S. tests, have been registered not only by U.S. manufacturers, but also by European and Japanese manufacturers. The result of the more-fuel-efficient vehicles, in terms of less petroleum consumption per mile of travel, will become evident as newer vehicles replace the older vehicles on the road.

Table 6-15 provides an indication of the lead time needed for equipment changes to be felt in the U.S. market. It also depicts the motor vehicle manufacturers' efforts to diminish the passenger car's role in air pollution. Figure 6.5 defines the emission control systems that have been installed on passenger cars sold in the United States and portrays the change in the U.S. auto population.

Use of motor vehicles

Personal consumption expenditures for user-operated transportation totaled $163 billion, 13% of total personal

TABLE 6–15
Passenger Cars with Emission Controls, United States

Emission Controls	1967	1972	1974	1975	1976	1977	1978
	Number of Passenger Cars ($\times 10^3$)						
Catalyst or equivalent, No$_x$, fuel evaporation, exhaust and crankcase controls	0	0	0	4,684	14,155	24,211	34,582
No$_x$, fuel evaporation, exhaust and crankcase controls*	0	726*	18,675	22,053	21,820	21,401	20,967
Fuel evaporation, exhaust and crankcase controls	0	16,213	18,607	18,476	17,937	17,241	16,274
Exhaust and crankcase controls	1,371	27,214	25,522	24,650	22,928	20,448	17,831
Crankcase control only	38,385	32,789	24,817	21,359	17,697	13,930	11,043
No controls	33,212	9,469	4,962	3,998	3,253	2,673	2,260
Total cars	72,968	86,411	92,583	95,220	97,790	99,904	102,957
	Percent of Passenger Cars						
Catalyst or equivalent, No$_x$, fuel evaporation exhaust and crankcase controls	0	0	0	4.9	14.5	24.2	33.6
No$_x$, fuel evaporation, exhaust and crankcase controls*	0	0.8	20.2	23.2	22.3	21.4	20.4
Fuel evaporation, exhaust and crankcase controls	0	18.8	20.0	19.4	18.3	17.3	15.8
Exhaust and crankcase controls	1.9	31.5	27.6	25.9	23.5	20.5	17.3
Crankcase control only	52.6	37.9	26.8	22.4	18.1	13.9	10.7
No controls	45.5	11.0	5.4	4.2	3.3	2.7	2.2
Total percent	100.0	100.0	100.0	100.0	100.0	100.0	100.0

*Improved control systems on some 1971 and 1972 models, and on all models for 1973 and after lowered total vehicle emissions of oxides of nitrogen. Data as of July 1, of each year; not model year.

SOURCE: Computed by the MOTOR VEHICLE MANUFACTURERS ASSOCIATION OF THE UNITED STATES, INC., from R. L. Polk & Co. data.

consumption expenditures in the United States in 1977. This represented 95% of the $172 billion that consumers spent for all modes of passenger transportation. Table 6-16 shows U.S. personal consumption expenditures for transportation for 1966–1977. The cost of operating a passenger car in the United States has risen from 8.6 cents/mi for 10,000 mi in 1950 to 24 cents in 1979. The historic pattern of passenger car operating cost is shown in Table 6-17.

Motor vehicle travel on U.S. roads in 1978 was a record 1548 billion vehicle miles, more than triple the vehicle miles of travel in 1950. Figure 6.1 showed that the rate of growth of vehicle travel on U.S. roads had slightly exceeded the rate of growth of the U.S. economy as measured by the U.S. gross national product valued in constant dollars. It has also exceeded the rate of growth of U.S. motor vehicle registration.

Table 6-18 shows that there may be a direct relationship between the economic situation of a country and the vehicular travel in a country. It will be noted that as the gross national product increases, vehicular travel increases. Between 1950 and 1978, U.S. passenger car travel grew from 364 billion vehicle miles to 1171 billion, an increase of 222%. Travel by trucks and truck combinations grew 284%, from 91 billion vehicle miles in 1950 to 348 billion in 1978. The pattern of vehicular travel on U.S. roads is shown in Table 6-19. The growth of total motor vehicle travel in selected countries is shown in Table 6-20.

Travel in U.S. urban areas—travel on all roads and streets

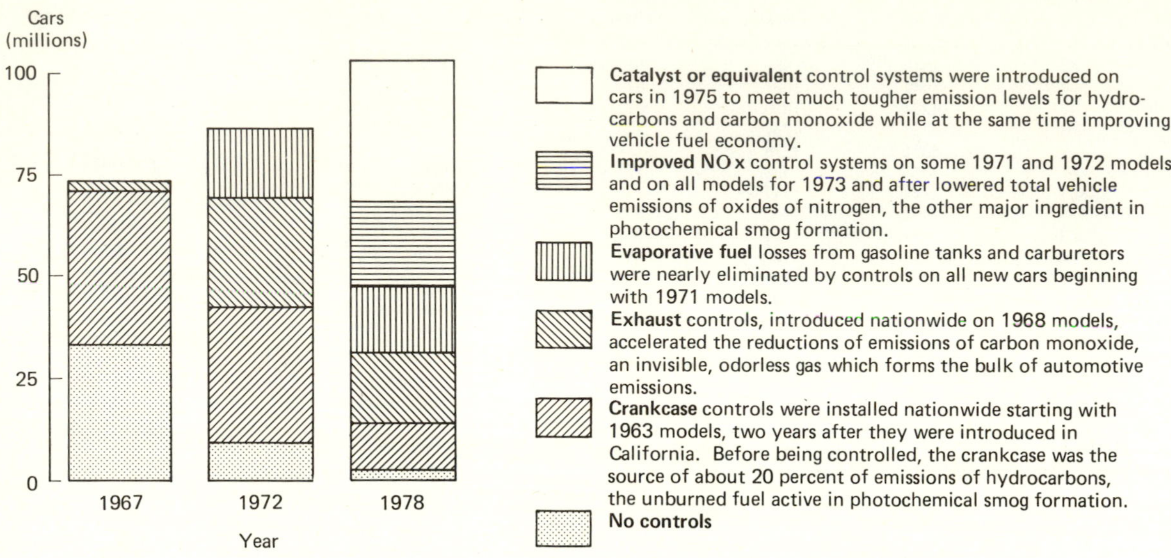

Figure 6.5. Emission control equipment on cars—U.S. SOURCE: Computed by the MOTOR VEHICLE MANUFACTURERS ASSOCIATION OF THE UNITED STATES, Inc., from R.L. Polk data.

TABLE 6–16
Personal Expenditures for Transportation, United States (Dollars × 10⁶)

	1966	1968	1970	1972	1974	1975*	1976*	1977
User-operated transportation								
New autos	$ 21,029	$ 24,638	$ 22,119	$ 32,106	$ 27,520	$ 30,030	$ 39,211	$ 46,259
Net purchases of used autos	4,067	4,919	5,675	7,300	8,824	10,193	13,562	15,504
Other motor vehicles†	1,540	2,304	2,549	5,454	4,731	5,681	8,744	10,233
Tires, tubes, accessories, and parts	3,434	3,944	4,587	5,691	6,911	7,490	8,210	9,495
Repair, greasing, washing, parking, storage, and rental	7,393	8,864	11,248	13,922	17,610	20,388	23,124	25,882
Gasoline and oil	15,962	18,422	21,997	24,879	36,431	39,509	42,825	46,457
Bridge, tunnel, ferry, and road tolls	495	563	643	745	764	798	841	879
Insurance premiums less claims paid	2,839	3,017	3,685	5,248	4,939	3,771	5,302	7,943
Total user-operated transportation	$ 56,759	$ 66,671	$ 72,503	$ 95,345	$107,730	$117,860	$ 141,819	$ 162,652
Purchased local transportation								
Transit systems	$ 1,343	$ 1,411	$ 1,573	$ 1,535	$ 1,733	$ 1,787	$ 1,945	$ 2,071
Taxicab	638	729	776	842	875	1,006	1,112	1,196
Railway commutation	140	153	172	177	200	206	224	230
Total purchased local transportation	$ 2,121	$ 2,293	$ 2,521	$ 2,604	$ 2,808	$ 2,999	$ 3,281	$ 3,497
Purchased intercity transportation								
Railway excluding commutation	$ 297	$ 227	$ 185	$ 176	$ 259	$ 254	$ 281	$ 292
Bus	429	475	496	523	617	605	608	640
Airline	1,329	1,838	2,166	2,637	3,484	3,595	4,206	4,780
Other	73	123	161	153	192	180	209	243
Total purchased intercity transportation	$ 2,128	$ 2,663	$ 3,008	$ 3,489	$ 4,552	$ 4,634	$ 5,304	$ 5,955
Total transportation	$ 61,008	$ 71,627	$ 78,032	$101,438	$115,090	$125,493	$ 150,404	$ 172,104
Total personal consumption expenditures	$464,793	$535,932	$618,796	$773,034	$889,603	$979,070	$1,090,244	$1,206,507

*Revised.
†New and net used trucks, recreation vehicles, etc.

SOURCE: U.S. BUREAU OF ECONOMIC ANALYSIS, *The National Income and Product Accounts of the U.S.: Revised Estimates, 1929–74,* and *Surv. Cur. Bus.,* July 1978.

TABLE 6–17
Passenger Car Operating Costs, United States*

	1950	1955	1960	1965	1970	1975	1979
Variable costs (cents/mi)							
Gas and oil	2.14	2.29	2.62	2.58	2.76	4.82	4.11
Maintenance	0.68	0.74	0.79	0.68	0.68	0.97	1.10
Tires	0.46	0.51	0.49	0.44	0.51	0.66	0.65
Total	3.28	3.54	3.90	3.70	3.95	6.45	5.86
Fixed costs ($/yr)							
Fire and theft insurance†	$ 15.79	$ 17.81	$ 30.38	$ 31.00	$ 44.00	$ 53.00	$ 74.00
$100 deductible collision insurance	—	—	—	—	102.00	141.00	168.00
Property damage and liability insurance‡	59.71	86.65	109.76	126.00	154.00	189.00	241.00
License and registration	15.47	16.83	22.40	24.00	24.00	30.00	90.00
Depreciation	442.05	477.36	646.00	626.00	729.08	773.00	42.00
Finance charge	—	—	—	—	—	—	296.00
Total	$533.02	$598.65	$808.54	$807.00	$1,053.00	$1,186.00	$1,811.00
Total variable and fixed cost							
At 10,000 mi/yr	$ 861.02	$ 952.65	$1,198.54	$1,177.00	$1,448.00	$1,831.00	$2,397.00
At 20,000 mi/yr	1,189.02	1,306,65	1,588.54	1,547.00	1,843.00	2,636.00§	3,188.00§
Cost per mile (cents)							
At 10,000 mi/yr	8.61	9.53	11.99	11.77	14.48	18.31	23.97
At 20,000 mi/yr	5.95	6.53	7.94	7.74	9.22	13.18	15.94

*Cars specified: 1950 and 1955, "car in $2000 price class"; 1960 and 1965, Chevrolet, 8-cylinder, Bel-Air 4-door sedan; 1970, Chevrolet, 8-cylinder, Impala 4-door hardtop; 1975 and 1979, Chevelle, 8-cylinder, Malibu Classic 4-door hardtop.
†$50 deductible in 1975; $100 deductible in 1979.
‡Property damage and liability insurance coverage: 1950 and 1955, $15,000/$30,000; 1960 and 1965, $25,000/$50,000; 1970 to date, $100,000/$300,000.
§For mileage in excess of 15,000, an additional depreciation allowance of $32.00 per thousand in 1975, and $41.00 per thousand in 1979.

SOURCE: AMERICAN AUTOMOBILE ASSOCIATION, *Your Driving Costs,* various issues.

TABLE 6–18
Gross National Product and Vehicle Travel, Selected Countries*

	Gross National Product (× 10⁹)	Vehicle-Kilometers (× 10⁶)†			
		Total	Cars	Buses	Trucks
Belgium	$ 53	38,343	33,510	403	4,430
France	304	229,600	192,000	1,600	36,000
Greece	17	13,296	7,030	1,011	5,228
Hong Kong	6	3,093	2,047	512	534
Hungary	25	13,047	8,208	789	4,050
Israel	12	8,820	5,345	408	3,067
Italy	160	184,558	158,670	1,680	24,208
Ivory Coast	3	4,571	1,897	357	2,317
Netherlands	68	55,675	51,700	525	3,450
Nigeria	26	17,355	10,851	4,591	1,913
Norway	23	14,730	12,600	270	1,860
Poland	85	26,423	9,700	3,123	13,600
Sierra Leone	0.5	828	389	106	333
Spain	74	55,524	40,311	1,041	14,172
United Kingdom	200	236,290	192,480	3,540	40,270

*Data for 1975.
†1.609 km = 1 mi.

SOURCE: INTERNATIONAL ROAD FEDERATION, *World Road Statistics 1973–1977;* U.S. DEPARTMENT OF STATE, *Special Report No. 33,* May 1977.

TABLE 6–19
Motor Vehicle Travel, United States,† (Vehicle-Miles × 10⁹)

	Passenger Cars		All Buses		Trucks and Combinations		All Motor Vehicles*
Year	Miles	Percent	Miles	Percent	Miles	Percent	Miles
1936	208.7	82.7	2.4	1.0	41.1	16.3	252.1
1940	249.6	82.6	2.7	0.9	49.9	16.5	302.2
1945	200.4	80.1	3.8	1.5	45.9	18.4	250.2
1950	363.6	79.4	4.1	0.9	90.6	19.7	458.2
1955	492.6	81.3	4.2	0.7	108.8	18.0	605.6
1960‡	588.1	81.8	4.4	0.6	126.4	17.6	718.8
1965	709.3	79.9	4.7	0.5	173.7	19.6	887.6
1970	890.8	79.5	5.0	0.4	214.7	19.2	1120.7
1975	1028.1	77.3	5.1	0.4	274.5	20.6	1330.1
1976	1075.8	76.2	5.8	0.4	308.0	21.8	1411.9
1977	1118.6	75.8	5.9	0.4	329.5	22.3	1476.6
1978	1171.1	75.6	6.1	0.4	347.9	22.5	1548.2

*Includes motorcycles 1970 to date.
†1 mi = 1.609 km.
‡Alaska and Hawaii included for first time in 1960.

SOURCE: U.S. FEDERAL HIGHWAY ADMINISTRATION, *Highway Statistics Summary to 1975,* and *Highway Statistics,* annual.

in urban places with population of 5000 or more—accounted for 55% of total highway travel in 1978, somewhat more than the 48% urban travel recorded in 1950. A partial reason for this relative increase in urban travel is that places defined as rural in 1950 had become urbanized by 1978. The pattern of growth of urban and rural travel is shown in Tables 6-21 and 6-22.

Average annual mileage per U.S. passenger car grew from 9020 mi in 1950 to 10,046 mi in 1978, an increase of 11%. The average mileage traveled by all vehicles grew from 9369 in 1950 to 10,059 in 1978. Table 6-23 indicates the growth in average miles of travel.

TABLE 6–20
Motor Vehicle Travel, Selected Countries (Vehicle-Kilometers and Vehicle-Miles × 10⁶)

	1975	1970
Australia		
km	103,719	65,890
mi	64,409	40,918
Canada		
km	174,370	136,206
mi	108,283	84,584
France		
km	229,600	169,000
mi	142,582	104,949
Germany, West		
km	293,846	267,721
mi	182,478	166,254
Italy		
km	184,558	146,423
mi	114,704	90,928
Japan		
km	286,342	193,608
mi	177,818	120,230
United Kingdom		
km	236,310	202,874
mi	146,749	125,985
United States		
km	2,139,970	1,804,669
mi	1,330,100	1,120,700

SOURCE: INTERNATIONAL ROAD FEDERATION, *World Road Statistics*.

Mode of domestic passenger travel—United States

The dominance of the highway vehicle in U.S. passenger transportation is indicated in Table 6-24. In 1969–1970, the private automobile and truck accounted for 92% of all person trips, school buses better than 4%, mass transit (including buses other than school buses) over 3%, and all other modes less than 1%. It will be noted from the table that while the private motor vehicle is the dominant mode of transportation for all sizes of incorporated and unincorporated areas, mass transit's percent of person trips increases as the population size of the incorporated area increases.

The average U.S. passenger car trip in 1969–1970 measured 8.9 mi one-way and carried 1.9 occupants per car. More than 36% of the passenger car trips were related to earning a living; 31% involved family business; 9% for educational, civil or religious activities; and 22% for social and recreational activities. Table 6-25 indicates average trip length and average occupancy by type of trip.

As indicated in Table 6-26, transit use in the United States, as measured by total revenue passengers, has increased each year since 1972, when it reached a low of 6.6 billion passengers, after declining steadily from the 1946 high of 23.2 billion riders. Preliminary data for 1978 show annual transit ridership at 7.6 billion passengers, 1 billion more than 1972. Events of the 1970s such as federal aid, environmental concerns, congestion, fuel shortages, and the opening of new systems and modernization of other transit systems have contributed to the turnaround.

Intercity passenger travel in the United States exceeded 1.5 trillion passenger miles in 1978, an increase of over 200% since 1950. Each year since 1950, passenger cars have accounted for nearly 85% of the total. The airways share of intercity travel has grown from 2% of the total in 1950 to an estimated 13% in 1978. The major portion of the airway traffic increase resulted from the very substantial

TABLE 6–21
Rural Motor Vehicle Travel, United States* (Vehicle-Miles × 10⁶)

		Motor Buses			Trucks			
Year	Passenger Cars	Commercial	School and Nonrevenue	All Buses	Single-Unit	Combinations	Total Trucks	All Motor Vehicles
1930	—	—	—	—	—	—	—	95,118
1935	—	—	—	—	—	—	—	110,241
1940	120,540	808	640	1448	—	—	30,207	152,195
1945	90,926	1328	577	1905	—	—	27,181	120,012
1950	181,095	1394	729	2123	—	—	56,780	239,998
1955	259,039	1290	1116	2406	—	—	69,096	330,541
1960†	303,283	1023	1232	2255	—	—	81,722	387,260
1965	333,412	1126	1445	2571	80,948	21,841	102,789	438,772
1970	406,449	1133	1686	2819	105,620	28,444	134,064	543,332
1971	428,943	1118	1783	2901	111,387	30,083	141,470	573,314
1972	435,957	1103	1884	2987	118,155	33,128	151,283	590,227
1973	444,264	1003	1915	2918	120,056	33,937	153,993	601,175
1974	427,309	1055	1930	2985	107,231	45,949	153,180	583,474
1975	440,898	1008	1950	2958	111,122	45,653	156,775	600,631
1976	461,501	1178	1979	3157	115,223	47,850	163,073	627,731
1977	475,263	1177	2041	3218	124,680	51,435	176,115	654,596
1978	500,656	1161	2066	3227	131,507	54,563	186,070	689,953

*1 mi = 1.609 km.
†The 1960 data include Alaska and Hawaii for the first time.

SOURCE: U.S. FEDERAL HIGHWAY ADMINISTRATION, *Highway Statistics Summary to 1975*, and *Highway Statistics*, annual.

TABLE 6–22
Urban Motor Vehicle Travel, United States* (Vehicle-Miles × 10^6)

Year	Passenger Cars	Motor Buses: Commercial	Motor Buses: School and Nonrevenue	Motor Buses: All Buses	Trucks: Single-Unit	Trucks: Combinations	Trucks: Total Trucks	All Motor Vehicles
1930	—	—	—	—	—	—	—	111,202
1935	—	—	—	—	—	—	—	118,327
1940	129,060	1136	73	1209	—	—	19,724	149,993
1945	109,472	1864	65	1929	—	—	18,760	130,161
1950	182,518	1877	81	1958	—	—	33,772	218,248
1955	233,596	1632	156	1788	—	—	39,721	275,105
1960†	284,800	1849	249	2098	—	—	44,687	331,585
1965	378,182	1893	318	2211	59,169	9478	68,647	449,040
1970	494,543	1810	414	2224	68,823	11,783	80,606	577,373
1971	525,212	1767	429	2196	73,009	12,558	85,567	612,975
1972	567,541	1647	475	2122	94,967	13,485	108,452	678,115
1973	592,191	1545	497	2042	99,072	14,082	113,154	707,387
1974	585,759	1555	520	2075	104,229	10,110	114,339	702,173
1975	609,574	1640	550	2190	107,772	9907	117,679	729,443
1976	636,678	1721	883	2604	133,572	11,305	144,877	784,159
1977	665,952	1760	909	2669	141,320	12,030	153,350	821,971
1978	693,575	1924	925	2849	149,071	12,765	161,836	858,260

*1 mi = 1.609 km.
†The 1960 data include Alaska and Hawaii for the first time.

SOURCE: U.S. FEDERAL HIGHWAY ADMINISTRATION, *Highway Statistics Summary to 1975*, and *Highway Statistics*, annual.

TABLE 6–23
Average Annual Mileage per Vehicle, United States, 1936–1978*

Year	Passenger Cars	Buses	Trucks	All Motor Vehicles
1936	8,622	19,089	10,098	8,879
1940	9,080	18,580	10,626	9,347
1945	7,771	23,521	9,270	8,094
1950	9,020	20,910	10,776	9,369
1955	9,359	17,658	10,697	9,615
1960	9,446	16,004	10,583	9,652
1965	9,387	15,215	11,587	9,677
1970	9,978	13,306	11,450	10,076
1975	9,634	11,140	10,648	9,644
1976	9,763	12,044	11,086	9,844
1977	9,839	11,973	11,145	9,926
1978	10,046	12,143	10,974	10,059

*1 mi = 1.609 km.

SOURCE: U.S. FEDERAL HIGHWAY ADMINISTRATION, *Highway Statistics Summary to 1975*, and *Highway Statistics*, annual.

decline in rail travel. Rail accounted for 6.4% of total intercity passenger miles in 1950 and 0.7% in 1978. Table 6-27 indicates the trend in U.S. intercity passenger travel by mode.

Mode of domestic freight shipments—United States

Expenditures for freight movement in the United States exceeded $190 billion in 1978, more than four times the $47 billion spent in 1960. The highway portion has increased from 67% in 1960 to 77% in 1978. Table 6-28 indicates annual freight expenditures by mode of transport. Between 1950 and 1978, the volume of intercity freight in the United States increased from 1063 billion ton-miles to 2458 billion. While the volume of freight moved by each mode increased,

TABLE 6–24
Person-Trips and Person-Miles by Mode, United States*

	Person-Trips (%): Passenger Cars or Trucks†	Person-Trips (%): Mass Transit Other Than School Bus	Person-Trips (%): School Bus	Person-Trips (%): All Other‡	Person-Trips (%): Total	Person-Miles (%): Passenger Cars or Trucks†	Person-Miles (%): Mass Transit Other Than School Bus	Person-Miles (%): School Bus	Person-Miles (%): All Other‡	Person-Miles (%): Total
Unincorporated	90.9	0.8	7.9	0.4	100	93.2	1.8	4.5	0.5	100
Incorporated										
Under 5000	94.6	0.7	4.2	0.4	100	93.3	2.5	2.7	1.5	100
5000–24,999	95.7	1.3	2.7	0.3	100	90.3	3.4	1.6	4.7	100
25,000–49,999	94.1	2.4	3.1	0.4	100	91.3	4.2	2.3	2.2	100
50,000–99,999	94.7	3.4	1.6	0.2	100	94.5	2.6	0.4	2.4	100
100,000–999,999	92.5	6.0	1.0	0.6	100	87.1	5.0	0.6	7.2	100
1,000,000 and up	73.8	23.9	1.7	0.6	100	78.5	17.7	1.0	2.8	100
All places	92.0	3.2	4.4	0.4	100	90.8	3.9	2.6	2.7	100

*Data for 1969–1970.
†Includes taxi passengers.
‡Includes travel by air, motorcycle, other.

SOURCE: Based on unpublished data from the 1969 Nationwide Personal Transportation Study, U.S. Department of Transportation, adjusted to 1969 highway vehicle miles of travel.

TABLE 6–25
Passenger Car Use by Purpose, United States*

Purpose of Travel	Percentage Distribution: Trips	Percentage Distribution: Travel	Average Trip Length One-Way (mi)	Average Occupants per Car
Earning a living				
To and from work	31.9	33.7	9.4	1.4
Business related to work	4.3	7.9	16.1	1.6
Total	36.2	41.6	10.2	1.4
Family business				
Medical and dental	1.8	1.6	8.4	2.1
Shopping	15.2	7.5	4.4	2.0
Other	14.0	10.2	6.5	1.9
Total	31.0	19.3	5.6	2.0
Educational, civic, or religious	9.3	4.9	4.7	2.5
Social and recreational				
Vacations	0.1	2.5	160.0	3.4
Visit friends or relatives	8.9	12.1	12.0	2.2
Pleasure rides	1.4	3.1	20.0	2.7
Other	12.0	15.3	11.4	2.6
Total	22.4	33.0	13.1	2.5
All purposes	100.0	100.0	8.9	1.9

*Data for 1969–1970.

SOURCE: U.S. FEDERAL HIGHWAY ADMINISTRATION, *Nationwide Personal Study* (1969). Report Nos. 1 and 7.

the percentage distribution between modes shifted. The rail portion of shipments declined from 56% in 1950 to 36% in 1978. Motor truck's share increased from 16% to 25% and pipelines increased from 12% to 24%. Figure 6.6 shows the volume growth trend for each mode.

TABLE 6–26
Transit Travel Trends, United States, 1940–1978

Calendar Year	Revenue Vehicles	Vehicle Miles Operated ($\times 10^6$)	Passengers ($\times 10^6$)
1940	75,464	2,596.0	13,098
1945	89,758	3,253.8	23,254
1950	86,310	3,007.6	17,246
1955	73,089	2,447.5	11,529
1960	65,292	2,142.8	9,395
1965	61,717	2,008.2	8,253
1970	61,350	1,883.1	7,332
1972	60,704	1,755.6	6,567
1975	62,226	1,989.7	6,972
1976	63,787	2,026.3	7,081
1977	63,287	2,021.3	7,286
1978*	64,013	2,028.3	7,616

*Preliminary.

SOURCE: AMERICAN PUBLIC TRANSIT ASSOCIATION, *Transit Fact Book*, 1978–1979.

Road and street mileage

Road and street mileage is partly a function of land area, land use, and population density. Table 6-29 provides data for selected countries. In the United States, road and street mileage in 1978 totaled 3.885 million miles, which was 23% more than the 3.160 million miles in existence in 1921 and 17% more than the total mileage of 1950. Vehicle miles of travel on U.S. roads and streets during the period 1921–1978 increased 28-fold, from 55 billion in 1921, to 1548 billion in 1978. Both improved design and construction

TABLE 6–27
Intercity Passenger Travel by Mode, United States

	Automobiles*	Motor Coaches*	Total Motor Vehicles*	Railways, Revenue Passengers	Inland Waterways†	Airways, Domestic Revenue Services	Total
			Passenger-miles by mode ($\times 10^9$)				
1950	438.3	26.4	464.7	32.5	1.2	10.1	508.5
1955	637.4	25.5	662.9	28.7	1.7	22.7	716.0
1960	706.1	19.9	726.0	21.6	2.7	34.0	784.3
1965	817.6	23.8	841.4	17.6	3.1	58.1	920.2
1970	1026.0	25.3	1051.3	10.9	4.0	118.6	1184.8
1975	1123.0	25.4	1148.4	10.1	4.0	148.0	1310.5
1976	1187.0	25.1	1212.1	10.2	4.0	163.9	1390.2
1977	1240.6	25.9	1266.5	10.4	n.a.	176.3	1453.2
1978‡	1297.7	25.1	1322.8	10.3	n.a.	204.3	1537.4
			Passenger-miles by mode (%)				
1950	86.19	5.20	91.39	6.39	0.23	1.99	100
1955	89.02	3.56	92.58	4.01	0.24	3.17	100
1960	90.03	2.54	92.57	2.75	0.34	4.34	100
1965	89.33	2.48	91.81	1.83	0.32	6.04	100
1970	86.59	2.13	88.73	0.91	0.33	10.01	100
1975	85.80	1.90	87.70	0.80	0.30	11.20	100
1976	85.40	1.80	87.20	0.70	0.30	11.80	100
1977	85.40	1.80	87.00	0.70	n.a.	12.10	100
1978‡	84.40	1.60	86.00	0.70	n.a.	13.30	100

*Includes intracity portions of intercity trips, strictly intracity trips with both origin and destination confined to same city, local bus or transit movement, and nonrevenue school and government bus operations.
†n.a., not available.
‡Preliminary.

SOURCE: ICC and TRANSPORTATION ASSOCIATION OF AMERICA.

TABLE 6–28
Freight Transportation Expenditures, United States

	Freight Expenditures (× 10^6)						
	1960	1965	1970	1975	1976	1977	1978
Highway freight expenditures							
Truck intercity							
ICC-regulated	$ 7,214	$10,068	$14,585	$ 22,000	$ 26,000	$ 31,000	$ 36,500
Non-ICC-regulated	10,744	13,560	18,968	25,400	30,245	36,356	43,069
Truck local	13,498	20,120	28,819	47,790	54,531	60,739	67,630
Bus	42	70	122	156	180	179	205
Total	$31,498	$43,818	$62,494	$ 95,346	$110,956	$128,274	$147,404
Air	$ 354	$ 708	$ 1,171	$ 1,838	$ 2,052	$ 2,357	2,654
Oil pipeline	895	1,051	1,396	2,220	2,532	3,209	5,452
Rail	9,028	9,923	11,869	16,509	18,648	19,557	20,993
Water	3,338	3,758	5,109	7,888	8,860	10,474	11,458*
Other	1,714	1,869	1,791	2,208	2,468	2,648	2,735*
Total all freight	$46,827	$61,127	$83,830	$126,009	$145,516	$166,518	$190,796*

*Preliminary.

Source: Transportation Association of America, *Transp. Facts Trends,* July 1978, and *Quart. Supple.*, Oct. 1979.

in many cases have accommodated the increased traffic volume.

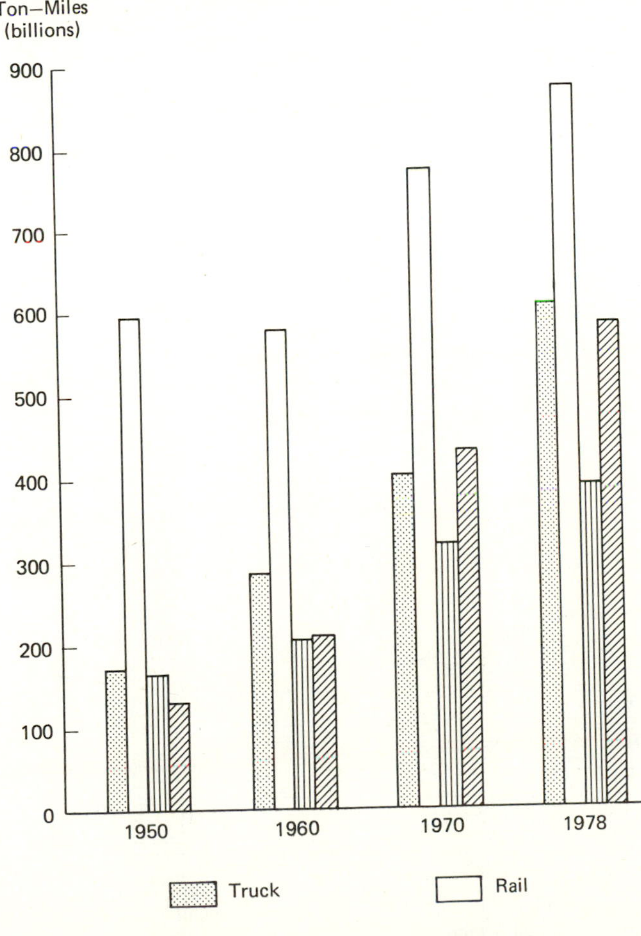

Figure 6.6. Intercity freight ton-mileage by mode—U.S. Source: Interstate Commerce Commission, American Trucking Associations, and Transportation Association of America.

TABLE 6–29
Road Mileage, Land Area, and Population Density, Selected Countries*

	System Length		Land Area		Population Density	
	mi (× 10^6)	km (× 10^6)	mi² (× 10^6)	km² (× 10^6)	Per mi²	Per km²
Belgium	71.4	114.8	11.8	30.5	832	322
France	494.6	795.8	211.2	547.0	251	97
Germany, West	291.8	469.6	96.0	248.6	641	247
Greece	22.7	36.6	50.9	131.9	180	69
Hong Kong	.7	1.1	.4	1.0	11,110	4444
Hungary	61.9	99.6	35.9	93.0	295	114
Israel	2.7	4.4	8.0	20.8	442	170
Italy	181.4	291.9	116.3	301.2	483	186
Ivory Coast	28.1	45.2	124.5	322.5	55	21
Netherlands	53.7	86.4	15.8	40.8	872	338
Nigeria	64.3	103.4	356.7	923.8	182	70
Norway	48.5	78.1	125.2	324.2	32	12
Poland	187.0	300.8	120.7	312.7	285	110
Sierra Leone	4.4	7.1	27.7	71.7	113	43
Spain	90.3	145.3	194.9	504.8	185	71
United Kingdom	214.8	345.5	88.7	229.8	630	243
United States	3,857.4	6,211.6	3,615.2	9,363.4	60	23

*Data for 1976.

Source: International Road Federation, *World Road Statistics, 1973–1977;* U.S. Bureau of the Census, *Statistical Abstract of the United States, 1977.*

In 1921, only 14% of U.S. road and street mileage was surfaced. In 1978, 82%—more than 3.2 million miles—was surfaced. "Surfaced" is defined as including all types of roads from soil-surfaced through bituminous and portland cement concrete. Table 6-30 and Figure 6.7 indicate the growth in total surfaced road mileage. In 1978 of the 3.203 million miles of roads and streets classified as surfaced, nearly 40%, 1.2 million miles, were soil, slag, gravel, or stone. Table 6-31 indicates that most of this was rural mileage under local control.

Road design and operational techniques have changed in the United States to permit increased traffic flow and to accommodate larger traffic volumes. One method of increasing traffic flow is to increase the number of traffic lanes. In 1956, the U.S. surfaced State Primary Road System of 420,041 mi had only 10,146 mi, 2.4%, of divided highways of four or more lanes. By 1977, this had increased

TABLE 6–30
Road Mileage and Surface Type, United States* (Miles × 10³)

	Nonsurfaced		Surfaced†		
Year	Miles	Percent	Miles	Percent	Total Miles
1904	2147	91	204	9	2351
1909	2165	90	245	10	2410
1914	2352	88	314	12	2666
1921	2713	86	447	14	3160
1925	2620	81	626	19	3246
1930	2405	74	854	26	3259
1935	2055	62	1255	38	3310
1940	1730	53	1557	47	3287
1945	1598	48	1721	52	3319
1950	1374	41	1939	59	3313
1955	1145	33	2273	67	3418
1960	989	28	2557	72	3546
1965	914	25	2776	75	3690
1970	783	21	2948	79	3731
1975	737	19	3101	81	3838
1976	722	19	3135	81	3857
1977	704	18	3163	82	3867
1978	682	18	3203	82	3885

*1 mi = 1.609 km.
†Surfaced includes all types of surfacing, from soil-surfaced through all types of hard surface.

SOURCE: U.S. FEDERAL HIGHWAY ADMINISTRATION, *Highway Statistics Summary to 1975*, and *Highway Statistics*, annual.

to 14.6% of the system's 476,779 mi, or 69,582 mi of divided highways. Mileage of four-lane or more of undivided highways on State Primary Systems had grown to 13,736 mi in 1977 from 7122 mi in 1956. Table 6-32 indicates the trend in traffic lanes of the surfaced mileage of State Primary Highway Systems.

Responsibility for the administration of the U.S. road system is divided among various governmental units. The trend in administrative control is shown in Table 6-33. In 1978, local governments had administrative responsibility for 74% of the U.S. roads and streets, including local city streets which accounted for 16%. State governments were responsible for 20% and the federal government for 6%.

TABLE 6–31
Road Mileage by System and Surface Type, United States, 1978*
(Miles × 10³)

	Nonsurfaced	Gravel, etc.	Paved†	Total Surfaced	Grand Total
Total mileage	682	1192	2011	3203	3885
Percent	17.6	30.7	51.8	82.4	100.0
Rural roads					
State primary	1	6	395	401	402
State secondary	14	27	150	178	192
Other state	14	31	64	95	109
Under state control	29	64	610	674	703
Percent	4.2	9.1	86.7	95.8	100.0
Under local control	495	1014	746	1760	2255
Percent	22.0	45.0	33.1	78.0	100.0
Under federal control	131	50	51	101	232
Percent	56.6	21.5	21.9	43.4	100.0
Total rural mileage	656	1128	1406	2534	3190
Percent	20.6	35.4	44.1	79.4	100.0
Municipal roads					
State primary	‡	‡	67	67	67
State secondary	‡	‡	19	20	20
Under state control	‡	1	86	87	87
Percent	0.3	0.6	99.1	99.7	100.0
Under local control	26	64	518	582	607
Percent	4.2	10.5	85.3	95.8	100.0
Total municipal mileage	26	64	604	668	694
Percent	3.7	9.2	87.0	96.3	100.0

*1 mi = 1.609 km.
†Paved includes all types of hard surfacing from bituminous treated to portland cement.
‡Less than 500 mi, or 0.05%.

SOURCE: U.S. FEDERAL HIGHWAY ADMINISTRATION, *Highway Statistics*, 1978.

Highway finance

Expenditures for U.S. highways by all forms of government in 1978 totaled $31.8 billion, seven times the $4.5 billion spent in 1950. While state highway agencies spent 61% or more than $19 billion in 1978, the proportion of

Figure 6.7. Total road and street mileage in the United States, by surface type (1900–1978). SOURCE: U.S. FEDERAL HIGHWAY ADMINISTRATION.

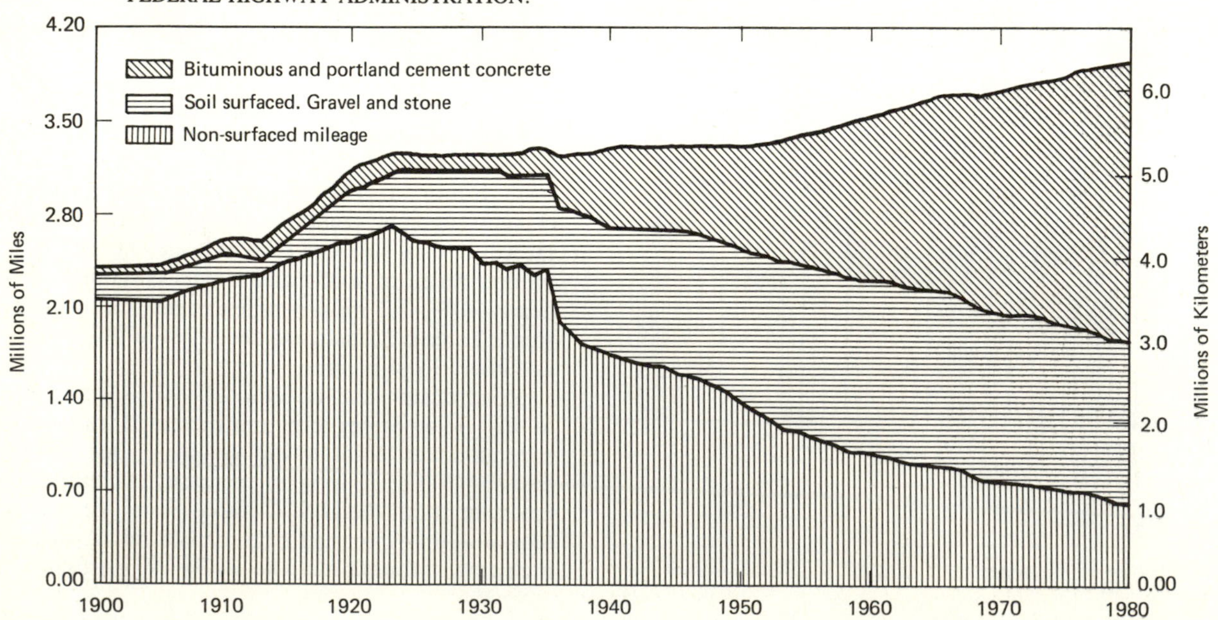

TABLE 6-32
Surfaced Mileage of State Primary Systems, United States

	Undivided				Divided			
					Access Control			Total Surfaced Mileage
Year	2 Lanes	3 Lanes	4 Lanes or More	One-Way Street	None	Partial	Full	
1956	397,480	5110	7122	183	6823	2264	1059	420,041
1960	405,799	4916	9426	343	8640	4767	6101	439,992
1965	408,268	3711	11,430	550	11,911	5644	19,382	460,896
1970	391,919	2945	11,557	442	15,501	6478	33,368	462,210
1975	392,888	1931	13,539	646	18,939	7222	40,182	475,347
1976	390,934	3233	14,156	615	19,209	7311	41,677	477,135
1977	389,711	2971	13,786	729	20,925	6468	42,189	476,779
1978	385,190	3127	13,902	822	19,963	5661	39,204	467,869

SOURCE: U.S. FEDERAL HIGHWAY ADMINISTRATION, *Highway Statistics Summary to 1975*, and *Highway Statistics*, annual.

TABLE 6-33
Road Mileage Trends by Administrative Control, United States, 1921–1978*

		Local Control			
Year	State Control	County, Town, and Township	Local City Streets	Federal Control	Total
1921	203	2722	235	†	3160
1925	275	2731	240	†	3246
1930	324	2685	250	†	3259
1935	523	2527	260	†	3310
1940	551	2396	270	70	3287
1945	576	2398	274	71	3319
1950	616	2337	287	73	3313
1955	661	2333	331	93	3418
1960	709	2346	379	112	3546
1965	751	2346	442	150	3690
1970	781	2275	486	188	3730
1975	795	2261	555	227	3838
1976	798	2264	561	234	3857
1977	789	2236	600	242	3867
1978	792	2256	608	231	3885

*1 mi = 1.609 km.
†Included with county, town, and township roads.

SOURCE: U.S. FEDERAL HIGHWAY ADMINISTRATION, *Highway Statistics Summary to 1975*, and *Highway Statistics*, annual.

total highway expenditures was down from their nearly 68% share in 1970. Local municipalities were responsible for spending $6.5 billion or 20%, while counties and townships spent $5 billion, or 16%.

The U.S. government is a major distributor of highway funds, but historically it has been directly responsible for spending only a small portion of those funds, 2.5% in 1978. Highway disbursements by expending agencies for selected years 1921–1978 are shown in Table 6-34.

Capital outlays accounted for more than 44%, or $14 billion, in 1978. Expenditures on highway maintenance approached $9 billion, or 28%. Administrative and miscellaneous expenditures, which represented about 7% in 1950, totaled 18% or $5.6 billion in 1978, while debt service added another $3 billion. Figure 6.8 illustrates the growth in expenditures since 1921. Total monies for both capital outlays and maintenance expenditures, measured in current

TABLE 6-34
Highway Expenditures by Agency, United States, 1921–1978 (× 10^6)

Year	Federal Government	State Agencies and D.C.	Counties and Townships	Municipalities	Total
1921	$ 6	$ 406	$ 636	$ 337	$ 1,385
1925	11	631	618	591	1,851
1930	14	891	751	779	2,435
1935	258	830	502	408	1,998
1940	549	1,115	535	489	2,688
1945	26	779	515	376	1,696
1950	72	2,564	970	865	4,471
1955	97	4,670	1324	1264	7,355
1960	202	7,125	1636	1799	10,762
1965	246	9,814	2065	2186	14,311
1970	431	14,100	2864	3440	20,835
1975	629	18,190	4409	5471	28,699
1976	733	18,222	4808	6015	29,778
1977	751	18,019	4875	6140	29,785
1978	807	20,170	5063	6470	32,510

SOURCE: U.S. FEDERAL HIGHWAY ADMINISTRATION, *Highway Statistics Summary to 1975*, and *Highway Statistics*, annual.

Figure 6.8. Total disbursements for highways, by function (1921–1978). SOURCE: U.S. FEDERAL HIGHWAY ADMINISTRATION.

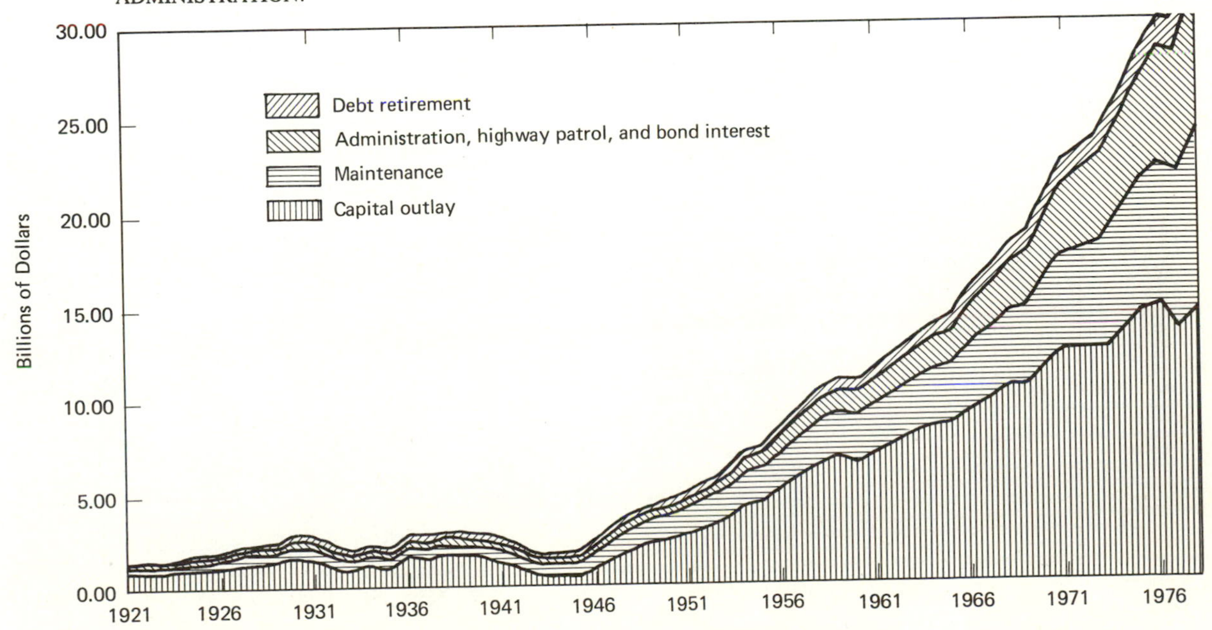

dollars, have increased greatly from amounts spent in the mid-1950s. However, when measured in terms of constant dollars per vehicle mile, they have declined. Tables 6-35 and 6-36 show this historic trend.

The relative importance of various sources of funds, both in terms of the collecting agency and the method of taxation, has shifted significantly over the years. In 1978, motor fuel and vehicle taxes provided 60%, or more than $20 billion of highway revenues, with property taxes and general fund appropriations contributing an additional nearly $7 billion, or 22%, of the more than $34 billion total. In 1921, property taxes contributed 62%, with bond issued proceeds adding an additional 25%, and motor fuel and vehicle taxes contributing 9%. Table 6-37 and Figure 6.9 indicate the shift in revenue sources. The primary source of these revenues historically has been property taxes at the urban and county level and motor fuel and vehicle taxes at the state level. The federal source is also motor fuel and vehicle taxes, which took a major jump upward in 1956 with the creation of the Highway Trust Fund.

State, county, and urban governments were the principal collecting agencies for highway revenues in 1921. States collected 25% of revenues, counties 45%, and urban government an additional 24%. In 1978, state governments were the principal collecting agencies accounting for 51% of revenues, followed by the U.S. government with 28%, and urban governments with 14%.

Table 6-38 illustrates the relative shift in collecting agencies. Table 6-39 provides highway expenditures in selected countries on a per capita basis. Expenditures in total and on a per capita basis have increased in each country since 1970.

TABLE 6–35
Highway Construction Costs, United States, 1922–1978

Year	Actual Capital Outlay (× 10^6)	Highway Construction Cost Index (1967 = 100)	Capital Outlay in 1967 Prices (× 10^6)	Outlay* (cents/vehicle-mile)
1922	$ 836	53.8	$1,554	2.28
1925	1,039	54.6	1,903	1.56
1930	1,522	43.6	3,491	1.69
1935	920	40.9	2,249	0.98
1940	1,450	36.4	3,984	1.32
1945	373	55.4	673	0.27
1950	2,297	66.6	3,449	0.75
1955	4,334	74.3	5,833	0.96
1960	6,290	80.1	7,853	1.09
1965	8,368	90.3	9,267	1.04
1967	9,661	100.0	9,661	1.00
1970	11,575	125.6	9,216	0.82
1975	14,398	203.8	7,065	0.53
1976	13,927	199.3	6,988	0.49
1977	13,117	216.4	6,061	0.41
1978	14,117	264.9	5,329	0.35

*Constant 1967 dollars.

SOURCE: MVMA calculations from U.S. Federal Highway Administration data in Tables HF-211, PT-201, HF-12, and PT-1.

TABLE 6–36
Highway Maintenance Costs, United States, 1935–1978 (× 10^6)

Year	Actual Maintenance Outlays (× 10^6)	Highway Maintenance and Operations Cost Index (1967 = 100)	Maintenance Outlays in 1967 Prices (× 10^6)	Outlays* (cents/vehicle-mile)
1935	$ 540	25.37	$2129	0.93
1940	610	27.43	2224	0.74
1945	796	37.42	2127	0.85
1950	1423	51.31	2773	0.61
1955	1881	64.09	2935	0.48
1960	2640	78.35	3370	0.47
1965	3289	89.66	3668	0.41
1967	3772	100.00	3772	0.39
1970	4720	116.78	4042	0.36
1975	7286	172.97	4212	0.32
1976	7735	188.08	4113	0.29
1977	8459	202.92	4168	0.28
1978†	8989	218.80	4108	0.27

*Constant 1967 dollars.
†Preliminary.

SOURCE: MVMA calculations from U.S. Federal Highway Administration data in Tables HF-211, PT-205, HF-12, and PT-5.

Figure 6.9. Total receipts for highways, by governmental units (1921–1978). SOURCE: U.S. FEDERAL HIGHWAY ADMINISTRATION.

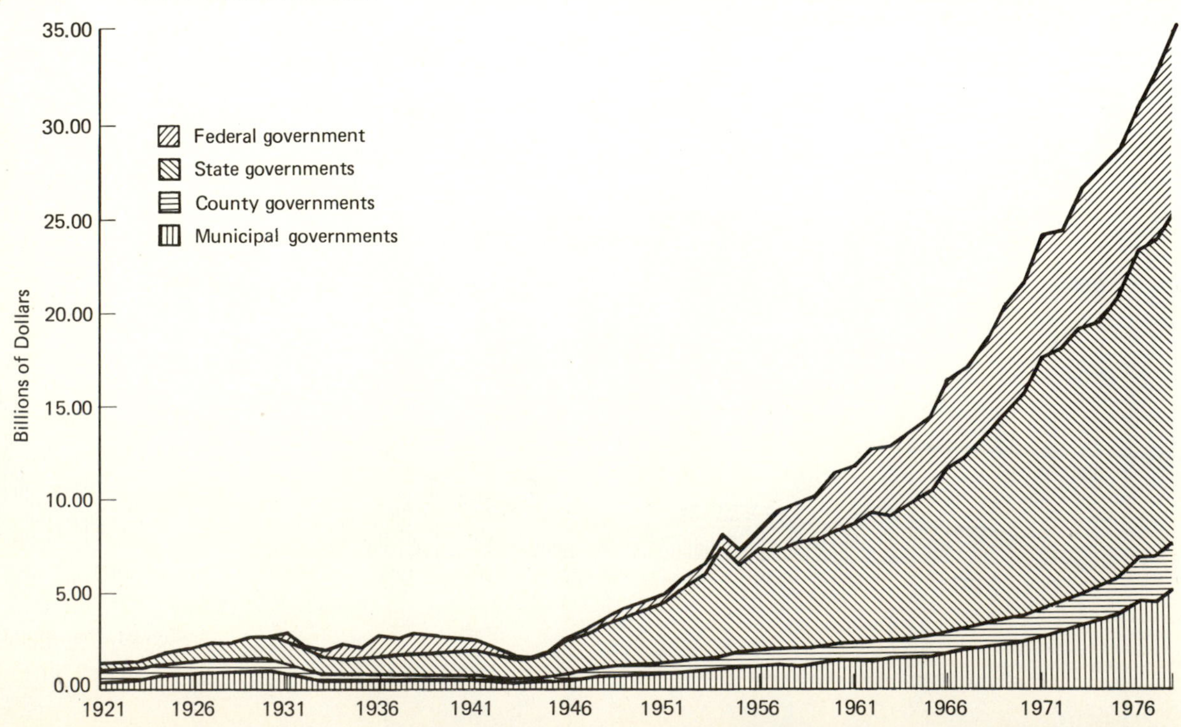

TABLE 6–37
Highway Receipts, United States, 1921–1978* (× 10^6)

	Federal		State		County		Urban		
Year	Receipts	Percent	Receipts	Percent	Receipts	Percent	Receipts	Percent	Total
1921	$ 92	6.5	$ 346	24.5	$ 636	45.1	$ 337	23.9	$ 1,411
1925	103	5.2	589	30.0	581	29.6	691	35.2	1,964
1930	112	4.1	1079	39.4	645	23.6	899	32.9	2,735
1935	480	23.3	909	44.0	322	15.6	352	17.1	2,063
1940	752	27.6	1250	46.0	307	11.3	410	15.1	2,719
1945	93	4.8	1212	62.9	286	14.8	338	17.5	1,929
1950	500	10.8	2,835	61.5	537	11.7	735	16.0	4,607
1955	791	10.8	4,587	62.4	810	11.0	1157	15.8	7,345
1960	3063	26.7	6,055	52.7	848	7.4	1519	13.2	11,485
1965	4079	28.2	7,623	52.8	1067	7.4	1669	11.6	14,438
1970	6144	28.2	11,737	54.0	1460	6.7	2406	11.1	21,747
1975	7676	26.3	15,105	51.8	2270	7.8	4109	14.1	29,160
1976	8038	26.1	16,126	52.3	2400	7.8	4267	13.8	30,831
1977	9198	28.0	16,644	50.7	2560	7.8	4425	13.5	32,827
1978	9692	27.6	17,755	50.6	2721	7.8	4913	14.0	35,081

*Includes borrowing, but excludes amounts allocated for collection expenses and nonhighway purposes.

SOURCE: U.S. FEDERAL HIGHWAY ADMINISTRATION, *Highway Statistics Summary to 1975*, and *Highway Statistics*, annual.

TABLE 6–38
Highway Receipts, United States, 1921–1978 (× 10^6)

	Motor Fuel and Vehicle Taxes		Tolls and Parking Fees		Property Taxes and General Fund Appropriations*		Bond Issue Proceeds		Miscellaneous Receipts†		
Year	Amount	Percent	Amount	Percent	Amount	Percent	Amount	Percent	Amount	Percent	Total
1921	$ 125	8.9	$ —	—	$ 872	61.8	$ 353	25.0	$ 61	4.3	$ 1,411
1925	387	19.7	—	—	1157	58.9	380	19.4	40	2.0	1,964
1930	811	29.7	12	0.4	1477	54.0	387	14.1	48	1.8	2,735
1935	766	37.1	17	0.8	1086	52.7	171	8.3	23	1.1	2,063
1940	1,092	40.1	43	1.6	1334	49.1	212	7.8	38	1.4	2,719
1945	1,106	57.3	56	2.9	657	34.1	57	3.0	53	2.7	1,929
1950	2,300	49.9	132	2.9	1397	30.3	655	14.2	122	2.7	4,606
1955	3,643	49.6	291	4.0	2004	27.3	1185	16.1	222	3.0	7,345
1960	7,634	66.5	572	5.0	1714	14.9	1219	10.6	346	3.0	11,486
1965	9,938	68.8	752	5.2	2150	14.9	1070	7.4	528	3.7	14,438
1970	14,294	65.7	1017	4.7	3490	16.0	1886	8.7	1060	4.9	21,747
1975	17,220	59.1	1358	4.6	6224	21.3	2239	7.7	2119	7.3	29,160
1976	18,397	59.7	1414	4.6	6621	21.5	2221	7.2	2178	7.0	30,831
1977	19,832	60.4	1474	4.5	7125	21.7	2003	6.1	2392	7.3	32,827
1978	20,761	59.2	1570	4.5	7811	22.3	2042	5.8	2897	8.3	35,081

*Prior to the Highway Trust Fund, all federal receipts were classified as general fund contributions. Excludes amounts allocated for collection expenses and nonhighway purposes.
†Includes investment income, miscellaneous taxes, and other receipts.

SOURCE: U.S. FEDERAL HIGHWAY ADMINISTRATION, *Highway Statistics Summary to 1975*, and *Highway Statistics*, annual.

TABLE 6–39
Annual Highway Expenditures, Selected Countries

	Highway Expenditures			
	Total (× 10^6)		Per Capita	
	1968	1976	1968	1976
Canada	$ 1,800*	$ 2,593†	$ 86*	$119†
France	1,980	4,792‡	40	92‡
Germany, West	2,910	6,695	50	109
Sweden	584	754	74	91
United Kingdom	1,265	2,360	23	42
United States	22,504§	29,778	109§	137

*1968 data.
†1973 data.
‡1975 data.
§1971 data.

SOURCE: Compiled by the MOTOR VEHICLE MANUFACTURERS ASSOCIATION OF THE UNITED STATES, from various sources.

Part B

VEHICLE OPERATING CHARACTERISTICS

ALEXANDER FRENCH, *Consultant*
Annandale, Virginia

In planning, designing, and developing facilities and procedures for the transportation of people and goods, it is necessary to understand operating capabilities as well as operating practices in customary use of the vehicles. Data on vehicle characteristics related to costs, energy requirements, and the capabilities of other modes are frequently necessary. Knowledge of physical dimensions and of the principles governing capabilities of vehicles is needed for the design of facilities for efficient operation.

Resistance to motion

The forces that must be overcome by motor vehicles if they are to move are rolling, air, grade, curve, and inertial resistance. Grade acts as a retarding force only when vehicles are on upgrades and inertia only when speed increases are involved. When vehicles are being stopped or slowed, all these resistances except downgrades and inertia help braking action. An additional resistance to motion during deceleration in gear is provided by engine compression forces.

Rolling resistance

Rolling resistance results from the frictional slip between tire surfaces and the pavement; flexing of tire rubber at the surfaces of contact; rolling over rough particles (i.e., stones or broken asphalt); climbing out of road depressions; pushing wheels through sand, mud, or snow; and internal friction at wheel, axle, and driveshaft bearings and in the transmission gears. For speeds up to 60 mph (96.5 km/h) the rolling resistance of modern passenger cars on high-type pavement is constant at about 27 lb/ton of weight (13.5 kg/mton).[1] For higher speeds these values increase by 10% for each 10 mph (16 km/h) increase in speed above 60 mph (96.5 km/h). Typical passenger car rolling resistances at low speed on low types of surfaces are given in Table 6-40.

TABLE 6-40
Rolling Resistances of Passenger Cars*

Uniform Speed		Badly Broken and Patched Asphalt		Dry, Well-Packed Gravel		Loose Sand	
mph	km/h	lb/ton	kg/ton	lb/ton	kg/ton	lb/ton	kg/ton
20	32.1	29	14.5	31	15.5	35	17.5
30	48.3	34	17.0	35	17.5	40	20.0
40	64.4	40	20.0	50	25.0	57	28.5
50	80.5	51	25.5	62	31.0	76	38.0

*Low-type road surfaces in poor condition

SOURCE: Computed using 27 lb/ton rolling resistance for high-type pavement and correcting for other pavement types using adjustment factors based on fuel consumption as given in Table 6B, p. 17, *Running Costs of Motor Vehicles as Affected by Road Design and Traffic*, Report 111, National Cooperative Highway Research Program (Washington, D.C.: HIGHWAY RESEARCH BOARD, 1971).

Air resistance

Air resistance is composed of the direct effect of air in the pathway of vehicles, the frictional force of air passing over the surfaces of vehicles (including the undersurface), and the partial vacuum behind the vehicle. For the typical modern car having a projected frontal cross section of 30 ft^2 (2.78 m^2), air resistance varies from zero at 10 mph (16 km/h) to 55 lb (25 kg) at 55 mph (88.5 km/h), approximately in proportion to the square of the velocity.[2] Equation (6.1) gives the air resistance force acting on an automobile:

$$R_a = 0.0006\,AV^2 \text{ (U.S. units)}$$
$$= 0.0011AV^2 \text{ (metric units)} \qquad (6.1)$$

where R_a = air resistance, lb or kg

A = frontal cross-sectional area, ft^2 or m^2

V = speed, mph or km/h

Grade resistance

Grade resistance is the force acting on a vehicle because it is on an incline. It equals the component of the vehicle's weight acting down the grade. Equation (6.2) gives the grade resistance force:

$$R_g = 20\,Wg \text{ (U.S. units)} = 10Wg \text{ (metric units)} \qquad (6.2)$$

where R_g = grade resistance, lb or kg

W = gross vehicle weight, tons or metric tons

g = gradient, %

Curve resistance

Curve resistance is the force acting through the front-wheel contact with the pavement needed to deflect a vehicle along a curvilinear path. This force is a function of speed because the faster an object is moving, the greater the force required to change its direction. Studies have shown the curve resistance of standard or intermediate-type passenger cars operating on high-type asphalt pavement to be as given in Table 6-41.[3]

[1] J. C. KESSLER AND S. B. WALLIS, "Aerodynamic Test Techniques," *SAE Trans.*, *75*, Sec. 3, p. 12 (1967).

[2] Ibid.

[3] PAUL J. CLAFFEY, *Running Costs of Motor Vehicles as Affected by Road Design and Traffic* (Washington, D.C.: Highway Research Board, 1971), p. 17.

TABLE 6-41
Curve Resistances of Passenger Cars*

Curvature		U.S. Units		Metric Units	
Degree	Radius (ft)	Speed (mph)	Resistance (lb)	Speed (km/h)	Resistance (kg)
5	1146	50	40	80.5	18
5	1146	60	80	96.5	36
10	573	30	40	48.3	18
10	573	40	120	64.4	54
10	573	50	240	80.5	108

*High-type road surfaces.

SOURCE: Determined from data on the effect of curvature on fuel consumption as reported in *Running Costs of Motor Vehicles as Affected by Road Design and Traffic*, NCHRP Report 111 (Washington, D.C.: HIGHWAY RESEARCH BOARD, 1971). The resistance forces were developed by evaluating the forces needed to produce the additional fuel consumption recorded for operation on curves.

Inertial resistance

Inertial resistance is the force that must be overcome to change speed. It is a function of vehicle weight (regardless of type of vehicle) and the rate of acceleration or deceleration. It may be computed from the following equation:

$$R_i = 91.1\ WA \text{ (U.S. units)}$$
$$= 28.0\ WA \text{ (metric units)} \qquad (6.3)$$

where R_i = inertial resistance, lb or kg

W = gross vehicle weight, tons or metric tons

A = acceleration rate, mph/s or km/h/s

Power requirements

Horsepower

Horsepower is the time rate of doing work, and the maximum an engine can deliver is a measure of its performance capability. The horsepower actually used by a motor vehicle for propulsion may be determined from Equation (6.4):

$$P = 0.0026\ RV \text{ (U.S. units)}$$
$$= 0.0036\ RV \text{ (metric units)} \qquad (6.4)$$

where P = horsepower actually used

R = sum of resistances to motion, lb or kg

V = speed, mph or km/h

The maximum horsepower output available for propulsion at a given engine speed equals the maximum gross brake horsepower at the flywheel for that engine speed less the horsepower consumption of engine accessories, such as the alternator, automatic transmission, power steering, and air conditioner. For vehicles with typical accessories, maximum horsepower available for propulsion at 60 mph (96.5 km/h) is about 50% of the manufacturer's nominal engine horsepower rating. This relationship may be used to examine maximum acceleration rates and maximum speeds on grades given nominal engine horsepower in relation to engine speed and reliable values of resistances (particularly rolling and air resistance).

TABLE 6-42
Representative Motor Vehicle Weights and Horsepower

Motor Vehicle Category	Empty Weight with Driver Aboard		Nominal Horsepower	Engine Speed for Given Horsepower (rpm)
	lb	kg		
Intermediate-type passenger car	4,000	1,814	195	4,800
Pickup truck	4,500	2,041	125	3,800
Two-axle, six-tire, single-unit truck	10,000	4,535	142	3,800
2S-2*	20,000	9,070	175	3,200

*Two-axle tractor and two-axle semitrailer.

Empty weights and nominal horsepower ratings representative of major categories of motor vehicles are given in Table 6-42.

Weight/horsepower ratio

Weight/horsepower ratios are useful for indicating the overall performance characteristics of vehicles, particularly for making approximate performance comparisons among different vehicle types. The weight/horsepower ratio (the number of pounds or kilograms of gross vehicle weight for each horsepower available for propulsion) is a direct measure of the sluggishness of vehicle operation. Because weight is a rough indicator of resistance to motion, the higher the weight/horsepower ratio, the more sluggish the action of the vehicle. A low weight/horsepower ratio means high performance because it reflects a high ratio of power capability to travel resistance.

It would be inappropriate here to present specific values of truck weight/horsepower ratios by vehicle class. Vehicle weight depends on the weight of the carried load. For the larger trucks and truck combinations, the load can vary from zero to an amount equal to twice the vehicle's weight. Furthermore, the horsepower available for propulsion depends on engine condition and size, transmission arrangement, and engine speed.

The weight/horsepower ratio is important in defining the hill-climbing capability of a vehicle. Table 6-43 provides recent data on actual sustained operating speeds on upgrades for a variety of vehicles. Also shown is the speed below which the slowest 12.5% of vehicles traveled. Based on the frequency of the vehicle types in the traffic streams, this can be used to help estimate the impediments to traffic flow and the proportions of potential passing maneuvers.[4] Additional information on the weight/horsepower ratios as a factor in highway design and vehicle operation can be found in the report of a 1979 study of truck operation on grades,[5] in a 1955 report on climbing-lane design,[6] and in *A Policy on Geometric Design of Rural Highways*.[7]

[4] *Time and Gasoline Consumption in Motor Truck Operation*, Research Report 9-A (Washington, D.C.: Highway Research Board, 1950).

[5] P. Y. CHING AND F. D. ROONEY, *Truck Speeds on Grades in California*, California Department of Transportation, June 1979.

[6] T. S. HUFF AND F. H. SCRIVER, "Simplified Climbing Lane Design Theory and Road-Test Results," *Vehicle Climbing Lanes*, Bull. item 104 (Washington, D.C.: Highway Research Board, 1955).

[7] *A Policy on Geometric Design of Rural Highways* (Washington, D.C.: American Association of State Highway Officials, 1965).

TABLE 6-43
Speeds on Upgrades*

Vehicle Type	Upgrade 1.78% Avg.	1.78% 12.5%	3.0% Avg.	3.0% 12.5%	4.0% Avg.	4.0% 12.5%	5.0% Avg.	5.0% 12.5%	6.0% Avg.	6.0% 12.5%	7.0% Avg.	7.0% 12.5%
Compact sedan												
mph			60	55					57	48		
km/h			96	83					91	77		
Standard sedan												
mph			62	56					60	52		
km/h			100	90					97	84		
Pickup truck												
mph			60	54					58	52		
km/h			96	87					93	84		
Pickup with canopy												
mph			57	52					54	46		
km/h			92	84					87	75		
Pickup with camper												
mph			53	43					47	38		
km/h			86	77					76	62		
Light 4-wheel drive												
mph			58	53								
km/h			94	85								
U.S. van												
mph			59	54					56	51		
km/h			95	86					91	83		
VW van												
mph			54	46								
km/h			86	75								
Vehicle/lt trlr												
mph			53	44								
km/h			85	71								
Vehicle/tr trlr												
mph			51	43					40	30		
km/h			82	70					65	48		
Motor home												
mph			53	46					44	35		
km/h			86	75					70	57		
Intercity bus												
mph			54	46								
km/h			86	73								
Two-axle truck												
mph	54	43	49	40	44	34	40	27	34	23	34	22
km/h	87	78	79	65	71	55	65	44	55	37	54	36
Three-axle truck†												
mph	56	49	48	39	43	31	38	26	33	19	33	23
km/h	90	79	77	62	69	50	62	41	53	31	54	38
Four-axle truck												
mph	55	48	48	34	42	31	38	28	32	21	26	17
km/h	89	77	77	55	67	50	61	45	52	34	42	28
Five-axle truck												
mph	50	42	43	32	38	24	35	23	32	18	30	15
km/h	81	68	70	51	61	39	56	37	52	29	49	24

*Sustained average and low 12.5% speeds observed in California for selected vehicle types on upgrades. Miles per hour reported to 0.01 have been converted to kilometers per hour to 0.01 and all values rounded to the nearest whole number, with the result that direct conversion of values in this table may differ by 1 in a few cases.
†Trucks shown as having three axles or more include both straight trucks and combinations.

SOURCE: P. Y. CHING AND F. D. ROONEY, *Truck Speeds on Grades in California*, California Department of Transportation, June 1979.

Figure 6.10 compares the 1978 and 1969 traffic mix on main rural roads and indicates that the increase in pickup and panel trucks has reduced the percentage of passenger cars and that the 3S2 combination (three-axle tractor and two-axle semitrailer) has become the predominant cargo hauler.

Figure 6.11 shows 1977 and 1969 comparisons of axle and gross weights of loaded trucks. In applying the data in Table 6-42 to other locations it is important to use a traffic mix by vehicle types that is representative of the area being analyzed.

Acceleration performance

Information on vehicle acceleration capabilities is needed for evaluation of minimum sight-distance requirements for passing and for determination of minimum lengths of acceleration lanes at interchanges. Normal roadway acceleration rates are a factor in designing cycle lengths of traffic signals, in computing fuel economy and travel-time values, and in estimating how normal traffic movement is resumed after a breakdown in traffic flow patterns.

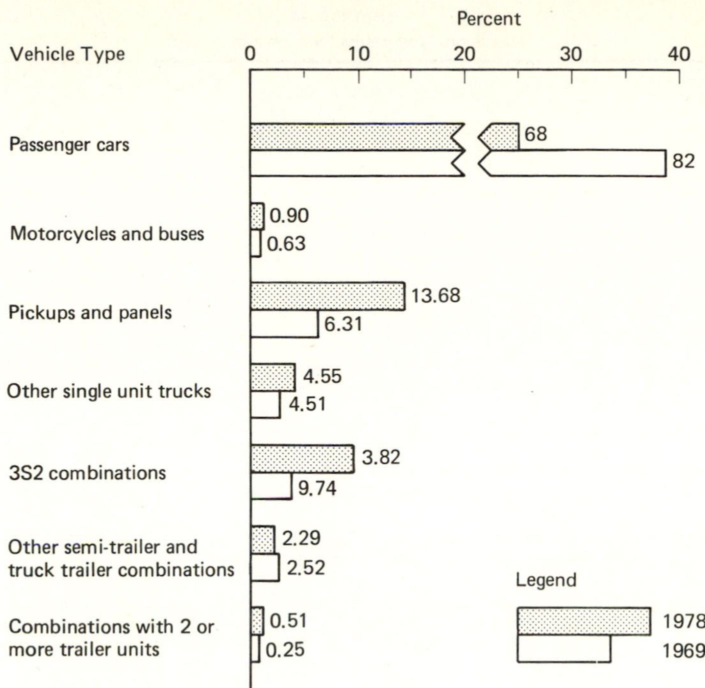

Figure 6.10. Change in traffic composition on main rural roads (1969–1978). SOURCE: U.S. DEPARTMENT OF TRANSPORTATION, FHWA, Highway Statistics Division, Washington, D.C.

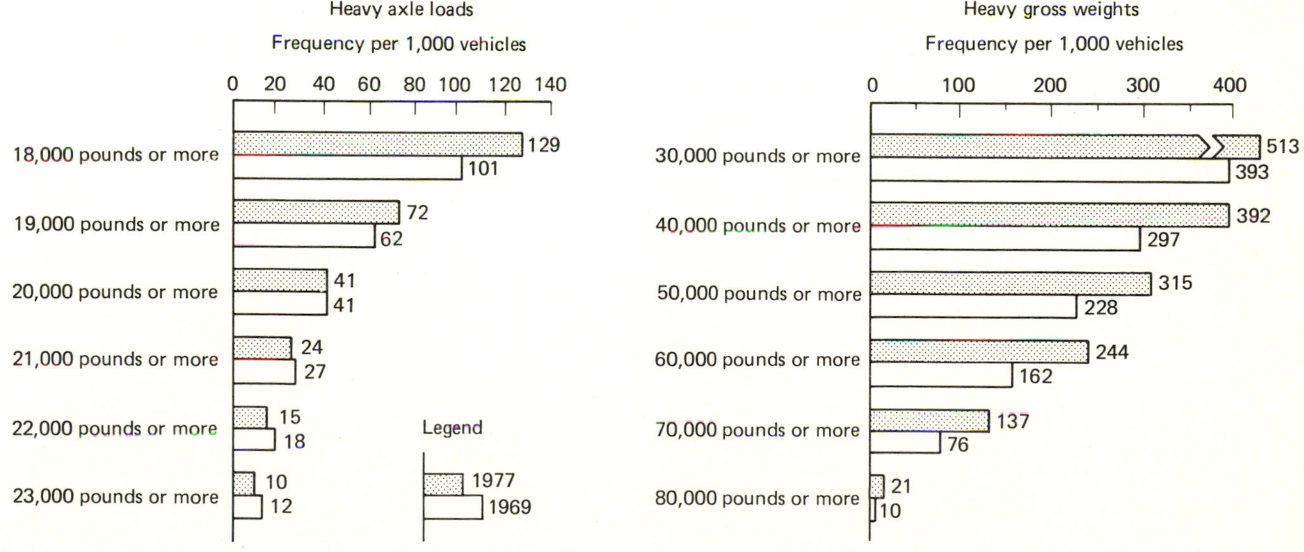

Figure 6.11. Decrease in frequency of heavy axle loads with increase in frequency of heavy gross weights (over 20,000 pounds) for trucks weighed on main rural roads, 1969–1977. SOURCE: *Ibid.* (Figure 6.10).

Maximum acceleration rates

Typical maximum level road acceleration rates for several groupings of passenger cars and for typical weight ranges of pickup trucks, of two-axle, single-unit trucks, and of tractor–semitrailer combination trucks are shown in Table 6-44 for standing starts to 15 mph (24 km/h) and 30 mph (48 km/h) speeds. Maximum level road acceleration rates for representative small, compact, intermediate, and large passenger cars, for pickup and two-axle, single-unit trucks, and for tractor–semitrailer combinations at normal weights for 10 mph (16 km/h) increases in speed at running speeds of 30, 40, 50, and 60 mph (48, 64, 80, and 97 km/h) are given in Table 6-45. The values in Tables 6-44 and 6-45 are for typical vehicles manufactured since 1965.

Maximum acceleration rates for operation on a series of

TABLE 6-44
Maximum Acceleration from Standing Start*

Vehicle Type	Typical Gross Vehicle Weight		Net Engine Propulsion Capability				Typical Maximum Acceleration Rate of Level Roads†			
			Given by Manufacturer		At 15 mph‡ (24 km/h)		To 15 mph (24 km/h)		To 30 mph (48 km/h)	
	lb	kg	hp	rpm	hp	rpm	mph/s	km/h/s	mph/s	km/h/s
Large car	4,800	2,177	350	4,400	60	1,420	10.0	16.1	7.0	11.3
Intermediate car	4,000	1,814	195	4,800	40	1,180	8.0	12.9	5.0	8.0
Compact car	3,000	1,361	120	4,400	32	1,490	8.0	12.9	5.0	8.0
Small car	2,100	952	42	3,900	17	1,900	6.0	9.7(2)	4.0	6.4(3)
Composite car§	4,000	1,814	—	—	—	—	8.0	12.9	5.0	8.0
Pickup truck	5,000	2,268	125	3,800	30	1,300	8.0	12.9(3)	5.0	8.0
Two-axle, single-unit truck	12,000	5,443	142	3,800	43	1,500	2.0	3.2(3)	1.0	1.6
Tractor–semitrailer truck	45,000	20,411	175	3,200	140	2,660	2.0	3.2(3)	1.0	1.6(4)

*If transmission is other than highest gear (or is automatic), gear position is shown in parentheses for 0–15 mph in the "To 15 mph" column and for 15–30 mph in the "To 30 mph" column.
†These data were observed for vehicles used in the operating cost research study conducted for NCHRP Project 2-5A. They were not included in the report of that project [*Running Costs of Motor Vehicles as Affected by Road Design and Traffic*, NCHRP Report 111 (Washington, D.C.: Highway Research Board, 1971)] since they were developed principally as part of the information needed for planning project activities.
‡Computed using typical graphs of engine speed vs. horsepower and known transmission and rear-axle ratios. The transmission and rear-axle ratios of the vehicles are given on pp. 7–8 of *Running Costs of Motor Vehicles as Affected by Road Design and Traffic*, NCHRP Report 111 (Washington, D.C.: Highway Research Board, 1971).
§The composite car represents the typical passenger car in traffic on American highways, circa 1970.

TABLE 6-45
Maximum Acceleration for 10-mph (16 km/h) Increments*

Vehicle Type	Typical Gross Vehicle Weight		Running Speeds†							
			30 mph (48 km/h)		40 mph (64 km/h)		50 mph (80 km/h)		60 mph (96 km/h)	
	lb	kg	mph/s	km/h/s	mph/s	km/h/s	mph/s	km/h/s	mph/s	km/h/s
Large car	4,800	2,177	5.0	8.0	4.0	6.4	3.0	4.8	2.5	4.0
Intermediate car	4,000	1,814	5.0	8.0	4.0	6.4	3.0	4.8	2.0	3.2
Compact car	3,000	1,361	4.0	6.4	3.0	4.8	2.2	3.5	1.1	1.8
Small car	2,100	952	2.0	3.2	1.2	1.9	0.7	1.1	—	—
Composite car‡	4,000	1,814	4.7	7.5	3.8	6.1	2.8	4.5	1.9	3.1
Pickup truck	5,000	2,268	2.0	3.2	1.8	2.9	1.5	2.4	0.7	1.1
Two-axle, single-unit truck	12,000	5,443	1.0	1.6	0.6	0.9	0.2	0.3	—	—
Tractor–semitrailer truck	45,000	20,411	0.8	1.3	0.4	0.6	—	—	—	—

*Determined, given the maximum running speeds on particular grades developed in connection with the research for NCHRP Project 2-5A and reported in *Running Costs of Motor Vehicles as Affected by Royal Design and Traffic*, NCHRP Report 111 (Washington, D.C.: Highway Research Board, 1971). This was done by computing the accelerations that can be achieved on level roads if the forces needed to overcome the resistances of the grades of the NCHRP study are used to produce acceleration.
†Transmission is in highest gear (or in automatic) except for the small car, which is in second gear at 30 mph and in third gear at 40 and 50 mph; for the two-axle, single-unit truck, which is in third gear at 30 and 40 mph; and for the tractor–semitrailer truck, which is in third gear at 30 mph and in fourth gear at 40 mph.
‡The composite car represents the typical passenger car in traffic on American highways, circa 1970.

upgrades are presented in Table 6-46. These data were developed from the values of Tables 6-44 and 6-45 by computation as noted in the footnotes to Table 6-46.

The relationships between distance traveled and speed achieved for automobiles accelerating at their maximum rate from a standing stop are given in Figure 6.12 for operation on level road and on 6 and 10% grades. Data are for the composite car described in Tables 6-44 to 6-46.

Passing sight distances. Minimum passing sight distances on two-lane, two-way roadways are a function of maximum acceleration rates because the more quickly vehicles can accelerate while passing, the shorter the road length traversed during passing and the shorter the passing sight distance required. The minimum passing sight distances used for design are those recommended by the American Association of State Highway and Transportation Officials.[8] The acceleration rates on which they are based are 1.40 mph/s (2.25 km/h/s) for an average passing speed of 34.9 mph (56.1 km/h), 1.43 mph/s (2.30 km/h/s) for 43.8 mph (70.5 km/h), 1.47 mph/s (2.37 km/h/s) for 52.6 mph (84.6 km/h), and 1.50 mph/s (2.41 km/h/s) for 62.0 mph (99.8 km/h).[9] At locations where maximum acceleration rates differ from those on which the AASHTO policy passing sight distances are based (i.e., on parkways limited

[8]Ibid, p. 612, Table 14-5.
[9]Ibid, p. 144.

TABLE 6-46
Maximum Acceleration on Upgrades*

Gradient (%)	Composite Passenger Car‡ 4000 lb (mph/s)	Composite Passenger Car‡ 1814 kg (km/h/s)	Pickup Truck 5000 lb (mph/s)	Pickup Truck 2268 kg (km/h/s)	Two-Axle, Six-Tire Truck 12,000 lb (mph/s)	Two-Axle, Six-Tire Truck 5443 kg (km/h/s)	Tractor–Semitrailer Truck 45,000 lb (mph/s)	Tractor–Semitrailer Truck 20,411 kg (km/h/s)
			Speed Change = 0–15 mph (0–24 km/h)					
2	7.8	12.6	7.8	12.6	1.6	2.6	1.6	2.6
6	6.7	10.7	6.7	10.7	0.7	1.1	0.7	1.1
10	5.8	9.3	5.8	9.3	(14)	(23)	(4)	(6)
			Speed Change = 15–30 mph (24–48 km/h)					
2	4.6	7.4	4.6	7.4	0.6	1.0	0.6	1.0
6	3.7	6.0	3.7	6.0	0.0	0.0	(23)	(37)
10	2.8	4.5	2.8	4.5	0.0	0.0	0.0	0.0
			Speed Change = 30–40 mph (48–64 km/h)					
2	4.2	6.8	1.6	2.6	0.6	1.0	0.3	0.5
6	3.4	5.5	0.7	1.1	(30)	(48)	0.0	0.0
10	2.5	4.0	(30)	(48)	0.0	0.0	0.0	0.0
			Speed Change = 40–50 mph (64–80 km/h)					
2	3.4	5.5	1.4	2.3	0.2	0.3	(45)	(72)
6	2.5	4.0	0.5	0.8	0.0	0.0	0.0	0.0
10	1.6	2.6	0.0	0.0	0.0	0.0	0.0	0.0
			Speed Change = 50–60 mph (80–96 km/h)					
2	2.4	3.8	1.0	1.6	(50)	(80)	0.0	0.0
6	1.5	2.4	0.2	3.2	0.0	0.0	0.0	0.0
10	0.6	1.0	0.0	0.0	0.0	0.0	0.0	0.0

*Computed, given the acceleration rates for level roads of Tables 6–44 and 6–45, by reducing the acceleration forces available on level roads by amounts equal to the corresponding grade resistances.
†Values given in parentheses in this table are typical maximum possible speeds in miles per hour (and kilometers per hour) for the given gradients.
‡The composite car represents the typical passenger car in traffic on American highways, circa 1970.

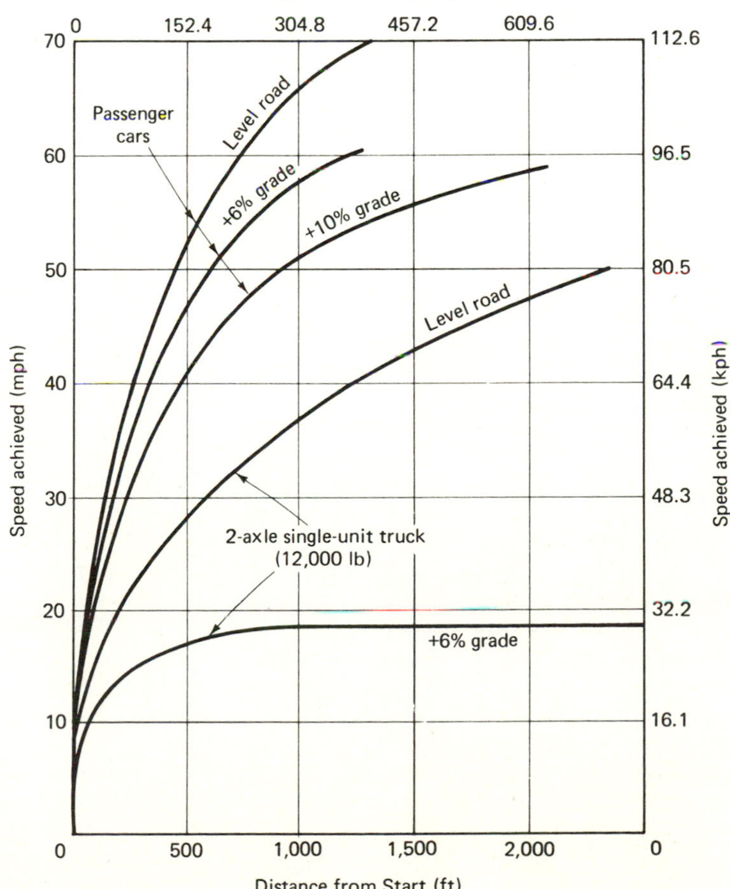

Figure 6.12. Speed-distance relationships observed during maximum rate accelerations. SOURCE: Tables 6-44, 6-45, and 6-46.

TABLE 6-47
Normal Acceleration and Deceleration Rates*

Speed Change		Accelerations		Decelerations	
mph	km/h	mph/s	km/h/s	mph/s	km/h/s
0–15	0–24	3.3	5.3	5.3	8.5
0–30	0–48	3.3	5.3	4.6	7.3
30–40	48–64	3.3	5.3	3.3	5.3
40–50	64–80	2.6	4.2	3.3	5.3
50–60	80–97	2.0	3.2	3.3	5.3
60–70	97–113	1.3	2.1	3.3	5.3

*Determined by equipping a passenger car with an accelerometer, matching the speed change rates of this car with other cars in traffic, and observing acceleration and deceleration rates. These data were obtained in connection with the research conducted for NCHRP Project 2-5A. They were not included in the report of this project, *Running Costs of Motor Vehicles as Affected by Road Design and Traffic*, NCHRP Report 111 (Washington, D.C.: Highway Research Board, 1971) because they were developed principally as part of the information needed for planning project operations.

to passenger cars only), minimum passing sight distances may be computed by using the formulas from the policy manual and the maximum acceleration rates given in Table 6-45.

Normal acceleration rates. Observed normal roadway acceleration rates for passenger cars from standing stop to 15 mph (24 km/h) and for 10 mph (16 km/h) increases in speed at running speeds of 20, 30, 40, 50, and 60 mph (32, 48, 64, 80, and 96 km/h) are given in Table 6-47. These acceleration rates were observed when drivers were not influenced to accelerate rapidly. They are typical of passenger cars starting up after a traffic signal turns green and those passing on four-lane divided highways. Observed normal deceleration rates of passenger cars are also given in Table 6-47.

Deceleration performance

Some deceleration of motor vehicles occurs automatically when the accelerator pedal is released because of the retarding effect of the resistance to motion, including engine compression forces. For controlled deceleration and for maximum rates of deceleration, however, vehicle brakes are used to restrain vehicle motion.

Deceleration without brakes

Deceleration rates without brakes are much greater at high running speeds because the resistances to motion, particularly air resistance, are greater. This is important in planning for the control of high-speed traffic. For example, at speeds of 70 mph (113 km/h) anything that causes a driver's foot to be removed from the accelerator will result in a rapid drop in speed of about 2.2 mph/s (3.5 km/h/s) without a brake-light warning to alert following motorists.[10]

An increase in one or more of the resistances to motion will cause a vehicle to decelerate automatically unless compensated for by an immediate increase in the throttle opening. For example, at points where a level or descending road changes to an upgrade, or where a straight road deflects onto a sharp curve, vehicles will decelerate appreciably unless the driver depresses the accelerator enough to offset the effect of the added resistance.

Deceleration with brakes

Information on the deceleration rates of motor vehicles with braking (both maximum rates and the observed rates for normal slowdowns) is needed by traffic engineers. Maximum rates are used for estimating minimum stopping distances in emergencies. Normal slowdown rates provide the basis for estimating reasonable time and road lengths for stops at signs and signals where frequent normal stops are necessary.

Maximum deceleration rates

Retardation forces developed in brake drums or disks determine the braking deceleration rates of motor vehicles as long as slippage does not occur between pavement and tire surfaces. When the available braking force cannot be carried to the pavement without skidding, deceleration rates are determined by the effective coefficient of friction at the tire surface of contact. This coefficient is a function of pavement type, tire condition, and whether the pavement is wet or dry. Representative values are given in Table 6-48 together with values recommended for highway design purposes. Because braking systems in good order can usually provide more braking force than can be carried to the pavement, maximum deceleration depends primarily on this coefficient of friction between pavement and tire surfaces.

Equation (6.5) relates the coefficient of friction between pavement and tires and running speed to minimum stopping distance:

$$S = \frac{V^2}{30}(f \pm g) \text{ (U.S. units)}$$

$$= \frac{V^2}{255}(f \pm g) \text{ (metric units)} \qquad (6.5)$$

where S = minimum stopping distance, ft or m

V = running speed, mph or km/h

f = coefficient of friction, tire to pavement

g = gradient

Normal deceleration rates

Observed normal deceleration rates for passenger cars on dry pavements are presented in Table 6-47 for stops from running speeds of 15 and 30 mph (24 and 48 km/h) and for 10-mph slowdowns (16 km/h) from 40, 50, 60, and 70 mph running speeds (64, 80, 97, and 113 km/h). Deceleration

[10]E. E. Wilson. "Deceleration Distances for High-Speed Vehicles," Proc. 20th Annu. Meet. Highway Res. Board (Washington, D.C.: Highway Research Board, 1940), pp. 393–397.

TABLE 6–48
Passenger Car Skidding Friction Coefficients

Surface Description	Dry Surface* New Standard Tires	Dry Surface* Badly Worn Tires	Wet Surface Recommended by AASHTO for Design†
	Running Speed = 11 mph (17.7 km/h)		
Dry bit. conc.	0.74	0.61	—
Sand asphalt	0.75	0.66	—
Rock asphalt	0.78	0.73	—
Port. cem. conc.	0.76	0.68	—
	Running Speed = 20 mph (32.2 km/h)		
Dry bit. conc.	0.76	0.60	0.40
Sand asphalt	0.75	0.57	0.40
Rock asphalt	0.76	0.65	0.40
Port. cem. conc.	0.73	0.50	0.40
	Running Speed = 30 mph (48.2 km/h)		
Dry bit. conc.	0.79	0.57	0.36
Sand asphalt	0.79	0.48	0.36
Rock asphalt	0.74	0.59	0.36
Port. cem. conc.	0.78	0.47	0.36
	Running Speed = 40 mph (64.4 km/h)		
Dry bit. conc.	0.75	0.48	0.33
Sand asphalt	0.75	0.39	0.33
Rock asphalt	0.74	0.50	0.33
Port. cem. conc.	0.76	0.33	0.33
All pavements	Running Speed = 50 mph (80.5 km/h)		0.31
	Running Speed = 60 mph (96.5 km/h)		0.30
	Running Speed = 70 mph (112.6 km/h)		0.29
	Running Speed = 80 mph (128.7 km/h)		0.27

*T. E. SHELBOURNE AND R. L. SHEPPE, "Skid Resistance Measurement of Virginia Highways," *Research Report 5–5, Highway Research Board* (Washington, D.C.: Highway Research Board, 1948), pp. 62–80.
†*A Policy on Geometric Design of Rural Highways* (Washington, D.C.: American Association of State Highway Officials, 1965), p. 136.

rates up to 5.5 mph/s (8.8 km/h/s) are reasonably comfortable for car occupants.[11]

Vehicle operating costs

In order for engineers to plan and design traffic control facilities that are compatible with economical vehicle operation, they must know how vehicle operating costs are related to road geometry, surface conditions, traffic flows, and speed-change requirements. Fuel consumption and related costs as averaged in Tables 6-14 and 6-17 are substantially affected by these physical factors.

The information on vehicle operating costs presented in the following paragraphs and in Tables 6-49 to 6-56 was obtained from Report 111 of the National Cooperative Highway Research Program.[12] These tables are based on data predating the fuel price changes and vehicle emission and fuel consumption rate regulations of the 1970s, and are the most comprehensive available. More recent spot checks for certain vehicle types and road conditions indicate that changes in relative differences in fuel consumption rates related to operating conditions are consistent with values in these tables. The mix of vehicles is specified in the notes to Table 6-49 and should be reviewed with respect to applicability to particular analytic needs. It has been found that when the panels, pickups, and vans are classed as passenger vehicles in accordance with recent usage trends, the values are usable and consistent with current fuel consumption rates. In addition, the assumptions that must be made for most analyses concerning speed distributions, acceleration practices, and so on, are sources of far greater uncertainty. The effects of these factors, as well as estimates of future fuel consumption rates, should be reviewed for each situation and new base values established for Table 6-49 categories where appropriate.

Fuel consumption

Vehicle fuel consumption is a major item of operating expense and one closely associated with road and traffic conditions. Table 6-49 presents the fuel consumption rates of the composite car for operation at various speeds on level roads and on gradients. The composite car reflects the vehicle distribution given in the first footnote of the table.

Table 6-50 gives the fuel consumed by the composite passenger car for stop–go and slowdown cycles in excess of that for continued operation at the given running speeds. Tabular values for stop–go cycles (upper values in each column of Table 6-50) do not include fuel consumption for

[11]Ibid.

[12]CLAFFEY, *op. cit.*, pp. 16–39.

TABLE 6–49
Fuel Consumption as Affected by Speed and Gradient*

Uniform Speed mph	Uniform Speed km/h	Level gal/mi	Level liters/km	2% gal/mi	2% liters/km	4% gal/mi	4% liters/km	6% gal/mi	6% liters/km	8% gal/mi	8% liters/km	10% gal/mi	10% liters/km
		Gasoline Consumption on Plus Grades†											
10	16	0.072	0.169	0.087	0.204	0.103	0.242	0.121	0.285	0.143	0.336	0.179	0.421
20	32	0.050	0.117	0.070	0.164	0.086	0.202	0.104	0.245	0.128	0.301	0.160	0.376
30	48	0.044	0.103	0.060	0.141	0.078	0.183	0.096	0.226	0.124	0.291	0.154	0.362
40	64	0.046	0.108	0.062	0.145	0.078	0.183	0.096	0.226	0.124	0.291	0.156	0.367
50	80	0.052	0.122	0.070	0.164	0.083	0.195	0.104	0.244	0.130	0.306	0.162	0.381
60	97	0.058	0.136	0.076	0.179	0.093	0.219	0.112	0.263	0.138	0.325	0.170	0.400
70	113	0.067	0.158	0.084	0.198	0.102	0.240	0.122	0.287	0.148	0.348	0.180	0.423

*The composite passenger car represented here reflects the following vehicle distribution: large cars, 20%; standard cars, 65%; compact cars, 10%; small cars, 5%.
†The values of this table are for straight high type pavement and free-flowing traffic. They should be increased about 20% for speeds of 30 mph (48 km/h) and 50% for speeds of 50 mph (80 km/h) when operation is on badly broken and patched asphalt pavement. They should also be increased for operation on curves: on 5° curves, increase about 3% at 30 mph (48 km/h) and 30% at 60 mph (97 km/h); on 10° curves, increase about 20% at 30 mph (48 km/h) and 100% at 50 mph (80 km/h).

TABLE 6–50
Excess Fuel Consumption for Stop and Slowdown Cycles, Automobiles*

Running Speed		Excess Gasoline Consumed by Amount of Speed Reduction before Accelerating Back to Speed											
		10 mph	16 km/h	20 mph	32 km/h	30 mph	48 km/h	40 mph	64 km/h	50 mph	80 km/h	60 mph	97 km/h
mph	km/h	gal	liters	gal	liters	gal	liters	gal	liters	gal	liters	gal	liters
10	16	0.0016†	0.0056†	—	—	—	—	—	—	—	—	—	—
20	32	0.0032	0.0121	0.0066†	0.0250†	—	—	—	—	—	—	—	—
30	48	0.0035	0.0132	0.0062	0.0235	0.0097†	0.0367†	—	—	—	—	—	—
40	64	0.0038	0.0144	0.0068	0.0257	0.0093	0.0352	0.0128†	0.0484†	—	—	—	—
50	80	0.0042	0.0158	0.0074	0.0280	0.0106	0.0401	0.0140	0.0530	0.0168†	0.0636†	—	—
60	97	0.0046	0.0174	0.0082	0.0310	0.0120	0.0454	0.0155	0.0587	0.0190	0.0719	0.0208†	0.0787†

*The composite passenger car represented here reflects the following vehicle distribution: large cars, 20%; standard cars, 65%; compact cars, 10%; small cars, 5%.
†Excess fuel consumed for stop–go cycles at given running speeds.

TABLE 6–51
Fuel Consumption as Affected by Speed and Grade, Two-Axle Six-Tire Trucks*

Uniform Speed†		Gasoline Consumption on Plus Grades of‡											
		Level		2%		4%		6%		8%		10%	
mph	km/h	gal/mi	liters/km	gal/mi	liters/km	gal/mi	liters/km	gal/mi	liters/km	gal/mi	liters/km	gal/mi	liters/km
10	16	0.074	0.174	0.120	0.282	0.175	0.411	0.225	0.529	0.289	0.680	0.357	0.840
20	32	0.059	0.139	0.112	0.263	0.167	0.393	0.214	0.503	0.295	0.694	0.394	0.927
30	48	0.067	0.158	0.121	0.284	0.181	0.426	0.232	0.546	0.305	0.717	—	—
40	64	0.082	0.193	0.141	0.332	0.210	0.494	—	—	—	—	—	—
50	80	0.101	0.238	0.159	0.374	—	—	—	—	—	—	—	—
60	97	0.122	0.287	—	—	—	—	—	—	—	—	—	—

*The composite two-axle, six-tire truck represented here reflects the following vehicle distribution: two-axle trucks at 8000 lb GVW: 50%; two-axle trucks at 16,000 lb GVW: 50%.
†Operation is in the highest gear possible for the grade and speed (fourth, third, or second). When vehicle approach speed exceeds the maximum sustainable speed on plus grades, speed is reduced to this maximum as soon as the vehicle gets on the grade.
‡The values of this table are for straight, high type pavement and free-flowing traffic. They should be increased about 7% at 30 mph (48 km/h) and 20% at 50 mph (80 km/h) for operation on a badly broken and patched asphalt surface. They should also be increased for operation on curves: on 5° curves, increase about 3% at 30 mph (48 km/h) and 23% at 50 mph (80 km/h); on 10° curves, increase about 21% at 30 mph (48 km/h) and 43% at 40 mph (64 km/h).

stopped delays. Fuel consumption while stopped may be computed by using the composite passenger car idling fuel consumption rate of 0.58 gal/h (2.20 liters/h).

Table 6-51 is similar in form to Table 6-49, but it provides fuel consumption values for a two-axle, six-tire, single-unit truck at an average gross vehicle weight of 12,000 lb (5443 kg).

Table 6-52 gives the excess fuel consumption for speed changes for the representative two-axle, six-tire, single-unit truck and is similar in form to Table 6-50. Average idling fuel consumption while stopped is 0.65 gal/h (2.46 liters/h) for this vehicle.

TABLE 6–52
Excess Fuel Consumption for Stop and Slowdown Cycles, Two-Axle Six-Tire Trucks*

Running Speed		Excess Gasoline Consumed by Amount of Speed Reduction before Accelerating Back to Speed ($\times 10^{-3}$)							
		10 mph	16 km/h	20 mph	32 km/h	30 mph	48 km/h	40 mph	64 km/h
mph	km/h	gal	liters	gal	liters	gal	liters	gal	liters
10	16	3.6†	13.6†	—	—	—	—	—	—
20	32	7.3	27.6	9.7†	36.7†	—	—	—	—
30	48	8.0	30.3	14.8	56.0	17.3†	65.5†	—	—
40	64	9.6	36.3	16.7	63.2	22.6	85.5		

*The composite two-axle, six-tire truck represented here reflects the following vehicle distribution: two-axle trucks at 8000 lb GVW: 50%; two-axle trucks at 16,000 lb GVW: 50%.
†Excess fuel consumed for stop–go cycles at given running speeds.

Tire wear

Tire wear costs in Tables 6-53 to 6-55 are based on 1969–1970 prices as indicated in the notes. Prices must be adjusted to current or forecast conditions in accordance with analytic objectives. Adjustment is affected by three principal variables: (1) the change in the price of tires for each vehicle type, (2) the change in durability of tires in general use, and (3) the change in vehicle mix. For example, if study year prices for the tires for the four vehicle types referred to in Table 6-53 are \$80, \$65, \$55, and \$45; if the vehicle mix is "large (including vans, campers, pickups, and panels)" 20%, "standard" 20%, "compact" 20%, and "small" 40%; and if average tire life is estimated to have increased from 25,000 to 40,000 mi, then an adjustment factor may be computed as follows:

$$\frac{(80 \times 20 + 65 \times 20 + 55 \times 20 + 45 \times 40)}{100 \times 40{,}000} \div \frac{(35 \times 20 + 30 \times 65 + 25 \times 10 + 15 \times 5)}{100 \times 25{,}000} = 1.08$$

Thus, all values in that table would be increased by 8% for the example analysis. As with changes in fuel consumption, it is expected that research in the 1980s will provide refinements in many operating cost factors. For credibility of analytic results, the effects of new relationships and sen-

TABLE 6–53
Tire Wear Cost Factors, Automobiles*

Uniform Speed		High-Type Concrete						High-Type Asphalt						Dry, Well-Packed Gravel	
		Straight		5°		10°		Straight		5°		10°		Straight	
mph	km/h	c/mi	c/km	c/mi	c/km	c/mi	c/km	c/mi	c/km	c/mi	c/km	c/mi	c/km	c/mi	c/km
20	32	0.09	0.06	0.11	0.07	0.17	0.11	0.27	0.17	0.32	0.20	0.51	0.32	1.03	0.64
30	48	0.19	0.12	0.43	0.27	0.82	0.51	0.36	0.22	0.82	0.51	1.56	0.97	1.05	0.65
40	64	0.29	0.18	2.17	1.35	4.83	3.00	0.43	0.27	3.22	2.00	7.16	4.45	1.07	0.66
50	80	0.32	0.20	4.44	2.76	14.34	8.91	0.45	0.28	6.25	3.88	20.10	12.48	1.10	0.68
60	97	0.31	0.19	7.64	4.74	—	—	0.46	0.29	16.34	9.99	—	—	—	—
70	113	0.30	0.18	—	—	—	—	0.44	0.27	—	—	—	—	—	—
80	129	0.27	0.17	—	—	—	—	0.43	0.27	—	—	—	—	—	—

*The composite passenger car represented here reflects the following vehicle distribution: large cars, 20%; standard-size cars, 65%; compact cars, 10%; small cars, 5%.
Tire costs were computed by using a weighted average cost of $119 for a set of four new, medium-quality tires based on the following unit tire costs by vehicle type (as noted in the northeastern states in 1969): large cars, $35 per tire; standard-size cars, $30 per tire; compact cars, $25 per tire; small cars, $15 per tire.
There are approximately 1500 g of usable tire tread in 80% of passenger car tires. This weight of usable tire tread was also recorded for the tires used in the tire wear test.
Tire wear costs are based on 1969–1970 prices. See the text for method of update.

sitivity should be related to the policy, planning and design issues of concern.

The excess tire costs for stop–go and 10 mph (16 km/h) slowdown speed-change cycles are shown in Table 6-54 for the composite passenger car for a series of running speeds on high-type road surfaces.

TABLE 6–54
Excess Tire Cost for Speed Changes, Automobiles*

Running Speed		Cost of Four Tires (cents per cycle)			
		Stop-Go Speed Change Cycles		10 mph (16 km/h) Slowdown Cycles	
mph	km/h	Concrete	Asphalt	Concrete	Asphalt
20	32	0.10	0.30	0.04	0.10
30	48	0.30	0.60	0.08	0.15
40	64	0.58	0.85	0.09	0.14
50	80	0.72	1.10	0.09	0.14
60	97	0.80	1.20	0.08	0.12
70	112	0.85	1.25	0.08	0.12

*The composite passenger car represented here reflects the following vehicle distribution: large cars, 20%; standard-size cars, 65%; compact cars, 10%; small cars, 5%.
Tire costs were computed by using a weighted average cost of $119 for a set of four new, medium-quality tires based on the following unit tire costs by vehicle type (as noted in the northeastern states in 1969): large cars, $35 per tire; standard-size cars, $30 per tire; compact cars, $25 per tire; small cars, $15 per tire.
There are approximately 1500 g of usable tire tread in 80% of passenger car tires. This weight of usable tire tread was also recorded for the tires used in the tire wear test.
Tire wear costs are based on 1969–1970 prices. See the text for method of update.

Tire wear cost values for the representative truck (a two-axle, six-tire, single-unit truck) for straight road operation at 45 mph (72 km/h) for curve operation and for operation on major urban arterials are given in Table 6-55.

Maintenance costs

Maintenance costs for vehicle components should be estimated for known or assumed study-year conditions and the effects on analytic results determined. These costs are expected to change significantly and are influenced by inflation and changes in design related to fuel conservation. In 1970, passenger car maintenance costs were estimated to be 1.15 cents/mi (0.71 cents/km) compared to over 4.0 cents/mi (1.89 cents/km) for 1979.[13,14] Although not directly comparable, the 1970 figure for pickup trucks was 1.42 cents/mi (0.88 cents/km) and the 1979 figure for pas-

[13]Ibid.

[14]JOSEPH E. ULLMAN, *Cost of Owning and Operating Automobiles and Vans 1979* (Washington, D.C.: FMWA/U.S. Department of Transportation, May 1979).

TABLE 6–55
Tire Wear Cost Factors, Two-Axle, Six-Tire Truck*

Type of Operation and Road Surface	Tire Wear Costs (per Axle)			
	Rear Axle—Four Tires (12,000 lb)	(5443 kg)	Front Axle—Two Tires (4000 lb)	(1814 kg)
	c/mi	c/km	c/mi	c/km
Uniform speed of 45 mph (72 km/h on high-type concrete	0.40	0.25	0.10	0.06
25–30 mph (40–48 km/h) on four-lane major street urban arterial with high-type concrete surface (3–4 stops per mile)	1.96	1.22	0.28	1.74
25 mph (40 km/h) on 30° curve with high-type surface	10.80	6.71	1.30	0.81
25 mph (40 km/h) on 60° curve with high-type surface	108.00	67.10	9.20	5.72

*Tire wear costs based on a cost of $120 per tire for a medium-quality, 10-ply 8.25 × 20 transport tire (1970 price in the northeastern states). Each tire has approximately 4500 g of usable tread before recapping is necessary. Value of the tire carcass when recapped was assumed to be $20.
Tire wear costs are based on 1969–1970 prices. See the text for method of update.

senger vans was 5.28 cents/mi (3.27 cents/km). The per mile maintenance costs for line-haul trucks tends to fall below pickups and vans, owing to the much greater mileage per year and other design and operating characteristics.

Oil consumption

Oil consumption results from oil contamination during use and oil loss through leakage and combustion. The combined oil consumption rates for contamination, leakage, and combustion for passenger cars and two-axle, six-tire, single-unit trucks are given in Table 6-56 for operation in free-flowing traffic on dust-free (high-type) roads.

TABLE 6–56
Engine Oil Consumption Rates*

Speed†		Passenger Car‡		Two-Axle, Six-Tire Truck§	
mph	km/h	qt/1000 mi	liters/1000 km	qt/1000 mi	liters/1000 km
30	48	0.97	0.57	2.77	1.63
35		0.97	0.57	2.77	1.63
40	64	1.12	0.66	2.84	1.67
45		1.28	0.75	3.00	1.76
50	80	1.45	0.85	3.16	1.86
55		1.64	0.96	3.33	1.96
60	97	1.78	1.05	3.50	2.06

*In free-flowing traffic on high-type roads. Oil consumption includes oil both for oil changes and for additions between oil changes.
†Minimum trip length = 10 mi (16 km).
‡An eight-cylinder Chevrolet sedan with an engine displacement of 283 in.^{3} represented the typical passenger car.
§A truck with a six-cylinder engine (engine displacement of 351 in.^{3}) represented the typical two-axle, six-tire truck.

Depreciation

The magnitude of motor vehicle depreciation cost, when defined as the quotient resulting from dividing the difference between original cost and scrap value by lifetime mileage, depends largely on nonhighway factors (new- and used-car-market values and user travel desires). Because the work of the traffic engineer has little effect on these factors, vehicle depreciation cost factors are not included here. The used-car-market price book generally sets remaining value up to about 5 years. A writeoff somewhere in the fifth to tenth years is commonly set.

Congestion costs

Highway congestion conditions affect vehicle operating costs for fuel and oil consumption, tire wear, and maintenance principally as a result of the speed changes and stopped delays associated with congestion. The frequency and severity of the speed changes and the duration of stopped delays caused by congestion vary widely from one congestion location to another. When it is desired to determine vehicle operating costs caused by congestion at a given location, the recommended procedure is to observe, at that location, both the frequency of speed changes by ranges of speed change and the frequency of vehicle stops by range of stop duration and to compute the resulting fuel and oil consumption, tire wear, and maintenance costs by using the speed-change and idling operating cost data given above. Similarly, the fuel conservation potential of alternative traffic control strategies and geometric designs can be estimated.

Petroleum conservation

As shown in Figure 6.13, nearly half of all energy used in the United States is derived from petroleum and 18% is consumed for highway transportation. This means about 40% of all petroleum used in the United States is used for highway vehicles. A comparison of several European countries having similar population densities to the United States showed nearly double the fuel efficiency on a miles per gallon basis.[15] Tables 6-57 and 6-58 show the range of energy use rates for passenger and freight transportation for each mode. The range of values depends on the analyst and the study procedures. Differences in loading as well as efficiency of vehicles within a class can result in substantial differences in terms of passenger miles and ton-miles per gallon or per Btu. Figure 6.14 compares passenger mile per gallon values for various types of vehicles and loadings. For comparisons among modes it is particularly important that load factors be on a passenger mile per vehicle mile basis rather than a spot occupancy or person trip per vehicle trip basis and that the amount of deadheading be accounted for. In addition, where an auto is used by individuals to and from terminals, the fuel used for the auto leg can be significant. Figure 6.15 shows that fuel efficiency during the first 2 mi (3.2 km) from a cold start is only about half the city driving rate, and not until about 10 mi (16 km) does it approach 90%.

Similar considerations are important in analyzing freight transportation alternatives. In addition, where new construction is involved, the petroleum consumption related to the construction itself, and added or reduced vehicle miles resulting from construction of the facility, may be sufficient to tip the balance.

Vehicle dimensions

Information on the various dimensions of motor vehicles are compared for 1968 and 1978 in Figure 6.16. These are useful for geometric design and parking layout. It is evident that maximum dimensions have changed very little. Table 6-59 provides parking dimensions for bicycles and various motor vehicles. The minimum values may require care in arrangement in the case of bicycles and motorcycles, and provide less than a fully opened door on one side and no opening on the other in the case of autos and light trucks, with bumpers touching.

[15]A. French and L. D. Wylie, *Highway Transport and Energy Problems in Europe* (Washington, D.C.: International Road Federation, June 1975).

TABLE 6–57
Energy Efficiency for Passenger Transportation Modes

Mode	Passenger-Miles/Gal	Seat-Miles/Gal	Btu/Passenger-Mile	Load** Factor Assumed	Source	Remarks
Auto	22	57	5,578	1.9	TSC (12)	Urban (1972)
	30	68	4,208	2.2	TSC (12)	Combined (1972)
	43	83	2,902	2.6	TSC (12)	Intercity (1972)
Small						
Work and related business	21.67	70*	5,768	1.6	FHWA (54)	
Shop and family business	41.39	63	3,020	2.3	FHWA (54)	
Social and recreation	74.93	94	1,668	2.8	FHWA (54)	
Subtotal	47.74	76	2,618	2.2	FHWA (54)	
Standard						
Work and related business	15.68	59	7,972	1.6	FHWA (54)	
Shop and family business	20.70	54	6,039	2.3	FHWA (54)	
Social and recreation	42.15	90	2,966	2.8	FHWA (54)	
Subtotal	24.51	67	5,100	2.2	FHWA (54)	
Bus	168		743		TSC (12)	School (1972)
	116	247	1,170	47	TSC (12)	Intercity (1972)
	48	180	2,891	24	DOT/NASA (17)	Urban (1972)
Rail	84		1,646		TSC (12)	Transit (1972)
	32	128	4,300	25	Mitre (16)	Urban (1970)
	51	138	2,730	37	Mitre (16)	Intercity (1970)
Air	16		7,766		TSC (12)	Domestic (1972)
	15.2	29		52.7	FEA (8)	Domestic (1970)
	19	34		56.4	FEA (8)	International (1972)
	14		9,700		Rice (15)	(Mid-1960's)
	18–28			60	Boeing (11)	700-statute mile range
Miscellaneous						
Bicycle			1,300		Hirst (19)	Total energy use
			97		EPA (20)	10 mph
			200		Rice (15)	5 mph
			500		EPA (20)	2.5 mph
Walking			300		Rice (18)	2.5 mph
Taxi†	8		15,600	0.7	DOT (51)	
Dial-A-Bus	15.6			3.0	HRB (21)	Peak hour
Van-pool	81	108	1,540	9.0	3-M Co. (59)	Peak hour
BART	88			40	BART (22)	Peak hour

*Small cars are assumed to average 3.5 passenger-seats and other cars 6.0 passenger-seats.
†The driver is assumed not to be a passenger.
**Passenger miles per vehicle mile (PM/VM)

Source: "Energy, Effects, Efficiencies, and Prospects for Various Modes of Transportation," *National Cooperative Highway Research Program Synthesis of Highway Practice,* No. 43 (Washington, D.C.: TRANSPORTATION RESEARCH BOARD, 1977).

TABLE 6–58
Energy Efficiency for Intercity Freight Transport Modes

Mode	Ton-Miles/Gal	British Thermal Unit/Ton-Mile	Source	Remarks
Heavy-duty truck (combinations)	57	2,400	Mooz (37)	Based upon 1967 data
	41	3,440	Mitre (16)	
	85	1,600	DOT/EPA (26)	Based upon 1972 ATA data
Railway	184	750	Mooz (37)	
	212	650	Smith (38)	Modification of Mooz (37) to eliminate data errors
	197	700	FEA (8)	Show efficiency decreasing from 650 in 1965 to 700 in 1972
Waterway	280	500	Mooz (37)	
	214	655	Smith (38)	Modification of Mooz (37) to eliminate data errors
	187	750	Mitre (16)	
Airplane	2.0	63,000	Mooz (37)	
	4.7	27,000	TSC (12)	
	3.3	37,500	Mitre (16)	
Pipeline	206	600	TSC (12)	Oil pipeline
	52	2,637	TSC (12)	Gas pipeline
	324	420	Mitre (16)	Oil pipeline

Source: "Energy, Effects, Efficiencies, and Prospects for Various Modes of Transportation," *National Cooperative Highway Research Program Synthesis of Highway Practice,* No. 43 (Washington, D.C.: TRANSPORTATION RESEARCH BOARD, 1977).

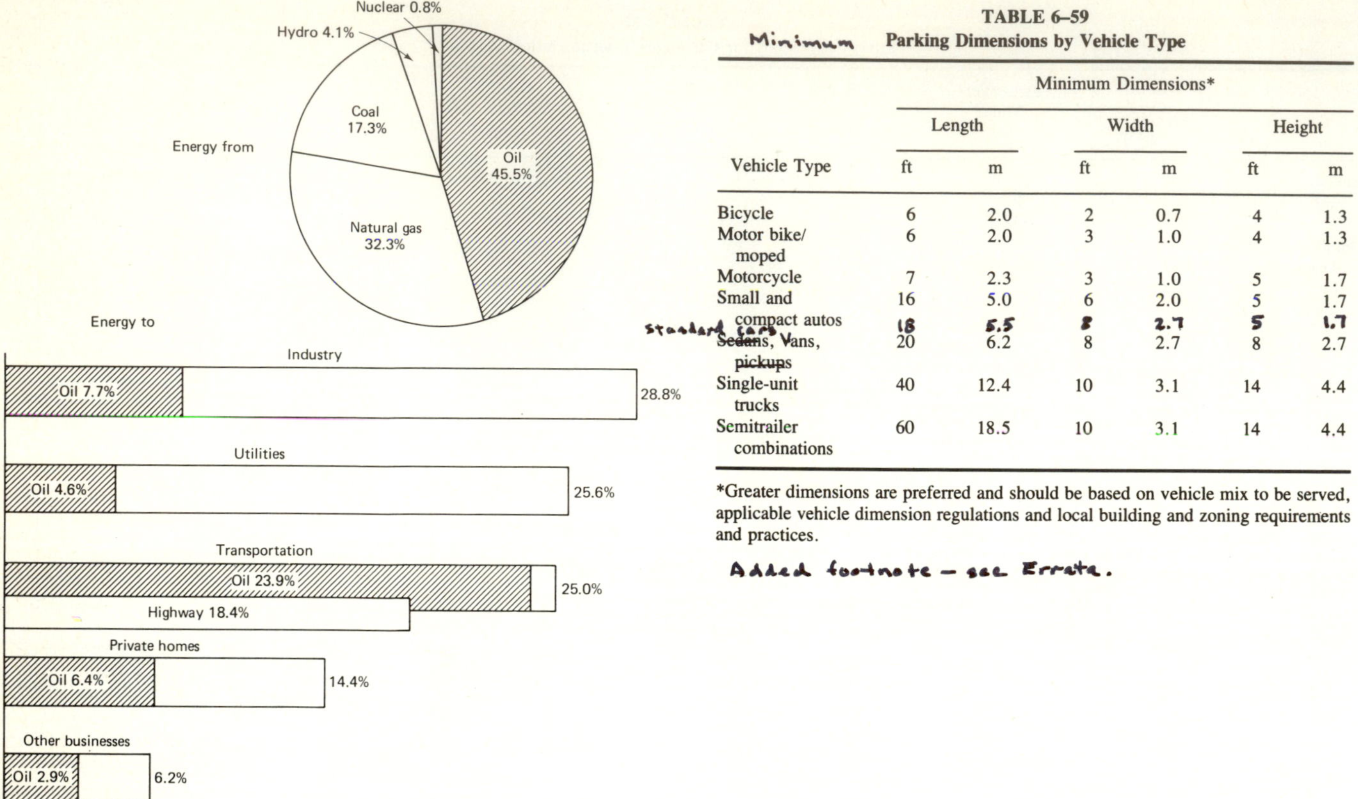

Figure 6.13. Sources and uses of energy. SOURCE: French, A. *Transportation Energy Considerations in the Urban Environment,* U.S. DOT/FHWA, Washington, D.C., May 1975.

TABLE 6–59
Parking Dimensions by Vehicle Type

	Minimum Dimensions*					
	Length		Width		Height	
Vehicle Type	ft	m	ft	m	ft	m
Bicycle	6	2.0	2	0.7	4	1.3
Motor bike/ moped	6	2.0	3	1.0	4	1.3
Motorcycle	7	2.3	3	1.0	5	1.7
Small and compact autos	16	5.0	6	2.0	5	1.7
Sedans, Vans, pickups	20	6.2	8	2.7	8	2.7
Single-unit trucks	40	12.4	10	3.1	14	4.4
Semitrailer combinations	60	18.5	10	3.1	14	4.4

*Greater dimensions are preferred and should be based on vehicle mix to be served, applicable vehicle dimension regulations and local building and zoning requirements and practices.

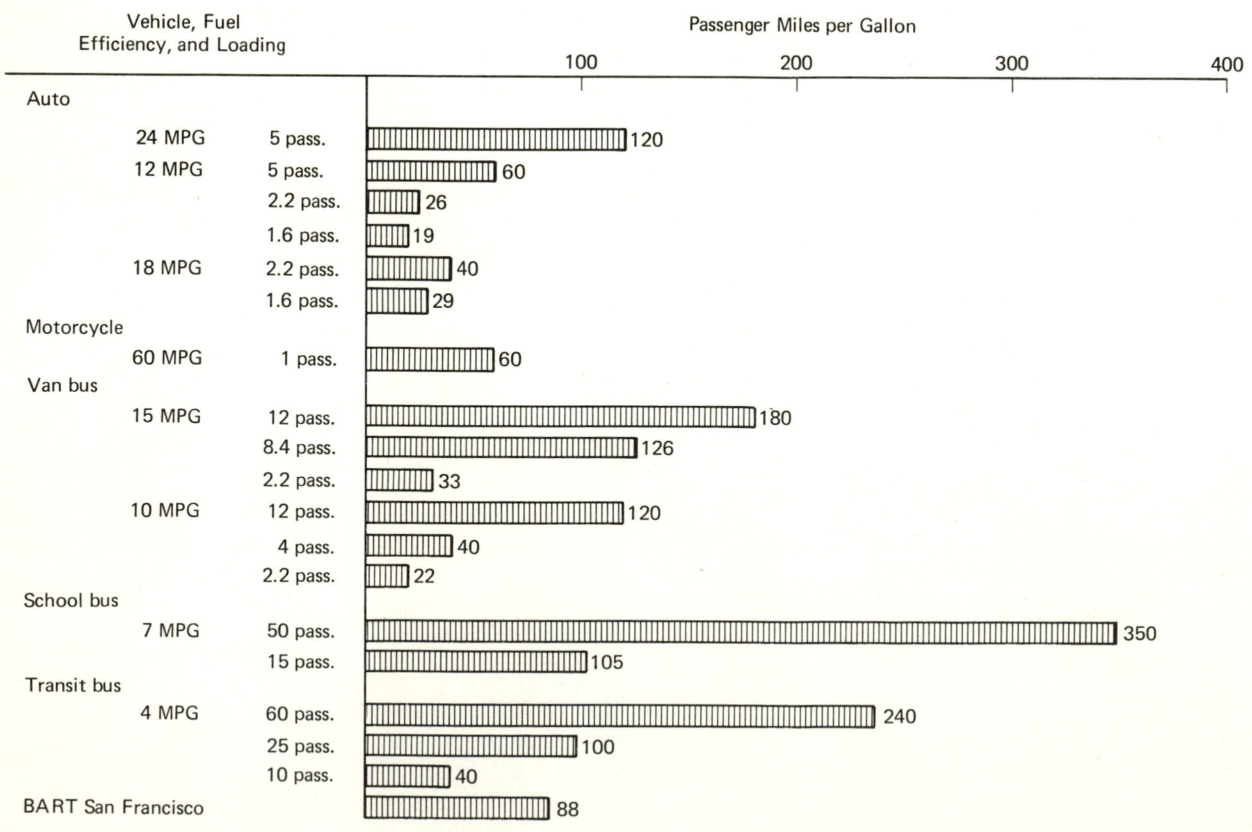

Figure 6.14. Comparative fuel efficiency. SOURCE: *Ibid.* (Figure 6.13).

Figure 6.15. Variation of fuel economy with trip length. SOURCE: T. Iura, W.U. Roessler, and H.M. White, *Research Plan for Achieving Reduced Automotive Energy Consumption,* Aerospace Report No. ATR-76 (7467)-1, National Science Foundation, Washington, D.C., 1976, Fig. 2-4.

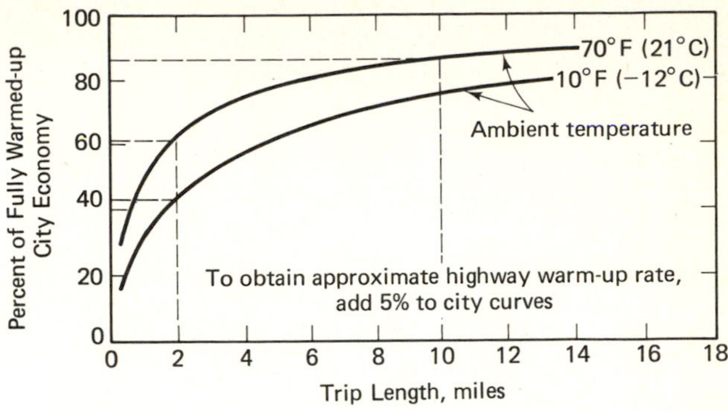

Figure 6.16. Changes in vehicle dimensions. SOURCE: MOTOR VEHICLE MANUFACTURERS ASSOCIATION, *Parking Dimensions 1978 Model Passenger Cars* and interpolation from graphs in previous handbook.

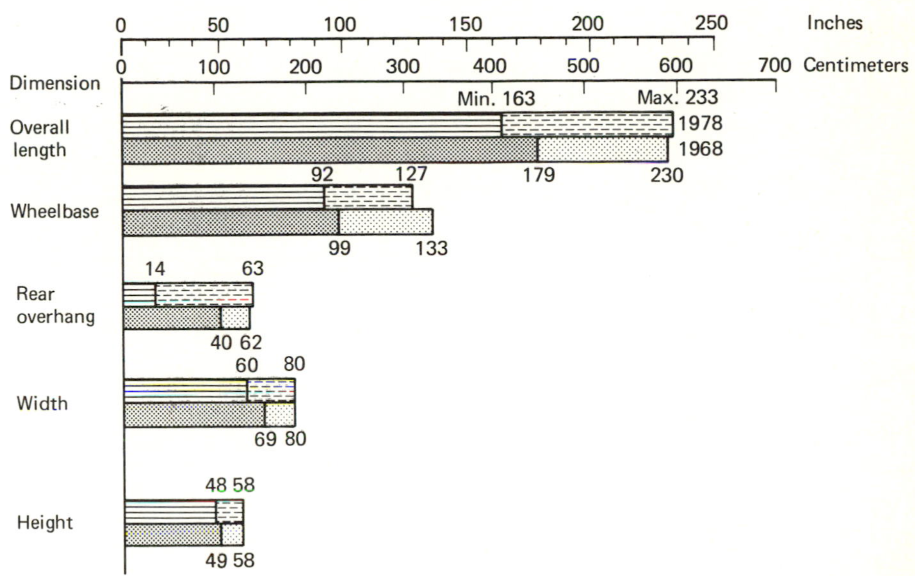

REFERENCES FOR FURTHER READING

CHING, P. Y., AND F. D. ROONEY, *Truck Speeds on Grades in California*. Sacramento, Calif. California Department of Transportation, June 1979.

CLAFFEY, P. J., *Running Costs of Motor Vehicles as Affected by Road Design and Traffic*. Washington, DC: Highway Research Board (NCHRP Report 111), 1971.

"Energy Effects, Efficiencies, and Prospects for Various Modes of Transportation," *National Cooperative Highway Research Program Synthesis of Highway Practices,* No. 43. Washington, DC: Transportation Research Board, 1977.

KENT, P. M., ET. AL., *1978 National Truck Characteristics Report*. Washington, DC: FHWA/U.S. Department of Transportation, November 1979 (prepublication draft tables).

MATSON, THEODORE M., WILBUR S. SMITH, AND FREDERICK W. HURD, *Traffic Engineering*. New York: McGraw-Hill, 1955.

Parking Dimensions: 1978 Model Passenger Cars (and previous editions). Detroit, MI: Motor Vehicle Manufacturers Association.

ODIER, LIONEL, "The Economic Benefits of Road Construction and Improvements," trans. from the French document *Les Intérêts économiques des travaux routiers* by Noel Lindsay. Paris: Bureau Central d'Etudes pour les Equipements d'Outre-Mer, 1962.

Parking Dimensions: 1974 Model Cars, Engineering Notes. Detroit, Mi.: Motor Vehicle Manufacturers Association (annual publication).

Policy on Design of Urban Highways and Arterial Streets. Washington, D.C.: American Association of State Highway Officials, 1973.

Policy on Geometric Design of Rural Highways. Washington, D.C.: American Association of State Highway Officials, 1965.

ROSE, A. B., *Energy Intensity and Related Parameters of Selected Transportation Modes: Passenger Movements*. Washington, D.C.: U.S. Department of Energy, January 1979.

SEGER, E. E., AND R. S. BRINK, *Trends of Vehicle Dimensions and Performance Characteristics 1960 through 1970*. Milford, Mi.: General Motors Proving Ground, 1971.

ULLMAN, JOSEPH E., *Cost of Owning and Operating Automobiles and Vans 1979*. Washington, D.C.: FHWA/U.S. Department of Transportation, May 1979.

WINFREY, ROBLEY, *Economic Analysis for Highways*. Scranton, Pa.: International Textbook, 1969.

7

URBAN TRANSIT

WOLFGANG S. HOMBURGER, *Research Engineer*
Institute of Transportation Studies
University of California
Berkeley, California

HENRY D. QUINBY*

Urban transit systems are the common carriers of passengers in cities. Unlike the modes described in the preceding five chapters, urban transit is not a distinct technology, but an operational and institutional concept. It uses highway and railroad engineering extensively, as well as the operations and management methods employed by common carriers in any of the other transportation modes.

This chapter is therefore concerned with providing information on the physical and operational characteristics of urban transit specifically. The reader is referred to other chapters for further details on railroad engineering, motor vehicle characteristics, travel demand and modal choice, planning considerations, and similar material.

After defining important terms used in urban transit, the chapter surveys the physical characteristics of such systems (right-of-way, vehicles, routes, stops, and performance), operational procedures, and the economic and management aspects that define the capability of transit and its contribution to urban mobility. References for further reading at the end of the chapter, and footnote sources, offer the reader opportunities for extended study of this topic.

Definitions

Special words and phrases used in urban transit systems may be defined under the headings of general function, technology, and types of service.

General function definitions

○*Urban transit* (also called *mass transit*) is a common carrier service provided for the carriage of passengers and their incidental baggage on established routes and fixed schedules at published rates of fares, and available to all persons wishing to avail themselves of the service.
○*Paratransit* is a service that deviates from the preceding definition in that it may not follow fixed routes or schedules, may not be available to the general public, or both. Examples include taxis, vanpools, club buses, and demand-responsive services.
○*Charter* service is based on contracts between a transit agency and individuals for occasional or regular hire of vehicles and drivers, is restricted to the use of the contracting party, and follows whatever route and schedule this party desires.

Technological definitions

○*Right-of-way* refers to the land used by the transit systems. It may be *shared* (street transit), *semiexclusive* (light rail transit, buses, and high-occupancy-vehicles on reserved lanes), or *exclusive* (rail rapid transit).
○*Guideway* or *infrastructure* refers to the right-of-way plus the special improvements required for operations (e.g., tracks, power distribution, control system).
○*Revenue vehicles* are the rolling stock operating on highways or guideways which furnishes the actual passenger transportation. The term *transit unit* designates an individually scheduled service, which may be a single vehicle or a train. The following major categories are commonly used:

> ○*Van:* A passenger vehicle on an automobile or light truck chassis, propelled by an internal combustion engine, with a capacity for 6 to 15 persons.
> ○*Minibus:* A vehicle less that 25 ft (7.5 m) long, propelled by an internal combustion engine, with a capacity for more than 15 persons.

*Mr. Quinby, author of a similar chapter in the first edition of this handbook, had begun work on this chapter at the time of his death on December 16, 1978. Mr. Homburger has attempted to follow the intent of Mr. Quinby as faithfully as possible, while also reflecting his own ideas and responding to suggestions from reviewers.

○*Transit bus:* A vehicle more than 25 ft (7.5 m) long, usually propelled by a diesel engine.
○*Trolley bus:* A transit bus propelled by electricity obtained from overhead wires.
○*Articulated bus:* A transit bus (diesel or electric) with a permanently attached semitrailer, with full interior passenger circulation.
○*Streetcar* or *light rail vehicle (LRV):* An electrically propelled rail vehicle operated singly or in trains on shared or semiexclusive right-of-way.
○*Rail transit car:* An electrically propelled vehicle usually operated in trains on exclusive right-of-way.
○*Commuter railroad car:* A standard railroad passenger car with high-density seating. It may be self-propelled (by electricity or diesel engines) or designed for haulage by locomotive.

○*Light rail transit (LRT)* refers to rail service at least partly on shared or semiexclusive right-of-way, designed so that other traffic can mingle safely with the LRT operation where desired.

○*Heavy rail transit (HRT)* (also called *rapid transit* in common parlance) refers to rail service on exclusive right-of-way, designed without need to accommodate any other type of traffic.

Service definitions

○*Local transit* is service on streets or other right-of-way making frequent stops and, hence, operating at relatively low speeds, serving adjacent land uses within acceptable walking distances.

○*Express service* is service that does not attempt to serve all land areas through which it passes, but offers faster speeds to a selected number of stops spaced more widely apart.

○*Basic service* comprises routes that operate all day (although the length of the "day" may vary from about 14 to 24 h), and at least 5 days/week.

○*Peak service* comprises routes that supplement basic service during peak demand periods only.

○*Special service* comprises irregular routes operated for special events or for seasonal traffic generators.

○*Short-haul transit* refers to service within major activity centers over short routes. Special technology is sometimes used (see Chapter 22).

Right-of-way characteristics

This section gives information on typical geometric characteristics and minimum right-of-way requirements for selected transit technologies. Although the values indicated (Table 7-1) reflect current practice, it should be borne in mind that individual circumstances of different applications vary. Preparation of specific, detailed geometric criteria is desirable for each new transit service and facility application; these standards should reflect the specific conditions of that application.

TABLE 7–1
Typical Basic Geometric and Right-of-Way Characteristics for Selected Transit Facility Types

Characteristic	Unit	Exclusive Busway	Light Rail Transit: In Street Center Reservation	Light Rail Transit: In Exclusive Right-of-Way	Rapid Transit
Access control		Full	Partial	Full	Full
Number of lanes or tracks		2	2	2	2
Widths					
a. Transit vehicle	ft	8.5	9.5	9.5	10.3
	m	2.6	2.9	2.9	3.1
b. Lane envelope clearance*	ft	12.0	11.0	12.5	13.5
	m	3.7	3.4	3.8	4.1
c. Track gauge	ft	—	4.71	4.71	4.71
	m	—	1.44	1.44	1.44
d. Emergency walkway	ft	†	None	2.5	2.5
	m			0.8	0.8
e. Minimum shoulders (each)†	ft	2.5	None	None	None
	m	0.8			
f. Border barriers or fencing (each)	ft	2.0	None	1.0	1.0
	m	0.6		0.3	0.3
g. Overall minimum right-of-way‡					
(1) Aerial	ft	33	—	24	26
	m	9.5	—	7.3	7.9
(2) At-grade	ft	33	22	30	32
	m	9.5	6.7	9.1	9.8
(3) Subway	ft	39	—	38	40
	m	11.9	—	11.6	12.2
Stations§					
a. Side platform width	ft	10	6	12	12
	m	3.0	1.8	3.7	3.7
b. Center platform width	ft	—	—	24	24
	m	—	—	7.3	7.3
c. Platform length	ft	120	400	400	500–600
	m	36	122	122	152–183
Minimums					
a. vertical clearance	ft	14	14	14	14
	m	4.3	4.3	4.3	4.3
b. design speed	mph	60	40	60	60–80‖
	km/h	97	64	97	97–130‖
c. horizontal curve radius (for new construction)	ft	400	200	500	400–600‖
	m	122	61	152	122–183‖
Maximum grade	%	4.0	10.0	5.0	4.0

*Overall vehicle clearance requirements on tangent line.
†Emergency walkway for busways is incorporated in busway shoulders.
‡Minima based on normal structural requirements for tangent-line sections without stations, and without station acceleration and deceleration lanes and tapers for busways. Special drainage provisions, side slopes, or retaining walls on cuts and fills, and any subway lateral ventilation requirements are excluded.
§Typical line stations. In CBDs, busway station requirements and rail platform widths may be greater.
‖Higher end of ranges for regional rapid transit.

SOURCE: Various databooks, inventories, reports, and criteria.

Streets and highways

Buses on public streets and highways can generally operate effectively within the ranges of geometric values set forth in Chapter 19 for freeways, expressways, arterials, collectors, and local streets. Care should be taken to check (1) the vertical clearances required for double-decker buses, (2) the swept paths and horizontal clearance requirements of transit vehicles both while turning and in tangent operations, and (3) acceleration characteristics of the transit vehicle, especially in relation to geometrics of acceleration lanes and merging areas.

Generally, the operation of buses 8 ft (2.4 m) or more in width is not desirable in traffic lanes less than 10 ft (3.0 m) wide; lanes 12 ft (3.65 m) wide are preferred for these buses. However, practical compromises, involving reduced speeds, must sometimes be made in situations in which buses must use narrower lanes.

Priority treatment of buses on streets and freeways. The speed, capacity, and reliability of buses can be enhanced by a variety of techniques, such as:

1. Exclusive or preferential transit lanes on sections of streets and freeways.
2. Exclusive transit turns at intersections.
3. Metered freeway entry with bus preference.
4. Passive traffic signal priority measures, such as cycle-length adjustments, split phases, and timing plans selectively favoring buses.
5. Active traffic signal priority measures, such as unconditional or conditional signal preemption by buses.
6. Exclusive transit streets, malls, or ramps.
7. Exclusive busways.

Frequently, the operation of the first three techniques mentioned above is limited to peak periods and/or directions where transit patronage is relatively high. Other high-occupancy vehicles (HOVs) are sometimes permitted to share use of preferential transit lanes, ramps, and bypasses.

If street and highway space is considered for the exclusive use of buses, one test of reasonableness is that the combined auto and transit passenger volumes in the direction(s) and for the period(s) involved will not be reduced substantially below existing levels. Another criterion sometimes considered is that the total travel or delay times for all persons involved are reduced.

Busways for exclusive bus use. Table 7-1 indicates typical basic geometric characteristics for exclusive busways. The technology of line, station, and terminal facilities for busways continues to undergo development. At the same time, some busways are being opened to carpool drivers; as a result, their design must allow for the presence of mixed traffic streams.

Busway stations normally require a loading–unloading lane separate from the through lane in each travel direction. Different platform berth layouts (described later in this chapter) have different geometric and right-of-way requirements. The number of loading berths to be provided depends on design patronage volumes, minimum bus headways, peak bus accumulation, plans of operation, loading and fare collection characteristics, types and locations of stations, berth design, and other factors. Busway stations also usually require acceleration and deceleration lanes and tapers for satisfactory transition between line and station operations.

Busway stations in central business districts (CBDs) usually require more elaborate facilities and space than do stations located elsewhere. If CBD penetration involves subway structures, then ventilation, delivery, and station design problems may be severe and costly. Because of this, CBD delivery is often provided by means of streets with curbside stops, or through elevated terminals.

Rail transit

Table 7-1 shows typical basic geometric characteristics for two types of streetcar (LRT) facilities and for rail transit.

Light rail transit. The right-of-way for light rail transit routes includes sections of shared, semiexclusive, and exclusive facilities. The last of these becomes similar to heavy rail transit design (discussed in the next section), except that power distribution systems and station platform lengths differ.

Shared, on-street track alignment is primarily determined by the geometry of the streets available for the route. Turning radii can be quite short, but track spacing at sharp curves must be increased so that front and rear overhangs of one vehicle do not collide with the center portion of a vehicle on the adjacent track. This may preclude simultaneous 90° turns at intersections of two narrow streets, and dictate single-track, alternate movement, or other design solutions.

Semiexclusive route sections can be placed in the median strip of wide arterials with crossings at grade. In this case, tracks are usually laid on open ballast between intersections, both for a low-cost comfortable profile and to prevent motor vehicles from encroaching on the tracks. Curve geometrics are usually designed for somewhat higher speeds (larger radii), but clearances of vehicles at curves can still be a problem.

Methods of priority treatment for buses, mentioned above, are sometimes applicable to streetcar operation. This applies particularly to signal priority measures and exclusive use of streets in downtown areas.

LRT can offer platform speeds and track capacities that are only moderately lower than heavy rail transit. More direct service with branch or parallel lines can often be provided; stops may be located more accessibly and spaced more closely to reduce walking distances. Thus, overall door-to-door travel times for urban trips up to perhaps 10 mi (16 km) may be in the same range as those provided on fully grade-separated urban rapid transit facilities. Attractive linear park treatments, such as along St. Charles and Carrollton Avenues in New Orleans and Beacon Street in Boston–Brookline, can provide additional amenities along and in the streetcar right-of-way located in street medians.

Heavy rail transit. Because of the enormous investment required for the infrastructure of fully separated rail transit, such routes are only built in corridors with very large traffic demand. This technology offers very fast, high-capacity service, but the network extent is necessarily limited by available funds, and feeder services are required to serve the rail routes.

Heavy rail transit alignments are based on very detailed studies of demand, station locations, and relative costs. Horizontal alignment is based on standards such as shown in Table 7-1.

The decision on vertical alignment is made primarily so

that the sum of land, construction, and environmental costs is minimized, although irregular topography also plays a role. Construction costs are least at grade, but this requires permanent occupancy of a strip of land and building of grade separations for all crossings. It is therefore generally feasible only in outlying areas where land is inexpensive, or in freeway medians where the cost of land and grade separations can be shared with the highway project. Elevated construction costs are perhaps twice as much as for facilities at grade, but the land below can be used for a street, for parking or industrial uses, or even for linear parks; BART in Albany and El Cerrito, CA., is an example of the latter. In densely built up areas, including CBDs, the adverse impacts of noise and reduction of daylight militate against elevated construction. A doubling, or even tripling, of costs occurs if underground alignments are considered. However, land costs are minimized by the use of street rights-of-way, easements under private property instead of outright purchase, and development of air rights over those parcels which must be acquired. Environmental deterioration is minimized, although it must be recognized that underground travel is not as attractive to passengers as moving in daylight. Construction costs are discussed further in a later section of this chapter.

An operational analysis determines the need for crossovers and storage tracks. The former are needed primarily for track maintenance purposes, while the latter provide opportunity for turning trains back short of the end of the line, or for storing disabled vehicles.

Commuter railroads. In some large metropolitan areas, such as New York, London, Paris, and Tokyo, a large burden of urban transportation is borne by intercity railroads. Many of the lines involved were located for intercity travel and, in generating urban land uses along their corridors, found themselves serving increasing numbers of local trips. Up to about 1920 some railroads added routes in the suburbs where they found sufficient demand. However, since that time many routes have been abandoned because of the high costs of railroad operation and the reluctance by management to allow long-distance passengers and freight customers to subsidize urban transportation.

Originally, railroads were usually laid out at grade with level highway crossings. In some cities, such crossings were eliminated later by changing the grade of the railroad, thereby providing it with a fully exclusive right-of-way. Passenger operation was, however, still sharing this facility with freight movements.

A major problem of urban railroad services is the location of the central terminals. There is almost always only one downtown access point per corridor, and this is often located at the edge of or outside the CBD. Typically, it is a stub terminal with inherent limitations to the number of train movements that can be handled per hour. In some cities with extensive electrified suburban lines, such as Brussels, Munich, Hamburg, and most recently Philadelphia, these drawbacks have been overcome by connecting terminals located on opposite sides of the CBD with underground tracks and one or more intermediate stations for direct access to the city center. Capacity is increased because trains no longer need to be reversed at crowded terminals. In Paris, suburban rail lines were diverted before reaching their old terminals into a new network of lines across the inner city. The resulting operations in these cities are a mixture of heavy rail transit in the center and commuter railroad outside it.

Vehicle dimensions, capacities, and accommodations

Typical ranges for key dimensional and capacity characteristics of transit vehicles currently in significant use are indicated in Table 7-2. Lengths and widths shown are external body dimensions. Heights are from pavement or top of rail to roof. The lower end of the ranges of number of seats shown and the upper end of the ranges for standees generally apply to vehicles used on high-volume routes in large cities. The largest numbers of seats and lowest number of standees occur on longer suburban routes, or where, for policy reasons, high levels of comfort are to be offered.

For rail vehicles, Table 7-2 also shows the maximum length of trains in common use, and the resulting total capacity per train.

Seats

Widths of seats per passenger typically vary from 16 to 24 in. (0.4 to 0.6 m) with 17 to 20 in. (0.43 to 0.50 m) typical of vehicles used in local and high-density service, and wider seats in buses and rail vehicles designed for longer suburban runs.

The spacing distance between backs on transverse seats typically varies from 26 to 34 in. (0.65 to 0.85 m), with the lower half of this range most common for vehicles used in high-density service.

Accordingly, the area per seated passenger typically varies from 2.9 to 5.7 ft^2 (0.27 to 0.53 m^2), with from 3.2 to 4.2 ft^2 (0.3 to 0.4 m^2) appropriate for local service vehicles.

Passenger seats are usually arranged transversely or longitudinally in relation to the vehicle body length. Transverse seating is usually preferred for passenger comfort, but vehicle narrowness, high planned proportions of standees, wheel housings, or other spatial considerations often impose longitudinal seating in portions or the entirety of vehicles. Pairs of transverse seats are occasionally notched (longitudinally offset from each other by several inches) to save space or improve comfort in reaching the seats farthest from the aisle. The dimensions of such seats fall within the ranges given above.

Standing area, aisles, and doors

The area per standing passenger under crush peak-period conditions can be as little as 1.6 ft^2 (0.15 m^2). The minimum area per standing passenger under easy standing conditions, used by various designers as a basis for peak period service scheduling, varies from perhaps 2.5 to 4.0 ft^2 (0.23 to 0.37 m^2).

Usually, minimum aisle widths on transit vehicles are

TABLE 7–2
Ranges of Geometric Dimensions and Passenger Capacities of Transit Vehicles

Transit Vehicle Type	Length ft m	Width ft m	Height ft m	Design Capacity of Single Unit: Seats	Standees	Total Passengers	Design Capacity of Maximum Train: Cars	Total Passengers
Van	15–18 4.5–5.5	5.5–7.2 1.7–2.2	7–9 2.0–2.8	10–16	—	10–16	—	—
Minibus	18–25 5.5–7.6	6.5–8.0 2.0–2.4	7.5–10 2.3–3.0	15–25	0–15	15–40	—	—
Transit bus								
Single unit	25–40 7.6–12.2	7.5–8.5 2.3–2.6	9–11 2.8–3.4	30–55	10–75	40–115	—	—
Articulated	54–60 16.5–18.3	8.0–8.5 2.4–2.6	9.5–10.5 2.9–3.2	35–75	30–125	95–185	—	—
Double-deck	30–40 9.1–12.2	7.5–8.5 2.3–2.6	13–14.5 4.0–4.4	50–85	15–50	90–130	—	—
Streetcar								
Single unit	40–55 12.2–16.8	6.5–9.0 2.0–2.7	10–11 3.0–3.4	20–60	40–80	75–130	3	225–400
Articulated	60–90 18.3–27.4	7.5–9.5 2.3–2.9	10–11 3.0–3.4	30–85	120–200	100–275	3	300–825
Rail transit car								
Steel wheel	45–75 13.7–23.0	8.5–11.0 2.6–3.4	10–13 3.0–4.0	40–85	50–250	100–330	8–10	1000–2700
Rubber-tired	48–60 15.2–18.3	8.0–9.5 2.4–2.9	11–12 3.4–3.7	35–55	70–130	110–170	9	1000–1500
Commuter railroad car								
Regular	65–85 20.0–26.0	9.5–10.5 3.0–3.2	12 3.7	80–110	20–120	100–200	10	1000–2000
Double-deck	65–85 20.0–26.0	10 3.0	14–16 4.3–4.8	110–165	20–150	160–270	10	1600–2700

SOURCE: *Lea Transit Compendium,* Vol. II (1975), Nos. 5, 6, 9; Vol. III (1976–1977), Nos. 5, 6, 9; M. A. SULKIN AND D. R. MILLER, *Some State-of-the-Art Characteristics of Rubber-Tired Rapid Transit* (Pasadena, Calif.: 27th California Transportation and Public Works Conference, 1975); various databooks and specifications.

between transversely positioned seats; here, aisle widths typically range from 21 to 31 in. (0.53 to 0.80 m).

On most transit vehicles, doorway widths per passenger lane for boarding and alighting vary from 22 to 30 in. (0.55 to 0.75 m), with the lower half of this range typical on vehicles used in local transit. In the United States, single-channel doors predominate. In some other countries, double-channel doors are used; in these cases the clear width per channel or lane is slightly less than for single-lane doors.

Seated and standing passenger capacities

To compute the seated and standing passenger capacities of specific transit vehicles from the data given above, the gross floor area (the product of the vehicle length and width) may be taken as a point of departure. From this must be subtracted:

- The thickness of the body shell, ducts, sashes, and related appurtenances, perhaps 5 to 10% of the gross floor area.
- The area taken up by operator's and/or conductor's seat or cab.
- The area taken up by on-board fare collection equipment, if any.
- The area that must be kept clear of standing passengers for the safe operation of the vehicle.

The resulting net floor area may then be apportioned between standing and seated passengers by selected ratios and areal allowances, based on management policy on levels of service and comfort. These ratios, also called passenger load factors, are discussed in the section on "Capacities" below. In designing the interior of transit vehicles, this policy also determines the dimensions and spacing of seats to be installed.

In rail vehicles, a trade-off is possible between passenger space and operational flexibility. Streetcars can be designed with a single end for driving and doors only on one side, thereby providing more space for seats and standees; however, route terminals must permit turning such vehicles through loops or turning "wyes." Heavy rail vehicles can also be simplified by having driving equipment at only one end and operating permanently in "married pairs"; this again results in a slight increase in the available passenger space.

Examples of specific contemporary vehicles

Table 7-3 summarizes dimensional, capacity, and passenger accommodation characteristics for six representative contemporary North American urban transit vehicles. The standee capacities shown are those given by the manufacturers and do not necessarily represent policies of operators who purchase these vehicles.

Vehicle performance

Acceleration, deceleration, and jerk

Maximum rates of acceleration, deceleration, and rate of change of acceleration and deceleration (jerk) in normal transit service must be related to the tolerance of a standee

TABLE 7–3
Selected Characteristics for Some Contemporary North American Urban Transit Vehicles

Characteristics	Unit	Urban Transit Bus, Nonarticulated, General Motors, RTS II, 1978	Urban Transit Bus, Articulated, AM General/MAN, SG-220-18-2A, 1978	Light Rail Vehicle, Articulated, Boeing-Vertol, for Boston MTA, 1976	Rail Transit Car, Steel Wheels Pullman-Standard, R-46, 1975*	Rail Transit Car, Rubber-Tires, Canadian-Vickers, for Montreal, 1975*	Regional Rail Transit Car, Rohr Corp., San Francisco BART, 1972*
Length of vehicle body	ft	40.0	59.66	71.0	75.0	56.5	71.0
	m	12.2	18.18	21.64	22.9	17.2	21.6
Maximum width of body	ft	8.5	8.5	8.85.2.70	10.0	8.3	10.5
	m	2.59	2.59		3.05	2.5	3.2
Height, wheels to roof	ft	9.9	10.34	11.33	12.1	12.0	10.5
	m	3.0	3.15	3.45	3.70	3.65	3.2
Seats		45†	73	52	73	40	72
Standees	Design/crush	23/47	37/72	167/230	142/277	118/169	60/156
Total passenger capacity	Design/crush	68/92	110/145	219/282	215/350	158/209	132/228
Maximum cars per train		—	—	3	8	9	10
Total train capacity	Design/crush	—	—	650/850	1690/2800	1420/1880	1320/2880
Width of seats	in.	17.5	17.0	17.5‡	18.0‡	17.5‡	22.0
	m	0.44	0.43	0.44‡	0.45‡	0.44‡	0.56
Spacing between backs of	in.	27.4	27.0	30.0‡	§	§	34.0
transverse seats	m	0.70	0.69	0.76‡			0.86
Area per seated passenger	in.^{2}	3.3	3.2	3.6‡	3.3‡	3.3‡	5.2
	m^2	0.31	0.30	0.34‡	0.31‡	0.31‡	0.48
Minimum aisle width	in.	22.5	22.0	44.8	39.0	19.0	30.0
	m	0.57	0.56	1.14	1.00	0.48	0.76
Clear doorway width per passenger	in.	30.0;22.0	24.6	27.0	25.0	25.5	27.0
lane	m	0.76;0.56	0.57	0.69	0.64	0.65	0.69
Doorways per side × lanes per door		1×2; 1×1	2×2	3×2	4×2	4×2	2×2
Passenger load factor	Design/crush	1.5/2.0	1.5/2.0	4.2/5.4	3.0/4.8	4.0/5.2	1.8/3.2
Empty weight	lb × 10^3	25.9	37.5	67.0	87.1	55.3	58.7
	kg × 10^3	11.7	16.95	30.4	39.5	25.1	26.6
Weight per passenger (design/crush)	lb	380/280	340/260	305/240	405/250	325/265	445/255
	kg	170/125	155/115	140/110	185/115	150/120	200/115
Rated power of engines (motors)	hp	225	235	410	460	400	560
	kW	168	175	313	342	298	418

*Data are average for the normal combination of "A" and "B" cars, or motorized cars and trailers, used to make up maximum length of trains.
†Maximum seating could be 47, but 2 seats were removed to provide more comfort for seated passengers.
‡Estimated, based on seat plans.
§Transverse seats not arranged in files, or no transverse seats.

SOURCE: General Motors Corp.; AM General Corp.; Boeing-Vertol Co.; AMERICAN PUBLIC TRANSIT ASSOCIATES, *Roster of North American Rapid Transit Cars: 1945–1976* (Washington, D.C.,: Jan. 1977).

who is not able to hold on to any kind of hand grip. This condition frequently occurs when passengers have both hands full (e.g., with bundles), when such passengers cannot reach a hand grip, or when a hand grip is not available. The jerk rate is more critical to passenger comfort, but the rates of acceleration and deceleration themselves are also important.

Acceleration and deceleration rates of from 3.0 to 3.5 mph/s (1.3 to 1.6 m/s^2) are usually considered appropriate upper limits under the mentioned conditions. A preferred maximum jerk rate is 2.0 mph/s^2 (0.9 m/s^3), and an allowable maximum jerk rate is about 50% above this value.

Speed–time–distance curves indicating maximum acceleration, cruising, and deceleration rates for two different types of transit vehicle are shown in Figures 7.1 and 7.2. Figure 7.1 provides data for a typical urban transit bus, and Figure 7.2 does the same for a modern rapid transit vehicle. Both figures represent operation with full seated loads on level traveled ways. Total loaded vehicle weight, grades, degree and type of moisture on the adhesion surfaces, wind speed and angle, air-conditioning power requirements, power transmission type, and other factors also affect vehicle performance.

Adhesion

Transit vehicles are required to come to stops more frequently than most other types of vehicles. The traction and braking efforts involved in such operation are therefore of paramount importance. The adhesion between vehicle wheels and the roadway or guideway surface determine the extent to which the tractive effort or braking force can be utilized. The maximum force that can be transferred between wheels and guideway surface is expressed by the formula

$$F = \mu \times W_n \qquad (7.1)$$

where F = friction (adhesion) force; same units as W_n

μ = dimensionless friction or adhesion coefficient

W_n = force normal to the guideway surface

On level surfaces, if power is applied through all axles, or if all wheels are braked, W_n is the gross weight of the vehicle. If only some axles are powered, or if brakes do not operate on all wheels, the value of W_n is only that portion of the vehicle weight transmitted through the powered or

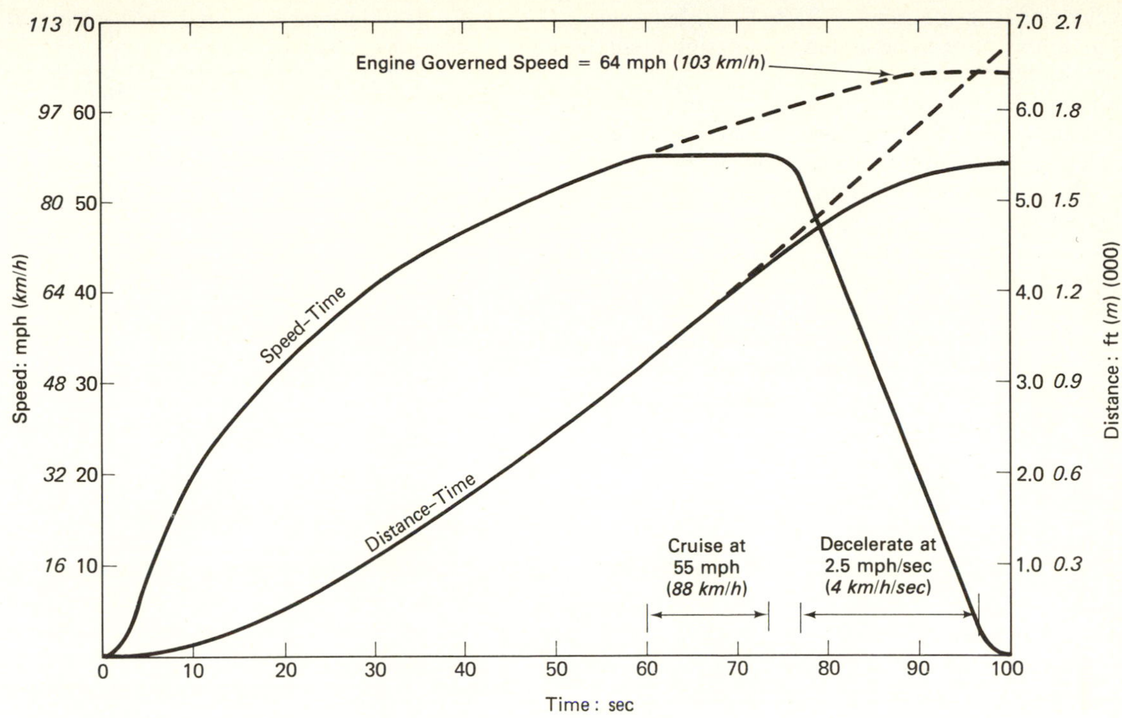

Figure 7.1. Speed-time-distance performance curves. Typical urban transit bus. Full seated load on level, tangent road, with all accessories, including air conditioning, in operation. SOURCE: GMC Truck & Coach Division, 1978.

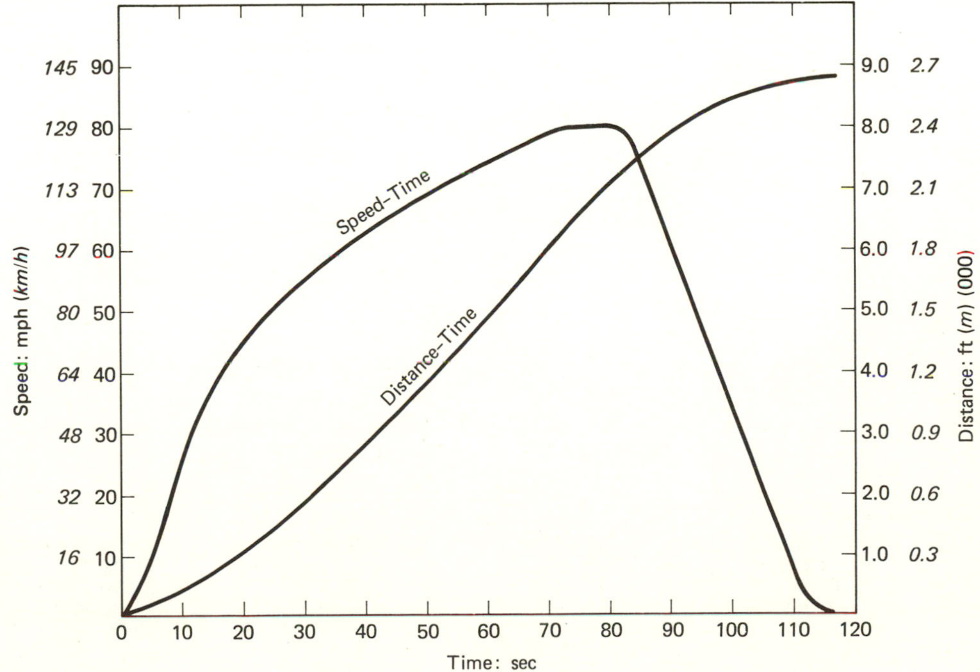

Figure 7.2. Speed-time-distance performance curves. Four-car San Francisco Bay Area Rapid Transit (BART) District train. Full seated load on level, tangent track. SOURCE: Parsons, Brinckerhoff-Tudor-Bechtel, general engineering consultants to BART.

brake wheels, and maximum tractive or braking effort is reduced.

Values for μ for rubber-tired vehicles on typical roadway surfaces are given in Chapter 6, Table 6-48. These values can also be applied as approximations for buses and for rubber-tired rail transit vehicles in clean condition. However, since the latter vehicles are guided positively, they tend to build up rubber deposits along narrow tracks of the guideway surface, with consequent reduction of the value of the friction coefficient. Steel wheels on dry steel rail develop values of μ in the range 0.25 to 0.30, but values as low as 0.18 may have to be assumed in design to allow for slippery conditions.

In addition to the types of materials used in the traveled way surface and wheels, the textures of the contact surfaces of these materials, the condition of the roadway or guideway (including slipperiness when damp or wet) and of the wheels, loaded vehicle weight, grades, and other factors influence adhesion characteristics.

To produce maximum tractive effort, all axles are powered in most modern rail transit trains. However, train formations of some large systems (e.g., London, Paris, Montreal) include nonmotorized trailers; these trade off some tractive effort in exchange for lower vehicle weight and lower vehicle and energy costs.

Velocities

In transit operations, the following speed terms are used:

○*Maximum speed*—the maximum vehicle performance capability with seated load on a level alignment.
○*Platform speed*—the service speed over a route, including allowance for passenger stops and traffic delays.
○*Schedule speed*—the average speed on a route when time spent at the terminals for layover is also included.

The platform speed for a trip on a route being designed or checked (V_p) can be computed from

$$V_p = \frac{D}{T_p} \tag{7.2}$$

where $T_p = \Sigma\, T_{ij}$ (sum of travel times between all stops along the route in seconds)

D = distance covered by the route, ft or m

$$T_{ij} = \frac{D_{ij}}{V_c} + V_c\left(\frac{1}{2a} + \frac{1}{2b}\right) + T_d(i) \tag{7.2a}$$

provided that

$$V_c < \frac{D_{ij}}{\sqrt{\dfrac{1}{2a} + \dfrac{1}{2b}}} \tag{7.2b}$$

and where D_{ij} = distance between stops i and j, ft or m

V_c = cruising (maximum) speed, ft/s or m/s

a = rate of acceleration, ft/s^2 or m/s^2

b = rate of deceleration, ft/s^2 or m/s^2

$T_d(i)$ = dwell time at stop i, s

The constraint in equation (7.2b) assures that the value for V_c used in formula (7.2a) can actually be achieved between stops i and j. The procedure assumes constant rates of acceleration and deceleration, which do not occur in practice. A more precise formulation, which includes consideration of jerk rates, is found in *Transit System Theory*.[1] The value of V_c is subject to maximum speed limits for highway vehicles. Computation of values for T_d are discussed later. Schedule speeds can be computed by adding the terminal layover times to the value of T_p in formula (7.2).

Table 7-4 shows typical ranges of maximum and platform speeds for different types of transit vehicles and services.

[1] ANDERSON, J. E. *Transit System Theory* (Lexington, Mass.: Lexington Books/ D. C. Heath, 1978), Chap. 2.

TABLE 7-4
Typical Vehicle Velocities and Stop Spacings

Transit Vehicle and Service Type	Maximum Performance Speeds	Platform Speeds	Linear Stop Spacing		
			CBDs	Non-CBD: Traditional Practice	Non-CBD: Some Modern Systems with Longer Stop Spacings
	mph km/h	mph km/h	ft m	ft m	ft m
Urban bus					
Local	50–65	8–14	500–1000	500–800	1000–1500
	80–105	13–23	150–300	150–250	300–460
Limited stop	50–65	12–18	500–1000	1200–3000	2000–5000
	80–105	20–30	150–300	360–900	600–1500
Express	50–65	16–32	*	4000–30,000	5000–15,000
	80–105	25–50		1200–9000	1500–45,000
Streetcar, local	40–60	8–15	500–1000	500–800	1000–1500
	65–95	13–25	150–300	150–250	300–460
Light rail transit	50–65	15–35	1000–2000	—	2000–5000
	80–105	25–55	300–600		600–1500
Heavy rail transit	50–70	15–35	1000–2500	1700–3500	3500–8000
	80–110	25–55	300–750	500–1000	1000–2500
Regional rapid transit	70–85	35–55	2000–3000	—	6000–30,000
	110–135	55–90	600–900		1800–9000
Commuter railroad	70–100	25–65	*	4000–15,000	8000–30,000
	100–160	40–105		1200–4500	2500–9000

*Usually stops at only one or two terminals in or adjacent to CBD.

SOURCE: Various specifications, plans, schedules, and other reports.

Vehicle weight and energy consumption

The ranges of weights for different types of urban transit vehicles are shown in Table 7-5, which also lists the ranges of weight/design capacity ratios; the latter is one measure of efficiency, because propulsion energy consumption depends more on vehicle weight than on any other factor.

TABLE 7–5
Ranges of Weight of Transit Vehicles

Transit Vehicle Type	Empty Weight (lb × 1000) (kg × 1000)	Weight/Unit Design Capacity (lb/psgr) (kg/psgr)
Van	5–7.5	200–650
	2.3–3.4	90–300
Minibus	7–17	200–700
	3.1–7.7	90–320
Transit bus		
Single unit	14–26	175–340
	6.3–12.0	80–155
Articulated	28–36	160–360
	13–16	75–165
Double-deck	15–28	200–230
	6.8–13.0	90–105
Streetcar		
Single unit	36–52	320–575
	16–24	145–260
Articulated	45–110	250–600
	20–50	115–275
Rail transit		
Steel wheel	35–90	200–500
	16–40	90–225
Rubber tired	44–75	275–450
	20–34	125–200
Commuter railroad car		
Regular	70–115	350–600
	32–52	160–275
Double-deck	100–125	400–750
	45–57	180–340

SOURCE: *Lea Transit Compendium*, Vol. II (1975), Nos. 5, 6, 9; Vol. III (1976–1977), Nos. 5, 6, 9; various other databooks and specifications.

Comparison of energy efficiency of different types of transit technology is very difficult. It must take into account a broad spectrum of factors involved in making the transit service possible, such as propulsion energy, the energy required to operate stations, control systems, and other appurtenances, and the energy required to construct and maintain the system and its vehicles. Total system analysis might also include energy consumed by passengers accessing a system. Finally, data must be obtained or assumed about the unit of productivity on the basis of which the comparison is to be made [often the passenger-mi (passenger-km) produced]. Widely varying results and interpretations have been reported,[2,3] reflecting disagreements about assumptions to be made and about the proper method of analysis.

Total energy consumed by transit vehicles in the United States amounts to roughly 420 million gal (1600 million liters) per year of diesel fuel and 2200 million kWh of electricity.[4] This is a very small proportion of total energy consumption by all transportation modes. The use of gasoline and propane in transit buses has become almost negligible; however, gasoline is still the fuel used in vans and small buses.

[2] CONGRESSIONAL BUDGET OFFICE, *Urban Transportation and Energy: The Potential Savings of Different Modes* (Washington, D.C.: Sept. 1977), 81 p.; and *Hearings before the Senate Subcommittee on Transportation* (Washington, D.C.: Oct. 1977), 334 p.

[3] MCCOY, M. "Transit's Energy Efficiency," *Transit J.*, *4*(4), 4–22 (Fall 1978).

System characteristics

Preceding sections of this chapter have been concerned with the capabilities and characteristics of fixed facilities and vehicles, which are component parts of transit systems. This and the following sections will deal with the complete system rather than its parts.

Kinds of routes

Geographically, several kinds of routes can be identified:

1. *Radial routes* radiate from the CBD. These are the "backbones" of a transit network and usually carry the largest numbers of passengers per unit length of route. They may have one terminal in the CBD, or may serve two different radial corridors by running through the CBD. Rail transit routes are almost always radial.
2. *Circumferential routes* provide service between different outlying areas without requiring travel through the CBD. By intercepting radial routes, they also serve as feeder/distributors for the latter. In very large metropolitan areas, complete circles are sometimes formed; in Europe, where these circles often connect a group of railroad terminals, such circular routes are sometimes served by rail transit.
3. *Crosstown routes* are similar to circumferential routes, except that the term is usually applied to short routes on fairly straight alignment, tangential to the CBD and perpendicular to radial routes.
4. *Feeder routes* connect certain outlying areas to radial routes where through routing to the CBD is infeasible.
5. *Shuttle routes* provide service between two major traffic generators, such as between the CBD and an outlying parking facility or railroad terminal.

Urban transit service

Service on the routes described above may be of one or more of the following types:

1. *Local service* serves all stops along a route. It is the basic and preponderant form of service in an urban transit network.
2. *Limited-stop and express service* becomes feasible when radial routes extend more than about 3 mi (5 km) from the CBD, and when patronage volumes thereon are large enough (especially with longer than average trip lengths) to sustain such service. Often such routes extend beyond the terminal of the complementing local route, operating

[4] AMERICAN PUBLIC TRANSIT ASSOCIATION, *'78–'79 Transit Fact Book* (Washington, D.C.: 1979), Table 17.

limited-stop or express in the inner area and as a local service beyond the terminal of the local line. Thus, in urban transit networks, there are sometimes two or more "rings" of local service, the inner ring being served directly by local routes and the outer ring(s) by routes that operate limited or express service in the inner ring. Such patterns are highly developed in cities such as Cleveland, Ohio, and in the San Francisco Peninsula suburban service of the San Mateo County Transit District. Often, limited-stop and express service is warranted only during peak periods, although special service, such as to airports, will be scheduled all day. Limited-stop service operates along city streets with stops mainly at major transfer points beyond the CBD. Express service involves even faster operation, often on freeways or other major highways parallel to the local route that it supplements.

3. *Secondary distribution* routes include internal service within major activity centers. They may also provide connections between such centers and transportation terminals or major parking facilities.

4. *Other types of transit routes* may be provided for special events, "owl" periods (consolidation of two or more daytime routes), outlying employment locations at shift-change times, and similar special situations which suggest the tailoring of service to the demand.

Paratransit

Paratransit covers a wide range of collective passenger movement types:

- School buses
- Social, health, and related special bus and van services
- Subscription (or "club") buses
- Community and neighborhood services by small buses and vans
- Jitneys
- Variable-route and route-deviation services by buses or vans
- Shared taxis and regular taxi services
- Vanpools and carpools
- Organized share-ride (hitchhiking) services

Many of these types of services are organized and/or operated by private companies, social agencies, or welfare organizations. Transit operators have been exploring opportunities which can be served by the equipment that is available to them.

A bus operating on a fixed route or schedule may, for example, be programmed to deviate from that route up to a certain distance to pick up and deliver passengers, and still operate within the general framework of the route and schedule involved. This is sometimes called flexible route service.

Still more freedom from route and schedule constraints is introduced by "dial-a-ride" service. Routes are determined dynamically by current demand, and schedules may only provide for vehicles meeting each other or fixed route service at some interval, such as once an hour; in some cases, there is no schedule at all. Service may focus at one or a few traffic generators ("many-to-few" service) or may be unconstrained within the area served ("many-to-many" service). Dial-a-ride service approaches the characteristics of on-call taxi service, except that several passengers and their individual origins and destinations are served on the same trip, often by a vehicle larger than a taxi. Adopted criteria for the maximum duration between phone calls for immediate service and vehicle arrival for pickup ("response time") usually help determine the size of the service area for individual dial-a-ride vehicles.

Manual or computer dispatching, or both, are required to translate passengers' calls for service into efficient temporal and spatial distribution of that service. Costs per passenger served are increased thereby. If fares are kept within or near the framework of customary transit fares, and/or if regular transit employees are used, flexible route (particularly dial-a-ride) services are likely to be considerably more expensive than fixed route transit service in relation to revenues generated.

Paratransit may be faced with special problems. Representation in policymaking may not be adequate at all levels of government, regulation may be unequal or inadequate, and transit labor contracts and labor relations may impose difficulties in successful paratransit implementation. There may be some organizational fragmentation in conducting and coordinating the many potential types of paratransit services in an urban institutional setting. Because many paratransit operations are small, there may be difficulty in attracting or retaining desirable management quality, and paratransit may suffer in competition with other agencies for funding support. Insurance coverage and costs for various types of paratransit may present additional challenges. On the other hand, none or only a few of these considerations may exist, and those that do may be overcome by effective strategies.

Paratransit should complement conventional transit service effectively and economically where the latter exists, each undertaking the functions best performed by it. Paratransit may have advantages when providing service in places and/or at times when conventional transit cannot provide them, meeting needs of special groups of travelers, helping to make more efficient use of existing or potential transportation resources, and providing economic service and other benefits. In some instances, paratransit has been operated in direct competition with conventional transit. In high-density corridors this may not be detrimental; but in medium- and low-density markets such competition has usually proved to be unsustainable.

Route systems

Many factors influence the overall transit route network configuration in an urban area. The configuration is defined in terms of time (periods and schedules of service), space (routes, stops, and fixed-facility geography), technology, service type, and other characteristics. Spatially and geographically, transit networks may vary widely in complexity and in interrelationships with other transportation networks.

They may take such forms as radial with a single center, radial with circumferential routes, regular or irregular grid pattern, trunk-and-feeders, multicenter (in metropolitan areas with two or more major cities), elongated spine, or combinations of such forms. The scope of this discussion does not permit more than a listing of influencing factors, but a number of them are treated elsewhere in this chapter. Major considerations in the evolution of a transit network include:

1. The overall area to be served, its geography, topography, and land use
2. Policies and master plans regarding land use and transportation
3. Service area coverage standards
4. Location of major traffic generators
5. Patronage volumes and patterns in time and space
6. Accessibility standards, and resulting stop and station locations
7. Service headway standards
8. Capacities of available systems and vehicles
9. Streets and other rights-of-way available for transit use
10. Land available for yards and maintenance facilities
11. Role of other urban transit systems
12. Interfaces with intercity transportation systems

Service area coverage

In order to reach a transit stop or station, patrons will usually travel up to the distance maxima shown in Table 7-6. A few patrons may travel considerably farther, but they are not typical. Acceptable walking distances from origin to boarding stop and from alighting stop to destination is usually taken to be 0.3 to 0.4 mi (0.5 to 0.6 km); such figures, of course, do not apply to the elderly and handicapped.

The acceptable walking distance is also affected by the quality of the transit service (patrons may walk farther for better service than for very poor service), perceptions of security en route and at the stop, available alternatives, quality of the traveled access ways, weather conditions, and other factors. The combined access time to/from transit stops at both ends of a trip may exceed the time spent on the transit vehicle itself, especially if the latter is relatively fast and involves no transfers.

TABLE 7–6
Typical Maximum Distance Traveled to Reach Urban Transit Stops and Stations

Access Mode	Most Patrons (mi) (km)	Some Patrons (mi) (km)
Walk	0.4–0.6	0.6–1.0
	0.6–1.0	1.0–1.6
Bicycle	1.0–2.0	2.0–3.0
	1.6–3.2	3.2–4.8
Feeder transit; motorcycle	2.0–4.0	4.0–8.0
	3.2–6.4	6.4–13.0
Auto		
Kiss-ride; taxi	3.0–4.0	4.0–6.0
	4.8–6.4	6.4–9.7
Park-ride	4.0–6.0	6.0–10.0
	6.4–9.7	9.7–16.0

SOURCE: HENRY D. QUINBY, "Coordinated Highway-Transit Interchange Stations," *Origin and Destination: Methods and Evaluation*, Highway Res. Rec. 114 (Washington, D.C.: Highway Research Board, 1966), pp. 99–121; various other reference data.

TABLE 7–7
Accessibility Standards for Urban Transit

Population Density (thousands/mi²) (thousands/km²)	Average Route Spacing: Radial Routes (mi) (km)	Average Route Spacing: Circumferential Routes (mi) (km)	Route Density (route-mi/mi²) (route-km/km²)
Over 12	0.40	0.60	4.00
Over 4.6	0.65	1.00	2.50
10–12	0.50	0.75	3.33
3.9–4.6	0.80	1.20	2.00
8–10	0.60	0.90	2.67
3.1–3.9	1.00	1.50	1.67
6–8	0.80	1.20	2.00
2.3–3.1	1.25	2.00	1.25
4–6	1.00	1.50	2.67
1.5–2.3	1.60	2.40	1.00
2–4	1.00	—	1.00
0.8–1.5	1.60		0.60
Under 2	2.00	—	0.50
Under 0.8	3.20		0.30

SOURCE: Adapted from MASSACHUSETTS BAY TRANSPORTATION AUTHORITY, *Service Policy for Surface Public Transportation* (Boston: 1975).

Area coverage or accessibility is also a function of the spacing of routes. Standards, such as those shown in Table 7-7, can be used to design adequate transit networks. These standards are usually modified to provide better accessibility (closer spacing of routes) where terrain hampers walking, and they do not apply to special services for the elderly or handicapped.

Transit stops

The spacing, location, design, and operation of transit stops (both intermediate line stops and terminals) have major effects on transit vehicle and system performance. (The term "stops" includes stations.) Stop spacing is a primary determinant of transit schedule and platform speeds. Stop location and spacing also affect door-to-door travel times and, hence, demand.

Spacing

Typical ranges of stop spacings for different modes and service types are shown in Table 7-4. Because of the general tendency toward overall reduction in door-to-door transit travel times and toward specific increase in transit vehicle speeds and utilization, the average distance between stops has been increased in some metropolitan regions on surface transit routes and in the planning of new rail transit facilities.

Research has been conducted on optimum spacing of rail

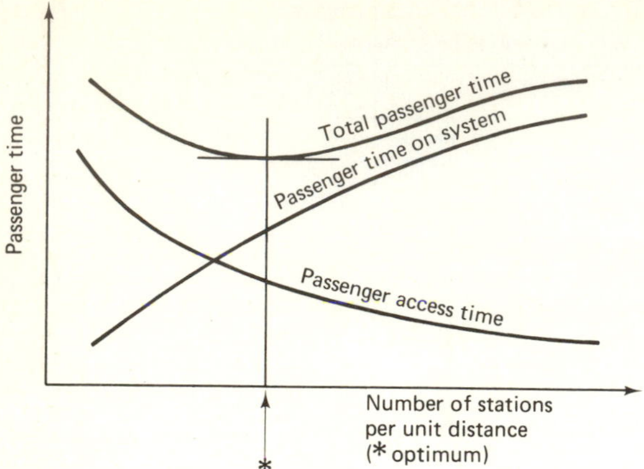

Figure 7.3. Passenger travel time as a function of the station spacing along a route. SOURCE: Adapted from V.R. Vuchic, *Interstation Spacing for Line-Haul Passenger Transportation*, Graduate Report, Berkeley Calif.: University of California, Institute of Transportation and Traffic Engineering, 1966, Fig. 11.

transit stations. Figure 7.3 illustrates the type of result that is sought with respect to optimizing passenger travel time.

Rail transit systems sometimes employ skip-stop operation to accelerate service, especially when existing stops may be spaced relatively closely. Half the trains along a route section in such operation do not stop at one group of stations; the other half bypasses other stations. All trains make important stops in CBDs and at major transfer and terminal points. Minimum possible train headways may be greater with skip-stop operation than without it. It is inconvenient for passengers who wish to travel between stations in different skip-stop groups, for they must transfer at a station where all trains stop. But these disadvantages may be more than balanced by the travel-time savings obtained.

Location

Bus stops. Bus stops on streets are usually located adjacent to the curb for direct, safe passenger access to and from sidewalks. The most common type—the box zone—is designated by pavement and curb markings indicating parking and stopping prohibitions for other motor vehicles. Pole-mounted signs also indicate the stop and provide information for waiting passengers. Where sidewalk width permits, shelters and benches are desirable at busy stops, especially where service headways exceed a few minutes. Shelter walls offer space for the transmission of more detailed information, such as maps and schedules, from transit management to the public, and for advertising.

Stops may be located either in the approach ("near side") or the exit ("far side") of an intersection or in midblock locations. The choice is made on the basis of turning movements of buses at the intersections, major turning movements of other traffic, the status of the cross street, transfer flows (if any), and the location of large traffic generators.[5]

Near-side stops are preferred where more traffic joins the street than turns off it, at intersections with one-way streets moving from right to left, and at locations where buses will make a right turn. Far-side stops are suggested where there are heavy turning movements off the street, at intersections with one-way streets moving from left to right, and where buses make left turns. The choice is also influenced by the time–space diagram of signal timing along the street (see Chapter 24), for judicious stop spacing can minimize delays experienced by buses because of red signal indications. The final choice also depends on the location of stops on intersecting bus routes or entrances to rail transit stations, and on the adequacy of the sidewalks.

Midblock stops are more rarely used, and never at major transfer points. They may be justified in long blocks at the center of which major traffic demand is generated, or where insufficient locations at adjacent intersections exist. The latter can happen if the number of buses per hour on all routes using a street exceeds the capacity of a single stop, and duplicate stops for different groups of routes are needed.

In locating bus stops, other factors to be considered include the origins and destinations of passengers, adjacent land uses and activities, truck loading and automobile parking needs, and physical factors, such as driveways, utility poles, trees, and hydrants.

Occasionally, special stops are needed in freeway rights-of-way. Many express routes use freeways only as a fast connection between the CBD and outlying areas, and are not designed to provide service along the freeway. However, some routes to outer suburbs, where low density of demand makes branch routes unfeasible, may need freeway bus stops. Additional needs for such facilities occur where freeway routes intersect important circumferential routes, usually near the perimeter of the CBD.

Where diamond interchanges exist, bus operators prefer to have buses leave via the off-ramp, stop at the intersecting street, and then reenter the freeway. This minimizes walking distances for passengers. At more complex interchanges, where buses would lose considerable time in reaching the street, special stops with approach and exit lanes and pedestrian path connections to the intersecting street are fitted into the interchange layout.[6] They should be located to provide quick and easy access to and from the through freeway lanes with a minimum of interference to through traffic. Acceleration and deceleration lanes are generally required.

Streetcar stops. Some of the considerations listed above for bus stops may in some degree also apply to streetcar stops. However, when the tracks are located adjacent to the street centerline, boarding and alighting areas must be accommodated within the roadway. Accordingly, locational considerations are somewhat different.

If the track area is paved for motor vehicle use, special protected islands are ideally located along the tracks at streetcar stops. If, much more preferably, the tracks are located in a center mall or median, then the stops are also located there. To utilize often-limited street cross-sectional

[5]INSTITUTE OF TRAFFIC ENGINEERS, *A Recommended Practice for the Proper Location of Bus Stops* (Washington, D.C.: 1967).

[6]AMERICAN ASSOCIATION OF STATE HIGHWAY OFFICIALS, *A Policy on Design of Urban Highways and Arterial Streets* (Washington, D.C.: 1973), pp. 486–494. See also Chapter 19 of this handbook.

width fully, the motor vehicle moving lanes alongside a central streetcar reservation may be eased over into the curb parking lane area in the vicinity of a streetcar stop, so that the platform at the stop may occupy the space thus made available. If cross-street traffic volumes approach expressway proportions, consideration can be given to grade separation of the streetcar tracks (and, perhaps, the stop platforms), by adjusting the vertical profile of the tracks, taking advantage of the steep grades (up to 10%) which can be negotiated by streetcars on short ramps.

Bus route terminals. Outer, intermediate, and many CBD bus route terminals usually consist of curbside box zones of sufficient length to accommodate the maximum number of terminal layover buses required. Routes generally terminate in a loop around one or more city blocks, and the layover point is located within or very close to that loop. In locating this terminal, care must be taken with respect to noise impact, space, and driver safety, in addition to the factors cited in the bus stop discussion earlier.

Sometimes, such terminal loops occur off-street, often as remnants of abandoned streetcar operations, in which case minimum curve radii of 40 ft (12 m) are appropriate, with loop lane widths from 15 to 20 ft (4.5 to 6 m). Storage space again must be provided for buses laying over, and also for a passenger waiting area.

Major bus terminals. Multiple-platform terminals are built in CBDs when many bus routes terminate near one point, perhaps with some routes passing through such terminals. They must usually be located off-street or in large plazas or other open spaces. Some urban bus terminals may be multimodal, involving also streetcars, rail transit, intercity rail and bus stations, and/or airport ground access.

The typical layout of a terminal includes entry and exit roadways (which may connect directly to a freeway, bridge, or tunnel), an internal network of roads, bus berths, pedestrian walkways, and often stairs and escalators leading to a passenger concourse and to adjacent streets and facilities (Figure 7.4).

The number of bus berths is calculated from estimates of expected bus volumes, dwell times at the berths, and the need for layover spaces. Berths are often of the parallel type for arriving commuter buses, of the shallow sawtooth type for departing commuter buses, and of the deep sawtooth type (requiring backing up on departure) for intercity buses. Table 7-8 lists data on some major bus terminals in the United States. Further information on terminal design is found in NCHRP Report 155.[7]

Rail transit and commuter railroad stations. Stations should be located so that good access and circulation is provided for the area to be served. When stations serve major urban centers (such as CBDs) and subcenters, they should usually be located to maximize convenience of pedestrian access. Stations that depend on automobiles and buses for substantial proportions of total passenger access should usually be located to optimize vehicular access and general vehicular circulation in the station vicinity.

Where access is expected to be by a number of modes, the station design must provide for safe circulation within the station area, separation of vehicular from pedestrian flows wherever possible, and the geometrics of loading and unloading areas, access roads, and parking facilities. The latter can be designed in much the same manner as other parking facilities (see Chapter 21). However, it is usual to divide the facility into a general area for unrestricted parking by patrons who will use the rail system ("park-ride") and a special area near the station entrance for short-term parking by vehicles waiting to pick up passengers arriving at the station ("kiss-ride"). Standard dimensions for stalls and aisles are used, but special areas striped for compact cars may be justified by site configuration or on the basis of special studies of the proportion of compact cars used by transit patrons. Bicycle lockers are also often furnished.

Space must be provided as close to the station entrance as possible for loading and unloading of feeder buses and taxis, connected to the street system by direct access roads. Parallel or shallow sawtooth berths are used. Since a rail transit station is often a terminal point for feeder buses, an area for bus layover may also be needed.[8]

Rail terminals. Streetcar terminals at street level are either of the stub end or loop type. In the former, only double-ended vehicles can be used, but space requirements are minimal. Loops, permitting the use of single-ended cars, are laid out either around a city block or on private property adjacent to the route. Grade-separated streetcar terminals are similar to rail transit terminnals except for platform heights. In all cases, consideration must be given to the possibility that the operating schedule will require some vehicles to lay over at the terminal, and that extra track space must be furnished for this purpose.

Rail transit terminals are similar to other rail transit stations, except for possible tail tracks for train reversal and storage, possible connections to storage yards, and space for dispatcher and train crews. In modern scheduling practice, trains begin their return journey immediately after unloading, but crews lay over by "dropping back" to a later train. Although a few rail transit routes end in loops—with some operational advantages—almost all rail transit terminals are of the stub end configuration. Crossovers are often located in front of the platform area. However, this limits capacity and reliability: two crossovers—one in front of the platform and one in a tail track area—are preferred.

Boarding–alighting times

Table 7-9 summarizes typical loading and unloading times per passenger per lane or channel of door space for transit vehicles. As can be seen, minimum times and maximum flow rates are obtained with high platforms (no steps to negotiate) and prepaid or postpaid fares. Pronounced

[7]Levinson, H. S. et al., *Bus Use of Highways: Planning and Design Guidelines*. Natl. Highway Res. Program Report 155 (Washington, D.C.: Transportation Research Board, 1975), Chap. 6.

[8]For further discussion, see Quinby, H. D. "Coordinated Highway-Transit Interchange Stations," *Highway Res. Rec. 114* (Washington, D.C.: Highway Research Board, 1966), pp. 99–121.

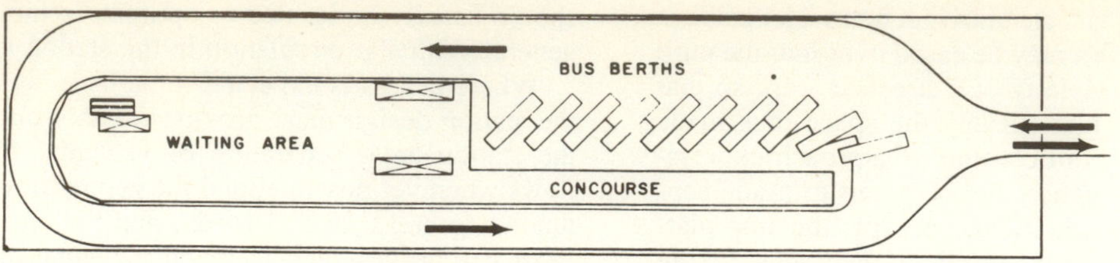

INTERCITY BUS LEVEL

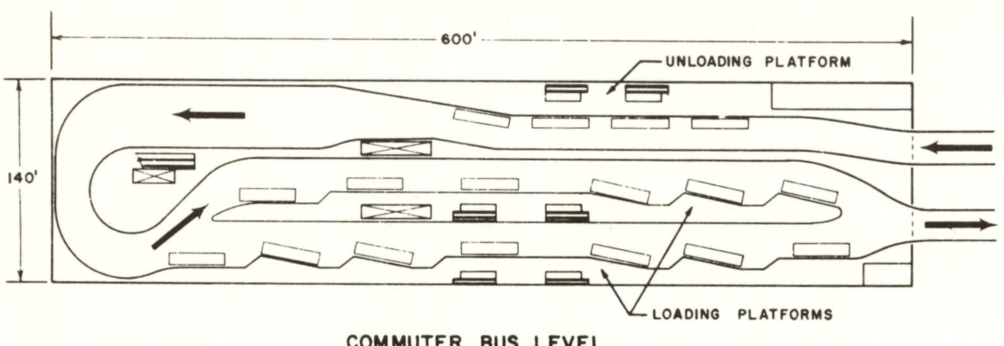

COMMUTER BUS LEVEL

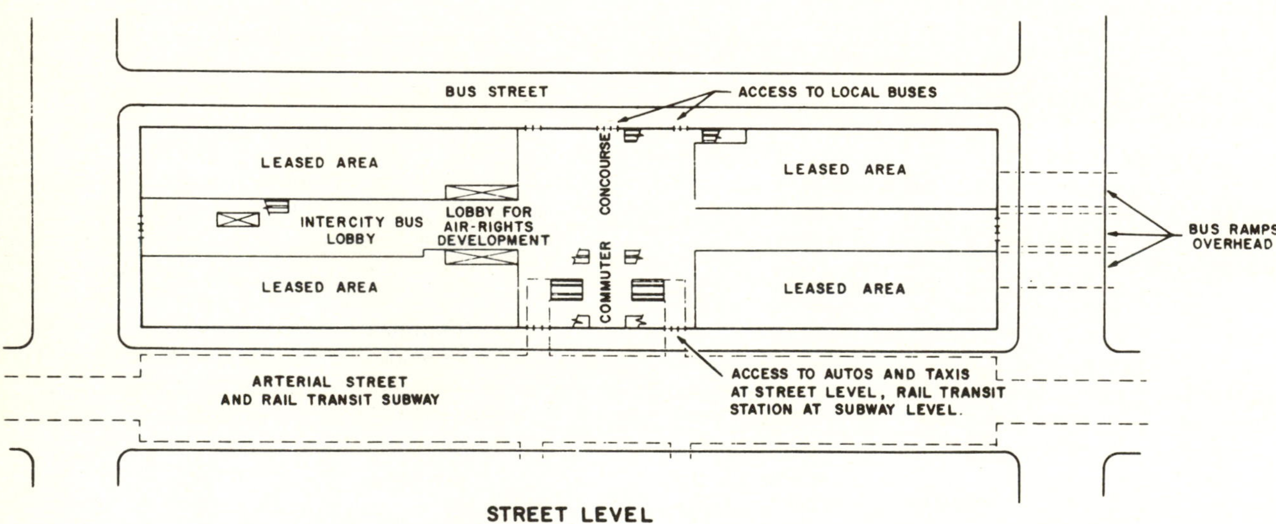

STREET LEVEL

Figure 7.4. Typical CBD bus terminal layout for a large city. SOURCE: Herbert S. Levinson, et al., *Bus Use of Highways: Planning and Design Guidelines,* National Cooperative Highway Research Program Report 155, Washington, D.C.: Transportation Research Board, 1975, Fig. 98.

crowding inside or immediately outside the vehicle may markedly increase the boarding–alighting times cited in this table.

Vehicle dwell times

The standing time of a transit vehicle making a passenger service stop comprises several components. Time must be allowed for the opening and closing of doors (usually from 1 to 4 s/stop), for the alighting and boarding of passengers, and sometimes for additional components, such as waiting to start, maneuvering into moving traffic (for buses only), or waiting ahead of the stop because of preceding vehicles or trains not having cleared the area.

Although passengers, especially in peak periods, tend to try to optimize their spatial distribution for boarding, alighting, or traveling on transit vehicles, imbalances in these functions frequently occur, resulting in varying demands for space at different doors. This imbalance factor must be taken into account when computing dwell time, either by identifying the passenger flow at the busiest door(s) or by adding 10 or 15% to the times obtained for the average value per door, lane, or channel.

TABLE 7–8
Principal Bus Terminals in the United States

Name of Terminal	Type of Bus Service	Number of Bus Levels	Number of Bus Berths	Contiguous Transportation Facilities	Direct Ramp Connections	Number of Passengers*,†		Number of Buses*,†	
						Daily	Peak Hour	Daily	Peak Hour
Port Authority Bus Terminal, New York, NY	Regional, intercity	3	184	Subways, local buses, auto parking	Lincoln Tunnel	105,500	32,600	3350	730
George Washington Bridge Bus Terminal, New York, NY	Regional, intercity	2	43	Subway, local buses	G.W. Bridge	20,000	4200	850	108
Greyhound Bus Terminal Clark and Randolph Sts., Chicago, IL	Mainly intercity	1	30	Subway, local buses	Garvey St. and Wacker Drive	10,000	n.a.	n.a.	n.a.
Transbay Terminal, San Francisco, CA	Regional, tour buses	1	37	Streetcars and buses, auto parking	Oakland Bay Bridge	35,000‡ 22,000§	16,000‡ 10,000§	1150‡ 900§	400‡ 250§
Market Street East Bus Terminal, Philadelphia, PA (planned)	Regional, intercity	2	70	Subway, railroad, streetcar, local buses, auto parking	Vine St. Expressway	n.a.	5900	n.a.	170

*Bus and passenger volumes for one direction only.
†n.a., not available.
‡1974 (before commencement of BART transbay service).
§1977 (after commencement of BART transbay service).

SOURCE: LEVINSON H.S. ET AL., *Bus Use of Highways: State of the Art,* National Cooperative Highway Res. Program 143, (Washington, D.C.: Transportation Research Board, 1973), Table 24. Transbay terminal data are from traffic counts by Institute of Transportation Studies, University of California, Berkeley, Calif., 1974, 1977.

TABLE 7–9
Average Boarding and Alighting Intervals for Transit Vehicles

Operation	Physical Conditions	Operational Conditions	Seconds/ Passenger/ Lane*
Boarding	High-level platform (rapid transit)	Fares paid at fare gates	1.0
		Fares paid off vehicle (at fare gates or by passes)	2.0
	Low-level or no platform (buses and streetcars)	Single-coin or token fare paid on vehicle	3.0†
		Multiple-coin fare paid on vehicle	4.0†
		Zone fares prepaid; tickets registered on vehicle	4.0–6.0
		Zone fares paid on vehicle	6.0–8.0†
Alighting	High-level platform	No ticket checking at vehicle doors	1.0
	Low-level or no platform	No ticket checking at vehicle doors	1.7
		Ticket checking or issue of transfers at vehicle doors	2.5–4.0

*A lane represents one file of persons, 22–24 in. (55–60 cm) wide. Assumes that all lanes are used equally; however, allowance is usually made for the fact that whereas some lanes are used to capacity, others operate below that flow rate.
†Where "exact fares" are required and drivers do not make change, times may be somewhat less.

SOURCE: LEVINSON H.S. ET AL., *Bus Use of Highway: Planning and Design Guidelines*, National Cooperative Highway Res. Program Report 155 (Washington, D.C.: Transportation Research Board, 1975).

Human–mechanical interfacing on a transit system is most critical in the immediate vicinity of vehicle doors at passenger stops. Human supervision of boarding and alighting, especially during peak periods, is essential. This supervision may be in the form of an onboard crew member (vehicle operator or train guard), assisted by mirrors and perhaps closed-circuit television, or by station personnel on platforms or at busy stops.

Lengths and capacity of bus loading zones

Table 7-10 shows the minimum lengths for bus loading zones at street curbs and in off-street facilities, such as bus terminals.

TABLE 7–10
Minimum Desirable Lengths for Bus Loading Zones*

Type of Bus Loading Zone	Length of Zone for Single Berth†		Additional Length for Second Berth	
	ft	m	ft	m
Curb loading zones				
Near side‡	$L + 65$	$L + 20$	$L + 5$	$L + 1.5$
Far side§	$L + 40$	$L + 12$	L	L
Midblock§	$L + 100$	$L + 30$	L	L
Off-street zones				
Parallel‖	$L + 40$	$L + 12$	$L + 5$	$L + 1.5$
Shallow sawtooth**	$L + 25$	$L + 7.5$	Not applicable	

*L = Length of longest bus using the loading zone.
†Based on side of bus positioned 1 ft (30 cm) from curb. If bus is to be positioned 6 in. (15 cm) from curb, 20 ft (6 m) should be added to near-side stops, 15 ft (4.5 m) to far-side stops, 35 ft (11 m) to midblock stops.
‡Add 15 ft (4.5 m) where buses are required to make a right turn, or 30 ft (9 m) if there is also heavy right-turn volume of other traffic.
§Based on roadways 40 ft (12 m) wide; add 15 ft (4.5 m) to length if roadway is only 32 ft (10 m) wide. These dimensions allow bus to leave loading zone without passing over street centerline.
‖Based on bus roadway plus loading zone width of 22 ft (6.75 m).
**Based on roadway plus loading zone width (to widest point of indentation) of 30 ft (9.2 m); length of zone measured parallel to axis of roadway.

SOURCE: Curb loading zones: HIGHWAY RESEARCH BOARD, *Highway Capacity Manual 1965* (Washington, DC: 1965), Table 11.8. Off-street zones: LEVINSON, H.S. ET AL., *Bus Use of Highways: Planning and Design Guidelines*, National Cooperative Highway Res. Program Report 155 (Washington, D.C.: Transportation Research Board, 1975), p. 40.

The capacity of a bus stop is defined as the maximum number of buses per hour that can use a stop with only a low probability (say, 0.025) of a bus having to queue to enter the stop and possibly blocking other traffic. An approximate formula for the capacity of a stop and the corresponding minimum headway is

$$F_{\max} = \frac{1800}{T_d} \quad \text{and} \quad H_{\min} = 2T_d \qquad (7.3)$$

where $T_d = A \times T_a + B \times T_b + T_c$ two-way flow at busiest door

$$T_d = \max \begin{Bmatrix} A \times T_a \\ B \times T_b \end{Bmatrix} + T_c$$ one-way flow through doors

and where $F_{\max}$ = max frequency (capacity), buses/h

$H_{\min}$ = min average headway, s

T_d = avg dwell time per bus, s

A, B = no. of alighting/boarding psgrs

T_a, T_b = avg alighting/boarding time, s/psgr (see Table 7-9)

T_c = sum of other delays at the stop

Multiple-berth stops do not have the same capacity per berth as single-berth stops, because buses may be delayed in entering or leaving an available berth by buses in adjacent berths. [In effect, the value of T_c in formula (7.3) must be increased to allow for this condition.] Where routes terminate, if buses lay over in a regular berth, T_c must also include the layover time.

If the number of buses to be accommodated along a street exceeds the capacity of the busiest stops, routes may be separated into two groups of about equal hourly volumes; different sets of stops are provided for each group of routes. If buses can pass each other along the street, the total street capacity for carrying transit buses approaches the sum of the capacities of the stops for each group.

Even higher capacities can be obtained by platooning buses. In such a project in São Paulo, Brazil,[9] bus routes are placed into three groups, and platoons are formed consisting of two buses from each group. The platoons arrive at each loading zone (which has six positions) together and leave together. Bus stop capacity can be expressed by

$$F_{\max} = \frac{3600 - 6p/(2 + n)}{(8 + 4n)/n} \qquad (7.4)$$

where $F_{\max}$ = maximum frequency (capacity), buses/h

n = average number of buses in a platoon

p = boarding passengers per hour at the stop

It should be kept in mind that this formula was developed for bus door designs and fare systems used in São Paulo and may have to be modified for conditions in other locations.

Capacity of rail transit stations

The capacity of rail transit stations is a function not only of dwell time, but also of train length, acceleration and decleration rates (including emergency deceleration), and methods of train control. The minimum headway can be estimated by drawing a distance–time diagram as shown in Figure 7.5. The "minimum safe separation" marked in this figure is based on an analysis of safe stopping distances by a following train in case the preceding train malfunctions. On some rail transit routes, the capacity bottleneck may occur at terminal stations if the track layout for reversing trains is inadequate.[10]

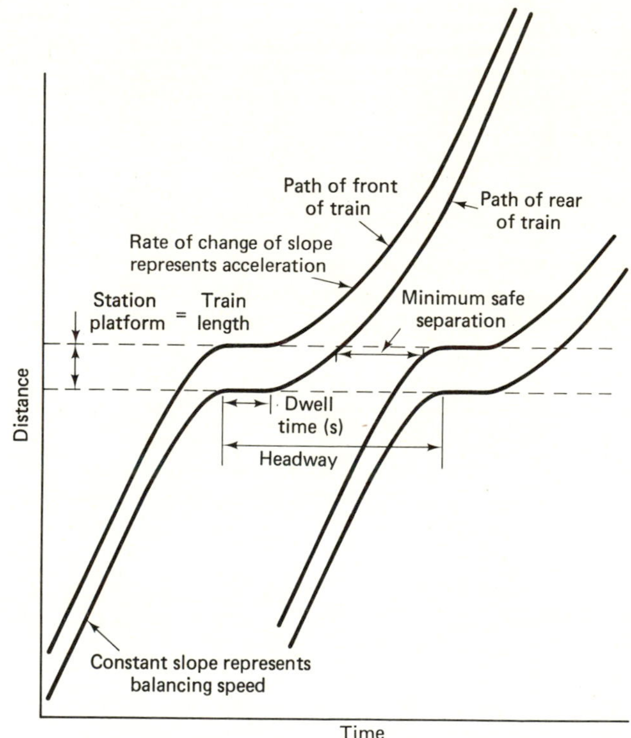

Figure 7.5. Distance-time diagram for rapid transit train headway and frequency analysis.

System performance

Service headways

Transit vehicle or train headways, and their reciprocal (frequencies) are affected by:

1. Patronage (demand) volumes in different time periods
2. Transit unit (vehicle or train) capacity
3. Minimum possible headway at busiest stop or station

[9]SZASZ, P. A. ET AL., *COMONOR Coordinated Bus Convoy*, CET Tech. Bull. No. 9 (São Paulo: Companhia de Engenharia de Tráfego, 1978), 80 pp.

[10]For detailed discussion of minimum train headways, see ANDERSON, *Transit Systems Theory*, Chaps. 4, 7.

TABLE 7–11
Typical Maximum Headway Policy

Time of Day	Maximum Headways								
	Arterial Routes			Feeder Routes			Express Routes		
	M–F*	Sat*	S&H*	M–F*	Sat*	S&H*	M–F*	Sat*	S&H*
6 A.M.–9 A.M.	15	30	30	30	60	60†	15	—	—
9 A.M.–4 P.M.	30	30	30	60	60	60†	—	—	—
4 P.M.–7 P.M.	15	30	30	30	60	60†	15	—	—
7 P.M.–12 A.M.	30	30	30	60†	60†	60†	—	—	—
12 A.M.–6 A.M.	60†	60†	60†	—	—	—	—	—	—

*M–F: Monday through Friday; Sat: Saturday; S&H: Sunday and holiday.
†Maximum headway if service is justified at all.

4. Maximum or policy headway
5. Headways of connecting routes

The first three factors are discussed elsewhere in this chapter. The maximum or *policy headway* is established by the governing board or regulatory agency as representing the minimum level of service that is considered adequate for various types of routes. A typical policy is shown in Table 7-11. Shorter headways are provided whenever demand justifies this.

When transit patrons know that the service they wish to use is scheduled at headways of about 10 min or less, they will usually arrive at the stop or station at random. Average waiting times of one-half the service headways may be assumed under these circumstances. Since the public is not concerned about precise timetables in such situations, headways are selected to correspond as precisely as possible to demand at the maximum load link. The resulting headway may be any integer or even fractional number of minutes.

When service headways lengthen to intervals greater than 10 min, some patrons will consult timetables and arrive at the transit stop shortly before the vehicle or train is scheduled to arrive. When headways exceed about 15 min, almost all patrons will do so. Transit schedules that use headways that are divisible into 60 min are more easily remembered by patrons and therefore minimize the need for timetables. Hence, headways of 12, 15, 20, 30, or 60 min are normally used, and other values are avoided. Good schedule adherence—particularly avoidance of running ahead of schedule—helps to minimize patron waiting time at stops. Such reliability requires careful supervision of line operations and of the scheduling process.

Capacities of transit facilities

Capacity of a route or of a group of routes on the same facility is almost always determined by conditions at stop areas rather than line conditions. The highest minimum headway value (lowest frequency) for any stop on a given facility represents the most critical situation and, hence, the minimum headway value that can be achieved. Headways in a given route section may also be affected by limiting conditions upstream or downstream.

The computation of minimum possible headways at a stop has been described by formula (7.3). Headways achieved in actual practice are shown in Tables 7-12 to 7-15 for various transit technologies.

When stops are made off the main line or artery, capacity is determined by the safe separation between transit units. Thus, on exclusive busways or bus lanes on freeways, with buses stopping only at multiplatform terminals or off-line bus stops, headways of 5 s can be achieved. Theoretically, rail systems could operate at headways of perhaps 60 s under similar conditions, but such situations are not found in practice.

On a single route, short headways in mixed traffic often

TABLE 7–12
Observed Peak-Hour Passenger Volumes on Urban Transit Buses, United States

City	Location	Buses/Hour	Headway (s)	Passengers/ Hour in Peak Direction	Passengers/Bus
City streets					
San Francisco	Market Street	155*	23	9900	58
New York	Hillside Avenue	170*	21	8500	50
Philadelphia	Market Street	143*	25	8300	58
Washington	K Street NW	130	28	6500	50
Chicago	State Street	151*	24	6100	40
Freeways					
New York†	I-495	490	8	21,600	44
Washington‡	Shirley Highway	110	33	5500	50
Chicago	North Lake Shore Drive	80	45	4000	50
New York	Long Island Expressway	89	40	3560	40
Philadelphia	Schuylkill Expressway	78	46	2800	36
Tunnel, bridges					
New York	Lincoln Tunnel	735	5	32,560	44
San Francisco§	Oakland Bay Bridge	360	10	14,900	41
Philadelphia	Ben Franklin Bridge	137	26	5065	37
New York	George Washington Bridge	108	33	4245	39
Washington	Memorial Bridge	100	36	4020	40

*Buses use more than one lane.
†Location is on New Jersey side of Hudson River.
‡Location is on Virginia side of Potomac River.
§Data from University of California, Institute of Transportation Studies.

SOURCE: LEVINSON, H.S. ET AL., *Bus Use of Highways: State of the Art,* National Cooperative Highway Research Program Report 143, (Washington, D.C.: Transportation Research Board, 1973), except data marked with §.

TABLE 7–13
Observed Peak-Hour Passenger Volumes on Streetcar (Light Rail Transit) Systems, 1978

City	Location	Cars or Trains/Hour	Headway (s)	Length of Cars or Trains ft	Length of Cars or Trains m	Passengers/Hour in Peak Direction	Passengers/Car or Train
On street							
Hong Kong	East edge of CBD	96	38	29.2	8.9	7975	83
Köln	Deutzer Brücke	32	113	101.7	31.0	6500	203
Basel	Post	70	51	*	*	5726	82
San Francisco	Market St.	65	55	46.0	14.0	4849	75
Melbourne	Princes Bridge	89	40	46.5	14.2	4394	49
Toronto	Queen St. E.	66	55	46.5	14.2	4201	64
In tunnel							
Köln	Neumarkt	48	75	101.7	31.0	10,000	208
Boston	Arlington Station	41	88	*	*	6722	164
Philadelphia	Juniper St. Station	20	180	46.0	14.0	3840	192

*Various lengths: in Basel—68.9–111.5 ft (21.0–34.0 m); in Boston—92.0 or 140.0 ft (28.0–42.7 m).

SOURCE: Survey by author.

TABLE 7–14
Observed Peak-Hour Passenger Volumes on Rapid Transit Systems, 1978–1980

City	Location	Trains/Hour	Headway (s)	Length of Trains ft	Length of Trains m	Passengers/Hour in Peak Direction	Passengers/Train
New York (IND)	53rd St./East River	29	124	600	183	48,070*	1660
Paris (Metro)	Gare de l'Est	37	97	294	89.5	40,160	1085
New York (IRT)	59th St./Lexington Ave.	24	150	510	155	35,120*	1460
Toronto	Bloor/Wellesley	30	120	450	137	31,784	1060
Montreal	Mount Royal Station	25	144	492	150	24,000	960
London (Tube)	Liverpool St. Station	30	120	413	126	23,000	770
Hong Kong	Nathan Road	20	180	300	91	20,000	1000
London (Underground)	Baker Street Station	28	129	423	129	17,000	610
Chicago	35th/Ryan	21	171	384	117	16,500	785
Stockholm	Skanstull	30	120	463	141	14,765	490
Boston	Andrew Station	17	212	280	85	13,045	770

*That these figures do not represent capacity is illustrated by the fact that higher volumes of passengers were carried before 1960. At the 53rd/East River location, 61,400 passengers were counted in the peak hour, on the Lexington Avenue line 44,500.

SOURCE: Survey by author.

TABLE 7–15
Observed Peak-Hour Passenger Volumes on Commuter Railroads, 1978

City	Location	Trains/Hour/Track	Headway (s)	Length of Trains ft	Length of Trains m	Passengers/Hour/Track (Peak Direction)	Passengers/Train
Paris (RER)	Auber-Châtelet	18	200	718	219	31,150	1730
London	Borough Market Jct.	30	120	515–798	157–243	28,520	950
München	Laim-Donnersbergbrücke	22	164	442–663	135–202	21,650	985
Paris (SNCF)	Paris Nord	17	212	604–732	184–223	17,420	1025
New York (LIRR)	Jamaica	15	240	1085	331	15,550	1035
Chicago (CNW)	Harvard Division	11	327	340–935	104–285	14,370	1300
Bruxelles	Sud-Nord	21	171	656–1066	200–325	12,600	600
New York (Conrail)	Park Avenue Tunnel	20*	180	255–970	78–296	12,000*	600
Zürich	Zürich-Oerlikon	15	240	1168	356	10,815	720

*Estimated from total count of three parallel tracks.

SOURCE: Survey by author.

lead to "bunching," the forming of groups of buses that travel part of the route together. This is difficult to control and results in infrequent service by groups of buses instead of frequent service by single units.

Passenger capacities for specific combinations of vehicles and facilities can be computed by using or assuming specific values for minimum headways and maximum vehicle or train loading applicable to the situation under study. The total passenger-carrying capacity of a facility (C_{pf}) is the product of the passenger-carrying capacity of each transit unit (C_u) and the capacity of the facility to carry these units, which is the maximum frequency (F_{max}).

Initial values for C_u and for F_{max} are given by Table 7-2 and formula (7.3), respectively. However, these values must be modified by consideration of the factors discussed next.

Passenger load factor. In transit operations, the passenger load factor is defined as the ratio of all passengers on a transit unit to the number of seats provided. In peak periods it is generally economically infeasible to provide a seat for every passenger. Therefore, the following load factors are often used:

- 0.90 if no standees are permitted by administrative or regulatory policy.
- 1.00 if the policy calls for no standees, but allows a few standees if demand fluctuates or service intervals become temporarily irregular.
- 1.25 to 1.50 for peak-period, peak-direction scheduling of urban bus and streetcar routes in North American practice.
- 1.50 to 2.00 for peak-period, peak-direction scheduling of urban bus and streetcar routes in some North American and many Latin American, European, and Asian cities, where vehicles are equipped with relatively few seats and much standing room.
- 1.50 to 6.50 for peak-period, peak-direction scheduling of urban rail transit trains, the value within this range depending on the standards of comfort acceptable in each instance.

One general rule is that the proportion of standees allowed should be inversely related to trip lengths. Passengers traveling less than 10 min (other than the physically handicapped and elderly) need not be seated, while attempts should be made to seat most or all passengers traveling more than 30 min on a vehicle.

Peak-hour factor. The peak-hour factor is a measure of consistency of demand, and is similar to the like-named factor used in highway capacity analysis (see Chapter 16). It is defined as the ratio of the passenger flow in 1 h to the hourly rate of passenger flow in the peak 15 min (i.e., four times the number traveling in this quarter hour). This factor ranges typically from 0.70 to 0.95, and may reach 1.00 in the centers of the largest metropolitan areas.

Unequal-loading factor. It is highly improbable that all vehicles in a stream of buses or streetcars or in a train will be loaded equally. In mixed-traffic situations, vehicles often bunch in groups of from two to perhaps five. Vehicles at the front of a bunch are usually loaded to capacity, but those toward the back often do not carry a full load. In trains, those cars farthest removed from platform access points are often less crowded than the average load for the entire train.

To allow for this, a modifying factor is introduced in capacity calculations. The value of this factor may be obtained from field observations. It is likely to be in the range 0.70 to 0.90. Only very occasionally, under conditions of extreme overcrowding, is the value likely to exceed 0.90.

Train length. Design and operational constraints must be recognized in capacity calculations of rail systems. Train length is one of these constraints. Streetcar trains should generally not exceed 280 ft (85 m) in LRT applications, and perhaps half this amount if most stops are in mixed traffic, where blocking cross streets during boarding/alighting could become a problem. Rail transit train lengths are constrained by station platform lengths. Also, given very long trains (as in some commuter railroad applications), the unequal-loading factor is likely to be near the low end of the range indicated above.

Number of lanes or tracks. The passenger capacity of an entire transit facility in one direction of travel is, subject to the limitations discussed below, the product of the capacity of a single lane or track and the number of lanes or tracks available in that direction. Lanes or tracks involved in such a multiplication must not interfere with each other or be subject to upstream or downstream bottlenecks. Where parallel tracks share a common platform, the design of that platform must be adequate to handle simultaneous boarding/alighting of two trains at the same rate of flow and with the same dwell times as is calculated for processing one train.

Route sections unaffected by stops. As mentioned above, in a few situations vehicles do not stop on the facility, and the minimum headway is determined by safe separation. In this case, standard traffic engineering studies should determine the distribution of headways and the average headway sustainable for an hour or operation, and the latter value should be used in calculating the capacity. Headways observed for only a few vehicles, closely bunched, are not a reliable basis for capacity computation.

Bottleneck identification. It must be kept in mind that the capacity of any section of route, facility, or service can be no greater than the most limiting set of conditions that affect the capacity directly or indirectly. The "bottleneck" is usually the stop with the longest dwell times on the facility being analyzed. However, it could be a terminal crossover, a highway traffic bottleneck, or some upstream or downstream network configuration feature. For example, consider two outer branches of a rail transit route. Each branch has a theoretical capacity of, say, 40 trains per hour. However, this is also the capacity of the trunk line from which these branches are served. Assuming that half the trains are routed to each branch, the maximum flow of trains on either branch can be only 20 per hour.

Demand and capacity. The analyst must check whether assumptions made in capacity analysis affect the demand for the service. Demand responds to both frequency of service and the comfort level defined by load factors. For example, it is unrealistic to assume that the capacity of a 50-seat bus is 100 persons (load factor of 2.0) if passengers to be served refuse to crowd into the vehicles to such an extent.

Capacity calculations

The calculation of the capacity of a facility can be summarized by the following steps, which are then illustrated by two examples:

1. Identify the controlling bottleneck.
2. Calculate the maximum frequency at this bottleneck (F_{max}).
3. Assume the number of seats per transit unit (S_u) from available or future vehicle fleet, the load factor (LF) from current system policy, and the peak-hour factor (PHF) and unequal loading factor (ULF) from field observation or prediction.
4. Calculate the passenger-carrying capacity of each unit (C_u) from

$$C_u = S_u \times \text{LF} \times \text{PHF} \times \text{ULF} \qquad (7.5)$$

5. Calculate the passenger-carrying capacity of the facility (C_f) from

$$C_f = C_u \times F_{max} \qquad (7.6)$$

EXAMPLE 1. CAPACITY OF AN EXCLUSIVE BUS FACILITY

It is planned to establish a downtown mall to be used only by pedestrians and buses. Several bus routes will use this street; about 50 buses are to be accommodated per hour in the peak direction. How can this flow be handled?

1. *Bottleneck identification*. The busiest stop is identified from present passenger trip patterns. It is found that during the peak 15 min in the afternoon peak, an average of 20 persons are expected to board each bus at this stop. Alighting will be through rear doors only, and will involve fewer passengers. Exact fares are used.

2. *Calculation of F_{max}*. Dwell time T_d is calculated from

$$T_d = B \times T_b + T_c \qquad \text{[see formula (7.3)]}$$

From Table 7-9, adjusting for use of exact fares, the value for T_b is selected as 2.5 s. Based on analysis of operations and traffic signal timing, a value for T_c of 10 s is assumed. Therefore,

$$T_d = 20 \times 2.5 + 10 = 60 \text{ s}$$

$$F_{max} = \frac{1800}{T_d} = \frac{1800}{60} = 30 \text{ buses/h for single berth stop}$$

This is inadequate; hence, assume two berth stops. For second berth, use T_c = 30 s to allow for delays caused by buses interfering with each other. For the second berth, T_d = 80 s and F_{max} = 22 buses/h. F_{max} for both berths = 30 + 22 = 52 buses/h, which is adequate.

3. *Input of other factors*. Based on buses now in use, S_u = 50 seats. LF = 1.50 from policy. PHF = 0.85 and ULF = 0.85 on present downtown street. However, it is anticipated that the mall will reduce bunching, and the ULF = 0.90 is achievable.

4. *Calculation of C_u:*

$$C_u = 50 \times 1.50 \times 0.85 \times 0.90 = 57.4 \text{ passengers/vehicle}$$

5. *Calculation of C_f:*

$$C_f = 57.4 \times 52 = 3000 \text{ passengers/h}$$

EXAMPLE 2. CAPACITY OF A PROPOSED RAIL TRANSIT LINE

In this case let us assume that the desired capacity is given, and that the required length of trains (and hence of station platforms) is to be calculated. The demand analysis indicates that 30,000 persons will travel in the peak direction in the peak hour. Cars with 60 seats are to be used, each car having four two-channel doors per side. A trial-and-error method is used, with the first assumption of eight-car trains and 2.5-min headways.

1. *Bottleneck identification*. At the busiest station, 4500 persons are expected to alight and board during the peak 15 min.

2. *Calculation of F_{max}*. The number of door channels per train is 8 cars × 4 doors × 2 channels/door = 64. Assume that the busiest doors handle 20% above the average number of passengers for all doors. Number of trains in 15 min = 6; hence, number of passengers in and out of the busiest doors is 4500/(6 × 64) × 1.2 = 14. T_a and T_b (from Table 7-9) taken to be 1.0 s. T_c (time to open and close doors) taken to be 5.0 s. Therefore,

$$T_d = 14 \times 1.0 + 5.0 = 19 \text{ s}$$

A distance–time diagram is drawn, reflecting acceleration and train control characteristics, and using the assumed train length and the calculated value of T_d. Let us assume that this produces a value for F_{max} of 35 trains/h. Headway = 1.7 min (<2.5 min), which is acceptable.

3. *Input of other factors*. S_u = 60 seats/car or 480 seats/train. LF = 3.0 from policy. PHF = 0.85 from estimated demand patterns. ULF = 0.90, assumed from study of platform layout designs.

4. *Calculation of C_u:*

$$C_u = 480 \times 3.0 \times 0.85 \times 0.90 = 1{,}100 \text{ psgrs/train}$$

5. *Calculation of C_f:* Note that the assumed headway gives 24 trains/h.

$$C_f = 1100 \times 24 = 26{,}400 \text{ psgrs/h}$$

Since this value of $C_f < 30{,}000$, another trial must be made. The first trial indicates that a shorter headway can be assumed and the demand can then be readily accommodated. Another trial might be with an assumed train frequency of 35 trains/h, as obtained at the end of step 2 of the first trial, and with seven-car trains.

Observed values for peak passenger volumes

Tables 7-12 to 7-15 list observed values for peak-hour, peak-direction passenger volumes for various transit technologies. These do not necessarily equal the capacities of these facilities, because there may be insufficient demand to achieve capacity flows. They are, however, an indication of some of the highest transit passenger flows reported. Additional, more detailed data for buses are found in the source cited in Table 7-12.

Travel time

Two types of travel time are of concern to analysts of transit system performance. Transit travel time is the time consumed in traveling within the transit system. Total trip time is measured from origin to destination of a trip.

Transit travel time. The rate of progress of transit vehicles or trains along their routes is the reciprocal of platform speed, which was defined earlier. Total system performance is often measured in terms of platform speed or transit travel time rate (min/mi, or min/km); maximizing platform speed or minimizing transit travel time rates not only indicate improved service to passengers but also implies decreased platform labor costs.

Transit travel time is a function of vehicle performance, stop spacing, dwell times, route geometry (alignment, grades), legal or design speed limits, and miscellaneous delays. Transit operations in mixed traffic are particularly susceptible to delay, whereas efficiently operated services on exclusive right-of-way should experience only delays connected with passenger stops.

Table 7-16 classifies bus transit travel time spent en route for a number of situations. It will be noted that fare collection procedures influence the proportion of total time spent at stops. As might be expected, the lowest proportion of travel time attributable to traffic delays occurs when buses operate outside the central area of the city.

Although average travel time is often used in analysis, deviations from the average are of great importance. Passengers are concerned about arriving at destinations on time, and may evaluate a transit service more in terms of the 95th or even 99th percentile travel time than of the mean value. Schedule makers must allow for late running in calculating layover time at terminals, and therefore also consider travel-time deviations. As might be expected, such deviations are largest in mixed-traffic situations, and least for operations in exclusive rights-of-way.

Total trip time. The total travel time for origin to destination, or door-to-door travel time, may include the following components:

1. Access time from trip origin to boarding transit stop
2. Time spent walking within larger transit stations
3. Waiting time for the next transit service
4. Travel time on the transit system
5. Transfer time, if a route change is involved
6. Access time from final alighting stop to destination

At change-mode points, such as rail transit stations where passengers may transfer between rail service and feeder buses or automobiles, the time involved (items 2 and 5) may become substantial. Transfer time (item 5) also includes a new waiting time (item 3), unless schedules are so closely coordinated that the connecting service departs as soon as passengers have arrived from the arriving service.

Access time depends on access mode. Walking speeds are assumed to be in the range 4 to 5 ft/s (1.2 to 1.5 m/s), bicycling about 10 mph (15 km/h). Speeds for auto and bus access must be measured from field conditions, and allowance must be made for walking between these access modes and the stop or station entrance. Waiting time is a function of service headways, as was discussed earlier in the chapter.

The combined effect of the various components of total trip time is illustrated in Figure 7.6. A home-to-CBD trip of 7.5 mi (12 km) is shown in a group of graphs, each involving a different mode or combination of modes of travel. Assumptions include walking speed of 3 mph (4.8 km/h), bus speed of 12 mph (19 km/h) except in the city center, where 8 mph (13 km/h) is used, auto travel speed of 20 mph (32 km/h), and rail transit travel speed of 25 mph (40 km/h). Arbitrary, though realistic, waiting and transfer times are included.

TABLE 7–16
Travel Time and Delay For Typical Bus Routes During Peak Periods

Size of Bus Crew†	City	Component of Journey Time* Spent: At Stops (%)	Between Stops: Moving (%)	Between Stops: Delayed (%)	Remarks
One	Adelaide, South Australia	27–23	60–59	13–18	Tickets purchased on bus
	Helsinki, Finland	10–9	62–64	28–27	Central area**
	Helsinki, Finland	13–11	80–85	7–4	Suburban route
	Oakland, California	17–20	57–55	26–25	Fares paid on bus
	Providence, Rhode Island	24.5	59.0	16.5	Fares paid on bus
	St. Louis, Missouri	17.9	69.3	11.8	Fares paid on bus
Two	Glasgow, Scotland	17	60	23	Outside city center
	London, England	12–14	66–60	22–28	Route 14
	Newcastle/Tyne, England	14	76	10	Outside city center

*Where two numbers are shown, the first refers to the A.M. peak, the second to the P.M. peak.
†Where crews of two are used, fare collection takes place while the bus is in motion.
**Much use of prepurchased tickets.

SOURCES: U.S. data from CALIFORNIA DEPARTMENT OF TRANSPORTATION, District 4, *Alameda-Contra Costa Transit District Bus Priority Techniques Study, Detailed Final Report (Draft)*, July 1979; WILBUR SMITH & ASSOCIATES, *Trade, Transit and Traffic*, Providence, R.I.: 1958; W. C. GILMAN & CO., *St. Louis Metropolitan Area Transportation Survey Report*, 1959. Other data compiled from R. A. CHAPMAN, H. E. GAULT, AND I. A. JENKINS, *Factors Affecting the Operation of Urban Bus Routes*, Transportation Operations Research Group. Working Paper No. 23, (Newcastle Upon Tyne: University of Newcastle, 1976).

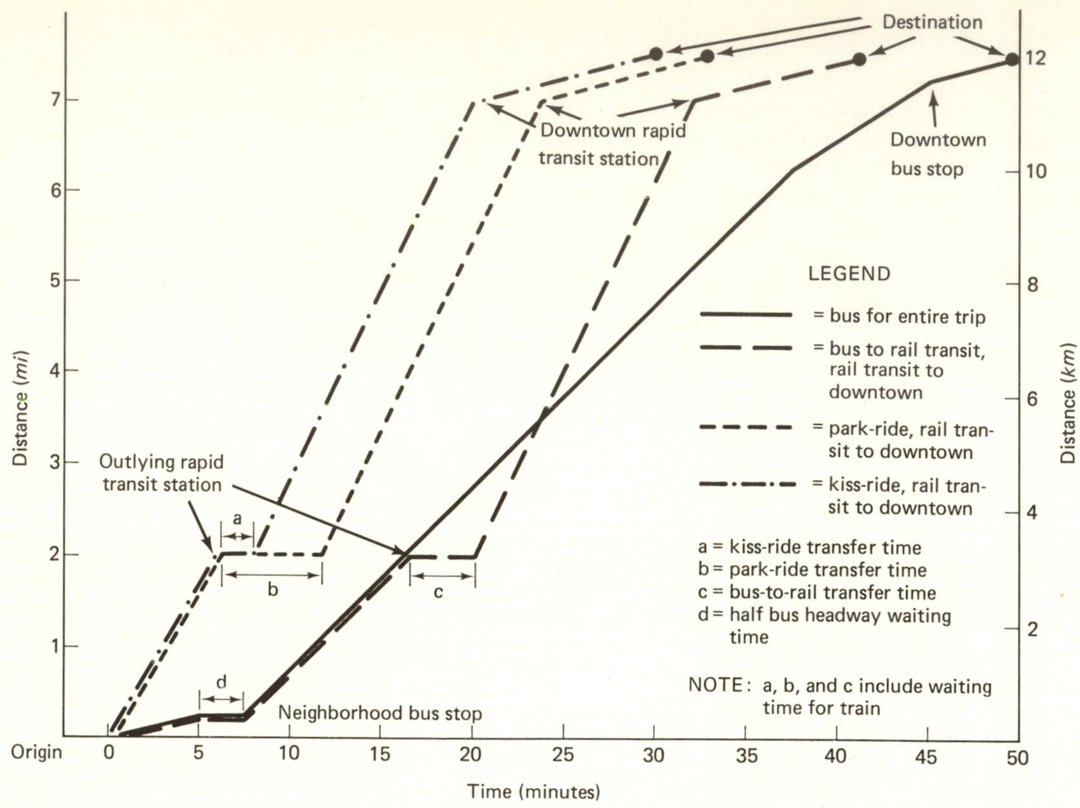

Figure 7.6. Components of total trip time for a typical trip (distance-time graphs) from outlying origin to downtown.

Transit operations

Organization

The principal operations activities of a transit system are best understood within the context of the organizational structure of such an activity. Figure 7.7 is a generalized arrangement of a typical organization, but many different schemes are possible.

In large systems, the four main departments may be broken into even more, with several deputy general managers, each responsible for two or more departments, reporting to the general manager. In small systems, there may be only an operations department, with other functions conducted by appropriate offices within municipal government; some functions, such as maintenance, fare collection and banking, and accident claims, may be contracted out to private industry.

There is a functional, sequential flow process in transit operations. It starts with goals and standards, established by the governing board. Staff undertake long-range and short-range planning, budgeting, implementation of service changes, actual operations, maintenance, and supporting services. Several of the most important aspects of operations are described in this section.

Figure 7.7. Typical transit agency organization.

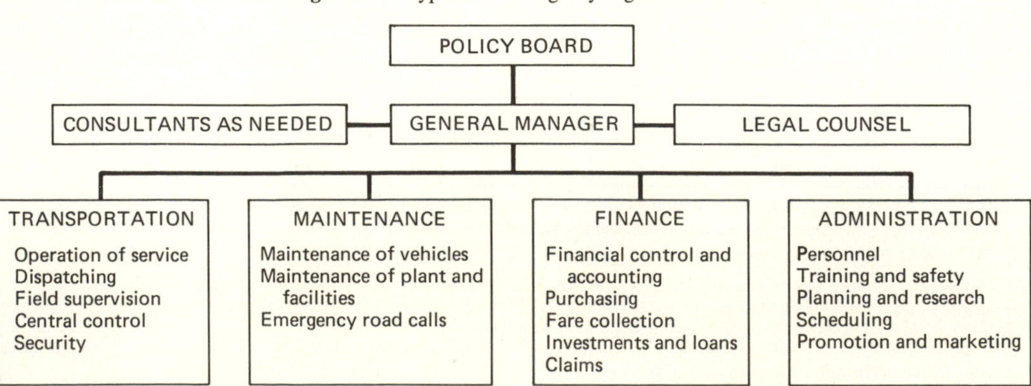

Conduct and supervision of operations

The conduct and supervision of transit operations is the function of the transportation department of a transit agency. Major activities include dispatching, supervision, central control, communications, and security.

Dispatching involves getting transit operators and vehicles into service properly and on time, receiving them when vehicle runs are completed for the day, and maintaining a variety of records required in this activity. Dispatchers manage the "extra board," which furnishes replacements for operators who are absent for any of a variety of reasons. They may keep constant running records of the status and availability of every vehicle for assignment to individual runs. Often, they supervise the makeup of pouches or outfits of transfers, schedule paddles, instructions, and so on, given to each operator initiating a vehicle run.

Field supervisors or inspectors are responsible for service reliability, eliminations of bunches and gaps in service, service restoration following accidents or other emergencies, handling disabled transit vehicles, reassigning vehicles and operators when necessary, and similar field operational activities. Such inspectors may cover an assigned district in a radio car or they may be stationed at critical transit intersections or in a central walkable zone. They work closely with the central control facility. Automatic vehicle monitoring, described below, can replace field inspectors to a very large extent.

The central control office is the nerve center of a transit system. It is in two-way communication by radio with all or most transit vehicles or trains on the system, and usually on separate radio channels with every field inspector, maintenance vehicle (including road-call trucks for disabled vehicles), top- and middle-management vehicle in the field, security police, revenue collection vehicles, and so on. Central control provides support, general direction, coordination, and, where necessary, appropriate strategies regarding any kind of emergency on the transit system; it also makes routine checks and serves as the field communications center of the transit system. Records are usually kept of all service delays, interruptions, and emergencies, and of all communications both ways on the radio system.

Automatic vehicle location monitoring is becoming increasingly feasible as necessary hardware components are developed and refined. Through such means, the central control facility can further centralize the direct management of field operations of a transit system. System communications are primarily conducted by two-way, multiple-channel UHF or VHF radio, by headway recorders which register times at which revenue transit vehicles pass key points in each direction, by special telephones, and by more sophisticated forms of automatic vehicle location and status equipment, including central control displays. Automatic counters, which record the number of passengers entering and leaving buses, can also be polled by wayside equipment, so that the total number of passengers on board can be reported to central control. (These data are also of value to the planning and schedule sections.)

Many transit vehicles are equipped with forms of "silent alarm" actuated covertly by operators when crime problems threaten or occur on or about their vehicles. Security activities include passenger protection or surveillance on vehicles, patrols of fixed facilities, formulation of felony and misdemeanor incidence analyses to improve surveillance routines, coordination with police and other security services, and special investigations and services related to security of the transit system.

Service scheduling

In an urban transit system, scheduling is a major function that follows from the various stages of planning and provides the detailed framework for the conduct of daily operations. Transit scheduling involves separate but closely related preparation of schedules of the service itself (timetables), the rolling equipment to furnish that service, and the daily and weekly tours of duty of the personnel to operate the rolling equipment involved. Inputs required for this process include patronage estimates, network information (bus travel times, schedules of connecting services), vehicle capacity and availability data, policy on headways and load factors, and provisions of the labor agreement concerning working conditions.

The scheduling process includes the following steps:

1. Define the distinct periods of passenger demand in the day; these are usually the morning peak, midday base, afternoon peak, evening, and (if operated) the "owl" period after midnight. Weekends are handled separately. Steps 2 to 7 will be repeated for each of these periods.
2. Obtain or calculate:
   - **a.** The passenger demand on the maximum load link ($P_{\max}$).
   - **b.** The cycle time for the route (T), the sum of the travel time for one round trip, and the time allowed at each terminal for "recovery" in case of late arrival and for operator rest.
   - **c.** The policy headway (h_p) and policy load factor (LF).
   - **d.** The number of seats per transit unit (S_u).
3. Calculate passengers per transit unit (C_u) from formula (7.5). In the off-peak periods, PHF and ULF may be taken to be 1.0 for most routes. On some heavily patronized routes, field studies may have to be made to obtain appropriate values.
4. Calculate the first estimate of the headway (h):

$$h = \frac{C_u}{P_{\max}} \tag{7.7}$$

5. Calculate the first estimate of the number of transit units required (N):

$$N = \frac{T}{h} \tag{7.8}$$

6. Increase N to the next highest integer (N'), and calculate the new headway (h'):

$$h' = \frac{T}{N'} \tag{7.9}$$

If $h' < h_p$, use h_p instead. Otherwise, round h' to a suitable value for schedule coordination, as discussed under "Service Headways" (h'').

7. Calculate final cycle time (T') and the extra time available to be distributed among terminals:

$$T' = n \times h'' \tag{7.10}$$

8. Prepare timetable, considering the following additional factors:
   a. Transition between peak and off-peak periods.
   b. Possible sharp fluctuation in demand within a period (e.g., during shift changes at factories).
   c. Connections with intersecting routes where numbers of transfers can be estimated to be substantial. (This is especially important when headways are long.)
   d. Schedule coordination of coinciding portions of routes to equalize headways.
   e. Opportunities for turning some trips back short of the terminals.
9. Prepare vehicle or train assignment diagrams.
10. Prepare operator assignments ("run cutting"), based on the applicable provisions of the labor agreement (discussed below).

The schedule department of a transit system also conducts field checks of passenger volumes past maximum and other load points and of transit vehicle running times at various times of day,[11] special surveys, and operator work signups. It may also house a relatively large reproduction activity because of the volume of scheduling and signup materials, public timetables and maps, forms, bulletins, and other materials requiring printing.

Until recent years schedule making has been largely or completely a manual process. The Run-Cutting and Scheduling (RUCUS) battery of programs,[12] for example, now makes it possible to computerize most of this process after a conversion and testing period; it requires initiation and maintenance of substantial input data in RUCUS formats, monitoring, and selective intervention by schedule makers. Although RUCUS may not reduce scheduling staff, it provides that staff with greater versatility and options, and better-formatted outputs. When successfully applied, it is claimed to reduce total transit system operating costs somewhat through more efficient scheduling of vehicles and operators. The degree of favorable results depends on individual transit systems' characteristics and the manner in which RUCUS is applied and maintained.

Fares and fare collection

Setting of fares and development of fare structures is a complex task. The policy prepared by the governing board guides the general form of fare systems, and the board also approves each element of the tariff. The level and structure of fares, of course, determine the passenger volumes attracted and the revenues generated. Fare collection procedures may also affect revenues produced, and are a factor in transit operating speeds, capacity of stops and stations, and operation costs.

Fare levels. The level of fares has often been found in planning studies to be a secondary factor affecting trip making and modal choice; in other words, the market is somewhat inelastic. The fact that most transit systems in the world are subsidized also means that the motive of maximizing profits is not a factor in establishing fare levels. Fare levels are therefore based on public policy in which the following factors are considered:

1. Requirement to produce a specific sum or a given proportion of operating costs, as determined by availability of subsidies.
2. Goal to maximize transit use and reduce automobile travel.
3. Social equity considerations applicable to the total ridership or various subgroups.
4. Competition from other modes or systems, if any.
5. Willingness of passengers to pay premium fares for special services.
6. Operational constraints, such as the disadvantages of collecting multiple-coin fares on board vehicles.

The first factor above can be seen as emerging from a policy judgment as to what proportion of total transit costs should be borne by its users and what can justly be charged to the general taxpayer.

Fare structures. Transit fares may be uniform throughout a route network, zoned between different geographical sectors of the service area, or related directly to the distance traveled; or no fare at all may be charged, at least to the passenger.

A uniform fare is self-descriptive. It tends to favor the longer passenger trip and penalize the shorter one, but it is simple to collect and to understand. It is nearly ubiquitous on the North American city transit systems.

Zone fares, of which there are numerous kinds, fall between uniform and distance-related fares in their ability to charge for the quantity of service consumed. A fine-grained zone-fare system approaches the equity of a distance-graduated fare but is usually cumbersome and expensive to administer with manual fare collection. Zones are often used for long-route sections extending beyond the central area of a flat-fare system. Or an entire route network can be divided by a series of concentric rings (representing fare-zone boundaries) centered on the CBD. Such a zone-fare system may increase fare revenue, but may also slow service if the system is administered by checking tickets at zone boundaries; it may also seem complex to the infrequent rider. In Europe, the purchase of season tickets good for one or more months and valid in some or all zones of a network provides the equity of zone fares with fast and convenient boarding or alighting. Stages or route segments, sometimes overlapping, may be used as zones, as in Lon-

[11] J. C. Oppenlander and P. C. Box, *Manual of Traffic Engineering Studies* (Arlington, Va.: Institute of Transportation Engineers, 1976), Chaps. 11, 12. See also Chapter 17 of this handbook.

[12] MITRE Corp., *Vehicle Scheduling and Driver Run Cutting (RUCUS) Package User Documentation,* Report MTR-6678 (McLean, Va.: May 1974); Ernest Nussbaum et al., *RUCUS Implementation Manual,* Report MTR-6949 (McLean, VA: MITRE Corp., July 1975).

don. A disadvantage of zone fares is that the fare is often relatively high for short trips that happen to traverse a zone boundary.

Fares graduated by distance provide the greatest equity to the passenger if distance traveled is the criterion. However, to measure distance traveled (and hence compute the fare), passengers must be checked both at the beginning and end of their trips. This procedure is cumbersome, time consuming, and expensive on surface transit vehicles with limited floor space. Distance-related fares find their most widespread current application, therefore, where automation can be applied economically, namely on rapid transit systems, as in San Francisco, Washington, and London, and on some commuter railroads as, for example, in New York, Chicago, Philadelphia, and the RER route in Paris. Passengers enter and leave "paid" areas in the stations of such systems by inserting magnetically encoded cards in automatic fare gates. The tickets are checked and the required fee is subtracted electronically.

Paper transfers may be issued between transit routes, with or without extra charge, usually at the time the fare is paid. Transfers may also be dispensed before exiting at rail stations for use on connecting surface routes. Some station layouts permit internal walking between different modes without additional payment or issuance of transfers. There has been a tendency on some systems to liberalize the use of transfers by extending the period of validity in any but the reverse direction of travel.

Various promotional and incentive schemes to increase transit patronage may be coordinated with the structure, collection, and level of fares. There is increasing interest in common tariffs and transfer privileges between the routes of different transit systems within the same metropolitan area. The Hamburger Verkehrsverbund (HVV), Federation of Hamburg Transit Systems, is the pioneering example of this. The HVV coordinates services, fares, and operating financial results for virtually all public transport in its region.

Special fares often apply to regular commuters, children, students, senior citizens, public employees, and handicapped persons.

Methods of fare collection. Generally, fare collection systems may be divided into manual and automatic methods. There is a great variety of collection systems in each of these categories.

Fares may be paid in cash, tickets, or tokens, by showing a prepaid pass or season ticket, by canceling a ticket on board the vehicle, or by magnetically encoded tickets. Most North American surface transit systems now require the payment of exact fares; vehicle operators do not carry or make change. The exact-fare system has practically eliminated assaults on drivers; however, it represents some inconvenience to passengers. Bulk sale of tickets or tokens off vehicles partly alleviates this inconvenience.

There is a worldwide trend toward more prepayment and automatic payment of fares and away from on-board and manual fare payment. In some European cities, in fact, surface vehicle operators have been relieved of all fare collection responsibilities, and fare gates have been removed from rail stations. Passengers either use season tickets or purchase tickets from machines at stops or stations. Fare payment is checked at random by roving inspectors. Underpayment or nonpayment, when discovered, subjects the offender to a substantial fare surcharge (and embarrassment) on the spot or, if there is failure to pay, to an even greater penalty in subsequent proceedings. The practicality of such a system varies with different social environments.

Use of prepayment and off-vehicle fare collection reduces dwell time at stops, with resulting higher travel speeds for passengers and better utilization of vehicles by the transit agency. In addition, use of prepayment schemes brings cash to the transit agency at an earlier date than conventional cash tariffs.

Maintenance

Although maintenance activities are not directly visible to the transit user, the success of transit systems often depends on the quality with which rolling stock and fixed facilities are maintained. The public becomes quickly aware of scheduled trips not made. A common reason for the failure of a system to fill all scheduled trips is the unavailability of sufficient pieces of rolling stock in acceptable running condition. Rail systems must also maintain tracks, guideway structures, and stations in a safe and sanitary state.

Maintenance of rolling stock. The most successful transit systems practice "preventive maintenance" in addition to taking care of problems as they arise. Each vehicle is scheduled for different levels of maintenance at various intervals of service. An example of a maintenance schedule for a bus fleet is given in Table 7-17.

Administration of vehicle maintenance programs of any appreciable size is usually computerized. By input from dispatchers, or from a computerized scheduling program, vehicles due any of the periodic maintenance activities can be identified. Fuel and oil consumption can be recorded and analyzed to identify possible deterioration of engine per-

TABLE 7–17
Typical Maintenance Schedule for a Bus Fleet

Frequency	Maintenance Activity
Preventive maintenance	
Daily	Clean inside of vehicle, fuel, inspect tires, check all lights. Check drivers' vehicle defect report form and take actions indicated by notations thereon.
Every second day	Wash vehicle exterior.
Every 500 mi (800 km)	Safety check: condition of brakes, lights, etc.; fuel, oil, water, or air leaks; condition of hoses; etc.
Every 5000 mi (8000 km)	Minor inspection of engine, chassis, brakes, electrical system, body, and interior; lubrication; test drive.
Every 10,000 mi (16,000 km)	Minor inspection plus: steam cleaning, tightening of bolts and lugs, brake adjustments, changing engine oil and filter, lubricating, test drive, etc.
At various intervals, as indicated by breakdown experience	Replace engine, transmission, starter, batteries, etc., with rebuilt or new components.
Response-maintenance as needed	Replace or repair failed or damaged components, including glass, upholstery, paint, body work, mechanical and electrical items, tires, etc.

formance. Spare parts inventories and purchasing requirements are also processed by computer.

There is also a need to store (park) vehicles when not in use. The location of bus or rail vehicle yards is usually combined with the site of maintenance facilities, and rooms for dispatchers and vehicle operators reporting for work are provided. Some systems also acquire or lease bus parking space near the CBD (perhaps under an elevated freeway or transit structure) where buses not needed in the middle of the day can be stored between the two commute peaks; such parking areas usually do not include any facilities for vehicle fueling or maintenance.

Maintenance of plant and fixed facilities. All plant and fixed facilities (including the maintenance shops themselves) must be kept clean and in working order. In rail systems, a major effort is also expended in maintaining the track and guideway. Such activity is subdivided into the following major parts:

1. Track inspection and replacement.
2. Inspection and maintenance of power distribution (third rail or overhead).
3. Mechanical maintenance, including ventilation and air-conditioning equipment, escalators, elevators, etc.
4. Trash collection, cleaning, repairing damage in stations and on right-of-way.
5. Inspecting and maintaining fire hoses, water lines, and related safety equipment.

To perform these activities efficiently, a right-of-way maintenance yard is provided, combined with a rolling-stock maintenance yard or at a separate location. Special-purpose vehicles, including a diesel-powered locomotive, are also needed.

Safety

Safety in urban transit concerns itself with two major problems: accidents and crimes. Some data on transit system accidents are given in Chapter 18.

Three types of accidents can occur in transit systems:

1. Vehicle collision accidents: Transit vehicles in mixed traffic may collide with other vehicles, pedestrians, or fixed objects; usually, vehicles overturning or leaving the roadway are included in this category. Rail transit vehicles may collide with other cars or trains, with service vehicles, or with pedestrians. (Some train collisions with pedestrians in rail stations are the result of suicide attempts.)
2. On-board passenger accidents: Passengers may suffer injury when entering or leaving vehicles, or while on board. A common cause of accidents is the closing of doors while passengers are moving through them.
3. Nonvehicle station accidents: Passengers or employees may be injured in bus or rail stations, especially on stairs and escalators.

The first two of these accident types can be reduced to some extent by safety training of vehicle operators; special emphasis in this training is placed on proper procedures for decelerating, opening and closing doors, and accelerating, since many accidents are caused during these parts of the operating cycle. Nonvehicle station accident problems must be addressed through design changes, such as better lighting and marking of obstacles, signing, and, in critical situations, redesign and reconstruction of the hazardous area.

Crimes may be classified into two major groups: those against persons and those against property. Either type may occur on transit vehicles or in transit stations/stops and their vicinity. In the first category, the most common crimes involve theft, ranging from picking pockets to assault and robbery. In the second category are included vandalism—damage to and destruction of transit property.

The effort to prevent crimes requires police patrol work. In small systems, municipalities may be requested to furnish this service and to respond to specific incidents when called by vehicle operators or the central controller. Rapid transit system, because of the large areas of special property (stations, parking areas, etc.) involved, usually must furnish their own protection, and therefore establish their own police force. They also avail themselves of closed-circuit television equipment to survey and control station areas.

Labor

Transit systems are highly labor-intensive. In the United States, for example, almost 80% of all operating costs for the industry was represented by payroll, taxes, and costs of fringe benefits; average earnings per employee in 1978 were estimated to be about $16,600.[13] The trends and implications of such statistics will be discussed in the next section of this chapter.

The majority of nonmanagement employees in the transit industry of the United States and many other countries is unionized. Over the years, the unions have gained major improvements in wage levels and working conditions. Labor contracts generally specify maximum number of hours of unpaid breaks, maximum length of "spread" (the time between first reporting to work and last leaving it), length of rest periods, overtime and night differentials, the minimum proportion of straight shifts to be scheduled, and other factors affecting platform costs. It is understandable that employees and their union representatives would prefer a system in which all worked straight shifts of 8 h. Passenger demand, on the other hand, calls for peak employee needs between 0600 and 0900, and again between 1600 and 1900, which would best be satisfied by scheduling many split shifts with large spreads and large unpaid breaks. Negotiating the compromise is often difficult and is bound to result in less-than-optimum labor costs. Part-time employment can alleviate some of these problems; it had almost disappeared from U.S. labor contracts until 1978, when the Seattle Metro Transit System was able to include a provision for some part-time bus operators in its settlement with the union. Other systems are striving for similar arrangements.

Strikes do occur at times, and invariably result in a shut-

[13]Based on data in AMERICAN PUBLIC TRANSIT ASSOCIATION, *'78–'79 Transit Fact Book* (Washington, D.C.: 1979), Tables 4, 13.

down of the system; operation with supervisory personnel is considered undesirable and unsafe. The laws governing many publicly owned transit systems prohibit strikes, but have not been effective in preventing them. If a strike lasts long enough for some members of the public to find alternative modes, such as carpools, which they then prefer to transit service, there will be a permanent drop in the patronage level.

Economic characteristics of transit systems

Urban transit system finances in industrialized nations have tended to follow a historic path consisting of three stages. In their early years, systems were profitable and attracted private capital for construction and operation. With the advent of competition from private automobiles, profits disappeared more or less rapidly. At this point, many systems became publicly owned and entered a stage in which it was felt both justifiable and practical to expect passengers to pay only for the cost of operation and perhaps make some contributions toward capital costs; however, government assumed the financing of most of the capital burden.

In recent years, operating expenses have risen more rapidly than inflation (lower half of Figure 7.8). At the same time, policies adopted because of increased concern about air pollution and energy conservation militated against raising fares appreciably, if at all. As a result, most systems in the United States and in many other countries entered a third financial phase, in which no attempt is made to have users pay the full amount of operating expenses. Government—national, state, or local, or a combination of these—assumes the responsibility of making up the deficits through subsidy grants.

Figure 7.8. Transit operating revenues and expenses, United States, 1950–1978. (Upper graph in current dollars; lower graph in 1967 dollars.)

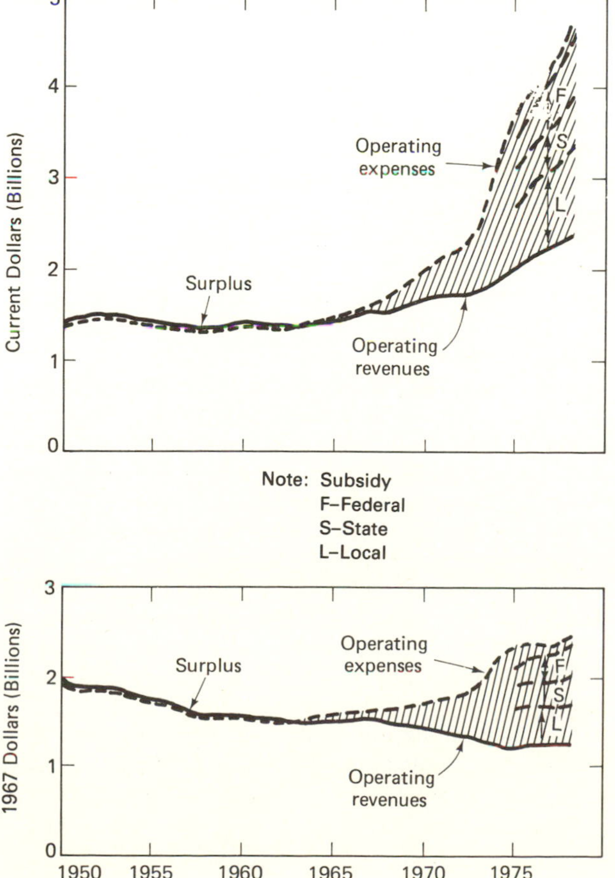

Figure 7.8 illustrates that the U.S. transit industry as a whole was in the second stage until the middle of the 1960s, but has since become dependent on government subsidies for operations. It should be kept in mind that industry average trends conceal the fact that there are still some profit-making privately owned bus systems in the United States, and that there are others which fully meet operating expenses from operating revenues.

The trend in average fares charged is shown in Figure 7.9. This trend also exceeded the rate of inflation (in other words, average fares increased in *constant cents*) until 1971. The rather sharp drop in constant money terms after that year can be explained by the increase in government subsidies available, which permitted fares to be kept at a lower level than would otherwise have been the case, and by the institution of special fares for the elderly and handicapped, mandated as a condition for receiving federal financial grants.

Despite this, however, the cost of transit trips is still often higher than that of driving an automobile. The average transit fare in the United States in 1978 was just above 38 cents, with many systems charging a basic adult fare in the 35- to 50-cent range. The average transit trip length in the

Figure 7.9. Trends in transit fares and employee earnings, United States, 1950–1978. SOURCE: American Transit Association, *Transit Fact Book*, Washington, D.C., annual; U.S. Bureau of the Census, *Historical Statistics of the United States, Colonial Times to 1970*, Series D722, Washington, D.C., 1975; U.S. Bureau of the Census, *Statistical Abstract of the United States* 1978, Washington, D.C., Table 686. (Some values estimated.)

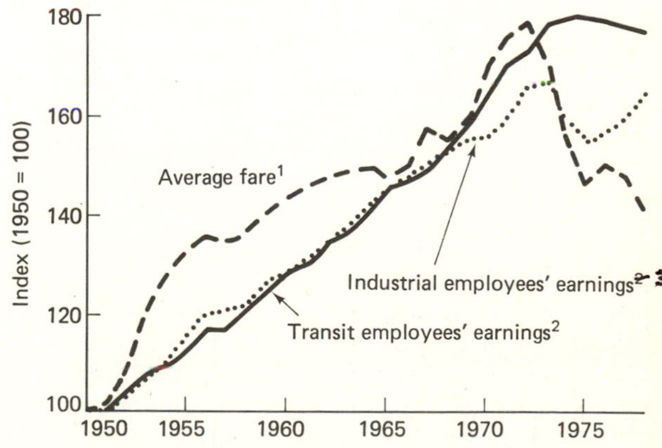

1 – Average fare in constant cents; includes transfer and zone charges, reduced fares, and fare-free rides.
Index 100 = 10.02 cents at 1950 dollar levels.

2 – Average annual earnings of all transit industry employees in constant dollars.
Index 100 = $3,480 at 1950 dollar levels.

3 – Average annual earnings of all US industry employees in constant dollars.
Index 100 = $3,000 at 1950 dollar levels.

United States is approximately 5.2 mi (8.4 km). Thus, the average fare per *passenger*-mile approximated 7.3 cents (4.5 cents per passenger-km) in 1978. Because total operating expenses were just twice passenger revenues for U.S. transit systems in that year, the actual operating cost per *passenger*-mile was about 15 cents (9 cents per passenger-km). In contrast, total operating cost per *vehicle*-mile in the United States in mid-1979 was 18.5 cents for subcompact cars, 21.7 cents for compact cars, and 24.6 cents for standard-size cars, respectively (11.5, 13.5, and 15.3 cents per vehicle-km, respectively), including depreciation, maintenance, tires, fuel, oil, parking, tolls, insurance, and user taxes devoted largely to financing the capital costs of road improvements.

Under such conditions, two people traveling together in a small automobile can often make an urban trip less expensively than by transit (except when parking costs are very high), and without the travel time, schedule, and route-stop constraints imposed by transit service. When more than two people share the ride, transit is placed in an even more unfavorable competitive light. Finally, transit suffers competitively because potential travelers, when choosing their mode, often consider only the out-of-pocket costs of driving an auto (about one-half of the total costs). When transit fares are below the levels indicated above, the economic attractiveness of using transit tends to improve, but then the need for outside subsidy of the transit agency is often increased.

Subsidies

Subsidies in one form or another have been found in transit system accounts for many years. For example, commuter railroad operation is generally a money-losing proposition, supported by profits made from freight and, perhaps, long-distance passenger business. Municipally owned utilities, such as gas and electricity supply, in several countries have assisted transit budgets, perhaps by cash transfers or by setting artificially low prices for electricity consumed by trains and streetcars. However, recent financial stringencies have required that large cash subsidies be made by national, state, or local governments.

Subsidies for capital investments are now common throughout the world. They are usually made by a higher level of government (national or state/provincial) and are accompanied by conditions as to the type of project to be financed and the size of the local contribution. In the United States, federal capital grants were initiated in 1965 and have increased in size considerably since then (Table 7-18).

The sources of subsidies for operating expenses, the methods of raising them, and the conditions attached to granting them vary greatly within any country and among different countries.[14] Each method is the result of the goals, needs, and political climate of the area involved.

Subsidies may be generated within the system or within the next larger organization of which the system is a part. This may involve transfer of utility profits, toll bridge revenues, or profits from other operations, such as freight transportation. Alternatively, the transit agency may have the power to levy taxes directly; for example, real estate, sales, income, fuel, and motor vehicle registration taxes are levied in various parts of the United States.

Subsidies may also be derived from local, state/provincial, or national governments. In some cases general funds are used, in others the proceeds of special taxes. To assure that these subsidies are truly needed and effectively spent, the granting agency usually attaches some conditions to the grants. Also, some programs provide specifically for subsidizing the money "lost" by the charging of concessionary fares to the elderly, the handicapped, students, or other groups.

TABLE 7–18
Federal Commitments to Mass Transit, United States, 1962–1978

	Commitments (dollars × 10⁶)				
Fiscal Year	Capital Grants	Operating Grants	Other Grants*	WMATA†	Total Commitments
1962	0	0	0.4	0.9	1.3
1963	0	0	19.9	2.7	22.6
1964	0	0	11.8	0.7	12.5
1965	50.7	0	9.4	0.5	60.6
1966	106.1	0	9.4	3.3	118.8
1967	120.9	0	12.3	2.8	135.9
1968	121.8	0	10.0	2.9	134.6
1969	148.3	0	25.0	6.4	179.7
1970	132.7	0	27.4	163.9	323.9
1971	283.7	0	57.4	180.0	521.1
1972	510.0	0	94.0	188.0	792.0
1973	825.7	0	152.3	179.2	1157.2
1974	966.0	0	114.3	164.9	1245.1
1975	1287.1	142.5	95.6	126.9	1652.0
1976	1953.8‡	433.5‡	131.6‡	126.4‡	2623.0‡
1977	1737.4	587.7	119.9	128.5	2577.0
1978	2051.6	763.6	143.1	66.8	3025.1

*Primarily research, development and demonstration planning, and training grants and administration.
†Washington Metropolitan Area Transportation Authority and predecessor agency.
‡Covers 15 months, because of change in beginning of fiscal year.

SOURCE: Correspondence from Congressional Budget Office, Washington, D.C.

Operating expenses

Transit systems are highly labor-intensive and, except for those involving fixed-rail facilities, require relatively little capital funding. As a result, the total expenses involved depend very much on labor costs and labor efficiency. As shown in Figure 7.9, the annual earnings in *constant* dollars of transit employees rose about 80% in the period from 1951 to 1973, after which they tended to stabilize at least temporarily. This rate of increase matched the trend in annual earning for all U.S. industrial employees until 1968, but exceeded it thereafter. Total operating expenses, shown in Figure 7.8, of course did not rise at the same rate, because the scale of system operations was declining during the same period.

In a study of six rail transit systems and about 100 bus systems in the United States,[15] the following formulas were

[14]INSTITUTE OF TRANSPORTATION ENGINEERS TECHNICAL COUNCIL COMMITTEE 6F7, "Transit Operating Subsidies," *ITE J.*, *49* (10), 40–48 (Oct. 1979).

[15]DELEUW, CATHER & CO., *Characteristics of Urban Transportation Systems: A Handbook for Transportation Planners*, Report URD.DCCO.74.1.4 (Washington, D.C.: U.S. Department of Transportation, May 1974), 111 p.

calibrated for rail transit operating cost per car-mile (C_r) and operating cost per bus-mile (C_b):

$$C_r = W\left(0.535 - 0.000004\,\frac{\text{annual car-miles}}{\text{fleet size}}\right) \quad (7.11)$$

$$C_b = W\left[2.5\,\frac{\text{bus-hours}}{\text{bus-miles}} - 0.00002(\text{fleet size})\right] \quad (7.12)$$

where W = local wage rate (\$/h)

Of course, the coefficients in these formulas may have to be adjusted for conditions that have changed since 1972, other than the wage-rate changes. Note that in formula (7.12) the first bracketed term is the travel time or the reciprocal of speed. This emphasizes the importance of attempting to maximize bus speeds in order to reduce operating expenses per vehicle-mile of service. In rail systems speeds are fairly constant, and therefore no speed term appears in formula (7.11).

Table 7-19 shows 1977 operating expense data per vehicle-mile (vehicle-km) for the Chicago Transit Authority. In comparing these figures, the different capacities and platform speeds of bus and rail modes should be borne in mind.

TABLE 7–19
Unit Operating Expenses, Chicago Transit Authority, 1977

Vehicle Type	Expense/Vehicle mi	Expense/Vehicle km	Percent of Total
Motor buses			
Maintenance of plant and equipment	\$0.61	\$0.38	22.3
Operating and garage expense, fuel	0.13	0.08	4.8
Transportation, including drivers	1.59	0.99	58.2
Administrative, and misc.	0.27	0.17	9.9
Depreciation	0.13	0.08	4.8
Total	\$2.73	\$1.70	100.0
Rail rapid transit			
Maintenance of way and structures	\$0.40	\$0.25	16.1
Maintenance of equipment	0.41	0.25	16.5
Power	0.13	0.08	5.3
Transportation, including train crews	0.99	0.62	39.9
Administrative, and misc.	0.28	0.17	11.3
Depreciation	0.27	0.17	10.9
Total	\$2.48	\$1.54	100.0

Capital costs

Capital costs are subject to many factors that differ from one system to another. Although basic bus costs are fairly similar, they do vary substantially with optional equipment ordered, and from year to year with inflationary pressures. Civil engineering construction for guideways, stations, terminals, and maintenance facilities are also functions of the topography and soil conditions of the site, of the prices of construction materials, and of the level of construction wages. The values in Tables 7-20 and 7-21 (for infrastructure and vehicles respectively) are only rough indications of costs incurred at the time the data were assembled.

System efficiency and effectiveness

The efficiency and effectiveness of any transportation system is always important. When, however, the more traditional measure of performance, the "bottom line" of the annual financial statement, can no longer be expected to be printed in black ink, other indicators must serve to justify investments and service levels, to determine priorities, and to evaluate performance. Efficiency measures are those which evaluate the quality of system management and operation; effectiveness indicators are used to quantify the success of systems to serve the public and to fulfill the policy objectives (other than internal efficiency) established for them.

Efficiency indicators relate the quantity of service to the resources required to accomplish this effort. Quantity of service may be measured in vehicle-miles or seat-miles (vehicle-km or seat-km), or in vehicle-hours or seat-hours. Some efficiency indicator trends for the U.S. transit industry are shown in Figure 7.10. Labor and vehicle utilization have remained relatively stable in the period since 1950. However, cost efficiency has declined steadily, and sometimes steeply; the reason can be found in the graph of annual earnings of transit employees in Figure 7.8.

TABLE 7–20
Capital Costs of Infrastructure for Two-Track Rail Systems
United States, 1974

Location Alignment	Typical Costs (\$ × 10^6): Guideway per mi	Guideway per km	Stations Each	Yards and Shops Each
Light rail systems				
Suburban				
At grade	2.9–5.3	1.8–3.3	0.02–2.8	12.0–45.4
Elevated	5.1–11.3	3.2–7.0	0.2–3.5	—
Depressed	6.5–15.2	4.0–9.5	0.2–3.6	—
Urban				
At grade	4.1–7.3	2.6–4.5	0.02–0.06	12.0–45.4
Elevated	18.1–23.7	11.2–4.7	0.2–0.7	—
Cut-and-cover	32.7–40.3	20.3–25.0	0.4–1.0	—
Core				
Elevated	19.5–27.8	12.1–17.3	1.3–4.6	—
Cut-and-cover	34.1–44.4	21.2–27.6	1.8–7.6	—
Heavy rail systems				
Suburban				
At grade	3.4–8.4	2.1–5.2	0.4–4.2	11.1–40.7
Elevated	5.2–13.1	3.2–8.1	0.7–5.2	—
Depressed	6.6–17.0	4.1–0.6	0.9–5.5	—
Urban				
Elevated	18.2–25.5	11.3–15.9	1.0–2.9	—
Cut-and-cover	32.8–42.1	20.4–26.2	4.0–10.0	—
Core				
Elevated	19.6–29.6	12.2–18.4	1.4–4.7	—
Cut-and-cover	34.2–46.2	21.2–28.7	5.0–12.0	—

SOURCE: DYER, T. K. *Rail Transit System Cost Study*, Report No. DOT-TSC-UMTA-75-22, Rev. 1 (Washington, D.C.: U.S. Urban Mass Transportation Administration, Mar. 1977), Table 1-2.

TABLE 7–21
Capital Costs of Selected Urban Transit Vehicles, United States

Vehicle	Typical Cost (\$ × 10^3)	Year	Source
Light rail vehicle, articulated	645	1977	(a)
Heavy rail transit car	475–730	1976–1977	(a)
Bus with air conditioning			
Articulated, 60 ft (18.3 m)	180	1977	(b)
Standard, 40 ft (12.2 m)	95–117	1979	(b)
Standard, 35 ft (10.7 m)	85	1979	(b)
Minibus, 25 ft (7.6 m)	52	1977	(b)

SOURCE: (a) RICHARD J. BARKER ASSOCIATES, INC., *The U.S. and International Market for Rail Equipment*, Report UMTA-DC-06-0213-78-1 (Washington, D.C.: U.S. Urban Mass Transportation Administration, Mar. 1978); (b) news reports in *Passenger Transport* and author's survey.

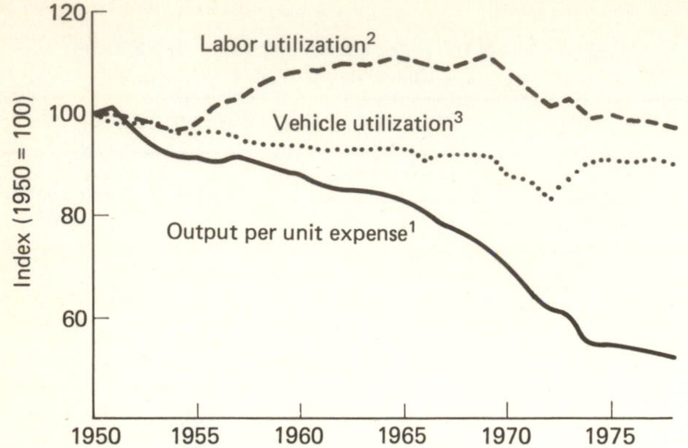

1 — Vehicle-miles (*vehicle-km*) per constant dollar of operating expense.
Index 100 = 2.17 veh-mi (*3.49 veh-km*) per 1950 dollar.

2 — Vehicle-miles (*vehicle-km*) per employee.
Index 100 = 12.5 veh-mi (*20 veh-km*) per employee.

3 — Vehicle-miles (*vehicle-km*) per vehicle owned or leased.
Index 100 = 34,900 miles (*56,000 km*) per vehicle

Figure 7.10. Trends in efficiency indicators, United States, 1950–1978. SOURCE: Compiled from data in American Public Transit Association, *Transit Fact Book*, Washington, D.C., annual.

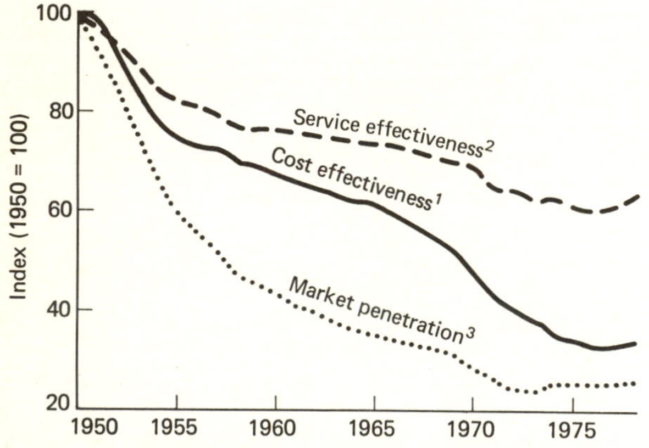

1 — Revenue passengers per constant dollar of operating expenses.
Index 100 = 10 psgrs per 1950 dollar.

2 — Revenue passengers per vehicle-mile (*vehicle-km*)
Index 100 = 4.6 psgrs/veh-mi (*2.9 pagrs/veh-km*).

3 — Revenue passengers per annum per capita of urban population.
Index 100 = 140 psgrs/annum per capita.

Figure 7.11. Trends in effectiveness indicators, United States, 1950–1978. SOURCE: Compiled from data in American Public Transit Association, *Transit Fact Book*, Washington, D.C., annual.

Three typical effectiveness indicators are plotted in Figure 7.11 for the U.S. transit industry. These all declined during the period since 1950, but at different rates. The effect of the rapid increase in automobile ownership in the United States in the decade of the 1950s is readily apparent from these trend lines. Other effectiveness measures sometimes used include accessibility indicators (percentage of population within a certain distance of a transit service) and quantity of service offered per capita of population.

There is considerable discussion in government circles about the need or desirability of setting efficiency and effectiveness criteria for transit systems as a condition of receiving subsidy grants. It is generally agreed that any system should always strive to improve its score in such indicators or, at least, to reverse past downward trends. However, selection of specific indicators as a tool for measuring management performance, let alone for distributing subsidies, is fraught with difficulty. For example, if vehicle-miles per unit cost is the principal or only efficiency criterion, a shrewd manager will increase service on fast routes in outlying areas and on express lines, while reducing service on the slowest, though perhaps best patronized lines. (Remember that the number of vehicle-miles produced per dollar varies with the platform speed of the service.) If vehicle-hours are used as the unit of output, the manager may make little effort to look for ways of accelerating service. If area coverage is an effectiveness indicator, this can be maximized by establishing a vast network of routes, all with minimal service; if per capita patronage is selected, the manager will do just the opposite, concentrating service in the densest area of the city. Any judgment on the performance of a transit system must therefore be based on a combination of factors selected to achieve desired goals.

To achieve higher efficiencies and effectiveness, a number of measures may be considered for application.[16]

Measures to improve efficiency

1. Improved selection and training of transit managers.
2. More freedom for transit management to manage, within broad policy guidelines; greater use of modern management techniques.
3. Better training programs, including sensitivity and motivational training for nonmanagement personnel; better motivational strategies for employees.
4. Better labor utilization through increased use of high-capacity transit vehicles.
5. Greater standardization of vehicle design for more efficient operation and maintenance; further improvements in design.
6. Joint bulk procurement of vehicles, spare parts, and other items, especially for smaller systems.
7. Prompt adjustment of services—additions, cutbacks, changes—in response to changing demands.
8. Increased efficiency in scheduling of operators and vehicles.
9. More productive and cost-effective labor contract provisions.
10. Compulsory arbitration when necessary and effective to avoid strikes; use of thoroughly qualified arbitrators jointly approved by transit management and labor leadership.
11. Selective use of part-time labor.
12. Improved field supervision of operations to reduce delays, gaps in service, and bunching; improved vehicle monitoring and control.
13. Simplified fare collection methods to accelerate passenger flow at bus stops and in stations.

---

[16]Partly derived from AMERICAN PUBLIC TRANSIT ASSOCIATION, *Survey of Transit Management Attitudes and Opinions* (Washington, D.C.: 1976).

Measures to improve effectiveness

1. Most of the efficiency measures listed above, in as much as they will result in better and, perhaps, lower-priced service.
2. Improved and new services to generate new demand (as distinguished from the response to demand changes), including the use of paratransit and experimental service strategies where appropriate.
3. Improved marketing strategies.
4. Improved transit information systems and communication between transit management and passengers.
5. Improved transit service through traffic engineering techniques, such as preferential lanes for buses and signal preemption.

Public policy measures to increase efficiency and effectiveness

1. Promotion of increased use of transit generally.
2. Long-range commitment of subsidies from government to permit long-range planning; clarification of goals and expectations of the grantors of such subsidies.
3. Subsidies of concessionary fares by other agencies, such as welfare and education programs.
4. Reduction in time and expense of requirements to obtain government grants for capital and operating expenses.
5. Selective disincentives to automobile use when good transit altėrnatives are available.
6. TSM techniques which result in more balanced demand by shifting peak trips to off-peak periods such as flextime work schedules.

REFERENCES FOR FURTHER READING

Books and Reports

ANDERSON, ARTHUR & CO. *Urban Mass Transportation Industry Uniform System of Accounts and Records and Reporting System*, Report UMTA-IT-06-0094-77-1. Washington, D.C.: Urban Mass Transportation Administration, 1977.

ANDERSON, J. EDWARD. *Transit Systems Theory*. Lexington, Mass.: Lexington Books/D. C. Heath, 1978.

CRESSWELL, ROY (ed.). *Passenger Transport and the Environment*. London: Leonard Hill (International Textbook Co. Ltd.), 1977.

DELEUW, CATHER & CO. *Characteristics of Urban Transportation Systems: A Handbook for Transportation Planners*, Report URD.DCCO.74.1.4. Washington, D.C.: U.S. Department of Transportation, May 1974.

DELEUW, CATHER & CO. *Light Rail Transit: A State of the Art Review*, Report UT 50009. Washington, D.C.: Urban Mass Transportation Administration, Spring 1976.

GRAY, G. E., and L. A. HOEL (eds.). *Public Transportation: Planning, Operations and Management*. Englewood Cliffs, N.J.: Prentice-Hall, 1979.

HOVELL, P. J., W. H. JONES, AND A. J. MORAN. *The Management of Urban Public Transport: A Marketing Perspective*. Westmead, England: Saxon House, 1975. (Also published in the United States at Lexington, Mass.: Lexington Books/D. C. Heath.)

INSTITUTE FOR DEFENSE ANALYSIS. *Economic Characteristics of the Urban Public Transportation Industry*. Arlington, Va.: Feb. 1972. (Prepared for U.S. Department of Transportation; available from U.S. Superintendent of Documents.)

JHK & ASSOCIATES. *Public Transportation: An Element of the Urban Transportation System*. Alexandria, Va.: May 1977. (A training course prepared for the U.S. Federal Highway Administration.)

LEVINSON, H. S., ET AL. *Bus Use of Highways*. Washington, D.C.: Transportation Research Board, National Cooperative Highway Research Program. *Report 143, State of the Art*, 1973; *Report 155, Planning and Design Guidelines*, 1975.

MCGEAN, THOMAS. *Urban Transportation Technology*. Lexington, Mass.: Lexington Books/D. C. Heath, 1976.

OLSON, C. L. *Independent Study of Personal Rapid Transit*, Report UMTA-CA-06-0090-77-1. Washington, D.C.: Urban Mass Transportation Administration, Dec. 1977.

PUSHKAREV, B. S. AND J. M. ZUPAN. *Public Transportation and Land Use Policy*. Bloomington, Ind.: Indiana University Press, 1977.

SMERK, GEORGE M. *Readings in Urban Transportation*. Bloomington, Ind.: Indiana University Press, 1968.

SMERK, GEORGE M. *Urban Mass Transportation: A Dozen Years of Federal Policy*. Bloomington, Ind.: Indiana University Press, 1974.

SOBERMAN, R. M. AND HAZARD, H. A. (EDS). *Canadian Transit Handbook*, Downsview, Ont: University of Toronto-York University Joint Program in Transportation, 1980.

TRANSIT DEVELOPMENT CORP. *Subway Environmental Design Handbook*, Report UMTA-DC-06-0010-74-1. Washington, D.C.: Urban Mass Transportation Administration, 1975.

TRANSPORTATION RESEARCH BOARD. *Light Rail Transit*, Spec. Report 161. Washington, D.C.: 1975. *Light-Rail Transit: Planning and Technology*, Spec. Report 182. Washington, D.C.: 1978.

TRANSPORTATION RESEARCH BOARD. *Paratransit*, Spec. Report 164. Washington, D.C.: 1976.

VUCHIC, VUKAN R. *Light Rail Transit Systems—An Evaluation*, Report DOT-TSC-310-1. Washington, D.C.: Urban Mass Transportation Administration, Oct. 1972.

VUCHIC, VUKAN R., ET AL. *Transit Operating Manual*. Harrisburg, Pa: Pennsylvania Department of Transportation, 1976, 5 pp.

WEIGELT, H. R., R. E. GÖTZ,AND H. H. WEISS. *City Traffic: A System Digest*. New York: Van Nostrand Reinhold, 1977.

Data Sources

AMERICAN PUBLIC TRANSIT ASSOCIATION. *Roster of North American Rapid Transit Cars: 1945–1980*. Washington, D.C.: 1980.

AMERICAN PUBLIC TRANSIT ASSOCIATION. *Transit Fact Book*. Washington, D.C.: Annual.

CALIFORNIA DEPARTMENT OF TRANSPORTATION, Division of Mass Transportation. *Trans Guide*. Sacramento, Calif.: 1976, with periodic updating.

CANADIAN URBAN TRANSIT ASSOCIATION. *Transit Fact Book*. Toronto. Annual.

N. D. LEA TRANSPORTATION RESEARCH CORP. *Lea Transit Compendium*. Huntsville, Al.: 3 vols, 1975–77.

UNION INTERNATIONAL DES TRANSPORTS PUBLICS. *UITP Handbook of Urban Transport*. Bruxelles. Approximately biannual.

U.S. URBAN MASS TRANSPORTATION ADMINISTRATION. *Innovation in Public Transportation. A Directory of Research, Development and Demonstration Projects*. Washington, D.C.: Annual.

Journals

Bus Ride. Spokane, Wash.: Friendship Publications. 8 issues/annum.

City and Suburban Travel. Los Angeles, Calif.: Transit Research Foundation. Monthly.

Mass Transit. Washington, D.C. Monthly (some issues consolidated).

Metropolitan (Metro). Redondo Beach, Calif.: Bobit Publishing Co. Bimonthly.

Modern Railroads/Rail Transit. Chicago: Cahners Publishing Co. Monthly.

Modern Tramway and Rapid Transit. Shepperton, England: Ian Allan Ltd. Monthly.

Passenger Transport. Washington, D.C.: American Public Transit Association. Weekly.

Railway Gazette International. London: IPC Transport Press Ltd. Monthly.

Revue de l'UITP (UITP Review). Bruxelles: Union Internationale des Transports Publics, Quarterly. In English, French, and German.

Stadtverkehr. Bielefeld, Germany: Werner Stock Verlag. Monthly (some issues consolidated). In German.

Transit Canada. Oshawa, Ontario: T. C. Publishing, Ltd. Bimonthly.

Transit Journal. Washington, D.C.: American Public Transit Association. Quarterly.

Verkehr und Technik. Berlin: Erich Schmidt Verlag. Monthly. In German.

8

HUMAN FACTORS IN TRANSPORTATION

SLADE HULBERT

TRACOR-MB Associates
San Ramon, California

Consideration of human factors as a professional activity dates to World War II work of behavioral scientists with design of man–machine systems. Transportation systems are a natural area for the interaction between engineers and psychologists. Modern transportation systems involve humans as vehicle operators, passengers, and pedestrians.

The human element of any transportation system is largely a "given" around which the other elements must be designed and operated. Safety considerations are important, but efficiency also plays a major role in the system design trade-offs that must be made. All too many of these trade-offs are made with insufficient information about human capabilities. As a result, system inefficiencies and breakdowns occur that could be prevented.

Transportation systems account for large numbers and proportions of injuries and deaths in every country. For the magnitude of the problems in the United States, see Table 8-1. Accident records are crudely generated and serve only as a broad indicator of the magnitude of the problems. This leaves system designers and operators (transportation engineers) to rely on what is known about human factors principles to achieve desired system performance. Unfortunately, the design responsibility in most transportation systems is badly fractionized among various subgroups. For example, vehicle design engineers and pathway designers commonly function independently from each other and from operating engineers, who in turn operate separately from transportation law makers and law enforcers. Those who train and select (license) operators form yet another independent subgroup. Each subgroup deals, for better or for worse, with human factors of the system users.

An accident is an indicator of system failure and as such it is a measure of effectiveness (MOE). In the United States, all accidental deaths in 1978 increased about 1300 from

TABLE 8-1
Accidental Deaths According to the International List of Causes of Death*

Type of Accident or Manner of Injury	1977†	1976	1975	1974
All accidental deaths	103,202	100,761	103,030	104,622
All transport accidents	53,286	50,644	49,838	50,659
Railway accidents	576	552	608	716
Motor vehicle	49,510	47,038	45,853	46,402
Traffic	48,457	46,012	44,820	45,314
Nontraffic	1,053	1,026	1,033	1,088
Other road vehicle	200	238	255	275
Water transport	1,357	1,371	1,570	1,579
Drowning (excluded from drownings below)	1,165	1,182	1,360	1,413
Other water transport	192	189	210	166
Air and space transport	1,643	1,445	1,552	1,687

*Deaths are classified on the basis of the eighth revision of "The International List of Diseases and Causes of Death," which became effective in 1968. This revision provides for a class of deaths due to injury when it cannot be determined whether the death was an accident, suicide, or homicide. There were 4433 deaths classified in this category in 1977.

SOURCE: *Accident Facts,* 1979 ed., National Safety Council, Chicago.

1977 and the largest increase occurred in motor vehicle deaths. However, according to the National Safety Council, the overall accidental death rate per 100,000 population was 47.9, the third lowest rate on record (*Accident Facts*, 1979). Between 1912 and 1978 accidental deaths per 100,000 population were reduced 41%, from 82 to 48. The 70% reduction from 79 to 24 in the non-motor-vehicle death rate was offset in part by the eightfold increase in the motor vehicle death rate, from 3 to 24. The reduction in the overall rate during a period when the nation's population more than doubled has resulted in 1,950,000 fewer people being killed accidentally than would have been killed if the rate had not been reduced. All these rates are adjusted to the age distribution of the population in 1940 to remove the influence of changes in the average age of the population through the years. In 1978, there were 27 times as many deaths as in 1910, but almost 330 times as many vehicles on the highways.

Trends in accidental death rates, as shown in Table 8-2, indicate that transportation is starting to climb back toward 1970 levels following the sharp decrease in 1973–74. A newsletter reported the following:[1]

> According to Joan Claybrook, Administrator of the National Highway Traffic Safety Administration, "people are dying on the nation's highways in epidemic proportions." At a news conference in Washington last week, she reported that the death count has shown "alarming increases" over the last 12 months. Fatalities in 1978 exceeded 50,000 for the first time in five years and the trend is continuing. In the first two months of this year, an estimated 6,267 fatalities were recorded, an *increase of 855 deaths or 16.4 percent* over the corresponding period in 1978.
>
> Claybrook released a four-year study of 1975–78 trends in the *Fatal Accident Reporting System*. A breakdown by vehicle type found that while there was a 12.6 percent increase in fatalities between 1975 and last year, passenger car deaths were up only seven percent. Heavy truck fatalities, however, increased more than 40 percent while motorcycle deaths rose 41 percent. An increase in deaths of 37 percent was found among occupants of pickup trucks and vans. Claybrook said that these statistics indicate the need for improving the safety of motorcycles and light and heavy trucks.

Human beings were essentially the same, yet their behavior must have changed for the worse during the 1977–1979 period. Generally, there is a trend for more or less steady improvement in the physical elements of transportation. During 1973–1974 some degree of decrease in risk taking or exposure to death by travel must have occurred. At any rate, such changes in behavior are pretty much of a mystery. Travelers of all types generally tend to operate within their limitations as long as they are provided with enough information from the transportation environment to make the proper decisions. In the highway mode, the concept of providing sufficient information has been termed "positive guidance," but the approach is equally applicable in all modes of transportation.

Transportation engineers can refer to behavioral scientists for information about human factors. A great deal of research has produced an ever-growing body of this useful information.[2] But when the necessary information is not available, it can be created by appropriate research. Here is where the human factors scientists can interact with transportation engineers in design decision making and system evaluation programs.

[1]*Highw. Vehicle Safety Rep.*, 5(16) (May 1979).

[2]D. Shinar, *Psychology on the Road: The Human Factor in Traffic Safety* (New York: Wiley, 1978), p 212.

TABLE 8–2
Trends in Accidental Death Rates, 1910–1978*

Year	Deaths per 100,000 population: All Accidents†	Motor Vehicle	Public (Non-Motor Vehicle)
1910	90	2	n.a.
1930	80	27	16
1950	60	23	10
1970	56	27	11
1972	55	27	11
1974	50	22	11
1976	47	22	10
1978	48	24	10

*n.a.—not available
†Also includes deaths in accidents at work and in the home.

Source: Adapted from *Accident Facts*, 1979 ed., National Safety Council, Chicago.

Drivers

Since the early 1930s psychologists have been engaged in research on vehicle operators. Early work was done on streetcar motormen and truck and cab drivers, but the private auto driver has been involved in the bulk of fatalities and received the most extensive study.

TABLE 8–3
How Sample of California Drivers Learned to Drive

Age Group	*N*	Percent How Learned to Drive*: 1	2	3	4	5	6	7
Under 20	1,921	47.1	0.9	11.9	0.7	9.9	29.1	0.4
20–24	2,168	60.3	2.0	9.5	1.1	6.0	20.2	0.9
25–29	1,831	74.7	3.2	6.9	1.7	4.2	8.7	0.6
30–34	1,755	85.5	4.3	3.4	1.4	1.3	3.8	0.3
35–39	1,820	90.5	4.1	1.8	1.3	0.5	1.6	0.2
40–44	1,848	89.8	4.0	1.8	2.1	0.3	1.5	0.6
45–49	1,587	93.1	2.7	1.1	1.3	0.1	1.4	0.3
50–54	1,443	92.6	3.7	0.6	1.1	0.2	1.5	0.3
55–59	1,022	93.8	2.7	0.8	1.3	0.1	1.1	0.2
60–64	774	92.0	4.3	1.2	1.2	0.5	0.8	0.1
65 and up	1,304	91.4	4.2	1.9	1.7	0.1	0.5	0.2
All ages	17,473	80.5	3.2	4.3	1.4	2.5	7.7	0.4

*1, taught by family, friends, and/or "picked up"; 2, paid instruction; 3, driver education (classroom plus on-the-road); 4, 1 above plus paid instruction; 5, 1 above plus classroom course only; 6, 1 above plus driver education; 7, miscellaneous and not stated.

Source: Albert Burg, "Characteristics of Drivers," in *Human Factors in Highway Traffic Safety Research*, T. W. Forbes, ed. New York: Wiley, 1972, p. 79.

There were more than 142 million licensed drivers in the United States[3] in 1978, but because of markedly different license standards among the states, there is very little homogeneity in driving ability among these drivers. Most drivers received no formal driver training (Table 8-3), and even those who did, received so little that by far the bulk of driving skill has been learned on a trial-and-error basis. This means that street and highway facilities must accommodate

[3]National Safety Council, *Accident Facts* (Chicago: 1979), p. 40.

all levels of competence, ranging from the rankest beginners to the most experienced and skillful. National and local programs are under way to improve the training that drivers receive and to standardize the driver license requirements among the states, but for some time to come the range of driver capabilities must be recognized as being so great as to cause major concern and as much consideration by traffic engineers as feasible.

The wide range of driver skills and perceptual abilities is partially offset by the fact that driving is a self-paced task. The pace (or rate of driving speed) can of course greatly change the "task load." One aspect of task load is how frequently the roadway environment must be visually scanned or sampled. Beginning drivers have a low sampling rate because they must search for salient cues, whereas experienced drivers have gradually learned which cues are salient and can respond quickly to minimal cues in a more efficient search pattern. This is dramatically evident when comparing eye-movement patterns of novices with those of experienced drivers.[4] Similar results have been obtained from aircraft pilots,[5] and it is a familiar experience for anyone who has ever attempted to teach another person to drive.

For the novice, the visual search pattern is more active and erratic and dwell times tend to be longer. For the experienced driver, visual search patterns are generally less active and dwell times much shorter because the central nervous system (CNS) processing takes place more rapidly and because the driver has learned what to expect. However, operator skill by itself is not enough for safe driving. Williams and O'Neill[6] reported a study of race drivers (in three states) which showed them to have significantly higher numbers of both accidents and violations compared to "normal" drivers.

With increasing age of the driver, the dwell times increase because of a slowdown in CNS process time, but this slowdown occurs gradually over many years and is adjusted by changes in pace and offset by additional learning. Alcohol and other drugs also slow down the CNS; this change, however, is rapid and may or may not be compensated for by a reduction in pace, depending on the degree of conscious awareness of the driver of the drug effects on his abilities. Alcohol is discussed in detail later in this chapter. Fatigue also slows CNS rate far more rapidly than age, but fatigue does have a large number of recognizable symptoms that drivers can use as a basis for deciding to reduce their pace. Kimball et al. clearly show this trade-off of pace for steering in a comparison of experienced drivers with novices.[7] Shinar et al.[8] reported that the novices (with fewer than 10 h of experience) also required more steering inputs to maintain "marginal control" of the vehicle steering task than did the experienced drivers. They also indicated that driving visual search patterns are different for drivers who take longer to detect hidden figures in paper-and-pencil tests; Goodenough's early work[9] indicated that low-accident groups found the hidden figures sooner than did high-accident groups.

Unfortunately, reduction of the driving pace only reduces a portion of the driving task load because the remainder of the task load is determined by other drivers, pedestrians, other roadway users, and sudden or unexpected changes in the roadway environment, such as illumination, alignment, traction, sight distance, and visibility.

Age and sex of drivers

Age and sex of drivers are important variables in that they are easily determined and can be used in driver licensing or other driver control efforts. Burg concludes the following[10] from the data presented in Table 8-4:

> The trend in recent years shows that:
>
> 1. Females are comprising an ever-increasing proportion of the driving population, with the male/female ratio approaching that which exists in the general population [and that]
> 2. Both old and young drivers comprise an increasing proportion of the total driving population.

TABLE 8–4
Age and Sex Distribution of Licensed Drivers in the United States by Year

Age Group	Percent of Total				
	1977	1972	1970	1965	1960
Under 20	10.1	10.3	10.2	9.8	7.2
20–24	11.8	11.3	11.1	10.4	11.2
25–29	11.8	10.8	10.1	9.6	12.7
30–34	11.2	9.8	9.5	10.1	12.5
35–39	9.0	9.5	9.8	11.1	11.6
40–44	8.2	9.6	10.4	10.8	10.3
45–49	8.5	9.6	9.8	9.7	9.1
50–54	8.3	8.7	8.6	8.5	7.8
55–59	6.8	6.7	6.8	6.8	6.2
60–64	5.1	5.2	5.2	5.2	4.7
65–69	4.4	3.9	3.9	3.7	3.1
70–74	2.9	2.7	2.7	2.6	2.1
75 and up	1.9	1.9	1.9	1.7	1.5
Total licensed drivers ($\times 10^6$)	121.9	118.2	111.0	98.0	87.0
Percent male	54	56	57	61	70
Percent female	46	44	43	39	30

SOURCE: ALBERT BURG, "Characteristics of Drivers," in *Human Factors in Highway Traffic Safety Research*, p. 76; *Accident Facts* (Chicago: National Safety Council, 1973), p. 54; *Accident Facts*, 1978, p. 54.

It is clear that raw numbers of reported accidents and traffic law violation convictions decrease with age; when exposure (miles driven) is taken into account, however, both young and old drivers have poorer driving records than middle-aged drivers. Also, there are differences in violation patterns related to age.[11] Young drivers' violations (e.g.,

[4]R. R. MOURANT AND T. H. ROCKWELL, "Strategies of Visual Search by Novice and Experienced Drivers," *Human Factors, 14*(4) 323–335 (1972).

[5]Ibid.

[6]A. S. WILLIAMS AND B. O'NEILL, "On-the-Road Driving Records of Licensed Race Drivers," *Accident Prev., 6,* 260–272 (1974).

[7]K. KIMBALL, V. ELLINGSTAD, AND R. HAGEN, "Effects of Experience on Patterns of Driving Skill," *J. Safety Res., 3*(3), 129–135 (Sept. 1971).

[8]D. SHINAR, E. D. MCDOWELL, N. J. ROCKOFF, AND T. H. ROCKWELL, "Field Dependence and Driver Visual Search Behavior," *Human Factors,* 20 (1978).

[9]D. R. GOODENOUGH, "A Review of Individual Differences in Field Dependence as a Factor in Auto Safety," *Human Factors, 18,* 53–62 (1976).

[10]ALBERT BURG, "Characteristics of Drivers," in *Human Factors in Highway Traffic Safety Research,* T. W. Forbes, ed. (New York: Wiley, 1972), p. 76.

[11]DAVE M. HARRINGTON AND ROBIN S. MCBRIDE, "Traffic Violations by Type, Age, Sex and Marital Status," *Accident Anal. Prev., 2*(1), 67–69 (1960).

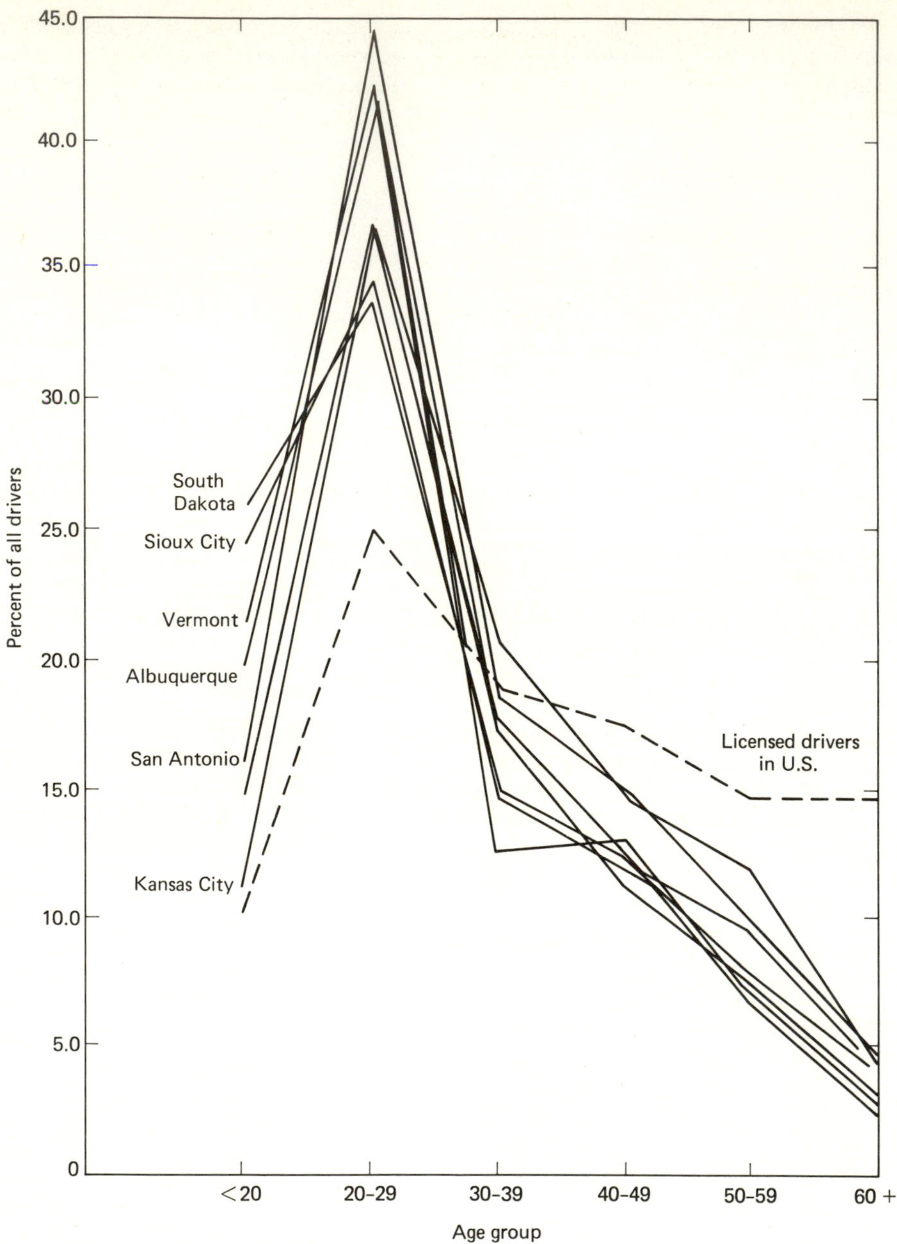

Figure 8.1. Age distribution of drivers using the road at night in seven areas of the United States. SOURCE: U.S. Department of Transportation, National Highway Safety Administration, *The Driver Education Program (DEEP) Study: A Report to the Congress,* Washington, D.C., July 1975, p. 21.

speeding) reflect a greater propensity for risk-taking behavior than older drivers' violations (e.g., signs, turning, passing, and right of way). This indicates decrements in physical and judgmental skills of both younger and older drivers. There is some evidence that accident type also varies with age, but this has not as yet been studied in detail. It is also clear that young drivers as a group do more nighttime driving than older drivers (see Figure 8.1) and nighttime fatal accidents occur about twice as often per mile as daytime. However, it is not clear whether more accidents occur at night because more inexperienced drivers are out or because of many other factors that obtain at night, such as lowered visibility, fatigue, and more alcohol. Transportation engineers can help improve the level of positive guidance at night and this does seem to pay off in many instances.

Miles driven (quantitative exposure to risk) is the single variable most highly correlated with accident and violation record. Accidents and convictions increase with increasing mileage, but not linearly.

Male drivers have more accidents and convictions than females; when miles driven is taken into account, however, the differences essentially disappear.

Married drivers have better driving records than single drivers for both males and females, at all age levels, and whether or not exposure (miles driven) is taken into account, although exposure does enter in and the relationship is less for older drivers.

Driver license laws and regulations in many states encourage young drivers to complete driver education and driver training courses. No special requirements are set for

TABLE 8–5
Improper Driving Reported in Accidents, 1977 (%)

Kind of Improper Driving	Fatal Accidents Total	Fatal Accidents Urban	Fatal Accidents Rural	Injury Accidents Total	Injury Accidents Urban	Injury Accidents Rural	All Accidents* Total	All Accidents* Urban	All Accidents* Rural
Total	100.0	100.0	100.0	100.0	100.0	100.0	100.0	100.0	100.0
Improper driving	75.9	74.0	76.2	82.5	81.9	83.4	83.4	82.0	86.3
Speed too fast†	30.1	15.4	37.2	16.8	8.6	36.4	17.7	10.4	33.6
Right of way	14.1	16.2	13.0	19.7	20.7	17.3	21.3	22.5	18.5
Failed to yield	8.3	10.0	7.3	12.8	13.6	10.8	14.8	15.8	12.1
Passed stop sign	3.3	2.6	3.7	2.8	2.3	4.0	2.5	2.1	3.5
Disregarded signal	2.5	3.6	2.0	4.1	4.8	2.5	4.0	4.6	2.9
Drove left of center	10.5	3.7	14.2	3.3	1.7	7.0	3.6	2.2	7.1
Improper overtaking	2.7	1.3	3.5	1.6	1.0	3.1	2.7	2.1	3.8
Made improper turn	0.9	0.7	0.9	2.1	2.2	1.9	3.7	4.0	3.0
Followed too closely	0.8	1.0	0.7	6.8	6.6	7.3	8.6	8.8	8.0
Other improper driving	16.8	35.7	6.7	32.2	41.1	10.4	25.8	32.0	12.3
No improper driving stated	24.1	26.0	23.8	17.5	18.1	16.6	16.6	18.0	13.7

*Principally property damage accidents but also includes fatal and injury accidents.
†Includes "speed too fast for conditions."

SOURCE: Reports of state and city traffic authorities as follows: urban—41 cities; rural—11 states; total—NSC estimates based on urban and rural reports.

Improper Driving by Type of Vehicle in Fatal Accidents, 1976 (%)

Kind of Improper Driving	All Vehicles	Type of Vehicle: Automobile	Motorcycle	Bus	Special Vehicle*	Truck
Total	100.0	100.0	100.0	100.0	100.0	100.0
Speed too fast†	37.4	37.0	51.7	12.9	22.6	34.2
Right of way	23.8	24.5	12.9	51.6	24.8	24.0
Failed to yield	17.0	17.2	8.0	45.2	19.7	17.8
Disregarded traffic controls	6.8	7.3	4.9	6.4	5.1	6.2
Improper lane or ran off road	21.7	22.2	17.7	8.1	24.8	21.9
Improper or erratic lane changes	0.8	0.7	0.8	1.6	1.5	1.0
Improper overtaking	2.6	2.5	3.1	1.6	1.5	2.8
Improper turn	1.5	1.5	0.5	3.2	3.7	2.1
Followed improperly	1.3	0.9	2.3	0.0	1.5	2.3
Other violation	10.9	10.7	11.0	21.0	19.6	11.7

*Includes emergency vehicles, farm equipment, snowmobiles, etc.
†Includes "speed too fast for conditions."

SOURCE: Based on National Highway Traffic Safety Administration, 1976 Fatal Accident Reporting System.

single versus married drivers, although insurance rates do differ.

Driver behavior and accidents

Some tabulations of types of improper driving as related to accidents have been made as shown in Table 8-5. These and other types of improper driving can be the results of either willful or inadvertent errors. Unfortunately, it is not easy to discover which type of behavior has caused an accident.

An October 1970 report by the U.S. Department of Transportation[12] deals with this difficult problem and concludes: "The negligence law usually treats 'driver error' as both avoidable and unreasonable, and imposes liability pursuant to an objective standard to which all drivers are held. But a review of the available research indicates that a significant gap exists between the standard of behavior required by the negligence law and the average behavior normally exhibited by most drivers."

The report also says: "You will note that the standard of care required is that exercised by a person of reasonable and ordinary prudence, rather than that exercised by a person of extreme caution or exceptional skill. While exceptional skill is to be admired and encouraged, the law does not demand it as a general standard of conduct."

Many programs of driver improvement seem to be based on an assumption of willful misbehavior and therefore concentrate on the multiple violator and accident repeater. However, studies by Campbell[13] show that there is little evidence to support this position. Most accidents involve drivers with good records who have not had any previous serious crashes. In other words, the old concept of the "accident-prone" driver is not supported by the facts.

Each year traffic accidents seem to be distributed among the states in about the same proportions per millions of

[12]U.S. DEPARTMENT OF TRANSPORTATION, *Driver Behavior and Accident Involvement: Implications for Tort Liability*, Insurance and Compensation Study, Washington, D.C., Oct. 1970, p. 190.

[13]B. J. CAMPBELL, "The Effects of Driver Improvement Actions on Driving Behavior," *Traffic Safety Res. Rev., 3*(3), 19–31 (1959).

vehicle-miles driven. Raw numbers of fatal crashes occur more frequently during the summer and fall when there is more travel. These facts all seem to point to the conclusion that the more driving we do, the more the chance of an accident occurring increases, and the more do occur. This would seem to argue for the major role of chance in the distribution of fatal crashes. Undoubtedly, chance factors are acting, but each accident was caused and therefore could have been prevented.

Since the majority of motor vehicle accidents occur in daylight on dry roads with sound vehicles, the causes seem to be with the drivers and the ways in which they interact with the roadway. The more that is understood about drivers, the more likely are traffic control and remedial efforts to be successful. Burg deals with this question and presents the following conclusions:

1. *Biographical descriptors:* A justification exists for differential licensing for both young and old drivers, and implementation of such a program is feasible. Not feasible, however, is differential licensing on the basis of such factors as marital status, education, or annual mileage, although research results would suggest such a move.

2. *Chronic medical conditions:* There is sufficient evidence relating certain severe medical conditions to accidents to suggest that short-term licensing of such individuals might prove beneficial. However, final action of this sort should not be taken without confirmation of present findings through a carefully controlled study.

3. *Hearing:* Present evidence suggests that the deaf driver may be at a disadvantage, and that special training programs and/or special aids might be of benefit; however, additional research again is needed before action is warranted.

4. *Loss of limb:* There is no evidence to justify taking any action in this area.

5. *Vision:* Research results indicate that vision is indeed related to driving. However, the magnitude of the relationship appears to be small, and the question of practical significance arises; however, it is interesting to note that Shinar[14] found that "nighttime accident involvement is related to poor visual acuity under nighttime levels of illumination, but unrelated to visual acuity under high (daytime) levels of illumination."

Burg states: "How much improvement in the traffic accident picture can be effected by more effective vision screening? By the same token, of what value are present licensing techniques such as written examinations and driver tests? These are questions that have no clear-cut answers, for definitive research has yet to be done, and other factors, such as 'face validity' and 'tradition' serve to confound the issue."[15]

Drivers can become involved in accidents even as innocent victims and yet be included in some records. Because of legal implications, many such records do not distinguish the "at fault" driver from those not at fault, which makes research in group behavior very difficult. Therefore, care must be exercised when examining studies of driving accident records to know what criteria were used.

[14]D. SHINAR, *Driver Visual Limitations, Diagnosis and Treatment,* Indiana Univ. Final Report No. DOT-HS-5-1275, Oct. 1977.

[15]BURG, "Characteristics of Drivers," pp. 91–92.

The driving task

Human beings as components in any transportation system have several important functions to perform in addition to actual control of the vehicle. For example, they must decide where and when they want to go, and they must choose their route and type of vehicle. These various functions that human beings perform are described in the generalized framework shown in Figure 8.2, which can be used to analyze any transportation system (or subsystem). Using such a framework will help to keep in mind the many interactions that are involved in even the most simple motor trip. Pretrip planning, for example, can be influenced by radio broadcast advisory information on traffic congestion. Many examples of the application of this framework are provided by Hulbert and Burg.[16]

Usually, however, the driving task is dealt with in a more narrow frame of reference that considers only the actual control of the vehicle along a roadway. From this viewpoint, research work has been done to describe human beings as a control element in a servo system. To date, several mathematical models have been developed to aid vehicle designers to produce automobiles with "good" handling characteristics so that drivers with less than average skill and strength can successfully accomplish the maneuvers they wish to perform.

These types of vehicle control maneuvers are influenced directly by the available information (cues) and the driver's ability to receive and process that information. A landmark study[17] reports on the information needs of drivers and classifies these needs into various categories that relate to pathway information and delineation which are primary needs and are related to route selection and tracking skills. The other major task is object avoidance, about which much less has been published. Traffic control devices can help in both of these tasks in many ways, as discussed by Hulbert,[18] for example, assigning right of way, warning of curves, and control of passing.

Tracking and object avoidance must be performed concurrently, but human beings have essentially a one-track (single-channel) mind, and therefore they must divide attention while driving. Most driving information comes to drivers visually in a stream of changing scenes from which they must sample (because they cannot take it all in) and select cues to make decisions about where they are going to be in the next instant and the next few seconds. This is a spatial commitment described as a fan-shaped zone extending in front of the moving vehicle. Figure 8.3 describes this zone, which, of course, varies in its exact shape but nevertheless is there and has been committed to by the driver.

The concept of the committed zone has been extended to a three-dimensional form. In this way, it is possible to

[16]SLADE F. HULBERT AND ALBERT BURG, "Human Factors in Transportation Systems," in *Systems Psychology,* Kenyon B. DeGreene, ed. (New York: McGraw-Hill, 1970), pp. 471–509.

[17]*Development of Information Requirements and Transportation Techniques for Highway Users,* Vol. 1 (Deer Park, N.Y.: Airborne Instruments Laboratory, 1967).

[18]SLADE F. HULBERT, "Driver Information Systems," in *Human Factors in Highway Traffic Safety Research,* T. W. Forbes, ed. (New York: Wiley, 1972), pp. 110–132.

	A. Trip planning		B. Making vehicle control decisions			C. Executing vehicle control decisions		D. Vehicle maintenance	
	a. Schedule	b. Route	a. Path	b. Speed	c. System failure	a. Acceleration	b. Direction	a. At home	b. En route
1. Input (Sources of information)									
2. Output (Range of performance)									
3. Evaluation of performance									
4. Selection and placement									
5. Training of personnel									

Figure 8.2. Generalized framework for analysis of human functions and their characteristics in transportation systems. SOURCE: Slade F. Hulbert and Albert Burg, "Human Factors in Transportation Systems," *Systems Psychology*, Kenyon B. De Greene, ed., New York: McGraw-Hill, 1970, p. 482.

Figure 8.3. Spacial commitment of driver in moving vehicle. SOURCE: Slade F. Hulbert, "Driver Information Systems," *Human Factors in Highway Traffic Safety Research*, T.W. Forbes, ed., New York: Wiley, 1972, p. 111.

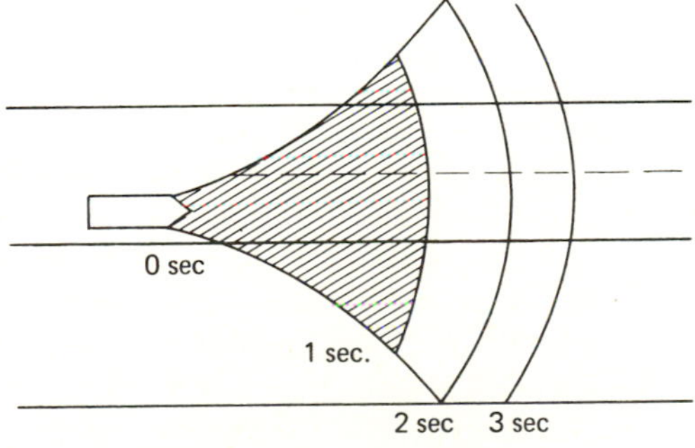

The exact configuration of this fan-shaped zone will depend on the vehicle speed, turning radius, and stopping distance as they interact with the driver's reaction time.

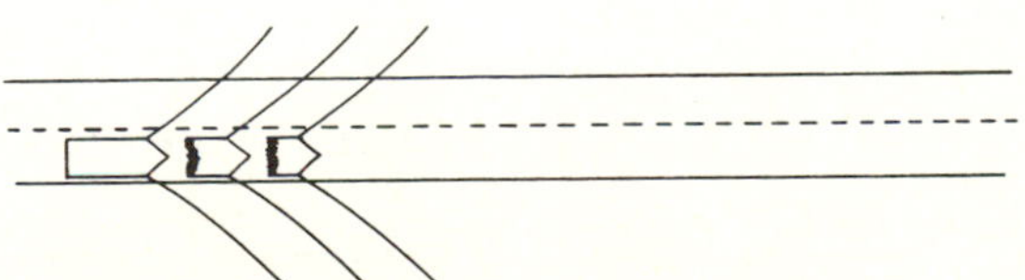

As each driver proceeds, the fan-shaped zone extends in front of his path and changes shape as velocity and pavement conditions vary.

portray the committed zone as it appears through the windshield to the driver. It has been concluded that "all portions of the driver's field of view are not of equal importance, nor are all portions equally easy for him to use, considering inherent constraints in the human visual system. Committed zone analysis is a promising tool; however; the size, shape and location of a committed zone will be determined by such statistical variables as vehicle velocities, accelerations, and road properties. Sizable samples of these statistics are available, but more studies must be conducted before the descriptions can be developed into normative samples. Then the relative importance of the committed zones will be known."[19]

As the time frame of the commitment increases, the commitment becomes more and more provisional because the driver has more time to receive new (updated) information and change path or speed. Each driver knows that this is the case (although perhaps not consciously) and behaves accordingly, which explains why urban freeway drivers move with only 1-s headway at speeds over 60 mph. Each driver knows that the driver ahead also has a committed zone stretching ahead and therefore cannot stop instantaneously. So we feel comfortable in making a similar spatial commitment allowing only 1 s for reaction time and assuming that we can stop as quickly as the driver ahead. If drivers did not behave this way, freeway volumes of as much as 1900 vehicles/lane/h could not be achieved. However, freeway accidents do occur and could be reduced by providing more information to the driver about headway and impending changes in headway.

[19]HYMAN FORBES, "Geometric Vision Requirements in the Driving Task," *1970 International Automobile Safety Conference Compendium* (New York: Society of Automotive Engineers, 1970), pp. 677–689.

Expectation and reaction time

The role of expectancy is paramount in understanding driver behavior, and this understanding leads to an improved ability on the part of traffic engineers to shape and configure the environment in order to make traffic safe and efficient. Drivers' reactions to various roadway environments have been and are being studied in many research projects, and the results can be applied and useful only if they are understood in the context of the human perception process and the way it affects and changes driver behavior. Expectation is an explantory concept that places all the many things that traffic engineers do in a somewhat different frame of reference that can be extremely useful in applying results of research to everyday engineering practice.

For example, the addition of a yellow phase to traffic signals clearly grew out of the fact that, as vehicle speeds increased, the driver's limited range of abilities had to be assisted. At the same time there has been an increase in the number of signal heads because of the recognition of the driver's limited rate of sampling of the visual environment, so that if the driver's visual attention happens to be away from one signal head, there are other signal heads available to see within a normal cone (or field) of attention. This increases the likelihood that at least one will be seen, and is sometimes called redundancy.

This is an obvious example of the evolution of traffic signals. If one considers recent trends to more complex, multiphase, multi-indication signal displays, it soon becomes evident that a conceptual and systematic understanding of driver behavior can be useful. For example, the addition of pedestrian heads to signals has become increasingly popular because they help to shorten the time that must be allotted to pedestrian movement. However, an understanding of driver behavior will lead to a recognition that drivers also can see the pedestrian heads and actually are using them as a pre-yellow indication in much the same way as the traffic funnel concept. Pedestrian heads thus provide a possible increase in accuracy of driver expectation of a change in the signal indication. Evidence that pedestrian heads do serve this function is contained in a small study of the accident records at signalized intersections where there was found a reduction in car-to-car collisions after installation of pedestrian heads, and also a lower frequency of these crashes than on a comparable roadway where pedestrian heads were not installed.[20] A recent study[21] of delay measurements at signalized intersections advocates standardizing the duration of the flashing "don't walk" message so that pedestrians could learn to expect how much time they had left at any intersection. This is an example of a human factors principle that also would help those drivers who are using the pedestrian head display as a pre-yellow.

The extreme importance of the role of expectation in driver reaction time was documented in the 1971 report by Johannsson and Rumar.[22] In a series of experiments they

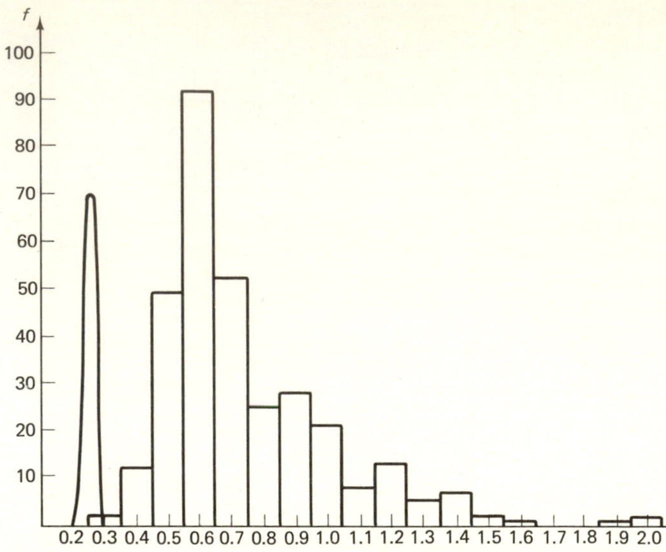

Figure 8.4. Brake-reaction-time distribution for 321 drivers on the road. SOURCE: G. Johansson and K. Rumar, "Drivers' Brake Reaction Time," *Human Factors, 13*(1), 26 (1971).

gathered data from 321 drivers who expected to have to apply their brakes. These data are shown in Figure 8.4. The median value is 0.66 s, the range being from 0.3 to 2.0 s.

For a smaller group of drivers they gathered data on the stimulus coming as a surprise and also on the stimulus being anticipated. Table 8-6 shows the results. Every driver had longer reaction time when the signal occurred completely unexpectedly. The range of times also was smaller for the anticipated signal, although not as much as might have been expected.

Using these results, Johannsson and Rumar calculated a "correction factor" which they then applied to the data shown in Figure 8.4 to estimate how much longer these reaction times would have been if the need for braking had occurred unexpectedly. This resulted in an estimated brake reaction time of 0.9 s or longer in 50% of the drivers. For 10% of the drivers the time would have been 1.5 s or longer and in a few cases it would have exceeded 2 s. These authors state in conclusion: "The distribution of brake reaction time obtained here is caused by interindividual differences (between drivers). It is not improbable to assume that the intraindividual (within drivers) distribution over various occasions could have the same form and range."

TABLE 8–6
Brake Reaction Time for Surprise and Anticipated Situation*

	Observations Number		Median (s)		Range (s)	
Subject	*sb*	*ab*	*sb*	*ab*	*sb*	*ab*
A	10	10	0.88	0.6	0.7–1.1	0.5–0.7
B	10	10	0.6	0.5	0.6–1.0	0.5–0.8
C	10	10	0.9	0.55	0.7–1.0	0.5–0.8
D	10	10	0.7	0.55	0.6–0.7	0.5–0.6
E	10	10	0.6	0.5	0.5–0.9	0.4–0.6
Total (mean)	50	50	0.73	0.54	0.5–1.1	0.4–0.8

**sb*, surprise braking situation; *ab*, anticipated braking situation.

SOURCE: G. JOHANSSON AND K. RUMAR, "Driver's Brake Reaction Times," *Human Factors, 12*(1), 99 (1971).

[20] LOS ANGELES CITY TRAFFIC DEPARTMENT, "Florence Avenue Study," Informal Staff Report, Mar. 1969. p. 5.

[21] S. L. COHEN AND W. R. REILLY, "Delay Measurement at Signalized Intersections," *Public Roads, 42*(3), 81–84 (Dec. 1978).

[22] G. JOHANNSSON AND K. RUMAR, "Driver Brake Reaction Times," *Human Factors, 13*(1), 22–27 (1971).

Hulbert and Beers, in a study of driver responses to "wrong way" signs, found that fully 5% of healthy, alert young drivers utterly and completely failed to see two sets of large red signs when they unexpectedly came upon them.[23]

The role of expectation in human perception cannot be overemphasized. Indeed, one might even conclude that a major task of traffic engineering is to use all devices and techniques available in order to shape and manipulate driver expectation so that there will be as few surprises as possible. Design and construction errors create many unfortunate surprises that traffic engineers must try to render harmless by the use of warning devices, delineation, channelization, stop signs, and other techniques; for example, in some regions, signs have been placed warning "Dangerous Intersection." This, it would seem, is a very general alerting device and may be the only appropriate one when a variety of "surprises" lie in wait.

Unfortunately, drivers often do not use information the way that engineers thought they would. Shinar[24] says: "Thus, drivers tend to use advisory speed signs before curves as a caution sign calling for close evaluation of the curve ahead, rather than slow down to the recommended speed."

Bleyl[25] found that flashing yellow signals did not slow drivers below the speed at which they drove when shown only a green ball indication.

Shared tasks

If our single central processing channel is occupied with one kind of information, it cannot be utilized to process additional information. Therefore, time spent reading a highway sign or looking at a pedestrian is time taken away from the tracking task. For this reason designers of roadways and vehicles have striven to make the tracking task easier, and after many years of trial and error, traffic control devices have been designed to be relatively unambiguous information generators, demanding a minimum of attention.

A recent review by this author of several thousand accident reports where attention had been cited as a causal factor revealed that distractions occur in three major categories:

1. Events within the car, such as infants, pets, and falling objects.
2. Events outside the car, such as rubbernecking, looking for street names or addresses, or looking at accidents.
3. Events within the driver, such as daydreaming, sudden pain, and loss of consciousness.

Drivers were remarkably candid about revealing what had distracted them just before the crash. Some things that transportation engineers could do about driver distraction are to use large street signs and attempt to reduce rubbernecking by use of glare screens that prevent a view of the other side of the road.

[23]S. Hulbert and J. Beers.

[24]D. Shinar, *Psychology on the Road, The Human Factor in Traffic Safety*, (New York: Wiley, 1978), p. 91.

[25]R. L. Bleyl, "Speed Profiles Approaching a Traffic Signal," *Highway Res. Rec. 386*, 1972, pp. 17–23.

Visual attention

Hulbert and Burg discuss visibility of vehicles that are on a collision course with each other.[26] Figure 8.5 shows that as these vehicles approach the point of collision, they do not change their bearing to each other. Visually, this means that they remain stationary in each other's field of view. If one or both of these nonmoving images is hidden by the vehicle corner post (or other obstruction), it will remain there. Some experienced drivers take this into account in some situations and vigorously move their heads to see around the blind spot. But unsuspecting drivers who are on a collision course unfortunately, because of the geometry of the situation, have lost one of the major cues (namely, an object moving in their field of view) just at a time when they most need it.

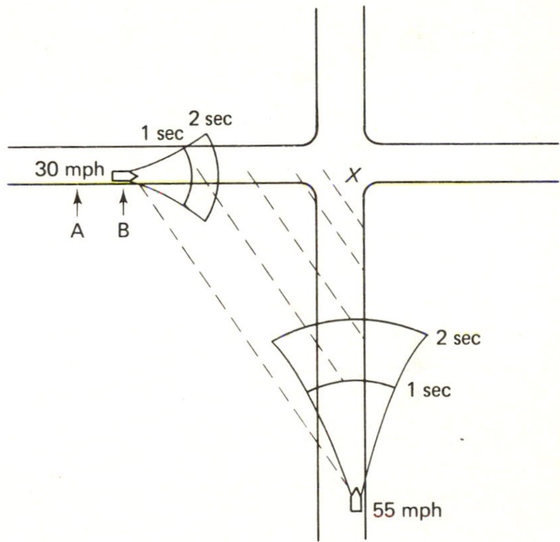

Figure 8.5. Committed zones for two vehicles approaching an intersection. Source: Slade F. Hulbert and Albert Burg, "Human Factors in Transportation Systems," *Systems Psychology*, Kenyon B. De Greene, ed., New York: McGraw-Hill, 1970, p. 485.

The second visual attention factor in the driving task is the way in which the driver's eyes function. When the head and eyes are moved from one object to another (at different places in the visual field), an involuntary blink often occurs that blocks out what otherwise would be a streaming or blurred image (just as when a moving picture camera is panned too fast). This wonderfully timed blink is so natural that drivers are not aware that often as they transfer their gaze, the blink actually blanks out the visual scene that lies between the two points of visual attention. This is important for the placement of the signs or signals, particularly where some vehicle turning movements are being made. Figure 8.6 shows how drivers waiting to make a left turn against

[26]Hulbert and Burg, "Human Factors in Transportation Systems."

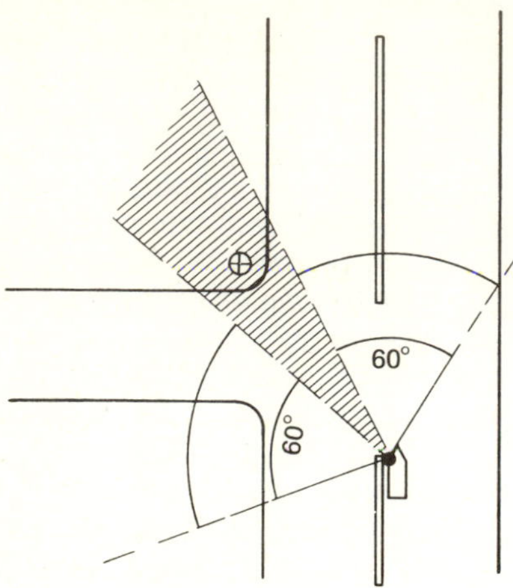

Figure 8.6. Change in visual field for left-turn situation.

oncoming traffic will rapidly shift their gaze from the oncoming stream (when they find an acceptable gap) over to their projected path as they execute their turn. In so doing, they will swing past a large segment of the visual field while their view is blocked by the involuntary blink. Assuming that the central field of attention is approximately 60°, the diagram shows how drivers can completely fail to see the crosshatched area, which is where many signs are placed or where a pedestrian may be crossing.

Robinson et al. studied drivers as they waited to cross a major highway and also as they made lane changes.[27] In the first case (stop and enter), visual search times ranged from 1.1 to 2.6 s. In the lane-change situation, times ranged from 0.8 to 1.6 s for mirror use and 0.8 to 1.0 s for "look-back" time. The more traffic, the greater number of "looks" and the "looks" tended to be longer (dwell time increased).

Alcohol, drugs, age, and fatigue

Buttiglieri et al. state: "Society today is a drug taking society."[28] The authors compared a 1959 survey with a 1968 survey and noted a fourfold increase in the percentage of people who reported using tranquilizers. Self-medication practices have increased considerably according to a 1967 report by the California Medical Association,[29] and many surveys describe the current popularity of stimulants, marijuana, and hallucinogens.

The National Safety Council states:

> Valium was the most frequently encountered drug (excluding alcohol) among drivers in fatal motor-vehicle accidents in Indiana during the period July 1, 1975 to July 1, 1976. Blood specimens from these drivers were analyzed for drugs, alcohol, and carbon monoxide in a study at the Indiana State Department of Toxicology and Valium was found in 9 percent of the specimens. Alcohol was found in 44 percent of the samples taken. Barbiturates were present in 3 percent of the specimens. Carbon monoxide was found in 17 percent of the drivers and in 61 percent of these cases alcohol was also present. The combination of alcohol and Valium was found in 5 percent of the driver specimens taken.

Still the most widespread tranquilizer is alcohol, the use of which dates to prehistoric times on a nearly worldwide basis. In the United States estimates are that at least 50% of drivers arrested while under the influence of alcohol are "problem drinkers" who are frequently on the road while drunk.[30]

Driver characteristics, alcohol, and drugs

Since alcohol can be relatively easily detected and measured in the blood, breath, and urine, it has been most widely studied in relation to traffic accidents. Buttiglieri et al. point out that the effects of alcohol on the human body are much more complex than was first assumed.[31] They point out that although there is a good deal of variation among individuals, for most people a blood alcohol level (BAL) up to 0.05% induces some sedation or tranquility. From a 0.05 to a 0.15% BAL, a lack of coordination may be apparent, as well as behavioral changes which seem to suggest stimulation of the brain (such as talkativeness, aggressiveness, and hyperactivity) but which actually result from the depression of brain centers that normally inhibit such behavior. As drivers' abilities are impaired by higher BALs, their self-judgment frequently worsens and they believe that they are performing normally or even better.[32]

To the extent that traffic engineering techniques can provide an improved means for letting drunk (or otherwise impaired) drivers know that their performance is poor, this unfortunate effect of alcohol perhaps can be offset. In this respect, raised pavement markers, for example, not only provide a stronger visual cue that is more easily processed by the driver but also a rumble effect that adds another cue when tracking performance exceeds an error limit. This benefit of raised pavement markers has been praised by drivers but not documented by research.

In a traffic safety monograph by the National Safety Council it was stated that approximately 90 to 95 million persons in the United States drink alcoholic beverages at least occasionally.[33] It has been estimated that 80% of men and 67% of women over the age of 21 drink. How often they drive while drinking is not precisely known. However, it is estimated by the National Safety Council that alcohol plays a role in at least 1 out of every 16 crashes annually,[34] and field studies have conclusively shown that the blood alcohol levels of drivers who were in serious or fatal crashes

[27]G. H. Robinson et al., "Visual Search by Automobile Drivers," *Human Factors, 14*(4), 315–323 (1972).

[28]Matthew Buttiglieri, Anthony J. Brunse, and Harry W. Case, "Effects of Alcohol and Drugs on Driving Behaviors," in *Human Factors in Highway Traffic Safety Research*, T. W. Forbes, ed. (New York: Wiley, 1972), p 303.

[29]California Medical Association, "Self-Medication Practices," *Calif. Med. 107*(5), 452–454 (Nov. 1967).

[30]U.S. Department of Transportation National Highway Safety Administration, *The Driver Education Evaluation Program (DEEP) Study: A Report to the Congress*, July 1975, p. 21.

[31]Buttiglieri et al., "Effects of Alcohol and Drugs on Driving Behaviors," p. 307.

[32]Ibid.

[33]National Safety Council, "On the Level," *Traffic Safety Monogr. No. 1* (Chicago: 1969).

[34]National Safety Council, *Accident Facts* (Chicago: 1972).

differ greatly from those drivers not involved in crashes.[35–38] In these studies only 1 to 4% of nonaccident drivers were found with a BAL at or above 0.10%, while from 48 to 57% of fatally injured drivers in one-car crashes were found to have BALs in excess of 0.10%. In multiple car crashes, similarly high BALs were found in 45% of fatally injured drivers.[39,40] Zylman has critically reviewed these studies and performed further analysis of the data which indicate the important role of traffic density, time of day, type of driver, and trip purpose.[41] For example, women were 26% of the control sample between noon and 3:00 P.M. but only 6% of the sample from 3:00 A.M. to 6:00 A.M. He expects there are some differences in drinking behavior between men and women. He speaks also of the importance of drinking and driving experience such that those who are experienced will be safer than beginners.

Drivers with BALs of 0.10% will not usually show any marked outward evidence of impaired driving capability. This was clearly revealed in initial research at UCLA ITTE, where drivers were intoxicated and their performance measured in the UCLA Driving Simulator.[42] It was only when a secondary visual task was added that the evidence of alcohol effects became clear. The underlying concept put forth by Moskowitz and Prey is that driving is a task that requires a division of attention.[43] In other words, the single-track mental system described earlier is used by alert drivers to sample the driving environment both outside and inside the vehicle and to look for cues that will enable them to predict and anticipate correctly what lies ahead. Jex et al. reported that drivers in a simulator at 0.10 BAL were poor at detecting roadside signs,[44] and Hicks found this to be true in actual nighttime driving.[45]

The divided-attention concept of why alcohol increases accident likelihood explains why simple reaction time may not be affected or may even be improved. Alcohol apparently narrows the field of attention, which can actually improve the ability to respond to a simple and expected change in the environment. The UCLA work showed that this holds true for auditory stimuli as well as for visual,[46] which is evidence that the behavioral impairment takes place in the central nervous system and in particular reduces the driver's information-handling capability. This concept helps to explain why visual acuity is not affected by BALs of 0.10%.

When the driving task is considered in terms of the impairment in mental processing and environment sampling rate decrease caused by alcohol, it is readily understood how drunk drivers can fail to drive safely. They can fail by completely "not seeing" obstacles or other vehicles because their visual scanning rate is simply too slow e.g. 29% fewer glances at 0.07% BAL. They can, and do, fluctuate speed greatly and erratically because their rate of speed monitoring is too slow to detect speed changes as efficiently as normal. Their steering performance may not vary greatly but it can demand nearly all of their limited attention, whereas normally (sober) they need devote only a fraction of attention to steering and have a great deal of attention available to detect and process other cues from the environment.

Similar effects on human performance are likely to occur as a result of fatigue, mental stress, age, and most certainly other drugs. It has been found that some tranquilizers interact with alcohol to produce a combined effect that is greater than the sum of their individual effects. Barbiturates in combination with alcohol can be lethal and even in small amounts can result in loss of consciousness. These and other unfortunate combination effects of medication are particularly dangerous and difficult to detect. Their frequency of use and role in traffic crashes is unknown, but police officials do report many instances of drivers' unknowingly falling victim to these combination effects.

The widespread use of marijuana has focused attention on its possible effects on driving skills. Survey results have indicated that marijuana users receive more traffic tickets than do nonusers.[47,48] Similar results have been derived from the traffic records of persons arrested for marijuana use, although the accident rate was not above average.[49] Of course, these findings are simply correlates of marijuana use and do not indicate a causal relationship. The user's own assessment of the effect of marijuana intoxication on driving performance is apparently related to age-related involvement in the current marijuana controversy—17% of a sample of student and other young marijuana users felt that their driving was impaired by the drug in comparison to 72% of a sample who began using marijuana some 20 years ago.[50]

One study compared the effects of alcohol (1.2 g/kg body weight) and smoked marijuana [22 mg of tetrahydrocan-

---

[35]R. L. Holcome, "Alcohol in Relation to Traffic Accidents," *J. Am. Med. Assoc., 3*(12), 1076–1085 (1939).

[36]G. H. Lucas, W. Kalow, J. D. McCowl, B. A. Griffith, and H. W. Smith, "Quantitative Studies of the Relationship between Alcohol Levels and Motor Vehicle Accidents," *Proceedings of the 2nd International Conference of Alcohol and Road Traffic, Toronto, 1955*, pp. 139–142.

[37]J. R. McCarroll and W. Haddon, "A Controlled Study of Fatal Automobile Accidents in New York City," *J. Chronic Dis., 15*(8), 811–826 (1962).

[38]R. F. Borrenstein, R. F. Crowther, R. P. Shumate, B. W. Zuri, and R. Zlyman, *The Role of the Drinking Driver in Traffic Accidents* (Indianapolis, Ind.: Indiana University Police Institute, Feb. 1964).

[39]R. A. Nillson, *Alcohol Involvement in Fatal Motor Vehicle Accidents* (San Francisco: California Traffic Safety Foundation, Sept. 1965).

[40]R. A. Nillson, *A Survey of Post-mortem Blood-Alcohols from 41 California Counties in 1966* (San Francisco: California Traffic Safety Foundation, Apr. 1967).

[41]Richard Zylman, "Analysis of Studies Comparing Collision-Involved Drivers and Non-Involved Drivers," *J. Safety Res., 3*(3), 116–128 (Sept. 1971).

[42]H. W. Case, Slade F. Hulbert, and H. A. Moskowitz, *Alcohol Level and Driving Performance*, Inst. Transport. Traffic Eng. Report No. 71-17 (Los Angeles, Calif.: University of California, Apr. 1971).

[43]H. Moskowitz and D. D. Prey, "The Effects of Alcohol Upon Auditory Vigilance and Divided Attention Tasks," *Quart. J. Study Alcohol, 29*(1), 54–63 (1968).

[44]H. R. Jex, R. J. DiMarco, and A. R. Wade, "Impairment of Moderate versus Heavy Drinkers in Simulated Driver Tests," paper presented at *10th Annual Conference on Manual Control, Wright-Patterson AFB, Ohio, Apr. 1974.*

[45]J. A. Hicks, *An Evaluation of the Effect of Sign Brightness on the Sign Reading Behavior of Alcohol-Impaired Drivers,* TCC Report No. 6, University of South Carolina, Traffic and Transportation Center, May 1974.

[46]Moskowitz and Prey, "Effects of Alcohol."

[47]J. L. Hochman and N. Q. Brill, "Marijuana Use and Psychosocial Adaption," unpublished paper delivered at American Psychiatric Association meeting, Washington, D.C., May 1971.

[48]B. D. Johnson, "Social Determinants of the Use of 'Dangerous Drugs' by College Students," Doctoral thesis, Columbia University, June 1971.

[49]A. Crancer and D. L. Quiring, "Driving Records of Persons Arrested for Illegal Drug Use," report 011, State of Washington, Department of Motor Vehicles, May 1968

[50]W. H. McGlothlin et al., "Marijuana Use among Adults," *Psychiatry, 33*(4), 433–443 (1970).

nabinol (THC)] on driving simulator performance. The alcohol dose significantly impaired simulator scores, whereas the marijuana usage produced minimal changes.[51] Moskowitz et al. have examined the effect of marijuana on attentional aspects of driving (i.e., the ability to attend to peripheral cues while carrying out central tracking tasks).[52] Smoked marijuana containing 15 mg of THC significantly impaired this function in laboratory tests of both the visual and auditory modalities. The extent of decrement was approximately equivalent to that produced by a blood alcohol level of about 0.07% (i.e., the consumption of about 5 oz of 80 proof liquor in less than 1 h).

Results of Moskowitz's work at UCLA[53] indicate that impairment caused by marijuana is different in nature from that caused by alcohol. Peripheral attention and vision are affected differently and perhaps more seriously.

An article on this topic reports[54] on a California study:

> Begun in 1976, this study involved testing for THC in blood samples taken from drivers "subjectively judged to be intoxicated." Out of a total of 19,000 blood samples submitted by the California Highway Patrol to certain laboratories for testing for alcohol content, about 1800 were randomly selected for the tests for THC.
>
> The tests showed that 16 percent of the impaired drivers had THC in their blood. For those between age 14 and 29, the percentage was 13 to 15; for drivers between age 30 and 60 years, the figure was 19 percent. The researchers suspected that these figures might be conservative, and that the actual incidence of marijuana use before driving might be much higher. One reason is that THC disappears rapidly from the blood. Also, any stoned driver who was stopped for suspected intoxication could choose breath or urine analysis and not be detected.

Age and driving

Age clearly changes driving behavior as well as other behavior. One study found that older drivers (51 years or more) had far more difficulty performing a simultaneous sign reading and steering task on a simple driving simulator device.[55] They also drove more erratically in city traffic as well as in the UCLA driving simulator, which represents 31 mi of free moving through rural roads, arterials, and residential roadways. Although not enough data have yet been collected, there is strong evidence that age will prove to interact with alcohol effects on divided attention tasks. There also may be a simple age effect that is to be expected if CNS processing time and ability are affected in the way many researchers believe age-related changes do come about.

[51]A. Crancer et al., "Comparison of the Effects of Marijuana and Alcohol on Simulated Driving Performance," *Science, 164*(3881), 851–854 (1969).

[52]H. Moskowitz, Slade F. Hulbert, and W. H. McGlothlin, "The Effects of Marijuana Upon Performance in a Driving Simulator," unpublished paper, Institute of Transportation and Traffic Engineering, University of California, Los Angeles, 1973.

[53]H. Moskowitz, "Marijuana and Driving," *Accident Anal. Prev., 8*, 21–26 (1976).

[54]J. Road, "Driving Stoned," *Driver Mag.*, 8 (Feb. 1979).

[55]J. Beers, H. W. Case, and Slade F. Hulbert, *Driving Ability as Affected by Age*, Inst. Transport. Traffic Eng. Report No. 70-19 (Los Angeles, Calif.: University of California, Los Angeles, Mar. 1970).

Sleep deprivation

Falling asleep at the wheel is a problem of major proportion in the cause of traffic accidents. The exact dimensions of this problem are not known; however, Hulbert states that available data indicate that from 35 to 50% of highway fatalities may well be caused by this factor.[56,57]

Alcohol, tranquilizers, antihistamines, barbiturates, and other substances promote drowsiness even in small doses for many persons. Driving in itself is soporific for some people. Trip habits and long stretches of superhighway keep drivers longer on the road.

All these factors are interacting to create a major source of driver impairment which is most clearly evident in single-vehicle crashes but probably also plays a part in many multiple-vehicle crashes.

One research method is to induce sleep loss to increase the likelihood of drowsiness at the wheel. Hulbert tested the effect of increasing the blood sugar level on sleep-deprived (24 h) drivers and found overwhelming evidence that increasing the sugar level prevented the drivers from falling asleep in using the UCLA driving simulator.[58]

Fifty percent of drivers in a study by Hulbert and Mellinger reported a tendency to fall asleep at the wheel even when they were not otherwise tired and had normal sleep.[59] Robert Yoss at the Mayo Clinic has studied drivers and aircraft pilots and concludes that many persons naturally are prone to such drowsiness.[60] He has been successful in correlating this unfortunate and dangerous tendency with a decrease in pupil size while looking into a pupilometer. Eventually, it may be feasible to screen out such drivers for medical treatment. At present, traffic engineers can only be aware that drugged and sleepy motorists need the most clear, unambiguous, and redundant traffic control devices that can feasibly be provided. Certain times and locations may be particularly likely to have these impaired drivers in the traffic stream. Accident record analyses and law enforcement efforts can help traffic engineers to locate such spots and perhaps can lead to effective countermeasures by the community as a whole.

Pedestrians

Even though approximately 400,000 pedestrians annually are being struck by vehicles (resulting in about 10,000 fatalities),[61] they are being killed at consistently decreasing

[56]Slade F. Hulbert, "Effects of Driver Fatigue," in *Human Factors in Highway Traffic Safety Research*, T. W. Forbes, ed. (New York: Wiley, 1972).

[57]Slade F. Hulbert (with A. and H. Eisenberg), "Asleep at the Wheel," *Readers Dig., 104*(619), 77–82 (Nov. 1973).

[58]Slade F. Hulbert, J. Beers, J. Herzog, and S. Blyden, *Blood Sugar Level and Fatigue Effects on a Simulated Driving Task*, Inst. Transport. Traffic Eng. Report No. 63-53 (Los Angeles, Calif.: University of California, Los Angeles, Oct. 1963).

[59]Slade F. Hulbert and R. L. Mellinger, *Effects of Fatigue on Skills Related to Driving*, School of Engineering Report 70-60 (Los Angeles, Calif.: University of California, Los Angeles, Jan. 1970).

[60]D. Yoss, "A Test to Measure Ability to Maintain Alertness and Its Application in Driving," *Mayo Clinic Proc., 44*(11), 769–783 (1969).

[61]Diane Chrzanowski Roberts, "Pedestrian Needs—Insights from a Pilot Survey of Blind and Deaf Individuals," *Public Roads, 37*(1), 29–31 (June 1972).

rates per vehicle-miles. This is largely attributable to improved roadways, more sidewalks, and special law enforcement efforts.

Many pedestrians are killed in urban areas; in the largest cities they account for one-half of motor vehicle–related deaths, and one-third in middle-sized cities. For 18 cities the daily fatality rates reach as high as 11 per day per city.[62]

Several studies agree that young and old pedestrians are particularly involved in more than their proportionate share of accidents.[63–66] Smeed[65] in England found that the amount of walking people do is related to their age and their accident rate. Old people (65 or older) were three times as likely to have an accident as young adults (30 to 39) for every mile walked; children under the age of 10 were eight times as likely to have an accident as young adults for every mile walked.

It seems that drivers do perceive these two groups as more vulnerable. Zuercher[67] in interviewing 417 drivers by showing them a picture of a pedestrian wanting to cross the street, found 47% to think a little girl is most vulnerable to traffic, 44% considered an elderly woman to be most vulnerable, and 9% judged a woman with a child, a middle-aged man, or a young man to be most vulnerable.

Children

One out of 10 deaths of children between the ages of 5 and 14 is a pedestrian traffic fatality. Child pedestrians receive most traffic engineering attention near school grounds, but the safety record at school crossings is excellent. Snyder and Knoblauch found only 2% of 2146 pedestrian accidents at school areas.[68] Small children are particularly vulnerable pedestrians because they are more easily hidden from the driver's view; conversely, from their lowly eye position there are more visual obstacles to obscure oncoming vehicles. A 1968 statistic shows that primary-grade children have three times the death and injury rate of children twice that age.[69] Sleight points out that only one of every four children killed and one in five injured were on their way to or from school.[70] Far more must be done away from school, where children have all the problems of other pedestrians in addition to the use of streets as play areas. It is particularly important to educate children to understand that drivers have difficulty seeing them.

Avery[71] concluded that the human functions needed to cross a street have a "developmental trend," so that prior to a certain age, a child cannot perform them adequately. Zwahlen[72] found that children are far more variable in estimating distance than are adults.

Children seem to employ a different strategy as they prepare to cross the street than do adults. Routledge et al.[73] state:

> Adults assess the crossing situation as they approach the kerb, while children pay little attention to the crossing situation until they arrive at the kerb, and are therefore less well prepared to take advantage of favourable traffic configurations. Having stopped at the kerb to wait for a gap in the traffic children are slower to start and seldom anticipate when they cross through a chosen gap, while adults take most advantage of gaps in traffic by anticipating their arrival. Children learn to adopt these adult strategies without instruction and indeed contrary to the way in which they have been taught. There appears to be a mismatch between the information they receive from parents, schools and safety programmes and the information they gain from their own experiences and from observation of adult pedestrians.

Elderly

It is clearly the elderly who are disproportionally the pedestrian victims. The elderly are particularly vulnerable probably because of decreases in their abilities to perceive oncoming cars and because of their lessened agility and speed of movement to dodge or cross the roadway quickly. Snyder found higher fatality rates for older pedestrians.[74] Sleight cites a study in St. Petersburg, Florida, where the proportion of residents over 65 is three times the national average. The study shows that the elderly experienced nearly 70% of deaths and one-half the traffic injuries although they made up less than 30% of the population.[75]

Walking rates

Walking rates are reported by Sleight from several studies where the average adult and elderly moved at approximately 4.5 ft/s (1.4 m/s). Children moved more rapidly, at approximately 5.3 ft/s (1.6 m/s).[76] Figure 8.7 shows the distributions of the observed speeds. Some engineers use a 4.0-ft/s (1.2-m/s) rate, but for the relatively slow walkers, speeds of from 3.0 to 3.25 ft/s (0.9 to 1.0 m/s) would be

---

[62]Robert B. Sleight, "The Pedestrian," in *Human Factors in Highway Traffic Safety Research,* T. W. Forbes, ed. (New York: Wiley, 1972), pp. 224–253.

[63]S. P. Baker, L. S. Robertson, and B. O'Neill, "Drivers Involved in Fatal Pedestrian Collisions," *Proceedings of the 16th Conference of the American Association for Automotive Medicine, Chapel Hill, N.C., Oct. 1972.*

[64]C. V. Zegeev, and R. C. Deen, "Pedestrian Accidents in Kentucky," *Transport. Res. Rec. 605,* 1976, pp. 26–28.

[65]R. J. Smeed, "Pedestrian Accidents," *Proceedings of the International Conference on Pedestrian Safety,* Vol. 2 (Haifa, Israel: Michlol, 1976).

[66]G. C. Avery, *The Capacity of Young Children to Cope with the Traffic System: A review,* Traffic Accident Research Unit, Department of Motor Transport, New South Wales, June 1974.

[67]R. Zuercher, "Communications at Pedestrian Crossings," *Proceedings of the International Conference on Pedestrian Safety* (Haifa, Israel: Michlol, 1976).

[68]Monroe B. Snyder and Richard L. Knoblauch, *Pedestrian Safety: The Identification of Precipitating Factors and Possible Countermeasures* (Silver Spring, Md.: Operations Research, Inc., Jan. 1971).

[69]Sleight, "The Pedestrian," p. 228.

[70]Ibid., p. 229.

[71]G. C. Avery, *The Capacity of Young Children to Cope with the Traffic System: A Review.*

[72]H. T. Zwahlen, "Distance Judgment Capabilities of Children and Adults in a Pedestrian Situation," paper presented at the 3rd International Congress of Automotive Safety, San Francisco, Calif., July 1974.

[73]D. A. Routledge, R. Repetto-Wright, and C. I. Howarth, "The Development of Road Crossing Skill by Child Pedestrians," *Proceedings of the International Conference on Pedestrian Safety* (Haifa, Israel: Michlol, 1976), p. 701.

[74]Snyder and Knoblauch, "Pedestrian Safety."

[75]Sleight, "The Pedestrian," pp. 229–230.

[76]Ibid., p. 234.

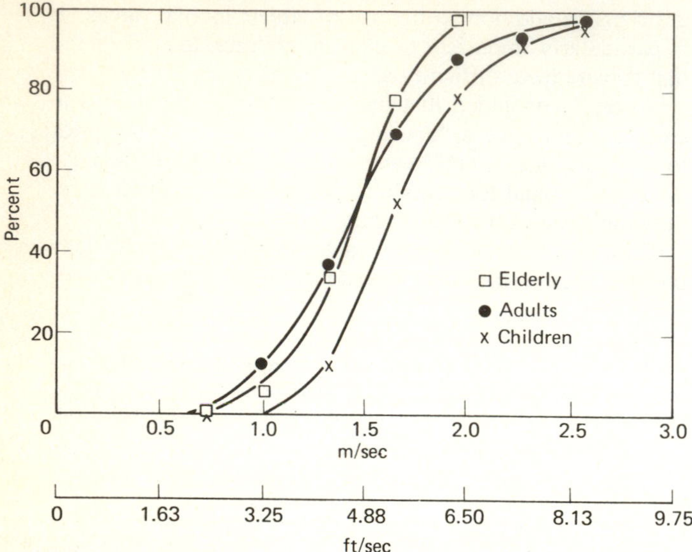

Figure 8.7. Typical speed of pedestrian movement at crossings. SOURCE: Robert B. Sleight, "The Pedestrian," *Human Factors in Highway Traffic Safety Research,* T.W. Forbes, ed., New York: Wiley, 1972, p. 235.

more appropriate. Weiner found an average rate for all individuals of 4.22 ft/s (1.29 m/s), however, and for women only 3.70 ft/s (1.13 m/s). When groups of pedestrians walked together, the rate dropped to 3.83 ft/s (1.17 m/s) for men and to 3.63 ft/s (1.11 m/s) for women.[77]

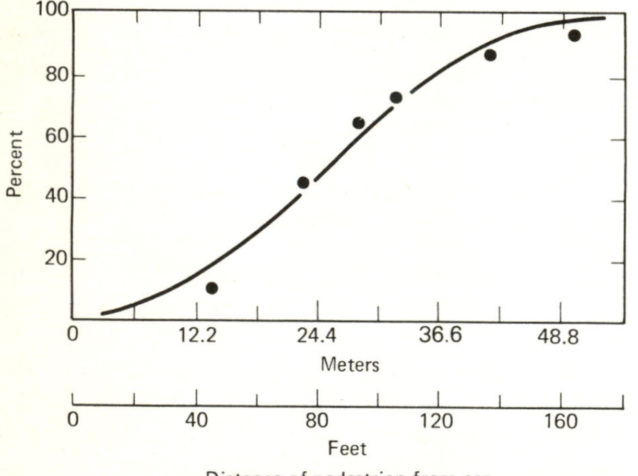

Figure 8.8. Percent of pedestrians accepting gaps of given size in crossing. (After Jacobs, 1968.) SOURCE: Robert B. Sleight, "The Pedestrian," *Human Factors in Highway Safety Traffic Research,* T.W. Forbes, ed., New York: Wiley, 1972, p. 237.

Gap acceptance

Pedestrian habits while crossing roadways have been studied and reported by Jacobs.[78] The so-called threshold gap (defined as the gap accepted by 50% of pedestrians) for 20-mph traffic is 84 ft (25.6 m). The distribution of gaps is shown in Figure 8.8.

Snyder found a high incidence of pedestrian accidents in the center city outside the CBD.[79] "Such areas have been characterized as crowded, high-crime slums and ghettos." It has been observed that large-city pedestrians at signalized intersections seem to respond more to gaps in traffic than to traffic signals. Police officers will even "turn away" when pedestrians cross narrow side streets against the light when no traffic is coming.[80] This tacit recognition of human judgment is akin to using the 85 percentile values for setting roadway speed limits.

Volume and density

Pedestrian volume is defined as the number of persons passing a given point in a unit of time. Pedestrian density can either be expressed in the number of pedestrians per square foot (square meter) or its reciprocal, the number of square feet (square meters) of area per pedestrian.[81] Since it is easier to visualize the latter, it will be used here. Needless to say, pedestrian volume and density are interrelated.

Normal free walking speed increases as more area becomes available to pedestrians (i.e., as the density decreases). However, flow volume increases as the area per pedestrian decreases, until a critical point is reached at which movement is highly restricted because of lack of space.[82] Figure 8.9 shows this critical point for three categories of pedestrian traffic. Studies of pedestrian flows concluded that flows of 20 pedestrians per foot width per minute (PFM) were possible under a wide variety of conditions. Twenty-five PFM was attainable under favorable conditions and as high as 30 PFM could be attained under highly favorable conditions.[83]

Figure 8.10 is a graphic representation of longitudinal and lateral spacings of pedestrians. As density increases, pedestrians maintain constrained spacing patterns to avoid brushing against others and to allow for pacing room. Spacing measurements suggest that average pedestrian areas greater than 25 ft^2 (2.3 m^2) per person are required before there is enough lateral space to freely bypass slower-moving pedestrians. Table 8-7 shows the distribution patterns for midtown Manhattan as an example of urban pedestrian traffic flow.

Various attempts to model pedestrian trip distribution have been evaluated in a paper by Rutherford,[84] who used a large study of 10,000 origin–destination interviews in Chicago to test a standard gravity model. He concludes that such a model, "with a few simple modifications," could be used to begin testing the impact of various CBD improvements, such as moving walks or PRTs.

[77] E. L. WEINER, "The Elderly Pedestrian: Response to an Enforcement Campaign," *Traffic Safety Res. Rev., 12*(4) (1968).

[78] G. D. JACOBS, *The Effect of Vehicle Lighting on Pedestrian Movement in Well-Lighted Streets,* RRL Report LR214, Road Research Laboratory, Crowthorne, England, 1968.

[79] SNYDER AND KNOBLAUCH, "Pedestrian Safety," p. 4-2.

[80] Ibid.

[81] JOHN J. FRUIN, *Pedestrian Planning and Design* (New York: Metropolitan Association of Urban Designers and Environmental Planners, Inc., 1971), p. 38.

[82] Ibid, p. 43.

[83] Ibid, p. 45.

[84] G. SCOTT RUTHERFORD, *Mathematical Models of Pedestrian Behavior,* (Washington, D.C.: G. S. Rutherford & Associates, Jan. 1979), p. 44.

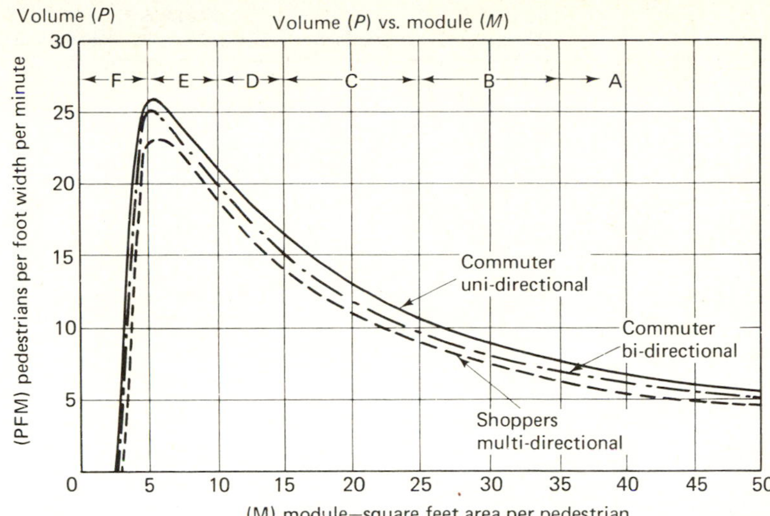

Figure 8.9. Level of service standards for walkways. SOURCE: John J. Fruin, *Pedestrian Planning and Design,* New York: Metropolitan Association of Urban Designers and Environmental Planners, Inc., p. 78.

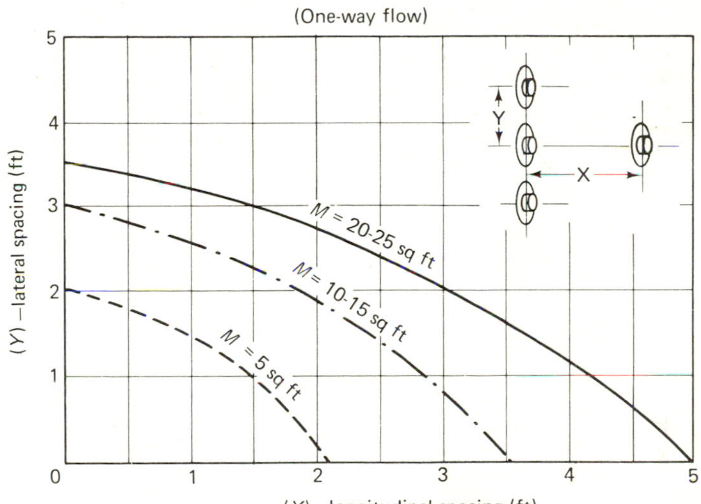

Figure 8.10. Average longitudinal and lateral spacing of pedestrians in a traffic stream. SOURCE: John J. Fruin, *Pedestrian Planning and Design,* New York: Metropolitan Association of Urban Designers and Environmental Planners, Inc., 1971, p. 48.

Observation of regulations

Sleight cites a safety campaign to reduce jaywalking in a city known to have a large proportion of elderly pedestrians.[85] The before and after proportion of legal crossings improved from 61% to 73% when police were stationed there, but it did not increase when there were no police. At the height of the campaign, however, the legal crossings jumped to 93% when police were present and 75% when police were absent.[86] Apparently, the effects of campaigns and crackdowns are short-lived and directly related to the presence of police.

Pedestrian crosswalks do have a safety benefit, apparently because of their influence on the motorists' expectancy of an encounter with a pedestrian. Uniform location of crosswalks at roadway intersections helps to increase driver expectancy but does make it difficult for drivers to cope with midblock crosswalks even though they often are equipped with flashers and sometimes a midblock signal. Studies by Jacob and Wilson,[87] Katz et al.,[88] and Older and Grayson[89] all support the safety benefits of crosswalks as decreasing the risk of an accident. However, the San Diego, California, study by Herms[90] of 400 unsignalized intersections does point out a possible disbenefit due to pedestrians becoming overconfident of the protection afforded them by the crosswalk.

A study by Katz et al.[91] in Israel highlights the human factors interacting between motorists and pedestrians by

[85]SLEIGHT, "The Pedestrian," p. 233.

[86]WEINER, "The Elderly Pedestrian."

[87]G. D. JACOBS AND D. G. WILSON, *A Study of Pedestrian Risk in Crossing Busy Roads in Four Towns,* RRL Report LR 106, Road Research Laboratory, Ministry of Transport, England, 1967.

[88]A. KATZ, A. ELGRISHI, AND L. GUTTMAN, *Proposed Warrants and Standards for Pedestrian Guard Rails,* Report No. 1: Pedestrian Behavior at Locations with Guardrails, Publ. No. 72/7, Road Safety Center, Technion Research and Development Foundation, Aug. 1972.

[89]S. J. OLDER AND G. B. GRAYSON, "An International Comparison of Pedestrian Risk in Four Cities," *Proceedings of the International Conference on Pedestrian Safety* (Haifa, Israel: Michlol, 1976).

[90]B. S. HERMS, "Pedestrian Crosswalk Study: Accidents in Painted and Unpainted Crosswalks," *High. Res. Rec. 406,* 1972, pp. 1–13.

[91]A. KATZ, D. ZAIDEL, AND A. ELGRISHI, "An Experimental Study of Driver and Pedestrian Interaction during the Crossing Conflict," *Human Factors, 17,* 514–527 (1975).

TABLE 8–7
Estimated Hourly Distribution of Person Travel in Midtown Manhattan by Surface Modes

Time	Percent of Daily Vehicular Flow*	Percent of Daily Pedestrian Flow†	Estimated Hourly PMT, Auto and Taxi Passengers‡	Estimated Hourly PMT, Bus Passengers§	Estimated Hourly PMT, Pedestrians	Pedestrian PMT as Percent of Total‖
4–5 A.M.	1.10	(0.03)	4,900	496	(288)	—
5–6	1.06	(0.03)	4,700	1,333	(288)	—
6–7	1.77	0.45	9,200	4,216	4,320	24
7–8	3.56	1.85	20,400	15,097	17,760	33
8–9	5.50	7.61	32,100	31,744	73,056	53
9–10	6.01	6.45	32,600	21,607	61,920	53
10–11	5.80	4.60	31,400	14,818	44,160	49
11–12	5.75	5.98	30,900	16,647	57,408	55
12–1 P.M.	5.52	11.76	29,700	17,763	112,896	70
1–2	5.50	11.90	29,900	17,980	114,240	70
2–3	5.75	8.38	31,300	19,809	80,448	61
3–4	5.86	6.60	32,400	22,010	63,360	54
4–5	6.17	8.05	36,400	26,691	77,280	55
5–6	6.39	11.36	39,600	31,372	109,056	61
6–7	6.03	5.32	38,300	22,258	51,072	45
7–8	5.12	3.09	33,500	12,927	29,664	39
8–9	4.54	2.27	29,700	9,362	21,792	36
9–10	3.86	(1.42)	25,100	6,851	(13,632)	—
10–11	3.81	(1.02)	25,000	6,541	(9,792)	—
11–12	3.92	(0.90)	25,400	5,673	(8,640)	—
12–1 A.M.	2.71	(0.50)	15,900	2,573	(4,800)	—
1–2	1.86	(0.30)	9,800	992	(2,880)	—
2–3	1.35	(0.10)	6,800	775	(960)	—
3–4	1.06	(0.03)	5,000	465	(288)	—
24 hr	100.00	100.00	580,000	310,000	960,000	1,850,000
Percent by each mode			31	17	52	100

*Based on NYC Department of Traffic courts.
†Based on averages from daily peaking, patterns extrapolated for nighttime hours.
‡VMT (vehicle miles of travel) reduced by percent trucks and buses by hour, multiplied by occupancy counts by hour.
§PMT (person miles of travel) for period 1–3 P.M. expanded by hour in relation to peaking pattern of bus travel across 61st Street.
‖—no percentages listed because pedestrian estimates before 6 A.M. and after 9 P.M. are not reliable.

SOURCE: BORIS S. PUSHKAREV AND JEFFREY M. ZUPAN, "Walking Space for Urban Centers," unpublished paper (New York: Regional Plan Association, Sept. 1971), p. 111.

documenting the fact that motorists slowed down more when the pedestrian did not look in the direction of the approaching motorist.

Signals

A 1973 study by Mortimer[92] in Detroit, Michigan, compared pedestrian behavior at signalized intersections with and without pedestrian indications ("ped heads") and found greater compliance, nearly 35% fewer illegal crossings, with ped heads installed. But pedestrian compliance varies widely as revealed in a study by Robertson[93] in seven U.S. cities. Only 42% complied in Buffalo, New York, whereas in Tempe, Arizona, compliance was 84%.

Current research is under way to improve the pedestrian's understanding of ped heads displays. There is much room for improvement in this relatively new type of traffic signal from the standpoint of the human factors involved in the complex interactions among motorists, pedestrians, and now joggers.

[92]R. G. MORTIMER, "Behavioral Evaluation of Pedestrian Signals," *Traffic Eng.*, *43*, 22–26, 1973.

[93]H. D. ROBERTSON, "Intersection Improvements for Pedestrians," *Proceedings of the International Conference on Pedestrian Safety* (Hafai, Israel: Michlol, 1976).

Accident characteristics

Snyder found that an unusually high proportion of urban pedestrian accidents occurred in the afternoon.[94] About half of the 2146 pedestrian accidents occurred in residential areas, 7% in mixed commercial–residential, and 40% in primarily commercial areas.[95] Only 2% occurred in school areas. About half the accidents studied occurred at or near intersections. Traffic flow was generally normal (56%) or light (27%). Most accidents (78%) occurred on two-way streets. Crossing distances were generally not too great—57% were less than 40 ft (12.2 m). Average speed of vehicles during times that accidents occurred was not high—95% were under 35 mph (56 km/h) and 58% were under 25 mph (40 km/h).[96] Hazlett and Allen point out that a 3-year study of 12 U.S. cities having 500,000 or more population found that 50% of nighttime traffic fatalities were pedestrian deaths.[97] They report a "critical visibility distance" associated with vehicle speed.[98] This can be related

[94]SNYDER AND KNOBLAUCH, "Pedestrian Safety," p. 4-2.

[95]Ibid, p. 4-4.

[96]Ibid.

[97]R. D. HAZLETT AND J. J. ALLEN, "The Ability to See a Pedestrian at Night: The Effects of Clothing, Reflectorization and Driver Intoxication," *Am. J. Optom. Arch. Am. Acad. Optom.*, *45*(4), 246–258 (1968).

[98]Ibid, pp. 246–258.

to the "committed zone" described earlier in the chapter. Their data indicate that unless pedestrians wear light-colored clothing, they will not be revealed by automobile headlights in time for the motorist to avoid striking them. Hazlett and Allen also studied reflectorized material and found that this greatly increased the visibility distance of simulated pedestrians.[99]

However, pedestrians do not realize how "invisible" they are. Allen et al.[100] asked pedestrians to judge when they were visible to approaching vehicles; many thought they could be seen as far away as 800 ft (240 m), whereas the truth was they were not visible until 175 ft (50 m) from the motorist.

This points up the need for education of pedestrians before they will be likely to accept reflectorized clothing or alter their walking habits.

Pedestrians and alcohol

Snyder found alcohol present in only 4% of 2146 accidents studied.[101] This does not necessarily conflict with the study by Haddon and Bradess of Westchester County pedestrian fatalities.[102] In this study blood samples were used. Haddon and Bradess clearly described the role of alcohol when it is present, in greatly increasing pedestrian fatalities. He found that those pedestrians killed were several times more likely to have high (0.10%) blood alcohol than a random sample of pedestrians taken at the same location and time of day and day of week.

Clayton et al.[103] in 1971 performed a study similar to Haddon's 1959 study and found similar results; namely, in the control group only 4% of the pedestrians had BALs equal or greater than 0.10%, but the accident group had 19% with that much alcohol in their blood. The same factors discussed earlier that caused alcohol and other drugs to reduce motorists' capabilities are active in pedestrian behavior.

Injuries

Injuries to pedestrians struck by vehicles relate directly to the profile of the vehicle and the size of the pedestrian. Some 89% of the pedestrians fatally struck by heavy trucks were killed by being run over by the wheels, whereas only 10% of those killed by passenger vehicles were run over by the wheels.[104] Modern styling of passenger vehicles results in adult pedestrians being tossed into the air when struck. Children, however, are more likely to be struck down and run over or propelled horizontally.[105] Studies by Robertson,[106] Severy,[107] and McKay[108] all find that many injuries are caused by pedestrians striking the pavement, and the studies suggest that vehicles be constructed of more yielding materials that would absorb the striking energy and perhaps even carry the pedestrian along until the vehicle can be stopped.

Sidewalks and underpasses

Traffic engineers are often pressured by the public for sidewalks and underpasses. Recently, overpasses have been provided, largely for children en route to school.

Underpasses and overpasses should provide ramps for walking bicycles, but they should discourage bicycle riding because it is hazardous for pedestrians. Spiral ramps seem to do this effectively. Spiral ramps are also a help to the elderly, who have difficulty climbing steps. If underpasses are used, they must be well-lighted, cleaned, and even patrolled in areas where there are likely to be thieves and indolents. Overpasses may create nuisances and hazards because of pedestrians who throw objects at cars passing below. Fencing is sometimes required to combat this unfortunate aspect of pedestrian behavior.

Zaidel et al.[109] report an important human factor principle regarding overpass (bridge) location and design. They state: "When a bridge is built in a natural and direct link between activity centers, most pedestrians will cross there, even if there is no strong need for a crossing aid. . . . The details of the bridge's architectural design will not have a significant effect, as long as the comfort of crossing the bridge is reasonable." They found the reverse to be true also: if the bridge is placed in an inconvenient location, it will not be used, especially by younger, healthy (unhandicapped) pedestrians.

Accident countermeasures

An important study by Snyder and Knoblauch on over 2000 pedestrian accidents in 13 major cities led to the following list of the five most frequent noted types of accidents.[110]

Dart-out (first half) (24%). A pedestrian, not in an intersection crosswalk, appears suddenly from the roadside.

Dart-out (second half) (9%). This is the same as the dart-out described for the first half above, except that the pedestrian covers half of a normal crossing before being struck.

[99]Ibid.

[100]M. J. Allen, R. D. Hazlett, H. L. Tacker, and B. V. Graham, "Actual Pedestrian Visibility and the Pedestrian's Estimate of His Own Visibility." *Am. J. Optom. Arch. Am. Acad. Optom., 47,* 44–49 (1970).

[101]Snyder and Knoblauch, "Pedestrian Safety," p. 4-4.

[102]W. Haddon and V. A. Bradess, "Alcohol in the Single Vehicle Accident—Experience of Westchester County, New York," *J. Am. Med. Assoc., 14,* 127–133 (1959).

[103]A. B. Clayton, A. C. Booth, and P. E. McCarthy, *A Controlled Study of the Role of Alcohol in Fatal Adult Pedestrian Accidents,* Transport and Road Research Laboratory, Suppl. Report No. 332, Crawthorne, England, 1977.

[104]J. S. Robertson, A. J. McLean, and G. A. Ryan, *Traffic Accidents in Adelaide, South Australia Summary, 1963–64,* Australian Road Res. Bd. Report No. 1, 1967.

[105]Ibid.

[106]Ibid.

[107]D. M. Severy, "Auto–Pedestrian Impact Experiments," *The Seventh Strapp Car Crash Conference, 1963.*

[108]G. M. McKay, "Automobile Design and Pedestrian Safety," *Int. Road Safety Traffic Rev.,* Summer 1965.

[109]D. Zaidel, A. Algarishi, and A. Katz, "Factors Affecting the Use of Pedestrian Overpasses," *Proceedings of the International Conference on Pedestrian Safety* (Haifa, Israel: Michlol, 1976).

[110]Snyder and Knoblauch, "Pedestrian Safety."

Intersection dash (8%). This category covers cases similar to dart-outs with regard to pedestrian exposure to view, but the accident occurs in or near a marked or unmarked crosswalk at an intersection.

Multiple threat (3%). The pedestrian is struck by car x after other cars blocking the vision of car x stopped in other lanes going in the same direction, and avoided hitting the pedestrian.

Vehicle turn merge with attention conflict (7%). The driver is turning into or merging with traffic; the situation is such that he attends to auto traffic in one direction and hits the pedestrian who is in a different direction from his attention.

Countermeasures were also proposed to cope with these pedestrian accidents as follows:[111]

Street parking redeployment. This countermeasure is aimed primarily at the dart-outs but would influence two other types as well. The objective is to use parking control to remove some of the visual obstruction, provide a partial barrier to physically control the pedestrian course, and increase the likelihood of detection. . . .

Two steps would be taken. First, parking would be removed from one side of the street, probably the left. Second, head-in diagonal parking would replace parallel parking on the right. In appropriate locations this would accomplish removal of visual obstructions from the left side of the road giving the driver increased view and more time to detect and react. The diagonal parking would provide a physical control that would tend to slow down the pedestrian as he ran across the street, but even more important, would angle him into traffic and direct his field of vision more in the direction of the threatening vehicles. . . .

Meter post barrier. In commercial areas with on-street parking meters, small fences or railings extending out a few feet from either side of the meter post could combine with parked cars to form a barrier to prevent dart-outs. . . .

Signal retiming or modification. One of the predisposing factors identified for the intersection dash was the inducement to risk taking coming from the traffic signal. Pedestrians are wrong to cross against the light. They should wait until they have the proper signal, but it is apparent that some will become impatient when they must wait. Countermeasures include:

- Resetting cycles to bring pedestrian waiting time in line with the norm, or lower if other considerations permit.
- If rush-hour volumes do not permit complete retiming, reduce pedestrian waiting periods during nonpeak hours. (Two-thirds of intersection dashes occurred before or after the 4:00 P.M. to 6:00 P.M. rush period.)
- Provide a signal indicating the waiting time remaining to green. . . .

One additional possibility is to consider complex signal heads such as those that display "DON'T WALK" and "WALK" simultaneously to different zones or portions of the crosswalk in order to reduce the total walk time for each walk period.

Accident types involving salient predisposing factors

Four other accident types involved specific predisposing factors. They account for about 7% of the cases and offer possibilities for extreme reductions. The basic descriptions and countermeasure recommendations for each follow:[112]

[111]Ibid, pp. 1-4 to 1-6.

[112]Ibid, pp. 1-8 to 1-9.

Vendor—ice cream truck (2%). The pedestrian is struck going to or from a vendor in a vehicle on the street. This is usually similar to a dart-out, with ice cream trucks being the most frequent attraction. This specific classification was given precedence over dart-out when assigning cases to types. The countermeasure is ice cream truck regulation and visual warning devices.

Pedestrian exiting from vehicle (1%). The pedestrian had been a passenger or driver and is struck while exiting from a vehicle: all vehicles are included. The countermeasures are vehicle exit visual warning devices, regulation of licensed public vehicles, and exit platform design. Parking redeployment would also help.

Bus stop–related (3%). This type includes cases in which the location or design of the stop appears to be a major factor in the causation, e.g., the pedestrian crosses in front of the bus standing at a stop on the corner, and the bus blocks the view of cars. It does not include those cases that may be considered as exiting from a vehicle, nor does it include cases in which the stop is only an attraction or distraction. The countermeasure is location of bus stops at the far side of the intersection.

Backing up (2%). The pedestrian is struck by a vehicle which is backing up. A case would not be so classified if the pedestrian were clearly aware of the movement of the vehicle; detection failure is important. This type was used even if the accident occurred off the street. The countermeasure is backup warning devices.

Bicyclist and bicycle use

Relatively little information on bicyclists and their characteristics is available in the literature on transportation engineering and highway operation. A study by the Institute of Transportation and Traffic Engineering, University of California, Los Angeles,[113] contains data on cyclist dimensions, velocity, and grade capability.

The average dimensions of a bicycle and cyclist pertinent to minimum design standards are:[114]

Handlebar width	1.96 ft (0.6 m)
Cycle length	5.75 ft (1.75 m)
Pedal clearance	0.5 ft (0.15 m)
Vertical space occupied by cycle/cyclist	7.4 ft (2.5 m)

Mean measured separation between handlebars of two cyclists riding abreast at a velocity of 10 mph is given as 2.5 ft (0.75 m).[115]

Measurements of bike speeds in Davis, California, have shown that speeds vary between 7 and 15 mph (11 and 24 km/h), with the average between 10 and 11 mph (16 and 18 km/h).[116]

Figure 8.11 shows the variation of grade as a function of velocity and cycle characteristics. The curves, used for illustrative purposes only, relate the maximal work rate K to velocity and percent grade. A value of $K = 0.6$ would be equivalent to playing tennis for over 8 h with frequent long rests, and a value of $K = 0.4$ would be equivalent to level bicycling for 8 h with occasional 50 to 10-min rests.[117]

[113]*Bikeway Planning Criteria and Guidelines,* Institute of Transportation and Traffic Engineering, University of California, Los Angeles, Apr. 1972.

[114]Ibid, p. 22.

[115]Ibid, p. 26.

[116]Ibid, p. 21.

[117]Ibid, p. B-7.

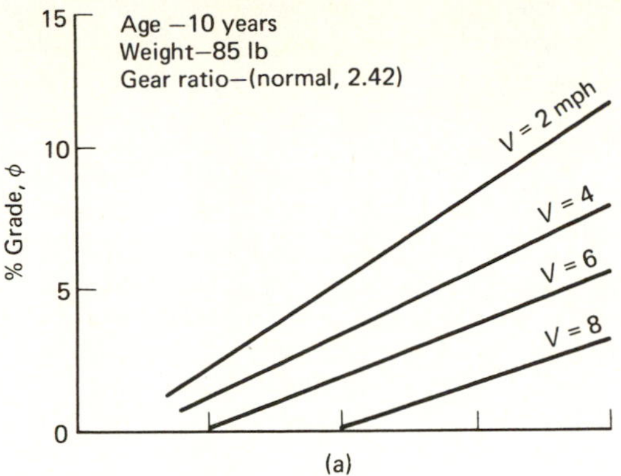

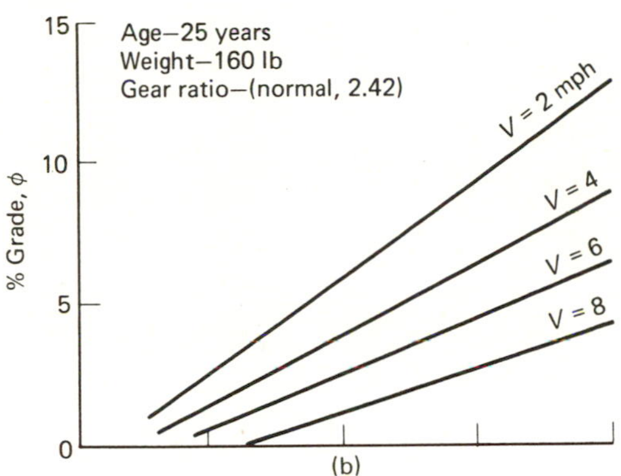

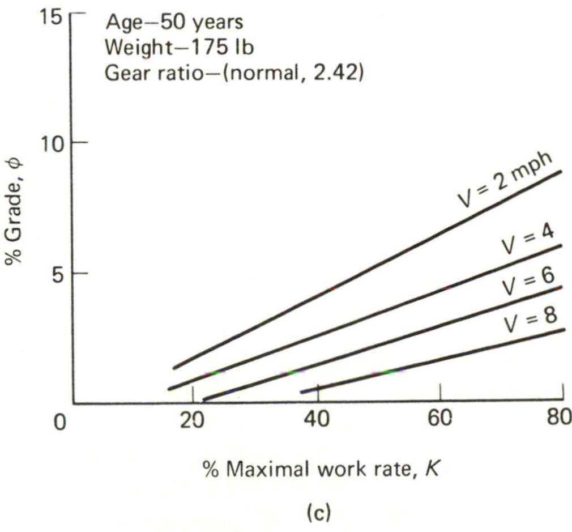

Figure 8.11. Example of grade capability for cyclists. SOURCE: "Bikeway Planning Criteria Guidelines," Los Angeles, Calif.: Institute of Transportation and Traffic Engineering, University of California, Apr. 1972, p. B-3.

The values are for a single gear ratio of 2.42 and for a male rider on a 35-lb (16-kg) bicycle that has 26-in. (0.66-m)-diameter wheels.

As an example of the use of such curves, for a design speed of 6 mph (10 km/h) and a work level K of 50%, the 10-, 24-, and 50-year-old can tolerate grades of 2.9, 3.5, and 2.2%. Similarly, on a 5% grade with a 50% energy expenditure, speeds of 3.8, 4, and 2 mph (6.1, 6.4, and 3.2 km/h) can be negotiated by the three age groups of cyclists.

Trends in bicycle accidents are reported in a study[118] covering data from 1973 through 1976. Two data sources were used by the U.S. Consumer Products Safety Commission. The first, the National Electronic Injury Surveillance System (NEISS), is based on a national sample of hospital emergency rooms that report product-associated accidents. The second is in-depth investigations of accidents attributed to bicycles. Figure 8.12 shows the projected numbers of bicycle-associated injuries over a 3½-year period. The seasonal trend is most apparent. Figure 8.13 shows the estimated distribution of accidents by age and sex. Note that approximately twice as many males as females are involved. Three percent of the accidents in the NEISS sample involved motor vehicles.

Vehicle design

Driver dimensions

Versace in a Ford Motor Company report states in considering driver dimensions:

> Published anthropometric data are seldom applicable because they were obtained under standardized postural conditions which were not related to design needs. . . . As a result, a fair amount of on-site validation and check out is required.[119]

He elaborates upon this fact in a later report,[120] in which he clearly points out the many, complex design trade-offs that are made in designing the driver package (a set of dimensions relative to the vehicle coordinate system, which define the shape and location of operator foot and hand controls, the seat, and interior accommodation room). For example: "Although tall persons tend to have long arms, and thus should reach farther, they also tend to have long legs and therefore position the seat farther away from the instrument panel."

And later: "By locating the instrument panel so far aft that even marginal drivers can reach it would result in it being so close for many others that knee clearance, particularly in entering and exiting the car, could become a matter of some concern."

At least seven variables are involved in the design of the package to accommodate the reach capabilities of motorists:

1. Horizontal seat
2. Vertical seat
3. Horizontal wheel
4. Vertical wheel
5. Back angle
6. Pan angle
7. Wheel angle

---

[118] J. D. FLORA AND R. D. ABBOTT, "National Trends in Bicycle Accidents," *J. Safety Res.*, *11*(1), 20–27 (Spring 1979).

[119] JOHN VERSACE, University of Michigan Short Course in Engineering, unpublished lecture notes, 1967.

[120] JOHN VERSACE, "Human Factors Measurements Related to the Setting of Automotive Safety Standards," *American Society for Quality Control, Administrative Applications Division Conference Transactions, Mar. 1970*, pp. 1D-1-1D-26.

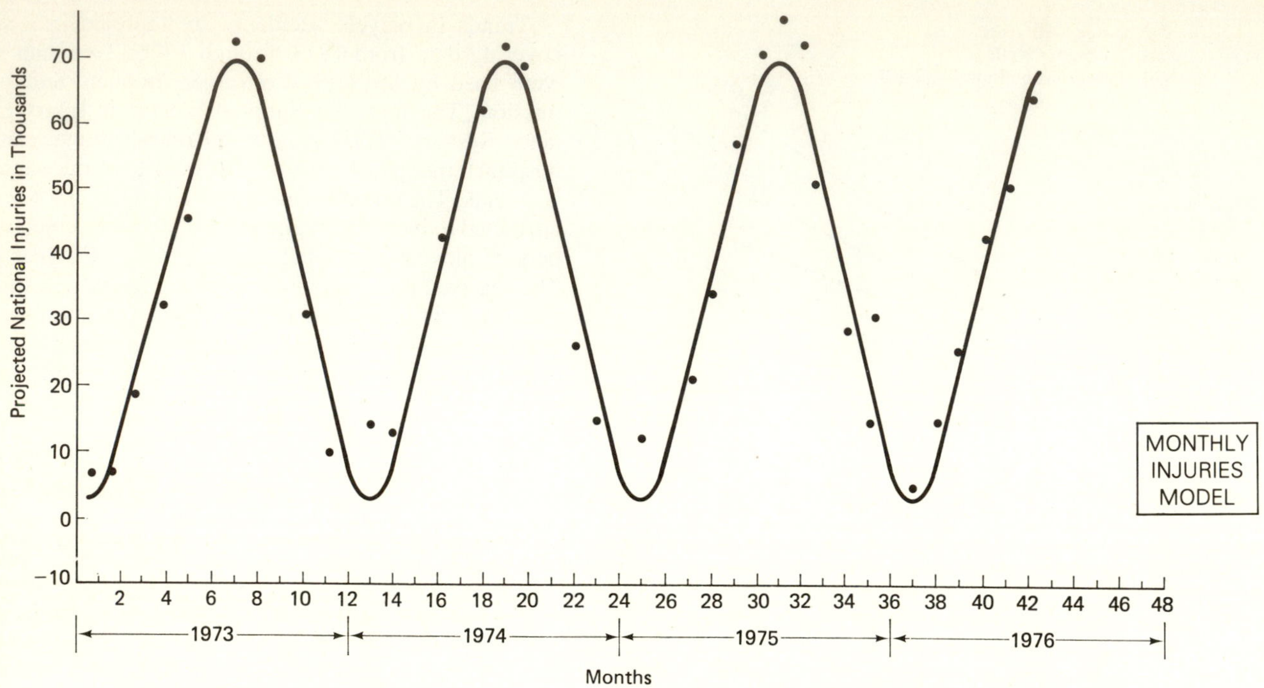

Figure 8.12. Estimated monthly injuries model with seasonal and trend effects. SOURCE: J.D. Flora and R.D. Abbot, "National Trends in Bicycle Accidents," *Journal of Safety Research,* Spring 1979, Vol. II, No. 1, pp. 20–27.

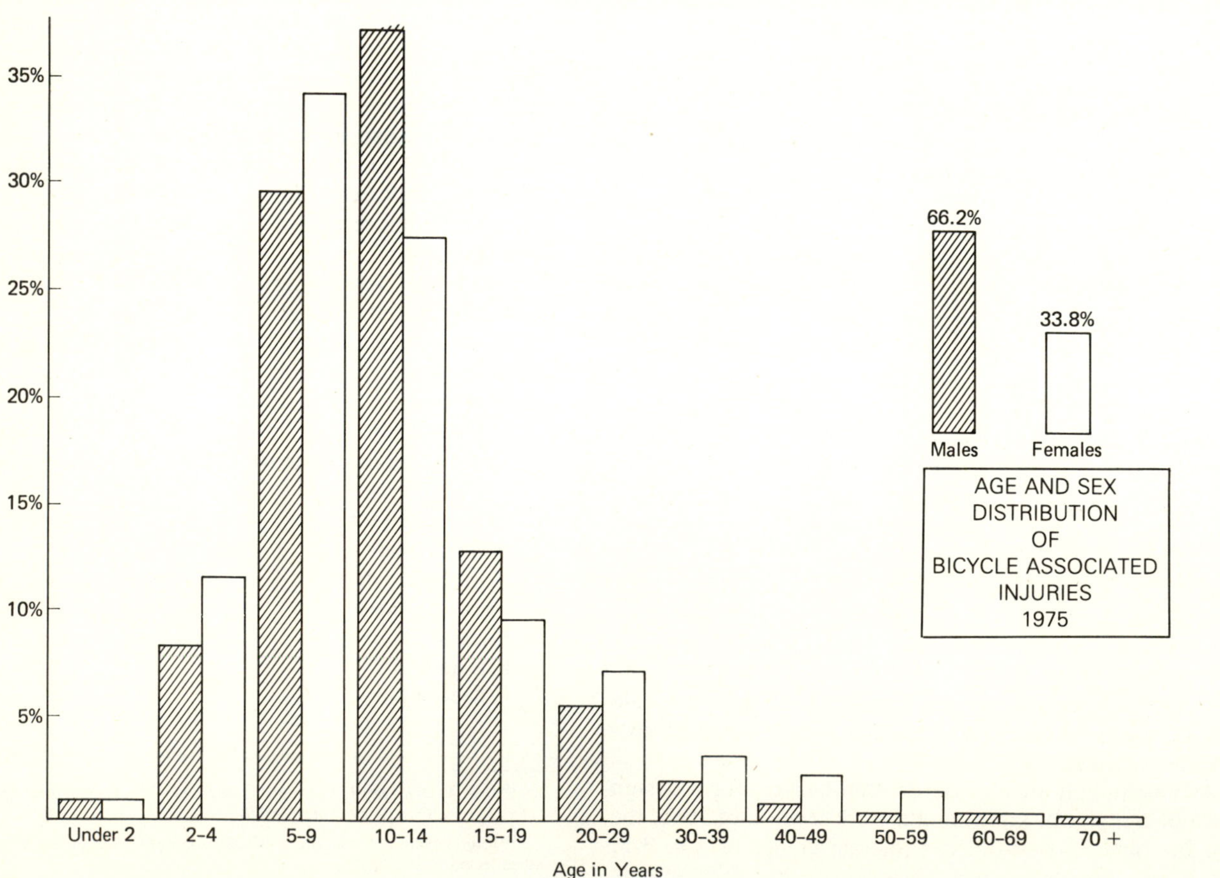

Figure 8.13. Age and sex distribution of bicycle-associated injuries, 1975. SOURCE: Ibid. Figure 8.12.

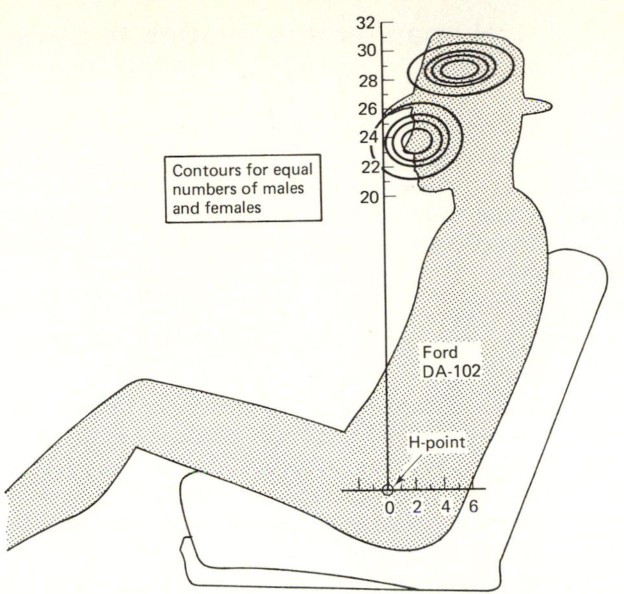

Figure 8.14. Distance from eye and top of head to hip point. SOURCE: John Versace, University of Michigan Short Course in Engineering, 1967.

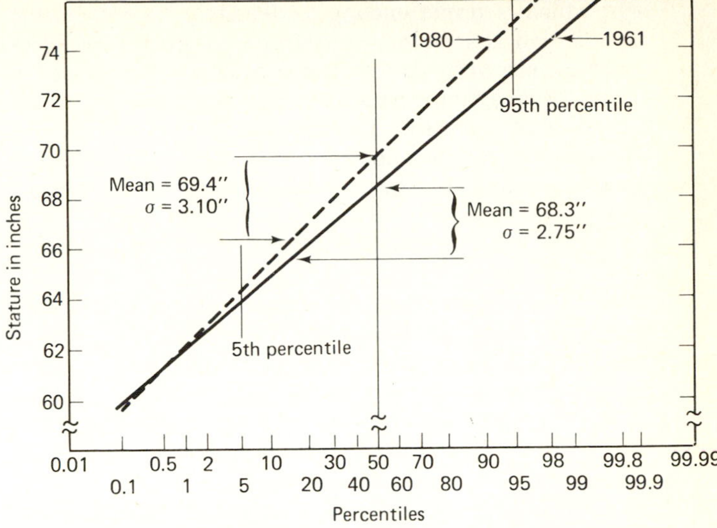

Figure 8.15. Civilian male stature in 1961 projected through 1980, age 15 years and above. SOURCE: J. Versace, University of Michigan Short Course in Engineering, 1967.

Figure 8.16. Glare-brightness relationship for light sources based on laboratory data with a high level of dark adaptation. SOURCE: J. Versace, University of Michigan Short Course in Engineering, 1967.

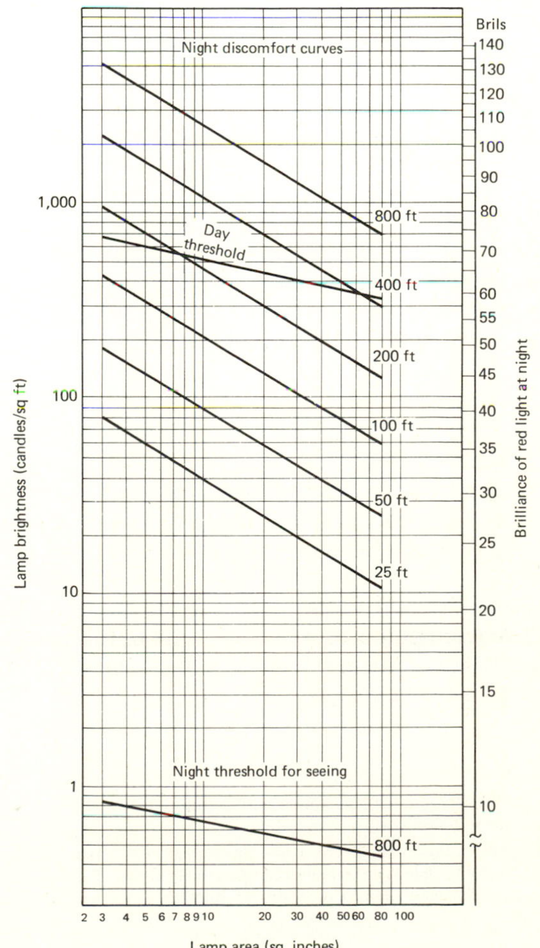

These seven parameters were included in multiple correlational analysis that resulted in the use of only *H* (hip point) for seat location and *W* (wheel placement) for steering wheel location in order to carry out the reach studies that otherwise would have been impractical (too numerous) to perform.

In similar fashion, other design trade-offs are assisted by careful planning of how to collect data from samples of drivers and use the results in driver package design. Figure 8.14 shows the *H* point relative to the car seat and the distance from eye and top of head to hip point *(H)*. Driver eye positions fall in a wide range of locations called an "eyellipse." These are then converted to a "tangent cutoff ellipse," which is the locus of instantaneous tangencies of sight lines drawn in such a way that each of those tangents will cut off some designated fraction of the population. Even this is not truly indicative of what drivers actually can see because it is a static representation and does not take account of how far drivers can and do move their heads and lean their bodies while driving.

Overlying these factors are some general trends. For example, for many years the U.S. Material Command has recognized that the distribution of human dimensions is not stationary in time—that people clearly are getting bigger. Figure 8.15 shows some projections of overall stature as a function of age, for males in 1961 as compared to 1980.

Vision

Discussing lights and vision, Versace points out that "the acceptable glare level of a light depends upon its brightness, size, and distance away."[121] Figure 8.16 shows that any

[121]JOHN VERSACE, University of Michigan Short Course in Enginering.

light which is bright enough to definitely be seen in the daytime will at some close distance be regarded as objectionable under very dark nighttime conditions. Because the human visual system responds to light approximately as the cube root of intensity, it takes about 10 times as much intensity for a light to appear twice as bright. And to assure positive absolute identification on a brightness scaling basis, intensity ratios greater than that are required. Brake lights are more intense than taillights by ratios often exceeding 30:1.

Glare is considered in two major categories, disabling (which interferes with vision) and discomfort (which causes irritation and distraction). Bennett[122] has reviewed some research aimed at fixed roadway lighting as seen by the driver. European standards do consider discomfort glare, but U.S. and Canadian engineers have encountered difficulties in tests of these procedures.

In vehicle lighting and signal light work, consideration has been directed to the effect of color on signal visibility. A signal light viewed at 400 ft (120 m) adjacent to an oncoming headlight is less identifiable if it is yellow than if it is red or green. Also to be considered in the color of signal lights are the penetrating quality in fog, the role of colorblindness, and the natural meaning of the color to the observer. Design changes, particularly those involving the signaling system, must be evaluated in terms of possible confusion in comprehension when there is a prolonged period in which both old and new systems are used concurrently on the road.

In a study of vehicle rear lighting Case et al. conclude that rear-end accidents involve tbe following driver when he is either "coupled" or "uncoupled" to the car ahead.[123] In the first case he is aware of the lead vehicle and is performing what is called "car following." As discussed earlier, very short headways can safely be accomplished, particularly by commuter drivers on freeway, because each driver is aware of the committed zone in front of each moving vehicle. When uncoupled, however, the following (overtaking) driver has a complex series of visual detection and driving decision tasks to perform in a relatively short time.

Vehicle rear lighting is most important in helping drivers to move from the uncoupled to the coupled condition. Current systems of vehicle rear lighting do not take advantage of the many ways in which drivers can detect the presence and position of vehicles ahead of them. Color differences, position, brightness, and intermittence are also used to some extent.

Engineers should follow with interest the development of vehicle rear lighting as it interacts with traffic signals and warning lights, particularly in rural areas, where such devices are visible at great distances.

[122]Corwin A. Bennett, "Discomfort Glare: A Review of Some Research," Kansas State University (no date).

[123]Harry W. Case, Slade F. Hulbert, and Oscar E. Patterson, *Development and Evaluation of Vehicle Rear Lighting Systems,* Inst. Transport. Traffic Eng. Report No. 68-24 (Los Angeles, Calif.: University of California, Los Angeles, May 1968).

Human factors relating to transit passengers[124]

This section briefly summarizes some human-factor aspects related to passengers in transit vehicles or, for that matter, in any common carrier system. Two major concerns are the spatial requirements inside vehicles for passengers and the environmental factors that affect human physiology and comfort.

Spatial requirements

Studies in anthropometry, in human engineering, and in pedestrian behavior and dynamics have defined the spatial requirements of human beings in relation to various levels of comfort or freedom (analogous to levels of service). For pedestrian traffic streams this was discussed earlier (see, e.g., Figure 8.9).

Persons standing in a queue or on board transit vehicles are separated by distances defined as average interperson spacings; these vary according to person density, which can be related to the level-of-service concept used in highway traffic analysis. As shown in Figure 8.17, the levels are defined as:

1. Level A, *free circulation zone,* interperson spacing of 4 ft (1.2 m) or more, allowing for free circulation through the queueing area or vehicle without disturbing others. In vehicles, standing areas are seldom of sufficient size for this spacing.
2. Level B, *restricted circulation zone,* interperson spacing of 3.5 to 4 ft (1.07 to 1.22 m), allowing for restricted circulation.
3. Level C, *personal comfort zone,* interperson spacing of 3 to 3.5 ft (0.92 to 1.07 m), permitting standing and restricted circulation by disturbing others; it is within the range of the personal comfort body buffer zone established by psychological experiments.
4. Level D, *no-touch zone,* interperson spacing of 2 to 3 ft (0.61 to 0.92 m), providing for standing without personal contacts with others; however, circulation is severely restricted, and forward movement is possible only as a group.
5. Level E, *touch-zone,* interperson spacing of 2 ft (0.61 m) or less; space is provided for standing, but contact with others is unavoidable and no circulation is possible.
6. Level F, the *body ellipse,* space occupancy of 2 ft^2 (0.22 m^2) or less; standing for short lengths of time is possible, but close unavoidable contact with others causes physical and psychological discomfort; in large crowds the possibility of panic exists.

Levels E and F are associated with crowded elevators. Standee space calculations in transit vehicles should be

[124]This section is based in part on lecture notes prepared by Ph. H. Bovy, École Polytechnique Fédérale de Lausanne, Switzerland, for a course at the University of California, Berkeley, in 1975.

Levels of Service For Queuing

Level of Service	Definition	Diameter (m)	Occupied space (m^2)
A	Free circulation	> 1.22	
B	Restricted circulation	1.07-1.22	1.17
C	Personal comfort zone	0.92-1.07	0.90
D	No touch zone	0.61-0.92	0.66
E	Touch zone	< 0.61	0.20
F	Body ellipse	0.61x0.46	0.22

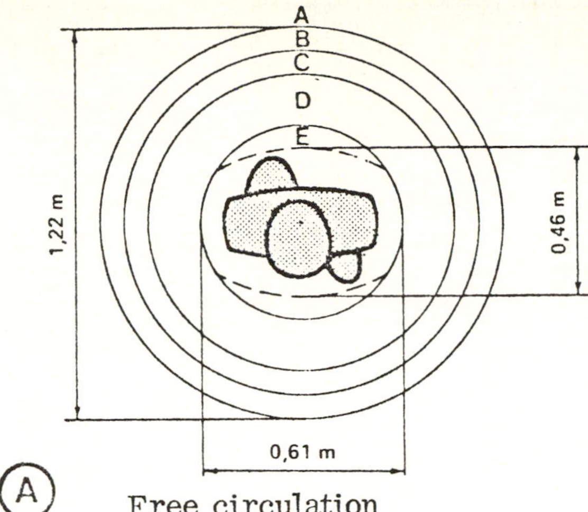

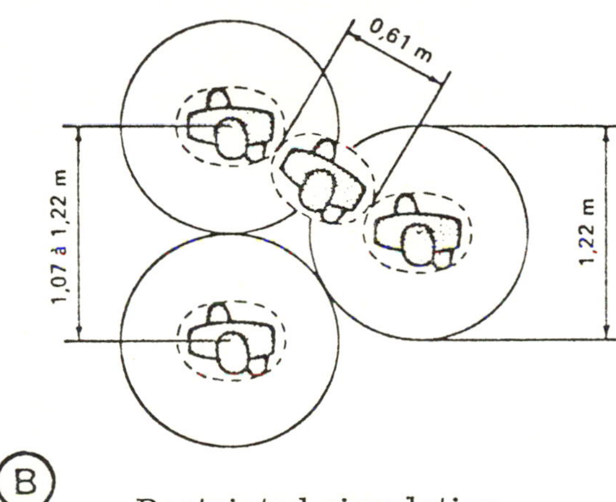

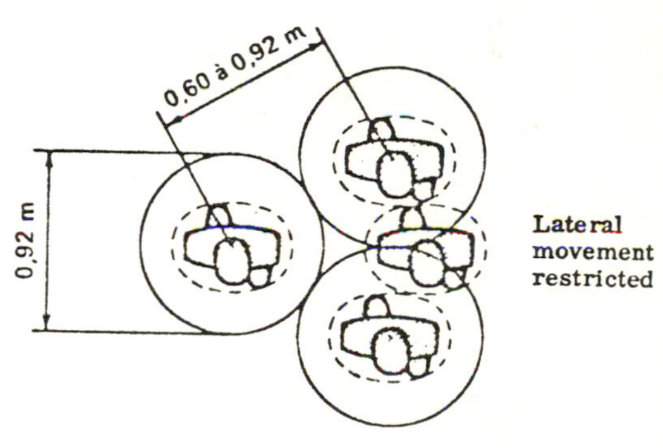

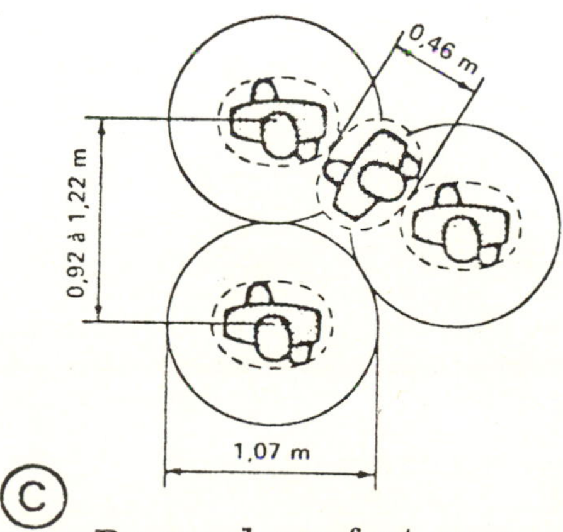

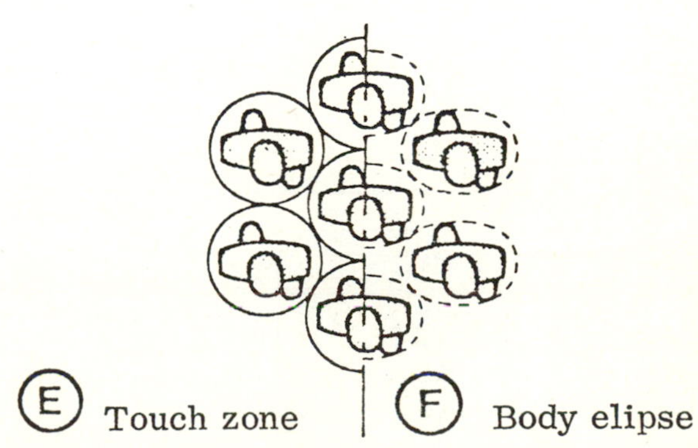

Figure 8.17. Comfort levels of service of groups of persons standing in queues or on vehicles. SOURCE: John F. Fruin, *Pedestrian Planning and Design,* New York: Metropolitan Association of Urban Designers and Environmental Planners, Inc., 1971, p. 38; Battelle Institute, *Recommendations en vue de l'amènagement d'une installation de transport compte tenu des donnèes anthropomètriques et des limites physiologiques de l'homme,* Geneva, 1973.

	COMMENTS	Dimensions (m)					Projected Surface (m^2)
		①	②	③	④	⑤	
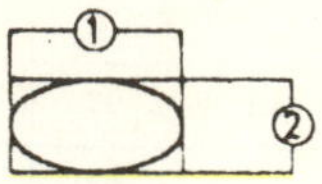	Thorax	~~(0.49)~~ 0.53	~~(0.26)~~ 0.31	—	—	—	~~(0.13)~~ 0.16
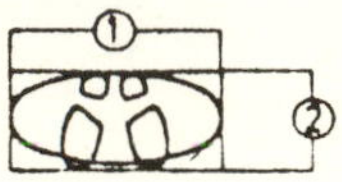	Thorax with feet	~~(0.61)~~ 0.66	~~(0.29)~~ 0.31	—	—	—	~~(0.17)~~ 0.21
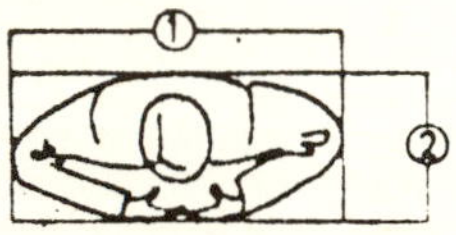	Horizontal arms with tips of fingers touching each other	0.95	0.43	—	—	—	0.40
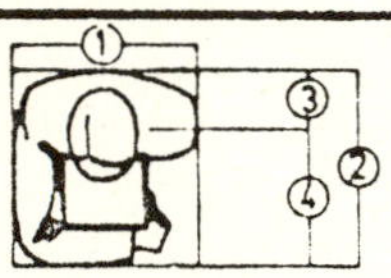	Person carrying parcel	0.53	0.57	0.16	0.41	—	0.30
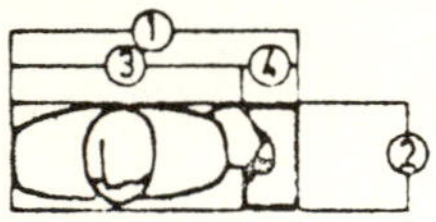	Person carrying one small piece of luggage	0.82	0.30	0.67	0.15	—	0.25
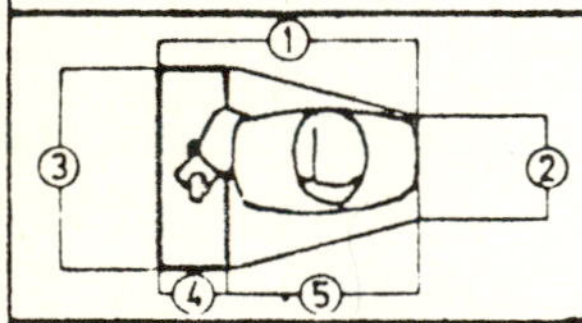	Person carrying one large piece of luggage	0.73	0.31	0.60	0.20	0.53	0.33
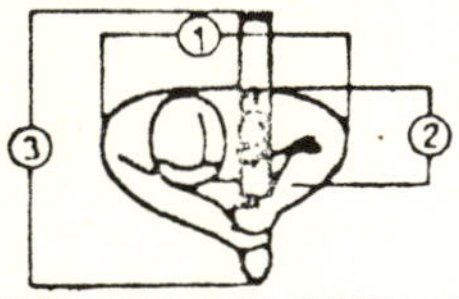	Person carrying skis (for aerial tramway design)	~0.70	~0.30	~0.75	—	—	~0.50
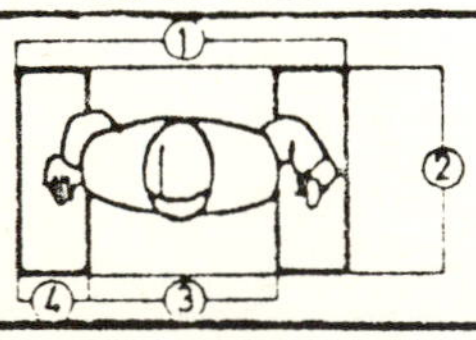	Person carrying two large pieces of luggage	0.93	0.60	0.53	0.20	—	0.56
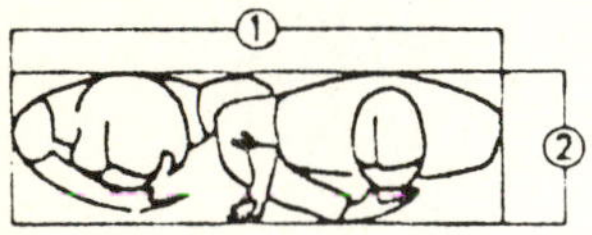	Couple	1.40	0.43	—	—	—	0.61
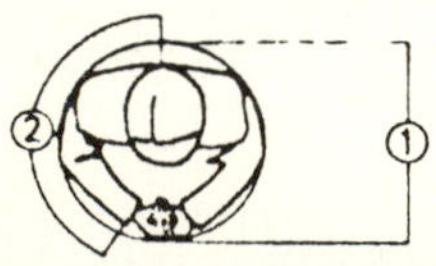	Person holding on to stanchion	0.58	0.905	—	—	—	0.26

Figure 8.18. Anthropometric measurements of pedestrians and standing passengers. SOURCE: Battelle Institute, *Recommendations en vue de l'amènagement d'une installation de transport compte tenu des donnèes anthropomètriques et des limites physiologiques de l'homme,* Geneva, 1973.

		Comments	Dimensions (m) ①	②		Projected Surface m²
1 Person	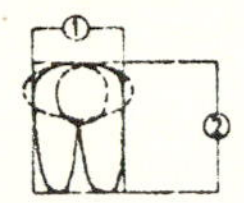	Minimum space requirement	~~(0.40)~~ 0.46	~~(0.60)~~ 0.66		~~(0.24)~~ 0.30
	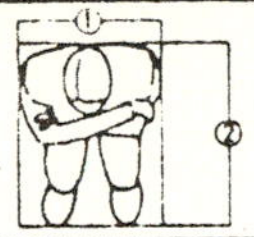	Normal, comfortable situation	0.66	0.82		0.54
	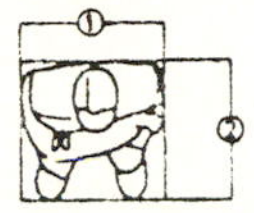	Person leaning	0.55	0.62		0.41
2 Persons	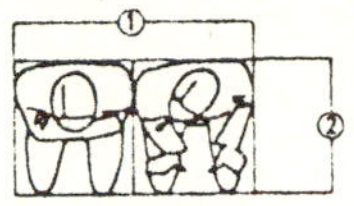	Uncomfortable arrangement	1.08	0.66		0.71
	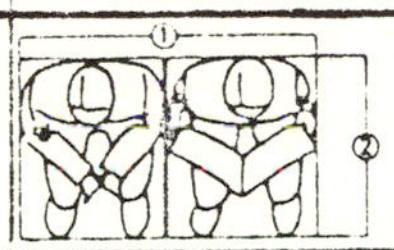	Comfortable situation	1.34	0.82		1.10

Figure 8.19. Anthropometric measurements of seated passengers. SOURCE: Battelle Institute, *Recommendations en vue de l'amènagement d'une installation de transport compte tenu de donnèes anthropomètriques et des limites physiologiques de l'homme,* Geneva, 1973.

based on level C, whereas queueing space in transit stations (at escalators, fare gates, etc.) should be at level B.

Width and depth dimensions of standees under various conditions are shown in Figure 8.18. Seated passengers require about half the space of standees under level A condition, or about 2.5 times the space under level E conditions, as shown in Figure 8.19.

The duration of trips is an essential parameter when defining passenger levels of service, as the physical and psychological comforts vary with time. Trips of less than 1 min can be sustained at level E with about 5 passengers/m^2; trips of more than 30 min in length should be furnished with seats for all passengers; long-distance travel in planes or trains requires lower seat densities than those needed for urban transit travel (Figure 8.20).

Physiological factors affecting comfort

A number of environmental factors determine how human beings and their faculties are affected in the confined environment of transportation vehicles. These factors may be categorized in three groups:

1. *Vehicle microclimate,* such as temperature, humidity, ventilation level, and noise level in the interior.
2. *Spatial components,* such as the amount of floor area and volume space per passenger, and the vehicle capacity.

Figure 8.20. Passenger space requirements versus travel time. SOURCE: P.H. Bovy, *Amènagement du territoire et transports,* Vol. 2, EPF-ITEP, Lausanne, Switzerland, 1974, Fig. 6.14e.

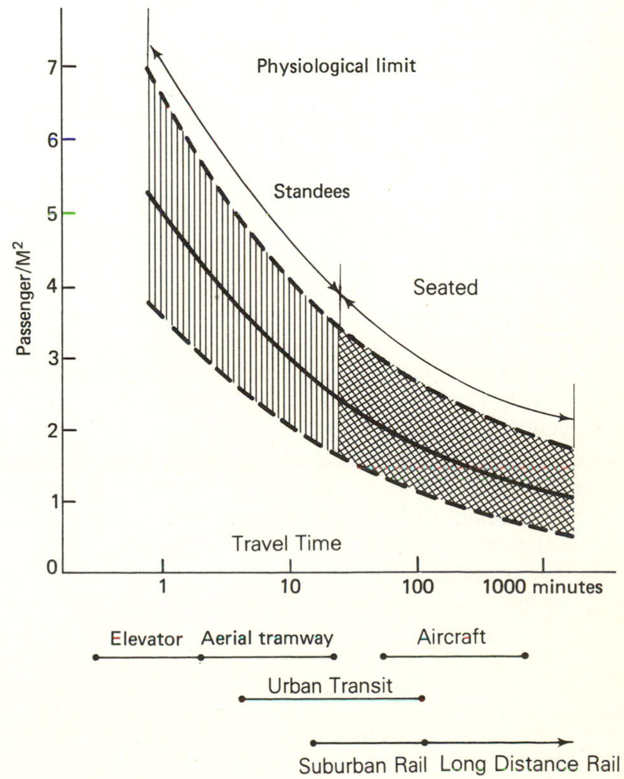

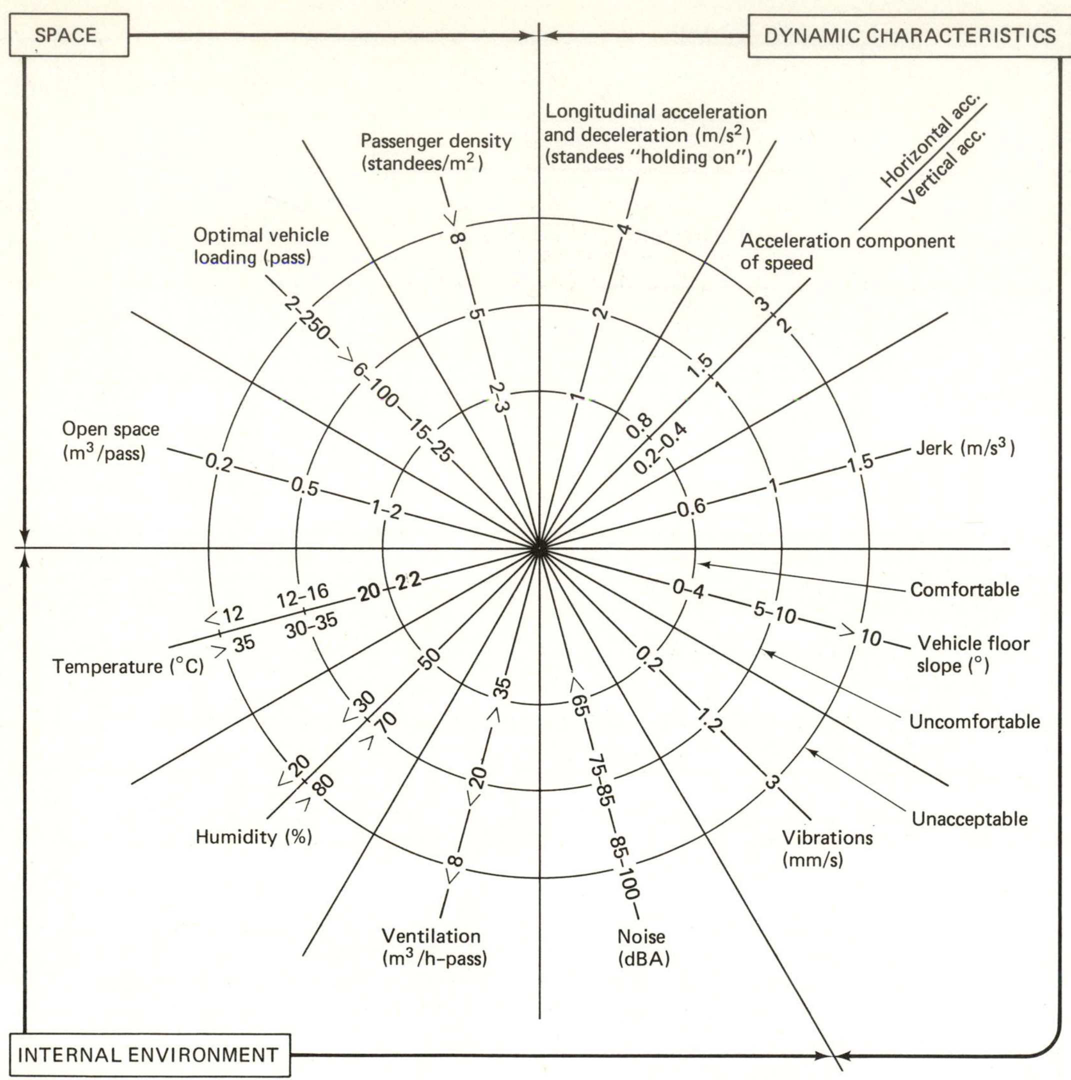

Figure 8.21. Principal recommendations for levels of comfort of urban public transport vehicles. SOURCE: Ibid. Figure 8.19.

3. *Vehicle dynamics,* such as longitudinal, horizontal, and vertical acceleration and deceleration, jerk, vibrations, and slope of the vehicle floor.

Values of these parameters for comfortable, uncomfortable, and unacceptable conditions have been quantified[125] as shown in Figure 8.21.

Psychological factors are observable but are generally not measurable. They are related to physiological factors, especially when the limits of comfort are reached. Psychological reactions to uncomfortable environments include travel sickness, claustrophobia, insecurity, and panic (in cases of system failure or accident of high-capacity vehicles such as ferries or wide-body aircraft).

[125]BATTELLE INSTITUTE, *Recommendations en vue de l'aménagement d'une installation de transport compte tenu des données anthropométriques et des limites physiologiques de l'homme* (Geneva: 1973). English summary published as *Synthesis of a Study on the Analysis, Evaluation and Selection of Urban Public Transport Systems* (Geneva, Battelle Research Center, Quaderno No. 8, Sept. 1974).

REFERENCES FOR FURTHER READING

ALLEN, MERRILL J., *Vision in Highway Safety,* Chilton Book Company, Philadelphia, 1970.

Factors Influencing Safety at Highway-Rail Grade Crossings, National Cooperative Highway Res. Program Report No. 50, Highway Research Board, Washington, D.C., 1968. (Note especially Appendix B.)

FORBES, T. W., *Human Factors in Highway Traffic Safety Research,* Wiley, New York, 1972.

KINKADE, ROBERT G., AND HAROLD P. VAN COTT, *The Human Engineering Guide to Equipment Design,* rev. ed., U.S. Superintendent of Documents, Washington, D.C., 1972.

RISTO NAATANEN AND HEIKKE SUMMOLA, *Road-User Behavior and Traffic Accidents,* North-Holland, Amsterdam/American Elsevier, New York, 1976.

Planning and Design Criteria for Bikeways in California, California Department of Transportation, 1978.

Proceedings, American Association for Automotive Medicine—22nd Conference, International Association of Accident and Traffic Medicine—VII Conference, American Association for Automotive Medicine, Morton Grove, Ill., 1978.

9

INTERCITY PASSENGER AND FREIGHT TRANSPORTATION

ROBERT BREUER

New York State Department of Transportation
Albany, New York

This chapter presents an overview of intercity passenger and freight transportation. It presents comparative data on travel, trips, and goods movement for several modes. The chapter provides a scale and context for individual modes, on the basis of which general prospects and policies can be evaluated. Highway transportation, particularly auto and truck usage, will be examined in further detail.

Intercity and rural travel

Intercity and rural travel are difficult to define consistently and precisely. Private auto use is generally estimated on the basis of related factors, such as gasoline sales. Common carriers such as air, rail, and bus are more easily measured, because records are kept according to regulatory agency requirements.

Furthermore, the distinction among intercity, rural, and urban travel is not clear cut; it varies because of reporting difficulties and inherent differences between modes. For example, the term "intercity travel" is often used synonymously with long trips, whether they are made between cities or not; it commonly includes all travel on certain modes, whether intraurban, urban–rural, or other. To overcome this difficulty data in this chapter will be defined as precisely as possible.

In 1970, 69.5% of the U.S. population lived in 275 urbanized areas or in urban places of 5000 persons or more outside urban areas, as defined by the U.S. Bureau of the Census. This chapter does not deal with travel in these urban areas, but with travel outside them.

Travel data presented in this chapter include all domestic travel by air carriers; travel by rail, excluding commuter travel (except where noted); and travel by bus, excluding school and local transit. Intercity travel by water and general aviation is included, although comparable data for these modes are not always available. Travel data include auto travel outside urban places. Some of this travel is between urban places; it also includes a large number of trips with one or both ends in the rural area.

Passenger travel by truck is also included. This mode is often overlooked in travel summaries, but it is not insignificant. Over 20% of U.S. households in 1974 owned one or more pickup trucks, vans, or recreational vehicles, most of which are registered as trucks.[1] Almost three-fourths of all trucks in 1972 were light trucks [under 10,000 lb (4560 kg) gross vehicle weight]. For over half of these the principal use was reported as personal transportation.[2]

Travel and trips

Intercity and rural travel is overwhelmingly by auto, as shown in Table 9-1. This mode, which accounts for almost 86% of all personal travel, is probably the least precisely measured. Auto person-miles of travel is an estimate derived from auto occupancy and vehicle-mile estimates; vehicle-miles on rural roads, in turn, is an estimate from vehicle counts, gasoline consumption, and other factors.

Aviation predominates with 83% of the total passenger travel by common carriers. Table 9-2 shows the amount of travel and trips for air, rail, and bus modes. Bus accounts for the majority of trips and has an average trip length of 74 mi (119 km); this is about the same as rail but is only about 10% of air travel trip length, which averages 739 mi (1189 km).

Table 9-2 includes all intercity air, rail and intercity bus travel as reported to federal regulatory agencies. A different perspective is presented in Table 9-3, which shows the

---

[1]MOTOR VEHICLE MANUFACTURERS ASSOCIATION, *Motor Vehicle Facts and Figures 1977*, Detroit, Mich., p. 38.

[2]U.S. BUREAU OF THE CENSUS, *Truck Inventory and Use Survey, 1972*, Vol. 2, U.S. Government Printing Office, Washington, D.C., 1974, Tables 4, 5.

TABLE 9–1
Intercity and Rural Travel, 1976

Mode	Passenger-Miles (× 10^9)	Passenger-Kilometers (× 10^9)	Percent
Auto	1187.0	1910.0	85.6
Bus	25.1	40.4	1.8
Rail*	5.9	9.5	0.4
Airline	152.3	245.1	11.0
General aviation	11.6	18.7	0.8
Water	4.0	6.4	0.3
Total†	1385.9	2230.0	100.0

*Excludes commutation, 4.5 billion passenger-miles (7.2 billion passenger-km).
†May not add because of rounding.

SOURCE: Auto, bus, rail, air, general aviation: *Transportation Facts and Trends,* 14th ed., Transportation Association of America, Washington, D.C., July 1978, p. 18; rail commutation and water: *National Transportation Statistics,* U.S. Department of Transportation, Transportation Systems Center, Cambridge, Mass., Sept. 1978, Table 6.

TABLE 9–2
Air, Rail, and Bus Travel and Trips, 1976

	Air	Rail*	Bus	Total
Person-miles (× 10^6)	152,300	5,900	25,100	183,300
Person-km (× 10^6)	245,100	9,400	40,400	294,900
Percent	83.1	3.2	13.7	100
Person-trips (× 10^6)	206.2	78.5	340.0	624.7
Percent	33.0	12.6	54.4	100
Average trip length				
Miles	739	75	74	294
Kilometers	1,189	120	119	473

*Excludes 4,500 (× 10^6) person-miles [7,200 (× 10^6) person-km] and 193.2 (× 10^6) passengers, commutation.

SOURCE: Person-miles (km), Table 1; person-trips, *Transportation Facts and Trends,* 14th ed., Transportation Association of America, Washington, D.C., July 1978, p. 19; commutation trips, *National Transportation Statistics,* U.S. Department of Transportation, Transportation Systems Center, Cambridge, Mass., Sept. 1978, pp. 30, 32.

TABLE 9–3
Long Trips by Mode [Trips of 100 Miles (161 km) or More Away from Home] 1977

	Air	Rail	Bus	Auto*	Other†	Total‡
Person-miles of travel (× 10^6)	126,118	3,871	8,902	230,708	12,866	382,466
Person-kilometers of travel (× 10^6)	202,924	6,228	14,323	371,209	20,701	615,385
Percent	33.0	1.0	2.3	60.3	3.4	100
Person-trips (× 10^6)	65.7	4.1	15.0	442.0	12.6	539.5
Percent	12.2	0.8	28	81.9	2.3	100
Average round-trip length						
Miles	1,920	944	593	522	1,021	709
Kilometers	3,089	1,519	954	840	1,643	1,141

*Includes truck.
†Includes different mode going and returning and other.
‡Components may not equal total due to rounding.

SOURCE: *1977 Census of Transportation, National Travel Survey,* U.S. Bureau of the Census, Washington, D.C., 1978, Table 2A.

amount of travel and trips in 1977 by mode for long trips; these are trips to destinations over 100 mi (160 km) away from home [or 200 mi (320 km) round trip]. Auto predominates with 60% of all such travel, although compared to Table 9-1, to a lesser extent. Although these are the longer, more infrequent trips and account for about one-fourth of all intercity and rural travel, they represent the majority of rail and aviation travel. When related to trip distance, as shown in Table 9-4, the auto share of total trips declines with increasing distance; for round trips over 2000 mi (3200 km) and for trips outside the United States, air accounts for the majority of the trips.

The National Travel Survey presents data on the use of trucks for personal transportation in United States. In 1977, truck trips were 9.5% of household trips over 100 mi (161 km) from home. Person travel by truck generally is not measured separately and is included with auto or overlooked in most summaries.

TABLE 9–4
Trip Length and Mode Used [Trips Over 100 Miles (161 km) Away from Home], 1977

Round-trip Distance		Household Trips	Percent of Household Trips by Mode*					
mi	km	(× 10^6)	Auto	Truck	Bus	Rail	Air	Other†
200–299	322–481	104.4	81.9	11.1	3.7	1.0	.9	1.4
300–399	482–643	50.4	78.8	11.3	3.8	0.7	3.4	1.9
400–599	644–964	53.1	70.8	10.9	5.2	1.3	8.8	2.9
600–799	965–1286	23.8	61.3	9.0	4.0	1.0	20.9	3.7
800–999	1287–1608	13.9	55.5	6.8	3.9	0.5	28.6	4.6
1000–1999	1609–3217	29.2	41.7	6.6	3.2	1.3	41.5	5.8
2000 and up	3218 and up	27.4	20.5	4.0	1.8	1.5	67.1	5.0
Outside U.S.		10.4	33.3	5.5	4.5	0.7	51.5	4.6
Total		312.5	66.0	9.5	3.8	1.0	16.7	2.9

*May not total 100 due to rounding.
†Includes different mode going and returning and other.

SOURCE: *1977 Census of Transportation, National Travel Survey,* U.S. Bureau of the Census, Washington, D.C., 1978, Table 4.

Purpose of travel

In 1977, U.S. households made an average of 7.2 long round trips per household [over 200 mi (322 km) round trip]. Thirty-seven percent of these were vacation trips, and because their average length was 976 mi (1570 km), they account for over 50% of the person travel reported in the National Travel Survey. The estimated annual number of long trips categorized by their main purpose, using a more detailed breakdown than vacation/nonvacation, is given in Table 9-5. The table also shows trip rates per household

TABLE 9–5
Purpose of Travel [Trips Over 100 Miles (161 km) Away from Home], 1977

Main Purpose of Trip	Person-Trips (10^3)	Person-mi (10^9)	Person-km (10^9)	Average Round-Trip Length mi	Average Round-Trip Length km	Person-Trips per Household
Visit relatives or friends	198,479	140,227	225,625	707	1,138	2.66
Business	94,800	75,179	120,963	793	1,276	1.27
Convention	10,604	11,897	19,142	1,122	1,805	0.14
Outdoor recreation	70,610	35,648	57,358	505	813	0.95
Entertainment	41,790	30,513	49,095	730	1,175	0.56
Sightseeing	28,237	27,965	44,996	990	1,593	0.38
Personal or medical	67,164	43,411	69,848	646	1,039	0.90
Shopping	3,665	988	1,590	270	434	0.05
Other	23,940	16,638	26,771	695	1,118	0.32
Total	539,289	382,466	615,388	709	1,141	7.24

SOURCE: *1977 Census of Transportation, National Travel Survey,* U.S. Bureau of the Census, Washington, D.C., 1978, Table 2A; trip length and trip rate computed (74,481 households from Table 1).

and average trip length. It is the combination of the two factors on which total travel is based; for example, convention trips represent less than 2% of the total trips per household in 1977, but their average length, 1122 mi (1805 km), was the highest of any trip purpose reported, which increased their significance in total travel. Business accounts for almost 20% of all such travel.

Income relationships

Long trips [over 100 mi (161 km) from home] are relatively infrequent compared to urban trip-making. For example, seven one-way trips per household *per day* is a typical urban trip rate, compared to seven long, round trips *per year*. Over 20% of households reported no long trips at all in a year's time. The long trip rate varies by income class, as shown in Figure 9.1. Less than half the households with income under $5000 report a trip over 100 mi (161 km) away from home, whereas more than 90% of households with incomes of $25,000 and over report such trips.

Travel costs money; and long trips require additional expenses, often for lodging and other needs. It is not surprising that the trip rate varies considerably with income, from 2.6 long trips per year for households with income under $5000, to over 20 for households with income over $50,000, as shown in Table 9-6. Travel increases similarly with income, with over 18,000 person-mi (29,000 person-km) per year for the highest household income class; this is over 10 times the rate of the lowest income group.

The mode of travel varies with income, as shown in Table 9-7. The proportion of travel by air increases with income, probably reflecting the ability to pay for more expensive air travel. Bus use shows an inverse correlation with income, while rail and auto do not exhibit a clear relationship. It is interesting to note that the ratio of truck trips to auto trips peaks at 0.17 for the $15,000 to $19,000 income class. Below that, ownership of a truck, usually a second

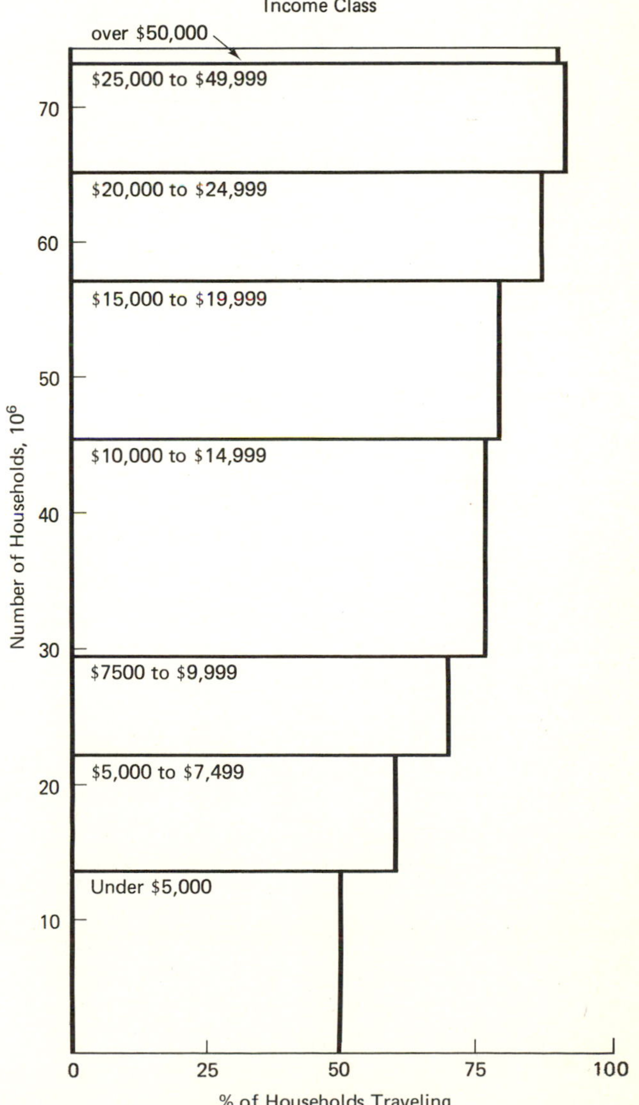

Figure 9.1. Percent of households reporting long trips (trips over 100 mi (160 km) from home), by income class. SOURCE: *1977 Census of Transportation, National Travel Survey,* U.S. Bureau of the Census, Washington, D.C., 1978, Table 1; percentages computed.

TABLE 9–6
Income and Trip Making [Trips Over 100 Miles (161 km) Away from Home], 1977

Family Income	Households (× 10³)	Person-Trips (× 10³)	Person-Trips/ Household	Person Travel mi (× 10⁹)	Person Travel km (× 10⁹)	Person Travel/Household P-mi	Person Travel/Household P-km
Under $4,999	13,593	35,218	2.6	24,051	38,698	1,769	2,847
$5,000–7,499	8,801	32,714	3.7	23,827	38,338	2,707	4,356
$7,500–9,999	7,055	33,205	4.7	22,680	36,492	3,215	5,173
$10,000–14,999	16,303	111,373	6.8	73,128	117,663	4,486	7,217
$15,000–19,999	11,859	101,586	8.6	66,214	106,537	5,584	8,984
$20,000–24,999	7,778	85,366	11.0	58,436	94,024	7,513	12,088
$25,000–49,999	8,150	120,813	14.8	96,890	155,896	11,888	19,128
$50,000 and over	944	19,014	20.1	17,240	27,739	18,262	29,385
Total	74,481	539,289	7.2	382,466	615,387	5,135	8,262

SOURCE: *1977 Census of Transportation, National Travel Survey*, U.S. Bureau of the Census, Washington, D.C., 1978, Tables 1, 3A; trip rates computed.

TABLE 9–7
Income and Mode Used [Trips Over 100 Miles (161 km) or More Away from Home], 1977

Family Income	Percent of Household Trips by Mode* Auto	Truck	Bus	Rail	Air	Other†
Under $5,000	68.2	6.9	9.4	1.2	10.7	3.7
$5,000–7,499	70.2	8.8	6.8	0.9	9.8	3.5
$7,500–9,999	68.2	10.3	4.7	1.0	12.7	3.1
$10,000–14,999	70.0	11.3	3.8	0.9	11.7	2.2
$15,000–19,999	68.2	11.6	3.3	0.8	12.8	3.2
$20,000–24,999	65.0	10.0	3.1	0.8	18.4	2.6
$25,000–49,999	60.8	7.5	1.9	1.5	25.5	2.7
$50,000 and over	52.5	5.2	1.5	1.5	35.4	3.8

*Includes different mode going and returning and other.
†May not total 100 due to rounding.

SOURCE: *1977 Census of Transportation, National Travel Survey*, U.S. Bureau of the Census, Washington, D.C., 1978, Table 5; percentages computed.

vehicle, is probably limited by income; above that, truck use may not fit the life-style.

Trends in travel

As was noted, travel per household is much greater for households with high income. One of the effects of the continuing growth in real household income over time is the fact that the growth of travel far outstrips that of population. The amount of intercity travel increased 216% between 1948 and 1976, as shown in Table 9-8. During that period, U.S. population grew 46%. Travel per capita grew from 2986 to 6447 mi (4804 to 10,373 km) per person in that period, or 116%.

A much more stable relationship is evidenced between the growth of travel and of the economy. Passenger-miles of travel per constant dollar of gross national product has been a remarkably stable index for almost three decades, as shown in Table 9-8; it was identical in 1954 and 1976. Whether this past relationship between intercity travel and the level of the economy will continue is uncertain because of two factors. First, energy supplies may be more limited and energy prices will certainly be much greater than they have been over the past several decades; transportation accounts for about a third of the nation's energy consumption, and its convenience and cost will be greatly affected by the energy situation. Second, the public is increasingly sensitive

TABLE 9–8
Trend of Intercity Travel per Capita and Gross National Products*

Year	Population (× 10⁶)	Passenger Travel (× 10⁹) mi	Passenger Travel (× 10⁹) km	Passenger Travel/Person mi	Passenger Travel/Person km	Gross National Product (constant 1977 dollars × 10⁹)	Ratio Passenger Travel/GNP mi/$GNP	Ratio Passenger Travel/GNP km/$GNP
1948	147	439	706	2986	4804	689	0.64	1.02
1950	152	504	811	3316	5335	754	0.67	1.08
1952	158	613	986	3880	6243	846	0.73	1.17
1954	163	668	1075	4098	6594	867	0.77	1.24
1956	169	746	1200	4414	7102	948	0.79	1.27
1958	175	758	1220	4331	6973	960	0.79	1.27
1960	181	781	1257	4315	6969	1041	0.75	1.21
1962	187	815	1311	4358	7012	1129	0.72	1.16
1968	192	893	1437	4651	7483	1235	0.72	1.16
1966	197	968	1576	4914	7907	1386	0.70	1.14
1968	201	1075	1730	5348	8605	1486	0.72	1.16
1970	205	1180	1899	5756	9210	1519	0.78	1.25
1972	209	1296	2085	6201	9261	1655	0.78	1.26
1974	212	1255	2019	5920	9525	1721	0.73	1.17
1976	215	1386	2230	6447	10373	1801	0.77	1.24

*Includes rail commutation; per capita rate and ratio computed.

SOURCE: *Transportation Facts and Trends*, 14th ed., Transportation Association of America, Washington, D.C., July 1978, p. 2.

TABLE 9-9
Intercity Travel Growth Projections

Mode	1975		1985		2000	
Passenger travel [mi (km) × 10^9]						
Air	148	(238)	232	(373)	472	(759)
Auto	1,123	(1,807)	1,371	(2,206)	1,830	(2,944)
Bus	25	(40)	27	(43)	31	(50)
Rail	5	(8)	6	(10)	6	(10)
Total	1,302	(2,093)	1,637	(2,632)	2,340	(3,763)
Person-trips (× 10^6)						
Air	282		430		866	
Auto	12,976		16,513		24,170	
Bus	239		268		412	
Rail	31		37		52	
Total	13,528		17,249		25,499	

SOURCE: *National Transportation Policies through the Year 2000*, Final Report, National Transportation Policy Study Commission, Washington, D.C., June 1979, Tables 27, 28; medium-growth scenario shown.

TABLE 9-10
Trends in Travel by Mode

Year	Auto	Airline	General Aviation	Bus	Rail	Total
Passenger-Miles (× 10^9)						
1940	292.7	1.2	0.1	10.2	24.8	329.0
1945	220.3	4.3	—	27.4	93.5	345.5
1950	438.3	9.3	0.8	22.7	32.5	503.6
1955	637.4	21.3	1.5	21.9	28.7	710.8
1960	706.1	31.7	2.3	19.3	21.6	781.0
1965	817.7	53.7	4.4	23.8	17.6	917.2
1970	1026.0	109.5	9.1	25.3	10.9	1180.8
1975	1123.0	136.9	11.1	25.4	10.1	1306.5
Passenger-Kilometers (× 10^9)						
1940	471.0	1.9	0.2	16.4	39.9	529.4
1945	354.5	6.9	—	44.1	150.4	555.9
1950	705.2	15.0	1.3	36.5	52.3	810.3
1955	1025.6	34.3	2.4	35.2	46.2	1143.7
1960	1136.1	51.0	3.7	31.0	34.8	1256.6
1965	1315.7	86.4	7.1	38.3	28.3	1475.8
1970	1650.8	176.2	14.6	40.7	17.5	1899.8
1975	1806.9	220.3	17.9	40.9	16.3	2102.3

SOURCE: *Transportation Facts and Trends*, 14th ed., Transportation Association of America, Washington, D.C., July 1978, p. 18; rail includes commutation.

to the unwanted side effects of transportation—noise, air and water pollution, and accidental death and injury—modifications of transportation vehicles and systems required by government regulation to mitigate these effects will increase the cost of transportation.

Intercity travel projections of the National Transportation Policy Study Commission, shown in Table 9-9, reflect these factors.[3] Increases of 80% and 88% between 1975 and 2000 are projected for passenger-miles (km) and person-trips, respectively. This is based on what the commission termed a "medium-growth scenario," with population and gross national product growth projections of 21% and 135%, respectively, for the same period. Low- and high-growth projections were also made by the commission, reflecting different assumptions of future population, economic, and social factors. Intercity travel growth ranges from 38% to 118%, respectively for the low- and high-growth scenarios over the same period.

Travel has not grown uniformly by mode, declining for some and increasing for others, as shown in Table 9-10. These differing trends reflect different technological, institutional, and other factors that were affecting each mode; these are discussed in detail in other chapters.

Air travel grew 100-fold between 1940 and 1975, in the wake of major improvements in speed, safety, efficiency, and system extent and convenience. General aviation increased in similar proportions for many of the same reasons. Auto travel increased by 283%, with increasing car ownership and road improvements. Rail usage was down 90% from its wartime peak, reflecting the competition from air, auto, and bus, as well as other complex industry factors. Bus usage remained relatively constant between 1945 and 1975.

These trends have meant dramatic changes in the proportional shares of the common-carrier market, as shown in Figure 9.2; where rail once was the major mode, air now predominates.

[3] *National Transportation Policies through the Year 2000*, Final Report, National Transportation Policy Study Commission, Washington, D.C., June 1979.

Expenditures for intercity travel

Intercity person travel expenditures or revenues were estimated at $78 billion for 1976. Table 9-11 shows the estimated distribution of these expenditures—revenues, intercity travel, and revenue or expenditure per unit distance by mode. From this estimate, intercity person travel accounts for 45% of total travel expenditures and 6% of total personal consumption expenditures.

Revenue or expenditure per mile varies considerably. Auto is one of the lowest cost modes at 5 cents/passenger-mi (3 cents/passenger-km) including all costs. Rail fares do not reflect fully the high cost per mile indicated because of heavy government subsidies to AMTRAK, the National Railroad Passenger Corporation. General aviation is a high-cost, special service not competing directly with other modes.

High-density corridors

Relatively short corridors, less than 500 mi (800 km) in length, with two or more large urban areas, exhibit different trip proportions than the national total. This is because (1) the urban areas have relatively frequent and direct air, rail, and bus service; (2) there are high highway volumes between and within the urban areas that discourage auto use; and (3) the time and cost of travel by car or air are high for a trip with one or both ends in the central business district.

The Northeast Corridor between Washington and Boston is the highest-density transportation corridor in the United States. Within it are the large metropolitan centers of Boston, Providence, New York, Philadelphia, Baltimore, and Washington. Table 9-12 shows the volume of trips and distance between selected city pairs in the corridor, and the modal shares of travel between them. Aviation use falls markedly with decreasing distance, as the speed advantage of air is lost in terminal and access time. Rail is quite significant at this distance. Less than half of the trips are by auto for the longer city pairs.

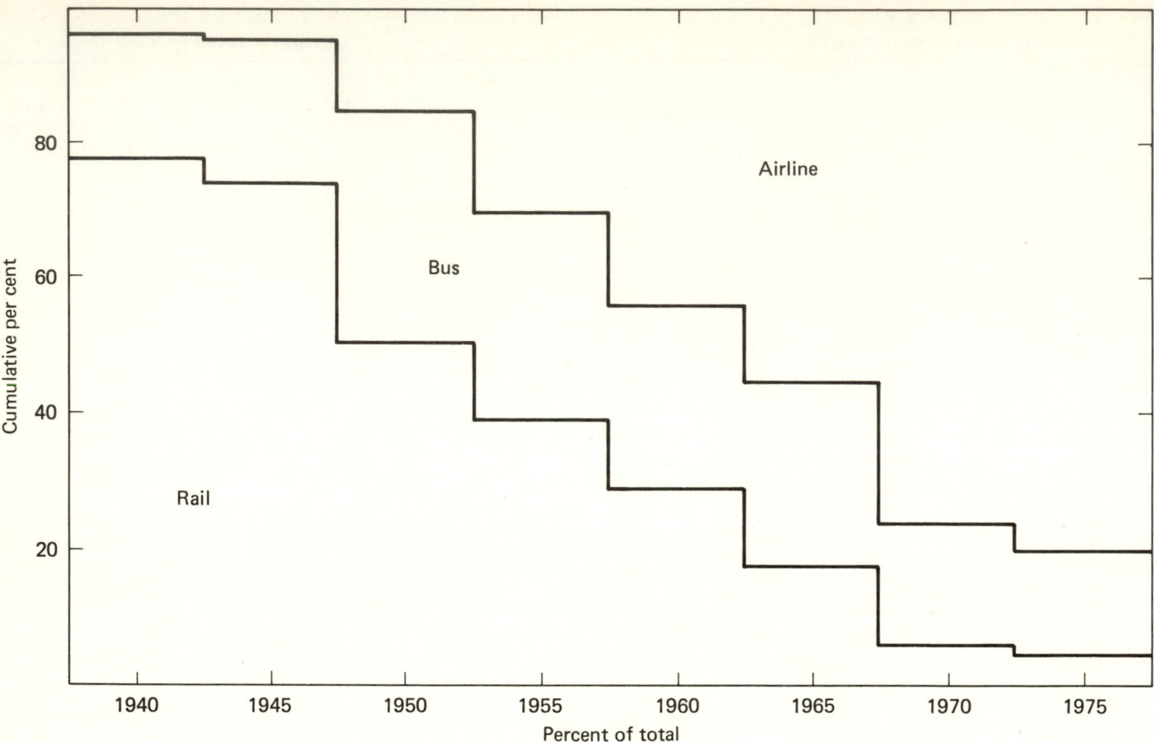

Figure 9.2. Trends in airline, rail, and bus share of intercity travel. SOURCE: *Transportation Facts and Trends*, 14th ed., Transportation Association of America, Washington, D.C., July 1978, p. 18.

TABLE 9–11
Intercity Travel Revenues/Expenditures by Mode, 1976

Mode	Revenue/Expenditure* ($ × 10^6)	Travel (× 10^9) P-mi	Travel (× 10^9) P-km	Revenue/Expenditure ($) Per P-mi	Revenue/Expenditure ($) Per P-km
Airline	12,394	152,300	245,100	0.081	0.051
Rail	601	5,808	9,345	0.104	0.064
Bus	1,026	25,100	40,400	0.041	0.025
Auto†	58,757	1,187,000	1,910,000	0.050	0.031
General aviation	5,048	11,600	18,700	0.435	0.270
Total	77,826	1,381,808	2,223,545	0.056	0.035

*Expenditures estimated for auto and general aviation; revenues for other modes.
†Intercity auto expenditure estimated by intercity proportion of total vehicle-miles; includes cost of new and used cars; tires; gasoline and oil; tolls, insurance, repair; washing, parking; operators' and registration fees (equals $0.110 per vehicle mile at 2.2 passengers/vehicle occupancy).

SOURCE: *National Transportation Statistics*, U.S. Department of Transportation, Transportation Systems Center, Cambridge, Mass., Sept. 1978, Fig. 3, 5; per mile (km) rates computed.

TABLE 9–12
Modal Shares in Northeast Corridor (Total and Selected City Pairs), 1974

City Pair	Distance mi	Distance km	Annual Number of Trips (× 10^3)	Modal Share (%) Auto	Bus	Air	Rail
Washingon–Boston	410	660	803	23.9	1.2	72.2	2.7
Washington–New York	220	350	6,065	45.4	8.8	29.6	16.2
Washington–Philadelphia	130	209	3,367	72.1	4.1	5.5	18.3
New York–Philadelphia	90	140	13,200	73.3	2.6	0.6	23.5
Total corridor*			71,256	75.5	3.8	7.9	12.8

*City pairs that can be served by rail.

SOURCE: *Demand Projections for the Northeast Corridor,* Final Report, prepared by Peat, Marwick, Mitchell & Co. for U.S. Department of Transportation, Transportation Systems Center, Cambridge, Mass., Jan. 1976, Table IV.4 (estimated from 1970 surveys).

When improvements are contemplated to certain modes—high-speed rail or airport access improvements, for example—a change in the amount and proportion of intercity modal use is often expected. A variety of models have been developed, some directly estimating modal use (predistribution) and others estimating modal shares to be applied to total city-pair demand estimates (postdistribution). Several models are discussed in *Intercity Passenger Demand Models: State of the Art,* New York State Department of Transportation. An example of a model developed to predict modal shares in the Northeast Corridor is shown in Figure 9.3.

Description: Stratified, abstract mode, cross-elasticity model–1971

Specification:

$$S_i = \frac{w_i}{\sum_i w_i} \qquad w_i = a_0 t^{a_1} c^{a_2} f'^{a_3}$$

$$f' = 1 - e^{-kf}$$

Calibrated Parameters:

		a_0	a_1	a_2	a_3	k
Business	air	1.1232	−3.384	−0.483	2.279	0.12
	rail	1.4813	−3.384	−0.483	2.279	0.12
	bus	0.3767	−3.384	−0.483	0	0
	automobile	1.0	−3.384	−0.483	0	0
Non-business	air	0.7767	−1.5821	−1.5821	2.0462	0.18
	rail	1.9881	−1.5821	−1.5821	2.0462	0.18
	bus	1.3872	−1.5821	−1.5821	0	0
	automobile	1.0	−1.5821	−1.5821	0	0

Variable Definition:

t = total average one-way door-to-door travel time in hours

c = total average one-way door-to-door travel price in dollars
automobile per person trip cost: business- - 2.3c/mile:
non-business- - 1.0c/mile

f = average number of one-way trips in one direction

Figure 9.3. Description of Northeast Corridor Model CN27. SOURCE: Peat, Marwick Mitchell & Co., *Demand Projections for the Northeast Corridor,* prepared for the U.S. Department of Transportation, Transportation Systems Center, Cambridge, Mass., Jan. 1976, Fig. II.1.

Small urban and rural passenger transportation

Travel in rural and small urban areas is almost exclusively by auto and personal-use truck. The importance of the private vehicle to nonmetropolitan residents can be deduced from the very high percentage of licensed drivers in small towns and cities and rural counties. Table 9-13 shows the inverse relationship between the size of place of residence and percent of residents licensed to drive. Fixed-route transit service is rare in low-density rural areas, except between some cities where intercity local transit routes traverse the rural area. Taxis provide some service in small communities.

TABLE 9–13
Persons 16 Years of Age and Older with Driver's Licenses by Places of Residence, 1969

	Persons with Driver's Licenses (%)		
Place of Residence	Males	Females	Total
Unincorporated areas	90.0	68.8	79.2
Incorporated places			
Under 5,000	90.9	67.4	78.8
5,000–24,999	90.5	66.9	78.2
25,000–49,999	87.8	66.4	76.6
50,000–99,999	86.2	59.5	71.8
100,000–999,999	84.5	54.5	68.3
1,000,000 and over	68.2	32.5	48.8
All incorporated places	85.4	58.1	70.9
All areas and places	87.0	61.5	73.6

SOURCE: *National Transportation Trends and Choices (to the Year 2000),* U.S. Department of Transportation, Washington, D.C., Jan. 1977, Table XIII.1.

The transportation problem in rural and small urban areas, with little or no transit service, is primarily one of the poor, aged, or handicapped, to whom an auto may not be an available alternative. Whereas 27% of the total population resides in nonmetropolitan areas, 40% of persons in low-income households in 1973 resided in such areas. Relatively, the elderly are probably the worst off: 20% of the nonmetropolitan residents over 65 had incomes below the poverty level in 1975; 20% of the elderly in all areas had health-related mobility constraints.

Many states and local communities have active programs of planning and providing rural transit services; the 1978 Surface Transportation Assistance Act provided a new federal program to fund such services. Fixed-route transit service, as noted above, is not usually a practical alternative for the dispersed origins in low-density rural areas. Door-to-door, demand-responsive systems are usually suggested, especially since the majority of potential riders are elderly or handicapped. Although operating cost per passenger-mile may be 50% greater, if demand is less than 100 passengers/mi^2 (40 passengers/km^2), the flexible routes provide superior service.[4]

Intercity freight transportation

This section presents background data on goods movement by intercity freight transportation modes. It focuses on the movement of *goods*—bulk and packaged commod-

[4] *National Transportation Trends and Choices (to the Year 2000),* U.S. Department of Transportation, Washington, D.C., Jan. 1977. p. 352.

ities—as opposed to freight vehicles, networks and operations, and so on. These concerns are discussed in greater detail in the chapters that deal with individual modes and systems.

As with intercity passenger travel, data for different modes are not always reported consistently and completely. Data for rail, pipeline, and air are relatively complete (only oil pipeline data are given; gas pipeline data are omitted). Domestic goods movement by water and truck are less precise estimates. The pickup and/or trip from an intercity air, rail, truck, pipeline, or water terminal is sometimes included in the modal data total, even if it is by different mode. Urban goods movement, which accounts for a considerable amount of freight transportation, is almost entirely by truck and is not included in this chapter's discussion.

Modal and commodity characteristics

The freight transportation industry carries an extraordinary variety of things in a great variety of ways. The total movement of goods, for which U.S. national statistics are presented in this section, is the summation of many individual shipment decisions in which characteristics of modes and services are matched with the requirements of specific shipments of goods.

Different modes have different locations which limit the extent of their service. There are 397[5] points served by trunk and regional service air carriers. There are approximately 170,000[6] mi (270,000 km) of oil pipelines, and 25,000[7] mi (40,000 km) of commercially navigable inland waterways, but these do not reach every part of the nation, and some waterways are unusable for periods of the year when they are frozen. The rail freight network extends 200,000 mi (320,000 km)[8] and reaches almost every area of the nation but still only a fraction of its commercial establishments; many establishments are located off a rail line. The highway network is the largest—3.8 million mi (6.1 million km)—and permits intercity truck shipments to nearly every location. Through the use of intermodal services, the area of air, water, pipeline, and rail service can be extended, but at the cost of extra handling; for some commodities this can be considerable and make intermodal transportation uneconomic.

For different modes there are dimension limitations (height, width, length and weight) as well as optimum sizes based on the capacity of a fully loaded vehicle or container. Generally, ships and barges can carry the largest, heaviest loads, followed by rail, truck, and air, although special vehicles and services provide exceptions to this general rule. Size and weight limitations are not applicable to pipelines, which are limited, on the other hand, to liquids and some solids in slurry form. Special vehicles, facilities, and services are available for specific types of shipments (refrigerated, cushioned), but generally perishable or fragile goods get more individual attention on air and truck modes than when shipped by rail or water.

Shipment by air is the fastest over long distances, followed by truck, rail, and water. Special rail services that minimize time lost in switching yards are offered in some cases to compete more favorably with trucks in speed. Pickup, delivery, and intermodal handling time also present a disadvantage for rail compared to truck, for origins and destinations off a rail line.

The cost of shipment and, for public carriers, the rates charged vary significantly by mode. Per mile costs are generally greatest for shipments by air, with truck, rail, water and oil pipelines following in that order.[9] Pickup, delivery, and handling can affect total door-to-door cost significantly, particularly for short movements where they make up a large percent of the total cost. More important, the choice of mode for a shipment will reflect all the preceding factors, plus other factors unique to each shipper. The size, distribution, and predictability of markets and the cost of goods tied up in transit or inventories all affect an individual shipper's decision; this explains why the same commodity will be moved in different ways by different shippers.

Amount of goods movement

In 1976, domestic intercity freight in the United States amounted to 5280 million tons. This was almost 25 tons for every man, woman, and child. A large portion of these were shipments of bulk commodities—petroleum and petroleum products, coal, ores, grain, and so on—that the consumer did not see until they were processed into energy or manufactured goods or disposed of.

TABLE 9–14
Domestic Intercity Freight Transportation by Mode, 1976

	Amount			Amount-Distance			Average Length of Haul	
Mode	Tons (× 10^6)	kg (× 10^9)	Percent	Ton-mi (× 10^9)	Tonne-km (× 10^9)	Percent	mi	km
Rail	1477	1340	28.0	799	1166	33	538	871
Truck	1974	1790	37.4	510	744	21	258	415
Oil pipeline	934	847	17.7	523	763	22	560	901
Water*	892	809	16.9	591	863	24	663	1066
Air	3	3	—	4	6	—	1200	1900
Total	5280	4790	100	2427	3543	100		

*Includes Great Lakes, rivers and canals, and domestic deep sea.

SOURCE: *Transportation Facts and Trends,* 14th ed., Transportation Association of America, Washington, D.C., July 1978, pp. 8, 10.

Tons and ton-miles (ton-km) by mode, both significant measures of goods movement, are shown in Table 9-14. Whereas tons is a measure of the amount of goods moved, ton-miles reflects the distance moved as well and is a measure of transportation service performed.

---

[5]Ibid., p. 230.

[6]Ibid., p. 291.

[7]Ibid., p. 254.

[8]Ibid., p. 156.

[9]*National Transportation Statistics,* U.S. Department of Transportation, Transportation Systems Center, Cambridge, Mass., Sept. 1978, p. 42.

TABLE 9-15
Shipments by Manufacturing Establishments: Distribution of Intercity Goods Movement by Mode, 1972

Shipper Group*	Percent of Ton-Miles (tonne-km) by: Rail	Truck	Air	Water	Other† and Unknown
Meat and dairy products	27.8	71.6‡	0	0.2	0.4
Canned, frozen, and other food products	66.8‡	27.8	0	5.0	0.4
Candy, beverages, and tobacco products	43.2	54.6‡	0	1.9	0.3
Textile mill and leather products	16.3	81.9‡	0.2	0	1.6
Apparel and related products	13.4	76.5‡	4.8	0.1	5.2
Paper and allied products	74.0‡	24.5	0	1.3	0.2
Chemicals, plastics, synthetic rubber, and fibers	63.2‡	26.3	0	10.0	0.5
Drugs, paints, and other chemical products	44.4	40.4	0.1	14.4	0.7
Rubber and plastic products	32.1	66.1‡	1.0	0.3	0.5
Lumber and wood products, except furniture	76.8‡	18.3	0	4.7	0.2
Furniture and fixtures	37.1	60.4‡	0.8	0.3	1.4
Stone, clay, and glass products	45.4	47.9	0	6.1	0.6
Primary iron and steel products	51.6‡	40.7	0	7.3	0.4
Primary nonferrous metal products	67.3‡	31.1	0	1.1	0.5
Fabricated metal products	23.3	73.1‡	0.4	2.1	1.1
Metal cans and products	50.5‡	47.4	0.6	0.8	0.7
Industrial machinery, except electrical	12.3	84.7‡	1.2	0.1	1.7
Machinery, except electrical and industrial	37.7	58.7‡	1.3	0.6	1.7
Communications products and parts	18.0	65.5‡	12.0	0.3	4.2
Electrical products and supplies	43.1	54.3‡	0.8	0.5	1.3
Motor vehicles and equipment	80.8‡	18.4	0.1	0.2	0.5
Transportation equipment, except motor vehicles	24.0	73.4‡	1.3	0.3	1.1
Instruments, photo equipment, watches, and clocks	34.4	59.7‡	3.6	0.3	2.1

*Shipments include all commodities, except petroleum and coal products, aggregated by shipper, not commodity group.
†Excludes pipeline.
‡Predominant mode.

SOURCE: *Transportation Facts and Trends,* 14th ed., Transportation Association of America, Washington, D.C., July 1978, p. 12.

Trucks accounted for 37% of all goods moved in 1976, followed by rail, oil pipeline, water, in that order; air was less than 1% of total tonnage. Because of its smaller average length of haul, 258 mi (415 km) less than one-half of that of other modes, truck was not the predominant mode, measured by ton-miles (ton-km). Rail, with 33% of the total, had the largest proportion. Water, oil pipeline, and truck account for 24, 22, and 21%, respectively, of the total; air, even though its average haul was 1200 mi (1900 km), was still less than 1% of the total.

Commodity types and modes used for their shipment

Table 9-15 shows the mode used for shipment by manufacturing establishment groups surveyed by the Bureau of the Census in the 1972 Census of Transportation. Rail accounted for more than half the goods movement for eight of the shipper groups.[10] These are firms that tend to ship products of high weight and bulk, which require less speed and are less prone to spoilage or breakage, and which are shipped long distances—all characteristics for which rail is advantageous.

Truck accounted for more than half the goods movement by 13 of the shipper groups. These establishments typically ship goods that are of lighter weight; of smaller size; shipped as individual units (i.e., furniture and fixtures); of higher value, for which transportation costs are a less important contribution to total cost (i.e., candy, beverages, and tobacco products); more prone to spoilage (i.e., meat and dairy products); more prone to breakage (industrial machinery); and generally travel shorter distances.

Air and water modes are minor as a percent of total goods movement for products of manufacturing groups, although it is of interest to note which establishment groups have any significant use of these modes. Air accounts for 4.8, 12.0, and 3.6%, respectively, of the apparel; communications products and parts; and instruments, photo equipment, watches, and clocks groups' shipments. These firms generally ship relatively lightweight, high-cost products requiring careful handling, where speed of shipment is often important and the higher shipping cost of air is sometimes economical.

Shipments by barge and ship usually are not made by manufacturing establishments, which accounts for their small share of ton-miles in Table 9-15. They account for 24% of total domestic goods movement; generally, they carry bulk commodities, such as petroleum and petroleum products; coal, sand, gravel and stone; iron ore, iron and steel; and logs and lumber. For these products the low cost of water transport more than makes up for its slower speed.

Regulated carriers

Freight transportation in the United States is provided by both public (i.e., for-hire) carriers and private companies shipping their own products. Public carriers may or may not

[10] Canned, frozen, and other food products; paper and allied products; chemicals, plastics, synthetic rubber and fibers; lumber and wood products, except furniture; primary iron and steel products; primary nonferrous metal products; metal cans and products; and motor vehicles and equipment.

TABLE 9–16
Federally Regulated Goods Movement by Mode, 1976

Mode	Ton-Miles ($\times 10^9$)	Tonne-km ($\times 10^9$)	Percent Regulated
Rail	799	1166	100
Truck	510	744	44
Oil pipeline	523	763	84
Water	591	863	8
Air	4	6	100
Total	2427	3542	62

SOURCE: *Transportation Facts and Trends,* 14th ed., Transportation Association of America, Washington, D.C., July 1978, p. 9. Percent by water computed from pp. 8 and 9.

be publicly regulated, depending on federal and state legislation. Regulated carriers are granted authority by government to serve specified intercity markets, for specified commodities, at specified rates. Federal economic regulation began with the railroads in the 1800s to ensure equitable treatment for all shippers, communities, and carriers. It now includes, in addition, all or part of freight transportation by truck, air, water, and pipeline.

Table 9-16 shows the percent of goods movement by mode that is federally regulated. Rail freight is totally regulated by the Interstate Commerce Commission (ICC). Air freight is similarly subject to regulation by the Civil Aeronautics Board. Those oil pipelines which are common carriers are subject to ICC regulation; a small proportion are not for-hire and therefore not subject to regulation. Almost all intercity domestic freight transportation by water is unregulated, conducted either by private carriers or carriers of exempt commodities.

Less than half the intercity goods movement by truck is subject to federal regulation by the ICC. The majority consists of private carriage, or the carriage of livestock, fish, and agricultural and horticultural products, exempt from ICC regulation. A small portion is intrastate/intercity movement, subject in some cases to state regulation.

Economic regulation of public carriers in the United States is undergoing intensive reexamination and change. Recent federal measures to ease market-entry, exit and ratemaking restrictions on regulated carriers are intended to achieve the cost and service advantages of a free market.

International trade

U.S. foreign trade measured by tonnage is almost entirely by ship. Foreign trade through U.S. coastal ports is increasing at a greater rate than domestic traffic and made up three-fourths of the total tonnage through coastal ports in 1974.[11] Commodities shipped in U.S. foreign waterborne commerce in 1974 are shown in Table 9-17. The largest export commodity groups were the grains—corn, wheat, and soybeans. Import tonnage exceeded exports by 86% and was dominated by petroleum and petroleum products.

[11] *National Transportation Policies through the Year 2000,* p. 383.

TABLE 9–17
U.S. International Waterborne Commerce, 1974

Commodity Group	Imports ($\times 10^3$)		Exports ($\times 10^3$)	
	Tons	Tonnes	Tons	Tonnes
Crude petroleum	215,994	195,945	130	118
Residual fuel oil	81,286	73,741	813	738
Coal and lignite	2,102	1,907	61,582	55,866
Iron ore and concentrates	50,859	46,138	2,495	2,263
Basic chemicals and products	7,096	6,437	8,747	7,935
Corn and wheat	84	76	59,497	53,974
Aluminum ores, concentrates	18,908	17,153	2	2
Coke, petroleum asphalt, solvents	7,843	7,115	9,313	8,449
Soybeans	*	*	15,170	13,762
Phosphate rock	178	161	12,395	11,244
Distillate fuel oil	12,082	10,961	103	93
Limestone	7,694	6,980	2,546	2,310
All others	93,157	84,510	94,013	85,287
Total	497,283	451,011	266,806	242,041

*insignificant quantity.

SOURCE: *National Transportation Trends and Choices to the Year 2000,* U.S. Department of Transportation, Washington, D.C., Washington, D.C., Jan. 1977, p. 384.

Freight revenues

Domestic freight revenues (and in the case of private transportation, expenditures) were estimated at $81 billion for 1976, as shown by mode in Table 9-18. This presents a different perspective on modal importance than tons or ton-miles, previously discussed.

Trucking accounted for 69% of all intercity and freight revenue/expenditures, a far greater proportion than the 21% of goods movement it represented. This is because its unit revenue/cost dollars per ton-mile (ton-km) was an average of 0.109 (0.075), considerably greater than that of rail 0.023 (0.016), and much greater than that of water and oil pipeline, 0.006 (0.004) and 0.004 (0.003), respectively. Bulk commodities, such as predominate on the water and pipeline systems, cannot absorb as high a unit cost as other, higher-value commodities. Air had the highest average unit revenue, 0.33 per ton-mile (0.221 per ton-km) and accounted for 2% of total intercity freight revenue.

Intermodal transportation

Technological and regulatory changes are increasing the potential for intermodal transportation, whereby two or more modes are used for a single shipment. By so doing, the advantages of each mode can be exploited to the maximum, resulting in faster, safer, and more economical shipment. Truck trailer-on-flat car (TOFC) benefits from rail's lower line-haul unit cost, and it eliminates the costly transfer of goods from truck to boxcar and back that was necessary for service off of a rail line.

A significant development for intermodal transportation was the creation of standard containers that can be loaded and sealed at the origin; shipped by truck, water, air, or rail; transferred once or even twice to another mode; and opened at the destination. Containers offer great advantages in reduced labor costs through highly mechanized loading

TABLE 9–18
Intercity Freight Revenue and Unit Cost, 1976

Mode	Revenue or Expenditure		Amount-Distance			Cost	
	$ × 10^6	Percent	Ton-mi (× 10^9)	Tonne-km (× 10^9)	Percent	$/ton-mi	$/tonne-km
Air	1,288	2	3.9	5.7	—	0.330	0.221
Rail*	17,951	22	790.0	1,153.1	33	0.023	0.016
Truck	56,008	69	510.0	744.4	21	0.109	0.075
Oil pipeline	2,532	3	523.0	763.4	22	0.004	0.003
Water	3,420	4	591.9	864.0	24	0.006	0.004
Total	81,119	100	2,418.8	3,530.6	100	0.034	0.023

*Class I railroads.

SOURCE: *National Transportation Statistics*, U.S. Department of Transportation, Transportation Systems Center, Cambridge, Mass., Sept. 1978, pp. 6, 9. (Dollars per ton-mile computed.)

and unloading onto vehicles and in reduced risk of pilferage and breakage at various points along the route. Restrictions on expansion of intermodal transportation can be attributed less to technological than to institutional factors. These include such problems as the establishment and division of joint or through rates, billing, liability, and responsibility, and have proven slower to adapt.

Freight trends

Intercity freight tonnage carried increased over 80% between 1948 and 1976, as shown in Table 9-19; ton-miles (ton-km) grew even faster—111% in the same time period. This reflects the rapid growth in water, oil pipeline, and air freight tonnage, which have greater average lengths of haul than other modes.

Both tons and ton-miles per person have increased over the same period, 25% and 45%, respectively. This reflects real income growth and the greater consumption of goods both directly—personal consumption—and indirectly—to build the schools and planes, and to supply the energy needed for their operation.

Tons and ton-miles per constant dollar of gross national product have declined, however, by 30% and 19%, respectively, in this period. The reasons for this phenomenon, which contrasts with the relatively constant relationship between person travel and gross national product, discussed previously, can only be conjectured. Among the possible explanations may be the lighter-weight materials, such as plastic and aluminum, that have been substituted for heavier materials in many products.

The trend of goods movement by mode (Table 9-20) shows striking differences during the 1948–1976 period. Rail accounted for almost 62% of the total in 1948 (after the World War II gasoline rationing effects had eased) but had fallen to just 36% by 1976. In absolute ton-miles (ton-km), rail was carrying 23% more in 1976, but this increase was so small compared to that of the other modes that its relative share declined. Truck and oil pipeline percentages more than doubled, water transport increased slightly in percentage, and aviation grew from a negligible to a small,

TABLE 9–19
Trend of Intercity Goods Movement and Related Factors*

Year	Tons† (× 10^6)	Ton-mi† (× 10^9)	Population (× 10^6)	Tons/Person	Ton-mi/Person (× 10^3)	Gross‡ National Product ($ × 10^9)	Tons/$GNP (× 10^3)	Ton-mi/$GNP
1948	2756	1045	147	18.7	7.10	689	4.00	1.52
1950	2860	1063	152	18.8	6.99	754	3.79	1.41
1952	3069	1145	158	19.4	7.25	846	3.63	1.35
1954	3047	1123	163	18.7	6.89	867	3.51	1.30
1956	3630	1356	169	21.5	8.02	945	3.84	1.43
1958	3196	1216	175	18.3	6.95	960	3.38	1.29
1960	3397	1314	181	18.8	7.26	1041	3.26	1.26
1962	3670	1371	187	19.6	7.33	1129	3.25	1.21
1964	4159	1543	192	21.7	8.03	1235	3.36	1.21
1966	4473	1747	197	22.7	8.87	1386	3.23	1.26
1968	4635	1838	201	23.1	9.14	1486	3.12	1.24
1970	4822	1936	205	23.5	9.44	1519	3.24	1.30
1972	4996	2072	209	23.9	9.91	1655	3.02	1.25
1974	5120	2212	212	24.2	10.43	1721	2.97	1.28
1976	5044	2209	215	23.5	10.27	1801	2.80	1.23

*Metric conversions: 1 ton = 0.9072 tonne; 1 ton-mile = 1.46 tonne-km.
†Does not include domestic deep sea.
‡In constant 1977 dollars.

SOURCE: *Transportation Facts and Trends*, 14th ed., Transportation Association of America, Washington, D.C., July 1978, pp. 2, 8, 10.

TABLE 9–20
Trend of Intercity Goods Movement by Mode (Percent of Ton-Miles)

Year	Rail	Truck	Oil Pipeline	Water*	Air
1948	61.9	11.1	11.5	15.5	—
1950	56.2	16.3	12.1	15.4	—
1952	54.4	17.0	13.8	14.8	—
1954	49.6	19.0	15.9	15.5	—
1956	48.4	18.4	17.0	16.2	—
1958	46.0	21.1	17.4	15.6	0.1
1960	44.1	21.8	17.4	16.7	0.1
1962	43.8	22.5	17.3	16.3	0.1
1964	43.2	23.1	17.4	16.2	0.1
1966	43.0	21.8	19.1	16.0	0.1
1968	41.2	21.5	21.3	15.8	0.2
1970	39.7	21.3	22.3	16.5	0.2
1972	37.7	22.7	23.0	16.4	0.2
1974	38.5	22.4	22.9	16.0	0.2
1976	36.2	23.0	23.7	16.9	0.2

*Does not include domestic deep sea.

SOURCE: *Transportation Facts and Trends,* 14th ed., Transportation Association of America, Washington, D.C., July 1978, p. 8.

although (as noted in the discussion of revenues) significant percentage.

As noted in the discussion of trends in person travel, both technological and institutional factors contributed to the various trends. The availability of bigger and better trucks and, more important, a much improved highway system, permitted truck ton-miles (ton-km) to expand fourfold in this period. A factor that both contributed to the growth in trucking and was one of its effects was the increasing trend to locate industrial and commercial establishments off rail lines at points accessible only to truck freight.

The past three decades have also seen major improvements in air freight, with greater capacity and lower unit rates; and in waterways, with extensions and enlargements of the internal and Great Lakes waterways and increased lock capacity to take larger ships and barge tows. Oil pipeline expansion can be related to the increased use of oil and its substitution for coal as a source of energy. All of these economic and technological changes have served to divert many commodities from rail to other modes. In addition, it is generally accepted that the railroad industry's inability to respond in innovative ways to its new competition, because of federal regulations (restricting rates and services and abandonment of uneconomical lines), labor rules, and management shortcomings, contributed to its declining share of the market.

As discussed earlier, forecasts of transportation growth were made by the National Transportation Policy Commission. The relative growth rates between 1975 and 2000 for the medium-growth scenario are shown in Table 9-21. Rail is expected to remain the dominant freight mode in terms of ton-miles (ton-km) through the year 2000. Most important for railroads is the increasing reliance expected to be placed on domestic coal as a substitute for imported oil as an energy source. A fivefold increase in coal ton-miles (ton-km) is forecast, based on major increases in coal production in the western United States, relatively distant from consuming regions.

TABLE 9–21
Forecast of Intercity Freight Growth, 1975–2000

Mode	Ratio of Ton-Miles
Rail	2.95
Truck	2.80
Water	3.35
Oil pipeline	2.43
Air freight	2.50
All	2.88

SOURCE: *National Transportation Policies through the Year 2000,* National Transportation Policy Study Commission, Washington, D.C., June 1979. Appendix Table 37; ratios computed; gas pipeline omitted.

Intercity highway vehicular travel

A different perspective on intercity travel, and one of major interest to transportation engineers, is that of highway vehicular travel. In contrast to intercity person and goods movement by highway, this section deals with autos and trucks, the vehicles that move people and goods outside urban areas.

Volume

Road classifications. Outside of urban areas, 1,650 million vehicle-miles (2656 vehicle-km) of travel per day were estimated in the United States in 1975. This was 7.7 mi (12.4 km) per day for each person (214 million), or 12.4 mi (20.0 km) for each registered vehicle in the United States (133 million). Table 9-22 shows the extent of rural highways and travel by functional classification of road.

Most rural traffic is carried on the higher classifications of roads. The rural arterial systems, which comprise about 8% of rural roads, carry over 60% of rural travel, as shown in Table 9-22. Also shown is average daily traffic by classification, as computed from mileage and vehicle-miles of travel. Average daily traffic on Interstate system routes was over 10,700, on principal arterials it was 4086.

Almost all interstate and many other rural principal arterials are of four lanes or more, which explains their considerably lower vehicle-miles per lane-mile figure, also shown in Table 9-22; average daily traffic is about twice vehicle-miles per lane-mile for minor arterial and collectors, which are generally two-lane roads.

Volumes are not high on most rural highways. Table 9-23 shows the length of the state rural primary system highway by volume class. About 24,800 mi (39,900 km) had average daily volumes of 10,000 or greater; this was 6% of all state rural primary highways. Because of these low volumes, capacity is a relatively minor concern on intercity and rural highways and is usually a local or seasonal phenomenon. Volume/capacity ratios were estimated for the National Highway Inventory and Performance Study. The extent and percent of rural highways with volume/capacity ratios exceeding 0.7 is shown in Table 9-24. Less than 4% of rural interstate highways had volume/capacity ratios in this range, where speeds begin to show the effect of congestion.

TABLE 9–22
Rural Road Length and Travel by Functional Classification of Road, 1975

Functional Classification of Road	Rural Roads mi (× 10³)	Rural Roads km (× 10³)	Rural Roads Percent	Daily Travel Veh-mi (× 10⁶)	Daily Travel Veh-km (× 10⁶)	Daily Travel Percent	Average Daily Traffic [veh-mi/mi (veh-km/km)]	Average Lane Volumes [veh-mi/lane-mi (veh-km/lane-km)]
Principal arterial								
Interstate	29.9	48.2	0.9	320.9	516.4	19.5	10,732	2,546
Other	81.1	132.2	2.6	335.5	539.8	20.3	4,086	1,581
Minor arterial	152.6	245.5	4.9	342.0	550.4	20.7	2,241	1,014
Collector								
Major	431.0	693.4	13.8	349.6	562.4	21.2	811	414
Minor	306.8	493.6	9.8	102.4	164.8	6.3	334	153
Local	2,127.9	3,423.8	68.0	200.2	322.0	12.1	94	—
Total	3,130.2	5,036.6	100.0	1,650.6	2,655.8	100.0	527	—

SOURCE: *Status of the Nation's Highways: Conditions and Performance,* Report of the Secretary of Transportation to the U.S. Congress Pursuant to Public Law 89-139, U.S. Government Printing Office, Washington, D.C. 1977, p. 59 (includes Puerto Rico); average daily traffic computed. Vehicle-miles per lane mile from *National Highway Inventory and Performance Summary,* Federal Highway Administration, Washington, D.C. 1977, p. II-3.

TABLE 9–23
Length of State Rural Primary System in Various Volume Groups, 1976

Average Daily Traffic (veh/day)	Rural Primary Systems mi	km	Percent
Less than 400	71,888	115,668	17.6
400–999	90,468	145,563	22.1
1,000–1,999	87,094	140,134	21.3
2,000–2,999	48,303	77,720	11.8
3,000–3,999	30,228	48,637	7.4
4,000–4,999	18,842	30,317	4.6
5,000–9,999	37,176	59,816	9.1
10,000–14,999	12,397	19,947	3.0
15,000–19,999	5,719	9,202	1.4
20,000–29,999	4,318	6,948	1.1
30,000–39,999	1,275	2,051	0.3
40,000 and over	1,097	1,765	0.3
Unclassified	16	26	—
Total	408,821	657,793	100

SOURCE: *Highway Statistics 1976,* Report FHWA-HP-HS-76, Federal Highway Administration, Washington, D.C.

TABLE 9–24
Rural Highways with Volume/Capacity Ratio Exceeding 0.7 in Peak Hour, by Functional Classification, 1975

Classification	Rural Highways mi	km	Percent
Interstate	992	1,596	3.6
Other principal arterials			
Multilane	179	288	1.3
2- or 3-lane	2,313	3,722	3.7
Minor arterial			
Multilane	102	164	2.2
2- or 3-lane	2,476	3,984	1.8
Major collector			
Multilane	49	79	2.0
2- or 3-lane	2,255	3,628	0.7
Minor collector			
Multilane	0	0	—
2- or 3-lane	474	763	0.3
Total	7,922	12,746	1.1

SOURCE: *National Highway Inventory and Performance Summary,* Federal Highway Administration, Washington, D.C., 1977, Table III–1; volume/capacity ratio in peak direction for multilane highways.

Vehicle classes. Table 9-25 presents data on the use of rural roads by different vehicle classes in 1975. Trucks made up 26% of rural travel, buses less than 1%, and autos (and motorcycles) the remainder. On main rural roads, the truck proportion was even higher, almost 29%. Tractor-trailers and larger combinations were 9.5% of main rural road travel but only 1% of local rural road travel. Bus travel on local rural roads consists mainly of school bus travel.

Table 9-25 also presents data on the average rural travel per vehicle (considering all vehicles registered in the United States, whether in rural or urban areas). The average rural travel per vehicle for truck combinations, 40,000 mi (65,000 km), stands out, being more than eight times that of auto.

Trends of traffic volume. Over the long term, traffic volumes on rural and intercity highways have and are expected to continue to increase. Figure 9.4 shows the trend of travel on main rural routes from 1936–1978 as reported to the Federal Highway Administration by state highway agencies. Through 1973, travel was increasing at a relatively constant rate of 4 to 5% per year.

The gasoline shortages and price rises of 1973–1974, and the reduction in the speed limit to 55 mph, all made intercity auto travel more costly, difficult, and time consuming than previously. A 6% drop in travel in a year's time was evidenced. Since 1974, rural travel has resumed its growth, at an average of 6% per year to 1978. The year 1979 brought new gasoline shortages and accelerated price rises, and whether the recent rate of increase will continue is not known. One effect of fuel price rises was the trend of American consumers to more-fuel-efficient cars; sales of more-efficient foreign cars have grown, and increases in fuel efficiency are mandated by law for American cars as well.

The National Transportation Policy Study Commission forecast increases of 22% and 60% from 1975 for auto vehicle-miles (km) of travel for 1985 and 2000, respectively; and 50% and 144% for truck vehicle-miles (km) of travel for the same periods. These forecasts are based on the assumption of higher prices for fuel but its continued availability in the future. With increased fuel efficiency assumed, the auto travel increases can be achieved in 1985 and 2000[12] with reduced fuel consumption from 1975 levels.

[12] *National Transportation Policies through the Year 2000*, Tables 27, 33; medium growth scenario.

Cyclical variations. Besides the long-term trend of rural road volume, there are annual, weekly, and daily cycles of traffic volume variation, corresponding to the pattern of activities for which travel is made. Figure 9.5 shows the annual variation of vehicle-miles (km) of travel on rural

TABLE 9–25
Rural Travel by Vehicle Class, 1975

			Trucks			
	Autos*	Buses†	Single Unit	Combinations	Total	Total
Annual vehicle travel						
Main rural roads						
Veh-mi (× 10^6)	329,050	1,858	90,410	44,317	134,727	465,635
Veh-km (× 10^6)	529,441	2,990	145,470	71,306	216,776	749,207
Percent	70.7	0.4	19.4	9.5	28.9	100.0
Local rural roads						
Veh-mi (× 10^6)	111,848	1,100	20,712	1,336	22,048	134,996
Veh-km (× 10^6)	179,963	1,770	33,326	2,150	35,475	217,209
Percent	82.9	0.8	15.3	1.0	16.3	100.0
All rural roads						
Veh-mi (× 10^6)	440,898	2,958	111,122	45,653	156,775	600,631
Veh-km (× 10^6)	709,405	4,759	178,795	73,456	252,251	966,415
Percent	73.4	0.5	18.5	7.6	26.1	100.0
Number of vehicles						
Registered in U.S. (× 10^3)	111,679	462	24,645	1,131	25,776	137,917
Annual rural travel per vehicle						
Veh-mi	3,948	6,403	4,509	40,365	6,682	4,355
Veh-km	6,352	1,030	7,255	64,947	10,751	7,007

*Includes motorcycles.
†Includes school buses.

SOURCE: *Motor Vehicle Facts and Figures, '77,* Motor Vehicle Manufacturers Association, Detroit, Mich., p. 60; rural travel per vehicle computed.

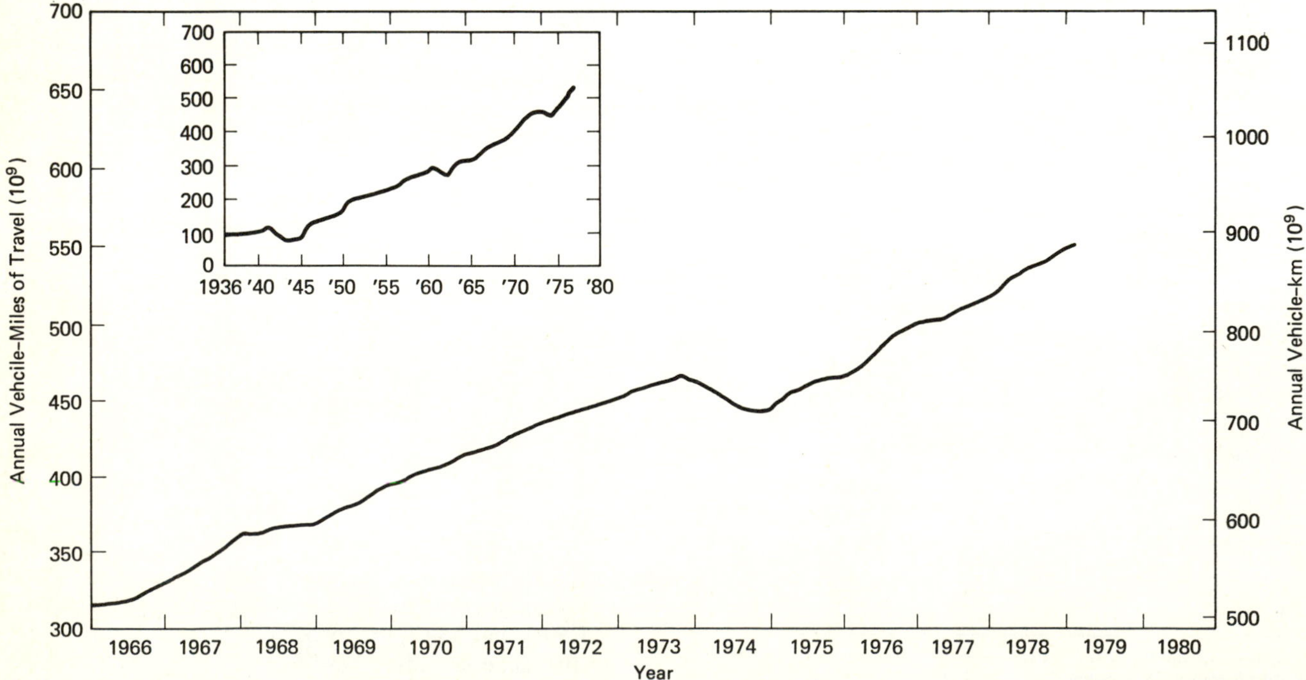

Figure 9.4. Trend in travel on main rural roads. SOURCE: *Traffic Volume Trends,* Federal Highway Administration, Washington, D.C., Feb. 1979, Fig. 2.

roads by month. These data are based on continuous traffic-counting locations throughout the United States as reported by the states to the Federal Highway Administration. The peak months for travel on main as well as local rural roads are July and August, when travel is 20% greater than the average. This is when many recreational and vacation trips are made to rural locations, as well as between cities. The low months for the year are January and February, when traffic is about 77% of the average. The pattern for main and local rural roads is about the same.

The variation in traffic volume on certain rural routes may be very different from these national averages, de-

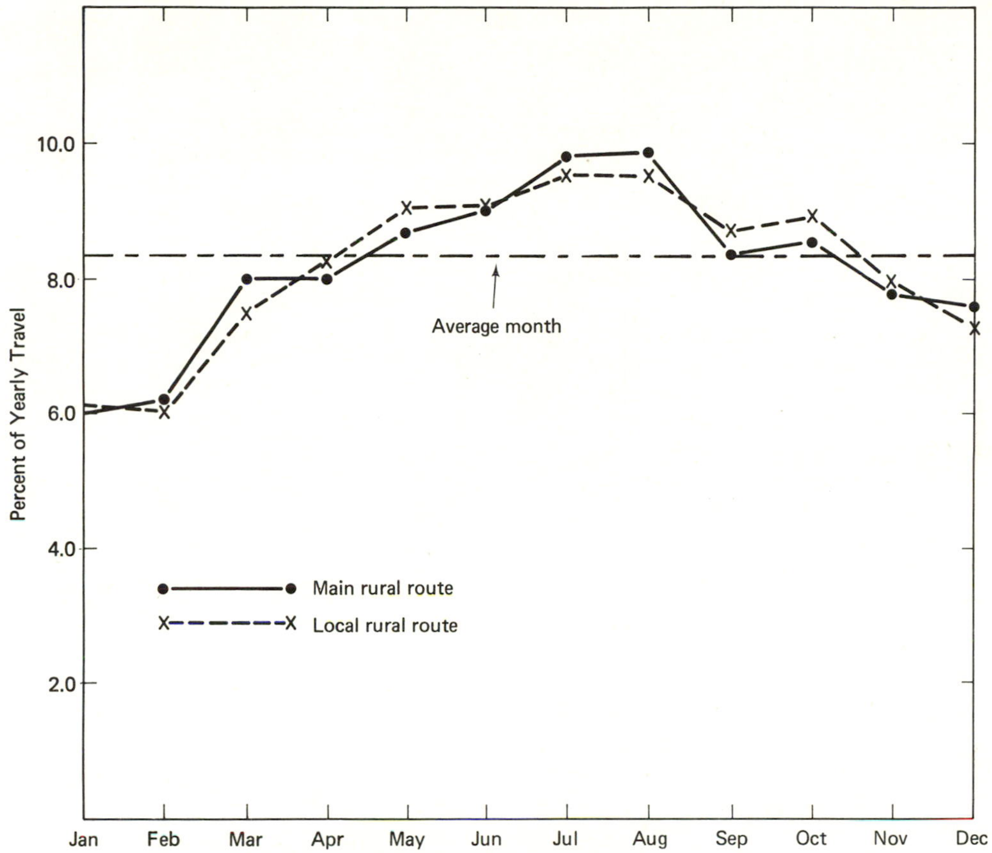

Figure 9.5. Variation in travel on rural roads by month, 1978. SOURCE: *Traffic Volume Trends,* Federal Highway Administration, Washington, D.C., Feb. 1979, Table 3.

	Vehicle Miles (10^9)					
	Main Rural		Local Rural		Total Rural	
		%		%		%
January	34.6	6.31	9.5	6.41	45.0	6.45
February	35.0	6.38	9.4	6.34	44.4	6.36
March	44.2	8.06	11.2	7.56	55.4	7.94
April	44.3	8.08	12.3	8.31	56.6	8.11
May	48.5	8.84	13.6	9.18	62.1	8.90
June	50.3	9.17	13.6	9.18	63.9	9.15
July	54.3	9.90	14.4	9.72	68.3	9.79
August	55.0	10.03	14.4	9.72	69.4	9.94
September	47.4	8.64	13.2	8.91	61.6	8.83
October	48.0	8.75	13.4	9.05	61.4	8.80
November	44.0	8.02	12.0	8.10	56.0	8.02
December	42.8	7.80	11.1	7.49	53.9	7.72

TABLE 9–26

Factors Used to Compute Annual Average Daily Traffic for Different Annual Volume Patterns in New York State

Volume Pattern Group	Jan.	Feb.	Mar.	Apr.	May	June	July	Aug.	Sept.	Oct.	Nov.	Dec.
	Month											
1	0.97	0.98	1.05	1.08	1.10	1.13	1.07	1.08	1.07	1.06	1.04	1.07
2	0.89	0.90	0.96	1.02	1.08	1.11	1.12	1.15	1.12	1.09	1.04	1.01
3	0.81	0.81	0.86	0.93	1.03	1.07	1.18	1.20	1.08	1.04	0.94	0.89
4	0.92	0.93	0.98	1.05	1.10	1.14	1.23	1.26	1.13	1.08	1.03	0.97
5	0.74	0.74	0.79	0.88	1.01	1.07	1.28	1.31	1.09	1.01	0.90	0.82
6	0.69	0.68	0.71	0.81	1.02	1.12	1.43	1.38	1.09	0.95	0.81	0.74
7	0.69	0.73	0.75	0.81	0.94	1.03	1.55	1.60	1.05	0.95	0.81	0.77
8	0.53	0.54	0.56	0.65	0.87	1.15	1.93	1.97	1.20	1.06	0.67	0.59

SOURCE: Internal Memorandum, New York State Department of Transportation, 1975. The Department conducts spring, summer, and fall counts on traffic control sections every 9 years to establish into which of the eight volume pattern groups the section falls. Counts in the other years can then be factored to estimate annual average daily traffic.

pending on the type of area and traffic it serves. Recreational area routes, particularly, exhibit greater peaks. A knowledge of the type of route and its volume variation cycle is essential to relating single traffic counts to an annual average. Patterns can be established for a route from seasonal counts in widely separated years, so that more-frequent, once-a-year counts can yield longer-term volume trends.

The New York State Department of Transportation found eight significantly different volume patterns, shown in Table 9-26. The Department performs machine counts on all traffic control sections in a periodic schedule: a one-time count every 3 years and a three-time count (spring, summer, and fall) every 9 years. The three-time counts are used to assign the traffic control sections to one of the established factor groups. The one-time counts can then be used to estimate changes in average annual daily traffic.

Rural routes also exhibit variations in traffic volume by day of the week. Figure 9.6 presents data from counts on three types of routes: local rural, main rural, and recreational. On a local route, Saturday and Sunday exhibit the lowest traffic count; Thursday traffic is highest of the weekdays, although not by much. Main rural routes, generally connecting large cities, show the most uniform pattern. A peak on Friday is about 50% greater than the lowest weekday and higher than both weekend days. On the major access route from New York City to the Catskill mountain resort area, Friday and Sunday are the peak days; volume on Sunday is nearly twice that of a typical weekday.

Variations in volume by hour form a daily pattern, as shown in Figure 9.7. The patterns are different for weekdays and weekend days and different route types. The local rural route is dominated by commuting traffic, with peaks from 8 to 9 A.M. and 5 to 6 P.M. on a weekday. On Saturday and Sunday the pattern is quite different, with a more even distribution which rises to its greatest level from noon to 6 P.M. The weekday patterns of an intercity route and a recreational route are both significantly different from that of the local rural route noted above; they do not exhibit the morning and afternoon commuting peaks, but rather a single, more gradual peak. On weekends, the intercity route shows its greatest peak on Saturday afternoon. The largest peak for the recreation access route is on Sunday afternoon.

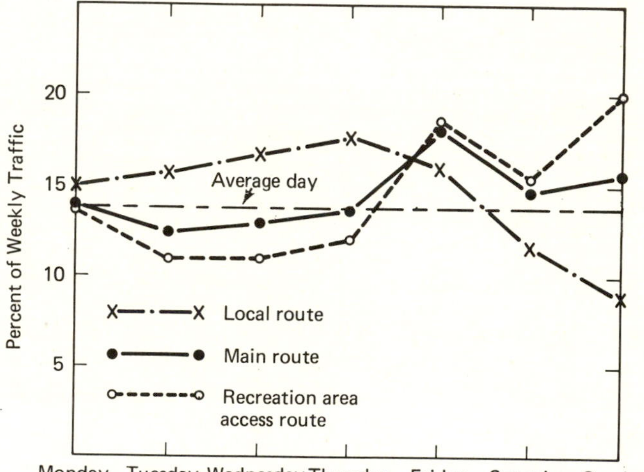

Percent of Weekly Total Traffic

Day of Week	Local Route (County Rte. 18)	Main Rural Rte. (Interstate 81)	Recreation Access Rte. (NY Rte. 17)
Monday	14.9	13.6	13.2
Tuesday	15.5	12.2	10.9
Wednesday	16.5	12.9	10.9
Thursday	17.4	13.4	11.9
Friday	15.7	18.0	18.2
Saturday	11.3	14.5	15.1
Sunday	8.7	15.4	19.9
Average Day	14.3	14.3	14.3

Figure 9.6. Variation in traffic on rural roads by day of week, 1978. SOURCE: Unpublished N.Y. State Department of Transportation counts, 1978.

Peak-hour traffic. The data presented above described some aspects of traffic volume variability on rural roads—by month, day of week, and hour of day. The peak volume hours of the year reflect the combination of all these variations, and it is these peaks that bear on the degree and frequency of those occurrences when volume exceeds the capacity of the facility and congestion is evidenced.

Figure 9.8 shows the percent of average daily traffic (ADT) equaled or exceeded for the peak hours of the year on typical rural roads. The peak two-way volume hour of the year was over 22% of two-way ADT; the peak one-way volume hour was over 24% of the one-way ADT. The 100th peak hour volumes (equalled or exceeded 100 times in a year) were about 14% and 13% of one- and two-way ADT, respectively. The "design-hour volume," which is used for

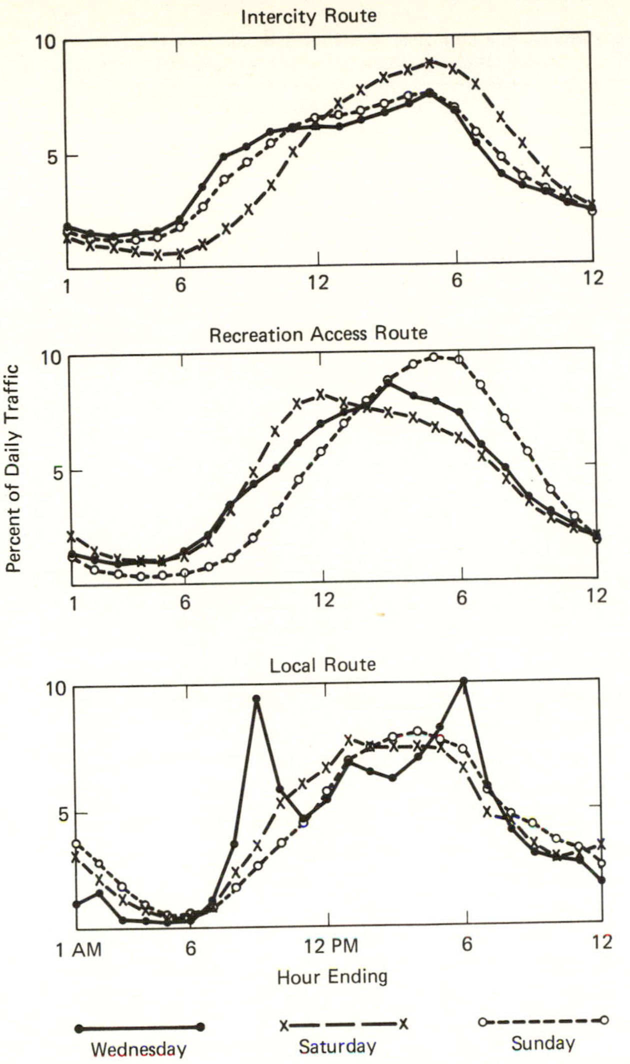

Hour of Day		Local Route			Intercity Route			Recreational Access Route		
		Wed	Sat	Sun	Wed	Sat	Sun	Wed	Sat	Sun
AM	12-1	1.0	3.0	3.7	1.5	1.2	1.6	1.2	2.0	1.1
	1-2	1.5	2.0	2.8	1.3	0.9	1.2	1.0	1.3	0.7
	2-3	0.3	1.2	1.7	1.2	0.7	1.1	0.9	1.0	0.5
	3-4	0.1	0.6	0.9	1.3	0.6	1.1	1.0	0.9	0.4
	4-5	0.1	0.3	0.4	1.4	0.5	1.2	1.0	0.9	0.4
	5-6	0.2	0.3	0.3	2.0	0.6	1.7	1.3	1.1	0.4
	6-7	1.0	0.8	0.8	3.4	0.9	2.7	2.0	1.7	0.6
	7-8	3.7	2.1	1.7	4.8	1.5	3.8	3.3	3.0	1.0
	8-9	9.9	3.5	2.6	5.2	2.3	4.5	4.1	4.7	1.9
	9-10	6.0	5.3	3.6	5.8	3.5	5.3	4.9	6.5	3.0
	10-11	4.7	6.1	4.6	6.0	4.9	6.0	6.0	7.6	4.4
	11-12	5.5	6.8	5.8	6.0	6.1	6.3	6.8	8.0	5.7
PM	12-1	7.2	8.0	7.1	6.0	7.0	6.4	7.2	7.6	6.8
	1-2	6.7	7.7	7.7	6.3	7.7	6.7	7.4	7.4	7.7
	2-3	6.4	7.7	8.1	6.7	8.1	7.0	8.7	7.1	8.6
	3-4	7.2	7.8	8.3	7.0	8.5	7.2	8.0	7.0	9.4
	4-5	8.5	7.6	8.0	7.4	8.8	7.4	7.7	6.6	9.6
	5-6	10.6	6.8	7.6	6.7	8.3	6.8	7.2	6.1	9.4
	6-7	6.0	4.9	5.8	5.1	7.7	5.7	5.8	5.3	8.3
	7-8	4.1	4.6	4.8	3.9	6.3	4.6	4.8	4.3	6.9
	8-9	3.1	3.3	4.3	3.3	5.1	3.8	3.6	3.3	5.4
	9-10	2.8	2.9	3.7	3.0	3.9	3.2	2.9	2.7	3.8
	10-11	2.8	3.1	3.4	2.6	2.9	2.6	2.3	2.1	2.5
	11-12	1.7	3.3	2.5	2.1	2.1	2.0	1.8	1.7	1.6

Figure 9.7. Variation in traffic by hour. SOURCE: Unpublished N.Y. State Department of Transportation counts, 1978.

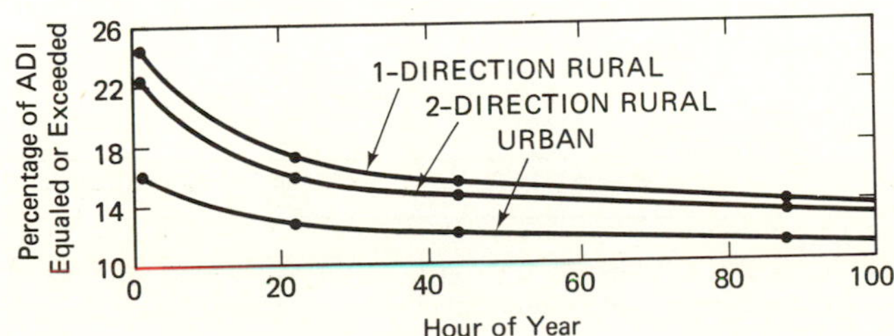

Figure 9.8. Percentage of average daily traffic during 100 highest hours of the year, selected rural roads, 1959–1960. SOURCE: *Highway Capacity Manual, 1965,* Special Report 87, Highway Research Board, Washington, D.C., Fig. 3.16.

capacity comparisons, is obviously a compromise between the highest peak of the year, for which design would often be quite costly and capacity would be required only once a year, and design for a volume for which congestion would be accepted a given number of times in a year but for which capacity could be provided at lower cost. Although the curves in Figure 9.8 are continuous, a relative "break" in the curve is observable at the 30th peak hour—where the percent of ADT is equalled or exceeded 30 h/yr. The 30th peak hour is utilized by many states as a design criterion for rural highways.

Figure 9.9 shows the percent of annual ADT (AADT) in the 30th highest hour for different types of rural facilities. The mean peak percentages of AADT were 13.5, 12.7, 12.7, and 13.6 for freeways, expressways, and highways with three or more lanes and for two-lane highways, respectively. As can be seen in the figure, however, there was considerable spread even within the same facility class in the percent of AADT in the 30th peak hour. Generally, the percentage of AADT in the highest hours is greater for highways with very low AADT and for highways in areas

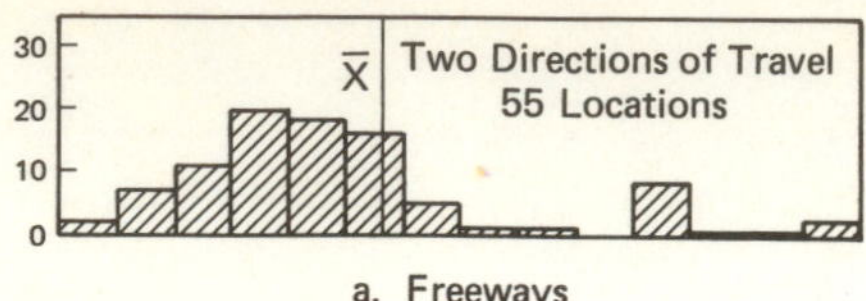

a. Freeways

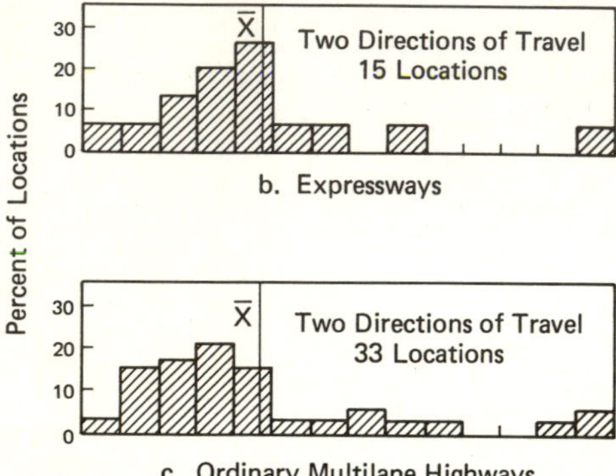

c. Ordinary Multilane Highways

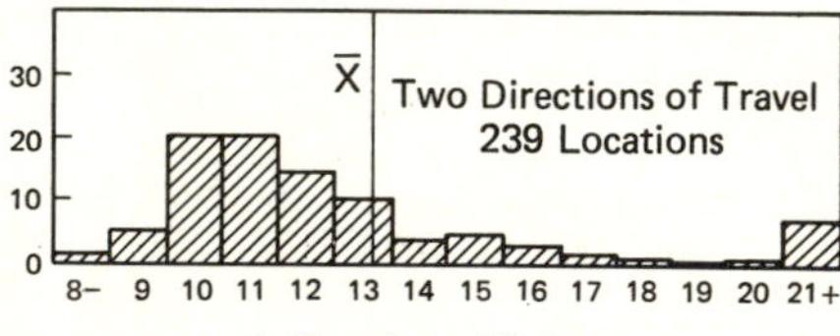

d. Two-Lane Highways

Percentage of AADT
in 30th Highest Hour

Figure 9.9. Relation of 30th peak-hour two-way volumes and annual average daily traffic, selected rural locations, 1961 and 1962. SOURCE: *Highway Capacity Manual, 1965,* Special Report 87, Highway Research Board, Washington, D.C., Fig. 3.17 to 3.20.

of low population or sparse development or subject to high seasonal variation. Over time, development or growth in the surrounding area tends to decrease the 30th-peak-hour percentage. The choice of an appropriate peak-hour factor should be based on studies of traffic on the specific highway, if possible, or on highways with similar characteristics.

Speed on rural highways. Speeds on rural highways were also estimated in the National Highway Inventory and Performance Study. These are theoretical speeds based on traffic volumes and composition and highway capacity and alignment. Table 9-27 shows the percent of miles of highway with speeds 55 mph or greater by highway classification, terrain, and number of lanes estimated from the factors described above. Of note is the general decrease in the percentage of mileage with speeds 55 mph or greater by decreasing functional classification. Terrain has a similar effect, with more mileage under 55 mph generally in mountainous terrain than in rolling or flat terrain. Congestion effects are implicit in these estimates, but are not generally large, based on the foregoing discussion of volume/capacity ratios.

Speeds are measured by the states on straight, open sections of roads, posted at the statewide speed limit, under free-flowing conditions, and data from these surveys are

TABLE 9–27
Rural Highways with Peak-Hour Operating Speed 55 mph (88 km/hr) or More by Highway Classification and Terrain, 1975

	Percent of Miles (km) by Terrain		
	Flat	Rolling	Mountainous
Interstate			
Multilane	91.6	83.3	67.5
2- or 3-lane	41.6	19.8	38.2
Other principal arterial			
Multilane	66.2	80.0	82.4
2- or 3-lane	62.5	45.8	16.5
Minor Arterial			
Multilane	72.0	72.2	88.4
2- or 3-lane	69.3	60.2	21.1
Major Collector			
Multilane	56.6	71.6	61.3
2- or 3-lane	63.1	63.9	19.6
Minor Collector			
Multilane	26.5	73.0	0
2- or 3-lane	56.5	58.7	26.6
All			
Multilane	81.0	81.0	74.4
2- or 3-lane	62.8	60.3	21.4

SOURCE: *National Highway Inventory and Performance Summary,* Federal Highway Administration, Washington, D.C., 1977, Table IV–1.

reported annually to the Federal Highway Administration. Table 9-28 shows median and 85th percentile speeds for selected vehicle types and highway classifications measured in New York State. In 1977, 50% of the autos were measured under these "ideal" conditions at speeds greater than 58.5 mph (94.1 km/h) on interstate routes. Median bus speeds were about the same (58 mph; 93.3 km/h) and truck speeds were somewhat lower (57 mph; 91.7 km/h). Fifteen percent of the vehicles in each class were measured at even higher speeds; 64, 64, and 62 mph (103, 103, and 100 km/h) respectively, for auto, bus, and truck. These measured speeds were in excess of the 55-mph (88-km/h) posted speed limit.

The effect of the national speed limit can be discerned, however, when current data are contrasted with data from 1970, when the speed limit was 65 mph (105 km/h) on

TABLE 9–28
Median and 85th Percentile Speed for Selected Vehicle Types in New York State, 1970 and 1977

	1977				1970			
	Interstate Routes		Touring Routes		Interstate Routes		Touring Routes	
	mph	km/h	mph	km/h	mph	km/h	mph	km/h
Autos								
Median	58.5	94.1	53.5	86.1	64.5	103.8	51.8	83.3
85th percentile	64.0	103.0	59.6	95.9	69.6	112.0	57.8	93.0
Trucks								
Median	56.9	91.6	52.5	84.5	61.0	98.1	50.5	81.3
85th percentile	61.9	99.6	58.5	94.6	65.8	105.9	56.1	90.3
Buses								
Median	59.0	94.9	50.7	81.6	63.2	101.7	52.3	84.2
85th percentile	64.1	103.1	55.8	89.8	69.2	111.3	61.1	98.3
All vehicles								
Median	58.0	93.3	53.2	85.6	64.0	103.0	51.6	83.0
85th percentile	63.5	102.2	59.4	95.6	69.4	111.7	57.6	92.7

SOURCE: *Data Blips,* Comparative Findings of the 1970–1977 Speed Studies, by Jerry Bala, Data Services Bureau, N.Y. State Department of Transportation, Albany, N.Y., undated.

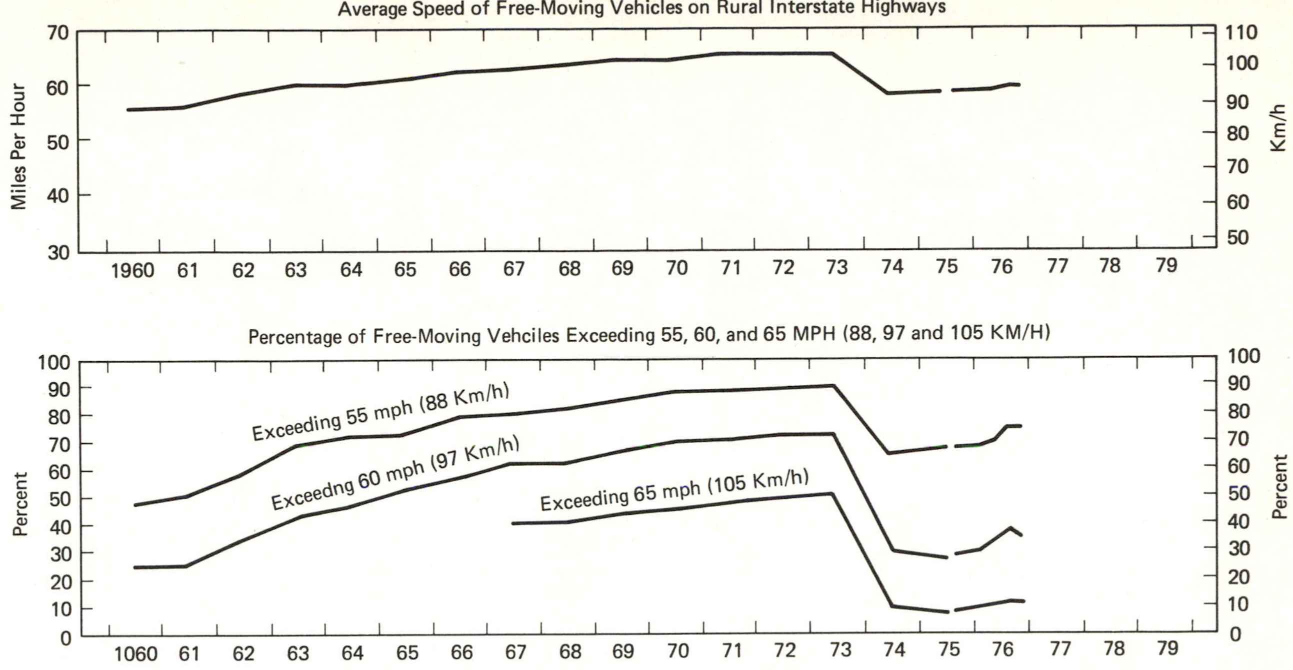

Figure 9.10. Speed trends on rural interstate highways. SOURCE: *Highway Statistics 1976*, Report FHWA-HP-HS-76, Federal Highway Administration, Washington, D.C.

interstate routes in New York State. At that time, median speeds were 65, 63, and 61 mph (104, 102, and 98 km/h) and 85th percentile speeds were 70, 69, and 66 mph (112, 111, and 106 km/h) for autos, buses, and trucks, respectively. A significant drop in speed is noticeable. Median speed on noninterstate routes was less than the speed limit in 1977 and was actually greater than in 1970 for each vehicle class. This probably reflects road improvements in the intervening years.

Average speed over the long term was increasing until the speed-limit change of 1974. Figure 9.10 shows average speed on interstate highways from 1960 to 1976. A gradual increase from 1960 to 1973 can be noted, with a drop in 1973–1974 and a gradual rise since then. The percentage of free-moving vehicles exceeding selected speeds is also shown in Figure 9.10. In 1973, almost 50% of vehicles exceeded 65 mph (105 km/h); in 1974, the figure was reduced to 10%. The number exceeding 55 mph (88 km/h) was 65% in 1974 and has increased somewhat since then. The federal government is pressing states to enforce the federally mandated 55-mph (88-km/h) speed limit vigorously to meet safety as well as energy-conservation goals, and this may affect future speeds.

The effect of the speed-limit reduction was evidenced not only in average speeds but also in speed distribution. Forty percent of the vehicles were moving at speeds between 55 and 65 mph (88 and 105 km/h) before the speed change; in 1976, this figure was almost 65%, as shown in Figure 9.9. This more pronounced "bunching" of speeds is believed to reduce vehicle maneuvering and accident potential.

For further reading

The Federal Highway Administration's *Nationwide Personal Transportation Study* contains reports on automobile occupancy (No. 1, April 1972), seasonal variations of automobile trips and travel (No. 3, April 1972), purposes of automobile trips and travel (No. 10, May 1974), and automobile ownership (No. 11, December 1974). For information on a state-by-state basis, see *Statewide Travel Demand Forecasting*, published by the Federal Highway Administration in 1973.

More recent data on highway travel, including the effects of the 1979 gasoline shortage are reported in *Highway Travel Trends During the 1970's*, Federal Highway Administration, July 1980.

10

URBAN TRAVEL CHARACTERISTICS

HERBERT S. LEVINSON, *Consultant and Professor of Transportation*

University of Connecticut

This chapter on urban travel characteristics contains information on trip generation, trip purpose, trip lengths, and travel modes; shows how population, density, income, car ownership, and age influence travel behavior; and summarizes central business district travel. It also shows how people respond to changes in transportation service or costs.

The information can be used by transportation engineers and planners to analyze current conditions, to evaluate traffic impacts of proposed developments, and to derive broad-gauged estimates of future travel demand. The various factors and relationships can help to formulate and assess traffic modernization programs and transportation system management plans. They can provide inputs into the urban transportation planning process to check the results of various transportation planning models and to assess key transport investment decisions. They can serve as a benchmark in evaluating changes in characteristics as they relate to revisions in transportation systems and/or availability of energy.

Urban transportation characteristics largely reflect physical, economic, and social conditions for a given point in time. Accordingly, an attempt has been made to introduce new material, such as the U.S. Bureau of the Census Annual Housing Survey (1976) and the U.S. Nationwide Personal Transportation Survey (1970). However, many of the characteristics are derived from the comprehensive urban transportation planning studies conducted during the 1960s—generally after 1965.[1]

The principal focus is on transportation characteristics of U.S. and Canadian cities; however, selective information is provided on cities throughout the world for comparative purposes.

[1]For data before 1965, see J. E. BAERWALD, ed., *Transportation and Traffic Engineering Handbook*, Prentice-Hall, Englewood Cliffs, N.J., 1976, Chap. 5; and H. S. LEVINSON, *Characteristics of Urban Transportation Demand, A Handbook for Transportation Planners*, Urban Mass Transportation Administration, Washington, D.C., Apr. 1978.

Characteristics of cities

The social, demographic and land-use characteristics of the modern North American urban region influence the travel behavior of its residents and demands for transportation facilities. This region is usually characterized by continuing growth in population and area of urbanization, a proliferation of commercial and industrial centers, an increase in car ownership that outpaces population growth, and a relative decline in certain types of central business district activities. These patterns were most pronounced during the 1950s and 1960s, although many of the trends continue, sometimes at a slower rate.

On a global basis, rates of national economic and population growth are translated into urban growth. In many cases, there are corresponding increases in car ownership, car use, transit ridership, and congestion.

Population and density

Each urban area reflects historical, social, and economic antecedents. Likenesses and differences among cities relate primarily to economic base, topography, and age.

Population density patterns generally reflect city age and the modes of intraurban transport that prevailed during formative years. Consequently, cities in Europe, Asia, and South America generally exhibit higher densities than do American cities. Table 10-1 compares densities in large American, European, and Asian cities during two periods—1920 or before, and 1960–1975.

Within the United States, New York, Chicago, Philadelphia, Boston, and San Francisco were the only large central cities with densities exceeding 13,000 persons/mi^2 (5000 persons/km^2) in 1975. In Canada, Montreal and Toronto had central city densities of approximately 17,000 persons/mi^2 (6600 persons/km^2). Central-city population

TABLE 10–1
Population and Density of Selected Major Cities

United States and Canada				
Central City	Year	Population	Area (mi^2)	Density ($persons/mi^2$)
New York (Manhattan)	1920	2,284,000	22	103,818
New York (Manhattan)	1975	1,429,033	22	64,956
New York City	1923	5,927,625	299	19,825
New York City	1975	7,481,613	300	24,944
Chicago	1923	2,886,971	195	14,805
Philadelphia	1923	1,922,788	127	15,141
Chicago	1975	3,099,391	223	13,911
Los Angeles	1975	2,727,399	464	5,879
Philadelphia	1975	1,815,808	128	14,131
Detroit	1975	1,335,805	138	9,675
Houston	1975	1,326,809	484	2,744
Montreal	1976	1,080,546	61	17,714
Baltimore	1975	851,698	78	10,877
Dallas	1975	812,797	270	3,006
San Diego	1975	773,996	323	2,397
San Antonio	1975	773,248	264	2,935
Washington, D.C.	1975	711,518	61	11,588
Toronto	1976	633,318	38	16,888

Rest of World				
Central City	Year	Population	Area (mi^2)	Density ($persons/mi^2$)
London (excluding outer ring)	1921	4,848,523	117	38,329
Greater London	1977	6,970,100	610	11,400
Paris	1921	2,856,986	30	95,233
Berlin	1905	2,033,900	29	70,134
Tokyo	1905	1,969,833	30	65,661
Moscow	1902	1,092,360	32	34,136
Glasgow	1921	1,034,174	30	34,472
Shanghai	1976	10,820,000	345	31,400
Tokyo	1977	8,323,000	222	37,500
Moscow	1960	6,046,000	338	17,900
Seoul	1975	5,510,000	142	38,800
Osaka	1960	5,158,010	123	41,935
Calcutta	1975	4,200,000	49	85,700
Bombay	1960	3,000,000	26	115,400
Buenos Aires	1970	2,972,453	79	38,600
Paris	1975	2,299,830	41	56,100
London (city)	1974	2,145,185	117	18,300
Berlin, West	1977	1,926,800	185	10,400
Rio de Janeiro	1975	1,800,000	49	36,700
Berlin, East	1977	1,118,142	156	7,200

SOURCE: Compiled from U.S. and world census data in:
JOHN C. WEAVER AND FRED E. LUKERMANN, *World Resource Statistics,* Briggs Publishing Co., Minneapolis, Minn., 1953;
UNIVERSITY OF CALIFORNIA, International Urban Research, Institute of International Studies, *The World's Metropolitan Areas,* University of California Press, Berkeley, Calif., 1959;
HERBERT B. DORAU AND ALBERT G. HINMAN, *Urban Land Economics,* Macmillan, New York, 1928;
HERBERT S. LEVINSON AND F. HOUSTON WYNN, "Effects of Density on Urban Transportation Requirements, Community Values as Affected by Transportation," *Highway Res. Rec. No. 2,* Highway Research Board, Washington, D.C., 1963, p. 40;
County and City Data Book, 1977: U.S. Department of Commerce, Bureau of the Census, and 1976 Census of Canada;
PETER HALL, *The World Cities,* World University Library, McGraw-Hill, New York, 1966;
UITP Handbook of Urban Transport, compiled by Lee H. Rogerson in collaboration with the Documentation Center of UITP, 1975, Brussels, Belgium;
The Statesmans Year Book, 1979–80, ed. John Paxton, St. Martins Press, New York;
J. MICHAEL THOMPSON, *Great Cities and Their Traffic,* Lowe and Brydone, Thetford, Norfolk, U.K., 1977;
Europe Year Book, 1979, A World Survey, Europe Publications, London.

density generally relates to the year when the city population first reached 350,000.

Population density reflects the types and mix of dwelling units in each city. The mix between single-family and multifamily units depends on the family life cycle, housing market conditions, and land cost and/or availability, as well as city age, economy, and topography. New York City, for example, contains a high proportion of five (or more)-family apartments; Baltimore and Philadelphia contain high proportions of row houses. Single-family houses predominate in Houston and Dallas despite a rise in apartment construction.

In most cities, net residential density declines exponentially with increasing distance/time from a principal city center:[2] that is,

$$d_x = d_0 e^{-bx} \tag{10.1}$$

where d_x = density at distance x from the city center

d_0 = density at distance 0 (central density)

b = density gradient

[2]A high rate of decline shows that the city is compact, whereas a low-density gradient (increasingly typical of North American cities) reflects a dispersed development pattern. See, for example, T. F. C. CLARK, "Urban Population Densities," *J. R. Stat. Soc., Ser. A, 114,* 490–496 (1951).

Car ownership increases with rising income and with decreasing density. The proportion of one-car households is approximately the same at all density levels; however, the proportion of multicar households is highest in suburban areas. The highest densities of car ownership (i.e., cars per square mile) are usually found in old central cities. Philadelphia and Boston, with almost 15,000 persons/mi^2 (5800 persons/km^2), average 4000 cars/mi^2 (1550 cars/km^2), but Los Angeles, with 6000 persons/mi^2 (2300 persons/km^2), averages fewer than 3000 cars/mi^2 (1150 cars/km^2).

Land use

Urban land uses in major U.S. metropolitan areas are summarized in Table 10-2. Generally, approximately 33% to 50% of all developed land is devoted to residential purposes; about 25% for streets; 6% for transportation, communication, and utilities (other than streets); 6% for manufacturing; and up to 5% for commercial uses. The proportion of land devoted to public open space and institutional uses generally ranges from 10% to 25%. These land-use studies indicate that street rights-of-way occupy one-fourth to one-third of all developed land regardless of

TABLE 10–2
Land Use in Selected Urban Areas, United States* (%)

Land Use	Los Angeles 1960: 5,776,000 Acres	Chicago, 1970: 2,973,650 Acres	New York Tristate Region, Intensively Developed Area, 1963: 2,344,480 Acres	Atlanta, 1961: 1,238,634 Acres	Buffalo, 1962: 996,941 Acres	Washington, D.C.–Md.–Va., 1968: 785,660 Acres	Philadelphia, 1960: 752,010 Acres	Minneapolis –St Paul, 1958: 569,458 Acres	Baltimore, 1963: 498,366 Acres
Developed land									
Residential	38.3	35.8	53.8	51.7	40.1	41.6	47.6	41.8	39.3
Commercial	4.2	3.5	4.0	3.9	4.5	4.7	3.8	3.0	2.8
Manufacturing	9.6	4.4	2.8	5.0	4.9	3.5	6.9	3.0	16.5
Transportation–communications–utilities	2.4	10.8	3.6	†	8.4	‡	3.8	8.1	—
Public and semipublic bldgs.	—	8.6	4.5	4.2	3.3	19.5	6.1	3.7	13.5
Open space	24.0	15.5	13.7	6.1	14.7	11.2	16.7	11.3	11.3
Parking and miscellaneous	—	0.3	—	—	—	—	—	—	—
Streets and alleys	21.5	19.4	17.6	29.1	24.1	19.5	15.1	29.1	16.6
	100.0	100.0	100.0	100.0	100.0	100.0	100.0	100.0	100.0
Total area									
Developed land	16.7	31.5	53.8	18.6	19.9	44.0	47.1	27.9	36.2
Vacant or not in urban use	83.3	68.5	46.2	81.4	86.1	56.0	52.9	72.1	63.8
	100.0	100.0	100.0	100.0	100.0	100.0	100.0	100.0	100.0

Land Use	Detroit, 1953: 436,121 Acres	Tucson, 1959: 390,631 Acres	Pittsburgh, 1958: 268,570 Acres	Nashville, 1957: 150,195 Acres	South Bend, 1967: 120,404 Acres	Chattanooga, 1960: 90,085 Acres	Average (Bartholomew) 53 Central Cities	33 Satellite Cities	11 Urban Areas
Developed land									
Residential	45.6	32.0	44.5	53.2	47.5	51.3	39.6	42.2	28.0
Commercial	2.5	7.4	3.5	3.1	2.2	3.9	3.3	2.5	2.6
Manufacturing	9.1	3.6	4.5	3.5	3.0	13.5	6.4	7.8	5.7
Transportation–communications–utilities	—	10.1	5.8	6.9	9.4§	—	4.8	4.6	6.2
Public and semipublic bldgs.	4.4	8.2	5.3	19.2	0.7	5.4	17.7**	15.3**	29.9**
Open space	5.4	5.7	11.4	—	8.4	2.0‖	—	—	—
Parking and miscellaneous	2.2	—	—	—	—	—	—	—	—
Streets and alleys	30.8	33.0	25.0	14.1	28.8	23.9	28.2	27.6	27.6
	100.0	100.0	100.0	100.0	100.0	100.0	100.0	100.0	100.0
Total area									
Developed land	48.1	12.6	43.4	49.1	31.3	39.7			
Vacant or not in urban use	51.9	87.4	56.6	50.9	68.7	60.3			
	100.0	100.0	100.0	100.0	100.0	100.0			

*1 acre = 4050 m^2.
§Service.
‡Included in streets.
†Included with manufacturing.
‖Recreational.
**Includes open space.

SOURCE: Specific data compiled from land-use and origin–destination studies in each urban area. Average data from HARLAND BARTHOLOMEW, *Land Uses in American Cities*, Harvard University Press, Cambridge, Mass., 1955. Data also from comprehensive metropolitan area transportation studies.

city size and density. This proportion has not changed appreciably even where freeways have been built. (In the Los Angeles and New York metropolitan areas, less than one-fourth of all land is devoted to streets, but within New York City's five boroughs, streets occupy more than one-third of all developed land).

L'Enfant's Washington, D.C., plan dedicated 49% of all land to arterial streets; Captain John Sutter's Sacramento plan reserved approximately 38% for street use.[3] In contrast, portions of Sacramento laid out between 1900 and 1930 allocated only 21% of their area to streets, and some new areas developed in North America since World War II have reserved only 15% of the subdivided land for transportation purposes.

Car ownership

Car ownership varies among cities throughout the world depending upon per capita incomes. The number of persons per car is reported as 82 in Bombay, 58 in Djakarta, 45 in Bogota, and 11 in Nairobi and Caracas (Table 10-3). In contrast, there was one passenger car for every two persons in the United States in 1978.

[3]K. MOSKOWITZ, "Living and Travel Patterns in Automobile Oriented Cities," *The Dynamics of Urban Transportation*, Symposium sponsored by the Automobile Manufacturers Association, Inc., Detroit, Mich., Oct. 23–24, 1962.

TABLE 10–3
Automobile Registrations in Selected Cities in Lesser Developed Countries

City	Year	Population (× 10⁶)		Registered Automobiles (× 10³)		Persons/Car		City's % of National Total	
		National	City	National	City	National	City	Population	Automobiles
Abidjan	1968	4.1	0.51	43.9	30.9	93	16.5	12.5	70.4
Bangkok	1966	31.7	2.50	99.0	72.0	320	34.8	7.9	72.8
Bogota	1969	20.2	2.34	146.0	52.0	138	45.0	11.6	35.6
Bombay	1966	475.0	5.00	420.0	61.0	1,131	82.0	1.1	14.5
Caracas	1966	8.9	1.72	420.0	151.5	21	11.3	19.3	36.1
Djakarta	1969	118.0	4.50	212.2	77.2	557	58.0	3.8	36.6
Nairobi	1965	9.5	0.45	70.0	41.6	135	10.8	4.7	59.4
San Jose (C.R.)	1966	1.5	0.19	27.2	13.0	56	14.2	12.3	48.1
São Paulo	1967	86.6	5.25	1,417.9	366.1	61	14.4	6.1	25.8
Tehran	1966	25.1	2.71	174.0	85.5	144	31.7	10.8	49.1

SOURCE: Automobile Manufacturers Association, *Facts and Figures*, and World Bank documents, as reported in *Urbanization Sector Working Paper*, World Bank, June, 1972.

Expressed in slightly different terms, almost 85% of all families in the United States own at least one automobile, and approximately 35% of the total family units own two or more automobiles. Approximately 73% of all family units in central cities and 84% in metropolitan areas owned one or more cars in 1976 (Table 10-4). (Although the estimates of car ownership vary among different sample surveys and sources, the range is not great, and all studies indicate the same general findings).

Effect of household characteristics. The effects of family size; age, occupation, and education of family head; housing tenure; and family income are shown in Table 10-5. Homeowners are more likely to own a vehicle than are renters, larger families than smaller families. Heads of households with some college education are likely to own at least one vehicle; probable two-car ownership is greatest in families where the head of household is between 25 and 54 years old; the lowest ownership is in the 65-and-over bracket. Seventy percent of families with incomes of $4000 to $5000 have cars; over 95% of all families with incomes over $12,000 own cars.

A more detailed distribution of U.S. car and truck ownership by household income for 1974 is shown in Table 10-6. Motor vehicle ownership rises with increasing income, especially the proportion of multicar households. These patterns provide a general guide to estimating car and truck ownership for various household income levels, provided that appropriate adjustments are made to reflect inflation.

Drivers' licenses in metropolitan areas. The proportions of persons 16 years of age and older with drivers' licenses in U.S. metropolitan areas of various size groups are shown in Table 10-7. These data, based upon the Nationwide Personal Transportation Survey, suggest a generally declining percentage with increasing population, except for very small towns. Income, density, socioeconomic conditions, and transit system characteristics probably account for the lower number of licensed drivers in the very large metropolitan areas.

Travel characteristics

The urban travel patterns and characteristics that follow were assembled from a variety of sources. These include (1) U.S. Census Travel Surveys, (2) comprehensive metropolitan area origin–destination and land-use studies, (3) Nationwide Personal Transportation Survey (U.S.), (4) Institute of Transportation Engineers Trip Generation Research, (5) usage characteristics of urban road and transit systems, and (6) special studies of urban goods movement. Collectively, these studies provide information on the nature of urban trip-making and travel behavior. They show how

TABLE 10–4
Households with Automobiles and Trucks, United States, 1976 (%)

Category	Automobiles					Light Trucks			
	None	One or More	One	Two	Three or More	None	One or More	One	Two or More
Region									
Northeast	21.9	78.1	44.8	26.4	6.9	89.7	10.3	9.5	0.8
North Central	13.4	86.6	47.8	31.1	7.7	78.7	21.3	19.3	2.0
South	16.0	84.0	49.1	27.8	7.1	73.4	26.6	24.3	2.3
West	13.8	86.2	50.2	28.3	7.7	72.0	28.0	24.7	3.3
Residence									
Metropolitan area	17.1	82.9	45.5	29.6	7.8	84.2	15.8	14.5	1.3
Central cities	26.7	73.3	45.4	22.5	5.4	89.0	11.0	10.2	0.8
Suburban rings	9.2	90.8	45.6	35.5	9.7	80.2	19.8	18.1	1.7
Outside metropolitan area	14.3	85.7	53.3	26.0	6.4	65.2	34.8	31.0	3.8
Total U.S.	16.3	83.7	48.0	28.4	7.3	78.2	21.8	19.7	2.1

SOURCE: U.S. Bureau of the Census, *Current Housing Reports, Annual Housing Survey: 1976*, Washington, D.C.

TABLE 10–5

Family Ownership of Vehicles, by Selected Family Characteristics, United States, 1972–1974

Category	Number of Families (× 10³)	Average Number of Vehicles Owned	Percent Owning at Least One Vehicle
Region			
Northeast	17,103	1.1	74
Northcentral	19,780	1.3	82
South	21,979	1.3	79
West	12,869	1.4	83
Urbanization group			
Total inside SMSA	50,076	1.2	78
Urban	44,868	1.2	76
Central city	23,541	1.0	67
Other urban	21,326	1.4	87
Rural	5,209	1.7	92
Outside SMSA	21,655	1.4	82
Urban	9,082	1.2	78
Rural	12,573	1.5	85
Family size			
1 person	17,080	0.6	53
2 persons	20,403	1.2	84
3 persons	11,563	1.5	87
4 persons	10,471	1.7	91
5 persons	6,392	1.8	92
6 persons or more	5,822	1.7	88
Age of family head			
Under 25	6,478	1.0	77
25–34	14,457	1.4	87
35–44	11,590	1.6	88
45–54	13,227	1.6	87
55–64	11,551	1.3	81
65 and over	14,428	0.8	58
Occupation of family head			
Self-employed workers	5,304	1.8	93
Salaried and wage earners	46,294	1.5	89
Professionals and Managers	13,467	1.6	94
Clerical and sales workers	7,517	1.3	85
Craftsmen and operatives	16,937	1.6	92
Laborers and service workers	8,372	1.1	77
Occupation of Family head			
Salaried and wage earners			
Armed forces personnel	855	1.5	96
Retired	11,667	0.7	56
All other and not reported	7,611	0.6	45
Education of family head			
Elementary			
1–8 years	16,148	1.0	66
High school			
1–3 years	11,524	1.3	79
Graduate 4 years	20,781	1.4	87
College			
1–3 years	9,800	1.4	89
Graduate 4 years	5,957	1.5	91
More than 4 years	4,726	1.5	93
No school and not reported	2,797	0.3	19
Housing tenure			
Homeowner	43,135	1.6	90
Renter	25,587	0.9	67
Not reported	3,010	0.3	27
Family income before taxes			
Under $3,000	10,277	0.5	38
$3,000–3,999	3,890	0.7	57
$4,000–4,999	3,680	0.9	71
$5,000–5,999	3,365	1.0	80
$6,000–6,999	3,574	1.2	83
$7,000–7,999	3,302	1.2	87
$8,000–9,999	6,449	1.4	91
$10,000–11,999	6,524	1.5	94
$12,000–14,999	7,659	1.7	96
$15,000–19,999	7,847	1.8	97
$20,000–24,999	3,461	2.0	98
$25,000 and over	3,372	2.1	98
Not reported	8,331	1.2	72
All families	71,731	1.3	79

SOURCE: U.S. BUREAU OF LABOR STATISTICS, *Consumer Expenditure Survey: Diary Survey, July 1972–June 1974*, Bull. 1959, Washington, D.C.

TABLE 10–6

Automobile Ownership by Household Income, United States, 1974 (%)

Household Income	No Car	One or More Cars	One Car	Two Cars	Three or More Cars	One or More Light Trucks	One or More Motor Vehicles
Under $3,000	56.8	43.2	37.0	5.5	0.7	7.8	46.2
$3,000–4,999	39.3	60.7	51.9	8.0	0.8	11.0	64.2
$5,000–7,499	24.0	76.0	60.4	13.6	2.0	14.3	79.4
$7,500–9,999	15.0	85.0	61.9	20.9	2.2	16.8	88.3
$10,000–14,999	8.3	91.7	54.9	32.4	4.4	22.2	93.9
$15,000–19,999	4.5	95.5	45.4	42.3	7.8	22.7	96.7
$20,000–24,999	3.1	96.9	36.8	46.9	13.2	19.2	97.4
$25,000 and over	3.3	96.7	29.5	45.7	21.5	17.2	97.2

SOURCE: U.S. DEPARTMENT OF COMMERCE, Bureau of the Census, "Consumer Buying Indicators, 1974 Survey of Purchases and Ownership," in *Motor Vehicle Facts and Figures*, Washington, D.C., 1977, p. 38.

TABLE 10–7

Persons 16 Years of Age and Older with Drivers' Licenses in SMSAs by Population Size Groups, United States, 1970

SMSA Population Size Group	Persons with Licenses (%)
Under 100,000	72.9
100,000–249,999	78.7
250,000–499,999	75.0
500,000–999,999	72.0
1,000,000–1,999,999	76.1
2,000,000–2,999,999	71.5
3,000,000 and over	65.1
All SMSAs	72.2*

*Percentage based on 92,395,824 persons.

SOURCE: Unpublished Table H-1.1, *Nationwide Personal Transportation Survey*, Bureau of the Census, Federal Highway Administration, Washington, D.C., 1969–1970.

the number, length, purpose, mode, and orientation of urban trips relate to (1) land-use patterns, (2) socioeconomic characteristics, and (3) available transportation services.

Summary patterns: United States and Canada

National overview. The U.S. Bureau of the Census Journey-to-Work Surveys are summarized in Table 10-8. In 1976, the following travel patterns characterized U.S. metropolitan areas (Table 10-8):

TABLE 10–8
Characteristics of Household Heads' Transportation to Work, United States, 1976 (%)

		Place of Residence							
		Inside SMSA*				Regions			
	Total U.S.	In Central Cities	Not in Central Cities	Total SMSA	Outside SMSA	Northeast	North Central	South	West
Principal means of transportation to work									
Drives self	70.9	66.0	75.9	71.8	68.8	64.6	72.5	71.7	74.4
Carpool	15.5	12.5	15.3	14.1	18.7	13.5	13.9	18.8	14.7
Mass transportation	5.5	13.2	3.6	7.6	0.5	13.5	3.8	2.6	3.5
Bicycle and motorcycle	0.7	1.0	0.7	0.8	0.7	0.3	0.7	0.7	1.5
Taxi	0.2	0.3	0.0	0.2	0.2	0.3	0.1	0.2	0.1
Walk	3.9	5.1	2.2	3.4	4.9	5.4	4.1	3.0	3.2
Other means	0.6	0.5	0.4	0.5	0.8	0.5	0.3	0.8	0.6
Works at home	2.6	1.1	1.6	1.4	5.4	1.8	4.3	2.2	1.9
Not reported	0.2	0.2	0.2	0.2	0.2	0.2	0.2	0.2	0.1
Total	100.0	100.0	100.0	100.0	100.0	100.0	100.0	100.0	100.0
Distance† from home to work									
Less than 1 mi‡	10.8	8.6	6.7	7.5	18.5	10.8	13.3	10.1	8.8
1–4 mi	26.4	32.9	20.5	25.7	27.9	25.9	27.5	25.8	26.3
5–9 mi	17.4	21.8	18.0	19.6	12.3	16.8	16.8	17.6	18.6
10–29 mi	27.1	23.4	35.4	30.4	19.7	28.6	25.6	26.9	28.1
30–49 mi	4.2	1.7	5.0	3.6	5.4	5.0	3.6	4.2	3.9
50 mi or more	1.3	0.6	1.1	0.9	2.4	1.5	0.9	1.6	1.4
No fixed place of work	11.2	9.2	12.0	10.8	12.0	9.9	10.7	12.0	12.0
Not reported	1.6	1.8	1.2	1.5	1.7	1.6	1.6	1.9	1.0
Total	100.0	100.0	100.0	100.0	100.0	100.0	100.0	100.0	100.0
Travel time from home to work									
Less than 15 min	31.3	29.4	25.6	27.2	40.6	28.6	33.5	30.8	31.8
15–29 min	30.7	36.4	32.9	34.2	22.6	29.0	29.8	31.6	32.5
30–44 min	13.7	13.8	16.7	15.5	9.7	15.5	12.8	13.6	13.3
45–59 min	4.8	4.6	5.7	5.2	3.8	6.4	4.4	4.4	4.2
60–89 min	3.4	3.5	3.7	3.6	3.0	5.9	2.9	3.0	2.5
90 min or more	1.0	1.0	0.9	1.0	1.2	1.8	0.6	1.0	0.9
Works at home	2.6	1.1	1.6	1.4	5.4	1.8	4.3	2.2	1.9
No fixed place of work	11.2	9.2	12.0	10.8	12.0	9.9	10.7	12.0	12.0
Not reported	1.2	1.0	1.1	1.0	1.6	1.0	1.3	1.4	0.9
Total	100.0	100.0	100.0	100.0	100.0	100.0	100.0	100.0	100.0
Households with vehicles available§									
Automobiles									
1	48.0	45.4	45.6	45.3	53.3	44.8	47.8	49.1	50.2
2	28.4	22.5	35.5	29.6	26.0	26.3	31.1	27.8	28.3
3 or more	7.3	5.4	9.7	7.8	6.4	6.9	7.7	7.1	7.7
None	16.2	26.7	9.1	17.1	14.3	22.0	13.4	16.0	13.7
Total	100.0	100.0	100.0	100.0	100.0	100.0	100.0	100.0	100.0
Trucks									
1	19.7	10.2	18.0	14.5	31.0	9.5	19.3	24.3	24.7
2	2.1	0.8	1.7	1.3	3.8	0.8	2.0	2.3	3.3
None	78.2	88.9	80.2	84.2	65.3	89.7	78.7	73.3	72.0
Total	100.0	100.0	100.0	100.0	100.0	100.0	100.0	100.0	100.0
Households (× 10^3)	74,005	22,930	27,522	50,452	23,553	16,544	19,723	23,741	13,997

*SMSA, Standard Metropolitan Statistical Area.
†Distance refers to one-way distance. 1 mi = 1.609 km.
‡Includes those who work at home.
§Statistics on automobiles available represent the number of passenger automobiles, wagons, which are owned or regularly used by any member of the household and which are ordinarily kept at home. The figures include leased automobiles, and company-owned automobiles kept at home. The data on trucks available represent the number of pickups and small panel trucks of 1-ton capacity or less which are owned or regularly used by any member of the household and which are ordinarily kept at home. Trucks used for business purposes were included only if also used for personal activities of household members.

SOURCE: U.S. BUREAU OF THE CENSUS, *Current Housing Reports, Annual Housing Survey: 1976,* Washington, D.C.

- 72% of all trips were as auto driver, 14% in a car pool, 8% by transit, and 6% by other means.
- The median distance of the journey to work was less than 9 mi.
- 61% of all trips were less than 30 min.

Commuter travel patterns in 20 large metropolitan areas are shown in Table 10-9. Overall, 76% of the commuters used cars and 18% transit; the remainder mainly walked. Median commuting distances were 7.9 mi for auto drivers, 9.5 mi for auto passengers, 8.8 mi for transit riders, and

TABLE 10–9
Mode of Travel of Commuting Workers* in Selected SMSAs, United States, 1976 (%)

SMSA†	Private Automobile or Truck					Public Transportation	Other Means	Walk
	Total by Automobile or Truck	Drive Alone	Share Driving	Drive Others	Ride with Someone			
Allentown–Bethlehem–Easton, PA-NJ								
Mode of transport (%)	89.9	70.5	6.2	4.4	8.8	1.8	0.4	7.9
Median time (min)	16.6	16.3	23.9	18.9	14.1	25.4	13.1	8.2
Median distance (mi)	5.4	5.4	9.3	4.9	3.9	4.0	2.2	0.6
Baltimore, MD.								
Mode of transport (%)	82.7	61.2	7.3	5.8	8.4	11.6	0.6	5.1
Median time (min)	23.1	21.9	32.9	27.3	22.4	39.7	15.8	9.1
Median distance (mi)	10.0	9.4	19.2	10.9	8.4	6.5	3.3	0.6
Birmingham, AL								
Mode of transport (%)	93.5	75.6	5.4	3.6	9.0	3.2	0.7	2.5
Median time (min)	20.7	20.2	31.1	23.6	19.8	33.7	12.0	8.1
Median distance (mi)	8.7	8.4	15.2	11.5	7.3	9.5	3.8	0.6
Buffalo, NY								
Mode of transport (%)	87.9	72.8	3.9	3.1	6.6	5.5	1.1	5.5
Median time (min)	17.9	17.8	23.4	19.6	15.4	27.3	19.1	0.9
Median distance (mi)	6.4	6.3	11.3	7.3	4.4	4.5	3.1	0.8
Cleveland, OH								
Mode of transport (%)	84.0	68.7	4.7	4.4	4.8	11.1	1.2	3.6
Median time (min)	21.2	21.0	25.5	25.8	19.6	32.7	29.8	8.2
Median distance (mi)	8.2	8.1	11.5	8.9	6.4	8.2	6.2	0.7
Denver, CO								
Mode of transport (%)	87.3	69.4	9.0	3.8	4.7	5.3	2.3	5.2
Median time (min)	19.5	19.0	23.6	20.4	18.1	28.4	16.1	9.4
Median distance (mi)	8.2	7.9	11.6	8.4	6.1	7.8	4.0	0.6
Grand Rapids, MI								
Mode of transport (%)	91.7	74.9	7.0	3.1	6.2	1.3	2.2	4.8
Median time (min)	16.0	15.5	21.1	19.3	13.9	23.2	14.4	7.6
Median distance (mi)	6.7	6.3	11.2	9.4	5.0	4.7	3.4	0.6
Honolulu, HI								
Mode of transport (%)	82.6	57.4	5.0	9.7	10.4	11.4	2.0	4.0
Median time (min)	21.4	20.8	26.9	25.5	19.8	29.0	16.4	9.3
Median distance (mi)	7.4	7.3	11.2	8.5	5.5	4.8	3.3	0.6
Houston, TX								
Mode of transport (%)	92.5	70.4	8.2	5.0	8.3	3.7	1.2	2.7
Median time (min)	21.7	20.9	27.3	26.1	21.4	35.8	14.1	7.5
Median distance (mi)	9.6	9.1	13.6	12.0	9.5	9.5	3.5	0.6
Indianapolis, IN								
Mode of transport (%)	93.3	71.3	5.4	6.5	9.7	3.0	0.6	3.2
Median time (min)	20.8	20.1	27.5	26.3	19.6	29.7	18.7	7.4
Median distance (mi)	7.7	7.5	13.9	9.4	5.7	4.8	3.5	0.6
Las Vegas, NV								
Mode of transport (%)	93.1	75.9	5.5	4.1	7.6	2.1	2.1	2.6
Median time (min)	16.6	16.4	19.3	17.6	16.6	90.0	16.5	8.3
Median distance (mi)	6.1	5.9	7.7	6.8	6.3	13.8	4.4	0.6
Louisville, KY–IN								
Mode of transport (%)	91.6	72.0	5.2	5.6	8.0	4.9	1.0	2.4
Median time (min)	20.4	19.7	28.4	24.3	19.0	31.2	17.8	9.6
Median distance (mi)	8.1	7.9	12.8	9.0	6.1	7.0	4.4	0.6
New York, NY								
Mode of transport (%)	47.0	36.3	3.7	2.4	4.0	44.4	0.7	7.9
Median time (min)	21.9	21.3	28.6	23.2	21.4	42.0	17.2	10.4
Median distance (mi)	8.6	8.3	13.3	9.7	7.4	9.4	3.8	0.6
Oklahoma City, OK								
Mode of transport (%)	95.1	76.4	6.6	4.5	6.9	0.7	1.4	2.7
Median time (min)	18.5	17.7	23.6	23.3	19.0	35.7	13.2	7.6
Median distance (mi)	7.3	6.9	11.1	10.5	6.8	8.5	2.8	0.6
Omaha, NE–IO								
Mode of transport (%)	90.1	68.1	6.9	5.2	9.1	4.7	1.3	3.9
Median time (min)	17.0	16.8	19.4	20.5	15.2	32.0	11.6	8.5
Median distance (mi)	5.9	5.9	7.0	6.5	4.5	5.0	3.0	0.6
Providence–Pawtucket–Warwick, RI-MA								
Mode of transport (%)	91.0	70.1	5.6	5.6	9.3	3.4	0.6	5.1
Median time (min)	17.1	17.2	25.7	17.8	12.8	22.3	13.9	8.1
Median distance (mi)	6.1	6.4	13.5	4.7	3.9	3.8	3.6	0.6
Raleigh, NC								
Mode of transport (%)	94.6	70.3	9.9	5.4	9.0	1.8	0.9	2.7
Median time (min)	17.6	17.0	21.3	22.6	16.3	21.7	17.1	8.7
Median distance (mi)	7.2	6.7	10.7	9.3	5.8	4.0	3.3	0.6
Sacramento, CA								
Mode of transport (%)	91.3	74.1	5.8	4.4	6.7	2.3	4.1	2.3
Median time (min)	18.0	17.6	21.4	21.6	17.3	30.3	13.8	8.1
Median distance (mi)	7.8	7.5	11.3	9.6	7.7	10.3	2.7	0.5

TABLE 10–9 (Continued)
Mode of Travel of Commuting Workers* in Selected SMSAs, United States, 1976 (%)

SMSA†	Private Automobile or Truck: Total by Automobile or Truck	Drive Alone	Share Driving	Drive Others	Ride with Someone	Public Trans-portation	Other Means	Walk
St. Louis, MO–IL								
Mode of transport (%)	90.4	68.3	8.0	5.0	8.6	4.6	1.2	3.8
Median time (min)	20.6	19.5	29.2	25.3	19.7	32.1	14.0	7.7
Median distance (mi)	9.0	8.3	16.4	10.7	7.8	7.2	2.8	0.6
Seattle–Everett, WA								
Mode of transport (%)	87.0	69.1	7.5	4.1	6.1	8.0	1.4	3.4
Median time (min)	20.1	19.6	26.6	23.6	18.2	32.1	16.2	9.2
Median distance (mi)	9.5	9.1	14.7	11.3	7.8	7.9	3.9	0.6

*Excludes those who work at home—less than 100% represented in total of all modes.
†SMSA, Standard Metropolitan Statistical Area. 1 mi = 1.609 km.

SOURCE: U.S. BUREAU OF THE CENSUS, *Current Population Reports, Selected Characteristics of Travel to Work in 20 Metropolitan Areas: 1976,* Washington, D.C.

0.6 mi for pedestrians. Median travel times were 9.2 min for pedestrians; 19.6 min for auto drivers; 22.7 min for auto passengers; and 39.5 min for transit riders. Transit accounted for 44% of all trips in New York City; about 11% to 12% in Cleveland, Baltimore, and Honolulu; and less than 10% in the other 17 cities summarized.

Travel characteristics of nonpedestrian person trips as reported in origin–destination surveys are summarized in Tables 10-10 to 10-13. These tables provide a basis for comparing results of surveys in other communities, and for cross-checking the reasonableness of forecasts. Salient findings and guidelines are as follows:

1. In most North American cities, more than two-thirds of all person-trips are made by car. The proportion of trips made by public transport tends to increase as the population and/or density increases. (The location of survey area boundaries influences the modal distribution since a "tight" cordon line generally produces a higher proportion of trips by transit; Tables 10-10 and 10-11).
2. Average car occupancy has been relatively constant in U.S. and Canadian cities at approximately 1.5 persons/car. The range is from 1.4 to 1.6 (Table 10-11). Energy-conservation efforts are likely to change this to an unknown degree.
3. Trucks in U.S. and Canadian cities constitute approximately 15% of all vehicle trips, ranging from 10% to 21% (Table 10-11).

Trip-generation overview. The typical urban resident in U.S. and Canadian cities averages about 2.5 trips/day in vehicles (Table 10-12). There is, however, a wide variation among cities, depending on city size, structure, economy, auto ownership levels, and year of study.

Generally, individuals in smaller communities report more trips than do residents in larger ones. The number of daily trips in vehicles decreases gradually as city size and/or density rises. There is, however, considerable variation among cities in the same population range; the year of study and sampling variability also influence trip rates.

In large cities, such as Chicago, Philadelphia, and Detroit, the urban resident averages 2 to 2.5 trips daily in

TABLE 10–10
Travel Modes of Urban Residents

Urban Area	Year	Study Area Population* (× 10³)	Daily Person-Trips (× 10³): Auto	Transit†	Percent: Auto	Transit†
New York, NY (tristate)	1963	16,302	19,840	9,730	67.1	32.9
Los Angeles, CA	1967	9,008	19,819	759	96.3	3.7
Chicago, IL (expanded area)	1970	7,593	15,961	2,655	85.7	14.3
Chicago, IL (1956 area)	1970	n.a.	10,974	1,976	84.7	15.3
San Francisco, CA	1965	4,400	8,953	933	90.6	9.4
Detroit, MI	1965	4,042	9,357	452	95.4	4.6
Philadelphia, PA	1960	4,007	6,477	1,283	83.5	16.5
Boston, MA	1963	3,584	6,351	1,500	80.2	19.8
Washington, DC	1968	2,714	5,222	657	88.8	11.2
Pittsburgh, PA	1967	2,601	3,712	763	83.0	17.0
Cleveland, OH	1963	2,140	4,477	539	89.3	10.7
Minneapolis–St. Paul, MN	1970	1,874	4,933	162	96.2	3.8
Dallas, TX	1964	1,821	5,062	198	96.2	3.8
Milwaukee, WI	1972	1,811	4,122	383	91.5	8.5
Toronto, ON	1964	1,800	3,124	753	80.6	19.4
Atlanta, GA	1972	1,640	3,662	425	89.6	10.4
Baltimore, MD	1962	1,608	2,150	455	82.5	17.5
Cincinnati, OH	1965	1,392	2,738	287	90.6	9.4
Buffalo, NY	1962	1,350	2,476	284	90.3	9.7
Miami, FL	1964	1,187	2,391	165	93.6	6.4
Denver, CO	1971	1,116	3,097	58	58.2	1.8
San Diego, CA	1966	1,180	2,839	107	96.4	3.6
Sacramento, CA	1968	774	1,943	108	94.8	5.2
Louisville, KY	1964	752	1,279	78	94.3	5.7
Indianapolis, IN	1964	763	1,462	167	89.8	10.2
San Juan, PR	1964	759	737	439	62.7	37.3
Columbus, OH	1964	734	1,821	90	95.3	4.7
Memphis, TN	1964	648	1,345	85	94.1	5.9
Southeast, VA	1962	602	1,213	141	89.6	10.4
Oklahoma City, OK	1965	574	1,636	87	95.0	5.0
Birmingham, AL	1965	559	1,440	86	94.3	5.7
Jacksonville, FL	1968	547	1,276	45	96.6	3.4
Springfield, MA	1965	531	1,034	119	89.7	10.3
Richmond, VA	1964	418	799	124	86.6	13.4
Tampa–St. Petersburg, FL	1965	396	908	19	97.9	2.1
Orlando, FL	1965	356	899	23	97.5	2.5
Lehigh Valley, PA	1964	345	629	59	91.4	8.6
Fresno–Clovis, CA	1971	295	857	32	96.4	3.6
Mobile, AL	1966	280	755	15	98.0	2.0
Peoria, IL	1964	261	782	10	98.7	1.3
Baton Rouge, LA	1965	245	568	47	92.3	7.7
Charleston, SC	1965	236	547	54	91.0	9.0
South Bend, IN	1967	222	636	39	94.3	5.7
Columbia, SC	1964	196	496	36	93.3	6.7
Stockton, CA	1967	170	401	18	95.8	4.2
Springfield, IL	1964	138	318	15	95.6	4.4

*n.a., not available.
†School bus included with transit where identified.

SOURCE: Comprehensive urban area transportation planning studies.

TABLE 10–11
Travel Modes, Car Occupancies, and Truck Trips, Selected Urban Areas

			Daily Person-Trips (× 10³)				Percent by:			Daily Vehicle Trips‡		
Urban Area*	Year	Study Area Population	Auto Driver	Auto, Truck, Taxi Passengers	Transit† Passengers	Total	Auto	Transit†	Average Car Occupancy	Truck-Trips	Total Vehicle-Trips	Percent Trucks
Los Angeles, CA	1967	9,008,400	14,098	5,721	759	20,578	96.3	3.7	1.41	1,612	15,710	10.2
Chicago, IL	1970	7,593,000	10,935	5,026	2,655	18,616	85.7	14.3	1.46	n.a.	n.a.	n.a.
Detroit, MI	1965	4,041,800	6,439	2,918	452	9,809	95.4	4.6	1.45	920	7,359	12.5
Philadelphia, PA	1960	4,007,000	4,309	2,168	1,283	7,760	83.5	16.5	1.50	990	5,299	18.6
Boston, MA	1963	3,584,400	4,444	1,907	1,500	7,851	80.2	19.8	1.43	878	5,322	16.4
Washington, DC	1968	2,714,000	3,407	1,815	657	5,879	88.3	11.2	1.53	446	3,853	11.6
Pittsburgh, PA	1967	2,601,400	2,528	1,184	763	4,475	83.0	17.0	1.44	449	2,977	15.1
Minne–St. Paul, MN	1970	1,874,400	3,014	1,919	162	5,095	96.2	3.8	1.64	489	3,503	14.0
Dallas, TX	1964	1,821,000	3,338	1,724	198	5,260	96.2	3.8	1.52	418	3,755	11.1
Milwaukee, WI	1972	1,811,000	2,897	1,225	383	4,505	91.5	8.5	1.42	529	3,416	15.5
Toronto, ON	1964	1,800,000	2,244	880	753	3,877	80.5	19.4	1.44	n.a.	n.a.	n.a.
Atlanta, GA	1972	1,640,000	2,501	1,161	425	4,087	89.6	10.4	1.46	n.a.	n.a.	n.a.
Baltimore, MD	1962	1,607,800	1,426	724	455	2,605	82.5	17.5	1.50	378	1,804	20.9
Buffalo, NY	1962	1,350,000	1,588	888	284	2,760	89.8	10.2	1.56	208	1,796	11.6
Cincinnati, OH	1965	1,392,000	1,759	979	287	3,025	90.6	9.4	1.55	397	2,146	18.4
Miami, FL	1964	1,187,300	1,533	858	165	2,556	93.6	6.4	1.56	163	1,696	9.6
Denver, CO	1971	1,116,000	2,133	964	58	3,097	98.2	1.8	1.45	n.a.	n.a.	n.a.
Indianapolis, IN	1964	762,900	1,011	451	167	1,629	89.8	10.2	1.45	175	1,186	14.8
Southeast Virginia	1962	602,000	799	414	141	1,354	89.6	10.4	1.52	119	918	11.3
Oklahoma City, OK	1965	574,000	1,077	559	87	1,723	95.0	5.0	1.52	148	1,255	12.0
Birmingham, AL	1965	559,100	961	479	86	1,527	94.3	5.7	1.51	n.a.	n.a.	n.a.
Springfield, MA	1965	531,000	725	309	119	1,153	89.7	10.3	1.43	81	806	10.0
Richmond, VA	1964	417,600	542	257	124	923	86.6	13.4	1.47	94	636	14.7
Orlando, FL	1965	355,600	594	305	23	922	97.5	2.5	1.51	84	678	12.3
Lehigh Valley, PA	1964	345,100	443	186	59	688	91.4	8.6	1.42	82	525	15.6
Mobile, AL	1966	279,700	450	305	15	770	98.0	2.0	1.57	87	543	16.0
Peoria, IL	1964	260,800	489	293	10	792	98.7	1.3	1.60	65	554	11.7
Baton Rouge, LA	1965	245,000	380	188	47	615	92.3	7.7	1.49	90	470	19.0
Charleston, SC	1965	235,500	380	167	54	681	91.0	9.0	1.44	65	445	14.6
Columbia, SC	1964	196,000	330	166	36	532	93.3	6.7	1.50	52	382	13.6

*Some urban areas appear at two dates.
†School bus included with transit.
‡n.a., not available.

SOURCE: Comprehensive urban area transportation planning studies.

TABLE 10–12
Generation of Travel by Urban Residents, Selected American Cities

Urban Area	Year	Population	Trips/Person	Persons/Car*	Trips/Dwelling	Persons/ Dwelling*	Cars/Dwelling*	Person-Trips by Car (%)
New York (tristate)	1963	16,302,000	1.81	3.89	5.61	3.09	0.79	67.1
Los Angeles, CA	1967	9,008,000	2.26	2.29	6.68	2.93	1.28	96.3
Chicago, IL	1970	7,593,000	2.45	2.83	7.20	2.94	1.04	85.7
San Francisco, CA	1965	4,400,000	2.25	n.a.	n.a.	n.a.	n.a.	90.6
Detroit, MI	1965	4,042,000	2.43	2.67	8.56	3.53	1.32	95.4
Philadelphia, PA	1960	4,007,000	2.03	3.69	6.26	3.08	0.84	83.5
Boston, MA	1963	3,584,000	2.23	3.36	7.33	3.30	0.98	80.2
Washington, DC	1968	2,714,000	2.17	2.58	7.19	3.32	1.29	88.8
Pittsburgh, PA	1967	2,601,000	1.72	3.02	5.71	3.32	1.10	83.0
Cleveland, OH	1963	2,140,000	2.34	2.88	7.72	3.29	1.14	89.3
Minneapolis–St. Paul	1970	1,874,000	2.72	2.62	8.02	3.27	1.25	96.2
Dallas, TX	1964	1,821,000	2.89	2.50	8.92	3.09	1.24	96.2
Milwaukee, WI	1972	1,811,000	2.49	2.60	7.90	3.19	1.23	91.5
Atlanta, GA	1972	1,640,000	2.49	2.10	7.20	2.90	1.38	89.6
Baltimore, MD	1962	1,608,000	1.66	3.61	5.56	3.34	0.92	82.5
Cincinnati, OH	1965	1,392,000	2.17	2.87	7.17	3.30	1.15	80.6
Buffalo, NY	1962	1,350,000	2.04	3.86	7.65	3.74	0.97	90.3
Miami, FL	1964	1,187,000	2.16	3.10	7.77	3.61	1.16	93.6
Denver, CO	1971	1,116,000	2.83	2.21	8.76	3.10	1.40	98.2
San Diego, CA	1966	1,103,000	2.67	2.38	7.40	2.77	1.16	96.4
Sacramento, CA	1968	774,000	2.65	n.a.	7.56	2.85	n.a.	94.8
Indianapolis, IN	1964	763,000	2.14	2.79	6.50	3.10	1.11	89.8
San Juan, PR	1964	759,000	1.53	5.02	7.51	4.85	0.99	62.7
Louisville, KY	1964	752,000	1.93	3.02	6.30	3.26	1.08	94.3
Columbus, OH	1964	734,000	2.60	2.78	8.45	3.25	1.17	95.3

TABLE 10–12 (Continued)
Generation of Travel by Urban Residents, Selected American Cities

Urban Area	Year	Population	Trips/Person	Persons/Car*	Trips/Dwelling	Persons/ Dwelling*	Cars/Dwelling*	Person-Trips by Car (%)
Norfolk, VA (SE VA)	1962	602,000	2.25	3.54	7.37	3.27	0.53	89.6
Birmingham, AL	1965	559,000	2.68	2.78	8.96	3.34	1.19	94.3
Oklahoma City, OK	1965	574,000	3.00	2.49	9.51	3.17	1.27	95.0
Jacksonville, FL	1968	547,000	2.41	2.70	7.83	3.25	1.20	96.6
Springfield, MA	1965	531,000	2.25	3.14	7.05	3.13	1.00	89.7
Fort Lauderdale, FL	1964	450,000	2.66	2.33	7.53	2.83	1.22	n.a.
Richmond, VA	1964	418,000	2.33	3.04	7.57	3.33	1.07	84.6
Orlando, FL	1965	356,000	2.59	2.59	8.39	3.24	1.25	97.5
Lehigh Valley, PA	1964	345,000	2.00	2.84	6.40	3.21	1.13	91.4
Fresno, CA	1972	295,000	3.00	2.27	8.25	2.74	1.21	96.4
Mobile, AL	1966	280,000	1.79	2.94	6.42	3.59	1.21	96.0
West Palm Beach, FL	1965	261,000	2.58	2.44	7.46	2.89	1.19	n.a.
Peoria, IL	1964	261,000	3.03	2.72	9.74	3.21	1.18	96.7
Baton Rouge, LA	1965	245,000	2.50	2.85	8.76	3.23	1.13	92.3
Charleston, SC	1965	235,500	2.55	3.20	8.30	3.25	1.01	91.0
Little Rock, AR	1964	223,000	3.09	3.05	9.89	3.20	1.10	95.7
South Bend, IN	1967	222,000	3.04	2.45	9.24	3.04	1.24	94.3
Columbia, SC	1964	196,000	2.96	2.83	9.42	3.17	1.12	93.3
Evansville, IN	1970	175,000	3.29	2.23	10.17	3.09	1.39	n.a.
Huntsville, AL	1964	123,000	2.87	2.52	9.20	3.21	1.27	94.5

*n.a., not available.
SOURCE: Computed from transportation studies in each urban area.

vehicles. In smaller cities, such as Oklahoma City and Little Rock, the urban resident averages 2.5 to 3 trips/day.

These differences are partially explained by the close relationship among car ownership, population density, and travel mode. The number of total person trips (in vehicles) decreases consistently with increasing population concentration and decreasing car ownership; however, the number of transit trips per capita increase. Many trips in high-density urban areas are pedestrian trips and are not reported in the basic trip data. When these pedestrian trips are superimposed on the trips in vehicles, there is probably a rising rate of total trip generation, and hence interaction in high-density environments.

Trip-purpose overview. All trips have some underlying reason: for example, a trip to work, to the doctor, or to visit a friend. Trip-purpose patterns therefore reflect the daily activities of urban residents.

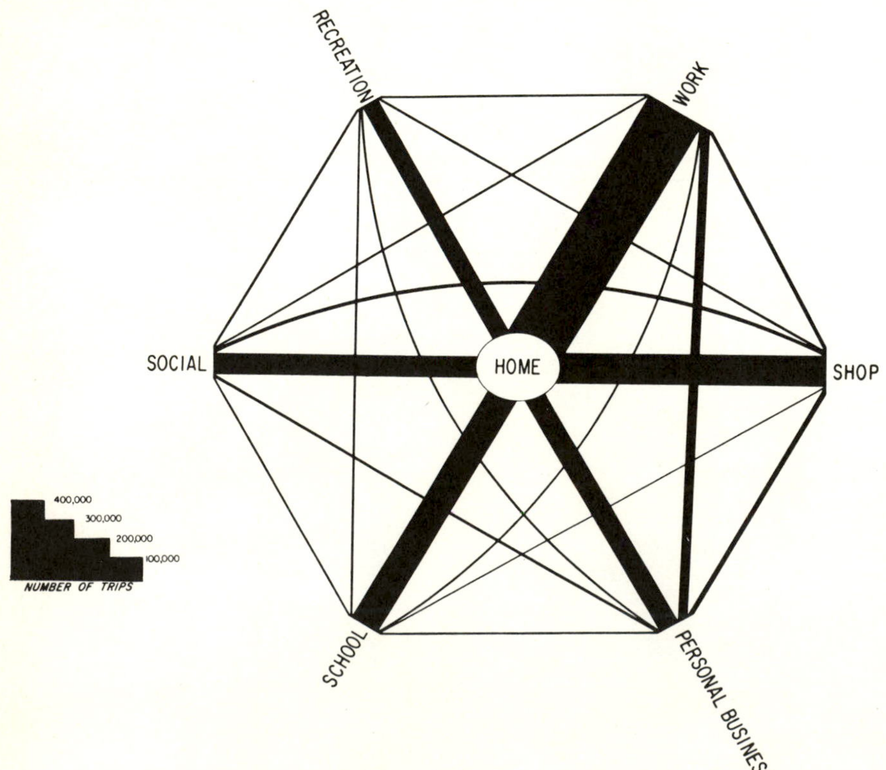

Figure 10.1. Trip purposes within typical urban area. This diagram shows the reasons for which trips are made in the Springfield, Mass. region on a typical 1965 day. More than three-fourths of the 1.15 million internal person trips were made either to or from home. SOURCE: Springfield Urbanized Area Comprehensive Transportation Study, Volume I, *The Land Use, Transportation and Travel Inventories,* Wilbur Smith & Associates 1969, p. 163.

1. The home or dwelling unit is the primary origin or destination of most trips (Figure 10.1). Generally, more than three-fourths of all urban trips are to or from home.
2. Table 10-13 summarizes the home-based trip purposes for urban areas in the United States and Canada. Approximately 30% of all trips are to or from work, 18% to or from shopping, 21% for social or recreational purposes, 12% for business purposes, 10% to and from school, and the remaining 9% are for other reasons.
3. The number of daily work trips per person remains about the same from city to city in the United States. It averages 0.7 trip/person, despite the variations in total trip making. This suggests that work trips are relatively inelastic and that it is the nonwork trips that increase with rising car ownership and income. An increase in the number of second wage earners will probably raise work trip rates in future years.

Summary patterns: Foreign cities

Transport data for selected cities throughout the world are summarized in Table 10-14. The heavy reliance on public transport in most cities reflects the low per capita incomes and car ownership levels. Because of the variety of sources, differences of definition, and limitations of data collection, care should be exercised in making comparisons among cities.

Origin–destination surveys for various cities in Europe, Asia, Australia, and South America provide additional information on trip rates and travel modes in relation to car ownership (Table 10-15).

1. Motor vehicle ownership in the cities shown ranges from about 3.4 persons/vehicle in Hobart, Australia (1963), to over 40 persons/vehicle in Bogota (1969) and Bombay (1962).
2. Total daily motorized trips/person ranges from 0.6 (Bombay) to 1.9 (Hobart).
3. Most trips in European, Asian, and South American cities with high population densities and low car ownership are generally made by public transport.

Trip generation: Guidelines and procedures

"Trip generation" defines the relationship between the activities of people in the urban setting and the travel they generate—it provides the vital link between land use and travel. The number, type, and frequency of urban trips reflects the character and intensity of urban land use and the socioeconomic characteristics and travel attitudes of urban residents. From a behavioral perspective, trip-generation models attempt to quantify choice of trip frequency and type.

Trip generation is important in many aspects of transportation planning and engineering. These include (1) com-

TABLE 10–13
Home-based Trips by Urban Residents According to Purpose (Weekday)

Urban Area	Year	Population	Home-based Trips as Percent of All Linked Trips	Percent by Purpose of Home Based Trips: Work	Business	Shopping	Social–Recreational	School	Other	Total Home-based Trips/Dwelling Unit
Los Angeles, CA	1967	9,008,000	73.6	30.4	—	17.6	—	—	52.0	4.70
Chicago, IL	1956	5,170,000	86.8	37.5	9.7	18.9	22.8	4.0	7.1	5.17
San Francisco, CA	1965	4,400,000	79.2	23.3	—	16.1	—	—	60.6	6.94
Detroit, MI	1965	4,042,000	77.6	20.8	22.2	19.8	22.2	17.0	—	6.64
Philadelphia, PA	1960	4,007,000	85.4	34.8	9.8	12.7	17.1	6.6	19.0	3.90
Boston, MA	1963	3,584,000	81.0	28.3	9.9	17.5	17.0	11.5	15.8	5.30
Washington, DC	1968	2,714,000	87.2	28.0	15.6	23.4	17.7	8.0	7.3	6.30
Milwaukee, WI	1972	1,811,000	80.0	41.2	—	—	—	—	58.8	6.32
Toronto, Canada	1964	1,800,000	88.7	48.5	8.9	17.3	16.2	4.6	4.5	5.64
Atlanta, GA	1972	1,640,000	80.8	31.4	—	—	—	—	68.6	5.82
Baltimore, MD	1962	1,608,000	88.0	39.7	8.1	15.1	15.6	12.0	9.5	4.58
Cincinnati, OH	1965	1,392,000	77.7	30.6	—	19.3	22.4	10.1	17.6	5.57
Miami, FL	1964	1,187,000	83.7	23.6	8.0	21.0	20.8	11.4	15.2	6.50
Denver, CO	1971	1,116,000	79.2	23.3	—	16.1	—	—	67.6	6.94
San Diego, CA	1966	1,103,000	70.6	23.5	—	19.5	—	—	51.0	5.22
Sacramento, CA	1968	774,000	73.9	26.1	—	17.3	—	—	56.6	4.06
Indianapolis, IN	1964	763,000	78.5	34.2	—	17.6	—	12.5	35.7	5.63
Southeastern VA (Norfolk)	1962	602,000	81.8	31.6	12.5	20.2	23.8	11.9	—	6.22
Oklahoma City, OK	1965	574,000	73.0	26.4	9.6	20.8	27.4	15.8	—	7.89
Birmingham, AL	1965	559,000	76.6	23.4	35.5	18.0	14.0	9.1	—	6.50
Springfield, MA	1965	551,000	81.1	30.1	9.6	16.5	18.3	13.6	11.9	5.37
Jacksonville, FL	1968	547,200	75.0	26.4	—	—	—	—	73.6	6.22
Richmond, VA	1964	418,000	80.3	34.2	13.0	16.6	18.1	11.0	7.1	5.51
Lehigh Valley, PA	1964	345,000	77.8	31.0	11.8	15.9	14.8	13.2	13.3	5.20
Fresno, CA	1971	295,000	69.3	24.8	—	18.3	—	—	56.9	5.94
Peoria, IL	1964	261,000	77.5	22.4	—	22.0	—	—	55.6	7.51
Charleston, SC	1965	235,500	78.8	26.4	—	—	—	—	73.6	6.22
Little Rock, AR	1964	223,000	83.2	25.8	8.9	20.1	31.2	14.0	—	8.23
Columbia, SC	1964	196,000	77.5	25.3	7.9	16.9	20.2	14.9	14.8	6.60

SOURCE: Computed from transportation studies in each urban area.

TABLE 10–14
Transport Data for Selected World Cities*

City	(1) Population, 1970 (× 10³)	(2) Income/Capita, (US$) 1970	(3) Rate of Growth 1960–1970: Population, (%)	(4) Rate of Growth 1960–1970: Autos (%)	(5) Number/1000 Population 1970: Autos	(6) Number/1000 Population 1970: Buses	(7) Number/1000 Population 1970: Commercial Vehicles	(8)‡ Import Duty %: Economy Cars	(9)‡ Import Duty %: Luxury Cars	(10) Modal Split of Motorized Trips (%)†: Autos	(10) Buses	(10) Other Motorized	(11)‡ Price of Regular-Grade Gasoline/ U.S. Gal	(12)‡ Bus Fare for a 3-mi Trip (U.S. cents)
Calcutta	7,402	270	2.2	7.2	13.0	0.3	4.0	150	150	8	34	58(3)	1.76	3
Bombay	5,792	390	3.7	8.2	13.5	0.3	4.5	150	150	11	41	48(5)	1.76	3
Madras	3,438	180	4.5	5.8	7.9	0.6	1.9	150	150	—(1)	54	46(8)	1.76	3
Seoul	5,536	440	8.5	22.0	6.3	0.9	3.5	100	150	8	89	3(7)	1.65	—
Jakarta	4,312	325	5.3	8.8	18.0	1.1	4.3	200	200	29	49	22(9)	0.44	4
Hong Kong	3,350	850	2.9	7.1	26.2	2.1	7.0	—	—	22	55	23(2)	1.10	4–10
Karachi	3,460	360	5.6	(0.6)	10.4	0.3	—	300	150	16	63	21(8)	0.89	1
Tehran	3,600	950	7.0	(15.4)	44.4	1.0	6.8	30	62	37	42	21(7)	0.35	3–8
Bangkok	3,090	525	6.2	12.0	49.7	1.2	16.3	80	80	29	59	12(7)	0.50	5
Singapore	2,110	1,100	2.6	6.7	73.0	1.3	17.9	25	25	24	43	33(5)	0.98	6.5
Kuala Lumpur	755	660	6.5	11.3	51.9	1.0	21.8	35	60	47	35	18(7)	1.40	5
Mexico City	8,600	1,275	5.8	10.5	78.3	1.3	9.0	212	212	19	65	16(3)	0.45	—
Buenos Aires	8,400	1,800	2.4	(12.1)	73.9	1.6	25.6	140	140	17	60	23(6)	1.29	—
São Paulo	8,400	785	6.4	—	62.3	1.3	10.6	70	105	26	60	14(4)	1.30	—
Bogota	2,551	760	7.3	—	22.0	1.4	25.0	350	350	17	71	12(6)	0.10	2.5
Caracas	2,277	1,600	5.4	8.3	91.0	0.6	27.3	135	135	46	35	19(3)	0.13	—
San José	435	430	5.4	10.9	47.9	1.0	34.0	100	100	23	74	3(10)	0.98	4
Cairo	6,500	275	5.7	—	—	0.3	—	100	200	—	—	—	—	2
Istanbul	2,800	810	6.0	12.2	21.0	0.2	13.1	25	25	57	28	15(4)	0.80	10
Casablanca	1,505	820	4.5	(6.1)	72.9	0.4	26.1	120	120	—	—	—	1.46	10–20
Lagos	1,448	555	7.9	15.5	22.8	1.0	8.3	75	150	12	—	88(2)	0.52	—
Kinshasa	1,134	660	12.1	—	—	0.4	—	20	20	33	58	9(7)	1.52	6
Tunis	746	500	2.5	6.0	57.6	0.5	12.1	33	33	15	75	10(9)	1.50	1.5
Beirut	600	1,000	2.9	9.1	153.0	2.3	17.3	32	32	60	10	30(7)	0.54	6
Nairobi	567	495	8.1	(6.8)	52.7	1.5	40.6	40	100	72	28	—(7)	1.12	10
Abidjan	424	500	11.0	(12.7)	75.5	1.7	35.4	58	58	40	47	13(10)	1.31	5
Dar es Salaam	350	710	9.0	—	33.0	0.6	17.3	75	150	7	40	53(4)	—	3.5
Lusaka	225	660	3.1	—	45.7	1.1	22.1	10	10	66	7	27(6)	—	11
Tokyo	14,900	2,775	3.4	16.0	83.3	1.3	134.5	40	40	35	8	57(5)	1.46	25
London	10,547	2,550	−0.7	5.2	222.0	0.6	22.0	15.4	15.4	59	24	17(8)	1.29	25
Paris	8,448	3,530	1.3	6.5	248.0	0.4	44.4	11	11	36	21	43(2)	1.40	30
Athens	2,416	—	3.0	12.8	60.8	2.5	18.2	25	25	—	—	—	2.15	10

*Because of the variety of sources, differences of definition and general weaknesses of collection, the data, although indicating orders of magnitude, have only limited comparability. Caution is accordingly required in their use. Data for columns 1, 2, 5, 6, and 7 are for 1970, except in the case of a few cities for which data for 1969 or 1971 had to be used. Rates of growth in columns 3 and 4 are for 1960–1970, except for a few cities where growth rates were available for a shorter period only. Growth rates in parentheses are for the country and not the city. For columns 8 and 9, a Toyota Corona was used to represent an economy car and a Mercedes-Benz 280 a luxury car. In column 10, the data are for different years, depending on the most recent traffic survey available to the World Bank. The various years are shown in the footnotes.

†(1) Included in "Other Motorized"; (2) figures for 1965; (3) figures for 1966; (4) figures for 1967; (5) figures for 1968; (6) figures for 1969; (7) figures for 1970; (8) figures for 1971; (9) figures for 1972; (10) figures—for 1973 for all three columns in each case.

‡Data for Oct. 1974.

SOURCE: *Urban Transport Sector Policy Paper*, World Bank, May 1975. The data in the table were obtained from several publications as indicated, supplemented by information in various urban and transport studies available in the World Bank. Information was also collected by World Bank missions and from government authorities. Since the sources and methods of data collection are extremely diverse, the table indicates only in rough measure conditions of urbanization and motorization. UNITED NATIONS, *World's Million Cities*, 1972 (for columns 1 and 2). MOTOR VEHICLE MANUFACTURERS ASSOCIATION, *Digest of Import Duties for Motor Vehicles Levied by Selected Countries*, 1974 (columns 5 and 6). WILFRED OWEN, Brookings Institution, *Automobiles and Cities—Strategies for Developing Countries*, Bank Staff Working Paper No. 162, Sept. 1973. Data supplied by World Bank missions and government authorities (columns 11 and 12).

prehensive long-range transportation plans (highway or transit), (2) short-range plans for an urban area, corridor, or facility and (3) assessing the impact of new developments, such as a regional shopping center, residential complex, or industrial park.

The basic approaches to trip generation, including methods of analysis and applications, are documented in many urban area transportation studies, in U.S. Department of Transportation publications,[4] and in Chapter 12.

[4]*Guidelines to Trip Generation Analysis*, Federal Highway Administration, Washington, D.C., 1967; *Trip Generation*, Federal Highway Administration, Washington, D.C., 1975; and Levinson, *Characteristics of Urban Transportation Demand*.

Trip rates: Trip production

Trip production reflects the number of trips generated at home. Trip production rates are expressed as a function of income, family size, population density, car ownership, and age of trip maker. Guidelines are given in Tables 10-16 to 10-21.

Population density. Increasing population density has a reductive effect on total trip making and a corresponding increase in transit use: (1) at high densities, many trips are made on foot that are made in vehicles at lower densities;

TABLE 10–15
Trip Characteristics of Selected Cities in Europe, Asia, Australia, and South America

City	Study Year	Population (Rounded)	Survey Area (mi²)*	Population Density (Persons/ mi²)*	Vehicle Registration (All Motorized Vehicles)	Persons/ Registered Vehicle	Total Daily Person-Trips (Internal)	Daily Motorized Person-Trips/ Person	Percent by Public Transport
1 Athens	1962	1,900,000	206	9,223	67,700	28.1	3,200,000	1.7	65
2 Bangkok	1972	4,067,000	1,116	3,644	250,000	16.3	4,498,000	1.1	70
3 Bogota	1969	2,339,600	1,512	1,547	55,000†	42.5	2,604,000	1.1	83
4 Bombay	1962	4,345,200	328	13,248	62,200	69.9	2,700,000	0.6	70
5 Brisbane	1960	593,700	375	1,583	151,600	3.9	1,011,200	1.7	45
6 Caracas	1966	1,719,000	n.a.	n.a.	151,000†	11.4	2,244,000	1.3	52
7 Hobart, Australia	1963	125,400	78	1,608	36,900	3.4	238,000	1.9	27
8 Kingston-upon-Hull, England	1967	344,900	385	8,955	52,700	6.6	498,000	1.4	17
9 Kuala Lumpur	1973	912,500	202	4,517	80,800	11.3	1,589,700	1.7	40
10 London	1961	8,826,600	941	9,380	1,454,000	6.1	14,396,000	1.6	54
11 London	1971	8,380,000	941	8,905	1,885,700†	4.4	12,550,000	1.5	40
12 Reading, England	1971	192,000	35	5,486	44,000†	4.4	589,800	3.1	60
13 Singapore	1968	1,536,000	186	8,258	98,920	15.5	2,150,000	1.4	64
14 Skopje	1965	220,000	42	5,238	10,600	20.8	163,200	0.7	74
15 Tel Aviv	1965	817,000	68	12,015	51,700	15.8	1,365,100	1.7	61

*1 mi² = 2.59 km². n.a., not available.
†Passenger cars.

SOURCE: Cities 1, 4, 5, 7, 10, 14: WILBUR S. SMITH, "Research and Worldwide Urban Transportation," *Highway Transportation Research, Education and Technology Annual*, Highway Res. Rec. 125, Highway Research Board, Washington, D.C., 1966, p. 30. Cities 2, 3, 6, 7, 8, 9, 13, 15: YACOV ZAHAVI, *Travel Characteristics in Cities of Developing and Developed Countries*, World Bank Staff Working Paper No. 230, Mar. 1976. City 4: YACOV ZAHAVI, "Can Transport Policy Decisions Change Urban Structures," *Transport. Res. Circ. No. 199*, Transportation Research Board, Washington, D.C., Feb. 1979. Cities 11, 12: "Consistency of Origin Destination Characteristics through Time," Committee 6F12, *ITE J.*, Oct. 1979.

(2) incomes are normally lower in high-density areas; and (3) car ownership is normally less.

Figure 10.2 shows how transit ridership relates to population density. In almost every case high density (in combination with low car ownership) tends to increase transit use. But the relationships are also influenced by factors such as service and fare differentials, concentrations of activities within the central area, and clustering of population along specific corridors that influence patronage and affect the plotted values.

Curves relating the percent of automobile driver trips to person trip-end density are shown in Figure 10.3 for the Penn–Jersey, Pittsburgh, and Chicago areas. These curves indicate that below a density of 10,000 trips/mi² (3900 trips/km²), approximately 57% of the total person-trips are expected to be made as auto-driver trips. Above this density, there is a dropping off of auto-driver trips at rates that appear to vary by area and by the cars/person ratio.

Pushkarev and Zupan explain the relationship among urban density, transit service, and transit demand as follows:[5]

1. Demand for public transportation depends upon its service and its price, but even more on the availability, convenience, and price of the competing mode—the automobile.
2. As urban density increases, the density of demand (number of passengers boarding per unit of area) also increases. This is because there are more people present to make each trip and each person makes fewer trips by auto.
3. At any given cost per passenger, more service per unit area is provided at higher density because demand is higher.

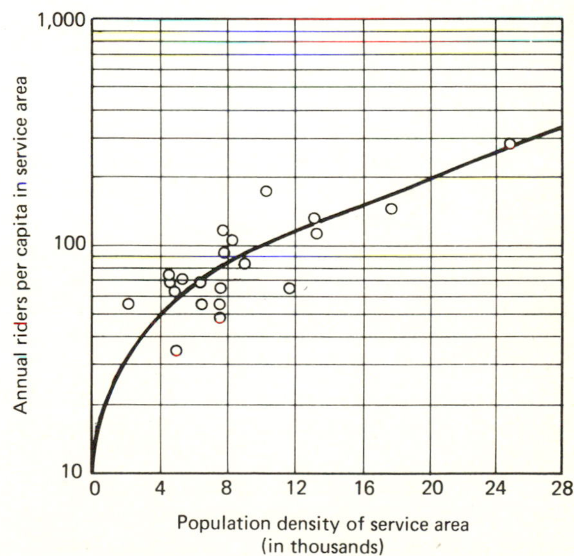

Figure 10.2. Transit riding habit in relation to population density. SOURCE: Levinson and Wynn, "Effects of Density on Urban Transportation Requirements," p. 58.

4. At any given service level, the cost per passenger is lowered with rising density.

Car ownership. The importance of car ownership on both the number of urban trips and the choice of travel mode is also widely recognized. Table 10-16 provides general guidelines for estimating the number of trips per person from the number of persons per car. These values can be used to check travel projections and to assess the effects of changing car ownership on average trip rates.

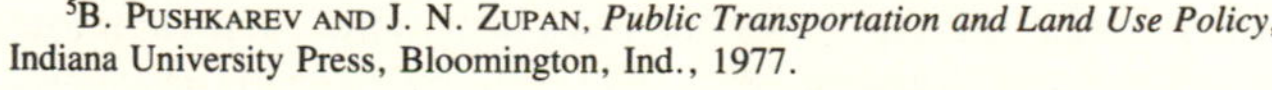

[5]B. PUSHKAREV AND J. N. ZUPAN, *Public Transportation and Land Use Policy*, Indiana University Press, Bloomington, Ind., 1977.

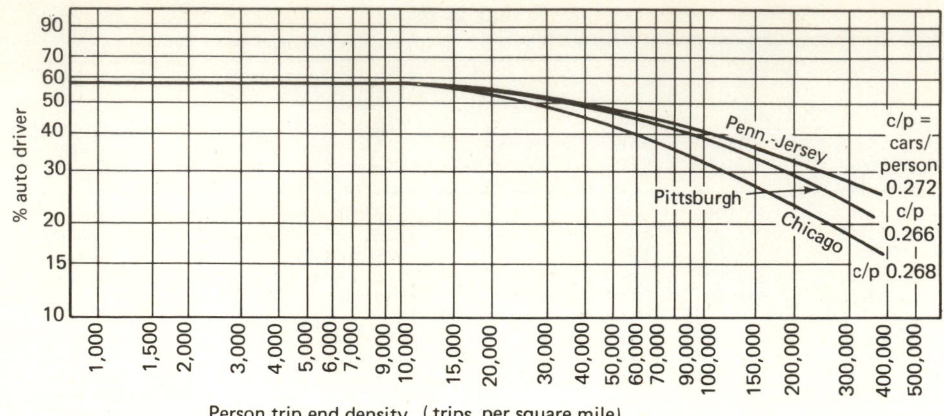

Figure 10.3. Percent automobile drive trips of total person trips vs. person trip end density. *Note:* 1,000 trips/sq mi = 385 trips/km^2. SOURCE: Tri-State Transportation Committee, *Interim Technical Report 4011-1320*. Proposed procedure for 1985 traffic estimates, February, 1965.

TABLE 10–16
Ranges of Overall Person-Trip Generation (Areawide), 1970–1976 Conditions

	Average Trips/Person Day	
Persons/Car	Range	Typical
2.0	2.5–3.5	3.0
2.5	2.1–3.1	2.6
3.0	1.8–2.8	2.3
3.5	1.6–2.6	2.1
4.0	1.5–2.5	2.0

SOURCE: Based on comprehensive urban transportation studies.

Typical relationships among car ownership, trip generation, and travel mode for selected cities are summarized in Table 10-17. Members of zero-car households made slightly under 1 person-trip per day, members of one-car households approximately 2 person-trips per day, and members of multicar households approximately 3 to 4 person-trips per day. However, the number of trips by public transport drops rapidly as car ownership rises. The first car generally has the most reductive effect on transit ridership. In large cities the number of daily person-trips by public transport decreases from approximately 0.6 in zero-car households to 0.3 for one-car households, and 0.2+ in multicar households. In smaller cities the overall rates of person trip making are approximately the same as for larger cities within a given level of car ownership. However, the proportion of trips by public transport is much less, even among zero-car households. It is important to note that a substantial proportion of travelers from zero-car households actually travel as automobile passengers. This implies a dependence on the neighbor (i.e., ride sharing as a means of traveling to work or to shop).

The different levels of trip making in households owning zero, one, and two or more cars, according to trip purpose, are shown in Table 10-18. Here, again, it is clear that a rise in multiple-car ownership brings with it a concomitant rise in auto-driver trips, particularly for nonwork trips. The increase in trip making, however, also depends on family size and number of people employed.

Household size and car ownership. The combined effects of automobile ownership and household size on the daily trips per household and daily trips per person are shown in Table 10-19. The larger the household size, the greater the total daily trip generation for any given level of car ownership. Also, for any given household size, the trips per household increase with increased car ownership. The trips per person generally increase rapidly with each level of car ownership and more gradually with family size.

These interactions can be summarized as follows: There is an increase in per capita trip generation with increases in car ownership, workers, and income per family; the per capita trip production declines slightly with each increase in family size. Although the aggregate number of trips gen-

TABLE 10–17
Trip Generation by Car Ownership in Selected Urban Areas

	Cars/Dwelling Unit			
Item	0	1	2	3+
Total trips/person				
London	0.93	2.03	2.56	3.06
Chicago	1.08	2.61	3.46	4.01
San Francisco	0.99	2.17	2.63	3.03
Detroit	0.70	2.08	3.20*	
Minneapolis	1.60	2.83	3.51	
Pittsburgh	1.12	1.70	2.40*	
Seattle	0.90	2.60	3.20	3.40
Indianapolis	0.93	2.13	2.88	2.25
San Juan	0.99	2.00	3.28*	
Springfield, MA	0.71	2.27	3.13*	
Knoxville	0.85	2.49	3.36	3.87
Lexington	0.76	2.06	2.91	3.26
Transit trips/person				
London	0.78	0.60	0.55	
Chicago	0.62	0.36	0.31*	
San Francisco	0.61	0.20	0.14	0.12
Detroit	0.42	0.25	0.24*	
Minneapolis	0.42	0.09	0.04	
Pittsburgh	0.74	0.38	0.26*	
Seattle	0.37	0.12	0.06	0.06
Indianapolis	0.32	0.09	0.04	0.10
San Juan	0.73	0.38	0.24*	
Springfield, MA	0.20	0.07	0.04*	
Knoxville	0.32	0.09	0.04	0.03
Lexington	0.28	0.10	0.07	0.05

*Two or more cars per dwelling unit.

SOURCE: Computed from origin–destination studies in each urban area. Data may vary slightly from those set forth in other tabulations. For Puget Sound and Minneapolis, data are based on persons over 5 years old in households.

TABLE 10–18
Effects of Car Ownership on Trip Purpose

Trip Purpose (All Modes)	Distribution (%) Zero-Car Households	One-Car Households	Multicar Households
Home-based work	35	26	21
Home-based shopping	19	16	14
Home-based social–recreational	15	17	18
Home-based school	9	7	9
Home-based other	12	13	14
Subtotal	90	79	76
Non–home-based	10	21	24
Total*	100	100	100
Trips/dwelling unit/day	1.8	7.0	12.0
Home based work trips per dwelling unit per day	0.6	1.8	2.5

*Totals represent averages for U.S. urban areas.

SOURCE: Purpose distribution is based on *OKI* (Cincinnati) *Urban Transportation Study*, 1965.

erated by each household increases as a household gets larger, the rate of increase generally slows down.

Income and car ownership. The combined effects of household income and car ownership on trip rates are shown in Table 10-20 and in Figures 10.4 and 10.5. These exhibits suggest that rising incomes gradually increase household trip making at such levels of car ownership.

1. Table 10-20 summarizes the trip rates by income and car ownership as reported in the Nationwide Personal Transportation Study for 1970.
2. Figure 10.4 gives average daily person-trips per household by number of autos per household versus income for various urban population levels. These were derived from a number of urban transportation planning studies in the period 1965–1974 and represent average 1970 conditions.[6] The income ranges are in terms of 1970 dollars. Therefore, where income is used to enter the table, it should be represented in terms of 1970 dollars.
3. Figure 10.5 provides a guide to estimating trips by purpose for various levels of income and car ownership. The data, although based on a specific area (Greater Cincinnati), can be used in other urban areas. However,

[6]ARTHUR SOSSLAU, AMIN B. HASSAM, MAURICE M. CARTER, AND GEORGE V. WICKSTROM, *Quick Response Techniques and Transferable Parameters—User's Guide*, National Cooperative Highway Res. Prog. Report 187, Transportation Research Board, National Research Council, Washington, D.C., 1978.

TABLE 10–19
Person-Trips per Dwelling Unit (DU) Related to Car Ownership and Household Size

Household Size	Daily Person-Trips/DU Chicago 1956	Chicago 1970	Puget Sound, 1961	Madison, Wis., 1962	Average	Average Daily Trips/Person
No cars/DU						
1	1.8	1.5	0.9	1.0	1.3	1.3
2	2.9	2.4	1.8	1.5	2.2	1.1
3	4.0	3.5	3.5	3.1	3.5	1.2
4	4.7	2.7	3.5	3.2	3.5	0.9
5	5.7	3.3	4.3	5.2	4.6	0.9
6–7	n.a.	n.a.	n.a.	n.a.	n.a.	n.a.
8+	n.a.	n.a.	n.a.	n.a.	n.a.	n.a.
All	3.0	2.1	1.4	1.6	2.0	n.a.
One car/DU						
1	3.5	3.8	3.2	2.7	3.3	3.3
2	5.5	5.7	5.1	5.1	5.5	2.8
3	7.2	7.6	7.8	7.2	7.4	2.5
4	8.9	8.8	10.0	8.0	8.9	2.2
5	10.2*	10.5	11.5	9.2	10.3	2.1
6–7	n.a.	n.a.	12.6	n.a.	12.6	1.9
8+	n.a.	n.a.	15.1	n.a.	15.1	2.2
All	6.9	6.7	6.9	6.6	6.8	n.a.
Two cars/DU†						
1	n.a.	n.a.	3.5	4.4	4.0	4.6
2	7.7	8.1	7.3	7.0	6.8	3.4
3	9.8	10.3	10.2	9.4	9.9	3.3
4	12.0	13.8	12.9	11.7	12.6	3.2
5	13.8	17.3	15.0	13.4	14.9	3.0
6–7	n.a.	n.a.	17.2	n.a.	17.2	2.6
8+	n.a.	n.a.	21.9	n.a.	21.9	3.1
All	10.9	12.0	11.0	10.9	11.3	n.a.
Three cars/DU†						
1	n.a.	n.a.	n.a.	n.a.	n.a.	n.a.
2	n.a.	n.a.	9.9	n.a.	9.9	5.0
3	10.9	12.3	11.1	n.a.	11.4	3.8
4	13.9	14.6	13.7	n.a.	14.1	3.5
5	16.4	22.0	17.2	n.a.	18.5	3.7
6–7	n.a.	n.a.	18.6	n.a.	18.6	2.9
8+	n.a.	n.a.	23.6	n.a.	23.6	3.0
All	14.5	16.8	14.0	n.a.	15.1	n.a.

*Last figure represents indicated household size or more.
†Data for Madison shown for two or more cars; Chicago, three or more cars.
.a. - not available.

SOURCE: Comprehensive transportation studies for each urban area.

TABLE 10–20
Auto Trips per Household by Income and Auto Ownership, 1970

	Income								All Incomes
Auto Ownership	Under $3,000	$3,000–3,999	$4,000–4,999	$5,000–5,999	$6,000–7,499	$7,500–9,999	$10,000–14,999	Over $15,000	
None	1.1	2.2	2.2	2.4	2.9	3.2	2.8	3.3	1.7
One	3.5	4.8	5.8	5.3	6.5	7.3	7.0	6.1	5.9
Two	5.5	8.9	9.3	7.8	8.0	9.3	8.7	10.5	9.1
Three or more	n.a.*	n.a.*	12.0	12.3	10.6	12.8	12.1	13.0	12.4
Total	2.2	4.2	5.4	5.2	6.6	8.0	8.1	9.5	6.2

*n.a., not available.

SOURCE: FEDERAL HIGHWAY ADMINISTRATION, *Nationwide Personal Transportation Study*, Report 11, "Auto Ownership," Washington, D.C., 1973, Table 26.

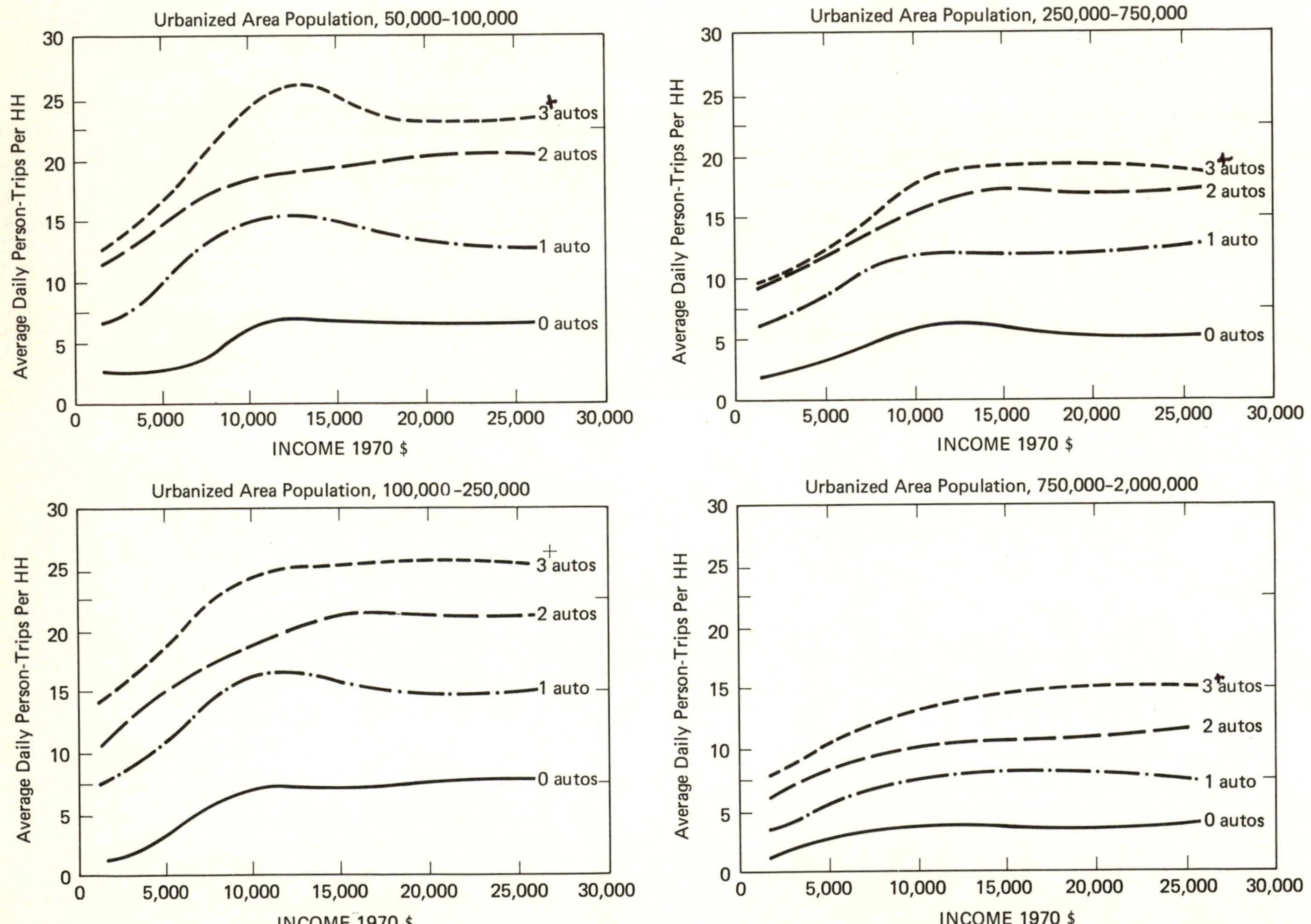

Figure 10.4. Average daily person trips per household, by number of autos per household vs. income, for various urban area populations. SOURCE: Arthur Sosslau, Amin B. Hassam, Maurice M. Carter, and George V. Wickstrom, *Quick Response Techniques and Transferable Parameters—User's Guide*, National Cooperative Highway Res. Prog. Report 187, Transportation Research Board, National Research Council, Washington, D.C., 1978.

in the case of work trips, it is suggested that the trip rates remain constant for each level of car ownership as income rises.

Age. The travel behavior patterns of various age-groups provide a basis for (1) identifying latent travel demands and (2) providing special mobility for the elderly. Total trip making reaches a maximum in the middle years, between 30 and 49, depending upon income.

Table 10-21 gives typical trip rates for elderly persons, based on the 1969 Nationwide Personal Transportation Study. Trip data for the "typical" urban resident are given for comparative purposes. The average elderly person makes about 1 trip each day as compared with about 2.5 for all

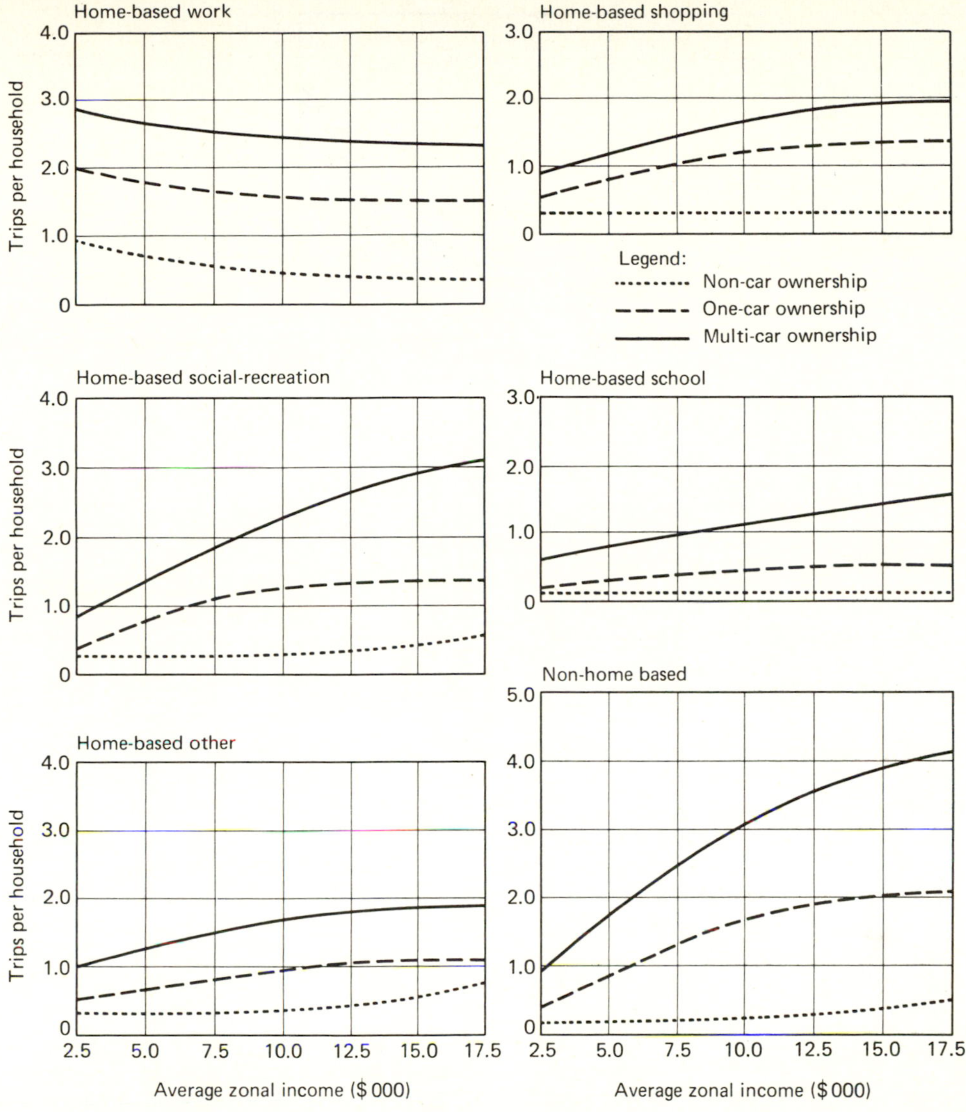

Figure 10.5. Trips per household by car ownership and income. SOURCE: *Ohio-Kentucky-Indiana Regional Transportation and Development Plan,* Wilbur Smith & Associates, p. 24.

TABLE 10–21
Estimated Trip-making Rates for Elderly Persons (Aged 65 Years or More)

Trip Purpose	Average Number of Trips/ Person/Day (Elderly)	Average Total Urban Population
Work	0.125	0.750
Shop	0.218	0.450
School/church	0.101	0.250
Other	0.504	1.050
Total (excludes walking trips)	0.948	2.500

SOURCE: Second column: *Nationwide Personal Transportation Study,* Federal Highway Administration, Washington, D.C., 1969. Third column: estimated from Table 10–10, based on 2.5 trips/person/day.

urban residents. Corresponding data for the Tri–State (New York) region show 0.8 daily trip by each elderly person.[7]

Additional analyses of age as a factor in urban travel behavior were conducted by Ashford and Holloway, based on origin–destination data for Milwaukee, Wisconsin, and Albany, Augusta, Columbus, Macon, and Savannah, Georgia. Principal findings are summarized as follows:[8]

1. CBD orientation (Figure 10.6): "Age had a direct influence on the percentage of a trip maker's CBD-oriented journeys. As the trip maker's age increases, the CBD becomes a more dominant attractor."[9]
2. Total travel: "The work trip increases in importance up to the age of general retirement and then rapidly declines, while shopping trips increase in relative importance with age and increase sharply for the elderly. The relative importance of school trips declines rapidly, becoming negligible above the age of 25. Miscellaneous trips reach

[7]J. K. MARKOVITZ, "Transportation Needs of the Elderly," *Traffic Quart.* 25(2), 240 (Apr. 1971).

[8]N. ASHFORD AND F. M. HOLLOWAY, "The Effect of Age on Travel Behavior," *Traffic Eng.*, *41*(7), 46–49, 67 (Apr. 1971).

[9]Ibid., p. 67.

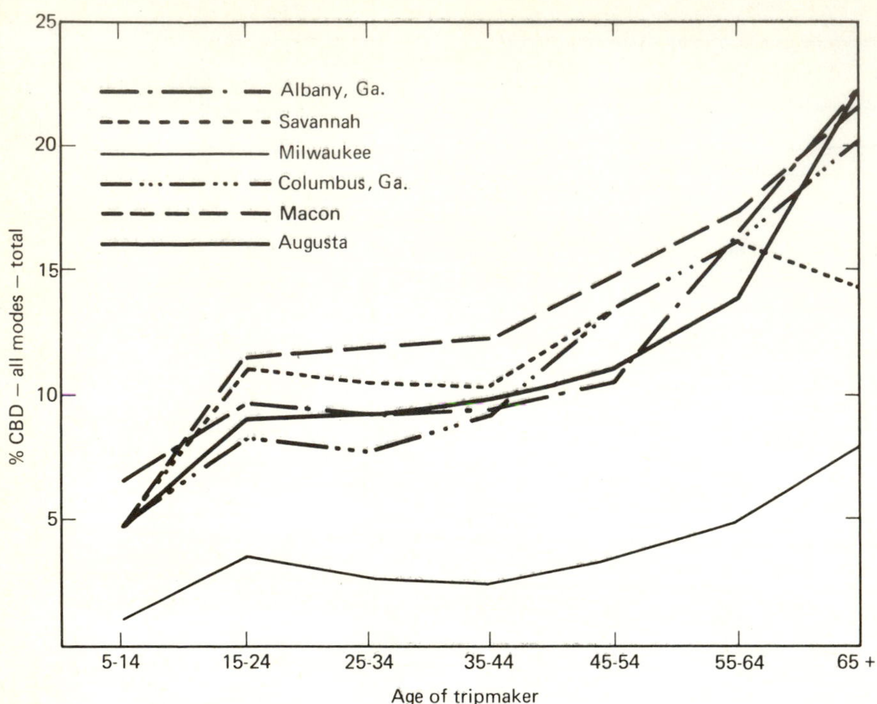

Figure 10.6. Percent of trips to CBD by various age groups, all modes, all home-base purposes. SOURCE: Norman Ashford and Frank M. Holloway, "The Effect of Age on Travel Behavior," *Traffic Engineering*, Vol. XLI, No. 7 (April 1971), p. 47.

a minimum in middle age and rapidly increase in importance for elderly persons."[10]

Physically handicapped. The physically handicapped make only about 1.1 daily trips per capita as compared with 2.20 for the general population. About 13.7% of these trips are made by taxi as compared with 0.3% for the general population. In contrast, only 2% of all trips by handicapped persons are made by school bus as compared with 8% for the general population.

Trip rates: Trip attraction

Each type of urban land generates person- and vehicle-trips in accordance with the nature and intensity of its use. Commercial land may generate more than 150 person-destinations per acre; public open space, fewer than 5. Trip attraction relates to the trips generated by nonresidential land for various trip purposes.

Trip-generation factors for use in estimating impact of new developments are set forth in Table 10-22. This table summarizes the average weekday vehicle trip ends (i.e., vehicles entering and leaving various land uses), as contained in the Institute of Transportation Engineers, "Trip Generation", report.[11] The full report contains definitions, procedures, and daily and weekend trip rates for a variety of land uses. Data were obtained from various local governmental agencies, consulting engineers, universities and colleges, and sections of the Institute of Transportation Engineers. Trip rates are expressed in terms of parameters, such as square feet of floor space (i.e., retail), employment (i.e., office), dwelling units (residential), enrolled students (schools), seats (theaters), or beds (hospitals). Data are presented for:

- Average weekday trip ends
- A.M. peak-hour trips in and out (highway peak)
- P.M. peak-hour trips in and out (highway peak)
- Peak hour of each generator (i.e., A.M. or P.M.) (may differ from highway peak hours)

The rates in this table are commonly used to estimate the transportation impacts of new land development. They can also be used to derive overall urban area trip attraction rates for various trip purposes. This usage requires factors for estimated vehicle occupancy and modal split.

Vehicular trip generation at regional shopping centers approximates 15 to 20 car destinations per day per 1000 ft^2 of gross leasable floor space. This varies among shopping centers according to their location, size, productivity, store type, and parking supply. There is a general trend for trip rates to decline as the size of center increases, especially up to 500,000 ft^2 (50,000 m^2) of gross floor space (Figure 10.7). Approximately 15% to 20% of these movements take place inbound and also outbound during peak shopping hours and about 10% during the P.M. rush hours.[12]

A 1 million-ft^2 regional shopping center would produce the following typical traffic "design" values:

Entering:	daily (avg)	15,500
	P.M. peak hour	1,400
	peak shopping	2,700
Exiting:	P.M. peak hour	1,800
	peak exit hour	4,200

[10] Ibid.

[11] *Trip Generation—An Informational Report*, 1976, and *Trip Generation Supplement No. 1*, Feb. 1979, Institute of Transportation Engineers, Washington, D.C.

[12] See, for example, C. H. BUTTKE, "An Approximation of Regional Shopping Center Traffic," *Traffic Eng.*, 42(7), 20–23 (Apr. 1972).

TABLE 10–22
Vehicle Trip Generation of Urban Land Use

Trip Generator†	Daily Trips In + Out			A.M. Peak Hour Trips		P.M. Peak Hour Trips		Peak Hour of Trip Generation		
	Min.	Avg.	Max.	In	Out	In	Out	In	Out	Time of Day
Shopping center/1000 gross ft²										
0–49,999 ft²	21.5	115.8	270.9	1.1	0.9	7.2	7.2	7.6	7.8	P.M.
50,000–99,000 ft²	25.5	79.1	161.3	2.9		2.4	2.7	9.1		P.M.
100,000–199,000 ft²	32.1	60.4	103.7	—		2.6	2.9	3.0	2.8	P.M.
200,000–299,000 ft²	18.0	49.9	92.0			2.1	2.3	2.7	2.5	P.M.
300,000–399,000 ft²	16.0	40.4	58.4	—		5.2		5.2		P.M.
400,000–499,000 ft²	29.0	47.6	90.0	—		5.7		5.0		P.M.
500,000–999,000 ft²	17.3	34.5	61.2	0.6	0.3	1.2	1.3	2.2	1.9	P.M.
1,000,000–1,249,000 ft²	16.4	31.1	57.0			1.4	1.8	0.7	4.2	P.M.
1,250,000 ft² and over	18.9	26.5	35.7	0.4	0.2	1.1	1.5	1.4	1.7	P.M.
Discount store										
7000–150,000 ft²	29.8	64.6	121.1	1.4	1.9	2.6	2.4			
Hardware or paint store										
1000 gross ft²	43.6	51.3	74.1	1.1		4.9		5.2		P.M.
Employee	45.9	53.2	58.2	5.1		5.1		5.4		P.M.
Employee (Sat.)	62.8	85.6	94.1							
Acre	467.0	546.0	906.0	11.6		51.8		55.6		P.M.
Supermarket										
1000 gross ft²	51.7	125.5	270.8			3.7	3.3	6.0	7.4	P.M.
Convenience market—24-hour										
1000 gross ft²	480.0	577.5	699.2							
Restaurant—quality										
Seat		1.2		0.0	0.0	0.1	0.1	0.2	0.2	P.M.
1000 gross ft²		56.3		0.8	0.5	2.8	1.7	5.1	4.4	P.M.
Restaurant-sitdown										
1000 gross ft²	47.9	164.4	551.2	—		9.9	4.0	13.0	9.2	P.M.
Restaurant-drive-in										
1000 gross ft²	37.6	55.3	82.8			17.0	14.6	44.4	41.9	Noon
New-car sales										
Site				33.0	19.5	19.0	40.5			
Service station										
Station	620.0	748.0	100.0	21.0		25.0		31.0		P.M.
Pump	103.0	133.0	170.0							
Car wash										
Site								59.6		Sat.
Highway oasis										
Site				34.0	43.0	27.0	55.5	40.0	64.5	P.M.
Truck stop										
Site				31.5	32.5	39.0	48.5	50.5	52.5	P.M.
Banks—walk-in										
1000 gross ft²		169.0		4.4		35.8		35.8		P.M.
Employee		44.5		1.2		9.4		8.7		P.M.
Banks—drive-in										
1000 gross ft²	160.0	192.0	270.0	5.4		6.5	12.3	18.3	12.8	P.M.
Employee	32.0	117.4	92.0	1.2		2.3	4.4	6.5	4.5	P.M.
Window	207.0	297.0	330.0	5.0		20.0	26.0	44.0		P.M.
Savings and loan—walk-in										
1000 gross ft²		61.0		1.3		5.3		9.		A.M.
Employee		30.5		0.7		2.7		4.8		P.M.
Savings and loan—drive-in										
1000 gross ft²		74.0		1.0		6.8		9.7		P.M.
Employee		49.0		0.7		4.6		6.4		P.M.
Window		445.0		6.0		41.0		58.0		P.M.
Insurance										
1000 gross ft²	10.1	11.5	12.5	2.3		2.4		2.4		P.M.
Employee	2.4	2.4	2.5	0.5		0.5		0.5		P.M.
Acre		91.8		18.3		17.9		18.3		A.M.
General office building										
Employee	2.4	3.6	11.2	0.6		0.6		0.6		P.M.
1000 gross ft²	3.6	12.3	43.5	1.9	0.4	0.3	1.9	1.9	0.4	A.M.
Acre	51.0	240.1	299.7	19.2		18.0				
Medical office										
1000 gross ft²	38.0	75.0	99.0						6.4	P.M.
Government office										
Employee		12.0		0.8	0.2			1.4	0.5	P.M.
1000 gross ft²		68.9		4.9	1.0			8.2	2.8	P.M.

TABLE 10–22 (Continued)
Vehicle Trip Generation of Urban Land Use

Trip Generator†	Daily Trips In + Out			A.M. Peak Hour Trips		P.M. Peak Hour Trips		Peak Hour of Trip Generation		
	Min.	Avg.	Max.	In	Out	In	Out	In	Out	Time of Day
Civic center										
Employee		6.1		0.5	0.1	0.2	0.5			
1000 gross ft^2		25.0		2.0	0.2	0.9	2.0			
Office park										
Employee	2.9	3.3	3.5	0.6		0.5		0.6		A.M.
1000 gross ft^2	9.4	20.6	30.3	9.4	0.3	0.3	1.8	2.0	0.3	A.M.
Acre		276.6		52.7		44.7		52.7		A.M.
Research center										
Employee	2.0	3.1	5.3	0.5		0.5		0.7		P.M.
1000 gross ft^2	4.3	9.3	9.8	1.3		1.5		1.6		P.M.
Acre		37.7		7.3		8.4		8.4		P.M.
Commercial airport										
Employee	11.6	16.8	26.6	1.0	0.7	1.4	1.5	0.5	0.6	A.M.
Flights/day	2.6	11.8	60.7	0.2	0.1	0.2	0.2	1.9	2.1	P.M.
Commercial flights/day		77.9	84.6	3.0	2.0	4.2	4.4	2.7	2.9	P.M.
General aviation airport										
Employee		6.5	122.0	—	—	—	—	0.2	0.3	P.M.
Flights/day	1.0	3.1	10.3	0.2	0.2			0.2	0.4	P.M.
Truck terminals										
Employee	4.2	47.3	7.0	0.3	0.4	0.3	0.3	0.3	0.4	A.M.
1000 gross ft^2		9.9		0.4	0.5	0.4	0.5	0.4	0.5	
Acre	66.2	81.9	100.1	3.1	4.6	3.0	3.4	3.1	4.6	
Industrial—general										
Employee	1.4	3.0	15.7	0.5		0.6		0.6		A.M.
1000 gross ft^2	0.5	5.4	52.0	0.8		1.0		1.0		A.M.
Acre	3.5	59.9	441.2	9.3		12.0		11.5		A.M.
General light industrial										
Employee	1.5	3.2	4.5	0.7	0.1	0.3	0.5	0.3	0.5	P.M.
1000 gross ft^2	1.6	5.5	16.9	0.8	0.2	0.3	0.6	0.3	0.7	
Acre	5.2	52.4	159.4	18.2	3.3	6.9	13.6	6.9	13.3	
General heavy industrial										
Employee	0.7	0.8	1.8	0.4		0.6		0.3		A.M.
1000 gross ft^2	0.4	1.5	1.8	0.5		0.2		0.7		A.M.
Industrial park										
Employee	1.4	3.9	8.8	0.5	0.2	0.6		0.2	0.5	P.M.
1000 gross ft^2	0.9	7.3	37.0	1.0		1.2			0.9	P.M.
Acre	13.9	56.1	441.2	7.9	2.8	10.0			8.0	P.M.
Manufacturing										
Employee	0.6	2.0	6.7	0.4		0.2	0.2	0.4		A.M.
1000 gross ft^2	0.5	4.0	52.0	0.8		0.8		0.8		A.M.
Acre	2.5	38.3	396.0	7.3		8.4		9.0		A.M.
Warehousing										
Employee	3.0	4.3	15.7	0.5		1.4		1.4		A.M.
1000 gross ft^2	1.5	5.0	17.0	0.6		1.6		1.6		P.M.
Acre	42.5	62.0	256.0	9.8		20.2		20.0		A.M.
Military base										
Employee	1.0	1.8	4.1							
Vehicle	0.6	0.9	2.3							
Elementary school										
Employee	4.5	13.1	26.4	2.9		0.3		3.4		A.M.
Student	0.5	1.0	1.8	0.2		0.0		0.3		
High school										
Student	0.7	1.4	2.5	0.3		0.2		0.3		A.M.
Employee	4.0	455.0	937.0					3.5		
Junior/community college										
Student	0.9	1.6	2.9	0.2	0.0	0.0	0.1	0.2	0.0	A.M.
University										
Student	1.4	2.4	3.9							P.M.
Library										
Employee	36.8	51.0	81.9					3.8	3.4	P.M.
1000 gross ft^2		41.8						3.0	2.7	P.M.
Hospital										
Employee	2.2	5.5	11.1					0.3	0.4	P.M.
Bed	3.0	12.2	32.8					0.5	0.9	P.M.
1000 gross ft^2		16.9						2.3		
Nursing home										
Bed	1.9	2.7	4.0		0.1		0.2	0.4		P.M.
Clinic (research and special cases)										
Employee		5.9							0.6	P.M.

TABLE 10–22 (Continued)
Vehicle Trip Generation of Urban Land Use

Trip Generator†	Daily Trips In + Out			A.M. Peak Hour Trips		P.M. Peak Hour Trips		Peak Hour of Trip Generation		
	Min.	Avg.	Max.	In	Out	In	Out	In	Out	Time of Day
Single family										
Person	1.2	2.5	4.8	0.1	0.2	0.2	0.1	0.2	0.1	P.M.
Vehicle	1.0	6.5	9.4	0.2	0.4	0.4	0.2	0.5	0.2	P.M.
Dwelling unit	4.3	10.0	21.9	0.3	0.6	0.7	0.4	0.7	0.4	P.M.
Acre		25.7		0.7	1.6	1.9	1.1	2.1	1.1	P.M.
Apartment										
Person	1.2	2.8	5.8	0.1	0.2	0.2	0.1	0.2	0.1	P.M.
Vehicle	2.9	5.1	8.6	0.1	0.2	0.2	0.1	0.2	0.1	P.M.
Dwelling unit	0.5	6.1	12.3	0.1	0.4	0.4	0.2	0.4	0.2	P.M.
Acre		22.2		1.2		2.2		2.2		
Low-rise dwelling unit	4.7	5.4	5.5	0.1	0.4	0.4	0.2	0.4	0.2	P.M.
High-rise dwelling unit	1.2	3.7	6.4	0.3		0.3		0.5		P.M.
Condominium										
Person	1.1	1.9	3.3	0.0	0.1	0.1	0.1			
Occupied unit	0.6	5.1	9.4	0.1	0.5	0.4	0.2			
Mobile home										
Person	1.6	2.5	3.6	0.4	0.2	0.2	0.1	0.2	0.1	P.M.
Vehicle	1.9	3.4	4.8	0.1	0.2	0.2	0.1	0.2	0.1	P.M.
Occupied dwelling unit	2.8	5.4	6.8	0.1	0.4	0.4	0.2	0.4	0.2	P.M.
Retirement dwelling unit	2.8	3.3	4.9	0.4		0.4		0.4		P.M.
PUD dwelling unit	6.2	7.9	10.0	0.3	0.5	0.5	0.4	0.5	0.4	P.M.
Recreational—general										
Employee–Weekday	8.3	22.8	183.7							
Employee–Saturday		162.2								
Parking space–Weekday	0.4	3.1	5.4							
Parking space–Saturday		6.6								
Park										
Employee	42.3	96.2	183.7							
Parking space	2.9	7.8	24.3							
City park										
Acre	1.0	6.0	8.0							
County park										
Employee	23.3	26.5	183.3							
Parking space	0.4	2.2	21.0							
Acre	0.2	5.1	61.2							
State park										
Employee	21.9	61.1	183.3							
Parking space	0.4	1.2	3.1							
Acre	0.1	0.6	16.6							
Golf course										
Employee	22.5	34.2	49.1							
Parking space	2.6	8.2	16.3							
Acre	2.5	9.1	22.7							
Racquet club										
Court	20.2	42.6	70.2	1.1		4.1		5.0		P.M.
1000 gross ft² building area	7.6	8.9	10.4			1.1		0.8		
Member–Weekday		0.6		0.0		0.1		0.1		
Member–Saturday		0.8								
Employee	19.6	35.6	78.5	1.3		2.9		5.3		
Hotel										
Employee	7.2	11.3	7.2	0.4	0.2	0.2	0.2	0.9		A.M.
Room	9.1	10.5	13.4	0.6	0.3	0.4	0.4	0.9		A.M.
Motel										
Employee	7.2	12.8	41.0	1.0		0.8		1.1		P.M.
Occupied room	4.7	10.1	14.6	0.7		0.6		0.8		P.M.
Resort hotel										
Employee		10.3		0.3		0.7		0.8		P.M.
Occupied room		10.2		0.3		0.7		0.8		P.M.

†1 ft² = 0.0929 m².

SOURCE: *Trip Generation—An Informational Report, 1976,* and *Trip Generation Supplement No. 1, Feb. 1979,* Institute of Transportation Engineers, Washington, D.C.

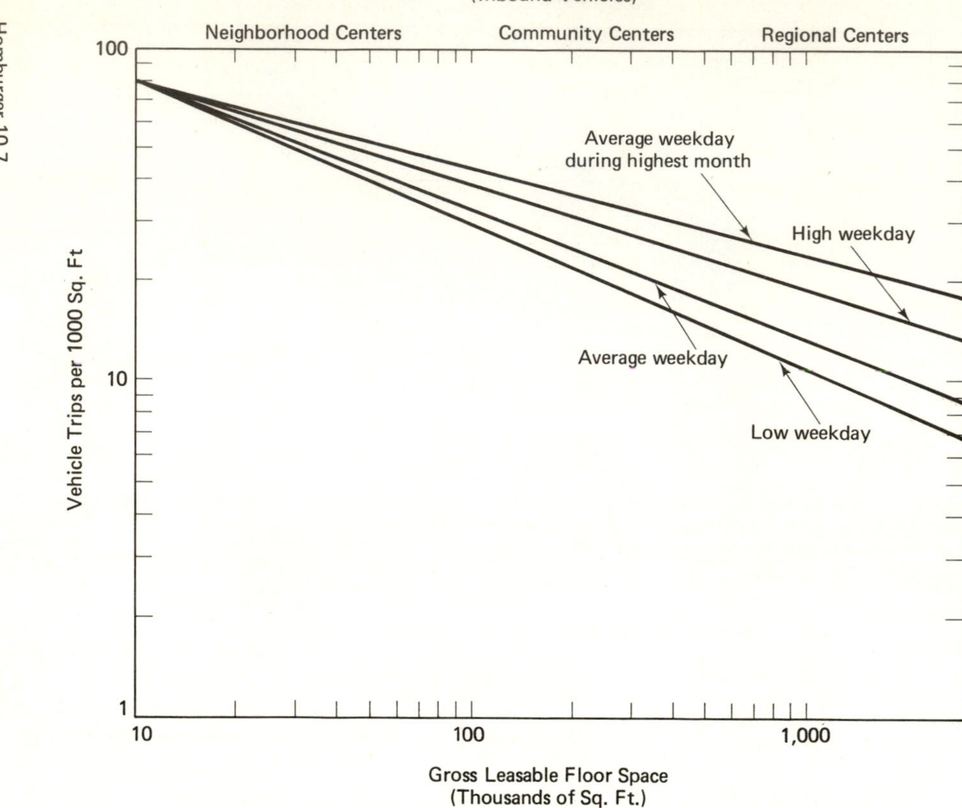

Figure 10.7. Daily vehicular trip rate to shopping centers. SOURCE: L. Hammel, Trip Generation Material Available at Tri-State Regional Planning Commission, Interim Technical Report 4418, New York, 1977.

Table 10-23 gives generalized monthly variations in entering traffic and dollar sales at regional shopping centers with more than 500,000 gross square feet of leasable area. The variations in traffic are less pronounced than those in dollar sales. This is because of the higher average purchases, especially in the pre-Christmas shopping season.

Car occupancy

Car occupancy—the number of passengers per car—is either determined by direct measurement or obtained through home-interview travel surveys. Cordon counts of vehicles and people entering and leaving the CBD are an important data resource. Cordon counts around downtown Providence in 1976, for example, showed an average occupancy of 1.40 persons per auto with 69% of the cars carrying one person; 24%, two people; and 7%, 3 to 6 people.[13] During the P.M. peak hour, car occupancy of vehicles leaving downtown Providence declined from 1.6 in 1957 to 1.5 in 1972 and 1.4 in 1976.

[13] *Downtown Providence—Traffic Circulation and Development Study,* Final Report, Wilbur Smith & Associates, New Haven, Conn., 1978.

TABLE 10–23
Monthly Variations in Traffic and Sales at Regional Shopping Centers

Month	Percent of Average Monthly Traffic Volume	Percent of Average Monthly Sales Volume
January	70	80
February	60	65
March	100	85
April	90	80
May	110	95
June	110	92
July	103	90
August	100	115
September	95	95
October	115	102
November	105	110
December	150	200

SOURCE: Traffic volume: *Two Regional Shopping Centers in Washington, 1971, and One in California, 1965,* Trip Generation Institute of Transportation Engineers Informational Report, Washington, D.C., 1976. Sales volume: DONALD E. CLEVELAND AND EDWARD A. MUELLER, *Traffic Characteristics of Regional Shopping Centers,* Bureau of Highway Traffic, Yale University, New Haven, Conn., 1961.

Urban car occupancies as reported in origin–destination surveys (United States) range from 1.4 to 1.7 on a typical weekday. Typical occupancies by trip purpose are shown as follows:

Type of Trip	Persons/Car
Work	1.2–1.3
Shopping	1.5–2.0
Personal business	1.5–1.6
School	2.0–3.0
Social–recreational	1.7–3.0

Occupancies for work and shopping trips increase as the number of persons per car increases (i.e., as car ownership in an urban area decreases). Social trip occupancies are the same for all levels of vehicle ownership, although fewer trips are made by families with low car ownership ratios.

Average automobile occupancies classified by major trip purpose and place of residence in standard metropolitan statistical areas (SMSA), as reported in the 1970 Nationwide Personal Transportation Survey, include weekend recreational trips and vacation trips. Consequently, they are somewhat higher than those reported in the various urban studies. Occupancies for all trip purposes range from 1.8 to 2.0, with the highest occupancies for educational, civic, religious, and social-recreational purposes (2.5 to 2.7 persons per car).

Vehicle occupancy distribution as a function of mean occupancy is shown in Figure 10.8. For example, if the mean occupancy is 1.5 persons per car, then 67% of the cars carry one person; 22%, two persons; 6%, three persons; and 5%, four persons.

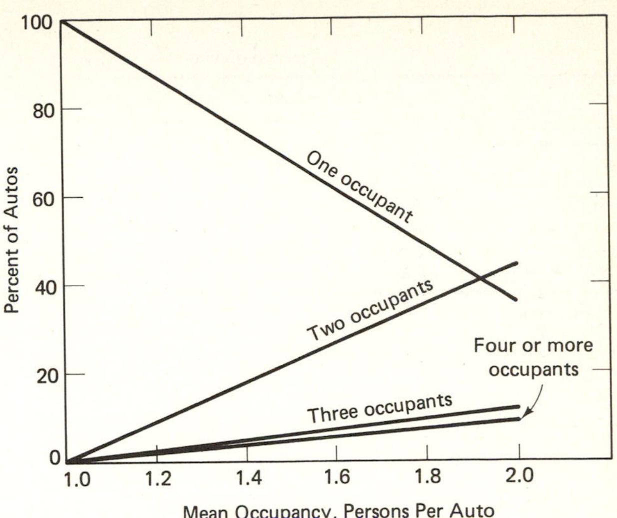

Figure 10.8. Vehicle occupancy distribution as a function of mean occupancy. SOURCE: Morin, D.A., Analysis of the Distribution of Automobile Occupancies. U.S. Department of Transportation, Federal Highway Administration, 1969.

Urban travel magnitudes

Investment levels and capacity requirements of urban highway and transit facilities should consider the total miles of travel as well as the number of trips. Person-miles of travel (PMT) and vehicle-miles of travel (VMT) are also useful in assessing the effectiveness of transportation improvements on air-quality levels and energy consumption. Therefore, person-miles of travel and vehicle-miles of travel are important planning parameters.

Total person travel. Table 10-24 summarizes the daily airline distance person-miles of travel, the person-miles per capita, and the average airline distance trip lengths in five major urban areas. (Airline distance is direct line as opposed to actual over-the-road miles). In the five cities shown, the airline distance person-miles per capita ranged from approximately 7 to 13 (11 to 21 person-km), and the average airline distance trip length, from 3.6 to 5.1 mi (5.8 to 8.2 km).

Airline trip lengths. Airline distance trip lengths by urban travel mode are shown for five major metropolitan areas in Table 10-25.

Travel Mode	mi	km
Auto (driver)	4.0–7.2	6.4–11.6
Auto (passenger)	3.6–7.2	5.8–11.6
Bus	2.5–4.3	4.0–6.9
Rapid transit	5.8–7.9	9.3–12.7
Commuter railroad	14.6–18.5	23.5–29.8

The increased length of rail transit trips results from (1) the greater speeds attainable, (2) the limited service coverage and greater distance between stations, and (3) the downtown focus of these trips. There also appears to be an increase

TABLE 10–24
Daily Urban Person Travel in Selected Urban Areas (Airline Miles)*

Study Area	Year	Population	Person-Miles (Airline)	Person-Trips (Destinations)	Airline Person-Miles/ Capita	Average Airline Trip Length (mi)
Chicago (eight-county area)	1970	7,593,000	95,647,000	18,616,000	12.6	5.1
Chicago	1956	5,169,700	49,164,000†	10,525,000	9.5	4.9
Philadelphia	1960	4,007,000	27,700,000	7,760,000	6.9	3.6
Minneapolis	1970	1,874,000	24,668,300	5,095,040	13.2	4.9
Washington	1955	1,568,500	11,536,000	2,589,000	7.4	4.5
Buffalo	1962	1,350,000	11,067,000	2,991,000	8.2	3.7

*1 mi = 1.609 km. Airline miles are straight line miles point to point.
†65,000,000 mi over the road.

SOURCE: Comprehensive transportation studies in each urban area.

TABLE 10–25
Average Urban Trip Lengths by Travel Mode in Selected Urban Areas (Airline Miles)*

Study Area	Year	Auto Driver	Auto Passenger	Taxi	Ferry	Bus–Car	Rapid Transit	Commuter Railroad	School Bus
Chicago	1956	4.3	4.5	—	—	3.6	7.2	14.6	—
	1970†	5.1	5.0	—	—	3.9	7.9	18.5	3.0
Minneapolis	1970	5.1	—	—	—	4.3	—	—	—
New York (tristate)	1963	4.0	3.6	2.1	4.5	2.5	5.8‡	17.6	—
San Diego	1975	7.2**	—	—	—	3.7	7.6§	—	—
Washington	1968‖	4.9	4.9	—	—	3.6	—	—	—

*1 mi = 1.609 km
†Expanded survey area.
‡NYCTA, 5.9; PATH, 4.9; SIRT, 6.2
§Express bus.
‖Nonwork.
**Average for drivers and passengers combined.

SOURCE: Comprehensive transportation studies in each urban area.

TABLE 10–26
CBD and Overall Trip Length Comparisons

Area	Year	Airline Trip Length (all modes) (mi)* All	CBD	Ratio
Chicago	1970	5.10	8.40	1.65
Philadelphia	1960	3.60	5.80	1.61
Minneapolis	1970	4.87	6.20	1.27

*1 mi = 1.609 km.

SOURCE: Comprehensive transportation studies in each urban area.

in trip lengths over time, although the increase may partially reflect a larger study area.

Trips to the city center are considerably longer than most other urban trips. This is apparent from Table 10-26, which sets forth comparative data for three cities; Chicago, Minneapolis, and Philadelphia. Person-trips to Chicago's Loop and Philadelphia's Center City are about 60% longer than overall trip lengths. In Minneapolis, without historic development along commuter rail lines, CBD trips are about 30% longer.

Comparative lengths of work trips and all trips are given in Table 10-27 for all modes (airline distance miles) and auto drivers (over-the-road miles). Work trips are generally 30 to 50% longer than other trips.

TABLE 10–27
Work versus Nonwork Trip Length Comparison*

	Work	All	Ratio Work/All
All modes (airline miles)			
Chicago, 1970	7.00	5.10	1.37
Minneapolis, 1970	6.57	4.87	1.35
Auto drivers (over-the-road miles)			
Boston	8.0	5.2	1.54
St. Louis	8.2	5.9	1.39
Seattle	7.6	5.1	1.49
Louisville	6.3	4.7	1.34
Oklahoma City	5.3	3.5	1.51
Colorado Springs	4.3	3.1	1.39
Stockton	4.2	2.9	1.45

*1 mi = 1.609 km.

SOURCE: Chicago and Minneapolis: comprehensive urban area transportation studies. Other data from PEAT, MARWICK, MITCHELL & CO., *An Analysis of Urban Area Travel by Time of Day*, various cities, 1972.

The relationship between airline distance and actual (over-the-road) trip lengths in selected urban areas is shown in Figure 10.9. The ratio depends on the configuration of the specific street network. It ranges from approximately 1.2 to 1.4; the higher figure reflects a complete grid, or irregular street system (Chicago, Pittsburgh), and the lower figure reflects radial–circumferential street systems (Detroit, Washington).

Vehicle-miles of travel. Over-the-road vehicle-miles of travel, vehicle trip lengths, and daily vehicle-miles of travel (VMT) (car and truck) per capita and per registered car are given in Table 10-28. These data are important in calibrating transportation system models and in checking the reasonableness of travel forecasts.

The following formulas based on regression analysis can serve as guides.[14]

$$\log(\text{VMT per vehicle}) = 0.99 + 0.07 \log P \qquad (10.2)$$

$$r = 0.66$$

$$\log[\text{avg trip length (mi)}] = 0.039 + 0.18 \log P \qquad (10.3)$$

$$r = 0.85$$

Note:
P is population
VMT refers to car plus truck VMT.

General vehicle trip length and VMT guidelines based on these formulas are: (1) total daily VMT/car should not exceed 30.0, and (2) average vehicle (car and truck) trip lengths should not exceed 6 mi except in very large urban areas.

Effect of population on trip lengths and trip times. The effect of population on trip length is shown in Figure 10.10. There is a general increase in trip length as urban population rises.

[14]LEVINSON, H. S. *Characteristics of Urban Transportation Demand, A Handbook for Transportation Planners*, Urban Mass Transportation Admin., Washington, D.C., April 1978, p. 19.

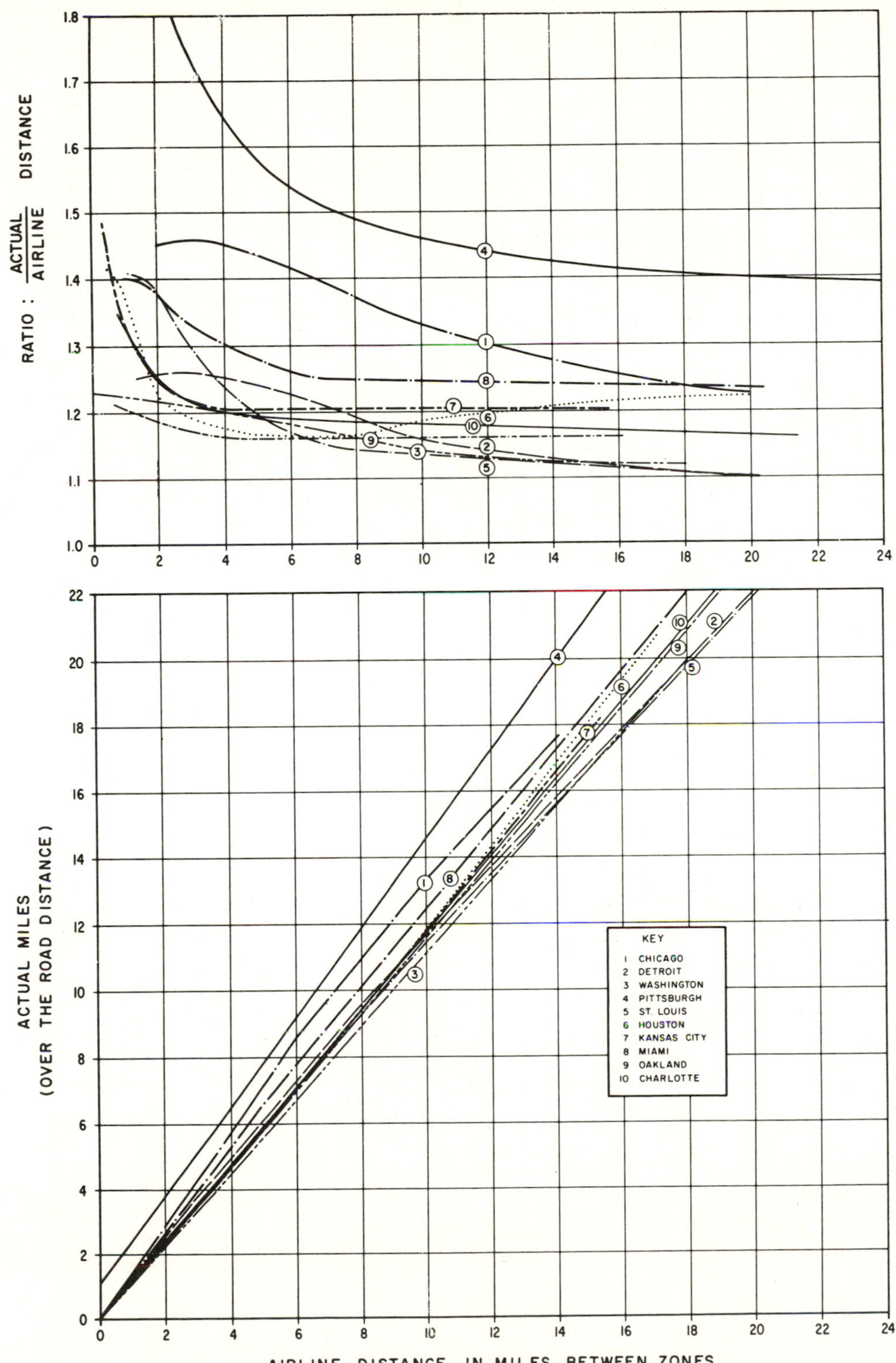

Figure 10.9. Trip length comparisons—airline mileage vs. over-the-road distance. SOURCE: H. S. Levinson and F. H. Wynn, "Some Aspects of Future Transportation in Urban Areas," Bulletin 326, Washington, D.C.: Highway Research Board, 1962, p. 8.

TABLE 10–28
Vehicle Travel in Selected Urban Areas (over-the-road miles)*,†,‡

Urbanized Area	Source	Year	Population	Trip Length (mi)	Daily VMT§/ Capita	Daily VMT§/ Car
New York–NY, NJ, CT	(1)	1972	19,100,000	—	9.7	—
New York–NY, NJ, CT	(1)	1963	16,302,000	8.0	8.8	34.2
Los Angeles, CA	(1)	1970	10,047,000	n.a.	14.3	28.1
Los Angeles, CA	(1)	1963	7,579,000	6.0	11.6	29.1
		1967	9,008,400	7.7	13.5	30.9
Chicago, IL	(5)	1970	7,543,000	n.a.	11.0	30.7
Chicago, IL	(1)	1956	5,170,000	5.9	7.0	26.9
Philadelphia, PA	(1)	1970	4,945,000	—	9.7	—
Philadelphia, PA	(1)	1960	4,007,000	4.9	7.2	26.6
San Francisco, CA	(1)	1965	4,400,000	n.a.	13.7	—
Boston, MA	(2)	1963	3,584,000	5.7	8.7	29.2
Detroit, MI	(1)	1965	4,042,000	5.7	10.4	27.9
Detroit, MI		1953	2,968,900	5.5	8.5	29.8
Washington, DC–MD–VA	(1)	1968	2,714,000	8.3	12.1	31.2
Washington, DC	(1)	1955	1,568,000	4.3	5.5	20.6
Houston, TX	(4)	1977	2,300,000	n.a.	17.8	n.a.
Dallas–Ft. Worth, TX	(4)	1970	2,200,000	n.a.	14.3	n.a.
St. Louis, MO	(2)	1965	2,175,000	6.3	9.1	—
St. Louis, MO	(1)	1957	1,276,000	4.7	6.6	22.9
Minneapolis–St. Paul, MN	(1)	1970	1,874,400	618	12.7	33.3
Milwaukee, WI	(5)	1972	1,811,000	5.9	11.1	28.6
Seattle, WA	(4)	1975	1,800,000	n.a.	13.1	n.a.
Seattle, WA	(2)	1961	1,350,000	5.5	8.9	24.6
Atlanta, GA	(5)	1972	1,640,000	7.7	13.8	28.9
Baltimore, MD	(3)	1962	1,601,000	5.8	n.a.	—
San Diego, CA	(1)	1975	1,555,000	7.2	13.4	31.0
Cincinnati, OH	(1)	1965	1,392,000	5.5	9.2	26.4
Buffalo, NY	(1)	1962	1,350,000	5.9	8.5	32.8
Denver, CO	(1)	1971	1,116,000	n.a.	12.2	27.0
Denver, CO		1970	1,000,000	n.a.	12.3	—
Kansas City, MO	(1)	1959	859,600	4.8	7.6	24.8
Louisville, KY	(1)	1964	768,900	n.a.	9.2	27.8
Honolulu, HI	(1)	1970	750,000	—	11.9	—
Springfield, MA	(1)	1965	531,000	5.0	8.9	27.9
Birmingham, AL	(1)	1965	559,100	5.0	10.1	28.1
Tucson, AZ	(1)	1973	407,000	n.a.	12.5	—
Tucson, AZ		1960	265,600	n.a.	8.4	23.3
Phoenix, AZ	(1)	1957	397,400	4.5	9.0	25.8
Nashville, TN	(1)	1959	357,600	4.2	7.5	25.1
Orlando, FL	(3)	1965	355,600	4.3	9.1	23.4
Peoria, IL	(1)	1964	260,800	4.1	9.6	—
Baton Rouge, LA	(3)	1965	245,100	3.3	7.7	—
South Bend, IN	(3)	1967	222,100	n.a.	9.5	23.3
Charlotte, NC	(1)	1958	202,300	3.4	6.9	22.6
Evansville, IN	(1)	1970	175,500	n.a.	10.3	23.0
Monroe, LA	(3)	1965	96,500	2.8	7.4	22.6
Champaign, IL	(3)	1965	94,200	n.a.	7.4	n.a.
Fort Smith, AR	(3)	1965	80,100	3.1	7.4	21.2
Great Falls, MT	(5)	1968	75,500	3.4	7.7	18.9

*1 mi = 1.609 km.
†Population as reported by urbanized area in relation to VMT: Generally, but not always transportation study area population.
‡n.a., not available.
§VMT = Vehicle Miles Traveled.

SOURCE: (1) WILBUR SMITH & ASSOCIATES, summaries of analysis of comprehensive urban area transportation studies, generally includes internal plus external car and truck trips. (2) PEAT, MARWICK, MITCHELL & CO., summaries. (3) Y. ZAHAVI, summaries—car trips only, except where noted. (4) Internal memorandum, Denver Council of Government Plan Restatement Model Output Reasonableness Check, Dec. 29, 1978. (5) INSTITUTE OF TRANSPORTATION ENGINEERS COMMITTEE 6F-1L, "Consistency of Origin-Destination (O&D) Characteristics through Time," *ITE J.*, Oct. 1979.

Trip times also increase as urban population increases. Regression analysis conducted by Voorhees et al. showed the following relationship between population and average work trip duration based on data for 23 cities, ranging from Beloit, Wisconsin, to Los Angeles, California:[15]

$$\log \bar{t} = -0.25 + 0.19 \log_e P \qquad (10.4)$$

where $\bar{t}$ = avg trip duration (min)

P = urban area population

This equation can be written

$$\bar{t} = 0.98P^{0.019} \qquad (10.5)$$

[15]A. M. VOORHEES, S. J. BELLOMO, J. L. SCHOFER, AND D. E. CLEVELAND, "Factors in Work Trip Lengths," *Highway Res. Rec. No. 141*, Highway Research Board, Washington, D.C., 1966, pp. 24–46.

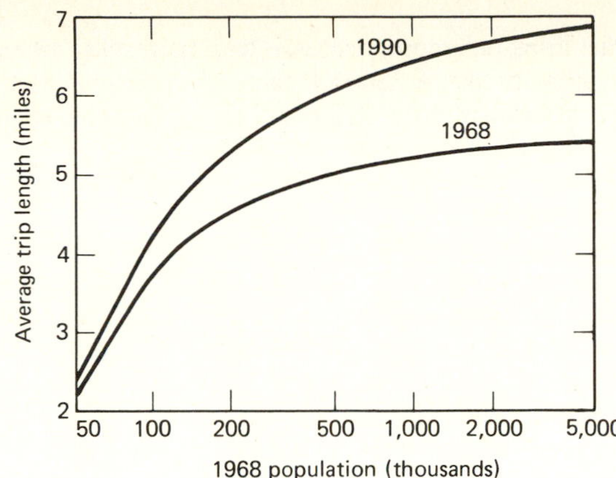

Figure 10.10. Average trip length in urban areas. SOURCE: Kassoff and Gendell, "An Approach to Multi-Regional Urban Transport Policy Planning," p. 83.

The standard error of the regression coefficient was 0.026, and the coefficient of determination (R^2) was 0.71.

The physical structure of an urban area appears to affect trip lengths and durations. Fort Worth, for example, had an average work trip length of 8.1 mi (13.0 km), and an average trip duration of 15.7 min. New Orleans, larger in population, but more compact, had an average work trip length of 2.5 mi (4.0 km), and an average trip duration of 7.4 min.

Travel time budgets. Zahavi has suggested that households have budgets in both monetary terms and time.[16] In 1970 about 0.75 to 0.85 person-hour per capita per day was spent in travel in large U.S. metropolitan areas.[17]

Urban truck travel

Urban goods movement reflects the diverse needs of the many establishments in the modern metropolis. There is a growing body of information on the characteristics and planning of urban goods movement.

Most urban goods movement takes place by motor truck. Two-thirds of the trucks registered are involved in local urban operations. Between 9 and 11 billion gallons of fuel are used each year in the urban goods movement process in the United States. This represents between 6% and 9% of U.S. total transportation fuel usage.[18]

Truck registrations. Truck ownership statistics for U.S. urban areas are shown in Figure 10.11. This chart reflects studies conducted between 1956 and 1965 for metropolitan areas ranging from approximately 50,000 to over 5,000,000 residents.

Urban motor truck registrations generally relate to the size of the urban area and its geographic setting. The higher per capita ownership of motor trucks in smaller cities largely reflects use for personal transportation purposes. As cities grow, the need for a personal truck diminishes because truck services are more readily available from "for-hire" sources, and the affluence level of residents is higher.

[16]Y. ZAHAVI, *Travel Characteristics in Cities of Developing and Developed Countries,* World Bank Staff Working Paper No. 230, Mar. 1976, p. 45; Y. ZAHAVI, *Travel Time Budgets and Mobility in Urban Areas: Final Report,* May 1974.

[17]Origin–destination studies in Philadelphia (1960), Detroit (1953), Minneapolis (1970), and Washington (1968). Values were 0.75, 0.75, 0.78, and 0.81, respectively.

[18]A. T. KEARNEY, *A Primer on Urban Goods Movement, Summary Report,* Washington, D.C., prepared for Urban Mass Transportation Administration, Apr. 1976.

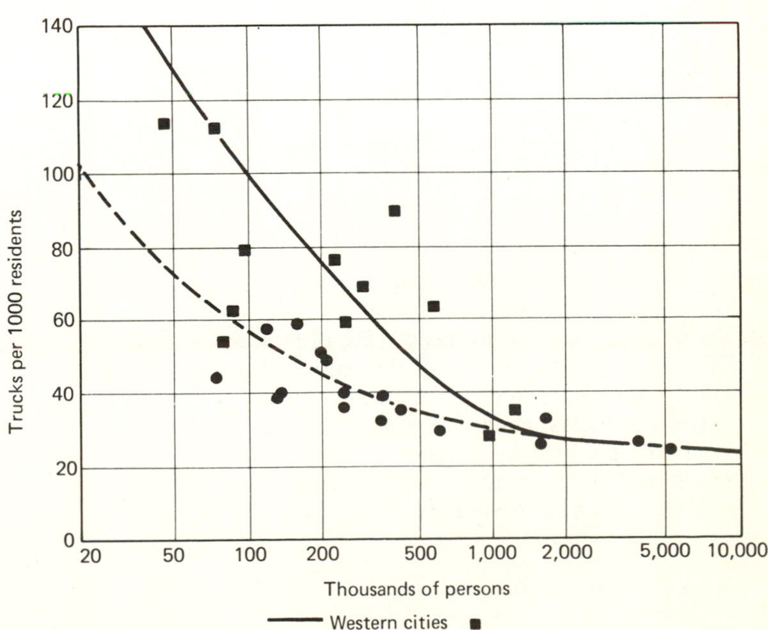

Figure 10.11. Registered trucks per capita. SOURCE: *Motor Trucks in the Metropolis,* prepared for Automobile Manufacturers Association by Wilbur Smith & Associates, 1969, p. 17.

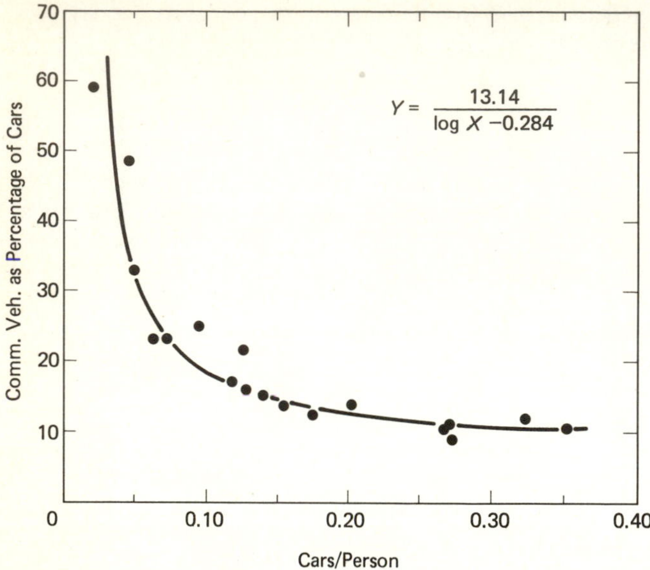

Figure 10.12. Proportions of commercial vehicles vs. cars/person. SOURCE: Y. Zahavi, Travel Characteristics in Cities of Developing and Developed Countries, Staff Working Paper No. 230, Mar. 1976. International Bank for Reconstruction and Development.

Truck ownership rates are also influenced by geographic differences of cities under 1 million residents. For urban areas of approximately 100,000 population in the East, South, and Midwest, the rate is approximately 60 per 1000 population; for Western cities, the rate is approximately 100 per 1000 residents. Above 1 million population, the ownership rate is consistent at approximately 25 to 30 registered trucks per 1000 persons.[19]

The relationship between commercial and passenger vehicles for cities throughout the world is shown in Figure 10.12. Commercial vehicles are a decreasing percentage of passenger cars as the cars per person increase.[20] This relationship can be expressed by

$$y = \frac{13.14}{\log x - 0.284} \tag{10.6}$$

where

$$x = \frac{\text{cars}}{100 \text{ people}} = \text{"motorization"}$$

$$y = \text{commercial vehicles per car}$$

Summary characteristics. The following characteristics typify truck travel in American cities:

1. Motor trucks account for about 15% of total daily trips. They represent up to 20% of the daily traffic on many city streets and expressways. Large trucks, including intercity vehicles, concentrate on expressways, whereas local delivery vehicles utilize city streets.
2. There are approximately 1.6 to 1.8 daily truck trips per acre of developed urban land.
3. Truck trips per capita decrease with increasing city size: for urban areas of 250,000 there are approximately 30 daily truck trips per 100 population; in urban areas of over 2,000,000, approximately 20.
4. There are approximately 2.0 daily truck-miles for each urban resident.
5. Light trucks dominate the urban traffic stream. They account for 68% of the trips and 65% of the truck miles. Medium trucks account for 27% of the trips and 25% of the miles; heavy trucks for about 5% of the trips and 10% of the miles. The mix of truck trips varies among cities; the proportion of heavy truck travel rises in larger and more industrialized activities.
6. Most truck trips are short, averaging less than 3 mi (5 km). Larger vehicles carrying heavier loads usually make longer trips. Typical urban truck trip lengths are:
   a. Light trucks: 2 to 3 miles (3 to 5 km)
   b. Medium trucks: 2 to 3 miles (3 to 5 km)
   c. Heavy trucks: 4 to 7 miles (6 to 11 km)
7. Typical stem driving speeds (time to the first stop and from the last stop) to the home terminal are:

Driving Conditions	min/mi	min/km
Congested areas	5.0	3.1
Normal urban conditions	3.3	2.0
Suburban areas	2.0	1.2
Expressways	1.3	0.8

Detailed characteristics. Detailed characteristics of urban truck travel in 11 urban areas are summarized in Tables 10-29 to 10-31. The 11 urban areas represented in these tabulations are Albuquerque, New Mexico; Baltimore, Maryland; Baton Rouge, Louisiana; Columbia, South Carolina; Lewiston, Maine; Little Rock, Arkansas; Manchester, New Hampshire; Monroe, Louisiana; Richmond, Virginia; Sioux Falls, South Dakota; and Winston-Salem, North Carolina.

1. Table 10-29 summarizes average daily truck usage. Light trucks represent two-thirds of the daily travel; medium and heavy trucks, one-third. On the average each truck made nearly 9 trips per day.
2. Table 10-30 summarizes daily truck travel according to industry classifications. Approximately 30% of the total daily travel represents trips by trucks engaged in the wholesale and retail trades. Another 17% represents trucks used in construction, and 15% represents trucks in personal use.
3. Table 10-31 indicates the trip purposes of trucks. The greatest number of trucks involve pickup and delivery operations.

Taxi and paratransit travel

Taxi travel by age group in the United States in 1970 is summarized in Table 10-32. People over 60 accounted for 9% of the total person-trips and 22% of the taxi trips, suggesting a higher use of taxis by the elderly.

A comparative analysis of users of 16 paratransit systems

[19]See *Motor Trucks in the Metropolis*, Wilbur Smith & Associates, Columbia, S.C., 1969.

[20]Y. ZAHAVI, *Travel Characteristics in Cities of Developing and Developed Countries*, pp. 20–21.

TABLE 10–29
Average Daily Truck Usage in 11 Urban Areas*

Truck Class	Trucks Making Trips		Daily Trips		Daily Truck-Miles		Daily Mileage		Daily Trips/ Truck†
	Number	Percent	Number	Percent	Number	Percent	Per Truck	Per Trip	
Medium	72,989	71.8	608,606	67.7	2,075,660	65.3	28.4	3.4	8.3
Medium-Heavy	28,691	28.2	289,810	32.3	1,104,742	34.7	36.5	3.8	10.1
Total	101,680	100.0	898,416	100.0	3,180,402	100.0	31.3	3.5	8.8

*The values are summations of trip values for the 11 areas shown in the source.
†These values are for trucks making trips on a typical weekday. When related to all trucks registered in the urban area, the average is 5.9 trips per day, since a proportion of the registered trucks are idle on any given day.

SOURCE: Comprehensive transportation studies by Wilbur Smith & Associates in Albuquerque, N.M.; Baltimore, Md.; Baton Rouge, La.; Columbia, S.C.; Lewiston, Me.; Little Rock, Ark.; Manchester, N.H.; Monroe, La.; Richmond, Va.; Sioux Falls, S.D.; Winston-Salem, N.C.

TABLE 10–30
Daily Truck Travel in 11 Urban Areas by Category of User and Class of Truck

User Category	Percent of Trucks Making Trips			Percent of Daily Trips			Percent of Daily Vehicle-Miles		
	Light	Heavy	All	Light	Heavy	All	Light	Heavy	All
Industry									
Agriculture	1.8	2.1	1.9	1.5	1.4	1.5	1.7	1.8	1.8
Construction	20.2	12.5	17.6	11.1	6.9	9.7	20.2	11.7	17.3
Manufacturing–processing	4.4	11.8	6.5	9.4	13.5	10.8	5.8	11.2	7.7
Transportation–public utilities	6.2	23.3	11.0	12.0	16.5	13.4	7.4	25.2	13.5
Wholesale–retail trade	20.9	36.4	25.3	33.2	45.7	37.4	26.9	37.0	30.3
Service and recreation	10.2	4.4	8.6	15.9	4.6	12.2	12.4	3.2	9.2
Government (public service)	2.9	6.5	3.9	3.8	9.1	5.5	3.7	7.4	5.0
Personal use	33.4	3.0	25.2	13.1	2.4	9.6	21.9	2.5	15.2
All users	100.0	100.0	100.0	100.0	100.0	100.0	100.0	100.0	100.0

SOURCE: See Source of Table 10–29.

TABLE 10–31
Percentage Distribution of Purposes for Urban Truck Trips in 11 Urban Areas

Trip Purpose at Trip Destination		Percentage of Total Daily Trips
Home base		19.3
Personal use		9.1
All pickup and delivery		41.1
Retail	17.3	
Wholesale	16.3	
Merchandise	7.5	
Mail and express		6.1
Construction		4.9
Maintenance and repair		8.0
Business use		7.2
Other		4.3
All purposes		100.0

SOURCE: See Table 10–29.

is given in Table 10-33. This table indicates that nondrivers, members of the households without cars, and the elderly are represented far beyond their population shares; however, the patterns vary among properties, depending upon specific local circumstances.

Hourly variations

The hourly variations of travel throughout the typical weekday reflect the basic purposes for which trips are made and the capabilities of the various travel modes. Vehicular travel on highways is normally less peaked than public transport (especially rail transit) because (1) more travel takes place during evenings and other off-peak times for nonwork purposes and (2) road capacity constrains peak-hour travel on many streets and highways.

TABLE 10–32
Proportion of Taxi Trips by Population Age Groups, 1970

Age Groups	Total Person-Trips (× 10^6)		Total Taxi Trips (× 10^6)		Percentage of All Trips Made by Taxi
	Number	Percent	Number	Percent	
5–13	21,020	14	42	11	0.2
14–15	5,271	4	11	3	0.2
16–20	15,527	11	—	—	0.1
21–25	14,652	10	44	11	0.3
26–29	10,046	7	40	10	0.4
30–39	23,905	16	72	18	0.3
40–49	24,070	17	48	12	0.2
50–59	16,685	12	50	13	0.3
60–64	6,391	4	45	11	0.7
65–69	3,236	2	26	7	0.8
70 and over	4,263	3	17	4	0.4
Total	145,066	100	395	100	0.3

SOURCE: FEDERAL HIGHWAY ADMINISTRATION, *Nationwide Personal Transportation Study Report No. 9*, Washington, D.C., 1973; A. RANDILL, H. GREENHALGH, and E. SAMSON. Data derived from National Personal Transportation Study by A. ALTSHULER, J. P. WOMACK, and J. R. PUCHER, in *The Urban Transportation System, Politics and Policy Innovation*, MIT Press, Cambridge, Mass., 1979.

Variations by mode. A composite of typical hourly variations by travel mode is shown in Figure 10.13 for Detroit, Washington, Chicago, Pittsburgh, and Toronto. Approximately 10% of all person travel takes place in the morning peak period, and again in the evening peak period. During these peaks, public transport carries a relatively large share of the total trips. Approximately 12% to 16% of all person trips by transit and from 8% to 10% by car take place in the peak hour. During the evening shopping period

TABLE 10–33
Characteristics of Demand-Responsive Transit Riders

	Date of Survey	Percentage of Users from Households with No Auto	Percentage of Users from Households with One Auto	Nondrivers (% of Users)	Youth (% of Users under 16)	Elderly (% of Users over 64)	Handicapped (% of Users)*
Ann Arbor, MI	2/75	26	35	45	20	4	0.6
Benton Harbor–St. Joseph, MI	11/74	41	38	64	9	17	Unknown
Beverly–Fairfax, CA	2/76	Unknown	Unknown	Unknown	Unknown	89	2.0
Columbus, OH	8/72	69	15	82	15	22	Unknown
El Cajon, CA	Unknown	Unknown	Unknown	Unknown	Unkown	33	0.6
La Habra, CA	10/75	Unknown	Unknown	Unknown	Unknown	19	0.4
Ludington, MI	9/74	54	27	68	7	41	2.9
Merced, CA	Unknown	Unknown	Unknown	Unknown	Unknown	Unknown	Unknown
Midland, MI	10/74	22	37	50	18	9	0.8
Niles, MI	5/75	58	28	Unknown	13†	30	1.7
Oneonta, NY	11/74	Unknown	Unknown	Unknown	13	21	Unknown
Rochester, NY	6/75	23	41	57	11	7	0.7
Santa Clara Co., CA	2/75	Unknown	Unknown	Unknown	55‡	3	Unknown
Xenia, OH	7/73	Unknown	Unknown	63	33‡	3	Unknown

*Figures refer to the nonambulatory handicapped.
†No attempt was made to compensate for "no response.".
‡Figures were obtained through interpolation.

SOURCE: REID EWING AND NIGEL WILSON, *Innovation in Demand-Responsive Transit,* MIT Center for Transportation Studies, Cambridge, Mass., Oct. 1976, Table 10, pp. 28–29.

Figure 10.13. Hourly variation of travel by mode. SOURCE: Compiled from data on five North American cities, Chicago, Detroit, Pittsburgh, Toronto, Washington.

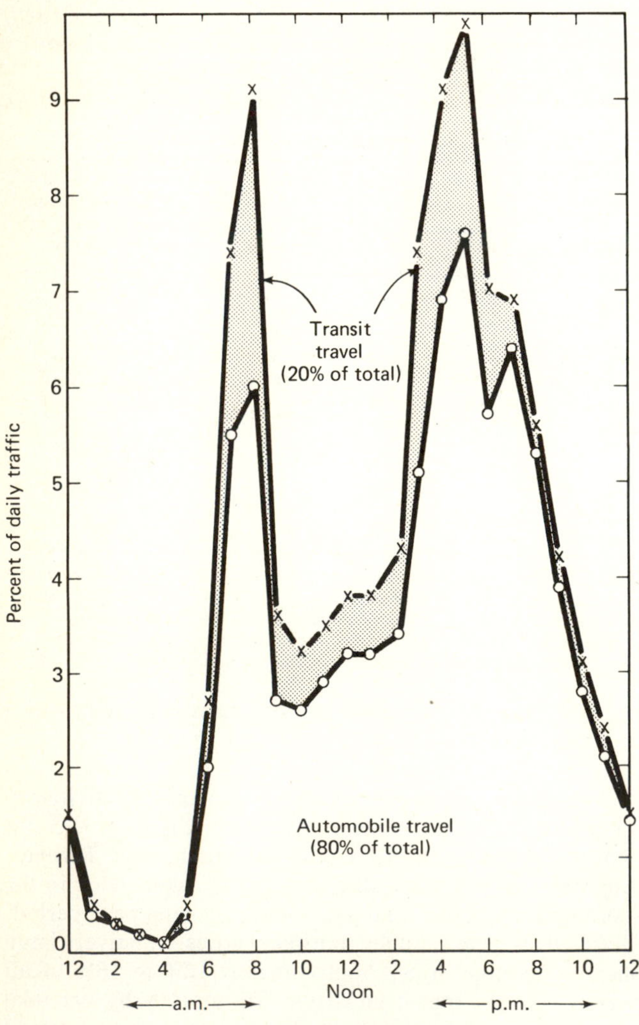

(7:00 to 8:00 P.M.) more trips in autos are made than during the morning peak hour, largely because of higher car occupancies. Approximately 80% of all person-trips are made by automobile.

Peaking characteristics of urban trips by mode are further detailed in Tables 10-34 and 10-35 and Figure 10.14.

1. Table 10-34 gives ratios of peak to 24-h travel for pedestrian, bus, taxi, car, rapid transit, and commuter rail trips in New York, Chicago, and three Connecticut cities.

TABLE 10–34
Peaking Characteristics in New York, Chicago, and Three Connecticut Cities

Location	Mode	Hour	Percent of 24-h Traffic in Peak Hour (Two Directions)
Manhattan cordon	Commuter rail	A.M.	23.7
	Subway	A.M.	16.7
	Bus	A.M.	10.0
Manhattan (midtown)	Pedestrian trips	Noon	11.9
Manhattan (excluding midtown)	Pedestrian trips		
	Department store	Noon	23.8
	Other buildings	P.M.	17.6
	Restaurant	Noon	19.0
	Apartment	P.M.	10.7
New York suburban area	Auto trips	P.M.	8.8
	Taxi trips	A.M.	8.2
Chicago, IL	Rapid transit	P.M.	13.9
	Bus	A.M.	11.8
Hartford, CT	Bus	P.M.	15.4
New Haven, CT	Bus	P.M.	12.0
Stamford, CT	Bus	P.M.	12.6

SOURCE: B. PUSHKAREV AND J. ZUPAN, *Urban Space for Pedestrians, A Report of the Regional Plan Association,* MIT Press, Cambridge, Mass., 1975; B. PUSHKAREV AND J. ZUPAN, *Public Transportation and Land Use Policy,* Indiana University Press, Bloomington, Ind., 1977; Chicago Transit Authority, 1970 survey.

TABLE 10-35
Hourly Variations in Weekday Rapid-Transit Ridership

Hour Beginning	Percent of Daily Ridership (Two Directions) Chicago (CTA), 1970	New York City (NYCTA), 1975	San Francisco (BART), 1977
12:00 Midnight	0.9	0.7	0.2
1:00 A.M.–5:00 A.M.	1.1	1.6	—
5:00 A.M.	1.7	0.8	0.2
6:00 A.M.	6.0	3.5	3.2
7:00 A.M.	13.3	10.8	13.6
8:00 A.M.	12.5	12.9	13.1
9:00 A.M.	4.0	6.4	4.9
10:00 A.M.	3.0	3.6	3.9
11:00 A.M.	2.8	3.0	4.1
12 Noon	2.7	3.1	4.6
1:00 P.M.	3.1	3.2	4.1
2:00 P.M.	4.0	4.4	4.6
3:00 P.M.	6.2	6.6	6.0
4:00 P.M.	12.5	11.0	9.9
5:00 P.M.	13.9	13.1	16.1
6:00 P.M.	4.8	5.9	3.9
7:00 P.M.	2.3	3.1	3.0
8:00 P.M.	1.6	2.1	1.6
9:00 P.M.	1.3	1.6	1.2
10:00 P.M.	1.2	1.5	0.9
11:00 P.M.	1.1	1.1	0.9
Total	100.0	100.0	100.0

SOURCE: Chicago: Chicago Transit Authority, OPX74263, May 1974, based on 24-h traffic checks taken in June 1970 at maximum use points on each route (10 locations). New York: Turnstile counts, NYCTA, Mar. 5, 1975; undistributed included with midnight hours. San Francisco: derived from "Draft, Summary Report," *BART Impact Study*, Metropolitan Transportation Commission, 1978, Fig. 12.

2. Table 10-35 gives hour-by-hour variations of rapid transit ridership in Chicago, New York, and San Francisco.
3. Figure 10.14 gives hourly variations of bus trips in eight cities.

Significant ranges for peak two-directional trips as a percent of daily trips, based on these exhibits, are:

Commuter rail	24%
Rapid transit	14–17
Bus—large cities	10–12
Bus—medium-sized cities	12–16
Bus—small cities	12–20
Pedestrians (CBD)	12–25
Auto	9

The Chicago Transit Authority reports that 21% of the inbound rapid transit trips take place from 8:00 to 9:00 A.M., and 24% of the outbound rapid transit trips occur from 5:00 to 6:00 P.M.

Peak-hour travel on specific facilities. Peak-hour travel on specific rail transportation and highway facilities

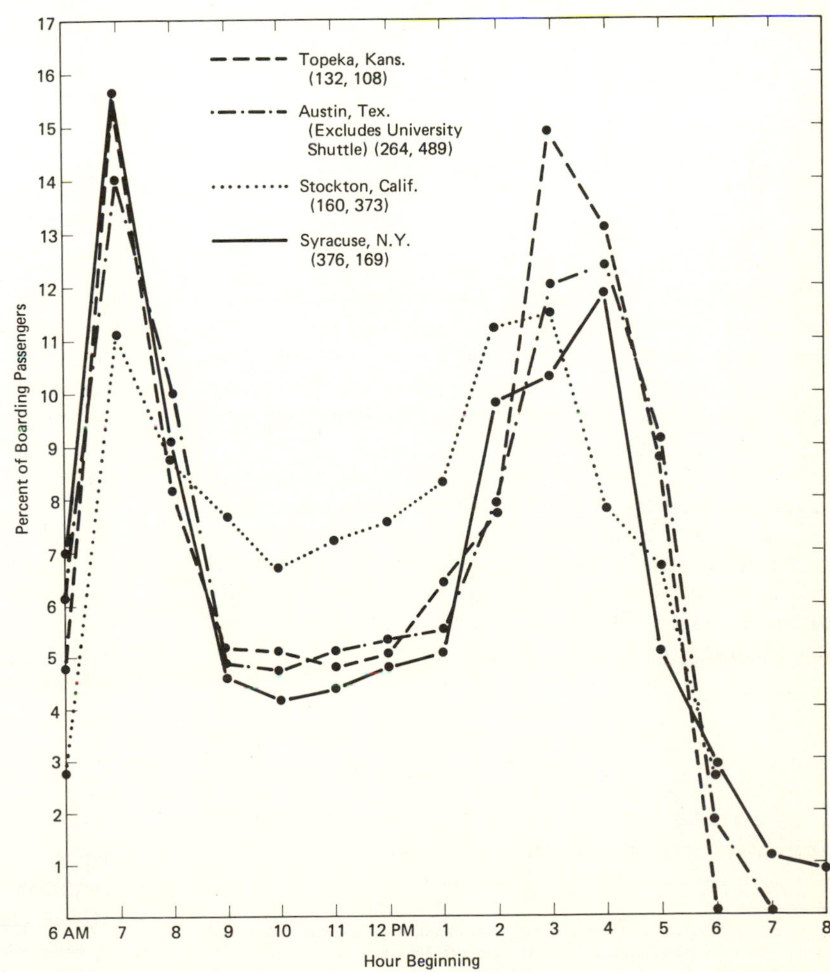

Figure 10.14. (a) Bus ridership by time of day for selected medium-sized urban areas (100,000 to 400,000 population). SOURCE: Report UTP PMM761.1, Analyzing Transit Options for Small Urban Communities, PMM and D.H. James, U.S. Department of Transportation, Jan. 1978.

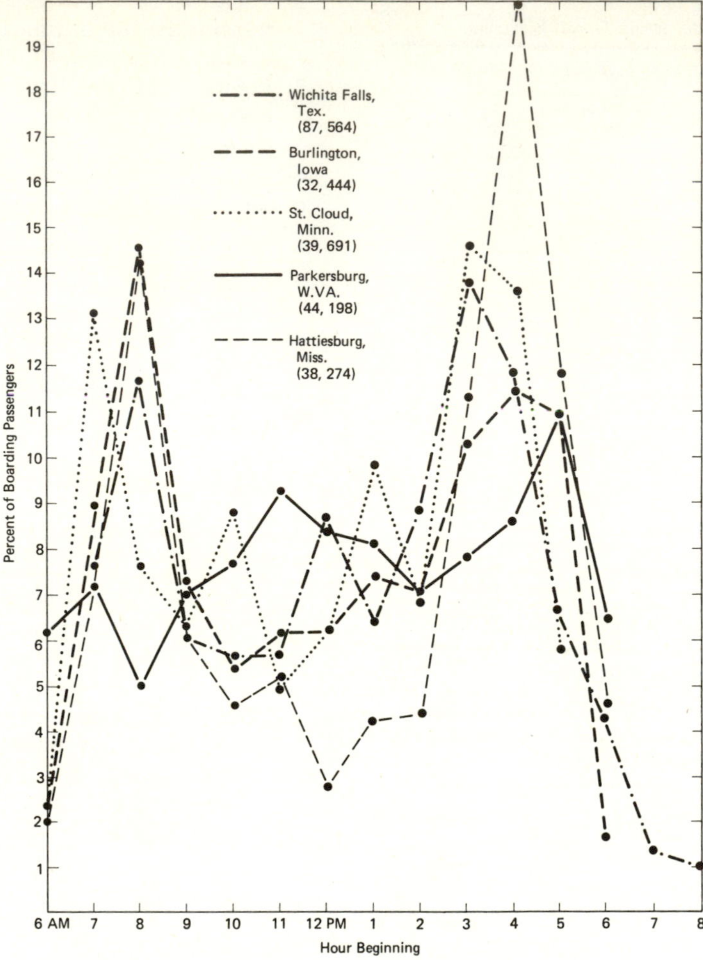

Figure 10.14. (b) Bus ridership by time of day in selected small urban areas (30,000 to 100,000 population). SOURCE: Ibid Figure 10.14.

are given in Tables 10-36 and 10-37, respectively. The peak-hour travel in the heavy direction approximates 25% for commuter railroads, 18% to 20% for rapid transit lines (except for a few routes), and 3% to 8% for urban express roads. These peaking patterns have not changed appreciably over the last two decades.[21]

Variations in truck traffic. Hourly variations in truck travel by class of truck and purpose of truck trip are shown in Table 10-38 and Figure 10.15, respectively. Truck travel remains relatively constant throughout the day, generally peaking at about 10:00 A.M. This peak reflects the increases in midmorning deliveries.

Central-business-district travel characteristics

The central business district (CBD) is the urban region's cultural, commercial, and financial center; the focus of its transportation system; and the area of greatest travel intensity.

A clear knowledge of downtown travel patterns is essential in assessing the capacity requirements of the urban transport system, developing CBD circulation improvement and transportation system management plans, and formulating regional transportation policy.

Summary patterns

Travel characteristics for a wide range of city centers throughout the United States and Canada are summarized in Tables 10-39 to 10-41.

1. Table 10-39 gives data on CBD area, employment, floor space, and person-destinations by mode for the 30 largest urbanized areas in the United States, ranked by population. Data are given for several points in time where information is available. CBD area and employment data are as reported in origin–destination or cordon count studies and may vary from that reported by the U.S. Bureau of the Census.

[21]Corresponding values reported in the first edition of the *Transportation and Traffic Engineering Handbook*, 1975, were over 20% for commuter railroads, 12% to 16% for rapid transit lines, and 4% to 8% for urban express roads.

TABLE 10–36
Peak-Hour Travel on Selected Rail Transportation Facilities, United States and Canada

Facility or Cordon	Estimated Daily Patronage at Maximum Load Point (Two-Way)	Peak-Hour Peak Direction Traffic at Maximum Load Point (One-Way)	
		Number	Percent of Daily Total
Suburban Railroads (1963)			
Long Island Railroad at Penn. Station	136,900 (P.M.)	31,600	23.1
Penn Central/New Haven Railroad at Grand Central	132,400 (A.M.)	33,800	25.5
New York City (1974)			
59th Street Cordon	1,305,560	170,540	13.0
Queens Cordon	791,170	130,610	16.5
Brooklyn Cordon	1,109,890	179,470	16.1
PATH—Lower Manhattan	82,500	29,000	24.2
PATH—Midtown	51,400	10,000	19.5
Chicago (1973)			
North–South (North Side)	120,000	14,000	11.7
North–South (South Side)	80,000	11,000	13.7
West–Northwest (NW Side)	72,000	14,000	19.4
West–Northwest (SW Side) (Douglas–Congress)	78,000	8,500	12.0
Lake–Ryan (West Side)	43,000	5,800	15.8
Lake–Ryan (South Side)	87,000	14,000	16.1
Ravenswood	45,000	6,600	14.7
Evanston	20,000	3,700	18.5
Skokie Swift	7,000	1,300	18.5
Philadelphia (1975)			
Market (subway–surface)			
Broad Street (N. of Market)	96,000	8,500	8.9
Market–Frankford (E. of Broad)	103,000	12,800	12.4
Market–Frankford (W. of Broad)	103,000	11,700	11.3
Camden–Lindenwold Line–Patco	41,000	8,000	19.5
Cleveland (1974)			
East–West Rapid (East Side)	10,000	1,900	19.0
East–West Rapid (West Side)	34,000	5,100	15.0
Toronto (1974–5)			
Yonge Street (N. of Bloor)	234,000	28,000	12.0
Yonge Street (S. of Bloor)	265,000	36,000	13.6
Bloor Street (W. of University)	193,000	23,000	12.0
Bloor Street (E. of Yonge Street)	184,000	22,000	12.0
University (S. of Bloor)	70,000	15,000	12.0
San Francisco (1975)			
BART (Concord Line)	32,000	6,200	19.4
BART (Daly City Line)	36,000	6,300	17.5

SOURCE: H. S. LEVINSON, *Characteristics of Urban Transportation Demand, A Handbook for Transportation Planners*, prepared for Urban Mass Transportation Administration, Washington, D.C., 1978.

TABLE 10–37
Peak-Hour Urban Freeway and Expressway Volumes

City and 1970 Urbanized Area Population	Facility	Number of Lanes	Year	Average Daily Traffic	Peak Directional Volumes	
					Vehicles	Percent of ADT
Atlanta, GA	I-20 E. of CBD at Moreland Ave.	6	1975	105,100	5,980	5.7
1,172,778	I-75 S. of CBD at University Ave.	6	1975	110,800	6,200	5.6
	I-20 W. of CBD at Mozley Drive	6	1975	78,600	4,450	5.7
	I-75 N. of CBD (N. of I-85)	6	1975	72,800	4,500	6.2
	I-85 N. of I-75 at Monroe Drive	6	1975	90,100	5,500	6.1
Boston, MA	I-93 at Stoneham Town Line	6–8	1975	80,300	6,270	7.8
2,652,575	S.E. Expwy at Southampton	6–8	1975	129,000	7,060	5.4
	Rt. 128 at Burlington Town Line	8	1975	86,400	5,660	6.6
Chicago, IL	Lake Shore Drive at 49th Street	6–8	1975	61,100	4,120	6.8
6,714,578	Lake Shore Drive at Aldine	8	1975	117,000	9,380	8.0
Denver, CO	I-25 between 38th Ave. and I-70	6	1974	145,000	7,500	5.2
1,047,311	I-225 between I-25 and Washington St.	6	1974	105,000	5,400	5.1
Detroit, MI	Ford Fwy. (I-94) at Chrysler Fwy.	6	1975	161,500	5,570	3.4
3,970,584	Jeffers Fwy. (I-96) at Warren		1974	72,100	4,850	6.7
	Southfield Fwy (M39) at Plymouth	6	1973	142,100	6,210	4.4
	Lodge (M10) at Pallister	6	1972	173,000	5,310	3.1
	Fisher Fwy. at Lodge	6–8	1972	118,100	5,310	4.5
Houston, TX	I-45—Gulf at Woodbridge	6	1976	106,600	4,910	4.6
1,677,863	US 59—S.W. at Montrose	10	1976	145,900	8,470	5.8
	US 59 S.W. at Rice Ave.	8	1976	162,700	6,730	4.1

TABLE 10-37 (Continued)

City and 1970 Urbanized Area Population	Facility	Number of Lanes	Year	Average Daily Traffic	Peak Directional Volumes	
					Vehicles	Percent of ADT
Houston, TX	I-45—North side of North Loop	8	1976	121,900	7,420	6.0
	I-10—East W. of Waco St.	8	1976	117,600	7,090	6.0
	I-610 West at Buffalo Bayou	8–10	1976	174,400	9,520	5.4
	I-10 North E. at North Main	8	1976	125,300	6,640	5.3
	I-610—Katy E. of Taylor St.	10	1976	109,500	7,600	6.9
	I-610—South West of Main	8	1976	100,300	6,700	6.7
Milwaukee, WI 1,252,457	N-S Fwy at Wisconsin		1975	90,310	5,260	5.8
	N-S Fwy at Greenfield		1975	96,770	5,780	6.0
	E-W Fwy at 26th St.		1975	93,280	5,000	5.4
	Airport Fwy at 68th		1975	62,300	3,520	5.7
New York City, NY 16,206,841	Long Island Expwy	6	1973	165,000	5,300	3.2
	FDR Drive	6	1974	117,000	4,400	3.8
	Holland Tunnel	4	1974	61,400	2,400	3.9
	Lincoln Tunnel	6	1974	97,300	4,900	5.0
	Brooklyn–Battery Tunnel	4	1974	46,700	3,400	7.3
San Francisco, CA 2,987,850	Oakland–Bay Bridge (I-80)	10	1973	184,000	8,120	4.4
	Southern Fwy (I-280)	8	1969–73	114,000	6,150	5.4
	Golden Gate Bridge (U.S. 101)	6	1969–73	92,000	5,720	6.2
Washington, DC–MD–VA 2,481,489	Shirley Hwy (N. of 4 Mile River)	8	1975	136,000	8,010	5.9
	Center Leg Fwy	8	1975	68,000	3,410	5.0
	I-95 Bridge (over Potomac)	8	1975	142,700	6,260	4.4
	Balt.–Wash. Pkwy (District Line)	6	1975	101,300	4,930	4.9
	Woodrow Wilson Bridge	6	1975	97,800	4,620	4.7

SOURCE: H. S. LEVINSON, *Characteristics of Urban Transportation Demand, A Handbook for Transportation Planners,* prepared for UMTA, Washington, D.C., 1978.

TABLE 10-38
Hourly Variations in Truck Trips on a Typical Business Day

Hour Beginning	Percentage Distributions		
	Light Trucks	Heavy Trucks	Total, All Trucks
6:00 A.M.	3.2	3.5	3.3
7:00 A.M.	6.5	7.0	6.7
8:00 A.M.	9.1	10.9	9.7
9:00 A.M.	10.1	11.6	10.6
10:00 A.M.	10.4	11.4	10.7
11:00 A.M.	10.1	10.9	10.4
12:00 Noon	7.9	7.5	7.8
1:00 P.M.	9.0	9.5	9.1
2:00 P.M.	8.5	8.8	8.6
3:00 P.M.	7.6	8.0	7.8
4:00 P.M.	8.2	6.4	7.6
5:00 P.M.	6.1	3.1	5.1
6:00 P.M.	2.7	1.0	2.2
Other	0.5	0.4	0.4
Total	100.0	100.0	100.0

SOURCE: Percentages derived from Table A-7L, "Truck Statistics," *Motor Trucks in the Metropolis,* by Wilbur Smith & Associates, Columbia, S.C. 1969, p. 185.

2. Table 10-40 gives cordon count data for the 20 largest United States urbanized areas. It summarizes the peak-hour one-way person movements and peak person accumulation by mode.
3. Table 10-41 gives employment and cordon count data for major Canadian city centers.

General characteristics. The following characteristics typify American and Canadian cities:

1. Most CBDs are located near the population center of the urban region, except where inhibited by topography. They generally occupy from 1.0 to 1.5 mi^2 of area and contain less than 40 million ft^2 of floor space. Approximately half of all downtown land is devoted to streets and parking, because of the many lots and garages in the downtown area.
2. There is a highly skewed distribution of CBD intensity. A few large U.S. city centers—New York, Chicago, Washington, San Francisco, Boston, and Philadelphia—far outstrip other centers when measured in terms of floor space, employment, person-destinations, and relative transit use.
3. Peak-hour cordon volumes are generally fewer than 100,000 persons. This implies corridor movements by all modes that are usually under 25,000 persons.
4. Per capita trip attractions to the city center generally decrease with increasing time and distance from the city center. Per capita attraction of workers is relatively constant in comparison.
5. In most cities, trips to the city center have grown at a slower rate than the overall growth in total metropolitan area trips. This usually results in a decline of trips between established neighborhoods and the city center and an increase in trips from suburban areas. As a consequence, there is generally an increase in average trip lengths and a decrease in public transportation use over time.
6. The number of people entering, leaving, or accumulated in the city center has remained relatively constant in many cities. In Boston, for example, the number of people accumulated downtown was about the same in

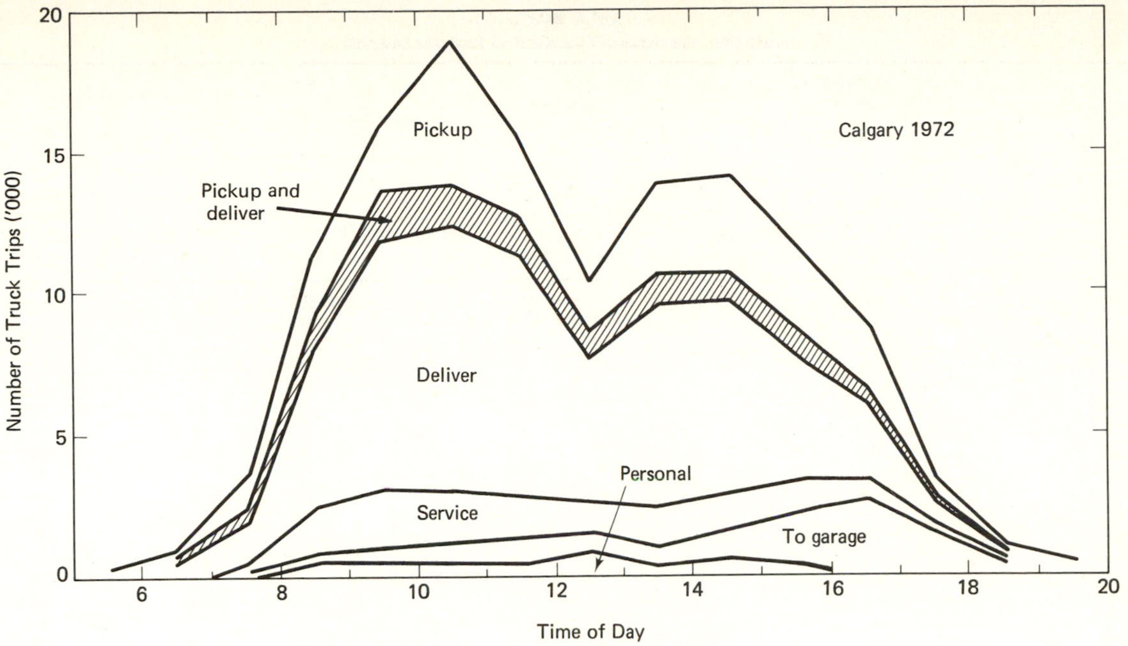

Figure 10.15. Truck trips by time of day, Calgary, 1972.

1927 and 1972; data for Chicago's Loop and Manhattan also show little long-term change. There are exceptions, depending upon the economy of the center and, in some cases, new freeway patterns that reduce the number of entrants. Sometimes, new commercial areas develop outside the traditional downtown cordon, (i.e., North Michigan Avenue, Chicago).

7. The importance of public transportation to the city center depends on (1) historic antecedents, (2) barriers and constraints to automobile travel, and (3) intensity of downtown land use and employment.
8. In cities with a high employment density, a major decline in public transport riding could seriously increase congestion and capital expenditure for transport.
9. In most American cities, one-half to two-thirds of all peak-hour vehicular traffic passes through the center, with origins and destinations either in adjacent areas or elsewhere in the urban region. In contrast, two-thirds to three-fourths of all rail transit riders have origins or destinations in the downtown area.

These general patterns and trends should be considered in estimating future travel demands and transportation system requirements.

Travel magnitudes and trip purposes. Generalized relationships between urban population and CBD trip destinations by purpose are shown in Figures 10.16 and 10.17. Travel to the CBD increases in magnitude as urban population rises, but at a decreasing rate. The proportion of trips for work purposes increases with size; more than half of all person-trips to the CBDs in urban areas of over 1 million persons are for work purposes.

1. The daily person-destinations in the CBD increase from approximately 40,000 in urban areas of up to 200,000 population to approximately 225,000 in urban areas with 2,000,000 inhabitants.
2. The proportion of work trips increases from approximately 33% in urban areas of 200,000 population to over 50% in the larger urban areas. This indicates that the city center increasingly becomes a work center as urban areas get larger.
3. In urban areas in the 2 million population category, approximately 55% of all downtown person-destinations are for work purposes, 15% for shopping, 15% for personal business, and 15% for social, recreational, and miscellaneous reasons.
4. Shoppers account for a higher proportion of total daily pedestrian trips than they represent of total person-trips to the CBD.

Internal movement patterns

Most person-trips within the CBD are made as pedestrians. Pushkarev and Zupan, for example, estimate that 52% of the total daily person-miles of travel in midtown Manhattan are by pedestrians, with the figure ranging up to 70% during noontime and P.M. peaks.[22]

[22]B. Pushkarev and J. Zupan, *Urban Space for Pedestrians, A Report of the Regional Plan Association,* MIT Press, Cambridge, Mass., 1975.

TABLE 10–39
Selected Characteristics of U.S. Central Business Districts

1970 Census Rank	Urbanized Area	1970 Population (× 10³)		1970 Central City Pop. Density (Persons/ mi²)	Central Business District								
									Daily Person-Trip Destinations			Destinations/ mi²	
										Percentage by:			
		Urbanized Area	Central City		CBD Area (mi²)	Year of O-D Survey	Employment (1,000's)	Floor Space (ft² × 10³)	No. (× 10³)	Auto	Transit	All Modes	Autos Only
1	New York–NY, NJ	16.207	7.895	26,343	9.0[a]	1963	1,752	800	2,405	11	89	267	29
					2.0[b]	1963	1,000	241	—	—	—	—	—
					1.0[b]	1963	500	—	—	—	—	—	—
2	Los Angeles, CA	8.351	2.816	6,073	0.6[c]	1960	130	42	158	45	55	250	114
					2.0[d]	1966	176[e]	76	—	—	—	—	—
3	Chicago, IL, IN	6.715	3.367	15,126	1.1	1956	300	92	466	29	71	439	128
4	Philadelphia, PA, NJ	4.021	1.949	15,164	2.2	1960	225	124	389	41	59	177	73
5	Detroit, MI	3.971	1.511	10,953	1.1	1953	114	50	253	56	44	234	132
						1974	—	—	62	65	35	—	—
6	San Francisco, CA	2.988	0.716	15,764	2.2	1965	282	88	423	63	37	192	71
						1970	304	—	—	—	—	—	—
7	Boston, MA	2.653	0.641	13,936	1.4	1963	246	—	400	50	50	290	145
						1972	263	96	—	—	—	—	—
8	Washington, DC, MD, VA	2.481	0.757	12,321	4.5[f]	1955	315	—	442	57	43	98	43
					1.7[g]	1955	212	—	266	55	45	156	86
9	Cleveland, OH	1.960	0.751	9,893	1.0	1963	117	47	123	59	41	123	73
10	St. Louis, MO, IL	1.883	0.622	10,167	0.8	1957	119	39	125	53	47	178	95
11	Pittsburgh, PA	1.846	0.520	9,422	0.5	1958	84	32	154	49	51	308	151
						1969	100	—	151	55	45	302	166
12	Minneapolis–St. Paul, MN	1.704	0.434	8,135	0.9	1958	90	—	188	73	27	209	153
						1970	—	—	166	80	20	184	147
13	Houston, TX	1.678	1.231	3,102	0.9	1953	—	—	141	69	31	157	109
						1960	120	61[i]	113	80	20	125	100
14	Baltimore, MD	1.580	0.906	11,568	0.8	1962	78	33	130	54	46	162	88
15	Dallas, TX	1.339	0.844	3,179	0.5[c]	1964	—	—	—	—	—	—	—
					1.5[c]	1964	135	31	164	86	14	109	94
						1970	116	61[i]	—	—	—	—	—
16	Milwaukee, WI	1.252	0.717	7,548	0.9	1963	—	31	140	66	34	155	102
						1972	91	—	134	78	22	149	116
17	Seattle–Everett, WA	1.238	0.531	6,350	0.6	1961	60	27	126	71	29	210	167
						1970	60	37	145	—	—	241	—
18	Miami, FL	1.220	0.335	9,763	0.9	1964	28	12	49	67	33	54	36
19	San Diego, CA	1.198	0.694	3,261	2.2	1966	56[h]	23	130	88	12	59	52
20	Atlanta, GA	1.173	0.497	3,779	0.6	1961	75	30	94	72	28	156	112
21	Cincinnati, OH, KY	1.111	0.452	5,794	0.5	1965	—	35	113	71	29	220	156
22	Kansas City, MO, KN	1.111	0.502	2,101	0.9	1957	65	30[h]	107	70	30	118	82
						1971	58	31	—	—	—	—	—
23	Buffalo, NY	1.087	0.463	11,205	0.9	1962	48	28	104	67	33	115	77
24	Denver, CO	1.047	0.515	5,406	0.5	1959	50	24	105	80	20	210	167
25	San Jose, CA	1.025	0.444	3,817	—	—	11	7	—	—	—	—	—
26	New Orleans, LA	0.962	0.592	6,846	1.5	1960	60	—	129	—	—	86	—
27	Phoenix, AZ	0.863	0.582	2,346	0.7	1957	21	—	65	89	11	93	83
28	Portland, OR	0.825	0.383	4,294	1.2	1970	54	—	133	81	19	110	90
29	Indianapolis, IN	0.820	0.743	2,113	—	1964	85	30	150	87	13	—	—
30	Providence, RI	0.795	0.179	9,482	0.5	1977	26	10	63	84	16	126	106

[a]Manhattan—South of 59th Street
[b]Midtown.
[c]Core.
[d]Cordon area.
[e]1966.
[f]Zero sector.
[g]CBD.
[h]1975
[i]1976

SOURCE: Compiled from Comprehensive Transportation Studies in each urban area and from information furnished by various cities.

Major internal linkages. Pedestrian destinations and trips in the CBD are mainly concentrated in the retail and commercial cores. They reflect two basic linkage patterns: (1) between principal transit stops or parking terminals and places of work and (2) between stores, restaurants, and offices within the commercial core. (In downtown Seattle, for example, about 56% of all walking trips were to or from parking or public transport facilities, while 44% were interbuilding trips).[23]

[23]*Center City Transportation Project: Urban Transportation Concepts,* Wilbur Smith & Associates, Columbia, S.C., 1970.

TABLE 10–40
U.S. Central Business District Cordon Counts

Rank (1970 Census)	Urbanized Area	1970 Urbanized Area Population	Year of Count	Peak-Hour Persons (× 10³)	One-way Movement (%)		Peak Accumulation*		
								Percent	
					Auto	Transit	Persons (× 10³)	Auto	Transit
1	New York, NY	16,206,841	1974	738	10	90	n.a.	n.a.	n.a.
			1971	805	8	92	2,056†	n.a.	n.a.
2	Los Angeles, CA	8,351,266	1970	99	69	31	148	67	33
			1974	93	63	37	152	62	38
3	Chicago, IL–IN	6,714,578	1971	210	19	81	283‡	14	86‡
			1974	200	10	82	295	17	83
4	Philadelphia, PA–NJ	4,021,066	1955	177	29	71	210	23	77
5	Detroit, MI	3,970,584	1956	66	49	51	n.a.	n.a.	n.a.
			1974	39	67	35	62	65	35
6	San Francisco, CA	2,987,850	1965	129	56	44	165	n.a.	n.a.
7	Boston, MA	2,652,575	1974	131	51	49	192	40	60
			1972	143	50	50	195	38	62
8	Washington, DC–MD–VA	2,481,489	1961–62	138	65	35	n.a.	n.a.	n.a.
			1968	159	71	29	n.a.	n.a.	n.a.
9	Cleveland, OH	1,959,880	1970	50†	56	44	92	41	59
10	St. Louis, MO–IL	1,882,944	1957	62	58	42	89	50	50
11	Pittsburgh, PA	1,846,042	1963	56	54	56	94	40†	60†
12	Minneapolis, MN	1,704,423	1974	n.a.	n.a.	n.a.	55	56	44
			1965	57	80	20	60	80	12
13	Houston, TX	1,677,863	1971	55§	86	14	56	86	14
				68‖	86	14	67	86	14
14	Baltimore, MD	1,579,781	1955	67	56	44	119	66	34
15	Dallas, TX	1,338,684	1964	62	81	19	86	84	16**
			1971	50	72	28	64	72	28††
16	Milwaukee, WI	1,252,457	1974‡‡	33	95	25	n.a.	n.a.	n.a.
17	Atlanta, GA§§	1,172,770	1962 (app.)	31	55	45	56	n.a.	n.a.
18	Cincinnati, OH	1,110,514	1962 (app.)	35	70	30	n.a.	n.a.	n.a.
19	Denver, CO	1,047,311	1977	34	70	30	46	60	40
20	New Orleans, LA	961,728	1966	36	56	40	55	54	46
30	Providence, RI	795,311	1977	19	79	21	26	71	29

*n.a., not available.
†Estimated.
‡CATS estimates 325,000 for 1970.
§Central traffic district—0.63 mi².
‖Central business district—1.53 mi.
**Larger CBD area.
††Cordon around core area.
‡‡Estimated, based on 12-h cordon count and peak-hour vehicle flow.
§§1976, Atlanta, 21,100 vehicles in A.M., or about 30,000 persons in cars.

SOURCE: Cordon counts in indicated cities.

TABLE 10–41
Selected Characteristics of Major Canadian City Centers (1970 Conditions)

Item	Vancouver	Toronto	Ottawa	Edmonton	Hamilton
1969 population	1,000,000	1,916,100	445,800	434,800	384,000
CBD employment	91,000*	118,000†	60,000	40,000	24,000
CBD cordon count of two-way daily person-trips by all modes	592,000	763,000	382,000	—	225,000
Percent by car	64	48	78	—	
Percent by transit	36	52	22		28
CBD cordon count of peak-hour peak-direction person-trips by all modes	45,000	76,000	35,000	25,000	20,000
Percent by car	60	32	60	65	—
Percent by transit	40	68	40	35	—
CBD peak person accumulation by all modes	53,000‡ 62,000§	105,000	52,000	—	—
Percent by car	51	24	56	—	—
Percent by transit	49	76	44	—	—

*Downtown peninsula.
†0.85-mi² CBD core; total CBD = 210,000.
‡Excluding pedestrians.
§Including pedestrians.

SOURCE: Cordon count and origin destination studies in each urban area, 1970–1975 conditions; Edmonton population is for 1971.

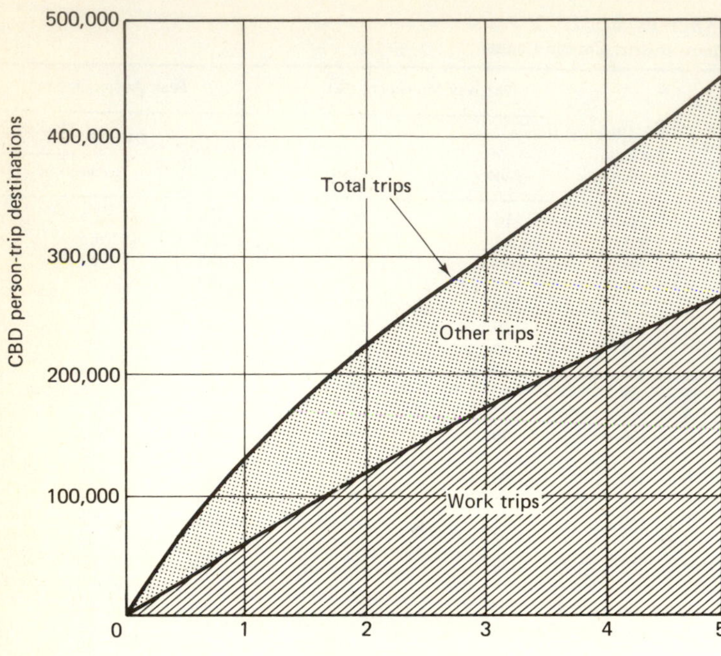

Figure 10.16. Generalized central business district trip generation. SOURCE: *Urban Transportation Concepts,* Wilbur Smith & Associates, Center City Transportation Project, Sept. 1970, p. 21.

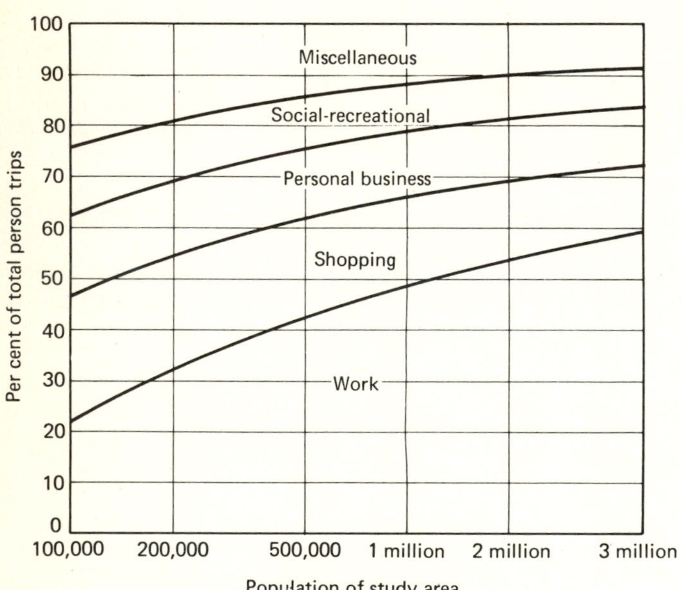

Figure 10.17. Central business district trip purposes. SOURCE: *Transportation and Parking for Tomorrow's Cities,* prepared under commission from the Automobile Manufacturers Association by Wilbur Smith & Associates, 1966, p. 55.

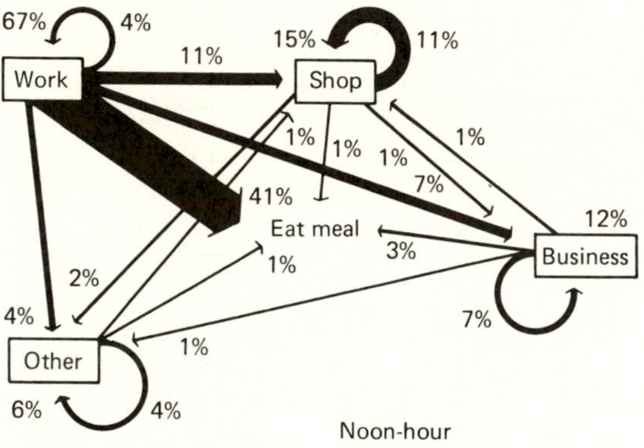

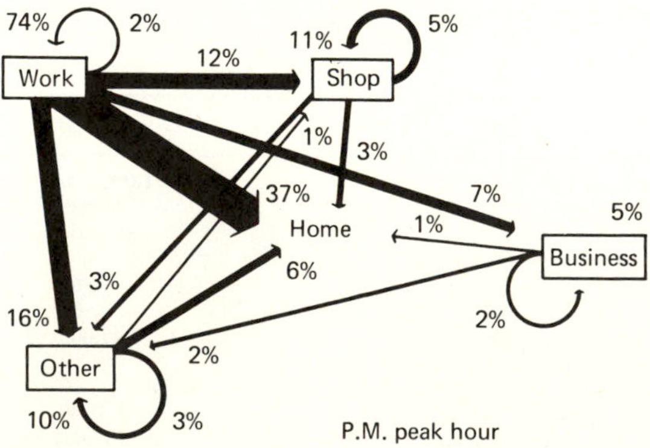

Figure 10.18. Pedestrian trip purposes, Boston City Center, 1963. SOURCE: Barton-Aschman Associates, *Traffic Circulation and Parking Plan, Central Business District Urban Renewal Area, Boston, Mass.,* p. 23.

Thus, the location of major garages, bus stops, and rail transit stations significantly influences the distribution of CBD walking trips. Comparatively little walking takes place between the core areas of intense demand and secondary activity concentrations on the edge of the CBD.

Pedestrian trip patterns observed in downtown Boston further illustrate these characteristics. During the noon hour, nearly half of all pedestrians reported "lunch" as their immediate trip purpose. During the evening peak hour, almost half reported "home" as their destination (Figure 10.18). The largest individual movements were from work to lunch and from work to home. Workers represented about two-thirds of all pedestrians at the noon hour and almost three-fourths of the total in the afternoon peak hour. During the lunch hours, over 60% of all pedestrian trips by workers represented lunch trips and 16% shopping trips. During the evening peak hour, 50% of all workers were on their way home and 16% were shopping.

Pedestrian flows. Pedestrian flows are far more localized than either automobile or transit patterns. The following examples illustrate the rapid decline in pedestrian volumes with increasing distance from the retail-office core.

1. Midday hourly pedestrian volumes in New York City concentrate along Fifth Avenue (about 25,000 persons per hour), while volumes along the Avenue of the Americas average 10,000 persons, and volumes on Eighth Avenue, 2000 ft to the west, are below 5000.
2. Evening peak-hour volumes in downtown Boston approximate 5000 people on Summer, Washington, and Tremont Streets near major subway entrances and drop to fewer than 2000 persons within a few blocks.
3. Ten-hour pedestrian volumes in Chicago's Loop (1971) exceed 60,000 persons on State Street but are below 7000 five blocks to the west on Franklin Street.
4. In Philadelphia, daily crosswalk pedestrian volumes exceed 25,000 persons in the core area but drop to 1000 persons within four blocks.
5. In Seattle (1970), daily crosswalk pedestrian volumes often exceed 20,000 persons in the core area but drop to 3000 persons within two blocks of the core area.
6. In Dallas (1968), daily crosswalk pedestrian volumes exceed 12,000 persons in the core area but drop to 3000 persons within three blocks.

Walking distances. Pedestrian walking distances reflect peoples' desire to minimize travel time and inconvenience. They vary according to city size and usually reflect the locations of rail or rapid transit stations, bus stops, and parking garages relative to major stores and offices.

Walking-distance patterns are generally consistent among cities of similar size (Figure 10.19). In Edmonton, median walking distance approximates 400 ft (120 m) and the 80th percentile is 1000 ft (300 m); in cities such as Dallas and Pittsburgh, median walking distance approximates 500 ft (150 m) and the 80th percentile is 1200 ft (360 m). In Boston, where pedestrian walking distances are influenced by locations of commuter railroad stations, 50% of all pedestrian trips are below 1000 ft (300 m) and 80% are below 2000 ft (600 m). Slightly longer walking distances are found in New York because of the block spacing and location of subway stations; the 80th percentile in Manhattan approximates 2500 ft (750 m).

Trip rates. Pedestrian trip rates for office buildings, restaurants, and retail stores in downtown Boston, New York, Providence, and Seattle are summarized in Table 10-42. The highest trip rates are for supermarkets and restaurants; the lowest for office buildings and hotels. High employment densities and large captive daytime populations contribute to the high trip rates in Manhattan.

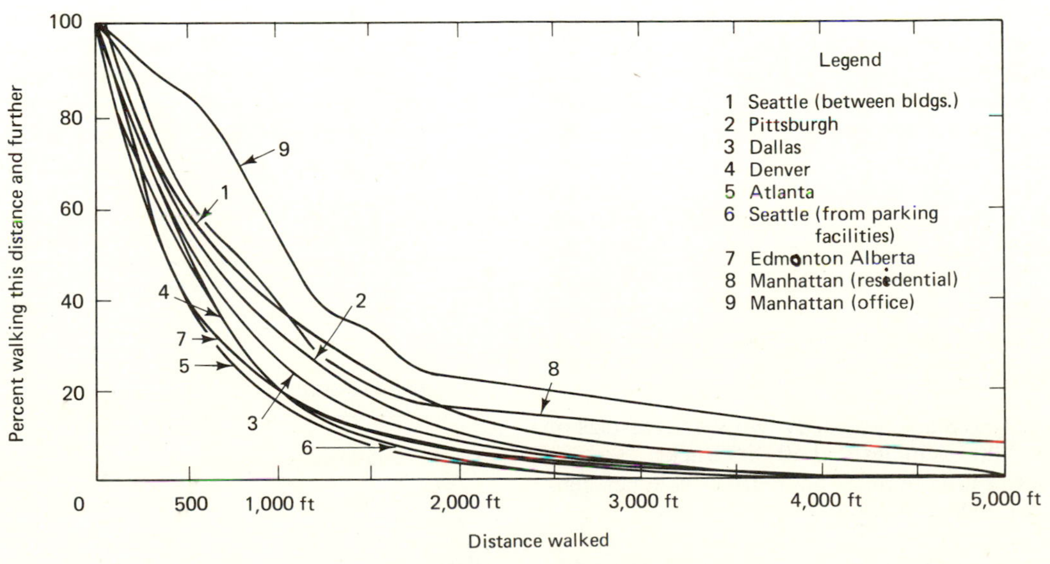

Figure 10.19. Walking distance in the city center. SOURCE: Parking surveys in Atlanta, Dallas, Denver, Pittsburgh. Pedestrian Surveys in Seattle, as reported in *Urban Transportation Concepts Center City Transportation Project,* Wilbur Smith & Associates, 1970. Edmonton: D. Hill, J. Bakkar, and B. L. Akens, *An Evaluation of the Needs of the Pedestrian in Downtown,* Traffic Research Corporation, 1964. New York: Regional Plan Association, as reported in B. Pushkarev and J. Zupan, *Urban Space for Pedestrians, A Report of the Regional Plan Association,* MIT Press, Cambridge, Mass., 1975.

TABLE 10–42
CBD Pedestrian Trip Rates

Type of Use	Location	Gross Floor Space (ft²)*	Hours	Destinations or Arrivals/ 1000 Ft²*	Source
Urban office buildings					
Mixed use	Manhattan	314,000	24	8.7	(1)
Headquarters	Manhattan	1,634,000	24	7.1	(1)
Headquarters	Manhattan	1,048,000	24	6.6	(1)
24 buildings	Seattle	5,241,000	24	7.7	(1)
40 Westminster (general)	Providence	286,000	7 A.M.–6 P.M.	10.3	(2)
Industrial Ntl. Bank (general)	Providence	350,000	7 A.M.–6 P.M.	13.7	(2)
Hosp. Trust (general)	Providence	538,000	7 A.M.–6 P.M.	13.1	(2)
Providence Journal (specialized)	Providence	162,000	7 A.M.–6 P.M.	14.2	(2)
State Capitol	Providence	146,000	7 A.M.–5 P.M.	8.9	(2)
Seven Office Bldgs.	Downtown Boston	11,600,000	7 A.M.–6 P.M.	7.5†	(3)
Restaurants					
Cafeteria	57th Street	7,200	10 A.M.–8 P.M.	246.0	(1)
Sandwich shop	Garment District	1,000	6 A.M.–3 P.M.‡	215.0	(1)
Restaurant	Times Square	12,000	9 A.M.–9 P.M.	86.5	(1)
Urban retail stores					
Delicatessen	Manhattan	2,500	10 A.M.–10 P.M.§	1230.0	(1)
Supermarket	Staten Island	7,500	9 A.M.–9 P.M.	142.5	(1)
Supermarket	Manhattan	5,100	9 A.M.–6 P.M.§	254.5	(1)
Supermarket	Manhattan	14,500	9 A.M.–9 P.M.‡	186.5	(1)
Junior dept. store	Manhattan	69,600	9 A.M.–9 P.M.‡	192.5	(1)
Dept. store	Manhattan	176,700	9 A.M.–9 P.M.‡	126.0	(1)
Boutique	Manhattan	3,400	11 A.M.–7 P.M.‡	102.5	(1)
Dept. store	Providence	431,000	8:45 A.M.–6 P.M.‡	244.0	(1)
Dept. store	Boston	792,000	7 A.M.–6 P.M.	18.3†	(2)
Hotel	Boston	644,000	7 A.M.–6 P.M.	4.3†	

*1 ft² = 0.0929 m².
†"Primary" destinations.
‡Weekday.
§Saturday.

SOURCE: (1) B. PUSHKAREV AND J. ZUPAN, *Urban Space for Pedestrians, A Report of the Regional Plan Association,* MIT Press, Cambridge, Mass., 1975. (2) *Downtown Providence Traffic, Circulation and Development Study,* Wilbur Smith & Associates, New Haven, Conn., 1978. (3) *Final Report, An Access Oriented Parking Strategy for the Boston Metropolitan Area,* Wilbur Smith & Associates, New Haven, Conn., 1972.

Truck travel

Motor truck movements are also concentrated in the city center and its environs. Light and medium truck trips dominate because tractor-trailers are more oriented to wholesale and warehouse areas that increasingly locate outside the city center in the United States.

Downtown cordon crossings. Truck traffic across the downtown cordon generally represents less than 12% of the total vehicles. This proportion reduces to 5% to 8% of the evening peak-hour, peak-direction traffic and increases to about 15% of the peak-truck-hour, peak-direction movement.

1. Most U.S. city centers have daily two-way crossings of less than 500,000 vehicles and 40,000 trucks.
2. During each peak commuter hour, truck volumes generally exceed 2000 vehicles.

Travel patterns and rates. On a typical weekday, 5% to 15% of the total truck trips in U.S. and Canadian metropolitan areas have destinations in the city center. This percentage generally drops with city size, reflecting the decentralization of urban activities. It is generally higher in cities elsewhere in the world, where commercial activities remain clustered in and around the city center.

Truck travel to, from, and within the CBD increases at a slower rate than overall urban population. There are approximately 40 daily CBD truck trips per 1000 persons in urban areas of 250,000, as compared with fewer than 15 in urban areas over 1 million.

The generation of truck trips and truck "stops" relates closely to the type and intensity of land use. Table 10-43

TABLE 10–43
CBD Truck Stops for Various Land Uses

	Average Daily Truck Stops/1000 ft² of Floor Space*	
Type of Establishment†	Range	Typical Value (Rounded)
Office	0.15–0.24	0.20
Retail		
Apparel	0.18–0.67	0.45
Department store	0.14–0.37	0.25
Furniture	0.19–0.60	0.30
Restaurant	2.70–6.10	3.60
Hotel	0.03–0.20	0.10
Manufacturing	0.35–0.68	0.50
Warehousing	0.35–0.53	0.50

*1 ft² = 0.0929 m².
†A truck "stop" is equivalent to a visit to a particular establishment.

SOURCE: Adapted from H. S. LEVINSON AND P. E. CONRAD, *Urban Truck Road Systems and Travel Restrictions,* Vol. 2, Appendices, prepared for FHWA by Wilbur Smith & Associates, Columbia, S.C., 1975.

summarizes salient truck-stop characteristics. These planning guidelines represent the number of actual stops or visits to particular establishments, rather than "trips" as defined in origin–destination surveys. There is about 0.25 truck stops per 1000 ft^2 (100 m^2) of floor space each day, with a wide variation by type of establishment. The highest unit generation (3.60 stops/1000 ft^2) is by restaurants and the lowest by office buildings and hotels.

TABLE 10–44
Purpose of Truck Stops in Downtown Areas

Location	Purpose of Truck Stop (%)				
	Pickup	Delivery	Pickup and Delivery	Service	Other
Dallas (1)	16	59	10	5	10*
Brooklyn (2)	18	82		†	
San Francisco (3)					
St. Francis Hotel	12	76	12	†	
Macy's Dept. Store	26	60	14	†	
Bank of America	26	61	13	†	
General estimates (4)				10–20	

*Correspondence and securities.
†Data not collected.

SOURCE: (1) ALAN M. VOORHEES & ASSOCIATES, INC., *Summary Report of Preliminary Goods Movement Data,* prepared for North Central Texas Council of Government, McLean, Va., 1972. (2) PHILIP HABIB, *Urban Goods Movement Planning,* Polytechnic Institute of New York, Brooklyn, N.Y., 1974–1975. (3) H. S. LEVINSON AND P.E. CONRAD, *Urban Truck Road Systems and Travel Restrictions,* prepared for FHWA by Wilbur Smith & Associates, Columbia, S.C., 1975. (4) RICHARD STALEY, "Service Trucks in the Urban Traffic Environment," *Proceedings of the Engineering Foundation Conference on Goods Transportation in Urban Areas,* Gordon Fisher, ed., June 1978, p. 653; HERBERT S. LEVINSON, "The View from the Service Truck—A Missing Link in Urban Goods Movement," *Proceedings of the Engineering Foundation Conference on Goods Transportation in Urban Areas,* Gordon Fisher, ed., June 1978, p. 657.

Trip purpose. Truck travel in the city center peaks between 9:00 and 11:00 A.M. with a secondary peak in the midafternoon. About 30% of all stops relate to delivery of perishable or high-value commodities or securities and are usually made before noon. Mail and parcel pickups dominate trips during the P.M. rush hour. Truck drivers try to avoid the noontime hours of high pedestrian concentrations.

Purposes of truck stops in three downtown areas are given in Table 10-44. Suggested guidelines are: delivery, 60% to 65%; pickup, 15% to 20%; pickup and delivery, 10% to 15%; and service, 5% to 10%.

CBD Parking characteristics

Parking patterns, practices and characteristics in the CBD reflect the types and intensity of downtown land-uses, economic functions, and reliance on public transport. Salient parking characteristics, based on studies conducted in major North American cities over the past several decades are summarized herein. Application of these and other parking characteristics in the formulation of policies and programs, and the design of facilities are given in Chapter 21, Parking and Loading Facilities.

Parking supply

The CBD parking spaces provided in cities located around the world (outside of the United States and Canada) are shown in Table 10-45. CBD parking spaces per thousand persons ranged from 4.1 in Barcelona, Spain to 115.8 in Strasbourg, France. The 24 cities shown averaged nearly

TABLE 10–45
CBD Parking Spaces in Relation to CBD Area and Metropolitan Area Population

City	Metropolitan Area Population	CBD Areas		CBD Parking Spaces Provided			Parking Space Ratios		
		Acres	Hectares	On-street	Off-street	Total	Spaces per 1,000 pop.	Spaces per Acre	Spaces per Hectare
Adelaide (Aust.)	746,000	455	184	6,003	8,074	14,077	18.9	30.9	76.5
Perth (Aust.)	470,000	1,485	600	8,103	19,400	27,503	58.5	18.5	45.8
Copenhagen (Den.)	1,400,000	1,455	588	17,141	2,025	19,166	13.7	13.2	32.6
Marseille (Fr.)	900,000	297	120	6,621	2,590	9,211	10.3	31.0	76.8
Nice (Fr.)	350,000	817	330	24,040	4,820	28,860	82.5	35.4	87.5
Strasbourg (Fr.)	250,000	2,426	980	26,550	2,386	28,939	115.8	11.9	29.5
Toulouse (Fr.)	375,000	1,435	580	8,435	8,175	16,610	44.3	11.6	28.7
Essen (Ger.)	727,000	89	36	2,122	4,941	7,063	9.7	79.4	196.4
Frankfurt (Ger.)	693,000	631	255	11,783	28,500	40,283	58.1	63.8	157.9
Hamburg (Ger.)	1,860,000	594	240	4,272	10,116	14,388	7.7	24.2	60.0
Coventry (Eng.)	330,000	275	111	621	3,067	3,688	11.2	13.4	33.2
Kingston Upon Hull (Eng.)	310,000	280	113	2,400	2,300	4,700	15.2	16.8	41.6
Leeds (Eng.)	512,000	2,297	928	2,105	7,665	9,770	19.1	4.3	10.5
Tel Aviv-Yafo (Isr.)	400,000	359	145	6,000	5,200	11,200	28.0	31.2	77.3
Rome (It.)	2,489,000	4,950	2,000	25,252	9,582	34,834	14.0	7.0	17.4
Rotterdam (Neth.)	732,000	371	150	3,300	6,617	9,917	13.6	26.7	66.1
Auckland (N.Z.)	500,000	641	259	13,300	14,571	27,871	55.8	43.5	107.7
Cape Town (So. Af.)	508,000	394	159	7,718	4,174	11,892	23.4	30.2	74.8
Durban (So. Af.)	510,000	433	175	3,404	3,841	7,245	14.2	16.7	41.4
Barcelona (Sp.)	1,696,000	507	205	6,130	883	7,013	4.1	13.9	34.2
Madrid (Sp.)	2,700,000	547	221	8,250	12,500	20,750	7.7	38.0	94.0
Gothenburg (Swed.)	405,000	248	100	2,367	3,167	5,534	13.7	22.3	55.3
Malmo (Swed.)	245,000	604	244	5,300	3,400	8,700	35.5	14.4	35.7
Zürich (Swit.)	440,000	621	251	7,000	6,400	13,400	20.5	21.6	53.4

SOURCE: Compiled from "Schemes for the Provision of Parking Spaces in Town Centers," *Theme 6, Eighth International Study Week in Traffic Engineering,* OTA, London, England, 1966.

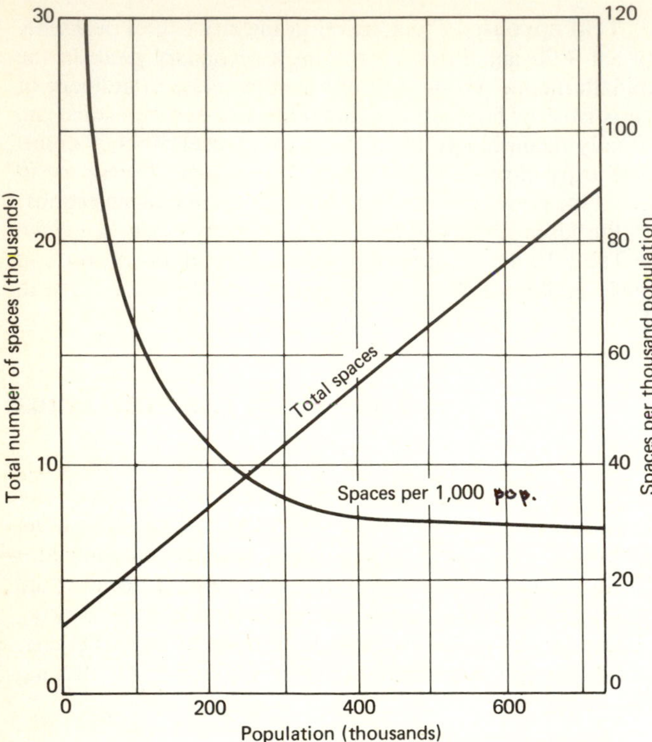

Figure 10.20. Number of parking spaces in the CBD vs. population. SOURCE: *Parking Principles,* Special Report No. 125, Washington, D.C.: Highway Research Board, 1971, p. 9.

30 CBD spaces per 1000 population. The number of spaces provided ranged from 4.3 per acre (10.5 per hectare) in Leeds, England to 79.4 per acre (196.4 per hectare) in Essen, Germany.

United States. The relationship between the number of CBD parking spaces provided in U.S. cities and urbanized area population is shown in Figure 10.20. As population rises, the supply of downtown parking also increases, but at a diminishing rate.

The number of CBD parking spaces provided by type of facility is summarized in Table 10-46 and Table 10-47. As urban population increases, the proportion of total spaces along the curb decreases, while the proportion of spaces provided in garages increases. The percentage of total spaces in off-street lots remains fairly constant, and peaks at a population of 300,000 and 400,000. Figure 10.21 shows the percentage distributions of parking spaces by curb, lot and garage as a function of urban population.

Local governments in the United States provide many parking spaces within their boundaries for use by residents

TABLE 10–46
Number and Percent of Total Parking Spaces Classified by Type of Facility—United States

Population Group of Urbanized Area	Type of Facility: Curb	Off-street: Lot	Off-street: Garage	Average Number of Total Spaces	Spaces per 1,000 Population
10,000–25,000	1,090 (43%)	1,530 (57%)	10 (0%)	2,630	150
25,000–50,000	1,430 (38%)	2,240 (59%)	140 (3%)	3,990	120
50,000–100,000	1,610 (35%)	2,790 (60%)	260 (5%)	4,660	70
100,000–250,000	2,130 (27%)	4,760 (62%)	820 (11%)	7,710	50
250,000–500,000	2,450 (20%)	7,910 (64%)	1,940 (16%)	12,300	30
500,000–1,000,000	3,200 (14%)	12,500 (56%)	6,900 (30%)	22,600	30
Over 1,000,000	8,000 (14%)	32,200 (55%)	18,600 (31%)	58,800	20

SOURCE: "Parking Principles," *Highway Research Board Special Report No. 125,* Washington, D.C., Highway Research Board, 1971, p. 9.

TABLE 10–47
Parking Spaces Classified by Type of Facility

Population Group of Urbanized Area	Curb: Metered (%)	Curb: Non-metered (%)	Curb: Special (%)	Lot: Public (%)	Lot: Private (%)	Garage: Public (%)	Garage: Private (%)
10,000–25,000	47	51	2	18	82	93	7
25,000–50,000	55	40	5	27	73	50	50
50,000–100,000	55	41	4	42	58	56	44
100,000–250,000	47	46	7	52	48	89	11
250,000–500,000	49	40	11	66	34	95	5
500,000–1,000,000	54	38	8	68	32	87	13
Over 1,000,000	27	46	27	67	33	84	16

SOURCE: *Parking Principles,* p. 10.

TABLE 10–48
Number and Type of Municipally Owned Off-street Parking Facilities—United States

City Population	No. of Cities Surveyed	In CBD: No. of Garages	In CBD: No. of Spaces	In CBD: No. of Lots	In CBD: No. of Spaces	Outside CBD: No. of Garages	Outside CBD: No. of Spaces	Outside CBD: No. of Lots	Outside CBD: No. of Spaces
Under 2,500	42	0	0	61	3,968	0	0	0	595
2,500–5,000	122	1	29	282	13,341	1	24	41	2,487
5,000–10,000	251	5	780	680	41,640	3	70	131	13,447
10,000–25,000	302	22	2,231	1,141	76,361	0	0	218	22,001
25,000–50,000	166	18	3,558	929	72,894	0	0	210	25,040
50,000–100,000	106	34	13,227	761	65,187	3	368	205	37,934
100,000–250,000	63	40	15,504	454	50,844	2	1,100	203	32,582
250,000–500,000	21	23	12,589	124	19,038	1	389	67	22,785
500,000–1,000,000	18	35	24,603	41	13,488	4	2,960	129	47,217
Over 1,000,000	6	26	20,382	47	17,444	6	2,248	325	67,766
Total	1,097	202	92,063	4,466	382,674	16	6,950	1,527	251,890

SOURCE: W.D. Heath, J.M. Hunnicut, M.A. Neale, and L.A. Williams, "Parking in the United States—A Survey of Local Government Action," *National League of Cities, Department of Urban Studies,* Washington, D.C., 1967, pp. 1–25.

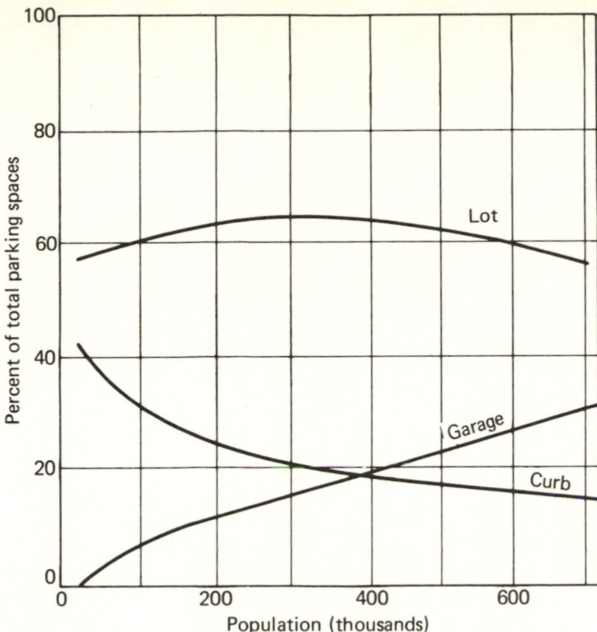

Figure 10.21. Percentage of all parking spaces in the CBD by type of facility. SOURCE: *Parking Principles*, p. 14.

and workers: in total, nearly 750,000 off-street spaces. Nearly 100,000 municipally owned spaces are provided in garages with the remainder in surface lots (see Table 10-48). As urban area population increases, the proportion of off-street parking space provided for public use also increases.

Canada. CBD parking supply patterns for 68 Ontario municipalities are shown in Table 10-49 and Figure 10.22 and Figure 10.23. These patterns are generally similar to those found in U.S. cities. As urban population rises, there is a decreasing rate of parking space growth; and a steady reduction in the proportion of on-street space.

Parking rates

United States. Parking rates in U.S. city centers are shown in Figure 10.24. The data shows that the "work type" rate increased from about 50 to 75 cents per day in cities such as Charlotte and Chattanooga to over $1.50 per day

TABLE 10–49
CBD Parking Space Inventories—Ontario

Population (× 10³)	Number of CBDs	Average Number of Spaces: Legal Curb	Off-Street	Total	Percent Curb
Over 1,000	1	1,080	23,070	24,150	4.5
300–500	2	1,120	11,050	12,165	9.2
200–300	2	690	5,735	6,425	10.7
75–150	7	705	2,270	2,975	23.6
25–75	17	625	1,170	1,795	34.9
10–25	29	440	730	1,170	37.6
Under 10	10	410	490	900	45.6

SOURCE: *Parking in Ontario's Centres*, Wilbur Smith & Associates, Columbia, S.C., July 1972.

in Pittsburgh and Philadelphia. Daily rates in large city centers such as New York, Chicago and San Francisco often exceed $5.00 per day. Inflation in the late '70's further increased these values.

Canada. The proportions of free and 'pay' parking in 68 Ontario city centers, according to municipality size are shown in Figure 10.25 and Table 10-50. In communities of less than 50,000, more than 66% of all parking space is free. This proportion contrasts with downtown Toronto where less than 25% of the supply represented free parking.

Usage patterns

Downtown parking characteristics for major U.S. urban areas are summarized in Table 10-51. This table shows the following ranges:

- peak accumulation: 74% to 91% of total space
- average walking distance: 399 to 895 feet
- average duration: 2 hours 6 minutes to 4 hours 40 minutes
- work parkers: 22% to 47%

Generally as urban population rises, walking distances get longer, duration (length of time parked) increases, and there is a corresponding increase in the proportion of trips for work purposes.

Location of parkers. Table 10-52 shows how usage of different types of parking facilities varies with urban population. The percentage of parkers at the curb in the CBD decreases greatly as the city size increases, while the amount of off-street parking increases. The percentage of parkers using garage facilities is very low in the smaller cities but increases in larger communities.

Trip purpose and parking duration. Parking durations reflect city size and trip purpose as shown in Table 10-53. As urban population increases, the parking durations for all trip purposes tend to increase.

The proportion of business and "other" trips remains relatively constant, while the proportion of work trips rises with city size as shown in Table 10-54. Work trips have the longest duration and average 5 to 6 hours in the larger cities, while shopping and personal business trips produce parking durations that are much shorter in length.

Walking distance. Average walking distance of parkers in the CBD reflects city size, trip purpose, topography, type of parking facility used, fee charged, and the length of time parked. Table 10-55 shows how trip purpose, type of facility and length of time parked influence the distance walked. (1) Work trips generally have the greater walking distance. (2) Curb parkers have shorter walking distances than off-street parkers, while off-street parkers using surface lots walk greater distances than those parked in garages. (3) For each city size, walking distance increases as the parker's duration in the CBD increases. In all instances, the walking distance increases substantially with an increase in city size (see Figure 10.26).

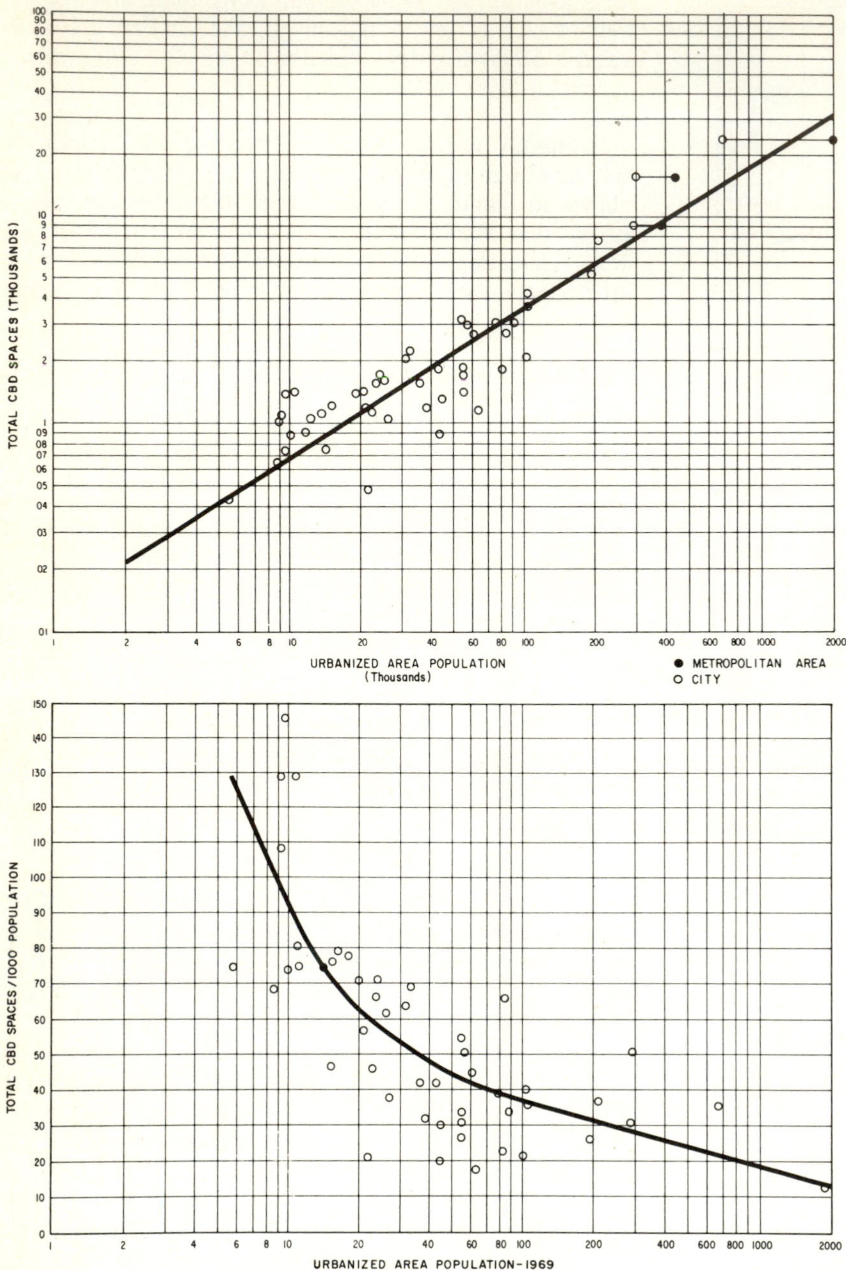

Figure 10.22. CBD parking spaces in relation to urbanized area population. SOURCE: *Parking in Ontario's Centres,* Wilbur Smith & Associates, Columbia, S.C., July 1972.

Parking turnover. Parking turnover is a measure of the utilization of a parking space and indicates the number of different vehicles that use the space during a specified time period. Table 10-56 gives turnover rates for different types of parking facilities for the 8 hour period 10:00 A.M. to 6:00 P.M. Curb parking turnover averages 3 to 9 times more than off-street parking. Parking garages usually have lower turnover rates than parking lots for reasons that include lower parking lot charges, personal preference for open-lot parking; and a larger supply, and greater dispersion of facilities.

Accumulation. Typical parking accumulations for various city sizes are shown in Figure 10.27. Accumulations remain relatively constant until about 3:00 P.M. when the exodus of parkers from the CBD begins. The typical accumulation curves in Figure 10.28 for several days of the week indicate that accumulations normally peak on Monday. The Wednesday accumulation curve is typical of midweek days.

Other characteristics of typical accumulation curves include:[24]

[24]"Parking Principles," *Special Report 125* (Washington, D.C., Highway Research Board, 1971), pp. 12–13.

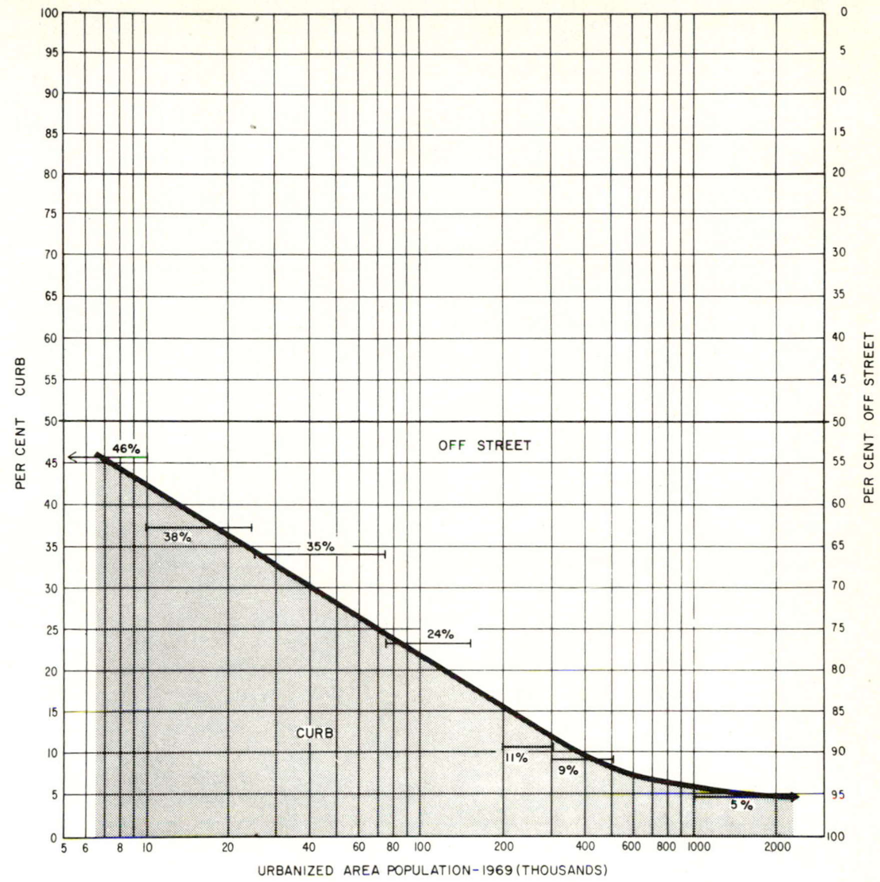

Figure 10.23. Curb and off-street parking by municipality size. SOURCE: *Parking in Ontario's Centres,* Wilbur Smith & Associates, Columbia, S.C., July 1972.

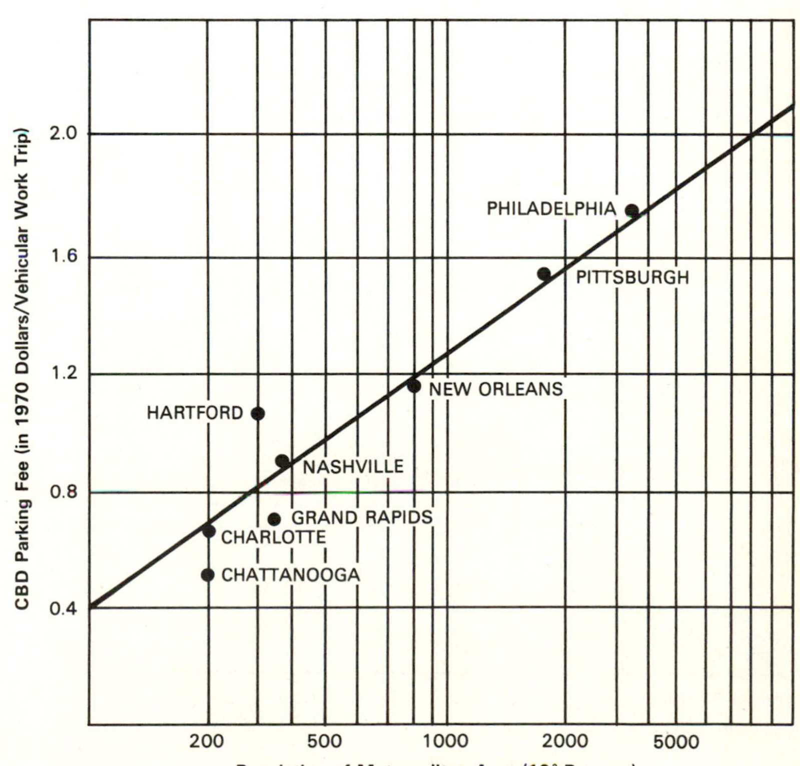

Figure 10.24. Variation of CBD parking fee with metropolitan area size—United States. SOURCE: Abdus-Samad and Grecco, 1972.
(See Errata No. 2 for complete citation.

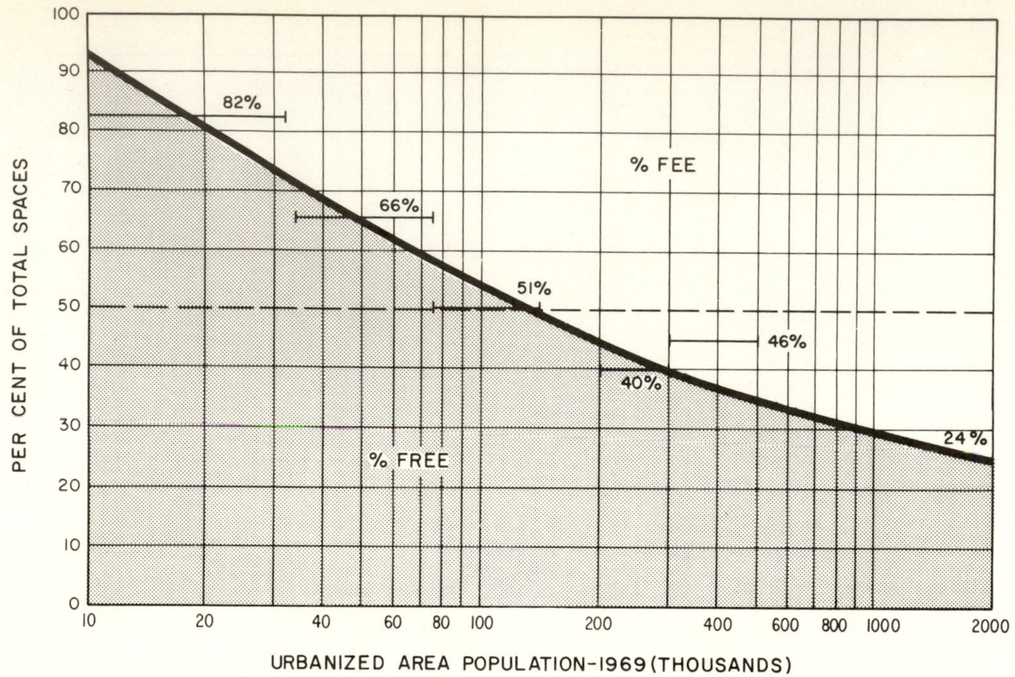

Figure 10.25. Pay and free parking by municipality size. SOURCE: *Parking in Ontario's Centres,* Wilbur Smith & Associates, Columbia, S.C., July 1972.

TABLE 10–50
Distribution of "PAY/FREE" CBD Off-Street Parking Spaces (68 Ontario Municipalities 1971–1972)

Generalized Population Categories (× 10³)	Number of CBD's	Type of Off-Street Parking "Pay"		"Free"		Total
Over 1,000	1	17,470	76%	5,600	24%	23,070
300–500	2	11,935	54%	10,165	46%	22,100
200–300	2	6,880	60%	4,590	40%	11,470
75–150	7	7,790	49%	8,100	51%	15,890
25–75	17	6,770	34%	13,120	66%	19,890
10–25	29	3,820	18%	17,350	82%	21,170
Under 10	10[1]	—	—	—	—	—
Total	68	54,665	48%	58,925	52%	113,590

[1]Insufficient data available to provide valid breakdown.

SOURCE: Same as Table 10–49.

TABLE 10–51
Downtown Parking Characteristics for Major U.S. Cities

Urban Area	Population	Study Year	Study Blocks	Total Spaces	Accumulation Peak	Accumulation Percent[1]	Average Walking Distance (Feet)	Average Duration	Trip Purpose (percent) Work	Shopping	Other
New Orleans, LA	845,237	1960	113	13,634	12,167	89.2	478	2h. 26m.	32	11	57
Buffalo, NY	1,034,370	1962	48	6,609	4,913	74.3	490	2h. 6m.	22	21	57
Atlanta, GA	1,259,292	1966	174	36,292	30,228	83.3	658	3h. 9m.	34	24	42
Boston, MA	1,753,700	1972	340	39,230	36,120	90.9	895	4h. 40m.	36	15	49
Baltimore, MD	2,070,670	1969	490	38,636	32,129	83.2	670	3h. 37m.	39	11	50
San Francisco, CA	3,000,000	1966	200	61,000	52,000	84.2	478	2h. 39m.	35	9	56
Los Angeles, CA	7,032,938	1967	237	81,452	60,500	74.3	399	3h. 10m.	47	11	42

[1]Percent of total spaces.

SOURCE: Parking studies in each urban area.

TABLE 10–52
Percent of Parkers Classified by Facility and Trip Purpose

Population Group of Urbanized Area	Curb					Off-street: Lot					Off-street: Garage				
	Shopping	Personal Business	Work	Other	Total Curb	Shopping	Personal Business	Work	Other	Total Lot	Shopping	Personal Business	Work	Other	Total Garage
10,000–25,000	30	22	11	16	79	8	1	10	2	21	0	0	0	0	0
25,000–50,000	22	30	8	14	74	5	5	13	3	26	0	0	0	0	0
50,000–100,000	19	24	7	18	68	5	7	12	7	31	0	0	1	0	1
100,000–250,000	11	24	6	11	52	9	9	17	7	42	1	1	3	1	6
250,000–500,000	10	23	8	13	54	6	7	18	3	34	3	3	4	2	12
500,000–1,000,000	3	12	9	9	33	5	8	23	3	39	5	5	15	3	28
Over 1,000,000	3	15	4	8	30	4	13	29	8	54	3	2	8	3	16

SOURCE: *Parking Principles*, pp. 12–13.

TABLE 10–53
Parking Duration by City Size—United States

Population Group of Urbanized Area	Length of Time Parked: 0–0.5 hr (%)	0.5–1 hr (%)	1–2 hr (%)	2–5 hr (%)	Over 5 hr (%)
10,000–25,000	60	14	10	10	6
25,000–50,000	59	15	10	9	7
50,000–100,000	60	15	10	10	5
100,000–250,000	46	14	11	13	16
250,000–500,000	38	15	17	15	15
500,000–1,000,000	24	12	13	18	33
Over 1,000,000	16	12	20	12	40

	Trip Purpose: Shopping (hr)	Personal Business (hr)	Work (hr)	Average All Trips (hr)
10,000–25,000	0.5	0.4	3.5	1.3
25,000–50,000	0.6	0.5	3.7	1.2
50,000–100,000	0.6	0.8	3.3	1.2
100,000–250,000	1.3	0.9	4.3	2.1
250,000–500,000	1.3	1.0	5.0	2.7
500,000–1,000,000	1.5	1.7	5.9	3.0
Over 1,000,000	1.1	1.1	5.6	3.0

SOURCE: *Parking Principles*, p. 14.

TABLE 10–54
Trip Purpose—United States

Population Group of Urbanized Area	Parkers by Trip Purpose: Work %	Shop %	Personal Business %	Other %
10,000–25,000	21	38	23	18
25,000–50,000	21	27	35	17
50,000–100,000	20	24	31	25
100,000–250,000	26	21	34	19
250,000–500,000	30	19	33	18
500,000–1,000,000	47	13	25	15
Over 1,000,000	41	10	30	19

SOURCE: *Parking Principles*, p. 14.

TABLE 10–55
Average Walking Distance by City Size†—United States

Population Group of Urbanized Area	Distance Walked By Trip Purpose: Shopping (ft)	Personal Business (ft)	Work (ft)	Other (ft)
10,000–25,000	200	200	270	190
25,000–50,000	280	240	400	210
50,000–100,000	350	290	410	260
100,000–250,000	470	390	500	340
250,000–500,000	570	450	670	380
500,000–1,000,000	560	590	650	500

	By Kind of Facility: Curb (ft)	Off-street: Lot (ft)	Off-street: Garage (ft)	Overall Average (ft)
10,000–25,000	210	210	—	210
25,000–50,000	250	350	100	280
50,000–100,000	280	380	240	280
100,000–250,000	370	540	330	420
250,000–500,000	390	760	700	550

	By Length of Time Parked: 0.5–1 hr (ft)	1–2 hr (ft)	2–5 hr (ft)	Over 5 hr (ft)
10,000–25,000	220	250	280	330
25,000–50,000	270	290	370	500
50,000–100,000	310	350	370	430
100,000–250,000	420	380	500	440
250,000–500,000	440	510	590	740
500,000–1,000,000	480	480	560	910
Over 1,000,000	520	560	680	900*

*Estimated from limited sample.
†From place parked to destination.

SOURCE: *Parking Principles*, p. 15.

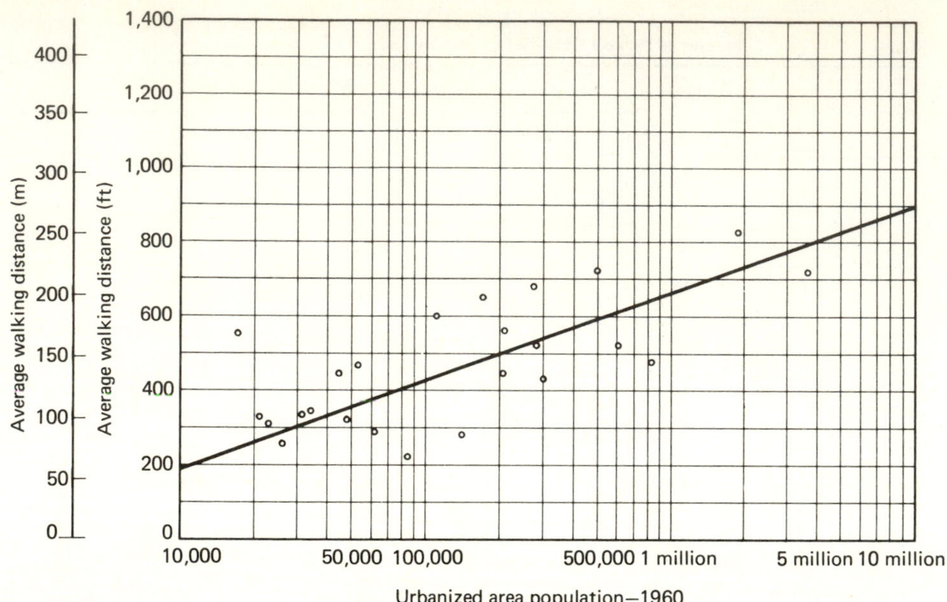

Figure 10.26. Average walking distances vs. population. SOURCE: Wilbur Smith & Associates, *Parking in the City Center*, The Automobile Manufacturers Association, 1965, p. 14.

TABLE 10–56
Parking Turnover Classified by Type of Facility—United States*

Population Group of Urbanized Area	Type of Facility						
	Curb				Off-street		
	Metered	Posted	Special	Average	Lot	Garage	Average
10,000–25,000	—	—	—	6.7	1.8	0.3	1.8
25,000–50,000	—	—	—	6.4	1.5	0.6	1.5
50,000–100,000	7.8	2.8	3.7	6.1	1.7	0.8	1.6
100,000–250,000	8.1	3.1	4.4	5.7	1.6	1.0	1.5
250,000–500,000	7.1	2.5	3.3	5.2	1.4	1.1	1.4
500,000–1,000,000	6.6	1.1	3.9	4.5	1.2	1.4	1.2
Over 1,000,000	5.5	3.6	2.9	3.8	1.1	1.0	1.1

*Parkers per 8-hr period between 10:00 a.m. and 6:00 p.m.

SOURCE: *Parking Principles*, p. 16.

1. Shopper and business trip accumulation peaks in mid-afternoon (about 3:00 P.M.) for smaller cities and in early afternoon (about 1:00 P.M.) for larger cities.
2. Work trips peak in late morning (10:30 A.M. to 11:00 A.M.) for all size cities.
3. Curb accumulation is nearly constant from 11:00 A.M. to 3:00 P.M. in larger cities and until 4:00 P.M. in smaller cities.
4. In larger cities, curb accumulation at 9:00 A.M. and 5:00 P.M. is about 40% of maximum accumulation. This figure is 80% for smaller cities.
5. Off-street parking accumulation peaks between 10:00 A.M. and 11:00 A.M. for all city sizes.

Parking demands

Present and future demands for parking space in the city center depend upon a variety of interrelated factors. These include (1) normal growths in population, motor vehicle registration and travel; (2) strength, economy, and growth prospects of the CBD (i.e., changes in employment, floor space, and/or retail sales); (3) public transport availability and use; (4) existing parking supply; and (5) public policies regarding cars, parking and transit.

The estimation of parking demand is sometimes difficult in planning needed parking facilities because the actual usage of available parking spaces is based on the system of parking supply that exists. The real demand for parking facilities is determined only from an evaluation of the parking preferences of the drivers who desire to satisfy various trip purposes in the downtown areas.

Table 10-57 gives the peak CBD parking accumulations for various purposes. It provides a basis for translating the total daily parkers into the number of peak-parkers for each type of purpose–an important step in assessing parking demands. For example, the peak-demand by work-related parkers approximates 0.75 spaces for each car parked for work purposes; the corresponding figure for non-work trips is 0.22 spaces.

Several trip generation studies have quantified parking space requirements for CBD commercial establishments and centers. The average values and ranges for the parking requirements in Table 10-58 are based on the gross floor area for different kinds of commercial establishments located in the downtown area.

Truck parking

Studies of trucks parking in the city center indicate that:

1. Trucks represent 10% to 15% of the vehicles parking at one time and 3% of the maximum parking accumulation.
2. In large cities, some 60% of all deliveries are made at the front entrance along the curb, approximately 30% in the rear entrance or side alley, and approximately 10% from off-street service entrances. There is a higher use of curb space where there are no alleys. For example,

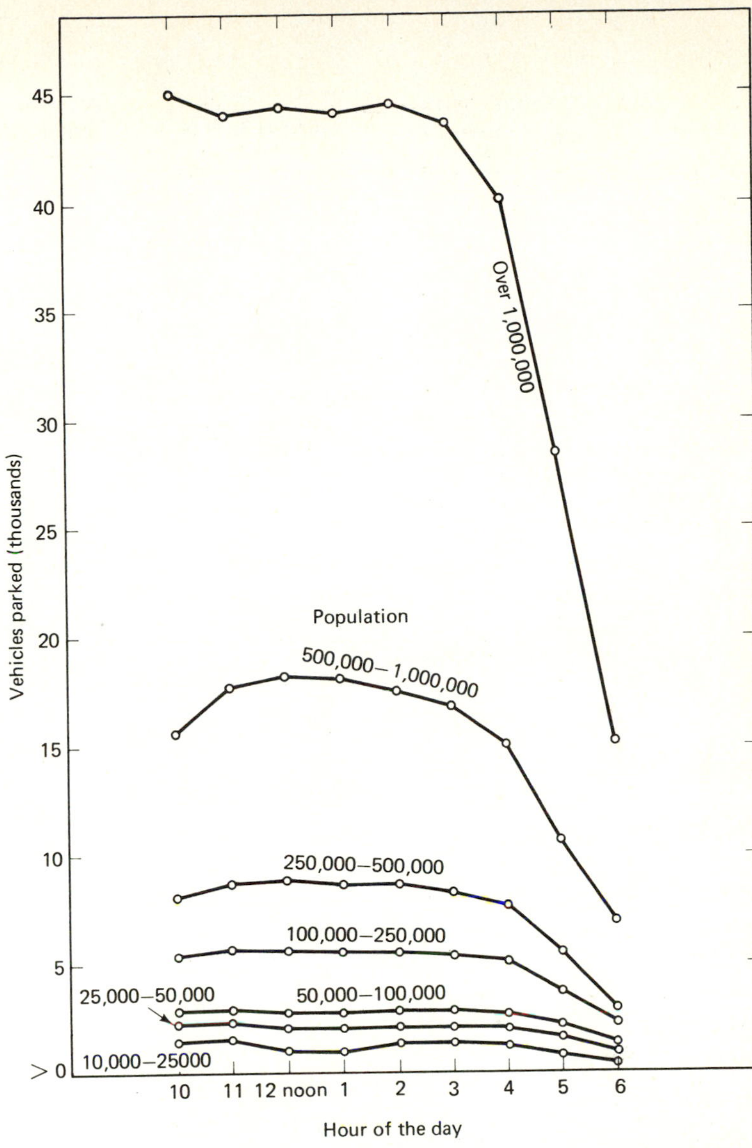

Figure 10.27. Hourly parking accumulation (central business district). SOURCE: *Parking Principles,* p. 12.

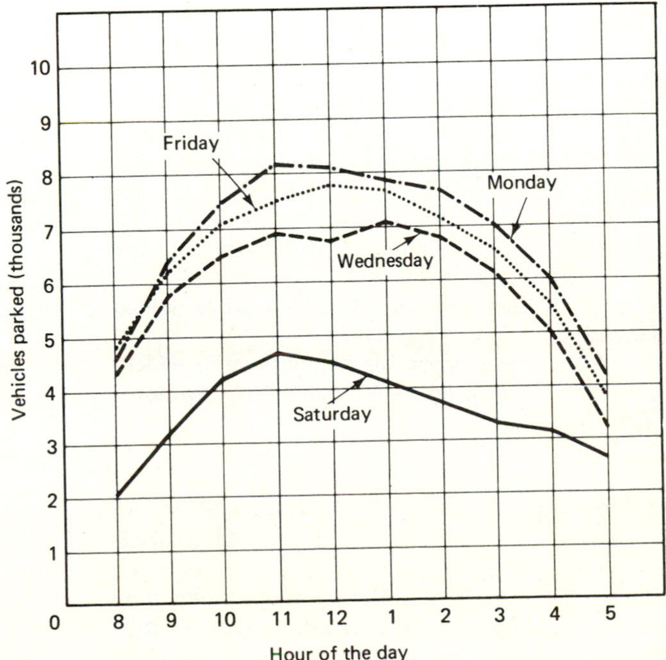

Figure 10.28. Typical CBD parking accumulation. SOURCE: Nashville Metropolitan Area Transportation Study—Downtown Parking, Nashville Parking Board, 1960, p. 57.

TABLE 10–57
Peak Parking Accumulation for Various Trip Purposes (Central Business Districts)

Trip Purpose	Ratio of Parkers in Peak (Maximum) Accumulation to Total Daily Parkers
Shopping	0.26
Business	0.18
Sales - Service	0.16
Load - Unload	0.11
Other	0.22
All non-work	0.22
All work	0.75

SOURCE: Estimate based on Table 5, *Parking in the City Center*, prepared for Automobile Manufacturers Association by Wilbur Smith & Associates, New Haven, Conn., 1965.

TABLE 10–58
Average Parking Space Requirements for Selected Downtown Establishments

Type of Establishment	Spaces per 1,000 ft²	
	Average	Range
Banks	5.4	1.8–10.8
Bus depots	4.8	1.7– 7.9
Libraries	4.1	3.9– 4.3
Medical buildings	3.8	1.1– 8.6
Grocery stores	3.7	1.4– 7.5
City-County offices	3.6	1.2– 6.0
Post offices	3.4	2.0– 4.9
Utility company offices	2.9	0.4–10.7
Drug stores	2.9	1.4– 5.5
Department stores	2.8	1.4– 5.1
Clothing stores	2.5	1.1– 6.3
Restaurants	2.1	0.9– 3.3
YMCA-YWCA	1.6	1.2– 2.2
Offices	1.5	0.4– 2.9
Auto sales	1.2	0.9– 1.5
Variety stores	1.1	0.6– 1.9
Hotels	0.6	0.4– 1.0
Furniture stores	0.6	0.3– 1.2

SOURCE: H. K. Evans, "Parking Study Applications," *Traffic Quarterly*, The Eno Foundation for Highway Traffic Control, Saugatuck, Conn., April 1963, p. 277.

in Dallas, 80% of all truck deliveries are made from the curb.

3. Average durations of downtown truck parkers were reported as 22 min in Dallas, 33 min in Chattanooga, and 55 min in New Orleans. Trucks using loading zones generally stay less than 1 h.
4. Durations of truck stops for service trips range from 30 to 90 min per stop, while pickup and delivery trips are generally less than 20 min per stop.
5. One-third of all trucks parking at curbs load or unload merchandise.
6. The percentage of trucks parking illegally varies widely among CBDs, ranging up to 80% in large downtown areas such as Boston.

Traveler response to transport system changes

There is a growing body of information describing how travelers react to changes in the transport system, such as increasing or reducing service or price, opening a new express bus or rail transit system, or implementing transportation system management actions. The following sections summarize some of these responses and may be used as a guide in assessing the travel behavior or usage impacts of similar actions.[25]

Impact of new facilities

The effects of opening new transit lines on urban travel demands are depicted in Figure 10.29 and in Tables 10-59 to 10-62.

1. Some 20% to 30% of the total ridership was reported as "new" or induced for Skokie Swift, Lindenwold, and BART (transbay) rail transit facilities. The other riders were derived about equally from car and bus.
2. Data for busways, bus lanes and ramps show a higher variability between diverted and induced trips.
3. About 25% of users of park and ride lots were auto drivers before the lots were available; however, there is a wide range among specific facilities (Table 10-62).

The ridership impacts of transit strikes in two properties are summarized in Table 10-63. About 10% to 20% of the work trips, and about 40% to 60% nonwork trips in New York City and Alameda–Costa County transit were suppressed. The automobile was the primary mode used by trips that were not suppressed by the strikes.

Travel elasticity

Various studies have attempted to establish the "elasticity" of auto and transit trips as a function of changes in costs or travel times. Pertinent findings are summarized in Tables 10-64 and 10-65.

1. A fare elasticity of -0.3 has been widely used by the transit industry in the United States. This implies that a 1% increase in fares would result in a 0.3% decrease in ridership (a shrinkage ratio of one-third) or a two-thirds realization of the additional revenue.

2. Transit fare elasticity ranges from -0.15 to -0.85, depending on city size. This pattern suggests that the smaller the city, the greater the elasticity with a change in fares.

3. Transit-time elasticities appear to be greater than those for fares (0.3 to 0.8). However, opportunities to substantially reduce these travel times are usually limited.

Elasticities of -0.2 to -0.6 have been calculated based upon parking toll increases and taxes. An automobile elasticity of -0.2 is considered representative of urban toll bridge price increases. American experience indicates that the demand for gasoline has been relatively price inelastic and that the decreased availability of fuel is more important than price in reducing travel demand.

---

[25]See, for example, R. H. PRATT AND ASSOCIATES, *Traveler Response to Transportation System Changes, A Handbook for Transportation Planners*. Prepared for Federal Highway Administration, Urban Planning Division, Washington, D.C., 1977.

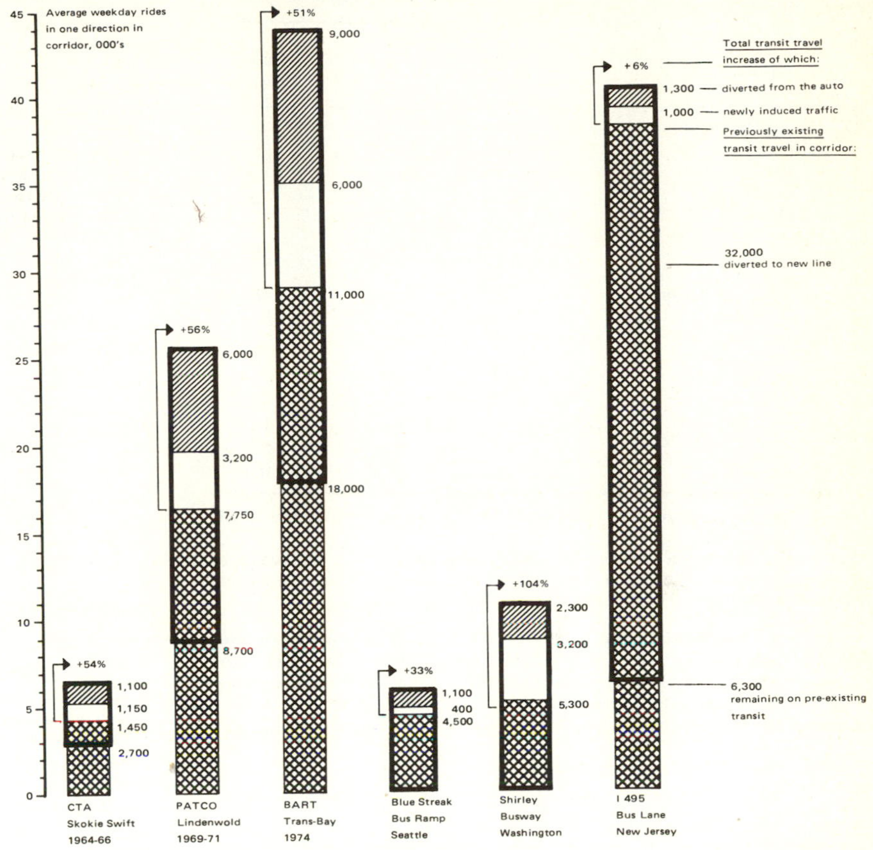

Figure 10.29. Effect of opening new transit lines on travel demand. SOURCE: B. Pushkarev and J. N. Zupan, *Public Transportation and Land Use Policy*, Indiana University Press, Bloomington, Ind., 1977. Their sources were as follows: Skokie Swift, adapted from Chicago Area Transportation Study data, Chicago Transit Authority, *Skokie Swift Mass Transportation Demonstration Project Final Report*, May 1968, p. 61. Lindenwold Line, RPA estimate developed from various published articles and unpublished bus ridership data from Transport of New Jersey; includes former PRSL rail riders. BART from California Department of Transportation unpublished tabulation, Fall 1974. The three exclusive bus facilities from Herbert S. Levinson, et al., *Bus Use of Highways, State of the Art*. National Cooperative Highway Research Program Report No. 143, Highway Research Board, Washington, D.C., 1973; also, Tri-State Regional Planning Commission, *Interstate 495 Exclusive Bus Lane Final Report*, New York, July 1972. *Note:* Figures for the I-495 bus lane refer only to the hours during which it is in operation.

TABLE 10–59
Modal Shifts and Trips Generated by BART (%)

Made trip before BART		73
Prior mode		
Drove alone	37	
Shared ride	18	
Bus	43	
Other	2	
Did not make trip before BART		27
Total		100

SOURCE: "Draft Summary Report," *BART Impact Study*, Metropolitan Transportation Commission, San Francisco, Calif., 1978; data for May 1976.

The short-term (one year) direct price elasticity of gasoline demand has been estimated to range from −0.2 to −0.3. Long-term price elasticity is estimated to range from −0.3 to −1.4, long-term being from 2.5 to 12 years. The Federal Energy Administration has estimated the 10 year price elasticity at −0.76.[26]

The elasticity data show considerable variability. Therefore, they should be used with caution in estimating the impacts of price and travel time changes on urban travel behavior.

[26]ALTSHULER, A., J. P. WOMACK, J. R. PUCHER, *The Urban Transportation System, Politics and Policy Innovation*, MIT Press, Cambridge, Mass., 1979, pp. 146–147.

TABLE 10–60
Changes in Person-Trips 1973–1977 as a Result of BART Service to San Francisco*

Location	Before BART, 1973	After BART, 1977
San Francisco–Oakland Bay Bridge		
6:30–9:00 A.M.		
Person-trips	47,860	57,620
Auto	54.7%	48.1%
Bus	45.3%	24.9%
BART	0.0%	27.0%
9:00 A.M.–4:00 P.M.		
Person-trips	46,690	59,420
Auto	89.7%	79.4%
Bus	10.3%	4.9%
BART	0.0%	15.7%
Caldecott Tunnel		
6:30–9:30 A.M.		
Person-trips	29,800	33,650
Auto	73.8%	66.4%
Bus	15.2%	2.2%
BART	11.0%	31.4%
9:00 A.M.–4:00 P.M.		
Person-trips	24,400	26,090
Auto	93.1%	87.0%
Bus	1.3%	0.0%
BART	5.5%	13.0%

*Inbound trips only.

SOURCE: "Draft Summary Report," *BART Impact Study*, Metropolitan Transportation Commission, San Francisco, Calif., 1978.

TABLE 10–61
Prior Travel Mode of Shirley Busway Users

Item	Percentage Distribution		
	"Choice" Transit Riders*	Carpool Drivers	Carpool Passengers
Did not make present trip†			
Used auto	30	22	18
Used bus	23	9	9
Other	4	1	2
Subtotal	57	32	29
Drove alone	19	23	16
Carpool			
Alternate driver in carpool	3	23	20
Drove in carpool	5	3	2
Passenger in carpool	3	4	4
Subtotal	13	30	26
Bus	8	12	24
Other (taxi, truck passenger, etc.)	5	3	5
Total	100	100	100

*Riders who had an automobile available for their work trip (includes 81% of all busway transit riders).
†Users who did not report a prior mode for their present trip (i.e., their prior condition involved a different residence or workplace). The modes shown are those for the comparable prior trip.

SOURCE: JAMES T. MCQUEEN, DAVID M. LEVINSOHN, ROBERT WAKSMAN, AND GERALD K. MILLER, *The Evaluation of the Shirley Highway Express-Bus-On-Freeway Demonstration Project,* Final Report, National Bureau of Standards, Technical Analysis Division, prepared for Urban Mass Transportation Administration, U.S. Department of Transportation, Project No. DOT-UT-306, Washington, D.C., Aug. 1975.

TABLE 10–62
Former Travel Modes of Users of Park-and-Ride Services (%)

Vancouver, B.C. (1)		Milwaukee, Wis. (2)	
(new express bus service)		(new express bus service)	
Drove	38	Drove	25
Bus	21	Transit	38
Carpool passenger	8	Carpool passenger	18
Other	33	Other	19
Washington, D.C. (3)		New Brunswick, N.J. (4)	
(new express bus service)		(new commuter rail station)	
Drove	25	Drove	11
Parked on street, rode bus	14	Bus	13
Walk	15	Other (includes rail users from another station)	76
Kiss-and-ride	9		
Carpool passenger	18		
Other	19		

SOURCE: (1) G. BROWN, *Analysis of User Preferences for System Characteristics to Cause a Model Shift,* Highway Res. Rec. 417, Highway Research Board, Washington, D.C., 1973. (2) PEAT, MARWICK, MITCHELL & CO., AND MARKET FACTS, *Fringe Parking and Intermodal Passenger Transportation: Operational Experiences in Five Cities,* Final Report, 1971. (3) T. B. DEEN, *A Study of Transit Fringe Parking Usage,* Highway Res. Rec. 130, Highway Research Board, Washington, D.C., 1961. (4) TRI-STATE TRANSPORTATION COMMISSION, *Park and Ride Rail Service, New Brunswick, New York City, Newark: A Final Report on the Mass Transit Department Project, October 27, 1963–April 20, 1965,* 1967.

TABLE 10–63
Transit-Strike Impacts on Transit Riders

Item	New York City	A.C. Transit
Population served by suspended service	8,000,000	1,000,000
Daily patronage	5,000,000	200,000
Number of working days during strike	9	45
Work trips suppressed (%)	15–20	9–21
Nonwork trips suppressed (%)	41	46–59
Alternate mode for trips not suppressed (%)		
Auto (driver or passenger)	51	68
Chartered bus	11	0
Taxi	12	4
Commuter train/BART	7	15
Walk	10	8
Hitchhike, bike, etc.	2	5
Stayed all night near work	7	0
Total	100	100

SOURCE: PEAT, MARWICK, MITCHELL & CO., *Assessment of the Impacts of the AC Transit Strike upon BART,* prepared for the Metropolitan Transportation Commission, Berkeley, Calif., 1975.

TABLE 10–64
Transit Travel Demand Elasticities

Type of Trip	Elasticity of Demand*			
		Price in Travel Time†		
	Price in Money	In-Vehicle	Access	Schedule Frequency
New York City subway trips (1950–1974 with fare in constant dollars)	−0.147	n.a.	n.a.	+0.240
Montreal transit trips (1956–1971)	−0.150	−0.270	−0.540‡	
Boston transit work trips (1964 cross-sectional data)	−0.170	−0.390	−0.709	n.a.
New York City bus trips (1950–1974 with fare in constant $)	−0.305	n.a.	n.a.	+0.634
Boston transit nonwork trips (1964 cross-sectional data)	−0.323	−0.593		n.a.
Bus trips in 17 urban areas 75,000–950,000 in population (1960–1970)	−0.533	n.a.	n.a.	+0.765
Bus trips in 13 Iowa cities 20,000–200,000 in population (1955–1965)	−0.850§		n.a.	n.a.
Boston auto work trips (1964)	−0.565	−0.820	−1.437	n.a.
Boston auto nonwork trips (1964)	−2.528	−1.020	−1.440	n.a.

*Elasticity of demand is the percent change in the number of trips with respect to a 1% change in the specified variable.
†n.a., not available or not applicable.
‡Waiting only.
§Average.

SOURCE: Lines 1 and 4: Regional Plan Association of New York: see B. PUSHKAREV AND J. ZUPAN, *Public Transportation and Land Use Policy,* Indiana University Press, Bloomington, Ind., 1977. Line 2: M. GAUDRY, *An Aggregate Time-Series Analysis of Urban Transit Demand: The Montreal Case,* Centre de Recherche sur les Transports, Montreal, 1974. Lines 3, 5, 8, 9: CHARLES RIVER ASSOCIATES, *Free Transit,* Lexington Books/D. C. Heath, Lexington, Mass., 1970 pp. 17–23. Line 6: J. H. BOYD AND G. R. NELSON, *Demand for Urban Bus Transit; Two Studies of Fare and Service Elasticities,* Institute for Defense Analyses, Arlington, Va., 1973, p. 7. Line 7: R. L. CARSTENS AND L. H. CSANYI, *A Model for Estimating Transit Usage in Cities in Iowa,* Highway Res. Rec. No. 213, Highway Research Board, Washington, D.C., 1968.

TABLE 10–65
Transit Service Headway Elasticities

Massachusetts Demonstrations*	Headway Elasticity	Months after Implementation
Boston–Milford suburban route (new headway approximately hourly)	−0.4	10–12
Uxbridge–Worcester suburban route (new headway hourly)	−0.2	7–9
Adams–Williamstown city route (new headway approximately hourly)	−0.6	1–3
Pittsfield city route (raised from 3 to 8 round trips daily)	−0.7	1–3
Pittsfield city route (raised from 10 to 15 round trips daily)	−0.6	1–3
Newsburyport–Amesbury (depressed area) city route (new headway 30 min peak/60 min midday)†	−0.4	6–8
Fall River (depressed area) city service (overall 20% service increase)	Nil	4–6
Fitchburg–Leominster city route (new afternoon headway 10 min, to match morning)†·‡	−0.3	6–8
Boston downtown distributor, phase 1 (new midday headway 5 min, to match peak)‡	−0.8	5–7
Boston downtown distributor, phase 2 (new headway 4 min base, 8 min midday)‡	−0.6	8–10
Boston rapid transit feeder route (new midday headway 5 min, to match peak)‡	−0.1	4–6
Other reported findings (126)		
Study of Milwaukee transit (1955–1970)	−3.8	—
Detroit city route (new headway 2 min base, 3½ min midday)§	−0.2	—
Chesapeake, Va., suburban service§	−0.9	—

*Arc elasticity calculated on the basis of revenue.
†Includes impact of minor route extension.
‡Approximate elasticity computed for full service day by using an unweighted average of peak and off-peak (or morning and afternoon) headway improvements.
§Arc elasticity calculated on the basis of ridership.

SOURCE: RICHARD H. PRATT, NEIL J. PEDERSON AND JOSEPH J. MATHER, *Traveler Response to Transportation System Changes—A Handbook for Transportation Planners*, prepared for U.S. Department of Transportation, Washington, D.C., Feb. 1977.

REFERENCES FOR FURTHER READING

HABIB, P., *Urban Goods Movement Planning*, Polytechnic Institute of New York, 1974–1975.

HAMMEL, L. V., *Trip Generation Material Available at Tri-State*, Interim Tech. Report 4410, Tri-State Regional Planning Commission, New York, June 1977.

KERCHOUSKAS, K. AND A. K. SEN, *Park and Ride* Planning Manual, Volume III, November, 1977, Final Report, DOT 05-60131, University of Illinois, Chicago Circle Campus.

MORIN, D. A., *Analysis of the Distribution of Automobile Occupancies*, U.S. Department of Transportation, Federal Highway Administration, Washington, D.C., 1969.

PEAT, MARWICK, MITCHELL & CO., AND D. N. JAMES, *Analyzing Transit Options for Small Urban Communities*, Urban Mass Transportation Administration, Washington, D.C., 1975.

REID, E., AND N. WILSON, *Innovation in Demand-Responsive Transit*, MIT Center for Transportation Studies, Cambridge, Mass., Oct. 1976.

SMITH, WILBUR & ASSOCIATES, prepared for Urban Mass Transportation Administration: Kassoff and Gendell, *An Approach to Multi-regional Urban Transport Policy Planning*, Washington, D.C.

SMITH, WILBUR & ASSOCIATES, *Transportation and Parking for Tomorrow's Cities*, prepared under Commission from the Automobile Manufacturers Association, 1966, p. 55.

Trip Generation, Federal Highway Administration, Washington, D.C., 1975; Urban Mass Transportation Association, Washington, D.C., 1978.

WEANT, R., *Parking Garage Planning and Operation*, Eno Foundation for Transportation, Westport, Conn., 1978.

11

STATEWIDE AND REGIONAL TRANSPORTATION PLANNING

ROGER L. CREIGHTON

Roger Creighton Associates Incorporated
Delmar, New York

This chapter is organized into six major sections. The first section traces the history of the field. The second section contains a formal definition of comprehensive statewide transportation planning and then qualifies that definition by looking at special subjects such as national planning and urban transportation planning. Steps, levels, and modes in the planning process are also considered. The third section contains information on organization: functions and powers of transportation departments, internal organization for statewide planning, and external organization. The fourth section deals with preparatory steps for statewide transportation planning—the process itself, stating goals, obtaining data, and preparing forecasts. The fifth section discusses modal studies. Coordination between the separate modal studies is taken up in the sixth section, which also presents coordination with land-use plans and implementation through capital programming.

History

The beginnings of statewide transportation planning in the United States can be traced to the Federal-aid Highway Act of 1921 and to the statewide highway planning surveys of the 1930s, both of which were intended to produce planned systems for entire states, even if only for a single mode. In the 1960s and 1970s a variety of new forces expanded the concerns of statewide transportation planning, giving it the essential multimodal characteristic which was lacking earlier. Among these forces were:

- The crisis in the railroads that followed the bankruptcy of the Penn-Central in 1970.
- The changes in air transportation that followed technical advances such as the wide-bodied jet.
- The example set by the establishment of the U.S. Department of Transportation in 1967.
- The need to prevent conflicting transportation policies and wasteful expenditures of funds by having government deal with all modes as components of a total transportation system.
- The changing viewpoint of the federal government on its role in regulation, particularly since the years 1976–1977.

Impelled by these and other forces, the number of state departments of transportation (hereafter, DOTs) increased from 3 in 1967 (Hawaii, New York, and New Jersey) to 40 at the end of 1978; at least 6 other states are studying the creation of DOTs. Not all present DOTs have significant implementation or even planning powers relative to all the modes. Nevertheless, the indications are clear that states are strongly and increasingly concerned with the coordination of all modes of transportation. Planning for the coordination and improvement of all modes will, therefore, be a substantial and growing activity in coming years.

The content and methodology of statewide transportation planning has been evolving rapidly. In the early 1970s, there was a strong thrust toward systems planning, as professionals attempted to transfer urban transportation planning skills to the larger problems at the state level.[1] Some of this found expression in the conference report of the 1974 Williamsburg Conference on Statewide Transportation Planning.[2] However, the pressure of events since that time has demanded that attention be paid to subsets of total transportation systems—for example, railroad branch-line abandonments or rural public transportation systems. These special problems come at the state DOT transportation planner from many different directions. There is, therefore, a need

---

[1]ROGER L. CREIGHTON, "Statewide and Regional Transportation Planning," in Institute of Traffic Engineers, *Transportation and Traffic Engineering Handbook*, Prentice-Hall, Englewood Cliffs, N.J., 1976, Chap. 13.

[2]*Issues in Statewide Transportation Planning*, Spec. Report 146, Transportation Research Board, Washington, D.C., 1974.

to be able to respond to these successive challenges while maintaining a sense of direction for all transportation improvements of a state, so that they should be coordinated, efficient, and consistent in their service to people and to the sound economic development of the state.

The 1979 Airlie House Conference on Statewide Transportation Planning brought forward a new dimension and relationship for the professional practice of statewide transportation planning. This is the dimension of management, and the need is for the closest possible relationships between the executive of a state DOT and the DOT's professional planning staff. The reason for this emphasis is that new forces—primarily external—keep beating in upon the transportation systems of a state. Top-level management can no longer simply administer set programs year after year. New problems must be anticipated and ever-more-scarce resources skillfully managed. In this kind of situation, the DOT executive needs a staff that can anticipate change (the "early warning" function), regularly report on the performances of the state's transportation systems (both public and private), and evaluate the impacts of alternative policy options.[3]

Definition

Statewide or regional transportation planning may be defined as an activity, or series of activities, that lead to recommendations for undertaking action:

1. To attain a series of goals, or to improve performance as measured by a series of criteria,
2. of different groups, for example people who use transportation facilities, shippers and receivers of goods, suppliers of transportation services, and particularly the public at large,
3. through coordinated changes in the construction, investment in management, technology, pricing, subsidy, and regulation,
4. of transportation facilities and services of all types,
5. for the movement of people and goods,
6. planned by means of an orderly, objective process that is based on measurement,
7. closely integrated with land-use, economic, environmental, and energy planning,
8. for the geographic area of a state, several states, or a region of some other type,
9. for a period that may vary from 10 to 30 years or more in length.

Clearly, statewide and regional transportation planning should be concerned with all modes of transportation, with many goals, with both public and private organizations, and using not only new construction but also the tools of pricing, regulation, and management in order to make improvements. Statewide transportation planning is seriously concerned with policies of population location and land development and with the energy, environmental, and economic implications of its actions.

[3]*State Transportation Issues and Actions,* Spec. Report 189, Transportation Research Board, Washington, D.C., 1980.

Areas of concerns

The preceding definition of statewide transportation planning is very broad and inclusive in its coverage. Theoretically, it covers decisions ranging from the weight of rail to be used in a railroad branch line to the policy decision of how much money should be allocated by a state to urban transit as opposed to rural secondary roads. Consequently, it is necessary to supplement the preceding definition by specifying more completely the subjects that are of direct concern and those that are of lesser concern.

Table 11-1 lists the subjects that are of concern to statewide transportation planning and those subjects that are of little or no direct concern. This table is based on work done in cooperation with the Pennsylvania Department of Transportation in 1971.[4] Such a table should be prepared by each state, and revised from time to time, since the needs and concerns of states may vary considerably.

Generally, Table 11-1 suggests that, for most modes, planning at the state level is concerned with the following questions.

- Level of public investment
- Corridor locations for highway, bus, and rail systems; terminal locations for air, rail, truck, and waterway systems
- Type of facilities within each mode (e.g., type of highway and type of airport)
- Level of service to be provided
- Timing of construction or other implementing action
- Pricing
- Regulation
- Safety (directly or indirectly)
- Relationships among transportation and land use, the economy, the environment, and energy

The products of statewide transportation planning consist principally of recommendations in the preceding areas.

Problems and issues

The preceding definitions and concerns are intended to ensure complete coverage of subjects that are of significant interest to those engaged in statewide transportation planning. However, such complete lists carry the danger that too much may be included within the professional's domain, leading to a dissipation of effort over too broad an area.

A useful supplement to the preceding definitions, therefore, is a list of those problems and issues that are currently facing a state in the field of transportation. A list of typical problems and issues is shown as Table 11-2.[5]

[4]CREIGHTON, HAMBURG, INC., *A Work Plan for Statewide Transportation Planning,* Vol. 1, Commonwealth of Pennsylvania, Department of Transportation, Harrisburg, Pa., June 1973.

[5]ROGER CREIGHTON ASSOCIATES INCORPORATED AND R. L. BANKS & ASSOCIATES, INC., *Freight Data Requirements for Statewide Transportation Systems Planning—Research Report,* NCHRP Report 177, National Cooperative Highway Research Program, Washington, D.C., 1977.

TABLE 11–1
Subject Matter of Statewide Transportation Planning (1971 PennDOT Definition)

Mode	Is Concerned with:	Is Not Directly Concerned with:
Highway	System design in principle for all systems; corridor location for primary and Interstate routes; investment levels by type, location, and timing (both intraurban and statewide); safety;* user costs,† environmental effects	Route location; engineering design; corridors of secondary highways; traffic engineering and control
Bus	Systems of routes (design and interline coordination); service levels (headways); generalized terminal location; safety;* pricing;† bus size	Detailed terminal location; scheduling
Air passenger and air freight	Systems of air routes and airports; generalized airport location, size, and investment; environmental effects; pricing,† airspace use‡	Detailed airport location; scheduling, internal operations; safety; air traffic control
General aviation	Systems of airports; generalized airport location, size, and investment; airspace use; environmental effects; pricing†	Detailed airport location; scheduling; internal operations; safety; air traffic control
Rail passenger	Rail passenger systems, generalized station locations; pricing;† service levels (headways); subsidies; grade-crossing elimination§	Scheduling and operations; safety
Rail freight	Extent and design of system, investment; terminals, especially trailer- and container-on-flatcar (TOFC/COFC); system speed and pickup frequency; rail–truck coordination; pricing;† grade-crossing elimination§	Scheduling and operations; safety
Truck	TOFC/COFC locations; expressway location; truck size; safety;* pricing†	Operations; details of TOFC/COFC locations; safety
Waterways	Investment and maintenance costs; systems as related to rail and highways	Operations; recreational use
Ports	Investment; coordination with rail, highway; interport coordination	Design; management; operations
Pipelines	Impact on rail, waterways, ports	Safety; management; operations

*Although safety is of concern in all modes, it is a dominant factor in highway-related modes because of the magnitude of the highway safety problem.
†Despite a PennDOT suggestion that pricing was not involved, pricing considerations were left in this part of the table. The economics of transportation according to mode is a fundamental determinant of modal use, particularly regarding the movement of freight.
‡Airspace use is meant in general intensity terms rather than in terms of control tower operations.
§The elimination of grade crossings is included to reflect overall concern within planning for future highways and railroads, not the specific engineering design details of each planned grade separation.

It is recommended that, prior to the initiation of a state's technical planning work program, and periodically thereafter, a list of current issues should be prepared. Conversations or meetings can be held, preferably with advisory committees, to develop such lists, preferably in priority order. This will then ensure that the most immediate and pressing needs are being met by staff work.

TABLE 11–2
Typical Statewide Transportation Problems and Issues

Rail freight transportation issues
- Light-density-line abandonments or retention
- Mainline abandonments or downgradings as a result of bankruptcies, mergers, or consolidations
- Electrification of high-density lines
- Urban rail rationalization
- Construction of bypass routes around urban areas
- Terminal/yard replacement or modernization
- Providing new (or improve existing) intermodal transfer facilities
- Poor ground access to freight yards for intermodal transfers
- Condition of roadbed, track, and structures on mainlines
- Condition of roadbed, track, and structures on light-density lines
- Disposal/retention of right-of-way of abandoned light-density lines
- Level/quality of service (speed, reliability, security, product safety)
- Developing, testing, and marketing new services
- Freight rates; regulatory modernization
- Taxation of roadbed, facilities
- Inability to raise new capital
- Safety at grade crossings
- Safety (derailments, hazardous materials)

Rail passenger issues (intercity service)
- High level of subsidies required
- Condition of roadbed
- Slow operating speeds
- Age of passenger coaches; availability
- Condition of railroad stations
- Unreliability of service

Highway freight transportation issues
- Poor maintenance of roadways (roughness)
- Traffic congestion (primarily urban)
- Limitations on vehicle size and weight
- High terminal costs
- Cargo security
- Need for regulatory modernization
- Safety of road system
- Inadequacy of highway system (lack of capacity, and lack of continuity of expressway and arterial systems)
- Vehicle safety (e.g., braking systems)
- Low standards of rural secondary roads
- Impact of larger vehicles on rural roads and bridges

Highway passenger transportation issues (intercity bus)
- Competition from subsidized rail passenger services
- Safety of roadways
- Urban traffic congestion
- Unsightly and unclean terminals
- Lack of coordination between scheduled services
- High costs of providing service to small communities in rural areas

Highway passenger transportation issues (automobile travel)
- Excessive trucking on highways; "double-bottom" trucks
- Poor maintenance of roads (roughness)
- Traffic congestion (primarily urban; some weekend/holiday recreational travel congestion)
- Safety of travel, of road system
- Unattractive roadside development
- Incompatibility between vehicle travel and roadside development
- Inadequacy of highway system (lack of capacity, lack of continuity of expressway and arterial systems)
- Poor construction and maintenance of rural secondary roads

Port/waterway issues (freight transportation)
- Need for new ports (especially offshore, deep-water ports for supertankers or hazardous-cargo ships)
- Lack of capital for port expansion, modernization
- Lack of capital for expansion, modernization of port terminal buildings
- Poor highway access to ports/terminals
- Poor rail access to ports/terminals
- Need to maintain/deepen harbors/channels/waterways
- Institutional obstacles to improving intermodal transfer facilities
- Need for regulatory modernization
- Need to upgrade existing waterways, expand lock capacity
- Equity of user fees

Aviation issues (air cargo)
- Need to modernize/expand air cargo terminals
- Regulatory modernization
- Cargo security

Aviation issues (passenger service)
- Security
- Safety
- Inadequate parking
- Poor ground access
- Poor public transportation connections
- Service to smaller urban areas

TABLE 11-2 (Continued.)

Pipeline transportation issues
- System capacity limitations
- Extensions into unserved areas
- Slurry pipelines
- Safety

Environmental, energy, economic, and social issues
- Environmental impacts—air pollution
- Environmental impacts—noise
- Environmental impacts—water pollution
- Environmental impacts—visual
- Regional/community development
- Stimulation of economic development
- Energy consumption by transportation

The listing of current problems and issues of a state will normally produce a cafeteria of problems. These will range from problems that are large-scale, industry-wide, and general to those that are small, extremely specific, and localized. This diversity of type, of mode, and of specificity versus generality immediately raises two serious questions. First, how can a state DOT's staff address so many diverse problems? Second, how can it bring a sense of coherence and even unity to the results of its work? A beginning of an answer to these two questions is given in succeeding parts of this chapter.

Qualification of the definition

The preceding definition of statewide transportation planning must be qualified in a number of respects. These qualifications are given below.

Urban transportation planning. Statewide transportation planning is in general concerned with all transportation throughout its defined area, including metropolitan and other urban areas. However, urban areas (both small and large) have their own distinct problems and generally require separate planning studies to be undertaken, using methods that have been well established, to produce plans that are quite detailed—especially when viewed from the state perspective (see Chapter 12). Hence, the urban transportation planning process is normally not considered to be a part of statewide transportation planning. However, there are certain products of the urban transportation planning process which are a definite concern of state-level planning.

1. Statewide planning should be concerned with the proposed timing and level of transportation investment in each urban area because this affects other urban areas as well as the state as a whole.
2. Statewide planning should be concerned with the pattern of planned freeway, rail, and other modal routes, as these leave each urban area because these routes become part of the statewide system.
3. Statewide planning may be concerned, in some cases, with the general location of airports, ports, and rail terminals [particularly container on flatcar (COFC) and trailer on flatcar (TOFC)—"piggyback" terminals] within or near urban areas because these may in some cases affect service to other cities and to the state as a whole.

Regional transportation planning. Some states in the United States (California and Connecticut, for example) are divided completely into regions, which may have substantial transportation planning duties assigned to them. Among these regions there may be metropolitan regions, such as the region of the Delaware Valley Regional Planning Commision, centered on Philadelphia, Pennsylvania, and Camden, New Jersey. Other regions may be predominantly rural. The fact that specific transportation planning functions are assigned to regions does not alter the earlier definition of statewide transportation planning, but it does emphasize the need to be careful in the allocation of responsibility so that there are neither duplications nor gaps in coverage.

Relationships to national transportation planning. How does statewide transportation planning relate to national transportation planning? Can this chapter be of assistance to planners working at the national level in smaller countries throughout the world? These two questions are important, but unfortunately open up subject areas that cannot be covered adequately in this chapter. Several observations can, however, be made.

First, this chapter is based primarily upon experience in the United States, and reflects the U.S. governmental organization, mixed private and public economy, technological development, and size (in terms of both population and area). The average state in 1970 had a population of 4,211,000 and a land area of 61,800 mi^2.[6] This size almost automatically means that substantial powers must be delegated to, or retained by, each state. For the highway function (at least for arterials) the state has been the logical unit of government for ownership, maintenance, and operations; for other modes the states have had mixed responsibilities, as shown in Table 11-3. Railroads, intercity bus lines, and airlines have been owned and operated privately, whereas inland waterways and intercity railroad passenger service (Amtrak) are federal responsibilities for the most part. Finally, the states depend to a great extent upon the federal government for financial aid, which comes with attendant guidelines and regulations.

TABLE 11–3
Percentages of States* Having the Powers Shown for the Functions Indicated

Function	Financial Control or Responsibility	Power to Give Technical Assistance Only	Power to Plan Only
Aeronautics	82.5	12.5	17.5
Highway	95.0	2.5	10.0
Rail	37.5	37.5	20.0
Waterways or ports	37.5	27.5	10.0
Transit	67.5	22.5	45.0
Regulation	25.0	2.5	12.5
Highway patrol	12.5	—	7.5
Motor vehicle	40.0	—	—
Toll facilities†	45.0	—	—

*38 states, the District of Columbia, and Puerto Rico.
†Toll roads, toll bridges, or ferries.

[6] *Statistical Abstract of the United States 1971*, 92nd ed., U.S. Bureau of the Census, Washington, D.C., 1971.

In the United States, therefore, state–national relationships in transportation planning are strongly affected by all these factors, some of which vary from state to state. New York and California differ from each other and from Delaware, Tennessee, and South Dakota. Each state must adapt to its own circumstances and with its own resources. Other major world powers, such as China, Brazil, Australia, the USSR, and India, which have large provinces or states, will have to organize provincial or state transportation planning according to their own circumstances.

Second, this chapter may be of direct assistance to those countries whose populations and areas are of the same order of magnitude as states in the United States. Venezuela, for example, has a population of approximately 18,000,000, which is close to that of New York or California. Some of the methods and principles described herein may be transferable, therefore, for application as national transportation planning.

Steps, levels, and modes

To complete the definition of statewide transportation planning, it is necessary to identify the most important stratifications of the subject. A basic understanding of the way the subject is divided into parts is helpful both to facilitate the presentation and to serve as the basis for assigning parts of the subject to different agencies as their particular responsibilities.

Three stratifications are most commonly used; these are (1) steps in the planning process, (2) levels of planning, and (3) modes.[7]

Steps. Most planning processes, whether business, governmental, military, or in the transportation field, have seven components or steps. These are are identified and briefly described below, as they may be applied to transportation planning.

Data collection. Data, especially quantitative data, are the material employed in planning, by means of which accurate and objective descriptions are obtained and which permit forecasts to be generated and tests of plans to be conducted. Obtaining such data is often, but not necessarily, the first step in the transportation planning process.

Forecasts. Forecasts describe future conditions which improved transportation facilities are intended to serve. In some cases forecasts are unaffected by what is being planned; in other cases transportation improvements may affect the future. In the latter case the planning process may include a feedback to determine the extent and nature of the impacts of changed transportation systems upon the economy of the state, or upon other sectors, such as population.

Goal Specification. The performance of a transportation system is measured against a series of goals. These should preferably be stated in writing at the outset of the transportation planning process.

Preparation of Alternative Plans. This is a deliberate step of describing proposed changes to transportation systems or services. Generally, one "plan" should be a "null" or "no-change" plan; this becomes a useful benchmark against which various improvements can be compared as to their performance.

Testing. Testing is the process of estimating how a proposed improvement will function. A wide variety of tests can be conducted, including cost estimation, traffic flow simulation, socioeconomic impact estimation, energy/environmental impact estimation, and public review.

Evaluation. This is the weighing of test results in the light of the goals and objectives that have previously been specified.

Implementation. The planning process concludes with the preparation of a recommendation for implementation which may be submitted to a state DOT executive, to a private firm's executive, or to a legislature.

Levels. The preceding steps of planning may be undertaken at any one of several levels of statewide transportation planning. Altogether, transportation planning may be said to have six levels:

- Policy planning
- Systems planning
- Corridor (project) planning
- Preliminary engineering
- Engineering design
- Planning for operations of existing systems or services

Except for policy planning, these levels are consistent with the "action plans" that most states adopted in the early 1970s. (An action plan is a formal document describing organization and procedures to be followed to ensure that highway projects are planned, from system planning through design, in full consideration of their social, environmental, and economic impacts.) Since statewide transportation planning is predominantly concerned with the first three levels, only those levels are defined below.

Policy Planning. This level is defined to include the process by which decisions are made relative to three broad subjects.

1. Allocation of resources—human, material, and energy—principally through the control of money. Examples include resource allocation by state budgets, by taxation, by fuel rationing, and by pricing (public or private).
2. Arrangements of institutions—who does what. Examples include takeovers of urban transit systems by public authorities and railroad reorganizations, such as the creation of Conrail, or deregulation.
3. Shared policies—decisions made in one sector, such as environmental regulations, that influence decisions made in another sector, such as transportation. Sectors include natural resources, the economy, energy, population, housing, land use, and the environment.

[7]RICHARD J. BOUCHARD ET AL., "Techniques for Considering Social, Economic, and Environmental Factors in the Planning of Transportation Systems," paper presented at the Annual Meeting of the Highway Research Board, Washington, D.C., Jan. 1972.

In general, policy planning does not deal with specific physical systems or transportation operations. Policy planning does, of course, have strong mutual interactions with systems and operations.

Systems Planning. Systems planning deals with the physical arrangement of networks of roads, railroads, transit lines, bus lines, waterways, and pipelines; it is also concerned with locations of airports and ports. The emphasis of systems planning is on the whole system rather than individual parts, and it is of greatest value where the location of components affects the usage and performance of other components in the system.

Corridor (or Project) Planning. In statewide transportation planning, corridor (or project) planning focuses upon single, large elements which are of state as opposed to local concern. An example might be an economic study of a major waterway (such as the New York State Barge Canal) or the determination of the optimum location of transportation facilities between cities, such as in the 1974 Sacramento–Stockton–San Francisco Corridor Study. Corridor planning will often review alternative modes as well as alternative locations of routes. Corridor planning is more detailed than system planning, but less detailed than preliminary engineering.

Modes. There are many ways of classifying modes of transportation. Figure 11.1 shows a useful method of classifying and comparing mode by (1) fixed facility type, (2) vehicle type, and (3) whether the mode serves passenger or freight. Subclassifications within the mode may include (1) functional classification (applied mostly to highways and

Figure 11.1 Modes classified by fixed-facility type, vehicle type, and by type of service rendered.

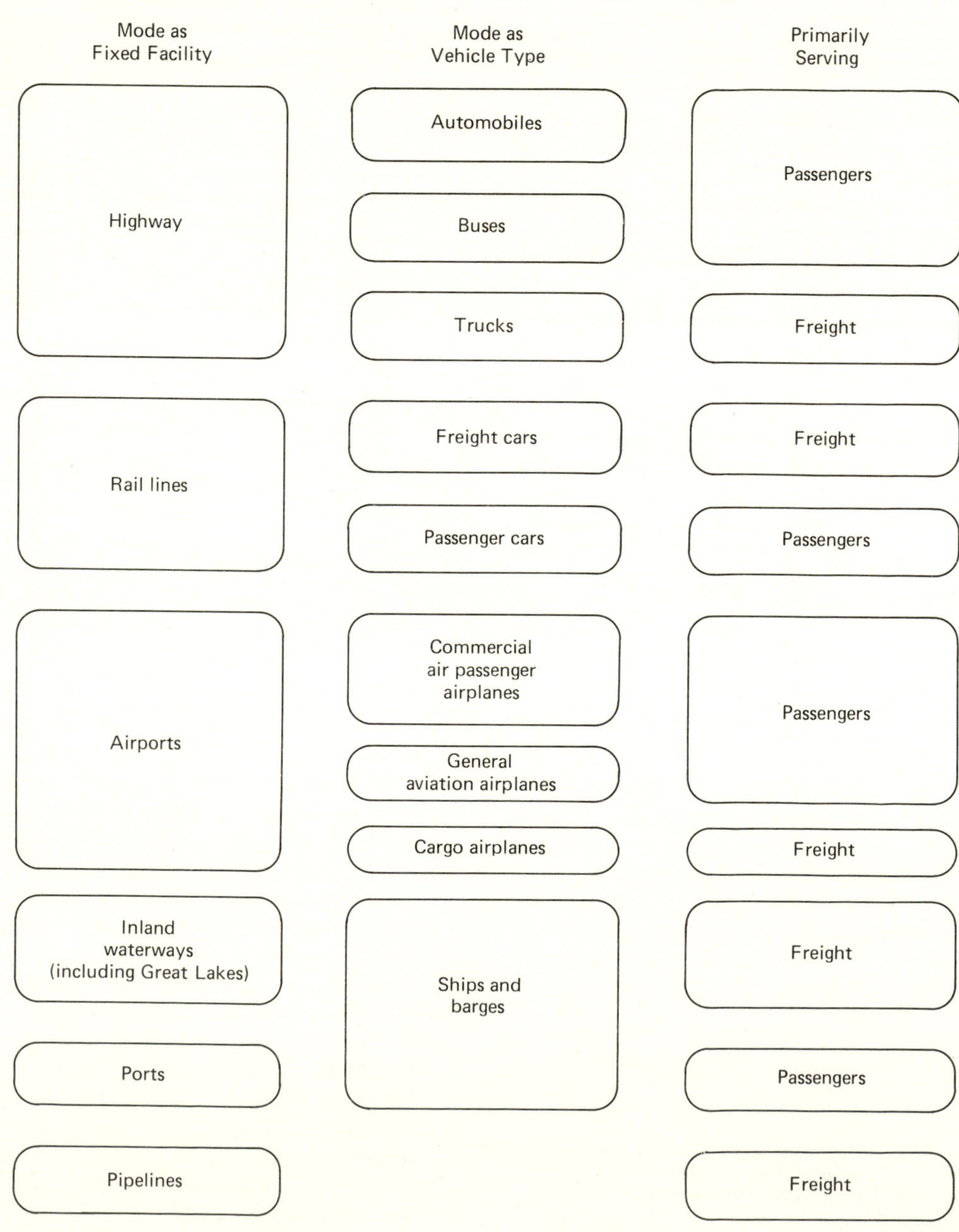

airports), (2) jurisdiction or ownership, and (3) product, as in the case of pipelines for gas, petroleum products, crude oil, and slurries.

Organization for statewide transportation planning

Although comprehensive statewide transportation planning might be undertaken by a state without specific legislative mandate, effective planning should have an adequate basis in legal authority. The concern here is for two kinds of authority: (1) authority to plan for all modes of transportation and (2) authority to implement plans. Without some kind of power for effectuation, planning is only an exercise.

Enabling legislation

In a 1974 survey, it was found that of 22 state departments of transportation, 21 had specific authorization to prepare comprehensive transportation plans. Six had already published plans, and the remainder were more or less actively engaged in preparing or revising comprehensive plans.[8] As of 1978, 14 states had prepared and published statewide transportation plans.[9]

Authority to carry out plans

Various kinds of authority have been given to the state transportation departments by which they can influence actions taken in the various modes. For convenience, four kinds of authority have been identified:

1. The power to construct, operate, and maintain. This is the strongest power, for it springs from ownership. All states have this power with respect to state highway systems, but few have it with respect to ports, airports, and canals.
2. The power to give financial aid. This power is important because it gives states the potential to exercise considerable influence on the design and operation of transportation facilities, while leaving day-to-day management to others. Tax relief is a form of financial grant.
3. The power to license and regulate. States may delegate to their departments of transportation the power to license and regulate private carriers in various fashions, including regulating:
   - **a.** A license to operate
   - **b.** Safety
   - **c.** Passenger fares and freight rates
   - **d.** Adequacy of service
   - **e.** Route(s) or territory served

   However, the power to license and regulate carriers has in most cases been held by state public service commissions or public utilities commissions, which are independent of state departments of transportation.
4. Power to license vehicles. The power to license vehicles permits states to regulate size of vehicle and various safety features.

In addition to the above, state departments of transportation may exercise certain other powers or undertake other functions, for example control or review over toll authorities, promotion of transportation, construction and operation of interstate bridges, conduct of research and demonstration studies, state highway patrol, and driver licensing.

A tabulation of DOT functions in 38 states, the District of Columbia, and Puerto Rico is maintained by the Iowa Department of Transportation and is updated annually.[10] This tabulation (see Figure 11.2) is summarized in Table 11-3. The three most common responsibilities of DOTs are highways (95%), aeronautics (82.5%), and transit (67.5%).

"Financial control or responsibility" for railroads, as shown in Figure 11.2, does not mean financial control or responsibility over *all* railroads in the indicated states. Instead, it is a power exercised by these states generally over only a few miles of state-owned rail lines.

Responsibility for regulation appears to be increasing as a function of state DOTs; in 1974 only one state DOT (New York) had this function. In 1978, 10 states had some form of regulatory power.

Internal organization

It is difficult to be dogmatic about internal organization for statewide transportation planning because so many organizational forms exist and because there are so many factors that influence the design of an organization. Among these factors are the intangibles of past organizational formats, personality, training and ability, and the often-inflexible Civil Service or personnel rules. Nevertheless, certain principles and factors can be stated.

First, statewide transportation planning should be the responsibility of a single group (division, subdivision, or bureau) which plans for all modes, at least on the policy and systems planning levels. In many cases work at the corridor (or project) planning level can be split off and assigned to a "line" division—for example, airport (as opposed to air systems) planning is often the responsibility of a Division of Aeronautics. A single organization is best able to develop and coordinate plans for all modes of transportation—again, at certain levels—and to advise the chief executive of the transportation department on plans and programs.

Second, the "development function" may, for some modes, become assigned to a planning division or bureau. The "development function" consists of duties related to the implementation of plans—for example, the administration of transit operating assistance and capital grants or the

[8] *Issues in Statewide Transportation Planning*, Spec. Report 146, Transportation Research Board, Washington, D.C., 1974.

[9] "Status of Statewide Multimodal Planning" (unpublished paper), Office of the Secretary, U.S. Department of Transportation, Jan. 1978.

[10] *State Departments of Transportation as of October, 1978*, Iowa Department of Transportation, Des Moines, Iowa.

	Aeronautics	Highway	Rail	Waterways or Ports	Transit	Regulation	Highway Patrol	Motor Vehicle	Other
Alaska	X	X		X	X T				Public Fac.
Arizona	X	X	P		P T			X	
Arkansas	P	X	P	P	P	Weight			Toll Roads
California	$X^{1,3}$	X T	X^3 P T		$X^{1,3}$	T	T		Fer., Toll Brgs.
Connecticut	X	X	X	X	X				
Delaware	X	X	X		X				Toll Roads
Dist. of Columbia	X	X			T			X	
Florida	X	X	P T	P	X				Toll Fac.
Georgia	X	X	P T	X	X				Toll Roads
Hawaii	X	X	T	X	T	T	T	X	
Idaho	X	X	P		P T	Wt./Size			Hwy. Safety
Illinois	X T	X T	X	P T	X T	T	T		Safety
Iowa	X	X	X	P T	X P T	X		X	Toll Bridges
Kansas	T	X	P	P	X				
Kentucky	X	X	P	P	T	X		X	Toll Fac.
Louisiana	X	X	P		X	Weight			Fer., Toll Brgs
Maine	X	X	T	X P	T				
Maryland	X	X	X T	X	X			X	Toll Fac. and Safety
Massachusetts	X	X	X	X P	X	T			Toll Roads
Michigan	X	X	X	X	X				Toll Bridges
Minnesota	X	X	X	X	X	X			
Missouri	X	X	X	X	X				
New Jersey	P T	X	X		X	In Process			
New Mexico	X	X			X	Enforcement		X	
New York	X T	X T	X T	X T	X T	X			
North Carolina	X P T	X	P		X^3 P T	Weight	X^5	X	Ferries
Ohio	X	X	T		T	X			Toll Fac.
Oklahoma	P T	X	P	P	P T				
Oregon	X	X	P	P	X		X^5	X	Parks
Pennsylvania	X P T	X P T	X P	X	X P T	P T	X	X	Toll Fac.
Puerto Rico	X	X		X	X	X		X	Toll Roads
Rhode Island	X	X	X^3		X^3	X		X	Hwy. and Safety
South Dakota	X	X	P		T	X^4	X^5		
Tennessee	X	X		X	X				
Texas		X			P T			X	Ferries
Utah	X	X	Safety		T	Motor Car			
Vermont	X	X	X	X	X	X		X	
Virginia		X			X			X	Toll Roads
Washington	X	X	P		P T	Weight			Fer., Toll Brgs
Wisconsin	X	X		P	X	X	X	X	

P = Planning Only
T = Technical Assistance
X = Financial Control or Responsibility

[1]Capital improvements only
[2]Funding for commuter lines only
[3]Partial funding

[4]Highway and airports only, exclusive of motor vehicles
[5]From highway revenues; under Dept. of Public Safety

Figure 11.2. Functions of state departments of transportation, October 1978. SOURCE; *State Department of Transportation as of October, 1978,* Iowa Department of Transportation, Des Moines, Iowa.

administration of contracts related to the subsidization of railroad branch lines. The New York State DOT, for example, has a Planning Division and a Development Division reporting to the Assistant Commissioner for Planning and Development. Both divisions have planning functions, although the Development Division's functions are more short-range and more corridor- or project-oriented. The danger exists, where planning and development are the functions of a single group, that the administrative pressures of the development function will reduce or eliminate the time available for planning. In general, the development function should remain with the statewide planning function only when the development function is comparatively limited, or for a minor mode. As soon as development becomes a strong and continuing activity, it is likely to acquire "line" status and to become a distinct division or bureau in its own right.

Third, within a statewide planning staff there can be a

variety of organizational arrangements. The exact organization will depend on the size of the state, the kinds of plans expected to be produced by the planning staff, the emphasis of federal programs, and other factors. In a large state the statewide staff may concentrate on policy and systems level work, with corridor or project planning handled by separate groups, some of which may be outside the planning division. In a small state the staff planning organization may carry plans down to the route location or project planning level of detail. Organizational possibilities include the following:

1. Set up a single group, without specializing, to develop plans for all modes; the accent is then on the total transportation system.
2. Employ existing modal specialists because of their experience, thus organizing along modal lines: highway planning, transit planning, railroad planning, and/or aviation planning.
3. Organize on functional lines: data collection, systems analysis, programming, policy planning, and corridor or project planning.
4. Organize on geographic lines.

Generally, organizations reflect compromises between these different viewpoints. In New York's organization (see Figure 11.3) the statewide planning section consists of four units. Originally conceived as being organized on nonmodal lines in the 1960s, this section has since begun to specialize on modal lines. Actual responsibilities of units within the sections may change from year to year. The section can also avail itself of services of specialists in other parts of the Department, such as computer programming and cartographic specialists.[11]

External organization

The function of statewide transportation planning, including the development function, must have regular channels for communications and coordination with (1) other agencies of state (and sometimes local) government and (2) the private sector of the transportation industry, plus persons who represent the public at large, or significant interest groups.

An example of how such external organization could be set up is shown in Figure 11.4.[12] This example is for rail planning in state governments, but it could equally serve as an organization chart for multimode planning. Note that two committees are proposed:

1. An intrastate coordination committee, designed to bring together representatives of different state agencies that have an interest in transportation.

[11]Correspondence and discussions with G. F. Young, Head, State Planning and Research Section, New York State Department of Transportation, Albany, N.Y.

[12]JWK International Corporation and Roger Creighton Associates Incorporated, *Rail Planning Manual*, Vol. 2, *Guide for Planners*, Federal Railroad Administration, Washington, D.C., July 1978.

Figure 11.3. Functional organization chart of state planning and research section, New York State Department of Transportation (unofficial). Source: Correspondence and discussions with G. F. Young, Head, State Planning and Research Section, New York State Department of Transportation, Albany, N.Y.

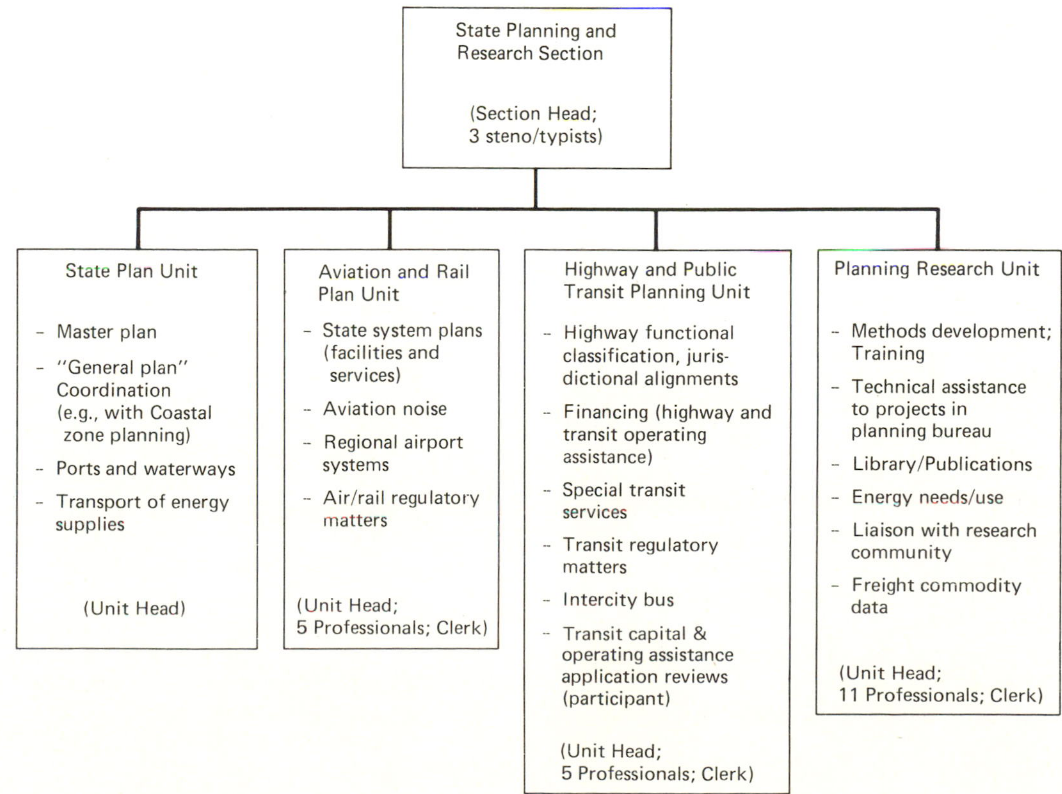

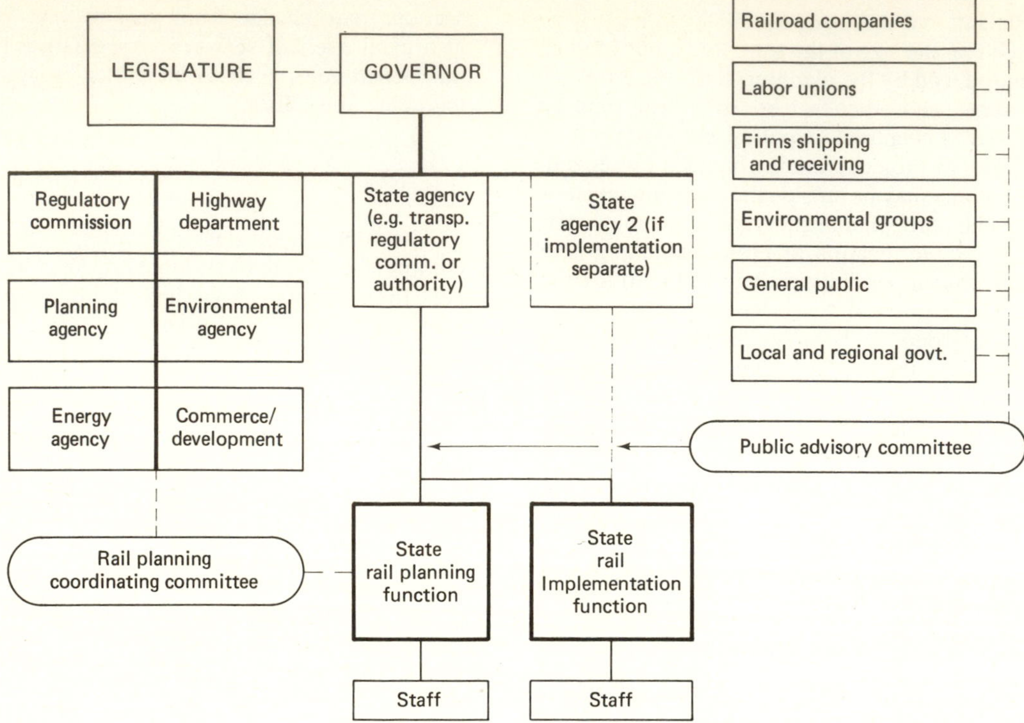

Figure 11.4. Organization for state rail planning and public participation. SOURCE: JWK INTERNATIONAL CORPORATION AND ROGER CREIGHTON ASSOCIATES, INCORPORATED. *Rail Planning Manual,* Vol. 2, *Guide for Planners,* Federal Railroad Administration, Washington, D.C., July 1978.

2. A public participation committee, designed to bring representatives of the private sector transportation industry, plus other interested groups, together for the purposes of reviewing plans, providing data, and sharing ideas and criticisms.

Pennsylvania, Iowa, Wisconsin, and New York are examples of states that have organized committees to advise on state rail planning. Rail advisory committees have ranged in size from 30 to nearly 100 members. Representation includes railroad companies, unions, shippers, the university community, environmental groups, regional planning agencies, and others. In Wisconsin the rail advisory committee's work was supported by regional commissions which formed their own groups to study particular rail problems.[13]

Initiating statewide transportation planning

For some states, and for those nations for which this chapter is relevant, a prime concern is how to get started with transportation planning at the state or national level. For states and nations that already have planning programs, the question is one of reexamining an existing planning program to determine how it can be made more effective. In either case the problem is one of assembling ideas, facts, and opinions on a variety of subjects and then synthesizing a work program that is responsive to needs. The process of assembly and synthesis is complex: certain steps and topics, however, are basic. These are presented below.

Developing the work program

Each state or nation that is developing or revising a program of transportation planning for its jurisdiction must begin by identifying the critical needs that must be addressed by planning. The topics presented earlier in this chapter provide the means for a successive screening that can identify which problems are most critical. (Implicit in the development of a work program and in identifying problems is the establishment of state or national goals. This is discussed subsequently.) The following procedure is therefore suggested.

1. Prepare a working definition of statewide transportation planning as it will apply to the particular state or nation.
2. Identify the concerns of planning, using Table 11-1 as a starting point. Which subjects are definitely of concern? Are these subjects within the jurisdiction of the agency to which the statewide planning function is attached? Should they be? Is it possible for the planning group to deal with each of the areas of concern? (Feasibility is a matter of technical competence, of time, and of staff size.)
3. Prepare a list of problems and issues currently affecting the state or nation, using Table 11-2 as a starting point. Be as specific as possible, and include locality of the problem, or some measure of the severity of the problem.
4. Develop a means for obtaining a widespread and inde-

[13]Ibid.

pendent review of the products of steps 2 and 3 preceding. One means is to have technical staff visit key officials in the public and private sectors. Another is to form one or more transportation advisory committees as described earlier.

5. Using the independent review process, finalize the list of planning concerns from step 2 and the list of problems and concerns from step 3. Establish priorities for these problems and concerns. Which must be dealt with immediately? Which can wait for a year or two?

The preceding five steps result in a statement of critical needs for planning work, in a priority order. This must now be converted into a work program that is within the technical personnel, budgetary, and time constraints of the agency (or agencies) responsible for planning.

To develop such a work program, a division of the total list of priority problems must be made, that is, a division into components that are amenable to attack by individuals, small teams of professionals, or consultants. To make this division, problems should be classified by mode, level, and step (in that order) using the stratifications described earlier.

Looking at the final products

As part of the process of initiating statewide transportation planning, it is necessary to look ahead at the final product or products that are expected to emerge. What will these products be? How will they help decision makers? If they can be defined, the development of a work plan will be that much easier.

Three types of planning products can be defined. First is the special report which is issued at the end of an investigation of a particular topic that, because of its unique nature or critical need, is prepared outside the stream of studies that lead to the preparation of a multimode, comprehensive statewide transportation plan. There may be many such studies. Examples include energy conservation or energy contingency plans, or plans for a particular waterway. In all such cases, the special nature of the problem being faced dictates the content of the work program, and this content is so diverse that it is unprofitable to generalize regarding how the work should be done.

The second type of planning product is the plan that is mandated by a federal law or regulation. An example of such a plan is the state rail plan which was mandated by the Railroad Revitalization and Regulatory Reform Act of 1976. The minimum required content of these plans is described in the FRA *Rail Planning Manual*.[14] Since the content of mandated plans is specified, the work programs to develop them are also reasonably well specified, and this makes the task of initiating such planning relatively simple, the more so when manuals have been prepared.

The third type of planning product is the multimode, comprehensive statewide transportation plan. What is significant about these plans is that they demonstrate a variety of approaches to planning, and these approaches naturally influence the work program of the transportation planning team.

Five major types of statewide transportation plans may be identified. These are briefly described below.

1. *The Reconnaissance Plan*. In the early years of DOT experience with statewide planning, a "reconnaissance" or "background" approach may be required. The purpose is to gain an understanding of the extent and characteristics of the various modes, how they work and whom they serve, and how they have developed over time. A number of early plans[15,16] contain such strong descriptive elements.

2. *The Policy Plan*. Several states have issued "policy plans" that contain statements of the goals and policies of the state with respect to transportation. Such statements tend to be qualitative rather than quantitative, and general rather than particular. One of the best of such statements was issued by the U.S. DOT in 1975.[17] Wisconsin's recent plan[18] is also a policy plan.

3. *The Plan as Program*. A number of state plans, including those of Rhode Island,[19] Georgia,[20] and Connecticut,[21] are strongly oriented toward programming in that they contain lists of projects which are intended to be implemented in scheduled order. Such a plan can be very useful, especially when updated annually (as Connecticut's is), in showing legislators or the public exactly which projects will be accomplished.

4. *The Comprehensive Plan*. This is the classic aim of transportation planning: to deal with all aspects of transportation in a coordinated fashion and to produce a document that reflects a state (or national) DOT's mastery of policy, of physical systems, of finance, and of regulation. Among plans that fall into this category are New York's 1973 plan[22] and Maryland's 1978 plan.[23] The California planning program was headed in this direction, but was terminated after substantial opposition developed.[24]

5. *The Sketch Plan*. This approach, an attempt to relate a multimode transportation plan to the economic, locational, energy, environmental, and "quality-of-life" sectors of a state, was followed in the preparation of the 1976 North Carolina Transportation Plan.[25] Four alternative futures

---

[14]Ibid.

[15]*Policies and Plans for Transportation in New York State*, New York State Department of Transportation, Albany, N.Y., 1968.

[16]*Transportation Policies for Pennsylvania*, Pennsylvania Department of Transportation, Harrisburg, Pa., 1970.

[17]*A Statement of National Transportation Policy*, U.S. Department of Transportation, Washington, D.C., Sept. 1975.

[18]*State Transportation Policy Plan*, Wisconsin Department of Transportation, Madison, Wis., Apr. 1979.

[19]*Rhode Island Transportation Plan—1990*, Rhode Island Statewide Planning Program, Department of Administration, Providence, R.I., Jan. 1975.

[20]*Georgia Transportation Plan*, Department of Transportation, Atlanta, Ga., May 1978.

[21]*Connecticut Master Transportation Plan 1979*, Connecticut Department of Transportation, Wethersfield, Conn., Dec. 1978.

[22]*Statewide Master Plan for Transportation*, Vol. 1, New York State Department of Transportation, Albany, N.Y., 1973.

[23]*1978 Maryland Transportation Plan*, Maryland Department of Transportation, Baltimore–Washington International Airport, Md., July 1978.

[24]William S. Weber, "The California Transportation Plan—Recommended Statewide Transportation Goals, Policies and Objectives," paper prepared for delivery to the Transportation Research Board, Jan. 1978.

[25]Barton-Aschman Associates, Inc., *Statewide Transportation Plan*, Phase I Summary Report and Phase I Technical Report, North Carolina Department of Transportation, Raleigh, N.C., 1976.

("historic trends," "managed growths," "voluntary conservation," and "managed conservation") were selected and described in terms of the density and location of population. The multimode transportation needs and implications of each future were examined. For an entire state, this was a formidable problem, which was carried out with thoroughness but at a general rather than detailed level. The approach merits study but must be examined from the viewpoint of whether it is sufficiently detailed in its result to be of significant assistance to the decision maker.

Any state or nation that is embarking on a new transportation program or revising its present program should carefully review the available alternative types of transportation plans, and then select that type which it finds will be most useful in promoting sound decision making and orderly implementation.

Alternative approaches to problem solving

When initiating or revising a statewide transportation planning program, decisions need to be made as to the approach or approaches to be used in solving problems that affect the entire area of a state. Here we are not concerned with the techniques that may be used to deal with specific, localized, or technical problems, but rather with methods that solve problems of large systems or deal with decisions as to the relative merits of components of those systems.

Basically, there are three approaches to solving problems of this type. First is the needs–standards approach, in which a standard is established (on the basis of judgment or experience) as the principal criterion for decision making. Second is the single-mode simulation–evaluation approach, in which performance of a system is simulated and evaluated in terms of various goals. Finally, there is the programming approach, in which given projects are prioritized, for example through the application of a cost–benefit ratio. These three approaches are described below.

Needs–standards approach. In this approach, standards are set for each mode of transportation. These may include standards of physical design (as of roadway geometrics): standards of service levels (capacity in relationship to demand, or frequency of mass transportation service), and safety standards. Surveys then measure existing conditions; forecasts estimate future demands. The difference between the standards and existing (or future) conditions is, by definition, the need. Generally, needs exceed financial resources, and, therefore, priority projects must be identified, which become the program for construction or other implementation. This approach is diagrammed in Figure 11.5.

The advantages of the needs–standards approach, which is basically the approach used in the National Transportation Planning Manuals of the U.S. DOT[26] are its simplicity, directness, credibility, and the fact that it can be done. The disadvantages are that the needs are a direct function of the

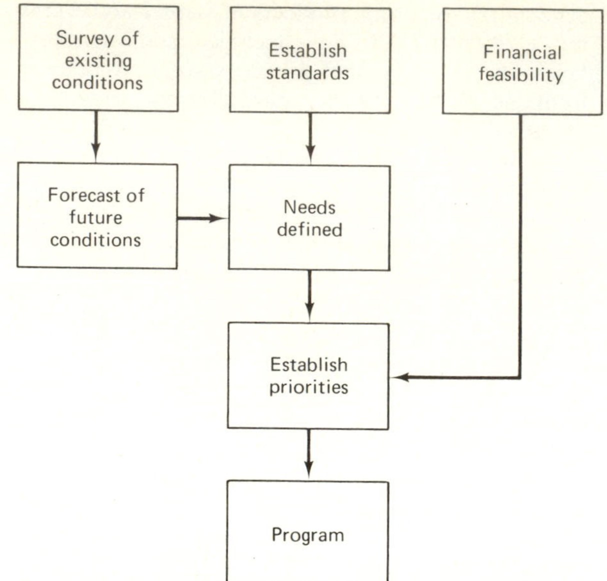

Figure 11.5. Needs–standards approach to statewide transportation planning. SOURCE: Roger L. Creighton, "Statewide and Regional Transportation Planning," in Institute of Traffic Engineers, *Transportation and Traffic Engineering Handbook,* Prentice-Hall, Englewood Cliffs, N.J., 1976.

standards that have been set, and the standards can be debated. Furthermore, the benefits to users and nonusers are not directly measured, and comparisons of intermodal investment productivity cannot be made directly. If the disadvantages of the method are explicitly recognized and are understood both by the planner and by the reader (or the general public), this method is a practical and honest approach. However, if the method is not understood, it may deceive the planner as well as the public, possibly producing a wasteful result.

Single-mode simulation–evaluation approach. The single-mode simulation–evaluation approach is derived from the urban transportation planning process. It typically contains four major elements, plus the elements of data collection and programming–implementation. The major elements are (1) the specification of goals or criteria, (2) the preparation of plans to improve performance in relationship to those goals or criteria, (3) the simulation of present and/or future performance of the planned system, and (4) the evaluation of the results.

The basic distinction between the needs–standards approach and the simulation–evaluation approach lies in the nature of the goals which are used. The standards employed in the needs–standards approach tend to be physically dimensioned, relating to the facility itself; the goals used in simulation–evaluation stem from performance *as observed by users or nonusers*. The sequence of steps used in single-mode simulation evaluation can be diagrammed in many ways, but a simple diagram containing the essential feedback steps is shown in Figure 11.6. Essential to this process are data that represent the behavior of the system being planned and permit future behavior to be represented. Quantitative data, instead of word data or descriptions, are needed.

[26]*National Transportation Planning Manual (1970–1990),* including Manual A (General Instructions); Manual B (National Highway Functional Classification and Needs Study Manual); and Manual D (Airports and Other Intercity Terminals), U.S. Department of Transportation, Washington, D.C., 1970, 1971.

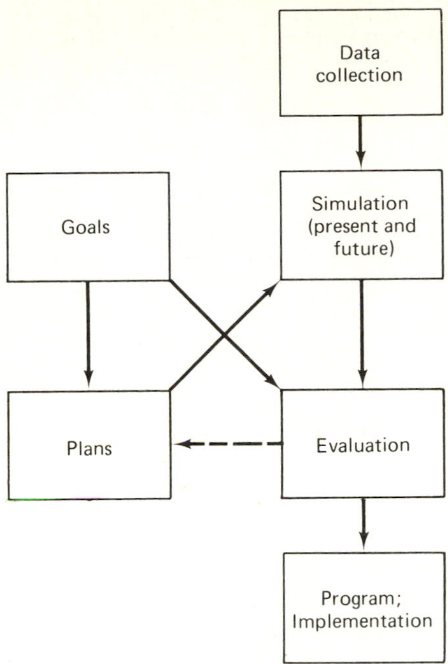

Figure 11.6. Single-mode simulation-evaluation approach. SOURCE: Roger L. Creighton, "Statewide and Regional Transportation Planning," in Institute of Traffic Engineers, *Transportation and Traffic Engineering Handbook,* Prentice-Hall, Englewood Cliffs, N.J., 1976.

The advantages of the single-mode simulation–evaluation approach are (1) that it evaluates plans directly in terms of user and nonuser goals, for example minimizing time and out-of-pocket costs and maximizing safety; (2) that it deals with and represents systems directly, thus leading to greater understanding; and (3) that it offers the ability to aggregate costs (e.g., time) on the same basis for several modes, thus permitting intermodal comparisons. The disadvantages of this approach are (1) its complexity and difficulty, (2) its large data requirements, and (c) the time that it takes. Some experience with single-mode simulation–evaluation has been gained, and is partially reported later in this chapter.

A variation of the single-mode simulation–evaluation approach is the multimode simulation–evaluation approach. This might be called a third-generation approach to statewide transportation planning. The demands for transportation, both of people and goods, are estimated for all parts of a state.[27] The demands are then allocated between modes, and simulation is undertaken for all modes, much as in the single-mode process described above, except that allowance is made for feedbacks, as planned changes in service levels affect the choices of mode.

The advantages of this variation are that it deals with all modes of transportation simultaneously and presumably permits more effective planning and coordination across all modes. The disadvantages are (1) its extreme complexity, (2) the inadequacy of necessary data, and (3) the fact that there is so little experience with it except for a few studies undertaken for foreign countries.[28]

Programming approach. This approach may be used independently, or in combination with either or both of the preceding approaches. The essence of this method is that it receives lists of projects from any of a variety of sources, arranges them in priority order through the application of one or more evaluation procedures, and then schedules them into construction (or other implementation) after careful study of resource availability.

The advantages of the programming approach are (1) its directness, (2) its plausibility, and (3) its direct connection with the "bottom line": funding and implementation. Programming can be accomplished either simply or with sophisticated evaluation procedures. Programming can be built into the process of intergovernmental cooperation, and into policy or political decision making; it is essentially a management tool.

The disadvantages of programming will become apparent if it is unsupported by other planning methodologies. Alone, programming can only react to the projects that are fed to it; it does not look at future demand or future systems. Basically, it is not a creative process, and in practice can become mechanical and uncritical. Hence, although programming is an important part of statewide transportation planning, it should not be accepted as the sole method of planning.

Standards and goals

When statewide transportation planning is being initiated, it is desirable to develop formal statements of the goals and standards that will be used (1) to judge the performance of existing transportation systems and services and (2) to evaluate proposed changes in those systems and services.

Standards and goals have two distinct meanings. A standard is a specific characteristic of a transportation facility, for example a pavement width, a volume/capacity ratio, or a transit or airline service frequency. A goal is a desired quality of a transportation facility seen from the viewpoint of a person or group of people in terms of its impact upon them. For example, safety is a desired quality, and people rank highways or air service in terms of risk of accident.

Examples of standards are those set up in the manuals of the 1970 National Transportation Needs Study.[29] Table 11-4 is an example of standards for rural arterials and collectors.

A basic difficulty with standards is in determining how much it is worth to attain them, or even to make improvements toward them. Here is where an approach that rates transportation system performance in relationship to the things (goals) people want for themselves or for their or-

[27] TRANSPORTATION RESEARCH INSTITUTE OF CARNEGIE-MELLON UNIVERSITY AND PENNSYLVANIA TRANSPORTATION TRAFFIC CENTER, *Methodological Framework for Comprehensive Transportation Planning,* Governor's Committee on Transportation, Pennsylvania State University, State College, Pa., 1968.

[28] JOHN R. MEYER, ed., *Techniques of Transportation Planning,* Vol. 2, *Systems Analysis and Simulation Models,* The Brookings Institution, Washington, D.C., 1971.

[29] *National Highway Functional Classification and Needs Study Manual (1970–1990),* (Manual B of the National Transportation Planning Study) U.S. Department of Transportation, Washington, D.C., 1970.

TABLE 11–4

Example of Certain Standards Established for the 1972 National Transportation Needs Study: Minimum Tolerable Conditions for Rural Arterials and Collectors

Functional Systems:	Rural Principal Arterials			Rural Minor Arterials								
ADT for Analysis Year:	All			Over 6000			2000–6000			Under 2000		
Terrain†:	F	R	M	F	R	M	F	R	M	F	R	M
Operating speed (peak hour) (mph)	55	50	45	50	45	40	50	45	40	40	40	35
Surface type		High			High			Inter.			Inter.	
Lane width (ft)		11			11			11			11	
Shoulder type		Stab.			Stab.			Stab.			Earth	
Graded right shoulder width (ft)	8	8	6	8	8	6	6	6	4	6	6	4
Safe speed‡ (mph)	65	55	45	60	50	40	60	50	40	60	50	40
Stopping sight distance (ft)	550	415	315	475	350	275	475	350	275	475	350	275
Maximum curvature (deg)	5	6	10	5	8	13	5	8	13	5	8	13
Maximum gradient§ (%)	3	4	8	3	5	9	3	5	9	3	5	9
Number of lanes		‖			‖			2			2	
Pavt. cond. rating (PSR or equivalent)		2.6			2.6			2.1			2.1	
Structures												
Width (ft)**	Traveled-way width + 6 ft						Traveled-way width + 4 ft					
Vertical clearance (ft)		14			14			14			14	
Loading		H-20			H-20			H-15			H-15	

Functional Systems:	Rural Collectors											
ADT for Analysis Year:	1000–6000*			400–1000			100–400			Below 100		
Terrain†:	F	R	M	F	R	M	F	R	M	F	R	M
Operating speed (peak hour) (mph)	—	—	—	—	—	—	—	—	—	—	—	—
Surface type		Inter.			Low			Low			Gravel	
Lane width (ft)		11			10			9			22-ft roadway	
Shoulder type		Earth			Earth			Earth			—	
Graded right shoulder width (ft)	4	4	4	4	4	4	2	2	2		—	
Safe speed‡ (mph)	50	45	35	50	40	30	50	40	30	40	35	25
Stopping sight distance (ft)	350	315	250	350	275	200	350	275	200		—	
Maximum curvature (deg)	8	10	18	8	13	23	8	13	23		—	
Maximum gradient§ (%)	4	5.5	10	4	6	11	4	6	11		—	
Number of lanes		2§			2			2			—	
Pavt. cond. rating (PSR or equivalent)		2.1			2.1			2.1			—	
Structures												
Width (ft)**	Traveled-way width + 2 ft									18	18	18
Vertical clearance (ft)		14			14			14			14	
Loading		H-15			H-15			H-15			H-15	

*Rural collectors with present ADT above 6000 should be multilane where necessary to maintain peak hour operating speeds of 40, 35, and 30 mph in flat, rolling, and mountainous terrain, respectively.
†F, flat terrain; R, rolling terrain; M, mountainous terrain.
‡Approximate speed on which minimum tolerable stopping-sight-distance curvature and gradients are based.
§Steeper grades may be considered tolerable if lengths are relatively short or climbing lanes are provided.
‖As necessary to maintain the operating speed specified.
**For bridges over 250 ft in length, widths 4 ft less than shown, but in no case less than the width of the approach traveled way will be considered adequate.

ganizations can provide an additional strength. Costs of making improvements can be related to reductions in costs to users or to gains in other recognized values, such as safety.

The following list of general goals may be used as a starting point for the development of more specific goals tailored to a particular region. For convenience, these goals have been divided into three groups, according to the viewpoint of the persons or groups most concerned with each goal. The three groups of viewers are (1) the users of transportation facilities, including individuals who themselves use transportation facilities or the shippers of goods;(2) the providers of transportation facilities, both public and private; and (3) the nonuser public, which is the total population playing the roles of residents, conservationists, and so forth. As a matter of procedure, goal statements should be developed at the staff level and then reviewed at the policy level of government. Once accepted at the policy level, goals can be used to evaluate either present conditions or proposed changes in facilities or services.

Transportation user goals. Common user goals include some or all of the following:

1. *Increased mobility*. Greater mobility is desired for all the population. In addition, special consideration must be given to increasing the mobility of older citizens, the handicapped, and those who cannot afford to drive or who are incapable of driving to work, to shopping and recreational facilities, or for other purposes.
2. *Increased dependability*. A dependable transportation system is desired which will be able to cope with bad weather and other adverse conditions and which will have a high percentage of on-time arrivals.
3. *Reduced time spent in travel*. Faster door-to-door transportation is desired for both people and goods. This includes time spent in transferring people and goods between transportation modes.
4. *Increased comfort*. The comfort of transportation can be increased by providing clean, air-conditioned, and well-maintained vehicles and terminals and by reducing congestion.
5. *Reduced accidents*. A major goal is to reduce fatalities, injuries, and property damage accidents for all modes of transportation.
6. *Reduce user costs*. User costs are monies spent for operating costs for private vehicles, fares on and operating subsidies for mass transportation systems, and prices for the shipment of goods, including losses and spoilage. Clearly, it is an important goal to keep these costs as low as possible.
7. *Enhance aesthetics*. People spend a significant portion of their time traveling to and between cities. The travel

experience should be kept as pleasant as possible for all modes of transportation by promoting beautification and the development of scenic facilities along rights-of-way and at terminals.

Goals of transportation agencies and companies. Public and private transportation groups may have the following goals:

1. *Reduce capital costs*. The construction of transportation facilities and the purchase of common carrier vehicles for the movement of people and goods are major investments. These should be kept as low as possible, consistent with the achievement of other desired goals.
2. *Reduce maintenance costs*. The costs of maintaining existing facilities and equipment should be kept as low as possible, consistent with the attainment of other goals, including the goal of reducing capital costs.
3. *Reduce operating costs*. Labor and energy costs are major components of the total cost of providing for the movement of goods and for the common carrier transportation of people. These costs should be kept as low as possible, consistent with the attainment of other goals.
4. *Profit*. For the private carriers, making a profit is an important goal; in fact, profit is an indication of organizational vitality and efficiency.
5. *Increase coordination*. All transportation facilities of a state should be planned to work as a system with the various modes interconnected for flexibility yet providing that efficiency which only specialization can produce.
6. *Preserve resources*. The transportation system should be planned so that natural resources, such as prime agricultural lands, forests, shorelands, lakes, and wildlife preserves, are conserved. In addition, new transportation facilities should avoid sites that have historic and aesthetic value.
7. *Economic growth*. Transportation is a vital ingredient in promoting economic development.

Community goals. Depending on local circumstances, community goals may be to:

1. *Increase accessibility*. A major statewide goal is to increase accessibility to all parts of the state and especially to those parts not adequately served by transportation.
2. *Reduce pollution*. The emission of noise, gaseous and particulate pollutants, and solid wastes from transportation sources should be kept below the levels set by state and federal law.
3. *Encourage desirable settlement patterns*. Because transportation affects the patterns of development within a state, it should be used to the extent feasible to promote desired forms of population settlement patterns and the desired location of economic activities.
4. *Reduce harmful environmental impact*. The construction of transportation facilities should be planned so that harmful impact on the natural environment, including marine life and wildlife, is minimized.

Data

The last of the requirements for initiating statewide transportation planning (as presented in this series) is the need for an adequate data base. For purposes of convenience, the data base is described here in two sections—one for freight planning and one for passenger planning.

Freight data. The study entitled *Freight Data Requirements for Statewide Transportation Systems Planning* was conducted by the National Cooperative Highway Research Program and published in 1977 as NCHRP Reports 177 and 178.[30,31] The following paragraphs summarize the principal findings:

The types of freight data that are needed may be classified in five groups.

1. *Traffic flow data,* including production and consumption of goods, commodity flows (by commodity type, origin to destination), traffic flows (origin to destination freight movements), vehicle flows, import/export movements, and routings of traffic.
2. *Carrier data,* describing carriers as firms in terms of finances, equipment, and its operations.
3. *Shipper/consignee attributes,* describing the shippers and receivers of goods.
4. *Physical and operating data,* describing the fixed facilities, vehicles (e.g., railcars or trucks), operating characteristics (e.g., schedules, speeds), capacities, and unit costs of the system.
5. *Direct and indirect impacts,* describing the varied effects of a freight transportation system on the economic, environmental, social, energy, and other dimensions of a state.

Requirements for the preceding types of data are shown graphically in Figure 11.7 according to the level of need—low, moderate, high, and very high. The three "priorities" shown in Figure 11.7 were determined by the amount of work already done by states that used these data; in general, Priority I needs are for initial stages of planning, Priority II for intermediate stages, and Priority III data needs are for advanced, more sophisticated, and more comprehensive planning work. These stages are defined below.[32]

1. *Initial stage*. Involvement largely limited to obtaining an initial familiarity with the freight transport system and its economic implications. Planning largely an individual response to particular problems or issues. Some broad-scale, policy-level planning. Data requirements limited to readily available secondary source data concerning network characteristics and use.

---

[30]Roger Creighton Associates Incorporated and R.L. Banks & Associates Inc., *Freight Data Requirements—Research Report*.

[31]Roger Creighton Associates Incorporated and R. L. Banks & Associates, Inc. *Freight Data Requirements for Statewide Transportation Systems Planning—User's Manual,* NCHRP Report 178, National Cooperative Highway Research Program, Washington, D.C., 1977.

[32]Roger Creighton Associates Incorporated and R. L. Banks & Associates, Inc., *Freight Data Requirements—Research Report*.

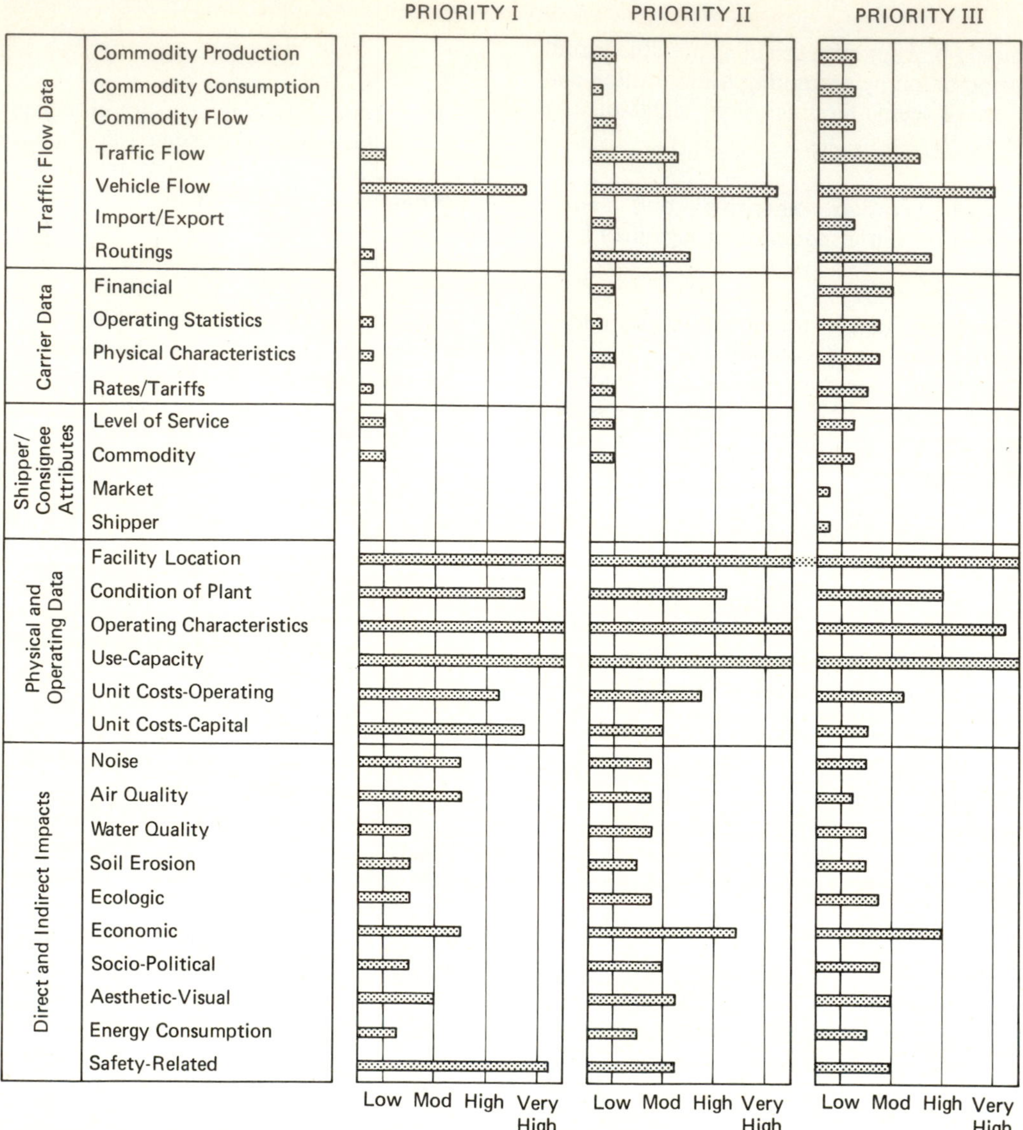

Figure 11.7. Data requirements for freight transportation planning, all modes. SOURCE: ROGER CREIGHTON ASSOCIATES INCORPORATED AND R. L. BANKS & ASSOCIATES, INC., *Freight Data Requirements for Statewide Transportation Systems Planning—Research Report,* NCHRP Report 177, National Cooperative Highway Research Program, Washington, D.C., 1977.

2. *Intermediate state.* Developing a system planning capability. Initial use of analytical techniques for forecasting demand, estimating modal choice, assessing economic effects, and estimating impacts for comprehensive freight planning. More sophisticated, quantitative response to particular problems or issues. Deeper understanding of factors influencing demand and mode choice. Data requirements mandate the acquisition and use of a majority of the listed data sources.

3. *Advanced stage.* Full development of a comprehensive freight transportation systems planning process. Full-scale application of the more sophisticated techniques for demand estimation, mode split, network analysis, economic evaluation, and impact estimation. Data requirements include the listed data sources plus other sets of primary and secondary data.

Another way of displaying the data needs discussed in NCHRP Report 177 is shown in Table 11-5. Here typical data requirements are spelled out, by data category, for the three stages of planning as defined above.

NCHRP Report 177 also examines five specific freight planning problems: demand forecasting, mode choice analysis, network analyses (simulation of traffic flows), economic evaluation, and impact estimation. Specific models are identified that have been used or proposed for solution of each of these planning problems; each model's particular data requirements are specified. Appendixes B to F contain a useful listing of models as well as their data requirements.

Professionals interested in locating data for use in their own planning programs should obtain a copy of NCHRP Report 178, which is a user's manual containing a catalog of 80 principal sources of freight data, 116 other sources of freight data, and 34 reference works. A typical documentation of a principal data source is shown in Figure 11.8. Report 178 is indexed so that users can find whether needed data are available or not, and has two sections deal-

TABLE 11–5
Data Required for Freight Systems Planning, by Category, by Stage

Data Category	Data Requirements
	Stage I
Traffic flow data	1. Estimates of annual state and national modal traffic flow data, in tons and ton-miles, compiled from secondary sources, such as the Carload Waybill Statistics, *Census of Transportation,* Waterborne Commerce of the U.S., FHWA truck survey data.
Modal forecasts	1. Historical trends and modal forecasts of national modal distributions by year, average length of haul in mileage blocks, average shipment size. Obtained from governmental agencies, trade associations, etc.
Network parameters	1. Schematic network maps showing link lengths and nodal characteristics.
National and state economic forecasts	1. Publications of state and federal governments, trade associations, and major industries forecasting economic growth, trends and outlook on a recurring basis.
Costs and rates	1. Average operating costs and revenues for different mileage and tonnage blocks (from published sources). 2. Typical unit capital costs for different modal investments. 3. Class rates.
Impact data	1. Fuel consumption and air pollutant emission rates, by mode.
	Stage II
Traffic flow data	1. Annual traffic flows between state regions and between state and national regions (states), by commodity types.
Modal forecasts	1. Projections made by major carriers serving the state. 2. Average shipment size and average value per ton, by commodity grouping. 3. Distance and transit time between zonal pairs, by mode.
Network parameters	1. Detailed maps for each mode, showing link distances, travel times, and interzonal routings.
State economy	1. Detailed economic growth forecasts, by county or substate region. 2. Historical data for various years on commodity production and consumption, by region assembled from various agencies.
Costs and rates	1. Operating costs and revenues, from sample surveys of waybills. 2. Average unit capital costs, from sample surveys of specific modal investments.
Transport time and time reliability	1. Sample surveys of total transit time (e.g., waybill studies). 2. Length of haul by shipment, line-haul time, transfer time, delivery time from analytic models. 3. Standard deviation of shipment times.
Impact data	1. Fuel consumption per horsepower-hour. 2. General operating characteristics (average vehicle size, operating speed, trips per day). 3. Air pollution emission rates for different power units. 4. Existing pollution levels. 5. Population near segment.
	Stage III
Traffic flow data	1. Disaggregate commodity traffic flows between county pairs and between counties and other states or multistate areas.
Modal forecasts	1. Shipment weights and value per ton, by detailed commodity grouping. 2. Transit time and rates (see below).
Network parameters	1. Network suitable for computer processing, detailed link parameters, and detailed node parameters.
State-level economic information	1. Inputs and outputs from specially developed economic model of the state's economy from state, national, or private sources.
Costs and rates	1. Detailed operating cost data (comparable to that available to carriers and regulatory agencies). 2. Detailed unit capital costs similar to those developed by Bechtel for USRA. 3. Tariff rules and schedules.
Transit time and time reliability	1. Time obtained through field measurements.
Impact data	1. Train performance calculators and other models that simulate operations. 2. Physical characteristics or route. 3. Ambient air, water, and noise levels along routes. 4. Air and noise dispersion models. 5. Accident rates, by mode and commodity grouping.

ing with primary data collection: Appendix A describes the organization and conduct of a shipper's survey and Appendix B describes how a physical systems inventory can be compiled from secondary data.

Passenger data. The need for and availability of data on passenger transportation at the state level has not been investigated as thoroughly as the subject of freight data. This stems in part from the fact that state DOTs until recently have not been engaged in quantitative planning for air, rail, or bus passenger systems. State planning for nonurban highways, which typically carry 90% or more of nonurban person-miles of travel, has generally had adequate data, particularly on facilities and traffic volumes, if not on statewide person-trip generation or origins and destinations. The needs for and supply of data for metropolitan transportation planning (which focuses mainly on person travel) have been investigated.[33] Because of the lack of research into data needs for nonurban and nonmetropolitan passenger planning, the following list must be regarded as preliminary.

1. *Network data.* Data on highway networks are generally adequate for most planning purposes in that link locations, widths, speeds, and pavement conditions are recorded. Aviation schedule data are available from airline companies. Rail schedules are available from Amtrak. Bus schedules are available from *Russell's Guide.*[34]

2. *Terminal data.* Airport data will be available if the state has completed a state aviation plan in accordance with FAA requirements. Rail and bus terminal data are generally not available; special surveys to measure their capacity, condition, and public services will often be needed.

3. *Person trip generation.* Population data are available from census sources to the MCD (minor civil division) or even tract level of detail. The generation of person-trips by mode (auto, light truck, air, rail, and bus) is not well measured as regards nonurban or intercity movements. These rates are subject to a high degree of variability depending upon (a) the availability of each mode, (b) the density of population and the configuration of urban settlements in a state, (c) income, and (d) occupation. Consequently, surveys of trip generation may be needed. If the major concern is air, bus, and rail travel, such surveys should be taken at the terminal. If the concern is highway travel, a sample survey at the home, by telephone or personal interview, is best.

4. *Origin–destination data.* Origin–destination data for state-level planning vary in quality and availability. For highway planning at the state level, very few origin–destination data are available; major surveys have not been funded in recent years, and most urban area cordon-line data sets are 10 to 15 years old. Whether such data are needed or not will have to be determined. The Civil Aeronautics Board obtains a 10% sample of airline tickets and publishes the results annually as a table of city-to-city move-

[33]CREIGHTON, HAMBURG, INC., *Data Requirements for Metropolitan Transportation Planning,* NCHRP Report 120, National Cooperative Highway Research Program, Washington, D.C., 1971.

[34]*Russell's Official National Motor Coach Guide,* Russell's Guides, Inc., Cedar Rapids, Iowa, 1978.

NCHRP PROJECT 8-17
Freight Data Requriements for Statewide Systems Planning
Data Source Documentation
Principal Data Source

I. Source Summary

1. TITLE: Annual Report Form F-1 Freight Forwarders – Class A	2. MODE: Rail, Highway 3. TYPE: Carrier
4. COLLECTED BY: Interstate Commerce Commission Bureau of Accounts	
5. FORM OF DATA: Hard copy, magnetic tape (Since 1971)	6. TIME PERIOD COVERED: Annual
7. ABSTRACT/KEY WORDS: This report is a primary source of *financial, operating and physical statistics* on the operations of freight forwarders.	
8. ISSUED BY: Each Class A freight forwarder (gross revenues exceed $100,000)	
9. FORM OF ISSUED DATA: Hard copy, magnetic tape (since 1973)	10. PRICE: Reimburse copy cost/ hard copy and magnetic tape.

II. Detailed Description

11. COVERAGE: All Class A freight forwarders

12: RELEVANT CONTENT OF SOURCE FILE:

ITEM (FROM REPORTING FORM)	CODING SCHEME OR UNITS
States in which traffic is originated and/or terminated	Name
Comparative balance sheet	Dollars
Income placement for the year	Dollars
Operating revenues by source	Dollars
Operating expenses by type	Dollars
Schedule of employees by occupation	Number/dollars
Description of motor vehicles owned	Number/dollars
Statistics - Tons of freight received from shippers	Tons
- Number of shipments received for shippers	Number

13: AVAILABLE SUMMARIES:

NAME: Transport Statistics in the U.S., Part B, Freight Forwarders

ISSUED BY: Superintendent of Documents, Government Printing Office, Washington, D.C. 20402

PRICE: $0.25 PUBLICATION CYCLE: Annually

ABSTRACT/KEY WORDS: A summary of Class A freight forwarders financial, operating and physical statistics. (*Carrier financial, operating statistics*)

14. DESCRIPTION OF COLLECTION PROCESS:

All Class A freight forwarders are required by the ICC to submit Form F-1 on a calendar year basis.

III. Evaluation/Constraints on Usage

15. SIGNIFICANT EXCLUSIONS OF DATA: None

16. FUTURE UPDATE OR EXTENSION PLANS: Program to continue indefinitely.

17. DATA AVAILABILITY/CONSTRAINTS ON DISSEMINATION: These data are publicly available.

18. EVALUATION/COMMENTS: These data are provided to the ICC by individual motor carriers whose collection processes may vary. Reports are audited by the ICC at irregular intervals.

For Class A freight forwarders the Form F-1 provides useful financial, operating and physical information for assessing financial viability, current results of operations and overall capability. These reports are the prime public source of cost data.

Figure 11.8. Example of documentation for a "Principal Data Source" catalogued in NCHRP Report 178. SOURCE: ROGER CREIGHTON ASSOCIATES INCORPORATED AND R. L. BANKS & ASSOCIATES, INC. *Freight Data Requirements for Statewide Transportation Systems Planning—User's Manual*, NCHRP Report 178, National Cooperative Highway Research Program, Washington, D.C., 1977.

ment. However, these data do not report the minor civil division of origin or destination. Bus and rail origin–destination data are not available except through the carriers.

5. *Miscellaneous data.* Planning requires a number of small data sets covering such subjects as travel cost, speed, reliability, quality of ride, safety, vehicle occupancy, access time (to a particular mode), access cost, energy consumption per vehicle-mile, and other topics. Most of these data can be obtained from secondary sources, but some surveys may have to be made.

Modal studies

In a chapter of this length, it is not possible to deal in depth with all the modes of transporting people and goods. Accordingly, four modes have been selected for examination: rail freight, intercity bus passenger service, aviation, and highways. Not covered are rail passenger transportation (primarily the responsibility of Amtrak in the United States); rural bus transportation for the elderly, handicapped, and other transportation-disadvantaged persons; pipelines; and water transportation. For those modes that are examined, discussion centers around (1) key facts and trends concerning the mode, (2) problems and issues, (3) the role of the state regarding that mode, and (4) comments on planning techniques.

The problems and issues described herein are issues as seen by the transportation planner or transportation executive working in government. This viewpoint tends to be technical, concerned with investment and allocation of governmental resources, and concerned with systems in the long run. The issues as seen by the carriers tend to be much more concerned with individual, short-range problems (such as costs of labor, franchises, and other management and operational problems) and are less frequently concerned with systems. It will be important for the future of the transportation industry that a shared view of issues and problems be taken, acknowledging the existence of both short- and long-range issues.

Railroad transportation

Key facts and trends. Railroads in the United States are an enormous industry. In 1975 they had a net investment (Class I railroads alone) of $29.5 billion and their operating revenues were $16.4 billion.[35] This compares with an estimated $21.9 billion available to all levels of government in the United States for highway purposes during the same year.[36] In terms of system length, there were about 200,000 mi of railroad lines in the United States in 1975 compared with 42,500 mi of Interstate highways and 270,000 mi of primary highways (including the Interstate highways).

Railroads are still the largest single mode for the transportation of intercity freight. In 1975, the number of tons of revenue freight originated on Class I railroads was estimated at 1.396 billion tons. Revenue ton-miles exceeded 752 billion. Tons originated have not changed significantly over the years, but ton-miles rose from the 447 billion ton-miles of 1929 to the level of 852 billion ton-miles in 1973 and dropped to 752 billion ton-miles in 1975. This implies that rails are hauling freight over longer distances, leaving more short-haul transportation to trucks.[37]

Problems and issues. The more important problems and issues, as seen from the public viewpoint, are:

1. *Railroad-grade-crossing elimination.*

2. *Redundant mainlines.* The aggregate route length of U.S. railroads in 1975 was approximately 200,000 mi, down from the all-time peak of 252,845 mi in 1920. (The U.S. rail system could decline to 150,000 mi in the next two decades.) Many of these miles are in redundant, near-parallel mainlines that were built in the era of intense competition of the late nineteenth century. Which mainlines should be eliminated is an important question, not only for the economy and efficiency of railroad operations, but also for the economies of states and localities.[38]

3. *Branch line discontinuation.* How extensive a system of branch lines is ultimately needed? Before all-weather highways formed an extensive intercity system (approximately 1920), railroads were the sole means of freight and passenger access to many small localities. But the need for such access has been declining. As a result, railroad branch lines have been discontinued steadily for many years, and streamlined procedures were adopted in the Railroad Revitalization and Regulatory Reform Act of 1976.[39] The disadvantages of branch line discontinuance are felt primarily by localities, which can lose employment and income.

4. *Urban rail rationalization.* In many cities, railroad mainlines, branch lines, yards, and interconnections form a complex web that occupies a great deal of land, creates unnecessary grade crossings, requires overpasses, and may cause substantial delays and increase the costs of railroad operation. The rationalization of such urban systems is an extremely difficult planning operation, but has long-term rewards.[40]

In addition to the preceding issues, which directly relate to the concerns of a state's economy and transportation system, there are many other issues that are indirectly a concern of the state. These are listed in Table 11-2.

Comments on planning. State rail planning received its greatest impetus from the passage of the Regional Rail Reorganization Act of 1973 (the 3R Act) and the Railroad Revitalization and Regulatory Reform Act of 1976 (the 4R

---

[35] *Yearbook of Railroad Facts,* 1976 ed., Association of American Railroads, Washington, D.C., 1976.

[36] *Statistical Abstract of the United States—1976,* Bureau of the Census, Washington, D.C., 1976.

[37] *Yearbook of Railroad Facts,* 1976.

[38] JWK International Corporation and Roger Creighton Associates Incorporated, *Rail Planning Manual,* Vol. 1, *Guide for Decisionmakers,* Federal Railroad Administration, Washington, D.C., Dec. 1976.

[39] JWK International Corporation and Roger Creighton Associates Incorporated, *Rail Planning Manual,* Vol. 2.

[40] Stanford Research Institute et al., *Urban Railroad Relocation: Nature and Magnitude of the Problem and Planning for Remedial Action—Executive Summary,* prepared for the Federal Railroad Administration, U.S. Department of Transportation, Washington, D.C., Aug. 1975.

Act). The 3R Act was passed primarily in response to the bankruptcy of the Penn-Central System and related only to the 17 states of the Northeast and Midwest regions; in that act, funds were set aside for state rail planning, mainly to deal with the problem of abandonment of light-density lines (branch lines). The 4R Act subsequently extended these provisions (and others) to cover the entire country. As in the 3R Act, the 4R Act's main emphasis, as far as statewide rail planning was concerned, was on the light-density-line problem.

Light-density lines are defined principally by tonnage carried. To put this in perspective, Category A mainlines are defined as those that (1) carry 20 million or more gross ton-miles per mile each year, (2) have three or more daily passenger trains per day in each direction, and (3) connect major transportation zones. Category B mainlines carry between 5 and 20 million gross ton-miles per mile per year. Category A branch lines carry between 1 and 5 million gross ton-miles per mile per year, and category B branch lines are here called light-density lines; they comprise approximately 25% of the nation's Class I route miles.[41]

The abandonment of a light-density line can cause significant changes and hardships to the localities it served. The potential impacts resulting from abandonment are diagrammed in Figure 11.9.[42] The types of impacts include displacements (people moving because of lost jobs), loss of income, increased costs to state and local government, losses in local tax bases, and the impacts caused by shifts in mode of transportation. These may include energy, air pollution, safety, and noise impacts (although these are often very small), and increases in transportation costs. The latter can reduce agricultural income.

Planning for light-density lines, including the important relationships of planning to FRA regulations and ICC abandonment procedures, is the subject of Chapter 2 of the FRA's *Rail Planning Manual*.[43] That chapter presents the following key components of light-density-line planning:

- Study design; relationship to FRA regulations and ICC abandonment process
- Data collection, including a minimanual on the conduct of a shipper's survey
- Community impact analyses, including methods for estimating primary and secondary job losses, wage losses, unemployment compensation, personal income losses, income and property tax losses, safety, and environmental impacts
- Financial analysis
- Implementation planning
- Monitoring the performance of light-density lines

In contrast with light-density-line planning, where the states have a definite role that is specified by the 3R and 4R acts, the state's role in planning for mainlines is generally complementary to the dominant role of the private carriers and the federal government. Nevertheless, states have definite interests to protect, including the enhancement of the state's economic growth, the preservation of railroads as profitable operations, avoidance of overuse of the highway system, the preservation of competition in transportation, and the minimization of energy use and adverse environmental impacts. To protect its interests, states may have to become deeply involved in studies of mainline operations, capital needs, rate changes, and regulatory changes.

Chapter 3 of the *Rail Planning Manual* (Volume II) deals with planning for mainlines. Topics covered include:

- Initiating mainline studies (study design, classification, zoning)
- Data collection, including a minimanual on physical system inventory
- Demand forecasting
- Network simulation
- Plan evaluation

Other aspects of state rail planning are documented in the FRA *Rail Planning Manual* (Volume II). Chapter 4 ("Special Topics") deals with railroad safety, national defense, rail passenger planning, urban rail rationalization, and other topics. There are other chapters covering (1) public participation, (2) implementation, and (3) relationship to the (multimode) statewide transportation planning process. The planner working in this field ought to obtain a copy of this manual before beginning to work in this specialized area.

Intercity bus transportation

With railroads steadily declining as a means of moving people between cities, and with air transportation being fairly inefficient in terms of cost and speed for trips of less than 150 mi or when attempting to serve small communities, buses remain an important and economical common carrier for passengers making trips of medium length. Bus service is the most ubiquitous form of common carrier transportation; over 15,000 communities in the United States are served by buses.[44]

Bus transportation is a major industry. In the United States, all Class I bus companies carried an estimated 100.3 million passengers in 1977, with a total of 12,560 million passenger-miles. (These are estimates for regular-route intercity service.) For the same year, there were 630 million vehicle-miles of service provided, with an average load of 19.9 passengers per bus. The average trip length was 125 mi—an increase from the 106 mi reported for 1970. The Class I carriers had a estimated 29,660 employees in 1977, and operated a fleet of 8270 buses.[45]

The people who use buses "tend to be drawn from the low income and non-professional occupational groups. The

[41]JWK International Corporation and Roger Creighton Associates Incorporated, *Rail Planning Manual*, Vol. 1.

[42]JWK International Corporation and Roger Creighton Associates Incorporated, *Rail Planning Manual*, Vol. 2.

[43]Ibid.

[44]*The Intercity Bus Industry—A Preliminary Study*, Interstate Commerce Commission, Washington, D.C., May 1978.

[45]*America's Number 1 Passenger Service*, American Bus Association (also, similar reports, under different titles, for 1974, 1976, and 1977), Washington, D.C., 1978.

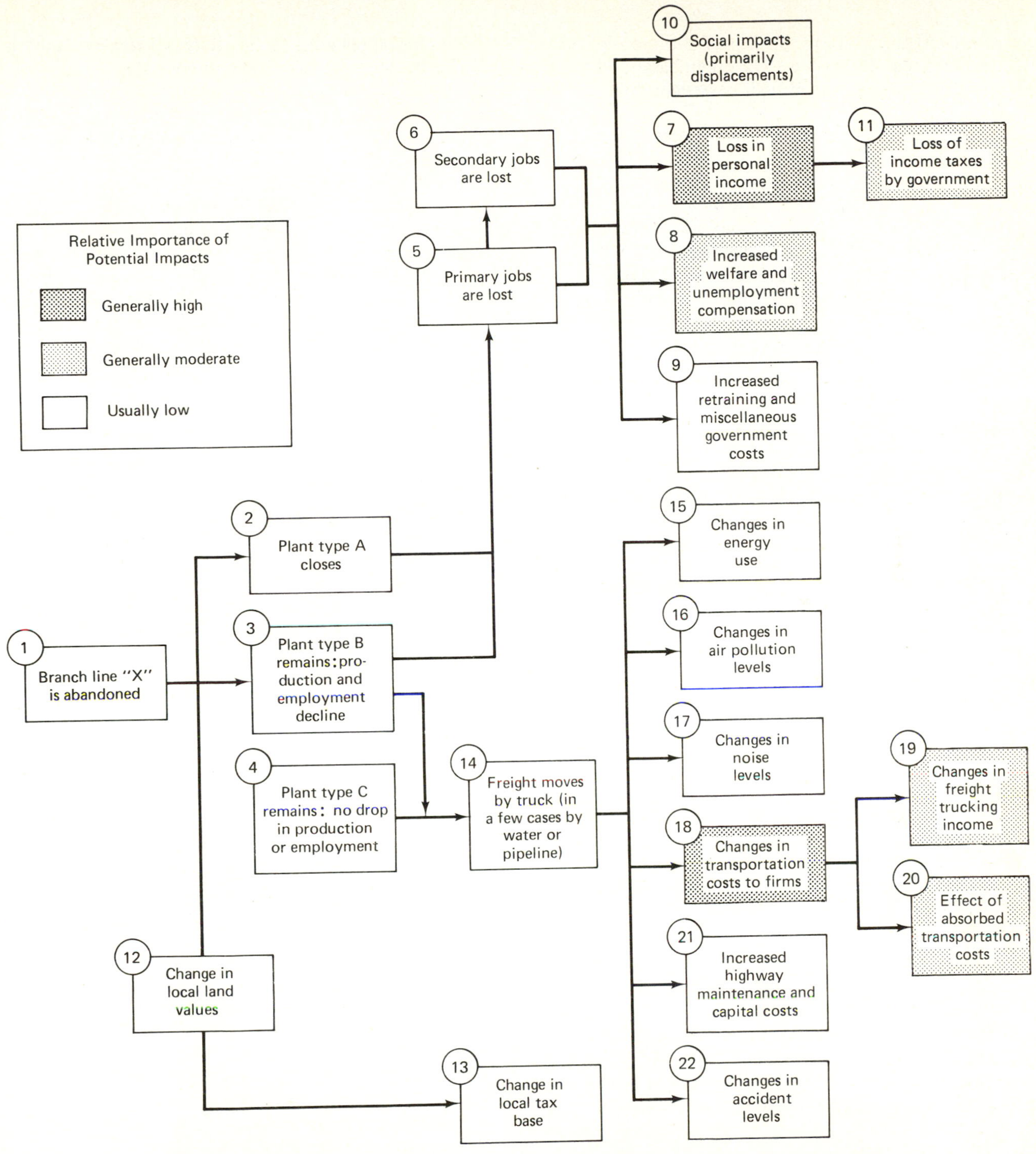

Figure 11.9. Potential impacts resulting from the abandonment of light-density lines. SOURCE: JWK INTERNATIONAL CORPORATION AND ROGER CREIGHTON ASSOCIATES INCORPORATED, *Rail Planning Manual,* Vol. 2, *Guide for Planners,* Federal Railroad Administration, Washington, D.C., July 1978.

relatively young and old, students, military personnel and retirees are heavy users. Moreover, a high proportion of trips taken are non-business-oriented and are for relatively short distances."[46] These findings are consistent with a service that is low in per mile cost; the 1976 revenue of all Class I carriers was slightly over 5 cents per passenger-mile.[47]

[46]Ibid., p. iii.

[47]*The Intercity Bus Industry.*

Approximately 65% of total operating revenues of Class I carriers in 1976 are estimated to be from regular-route passengers. Charter service generates approximately 16.3%, and package express generates 15.2%.[48]

Public problems and issues. Historically, bus passenger miles (all Class I carriers, regular-route intercity service)

[48]Ibid.

peaked in 1950 at 17 billion, up from 7.3 billion in 1939. Since 1965 (except during the 1974 oil embargo) there has been a fairly steady decline in both passenger miles and in passengers carried.[49]

Although operating revenues have generally increased during this period as a result of higher fares, increased charter revenues, and package express revenues, costs have risen even faster. Profit margins of the industry have shrunk. The point has been reached where some discontinuances of service on low-volume lines have occurred, and where the ability of the companies to replace their buses is threatened. Such economic forces and trends, similar to those that have attacked the urban transit industry and the railroads, accentuate a number of issues that currently face the states.

Public Subsidies. Some states (Michigan and Pennsylvania) have already provided some subsidies to particular intercity bus routes that serve communities threatened with loss of service.[50,51] There is a possibility that the need for such subsidies may increase over time. States will basically have to decide whether they should provide certain communities, primarily the smaller communities, with service at public expense, and how much it is worth.

Terminals. The location and condition of bus terminals are matters that deserve the attention of transportation planners at the state level. A survey of all bus terminals in the 14 Appalachian counties of New York State found one-third with fair-to-poor "general environment rating," a composite of cleanliness, lighting, ventilation, general physical condition, and rest-room cleanliness. Three of 12 cities had two separate bus terminals, making interline transfer difficult. Only one city had off-street parking available.[52] If buses are to maintain their ridership, certain basic facilities ought to be provided to the traveling public; such facilities should (1) facilitate interline transfer, (2) facilitate local travel connections by car and local transit, and (3) meet basic standards of cleanliness in their rest rooms, waiting areas, and food services. If private bus companies cannot provide these services, the public may have to do so.

Deregulation. If deregulation were to occur in a fashion that would permit rates to change, service to be discontinued, and free entry into the market by new bus companies, the entire character of present intercity bus services might change substantially. Service to smaller communities in low-density areas might contract sharply, and the number of small bus companies could increase. Needs for state subsidies would probably rise if the states determined that service to small communities is necessary in the public interest.

[49]National Association of Motor Bus Owners, *1926–1976—One Half Century of Service to America*, National Association of Motor Bus Owners, Washington, D.C., 1976.

[50]*The Intercity Bus Industry*.

[51]William C. Underwood, Director Mass Transit Systems, Department of Transportation, Harrisburg, Pa., unpublished data furnished the author, Jan. 1979.

[52]Creighton, Hamburg, Inc., *Transportation in the Appalachian Region of New York State: Phase II*, New York State Department of Transportation and New York State Office of Planning Coordination, Albany, N.Y., 1970.

Systematic planning for intercity bus transportation is in its beginning stages at the state level. Wisconsin,[53] Michigan,[54] and Iowa[55] appear to have done the most work. Michigan and Pennsylvania have subsidy programs for intercity bus transportation.[56] Michigan's program is by far the largest. (This statement does not include subsidies to commuter bus operations, which are widespread, for example, in New Jersey.) Michigan's program includes demonstration grants to bus routes in low-density areas of the state, purchase of buses with low-interest leases to private bus companies, and the construction of two bus terminals, including an intermodal terminal in Kalamazoo.[57] A National Cooperative Highway Research Program study on intercity bus transportation planning was started in 1979; it should be a major impetus for improvements in state-level planning technique.

At present, factual data on origin and destination travel patterns, trip purpose, passenger characteristics, and volumes of intercity bus travel are generally inadequate. Yet means for collecting these data are simple and relatively inexpensive. Interviews can be taken at bus terminals or forms can be distributed to passengers. These forms may either be mailed back or picked up by the driver or by survey personnel at destination terminals. Surveys should always obtain information on the exact location of each passenger's origin and destination so that the data can be used not only for intercity system planning but also for the improvement of intraurban service to bus terminals.

Planning at the state level for intercity bus transportation must mainly deal with two classes of problems: (1) the problem of maintaining service to small urban settlements in low-density regions and (2) the problem of working with the intercity bus companies to improve the efficiency of bus service and increase its attractiveness to the traveling public.

In many ways, maintaining service in low-density regions is comparable to maintaining freight service on light-density lines. Costs are known, and rising. Revenues are inadequate to cover costs, because of low density. Cross-subsidies within a private firm, by which service was formerly maintained, can no longer be counted on as the profit margins of the entire industry are squeezed. The question then becomes one of how important it is, as a public service, to maintain one or two trips per day to isolated communities. A state will have to evaluate the equity of claims from small communities against other transportation needs, all in the light of available fiscal resources.

Planning to improve service levels, efficiency, and profits of the intercity bus industry across an entire state is an equally difficult task. This activity must deal with (1) state/federal subsidies to competing modes, such as rail; (2) improvement of terminals and especially intercity terminals;

[53]*Intercity Bus Transportation in Wisconsin*—Vol. 4, *Future Demand for Service*, Wisconsin Department of Transportation, Madison, Wis., Sept. 1977.

[54]*Michigan Intercity Bus Study—Ridership and Travel Characteristics*, Michigan Department of State Highways and Transportation, Lansing, Mich., Nov. 1977.

[55]Engineering Research Institute of Iowa State University, *Intercity Passenger Carrier Improvement Study*, Iowa Department of Transportation, Ames, Iowa.

[56]*The Intercity Bus Industry*.

[57]*Ibid*.

(3) coordination with urban bus services; (4) possible competition from subsidized rural social-service bus operations; and (5) use of transportation systems management (TSM) techniques or other devices to increase the speed of bus travel.

Air transportation

The growth of air travel in the United States has been phenomenal. Between 1950 and 1960 the number of public carrier air passenger-miles of domestic intercity travel (PMT) in the United States more than tripled, from 9.3 billion PMT to 31.7 billion PMT. Between 1960 and 1973 air travel quadrupled, from 31.7 billion PMT to 122.6 billion PMT. Estimates for 1978 put the level at 172.1 billion PMT.[58]

Almost all forecasts indicate continued rapid growth in all components of air transportation. The Federal Aviation Administration[59] foresees domestic airline passenger miles in the United States rising to 314.6 billion by 1985, nearly 10 times the 1969 level. International air travel using United States air carriers, according to the Federal Aviation Administration (FAA), will rise from the 19.0 million enplaned passenger level of 1973 to 38.3 million in 1990. This is a twofold increase. General aviation aircraft are expected to increase in number from 145,000 in 1973 to 310,800 in 1990, and domestic air freight ton-miles are expected to grow from 3.662 billion ton-miles in 1973 to 8.784 billion ton-miles in 1990. These FAA forecasts are somewhat more conservative than industry forecasts of 1969.[60]

The impact of rapid increases in the cost of flying, caused in part by escalating fuel costs since 1979, may require that many forecasts be reexamined. Nevertheless, there is a need for active state concern for air transportation because it is clear that growth in demand will press strongly against the supply of facilities and of airspace.

Problems and issues. Problems and issues as seen from the public viewpoint are:

1. *Airspace and airport congestion in the large metropolitan centers.* "Experience has shown that planning for airports in the larger metropolitan areas is a much more complex task than planning for airports in the smaller communities. This is due, logically, to the greater demand for aeronautical services in the larger cities and the requirement to provide a sufficient number of adequate airports in densely populated areas. In addition, the aeronautical problems related to the use of the airspace, the problems of insufficient land, congestion of surface transportation, objections to aircraft noise, etc., highlight the complexities of metropolitan area airport planning."[61]

2. *Changes in commercial passenger service to smaller urban centers.* Faced with rising costs, provided with the capacities and speeds of larger jet aircraft, and given the changes made possible by fuel crises and deregulation, the certificated air carriers have been revising their routes and schedules significantly. Between 1969 and 1978, for example, departures of certificated airlines from airports in the 13 Appalachian counties of New York State declined by 68%, while passenger boardings increased from 12 to 25% per departure. To fill in the gap, commuter airlines increased their departures from zero to 400 per week in the same region.[62] In another example, 22 airports in the 13-state Appalachian region had increased departures of commuters and trunk-line aircraft, while 25 airports had decreased departures.[63] These are symptoms of significant changes in air passenger service, with the smaller airports generally having the greatest change.

3. *Preservation of general aviation airports.* This need is greatest in and near urban areas, where competition for land becomes intense.

Comments on planning. The preparation of state aviation plans is now a fairly standardized type of operation, following general procedures recommended by the Federal Aviation Administration.[64–67] In some cases, state-level planning has been subdivided into regional-plus-state operations, permitting greater detail to be developed in each region of the state and allowing for greater public participation[68] (see Chapter 2).

In general, the planning process, whether statewide or regional, consists of the following basic steps.

- Specification of goals and objectives; identification of problems and issues.
- Collection of data.
- Forecasts of air carrier passenger enplanement demands, general aviation activity, and air cargo activity.
- Airport capacity analysis.
- Aviation system requirements (needs).
- Development of alternative solutions to future needs.
- Evaluation and selection of alternatives.
- Recommendation of plan.
- Financial resource estimation.
- Program of projects to implement plan.

These steps should be undertaken in cooperation with an advisory panel representing (1) certified carriers, (2) com-

[58]*FAA Aviation Forecasts, Fiscal Years 1979–1990* Federal Aviation Administration, Washington, D.C., Sept. 1978.

[59]Ibid.

[60]*Industry Report ATA Airline Airport Demand Forecasts,* Air Transport Association of America, Washington, D.C., 1969.

[61]*Airport User Traffic Characteristics for Ground Transportation Planning,* Institute of Transportation Engineers, Arlington, Va., 1976.

[62]Data supplied by the New York State Department of Transportation.

[63]*Report on Airline Service, Status on March 1, 1979,* Civil Aeronautics Board, Washington, D.C., Apr. 1979.

[64]*Planning the State Airport System,* Federal Aviation Administration, Washington, D.C., June 1972.

[65]*Planning the Metropolitan Airport System,* Federal Aviation Administration, Washington, D.C., May 1970.

[66]*National Transportation Planning Manual:* Manual D: *Airports and Other Intercity Terminals,* U.S. Department of Transportation, Washington, D.C., 1971.

[67]*Airport Site Selection,* U.S. Department of Transportation, Washington, D.C., 1977.

[68]*Guidelines for Regional Aviation System Planning,* New York State Department of Transportation, Albany, N.Y.

muter and air taxi airlines, (3) general aviation interests, (4) local government, (5) environmental interests, and (6) economic interests, such as chambers of commerce.

The process described above is basically a "needs–standards" process, in which needs are estimated on the basis of present usage and forecasts of future passenger and cargo demand. The standards have to do with the capacity of airspace, the capacity of the terminal, and the capacity of "landside" facilities, including roads, parking, and truck loading docks. The determination of these capacities is a technical task, and reference should be made by the interested professional, to the *Airport Capacity Handbook,*[69] *Airport User Traffic Characteristics for Ground Transportation,* and similar works.

The nature of aviation issues is such that great care must be taken to relate aviation planning to environmental and land-use factors. In growing urban areas, airports were originally located at some distance from development, but development has steadily spread out to and often around the airports. As a result, noise and air pollution, which formerly bothered few people, have become a considerable nuisance to many. Land-use controls have rarely been effective at keeping development away, and state aviation budgets have not been sufficient to purchase enough land. Hence, suits and protests have been frequent. Smaller, privately owned general aviation airports, with generally marginal resources, often are sold when the time is ripe. If existing airports are to be kept for general aviation, it may be necessary to provide some form of financial relief.

Highway transportation

The dominant transportation mode in the United States is the highway system, over which moves 95% of all person-miles of travel and approximately 25% of all ton-miles of freight. The most important roads in the highway system—roads functionally classified as arterials (including Interstate highways)—are generally the responsibilities of state departments of transportation, which in a few states also have responsibility for principal collectors.

From 1890, when state government first began to support road construction, highway planning and improvement evolved through different cycles. Federal aid began in 1916, and the Federal-aid system connecting urban areas (but not inside them) was the primary focus for construction between 1921 and 1934. Statewide highway planning was funded by the Hayden-Cartwright Act of 1934. The move to "get the farmer out of the mud" spanned the Depression. Urban areas began to receive intensive highway funding and planning after 1945, and urban expressway construction was extremely important in the 1950s and 1960s. Construction of the Interstate system dominated the attention of state highway departments from 1956 to the late 1970s, when it approached completion.

As highways have been extended, improved in speed and safety, and increased in capacity, startling changes have come about in national settlement patterns and travel habits.

[69]AIL-CUTLER HAMMER, *Airport Capacity Handbook,* Federal Aviation Administration, Washington, DC, June 1969.

Suburbs have spread out at lower and lower densities. Bus transportation in urban areas has declined. Truck transportation grew phenomenally, and industry has located more and more away from rail lines.

What will the next two decades bring for highway transportation and planning? The answer to this is by no means clear. The following factors must be taken into account. Energy prices increased substantially in 1973–1974 and again in 1979, although in the years between they were nearly constant in real dollar terms.[70] The automobile fleet is increasingly composed of smaller cars, with more efficient engines. In part because of this, and in part because of inflation, real-dollar receipts from gasoline taxes have declined by at least 20% for most states.[71] Rail, truck, and intercity bus deregulation are being considered seriously by the federal government. Despite the energy and economic problems of 1979–1980, many economists are predicting continued increases in travel demand, both for passengers and for freight.

Probably the highway systems of most states will not change substantially in the next decade, at least in terms of center-line miles. However, continued adaptation and improvement of that system will be made and must be planned so as to deal with the following problems and issues.

Problems and issues. Major problems and issues as seen from the public viewpoint are:

1. *Deterioration of the physical highway plant.* Deterioration of roads has resulted from reduced funds (measured in constant dollars or real purchasing power) being available for maintenance and reconstruction. Bridge replacement needs are acute, particularly small bridges in rural areas.
2. *Increased truck travel; larger trucks.* Trucks, using the Interstate system in large numbers, have steadily increased their share of domestic freight transportation. Trucks also are becoming larger and heavier.
3. *Reduced financial resources.* Gasoline taxes, based on rates per gallon, have decreased in real purchasing power. Alternative revenue sources (except for bonding) have not been found.
4. *Long lead times to implement highway construction projects.* Long lead times result from community participation and environmental review requirements, and have resulted in higher costs.
5. *Coordination with nonhighway modes.* As the dominant mode, highways provide the connections to and between other modes. This requires access roads to airports, bus terminals, rail terminals (including TOFC/COFC or "piggyback" terminals), and parking lots for carpools and vanpools.

Comments on statewide highway planning. A variety of planning techniques are available to help states establish their highway construction policies. Several of these are described below, beginning with highway classification studies and needs studies.

[70]"*State Transportation Issues and Actions,* Spec. Report 189, Transportation Research Board, Washington, D.C., 1980.

[71]Ibid.

Highway Classification. Highway classification is an important first step in statewide highway planning. It has several purposes: one is to define the systems to be examined in highway needs studies. A second purpose is to provide a basis for dividing the total road system among political jurisdictions (town, county, and state) and for use in establishing the various federal-aid systems. Third, classification may be used as the means for eliminating local roads from a network so that planning attention can be devoted to more important highways. Finally, classification studies provide the basis for determining the level of future highway expenditures and for the allocation of funds between states and among Federal-aid highway networks.

Needs Study: A Method of Highway Planning. After a classification study has been completed, a sensible method of statewide highway planning can be carried out in conjunction with a long-range evaluation of highway needs. This is the approach used in Manual B of the *U.S. National Transportation Planning Study*. According to this manual:

The functional classification process, the process by which streets and highways are grouped into classes or systems according to the character of service they are intended to provide, has been widely used in conjunction with needs estimates to outline long-range highway plans. In this study, focus is being aimed at the development of nationwide 1990 functional plans in concert with 1990 nationwide needs evaluation.[72]

The first step in the needs-study approach to highway planning is to complete a present-day highway classification study.[73] Once the rural highway system has been classified according to type and into prescribed systems, a forecasting operation must be conducted. Working from consistent national, or state, population forecasts, planners should estimate the growth of cities of various sizes throughout a state, together with the populations of surrounding rural areas. Future urban area boundaries should be located, say, for a planning period of 20 years.

Given the new sizes of cities and the present highway network, the highway planner must reexamine the network to determine where changes should be planned so that future travel between enlarged cities and towns can be accommodated. In many ways this is simply a reclassification based on changed population and land use. Manual B states:

The (future) functional classification will differ from the 1968 classification in two basic respects: (1) it will be based on projected 1990 population, land use, and travel; and (2) it will include, in addition to existing facilities, such projected totally new facilities as will be needed to serve 1990 land use and travel.[74]

According to Manual B, the additional new miles of rural highways are expected to be (1) presently unbuilt Interstate mileage, (2) belts and bypasses for smaller cities, (3) some new routes needed to serve new recreational areas or new towns, and (4) replacement or expanded facilities on new rights-of-way.

It can be seen that this is a fairly conservative approach to rural highway planning:

Studies conducted over the years have indicated a large degree of stability in the routes and corridor locations of arterial systems. To a considerable extent, centers of the lower size range of places served by these systems . . . are not undergoing great or rapid change. Furthermore . . . if all centers were growing in (the same) proportion . . . such growth would not affect the functional relationships in the road network.[75]

The same argument applies to rural collector routes.

Manual B is careful to point out that new routes, introduced into the existing network, will be likely to affect the travel choices of people and thus change traffic volumes and functional uses of other routes. Such changes in traffic volumes will have to be estimated carefully, and estimates of new needs must be adjusted accordingly.

Once a future classification plan has been prepared, the needs study proper can be completed for both rural and urban areas. For each link, or for a sample of links, studies are made to determine the costs of bringing these links up to a predetermined standard. The costs may either be to overcome an existing deficiency, called a "backlog" need, or to overcome a future deficiency, called an "accruing" need. Costs of maintenance and future repairs are also estimated. The product of these studies can be used directly in capital programming.

Simulation Approach to Rural Highway System Planning. Simulation has been used by state transportation and highway departments in the United States as a means for preparing and testing rural highway plans. As of mid-1971, 14 states had used simulation to assign traffic to statewide highway networks and 8 were in the process of developing or applying assignment techniques.[76] Simulation offers a way of estimating traffic on all links in a state's highway network, and it is one of the few methods of estimating the consequences of inserting new links within an existing system. It also offers the potential for determining certain consequences of vehicular travel (accidents, travel time, operating costs, and air pollution) that are obtainable only with difficulty by other techniques.

An early user of simulation in statewide highway planning was Connecticut.[77,78] The basic process used by Connecticut is illustrated in Figure 11.10. The Connecticut process is similar to the planning processes used in many urban areas. It involves data collecting, forecasting of trip ends (taking into account population, employment, land use, and vehicle registrations), and the assignment of trips by using a mathematical model (in this case the gravity model) over a network. The basic network consisted of the existing net-

[72] *National Highway Functional Classification and Needs Study Manual*, U.S. Department of Transportation, Washington, D.C., 1970.

[73] *1968 National Highway Functional Classification Study Manual*, (Manual B of the National Transportation Board Study) U.S. Department of Transportation, Washington, D.C., 1969.

[74] Ibid.

[75] *National Highway Functional Classification and Needs Study Manual*.

[76] Philip I. Hazen, "A Comparative Analysis of Statewide Transportation Studies," *Intermodal Transportation Planning at the State, Multistate and National Scale*, Highway Res. Rec. 401, Highway Research Board, Washington, D.C., 1972.

[77] *Planning for the Future—Connecticut's Major Corridor Needs, Present to Year 2000*, Connecticut Highway Department, Sept. 1968.

[78] *Planning for the Future—Connecticut's Major Arterial Needs, Present to Year 2000: Part II*, Connecticut Highway Department, Sept. 1969.

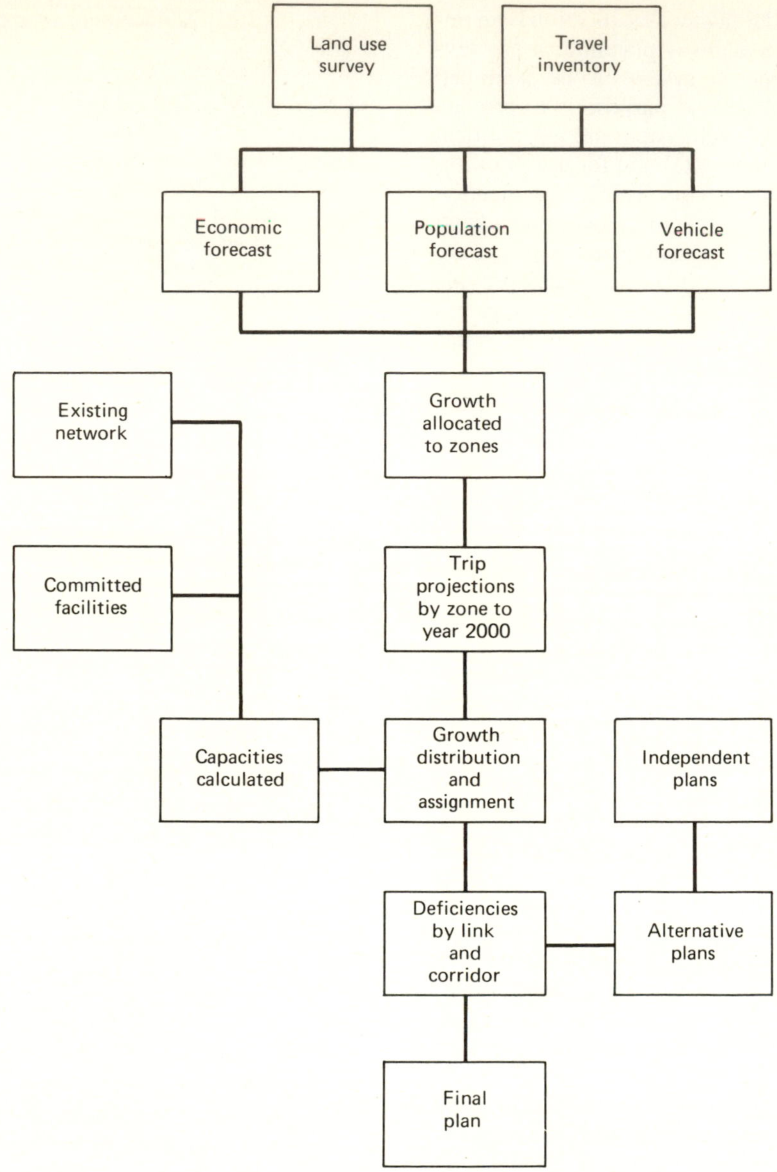

Figure 11.10. Connecticut highway planning process. SOURCE: *Connecticut Master Transportation Plan 1979,* Connecticut Department of Transportation, Wethersfield, Conn., Dec. 1978.

work plus the committed network, that is, those facilities that were programmed plus those facilities which, for various reasons, were considered to be definitely "committed." Traffic was then assigned to the existing and committed highway network for every decade from 1970 through 2000.

Capacities of the existing and committed highway networks were calculated, as were the differences between demand (as determined by the assignments for each decade) and capacities. Thus, deficiencies were known for each decade. These deficiencies were obtained for highway links grouped by a series of screenlines created by a variable-width grid superimposed on a map of the state. Finer grid intervals were used in higher-density corridors.

Deficiencies by decade were used to develop two different sketch plans, one based on needs for additional lanes in each corridor, the other based on an analysis of link deficiencies on the network, with emphasis on the expressway network. In addition, a composite of regional plan highway proposals was examined along with the Connecticut Highway Department's then-existing long-range proposals. Traffic volumes for the year 2000 were assigned to all four of these plans. As noted in the report: "Through the continuous process of testing and analyzing various combinations of proposed facilities, a plan evolved which best appeared to satisfy traffic demand of the 2000 decade."[79]

Truck Weight Studies. Truck weight studies are generally made each year by the states to provide data for use in the design of highway pavements, for allocations of highway costs in relation to usage and revenue, and for a variety of other studies, including goods movement. In the words of the *Guide for Truck Weight Study Manual:*[80]

[79] *Planning for the Future,* Sept. 1968.

[80] *Guide for Truck Weight Study Manual,* Federal Highway Administration, U.S. Department of Transportation, Washington, D.C., Apr. 1971.

Truck weight data are obtained either by using permanent platform scales, most of which are capable of weighing an entire truck, or portable scales, generally used in pairs to weigh one axle of a truck at a time. The permanent scales are located on main roads entering a state so that a significant percentage of the truck traffic entering that state is intercepted. Portable truck weight stations can be set up in order to obtain a wider sample of data at different locations throughout a state and on different kinds of roads having different percentages of truck traffic.

Procedures for locating weight stations, sampling and classifying the stream of trucks, and conducting both weighing and driver interviewing are contained in that report.

Coordination and programming

A persistent difficulty with transportation planning at the state or national level is the problem of coordinating the large number of separate studies, actions, and decisions that are constantly ongoing as the state, private transportation companies, and local governments adjust transportation systems to provide better and more efficient services. The problem of coordination is demonstrated by the following items.

- *The variety of goals and viewpoints.* Earlier in this chapter were listed 18 goals, categorized by the viewpoint of three groups who are major actors influencing transportation decision making.
- *The variety of objectives of different "dimensions" of a state* (see Figure 11.11).[81]
- *The large number of issues facing transportation planners at the state level* (see Table 11-2). These issues range up and down the scale, from large-scale problems/issues affecting the entire state to small-scale and localized problems.

Faced with this large number of issues, and at the same time with competing and often conflicting objectives, the transportation planner and the policymaker must decide not only which issue to address first, but the more difficult problem of determining whether a recommendation for action emanating from one study will be wise when taking into account relevant objectives selected from the range of objectives that exist. The following three examples illustrate this difficulty.[82]

1. The plan for a major interstate highway is stalled because it conflicts with environmental objectives. However, failure to build the highway may be a significant factor contributing to urban economic decline, both in the short run and in the long run.
2. A plan for rail freight transportation correctly permits the elimination of a few light-density lines in a state. However, the plan is silent on positive state action that is needed (a) in industrial location policy and (b) in rate making. Action in these two fields could increase rail utilization and hence support the rail industry.

Dimensions	Objectives
Economy	Maintaining technological efficiency Increased economic activity Reduction of trade deficits Increased productivity Reduction of unemployment Promote free enterprise
Society	Increased personal real income Reduction of poverty Security Health Adequate housing Increased educational opportunities Equitable distribution of wealth Equal employment opportunities Increased cultural and recreational opportunities
Land Use	Preservation of prime agricultural lands Preservation of scenic areas Coastal zone preservation Preservation of historical buildings and sites Making urban areas attractive, functional and economic Eliminating urban decay Preserving adequate park and open spaces
Natural Resources	Efficient use of energy Preservation of wildlife habitats Preservation of natural environment and reduction of pollution Preservation of endangered species

Figure 11.11. Objectives of different dimensions of a state. SOURCE: ROGER L. CREIGHTON, *Statewide Transportation Planning: Detailed Studies Unifying Controls, and Performance Monitoring,* In Spec. Rpt. 183, Transportation Research Board, Washington, D.C., 1978.

3. A plan for statewide rail and air passenger service discloses that there will be shortfalls in operating costs if service is improved as indicated by the plan. Should these funds come from state highway sources, replacing maintenance or capital activities in the highway sector?

In cases such as these, it is clear that improvements in performance in terms of one objective mean losses in terms of other objectives. Many such decisions must be made each year. How can coordination be attained in this kind of situation?

A practical response to this problem is through the imposition of certain unifying controls applied within a regular statewide transportation planning cycle. Among these controls, the programming activity is of outstanding importance. The following two sections therefore deal separately with the subject of (1) coordination through a regular statewide transportation planning cycle embodying unifying controls and (2) programming.

Coordination through the statewide transportation planning cycle

Figure 11.12 shows a graphic conception of statewide transportation planning cycle.

The statewide transportation planning cycle recognizes that technical planning must respond to a wide variety of critical issues such as might be selected from those listed in Table 11-2. These issues may be as unique as planning for a single waterway in a state or they may be more gen-

[81] ROGER L. CREIGHTON, *Statewide Transportation Planning: Detailed Studies Unifying Controls, and Performance Monitoring,* In Spec. Rpt. 183, Transportation Research Board, Washington, D.C., 1978.

[82] Ibid.

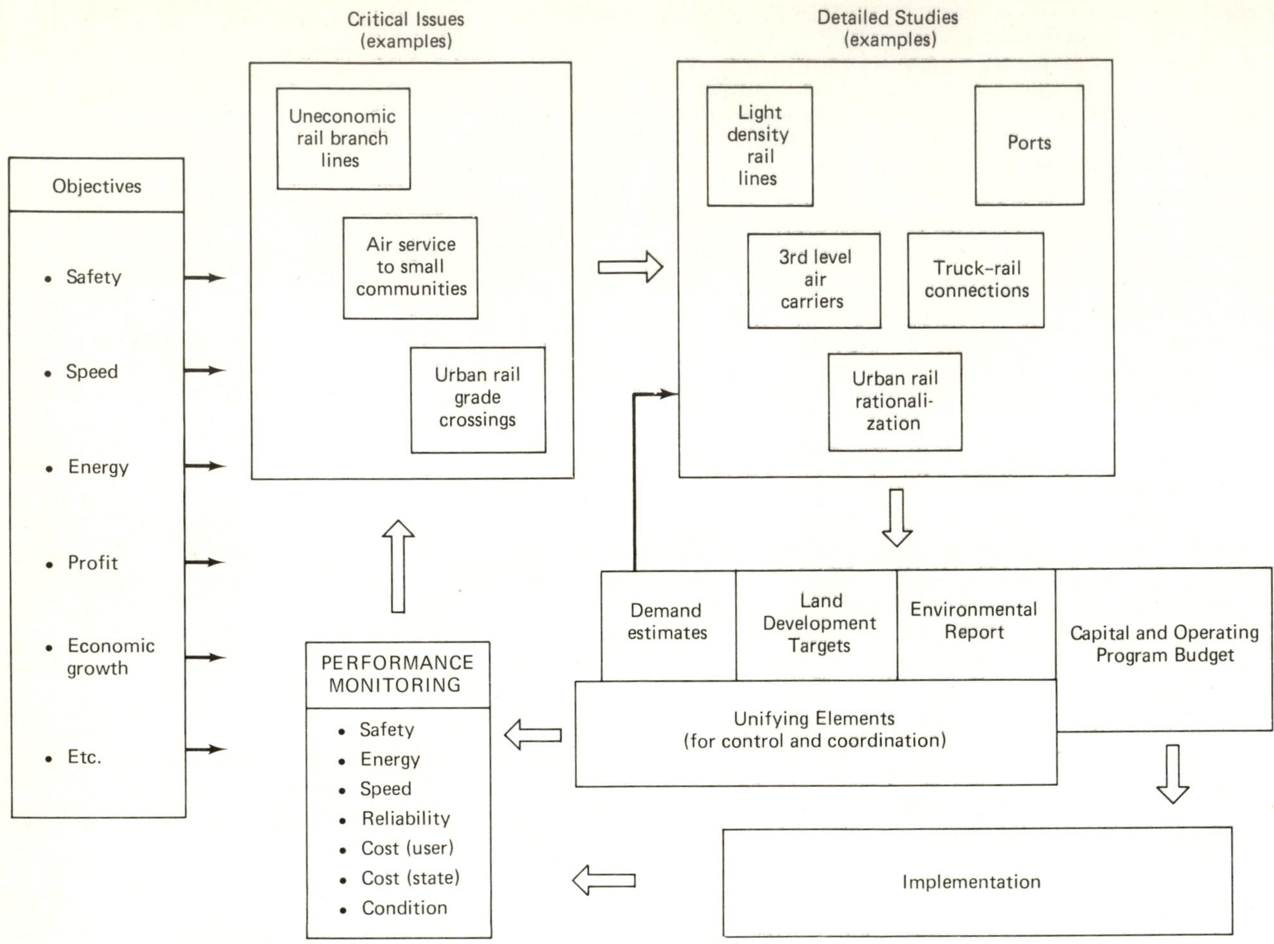

Figure 11.12. Statewide transportation planning cycle. SOURCE: Roger L. Creighton, *Statewide Transportation Planning: Detailed Studies Unifying Controls and Performance Monitoring*, Transportation Research Board, Washington, D.C., 1978.

eralized, such as the need to prepare a plan for general aviation airports throughout an entire state or developing nation. Whether dealing with a single mode or with a highly localized problem, the problem of coordination remains.

However, in responding to critical issues through detailed studies, several requirements should be imposed by the state department of transportation to ensure coordination.

- The studies would have to accept state-generated population and economic growth projections, by appropriate geographical subarea, as input to any demand estimates prepared by detailed study.
- Each detailed study would have to produce selected, prespecified estimates of economic, social, environmental, and energy impacts. These estimates would relate to certain unifying controls identified below.
- Each detailed study would have to produce a cost estimate, both for capital and operating costs, to fit into the state DOT's programming process.

The preceding requirements imposed on any detailed or single-mode studies fit into the unifying controls that would have to be maintained by each state DOT (in collaboration with other state agencies) as the means for judging the desirability of recommendations coming from each detailed study. There are four important unifying controls.[83]

1. *Transportation demand estimates*. It is the custom for many detailed transportation studies to develop their own estimates of passenger or freight demand; sometimes these estimates are based on differing assumptions as to the future population and economic growth of the state. Such practice is clearly the opposite of coordination. Therefore, it is important for state DOTs to maintain, as a unifying force, a common step of travel demand estimates (passenger and freight) based on a common set of population and economic forecasts for the state.

2. *State development plans*. It is commonly accepted that transportation must serve the development plans of the state, by which is meant plans for the distribution of population and economic activities, density of development in different parts of the state, and the preservation of natural resources. The more specific and detailed these development targets can be, the more useful they will be as the basis for criticizing detailed transportation studies and their demands for land or impacts on economic growth and population location.

[83]Ibid.

3. *Environmental plans*. Maintaining and improving the environment of the state is an important goal that may influence decisions in the transportation field. A statewide environmental report should be prepared describing (a) present conditions of the environment in terms of air quality, water quality, wildlife, endangered species, and (if environment is very broadly defined) social, economic, and "built environment" conditions within which the population of the state resides. It is desirable for the subject of energy to be dealt with in the environmental report since the consumption of energy is a major source of pollution.

4. *A capital and operating program*.

The preceding are the unifying elements which, in the statewide transportation planning cycle, touch almost every detailed study in one way or another and hence provide a common framework for evaluating the recommendations of those detailed studies.

The final activity of the statewide transportation planning cycle is the conduct of performance monitoring. All the separate modes and systems of transportation in a state should be monitored regularly to determine their performance levels. Performance should be measured in terms of a relatively small number of key objectives, including:

- Safety
- Energy consumption
- Speed and travel
- Reliability
- Costs to users
- Costs to the state
- Condition

The monitoring activity would produce data that would help to define and identify the important issues needing detailed study. This, then, completes the cycle of statewide transportation planning.

There are four advantages of this approach to planning and coordination. First, it recognizes the inevitability of detailed studies that address individual modes and individual issues. Second, it provides a means whereby a state DOT can consciously control and evaluate detailed studies on a uniform and objective basis. Third, it provides a recognized place in the planning cycle for performance monitoring. Finally, the entire cycle is readily implementable in state DOTs with only minor organizational changes.

Programming as a control

For all those modes of transportation for which a state DOT makes some direct financial contribution, by a grant, an operating subsidy, or a direct act of construction, programming is an excellent means of exercising some form of coordination and control. Programming is defined here as the "scheduling of project starts and completions, according to an evaluation of their relative importance, within available financial resources, and according to Department policies."[84] Programming, also called project programming or priority programming, is partly a planning function and partly a top-level DOT management function. Most frequently, it has been used as a means for scheduling the construction of highway projects, but the process itself, if carefully conceived, is inherently capable of dealing with projects for multiple modes.[85,86] In either case, however, the externalities of programming must be recognized, for they are as important as the internal processes of ranking projects according to their priorities.

Programming: the context. The setting for programming is shown in Figure 11.13 in a diagram taken from a report prepared for the Kentucky Department of Transportation.[87] The key elements of the diagram are discussed below.

1. The "Office of the Secretary" represents the Secretary of the Kentucky Department of Transportation, the chief executive. In a broader sense, however, it represents a linkage to the governor and legislature of the commonwealth, since the Secretary is the point of contact to the governor and legislature on all important policy matters.

2. "Financial policy planning" represents an ongoing staff activity, undertaken at the request of the Secretary, which (among other things) develops estimates of financial resources, prepares guidelines for allocations between modes and their categorical program (e.g., Interstate, bridge reconstruction, rural transit), and prepares critical evaluations of the worth of existing programs.

3. The "action pipeline" is the sum of all those processes by which transportation system plans are prepared, projects planned, engineering designs prepared, bids let, construction undertaken, and completed facilities operated and maintained.

4. "Monitoring" is the activity by which the progress of projects through the action pipeline is observed, the passage of key milestones recorded, and changes in project cost or scope noted. Monitoring reports are forwarded not only to top management, but to the managers of the various planning and design groups within the DOT.

5. "Fiscal reporting" is the recording of obligations and payments for projects within the project pipeline, with reports being directed both to top management and to other responsible needs of divisions and bureaus in the DOT.

The programming activity has important direct relationships with these elements. First, it must accept and work within the financial policy guidelines given to it by the executive of the DOT. Some of these guidelines can be set by the DOT executive himself, but many of them are dictated by state budgets, executive policies, and legislation, whereas others are determined by federal laws, appropriations, and regulations. For example, Figure 11.14 shows the Kentucky Department of Transportation's 1977–1978

[84] Roger Creighton Associates Incorporated, *Management Study of Project Programming—Final Report,* prepared for Kentucky Department of Transportation, May 1978.

[85] *Evaluating Options in Statewide Transportation Planning/Programming, Techniques and Applications,* NCHRP Report 199, National Cooperative Highway Research Program, Washington, D.C., Mar. 1979.

[86] *Priority Programming and Project Selection,* NCHRP Synthesis 48, National Cooperative Highway Research Program, Washington, D.C., 1978.

[87] Roger Creighton Associates Incorporated, *Management Study of Project Programming*.

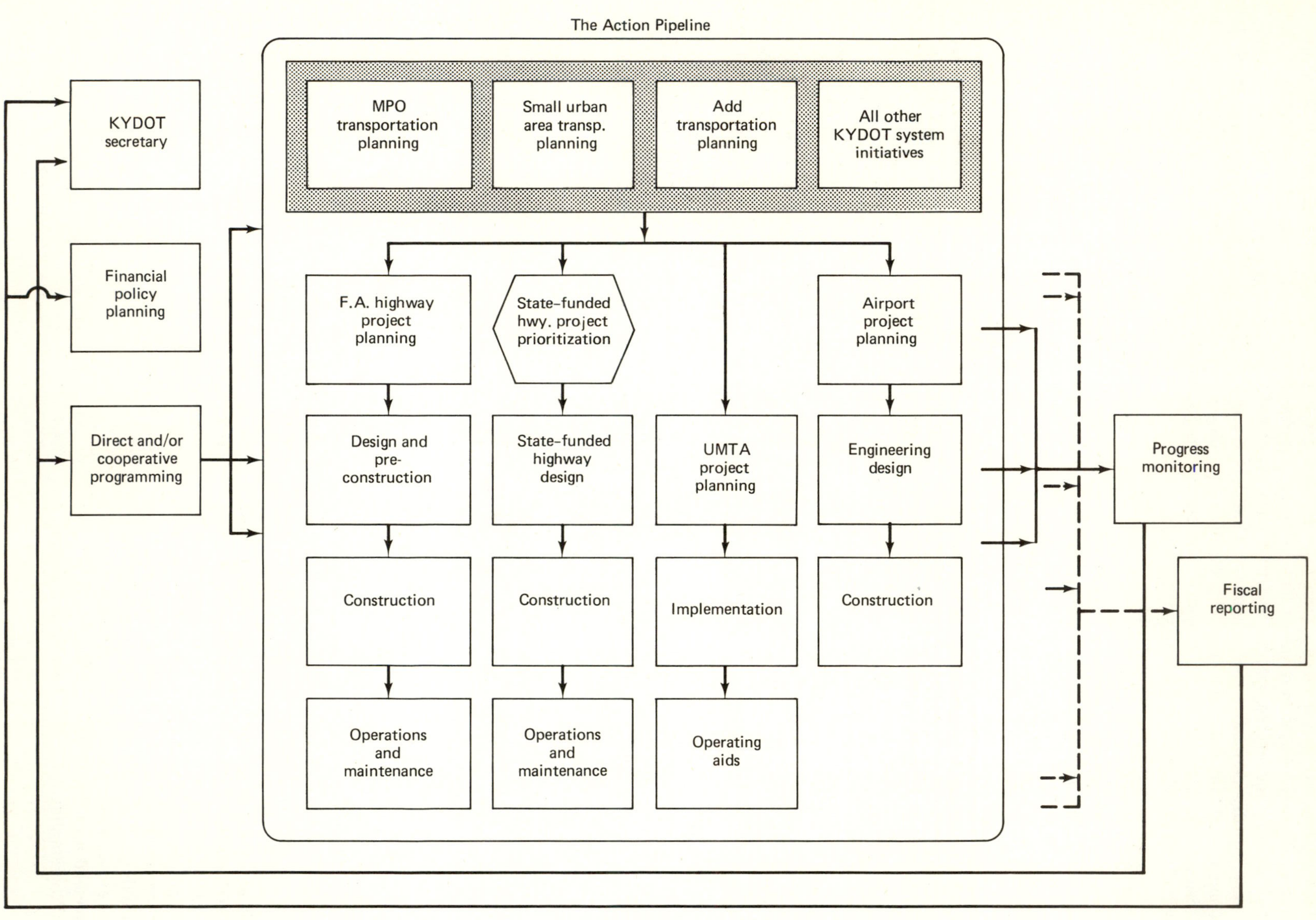

Figure 11.13. Overview of programming as it relates to the KYDOT action pipeline. SOURCE: ROGER CREIGHTON ASSOCIATES INCORPORATED, *Management Study of Project Programming*.

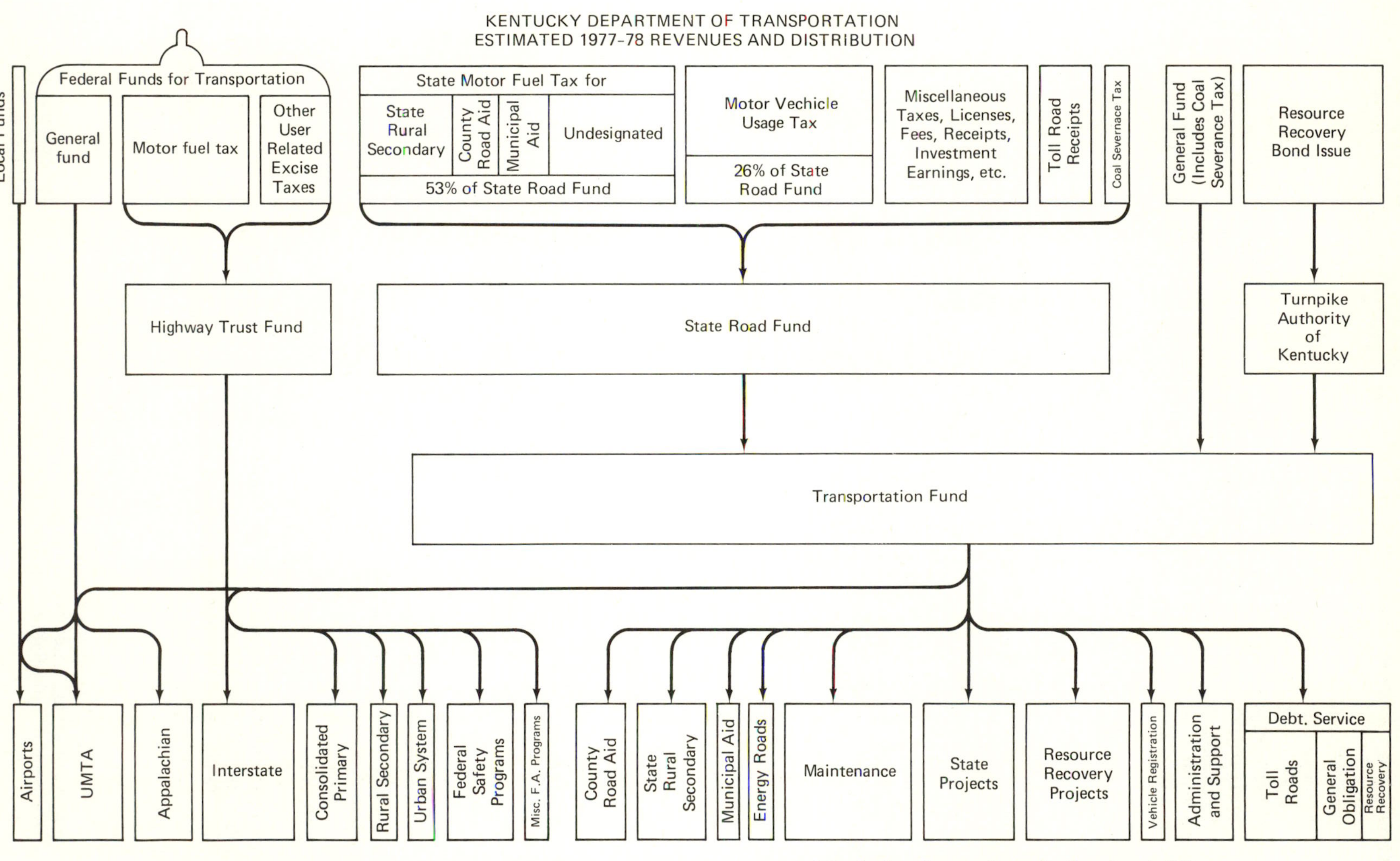

Figure 11.14. Kentucky Department of Transportation estimated 1977–1978 revenues and distribution. SOURCE: Kentucky Department of Transportation, "Estimated 1977–78 Revenues and Distribution," unbound graphic provided by the Kentucky Department of Transportation, 1978.

estimated revenues and distribution of funds.[88] The large majority of the object categories are nondiscretionary.

Second, programming must maintain a constant interaction with the "action pipeline" within which projects are generated, developed, refined, and finally passed to construction or other forms of implementation. The progress of projects through this pipeline is by no means at a uniform rate of speed. Some types of project may take 10 years to get to construction because of delays caused by legal action or environmental reviews. Other projects may take only a year or two. Because programming is, in part, a matching of projects to available fiscal resources, these shifts must be constantly monitored. For this reason, programming personnel must receive regular reports on the status of projects and on fiscal encumbrances.

The preceding conception is oversimplified, primarily because the "action pipeline" is not a single kind of planning, but a broad array of different planning processes. Federal-aid highway planning, state-funded highway planning, transit planning, aviation planning, and rail planning may all be involved. Furthermore, the systems themselves may be developed by different organizations, such as MPOs, COGs, small urban-area planning teams, area development districts (ADDs), or regional planning agencies. Each of these planning groups may consider that it has a programming responsibility. Hence, the coordination of local with state programs becomes an additional task, in which the state DOT must play a leading role.

The preceding is a reasonable description of the complexities that are the context within which a state DOT's programming function must exist. These departmental and external realities must be recognized; programming is an institutional as well as a technical process.

Programming: the process. The process of programming, from the viewpoint of its practical inner workings, is nearly as complicated as the external world to which programming is linked. At the core of the process only a few basic questions need to be answered to set up a program. These questions are:

- Is project 1 more important than projects 2, 3, and 4? If so, it should be scheduled ahead of 2, 3, and 4.
- Is there enough money to implement projects 1, 2, 3, and 4? If not, only those projects should be programmed for which there is enough money; the rest will have to be put off.
- Are there external factors (such as equity of geographical distribution) that should alter priorities?
- Are there separate funds set aside for several series of projects? If so, the programming process can deal separately and in parallel with several series.

These questions can be answered by a sequence of manual calculations, or in the black box of a computer. The calculations can be simple, or sophisticated economic procedures. Either way, a stream of information is needed as input to the decision process. The more important of these inputs are described below.

Financial Policy. Financial policy that sets the number of dollars available for any given "program fund" or "categorical program" is determined by a number of governmental bodies, including the Congress, the U.S. Department of Transportation, the state legislature, and the state administration. For example, Table 11-6, developed from the Kentucky Department of Transportation Division of Account's "Obligation Reporting Form," shows 33 different federal-aid funds for highways alone. These 33 funds do not include other highway funds which are established by the Kentucky legislature. Unfortunately, the dollar amounts available for these funds are only known for a short time in advance of availability; even the near-term (5-year) future funding levels need to be estimated, and this is one of the duties of personnel in a programming unit of a state DOT.

Project Initiation. In the Kentucky DOT, the initiation of a project is a tightly controlled event. Before a project can be considered for any type of planning or engineering investigation or design, it must be approved first by one of three officials (State Highway Engineer, Transportation Planning Engineer, or the Deputy Commissioner for Rural and Municipal Aid), depending upon the type of project. Subsequently, it is approved by the Secretary of the Kentucky DOT. This authorizing signature permits the project to be considered for programming, for entry into the plan-

TABLE 11–6
Federal Aid Highway Programs Funds

23 USC Section	Year of FA Highway Act	Section of Act	Fund Name
		Apportionments	
104b(1)	1976	105a	Consolidated Primary
104b(1)	1973	104a	Primary, Rural Areas
147b	1976	105a	Priority Primary
104b(2)	1975	104a	Secondary, Rural Areas
104b(6)	1976	105a	Urban System
104b(3)	1973	104a	Urban Extension
104b(5)	1973	102	Interstate
104b(5)	1976	106	Interstate Reconstruction
104a	—	—	HPR (23 USC 307c)
104f(1)	—	—	Metropolitan Planning (23 USC 134)
104	1976	104a	Transition Quarter
152b	1973	209a	High Hazard Locations
153b	1973	210a	Elimination of Roadside Obstacles
152-3d	1976	202	High Hazard and Roadside Obstacles
405	1973	230c	Safer Roads Demonstration
402	1976	202(1)	Highway Safety Program
	1976	202(2)	Highway Safety R&D
219	1975	101(6)	Off-System Roads
219	1976	105a	Safer Off-System Roads
130	1976	203b	Rail-Highway X-ings on a FA System
130	1976	203c	Rail-Highway X-ings Off System
202a	1976	105a	Forest Highways
148d	1976	105a	Great River Road (Scenic Highway)
		Allocated Funds (Not by Apportionment)	
320d	1976	137	Bridges on Federal Dams
125	1976	119a	Emergency Relief
143	1976	105a	Economic Growth Center
144	1976	202	Bridge Replacement
131	1976	105a	Control of Outdoor Advertising
136	1976	105a	Control of Junkyards
319b	1976	105a(13)	Landscaping
151c	1976	202	Pavement Marking Demonstration
		Other Federal Funds Not under 23 USC	
			Appalachian Development Highways
			Appalachian Access Highways

SOURCE: KYDOT Division of Accounts' Obligation Reporting Form.

[88]Kentucky Department of Transportation, "Estimated 1977–78 Revenues and Distribution," unbound graphic provided by the Kentucky Department of Transportation, 1978.

ning–design–construction–operation pipeline, and where necessary, for federal reviews. The authorization form and the project number are the "tags" used for monitoring and fiscal control.

Programming Operations. The actual work of developing a program consists of the following discrete operations.

- Projects are sorted into categories corresponding to the categories of funds that are available.
- Projects within each category are prioritized. Prioritization may be done by one or more ranking methods, such as cost–benefit ratios, need (as determined by safety, condition, failure to meet geometric or service standards, index of congestion), or some combination of indexes.
- High-priority projects of a given type are matched with funds available for that type of project, year by year, for as many years (2 to 5) as this is realistic.
- The previous steps are repeated for all categories of projects and funds.
- The resulting program is reviewed by senior DOT officials to determine if the results are reasonable from the viewpoint of geographic distribution, urban–rural distribution, and other practical criteria.

The resulting program may be published annually, or biennally, and for time periods of different lengths. Some departments are wary of being too specific about publishing the year in which they expect to go into contract letting on projects, and hence may publish those anticipated to be let in the first two years, with all others grouped in the "next five year period."

Revision. Programming is a nearly continuous process. If the state is large, some of the decision making may be delegated to regions, particularly for smaller projects. Metropolitan planning organizations (MPOs) have a role to play, by developing their transportation improvement programs (TIPs) with their "Annual Elements." All this implies a cycle, which may be a full year in length, for the development of a program.

Revisions during the year may be necessary, because projects may be delayed by court proceedings, or emergencies (floods, earthquakes, etc.) may absorb available funds. Further, there may be slowdowns in planning, design, right-of-way acquisition, or other DOT activities. The possibility of delay requires a monitoring process to report progress on all projects, so that reassignments of funds can be made to other projects.

REFERENCES FOR FURTHER READING

Evaluating Options in Statewide Transportation Planning/Programming, Techniques and Applications, NCHRP Report 199, National Cooperative Highway Research Program, Washington, D.C., Mar. 1979.

Issues in Statewide Transportation Planning, Spec. Report 146, Transportation Research Board, Washington, D.C., 1974.

JWK INTERNATIONAL CORPORATION AND ROGER CREIGHTON ASSOCIATES INCORPORATED, *Rail Planning Manual*, Vol. 2, *Guide for Planners*, Federal Railroad Administration, Washington, D.C., July 1978.

National Transportation Policies through the year 2000, National Transportation Policy Study Commission, Washington, D.C., June 1979.

Priority Programming and Project Selection, NCHRP Synthesis 48, National Cooperative Highway Research Program, Washington, D.C., 1978.

State Transportation Issues and Actions, Spec. Report 189, Transportation Research Board, Washington, D.C., 1980.

A Statement of National Transportation Policy, U.S. Department of Transportation, Washington, D.C., Sept., 1975.

12

URBAN TRANSPORTATION PLANNING

DAVID K. WITHEFORD

Engineer of Traffic and Operations
Transportation Research Board, National Academy of Sciences
Washington, D.C.

Urban transportation planning is an activity that has been going on for centuries, shaping cities and the ways that communities live. Even so, it is still part art and part science. As new techniques are brought to bear, the processes improve. More important, they change as the needs of society change. The resulting dynamics, which affect the work and lives of all transportation professionals, offer an engrossing career challenge to many of them. This changing nature creates some difficulty in presenting this chapter, because it can become quickly dated. The objective, therefore, is primarily to highlight existing practice and, secondarily, to indicate changes likely for the future.

There have been a number of relatively recent changes. Whereas environmental considerations have been a recognized issue in urban transportation planning for over a decade, energy questions only recently entered the picture as a result of threatened fuel shortages, rising fuel costs, and relatively declining incomes from fuel-tax sources. Inflation in construction costs has also had an impact. Joining with such issues is the host of broad social questions concerning transportation equity for special groups and increased involvement of the public in all matters affecting their welfare. Together, these forces have changed urban transportation planning. In the United States, at least, an era of urban freeway planning and construction has ended. A more austere era of planning to optimize the capacity of existing urban systems has clearly begun.

Reflecting such changes, this chapter emphasizes short-range more than long-range planning in first describing the planning process and then the variety of projects or studies that can be called urban transportation planning. Following a section concerned with organization for planning, the chapter ends with a review of new directions and emerging issues. Throughout, the chapter identifies examples of planning projects and lists selected references. The large body of literature defies cataloging in this publication, however. The purpose of citations is thus primarily to indicate the types of materials and sources that are available for more detailed study.

Development of urban transportation planning

Urban transportation planning in the United States has been an evolutionary process. Beginning in the 1920s and 1930s, it became increasingly formalized through the home-interview studies conducted in more than 100 cities during the decade following World War II. The concept of small sample home interviews was augmented with cordon-line roadside surveys to derive patterns of urban travel. Traffic usage of future urban highway projects was predicted by manually assigning origin–destination (O.D.) movements to the alternatives being studied.

Because better estimating methods were needed to forecast design-year travel, the early 1960s brought studies investigating land use and traffic relationships. Improved methods of forecasting future population and its distribution, trip-generation analysis relating travel to underlying household characteristics (such as car ownership), and planning for networks instead of single routes all emerged. The growing availability of data processing systems facilitated procedures, while the increasing capabilities of electronic computers encouraged study of more plan alternatives. Also, criteria for determining whether plans met broad community objectives (a concept not generally introduced until the mid-1960s) could be increasingly quantified and brought into the plan evaluation process.

Direction and funding for the development of urban transportation planning in the United States has been supplied principally through federal legislation. The Federal-aid Highway Act of 1944 first permitted the use of federal funds for urban highway facilities. Later, the 1962 Federal-aid Highway Act required that federally assisted highway projects must be "based on a continuing comprehensive transportation planning process carried on cooperatively by states and local communities. . . . " This "3C" philosophy of *continuing, comprehensive,* and *cooperative* urban transportation planning best describes the status in the late 1960s.

Significant changes next came about after the passage of the Clean Air Act, the Urban Mass Transportation Assistance Act of 1970, and more recent federal highway acts. These made transit planning more feasible, permitted fund transfers from highway to transit programs, and caused planning to deal with social and environmental considerations more explicitly. Joint regulations promulgated in 1975 by the Urban Mass Transportation Administration (UMTA) and Federal Highway Administration (FHWA), and others prepared later by FHWA and the Environmental Protection Agency (EPA), caused transportation planning to be aimed at short-range needs as much if not more than at long-range needs.

Elements of urban transportation planning

Urban transportation planning can be described as a systematized approach to the solution of urban mobility problems. Because transportation solutions are generally costly in public funds and important in their community impacts, they need to be carefully planned. A systems approach helps to ensure that alternative possibilities are selected and evaluated judiciously, that recommendations are offered with evidence showing that they are appropriate to the problems being addressed, and that solutions are valid. What follows next is a discussion of the planning process—including its principles, constraints, and applicability—that will indicate how a systematic approach can be applied to both short- and long-range planning problems.

Planning principles

Planning is generally carried out by the professional staffs of public agencies. One guiding principle for their activities is that planning should be responsive to community or constituency needs. First and foremost then, goals and objectives for planning projects should be established consistent with the aims of some "client" group. Next, the planning process should be designed and be directed toward achieving chosen objectives. Third, the planning effort should be commensurate with the scale of projects being planned. Apart from electing to test and adopt "no-build" alternatives, it would be unwise generally to spend more in planning than in solving transportation problems; yet planning decisions that involve large capital expenses will merit extensive data gathering and analytical procedures. Fourth, the planning process should be dynamic in responding to changing needs. The importance in the United States of principles such as these is demonstrated by the 1962 Federal-aid Highway Act emphasis on continuing, comprehensive, and cooperative planning.

Planning constraints

Planning processes are shaped not only by principles, but also by constraints. These can be grouped into four areas: money and personnel, planning techniques, institutional considerations, and existing facilities.

Money and personnel. How well planning can be executed depends clearly on funding commitments and the expertise that can be brought to bear. Many communities will find it impractical to undertake comprehensive planning studies, simply because there will be insufficient funds to support a program or staff (or consultants) to do the work. Recognition of the reduced planning needs and capabilities of smaller urban areas recently prompted U.S. federal transportation agencies to provide data and procedures that make studies easier to carry out.

Planning techniques. Planning techniques range from simple extrapolation and factoring procedures to the most complex forms of regional growth models. Yet techniques are still sometimes a constraint on the quality of planning. For example, many traditional techniques are of little help in evaluating road pricing or the equity of transportation service to special population groups. Although research into travel behavior and travel modeling is leading toward development of more responsive methods, these have not yet been demonstrated as being suitable for broad use. The characteristics of existing techniques constrain planning effectiveness in other ways. Some are "data-hungry," requiring costly data on households and trip making. Other alternatives of using either "default" or mean values for selected parameters introduce risks of forecasting errors that must either be ignored or evaluated by sensitivity testing.

Institutional considerations. Organizational constraints affect the planning process. The typical planning project involves state, regional, and local governments and, occasionally, private institutions. Interaction among multiple agencies introduces problems of leadership, cost sharing, and coordination of both planning inputs and program implementation. Legislative or regulatory requirements that prescribe specific planning procedures or attention to specific community problems may impede the development of solutions acceptable at the local level. Last, commitments already made for future improvements and the availability of funds for construction can be constraints postponing implementation of even short-range solutions.

Existing facilities and physical constraints. A very real constraint to planning is the present investment in plant, equipment, or facilities. Most plans necessarily add to an extensive present network of facilities, or modify and supplement existing practices. Most solutions are constrained to some extent, therefore, by the characteristics and capabilities of existing services. Other physical features of urban development also act as constraints. Planned new facilities or services must take into account topographic and man-made impediments such as rivers, steep terrain features, railroads, and high-density urban development. Neighborhood patterns and regional facilities such as reservoirs, cemeteries, and parks also limit the range of feasible solutions.

Planning processes

Figure 12.1 identifies a number of steps common to most planning processes. The degree and complexity of effort in each of the seven tasks will depend on the type of planning project. The discussion that follows offers more detail than will be appropriate for the simplest planning project, for example, but less detail than is demonstrated by the long-range regional studies characteristic of the last two decades.

Goals and objectives. Urban transportation planning calls for more than just providing for the safe and efficient movement of people and goods. It involves the planning of transportation facilities or operations responsive to the goals of the community being served.

Identifying goals and seeing that plans are responsive to them can be difficult. One way to bridge gaps between community viewpoints and the planner's technical processes is to set up an interlocking set of guides that proceed from the general to the particular. A hierarchy of values, goals, objectives, criteria, and standards has been suggested, in which:

1. *Values* are basic social drives that govern human behavior. They include the desire to survive, the need to belong, the need for order, and the need for security.

Figure 12.1. Major steps in the urban transportation planning process.

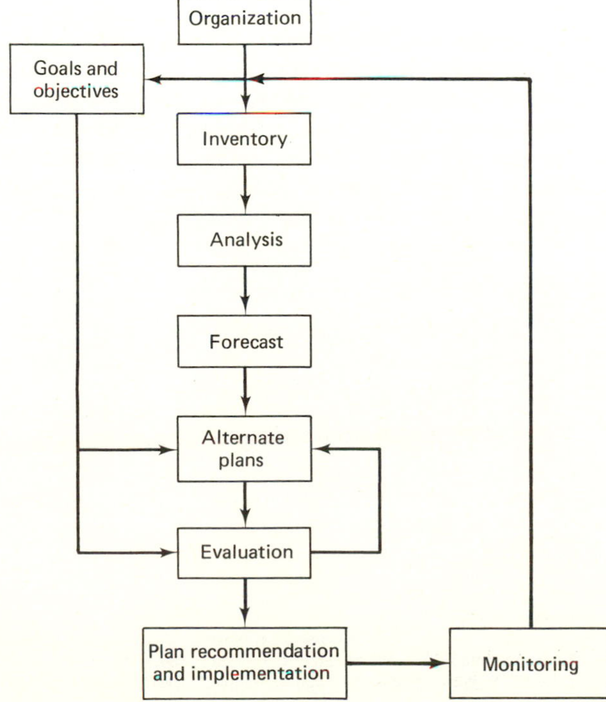

2. *Goals* define conditions to be achieved, as environments favorable to maximizing values. They can be stated, although the degree of their achievement may not be definable. "Equal opportunity," for example, is a goal based on the values of security and belonging.
3. *Objectives* are specific, attainable, and measurable. In relation to the goal of equal opportunity, a transportation objective might be equal public transportation costs for all citizens regardless of location within the city.
4. *Criteria* are the measures or tests to show whether or not objectives are attained. For example, the ratio of transit fares to personal income may be the criterion for determining whether or not the foregoing equal-transportation-cost objective has been met.
5. *Standards* establish a performance level that must be equaled or surpassed. To continue with the previous example, transit service within ¼ mi of every residence would be a standard.[1]

For illustration, the three fundamental goals of accessibility, opportunity, and efficiency could be a starting point. In relation to them, the following objectives could be listed:

1. Reduce transportation costs by reducing accident rates and severity, unit costs of vehicle operation, and time spent in travel.
2. Provide transportation facilities for nonauto users.
3. Foster compatibility of transportation and adjacent land uses.
4. Minimize disruption of existing communities in new facility construction.
5. Reduce air pollution, noise, and other nuisances from transportation activities.

Criteria and standards would be established accordingly.

Another suggested approach is to set several levels of objectives, again in a hierarchical relationship. The levels, which become increasingly specific, would be set up as follows:

1. *Policy objectives*
   a. *Global:* Objectives about society as a whole (e.g., promote equality between all sectors of society).
   b. *Primary:* General objectives unique to one institutional sector, in this case transport (e.g., improve accessibility).
2. *System objectives*
   a. *Intermediate:* Strategic objectives which refer to concrete actions (e.g., give priority to buses).
   b. *Project:* Objectives referring to particular schemes of action (e.g., increase capacity on a specific street).[2]

[1] Edwin N. Thomas and Joseph L. Schofer, *Strategies for the Evaluation of Alternative Transportation Plans*, NCHRP Report 96 (Washington, D.C.: Highway Research Board, 1970), p. 40.

[2] *Transportation Requirements for Urban Communities: Planning for Personal Travel* (Paris: Organisation for Economic Co-operation and Development, 1977), p. 27.

Structuring objectives in a hierarchy downward from the political and general to the technical and specific should, at the end of the planning process, facilitate the transfer of the planner's recommendations from the technical arena to the usually broader political arena of the decision maker.

The preceding discussion suggests that freedom of choice exists in framing objectives, but that is not always possible. Sometimes the choice of objectives is mandated by law, and the planning process must respond to imperatives such as environmental protection or energy conservation. In the United States in recent years, for example, urban transportation planning agencies have spent increasing proportions of their time responding to requirements related to future air quality standards.

Inventories. Sound planning almost always requires an assessment of present service as a basis for selecting future improvements. So the second stage of any urban transportation planning process, for large or small projects, is likely to involve inventories or the assemblage of data. Information may be required on travel facilities, travel characteristics, distributions of population and land use, and economic activity. Needs obviously will vary according to the scope and nature of projects, past planning activity, costs of data collection, and so on.

Travel Facilities. Assessing the physical nature and performance of existing travel facilities is particularly essential before using and augmenting the present systems in the planning process. Classifying highways and streets by jurisdiction and function identifies primary and secondary networks. Physical inventories provide inputs for analysis of system spacing, system coherence and unity, route capacity, and potentials for improvement. Speed and delay studies indicate quality of service. Accident compilations identify safety problems. Transit service quality can be gauged by analysis of route maps and service schedules. Equipment inventories and analysis of management policies may also be necessary. In addition, vehicle occupancy and schedule adherence checks can establish present levels of transit performance.

For some studies, parking and terminal facility surveys will be desirable. Quantifying parking demand and supply in CBDs and other centers makes it possible, for example, to assess the potential for gaining street capacity through curb parking prohibition. Mode transfer terminal problems (at airports, railroad stations, and freight yards) may require definition by analysis of data before solutions can be advanced.

Travel Characteristics. Estimates of present traffic volumes give a base condition against which travel survey data may be checked, to which new trip generation may be added, or trip distribution and traffic assignment models calibrated and validated. Manual classification counts, machine counts, and hourly screenline volume counts are sources of needed data.

Comprehensive data on person travel—trips by mode, by time, by purpose, by land use, and so on—usually require home-interview surveys on a sampling basis. Small-sample cluster survey techniques have been described for use in attitude surveys,[3] or the U.S. Census may be a source of some travel data. External trips (those crossing study-area boundaries) and truck and taxi travel are also surveyed on a sampling basis. Because of the considerable effort involved in designing samples, collecting data, and processing results into machine-usable form, such surveys may outweigh in cost almost all other elements in transportation planning.

Population and Land Use. It is essential to understand relationships among travel facilities, travel characteristics, and urban land use. For simple studies or projects, relationships drawn from previous studies may be adopted. For larger undertakings, inventories of population and land use may accompany the facility and travel inventories.

Current and past population data may be needed. Present population distribution, density, average income, type of dwelling, and car ownership may provide data for travel models. Historic patterns of distribution, migration, density, and growth trends combined with present conditions aid in preparing population forecasts. A number of land-use inventories may be useful:

1. Historic development trends such as patterns of urbanization by decade.
2. Topography and physical constraints on development.
3. Acres of land in urban use, by detailed type of use.
4. Acreage of vacant land, classified by unusable and usable, and by public and private ownership.
5. Location of major travel generators.
6. Identification of neighborhood and community boundaries (social as well as political or physical).
7. Nature of existing land-use controls: zoning, official maps, subdivision regulations.
8. Identification of redevelopment areas.

Economic Activity. Historic and present community patterns of investment in manufacturing, services, redevelopment, and other real estate point the way to the future. So does information on past and present employment by industry or activity. Transportation facility investment levels and estimates of available resources can be useful indicators to the regional transportation planner.

Analysis. Analysis of inventory data will follow in a variety of ways, depending on the scope of the particular project:

1. To identify the scale of present system inadequacies.
2. To identify the bases from which to forecast future land use and travel.
3. To develop inputs from which to derive population/land use/travel relationships.
4. To develop inputs from which to calibrate travel.

---

[3]Lawrence M. Levinson and Marvin C. Gersten, "Transportation Attitude Surveys for Modal-Split Forecasting as Part of Long-Range Transit Planning," *Transport. Res. Rec. 508* (Washington, D.C.: Transportation Research Board, 1974), pp. 13–22.

Data Coding and Validity Checks. When data are reduced to machine-processing form, analysis will be simplified and aided if:

1. Geographic coding of study area zones and network link coding are interrelated.
2. Land-use category coding is consistent between land use and travel survey data files.

As an example, interrelating zone boundaries and census boundaries may help other planning agencies to treat transportation study files as a data bank.

Other initial analysis procedures are to validate data file accuracy and compile tabulations. Consistency checks should be made of both field-recorded information and keypunched records. Further, because most travel data are samples that must be expanded to average weekday travel, the expanded data files should be verified. Data-based estimates of vehicle-miles of travel should be compared to estimates derived from other sources. Also, if land use and population coding systems are compatible as noted above, expanded sample household data can be checked against census information.

Network Analysis. For many undertakings, for either highways or transit, a network of facilities must be defined and its capabilities assessed by comparing capacity to traffic volumes on a link-by-link basis. Volume/capacity assessments may be made manually and presented graphically, or they may be produced by computer analysis after networks are designated and coded for such processing. In the latter event, each link in the chosen network will be identified by a pair of node numbers representing its terminal intersections. These may be designed to facilitate later mapping by computer or summaries by geographic area. Normally, at least the following link characteristics will be recorded: type of route, length, average speed, travel time, average daily traffic, and capacity. An example of a highway network section and its coding information is shown in Figure 12.2.

The coded networks, which must first be checked by verifying the reasonableness of computer-selected paths connecting all zones, can then be employed for several purposes: to depict the quality of existing travel service, to serve as the framework upon which trip distribution and modal split models are tested, and to be the base to which alternative future transportation proposals are added.

Four-Step Planning Procedure. To explain and develop land use/travel relationships, four steps of trip generation, trip distribution, modal split, and traffic assignment are typically followed.

1. *Trip generation.* In major urban studies, trip generation mathematically relates survey-reported trip making to household characteristics and other land-use types, using statistical procedures to establish trip rates, such as person-trips per household. The trip-distribution procedure usually determines the necessary level of detail. In some studies, trip generation expressed as auto driver trips per 1000 ft^2 of floor space will be satisfactory. Even more simply, reported trip rates published in *Trip Generation*[4] or other sources may be applied to a land-use data base.

2. *Trip distribution.* The preceding step of trip generation typically develops a tabulation of trip origins or trip attractions by small areas. Trip distribution links trip origins to destinations in order to produce estimates of network travel. Several models may be used: among these are the Fratar method, the intervening opportunities model, and the gravity model. In the latter technique, which is most commonly used, trip volumes from zone A to zone B are calculated as a direct function of the product of trip-end quantities in both zones and as an inverse function of the time or distance separating them. Typically, trips will be stratified into groups by trip purpose and the distribution for each group will be determined independently. Groupings might include:

- Home-based trips to work, shopping, social-recreation, schools, and all other purposes
- Nonhome-based trips (neither origin nor destination at home)
- Truck trips
- Taxi trips

The model's performance is first verified by using the network and traffic assignment techniques to see if model-produced O-D patterns and network loadings are comparable to those obtained from trip surveys and their assignment to the network. Once calibrated, the model is then ready to develop travel patterns based on forecast data for the target planning year.

3. *Modal split.* The trip-generation and trip-distribution steps may or may not be concerned with the problem of converting person-trips into automobile trips or transit passenger trips. Where mode choice is essential, several procedures are available to determine the split either before or after the trip-distribution step.[5] Trip diversion based on travel-time differences between modes is the basis for some methods, but it is being supplanted by techniques relying heavily on trip-maker or household characteristics.

4. *Traffic assignment.* The fourth step brings the outputs from preceding tasks to a coded transportation network. The estimates from the trip-generation step are loaded on the network from zone-level "loading nodes." They are then routed over those links giving the shortest time paths to zonal destinations as determined by the trip-distribution model. If certain links become overloaded as a result of assignments, the model may use "capacity-restraint" procedures to limit the volumes, usually by increasing link travel times or reassigning subsequent trips to alternative paths. When the process is done, the results can be produced as tabulations of link loadings or plotted graphically. Depending on available subroutines, other results, such as link and area volume/capacity ratios, vehicle-miles, and vehicle-hours of travel, or tabulations of O-D matrices using selected

[4] *Trip Generation* (Arlington, Va.: Institute of Transportation Engineers, 1979).

[5] ARTHUR B. SOSSLAU ET AL., *Quick Response Urban Travel Estimation Techniques and Transferable Parameters—User's Guide,* NCHRP Report 187 (Washington, D.C.: Transportation Research Board, 1978), pp. 63–87.

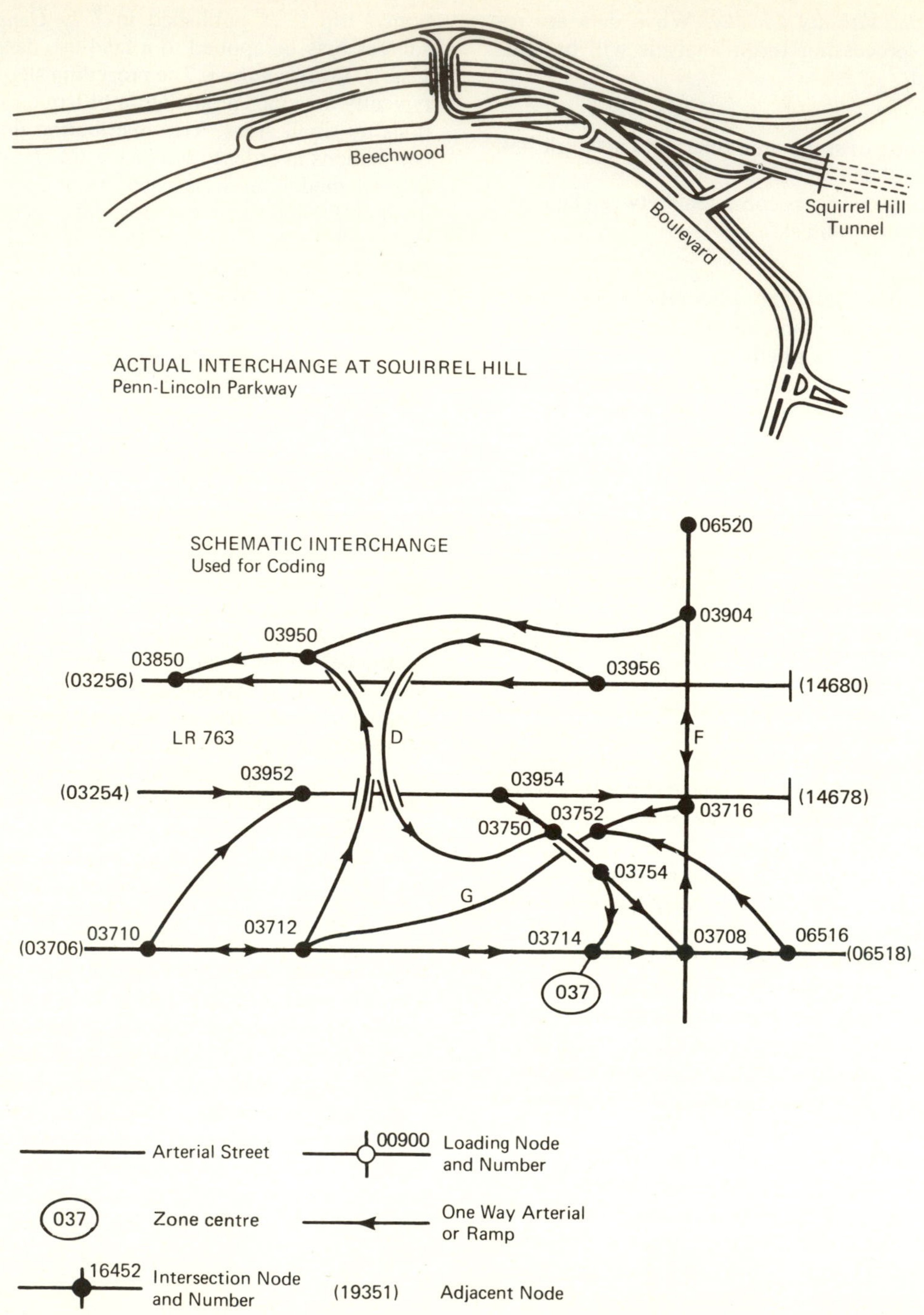

Figure 12.2. Example of network coding procedures. SOURCE: Southwestern Pennsylvania Regional Planning Commission.

links, may also be derived. Similar procedures apply to person-trips assigned to transit networks.

Alternative Analysis Procedures. Because the four-step process demands considerable staff expertise and time, its use is limited largely to the kinds of questions addressed by long-range planning studies. Even there, the process is flawed in two respects. First, the trip-generation, trip-distribution, and modal split techniques tend to project into the future the same forces that influence travel demand today. Second, the procedures do not lend themselves to exploring the impacts of many current policy issues, such as road pricing or inducing greater transit usage.

Because transportation planners must deal more and more with short-range issues and policies, analytical procedures that permit quick and inexpensive responses are becoming increasingly valuable. These changing procedural needs have stimulated research into new methodologies, and several techniques are emerging as a result.

One of the new techniques—disaggregate demand modeling—can be described as designed to identify the travel needs, rather than to measure present demands, of different parts of the community. Specialized travel needs, such as those of the handicapped or elderly, may be determined by surveys of their requirements. These are then translated into transportation service needs that should be satisfied. The approach can be applied to other population subgroups stratified according to area of residence, car ownership, income level, and so on. Since many current planning issues relate to specific needs of specific population groups, the disaggregate demand models permit evaluations that would be either impossible or too costly to assess by the conventional four-step process. They have had particular applicability in modal choice analyses.

A second procedure that is rapidly becoming more feasible is the use of "default values." Derived from accumulated experience in many urban travel surveys, default values are proved mean or median values of parameters for use in place of values derived from new surveys. They facilitate both manual and computer analysis of trip generation, distribution, and modal choice problems. The publication *Transportation Planning for your Community; System Planning*[6] suggests that they be employed for many types of current planning studies.

Forecasting. Forecasting follows analysis in most planning processes. Although 20-year plans are still appropriate for some studies, requirements are perhaps less of a burden than they used to be. Generally speaking, target years or planning horizons are closer to the present. Furthermore, because plan objectives are more limited, the size of the investment decision that hinges on the forecast outcome is smaller. The importance of accuracy is thus lessened at the same time that its likelihood is enhanced.

In many cases, forecasts by small areas are needed to generate future travel estimates, and something more than a simple extrapolation of growth rates will probably be required. Forecasts of population and dwelling units are most important, although in some cases land-use patterns will also be projected. Needed data on future household incomes, autos owned, and employment by type may sometimes be obtained from published sources or files of other agencies.

Techniques for zone-level forecasting vary in complexity. *Transportation Planning for your Community; Monitoring and Forecasting*[7] suggests these seven simple steps, for instance:

1. Determine an area-wide control total.
2. Determine a dwelling unit control total based on household data.
3. Prepare a dwelling unit forecast by subarea, based on the base-year inventory and proposed residential development.
4. Evaluate and resolve differences between items 2 and 3.
5. Make modifications needed for preparing revised subarea estimate.
6. Recalculate the forecast dwelling units per subarea.
7. Determine forecast population by subarea.

Similar procedures may be followed to derive future employment by subarea.

Where the objective is to plan long-range regional improvements requiring major capital investments, travel forecasts merit more detailed attention. Future land use may be based on projections or on formal plans. Population growth forecasts will be carefully estimated, based on development patterns, densities, and migration characteristics. Economic activity and employment forecasts may be derived by modeling. Internal checks between forecasted area totals and accumulated totals from subarea estimates will be essential. For example, the total number of automobiles aggregated from household car ownership forecasts should not exceed the number of licensed drivers derived from area population and driver registration trends.

Alternate plan development. Like forecasts, the level of detail in posing alternatives depends very much on project scale and the formality of the planning process. On the one hand, alternative selection may require hypothesizing different patterns of future urban land use and designing diverse networks of major facilities. Such alternative concepts may be shaped by various "plan-forms" (radial corridors, linear cities, dispersed or "spread" cities, satellite nucleations around a central city) or by different patterns of population densities. The forms of transportation may themselves be determinants, featuring network alternatives (highways versus public transportation, arterials versus freeways, grid versus radial patterns, minimum versus maximum construction). Principles for designing such arterial and freeway networks can be found in ITE publications.[8] On the other hand, planning may be oriented to current issues and policy questions, such as alternatives to optimize the values of existing facilities. Such solutions will often be examined at corridor and subregional levels, where alternatives might range from bypass routes to reverse-lane operations on a single facility. The breadth of options is indicated in Table 12-1, which shows one set of options to reduce demand and another to increase capacity.[9]

Plan testing and evaluation. The purpose of plan evaluation is to determine how well proposed solutions perform in meeting chosen planning objectives. Since more than one objective will probably have to be satisfied, and some objectives may conflict with one another, the recommendation of solutions may become difficult. "Transport Requirements for Urban Communities: Planning for Personal Travel"[10] suggests two choices for dealing with such difficulties: setting up multiple criteria or indicators of plan effectiveness,

---

[6]U.S. Federal Highway Administration. Office of Highway Planning. "Transportation Planning for your Community; System Planning." Washington, D.C.: Government Printing Office, 1980. (GPO SN 050-001-00181-1)

[7]U.S. Federal Highway Administration. Office of Highway Planning. "Transportation Planning for your Community; Monitoring and Forecasting." Washington, D.C.: Government Printing Office, 1980. (GPO SN 050-001-00183-7)

[8]*System Considerations for Urban Arterial Streets* (Washington, D.C.: Institute of Traffic Engineers, 1969); *System Considerations for Urban Freeways* (Washington, D.C.: Institute for Traffic Engineers, 1967).

[9]Neilon J. Rowan, Donald L. Woods, and Vergil G. Stover, *Alternatives for Improving Urban Transportation* (Washington, D.C., Federal Highway Administration, 1977).

[10]*Planning for Personal Travel*, p. 57.

TABLE 12–1
Alternative Choices for Transportation Improvements

Reducing Vehicle Demand	Increasing Capacity
Transportation pricing	Build new facilities
Peak-period dispersion	Improve traffic operations
Ride sharing	High-occupancy-vehicle priority
Improve public transportation	Improve pedestrian facilities
Facilitate bicycle travel	Improve goods movement

SOURCE: NEILON J. ROWAN, DONALD L. WOODS, AND VERGIL G. STOVER, Modified from *Alternatives for Improving Urban Transportation,* (Washington, D.C.: Federal Highway, 1977).

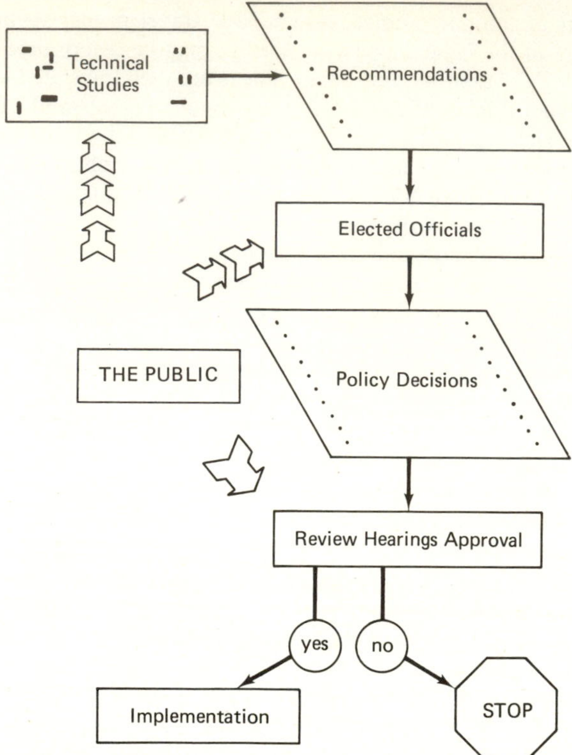

Figure 12.3. Decision process for transportation planning. SOURCE: Richard M. Sokesman, "Developing Transportation and Land Use Alternatives in Toronto," *Transportation and Land Use Planning Abroad,* Special Report 168, Washington, D.C.: Transportation Research Board, 1976.

or raising the decision making from the technical level to the political level.

Useful indicators of effectiveness fall into two classes, those applicable to transport system attributes and those relevant to broader social issues. Three subsets of indicators for system analysis include performance indicators (speed, capacity, fares, and comfort, for example), cost indicators (charges for personnel, capital, equipment, and operating services), and safety and environmental indicators (accidents, noise, air pollution, etc.).

Three sets of indicators for policy questions include social indicators (accessibility for population groups, or impacts on selected segments of the population), land-use-effect indicators (blighting, growth stimulus, severance of neighborhoods, changing land values), and economic effect indicators (investment required, changes in productivity, and market penetration).

Shifting the level for decision making recognizes the changing nature of planning and increasing citizen involvement in a participatory process. The planner assembles alternative evaluations related to the more complex objectives and refers them to policymakers, who can then make a choice with full awareness of the trade-offs.

The broad range of available techniques for evaluation falls into three groups. Manual methods are suitable for all the analysis steps of trip generation, distribution, mode choice, and assignment. Examples of projects to which they can be applied include "a transit-route extension; increasing frequency of service along a route; assessing the impact of a proposed major development on the surrounding street system; evaluation of system needs within a single corridor. . . ."[11]

Computer methods are the second group. In the U.S., most stem from the Urban Transportation Planning System (UTPS) developed by UMTA and FHWA. The direction in packaging these programs has been toward extending their applicability to smaller areas, and simplifying them to encourage broader use.

NCHRP Report 186 describes the third group as pivot-point sensitivity methods: "Elasticity and sensitivity-type relationships provide a rapid means of evaluating issue-oriented changes such as parking costs, system extensions, carpooling, and system capacity. . . . Most elasticity relationships have been provided by calibration of a model against some known condition and exercising the model to produce sensitivity relationships. These methods hold more promise for transferability, and unquestionably can provide answers to policy issues more quickly than the four-step process—computerized or manual. The results are more general relative to system description than the specific facility-related processes."[12]

Evaluation techniques should be compatible with the problems being solved. This means using techniques that provide responses appropriate in their timeliness, in the levels of effort required, and in their relevance to planning objectives and criteria.

Decision making and implementation. At this stage in the planning process, it is time for decisions and actions to implement plans. Figure 12.3 emphasizes the essential element of public participation and community input in shaping this activity. Public input can occur at three stages. First, in the technical studies themselves, citizen participation can occur through citizen advisory groups in the framing of objectives. Second, in considering recommendations, elected officials reflect the views of their constituents. Third, through review and the public hearing processes legally required for certain transportation planning activities, the public has a direct opportunity to make its views heard. Sometimes, technically acceptable alternatives may be rejected and sent back for restudy.

[11]ARTHUR B. SOSSLAU ET AL., *Travel Estimation Procedures for Quick Response to Urban Policy Issues,* NCHRP Report 186 (Washington, D.C.: Transportation Research Board, 1978), p. 26.

[12]SOSSLAU, *Travel Estimation Procedures,* p. 26.

Given approval of recommended solutions, in the U.S. regional plans must next be turned into Transportation Improvement Programs (TIPs) and their Annual Elements (AEs). Factors to consider are funding, coordination of different agency efforts, and selection of project priorities. *Transportation Planning for your Community; the Manager's Guide* prescribes seven elements for programming:[13]

1. Form a programming committee.
2. Assign administrative responsibility of public elements of the urban transportation system.
3. Identify candidate improvement projects.
4. Determine the plan to fund candidate improvement projects.
5. Assign priorities to candidate improvement projects.
6. Allocate and schedule projects.
7. Monitor, adjust, and evaluate the programs.

A committee, preferably of representatives already involved in the planning process, will best guide development of annual and longer-range programs through ensuring the needed coordination of different agencies. Responsibility for executing appropriate parts of the programs will be negotiated among the agencies charged with their implementation. Next or concurrently, the ability to finance programs and to prioritize them in succeeding annual increments will be determined by a review of existing and potential fund sources and forecasts of expected revenues. Priorities for projects will also be set. These may be based on considerations such as meeting the most serious deficiencies first, providing earliest maximum benefits, or following ongoing staged-construction sequences. Apart from desirable priorities, project schedules will also be influenced by time allowances for preimplementation activities such as public hearings, environmental impact studies, and detailed design development.

The end result will be a project listing and budget coordinated for the various participating governmental jurisdictions. Another consideration is essential: since construction timetables may be upset by delays, or unforeseen emergencies may arise, or shifts of emphasis may change priorities, the programming process should include a procedure for annual reviews. These reviews should include program monitoring and evaluation as each annual element is added to keep multiyear transportation improvement programs advancing.

Monitoring. One more step in the UTP process, which indeed implies that the process really has no end, is monitoring. This activity usually means keeping up with change. One kind of change to keep up with, of course, is change in planning techniques. Procedures do change, with emphasis shifting from public and legislative pressures, and with improving modeling and computer capabilities. Agency staffs need to keep current in these respects.

The most important changes are those that may affect the validity of previously adopted plans. A major purpose of monitoring is to ascertain whether what is happening in urban area development is consistent with or contrary to what was anticipated. If contrary, forecasts—and plans—may require revision. Thus, at least the following data bases should be kept reasonably current:

1. Traffic volumes and transit ridership figures
2. Transportation facility characteristics
3. Population, employment, and land use

The effort that should go into maintaining current data bases is impossible to generalize. It will clearly vary with community size, the relative proportions of long- and short-term planning, funds available, and so on. One determinant of monitoring need may be found only after some monitoring is done; the more that reality deviates from forecasts as time passes, the greater will be the need for subsequent monitoring efforts. Typically, the frequency of updating most elements in the data base, such as the three mentioned above, can be at 2-year intervals.

Costly surveys are unnecessary for most update requirements. Instead, ongoing routine work by other agencies will probably be the major information source. Figure 12.4 illustrates, for example, sources at three levels of government for seven categories of data.

A second purpose of monitoring is to evaluate the ef-

Figure 12.4. Potential sources of data for monitoring. SOURCE: R.D. Worrall and S. Robertson, "Development of Information System for the Urban Transportation Planning Process," Peat, Marwick, Mitchell & Co., May 1973. Washington, D.C.

AGENCY	Land Use	Population	Employment	Demographic	Roadway facilities	Public transportation	Travel
FEDERAL							
Bureau of Census		X	X	X			X
U.S. Dept. of Transportation				X			X
STATE							
Dept. of Transportation					X	X	
State Planning Agency	X	X	X	X			
Revenue Office			X				
Motor Vehicle Dept.			X	X			
Employment Security		X					
LOCAL							
Planning and Zoning	X	X	X	X			
Traffic Department					X	X	X
Utility Departments		X					
Building and Permits		X		X			
Chamber of Commerce	X	X	X				
Public Transp. Agencies						X	X

[13]U.S. Federal Highway Administration. Office of Highway Planning. "Transportation Planning for your Community; The Manager's Guide for Developing a Planning Program." Washington, D.C.: Government Printing Office, 1980. (GPO SN 050-001-00186-1)

TABLE 12–2
Surveys to Evaluate Parking Policy Implementation

Regular Surveys	Occasional Surveys
Parking supply	Pedestrian flows
Parking usage (arrivals, departures, duration, occupancy, trip purpose)	Noise and pollution levels
Traffic flow and composition	Time taken to park and reach destination
Traffic speed	Changes in operation of land uses, including retail turnover, mode, origin and frequency of customers
Bus speed and regularity	Reasons for changes in land use
Accidents	Attitude to parking controls
Origins and destinations of parked and moving cars	
Factors influencing need to use a car	
Land-use changes	
Levels of enforcement and compliance for parking controls	
Running costs of parking controls	

SOURCE: D. BAYLISS ET AL., *Case Study on London* (Paris: Organisation for Economic Cooperation and Development, 1976), pp. 24–25.

fectiveness of implemented plans. Here the objective is to determine whether policies need to be extended or modified. Table 12-2 shows the types of surveys recommended for a parking control program in London, England. The types of data are grouped by those that should be collected regularly (some probably are by one agency or another) and those that may be collected only occasionally. This is clearly a significant effort to monitor parking policy implementation, but then the program affects one of the most heavily used street networks in the world. Furthermore, many of the recommended surveys would also benefit other planning projects.

Relationships between planning elements and UTP projects

It may be helpful to summarize what has been presented so far and relate it to different types of transportation planning activity. Table 12-3 describes three classes of projects and indicates the importance of different elements in each class. There is always risk in easy generalization, but the significance of principles and constraints as well as the process emphasis appropriate to short-, medium-, and long-range planning studies shows approximately the different levels of planning complexity.

Urban transportation planning ranges across a broad spectrum, from back-of-the-envelope analyses to multiyear, multimillion dollar undertakings carried out by large permanent staffs using the most advanced theories and technology. A later section gives some examples of different projects in each of the three categories and describes some of their salient characteristics.

Tools for transportation system planning

Travel modeling and forecasting are critical elements in the urban transportation planning (UTP) process. Typically, the procedure will involve the four steps of trip generation, trip distribution, modal split, and traffic assignment. They can be carried out either manually or by computer, depending on funding, staffing, project scope, and other considerations. This section briefly describes the two options and notes where to find more detailed information.

Computer techniques

Computers play an increasingly important role in the UTP process. While some of the largest planning groups have prepared their own software to suit uniquely developed models, federal agencies have developed and improved upon standardized computer packages for application to studies of all sizes. For example, the readily available current Urban Transportation Planning System (UTPS) package can be applied in study areas as small as 25,000–50,000

TABLE 12–3
Relationships between Planning Elements and Different Types of UTP Projects

Element	Planning Study Type: Short Range	Planning Study Type: Intermediate Range	Planning Study Type: Long Range
Project characteristics			
Implementation schedule	1–5 years	5–10 years	10 years or more
Solution cost range	$100,000–$5,000,000	$5,000,000–$10,000,000	$10 million and up
Complexity of study process	Minimal	Minimum data, analytical	Full process
Project funding status	Probably available	May be assured	Probably unknown
Planning principles			
Goals and objectives re "client"	Probably defined in advance	Important to develop	May need to *lead* client
Process guided by goals and objectives	Important	Important	Very important
Effort consistent with scale	Very important	Important	May not be a factor
Dynamic and continuing	Not a factor	Probably important	Very important
Planning constraints			
Money and personnel	Significant	Possibly significant	May not be a factor
Planning techniques	Significant	Possibly significant	Not a factor
Institutional considerations	Very significant	Significant	Should not be a factor
Existing facilities	Very significant	Significant	Significant
Planning processes			
Goals and objectives	Will be understood	Specify clearly	Specify clearly
Inventories	Existing data base	Modest	Significant effort
Analysis	Default values	Simple models	Sophisticated and innovative
Forecasting	Not a factor	Simple models	Sophisticated and innovative
Alternate plan development	Limited scope	May be significant	Broad opportunity
Plan test and evaluation	Manual	Range of methods	Sophisticated process
Plan implementation	Programming significant	Suggest with plan	Staging, not programming
Monitoring	Not a factor	May be significant	Essential

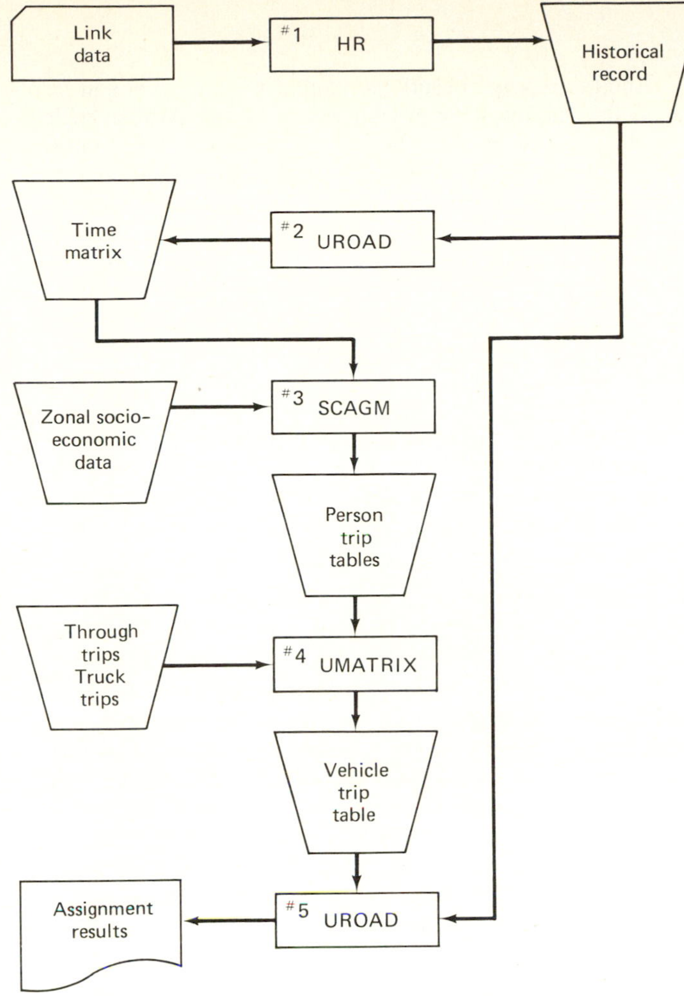

Figure 12.5. Simplified chain of UTPS programs for four-step transportation planning. SOURCE: Urban Mass Transportation Administration, Washington, D.C.

population. Figure 12.5 shows how a minimum battery of five programs can be employed with highway network data files to perform the following functions:

1. HR: Produce a computerized network description (historical record) from coded highway link data.
2. UROAD: Produce a matrix of travel times between all zones.
3. SCAGM: Apply trip-generation rates and a gravity model to produce a trip table.
4. UMATRIX: Convert person-trips to vehicle-trips and incorporate through-trips and truck-trips.
5. UROAD: Convert the production-attraction table to origin–destination format and assign trips to the network.

A feature of the UTPS package is its flexibility with respect to certain data inputs. This is accomplished by using standard values of parameters where existing data bases are inadequate. A listing of available parameters is provided in *Characteristics of Urban Transportation Systems* (CUTS),[14] a computer-printed reference periodically updated by UMTA as new information becomes available.

CUTS provides data in self-descriptive tables for the following modes: rail transit, bus transit, automobile-highway systems, pedestrian assistance systems, and activity center systems. The following seven supply parameters are covered:

1. Speed (average, maximum)
2. Capacity, or service volume (vehicle, person)
3. Operating cost (vehicle)
4. Energy consumption (vehicle or source)
5. Pollution (emissions, noise)
6. Capital cost (land, construction, vehicle acquisition)
7. Accident frequency

The tables sometimes present three levels of detail. The first, called a default value, is a typical mean design figure, derived from substantial empirical observations, to be used where site-specific data are unavailable. The second level is a range of values, giving low and high estimates and conditions where they apply, which permits sensitivity testing and gives the user a choice if it seems appropriate. When neither the default value nor range of values is adequate, the theoretical value, which is by definition generally derivable from mathematical formulas, can be used. All may be used with either manual or computer techniques.

Simulation models

Another class of computer models, of growing interest to transportation planners for TSM strategy evaluations, are the operational and simulation models. Research at the University of California, for example, has led to models that integrate three activities: demand–supply modeling, impact assessment, and demand forecasting.[15] Model inputs consist of capacity-related design features, origin and destination demand patterns, and existing control states. The simulation submodel is used first to predict impacts under present operating conditions. The optimization submodel then develops an improved operating strategy and recalls the simulation submodel to estimate impacts with new conditions. One such model has been described as follows:

> The FREQ6PE model is a macroscopic decision model of a freeway corridor and is used primarily for the evaluation of priority entry and normal entry control on a directional freeway. The model can also be used for evaluating design improvements with or without freeway entry control. The user selects the type of entry control combined with design changes, if desired, and the model through a linear programming optimization process selects the ramp control plan. The model predicts a timestream of impacts and traveller responses due to the interaction between ramp control strategy and traveller responses.

Figure 12.6 shows some of the results from applying the model to a 10-mi section of the Eastshore Freeway in the San Francisco Bay area. The total assessment covers travel time, fuel, emissions, and noise impacts, and the demand forecasting model provides short-term and long-term trav-

[14] *Characteristics of Urban Transportation Systems* (Washington, D.C.: Urban Mass Transportation Administration), issued irregularly.

[15] ADOLF D. MAY, "The Role of Operational Planning Models in Transportation System Management" (unpublished paper at FHWA Conference, University of Maryland, Oct. 1978).

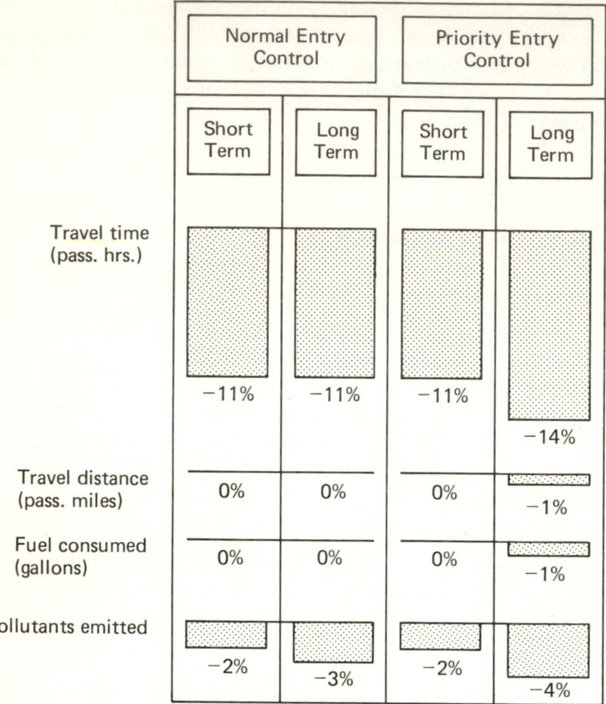

Figure 12.6. Percent change in measures of effectiveness. SOURCE: A.J. Kruger and A.D. May, *Further Analysis and Evaluation of Selected Impacts of Traffic Management Strategies,* Washington, D.C.: U.S. Department of Transportation, 1977.

eler responses. For this particular test of afternoon peak periods, based on the assumptions of metering rates, sensitivities for route diversion and modal shifts and other parameters, it was determined that entry controls would be needed at six ramps between 4:00 and 5:15 p.m.

The same model has been applied to other problems, such as effects of changes in speed limits and metering rates, evaluations of pricing measures and priority-lane operations, and trade-offs between traveler equity and system performance. Other models, developed or under development, deal with arterial networks, residential areas, downtown areas, and rural highways.

Manual techniques

Many study situations will not warrant computer usage. Even where computer packages are available, simpler manual methods may be more appropriate. Some are suggested in *Achieving a Long-Range/Short-Range Planning Balance with an Appropriate Level of Effort.*[16] This review of planning rationale for smaller urban areas identifies manual techniques suitable for six areas of work: areawide and subarea planning, site-specific techniques, transit planning (long and short range), air quality analysis, land-use forecasting, and traffic engineering studies. Typical values for data points useful in such studies can be found in Chapter 10.

[16]CHRISTOPHER FLEET, ~~ATHONY~~ ANTHONY KANE, AND GEORGE SCHOENER, *Achieving a Long-Range/Short-Range Planning Balance with an Appropriate Level of Effort* (Washington, D.C.: Federal Highway Administration, 1978).

Another report[17] describes manual methods that can be applied to the four-step procedure, giving the basis of their development, data required for use, features, and limitations. The report suggests their application to subarea or corridor studies, but indicates that they can also be useful in small regions, such as those containing fewer than 80 zones and a network of fewer than 200 links. In all, the report covers the following aspects of transportation planning: trip generation, trip distribution, mode choice, auto occupancy, time-of-day distribution, traffic assignment, capacity analysis, and development density/highway spacing relationships. To illustrate the broad potentials of the recommended techniques, three quite different scenario applications are included; the sample studies are: a site-development impact analysis in Boise, Idaho; a corridor analysis in Columbus, Ohio; and a land use/highway spacing study in Fairfax, Virginia.

Other guides

Two other series of U.S. government publications offer comprehensive guidance in solving urban transportation planning problems. One, *Transportation Planning for your Community,* is available in a seven-part series.[18] The second, *Analysing Transit Options for Small Urban Communities,* is a three-volume UMTA manual that provides an analytical framework and supporting analytical techniques.[19] In addition, of course, numerous texts on urban transportation planning are available.

Examples of urban transportation planning

Where a permanent agency staff is engaged in urban transportation planning, its efforts will probably be diffused over many activities rather than focused, as they would have been a few years ago, on the development of an areawide transportation plan of major facilities. Typical concerns could fall into short-, middle-, and long-range programs. The short-range items will generally be specific project-oriented tasks, identified with a single site, a single mode, or a single route. Middle-range work will include projects of large scope and funding or an assemblage of separate but coordinated projects with designated priorities. Long-range activities will usually be those involving large capital investments extending over many years.

[17]SOSSLAU ET AL., *Quick-Response Urban Travel Estimation Techniques and Transferable Parameters—User's Guide.*

[18]U.S. Federal Highway Administration. Office of Highway Planning. "Transportation Planning for your Community." Washington, D.C.: Government Printing Office, 1980. A series of 2 guides and 5 technical manuals:

1. A Guide for the Decision Maker GPO SN 050-001-00192-6
2. The Manager's Guide for Developing a Planning Program GPO SN 050-001-00186-1
3. Traffic Planning GPO SN 050-001-00185-3
4. Transit Planning GPO SN 050-001-00182-9
5. System Planning GPO SN 050-001-00181-1
6. Monitoring and Forecasting GPO SN 050-001-00183-7
7. Programming Projects GPO SN 050-001-00184-5

[19]*Analyzing Transit Options for Small Urban Communities* (Washington, D.C.: Urban Mass Transportation Administration, 1978).

Short-range or project planning activities

The following types of short-range projects in urban transportation planning are of two kinds. Some are examples of studies carried out by public agencies; others are illustrative of planning principles or recommended solutions to general problems.

Transportation for selected groups. Mobility of the elderly and the handicapped poses special problems, and sometimes solutions involve specialized equipment. But useful and quickly obtained answers to some problems may be derived from projects such as the following example.

Under funding from federal and local transportation organizations, the Department of Human Resources of the Metropolitan Washington Council of Governments compiled a directory of special transportation services in the Washington area. Developed to help elderly, handicapped, and others with special needs to find the agency best able to provide needed transportation services, the directory serves also as an information source for planners concerned with transportation for such population groups. It lists 94 agencies of different kinds providing transportation services, with a tabulation for each agency such as that shown in Figure 12.7. Not just a reference source, a report such as this one conveys what levels of service exist and may be a basis for designing improvements.

Studies of transportation/land use interactions. Of particular interest to transportation planners are sites that are regional attractors of traffic, such as warehouse areas, airports, and major shopping centers. Activities such as these frequently impose heavy burdens on the adjacent traffic facilities as well as requiring large land areas for their operation. Thus, a research study on shopping center trip generation should have considerable interest for planners.

In "Parking Demand at the Regionals,"[20] the author points out that regional shopping centers, those with 800,000 ft^2 or more (67,000 m^2) of gross leasable area (GLA) almost invariably require special trip-generation and parking-demand studies. Urban zoning requirements typically have specified 5.5 parking spaces per 1000 ft^2 (6.3 per 100 m^2) of GLA for these land uses, but newer studies suggest that changing patterns of both travel and center activities cause peak parking demands lower than those that used to occur. A ratio of 5.0 per 1000 ft^2 (5.75 per 100 m^2) is likely to be adequate in most circumstances. At existing centers, therefore, several opportunities arise as a result:

1. Additional floor space can be developed.
2. Additional landscaping and amenities can be provided.
3. Peripheral land may be available for street widening.
4. Commuter "park-and-ride" facilities may be installed.

Each of these opportunities can be employed in the interest of better urban transportation planning. Planners wanting to take advantage of such opportunities should verify by survey that local travel and shopping center characteristics will permit a reduction in parking requirements. In any case, these national survey findings do suggest that local planning agency research and analysis can lead to more productive use of land and travel facilities.

	District of Columbia
Organization:	Frienship House Senior Program 619 D Street, S.E. Washington, D.C. 20003
Contact Person:	Mrs. Melvina Brown, Project Director Nutrition Program Mrs. Edith Beckwith, Project Director Project Link
Telephone Number:	(202) 547-8880
Eligibility Requirements:	55 years and older
Geographic Area Served: (description of routes and shedules)	District of Columbia Service Area = 5
Operating Hours:	10.00 A.M. - 2.00 P.M. Monday to Fiday
Trip Purposes:	Shopping, medical and recreational purposes and luncheon meals
Fare:	Free
Service Type:	Scheduled for hot meal program; other uses demand-scheduled
Number of Vehicles:	2
Type of Vehicles:	Vans
Capacity of Vehicles:	1 15-passenger, 1 14 -passenger
Number of Persons Served:	Week - 185
User Characteristics:	100% elderly (35% handicapped)
Length of Time Providing Service:	Since 1974
Type of Service Provided:	Non-profit.

Figure 12.7. Excerpt from *Directory of Special Transportation Services, Metropolitan Washington Area,* Washington, D.C.: Metropolitan Washington Council of Governments, 1977, p. 15.

Goods movement studies. Truck travel in cities produces nuisances in the form of noise, vibration, congestion, and air pollution. Cities have consequently restricted the times and places of truck travel, in some cases quite severely. Figure 12.8 shows, for example, how the city of Stockholm, Sweden, limits movement of trucks over 3½ tons (3200 kg) gross weight, except on certain designated routes and access roads to terminals or industrial sites. The time limitations led to a study recently of the possibilities for consolidated distribution of goods between wholesalers and retailers. As described in "Distribution of Goods in Urban and Metropolitan Areas,"[21] planning to develop new goods distribution patterns requires investigating complex

[20]Richard C. Gern, "Parking Demand at the Regionals," *ITE J., 48*(9), 19–24 (1978).

[21]Gunnar Kullstrom, "Distribution of Goods in Urban and Metropolitan Areas," AIT 13th International Study Week, 1978.

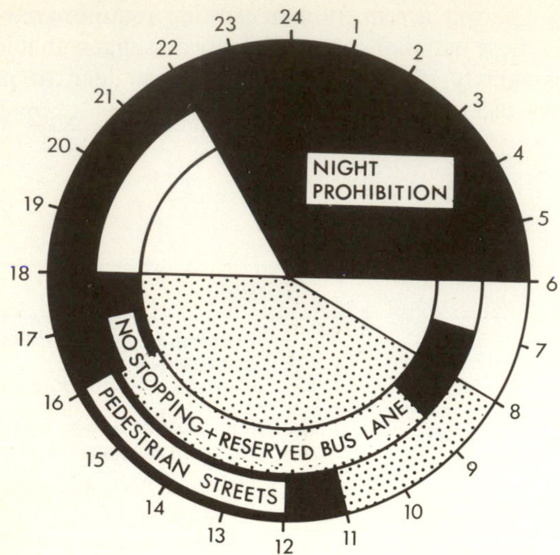

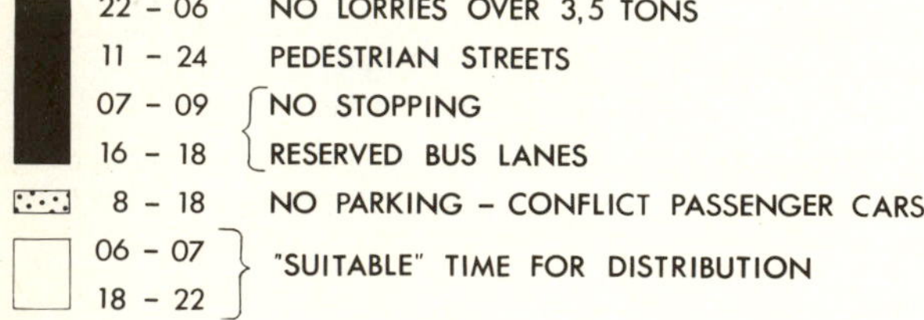

NOTE: THERE IS NORMALLY A LIMITED NUMBER OF PEDESTRIAN STREETS AND RESERVED BUS LANES IN AN INNER URBAN AREA

Figure 12.8. Time restrictions on truck activity, Stockholm, Sweden. SOURCE: Gunnar Kullström, "Distribution of Goods in Urban and Metropolitan Areas," AIT 13th International Study Week, 1978.

alternatives for routing between shippers and receivers, both considering or excluding intermediate handling at terminals. This study proposed several theoretical models and noted that the economic feasibility of any scheme depended on many factors, such as "volume of commodity, weight of commodity, frequency of delivery, delivery time constraint, handling devices of delivery vehicle, design of goods reception, owner relationships."

To gain more insights into the character of urban goods movement and to develop methods of assessing relevant public policy decisions, the Transport and Road Research Laboratory of Great Britain has conducted a series of studies. The first test site was Swindon, a well-defined community of about 125,000 population that experiences about 4000 daily trips of trucks exceeding 8.5 tons (7700 kg) gross vehicle weight. The investigations included surveys and the development and application of a model.

The surveys produced a detailed record of the movement of goods vehicles in Swindon, together with other information. "Two main types of data inputs to the model were required: first, factual information about existing goods vehicle movements, the road network, traffic and environmental conditions in the area and the nature of companies operating vehicles; and second, information of a more sub-

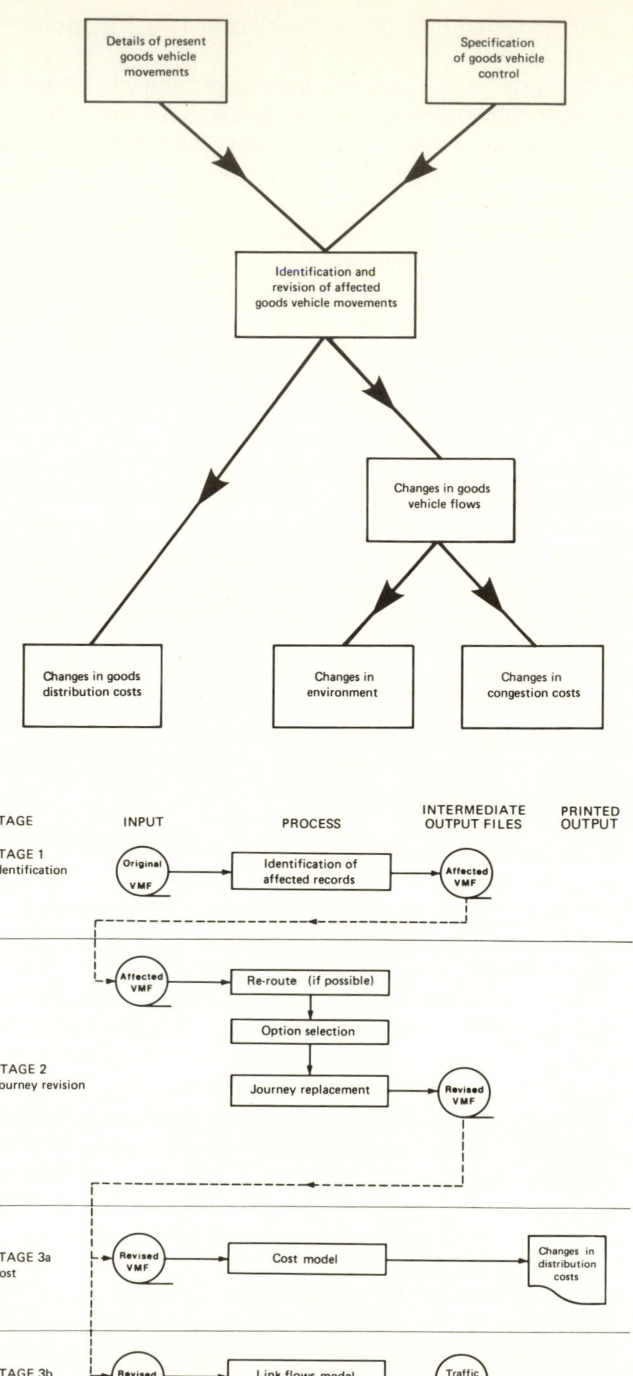

Figure 12.9. Schematic representation (top) and flow diagram (bottom) of Swindon Freight Model. SOURCE: R.H. Purcell et al., "The Swindon Freight Study," *Traffic Engineering and Control,* 18(4), 162–165, April 1977.

jective nature about the motives of transport operators and their likely reaction to controls."[22]

The model, diagrammed in Figure 12.9, was designed to simulate goods movements and quantify the effects of controls, using survey results and a coded network:[23]

> The model first processes records of individual vehicle movements obtained from the surveys and identifies any journey affected by the controls proposed by the model-user. Following the identification of affected journeys, the model revises them in a way which enables the distribution of goods to be fully maintained. For each control situation, therefore, the model establishes a new pattern of vehicle movements and calculates the changes in traffic flows, the changes in goods distribution costs, the changes in the costs of congestion to all road traffic and the environmental changes resulting from the control.

The model was designed to function under three sets of options, reflecting transport-operator choice patterns for rerouting and so on, with vehicle controls tested across nine gross vehicle weight classes. The policy alternatives tested were (1) to prohibit entry totally into designated areas (four sets from subareas to the whole area were chosen) or (2) to prohibit entry for all but those vehicles with destinations within the same sets of areas. The results showed that a policy of "no entry except for access" applied to the whole town was the most cost-effective solution for Swindon's goods movement problems, largely because of the availability of "environmentally insensitive roads" outside but close to the built-up area.

Residential development projects. As long as suburban growth continues, or as urban redevelopment encourages redesign, the planning of residential area streets will be important in urban transportation. A Swedish paper, "Planning Principles for New Residential Areas,"[24] compares practices in five different nations. Table 12-4 excerpts some of the data presented.

An illustration of a Dutch "Woonerf," particularly suitable for high-density townhouse or other "in-town" developments, is given in Figure 12.10. For more typical American situations, the ITE publication *Recommended Practices for Subdivision Streets*[25] provides specifications for design elements and other material relevant to the design of subdivision streets for capacity and safety.

In both urban and suburban design, site-specific traffic planning is more and more needed. Questions such as the following should be asked and answered:

1. Can approach streets accommodate new traffic demands generated by the development?
2. Are modifications to existing operation necessary?
3. Do internal circulation patterns prevent internal congestion from spreading into surrounding streets?
4. Are parking provisions adequate, or can overflows be handled within reasonable distances?
5. Can goods movement needs (e.g., moving vans) be accommodated without congestion?
6. Are pedestrian–vehicle conflict situations properly treated?

Transit system evaluation studies. Especially in smaller urban areas, it may be desirable to monitor the performance of transit systems on a regular if not an annual basis. Transportation planning agencies or others may find it useful to assemble and analyze data such as those described in a 1978 *ITE Journal* article.[26]

This study of 10 transit systems in Pennsylvania considered many performance indicators and concluded that at least three were essential. The system characteristics are summarized in Table 12-5; variation among them in the three performance measures is shown in Figure 12.11. The most important indicator is operating ratio (the ratio of revenues to expenses), the basic measure of system profitability. The 10 systems achieved a mean value of 67% for expenses recovered out of generated revenues. Another important measure is total cost per passenger. Here the mean value was $0.525 per passenger for the 10 Pennsylvania systems. Average speed is the third major measure, as it determines vehicle requirements for each route, given a desired headway interval.

The resulting measures of efficiency and effectiveness are useful not only for system planning purposes but also may serve to assure equity in allocating financial assistance.

Bikeway planning. In many of the world's urban areas, bicycles are a significant transportation mode. For example, in some European cities with favorable terrain and climatic conditions they account for 15% or more of daily trip making. Even in the most motorized nation (United States), about 40% of the population may own bicycles. Facilities for bicycle use are, therefore, a proper urban transportation planning consideration.

Two publications deal with the planning and design of bikeways: *A Bikeway Criteria Digest*[27] and *Planning and Design Criteria for Bikeways in California*.[28] Both offer guidance for planning and locating such facilities, stressing that usage is generally either recreational or utilitarian and usually accommodated through shared use of existing streets and highways. Bikeway planning must also consider the need for bicycle security and storage at the nonhome end of many trips; without appropriate provisions, bikeways may simply not be used. Bikeway objectives are generally the enhancement of user convenience and safety. Bikeways do not necessarily have to be separate facilities; in fact,

---

[22]R. H. PURCELL ET AL., "The Swindon Freight Study," *Traffic Eng. Control, 18*(4), 163 (Apr. 1977).

[23]PURCELL, "The Swindon Freight Study," p. 163. A reference for U.S. practice can be found in DENNIS L. CHRISTIANSEN, *Urban Transportation Planning for Goods and Services* (Washington, D.C.: Federal Highway Administration, 1979).

[24]STIG NORDQVIST, "Planning Principles for New Residential Areas." Nordplan, Stockholm, Sweden, 1978.

[25]*Recommended Practices for Subdivision Streets* (Washington, D.C.: Institute of Traffic Engineers, 1965).

[26]DENNIS F. MCCROSSON, "Choosing Performance Indicators for Small Transit Systems," *Transport. Eng., 48*(3), 26–30 (Mar. 1978).

[27]*A Bikeway Criteria Digest* (Washington, D.C.: Federal Highway Administration, 1977).

[28]*Planning and Design Criteria for Bikeways in California* (Washington, D.C.: Federal Highway Administration, 1979).

TABLE 12–4
Design Considerations for Residential Streets

Design Aspect	West Germany (Richtlinien für die Anlage von Stadtstrassen, 1971)	Netherlands (Woonerf Regulations, 1976)	Sweden (SCAFT, 1968, and Stadens Trafiknät, 1977)	U.K. (Residential Roads and Design Bulletin 32, 1977)	U.S. (Recommended Practices for Subdivision Streets, 1967)
Differentiation	Wohnwege Anliegerstrassen Sammelstrassen Verkehrsstrassen Hauptverkehrsstrassen Schnellverkehrsstrassen Autobahnen	Recommended	Access way Approach road Local distributor District distributor Regional distributor National distributor	Access road Local distributor District distributor Primary distributor	Recommended
Separation, segregation	Not explicitly recommended as a system, but access ways where motor vehicles are left out are proposed	No recommendations	Recommended	Not recommended as a general rule. But: "Where community facilities are part of the development, the opportunity should be taken to serve them with pedestrian routes segregated from distributor roads"	Not explicitly recommended. But: "In general, while vehicular flow must be outward-oriented . . . pedestrian travel should be inward-oriented . . ."
Integration, shared surfaces	No recommendations	Recommended. May be applied to all streets with less than 300 vehicles per hour during peak period. Special regulations adopted	The system is recommended for testing	Shared surfaces proposed in several local planning-guides for some cul-de-sacs or short loops. No legal precedence for pedestrians over motor vehicles	
Reducing speed Maximum street length access road	200 m	500 m	150–200 m "Longer streets may be accepted if efficient speed-reducing obstacles are applied"	"A main aim should be to create conditions under which the great majority of drivers will normally drive with care and maintain low speeds . . . This will have indications for the travel distance . . ."	Maximum lengths of cul-du-sacs 300 m
Street entrance design	No recommendations	"The entrance and exits of a Woonerf must be so designed that they can be clearly recognized"	No recommendations	". . . the design of carriageways and their surrounds may be varied to mark the transition from one type of road to another"	No recommendations
Narrowing width	Minimum width of roadway 4.5 m	Streets should not be narrower than allowing a minimum distance of 0.6 m between vehicle and building. Minimum road width 2.8 m when used only by small vehicles, 3.2 m when used by larger vehicles	Minimum width of roadway 4.5–5.0 m. The width may be reduced to 2.75 m along short sections to reduce speeds	". . . a width of 4.1 m will still provide two-way flow for the majority of residential traffic". Narrow gateways may be used to encourage low speed. 2.75 m enough for fire service, etc.	Minimum width 6.6 m. Narrowing width to reduce speed is not explicitly recommended
Humps	No recommendations	Studies for an optimal design of humps are in progress	Suggested, but no design recommendations	Legally restricted; studies are in progress	No recommendations
Staggering of the roadway, tight bends	No recommendations	Recommended, should be fairly severe	Recommended	Recommended	No recommendations
Changing material of road surface or painting	No recommendations	Extensively used	Recommended	Recommended	No recommendations
Halting and parking	Parking as near entrances as possible. Maximum distance 200 m	All vehicles may halt up to all entrances. Parking only permitted in defined parking places. Parking areas can be designed so that they can be used as play areas during the day	Maximum distance between halting and entrance: Handicapped, fire vehicle 0 Taxi, ambulance, furniture removal van 25 m Mail van, refuse collection vehicle, tanker lorry 50 m Maximum distance to residents' and visitors' halting 100m Maximum distance to residents' and visitors' parking 300m	Parking spaces for residents, visitors and emergency vehicles as near to the dwelling entrance as possible	No recommendations

SOURCE: STIG NORDQVIST, "Traffic Safety. Planning Principles for New Residential Areas," Nordplan, Stockholm. Meddelande 1978:4.

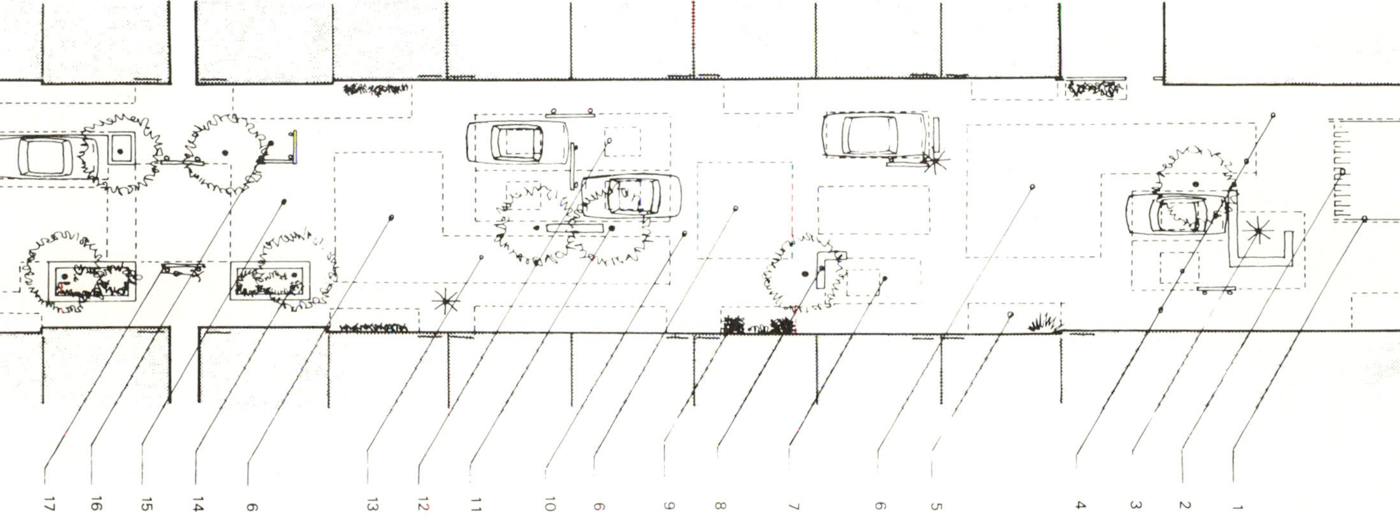

Figure 12.10. Plan and illustration of a Dutch "Woonerf." SOURCE: ~~Woonerf~~ Royal Dutch Touring Club, 1977.

TABLE 12–5
Small Transit Systems, Pennsylvania Sample Population*

Transit System	Urban Area	1970 Population	1975 Patronage	Fleet Size
AMTRAN	Altoona	74,396	1,552,532	33
BARTA	Reading	200,744	3,782,521	66
CAT	Harrisburg	293,654	4,480,256	98
COLTS	Scranton	240,513	2,936,874	40
EMTA	Erie	212,261	5,345,448	61
CCTA	Johnstown	97,003	1,505,184	35
LANTA	Allentown	346,310	3,859,097	71
LCCTA	Lancaster	254,491	1,681,004	35
LCTA	Wilkes-Barre	240,190	5,001,880	46
WMSPT	Williamsport	52,524	901,034	16

*Each system is publicly owned and the direct recipient of federal financial operating assistance. All are subject to the same state and federal regulations.

SOURCE: DENNIS F. MCCROSSON, "Choosing Performance Indicators for Small Transit Systems," *Transport. Eng.*, *48* (3), 27 (Mar. 1978).

vigorous education and enforcement activities may serve their objectives better than physical facilities.

Systematic planning can start by posing and answering the following questions:

1. What is needed now and in the future?
2. Where should bikeways be located?
3. When should bikeways be built?
4. Who should build them?
5. Who should finance them?

The process, which can best be conducted by local agencies, begins by identifying problems, such as accident locations, congestion, or unmet recreational travel demands, and then setting specific objectives. Estimates of potential bicycle usage should follow, derived from surveys of ex-

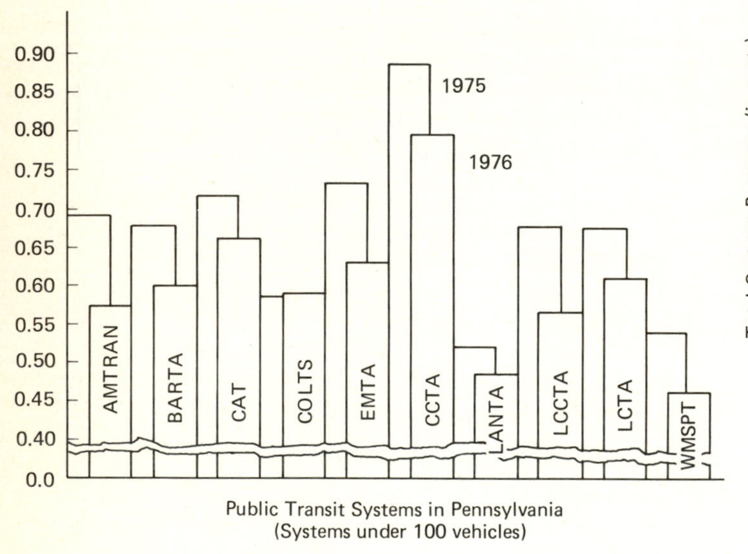

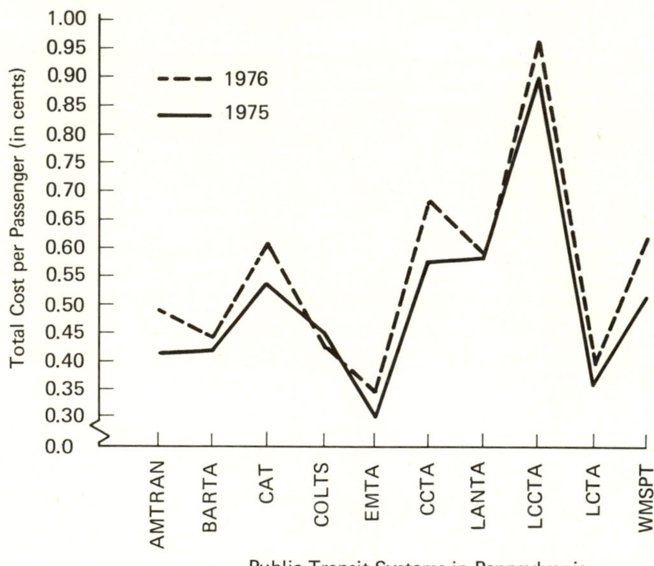

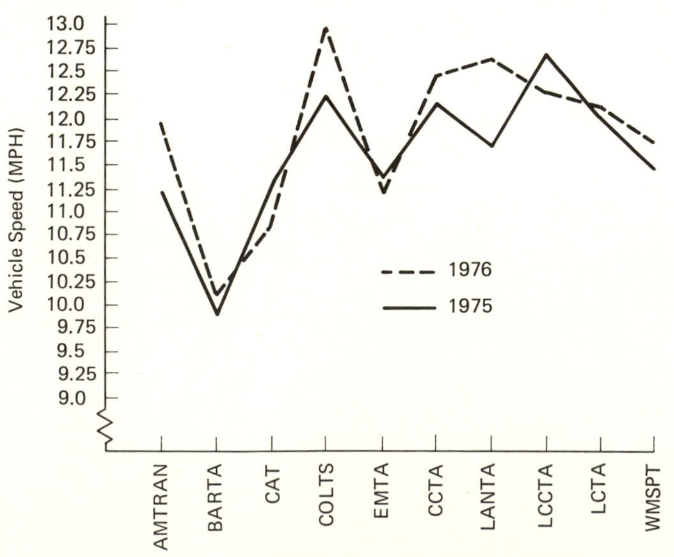

Figure 12.11. Performance characteristics of small transit systems in Pennsylvania. SOURCE: Dennis F. McCrosson, "Choosing Performance Indicators for Small Transit Systems," *Transportation Engineering*, 48(3), 26–30, March 1978.

isting facilities, trip generators, bicycle registration levels, public attitudes, and civic groups. Trip lengths, trip purposes, and other characteristics of potential users (such as age, occupation, etc.) will help determine the probable use of specific facilities.

A parallel step may be to prepare map overlays depicting both obstacles and opportunities. Obstacles may be terrain features (rivers, lakes, steep grades), busy highways, or other land-use impediments. Opportunities are parks, greenbelts, rights-of-way (utilities, railroads, highways) with adequate space for parallel routes, and favorable grades. Trip attractors for recreational or utilitarian (work, school, or shopping) trip making can be pinpointed. For later implementation and programming consideration, it may also be useful to depict planning districts or subareas where bikeway system elements can be planned to meet local needs. All such information leads to identification of suitable service corridors.

Experience shows the importance of certain location criteria. Selected alignments must be tested for their potential use, system connectivity, adequacy of facility width, safety aspects, grades and sight distance, and quality of pavement surfaces. Environmental quality appropriate to the type of expected usage is important. Directness to destinations will count more for utilitarian usage than will esthetic qualities of scenery or the noise and air pollution of high traffic corridors. On the other hand, separate facilities that avoid traffic and maximize pleasing scenic values are more important for recreational routes. Other general considerations are competing uses (vehicle–bicycle, pedestrian–bicycle, residential area–bicycle, etc.) and security. Bicycle paths separate from other facilities may encourage assaults on users.

The last and most essential considerations are costs and funding sources. Costs will depend primarily on the design characteristics, especially for off-street facilities. Funding may come from local, county, or state levels (depending possibly on how much support is generated through community involvement in the planning process) or perhaps even from the national government, depending on the location and primary purpose of the bikeway facilities.

Energy contingency planning. Metropolitan planning agencies are well situated to develop urban responses to energy shortages, especially when they concern transportation fuel supplies. The North Central Texas Council of Governments undertook such a study in *A Metropolitan Transportation Plan for National Energy Contingencies*.[29] Plan objectives were to develop locally effective short-range responses designed to be implementable within 3 months after a near-term supply interruption and to encourage voluntary rather than mandatory actions.

The study approach looked first at the impact of the 1973–1974 shortages on national and local transportation patterns. Based on then-current allocation and rationing contingencies, the study next outlined those regulations with greatest implications for the region's transportation and examined the problems they would cause. Strategies developed and evaluated as a result led to the following 11 recommendations:

1. Establish public transportation priorities in fuel allocation.
2. Maintain the present metropolitan carpool programs.
3. Expand or develop fuel storage capacity.
4. Designate a local energy coordinator.
5. Encourage flexible work hours.
6. Increase bus availability.
7. Modify state law to permit public use of school buses.
8. Investigate role of and impact of or on taxicabs in energy shortage.
9. Develop regional park-and-ride/exclusive lane plan.
10. Draft contingency agreements.
11. Begin intergovernmental dialogue regarding energy contingencies.

In concluding remarks, the study report noted: "While even the complete execution of these recommended strategies cannot guarantee that transportation problems will not occur in North Central Texas, they will equip the area with a preparedness which few other areas may have. It must be remembered that these are merely temporary short-term solutions to the energy problem. Future study should address the area of long-range implications in their policy decision and strive to implement them in conjunction with the continued growth of North Central Texas." The report led to early action on several of the recommendations, including those on transit fuel storage, enabling legislation for school bus usage, and taxi service studies.

Impact assessment surveys. Transportation planning bodies are likely to be involved in developing environmental impact statements for elements of a transportation plan. A starting point can be an overall survey of a plan's area-wide impacts, as the Pennsylvania Department of Transportation did for the Interim Plan Update of the Harrisburg Area Transportation Study.[30]

Beginning with source materials available from federal or state agencies, this evaluation identified the probable adverse impacts of individual projects. Impacts were classified as "probable" where a project corridor or alignment could involve property acquisition or clearly affect one of eight environmental parameters because of proximity. Impacts were classed as "possible" where the degree of encroachment or need for acquisition could not be determined from the reference materials. Results of the survey, measured against these parameters, are summarized in Table 12-6 on a project-by-project basis. For decision makers, the involved technician, or the interested layman the summary clearly identifies where further analysis may be needed and the types of assessment necessary. Similar reports were made on air quality and minority-group impacts.

The nature of detailed investigations is suggested by a

[29]*A Metropolitan Transportation Plan for National Energy Contingencies* (Arlington, Tex.: North Central Texas Council of Governments, 1977).

[30]*Interim Plan Update, Environmental Assessment, 1978* (Harrisburg, Pa.: Pennsylvania Department of Transportation, 1978).

TABLE 12–6
Survey of Potential Impacts of Highway Projects*

Project Description	Recreational Facilities	Agricultural Land	Woodland	Surface Water	Slopes	Floodplains	Historic Sites	Community Facilities†
I-83 widened to six lanes and reconstruct interchange, Simpson Ferry Road to Third Street, Lemoyne	○	—	—	—	—	—	—	—
I-83 South Bridge widened to six lanes and reconstuct interchanges, Third Street, Lemoyne to 19th Street, Harrisburg	—	—	—	●	—	●	—	—
I-83 safety improvements, signing, lighting from Fishing Creek Road to Simpson Ferry Rd.	—	—	—	—	—	—	—	—
Grade separated interchange at U.S. 15 and Winding Hill Road	—	—	—	—	—	—	—	—
Simpson Ferry widening, four-lane arterial upgrading from St. Johns Road to U.S. 15								●-S ○-FH ○-MU ●-CM
Clarks Ferry Bridge, four-lane relocation and approaches	○	—	—	●	—	●	—	—
I-81 Spur, two-lane freeway connecting U.S. 11 with I-81	○	●	●	○	●	○	○	○-S ●-S ○-FH ○-MU
Cameron Street improvements, upgrading between Dauphin and Paxton Streets	○					●		○-C ○-FH ●-S
PA 441, four-lane arterial upgrading from Paxton Street to 40th Street	●		●	○	○	○		○-MU
TR 39, two-lane upgrading from U.S. 22 south to West Hanover Township Line		●	○					○-FH ○-CM

*●, probable impact; ○ possible impact.
†MU, municipal building and sewage treatment plants; FH, fire houses and hospitals; S, schools; C, churches; CM, cemeteries.

SOURCE: *Interim Plan Update, Environmental Assessment, 1978*, (Harrisburg, Pa.: Pa. Department of Transportation, 1978).

list of eight requirements for impact studies given in NCHRP Report 156, *Transportation Decision Making: A Guide to Social and Environmental Considerations*.[31] The requirements are:

1. Indicate how particular interests are affected by transportation proposals.
2. Give as much importance to social, economic, and environmental impacts as to transportation impacts.
3. Document associated uncertainty.
4. Deal with qualitative information.
5. Be sensitive to people's perception of impacts.
6. Address indirect impacts.
7. Determine the time frame in which particular impacts are likely to occur.
8. Assign priorities to studies of particular impacts.

The interests that may be affected by a transportation decision could be people, institutions, or resources of many kinds. The variety of possible impacts that may occur is likely to be broad. Table 12-7 gives a checklist under seven broad headings: operational, activity distribution, monetary, social, environmental, aesthetic, and institutional impacts. Whether they are measured quantitatively or qualitatively, crudely or precisely, assessment of impacts is important in assuring a responsive planning process.

Middle-range planning

The varying character of urban transportation planning tasks makes it difficult to set arbitrary boundaries for short-, middle-, and long-range planning. The nature of the projects and their funding requirements, for example, may be the best determinants. The two types of activities identified here under middle-range planning are listed primarily because of their probable time to full implementation.

Transportation system management. In the last half of the 1970s, the term "transportation system management" (TSM) entered the transportation planner's vocabulary. Metropolitan planning organizations in the United States now prepare not only long-range "3C" plans, but also a "transportation systems management element." This element is aimed at using existing transportation facilities efficiently through traffic engineering, public transportation, regulatory, pricing, management, operational, and other improvements. Employment of these strategies has been formalized because of environmental considerations, public disenchantment with urban highway construction, capital shortages, new emphasis in transportation goals, and most recently, energy shortages.

As with other planning, the TSM process begins with identifying goals and objectives and concludes with programming of chosen strategies. Unlike long-range transportation planning, however, TSM planning is not capital-intensive. It can be as much concerned with modifying travel demand as with designing facilities to meet forecasted de-

[31]MARVIN L. MANHEIM ET AL., *Transportation Decision Making: A Guide to Social and Environmental Considerations,* NCHRP Report 156 (Washington, D.C.: Transportation Research Board, 1975), p. 65.

TABLE 12–7
Checklist of Impact Types

Operational Impacts

Network	Facility	Service by Mode		
		Accessibility	User	Goods
Network integration	Short-run operating conditions	Public services	Total trip speed	Goods distribution
System operation	Long-run operating conditions	Jobs	Travel time	Freight costs
Effect on arterial and local street systems	Relation to future technology plans and development	Recreation	Trip length	Delivery services
Safety	Safety	Commercial industry	Accident record	Terminal location and operation
	Modal coordination	Churches	Operating cost	
		Medical	Trip reliability	
		Shopping	Comfort, convenience, and other qualitative factors	
		Cultural	Level of service	
		Friends	Usage	
		Relatives	Parking	
		Social services		

Activity Distribution Impacts

Land Use		Development Type		Development Opportunities	
Parkland	Commercial	Population	Production	Joint development	Rezoning
Open space	Industrial	Employment	Markets	Short-term	Capital program
Residential	Institutional	Industry		Long-term	

Monetary Impacts

Agency Costs	User Costs	Neighborhood Costs	Community Costs	Displacee Costs
Right-of-way	Operating	Property values	Income	Replacement costs
Construction	Maintenance	Rents	Production value	Mortgages and investments
Auxiliary facilities	Parking	Assessments	Jobs	Rents
Replacement housing	Insurance	Taxes	Assessment, taxes	Title fees
Replacement of facilities	Accident	Pollution	Provision of services	Moving expenses
Maintenance	Time	Blight	Regional economy	Clientele loss or gain
Revenue sources	Fares	Accessibility		
Relocation services				
Cost of capital				

Social Impacts

Community Boundaries	Community Character	Community Function	Community Economy	Community Accessibility
Religious	Cohesion and stability	Safety	Housing supply	Church
School	Structure	Housing quality	Employment	School
Political ward	Identity	Public services	Land values	Entertainment
Ethnic district	Goals	Employment levels	Zoning	Friends
Neighborhood	Attitudes	Industrial and farming processes		Relatives
	Population composition	Pedestrian circulation		Shopping
				Recreation
				Parks
				Jobs
				Community services

Environmental Impacts

Effects of Traffic			Effects of Roadway Structure		
Air Pollution		Noise	Water	Natural Resources	
Real estate values	Mental depression	Psychological effects	Drainage	Animal life	Access to light
Material deterioration	Balance of nature	Ability to concentrate	Diversion	Animal migratory paths	Glare
Power demands	Dust	Sleep	Erosion	Plant life	Soils
		Nuisance	Access to light	Cultivated areas	Energy consumption
				Uncultivated areas	

Esthetic Impacts

View of the Facility		View from the Facility	Natural Beauty
Lighting	Architectural quality	Location	Open spaces
Dark areas	Image ability	Perception sequence	Greenery
Cold light	Dimensional balance	Design	Park system
Monotony	Beauty	Rhythm	Boulevards or gardens
Location	Orientation	Signing	Lakes
Obstruction of sunlight	Psychological barrier		Wildlife habitats
Change of air currents			
Visual barrier			

TABLE 12-7 (Continued.)

Institutional Impacts				
Administrative			Community	
Governmental		Private	Historical Sites	Cultural Sites
Budgets Revenues Commitments Priorities Laws Ordinances	By-laws Goals and programs (national defense, conservation, recreation, etc.) Regional access	Educational Religious Military Corporate Industrial		

SOURCE: MARVIN L. MANHEIM ET AL., *Transportation Decision-Making—A Guide to Social and Environmental Considerations*, NCHRP Report 156 (Washington, D.C.: Transportation Research Board, 1975), p. 67.

mands. Other unique aspects of TSM planning are its identification of multiple objectives and its assembly of diverse strategies into mutually supporting combinations. Figure 12.12 illustrates four sets of strategies, for example, grouped according to their influence on the supply and demand sides of the travel equation. The TSM actions in the right column reflect a wide range of possible actions. The impacts of different choices is shown in the illustration against an ordinate representing system disutility function (minutes per mile spent in travel), and an abscissa representing travel demand (vehicle-miles of travel). Curves of supply and demand for any system, with the demand curve sloping downward and supply curving upward, show system equilibrium at any time with their crossing point. The four segments labeled A through D show the general effects of applying to the prevailing equilibrium the similarly labeled strategy groups. For example, increasing system supply without modifying demand (shifting the supply curve to the right, strategy B) moves the equilibrium point down and to the right, indicating lower disutility and enhanced mobility. On the other hand, shrinking supply and reducing demand by applying strategy C serves to reduce travel, providing benefits of lower fuel consumption and lower pollutant production levels.

The cost effectiveness of applying different TSM tactics is given in Table 12-8, which relates predicted city-wide reductions in vehicle-miles or vehicle-hours of travel to the costs of achieving them. Costs range from a low of $0.01 per vehicle-mile for increased ride sharing to a high of $8.00

TSM Action class	Impact on: Highway supply	Automobile demand	Examples of TSM actions
A	—	Reduce	Encourage ridesharing Transit marketing Express bus/park-ride Transit route and schedule improvements Paratransit systems Bicycle and pedestrian facilities Pricing (transit fare reductions) Pricing (reduced taxes, tolls, fees, and fares for HOV's, or increases for autos) Work rescheduling (4-day week)
B	Enhance	—	General traffic engineering Freeway traffic management Truck restrictions and enhancements Work rescheduling (staggered hours and flexitime)
C	Degrade	Reduce	Preferential treatment for HOV's (take-a-lane) Auto restricted zones Parking supply reduction
D	Enhance	Reduce	Preferential treatment for HOV's (add-a-lane)

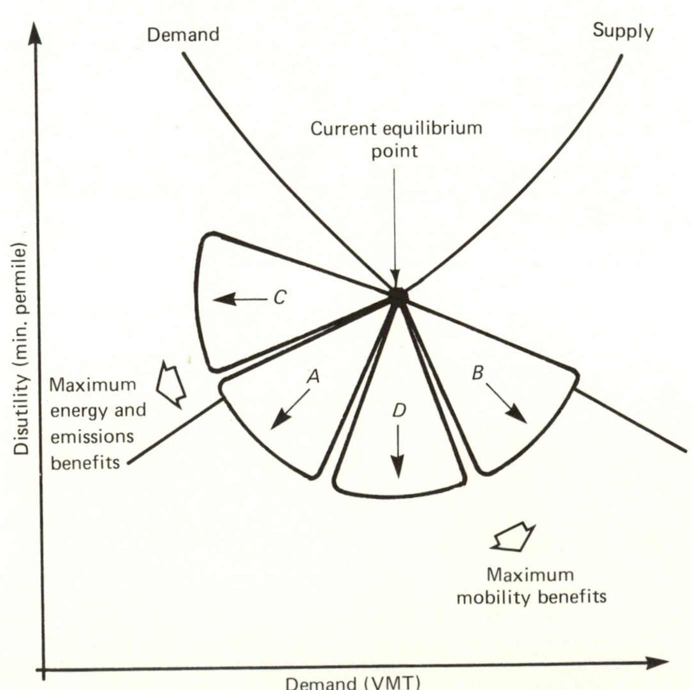

Figure 12.12. Equilibrium shifts from TSM actions. SOURCE: Fred A. Wagner and Keith Culbert, *TSM: An Assessment of Imports*, Washington, D.C.: Urban Mass Transportation Administration, 1978, pp. 7, 8.

TABLE 12–8
Cost Effectiveness of Selected TSM Programs*

TSM Action	Areawide Percent Reduction: VMT	Areawide Percent Reduction: Travel Time	Annual Cost	Cost per: VMT Reduced	Cost per: VHT Reduced
Ridesharing					
Current program	0.2		$200,000	2 cents	
Expanded program	1.0		$400,000	1 cent	
Express bus	0.3		$5–7 million	40 cents	
Local bus (50% increase)	0.3		$6–5 million	43 cents	
Work rescheduling		0.4	$200,000		25 cents
Signal timing optimization		6.0	$250,000		2 cents
Computerized traffic control		1.5	$800,000		27 cents
Freeway surveillance and control		0.5	$1 million		$1.00
Truck restrictions/ enhancements		0.2	$200,000		50 cents
Comprehensive preferential treatments	0.1	(+0.4 increase)	$800,000	16 cents	(VHT increase)
Exclusive HOV lanes	0.1	0.4	$5–8 million	$1.30	$8.00

*Base conditions for urban area of 1 million: annual VMT ≃ 5000 million (VMT, vehicle miles of travel); annual VHT ≃ 200 million (VHT, vehicle hours of travel).

SOURCE: FRED A. WAGNER AND KEITH GILBERT, *Transportation System Management: An Assessment of Impacts* (Washington, D.C.: Urban Mass Transportation Administration, 1978), p. 37.

per vehicle-hour of time saved by providing exclusive lanes for high-occupancy vehicles.

The value of forming combinations of solutions is supported by conclusions from another study. "If there is a recommended course of action . . . it would emphasize the potential cost effectiveness of a package of TSM measures that combines preferential entry [to freeways], carpool matching, time-of-day pricing, variable working hours, and the procurement of paratransit services through competitive bidding. These actions appear to be mutually reinforcing opportunities to make use of slack or underutilized capacity—in the shoulder period of the peak, in the local road system, and in equipment of private taxi and charter-bus operators."[32]

[32]DAVID W. JONES, JR., AND EDWARD C. SULLIVAN, "TSM: Tinkering Superficially at the Margin," *Transport. Eng. J.*, *104*(TE6), 832 (1978).

As a planning process, TSM is still evolving; as implemented programs, TSM activities are largely unevaluated. Funding for both planning and implementation is available, but institutional problems can arise in getting projects implemented by different agencies within each community. One reason for taking TSM out of the short-range category and presenting it here as a middle-range planning activity is the likely time to complete implementation of projects.

Air quality planning projects. In the United States in the late 1970s, the passage of the Clean Air Act required the U.S. Environmental Protection Agency and the U.S. Department of Transportation to prepare and issue transportation–air quality planning guidelines. These guidelines were designed to assist local agencies in developing transportation system components for plans aimed at eliminating excessive photo-chemical oxidants and/or carbon monoxide. They described an "acceptable planning process . . . that must result in the expeditious development and implementation of all reasonably available measures . . . determined through an analytical, participatory and negotiatory process."[33] In most areas, metropolitan planning organizations were designated as the lead agencies in establishing programs.

An example of the resultant planning effort is reported in *Selected Estimates of Effects of Strategies to Control Air Quality*.[34] This study examined the effect on auto-travel demand of gasoline tax increases, transit fare reductions, cutbacks in off-street parking space, and termination of commuter discounts at Hudson River toll facilities. The emissions benefits were then derived by modeling.

The results are summarized in Table 12-9, which shows how increasing the gasoline tax affects suburban more than city travel, while a 40% cut in transit fares has precisely the opposite regional impact. Changing commuter toll rates has little traffic impact at all, but restricting off-street park-

[33]*Transportation—Air Quality Planning Guidelines* (Washington, D.C.: U.S. Environmental Protection Agency and U.S. Department of Transportation, June 1978).

[34]*Selected Estimates of Effects of Strategies to Control Air Quality*, Interim Tech. Report 2405 (New York: Tri-State Regional Planning Commission, Nov. 1978).

TABLE 12–9
Air Quality Impacts of Selected Traffic Strategies

Strategy	Percent Change: Vehicle Miles of Travel: N.Y. City	Suburbs	Total	Hydrocarbons and Carbon Monoxide: N.Y. City	Suburbs	Total
Gas tax increase						
10 cents	−1.2	−2.6	−2.1	−1.7	−3.1	−2.7
30 cents	−3.8	−7.9	−6.3	−5.3	−9.5	−8.2
Transit fare cut, 40%	−6.7	−0.4	−2.7	−9.4	−0.5	−3.5
Elimination of toll discounts, Hudson River crossings	−0.4	—	—	−0.6	—	—
Off-street parking reductions						
15% CBD cut	−2.9	—	—	−2.9 to 4.1	—	—
25% CBD cut	−4.1			−4.1 to 5.7		
35% CBD cut	−8.0	—	—	−8.0 to 11.2	—	—
Truck retrofit program	—	—	—	−8.2 (HC) −18.7 (CO)	−5.6 (HC) −13.7 (HC)	−6.7 (HC) −15.9 (HC)

SOURCE: Adapted from Table 13, *Selected Estimates of Effects of Strategies to Control Air Quality*, Interim Tech. Report 2405 (New York: Tri-State Regional Planning Commission, Nov. 1978).

ing is shown to bring about the largest reduction in travel, during off-peak hours.

A mobile source emissions model applied to the predicted travel demands produced estimates of changes in the levels of hydrocarbons and carbon monoxide. This part of the table also shows the effect on emissions projected to result from a truck retrofit program. Not surprisingly, the most effective measures are transit fare reductions, off-street parking limitations, and the truck retrofit program. The summary of the report stresses that these results are only part of the picture; they do not represent all the impacts of the selected strategies. For instance, although the truck retrofit program could produce major benefits by 1987, its implementation depends heavily on physical, economic, and political feasibility.

Long-range planning

Objectives and approaches. The fundamental objective of the long-range urban transportation study is to develop a transportation plan serving the community of the future. Definitions of a plan may vary. Some plans may include parking and terminal recommendations with proposals for new transit and highway facilities. Some single-mode plans may include "immediate action" programs for arterial improvements, together with 20-year or even longer-range freeway development plans. Some may detail precise highway locations with pinpointed ramp connections. Others may deal only in "corridors" and undetermined alignments.

Generally, the long-range studies do not concern precise locations or precise answers for design-hour volumes as much as the density and configuration of future freeway, arterial, and transit systems. Such plans scale—in mileage, construction cost, and environmental impacts—the facilities required to meet the travel expectations of a future population.

The approach is through systems analysis: studying the behavior of separate systems and the interactions between them. Thus, the influence of land-use alternatives on transportation solutions and the effect of different transportation alternatives on urban development patterns may be equally important. The total analysis framework includes consideration of two subsystems, person transport and goods transport, even though historically the latter has not received much attention. In each subsystem, studying passenger vehicle movement and storage (parking) and goods movement and storage (truck transfer and terminal facilities) may require analysis of the services, influences, and costs of several different transport modes.

Long-range studies in developing countries. At this time, the greatest need and greatest applicability for long-range urban transportation studies appears to be in the developing nations of the world. In these nations, population growth and urban migration rates together force growth on cities already medium-sized to large. The resultant pressures require all kinds of public services to augment presently inadequate facilities. Although transportation services may not be the greatest need, they must be provided if employment and other vital social and public health needs are to be met. Thus, transportation planning is essential. It may follow conventional forms in some respects, although departures will occur from the techniques applied in industrialized nations. One recent study exemplifies the problems and shows the parallels.

New Town Planning. Sadat City will be a new industrial center west of the Nile Delta in Egypt, designed and developed to meet the following two goals (representative perhaps for many nations): to bring about population redistribution from crowded urban centers and to develop large-scale industrialization. Designing for a target population of 500,000 in the year 2000 and projections of substantial manufacturing activity in metallurgical, textile, and transportation industries, a team of consultants developed land-use and transportation plans. Transportation objectives—to minimize travel needs and to provide efficient and high levels of service—were to be achieved by high-density land-use development and emphasis on public transport.

The transportation plan that evolved in conjunction with the land-use development plan considers the location of major industries and access to external transportation facilities (highway, rail, and canal) as well as the objectives of minimizing travel while making it efficient. A concept of "hierarchical spines" has emerged, providing maximum accessibility through an interconnected network of public transportation, pedestrian, and bicycle facilities. Buses operating on exclusive rights-of-way are the primary transportation service, because public transportation should serve nearly two-thirds of all trip making. In contrast to Western cities, private vehicles will accommodate less than one-fifth of total travel.

The planning process used to evaluate the plan is shown in Figure 12.13. The essential feature is the use of default values within the four-step process. Definition of 45 traffic zones and their forecast population and employment levels came first, followed by trip productions and attractions by modes using relationships derived from a transportation study in nearby Cairo. These included such factors as modal split, percent of trips in peak hours, percent of population employed, and absenteeism rates. Next, a form of gravity model using calibration constants based on previous models used in two other Egyptian cities provided the zone-to-zone distribution of private vehicle and public transport trips. Relationships between income and car ownership in Cairo and projections of income to the target year produced the modal split estimates. They next were modified at the zone level by considering walk trip possibilities and the proposed high quality of bus service. Some of the resulting forecast figures were as follows:

Target-year car ownership: 50 per 1000 population

Total person-trips by public transport: 63%

Total person-trips by private vehicle: 17%

Total person-trips by pedestrian and bicycle: 20%

An all-or-nothing minimum-time-path procedure with no capacity restraints assigned trips to the designated street and transit networks. Figure 12.14 shows the resulting loadings on the three levels of facilities in the total transit system. External trips, derived from separate forecasts, were man-

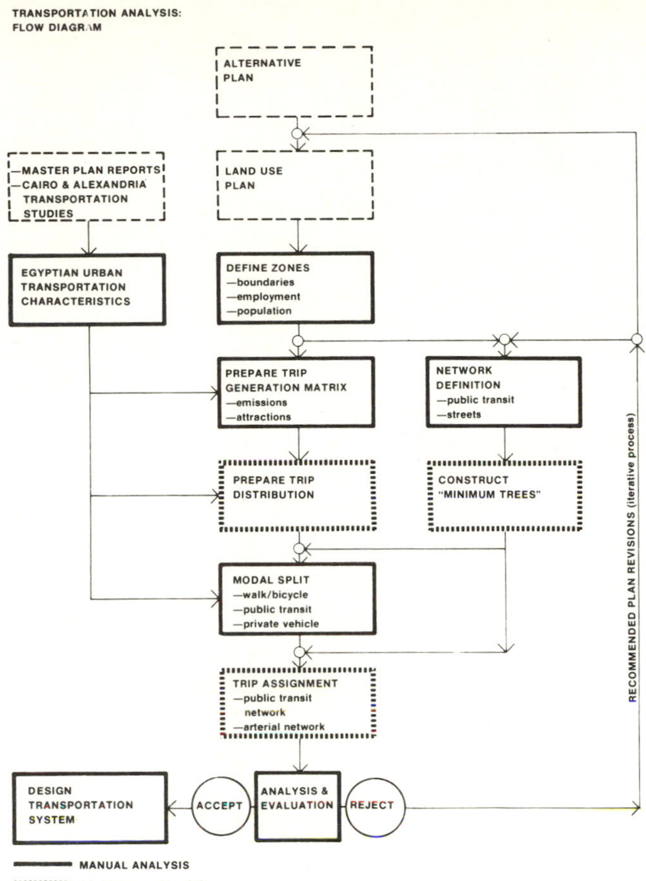

Figure 12.13. Flow diagram for transportation analysis, Sadat City, Egypt. SOURCE: Ronald E. Tadross, "Travel Forecasting: Sadat City, Egypt New Town," *ITE Journal*, 48(9), Sept. 1978.

ually assigned to paths connecting them to internal origins and destinations calculated according to employment distribution.

Two unusual features of the transportation planning work for Sadat City, besides the spine form of development and reliance on exclusive busways, are the special provisions to segregate animal-drawn vehicles from motorized traffic and the fact that development frontage will not be allowed on arterial streets. Because the highest two-way traffic volume is 1600 passenger car equivalents per hour, only three grade separations are necessary in the city, at points where major arterials cross the central busway and pedestrian mall.

Comprehensive Transport Study. A long-range transportation planning study done by Wilbur Smith & Associates for the Hong Kong Public Works Department[35] shows how the urban transportation planning process deals with the unique characteristics of a large and heavily urbanized community. This study produced a report of over 400 pages, 150 tables, and 100 figures, which collectively describe the data, analyses, forecasts, alternatives, and recommendations for a plan to meet the 1991 transport needs of the region. Excerpts here emphasize the public transport aspects of the plan.

1. *Background*. Hong Kong has a total area of 1044 km^2 supporting a population of over 4,000,000, with 80% of that population concentrated in the 129-km^2 area of Hong Kong Island, Kowloon, and New Kowloon. In 1973, one-seventh (118,000) of all households had a car available for personal use, thus making public transport the dominant form of travel. The magnitude of travel shows in the following estimates of annual journeys in 1974: a total of 2.25 *billion* trips, less than 10% of which were in private cars, nearly 2 billion of which (87%) were made on public transport. Figure 12.15 suggests the volume and diversity of this travel, which with increasing population and increasing incomes, continues to grow.

2. *Study surveys and inventories*. While previous studies provided some data bases, the most recent study included a survey of 25,000 households. Other data bases came from surveys of goods vehicle movement, cross-harbor screenlines, taxis, and transient visitors. Annual traffic counts, road network inventories, transit, and travel-time studies provided additional information. Historical data revealed the growth in registered vehicles from 17.1 in 1961 to 45.5 vehicles per 1000 persons in 1974. Table 12-10 summarizes and compares selected travel characteristics of Hong Kong and other cities.

3. *Transport demand models and projections*. The modal diversity and complications of geography in Hong Kong call for a complex array of models to analyze present travel and prepare projections. Figure 12.16 shows the relationships among data inputs, analytical steps, and the 15 resulting models. The interactance or gravity model, which requires development and validation of several parameters, is essential to the trip distribution. As well as reflecting the usually differing characteristics of trip making according to trip purpose and mode, the Hong Kong models also had to account for different trip-length distributions of three distinct groups of trips: those on Hong Kong Island, those on the mainland, and cross-harbor trips. The patterns shown here in Figure 12.17 also demonstrate how closely the calibrated models reproduced the observed trip distribution.

Beginning with 1991 population estimates of 5,850,000, three land-use alternatives reflecting possible policy choices, and densities and employment distribution assumptions combined with household income and school student forecasts, the 1991 forecasts of trip generation, modal split, goods vehicle movement, and generalized corridor travel demands were made. Total Hong Kong trip making, growing from 1.32 to 1.49 daily person-trips, will reach a total of 8,730,400 daily trips.

4. *Alternative transport policies and plans*. When it is unlikely that the stock of physical facilities can be increased to meet an unrestrained growth in private car travel demand and where, as a result, public transport use must be encouraged, transportation planning must consider policy choices that affect travel demand as well as those that affect facility supply. Thus, the Hong Kong study exhibits a variety of policies to restrain usage of private vehicles and encourage transit usage. The study reached these conclusions:

[35]*Hong Kong Comprehensive Transport Study*, prepared for the Hong Kong Government by Wilbur Smith & Associates (Columbia, S.C.: 1976).

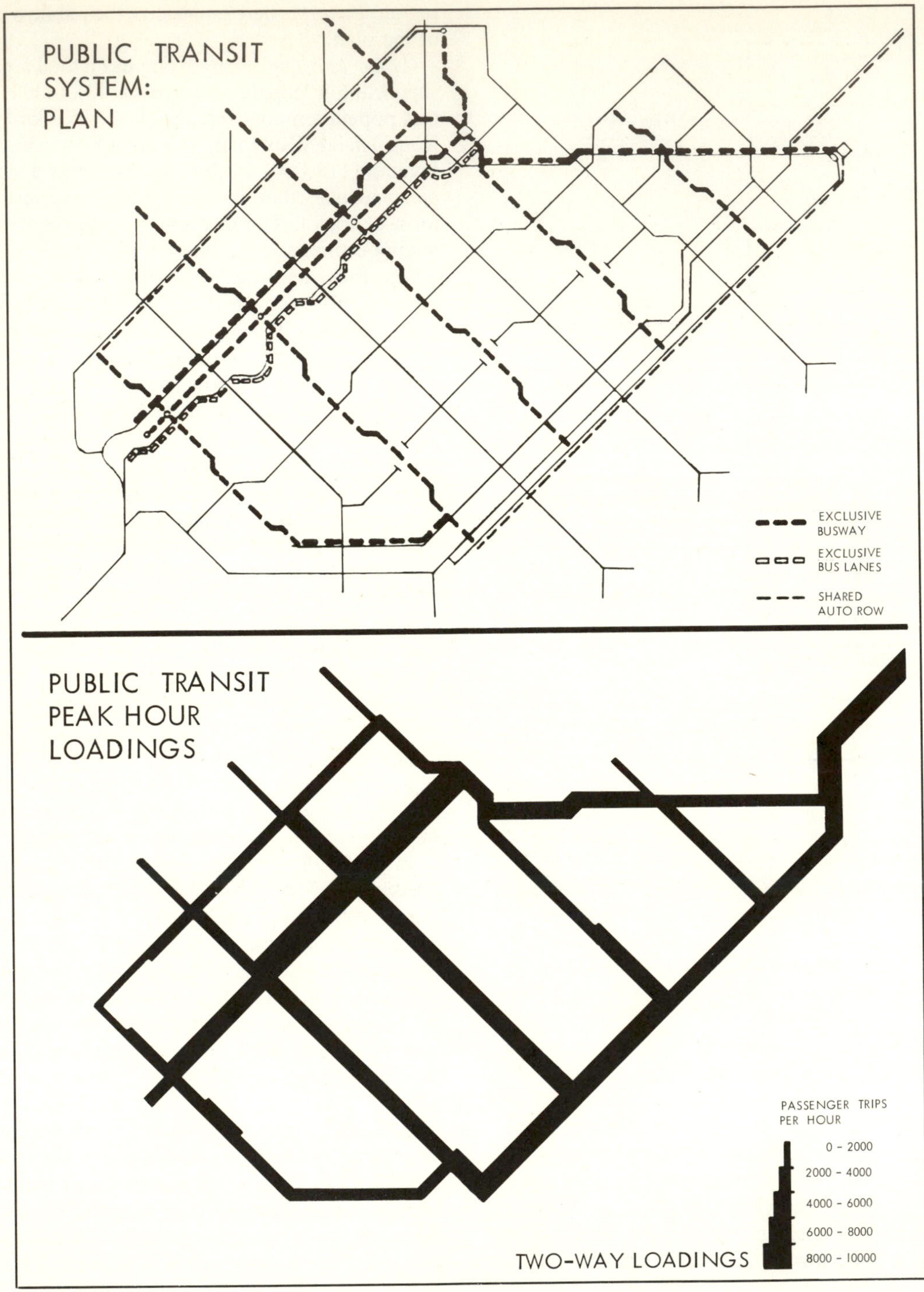

Figure 12.14. Public transit system, Sadat City: plans and peak-hour loadings. SOURCE: P.C. Byrne, R.E. Tadross, and S. Grove, "Sadat City" (unpublished).

1. Although road pricing and area licensing (the Singapore approach) offer advantages, they were not yet sufficiently proved to be investigated further for this study.
2. Fuel taxes and toll systems were not adopted because of their general rather than specific impacts and the space needs for toll plazas, respectively.
3. Ownership restraints through garaging control were seen as a localized rather than general method for limiting car ownership. Licensing fees were seen as a suitable restraint.
4. Usage restraint could be achieved through parking charges and taxi fee structures.
5. Unlike Western cities, no encouragement through adjusted or unified fare structures is necessary to divert auto drivers to public transport or to obtain balance between alternative transit modes.

Figure 12.15. Multiple modes of travel in Hong Kong. SOURCE: Wilbur Smith & Associates, *Hong Kong Comprehensive Transport Study,* Columbia, S.C., 1976.

6. Special studies would be needed to balance fare structures between existing systems and the proposed rail transit facility.

In the area of physical facilities, the plan designated three transport system alternatives. All include the current or committed facilities, including new rail transit (Metro). Variations between alternatives occur in the extents of the commuter rail (Metro) and tram (light rail) networks, ferry systems, and highway improvements. Bus and public light bus (PLB) networks are largely similar for all three alternatives. Total estimated construction costs range between \$11 and \$15 billion, with costs roughly split evenly between Metro and roads in the lowest-cost system, and costs split 2:1 favoring rail systems in the highest-cost system.

5. *Plan evaluations and recommendations.* The study tested plan alternatives by travel model and network assignment techniques, presenting detailed results in the re-

TABLE 12–10
Summary of Travel Characteristics in Selected Areas

Survey Area	Survey Year	Population	Persons/ Household	Cars/ 1000 Persons	Total Trips/ Person	Car Trips/ Person	Modal Split* (%)	Average Car Occupancy
Hong Kong	1973	4,191,100	4.66	30	1.27	0.19	73	1.56
Singapore	1968	1,537,000	5.93	41	1.11	0.20	52	1.66
Kuala Lumpur	1973	913,000	5.82	72	1.76	0.49	37	1.63
London	1971	8,372,000	2.84	225	1.50	0.88	41	1.27
Copenhagen	1967	1,107,000	2.63	185	1.64	0.77	31	1.34

*Public transport trips as a percentage of total trips.

SOURCE: WILBUR SMITH & ASSOCIATES, *Hong Kong Comprehensive Transport Study* (Columbia, S.C.: 1976), p. 72.

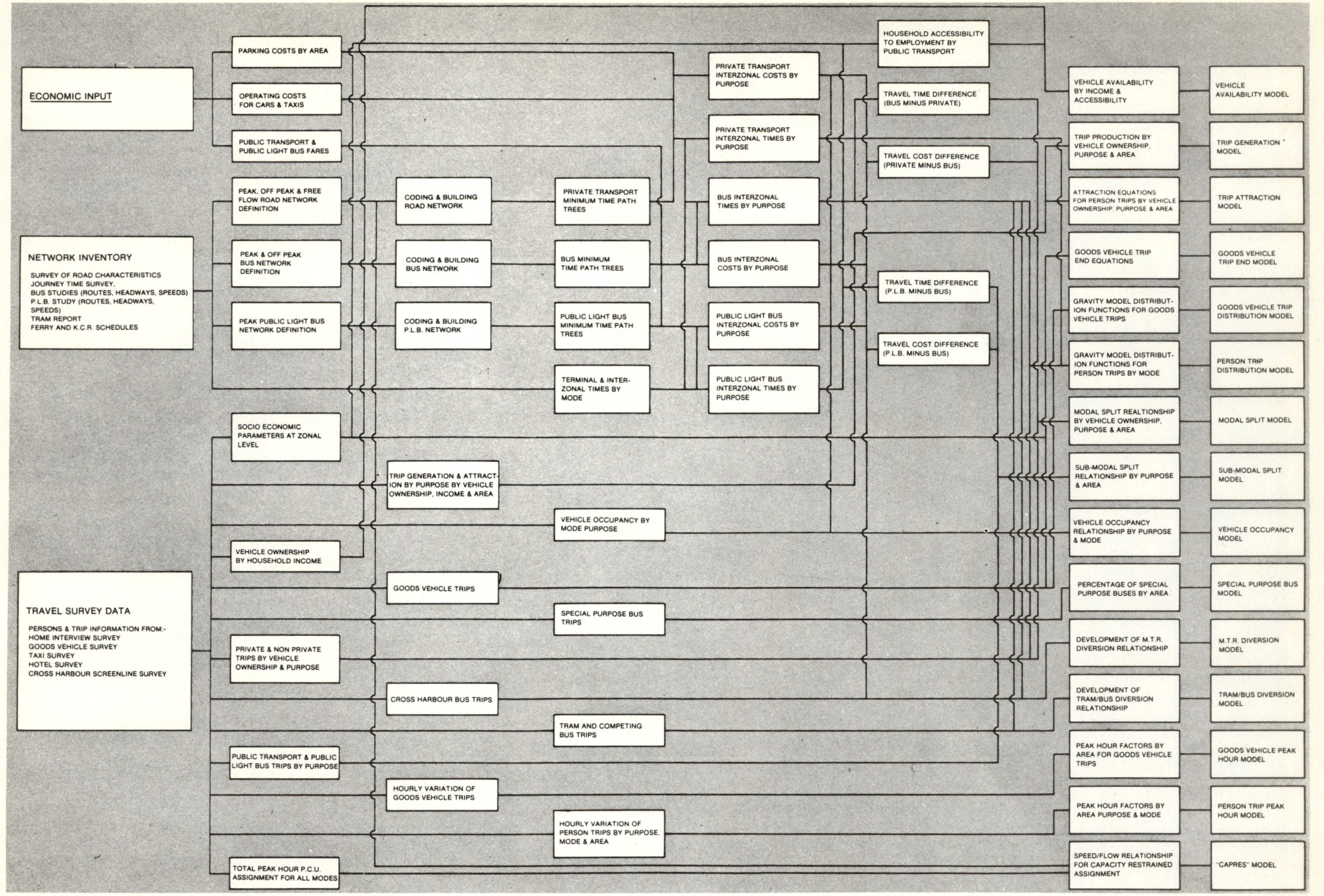

Figure 12.16. Transportation planning methodology, Hong Kong. SOURCE: Wilbur Smith & Associates, *Hong Kong Comprehensive Transport Study*, Columbia, S.C., 1976.

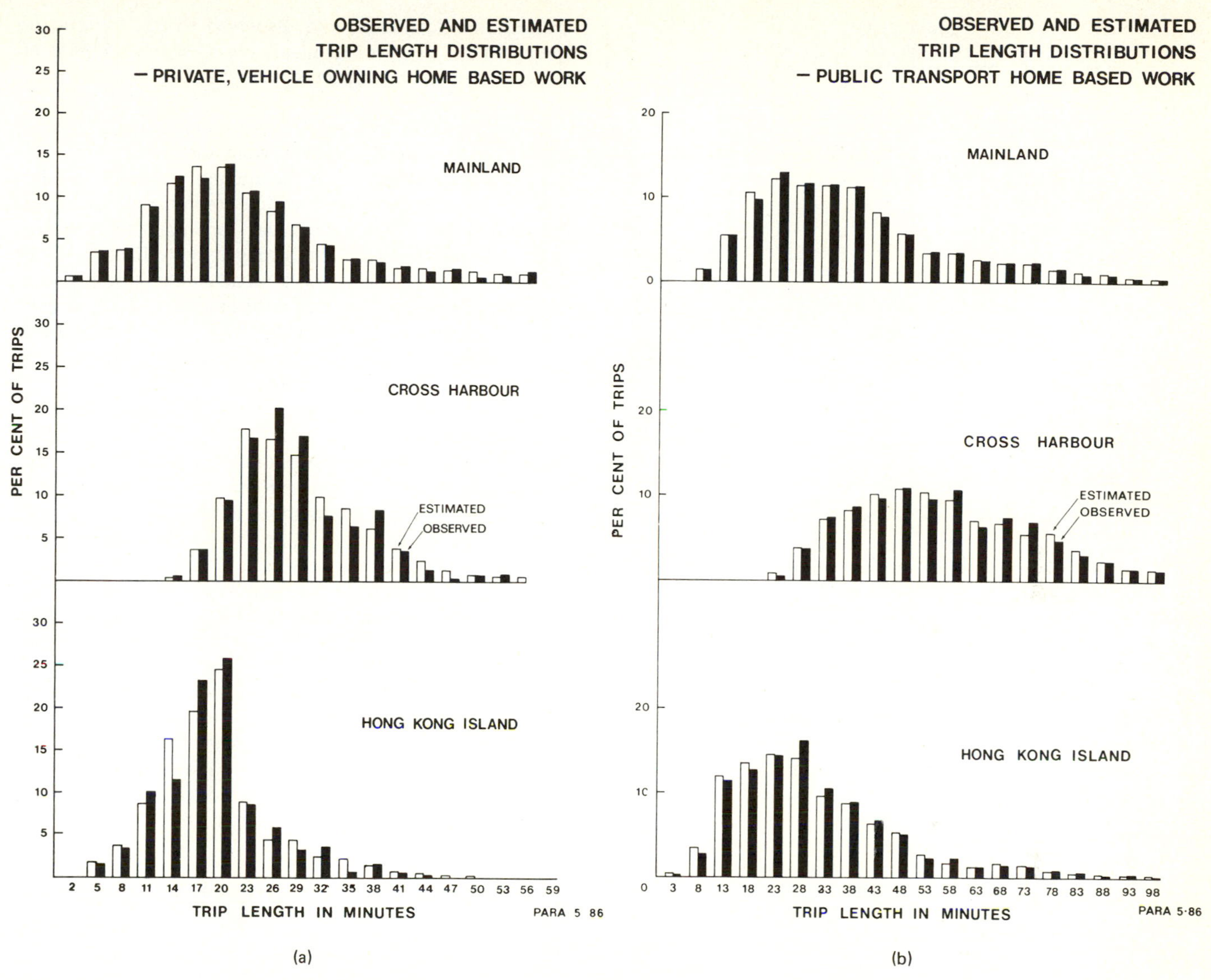

Figure 12.17. Observed and estimated trip length distributions: (a) private; vehicle owning, home based work; (b) public transport, home based work. SOURCE: Wilbur Smith & Associates, *Hong Kong Comprehensive Transport Study,* Columbia, S.C., 1976.

port. The example in Table 12-11 illustrates resulting volumes of passengers, passenger- and vehicle-kilometers, vehicle speeds, and revenues for three major modes. Other tables show the effects of vehicle restraint policies; for example, a combination of high taxi and parking charges should cut 1991 daily private vehicle trips from 1,404,600 to 1,236,200, 12% below the trip-making level associated with low taxi and parking charges.

To hold down the growth in private travel while recommending heavy investment in both road and rail transit facilities, the study report recommends private vehicle restraint programs (relying on increases in license fees, parking, and taxi fees). Even with big capital investments, though: "Buses will continue to be the principal means of public transport in the future as they have been in the past. Rail and ferry services cannot be expected to meet completely the varied needs of the traveling public. Along with PLBs, buses can provide the flexibility in route structures and operating characteristics vital to an ever-changing environment."

Long-range studies in North America. The recent thrust of transportation planning in the mature, auto-oriented large cities of North America is well illustrated by *Choices for the Future,* a summary report on the review of transportation plans for metropolitan Toronto, Canada.[36] This report not only discusses long-range planning activities but also shows how planning organizations must nowadays be as much concerned with short-term and special project planning.

[36] *Choices for the Future—Summary Report* (Toronto: Metropolitan Toronto Transportation Plan Review, Jan. 1975).

TABLE 12–11
Summary Statistics for Buses, PLBs, and Ferries in 1991*

Item	Buses	PLBs†	Ferries
Operations			
Number of vehicles‡	2221	1751	114
Annual vehicle-kilometers ($\times 10^9$)§	162.7	193.2	117.6
Annual vehicle-hours ($\times 10^3$)§	9842	8605	574
Average speed (km/h)§	16.5	22.5	20.5
Ridership			
Annual passengers ($\times 10^9$)	1344	308	213
Passengers/vehicle-kilometer	8.3	1.6	18.1
Annual rides/capita	230	53	36
Revenue			
Annual cash fare revenue ($\$ \times 10^9$)	947	534	328
Average fare/passenger (cents)	70	173	155
Gross revenue/vehicle ($\$ \times 10^3$)	426	305	2880
Gross revenue/vehicle-kilometer ($)	5.82	2.76	27.91
Gross revenue/vehicle-hour ($)	96	62	572

*Daily values multiplied by 355 to obtain annual totals. Assumes 1991 System 3.
†PLBs are 14-passenger public light buses, licensed but unregulated, most of which operate on established routes.
‡Vehicles include a 10% allowance for PLB and ferry spares and an 18% allowance for buses.
§Includes layover, deadheading, garage, and charter times and distances for buses, and layover and dead time for ferries.

SOURCE: WILBUR SMITH & ASSOCIATES, *Hong Kong Comprehensive Transport Study* (Columbia, S.C.: 1978), p. 237.

Studies in the 1960s had led to the adoption in 1966 of a long-range transportation plan for metropolitan Toronto. Since then, much of the transit system had been constructed, but several links in the expressway system had been canceled. With questions arising about the plan's continuing validity, a Plan Review Body was established in 1972 to explore the plan's strengths and weaknesses. The Plan's Review Body set four objectives:

1. To develop feasible land-use and transportation alternatives for 1981 and 2000, with explanation of their implications.
2. To provide analysis and information with respect to those elements of the 1966 Plan for which irrevocable decisions have not already been made.
3. To make recommendations for possible short-term improvements to the existing transportation system.
4. To develop a continuous planning process incorporating public participation.

Funding for the review came from the provincial government (75%) and the Metropolitan Toronto Planning Board (25%). An appointed study director hired staff in addition to other staff appointed to the study by these two agencies. Over a 2½-year period, the study operated under the general direction of a technical committee, preparing and publishing a total of 58 reports on different phases of the work. Throughout, communication with the public and civic groups was highly important to "air the issues surrounding transportation decisions" and to obtain perspectives on community views.

For the long-range planning studies the project developed a series of transportation and land-use alternatives. Six transportation systems were made up from combinations of four elements: freeways, intermediate-capacity transit systems (ICTS), commuter rail, and special services. Fourteen land-use alternatives were posed under several classes of centralized, multicentered, and dispersed forms. Criteria for testing included travel demand, costs, socioeconomic effects, environmental impact, development effects, and phasing.

Based on the criteria, preferred combinations of land use and transportation alternatives were identified. The summary report emphasizes that "no attempt was made to select a single transportation and land use combination as the best choice." However, the study did conclude that the most likely alternatives were the strongly centralized and one involving some central growth but also extending low-density suburban areas (first and third in Table 12-12, respectively). In each case, the transportation alternative best balanced across the four facility types appeared most desirable to follow.

The Plan Review also covers short-term improvements, considering the following options: dial-a-bus, transportation for handicapped, staggered work hours, carpooling, express bus service, and restrictions on auto use. With respect to the last, the reports recommended against such restrictions until the consequences could be thoroughly analyzed. On the other hand, carpooling was favorably recommended, based on studies of various schemes listed in Table 12-13.

In addition to both long-term considerations and what could be called TSM elements, the study examined special problems involving major facilities and selected regions in the metropolitan area. Recommendations were offered regarding specific and general arterial street expansions, specific extensions or additions to rail transit systems, treatment of terminal facilities, the relation of central area employment and transit needs, and the general needs for street and highway improvement in the northwestern sector of Toronto.

Management of urban transportation planning

Every city must house the activity of urban transportation planning in some part of its government structure, and a variety of organizational and administrative arrangements has developed in the United States. Generally, ad hoc, semiindependent staffs, or regional planning commissions or councils of government, and occasionally contract study organizations manage the function, although in the 1960s state agencies were sometimes involved. In the late 1970s, largely as a result of federal legislation, the range has narrowed and regional planning agencies usually carry out the role. This section describes alternative organizational structures and appropriate administrative procedures.

Organizational arrangements

No single form of structure connected to any particular groupings of planning agencies can be prescribed as the one right way to organize the transportation planning process. The form should be determined according to local community needs for both planning and plan implementation.

Housing the process. In general, the organization should be such as to bring together community leaders,

TABLE 12–12
Summary of Preferred Land-Use and Transportation Combinations and Related Decisions

Development Objective	Preferred Combination	Description	Land-Use Strategies	Supporting Transportation Elements
Centralization	M3	Highest level of central area growth	Oppose development controls in the central area Support full-scale development of Metro Centre Centralize government functions	Modest expansion of GO Transit to Streetsville and Richmond Hill; increased capacity of Lakeshore GO Eglinton Transit Allendale and Don Mills high-capacity transit Scarborough Town Centre/Malvern ICTS Road improvements in the Northwest Major Metro Centre Transportation Terminal Don Valley Parkway Extension
Bi-nodal	06	Downsview Airport, major center	Support development controls in the Central Area Prepare proposals for the development of the Downsview Airport site Locate Metro offices in Downsview	Modest expansion of GO Transit to Streetsville and Richmond Hill; modest increase in capacity of Lakeshore GO Sheppard/Wilson Transit Scarborough Town Centre/Malvern ICTS Road improvements in the Northwest Highway 407 Spadina Expressway extension to Highway 407
Subcenter	D3	Subregional centers at North York, Mississauga, and Oshawa Several local centers	Support development controls in the Central Area Support high-density development at sites with good transit access Decentralize government functions	Modest expansion of GO Transit to Streetsville and Richmond Hill; modest increase in capacity of Lakeshore GO Eglinton Transit Scarborough Town Centre/Malvern ICTS Road improvements in the Northwest Highway 403 As per D3 except for Highway 403
Corridor development	G2	Eglinton Development Corridor	Support development controls in the central area	
	F1	Lakeshore Development Corridor	Support development controls in the central area	As per D3 plus Major capacity increase of Lakeshore GO (possible electrification) Major Metro Centre Transportation Terminal
Metro dispersion	C3	Toronto Centered Region concept with minor adjustments	Support development controls in the central area Support intensive use of commercial and industrial areas of Scarborough Oppose high-density redevelopment	As per D3 plus Support more regional freeways
Regional dispersion	L3	Decentralization with development in Highway 407 corridor	Support development controls in the Central Area Discourage extensive residential redevelopment in Metro	As per D3 plus Support early construction of Highway 407 Don Valley Parkway Extension Spadina Expressway Extension to Highway 407

SOURCE: *Choices for the Future* (Toronto: Metropolitan Toronto Transportation Plan Review, Jan. 1975), Table 4.1.

planning staffs, and those agencies charged with plan implementation and facility operation. One recent survey of transportation planning agencies for large metropolitan areas found it useful to classify the organizations in the following four types:

1. Multifunction implementing agency (i.e., concerned with all planning activities and typically carrying out all metropolitan planning organization functions).
2. Multifunction advisory agency (i.e., concerned with broad planning but not usually with the funding of improvements).
3. Single-function implementing agency (i.e., concerned not only with transportation planning but also with plan implementation).
4. Single-function advisory agency (i.e., a transportation planning agency with no implementing authority).[37]

In smaller cities, the transportation planning process may not be formalized to the extent of being even permanently

[37]JERRY L. EDWARDS AND EDWARD A. BEIMBORN, "Future Relationships Between Long- and Short-Range Urban Transportation Planning," *Traffic Quart.*, *32*(4), 531–544 (Oct. 1978).

TABLE 12–13
Carpooling Schemes

Type	Implementable by Government	Implementable by Private Employers
Incentive in nature	Priority lanes and roads for carpools Carpool matching service Advertising and promotion Development of promotional programs for employers Relatively low-priced parking for carpools in municipal parking lots Income tax relief to participants in carpools*	Reduced rate/no-charge parking for carpools Preferential parking location Carpool matching service Time allotment for meetings to arrange pools Supply of pool vehicles Flexibility in hours of work
Restrictive in nature	Road prohibitions and restrictions to non-carpool vehicles Higher-priced parking for nonpool vehicles in municipal lots Regulation of parking rate structure in commercial parking lots to favor carpools Regulations to discourage employers providing unlimited free or low-cost parking Gasoline rationing*	Higher parking rates for nonpool vehicles Limited supply of parking spaces

*Not applicable at the local level.

SOURCE: *Choices for the Future* (Toronto: Metropolitan Toronto Transportation Plan Review, Jan. 1975).

staffed; instead, it may be assigned to an existing agency, perhaps even to only one staff member.

Structuring the process. Several means bring direction and guidance from interested parties into the planning process. Most commonly, four groups of participants are established: policy guidance, technical guidance, study staff, and citizens' advisory groups. Interactions among the four may vary, as Figure 12.18 illustrates.

Policy Guidance. Typically provided through a committee holding regular meetings, policy guidance should come from the following groups or their representatives: local elected officials, the state transportation agency, executives of local transportation and planning agencies.

The function of a policy committee has been described as carrying out the following actions:[38]

- Designate agencies, firms, or persons to carry out urban transportation planning responsibilities.
- Administer or delegate the administration of urban planning program.
- Review and adopt the program.
- Determine funding for the program.

[38]U.S. Federal Highway Administration. "Transportation Planning for your Community; The Manager's Guide for Developing a Planning Program."

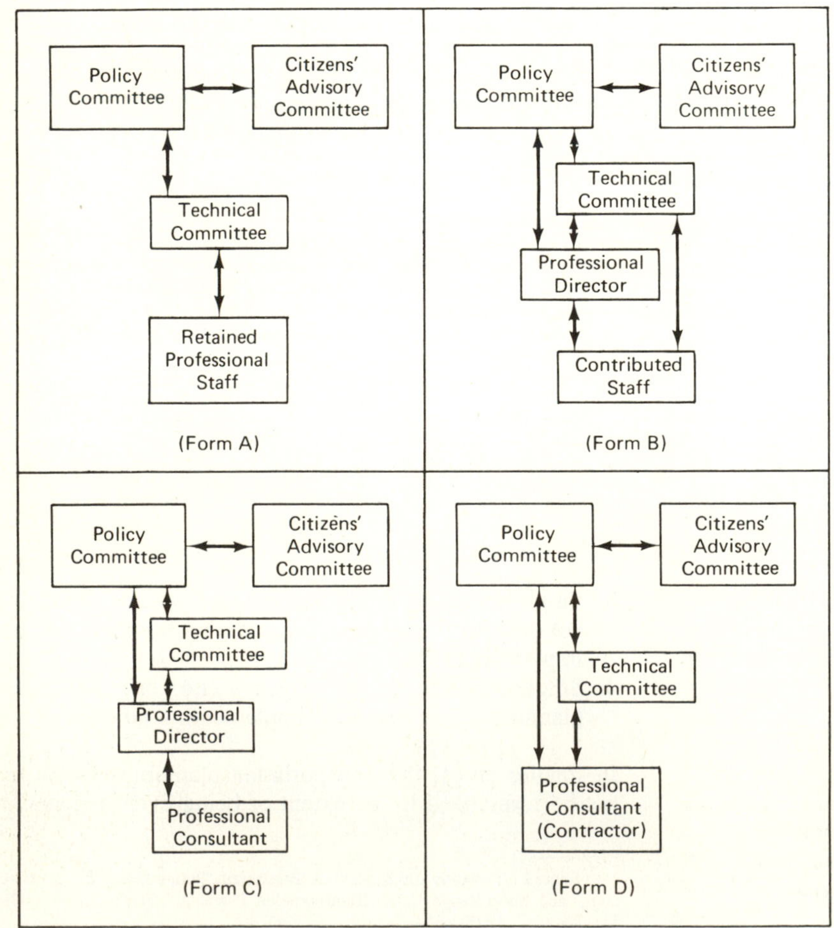

Figure 12.18. Alternative structures for study management. SOURCE: R.J. Hensen and W.L. Grecco, "Evaluation of the Effectiveness of Transportation Planning in the Smaller Urban Area," Traffic Quarterly, 24(3), 398, 1970, By permission of Eno Foundation for Transportation, Inc.

○ Adopt guidelines for the program.
○ Adopt urban transportation policy, goals, and objectives.
○ Receive advice from citizens and technical staff on urban area transportation issues.
○ Review and endorse plans, programs, and other recommendations.
○ Inform the public of important transportation issues, policies, and plans.

Technical Guidance. Technical guidance for the study may also come from an appointed committee holding regular meetings. This group should also represent concerned agencies, such as local and state highway operating agencies, municipal managers, planning agencies, and public transportation operators. Activities include deciding technical questions related to planning procedures and alternative selection, coordinating the technical service contributions from participating agencies, and making recommendations to the policy group. Such recommendations might cover:

1. The form of transportation planning activities.
2. Funding for transportation planning activities.
3. Statements of policy, goals, and objectives.
4. Transportation plans and programs.

Planning Staff. Obviously, the size and nature of the staff relates to the scale of planning needs, which will be determined by the size of the community, existing planning capabilities, and the extent of transportation problems. The distribution of staffing needs for typical studies is given in Figure 12.19, which depicts a scale of personnel needs for different work phases. It emphasizes that personnel needs will be most intensive for short periods during data collection and initial data processing. Personnel needs for later analysis, forecasting, and evaluation will be low (and usually requiring higher levels of technical skill) but will extend over longer periods.

For any particular planning situation, staff needs will depend on either the availability of data and contributed services from other planning agencies, or the need to mount significant efforts in their absence.

Citizens' Advisory Groups. Although participation in the planning process of elected officials, or their representatives, should ensure that local concerns are addressed, citizen advisory groups can help not only in planning but also in plan implementation. Such groups should represent business, industry, and labor, civic groups concerned with community enhancement, and communications media. Their function is essentially twofold: to inform the other study participants of public thinking, and to pass information from the planning process to the community.

The importance of citizen involvement with respect to air quality and transportation planning in the U.S., for example, is demonstrated in the Clean Air Act of 1977, which specified that 1979 State Implementation Plans shall evidence public involvement and consultation in accordance with Section 174 (relating to planning procedures).

Among publications describing how best to incorporate citizen involvement are two ITE Informational Reports and an NCHRP Report.[39] The latter describes the challenge of a successful participatory process in the following terms:

> At its root, the participatory process is a humanistic, political enterprise set firmly in the midst of the technical, political process of transportation planning and decision making. To carry out such an enterprise requires skilled professionalism. But success finally rests on the humanistic resources: common sense and sensitivity both to individuals' concerns and to broad public interests. . . . Although transportation agencies possess the technical expertise and the mandate to provide transportation, they are no less a part of the political aspects of the transportation planning process as are citizens. The test for both agencies and communities is to use the process to integrate humanistic insights with technical expertise via decisive actions satisfying both. Then agencies fulfill their responsibility to serve public interests through transportation, and communities fulfill their goal to protect and enhance their well-being. The participation of citizens with transportation professionals in planning is the means to this end.

[39] *Methods for Citizen Involvement* (Arlington, Va.: Institute of Transportation Engineers), unpublished; Kathleen Stein Hudson and Timothy J. Lindon, *Guidelines on Citizen Participation in Transportation Planning* (Washington, D.C.: American Association of State Highway and Transportation Officials, 1978).

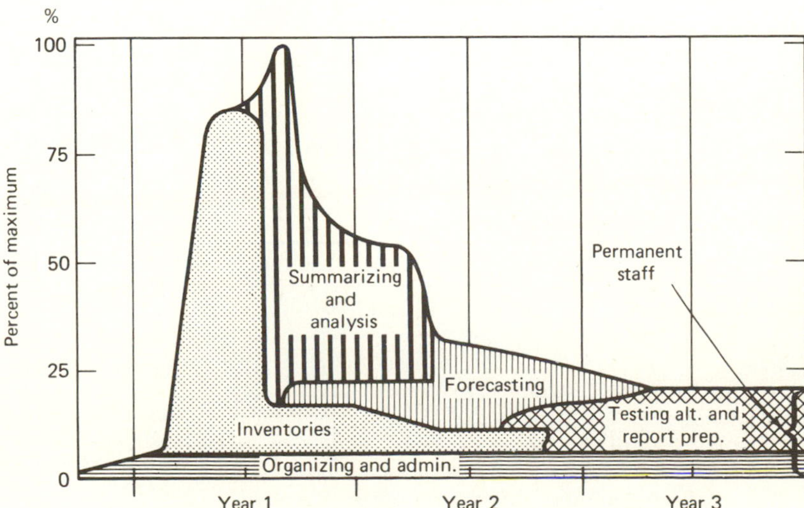

Figure 12.19. Personnel needs of a major transportation study expressed as a percent of maximum. SOURCE: Clyde E. Sweet, Jr., *Guidelines for the Administration of Urban Transportation Planning*, Washington, D.C.: Institute of Traffic Engineers, 1969, p. 26.

Administration of urban transportation planning activities

Any effective planning program requires appropriate staffing, adequate funding, and management guided by principles such as those enumerated below.

Management principles. (1) The planning process must be dynamic and responsive to community needs. Study staff and guiding committees should be alert to changes in those needs and jointly adjust planning objectives accordingly. (2) When the planning process calls for contributed services from different agencies, scopes of work and delivery schedules should be carefully planned and agreed to. Schedules for sequential tasks in the planning process should be realistic so that reporting deadlines can be achieved. (3) Progress reporting procedures should be set up so that performance is checked. (4) In addition to reports emanating from plan process tasks that call for technical or policy committee approvals, informational reports for citizen advisory committees should be periodically produced. Such reporting may be built into the planning process through requirements of planning grants.

Funding and study costs. In the United States in recent years, funds have been available from the Federal Highway Administration and the Urban Mass Transportation Administration of the DOT and from the Department of Housing and Urban Development. Traditionally sources for long-range planning support, the first two at least are now funding sources for short-range planning studies as well. In addition, resources for planning to meet air quality standards have become available from the Environmental Protection Agency.

Local sources include legislatively mandated returns of state-collected fuel-tax revenues to cities, as well as funding obtained through local tax bases. Where local support of a state and federally supported project is required, staff work contributed by local agencies may be an acceptable substitute for funding.

Given the diversity in planning activities, it is meaningless to cite typical costs except in relative terms. The important value of contributed data or available data sources can be demonstrated by the relationships between different phases of the planning process. Note, in Table 12-14, that data collection and preparation costs amount to virtually half of the total. Administration and reporting costs account for another 20%, and analytical and evaluative efforts account for roughly one-third of the total costs. As with the personnel needs shown in Figure 12.19, this cost distribution may reasonably represent current patterns.

TABLE 12–14
Distribution of Transportation Study Costs

Study Phase	Percent of Total Costs
Data collection and preparation	49
Developing and testing models	6
Forecasting	6
Traffic assignments	4
Analysis of alternatives	15
Report preparation	7
Other	13
Total	100

SOURCE: THOMAS J. HILLEGASS, "Urban Transportation Planning—A Question of Emphasis," *Traffic Eng. 20*(7), 47 (1969).

Balancing long-range and short-range efforts. Current federal regulations affecting U.S. planning activities call for developing Unified Planning Work Programs (UPWP) as a prerequisite condition for federal assistance in transportation planning. The work program should specify all planning and supporting efforts to be accomplished in a given fiscal year, and demonstrate coordination of efforts among participating agencies.

The Unified Work Program for the Washington metropolitan area in Fiscal Year 1979 shows nearly $4 million in FHWA, UMTA, state, and local funds to be expended by several agencies. The program organizes activities into three major areas:[40]

> Long-range transportation planning activities . . . contribute to refinements of the long-range regional transportation plan and provide input to other functional planning areas such as land use, air quality, housing, energy, and water resources. Short-range transportation planning activities . . . are more immediate action oriented and focus on short-term improvements to the existing transit, highway and commuter rail system. Continuing transportation planning activities . . . focus on monitoring and providing data and analytical services to local, regional and state transportation agencies.

An appendix describes the Work Program tasks under six major categories (see Table 12-15). Note that the distribution of funding across the six major areas gives the major emphasis to short-range planning, apart from the item of state and local services. The services activities are "technical assistance for a variety of tasks requested by the state in support of project development, corridor studies, or other state planning activities, as requested. This assistance will include traffic impact analysis for alternatives, field data collection, technical evaluation, monitoring activities, and other related transportation planning activities."[41]

The emphasis shown on short-range and "response" services in the Washington planning program raises the pertinent question of how to strike a balance between short- and long-range planning. A recent FHWA publication offers an illustration for general guidance (Figure 12.20).[42] The suggested determinants affecting the assignment of effort and resources are size of area, complexity of problems, community growth potential, and the nature of feasible solutions. Table 12-16 suggests a distribution of effort for two hypothetical cases. Obviously, the order of magnitude in the total planning effort will be vastly different between the two examples. In the small-city cases, planning will emphasize simple methods. In the larger areas, computer modeling may be applied to analytical findings based on extensive surveys.

Figure 12.20 and Table 12-16 both show the opportunity for designing flexibility into the planning process. They thus reflect a major policy advance in the United States over

[40]*Fiscal Year 1979 Unified Work Program* (Washington, D.C.: Metropolitan Washington Council of Governments, Mar. 1978), p. i.

[41]*FY79 Unified Work Program*, p. A-19.

[42]FLEET ET AL., *Achieving a . . . Balance*.

TABLE 12–15
Distribution of Fiscal Year 1979 Program Funding by Major Activities and Funding Sources, Washington Metropolitan Council of Governments

Activity	UMTA/Local	FHWA/State	Total
Long range	120,000	40,000	160,000
Short range	220,000	190,000	410,000
Surveillance	80,000	80,000	160,000
Technical methods	125,000	65,000	190,000
Services	180,000	300,000	480,000
Related	—	100,000	100,000
Total	725,000	775,000	1,500,000

SOURCE: *Fiscal Year 1979 Unified Work Program* (Washington, D.C.: Metropolitan Washington Council of Governments, Mar. 1978), p. A-21.

TABLE 12–16
Alternative Distributions of Effort between Long-Range and Short-Range Planning

	Percent of Effort	
Activity	Small City with Slow Growth, Simple Problems; Traffic Engineering Solutions Adequate	Rapidly Growing Large City with Complex Problems; Major Facilities Required
Long-range planning	15	35
Short-range planning	50	35
Short-range programming	25	15
Monitoring	10	15

SOURCE: CHRISTOPHER FLEET, ANTHONY KANE, AND GEORGE SCHOENER, *Achieving Long-Range/Short-Range Planning Balance with an Appropriate Level of Effort* (Washington, D.C.: Federal Highway Administration, 1978), p. 11.

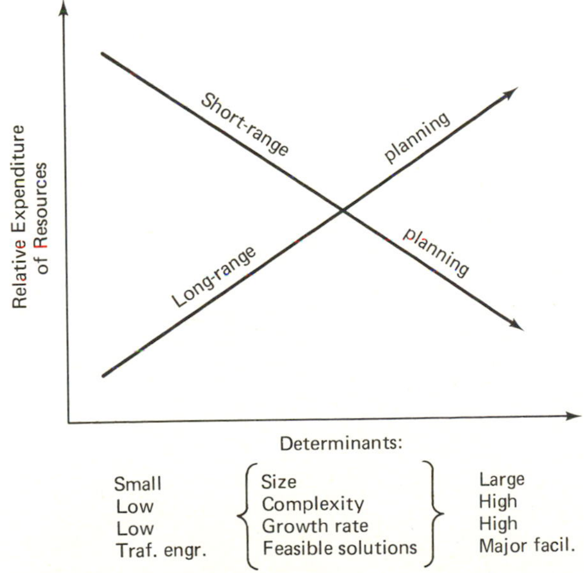

Figure 12.20. Balancing effort between short-range and long-range planning. SOURCE: Christopher Fleet, Anthony Kane, and George Schoener, *Achieving a Long-Range/Short-Range Planning Balance with an Appropriate Level of Effort,* Washington, D.C.: Federal Highway Administration, 1978.

procedures of several years ago, in suggesting that the planning process can become more responsive to the community it serves. This flexibility lowers the likelihood of producing plans that merely gather dust and enhances the likelihood of implementation. The impact of the most recent federal regulations, therefore, although perhaps more onerous in prescribing planning process requirements, should lead not only to better planning but also to better programs for each community.

Role of the transportation professional

The transportation professional can and should play an important part in every one of the urban transportation planning studies previously described. Opportunities exist from the lowest technical levels to the highest management positions.

In the long-range studies, for example, the selection and description of an arterial network is basic to the planning process. Volumes, speed characteristics, capacity limitations, and system classifications are needed, and transportation engineering personnel are essential to this inventory function. Traffic engineers may also be responsible for parking and accident studies, as well as for taking part in travel survey design and operation. Estimating capacity or other deficiencies in existing networks and setting performance standards for network elements are clearly engineering assignments. Screenline accuracy checks, traffic assignment, network construction, and even trip model development and calibration may also be done by engineers. Analyzing spacing, network configurations, interchange location, capacity designation, speed, and other design standards and coordinating with transit network schemes are logical additional functions. In the evaluation stage, reviewing link volume/capacity ratios, calculating benefit/cost ratios, and evaluating quality of service are tasks for accomplishment by engineering personnel. Finally, in the long-range study, transportation engineering skills can be applied to jurisdictional assignment of projects, coordination of arterial and freeway improvements, and designation of priorities.

Many of the foregoing tasks also apply in the monitoring activities of metropolitan planning organizations. Staff engineers should be sensitive to the needs of local traffic and transit agency staffs. For instance, planning staffs can provide operating agencies with data collection services, research studies, and forecasts of construction program impacts.

Much short-range planning work clearly belongs to transportation professionals, for example, as in many TSM studies and studies of major generators and passenger terminal or transfer facilities. Testing the adequacy of local access to "park-and-ride" transit terminals and ensuring adequate internal circulation at such sites illustrate transportation engineering contributions. Obviously, the engineer should also have a part in other planning, as for example, in analyzing traffic generation for joint development or multiple-use projects.

Local traffic personnel outside the planning agencies can assist planners during inventory stages by providing data on volumes, parking, control devices, and in selecting the functional arterial network. The technical advisory committee of the planning agency should include a representative from the traffic engineer's office.

In return, the city traffic engineering personnel can benefit from planning information and capabilities. Planning sources often provide details unavailable elsewhere. Network capacity inputs, O-D patterns, and even land-use information may be of value. Traffic assignments may test the effects of necessary street closings, and so on, anticipated by the city. Moreover, short-range planning projects may support the city traffic engineer in providing immediate-action answers to congestion problems.

New directions and issues

Planning requires looking ahead, and looking ahead requires awareness of trends and understanding of their implications. Because changes in urban living are constantly occurring and directly affect the character of urban transportation planning, this section identifies several trends and their likely effects on planning procedures. A distinction is made between transportation considerations affecting cities of the industrialized nations from those of developing countries.

In developed nations

Urban transportation trends in the industrialized world include:

1. Continuing growth in car ownership.
2. Continuing decline in public transportation usage.
3. Decline of travel to central business districts with respect to total urban travel.

Broadly speaking, the effects of improved travel facilities are to "increase the accessibility to parts of the city. Analyses of the changes which these improvements have brought about show that they do increase the total amount of travel but in such a way that the time spent on travel remains fairly constant over the year."[43] Development trends show lower densities and continuing dispersion of urban activities over larger areas. These trends seem likely to continue, although in varying degree among the different industrialized nations.

Several influences of a social, economic, and technical nature may be worth noting. In the United States, there is the decline of central city population in the largest metropolitan areas. The pattern is not peculiarly American; the population of London, England, has declined from 8,000,000 in the 1960s to about 7,000,000 at present. Other demographic influences in the United States include the general aging of the population and an increase in part-time employment, both of which could reduce the volume and duration of work-trip peak periods. A significant social consideration is increased public concern for transportation equity (i.e., meeting the travel needs of those whose mobility may be restricted because of poverty, health, or other reasons).

Economic influences affecting transportation include the rising costs and threatened shortages of fuel supplies. Less obvious is the shortage of capital for construction of new travel facilities. Funding for developing new technology in person movement has dwindled, for example, so that emerging technical innovations in automated people movers have been shelved. Concern is directed instead toward improved efficiency in the use of present facilities and equipment, through lower fuel consumption rates, higher levels of vehicle occupancy, or other more intensive uses of street and highway systems.

In developing nations

Present conditions and trends in urban transportation are quite different in cities of developing nations. Large cities often experience population growth rates of 4 to 7% per year. Although low in automobile use, these cities experience severe congestion because of mixed travel modes and shortage of road space, which frequently accounts for only half of the total urban area typically devoted to roads in the industrialized world.

Added to impacts from soaring population growth, demands for mobility increase with increasing personal incomes. The mere fact that population growth expands distances between housing and necessary destinations also causes increased travel.

At the same time, economic constraints restrict the development of facilities. Rising fuel costs limit vehicular and transit travel growth. Increasing road costs (partly due to increasing land costs) limit the possibilities for adding network capacity. Because capital shortages prevent the development of major highway or transit systems, transportation improvements fail to keep pace with needs in some of the world's largest and most rapidly growing cities. The World Bank has noted that the primary emphasis for physical facilities will "be placed on low cost public transport providing greater access to job opportunities and on facilities for commercial traffic, cyclists and pedestrians."[44]

Impact on urban transportation planning

The growth patterns in the cities of developed nations have clearly affected the transportation planning process. Planners deal now with a wider spectrum of issues in shorter time frames; concerned individuals and groups also participate in the process, in contrast to the more isolated technical procedures of an earlier time.

Recognizing such changes, a study group sponsored by the Organization for Economic Cooperation and Development (OECD) has suggested the following needs for planning process improvement.

1. The methods for setting objectives need modification [a proposed approach was described earlier under "Goals and Objectives"].

2. Forecast models should:

a. Reflect the dynamic nature of urban transportation (as in the feedbacks between supply and demand);

b. Deal especially with particular interest groups in the population through disaggregate demand techniques;

[43] *Planning for Personal Travel*, p. 52.

[44] *Urban Transport Sector Policy Papers*, (Washington, D.C.: World Bank, 1975), p. 14.

c. Be amenable to sensitivity testing so that error probabilities can be weighed.

3. The "activity requirements" of population groups, rather than observable travel demands, must be studied so that transportation services meet real needs rather than answering only apparent travel demands.

4. Wider ranges of objectives require plan evaluation to employ new measures of effectiveness.

5. Evaluations should describe trade-offs to the decision makers. "What is ultimately presented to the policymaker is not a single result for each alternative evaluated . . . but a set of comparable assessments for each alternative between which the decision-maker can choose."[45]

The dynamic character of urban travel growth in developing countries also forces changes in accepted transportation planning techniques. The rates of change in population and uncertainty of economic forecasts, especially when there are likely to be no historic data files upon which to base extrapolations, make planning difficult. Transferability of travel relationships, as in the Cairo–Sadat City example, may ease some of these problems but cannot be thoughtlessly applied. In many areas, of course, the time and cost of typical planning studies are unaffordable luxuries. Accordingly, planning studies may take on more of the forms suggested in NCHRP Report 186,[46] which outlines techniques appropriate for obtaining quick responses to policy issues.

In conclusion, it is clear that as planning problems change, so must planning techniques. The combination of changing problems and changing techniques means that challenging opportunities will exist in transportation planning for many years to come.

[45] *Planning for Personal Travel*, p. 57.

[46] SOSSLAU, *Travel Estimation Procedures*.

13

ENVIRONMENTAL CONSIDERATIONS

JOHN D. EDWARDS, JR., *President*

Traffic Planning Associates, Inc.
Atlanta, Georgia

Background on environmental issues

In the early years of transportation development in the United States, the primary concern was the ability to move people and goods rapidly and efficiently. Little regard was given to the side effects of transportation on the environment or to the depletion of natural resources. Even recent improvements in transportation systems have not been without some compromises to the environment, especially in urban areas. The stage has now been reached, however, where the complexity of society demands a broader consideration of transportation impact. Other criteria—in addition to efficiency—have risen in importance in judging the value and the impact of transportation improvements: safety, aesthetics, and effects on the social and physical environment. Realizing the tremendous impact that transportation systems have on each individual and on the areas in which they live, transportation engineers must be more concerned with the compatibility of these systems with societal and environmental systems.

The environment and the national interest

Partially in response to the drastic effect of transportation improvements on the environment, and partially due to shifting priorities in the national life style within the United States, there has been a growing concern about the impacts of transportation. Opposition to transportation improvements, initially in urban areas, is one sign of this concern. These efforts, primarily emphasizing the negative aspects of transportation impacts, intensified in the middle to late 1960s and finally resulted in legislative action by the Congress beginning with the Clean Air Act of 1965 and followed by the National Environmental Policy Act in 1969, the 1970 Clean Air Act, the 1970 Federal-aid Highway Act, the National Air Quality Standards (1971), the 1977 Clean Air Act Amendments, and Noise Standards and Procedures (1972) published by the Federal Highway Administration (FHWA).

No transportation improvement is without both positive and negative effects on the environment, Certain impacts, such as changes in air quality, topography, visual appearance, and noise can be effectively quantified and evaluated. Others, such as aesthetics, effects on established neighborhoods, and social impacts, are more difficult to measure. Environmental considerations discussed in this chapter are limited to those elements and factors that have readily definable quantitative limits.

Clear and concise definitions are a prerequisite to understanding environmental considerations. Although pollution is an adverse impact, pollution and adverse impact are discussed separately because pollution is readily measurable (there are technologically defined measures of pollution which are recognized by both the technological community and by the legislative bodies on a national scale), whereas other adverse impacts are more amorphous.

Pollution generally results from the addition of some man-made impurity to air, water, or to some other element of nature. Pollution, as a chemical agent, can be quantified and measured as to level and effect. Air pollution is an obvious kind of pollution and readily available criteria can be used to measure the level of air pollution. Noise pollution is also readily measurable, although standards for measuring the nonacceptable levels are more subjective.

Adverse impact is subjective. Quantitative criteria are not generally applicable. Adverse impacts include such disparate elements as "visual pollution," depletion of natural resources, undesirable land uses, traffic congestion and accidents, and inefficient space utilization, which result in waste or spoilage of the natural endowment. Although they do not permanently damage the balance of nature, they do cause problems, displeasure, anxiety, and grief to society.

Adverse impact is measured on a scale that varies from

individual to individual. What may be pleasure or profit to one is misery and loss to another. The broad area of concern and the lack of unanimity on degree of the adversity make even general subjective measures of the problem difficult.

Legislative approaches to improving the environment

The Clean Air Act of 1965 was the first federal attempt to legislate transportation operations to improve the environment. Since those initial efforts there has been a steady stream of federal and state amendments, adjustments, and changes. Some of the more significant efforts in this regard are summarized here.

The Environmental Policy Act was passed by the U.S. Congress in 1969 as a result of concentrated efforts of environmental groups within the United States. This act deals with all federally funded projects involving possible environmental impacts—whether actual construction is involved or not. The basic purpose of the act is to provide a detailed statement on projects and proposals that will have a potential impact on the human environment. Referred to as Environmental Impact Statements (EIS), these required documents for a sizable construction project in an urban area can run to several thousand pages.

The Environmental Impact Statement (EIS) must include:[1]

1. the environmental impact of the proposed action,
2. any adverse environmental effects . . . ,
3. alternatives to the proposed action,
4. the relationship between local short-term uses of man's environment and the maintenance and enhancement of long term productivity, and
5. any irreversible, irretrievable commitments of resources . . . .

The processing of the environmental statement outlined above for a highway location is illustrated in Figure 13.1. The procedure provides for a location and design public hearing at each stage of the highway project.

[1]"Guidelines for Implementing Section 102(2)(C) of the National Environmental Policy Act of 1969," *Policy and Procedure Manual 90-1* (Washington, D.C.: U.S. Department of Transportation, Federal Highway Administration, 1971), p. 1.

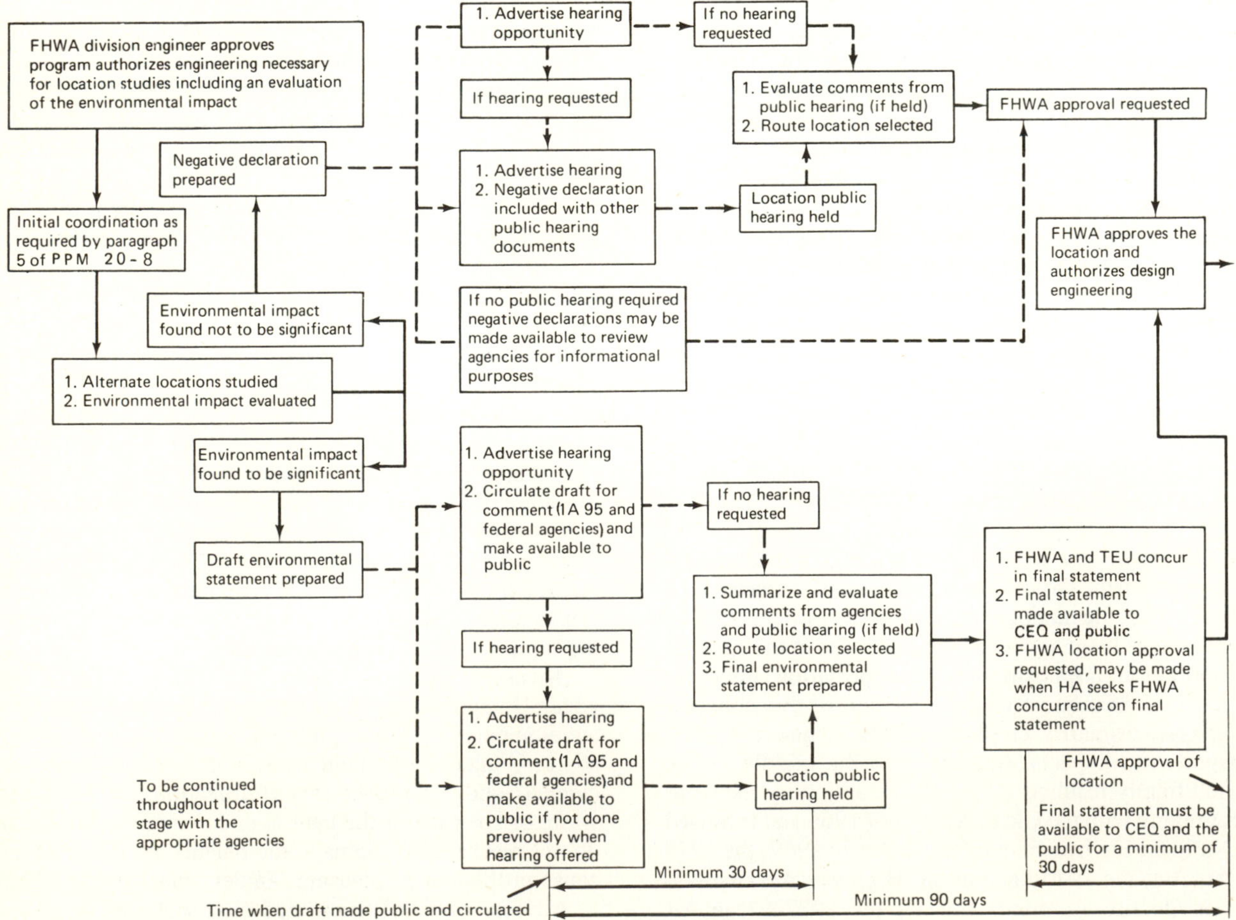

Figure 13.1. Flowchart for processing an environmental impact statement. SOURCE: "Guidelines for Implementing Section 102(2)(C) of the National Environmental Policy Act of 1969, Section 1653(f) of 49 U.S.C.," Policy and Procedural Manual 90-1, U.S. Department of Transportation, Federal Highway Administration, August 24, 1971, App. C.

For Federal-aid transportation projects, the impact categories that must be covered by the EIS include:[2]

○ *Social impacts:* community cohesion, accessiblity of facilities and services, and displacement of people.
○ *Economic impacts:* employment, income, residential activity, effects on property taxes, regional and community plans and growth, and resources.
○ *Environmental impacts:* environmental design, aesthetics and historic values, terrestrial ecosystems, aquatic ecosystems, air quality, and noise and vibration.

Responsibilities for public hearing and environmental review procedures have also been established at the state level by several reorganization acts establishing state departments of transportation. An example of this approach is illustrated by the legislation that established the Pennsylvania Department of Transportation (Penn DOT) and specified that the department

> shall consider the following effects of the transportation route or program: (1) residential and neighborhood character and location; (2) conservation including air, erosion, sedimentation, wildlife and general ecology of the area; (3) noise, air and water pollution; (4) multiple use of space; (5) replacement housing; (6) displacement of families and business; (7) recreation and parks; (8) aesthetics; (9) public health and safety; (10) fast, safe and efficient transportation; (11) civil defense; (12) economic activity; (13) employment; (14) fire protection; (15) public utilities; (16) religious institutions; (17) conduct and financing of government including the effect on the local tax base and social service cost; (18) national and historic landmarks; (19) property values; (20) education including the disruption of school district operations. . . . [3]

Air pollution standards

Air pollution control standards have existed for a number of years, generally as part of the municipal codes in several U.S. cities and in at least one state. One of the earlier efforts at control was an antipollution ordinance passed in 1958 by the City of Newark, N.J. The ordinance provided that no motor vehicle shall be operated which causes a nuisance by emitting obnoxious or excessive smoke, gases, vapor, or fumes, and that no gasoline or diesel-fueled bus shall be permitted to operate while discharging polluting gases. Other attempts at municipal air pollution control were made in Toledo, Ohio; Chicago, Illinois; and elsewhere. The problem with municipal ordinances is the difficulty of enforcement of the subjective standards stated in the ordinances.

California has generally led the way in the development of air pollution control standards within the United States. Standards were adopted and modified over a period of several years in the early and middle 1960s.

In 1977, the Congress passed the Clean Air Act Amendments, which made more precise the requirements of previous federal legislation. The new legislation designates areas—particularly national parks, wilderness areas, etc.—which do not have violations of the National Ambient Air Quality Standards as areas of "prevention of significant deterioration" (PSD) in air quality. Those areas already violating the standards are designated as nonattainment areas. A State Implementation Plan (SIP) is required for every state. The Environmental Protection Agency (EPA) provides grants to pay for the reasonable costs of developing a plan for the planning requirements for nonattainment areas.

The act established a designation of nonattainment areas for locations with violations of the air quality standards and also established a schedule of deadlines to comply with the standards. In nonattainment areas, state and local officials are responsible for developing a state/local organization to prepare the needed air quality control plan. The act requires the state/local officials to allocate sufficient resources, compliance schedules, and enforcement actions necessary to meet the national air quality standards. Although the entire act is of general importance to transportation engineers, the following confines itself to sections of the act with particular significance.

Measures including transportation controls will be included in the SIP. The measures will not be limited to transportation controls, but will include administrative and legal requirements. The SIP preparation procedure has 11 requirements, which include a SIP plan subjected to public notice and hearing; a schedule of reasonable further progress in meeting standards; a comprehensive emissions inventory; identification of personnel requirements for plan implementation and provisions for necessary staffing; evidence of public, local government, and state legislative involvement in the implementation process; adequate legal authority for implementation; and in the case of 1987 extensions for carbon monoxide (CO) and oxidants, provision for an inspection and maintenance program. Extension of the 1982 time limit for areas unable to meet CO or oxidant standards is allowed, provided that commitments for improving public transit and for an inspection and maintenance program are made and all reasonable measures will not result in attainment.

Indirect source review (ISR) has been delayed pending a more definitive analysis of impacts. Federally assisted projects that provided major indirect sources are being evaluated to assure conformance with air quality plans. Restriction of EPA and DOT funding for areas not meeting the CO and/or oxidant standards will be applied to areas needing transportation control plans where reasonable efforts to develop plan submissions are not apparent.

Vehicle emission standards are expected to reduce drastically the amount of air pollution from all sources. The goal of the Federal Motor Vehicle Control program is to eliminate 97% of the hydrocarbons and 96% of all carbon monoxide from automobile exhausts by the 1980 models.

As a result of legislation in the mid 1960s and 1970s, air pollution levels have already declined in a number of U.S. cities. Air quality trends for carbon monoxide between 1972–1973 and 1975–1976 are illustrated in Figure 13.2 for eight cities: Atlanta, Boston, Denver, Phoenix, Portland, Riverside (California), Salt Lake City, and Seattle. An average reduction of 46% in violations of the carbon monoxide standards resulted. Excluding Atlanta, the seven cities showed an average reduction of 22% in violations of the

---

[2] *Environmental Assessment Notebook Series* (Washington, D.C.: U.S. Department of Transportation, 1975).

[3] Act No. 120, SB408, General Assembly of the Commonwealth of Pennsylvania, 1970, p. 13.

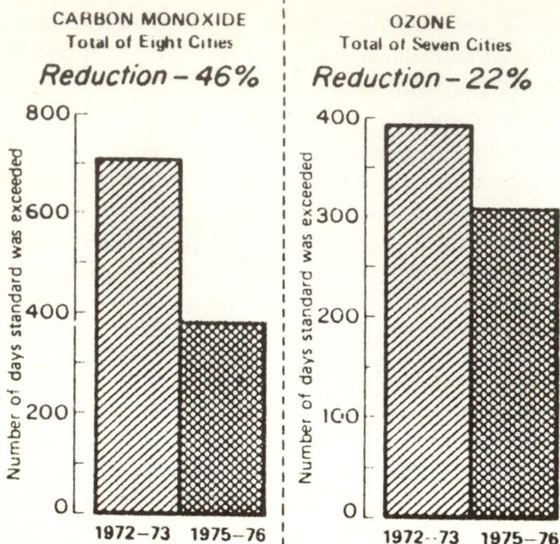

Figure 13.2. Trends in two measures of air quality between 1972–1973 and 1975–1976. (Based upon measurements from representative groups of cities averaged over two-year periods for violations of air quality standards for carbon monoxide and ozone.) SOURCE: Council on Environmental Quality, 8th Annual Report, Dec. 1977, Chap. 1.

ozone standard. The Council on Environmental Quality expects that all but a few urban areas will attain air quality standards for carbon monoxide and photochemical oxidants by 1990. Improvements in motor vehicle emission control devices are expected to make the greatest contribution to reduction of these pollutants from motor vehicles.

Noise regulation and legislation

The existing local legislation in the United States related to motor vehicle noise is subjective in character. A majority of states and cities utilize elements of the *Uniform Vehicle Code* published by the National Committee on Uniform Traffic Laws as a basis for noise regulation, even though this code is relatively vague about vehicular noise. The code states:

> Every motor vehicle shall have at all times mufflers in good working order and in constant operation to prevent excessive or unusual noise and annoying smoke, and no person shall use a muffler cut-out bypass or similar device on a motor vehicle on the highway.[4]

The passage implies that there is no objective measure of permissible noise. Enforcement depends to a great extent on the police officer's judgment of what is excessive or unusual noise. As a result, in several localities the courts have declared that local noise regulations are unconstitutional.

The lack of an objective standard for excessive noise has been recognized by a number of enforcement agencies and has promoted some interest in revising legislation to specify an objective measure of motor vehicle noise. Generally, these efforts center around the use of a sound-level meter. At least nine U.S. cities and two states had noise ordinances. In the case of the states, statutes have been repealed primarily because the ordinances were either unenforceable or required excessive amounts of police personnel. Trying to isolate the noise emitted from one particular vehicle out of many vehicles and applying such regulations on a city-wide basis presents enforcement problems. Nonresidents driving through the area who may be unfamiliar with the regulations are particularly affected. Table 13-1 summarizes some of the early efforts at legal restriction on noise.

In 1970, Congress passed the Noise Pollution and Abatement Act (PL 91-604), which provided the initial step toward establishing measures and standards for noise, but the 1972 Noise Control Act required that national noise emission standards be promulgated. The act specifically required noise emission standards which reflect the degree of noise reduction that may be achieved through the application of the best available technology. The final standards, which were to be applied to trucks in use, were essentially the standards proposed and shown below:

1. 90 dBA at 50 ft (15.2 m) at speeds greater than 35 mph (56.3 km/h)
2. 86 dBA at 50 ft (15.2 m) at speeds less than 35 mph (56.3 km/h)
3. 80 dBA at 50 ft (15.2 m) on level streets less than 35 mph (56.3 km/h)
4. 88 dBA at 50 ft (15.2 m) on stationary runup[5]

Additionally, the FHWA has promulgated standards which require that highways constructed with federal funds provide certain noise limits for abutting lands. These levels, shown in Table 13-2 apply to the highway design year and strike a balance between the desirable and the feasible.

Scope of environmental considerations

The environmental impacts produced by each mode of transportation vary in terms of intensity and in terms of its surroundings. A railroad has a much greater and more visible impact than a pipeline, which is odorless and noiseless. Yet under certain circumstances even a pipeline can have significant environmental impacts. This chapter primarily deals with the environmental impacts of surface transportation, although limited data are presented on airports and air transportation. The surface transportation modes include auto, truck, bus, and rail. Mention is made of the pipeline but little information is available on air pollution or the noise aspects of this mode. Primary emphasis is placed on the private automobile, truck, and transit modes, particularly as they affect urban areas.

---

[4]W. E. CLARKE, W. J. GALLOWAY, AND J. S. KERRICK, *Highway Noise Measurement Simulations, and Mixed Reaction,* NCHRP Report No. 78 (Washington, D.C.: Highway Research Board, 1969).

[5]ENVIRONMENTAL PROTECTION AGENCY, "Noise Abatement: Interstate Motor Carrier Noise Emission Standards, 40 CFR Part 202," *Fed. Reg. 38* (Washington, D.C.: U.S. Government Printing Office 1974), p. 144.

TABLE 13–1
Legal Restrictions on Motor Vehicle Noise*

Location or Agency	Autos	Trucks and Buses	Motorcycles
Cincinnati, Ohio (1)	95 dBA at 20 ft = 88 dBA at 50 ft		
Beverly Hills, Calif. (1)	95 dBA at 5 ft = 77 dBA at 50 ft		
Peoria, Ill. (1)	95 dBA at 50 ft		
Milwaukee, Wis. (1)	95 dBA at 20 ft = 82 dBA at 50 ft		
Memphis, Tenn. (1)	90 dBA at 20 ft = 77 dBA at 50 ft		
New York	88 dBA at 50 ft	88 dBA	88 dBA at 50 ft
Committee on Problem of Noise, U.K. (2)	79 dBA at 50 ft	79 dBA at 50 ft	84 dBA at 50 ft
Ministry of Transport, U.K. (3)	84–85 dBA at 50 ft	89 dBA at 50 ft	Cylinder capacity $\leq$ 50 cc: 77 dBA at 50 ft 50 $<$ Capacity $\leq$ 125 cc: 82 dBA at 50 ft Capacity $>$ 125 cc: 86 dBA at 50 ft 93 dBA in special test shed
Bermuda (4)			
Germany	75 dBA at 50 ft	Load over 2.5 tons: 80 dBA at 50 ft = dBA at 50 ft Load less than 2.5 tons: 75 dBA at 50 ft = 73 dBA at 50 ft	73–75 dBA at 50 ft = 71–73 dBA at 50 ft
South Africa (4)	85 dBA at 50 ft for all vehicles to be reduced to 80 dBA at 50 ft		
Sweden (4)	65 dBA	69 dBA	69 dBA
Canada (4)	$\leq$ 30-mph zones: 80 dBA at 15 ft (73 dBA at 15 ft) $>$ 30-mph zones: 87 dBA at 15 ft (80 dBA at 50 ft)	$>$ 3 tons (*see* autos) $\leq$ 30-mph zone: $>$ 3 tons: 87 dBA at 15 ft; 80 dBA at 50 ft Tractor-trailers: 87 dBA at 15 ft; 80 dBA at 50 ft $>$ 30-mph zone: $>$ 3 tons: 92 dBA at 15 ft; 85 dBA at 50 ft Tractor-trailers: 95 dBA at 15 ft; 88 dBA at 50 ft	$\leq$ 30-mph zones: Day: 85 dBA at 15 ft (78 dBA at 50 ft) Night: 82 dBA at 15 ft (75 dBA at 50 ft) $>$ 30-mph zones: 90 dBA at 15 ft (83 dBA at 50 ft)
California (5)	80 dBA at 50 ft	1975–1977: 83 dBA at 50 ft 1978–1981: 83 dBA at 50 ft† 80 dBA at 50 ft‡ After 1981: 80 dBA at 50 ft	To 1981: 83 dBA at 50 ft 1982–1985: 80 dBA at 50 ft 1986–1989: 75 dBA at 50 ft After 1989: 70 dBA at 50 ft

*1 ft = 0.305 m; 1 ton = 907.2 kg.
†Vehicles exceeding 8500 lb (3655 kg) gross weight.
‡Vehicles rated at or below 8500 lb (3655 kg) gross weight.

SOURCE: (1) *Pollution of Michigan Urban Atmosphere by Highway Generated Noise;* Res. Report 68G (Lansing, Mich.: Department of State Highways, 1970), p. 162. (2) COMMITTEE ON THE PROBLEM OF NOISE, *Noise, Final Report* (London: HMSO, 1963). (3) W. BURNS, *Noise and Man* (London: John Murray, 1969). (4) *A Brief Study of a Rational Approach to Legislative Control of Noise*, Acoustics Section, Division of Applied Science (Ottawa: National Research Council, 1968). (5) California Vehicle Code, Section 27202–27206 (Sacramento); years refer to dates of manufacture.

TABLE 13–2
Federal Highway Administration Noise Standards for New Highway Construction

Activity Category	Design Noise Level (dBA) L_{eq}	L_{10}	Description of Activity Category*
A	57 (exterior)	60 (exterior)	Tracts where serenity and quiet are especially important
B	67 (exterior)	70 (exterior)	Residences, motels, schools, churches, hospitals, etc.
C	72 (exterior)	75 (exterior)	Developed lands other than those above
E	52 (interior)	55 (interior)	Building interiors

*Either L_{eq} or L_{10} may be used—not both—and an hourly measure applies. The land-use descriptions are further qualified in the reference, and a category D is also reserved for underdeveloped land. The interior noise levels may be established by subtracting from outdoor levels the attenuation expected of the particular wall and window constructions involved.

SOURCE: FEDERAL HIGHWAY ADMINISTRATION, *Procedures for the Abatement of Highway Traffic Noise and Construction Noise*, Fed. Reg. 41(80) (Washington, D.C.: U.S. Government Printing Office, 1976).

Transportation modes with significant impacts

Each transportation mode impacts society and the environment in a different way. The private automobile has far-reaching positive economic impact, but can have very negative environmental impact as well. The pipeline has very positive economic impact but relatively minimal negative environmental impact. More confusing, negative impacts may be related only to the type of environment—for example, a railroad has little negative noise impact in rural areas. Table 13-3 summarizes possible impacts by mode.

Air pollution impacts

The major sources of pollution are nature, stationary fuel combustion, industrial processes, transportation, solid waste, and miscellaneous sources, such as forest fires, managed burning, coal refuse burning, and structural fires. Stationary fuel combustion is created by electric utilities, industrial plants, and residential, commerical, and institutional activities. Industrial processes can be divided

TABLE 13–3
Significant Impacts of Transportation Facilities

Mode of Transportation	Positive Impacts	Negative Impacts
Automobile and track	Employment Accessibility Mobility Stimulates "desirable" development	Noise Air pollution Stimulates "undesirable" development
Urban transit	Mobility Energy efficiency	Noise Air pollution
Air transportation	Mobility Speed	Noise Air pollution
Rail transportation	Mobility (particularly freight)	Noise Air pollution
Pipeline	Mobility (liquid freight)	Odor

SOURCE: John D. Edwards, Jr.

TABLE 13–4
1976 U.S. Manmade Emissions (Million Tons/Year)*

Substance	Total All Manmade Sources	Total All Transportation† Sources	Highway Vehicles‡ Only
Total suspended particulates (TSP)	13.4	1.2	0.8
Sulfur oxides (SO_x)	26.9	0.8	0.4
Carbon monoxide (CO)	87.2	69.7	61.4
Hydrocarbons (HC)	27.9	10.9	9.3
Nitrogen oxides (NO_x)	23.0	10.1	7.8

*1 ton = 907.2 kg.
†Transportation includes highway vehicles, aircraft, railroads, vessels, farm equipment, and others.
‡Highway vehicles include passenger cars, trucks, and buses.

SOURCE: U.S. Environmental Protection Agency.

into six types; chemicals, petroleum refining, metals, mineral products, oil and gas production and marketing, and industrial organic solvent use. Transportation involves vehicles both on and off the highway. Solid waste includes disposal and sewage disposal plants.

Air pollution defined. Pure air rarely exists, even in undeveloped areas. For example, it is estimated that on a global basis, nature accounts for more than 90% of carbon monoxide (CO) in the air. Therefore, air pollution must relate to *excess CO* or other harmful substance in the atmosphere. Controlling legislation is directed for the most part to reduction of man-made pollution created by stationary sources and by transportation sources. Air pollution, like other forms of pollution in the United States, is caused by the multiplicative effect of population growth and increasing per capita demands for goods and services. In the process of meeting these demands, millions of tons of gaseous and particulate pollutants are dumped into the atmosphere. These pollutants soil, produce corrosion, and may be harmful to both plants and animals. Pollution has been defined as "an undesirable change in the physical, chemical, or biological characteristics of our air, land, and water that may or will harmfully affect human life or that of any other desirable species, or industrial process, living conditions, or cultural assets; or that may or will waste or deteriorate our raw material resources."[6]

Transportation's share of air pollution. Some transportation sources emit pollutants in relatively large quantities, but all pollutants are not equally harmful. About 70% of man-made carbon monoxide is attributed to highway vehicles; and carbon monoxide comprises a large portion of pollution by weight, 87.2 million tons annually in the United States. Yet carbon monoxide in the air is not as harmful to human beings as are sulfur oxides (SO_x), which are emitted for the most part by power plants and factories at a rate of 26.9 million tons annually. Table 13-4 indicates the relative magnitude of major pollutants annually for the United States.

Motor vehicles emit about 33% of man-made hydrocarbons (HC) and nitrogen oxides (NO_x), about 6% of total suspended particulates, but only 1.5% of sulfur oxides. Transportation air pollution is primarily concentrated around the major metropolitan areas and is caused principally by urban traffic. Transportation-related pollution accounts for an average of 60% of the total pollutants in the atmosphere for the major metropolitan areas in the United States. Of this, the private automobile contributes from 90 to 95% of the air pollution.

Kinds of pollutants. Carbon monoxide (CO), a by-product of the internal combustion engine, drives out the oxygen in the bloodstream. A high concentration over a short exposure time can kill; a small amount can cause dizziness, headaches, fatigue, and slow driving reactions. Moderate concentrations often exist in tunnels, garages, and heavy traffic. It is especially dangerous for people with heart disease, asthma, anemia, and so on.

Sulfur oxide (SO_x) is a by-product of the combustion process in factories and power plants that burn coal or oil containing sulfur. This pollutant by itself is usually not harmful, but when it is mixed with other pollutants and with moisture, it irritates the eyes, nose, and throat, damages the lungs, kills plants, rusts metals, and reduces visibility.

Oxide of nitrogen is produced by burning fuels that convert nitrogen and oxygen to nitric oxide (NO). The greatest toxic potential is the tendency of nitric oxide (which is not an irritant) to oxidize to nitrogen dioxide (NO_2), which is a major component of smog.

Hydrocarbons are unburned chemicals in combustion, such as car exhaust, which react in the presence of sunlight to produce smog. Hydrocarbons have produced cancer in animals and may be a cancer-producing element in cigarette smoke. They are primarily of concern because of their role in the formation of photochemical oxidants.

Particulates are smoke, fly ash, dust, and fumes that are solid and liquid matter in air. They may settle to the ground or may stay suspended. They soil clothes, dirty window sills, scatter light, and carry poisonous gases to the lungs. They come from autos, fuels, smelters, building materials, fertilizers, and elsewhere.

Photochemical smog is a mixture of the gases and particles described above from products of gasoline and other burning fuels that are oxidized by the sun. It irritates the eyes, nose, and throat, makes breathing difficult, and damages crops and material.

[6]*Report of the Committee on Pollution* (Washington, D.C.: National Academy of Science, National Research Council, 1970).

Measures of air quality. Several sources of air pollution justify special definition. An "area source" is one that individually does not contribute significantly to the air pollution problem but collectively becomes a problem. Individual homes may not be a problem; but many homes, collectively, may be one.

A point source is one specific identifiable location of pollution. Some area and point source categories include:

- Transportation: motor vehicles, aircraft, fuel handling and shipment
- Stationary: power plants, homes, industry—through burning of fuel
- Industrial process: chemical processes, petroleum refining, surface coating
- Solid waste disposal: incineration, open burning of wastes
- Miscellaneous: forest fire, dust from agricultural operations

Several measures of air quality have been developed for use by the various governmental agencies in quantifying the characteristics of air pollution. Air quality standards promulgated by EPA specifies carbon monoxide (CO) levels of 9 parts per million (ppm) maximum 8-h concentration and 35 ppm maximum 1-h concentration not to be exceeded more than once per year; for ozone, a standard of 0.12 ppm maximum 1-h concentration. Standards for hydrocarbons are 0.24 ppm for a 3-h average concentration from 6 to 9 A.M., and for nitrogen dioxide, 0.05 ppm annual aeromatic means.

The automobile and air quality. The initial concern with air quality, particularly in urban areas, was due to the smog alerts that Los Angeles experienced in the 1950s and 1960s. In 1960 the U.S. Public Health Service conducted air quality surveys at Continuous Air Monitoring Program (CAMP) sites, which provided much of the background information on urban air quality. These CAMP sites measured levels of carbon monoxide, nitrogen dioxide, particulates, and sulfur dioxide. Some general conclusions about air pollution characteristics can be drawn.

1. The highest concentrations of pollutants were found in the winter months.
2. In Washington, D.C., the carbon monoxide (CO) level varied from 8 to 12 ppm during winter compared to 5 to 8 ppm during the summer.
3. CAMP-site air pollution data could be compared with health and mortality statistics to determine general impacts of air pollution.
4. Transportation corridor pollution levels were measured and CO levels were found to be considerably higher along arterials and expressways than within the community as a whole.
5. CO concentrations were found to be 20 to 28 ppm during peak hours on arterials and expressways, considerably higher than the 9-ppm 8-h standard.
6. CO concentrations in downtown areas were found to range from 25 to 40 ppm during A.M. and P.M. peak hours—approaching or exceeding the 35-ppm 1-h concentration standard.

These conditions were reported from CAMP sites in the early to mid-1960s. Clearly there was a problem impending in the urban areas on air pollution, and this problem was related to the automobile.

The air pollution problem is closely related to the characteristics of use of the automobile. Perhaps the most graphic example of this is a comparison of vehicular movement by hour and air pollution levels in the urban area. Figure 13.3 illustrates the hourly variation in traffic volumes entering and leaving the central business district of Los Angeles and the concentration of NO_x and CO in the atmosphere for this area during the comparable hours for a period in the early 1960s. The peak concentration for both CO and NO occurs between 7:30 and 8:00 A.M., with concentration levels from 15 and 18 ppm, respectively. The pollution level drops during the late morning hours for NO to only 1 to 2 ppm—during this period sunlight tends to dissipate the NO. Nitrogen oxide levels increase again toward late afternoon. Carbon monoxide concentrations decrease to 10 ppm, where they level out throughout the evening with very little variation until the following morning peak hour. Although these relationships may not be representative of the Los Angeles condition today, the direct correlation between the automobile and pollution is apparent. Transportation impact on air quality, particularly in urban areas, is related most directly to private vehicle use. In terms of numbers of vehicles, this is generally the predominant form of transportation, particularly in the industrialized countries of the world.

Pollution levels vary considerably, depending on the time of day and the atmospheric conditions within the urban area. In most cities the peak condition for carbon monoxide concentration follows very closely the chronological sequence of peak-hour vehicular operations.

There is a considerable difference in arterial and expressway carbon monoxide concentrations. A study[7] completed by the California Vehicle Pollution Laboratory indicates that the hydrocarbon level varies with the average speed of the vehicle. Other tests indicate that for average freeway operating conditions, the concentration was from 350 to 400 ppm, whereas for average operating conditions on arterial streets the HC concentration was from 580 to 590 ppm. The HC emissions were 100 ppm for an engine idling, 540 ppm for acceleration, 485 ppm under cruising conditions, and 5000 ppm during deceleration.[8]

The frequency of stopping and starting (e.g., on a major signalized arterial street) associated with lower average speeds also has a very dramatic effect on HC and CO emissions. Figure 13.4 illustrates the CO emissions for an automobile at speeds of from 10 to 40 mph (16 to 64 km/h) for three different time periods: pre-1968, 1970, and 1977. At 40 mph (64 km/h) for 1977 vehicles, the emission is approximately 37 grams (g) per mile, but at 10 mph (16 km/h) it is approximately 96 g/mi, that is, more than twice

[7]C. Chipman, *Comparison of Auto Exhaust Emissions: Freeway vs. Average Type of Driving* (Los Angeles, Calif.: California Vehicle Pollution Laboratory, 1964), p. 64.

[8]Chipman, *Comparison of Auto Exhaust Emissions*, p. 67.

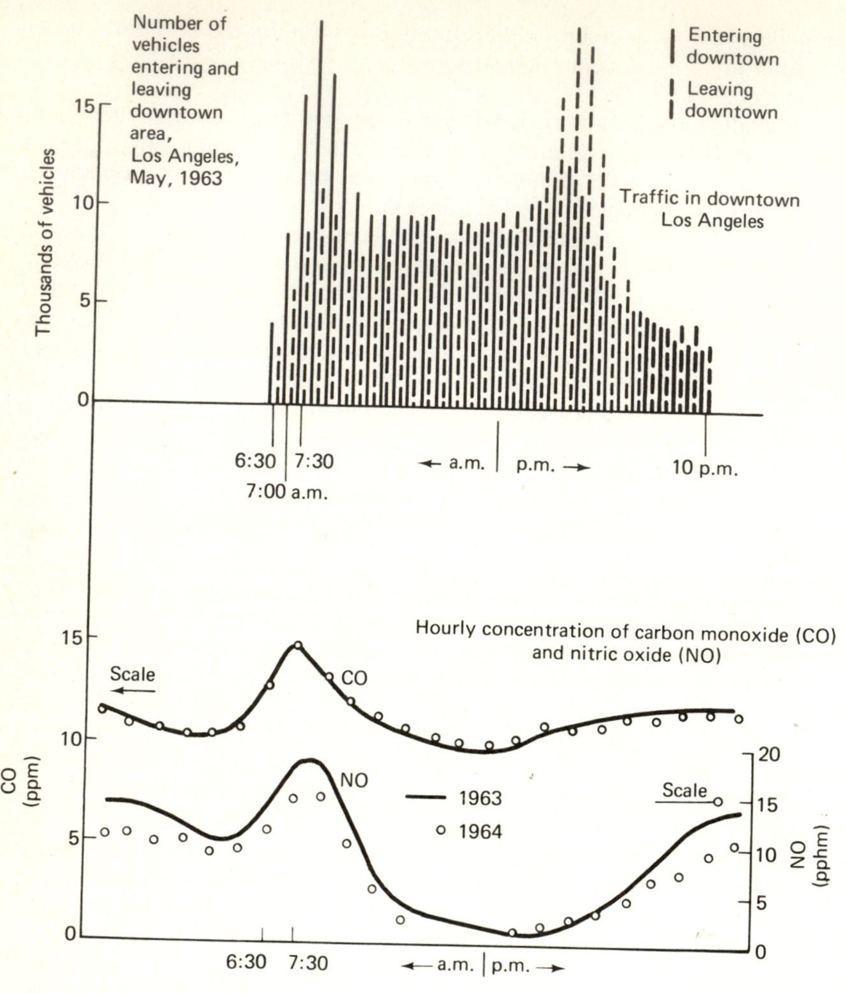

Figure 13.3. Hourly variation in pollution levels. SOURCE: C. Chipman, *Comparison of Auto Exhaust Emissions, Freeway's Average Type of Driver;* Los Angeles, Calif.: California Vehicle Pollution Laboratory, 1964, p. 64.

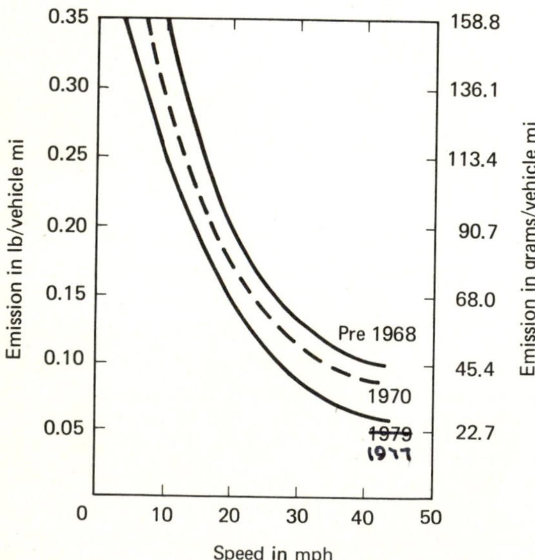

Figure 13.4. Carbon monoxide vehicular emission vs. speed. SOURCE: Second Report, Secretary of HEW to U.S. Congress pursuant to P.L. 88-206 Clean Air Act, Feb. 19, 1965, Table 1; U.S. Environmental Protection Agency, *Mobile Source Emission Factors,* Final Document, EPA 400/9-78-006, Washington, D.C.: 1978, Tables F-3, F-21.

the emission at 40 mph (64 km/h). The pre-1968 curve shows a more drastic difference—45 g/mi at 40 mph (64 km/h) vs. 160 g/mi at 10 mph (16 km/h)—almost four times as much. The family of curves shows considerable improvement in carbon monoxide emissions over time, with 1977 levels at 40 mph (64 km/h) at almost one-half of the pre-1968 levels.

Figure 13.5 illustrates the relationship between speed and hydrocarbon (HC) emissions. These curves are similar to those of CO emissions, with 1977 HC emissions at 10 mph (16 km/h), approximately three times the emissions measured at 40 mph (64 km/h). A comparison of the curves, however, indicates an increase in the emission rates for 1970 over the pre-1968 levels, but a decline as of 1977—emissions in the range 40 mph (64 km/h), roughly one-half of the pre-1968 conditions.

Contrary to the declines in emissions for hydrocarbons and carbon monoxide, emissions for nitrogen oxide increase with increasing speed. Nitrogen oxide emissions (see Figure 13.6) for cars equipped with no emission controls (pre-1968) range from 1.1 g/mi at 10 mph (16 km/h) up to 4.536 g/mi at 40 mph (64 km/h). The emissions for 1977 show an increase to 2.6 g/mi at 10 mph (16 km/h); at 40 mph (64 km/h) the 1977 emissions are about one-tenth less than the pre-1968 conditions.

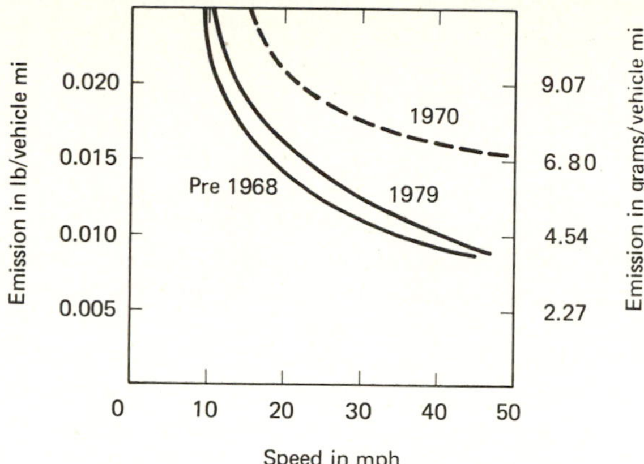

Figure 13.5. Hydrocarbon vehicular emission vs. speed. SOURCE: Second Report, Secretary of HEW to U.S. Congress pursuant to P.L. 88-206 Clean Air Act, Feb. 19, 1965, Table 1; U.S. Environmental Protection Agency, *Mobile Source Emission Factors,* Final Document, EPA 400/9-78-006, Washington, D.C.: 1978, Tables F-3, F-21.

Replace. See Errata No. 2

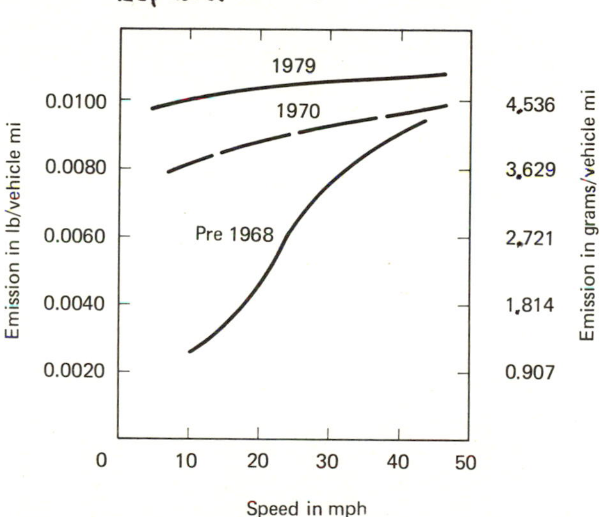

Figure 13.6. Nitrogen oxide vehicular emission vs. speed. SOURCE: Second Report, Secretary of HEW to U.S. Congress pursuant to P.L. 88-206 Clean Air Act, Feb. 19, 1965, Table 1; U.S. Environmental Protection Agency, *Mobile Source Emission Factors,* Final Document, EPA 400/9-78-006, Washington, D.C.: 1978, Tables F-3, F-21.

Replace. See Errata No. 2

Higher operating speeds and improved operating conditions provided by freeways do not reduce emissions of nitrogen oxide. These emissions may be reduced by the recirculation of the exhaust gas through the carburetor. The results are reduced power and more expensive operating conditions. Vehicle age is a factor in the level of pollution primarily because of innovations in antipollution equipment rather than lack of maintenance. Hydrocarbon emissions from improper carburation, combustion, and crankcase fumes amount to approximately 7% of the total hydrocarbon emissions. The installation of blow-by equipment on all vehicles, as required by California after 1961, has almost eliminated this element.

Surprisingly, studies and reports[9] by the Automobile Club of Southern California indicate that automobile maintenance has very little, if any, effect on hydrocarbon emissions. The studies indicate that although there may be some increase in emissions, these malfunctions are generally promptly corrected by the owner because they adversely affect the operating characteristics of the vehicles.

Truck emissions. Although trucks generally account for about 20% of total vehicle-miles of travel, and for as much as 50% of the traffic volume on truck routes, they play a relatively minor role in air pollution, for several reasons. Most large trucks, which account for the greatest vehicle-miles of operation, are powered by diesel engines. The total pollution produced by diesel engines is considerably less than that of gasoline. Figure 13.7 shows that a gasoline engine produces 13.7 times more emissions than a diesel engine of comparable size (piston displacement). Also, truck travel is more constant throughout the day, with less peaking occurring during normal morning and afternoon commuting hours. Since air pollution has a temporal as well as geographic dimension, the time distribution of truck travel tends to lessen the impact of emissions by these vehicles.

Noise pollution impacts

Noise has often been described as unwanted sound, sound without value, or vibrational energy out of control. Noise has become a national concern and an increasing problem.

[9] LOUIS J. BINTZ, *Report on the Status of Automotive Air Pollution in the Los Angeles Basin* (Los Angeles, Calif.: Automobile Club of Southern California, Jan. 1967).

Pollutant emitted	Pollutant quantity in cu ft/1,000 lb/fuel: Diesel	Gasoline	Ratio: Gasoline/diesel
Carbon monoxide	123	7,100	58:1
Oxides of nitrogen	337	305	0.9:1
Hydro carbons	93	183	2:1
Totals	553	7,588	13.7:1

Figure 13.7. Comparison of diesel and gasoline engine emissions. SOURCE: M.D. Harmelink and W.J. Peck, *Transportation Air Pollution,* DHO Report No. RR169; Downview, Ontario: Department of Highways, 1971, p. 31.

Generally, noise has three sources: transportation noise, occupational or industrial noise, and community background noise. Because any noise is capable of producing both physical and psychological damage, all sources are of concern in the urban environment.

Typical sound sources. Although aircraft noise may first come to mind when transportation noises are being discussed, noise from surface vehicles such as automobiles, trains, trucks, and motorcycles, and industrial or occupational noises are more widespread and more significant. Most occupational or industrial noise results from metal-to-metal contact or from high-speed equipment (blowers, for example) and is a serious problem in the steel, paper, textile, and petrochemical industries. In this chapter noise pollution is related primarily to transportation noise and comparisons with community noise levels.

The measurement of sound, particularly noise, is a very complex procedure because of the uneven response of the human ear to all sound frequencies, the mixture of frequencies found in the real world, the psychological aspects of annoyance with sound, and the mathematical difficulties of comparing the level of one source to another. Sound measurement and comparison has evolved through a series of scales, beginning with the sound pressure level[10] (SPL), which attempts to adjust all frequencies of sound to an even response level for the human ear. Sound levels in SPL are expressed in phons; a just barely audible sound of 1000 Hz represents *0 phons*. A useful rule in SPL measures is that loudness doubles with every 10-phon increase.

Another effort to develop usable measures of sound involves using a weighted sound curve which attempts to relate the actual response of the ear to mixed frequencies. Subtracting some decibels below 500 Hz and above 8000 Hz can produce a weighted sound level which to some extent correlates to the sound's loudness. Several weightings—A, B, and C—have been proposed, but A-weighted levels are the most widely accepted. All weighted scales are logarithmic in function. The A-weighted scales also take into account the masking of one sound by another. For a detailed comparison of sound measures, the reader is referred to the *Handbook of Noise Assessment*.[11] Table 13-5 provides examples of typical sound sources.

Transportation sound sources. Sound levels illustrate the relative amounts of noise generated by selected sound sources as compared to human response and hearing effects. Comparative sound levels for transportation equipment are presented in Table 13-6. These sound levels, except for aircraft, generally fall within the range 80 to 110 dBA—considerably lower than the average disco.

[10]The term "level" is used to indicate a logarithmic instead of a linear scale. It so happens that the physiological response of the auditory system is essentially exponential; this is another reason for the decibel scale.

[11]Daryl N. May, *Handbook of Noise Assessment* (New York: Van Nostrand Reinhold, 1978), pp. 12–13.

TABLE 13–5
Sound Levels and Human Response

Activity or Location	Noise Level (dBA)	Hearing Effects: Response	Hearing Effects: Conversational Relationships
	150		
Carrier deck jet operation			
	140		
		Painfully loud	
	130	Limit amplified speech	
Jet takeoff (200 ft; 61m)	120		
Discotheque		Maximum vocal effort	
Auto horn (3 ft; 0.9 m)			
Riveting machine	110		
Jet takeoff (2000 ft; 610 m)			
Shout (0.5 ft; 0.2 m)	100		Shouting in ear
N.Y. subway station		Very annoying	
Heavy truck (50 ft; 15.2 m)	90	Hearing damage (8 h)	Shouting at 2 ft (0.6 m)
Pneumatic drill (50 ft; 15.2 m)	80	Annoying	Very loud conversation, 2 ft (0.6 m)
Freight train (50 ft; 15.2 m)			
Freeway traffic (50 ft; 15.2 m)	70	Telephone use difficult	Loud conversation, 2 ft (0.6 m)
		Intrusive	
Air conditioning unit (20 ft; 6.1 m)	60		Loud conversation, 4 ft (1.2 m)
Light auto traffic (100 ft; 30.5 m)	50	Quiet	Normal conversation, 12 ft (3.7 m)
Living room			
Bedroom	40		
Library			
Soft whisper (15 ft; 4.6 m)	30	Very quiet	
Broadcasting studio	20		
	10	Just audible	
	0	Threshold of hearing	

Source: U.S. Environmental Protection Agency, *Noise Pollution*, (Washington, D.C.: U.S. Government Printing Office, Aug. 1972), p. 6.

TABLE 13–6
Comparative Transportation Sound Levels

Miscellaneous Vehicles	Maximum Noise at Operator's Ear (dBA*)
Bus	82–96
Truck	81–92
Tractor	85–113
Diesel locomotive	88–100
Jet airliner (takeoff power)	140–160
River barge tow boat, 919 tons gross (engine room)	101–112
Power boat, at seat nearest motor (cruising speed)	83–104
Outboard motor	85
Street sweeper	96
Crane	85–113
Diesel shovel	91–107
Electric shovel	83–91
Bulldozer	102–106
Road grader	97–100

*A, weighted sound level.

SOURCE: JAMES H. BOTSFORD, "Damage Risk," *Transportation Noises—A Symposium on Acceptability Criteria* (Seattle, Wash.: University of Washington Press, 1970), pp. 110–111.

Measurement of noise. The measurement of noise and the correlation of that noise to human annoyance is a very complex procedure. Extensive research has been completed to quantify the most significant measures of loudness. Two approaches have been utilized; research on how an individual judges loudness and noise from a psychological viewpoint and experiments on groups of people in order to determine how they judge the acceptability of various sounds on category judgment scales.

Community response to noise. Although community response to noise, especially highway-related noise, must certainly be negative, a certain amount of transportation noise is unavoidable. Quantifying objectionable transportation noise levels is difficult because of the extreme variability of human response to noise and, even more important, human response to sound. Any evaluation of community response to noise must consider the following elements:

1. The attitudes of the sample upon which the response is based.
2. The socioeconomic background of the sample (collectively and individually).
3. The presence of other negative stimuli that could be associated with the sound source.
4. The physiological characteristics of each individual in the sample with respect to his or her exposure to sound.

Early studies of freeway noise found that persons judge freeways not so much by noise generation or other assumed factors as by attributes such as accessibility, the advantages of a freeway location, and the appearance of the freeway. Some factors that are generally assumed as being adverse—for example, the appearance of the freeway or the high lighting level associated with most freeways—were reacted to favorably on the part of many respondents, even by those who lived near the freeway. Significantly, those who expressed annoyance at noise levels were doing so on the basis of an average of only 1 dBA increase above the mean level of those who expressed no annoyance at freeway noise.

Sound sources, when viewed in proper perspective, must be related to the prevailing community background noise level. Extensive research indicates that for each community there is a noise signature that corresponds to the type and spatial arrangement of industrial activities, transportation corridors, and land-use patterns within the region as well as atmospheric conditions and the topography.

A study in Ottawa, Canada, attempted to develop a predictive equation to determine the background noise at any given point in the community[12] (see Figure 13.8). For the weekday patterns, the 8:00 A.M. and the 5:00 P.M. peak hours are indicated, with the A.M. peak showing more prominently. Instantaneous peaks of 65 dBA were common through the daylight hours during the week, with the mean level between 50 and 55 dBA. This is contrasted to a mean noise level of from 45 to 50 dBA on Saturdays and Sundays.

Further research suggests that the background noise level within a community is not greatly affected by an increase in city size.[13] Noise levels in a city 100 mi (161 km) in diameter would only increase 4 dBA over a city 10 mi (16.1 km) in diameter. Traffic movement in an urban area does

[12]G. J. THIESSEN, *Community Noise Levels, Transportation Noises—A Symposium on Acceptability Criteria* (Seattle, Wash.: University of Washington Press, 1970), p. 24.

[13]THIESSEN, *Community Noise Levels, Transportation Noises*, p. 26.

Figure 13.8. Sound signature for Ottawa, Canada. SOURCE: James D. Chalupnik, *Transportation Noises: A Symposium on Acceptability Criteria;* Seattle, Wash.: University of Washington Press, 1970, p. 27.

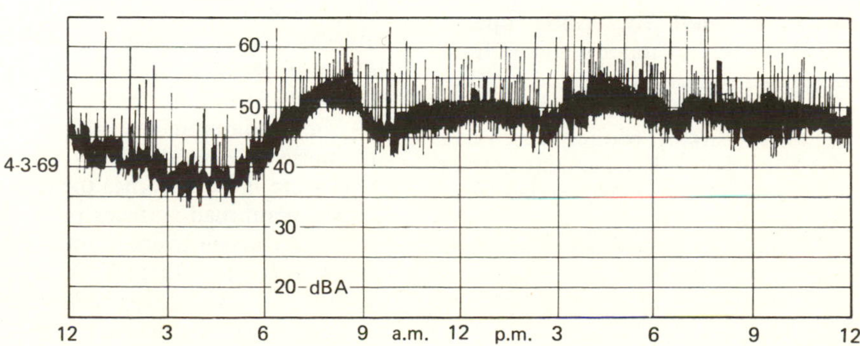

not drastically change the background noise level. Research studies indicate that doubling of the density of traffic would increase the background noise by only 3 dBA.

Automobile noise characteristics. In spite of the apparent lack of formal complaints, traffic noise is the most significant element of noise in the urban environment. In a 1971 survey of 1200 persons, 55% of the respondents mentioned traffic noise as the primary element of annoyance in their neighborhood, whereas only 15% mentioned aircraft noise as a primary element.[14]

The noise emission level in dBA at a 50-ft (15.2-m) distance from a typical passenger automobile on an average roadway surface is found to be[15]

$$L_{auto} = 16 + 30 \log V$$

where V is the auto speed in mph. This yields sound levels (rounded off to the nearest interval) over the range of typical speeds shown in Table 13-7.

TABLE 13–7
Automobile Noise vs. Speed

Speed		Noise Level (dBA)
km/h	mph	
48	30	60
64	40	64
80	50	67
60	60	69
113	70	71

SOURCE: W. J. GALLOWAY, W. E. CLARKE, AND J. S. KERRICK, *Highway Noise Measurement, Simulation and Mixed Reaction*, NCHRP Report 79 (Washington, D.C.: Highway Research Board, 1969).

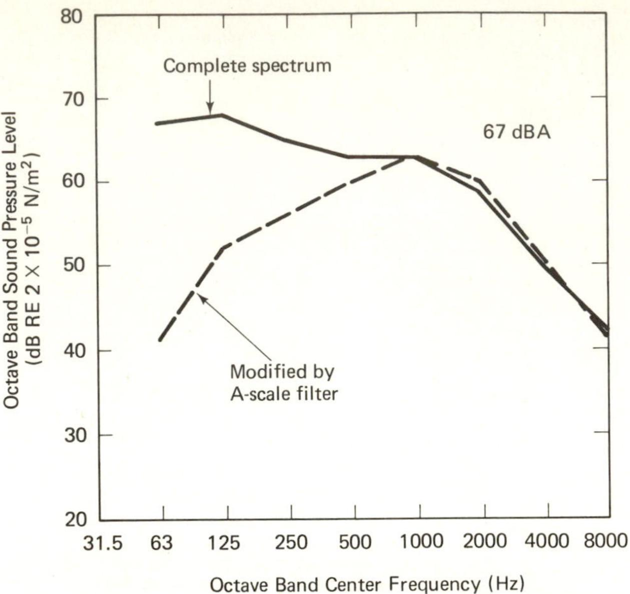

Figure 13.9. Generalized sound spectrum of typical passenger automobile. SOURCE: W.J. Galloway, W.E. Clarke, and J.S. Kerrick, *Highway Noise Measurement, Simulation and Mixed Reaction,* Report No. 78; Washington, D.C.: Highway Research Board, 1969, Fig. 13.5.

The octave-band-frequency spectrum at a 50-ft (15.2-m) distance for a typical automobile moving at 50 mph (80 km/h) is shown by the solid curve in Figure 13.9. The spectrum shape does not vary significantly for the speed range 35 to 65 mph (56 to 105 km/h), although, of course, the noise level changes with speed as indicated. The spectrum shape does change slightly as a function of road surface.

If the total noise of the typical auto (the solid curve of Figure 13.9) were passed through the A-scale filter of a sound-level meter, the resulting octave-band contributions would be approximately the relative importance of the various octave bands in terms of their contributions toward the loudness or disturbance of the noise to people. It is seen that the center-frequency region, 500 to 2000 Hz, is the strongest contributor in terms of A-scale readings.

Auto noise levels as affected by traffic operations. Noise from motor vehicles in motion comes from two major sources: the engine exhaust system and the tire-roadway system. Major engine-exhaust noise sources consist of the intake noise at the carburetor, cooling fans, valve lifters, gear boxes, and exhaust noise. Exhaust noise, when properly muffled (as with factory-installed equipment), probably contributes no more than 10 to 15% to the overall noise signature of the vehicle.

Tire–roadway noise is present for all vehicles in motion and is the dominant source of noise under certain operating conditions. The tire–roadway interaction produces a sound signature primarily attributable to the pattern and depth of tire tread, roughness of the road surface, wetness, tire stiffeners, tire loading, and the suspension system of the vehicle.

Speed produces variations in noise. Table 13-7 illustrates that for an individual automobile, the higher the speed, the louder the noise. Under conditions of maximum acceleration, automobiles were found to produce approximately 8 dBA higher noise levels than for normal cruise conditions at the same speed. This would be significant for ramp approaches to main highways, where high acceleration is required to enter the high-speed traffic lanes.

Traffic volumes as well as speed play an important role in noise production. Figure 13.10 illustrates the relationship among speed, volume, and sound level. It is important to note that these curves represent *uninterrupted flow*—not stop-and-start conditions. The range in sound level for 1000 vehicles per hour (vph) is about 10 dBA between speeds of 20 and 70 mph (32 and 117 km/h). From the chart, 10,000 vph will produce about the same sound level (63 dBA) at 20 mph (32 km/h) 1000 vph will produce at 70 mph (117 km/h).

The condition of the road surface makes a difference in the noise level produced by automobiles at higher speeds, where tire noise becomes the dominant noise. Very rough, coarse-grain road surfaces produce higher noise levels, up to 5 dBA above average road surfaces; and very smooth, fine-grain road surfaces produce lower noise levels, as much as 5 dBA below average road surfaces. Table 13-8 provides general guidelines for road surface types. There is no stan-

[14]D. R. JOHNSON AND E. G. SANDERS, The Evaluation of Noise from Freely Flowing Traffic, *J. Sound Vib.*, (July 1968), p. 28.

[15]BOLT, BERANEK AND NEWMAN, INC., *Traffic Noise Sources, Fundamentals and Abatement of Highway Traffic Noise* (prepared for U.S. Department of Transportation, Office of Environmental Policy, June 1973), Chap. 2, p. 1.

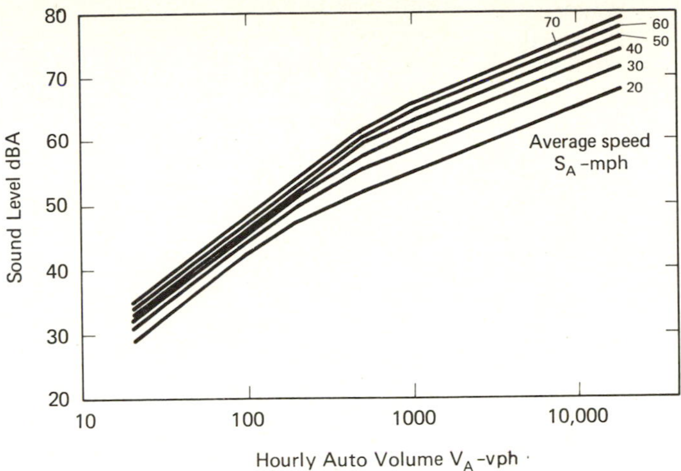

Figure 13.10. Sound levels as a function of volume and speed. SOURCE: M.D. Harmelink, *Noise and Vibration Control for Transportation Systems,* Road Research Report 168; Toronto, Ontario: Department of Highways, 1970, Fig. 18.

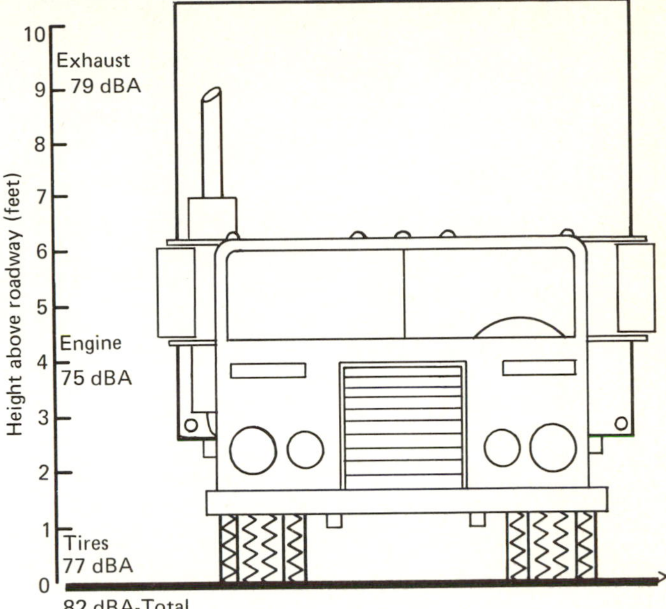

Figure 13.11. Truck noise component sources and height. SOURCE: Bolt, Beranek and Newman, Inc., *Fundamentals and Abatement of Highway Traffic Noise,* Washington, D.C.: Federal Highway Administration, June 1973, Fig. 2.5.

TABLE 13–8
Auto Noise and Road Surface Type

Surface Description	Add to Auto Noise Level (dBA)
Very rough surface	+5
Medium rough surface	+2
Average surface	0
Medium smooth surface	−2

SOURCE: BOLT, BERANEK AND NEWMAN, INC., *Fundamentals and Abatement of Highway Traffic Noise* (Washington, D.C.: Federal Highway Administration, 1973), pp. 2–3.

dard for rating roadway surface roughness or smoothness, but for any noise, the surface smoothness can be a small factor in noise control design.

Experiments comparing a new vehicle with a 2-year-old vehicle of the same model indicate that the difference in noise levels in relation to vehicle age is primarily caused by exhaust system wear and body rattles. The average difference in noise levels (over all ranges of speed) of from 3 to 5 dBA indicates a relatively small change in noise as related to age.

The loudest sounds are generated at intersection areas by stopping and starting vehicles. These noise sources consist of braking noises, including tire–roadway and brake system (primarily in deceleration and engine exhaust noise) and tire–roadway interaction (primarily in acceleration). Generally, deceleration at intersections is controlled and without tire skid, so that the acceleration phase of intersection produces the greater sound level.

Truck noise characteristics. There are significant variations in the noise signature of individual vehicle types. Trucks, especially large diesel units, although a relatively small proportion of the total traffic stream, contribute significantly to the noise produced by traffic. Diesel trucks are inherently more noisy than passenger cars, producing a noise level about 15 dBA higher in each type of vehicle operating condition. The noise source for large diesel trucks (see Figure 13.11) is a composite of contributions from the engine exhaust system and the tire–roadway interaction, but the engine and exhaust noise tends to be dominant at low operating speeds, and tire–roadway interaction dominates at high operating speeds. A comparison of passenger car noise with truck noise is given in Figure 13.12.

Another interesting characteristic of noise production by trucks is its variation based upon the operating conditions. Figure 13.13 presents data for a truck during cruise at level (1900 rpm), climbing an upgrade (2100 rpm), and acceleration and descending a downgrade (1600 rpm). There is a 20-dBA difference in sound levels between downgrade and upgrade operating conditions, and generally there is a range of 5 to 10 dBA in noise level based only on speed variations.

Motorcycle noise characteristics. Motorcycles are often cited as the prime violators of noise restrictions. Measurements show no particular correlation between the amount of power developed or the size of the vehicle and the amount of noise output. Exhaust-level muffling is highly variable for each manufacturer's product and is much more variable in the hands of the users.

Rail transit noise characteristics. Noise levels for the rail public transportation facilities in Table 13-9 are based on current experience with equipment operated in Germany, England, Toronto, and Philadelphia. A range of noise levels upward from 78 dBA has been recorded, depending on the observer's location, the type of equipment, and the location whether above or below ground. These noise levels are representative of most of the noises associated with existing public transit systems. For comparison, noise levels on the Montreal Metro, a modern transit system utilizing rubber

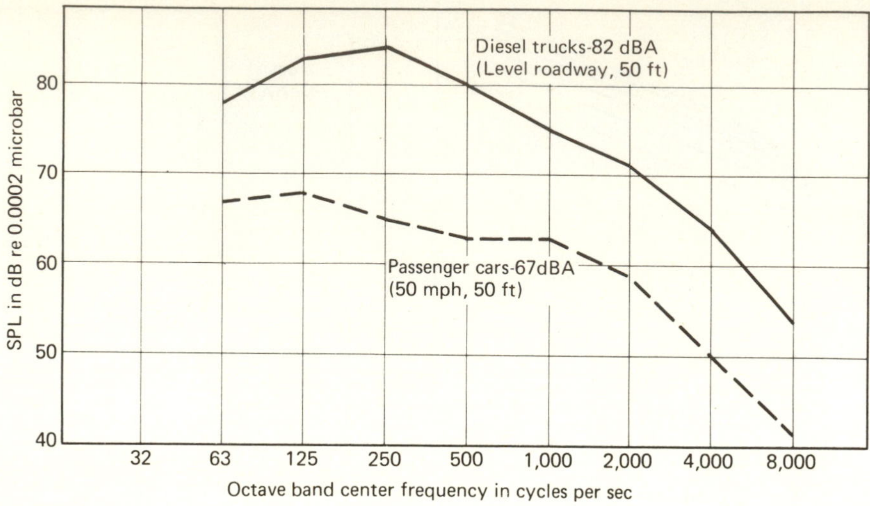

Figure 13.12. Comparison of truck and auto noise for acceleration. SOURCE: W.E. Clarke, W.J. Galloway, and J.S. Kerrick, *Highway Noise Measurement, Simulation and Mixed Reactions,* NCHRP Report 78, Washington, D.C.: Highway Research Board, 1969, p. 42.

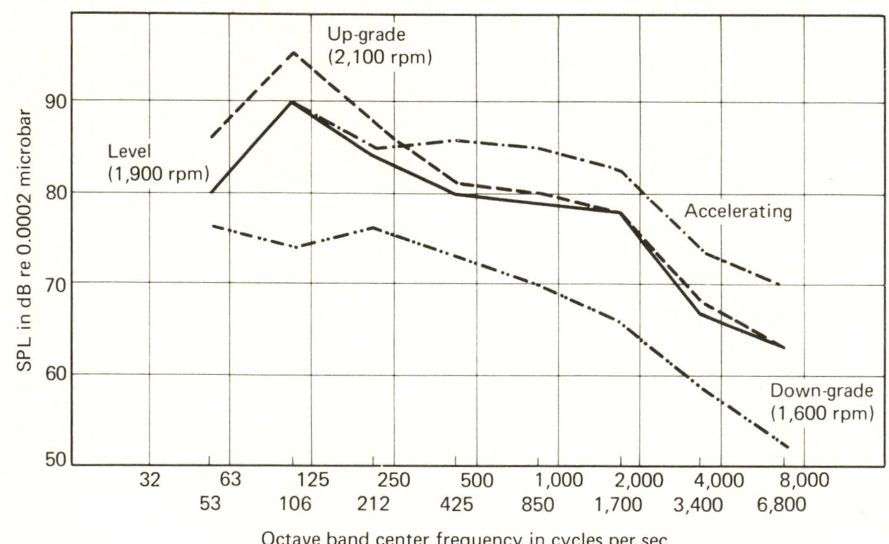

Figure 13.13. Sound level of truck operating conditions. SOURCE: W.E. Clarke, W.J. Galloway, and J.S. Kerrick, *Highway Noise Measurement, Simulation, and Mixed Reactions,* NCHRP Report 78, Washington, D.C.: Highway Research Board, 1969, p. 39.

tires on concrete rail, are generally in the range 60 to 80 dBA.

The three basic rail–wheel systems in use today are the conventional steel wheel–rail, the rubber tire on concrete, and the rubber tire on monorail. The severity of the noise problems encountered are primarily determined by the rail–wheel system involved. Surface rail lines generally provide a quieter ride for the passenger because of the lack of noise reflected back into the train, but produce more noise for the nonuser than an underground line because of the absence of a noise enclosure. Structure-borne noise is still a problem with underground lines, as it can be transmitted through the soil from all surfaces of the subway structure into adjacent structures for a considerable distance. Aerial structures pose special noise and vibration problems and should be avoided in noise-sensitive areas.

Aircraft noise characteristics. The present aircraft noise problem is primarily concentrated around airports and results from the rapid growth of air transportation after the end of World War II and the advent of the jet aircraft in the late 1950s. The supersonic jets (SST) have noise impacts far beyond the immediate environs of the airport, of course, and may pose a broader problem if usage becomes more widespread.

The intensity and frequency distribution, duration, and time characteristics of aircraft noise are relevant. Clearly recognizable physical differences exist between jet engine

TABLE 13–9
Typical Noise Levels Produced by Rail Transit Systems

Investigator or Reporter	System		Internal Noise Levels	External Noise Levels				
Davis (1) (all subways)	Philadelphia	30 mph:	103 phons = 98 dB; vibration high					
	Boston	30 mph:	97 phons = 95 dB; vibration high					
		45–50 mph:	90 phons = 86 dB;					
	New York	30 mph:	98 phons = 94 dB; vibration medium	Station platform	103–108 phons = 98–100 dB			
	Chicago	30 mph:	98 phons = 92 dB; vibration low	Station platform	99–106 phons = 92–100 dB			
	London	30 mph:	93 phons = 87 dB; vibration medium					
		45–50 mph:	91 phons = 86 dB;					
	Berlin	30 mph:	85 phons = 86 dB; vibration low	Station platform	92–98 phons = 88–94 dB			
		40 mph:	91 phons = 86 dB;					
	Hamburg	30 mph:	87 phons = 80 dB; vibration low	Station platform	95–105 phons = 88–97 dB			
	Paris (rubber)	30 mph:	89 phons = 86 dB; vibration medium	Station platform	93–101 phons = 88–96 dB			
	Toronto	30 mph:	90 phons = 85 dB; vibration low	Station platform	93–94 phons = 87 dB			
		45–50 mph:	90 phons = 86 dB;	Inside adjacent houses	Up to 64 dB			
				25 ft	50 ft	75 ft	100 ft	over 100 ft
Lord (2)	Toronto	40 mph:	78 dBA	84 dBA	79 dBA	76 dBA	—	—
	British Rail suburban train	40 mph:	71 dBA	88 dBA	83 dBA	78 dBA	—	—
	London Transport Metro Line	40 mph:	78 dBA in open, 82 dBA in tunnel	87 dBA	—	—	—	—
	Alweg monorail	40 mph:	81 dBA	80 dBA	75 dBA	68 dBA	—	—
	Safege Monorail	40 mph:	68 dBA	84 dBA	78 dBA	76 dBA	—	—
Embleton and Thiessen (3)	Freight trains near Ottawa, Ontario							
	Diesel engine:			100–110 dBA	—	—	88–100 dBA	74–84 dBA at 800 ft
	Track noise at 40 mph:			95–98 dBA	—	—	89–93 dBA	79–83 dBA at 800 ft
	Whistles			116 dBA	—	—	104–107 dBA	92–97 dBA at 400 ft
Botsford (4)	Philadelphia subway		Below ground: 82–95 dBA Above ground: 78–90 dBA	Boarding platform: Below ground: 93–98 dBA Above ground: 83–93 dBA				

SOURCE: (1) E. W. DAVIS, *Comparison of Noise and Vibration Levels in Rapid Transit Vehicle Systems* (Operations Research, Inc., for National Capital Transportation Agency, Washington, Apr. 1964). (2) *Manchester Rapid Transit Study* (De Leuw, Cather and Partners/Hennessy, Chadwick, O Heocha and Partners for City of Manchester, Ministry of Transport, and British Railways, Aug. 1967). (3) T. F. W. EMBLETON AND G. J. THIESSEN, "Train Noises and Use of Adjacent Land, *Sound*, *1*(1), 10–16 (1962). (4) J. H. BOTSFORD, Damage Risk, *Transportation Noises—A Symposium on Acceptability Criteria* (Seattle, Wash.: University of Washington Press, 1970), pp. 103–113.

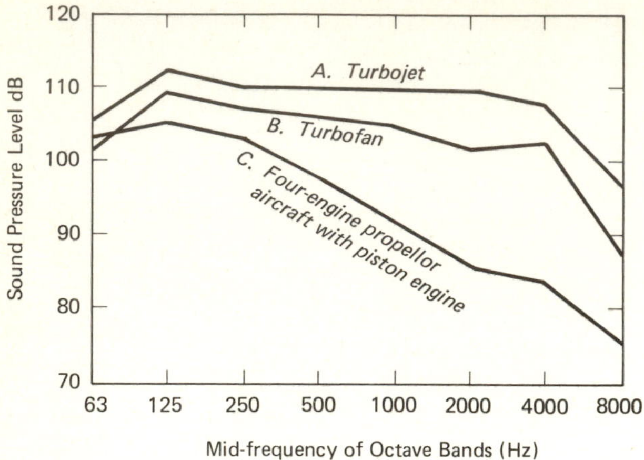

Figure 13.14. Frequency spectra of aircraft types in flight. SOURCE: W. Burns, *Noise and Man,* London: John Murray, 1968, Fig. 42.

noise and the noise produced by propeller-driven aircraft. Figure 13.14 compares the noise levels of differing aircraft types in flight measured at 50 ft (15.2 m). The noise of any type of aircraft engine increases with increased power. Since takeoff demands maximum power, noise output is greatest in this flight condition. However, the noise characteristics of jet- and piston-engined aircraft differ not only at maximum power conditions, but also markedly under reduced power or idling conditions; piston engine noise levels are significantly lower than jet engine noise levels on takeoff, landing, or taxiing.

Noise from large piston-engined aircraft originates chiefly in the engine exhaust and the propellers, with aerodynamic noise and mechanical engine noise as less important sources. The noise at takeoff is considerable, but high frequencies are less noticeable than in the case of the jet engine, as shown in Figure 13.14. Jet engine noise comes from several sources, including the noise of the jet itself, the compressor, and the turbine. The characteristic roar of a jet engine is produced by the violent mixing of the exhaust gases with the air into which they are discharged, and depends markedly on the velocity of the actual jet relative to the surrounding air.

Visual impacts

The visual impact of the highway environment is the basis on which most of the driving public judges a good or bad road. There are miles and miles of scenic areas made accessible through the development of modern roadways, but the good areas tend to be forgotten when the motoring public is exposed to the bad areas (see Figure 13.15). Many unsightly areas tend to occur along arterial streets in most urban areas. Unfortunately, the majority of the motoring public is exposed to these areas every day during their commute to work, whereas they may only see the good areas infrequently when they are vacationing. Negative visual impacts seem to be primarily associated with roadways in the public's mind. However, they relate to other modes of transportation as well. Many miles of railroads in urban areas are lined with abandonded, deteriorated industrial facilities. More important, many rail passenger stations constructed many years ago tend to be dilapidated and in need of either renovation or abandonment. This is particularly true in the northeastern United States, where commuter rail facilities were extensively used in past years but have since been forgotten.

Streets and roads. One of the reasons for the poor visual appearance of streets and roadways is the "fractured responsibility" of persons and agencies for a particular section of road. Whereas a state or county highway agency may be responsible for the paving and cross-section elements, the control of signs, building conditions, and adjacent development may well be within the purview of a city planning department or zoning commission—or completely controlled by private hands. A major element is the negative impact of overhead utilities along the right-of-way, which generally are the responsibility of the local utility. An ex-

Figure 13.15. Visual characteristics of strip commercial development. SOURCE: Traffic Planning Associates, Inc.

BEFORE

AFTER

Figure 13.16. Comparison of before and after urban street environment (Buckhead, Atlanta, Ga.). SOURCE: Before, North Georgia Chapter, American Institute of Architects, *The Mess We Live In,* Atlanta, Ga.: North Georgia Chapter, American Institute of Architects, 1960, Fig. 16; After, Traffic Planning Associates, Inc.

ample of a real before-and-after condition is illustrated in Figure 13.16.

Considerable study of the visual quality of streets and freeways in urban areas has been done. Appleyard et al.[16] analyzed the aesthetics of existing streets and highways and focused upon the possibilities for reestablishing an understandable urban scale through sensitive design of the urban expressway. Their research included four phases: the fundamentals of the highway experience, recording visual highway sequences, the analysis of existing highway sequences, and the development of visual study design procedures. The objective of the research was to develop a procedure through which expressway design, and hence all roadway design, could be made to reflect a conscious aesthetic effort.

Quoting from another study, Visual Survey and Design Plan[17]:

> Our streets, especially commerical streets, are crowded corridors where automobiles and pedestrians are hopelessly intermingled and where ugly, unplanned, uncoordinated street furniture completes the visual confusion. The graphics of an area should be integrated with the architecture and landscape of the area so as to achieve visual unity and individual identity. Traffic signs, store signs, lettering outside and inside buildings as well as letters on traffic lights, sidewalks, and benches should all show a relationship of form and color. Planned graphics will not be pleasing to the eye, but will guide the motorist and pedestrian through the area efficiently.

The efforts of urban design professionals to achieve coordination in signing includes the consideration of traffic signs as well as other graphics. "Street Graphics,"[18] a report published by the American Society of Landscape Architects, adds:

> While the street graphics controls proposed herein function within the performance standards of a legal framework to help produce a more pleasing aesthetic result, it is hoped that this study will go beyond legalities to really interest sign manufacturers and their clients and to help strengthen decisions of our courts which are coming more and more to recognize amenity as a *legitimate basis* for public concern and regulation.

Recognition of the sign control problem has received attention in the past from the Federal Highway Administration through the allocation of a 5% additional funding for state highway departments which exercise controls on billboards within 800 ft (244 m) of the Interstate System right-of-way.[19]

Traffic control devices. In recent years the National Advisory Committee on Uniform Traffic Control Devices has been very active in establishing uniform signs and pavement markings throughout the United States. These uniform standards were developed to assure that highways are signed and marked in accordance with an overall plan. Many of the ideas for uniformity and symbolism came from countries in western Europe, where urban development is more dense and the need for communication is more intense. Uniformity has received international support from a broad range of professional groups.

Some groups have strongly objected to multiple signing or oversigning. Harold Lewis Malt, a landscape architect, made the following comment:

> When three, four, five or ten traffic signals are required at one intersection to let the motorist know who has the right-of-way, then it is clear that something is wrong with the design of the signal, the design of the installation, or the design of the intersection—perhaps, all three. This kind of design is deliberate. It results from the theory that communicating a message with more than one sign or signal helps minimize the background "noise" of all the competing stimuli on the urban scene. In other words, redundancy is considered desirable. Although usual engineering practice

[16]DONALD APPLEYARD, KEVIN LYNCH, AND JOHN R. MYER, *The View from the Road* (Cambridge, Mass.: MIT Press, 1964), p. 38.

[17]NORTH GEORGIA CHAPTER, AMERICAN INSTITUTE OF ARCHITECTS, *Visual Survey and Design Plan* (Atlanta, Ga.: American Institute of Architects, 1965).

[18]W. R. EWALD AND D. R. MANDELKER, *Street Graphics* (Washington, D.C.: ASLA Foundation, 1971), p. 23.

[19]*Congressional Record,* Federal Aid Highway Act.

tolerates some over-design as a factor, redundancy may cause chaos and confusion in the hands of an unskillful engineer.

In Buffalo, New York, there are estimated to be 45,000 traffic signs displayed on light standards and makeshift supports. In a single year, 1966, the City's Bureau of Signs and Meters rehabilitated 5,304 traffic signs, fabricated 6,600 new signs, installed 963 concrete foundations, and erected 853 street name signs. This pattern exists in other cities of the country. In a recent study in the District of Columbia alone, there was an inventory of 34,100 parking signs estimated to carry over 51,000 parking messages.[20]

The point that some urban design professionals are raising is that the sheer number of traffic signs on many streets and highways constitutes visual pollution and contributes to confusion and, possibly, to accidents. At the same time, many of the signs are not necessarily contributing to the efficient flow of traffic. Additional research on better ways of communicating more effectively with motorists is needed.

Freeways. Freeways offer an opportunity to enhance the environment as well as to furnish a necessary transportation service. They can provide a green belt space in developed areas where space is nonexistent, and with careful design can be used to provide structure to the community. Figure 13.17 is an example of a freeway used as an asset to the physical environment as well as a major transportation facility.

Generally, the visual impact created by a freeway is the result of the highway designer's appreciation for visual amenities. Few highway design professionals have done a comprehensive job of considering the total improvement corridor where highway improvements have been made, particularly in urban areas. Whatever the causes of adverse visual impact, most of the problems can be solved by good design, by the proper consideration of the total environment, and by the use of joint development proposals that complement the proposed facility.

The detrimental visual aspects of freeways can be divided into two basic areas: (1) the physical characteristics of the facility itself, such as ramps, structures, barriers, medians, retaining walls, and other elements that clash with the environment; and (2) land development patterns for which the freeway has served as a catalyst. Examples of visually negative freeway characteristics are especially evident along segments constructed in the early days of freeway development before there was much experience in freeway design. Many of these facilities have design deficiencies such as narrow barrier-type medians, high retaining walls, abutment-type bridges, prolonged elevated structures, and heavily signed transition areas, which create a negative visual reaction on the part of the motorist.

Parking lots. The improper design of large parking areas for major traffic generators can have strong adverse visual impacts. Such areas have traditionally been barren, lacking even a sprig of green or any other landscaping to make them more attractive and more functional. By contrast, Figure 13.18 illustrates a well-landscaped parking area.

Landscaped islands and other channelization and orientation elements have real functional uses in traffic operations. It is very difficult for a motorist driving through a maze of parked cars to locate an egress point. The use of

[20]Harold Lewis Malt, *Furnishing the City* (New York: McGraw-Hill, 1970), p. 178.

Figure 13.17. Freeway that enhances the environment. Source: J.O. Simonds, ed., *The Freeway and the City,* Washington, D.C.: U.S. Government Printing Office, 1968, p. 40.

Figure 13.18. Well-landscaped parking lot. SOURCE: Traffic Planning Associates, Inc.

islands as a channelizing device helps to reduce high-speed diagonal maneuvers across parking areas, provides direction for motorists, and reduces parking lot accidents. Large parking lots should be divided into a series of smaller lots (generally not exceeding 400 to 500 cars each) in order to obtain more efficient use, safer operation, and better traffic circulation.

Railroad transportation facilities. Although there are literally thousands of miles of rail in the world that offer the rail passenger dramatic and exciting visual scenery, there are major problem areas, especially in older urban areas. However, the visual impact of the rail and trackbed, no matter how negative as a result of abutting properties, are generally insignificant to the rider. As long as the quality of service is adequate and the cars and stations are pleasing in appearance, negative impacts are held to a minimum. Recent improvements in railroad passenger equipment in the United States by Amtrak have encouraged the interest of the public in rail passenger transportation. Much more emphasis is needed, particularly in terminal facility restoration and reconstruction.

Urban transit. The visual impacts of urban transit generally relate to either street and road impacts or rail transportation impacts, depending on the type of urban transit. Bus transit, with the exception of rapid busways, operates over the urban street system or the rural highway system. Visual impacts covered under streets and roads therefore apply. In the case of older rail mass transit, the comments made relative to rail transportation generally apply.

The construction of new rail rapid transit systems has generally stressed the importance of a positive visual impact. As a result, planning and design has generally placed more emphasis on the facility being compatible with the environment and in stimulating a positive attitude toward the facility. A more detailed discussion is presented in the section "Technological Approaches."

Impacts on land development

The subject of transportation impacts on land development is so broad that it is difficult to touch on the subject in a limited way. Transportation and land-use impact upon the broad social–economic–environmental spectrum of society. The following sections discuss the most significant of these impacts related to environment.

Highways and commercial development. Land development patterns are dramatically influenced by the accessibility provided by highways and streets. High-intensity development of many roadside businesses is frequently stimulated at major intersections and interchanges. This overuse of the land usually creates a negative visual impact. Strip commercial development, coupled with the lack of sign control and the lack of access control, is characteristic of too many highway-oriented commercial districts. The lack of land-use control along a new highway can result in adverse impact on the development of a quality environment. The negative effect of "strip" development along a street or highway may be measured in visual, accident, and congestion impacts. An "affiliated commercial area" on either side of the highway must be served by a network of streets. The traffic generated on these cross streets and at major access points to the development must enter the highway at a number of closely spaced intersections. The most significant detrimental impact is the reduction in capacity for through traffic caused by the number of turning movements generated by the highway commercial businesses. Although accidents cannot be considered pollution in the normal sense, accident zones related to strip commercial development create a major negative impact related to transportation.

Traffic and existing development. Strip commercial development, which may occur in response to accessibility or traffic volumes, may adversely affect the existing development in adjacent areas. Strip development requires visual exposure to the major traffic corridor along which it is located. Sites that provide direct visual exposure are highly sought by most highway-oriented establishments. Thus, the development corridor is relatively narrow, usually only one lot deep along the highway. There is little effort to encourage development to spread laterally to adjacent areas, which would tend to concentrate the negative impacts in one area.

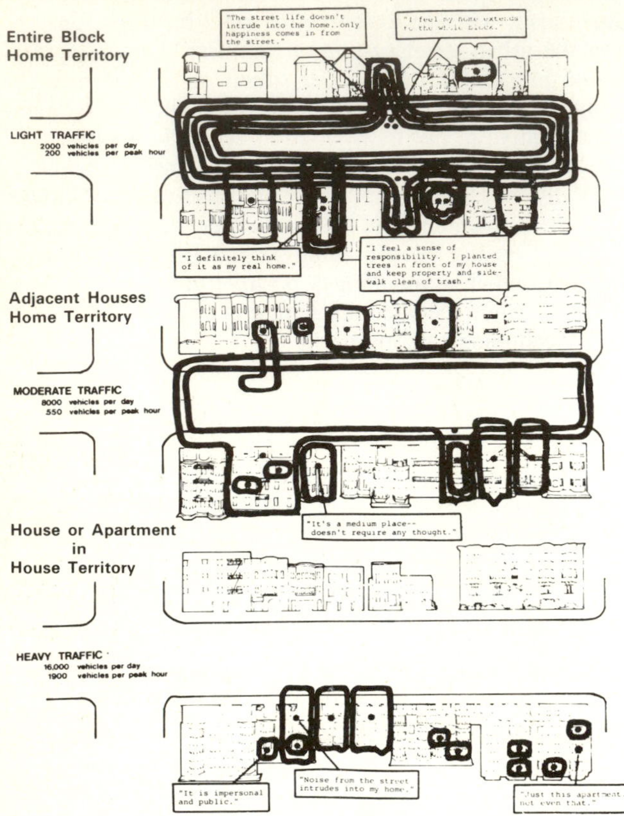

Figure 13.19. Defined home territory. (Lines show areas people indicated as their "home territory.") SOURCE: Donald Appleyard, Sue Guerson, and Mark Untell, *Livable Urban Streets*, Washington, D.C.: Federal Highway Administration, 1976, p. 20.

Because of the linearity of development, these areas tend to extend for miles along some major arterial routes. Their attendant negative aspects include the exposure of a large amount of residential area to commercial operations. This is especially harmful in the case of restaurants because of the long and late hours of operation.

Traffic and neighborhood preservation. Recent studies have indicated that there are significant interrelationships between the levels of traffic movement through a neighborhood and the attractiveness of that neighborhood for residential use. This is especially significant in neighborhoods near central business districts, because they are likely to be exposed to heavy traffic with no origin or destination in the area—simply using local streets as a cut-through. Appleyard, in his studies of traffic volume levels in San Francisco neighborhoods, found that, as the traffic increased, the desirability of the area as a living place decreased and the market for residential use became more and more limited.[21] Figure 13.19 illustrates the progressive nature in traffic volumes and its impact on the desirability of a residential area.

The negative aspects associated with increases in traffic volumes are noise, air pollution, and accident potential. Noise restricts the ability of separate blocks in the neighborhood to communicate—the higher the noise level, the greater the constraint on communication. Air pollution and accident potential and hazard are mostly psychological. The perception of the resident, whether correct or not, is usually the basis for judging an area desirable or undesirable. Rarely are these judgments based on objective evaluation of data. Visual impact, subjective influences such as annoyance at traffic, and other influences have considerable impact on the desirability of a particular area.

Traffic and urban sprawl. Much has been written about the adverse effects of urban sprawl. The literature generally treats urban sprawl as inefficient and wasteful of natural resources, resulting in unattractive development. It is said that urban sprawl results in excessive expenditures for utility and transportation facilities and does not allow proper timing of land development, which, in turn, results in undesirable development patterns. An objective evaluation of the pros and cons of urban sprawl is, however, not that simple.

The spread of urban sprawl in North America corresponds in time with the rapid increase in automobile usage in the United States and Canada and the corresponding decline in mass transit patronage. Urban sprawl lowers the density of development for the metropolitan area. Trends in density for 21 North American cities are illustrated in Figure 13.20. This Wilbur Smith study found that density patterns primarily reflect the city's age and the mode of intraurban transport that dominated the transportation picture during the city's formative years.[22] The family of curves representing different points in time clearly indicates a continuing trend toward decentralization for most cities; however, there are a few notable exceptions, such as Los Angeles, and New Orleans. In every land, pedestrian-oriented cities have always been tightly clustered, and cities built before mechanical transportation have been typified by high density. Thus, comparison of recently built North American cities with large older cities throughout the world provides insight into the changes that new forms of transport have wrought on the patterns of urban living. Cities in Europe, Asia, and South America of similar population are universally more dense.

Decreasing residential densities in the United States are related to a number of factors:

1. The availability of mortgage money to finance up to 90% of the cost of a single-family house.
2. The income tax advantage provided by the U.S. government for those persons financing homes (through the deduction of mortgage interest cost).
3. The reduction of the local tax burden by living outside the incorporated limits of the larger cities.
4. Improved accessibility within the cities provided by freeways and major arterial systems.
5. Increased vehicular ownership provided by higher incomes.

[21]DONALD APPLEYARD, SUE GUERSON, AND MARK UNTELL, *Livable Urban Streets* (Washington, D.C.: Federal Highway Administration, 1976), p. 21.

[22]WILBUR SMITH & ASSOCIATES, *Transportation and Parking for Tomorrow's Cities* (Detroit, Mich.: Automotive Manufacturers Association, 1966), pp. 15–18.

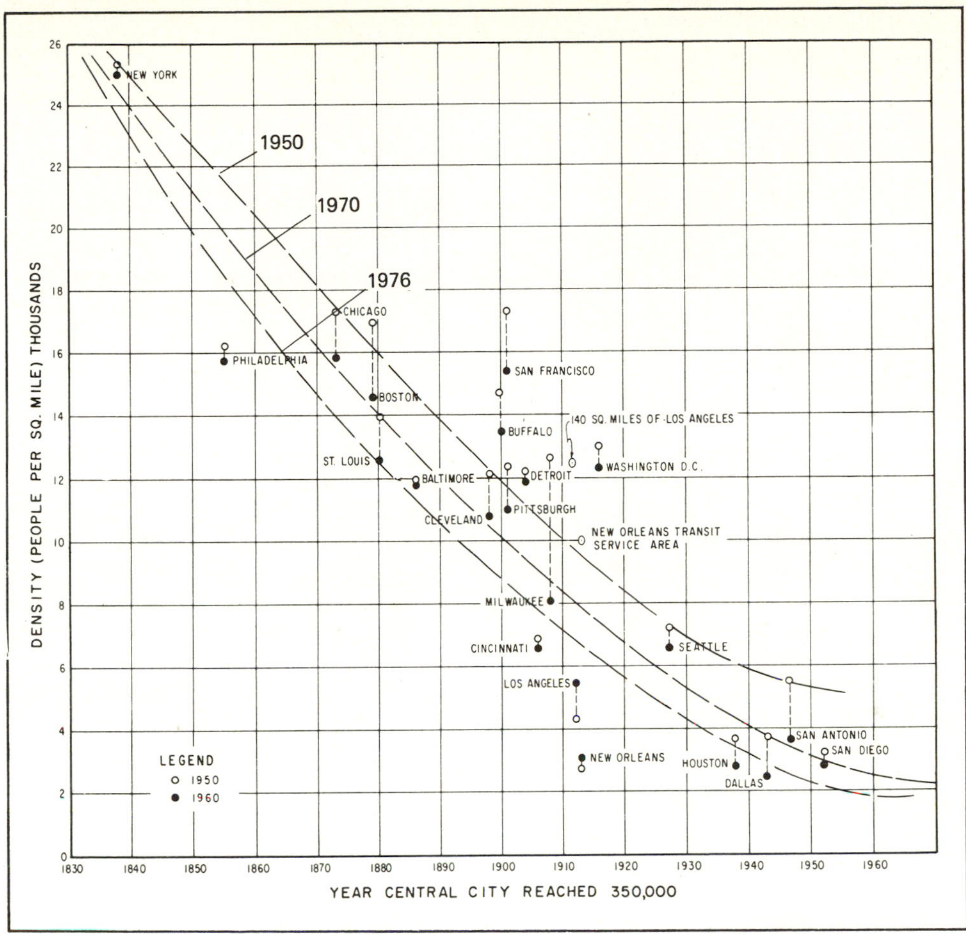

Figure 13.20. City age and population density. SOURCE: Wilbur Smith & Associates, *Transportation and Parking for Tomorrow's Cities,* Detroit, Mich.: Automotive Manufacturers Associations, 1966, p. 15. 1970 and 1976 curves by Traffic Planning Associates, Inc., from data supplied by the U.S. Bureau of the Census, *Statistical Abstract.*

Although there are other factors that play a role, reliance on the automobile has been most significant in this trend. An example of comparative land utilization of a highway-dominated "centralized" land-use plan with a low-density "sprawl" land-use plan is illustrated by the planning efforts for southeastern Wisconsin (Milwaukee). Densities in Milwaukee decreased from 12,500 persons/mi^2 in 1950 to 7500 persons/mi^2 in 1976. The area is expected to have a population density of 4400 persons/mi^2 for the "1990 centralized plan" as compared to 2700 persons/mi^2 for the "sprawl" plan.[23] Thus, even for the centralized plan, densities for 1990 were anticipated to decline to 60% of the 1976 level.

For the centralized plan, which involves a mass transportation network, the total land for transportation was estimated at 66.5 mi^2 or approximately 30% of the total land area. For the "sprawl" alternative 94.6 mi^2 or approximately 40% of the total urbanized area was required for transportation.[24] Vehicle hours of operation and operating costs per day for the "centralized plan" as compared to the "sprawl plan" were estimated at $20.3 billion and $22.31 billion respectively, a difference of approximately $2 billion per day. The comparative costs of transportation system cooperation with different densities and patterns of development is very significant.

[23]SEWRPC, *Planning Report No. 7, Land Use Transportation Study,* Vol. 3, *Recommended Regional Land Use and Transportation Plans—1990* (Waukesha, Wis.: Southeastern Wisconsin Regional Planning Commission, 1966), pp. 69–71.

[24]SEWRPC, *Recommended Land Use and Transportation Plans,* p. 71.

Technological approaches to improving the environment

The legislative approach to improving the environment is limited to broad policymaking. Extensive technical detail is necessary to provide a precise guide for implementation. Therefore, technological approaches supplementing legislation are required for implementation. Recently, considerable technical work has been done on methods of alleviating air pollution and noise problems.

Air pollution control packages

The objectives of the air pollution control packages are as follows:

TABLE 13–10
Transportation-related Air Pollution Problems

Type of Problem	Pollutant	Air Quality Standard	Typical Impact Area	Selected Travel Factors Contributing to Problem
Localized	Carbon monoxide	8-hour 10,000 g/m³ (9 ppm) 1-hour: 40,000 g/m³ (35 ppm)	Intersections Locations adjacent to freeways and arterials	High vehicular traffic volumes Stop-and-go traffic flows (e.g., idling)
Regional	Photochemical oxidant	1-hour: 160 g/m³ (0.08 ppm)	Overall urban area (based on oxidant concentrations measured at specific locations)	High vehicular traffic volumes Low speeds

SOURCE: PEAT, MARWICK, MITCHELL & CO., *Air Quality Impacts of Transit Improvement, Preferential Lane, and Carpool/Vanpool Programs* (prepared for EPA, Report 400/2-78-002a, Mar. 1978).

1. To identify transportation control measures for reducing air pollution emissions and meeting National Ambient Air Quality Standards.
2. To evaluate the travel and emissions impacts of individual control measures and packages of such measures.
3. To suggest approaches for selecting, analyzing, and evaluating impacts of TSM and longer-range control measures.

Each of these points is discussed below following a brief overview of the relationship between travel and air pollution within the urban areas.

Localized and regional problems. Relatively few urban areas over 200,000 in the United States meet National Ambient Air Quality Standards (NAAQS) for ozone or carbon monoxide. As illustrated in Table 13-10 transportation-related air quality problems are of two general types: localized and regional. Localized transportation-related air quality problems generally result in CO concentrations exceeding either the 1-h or, more likely, the 8-h CO air quality standards. Factors contributing to this problem include high vehicular traffic volumes occurring under congested traffic conditions frequently found in densely developed portions of urban areas.

Factors affecting emissions and concentrations. The relationship between the amount of travel and air pollution emissions and concentration is complex. The assumption is frequently, but invalidly, made that reductions in vehicle miles of travel (VMT) translate directly into a comparable reduction in CO, HC, and other emissions. This assumption should only be used for "ballpark" estimates of emission reductions. In addition to associated emission levels, air pollution concentrations are significantly affected by topography, the physical characteristics of the highway facilities and adjacent development, and meteorological conditions such as wind direction, wind speed, stability class, and mixing depth, together with the previously noted ambient temperature and humidity. Concentrations may be several times higher under extremely poor dispersive conditions. Prevailing meteorological conditions are a very critical factor in determining the localized CO impact actually realized.

TABLE 13–11
Transportation Control Measures Reasonably Available

Category	Major Element
Mechanical	Inspection and maintenance programs Vapor recovery Alternative fuels or engines Other fleet vehicle controls Light-duty vehicle retrofit Extreme-cold-start emissions reduction programs
Economic policy issue	Auto restricted zone Parking management Staggered work hours Pricing strategies
Transportation operations	Improved public transit Exclusive bus and carpool lanes Areawide carpool programs Long-range transit improvements On-street parking controls
Transportation construction/ capital improvements	Park and ride (fringe parking lots) Pedestrian malls Bicycle lanes and storage facilities Traffic flow improvements

SOURCE: U.S. ENVIRONMENTAL PROTECTION AGENCY AND U.S. DEPARTMENT OF TRANSPORTATION, *Transportation—Air Quality Planning Guidelines* (June 1978).

The Transportation Air Quality Planning Guidelines[25] stipulate that SIP revisions "must provide for expeditious implementation of reasonably available control measures." The transportation control measures considered by EPA to be readily available include those listed in Table 13-11. The VMT and emissions impacts of selected individual transportation control measures are categorized into several major elements. The sources of and the urban areas for which the estimates were prepared are also indicated. Of particular interest are those measures that are the purview of the transportation engineer. Most of the individual control measures identified are estimated to reduce weekday, areawide VMT, CO, and HC emissions by 1% or less. The control measures likely to reduce weekday, areawide VMT and/or emissions by more than 1.5% include inspection and maintenance, 4 to 8%; vehicle retrofits, 0.3 to 9.3%; employee-based carpool/vanpool programs, 2.5%; driving ban (1 day/week),

[25]U.S. ENVIRONMENTAL PROTECTION AGENCY AND U.S. DEPARTMENT OF TRANSPORTATION, *Transportation Air Quality Planning Guidelines* (Washington, D.C.: U.S. Government Printing Office, June 1979), p. 2.

6 to 8%; parking management, 0.6 to 5.7%; staggered work-hours, 2%; major increases in gasoline prices, 1.5 to 13.8%; and idling controls, 5%.

The reduction in emissions available from individual control measures are presented in Table 13-12. These reductions are based upon individual studies in the selected cities and illustrate HC and CO (8-h) emissions. Inspection and maintenance is the most effective in reducing HC emissions (8.1%), and reserved bus lanes and HOV lanes on freeways are most effective in CO emissions (10 to 15% for peak hours). For reducing vehicle-miles of travel, parking rate increases of $1 to $2 per day show a 29 to 30% decrease in travel.

Reducing emissions through transportation/land use planning. Preparing a transportation–land use plan provides the opportunity to coordinate the development of the transportation system with land-use policies. Hopefully, it will result in maximizing the efficiency of the transportation system while minimizing the adverse influence on the environment, for example, air pollution emissions. One goal of the transportation planning process is to minimize the amount of travel required within the region and yet provide an acceptable level of service. The evaluation of alternative regional land-use plans has frequently provided a basis for reducing the amount of pollution by simply reducing the amount of travel. One of the best examples of this approach

TABLE 13–12
Estimated Impacts of Selected Transportation Control Measures*

Measure	Reduction by Percentage			Study Location
	Weekday Vehicle-Miles Travel	Emission†		
		HC	CO (8 h)	
Mechanical				
Inspection and maintenance	n.a.	8.1	n.a.	Washington
	n.a.	4.7	6.4	Baltimore
	n.a.	1.0	6.0	N.Y. Metro
Idling controls	n.a.	1.5	3.4	Upstate N.Y.
Retrofits				
Light-duty vehicles	n.a.	3.2	9.3	Baltimore
Light-duty trucks	n.a.	.2	.3	Baltimore
Heavy-duty gas trucks	n.a.	1.6	6.3	Baltimore
Economic policy				
Pricing strategies				
Transit				
10% (5¢) fare decrease	0.22	n.a.	n.a.	Albany
10¢ fare decrease	0.70	.3	n.a.	Baltimore
Auto				
CBD parking rate increase				
$1	0.3	n.a.	n.a.	Washington
$2	0.6	n.a.	n.a.	Washington
$3	0.9	n.a.	n.a.	Washington
Parking rate increase				
Commercial rates	14.0	n.a.	n.a.	Washington
Commercial rates + $1	29.0	n.a.	n.a.	Washington
Commercial rates + $2	30.0	n.a.	n.a.	Washington
Areawide parking rate increase				
$1	0.8	n.a.	n.a.	Washington
$2	1.7	n.a.	n.a.	Washington
$3	2.5	n.a.	n.a.	Washington
Parking surcharge				
$1	0.8	0.3	0.3	Baltimore
$2	1.1	0.8	0.7	Baltimore
Outlying parking cost	4.8	2.7	1.5	Baltimore
Increasing gas prices				
20¢/gal	1.5	n.a.	n.a.	Baltimore
Double	5.1	n.a.	n.a.	Washington
Quadruple	13.8	n.a.	n.a.	Washington
Toll for one-person car				
50¢	0.2	n.a.	n.a.	Washington
$1	0.4	n.a.	n.a.	Washington
Vehicle ownership tax				
$100 per vehicle	0.1	n.a.	n.a.	Washington
$200 per vehicle	0.2	n.a.	n.a.	Washington
$400 per vehicle	0.4	n.a.	n.a.	Washington
Carpool cost subsidy				
2.5/passenger-mile	0.3	n.a.	n.a.	Washington
5.0/passenger-mile	0.7	n.a.	n.a.	Washington
Carpool tax rebates				
$250/yr	0.05	n.a.	n.a.	Washington
$500/yr	0.1	n.a.	n.a.	Washington
Auto restricted zones				
One-day-a-week ban	8.8	n.a.	n.a.	Washington
Auto restricted zones	0.4	n.a.	n.a.	Washington
Preferential parking—carpools	0.0	n.a.	n.a.	Washington
Staggered work hours	3.7	2.0	n.a.	Baltimore
Flexible working hours	4.0	n.a.	n.a.	Washington

TABLE 13–12 (Continued.)

Measure	Reduction by Percentage: Weekday Vehicle-Miles Travel	Emission†: HC	Emission†: CO (8 h)	Study Location
Transportation operations				
Improved public transit				
10% increase in bus service	0.02	n.a.	n.a.	Albany
Increased frequency to CBD	0.1	n.a.	n.a.	Washington
Increased frequency, express bus to CBD	0.3	n.a.	n.a.	Washington
Increased frequency, extended coverage	1.1–2.2	n.a.	n.a.	San Diego
Reserved bus lane on arterial	n.a.	n.a.	15‡	n.a.
Carpool/vanpool				
Matching and promotion	0.4	n.a.	n.a.	Washington
Carpool/vanpool program	1.5	1.3	1.3	500,000 pop.
Vanpooling	1.2	n.a.	n.a.	Washington
Carpool locator	0.4	.2	n.a.	Baltimore
Employer matching	1.0	n.a.	n.a.	Chicago
Employer matching	1.2	n.a.	n.a.	Numerous areas
Areawide programs	0.12	n.a.	n.a.	Numerous areas
Meet-and-ride program	1.0	n.a.	n.a.	Chicago
Traffic flow improvements				
Preferential traffic control	0.1	n.a.	n.a.	Washington
Increase speeds by 1%	n.a.	1.0	1.0	Washington
HOV preferential lanes	2.5	n.a.	n.a.	Albany
HOV lane on freeway	0.2	0.1	n.a.	Baltimore
	0.6	n.a.	n.a.	Washington
	n.a.	n.a.	10.0‡	n.a.
On-street parking controls				
Reduced parking supply in CBD	0.5	n.a.	n.a.	Washington
Transportation construction/capital improvements				
Park-and-ride lots				
6 Park-and-ride lots	0.8	n.a.	n.a.	Syracuse
6 peripheral park-and-ride lots	0.5	n.a.	n.a.	Syracuse
Pedestrian malls	0.3	n.a.	n.a.	Syracuse
	+1.9	n.a.	n.a.	Syracuse

*n.a., not available.
†CO, carbon monoxide; HC, hydrocarbons.
‡Peak-hour concentration.

SOURCE: U.S. ENVIRONMENTAL PROTECTION AGENCY AND U.S. DEPARTMENT OF TRANSPORTATION, *Transportation—Air Quality Planning Guidelines* (Washington, D.C.: June 1978), pp. 111–14, 19.

of reducing adverse influence is exemplified by the transportation–land use plan, previously discussed, that was prepared by the Southeastern Wisconsin Regional Planning Commission.

Another approach used in evaluating transportation plans is illustrated by Table 13-13, which shows, for two alternative land-use patterns and three highway networks, the estimated reduction that can be achieved in various vehicular emissions over the base network. The table includes emissions based on pre-1968 emissions standards and an assumed post-1975 emission rate. The "A Sprawl" land-use plan, coupled with four major radial freeways and an inner loop, results in an estimated 35% decrease in CO, a 14% decrease in HC, and a 154% increase in NO using 1968 emission rates for automobiles. Using 1975 EPA standards, the emissions rates are further reduced. The table suggests that criteria for evaluating alternative regional transportation networks should include air pollution as a factor.

TABLE 13–13
Changes in Air Pollution Related to City Form and Highway Network

Urban Pattern	Highway System	Base Network	Reductions (−) for Different Highway Systems as Compared to a Base Highway Network (%): Pre-1968 Emission Rate: CO	Pre-1968: HC	Pre-1968: NOx	Post-1975 Emission Rate: CO	Post-1975: HC	Post-1975: NOx
A Sprawl	2 Freeways along major radials	1 Basic arterial grid	−13	−4	+82	−9	−29	+52
A Sprawl	4 Additional radial freeways and an inner beltway for maximum coverage	1 Basic arterial grid	−35	−14	+154	−31	−19	+160
B Moderate corridors	3 Major radial freeways with outer beltway and inner loop added	2 Freeways along major radials	−11	+5	+30	+5	+5	+26

SOURCE: S. J. BELLOMO AND EDWARD EDGERBY, *Ways to Reduce Air Pollution through Planning, Design and Operations* (Washington, D.C.: Highway Research Board, unpublished paper, 1971), Table 10, p. 24.

Integrating land use and transportation planning

Chapters 11 and 12 contain discussions of land-use considerations. Land use and transportation planning can be coordinated to reduce the adverse impact of traffic in several ways:

1. Land-use patterns can be established to encourage transit usage and thereby reduce vehicular emissions. The development of land-use plans to encourage transit usage generally involves higher densities along existing or proposed transit corridors. This increased density provides the market for transit ridership to the CBD. The result may be a higher proportion of transit ridership and a consequent reduction in the use of the private vehicle. This translates to lower air pollution and noise.
2. The transportation network can be designed to minimize vehicular hours of travel, thereby reducing emissions and noise. Systems planning usually strives to minimize vehicle-miles and vehicle-hours of travel. The proper balance of freeways, arterial streets, and public transit will result in a compromise situation in which vehicle-miles and vehicle-hours are minimized consistent with capital investment and operating costs for highways and transit. Reductions in vehicle-hours of operation will reduce air pollution and noise.
3. Land-use plans can be coordinated with transportation plans to reduce the exposure of residential areas to heavy movement. Transportation networks should be selected in such a way that existing residential areas are protected and that a framework for logical development of future residential areas is provided. The design of the network with adequate spacing allows the development of the residential areas between the major segments. The network must have sufficient capacity, however, to eliminate through traffic in the residential areas. This design minimizes transportation noise levels within neighborhoods and reduces the number of accidents.
4. Land-use controls can be established to preserve capacity and minimize ribbon commercial development along major radial routes. Heavy traffic flow can serve as a catalyst for ribbon development and frequently reduces capacity on the major arterial facility. Land-use controls, when properly applied, can restrict undesirable development and/or can provide design solutions such as control of access or driveway design that minimize the detrimental aspects of the development. The result is the protection of capacity on major arterial routes, the reduction of accident rates within these corridors, the improvement to visual appearance by sign controls, and the removal of "zoning pressure" on adjacent residential development.

Transportation noise control

While air pollution must primarily be attacked through regional, statewide and national controls, transportation noise can be approached in a more localized manner. Through the careful design of new facilities and with the application of ameliorative measures to existing facilities, it is possible to reduce noise levels. The technical approaches suggested here emphasize the application of design and planning techniques to freeways, highways, and airports for the protection of adjacent areas.

Techniques of highway noise abatement. Reductions of the undesirable effects of highway-generated noise involves a comprehensive approach which includes vehicle noise reduction, improved highway design, and land-use control. The first two components can be most effectively addressed by private industry and governmental agencies, but the third is traditionally an area of local governmental responsibility. Cooperation among all levels of government, industry, and the public in implementing the three-part approach is essential to achieving noise reduction because of the limitations of each noise control element when applied separately.

Noise reduction includes the development of quieter cars and trucks. Significant progress is being made in research to reduce vehicle engine and exhaust noise, but tire design, the major source of high-speed traffic noise, may place limits on further improvements. Because of enforcement problems, it would appear that any efforts at vehicular noise control must be made on at least a statewide basis. There is a need for promulgating objective standards that bear a direct relationship to goals and objectives on noise control.

Improved highway design involves greater attention to noise impacts in choosing the route and layout of new highways. In February 1978 the Federal Highway Administration issued standards for highway noise levels in its Policy and Procedure Memorandum PPM 90-2, "Noise Standards and Procedures."[26] These standards are not a complete solution to highway noise, but "represent a balancing of that which may be desirable and that which may be achieved." PPM 90-2 urges highway agencies to strive for even lower noise levels where they can "be achieved at a reasonable cost, without undue difficulty, and where the benefits appear to clearly outweigh the costs and efforts required."[27] PPM 90-2 requires consideration of noise-abatement measures for developed areas near new highways, but does not regulate noise in undeveloped areas or along existing roads. Rather, it recognizes a dual responsibility, where highway agencies have the responsibility for taking measures that are prudent and feasible to assure that the location and design of highways are compatible with existing land use. Local governments, on the other hand, have responsibility for land development control and zoning.[28]

Thus, land-use control will continue to be a crucial component of the three-part approach to noise control. Local governments will continue to have the responsibility for discouraging the development of noise-sensitive land uses (such as homes and schools) in highway noise-impacted

---

[26] Federal Highway Administration, *Noise Standards and Procedures, Planning and Procedure Manual 90-2*, Pt. 1 (Washington, D.C.: U.S. Government Printing Office, Feb. 1978).

[27] Federal Highway Administration, *Noise Standards and Procedures, Manual 90-2*, p. 16.

[28] Federal Highway Administration, *Noise Standards and Procedures, Manual 90-2*, p. 17.

TABLE 13–14
Design Noise Level/Land-Use Relationships

Land-Use Category	Design Noise Level, L_{10}	Description of Land-Use Category
A	60 dBA (exterior)	Tracts of lands in which serenity and quiet are of extraordinary significance and serve an important public need, and where the preservation of those qualities is essential if the area is to continue to serve its intended purpose. Such an area might include amphitheaters, particularly parks or portions of parks, or open spaces that are dedicated or recognized by appropriate local officials for activities requiring special qualities of serenity and quiet.
B	70 dBA (exterior)	Residences, motels, hotels, public meeting rooms, schools, churches, libraries, hospitals, picnic areas, recreation areas, playgrounds, active sports areas, and parks.
C	75 dBA	Developed lands, properties, or activities not included in categories A and B.
D		For requirements on underdeveloped lands, see paragraphs 5a(5) and (6) of source reference.
E	55 dBA (interior)	Residences, motels, hotels, public meeting rooms, schools, churches, libraries, hospitals, and auditoriums.

SOURCE: U.S. DEPARTMENT OF TRANSPORTATION, Federal Highway Administration, *Noise Standards and Procedures, Policy and Procedure Memorandum 90-2* (Washington, D.C.: U.S. Government Printing Office, Feb. 8, 1978).

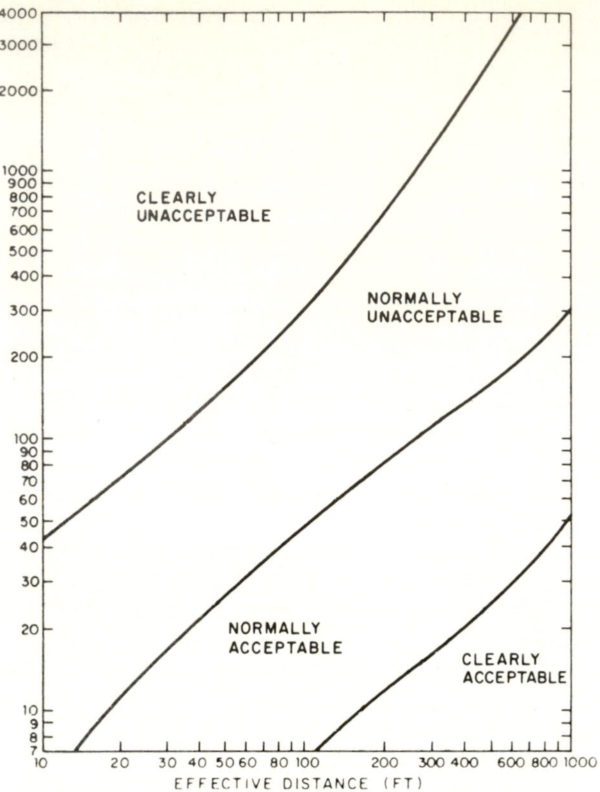

Figure 13.21. HUD guidelines for site noise. SOURCE: Bolt, Beranek and Newman, Inc./HUD, *Noise Assessment Guidelines*, Washington, D.C.: U.S. Government Printing Office, 1971, p. 10, Fig. 3.

areas and for ensuring that any such development that does occur is planned to minimize the adverse effects of noise. In an effort to provide some reasonable guidelines for the design of "quieter" highways, FHWA has developed guidelines for maximum sound levels for an array of land-use types, as shown in Table 13-14. Guidelines for evaluating housing sites have been established by the U.S. Department of Housing and Urban Development (HUD). These guidelines cover air, highway, and rail transportation noise sources and include procedures for calculating noise levels. Presumably, no federal loan guarantees or other governmental-financed assistance will be available for housing sites that do not meet the standards. Figure 13.21 illustrates the application of the guidelines for site exposure to truck noise. Adjustments are made for road grade, sound barriers, and stop-and-go traffic.

Design techniques to reduce noise have been developed primarily for highways in urban areas. The application of these physical features covers noise production, primarily on freeways, for the private vehicle, trucks, and rubber-tired urban and intercity transit. A wall, a building, an earth berm, a hill, or some other type of solid structure, if large enough, can serve as a partial barrier to sound and can provide a moderate amount of sound reduction to an area located within the "shadow zone" provided by the barrier. Sound barriers do not cast as sharply defined shadows as do light barriers. The dimensions of a barrier are many, many times longer than the wavelength of light. Because wavelengths of sound are usually somewhat comparable to the dimensions of the barrier, the actual cut-off of sound is "fuzzy." Figure 13.22 shows the effect and the limitations of a sound barrier. Even though the receiver appears to be located in the shadow zone of the wall, and even though the receiver cannot see the sound source, some sound may be heard in this shadow zone. It is a fundamental fact of acoustics, however, that the larger the angle of the deflection, the less sound will be heard at the receiver location. Thus, the design of an effective sound barrier must be of sufficient height or length to make the deflection angle large.

Long lines of barriers may be required to achieve sub-

Figure 13.22. Diagram showing effects and limitations of a barrier. SOURCE: U.S. Department of Transportation, Federal Highway Administration, *The Audible Landscape: A Manual for Highway Noise and Land Use*, Washington, D.C.: U.S. Government Printing Office, 1974, p. 55.

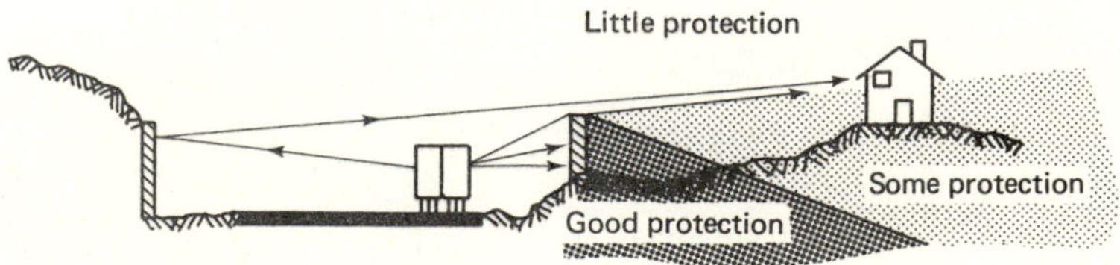

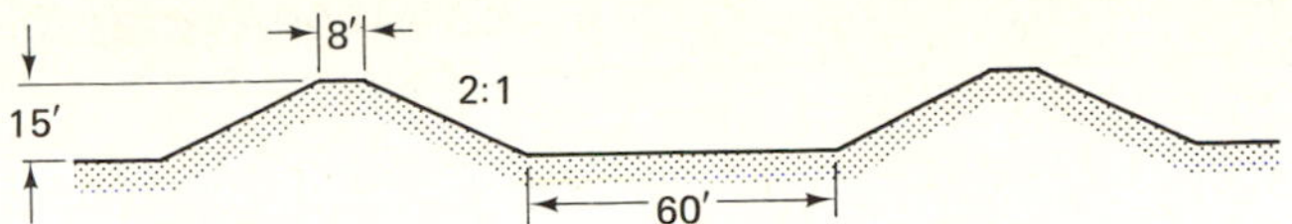

Figure 13.23. Cross section of a typical berm. SOURCE: U.S. Department of Transportation, Federal Highway Administration, *The Audible Landscape: A Manual for Highway Noise and Land Use*, Washington, D.C.: U.S. Government Printing Office, 1974, p. 55.

stantial noise reduction from a highway. The barrier attenuation changes for various portions of the roadway because of the various distances involved. Wind and thermal gradients introduce additional bending of the sound waves diffracted over the top of a barrier, and this tends to produce lower attenuation than that calculated. A detailed discussion of barrier types, design, and sound impacts is included in NCHRP Report 117.

Although walls have been shown in the foregoing illustrations of barriers, other forms, such as earth berms, hills, cuts, embankments, or any other type of natural or constructed solid structure, may serve as barriers. Figure 13.23 illustrates a typical berm structure. The barrier must have adequate mass and solidity to prevent appreciable sound transmissions through the barrier itself.

Studies have been carried out on noise penetration into a community bordering a noise source. The findings are not very precise or consistent, possibly because of variations in geometry, house sizes, lot sizes, house spacing, and so on. It appears reasonable, however, to follow the conclusions of the NCHRP Report 117, which allow a 5-dBA reduction in the sound level provided by the first row of buildings and 10 dBA as the maximum reduction provided by the multiple rows of buildings.

Other noise-reducing techniques. Other noise-reducing techniques include increasing the distance between the noise source and the receiver, placing nonresidential land uses such as parking lots, maintenance facilities, and utility areas between the source and the receiver, and orienting the residences away from the noise. Noise can be effectively reduced by increasing the distance between a residential building and a highway. Distance itself reduces sound; doubling the distance from a noise source can reduce its intensity by as much as 6 dBA. In the case of high-rise buildings, distance may be the only means, besides acoustical design and construction, of reducing noise impacts. This is because it is nearly impossible to provide physical shielding for the higher stories from adjacent noise.

A heavy, dense growth of woods provides a small but useful amount of attenuation. NCHRP Report 117 suggest the use of 5-dBA attenuation for each 100-ft (30.5-m) depth of woods of sufficient density that no visual path exists through it. The woods should extend at least 15 ft (4.6 m) above any line of sight between highway traffic sources and all portions of the neighboring buildings to be protected. For an additional depth of 100 ft (30.5 m) or more, an additional 5-dBA attenuation can be assumed, but the total attenuation claimed for all such plantings should not exceed 10 dBA in any configuration.

Noise abatement through land-use control

There are two basic types of tools available for prevention of noise incompatible with land use: design techniques that reduce noise impacts and the technological controls available to local governments. Some controls available include zoning, subdivision control, building codes, health codes, municipal ownership or control of the land, financial incentives, and technical advisory services. Usually, the best solution for the municipality will be a combination of several techniques chosen to cover the widest possible range of noise incompatibility situations. For more detail, the reader is referred to "The Audible Landscape."[29]

In evaluating control techniques, these factors must be kept in mind:

1. The authority for creation and enforcement of local laws and regulations comes from the "police powers" which are delegated to the local governments by the state. The enabling acts, through which the various states delegate the police powers, differ from state to state, and the ability of the local government to enact laws is limited to items specifically contained in the appropriate enabling act. The legality under individual state enabling acts must be determined and resolved before any control technique is seriously considered.
2. Administrative costs associated with the use of each technique also vary across local governments. In general, it is most efficient to choose a strategy that is consistent with ongoing programs.
3. Variations in terrain, traffic, population density, and noise sensitivity occur within as well as between municipalities. Regulations must be flexible enough to allow the exercise of sound administrative judgment to treat each situation individually.

Despite the foregoing limitations, the variety of available techniques is great enough to ensure that most communities will be able to find a combination of techniques appropriate to control local problems while remaining consistent with both state law and the administrative structure of the municipality. Zoning is a commonly used local administrative technique to direct land use in accordance with a plan for orderly community growth. The zoning ordinance, or bylaws, specifies what type of land use is permitted in each zoning district. Zoning specifications have been used to

[29]U.S. DEPARTMENT OF TRANSPORTATION, Federal Highway Administration, *The Audible Landscape; A Manual for Highway Noise and Land Use* (Washington, D.C.: U.S. Government Printing Office, 1974), p. 55.

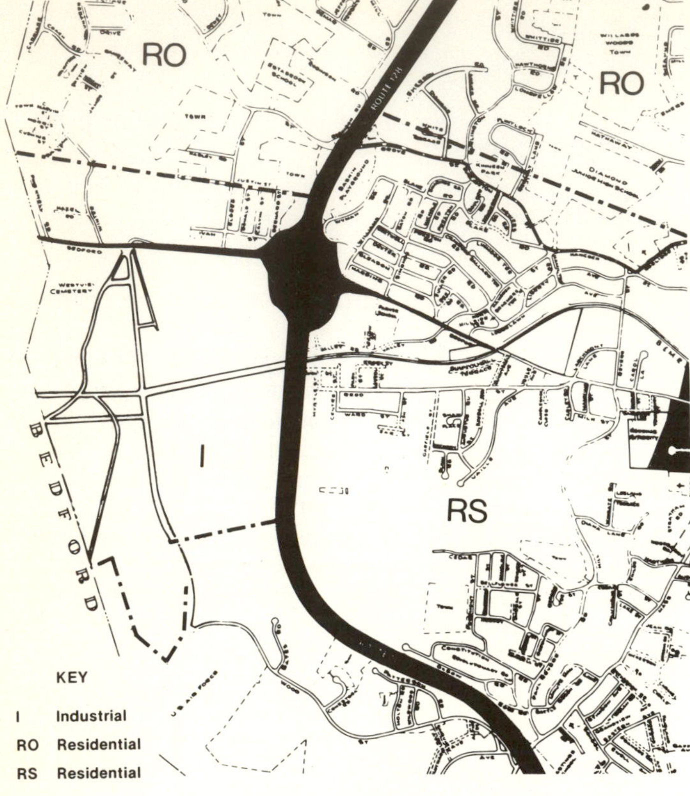

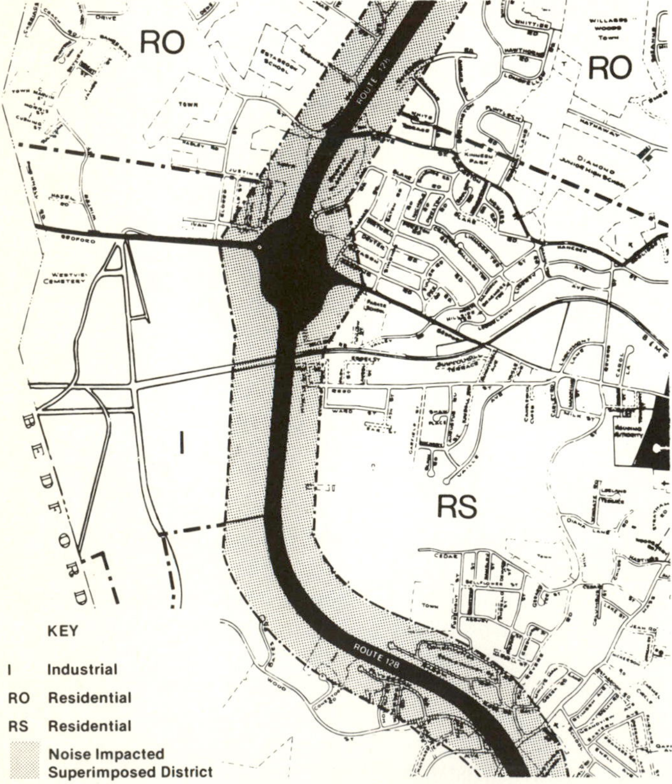

Figure 13.24. Identification of noise-impacted area by overlay zone. SOURCE: U.S. Department of Transportation, Federal Highway Administration, *The Audible Landscape: A Manual for Highway Noise and Land Use,* Washington, D.C.: U.S. Printing Office, 1974, pp. 9–11.

control signs, off-street parking facilities, lot size, frontage, maximum building height, and ratio of open space to developed land. These precedents make zoning a useful tool for noise control in most localities.

A simple approach is the creation of an "overlay zone," which is a special-purpose zone superimposed over the regular zoning map. Often, such zones are called "superimposed districts," and they are used for a variety of reasons, including wetlands protection and airport compatibility. In the case of noise control, the overlay zone could be all land that is exposed to noise over a certain level such as 65 dBA, or it could be defined more easily, but less appropriately, as all land within a certain distance from the highway, say 500 ft (152 m). Land that falls in such a zone would be subject not only to the regulations pertaining to the regular zone in which it lies, but also to the additional regulations pertaining to the overlay zone. Such a technique is much less cumbersome legally and administratively than the creation of an entire series of special zones (single-family residential, multifamily residential, commercial, etc.) in the noise-impacted portion of the community. Figure 13.24 illustrates a typical overlay zone.

Urban transit and rail transportation noise suppression

Urban transit noise primarily comes from diesel-powered buses in most urban areas; but rubber-tired transit is a minor element of the noise problem. The previous discussion for diesel trucks presents a considerably higher noise level than is attributable to transit. The small number of transit vehicles in the total traffic stream suggest that transit noise is not a major problem.

Rail transportation includes both passenger and freight vehicles, although commuter rail transit presents the most significant problem in urban areas. In most countries railroads do not represent a widespread noise problem. This is particularly true in the United States, where the most mileage is in rural areas. In some countries, notably Japan, where high-speed rail transportation is in common use, railway noise poses serious community noise problems. The application of technology for noise supression to rail transit focuses on equipment improvements as well as improvements to the roadbed. This is particularly true of rail rapid transit operations in urban areas where sharp grades and curves are necessary. Table 13-15 presents a list of noise sources and suggests corrective devices or techniques.

Aircraft and airport noise evaluation

In our earlier discussion of noise levels, the range of commonly used noise measures was described. For aircraft noise and aircraft noise-impacted areas, there are several additional noise measures: the composite noise rating (CNR) is based upon perceived noise in decibels, which takes into account the duration of noise; the calculation of CNR essentially involves adding together all the single-event noise levels for a 24-h period; the noise exposure forecast (NEF)

TABLE 13–15
Rail Transportation Noise and Vibration Sources

Source of Noise and/or Vibration	Causes of Noise or Vibration Generation	Methods of Suppression
Power conducting and generating equipment, brakes, fans, (vehicle and structure)	Pickup and conduction of electric power, motor sliding or rolling contact; vibration similar to wheel on rail; generally 10–15 db below present train noise levels	Vibration isolation; low density, low sound velocity contact(s); damping material applied to radiating bars and contacts; acoustic isolation of contact bar from support structure; graphite lubrication
	Generating equipment; mechanical engine or electrical machine without moving parts (transformer)	Vibration isolation from support, damping procedures, or noise-absorbent enclosures
	Compressors; thumping effect, noise of escaping air	Compressor design changes, vibration isolation, acoustic enclosure, redesign of air-release, orifices, air escape chamber
	Ventilating and cooling fans; for vehicle and for ventilation of underground structure	Design, decrease of air velocity, vibration isolation, location, baffling and dust acoustic treatment, silencer installation
	Gear noise; fairly major source of propulsion noise	Stiffened areas around thrust bearings, lubrication, maintenance, vibration isolation
	Bearing noise	Precise manufacturing; lubrication, maintenance of alignment important
	Diesel locomotives; engine and exhaust important source	Acoustical absorption around engine compartment; muffler design and maintenance
	Brakes, brake shoes; hissing, squealing; important source	Asbestos composition brake shoes (reduce from 95 dB to 90 dB); use of dynamic braking down to low speed; vibration isolation from car body
	Coupling	Reduction of slackness of components, lubrication
Wheel and rail noise (vehicle/track)	Impacts due to continual striking of rail by rolling wheels, many factors affect it, produce varying effects. The most important source of rail noise and vibration	
	Rolling of wheel on rail; nonuniformity of wheel and rail; worse on joints, special trackwork (switches)	Reduce unsprung weight; reduce total weight; heat treated rail (more wear resistant); continuous welded rail (smoother, no joints); rail lubrication; elastomeric material between wheel and rail
	Rail corrugation and wheel irregularities can occur to aggravate the problem	Rail and wheel grinding. This also reduces rail and wheel life; however, maintenance is costly
	Insulated rail joints (for electrical isolation in power and signal circuits)	Problem not yet solved; diagonal joint or pre-assembled glued joint should be tried
	Wheel and rail squeal on curves due to wheel stoppage; bearing of wheel flange on rail, wheel movement across rail head, or rail and wheel resonance because of structure of car truck (4 wheels of each truck being rigidly fixed in relation to one another); wheel skidding on the rail is caused on curves because of different outer and inner wheel path lengths	Rail lubrication on curves; flatter curve design where possible; reduce total vehicle weight Damping material on trucks Changes in truck design No control method yet available, except design for elimination of retaining rail
	All of above may be transmitted to structure through track fastenings (devices for fastening track to structure)	Design vibration isolation of rail from supporting structure by rubber or elastomeric pads
	Roadbed, as carrier of noise and vibration; ties and ballast vs. concrete	Ties and ballast more absorptive; concrete cheaper: with concrete, pads to isolate roadbed from main structure can be used (lead-asbestos) in special areas
	Resonance of car wheel at natural frequency (~600 Hz)	Constrained damping on wheels
Vehicle	Aerodynamic noise, especially air turbulence in tunnels	Vehicle design; laying boards over ties
	Rubbing together of car-vestibule end frames	Design, vibration isolation
	Vibration of side panels of vehicle, due to transmission of structure-borne noise from beneath (wheel, rail, truck)	Acoustic materials, damping

SOURCE: M.D. HARMELINK, *Noise and Vibration Control for Transportation Systems* (Downsview, Ontario: Department of Highways, 1970), Table 18.

is a more precise and refined procedure for noise-impact forecasting; the community noise equivalency level (CNEL) uses the foregoing levels in a simplified way and also involves community background noise; day–night average sound level (L_{dn}) allows a comparison of noise levels from a variety of urban sources with aircraft-generated noises. The level of precision for L_{dn} is comparable to NEF and CNR. Table 13-16 compares the noise measures used in airport impact evaluations.

Airports in the United States are generally required by the Federal Aviation Agency (FAA) to use one or more of the established cumulative measures of noise assessment when determining the environmental impacts of proposed airport improvements. These measures are also used by HUD in a determination of qualification for financial assistance to housing projects.

Control of jet engine noise rests entirely with the federal government. Control of aircraft in flight—when modifications in takeoff and landing procedures can reduce noise—again remains with the federal government but is also affected by individual airline flight rules and ultimately by the pilot's own discretion. Achieving significant reductions in aircraft engine noise has been slow in coming, partly because of the low turnover rate of older, noisier aircraft and the substantial cost of reequipping airline fleets with quieter

TABLE 13–16
Comparison of Measures and Levels Used in Airport Noise Evaluation

CNR	NEF	CNEL and L_{dn}	Description of Expected Response
100	30	65	Essentially no complaints would be expected. The noise may, however, interfere occasionally with certain activities of the residents.
100–115	30–40	65–75	Individuals may complain, perhaps, vigorously. Concerted group action is possible.
115	40	75	Individual reactions would likely include repeated, vigorous complaints. Concerted group action might be expected.

SOURCE: *Environmental Comment, Airport Environs; Noise-Polluted Land, Measurement of Aircraft Noise* (Washington, D.C.: Urban Land Institute, Mar. 1979), p. 4.

aircraft. Operating procedures cannot solve the problem; at best, they can reduce noise only marginally. When safety is also considered, a few truly effective procedures can be fully implemented.

Most airports with severe noise problems involve a high concentration of residential development which grew up around it, often to within a few hundred feet of the runways. Primary examples of this situation are Los Angeles International, New York's John F. Kennedy International, Chicago's O'Hare, and Boston's Logan International airports. In each case, except perhaps the latter, the airport was originally located a substantial distance from existing urban development. As the urban area developed outward, the axis between the airport and existing urban development became a natural focus for suburban residential uses. Today, each of the noted airports is well within the boundaries of the urbanized region it serves. From a planning perspective, the ideal land use around an airport would consist of aviation-related industrial and commercial/service functions as well as open space or other public uses not sensitive to high noise levels. For a variety of reasons, however, this kind of land use has not developed around airports; therefore, airport operators must attempt to generate it.

Visual elements of transportation

Transportation facilities directly affect the quality of the environment, for better or for worse, because of the physical predominance of the facilities. Inevitably, they interact with personal and community aspirations in such areas as conservation of existing development, impact on new development, preservation of historic sites, improved housing, schools and neighborhoods, cleaner air, and general community well-being. And inevitably, the potential for conflict between transportation and these other values is greatest in America's densely populated urban areas.

Traffic control devices

The urban design profession is increasingly concerned with the coordination of information systems for the pedestrian and the motorist, resulting in a more systematic means of visual communication. This usually involves the design or selection of a graphics system, the combination of information systems (street name, directional signs, regulatory signs, parking control signs, etc.) within a standardization structure for simplicity and aesthetic reasons. Figure 13.25 illustrates one attempt at the design of an information system that incorporates a number of information sources. In this system, vehicular signals and pedestrian signals are combined within one structural element. Lane signs and a standard traffic signal head are mounted within the space frame. The space frame is also part of a combination lighting standard and sign system for parking regulation and has a trash receptacle. The objective is to combine many separate and uncoordinated street elements into a unified whole. The application of this technique has been restricted primarily to the CBD.

Freeway planning and design

Personal mobility remains a cherished right in a free society and essential to the pursuit of each individual's goals. Highway transportation is the basis for the unprecedented degree of personal mobility enjoyed today, as well as for the scope and dependability of freight movement. Maintaining mobility in a growing economy clearly requires a balance of transportation which includes freeways as well as other modes. On the other hand, highway transportation cannot be allowed to function apart from or in conflict with its environment. The question is not, for example, whether to preserve a historic site or to build a highway. Rather, the question is: How do we provide needed mobility and, in the

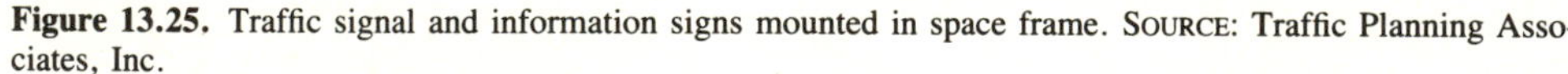

Figure 13.25. Traffic signal and information signs mounted in space frame. SOURCE: Traffic Planning Associates, Inc.

same process, contribute to other important social goals—such as the preservation of historic sites? In the report "The Freeway and the City," eight distinguished professionals have drawn upon their experience, as independent and concerned observers of the urban scene, to develop thinking on the principles and potentials of highway planning and design. Some of the more important principles are as follows:[30]

1. *Where appropriate the urban freeway can provide a logical and useful boundary between different land use areas.* Such a separation is welcome, for example, between a heavy industrial complex and a recreation area, or between a residential neighborhood and a regional shopping center with its attendant traffic and extensive parking areas.
2. *Sufficient cross-freeway vehicular and pedestrian connections must be provided and strategically located.* Overpasses or underpasses should maintain adequate communication between one side and the other. Cross street communication is maximum where a tunnel or continuous overhead structure is provided, and can be facilitated by narrowing the highway in the section to be crossed. The crossings, as important connecting elements for the adjacent land, should be coordinated with comprehensive land use and local thoroughfare plans.
3. *An urban highway should be so located and designed as to enhance rather than destroy a city's best attributes.* Such attributes include:
   - **a.** a safe, clean, and healthful living environment,
   - **b.** unified neighborhoods, communities, shopping districts, institutional centers, industrial districts, and recreation areas,
   - **c.** a dynamic and cohesive central core or cores,
   - **d.** interrelated systems of vehicular and pedestrian movement,
   - **e.** a system of parks and open spaces,
   - **f.** historic areas and landmarks,
   - **g.** topographics superlatives, and
   - **h.** a composite of all those cultural and environmental components and qualities which together yield a satisfying way of life.
4. *Expressways should blend into the community.* This is especially true in regard to their effect upon the established street pattern, natural topographic features, landmarks, prominent buildings, parks, and other physical elements.
5. *Every urban expressway should be an aesthetic statement.* All policies or regulations relating to highway development must provide that flexibility and freedom of choice essential to creative design.
6. *Beauty in freeway design is a result of the sum total of carefully planned and sensitively handled elements.* Full consideration must be given to location, alignment, cross section, scale, environmental impact, architectural detailing, and landscape development. The beauty of a highway is often enhanced by utmost simplicity in the design of the roadway and bridges, and in such appurtenances as guardrails, signs, and lighting standards.
7. *By location and design, urban thoroughfares should be pleasant to drive.* Contributing factors include an ease in finding direction, apparent directness of routing toward desired destinations, and a sense of smooth uninterrupted flow, in harmony with the landscape forms and well related to architectural features.
8. *The urban highway should provide a variety of visual experiences.* Views of similar features from similar distances and elevations with similar enframement or lack of enframement are bound to be monotonous. Visual interest and scenic richness are achieved by providing a variety of subjects seen from a variety of viewing situations with each vista considered as one element of a studied and interrelated visual experience. It is the conscious playing of the near against the far, the light against the dark, the natural against the architectural, that has produced our most handsome scenic highways.
9. *Freeways entering the city should, by their location and design, present each city in its most interesting light.* This is a relatively new type of visual experience. The views from the highway should not be abrupt or fragmented. As a vehicle moves into, through, or out of the city, its various features should be introduced, enframed, and so related to the viewer as to give him a sense of what the place is really about. Where feasible, curvilinear highway alignments, in comparison with long, straight tangents, provide more attractive and varied views.
10. *The freeway should make visible the most specific features of the cityscape.* It is not enough that landmarks, activity centers, and topographic superlatives be left undisturbed. The freeway should relate to each in such a way as to identify and reveal to the motorist its special character. Where the highway passes close to a historic landmark, the highway improvement should include screening where this is indicated, or the development of an appropriate foreground and enframement of the feature as viewed from the road.
11. *On a freeway, the visual effects will be comprehensible to its users only if their high speed of travel is borne in mind.* Compared to streets, expressways require a very different scale. Signs, views, and variations in grade or alignment and landscape development must be designed to the viewer's trajectory, speed, and range of perceptual capacity.
12. *The driver of a vehicle traveling at a relatively high speed can only experience those views positioned almost directly ahead of him.* The driver's eyes are focused on the road ahead and his attention centers on his driving. Only for very short glimpses can he safely take his eyes from the road, and these can be only a few degrees to the right or left. As vehicle speed increases, the driver's eyes focus farther and farther ahead, and his angle of vision becomes narrower and narrower. At 25 mph (40 km/h) his total horizontal angle of vision is about 50° to either side, and the eyes focus at a point about 600 ft (183 m) ahead, but for 60 mph (97 km/h) the focus may be nearly 2,000 ft (610 m) ahead, while the angle of vision has shrunk to less than 20°.
13. *What is seen of an expressway from the city is as important as what is seen of the city from the expressway.* Visual aspects of arterial highway location and design should be considered from the points of view both of the user and of the communities traversed, generally favoring the group most affected in any specific instance. For example, an expressway in a scenic corridor should favor the user while a freeway in a built-up section of the city might favor residential neighbors.[31]

Opportunities for transportation energy conservation

Five general categories of conservation options for transportation modes are listed in Table 13-17. Automobiles offer the greatest potential for energy conservation. This can be done through technological improvements and/or attitude changes. The most important options for the transportation

[30]John O. Simonds, eds., *The Freeway and the City: Principles of Planning and Design* (Washington, D.C.: U.S. Government Printing Office 1970), pp. 27–29.

[31]Simonds, *The Freeway and the City.*

TABLE 13–17
Summary Assessment of Transportation Energy-Conserving Options

Approach	Time Frame*	Benefit†	Means‡				Likelihood of Implementation§
			R	A	E	T	
Shifts among modes							
Auto commuters to express buses	M	L		×	×		M
Auto commuters to mass transit	M	L	×	×	×		M
Intercity auto to bus and rail	M	L	×	×	×		L
Short-haul air to bus and rail	M	L	×	×	×		L
Short-haul air to TLV systems	L	L	×	×		×	M
Conventional jet to wide-body jet	M	L	×	×	×		M
Short-trip auto to human-powered systems	M	L		×	×		M
Intercity trucking to rail	M	L	×			×	M
Increased load factor							
Carpooling	S	H	×	×	×		M
Air	M	M	×		×		M
Truck	M	M	×		×		L
Rail	M	L	×		×		L
Tankers	M	L			×	×	L
Urban mass transit	M	L	×	×	×		L
Reduced demand							
Telecommunications	L	L			×		H
Improved land use and urban planning	L	H	×		×		H
Fuel tax or surcharge	M	H	×		×		H
More efficient trip planning	S	M		×			M
Increased energy-conversion efficiency							
Smaller autos	L	H	×	×	×		H
Reduced drag	L	H			×	×	L
More efficient engines	L	M			×	×	H
Better maintenance	M	M	×	×	×	×	H
Hybrid auto systems	L	H			×	×	L
Reduced accessory load	S	M	×	×	×		L
Reduced performance demand	S	M	×	×	×		M
Improved usage patterns							
Traffic management	M	M	×	×			H
Better driving techniques	M	M		×	×		H
Improved aircraft operations	S	L	×	×		×	M

*Time frame: time required to implement progam so that at least 50% of maximum practical benefit in energy reduction for the particular approach could be achieved. S, <1 year; M, 1–5 years; L, >5 years.

†Benefit: % reduction in total transportation energy consumption, accounting for resulting energy changes in all sectors: L, <1% of transportation energy; M, 1–5% of transportation energy; H, >5% of transportation energy.

‡Means: R, regulation; A, attitude (voluntary actions from influencing public opinion); T, technology; E, economic (includes taxes and fees imposed by regulatory bodies).

§Likelihood of implementation: The probability that a particular approach will be implemented within the next 10 years: L, <10% probability; M, 10–50% probability; H, >50% probability.

SOURCE: U.S. DEPARTMENT OF TRANSPORTATION, *Energy Primer* (Washington, D.C.: U.S. Government Printing Office, 1975), p. 8.

engineer are those options listed in the table under "Improved Usage Patterns." This includes the traditional traffic engineering improvements, such as one-way streets, parking restrictions, improved signal coordination, and intersection improvements. The percent reduction in energy use for an urban region is estimated to vary from 1.0 to 4.0% depending on the type of traffic flow improvement implemented (see Figure 13.26). Other changes in the manner of auto operation—cruising at lower speeds, accelerating more slowly, and using brakes less—can lead to lower gasoline consumption as well. Table 13-18 summarizes the categories of possible actions and the resulting environmental effects. Furthermore, encouraging more efficient use of existing modes and transportation systems is the only conservation strategy that can be employed for results in the near future. In a moderate time frame, mode shifts could be effected, but they would not allow significant energy savings, since without enormous capital expenditures for system expansion they could not bear substantial traffic shifted from automobiles.

Several strategies could be used to achieve energy savings by the end of 25 years: more efficient propulsion systems and alternative fuels could be developed, congestion could be reduced through traffic engineering, and land use could be planned with reducing the need for travel in mind. Economic processes, without governmental regulation except in the form of fees or taxes, are also effective for the implementation of most of the conservation options.

Many alternatives to commuting by auto have been advanced: they include use of express commuter buses, urban mass transit, carpooling, and bicycling or walking. Express commuter buses (whose use is limited, since they are feasible only between clearly delineated origin–destination pairs) are theoretically five times as energy efficient as a four-member carpool traveling in a standard (six-passenger) car. The carpool, however, costs 20 to 40% less per passenger and a dimension other than cost must be included: feasibility of implementation. The limited capability of the bus manufacturing industry to increase production is a constraint. The same problems of time and money for new equipment appear when the alternative of shifting automobile traffic to urban mass transit is proposed.

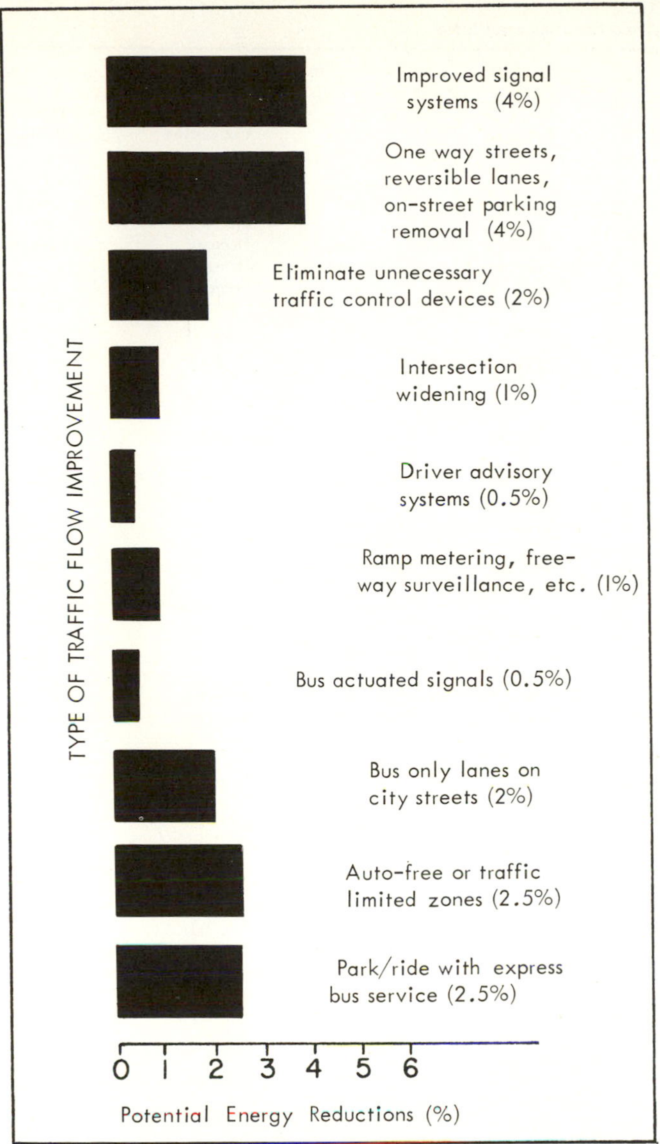

Figure 13.26. Comparison of energy reduction by type. SOURCE: U.S. Department of Transportation, *Energy Primer,* Washington, D.C.: U.S. Government Printing Office, 1975, Table 3.

Shifts among intercity travel modes offer as many potentials and pitfalls. So many vehicle-miles are traveled by intercity automobiles that even doubling intercity bus and rail travel (with all attendant implementation problems) would reduce intercity automobile travel by only 4% and result in 0.4% reduction of the 1970 transportation energy consumption. Similarly, because short-haul air traffic accounts for so few passenger-miles, shifting even 50% of that traffic to bus and rail would save only 0.6%. Shifting 50% of all air traffic (both long and short haul) from conventional to wide-body jets would produce slightly higher savings of 0.9%, and shifting 10% of the intercity trucking to rail would effect an energy savings of 0.6% of the 1970 base.

The energy efficiency of a mode may be improved if the load factor (proportion of actual load to capacity) per trip is increased. This will decrease the number of individual vehicle trips, with a resulting reduction in vehicle-miles traveled. Load factor in private automobiles may be increased by carpooling. Increasing load factors of common carriers would be easier than carpooling. Governmental machinery for regulation already exists. Unscheduled services (charter buses and planes, oil tankers, etc.) already have high load factors because of their schedule flexibility. Off-peak service could be reduced, secondary loads could be given lower time priority, and price incentives could attract travelers, thereby increasing load factors of scheduled services.

Reducing personal travel demands could save a great deal of transportation energy, but this strategy has far-reaching social effects. The dependence of Americans on the automobile has already been discussed. Steps to reduce travel demand are a desirable long-range goal. Three types of strategies that could be used are: raising gasoline taxes and/or taxing motorists on a mileage basis, development of communication systems as a substitute for travel, and land-use changes that place origins and destinations (i.e., homes and places of work) in closer proximity.

Improving automobile fuel economy offers the greatest opportunities for conserving energy—reducing power demands in smaller, lighter vehicles, and reductions in tire and aerodynamic drag.

The other major means of improving energy conversion efficiency is to increase the efficiency of the propulsion system itself. Available options for doing this include the development and use of more efficient engine and transmission systems, and enforcement of more stringent vehicle maintenance requirements.

Direct regulation would not be necessary to implement the options discussed above; economic incentives would probably suffice. It would be several years, however, before implementation of the options would be noticeably effective, owing to the slow change of the fleet mix.

Summary of environmental and energy impacts. Fortunately, improvements in energy efficiency also have environmental benefits. Thus, it is possible and likely that reductions in energy consumption will also help to improve environmental conditions. A number of actions to reduce energy consumption have been identified, and the environmental consequences have been quantified. These actions are listed in Table 13-18.

Improving the environment by innovative transportation modes

Another possibility for improving the environment is through the use of new transportation modes and methods of propulsion. The success of the new propulsion systems will depend on how attractive these systems are to the traveling public on a mass basis, because any propulsion system must be mass-produced to be economically feasible. Table 13-19 contains a description of alternative propulsion systems in addition to the internal-combustion gasoline engine. All 11 alternative systems shown have been studied in some

TABLE 13–18
Summary of Energy-Consumption Actions and Environmental Effects

Action Group	Action	Regional Energy Reduction (%)	Environmental: Air Pollution	Noise	Congestion	Land-Use* Patterns
Measures to improve flow of high-occupancy vehicles	Bus-actuated signals	0–0.5	Decrease	Decrease	Decrease	NE
	Bus-only lanes on city streets	0–2.0	Decrease	Decrease	Decrease	NE—minor
	Reserved freeway bus or bus/carpool lanes and ramps	1.0–3.0	Decrease	Decrease	Decrease	NE—minor
	Bus priority regulations at intersections	0–0.5	Decrease	Decrease	Decrease	NE
Measures to improve total vehicular traffic flow	Improved signal systems	1.0–4.0	Decrease	Decrease	Decrease	NE
	One-way streets, reversible lanes, no on-street parking	1.0–4.0	Decrease	Decrease	Decrease	NE—minor
	Eliminate unnecessary traffic control devices	0–2.0	Decrease	Decrease	Decrease	NE
	Widening intersection	0–1.0	Decrease	Decrease	Decrease	NE—minor
	Driver advisory system	0–0.5	Decrease	Decrease	Decrease	NE
	Ramp metering, freeway surveillance, driver advisory display	0–1.0	Decrease	Decrease	Decrease	NE
	Staggered work hours	0	Decrease	Decrease	Decrease	NE
Measures to increase car and van occupancy	Carpool matching programs	3.0–6.0	Decrease	Decrease	Decrease	NE
	Carpool public information	2.0–4.0	Decrease	Decrease	Decrease	NE
	Carpool incentives	4.0–6.0	Decrease	Decrease	Decrease	NE
	Neighborhood ride sharing	0–1.0	Decrease	Decrease	Decrease	NE
Measures to increase transit patronage	Service improvements	1.0–3.0	Decrease	Decrease	Decrease	NE
	Fare reductions	4.0–6.0	Decrease	Decrease	NE	NE
	Traffic-related incentives	1.0–5.0	Decrease	Decrease	Decrease	NE
	Park-and-ride with express bus service	0.5–2.5	Decrease	Decrease	Decrease	Minor
	Demand responsive service	0–1.0	Decrease	Decrease	Decrease	NE
Measures to encourage walk and bicycle modes	Pedestrian malls	0.5–2.5	Decrease	Decrease	Decrease	Minor/major
	Second-level sidewalks	0.5–2.0	Decrease	Decrease	Decrease	Minor
	Bikeway system	0.5–2.0	Decrease	Decrease	Decrease	Minor
	Bicycle storage facilities	0–1.0	Decrease	NE	NE	NE
	Pedestrian-actuated signals	0–0.5	NE	NE	Decrease	NE
	Bicycle priority regulations at intersections	0–0.5	NE	NE	Decrease	NE
Measures to improve the efficiency of taxi service and goods movement	Improve efficiency of taxi service	0–2.0	Decrease	Decrease	Decrease	NE
	Improve efficiency of urban goods movement	0–1.5	Decrease	Decrease	Decrease	Minor
Measures to restrict traffic	Auto-free or traffic limited zones	0.5–2.5	Decrease	Decrease	Decrease	Minor/major
	Limiting hours or location of travel	0–3.0	Decrease	Decrease	Decrease	Minor/major
	Limiting freeway usage	0–1.0	Decrease	Decrease	Decrease	Minor
Transportation pricing measures	Bridges and highway tolls	1.0–5.0	Decrease	Decrease	Decrease	NE
	Congestion tolls and road cordon tolls	1.0–5.0	Decrease	Decrease	Decrease	NE
	Increased parking costs	0.5–3.0	Decrease	Decrease	Decrease	NE
	Fuel tax	2.0–6.0	Decrease	Decrease	Decrease	NE
	Mileage tax	2.0–6.0	Decrease	Decrease	Decrease	NE
	Vehicle-related fees	2.0–10.0	Decrease	Decrease	Decrease	NE
Measures to reduce the need to travel	Four-day workweek	1.0–6.0	Increase/decrease	Increase/decrease	Decrease	NE—minor
	Zoning	1.0–10.0	Decrease	Decrease	Decrease	Major
	Home goods delivery	0–1.0	Decrease	Increase/decrease	Decrease	NE
	Communications substitutes	0–1.0	Decrease	Decrease	Decrease	Major
Energy restriction measures	Gas rationing without transferable coupons	10.0–25.0	Decrease	Decrease	Decrease	Minor/major
	Gas rationing with transferable coupons	10.0–25.0	Decrease	Decrease	Decrease	Minor/major
	Restriction of quantity of sales on a geographic basis	5.0–20.0	Decrease	Decrease	Decrease	Major
	Ban on Sunday and/or Saturday gas sales	2.0–10.0	Decrease	Decrease	Decrease	Minor
	Reduced speed limits	0–2.0	Decrease	Decrease	NE	NE

*NE, no effect

SOURCE: U.S. DEPARTMENT OF TRANSPORTATION, *Energy Primer* (Washington, D.C.: U.S. Government Printing Office, 1975), pp. 65–67.

detail as a part of research undertaken by the various automobile manufacturers. The electric propulsion system is the least polluting, but it is impractical for the private automobile at the present time because of the lack of efficient batteries. Perhaps the most practical low-emission propulsion is the modified diesel engine, which uses gasoline or diesel fuel as a power source and has emissions relatively low in hydrocarbons, carbon monoxide, and nitrogen oxide. The major drawbacks to the modified diesel engine are odor, smoke, and noise.

TABLE 13–19

Alternative Propulsion Systems and Their Applicability to Motor Vehicles

Propulsion System	Power Source	Principal Applications	Applicability to Motor Vehicles	Feasibility as Alternative to Gasoline Internal Combustion Engine	Air Pollution Problems
Diesel	Diesel fuel, kerosene	Trucks, buses, trains, auxiliary power for other systems (G.V.T.), boats	Engine has been fully tested; poorer acceleration performance than gasoline engine	Economical in larger sizes, less so in auto	Smoke and odor are principal concerns Low emissions of HC, CO, NO_x Emission could be controlled by design
Stratified charge	Gasoline or diesel fuel	Any vehicle now using an I.C.E.	Available in some cars Advanced version being tested by UPS, Texaco, and others for trucks	Economical version of I.C.E.; fuel efficient Advanced version can use rough-cut fuel	Low emissions
Gas turbine	Gasoline and other petroleum fuels	Cars, trucks, buses, trains, aircraft, TACV, boats, hovercraft	Chrysler field-tested 50 turbine cars and found them reliable and operationally economical as new cars, but has not continued production	Reasonable alternative in larger sizes; trucks, buses, but not economical for use in auto; high temperatures at constant operations require development of new materials	Low emission of CO and HC NO_x could be controlled by design Future emission possibilities in g/mi: HC 0.5–1.2, CO 3.0–7.0, NO_x 0.15–0.4
Natural gas propane engine	Natural gas fuel	Alternative to gasoline I.C.E. (I.C.E. can be modified)	Runs well, with somewhat poorer acceleration performance than gasoline I.C.E. Refueling less convenient than with gasoline engine Longer valve life	Initial cost probably higher, although could drop if production increased Cost of modifying gasoline I.C.E. = \$500 Propane supply probably insufficient for automobile population	Natural gas is one of the cleanest fuels CO can be considerably reduced No NO_x, virtually no HC or sulfur oxides Future emission possibilities in g/mi: HC 1.5, CO 3.0–5.0, NO_x 1.5
Steam	Steam-powered Rankine engine burns fuel	Cars, trains, boats	Lear Jet had devoted time and money to development of steam car, but has now stopped work Minto developed a Freon engine that operates like steam engine, sold licensing rights in Japan	Research has proved that steam car is an uneconomical alternative to auto	Burns fuel more cleanly than I.C.E., thus emitting less pollutants Future emission possibilities in g/mi: HC 0.2–0.7, CO 1.0–4.0, NO_x 0.15–0.40
Wankel	Several fuel types	Cars, trucks	Powers several production cars Engine has relatively short life	Shape of engine parts, rubbing surface requiring special treatment, and many seals being required make this car inherently expensive to produce	Worst possible engine from the viewpoint of pollutant emission Future emission possibilities in g/mi: HC 1.8, CO 2.3, NO_x 2.2
Stirling	Any organic fuel	Cars, trucks, buses, boats	Philips Research Laboratory and Ford developed modern Stirling engine High efficiency	Higher material costs, more expensive manufacturing, low production, and large size indicate high price Not economical at present for use in auto Problem of sealing and working fluid not yet solved	Very low emission of pollutants Future emission possibilities in g/mi: HC 0.006, CO 0.3, NO_x 2.2
Hybrid	Combines attributes of internal combustion and electrical engine	Cars, buses, trains	Overall efficiency is estimated to equal present engines Mercedes Benz developed a workable system for buses	Initial costs are high and could not hope to compete with auto unless technological breakthrough is made Operating cost may be lower	Emits no pollutants when operating electrically
Direct feed electric	Electricity	Subways, trains, belted cable systems	Roadway powered vehicle under test by Lawrence Livermore Laboratory	Not feasible until powered roadways are developed and constructed	Virtually pollution-free except for pollutants that may result from generating source
Battery electric	Electricity	Possible alternative to gasoline I.C.E.	Cannot compete with I.C.E. on an equal performance basis but will satisfy city driving needs Reliable operation and power availability	Uneconomical at present because of short range, low speed, recharging constraints on present-day lead batteries Requires development of high energy and power density batteries	Same as above
Linear electric	Electricity	Maglev, trains, rail transit, hybrid vehicles	Efficiency very high	Probably less feasible than direct-feed, and will need powered roadway	Same as above

SOURCE: Based on: M. D. HARMELINK and W. J. PECK, *Transportation Air Pollution*, DHO Report No. RR 169 (Downview, Ontario: Department of Highways, 1971), p. 31. Revised by H. W. BRUCK, E. DEAKIN, and L. MONEY, 1981.

14

*ECONOMIC CONSIDERATIONS**

IAN G. HEGGIE AND SIMON THOMAS

Transportation Consultants
Oxford, England

This chapter deals with the contribution of economics to the identification of transport engineering problems and the evaluation of their solution. It is concerned with economics as a technique for resource allocation rather than with economics as a measure of financial cost effectiveness. It measures resource costs and social benefits rather than the revenues and expenditures associated with private-enterprise investments. In this form it is called social benefit–cost analysis.

The introduction deals with fairly general economic issues: the relationship between economics and design and the objectives of economics. The second and largest section deals with the impact of transport improvements. It includes initial and recurrent expenditure, vehicle operating costs, the value of time savings, and the value of reduced accidents.

The third section deals with the identification of alternatives for detailed study. It covers the identification of projects and policies and the use of rules of thumb for establishing rough priorities.

The fourth section deals with detailed economic evaluation: how benefits and costs are defined, what role prices play in an evaluation, what discounting is, how budget constraints are dealt with, and what length of evaluation period should be used.

The fifth section turns to the treatment of noncomparable effects and discusses various ways of presenting the results of an evaluation.

The sixth section gives some practical examples of an economic assessment. They include a simple airport runway extension, the addition of new berths to a port, a traffic management scheme, and an urban bypass.

The final section concludes with a summary and references for further reading.

Introduction

Economics and transportation engineering

An economic analysis should not be carried out as an afterthought. It should be used as part of a continuous process, starting with the objectives of the proposed transportation project (can these objectives be satisfied in any other way?), running through the entire planning and design process, and only ending, as a final summing up, with the overall evaluation. It should consider the following questions:

1. *Project identification*. Which projects or policies should be considered as possible solutions to a particular transport need?
2. *Establishing rough priorities*. Which projects and policies should be considered in detail?
3. *Detailed evaluation*. Which costs and benefits are relevant to the evaluation, how should they be measured, and how can they best be presented as an index of priority?
4. *Project selection*. Should this project be selected, should it be rejected, or should it be postponed?

Economics is often overlooked as an aid to transportation planning and design. Yet any transportation engineering problem involves a whole series of essentially economic decisions. In the area of design, for example, the transportation engineer must choose materials, select an overall de-

*Many publishers, individuals and organizations have kindly allowed us to use material for which they hold the copyright. We are most grateful for their permission and would like to acknowledge the following for permission to use material: Economist Intelligence Unit, Her Majesty's Stationery Office, Ministry of Overseas Development (G.B.), McGraw-Hill Book Company (U.K.), Royal Statistical Society, Rendel Palmer & Tritton, and Transport and Road Research Laboratory.

sign concept, and then combine the component parts of the scheme into an effective, and economical, whole. A river crossing could thus be by ferry boat, causeway, or bridge. In the latter case it could be in steel, concrete, or timber. It could be suspended, arched, or simply supported. What should the engineer choose?

The range of choice is not usually as large as this. Some solutions will be physically infeasible (e.g., by lack of suitable foundations for an arched bridge), but important choices will remain. In the absence of a rigorous economic analysis, the designer may make these choices on the basis of:

1. Experience, which may or may not cover an adequate range of options.
2. Preconceptions as to what is desirable (e.g., one solution uses less material).
3. An innate view of mathematical or structural elegance (e.g., an arch is a more elegant structural form).

Economics avoids the need for these arbitrary rules by providing a tangible criterion—cost—for choosing between alternative solutions. In many cases this can be done quite simply by drawing envelopes of cost curves of, for example, steel girder bridges versus reinforced concrete bridges versus prestressed concrete bridges. By plotting cost (y) against span length (x) the engineer can choose which type is most economic over a given range of span lengths.

In practice, the engineer does not usually carry the economic analysis to this level of detail, although curves like this commonly form part of the standard highway design repertoire. It is more a question of the economic attitude of mind that asks: Is this the only possible solution, and if not, is there a better one? It is this general principle which eventually ensures that the final design is the most economical and the one which, if justified in aggregate terms, offers best value for money.

Optimum allocation of scarce resources

Economics makes the presumption that resources are scarce. The main task of economics is thus to ensure that these scarce resources are allocated to produce maximum value. There are two dimensions to the problem: first, resources must be allocated between competing ends, and second, they must be allocated over time.

The efficient allocation between competing ends is generally handled by the market economy, which sets prices indicative of the amount of money people are willing to pay rather than go without the item (i.e., it defines the value—not the cost—of producing the item). The change in value associated with a new or improved product, such as an improved road alignment, is nevertheless not a simple function of the fall in price. Following Dupuit,[1] it is equal to the difference in consumers' surplus. This is shown in Figure 14.1. DD is the demand curve and is a function of quantity and price (all other things being held equal). In the case of

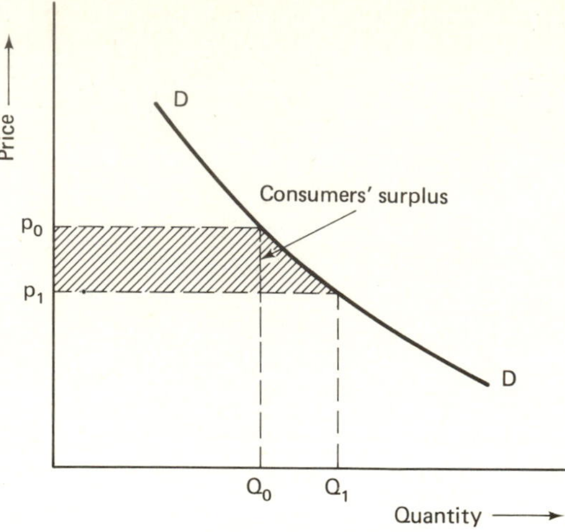

Figure 14.1. Consumers' surplus illustrated.

transport, Q will represent the volume of traffic and p its price or cost. At price p_0 the level of demand is Q_0. If price falls to p_1, corresponding to a reduction in travel cost, the volume of demand will increase from Q_0 to Q_1. This gives rise to an increase in consumers' surplus. It is made up of two elements:

1. Benefits to existing consumers $= p_0Q_0 - p_1Q_0$
   $= Q_0(p_0 - p_1)$.
2. Benefits to new consumers $= \frac{1}{2}(p_0 - p_1)(Q_1 - Q_0)$, assuming that DD is linear over the range of prices involved.

The first item corresponds to the usual financial measure of increased revenue; the second is ignored in a financial calculation because it produces no revenue surplus. It is included in an economic analysis because it does represent a benefit to consumers.[2]

The efficient allocation of resources over time must take account of the fact that a dollar today is worth more than a dollar next year, or the year after. The reason is that a dollar received now could be invested to earn interest and so would be worth more in a year's time.

The simplest way of allowing for the time dimension is to define a series of weights, $w_1, w_2, \ldots, w_n$, to describe the unit value today of a dollar in each of n future time periods. The present aggregate weighted value of a stream of resource expenditures, consumer benefits, or net benefits can then be written

$$w_0R_0 + w_1R_1 + w_2R_2 + \ldots + w_nR_n$$

where $R_0, R_1, R_2, \ldots, R_n$ represent the resource expenditure, the consumer benefit, or the net benefit in each time period. If the weight for R_0 is set equal to 1 (by dividing throughout by w_0), the sum above is reduced to what is called its "present value."

In many cases the "rate of discount" to be used will be provided by the central finance ministry and can be taken as a fixed parameter by the transportation engineer.

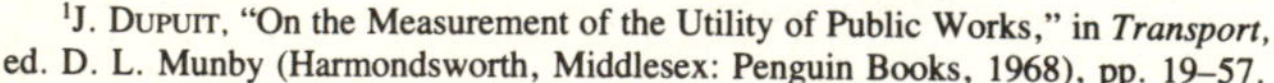

[1] J. Dupuit, "On the Measurement of the Utility of Public Works," in *Transport*, ed. D. L. Munby (Harmondsworth, Middlesex: Penguin Books, 1968), pp. 19–57.

[2] I. G. Heggie, *Transport Engineering Economics* (London: McGraw-Hill, 1972), Chap. 2.

The essential task of the economic evaluation is thus to fix priorities by determining value for money. It does so by quantifying resource costs and consumer benefits, discounts them both to their present value, and compares them in an attempt to arrive at an unambiguous index of priority.

Economic efficiency and distribution

Economics is not concerned solely with the optimum allocation of resources, but with wider questions of equity and the distribution of costs and benefits among individuals, regions, etc. It is thus concerned with the question: Who does what, to whom, and at whose expense? In a sense this concern complements the intertemporal considerations noted above. A dollar to one person is not necessarily worth the same amount to another. Since economics assumes that marginal values decline as income increases, interpersonal differences in income may thus affect any overall measure of consumer benefit.

Questions of distribution nevertheless go beyond mere differences in income. Institutional constraints usually prevent beneficiaries, defined in the broadest sense, from compensating people who are adversely affected. It is therefore often appropriate to separate the impact of a transport improvement into its effect on different interest groups, in addition to its effect on different income groups.

Impact of transport improvements

Transport projects can have both direct and indirect effects. The former are localized, are directly related to the scheme in a simple causal fashion, and are readily identifiable. The latter are more tenuous. The causal processes are less obvious and must usually be identified by going beyond the boundaries of the transport scheme itself. There is usually a strong relationship between the size of a scheme and the incidence of such indirect effects.

Indirect impacts

Some transport schemes are specifically designed to encourage such impacts. The large regional development scheme, based on a new port with port-based industries, or feeder roads and penetration tracks in virgin territory, are typical examples. A major road improvement to encourage the relocation of industry, is another. In both cases the benefits of the schemes, and sometimes their costs, cannot be evaluated with reference to the transport impacts alone. Indeed, since some schemes are specifically designed to open up new areas presently lacking transport services, there may be no existing transport costs the scheme could reduce.

Consider the following example. A new deep-water port is proposed with the object of attracting new port-based industries to an area of relatively high unemployment. How should it be evaluated?

The first step is to ask whether a port is the best answer and then to establish different possible levels of service, such as the depth of water and complementary facilities provided, considering which industries might be attracted to the port at each level. For each firm or industry likely to be attracted to the new port the economic evaluation should ask: Where would this industry have gone otherwise, and what *net* benefit is it likely to bring to the port authority, the region, and the country as a whole? If industry is simply diverted from one part of the country to another, it may generate few, if any, net benefits. The gain in new port revenue may be offset by a loss of revenue elsewhere, and any benefits associated with new employment may similarly be offset by redundancies elsewhere. It is the overall balance that counts. The evaluation should thus compare the cost of the proposed scheme (including the cost of any complementary facilities) with:

- ○ Net gain to shipping companies, if thought relevant (if a scheme reduces shipping costs, it is often appropriate to revise charges to recapture some of these benefits as increased port revenue[3]).
- ○ Net port revenue (gross revenues of the port, less any loss of revenue at other ports).
- ○ Indirect reduction in ports costs (reduced costs of other ports no longer handling diverted traffic).
- ○ Net gain to the local economy (in an input–output sense; value of output less resource costs of all inputs).

The first two items would generally be classified as direct effects. The latter two are indirect, because they are not obviously part of the scheme being examined and can arise in a wide variety of transport schemes. For example, a runway extension at a small airport may reduce airline costs as its main benefit but may also encourage tourist travel or stimulate the growth of specialized high-value industries. Similarly, a major road improvement may divert traffic from the railways and cause some branch lines to close. This could lead to the relocation/closure of some industries and to the decline of rail-based communities. Since indirect effects can be important, they should therefore only be omitted when they are known to be nonexistent or unimportant.

Direct impacts

These generally fall into five categories: initial and recurrent costs, vehicle operating costs, savings in travel time, accident costs, and environmental and wider considerations.

A U.K. Consultation Document[4] estimated the benefits from the average trunk road (intercity) scheme as follows:

Benefit	Percent of All Benefits
Vehicle operating-cost savings	0
Travel-time savings	
Work	51
Nonwork	29
Accident savings	20
	100

[3]I. G. Heggie, "Charging for Port Facilities," *J. Transport Econ. Policy, 8*(1), 1–23 (1974).

[4]*Transport Policy: A Consultation Document,* Vol. 2 (London: H.M.S.O., 1976), p. 99.

This pattern is fairly typical of a wide range of freeway and expressway projects in the United Kingdom. Time savings are considered immensely important; other benefits, such as accident reduction, moderately important; and vehicle operating-cost savings relatively unimportant. (The latter are very much more important when roads are upgraded from earth or gravel to bitumen, or from signalized streets to expressways). Each of these types of benefit is considered below.

Initial and recurrent costs. These consist of construction costs (including land acquisition), maintenance and other recurrent costs, and the cost of disrupting traffic while the new scheme is introduced. The only cautionary notes relate to the cost of land acquisition and maintenance/recurrent costs. The former should be based on the value of the land in its best alternative use (if there is no alternative, the value is zero). Market prices should only be used when there is a free market in land. Maintenance and other recurrent costs are sometimes estimated on the basis of convenient fictions such as "1% of construction costs per annum." This is not a satisfactory procedure. To the extent possible, they should always be based on historical precedent and should represent the net cost of running the new facility (i.e., the difference in cost between running it with and without the proposed new scheme).

Vehicle operating costs. Most transport schemes affect vehicle operating costs. Some reduce costs by reducing fuel use, whereas others increase vehicle costs in order to produce another type of benefit. Traffic management schemes—which often sacrifice vehicle costs to save travel time—are an example.

The quantification of vehicle operating cost savings is relatively straightforward. An estimate of annual running costs per vehicle with the scheme is subtracted from a similar estimate without the scheme. The consumers' surplus (see "Optimum Allocation of Scarce Resources") is then calculated by multiplying this difference by (1) the volume of traffic likely to use the scheme *without* the improvement and (2) half the volume of traffic induced by the improvement. Diverted traffic is dealt with in the same way as induced traffic, by assuming that it is continuously diverted from other routes. When diversion is discrete (i.e., when a block of traffic diverts at a given cost level), the benefit is calculated by multiplying the difference in cost by the whole of the diverted traffic.

Operating costs are normally grouped under the following headings:

- Fuel consumption
- Lubricants
- Vehicle maintenance (labour and parts)
- Capital consumption (depreciation)
- Interest on capital employed
- Wages
- Overheads

Items such as insurance and licence fees/taxes are not included in this list. Insurance is a proxy for accident costs and should be dealt with explicitly in terms of those costs; licence fees/taxes represent a contribution toward the fixed and running costs of facilities which will already have been included in estimates of the initial and recurrent costs of the facility.

Vehicle operating costs are readily available from shipping companies, airline operators, aircraft manufacturers, and for highways, from organizations such as the American Association of State Highway and Transportation Officials (AASHTO),[5] the World Bank,[6] and the U.K. Transport and Road Research Laboratory.[7] Government transport departments have their own official figures which they periodically update for use in transport evaluations (see Chapter 6).

Savings in travel time. This is usually the single most important benefit and must therefore be very carefully evaluated because of the significant impact on the overall ranking of schemes. Time savings fall into three main categories: savings to commercial vehicles (i.e., trucks, aircraft, ships), savings to business travelers, and savings to people traveling in their own time. Several organizations publish recommended figures for use in economic evaluations (see Tables 14-1[8] and 14-2[9]).

In the case of commercial vehicles, it is often assumed that any time saving will be translated into additional output by the crew and perhaps by the vehicle itself. These assumptions must be interpreted with caution. Drivers and vehicles cannot always be automatically switched from one task to another—even in the long run—and half or more of a vehicle's time is usually taken up loading, servicing, and waiting. A half-hour saving may thus have no value,[10] or a disproportionately high one, depending on what the operator can do with it. The best procedure is to use the published figures as a guide, but then to look more closely at how the transport scheme affects the operators involved in order to adjust the published figures downward or upward.

Business travel time is dealt with in the same way as that of commercial vehicles; the same general qualifications apply, but are more substantive.[11] Not only are there limits on the way such savings can be translated into extra output, but (1) quite a lot of business travel is done in the traveler's own time, so that the saving is not necessarily translated into extra working time; and (2) some businesspeople work while traveling, particularly when doing so by rail or air, so that their travel time cannot wholly be treated as "lost time." When these factors are taken into account, the value of business travel time can be quite dramatically reduced. For example, in a recent airport study in Australia, the

---

[5] *A Manual on User Benefit Analysis of Highway and Bus Transit Improvements* (Washington, D.C.: American Association of State Highway and Transportation Officials, 1977).

[6] J. de Weille, *Quantification of Road User Savings* (Baltimore: Johns Hopkins Press, 1966).

[7] R. F. F. Dawson and P. Vass, *Vehicle Operating Costs in 1973*, Report 661 (Crowthorne, England: Transport and Road Research Laboratory, 1973).

[8] *Value of Time and Vehicle Operating Costs for 1979*, Highway Econ. Note 2 (London: Department of Transport, 1980).

[9] *A Manual on User Benefit Analysis*, pp. 15–20.

[10] A. Woolterton and M. White, "Freight Transport in St. Helens: The Value of Road Improvements," *Traffic Eng. Control, 19*(7), 343–345 (1978).

[11] R. C. Carruthers and D. A. Hensher, "Resource Value of Business Air Travel Time," in *Modal Choice and the Value of Travel Time*, ed. I. G. Heggie (Oxford: Oxford University Press, 1976), pp. 164–185.

original value of 150% of the average wage rate (based on the U.K. Roskill Commission central value) was reduced to 65% of the average wage rate for domestic passengers and 30% for international passengers.[12]

The sensible procedure is again to use accepted values as a starting point (e.g., wage rate plus an allowance for overheads), but then to modify this for the particular scheme being evaluated and the context in which the time savings accrue.

Finally, there are savings in nonworking time. These are commonly expressed as a proportion of the average hourly wage rate, on the assumption that people's willingness to pay for time savings is positively related to their income (because of the declining marginal utility of money as incomes rise and the fixed constraint of the 24 hour day), measured by the wage rate. It follows that high-income travelers, such as air passengers, are thought to attach more value to time savings than are low-income ones, such as bus passengers, and that the unit value of time savings will increase as real incomes rise in the future. Estimated value of travel time tends to lie in the range one-fourth to one-third of the average hourly wage rate, measured in terms of average household income. This value is increased each year to reflect increases in real income; in practice it is increased in line with actual and forecast increases in GNP (gross national product).

Estimated values are derived from studies of mode choice and route choice. This procedure and the implicit assumptions built into the analysis have, however, been severely criticized in recent years.[13,14] It is felt that (1) small time savings may not have the same unit value as large time savings, as already recognized in the United States, (2) their value may be a function of journey length, and (3) the assumption that unit values increase in line with GNP may be mistaken.[15] Research has nevertheless not yet provided a set of alternative values for use in economic evaluation. Recommended values such as those presented in Tables 14-1 and 14-2 must thus be used, but should be applied with caution. It is also worth separating time savings from the rest of the evaluation—to show that they are not strictly comparable with money cost savings—perhaps also distinguishing between large and small time savings.

Accident costs. This is particularly relevant in the case of highways and is one of the more important items in the evaluation. Accident costs are again usually available in the form of recommended values.[16,17] Some example values are set out in Tables 14-3 and 14-4. However, the method of establishing such values is not without its critics. The procedures generally use a value based on the individual's gross or net output and then add a lump sum to reflect the subjective cost of casualties. Some economists argue that this approach looks at the problem too retrospectively. It asks, "How much will I save by carrying out an improvement?" rather than "How much are people willing to pay to reduce the risk of being involved in an accident?". The latter will usually give a higher value, because it applies to the whole of the traveling population rather than the small group likely to be involved in an accident. Until this issue is resolved, however, and another set of recommended values is avail-

TABLE 14–1
Recommended Value of Time in the United Kingdom*

Time	1979 Values
Working	
Car drivers	411
Car passengers	329
Rail passengers	440
Bus passengers	273
Underground passengers	400
Heavy-goods-vehicles occupants	300
Light-goods-vehicles occupants	258
Bus drivers	277
Bus conductors	271
Nonworking	
In-vehicle time	55
Walk/wait time	110

*Pence/hour, average 1979 prices; £1 = $2.

TABLE 14–2
Recommended Value of Time in the United States*

Person-Time (person-hour)	In-Vehicle Time	Waiting or Walking Time
Low time savings (0–5 min)		
Average trips	0.21	5.85–7.80†
Work trips	0.48	5.85–7.80†
Medium time savings (5–15 min)		
Average trips	1.80	5.85–7.80†
Work trips	2.40	5.85–7.80†
High time savings (over 15 min)		
Average trips	3.90	
Work trips	3.90	
Commercial vehicles (vehicle-hour)	*Overall time*	
Single unit truck	7.00	
3-S2 diesel truck	8.00	

*Dollars/person-hour or vehicle-hour, 1975 prices.
†Depends on out-of-vehicle comfort and safety.

TABLE 14–3
Averge Cost per Accident, by Class of Road and Type of Accident in the United Kingdom*

Class of Road / Type of Accident	Urban** Roads	Rural† Roads	Motorways	All Roads
Fatal accident	107,500	119,300	122,800	112,700
Serious accident	5,470	7,220	7,370	6,020
Slight accident	710	1,240	1,370	810
Average injury accident	3,720	8,420	8,370	4,820
Damage only accident	330	410	480	350
Average accident cost per injury accident°	5,860	10,300	10,540	6,900

*£'s per accident at 1979 prices, using a 5% discount rate.
**Roads subject to 30/40 mph speed limit.
†Roads not subject to 30/40 mph speed limit.
°Includes an allowance for damage only accidents.

SOURCE: "Road Accident Costs" (London: Department of Transport Highway Economics Note No. 1, Dec. 1979).

[12]Ibid, p. 181.

[13]HEGGIE, *Modal Choice and the Value of Travel Time;* see the Introduction, in particular.

[14]I. G. HEGGIE, "Economics and the Road Programme," *J. Transport Econ. Policy, 13*(1), 52–67 (1979).

[15]T. SCITOVSKY, *The Joyless Economy* (Oxford: Oxford University Press, 1976), pp. 161–165.

[16]R. F. F. DAWSON, *Current Cost of Road Accidents in Great Britain,* Report 396 (Crowthorne, England: Transport and Road Research Laboratory, 1971).

[17]*A Manual of User Benefit Analysis,* pp. 63–68.

TABLE 14-4
Societal Costs of Motor Vehicle Accidents in the United States*

Cost Component	Severity of Injury: Fatal	Survival uncertain	Survival probable	Not life threatening	Moderate	Minor	Property damage only
Production/ Consumption	275,365	164,645	72,210	2,070	1,175	85	—
Medical	565	17,345	7,450	1,620	615	100	—
Other	11,245	10,250	7,295	4,395	2,560	2,007	518
Total	287,175	192,240	86,955	8,085	4,350	2,190	520

*($'s per fatality and injury, or per vehicle for property damage, at 1975 prices using a 7% discount rate)

SOURCE: FAIGIN, B.M. "Societal Costs of Motor Vehicle Accidents" (Washington, National Highway Traffic Safety Administration, 1976).

able, the current recommended values must be used (see Chapter 18).

Wider considerations. The impacts described above are clearly not exhaustive. They include all the major quantifiable impacts but ignore the qualitative ones which must be evaluated subjectively or dealt with outside the usual economic evaluation. The final number or set of numbers produced by an economic evaluation will therefore not point to a unique and unequivocal decision. The results of the evaluation have to be set alongside a variety of other considerations, whether strategic or nonmonetary, before the policymaker can reach a final decision. The economic evaluation must thus be seen in context, with its measures of priority contributing to only one part of the overall process of choice and decision.

Identification of alternatives for detailed study

There are three parts to the identification of transport alternatives: the statement of objectives, the evaluation of resources and constraints, and the specification of feasible solutions for further study. This amounts to asking: What are we trying to do, what resources are at our disposal and how should we mobilize them to meet these objectives?

In principle, such a search procedure could produce an almost infinite number of possible solutions. It must thus be combined with a "screening process" to establish rough priorities by eliminating schemes that lie too far outside some minimum criterion of choice. This is where rules of thumb are important. They are quick and easy to apply and are generally accurate enough—provided that they are used with discretion—to identify rough priorities.

Identification of projects and policies

This is an innovative activity in which the engineer "invents" possible solutions. It is largely unstructured and follows the general principles of lateral thinking.[18]

It is unwise to introduce too much structure, since it is likely to undermine the innovative content and lead to a system based on checklist elimination. In this, the engineer does not innovate, but responds passively to suggestions from the public or their elected representatives, and subjects them to a series of structured checks:

- Will the proposed scheme solve a specific problem?
- Will the problem still remain after current projects are completed?
- How well does the proposed scheme solve this problem?

and so on

This structured approach is not recommended. An effective procedure for identifying possible alternatives must ask where the problems are and which are most important, and must complement this by considering different solutions.

A better approach is embodied in Figure 14.2. This shows how a loosely structured consideration of objectives/resources/constraints can be used to direct attention to the main pressure points on a sector or on one of its components. In generating these alternatives the engineer must also consider a wide range of possible solutions, including:

1. Getting better use out of existing facilities by improved management.
2. Encouraging use of other, underutilized modes of transport.
3. Using different means of communication, such as telephones and closed-circuit TV.

Other options include the staged implementation of schemes, variations in design standards, and alternative materials.

Such a search procedure is often helped by the use of simple indices of performance (these cannot indicate when a new facility is required and must be used with discretion). In the case of highway schemes, for example, the engineer could use Highway Sufficiency Ratings, indices of accidents (either aggregate costs or their number and severity), measures of traffic delay (in aggregate or by class of vehicle), or measures of pedestrian delay or hazard. A harbor scheme can use a similar index of delay—or transit time—for each component of the port as well as for individual commodities. Similar indices can be developed for other transport facilities or for their impact (e.g., noise-level indices), to try and identify where the system, or its environment, is overloaded.

Rules of thumb for rough priorities

Having established a prima facie case for a particular transport scheme, the next step is to decide whether or not it warrants further study. This needs a rough rule of thumb which can say (1) whether the scheme is definitely not worth considering, (2) whether it is definitely worth doing, or (3) whether it is marginal and should be evaluated in more detail before a decision can be taken. Most schemes fall into categories (1) and (3).

[18] E. DE BONO, *The Use of Lateral Thinking* (Harmondsworth, Middlesex: Penguin Books, 1967).

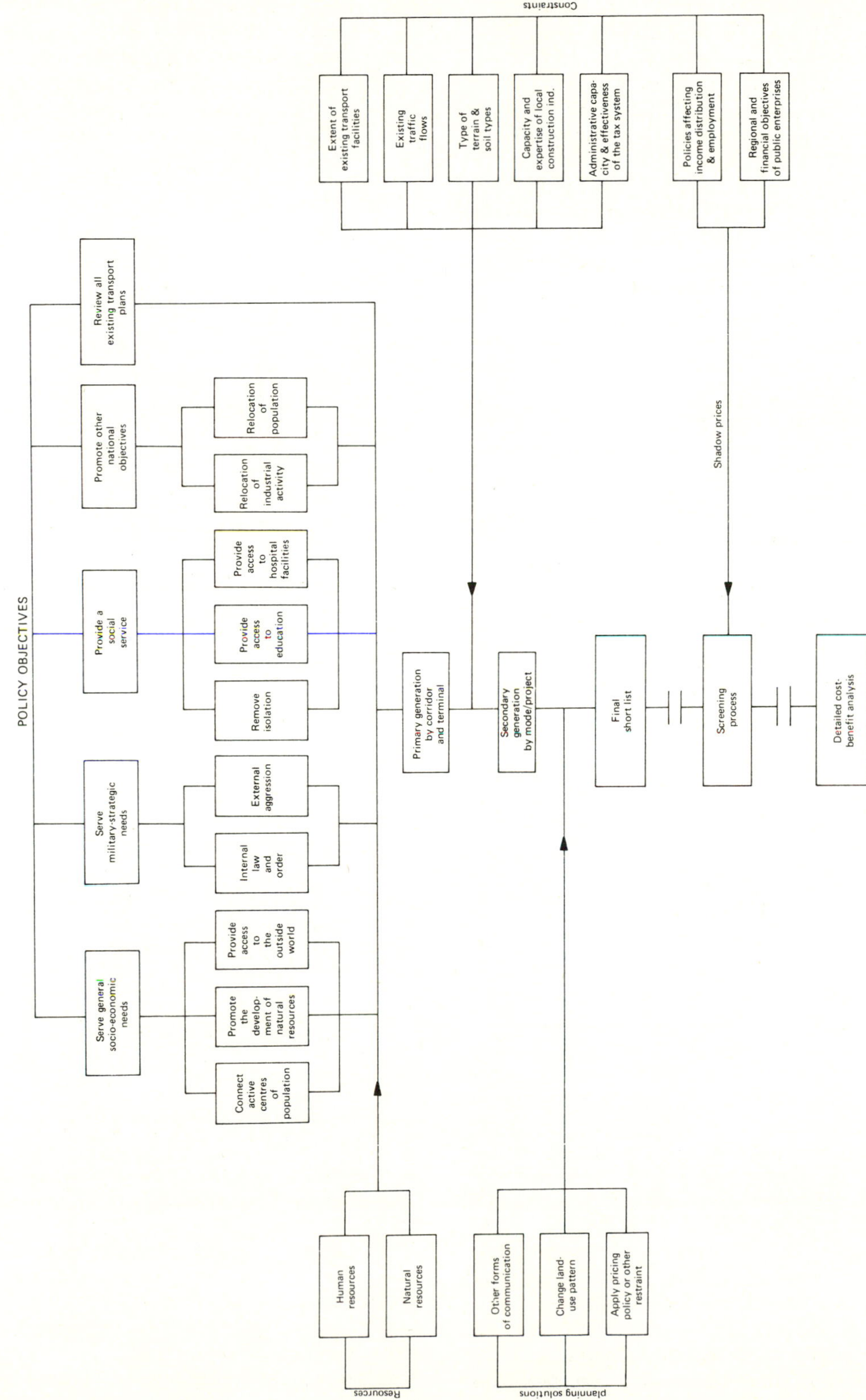

Figure 14.2. Translating policy objectives and constraints into schemes meriting detailed appraisal. SOURCE: I.G. Heggie, *Transport Engineering Economics*, London: McGraw-Hill, 1972.

The simplest and perhaps most common rules of thumb are based on total transport costs and on first-year rates of return, calculated by using average cost figures. They may be presented as a graph relating, say, the volume of traffic using a particular highway segment, or a particular type of intersection, to the total cost of using that facility.[19] The graph shows the cost profile on the existing facility, exclusive of any nonrecurrent sunk costs, together with the cost profiles of various levels of improvement, including the capital cost of improvement. Such graphs enable the engineer to decide, given the present volume of traffic using the facility, what standard of improvement (if any) should be studied in detail. Similar graphs can be drawn for other transport modes: for example, relating shipping costs to the depth of water in a harbor, or relating airline costs to the number and length of runways at an airport.

The foregoing examples are fairly simple, and more complex screening devices are usually desirable in practice. An example for a rural low-volume gravel road is shown in Table 14-5. It is based on marginal benefit–cost ratios (i.e., the change in value per current dollar associated with a 1-year postponement of the scheme) and takes account of the varying growth and composition of traffic.

TABLE 14–5
Tabulation of Data for Screening Proposed Road Improvements

Base Year Traffic Volume (A A D T)	Planning Period Indicated* For Traffic Compositions† Of:			
	C1	C2	C3	C4
60	3/2	3	3	3
70	2	3	3	3
80	2	3/2	3	3
90	2	2	3/2	3
100	2	2	2	3/2
110	2/1	2	2	2
120	1	2/1	2	2
130	1	1	2/1	2
140	1	1	1	2
150	1	1	1	2/1
160	1	1	1	1
170	1/0	1	1	1
180	0	1	1	1
190	0	1/0	1	1
200	0	0	1	1
210	0	0	1/0	1
220	0	0	0	1

*0 = constuct now.
1 = construct during first planning period.
2 = construct during second planning period.
3 = construct beyond second planning period.

†C1 = 15% cars, 55% truck/trailers, tankers and large buses, rest regular trucks.
C2 = 20% cars, 25% truck/trailers, tankers and large buses, rest regular trucks.
C3 = 20% cars, 5% truck/trailers, tankers and large buses, rest regular trucks.
C4 = 30% cars, 5% truck/trailers, tankers and large buses, rest regular trucks.

SOURCE: I.G. Heggie, *Transport Engineering Economics*

With computerized evaluation methods, the foregoing graphical or tabular techniques are rapidly becoming redundant. The engineer simply uses general data and produces a specific, although necessarily rough and ready, answer. This enables several different configurations and design standards to be rapidly compared, to decide which ones justify further investigation.

[19]HEGGIE, *Transport Engineering Economics*, pp. 136–143.

Detailed economic evaluation

An economic evaluation provides three types of information: whether the scheme is worthwhile, when it should be implemented, and how desirable it is compared with alternative schemes. It is thus an accounting exercise in which the benefits and costs of the scheme are first identified and quantified, reduced to a uniform and comparable unit of account, and compared to arrive at an index of priority.

Defining benefits and costs

The first step is to define benefits and costs. This is usually done by considering what would happen without the proposed scheme and what is likely to happen with it. The difference in costs and operating characteristics between the "with" and "without" conditions defines the appropriate levels of benefits and costs.

A highway scheme is thus usually evaluated by calculating:

1. The volume of traffic likely to use the highway without any improvement.
2. The cost to operate vehicles over the unimproved highway during a finite evaluation period (usually taken as 20 to 30 years), bearing in mind that vehicle speeds will change as the flow increases.
3. The cost of upgrading the highway (in terms of initial capital costs and increased maintenance costs).
4. The volume of traffic likely to use the highway once it has been improved.
5. The cost to operate vehicles over the improved highway.
6. Other indirect costs and benefits, such as noise pollution and positive effects on industry, caused by the highway improvement.

The benefits of the scheme can now be calculated as follows, using the formula in the section on vehicle operating costs:

$$\text{benefits} = [1 + \tfrac{1}{2}(4 - 1)](2 - 5) + \text{appropriate elements of } 6 \qquad (14.1)$$

The costs can be similarly calculated as

$$\text{cost} = 3 + \text{appropriate elements of } 6 \qquad (14.2)$$

The foregoing benefits and costs are calculated separately for each year of operation. Certain items will clearly recur from year to year, whereas others will only appear in individual years or during a finite period of time. An example of the cost profile attributable to building a new port jetty is illustrated in Table 14-6.

The above "with" or "without" principle applies to any type of transport evaluation: what would port congestion (and hence total shipping costs) be with and without additional berths, or what would aircraft delays be with and without a given increase in runway capacity? The rule must nevertheless be used with discretion:

1. The definition of what is likely to happen "without" the proposed scheme must be realistic. There is no point

TABLE 14–6
Example of the Cost Profile Attributable to a Port Extension*

	Capital [(a)]		Maintenance				Operating Costs		Total†			
									Assumption I		Assumption II	
Year	Jetty	Warehouses	Jetty		Warehouses		Fixed	Variable	Case A	Case B	Case A	Case B
1977								0.235/tonne				
1978												
1979	4,134.3	14,919.7							19,054.0		19,054.0	
1980	6,890.6	24,866.2							31,756.8		31,756.8	
1981	2,756.2	9,946.5	162.3‡	(222.0)§					12,865.0		12,924.7	
1982			295.6	(233.1)	764.0	(572.1)§	400.2	31.1	1,490.9		1,236.5	
1983				(244.2)		(602.4)		113.0	1,572.8		1,359.7	
1984				(255.2)		(632.7)		233.3	1,693.1		1,521.4	
1985				(266.2)		(663.0)		281.5	1,741.3		1,610.9	
1986				(277.3)		(693.3)		286.8	1,746.6		1,657.6	
1987				(288.3)		(723.6)		286.8	1,746.6		1,698.9	
1988				(299.4)		(754.0)			1,746.6		1,740.4	
1989				(310.4)		(784.3)			1,746.6		1,781.7	
1990				(321.5)		(814.6)			1,746.6		1,823.8	
1991				(332.5)		(844.9)		286.8 (406.3)§	1,746.6	1,866.1	1,864.4	1,983.9
1992				(343.5)		(875.2)		286.8 (406.3)	1,746.6	1,866.1	1,905.7	2,025.2
1993				(354.6)		(905.5)			1,746.6	1,866.1	1,947.1	2,066.6
1994				(365.6)		(935.8)			1,746.6	1,866.1	1,988.4	2,107.9
1995	2,920.7 (0)§			(376.7)		(966.1)			4,667.3	4,786.8	2,029.8	2,149.3
1996	4,442.8 (0)	9,597.0 (0)§		(387.7)		(996.4)			15,786.4	15,905.9	2,071.1	2,190.6
1997		9,597.0 (0)		(398.7)		(1026.7)			11,343.6	11,463.1	2,112.4	2,231.9
1998				(409.8)		(1057.0)			1,746.6	1,866.1	2,153.8	2,273.3
1999			295.6	(420.8)	764.0	(1087.3)			1,746.6	1,866.1	2,195.1	2,314.6
2000			295.6	(431.9)	764.0	(1117.6)			1,746.6	1,866.1	2,236.5	2,356.0
2001			295.6	(442.9)	764.0	(1147.9)			1,746.6	1,866.1	2,277.8	2,397.3
			295.6		764.0				1,746.6	1,866.1		
			295.6		764.0				1,746.6	1,866.1		
2010			295.6		764.0		400.2	286.8 (406.3)	1,746.6	1,866.1		

*$ × 10^3 at 1979 prices.
†Assumption I: equipment life = 15 years, evaluation period up to 2010; assumption II: equipment life = 20 years, evaluation period up to 2001; case A: exports rise to 1.2 mtonnes/yr; case B: exports rise to 1.2 mtonnes/yr and to 1.7 mtonnes/yr after 1990
‡Maintenance on first loader and conveyor only.
§Figures in brackets apply if equipment is replaced after 20 years.

in pretending that all decisions are of an all-or-nothing variety. For example, it would be unrealistic to pretend that the "without" condition for a port consisted of no new berths for 20 years, whereas the "with" condition consisted of adding 10 new berths now. The scheme may very well give a high rate of return when set out this way, but would probably imply queuing delays of up to 6 months or more by the time the 20 years was reached. In practice, the real options reduce to a limited number of discrete choices which have to be evaluated on an incremental basis (see the section "Incremental Analysis"): Should one new berth be added every 2 years, or groups of berths (to achieve economies of scale) at somewhat longer intervals? The with and without options should not therefore be defined as "nothing at all" versus "everything at once," but nothing versus one strategy, and then that strategy versus others. Only in this way can an optimum scheme be developed.

2. Benefits and costs must be carefully defined to avoid double counting. Savings in vehicle operating costs cannot be added to changes in property values. The former cause the latter, which represent the capitalized value of these, and perhaps other, benefits. One *or* the other measure should be used, not both.

3. Some benefits and costs arise due to interdependence between projects. The effect of the project may then depend on whether, and in what way, some other project is implemented. For example, the economies of scale associated with using large supertankers are dependent on whether all their ports of call have sufficient draft and appropriate mooring facilities. The benefits of dredging one port will thus depend on what is done in the other ports of call; the scheme is interdependent and can be evaluated only by considering all the ports of call as a single combined project.

What is the right price?

Prices affect an economic evaluation in the following ways:

1. The prices used to evaluate resource inputs determine the magnitude of net benefits.
2. The price charged for use of a facility, such as tolls, landing fees, harbor dues, and so on, affect the level of demand and hence the amount of traffic using it.
3. The price charged affects the way in which net benefits are distributed among the various groups affected by the project.

The ideal price at which to value resource inputs is based on their marginal opportunity cost: the value of the item in its next best use. The value of output is determined by asking how much people are prepared to pay rather than go without the item (see "Optimum Allocation of Scarce Resources").

In a reasonably functioning market system, market prices provide a reasonably good measure of marginal opportunity costs. There is, however, one qualification. Taxes and subsidies should be "netted out" of all prices before they are used to calculate costs and benefits. The reason is that taxes appear as a "cost" when resource expenditures are added together, but reappear as a "benefit" when the increase in government income is taken into account. Taxes are simply transfer payments and will always cancel out in a social benefit–cost analysis. It is therefore customary to remove them from the calculations and to perform the analysis excluding all such payments. The same argument applies in the case of subsidies.

Few, if any, countries have a perfectly functioning market system, so that other price distortions will also arise. For example, many transport improvements increase the efficiency of the transport sector by reducing the number of vehicles (e.g., trucks, ships, trains, etc.) required to produce a given level of output. This usually leads to the displacement of labor. The "savings" produced by the scheme thus include savings in wage payments. In a full-employment economy this is reasonable, because redundant labor can usually find alternative employment at a similar wage rate elsewhere in the economy. Where there is already unemployment, this will not be so, and some of the displaced labor may simply become permanently redundant. In such cases the person's wage is not "saved," since he continues to cost the economy enough resources to keep him alive.

When the foregoing type of distortions are present, it is desirable to use shadow prices.[20–22] These are difficult and time consuming to prepare, however, and should only be attempted when absolutely essential. Furthermore, shadow prices create their own distortions which may very well be worse than the original ones they are trying to avoid.[23]

A further complication is that some of the inputs and outputs will have no declared market price. They may either constitute a nonmonetary item, such as noise nuisance or visual intrusion, in which case they must be dealt with in the way described for "Wider Considerations," or they may simply be outside the market system. The latter effects may, in principle, be marketable like savings in travel time, but may not—for various institutional reasons—be bought and sold in the market place. In such cases surrogate prices are required and are estimated, as with travel time, by studying people's choices and the implicit values inherent in their choice.

The price charged for using a facility will affect the economic evaluation in two ways. It determines the level of demand, and hence the number of users, as well as the distribution of benefits. Often, the price charged will not be efficient, and will be below the value users derive from it. For example, the road tax paid by motorists is often well below the benefits they derive from using a particular segment of improved road, whereas the charges levied for use of airports and ports[24] are often nominal, and not related either to the cost of the services or to their value.

These anomalies may not matter. However, when international traffic uses a facility, it can result in people of country *A* paying for a facility that primarily benefits people of country *B*. This is particularly true of harbor facilities. Most major ports serve international traffic used by members of the various shipping conferences. When a port is improved, the conference averages the benefits and effectively applies them to all the ports included in its itinerary (alternatively, the companies in the conference may simply keep savings in the form of higher profits). To avoid this the improvement in facilities has to be linked to a revised tariff structure to ensure that the people paying for the improvement recover sufficient benefits to cover its costs.

Discounting

Once all the benefits and costs have been quantified, they must be turned into an index of priority. First, however, they must be reduced to their present values. In the section of "Optimum Allocation of Scarce Resources," it was shown that the present value of a stream of benefits and costs could be written as

$$\text{present value} = R_0 + \frac{w_1}{w_0}R_1 + \frac{w_2}{w_0}R_2 + \cdots + \frac{w_n}{w_0}R_n \quad (14.3)$$

where $R_0, R_1, R_2, \ldots R_n$ = net benefits in each year $0, 1, 2, \ldots, n$

$\frac{w_1}{w_0}, \frac{w_2}{w_0}, \ldots, \frac{w_n}{w_0}$ = "discount factors" applicable to each year.

Discount factors are generally expressed as an annual rate of return. For simplicity, they are held constant over time, and the rate of return is called the "discount rate." The discount factor, where r is the discount rate, is written as $(1 + r)^{-i}$, where i represents the particular year in question. The discount factors above thus become

$$\frac{w_0}{w_0} = 1, \quad \frac{w_1}{w_0} = (1 + r)^{-1},$$
$$\frac{w_2}{w_0} = (1 + r)^{-2}, \ldots, \frac{w_n}{w_0} = (1 + r)^{-n} \quad (14.4)$$

The net present value of this stream of net benefits is thus

$$\text{net present value (NPV)} = R_0 + \frac{R_1}{1 + r} + \frac{R_2}{(1 + r)^2} + \cdots + \frac{R_n}{(1 + r)^n} \quad (14.5)$$

This is the inverse of the compound interest amount and can be rationalized as follows. If r represents a possible rate of return on capital, a given sum R will grow to $R(1 + r)$ after 1 year, $R(1 + r)^i$ after i years, and so on. The present value of the sum $R(1 + r)^i$ in year i is R, since that was the

[20] I. M. D. Little and J. M. Mirlees, *Project Appraisal and Planning for Developing Countries* (London: Heineman Educational Books, 1974).

[21] I. M. D. Little and M. F. Scott, eds., *Using Shadow Prices* (London: Heineman Educational Books, 1974).

[22] I. G. Heggie, "Subsidy and Counter Subsidy: The Case for Accounting Prices," *Logist. Transport. Rev.*, *10*(1), 3–22 (1974).

[23] I. G. Heggie, "Practical Problems of Implementing Accounting Prices," in *Using Shadow Prices*, pp. 230–246.

[24] Heggie, "Charging for Port Facilities," pp. 1–5.

starting amount. The discount factor required to reduce $R(1 + r)^i$ to this present value is clearly $(1 + r)^{-i}$.

There are two ways of using the foregoing formula. Either a predetermined figure r can be used to reduce the stream of benefits and costs to its NPV (as illustrated above), or the formula can be used to calculate what value of r reduces the NPV to zero. The latter procedure solves for r to arrive at the solution rate of interest for one or more "internal rates of return" (IRRs). Both procedures are commonly used, although there are a number of technical reasons for preferring the NPV.

Discount rates

There are various ways of defining the discount rate, which is not simply equal to the market interest rate. The latter is more influenced by government monetary policy and short-term balance of payment conditions than it is by the long-term availability of investment resources.

The most usual methods are based on the "social time preference rate" (STPR) and the social opportunity cost of capital (SOC). The former represents the way people value present versus future consumption (it represents their preference for consumption now rather than in the future); the latter is equal to the marginal social productivity of capital (the output foregone by not investing in something else).

The engineer need not really be concerned with these complexities. The government should specify which discount rate it wishes to see used in an economic evaluation. This is desirable for consistency and because the government is the only organization able to form an effective judgment about the various components of the discount rate. Actual rates in the United Kingdom usually lie between 6 and 10%. In less developed countries, discount rates of 10 to 15% are common.

Incremental analysis

The simplest rule for using the NPV is that all projects whose NPV $\geqslant 0$ should be implemented. In the case of the IRR, the rule is that all projects whose IRR $\geqslant$ the minimum acceptable rate of return should be implemented. The rules above apply only when the choice involves "all or nothing." It does not apply when projects are interdependent or when they are incompatible.

Interdependent projects interact with each other. For example, a nonlinear value of time, as shown in Table 14-2, will usually make "linked" bus-lane schemes interdependent. The benefit produced by each separately will be less than that produced in combination. The order in which schemes are combined will similarly affect the incremental benefits and costs. When projects are interdependent, they should thus be analyzed as follows. Find the best initial investment (i.e., the component with the highest NPV or IRR) and then extend investment to other members of the interdependent group in descending order of priority until the NPV of the increment being considered is just equal to zero or its IRR is just equal to the minimum acceptable rate of return.

Incompatibility occurs when the choice of one project, or one version of a project, precludes the choice of another; incompatible projects are thus mutually exclusive. This is a common occurrence in highway projects: a dual three-lane highway is incompatible with a dual two-lane one; the choice of one precludes the choice of the other. There would clearly be no difficulty in this example if only one satisfied the investment criterion. The difficult cases occur when both satisfy the criterion. Incremental analysis must then be applied.

The schemes will nearly always differ in cost and should be ranked in order of cost: $A, B, C, D, \ldots$ starting with the smallest. They are then considered in order:

1. Is the NPV of $A \geqslant 0$? If so, continue.
2. Is the incremental NPV $(B - A) \geqslant 0$ (this is calculated by taking the increased cost of B and subtracting it from the increased benefits)? If so, continue.
3. Continue until either the whole package of schemes is accepted, or until the analysis reaches the project whose incremental NPV is just equal to zero.

The analysis above applies equally to the IRR. The incremental IRR is calculated (the IRR of the stream of differences $B - A$, etc.) until the marginal interdependent project is reached with an IRR that is just equal to the minimum acceptable IRR.

The incremental analysis is illustrated in Figure 14.3. It shows three incompatible schemes A, B, and C (they could represent dual two-, three-, and four-lane roads). The NPV of C, $Y_c - X_c$, is clearly $\geqslant 0$. However, the incremental NPV of C over B, $(Y_{C-B} - X_{C-B})$ and that of B over A, $(Y_{B-A} - X_{B-A})$ is < 0. Scheme A is thus the preferred solution. The extra benefit for schemes B and C does not cover the extra cost.

It is worth pointing out in Figure 14.3 that the NPV criterion, NPV $\geqslant 0$, is the same as saying $B/C \geqslant 1$. The incremental NPV criterion is the same as saying $\Delta B/\Delta C \geqslant 1$.

Figure 14.3. Diagram illustrating incremental analysis.

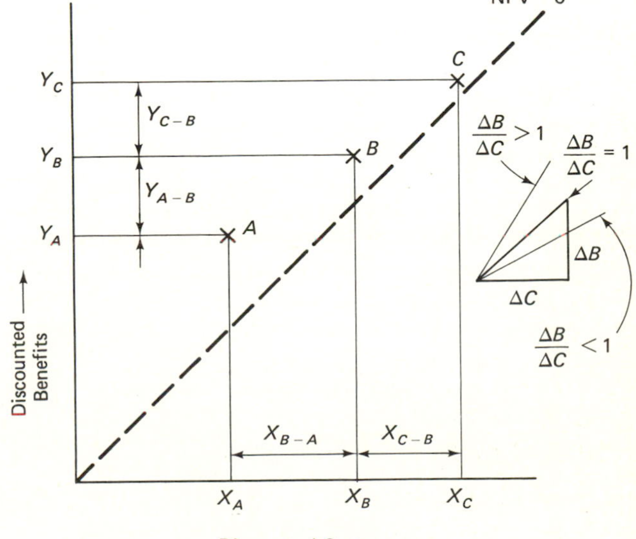

Budget constraints

A budget constraint is a form of incompatibility. Selecting one project and adding it to the list of those already selected precludes the selection of another. When resources are limited—as they invariably are—projects should thus be ranked in terms of their incremental IRR or NPV.

In practice, such ranking is rather cumbersome with the IRR. As a result, budget ranking is generally done using the incremental NPV, expressed as a benefit–cost ratio, B/C. This index, which defines the "present-value-per-current-dollar" ratio for each project, is then used as a ranking criterion, and schemes are ranked and selected, starting with the project with the highest B/C ratio, until the budget is exhausted. However, when projects vary in size, a small project with a high B/C ratio should not displace a larger one with a smaller ratio unless the sum of its NPV and that of the new project admitted to take up the surplus funds is greater than that of the larger project.

Benefit/cost ratios can, unfortunately, be ambiguous, since they depend on the precise way in which benefits and costs are defined. Which items should be treated as costs and placed in the denominator, and which should be treated as negative benefits and placed in the numerator? Reduced maintenance costs usually fall into this category. They usually appear in the numerator as a benefit (i.e., the numerator represents net benefits) but could equally well appear in the denominator as a cost saving, thus altering the overall B/C ratio and hence the general ranking of projects.

This ambiguity is fortunately not as serious as it seems. The decision of whether to place maintenance expenditure in the numerator or denominator represents an explicit policy choice. A benefit/cost ratio measures the *output* of a scheme relative to the *input* of scarce resources. If maintenance expenditure is in scarce supply, it should appear in the denominator; if not, it should appear in the numerator.

Although the B/C ratio provides a reasonable rough and ready rule for deciding investment priorities when there are budget constraints, it is by no means perfect. It will only select the optimum set of projects when the budget in *one* period is constrained. This is unrealistic, because a project that is not accepted in one period does not have to be rejected for all time: it can be postponed. The general problem of deciding priorities thus reduces to the question of deciding *when* to implement the project and, given that, whether it should be implemented at all.

This criterion is quite different from the B/C ratio, because a project with a high B/C ratio may lose little value if postponed, while one with a low B/C ratio may lose all its value. To maximize the aggregate NPV of both projects, the first project should thus be postponed in order to implement the second as soon as possible. This is clearly a mathematical programming problem which can be solved to find the best time to implement a project. In the commonest practical case, where net benefits are steadily increasing over time, it gives a result that simplifies to the following simple rule: *do not implement a project until the first year rate of return is equal to, or exceeds, the discount rate.*

When the stream of net benefits is not steadily increasing, this rule has to be amended as follows:

1. When it is constant or declining, implement the project now or not at all (unless the discount rate is declining).
2. When it fluctuates, derive the optimal conditions from the more general expression[25]

$$\text{NPV}[i - 1] \geqslant \text{NPV}[i] \geqslant \text{NPV}[i + 1]$$

where i is the year in which implementation begins.

Length of evaluation period

It is conventional to evaluate transport facilities over a finite period of time, and to ignore any benefits and costs that fall outside this period. In the case of highways, the period is commonly taken as 20 to 30 years; in the case of more permanent facilities such as docks and railways, it is often as long as 50 years.

The reason for these conventions is rarely made explicit, even though the finite nature of the evaluation period can affect the aggregate NPV of a project, as the following example shows.

Growth of benefits		2%	4%
Discount rate		12%	6%
Discounted benefits after	20 years	8.5136	16.3514
Discounted benefits after	30 years	9.4269	22.3965
Discounted benefits after	35 years	9.6442	24.9986
Extra benefits as a proportion of benefits after 20 years	20–30 years	+10.7%	+37.0%
	30–35 years	+2.6%	+15.9%

Variations in conventions within a sector (e.g., highways), or between sectors (e.g., highways versus ports) may thus affect overall priorities and may also affect the allocation of resources between sectors. Conventions must, therefore, be justified and used consistently, with suitable caveats when intermodal comparisons, using different evaluation periods, are involved.

The length of the evaluation period can be justified in several different ways. The most convincing relates to uncertainty: "It is rash to assume . . . that a capital asset, although it lasts forever, will have a value forever. . . . To guard against obsolescence, it is necessary to limit the period of time over which benefits (and costs) are counted."[26]. The substance of this argument is that assets are designed to serve a specific need, and over an extended period of time, changes in technology provide new ways of satisfying these needs, while the needs themselves will also change. In due course the asset may thus:

[25]Heggie, *Transport Engineering Economics*, pp. 136–140.

[26]C. D. Foster and M. E. Beesley, "Estimating the Social Benefit of Constructing an Underground Railway in London," in *Transport*, ed. D. L. Munby (Harmondsworth, Middlesex: Penguin Books, 1968), pp. 223–244.

1. Be rendered redundant.
2. Be rendered partly redundant and require adaptation before it again produces a reasonable stream of benefits.

The length of the evaluation period must thus be chosen to reflect the uncertainty associated with the future use of an asset. It follows that an asset has no residual value at the end of this period other than its scrap value. Anything greater than this implies continued use and should be accounted for by increasing the length of the evaluation period.

The choice of the evaluation period will be partly subjective and will relate to expected changes in technology, consumer tastes, and so on. It will vary between facility and between the individual components of each facility. For example, a high-volume, high-standard highway will usually have a longer useful life than a low-volume, local highway because interregional flows are usually more stable than local ones and there is less likelihood of alternative routes being constructed, whereas earthworks and structures usually have a longer useful life than pavements and culverts (i.e., they are less affected—although not wholly unaffected—by changes in axle weights, lane widths, speeds, etc.).

The same arguments apply to ports, airports, and railways. In an airport, for example, cargo and passenger handling techniques are changing rapidly (hence short evaluation periods), whereas runway lengths and load-bearing capacity are now changing relatively slowly (hence longer evaluation periods). Indeed, the whole concept of evaluation periods is not all that different from the business economist's concept of "payback period." The more variable the market or the technology, the shorter the asset's guaranteed useful life and hence the shorter its required "payback period."

To ensure consistency, evaluation periods should be specified by national or local governments, or by organizations embodying a national perspective.

Treatment of noncomparable effects

The section on "Detailed Economic Evaluation" implies that all costs and benefits can be expressed in terms of a common financial unit. The results are then presented as a single index, often as a benefit–cost ratio, for purposes of ranking and selection.

In a market economy, in which all items, including environmental effects, are traded at realistic prices, this procedure is readily applicable. The real world, however, does not work like this. A number of important impacts, such as noise nuisance and visual intrusion, are not traded in the marketplace and do not have a clear "declared" price. The evaluation—to the extent that these impacts can be expressed in monetary terms—will therefore use a proxy or some other indirect measure of impact. This usually involves assumptions, for example that studies of mode choice provide genuine insight into the way people value travel time, and value judgments. The resulting measure cannot thus be strictly comparable with direct measures of impact such as changes in vehicle operating costs.

The issue of comparability is important. If the various measures of impact are simply added (1) they are all implicitly given the same status, and (2) the resulting index will obscure the need to review the various assumptions/value judgments employed at the higher level of decision making where these decisions should properly be made.

The only effective way to deal with comparability is to use an impact tableau. This presents each impact category separately, using homogeneous units to measure the impacts within each category and, by implication, heterogeneous units between categories. Impacts such as noise nuisance, time saved, and vehicle operating costs would thus be presented separately.

Such a tableau has one dimension. There are occasions when a two-dimensional tableau is desirable. For example, the agency undertaking the evaluation may wish to know something about the incidence of impacts: Which costs are borne by central government, which by local government, and how are benefits/costs distributed between users and nonusers of the facility?

This suggests a two-dimensional benefit/cost tableau. The x axis might display the incidence of the benefits–costs; the y axis might show the nature of the impact. The standard benefit/cost ratio thus becomes a ratio of matrices instead of a ratio of two numbers. A simple example will illustrate this.

Consider the following highway schemes (all values are discounted to the beginning of each scheme):

	Scheme A	Scheme B
Capital costs		
Borne by central government	80	40
Borne by local government	20	10
Noise nuisance	20	20
Recurrent maintenance expenditure	50	100
Benefits		
Resource savings	60	60
Value of time savings	120	120

The usual benefit/cost ratio gives values of:

1. Net benefit/cost for

$$A\colon\ (120 + 60 - 50) \div (80 + 20 + 20) = 1.08$$

$$B\colon\ (120 + 60 - 100) \div (40 + 10 + 20) = 1.14$$

2. Total benefit/cost for

$$A\colon\ (120 + 60) \div (80 + 20 + 20 + 50) = 1.06$$

$$B\colon\ (120 + 60) \div (40 + 10 + 20 + 100) = 1.06$$

Item 1 is the ratio usually calculated in such evaluations and suggests that B is preferable to A. Ratio 2, on the other hand, gives both schemes the same priority.

The matrix presentation is as follows:

	Scheme A				Scheme B			
	Government				Government			
	Central	Local	Users	Nonusers	Central	Local	Users	Nonusers
Net benefit/cost								
Resource savings		−50	60			−100	60	
Time savings			120				120	
Capital cost	80	20			40	10		
Noise nuisance				20				20
Total benefit/cost								
Resource savings			60				60	
Time savings			120				120	
Capital cost	80	20			40	10		
Recurrent cost		50				100		
Noise nuisance				20				20

In this format, decisions about priorities will be dependent on the perspective of the individual decision maker. For example, central government may favor B because it will pay less, local government may favor A because *it* will pay less, while both will probably agree that neither scheme appears to have quite the same priority as when all impacts were aggregated and presented as a single benefit–cost ratio. The foregoing matrix format includes more information—and more relevant information—and is therefore likely to lead to better-informed decisions.

The matrix format above is merely illustrative. The precise format used in any particular evaluation will depend on the type of scheme involved and on the interests of the people who interpret its results. It can clearly either be expanded or contracted, and can be adapted along the lines of a comprehensive assessment framework[27] or a planning balance sheet[28] to embrace noneconomic objectives and wider environmental considerations. A complete description of the former method, together with a fully worked example, is set out in ref. 27.

Uncertainty

All aspects of life are uncertain, some more so than others. This creates problems, since an economic evaluation rarely reduces to simple choices between equally certain outcomes. The engineer is rarely faced with a straightforward choice between certain values for A and B; it is often a case of deciding between A, with a relatively narrow variance around its NPV, and B, with a higher variance and perhaps even a higher NPV. The engineer must then decide how to weight this uncertainty in order to assign priorities.

Any analysis of uncertainty should cover the following aspects. First, how can it be quantified; second, how does it or should it—affect the design, and finally, how can the results be made intelligible to the ultimate decision maker?

Sensitivity analysis

It is always tempting to avoid an explicit evaluation of uncertainty by basing the analysis on a "conservative" estimate of the uncertain variables. This is dangerous, since the engineer will not always know whether a conservative estimate—in the sense that it is supposed to lead to an underestimate of net benefits—requires a value that is higher or lower than the most likely estimate. For example, in a road evaluation, it is quite easy for a low, and hence conservative estimate of vehicle speed, to lead to an *overestimate* of traffic benefits! Unless the engineer knows how the estimate affects the mechanics of the evaluation, it is not possible to tell whether conservatism implies a value that is higher or lower than the "best estimate."

Faced with this problem, it is nearly always preferable to base an evaluation on the most likely value of each parameter.

The simplest way of then allowing for uncertainty is by means of sensitivity analysis: by systematically varying the value of each parameter to decide how important it is. The range of variation can either be a specified amount, say 10% above and below the central estimate, or can be related to the inherent uncertainty associated with the central estimate itself. In the latter case, the ranges would thus represent "high" and "low" values, not necessarily uniformly distanced from the most likely value. An example of sensitivity analysis is shown in Figure 14.4. Three variables are being tested for their impact on the overall NPV: (1) the discount

Figure 14.4. Example of sensitivity analysis.

– – – – = Assumption I: equipment life = 15 yrs; evaluation period = 30 yrs.

——— = Assumption II: equipment life = 20 yrs; evaluation period = 20 yrs.

Case A = Exports rise to 1.2m tonnes p.a.

Case B = Exports rise to 1.2m tonnes p.a. and to 1.7m tonnes p.a. after 1990.

Net Present Value ($'000)

Discount Rate

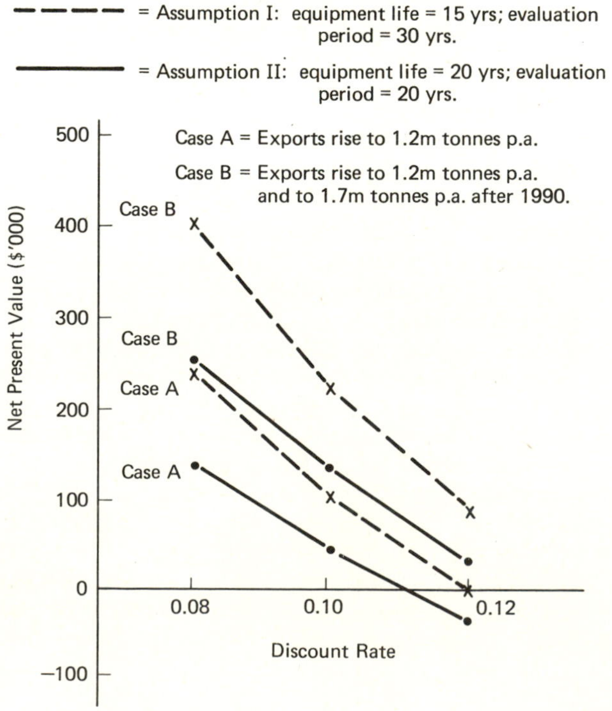

[27] *Trunk Road Proposals: A Comprehensive Framework for Appraisal* (London: H.M.S.O., 1979).

[28] Nathaniel Lichfield & Associates, *Stevenage: A Cost–Benefit Analysis of Alternative Public/Private Modal Split* (Stevenage, England: Stevenage Development Corporation, 1969), Chap. 4.

rate, (2) the length of evaluation period (assumption I = 30 years, assumption II = 20 years), and (3) the volume of traffic (case A = low, case B = high).

The foregoing sensitivity analysis quickly shows which estimates are most important and gives the engineer a general idea of (1) which aspects justify further work to narrow the range of uncertainty and (2) the qualitative uncertainty associated with the scheme as a whole.

When a quantitative evaluation of uncertainty is required,[29] a full simulation must usually be carried out (although it is possible to evaluate uncertainty using mathematical expectations, it is usually too complicated for all but the simplest applications). This is done by substituting either actual or synthetic distributions to replace the high, low, and most likely values for each parameter, and then combining values sampled from each distribution by means of random number tables into an aggregate distribution of NPV, or whatever other index of priority is used.

Impact on engineering design

It is generally not enough only to measure the uncertainty associated with the overall design. An analysis of uncertainty should also be used to guide the design as a means of ensuring against uncertainty.

There are two obvious ways in which the engineer can reduce the impact of uncertainty. The facility can be designed for flexibility, so that it can be adapted in the face of changing demands, or it can be built in stages so that part of the decision can be postponed until the future is more certain. Both strategies nevertheless increase costs, so that the engineer has to decide whether a given increase in cost is worth a measurable reduction in uncertainty.

Designing for flexibility is a relatively easy concept. For example, in the context of port design, the berths handling growing traffic should be located alongside those with traffic that is declining (thus permitting a gradual change of use); and special-purpose berths should be capable of adaptation to handle other cargoes (especially if demand for the special-purpose cargo is highly uncertain). Staged construction is often an equally feasible option. A rail scheme does not have to include upgrading, increased train frequencies, *and* a reorganized bus feeder service. The improvements can be introduced one at a time, so that subsequent stages can be reevaluated and adapted as demand develops.

The engineer can thus do a great deal to reduce the importance of uncertainty and should treat this aspect on a par with the other objectives of the design process.

Overall assessment

The section on sensitivity analysis concluded with a brief summary of how overall uncertainty can be evaluated. The end result will be a distribution of NPV, or of some other index such as aggregate delay to traffic, showing the shape of the distribution and how it relates to the mean value. When using mathematical expectations, it will usually result in values for the mean and variance only.

The next question involves what to do with this information. Although most decision makers are averse to uncertainty and prefer schemes with a reasonably certain outcome, they cannot usually say (although attempts have been made to measure it) how reduced risk is traded against increased cost. If this could be done, the engineer would be able to produce a weighted index of performance, or a weighted NPV, giving a neutral measure of priority. Since, however, this cannot be done with any respectability, the engineer must present this information in a reasonably intelligible way, and leave the decision maker to decide.

Now decision makers do not usually respond favorably to a probability distribution showing the range of possible NPV's associated with a project. They usually require the information in a simpler form. What they want to know is: "What is most likely to happen?" and "What might happen if something goes badly wrong or performs better than expected?" This information, suitably qualified, can usually be provided by carrying out a sensitivity analysis. A full analysis of uncertainty is not usually necessary unless the NPV relationships, and the intercorrelations between them, are so complex that sensitivity analysis—which by its very nature only gives a partial measure of uncertainty—becomes unreliable. In the absence of this, a most likely estimate based on an efficient measure of central tendency, combined with a qualitative description of uncertainty based on sensitivity analysis, should be sufficient.

Examples of application

The following illustrations covering a simple airport runway extension, the addition of new berths in a port, a traffic management scheme, and an urban bypass illustrate how the foregoing economic considerations are used to decide (1) which of alternative designs represents best value for money, (2) whether the best scheme is worthwhile, and (3) whether the scheme should be introduced now or later. The examples are extremely simple, but show the sort of considerations the transportation engineer should bear in mind when planning and designing a scheme, and how these translate into a numerical format as a means of deciding priorities.

Feasibility of a runway extension

The evaluation of an airport extension at Nicosia in Cyprus was carried out in 1968[30,31] and provides a useful illustration of macro economic effects.

Nicosia's main runway had a limited length of 8000 ft (2438 m), which imposed restrictions on certain types of aircraft under particular climatic conditions. It was feared

[29]HEGGIE, *Transport Engineering Economics*, pp. 240–246.

[30]J. G. ODY, "Application of Cost–Benefit Analysis to Airports," *J. Transport Econ. Policy*, *3*(3), 322–332 (1969).

[31]BRITISH AIRPORTS AUTHORITY, RENDEL PALMER & TRITTON, ECONOMIST INTELLIGENCE UNIT, "Nicosia Airport: The Feasibility of Extending the Runway and Improving Other Operational Facilities" (unpublished consultants' report, 1968).

that these restrictions would discourage further growth in tourist traffic to Cyprus and, conversely, that the runway extension might:

1. Encourage more tourist traffic.
2. Increase air freight traffic by inducing additional agricultural and industrial export traffic.
3. Increase airport revenue.

The first of a two-part evaluation considered the influence of runway length on aircraft operation and the impact of different extensions. Lengths between 8000 ft (2438 m) and 10,500 ft (3200 m) were examined. An eventual length of 9700 ft (2957 m) was chosen based on cost and air traffic characteristics of present and proposed aircraft types.

The second part evaluated three ways of providing the additional 1700 ft (518 m) of runway. The cost of each scheme was estimated on a net basis, excluding any expenditure that would have to be incurred regardless of whether or not the extension was built, while benefits were calculated as net gains to the Cyprus economy. This was done by eliminating the import content of any monetary gains and separating out the cost of any scarce resources which might simply be diverted from other productive uses in the island. Potential benefits fell into two categories: maintaining the growth of tourist traffic (each tourist "lost" because of the perceived difficulty of using the short runway would lose an average of £63 ($126) at a net cost of £37 ($74) to the local economy); and increased airport revenue, calculated on a net basis, associated with this traffic. Other types of benefits were also examined but turned out to be negligible or illusory.

The results of the evaluation were expressed in two ways: as a table listing the qualitative differences between the three schemes, and as a matrix of benefits and costs. These are shown in Tables 14-7 and 14-8.

It is fairly clear from these tables that (1) the cheapest scheme *B* represents the preferable option, since the incremental benefits *A–B*, *C–B*, and *A–C* are zero; (2) with a *B*/*C* ratio of well over 1.0, it is certainly worth implementing; and (3) with a first-year rate of return of at least 15.2% and a discount rate of 8%, it should be implemented as soon as possible.

Port improvement scheme

The desirability of extending the port facilities at Port Swettenham (now called Port Klang), Malaysia was evaluated in 1967–1968.[32,33] It illustrates the measurement of time savings, the optimum phasing of an investment program, and the importance of pricing policy when benefits and costs are passed indirectly to the final consumer.

[32] I. G. Heggie and C. B. Edwards, "Port Investment Problems: How to Decide Investment Priorities," *Conference on Engineering Problems Overseas* (London: Institution of Civil Engineers, 1968), pp. 31–49.

[33] Economist Intelligence Unit, "Port Swettenham Feasibility Study," Vols. 1, 3 (unpublished consultants' report, 1968).

TABLE 14–7
Qualitative Evaluation of Runway Extension*

	Proposal A	Proposal B	Proposal C
	Operational features		
1.	No new noise problem	Noise problem on approach over southern part of Nicosia	No noise problem for landing
2.	Subsidiary runway is 6000 ft long	Subsidiary runway is 8000 ft long	Takeoff runway is 9700 ft long; landing runway is 8000 ft long
3.	Severe restrictions on operations during construction; 14/32 runway closed for 10 months	Minor restriction only of operations on existing main runway during extension on 09/27 runway	As for B, with improvement of 14/32 runway after extended 09/27 runway opened to traffic
4.	Main runway ultimate capacity will be affected by necessity for backtracking between existing 32 threshold and new taxiway turning loop (820 ft)	Main runway ultimate capacity will be affected by necessity for backtracking between new apron turn-out and taxiway turning loop at end of extension (5400 ft)	Total capacity for separate landing and takeoff runways is much greater than for A or B, and is limited only by capacity of runway intersection
5.	I.L.S. localizer can be easily sited on projected centerline for landings in normal 32 direction	No site available on projected centerline for I.L.S. localizer without very extensive earthworks; offset, uncategorized I.L.S. is the only viable alternative	As for A
6.	New approach procedure for landings on 32 threshold would be similar to existing pattern	Entirely new approach procedure required for landings on 27 threshold	Existing approach procedure remains unchanged
7.	Control tower requires improvement for full visibility to extended threshold	As for A, but also for line of sight to new 27 threshold	As for B
	Construction and maintenance		
8.	Construction work subject to restriction before temporary closure of 14/32 runway	Construction work subject to restriction before temporary closure of 09/27 runway	Construction work relatively free of restriction, except on runway intersection
9.	Occasional use of 09/27 runway will not justify strengthening for some years	Occasional use of 14/32 runway will not justify strengthening for some years	14/32 runway is strengthened for main landing use
10.	Main runway maintenance may become a problem, as subsidiary runway is only 6000 ft long	Main runway maintenance will be easier as subsidiary runway is 8000 ft long	Necessary to maintain both runways, but each runway could be used for both landings and takeoff
	Land acquisition and access		
11.	Approximately 18.5 ha of agricultural land required	Approximately 2.3 ha of agricultural land required; remaining area is on rocky ground and under government control	As for B
12.	Requires no modifications to existing airport access	Requires additional minor access road to southeastern part of airport	As for B

*1 ft = 0.305 meters.

Source: British Airports Authority et al., "Nicosia Airport: The Feasibility of Extending the Runway and Improving Other Operational Facilities" (unpublished consultants' report, 1968), pp. 84–85.

TABLE 14–8
Discounted Benefits and Costs: Nicosia Airport Runway Extension*

	Scheme		
	A	B	C
Benefits			
Marginal increase in airport revenue			
Minimum forecast	228	228	228
Maximum forecast	343	343	343
Marginal increase in tourist expenditure			
Minimum forecast	7,812.8	7,812.8	7,812.8
Maximum forecast	11,715.7	11,715.7	11,715.7
Costs			
Net construction costs†	1,850,000	1,795,000	2,030,000
Increased operating and maintenance costs	267,400	267,400	303,400
Land acquisition, valued at opportunity cost		Not included	
Net benefit/cost ratios			
Minimum	4.20	4.33	3.81
Maximum	6.37	6.57	5.79
Total benefit/cost ratios			
Minimum	3.80	3.90	3.45
Maximum	5.70	5.85	5.17
First-year rate of return (%) (1972)			
Minimum	14.8	15.2	13.4
Maximum	22.2	22.8	20.1

*£ × 10^3 base year 1970; discount rate = 8%; £1 = $2.
†Excluding taxes and duties.

SOURCE: Based on BRITISH AIRPORTS AUTHORITY ET AL., "Nicosia Airport: The Feasibility of Extending the Runway and Improving Other Operational Facilities" (unpublished consultants' report, 1968), p. 81.

The port was suffering from growing congestion against the background of a changing pattern of traffic (more liquid and less dry cargo) and a change in the traditional methods of handling cargo. Furthermore, the port was divided into two halves (the old and the new port) and operated an elaborate system of berthing priorities.

The object of the evaluation was to decide how many new berths to construct, when to build them, and what special handling facilities should be provided. The variables were the future volume and type of traffic, the methods and rates of handling cargo, the physical constraints imposed by the port layout, and the priority system for ships. This posed an enormous analytical problem, so that a model was developed to simulate various possible solutions and calculate their consequences.

The main, and only really important, impact of the proposed scheme was to reduce the turnaround time of ships by reducing waiting time (in 1966 ships lost an average of 7000 h of potential working time due to delays). The simulation model thus calculated the likely level of ship delay for different sets of facilities introduced together, or in sequence, between 1972 and 1977 (1972 being the earliest date for commissioning new wharves).

The economic evaluation clearly had to compare the capital and recurrent costs of providing additional facilities with the benefits of reduced congestion. Benefits to cargo were also evaluated but were relatively small in relation to the cost of delays to shipping.

The cost of delays clearly depends on the types of traffic using the port [i.e., whether bulk (chartered) or liner traffic] and on the type of vessels involved. Valuing delays to bulk traffic is usually straightforward, because most vessels are on time charter. Delays to liner traffic are more difficult to evaluate and are usually based on the long-run average cost of operating a typical liner vessel.[34] This is not particularly satisfactory, and it is better to examine how the delays in a particular port affect the operation of shipping companies and how this, in turn, affects the costs they are likely to pass on to users through the liner conference tariff. In the example above, the valuation of benefits was based on an analysis of shipping company operations:[35]

> The pattern that . . . emerges (with scheduled services), as far as anticipated delays are concerned, is of shipping companies taking them into account and of rescheduling their fleet operations on the basis of an assumed reduction in their overall shipping space. If ships are only infrequently delayed, the companies use overtime and week-end working to make up anything up to three days of lost time.
>
> If there is the prospect of more than 3 days being lost, temporary rescheduling will take place or traffic will be diverted through another port. . . . Delays due to congestion, even if they are anticipated, are very rarely considered permanent. The shipping companies therefore make up their extra space by chartering occasional extra capacity or by bringing a "mothballed" vessel back into service. . . .
>
> Beyond a certain point the shipping company (therefore) has to add another schedule to its regular services and has to incur the costs of a complete round trip in doing this.

This implies a nonlinear cost function. However, since the shipping companies recover these costs by passing them on to the local economy through a flat freight surcharge, the analysis averaged the foregoing costs on the assumption that they would be incurred *ex post facto* as a fixed surcharge.

The computer simulation was finally used to test several ways of extending the port facilities. The two crucial variables were:

1. How many new berths should be commissioned in 1972.
2. How many additional berths should be added between then and 1977.

These options were quickly reduced to the choice between three, four, or six new berths in 1972, followed by a further one or two in 1975, 1976, or 1977. Various configurations were tested and ranked on the basis of total port costs. These were defined as the sum of construction and maintenance costs, the costs of delays to ships and cargo, and the cost of diverting some traffic to Singapore. The results are set out in Table 14-9.

First-year rates of return were not calculated explicitly in the study, but can be estimated for the highest-priority ranking as follows:

Plan	First-Year Rate of Return
Add four berths in 1972	Very large
Add two further berths in 1976	12.6%

[34]R. O. GOSS, "The Turn-round of Cargo Liners and Its Effect on Sea Transport," *J. Transport Econ. Policy, 1*(1), 75–89 (1967).

[35]ECONOMIST INTELLIGENCE UNIT, "Port Swettenham Feasibility Study," Vol. 2, p. 237.

TABLE 14-9
Alternative Port Schemes Ranked According to Total Port Costs

Number of New Berths and Date of Construction	Priority Ranking	Difference in Present Values between Priority and Other Rankings (M$)*
4 in 1972 + 2 in 1976 = 6	1	—
4 in 1972 + 2 in 1975 = 6	2	300,000
4 in 1972 + 2 in 1977 = 6	3	400,000
6 in 1972	4	700,000
3 in 1972 + 3 in 1975 = 6	5	1,100,000
3 in 1972 + 2 in 1975 = 5	6	1,300,000

*M$ = US$ 0.326.

SOURCE: I.G. HEGGIE AND C.B. EDWARDS, "Port Investment Problems: How to Decide Investment Priorities," *Conference on Engineering Problems Overseas* (London: Institution of Civil Engineers, 1968), p. 43.

The NPV of the best scheme, discounted at 10%, was very high because of the exponential nature of the delay function. The economic evaluation therefore had to consider only two broad issues: which configuration would produce best value for money, and whether any part of it should be delayed to increase this value. The figures above show that the priority 1 scheme represented best value for the money.

Traffic restraint scheme

The following traffic restraint scheme was introduced experimentally in Nottingham, U.K., in August 1975.[36] It illustrates the application of cost–benefit analysis to a management scheme involving little or no capital investment. It was introduced only in the western sector of the town and was discontinued before it could be extended to cover the whole town, as originally planned. The overall object of the scheme was to replace much of a previously planned highway construction program with improved bus services combined with a traffic management and car restraint scheme.

The scheme was based on four key features:

1. Zone exit controls, using traffic signals, which limited the rate at which traffic could leave residential zones.
2. Collar controls, again using traffic signals, which limited the amount of traffic entering and passing through the central area of the city.
3. Bus priorities to prevent bus passengers being delayed.
4. Park-and-ride facilities linked to specially provided peripheral car parks.

The aim was to reduce delays to buses in order to provide a more attractive alternative to the private car. It was accepted that to achieve this, selective delays would have to be imposed on nonbus traffic, and it was hoped this would encourage motorists to transfer to public transport.

During the experimental period, the zone exit and collar controls and bus priorities were only operated from 07.30 to 09.30. The park-and-ride services operated on a 7½-min headway during both peak periods and were serviced by regular buses during the rest of the day.

The scheme was comprehensively evaluated by means of home-interview surveys, roadside interviews, traffic counts, and various other indicators. It was then evaluated

TABLE 14-10
Capital and Total Running Costs for the Zones and Collar Experimental Scheme*

Item	Costs (£) Capital	Running
Minor roadworks and markings	29,000	20,500†
New traffic signals, detectors, signs, etc.	104,000	
Sign and signal equipment maintenance		25,000
Park-and-ride sites		
Rent and rates		23,000
Construction	141,000	18,000†
Staffing and maintenance		11,800
Park-and-ride coaches		
Leasing and operating		168,400
Proportionate cost of bus depot	16,300	
Publicity costs		14,500
Police enforcement (estimate only, made prior to scheme)		8,500‡
Planning costs + assessment needed to develop the scheme	40,000‡	
Totals	330,300	289,700
Park-and-ride revenue		−5,600
Net cost		284,100

*£1 = $2.
†Loan charges on borrowed capital.
‡Crude estimates only.

SOURCE: R.A. VINCENT AND R.E. LAYFIELD, *Nottingham Zones and Collar Study: Overall Assessment*, Report 805 (Crowthorne, England: Transport and Road Research Laboratory, 1977), p. 19.

TABLE 14-11
Value of Changes Attributable to the Scheme during the Morning Peak Period*

	Value (£/year)
Change estimate for	
Time savings to passengers in buses	+8,000
Reduced car running costs for park-and-ride users	+11,000
Interchange time losses for P&R users	−3,000
Disbenefits to car users due to zone exit controls	−16,000†
Disbenefits to commerical vehicle operators due to zone exit controls	−9,000†
Disbenefits to car users due to collar controls	−26,000†
Disbenefits to commerical vehicle operators due to collar controls	−13,000†
Time lost by car users diverted from closed-off zone exits‡	−4,000§
Extra running costs for cars diverted from closed-off exits‡	−2,000§
No significant changes for	
Road accidents	—
Nonusers of P&R service‖	—
Suppressed or generated journeys	—
Bus operating costs**	—
Net benefit	−54,000

*£1 = $2.
†Estimates ± 25% approximately.
‡No allowance for commercial traffic—mainly minor residential streets.
§Details of origins and destinations not known, estimates ± 50% approximately.
‖If a P&R service removes cars from the roads, remaining traffic could benefit; in this experiment, no appreciable effect was attributable to P&R.
**Theoretically, improved journey times could have allowed a savings of two buses, but this would have required rescheduling and may not have been practicable.

SOURCE: R.A. VINCENT AND R.E. LAYFIELD, *Nottingham Zones and Collar Study: Overall Assessment*, Report 805 (Crowthorne, England: Transport and Road Research Laboratory, 1977), p. 20.

[36] R. A. VINCENT AND R. E. LAYFIELD, *Nottingham Zones and Collar Study: Overall Assessment*, Report 805 (Crowthorne, England: Transport and Road Research Laboratory, 1977).

by comparing the capital and running costs of the scheme, with estimates of the annual benefits–costs during the morning peak. The results are set out in Tables 14-10 and 14-11. This shows that the scheme produced disbenefits to private and commercial traffic which substantially outweighed the measured benefits to bus passengers. Since net benefits were negative, no benefit–cost ratio or any other index of priority was calculated.

Although Table 14-10 includes all the items explicitly included in the objective of making a transfer of passengers from car to bus travel, it excludes the important objective of improving environmental conditions—either for householders or pedestrians—by reducing the overall flow of traffic. This was one of the prime objectives of the Nottingham scheme. The aim was to reduce the flow of car traffic to 15 to 20% below the peak flow in October 1973.[37] Objectives like this are almost impossible to evaluate, except in subjective terms.

Had the foregoing scheme been presented as one of environmental enhancement, the table would have had to include a number of objective measures of environmental improvement, such as changes in the number of properties subject to certain noise contours, variations in pedestrian hazards, and so on. The final decision would then have been a subjective one: Are the changes in these indicators "worth" an annual operating cost of £284,100 ($568,200), together with a net disbenefit to traffic of £54,000 ($108,000) per year?

Designing an urban bypass

The following example uses COBA,[38] a computerised cost–benefit model developed by the U.K. Department of Transport, to evaluate 20 different designs—all on one alignment—of a bypass for Swaffham in Norfolk. The total number of feasible designs clearly exceeds the 20 illustrated here. The example simply shows how the techniques of

[37]B. T. Collins, "Transportation Developments in Nottinghamshire," *Transport, 36* 10 (1975).

[38]*Report of the Advisory Committee on Trunk Road Assessment* (London: H.M.S.O., 1977), Chap. 15.

TABLE 14–12
Evaluation of Alternative Bypass Schemes for Swaffham in Norfolk*

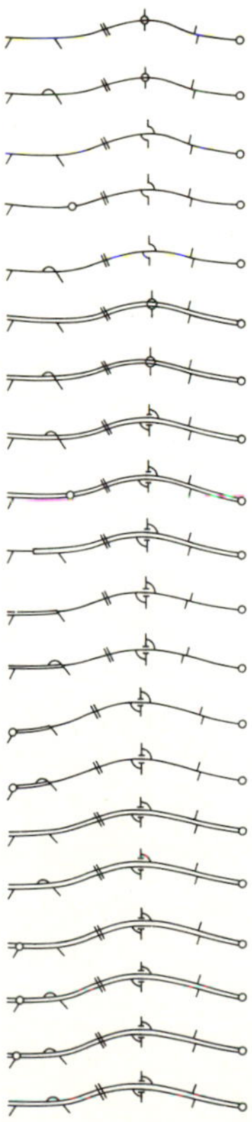

No.	Description	Diagram	Cost (£)	NPV (£)	NPV/Cost	NPV/C	FYRR† (%)
1	Single carriageway throughout. At grade junction at old A47. Roundabout at A1065.		1,510,134	−91,216	649,132	−0.1405	5.9
2	As 1 above but grade separation at old A47.		1,614,455	−91,878	693,968	−0.1324	5.9
3	Single carriageway throughout. At grade junction at old A47. Grade separation at A1065.		1,591,137	7,888	683,951	0.0115	6.9
4	As 3 but with roundabout at old A47.		1,602,137	−86,566	688,680	−0.1257	5.9
5	As 3 but with grade separation at old A47.		1,695,457	13,691	728,787	0.0188	6.9
6	Dual carriageway from at grade junction at old A47. Roundabout at A1065.		2,065,382	−149,706	887,800	−0.1686	5.4
7	As 6 but with grade separation at old A47.		2,220,050	−169,449	954,292	−0.1776	5.3
8	Dual carriageway from grade-separated junction at old A47. Grade separation at A1065.		2,256,525	−170,505	969,962	−0.1758	5.2
9	As 8 but with roundabout at old A47.		2,110,087	−131,415	907,016	−0.1449	5.5
10	As 8 but at grade junction at old A47.		2,101,823	−30,121	903,470	−0.0333	6.3
11	As 3 but dualing to A1122 from old A47. At grade from junctions at A1122 and old A47.		1,888,331	203,581	811,700	0.2508	8.1
12	As 11 but with grade separation at old A47.		1,992,738	199,417	856,537	0.2328	8.0
13	As 11 but with roundabout at A1122.		1,883,261	98,963	889,521	0.1222	7.2
14	As 13 but with grade separation at old A47.		1,987,568	94,799	854,357	0.111	7.2
15	As 10 but with dualing from old A47 to A1122. At grade junctions at A1122 and old A47.		2,399,019	125,411	1,031,219	0.1216	7.1
16	As 15 but with grade separation at old A47.		2,553,720	146,264	1,097,711	0.1332	7.2
17	As 15 but with roundabout at A1122.		2,393,949	26,893	1,029,040	0.0261	6.4
18	As 17 but with grade separation at old A47.		2,548,636	47,746	1,095,532	0.0436	6.6
19	Firm program scheme but with grade separation at old A47. Duals to A1122 and roundabout at A1122.		2,108,776	156,139	906,458	0.1723	7.5
20	As 19 but with at grade junction at A1122.		2,113,860	260,756	908,638	0.2870	8.3

*£1 = $2.
†First-year rate of return.

Source: *Report of the Advisory Committee on Trunk Road Assessment* (London: H.M.S.O., 1977), pp. 70–71.

economic assessment are used to choose between competing alternatives.

In practice, an experienced engineer would not carry out so many evaluations on one alignment. An optimum solution would be identified long before then, and the impact of varying the alignment would probably also be explored.

The 20 schemes are summarized in Table 14-12. For each variation there is a brief description, a sketch map, the overall cost, the NPV, the present value of these costs, the NPV/*C* ratio, and the first-year rate of return.

The schemes have been grouped as follows: schemes 1 to 5 investigate the effect of varying the junction configuration on a single carriageway scheme; schemes 6 to 10 carry out a similar exercise with a dual carriageway from the western junction with the existing A47; schemes 11 to 14 investigate various possibilities at the western end of the alignment assuming a single carriageway elsewhere; and schemes 15 to 20 undertake a similar evaluation assuming a dual carriageway elsewhere.

The difference between schemes 1 and 3 illustrates the difference between grade-separated junctions and a roundabout. Schemes 1 to 5 similarly show the great variation in net returns caused by variations in junction design. The difference between schemes 3 and 11 shows how a short stretch of dual carriageway can affect the net returns; the NPV/*C* ratio increases from 0.012 to 0.251. The dualing of scheme 1, however (shown as scheme 6), worsens the NPV/*C* ratio. This illustrates the complicated way in which decisions about junction design interact with those on dualing. It is worth noting that alternatives with similar costs can yield very different NPVs. Cost-effectiveness analysis is thus no real substitute for cost–benefit analysis when benefits vary.

Scheme 20 was finally selected as the preferred solution. It has a NPV/*C* ratio of 0.2870 and a first-year rate of return of 8.3%. This implies that it is the "best solution," but should be implemented only if the discount rate is 8% or less. Otherwise, it should be postponed until the first-year rate of return rises to equal, or exceed, the discount rate.

Summary

This section is presented as a checklist. It itemizes the key issues raised by an economic evaluation and the principal qualifications the transportation engineer should bear in mind when carrying one out.

1. Economics provides a method for choosing between competing alternatives. Very few transportation engineering problems have only one solution. Economics helps to rank solutions to achieve best value for money.
2. Transport schemes may have macro and micro economic impacts. These must be clearly distinguished, and any assumptions made during their quantification or evaluation must be clearly stated.
3. Treat "recommended values" with caution and always ask how appropriate they are in the context of each application.
4. Include *all* expected costs and benefits. If no numerical value is available, present the information descriptively. Avoid double counting.
5. Present the results of an evaluation in a simple and intelligible way. Present *all* relevant information. Avoid implicit value judgments, and do not aggregate noncomparable units of measurement (e.g., fuel savings and increased agricultural output) before the decision maker has seen them.
6. If at all possible, qualify the results of an evaluation by means of sensitivity analysis.
7. Never use economics to "justify" a scheme; it should only be used to evaluate and rank possible solutions.

REFERENCES FOR FURTHER READING

General

Coburn, T. M., M. E. Beesley, and D. J. Reynolds, *The London–Birmingham Motorway,* Tech. Pap. 46 (Crowthorne, England: Road Research Laboratory, D.S.I.R., 1960).

Flowerdew, A. D. J., "Choosing a Site for the Third London Airport: The Roskill Commission's Approach," in *Cost–Benefit Analysis,* ed. R. Layard (Harmondsworth, Middlesex: Penguin Books, 1972), pp. 429–451.

Harrison, A. J., *The Economics of Transport Appraisal* (London: Croom Helm, 1974).

Heggie, I. G., *Transport Engineering Economics* (London: McGraw-Hill, 1972).

Hutchinson, B. G., *Principles of Urban Transport Systems Planning* (New York: McGraw-Hill, 1974), Chap. 10.

Lane, R., T. Powell, and P. Prestwood Smith, *Analytical Transport Planning* (London: Duckworth, 1971), Chap. 5.

Manheim, M. L., *Fundamentals of Transportation System Analysis:* Vol. 1, *Basic Concepts* (Cambridge, Mass.: MIT Press, 1979), Chap. 9.

Munby, D. L., ed., *Transport* (Harmondsworth, Middlesex: Penguin Books, 1968).

Report of the Advisory Committee on Trunk Road Assessment (London: H.M.S.O., 1977).

Sharp, C. H., *Transport Economics* (London: Macmillan, 1973).

Stopher, P. R., and A. H. Meyburg, *Transportation Systems Evaluation* (Lexington, Mass.: Lexington Books, 1976).

Less Developed Countries

Adler, H. A., *Economic Appraisal of Transport Projects* (Bloomington, Ind.: Indiana University Press, 1971).

Dasgupta, P., A. Sen, and S. Marglin, *Guidelines for Project Evaluation* (New York: U.N. International Development Organisation, 1972).

Little, I.M.D., and J. A. Mirlees, *Project Appraisal and Planning for Developing Countries* (London: Heineman Educational Books, 1974).

Squire, L., and H. G. van der Tak, *Economic Analysis of Projects* (Baltimore, Md.: Johns Hopkins University Press, 1975).

15

TRAFFIC FLOW THEORY

MATTHEW J. HUBER, *Associate Professor*

Department of Civil and Mineral Engineering
University of Minnesota
Minneapolis, Minnesota

Traffic flow theory is concerned with the application of the laws of mathematics, probability theory, and physics to the description of traffic behavior. Transportation engineers have developed many empirical solutions to the problems of operating transportation systems. Subsequent studies in traffic flow theory have verified that many approaches developed by experiment and observation are the best solution. In other instances, traffic flow theory has given further insight to transportation problems and allowed for more sophisticated and precise solutions.

The prediction of the number of vehicles to be stored in a separate turning lane or the estimate of probable vehicular delay at an intersection are two examples of the application of traffic flow theory to design problems.

Analysis of traffic stream flow gives the designer more understanding of the capacity limitations of roadways and enables the user to estimate traffic behavior when a bottleneck situation is created. The analysis of car-following models can be used to estimate the impact of improved vehicular control devices on traffic stream flow.

While traffic flow theory was begun as early as the 1930s, the greatest advances have taken place since the 1950s. New developments continued in the 1970s, but more effort is now being devoted to adapting traffic flow theory to the solution of current problems in transportation system operation than to development of new theoretical models.

This chapter is a brief introduction to the techniques of traffic flow theory and an introduction to the literature. The references for further reading at the end of this chapter and the references cited in the footnotes will provide the user with further material for study.

Measurement of flow, headway, speed, and concentration

Flow, headway, speed, and concentration are the four most frequently used characteristics of the behavior of a group of vehicles. Chapter 17 presents details on the measurement and collection of these variables. This section provides precise definitions of these variables and the relationship between the method of data collection and variable measurement.

Measurements at a point

The simplest way to collect traffic flow data is to collect information at a point along a roadway over an extended period of time. Figure 15.1 shows a time–space plot of the paths of vehicles within a time–space domain. An observer (or detector) is located at point A and counts the number of vehicles passing point A in time T. The time headway between vehicles and the velocity (with the aid of radar or a speed trap) may also be measured at point A.

Flow is the rate at which vehicles pass a point on a roadway and is expressed in vehicles per unit of time. Consider Figure 15.1, where N vehicles cross line A–A' in time T and the flow is computed as

$$q = \frac{N}{T} = \frac{5 \text{ vehicles}}{20 \text{ seconds}} = 0.25 \text{ veh/s} = 900 \text{ veh/h} \tag{15.1}$$

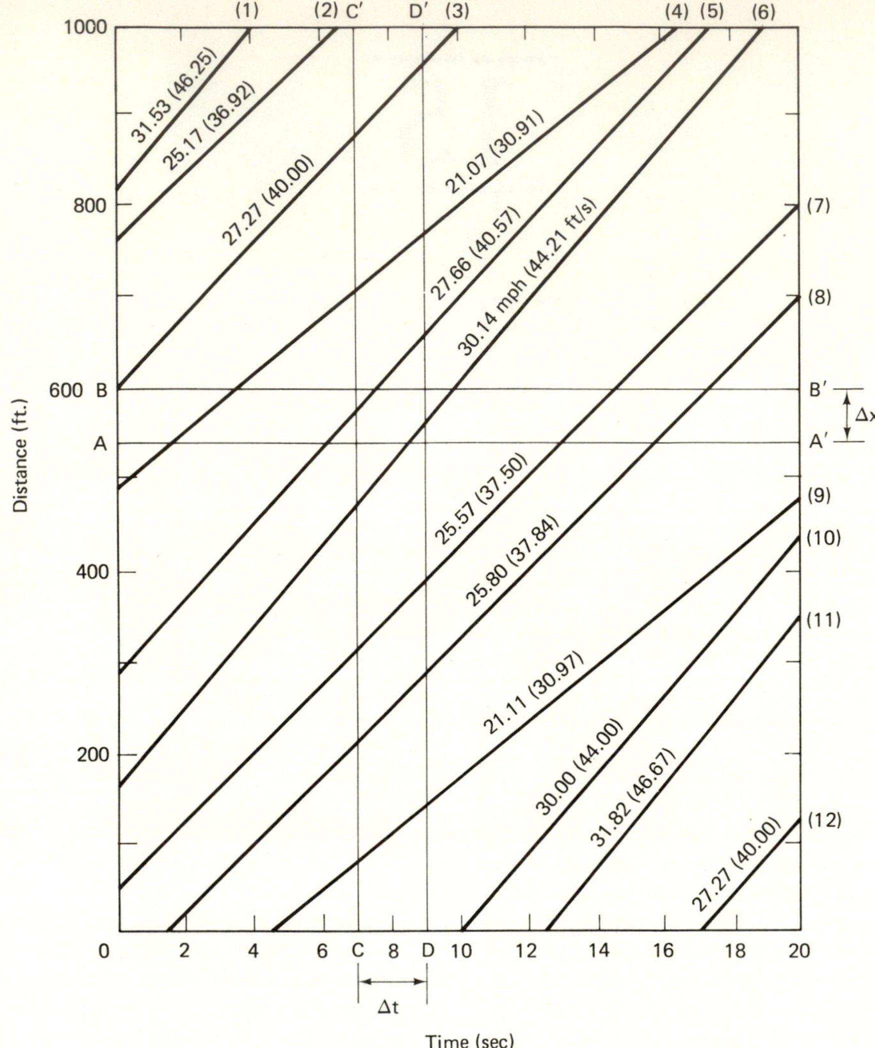

Figure 15.1. Time-space plot of vehicle paths within time-space domain.

Time headway h_t is the time between successive vehicles passing a point and is expressed in seconds. In Figure 15.1, a timer is begun at time 0.0 s, continuing for 20.0 s, and the times at which vehicles pass observation point A–A' are as follows:

Vehicle Number	Time of Passing (s)
4	1.62
5	6.16
6	8.60
7	13.07
8	15.77

Headways are observed to be

$$h_{4-5} = 4.54 \text{ s}$$

$$h_{5-6} = 2.44 \text{ s}$$

$$h_{6-7} = 4.47 \text{ s}$$

$$h_{7-8} = 2.70 \text{ s}$$

$$h_{8-4} = \underline{5.85 \text{ s}}$$

$$\text{Total: } \sum h_t = 20.00 \text{ s}$$

Since there are five vehicles, only the first four headways above are directly determined. The final headway may be calculated as shown in Figure 15.2. Since the time for beginning and ending the count interval is arbitrary (random) with regard to the passage of vehicles, the time gap defined by start time to first passage plus last passage to end time may also be considered as a headway.

Average time headway $\bar{h}_t$ is the average of all headway times h_t and is usually expressed as seconds per vehicle:

$$\bar{h}_t = \frac{\sum h_t}{N}$$

But $\Sigma\, h_t$ equals the counting period T, so that

$$\bar{h}_t = \frac{T}{N} = \frac{1}{q} \tag{15.2}$$

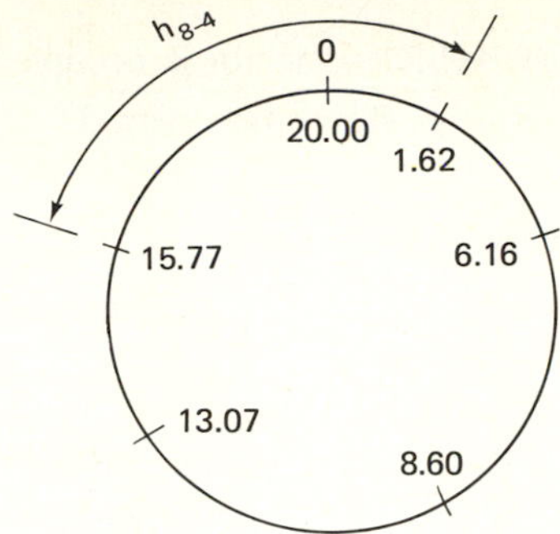

Figure 15.2. Definition of time gap between first and last vehicle in counting interval.

For the five vehicles observed at point A, the mean headway is

$$\frac{20.00 \text{ s}}{5 \text{ veh}} = 4.0 \text{ s/veh}$$

Speed is an important measure of traffic performance at a particular point or along a route.

Time mean speed $\bar{u}_t$ is the arithmetic mean (average) of the spot speeds:

$$\bar{u}_t = \frac{1}{N} \sum_{i=1}^{N} u_i \tag{15.3}$$

For the five vehicles observed at point A in Figure 15.1, the sum of the vehicle speeds (as determined by radar) is

$$\sum u_i = 21.07 + 27.66 + 30.14 + 25.57 + 25.80$$
$$= 130.24$$

and

$$\bar{u}_t = \frac{1}{5}(130.24) = 26.05 \text{ mph } (41.92 \text{ km/h})$$

Space mean speed $\bar{u}_s$ is the harmonic mean of the speeds observed at a point:

$$\bar{u}_s = \frac{N}{\sum_{i=1}^{N} 1/u_i} \tag{15.4}$$

For the five vehicles observed at point A in Figure 15.1, the sum of the reciprocals of the spot speeds is

$$\sum \frac{1}{u_i} = \frac{1}{21.07} + \frac{1}{27.66} + \frac{1}{30.14} + \frac{1}{25.57} + \frac{1}{25.80}$$
$$= 0.1947$$

and

$$\bar{u}_s = \frac{5}{0.1947} = 25.68 \text{ mph } (41.33 \text{ km/h})$$

In all instances (except the case of uniform speed), the space mean speed is lower than the time mean speed. The relationship between time mean speed and space mean speed was first developed by Wardrop[1] and is

$$\bar{u}_t = \bar{u}_s + \frac{\sigma_s^2}{\bar{u}_s}$$

where σ_s^2 is the variance about the space mean speed.

Speed trap measurements require observation at a second point on the roadway (B–B' in Figure 15.1) and a record of the time Δt_i required to travel the trap length Δx from which individual speeds may be calculated. The trap length Δx in Figure 15.1 is 60 ft and the time Δt_i is calculated as follows:

Vehicle Number	Time Passing A–A'	Time Passing B–B'	Trap Time (s)	Velocity (mph)
4	1.62	3.56	1.94	21.07
5	6.16	7.64	1.48	27.66
6	8.60	9.95	1.36	30.14
7	13.07	14.67	1.60	25.57
9	15.77	17.36	1.59	25.80
			7.97	130.24

The *time mean speed,* as before, from equation (15.3) is

$$\bar{u}_t = \frac{1}{5}(130.24) = 26.05 \text{ mph } (41.92 \text{ km/h})$$

The space mean speed $\bar{u}_s$ is defined as

$$\bar{u}_s = \frac{\Delta x}{\overline{\Delta t_i}}$$

where

$$\overline{\Delta t_i} = \frac{\sum_{i=1}^{N} \Delta t_i}{N}$$

so that

$$\bar{u}_s = \frac{\Delta x}{\left(\sum_{i=1}^{N} \Delta t_i/N\right)} = \frac{N\,\Delta x}{\sum_{i=1}^{N} \Delta t_i} \tag{15.5}$$

In the example used above,

$$\bar{u}_s = \frac{5 \times 60}{7.97} = 37.64 \text{ ft/s} = 25.66 \text{ mph}$$

The slight difference in $\bar{u}_s$ (25.66 mph versus 25.68 mph, previously calculated) occurs because times Δt_i are measured to ± 0.005 s; more precise timing (hardly possible with manual timing methods) would give identical results.

In equation (15.5), the numerator is the total distance traveled by the N vehicles within the roadway length and the denominator is the total time the N vehicles are observed within the roadway length. *Space mean speed* can then be expressed as

[1] J. G. Wardrop, "Some Theoretical Aspects of Road Traffic Research," *Proc. Inst. Civ. Eng., Pt. II* (2), 325–362 (1952).

$$\bar{u}_s = \frac{TT}{TTT} \quad (15.6)$$

where TT = total travel distance

TTT = total travel time

Density, k, is the concentration of vehicles on a roadway and is expressed as the number of vehicles per length of roadway. Assume that traffic is made up of substreams each at density k_i with its own constant speed u_i. For each substream, $k_i = q_i/u_i$. The density of the traffic stream $k = \Sigma k_i$, so that

$$\bar{u}_s = \frac{\Sigma k_i u_i}{k}$$

Since $k_i u_i = q_i$,

$$\bar{u}_s = \frac{\Sigma q_i}{k} = \frac{q}{k} \quad (15.7)$$

and

$$k = \frac{q}{\bar{u}_s} \quad (15.8)$$

The relationship among flow, density, and speed is defined in terms of $\bar{u}_s$, the space mean speed.

Density may be measured on a per lane basis or for all lanes on a facility. Since density is defined as above, it is not possible to measure this variable directly from measurements at a point. Instead, density can be estimated from point measurement using the relationship given by equation (15.8). In the example taken at point *A* on Figure 15.1, the density would be calculated as

$$k = (900 \text{ veh/h})/(25.68 \text{ mph}) = 35.05 \text{ veh/mi}$$

$$= (900 \text{ veh/h})/(41.33 \text{ km/h}) = 21.78 \text{ veh/km}$$

Since it is not possible to measure density directly at a point, a measure called *lane occupancy* has been developed for freeway surveillance. Let *R* be the ratio of length of vehicles on a roadway section to the length of the section:

$$R_1 = \frac{\Sigma \text{ vehicle lengths}}{\text{length of roadway section}} \quad (15.9)$$

This ratio divided by L_m, the average length of a vehicle expressed in miles, will give an estimate of the density.

As an example, suppose that six vehicles with lengths of 18, 20, 45, 15, 18, and 22 ft are distributed along a 1000-ft (305-m)-long section of one lane on a highway.

$$R_1 = \frac{138}{1000} = 0.138$$

If the average length of a vehicle is taken as 23.0 ft (7.0 m) [equals 0.00436 mi (0.00701 km)], the computed density will be 31.7 veh/mi (19.7 veh/km).

It is not practical to measure the lengths of vehicles as required by equation (15.9). However, it is possible to estimate the time that a vehicle "occupies" a presence detector so that we can measure the ratio

$$R_2 = \frac{\text{sum of times vehicle detector is occupied}}{\text{total time of observation period}} = \frac{\Sigma t_o}{T} \quad (15.10)$$

Density for a given lane may then be estimated by

$$k = R_2 \frac{5280}{L_e} = \frac{\Sigma t_o 5280}{TL_e} \quad (15.11)$$

where L_e is the effective length of the vehicle in feet and *k* is the density in veh/mi. The effective length of a vehicle is the length of the vehicle as detected by the presence detector. Assume that the detector is a simple buried loop that is activated by the presence of any part of a vehicle. The loop is 20.0 ft (6.1 m) long and the distance between bumpers on the vehicle being detected is 15.0 ft (4.6 m). The detector is actuated as soon as the front bumper enters the detector and remains on until the rear bumper has left the detector, so that the effective length L_e is (15.0 + 20.0) = 35.0 ft (10.7 m).

As an example, consider a detector that is occupied as follows during a 60-s period.

0.38 s	0.45 s	0.35 s
(T) 0.52 s	(T) 0.55 s	0.42 s
0.30 s	0.41 s	(T) 0.60 s
		0.40 s

The (T) indicates that the observed vehicle is a truck. The significance of this will be introduced later. For these data, $\Sigma t_o = 4.38$ s and $N = 10$. If the average effective length is taken as 30.0 ft (9.1 m),

$$k = \left(\frac{4.38}{60.0}\right)\left(\frac{5280}{30.0}\right) = 12.85 \text{ veh/mi}$$

In metric units:

$$k = \frac{\Sigma t_o 1000}{TL_e(\text{m})} = \left(\frac{4.38}{60}\right)\left(\frac{1000}{9.1}\right) = 8.02 \text{ veh/km} \quad (15.12)$$

Average speed $\bar{u}_s$ can be estimated from the relationship $\bar{u} = q/k$, to give

$$\bar{u}_s = \frac{NL_e}{\Sigma t_o} \quad (15.13)$$

where $\bar{u}_s$ is the estimated speed in ft/s (m/s). In this example, $\bar{u}_s = 10(30)/4.38 = 68.49$ ft/s (46.70 mph)

or $\bar{u}_s = [10(9.1)]/4.38 = 20.78$ m/s (74.79 km/h).

Equations (15.11) to (15.13) can lead to errors if the mix of trucks and cars in the traffic stream is varying. This can be compensated for by distinguishing between cars and trucks and using a value L_c and L_t for the effective length of cars and trucks separately. The estimate of velocity then becomes

$$\bar{u}_s = \frac{N_t L_t + N_c L_c}{\sum t_o} \tag{15.14}$$

Using the previous data and considering those vehicles labeled with a (T) as a truck with an effective length L_t of 45 ft, while cars have an effective length L_c of 20 ft, $N_t = 3$, $N_c = 7$:

$$k = \frac{3 + 7}{3(45) + 7(20)} \left(\frac{4.38}{60.0} \right) 5280 \tag{15.15}$$
$$= 14.02 \text{ veh/mi}$$

Measurements along a length

Measurements along a length of roadway are usually made by photographic methods from a high vantage point. Lines C–C' and D–D' on Figure 15.1 represent the type of information that can be observed from a photograph. A pair of photographs separated by time Δt is required to calculate velocities.

Density k can be determined directly from the scaled distance and vehicle count, where

$$k = \frac{N}{\ell} \tag{15.16}$$

where N is the number of vehicles counted and ℓ the length of the section in miles (kilometers). In Figure 15.1, the distance ℓ is 1000 ft (0.1894 mi) and the number of vehicles (N) along the section of roadway is 7, so that

$$k = \frac{7}{0.1894} = 36.96 \text{ veh/mi}$$

Speed u cannot be measured directly from a single observation, but requires two observations Δt seconds apart. Line D–D' represents the position of vehicles on a second photograph. Each vehicle travels a distance s_i in the constant time Δt, so that

$$u_i = \frac{s_i}{\Delta t}$$

$$\bar{u}_s = \frac{1}{N} \sum_{i=1}^{N} u_i = \frac{1}{N} \sum_{i=1}^{N} \frac{s_i}{\Delta t} = \frac{1}{N\,\Delta t} \sum_{i=1}^{N} s_i \tag{15.17}$$

In equation (15.17) the numerator is the total distance traveled by the N vehicles (TT) and the denominator is the total travel time (TTT) for the N vehicles, so that by equation (15.6) the resulting mean is *space mean speed.*

From Figure 15.1 the following positions are observed on the two photographs taken 2.0 s apart; the distance s_i that each vehicle travels is the difference in position:

Vehicle	Position 1	Position 2	s_i (ft)
3	880.0	960.0	80.0
4	706.4	768.2	61.8
5	574.0	655.1	81.1
6	469.5	557.9	88.4
7	312.5	387.5	75.0
8	208.1	283.8	75.7
9	77.4	139.4	62.0
			$\Sigma s_i = 524.0$

$$\bar{u}_s = \frac{524.0}{7(2.0)} = 37.4 \text{ ft/s} = 25.5 \text{ mph}$$

Flow q cannot be measured along a length, but is computed from the previously obtained values of density and average speed, so that

$$q = k\bar{u}_s \tag{15.18}$$

For the data calculated from Figure 15.1,

$$q = 36.96 \times 25.5 = 942 \text{ veh/h}$$

Definitions independent of the method of measurement

The previous sections have considered the definition of flow characteristics (1) as measured for a long time at a point or short distance and (2) as measured over a long distance at an instant or for a short time interval. Had a point other than A–A' or a time other than C–C' been selected, the variables observed would have had different numerical values. Edie[2] has developed procedures that will permit measurements for platoons of vehicles observed over a fixed distance or for a fixed period of time or for a combination of both.

Consider the space–time diagram of Figure 15.1 with the trajectories of the 12 vehicles as shown. Within the space–time domain, the flow rate q is defined as

$$q = \frac{\sum x_i}{A} \tag{15.19}$$

the density

$$k = \frac{\sum t_i}{A} \tag{15.20}$$

and the speed

$$\bar{u}_s = \frac{\sum x_i}{\sum t_i} \tag{15.21}$$

where x_i = distance traveled by the ith vehicle within the space–time domain

t_i = time taken by the ith vehicle to traverse the space–time domain

A = area of the space–time domain

The three definitions above are independent of measurement methods, are independent of the statistical procedures used for analysis, and yield consistent results.

The following numerical example is based on the 12 trajectories shown in Figure 15.1.

total distance traveled, $\sum x_i = 5740$ vehicle-feet

total time, $\sum t_i = 148$ vehicle-seconds

area of domain, $A = 20{,}000$ feet-seconds

$$q = \frac{\sum x_i}{A} = \frac{5740 \text{ veh-ft}}{20{,}000 \text{ ft-s}} = 0.29 \text{ veh/s}$$

$$= 1033.2 \text{ veh/h}$$

$$k = \frac{\sum t_i}{A} = \frac{148 \text{ veh-s}}{20{,}000 \text{ ft-s}} = 0.0074 \text{ veh/ft}$$

$$= 39.07 \text{ veh/mi}$$

$$\bar{u}_s = \frac{\sum x_i}{\sum t_i} = \frac{5740 \text{ veh-ft}}{148 \text{ veh-s}} = 38.78 \text{ ft/s}$$

$$= 26.44 \text{ mph}$$

Figure 15.3 shows the space–time diagram for a platoon of N vehicles traveling a distance X in time T. Data of this type could be developed by timing individual vehicles within a platoon while traveling from one intersection to the following intersection. The trajectories of vehicles O and N and the distance X define the area of the space–time domain. Assuming the trajectories of vehicles O and N to be straight lines (constant velocity), the area of the space–time domain is defined as

$$A = TX - \frac{X^2}{2}\left(\frac{1}{u_O} + \frac{1}{u_N}\right) \qquad (15.22)$$

where T = total time

u_O, u_N = average velocities of vehicles O and N in traversing distance X

Applying equations (15.19) to (15.21), the following definitions apply to the platoon of vehicles:

$$q = \frac{\sum X_i}{A} = \frac{NX}{TX - (X^2/2)(1/u_O + 1/u_N)} \qquad (15.23)$$

Figure 15.3. Trajectories for a group of N vehicles traveling distance X.

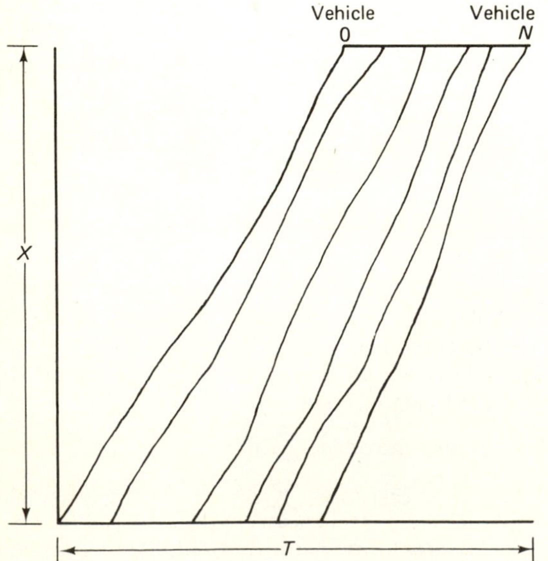

$$k = \frac{\sum t_i}{A} = \frac{X\sum 1/u_i}{TX - (X^2/2)(1/u_O + 1/u_N)} \qquad (15.24)$$

$$\bar{u}_s = \frac{\sum X_i}{\sum t_i} = \frac{N}{\sum 1/u_i} \qquad (15.25)$$

The flow rate q is independent of the velocity of intermediate vehicles. Density k and mean speed $\bar{u}_s$ are dependent upon the velocities of each vehicle.

The space–time diagram for a group of N vehicles bound by a time period T and the trajectories of vehicles O and N are shown in Figure 15.4. Data of this type would follow from plotting the positions of the vehicles within the platoon as shown on two aerial photographs taken at a time interval T. The area of the space–time domain is defined as

$$A = TX - \frac{T^2}{2}(u_O + u_N) \qquad (15.26)$$

The stream flow calculations are defined as

$$q = \frac{\sum X_i}{A} = \frac{T\sum u_i}{TX - (T^2/2)(u_O + u_N)} = \frac{\sum u_i}{X - (T/2)(u_O - u_N)} \qquad (15.27)$$

$$k = \frac{\sum t_i}{A} = \frac{NT}{TX - (T^2/2)(u_O + u_N)} = \frac{N}{X - (T/2)(u_O - u_N)} \qquad (15.28)$$

$$\bar{u}_s = \frac{\sum X_i}{\sum t_i} = \frac{T\sum u_i}{NT} = \frac{\sum u_i}{N} \qquad (15.29)$$

Figure 15.4. Trajectories for a group of N vehicles over time T.

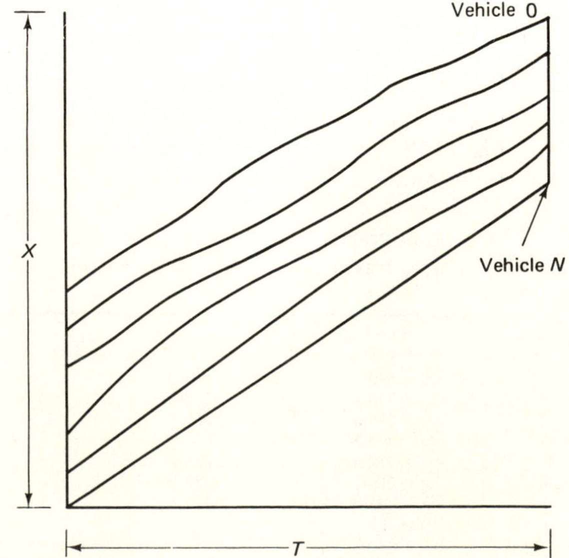

The density k is independent of the velocities of intermediate vehicles, whereas flow rate q and mean speed $\bar{u}_s$ are dependent upon the speed of all vehicles. In applying equations (15.23) to (15.25) and equations (15.27) to (15.29), the summations of distance, velocity, and time include values for only one (or the average) of the zeroth and N^{th} vehicles whose trajectories define the area of the domain.

Statistical distribution of traffic characteristics

Statistical distributions are useful in predicting events where events occur randomly. An event is said to occur randomly when each small increment of time (or space) is equally likely to contain an event. The event may be the arrival of a vehicle at a left-turn lane at a rural intersection. As long as the flow rate q is constant, each half-second interval is as likely as every other half-second interval to contain a vehicle arrival.

As a further example, consider the distribution of occupied parking spaces in a parking garage. The event (a parked vehicle) would be random if every space had the same opportunity of being occupied. This would probably not be a random event because experience shows that spaces near pedestrian exits and on the lower levels are more likely to be occupied than spaces more distant from pedestrian exits or on the upper levels.

Statistical distributions can be classified in two general categories:

1. Counting or discrete distributions
2. Interval or gap distributions

Counting distributions

Counting of the number of events that occur in a given time period is relatively easy and has been a useful tool of the transportation engineer. This section will consider four counting distributions that have been used in transportation studies:

1. Poisson distribution
2. Binomial distribution
3. Negative binomial distribution
4. Generalized Poisson distribution

Poisson distribution. The Poisson distribution is used to describe discrete events that are truly random, and historically was the first distribution to be applied to an analysis of vehicle flow. The distribution gives the probability of x events during a single trial using the single parameter m, where m is the average number of events in each trial.

The Poisson distribution is stated as:

$$P(x) = \frac{m^x e^{-m}}{x!} \qquad x = 0, 1, 2, \ldots \qquad (15.30)$$

or

$$P(x) = \frac{(\lambda t)^x e^{-\lambda t}}{x!} \qquad (15.31)$$

where for traffic counting

$P(x)$ = probability that x vehicles will arrive during a counting interval t

λ = average rate of arrival, veh/s (= flow rate)

t = duration of each counting interval, s

$m = \lambda t$ = average number of vehicles during a period of duration t

e = natural base of logarithms

The only parameter that must be estimated is the arrival rate, λ. Calculations may be simplified by noting that

$$P(0) = e^{-m} = e^{-\lambda t} \qquad (15.32)$$

and

$$P(x) = \frac{m}{x} P(x - 1) \qquad (15.33)$$

For the Poisson distribution, the mean and the variance are each equal to m, so that the ratio mean/variance = 1.0.

Binomial distribution. As traffic flow becomes congested, the flow becomes more uniform, so that the variance of the number of vehicles per interval is decreased. Consequently, the ratio mean/variance is greater than 1.0.

The binomial distribution gives the probability of x events in n trials and may be stated as

$$P(x) = \frac{n!}{x!(n - x)!} p^x q^{n-x} \qquad x = 0, 1, 2, \ldots \qquad (15.34)$$

where $P(x)$ = probability of x events in n trials

n = number of trial (each 1-s interval is a trial)

x = number of events in n trials

p = probability of an event on any given trial = probability that any 1-s interval will contain a vehicle

q = probability of a failure on any given trial = $1 - p$ = probability that any 1-s interval does not contain a vehicle

The two parameters of the binomial distribution are estimated as follows:

$$p = \frac{\bar{x} - s^2}{\bar{x}} \qquad (15.35)$$

$$n = \frac{\bar{x}^2}{\bar{x} - s^2} \qquad (15.36)$$

where $\bar{x}$ = mean number of events per n-second interval

s^2 = variance in the number of events per n-second interval

Calculations may be simplified by noting that

$$P(0) = q^n \qquad (15.37)$$

and

$$P(x) = \frac{n+1-x}{x}\frac{p}{q}P(x-1) \qquad (15.38)$$

The mean value of x is np and the variance of x is npq.

Negative binomial distribution. The negative binomial distribution follows from the binomial distribution and gives the probability that x failures occur in n trials before getting k events. For example, consider a traffic stream made up of a mixture of cars and trucks. The passage of each vehicle is a trial. The passage of a passenger car will be considered a failure, while the passage of a truck will be considered a successful event. The negative binomial distribution may be used to give the probability that six passenger cars will be observed ($x = 6$) before the third truck arrives ($k = 3$). The total number of trials n equals $x + k$ ($6 + 3 = 9$).

The negative binomial distribution may be stated as

$$P(x) = \frac{(x + k - 1)!}{x!(k - 1)!} p^k q^x, \quad x = 0, 1, 2, \ldots \qquad (15.39)$$

where $P(x)$ = probability of x failures in n trials before getting k successful events

p = probability of success on any given trial

$q = 1 - p$

k = number of successes in n trials where the last trial is a success

Calculations may be simplified by noting that

$$P(0) = p^k \qquad (15.40)$$

and

$$P(x) = \frac{x + k - 1}{x} q P(x - 1) \qquad (15.41)$$

The mean value of x is kq/p and the variance of x is kq/p^2.

Assume that 10% of the vehicles in a traffic stream are trucks ($p = 0.10$, $q = 0.90$). Then the probability that six passenger cars ($x = 6$) will be observed before the third truck ($k = 3$) is observed can be derived by equation (15.39):

$$P(6) = \frac{(6 + 3 - 1)!}{6!(3 - 1)!}(0.1)^3(0.9)^6 = 0.0149$$

When traffic counts are made downstream from a traffic signal, there will be periods of high flow and low flow, and the variance in the number of vehicles per counting period will be greater than that for random flow. For this case, the mean/variance ratio will be less than 1.0 and the negative binomial distribution may be used. When used in this manner to calculate the probability that x vehicles will be observed during some counting period, there is no real physical analogy among successful events, failures, and number of trials. In this instance the two parameters of the negative binomial distribution are estimated as follows:

$$p = \frac{\bar{x}}{s^2} \qquad (15.42)$$

$$k = \frac{\bar{x}^2}{s^2 - \bar{x}} \qquad (15.43)$$

Generalized Poisson distribution. Another counting distribution for the case where flow is between uniform and purely random has been suggested by Haight et al.,[3] because of its association with the Erlang distribution, which in turn is a useful interval distribution.

The generalized Poisson distribution is given by

$$P(x) = \sum_{j=xk}^{(x+1)k-1} \frac{e^{-\lambda t}\lambda t^j}{j!} \qquad (15.44)$$

where $P(x)$ = probability that x vehicles will arrive during a counting interval t

k = number of terms of the Poisson series associated with x

λ = average rate of arrival, vehicles/time (= flow rate)

t = duration of counting interval

Although equation (15.44) is somewhat complex, the interpretation is fairly simple. The probability of no cars in the time interval t is given by the first k terms of some Poisson series. The probability of one car is the sum of the second k terms of the same Poisson series, the probability of two cars would be the sum of the third k terms, and so on.

Assume a value of $\lambda t = 2.0$, giving the following results for the Poisson distribution, equation (15.31):

x	$P(x)$	x	$P(x)$
0	0.1353	5	0.0361
1	0.2707	6	0.0120
2	0.2707	7	0.0034
3	0.1804	≥8	0.0012
4	0.0902		mean ($\bar{x}$) = 2.0

For $k = 3$, the result would be

x	$P(x)$
0	0.6767
1	0.3067
≥2	0.0166
mean ($\bar{x}$) = 0.3399	

The selection of the two parameters λt and k can be done by calculating the mean and variance and then using the nomograph contained in Haight et al.'s work. If k is chosen, the other parameter, λt, can be estimated from the relationship

[2] L. C. Edie, "Discussion of Traffic Stream Measurements and Definitions," *Proc. 2nd Int. Symp. Theory Traffic Flow*, London, 1963, pp. 139–154.

[3] Frank A. Haight, Bertram F. Whisler, and Walter W. Mosher, Jr., "New Statistical Method for Describing Highway Distribution of Cars," *Proc. Highw. Res. Bd.*, *40*, 557–564 (1961).

$$\lambda t = \bar{x}k + \frac{1}{2}(k - 1) \qquad (15.45)$$

where $\bar{x}$ is the sample mean.

Summary of counting distributions. The following guidelines may be used in selecting the appropriate counting distribution for traffic flow.

1. In light traffic where mean/variance $\approx$ 1.0, use the Poisson distribution. The only parameter, $m = \bar{x}$.
2. In congested traffic where the mean/variance ratio is substantially greater than 1.0, use the binomial distribution where parameters are estimated by equations (15.35) and (15.36). The generalized Poisson distribution may also be used where the parameters are obtained by use of the nomograph just mentioned.
3. Where there is a cyclic variation in flow or where the mean flow is changing during the counting period, giving a mean/variance ratio substantially less than 1.0, use the negative binomial distribution where parameters are estimated by equations (15.42) and (15.43).

Interval distributions

If vehicles arrive in some pattern given by the counting distribution, it follows that there is also a distribution of intervals or gaps between the arrivals of successive vehicles. These intervals will be in time units and are continuous variables as opposed to the discrete variables obtained from counting distributions. Three interval distributions are discussed:

1. Negative exponential distribution
2. Shifted exponential distribution
3. Erlang distribution

Negative exponential distribution. The negative exponential distribution is the elementary interval distribution and follows directly from the Poisson distribution, equation (15.31). If there is no vehicle arrival in a time interval t, there will be headway h of at least t seconds between the last previous arrival and the next arrival. Using equation (15.32), we write

$$P(0) = P(h \geqslant t) = e^{-\lambda t} \qquad (15.46)$$

But $\lambda = 1/\bar{t}$, where $\bar{t}$ is the mean headway, so we may express equation (15.46) as

$$P(h \geqslant t) = e^{-t/\bar{t}} \qquad (15.47)$$

The cumulative distribution function of the negative exponential distribution may be written as

$$P(h \leqslant t) = 1 - e^{-\lambda t} = 1 - e^{-t/\bar{t}} \qquad (15.48)$$

The probability density function of the negative exponential distribution is

$$f(t) = \lambda e^{-\lambda t} \qquad (15.49)$$

with mean and variance equal to

$$\bar{t} = \frac{1}{\lambda} \qquad (15.50)$$

$$\sigma^2 = \frac{1}{\lambda^2} \qquad (15.51)$$

The single parameter of the negative exponential distribution may be estimated from either the counting distribution (λ) or from the mean of observed gaps ($\bar{t}$).

Shifted negative exponential distribution. Small time headways are very unlikely to occur in vehicles observed in a single traffic lane, but the negative exponential distribution predicts the highest probabilities for short time headways. One approach is to introduce a minimum allowable headway, a region in which headways are prohibited. This can be accomplished by shifting the negative exponential distribution to the right a distance c.

For the shifted negative exponential function, the cumulative distribution function is

$$P(h \leqslant t) = 1 - e^{-[(t-c)/(\bar{t}-c)]} \quad \text{for } t \geqslant c \qquad (15.52)$$

The probability density function is

$$f(t) = \begin{cases} 0 & \text{for } t < c \\ \dfrac{1}{\bar{t} - c}\, e^{-[(t-c)/(\bar{t}-c)]} & \text{for } t \geqslant c \end{cases} \qquad (15.53)$$

The mean and variance of the shifted negative exponential distribution are

$$\bar{t} = \frac{1}{\lambda} \qquad (15.54)$$

$$\sigma^2 = (\bar{t} - c)^2 \qquad (15.55)$$

Erlang distribution. The shifted negative exponential distribution makes the probability of a headway less than c equal to zero. A more desirable distribution, one that would have a very low, but not zero, probability of a small headway, is the Erlang distribution. The Erlang distribution is the interval distribution associated with the generalized Poisson distribution in the same manner that the negative exponential interval distribution is associated with the Poisson counting distribution.

The probability density function of the Erlang distribution can be stated as

$$f(t) = \lambda e^{-\lambda t} \frac{(\lambda t)^{k-1}}{(k - 1)!} \qquad (15.56)$$

The mean and variance of the Erlang distribution are

$$\bar{t} = \frac{k}{\lambda} \qquad (15.57)$$

$$s^2 = \frac{k}{\lambda^2} \qquad (15.58)$$

The cumulative distribution function of the Erlang distribution is

$$P(h \leq t) = 1 - e^{-\lambda t} \sum_{n=0}^{k-1} \frac{(\lambda t)^n}{n!} \qquad (15.59)$$

For $k = 1$, this reduces to $1 - e^{-\lambda t}$, the negative exponential distribution.

For $k = 2$,

$$P(h \leq t) = 1 - e^{-\lambda t}[1 + \lambda t]$$

For $k = 3$,

$$P(h \leq t) = 1 - e^{\lambda t}\left[1 + \lambda t + \frac{(\lambda t)^2}{2}\right]$$

For $k = 4$,

$$P(h \leq t) = 1 - e^{-\lambda t}\left[1 + \lambda t + \frac{(\lambda t)^2}{2} + \frac{(\lambda t)^3}{3!}\right]$$

If the mean and variance of the headway distribution are known from observed data, the parameters may be estimated from

$$\lambda = \frac{\text{mean}}{\text{variance}} \qquad (15.60)$$

$$k = \frac{(\text{mean})^2}{\text{variance}} \qquad (15.61)$$

Applications of statistical models

This section presents some examples of the application of statistical models to a set of observed vehicle arrivals in a single lane on Interstate 494, furnished by the Minnesota Department of Transportation. The number of vehicles *(x)* counted per 15-s interval is given in column 1 of Table 15-1 and the observed frequency *(f)* of each count is given in column 2. There is a total of sixty-four 15-s observations. For these data,

$$\Sigma f = 64$$

$$\Sigma f \cdot x = 478.0$$

$$\Sigma f \cdot x^2 = 3822$$

$$m = \lambda t = \frac{478}{64} = 7.46875 \text{ veh/15 s}$$

$$s^2 = \frac{3822 - (478)^2/64}{63} = 3.99901 \text{ veh/15 s}$$

Poisson distribution. The single parameter of the Poisson distribution is the mean m. The values $P(x)$, determined by applications of equations (15.32) and (15.33), are presented in column 3 of Table 15-1. The theoretical frequencies, 64 × $P(x)$, are presented in column 4. It will be observed that the fit of frequencies is poor. There is an overestimate of theoretical frequencies for low and high counted vehicles per interval and an underestimate of the theoretical frequencies for the intermediate range of counted vehicles per interval.

Binomial distribution. The mean/variance ratio is

$$\frac{7.46875}{3.99901} = 1.868$$

Since the ratio is greater than 1.0, the binomial distribution is fitted to these data. The parameter n is estimated from equation (15.36):

$$n = \frac{\bar{x}^2}{\bar{x} - s^2} = \frac{(7.46875)^2}{7.46875 - 3.99901} = 16.08$$

Since n must be an integer value, use $n = 16$. Also, since mean $= np$, the second parameter

$$p = \frac{7.46875}{16} = 0.46680$$

The values $P(x)$ are determined by application of equations (15.37) and (15.38) with the parameters p and n determined above. Values of $P(x)$ and theoretical frequencies are shown in columns 5 and 6 of Table 15-1. The fit is much improved over the entire range of the variable x.

Generalized Poisson distribution. If the mean/variance ratio is greater than 1.0, an alternative counting distribution is the generalized Poisson. The two parameters of the dis-

TABLE 15–1
Analysis of Counting Distribution Data

Vehicles/15-s Interval, x	Observed Frequency, f		Poisson $P(x)$	Poisson Theoretical Frequency		Binomial $P(x)$	Binomial Theoretical Frequency		Generalized Poisson $P(x)$	Generalized Poisson Theoretical Frequency	
0	0		0.00057	0.04		0.00004	0.00		0.00000	0.0	
1	0		0.00426	0.27		0.00060	0.04		0.00014	0.01	
2	0	3	0.01592	1.02	8.61	0.00393	0.25	4.24	0.00191	0.12	3.64
3	3		0.03962	2.54		0.01604	1.03		0.01190	0.76	
4	0		0.07398	4.74		0.04563	2.92		0.04290	2.75	
5	8		0.11052	7.07		0.09588	6.14		0.10056	6.44	
6	10		0.13757	8.80		0.15389	9.85		0.16524	10.58	
7	11		0.14678	9.39		0.19247	12.32		0.20071	12.85	
8	10		0.13703	8.77		0.18956	12.13		0.18741	11.99	
9	11		0.11372	7.28		0.14751	9.44		0.13864	8.87	
10	9		0.08493	5.44		0.09040	5.79		0.08324	5.33	
11	1	11	0.05767	3.69	14.08	0.04317	2.76	9.88	0.04136	2.65	9.63
12 or more	1		0.07743	4.95		0.02088	1.33		0.02599	1.65	
Totals	64		1.00000	64.00		1.00000	64.00		1.00000	64.00	

tribution are λt and k. The parameter k is estimated from the appropriate chart cited by Haight et al., in this instance, $k = 2$. The second parameter, λt, is found from equation (15.45).

$$\lambda t = \bar{x}k + \tfrac{1}{2}(k - 1)$$

$$= (7.46875)2 + \frac{1}{2}(2 - 1) = 15.43750$$

Values of $P(x)$ are then found by application of equation (15.44):

$$P(x)_{gp} = \sum_{j=xk}^{(x+1)k-1} \frac{e^{-\lambda t}\lambda t^j}{j!}$$

When $x = 0$, the range of j is 0 to 1, and the $P(0)_{gp}$ is $P(0)_p + P(1)_p$ of a Poisson distribution with a mean m equal to 15.43750. When $x = 1$, the range of j is 2 to 3 and the $P(1)_{gp}$ is $P(2)_p + P(3)_p$ of a Poisson distribution with the foregoing mean. The subscripts gp and p refer, respectively, to probabilities of the generalized Poisson and Poisson distributions. By equation (15.32),

$$P(0)_p = e^{-15.43750} = 1.97505 \times 10^{-7}$$

By equation (15.33),

$$P(1)_p = \frac{15.43750}{1} \times 1.97505 \times 10^{-7}$$

$$= 3.04899 \times 10^{-6}$$

$$P(2)_p = \frac{15.43750}{2} \times 3.04899 \times 10^{-6}$$

$$= 2.35344 \times 10^{-5}$$

$$P(3)_p = \frac{15.43750}{3} \times 2.35344 \times 10^{-5}$$

$$= 1.21104 \times 10^{-4}$$

and so on. Then, by equation (15.44),

$$P(0)_{gp} = 1.97505 \times 10^{-7} + 3.04899 \times 10^{-6}$$

$$= 3.24650 \times 10^{-6} = 0.00000$$

$$P(1)_{gp} = 2.35344 \times 10^{-5} + 1.21104 \times 10^{-4}$$

$$= 1.44638 \times 10^{-4} = 0.00014$$

and so on.

Values of $P(x)_{gp}$ and theoretical frequencies of the generalized Poisson distribution are shown in columns 7 and 8 of Table 15-1. Again, the fit to the observed data is good, indicating that the generalized Poisson may be used as an alternative to the binomial distribution.

Application of observed data to gap distribution. This section illustrates the calculations for gap distribution associated with the data presented in Table 15-1 for counting distributions. Since the mean number of vehicles observed every 15 s equals 7.46875 vehicles ($= \lambda t$), it follows that $\lambda = 7.46875/15 = 0.49792$ veh/s and $\bar{t} = 1/\lambda = 2.00835$ s. Theoretical headways, based upon parameters calculated from counting distribution observations, are calculated for the negative exponential, the shifted negative exponential, and the Erlang distributions.

Negative exponential distribution. The single parameter is λ and the following probabilities are calculated for headways (h) in seconds using equation (15.38):

$$P(h \leq 0 \text{ s}) = 1 - e^{-0.49792(0)} = 0.00000$$

$$P(h \leq 0.5 \text{ s}) = 1 - e^{-0.49792(0.5)} = 0.22039$$

$$P(h \leq 1.0 \text{ s}) = 1 - e^{-0.49792(1.0)} = 0.39221$$

$$P(h \leq 1.5 \text{ s}) = 1 - e^{-0.49792(1.5)} = 0.52616$$

and so on.

It follows that the probability of a headway between 0.0 and 0.5 is (0.22039 − 0.00000) = 0.22039. Similarly, the probability of a headway between 0.5 and 1.0 s is (0.39221 − 0.22039) = 0.17189. The probability of a headway greater than 1.5 s is (1.0 − 0.52616) = 0.47384. The expected distribution of headways, assuming the negative exponential distribution is shown in Figure 15.5(a). It will be observed that lesser headways are the most frequently expected.

Shifted negative exponential distribution. Two parameters are required for application of equation (15.52). The mean headway $\bar{t}$ has been calculated as 2.00835 s and the shifted parameter c is assumed to be 1.0 s, so that

$$P(h \leq 1.0 \text{ s}) \text{ (by definition)} = 0.00000$$

$$P(h \leq 1.5 \text{ s}) = 1 - e^{-[(1.5 - 1.0)/1.00835]} = 0.39095$$

$$P(h \leq 2.0 \text{ s}) = 1 - e^{-[(2.0 - 1.0)/1.00835]} = 0.62906$$

and so on.

There are no expected headways less than 1.0 s; the probability of a headway between 1.0 and 1.5 s is (0.39095 − 0.00000) = 0.39095 s. The probability of a headway greater than 1.5 s is (1.0 − 0.39095) = 0.60905. The expected distribution of headways, assuming the shifted negative exponential distribution, is shown in Figure 15.5(b). While headways less than 1.0 s have been eliminated, the distribution is seen to be very compact with the greatest expected probability for those headways just greater than the shift limit, 1.0 s.

Erlang distribution. In analyzing the counting distribution, it was found that the value of $k = 2.0$. The value of λ to be used is the same as for the negative exponential, 0.49792, so that by equation (15.59),

$$P(h < t) = 1 - e^{-0.49792t}[1 + 0.49792t]$$

$$P(h \leq 0.0) = 1 - e^{-0}[1 + 0] = 0.00000$$

$$P(h \leq 0.5) = 1 - e^{-0.49792(0.5)}[1 + 0.49792(0.5)] = 0.02630$$

$$P(h \leq 1.0) = 1 - e^{-0.49792(1.0)}[1 + 0.49792(1.0)] = 0.08957$$

$$P(h \leq 1.5) = 1 - e^{-0.49792(1.5)}[1 + 0.49792(1.5)] = 0.17225$$

and so on.

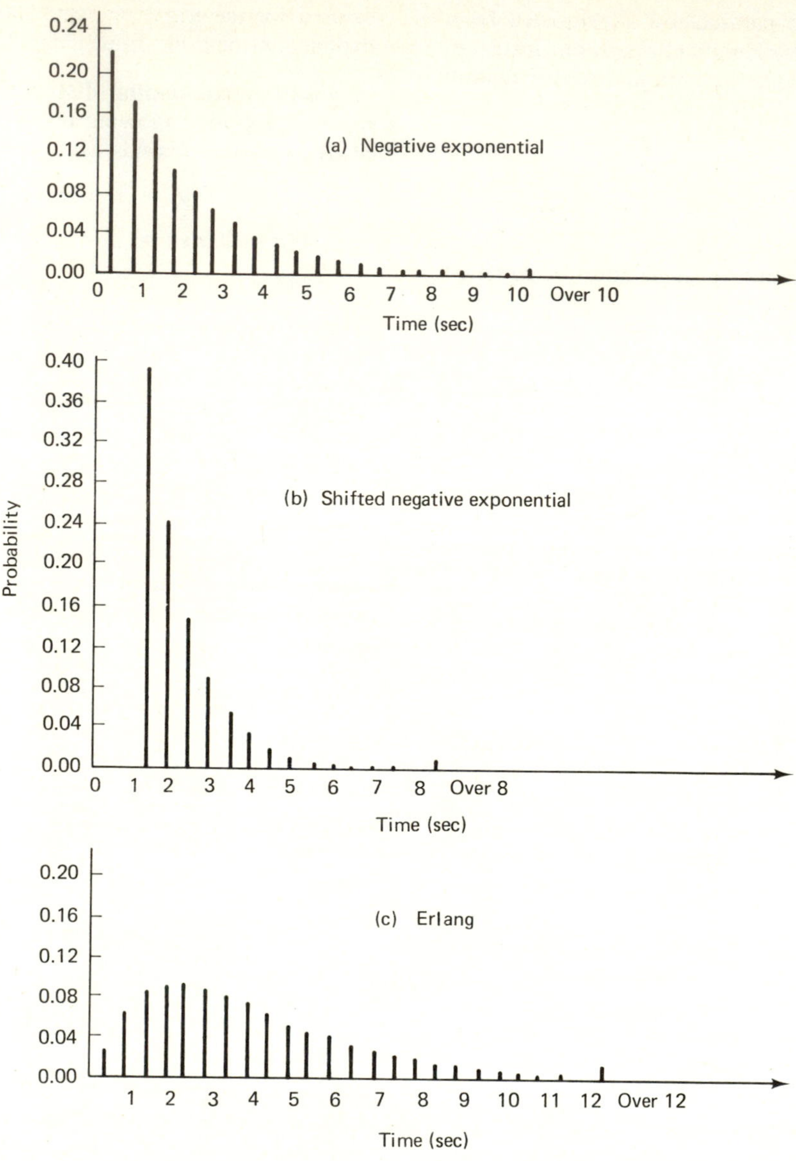

Figure 15.5. Gap distributions.

The Erlang distribution of gaps is an improvement in that it allows for minimum headways to occur but their expected frequency is less than those obtained by the negative exponential distribution. The probability that a headway is between 0.0 and 0.5 s is (0.02630 − 0.00000) = 0.02630, and the probability that a headway is between 0.5 and 1.0 s is (0.08957 − 0.02630) = 0.06328. The expected distribution of headways, assuming the Erlang distribution, is given in Figure 15.5(c).

Traffic stream models

For some types of traffic analysis and design, when considering uninterrupted flow, it is useful to use a functional relationship between the mean value of the characteristic under study and some other characteristic. The relationship among the three variables u, k, and q is called a traffic stream model. A dimensional analysis of the three variables gives the following relationship:

$$q(\text{veh/h}) = u(\text{mph})k(\text{veh/mi})$$

or (15.62)

$$q(\text{veh/h}) = u(\text{km/h})k(\text{veh/km})$$

where q = mean rate of flow

u = space mean speed

k = mean density

Other terms requiring definition are as follows:

q_m = maximum flow rate

u_f = free speed or speed at free-flow conditions

u_m = speed at which the flow rate is a maximum

k_j = jam density or density at which all vehicles are stopped

k_m = density at which the flow rate is a maximum

Speed–density models

It has been observed that, as the density of vehicles in a lane or on a roadway increases, drivers tend to decrease speeds. Knowing concentration and speed, it is possible to compute flow. Speed–density models described in this section include:

1. Linear model (Greenshields)
2. Logarithmic model (Greenberg)
3. Generalized single-regime models
   a. Pipes–Munjal
   b. Drew
   c. Bell-shaped curve
4. Multiregime models

The various models have evolved as further data have become available and as shortcomings in earlier models have become apparent. While the Greenshields linear model lends itself to simplicity in mathematical manipulation, it does not give realistic values of k_j, nor does the assumption of linearity agree with many of the observed data. The Greenberg logarithmic model gives more realistic values of k_j and provides a better fit to observed data but gives poor estimates of velocity at low values of density. A similar model by Underwood gives a good fit to the observed data and a better estimate of the velocity at low values of density, but gives poor estimates of velocity at high speed. Multiregime models have been introduced to overcome the shortcomings noted above by using different models for various portions of the speed–density curve.

Although no single model is a "best" model, it would appear that the Greenshields model is the simplest to use, provides insight into the behavior of traffic streams for uninterrupted flow, and gives a satisfactory fit to observed data over a sufficient range to make the results useful. Details of the various speed–density models are given in the following discussion.

Linear model. Greenshields,[4] in an early investigation of traffic characteristics, proposed a linear relationship between speed and density that can be expressed as

$$u = u_f\left(1 - \frac{k}{k_j}\right) \qquad (15.63)$$

The model is simple to use and investigators have found good correlation between the model and field data, but a linear relationship does not always exist over the entire range of observations. Some observers have suggested models that take the form shown in Figure 15.6.

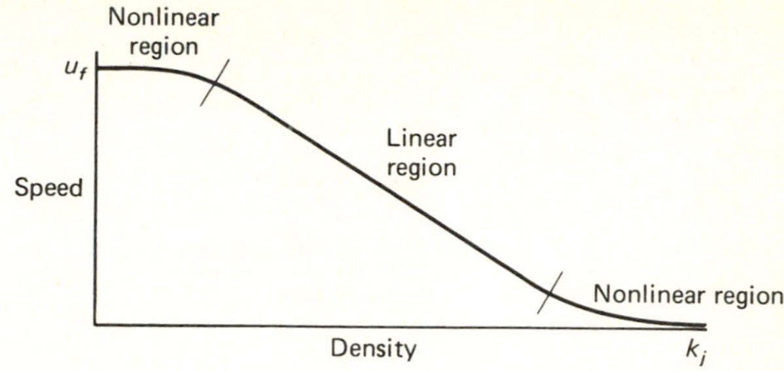

Figure 15.6. General type of speed-density curve obtained by field data.

Logarithmic model. Greenberg[5] developed a speed–density model of the form

$$u = u_m \ln\left(\frac{k_j}{k}\right) \qquad (15.64)$$

This model shows good agreement with field data for congested flows, but is less satisfactory at low values of density, as may be seen by letting $k \rightarrow 0$ in equation (15.64).

Underwood[6] proposed a model of the form

$$u = u_f e^{-k/k_m} \qquad (15.65)$$

The shortcoming of this model is that it does not represent zero speed at high concentrations.

Generalized single-regimes models. Pipes[7] and Munjal[8] proposed a family of models of the form

$$u = u_f\left(1 - \frac{k}{k_j}\right)^n \qquad (15.66)$$

where n is a real number greater than 1. When $n = 1$, the relationship reduces to equation (15.63).

Drew[9] proposed the following form for the speed–density relationship:

$$u = u_f\left[1 - \left(\frac{k}{k_j}\right)^{(n+1)/2}\right] \qquad n > -1 \qquad (15.67)$$

When $n = 1$, this reduces to equation (15.63). When $n = 0$, the speed–density relationship becomes

[4] B. D. GREENSHIELDS, "A Study of Traffic Capacity," *Proc. Highw. Res. Bd., 14*, 448–477 (1935).

[5] H. GREENBERG, "An Analysis of Traffic Flow," *Oper. Res., 7* (1), 79–85 (1959).

[6] R. T. UNDERWOOD, "Speed, Volume and Density Relationships," in *Quality and Theory of Traffic Flow*, Bureau of Highway Traffic, Yale University, New Haven, Conn., 1961, pp. 141–188.

[7] L. A. PIPES, "Car-Following Models and the Fundamental Diagram of Road Traffic," *Transport. Res., 1* (1), 21–29 (1967).

[8] P. K. MUNJAL AND L. A. PIPES, "Propagation of On-Ramp Density Perturbations on Unidirectional and Two- and Three-Lane Freeways," *Transport. Res., 5* (4), 241–255 (1971).

[9] D. R. DREW, "Deterministic Aspects of Freeway Operations and Control," *Freeway Characteristics, Operations and Accidents*, Highway Res. Rec. 99, Washington, D.C., 1965, pp. 48–58.

$$u = u_f\left[1 - \left(\frac{k}{k_j}\right)^{1/2}\right] \qquad (15.68)$$

and is often referred to as the parabolic model.

Drake et al.[10] proposed the use of the bell-shaped or normal curve as a model of speed–density using the form

$$u = u_f e^{-1/2(k/k_m)^2} \qquad (15.69)$$

Multiregime models. Edie[11] developed a model of speed–density which is a composite of equations (15.64) and (15.65). Equation (15.65) is used at low values of density and (15.64) at high values of density.

Flow–density relationships

The flow–density relationship shown in Figure 15.7 is sometimes called the fundamental diagram of traffic or the q–k curve. When there are no vehicles on the roadway ($k = 0$), it is evident that the flow is zero ($q = 0$), so that the curve must pass through the origin as represented by point A. The slope of the radius vectors from A to points B, C, and D represents speed u, corresponding to the volume and density conditions represented by the point at the end of the curve ($u = q/k$). Furthermore, the slope with which the curve leaves the origin A is the free-flow speed u_f.

Observations of queues stopped at traffic signals show that it is possible to have high concentrations of traffic when there is no flow, so that the curve has a point of maximum density k_j with zero flow. This is represented by point E in Figure 15.7.

Since there are observable flows at intermediate densities, it follows that there must be at least one point of maximum flow between the two zero points, point C in Figure 15.7.

Points B and D are arbitrary points which represent non-congested and congested conditions, respectively.

The numerical values of Figure 15.7 are for illustrative purposes only and are not assumed to represent conditions that may be expected from field observations. The maximum flow rate, q_m is 2400 veh/h and the jam density is 200 veh/mi. The density k_m at q_m is read from the diagram as 100 veh/mi. The speed u_m at maximum flow is the slope of the radius vector from the origin A to point C, so that $u_c = u_m = 2400/100 = 24.0$ mph.

At point B, the volume q is 1800 veh/h, the density k is 50 veh/mi, and the velocity $u = 1800/50 = 36.0$ mph.

Assume the volume at point D is 1224 veh/h, the density is 170 veh/mi, and the computed velocity $u = 1224/170 = 7.20$ mph.

This section will deal with two models of flow–density relationship, (1) the parabolic model and (2) the logarithmic model.

[10] J. S. Drake, J. L. Schofer, and A. D. May, Jr. "A Statistical Analysis of Speed Density Hypothesis," *Traffic Flow Characteristics*, Highway Res. Rec. 154, Washington, D.C., 1967, pp. 53–87.

[11] L. C. Edie, "Car-Following and Steady-State Theory for Non-congested Traffic," *Oper. Res.*, 9 (1), 66–75 (1961).

Parabolic model. The parabolic flow–density model follows directly from Greenshield's model of speed–density. Substituting equation (15.63) for u in equation (15.62), we get

$$q = uk = u_f\left(k - \frac{k^2}{k_j}\right) \qquad (15.70)$$

which is plotted in Figure 15.8(b), where q is a parabolic function of k. Differentiating equation (15.70), setting $dq/dk = 0$ and $k = k_m$, to obtain conditions of maximum flow, we get

$$\frac{dq}{dk} = u_f\left(1 - \frac{2k_m}{k_j}\right) = 0$$

Since u_f is not equal to zero,

$$1 - \frac{2k_m}{k_j} = 0$$

so that

$$k_m = \frac{k_j}{2}$$

Since the speed associated with the density k_m is the optimum u_m, we can substitute $k_m = k_j/2$ for k in equation (15.63), so that

$$u_m = u_f\left(1 - \frac{k_j}{2k_j}\right) = \frac{u_f}{2}$$

Therefore,

$$q_m = u_m k_m = \frac{u_f k_j}{4} \qquad (15.71)$$

which is shown in Figure 15.8(a) as a rectangle of maximum area.

Logarithmic model. The logarithmic model of flow–density follows directly from Greenberg's model of speed–density. Substituting equation (15.64) for u in equation (15.62), we get

$$q = uk = ku_m \ln\left(\frac{k_j}{k}\right) \qquad (15.72)$$

Differentiation of equation (15.72) to obtain conditions for maximum flow gives the results

$$k_m = \frac{k_j}{e} \qquad (15.73)$$

and

$$q_m = u_m \frac{k_j}{e} \qquad (15.74)$$

In this model, u_m is a parameter in equations (15.64), (15.72), and (15.74); that is, u_m is specified and determines the other characteristics.

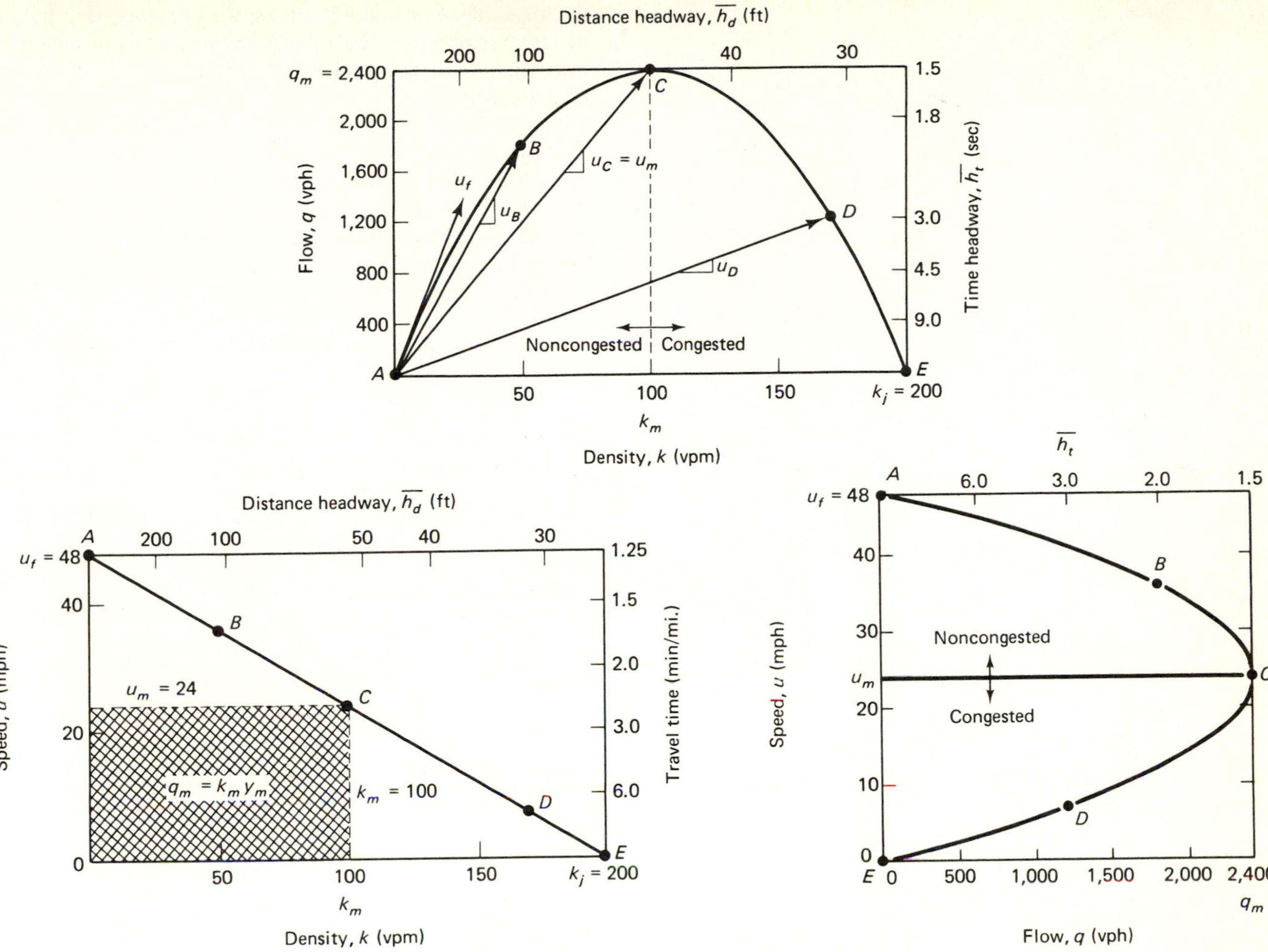

Figure 15.7. Flow-density relationship.

In Underwood's logarithmic model, equation (15.65), substitution into equation (15.62) gives

$$q = ku_f e^{-k/k_m} \tag{15.75}$$

Again, differentiation of equation (15.75) and analysis of boundary conditions gives the results

$$u_m = \frac{u_f}{e} \tag{15.76}$$

and

$$q_m = k_m\left(\frac{u_f}{e}\right) \tag{15.77}$$

For this model, k_m is a parameter that is specified.

Speed–flow models

Once a speed–density model has been determined, a speed–flow model can be determined from it. The free-flow speed u_f at zero concentration is the maximum obtainable speed, as shown in Figure 15.8(a). There will be a second point of zero flow, corresponding to zero speed at maximum density k_j. Between zero and maximum speeds, the diagram will form some type of loop toward maximum flow.

The speed–flow curve associated with Greenshield's model, equation (15.63), is developed below. From equation (15.63),

$$u - u_f = u_f\left(\frac{-k}{k_j}\right)$$

so that

$$k = k_j\left(1 - \frac{u}{u_f}\right)$$

Substituting this expression for k in equation (15.62) gives

$$q = uk = uk_j\left(1 - \frac{u}{u_f}\right) = k_j\left(u - \frac{u^2}{u_f}\right) \tag{15.78}$$

which results in a parabolic speed–flow curve as shown in Figure 15.8(c). The general form of the relationship shown in Figure 15.8(c) is fundamental to the discussion of the capacity for uninterrupted flow developed in Chapter 16.

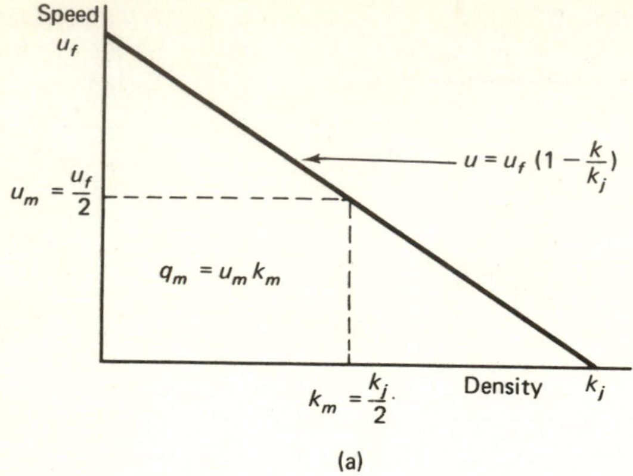

(a)

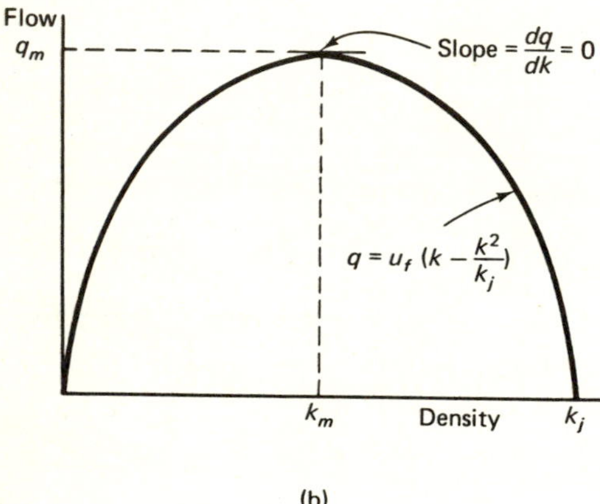

(b)

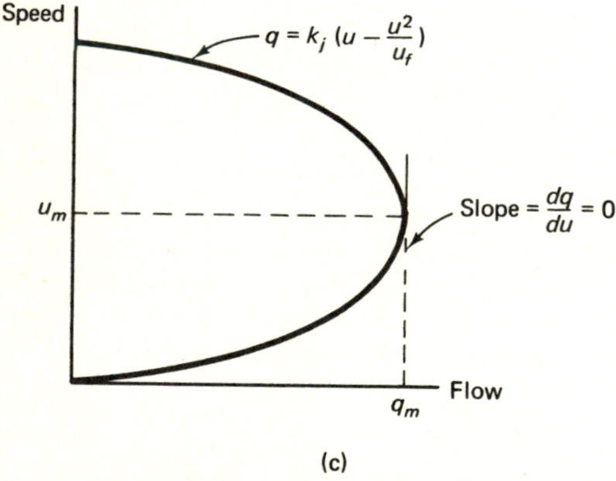

(c)

Figure 15.8. Relationships among the fundamental stream flow characteristics for the linear speed-density model.

Shock waves in traffic

Of particular interest in the study of traffic phenomena is the behavior of shock waves in the traffic stream. A shock wave may be defined as the motion of propagation of a change in density and flow. Consider, for example, behavior of a traffic stream that encounters a bottleneck caused by a disabled vehicle partially blocking the roadway. Vehicles are required to reduce their speed to pass the bottleneck. If the flow and density are relatively large, the point at which vehicles must reduce their speed, as evidenced by the appearance of brake lights on the vehicles, will be seen to move upstream. The movement of the point where the brake lights appear, relative to the roadway, is the movement of the shock wave.

Gerlough and Huber[12] present a discussion of shock wave analysis which is based on the work of L. A. Pipes.[13] Two distinct densities of traffic k_1 and k_2, moving along a straight highway are separated by a vertical line S which has a velocity u_w. The velocity u_w is considered positive if it moves in the direction x as shown in Figure 15.9(a). The following notation applies:

u_1 = space mean speed of vehicles in region A

u_2 = space mean speed of vehicles in region B

$U_{r1} = (u_1 - u_w)$ = speed of vehicles in region A relative to the moving line S

$U_{r2} = (u_2 - u_w)$ = speed of vehicles in region B relative to the moving line S

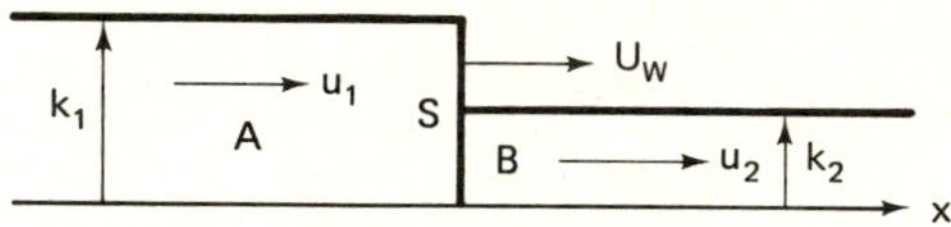

(a) Movement of two concentrations

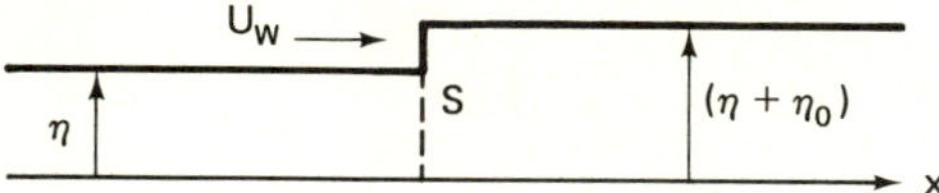

(b) Small discontinuity in concentration

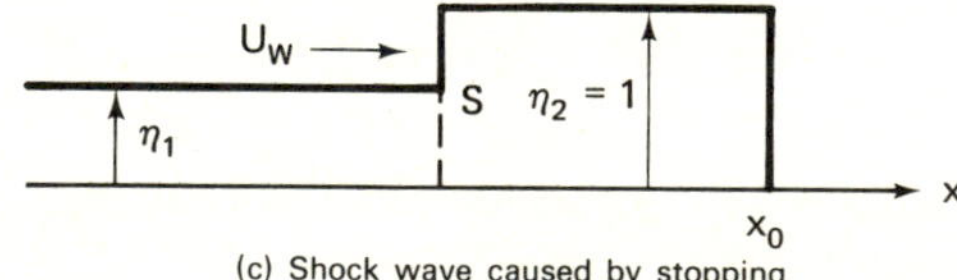

(c) Shock wave caused by stopping

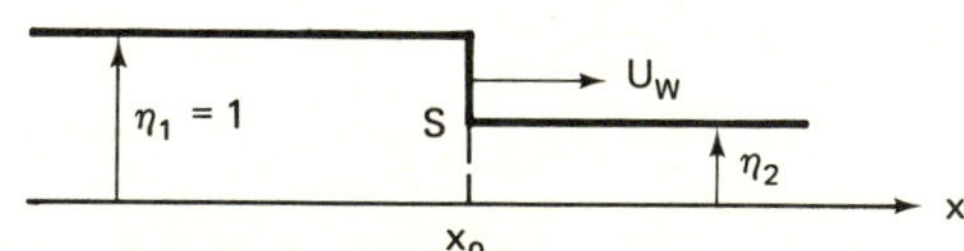

(d) Shock wave caused by starting

Figure 15.9. Schematic diagram for analysis of shock waves. SOURCE: L.A. Pipes, as reported in D.L. Gerlough and M.J. Huber, *Traffic Flow Theory*, Special Report 165, Transportation Reseach Board, Washington, D.C., 1975, pp. 112–116.

Over a time t both u_1 and u_2 will gain on S, the distance gained being $U_{ri}t$, and the number of vehicles N crossing the dividing line S from region A to region B is

[12]D. L. GERLOUGH AND M. J. HUBER, *Traffic Flow Theory*, Spec. Report 165, Transportation Research Board, Washington, D.C., 1975, pp. 112–116.

[13]L. A. PIPES, *Hydrodynamic Approaches—Part I: An Introduction to Traffic Flow Theory*, Spec. Report 79, Highway Research Board, Washington, D.C., 1961, pp. 3–5.

$$N = U_{r1}k_1t = U_{r2}k_2t \qquad (15.79)$$

so that

$$(u_1 - u_w)k_1 = (u_2 - u_w)k_2 \qquad (15.80)$$

This can be rewritten as

$$u_2k_2 - u_1k_1 = u_w(k_2 - k_1) \qquad (15.81)$$

Recalling that $q = uk$ and substituting in equation (15.81), we obtain

$$u_w = \frac{q_2 - q_1}{k_2 - k_1} \qquad (15.82)$$

Equation (15.82) demonstrates that the speed of the shock wave u_w is the slope of the chord between points A and B on the flow–density curve, where A and B are the points represented by k_1, q_1 and k_2, q_2, respectively, on the curve.

If the rates of flow and density are nearly equal, as for a wave of discontinuity,

$$q_2 - q_1 = \Delta q, \qquad k_2 - k_1 = \Delta k$$

so that equation (15.82) becomes

$$u_w = \frac{\Delta q}{\Delta k} = \frac{dq}{dk} \qquad (15.83)$$

In the following discussion, we assume Greenshield's model,

$$u_i = u_f\left(1 - \frac{k_i}{k_j}\right) \qquad (15.63)$$

and let

$$\eta_i = \frac{k_i}{k_j} \qquad (15.84)$$

We can now write

$$u_1 = u_f(1 - \eta_1) \quad \text{and} \quad u_2 = u_f(1 - \eta_2) \qquad (15.85)$$

where u_f is the free-flow speed and η_1 and η_2 are the normalized densities on both sides of the boundary line S. Substitution of equation (15.85) into equation (15.82) and simplifying gives the result

$$u_w = u_f[1 - (\eta_1 + \eta_2)] \qquad (15.86)$$

which is the velocity of the shock wave in terms of the normalized densities on either side of the moving discontinuity.

The case of nearly equal densities. Figure 15.9(b) is an illustration of the case where η_1 and η_2 are nearly equal to each other. If we let

$$\eta_1 = \eta, \quad \eta_2 = \eta + \eta_0 \qquad \text{where } (\eta + \eta_0) < 1$$

and substitute in equation (15.86), the result is

$$u_w = u_f[1 - (2\eta + \eta_0)] = u_f[1 - 2\eta] \qquad (15.87)$$

since η_0 is small enough to be neglected. In the case of nearly equal densities, the shock wave is called a wave of discontinuity.

Stopping waves. Figure 15.9(c) illustrates the case for traffic stream with a normalized density η_1, mean speed u_1, that is brought to a stop by a traffic signal at position $x = x_0$. The stream then assumes a saturated density of $\eta_2 = 1$. Substitution into equation (15.86) gives the result

$$u_w = u_f[1 - (\eta_1 + 1)] = -u_f\eta_1 \qquad (15.88)$$

which indicates that the shock wave of stopping moves upstream with a velocity $u_f\eta_1$. If the signal turns red at a time $t = 0$, then at time t later the length of the line of stopped cars will be $u_f\eta_1t$ measured from x_0.

Starting waves. In Figure 15.9(d) assume that at time $t = 0$ a line of vehicles has accumulated behind a signal located at $x = x_0$. The stopped vehicles have a saturated density of $\eta_1 = 1$. At $t = 0$ the signal at x_0 turns green, permitting vehicles to move forward at a velocity u_2. Since $u_2 = u_f(1 - \eta_2)$ it follows that the density of the starting vehicles is

$$\eta_2 = \left[1 - \left(\frac{u_2}{u_f}\right)\right] \qquad (15.89)$$

A starting shock wave forms as soon as the vehicles start to move. Substituting $\eta_1 = 1$, $\eta_2 = \eta_2$ into equation (15.86), the velocity of the shock wave is seen to be

$$u_w = u_f[1 - (1 + \eta_2)] = -u_f\eta_2 \qquad (15.90)$$

and then, in turn, substituting equation (15.89) in (15.90) gives

$$u_w = -(u_f - u_2) \qquad (15.91)$$

Assuming that vehicles depart at a velocity u_2 equal to $u_f/2$, the starting shock wave travels backward with a speed essentially equal to $-u_f/2$.

Numerical application of shock wave analysis

Figure 15.10 illustrates a flow–density curve based on Greenshield's model for which $u_f = 48.0$ mph and $k_j = 200$ veh/mi, so that $q_m = 48/2 \times 200/2 = 2400$ veh/h. Point B represents conditions for free-flow traffic when $\eta_B = 50/200 = 0.25$. At point B the wave of discontinuity is propagated with a speed [by equation (15.87)] of $48[1 - 2(0.25)] = 24.00$ mph (38.16 km/h) downstream. Point D represents conditions for congested flow where $\eta_0 = 170/200 = 0.85$ and the wave of discontinuity is propagated with a speed of $48[1 - 2(0.85)] = -33.60$ mph (-54.06 km/h) upstream.

At point C, the point of maximum flow $\eta_c = 100/200 = 0.5$ and the wave of discontinuity is propagated with a speed of $48[1 - 2(0.5)] = 0.0$.

Slow-moving-vehicle example. The following example was originally suggested by Edie and is based on an example used by Gerlough and Huber[14] and by Wattleworth.[15] Traffic

[14] Gerlough and Huber, *Traffic Flow Theory,* pp. 114–115.

[15] J. A. Wattleworth, "Traffic Flow Theory," in *Transportation and Traffic Engineering Handbook,* J. E. Baerwald, M. J. Huber, L. E. Keefer, eds., Prentice-Hall, Englewood Cliffs, N.J., 1976, p. 283.

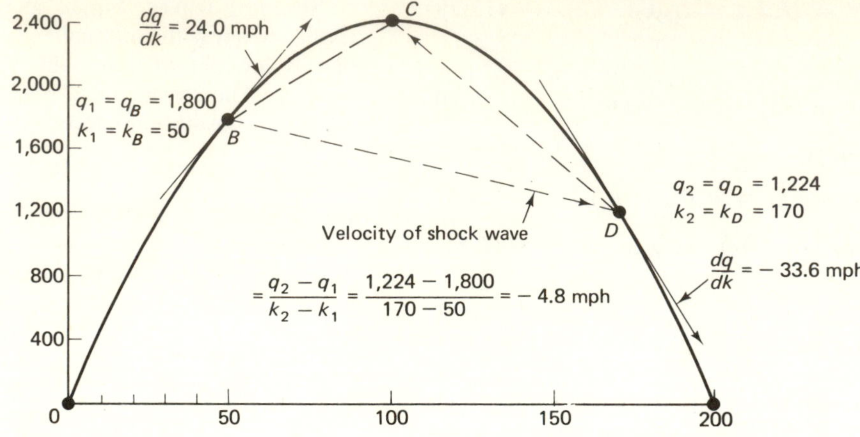

Figure 15.10. Kinematic and shock wave measurements related to flow-density curve.

on a single-lane roadway is flowing at 1800 veh/h at a speed of 36.0 mph (57.9 km/h) (point *B*, Figure 15.10). A slow-moving truck (7.2 mph (11.6 km/h) enters the roadway and travels for 1.8 mi (2.9 km) before exiting. Because vehicles are unable to pass the truck, a platoon forms at a flow rate of 1224 veh/h and density of 170 veh/mi (106 veh/km) as shown at point *D*. The rear of the platoon, the point at which free-flow vehicles join the congested platoon, moves at a velocity determined from equation (15.87) where $\eta_1 = 0.25$, $\eta_2 = 0.85$, so that

$$u_w = 48[1 - (0.25 + 0.85)]$$
$$= -4.80 \text{ mph } (-7.72 \text{ km/h})$$

While the rear of the platoon is moving backward at this speed, the front of the platoon is moving forward at the truck speed, so that the platoon is growing at a rate of 7.20 − (−4.80) = 12.0 mph (19.3 km/h). The truck requires 15 min to reach the point of exit. The length of the platoon is ¼ h × 12.0 mph = 3.0 mi (4.8 km). Since k_o is 170 veh/mi, there will be 510 vehicles in the congested platoon.

After the truck leaves the roadway, the flow increases to the point represented by point *C*, where $\eta_c = 0.50$. The wave generated by chord D–C by equation (15.86) is $u_w = 48[1 - (0.85 + 0.50)] = -16.80$ mph (−27.0 km/h). This second shock wave overtakes the first shock wave at −16.80 − (−4.80) = −12.0 mph (19.3 km/h). The time to dissipate the 3.0-mi congested platoon is 3.0 mi/12.0 mph = ¼ h. The point at which the congested platoon is dissipated is 0.25 h × −16.80 mph = −4.20 mi (−6.8 km) upstream from the exit point of the truck.

There is now a shock wave formed by the transition from the conditions at point *C* to the conditions at point *B*. From equation (15.86) the velocity of this shock wave is

$$u_w = 48[1 - (0.50 + 0.25)] = 12.0 \text{ mph } (19.3 \text{ km/h})$$

The time for this shock wave to return to the truck's exit point is 4.20 mi/12.0 mph = 0.35 h.

Total elapsed time, from the time the slow-moving vehicle enters the traffic stream until normal flow (point *B*) returns at the exit point, is

slow-moving vehicle on roadway	=	0.25 h
dissipate platoon congestion	=	0.25 h
normal flow at truck exit	=	0.35 h
total elapsed time		0.85 h

Stopping-wave example. Again, assume that traffic flow conditions are represented as shown by point *B* in Figure 15.10. Further, assume that traffic is stopped by a traffic incident for a duration of 3.0 min ($^1/_{20}$ h). By equation (15.88) the shock wave of stopping is

$$u_w = -48(0.25) = -12.0 \text{ mph } (-19.3 \text{ km/h})$$

The length of the stopped queue, at the time the incident is cleared ($t = {}^1/_{20}$ h), is $^1/_{20}$ h × 12.0 mph = 0.60 mi (1.0 km). The number of vehicles in the queue will be 0.60 mi × 50 veh/mi = 30 vehicles.

Starting-wave example. Assume that vehicles initially move at a speed of 24.0 mph when departing from the point of blockage (u_2 = 24.0 mph = 38.6 km/h). Then, by equation (15.91), the starting wave will move with a velocity

$$u_w = -(48.0 - 24.0) = -24.0 \text{ mph } (-38.6 \text{ km/h})$$

This starting wave will overtake the stopping wave at a relative velocity of −24.0 − (−12.0) = −12.0 mph (−19.3 km/h). The time to overtake the queue of 0.60 mi = 0.60/12.0 = 0.05 h, and the point on the roadway will be 0.05 h × 24 mph = 1.20 mi (1.93 km) upstream from the point of blockage.

Car following and acceleration noise

Traffic stream models, previously discussed, were based upon the relationships between the mean values of the characteristics flow *q*, density *k*, and speed *u*. From these relationships, it is possible to determine the behavior of vehicles in a stream of traffic. This type of analysis is referred to as a macroscopic analysis of traffic flow.

Car-following analysis is an effort to understand the behavior of a single-lane traffic stream by examining the manner in which individual vehicles follow one another, and from the behavior of pairs of vehicles, to deduce the behavior of a stream of traffic.

Development of a car-following model

Car-following models are developed from a stimulus–response relationship, where the response of successive drivers in the traffic stream is to accelerate or decelerate in proportion to the magnitude of the stimulus at time t and is begun after a time lag T, so that

$$\text{response } (t + T) = \text{sensitivity} \times \text{stimulus } (t)$$

Consider one vehicle following another in heavy traffic and unable to change lanes or pass. It is assumed that it will be spaced at a distance $s(t)$, as shown in Figure 15.11(a), so that if the first vehicle must stop suddenly, the second can be brought to a stop without striking the first vehicle. There is a reaction time T between the time the lead driver initiates a stop and the time the second driver initiates a stop.

The relative positions of the two vehicles after the stopping maneuver are shown in Figure 15.11(b), where

$x_n(t)$ = position of vehicle n at time t

$s(t)$ = spacing between vehicles at time t = $x_n(t) - x_{n+1}(t)$

d_1 = distance traveled by vehicle $(n + 1)$ during reaction time $T = Tu_{n+1}(t)$

d_2 = distance traveled by vehicle $(n + 1)$ during deceleration = $[u_{n+1}(t + T)]^2/2a_{n+1}(t + T)$

d_3 = distance traveled by vehicle n during deceleration = $[u_n(t)]^2/2a_n(t)$

L = distance from front bumper to front bumper at rest

$u_i(t)$ = velocity of vehicle i at time t

$a_i(t)$ = acceleration of vehicle i at time t

The desired spacing at time t, such that no collision will occur, is then

$$s(t) = x_n(t) - x_{n+1}(t) = d_1 + d_2 + L - d_3 \quad (15.92)$$

Defining the velocity of a vehicle as $u(t) = dx(t)/dt = \dot{x}(t)$ and the acceleration as $a(t) = d^2x/dt^2 = \ddot{x}(t)$ and substituting the appropriate relationships for d_1, d_2, and d_3 in equation (15.92) gives

$$s(t) = x_n(t) - x_{n+1}(t) = T\dot{x}_{n+1}(t) + \frac{\dot{x}^2_{n+1}(t + T)}{2\ddot{x}_{n+1}(t + T)} + L - \frac{\dot{x}^2_n(t)}{2\ddot{x}_n(t)} \quad (15.93)$$

Figure 15.11. Position of lead and following vehicles—emergency stop condition.

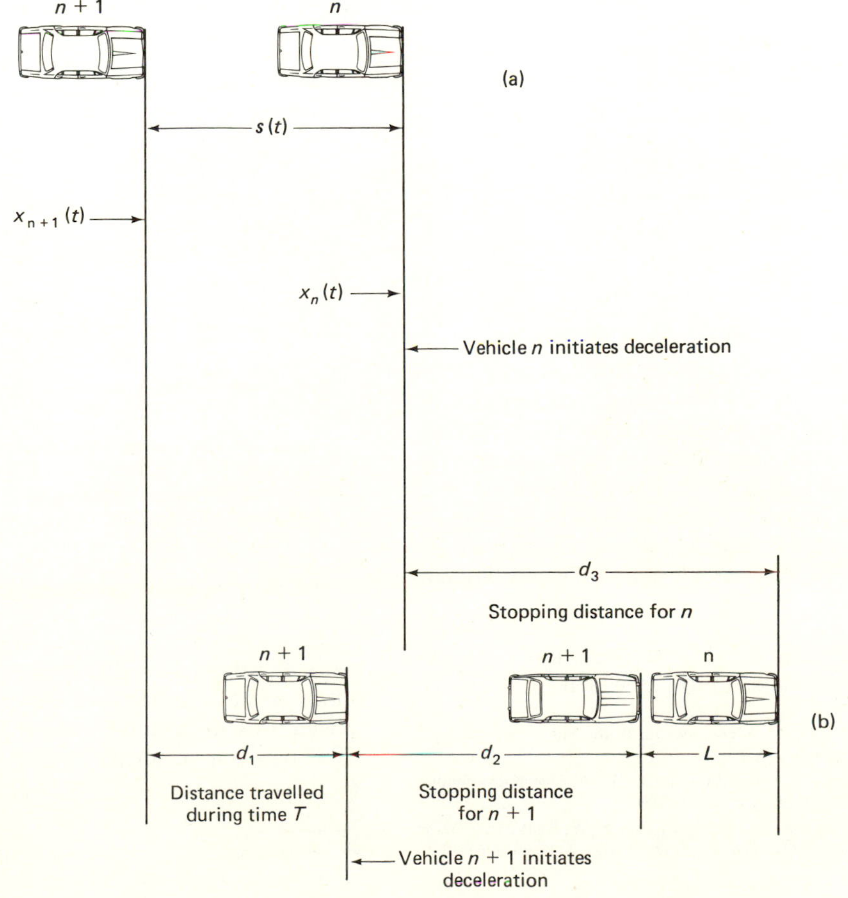

If the stopping distances of the two vehicles are assumed equal, so that $d_2 = d_3$, the spacing reduces to

$$x_n(t) - x_{n+1}(t) = T\dot{x}_{n+1}(t + T) + L \quad (15.94)$$

Differentiating with respect to (t) yields

$$\dot{x}_n(t) - \dot{x}_{n+1}(t) = T[\ddot{x}_{n+1}(t + T)] \quad (15.95)$$

so that the acceleration of the $(n + 1)$st vehicle at time $(t + T)$ becomes

$$\ddot{x}_{n+1}(t + T) = T^{-1}[\dot{x}_n(t) - \dot{x}_{n+1}(t)] \quad (15.96)$$

The response of the $(n + 1)$st driver, which takes place at time $(t + T)$, is to accelerate (decelerate) by an amount proportional to the positive (negative) difference in the relative velocity of the nth and $(n + 1)$st driver and the measure of sensitivity is given by T^{-1} (seconds).

A numerical solution of equation (15.96) for the case where $T = 1.0$ s, with two vehicles starting from a stopped position at a traffic light, shows that the second vehicle will follow the first at a safe distance, attaining the proper speed and velocity about 7 or 8 s after the first vehicle starts.

Kometani and Sasaki[16] have extended the application of equation (15.96) to the case where a queue of vehicles departs from a signal. By application of the Laplace transform to the solution of the car-following model, they demonstrated that the behavior of vehicles farther along the stream of traffic would be unstable, resulting in a collision if drivers behaved according to the car-following law of equation (15.96).

Chandler et al.[17] generalized equation (15.96) in the form

$$\ddot{x}_{(n+1)}(t + T) = \alpha[\dot{x}_n(t) - \dot{x}_{n+1}(t)] \quad (15.97)$$

where α is the sensitivity factor. This is a linear car-following model because the response is directly proportional to the stimulus.

Traffic stability

Although there are more complex car-following models than that given by the linear car-following model, the linear model is most amenable to a theoretical analysis of stability. Two types of stability are considered, local and asymptotic stability. Local stability is concerned with a response of a following vehicle to the lead vehicle in front of it. Asymptotic stability is concerned with the manner in which a fluctuation of motion of a lead vehicle is propagated through a line of traffic.

Local stability. Herman et al.[18] have identified the following situations for local stability, in which

$0 \leq (C = \alpha T) < \frac{1}{e}$ spacing is nonoscillatory

$\frac{1}{e} \leq (C = \alpha T) < \frac{\pi}{2}$ damped oscillation of spacing

$(C = \alpha T) = \frac{\pi}{2}$ spacing is oscillatory with undamped oscillation

$(C = \alpha T) > \frac{\pi}{2}$ increasing amplitude in oscillation of spacing

The responses for different values of C are given in Figure 15.12.

Asymptotic stability. The limit for asymptotic stability has been investigated and reported by Chandler et al.[19] A line of traffic is asymptotically stable only when $C = \alpha T < ½$, which may be compared with the limit for local stability, where $C = ½$ indicates that the spacing is oscillatory but dampens very quickly (Figure 15.12). The fluctuation in the motion of the lead vehicle is propagated through the line of vehicles at a rate of α^{-1} seconds per vehicle.

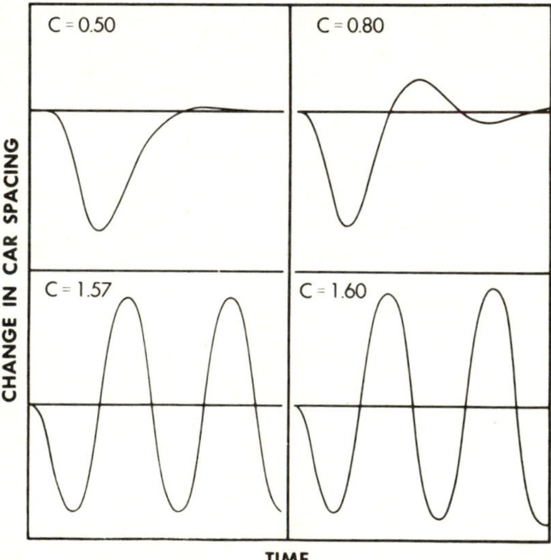

Figure 15.12. Change in car spacing of two cars for different values of $C = \lambda T$ when the first car maneuvers. For $C = 0.50$ and 0.80, the spacing is oscillatory and damped; for $C = 1.57$, oscillatory and undamped; for $C = 1.60$, oscillatory with increasing amplitude. SOURCE: R. Herman, E.W. Montroll, R.B. Potts, and R.W. Rothery, "Traffic Dynamics: Analysis of Stability in Car-Following," *Operations Research,* 7(1), Jan.–Feb., 1959, p. 94.

Figure 15.13 is an illustration of the spacing of successive pairs of vehicles for different values of αT and for a condition where the first vehicle decelerated and then accelerated back to its initial velocity, with an initial spacing of 70 ft between vehicles.

[16]E. KOMETANI AND T. SASAKI, "A Safety Index for Traffic with Linear Spacing," *Oper. Res.*, 7 (6), 704–720 (1959).

[17]R. E. CHANDLER, R. HERMAN, AND E. MONTROLL, "Traffic Dynamics—Studies in Car Following," *Oper. Res.*, *6* (2), 165–184 (1958).

[18]R. HERMAN, E. W. MONTROLL, R. B. POTTS, AND R. W. ROTHERY, "Traffic Dynamics: Analysis of Stability in Car Following," *Oper. Res.*, 7 (1), 86–106 (1959).

[19]CHANDLER ET AL., "Traffic Dynamics in Car Following."

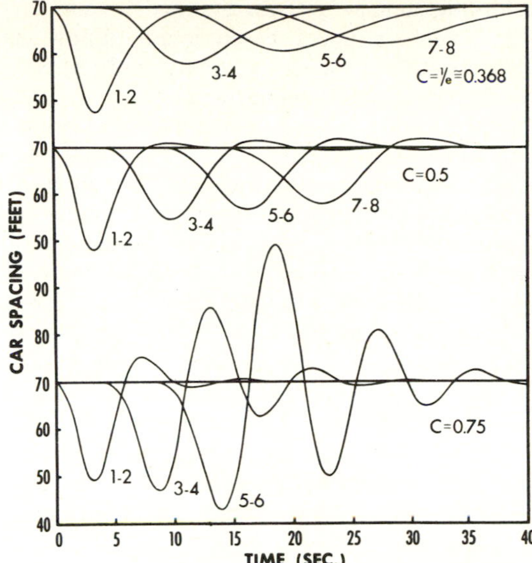

Figure 15.13. Car spacing of a line of cars for various values of $C = \lambda T$. The cars were originally spaced at 70 ft, the lead car then decelerated and then accelerated back to its original velocity, and the curves illustrate the propagation of the fluctuation down the line of cars. SOURCE: R. Herman, E.W. Montroll, R.B. Potts, and R.W. Rothery, "Traffic Dynamics: Analysis of Stability in Car-Following," *Operations Research,* 7(1), Jan.–Feb., 1959, p. 95.

General expression for car-following models

In the linear car-following model, equation (15.97), it is assumed that the response α is independent of the spacing between two vehicles, that a vehicle at 500 ft behind a lead vehicle would respond in the same manner as if 50 ft behind. Gazis et al.[20] developed a more realistic model, in which the sensitivity is inversely proportional to the spacing, so that

$$\ddot{x}_{n+1}(t + T) = \frac{\alpha_o}{[x_n(t) - x_{n+1}(t)]}[\dot{x}_n(t) - \dot{x}_{n+1}(t)] \quad (15.98)$$

where the units of α_o are distance/time.

Continuing development of car-following models led to generalized form of the equation as

$$\ddot{x}_{n+1}(t + T) = \alpha_o \frac{\dot{x}^m_{n+1}(t + T)}{[x_n(t) - x_{n+1}(t)]^{\ell}}[\dot{x}_n(t) - \dot{x}_{n+1}(t)] \quad (15.99)$$

where ℓ and m are constants.

First proposed by Gazis et al,[21] the general expression has been further examined by May and Keller[22] for the case of noninteger values of l and m. For the case where $l = 0$, equation (15.99) becomes equation (15.97), the linear model, while for $l = 1$, $m = 0$, equation (15.99) reduces to equation (15.98).

From car-following to traffic stream models

The relationship between car-following models and traffic stream models was first developed by Gazis et al.[23] who assumed a lead vehicle in a stream of cars proceeding at a velocity u while each following vehicle proceeds at the same velocity and at a spacing dictated by an appropriate car-following law. While the platoon of vehicles is moving in this steady state, it is possible to calculate flow rate q, density k, and velocity u, from which it is possible to develop conditions of traffic flow. The procedure is to integrate an expression for the acceleration of the $(n + 1)$st vehicle, which in turn is the velocity of the traffic stream u. The resulting equation can then be solved for known boundary conditions, leading to values of q and k. The development of the procedure is shown in detail because it clearly illustrates the relationship between car-following and traffic stream models.

Consider the application of the procedure to the model given by equation (15.98):

1. Express the acceleration for the $(n + 1)$st vehicle as

$$\ddot{x}_{n+1}(t + T) = \alpha_o \frac{\dot{x}_n(t) - \dot{x}_{n+1}(t)}{x_n(t) - x_{n+1}(t)} \quad (15.98)$$

2. Integrate the expression to obtain the velocity of the $(n + 1)$st vehicle (the velocity of the traffic stream):

$$\begin{aligned} \dot{x}_{n+1}(t + T) &= u \\ &= \alpha_o \ln [x_n - x_{n+1}] + C_o \quad (15.100) \end{aligned}$$

Because at steady state the velocity at time $(t + T)$ is the same as the velocity at time t, the lag time T can be dropped. It will also be seen that $[x_n - x_{n+1}]$ is the average spacing between vehicles, $s\ (= 1/k)$, so that equation (15.100) may be rewritten as

$$u = \alpha_o \ln \left(\frac{1}{k}\right) + C_o \quad (15.101)$$

3. The constant of integration C_o is determined by solving equation (15.101) for a known condition—in this case when $u = 0$, $k = k_j$, so that

$$0 = \alpha_o \ln \left(\frac{1}{k_j}\right) + C_o$$

[20] D. C. GAZIS, R. HERMAN, AND R. B. POTTS, "Car-Following Theory of Steady State Flow," *Oper. Res.*, 7 (4), 499–505 (1959).

[21] D. C. GAZIS, R. HERMAN, AND R. W. ROTHERY, "Nonlinear Follow-the-Leader Models of Traffic Flow," *Oper. Res.*, 9 (4), 545–567 (1961).

[22] A. D. MAY, JR., AND H. E. M. KELLER, "Non-integer Car-Following Models," *Mathematical and Statistical Aspects of Traffic,* Highway Res. Rec. 199, Washington, D.C., 1967, pp. 19–32.

[23] GAZIS ET AL., "Car-Following Theory of Steady State Flow."

and

$$C_o = -\alpha_o \ln \left(\frac{1}{k_j}\right) \tag{15.102}$$

4. Express u in terms of k in equation (15.101) using the value of C_o, so that

$$\begin{aligned} u &= \alpha_o \ln \left(\frac{1}{k}\right) - \alpha_o \ln \left(\frac{1}{k_j}\right) \\ &= \alpha_o \ln \left(\frac{k_j}{k}\right) \end{aligned} \tag{15.103}$$

5. Recalling that $q = uk$ leads to

$$q = \alpha_o k \ln \left(\frac{k_j}{k}\right) \tag{15.104}$$

6. To determine the proportionality constant α_o, refer to Figure 15.8 and observe that the slope $dq/dk = 0$ at maximum volume q_m. Differentiation of equation (15.104) gives

$$\frac{dq}{dk} = \alpha_o \ln \left(\frac{k_j}{ke}\right) = 0 \tag{15.105}$$

Assuming that the α_o is nonzero and defining k_m as the density at maximum volume, it follows that

$$\ln \left(\frac{k_j}{k_m e}\right) = 0$$

so that

$$\frac{k_j}{k_m e} = 1$$

and $k_m = k_j/e$, the same result as that found in developing equation (15.73). Defining u_m as the velocity associated with q_m and substituting together with k_m in equation (15.103) leads to

$$u_m = \alpha_o \ln \left(\frac{k_j e}{k_j}\right) = \alpha_o \ln (e)$$

so that

$$\alpha_o = u_m \tag{15.106}$$

and equation (15.103) then becomes

$$u = u_m \ln \left(\frac{k_j}{k}\right) \tag{15.107}$$

which is the same as Greenberg's model, equation (15.64).

The Greenberg model, based on a fluid-flow analogy, is mathematically equivalent to equation (15.98) based on the principles of a car-following model.

May and Keller[24] have shown the relationship between several models developed from traffic stream analysis and from the car-following model given in equation (15.99) for different values of l and m. Only those combinations shown in Table 15-2 and enclosed by the dashed line in Figure 15.14 have been verified by field observations. The case $m = 0$, $l = 0$ has been developed by Pipes[25] and analyzed for stability by Chandler et al.[26] The Greenberg[27] model and the Gazis et al.[28] model follow from the case where $m = 0$ and $l = 1$. The Drew[29] model follows from the case where $m = 0$ and $l = 3/2$. The Greenshields[30] model is for the case where $m = 0$ and $l = 2$, while the Edie[31] and Underwood[32] models result when $m = 1$ and $l = 2$. The bell-shaped curve of Drake et al.[33] occurs when $m = 1$ and $l = 3$.

TABLE 15–2
Steady-State Flow Equations for Various m, l Combinations

l	Equation of State
	$m = 0$
0	$q = \alpha[1 - k/k_j]$ $\alpha = q_m = 1/\text{reaction time}$
1	$q = \alpha k \ln [k_j/k]$ $\alpha =$ velocity at optimum flow (u_m)
$\frac{3}{2}$	$q = \alpha k[1 - (k/k_j)^{1/2}]$ $\alpha =$ velocity at free flow (u_f)
2	$q = \alpha k[1 - k/k_j]$ $\alpha = u_f$
	$m = 1$
2	$q = \alpha k e^{(k/k_0)}$ $\alpha = u_f$; $k_0 =$ density at optimum flow
3	$q = \alpha k e^{1/2(k/k_0)2}$ $\alpha = u_f$

SOURCE: Adapted from A. D. MAY AND H. E. M. KELLER, "Noninteger Car-Following Models," *Mathematical and Statistical Aspects of Traffic*, Highway Res. Rec. 199, (Washington, D.C.: Highway Research Board, 1967), p. 23.

Application of car-following models

Car-following models have been used to evaluate aids to drivers in car following, to examine the behavior of platoons of buses as they may be operated on an exclusive

[24] MAY AND KELLER, "Non-integer Car-Following Models."

[25] L. A. PIPES, "An Operational Analysis of Traffic Dynamics," *J. Appl. Phys.*, *24* (3) 274–281 (1953).

[26] CHANDLER ET AL., "Traffic-Dynamics, Studies in Car Following."

[27] GREENBERG, "An Analysis of Traffic Flow."

[28] GAZIS ET AL., "Car-Following Theory of Steady State Flow."

[29] DREW, "Deterministic Aspects of Freeway Operations Control."

[30] GREENSHIELDS, "A Study of Traffic Capacity."

[31] EDIE, "Car-Following and Steady-state Theory for Non-congested Traffic."

[32] UNDERWOOD, "Speed, Volume and Density Relationships."

[33] DRAKE ET AL., "A Statistical Analysis of Speed Density Hypothesis."

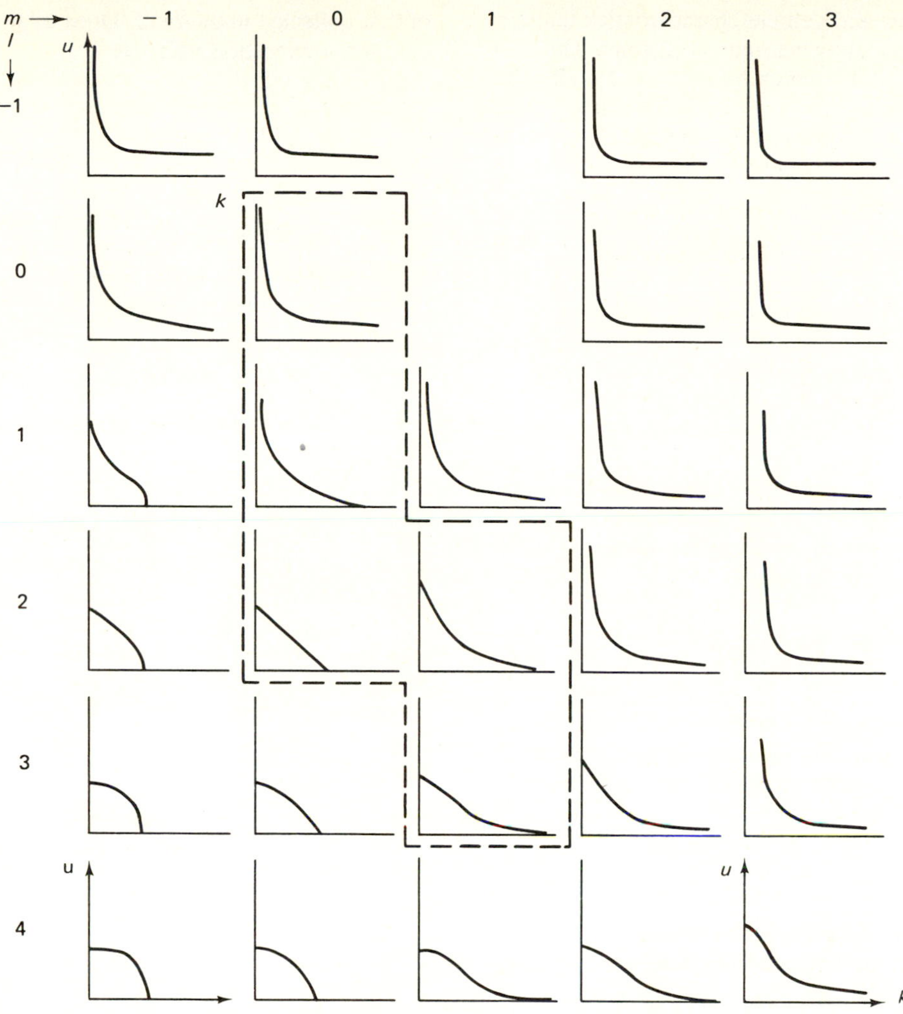

Figure 15.14. Matrix of speed-density relations for various *m, l* combinations of the general car-following equation. Only those models within the dashed line are included in Table 15.2. SOURCE: D. May, Jr., and H.E.M. Keller, "Non-integer Car-Following Models," *Mathematical and Statistical Aspects of Traffic*, Highway Res. Rec. 199, Washington, D.C., 1967, p. 24.

lane of a freeway, to anticipate the effect of smaller vehicles on the flow and speed of downstream traffic, and to examine safety in car following.

Fenton and Montano[34] performed experiments in which added information about the lead vehicle was given to drivers by a tactile device built into a single control stick used to maneuver the vehicle (accelerate, decelerate, change direction.) Bierley[35] experimented with improved visual displays and showed spacing in one instance and spacing plus relative velocity in the second case. Both reports do show some improvement in car-following ability.

A series of experiments with buses used to perform car-following experiments were reported by Rothery et al.[36] It was found that the reciprocal spacing model, equation (15.98), gave the best fit to the observed data. In experiments on platoons of buses ranging from 2 to 10 vehicles, it was found that maximum flows could be developed at a rate of 1450 buses/h at a constant speed of 33 mph.

The impact of small vehicles, 10 ft (3 m) in length, on reducing congestion was estimated from computer simulation of a single lane of traffic and reported by McClenahan and Simkowitz.[37] Driver behavior was based on a car-following model plus a model of lead-car behavior as the vehicles move through a street with fixed time cycles. The simulation showed that flow increased by 70% and the velocity by 57% if all small cars (10 ft or 3 m) are substituted for all long cars (20 ft or 6 m) and congestion is such that there is a queue of 15 vehicles at each traffic signal.

Fox and Lehman[38] simulated car-following behavior to

[34]R. E. FENTON AND W. B. MONTANO, "A Study of Driver-Aided Car Following," *Proc. 4th Int. Symp. Theory Traffic Flow, Karlsruhe, 1968,* pp. 1–7.

[35]R. L. BIERLEY, "Investigation of an Inter-vehicle Spacing Display," *Driver Characteristics, Night Visibility and Driving Stimulation,* Highway Res. Rec. 25, Washington, D.C., 1963, pp. 58–75.

[36]R. ROTHERY, R. SILVER, R. HERMAN, AND C. TONER, "Analysis of Experiments on Single-Lane Bus Flow," *Oper. Res., 12* (6) 913–933 (1964).

[37]J. W. MCCLENAHAN AND H. J. SIMKOWITZ, "The Effect of Short Cars on Flow and Speed in Downtown Traffic: A Simulation Model and Some Results," *Transport. Sci., 3* (2), 126–139 (1969).

[38]P. FOX AND F. G. LEHMAN, *Safety in Car Following—A Computer Simulation,* Newark College of Engineering, Newark, N.J., 1967, 173 pp.

investigate those driver and vehicle characteristics that are most important in eliminating rear-end collisions. The car-following model used is that given by $m = 1, l = 2$. The simulation demonstrated that most critical variables were (1) driver reaction time, (2) desired spacing, and (3) threshold boundary for relative perception.

Acceleration "noise"

It is reasonable to assume that a driver will attempt to maintain a uniform velocity when traveling along a roadway. But because of traffic and roadway conditions, or inattention to the driving task, the driver will vary the speed (and thus the acceleration) while proceeding along a roadway.

The standard deviation σ of the acceleration about the mean acceleration is defined as the acceleration "noise." The mathematical definition of this quantity, assuming mean acceleration to be zero, is

$$\sigma = \left\{\frac{1}{T}\int_{0}^{T}[a(t)]^2\,dt\right\}^{1/2} \tag{15.108}$$

where $a(t)$ is the acceleration (positive or negative) at time t and T is the total time in motion. An alternative form in which acceleration is sampled at successive time intervals (Δt) becomes

$$\sigma = \left[\frac{1}{T}\Sigma\,[a(t)]^2\,\Delta t\right]^{1/2} \tag{15.109}$$

Jones and Potts[39] measured acceleration noise over different roads, varying traffic conditions and different drivers. They reported the following conclusions:

1. For two roads through hilly country, σ is much greater for a narrow 2-lane road than for a 4-lane dual highway.
2. For a road in hilly country, σ is greater for a downhill journey than for an uphill one.
3. For two drivers driving different speeds below the design speed of a highway, σ is much the same.
4. If one or both drivers exceed the design speed, σ is greater for the faster driver.
5. Increasing traffic volume increases σ.
6. Increasing traffic congestion produced by parking cars, stopping buses, cross traffic, crossing pedestrians, etc., increases σ.
7. The value of σ may be a better measure of traffic congestion than travel times and stopped times.
8. High values of σ indicate a potentially dangerous situation.

Although Jones and Potts caution against the use of arbitrary interpretation of values of σ, they make the observation that $\sigma = 0.7$ ft/s^2 is a low value and $\sigma = 1.5$ ft/s^2 is a high value.

Calculation of acceleration noise. Equations (15.108) and (15.109) do not lend themselves to ease of calculation of data collected in the field. Drew et al.[40] derive an expression for acceleration noise as

$$\sigma = \left[\frac{(\Delta u)^2}{T}\sum_{i=1}^{K}\frac{n_i^2}{\Delta t_i} - \left(\frac{V_T - V_0}{T}\right)^2\right]^{1/2} \tag{15.110}$$

where T = total time in motion for subject trip segment

Δu = constant increment of velocity change (mph) (2 mph is suggested)

Δt_i = time interval (seconds) for a change in velocity of magnitude $n_i\,\Delta u$ (n is an integer)

V_o, V_T = velocity at the start and end of trip segment

K = number of segments of uniform acceleration

For a long trip, or a trip where V_T and V_0 are nearly identical, the second term of the equation can be neglected.

An example of calculation of acceleration noise for a vehicle in urban traffic is shown in Table 15-3. For this example, $\Delta u = 2.0$ mph and the total time in motion is 30.0 s. Between zero and 8 s, the vehicle accelerates from 20 mph to 24 mph, so that $n = 4.0/2.0 = 2.0$ and $\Delta t = 8.0$ s. Successive changes in velocity are evaluated similarly.

TABLE 15–3
Example of Calculation of Acceleration Noise*

Interval	Elapsed Time (s)	Velocity at End of Interval (mph)	n_i	Δt_i/ second	$n_i^2/\Delta t_i$
0	0	20	—	—	—
1	8	24	2	8	0.50
2	12	22	1	4	0.25
3	17	24	1	5	0.20
4	24	20	2	7	0.57
5	30	24	2	6	0.67
Total				30	2.19

$^*\sigma = \left[\frac{(2)^2}{30}(2.19) - \left(\frac{20 - 24}{30}\right)^2\right]^{1/2} = 0.52$ mph/s $= 0.77$ ft/s^2.

Queueing models

Delay resulting from congestion is commonly observed in many types of transportation systems. Vehicles wait in line for an opportunity to make a left turn, riders form a line to board a transit bus, and aircraft form a queue on a taxiway while awaiting permission to take off.

The length of time a user must wait, the number of units waiting in line, or the proportion of time that a facility might be empty (parking stall) are all examples of the type of problems that may be solved with the use of queueing models.

[39] T. R. Jones and R. B. Potts, The Measurement of Acceleration Noise—A Traffic Parameter," *Oper. Res., 10* (6), 745–763 (1962).

[40] D. R. Drew, C. L. Dudek, and C. J. Kreese, "Freeway Level of Service as Described by an Energy-Acceleration Noise Model," *Geometric Aspects of Highways*, Highway Res. Rec. 162, Washington, D.C., 1967, 30–85.

Fundamentals of queueing theory

The elements of a single-channel queueing system are illustrated in Figure 15.15. Of interest are such items as the number of units in the queue, the probability that there are no units in the queue, or the average time a unit waits in the queue. The queue is the number of units waiting to be served (5 units in Figure 15.15). The arrival rate of units is termed λ and the average service rate is μ.

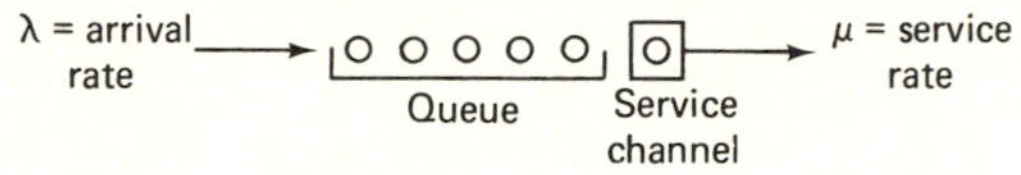

λ = arrival rate → Queue (○ ○ ○ ○ ○) → Service channel (○) → μ = service rate

Figure 15.15. Schematic of a single-channel queueing system.

To predict mathematically the characteristics of a queueing system, it is necessary to specify the following system characteristics and parameters:

1. Arrival pattern characteristics: (a) average rate of arrival λ and (b) statistical distribution of time between arrivals.

2. Service facility characteristics: (a) average rate of service μ, (b) statistical distribution of service time, and (c) the number of units that can be served simultaneously, or number of channels available (1 in Figure 15.15). Arrivals and service may be random where the time between arrivals at a ticket booth and the time it takes to collect a parking fee are both described by the negative exponential distribution. There may be a combination of statistical distributions, as for random arrivals of vehicles at a metered entrance ramp followed by uniformly distributed service times as a vehicle is permitted to enter every 9 s.

3. Queue discipline characteristics, such as the means by which the next unit is to be served: A common discipline is first in, first out (FIFO), such as is usually observed at a traffic signal or a freeway entrance ramp. Other disciplines may occur: for example, last in, first out (LIFO). This condition may occur on a two-lane approach to a signalized intersection where vehicles in the left lane are queued up behind a left-turning vehicle as the right lane empties. The last vehicle in the left lane is the first vehicle to enter the right lane and the queue is emptied from the rear as successive vehicles enter the right lane to bypass the delayed left-turning vehicle.

Single-channel queue. The formulas developed here are based on the assumption that interarrival and service times are exponentially distributed and the queue discipline is first in, first out. Since the arrival rate is λ, the interval between arrivals is $1/\lambda$. If the service rate is μ, the average service time is $1/\mu$. The ratio $\rho = \lambda/\mu$, called the traffic intensity or utilization factor, must be less than one ($\rho < 1$) for the following relationships to apply; otherwise, the queue will continue to grow indefinitely.

1. *Number of units in system.* The number of units in the system includes the number in queue plus the number being served. The probability of no units (an empty system) is

$$P(0) = 1 - \rho \qquad (15.111)$$

The probability of n units in the system is

$$P(n) = \rho^n P(0) \qquad (15.112)$$

2. *Average queue length, E(m).* The average number of units waiting to be served (average queue length) is

$$E(m) = \frac{\rho^2}{1-\rho} = \frac{\lambda^2}{\mu(\mu-\lambda)} \qquad (15.113)$$

3. *Average number in tbe system, E(n).* The average number in the system is the sum of those in queue plus the number being served.

$$E(n) = \frac{\rho}{1-\rho} = \frac{\lambda}{\mu-\lambda} \qquad (15.114)$$

4. *Variance of the number in the system,* var(n). The variance of the number in the system is

$$\text{var}(n) = \frac{\rho}{(1-\rho)^2} = \frac{\lambda\mu}{(\mu-\lambda)^2} \qquad (15.115)$$

5. *Average waiting time, E(w).* The average time an arrival spends waiting before service begins is

$$E(w) = \frac{\lambda}{\mu(\mu-\lambda)} \qquad (15.116)$$

6. *Average time in system, E(v).* The average time, including waiting plus the time being served, is

$$E(v) = \frac{1}{\mu-\lambda} \qquad (15.117)$$

Example of Queueing Calculations for a Single Channel. The exit from a parking facility is through a single exit, where variable fees are collected and change made. Vehicles arrive at a rate λ of 120 veh/h. The time to collect fees is exponentially distributed with a mean duration ($1/\mu$) of 18 s. What are the characteristics of the operation?

$$\lambda = \frac{120}{60} = 2 \text{ veh/min;}$$

$$\mu = \frac{60}{18} = 3\tfrac{1}{3} \text{ veh/min;}$$

$$\rho = \frac{2}{3\tfrac{1}{3}} = 0.60$$

1. The probability of an idle booth $(1 - 0.60) = 0.4$.
2. The probability that n vehicles will be in the system is:

	$P(x = n)$	$P(x \leq n)$
$P(0)$	0.4	0.4
$P(1)$	0.24	0.64
$P(2)$	0.144	0.784
$P(3)$	0.0864	0.8704
$P(4)$	0.05184	0.92224
$P(5)$	0.031104	0.953344

3. If the garage operator wishes to be certain with 0.95 probability that departing vehicles will not interfere with other operations, it will be necessary to provide space for five vehicles, four of which are in queue.

4. $E(m) = \dfrac{(0.6)^2}{1 - 0.6} = 0.90$ vehicle in queue on the average.

5. $E(n) = \dfrac{0.6}{1 - 0.6} = 1.50$ vehicles in system on the average.

6. $E(w) = \dfrac{2}{(10/3)\,(10/3 - 2)} = 0.45$ min average time waiting for service.

7. $E(v) = \dfrac{1}{(10/3) - 2} = 0.75$ min average time in the system.

Multiple-channels queue. A parking lot may be considered as an example of a system with parallel service channels where the K parking slots represent the service channels. Figure 15.16 shows the schematic of a multiple-channel queueing system. It is assumed that the service rate μ_K of each of the K channels is identical. Arrivals are random with rate λ, and $\rho = \lambda/\mu_K$. Further, ρ/K is defined as the utilization factor for the entire facility, representing the mean proportion of busy channels (full parking spaces). For the multiple-channels case, the value of ρ may be greater than 1, but the following formulas apply only for the case where the utilization factor $\rho/K < 1$.

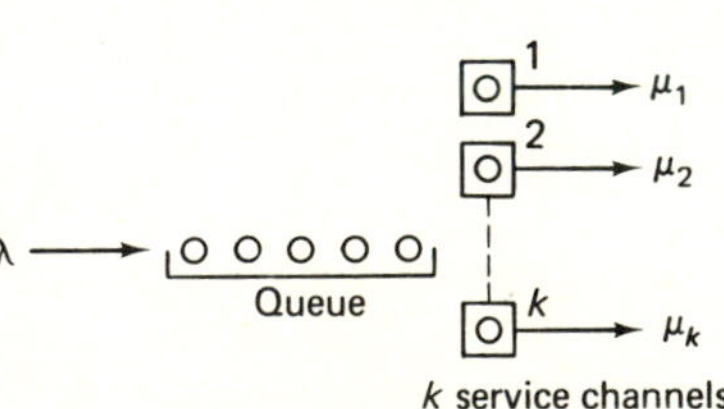

Figure 15.16. Schematic of a multichannel queueing system.

1. Probability of no units in system:

$$P(0) = \frac{1}{\displaystyle\sum_{n=0}^{K-1} \frac{\rho^n}{n!} + \frac{\rho^K}{K!(1 - \rho/K)}} \qquad (15.118)$$

2. Probability of n units in system:

$$P(n) = \begin{cases} \dfrac{\rho^n}{n!} P(0) & \text{for } n \leqslant K \qquad (15.119) \\[2ex] \dfrac{\rho^n}{K^{n-K}K!} P(0) & \text{for } n \geqslant K \qquad (15.120) \end{cases}$$

3. Average queue length:

$$E(m) = \frac{P(0)\rho^{K+1}}{K!K}\left[\frac{1}{(1 - \rho/K)^2}\right] \qquad (15.121)$$

4. Average number in system:

$$E(n) = \rho + E(m) \qquad (15.122)$$

5. Average time an arrival spends in the system:

$$E(v) = \frac{E(n)}{\lambda} \qquad (15.123)$$

6. Average waiting time (time spent in queue):

$$E(w) = E(v) - \frac{1}{\mu} \qquad (15.124)$$

Example of Queueing Calculations for Multiple Channels. Assume that the parking facility is operated with two exits, each capable of serving 3⅓ veh/min (μ). The arrival rates are as previously listed ($\lambda = 2$ veh/min, $\rho = 0.60$).

1. Probability of an idle booth, $P(0)$:
$P(\chi \leqslant \eta)$

$$P(0) = \frac{1}{\displaystyle\sum_{n=0}^{1} \frac{(0.6)^n}{n!} + \frac{(0.6)^2}{2(1 - 0.6/2)}}$$

$$= 0.5385$$

2. $P(1) = \dfrac{0.6}{1}(0.5385) = 0.3231$ 0.8615

$P(2) = \dfrac{(0.6)^2}{2}(0.5385)$

$= \dfrac{(0.6)^2}{(2)^{2-2}(2)}(0.5385) = 0.0969$ 0.9585

$P(3) = \dfrac{(0.6)^3}{(2)^{3-2}(2)}(0.5385) = 0.0291$ 0.9875

3. If the garage operator continues to be satisfied with 0.95 probability that departing vehicles will not interfere with other operations, the two booths are all that are necessary to provide space for the exiting vehicles.

4. $E(m) = \dfrac{0.5385(0.6)^3}{2(2)}\left[\dfrac{1}{(1 - 0.6/2)^2}\right] = 0.0593$ vehicle waiting on the average.

5. $E(n) = 0.60 + 0.0593 = 0.6593$ vehicle in system on the average.

6. $E(v) = 0.6593/2 = 0.3297$ min average in the system.

7. $E(w) = 0.3997 - \dfrac{1}{10/3} = 0.0297$ min average waiting for service.

By opening a second channel, the number of vehicles and the time spent waiting are both reduced. If there are no vehicles in the system, both booths are idle; if there is one vehicle in the system, there is one idle booth, so that the proportion of time that one or more booths will be idle is $(0.5385 + 0.3231) = 0.8651$.

Delays at intersections

Applications of queueing theory to problems represented by traffic situations are more complex than those developed for single and multiple channels. The time a unit waits in line at an unsignalized intersection is a function of a combination of gap acceptance characteristics, the passage of gaps in the main stream, and the characteristics of the waiting stream of traffic. There is a difference between the behavior of pedestrians and vehicles crossing an intersection, because pedestrians can accept a gap as a cluster, whereas a vehicle cannot accept a gap until it has waited to be first in line at the intersection.

This section will consider the definitions of blocks and gaps, pedestrian delay, and vehicular delay at unsignalized intersections and vehicular delay at signalized intersections.

Blocks, gaps, intervals, and lags. A stream of traffic may be considered as the passage of a succession of vehicles, or a succession of gaps, or a succession of blocks, as shown in Figure 15.17, where the time of arrival of main-street vehicles is shown on a time scale (events 2 to 9). Event 1 is the arrival of a cross-street vehicle. Raff[41] and Oliver[42] have considered the problem of defining the inter-vehicle intervals that might be considered as acceptable to a crossing or merging vehicle.

Intervals 2 to 9 are time intervals h between the arrival of main-street vehicles at the projected path of the crossing side-street vehicle. Interval 1, a lag, is defined as the time from the arrival of the side-street vehicle to the passage of the next main-street vehicle. If h is greater than the critical headway τ, the waiting driver or pedestrian will cross; otherwise, the driver will continue to wait.

Intervals 2, 6, 7, and 9 are each greater than τ, but only a portion of these four intervals is available for crossing. Raff has defined the time when no crossing is possible as a "block"; conversely, the remaining time is defined as "antiblocks." Oliver defined any time interval ($h > \tau$) as a gap and the remaining intervals as nongaps. Time intervals 2, 6, 7, and 9 are each a gap; time intervals 3, 4, and 5 are grouped into a single nongap; intervals 1 and 8 are also nongaps. The number of vehicles in an intergap headway (events 2 to 6) is defined as the number occurring just after the vehicle (or event) defining the start of a gap, but including the last vehicle that defines the end of the nongap. For example, the first intergap headway in Figure 15.17 contains four vehicles (3, 4, 5, and 6); the second intergap headway contains one vehicle, 7.

Pedestrian delay at unsignalized intersections. Pedestrian delay at an unsignalized intersection was first treated by Adams[43] in 1936. He assumed that pedestrian and vehicle

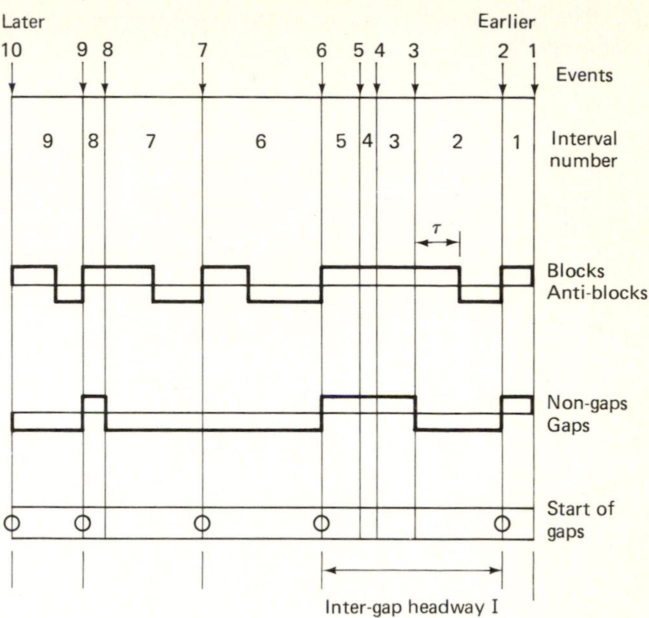

Figure 15.17. Definitions of time interval for stream flow.

arrivals are random (Poisson-distributed) and verified his results with field observations. If it is assumed that the main-street flow is q (veh/s) and that a minimum interval τ (the critical gap in seconds) is required between successive arrivals on the main street for a pedestrian to cross safely, by equation (15.46) the probability that a pedestrian will pass without delay is

$$P(h > \tau) = e^{-q\tau} \tag{15.125}$$

while the probability that a pedestrian will be delayed is

$$P_d = 1 - e^{-q\tau} \tag{15.126}$$

Of particular interest is the time a pedestrian must wait (block time) for an appropriate antiblock in order to cross the roadway. Roadway events are considered relative to the passage of vehicles over an elapsed time t, during which the number of events is the accumulated volume qt. Further, the mean headway $1/q$ is defined as T.

The average duration (seconds) of all gaps is

$$T + \tau \tag{15.127}$$

The average duration of all nongaps is

$$T - \frac{\tau e^{-q\tau}}{1 - e^{-q\tau}} \tag{15.128}$$

The average duration of all blocks is

$$(T/e^{-q\tau}) - T \tag{15.129}$$

The average duration of all antiblocks is T

The average delay for all pedestrians $E(d)$ is

$$\frac{1}{qe^{-q\tau}} - T - \tau \tag{15.131}$$

[41]M. A. Raff, *A Volume Warrant for Urban Stop Signs*, Eno Foundation for Highway Traffic Control, Saugatuck, Conn., 1950, pp. 62–75.

[42]R. M. Oliver, "Distribution of Gaps and Blocks in a Traffic Stream," *Oper. Res., 10* (2) 197–217 (1962).

[43]W. R. Adams, "Road Traffic Considered as a Random Series," *J. Inst. Civ. Eng., 4,* 121–130 (1936).

The average delay for only those pedestrians who are delayed $E(d_d)$ is

$$\frac{1}{qe^{-q\tau}} - \frac{\tau}{1 - e^{-q\tau}} \qquad (15.132)$$

As an example of the application of these formulas, consider the case in which pedestrians are crossing a wide street where the critical gap τ = 10.0 s. The flow rate is 720 veh/h, so that q = 0.2 veh/s and $T = 1/q$ = 5.0 s. The proportion delayed, by equation (15.126), is

$$1 - e^{-0.2(10)} = 0.86$$

The average duration of all gaps, by equation (15.127), is

$$5.0 + 10.0 = 15.0 \text{ s}$$

The average duration of all nongaps, by equation (15.128), is

$$5.0 - \frac{10e^{-0.2(10)}}{1 - e^{-0.2(10)}} = 3.43 \text{ s}$$

The average duration of all blocks, by equation (15.129), is

$$\left[5/e^{-0.2(10)}\right] - 5 = 31.95 \text{ s}$$

The average duration of all antiblocks, by equation (15.130), is 5.0 s.

The average delay to all pedestrians, by equation (15.131), is

$$\frac{1}{0.2e^{-0.2(10)}} - 5 - 10 = 21.95 \text{ s}$$

The average delay per delayed pedestrian, by equation (15.132), is

$$\frac{1}{0.2e^{-0.2(10)}} - \frac{10}{1 - e^{-0.2(10)}}$$
$$= 36.95 - 11.57$$
$$= 25.38 \text{ s}$$

The formulas developed above will also give the delay for crossing vehicles if the cross-street traffic volume is so low that there are no queues formed, so that any waiting vehicle can cross if the gap is sufficiently large.

Tanner[44] considered the problem of the distribution of the size of pedestrian groups crossing together. The average size of a group crossing together is

$$E(n_c) = \frac{pe^{p\tau} + qe^{-q\tau}}{(p + q)e^{(p-q)\tau}} \qquad (15.133)$$

where p is the pedestrian flow rate and q is vehicular flow. The average number of pedestrians waiting to cross is

$$E(n_w) = \frac{p}{q}(e^{q\tau} - q^{\tau} - 1) \qquad (15.134)$$

[44]J. C. TANNER, "The Delay to Pedestrians Crossing a Road," *Biometrika, 38,* 383–392 (1951).

In the previous discussion of pedestrian delay, it is assumed that distributions of headways on the main street were negative exponential. Mayne[45] generalized Tanner's results to include an arbitrary distribution of main-street headways. Weiss and Maradudin[46] and Herman and Weiss[47] applied renewal theory, which permits the consideration of "yield sign" delay where the critical lag of a crossing vehicle is a function of whether the vehicle is moving or stopped. They also considered the case for the impatient driver, where the probability of accepting a gap of given size increases with time. Assuming Poisson-distributed main-street flow with mean headway T and a shifted exponential gap acceptance, the mean delay to side-street traffic is

$$E(d) = \frac{e^{q\tau} - 1}{q} - \tau + \frac{1}{b}[e^{q\tau} - 1 - q^{\tau}$$
$$+ (\frac{q}{q + b})^2(1 + q\tau + b\tau)(1 - e^{-q\tau}) \qquad (15.135)$$
$$+ e^{-q\tau}(\frac{q}{q + b} + q\tau)]$$

in which τ is the minimum acceptable gap and b the parameter of the shifted exponential gap acceptance distribution, which equals $1/(T - \tau)$. Equation (15.135) may be compared to equation (15.131), where the gap acceptance is constant.

For the "yield sign" problem, where a moving vehicle requires a gap of τ_1 and a stopped vehicle requires a gap of τ_2, Weiss and Maradudin find the mean delay to be

$$E(d) = \frac{e^{q\tau_2}}{q}(1 - e^{-q\tau_1}) + e^{-q\tau_1}(\tau_2 - \tau_1) - \tau_2 \qquad (15.136)$$

Vehicular delay at unsignalized intersections. The preceding section considers delay only to a first-in-line vehicle and makes no allowance for waiting in a queue prior to being first in line. Major and Buckley[48] considered an inexhaustible queue of vehicles on a side street under the following conditions: when a main-street headway is less than τ, no vehicle enters; when a main-street headway is between τ and 2τ, one vehicle enters; when a main-street headway is between 2τ and 3τ, two vehicles enter; and so on. The number of vehicles N that can enter from the side street is found as follows:

Size of Headway	Number of Vehicles Entering Headway	Number of Headways This Size per Unit Time
Less than τ	0	$q(1 - e^{-q\tau})$
τ–2τ	1	$q(e^{-q\tau} - e^{-2q\tau})$
2τ–3τ	2	$q(e^{-2q\tau} - e^{-3q\tau})$
3τ–4τ	3	$q(e^{-3q\tau} - e^{-4q\tau})$
etc.		

[45]A. J. MAYNE, "Some Further Results in the Theory of Pedestrian and Road Traffic," *Biometrika, 41,* 375–389 (1954).

[46]G. H. WEISS AND A. A. MARADUDIN, "Some Problems in Traffic Delay," *Oper. Res., 10* (1) 74–104 (1962).

[47]R. HERMAN AND G. H. WEISS, "Comments on the Highway Crossing Problem, *Oper. Res., 9* (4), 828–840 (1961).

[48]N. G. MAJOR AND D. J. BUCKLEY, "Entry to a Traffic Stream," *Proc. Australian Road Res. Bd.,* 206–228 (1962).

The number of vehicles that will enter or cross the main-street flow per unit of time (capacity of cross flow) is

$$N = q(e^{-q\tau} - e^{-2q\tau}) + 2q(e^{-2q\tau} - e^{-3q\tau}) + 3q(e^{-3q\tau} - e^{-4q\tau}) + \cdots$$
$$= qe^{-q\tau} + qe^{-2q\tau} + qe^{-3q\tau} + \cdots$$

from which

$$N = \frac{qe^{-q\tau}}{1 - e^{-q\tau}} \qquad (15.137)$$

A more realistic assumption is that the headway for following vehicles is β_2, so that two vehicles require a headway of $\tau + \beta_2$, and three vehicles require $\tau + 2\beta_2$, and so on. Provided that $\beta_2 \leqslant \tau$, equation (15.137) becomes

$$N = \frac{qe^{-q\tau}}{1 - e^{-q\beta_2}} \qquad (15.138)$$

Ashworth[49] modified the approach used by Major and Buckley by assuming that the critical gap of the driver is τ_1 whereas that of the second driver is τ_2 seconds. Further, he assumed a move-up time equal to a constant β_2 seconds, during which time, following the departure of the vehicle at the head of the queue, the second vehicle moves into the front position but is unable to take advantage of any suitable gap offered. With these assumptions, he gives the average waiting delay at the head of the queue for those vehicles actually delayed:

$$E(d_d) = l + (e^{q\tau_2 - 1})\left(T - \frac{\tau_2 e^{-q\tau_2}}{1 - e^{q\tau_2}}\right) \qquad (15.139)$$

where

$$l = \frac{1 + q(\tau_1 - \beta_2) - e^{q(\tau_1 - \tau_2 - \beta_2)}(1 + q\tau_2)}{q[1 - e^{q(\tau_1 - \tau_2 - \beta_2)}]}$$

and $T = 1/q$.

The average waiting delay for all vehicles (provided that $\tau_2 > \tau_1 - \beta_2$) is

$$E(d) = \tau_1 - \tau_2 - \beta_2 + T\,[e^{q\tau_2} - e^{q(\tau_1 - \beta_2)}] \qquad (15.140)$$

Equations (15.140) and (15.139) may be compared to (15.131) and (15.132), respectively, where the latter two equations consider delay for the pedestrian case.

Signalized intersections. Queueing at a signalized intersection occurs during the red phase on each approach, and queues become longer as the approach volume nears the capacity of the approach. This section will consider a continuum model and several probability models.

Vehicles are considered as consisting of identical passenger car units (PCU). A truck, for example, may be considered as 1.5 or 2 PCU and a turning vehicle may be assigned a value depending on the type of maneuver and delays to that maneuver (such as pedestrians).

The following notation, after Allsop,[50] is used. Let

c = cycle time, s

g = effective green time, s

r = effective red time, s

q = average arrival rate of traffic on the approach, PCU/s

$I = \dfrac{\text{variance}}{\text{mean}}$ of number of PCU arriving in one signal cycle

s = saturation flow on the approach, PCU/s

d = average delay to PCU on the approach, s

Q_0 = overflow, PCU

$\lambda = g/c$, proportion of the cycle that is effectively green

$y = q/s$, ratio of average arrival rate to saturation flow

$x = qc/gs$, ratio of average number of arrivals per cycle to the maximum number of departures per cycle

Then $r + g = c$ and $\lambda x = y$. The ratio x is called the degree of saturation of the approach and y will be called the flow ratio of the approach.

The effective green time is the portion of the cycle time during which PCU are assumed to pass the signal at a constant rate s as long as there are vehicles waiting on the approach. Greenshields et al.,[51] for example, reported that the total time for a queue of n stopped vehicles to pass a signal can be given by

$$\text{total time} = 14.2 + 2.1(n - 5) \text{ seconds} \qquad (n \geqslant 5)$$

Had all the vehicles departed at the saturation rate s (1/2.1), the first five vehicles would have required 10.5 s, so that the effective green is the signal green time less 3.7 s. In most studies, it is assumed that a waiting queue of vehicles will take advantage of the yellow clearance interval, although the effective green time may be adjusted to reflect particular operating conditions.

Continuum model for pretimed signals. A representation of a continuum model proposed by May[52] is shown in Figure 15.18. The vertical axis represents the cumulative arrivals qt and the horizontal axis the time t. Case I represents the behavior when the capacity of the green interval exceeds the arrivals during the green + red time. Case II is concerned with the instance when the discharge during the green phase is equal to the arrivals during the green + red period. In Figure 15.18, the vertical distance c–a represents the number of vehicles that have accumulated since the signal entered the red phase. The horizontal distance a–b represents the total time from arrival to departure for any given vehicle.

May developed the following measures of queue behavior:

---

[49]R. Ashworth, "The Capacity of Priority Type Intersections with a Non-uniform Distribution of Critical Acceptance Gaps," *Transport. Res.*, *3* (2) 273–278 (1969).

[50]R. E. Allsop, "Delay at a Fixed-Time Signal I: Theoretical Analysis," *Transport. Sci.*, *6* (3), 260–285 (1972).

[51]B. D. Greenshields, D. Schapiro, and E. L. Erickson, *Traffic Performance at Urban Intersections*, Bureau of Highway Traffic, Yale University Press, New Haven, Conn., 1947.

[52]A. D. May, Jr., "Traffic Flow Theory—The Traffic Engineer's Challenge," *Proc. Inst. Traffic Eng.*, 290–303 (1965).

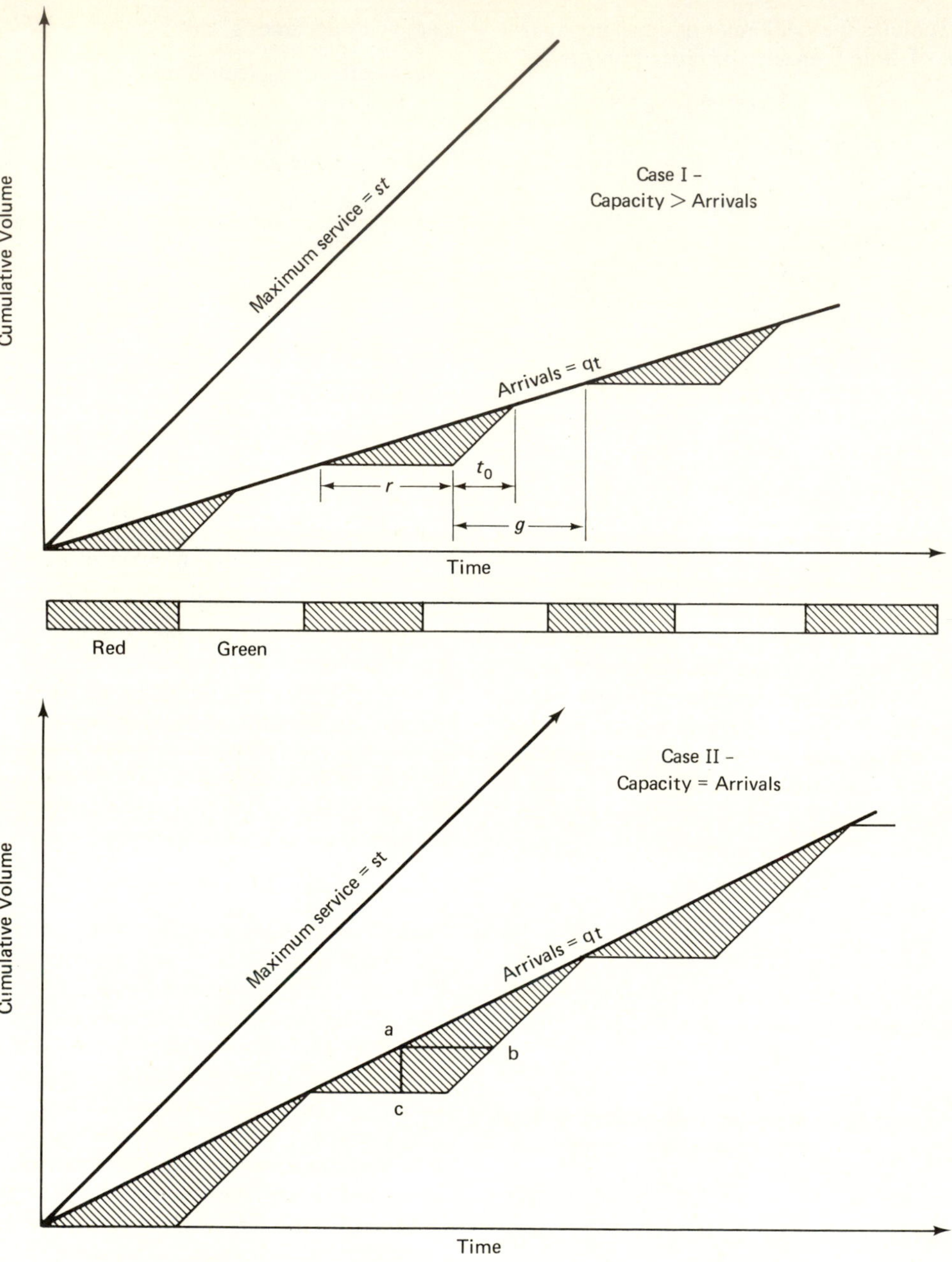

Figure 15.18. Representation of queueing at signalized intersection.

1. Time after start of green that queue is dissipated (t_0)
2. Proportion of cycle with queue (P_q)
3. Proportion of vehicles stopped (P_s)
4. Maximum number of vehicles in queue (Q_m)
5. Average number of vehicles in queue ($\overline{Q}$)
6. Total vehicle hours of delay per cycle (D)
7. Average individual vehicles delay (d)
8. Maximum individual vehicular delay (d_m)

The formulas for these two cases are developed from simple geometric relationships.

1. For any given cycle, it is evident that at time t_0 after the start of green, the arrivals equal the discharge:

$$q(r + t_0) = st_0$$

Letting $y = q/s$ yields

$$t_0 = \frac{yr}{1 - y} \tag{15.141}$$

2. Proportion of cycle with queue is equal to queue time/cycle length:

$$P_q = \frac{r + t_0}{c} \tag{15.142}$$

3. Proportion of vehicles stopped is equal to vehicles stopped/total vehicles per cycle:

$$P_s = \frac{q(r + t_0)}{q(r + g)} = \frac{t_0}{yc} \tag{15.143}$$

4. The maximum vehicles in queue will be seen by inspection to be the height of the triangle at r units after start of red:

$$Q_m = qr \tag{15.144}$$

5. The average number of vehicles in the queue, over the total length of cycle c, is

$$\overline{Q} = \frac{(qr/2)r + (qr/2)t_0 + 0(q - t_0)}{r + t_0 + q - t_0}$$

which yields

$$\overline{Q} = \frac{r + t_0}{c}\frac{qr}{2} \tag{15.145}$$

6. The total vehicle time of delay is given by the area of the triangle

$$\begin{aligned} D &= \frac{qr}{2}(r + t_0) \\ &= \frac{qr}{2}\frac{r}{1 - y} \\ &= \frac{qr^2}{2(1 - y)} \end{aligned} \tag{15.146}$$

7. The average individual delay is given by dividing the total delay by the number of vehicles:

$$\begin{aligned} d &= \frac{qr^2}{2(1 - y)}\frac{1}{qc} \\ &= \frac{r^2}{2c(1 - y)} \end{aligned} \tag{15.147}$$

8. The maximum individual vehicular delay will be seen from Figure 8.16 to be

$$d_m = r \tag{15.148}$$

If the departures $sc <$ arrivals qc, the queue grows with each successive cycle and the foregoing formulas are not applicable.

Probability models for pretimed signals. Several models have been used to describe the arrivals at intersections. The simplest approach is to use regular arrivals as in the continuum model. Beckmann et al.[53] used binomial arrivals, and the Poisson model has been used by Adams,[54] Webster,[55] and Wardrop.[56] Newell[57] used a model in which the arrivals were assumed to have a shifted exponential distribution.

Most models for the departure of PCU from a traffic signal queue assume departures at equal time intervals $1/s$. Other departure models have been proposed, but the choice of departure model does not affect delay calculations as does the choice of arrival model.

Allsop[58] shows that if arrivals are regular at intervals $1/q$ (a step function rather than the continuous functions as shown in Figure 15.18), the average delay per vehicle in seconds is

$$d = \left[\frac{1}{2c(1 - y)}\right]\left(r - \frac{1}{2s}\right)^2 + \frac{y(2 - y) + \theta(1 - y)^2}{12q^2} \tag{15.149}$$

where θ is in the range

$$-\frac{1}{3 \times 3^{1/2}} < \theta < \frac{1}{3 \times 3^{1/2}}$$

and c, q, r, s, and y are as previously defined. The first term of equation (15.149) is the same as that developed by Wardrop:

$$d = \frac{\left(r - \frac{1}{2s}\right)^2}{2c(1 - y)} \tag{15.150}$$

If q is allowed to increase indefinitely (the ratio $y = q/s$ remaining constant) in equation (15.149) the average delay per vehicle will tend to $d = r^2/[2c(1 - y)]$, the result given in equation (15.148) from a continuum model.

Webster used computer simulation to develop a formula for delay:

$$d = \frac{c(1 - \lambda)^2}{2(1 - \lambda x)} + \frac{x^2}{2q(1 - x)} - 0.65\left(\frac{c}{q^2}\right)^{1/3} x^{(2 + 5\lambda)} \tag{15.151}$$

Because $c(1 - \lambda) = r$ and $\lambda x = y$, the first term is the same as that obtained by assuming continuous flow, equation (15.148). Allsop demonstrates that the second term may be obtained by assuming that a queue with constant service $1/\lambda s$ is interposed between the signal and the arriving traffic, where the mean waiting time is $x^2/[2q(1 - x)]$. The third term is a correction term representing 5 to 15% of the total delay, so that equation (15.151) may be simplified to

$$d = \frac{9}{10}\left[\frac{c(1 - \lambda)^2}{2(1 - \lambda x)} + \frac{x^2}{2q(1 - x)}\right] \tag{15.152}$$

Hutchinson[59] made numerical comparisons of the delay expressions listed in this section on probability models and concluded that the results are sufficiently similar that convenience and simplicity of calculations may dictate the choice of model.

Queueing models at bottlenecks

A bottleneck on a roadway may result in a partial or total reduction in traffic flow. The case of total reduction is the

[53] M. Beckmann, C. B. McGuire, and C. B. Winsten, *Studies in the Economics of Transportation*, Yale University Press, New Haven, Conn., 1956.

[54] Adams, "Road Traffic Considered as a Random Series."

[55] F. V. Webster, *Traffic Signal Settings*, Road Res. Tech. Pap. No. 39, Great Britain Road Research Laboratory, 1958.

[56] Wardrop, "Some Theoretical Aspects of Road Traffic Research."

[57] G. F. Newell, "Statistical Analysis of the Flow of Highway Traffic through a Signalized Intersection," *Quart. Appl. Math.*, *13*, 353–369 (1956).

[58] Allsop, "Delay at Fixed Time Traffic Signal I: Theoretical Analysis."

[59] T. P. Hutchinson, "Delay at a Fixed Time Signal II: Numerical Comparisons of Some Theoretical Expressions," *Transport. Sci.*, *6* (3), 286–305 (1972).

same as that for a traffic signal. The bottleneck may be considered the server and the queue of delayed vehicles the customers.

May[60] applied the technique of continuum flow to the problem of the temporary bottleneck (i.e., a roadway blocked by a rail crossing or a single lane blocked by an accident). The problem may be represented by the behavior of a queue during one cycle of a traffic signal (Figure 15.18), where the duration of the delay or blockade is equivalent to the length of the red interval r and the time for the queue to dissipate after the blockade is removed is the same as time t_o in Figure 15.18.

The following notation, similar to that used for signalized intersections, will be used for May's roadway model. Let

q = average arrival rate of traffic (vehicle per minute) upstream of the bottleneck

s = saturation flow rate or capacity (vehicles per minute) of uninterrupted flow

s_r = flow rate (vehicles per minute) at bottlenecks during blockade ($s_r < q < s$)

r = duration of blockade, min

t_o = time for queue to dissipate after blockade is removed, min

t_q = total elapsed time from start of blockade until free flow resumes ($= r + t_o$), min

The value of s_r may be zero when the roadway is completely blocked, as for an at-grade railroad crossing, or some value ($s_r < q$) when the roadway is partially blocked by a disabled vehicle. May developed the following set of relationships:

duration of queue,

$$t_q = r\left(\frac{s - s_r}{s - q}\right) \tag{15.153}$$

number of vehicles affected,

$$N = qt_q \tag{15.154}$$

maximum number of vehicles in queue,

$$Q_m = r(q - s_r) \tag{15.155}$$

average number of vehicles in queue,

$$\overline{Q} = \frac{Q_m}{2} \tag{15.156}$$

total vehicle minutes of delay,

$$D = \frac{r(q - s_r)tq}{2} \tag{15.157}$$

average minutes vehicle delay,

$$d = \frac{r}{2}\left(1 - \frac{s_r}{q}\right) \tag{15.158}$$

[60]MAY, "Traffic Flow Theory—The Traffic Engineer's Challenge."

maximum minutes individual delay,

$$d_m = r\left(1 - \frac{s_r}{q}\right) \tag{15.159}$$

May and Keller[61] have applied a similar technique to analyze the behavior of queueing vehicles during rush-hour traffic. For this problem it is assumed that the capacity flow of the roadway s remains constant but that the demand q varies from some value less than s, equals s, and then reaches a maximum rate $q_2 > s$. They consider two cases for the shape of the demand curve:

1. Trapezoidal—demand increases at constant rate to maximum q_2, remains at q_2 for a fixed time, and then decreases as a constant rate to a constant post-peak demand.
2. Triangular—demand increases at constant rate to q_2 and then immediately decreases at a constant rate to a constant post-peak demand.

By analysis, similar to that used for bottlenecks, it is possible to calculate values of delay, queue length, and duration of queue.

McNeil[62] assumed that the bottleneck is a queueing model with random (Poisson) arrivals and a uniform service time for a single queue. The service time for the first vehicle in the queue b_1 is the time it is delayed s_1 plus the time a_1 for its effective length (front bumper to front bumper of following vehicle) to clear the block point. The time s_1 could vary from a few seconds in the event of a short delay to several minutes in the event of a vehicle breakdown.

Each subsequent vehicle in the queue is assumed to have a service time b_1 which is made up of the departure period s_i plus the time a_i for each vehicle to clear its own effective length. The departure period s_i, $i = 1, 2, 3, \ldots$, is a sequence of independent identically distributed variables with a mean value corresponding to the headway at the maximum flow rate. The value of a_i is constant for all vehicles, including the first, and is the effective length over the mean velocity V. The first and subsequent vehicles are each assumed to resume speed V instantly after passing the point of blockage.

The results of this model are as follows. Let

$E(b) = E(a) + E(s)$

= mean service time of all vehicles after the first

$E(b_1) = E(a_1) + E(s_1)$

= mean service time of first delayed vehicle

q = normal arrival rate at the bottleneck (vehicles per minute)

$\rho = qE(b)$

$\rho_1 = qE(b_1)$

$\rho_A = qE(a)$

[61]A. D. MAY, JR., AND H. E. M. KELLER, "A Deterministic Queueing Model," *Transport. Res., 1*, 117–128 (1967).

[62]D. R. MCNEIL, "Growth and Dissipation of a Traffic Jam," *Transport. Res., 3*, 115–121 (1969).

where $C_1^2 = \mathrm{var}(b_1)/E^2(b_1)$

$C_b^2 = \mathrm{var}(b)/E^2(b)$

Then

$$E(N) = 1 + \frac{\rho_1}{1 - \rho} = \text{total number of vehicles affected} \quad (15.160)$$

$$\begin{aligned} E(W) &= E(s_1) + \tfrac{1}{2}qE(s_1\, b_1) \\ &\quad + \tfrac{1}{2}\rho_1 [(2 + \rho_1 + \rho_1 C_1^2)E(s) + q \operatorname{cov}(s, b)] \\ &\quad (1 - \rho)^{-1} \\ &\quad + \tfrac{1}{2}\rho\rho_1 E(s)(1 + \rho C_b^2)(1 - \rho)^{-2} \\ &= \text{total vehicle delay time (vehicle-minutes)} \end{aligned} \quad (15.161)$$

where cov (s, b) is the covariance between the headway s and the service time b, and

$$\begin{aligned} E(t_q) &= E(s_1) + E(s)E(n - 1) \\ &= \text{duration of queue} \end{aligned} \quad (15.162)$$

REFERENCES FOR FURTHER READING

ASHTON, W. D., *The Theory of Road Traffic Flow*. New York: Wiley, 1966.

DREW, D. R., *Traffic Flow Theory and Control*. New York: McGraw-Hill, 1967.

GAZIS, D. C., *Traffic Science*. New York: Wiley, 1974.

GERLOUGH, D. L., AND M. J. HUBER, *Traffic Flow Theory*, Spec. Report 165. Washington, D.C.: Transportation Research Board, 1975.

HAIGHT, F. A., *Mathematical Theories of Traffic Flow*. New York: Academic Press, 1963.

WOHL, M., AND B. V. MARTIN, *Traffic System Analysis for Engineers and Planners*. New York: McGraw-Hill, 1967.

16

HIGHWAY CAPACITY AND LEVELS OF SERVICE

ARTHUR A. CARTER, JR., *Chief*

Traffic Characteristics Branch, Office of Traffic Operations
Federal Highway Administration, Washington, D.C.
and

DAVID R. MERRITT, *Highway Engineer*

Traffic Characteristics Branch, Office of Traffic Operations
Federal Highway Administration, Washington, D.C.
and

CARLTON C. ROBINSON, *Executive Vice President for Operations*

Highway Users Federation for Safety and Mobility
Washington, D.C.

Capacity: general

Broadly speaking, the capacity of a traffic facility is the measure of its ability to accommodate a stream of moving vehicles. It is a rate instead of a quantity and is not directly comparable to the capacity of a container or enclosed space. All flow rates, including maximum "capacity," of a facility can be affected by a number of factors—the roadway, vehicle performance characteristics, operational controls, and environmental elements. The basic determinant, however, is the driver and the summation of control decisions made by a group of drivers under the particular roadway, traffic stream, and environmental conditions present. Thus, highway capacity is inherently variable because the control decisions made by members of any large group of drivers and even by the same driver in two successive time periods will not be identical.

This characteristic of variability, incidentally, makes it difficult to combine capacity estimates from different countries. Although concepts may be similar, specific values are likely to vary considerably because of driver behavior differences. This chapter is based principally on American findings and procedures. Where procedures from other countries are included, they are identified.

Capacity defined

The term "highway capacity" has two meanings, one broad and the other specific. In the broad sense, it is an abbreviation for "highway capacity and levels of service," covering the whole range of traffic performance on a highway facility, from very low volumes up to the maximum volume reasonably attainable.

More specifically, "highway capacity" refers to the maximum number of vehicles that a highway element can be expected to accommodate under a given set of conditions. Under ideal roadway and environmental conditions and with the most homogeneous group of drivers and vehicles ever likely to occur in normal highway usage, the capacity of a single traffic lane is approximately 2400 passenger vehicles per hour. This volume would be produced by average headways of 1.5 s. Such average headways have been observed for short time periods and, on rare occasions, for an entire hour in the central lanes of a freeway built to high design standards. The combinations of circumstances that permit these high flow rates are extremely rare and, if momentarily present, would result in a highly unstable condition. This seldom-reached value is rarely used in calculations. Rather, it is taken as the absolute upper bound of capacity flow rates.

A more useful value than that described above is the *maximum number of vehicles that have a reasonable expectation of passing over a given roadway in a given time period under the prevailing roadway and traffic conditions*. This is the definition of capacity published by the Transportation Research Board in the *Highway Capacity Manual, 1965*[1] and generally followed in American practice. The capacities of various roadway configurations determined by observation under "ideal" prevailing conditions are given in Table 16-1. Although these values could change if there were a radical change in vehicle characteristics, driver competence or other external factors, observations over 50 years

[1]*Highway Capacity Manual, 1965*, Spec. Report 87, Highway Research Board (now Transportation Research Board) (Washington, D.C.: Highway Research Board, 1965), p. 5.

TABLE 16-1
Capacity under Ideal Conditions

Highway Type	Capacity Passenger Cars/Hour
Moving traffic	
Two or more lanes in one direction	2000 average per lane
Two lanes in two directions	2000 total both directions
Three lanes in two directions	4000 total both directions
Getaway from a stopped condition	1500 per lane (no opposing traffic)

SOURCE: *Highway Capacity Manual, 1965*, Special Report 87 (Washington, D.C.: Highway Research Board, 1965), pp. 76–77.

in the United States as well as recent studies in other parts of the world suggest that they are relatively stable.

Even the values in Table 16-1 are of only limited use because the "ideal" conditions necessary to sustain these capacity flows are usually not present. The more typical problem is to determine the capacity of a facility when some factors are less than ideal. In any event, when a facility is serving capacity-level volumes, the quality of service provided to the user is poor in terms of safety, freedom to maneuver, and speed.

Levels of service and service volumes

Normally, the engineer's problem is to determine the *service volume* that can be accommodated while providing the user with a specified *level of service* that is better than that obtained under capacity operation.

The objective of a transportation facility is to accommodate a *quantity* of traffic demand with an acceptable *quality* of service. The quality is apparent to the user in terms of freedom to follow a chosen path and speed, and the relative ease and physical and mental comfort of operation. Even though not directly conscious of it, drivers are also affected by the degree of hazard to which they are subjected, the relative probability of failure to meet their transportation objectives, and the total cost of the service. All of these measures of quality vary as some function of the ratio of the rate of flow to the capacity of the facility. Some, such as driver comfort, are largely unmeasured—and perhaps unmeasurable. Others, such as speed capability, are better established.

Figure 16.1 shows, in two different forms, the relationships of some of the better understood measures of quality of flow to the volume/capacity ratio and to the various levels of service for uninterrupted flow conditions. The relationships among speed, volume, and density implicit in the figures are precisely correct only if space mean speed is utilized, as in Figure 16.1(a). The relationships are conceptually but not precisely correct for the speed measures normally used in practice, such as operating speed, shown in the familiar speed–volume curve format of Figure 16.1(b). Because most speed measurements in the field are taken at a point, they reflect average speed, or time mean speed. Further, most capacity and service level descriptions in current American practice are in terms of operating speed. *Operating speed,* as defined in the *Highway Capacity Manual, 1965* and used herein, is the *highest overall speed at which a driver can travel on a given roadway under favorable weather conditions and prevailing traffic conditions without at any time exceeding the safe speed as determined by the design speed.* Its value will always be higher than either of the mean speed values but less than (or equal to) the design speed, which is the maximum safe speed at which vehicles can travel on the highway as designed.

Neither this figure, nor the basic speed–volume relationships on which the level of service criteria that follow are based, reflect the influence of an enforced speed limit. Rather, they represent basic driver desires. With respect to the national 55 mph (89 km/h) speed limit in the United States, it is assumed that, although many drivers tolerate it, most still would like to drive faster. That is, they visualize a quality of service, with respect to speed and travel time, better than that which is legally attainable. In fact, some violate the law to attain that level.

Level of service as used in this chapter is *a qualitative measure that incorporates the collective factors of speed, travel time, traffic interruptions, freedom to maneuver, safety, driving comfort and convenience, and operating costs provided by a highway facility under a particular volume condition.* The maximum volume associated with a particular level of service is termed the *service volume.*

It would be desirable to know and make use of all of the foregoing factors in defining specific levels of service and associated service volumes. The present state of the art and the practicalities of traffic measurement prevent this. In dealing with uninterrupted flow conditions, speed and volume have been the criteria most frequently cited because they are relatively simple to measure and understand. Density, however, is being increasingly used as a substitute for volume in certain applications because it reflects the phenomenon of headway, which is the only variable other than speed over which the individual driver has functional control. Because most of the factors cited presumably vary as a continuous, rather than a step, function of volume, speed, or density, division of the continuum into steps or ranges is based on a combination of theoretical and practical considerations. For computational purposes, volume is represented by the volume/capacity ratio in the *Highway Capacity Manual, 1965* procedures.

The practice of describing and labeling the various levels of service greatly facilitates communication both within and outside the profession and has been generally accepted. Its principal danger lies in the attribution of a precision to the commonly cited boundary points of service levels that is unjustified by either the state of current knowledge or the basic characteristics of highway traffic flow phenomena. The level-of-service descriptions that follow and the criteria given in later sections should be considered with that caution in mind.

The description, measurement, and illustration of the several service levels is easiest for freeways, because the range of speeds and volumes included is greatest. It is rather difficult to do for urban arterials, because of the limited speed range, and must be handled in a different way for intersections where speed has only indirect meaning. For illustrative purposes, therefore, freeways are shown here.

Level of service A is the highest quality of service a particular class of highway can provide. It is a condition of free flow in which there is little or no restriction on speed

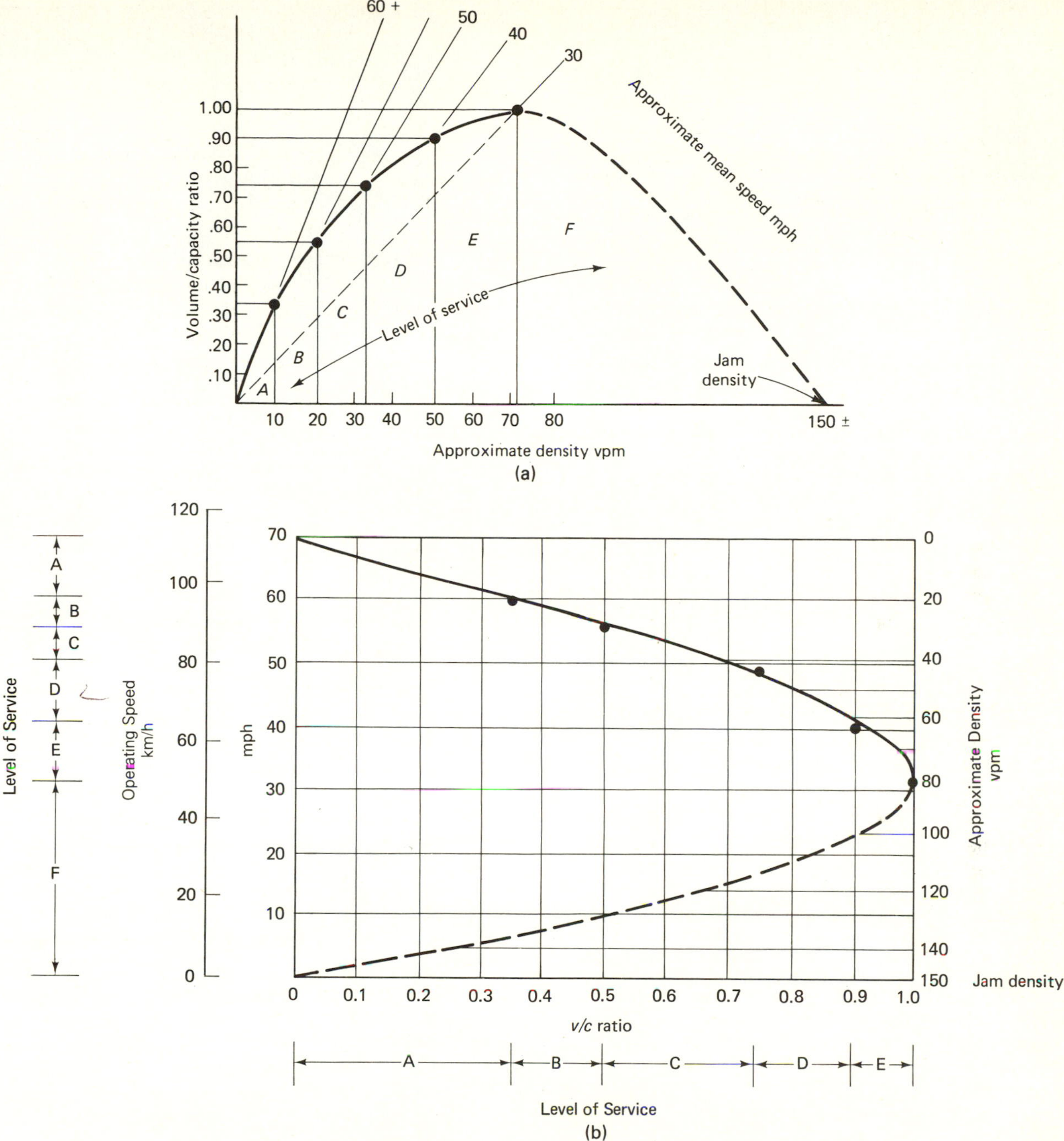

Figure 16.1. (a) Conceptual relationship of levels of service to some measures of quality under uninterrupted flow conditions (basic form). (b) Conceptual relationship of level of service to some measures of quality of flow under ideal uninterrupted flow conditions (approximate form, based on familiar speed-volume curve).

or maneuverability caused by the presence of other vehicles. As shown in Figure 16.1(b), operating speed is in the highest range and density is low. On a freeway, lane density is approximately 10 vehicles per mile (6 veh/km), and the volume/capacity ratio is typically about 1:3. Because speeds are high and volumes low, the occurrence rate of some kinds of accidents may be higher than at other service levels and the total economic cost of providing the service may be excessive. Figure 16.2 shows a typical freeway operating at level of service A.

Level of service B is a zone of stable flow. However, as shown in Figure 16.1(b), operating speed is beginning to be restricted by other traffic. Under freeway conditions, lane density is under 20 veh/mi (12 veh/km), restriction on maneuverability is still negligible, and there is little probability of major reduction in speed or flow rate. This level of service approximates typical design volumes for high-type rural highways, including freeways (see Figure 16.3).

Level of service C is still a zone of stable flow but at this volume and density level most drivers are becoming

Figure 16.2. Level of service A as viewed looking up stream on a typical freeway indicating no physical restrictions on operating speeds. SOURCE: Illinois Department of Transportation.

Figure 16.3. Level of service B as viewed looking up stream on a typical freeway indicating stable flow with few restrictions on operating speed. SOURCE: Illinois Department of Transportation.

Figure 16.4. Level of service C as viewed looking up stream on a typical freeway indicating stable flow, higher volume, and more restrictions on speed and lane changing. SOURCE: Illinois Department of Transportation.

Figure 16.5. Level of service D as viewed looking up stream on a typical freeway indicating approaching unstable flow, little freedom to maneuver, and condition tolerable for short periods. SOURCE: Illinois Department of Transportation.

Figure 16.6. Level of service E as viewed looking up stream on a typical freeway indicating unstable flow, lower operating speeds than level D and some momentary stoppages. SOURCE: Illinois Department of Transportation.

Figure 16.7. Level of service F as viewed looking up stream on a typical freeway indicating forced flow operation at low speeds where the highway acts as a storage area and there are many stoppages. SOURCE: Illinois Department of Transportation.

restricted in their freedom to select speed, change lanes, or pass. Operating speeds are still in the range of two-thirds to three-fourths of maximum; lane density reaches from 30 to 35 veh/mi on freeways (19 to 22 veh/km). This service level is frequently selected as being an appropriate criterion for design purposes, particularly for urban freeways, where the cost of providing the higher service level during peak periods may be prohibitive (see Figure 16.4).

Level of service D approaches unstable flow. Tolerable average operating speeds are maintained but are subject to considerable and sudden variation. Freedom to maneuver and driving comfort are low because lane density may reach as high as 45 to 50 veh/mi (28 to 31 veh/km), and the probability of accidents has increased. Most drivers would consider this service level undesirable (see Figure 16.5).

The upper limit of level of service E is the capacity of the facility. Operation at this level of service is unstable, and speeds for uninterrupted-flow highway types are about 30 mph (48 km/h) but will fluctuate widely from point to point. There is little independence of speed selection and maneuverability. Lane density normally reaches about 70 to 75 veh/mi (43 to 47 veh/km). Since headways are short and operating speeds subject to rapid fluctuation, driving comfort is low and accident potential high. Although circumstances may make operation of facilities under these conditions necessary, it is clearly unsatisfactory and should be avoided whenever feasible (see Figure 16.6).

Level of service F describes forced-flow operations. Speed and rate of flow are below the levels attained in level E and may, for short time periods, drop to zero. Density, on the other hand, continues to increase, eventually reaching "jam density" of about 150 veh/mi (93 veh/km) in stoppages. The output volume at the head end of these stoppages will revert to the approximately 1500 veh/h per lane "getaway" rate from a stopped condition, and a queue will continue to grow upstream as long as the arrival rate continues to exceed this discharge rate. (The fact that density is a continuous function through all levels, whereas the same volume may occur at two different speeds, one in a better level than capacity and one in level F, causes some users to prefer density to volume as a measure, for some applications.) Figure 16.7 shows, pictorially, the operating conditions on a typical freeway under service volumes associated with the level of service F.

The values given above for freeways are typical for high-standard, multilane facilities as well. Values for two-way, two-lane rural roads and urban arterials are given in subsequent sections.

Time period

The number of vehicles that will pass a particular point on a highway facility is determined not only by the capacity of that section but also by the capacities of other portions of the system that meter traffic to and from the section and (very important) by the demand for service which may or may not be present. As the time period under consideration is lengthened, the latter factor increasingly becomes the determinant.

It is known that traffic demand is generally cyclical on a daily, weekly, and seasonal basis and subject to other peaks caused by external influences. It is of little value to know the "annual capacity" of a facility based on 8760 consecutive hours of maximum demand, because such a pattern of demand will not occur. At the other extreme, even with maximum demand present, there will be random variations in the rate of demand during successive short time periods: for example, 1 min.

As a practical matter, the repetitive nature of the daily routines of life, with the attendant morning and evening peak periods of travel demand, presents a need for decisions based on these cyclical patterns. Therefore, most capacity computations are made on the basis of an intermediate time period which is usually 1 h, with adjustments as necessary to account for expected variations within the hour.

Peak-hour factor. The traffic demand on a specific facility within a 1-h period is subject to fluctuations, depending on the relationship of that facility to traffic generators and other elements of the transportation system. Observations of traffic flow on urban streets and on freeways have shown that 12 successive 5-min periods or 4 successive 15-min periods will rarely, if ever, be subject to equal demand, no matter what the apparent consistency of demand. The practical effect of this demand variation is to reduce the number of vehicles that can be served during a 1-h period without subjecting those in the maximum demand period within that hour to a lowered level of service.

The *peak-hour factor* (PHF) is a measure of these short-term variations in demand. It is defined as *the ratio of the total volume occurring during an hour to the peak rate of flow during a selected short time period within that hour, the latter expressed as an expanded hourly flow rate.*

In American practice, the PHF adjustment is made for freeways and expressways on a 5- or 6-min basis, and for urban signalized intersections it is applied on a 15-min basis. There is some rationale for this practice, but it is largely dictated by the format of available research and operational data.

EXAMPLE 16.1:

This example shows the computation of a 5-min peak-hour factor (PHF_5).

If during	1st	5 min,	flow equals	15
And during	2nd	5 min,	flow equals	16
And during	3rd	5 min,	flow equals	18
And during	4th	5 min,	flow equals	17
And during	5th	5 min,	flow equals	21
And during	6th	5 min,	flow equals	25*
And during	7th	5 min,	flow equals	23
And during	8th	5 min,	flow equals	20
And during	9th	5 min,	flow equals	17
And during	10th	5 min,	flow equals	15
And during	11th	5 min,	flow equals	13
And during	12th	5 min,	flow equals	10
Total hour volume equals				210

$$\text{and } PHF_5 = \frac{\text{volume}}{12 \times \text{peak flow rate}} = \frac{210}{12 \times 25} = \frac{210}{300} = 0.70$$

*maximum (peak) flow rate

All the influences that affect the PHF are not quantified; it is known, however, that the PHF is a function of the type and diversity of traffic generators being served by the facility, the spatial relationship of the facility to those generators, and capacity restraints elsewhere in the system. Peak-hour factors have been shown to be closely correlated with metropolitan area population. Table 16-2 shows the average 5-min peak-hour factors (PHF_5) compiled from freeway facilities in 31 American cities of various sizes.

TABLE 16–2
Average 5-Minute Peak-Hour Factor on American Freeways

Metropolitan Area Population	PHF_5*
100,000	0.77
500,000	0.80
1,000,000	0.85
5,000,000	0.88

*Standard deviation = 0.05.

SOURCE: D.R. DREW AND C.J. KEESE, "Freeway Level of Service as Influenced by Volume and Capacity Characteristics," *Freeway Characteristics, Operations and Accidents,* Highway Research Record 99 (Washington, D.C.: Highway Research Board, 1965). p. 4.

Fifteen-minute peak-hour factors (PHF_{15}) have been compiled for a large number of urban signalized approaches, as shown in Table 16-3. Although some intersections produced values near the theoretical maximum of 1.0, the observed values clustered between 0.80 and 0.95, with an average of 0.853 and a standard deviation of 0.06.

The use of the peak-hour factor to account for variations in demand during the peak hour is essential to the correct solution of many traffic design and operations problems. Most commonly, it is used to modify the service volume of the location under study. It has the effect of lowering the service volume such that the maximum flow during a short period in that hour will not have a lower level of service than that which is expected. Whenever possible, a locally determined PHF should be used, because many characteristics of this measure are still unknown and the average values in Tables 16-2 and 16-3 can be inappropriate to specific situations.

TABLE 16–3
Distribution of 15-Minute Peak-Hour Factors at Selected Urban Intersections*

PHF_{15}	Frequency
0.40–0.45	0
0.45–0.50	1
0.50–0.55	3
0.55–0.60	4
0.60–0.65	7
0.65–0.70	10
0.70–0.75	55
0.75–0.80	58
0.80–0.85	158
0.85–0.90	224
0.90–0.95	211
0.95–1.00	42

*Mean = 0.853; standard deviation = 0.06.

SOURCE: O.K. NORMANN, "Variations of Flow at Intersections as Related to Size of City, Type of Facility and Capacity Utilization." *Traffic Characteristics and Intersection Capacities, II Intersection Capacity,* Highway Res. Bd. Bull. 352, (Washington, D.C.: Highway Research Board, 1962), p. 65.

Freeways

Service volumes

The simplest and perhaps best understood traffic flow situation is the freeway or expressway roadway at locations well removed from conflict points such as on- and off-ramps. This is considered true "uninterrupted flow." There the quality of service is determined by vertical and horizontal alignment, cross-section dimensions, traffic volumes, peak-hour factor, composition of the traffic stream, and weather and lighting conditions.

Table 16-4 gives the operating speeds and volume/capacity ratios that have been established as the criteria for each service level, as well as the maximum service volumes that can be accommodated under ideal conditions. Although operating speed and volume/capacity ratio are related, each measures a different aspect of the service provided to the user and each is considered a separate criterion that must be satisfied if that level of service is to be provided.

TABLE 16–4
Operating Criteria and Maximum Service Volumes on Freeways (One Direction)*

				Basic Values for "Ideal" 70-mph (112 km/h) Average Highway Speed (AHS)						
				Volume/Capacity Ratio (*v/c*)			Maximum Service Volume (Passenger Cars/Lane)		Volume/Capacity Ratio (*v/c*) Any Number of Lanes:	
Level of Service	Description	Operating Speed mph	Operating Speed km/h	2 Lane One Direction	3 Lane One Direction	4 Lane One Direction	2-Lane, One Direction (Average/Lane)	Each Added Lane	60 mph (97 km/h) AHS	50 mph (80 km/h) AHS
A	Free flow	≥60	≥97	≤0.35	≤0.40	≤0.43	700	1000	—†	—†
B	Stable flow	≥55	≥89	≤0.50	≤0.58	≤0.63	1000	1500	≤0.25	—†
C	Stable flow	≥50	≥80	≤0.75 × PHF_5	≤0.80 × PHF_5	≤0.83 × PHF_5	1500 × PHF_5	1800 × PHF_5	≤0.45 × PHF_5	—†
D	Approaching unstable flow	≥40	≥64	≤0.90 × PHF_5	≤0.90 × PHF_5	≥0.90 × PHF_5	1800 × PHF_5	1800 × PHF_5	≤0.80 × PHF_5	≤0.45 × PHF_5
E	Unstable flow	<40	<64	≤1.00	≤1.00	≤1.00	2000	2000	≤1.00	≤1.00
F	Forced flow	<30	<48	←	Not meaningful	→	<2000	<2000	Not meaningful	Not meaningful

*Conditions: all passenger cars; 12-ft (3.7-m) lanes; 6-ft (1.8-m) lateral clearance (min.); level terrain.
†This level of service not attainable at this speed if 70 mph (112 km/h) is assumed to be ideal.

SOURCE: *Highway Capacity Manual, 1965,* Spec. Report 87 (Washington, D.C.: Highway Research Board, 1965), p. 252–253.

The service volumes given in Table 16-4 are maximums that have a high probability of being accommodated at the designated service level when all factors conducive to high-volume production are present; that is, conditions are "ideal." The following section provides means to adjust service volume estimates for situations in which conditions are less than ideal. The procedure is expressed by the formula

$$SV = MSV\ (W)\ (SM) \qquad (16.1)$$

where SV = service volume of the specific highway under consideration, one direction

MSV = maximum service volume for the level of service under consideration, one direction

W = adjustment factor for lane width and lateral clearance

SM = adjustment factor for slow-moving vehicle categories combined (may be replaced by individual adjustment factor *T* for trucks, *B* for buses, or *R* for recreational vehicles where only one category is significant)

Factors affecting service volumes

Design speed—average highway speed. Horizontal alignment, superelevation, and sight distance are correlated in design through designation of a "design speed" (see Chapter 19). *A weighted average of design speeds for all subsections of a section of highway* is termed the average highway speed (AHS). Table 16-4 gives service volumes and other characteristics for roadways with average highway speeds of 70 mph (113 km/h) or greater. Freeways with 60 mph (97 km/h) average highway speed cannot, by definition, provide level of service A and will provide levels of service B through D at volume/capacity ratios considerably lower than those on a 70-mph (113 km/h) design. Freeways or expressways of 50 mph (80 km/h) or lower average highway speed are not common. They handle even less traffic at a given level of service.

Figure 16.8 shows the relationship between operating speed and volume/capacity ratio on freeways of different average highway speed designs.

Lane width and lateral clearance. Narrow lanes and intermittent hazardous obstructions near the edge of the travel lanes increase driver tension and frequently cause drivers to select larger-than-normal headways and/or lower speeds. When this occurs, service volumes for all levels of service are lowered. Table 16-5 presents adjustment factors to be applied as multipliers to the basic capacity and service volume values given in Table 16-4, to reflect the influence of these restrictions.

Generally, low curbings or continuous regular features, such as safety shape barriers, do not cause as severe a driver reaction as do intermittent obstacles. Accordingly, the factors given in Table 16-5 may be modified by assuming that continuous, low obstacles are about 2 ft (0.6 m) farther from the lane edge than the actual distance. A paved shoulder adds to driver comfort and when such a shoulder of at least 4 ft (1.2 m) is available, it can be assumed to add 1 ft (0.3 m) to the effective width of any adjacent lane less than 12 ft (3.7 m) wide.

Traffic composition and grades. The effect of grade on level of service is caused by the differential speeds of

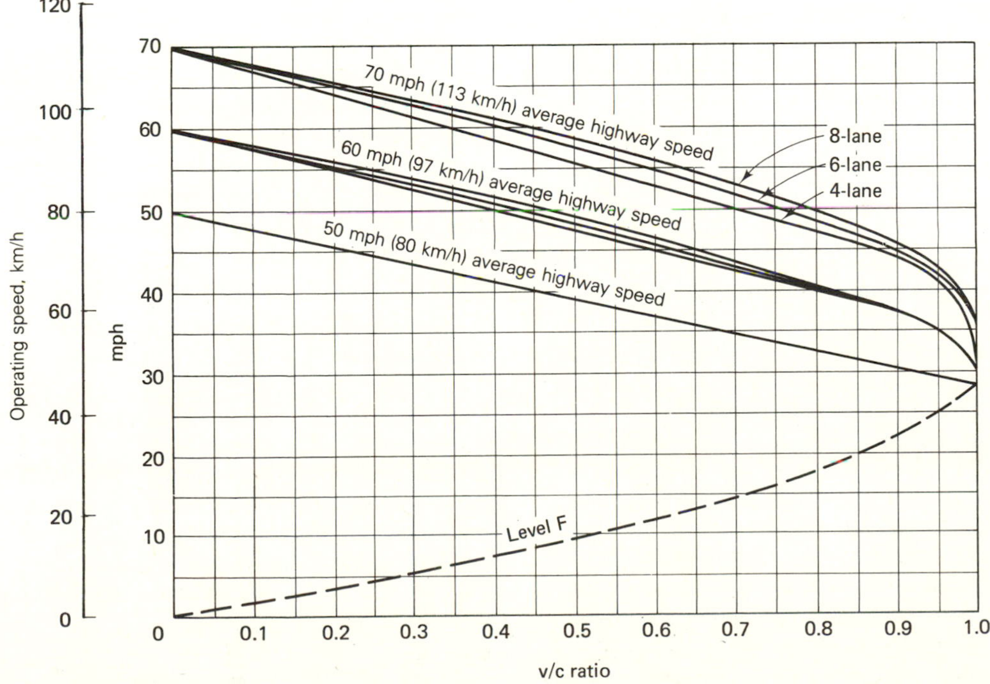

Figure 16.8. Relationship between operating speed and volume/capacity ratio on freeways. SOURCE: *Highway Capacity Manual, 1965,* Special Report 87, Washington, D.C.: Highway Research Board, 1965, p. 264.

TABLE 16–5
Adjustment Factors (*W*) for Narrow Lanes and/or Restricted Lateral Clearances on Freeways

Distance from Traffic Lane Edge to Obstruction		Obstruction on One Side Only				Obstruction on Both Sides			
ft	m	12-ft (3.7-m) Lanes	11-ft (3.4-m) Lanes	10-ft (3.0-m) Lanes	9-ft (2.7-m) Lanes	12-ft (3.7-m) Lanes	11-ft (3.4-m) Lanes	10-ft (3.0-m) Lanes	9-ft (2.7-m) Lanes
		Two-Lane Roadway (of Four-Lane Divided Highway)							
6	1.83	1.00	0.97	0.91	0.81	1.00	0.97	0.91	0.81
4	1.22	0.99	0.96	0.90	0.80	0.98	0.95	0.89	0.79
2	0.61	0.97	0.94	0.88	0.79	0.94	0.91	0.86	0.76
0	0	0.90	0.87	0.82	0.73	0.81	0.79	0.74	0.66
		Three-or-More-Lane Roadway (of Six-or-More-Lane Divided Highway)							
6	1.83	1.00	0.96	0.89	0.78	1.00	0.96	0.89	0.78
4	1.22	0.99	0.95	0.88	0.77	0.98	0.94	0.87	0.77
2	0.61	0.97	0.93	0.87	0.76	0.96	0.92	0.85	0.75
0	0	0.94	0.91	0.85	0.74	0.91	0.87	0.81	0.70

SOURCE: *Highway Capacity Manual, 1965*, Spec. Report 87 (Washington, D.C.: Highway Research Board, 1965), p. 256.

components of the traffic stream. The extent of this effect is determined by the length and steepness of the grade and the hill-climbing abilities of the vehicles, which, in turn, are determined by their weight/horsepower ratios. Grades up to 2% have negligible effect on standard American passenger cars (weight/horsepower ratios of from 30 to 45 lb/hp) (14 to 20 kg/hp) or modern intercity buses. The effect of such grades is frequently ignored in capacity computations when truck percentages are low, even though they have been found to have a small but discernible effect on capacity (level of service E), service volumes with a negative grade being noticeably beneficial.[2] Most American passenger cars and intercity buses can sustain speeds of from 30 to 40 mph (48 to 64 km/h) on long grades up to 7%, so that even such grades are considered to have negligible effect on capacity (level of service E) when only passenger cars or a low proportion of buses are involved. However, where significant numbers of trucks or recreational vehicles are present, both capacities and service volumes will be greatly affected. Each slow-moving-vehicle type is discussed separately below.

Trucks. The principal effect of grades is on trucks, which have high weight/horsepower ratios. Hill-climbing abilities of trucks in the 200-, 300-, and 400-lb/hp (91-, 136-, and 181-kg/hp) classes are shown in Figure 16.9.

On a freeway or multilane highway, the results of slowing of one component of the traffic stream are complex and not completely understood. At the lower volume/capacity ratios on relatively flat grades with a low percentage of trucks, the effect on average running speed is insignificant and only the increased accident hazard affects level of service. In fact, because of the combined effects of the 55-mph (89-km/h) national speed limit in the United States, and the gradually improving performance of trucks, passenger cars and trucks can perform more and more nearly alike under these conditions. The result is more passing of passenger cars by trucks. As the percentage of trucks and/or the length or steepness of the grade increases, however, faster vehicles tend to avoid the right lane completely and disproportionately increase the volume/capacity ratio of the remaining lane or lanes. This brings a lowering of speed and service level for the faster vehicles, largely passenger cars.

Buses. Operating characteristics of intercity and express buses approximate those of passenger cars under most circumstances. Only their added length has an appreciable effect on capacity. A variety of research[3,4] indicates that, on freeways and expressways with grades under 4%, such a bus is equivalent to between 1.4 and 1.7 passenger cars, averaging 1.6 passenger cars. This small effect is frequently disregarded, particularly because bus percentages in the traffic stream typically are very small. On occasion, however, a combination of heavy grades and substantial bus volumes may warrant their consideration.

Recreational Vehicles. In recent years, recreational vehicles have become a highly significant element of the traffic flow in certain parts of the world. They include campers, passenger cars and pickups with trailers, motor homes, and the like. Some are underpowered or unwieldy and are often operated by drivers relatively unfamiliar with either the route or the vehicle. The result is a third slow-moving-vehicle category to be considered. Thus far, only limited research has been done on their influence on freeway and multilane highway flow.

Adjustments have been developed for the effects of slow-moving vehicles both on specific individual grades and over extended sections of level, rolling, or mountainous terrain. These are derived by means of a unit called the passenger car equivalent, which represents the number of passenger cars displaced by the slow-moving vehicles on any particular grade or terrain. These equivalents, which are presented in detail in the *Highway Capacity Manual, 1965*, are not used directly as adjustment factors. Rather, they are converted to a slow-moving vehicle adjustment factor by the general expression:

[2]K. Moskowitz and L. Newman, "Notes on Freeway Capacity," *Highway and Interchange Capacity*, Highway Res. Rec. 27 (Washington, D.C.: Highway Research Board, 1963), pp. 44–68.

[3]*Highway Capacity Manual, 1965*, pp. 343–45.

[4]E. A. Hodgkins, "Effect of Buses on Freeway Capacity," *Freeway Operations*, Highway Res. Rec. 59 (Washington, D.C.: Highway Research Board, 1964), pp. 66–82.

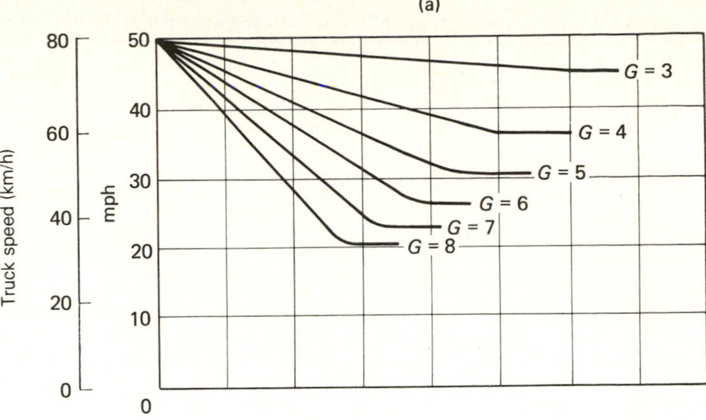

Figure 16.9. (a) Deceleration curves for trucks with weight/horsepower ratio = 200.

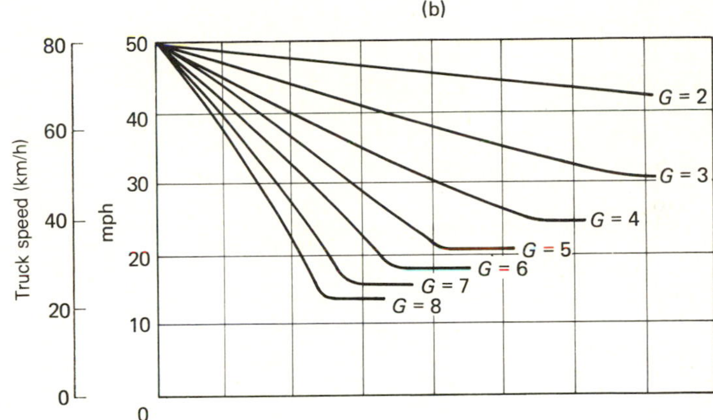

(b) Deceleration curves for trucks with weight/horsepower ratio = 300.

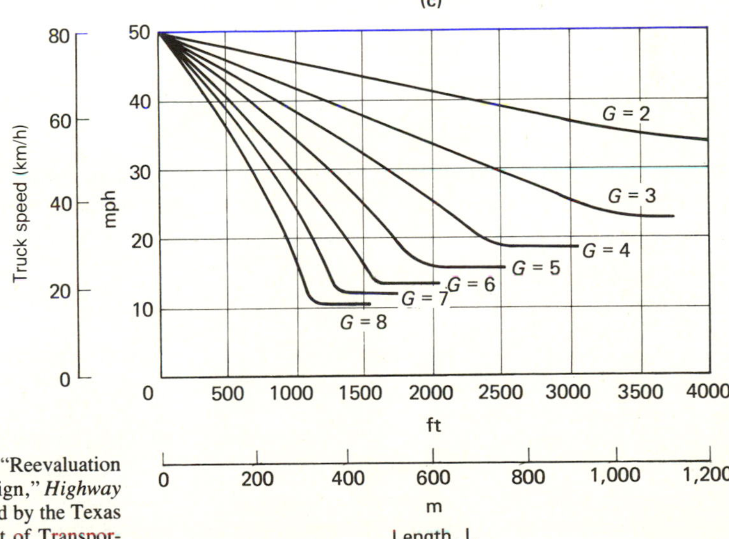

(c) Deceleration curves for trucks with weight/horsepower ratio = 400.

SOURCE: John C. Glennon and Charles A. Joyner, Jr., "Reevaluation of Truck Climbing Characteristics for Use in Geometric Design," *Highway Design Criteria—Research Study No. 2-8-68-134*, sponsored by the Texas Highway Department in cooperation with U.S. Department of Transportation (College Station, Texas: Texas A & M University, 1969) pp. 19, 20, 21.

$$SM = \frac{100}{100 - P_T + E_T P_T - P_B + E_B P_B - P_{RV} + E_{RV} P_{RV}} \tag{16.2}$$

where SM = slow-moving vehicle factor

P_T, P_B, P_{RV} = percentages of trucks, buses, and recreational vehicles, respectively

E_T, E_B, E_{RV} = passenger car equivalents of trucks, buses, and recreational vehicles, respectively

TABLE 16-6
Adjustment Factors for Trucks (*T*), Buses (*B*), and Recreational Vehicles (*RV*) on Freeways and Multilane Highways

Individual Grades		Trucks (*T*)								Buses (*B*)								Recreational Vehicles (*RV*)			
		Levels of Service A, B, and C				Levels of Service D and E				Levels of Service A, B, and C				Levels of Service D and E				Levels of Service A and B			
		Percentage of Trucks				Percentage of Trucks				Percentage of Buses				Percentage of Buses				Percentage of (*RV*)			
Grade (%)	Length mi (km)	3%	5%	10%	20%	3%	5%	10%	20%	3%	5%	10%	20%	3%	5%	10%	20%	3%	5%	10%	20%
Under 2	All	0.97	0.95	0.91	0.83	0.97	0.95	0.91	0.83	0.97	0.95	0.91	0.83	0.97	0.95	0.91	0.83	0.96	0.94	0.88	0.79
2	½ (0.8)	0.89	0.87	0.77	0.71	0.89	0.87	0.77	0.71	0.97	0.95	0.91	0.83	0.97	0.95	0.91	0.83	0.96	0.94	0.88	0.79
	1 (1.6)	0.85	0.83	0.71	0.63	0.85	0.83	0.71	0.63	0.97	0.95	0.91	0.83	0.97	0.95	0.91	0.83	0.96	0.94	0.88	0.79
	2 (3.2)	0.85	0.80	0.67	0.50	0.85	0.80	0.67	0.50	0.97	0.95	0.91	0.83	0.97	0.95	0.91	0.83	0.96	0.94	0.88	0.79
	4 (6.4)	0.85	0.77	0.59	0.42	0.85	0.77	0.59	0.42	0.97	0.95	0.91	0.83	0.97	0.95	0.91	0.83	0.96	0.94	0.88	0.79
3	½ (0.8)	0.79	0.74	0.71	0.63	0.79	0.74	0.71	0.63	0.97	0.95	0.91	0.83	0.97	0.95	0.91	0.83	0.96	0.94	0.88	0.79
	1 (1.6)	0.79	0.74	0.67	0.50	0.79	0.74	0.67	0.50	0.97	0.95	0.91	0.83	0.97	0.95	0.91	0.83	0.96	0.94	0.88	0.79
	2 (3.2)	0.79	0.71	0.59	0.42	0.79	0.71	0.59	0.42	0.97	0.95	0.91	0.83	0.97	0.95	0.91	0.83	0.96	0.94	0.88	0.79
	4 (6.4)	0.79	0.69	0.50	0.33	0.79	0.69	0.50	0.33	0.97	0.95	0.91	0.83	0.97	0.95	0.91	0.83	0.96	0.94	0.88	0.79
4	½ (0.8)	0.75	0.71	0.71	0.56	0.74	0.71	0.71	0.56	0.97	0.95	0.91	0.83	0.97	0.95	0.91	0.83	0.96	0.94	0.88	0.79
	1 (1.6)	0.75	0.69	0.59	0.42	0.74	0.69	0.59	0.42	0.97	0.95	0.91	0.83	0.97	0.95	0.91	0.83	0.96	0.94	0.88	0.79
	2 (3.2)	0.75	0.67	0.50	0.33	0.74	0.65	0.50	0.33	0.97	0.95	0.91	0.83	0.97	0.95	0.91	0.83	0.96	0.94	0.88	0.79
	4 (6.4)	0.75	0.63	0.42	0.28	0.74	0.61	0.40	0.26	0.97	0.95	0.91	0.83	0.97	0.95	0.91	0.83	0.96	0.94	0.88	0.79
5	½ (0.8)	0.74	0.67	0.63	0.45	0.72	0.67	0.63	0.45	0.92	0.87	0.77	0.63	0.97	0.95	0.91	0.83	0.95	0.92	0.85	0.75
	1 (1.6)	0.74	0.65	0.53	0.36	0.72	0.63	0.53	0.36	0.92	0.87	0.77	0.63	0.97	0.95	0.91	0.83	0.94	0.91	0.83	0.71
	2 (3.2)	0.74	0.61	0.43	0.28	0.72	0.59	0.42	0.26	0.92	0.87	0.77	0.63	0.97	0.95	0.91	0.83	0.94	0.90	0.81	0.68
	4 (6.4)	0.70	0.56	0.36	0.24	0.69	0.53	0.32	0.22	0.92	0.87	0.77	0.63	0.97	0.95	0.91	0.83	0.93	0.88	0.79	0.66
6	½ (0.8)	0.72	0.67	0.59	0.42	0.70	0.67	0.59	0.42	0.85	0.77	0.63	0.45	0.92	0.87	0.77	0.63	0.93	0.88	0.79	0.66
	1 (1.6)	0.72	0.63	0.48	0.33	0.70	0.61	0.45	0.33	0.85	0.77	0.63	0.45	0.92	0.87	0.77	0.63	0.91	0.85	0.75	0.60
	2 (3.2)	0.72	0.59	0.40	0.26	0.70	0.54	0.37	0.25	0.85	0.77	0.63	0.45	0.92	0.87	0.77	0.63	0.90	0.84	0.72	0.56
	4 (6.4)	0.65	0.53	0.34	0.21	0.64	0.48	0.31	0.19	0.85	0.77	0.63	0.45	0.92	0.87	0.77	0.63	0.89	0.83	0.71	0.56
Extended* sections	Level terrain	0.97	0.95	0.91	0.83	0.97	0.95	0.91	0.83	0.98	0.97	0.94	0.89	0.98	0.97	0.94	0.89	0.96	0.93	0.87	0.77
	Rolling terrain	0.92	0.87	0.77	0.63	0.92	0.87	0.77	0.63	0.94	0.91	0.83	0.71	0.94	0.91	0.83	0.71	0.92	0.87	0.78	0.63
	Mountainous terrain†	0.83	0.74	0.59	0.42	0.83	0.74	0.59	0.42	0.89	0.83	0.71	0.56	0.89	0.83	0.71	0.56	0.89	0.83	0.70	0.54

*Includes upgrades, downgrades, and level sections.
†Combinations of length, steepness, and frequency of grades sufficient to reduce trucks to crawl speeds (see Figure 16.9).

SOURCE: Truck and bus data: *Highway Capacity Manual, 1965*, Spec. Report 87 (Washington, D.C.: Highway Research Board, 1965), pp. 257–261. Recreational vehicle data: A. WERNER, "Effect of Recreational Vehicles on Highway Capacity," unpublished thesis, University of Calgary, 1974 [portions published in A. WERNER, J. F. MORRALL, AND GORDON HALLS, "Effect of Recreational Vehicles on Highway Capacity," *Traffic Eng. 45*(5), 20–25 (May 1975)].

Like all adjustment factors, this is a multiplier applied to basic capacity and service volume values.

Table 16-6 is a two-part table presenting adjustment factors for each type of slow-moving vehicle, both for "individual grades" and for "extended roadway sections." The truck and bus portions are condensed versions of the information in the *Highway Capacity Manual, 1965*. The recreational vehicle data are taken from the Canadian two-lane highway study referenced in footnote 13 later in this chapter. This approximation was made because the only conveniently available multilane data applied to the "worst-case" vehicles rather than the average vehicles reflected here. In actuality, on freeways and other multilane highways, recreational vehicle performance probably would be somewhat better than these adjustments would indicate.

In practice, in many situations trucks are the predominant slow-moving-vehicle category, with buses and recreational vehicles negligible. For such cases, Table 16-6 can be used to obtain the truck factor directly. Similarly, in those few situations where only bus volumes or only recreational vehicle volumes are heavy, it can be used to obtain those individual factors.

The separate adjustment factors for trucks, buses, and recreational vehicles should *not* be multiplied together. This simplification, which was condoned in the past, no longer appears wise. Rather, where two or three slow-moving classes exist in the traffic stream, the foregoing combined *SM* value should be developed. This involves selection of the appropriate adjustment factors from Table 16-6, their conversion to passenger car equivalents by means of Table 16-7, and substitution into equation (16.2). (Those familiar with *Highway Capacity Manual, 1965* will note that use of the conversion table is the reverse of that in the manual. The reason is that, here, the basic values tabulated are the adjustment factors rather than the equivalents; experience has shown a tendency for misuse of tabulated equivalents.)

Variations in flow rate. As previously discussed, the rate of flow during short time periods within the hour is seldom constant (see "Peak-hour factor"). At levels of service A and B, intervehicular influence is so small that these short fluctuations have little practical effect on overall operating speed or other measures of service. As volume and density increase, however, it becomes necessary to consider the effects of these short-term variations because a drastic reduction in speed or an instability in one time period can

TABLE 16–7

Relationship between Adjustment Factors for Trucks (*T*), Buses (*B*), and Recreational Vehicles (*RV*) and Passenger Car Equivalents*

Passenger Car Equivalent (E_T, E_B, or E_{RV})	Truck, Bus, or Recreational Vehicle Adjustment Factor (*T*, *B*, or *RV*)														
	Percentage of Trucks, Buses, or Recreational Vehicles														
	1	2	3	4	5	6	7	8	9	10	12	14	16	18	20
2	0.99	0.98	0.97	0.96	0.95	0.94	0.93	0.93	0.92	0.91	0.89	0.88	0.86	0.85	0.83
3	0.98	0.96	0.94	0.93	0.91	0.89	0.88	0.86	0.85	0.83	0.81	0.78	0.76	0.74	0.71
4	0.97	0.94	0.92	0.89	0.87	0.85	0.83	0.81	0.79	0.77	0.74	0.70	0.68	0.65	0.63
5	0.96	0.93	0.89	0.86	0.83	0.81	0.78	0.76	0.74	0.71	0.68	0.64	0.61	0.58	0.56
6	0.95	0.91	0.87	0.83	0.80	0.77	0.74	0.71	0.69	0.67	0.63	0.59	0.56	0.53	0.50
7	0.94	0.89	0.85	0.81	0.77	0.74	0.70	0.68	0.65	0.63	0.58	0.54	0.51	0.48	0.45
8	0.93	0.88	0.83	0.78	0.74	0.70	0.67	0.64	0.61	0.59	0.54	0.51	0.47	0.44	0.42
9	0.93	0.86	0.81	0.76	0.71	0.68	0.64	0.61	0.58	0.56	0.51	0.47	0.44	0.41	0.38
10	0.92	0.85	0.79	0.74	0.69	0.65	0.61	0.58	0.55	0.53	0.48	0.44	0.41	0.38	0.36
11	0.91	0.83	0.77	0.71	0.67	0.63	0.59	0.56	0.53	0.50	0.45	0.42	0.38	0.36	0.33
12	0.90	0.82	0.75	0.69	0.65	0.60	0.57	0.53	0.50	0.48	0.43	0.39	0.36	0.34	0.31
13	0.89	0.81	0.74	0.68	0.63	0.58	0.54	0.51	0.48	0.45	0.41	0.37	0.34	0.32	0.29
14	0.88	0.79	0.72	0.66	0.61	0.56	0.52	0.49	0.46	0.43	0.39	0.35	0.32	0.30	0.28
15	0.88	0.78	0.70	0.64	0.59	0.54	0.51	0.47	0.44	0.42	0.37	0.34	0.31	0.28	0.26
16	0.87	0.77	0.69	0.63	0.57	0.53	0.49	0.45	0.43	0.40	0.36	0.32	0.29	0.27	0.25
17	0.86	0.76	0.68	0.61	0.56	0.51	0.47	0.44	0.41	0.38	0.34	0.31	0.28	0.26	0.24
18	0.85	0.75	0.66	0.60	0.54	0.49	0.46	0.42	0.40	0.37	0.33	0.30	0.27	0.25	0.23
19	0.85	0.74	0.65	0.58	0.53	0.48	0.44	0.41	0.38	0.36	0.32	0.28	0.26	0.24	0.22
20	0.84	0.72	0.64	0.57	0.51	0.47	0.42	0.40	0.37	0.34	0.30	0.27	0.25	0.23	0.21
22	0.83	0.70	0.61	0.54	0.49	0.44	0.40	0.37	0.35	0.32	0.28	0.25	0.23	0.21	0.19
24	0.81	0.68	0.59	0.52	0.47	0.42	0.38	0.35	0.33	0.30	0.27	0.24	0.21	0.19	0.18
26	0.80	0.67	0.57	0.50	0.44	0.40	0.36	0.33	0.31	0.29	0.25	0.22	0.20	0.18	0.17
28	0.79	0.65	0.55	0.48	0.43	0.38	0.35	0.32	0.29	0.27	0.24	0.21	0.19	0.17	0.16
30	0.78	0.63	0.53	0.46	0.41	0.36	0.33	0.30	0.28	0.26	0.22	0.20	0.18	0.16	0.15
35	0.75	0.60	0.49	0.42	0.37	0.33	0.30	0.27	0.25	0.23	0.20	0.17	0.16	0.14	0.13
40	0.72	0.56	0.46	0.39	0.34	0.30	0.27	0.24	0.22	0.20	0.18	0.15	0.14	0.12	0.11
45	0.69	0.53	0.43	0.36	0.31	0.27	0.25	0.22	0.20	0.19	0.16	0.14	0.12	0.11	0.10
50	0.67	0.51	0.40	0.34	0.29	0.25	0.23	0.20	0.18	0.17	0.15	0.13	0.11	0.10	0.09
55	0.65	0.48	0.38	0.32	0.27	0.24	0.21	0.19	0.17	0.16	0.13	0.12	0.10	0.09	0.08
60	0.63	0.46	0.36	0.30	0.25	0.22	0.19	0.17	0.16	0.15	0.12	0.11	0.10	0.09	0.08
65	0.61	0.44	0.34	0.28	0.24	0.21	0.18	0.16	0.15	0.14	0.12	0.10	0.09	0.08	0.07
70	0.59	0.42	0.33	0.27	0.22	0.19	0.17	0.15	0.14	0.13	0.11	0.09	0.08	0.07	0.07
75	0.57	0.40	0.31	0.25	0.21	0.18	0.16	0.14	0.13	0.12	0.10	0.09	0.08	0.07	0.06
80	0.56	0.39	0.30	0.24	0.20	0.17	0.15	0.14	0.12	0.11	0.10	0.08	0.07	0.07	0.06
90	0.53	0.36	0.27	0.22	0.18	0.16	0.14	0.12	0.11	0.10	0.09	0.07	0.07	0.06	0.05
100	0.50	0.34	0.25	0.20	0.17	0.14	0.13	0.11	0.10	0.09	0.08	0.07	0.06	0.06	0.05

*Computed by $100/(100 - P + EP)$.

be expected to influence the service in one or more following periods and thus affect the overall level of service during the hour. As the flow increases to capacity levels, these short-term fluctuations are dampened by the capacity restraint and the facility increasingly operates under an artificial peak-hour factor which approaches but rarely actually reaches 1.0.

It is frequent practice, but not universal, to apply the service definitions of levels of service C and D on freeways to the 5-min period within the hour that is accommodating the maximum rate of flow. This is accomplished by multiplying the limiting volume/capacity ratio and service volume by an appropriate 5-min peak-hour factor (PHF_5). As previously indicated, PHFs between 0.75 and 0.95 have been found appropriate for urban freeways. One study of uncongested urban interstate freeways found an average value of 0.82.[5] Peak-hour factors on nonmetropolitan freeways have not been extensively studied but probably lie in the lower portion of the range cited above. The PHF adjustment for levels of service C and D is included in Table 16-4.

Weather and visibility. When drivers' visibility is restricted by darkness or inclement weather, their choice of speed and headway can be expected to be affected. The effect of this phenomenon on freeway capacity has not been extensively documented. A Connecticut[6] study of traffic performance under various levels of lighting suggests little significant difference in speeds with the average illumination range between 0.2 and 0.8 footcandles (2 to 8 lux).

Rain, which decreases both visibility and surface friction available for stopping, can be expected to lower service volumes at all levels of service. A Texas study indicates a reduction of about 10% in capacity (level of service E) on freeways. British research[7] found a 14% reduction on very

[5] *An Investigation of Peak Hour Factors,* Missouri State Highway Department, Mimeo, 1970.

[6] *Effect of Illumination on Operating Characteristics of Freeways,* National Cooperative Highway Res. Program Report No. 60 (Washington, D.C.: Highway Research Board, 1968), 150 pp.

[7] *Research on Road Traffic,* Road Research Laboratory (London: Her Majesty's Stationery Office, 1965), p. 213.

slippery pavement (wood block) but no corresponding reduction on rougher pavements. Snow and icy pavements can, in the extreme, reduce the capacity of a facility to zero. Any combination of visibility and surface conditions that reduces average freeway speeds to below 40 mph (64 km/h) can be expected to have very significant reducing effects on capacity. When these conditions occur frequently during periods of maximum demand, special studies should be undertaken to develop appropriate adjustment factors.

EXAMPLE 16.2:

Determine the service volume for level of service C, (SV_C), and level of service E, (SV_E), (capacity) for one roadway of an urban freeway of three lanes in one direction on a 3%, 1-mi (1.6-km) grade. The roadway has 11-ft (3.4-m) lanes, a 10-ft (3.0-m) right shoulder, and a continuous median barrier 4 ft (1.2 m) from the left lane edge. The facility was designed for an average highway speed of 70 mph (113 km/h) and carries 5% trucks and 1% intercity buses. The peak hour factor is 0.91.

Solution: *W* for three 11-ft (3.4-m) lanes, 10-ft (3.0-m) right clearance, and 4-ft (1.2-m) left clearance = 0.95 (Table 16-5). (Because the median barrier is continuous, a 2-ft (0.6-m) added distance could be assumed and the factor changed to 0.96. Such refinement is seldom warranted in planning applications because volume estimates are seldom this precise.)

T for 5% trucks on a 1-mi (1.6-km), 3% grade = 0.74 for both levels of service (Table 16-6). The small percentage of buses can be considered as passenger cars.

$$MSV_E = 2000 \times 3 = 6000 \text{ (Table 16-4)}$$

$$SV_E = (MSV_E)\ (W)\ (T)$$

$$SV_E = 6000 \times 0.95 \times 0.74 = 4218$$

$$MSV_C = 1500 + 1500 + 1800 \text{ (Table 16-4)}$$

$$SV_C = (MSV_C)\ (PHF_5)\ (W)\ (T)$$

$$SV_C = 4800 \times 0.91 \times 0.95 \times 0.74 = 3066$$

$$\text{Limiting } v/c \text{ ratio} = \frac{3066}{4218} = 0.73$$

From Figure 16.8 it can be seen that with a v/c ratio of 0.73 and a 70-mph (113-km/h) average highway speed design, the operating speed would be about 52 mph (84 km/h), slightly above the controlling criterion of 50 mph (80 km/h) for service level C. Had the average highway speed been 60 mph (97 km/h), the operating speed at v/c = 0.73 would be well below the criterion speed. To prevent this, a v/c ratio of 0.43 would be required, with a resulting reduction in SVc to 1800 veh/h (0.43 × 4200).

Freeway incidents: maintenance activities and accidents. The adverse influence of maintenance operations and accidents on freeway traffic flow is typically greater than could be accounted for by the adjustments previously given, for three principal reasons. First, one or more lanes may be temporarily blocked. Second, the curiosity or "gapers' block" factor usually develops—drivers simply slow down to "see what's going on." Third, whenever traffic is brought to a stop, its getaway rate from the resulting queue is less than the capacity flow rate. Table 16-8 presents flow rates that have been reported for a variety of impediments.

TABLE 16–8
Typical Capacity Flow Rates (vehicles/h), Past Freeway Incidents

Number of lanes, one direction (normal operation):	2	3 or 4	4
Number of lanes open, one direction:	1	2	3
Type of operation (1)			
Median barrier or guard-rail repair	1500	3200	4800
Pavement repair, mudjacking, pavement grooving	1400	3000	4500
Striping, resurfacing, slide removal	1200	2600	4000
Pavement markers	1100	2400	3600
Middle lanes—any reason	—	2200	3400
Accidents (2)			
Incident occurring in moving traffic lane with one lane blocked	1300	2700	4300
Number of lanes in one direction:	2	3	4
Accidents (2)			
Incident occurring on shoulder with no lanes blocked	3000	4600	6300

SOURCE: (1) C. E. FORBES ET AL., *Reducing Motorist Inconvenience Due to Maintenance Operation on High-Volume Freeways*, Spec. Report 116 (Washington, D.C.: Highway Research Board, 1971), pp. 181–188. (2) M. E. GOOLSBY, *Influence of Incidents on Freeway Quality of Service*, Highway Res. Rec. 349 (Washington, D.C.: Highway Research Board, 1971).

Ramp junctions: merging and diverging

The preceding sections have dealt with continuous movement of traffic, essentially in single lines without entrance or exit of traffic from the flow. In practice, of course, such "clean" flows are frequently interrupted at interchanges, particularly in urban areas. The situation at any such interface of two streams of traffic is a distinctly different phenomenon.

On-ramps. A basic merge situation is one in which a single entering traffic lane merges with another and leaves the merging area as a single lane. Here drivers are required to perceive and enter a gap in an intersecting traffic stream. Geometric conditions, including sight distance, angle of intersection, space available for the maneuver, and grades, have an important effect on the size of gap a driver will accept. The volume of traffic in the intersected stream will determine the frequency of gaps of the appropriate size (and the delay awaiting these gaps), and the volume of traffic in the intersecting stream will determine queuing delays.

Under ideal geometric circumstances with ample sight distance, a small angle of convergence and space for both streams to adjust to a nearly equal speed prior to intersecting, a merge rate equal to or exceeding the free-flowing rate can be accommodated at each service level. Observations of single-lane merging areas have revealed short-time merging rates up to 2300 veh/h. These rates can seldom be sustained for a full hour nor reliably predicted; thus, the Highway Capacity Committee, Transportation Research Board, has recommended a value of 2000 veh/h as the hourly volume

TABLE 16-9
Maximum Service Volumes for Single-Lane Merging and Diverging Areas on Freeways

Level of Service	Description	Approximate Freeway Speed		Maximum Service Volume*	
		mph	km/h	Merge	Diverge
A	Free flow	60	97	1000	1100
B	Some speed adjustment	55	89	1200	1300
C	Speed adjustment—limit of free flow	50	80	1700 × PHF†	1800 × PHF†
D	Occasional queuing on ramp	40	64	1800 × PHF†	1900 × PHF†
E	Unstable—frequent queuing	20–30	32–48	2000	2000
F	Stop and go	—	—	<2000	<2000
	(alternate feed merge)	—	—	≈1800	n.a.

*Passenger car total on ramp plus first freeway lane per hour. With favorable geometrics, flow can contain a small percentage of trucks.
†Peak-hour factor.

SOURCE: *Highway Capacity Manual, 1965*, Spec. Report 87 (Washington, D.C.: Highway Research Board, 1965), pp. 192–196.

that has a reasonable expectation of being served (capacity) on a properly designed freeway merging area. Recommended values for other service levels commonly used are given in Table 16-9.

It should be noted that the values cited above do not take into consideration the percentage split between the two traffic streams. On a theoretical basis, total delay to ramp vehicles will be greatest when ramp volume is near 40% of total volume.[8] At either higher or lower proportions of ramp traffic, total delay decreases. (Average delay for ramp vehicles only increases as freeway volume increases.) From simulation studies, it would appear that, at service level D (1800 veh/h total on ramp and lane 1) average delay with 720 ramp vehicles (40%) would be 60 s; with 200 or 1150 ramp vehicles, average delay would be 20 s.[9] These theoretical results seem to be consistent with observational studies.[10]

The merge values in Table 16-9 are also predicated on the total downstream volume on the freeway (all lanes) not exceeding established freeway service volume levels. In practice, this will frequently be the limiting condition when ramp volumes are a high proportion of total volume.

Ramp geometrics affect capacity and other levels of service. The relationship of angle of entry, length, and type of acceleration lane to the critical gap (t), and the critical gap to maximum service volumes for level of service D are given in Figure 16.10.

Estimation of ramp service volumes in a freeway merging situation requires that the freeway lane 1 volume and composition immediately upstream of the merging area be known or estimated. The lane 1 volume is the volume in the right-hand through lane in the ramp terminal area. A variety of formulas and nomographs to assist the engineer in this determination are given in Chapter 8 of *Highway Capacity Manual, 1965*. For example, for the simple case of a single ramp entrance well separated from other ramps operating at level of service A to C, the formulas given are:

2-lane roadway of freeway:
$$V_1 = 136 + 0.345V_f - 0.115V_r \tag{16.3}$$

3-lane roadway of freeway:
$$V_1 = -121 + 0.244V_f \tag{16.4}$$

4-lane roadway of freeway:
$$V_1 = -312 + 0.201V_f + 0.127V_r \tag{16.5}$$

where V_1 = lane 1 volume upstream of merge
V_f = total volume upstream of merge
V_r = on-ramp volume

While recent research, reported in the "interim materials" referred to at the end of this chapter, has shown the need for overall refinement of these merging criteria, it has also suggested that, in the meantime, the various formulas and nomographs be used for all levels of service, not just A through C as indicated in the manual.

Research data from 49 study sites on American freeways[11] produced the lane distribution curves in Figure 16.11. The report[12] provides a means to correct the values in Figure 16.11 for the influence of adjacent upstream ramps.

The highway designer who must estimate lane 1 volumes should use these formulas and nomographs cautiously and should provide a generous factor of safety. In analyzing existing situations, lane 1 volumes should be obtained by actual count.

Off-ramps. Diverge points are locations where parts of the traffic flow leave the freeway at off-ramps. These are less troublesome than merge points, because gap acceptance is not a key element. Nevertheless, they are friction-producing points because of the erratic driving that tends to occur in their vicinity. As indicated in Table 16-9, diverge service volumes slightly exceed equivalent merge volumes.

Just as is true for on-ramp merge points, *Highway Capacity Manual, 1965* provides a variety of formulas and equivalent nomographs for the off-ramp diverge case. Again, the recent research has shown them to be reasonably applicable at all levels of service, not just at levels A through C.

EXAMPLE 16.3:

Given a four-lane freeway and a total volume on two lanes in one direction of 3000 veh/h. A diamond interchange is being added to the freeway and the estimated traffic on the one-lane entrance ramp is 300 veh/h. The peak-hour factor for this area is 0.83. Find the level of service at the

[8]ROBERT DAWSON AND HAROLD MICHAEL, "Analysis of On-Ramp Capacities by Monte Carlo Simulation," *Statistical and Mathematical Aspects of Traffic*, Highway Res. Rec. 118 (Washington, D.C.: Highway Research Board, 1966), pp. 1–20.

[9]JOSEPH W. HESS, "Capacities and Characteristics of Ramp-Freeway Connections," *Highway and Interchange Capacity*, Highway Res. Rec. 27 (Washington, D.C.: Highway Research Board, 1963), pp. 86–89.

[10]See DAWSON AND MICHAEL, "Analysis of On-Ramp Capacities"; K. A. BREWER, "Analysis of a Signal-Controlled Ramp's Characteristics," *Traffic Flow Characteristics*, Highway Res. Rec. 308 (Washington, D.C.: Highway Research Board, 1970), pp. 48–61; HESS, "Capacities and Characteristics."

[11]D. R. DREW AND C. J. KEESE, "Freeway Level of Service as Influenced by Volume and Capacity Characteristics," *Freeway Characteristics, Operations and Accidents*, Highway Res. Rec. 99 (Washington, D.C.: Highway Research Board, 1965), pp. 1–39.

[12]Ibid.

Critical gap t based on entrance ramp geometrics

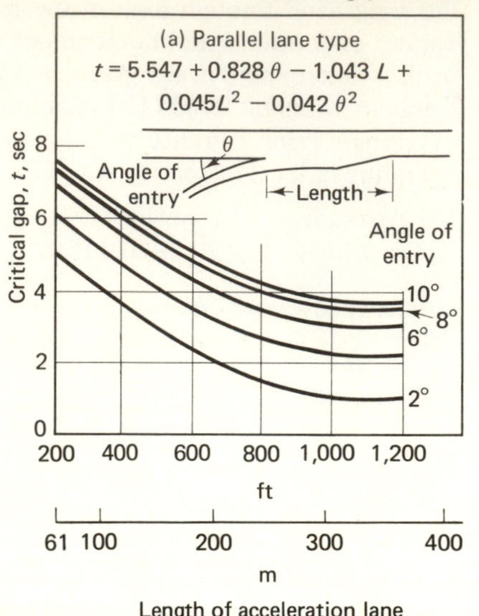

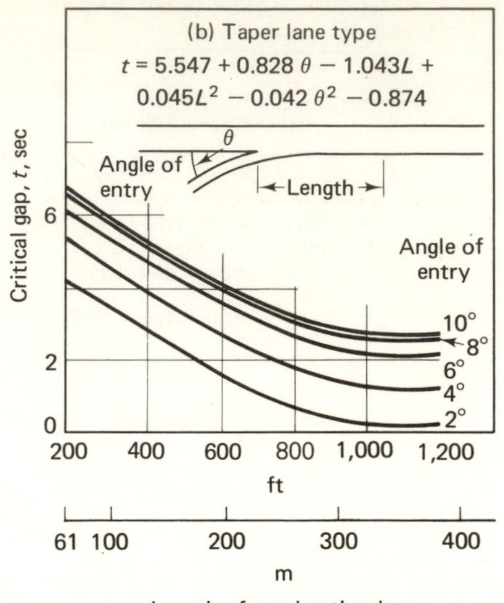

Relation of service volume to critical gap t

Ramp service volume q_r, vph: 40, 60, 90, 120, 150, 200, 250, 300, 400, 500, 700, 900

$t = 6$, $t = 5$, $t = 4$, $t = 3$

600 vph, 1,000, 1,400, 1,800

Freeway outside-lane volume q vph

Note: Derivation by Drew was for a probability of 0.33 of an arriving ramp vehicle joining a queue. The relationship to level of service D is by the author.

Figure 16.10. Relationship of ramp geometrics to level D service volumes. SOURCE: Donald R. Drew, *Traffic Flow Theory and Control,* New York: McGraw-Hill, 1968, pp. 218–219.

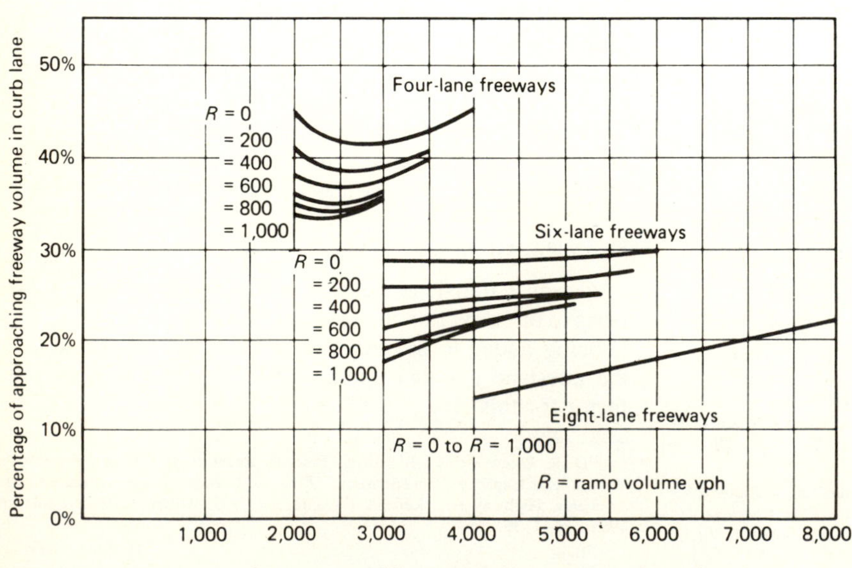

Figure 16.11. Lane distribution on freeways immediately upstream of an isolated on-ramp. SOURCE: Donald R. Drew, *Traffic Theory and Control,* New York: McGraw-Hill, 1968, p. 94.

ramp junction area assuming level terrain, adequate geometrics, and a minimal number of trucks in the traffic streams.

Solution: Substitute the appropriate values in equation (16.3) for a two-lane roadway and solve for lane 1 volume upstream of the ramp.

$$V_1 = 136 + 0.345(3000) - 0.115(300) = 1000 \text{ veh/h}$$

At the downstream end of the ramp, the total volume in lane 1 will be the computed upstream lane 1 volume plus the on-ramp, or 1000 + 300 = 1300 veh/h.

From Table 16-9, the maximum service volume for a merging condition for level of service C is 1700 × 0.83 = 1411 veh/h. The computed volume is less than this maximum volume but greater than the 1200 specified for level of service B; thus, the addition of this on-ramp will be expected to produce operation at level of service C.

Weaving

Where two traffic streams moving in the same general direction merge and then again diverge in a relatively short distance, crossings of portions of the traffic streams must occur. This is known as weaving. It may be found where separate freeways join and again divide, or where an on-ramp is followed by a nearby off-ramp. Typically, some, if not all, of the legs are multilane, and much of the traffic is not involved in the weaving movement.

In an ideal, balanced design, sufficient length and width of the weaving section are provided so that speeds of the nonweaving traffic will not be adversely affected. When space is not available or the traffic volumes are relatively high, it can be expected that the speed of the nonweaving as well as the weaving traffic through the weaving section will be somewhat lower than on the open road. The weaving analysis method uses a k factor that is applied to the smaller weaving volume to account for this congestive effect.

In Figure 16.12, the weaving influence factor k relationship is shown together with the "quality of flow" curves, which are designated by Roman numerals. They in a general sense denote the level of service to the weaving vehicles. The level of service to the nonweaving vehicles is also lower than on the open road, but in a balanced design they are related.

A k factor of 1 denotes that the weaving vehicles have no adverse effect on the traffic stream. A maximum factor of 3 is recommended in *Highway Capacity Manual, 1965,*

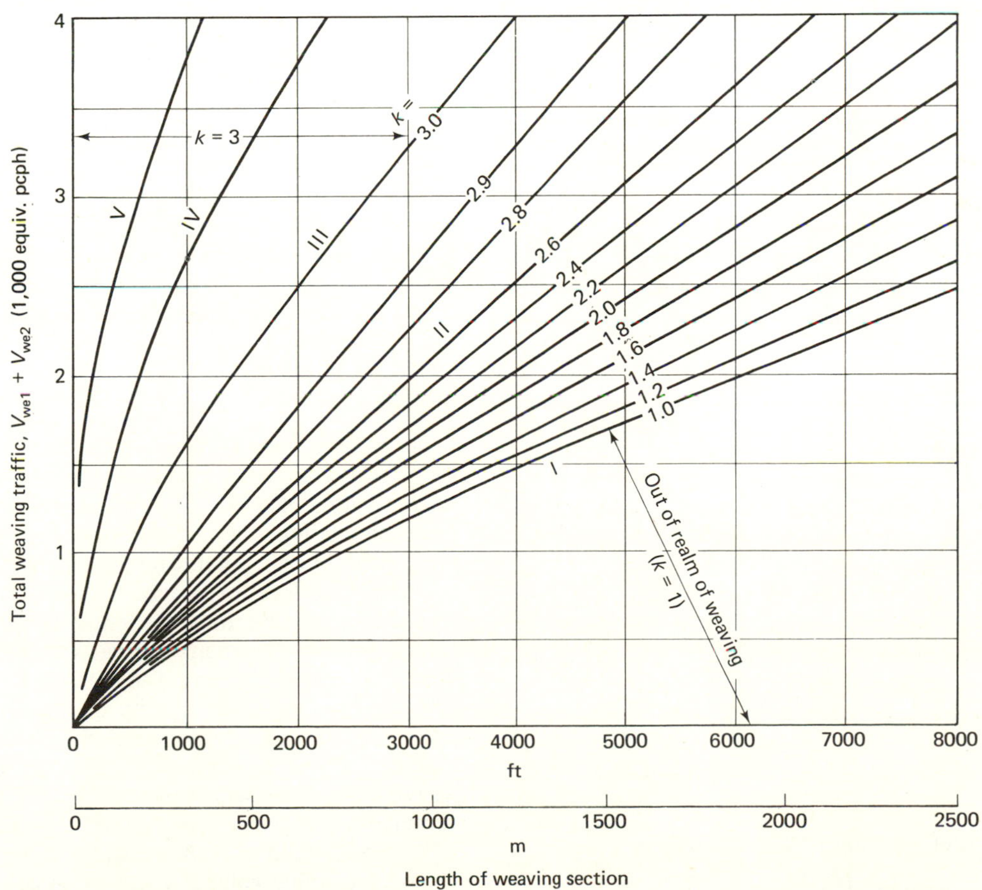

Figure 16.12. k values for weaving sections. SOURCE: *Highway Capacity Manual, 1965,* Special Report 87, Washington, D.C.: Highway Research Board, 1965, p. 166.

although additional curves are shown for lower "quality of flow" conditions. These hint that higher factors might well be appropriate for these curves.

Quality of flow I is representative of operating conditions much like those on a normal section on freeways. Weaving will take place at or above 50 mph (80 km/h).

Quality of flow II involves some minor restrictions and freeway weaving speeds between 45 and 50 mph (72 and 80 km/h).

Quality of flow III has weaving speeds between 40 and 45 mph (65 and 72 km/h) and may vary considerably between individual vehicles and adjacent time periods.

Quality of flow IV indicates weaving speeds falling as low as 30 to 35 mph (48 to 56 km/h). Occasional slowdowns and restrictive maneuvering space can be expected by the driver.

Quality of flow V is considered to be the capacity of the weaving section. Speeds may frequently drop to under 20 mph (32 km/h), and turbulent, extremely congestive forced-flow operating conditions are present, sometimes including alternate feed from the entrances.

The quality of flow levels shown in Figure 16.12 are identical for all types of highways; however, the corresponding levels of service, which vary depending on the type of highway, may differ. *Highway Capacity Manual, 1965* recommends the relationships given in Table 16-10 to equate quality of flow to level of service on any particular highway type. It should be noted that pure weaving on highway types other than freeways is also shown, although it is less likely to be found on nonfreeway facilities.

TABLE 16–10
Recommended Relationships between Level of Service on Weaving Sections and Overall Quality of Flow on the Facility

Level of Service	Freeway and Multilane Rural	Freeway Interchange Roadways	Two-Lane Rural	Urban Arterial
A	I or II	II or III	II	III or IV
B	II	III	II or III	III or IV
C	II or III	III or IV	III	IV
D	III or IV	IV	IV	IV
E	IV or V	V	V	V
F		Unsatisfactory		

SOURCE: *Highway Capacity Manual, 1965*, Spec. Report 87 (Washington, D.C.: Highway Research Board, 1965), p. 173.

It is important to remember that in the design of a weaving section, the operating level of the weaving section should be made compatible with the general level of service of the entire highway, of which the weaving section is only a part. In using Table 16-10, where two operating levels are shown, the first is the desirable and the second is considered to be minimum value for design of the weaving section.

The length, weaving volume, and k relationships are shown in Figure 16.12. Volumes are expressed in *equivalent passenger cars per hour* (pc/h) for this length relationship, where

V_{we} = total weaving traffic volume, pc/h

V_{we1} = larger weaving volume, pc/h

V_{we2} = smaller weaving volume, pc/h

and where $V_{we} = V_{we1} + V_{we2}$.

The width of the weaving section is expressed in terms of the number of lanes at a specified level of service. It is calculated by using the following equations, in which volumes are expressed *directly in mixed traffic* except in extreme cases:

$$V_t = V_{o1} + V_{o2} + V_{w1} + V_{w2} \tag{16.6}$$

where V_t = total volume (weaving plus nonweaving traffic entering the section in veh/h of mixed traffic)

V_{o1} = one of the two outer flows, not involved in weaving, veh/h of mixed traffic

V_{o2} = other of the two outer flows, not involved in weaving, veh/h of mixed traffic

V_{w1} = larger weaving volume, veh/h of mixed traffic

V_{w2} = smaller weaving volume, veh/h of mixed traffic

$$N = \frac{V_t + (k - 1)V_{w2}}{SV} \tag{16.7}$$

where N = number of lanes

V_t = total volume, as before

k = weaving influence factor

V_{w2} = smaller weaving volume, as before

SV = service volume for a free-flowing lane outside the weaving section on the type of facility for the selected level of service, veh/h

A variety of difficulties, both theoretical and practical, have been identified during the years that this basic procedure has been in use. The recent research efforts in this area have produced two different more refined procedures, both of which have been released for trial use and evaluation among the "interim materials" referred to at the end of this chapter. They offer promise of proving more accurate than the method presented herein.

EXAMPLE 16.4:

A six-lane freeway intersects with a four-lane freeway for a short distance, forming a weaving section. The traffic volumes are as shown. Trucks constitute 5% of each of the traffic stream flows. Find the distance required between the merge and diverge points and the number of lanes required to provide for level of service C on this section.

Solution: To determine the length of the weaving section from Figure 16.12, an appropriate quality of flow criterion should be selected. Using Table 16-10 for level of service C on a freeway, either quality of flow II or III could be used. The desirable curve labeled II will be used in this example. Prior to using Figure 16.12, the mixed traffic weaving volumes, which include 5% trucks, must be converted to passenger cars per hour from Table 16-6 as follows: (700 + 900)/0.95 = 1684 pc/h. From Figure 16.12, using this total weaving volume and projecting across to curve II, where a k value of 2.6 is noted, the length of the weaving section required is read as 2500 ft.

The width of the weaving section in "number of lanes," N, is found by substituting the appropriate values into equation (16.7) as follows, where SV = 1326 was obtained from Table 16-4 by averaging the maximum service volumes for level of service C assuming a PHF of 0.85:

$$N = \frac{V_t + (k - 1)V_{w2}}{SV}$$

$$= \frac{2500 + 900 + 700 + 1600 + (2.6 - 1)(700)}{1326}$$

$$= 5.1 \text{ lanes}$$

Although the required width is computed as 5.1 lanes for level of service C, in this case probably five lanes would be provided through the weaving section, knowing that during the peak periods the level of service would drop slightly into level of service D operation.

Multilane rural highways without access control

Service volumes

A divided, multilane highway without access control can operate identically with a freeway in sections where crossing opportunities and marginal influences are negligible. At the other extreme, an undivided roadway with heavy crossing, turning, and entering movements operates in an entirely different manner, and its capacity and service volumes are usually controlled by the characteristics of frequent major intersections.

Intermediate to these is the multilane roadway, usually undivided, with frequent turning opportunities at driveways and intersections that offer the potential for occurrence of interference. The quality of service on this class of road is determined by the alignment, grades, cross section, volume, and composition of traffic, just as in the freeway case. When operating at level of service E, capacity, these roads may, in some cases, carry traffic volumes comparable to a freeway; however, this condition would be extremely unstable and these maximum volumes might well not be attainable in all cases.

Although flow is still classified basically as "uninterrupted," at better service levels, the potential for interferences generally results in significantly lower maximum service volumes than on freeways. The criteria for each service level and the associated maximum service volumes are given in Table 16-11. For specific multilane highways, the formula used looks the same as that for freeways, previously described in detail:

$$SV = MSV\,(W)(SM) \tag{16.8}$$

However, the level of service criteria and absolute values of lane width and lateral clearance adjustments differ, so that equation (16.8) produces different results than does (16.1).

Factors affecting service volumes

Design speed—average highway speed. Table 16-11 shows the marked reduction in maximum service volume at all levels below capacity that accompanies lower design standards. The better levels of service cannot be provided, by definition, and the maximum service volumes at lower levels are affected by driver reaction to restrictions in sight distance and to existence of curves and other impediments. The relationship of volume/capacity ratio, operating speed, and average highway speed on a typical rural multilane highway is shown in Figure 16.13.

Lane widths and lateral clearance. On divided, multilane rural roads the effects of reduced lane widths and/or lateral clearances are the same as on freeways, and the adjustment factors previously given may be used. Factors for undivided roads are given in Table 16-12. The factors at the bottom of the table should be used only when an obstruction, such as a bridge member or center-line barrier, is introduced into the center of a normally undivided roadway.

Traffic composition. The effect of trucks, buses, and recreational vehicles on capacity and service volumes of multilane highways is similar to that on freeways. Thus, the

TABLE 16–11
Operating Criteria and Maximum Service Volumes on Multilane Rural Highways*

Level of Service	Description	Operating Speed		Average Highway Speed (AHS)					
				70 mph (113 km/h)		60 mph (97 km/h)		50 mph (80 km/h)	
		mph	km/h	Volume/Capacity Ratio (*v/c*)	MSV Pass. Cars/h/lane	Volume/Capacity Ratio (*v/c*)	MSV Pass. Cars/h/lane	Volume/Capacity Ratio (*v/c*)	MSV Pass. Cars/h/lane
A	Free flowing	⩾60	⩾97	⩽0.30	600	—†	—†	—†	—†
B	Stable flow	⩾55	⩾89	⩽0.50	1000	⩽0.20	400	—†	—†
C	Stable flow	⩾45	⩾72	⩽0.75	1500	⩽0.50	1000	⩽0.25	500
D	Approaching unstable flow	⩾35	⩾56	⩽0.90	1800	⩽0.85	1700	⩽0.70	1400
E	Unstable flow	≈30	≈48	1.00	2000	1.00	2000	1.00	2000
F	Forced flow	<30	<48	← Not meaningful →					

*Conditions: all passenger cars; 12-ft (3.7-m) lanes; 6-ft (1.8-m) lateral clearance (min.); level terrain.
†This level of service not attainable at this speed.

SOURCE: *Highway Capacity Manual, 1965,* Spec. Report 87 (Washington, D.C.: Highway Research Board, 1965), p. 284.

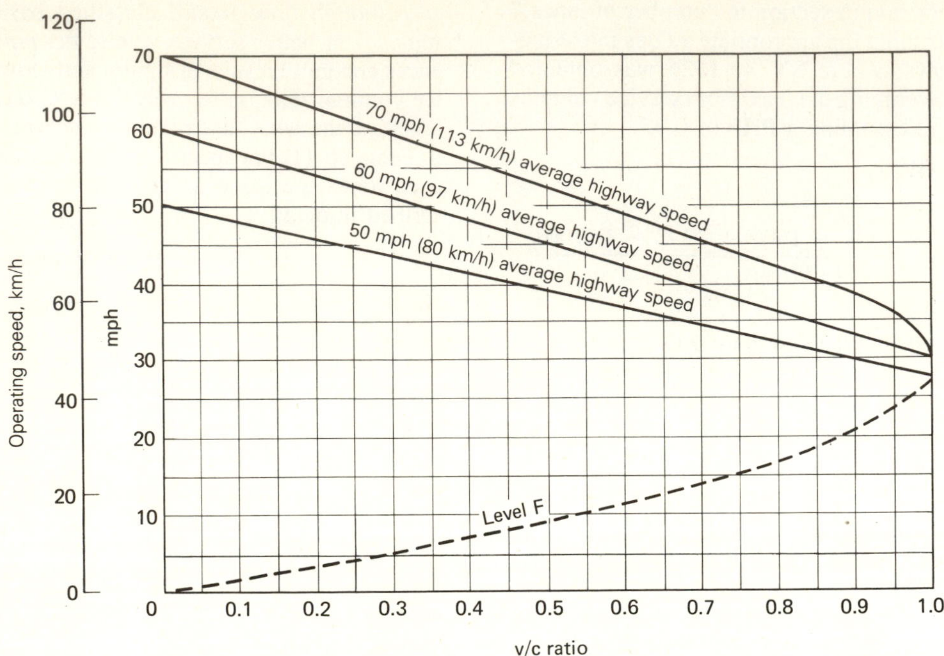

Figure 16.13. Relationship between volume-capacity ratio and operating speed on rural multilane highways. SOURCE: *Highway Capacity Manual, 1965,* Special Report 87, Washington, D.C.: Highway Research Board, 1965, p. 294.

TABLE 16–12
Adjustment Factors *(W)* for Restricted Lane Widths and Lateral Clearances on Undivided Multilane Highways*

Distance from Traffic Lane to Obstruction on Right Side Only		Two Lanes in Each Direction				Three or More Lanes in Each Direction			
ft	m	12-ft (3.7-m) Lanes	11-ft (3.4-m) Lanes	10-ft (3.0-m) Lanes	9-ft (2.7-m) Lanes	12-ft (3.7-m) Lanes	11-ft (3.4-m) Lanes	10-ft (3.0-m) Lanes	9-ft (2.7-m) Lanes
6	1.8	1.00	0.95	0.89	0.77	1.00	0.95	0.89	0.77
4	1.2	0.98	0.94	0.88	0.76	0.99	0.94	0.88	0.76
2	0.6	0.95	0.92	0.86	0.75	0.97	0.93	0.86	0.75
0	0	0.88	0.85	0.80	0.70	0.94	0.90	0.83	0.72
With additional obstruction on left side									
6	1.8	n.a.	n.a.	n.a.	n.a.	n.a.	n.a.	n.a.	n.a.
4	1.2	n.a.	n.a.	n.a.	n.a.	n.a.	n.a.	n.a.	n.a.
2	0.6	0.94	0.91	0.86	n.a.	0.96	0.92	0.85	n.a.
0	0	0.81	0.79	0.74	0.66	0.91	0.87	0.81	0.70

*n.a. = not applicable; use adjustment for right side only.

SOURCE: *Highway Capacity Manual, 1965,* Spec. Report 87 (Washington, D.C.: Highway Research Board, 1965), p. 286.

procedures and adjustment factors used for freeways are commonly used (Table 16-6). It should be noted that these factors are based on 200-lb/hp (91-kg/hp) trucks, high-performance intercity buses, and typical recreational vehicles. These are common on many multilane rural highways other than freeways, but they may not be appropriate in all cases. The adjustment factors for trucks on two-lane highways, given in a later section, are based on the performance characteristics of a 325-lb/hp (147-kg/hp) truck, to include the influence of typical American farm vehicles. Should this be the predominant type of vehicle expected on a particular multilane highway under study, appropriate adjustment factors should be utilized: on level to moderate rolling terrain, an equivalency of 3; in rolling terrain, 5; and mountainous terrain, from 10 to 12. For specific grades, reference to Figure 16.9 will assist in selecting appropriate factors. The factors given in a later section on two-lane roads should not be used because those factors also reflect the effect of passing restrictions on two-way roadways.

Variations in flow. Few data are currently available on peaking characteristics on ordinary rural highways. Thus, a specific adjustment for peak-hour factor is not usually made in level-of-service computations for such highways. It is commonly assumed that flow variations within the hour will not adversely affect levels A, B, and C at the maximum service volumes listed. The maximum service volumes given for level of service D will, however, result in a strong likelihood of delays and breakdown in flow if any significant peaking takes place. When this is known to be the case, the service volume D should be considered the maximum rate of flow that can be accommodated during a *short period* of maximum demand. If a peak-hour factor is known or can be reliably estimated, a downward adjustment in maximum service volume should be made by following the procedures given in preceding sections.

Roadside development and intersections. The procedures described above, based on uninterrupted traffic flow characteristics, can reasonably be applied where major intersections and/or roadside entrances are at least 1 mi (1.6 km) apart and speed limits are 40 mph (64 km/h) or greater. When this is not the case, procedures given later for urban arterials are more appropriate.

EXAMPLE 16.5:

Determine the level of service provided on a rural four-lane undivided highway with 11-ft (3.4-m) lanes, no shoulders, and obstructions at the pavement edge. Average highway speed is 60 mph (97 km/h) and there is a 1-mi (1.6-km), 6% grade. The existing demand volume is 1600 veh/h in the peak direction, with 10% trucks and insignificant buses and recreational vehicles. Determine the level of service with and without an added climbing lane.

Solution: Without a climbing lane:

(Assume level of service E)

Service volume (SV_E) = 2000 $(N)(W)(T)$

Number of lanes (N) = 2

Width adjustment (W) = 0.85 (Table 16-12)

Truck adjustment (T) = 0.45 (Table 16-6)

Substituting, SV_E = 2000(2)(0.85)(0.45)

= 1530 veh/h

Then, apparent v/c ratio $= \frac{1600}{1530} = 1.05$

Since the v/c ratio cannot exceed 1.00 in practice, this indicates that the roadway on this grade could not accommodate the demand volume, and level of service F would prevail.

Solution: With a climbing lane:

(Assume level of service D)

Service volume (SV_D) = 1700 $(N)(W)(T)$

Number of lanes (N) = 3

Width adjustment (W) = 0.90 (Table 16-12)

Truck adjustment (T) = 0.45 (Table 16-6)

Substituting, SV_D = 1700(3)(0.90)(0.45)

= 2065 veh/h

The v/c ratio $= \frac{1600}{2065} = 0.77$

Comparing the calculated v/c ratio with the operating criteria in Table 16.11 for a 60-mph (97-km/h) average highway speed, the level of service is found to be D, as originally assumed. If the resulting level of service had been different from that assumed, a second trial computation would be necessary.

Two-lane, two-way rural highways

Service volumes

The overriding distinction between traffic operations on a two-lane, two-way roadway and on those roadway types previously discussed lies in the passing maneuver, which must utilize a lane assigned to traffic traveling in the opposite direction. The resulting interaction requires that service volumes and capacities on two-way roadways be considered as total rather than one-way or one-lane values. Nevertheless, flow is still classified as basically "uninterrupted."

The need to pass in order to sustain a desired speed is a function of the amount of traffic in the lane and the distribution of speeds. The duration of the gap in opposing traffic required for the passing maneuver is a function of the speed and relative speed of passed and passing vehicles. The ability to pass is controlled further by the existence or nonexistence of a sight distance sufficient to detect and utilize an available gap with safety. When passing sight distance is not available, all vehicles as they overtake will form into a queue traveling at the speed of the slowest vehicle in the stream.

The capacity and service volumes of a two-way, two-lane roadway are thus seen to be functions of the flow rates in each direction, the speed of travel, the variance in speed in the traffic stream, and the availability of passing sight distance. The variance of speed is, in turn, principally established by the presence of trucks or other low-performance vehicles and of grades.

The reduction of marginal frictions through control of access undoubtedly affects service volumes on this kind of roadway, but since data are not available to quantify this effect, it has not been possible to give separate treatment to controlled and noncontrolled access facilities of this class. In general, the procedures given below are appropriate to roads having minor potential frictions, infrequently spaced. On sections having frequent turning and/or entering movements or having major crossing movements more frequent than one per mile (1.6 km), the procedures in a later section on urban streets should be used.

Again, it must be emphasized that the capacities and service volumes quoted for two-lane, two-way highways are totals for both directions combined, not by lane or directional values.

The basic computational formula again looks the same as for the better highway types:

$$SV = MSV(W)(SM) \tag{16.9}$$

but here the specific values have considerably different meanings. SV and MSV apply to total two-directional traffic, with allowance for passing sight distance, and the adjustment factors are different in absolute value.

TABLE 16-13
Operating Criteria and Maximum Service Volumes on Two-Lane, Two-Way Rural Highways*†

Level of Service	Description	Operating Speed mph	Operating Speed km/h	Passing Sight Distance (%)	Average Highway Speed (AHS): 70 mph (113 km/h) v/c(1)	70 mph (113 km/h) MSV(2)	60 mph (97 km/h) v/c(1)	60 mph (97 km/h) MSV(2)	50 mph (80 km/h) v/c(1)	50 mph (80 km/h) MSV(2)	40 mph (64 km/h) v/c(1)	40 mph (64 km/h) MSV(2)
A	Free flow	≥60	≥97	100	≤0.20	400	—	—	—	—	—	—
				80	≤0.18	360	—	—	—	—	—	—
				60	≤0.15	300	—	—	—	—	—	—
				40	≤0.12	240	—	—	—	—	—	—
				20	≤0.08	160	—	—	—	—	—	—
				0	≤0.04	80	—	—	—	—	—	—
B	Stable flow	≥50	≥80	100	≤0.45	900	≤0.40	800	—	—	—	—
				80	≤0.42	840	≤0.35	700	—	—	—	—
				60	≤0.38	760	≤0.30	600	—	—	—	—
				40	≤0.34	680	≤0.24	480	—	—	—	—
				20	≤0.30	600	≤0.18	360	—	—	—	—
				0	≤0.24	480	≤0.12	240	—	—	—	—
C	Stable flow	≥40	≥64	100	≤0.70	1,400	≤0.66	1,320	≤0.56	1,120	—	—
				80	≤0.68	1,360	≤0.61	1,220	≤0.53	1,060	—	—
				60	≤0.65	1,300	≤0.56	1,120	≤0.47	940	—	—
				40	≤0.62	1,240	≤0.51	1,020	≤0.38	760	—	—
				20	≤0.59	1,180	≤0.45	900	≤0.28	560	—	—
				0	≤0.54	1,080	≤0.38	760	≤0.18	360	—	—
D	Approaching unstable flow	≥35	≥56	100	≤0.85	1,700	≤0.83	1,660	≤0.75	1,500	≤0.58	1,160
				80	≤0.84	1,680	≤0.81	1,620	≤0.72	1,440	≤0.55	1,100
				60	≤0.83	1,660	≤0.79	1,580	≤0.69	1,380	≤0.51	1,020
				40	≤0.82	1,640	≤0.76	1,520	≤0.66	1,320	≤0.45	900
				20	≤0.81	1,620	≤0.71	1,420	≤0.61	1,220	≤0.35	700
				0	≤0.80	1,600	≤0.66	1,320	≤0.51	1,020	≤0.19	380
E	Unstable flow	≈30	≈48	Any	≤1.00	2,000	≤1.00	2,000	≤1.00	2,000	≤1.00	2,000
F	Forced flow	<30	<48	Any	← Not meaningful →							

(1) Volume/Capacity Ratio
(2) Maximum Service Volume pass. car/h (total both directions)

*Conditions: all passenger cars; 12-ft (3.7-m) lanes; 6-ft (1.8-m) lateral clearance (min.); level terrain.
†Dashes indicate level of service is not attainable at this speed.
SOURCE: *Highway Capacity Manual, 1965,* Spec. Report 87 (Washington, D.C.: Highway Research Board, 1965), pp. 302–303.

Factors affecting service volumes

Passing sight distance. Since maintenance of the stipulated operating speed requires a high degree of freedom to pass slower vehicles with minimum delay, any restriction on passing sight distance will have a marked effect on potential service volume. This effect is greatest at the better service levels and becomes less as the service level decreases, because the difference between the stipulated operating speed and the average speed of trucks and other slower-moving elements of the traffic stream becomes smaller.

Table 16-13 shows the approximate effect of restricted passing sight distance on maximum service volumes at each service level. In this table, the limitation of passing sight distance is expressed as the percentage of the length of the section under study that *provides* passing sight distance (see Chapter 19 for a definition and measurement of passing sight distance). This method is also used in *Highway Capacity Manual, 1965*. It should be noted that some publications in common use base sight-distance restriction on the obverse definition: the percentage of roadway that does *not* provide the stipulated sight distance.

Design speed—average highway speed. As before, the weighted average design speed of the highway is called the average highway speed. It affects the maximum service volumes in two ways: (1) it limits the operating speed of passenger vehicles and thus may make attainment of the better service levels impossible, and (2) it affects the average speed of trucks and slower-moving vehicles and thereby influences the need for passing maneuvers. When combined with limitations on passing sight distance, which is often the case, a lower average highway speed design will have substantially lower maximum service volumes at all service levels better than capacity level E. The approximate effect of these combined factors is shown in Table 16-13.

Similarly, Figure 16.14 presents a representative group of typical speed–volume curves combining the several factors, as condensed from the several charts in *Highway Capacity Manual, 1965*.

Lane width and lateral clearance. Because traffic in adjacent lanes of a two-lane, two-way roadway is moving in opposite directions, the effects of narrow lanes and/or restricted lateral clearances on vehicle-operator performance is more pronounced than on one-way or multilane roadways.

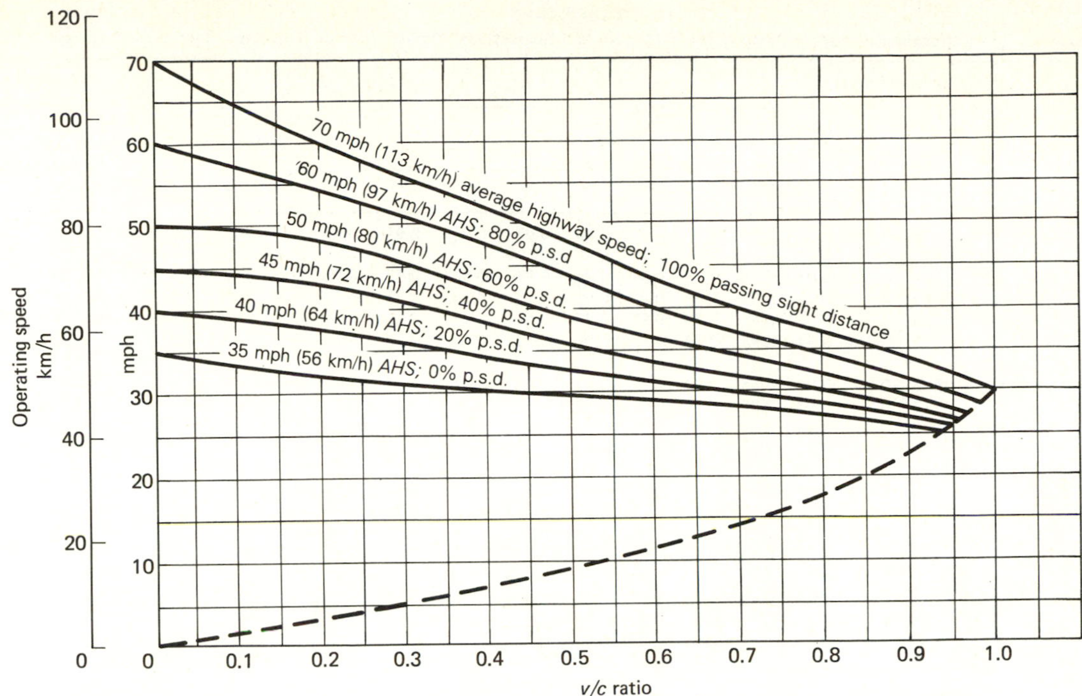

Figure 16.14. Typical relationships between overall volume-capacity for both directions of travel and operating speed on two-lane rural highways. SOURCE: Adapted from *Highway Capacity Manual, 1965*, Special Report 87, Washington, D.C.: Highway Research Board, 1965, p. 63.

The effect is also slightly more pronounced at the better service levels, as indicated in Table 16-14.

Traffic composition and grades. The combination of grades and trucks, or other nonpassenger car traffic categories, has a major effect on traffic operations on two-lane, two-way highways. It is considerably greater than that on freeways and other multilane highways, previously discussed. This section presents typical adjustment factors for the several vehicle types; details regarding passenger car equivalents and slow-moving vehicle adjustment factors appear in *Highway Capacity Manual, 1965*.

Trucks. Passenger car equivalents of trucks vary from a value of 2 on grades under 2% to a value of over 100 on long 7% or greater grades at or near capacity volumes. These equivalents are based on the hill-climbing ability of loaded trucks in the 325-lb/hp 147-kg/hp category. Higher-performance trucks would have less effect on service volumes.

Table 16-15 (top) gives truck adjustment factors for representative percentages of trucks on selected individual grades, and Table 16-15 (bottom) gives the general effects of trucks over extended sections with varying grades. It should be noted that a critical grade within the section may control the capacity of the entire section to a level below that obtained by using the latter generalized values.

Normally, the computation for truck effect is based on the total percentage of trucks in the two-way traffic stream and with the assumption that the effect of plus and minus

TABLE 16–14
Adjustment Factors (*W*) for Narrow Lanes and/or Restricted Lateral Clearances on Two-Lane, Two-Way Rural Highways

Distance from Traffic Lane Edge to Obstruction		Obstruction on One Side Only*								Obstructions on Both Sides*							
		12-ft (3.7-m) Lanes		11-ft (3.4-m) Lanes		10-ft (3.0-m) Lanes		9-ft (2.7-m) Lanes		12-ft (3.7-m) Lanes		11-ft (3.4-m) Lanes		10-ft (3.0-m) Lanes		9-ft (2.7-m) Lanes	
ft	m	Level B	Level E	Level B	Level E	Level B	Level E	Level B	Level E	Level B	Level E	Level B	Level E	Level B	Level E	Level B	Level E
6	1.8	1.00	1.00	0.86	0.88	0.77	0.81	0.70	0.76	1.00	1.00	0.86	0.88	0.77	0.81	0.70	0.76
4	1.2	0.96	0.97	0.83	0.85	0.74	0.79	0.68	0.74	0.92	0.94	0.79	0.83	0.71	0.76	0.65	0.71
2	0.6	0.91	0.93	0.78	0.81	0.70	0.75	0.64	0.70	0.81	0.85	0.70	0.75	0.63	0.69	0.57	0.65
0	0	0.85	0.88	0.73	0.77	0.66	0.71	0.60	0.66	0.70	0.76	0.60	0.67	0.54	0.62	0.49	0.58

*Includes allowance for opposite traffic.

SOURCE: *Highway Capacity Manual, 1965*, Spec. Report 87 (Washington, D.C.: Highway Research Board, 1965), p. 303.

TABLE 16–15
Approximate Adjustment Factors for Trucks *(T)*, Buses *(B)*, and Recreational Vehicles *(RV)* on Two-Lane, Two-Way Highways

			Levels of Service A and B										Level of Service C†						Levels of Service D and E†					
Grade	Length		Percentage of Trucks				Percentage of Recreational Vehicles				Percentage of Buses		Percentage of Trucks				Percentage of Buses		Percentage of Trucks				Percentage of Buses	
(%)	mi	km	3%	5%	10%	20%	3%	5%	10%	20%	3%	5%	3%	5%	10%	20%	3%	5%	3%	5%	10%	20%	3%	5%
0–2	All		0.97	0.95	0.91	0.83	0.96	0.94	0.88	0.79	0.97	0.95	0.97	0.95	0.91	0.83	0.97	0.95	0.97	0.95	0.91	0.83	0.97	0.95
3	½	0.8	0.79	0.69	0.53	0.36	0.96	0.94	0.88	0.79	0.97	0.95	0.97	0.69	0.53	0.36	0.97	0.95	0.85	0.77	0.63	0.45	0.97	0.95
	1	1.6	0.68	0.56	0.38	0.24	0.96	0.94	0.88	0.79	0.97	0.95	0.63	0.50	0.33	0.20	0.97	0.95	0.64	0.51	0.34	0.21	0.97	0.95
	2	3.2	0.63	0.50	0.33	0.20	0.96	0.94	0.88	0.79	0.97	0.95	0.56	0.44	0.28	0.17	0.97	0.95	0.54	0.42	0.27	0.16	0.97	0.95
	4	6.4	0.60	0.48	0.31	0.19	0.96	0.94	0.88	0.79	0.97	0.95	0.52	0.40	0.25	0.15	0.97	0.95	0.51	0.39	0.25	0.14	0.97	0.95
4	½	0.8	0.69	0.57	0.40	0.25	0.96	0.94	0.88	0.79	0.97	0.95	0.64	0.51	0.34	0.21	0.97	0.95	0.64	0.51	0.34	0.21	0.97	0.95
	1	1.6	0.57	0.44	0.29	0.17	0.96	0.94	0.88	0.79	0.97	0.95	0.49	0.37	0.23	0.13	0.97	0.95	0.47	0.35	0.21	0.11	0.97	0.95
	2	3.2	0.53	0.41	0.26	0.15	0.96	0.94	0.88	0.79	0.97	0.95	0.45	0.33	0.20	0.11	0.97	0.95	0.42	0.30	0.18	0.10	0.97	0.95
	4	6.4	0.51	0.39	0.25	0.14	0.96	0.94	0.88	0.79	0.97	0.95	0.43	0.31	0.19	0.10	0.97	0.95	0.39	0.28	0.17	0.09	0.97	0.95
5	½	0.8	0.59	0.47	0.30	0.18	0.95	0.92	0.85	0.75	0.92	0.87	0.51	0.39	0.24	0.14	0.94	0.91	0.48	0.36	0.22	0.12	0.97	0.95
	1	1.6	0.51	0.39	0.25	0.14	0.94	0.91	0.83	0.71	0.92	0.87	0.42	0.30	0.18	0.10	0.94	0.91	0.38	0.27	0.16	0.08	0.97	0.95
	2	3.2	0.48	0.36	0.22	0.12	0.94	0.90	0.81	0.68	0.92	0.87	0.38	0.27	0.16	0.08	0.94	0.91	0.35	0.24	0.14	0.07	0.97	0.95
	4	6.4	0.46	0.34	0.20	0.11	0.93	0.88	0.79	0.66	0.92	0.87	0.37	0.26	0.15	0.08	0.94	0.91	0.33	0.22	0.13	0.07	0.97	0.95
6	½	0.8	0.51	0.39	0.25	0.14	0.93	0.88	0.79	0.66	0.85	0.77	0.42	0.30	0.18	0.10	0.87	0.80	0.38	0.27	0.16	0.08	0.92	0.87
	1	1.6	0.46	0.34	0.20	0.11	0.91	0.85	0.75	0.60	0.85	0.77	0.36	0.25	0.15	0.08	0.87	0.80	0.33	0.22	0.13	0.07	0.92	0.87
	2	3.2	0.43	0.31	0.19	0.10	0.90	0.84	0.72	0.56	0.85	0.77	0.34	0.24	0.14	0.07	0.87	0.80	0.30	0.20	0.11	0.06	0.92	0.87
	4	6.4	0.40	0.29	0.17	0.09	0.89	0.83	0.71	0.56	0.85	0.77	0.33	0.22	0.13	0.07	0.87	0.80	0.27	0.18	0.10	0.05	0.92	0.87
7	½	0.8	0.43	0.31	0.19	0.10	0.93	0.88	0.79	0.65	0.75	0.65	0.35	0.24	0.14	0.07	0.75	0.65	0.31	0.21	0.12	0.06	0.79	0.69
	1	1.6	0.39	0.28	0.16	0.08	0.90	0.84	0.72	0.57	0.75	0.65	0.31	0.21	0.12	0.06	0.75	0.65	0.27	0.18	0.10	0.05	0.79	0.69
	2	3.2	0.36	0.25	0.15	0.08	0.90	0.84	0.72	0.56	0.75	0.65	0.29	0.20	0.11	0.06	0.75	0.65	0.25	0.17	0.09	0.05	0.79	0.69
	4	6.4	0.35	0.24	0.15	0.08	0.89	0.83	0.71	0.56	0.75	0.65	0.28	0.18	0.10	0.05	0.75	0.65	0.24	0.16	0.09	0.05	0.79	0.69

		Level of Service A: Percentage of Vehicles				Levels of Service B and C: Percentage of Vehicles				Levels of Service D and E: Percentage of Vehicles			
	Extended Sections*	3%	5%	10%	20%	3%	5%	10%	20%	3%	5%	10%	20%
Trucks	Level terrain	0.94	0.91	0.83	0.71	0.96	0.93	0.87	0.77	0.97	0.95	0.91	0.83
	Rolling terrain	0.92	0.87	0.77	0.63	0.89	0.83	0.71	0.56	0.89	0.83	0.71	0.56
	Mountainous terrain	0.85	0.77	0.63	0.45	0.79	0.69	0.53	0.36	0.75	0.65	0.48	0.31
Buses	Level terrain	0.97	0.95	0.91	0.83	0.97	0.95	0.91	0.83	0.97	0.95	0.91	0.83
	Rolling terrain	0.92	0.87	0.77	0.63	0.92	0.87	0.77	0.63	0.92	0.87	0.77	0.63
	Mountainous terrain	0.87	0.80	0.67	0.50	0.87	0.80	0.67	0.50	0.87	0.80	0.67	0.50
Recreational vehicles	Level terrain	0.97	0.94	0.89	0.81	0.96	0.93	0.87	0.77	0.98	0.97	0.94	0.89
	Rolling terrain	0.94	0.90	0.82	0.69	0.92	0.87	0.78	0.63	0.94	0.90	0.81	0.68
	Mountainous terrain	0.89	0.83	0.71	0.56	0.89	0.83	0.70	0.54	0.89	0.83	0.70	0.54

*Includes upgrades, downgrades, and level sections.
†Data not available for recreational vehicles; can be approximated by extrapolation of related values for levels A and B.

SOURCE: *Highway Capacity Manual, 1965,* Spec. Report 87 (Washington, D.C.: Highway Research Board, 1965), pp. 304–307; A. WERNER, "Effect of Recreational Vehicles on Highway Capacity," unpublished thesis, University of Calgary, 1974, pp. 198–201.

grades is the same. When the percentage of trucks in the two directions is appreciably different or when truck travel loaded in one direction and return empty, this simplification is not entirely valid.

Buses. Again, as with multilane highways, the influence of typically low volumes of buses may be ignored. Where, however, bus volumes are relatively high or grades severe, Table 16-15 gives bus adjustment factors both for individual grades and extended sections.

Recreational Vehicles. The influence of recreational vehicles is particularly noticeable where they appear in concentration in recreational areas, usually served by two-lane, two-way roads. Recent research in Canada[13] has developed passenger car equivalents for individual grades up to 11% for the better levels of service, and for extended roadway sections for all levels of service. Recreational vehicle adjustment factors developed from them appear in Table 16-15.

These slow-moving-vehicle adjustment factors are handled and applied in the same manner as are those for free-

[13] A. WERNER, "Effect of Recreational Vehicles on Highway Capacity", unpublished thesis, Department of Civil Engineering, University of Calgary, 1974 [portions published in A. WERNER, J. F. MORRALL, AND GORDON HALLS, "Effect of Recreational Vehicles on Highway Capacity," *Traffic Eng.*, *45*(5), 20–25 (May 1975)].

ways and multilane highways, previously described. As before, the individual factors should be used directly only where just one type of vehicle is involved. Where two or three are involved, a combined adjustment factor *SM* should be developed as there explained, making use of conversion Table 16-7 as before.

Variations in flow rate. As yet, little is known about any generalized influence of traffic flow variation (peaking) on two-lane, two-way highways. If such an influence is apparent in a particular situation, however, it should be taken into account.

EXAMPLE 16.6

Determine the service volume for level of service B on a rural two-lane, two-way highway with 10-ft (3.0-m) lanes, 4-ft (1.2-m) shoulders, and with obstructions at the edges of the shoulders. The average highway speed is 60 mph (97 km/h) with 60% available passing sight distance. There is a 1-mi, 5% grade with 10% trucks and 5% recreational vehicles in the traffic stream.

Solution: For level of service B,

$$SV_B = (MSV_B)(W)(SM)$$

where $MSV_B = 600$ (Table 16-13)

$W = 0.74$ (Table 16-14)

The adjustment factor for slow-moving vehicles (*SM*) is computed by first determining the adjustment factors for the trucks and recreational vehicles from Table 16-15, then using this result and Table 16-7 to find the passenger car equivalents, and finally substituting these into equation (16.2). The adjustment factors here are 0.25 for trucks and 0.91 for recreational vehicles. The corresponding passenger car equivalents, from Table 16-7, are 31 for trucks and 3 for recreational vehicles. Then:

$$SM = \frac{100}{100 - P_T + E_T P_T - P_{RV} + R_{RV} P_{RV}}$$

$$= \frac{100}{100 - 10 + 31(10) - 5 + 3(5)} = 0.24$$

Substituting yields:

$SV_B = (600)(0.74)(0.24) = 107$ veh/h, total for both directions

Urban arterials

Thus far, all freeway and rural flows that have been discussed have been described as basically "uninterrupted." In urban areas, however, flow is typically, although not always, "interrupted" on nonfreeway facilities.

This distinction between operation on a rural and an urban facility is created by the added frequency of marginal frictions, intersections, turning movements, pedestrians, and the like on the typical urban arterial or street. When these are not present in a situation under study, even though in an urban area, the procedures given in the preceding sections are appropriate and should be used.

Urban arterials are usually considered as those that have signalized intersections at less than 1-mi (1.6 km) intervals and sight distances and marginal frictions that hold the average (and usually legal maximum) speed to 35 mph (56 km/h) or less. Under these conditions, marginal frictions and interruptions play a more significant role than do stream frictions in determining capacity and service levels.

Traffic signal control at the major intersections is normally the capacity-controlling factor. At volume levels below capacity, the interrelationship between adjacent signals frequently sets the maximum possible average speed irrespective of flow rate. Marginal frictions, bus operation, and midblock turning movements may further reduce these speeds, which are essentially independent of the rate of flow on the arterial.

Service volumes

Because signalization of major intersections is usually the practical determinant of capacity and service volumes, the most frequently used method of evaluating arterial service is to analyze the signalized approaches and assume that the results are representative of the entire section.

This is not entirely satisfactory at best and is totally unrealistic when number or width of lanes, parking control, or geometrics differ between intersection approaches and midsection locations. It also is misleading where midblock features such as parking facility driveways produce intermediate congestion points.

The use of operating, running, or average speed as a measure of service level also poses serious problems on arterials. Since top speeds are limited by environmental or legal factors, there is little apparent change in average overall speed through the range of densities up to 40 or 50 veh/mi (25 to 31 veh/km) which are associated with levels of service A through D on other facilities, although momentary speeds may fluctuate widely.

Other, more sensitive, measures of service level have been suggested but are not currently widely used or completely understood. Particularly promising are various measures of delay. One such potential measure is the delay ratio, defined as the *ratio of amount of delay time to the total travel time on a section of roadway during a specified time period.*[14] In the cited study, delay ratios equal to or less than 0.05, 0.15, 0.25, 0.40, and 0.60 were proposed as upper limits of levels of service A through E. Even here, however, the problem of defining the "no-delay" condition still exists.

Several measures of smoothness of flow have been proposed. The first, acceleration noise, is the standard deviation of a vehicle's accelerations over time:

[14] WALTER E. PONTIER ET AL., *Optimizing Flow on Existing Street Networks*, National Cooperative Highway Res. Report No. 113 (Washington, D.C.: Highway Research Board, 1971).

$$\sigma_a = \left(\frac{1}{T} \int_0^T a^2 dt \right)^{1/2} \qquad (16.10)$$

where σ_a = acceleration noise

T = running time (overall time minus delay time)

a = acceleration

The mean velocity gradient (G) is the *ratio of acceleration noise to mean velocity*. The principal difficulty with these measures is the relatively high cost of data collection. Also, one study[15] found a highly correlated linear relationship between mean velocity gradient and travel time on urban arterials, indicating that the more easily measured travel time or its reciprocal, speed, was as accurate an index of quality of flow as mean velocity gradient.

Still another promising measure of quality of flow is the energy ratio,[16] defined as the ratio of *effective kinetic energy to measured (free flow) kinetic energy in the traffic stream:*

$$N = \frac{(Ku)^2}{(Ku_f)^2} = \frac{(u)^2}{(u_f)} \qquad (16.11)$$

where N = energy ratio

u = effective speed (distance/time)

u_f = free-flowing (spot) speed

K = density

This more easily obtained measure of smoothness of flow is also highly correlated with acceleration noise.

The Highway Capacity Committee, Transportation Research Board, although recognizing the disadvantages, has recommended average overall speed as the principal measure of service levels on urban arterials. These values are given in Table 16-16.

The volume/capacity ratios listed in Table 16-16 were selected to be consistent with intersection load factor values discussed later in the section on signalized intersections.

Another approach, suggested by one of the authors, is described below. It is more satisfying in some respects than the one described above but has not been either tested or accepted generally in the field.

By definition, traffic on an arterial is regimented by traffic signals and proceeds through a section in a series of platoons separated by time gaps with few if any vehicles. If, for the base condition, it is assumed that the traffic signals have a 50:50 cycle split and traffic flow is limited by the known performance of a line of cars starting from a stopped condition, then capacity, or the upper limit of level of service E, is 50% of 1500, or 750 veh/h. At 10 to 11 mph (16 to 18 km/h), a criterion slightly below that established by the Highway Capacity Committee, the approximate density would be in the range 70 to 75 veh/mi (43 to 47 veh/km).

[15]Ibid., p. 100.

[16]D. L. Cooper and R. J. Walinchus, "Measures of Effectiveness for Urban Traffic Control Systems," *Highway Capacity and Quality of Service*, Highway Res. Rec. 321 (Washington, D.C.: Highway Research Board, 1970), pp. 46–59.

TABLE 16–16
Operating Criteria for Urban Arterials

Level of Service	Description	Average Overall Speed mph	Average Overall Speed km/h	Volume/ Capacity Ratio	Associated Load Factor
A	Free flow	≥30	≥48	≤0.60	0.0
B	Stable flow	≥25	≥40	≤0.70	≤0.1
C	Stable flow	≥20	≥32	≤0.80	≤0.3
D	Approaching unstable flow	≥15	≥24	≤0.90	≤0.7
E	Unstable flow	≈15	≈24	≤1.00	≤1.0
F	Forced flow	<15	<24	Not meaningful	

Source: *Highway Capacity Manual, 1965*, Spec. Report 87 (Washington, D.C.: Highway Research Board, 1965), p. 323.

TABLE 16–17
Maximum Lane Service Volumes on Urban Arterials Based on 50% Cycle Split and Average Density and Speed Criteria

Level of Service	Average Overall Speed mph	Average Overall Speed km/h	Density vehicles/mi	Density vehicles/km	Approximate Volume*/ Lane (vehicles/h)
A	≥30	≥48	10	6	<300
B	≥25	≥40	20	12	500
C	≥20	≥32	30	19	600
D	≈15	≈24	45	28	675
E	≈10	≈16	75	47	750
F	<10	<16	>75	>47	Variable

*The speed–density–volume relationships implicit to this table are correct only if space mean speed is used. Average overall speed as usually measured only approximates this value.

This is the range of densities commonly associated with level of service E on free-flowing facilities. Using this same approach with the other service levels results in the relationships given in Table 16-17.

Factors affecting service volumes

Arterial performance is affected by a wider variety of factors than is freeway or rural flow, but quantitative means of estimating the effects of many of these factors on arterial service volumes are not readily available. Some of these factors are discussed below.

One-way operation. One-way operation is generally more efficient than two-way operation for a given street width. Based primarily on data for signalized intersection approaches, it would appear that the capacity advantage of one-way operation ranges from 10 to 20%. This advantage is caused primarily by the elimination of opposing flow conflicts, particularly where left turns occur, and frequently, the simplification of intersectional controls. Other factors, such as signal progression, advantageous lane dimensions, multilane operation, and changes in patterns of turning movements, may or may not be present in a particular case and each situation should be studied individually.

Lane configuration and width. Major contributors to traffic delays are left-turn and, to a lesser extent, right-turn movements. Higher service volumes can be accommodated if these movements are removed from the main through lanes by channelization or lane assignment.

The effect of lane markings and lane width on urban arterial flow is a subject of some uncertainty. Current basic American and British practice considers the carrying capacity of an arterial approaching a signalized intersection to be a function of approach width, irrespective of lane configuration. Australian practice considers the carrying capacity to be a function of number of lanes irrespective of width, within limits of 6.5 to 15 ft. (2.0 to 4.6 m). If, however, all parameters of level of service are considered, including driving comfort, it seems appropriate to consider lane width and configuration as factors. At capacity flow levels, available data indicate about a 40-veh/h increment per foot of lane width (12 veh/h per meter).[17] This is substantially less than the effect of lane width on freeways and rural highways, which is not unreasonable in view of the lower speed on arterials.

Signalized intersections. The operation of closely spaced signalized intersections and the related extent of progressive timing will usually be a principal determinant of arterial capacities and service volumes. These may be estimated by methods given later in the section "Intersections." The cross-street volumes will be another significant factor, owing to their influence on cycle splits.

Coming into increasing use in the United States is the "critical movement method" or "critical lane method" of intersection analysis, for relatively fast overview analyses of entire intersections. A brief description of this method is given at the end of the chapter.

Unsignalized intersections. Turning movements and crossing volumes can reduce arterial service volumes. As discussed later in the "Intersections" section, the influence depends upon the type of control present, if any. Typically, such intersections will be operating considerably below capacity; otherwise, local pressures would have required signalization.

Midblock driveways. Both right and left turns into and from driveways reduce arterial service volumes. Residential driveways can usually be ignored, but heavily used commercial driveways become, for practical purposes, unsignalized intersections.

Curb parking or loading. The area occupied by parked vehicles is not available for traffic movement. The effect on capacity and service volumes is thus equivalent to a reduction in effective width of at least 6 to 8 ft (1.8 to 2.4 m). Often, however, it is considerably greater, up to some 12 to 14 ft (3.7 to 4.3 m) or more, as in areas of heavy parking turnover, where a sporadic interruption in the adjacent lane will result from vehicles entering or leaving parking spaces.

Even where parking or loading is legally prohibited, momentary stops to discharge passengers, transit movements, and the possibility of illegal parking decrease the operational desirability of a curb lane. The proximity to pedestrians and to fixed objects in the border area and, frequently, an irregular cross slope to accommodate drainage further decrease the attractiveness of a curb lane. In Australian practice, the curb lane of multilane approaches (over two lanes) is penalized up to 60%, depending on parking enforcement practices, prevalence of right turns, and downstream roadway conditions.

Double parking. Double-parked trucks or passenger cars can drastically reduce the carrying capacity of an arterial because they occupy at least one lane and, on narrow streets, may require traffic to await gaps in opposing traffic before traffic can proceed.

Pedestrians. Light volumes of pedestrian traffic have marginal effect on service volumes since, by custom if not by law, they frequently adjust their crossing pattern to available gaps in the traffic stream. As pedestrian volumes increase, the effect is more pronounced because their presence interrupts both through movements and intersectional turning movements. Unregulated midblock crossings will have further adverse effects.

Trucks and through buses. Unless significant grades are present, trucks and express buses can operate at speeds comparable to passenger vehicles on arterials. Their effect on capacity and service volumes is caused primarily by their added size and somewhat lower acceleration capabilities. A passenger car equivalency of 2 is frequently used for trucks. As mentioned previously, research has shown that the equivalency of a transit bus in express service on freeways and expressways is about 1.6. This value can be accepted as an approximation for urban arterials as well. Australian[18] practice also uses an equivalency of 2.0.

Local transit buses. Transit buses in local service present a different case, depending on whether or not bus loading bays, bus zones in a parking lane, or curb stops in a normal driving lane are provided. The location of a bus stop in relation to a signalized intersection is also important and is treated in a later section.

In summary, methods of estimating capacity and service volumes on urban arterials are largely subjective because of the complex interrelationships involved and the paucity of scientific measurements in the past. Currently, considerable research into this subject is finally under way, but pending its successful completion and reporting, most capacity estimates are made in practice by relying on the signalized intersection procedures that follow.

Intersections

Any location at which two traffic streams cross is, in fact, an "intersection." In this broad sense, the weaving sections previously described are technically intersections. In normal practice, however, an intersection is usually con-

[17]Highway Res. Rec. 289 (Washington, D.C.: Highway Research Board, 1969), pp. 5, 15.

[18]Australian Road Research Board, *Signalized Intersections—Capacity Guide*, Res. Report 79, Melbourne, Australia, Apr. 1978, p. 4.

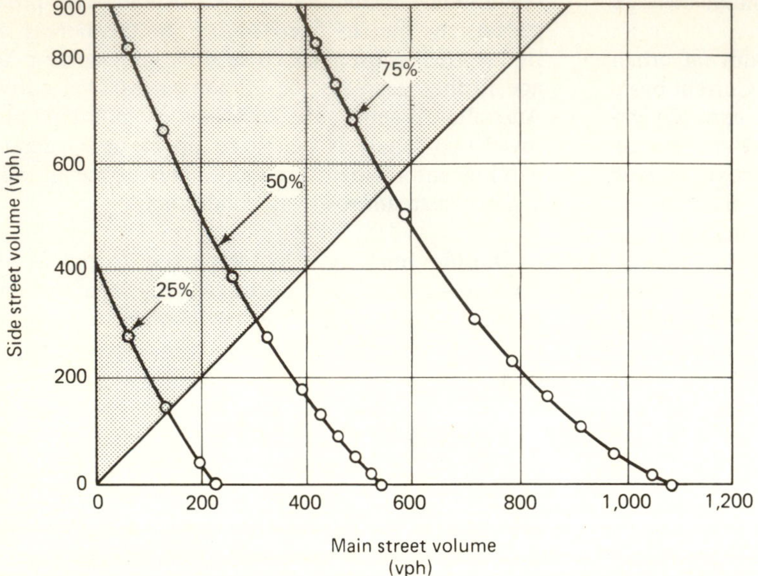

(a) Critical lag 4.6 sec

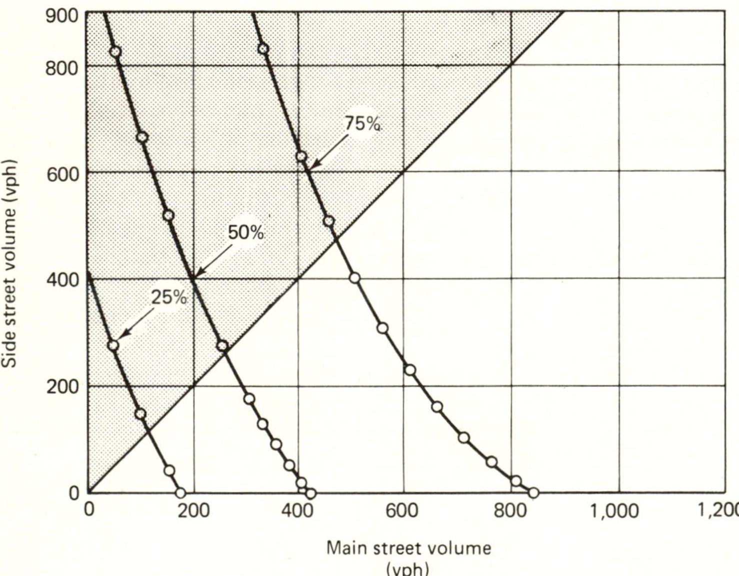

(b) Critical lag 5.9 sec

Figure 16.15. Volumes for which 25%, 50% and 75% of side-street vehicles are delayed. SOURCE: Morton S. Raff, *A Volume Warrant for Urban Stop Signs*, Naugatuck, Conn.: The ENO Foundation for Highway Traffic Control, 1950, pp. 94, 98.

sidered to be the at-grade crossing of two or more streets or highways at or near a single point.

Traffic performance at intersections, and identification of the factors involved, varies considerably depending upon the controls present—no control, yield, stop, traffic signals, or a traffic circle.

Uncontrolled intersections

Basic intersections. The intersection of two roadways at an angle of approximately 90° without any control devices present is probably the most common of all intersections. Relatively few studies have been undertaken as to either capacity or service volume values under these conditions, undoubtedly because safety considerations usually require installation of control devices at volume levels well below those that would significantly affect delay or other conventional measures of service. However, some analyses of delay have been made.

The probability of an approaching vehicle being delayed and the amount of delay at an uncontrolled intersection depends on the traffic volumes on the various approaches, the sight distances available, and the gap size acceptable to approaching drivers. The latter, in turn, is undoubtedly influenced by grades, speed of traffic, and the geometry of the intersection. A landmark study of these relationships showed that where random arrivals are assumed and volumes are sufficiently low so that queues usually will not occur, the probability that the vehicle on the lower volume street will be delayed is given by the formula[19]

$$P = 1 - \frac{e^{-2.5q_s}e^{-2qt}}{1 - e^{-2.5q_s}(1 - e^{-qt})} \qquad (16.12)$$

where P = probability of delay

e = Napierian base

q_s = side-street flow rate

q = main-street flow rate

t = critical lag (time spacing between arrival of side-street and main-street vehicles such that the number of rejected lags larger and the number of accepted lags smaller will be equal)

The percentage of side street vehicles delayed for various main- and side-street volumes is given in Figure 16.15 for critical lags of 4.6 and 5.9 s, which may be the typical range for urban intersections.

Another useful criterion is the mean delay to side-street vehicles, which is given by the formula

$$\bar{d} = q^{-1}(e^{qt} - qt - 1) \qquad (16.13)$$

where $\bar{d}$ = mean delay caused by blockage, s

e = Napierian base

q = main-street flow rate

t = critical gap (time spacing between arrival of succeeding main-street vehicles, which half of the side-street drivers will accept and half reject)

These values are plotted in Figure 16.16.

It should be noted that formula (16.13) gives only the delay caused by blockage by main-street cars. Time lost in deceleration and acceleration and any delay in queue awaiting a first-in-line position are not included. If queueing can be expected on the side street, the average delay, including the queueing delay, can be estimated from the formula

$$\bar{d}_t = \frac{1}{\mu - \lambda} \qquad (16.14)$$

where $\bar{d}_t$ = average total delay, s

μ = average service rate $1/\bar{d}$(Figure 16.16), veh/s

λ = side-street arrival rate, veh/s

The expected number of vehicles in the queue can be estimated from the formula

$$N = \frac{\lambda}{\mu - \lambda} \qquad (16.15)$$

where N is the expected number in the queue and μ and λ are as before.

[19]MORTON S. RAFF, *A Volume Warrant for Urban Stop Signs* (Saugatuck, Conn.: The ENO Foundation for Highway Traffic Control, 1950), p. 48.

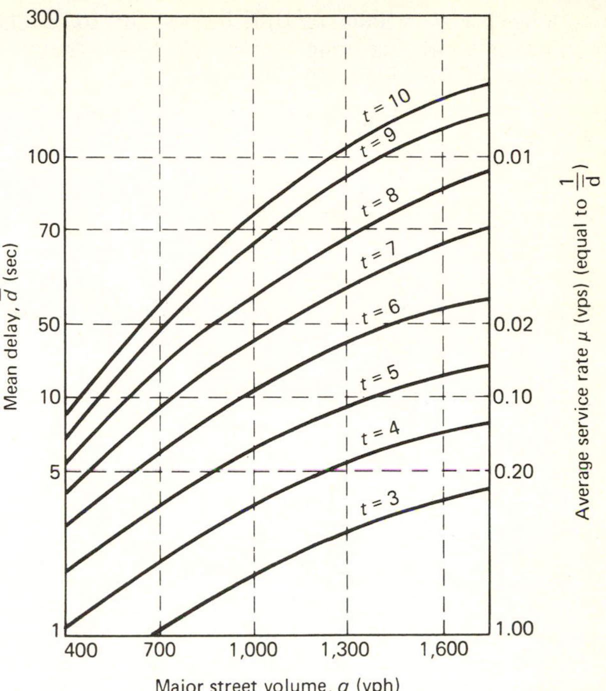

Figure 16.16. Mean delay to side-street vehicles without queuing. SOURCE: Vasant H. Surti, "Operational Efficiency Evaluation of Selected At-Grade Intersections," *Highway Capacity and Quality of Service*, Highway Research Record 321, Washington, D.C.: Highway Research Board, 1970, p. 68.

None of the values from formula (16.15) is an exact parallel of the speed or density criteria used in earlier sections to define various service levels. The engineer may, however, find them useful in evaluating service provided at an uncontrolled intersection. Because the flow rates on both main and side streets are significant to these formulas, flow variations within the peak hour should be considered, particularly since main- and side-street peak periods within the hour may not coincide.

Although capacities of unsignalized intersections are probably of more academic than practical interest in many localities, because of the usual need to provide some form of controlled operation at well below capacity level, capacity analysis procedures do exist. One rudimentary method, where no stop or yield sign controls exist, is to assume a signalized intersection with green time in proportion to main- and cross-street volumes and geometrics. Another is a recent adaptation of work done abroad, currently under trial evaluation among the "interim materials" referred to at the end of this chapter. It offers promise of greater precision.

Traffic circles (rotaries). The traffic circle or rotary is a special case of uncontrolled intersection, incorporating a series of short weaving sections intended to maintain flow while crossing movements are occurring. Many such sections are too short for effective analysis by means of *Highway Capacity Manual, 1965* procedures.

In such short weaving sections in traffic circles (or roundabouts, as they are known in Great Britain), maximum flow (capacity) has been found by British research[20] to be related to entrance width, weaving section width, and length and proportion of weaving traffic as follows:

$$\text{U.S. units: } V_{max} = \frac{108w(1 + m/w)(1 - P/3)}{(1 + w/l)} \qquad (16.16a)$$

$$\text{Metric units: } V_{max} = \frac{354w(1 + m/w)(1 - P/3)}{(1 + w/l)} \qquad (16.16b)$$

where V_{max} = maximum flow through weaving section, passenger car units per hour

w = width of roadway in the weaving section, ft (or m)

l = length of weaving section, ft (or m)

m = average width of entrances to weaving section $\left(\frac{m_1 + m_2}{2}\right)$, ft (or m)

P = proportion of weaving traffic to total traffic in the weaving section

Measurements are taken as shown in Figure 16.17.

It has been found that this formula overestimates the capacity of small circles and the constant 108 (or metric, 354) should be reduced to 92 (or metric, 302) for circles having computed capacity below 4000 veh/h. The values above are maximums and are attained only with long queues and at slow speeds (about 10 mph or 16 km/h). Values of approximately 80% of the above are considered satisfactory for design purposes (possibly level of service D). U.S. research[21] has resulted in the following formula for short-weaving-section capacity:

$$V_{max} = \frac{R + 1}{R}\left(\frac{3600}{t}\right)\log (R + 1) \qquad (16.17)$$

where R = ratio of major weaving flow to minor weaving flow

t = critical gap, s

Results of this formula are given in Figure 16.18. Although length and width of weaving section do not appear in this formula, they undoubtedly affect the value of t, which might increase from 2 to 5 or more with restricted designs. Empirical studies are required to determine the proper value for a specific design.

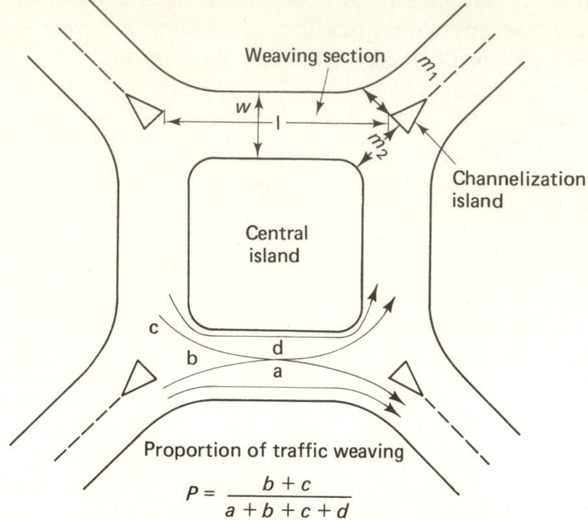

Figure 16.17. Relevant dimensions of weaving section and proportion of weaving traffic for use in capacity formula at traffic circle with square island. SOURCE: *Research on Road Traffic,* London: with permission of the Controller of Her Majesty's Stationery Office, 1965, p. 221.

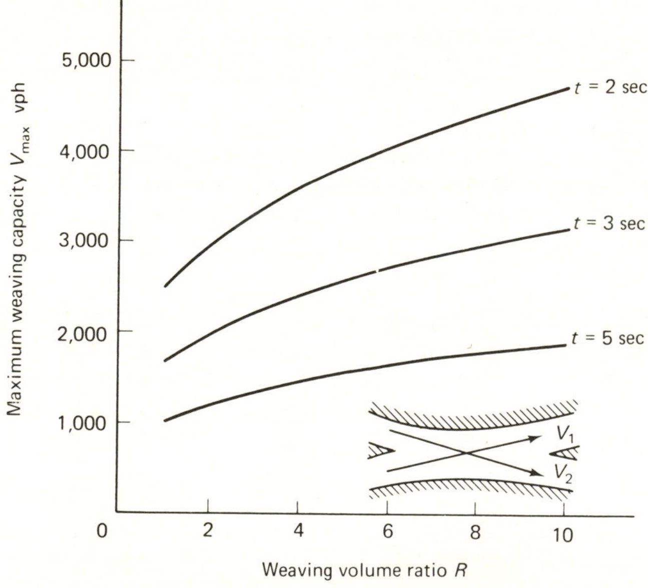

Figure 16.18. Traffic circle capacity as a function of weaving ratio and acceptable gap. SOURCE: Martin Wohl and Brian V. Martin, *Traffic System Analysis for Engineers and Planners,* New York: McGraw-Hill, 1967, p. 417.

Yield- and two-way stop-sign-controlled intersections

The principal effect of yield and stop-sign control is to assure that right of way will be assigned to the selected street and, in the case of stop signs, that all vehicles on the "minor" street will stop before entering the intersection. These rules affect the total intersection performance both in the initial delay imposed and in the increase in gap size required by vehicles entering from a stopped position. Observations of queues of vehicles that each come to a stop at a stop sign have shown that the median minimum departure headway (with no cross-street interference) is 4 s.[22]

[20]*Research on Road Traffic,* pp. 220–28.

[21]E. B. SHROPE, "Testing a Traffic Circle for Possible Capacity," *Proc. Highway Res. Bd., 31* (1952).

[22]JACQUES HEBERT, "A Study of Four-Way Stop Intersection Capacities," *Highway and Interchange Capacity,) Highway Res. Rec. 27 (Washington, D.C.: Highway Research Board, 1963), pp. 130–147.*

This provides a maximum stop sign capacity of 900 vehicles per lane per hour, provided that a continuous queue exists, no cross-street traffic is present, and all vehicles obey the stop regulation. Since such a combination of circumstances is rare, this value is of more academic than real interest.

An intersection with two-way stop- or yield-sign control may be analyzed for average delay and queue length by using equations (16.14) and (16.15) and appropriate critical gap values. These equations are based on a Poisson or random distribution of arrivals which is appropriate for low-volume conditions (fewer than 400 to 600 vehicles per lane per hour). As density increases, other distributions are more descriptive (see Chapter 15).

Because traffic volumes and densities at stop- or yield-sign-controlled intersections are likely to be in the higher range or be affected by nearby traffic signals, the foregoing formulas should be applied with discretion. Results of simulation studies given later in this section may be more appropriate for higher volumes because the assumption of Poisson distribution was not followed.

The size of the critical gap value is important. Factors that affect this value are not well understood and, whenever possible, they should be determined from observations at the intersection under study (see Chapter 17). Table 16-18 gives a range of values determined from past studies.

The average *waiting* delay to side-street vehicles at a stop-sign-controlled intersection (deceleration–acceleration delay not included) has been obtained from computer simulation.[23] In the model used, a two-way, two-lane street intersected a four-lane, two-way major street. Arrivals followed a modified binomial distribution, and critical lags of 5.8 s and 4.8 s were assumed. The volumes simulated were below approach capacity in all cases and a "backlog" limit of 20 vehicles was established. The resulting average waiting delays are shown in Figure 16.19. An acceleration–deceleration delay of 8.9 s was found in addition to the waiting delay, based on approach speeds of 30 mph (48 km/h) and 3 ft/s^2 and 6 ft/s^2 (0.9 m/s^2 and 1.8 m/s^2) for acceleration and deceleration, respectively. No delay was imposed on main-street vehicles by the side-street traffic. When average total delay to all vehicles was considered, including the acceleration–deceleration delay and turning delays to main-street vehicles (7% right and 7% left turns), results were as shown in Figure 16.20.

The values in Figures 16.19 and 16.20 may be used to

[23]R. M. Lewis and H. L. Michael, "Simulation of Traffic Flow to Obtain Volume Warrants for Intersection Control," *Traffic Flow Theory*, Highway Res. Rec. 15 (Washington, D.C.: Highway Research Board, 1963) p. 39.

TABLE 16–18
Observed Values of Critical Gaps at Urban Intersections

Situation-Location*	Gap (seconds)	Source
Minor street with major one-way street (England)	8.0	1
Minor street with stop sign (New Haven)	6.1	2
Open intersection, no control (New Haven)	2.9	2
Blind intersection, no control (Hartford)	2.8	2
Stop sign, 34 ft one-way street	4.6	3
Stop sign, 34 ft one-way through street	4.7	3
Stop sign, 41 ft two-way street	5.9	3
Stop sign, 63 ft two-way street	6.0	3
Yield sign	6.2	4
Stop sign	6.5	4
Stop sign (through vehicles)	5.8	5
Stop sign (left turns)	6.2	5
Stop sign (right turns)	5.4	5
Left turn through opposing	4.2	6
Left turn through opposing (moving)	4.4	7
Left turn through opposing (from stop)	4.6	7
60° intersection—stop sign (right turns)	5.5	8
60° intersection—stop sign (left turns)	7.0	8
T intersection—stop sign (right turns)	5.7	8
T intersection—stop sign (left turns)	7.2	8
Stop sign—into one-way street (right turns)	4.0	8
Stop sign—into one-way street (left turns)	5.6	8

*Parking conditions vary.

Source: (1) *Research on Road Traffic* (London: Her Majesty's Stationery Office, 1965), p. 228. (2) Bruce D. Greenshields et al., *Traffic Performance at Urban Street Intersections* (New Haven: Yale Bureau of Highway Traffic, 1944), pp. 67–70. (3) Morton Raff, *A Volume Warrant for Urban Stop Signs* (Saugatuck, Conn.: ENO Foundation, 1950), pp. 31–35. (The values given are for critical lag.) (4) De Leuw, Cather & Co., *Effect of Control Devices on Traffic Operations*, NCHRP Report 11 (Washington, D.C.: Highway Research Board, 1964), p. 27. (5) H. H. Bissell, "Traffic Gap Acceptance for a Stop Sign," Master's thesis, University of California, Berkeley, 1960. (6) F. J. Kaiser, Jr., "Left Turn Gap Acceptance," Student thesis manuscript, Yale Bureau of Highway Traffic, 1951. (7) Olin K. Dart, "Left-Turn Characteristics at Signalized Intersections on Four-Lane Arterial Streets," *Characteristics of Traffic Flow*, Highway Res. Rec. 230 (Washington, D.C.: Highway Research Board, 1968), p. 45. (8) Vasant H. Surti, "Operational Efficiency Evaluation of Selected At-grade Intersections," *Highway Capacity and Quality of Service*, Highway Res. Rec. 321 (Washington, D.C.: Highway Research Board, 1970), p. 60.

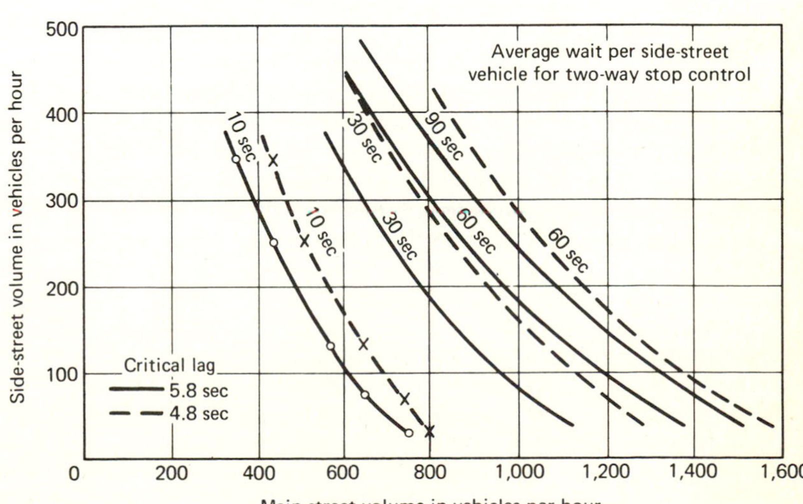

Figure 16.19. Waiting delay to side-street vehicles at stop-sign-controlled intersections. Source: Russell M. Lewis and Harold L. Michael, "Simulation of Traffic Flow to Obtain Volume Warrants for Intersection Control," *Traffic Flow Theory*, Highway Reseach Record 15, Washington, D.C.: Highway Research Board, 1963, p. 39.

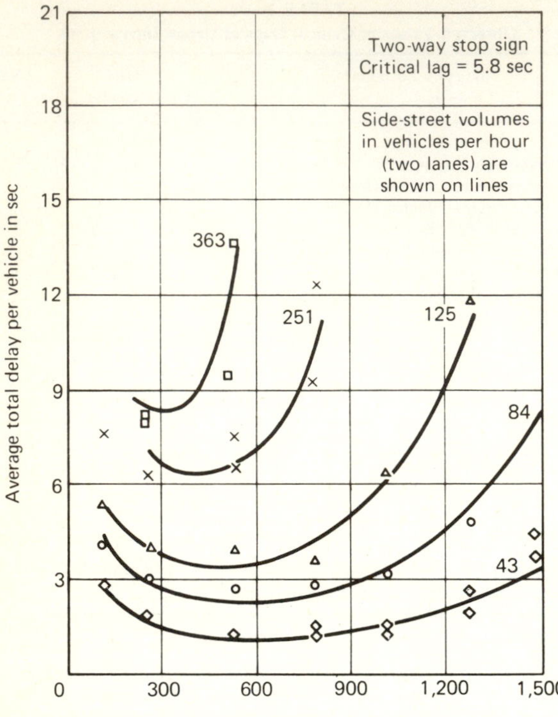

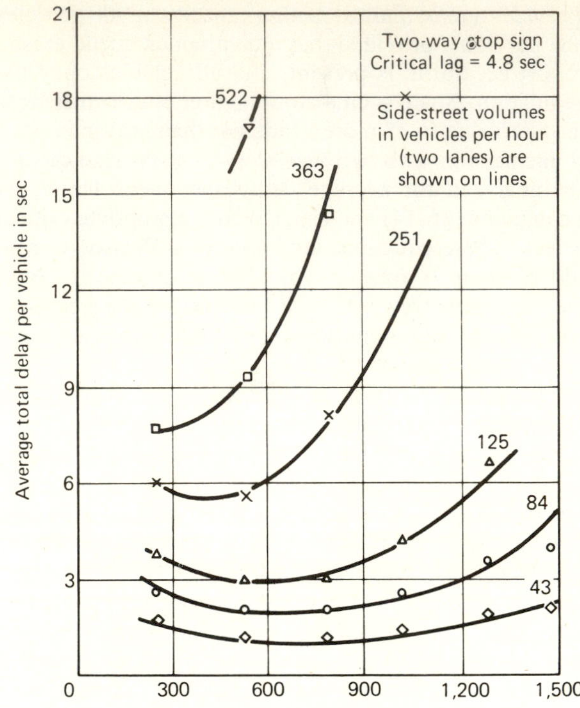

Figure 16.20. (a) Average total delay to all vehicles at stop-sign-controlled intersection (critical lag = 5.8 s). (b) Average total delay to all vehicles at stop-sign-controlled intersection (critical lag = 4.8 s). SOURCE: Russell M. Lewis and Harold L. Michael, "Simulation of Traffic Flow to Obtain Volume Warrants for Intersection Control," *Traffic Flow Theory,* Highway Research Record 15, Washington, D.C.: Highway Research Board, 1963, p 35, 36.

estimate service volumes at levels of service which are better than level of service E (capacity).

Four-way-stop intersections

The interaction of vehicles at a four-way stop is complex. The criteria of gap acceptance are no longer appropriate since vehicles on all approaches of the intersection will be at a stop or expected to stop. Departure headways of 4 s can be expected for single vehicles (900 veh/h) and approximately 4.5 s for pairs of vehicles entering together (1600 veh/h). When traffic is present on all approaches, median headways of 7.32 s have been observed at four-way-stop intersections of two-way, two-lane suburban streets and median headways of 8.08 s for vehicles crossing a four-lane intersecting street.[24] Based on these values and a tendency for the median headway to decrease on the major street when the split of traffic deviates from 50:50, the capacity of an intersection (all approaches) has been computed as shown in Table 16-19. The capacities in Table 16-19 would be obtained only with nearly constant queues on all approaches. Left turns do not appear to affect these values adversely, and a high percentage of right turns probably acts to increase them.

[24]Ibid.

TABLE 16–19
Estimated Capacity of Four-Way Stop Intersection of Two-Way, Two-Lane Streets

Cross Volume Split	Capacity (Total from All Approaches) (vehicles/h)
50/50	1900
55/45	1800
60/40	1700
65/35	1600
70/30	1550

SOURCE: *Highway Capacity Manual, 1965,* Spec. Report 87 (Washington, D.C.: Highway Research Board, 1965), p. 158.

Signalized intersections

Generally, those intersections that are significant from a capacity standpoint are either already signalized or prime candidates for signalization. Therefore, most current intersection-capacity criteria apply to signalized intersections.

The capacity and service volumes that a signalized intersection can accommodate are dependent on the intersection geometrics, signal operation, and traffic factors. In the first category, the approach width is most critical. The existence of parking, one-way vs. two-way operation, and lane configuration are also important. Other factors, such as grades and turning radii, are undoubtedly significant, but must be handled by judgment in the absence of specific criteria.

In the second category, the proportioning of green time is the single most important factor. Cycle length, phasing, and "lost-time" features are somewhat less significant.

Traffic factors include the pattern and composition of arriving traffic, turning movements, presence of pedestrians, and general driver characteristics. The latter appear to be related to the size of and location within an urban area and, although not well quantified, can be estimated from those factors. The pattern of traffic arrivals is strongly influenced by nearby traffic signals and their coordination.

Of major concern in evaluating intersection capacity and service volume is the proper measure to describe traffic performance at intersections. Speed, density and volume (or v/c ratio), the criteria used in free-flowing traffic situations, are not directly applicable and surrogate measures must be employed. Several offer potential for the future, but have complications that have impeded current application. These include delay, queue length, and cycle failures.

Delay. Although some form of delay would probably be the most satisfactory measure, its determination under field conditions is arduous, and since it is defined in a variety of ways, it is subject to frequent misinterpretation.

Recent research[25] has been directed at this problem, both to draw user attention to the several different delay measures in use in the field, all loosely described simply as "delay," although the absolute values differ, and to evaluate the several delay determination methods. The work examined both the relative accuracy and the relative ease of field data gathering of the following delay measures: stopped delay (point sample), percent of vehicles stopping, time-in-queue delay, and approach delay.

Stopped delay was found to be the most practical method for field use. Basically, it involves recording, at specified intervals, the number of fully stopped vehicles on an approach. It was determined, however, that the *stopped time* directly obtained by this method needed to be adjusted by the factor 0.92 to represent actual stopped delay more accurately.

Approach delay was found to provide the best representation of overall intersection performance, although it is difficult to record in the field. Important from an applications standpoint, it was established that approach delay can be approximated by multiplying the stopped-delay value, easily obtained, by the factor 1.3.

It is hoped that the availability of this new insight into delay in its several forms may soon result in more widespread empirical analyses of delay in the field.

A variety of other measures of delay have been developed through theory and/or simulation. A British method is the well-known Webster equation,[26] which calculates the average delay per vehicle on an approach to a fixed-time signalized intersection, described as equivalent to approach delay. This delay can be computed from a simplification of the basic Webster equation as follows:

$$d = \left(Cf_1 + \frac{f_2}{q} \right) \frac{100 - f_3}{100} \tag{16.18}$$

where d = average delay per vehicle on approach, s

C = cycle length, s

$f_1 = \dfrac{(1 - G_E/C)^2}{2(1 - q/s)}$ (see Table 16-20)

G_E = effective green time, s, as discussed below

q = approach flow, veh/s

[25] W. R. Reilly, C. C. Gardner, and J. H. Kell, *A Technique for Measurement of Delay at Intersections*, prepared for Federal Highway Administration (San Francisco, Calif. and Tucson, Ariz.: JHK Associates, 1976).

[26] F. V. Webster and B. M. Cobbe, *Traffic Signals*, Road Research Laboratory, Ministry of Transport Road Res. Tech. Pap. No. 56 (London: Her Majesty's Stationery Office, 1966).

TABLE 16–20

Tabulation of $f_1 = \dfrac{(1 - G_E/C)^2}{2\,(1 - q/s)}$

	G_E/C												
$x^{(1)}$	0.1	0.2	0.30	0.35	0.40	0.45	0.50	0.55	0.60	0.65	0.70	0.80	0.90
0.1	0.409	0.327	0.253	0.219	0.188	0.158	0.132	0.107	0.085	0.066	0.048	0.022	0.005
0.2	0.413	0.333	0.261	0.227	0.196	0.166	0.139	0.114	0.091	0.070	0.052	0.024	0.006
0.3	0.418	0.340	0.269	0.236	0.205	0.275	0.147	0.121	0.098	0.076	0.057	0.026	0.007
0.4	0.422	0.348	0.278	0.246	0.214	0.184	0.156	0.130	0.105	0.083	0.063	0.029	0.008
0.5	0.426	0.356	0.288	0.256	0.225	0.195	0.167	0.140	0.114	0.091	0.069	0.033	0.009
0.55	0.429	0.360	0.293	0.262	0.231	0.201	0.172	0.145	0.119	0.095	0.073	0.036	0.010
0.60	0.431	0.364	0.299	0.267	0.237	0.207	0.179	0.151	0.125	0.100	0.078	0.038	0.011
0.65	0.433	0.368	0.304	0.273	0.243	0.214	0.185	0.158	0.131	0.106	0.083	0.042	0.012
0.70	0.435	0.372	0.310	0.280	0.250	0.221	0.192	0.165	0.138	0.112	0.088	0.045	0.014
0.75	0.438	0.376	0.316	0.286	0.257	0.228	0.200	0.172	0.145	0.120	0.095	0.050	0.015
0.80	0.440	0.381	0.322	0.293	0.265	0.236	0.208	0.181	0.154	0.128	0.102	0.056	0.018
0.85	0.443	0.386	0.329	0.301	0.273	0.245	0.217	0.190	0.163	0.137	0.111	0.063	0.021
0.90	0.445	0.390	0.336	0.308	0.281	0.254	0.227	0.200	0.174	0.148	0.122	0.071	0.026
0.92	0.446	0.392	0.338	0.312	0.285	0.258	0.231	0.205	0.179	0.152	0.126	0.076	0.029
0.94	0.447	0.394	0.341	0.315	0.288	0.262	0.236	0.210	0.183	0.157	0.132	0.081	0.032
0.96	0.448	0.396	0.344	0.318	0.292	0.266	0.240	0.215	0.189	0.163	0.137	0.086	0.037
0.98	0.449	0.398	0.347	0.322	0.296	0.271	0.245	0.220	0.194	0.169	0.143	0.093	0.042

Source: *Research on Road Traffic* Road Research Laboratory (London: Her Majesty's Stationery Office, 1965), p. 301.

(1) where $x = \dfrac{C}{G_E} \cdot \dfrac{q}{s}$

TABLE 16–21*

Tabulation of $f_2 = \dfrac{x^2}{2(1 - x)}$

x (tenths)	x (hundredths) 0.00	0.01	0.02	0.03	0.04	0.05	0.06	0.07	0.08	0.09
0.1	0.006	0.007	0.008	0.010	0.011	0.013	0.015	0.017	0.020	0.022
0.2	0.025	0.028	0.031	0.034	0.038	0.042	0.046	0.050	0.054	0.059
0.3	0.064	0.070	0.075	0.081	0.088	0.094	0.101	0.109	0.116	0.125
0.4	0.133	0.142	0.152	0.162	0.173	0.184	0.196	0.208	0.222	0.235
0.5	0.250	0.265	0.282	0.299	0.317	0.336	0.356	0.378	0.400	0.425
0.6	0.450	0.477	0.506	0.536	0.569	0.604	0.641	0.680	0.723	0.768
0.7	0.817	0.869	0.926	0.987	1.05	1.13	1.20	1.29	1.38	1.49
0.8	1.60	1.73	1.87	2.03	2.21	2.41	2.64	2.91	3.23	3.60
0.9	4.05	4.60	5.28	6.18	7.36	9.03	11.5	15.7	24.0	49.0

*Use Table as follows: *Example:* if $x = 0.24$, $x = 0.2 + 0.04$; enter row 0.2 and column 0.04; then $f_2 = 0.038$.

SOURCE: *Research on Road Traffic* (London: Her Majesty's Stationery Office, 1965), p. 302.

s = saturation flow, veh/s, as discussed below

$$f_2 = \frac{x^2}{2(1 - x)} \quad \text{(see Table 16-21)}$$

$$x = \frac{C}{G_E} \cdot \frac{q}{s}$$

$$f_3 = \frac{0.65(C/q^2)^{1/3} x^{\,2+5(G_E/C)}}{Cf_1 + f_2/q} \quad \text{(see Table 16-22)}$$

The effective green time G_E is the time available for flow at the rate s. It is thus equal to the green time plus yellow time minus the time loss in queue startup and the time taken for the last vehicle to cross the intersection. Studies of queues at urban intersections suggest that the queue startup value averages about 3.7 s and the last vehicle value about 2.0 s (depending on speed and intersection geometrics).

The saturation flow rate s is the maximum rate at which vehicles enter the intersection in a single lane after the queue startup delay has been eliminated and while a continuous demand exists. Studies of intersection performance in the United States indicate that under ideal circumstances, headways between successive passenger vehicles stabilized at between 2.1 and 2.0 s, yielding values of s of 0.48 and 0.50 veh/s, or 0.49 averaged.

To use this procedure, demand flow rates for the approach, saturation flow rate, and effective green time must either be obtained from field measurements or be estimated.

Using the values given above and a 120-s cycle (30 cycles/h) with a 50% split, it is seen that the theoretical hourly capacity of a single-lane signal approach under ideal conditions is approximately $30G_Es$, or $30(60 - 3.7 - 2.0)(0.49) = 800$ passenger vehicles per hour, or 1600 passenger vehicles per hour of green. Such a flow rate would be accompanied by a high average delay (exceeding 4 min per vehicle). A value of 90% of the above, approximately 1450 passenger vehicles per hour of green, has been suggested as a more realistic value.

The computed delay from the preceding formulas at a representative intersection is shown in Figure 16.21. It can be seen that average delay increases very rapidly as volume

TABLE 16–22

Values of $f_3 = \dfrac{0.65\,(C/q^2)^{1/3}x^{2\,+\,5\,(G_E/C)}}{Cf_1 + f_2/q}$

x	G_E/C	qC 2.5	5	10	20	40
0.3	0.2	2	2	1	1	0
	0.4	2	1	1	0	0
	0.6	0	0	0	0	0
	0.8	0	0	0	0	0
0.4	0.2	6	4	3	2	1
	0.4	3	2	2	1	1
	0.6	2	2	1	1	0
	0.8	2	1	1	1	1
0.5	0.2	10	7	5	3	2
	0.4	6	5	4	2	1
	0.6	6	4	3	2	2
	0.8	3	4	3	3	2
0.6	0.2	14	11	8	5	3
	0.4	11	9	7	4	3
	0.6	9	8	6	5	3
	0.8	7	8	8	7	5
0.7	0.2	18	14	11	7	5
	0.4	15	13	10	7	5
	0.6	13	12	10	8	6
	0.8	11	12	13	12	10
0.8	0.2	18	17	13	10	7
	0.4	16	15	13	10	8
	0.6	15	15	14	12	9
	0.8	14	15	17	17	15
0.9	0.2	13	14	13	11	8
	0.4	12	13	13	11	9
	0.6	12	13	14	14	12
	0.8	13	13	16	17	17
0.95	0.2	8	9	9	9	8
	0.4	7	9	9	10	9
	0.6	7	9	10	11	10
	0.8	7	9	10	12	13
0.975	0.2	8	9	10	9	8
	0.4	8	9	10	10	9
	0.6	8	9	11	12	11
	0.8	8	10	12	13	14

SOURCE: *Research on Road Traffic* Road Research Laboratory (London: Her Majesty's Stationery Office, 1965), p. 303.

exceeds about 80% of theoretical capacity and becomes nearly asymptotic above 90% of theoretical capacity.

Queue length. Another possible measure of traffic performance at signalized intersections is the length of queues developed. Average queue length is approximated by the larger result of the two formulas

$$n = qR \tag{16.19}$$

and

$$n = q\left(\frac{R}{2} + d\right) \tag{16.20}$$

where n = average queue length, number of vehicles

q = approach flow, veh/s

R = red time, s

d = average individual delay from equation (16.18)

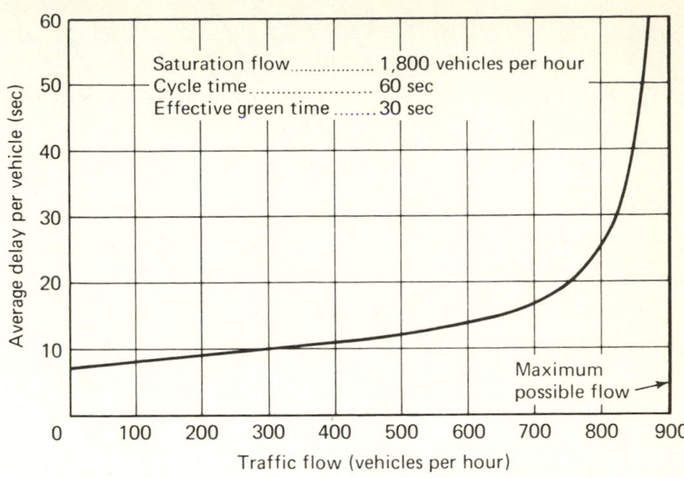

Figure 16.21. Typical delay/volume curve relationship on a signalized approach (British). SOURCE: *Research on Road Traffic,* London: with permission of the Controller of Her Majesty's Stationery Office, 1965, p. 304.

TABLE 16–23
Estimate of Queue Length at Start of Green Which Will Not Be Exceeded in More Than 1% of Cycles

		qC				
x	G_E/C	2.5	5.0	10.0	20.0	40.0
0.3	0.4	6	9	14	23	38
	0.6	5	6	11	17	28
	0.8	3	5	7	12	17
0.5	0.2	7	9	17	29	53
	0.4	6	9	14	23	38
	0.6	5	7	11	17	28
	0.8	4	5	7	12	18
0.7	0.2	9	12	17	28	50
	0.4	9	9	15	23	38
	0.6	8	9	12	18	28
	0.8	7	7	8	12	18
0.8	0.2	13	15	19	28	50
	0.4	12	13	17	24	39
	0.6	12	13	14	20	28
	0.8	11	12	12	15	18
0.9	0.2	29	25	29	38	55
	0.4	28	24	27	33	46
	0.6	27	24	26	28	42
	0.8	27	23	24	25	29
0.95	0.2	40	36	38	47	65
	0.4	40	34	37	44	55
	0.6	40	32	30	42	48
	0.8	39	32	34	36	40
0.975	0.2	82	70	79	69	93
	0.4	83	66	75	65	82
	0.6	82	70	69	59	79
	0.8	79	65	66	57	79

SOURCE: *Research on Road Traffic* Road Research Laboratory (London: Her Majesty's Stationery Office, 1965), p. 308.

A value of perhaps greater significance is the maximum probable queue length. This can be estimated from Table 16-23, in which the parameters *C*, *G*, *q*, and *x* are as defined for equation (16.18).

Cycle failures. The "load factor," which is described in more detail later among the factors affecting capacity, is utilized in the *Highway Capacity Manual, 1965* method as the most convenient available measure of intersection approach service, although it is admittedly rather artificial. It is the percentage of "loaded," or fully utilized, signal phases (i.e., cycle failures) on a particular intersection approach during the hour under consideration, determined by field observations or estimates.

Using another method, the percentage of cycles during which more vehicles arrive than depart can be estimated from the chart in Figure 16.22. Traffic arrivals are assumed to be Poisson-distributed. The departure rate is taken as 0.5 vehicles/s with an assumed 4-s lost time per phase. It should be noted that failures estimated by this method do not include the effect of queues carried over from previous cycle failures. It thus overestimates the possibility of vehicles being served during the cycle in which they arrive. Since overestimation becomes more serious as probability of failure increases, this estimate is reasonable only under the better level-of-service conditions.

The relationships between the failure rate determined by this method and levels of service computed by the *Highway Capacity Manual, 1965* method for a representative condition are shown in Figure 16.23.

The relationship between failure rate and average individual delay computed by the method given previously in this chapter is shown in Figure 16.24.

At this time there is no general agreement as to which of the measures of intersection performance is most appropriate. In fact, differing measures may be the most suitable in different specific cases. The distributions of vehicle arrivals assumed in the methods just described may not be descriptive of a specific case at hand, particularly an urban situation with other nearby signals. Other distributions might well be more appropriate. Once ongoing research is complete, it is likely that some measure of delay will prove to be the best basic measure.

Factors affecting signalized intersection capacity

Determination of signalized intersection capacity involves a substantial number of factors. In the *Highway Capacity Manual, 1965* procedures, some are automatically taken into account by proper selection of charts and curves;

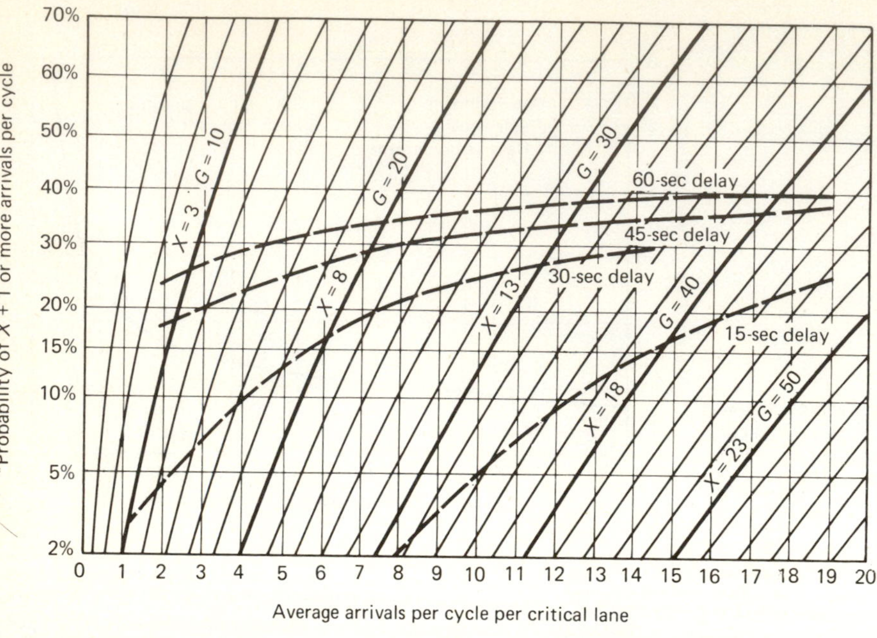

Figure 16.22. Probability of more vehicles arriving (X) than can be served during the green interval (G), SOURCE: Donald R. Drew, *Traffic Flow Theory and Control*, New York: McGraw-Hill, 1968, p. 140.

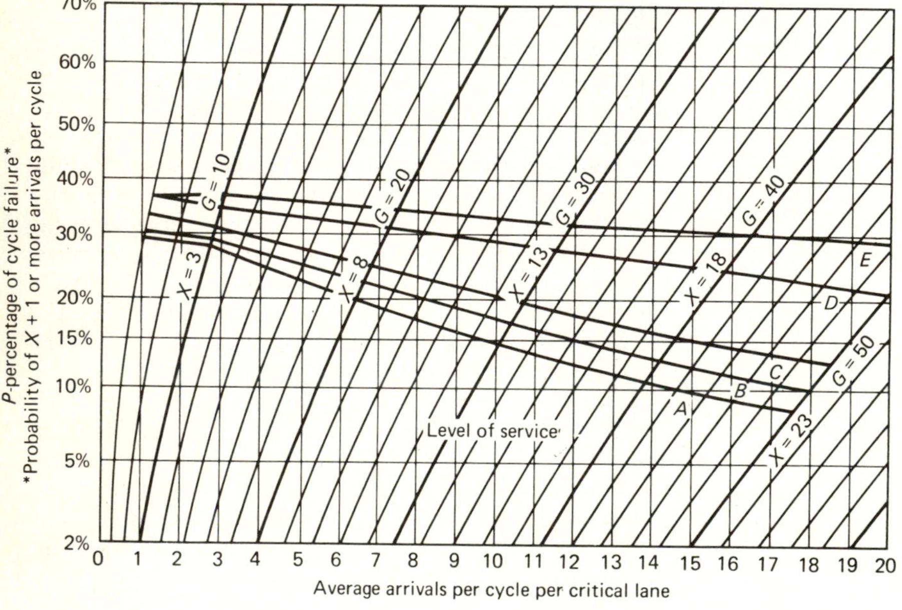

Figure 16.23. Typical relationship of computed cycle failure and level of service at a signalized intersection approach. SOURCE: John E. Tidwell, Jr., and Jack B. Humphreys, "Relation of Signalized Intersection Level of Service to Failure Rate and Average Individual Delay," *Highway Capacity and Quality of Service*, Highway Research Record 321, Washington, D.C.: Highway Research Board, 1969, p. 23.

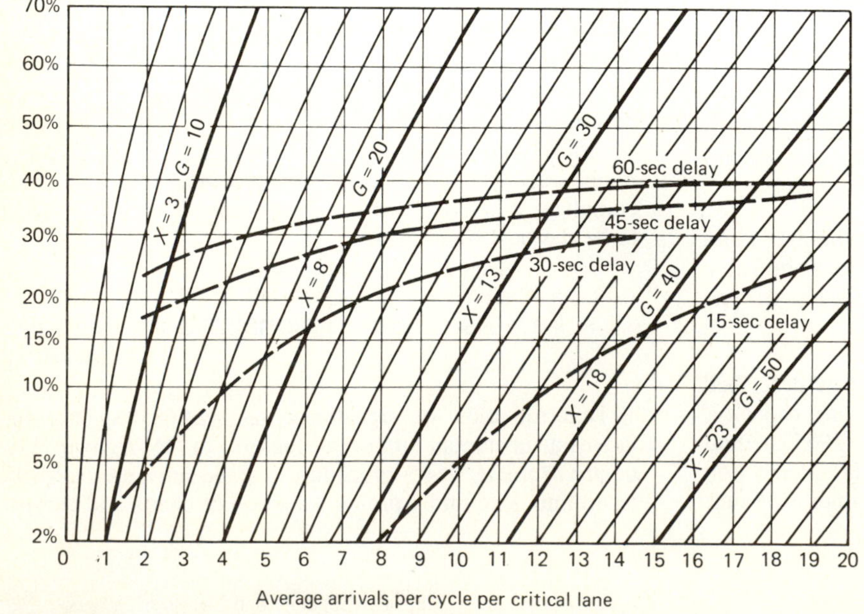

Figure 16.24. Typical relationship of a computed cycle failure and computed average individual delay at a signalized intersection approach. SOURCE: John E. Tidwell, Jr., and Jack B. Humphreys, "Relation of Signalized Intersection Level of Service to Failure Rate and Average Individual Delay, Highway Capacity and Quality of Service, Highway Research Record 321, Washington, D.C.: Highway Research Board, 1969, p. 27.

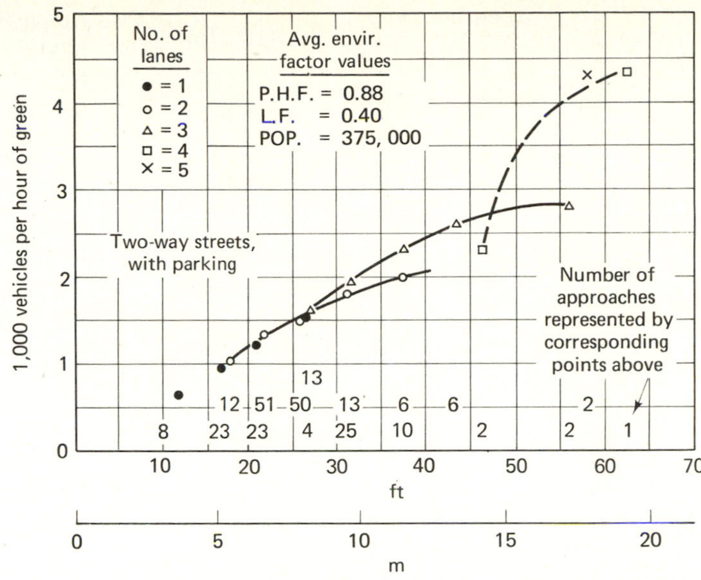

Figure 16.25. Efficiencies of signalized intersection approaches related to lane configuration. SOURCE: *Highway Capacity Manual, 1965,* Spec. Report 87, Washington, D.C.: Highway Research Board, 1965, p. 129.

the remainder are handled as multipliers. Other methods also exist in the United States and abroad.

Approach width. The width available for approach traffic is critical to intersection capacity; it may be considered either as total approach width or by lane and lane width. American and British practices favor the former, but Australian methods are developed around the latter. Unquestionably, the lane configuration has a bearing on performance; only its relative importance is in question. Figure 16.25 shows the relative efficiency of different lane configurations from an American study.

A comparison of American, Australian, and British methods for considering width is shown in Figure 16.26. The British value for saturation flow (veh/h) for approach widths greater that 17 ft (5.2 m) is $160w$, where w is the width in feet, or $525w$, where w is in meters, measured from curb to center line or edge of center island. This value is reduced 6% for off-peak conditions. An approximate American figure (based on a two-way street, no parking, no turns, no trucks, outlying location in metropolitan area of 250,000, PHF 0.85) is $s = 125w + 185$, with w in feet (or $s = 410w + 185$, with w in meters). The Australian calculations are based on central values for lanes 10 to 12 ft wide, with negative and positive adjustments for narrower and wider lanes, respectively.

Number of lanes. Where analysis is made on a "by-lane" basis, the number of approach lanes is, of course, important. The relative flows in the several lanes are established, typically, by applying factors to a base condition.

Parking. Parked vehicles in the vicinity of a signalized intersection reduce the space available for traffic movement and thus the carrying capacity of the intersection. Temporary blockage of an adjacent lane while vehicles enter or leave curb spaces will also reduce capacity.

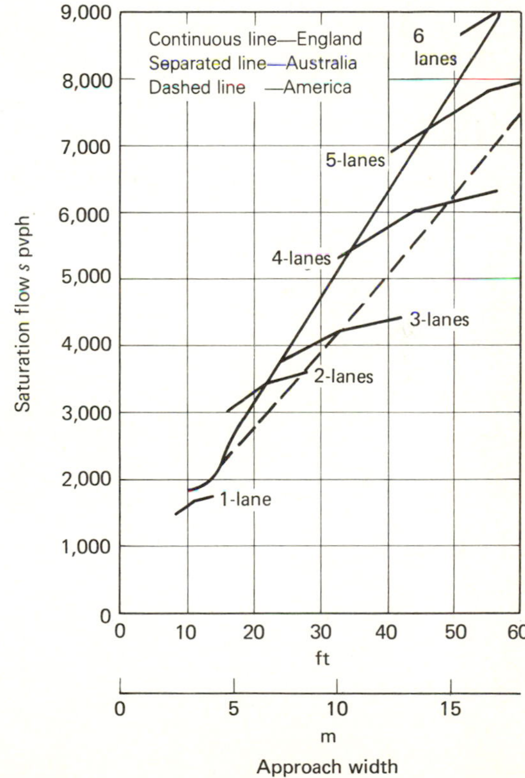

Figure 16.26. Saturation flow related to approach width at a signalized intersection. SOURCE: Alan J. Miller, "On the Australian Road Capacity Guide," *Highway Capacity,* Highway Research Record 289, Washington, D.C.: Highway Research Board, 1969, p. 7.

In the British system,[27] the effect of a parked vehicle at z ft from the intersection stop line is considered as a width reduction equaling

[27]*Research on Road Traffic,* p. 219.

U.S. units: $$w^l = 5.5 - \frac{0.9(z - 25)}{G} \qquad (16.21a)$$

Metric units: $$w^l = 1.68 - \frac{0.9(z - 7.62)}{G} \qquad (16.21b)$$

where w^l = width loss caused by parked vehicle, ft (or m)

z = clear distance between stop line and parked vehicle, ft or m

G = green time, s

If $z < 25$ ft (7.6 m), the second term is disregarded and the width loss is 5.5 ft (1.7 m).

In the Australian[28] system, which considers capacity by lane, the capacity of the curb lane is reduced as follows:

1. No parking permitted, one and two lanes—no reduction (100% utilization).
2. No parking permitted, three or more lanes, with no standing allowed—40% reduction (60% utilization).
3. No parking permitted, three or more lanes, with standing allowed—60% reduction (40% utilization).

The effect of parking in the American method is accounted for by a series of basic curves for different conditions (see Figures 16.27 to 16.31). An analysis of these curves shows the effect of a lane of parking to range from an equivalent width reduction of 6 to 8 ft (1.8 to 2.4 m) on relatively narrow streets up to as much as 15 ft (4.6 m) on wide approaches.

One-way vs. two-way operation. The principal benefit of one-way operation is to permit left turns (right turns in left-side-driving countries) to be made without interference

[28]AUSTRALIAN ROAD RESEARCH BOARD, *Signalized Intersections—Capacity Guide*, p. 21.

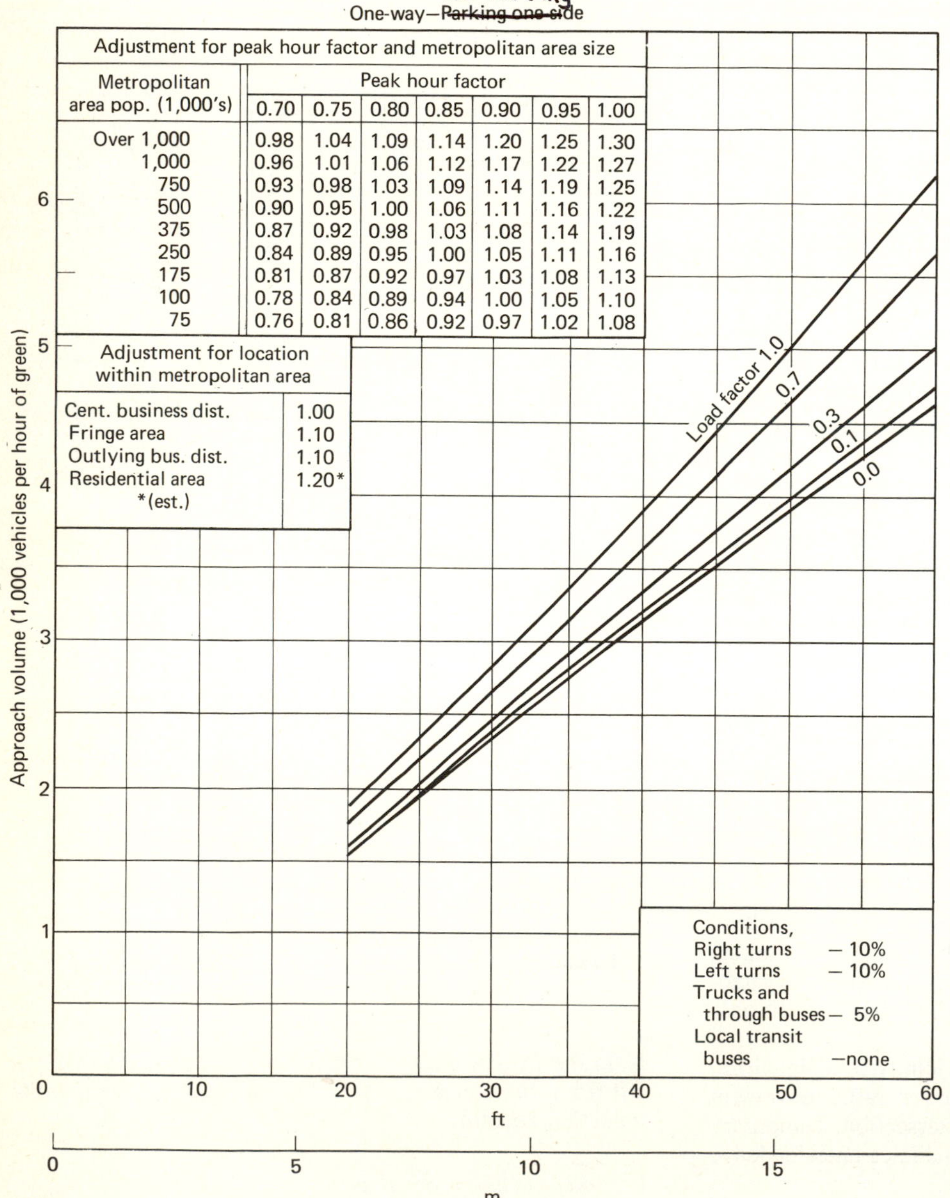

Metropolitan area pop. (1,000's)	0.70	0.75	0.80	0.85	0.90	0.95	1.00
Over 1,000	0.98	1.04	1.09	1.14	1.20	1.25	1.30
1,000	0.96	1.01	1.06	1.12	1.17	1.22	1.27
750	0.93	0.98	1.03	1.09	1.14	1.19	1.25
500	0.90	0.95	1.00	1.06	1.11	1.16	1.22
375	0.87	0.92	0.98	1.03	1.08	1.14	1.19
250	0.84	0.89	0.95	1.00	1.05	1.11	1.16
175	0.81	0.87	0.92	0.97	1.03	1.08	1.13
100	0.78	0.84	0.89	0.94	1.00	1.05	1.10
75	0.76	0.81	0.86	0.92	0.97	1.02	1.08

Figure 16.27. Urban intersection approach service volume, in vehicles per hour of green signal time, for one-way streets with no parking. SOURCE: *Highway Capacity Manual, 1965*, Spec. Report 87, Washington, D.C.: Highway Research Board, 1965, p. 134.

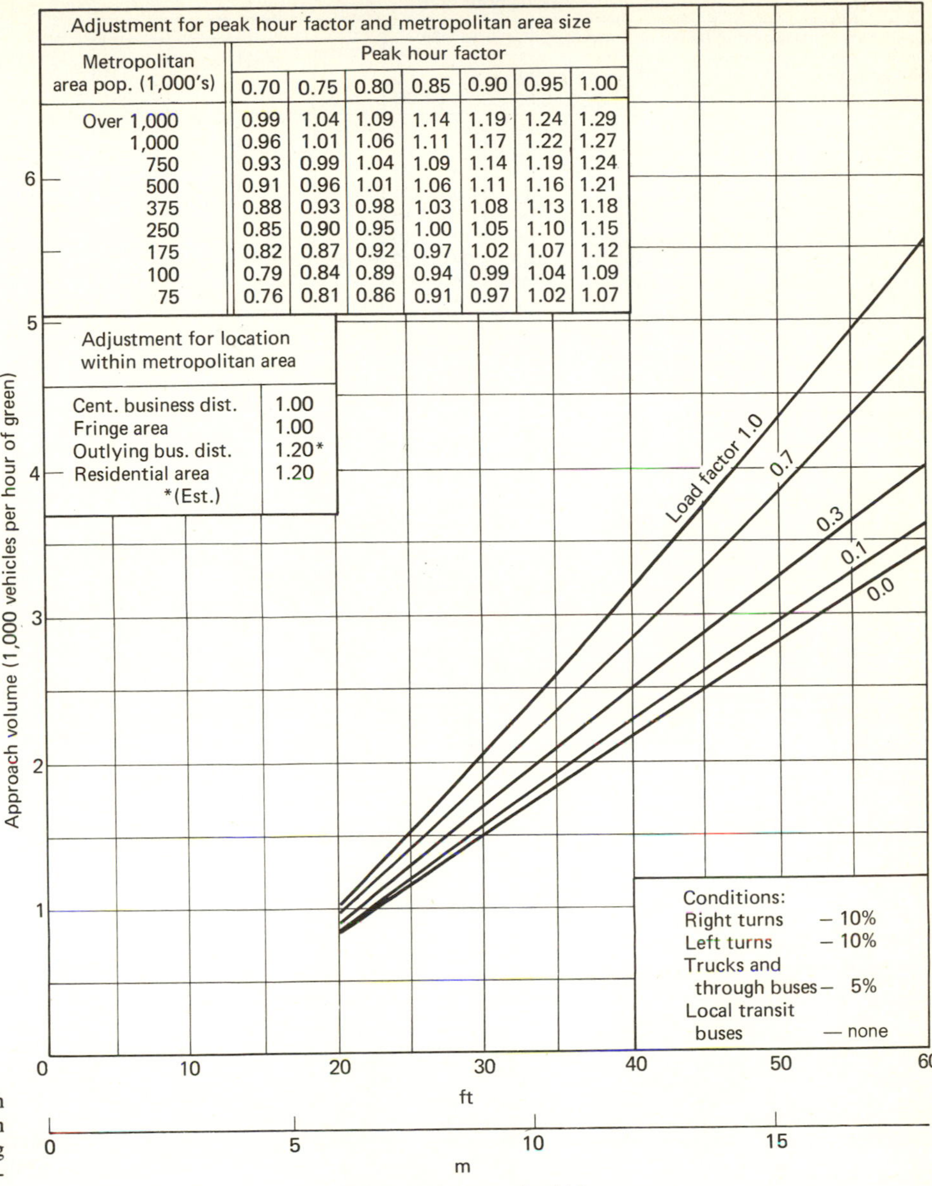

Adjustment for peak hour factor and metropolitan area size

Metropolitan area pop. (1,000's)	Peak hour factor 0.70	0.75	0.80	0.85	0.90	0.95	1.00
Over 1,000	0.99	1.04	1.09	1.14	1.19	1.24	1.29
1,000	0.96	1.01	1.06	1.11	1.17	1.22	1.27
750	0.93	0.99	1.04	1.09	1.14	1.19	1.24
500	0.91	0.96	1.01	1.06	1.11	1.16	1.21
375	0.88	0.93	0.98	1.03	1.08	1.13	1.18
250	0.85	0.90	0.95	1.00	1.05	1.10	1.15
175	0.82	0.87	0.92	0.97	1.02	1.07	1.12
100	0.79	0.84	0.89	0.94	0.99	1.04	1.09
75	0.76	0.81	0.86	0.91	0.97	1.02	1.07

Adjustment for location within metropolitan area

Location	
Cent. business dist.	1.00
Fringe area	1.00
Outlying bus. dist.	1.20*
Residential area	1.20

*(Est.)

Figure 16.28. Urban intersection approach service volume, in vehicles per hour of green signal time, for one-way streets with parking one side. SOURCE: *Highway Capacity Manual, 1965,* Spec. Report 87, Washington, D.C.: Highway Research Board, 1965, p. 134.

from opposing traffic. Both right and left lanes, however, are curb lanes on a one-way approach and subject to adverse influence of parking and pedestrian activity.

In the British system, the effect of one-way street operation is accounted for by considering all turns as nonconflicting turns, which, in that system, are equivalent to through vehicles.

In the Australian system, all turns from one-way streets are treated as nonconflicting and the curb-lane reductions given previously are applied to both curb lanes.

In the American system, separate curves are given for one-way and two-way operation (again see Figures 16.27 to 16.31). The effect of left-turning vehicles under one-way operation is considered to be one-half as great as under two-way conditions (equivalent to right turns). The added capacity caused by removal of parking on a second (usually left) side of a one-way street is shown to be only about one-half as great as the increment gained from removal on one side only.

Load factor. In American practice, the measure most commonly used to describe intersection performance is the load factor, which the *Highway Capacity Manual, 1965* defines as *the ratio of the number of green phases that are loaded or fully utilized by traffic (usually during the peak hour) to the total number of green phases available for that approach during the same period.* A green phase is considered loaded when (1) there are vehicles ready to enter the intersection in all lanes when the signal turns green and (2) they continue to be available to enter in all lanes during the entire phase with no unused time or exceedingly long spacings between vehicles caused by lack of traffic. The

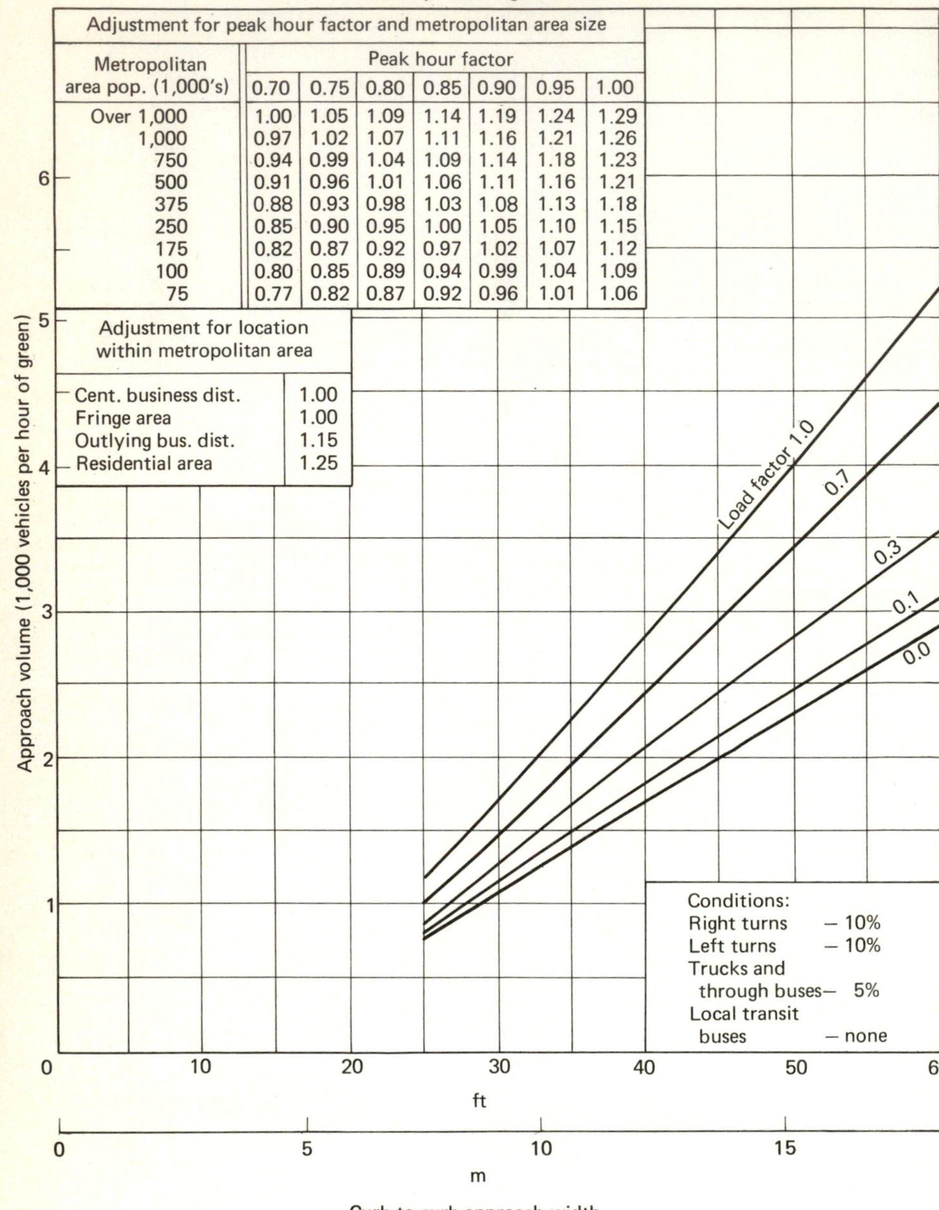

Adjustment for peak hour factor and metropolitan area size							
Metropolitan area pop. (1,000's)	Peak hour factor						
	0.70	0.75	0.80	0.85	0.90	0.95	1.00
Over 1,000	1.00	1.05	1.09	1.14	1.19	1.24	1.29
1,000	0.97	1.02	1.07	1.11	1.16	1.21	1.26
750	0.94	0.99	1.04	1.09	1.14	1.18	1.23
500	0.91	0.96	1.01	1.06	1.11	1.16	1.21
375	0.88	0.93	0.98	1.03	1.08	1.13	1.18
250	0.85	0.90	0.95	1.00	1.05	1.10	1.15
175	0.82	0.87	0.92	0.97	1.02	1.07	1.12
100	0.80	0.85	0.89	0.94	0.99	1.04	1.09
75	0.77	0.82	0.87	0.92	0.96	1.01	1.06

Adjustment for location within metropolitan area	
Cent. business dist.	1.00
Fringe area	1.00
Outlying bus. dist.	1.15
Residential area	1.25

Figure 16.29. Urban intersection approach service volume, in vehicles per hour of green signal time, for one-way streets with parking both sides. SOURCE: *Highway Capacity Manual, 1965,* Spec. Report 87, Washington, D.C.: Highway Research Board, 1965, p. 135.

load factor is relatively easy to determine in the field and is related in some manner to the several delay measures that exist, but in a way that has thus far defied easy measurement. The relationship between load factor and delay based on a simplified simulation model is given in Figure 16.32. The intersection modeled had a capacity of 600 veh/h, a 60-s cycle divided into two equal phases, a Poisson arrival distribution, and a minimum departure headway of 3 s. It can be seen that both the magnitude and variation of average individual delays increase rapidly at load factors above 0.5.

For computations, the Highway Capacity Committee has established the approximate relationships between load factor and service levels shown in Table 16-24. The families of curves in each of Figures 16.27 to 16.31 represent levels of service A through E by means of load factor, through these relationships. For example, a load factor of 0.3 rep-

TABLE 16–24
Relationship of Load Factor to Level of Service

Level of Service	Description	Load Factor
A	Free flow	0.0
B	Stable flow	≤0.1
C	Stable flow	≤0.3
D	Approaching unstable flow	≤0.7
E	Unstable flow	≤1.0*
F	Forced flow	—

*Usually ≤0.95 in the absence of an exceptionally effective signal progression.

SOURCE: *Highway Capacity Manual, 1965,* Spec. Report 87 (Washington, D.C.: Highway Research Board, 1965), p. 131.

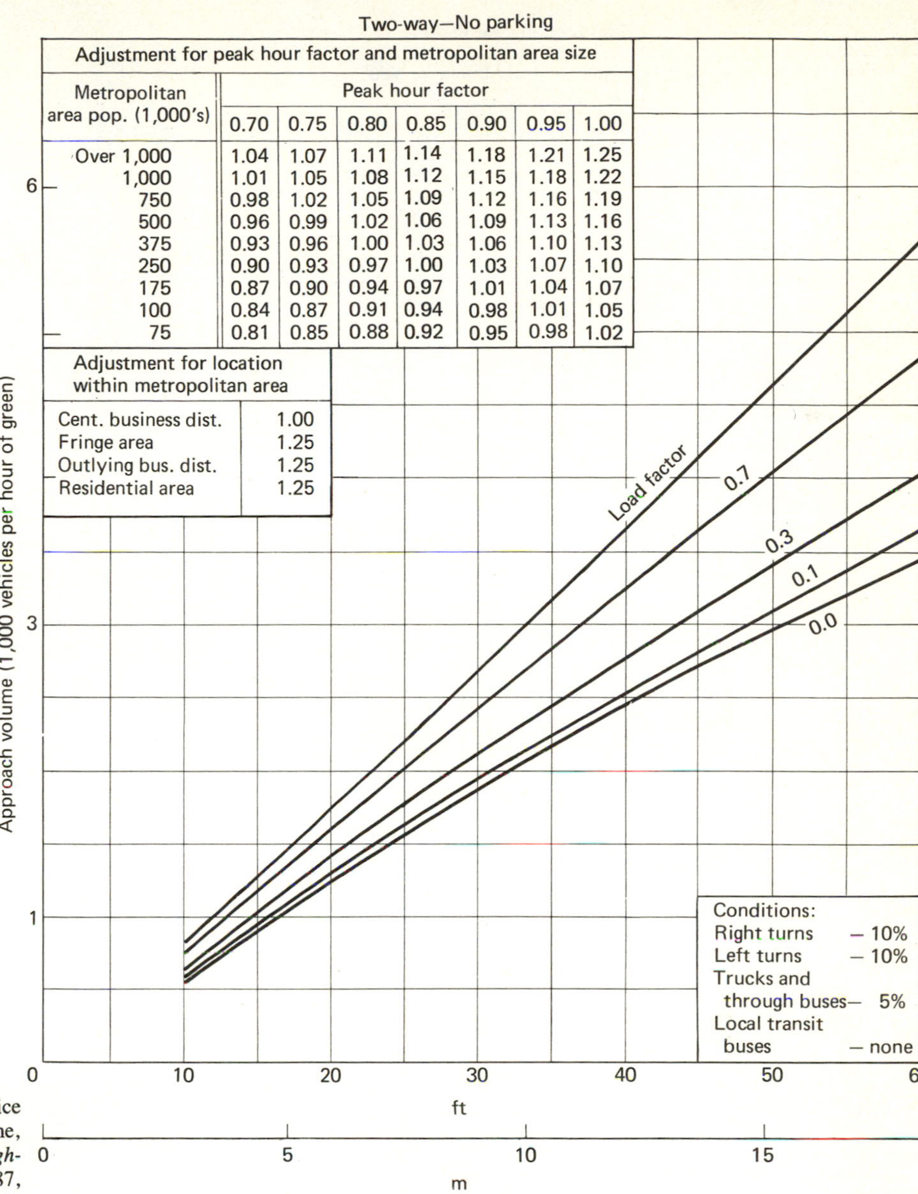

Adjustment for peak hour factor and metropolitan area size

Metropolitan area pop. (1,000's)	Peak hour factor 0.70	0.75	0.80	0.85	0.90	0.95	1.00
Over 1,000	1.04	1.07	1.11	1.14	1.18	1.21	1.25
1,000	1.01	1.05	1.08	1.12	1.15	1.18	1.22
750	0.98	1.02	1.05	1.09	1.12	1.16	1.19
500	0.96	0.99	1.02	1.06	1.09	1.13	1.16
375	0.93	0.96	1.00	1.03	1.06	1.10	1.13
250	0.90	0.93	0.97	1.00	1.03	1.07	1.10
175	0.87	0.90	0.94	0.97	1.01	1.04	1.07
100	0.84	0.87	0.91	0.94	0.98	1.01	1.05
75	0.81	0.85	0.88	0.92	0.95	0.98	1.02

Adjustment for location within metropolitan area

Location	Factor
Cent. business dist.	1.00
Fringe area	1.25
Outlying bus. dist.	1.25
Residential area	1.25

Figure 16.30. Urban intersection approach service volume, in vehicles per hour of green signal time, for two-way streets with no parking. SOURCE: *Highway Capacity Manual, 1965,* Spec. Report 87, Washington, D.C.: Highway Research Board, 1965, p. 135.

resents level of service C. Admittedly, these are rather artificial and less than adequate. Hopefully, current research will result in better indicators of intersection levels of service, probably incorporating a more manageable measure of delay.

Peaking characteristics. In American practice it is customary to consider the variation of flow within the hour in developing capacity and service volume values. A 15-min peak-hour factor (PHF_{15}) is usually used for this adjustment. The 15-min PHF is the ratio of the volume in a full hour to four times the flow occurring in the highest 15 consecutive minutes. Use of this factor has the effect of developing capacity and service volumes on the basis of peak period rather than hourly flow rates. It has been found that traffic distributions in these peak periods are more likely to be random (and thus more consistent with theoretical models) than is the case with full peak-hour flows.

City size and driver characteristics. Some studies of traffic performance at intersections have found a consistent pattern of higher capacities for locations in large metropolitan areas than for similar intersections in rural areas or smaller communities. In metropolitan areas of 1 million population, capacities were found to be about 5% greater than in communities of 500,000; in areas of 250,000 population, capacities were found to average about 5% less. The reasons for this might be a more hurried pace of life, different speed characteristics, or greater driver experience, the larger the city. The relationship is not consistent, however, and other studies, both in the United States and abroad, have failed to detect a similar relationship. The *Highway*

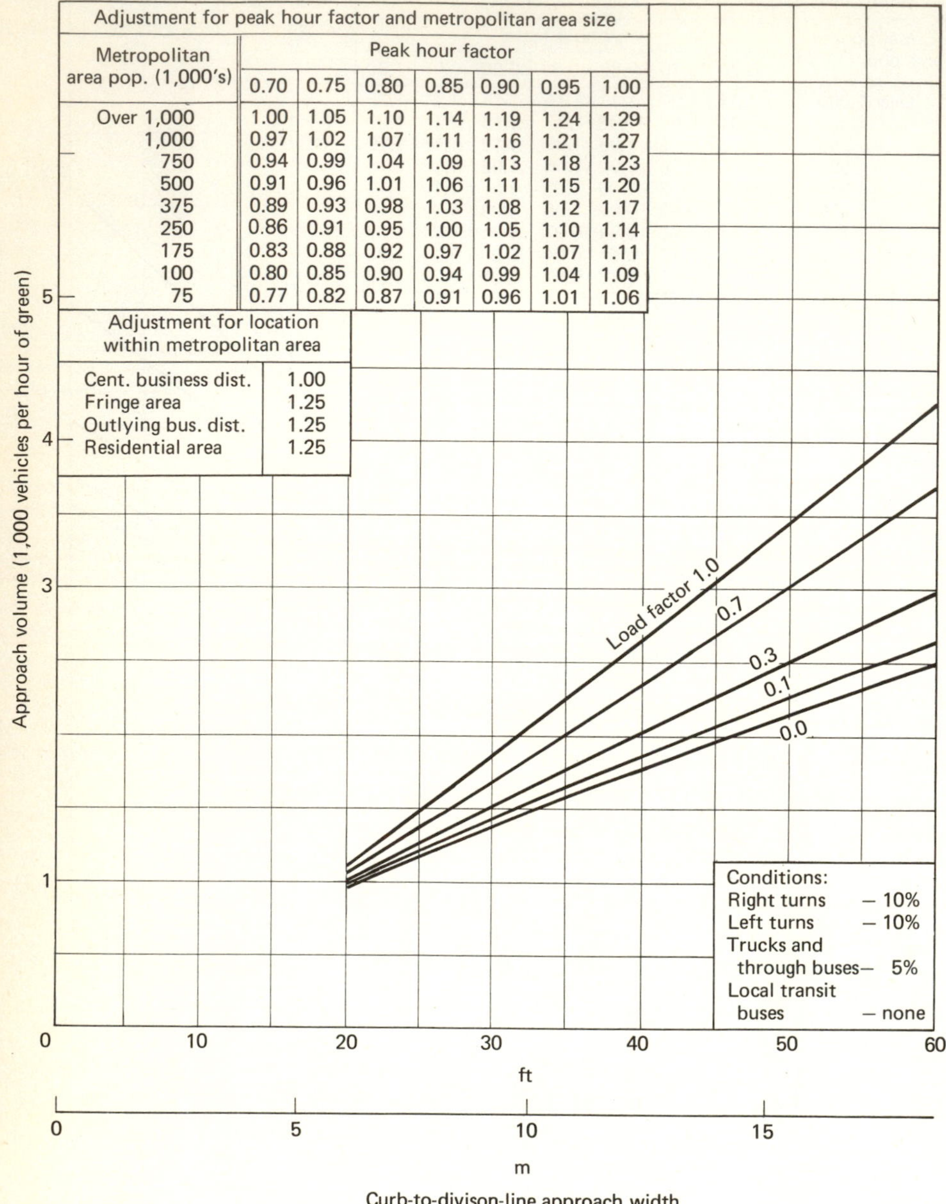

Adjustment for peak hour factor and metropolitan area size

Metropolitan area pop. (1,000's)	Peak hour factor 0.70	0.75	0.80	0.85	0.90	0.95	1.00
Over 1,000	1.00	1.05	1.10	1.14	1.19	1.24	1.29
1,000	0.97	1.02	1.07	1.11	1.16	1.21	1.27
750	0.94	0.99	1.04	1.09	1.13	1.18	1.23
500	0.91	0.96	1.01	1.06	1.11	1.15	1.20
375	0.89	0.93	0.98	1.03	1.08	1.12	1.17
250	0.86	0.91	0.95	1.00	1.05	1.10	1.14
175	0.83	0.88	0.92	0.97	1.02	1.07	1.11
100	0.80	0.85	0.90	0.94	0.99	1.04	1.09
75	0.77	0.82	0.87	0.91	0.96	1.01	1.06

Adjustment for location within metropolitan area

Cent. business dist.	1.00
Fringe area	1.25
Outlying bus. dist.	1.25
Residential area	1.25

Figure 16.31. Urban intersection approach service volume, in vehicles per hour of green signal time, for two-way streets with parking. SOURCE: *Highway Capacity Manual, 1965,* Spec. Report 87, Washington, D.C.: Highway Research Board, 1965, p. 136.

Capacity Manual, 1965 frequently followed in American practice, provides correction factors that combine the effect of area population and peak-hour factor. These are given in tables appearing in Figures 16.27 to 16.31. British and Australian practices do not utilize an adjustment for this characteristic.

Location within city/adjacent development. The culture and peripheral activities surrounding an intersection can also affect performance. In a busy central business district, the presence of many pedestrians, loading and unloading, and frequent parking maneuvers near the intersection have a deleterious effect on capacity. These factors are less frequent in fringe and outlying business districts and nearly absent in residential and rural areas. Thus, the functional capacity and service volume of two physically identical intersections can be markedly different depending on these influences. The *Highway Capacity Manual, 1965* uses a central business district base, and provides gross adjustments for other locations in the range 10 to 25%. Because of the large increments between these adjustment values, which so significantly influence the solution, they should be applied with considered engineering judgment. These adjustment factors also are given in tables incorporated in Figures 16.27 to 16.31.

Turning movements. Under most conditions, turning movements have an adverse affect on intersection capacity.

Right-turning vehicles have some effect because, typically, a short-turn radius requires slowing considerably below through traffic speeds. Also, the potential or actual presence of pedestrians will affect headways and performance.

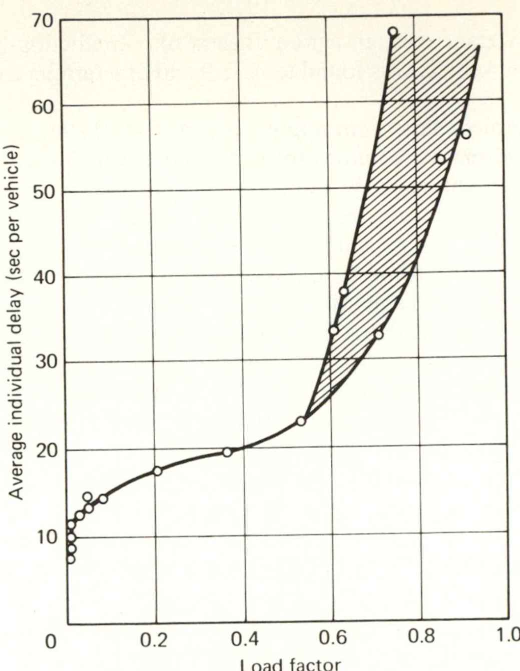

Figure 16.32. Average individual delay related to load factor. SOURCE: Adolf D. May, Jr., and David Pratt, "A Simulation Study of Load Factor at Signalized Intersections," *Traffic Engineering, 38*(5), 44, 1968.

The British capacity computation procedure accounts for this effect only in the selection of a saturation flow value; nonconflicting-turn vehicles are considered through vehicles.

The Australian method considers a nonconflicting-turn passenger vehicle to be equivalent to 1.25 through passenger vehicles and a similar truck to be equivalent to 2.5 passenger vehicles.

The American system increases or reduces the capacity and service volumes around a central value of 10% turns by a factor which, for two-lane approaches (16 to 24 ft, or 4.9 to 7.3 m) is equal to 0.5% per percent of right turns up to 30%. Above three lanes (34 ft or 39 ft, depending upon the parking conditions; i.e., 10.4 or 11.9 m), no adjustment is made. Adjustment factors for right turns and for left turns on one-way streets are given in Table 16-25. Special procedures are used when a separate turning lane or separate turning phase is provided, as discussed later.

Where left turns must be made across opposing traffic flows on two-way streets, such left-turning vehicles not provided with a separate lane or phase must await gaps in the approaching traffic and thus create delays to themselves and to those following in the same lane. Again, methods of computing their effect on approach capacity differ from country to country.

The British system, in a suburban condition in which saturation flow equals 160 passenger vehicles per hour of

TABLE 16–25
Adjustment Factors for Right Turns (and Left Turns from One-Way Streets)

	Adjustment Factor					
	With No Parking*			With Parking†		
Turns (%)	Approach Width ≤15 ft (≤4.6 m)	Approach Width 16–24 ft (4.9–7.3 m)	Approach Width 25–34 ft (7.6–10.4 m)	Approach Width ≤20 ft (≤6.1 m)	Approach Width 21–29 ft (6.4–8.8 m)	Approach Width 30–39 ft (9.1–11.9 m)
0	1.20	1.050	1.025	1.20	1.050	1.025
1	1.18	1.045	1.020	1.18	1.045	1.020
2	1.16	1.040	1.020	1.16	1.040	1.020
3	1.14	1.035	1.015	1.14	1.035	1.015
4	1.12	1.030	1.015	1.12	1.030	1.015
5	1.10	1.025	1.010	1.10	1.025	1.010
6	1.08	1.020	1.010	1.08	1.020	1.010
7	1.06	1.015	1.005	1.06	1.015	1.005
8	1.04	1.010	1.005	1.04	1.010	1.005
9	1.02	1.005	1.000	1.02	1.005	1.000
10	1.00	1.000	1.000	1.00	1.000	1.000
11	0.99	0.995	1.000	0.99	0.995	1.000
12	0.98	0.990	0.995	0.98	0.990	0.995
13	0.97	0.985	0.995	0.97	0.985	0.995
14	0.96	0.980	0.990	0.96	0.980	0.990
15	0.95	0.975	0.990	0.95	0.975	0.990
16	0.94	0.970	0.985	0.94	0.970	0.985
17	0.93	0.965	0.985	0.93	0.965	0.985
18	0.92	0.960	0.980	0.92	0.960	0.980
19	0.91	0.955	0.980	0.91	0.955	0.980
20	0.90	0.950	0.975	0.90	0.950	0.975
22	0.89	0.940	0.980	0.89	0.940	0.980
24	0.88	0.930	0.985	0.88	0.930	0.985
26	0.87	0.920	0.990	0.87	0.920	0.990
28	0.86	0.910	0.995	0.86	0.910	0.995
30+	0.85	0.900	1.000	0.85	0.900	1.000

*No adjustment necessary for approach width of 35 ft (10.7 m) or more; that is, use factor of 1.000.
†No adjustment necessary for approach width of 40 ft (12.2 m) or more; that is, use factor of 1.000.

SOURCE: *Highway Capacity Manual, 1965,* Spec. Report 87 (Washington, D.C.: Highway Research Board, 1965), p. 140.

green per feet of width for widths above 16 ft (4.9 m), considers one conflicting turn vehicle to be equivalent to 1.75 through vehicles. For central London conditions, a saturation flow of 115 passenger vehicles per foot (377 per meter) of width per hour of green is assumed with 25% commercial vehicles and 10% conflicting turns. Each 1% of conflicting turns above or below 10% is considered to change this value by ±0.6% up to a maximum reduction of 18%.

The Australian system provides a formula for computing the effect of conflicting turns as follows:

$$E = \frac{1.5}{f\frac{SG_E - qC}{S - q} + \frac{4.5}{G_E}} \qquad (16.22)$$

where E = the through car equivalent of a conflicting turn passenger car; for commercial vehicles add 1 to the result.

f = a function of opposing flow
= 1 at low flows and 0.45 at q = 800

S = saturation flow of opposing traffic, veh/s

q = flow of opposing traffic, veh/s

C = cycle length, s

G_E = effective green, s

The average through car equivalent of a conflicting-turn passenger vehicle was found to be 2.9 and of a turning truck 3.9.

The American system applies a correction factor to capacity and service volumes for left-turning vehicles which, for average approach widths from 16 to 34 ft (4.9 to 10.4 m) of clear approach, equals 1% per percent of left turns up to 20%. A central value of 10% is used and adjustment factors vary according to approach width. Adjustment factors are given in Table 16-26.

It should be noted that the American system, as presented in *Highway Capacity Manual, 1965,* does not directly consider the delaying effect of increases in opposing traffic. It is applied as a percentage correction related to approach volume only. The effect of a fixed *percentage* of left-turn vehicles thus apparently decreases as volume increases, whereas the opposite effect is found by the Australian method, as shown in Table 16-27. It seems highly probable that the results of the Australian methods are more reliable in this respect.

This flaw in *Highway Capacity Manual, 1965* has been recognized, and users are now advised to apply the so-called "1200 rule," that is, a capacity limit of 1200 left-turning plus opposing vehicles per hour of green signal indication for all ordinary intersection approaches.

In the case where there are separate left or right turning lanes with separate signal control, the basic computation procedure is modified somewhat. The width of each such

TABLE 16–26
Adjustment Factors for Left Turns on Two-Way Streets

	Adjustment Factor					
	With No Parking			With Parking		
Turns (%)	Approach Width ≤15 ft (≤4.6 m)	Approach Width 16–34 ft (4.9–10.4 m)	Approach Width ≥35 ft (≥10.7 m)	Approach Width ≤20 ft (≤6.1 m)	Approach Width 21–39 ft (6.4–11.9 m)	Approach Width ≥40 ft (≥12.2 m)
0	1.30	1.10	1.050	1.30	1.10	1.050
1	1.27	1.09	1.045	1.27	1.09	1.045
2	1.24	1.08	1.040	1.24	1.08	1.040
3	1.21	1.07	1.035	1.21	1.07	1.035
4	1.18	1.06	1.030	1.18	1.06	1.030
5	1.15	1.05	1.025	1.15	1.05	1.025
6	1.12	1.04	1.020	1.12	1.04	1.020
7	1.09	1.03	1.015	1.09	1.03	1.015
8	1.06	1.02	1.010	1.06	1.02	1.010
9	1.03	1.01	1.005	1.03	1.01	1.005
10	1.00	1.00	1.000	1.00	1.00	1.000
11	0.98	0.99	0.995	0.98	0.99	0.995
12	0.96	0.98	0.990	0.96	0.98	0.990
13	0.94	0.97	0.985	0.94	0.97	0.985
14	0.92	0.96	0.980	0.92	0.96	0.980
15	0.90	0.95	0.975	0.90	0.95	0.975
16	0.89	0.94	0.970	0.89	0.94	0.970
17	0.88	0.93	0.965	0.88	0.93	0.965
18	0.87	0.92	0.960	0.87	0.92	0.960
19	0.86	0.91	0.955	0.86	0.91	0.955
20	0.85	0.90	0.950	0.85	0.90	0.950
22	0.84	0.89	0.940	0.84	0.89	0.940
24	0.83	0.88	0.930	0.83	0.88	0.930
26	0.82	0.87	0.920	0.82	0.87	0.920
28	0.81	0.86	0.910	0.81	0.86	0.910
30+	0.80	0.85	0.900	0.80	0.85	0.900

SOURCE: *Highway Capacity Manual, 1965,* Spec. Report 87 (Washington, D.C.: Highway Research Board, 1965), p. 141.

TABLE 16–27
Effect of Saturation Flow and Opposing Flow on Capacity Reduction Factors for 10% Left Turns on Two-Way Streets with No Parking

Number of Lanes	Saturation Flow for Entering and Opposing Directions, (veh/h of green)	Opposing Flow, q (veh/h of green)	E_1*	Approach Volume at Load Factor = 1 (veh/h of green): Total	Left Turns	Approach Reduction Factors for 10% Left Turns: Australia Data	U.S. Data
		For Low Opposing Flow					
1	1800	200	1.7	1,682	168	0.93	0.77
2	3600	400	2.1	3,243	324	0.90	0.91
3	5400	600	2.4	4,736	474	0.88	0.95
		For Higher Opposing Flow					
1	1800	400	2.3	1,593	159	0.89	0.77
2	3600	800	3.1	2,970	297	0.83	0.91
3	5400	1200	4.1†	4,125	413	0.76	0.95‡

*Based on E_{rt} values from Appendix B, *Australian Road Capacity Guide*, for $C = 60$ and $g/c = 0.6$.
†From correspondence with Alan Miller.
‡Left-turn capacity is exceeded, because $q + LT > 1200$.

SOURCE: Y. B. CHANG AND D. S. BERRY, "Examination of Consistency in Signalized Intersection Capacity Charts of the Highway Capacity Manual," *Highway Capacity*, Highway Res. Rec. 289 (Washington, D.C.: Highway Research Board, 1969), p. 19.

lane is deducted from the overall approach width, and the remaining width is handled as before except that the percentage of turning traffic in the directions deducted is taken as zero. Each separate turning lane volume is then determined using the following equation,[29] derived from *Highway Capacity Manual, 1965:*

$$V = V_{TL}\left(\frac{G}{C}\right)\frac{W}{K[1 - 0.1(T - 5)]\,[1 + 0.8(N - 1)]} \tag{16.23}$$

where V = volume of turning traffic, veh/h

V_{TL} = turning lane service volume:

800 veh/h of green for service levels A, B, C

1000 veh/h of green for service level D

1200 veh/h of green for service level E

G/C = ratio of green signal time for the turning phase to the total cycle time

W = width of turning lane, ft (or m) [if over 12 ft (3.7 m), use 12 ft (3.7 m)]

K = 10 if W is in ft; 3 if W is in meters

T = percentage of trucks in turning-lane flow

N = number of turning lanes in the turn direction

The manual also provides procedures for separate turning lanes without separate signal control. For left turns, the "1200 rule" previously mentioned for ordinary approaches is applied. For right turns, the foregoing method for separate signal-controlled locations is used if pedestrian volumes are light. If heavy, the hourly turning volume is approximated by 600 × G/C.

Trucks and through buses. The larger size and lower acceleration ability of trucks, through buses, and other commercial vehicles reduce the capacity of a signalized intersection carrying mixed traffic.

The British method adjusts the flow rate by converting all traffic to equivalent passenger car units (PCU) by the following factors:

Heavy and medium commercial vehicle = 1¾ PCU

Light commercial vehicle = 1 PCU

Bus = 2¼ PCU

Tram = 2½ PCU

The Australian approach is the same in concept. The factors:

Through truck = 2.0 PCU

Nonconflict-turning truck = 2.5 PCU

Conflict-turning truck (average) = 3.9 PCU

The American method applies a factor that reduces or increases the capacity and service volumes 1% for each percentage of trucks and through buses in the approach stream above or below 5%. This value is based on observations of performance with truck percentages below 20%. There is some indication[30] that this overestimates the effect of trucks when they constitute over 20% of approach traffic. Table 16-28 gives truck adjustment factors.

TABLE 16–28
Truck and Through-Bus Adjustment Factors

Trucks and Through Buses (%)	Correction Factor	Trucks and Through Buses (%)	Correction Factor	Trucks and Through Buses (%)	Correction Factor
0	1.05	7	0.98	14	0.91
1	1.04	8	0.97	15	0.90
2	1.03	9	0.96	16	0.89
3	1.02	10	0.95	17	0.88
4	1.01	11	0.94	18	0.87
5	1.00	12	0.93	19	0.86
6	0.99	13	0.92	20	0.85

SOURCE: *Highway Capacity Manual, 1965*, Spec. Report 87 (Washington, D.C.: Highway Research Board, 1965), p. 142.

Local transit buses. The effect of a transit bus utilizing a bus stop at a signalized intersection is complex, depending on the frequency of buses, frequency and duration of stops, existence of a curb zone that can be utilized by right-turn vehicles when a bus is not present, and size and location of the stop in relation to the intersection. This effect is not well quantified, and the British and Australian methods are silent on the subject. The American *Highway Capacity Manual, 1965* presents a series of four nomographs to de-

[29] LOUIS J. PIGNATARO, *Traffic Engineering Theory and Practice* (Englewood Cliffs, N.J.: Prentice-Hall, 1973), p. 224.

[30] D. W. GWYNN, "Truck Equivalency," *Mathematical and Statistical Aspects of Traffic*, Highway Res. Rec. 199 (Washington, D.C.: Highway Research Board, 1967), p. 79.

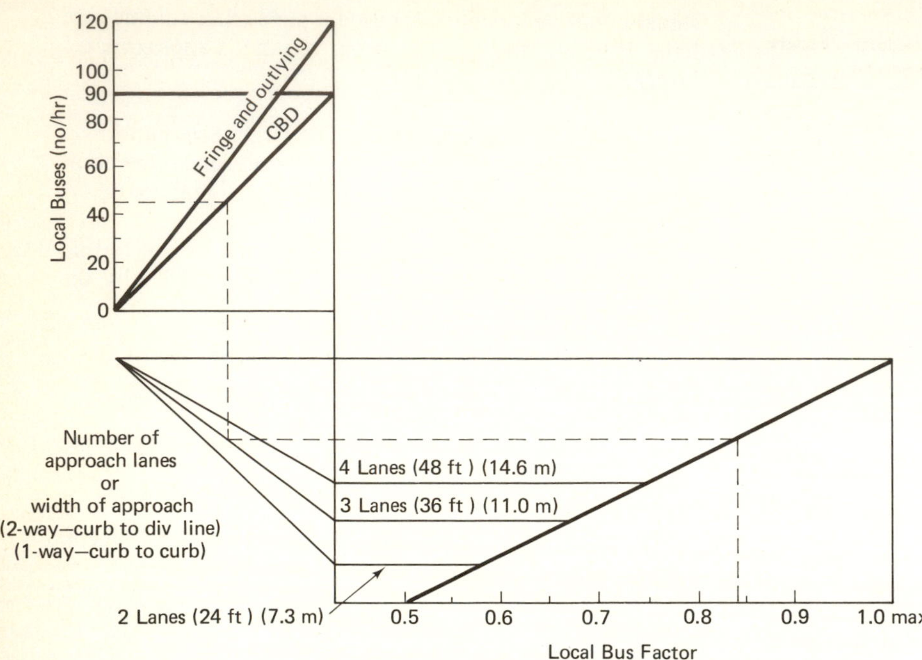

Figure 16.33. Local bus factor for near-side bus stop on street with no parking. SOURCE: *Highway Capacity Manual, 1965*, Spec. Report 87, Washington, D.C.: Highway Research Board, 1965, p. 143.

velop correction factors. These are rationalizations based on limited data. For the simplest case, a near-side bus stop on a two-lane approach with no parking, the factor is approximately a 0.4% volume reduction per bus per hour. Figure 16.33 presents, as an example, the nomograph for this basic case.

Signal timing. The effective green time available for movement is a critical determinant of the capacity of a signalized intersection approach. The total green time available in an hour is a function of both the cycle length and the green phase length. The British and Australian methods take both into account. The American method uses only the *G/C* ratio (green time/cycle time ratio), assuming that within the commonly used range of cycle lengths, cycle time as such is not a factor. This point remains controversial. In any case, frequently, cycle length is determined by considerations broader than simply performance at the specific intersection under study.

In comparing and using the various methods presented here, it is important to note that effective green time is determined differently. In British and Australian methods, the effective green is considered to be the green plus clearance periods minus lost time at the beginning and end of each green phase. In the American system, the actual green time excluding the clearance period is used in determining the *G/C* ratio, although the values given assume some passage during the clearance interval. The values are similar but by no means identical. The capacities and service volumes determined from calculations are in terms of flow per hour of green and are reduced to hourly volumes by multiplying by the *G/C* ratio.

Present methods have various inadequacies. The American method is based on fixed-time signals, and can be applied only approximately to actuated installations. Foreign methods concentrate on "saturation flow," or capacity, with relatively little coverage of better levels of service. Ongoing research may resolve some of these difficulties.

Grades. *Highway Capacity Manual, 1965* is largely silent regarding the influence of grades on intersection performance, yet it seems quite apparent that a negative grade on a signalized intersection approach will increase and a positive grade decrease the approach capacity. British research has found a 3% increase or decrease for each 1% of negative or positive grade in the range −5 to +10%.

Intersection-approach service volume computations

Figures 16.27 to 16.31 give the basic service volumes used in the American method, from *Highway Capacity Manual, 1965,* to which adjustments must be applied. Consideration of parking and of one-way vs. two-way is inherent in selection of the appropriate chart, while the load factor, representing the level of service desired, is inherent in the family of curves on each chart (see Table 16-24). Adjustment factors for several other variables—peaking, city size, and location—are tabulated on the charts. Still other adjustments that must be applied are the *G/C* ratio and factors for turns, trucks, and transit buses.

EXAMPLE 16.7:

Given a 25-ft (7.6-m) signalized approach on a two-way street with no parking, 15% left turns, 5% right turns, and 10% trucks on a level grade in an outlying business district of a city of 500,000 population. The signal operates on a fixed-time, 60-s cycle with 26-s green and 4-s clearance periods. Determine the volume that can be handled on the approach at level of service C and, by the British method, the average delay per vehicle at that volume.

Solution: Determine the service volume as follows. For level of service C, the load factor = 0.3 (Table 16-24). For an approach width of 25 ft (7.6 m), approach volume per hour of green time = 1800 (Figure 16.30). Assume a peak-hour factor of 0.85; then for a population of 500,000, the adjustment factor = 1.06 (Figure 16.30). Further, the:

$$\text{Location adjustment} = 1.25 \text{ (Figure 16.30)}$$

$$\text{Right turn adjustment} = 1.01 \text{ (Table 16-25)}$$

$$\text{Left turn adjustment} = 0.95 \text{ (Table 16-26)}$$

$$\text{Truck adjustment} = 0.95 \text{ (Table 16-28)}$$

$$\frac{G}{C} = \frac{26}{60} = 0.433$$

The adjusted service volume is:

$$SV_C = 1800(1.06 \times 1.25 \times 1.01 \times 0.95 \times 0.95 \times 0.433) = 940 \text{ veh/h}$$

Compute the delay by the British method as follows:

$$s = \text{saturation flow} = 160 \text{ PCU/ft/h} = 525 \text{ PCU/m/h}$$

Then 160 × 25 (or 525 × 7.6) = 4000 PCU/h = 1.11 PCU/s.

$$q\text{ (PCU)} = 940[0.75 + 0.15\,(1.75) + 0.10\,(1.75)] = 1116 \text{ PCU/h or } 0.310 \text{ PCU/s}$$

$$G_E = \text{effective green time} = \text{green} + \text{clearance} - \text{lost time}$$

Assuming a 6s lost time, $G_E = 26 + 4 - 6 = 24$ s.

$$x = \frac{Cq}{G_E S} = \frac{60(0.310)}{24(1.11)} = 0.698$$

$$\frac{G_E}{C} = \frac{24}{60} = 0.40$$

$$f_1 = 0.250 \quad \text{(Table 16-20)}$$

$$f_2 = 0.807 \quad \text{(Table 16-21)}$$

$$f_3 = 7.5 \quad \text{(Table 16-22)}$$

Substituting in the delay formula yields

$$d = \left(Cf_1 + \frac{f_2}{q}\right)\left(\frac{100 - f_3}{100}\right)$$

$$= \left(60 \times 0.250 + \frac{0.807}{0.310}\right)\left(\frac{100 - 7.5}{100}\right) = 16.3$$

Comparing the results of the delay computation using the British method with the simulation results shown in Figure 16.32, it is seen that an average individual delay of 16.3 s corresponds to a load factor of about 0.2, which is close to the level of service C load factor of 0.3 originally established in the problem. This indicates reasonably close correlation between the British and U.S. methods.

Intersection critical movement analysis

Critical movement analysis,[31] sometimes called "critical lane analysis," is a technique developed for use in certain highway planning applications to determine the level of service of entire signalized intersections. Since only a minimal amount of field and traffic information is required and the original computation procedure is simpler, faster, and maybe more easily understood when compared to most other methods, it is sometimes described as a shortcut method. It has been used recently to compare various alternative traffic improvements and to evaluate traffic impacts of land development proposals on the surrounding highway system.

Critical movement analysis is based on the principle that the level of service of an intersection can be predicted by analyzing the several traffic movements occurring during each signal phase. For each phase of signal cycle, there are either conflicting or simultaneous traffic flow movements which can be identified from the signal phasing diagram. The magnitude of these conflicting or simultaneous flows is measured by using the traffic volume information. The highest traffic volume obtained in a given phase, either by comparing the simultaneous single-lane traffic flow volumes or by the addition of each left-turn volume to its opposing flow volume, is called the control or "critical volume." When the critical volumes for each phase are added together, the total volume represents, in effect, a single lane of traffic moving through the intersection. Observations of traffic flow characteristics at various intersections over a period of years have confirmed that a signalized intersection can physically accommodate only about 1500 to 1800 passenger cars per hour acting as if it were theoretically moving continuously through the intersection in one lane.

When the summation of the critical volumes for all the signal phases is compared with a basic value for the capacity of the intersection as just described, the relative degree of usage of the intersection and a level of service can be determined.

In the basic critical movement analysis technique, it is assumed that optimal signalization exists at the intersection, that the approaching through traffic divides equally into all the through traffic lanes available on each approach, and that there are no other adverse traffic operational influences, such as restrictive geometrics, pedestrians, trucks and buses, and so on. More recently, various users have developed a variety of adjustment factors to account for such variations as lane width, distribution of approaching traffic, trucks and buses, number of approach lanes, separate left-turn lanes, pedestrians, signal phasing, traffic peaking characteristics, and the effect of parked vehicles. These have added a greater degree of sophistication to the basic method, but have resulted in a wide variety of adaptations of the basic method in use in the field.

Procedure. The basic intersection geometrics for each approach such as number of through and right- or left-turn

[31]H. B. McInerney and S. G. Peterson, "Intersection Capacity Measurement through Critical Movement Summation: A Planning Tool," *Traffic Eng.*, 41(4), 45–48 (Jan. 1971).

lanes, and signal phasing must be given or assumed along with the traffic movement and volume information for the intersection. The critical movement analysis procedure consists of determining the critical volumes for each signal phase and then adding them together to determine a level of service. Typical cases are as follows:

1. To determine the critical volume for an intersection approach with a separate left-turning lane, first compute the volumes of the through traffic by substracting from the total approach volume the volume of turning traffic. The critical through-lane volume is then the total through-traffic volume divided by the number of lanes on the approach. Instead of this division, a refinement developed by one user makes use of a multiplier called the lane use factor, as shown in Table 16-29.

TABLE 16–29
Lane Use Factor

Number of Lanes on Approach	Lane Use Factor
1	1.0
2	0.55
3	0.40
4	0.30

Next, compute the critical volume for the separate turning lane. If there is no separate signal phase, the critical volume will be the largest total traffic volume obtained by adding the left-turning volume to the opposing-flow volume. The critical volume for the signal phase, which includes both the through and turning traffic, will be the higher computed volume (i.e., either the through-lane critical volume or the turn-plus-opposing critical volume).

In the case where there is a separate turning phase for left-turning traffic, the critical volume for that phase will be the larger of the left-turning volumes that move during the phase.

2. To determine the critical volume where there are no separate turning lanes on the approach, the total approach volume is adjusted to account for the left-turning vehicular conflict effects by adding the left-turn volume to the opposing-flow volume and distributing this total volume over all the lanes on the approach. Various users have adopted differing methods for estimating the redistribution of the traffic on the approach. In all cases, the critical volume is still the highest volume movement during that signal phase.

3. For a two-lane, two-way intersection approach, the critical movement analysis is not as simple as in the case of the multilane approach. The actual traffic operations should either be observed in the field, if an existing condition is being analyzed, or assumed in the case of predicting a future level of service to determine the amount of bypassing of the left-turning vehicles by the through traffic. An estimate of this bypassing effect should be made and the volumes adjusted accordingly to reflect the actual operating conditions.

In the above cases, to determine the level of service of the intersection, the critical volumes for each signal phase are added together and this volume sum is compared with basic level of service criteria. The criteria developed by one user are shown in Table 16-30; there the maximum for level E (capacity) is given as 1600 *vehicles* per hour. Somewhat different criteria would be found in some of the other refined methods. For instance, in the "Critical Movement Analysis" section of the TRB *Interim Materials on Highway Capacity*,[32] limits for level E for operations and design applications are given as:

TABLE 16–30
Level of Service Criteria based on a Typical Procedure*

Level of Service	Maximum Sum of Critical Volumes for All Phases (vehicles/h)
A	≤1000
B	1150
C	1300
D	1450
E	1600
F	>1600

*Caution note: criteria differ in several alternative procedures in current use.

SOURCE: *Guidelines for the Analysis of the Traffic Impact of Development Proposals,* The Maryland–National Capital Park and Planning Commission, Prince Georges County, Md., 1977.

Two-phase signal control, 1800 *passenger cars* per hour

Three-phase signal control, 1720 *passenger cars* per hour

Four-phase signal control, 1650 *passenger cars* per hour

These reflect the principle that generally the comfort, convenience, and safety benefits of multiphasing are only obtained through a slight loss in capacity.

EXAMPLE 16.8:

Determine the level of service of the intersection shown, given a three-phase signal operation with the existing p.m. peak traffic volumes as shown, using the critical movement analysis method.

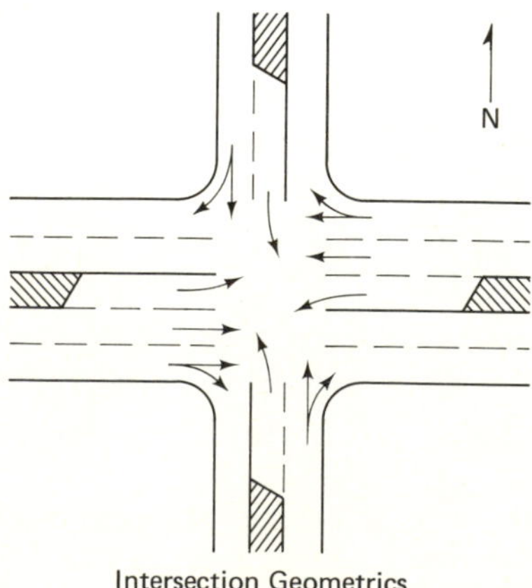

Intersection Geometrics

[32] "Interim Materials on Highway Capacity," *Transport. Res. Circ. No. 212* (Washington, D.C.: Transportation Research Board, Jan. 1980), p. 11.

Phase Diagram		(1) Movement	(2) Through and Right-Turn Volume	(3) Lane Use Factor	(4) Lane Volume: (2) × (3)	(5) Opposing Left-Turn Volume	(6) Critical Lane Volume: (4) + (5)
A		NB SB	175 + 25 250 + 25	1.0 1.0	200 275	100 75	300 350*
B		EB WB	— —	— —	200 300	— —	200 300*
C		EB WB	700 + 100 900 + 100	0.55 0.55	440 550	— —	440 550*

*Highest or critical lane volume.

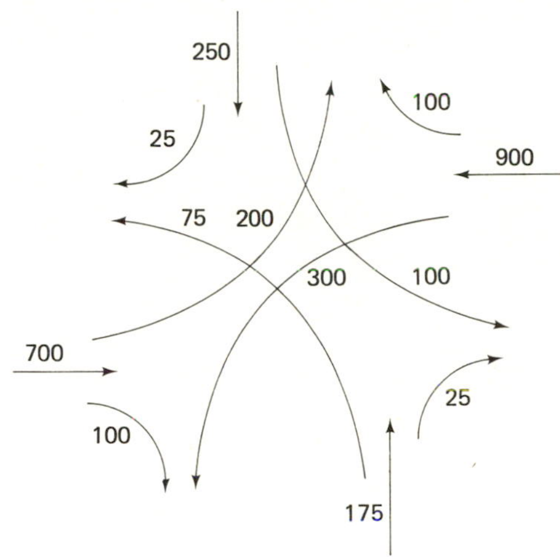

Existing PM Peak Traffic Volumes

Solution: Set up the three-phase signal plan with appropriate traffic volumes, determine the critical volumes for each phase, and add the critical volumes for the three phases together, as in the tabulation that follows. In this case, the basic method is slightly modified by using a lane utilization factor and level of service criteria previously described, as shown in Tables 16-29 and 16-30.

The summation of critical lane volumes for each signal phase is 350 + 300 + 550 = 1200. Comparing this total volume with the level of service criteria in Table 16-30, the intersection is found to be operating at level of service C *under these particular criteria*. It is important to note that some of the other current versions of this method, because of differing criteria and service volume scales, might indicate a different level of service. The establishment of uniformity appears to be a very desirable goal.

Summary

Although highway capacity and levels of service have been studied for over 50 years, many questions remain unanswered. The analysis methods reported herein are adequate for gross examination but seldom provide the knowledgeable user with a complete sense of ease when a precise answer is required. In no area is this more true than with signalized intersections. The complexity of factors involved and the inherent variability of traffic phenomena have thus far limited both theoretical and empirical approaches to precise solution. In time this may be corrected. Until then, engineers are well advised to use the content of this chapter and the sources referred to as a guide to the application of their mature judgment in estimating the capacity and service that a highway facility can provide.

As noted earlier, international findings in this field are likely to differ from American findings, as a result of driver behavior differences if for no other reason. Therefore, disagreement between results obtained by an American method and its equivalent from another country does not mean necessarily that either is in error; it may simply identify behavior differences. It follows, then, that foreign procedures should be used with caution in specific American problem solutions, and vice versa.

At the time that this handbook was sent to press, a new, greatly revised edition of the *U.S. Highway Capacity Manual* was in preparation, to be released on a chapter-by-chapter basis during the mid-1980s; certain "Interim Materials on Highway Capacity"[33] were already in circulation for initial evaluation. Users of this chapter are advised to be alert for such releases and to become familiar with these new techniques as issued.

[33]Ibid.

17

TRAFFIC STUDIES

PAUL C. BOX, *President*
Paul C. Box and Associates, Inc.
Skokie, Illinois

This chapter contains brief descriptions of basic traffic engineering studies, which are conducted to gather facts on traffic conditions. They must be set up and carried out so that the information is timely, reasonably accurate and unbiased, and at costs consistent with the magnitude of the problem, available funds, and personnel. Methods of data collection and analysis are presented. More detailed descriptions of studies, equipment, and forms are given in the *Manual of Traffic Engineering Studies (MTES)*.[1] Applications are discussed in other chapters.

Studies may be classified as *administrative*, which is the assembly of data already available in office files or *field*, which involves measurements or observations of existing conditions. They may be *static inventories* or *dynamic traffic studies* involving operational measurements.

Where statistical techniques are used to summarize the field studies, details are given. More complete coverage of statistical analysis is found in the *MTES*.

Inventories

An inventory is an accounting, tabulation, listing, or graphic display of information describing existing conditions. It must be readily available and periodically updated. Some inventories, such as traffic and parking regulations, parking facilities, and transit routes, may require frequent updating, whereas others, such as street widths, will be changed less frequently. Some of the more pertinent *inventories* are as follows:

1. *Public streets and highways*
   a. Rights-of-way
   b. Roadway and shoulder widths
   c. Location of curbed sections
   d. Condition of surface
   e. Location of structures, such as bridges, overpasses, underpasses, and major culverts
   f. Overhead structure clearances
   g. Railroad crossings
   h. Locations of critical curves or grades
   i. Identification of routes by governmental unit having maintenance jurisdiction
   j. Functional classifications
   k. Street lighting
2. *Land uses and zoning controls*
3. *Traffic generators*
   a. Schools
   b. Parks
   c. Stadiums
   d. Shopping centers
   e. Office complexes
4. *Laws, ordinances, and regulations*
5. *Traffic control devices*
   a. Traffic signs
   b. Signals
   c. Pavement markings
6. *Control device detail*
   a. Type of device
   b. Size, legend and color combination
   c. Authority for erection
   d. Installation date
   e. Dates of replacement, relocation, or revision
   f. Records of outages
   g. Condition of equipment
7. *Transit system*
   a. Routes—by street
   b. Location and lengths of stops and bus layover spaces
   c. Locations of off-street terminals
   d. Change-of-mode facilities, including parking, and passenger pickup/dropoff (P/D) areas

[1] PAUL C. BOX AND JOSEPH C. OPPENLANDER, *Manual of Traffic Engineering Studies*, 4th ed. (Arlington, Va.: Institute of Transportation Engineers, 1976).

8. *Parking facilities*—done principally for the central business district (CBD) of a city
   a. Available curb and off-street spaces, by location, time limits, and hours of application
   b. Parking meter locations
   c. Special zones, such as for truck loading, passenger P/D, taxi stands, etc.

Administrative studies may utilize records of the engineering, public works, or planning departments to supply substantial portions of the data. Other sources include county and state agencies, transit operators, and school administrators. Some duplication of records may be useful among governmental departments to ensure accessibility, but unnecessary duplication should be avoided. For example, urban traffic engineers need an updated inventory of rights-of-way and official names of all public roads in their area. However, records of lot numbers resulting from re-subdivisions that do not change street alignments would seldom be used by a city traffic engineer.

Generally, significant portions of an inventory will require field survey, taking measurements and notes as needed. Aerial photography at scales of 600 to 1200:1 is useful. Photo logging, using still or motion pictures taken from an instrumented vehicle, may facilitate inventories. Also, they form an excellent record of conditions at the time the photographs were taken. Data are sometimes gathered cooperatively by staffs of several agencies.

Many data can be effectively portrayed on *jurisdiction maps*. Examples include:

- Functional street classification
- Intersection controls
- One-way streets
- Weight limits and truck routes
- Overhead structure clearances
- Transit routes and stops
- Speed limits
- Snow emergency routes
- Daily traffic volumes
- Land use

Specialized *area maps* are useful to show detailed features, such as:

- Interconnected traffic signal systems
- Curb parking regulations
- Location of parking meters
- Off-street parking facilities
- Street light systems
- Roadway widths
- Right of way widths

Some inventories are best maintained in *card files* such as traffic signal descriptions, timing and offsets, and parking regulations.

The use of automated data processing (ADP) systems will facilitate accessibility to most inventories and data files, especially in larger agencies. However, the convenience of entry and revision available with map records, cards, and other direct file material should not be overlooked by administrators of agencies of any size.

The histories of intersections or street and highway sections should be readily available. Depending upon the type of records and size of the agency, separate file folders for each intersection and each different street and highway may be useful for storage of information, such as special traffic studies, condition and collision diagrams, citizen complaints and responses, special reports, details of physical improvement changes, dates of major control device changes, and, of course, dates of closure as in the case of a bridge shut down for repair or reconstruction.

The continuous updating of inventories is an important responsibility. Work-order control systems, mandated entry and revision routines, and other management devices are essential to this process. Even so, human errors of omission always exist. For this reason, *periodic resurveys* to update inventory records, usually at 5 or 10-year intervals, are necessary as well.

Availability and timeliness of data is important. As the size of an agency increases, the "compartmentalization" of individual functions increases and complicates the problem of record keeping. For example, the person responsible for traffic signal records may not be in a position to receive information on a bridge closing that might affect traffic flow on one leg of an intersection and invite temporary revision of timing.

Volume studies

Volume counts are *dynamic traffic studies*. They include a tabulation, generally by such time intervals as 15 min, 30 min, 1 h, or 1 day, of the number of pedestrians or vehicles passing a specific point. Depending upon the collection method, data may be subclassified into pedestrian age groups, vehicle types, occupancy, direction, or turning movement.

Methods and equipment

The manual count is the most basic and generally most useful of the volume collection procedures. It allows data to be collected on travel directions and turning movements at intersections or driveways, and can give subclassifications of vehicle types or sizes. Manual counts may be taken for any desired time interval, such as by signal cycles, 5-min periods, and so on. Furthermore, the checker may tabulate other useful information, such as queue lengths, obedience to control devices, and unusual events contributing to delay. Traffic-counting personnel may, after brief training, be able to identify significant deficiencies in signal timing or control-device placement.

Many traffic analyses, such as those relating to capacity, design, channelization, and delay, are most specifically involved with *peak-hour conditions*. Many situations can be adequately described by counts that are taken during the single heaviest hour of morning traffic and of evening traffic. Because of the large amount of secondary data that may be

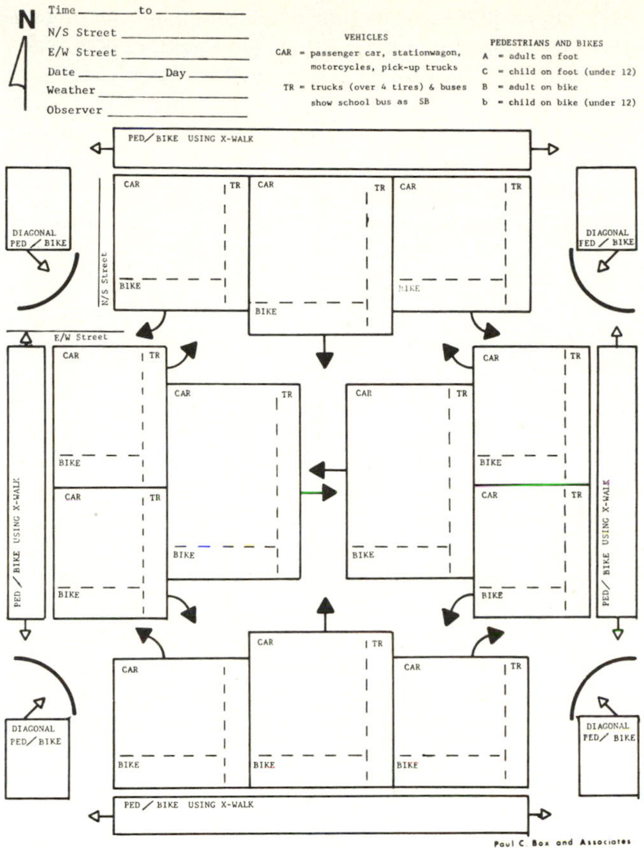

Figure 17.1. Field sheet for pedestrian and/or vehicle counts. SOURCE: Paul C. Box and Associates.

obtained, manual traffic counts often are markedly superior to any mechanical means of counting. For example, four mechanical counters are required to count traffic approaching a typical intersection. Even then, such an application would yield no data on turning movements, which are especially significant in design, channelization, lane marking, and the application of control devices.

Generally, checkers should not be asked to work for more than 3 or 4 h without a substantial break. Thus, checks for traffic signal warrants at an intersection, which may require 8 to 12 h of total counting, are generally performed by rotating teams of personnel or by counting portions on successive days.

The number of persons needed at a given location depends upon the total volume, the complexity of turning movements and overlaps (such as right turn on red), the subclassification of vehicles required, and the degree to which secondary notations such as pedestrian volumes, queue lengths, or obedience to control devices are to be made.

The type of manual counting equipment available also affects the selection of personnel. In its simplest form, equipment for a manual count involves a timepiece, two pencils with erasers, and a tablet. More often, a special field tabulation sheet such as shown in Figure 17.1 is employed.[2]

[2]For other forms, see the *Manual of Traffic Engineering Studies*.

Vehicles or pedestrians are recorded by tally marks in appropriate boxes. More sophisticated methods include mechanical tally counters, which may be ganged on a counter board and enable one person to count traffic from all directions at a moderate-volume intersection without taking the eyes from the road scene. However, the volume that can be counted will depend upon the degree of vehicle classification utilized.

Where counts are needed for extended periods of time, there are several types of automatic recording devices.[3] The simplest of these is the junior counter. This typically utilizes a road tube across the full width of a street or highway. The counter has a continuous serial recording and a reading that must be taken at the beginning and end of the count. These counters are typically used by agencies gathering 24-h data for calculation of average daily traffic volumes on the major street and highway network. Such counts may be taken on a seasonal basis to develop approximate adjustment factors.

A special version of the junior counter, called the period counter, has a time clock that may be set to turn on at a specific time, run for a definite length of time, and then shut itself off.

The senior counter contains a clock, reset-type counter, a stamping and/or punching machine, and a roll of tape or circular chart. In one type, a printing mechanism actuated by a clock transfers the count from the register to a paper tape at predetermined intervals. Commonly, subtotals are printed each 15 min and the register is automatically reset to zero every hour. A machine-readable code may also be printed with magnetic ink. The circular graphic chart senior counter may count volumes at intervals of 5, 10, 15, 20, 30, or 60 min, for up to 7 days duration. The distance a recording pen moves from the center of the chart is proportional to the volume, and the rotation is a function of time. A punched-tape counter records the volume in binary code on a special tape. This can be analyzed manually or processed by a translating device to generate punch cards or tapes for computer storage.

Permanent-type counting stations are established on urban and rural portions of the Interstate system and at key locations along other major highways. The continuous recording provides hourly data for every day of the year. These counts are useful in comparing hourly volumes among different weekdays, and in developing reliable monthly and seasonal variation factors. Trend data in annual volumes are also produced.

Some installations have only a sensor (detector) located at the counting station, with the impulses transmitted to a central location for recording. The transmission may be via a leased telephone line, radio, or other means, depending upon the requirement, availability, and costs.

Many types of detectors are available. For temporary counts utilizing junior or senior models, the pressure-type road tube or electrical contact tape is typically used. For permanent installations, the inductive loop has widespread application. Photoelectric detectors are sometimes used,

[3]INSTITUTE OF TRAFFIC ENGINEERS' COMMITTEE 7-G, Information Report, "Volume Survey Devices," *Traffic Eng.*, *31*(6), pp 44–51 (Mar. 1961); "Special Purpose Traffic Survey Devices," *Traffic Eng.*, *36*(5), pp 29–41 (Feb. 1966).

particularly in identifying vehicles above certain heights. Multiple beams may be used to count total vehicles.

The inductive loop detector works on the principle that the passage of a motor vehicle causes a disturbance in an electrical field or a change in the induction of the loop. The change in potential is amplified and an impulse sent to the counter.

A flexible tube stretched across the road utilizes the pneumatic pulse of air created by wheels passing over it. This closes an electrical circuit. The counts register one vehicle for each passage of two axles. Vehicles having more than two axles introduce an *overcount error*. The error increases with the proportion of multiaxle trucks. It can be compensated by computing correction factors from manual classification counts. However, some engineers prefer the original count because multiaxle vehicles occupy more space than two-axle vehicles. Such an unadjusted count is sometimes referred to as the "equivalent passenger car count."

Road tubes are also subject to *undercounting error* due to simultaneous vehicle passage in adjacent lanes. In urban areas, the counter can be rendered inactive by a vehicle parked with wheels on the tube. Also, the tube is subject to damage by sliding wheels or pavement imperfections. It cannot be used on a gravel road or during a period of snowfall. Tube placement is important because a fixed object such as a tree or pole is needed to anchor the recorder, and the tube must be clear of the turning paths of vehicles at a driveway or intersection.

Photographic equipment is sometimes used for counting. It requires a special camera and an elevated position. Time-serial pictures are taken to give either periodic or nearly continuous coverage of traffic flow. Because of the expense of the equipment and the necessity for security, normally the camera is attended. The film of traffic movement is generally taken at speeds of 60 to 300 frames per minute. The volume is then counted manually by projecting the film, frame by frame, on a screen. Data reduction is expensive and time consuming. The cost generally limits its application to research studies.

The *moving-vehicle* method of traffic counting utilizes a test vehicle and the volumes met by, overtaken by, and overtaking this vehicle are used to estimate volume on a road section. A 30-min sample on a street carrying 300 vehicles per hour has been found to have a typical error of 10% of the average volume. Greater errors may be expected on low-volume streets.[4]

The *vehicle-miles traveled* study, (vmt), most appropriate in networks, can be accomplished indirectly by aerial photographic samples of density and test vehicle estimation of average speed. These values are multiplied to give an estimate of volume, which in turn is multiplied by the length of the route.

Spot counts

Manual spot counts typically are conducted at intersections or major generator driveways. Periodic spot counts are desirable during the A.M. and P.M. peak hours at all major–major intersections (one major street intersecting another major street) every 3 years. Counts at other potentially important intersections such as that of a major street with a collector street are desirable at not less than 5-year intervals. The counts are used to check for needs of change in control devices, appropriateness of signal timing, need for improvements such as added turn lanes, or special signal phasing. Current counts are essential if the highway section is being studied for significant physical revision.

Spot counts normally involve a limited breakout of *vehicle classifications*. Typically, the "passenger vehicle" category is deemed to include also motorcycles, station wagons, and all two-axle, four-tire vehicles. The "truck" category then includes all vehicles having more than four tires, any passenger vehicle pulling a trailer, and so on. Such simplified classification is normally adequate for operational studies, including those for design and capacity. In general, a minimum number of vehicle classifications should be established and checkers should be instructed that the total physical count is more important than an occasional misclassification.

More detailed information on vehicle classification is needed for *pavement design* purposes. Here the classification of trucks must be in at least two groups, with the single-unit type separate from tractor–trailer combinations. A third heavy-vehicle grouping, comprising the large trash or cement truck, may also be utilized.

Figure 17.2. Example of graphic summary sheet for peak-hour turning movements.

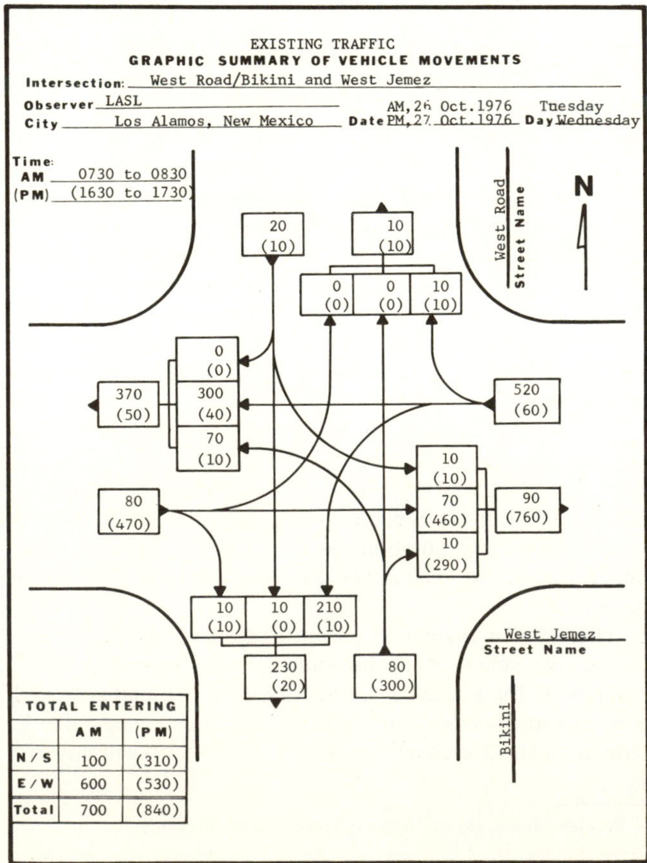

[4] R. C. Blensley, "Moving Vehicle Method of Estimating Traffic Volumes," *Traffic Eng.*, 27(3) pp. 127–29, 147 (Dec. 1956).

Daily variation data may be obtained from manual short counts. Traffic at a given location is counted for 5 min out of each of several hours of several days of the week. The observers make a circuit of as many as six locations, utilizing 5 min for travel between locations. The resulting total at each spot is then multiplied by 12 to give the estimated total hourly flow. This procedure has been shown to yield estimates to within several percent of the true total.

Temporary automatic (machine)-type counts are taken at spot locations to give estimates of daily traffic along sections of street or highway. It is usually desirable to apply day-of-week and seasonal adjustment factors.[5]

[5]Box and Oppenlander, *Manual of Traffic Engineering Studies*, pp. 29–35.

Passenger car and van occupancy studies are made to obtain information on passenger-miles of travel (for planning purposes) and car pooling (for traffic system management purposes).

Spot count data are normally tabulated by 15-min interval with hourly summations. For manual counts, the tabulation normally involves each of the turning movements. A graphic presentation is typically prepared for the A.M. and P.M. peak-hour data, with volumes rounded to the nearest 10 vehicles (see Figure 17.2).

Hourly variation graphs are often prepared showing the percent of daily traffic as taken from automatic recording counts. An example of hourly and of daily variation in volume is given in Figure 17.3.

Figure 17.3. Typical time-based distributions of traffic volumes. Source: Paul C. Box and Joseph C. Oppenlander, *Manual of Traffic Engineering Studies*, 4th ed. (Arlington, Va.: Institute of Transportation Engineers, 1976), Fig. A-1.

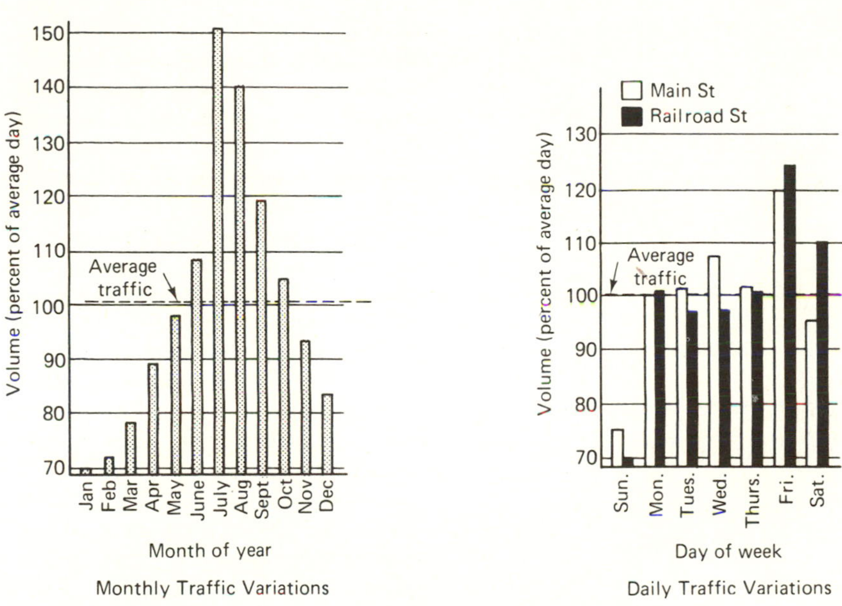

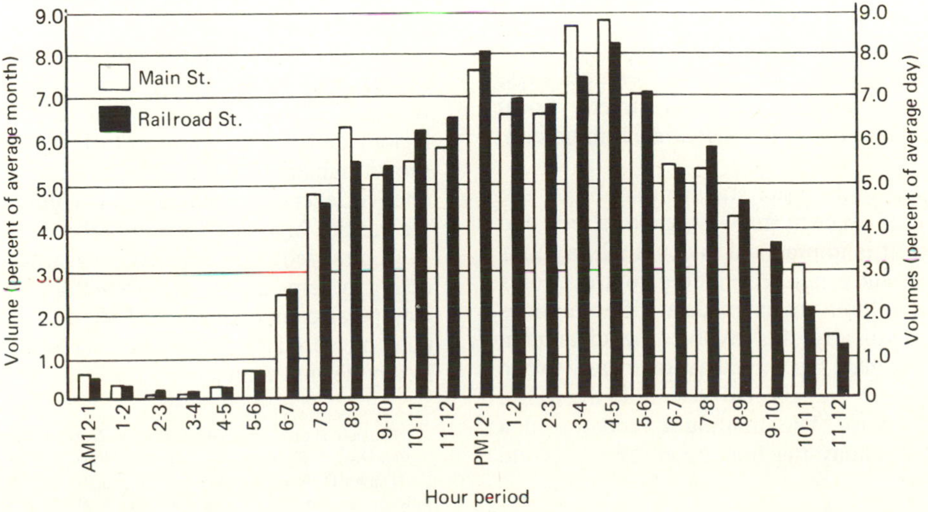

Areawide studies

It is desirable to obtain estimates periodically of the annual traffic volume on the major traffic street and highway network of cities, counties, and states. Such information is used to establish patterns of use and of growth.

Extensive counts for all links of a large area are of course impractical. Short counts, be they 1 h or 1 day long, may be considered as "samples." These can be expanded and adjusted for hourly, daily, and seasonal variation by use of a continuous master station. The conversion of short time (ST) counts to long time (LT) counts may be made as follows:

$$\text{Sta. A estimated LT count} = (\text{Sta. A ST count}) \times \frac{\text{Master Sta. LT count}}{\text{Master Sta. ST count}}$$

where

$$\frac{\text{Master Sta. LT count}}{\text{Master Sta. ST count}}$$

Sta. A ST count = known ST count at location in question

Sta. A LT count = unknown LT count at location in question

Master Sta. B ST count = known ST count at a nearby location covering the same specific period as the short-time count at Sta. A; usually a part of the Master Sta. LT count

Master Sta. LT count = known LT count at the same nearby location, for the same LT period as desired for Sta. A

In the same way that 1 or 2-h counts may be converted to average all-day counts, a 1-day count may be converted to an average weekly count or a monthly or annual count. Similarly, an average winter count may be converted to an average summer count. It is first necessary to classify the streets or highways by function. The four basic urban street classifications often used are freeways or expressways, major streets, collector streets, and local streets. Local streets may be further designated as residential, commercial, or industrial.[6]

In *urban studies,* several master stations may be set up, with at least one located on each freeway, major street, and collector street. Since it is impractical to count all locations simultaneously in the study area, continuing control counts are made to place the volume counts made at different times on a common basis. Typically, this involves the adjustment of sample counts to estimate the annual average daily traffic (AADT). Control stations are selected to sample the traffic movement on the system. The minimum recommended schedule is a 1-day weekday machine count every second year. Minor control stations are located to sample typical streets in the system. A minimum of three stations on each class of street should be established in a small city.

Key count stations are selected control stations used to obtain hourly, daily, and seasonal variations. At least one key station should be selected for each class of street. These stations are counted as follows: one nondirectional, 7-day machine count is performed annually, and one nondirectional 1-day weekday machine count is made monthly or quarterly.

Coverage counts are used to estimate AADT volumes throughout the street system. On freeways and expressways, and major and collector streets, one nondirectional weekday count is taken within each control section. Since only the 24-h total is needed, nonrecording counters may be satisfactory. The counts should be repeated every 4 years or less. On local streets, a one-day nondirectional machine count may be made for every mile.

Vehicle classification counts are made manually and are usually limited to a 14-h weekday period from 0600 to 2000 hours, with directional data being recorded for each hour.

As a part of urban transportation planning, it is often necessary to count the traffic on each of the links or sections of the traffic assignment network. In general, two 1-day directional counts should be made on each link. Peak-period directional counts may be made at major control stations.

Rural counting programs vary considerably, depending on the type and size of the area to be covered. Generally, the highways are classified into categories such as farm service routes, general-purpose routes, recreational routes, winter resort routes, and so on. The classification is based on land-service function, character of origins and destinations of traffic using the roads, continuity, and administrative classification. One authority recommends use of a few control stations for each class of road. Traffic is counted continuously through the year at each of these stations.[7] Less important stations are counted 2 to 4 days per year. Standard errors of less than 10% for roads with AADTs greater than 500 vehicles per day are expected. At 100 vehicles per day, the standard error is about 20% (i.e., at about two-thirds of the coverage stations, the true value of the AADT deviates from the estimate by less than 0.20 × true AADT).

In order that all traffic counts made within the area be comparable, the AADT is usually computed for each highway section by using appropriate multiplicative conversion factors developed from control stations. The results are shown numerically on highway survey maps that use distinctive legends to indicate the volume ranges into which the various highway sections fall.

Centralized statewide digital traffic reporting and processing systems are in use. Detectors are connected to minicomputer components and linked to a central digital computer by leased telephone lines. The data can be summarized in any desired manner.[8]

[6]National Committee on Urban Transportation, *Determining Street Use* (Procedure Manual 1A) (Chicago: Public Administration Service, 1958).

[7]Federal Highway Administration, *Traffic Volume Counting Manual* (Washington, D.C.: U.S. Government Printing Office, 1970).

[8]Emory C. Parrish, Edwyn D. Peterson, and Ray Threlkeld, "Georgia's Program for Automated Acquisition and Analysis of Traffic Count Data," *Mathematical and Statistical Aspects of Traffic,* Highway Research Rec. No. 199 (Washington, D.C.: Highway Research Board, 1967), pp. 42–61.

Cordon counts

Cordon counts are made to obtain information on the total number of specific types of motor vehicles and/or passengers inside an area and the number entering and leaving the area by time of day. Cordon counts are used to study traffic movements into and out of CBDs, other small areas of special interest, or entire cities or metropolitan areas. They may be a part of a comprehensive origin-destination (O-D) survey, or they may be used at regular intervals to develop trend statistics.

The cordon line is defined as the boundary of the area being studied. Adjustments to the line may be made to reduce the number of streets crossing it. Counting stations are established at the cordon line on all intercepted streets except that counts are seldom made on local streets known to be carrying negligible traffic volumes.

Appropriately classified directional counts are made at each station for 12 to 24-h periods, depending on the information desired. If possible, all stations should be counted on the same day; however, if a set of control stations is being maintained, counting may be spread over several weeks. All volumes are then adjusted to a common day using the control counts.

The *analysis* of cordon counts will depend on the information desired. For instance, the data may be broken down by hours and checked against the results of home interviews in an O-D survey. In studies of CBDs, the accumulation of vehicles within the cordon is of primary interest and is often shown graphically. Information on the number of vehicles in the area at the beginning of the study is obtained by an accumulation study. At equal intervals (usually every 15 min or every hour) the net number of vehicles entering or leaving the area is added to or subtracted from the number calculated at the end of the previous period. Information on hourly volumes crossing the cordon line in both directions is often used to present the results of this study.

Because the personnel requirement for cordon counts is extremely high, its use is generally limited to major transportation studies.

Screen line counts

These studies are made to determine the traffic crossing a major geographical barrier or moving between two areas. Some screen line studies are conducted at regular intervals so that long-range trends in traffic volumes at the screen line may be determined. The studies are also used to check the accuracy of an O-D survey. A screen line drawn across an area will intercept trips moving from one side of the line to the other. The line may be naturally defined by a river, ridge, railroad, or other geographical barrier. If established artificially, it is usually drawn so as to keep the number of crossing highways to a minimum.

The studies are conducted in the same manner as cordon counts. Analysis and presentation of the data depend on the purpose of the study. Trend charts and modified flowcharts may be drawn. For an O-D survey check, the measured volumes are compared to the estimated volumes produced from the interview data, and used to develop appropriate adjustment factors.

Pedestrian counts

Practically all pedestrian counting historically has been performed manually. At high-density crossings, such as those in CBD areas, manual counting may be impractical. Photographic equipment has been used successfully for such locations.

A mechanical counter has been developed for sidewalk counting. It consists of battery-powered switching mats glued to the sidewalk, covered by an overlay, and utilizing a traffic counter and summator.[9]

Pedestrian counts typically are taken to determine crosswalk usage as related to need for special traffic signal pushbuttons at intersections. Counts separating school children from adults are also sometimes taken.

Speed studies

In this section, spot speed studies and route speed studies are described. Information on study techniques and analysis is presented also.

Spot speed studies

This study is used to measure speed at a specific location. The speed characteristics have many applications, including:

- Establishing speed zones.
- Setting signal clearance intervals.
- Checking complaints on speeding.
- Checking for enforcement needs.
- Checking the need for posting advisory safe speed.
- Analyzing accident experience.
- Making before-and-after studies to evaluate a change in conditions.
- Checking speed trends by periodic studies at the same point.

Because of the widespread availability of radar, nearly all speed checks are today conducted with such electronic equipment. The radar meter operates on the principle that a radio wave reflected from a moving target undergoes a frequency change proportional to the speed of the target. Graphic recorders are available to provide a permanent record of the speeds; however, low speeds may be difficult to distinguish on the charts, which are designed for enforcement purposes. Therefore, tabulation directly from the meter readout is most often utilized in traffic engineering studies.

To avoid bias, it is imperative that approaching drivers not be aware of the checks. The radar set is generally kept inside a vehicle, so that it is not visible in the detection zone.

---

[9]Box and Oppenlander, *Manual of Traffic Engineering Studies*, p. 17.

Radar can operate up to a ¾-mile range, but it is difficult to distinguish among vehicles at such distances. Also, topography may intervene. Most radar readings are taken at distances of several hundred feet (100 to 150 m) from the approaching vehicle. The angle between the radar beam and the path of the approaching vehicle should be as small as practical. Individual radar unit operating instructions provide factors for calibration.

Spot speeds may be taken by using a stopwatch to check the time required for a vehicle to traverse a known short distance. Chapter 6 of the *MTES* describes this method and contains an illustration of a field sheet.[10]

The minimum sample size for a speed check is 30 vehicles. Such a small sample should be used only for extremely low volume conditions. Normally, 50 to 100 or more vehicles are checked. The equation for calculation of sample sizes for different conditions is[11]

$$N = \left(\frac{KS}{E}\right)^2 \qquad (17.1)$$

where N = minimum sample size

K = constant corresponding to the desired confidence level

S = estimated sample standard deviation (mph or km/h)

E = acceptable error in the speed estimate (mph or km/h)

A typical *standard deviation* is 5 mph (8 km/h). A K value of 2 is often used. It provides a confidence level of about 95%. The acceptable error usually ranges from 1 to 5 mph (1.6 to 8 km/h). If an error of 1 mph (1.6 km/h) is utilized, with a K value of 2 and an S average of 5 mph (8 km/h), the required sample size is 100. Statistically, these values indicate that under the stated conditions the probability is not more than 5% (1 in 20) that the mean speed derived from a sample of 100 will vary from the time mean speed by more than 1 mph (1.6 km/h). Raising the K value to 3 (setting a confidence level at 99.7%) increases the sample size to 225.

These calculations relate to sample sizes for mean or *average* speeds. If, instead, a sample size is desired for the P85 (85th percentile speed), the following formula is appropriate:

$$N = \frac{K^2S^2(2 + U^2)}{2E^2} \qquad (17.2)$$

where N, K, S and E are as in equation (17.1)

U = constant corresponding to the desired speed statistic (i.e., for P85, use 1.04)

[10] Box and Oppenlander, *Manual of Traffic Engineering Studies*.

[11] Ibid.

Solution of this equation for the same E value as in the mean speed check and with a K of 2 yields a sample size of 150. A K value of 3 requires a sample size of about 350.

Speed studies should be made during good weather conditions and are generally taken in off-peak times such as 0900 to 1130, 1330 to 1630, or 1900 to 2200 h. With low volumes, speed checks may be needed on more than one day to obtain the necessary sample size.

All readings should be representative of the free-flowing conditions of the traffic stream. With low volumes it is usually possible to check nearly all vehicular speeds. At higher volumes, a sampling procedure is needed. Recommendations are:

1. Observe every *n*th vehicle (second, third, etc.). Do *not* always observe the first vehicle in a platoon because the following vehicles may be restricted to travel at the speed of the lead vehicle.
2. Select trucks for speed observation in proportion to their presence in the traffic stream.
3. Avoid sampling a large proportion of high-speed vehicles.

Analysis and presentation of spot speed data

In analyzing spot speed data, several characteristics can be developed. Some values are computed directly from the data and others are most easily determined from a graphic presentation. The first step in tabulation is to establish a frequency distribution. This involves selection of a group or class size. If too few or too many groups are selected, detail is lost in the data reduction. In general, the appropriate number of classes ranges from 8 to 20. After the field data have been collected, the range in measurements is determined by subtracting the lowest from the highest values. This range is divided by 8 and by 20 to estimate, respectively, the maximum and minimum class sizes that are reasonable for the observed data. A convenient class size is then selected within the limits of the minimum and maximum values. After the class size has been determined, the class limits are selected to define completely the actual sample values within each class. These limits are written to the same precision as the original data. The midvalue or class mark is the middle point of the class.

A typical frequency table is illustrated in Table 17-1. (The following discussion and illustration, although given in mph, are equally valid in km/h.)

After the class limits have been recorded in the frequency table, each field observation is placed in its appropriate class. Adding the number of entries in each class gives the frequency of occurrences for each size classification in the speed check. The resulting table of occurrence in the various classes is defined as a *frequency distribution*. The sum of the occurrences in the several classes is equal to the sample size.

Examination of Table 17-1 will show that the P85 speed (that speed at or below which 85% of the vehicles are mov-

TABLE 17–1
Frequency Distribution for Spot Speed Data

Class Boundaries	Class Midvalues (u_1)	Class Frequencies* f_1	Relative Frequencies	Cumulative Frequencies Number	Cumulative Frequencies Relative
27.5	28.5	0	0.000		
29.5	30.5	1	0.005	0	0.000
31.5	32.5	2	0.011	1	0.005
33.5	34.5	14	0.075	3	0.016
35.5	36.5	7	0.038	17	0.092
37.5	38.5	20	0.108	24	0.129
39.5	40.5	38	0.204	44	0.237
41.5	42.5	29	0.156	82	0.441
43.5	44.5	35	0.188	111	0.597
45.5	46.5	15	0.081	146	0.785
47.5	48.5	12	0.065	161	0.866
49.5	50.5	9	0.048	173	0.930
51.5	52.5	4	0.022	182	0.979
53.5	54.5	0	0.000	186	1.000
55.5					
Total		186	1.000		

*As recorded in the samples.

SOURCE: PAUL C. BOX AND JOSEPH C. OPPENLANDER, *Manual of Traffic Engineering Studies,* 4th ed. (Arlington, Va.: Institute of Transportation Engineers, 1976), Table A-1.

TABLE 17–2
Summary Calculations for Classed Spot Speed Data

Class Boundaries	Class Midvalues, u_1	Class Frequencies f_1	f_1u_1	$f_1u_1^2$	$u_1-\bar{x}$	$(u_1-\bar{x})^2$	$f_1(u_1-\bar{x})^2$
27.5	28.5	0	0	0	−13.8	—	—
29.5	30.5	1	31	930	−11.8	139	139
31.5	32.5	2	65	2,113	−9.8	96	192
33.5	34.5	14	483	16,664	−7.8	61	854
35.5	36.5	7	256	9,326	−5.8	34	238
37.5	38.5	20	770	29,645	−3.8	14	280
39.5	40.5	38	1,539	62,330	−1.8	3	114
41.5	42.5	29	1,233	52,381	+0.2	0	0
43.5	44.5	35	1,558	69,309	+2.2	5	175
45.5	46.5	15	698	32,434	+4.2	18	270
47.5	48.5	12	582	28,227	+6.2	38	456
49.5	50.5	9	455	22,952	+8.2	67	603
51.5	52.5	4	210	11,025	+10.2	104	416
53.5	54.5	0	0	0	+12.2	—	—
55.5							
Total		186	7,877	337,335			3737

SOURCE: Modified from PAUL C. BOX AND JOSEPH C. OPPENLANDER, *Manual of Traffic Engineering Studies,* 4th ed. (Arlington, Va.: Institute of Transportation Engineers, 1976), Table A-2.

ing) is about 47.5 mph. The cumulative relative frequencies given in the last column reaches 0.866 = 86.6% with the 161st vehicle, and the upper class speed limit that includes the 161st is 47.5 mph (76.5 km/h).

Several measures of speed are commonly utilized in traffic engineering analysis. These include the time mean speed ("average"), the median speed, the P85, and the 10-mph (15-km/h) pace.

The *time mean* speed is obtained by dividing the sum of all the speeds in the sample by the number of vehicles in the sample. The general expression for the mean of unclassed data is represented by the equation

$$\bar{X} = \frac{\Sigma X_i}{N} \tag{17.3}$$

where $\bar{X}$ = arithmetical mean

ΣX_i = sum of all observed spot speeds

N = number of observations

If the measurements have been placed into classes, such as in Table 17-1, the computation of time mean speed is as shown in Table 17-2 and as follows:

$$\bar{x} = \frac{\Sigma(f_i u_i)}{\Sigma f_i} \tag{17.4}$$

where $\bar{x}$ = arithmetical mean

$\Sigma(f_i u_i)$ = sum of products of frequency and class midvalue for all classes

Σf_i = sum of frequencies of all classes

$$\bar{x} = \frac{\Sigma f_1 u_1}{\Sigma f_1} = \frac{7877}{186} = 42.3$$

The time mean speed is distinct from the space mean speed. The latter is obtained by dividing the sum of all travel times into the sum of all travel distances in the sample. It is used in certain gap and density studies.

The *median speed* (P50) is the speed below which one-half the vehicles in the sample travel and above which the other half travel. The median is a useful measure, because it is less affected by extreme values than is the time mean speed.

The *pace* is the speed range within defined limits, usually 10 mph (16 km/h), which contains the largest number of observations. This can be extracted from Table 17-2 directly by inspection. It is the range from 38 through 47 mph (sixth through tenth classes) in this sample.

An important measure of variability is the *standard deviation,* which is the positive square root of the variance. The variance is the sum of the squares of the deviations of the observations from the mean, divided by the total number of observations less one. Therefore, the expression for standard deviation is written in the following form for unclassed data:

$$s = \sqrt{\frac{\Sigma(X_i - \bar{X})^2}{N - 1}} \tag{17.5}$$

where s = standard deviation

$\bar{X}$ = arithmetic mean

X_i = ith observation

N = number of observations

(using equation 17.5) $s^2 = \frac{3737}{185} = 20.2$ and

$$s = \sqrt{20.2} = 4.5$$

Equation (17.6) for standard deviation is applicable when the information is classed:

$$s = \sqrt{\frac{\Sigma (f_i u_i^{\ 2}) - \frac{\Sigma (f_i u_i)^2}{\Sigma f_i}}{(\Sigma f_i) - 1}} \qquad (17.6)$$

$$\text{(using equation 17.6) } s^2 = \frac{337{,}335 - \frac{(7877)^2}{186}}{185} = 20.3$$

$$s = \sqrt{20.3} = 4.5$$

The standard deviation reflects the dispersion of the observations around the mean. Although the computational procedures are somewhat involved, the standard deviation is a reliable variability measure for statistical analysis.

If the data exhibit approximately a normal distribution, multiples of the standard deviation represent limits on either side of the mean within which will appear various percentages of the total observations in a selected sample. Under these conditions, 1, 2, and 3 standard deviations about the mean will contain respectively, 68.3, 95.5, and 99.7% of the observations.

The *cumulative frequency* diagram is prepared by plotting a graph with the class boundary of each class as the abscissa and the corresponding cumulative frequency of the class as the ordinate. The higher class boundary is matched with the corresponding cumulative frequency when the frequency summation is from the small to the large values of the study variable. However, the lower-class boundary is selected for this matching if the cumulative frequency is summed from the large to the small observations. A smoothed S-shaped curve is used to connect the plotted points between two extreme class boundaries having cumulative frequencies of 0% and 100%. Such a diagram is shown in Figure 17.4, using the data in Table 17-1. This curve is characteristic of the cumulative frequency for a normal distribution.

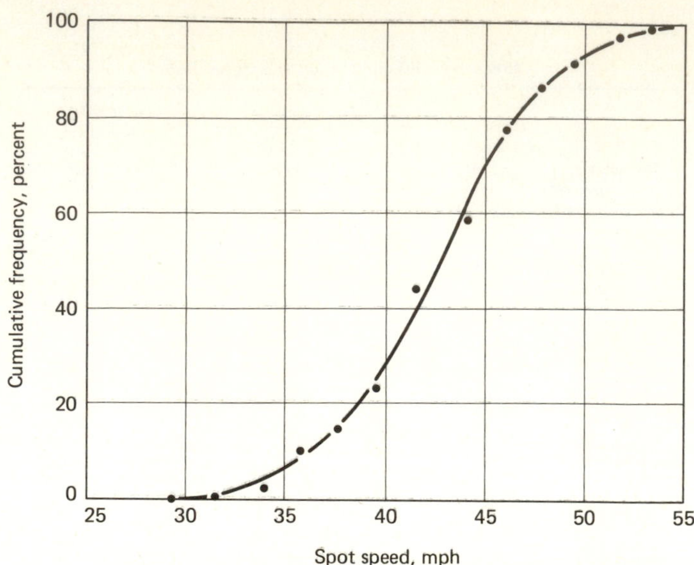

Figure 17.4. Cumulative frequency distribution of spot speeds (Rural area, two-lane highway). SOURCE: Paul C. Box and Joseph C. Oppenlander, *Manual of Traffic Engineering Studies*, 4th ed. (Arlington, Va.: Institute of Transportation Engineers, 1976), Fig. A-7.

Comparing averages for two speed studies

In order to determine whether or not the difference between the mean speed of two spot speed studies is significant, it is necessary to estimate the standard deviation of the difference in means by using the equation

$$s_d = \sqrt{s_{\bar{x}_1}^2 + s_{\bar{x}_2}^2} \qquad (17.7)$$

where s_d = standard deviation of the difference in means

$s_{\bar{x}_1}^2$ = variance of the mean for study 1

$s_{\bar{x}_2}^2$ = variance of the mean for study 2

If the absolute value of the difference in sample mean speeds is greater than almost twice the standard deviation of the difference in means; that is, if

$$|\bar{x}_1 - \bar{x}_2| > 2s_d$$

where $\bar{x}_1$ = mean speed of study 1

$\bar{x}_2$ = mean speed of study 2

$|\cdot|$ = absolute value

it can be said with 95% confidence that the observed difference in mean speeds is statistically significant and not caused by chance. An example is shown in Table 17-3, (data not shown).

TABLE 17–3
Significant Differences in Means

Parameter	Study 1	Study 2
Mean speed, $\bar{x}$ (mph)	17.3	19.0
Standard error of mean	0.34	0.50

$$s_d = \sqrt{(0.34)^2 + (0.50)^2} = 0.605$$

$$|\bar{x}_1 - \bar{x}_2| = (17.3 - 19.0) = 1.7$$

Since 1.7 > 2(0.605), the difference is significant.

Intersection speed studies

Special spot speed studies are sometimes made at intersections. A graphic pen recorder with a moving chart can provide an accurate mechanical method. The observer marks out the approach lanes at 20-ft (10-m) intervals starting about 150 ft (50 m) ahead of the intersection and continuing about 20 ft (10 m) into the intersection. The marks should be relatively inconspicuous to the drivers of approaching cars. As a vehicle crosses each line, the observer presses the corresponding button to actuate a pen. The moving chart provides a time scale from which the speed trajectory pattern of the car can be computed. A sample of 50 to 100 vehicles should be taken for each approach. A full stop should be indicated by actuating a special pen, since it will otherwise not be recorded.

If the approach being studied is signalized, counts are made to show the number of vehicles entering during green, yellow, and red signal intervals. A special pen actuated by the signal circuits can be used to indicate the signal phase at any time.

Safe speed studies

Studies may be conducted to determine safe speed of a horizontal curve and whether advisory signs need to be posted. Several trial runs are made through the curve in a test vehicle equipped with a ball-bank indicator. The ball-bank reading is a measure of the amount of overturning force (side friction) on the vehicle. Readings of 14° for speeds below 20 mph (30 km/h), of 12° for speeds between 20 and 35 mph (50 km/h) and of 10° for speeds above 35 mph are the usually accepted limits beyond which riding discomfort will be excessive and loss of vehicle control may occur. The reading at which loss of control will most certainly occur is a complex variable dependent on type and condition of pavement surface, inflation and condition of tires, condition of steering mechanism, and driver skill.

Route speed studies

Information desired on speeds over a route with length L (miles or kilometers) may be simply the overall speed, $\bar{u}$ (mph or km/h), which is obtained from

$$\bar{u} = \frac{60L}{t} \tag{17.8}$$

where t is the travel time (minutes).

The description of travel-time studies is given in the next section. The moving-vehicle method may also be used to obtain overall route speeds. The traffic volume for the ith direction of traffic, q_i, in a highway section is first computed from

$$q_i = \frac{N_i + F_i - S_i}{T_i + T_j} \tag{17.9}$$

The space mean speed for one-way stream, $\bar{u}$ (mph or km/h), is then given by

$$u_i = \frac{L}{T_i - \dfrac{(F_i - S_i)}{q_i}} \tag{17.10}$$

where T_i = travel time (hours) of the test vehicle through the section when moving in direction i (the opposite direction is called j)

N_i = number of vehicles moving in direction i met by test vehicle when moving in the opposite direction j

F_i = number of vehicles moving in direction i that overtake the test car when it is moving in direction i

S_i = number of vehicles moving in direction i that are passed by the test car when it is moving in direction i

L = length of section

On a one-way street, q_i is obtained by a spot count and this equation is used to obtain the average speed. When the average speed while moving (the running speed) is desired, time spent at rest is deducted from the denominator of the formula.

If more detailed information is required on the speed profile over L, it is convenient to describe speed by both the average speed and the measure of its dispersion called "acceleration noise." Practically, acceleration noise is obtained by measuring the times between successive speed changes of 2 mph, Δt_i. When the duration of the study is T, the acceleration noise A is found from[12]

$$A = 1.47 \frac{1}{T} \sum_i \frac{1}{\Delta t_i} \tag{17.11}$$

Travel time and delay

Route studies

A travel-time study measures the time required to traverse a route. If information is also obtained on the location, duration and cause of delays, it is called a speed and delay study. Studies limited only to moving time are called running-time studies.

Travel-time data are needed to evaluate existing levels of service in transportation planning and in economic studies. When secured on an annual or other continuing basis, trends in the level of service are identified.

For congested streets, speed and delay data are used in traffic control selection or revision. This information may also indicate locations where other traffic studies are needed to determine the proper improvement. The data may be used in before-and-after studies to determine the effectiveness of changes in parking prohibitions, signal timing, one-way streets, or turn prohibitions. Delay may be considered to be made up of fixed delay caused by traffic design and control, plus operational delay caused by traffic interference.

Several techniques can be used to obtain travel-time information,[13] as follows:

---

[12] T. R. Jones and R. B. Potts, "The Measurement of Acceleration Noise: A Traffic Parameter," *Oper. Res., 10*(6) pp. 745–763 (1962).

[13] Box and Oppenlander, *Manual of Traffic Engineering Studies*, pp. 93–105.

TRAVEL TIME AND DELAY STUDY
TEST CAR TECHNIQUE
FIELD SHEET

DATE ______ WEATHER ______ TRIP NO. ______

ROUTE ______ DIRECTION ______

TRIP STARTED AT ______ AT ______ (LOCATION) ______ (MILEAGE)

TRIP ENDED AT ______ AT ______ (LOCATION) ______ (MILEAGE)

CONTROL POINTS	
LOCATION	TIME

STOPS OR SLOWS		
LOCATION	SEC DELAY	CAUSE

TRIP LENGTH ______ TRIP TIME ______ TRAVEL SPEED ______

RUNNING TIME ______ STOPPED TIME ______ RUNNING SPEED ______

SYMBOLS OF DELAY CAUSE: S—TRAFFIC SIGNALS SS—STOP SIGN LT—LEFT TURNS PK—PARKED CARS DP—DOUBLE PARKING T—GENERAL PED—PEDESTRIANS BP—BUS PASSENGERS LOADING OR UNLOADING

COMMENTS ______

RECORDER ______

Figure 17.5. Sample travel-time and delay study field sheet—test car technique. SOURCE: Paul C. Box and Joseph C. Oppenlander, *Manual of Traffic Engineering Studies,* 4th ed. (Arlington, Va.: Institute of Transportation Engineers, 1976), Fig. 7-3.

1. In the *test vehicle method,* a series of "runs" are made through the section to obtain representative travel times. Two driving strategies may be used. In the "floating car" technique, the driver attempts to approximate the median speed by passing as many vehicles as pass him. Some inaccuracies arise, especially on multilane highways during periods of congested flow, and on roads with very low volumes. The second driving strategy is the "average speed" technique, in which the driver travels at a speed that, in his opinion, is representative of the speed of the traffic at every point and time. Tests of the latter method have shown excellent correlation with actual average travel times.[14]

Data are recorded by an observer in the vehicle or by a mechanical recorder. The use of an observer with two stopwatches is the most common method. The observer starts the first stopwatch at the beginning of the test run and allows it to run continuously, recording the cumulative lapsed time at successive control points and delay points along the route. The second stopwatch is used to determine the length of individual stopped-time delays at each delay point. The time, location, and cause of the delays is recorded on forms (see Figure 17.5) or by voice-recording equipment. It is possible for a driver alone to obtain the desired information by using voice-recording equipment and a stopwatch mounted on the dashboard of the vehicle, thus eliminating the need for an observer. However, it can be hazardous due to distraction from the driving task.

The sample size is based on the specific need for the information. The following suggested ranges of permitted errors in the estimate of the mean travel speed are related to the survey purpose:

- Transportation planning and highway needs studies: ±3.0 to ±5.0 mph (±5.0 to ±8.0 km/h)
- Traffic operation, trend analysis, and economic evaluations: ±2.0 to ±4.0 mph (±3.5 to ±6.5 km/h)
- Before-and-after studies: ±1.0 to ±3.0 mph (±2.0 to ±5.0 km/h)

Although the determination of sample-size requirements is difficult for travel times or travel speeds, the information given in Table 17-4 provides approximate values.

TABLE 17–4
Approximate Minimum Sample-Size Requirements for Travel-Time and Delay Studies with Confidence Level of 95.0%

Average Range in Travel Speed (mph)	Minimum Number of Runs for Specified Permitted Error (mph)				
	± 1.0	± 2.0	± 3.0	± 4.0	± 5.0
2.5	4	2	2	2	2
5.0	8	4	3	2	2
10.0	21	8	5	4	3
15.0	38	14	8	6	5
20.0	59	21	12	8	6

Average Range in Travel Speed (km/h)	Minimum Number of Runs for Specified Permitted Error (km/h)				
	± 2.0	± 3.5	± 5.0	± 6.5	± 8.0
5.0	4	3	2	2	2
10.0	8	4	3	3	2
15.0	14	7	5	3	3
20.0	21	9	6	5	4
25.0	28	13	8	6	5
30.0	38	16	10	7	6

SOURCE: PAUL C. BOX AND JOSEPH C. OPPENLANDER, *Manual of Traffic Engineering Studies,* 4th ed. (Arlington, Va.: Institute of Transportation Engineers, 1976), Table 7–1.

After the first group of travel speeds has been computed, the sets of absolute *differences* between the first and the second values, the second and the third values, and so on, are obtained. The final difference involves the next-to-last and last values in the series of overall travel speeds. These differences are summed, and the total is divided by the number of differences to provide the average range in travel speeds for the initial data. This procedure is represented by the following equation:

$$R = \frac{\Sigma S}{N - 1} \qquad (17.12)$$

[14]WILLIAM WALKER, "Speed and Travel Time Measurement in Urban Areas," *Traffic Speed and Volume Measurements,* Highway Res. Board Bull. 156 (Washington, D.C.: Highway Research Board, 1957), pp. 27–44. See also FELIX J. RIMBERG, "Urban Travel Time Measurement by Taxicab Speed Studies," *Traffic Eng.,* *31*(9), pp. 43–44 (June 1961).

where R = average range in travel speed (mph or km/h)

ΣS = sum of values for all speed differences

N = number of completed test runs

If the required sample size is greater for the range found than the number of vehicles sampled, additional studies must be performed under similar traffic and environmental conditions.

2. The "test" *moving-vehicle method* of volume counting also can be used to obtain travel times by following "test" vehicle procedures and computing the results with equation (17.10).

3. In the *license plate method,* travel-time information can be obtained by stationing one or more observers at each entrance and exit of the study section to record the time and license number (last three digits) of each vehicle as it passes the observation point. The numbers are matched later and the travel time for each vehicle (the difference between the two recorded times) is determined.

The equipment used in this technique consists of synchronized stopwatches and recording forms (such as shown in Figure 17.6) or voice recorders with or without audible time signals. Large sets of these data can be analyzed economically by ADP; however, hand reduction is quite tedious. A sample of 50 matches usually provides sufficient accuracy for most purposes.

4. *Direct observation and timing* of vehicles through an area is feasible if the observer can see both the entrance and exit points.

5. An *interview technique* is useful when a large amount of information is needed with little expense for field observations. Employees of private establishments or municipal agencies are asked to record their travel time to and from work on a particular day.

Travel-time information may be presented as the mean total time to travel a given distance or the mean overall speed maintained over that distance. In a study of travel from one point in all directions, isochronal charts are often drawn. These show the distance from a common origin (often the CBD) that can be reached in a given time. A typical chart is shown in Figure 17.7. Congested areas are evident wherever the isochrons are close together. Free-flowing freeways and major streets are evident where the lines become long "fingers" leading away from the common origin.

Another method of presenting travel-time data is to compute the *vehicle delay rate*. This consists of computing the mean travel time in minutes per mile and comparing this value with a standard adapted for the type of street. The difference between the two values (minutes/mile) is the delay rate. The delay rate multiplied by the volume gives a vehicle delay rate in vehicle-minutes per mile. These vehicle delay rates may be plotted on a map by using color codes or by using flow map techniques in which the width of the line represents the magnitude of the vehicle delay rate.[15]

Data gathered in speed and delay studies are subject to a wide variety of analyses. Figure 17.8 presents some of the more typical analyses. Overall speed, running speed, average delay, intersectional delay, midblock delay, and duration and frequency of each type (cause) of delay by time and location are considered significant.

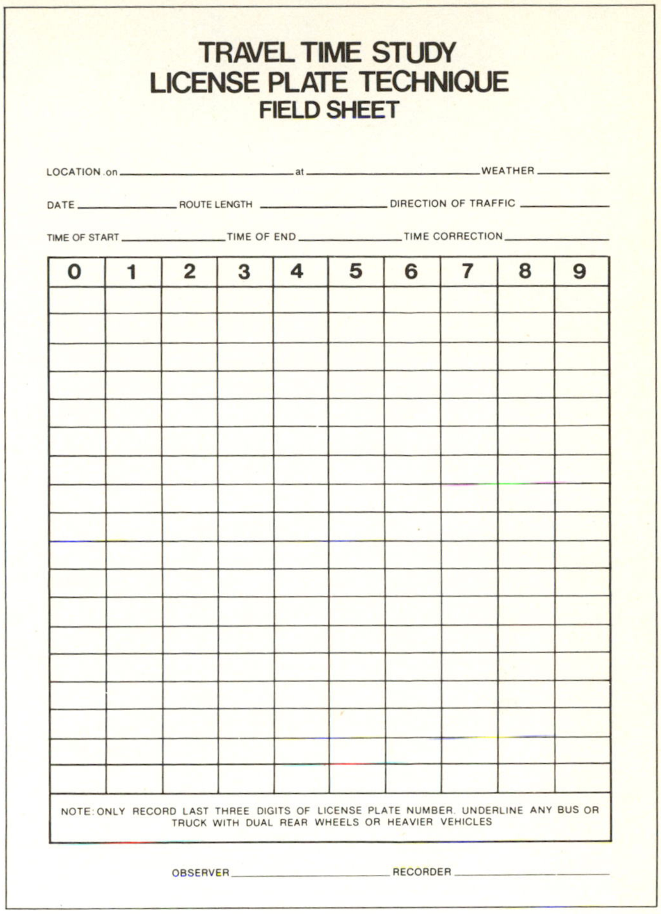

TRAVEL TIME STUDY
LICENSE PLATE TECHNIQUE
FIELD SHEET

LOCATION on ______ at ______ WEATHER ______

DATE ______ ROUTE LENGTH ______ DIRECTION OF TRAFFIC ______

TIME OF START ______ TIME OF END ______ TIME CORRECTION ______

0	1	2	3	4	5	6	7	8	9

NOTE: ONLY RECORD LAST THREE DIGITS OF LICENSE PLATE NUMBER. UNDERLINE ANY BUS OR TRUCK WITH DUAL REAR WHEELS OR HEAVIER VEHICLES

OBSERVER ______ RECORDER ______

Figure 17.6. Sample travel-time field sheet—license plate technique. SOURCE: Paul C. Box and Joseph C. Oppenlander, *Manual of Traffic Engineering Studies,* 4th ed. (Arlington, Va.: Institute of Transportation Engineers, 1976), Fig. 7-4.

Intersection delay studies

If travel-time or speed and delay study indicates that certain intersections have undue amounts of delay and need more intensive study, an intersection delay study will provide data on the amount of delay on one or more approaches.

This study is useful in design and in determining needed traffic control, such as prohibition of parking or turning movements, modified right-of-way controls, additional lane lines and channelization, or signal timing changes.

The basic values that are normally computed from an intersection delay study include total delay for each approach, average delay per vehicle, average delay per stopped vehicle, and percentage of vehicles delayed.

Methods for field measurement of intersection travel time and delay are varied. The travel-time study, when adapted to intersection delay, measures the travel time from a point in advance of the intersection to a point in or beyond the

[15]NATIONAL COMMITTEE ON URBAN TRANSPORTATION, *Determining Travel Time* (Procedure Manual 3B) (Chicago: Public Administration Service, 1958).

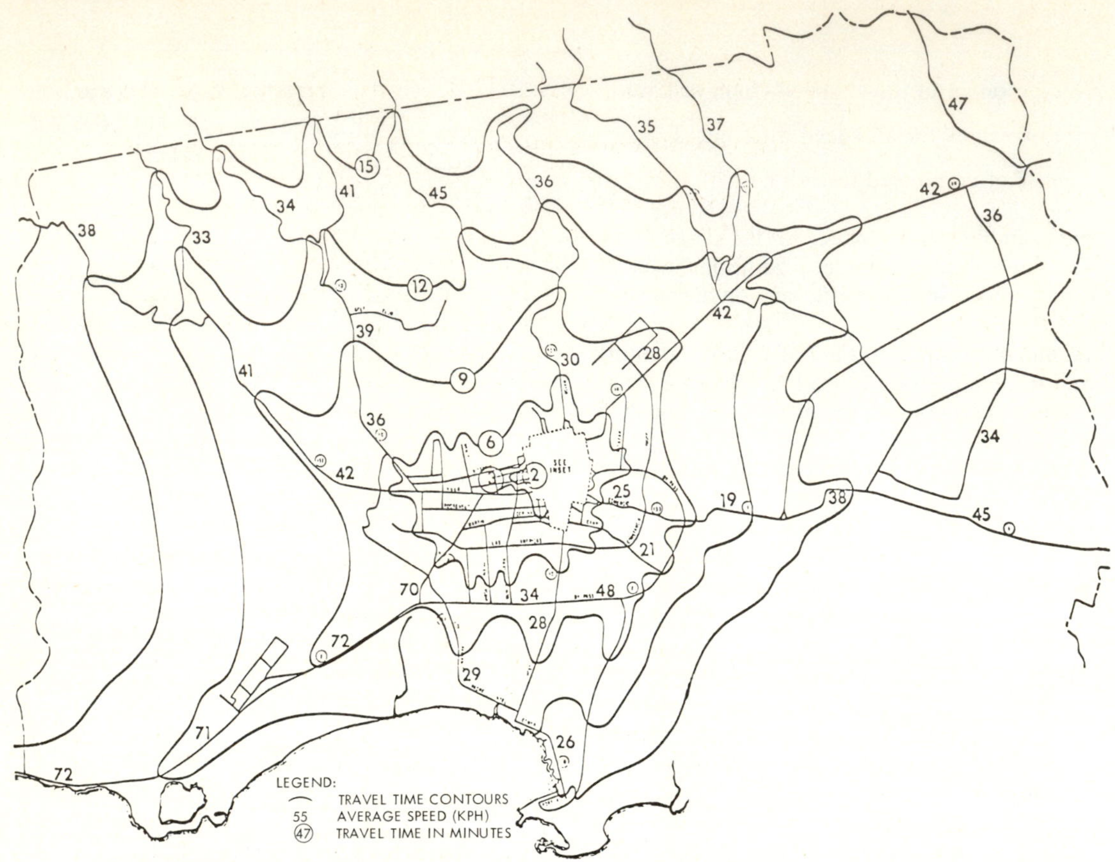

Figure 17.7. Travel-time contours and average speed, Ponce, Puerto Rico, 1970. SOURCE: The Recommended Plan and Growth Analysis, *Ponce Transportation Study,* Wilbur Smith & Associates, 1973.

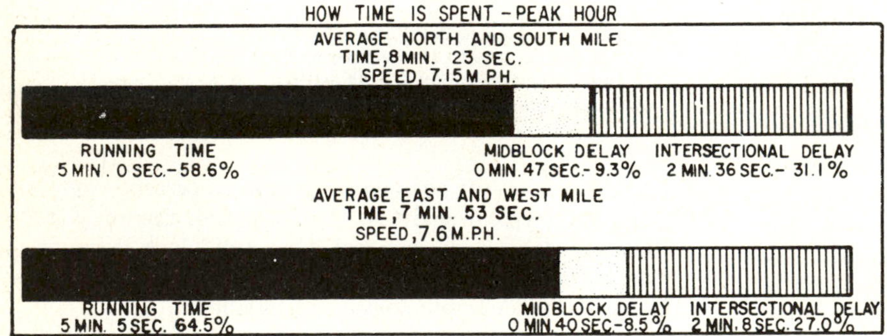

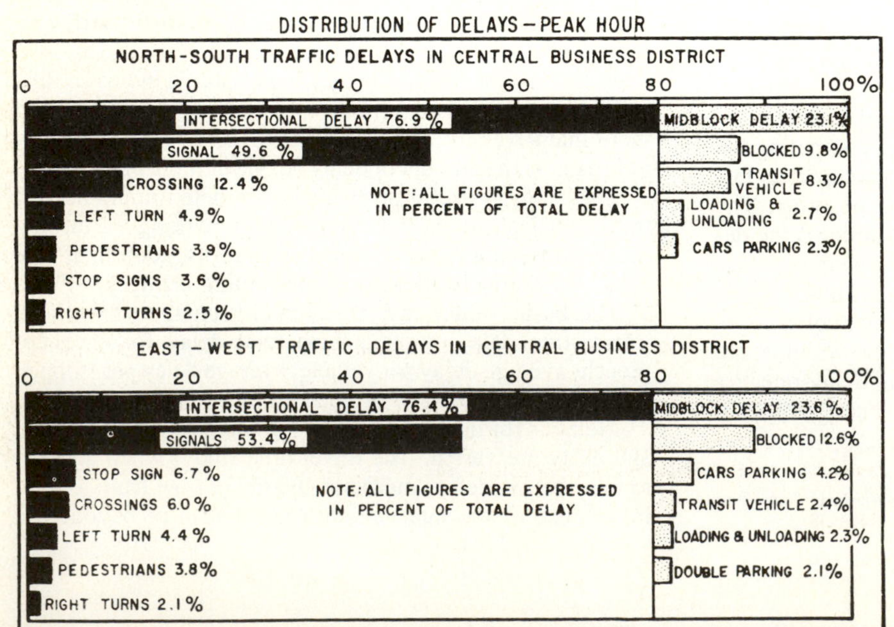

Figure 17.8. Typical graphical speed and delay analysis.

intersection on one or more approaches. The direct methods used to obtain the data are as follows:

- Test cars operated between key points.
- License plate numbers and times recorded at key points.
- Time-lapse photographs taken from a vantage point to permit the timing of each vehicle shown on the film.
- Strip-chart records actuated by road tubes or observers operating switches.
- Observers stationed at a vantage point tracing individual vehicles through an intersection and recording times at critical points.[16]

All of these methods may require extensive personnel or time for the collection and analysis of the data.

A method that gives an estimate of the average travel time for all vehicles on the approach is based on the flow–density–speed relationship.[17] This method requires one observer with a stopwatch for each approach studied. The observer records the number of vehicles occupying the approach area at periodic intervals, for example, every 15 s. The length of the observed approach area should extend from a point farther back than the tail end of any expected queue, to a point at which no additional delay is incurred, possibly the far side of the intersection. This density sample, accompanied by volume counts, is used to estimate both the total travel time and the average travel time through the approach area. To avoid systematic error the sampling interval should not be an even subdivision of the length of the signal cycle. The total vehicle-seconds of travel time is obtained by multiplying the total number of vehicles recorded (sum of periodic observations) by the sampling interval (seconds). The average travel time is obtained by dividing by the number of vehicles entering the approach. This can be expressed by

$$T = \frac{Nt}{V} \tag{17.13}$$

where T = average travel time through the study area

N = total density count; the sum of vehicles observed during the periodic density counts each t seconds

t = time interval between density observations, s

V = total volume entering study area during the total elapsed study period

Five minutes of data for such a travel-time study are shown in Table 17-5. In this example, the total volume in the 5-min period was 44 vehicles *(V)*. There were 61 *(N)* vehicles recorded during observations made at 15-s intervals *(t)*. The average travel time was 20.8 s, as shown in the table.

TABLE 17–5
Field Data from Intersection Delay Study*

Time (minute beginning)	Number of Vehicles Seen at:							
	+00 s		+15 s		+30 s		+45 s	Volume
1700	0		0		2		4	11
1701	7		2		0		1	7
1702	3		6		3		0	5
1703	0		4		9		9	11
1704	3		0		2		6	10
Total for period	13	+	12	+	16	+	20	44

*N = 61; t = 15; V = 44; $T = (61 \times 15)/44 = 20.8$ s.

A variation of this technique involves counting the standing vehicles on each approach, and calculating the total vehicle hours of delay for each clock hour (usually peak volume conditions).[18] A delay measure has been considered for many years as a potential warrant for traffic signal installation in the United States, and has been employed in other countries.

Other traffic stream studies

Although volume and speed studies are the basic tools of the traffic engineer, there are several other characteristics of traffic streams that are measurable and may be used directly for some purposes or that can be used to estimate volume, speed, or both. This section introduces the measurement of density, gaps, and vehicle spacing.

Density studies

Density at any instant may be obtained by observation or by photography. Density can also be computed from input/output studies or from studies providing joint information on volumes and speed. In observational studies, frequent samples of density counts are made on a road section. The average is taken as an unbiased estimate of the mean density during the sampling period. In photographic studies, spacing can be obtained by direct measurement of the distance between vehicles.

Occupancy studies

The availability of detectors that can signal the presence of a vehicle at the detector location has led to the use of an occupancy measure. The occupancy O is defined as the percent of time that a vehicle is over the detector. After accounting for effective detector length, it can be easily seen that the occupancy is related to the average density and the average vehicle length. For example, a single lane with

[16] Box and Oppenlander, *Manual of Traffic Engineering Studies*, pp. 106–112.

[17] David Solomon, "Accuracy of the Volume–Density Method of Measuring Travel Time," *Traffic Eng.*, *27*(6), pp.261–262, 288 (Mar. 1957). Also George Sagi and L. R. Campbell, "Vehicle Delay at Signalized Intersections," *Traffic Eng.*, *39*(5), 32–40 (Feb. 1969).

[18] William R. Reilly and Craig C. Gardner, *A Technique for Measuring Delay at Intersections*, (Reports FHWA-RD-76-135,136,137) (Washington, D.C.: US Federal Highway Administration, Sept. 1976). A summary appeared in *Transportation Res. Rec. 644*, 1977, pp. 1–7.

a flow of 1000 vehicles per hour with average lengths of 19 ft (6 m) operating at 30 mph (50 km/h) over a detector with a 6 ft (2 m) effective detection length would register an occupancy of

$$\frac{(19 + 6)(1000)(100)}{(30)(1.47)(3600)} = 16\%$$

$$\left[\frac{(6 + 2)(1000)(100)}{(50)(1000)} = 16\% \qquad \text{metric units}\right]$$

Gap studies

Time headways (measured from the arrival of the front ends of successive vehicles) or gaps between vehicles (measured from the arrival of the rear of a vehicle to the front of the following vehicle) are important to traffic engineers. The frequency of adequate gaps is used in warrants for traffic officer protection at school crossings and for traffic controls at other pedestrian crossings. Gaps are also important in capacity computations, in determining weaving from lane to lane, merging, and in warrants for stop-sign control.

Peak-hour gap availability may also be used to check for possible future control needs at a proposed new intersection or high-volume driveway. Typically, gaps of about 6 s are needed to allow the critical left-turn entry into the traffic stream of a major street. In this application, gaps occurring simultaneously across both directions of travel may be counted in groups, such as:

- 6 to 11 s
- 12 to 17 s
- 18 to 23 s
- 24 s and over (list actual gap value)

The available gaps are calculated by allowing one for each tabulated in group 1, two for each in 2, three for each in 3, and one for each 6 s of each gap listed under group 4. The summation of these is called the *total effective gaps*. If the volume of traffic projected to turn left on or cross the major street is somewhat less than the number of effective gaps, no control is likely to be needed. In practice, more vehicles can exit than the number of available gaps, because when several vehicles are standing in a queue awaiting exit, the second and third drivers will accept shorter gaps. Thus, a 15-s gap usually can accommodate three waiting cars.

Ordinarily, right turns are not critical, because available gaps are needed in only one direction of flow, and for a given volume these are far more frequent than the simultaneous available gaps in both directions.

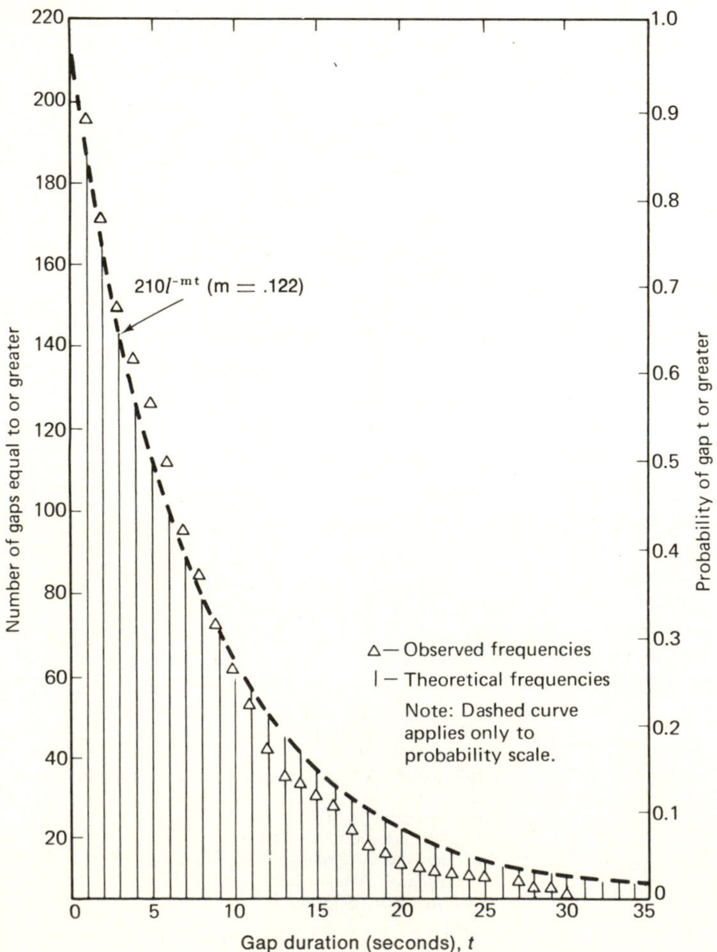

Figure 17.9. Observed and theoretical gap distributions. SOURCE: D.L. GERLOUGH and F.C. BARNES, *Poisson and Other Distributions in Traffic* (Saugatuck, Conn.: ENO Foundation for Transportation, 1971), p. 37.

An excellent timing device is a digital or strip-chart recorder that is actuated by a detector or human observer. Cumulative records of the successive times of arrival of vehicles may be subtracted to compute gaps. Stopwatches or metronomes may also be used to measure individual gaps. With data grouped in the 1–4 format, one person with a stopwatch can tabulate gaps and count directional flows having a combined volume of up to 1500 vehicles per hour. This assumes no requirement for vehicular classification.

Gap studies are facilitated by electronic digital readout stopwatches, inexpensive models of which are available.

Time-lapse photography and closed-circuit television systems also can provide records from which gaps may be measured. Figure 17.9 shows the recordings of a gap study plotted in an inverse cumulative form and fitted to a theoretical probability distribution.

Gap acceptance studies

When two traffic streams conflict, it may be desired to observe the gaps in one stream which are accepted or rejected by drivers in the other stream. There are several possible measures that may be used to describe the observations. The shortest gap length accepted by half of the drivers is the median acceptable gap. The critical gap is defined as the gap length for which the number of shorter accepted gaps is equal to the number of longer rejected gaps. The fact that a given driver can only accept one gap but may reject any number of gaps can be taken into account.

Acceleration and deceleration studies

Occasionally, the engineer is interested in accelerations or decelerations at a specific location. When the acceleration is nearly constant, a study of this type can be made by timing the arrival of the vehicle at four or five marked locations, preferably located so that the elapsed time between locations is about 2 s (for stopwatch observations). Three or four stopwatches are used, all being started at the first location and one stopped at the vehicle's arrival at each succeeding checkpoint. The trajectory of the vehicle is then plotted on a time–space (x, t) diagram by drawing a smooth curve between the points. The velocity, the time derivative (dx/dt), is obtained graphically by drawing a tangent to the curve at several locations. This, in turn, is plotted in a dx/dt vs. t diagram, a curve is drawn, and the acceleration is the slope of the velocity–time curve.

Intersection and driveway studies

Many previously discussed studies deal with data collection at intersections or high volume driveways (which are really T-type intersections). These include the inventory of intersection controls, turning-movement volume counts, intersection delay studies, and approach speed studies. Other specialized intersection studies include capacity, signal timing, queue studies, traffic conflicts, measurements of sight distance, and new development impact.

Capacity studies at signalized locations

Operational studies of load factors and peak-hour factors can be made using the Normann method described in the *Highway Capacity Manual.*[19] (These factors are described in Chapter 16.) The load factor can be measured by direct observation of the use of available green time during each signal phase. It can be accomplished as a special part of a queue length study. The peak-hour factor is obtained by counting volumes on each approach separately for each 15 min of the peak hour (machine counts are very suitable for this) and calculating as follows:

$$\text{peak-hour factor} = \frac{\text{peak-hour volume}}{4 \times (\text{peak 15-min volume})}$$

Traffic conflicts studies

This technique relates projected accident hazard to the frequency of observed intersectional vehicular conflicts of various types.[20] The existence of a conflict is inferred from an easily identifiable driver response. These responses include the application of the brake pedal (illuminated brake light) and lane changes. The causes of the action are categorized as left-turn conflicts, cross-traffic conflicts, or rear-end conflicts. The number of conflicts and the traffic volume are counted. Relationships developed from experience are used to evaluate the accident potential of the intersection.

Although some studies have concluded that the technique is a reliable tool for predicting accident potential, other researchers have questioned the degree to which this can be supported. Modifications of the technique have been successfully used with reduced personnel requirements.[21]

Queue studies

Two types of queue studies can be made at signalized intersections: queue discharge and queue length.

In the *queue discharge* study, several green phases are observed. A stopwatch is started when the green phase begins and stopped when the last vehicle in the delayed queue is discharged or when the phase ends. The number of vehicles entering the intersection and the time of the last vehicle's entrance are used to establish the discharge capacity. These data can be used in capacity estimates.

---

[19]*Highway Capacity Manual, 1965,* Special Report 87 (Washington, D.C., Highway Research Board, 1965).

[20]Stuart R. Perkins, *Traffic Conflicts Technique Procedure Manual,* Research Publication GMR-895 (Warren, Mich.: General Motors Research Laboratories, Aug. 1969); Stuart R. Perkins and J. J. Harris, "Traffic Conflict Characteristics—Accident Potential at Intersections," *Traffic Safety and Accident Research,* Highway Res. Rec. 225 (Washington, D.C.: Highway Research Board, 1968), pp. 35–47; William T. Baker, "An Evaluation of the Traffic Conflicts Technique," *Traffic Records,* Highway Res. Rec. 384 (Washington, D.C.: Highway Research Board, 1972), pp. 1–8.

[21]C. V. Zegeer and R. C. Dean, "Traffic Conflicts as a Diagnostic Tool in Highway Safety," Transportation Res. Rec. 667 (Washington, D.C.: Transportation Research Board, 1978), pp. 48–57.

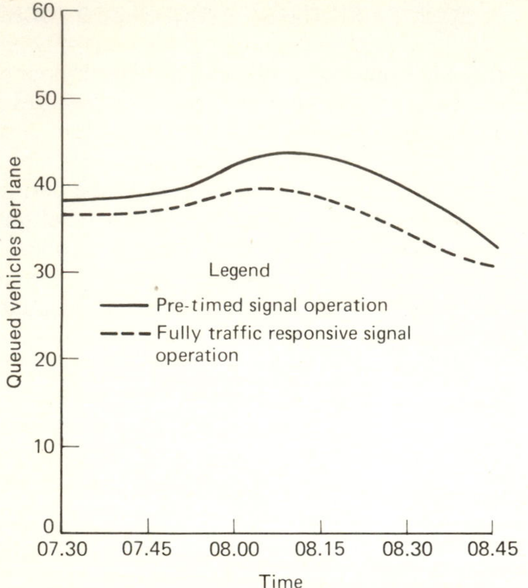

Figure 17.10. Comparison of effect of pretimed and traffic responsive traffic signal operations. SOURCE: *Improved Street Utilization through Traffic Engineering,* Special Report No. 93 (Washington, D.C.: Highway Research Board, 1967), p. 133.

In the *queue length* study, the instantaneous number of vehicles in a standing or slowly moving queue is counted in the field or from photographs. When the count is made at a signalized intersection, it should be made at the start of the green interval for each approach being studied, and also made at the end of the yellow interval. A notation should be made if the queue is completely discharged during the movement phase. At unsignalized intersections the counts are usually made at equal intervals of time such as 30 s or 1 min. This study is an important source of data for the calculation of load factors in highway capacity studies and to estimate intersectional delay. It can also be used to measure the effectiveness of a change in traffic signal control, through an analysis such as that shown in Figure 17.10.

Queue length studies have an important application in determining the appropriate locations for secondary street intersections or major driveways when they will be in proximity to a signalized intersection. The study is performed by establishing potential access locations at varying distances from the stop line of the controlled intersection and observing the extent to which queue lengths reach or pass these locations. It is often possible to select existing features, such as fire hydrants, sign posts, poles, or other references. The study should be conducted during the peak hour of heaviest loading. The expected proportion of the hour during which entry or exit to each potential location will be blocked by backup of standing traffic is computed from the data. Separate stopwatches may be used for each of the reference points and operated continuously during periods when traffic backup blocks each location for a direct measure of the total blockage during the study period. The blockage time for each location is divided by the total length of study to produce the percent of time blocked.

There are no hard-and-fast rules, but time blockages that do not exceed 10 to 15% are not considered serious. On the other hand, blockages of 25 to 50% would raise serious questions as to the feasibility of full access at that location (this does not necessarily preclude right turn-in and right turn-out access).

New development impact

From the capacity standpoint, the effect of a new traffic generator is generally most pronounced at the nearest controlled intersections. The special studies needed to assess this impact are discussed in the *ITE Driveway Guidelines* and are summarized as follows:[22]

1. Estimate the peak-hour traffic to and from the development.
2. Estimate the directional distribution of this traffic.
3. Assign appropriate volumes of turns in and out at the various access points.
4. Sum the volumes approaching critical intersections.
5. Take current peak-hour turning movement counts at the critical intersections.
6. Add the generated traffic and perform capacity analysis (use of the critical lane method expedites the analysis).[23]
7. If a significant worsening of the existing level of service would be produced, calculate additional lane requirements or revision of signal operation to result in an acceptable operation.

It is important that the generated traffic assumed to be added to the intersections be realistic. Certain types of development, such as residential, office, or industrial, will add about the same amount of generated traffic as the volumes estimated to use their access points. However, other developments, such as shopping centers, service stations, motels, and similar service-oriented facilities, will draw some portion of their volumes from existing traffic, and it may be of significant magnitude. For shopping centers of up to 100,000 ft^2 (9000 m^2) of gross leasable area located along shopping corridors, studies have shown about one-half of the driveway volume to be nongenerated (i.e., diverted from that already passing by on the street system). The assignment of total driveway traffic as a measure of impact in such cases would grossly exaggerate any improvement needs at nearby intersections.

Sight distance studies

Sight distance measurements are frequently used in operational studies, such as the setting of "no-passing" zones. Eye heights of 3.5 ft (1.0 m) and obstacle heights of 4.25 ft (1.3 m) are being used. For continuous measurement of sight distances, a pair of vehicles, equipped with communication and distance-measuring devices, can be used. The

[22] *Guidelines for Driveway Design and Location,* Recommended Practice (Arlington, Va.: Institute of Transportation Engineers, 1974).

[23] *Interim Materials on Highway Capacity,* Transportation Res. Circ. 212 (Washington, D.C.: Transportation Research Board, 1980).

rear vehicle can keep the front vehicle barely in sight and command cumulative distance measures at selected check points. The recorded difference is the sight distance. Lines of sight may also be measured on foot using tapes or measuring wheels.

At low-volume intersections, the relative need for control and the selection between yield and stop signs often are dependent on sight distance. See the *MTES* for a sight-angle board layout and application.[24]

School studies

Studies related to schools may be grouped into three categories; walking routes, street crossings, and operations adjacent to and on the school site.[25] The most critical studies are related to crossings—particularly of high-volume streets.

Crossing protection criteria depend on an appraisal of street widths, vehicular speeds and volumes, pedestrian volumes, and gaps in the traffic stream. Field studies are required to determine the extent of pedestrian delay prior to making a decision regarding control.

The minimum length of gap that will permit a group of pedestrians to cross a street of width *(W)* depends on group size, perception time, reaction time, and walking time. It must equal the time needed by the group to cross the roadway without coming in conflict with passing vehicles. This minimum gap time, G, is computed from the following equation:

$$G = \frac{W}{V} + P + K(N - 1) \qquad (17.14)$$

where W = width of the pavement to be crossed, ft or m

V = juvenile pedestrian walking speed (usually taken at 3.5 ft/s or 1 m/s)

P = pedestrian perception and reaction time, which is the number of seconds required for a juvenile to look both ways, make a decision, and start to walk across the street (usually taken at 3.0 s)

N = number of rows of pedestrians (see below)

$K(N-1)$ = total added time required for the entire group to enter the roadway, seconds; K is the time between the rows (usually taken as 2.0 s)

The pavement width is measured curb to curb. If the roadway is divided and the center island is wide enough for the maximum-size group of pedestrians to stand on it in safety, the width of only one roadway is used for W. This information is obtained at the same time the pedestrian group size study is made, and the pertinent data are recorded at the top of a form such as shown in Figure 17.11.

It is recommended practice to assume for the size of

[24]Box and Oppenlander, *Manual of Traffic Engineering Studies*, pp. 87 and 89.

[25]George R. Bonnett, "Effective School Pedestrian Transportation Studies," *Public Works*, p. 75 (June 1978); *Manual on Uniform Traffic Control Devices*, Traffic Controls for School Areas (Washington, D.C.: Federal Highway Administration, 1978); *A Program for School Crossing Protection*, ITE Recommended Practice (Arlington, Va., Institute of Transportation Engineers, 1972); Fred L. Orcutt and Hollis A. Walker, "Traffic Engineering for Pedestrian Safety," *Transport. Eng.*, pp. 16–22 (Jan. 1978). "Traffic Safety Planning on School Sites," Michigan Section ITE, Committee on Traffic Engineering around Schools, *ITE J.*, pp. 22–29 (Aug. 1978).

Figure 17.11. Sample pedestrian-group-size study field sheet. Source: *A Program for School Crossing Protection* (Arlington, Va.: Institute of Transportation Engineers, 1971), p. 17.

STUDY DATE 3/25/74 TIME: From 8 a.m. To 9 a.m. LOCATION 4th and L

CROSSWALK ACROSS 4th Street CURB-TO-CURB DISTANCE 40'

DIVIDED ROADWAY Yes No WIDTH OF ISLAND NA

Group size	Number of groups: Tally	Number of groups: Total	Cumulative	Computations
5 or fewer	/	1	1	60 x .85 = 51
6-10	𝍸	5	6	
11-15	𝍸 𝍸 //	12	18	
16-20	𝍸 𝍸 𝍸 ///	18	36	
21-25	𝍸 𝍸 ///	13	49	85% = 26-30 pedestrians
26-30	𝍸 //	7	56	
31-33	///	3	59	
36-40	/	1	60	
41-45				
46-50				
	TOTAL NUMBER OF GROUPS	60		

PEDESTRIAN DELAY TIME STUDY

Study date 26 Mar 81 Location 4th and D Crosswalk across D street

End of survey (to nearest minute) 0857	Number of rows. "N" 6
Start of survey (to nearest minute) 0802	Roadway width. "W" 40 ft.
Total survey time (minutes) 55	Adequate gap time. "G" 24 secs.

Gap size (seconds)	Number of gaps: Tally	Number of gaps: Total	Multiply by gap size	Computations
8–23	Discard gaps of less than 24 seconds from study.			
24	/	1	24	
25	////	4	100	
26	///	3	78	
27	//	2	54	T = total survey time x 60
28	/	1	28	
29	///	3	87	
30	~~////~~	5	150	T = 55 x 60
31	//	2	62	
32	////	~~5~~ 4	128	T = 3300 secs.
33		0	—	
34	///	3	102	
35	////	4	140	
36		0	—	
37	/	1	37	$D = \frac{T - t}{T} 100$
38				
39				$D = \left(\frac{3300 - 990}{3300}\right) 100$
40				D = 70
41				
42				
43				
"t" (total time of all gaps equal or greater than "G")			990 secs.	D = 70 %

Figure 17.12. Sample pedestrian-delay-time study field sheet. SOURCE: *A Program for School Crossing Protection* (Arlington, Va.: Institute of Transportation Engineers, 1971), p. 20.

group crossing the street the 85th percentile of all group sizes observed in the field. The size of each row (number of pedestrians walking abreast) is also measured; it is often found to be five persons. The number of rows *(N)* is then calculated by dividing the group size by the row size and rounding up to the next integer. *N* is taken as an integer because one pedestrian in excess of an even five will make an additional row and will require extra clearance time. School crossing pedestrian counts are made on a normal school day during the heaviest hour of crossing activity in the morning and in the afternoon.

The field study includes measurement of the gaps between the passing vehicles. A convenient form is shown in Figure 17.12. The gaps that are equal to or greater than the acceptable gap time for the established 85% gap are the periods when the children may cross the roadway safely. The time intervals between the acceptable gaps are delay time, the sum of which is the actual pedestrian delay. If only part of the roadway is to be crossed during a given gap, only the traffic flow in those lanes to be crossed are considered. The total available crossing time is the sum of all time by which each gap was equal to or greater than the acceptable gap. This total *(t)* is subtracted from the total survey time *(T)*. The following equation is then used to determine the percentage of potential pedestrian delay, *D:*

$$D\ (\%) = \frac{T - t}{T} \times 100 \qquad (17.15)$$

Methods of calculating delay at signalized intersections are similar, but substitute cycle length *C* for *T* and measure only the gaps between vehicles turning both right and left across the crosswalk under study.[26]

Public transit studies

The purpose of transit studies is to evaluate the service within a given area and to estimate the use of mass transit. Major regional transportation studies develop information on transit service and needs. Special studies may focus on local problems, such as the location of bus stops or the effect of one-way streets on transit routing. A number of

[26] *A Program for School Crossing Protection;* ORCUTT AND WALKER, "Traffic Engineering for Pedestrian Safety," pp. 16–22.

transit studies are described in detail in *Measuring Transit Service*[27] and *Urban Mass Transportation Travel Surveys*.[28] Forms are given in the *MTES*.[29]

Operations inventory

An inventory of public transit service supplies essential background information for other transit studies and for the evaluation of the service. The physical data include location of stops and transfer points. Additional information is needed on schedules indicating the frequency and hours of service on each route, the trip times between various points on the system, a summary of the rolling stock (showing its capacity, age, and condition), and the schedule of fares.

Operations studies

These studies provide data on passenger volumes, transit vehicle trip characteristics, vehicle occupancy, travel times, and adherence to schedules. The studies are of value when the data developed lead to improvement in the routing and scheduling. Traffic engineers need some of these data in studying the location of bus stops, turn prohibitions, and one-way street systems. The data are useful in the investigation of street operating plans that favor transit vehicles, such as signal timing and designation of exclusive bus lanes.

Three types of studies are used to determine transit operation characteristics: load checks, boarding and alighting checks, and speed and delay studies.

Transit load checks are made by observers stationed at one or more points along the routes. Generally, one point is at the maximum loadpoint, where the number of passengers carried is known to be the greatest. If two or more points along one route are studied simultaneously, the travel time of each transit vehicle between these points can be measured. Each observer records vehicle identification, time of arrival and/or departure, number of persons on board the vehicle when arriving, number of persons alighting, and number of persons boarding.

Boarding and alighting checks are conducted by observers traveling on transit vehicles. Each observer records the number of persons boarding and alighting at each stop, the number of persons on board between stops, the time the vehicle passes certain time check points on route, and sometimes the types of fare paid (cash, school tickets, transfers). On lightly traveled transit runs, the observer may be able to keep track of each passenger in order to relate the passenger's boarding stop to his alighting stop to provide information on the transit portion of that person's trip.

Transit *speed and delay studies* parallel similar studies for the entire vehicle stream described earlier in the chapter. Data are obtained by observers riding on the transit vehicles at various hours of the day. The time that each vehicle passes a check point and the cause and duration of delays are recorded. In addition to the types of delays found in general traffic speed and delay studies, the transit study also shows delays caused at bus stops by passengers alighting and boarding, and delays at time checkpoints if the vehicle has arrived ahead of schedule.

Prototype on-board electronic sensing and communication equipment has been developed that makes it possible to conduct these studies continuously as a part of transit operations management.

Planning studies

Planning studies are conducted in order to determine the origins, destinations, and characteristics of transit patrons. The home interview study described in the O-D section of this chapter is generally inadequate for a detailed description of transit user characteristics and trip making. The transit operations studies do not give any information about the portion of a passenger's trip between origin and boarding place, the alighting stop, and final destination. In the *transit interview* study, a questionnaire is handed to each boarding passenger on one or more routes, with the request that it be completed and returned to the driver or survey supervisor when alighting. Because this procedure may cause delays near the vehicle doors and inconvenience to passengers, prepaid postcards are sometimes handed out. A return of 30 to 50% of the cards may be expected.

The following questions are usually asked:

- Location of trip origin and destination (but not home address)
- Mode of access to transit line, and mode of travel between the transit system and the destination
- Frequency of making the trip
- Trip purpose

If important to the purposes of the study, the questionnaire may also request information about availability of a car, family income, and other social data.

Parking studies

Parking studies generally are conducted to identify inadequacies or to develop proposals to improve parking supply in a specific area. The study scale may vary from the preparation of a citywide parking program to the determination of the loading zone requirements for a single store.

The following types of information are almost always required in the study of a particular area such as a CBD:

1. Parking supply inventory
2. Characteristics of current parking usage
3. Parking demand estimates
4. Legal, financial, and administrative factors

Detailed descriptions of the conduct of parking studies, including those dealing with specific problems (e.g., employee parking, parking lot analysis, etc.), are described in

---

[27] NATIONAL COMMITTEE ON URBAN TRANSPORTATION, *Measuring Transit Service* (Procedure Manual 4A) (Chicago: Public Administration Service, 1958).

[28] Urban Transportation Systems Associates, *Urban Mass Transportation Travel Surveys* (Washington, D.C.: Federal Highway Administration, Aug. 1972).

[29] BOX AND OPPENLANDER, *Manual of Traffic Engineering Studies*.

Block and Curb Face Numbering System

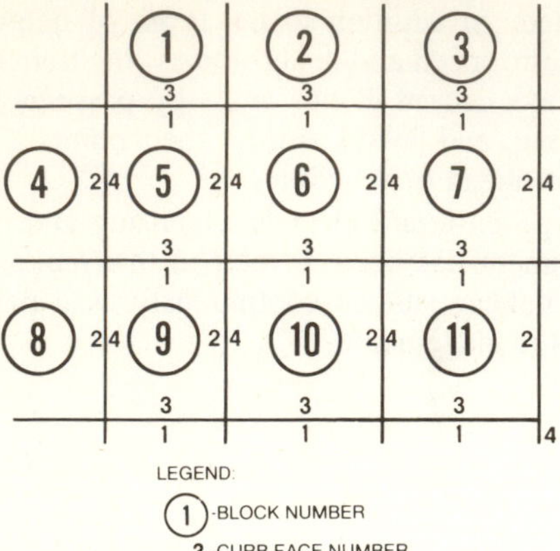

PARKING FACILITY NUMBERING

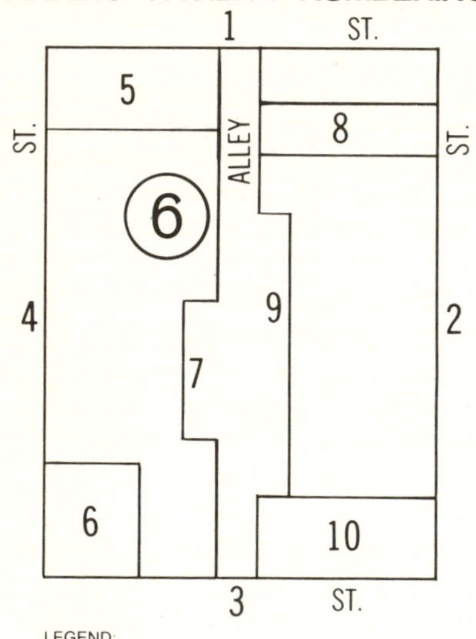

LEGEND:
(6) -BLOCK NUMBER
1 to 4 -CURB FACE NUMBERS
5 to 10 -OFF-STREET FACILITY NUMBERS

Figure 17.13. Block and facility numbering. SOURCE: Paul C. Box and Joseph C. Oppenlander, *Manual of Traffic Engineering Studies,* 4th ed. (Arlington, Va.: Institute of Transportation Engineers, 1976), Figs. 10-1 and 10-2.

Conducting a Limited Parking Study and *Conducting a Comprehensive Parking Study,*[30] and in *Parking Principles.*[31] The *MTES* includes details of various study techniques and numerous forms for both field and office tabulation.[32]

As a first step, the area to be studied must be delineated. The limits include not only the source of the parking problem itself (the business district, industrial park, etc.) but also the surrounding area within a reasonable walking distance. This may vary from 300 to 1500 ft (100 to 500 m). Each *block* in the study area is identified by code number. Secondary numbers are then used for each block face and off-street facility (see Figure 17.13).

Curb spaces are inventoried by observers who traverse all streets (and often alleys) in order to estimate or measure the prohibited parking zones, truck and passenger loading zones, parking spaces subject to time limits, and unrestricted spaces. Each off-street facility is classified as to whether it is private (e.g., employee parking only, not open to the public), commercial, public with restriction and/or charges, or public unrestricted. The capacity and parking fees are also noted.

The inventory is tabulated and graphical representations of curb parking are often superimposed on maps of the area (see Figure 17.14).

Occupancy studies

In parking occupancy studies the number of spaces used at various times are counted to identify the location and duration of high demand usage and surplus parking supply.

Curb space occupancy can be measured by observing each block face at regular intervals, counting the number of spaces occupied, including commercial vehicles in loading zones or prohibited spaces, and vehicles double-parked. Observers generally walk, but will travel in vehicles if the study area covers more than a few blocks. The interval between successive observations of each facility depends on the needs of the study. Generally, one count every hour is sufficient. In small communities, from two to five counts may adequately span the business day, and one or two Saturday checks are also required.

Off-street occupancy can also be obtained by counting the number of vehicles parked at regular intervals. Another method is to use observers or recording traffic counters to conduct a cordon count of a single facility. If it is very large, such as a shopping center, and if it is of interest to compare the occupancy of different sections, visual counts may still be required. Parking tickets used in public facilities are a useful source of occupancy data if the times of arrival and departure are indicated on the tickets.

Parking space occupancy data are summarized in tabular form and can also be shown graphically on maps. The number of parked vehicles is summarized for each hour, and the peak hour of parking accumulation is identified. The percentage of the available parking space-hours used by parked vehicles may also be shown. Comparisons can be made between legal parking, loading, and illegal parking, using space-hours as the common unit.

Duration and turnover studies

Parking duration and turnover studies are conducted to check the length of time vehicles are parked and the rate of space usage in a facility (called the turnover). Time limits for curb and off-street public facilities, and the geometric and operational design, are influenced by such information.

These data can be obtained by observing spaces at frequent and regular intervals and noting the license plate number for each vehicle parked at the time of observation (see Figure 17.15 for an example). Because most curb parking has a relatively short duration, some vehicles will park and

[30]National Committee on Urban Transportation, *Conducting a Limited Parking Study* and *Conducting a Comprehensive Parking Study* (Chicago: Public Administration Service, 1958).

[31]*Parking Principles,* Special Report 125 (Washington, D.C.: Highway Research Board, 1971), pp. 75–88.

[32]BOX AND OPPENLANDER, *Manual of Traffic Engineering Studies.*

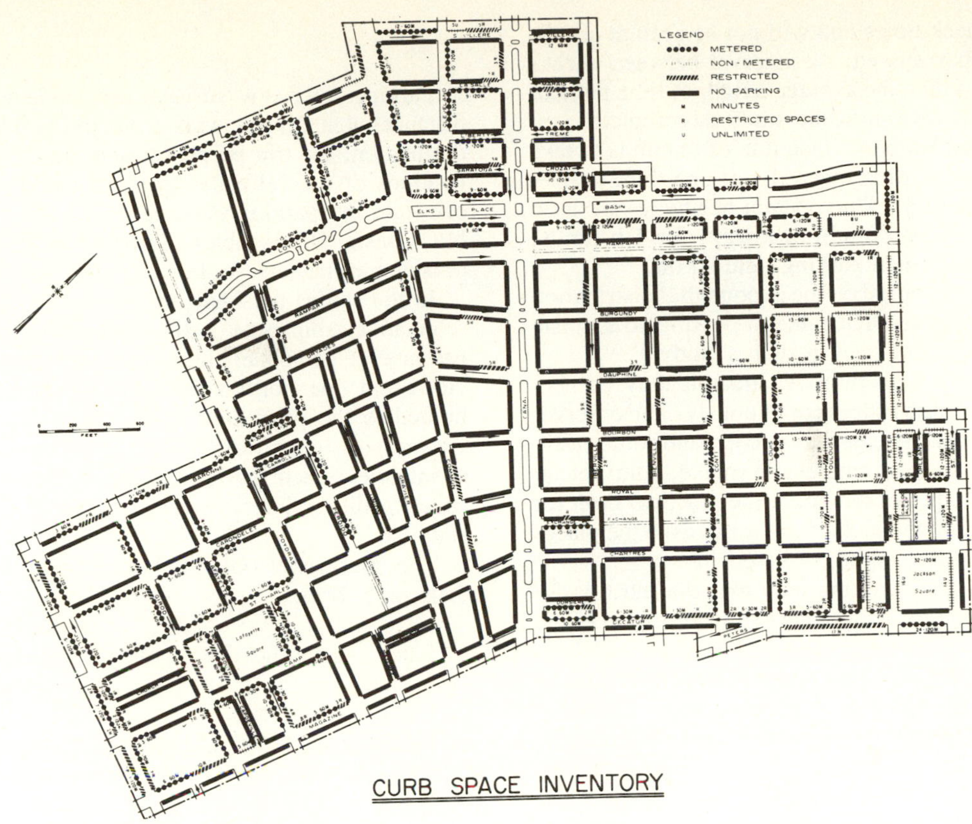

Figure 17.14. Sample curb space inventory map. SOURCE: Paul C. Box and Joseph C. Oppenlander, *Manual of Traffic Engineering Studies,* 4th ed. (Arlington, Va.: Institute of Transportation Engineers, 1976), Fig. 10-4.

Figure 17.15. Field data sheet used to record and identify the number of parked cars. SOURCE: Paul C. Box and Joseph C. Oppenlander, *Manual of Traffic Engineering Studies,* 4th ed. (Arlington, Va.: Institute of Transportation Engineers, 1976), Fig. 10-6.

LICENSE PLATE CHECK FIELD DATA SHEET

City ______ Date 10 MAY 1978 Recorded by JONES Side of Street W

Street WRIGHT between 5th and 6th

Codes: 000 last three digits of license number. ✓ for repeat number from prior circuit. __ for empty space

Space and Regulation	Time circuit begins										
	07	0730	08	0830	09	0930	10	1030	11	1130	1200
5th											
X-WALK	—	—	—								
NPHC	—	—	—								
1 HR M	—	713	✓	✓/TK							
" M	631	✓	(✓)	971							
" M	512	342	✓	014							
DRIVEWAY	—	—	—	—							
"	—	—	—	613							
1 HR M	—	—	418	✓							
"	117	220	✓	989							
"	—	148	096	✓							
FIRE HYD	—	—	—	—							
1 HR M	042	—	216	✓							
N PHC	—	—	—	T14							
X-WALK	—	—	—	—							
6th											

unpark between check times and will not be seen at all. To minimize the number missed, the interval between checks should be much less than the average length of time parked. Because this is unknown until the study is completed, rational estimates must be made. One rule of thumb is to take checks at headways (starting intervals) of one-third to one-half the posted time limit. Thus, 5-min headways are used for 15-min limits, 20 or 30-min headways for 1-h limits, 2-h headways for unlimited parking, and so on.

There is a technique based on the exponential distribution of the length of time parked that makes it possible to estimate the percent of parkers not seen in such a study.[33]

In some extremely high turnover areas it may be necessary to observe the curb spaces continuously. The observer identifies the cars by the spaces they occupy and some easily recognized characteristic of the vehicle (make, color, etc.). Ten to twenty spaces per observer are the practical limit for this study, which *also* may include notations as to the places of business walked to by some drivers.

Commercial off-street parking durations are most easily obtained by analyzing parking tickets showing times of arrival and departure. Durations can also be measured by continuous observation of a part or all of the facility or by recording license plate numbers at periodic intervals. Turnover can be obtained by counting entering or leaving traffic at exits, provided that the beginning and ending accumulations are also known.

In periodic check parking studies, the time parked is estimated by multiplying the number of times a vehicle is seen by the time interval between checks. Because of the missed parkers, the average duration calculated from these data is higher than actual.

Success in the use of colored aerial photographs in CBD parking studies has been reported.[34] In this case, occupancy and duration were satisfactorily obtained at cost savings exceeding 70%. Also, the photographs of the CBD have been useful for other planning studies.

Parking durations and turnover are generally summarized in tables, by type of facility (curb, by different time limits; and off-street, by retail lot, employee lot, etc.).

Parking *turnover is calculated* by dividing the number of *different* vehicles parked in a particular facility by the number of spaces. A turnover value must be related to a specific study period, such as 8, 10, or 12 h, so the unit is vehicles/space for K hours.

Truck loading studies

The allocation of freight zones at the curb requires data on the daily needs of individual merchants (such as the number and size of deliveries). Generally, a truck loading zone can be used by *all* properties in a given block. The hours of parking restriction for truck use only are typically limited to the business day, such as 0700–1800 h.

[33]D. E. Cleveland, "Accuracy of the Periodic Check Parking Study," *Traffic Eng.*, *33*(12), pp. 14–17 (Sept. 1963).

[34]Thomas A. Syrakis and John R. Platt, "Aerial Photographic Parking Study Techniques," *Parking*, Highway Res. Rec. 267 (Washington, D.C.: Highway Research. Board, 1969) pp. 15–28.

Interviews

Parking interview surveys are made to determine the distances that drivers walk from the parking space to the destination, the trip purposes, and the origins or next destinations of the vehicular trips. These studies are used to calculate the parking *demand* of an area, on a block-by-block basis. Occupancies, durations, and turnovers can be obtained at the same time.

In the study, personal interviews are conducted at representative samples of curb and off-street parking facilities. Because of personnel limitations, the area may be subdivided and one portion studied at a time. Work is often limited to the peak hour of parking demand. Each interviewer is assigned from 12 to 15 curb spaces and attempts to interview each driver parking in these spaces. At off-street facilities, interviewers are often placed at entrances and exits.

The interviewer obtains the following data and records them on a form:

1. Place where the driver plans to go while vehicle is parked.
2. Purpose of the trip.
3. Origin of trip which has brought the driver to the parking space (nearest street intersection and city).

The interviewer records the times of arrival and departure and may also note the location of the parking space used and the number of occupants.

If the purpose of the study is to check the parking generation characteristics of a particular building, the interviews may be conducted at entrances to the generator. The following information is secured:

1. Mode of travel (whether by car, bus, train, taxi, etc.)
2. If by car, whether a driver
3. If a driver:
   a. Where parked
   b. Trip purpose
   c. Trip origin

A *postcard survey* requests the same information as an interview. Prepaid, return-addressed postcards are placed under the windshields of vehicles parked in the study area. In off-street facilities, attendants may distribute the cards to their customers. Each postcard is given an identifying number to indicate the location of the parking space where it was issued. Distribution is usually made during the peak hour, as rapidly as possible. Figure 17.16 shows a sample card. Experience shows that about one-third of the postcards are returned. The value of this survey is limited by the fact that response biases may cause expansion of the data to be unreliable.

An alternative technique exists for interviews of *employees* at specific buildings or industrial plants. Here, cards are handed out and collected by office managers, shift foremen, and so on. Figure 17.17 shows an example of such a card.

Note that the interview cards do not ask for home address, but rather the nearest street intersection. This simplifies

______ PARKING SURVEY

Dear Motorist:
Please help improve parking in this community by answering these questions and mailing this post-paid card *today*.
Please do *not mark* in gray boxes!

4 9 9 2

I parked my car at this location today because (check one):

1 - I am employed or have my business downtown
2 - I am on a shopping trip (primary reason to be here)
3 - I am on a personal business trip (bank, doctor, etc.)
4 - Other reason (Please Specify) ______

After parking my car here, I walked to (please give address or name of building visited): ______

I drove to this parking space from: (place where trip started): (Nearest street intersection) ______

(City) ______

The length of time I parked here today was about:
______ (hours) and ______ (minutes)

Comments: ______

THANK YOU FOR YOUR COOPERATION

Figure 17.16. Sample parking postcard (mailback). SOURCE: Paul C. Box and Joseph C. Oppenlander, *Manual of Traffic Engineering Studies,* 4th ed. (Arlington, Va.: Institute of Transportation Engineers, 1976), Fig. 10-9.

Figure 17.17. Example of a handout card.

A traffic survey is being conducted in this area. Please answer the following questions and return the card to the office today before you leave.

1. Please check how you arrived:
   a. Drove automobile ____
   b. Rode with someone else ____
   c. Came by public transit ____
   d. Other means ____

IF YOU DROVE AN AUTOMOBILE, PLEASE ANSWER THE FOLLOWING QUESTIONS ALSO

2. Where do you live:
   a. City ______
   b. Nearest street intersection to your home ______

3. About what time did you arrive and when do you expect to depart:
   a. Arrived ______ Leave ______

THANK YOU FOR YOUR ASSISTANCE!

plotting the trip origin *and* increases the likelihood of returns by persons who object to giving out their home addresses. Information on the city of origin is also usually needed.

Destinations of parkers within the study area are often shown graphically on maps. The trip purposes and distances walked are generally tabulated. Origins or destinations of vehicle trips to or from the study area are plotted on maps or on desired line charts.

Attempts have been made to use general O-D data.[35] Unfortunately, the zone sizes are often too large. Parking demand estimates should use individual blocks.

Because of the large amounts of data that are collected, most parking studies include considerable use of ADP. Such data-processing systems may also have application for limited analysis.[36]

Special parking studies

Zoning regulations for off-street parking supply should be based upon realistic needs.[37] Spot checks of parking demand should be made at peak times for typical land uses, such as:

- Residential, single-family
- Apartments, efficiency or one-bedroom
- Apartments, two- or three-bedroom
- Restaurants
- Office buildings
- Shopping centers, neighborhood size
- Shopping centers, community size
- Shopping centers, regional size
- Banks
- Industrial plants

In making such checks, it is important to consider seasonal and day-of-week variations as well as the hourly changes. Residential uses peak between 0100 and 0500. Restaurants peak at noon (drive-in, CBD) or in the early evening (sitdown, outlying area). Offices have the heaviest parking demand on Monday morning about 1000 h, while shopping centers typically reach peaks on Saturday late morning through early afternoon. Banks peak on Friday evenings or Saturday mornings near each month's end.

Other special studies involve gathering information on *potential sites* for off-street parking development (dimensions, assessed value, and current use, if any). If a city has a parking agency or department responsible for curb and off-street public facilities, data are often gathered on gross revenues plus maintenance, operating, and collection costs. Financial statistics to show trends in net revenues are useful.

[35] LAWRENCE L. SCHULMAN AND ROBERT W. STOUT, "A Parking Study through the Use of Origin–Destination Data," *Parking Analyses,* Highway Res. Rec. 317 (Washington, D.C.: Highway Research Board, 1970), pp. 14–29.

[36] PEAT, MARWICK, MITCHELL & COMPANY. *A Guide to Parking System Analysis* (Washington, D.C.: Federal Highway Administration, 1972).

[37] *Parking Principles,* p. 32.

Transportation planning studies

These studies include all the major operational surveys described in this chapter: volume, speed, travel time, transit, and so on. Inventories of the transportation network are also obtained. Other data are gathered on the characteristics and economic status of the current population. Land-use types and intensities are inventoried. Detailed surveys are made of existing travel demand and its characteristics. This includes information on person and truck movement by location, mode, purpose, land use, and time of day. Population land use and economic studies are outside the scope of this chapter. For further information, see Chapters 11 and 12 and references listed in these chapters. Forms and details of field procedures are given in the *MTES*, including discussions of advantages and disadvantages of various study methods.[38]

Origin-destination studies

The comprehensive O-D study is the most complex traffic survey. Limited studies of this type are occasionally conducted utilizing certain parts of the comprehensive study. This section deals primarily with the larger study. For a summary and discussion of how the information derived from these studies is used, see Chapters 9 through 12. Detailed information on the conduct of this survey is contained in several references.[39]

The major purpose of an O-D survey is to obtain information on existing travel practices so that efficient transportation of people and goods can be planned and provided. The facts obtained from such a study include:

1. Where people begin and end their trips
2. How they travel (private automobile, public transit, truck, etc.)
3. When they travel (time of day)
4. Why they travel (work, shop, eat, etc.)
5. Where they park if they are vehicle drivers

Planning agencies need O-D data to aid in the planning of major street systems, freeway location and design (number of lanes, location of interchanges, etc.), major bridge locations, public transit improvements, and terminal facilities (off-street parking, bus, and truck terminals).

Facilities should be designed to meet future needs as well as those that exist at the time of data collection. O-D data are projected to the planning or design year in conjunction with projections of future economic and population growth, vehicle ownership and usage, land use, and similar factors as described in Chapter 12.

Census data may be available on trips made to work, by mode of travel. There has been some use of O-D surveys conducted at the place of employment. This technique has the advantage of simplicity in data collection, but it is limited because it samples only workers and usually obtains only work-trip data. Postcard surveys with appropriate follow-up techniques are also used.

The first step in conducting an O-D survey is to define the survey area by means of a *cordon line*. There are three general types of person-trips studied in different surveys: (1) the external–external trips, where both the origin and destination are outside the survey area (through trips); (2) external–internal trips with one end of the trip outside the area and the other within; and (3) internal–internal trips with both origin and destination within the area. For convenience, trips made by taxicab and trucks housed in the survey area are studied separately.

External study

The main external study determines the origins and destinations of groups (1) and (2) above, those persons traveling through, entering, or leaving the study area by motor vehicle. Special studies are sometimes made at air, bus, and rail terminals.

The most widely used method of conducting an external highway study is the *roadside interview*. Stations are established at the cordon line on all major roads entering the survey area. A large sample of vehicles is stopped and the drivers are asked the origin and destination of their trips. In some studies, they are asked the purpose of their trips, the location of internal stops made, and what route they are taking. Figure 17.18 shows a typical form.

In the *return-postcard* method, the drivers are handed prepaid postcards and are requested to list the origin and destination of their trips and return the cards by mail.

In limited studies of small areas, other methods can be used. *License plate studies* may be made. Observers are stationed at each entrance and exit of the area, and they record the license number of each vehicle passing the location. A questionnaire may be mailed to the owner of the vehicle within a few days after the field check.

The *vehicle-intercept* method also requires stations at all entrances and exits to the area. In this case, each entering vehicle is stopped and a precoded or colored card is handed to the driver (or affixed to the car, thus eliminating the need for stopping the vehicle a second time). In a variation of this method, when one entering station is studied, drivers are asked to turn on their headlights until they pass an exit station.

Internal study

The internal study provides information on trips made by residents of the area, which usually comprise the bulk of the travel in the area.

The *home interview* survey, developed by the FHWA, is the most commonly used form of internal survey. Dwelling unit samples distributed over the entire area in proportion to housing density are carefully selected, preliminary con-

[38] Box and Oppenlander, *Manual of Traffic Engineering Studies*, pp. 113–128.

[39] National Committee on Urban Transportation, *Conducting a Home Interview Origin–Destination Survey* (Procedure Manual 2B) (Chicago: Public Administration Service, 1958); U.S. Federal Highway Administration, *Urban Origin–Destination Surveys* (Washington, DC: 1973).

METROPOLITAN AREA TRAFFIC SURVEY
EXTERNAL TRIP REPORT

Card number 3 Station ________ Date _____ Hour period beginning _____ a.m. p.m. Inbound 1 Outbound 2

1	2	3	4	5	6	7	8	9	10		11	
Serial number	Vehicle type	No. in vehicle	Where did this trip begin?	Where will this trip end?	Trip purpose	Where is car owned or garaged	Control points passed	Route exit or entrance	Intermediate stop		Exp. factor	
									Location	Purpose	Hour	24 hour
						In area 1 Out area 2						
						In area 1 Out area 3						
						In area 1 Out area 3						
						In area 1 Out area 3						
						In area 1 Out area 3						
						In area 1 Out area 3						

Figure 17.18. External trip interview form. SOURCE: Federal Highway Administration.

tacts are made with the households, and interviewers are assigned the task of personally contacting the people living in these dwellings. Information obtained includes social and economic data on the household residents plus data on all trips made by all residents over 5 years of age on the previous weekday (see Figure 17.19).

Several other forms of internal surveys have been used. One is the controlled postcard survey, in which the vehicle owners of the area are sent postcards and are requested to list their trips for one day and to return the cards by mail.[40] The use of television as a replacement for the interview has been attempted.[41]

In the multiple cordon survey, concentric cordon circles are established within the urban area. Drivers are stopped to be interviewed or given premarked cards which are surrendered at the next interception point.

Special studies

Additional information is obtained on truck, taxi, and transit trips. The truck and taxi data are obtained by interviewing commercial organizations because much of the data are available from office records. A manual is available on transit surveys.[42]

Analysis and presentation of data

Origin–destination surveys produce large amounts of data that are analyzed by using computers. Each trip is first coded by assigning numerical codes indicating the specific zones of origin and destination for the trip. Appropriate codes are used for the other information obtained in the study.

The data are expanded to a 100% sample for an average weekday in both the external and internal phases. The expanded data are then compared to the actual screen line counts and possibly adjusted to match these counts. The data are then summarized and O-D tables are prepared show-

[40]R. C. BARKLEY, "Origin–Destination Surveys and Traffic Volume Studies," *Bibliography 11* (Washington, D.C.: Highway Research Board, 1951). See also HOWARD MCCANN AND G. MARING, "Evaluation of Bias in License Plate Traffic Survey Response," *Travel Analysis*, Highway Res. Rec. 322 (Washington, D.C.: Highway Research Board, 1970), pp. 77–83.

[41]WILLIAM R. MCGRATH AND CHARLES GUINN, "Simulated Home Interview by Television," *Origin and Destination Techniques and Evaluations*, Highway Res. Rec. 41 (Washington, D.C.: Highway Research Board, 1963), pp. 1–6.

[42]URBAN TRANSPORTATION SYSTEMS ASSOCIATES, *Urban Mass Transportation Travel Surveys*, Washington, D.C., 1972.

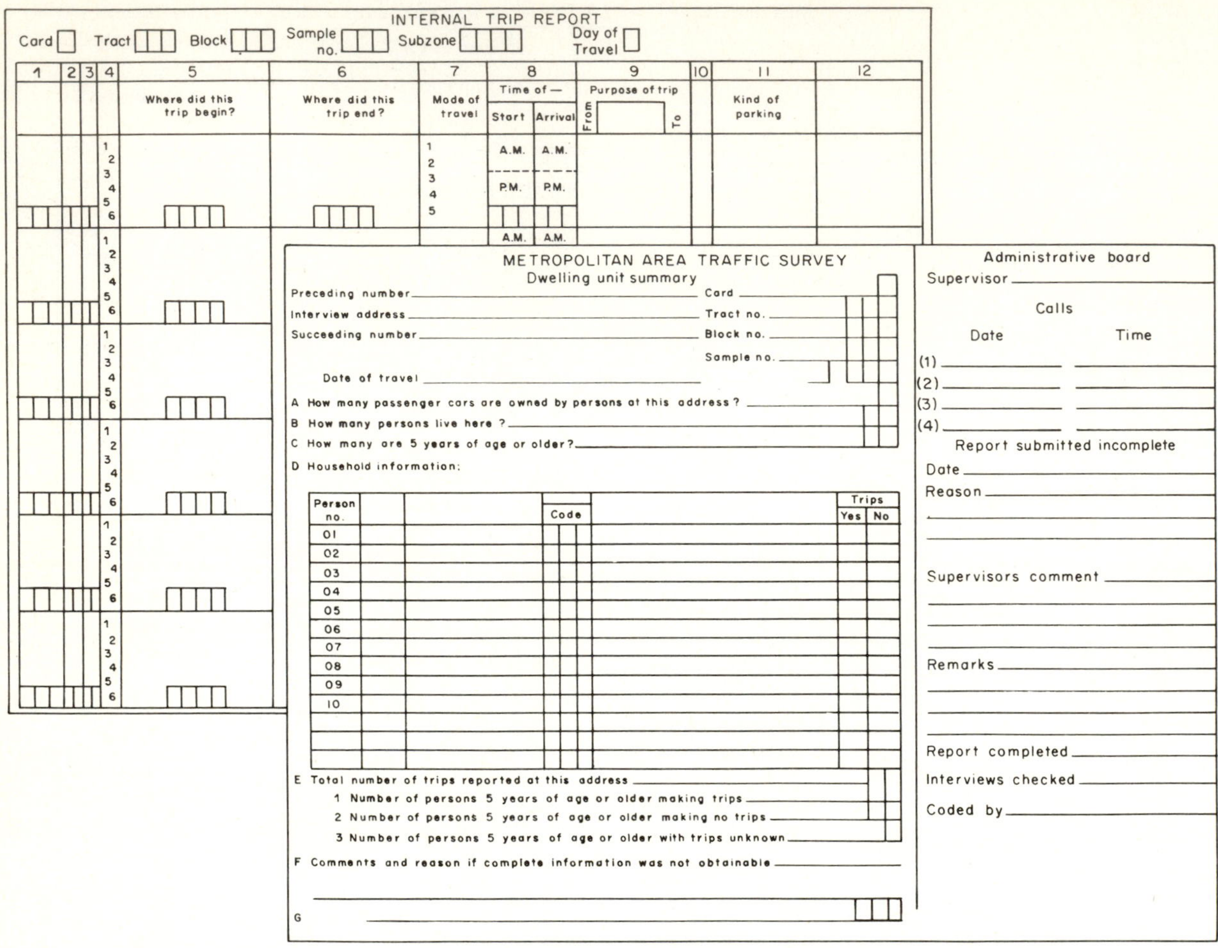

INTERNAL TRIP REPORT

Card | Tract | Block | Sample no. | Subzone | Day of Travel

1	2	3	4	5	6	7	8		9	10	11	12
				Where did this trip begin?	Where did this trip end?	Mode of travel	Time of — Start	Arrival	Purpose of trip From / To		Kind of parking	
			1 2 3 4 5 6			1 2 3 4 5	A.M. / P.M.	A.M. / P.M.				

METROPOLITAN AREA TRAFFIC SURVEY

Dwelling unit summary

Preceding number ____ Card ____

Interview address ____ Tract no. ____

Succeeding number ____ Block no. ____

Sample no. ____

Date of travel ____

A How many passenger cars are owned by persons at this address? ____

B How many persons live here? ____

C How many are 5 years of age or older? ____

D Household information:

Person no.			Code				Trips Yes	No
01								
02								
03								
04								
05								
06								
07								
08								
09								
10								

E Total number of trips reported at this address ____

1 Number of persons 5 years of age or older making trips ____

2 Number of persons 5 years of age or older making no trips ____

3 Number of persons 5 years of age or older with trips unknown ____

F Comments and reason if complete information was not obtainable ____

G ____

Administrative board

Supervisor ____

Calls

Date Time

(1) ____ ____

(2) ____ ____

(3) ____ ____

(4) ____ ____

Report submitted incomplete

Date ____

Reason ____

Supervisors comment ____

Remarks ____

Report completed ____

Interviews checked ____

Coded by ____

Figure 17.19. Internal trip interview form and dwelling unit summary. SOURCE: Federal Highway Administration.

ing the number of trips between each pair of zones. These tables indicate the total person travel on an average weekday.

Extensive use is made of graphic presentation in summarizing O-D data. In a desire line chart, straight lines are drawn between zones of O-D with the width of line proportional to the number of trips made between those points on an average day. Desire line charts usually separate the type of trip into through trips, local trips, and internal trips. Desire line charts may also be prepared for special zones that contain high-volume generators, such as the CBD or large industrial tracts. Other data obtained in the survey are also presented graphically on maps, such as population distribution, land use, and trip density.

Observance of control devices

The level of public obedience is one test of the effectiveness of regulations and devices, the adequacy of publicity and education dealing with these controls, and the level of enforcement. Results of these studies may lead to recommendations for changes in control devices or for increases in education and enforcement efforts.

Since the objective is to count persons violating traffic regulations, it is important that observers act in an *inconspicuous* manner. Use of clearly visible equipment should be avoided, and unmarked cars should be used.

Samples of 100 are often adequate to indicate observance, except when violations are rare. The following equation may be used to calculate appropriate sizes:[43]

$$N = \frac{pqK^2}{E^2} \tag{17.16}$$

where N = minimum sample size

p = proportion of drivers or pedestrians that observe the regulation

q = proportion of drivers or pedestrians that do not observe the regulation

K = constant corresponding to the desired confidence level

E = permitted error in the proportion estimate of observance

[43] BOX AND OPPENLANDER, *Manual of Traffic Engineering Studies*, pp. 180–187.

The selection of 0.5 for p and q provides a *conservative* estimate of the sample size. The size requirement becomes less as the value of p decreases or increases from 0.5. The sum of p and q is always equal to 1.0.

The constant K that is used depends on the desired level of confidence. The value of 2 for K is often selected for a confidence level of 95.5%, which is about 1 possibility in 20 that the proportion of violations found would occur by chance alone. The permitted error E is based on the precision that is required for this estimate. This measure is an absolute tolerance which is specified as plus and minus a selected value. The permitted error may generally range from ± 0.01 to ± 0.10 (1 to 10%).

As an illustration, assume a 10% violation rate, a 5% permitted error, and a K value of 2:

$$N = \frac{0.9(0.1)(2)^2}{(0.05)^2} = 144$$

Speed limits

Observance of speed regulations is measured by spot speed studies (see the preceding section on "Speed Studies"). The percentage of vehicles traveling above the legal or posted speed limit is calculated from the field data. Before-and-after spot speed studies can be used to determine the effectiveness of a change in speed regulations or education and enforcement practices. The checks are usually made during off-peak hours.

Traffic signals

A signal observance study is particularly concerned with the response of drivers approaching the signal during the clearance interval and red phase. Care must be taken to consider perception-reaction times in classifying violations of traffic signals.

The behavior of pedestrians in response to green, yellow, and red indications of vehicular signals may be studied, as well as obedience to any Walk, flashing Don't Walk, and steady Don't Walk indications.

Another type of study concerns RTOR (right turn on red) and the proper yielding of such drivers to pedestrians and other vehicular traffic. The measure of violation is the observed slowing or brake-light applications of through traffic, or interference with pedestrians.

Signal observance studies are appropriate during both peak and off-peak hours.

Other traffic regulations

Many traffic regulations require simple responses by motorists and pedestrians. These include turn prohibitions, use of pedestrian crosswalks, and the yielding of the right-of-way by drivers to pedestrians or to other drivers at uncontrolled approaches. Samples are taken to cover all applicable periods of the day. The percentage of drivers or pedestrians disobeying the regulations is computed and used for analysis and comparison purposes.

In some cases, at stop signs, for example, there may be several actions of interest (stop, crawling stop, slowing, no response). Each of these categories must be counted, as may the condition of through traffic flow for each response (conflict or no conflict). At yield signs, similar tabulations are made and the direct measure of violation is interference with through traffic. This is evidenced by brake-light applications or visible slowing of drivers on the protected street.

Parking regulations

The principal parking violations include overtime, prohibited parking, standing or stopping, and double parking. Occasionally, studies may be made of truck loading zones (proportion of time occupied by commercial vehicles or passenger cars actually engaged in loading or unloading, compared with use for "parking" private vehicles).

The types of forms used, hours of study, and degree of detail are all related to the purpose of the study. A "standard" parking technique, such as the license plate check, will produce data on most violations (see the "Parking Studies" section of this chapter, and the *MTES*[44]).

Traffic accident studies

Uses of data

Accident data, tabulated and analyzed, may be used by traffic engineers in the following ways:

- To define and identify high-accident locations.
- To make before-and-after studies where improvements have been made or where specific control devices have been changed.
- To justify action on public requests for installations of traffic control devices.
- To aid in evaluating different geometric designs, and in determining and developing proper design of streets, intersections, driveways, and traffic control devices to best accommodate *local* conditions.
- To establish ranking, programming, and scheduling of improvements at high-accident locations, as based on numbers (or costs) of accident types preventable by traffic engineering measures.
- To justify expenditures for major improvements that offer effective accident reduction.
- To develop changes in traffic regulations and zoning codes.
- To identify the need for:
  - a. Improved police traffic surveillance
  - b. Sidewalk and bikeway construction
  - c. Parking restrictions
  - d. Improved roadway lighting

[44]Box and Oppenlander, *Manual of Traffic Engineering Studies*.

○To identify certain driver/pedestrian actions causing accidents which might be prevented through public education.
○To assist in acquiring funds for comprehensive traffic safety programs in the community or state.

Accident reports

The primary sources of accident data are the local (city or county) and state police agencies. Also, many of the agencies routinely receive station reports or "desk complaints" whereby minor accidents are reported by the involved drivers, but on-the-scene investigation is not performed.

A secondary source of accident data involves copies of the driver financial responsibility reports that are required in many states. Many central state accident record bureaus are established to collect driver reports, and *some* of the accident reports from the various police agencies. Unfortunately, reports are not received for accidents below a specific dollar limit of accident cost, and consequently valuable data are lost.

The number of accidents is an important consideration in statistical validity of findings. For traffic engineering purposes, every attempt should be made to secure copies of *all* accident reports prepared by police agencies in the responsible jurisdiction. Usually, this is best performed in the city or county by having the police routinely copy every accident report and forward this copy to the traffic engineering office.

The three general types of report forms include the "closed box," the narrative, and the combination form. Figure 17.20 illustrates a common form of the latter type, and shows the kinds of information typically included.

For engineering analysis, one of the most important parts of the form is the sketch showing original paths of vehicle travel. Trained police officers use sufficient detail in the sketch to indicate the precollision movements reliably. Also important is the narrative portion of the form, in which officers provide information on other, noncontacted vehicles whose action may have contributed to the accident, or information such as end-of-queue conditions (as when a rear-end accident occurs in a backup of traffic from a control device).

Accident files

An accident report is nearly worthless to a traffic engineer unless he can identify the location as to specific intersection or point along a roadway. Most police agencies file accidents by serial number. Even with secondary references, it is much more difficult to extract reports from such a system than is the case if the reports are filed directly by location. Conversely, from the standpoint of police retrieval of a specific accident report for use in court or by insurance companies, the serial method of filing may be superior. Thus, there are definite advantages in the traffic engineering office receiving copies of the police accident reports, and setting up a separate location-type file. There are several methods of establishing such a file for either the original accident reports or copies.[45]

Prior to filing, accident data may be entered into a variety of data-processing systems. Normally, the data are interpreted, coded, and punched on cards. The information may then be transferred from the cards onto magnetic tape or disk.[46]

With electronic data processing, a number of tabulations may be available, including:

○Periodic printout listing of accidents by location.
○Periodic listing of "high-accident" locations.
○Detailed tabulations of data relating to high-accident locations which may be suitable for preparation of collision diagrams.
○Special summaries relating accident frequency or rates to highway type, geometric features, pavement conditions, and day or night conditions.

Data-processing systems, especially at the centralized state level, usually contain severe limitations. In many cases, the coding is only for accidents on the numbered state route system, and accident data may not be readily available for secondary routes, county roads, and city streets. Computer-generated information is usually not sufficiently detailed to permit thorough engineering analysis of intersections or roadways. There may be a considerable time lag between accident occurrence and date of availability. Contributing circumstances may not be properly related, particularly to intersections and noncontacted vehicles.

Relatively small numbers of accidents (up to 5000 to 10,000 a year) can readily be handled by manual systems. However, large numbers of accidents are much more efficiently accommodated by electronic processing systems. With such systems, it is imperative that direct and ready access be available to microfilmed or full-size copies of the accident report forms.

Inventory sections

Inventories are listings of accidents, keyed to general locations such as intersections, individual blocks of a city, or sections of rural highway.[47] The "location" must be clearly defined, and should be keyed to the operational practices of various agencies. The definitions need not be the same for all agencies; however, they should be mutually compatible and permit the effective grouping of data.

There are two general types of locations:

○A spot, such as an intersection or short bridge.
○A road section, which might be as short as 50 ft (15 m) or as long as 10 mi (16 km).

---

[45]Ibid., p. 44.

[46]T. K. Datta and R. J. Rogers, "Computerized Street Index for Michigan Accident Location Index System," Transportation Research Record 706 (Washington, D.C.: Transportation Research Board, 1979), pp. 20–22.

[47]*Highway Location Reference Methods,* NCHRP Synthesis Report 21 (Washington, D.C.: Highway Research Board, 1974).

POLICE REPORT OF MOTOR VEHICLE TRAFFIC ACCIDENT

National Safety Council
Chicago

DO NOT WRITE IN THIS SPACE
No.

TIME
DATE OF ACCIDENT .... 19 .... Day of Week .... Hour .... A.M. .... P.M. ....

LOCATION
PLACE WHERE ACCIDENT OCCURRED: County .... City, town or township .... State ....
If accident was outside city limits, indicate distance from nearest town .... miles North S E W of .... City or Town
ROAD ON WHICH ACCIDENT OCCURRED .... Give name of street or highway number (U.S. or State). If no highway number, identify by name.
AT ITS INTERSECTION WITH .... Name of intersecting street or highway number
IF NOT AT INTERSECTION .... feet North S E W of .... Show nearest intersecting street or highway, house no., bridge, RR crossing, alley, driveway, culvert, milepost, underpass, or other landmark.

VEHICLE NO. 1
VEHICLE .... Year Make Type (sedan, truck, taxi, bus, etc.) .... License Plate .... Year State Number
Parts of vehicle damaged .... Vehicle removed to: .... By: ....
OWNER .... Print or type FULL name .... Address .... Street or R.F.D. City and State
DRIVER .... Print or type FULL name .... Address .... Street or R.F.D. City and State
Regular Operator's License ☐ Other Type License ☐
Driver's License .... State Number .... Specify Type and/or Restrictions .... Date of Birth .... Month, Day, Year
OCCUPANTS
Front Center .... Name .... Address .... Street or R.F.D. City and State
Front Right .... Address ....
Rear Left .... Address ....
Rear Center .... Address ....
Rear Right .... Address ....

AGE	SEX	INJURY

Total number vehicles involved ....

VEHICLE NO. 2 or PEDESTRIAN
VEHICLE .... Year Make Type (sedan, truck, taxi, bus, etc.) .... License Plate .... Year State Number
Parts of vehicle damaged .... Vehicle removed to: .... By: ....
OWNER .... Print or type FULL name .... Address .... Street or R.F.D. City and State
DRIVER (or Pedestrian) .... Print or type FULL name .... Address .... Street or R.F.D. City and State
Regular Operator's License ☐ Other Type License ☐
Driver's License .... State Number .... Specify Type and/or Restrictions .... Date of Birth .... Month, Day, Year
OCCUPANTS
Front Center .... Name .... Address .... Street or R.F.D. City and State
Front Right .... Address ....
Rear Left .... Address ....
Rear Center .... Address ....
Rear Right .... Address ....

AGE	SEX	INJURY

FIRST AID GIVEN BY: .... Injured Taken to: ....
DAMAGE TO PROPERTY OTHER THAN VEHICLES .... Name object and state nature of damage
Name and address of owner of object struck ....

CODE FOR INJURY
(Use only the most serious one in each space for injury.)
K–Dead before report made.
A–Visible signs of injury, as bleeding wound or distorted member; or had to be carried from scene.
B–Other visible injury, as bruises, abrasions, swelling, limping, etc.
C–No visible injury but complaint of pain or momentary unconsciousness.
O–No indication of injury.

WITNESSES
Name .... Address ....
Name .... Address ....

AGE	SEX

KIND OF LOCALITY (Check one)
☐ Apartments, Stores, Factories
☐ One-family homes
☐ Farms, Fields
☐ No marginal development

ROAD SURFACE (Check one)
☐ Dry
☐ Wet
☐ Snowy or Icy
☐ .... Specify other

LIGHT CONDITIONS (Check one)
☐ Daylight
☐ Dawn or dusk
☐ Darkness

ROAD TYPE (Check one or more)
Driver 1 2
☐☐ 1 driving lane
☐☐ 2 driving lanes
☐☐ 3 driving lanes
☐☐ 4 or more lanes
☐☐ Divided roadway
☐☐ Expressway, parkway, toll road

WEATHER (Check one)
☐ Clear
☐ Raining
☐ Snowing
☐ Fog
☐ .... Specify other

TRAFFIC CONTROL (Check one or more)
☐ Stop sign
☐ Stop-and-go signal
☐ Officer or watchman
☐ R.R. gates or signals
☐ .... Specify other
☐ No traffic control

ROAD CHARACTER (Check two)
☐ Straight road
☐ Curve
☐ Level
☐ On grade
☐ Hillcrest

WHAT DRIVERS WERE GOING TO DO BEFORE ACCIDENT
Driver No. 1 was headed ☐ ☐ ☐ ☐ on .... (Street or highway)
North S E W
Driver No. 2 was headed ☐ ☐ ☐ ☐ on .... (Street or highway)
Driver 1 2 (Check one for each driver)
☐☐ Go straight ahead
☐☐ Overtake
☐☐ Make right turn
☐☐ Make left turn
☐☐ Make U turn
☐☐ Slow or stop
☐☐ Start in traffic lane
☐☐ Start from parked position
☐☐ Back
☐☐ Remain stopped in traffic lane
☐☐ Remain parked

WHAT PEDESTRIAN WAS DOING
Pedestrian was going ☐ ☐ ☐ ☐ (Check one) N S E W
☐ Along
☐ Across or into .... (Street name, highway No.) From .... To .... (N.E. corner to S.E. corner, or west to east side, etc.)
☐ Crossing or entering at intersection
☐ Crossing or entering not at intersection
☐ Getting on or off vehicle
☐ Walking in roadway—with traffic
☐ Walking in roadway—against traffic
☐ Standing in roadway
☐ Pushing or working on vehicle
☐ Other working in roadway
☐ Playing in roadway
☐ Other in roadway
☐ Not in roadway

CONTRIBUTING CIRCUMSTANCES
Driver 1 2 (Check one or more for each driver)
☐☐ Speed too fast
☐☐ Failed to yield right of way
☐☐ Drove left of center
☐☐ Improper overtaking
☐☐ Passed stop sign
☐☐ Disregarded traffic signal
☐☐ Followed too closely
☐☐ Made improper turn
☐☐ Other improper driving
☐☐ Inadequate brakes
☐☐ Improper lights
☐☐ Had been drinking

SHOW NORTH BY ARROW

INDICATE ON THIS DIAGRAM WHAT HAPPENED

Street or highway
Street or highway
Street or highway

DESCRIBE WHAT HAPPENED:
(Refer to vehicles by number) ....

POLICE ACTIVITY
Time notified of accident .... Date Hour ☐ A.M. ☐ P.M.
What was the source of accident information? .... (Officer at scene, No. 1 driver contacted station, both drivers contacted station, etc.)
Arrests
Name .... Charge ....
Name .... Charge ....
Other action taken: ....
SIGN HERE .... Officers rank and name .... Badge No. .... Department .... Date of report

Figure 17.20 Sample of traffic accident report form.

When developing inventory sections, it is important to realize that data from short links can readily be added together, whereas subdivision of data from sections of excessive length is much more difficult.

High-accident locations

These are locations where the frequency, as related to some estimate of exposure, is higher than the average for other similar locations or conditions.

For a spot, an appropriate exposure measure is the number of vehicles entering during a specific time period, usually expressed as MEV (million entering vehicles).

In the case of a road section, the travel during a selected period, expressed as 100 MVM or 100 MVK (million vehicle-miles or vehicle-kilometers) is the usual basis.

When accidents are related to exposure, a *rate* is calculated (see "Accident Rate Calculations").

In defining high-accident locations, the primary criterion should be developed around frequencies, or numbers of accidents during selected time periods, with weighting by exposure as a secondary check. Statistical measures should be used to determine whether a suspected "high"-accident location is actually abnormal, or whether the difference is due to chance variation.

In cities, a simplified type of comparison is sometimes used. Because annual traffic volume data are seldom if ever available for all intersections in a community, the annual numbers of accidents may be directly related to the number of intersections of the same functional classification in the city. There are six basic intersection types associated with unlimited access streets. Table 17-6 is an illustration of such a tabulation. Using the data, intersections having higher accident frequencies than the average for that functional classification can be singled out for special attention.

Funds for improvement that would affect significant accident reductions (such as 20 to 30%) would clearly do the most good at the highest-frequency locations. This is not to imply that simple, inexpensive improvements at lower-frequency sites may not be extremely cost-effective. Midblock or route section accident rates may also be tabulated on a rate per MVM ranking.

Four general systems for identification of hazardous locations as used on *state* highway systems are summarized below:

1. *Number method:* Locations are selected having more than a defined minimum number of accidents per unit length of highway.

TABLE 17–6
Example of Intersection Accident Frequency Tabulation

Type of Intersection	Number of Intersections	Number of Accidents in 3 Years	Annual Average Accidents/ Intersection
Major/major	14	721	17.1
Major/collector	9	121	4.5
Major/local	98	416	1.4
Collector/collector	6	16	0.9
Collector/local	62	70	0.4
Local/local	300	50	0.06

2. *Accident rate:* Locations are selected on the basis of exposure with roadway sections utilizing accidents per 100 MVM and intersections or spots utilizing numbers of accidents per MEV.
3. *Rate-quality control:* This utilizes a statistical test to determine the probability of the rate per 100 MVM or MEV being significantly higher than the average for similar locations.
4. *Number rate:* This utilizes both numbers of accidents and exposure rates. As an example, in one state, a spot is selected for a study when the number of accidents exceeds four per year and the rate per 100 MEV exceeds 150. A road section is selected when the accidents per mile per year exceed 1.5 and the accidents per 100 MVM exceeds 280.

The values for the numbers and rates to be used in each of these methods are generally developed through local experience.

The spot map has been utilized for noting general concentrations of accidents, but it is of greatest value for special situation-type studies. These include pedestrian accidents (especially as related to lighting conditions and thus on a day-or-night basis), parked-car accidents, or police patrol districts.

For traffic engineering purposes, the spot map should utilize a print of the street or highway system based upon a functional classification; that is, freeways, major routes, and collector streets, should be separately coded from the local streets.

Colored pins are used to represent various kinds or severities of accidents. At high-frequency locations, "multiplier" pins may be required, where one pin typically represents 10 accidents.

Detailed accident analysis

A desirable procedure for detailed examination of a high-accident location is:

1. Obtain copies of accident data (desirably the reports) for all accidents reported during the latest two years. If a before-and-after study of a traffic improvement is being performed, it is desirable to have at least 2 years of data during the "before" period, and at least 1 year (preferably 2 to 3 years) in the "after" period.
2. Prepare a collision diagram.
3. Prepare a condition diagram or inventory sketch, if needed.[48]
4. Obtain other pertinent traffic data:
   a. Intersection peak-hour turning movement counts.
   b. Speed checks on approaches if this may be a factor.
   c. Observance or control violation studies, if indicated by the pattern of accidents.
5. If an uncontrolled intersection with a pattern of right-angle collisions, make a safe approach speed analysis.[49]

---

[48] Box and Oppenlander, *Manual of Traffic Engineering Studies*, Chap. 2.
[49] Ibid., Chap. 6.

6. Field-check the location. On-site observation is essential to detect hazards not apparent on the condition diagram, or not clearly identified from the accident patterns of the collision diagram, to note abnormal traffic flow, and to check the visibility and placement of control devices. At signalized intersections, the adequacy of signal timing and phasing may require consideration. Night observation to check visibility of obstacles and reflectorization of control, guidance, or warning devices is often desirable.
7. Utilize the data to select the most appropriate treatment for the location.
8. After improvements have been installed, check back by performing a before-and-after study.

Although collision diagrams can be prepared for mid-block or route sections, they are used most often at intersections. The more important elements of the diagram—from a traffic engineering standpoint—include the following:

- What the drivers were going to do prior to the accident (such as make a left turn into a specific driveway, a right turn at a particular intersection, etc.);
- Vehicle paths prior to the accident, giving directions of original approach and graphically portraying the beginning of any *intended* turning movement; and,
- Notation of any unusual conditions of weather or road surface, and an indication if the accident occurred at night.

On the diagram for each individual accident, it is also desirable to show the day of the week, plus the date and time of occurrence. All intersection-related accidents should be shown, irrespective of actual location. The diagram is not to scale, and a rear-end collision occurring well away from a controlled intersection, at the end of backup of traffic to the control device, is diagrammed as though it occurred at the intersection.

Another important factor concerns the noninvolved or noncontacted vehicle or pedestrian.[50] In this case, "noninvolved" means that the traffic unit was not physically struck, and therefore is not directly identified on the accident report, but did perform an action creating circumstances leading to the accident.

Figure 17.21 diagrams six of the most common types of noninvolved vehicular accidents. A dashed line has been used to indicate the general intended path of the noninvolved unit, regardless of whether the turn has commenced or not.

Figure 17.22 shows a collision diagram for an urban intersection. Many modifications and simplified versions of the diagram are possible. For example, all accidents of a given pattern (such as eastbound, straight ahead, rear-end) can be denoted by a single line, and the number of such accidents can be indicated on the line without regard to dates or times. Separate lines and arrows may be used for this particular type of accident where injuries of fatalities

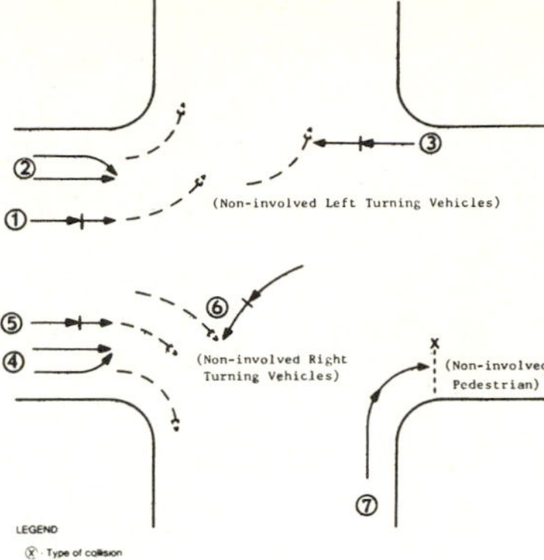

Figure 17.21. ~~Six~~ Seven of the most common types of noninvolved vehicle or pedestrian accidents.

are involved. Clearly, such abbreviated diagrams offer far fewer data to the analyst than does the complete diagram.

For a fuller discussion of collision diagrams and non-involved vehicle elements, see the *MTES*.[51]

Accident rate calculations

There are three basic types of comparisons:

1. Parallel study (between different locations or areas for the same period of time).
2. Before-and-after study (between different time periods at the same location or in the same area).
3. Condition study (between physical features of the roadway, regardless of the location or time of occurrence).

In making comparisons, a measure of any change in exposure should be incorporated. The standard equation for calculation of accident rate is:

$$\text{rate} = \frac{\text{number of accidents} \times \text{basis}}{\text{exposure}} \tag{17.17}$$

Studies have shown that traffic accident rates sometimes increase with volume. Thus, a six-lane freeway with 100,000 vehicles per day may have a higher number of accidents per 100 MVM than a four-lane freeway carrying only 20,000 vehicles per day. Accident rates are a measure, but *not* an absolute expression.

Rates on any given basis can also be computed by using a weighted severity factor. These factors arbitrarily assume some relationship between the basic PDO (property-damage-only) type of accident, which is given a weight of 1, and injury or fatal-type accidents. Alternatively, the factors can relate to the number of persons killed or injured.

It is usually considered preferable to use the number of fatal, injury, and PDO *accidents* for the calculations. The number of persons riding in a vehicle who might be killed

[50] Paul C. Box, "Non-involved Vehicle Accident Elements," *Public Safety Syst.*, Sept.–Oct. 1970.

[51] Box and Oppenlander, *Manual of Traffic Engineering Studies*, Chap. 4.

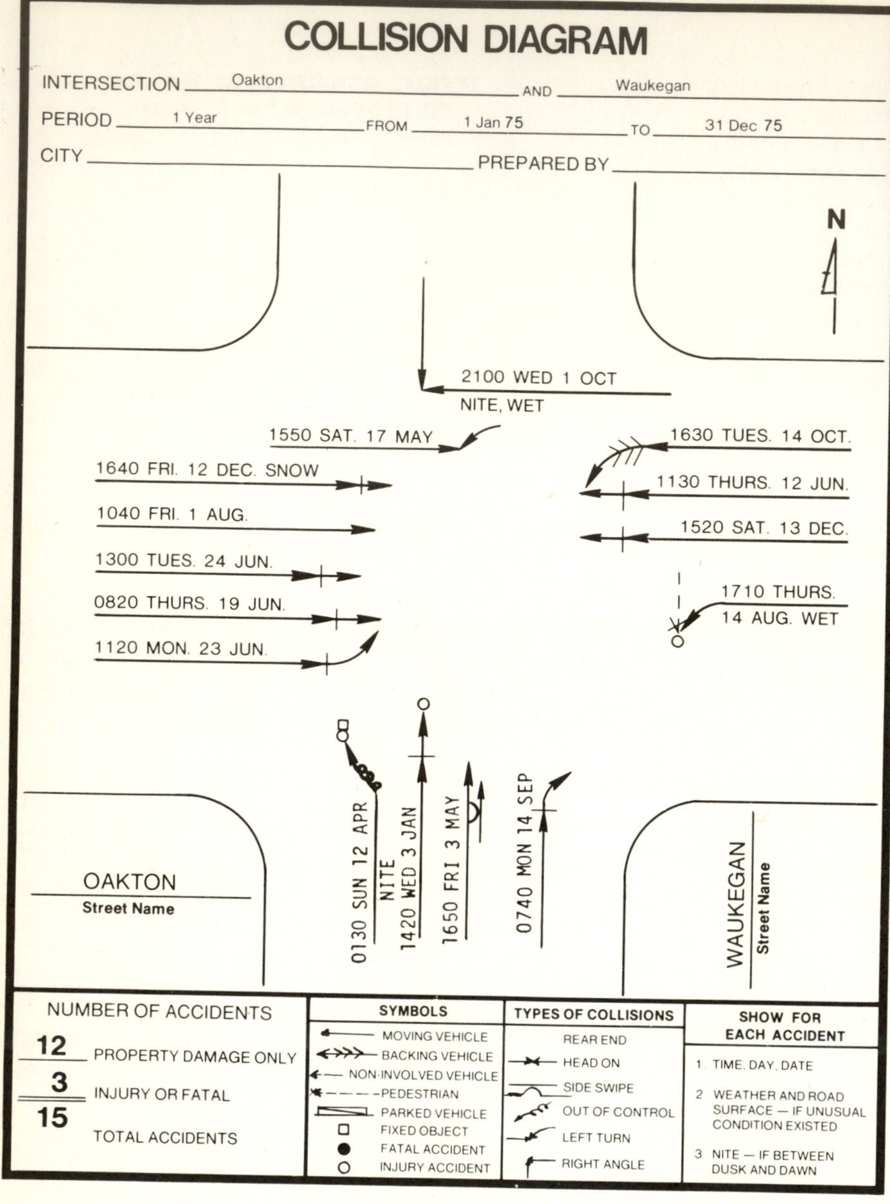

Figure 17.22. Example of a collision diagram.

or injured in a given accident tends to be random, and has practically no relationship to the conditions involved in the accident.

Another approach is to use EPDO (equivalent property-damage-only). In this system, the severity weight is equal to the estimated direct cost of an injury accident divided by that of a PDO accident, or of a fatal accident cost divided by that of an average PDO accident. In various studies, great differences have been found in assignable accident costs. For this reason, utilization of the EPDO concept is most appropriate when making direct comparisons, as in before-and-after studies.

The number of EPDO accidents is equal to the sum of the PDO accidents, plus the number of injury accidents times their severity weight, plus the number of fatal accidents times their severity weight. The EPDO *rate* is the number of EPDO accidents divided by some measure of travel exposure.

Before-and-after analyses

This basic study best measures the value of most traffic engineering improvements. It is appropriate to use when it is reasonable to assume that "before" conditions would be repeated in the "after" period if the improvement had not been made. The study utilizes a change in number, rate, or percentage. The percentage change using numbers (N) of accidents is equal to:

$$\frac{(\text{N in "after" period}) - (\text{N in "before" period})}{\text{N in "before" period}} \times 100$$

If there was a change in exposure (traffic volume), the direct percentage change of the number of accidents would not be the best method of expressing the difference. In this case, the accident *rate* can be calculated in the "before" period and separately in the "after" period. The percentage change is then calculated using these rates rather than the numbers of accidents.

In comparing the results of a before-and-after study, it is imperative that the statistical significance of the findings be related. This is readily and simply accomplished utilizing the chi-square relationship, which is used to minimize the chance of calling a reduction significant when it really is not; plus the Poisson distribution, which is used to minimize the chance of calling a reduction not significant when it probably is.

Curves for determining the statistical significance of percentage reductions are given in the *MTES*.[52] Reference to these curves shows that securing the largest practical accident sample size is important.

REFERENCES FOR FURTHER READING

Better Transportation for Your City (1958). National Committee on Urban Transportation, Public Administration Service, 1313 East 60th Street, Chicago, Ill. Supplemented by Series of Procedure Manuals (1958):

1A. *Determining Street Use.*
2A. *Origin-Destination and Land Use.*
2B. *Conducting a Home Interview Origin–Destination Survey.*
3A. *Measuring Traffic Volumes.*
3B. *Determining Travel Time.*
3C. *Conducting a Limited Parking Study.*
3D. *Conducting a Comprehensive Parking Study.*
4A. *Measuring Transit Service.*
5A. *Inventory of the Physical Street System.*

[52]Ibid., App. B.

BOX, PAUL C., "Analysis of Traffic Impact for New Developments—Parts 1 and 2," *Public Works,* Feb. and Mar., 1981, Ridgewood, N.J., pp. 61–65 and 87–90.

BOX, PAUL C., "Preparation of Collision Diagrams," *Public Safety Syst.*, July–Aug. 1970.

DICKEY, JOHN W., *Metropolitan Transportation Planning*. New York: McGraw-Hill, 1975 (esp. Chap. 5).

GERLOUGH, DANIEL L., AND FRANK C. BARNES, *Poisson and Other Distributions in Traffic*. Saugatuck, Conn.: ENO Foundation for Transportation, 1971.

GREENSHIELDS, BRUCE D., AND FRANK M. WEIDA, *Statistics with Applications to Highway Traffic Analysis,* rev. by Daniel L. Gerlough and Matthew J. Huber. Westport, Conn.: ENO Foundation for Transportation, 1978.

HUTCHINSON, BRUCE G., *Principles of Urban Transport Systems Planning*. New York: McGraw-Hill, 1974 (esp. Chap. 6).

MICHAELS, RICHARD M., "Two Simple Techniques for Determining Significance of Accident Reducing Measures," *Traffic Eng.*, p. 45 (Sept. 1966).

MORIN, DONALD A., "Application of Statistical Concepts to Accident Data," *Public Roads,* p. 135 (Apr. 1967).

RIGBY, J. P., AND P. J. HYDE, *Journeys to School: A Survey of Secondary Schools in Berkshire and Surrey,* Laboratory Report 776. Crowthorne, England: Transport and Road Research Laboratory, 1977.

SCHWAR, JOHANNES F., AND JOSE PUY-HUARTE, *Statistical Methods in Traffic Engineering*. Columbus, Ohio: Department of Civil Engineering, The Ohio State University, 1965.

18

TRANSPORTATION SAFETY

EDMUND J. CANTILLI

Polytechnic Institute of New York
Brooklyn, New York

Accidents (more correctly termed "incidents") are still thought of by some persons as "acts of God," or the result of luck or chance. Accident occurrence is considered to be "perhaps the last folklore subscribed to by rational men, including well-educated professionals who have been trained to identify and reject folklore in their own areas of competence."[1] The word "disaster," applied to the more catastrophic accidents, comes from the Latin for "evil star."

Accidents are *not* as uncontrollable as the weather, nor do they defy systematic study. Yet the greater part of the analysis that is performed with accident data in transportation is at the "macro" scale, and includes the tabulation of numbers and rates unrelated to true risk, which is often meaningless to the general public, including drivers and passengers. This is so because "micro" analysis is laborious and time-consuming, and requires the efforts of experienced engineers with good judgment. In addition, micro analysis is still a manual, individualized activity, and has not been systematized or applied to any great degree to automated data-processing procedures.

Often, solutions are proposed which appear to be based on a single panacea. Researchers or investigators may seek a "primary cause" or "proximate cause." But there *is* no single cause of any accident. A solution to the overall problem (which increases in scope and complexity almost daily) requires knowledge of the many causative factors that come together in combination, apparently coincidentally yet with traceable logic, to create the rare situation that leads to an incident.

Thus, when accidents are seen as true *incidents,* which result from a combination of circumstances or a chain of related events, they lend themselves to engineering study and systematic analysis. Engineering solutions (which must include some comprehension of operator, passenger, and pedestrian psychology) require knowledge of the characteristics of occurrence of accidents generally and in each transportation mode, of the major incident-producing conditions in each mode, and of the analytical tools and methods for both preventive activities and for accident investigation and analysis.

Transportation safety today

Since the beginning of the twentieth century, about 3 million people have lost their lives in transportation accidents in the United States alone; many millions more have suffered injuries; and the economic cost, or waste, is in the inestimable billions of dollars. Worldwide, the number of deaths connected with transportation may approximate 300,000 every year.

The last quarter of the twentieth century finds all transportation modes in a state of crisis. As population increases, transportation activity, economic restraints, and potential and actual conflicts all increase, but technical or procedural improvements do not take place at the same rate.

The crisis conditions associated with transportation are in *operation* and *maintenance, environmental impact,* and *fuel availability*. Each of these conditions affects personal safety. Increases in transportation operations expose operators, passengers, pedestrians, and bystanders to greater risks of injury and death. Declines in the quantity and quality of maintenance produce greater risk and incidence of failure. The use of fossil fuels, and spillages in the oceans, lakes, and rivers, affect ecosystems as large as the ocean, and as small as a forest, and eventually human health and well-being. Incidents involving the transport of hazardous materials release quantities of dangerous chemicals and other damaging materials into the atmosphere and onto the ground. Changes in the distribution, availability, and consumption of various fuels require transport over ever-in-

[1] WILLIAM HADDON, JR., EDWARD A. SUCHMAN, AND DAVID KLEIN, *Accident Research—Methods and Approaches,* Harper & Row, New York, 1964.

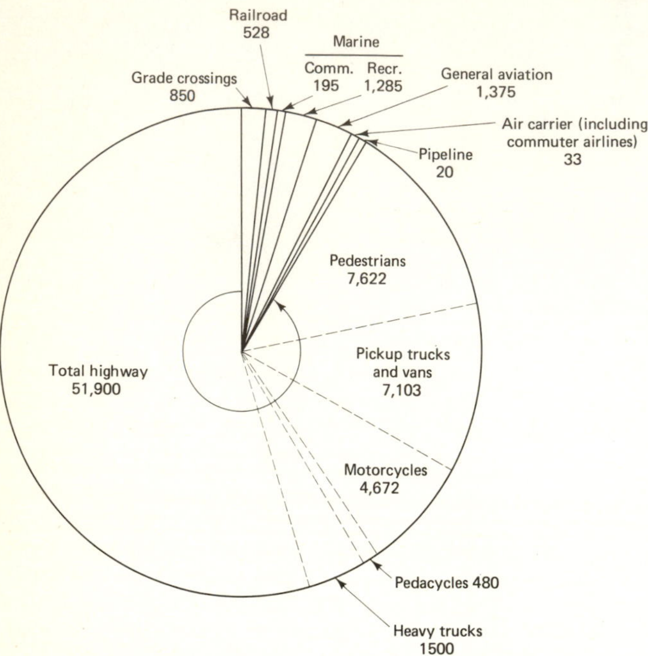

Figure 18.1. Distribution of transportation accidents, 1978. (Numbers are approximate.) SOURCE: Adapted from News release, National Transportation Safety Board, Washington, D.C., May 12, 1979.

creasing distances and into populated areas, at increasing risk.

Engineers must be in the forefront of accident *prevention*. Transportation is *movement;* engineers must be concerned with the safety of that movement, and be aware of the consequences of a lack of safety in design, construction, and operation. The immediate consequences are contained in the following statistics, which describe the current state of transportation safety in terms of incidents, injuries, and deaths resulting from transportation operations.

Figure 18.1 illustrates the distribution of approximately 56,430 fatalities in the United States by transportation mode for the year 1978. Motor vehicle traffic fatalities exceeded 50,000 for the first time in 5 years. The fatality *rate* also rose for the second straight year—from 3.24 deaths per 100 million vehicle-miles in 1977, to 3.27. General aviation fatalities reached 1690, the highest in more than 15 years. Waterborne transportation fatalities dropped to 179, the lowest number since 1973. Although recreational boating fatalities increased, this category experienced a record low fatality rate of 9.4 per 100,000 boats. Deaths resulting from incidents involving the transportation of hazardous materials were at a record high of 46.

Trends

Long-established trends of the numbers of accidents and fatalities continued upward after an abrupt decline occasioned by the fuel crisis of 1973–1974. Since most transportation accidents and fatalities are highway vehicle related, the reductions in highway travel caused by the fuel shortages were reflected in the improved statistics.

Figure 18.2 shows that the upward trend has been consistent since 1975, as more and more transportation activity creates more and more potential for error and conflict. Total transportation fatalities in 1978 increased by almost 4% over 1977, and continued an upward trend begun in 1976, after the 5-year low occasioned by the "energy crisis" of 1973–1974. Transportation fatalities had reached an all-time high of 58,400[2] in 1972, but fatalities represent only the tip of the iceberg. Transportation *accidents* in 1978 were reported to be more than 17,700,000, causing more than 2,000,000 injuries and costing approximately *$35 billion.*[3]

Causes and problem areas

In general, transportation accidents are caused by failure of one of the three major elements of a transportation system: the human (driver, pilot, engineer), the vehicle, or the guideway/environment. Improvements in each of these areas can be expected to improve safety generally, and to reduce the potential for failure.

In highway transportation, few accidents have been traced directly to mechanical failure of vehicles. Fewer still have been attributed to "failure" of the roadway, except for occasional direct involvement of potholes and other pavement conditions or defective traffic control devices, even though transportation engineers know there is a clear relationship between poor or substandard design or control measures and accident causation. The cause-and-effect relationships have yet to be established because the driver is expected to comprehend design and control inadequacies and compensate for them in the driving task. The resultant attribution of large percentages of highway accidents to driver failure (from 60 to 90% in many studies) does not serve the cause of safety. Human failure can as easily be said to be the cause of *all* accidents, because it is human beings who not only drive or steer vehicles, but who design and construct them, and design, construct, and operate the facilities that are used by vehicles of every mode. All too often blaming the driver simply hides the real cause.

The basic causes of transportation safety problems are those forces or situations that bring about overcrowding of the airways; a decline in maintenance of railroads, roadways, and bridges; reduced enforcement of necessary regulations; lack of attention to clear and apparent hazards; and ineffective inspections, training, or motivation of operating and maintenance personnel.

In addition, each transportation mode has clearly defined problem areas which can be attacked and concentrated upon, and which allow for limited, albeit highly effective, solutions when scarce resources are allocated properly.

---

[2] *Transportation Safety Information Report* (Oct., Nov., and Dec. 1978; Annual Summary), Research and Special Programs Administration, Transportation Systems Center, U.S. Department of Transportation, Washington, D.C., Mar. 1979.

[3] *Accident Facts, 1978 Edition,* National Safety Council, Chicago, June 1978.

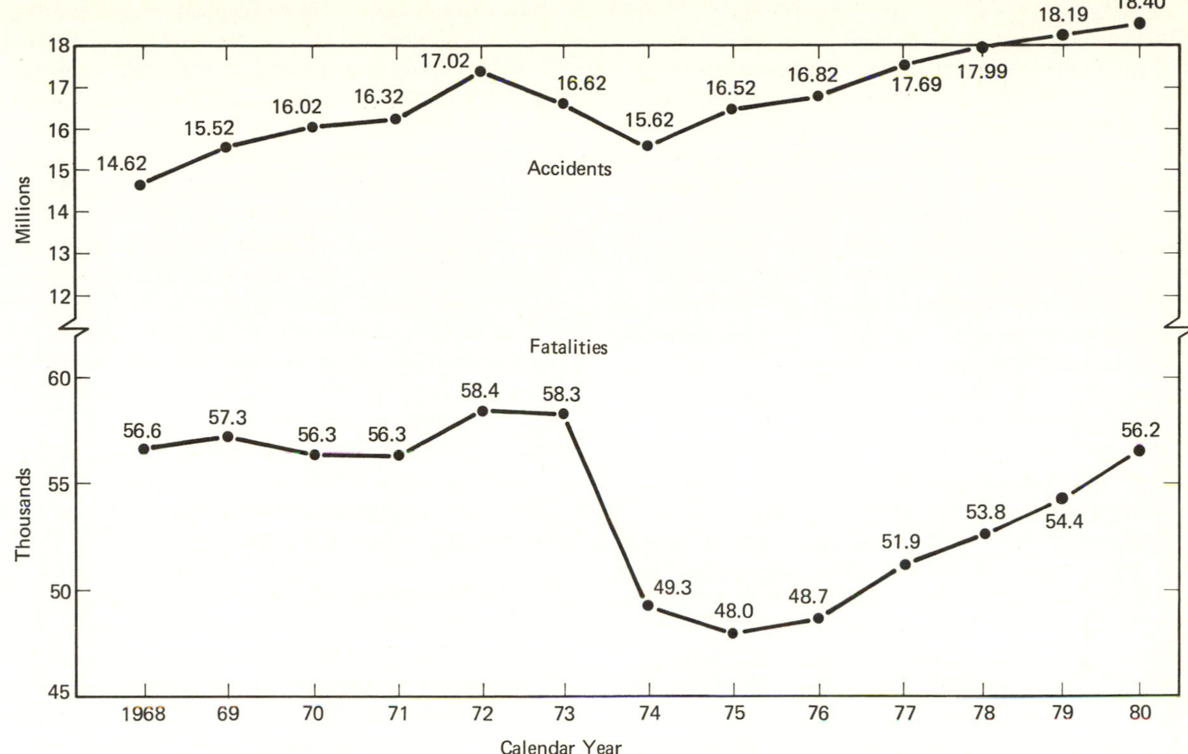

Figure 18.2. Transportation accidents and fatalities, 1968–1980. (Does not include waterborne transportation data.) SOURCE: *Transportation Safety Information Report,* Oct., Nov., and Dec. 1978, Annual Summary, U.S. Department of Transportation, Washington, D.C., March 1979. (1979–80 data added by author.)

Solutions

Solutions to transportation safety problems historically have been actions based in legislation, regulation, enforcement, education, and engineering. In recent years attempts also have been made to understand the psychology of unsafe behavior.

In *legislation,* governmental administrative structures and regulatory agencies are created, and money is appropriated for safety activities.

In *regulation,* rules are developed and promulgated which are intended to control the movements of vehicles of all modes in a safe manner. Regulation and certification of structures, vehicles, or personnel involved in transportation are also important regulatory-agency activities in the field of safety.

In *enforcement,* rules at various governmental levels are enforced by inspectors, examiners, and police, to ensure that safety regulations and legislation are carried out.

In *education,* classes in public and private schools at all levels teach many aspects of transportation safety. Special courses are designed to aid specialists and operating personnel in the performance of their daily safety-related duties. Governmental agencies present instructional material in the attempt to improve skills and awareness. Public information programs instruct the public in the driving of motor vehicles, the proper handling of bicycles and other transportation devices, and in some aspects of safety as passengers on public transport vehicles.

In *engineering,* safety begins in conceptual planning and proceeds into the design of vehicles, guideways (or traveled ways), and control systems of every mode. Safety is incorporated into the construction of transportation facilities. Finally, engineering is involved in daily operations and the maintenance of safety-related devices.

Transportation engineering solutions to major safety problems in the United States involve the federal government even though actual corrective action is, of necessity, taken at the state and local levels, because states and local agencies vary in their capacity and commitment to the time-consuming efforts required in safety work. Unfortunately, funds provided to local jurisdictions and state agencies from federal sources may be dissipated by spreading them over "safety" activities as varied as the TOPICS (Traffic Operations to Improve Capacity and Safety) program, correcting congested and unsafe intersections, driver-training programs (whose efficacy has never been proven), and the enforcement of unrealistic regulations. The lack of an overall, comprehensive approach has made transportation safety efforts less effective than they might be.

The U.S. Department of Transportation, through its several administrations, exercises some control over the design aspects of all transportation modes. The degree of such control varies considerably with each mode.

Study approaches

There are three categories of engineering studies related to transportation safety: the before-the-fact preventive approach; the alternative approach, which seeks to reduce accident severity; and the after-the-fact study of accidents and accident occurrence. It can be said that the study of accidents *is* a preventive point of view, in that lessons learned from the occurrence of a specific accident or a specific *type* of accident are applied toward the prevention of future accidents; however, in all modes the accident-study approach and the preventive approach have developed separately, with the latest body of techniques in preventive safety study having been developed as *transportation system safety*.[4] This concept is discussed later.

Accident prevention. In general, preventive measures start in design, at which stage engineers attempt to foresee situations that may lead to accidents and the consequences of the accident itself. This divides into two areas: design of the vehicular "environment" and design of the vehicle itself.

The environment, as a concept, includes a "guideway," whether physical or defined in space; the areas contiguous to the guideway; the physical features within that contiguous area, such as natural features or man-made structures and other physical elements; the control devices within or near the guideway or a part of the system itself; operating regulations which govern the system; and other vehicles making up the traffic stream.

Vehicle design engineers attempt to provide a structure that accomplishes its intended purpose, vehicular control devices that will function under all foreseeable circumstances, and the "fail-safe" concept, most notably applied in aircraft and aerospace vehicle design, which provides a "fall-back" system or device in the event of malfunction of critical elements of the system.

The next state at which preventive concepts are applied is in construction of the environment and the vehicle, during which proper materials and methods are used to further the intention of preventing accidents or preventing severe consequences should accidents occur.

Prevention is then exercised as an engineering point of view in the operation of a transportation facility or system. Prevention of accidents and minimization of severity should be kept in mind in designing routes and schedules, creating operating procedures and personnel tasks, and in scheduling inspections and reviews of operating activities and experience.

Prevention is also the basis of adequate maintenance schedules and procedures in the upkeep of both the vehicular environment and vehicles themselves. Each transportation mode stresses specific preventive activities.

Finally, training and licensing (or certification) procedures for operating and other personnel involved in all modes is, basically, a preventive approach to transportation safety. Transportation engineers may have some input into the training and licensing aspects of transportation safety, but the degree of technical control over these aspects of safety activity is governed by political, economic, and legislative influences over each transportation mode.

Accident impact attenuation. This approach involves means for reducing the severity of the results of an incident. As an engineering approach it is not well advanced, and the degree of interest and activity in attenuation is different in each mode. The seatbelt is a notable example of this approach. It is one thing to prove their usefulness and yet another to convince drivers and passengers to use them. Some devices, such as air bags and helmets for motorcyclists, become items of major controversy. Cleared slopes for runaway vehicles, breakaway signs and energy attenuators are used. Strict regulations control seating and standing activities of airline passengers. Intercity buses are permitted no standees, but urban transit riders are usually free to ride either sitting or standing.

Accident study and analysis. Accident analysis on the macroscale considers accident occurrence in a town, city, county, region, state or country, or worldwide. On the *microscale,* concentration is on accidents occurring on a specific network, facility, or location (airport, train station, or highway exit, interchange, curve, or intersection).

Macroscale Analysis. On the macroscale, accident data are summarized in tabular or chart form, (see Charts 1 through 19), providing a record of the performance of a region or a country in terms of one or more transportation modes. Accident occurrence, severity (in terms of fatalities, injuries, or property damage), and *rates* provide a statistical illustration of safety performance.

Rates are intended to provide a yardstick of safety related to the amount of exposure to danger involved in the transport mode. For instance, the common rate used in highway traffic safety is "accidents (or injuries or fatalities) per 100 million vehicle-miles," on the assumption that the number of vehicles, multiplied by the number of miles (estimated) driven by those vehicles, is a reasonable measure of the exposure to danger of the occupants of the vehicles.

At highway intersections, a rate based on number of vehicles entering the intersection is more appropriate.

Macroscale studies are rarely intended to point toward solutions to safety problems (except when a town's experience with nighttime accidents is out of proportion to expected numbers in comparable towns, say). But it is necessary to understand trends in accident occurrence, and to attempt to relate them to economic and other phenomena.

Microscale Analysis. Microscale accident studies can be subdivided into the study of individual accidents, known as "accident reconstruction," and the study of "high-accident locations," as they are known in traffic engineering. In this latter analysis, patterns of occurrence and type are analyzed for clues to causation, generally related to design and control elements at the location in question.

Accident reconstruction is performed in all transportation modes and practiced at all governmental levels. The National Transportation Safety Board, an independent federal

[4] Michael Horodniceanu and Edmund J. Cantilli, *Transportation System Safety,* D.C. Heath, Lexington, Mass., 1979.

agency, investigates major accidents in all modes within the limits of its funding. Each modal segment of the industry has its own methods, personnel, and forms for recording the results of an investigation. In air transportation accidents, the technique of accident reconstruction has reached its highest levels of detailed efficiency.

Locational Analysis is conducted at high-accident-frequency locations. The studies are based upon the individual accident report as a basic document. This procedure has been developed to its fullest in highway traffic safety, because the method requires relatively large numbers of accidents to occur at or near the same location, or for relatively large numbers of the same *type* of accident to occur on a facility or stretch of roadway.

Highway safety

Trends

Highway traffic accidents, injuries, and deaths continue as the major safety problem in transportation.

Passenger automobiles are the type of vehicle having the largest percentage of fatalities.

Trucks have a greater involvement in multiple-vehicle crashes than does any other vehicle type.

Most fatal accidents involving *motorcycles* result in the death of the motorcycle occupant rather than an occupant of the other vehicle involved. Similarly, in fatal collisions involving a truck and another vehicle, the fatality usually occurs in the other vehicle.

The largest percentage increases in motor vehicle traffic fatalities from 1977 to 1978 were in the categories of *pickup truck and van occupants* (13%) and *motorcyclists* (9.6%). In these two categories, increases in the popularity of these vehicles are reflected in accident figures.

Figure 18.3 shows the continuing upward trend of motor vehicle accidents, interrupted briefly by the fuel shortage of 1973–1974. Fatalities show an even greater rate of decline during the fuel shortage, but an even greater rate of increase since 1975.

As the number of vehicle-miles traveled increases (Figure 18.4), and fatalities remain relatively stable (except for the fuel shortage period of 1973–1974), fatality *rates* show a long-term decline. The 3-year period 1976–1978, however, showed a gradual increase.

Over a longer period of time, with data from 1925 (see

Figure 18.3. Motor vehicle accidents and traffic fatalities, 1968–1980. SOURCE: *Transportation Safety Information Report,* Oct., Nov., and Dec. 1978, Annual Summary, U.S. Department of Transportation, Washington, D.C., March 1979. (1979–80 data added by author.)

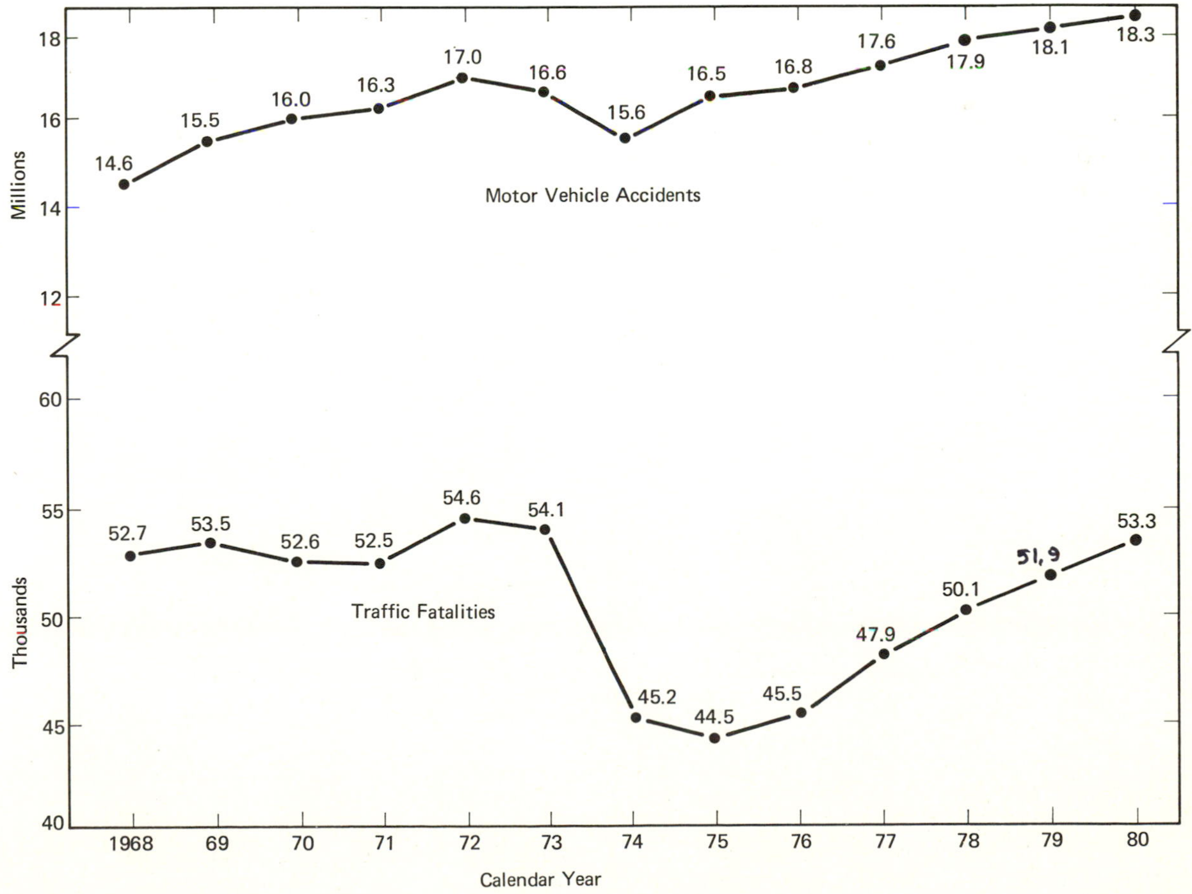

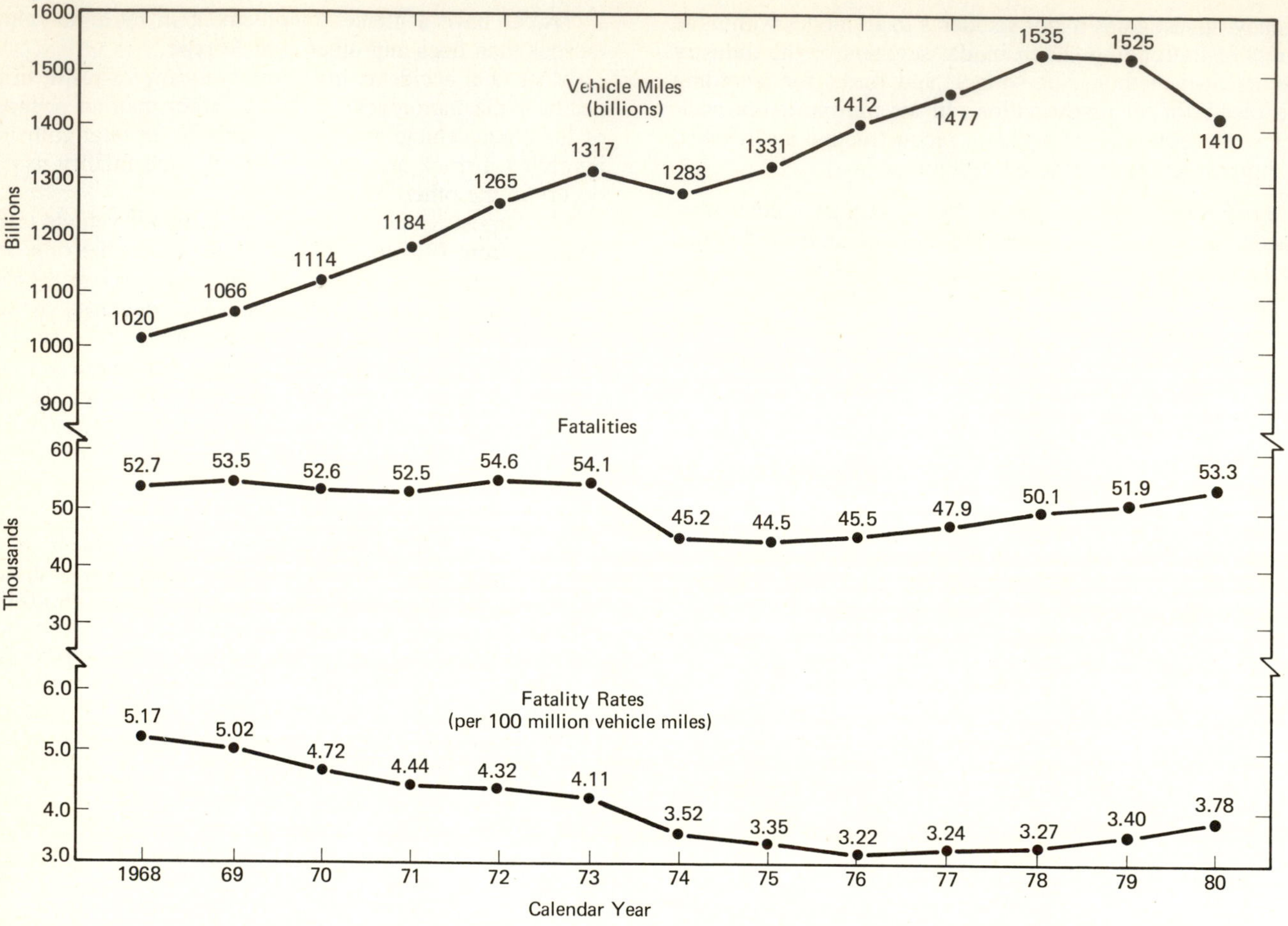

Vehicle Miles (billions)

Billions: 1600, 1500, 1400, 1300, 1200, 1100, 1000, 900

1968: 1020; 69: 1066; 70: 1114; 71: 1184; 72: 1265; 73: 1317; 74: 1283; 75: 1331; 76: 1412; 77: 1477; 78: 1535; 79: 1525; 80: 1410

Fatalities

Thousands: 60, 50, 40, 30

1968: 52.7; 69: 53.5; 70: 52.6; 71: 52.5; 72: 54.6; 73: 54.1; 74: 45.2; 75: 44.5; 76: 45.5; 77: 47.9; 78: 50.1; 79: 51.9; 80: 53.3

Fatality Rates (per 100 million vehicle miles)

6.0, 5.0, 4.0, 3.0

1968: 5.17; 69: 5.02; 70: 4.72; 71: 4.44; 72: 4.32; 73: 4.11; 74: 3.52; 75: 3.35; 76: 3.22; 77: 3.24; 78: 3.27; 79: 3.40; 80: 3.78

Calendar Year

Figure 18.4. Motor vehicle traffic fatality rates, 1968–1980. SOURCE: *Transportation Safety Information Report,* Oct., Nov., and Dec. 1978, Annual Summary, U.S. Department of Transportation, Washington, D.C., March 1979. (1979–80 data added by author.)

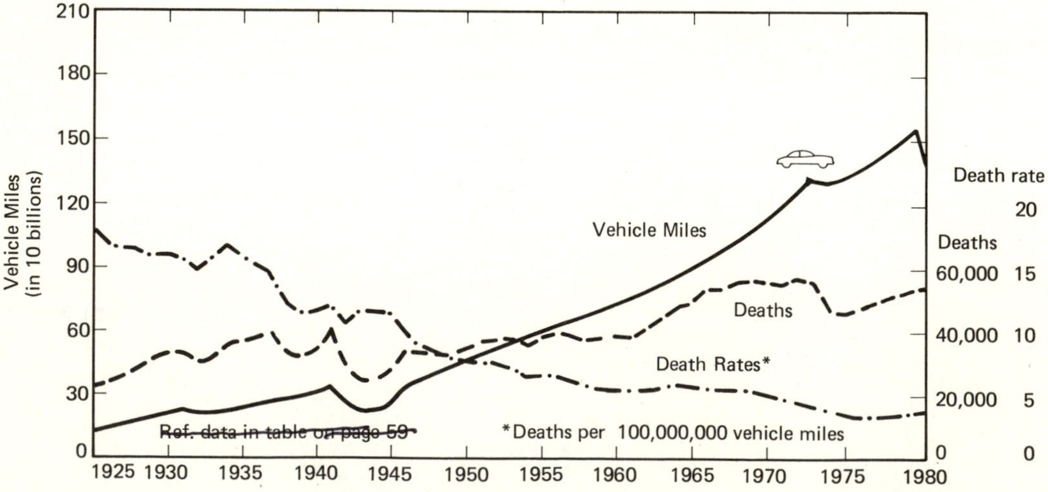

Figure 18.5. Travel, deaths, and death rates. SOURCE: *Accident Facts, 1978 Edition,* National Safety Council, Chicago, June 1978. (1979–80 data added by author.)

Figure 18.5), the general, long-term trends can be seen more clearly. The fuel shortage of 1973–1974, and imposition of the 55-mph speed limit, are seen to have had very temporary and limited effects on the general upward trend of vehicle-miles driven and number of deaths. The trend in the death *rate* may or may not have stabilized at a rate below 3.5 per 100 million vehicle-miles or may be increasing again.

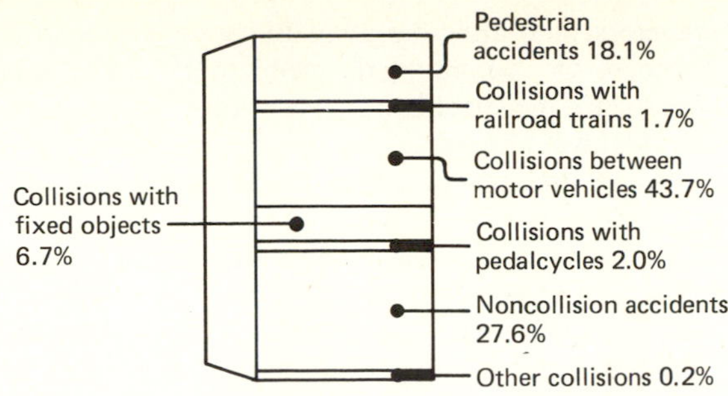

Figure 18.6. Percent traffic fatalities by causes, 1977. SOURCE: *MVMA Motor Vehicle Facts and Figures '78,* Motor Vehicle Manufacturers' Association of the United States, Inc., Detroit, Mich., 1979.

Causes and problem areas

Fatalities in 1977 were distributed as shown in Figure 18.6. Collisions between motor vehicles are seen to be the largest single category of traffic fatalities. "Noncollision" accidents (many of which involve collision with a fixed object) are second.

Identifiable problem areas in highway traffic safety include:

- Pedestrian–vehicle conflicts
- Vehicle–vehicle conflicts
- Interactions of differently sized vehicles
- Inadequate or impaired driving ability
- Railroad–highway grade crossings
- Inadequate communication with the driver (signs, markings, signals), and between drivers
- Deterioration of physical plant (reduced maintenance on highways and bridges)
- Roadside safety hazards

About 18% of the motor-vehicle-related deaths are pedestrian deaths (about 8000 in 1978).

Intersection accidents account for the major proportion of urban accidents.

The trend toward smaller automobiles and larger trucks has created a major problem on the highways, a problem that is aggravated by increases in motorcycle use; on many roads, bicycles and mopeds are added to the problem.

A majority of accidents are still attributed to "human error," or driver impairment through the use of alcohol or other drugs, even though it is clear that only minor advances can be expected in controlling this problem. At the same time, improvements in vehicle design and control, and highway design and control measures, have not been exhausted.

The railroad–highway grade crossing problem is one that should be clearly understood by transportation engineers and treated as an illogical intersection of two vastly different modes. Although it is economically impractical to eliminate all grade crossings within a brief time period, grade separation is the only positive engineering solution available and should be scheduled over a reasonable period. Other treatments for rail–highway grade crossings are interim solutions at best.

Poorly designed, placed, and maintained signs, poorly timed signals, and poorly maintained or nonexistent markings still abound in many areas of the country. It was stated in 1979[5] that bridges in the United States "are collapsing at the rate of one a day." And by 1979, 12 years after the U.S. House of Representatives' Subcommittee on Federal-aid Highways hearings pointed out the roadside-hazards or "booby-traps" problem on high-speed roads, deaths attributable to this kind of single-vehicle accident were again approaching 17,000 per year.[6]

Solutions

In highways, the U.S. Federal Highway Administration traditionally exercises control over the design, operation, traffic control, and maintenance aspects of federally aided highways and roads. Control is exercised through adopted standards and guidelines, applied at various state and municipal levels, and is more stringent for federally supported or subsidized classifications of roads than it is for local streets. FHWA also provides Federal-aid funds for safety construction and support programs.

The National Highway Traffic Safety Administration has concentrated its efforts on the development of safer vehicles, in terms of the structural design of motor vehicles and the restraint systems (including airbags and seatbelt/shoulder harnesses) designed for the safety of vehicle occupants. NHTSA works with the automobile manufacturing industry to improve the crashworthiness of motor vehicles. NHTSA also provides Federal-aid funds to states for non-highway-oriented safety programs.

Solutions to pedestrian–vehicle conflicts require the recognition, by legislators and engineers especially, that the interface between pedestrians and motor vehicles is an artificial one, and therefore inherently a highly dangerous one. The onus for safety is *not* entirely on the pedestrian, although the consequences almost inevitably are. The problem seems to have no likely solution, because pedestrians may decide to cross a traffic stream wherever they may choose, exposing themselves to danger.

Unfortunately, the traffic engineer has generally designed for the safe and expeditious movement of *vehicular traffic,* which has not been conducive to the safe movement of pedestrians. Traffic signals adjusted to the requirements of vehicles may not allow for children or the elderly to cross a road safely; pedestrian overpasses or underpasses which require the pedestrian to expend a great deal of energy in climbing stairs may not attract usage and will, therefore, often not contribute to safety.

Many vehicle–vehicle conflicts can be removed with the construction of highway interchanges, but the impracticability of converting every street crossing to an interchange leaves a major problem. Intersections at grade require the voluntary obedience of every driver. When such obedience breaks down, accidents ensue. Design and traffic control

[5]Statement made by JOHN S. HASSEL, Deputy Administrator, Federal Highway Administration, U.S. Department of Transportation, at *First National Symposium on Transportation System Safety,* Washington, D.C., May 7–9, 1979.

[6]*MVMA Motor Vehicle Facts and Figures '78,* Motor Vehicle Manufacturers' Association of the United States, Inc., Detroit, Mich., 1979.

improvements aid in the solution to this problem, but enforcement of legitimate and logical regulations is absolutely necessary to underpin voluntary obedience.

Vehicle size disparities have become greater over the years, and are therefore more dangerous. The lack of coordination between federal agencies, such as the National Highway Traffic Safety Administration and the Federal Highway Administration, have led to a worsening of the situation. Trucks have become wider and longer and higher off the ground, and private cars have become smaller and lighter and closer to the ground. Vehicle–vehicle conflicts then become more dangerous, and vehicle–roadway interactions become more difficult to control.

The *driver* continues to be blamed for most accidents. Although this may be true when considering "proximate cause" as the point at which a driver has made an incorrect decision in response to a given situation, it is not a determination that provides for practical solutions, unless engineers consider everything that led to the incorrect decision.

Improved driving ability would be the response to pure driver fault, but programs for improving driving ability through high school driver training programs have not been proven to be effective. In addition, driver licensing or testing programs are not sufficiently rigorous, nor is there any hope of their becoming sufficiently rigorous to produce desired changes in accident statistics. The range of reactive abilities of drivers is so wide as to make the design of vehicles and highway facilities for an "average" driver rather inadequate, just as the design of safe stopping distances on the basis of average driver eye height, in an era of vast ranges due to vehicle design, is becoming increasingly unrealistic.

Railroad–highway grade crossings represent a problem with a known solution: grade separation. However, cost is seen as an obstacle to the speedy realization of this solution. Yet means do exist for assessing the relative hazard at each crossing in any jurisdiction. From this point it is a simple step to the rational listing of crossings for priority of replacement. However, there are jurisdictional and political obstacles to this solution.

Communication problems are well understood and not beyond the technical capabilities of transportation engineers. However, lack of funds, and unsystematic approaches to the identification and solution of individual problems, delay needed improvements in this area. The installation of high-technology experimental systems at some locations, while poor or unmaintained installations of standard control systems are contributing to accident causation somewhere else, illustrates a lack of comprehensiveness in approach.

Lack of maintenance is a major problem of the current period. Deterioration of roads (including the Interstate highway system) is related to increases in fatalities. Filling potholes, repairing guardrails, rehabilitating deteriorated bridges, correcting illegible signs or replacing them, are all basic activities in a solution of the safety problem. Research into complex and subtle control devices and futuristic systems seems inappropriate when the existing physical plant is deteriorating at a rapid and unchecked rate.

Roadside hazards remain a major problem after more than a decade of awareness on the part of highway designers and operators, and after the availability of the technology and the means for eliminating the problem. In spite of money appropriated for the specific purpose of removing or treating roadside highway hazards, the number of annual single-vehicle accidents where vehicles encroach on the roadside appears to be returning to the figure of 17,000 which occurred in 1967. Transportation engineers should be the first to recognize this problem, because it is one of the few (railroad–highway grade crossings being another) which lends itself to logical engineering solutions through identification, design, and proper resource allocation.

Study approaches

Accident prevention. Highway engineers design the vehicular environment on the basis of standards created for safe operation at design speed. Vertical and horizontal geometry, pavement surface texture and roadside features are all designed to standards that emanate from the Federal Highway Administration and professional groups such as the Institute for Transportation Engineers and the American Association of State Highway and Transportation Officials. Traffic control features are also standardized and designed in the interests of safety.

The role of the National Highway Traffic Safety Administration in accident prevention in the United States has already been discussed. Federal agencies are also involved in the improvement of driver training and licensing.

State departments of transportation are involved in preventive efforts in maintenance and rehabilitation of highways, and the installation and maintenance of traffic control devices. State motor vehicle departments also engage in preventive efforts when improving licensing procedures, controlling poor drivers, developing alcohol programs, and disseminating literature and posters in the cause of safety education.

State motor vehicle inspection programs are of course intended to be major preventive efforts in the reduction of accident occurrence, but relatively few accidents are attributed to vehicle malfunction.

Accident impact attenuation. In the mid-1960s, as the numbers of traffic accidents climbed, and deaths rose toward 60,000 per year, the public, legislators, and those engineers and administrators involved in highway operations took an interest in the problem from two aspects: the design of the vehicle and the design of the highway. The National Highway Traffic Safety Administration has concentrated on the design of the interior and the structure of the passenger car, bus, and truck, to alleviate the extent and characteristics of the injuries that occur as a result of the "secondary impact" of a passenger within a vehicle, when striking the interior of the vehicle. This has led to regulations requiring padding of interiors, recessing of knobs and handles, and development of "collapsible" steering-wheel-and-column assemblies, on the one hand, and seatbelts and the development of air bags and other "passive restraint" systems, on the other hand. This work is not yet complete, since both "active" restraint (requiring the conscious action of a driver) and "passive" restraint (which takes place without thought or action of the driver) as concepts, have their partisans and opponents. This problem is clearest when considering motorcycle safety. Decreases were recorded in head-injury-related deaths after passage of laws requiring the use of helmets in many states, and subsequent increases in such deaths occurred after a number of states were prevailed upon to repeal such laws.

In the area of structural improvements to vehicles for safety, NHTSA has required "roll-over" bars to prevent the tops of passenger vehicles from crushing occupants, side rails through doors to absorb right-angle impacts, and, in conjunction with the Environmental Protection Agency, devices to reduce air pollution for the improvement of environmental safety.

The Federal Highway Administration has improved safety standards in the design of roadsides, gores, and medians to reduce the problem of single-vehicle accidents. Positive dividers on high-speed roads have reduced head-on collisions, the most severe accident possible, to a considerable degree. Guardrails, protecting vehicles from bridge abutments and piers and other roadside obstacles, are standard treatment for which guidelines and recommended practices exist.[7,8,9] The attenuation of single-vehicle impacts against fixed objects in roadsides and gores has been recommended, and funds have been made available to states and local jurisdictions. Designs have been developed for "breakaway" traffic sign and street-light poles, to eliminate the deceleration stresses of unyielding structures.

[7] *Guardrail Performance and Design,* NCHRP Report 115, Highway Research Board, Washington, D.C., 1971.

[8] *Location, Selection, and Maintenance of Highway Traffic Barriers,* NCHRP Report 118, Highway Research Board, Washington, D.C., 1971.

[9] *Highway Guardrail—Determination of Need and Geometric Requirements—with Particular Reference to Beam-Type Guardrail,* Special Report, 81, Highway Research Board, Washington, D.C., 1964.

Accident study and analysis. At the *macroscale,* accident statistics are gathered and summarized in a manner that will allow for generalized conclusions to be drawn as to where, when, and under what conditions accidents are occurring. This can be done at any level, from the national, to the state, county, or municipal, to the road network or facility (such as a major route or a turnpike). At the broadest level, such statistical summaries will provide information that may lead to legislation or regulatory measures intended to alleviate an aspect of the total problem. By this means the 55-mph maximum speed was seen as not only a fuel-conservation measure, but as a device for reducing highway fatalities.

At the state level, summaries provide a basis for comparison among states, and for comparison of regions within a state with the "norm" for the state as a whole.

The State of New York's *Motor Vehicle Statistics—1977 Accident and Operational Statistical Data,* a typical state document, presents summaries of "accident statistics," a breakdown of how, where, and when accidents occur, statewide, by type and condition of variables. Figure 18.7 shows proportions of state accidents by roadway surface condition, light conditions, and weather conditions at time of accident.

Data describing pedestrian accidents, motorcycle accidents, and bicycle accidents are included, as are accidents involving school buses and county accident data. Data for specific towns and villages are available upon request to the Department of Motor Vehicles.

At the *microscale,* accident reconstruction requires the drawing of inferences concerning the interactions of speed, position on the road, driver reaction, comprehension and obedience to traffic control devices, and evasive tactics.

The objectives of the accident reconstruction procedure[10] are to determine all the physical factors that clearly define

[10] RUDOLF LAMPERT, *Motor Vehicle Accident Reconstruction and Cause Analysis,* The Michie Company, Charlottesville, Va., 1978.

Figure 18.7. Typical results of macro-scale accident analysis—accidents as a function of road, light, and weather conditions. SOURCE: *Motor Vehicle Statistics—1977 Accident and Operational Statistical Data,* State of New York, Department of Motor Vehicles, Albany, N.Y., 1978.

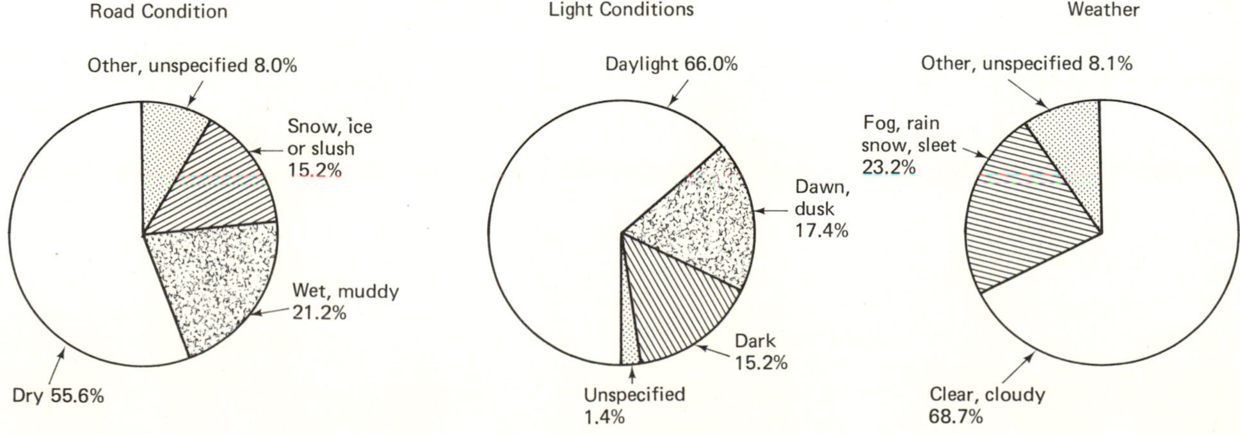

the collision and the production of injuries to human beings, plus all the physical factors that were involved in possibly leading to the accident. This includes both "pre"-accident factors, such as speed, direction, and characteristics of the vehicle; attitude and ability of the operator; and condition of the guideway and other environmental factors; and "post"-accident factors, such as final resting place of the vehicle or vehicle parts and passengers; skid marks or other evidence of maneuvering at the time of the accident; and degree of damage or injury incurred.

Data will often be insufficient for drawing reliable conclusions, in which case additional information will be obtained from personal observation or published sources. If measurements are lacking but photographs are available, reconstruction may require elementary photogrammetry to obtain mapping data.

Essential to accident reconstruction is the ability to recognize the different kinds of tire marks on the road, such as braking skidmarks, steering yaw marks, acceleration scuffs, and collisions scrubs. Certain aspects of vehicle damage must also be recognized, including contact damage areas, static and moving contact points, and the direction of thrust or force.

Accident reconstruction uses basic engineering knowledge of vehicle motion analysis, force analysis, and mechanical energy. The basic relationship for straight-line motion is

$$V = \frac{S}{t} \tag{18.1}$$

where V = velocity

S = distance

t = time

$$a = \frac{\Delta V}{\Delta t} = \frac{V_2 - V_1}{t_2 - t_1} \tag{18.2}$$

where a = acceleration or deceleration of the vehicle

t_1 = time at beginning of velocity change

t_2 = time at end of velocity change

V_1 and V_2 are the velocities at times t_1 and t_2

Force analysis requires knowledge of mass in slugs (kilograms) measured as lb-s^2/ft (newton-s^2/m).

where m = meters

s = seconds

lb = pounds

kg = kilograms

The basic equation is

$$F_R = ma \tag{18.3}$$

where F_R = resultant force acting on the body

m = mass of the body

The weight of the body, W, may be expressed as mg, where g is the acceleration due to gravity.

In rotation,

$$M_R = Ie \tag{18.4}$$

where M_R = net or resultant moment

I = mass moment of inertia

e = angular acceleration

Mechanical energy may be potential or kinetic. The potential energy E_p of a weight W at a height h is given by

$$E_p = Wh \tag{18.5}$$

The kinetic energy E_K of a vehicle of mass m moving at a velocity V is given by

$$E_K = \frac{1}{2}mV^2 \tag{18.6}$$

In a collision, the change in kinetic energy of a vehicle or a body is

$$\Delta E_K = \frac{1}{2}m(V_1^2 - V_2^2) \tag{18.7}$$

where V_1 = velocity immediately before impact

V_2 = velocity immediately after impact

Consideration of friction must also be brought into the analysis. In most collisions, skidding due to locked brakes occurs. The friction factor f between the tires and the roadway surface determines the size of the retarding force which, acting through the length of the skid d, absorbs kinetic energy. This relationship is described by

$$d = \frac{V_1^2 - V_2^2}{2gf} \tag{18.8}$$

If V_2 is taken to be zero, the "skid-to-stop" distance is calculated or, by expressing (18.8) in terms of V_1, one can calculate the initial speed before a skid-to-stop:

$$V_1 = \sqrt{2gfd} \tag{18.9}$$

It is usually convenient to express V_1 in mph or km/h and d in ft or m; the following versions of (18.9) include the required conversion factors and the value of g, the acceleration due to gravity:

$$V_1 = \sqrt{30fd} \tag{18.9a}$$

(V_1 in mph, d in ft)

$$V_1 = \sqrt{254fd} \tag{18.9b}$$

(V_1 in km/h, d in m)

For example, suppose that a vehicle skids 50 ft (15.2 m) with a friction factor of 0.7; its skid-to-stop speed calculated from this formula is 32 mph or 52 km/h. However, in most accidents a collision occurs before skidding has stopped the vehicle. Because of this, the speed at the beginning of the skid will be greater than the speed estimated for a skid-to-stop. If the speed at the end of a skid is estimated from statements, damage done in the collision, or other evidence, that speed must *not* be added to the skid-to-stop speed, but combined as follows:

$$V = \sqrt{V_1^2 + V_2^2} \tag{18.10}$$

where V = speed at the beginning of the skid

V_1 = skid-to-stop speed based on skid mark length

V_2 = speed at the end of the skid

In the example given above, if, instead of stopping at the end of the skid, the vehicle fell into a ditch with a "take-off" speed of 35 mph (56 km/h), its speed at the beginning of the skid would have been

$$V = \sqrt{32^2 + 35^2} = 47 \text{ mph or } \sqrt{52^2 + 56^2} = 76 \text{ km/h}$$

In estimating collision speeds, the concept of conservation of momentum is useful in deriving speed changes. Momentum equals mass × velocity or weight × speed. Like velocity, it is a vector quantity, requiring that its direction be specified. The total momentum of two colliding vehicles is the same before and after the collision. Kinetic energy, however, is lost, doing the damage. The general equation is

$$W_1V_1 + W_2V_2 = W_1V_1' + W_2V_2' \tag{18.11}$$

where the subscripts 1 and 2 indicate vehicles 1 and 2, and V and V' are speeds before and after impact, respectively.

This equation neglects the coefficient of resolution, which is very small in most vehicle collisions. As simplified, the equation provides a general approximation of the velocity changes that occur during a collision.

Equation (18.11) is most easily solved graphically, as shown in Figure 18.8. In this diagram the length of each vector represents the amount of momentum (weight × speed), and the direction represents the direction of the motion of the body. If we know the velocities and their directions *after* the collision and the directions of velocities *before* the collision, the momentums and, therefore, the velocities *before* the collision can be approximated.

A checklist for the collection of data in an investigation of an automobile accident includes *environmental factors,* such as:

- Roadway geometrics
- Road surface conditions
- Traffic control devices

After Collision Data:

$V_1' = 30$ $W_1 = 3.5 \times 10^3$ $V_1'W_1 = 105$

$V_2' = 45$ $W_2 = 2.0 \times 10^3$ $V_2'W_2 = 90$

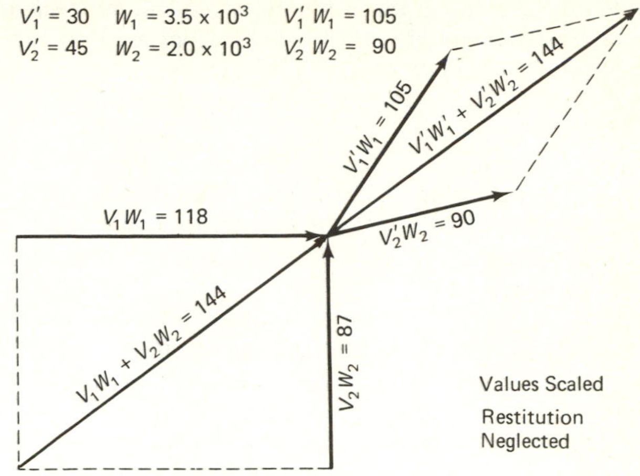

Before Collision Calculations:

$V_1W_1 = 118$ $V_1 = 118/3.5 = 33.7$

$V_2W_2 = 87$ $V_2 = 87/2.0 = 43.5$

Figure 18.8. Graphical solution to the momentum exchange between two vehicles in an angle collision. The combined momentum of vehicles *before* collision is equal in amount and direction to the combined momentum *after* collision. SOURCE: Institute of Traffic Engineers, *Transportation and Traffic Engineering Handbook,* Prentice-Hall, Englewood Cliffs, N.J., 1976.

- Traffic regulations in force
- Roadside environment (devices, obstructions)
- Ambient conditions (weather, wind, noise, temperature)
- Visibility restrictions
- Markings caused during accidents (tire prints, skid marks, metal-caused gouges)

vehicle factors, such as:

- Vehicle identification numbers, mileage, inspection dates, equipment information
- Condition of vehicle before crash, such as brake systems, tires, windshield, etc.
- Damage caused by collision
- Brake system condition
- Condition of steering system
- Conditions of tires, suspension, lights

and *human factors,* such as:

- Position of occupant
- Weight, height, age, sex
- Driver education, experience, familiarity with area
- Use of alcohol, drugs
- Extent and degree of injuries
- Driver responses (as determined)

Locational Analysis. An engineering locational analysis is usually made where accidents of a similar type occur at the same location, or at similar locations. To be most effective this kind of study must be done systematically and comprehensively.

Locations are selected, accident occurrence is analyzed, recommendations are made for improvement, the benefits of the improvement are estimated, locations are prioritized for maximum benefit and orderly improvement, and the effects of the improvements are measured after they have been made.

Because all analyses depend so completely on the basic document, the traffic accident report, deficiencies in this basic data source may make it difficult to locate accidents properly; the data may be incomplete, and minor accidents may be omitted.

The high-accident-location analysis procedure is described in detail in the *Manual of Traffic Engineering Studies*,[11] which provides forms and a procedural guide to the completion of a study.

Locations are generally selected on the basis of numbers of accidents occurring within a given period, usually five in 1 year at a specific location. However, severity should be considered in choosing locations. Severity is usually indicated by classifying accidents as *fatal, personal injury*, or *property damage only*. However, there is a range of severity represented by the term "personal injury," just as there is a wide range in the "property damage" category. Schemes exist[12,13] for weighting traffic accidents by severity, and analysts should so weight all accidents in the data base.

This severity-weighting process allows for ranking specific locations in three ways: by numbers of accidents, by total severity (a summation), and by a combination of frequency and severity (multiplication). Rates can be developed for each of these values. A comparison of ranking systems is given in Table 18-1.

[11]*Manual of Traffic Engineering Studies* (latest ed.), Institute of Transportation Engineers, Arlington, Va.

[12]EDMUND J. CANTILLI, "Statistical Evaluation of Traffic Accident Severity," *Bull. 208*, Highway Research Board, Washington, D.C., 1959.

[13]S. P. BAKER ET AL., "Injury Severity Score: A Method for Describing Patients with Multiple Injuries and Evaluating Emergency Care," *J. of Trauma, 14* (1974).

Locations are defined by a means that identifies similar characteristics producing (generally) similar types of accidents. *Intersections*, segments of streets *between intersections*, *merging* areas, *divergence* areas (gores), *weaving* areas, *on-ramps*, *off-ramps*, and so on, are commonly used as convenient locations. Long tangent sections may be divided into smaller segments as related to roadside features, such as bridges. Segments should not be less than 0.1 mi (0.2 km) long.

Locations should be characterized by type, such as:

Urban
- two-lane
- four or more lanes (undivided)
- four or more lanes (divided)
- freeway

Rural
- two-lane
- four or more lanes (undivided)
- four or more lanes (divided)
- freeway

and by control features, such as:

- No control
- YIELD sign
- Two-way STOP signs
- Three or four-way STOP signs
- Traffic signals
- Grade separation

Many factors contribute to the risk at a given location, including:

- Physical characteristics, such as geometric design and sight distances
- One-way or two-way traffic movement
- Irregular movements, such as turning or backing
- Speed
- Quality of traffic flow
- Size and performance characteristics of vehicles
- Volume of traffic
- Visibility conditions
- Clarity, comprehensibility of control devices

TABLE 18–1
Examples of Different Methods of Ranking Highway Sections According to Accidents Reported*

Line	Section Number										Total	Average
	1	2	3	4	5	6	7	8	9	10		
Basic Data												
Length in miles (km)	2.5	3.2	2.8	5.0	1.0	1.4	3.3	4.0	2.0	3.0	28.2	2.8
Average daily traffic $\times$ 10^{-2}	40	36	35	30	28	28	25	23	20	22	—	—
Total accidents	23	12	10	7	2	5	7	9	15	8	98	9.8
Fatal accidents	0	0	0	0	1	0	0	0	0	0	2	0.3
Injury accidents	4	2	2	0	0	0	0	1	3	2	15	2.6
Property damage only	19	10	8	7	1	5	7	8	12	6	81	8.4
Rates												
Accidents per mile (km)	9.20	3.75	3.57	1.40	2.00	3.57	2.12	2.25	7.50	2.67	—	3.5
Vehicle-miles (km) $\times$ 10^{-6} = M	3.65	4.20	3.58	5.48	1.02	1.43	3.01	3.36	1.46	2.41	29.60	2.96
Accident rate, R_s	6.30	2.86	2.79	1.28	1.96	3.50	2.33	2.68	10.27	3.32	—	3.3
Ranking by:												
Accidents	1	3	4	7	10	9	8	5	2	6		
Accidents/mi (km)	1	3	4	10	9	5	8	7	2	6		
Accident rate	2	5	6	10	9	3	8	7	1	4		
Number-rate selection	1	0	0	0	0	0	0	0	2	0		
Out of control	2	0	0	0	0	0	0	0	1	0		

*Accidents counted for 365 days.

SOURCE: Adapted from Institute of Traffic Engineers, *Transportation and Traffic Engineering Handbook*, Prentice-Hall, Englewood Cliffs, N.J., 1976, p. 386, Table 9.1.

○Roadside obstacles
○Physical condition of the roadway
○Environmental conditions

The concept of *benefit/cost* study, when applied to accident studies, has undergone considerable revision in recent years. Although estimates are still provided for the "value" of a human life and the "cost" of each person injured in traffic accidents, the general public is not likely to accept the equation of human life or suffering to dollar figures. Court cases involving benefit/cost trade-offs in vehicular design have awakened elements of the public to this engineering practice which is common in traffic engineering. It is more acceptable to consider the *cost effectiveness* of traffic improvements in terms of lives saved (potentially) and injuries avoided, per unit expenditure.

The results of improvements made are determined by the measurement of the ultimate criterion: reduction in accidents (or fatalities, or injuries). However, a 1-year study of accidents "before" and "after" an improvement may not appear to be statistically conclusive, owing to the random nature of accident occurrence. If there has been more than a 10% increase or decrease in traffic between the before and the after periods, a correction should be made in the number of accidents afterward. The difference in accidents per 12 months before and after should be divided by the number of accidents before, to get the fractional decrease or increase (from before to after).

Confidence in this figure depends on how much experience it represents. A reduction from 3 to 2 is 33%, but it is much more likely to be a matter of chance than a reduction from 30 to 20. There are statistical procedures for determining the significance of a difference. For practical purposes, the curve in Figure 18.9 will serve. It shows that a reduction from 3 to 2 is not significant, but a reduction from 30 to 20 is. The same procedure can be used to determine whether or not an increase (corrected for traffic volume) really represents an unsuccessful improvement or may be caused by chance.

If the fractional (or percent) saving in accidents is not significant, more experience is needed. This may be obtained by lengthening the period before or after, or both, to give a greater number of events. If similar treatment is given to a number of locations, the before and after data for all locations so treated can be pooled, to get an average improvement for the group. The larger number of cases will give a more reliable figure for the effect of the improvement.

In summary, *locational analysis* in traffic engineering requires collection of accident report forms for a given study location, covering a period of at least 1 year, and for accidents in excess of 5. The greater the number of accidents at a given location, the greater the possibility of finding patterns of occurrence that may be tied to alterable variables such as geometry, control measures, or regulation. Five is an arbitrary number selected on the basis of experience.

The data on accident report forms are transferred to and summarized in three documents: a summary sheet, a collision diagram, and a condition diagram.

The *summary sheet* collects the data available from the individual report forms into tables showing accident occurrence by hour of day, day of week, month, year; weather conditions; roadway conditions; type of accident (sideswipe, angle, rear-end); type of vehicles involved; action of driver; and any other available information recorded on the report form which may be of value.

The *collision diagram* provides a graphic presentation of approximate locations of accidents, by type, within the high-accident-frequency location being studied. The symbols offer instant recognition of patterns of occurrence (rear-end accidents at the southwest corner of the intersection, for instance), which allows the analyst to seek clues to causation.

The *condition diagram* is a scale drawing of the location, with all physical features in and near the location recorded on it, including traffic control devices, markings (and condition thereof), utility poles, and building lines.

This material, together with usual traffic engineering data, such as signal timing, speed of traffic, traffic volumes, and vehicle classification, provide the safety analyst with complete knowledge of the location from available records. At this point the analyst must visit, observe and become familiar with the location itself, its normal and peak-hour operating characteristics, and the difficulties that drivers, both regular and occasional users, may find in traversing the location under study.

Engineering judgment then comes into play. Insight on the part of the analyst is of greater importance than mechanical means of benefit/cost analysis based upon generalized studies of the efficacy of design or control changes in other locations. The advantage of studying individual high-accident locations lies in its specificity to a given location, with its peculiar problems, such as signal visibility or signal timing, visibility of traffic approaching from a given direction, or skid resistance of pavement.

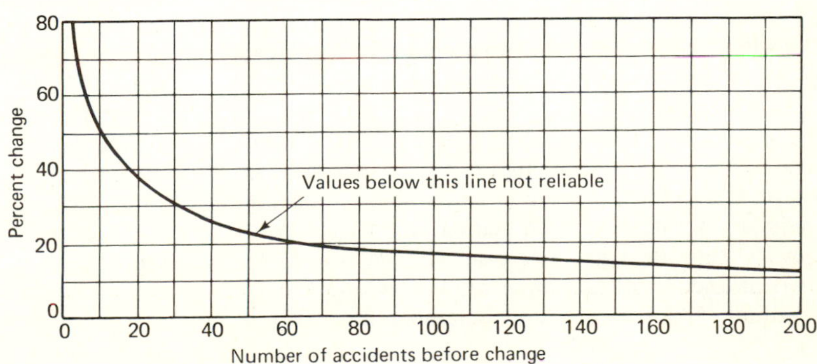

Figure 18.9. Chart for evaluating reliability of percent change in accidents at a location. SOURCE: Institute of Traffic Engineers, *Transportation and Traffic Engineering Handbook*, Prentice-Hall, Englewood Cliffs, N.J., 1976.

TABLE 18-2
Safety Benefits of Rural Improvements

Rank	Improvement	Annual Accident Reduction (%) Accidents	Injuries	Fatalities	Benefit/Cost Ratio
1	Shoulder widening or improvement	29	20	41	28.83
2	Installation of striping and/or delineators	13	20	46	26.49
3	Skid treatment/grooving	48	30	74	20.12
4	Installation or upgrading of traffic signs	23	33	27	15.03
5	Signing and/or marking	0	42	35	14.94
6	Installation or improvement of median barrier	3	6	91	13.73
7	Localized lighting installation	9	9	73	13.24
8	Installation or improvement of road-edge guardrail	13	15	59	10.97
9	Flashing lights replacing signs only—railroad crossing	94	93	99	9.41
10	Signs/striping combination	24	26	27	8.60
11	Breakaway signs or lighting supports	35	44	100	7.25
12	Traffic signals, installed or improved	18	32	49	6.36
13	Skid treatment/overlay	17	27	30	6.09
14	Automatic gates replacing signs only	99	99	100	5.44
15	Channelization, including left-turn bays	23	29	65	3.94
16	Pavement widening, no lanes added	25	38	87	3.68
17	Sight distance improved	31	38	36	2.97
18	Combination of channelization and signal installation or improvement	31	35	50	1.78
19	Automatic gates replacing active devices	81	75	96	1.13
20	Combination of horizontal and vertical alignment changes	21	32	69	0.91
21	Replacement of bridge or other major structures	44	60	47	0.09
22	Lanes added, without new median	17	11	31	0.80
23	Widening existing bridge or other major structures	65	74	33	0.41

SOURCE: THOMAS A. HALL, "Safety Benefits from the Categorical Safety Programs," *Transport. Eng.*, Feb. 1978.

The advantage of specificity happens to be the greatest disadvantage of the procedure, also, since it is time-consuming and costly. For this reason, although it is extremely effective in reducing accident occurrence when practiced properly by well-trained personnel with good judgment, it is rarely practiced in a systematic, comprehensive fashion by state or local jurisdictions.

It is helpful—but only helpful—to be cognizant of the results of studies that evaluate the safety benefits of the various possible improvements that can be made in highway transportation. Table 18-2 provides a recent example. It is necessary to realize that, although each of these improvements has proven effective, it is not necessarily applicable to every accident location under study.

Air safety

Trends

Air transportation is comprised of two diverse elements: air carriers (or "commercial" aviation) and general aviation. General aviation (or "private" flying) accounts for the greatest part of the air safety problem, with 10 times as many fatalities as air carriers.

U.S. air carriers recorded 163 fatalities in 1978 compared with 655 in 1977. Annual figures vary widely for two reasons: single accidents involve large numbers of people, and individual aircraft have been getting larger in terms of passenger-carrying capacity. For example, on March 27, 1977, two airliners collided on a runway in the Canary Islands, killing 583 persons; on September 25, 1978, a Boeing 727 air carrier jet and a single-engine private plane collided and crashed into a residential area, killing 144 persons in both planes and on the ground; and on May 25, 1979, an airliner lost an engine on takeoff in Chicago, with 272 fatalities.

Air carrier miles flown reached a record high in 1978, while the accident *rate* per million miles flown reached a record low.

The history of air accidents shows a definite trend downward (Figure 18.10). In fact, fatal accident rates, based on increasing numbers of miles flown, indicate a declining trend (Figure 18.11). However, as individual aircraft have gotten larger, the numbers of fatalities, and of fatal accidents, show a definite upward trend, in spite of the wide fluctuations from year to year, since 1975.

Rates are based on *miles flown* for air carriers because route-miles are known and available.

General aviation, in 1978, recorded 4609 accidents, 795 fatal accidents, and 1690 fatalities. This was an increase of 7.5, 13.2, and 17.7%, respectively, over the previous year. Fatalities in 1978 in this category were the highest in 15 years. Figure 18.12 shows a general increase in numbers of fatal accidents, fatalities, and accidents in this category, since 1972.

Fatal accident *rates* in this category (Figure 18.13) show a general decline since 1968 (except for 1978), related to the extremely rapid increase in aircraft hours flown even while fatal accidents increased.

General aviation is not a homogeneous grouping of modal type, however, and the safety problem within this category is greatest for so-called "personal" aircraft, or recreational flying (see Figure 18.14).

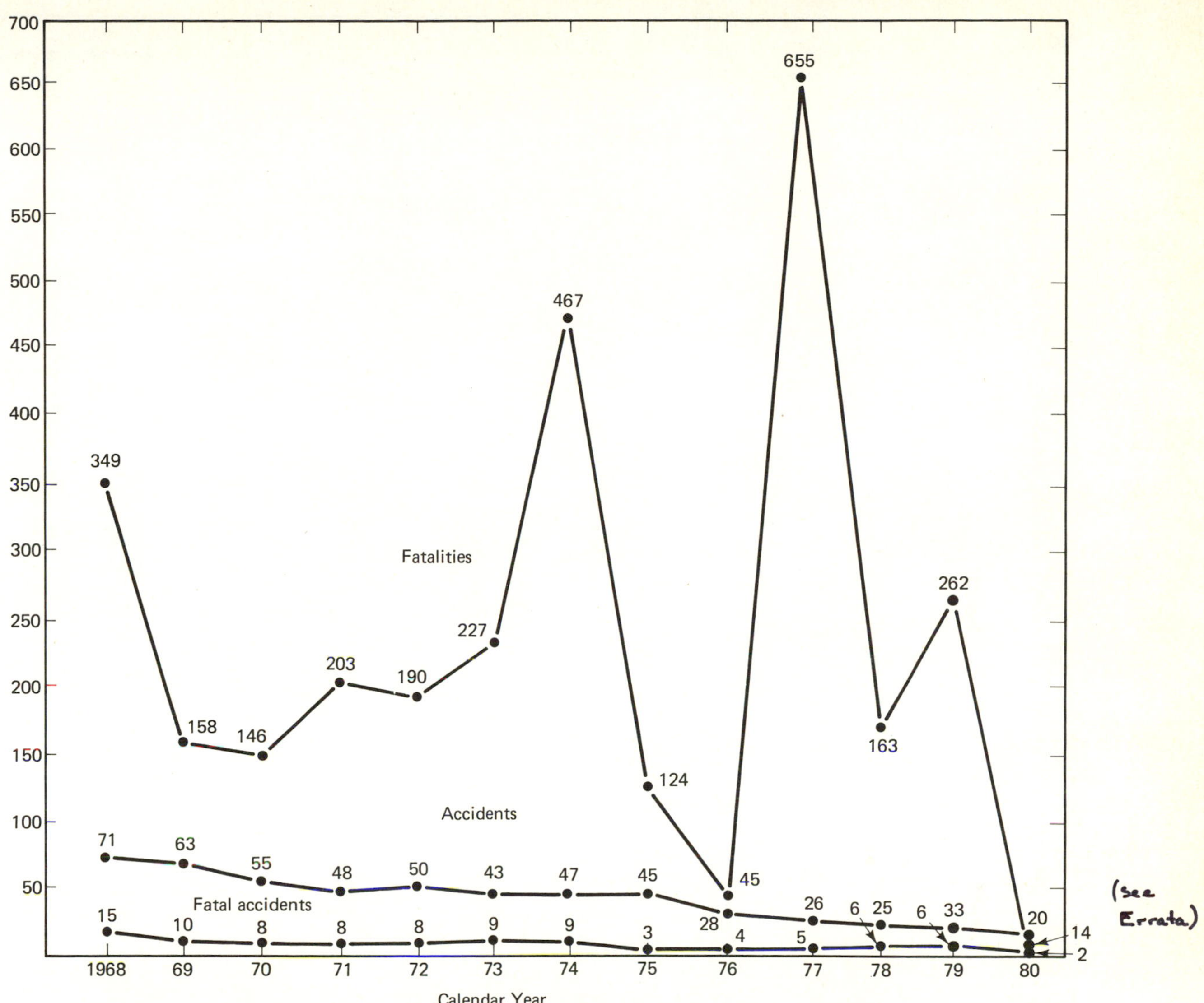

Figure 18.10. Air carrier accidents, fatalities, and fatal accidents, 1968–1980. SOURCE: *Transportation Safety Information Report,* Oct., Nov., and Dec. 1978, Annual Summary, U.S. Department of Transportation, Washington, D.C., March 1979. (1979–80 data added by author.)

Rates are based on *hours flown* in general aviation because of the nature of many flights (unscheduled, recreational, or instructional) and the wide variety of aircraft types.

Causes and problem areas

Most flight-related accidents occur in the vicinity of airports, either on approach to landing or on takeoff; and most aircraft accidents and fatalities involve the private or recreational flying aspect of general aviation.

Major accidents involving air carriers underline the need for preventive efforts in design and maintenance, even though these areas are far advanced in aviation as compared to other transportation modes; improved communication between pilot and control towers; improved communication between aircraft in the same airspace; the need to reconsider the mixing of air carriers and general aviation in the same airspace (because of differences in size, maneuverability, speed, visibility, and personnel capabilities); and the need to provide greater automation and electromechanical control over aircraft.

In general aviation, accidents and fatalities are attributed to lack of technical knowledge by private pilots, poor training and lesser certification (licensing) requirements than for air carrier pilots, the inadequacy of pilots in relation to weather conditions, and performance impairment due to alcohol or drugs (similar to the highway traffic safety problem).

Although there are wide differences of training and capability among pilots of recreational, sport, crop dusting, corporate, and the other aircraft that comprise the grouping known as "general aviation," overall lesser capabilities and knowledge are blamed for the safety problems of this group.

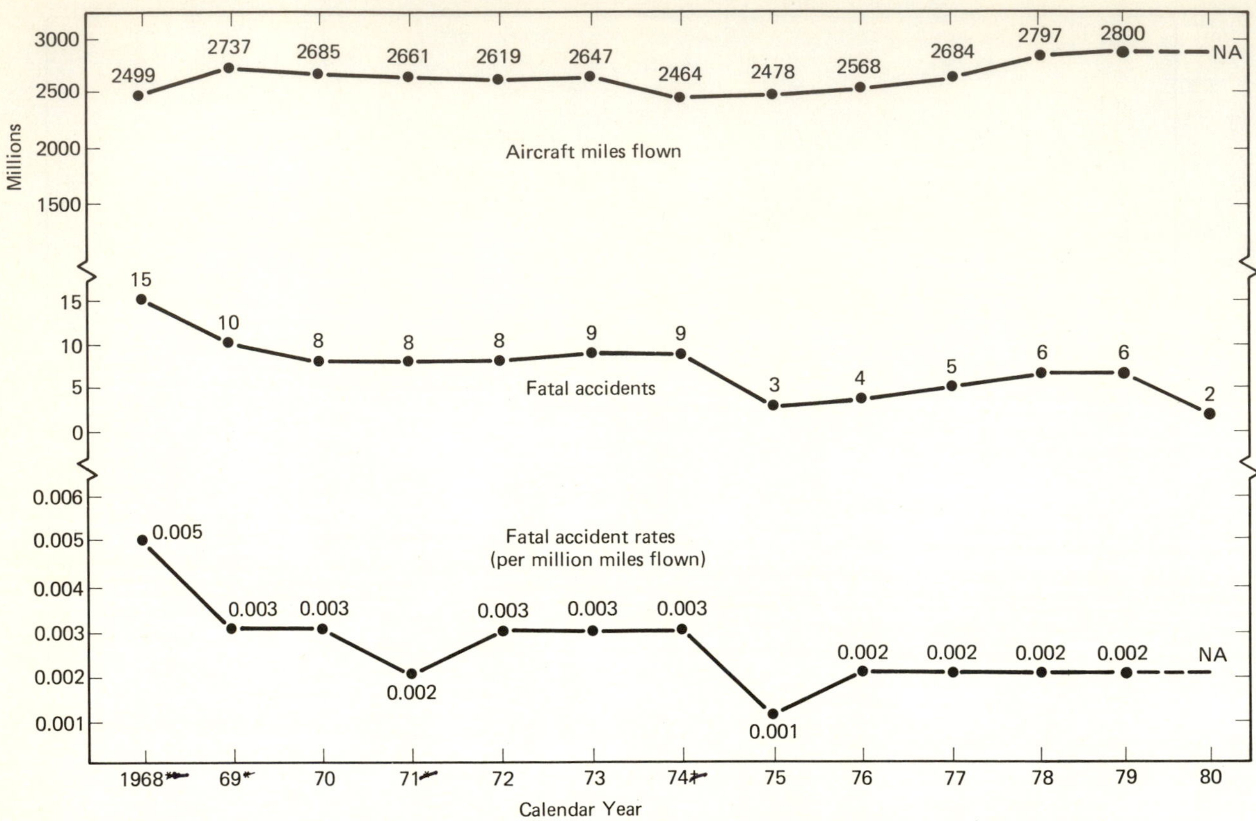

Figure 18.11. U.S. air carrier fatal accident rates, 1968–1980 (all operations). SOURCE: *Transportation Safety Information Report,* Oct., Nov., and Dec., 1978, Annual Summary, U.S. Department of Transportation, Washington, D.C., March 1979. (1979–80 data added by author.)

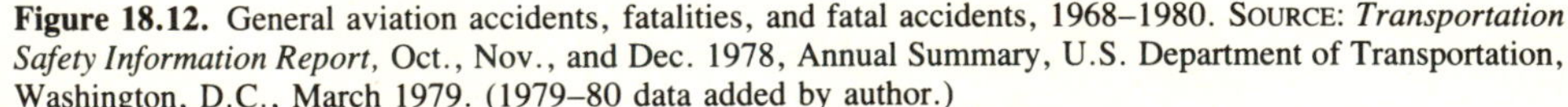

Figure 18.12. General aviation accidents, fatalities, and fatal accidents, 1968–1980. SOURCE: *Transportation Safety Information Report,* Oct., Nov., and Dec. 1978, Annual Summary, U.S. Department of Transportation, Washington, D.C., March 1979. (1979–80 data added by author.)

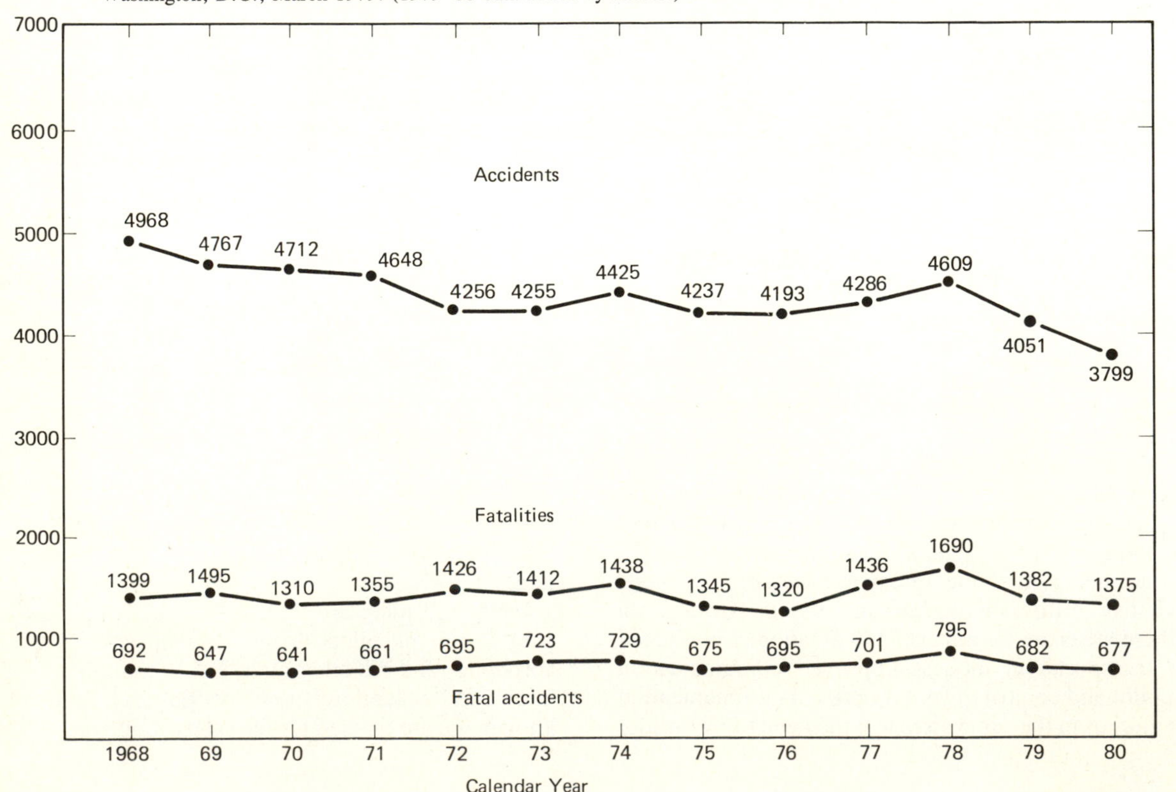

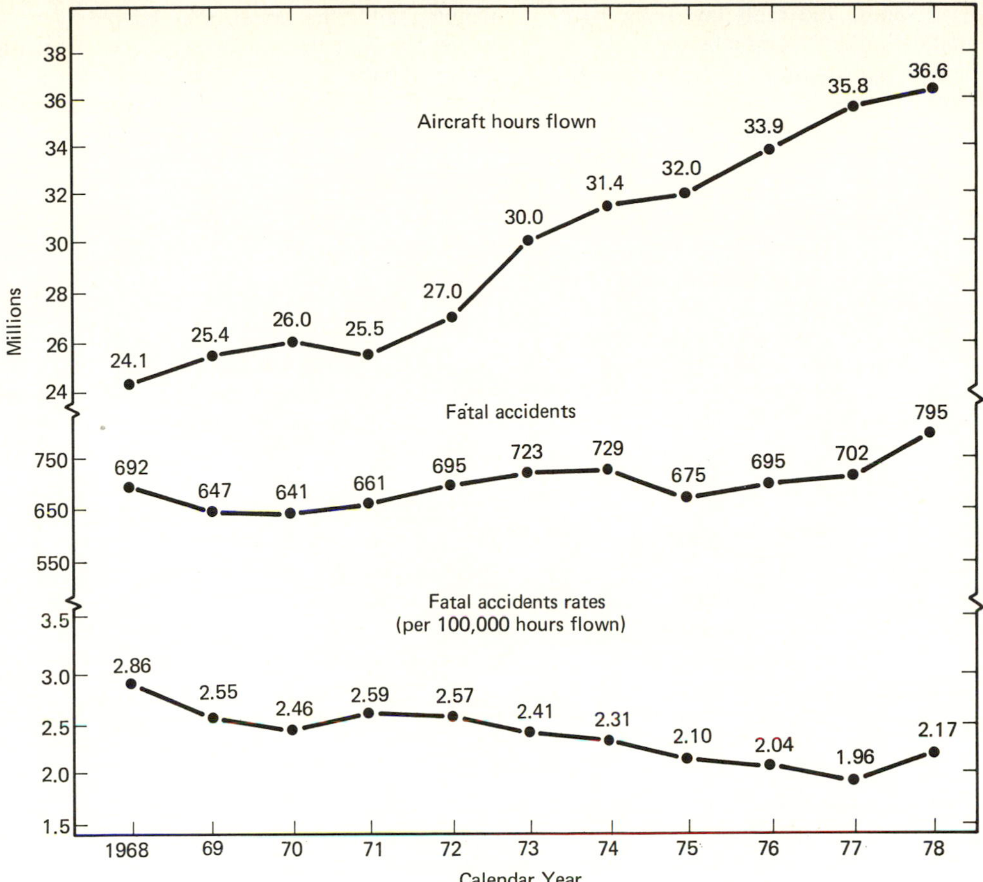

Figure 18.13. U.S. General aviation fatal accident rates, 1968–1978. SOURCE: *Transportation Safety Information Report,* Oct., Nov., and Dec. 1978, Annual Summary, U.S. Department of Transportation, Washington, D.C., March 1979.

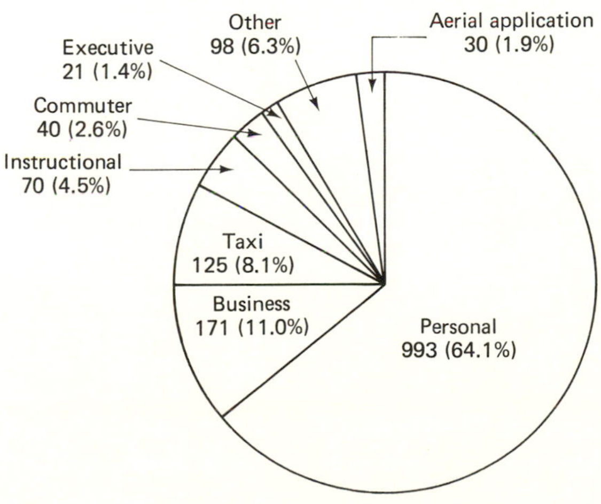

Figure 18.14. General aviation fatalities by aircraft classification, 1978. SOURCE: *Transportation Safety Information Report,* Oct., Nov., and Dec. 1978, Annual Summary, U.S. Department of Transportation, Washington, D.C., March 1979.

Solutions

The Federal Aviation Administration exercises the greatest control over the safety aspects of a transport mode of any governmental agency, as it has since the earliest beginnings of commercial and private flying.

The FAA is involved in the design of aircraft and the certification of both aircraft and pilots. The agency also issues design standards for airport runways and taxiways, and essentially operates (as one of the few Federal transportation operating agencies) the "airways," providing the rules and traffic control measures by which aviation must abide.

Since most air carrier and general aviation accidents occur at or near airports, engineers must concentrate on better communication and better control in the landing and takeoff aspects of air transport. Engineering efforts are constantly under way in the improvement of automatic devices for these operations, but difficulties are heightened by the mixing of aircraft of every size and maneuvering capability, with pilots of different levels of training in the same airspace. The problems involved in the San Diego crash referred to earlier were communication problems, primarily, between ground controllers and each plane, and between the planes themselves. In the case of the collision of the two airliners in the Canary Islands, the fault lay again with inadequacies of communication and comprehension.

Although vehicle design, construction, and maintenance have reached their highest levels in air transportation, a commercial jet lost an engine while taking off from Chicago's O'Hare Field on May 25, 1979. In this case, subsequent investigation by the National Transportation Safety Board found design and incorrect maintenance procedures to be at fault.

With general aviation, lesser levels of governmental control over aircraft design and construction, and pilot instruction, certification, and supervision, account for the greatest part of the problem. It is necessary to make such controls more stringent to prevent error and misunderstanding due to lack of knowledge or experience.

Study approaches

Accident prevention. The Federal Aviation Administration is directly involved in efforts at accident prevention. These reach into participation in the design of aircraft structures, engines, certification of such structures and aircraft generally, and training and certification of pilots and other personnel.

Traffic control is in the hands of FAA personnel, and improvements in air traffic control and airport design are all directed at prevention of incidents.

State and local agencies have a lesser role in air accident prevention efforts, since the major aspect of local involvement in air transportation is in the construction, operation, and maintenance of airports.

Accident impact attenuation. In aviation, little attention is directed at means of attenuating, or reducing the severity of a crash, since it is felt that developing a structure which is at all resistant to the forces involved in a crash would make the aircraft uneconomical to fly. Impact attenuation is therefore concentrated on seatbelts for passengers, and attention is aimed at prevention of the incident. However, it is well known that more than half of the persons involved in air crashes survive the impact, only to be asphyxiated by fumes and/or burned to death in the fire that follows.

Accident study and analysis. *Macro-analysis* of accidents is largely in terms of general aviation, which experiences greater numbers of accidents than does air carrier aviation. Analysis on this level reveals patterns of occurrence that lead to conclusions concerning the adequacy of training of pilots, the adequacy of technical knowledge of the pilots, and the adequacy of aircraft certification procedures.[14]

Micro-analysis, or the study of individual accidents in depth, is at its highest level of competence in aviation. Aircraft accidents are reconstructed from the evidence remaining after the crash, the statements of survivors and witnesses, and the evidence provided by flight recorders (recording the aircraft's flying functions for a brief period before the crash) and voice tapes of the cockpit conversations.

Marine safety

Trends

Marine transportation also covers two widely disparate categories: "waterborne" transportation, which includes what might be termed "commercial" ships and boats, operating on the high seas, along the coasts, lakes, rivers, and canals; and "recreational boating," which is the private, "amateur" aspect of marine transportation.

Classification of waterborne transportation accidents is not as clearly defined as in other transportation modes. For instance, in 1978 there were 498 waterborne fatalities, of which 179 were related to vessel accidents such as collision, fire, or explosion, and 319 deaths were "job-related" accidents aboard ship.

In another approach to categorization, 343 of the total fatalities occurred on board vessels that had not been inspected by the U.S. Coast Guard, and 155 occurred on board inspected vessels.

Trends in *waterborne* accidents and fatalities (Figure 18.15) show the clear upward direction of the number of accidents and of vessels involved. Annual fatalities fluctuate around the 200 mark, with a slight upward trend overall. There is no universally accepted means of calculating rates in marine safety for the waterborne classification.

In *recreational boating,* the fatality rate per 100,000 boats dropped to a record low of 9.4 for 1978. On the other hand, property damage in this category reached a record high of more than $12.3 million.

Figure 18.16 shows the increase in the accident trend line since 1972. Number of fatalities has held relatively steady except for the peak year of 1973. The annual number of injuries decreased to about 1800 after the peak of 2136 in 1975.

Although the number of fatalities leveled off, the increase in the number of boats (Figure 18.17) brought the fatality *rate* per 100,000 boats down from a high of 20.2 in 1971 to 9.4 in 1978.

Causes and problem areas

The huge disparity and wide range of vessel sizes and characteristics present a basic problem of designing and enforcing control measures. As with all modes, most accidents occur in the approaches to, and in the vicinity of, port or berthing facilities, where lanes of movement become crowded and requirements for higher skill levels increase. The improvement of waterborne vessel safety is impeded by questions of state and international jurisdiction, a wide range of certification and training requirements for personnel, and the physical difficulties inherent in moving vessels through greatly varying water and weather conditions.

[14]*The Accident Prevention Program,* FAA-P-8740-8, AFS-800-0478, Federal Aviation Administration, U.S. Department of Transportation, Washington, D.C.

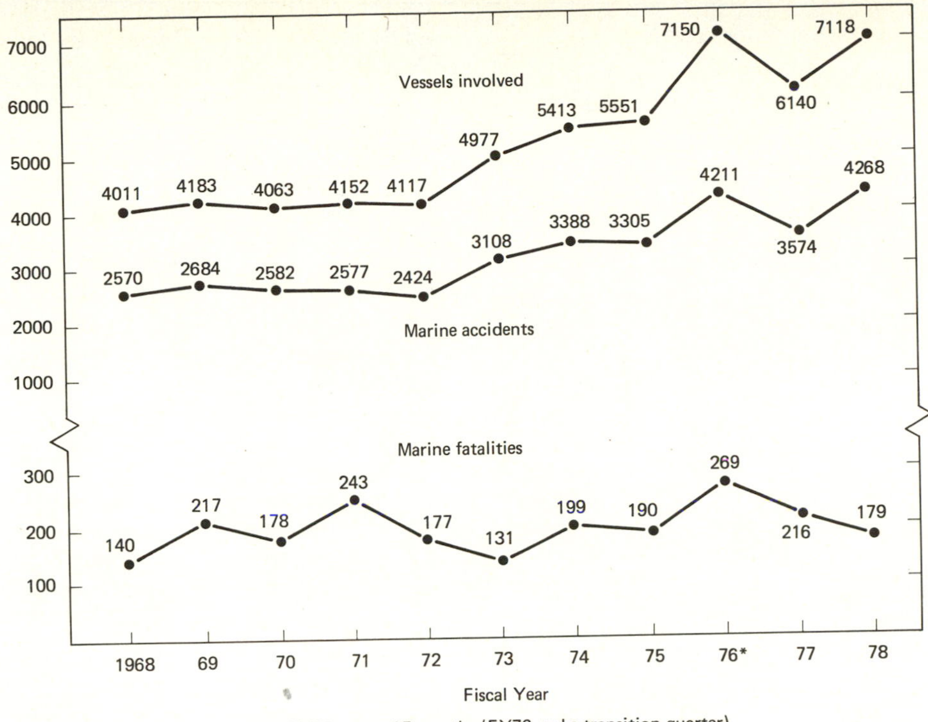

*FY76 covers 15 months (FY76 and a transition quarter).

Figure 18.15. Waterborne accidents and fatalities, 1968–1978. SOURCE: *Transportation Safety Information Report,* Oct., Nov., and Dec. 1978, Annual Summary, U.S. Department of Transportation, Washington, D.C., March 1979.

Figure 18.16. Recreational boating fatalities, injuries, and accidents, 1968–1978. SOURCE: *Transportation Safety Information Report,* Oct., Nov., and Dec. 1978, Annual Summary, U.S. Department of Transportation, Washington, D.C., March 1979.

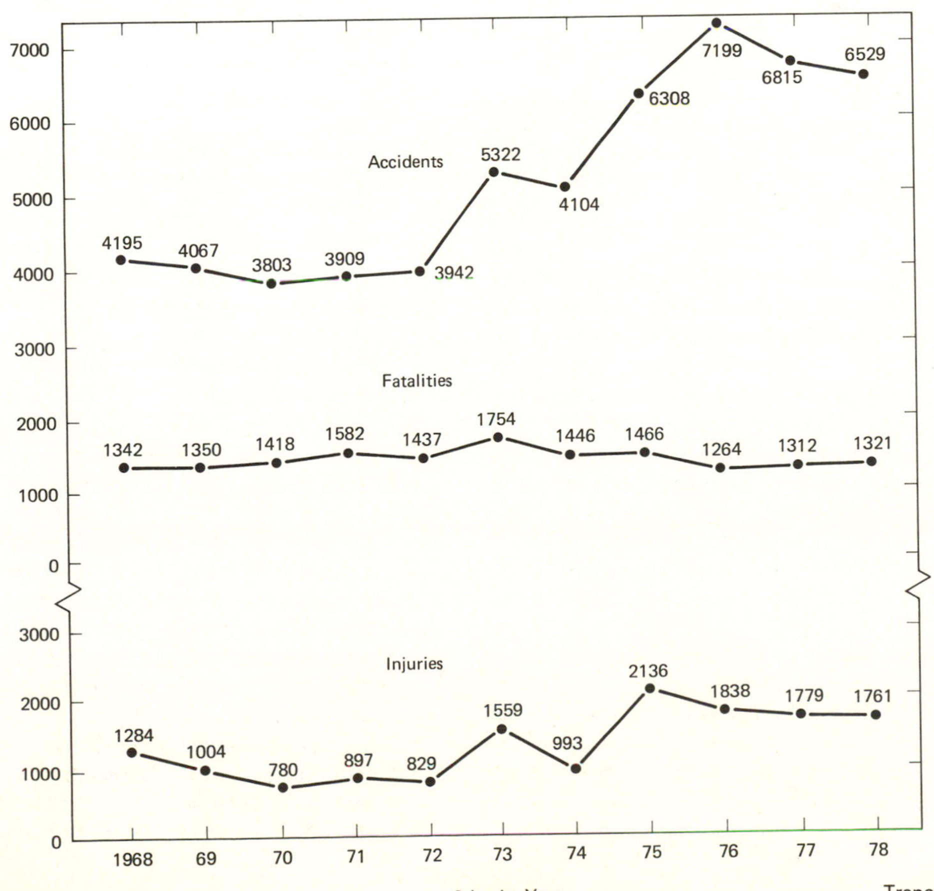

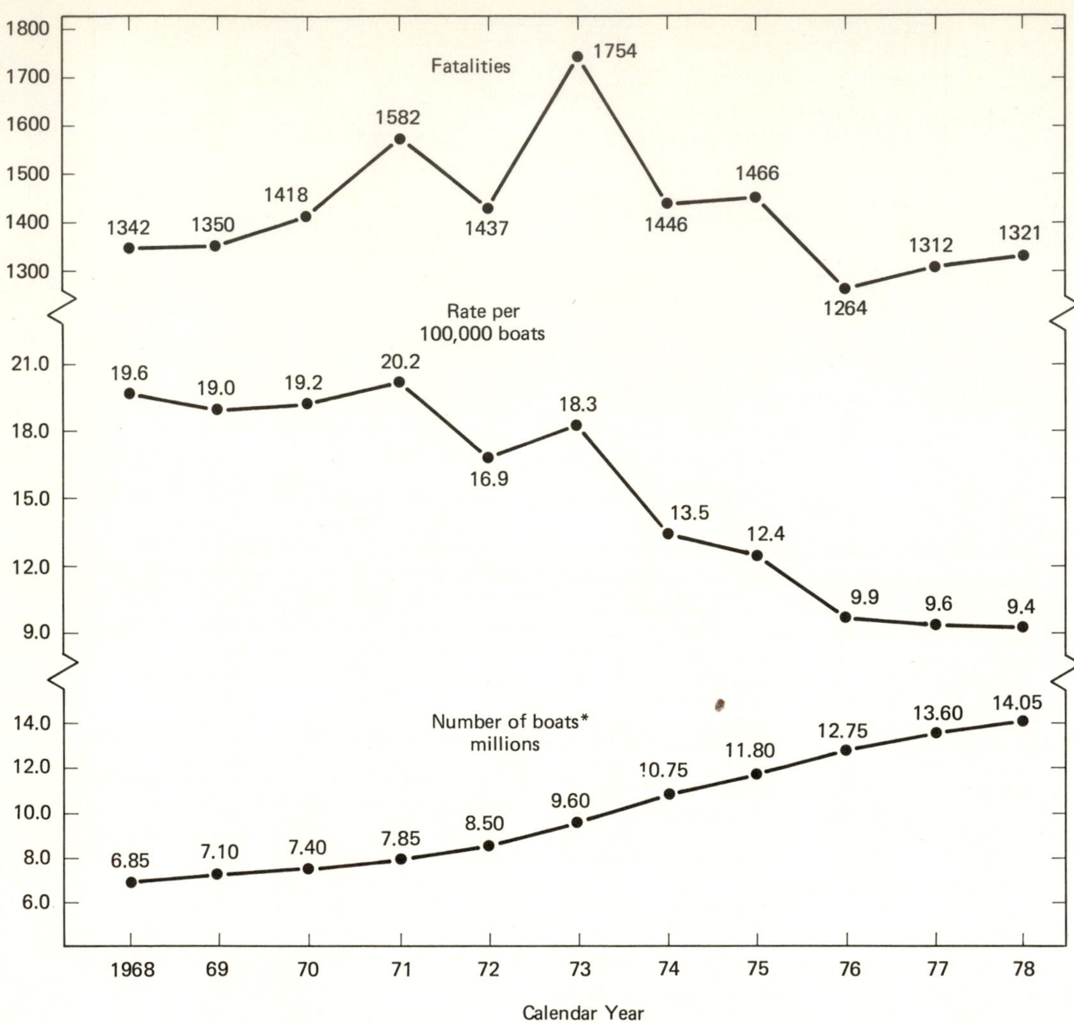

Figure 18.17. Recreational boating fatality rates, 1968–1978. SOURCE: *Transportation Safety Information Report,* Oct., Nov., and Dec. 1978, Annual Summary, U.S. Department of Transportation, Washington, D.C., March 1979.

Recreational boating safety is a major, separate, and distinct problem area in marine safety. Problems with this classification include weak jurisdictional control by the Coast Guard, lack of requirements for training and certification of operators, "amateur" operators (as in highway traffic) subject to alcohol and drug abuse, poorly defined and controlled "ways" or lanes separating the marine vessel/boat classifications, and inadequate adherence to accepted rules.

Solutions

In marine transportation, the Federal role is mixed, owing to the wide disparity in sizes of vessels and the numbers of jurisdictions. The U.S. Coast Guard inspects and exercises some control over design and construction, licensing and certification, but within a confusion of rules, international agreements, and limited jurisdiction.

Coast Guard control over *pleasure boating,* the area where safety is a major problem, is minimal, being limited to providing optional boating safety instruction and informative leaflets.

Waterborne vessels (as differentiated from pleasure boats) constitute the smaller part of the accident problem, but the wide disparities in Coast Guard jurisdiction, in its obligations to inspect and certify, are related to many of the problems. Limitations and constraints of funding and personnel restrict the ability of the Coast Guard to cover the many types of vessels along the coasts and on lakes, rivers, and canals. Solutions involve expansion of the jurisdiction of the Coast Guard, because the problems are understood and dealt with efficiently by that agency.

Another major area of concern in the waterborne category involves spillage of petroleum products on the high seas and in lakes and rivers. Much of this problem is related to skimpy design standards for vessels and the excessive sizes of many such vessels. Extreme size, combined with underpowering and consequent retarded maneuvering capability, leads to disasters.

In the area of recreational boating, the major problem is a lack of control by agencies such as the Coast Guard, combined with poorly or untaught users of powered craft. The problem of "amateur" boatsmen is aggravated when alcohol is involved and when craft are used in the vicinity of bathers. Greater control over such boats is absolutely essential to reduce the numbers of fatalities related to this type of water transport.

Study approaches

Accident prevention. The U.S. Coast Guard's efforts are mainly preventive in nature, although the agency serves as an investigatory arm of the National Transportation Safety Board, which otherwise performs its own safety investigations in all other modes. With powers of inspection and some certification, search and rescue, the Coast Guard spends a great deal of its efforts in preventive work.

In recreational boating the Coast Guard's efforts are essentially preventive in nature, holding voluntary classes in boat safety and attempting to apprise the public of proper seamanship and intelligent boating practices.

State and local agencies are involved to a lesser degree, related to the provision of harbor facilities and the operation of municipal ferries.

Accident impact attenuation. Little is done in this area, except for traditional use of pads at the bows of tugs and similar considerations. The structure of a ship or a boat is not intended to resist the impact of another ship's bow, except in naval vessels.

Accident study and analysis. *Macro-analysis* of accident occurrence is almost nonexistent, and is confined to recreational boating statistics on a national scale.

Micro-analysis is represented by the investigations made by the Coast Guard within the limitations of personnel and budgetary considerations.

Rail transportation safety

Trends

Rail transportation is also divided into two groupings: railroad and rail rapid transit. Rapid transit represents a separate application of the railroading mode, in that each rail rapid transit facility was built differently in small and large details; each is a finite, limited installation where both rolling stock and physical plant belong to a single operating agency. Generally, railroads in the United States have been privately owned, whereas rapid transit has been publicly owned.

Railroad accidents reached a 10-year high in 1978, at 11,459.

Derailments caused 80.2% of railroad accidents and 63.2% of the fatalities in 1978. Collisions caused 67.7% of the injuries.

Railroad accidents show a general upward trend (Figure 18.18) in spite of sharp declines in 1971 and 1975. Grade-crossing fatalities have increased since 1975, after a steady decline since 1968. Railroad fatalities have shown a slight increase since 1976, after reaching a record low point that year.

Accident *rates* (Figure 18.19) show a steep increase since 1972, following the increase in accidents, and reflecting the decline in train-miles traveled.

In *rail rapid transit,* fatalities, injuries, and accidents diminished again in 1978, just as there was a reduction from 1976 to 1977. Fatalities fell from 70 in 1977 to 37 in 1978, a drop of 47.1%. Accidents were reduced, from 7220 in 1977, to 6555 in 1978. Injuries also were reduced, from 7681 to 6659. Figure 18.20 shows monthly fluctuations for the period January 1977 to December 1978.

Accident data for rail rapid transit were not available for the industry before January 1977. Through the influence of the American Public Transit Association, an industry organization, and the Urban Mass Transportation Administration of U.S. DOT, these data have now been made available on a monthly basis.

Causes and problem areas

The safety problems of railroads are almost entirely due to economic decline. Bankruptcy, and losses in both passenger and freight movements since World War II, have led to reductions in maintenance and personnel, leading to a deterioration of both fixed plant and rolling stock. More than 7000 derailments were estimated[15] for the year 1976 in the United States, most of them attributed to poorly maintained tracks and roadbeds. Little research and development of improved methods and devices has taken place in the railroad industry for at least 50 years. Methods of operation and maintenance, except in a few instances, are the same as they were generations ago.

Rail rapid transit's safety problems are quite specific to each property. The older systems (New York City, Chicago, Boston) have problems similar to those of railroading, in that losses of revenue and inadequate subsidies have led to deterioration in maintenance and postponement of rehabilitation. Crime and vandalism are also major problems of the older systems.

The newer systems (BART in San Francisco and the Metro in Washington, D.C.) suffer from problems of implementation of new technologies (automation) and a lack (until recently) of disseminated state-of-the-art information concerning the histories and operational problems of existing systems.

All rail rapid transit operators agree that their major safety problems, in terms of numbers (if not severity), are those related to the movement of pedestrians through corridors, on platforms, boarding and alighting from trains, and up and down stairways and escalators.

[15] Elwood T. Driver, Vice Chairman, National Transportation Safety Board, quoted in the *New York Times,* 1978.

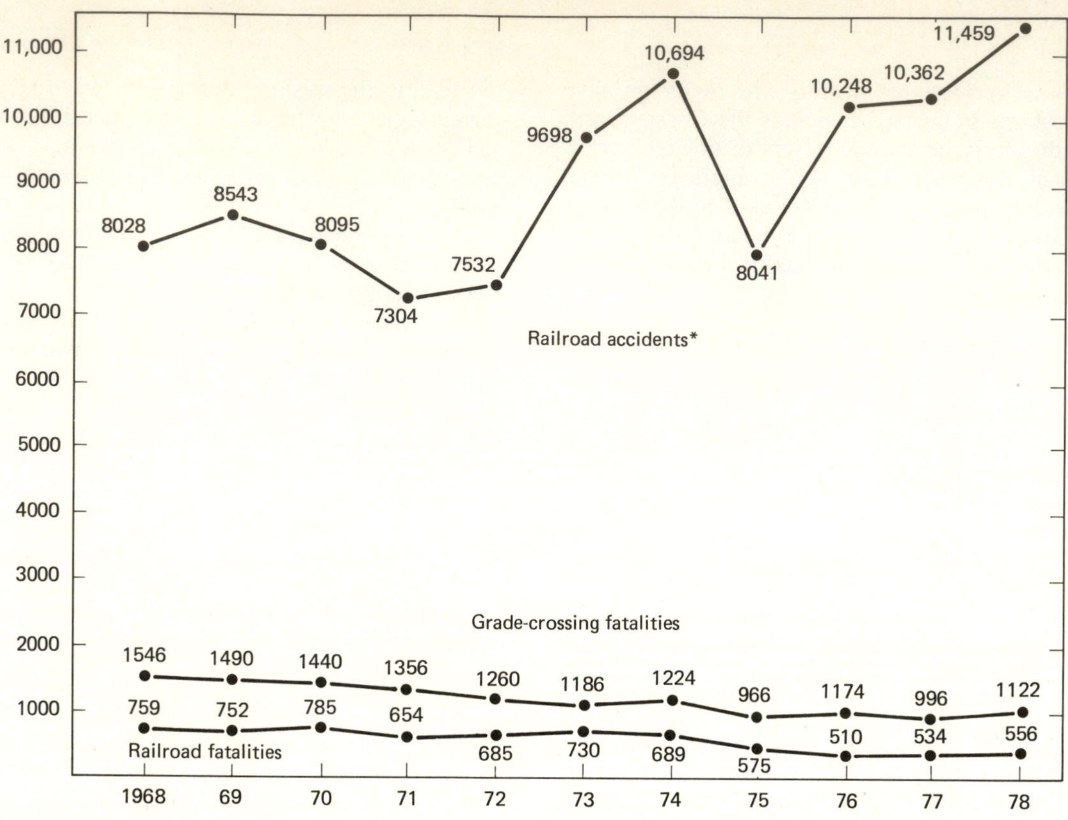

*Train accidents only, excludes train-service and non-train accidents

Figure 18.18. Railroad accidents and fatalities and grade crossing fatalities, 1968–1978. Source: *Transportation Safety Information Report,* Oct., Nov., and Dec. 1978, Annual Summary, U.S. Department of Transportation, Washington, D.C., March 1979.

Figure 18.19. Railroad accident rates, 1968–1978. Source: *Transportation Safety Information Report,* Oct., Nov., and Dec. 1978, Annual Summary, U.S. Department of Transportation, Washington, D.C., March 1979.

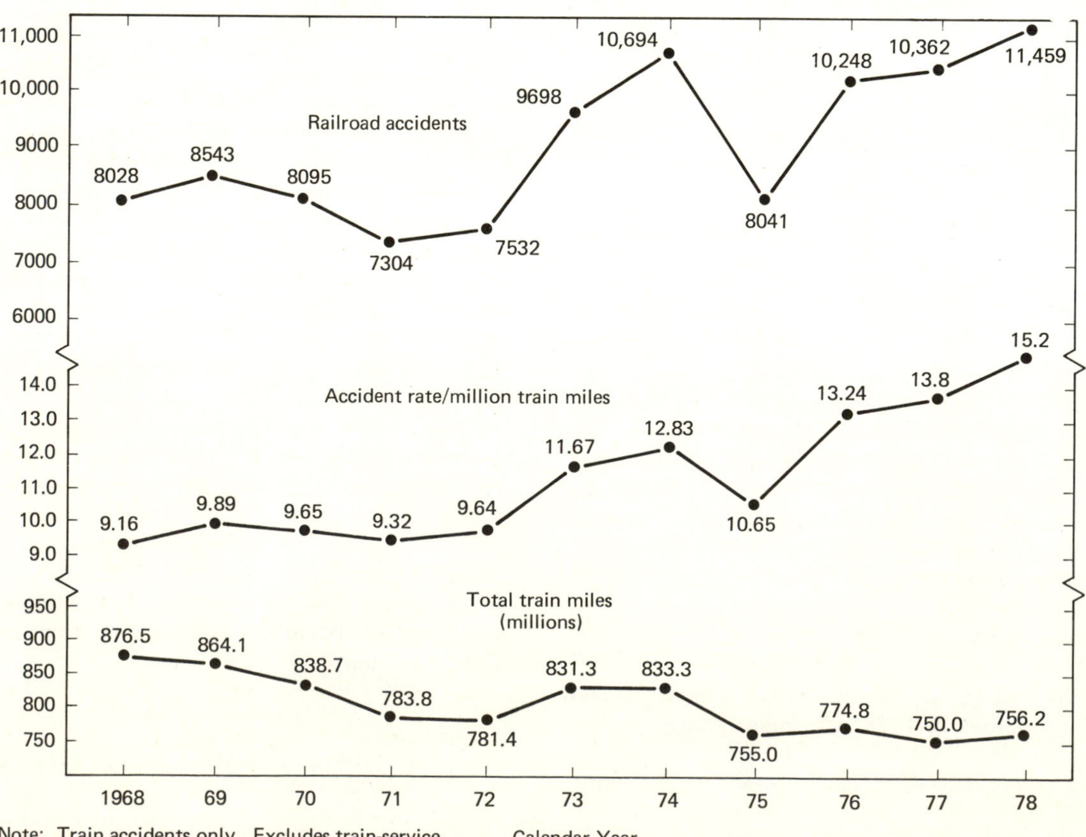

Note: Train accidents only. Excludes train-service and non-train accidents.

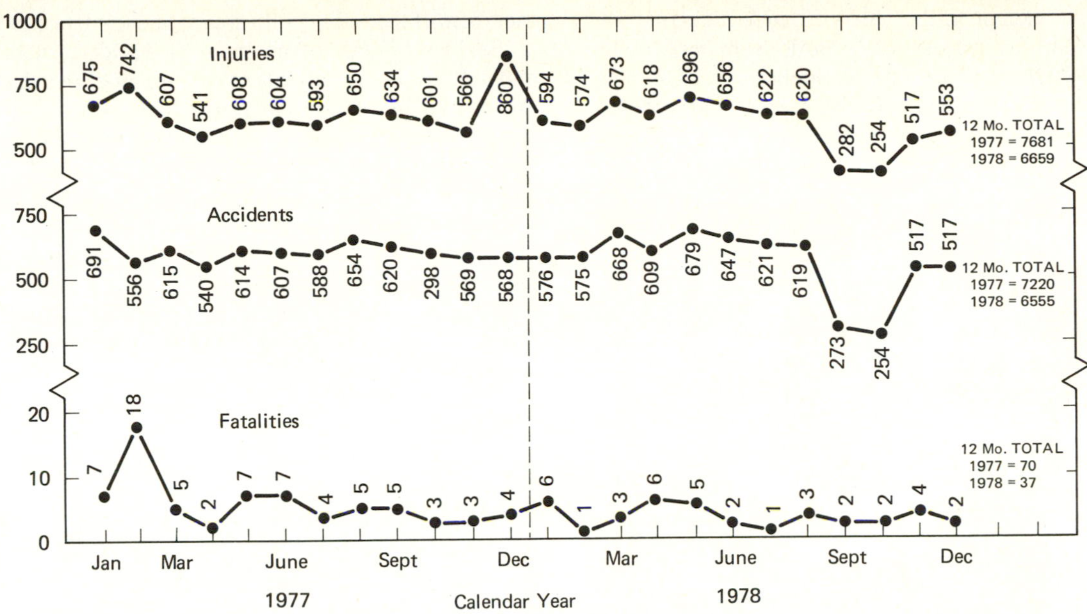

Figure 18.20. Rail rapid transit fatalities, accidents, and injuries, 1977–1979. SOURCE: *Transportation Safety Information Report,* Oct., Nov., and Dec. 1978, Annual Summary, U.S. Department of Transportation, Washington, D.C., March 1979.

Solutions

In *rail systems,* the Federal Railroad Administration has only recently acquired greater responsibility for control of safety, in terms of inspection and requirements for physical and control-measure improvements.

Maintenance of the guideway, or traveled way, of any transport mode is an essential part of the operating safety of a system, and cannot be compromised for budgetary reasons. Governments have been slow to provide solutions to this problem, since subsidies generally lead to greater and greater government involvement in operation and maintenance. But the safety of users and the general public must be accepted as paramount.

In recent years the government has entered into some attempts to revitalize the railroad industry. It has expanded the authority of the Federal Railroad Administration in areas of safety, but other national economic and energy concerns have led to fragmented efforts.

In *rail rapid transit,* the Urban Mass Transportation Administration exercises some control over safety, as it is related to Federal-aid funds which are allocated to the various operating agencies. UMTA has worked with such agencies on a voluntary basis in the improvement of safety, introducing the concept of *system safety* in 1979, with a requirement that System Safety Program Plans be developed by operating agencies.

Crime and vandalism, which are expressions of social problems, are not easily solved by one agency in a given area. Some of the newer systems have installed automatic television surveillance systems and other means of communication which greatly expand the coverage of individual police officers.

Problems on platforms, stairways, and escalators can be dealt with by engineering changes, which, however, are subject to economic considerations.

Study approaches

Accident prevention. Preventive efforts have lagged in both governmental and private circles until relatively recently. Declines in maintenance, the first bastion of accident prevention, have created a major safety crisis in both railroading and the older rapid-transit systems. Preventive efforts have increased with the granting of greater powers to the Federal Railroad Administration and the creation of the Urban Mass Transportation Administration, which has mounted efforts to introduce the system-safety concept into rail rapid-transit properties, as previously noted.

Local agencies' efforts have been limited to the efforts of operating agencies (generally special autonomous authorities).

Accident impact attenuation. An interest in impact attenuation has arisen in railroading in recent years as a result of efforts of the National Transportation Safety Board. Because of the mounting numbers of incidents involving the spillage or explosion of hazardous materials, the NTSB has investigated the need for tank-car redesign to prevent damage and leakage of vapors, liquids, and gases.

Accident study and analysis. In railroads and rail rapid transit, *macro-analysis* is limited to the tabulation of statistics and the observation of trends.

Micro-analysis, the study of individual accidents, is generally inadequate except in the case of major incidents involving deaths or the release of hazardous materials. In these cases, NTSB conducts the accident investigations, reporting its conclusions concerning causes and recommended improvements for prevention.

Pipeline safety

Trends

Pipeline accidents involve leaks and failures of facilities carrying liquid or gas. Accidents or incidents involving pipelines rose to a record high of 2366 in 1978. The number of injuries was 472 in 1977 and 429 in 1978, and fatalities went from 39 to 35.

Figure 18.21 shows the upward trend of gas pipeline failures, whereas a long downward trend for liquid pipelines was apparently reversed in 1976.

Fatalities in gas pipeline safety have fluctuated widely, whereas liquid pipeline fatalities hold steady at a low level.

Causes and problem areas

Pipelines may be termed the only purely goods-movement transportation mode, which limits the effects of hazards and accidents to employees and those bystanders or members of the public who are in the vicinity of the accident.

Besides failures of mechanical devices, such as pumps and valves, most incidents involving pipelines that carry gas are caused by external factors, such as a bulldozer excavating for some other purpose and striking the buried pipeline. Corrosion and construction defects follow in terms of causative factors in pipeline incidents.

Some control is provided through USDOT's Research and Special Programs Administration (RSPA), which has a pipeline and materials handling group. Pipelines come under federal supervision when they cross state lines; major projects such as the Alaska Pipeline are closely supervised by federal agencies.

Solutions

Problems in this mode can be solved by the application of engineering knowledge, especially in fail-safe pumping and metering systems, and in means of identifying buried pipelines to prevent unintentional disturbance.

Study approaches

Accident prevention. Pipeline transportation has a better record than other modes in terms of preventive efforts, since the industry lends itself better to the techniques of

Figure 18.21. Liquid and gas pipeline leaks, failures and fatalities, 1968–1978. SOURCE: *Transportation Safety Information Report,* Oct., Nov., and Dec. 1978, Annual Summary, U.S. Department of Transportation, Washington, D.C., March 1979.

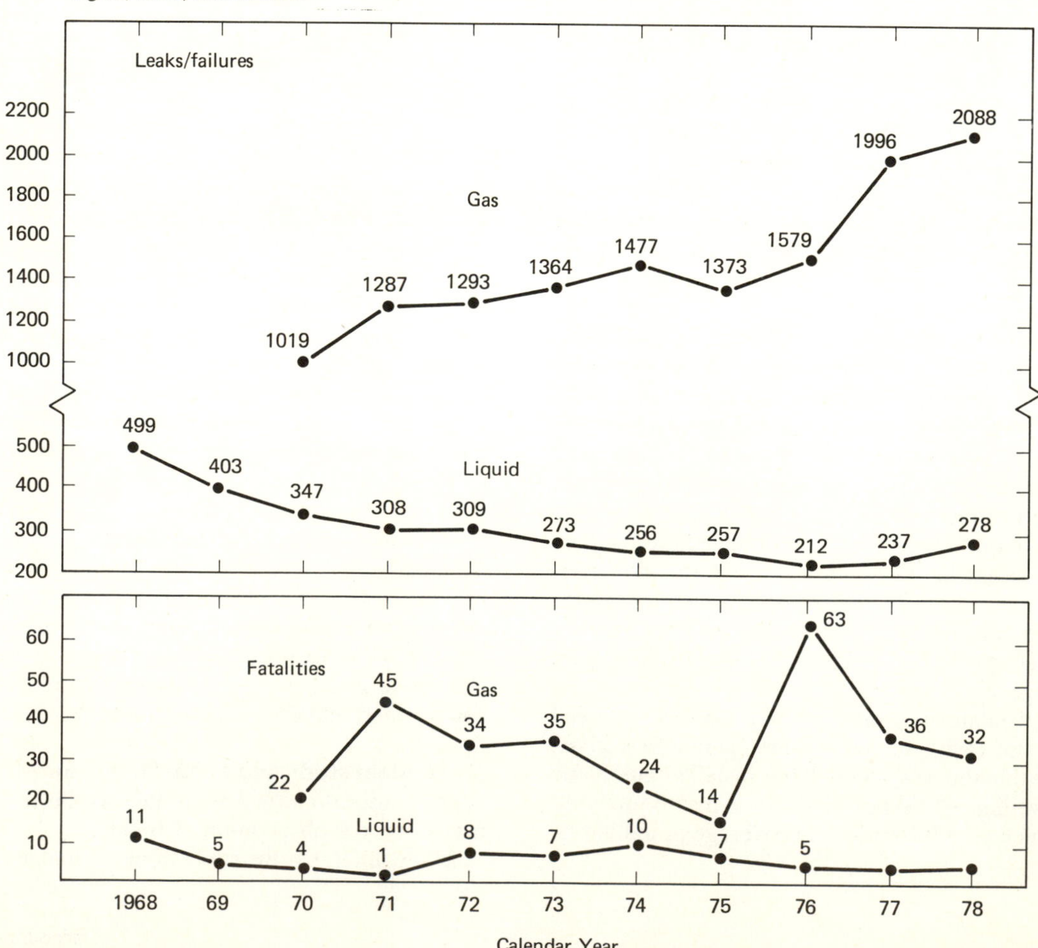

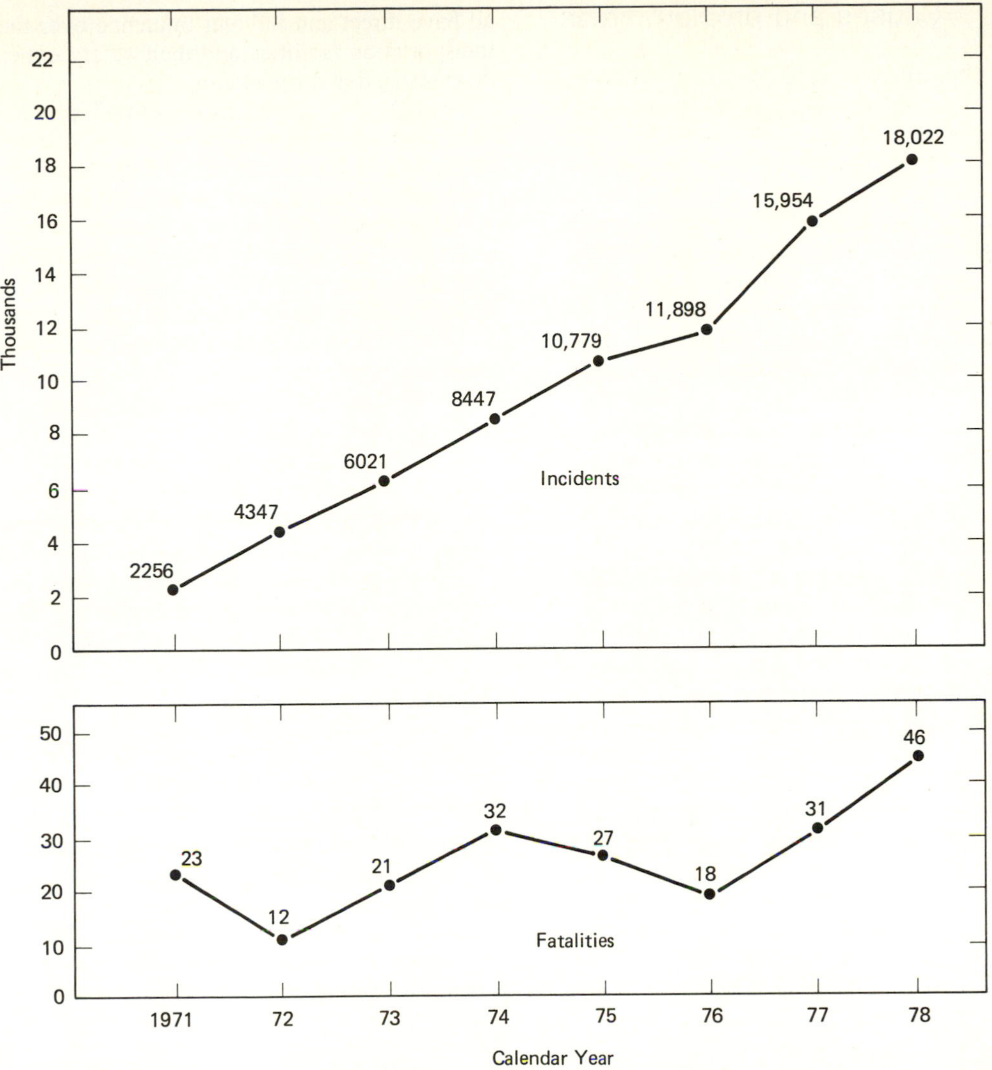

Figure 18.22. Hazardous materials incidents and fatalities, 1971–1978. SOURCE: *Transportation Safety Information Report,* Oct., Nov., and Dec. 1978, Annual Summary, U.S. Department of Transportation, Washington, D.C., March 1979.

system safety. This is because the pipeline transportation industry does not deal with passengers, and the hardware-oriented statistical and engineering techniques of traditional *system safety* lend themselves most easily to such a situation.

Local controls are limited to the granting of permits for construction.

Accident impact attenuation. This aspect is considered in the design stage, through application of *system safety* techniques.

Accident study and analysis. On the *macro scale,* pipeline accidents are relatively few and far between, and therefore do not lend themselves to the study of patterns, except in rare cases.

At the *micro scale,* individual accidents are investigated in detail for clues to causative factors that can be improved.

Transportation of hazardous materials

Trends

Accidents involving the transport of hazardous materials (HAZMAT) are an intermodal safety problem. The number of accidents in this field reached an all-time high in 1978, with 18,022 incidents; these incidents resulted in a record 46 fatalities. Tank trucks and trailers accounted for 1860 hazardous materials incidents, while more than 800 railroad tank car incidents were reported by rail carriers in 1978. Incidents have risen at an almost steady (and high) rate (Figure 18.22) since 1971, while fatalities have fluctuated between 12 and 46. The 3 years 1976–1978, however, show a steep upward trend.

Causes and problem areas

The movement of hazardous freight or cargo involves all modes and has become a major safety problem in the world since World War II. Before that war, only about 1000 different materials being transported were classified as hazardous.

Of concern to transportation engineers is both *operational* and *environmental* safety. Operational safety deals with the safety of persons or property on or near the transportation facility itself. Environmental safety is concerned with the well-being of human beings, animals, plants, and entire ecosystems (including the global ecosystem, which sustains all life).

As an outcome of technological development since World War II all manner of hazardous materials are transported, from volatile liquids and gases, which can be dissipated through explosion and burning, to radioactive materials, whose effects can linger for thousands of years.

The problems involved in transporting hazardous materials by any mode include choices in routing of vehicles and related risk-exposure considerations, design of vehicles to contain the material and to withstand impacts and stresses safely, assessment of the physical and control state of the guideway or environment over which the vehicle must pass, training and competence of operating personnel, knowledge of the nature of the cargo and its effects once released, emergency arrangements for quick action along the route, and information dissemination along the route. These developments make it difficult to produce a standard classification system.

A major problem concerns the variations among states and regions relative to all the problems noted above. Better coordination on a national scale is required to produce stronger policies and standards.

Solutions

Transportation of hazardous materials (HAZMAT) is coming under greater and greater scrutiny by Federal agencies, but because the problem crosses agency and administration lines of concern and authority, and because much of the problem is within the individual states themselves (Federal officials do not approve highway or rail routes for all shipments), or cross international lines, efforts are scattered and uncoordinated. A Materials Handling Bureau (MTB) exists in RSPA, however.

There is greater effort currently from federal departments in taking an active role in coordination and developing uniformity. U.S. DOT participates actively in international standardization and compliance. The MTB provides representation to the United Nations on the international transport of dangerous cargoes.

The U.S. Coast Guard and the International Atomic Energy Agency (IAEA), together with other agencies such as the Federal Aviation Administration, take an active role in various international compliance programs.

In addition to federal efforts, states and local authorities all have direct and indirect influence over the operation of transportation facilities and their safety experience, within their respective jurisdictions.

Solutions, however, to HAZMAT problems mentioned previously involve each of the critical areas: legislation, regulation, enforcement, education, and engineering.

Problems here are modal and intermodal. In each transportation mode, systematic planning is required to consider all aspects of the movement of dangerous materials over long distances, through intersections, switch points, ports, or locks. In addition, the design of vehicles and vessels must be related to the specific problems of that particular transport mode. Personnel involved must be trained specifically for the tasks at hand. Emergency crews must be trained, available, and alerted.

In addition, all such hazardous materials must be transferred, at some point, whether at a seaport, an airport, a tank farm or tank terminal, from transport mode to transport mode, or from transport mode to holding tanks. This transfer creates special problems, depending upon the volatility or other characteristics of the material carried, and must be considered in designs and operational methods.

Finally, whether the ultimate destination of a hazardous material is a final holding tank, an industrial complex, a dumping ground, or sea location, eventual and long-range problems to the environment and the people affected by that environment, whether immediately or in the near or far future, must be considered and designed for by engineers.

Engineers must make trade-offs between costs and degree of safety when dealing with hazardous cargoes. Avoiding dense population centers will add circuity to routes. Many modal systems are poorly maintained. Decisions (risk analysis) must be made between few large shipments and many smaller ones.

Study approaches

Accident prevention. In the transportation of hazardous materials, minimal efforts have gone into prevention, at every level, until relatively recently. The plethora of jurisdictions, modes, vehicle types and qualities, philosophies of risk management, and operator interests and capabilities have all served to retard efforts at systematically reducing risks to lives and property while transporting (and eventually storing or dumping) dangerous materials.

The prevention of accidents involving the transport of dangerous materials relates directly to the prevention efforts of each mode, with the added need for consideration of intermodal conflicts (rail–highway grade crossings, for instance), and the characteristics and qualities of the materials being transported.

In the first respect (intermodal conflicts), little additional preventive effort has been made except in certain rule-making (tanker trucks must stop at a grade crossing). In the second case (character of materials), preventive efforts involve the research conducted and funded by federal agencies, which is intended to improve containment of dangerous materials in transport vehicles.

Accident impact attenuation. Federal requirements which provide for apprising the Surgeon General of the routing of certain materials, plus the selection of routes through less-populated states and local jurisdictions are efforts toward impact reduction.

The availability of the CHEMTREC system, which provides a central location for information concerning the characteristics of specific chemical compounds, is another. CHEMTREC, the Chemical Transportation Emergency Center, is a 24-h service operating through the Manufacturing Chemists' Association. The service provides information concerning the nature of various chemicals for emergency response, and notifies shippers involved in specific incidents.

U.S. DOT and other government agencies provide guidelines for action during an incident. The "Chem-Card," which DOT distributes to many truck drivers, provides a brief description of a specific hazardous material, plus guidelines for emergency action.

Accident study and analysis. On the *macro scale,* incident data are collected by Federal authorities, but this effort is not yet at a high level of comprehensiveness or efficiency.

On the *micro scale,* major incidents are investigated by NTSB and recommendations are made for improvement.

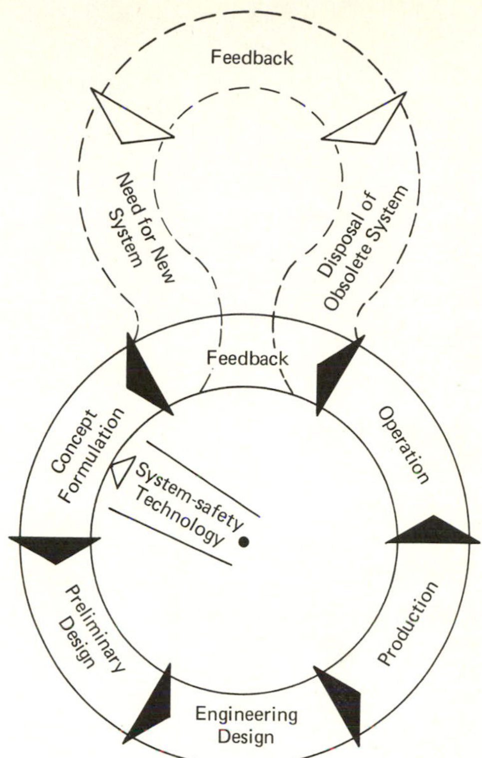

Figure 18.23. Transportation activity cycle (TAC) ring. SOURCE: Michael Horodniceanu and Edmund J. Cantilli, *Transportation System Safety,* D.C. Heath, Lexington, Mass., 1979.

Transportation system safety

Although all transportation modes may be said to be subjected to preventive activities, the efforts in every mode are limited and fragmented. Preventive efforts are quite apparent in the design stages, but such efforts should reach back even earlier, into the concept formulation and planning stages, when new facilities or portions of new facilities are being considered and debated.

In the design stage of most transportation facilities, safety is still at a point where prevention is seen as the proper application of previously developed standards, with little thought given by the design engineer to how such standards may apply to a specific condition in a specific location, under the very particular conditions that prevail.

In the engineering and construction phases, generally, preventive efforts consist in performing the intended work as closely to design specifications as possible, again with little engineering judgment applied to modifications that may be called for by the specific conditions prevalent at the location.

In operating stages, procedures and devices developed many years earlier, under totally different conditions from those prevailing today, are often left unreviewed and unimproved, leading to unsafe conditions, outright hazards, and, eventually, accidents.

In addition, in few transportation modes are the lessons to be learned from current operational and maintenance experience ever fed back and integrated into improvements in the design of new facilities or segments of facilities, or the vehicles that use those facilities.

To bring together all these sporadic and diffuse (and therefore often ineffective) efforts in preventive safety activity, the concept of *transportation system safety* (TSS) was developed.[16]

The engineering approach known as "system safety" was developed by the National Aeronautics and Space Agency (NASA) and the Department of Defense (DOD) as a means of ensuring the reliability, maintainability, and availability of hardware systems. By expanding the concept to include the human being, and by adding management tools and existing analytical procedures used in transportation engineering to the body of knowledge developed earlier, a methodology has been developed which is more closely applicable to the special problems of private and public transportation.

Comprehensiveness is the primary focus of the TSS approach, as shown in the "TAC" ring of Figure 18.23. Each stage of a transportation system's "life cycle" must be considered from the engineering preventive point of view, using "system-safety" technology. A transportation system, whether a network of roads, a rapid-transit line, or an airline route, may be considered as moving through a life cycle, or activity cycle, made up of the following segments:

○Concept formulation (and planning)
○Preliminary design

[16]HORODNICEANU AND CANTILLI, *Transportation System Safety,* D.C. Heath & Co., Lexington, Mass., 1979.

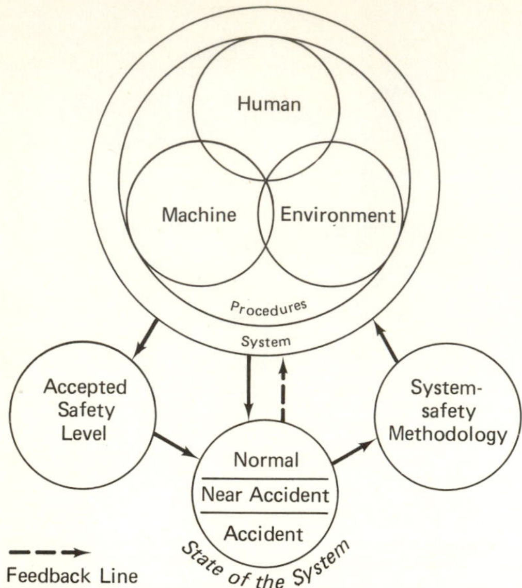

Figure 18.24. Human-machine-environment interactions. SOURCE: Michael Horodniceanu and Edmund J. Cantilli, *Transportation System Safety*, D.C. Heath, Lexington, Mass., 1979.

- Engineering design
- Production, construction, or installation
- Operation (and maintenance)

Later, a system, subsystem, or part of a system may be "disposed" of and replaced (rarely is an entire system scrapped, as in the military, which is the source of this concept). Under *all* circumstances, however, there is the need for "feedback" to link the lessons learned in the *operating* stage with the knowledge needed in the planning and design stages.

Comprehensiveness is also emphasized in the illustration (Figure 18.24) of the relationships of the various elements that influence safety in transportation. The human being, the machine or vehicle, and the environment define a transportation system, and their interactions define the state of safety in a mode or a system. For example, in the highway mode, the *human being* is the driver, the passenger, the pedestrian, the bystander, and the general public; the *machine* is the vehicle, of whatever type, including nonpowered; and the *environment* includes the road, traffic control devices, other vehicles in the traffic stream, the roadsides, conditions of light and weather, regulations, and any other factors that in any way influence the safety of human beings on or near the facility.

The tools assembled for safety analysis as part of TSS include *accident investigation* and *accident analysis,* from current transportation engineering activities; *accident cause–consequence analysis* (ACCA), a modification of a system-safety procedure known as "failure mode effects criticality analysis," which is a means of considering the various scenarios that might lead to a given incident, and the criticality of each step in the ultimate "failure" or accident; human-factors analysis (HFA), a way of bringing together concepts of physiological and psychological "error" into the analytical process; *fault-tree analysis* (FTA), another system-safety tool that provides a means of tracing both the path of a given "top undesired event," such as a single-vehicle roadside accident (see Figure 18.25), from its beginnings, and the probability of its occurrence from the various probabilities of failure that could lead to it; *procedure analysis* (PRA), a management tool for checking the adequacy and applicability of existing procedures, and the need for new procedures, in the operation of facilities; and the *investigation and review* process, a systematic audit and inspection program to uncover hazards.

The proper application of TSS methodology will require major improvements in existing safety-related data bases in all transportation systems, which are becoming more complex and heavily traveled every year.

Only through such a systematized approach can transportation engineers hope to grasp some control over the problem of transportation safety, which involves so many diverse modes, human and mechanical capabilities, and specialized activities.

The future of transportation safety

With increasing transportation activity creating greater risk through increases in conflicts and exposure to error, transportation engineers must approach safety considerations in an engineering manner: a systematic and logical manner that assesses risks, identifies hazards and hazardous conditions, eliminates or reduces the potential for harm done by the hazards, investigates the accidents and incidents that *do* happen for the lessons to be learned from them, and changes designs, personnel training, and procedures to prevent the occurrence or recurrence of accidents.

Organizations involved in transportation safety

Many organizations, public and private, are involved in some aspect of transportation safety. Generally, they are modally specialized. The major governmental agencies involved on a comprehensive level in the U.S. are federal and state, with most funding coming from the federal level. Cities and counties also provide for safety work from their own budgets.

Private organizations are generally consulting firms, interest groups, and nonprofit safety organizations, modally oriented.

Worldwide

On a global basis, the United Nations' *World Health Organization* collects and publishes statistics concerning death by accident, particularly motor vehicle accidents.

A more recently organized privately sponsored organization is the *World Safety Organization,* with headquarters in Manila, the Philippines. This organization sponsors annual meetings, and its interests go beyond transportation to include industrial hygiene and job safety.

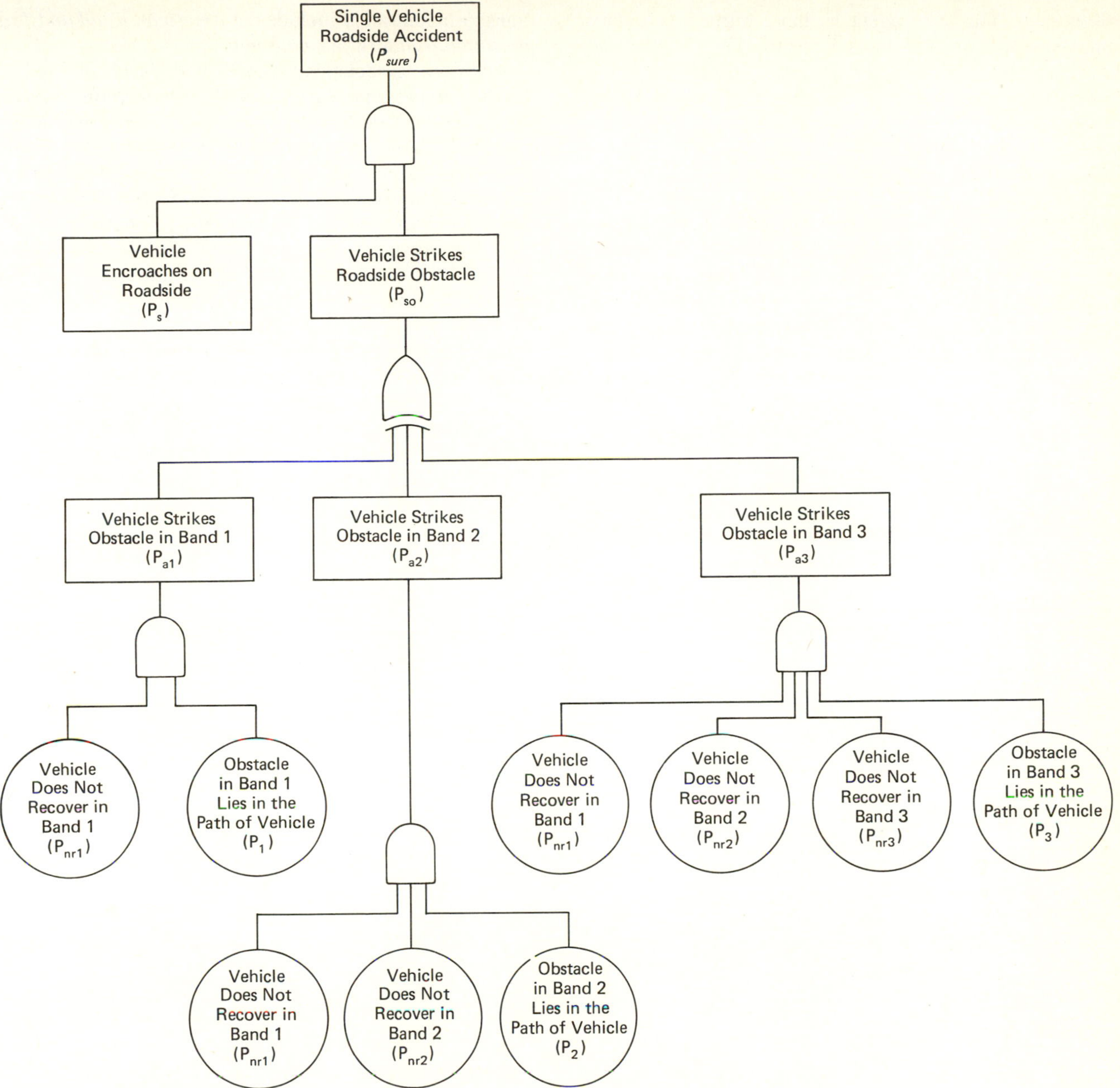

Figure 18.25. Single-vehicle roadside accident fault tree. Note: "Band 1" etc., refers to bands of specified width from edge of road outward; "P" etc., refers to probability of occurrence of the situation described. SOURCE: Michael Horodniceanu and Edmund J. Cantilli, *Transportation System Safety*, D.C. Heath, Lexington, Mass., 1979.

United States

At the national level, the role of the modal administrations in the U.S. Department of Transportation has already been mentioned. In addition, the following federal agencies all have some impact on aspects of transportation safety:

- National Transportation Safety Board
- U.S. Maritime Administration
- Interstate Commerce Commission
- National Aeronautics and Space Administration
- Environmental Protection Agency
- Department of Energy
- Department of Health and Human Services
- Department of the Interior
- Department of Defense

At the state level, most states followed the lead of the 1967 federal reorganization and developed "Departments of Transportation," although many of them are based upon the previous Highway Department or Public Works Department. Some states have special offices for traffic safety, and all states have been mandated to create a *Governor's State Highway Safety Committee,* headed by the governor's representative. The state agencies have formed voluntary organizations to carry this work forward. They include the *American Association of State Highway and Transportation Officials* (AASHTO) and the *Governors' Highway Safety Representatives*.

At county and municipal levels, safety is involved in the work of highway engineers and traffic engineers, with some special emphasis on traffic safety in many localities.

Privately, the *National Safety Council* is the major general safety organization, partially supported by the federal government, with some activities in transportation safety, principally the collection of statistics and the publication of literature and material on driver (motor vehicle) safety and motor vehicle fleet safety. Industrial safety, or the safety of the workplace (transportation yards and shops), is covered in the NSC's activities.

Engineering consultant groups involved in questions of transportation safety include the *American Road and Transportation Builders' Association*.

Engineering societies, such as the *American Society of Civil Engineers*, the *Institute of Transportation Engineers*, the *American Society of Mechanical Engineers*, and the *American Society of Automotive Engineers* are all involved to varying degrees in transportation safety. The *American Society of Safety Engineers* and the *System Safety Society* are specifically oriented toward general safety.

Other organizations include the *Citizens for Highway Safety*, the *American Association for Automotive Medicine*, and the *National Association of Women Highway Safety Leaders*, among many others.

Among the most recent organizations formed is the *Institute for Safety in Transportation*, which addresses safety in all transportation modes, and has as a goal the removal or treatment of safety hazards.

19

GEOMETRIC DESIGN

C. L. KING, *Highway Engineer*

Federal Highway Administration
Washington, D.C.,
and

WILSON B. HARKINS, *Senior Highway Design Engineer*

Federal Highway Administration
Washington, D.C.

The term "geometric design" pertains to the dimensions and arrangements of the visible features of the highway. This includes pavement widths, horizontal and vertical alignment, slopes, channelization, interchanges, and other features the design of which significantly affect highway traffic operation, safety, and capacity. Structural design related to vehicle loads rather than to traffic operations is not included.

The guiding precepts for geometric design have changed significantly over the years. Once, the objective was simply to provide a traversible way between two points. Now many factors must be considered in designing a highway: safety, economy, environmental concerns, energy conservation, and social effects.

Although emphases shift from time to time, the goal of good geometric design remains the same: to provide a safe, efficient, and economical system of highways, consistent with the volumes, speeds, and characteristics of the vehicles and drivers who use them. Highways constructed today will serve well into the future; consequently, designs must anticipate future vehicular characteristics and operational patterns.

Upgrading design standards and criteria to meet changing conditions has been made possible largely through a feedback and evaluation of operational information. No design can be completely evaluated until it has been subjected to traffic. If a facility does not operate as expected, it is imperative to find out why. Not only should the immediate problem be solved, but the answer should also be brought to the attention of the designer for consideration in future designs. This feedback should not be left to chance. There should be a systematic operational evaluation of existing and newly constructed facilities within any highway organization. Subsequently, many operational problems can be eliminated at the design stage, thus reducing the accident potential and providing cost savings for future remedial construction.

A complete international coverage of geometric design reflecting the practice of all countries would take several volumes. Thus, this chapter covers only the important details relating to standards and guides used in the United States and Canada. A survey of other representative countries indicates that, for the most part, design values are similar.

Design types of highways

The most widely accepted design criteria in the United States are those developed by the American Association of State Highway and Transportation Officials (AASHTO). Although every state and many countries, cities, and other governmental bodies have developed their own standards, they are based largely on AASHTO standards for two reasons: (1) AASHTO design policies, standards, and guides have been developed and approved by every state; and (2) the Federal Highway Administration (FHWA) has made them the applicable standards for design and construction of Federal-aid highways. AASHTO design criteria are also used as the basis for design standards used by many other countries.

General highway design standards, policies, and guides have been developed separately for (1) freeways, sometimes divided into Interstate freeways and other freeways; (2) arterial highways other than freeways; and (3) collector roads (secondary roads) and local roads and streets. These three general types of highways (and their rural–urban and sometimes suburban subdivisions) can be considered a form of system classification originating with Federal-aid funding distinctions, but more properly they are groupings of streets and highways for which geometric design values can be clearly separated. A brief description of the highways included in each type and the principal documents that are available for design guidance follows.

Freeways. Includes Interstate highways and all other fully controlled access facilities regardless of the system of which they are a part. Design standards and criteria are found in three publications: *A Policy on Geometric Design of Rural Highways*[1] furnishes basic design criteria and values for all types of rural highways, including freeways. Criteria for a range of conditions are described, sometimes with both minimum and desirable values for general alignment, profile, sight distance, and other design values. *A Policy on Design of Urban Highways and Arterial Streets*[2] supplements the rural policy and provides separate urban values for freeways, expressways-at-grade, arterial highways, and major streets. These two publications are being revised and combined into a single policy covering design of both urban and rural highways. Many of the criteria contained in this chapter are taken from the latest draft of this publication. *Geometric Design Standards for the National System of Interstate and Defense Highways*[3] was specifically developed for Interstate system highways, but it may also be used for design of other freeways.

Arterial highways. Includes the more important highways other than freeways. Design standards and criteria are found in the AASHTO design policy cited above and in *Geometric Design Standards for Highways Other than Freeways*,[4] which is a summary of the principal design controls for urban and rural highways without access control. Generally, the design controls are expressed as minimum values.

Local roads and streets. Includes all other highways. Design standards and criteria also are found in the AASHTO policy cited above and in the *Geometric Design Guide for Local Roads and Streets*,[5] which is applicable for both rural and urban design. *Recommended Practices for Subdivision Streets*[6] also contains standards and criteria for design of urban local and collector streets.

Standards for resurfacing, restoration, and rehabilitation. Although resurfacing, restoration, and rehabilitation projects do not constitute a highway type, they do have a close relationship to the designs for the various types of highways. It is apparent that, at least for the foreseeable future, available funding will be insufficient to improve existing facilities to current geometric standards at a rate comparable to that at which existing pavements are deteriorating. To alleviate this condition increasing amounts of current funding are being used on resurfacing, restoration, and rehabilitation projects. For this reason the need for criteria on these type projects is gaining importance and prominence. Although it would be desirable to include resurfacing, restoration, and rehabilitation values or guidelines in this chapter, criteria are still evolving, and it will require several years of testing and evaluating before proven guidelines appropriate for inclusion are available.

[1]*A Policy on Geometric Design of Rural Highways* (Washington, D.C.: American Association of State Highway Officials, 1965).

[2]*A Policy on Design of Urban Highways and Arterial Streets* (Washington, D.C.: American Association of State Highway Officials, 1973).

[3]*Geometric Design Standards for the National System of Interstate and Defense Highways* (Washington, D.C.: American Association of State Highway Officials, 1967).

[4]*Geometric Design Standards for Highways Other than Freeways* (Washington, D.C.: American Association of State Highway Officials, 1969).

[5]*Geometric Design Guide for Local Roads and Streets* (Washington, D.C.: American Association of State Highway Officials, 1970).

[6]*Recommended Practices for Subdivision Streets* (Washington, D.C.: Institute of Traffic Engineers, 1965). (Currently being revised.)

Design controls and criteria

In geometric design, various controls and criteria are employed to ensure that the facility will accommodate the expected traffic requirements and to encourage consistency and uniformity in operation. To some degree these controls and criteria are applicable to all streets and highways.

Control of access

Definition. Control of access is the condition in which the right of owners or occupants of abutting land or other persons to access, light, air, or view in connection with a highway is fully or partially controlled by public authority.[7] There are two degrees of access control:

1. *Full control of access.* Where the authority to control access is exercised to give preference to through traffic by providing access connections only with selected public roads through the prohibition of crossings at grade or direct private driveway connections.
2. *Partial control of access.* Where the authority to control access is exercised to give preference to through traffic to a degree that, in addition to access connections with selected public roads, there may be some crossings at grade and some private driveway connections.

Application. Access control is accomplished either by obtaining access rights (usually when the right-of-way is purchased) or by using frontage roads. When a freeway is developed on new location, of course, adjoining property owners have no inherent right to direct access to a highway that does not exist.

Highway function should determine the degree of access control needed. Freeways whose main function is to provide mobility should have full control of access. Urban arterial streets and major rural highways should have as great a degree of access control as is feasible.

The principal operational difference between a highway with and without control of access is in the amount of interference with through traffic by other vehicles and pedestrians. With access control, entrances and exits can be located at points best suited to enable vehicles to enter and leave safely without interfering with through traffic. Vehicles are prevented from entering or leaving elsewhere so that regardless of the type or intensity of development of the roadside areas, the efficiency and capacity of the high-

[7]Unless otherwise noted, all definitions of highway terms in this chapter are taken from *AASHTO Highway Definitions* (Washington, D.C.: American Association of State Highway Officials, 1968).

way are maintained at a high level and the accident hazard remains low.

When there is no control of access on some new or improved arterial streets, such as a bypass route, the concentrated flow of traffic can be expected to attract roadside businesses with resultant traffic interference, reduction in capacity of the highway, and increase in accident hazard. As traffic increases and roadside businesses multiply, the hazard increases and considerable congestion may develop. Any remedial treatment may be frustrated by the high value of the roadsides. It is, therefore, desirable to obtain access control initially before land values have increased. In designing arterial streets and highways without access control, initial allowance, such as extra lanes or a two-way left-turn lane, should be made for potential roadside commercial development and its effects on the operation of the facility.

In summary, points of access on streets and highways should be carefully planned to the extent possible. Access should not be allowed at locations where entering and leaving vehicles will create a hazard (such as at locations where sight distance is limited or at a point too close to another intersection). On other than freeways, location of access points should be controlled by curb-cut regulations, driveway permits, zoning restrictions, or frontage roads.

Design speed

Definition. A speed determined for design and correlation of the physical features of a highway that influence vehicle operation: the maximum safe speed maintainable over a specified section of highway when conditions permit design features to govern.

Application. Some features, for example, curvature, superelevation, sight distance, and gradient, are directly related to and vary appreciably with design speed. Pavement and shoulder widths and clearances to walls and rails are less directly related to design speed, but because they can affect vehicle speeds, higher standards for them should be used on highways with higher design speeds. Thus, nearly all geometric design elements of the highway are affected by the selected design speed.

Basis for selection. Design speed selection is influenced by the character of terrain, the density and character of the land use, the classification and function of the highway, the traffic volumes expected to use the highway, and by economic and environmental considerations. Usually, a highway in level terrain warrants a higher design speed than one in mountainous terrain; one in a rural area, a higher design speed than one in an urban area; an arterial highway, a higher design speed than a local road; and a high-volume highway, a higher design speed than one carrying low traffic volumes. Except for local roads and streets in urban areas, the design speed should be as high as possible commensurate with economic and environmental considerations.

Table 19-1 shows typical minimum design speeds for various highway classifications, types of terrain, and various volumes of traffic. These are minimum design speeds for the various conditions of terrain and traffic volumes. Higher than minimum design speeds are used, up to 90 mph (145 km/h) in the United States and 140 km/h (87 mph) in some European countries. Recent changes in the maximum speed limits to 55 mph (90 km/h) in the United States have somewhat reduced the use of design speeds above 70 mph (110 km/h), but it remains desirable to provide as high a design speed as feasible. Design speeds for freeways as shown in Table 19-1 continue to be applicable in that even though vehicles are traveling somewhat slower, highways with higher design speeds are safer. In most other countries speed limits have not been reduced in response to the "energy crisis."

TABLE 19–1
Typical Minimum Design Speeds for Various Types of Highways [mph (km/h)]

Freeways		
Terrain	Rural	Urban
Level	70 (115)	50 (80)
Rolling	60 (95)	50 (80)
Mountainous	50 (80)	50 (80)

Arterial Highways—Rural		
Terrain	Current ADT 50–750, DHV Less Than 200	DHV 200 and Over
Level	50 (80)	70 (115)
Rolling	40 (65)	60 (95)
Mountainous	30 (50)	40 (65)

Arterial Highways	
Urban	Suburban
30–40 mph (50–65 km/h) for all types of terrain and for all traffic volumes	40–50 mph (65–80 km/h) for all types of terrain and for all traffic volumes

Local Roads and Streets—Rural				
Terrain	Current ADT Less Than 50	Current ADT Less Than 250	Current ADT 250–400	Current ADT Greater Than 400, DHV Greater Than 100
Level	30 (50)	30 (50)	40 (65)	50 (80)
Rolling	20 (30)	30 (50)	30 (50)	40 (65)
Mountainous	20 (30)	20 (30)	20 (30)	30 (50)

Local Roads and Streets—Urban	
Collector Streets	Local Streets
30–40 mph (30–65 km/h) for all types of terrain and for all traffic volumes	20–30 mph (30–50 km/h) for all types of terrain and for all traffic volumes

Other speeds to be considered

Average running speed. For all traffic or component thereof, the summation of distance divided by the summation of running times.

Because 50% of all vehicles travel at speeds very close to the average running speeds shown in Table 19-2, they are used as a basis for design of geometric features, such as interchange radii, speed-change lanes, and superelevation of above-minimum curves.

TABLE 19-2
Relationship of Average Running Speed to Design Speed

Design Speed		Average Running Speed for Low-Volume Conditions	
mph	km/h	mph	km/h
30	50	28	45
40	65	36	58
50	80	44	71
60	95	52	84
65	105	55	88
70	115	58	93
75	120	61	98
80	130	64	103

Operating speed. The highest overall speed at which a driver can travel on a given highway under favorable weather conditions and under prevailing traffic conditions without any time exceeding the safe speed as determined by the design speed on a section-by-section basis.

Operating speed is usually about 5 mph (8 km/h) higher than the average running speed for low-volume conditions on free-flow facilities. It is used as a measure of level of service for those highways that provide uninterrupted flow conditions (usually rural only) for vehicular travel and is therefore useful in determining the level of service provided by a specific traveled way.[8]

Average overall travel speed. The summation of distances traveled by all vehicles over a given section of highway during a specified period of time, divided by the summation of overall travel times.

Average overall travel speed is used as a measure of level of service for interrupted flow conditions (urban arterial and downtown streets) and is therefore useful in determining the level of service of a specific traveled way in urban areas.

Design volume

Definition. A volume determined for design, representing traffic expected to use the highway. Current or estimated average daily traffic (ADT) may be used for designing local roads and streets. For more important two-lane highways, the design hourly volumes (DHV) concept is used—usually the thirtieth highest hourly volume that is expected to occur in some future design year. For multilane highways, use is made of the directional design hourly volumes (DDHV) for some future design year.

Application. The design volume represents the "load" that the highway must accommodate and it determines to a large degree the type of facility, required roadway widths, as well as other geometric features.

Determination. Determination of the design volume begins with the current or estimated ADT. This value is generally determined from planning studies. For all except local roads and streets (for which ADT may or may not be projected to some future year), the ADT is then projected to some future year, usually from 5 to 20 years beyond the estimated construction year. The DHV is then established by multiplying this future ADT by a *K* factor.

The *K* factor is the ratio of the DHV to the ADT. On the average main rural highway the *K* factor is about 15%[9] and for urban arterial streets about 11% of the ADT. A characteristic of the *K* factor is that for a particular facility it generally decreases only slightly over time with increases in the ADT. Therefore, the *K* factor determined for current traffic volumes need only be adjusted slightly, if at all, when used to determine future design hourly volumes. For two-lane highways, the DHV is used for design.

The directional design hourly volume (DDHV) is determined by multiplying the DHV by a directional factor (*D*). The *D* factor is the percentage of traffic in the dominant direction of flow during the design hour. On highways with more than two lanes, and on two-lane roads with important intersections, directional traffic estimates are essential. Traffic distribution by direction during peak hours is usually considered to remain unchanged throughout the week and year. Traffic data for rural and outlying urban highways show about 60 to 80% of peak-hour traffic in one direction, with an average *D* value of about 67%. In and near central business districts, particularly in large cities, *D* values approach 50%. Representative *D* values in large cities are: in downtown areas, about 55% on radial routes and inner belt lines; about 60% in intermediate areas; and 65 to 75% on radial routes in outlying areas.

The percentage of truck and bus traffic during the design hour, the *T* factor, should also be estimated so that allowances in the geometric design criteria can be made.[10] Vehicles of different sizes and weights have different operating characteristics, and the effect on traffic operation of one truck or bus is often equivalent to several passenger vehicles, depending on the gradient and the operating characteristics of the trucks (see Chapter 16). On rural highways *T* values range up to 7 to 9%.[11] On principal urban highways *T* values may reach 10%, particularly where local bus lines utilize the same route. On other urban routes which carry traffic primarily between the suburbs and the central business district (CBD), *T* values do not generally exceed 5%. A *T* value established on the basis of current traffic generally can be assumed to be applicable to future traffic volumes. The effects of trucks and buses in the traffic stream are allowed for by either decreasing the service volume or capacity or by increasing the equivalent passenger car volume.

In summary, it is necessary to know the traffic elements shown in Table 19-3 for design purposes for various type highways.

Design vehicle

Definition. A selected motor vehicle, the dimensions and operating characteristics of which are used in highway design. For purposes of geometric design, the selected de-

[8]"Traveled way" is defined in the upcoming "Cross Section" discussion.

[9]*A Policy on Geometric Design of Rural Highways*, p. 56.

[10]In Europe, use is made of the passenger car unit (pcu) which corresponds to a private car. For other vehicles, a pcu equivalent is applied.

[11]*A Policy on Geometric Design of Rural Highways*, p. 70.

TABLE 19–3
Summary of Traffic Elements Needed for Design Purposes

Type of Highway	Traffic Elements Required for Design
Local roads and streets	ADT, current or estimated average daily traffic
Two-lane arterial highways	ADT, current and estimated (for some future year) average daily traffic DHV, design hourly volume for some future year *T*, percentage of trucks during design hour
Multilane arterial highways and freeways	ADT, current and estimated (for some future year) average daily traffic DDHV, directional design hourly volume for the through lanes and turning movements *T*, percentage of trucks during design hour

sign vehicle should be one with dimensions and minimum turning radius as large or larger than almost all vehicles expected to use the highway.

Application. Design vehicle characteristics are used to develop sight distance, intersection design, cross section, and other geometric design criteria. Seven design vehicles are used for purposes of geometric design, one of which is selected with dimensions and turning characteristics equal to or greater than those of the largest vehicles expected in appreciable numbers (see Table 19-4). Similar data for vehicles of local or regional significance may be used to establish other design vehicles.

The minimum turning path for the specific design vehicle is particularly important. The generally circular path of the front overhang and the elliptical path of the inner rear wheel usually govern for design. Proper clearance beyond these paths must be provided to allow for a factor of safety. The outer front wheel is assumed to follow a circular arc which is the minimum turning radius as determined by the vehicle steering mechanism. A typical turning path of a WB-50 design vehicle is shown in Figure 19.1.[12] The minimum outside and inside wheel paths generally used are as follows:

[12]For others, see *A Policy on Design of Urban Highways*, pp. 268–276; and the new AASHTO policy on design of rural and urban highways when it is published.

Design designation

Design designation indicates the major controls for which a given highway is designed. It is largely independent of highway systems. The following tabulation is an example of a design designation for a freeway.

Design year	1995
Average daily traffic (current year)	20,100
Average daily traffic (design year)	39,600
Design hourly volume	4,400
Directional distribution of traffic	67%
Trucks	5%
Design speed	60 mph (95 km/h)
Control of access	full
Design level of service	C
Buses (current year)	200
Buses (design year)	300

Other necessary information for geometric design includes:

1. Pedestrian volumes and locations of crossings
2. Type, location, and nature of parking, if any required
3. Transit operation
4. Applicable design vehicle
5. Vehicle occupancy
6. Turning movements

Design elements

A number of design elements are common to all types of streets and highways. Reference to these elements will be made throughout the chapter.

TABLE 19–4
Design Vehicle Dimensions*

Design Vehicle		Dimensions (ft)					
Type	Symbol	Wheelbase	Front Overhang	Rear Overhang	Overall Length	Overall Width	Height
Passenger car	P	11	3	5	19	7	—
Single-unit truck	SU	20	4	6	30	8.5	13.5
Single-unit bus	Bus	25	7	8	40	8.5	13.5
Articulated bus	A-Bus	18 + 24 = 42	8	10	60	8.5	10.5
Semitrailer—combination intermediate	WB-40	13 + 27 = 40	4	6	50	8.5	13.5
Semitrailer—combination large	WB-50	20 + 30 = 50	3	2	55	8.5	13.5
Semitrailer—fulltrailer combination	WB-60	9.7 + 20.0 + 9.4† + 20.9 = 60	2	3	65	8.5	13.5

*Metric conversion factor: multiply value by 0.305 m/ft.
†Distance between rear wheels of front trailer and front wheels of rear trailer.

Design vehicle type	P		SU		A-bus		Bus		WB-40		WB-50		WB-60	
Minimum turning radius [ft (m)]	24	(7.3)	42	(12.8)	38	(11.6)	42	(12.8)	40	(12.2)	45	(13.7)	45	(14.7)
Minimum inside radius [ft (m)]	14.9	(4.7)	27.8	(2.7)	21	(6.4)	24.0	(7.1)	17.7	(6.1)	16.6	(6.0)	21.4	(6.9)

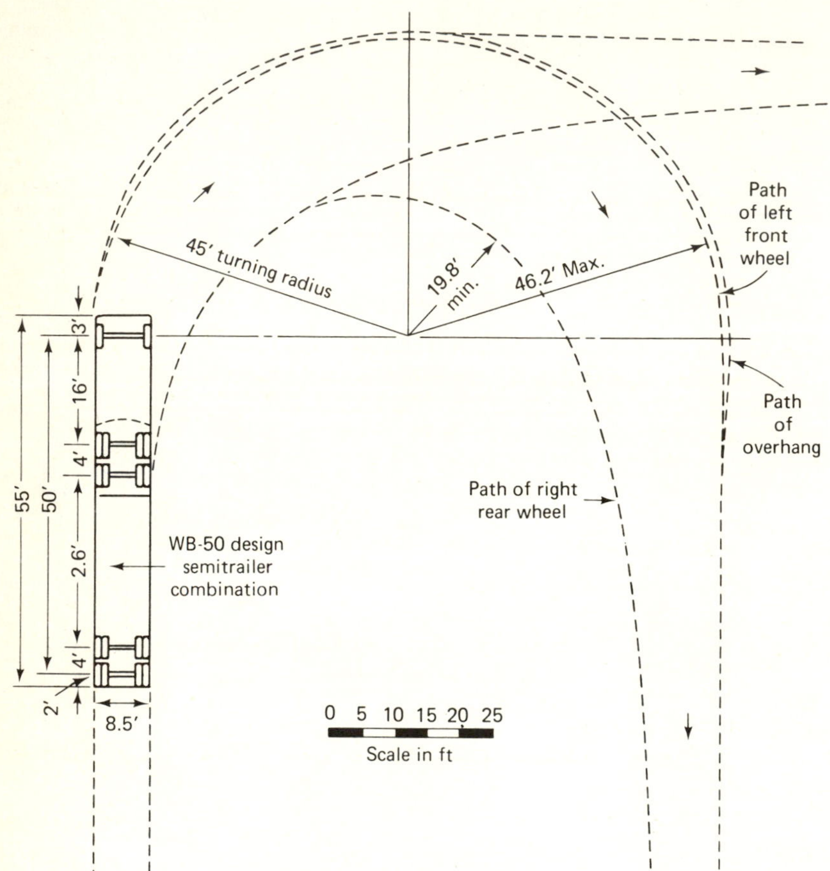

Figure 19.1. Minimum design path of typical design truck (WB-50 design vehicle). (Metric conversion factor: multiply value by 0.305 m/ft.) SOURCE: *A Policy on Geometric Design of Rural Highways*, Washington, D.C.: American Association of State Highway Officials, 1965, p. 84.

Sight distance

Stopping sight distance. Sight distance is the length of highway visible to the driver. Sight distance everywhere along a highway should be adequate for all but a few of the fastest drivers to come to a safe stop before reaching an object. Stopping sight distance used for design is the sum of two distances: (1) the distance a vehicle travels after the driver sights an object and begins braking and (2) the distance it travels during braking.

The stopping sight distance (SSD) in feet is determined from the formula

$$SSD = 1.47PV + \frac{V^2}{30(f \pm g)} \qquad (19.1)$$

where V = speed from which stop is made, mph

P = perception-reaction time, s

f = coefficient of friction (for wet pavement used for design)

g = percent of grade divided by 100 (added for upgrade and subtracted for downgrade)

If vehicle speed is in km/h, the stopping sight distance in meters is

$$SSD = 0.278PV + \frac{V^2}{225(f \pm g)} \qquad (19.2)$$

The range of minimum stopping sight distances for highways having various design speeds is shown in Table 19-5. Minimum distances assume that the vehicle is traveling at less than the design speed (the assumed speeds on which the minimum stopping distances are based). Longer distances assume that the vehicle is traveling at the design speed.

Stopping sight distance is measured from a "seeing" height of 3.5 ft (1.05 m) to an object height of 0.5 ft (15 cm). Desirable stopping sight distance values should be used for design whenever possible. Stopping sight distance values less than the minimum should never be considered.

Decision sight distance. Where conditions encountered by the driver are complex, there is often a need to provide sufficient space for a driver to do more than come to a stop. This space, termed decision sight distance, is defined as the

TABLE 19–5
Minimum Stopping Sight Distance on Wet Pavements*

Design Speed mph	Design Speed km/h	Assumed Speed for Condition mph (km/h)	Brake Reaction Time (s)	Brake Reaction Distance (ft)	Coefficient of Friction, *f*	Braking Distance on Level (ft)	Stopping Sight Distance Computed (ft)	Stopping Sight Distance Rounded for Design (ft)
20	30	20 (30)	2.5	73	0.40	33	106	120
30	50	28 (45)–30 (50)	2.5	103–110	0.35	75–86	178–196	200–200
40	65	36 (55)–40 (65)	2.5	132–147	0.32	135–167	267–314	275–325
50	80	44 (70)–50 (80)	2.5	161–183	0.30	215–278	376–461	375–475
60	95	52 (85)–60 (95)	2.5	191–220	0.29	311–414	502–634	525–650
65	105	55 (90)–65 (105)	2.5	202–238	0.29	348–486	550–724	550–725
70	115	58 (95)–70 (115)	2.5	213–257	0.28	400–583	613–840	625–850
75	120	61 (100)–75 (120)	2.5	224–275	0.28	443–670	667–945	675–950
80	130	64 (105)–80 (130)	2.5	235–293	0.27	506–790	741–1083	750–1100

Metric conversion factor: multiply value by 0.305 m/ft.

TABLE 19–6
Decision Sight Distance*

Design Speed mph	Design Speed km/h	Times (s) Premaneuver: Detection and Recognition	Premaneuver: Decision and Response Initiation	Maneuver (lane change)	Summation	Decision Sight Distance (ft) Computed	Rounded for Design
30	50	1.5–3	4.2–6.5	4.5	10.2–14	449–616	450–625
40	65	1.5–3	4.2–6.5	4.5	10.2–14	598–821	600–825
50	80	1.5–3	4.2–6.5	4.5	10.2–14	748–1027	750–1025
60	95	2–3	4.7–7.0	4.5	11.2–14.5	986–1276	1000–1275
70	115	2–3	4.7–7.0	4.0	10.7–14	1098–1437	1100–1450
80	130	2–3	4.7–7.0	4.0	10.7–14	1255–1643	1250–1650

*Metric conversion factor: multiply value by 0.305 m/ft.

SOURCE: McGee, H. W., Moore, W., Knapp, B. G., and Sanders, J. H. *Decision Sight Distance for Highway Design and Traffic Requirements*, U.S. Department of Transportation, FHWA, Washington, D.C. 1978.

distance at which drivers can detect a signal or hazard in a cluttered or visually noisy roadway environment, recognize it, and perform the required actions safely. Its values are substantially longer than those for stopping sight distance.

Locations where it is desirable to provide decision sight distance are: (1) complex interchanges and intersections; (2) any locations where unusual or unexpected maneuvers are required; (3) any variation in cross sections, such as toll plazas and lane drops; (4) where roadway elements, traffic and signs, signals, and other traffic control devices compete; and (5) areas where an unexpected maneuver may be required.

Table 19-6 shows a range of decision sight distances based on most complex situations. In measuring decision sight distance, the 3.5-ft (1.05-m) seated eye height criterion used to measure stopping sight distance is retained. However, the 6-in. (15 cm) object height is not retained and a zero height of object is adopted. Table 19-6 also shows the factors used to compute decision sight distances.

Passing sight distance. Passing sight distance is applicable only on two-lane, two-way highways. Passing sight distance is the length of highway ahead necessary for one vehicle to pass another before meeting an opposing vehicle which might appear after the pass began. Passing sight distances used for design, given in Table 19-7, are based on various traffic behavior assumptions.[13]

TABLE 19–7
Minimum Passing Sight Distances

Used for Design: Design Speed mph	km/h	Minimum Passing Sight Distance ft	m	Used for Pavement Marking: 85th Percentile Speed mph	km/h	Minimum Passing Sight Distance ft	m
20	30	800	245	—	—	—	—
30	50	1100	335	30	48	500	152
40	64	1500	457	40	64	600	183
50	80	1800	549	50	80	800	244
60	97	2100	640	60	97	1000	305
65	105	2300	701	—	—	—	—
70	113	2500	762	70	113	1200	366
75	121	2600	793	—	—	—	—
80	129	2700	823	—	—	—	—

Passing sight distances for purposes of pavement marking are also given in Table 19-7. No-passing zone markings, given in the *Manual on Uniform Traffic Control Devices,*[14]

[13] "A Policy on Design of Rural Highways." pp. 140–145. Also refer to the new AASHTO policy on rural and urban highways when it is published.

[14] FEDERAL HIGHWAY ADMINISTRATION, U.S. DEPARTMENT OF TRANSPORTATION, *Manual on Uniform Traffic Control Devices for Streets and Highways*, (Washington, D.C.: Government Printing Office, 1978), p. 3B–8.

are based on different assumptions which result in lower values. No-passing zones are based on the 85th percentile speed during low-volume conditions, which is slightly less than the design speed.

Sight distance adequate for passing should be provided frequently in design of two-lane highways, and each passing section should be as long as feasible. Although the frequency and lengths of such passing sections depend on physical and cost considerations and cannot be reduced to a standard, the importance of providing passing opportunities on as much of the length of a two-lane highway as possible cannot be overemphasized. The percentage of the highway where passing can take place affects not only capacity, but also the safety, comfort, and convenience of all highway users.

For purposes of design, passing sight distance for both horizontal and vertical restrictions is measured from a "seeing" height of 3.5 ft (1.05 m) to an object height of 4.25 ft (1.3 m). For purposes of marking pavement, it is measured from a "seeing" height of 3.75 ft (1.15 m) to an object height of 3.75 ft (1.15 m).

Intersection sight distance. Intersections should be planned and located to provide as much sight distance as possible. In achieving a safe highway design, as a minimum, there should be sufficient sight distance for the driver on the minor highway to cross the major highway without requiring approaching traffic to reduce speed. Minimums for different design speeds are shown in Table 19-8. Stop controls are assumed; other forms of traffic control have different intersection sight distance requirements.

TABLE 19–8
Suggested Corner Sight Distance at Intersections*

Design speed mph (km/h)				
20 (32)	30 (48)	40 (64)	50 (80)	60 (97)
Minimum corner intersection sight distance* ft (m)				
200 (61)	300 (91)	400 (122)	500 (152)	600 (183)

*Corner sight distance measured from a point of the minor road at least 15 ft (4.6 m) from the edge of the major road pavement and measured from a height of eye of 3.5 ft (1.05 m) on the minor road to a height of object of 4.25 ft (1.3 m) on the major road.

Procedures for checking plans. It is often desirable during the preliminary design stage to determine graphically the sight distances and record them at frequent intervals. Methods for scaling sight distances and a typical sight distance record which should be shown on final plans are shown in Figure 19.2. For two-lane highways, passing sight distance, in addition to stopping sight distance, should be shown.

Horizontal sight distance on the inside of curves may be limited by obstructions such as buildings, plant growth, or cut slope. Horizontal sight distance is measured along a straight edge, as indicated in the upper left in Figure 19.2.

Figure 19.2. Scaling and recording sight distances on plans. (Metric conversion factor: multiply values by 0.305 m/ft.) SOURCE: Adapted from *A Policy on Geometric Design of Rural Highways*, Washington, D.C.: American Association of State Highway Officials, 1965, p. 150.

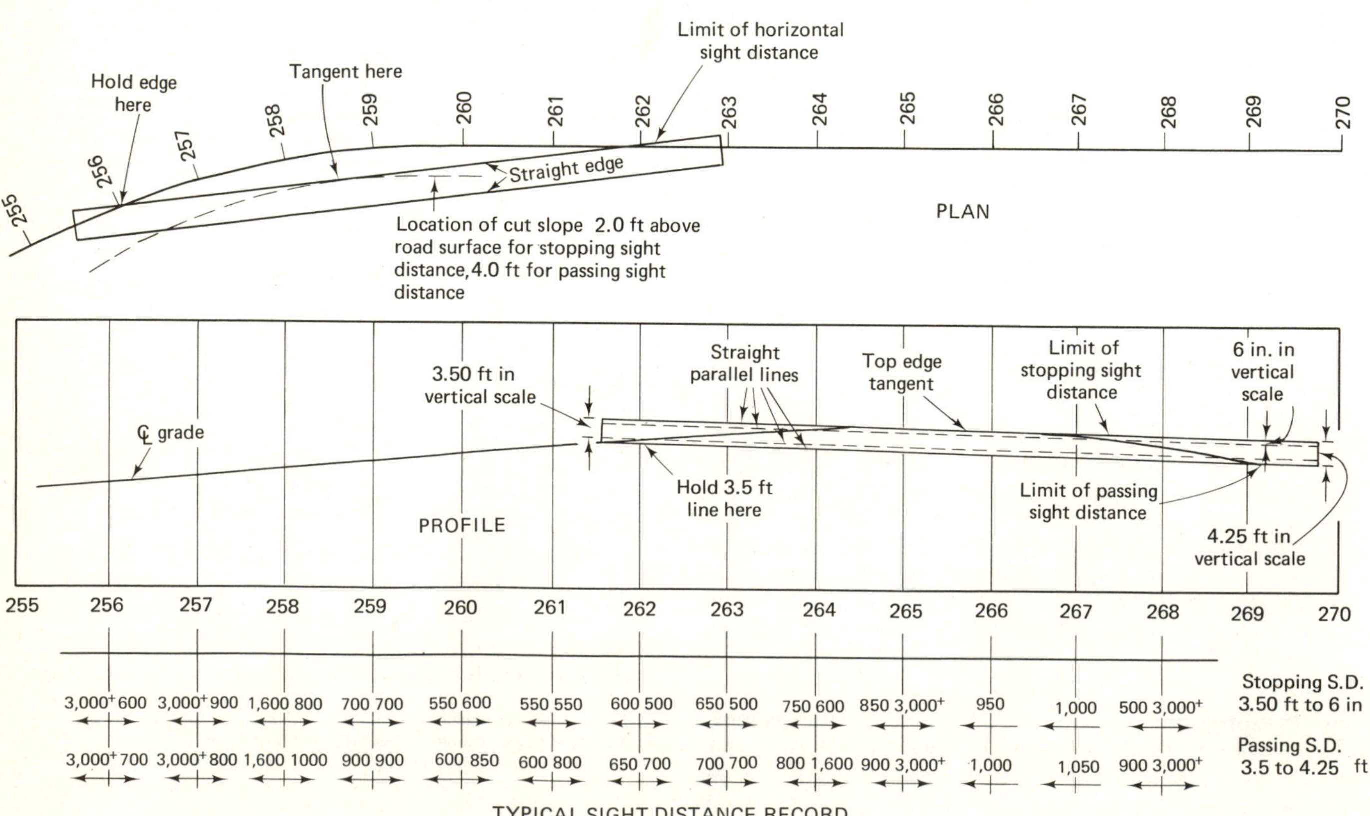

The cut slope obstruction is shown on the work sheets by a line representing the proposed excavation slope at a point about 2.0 ft (0.6 m) (average of 3.5 ft and 0.5 ft) above the road surface for stopping sight distance and about 4.0 ft (1.2 m) for passing sight distance. The stopping sight distance should be measured from center-to-center of the same traffic lane; the passing sight distance should be measured from the center of inside lane to center of outside lane.

Vertical sight distance may also be scaled, as shown in Figure 19.2. A transparent straightedge is used with a scaled width of 4.25 ft (1.3 m). Lines are drawn 6 in. (15 cm) and 3.5 ft (1.1 m) from the upper edge, in accordance with the vertical scale. The 3.5-ft line is placed on the station from which the vertical sight distance is desired, and the strip is pivoted about this point until the upper edge is tangent to the profile. The distance between the initial station and the station on the profile intersected by the 6-in. line is the stopping sight distance. The distance between the initial station and and the 4.25-ft line is the passing sight distance.

Sight distance design records are useful on two-lane highways for determining the percentage of highway length on which sight distance is restricted to less than the passing minimum—an important criterion in evaluating the overall design and the capacity. Where a computer is used in the design, it can be programmed to determine the proportion of passing sight distance.

Vertical alignment

Vertical alignment consists of tangent grades and vertical curves. Although there are no exact relationships, maximum grades and curvatures are generally related to design speed. Widely accepted criteria follow.

Vertical curves. In U.S. practice, vertical curves are parabolic. In Europe, circular curves are used. Parabolic curves are identified by their lengths and the algebraic difference of the grades they connect. The minimum length of vertical curve may be computed from the formula

$$L = KA \tag{19.3}$$

where L = length of vertical curve, ft

K = a constant for design

A = algebraic difference in grades, %

or, if L is in meters,

$$L = \frac{KA}{3.28} \tag{19.4}$$

K is constant for each design speed, and its selection for crest vertical curves is based on sight distance requirements. For sag vertical curves, K is based on headlight sight distance, which is assumed to be the length of a light beam from a source to the point of its intersection with the roadway surface. The source is considered to be 2.0 ft (0.6 m) above the pavement on a 1° upward divergence from the longitudinal axis of the vehicle to where the beam intersects the roadway surface. The formula computes minimum lengths of vertical curve in each case, but K values vary for each

TABLE 19–9
Design Controls for Vertical Curves: *K* Values*

Design Speed		Crest Curves			Sag Curves	
		Stopping Sight Distance		Passing Sight Distance	Stopping Sight Distance	
mph	km/h	Minimum	Desirable		Minimum	Desirable
20	30	10		160	18	
30	50	30		390	35	35
40	65	55	80	725	55	70
50	80	100	170	1050	80	110
60	95	200	320	1425	125	155
65	105	215	395	1710	130	180
70	115	280	545	2020	150	215
75	120	325	680	2185	165	240
80	130	400	910	2355	185	285

*Metric conversion factor: multiply values by 0.305 m/ft.

design speed and condition. Table 19-9 gives K values to be used for the three controls.

Grades. Maximum grades recommended for road design are mostly governed by their influence on truck speeds. Table 19-10 summarizes typical maximum grade controls for various classes of highways.

General controls. In addition to grade and vertical curvature controls, additional considerations in designing vertical alignment include:

1. Smooth grade lines with gradual changes, consistent with the class of highway and character of terrain, should be provided. Figure 19.3(a) shows an undesirable design

TABLE 19–10
Maximum Grades

Design Speed		Maximum Gradient (%)		
mph	km/h	Other Than in Mountainous Terrain		Mountainous Terrain
		Freeways		
50	80	5		7
60	95	4		6
70	115	3		5
		Arterial Highways*		
		Flat	Rolling	Mountainous
30	50	6	7	9
40	65	5	6	8
50	80	4	5	7
60	95	3	4	6
65	105	3	4	6
70	115	3	4	5
75	120	3	4	—
80	130	3	4	—
		Local Roads and Streets†		
		Flat	Rolling	Mountainous
20	30	7	10	15
30	50	7	9	13
40	65	7	8	11
50	80	6	7	9
60	95	5	6	—

*Short grades less than 500 ft (150 m) in length and one-way downgrades may be 1% steeper. For extreme cases, in urban areas and at some underpasses and bridge approaches, steeper grades for relatively short lengths may be considered. For low-volume rural highways, grades may be 2% steeper.
†For highways with ADT's below 250, grades of relatively short lengths may be increased to 150% of value shown.

(a)

(b)

Figure 19.3. Examples of highways showing the visual effects of (a) using short vertical curves and (b) the more desirable practice of using a smooth grade line with gradual changes. SOURCE: (a) Bob L. Smith, Professor of Civil Engineering, Kansas State University. (b) U.S. Department of Transportation, Federal Highway Administration.

in which short vertical curves are used in conjunction with relatively short tangent gradients. Figure 19.3(b) shows a much better alignment where long sweeping vertical curves are used in spite of the rugged terrain conditions.

2. "Roller-coaster" or "hidden-dip" profiles should be avoided. The profile in Figure 19.4(a) is aesthetically unpleasant and probably hazardous. Figure 19.4(b) shows the preferable use of a long, rolling grade line.
3. Broken-back grade lines (two vertical curves in the same direction separated by a short piece of tangent) should be avoided. Figure 19.5(a) shows an undesirable design of this type; Figure 19.5(b) illustrates a design that avoids a broken-back grade line. On long grades it may be preferable to place the steepest grades at the bottom if the terrain is such that a choice can be made.
4. Grades through at-grade intersections on highways with moderate or steep grades should be reduced whenever possible.

(a)

(b)

Figure 19.4. Example of highways with (a) a "roller-coaster" grade line and (b) the much more desirable profile with a long vertical curve. SOURCE: (a) Bob L. Smith, Professor of Civil Engineering, Kansas University. (b) U.S. Department of Transportation, Federal Highway Administration.

Figure 19.5. Example of (a) a vertical alignment with a "broken-back" grade line and (b) a much more desirable alignment in which a broken alignment has been avoided. SOURCE: (a) Bob L. Smith, Professor of Civil Engineering, Kansas State University. (b) U.S. Department of Transportation, Federal Highway Administration.

(a)

(b)

Horizontal alignment

Horizontal alignment consists of tangents and horizontal curves. In U.S. practice, horizontal curves are circular curves with a constant radius often connected to the tangents with transitions (either compound, single circular or spiral curves). Criteria for determining maximum curvature are based on the laws of mechanics, with design values depending on practical limits for superelevation and friction factors representative of pavement surfaces. The basic formula for determining horizontal curvature is

$$e + f = \frac{V^2}{15R} \tag{19.5}$$

where e = rate of roadway superelevation, ft/ft (m/m)

f = side friction factor

V = vehicle speed, mph

R = radius of curve, ft

or if V is in km/h and R is in meters, the formula is

$$e + f = \frac{V^2}{127R} \tag{19.6}$$

Maximum superelevation. Maximum superelevation rates are controlled by several factors which may vary widely: (1) frequency and amount of snow and ice; (2) type of area, whether rural or urban; and (3) frequency of slow-moving vehicles. Maximum e values range upward to 0.10 for highways in rural areas where there is no snow and ice. Where snow and ice conditions prevail, e values normally range from 0.08 to 0.10. Although uncommon practice, much higher e values could be desirable at special locations (on a one-way, downgrade ramp, for example).

The most commonly used e value is 0.08 for all highway classifications in rural areas and for freeways in developed areas. For other highways in urban areas, superelevation is not generally used, although e values up to 0.06 are sometimes applicable. In other countries, superelevation is expressed as a percentage and the maximum used is most commonly 7% (or e = 0.07).

Maximum degree of curvature. The other variable that influences maximum curvature is the side friction factor (f), which is assumed to be 0.16 for 30 mph (50 km/h) and 0.01 less than this value for each 10-mph (15-km/h) increase in design speed up to 0.14 at 50 mph (80 km/h). A 0.02 decrease for each 10-mph change in speeds above 50 mph (80 km/h) is assumed, which results in a 0.08 value for f at 80 mph. The maximum radii and degree of curvature for the various design speeds for maximum e values of 0.06 to 0.10, computed from the basic horizontal formula and the side friction factors given above, are shown in Table 19-11.

In addition to the controls on maximum curvature to satisfy the requirements outlined above, the need to provide minimum stopping sight distance around curves may be a control when sight distance cannot be otherwise provided by removing the sight obstruction. Figure 19.6 shows the required middle ordinates (m) for clear sight areas for various degrees of curve (D) based on the range of lower values for stopping sight distance. The figure may be used to determine the minimum radius (R) or degree (D) of the curve necessary to provide sufficient sight distance (S) from Table 19-8 for each design speed (V). The figure applies only when the horizontal curve is longer than the sight distance required. For other cases (including other than a vertical cut slope obstruction), either a graphic check as described previously or a more detailed analytical check should be made.

TABLE 19–11
Maximum Degree of Curve and Minimum Radius for Design*

Maximum e	Design Speed [mph (km/h)] 20 (35)	30 (50)	40 (65)	50 (80)	60 (95)	65 (105)	70 (110)	75 (120)	80 (130)
	Minimum Radius (ft)								
0.04	127	302	573	955	1528				
0.06	116	273	509	849	1348	1637	2083	2546	3274
0.08	107	252	468	764	1206	1528	1910	2292	2865
0.10	99	231	432	694	1091	1348	1637	2083	2546
	Maximum Degree of Curve								
0.04	45	19.0	10.0	6.0	3.75				
0.06	49.25	21.0	11.25	6.75	4.25	3.5	2.75	2.25	1.75
0.08	53.5	22.75	12.25	7.5	4.75	3.75	3.0	2.5	2.0
0.10	58	24.75	13.25	8.25	5.25	4.25	3.5	2.75	2.25

*Metric conversion factor: multiply values by 0.305 m/ft.

Superelevation rates. For curves of less than the maximum degree of curvature, the rate of superelevation is proportioned between the maximum curve for which superelevation is not required and the maximum curve for the selected maximum rate of superelevation. The superelevation rates (e) for various degrees of curvature for a maximum e value of 0.08 are presented in Table 19-12.[15]

Superelevation runoff and transition curves. Transition curves used in the United States are either a series of compounded circular curves or a spiral curve. Spirals provide a natural, easy-to-follow driving path, can enhance highway appearance, and provide a desirable arrangement for superelevation runoff.

Spirals are identified by their length, which is usually governed by the distance required for superelevation runoff. Lengths required for superelevation runoff and consequently spiral lengths are generally from 100 to 250 ft (30 to 75 m), the lengths increasing with higher design speeds. Table 19-12 also presents recommended lengths of superelevation runoff or spiral curves for a maximum e value of 0.08.

Without spirals, a large portion of the superelevation runoff must be placed on the approach tangents. In general, from 50 to 100% of the length of superelevation runoff can be considered suitable. For more precise control, from 60 to 80% of the runoff should be located on the approach tangents.

[15]Similar tables for other maximum e values are found in *A Policy on Geometric Design of Rural Highways, pp. 168–71, and the new AASHTO policy on rural and urban highways when it is published.*

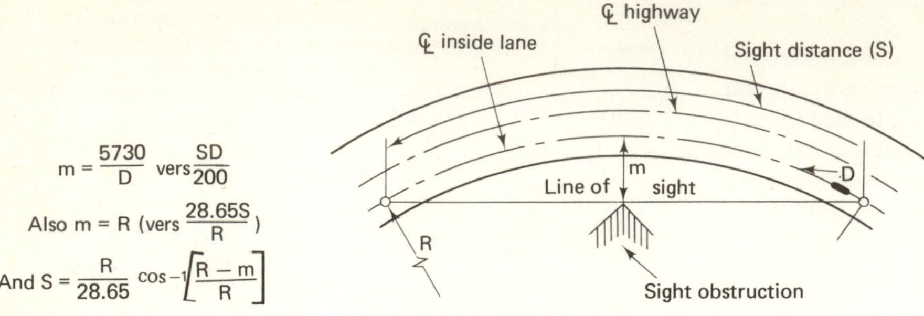

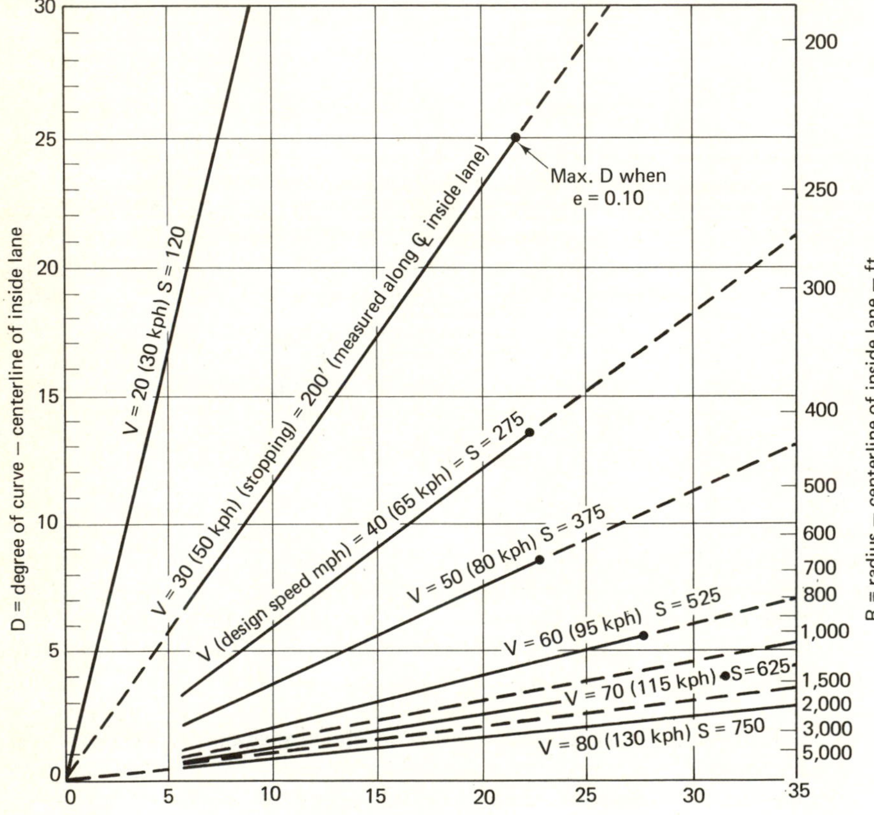

Figure 19.6. Range of lower values for stopping sight distances on horizontal curves. (Metric conversion factor: multiply values by 0.305 m/ft.)

General controls for horizontal alignment. In addition to the specific design elements for horizontal alignment, there are several other general controls:

1. Consistent with topography, alignments should be as direct as possible. Two-lane road alignments should provide as many safe passing sections as possible.
2. Maximum curvatures should be avoided whenever possible.
3. Consistent alignment should be sought. Sharp curves at the end of long tangents or at the end of long flat curves should be avoided.
4. Short lengths of curves should be avoided even for very small deflection angles.
5. Flat curvatures should be provided on long fills.
6. Compound circular curves with large differences in radii should be avoided.
7. Direct reverse curves should be avoided: A tangent length should be used between them.
8. "Broken-back curves" (two curves in the same direction on either side of a short tangent or large radius curve) should be avoided.

General controls for coordination of horizontal and vertical alignment. Although each is usually designed by a separate process, the effect that the horizontal and vertical alignments have together needs to be assessed. The following are some general controls:

1. A more pleasing facility generally results where both horizontal and vertical curvature are incorporated into the design. This curvature should be gentle for the most desirable results.
2. A sharp change in horizontal alignment should not be

TABLE 19–12
Values for Design Elements Related to Design Speed and Horizontal Curvature*

		V = 30 mph (50 km/h)			V = 40 mph (65 km/h)			V = 50 mph (80 km/h)			V = 60 mph (95 km/h)			V = 65 mph (105 km/h)			V = 70 mph (115 km/h)			V = 75 mph (120 km/h)			V = 80 mph (130 km/h)		
		e	L (ft)		e	L (ft)		e	L (ft)		e	L (ft)		e	L (ft)		e	L (ft)		e	L (ft)		e	L (ft)	
D	R (ft)		Two Lanes	Four Lanes		Two Lanes	Four Lanes		Two Lanes	Four Lanes		Two Lanes	Four Lanes		Two Lanes	Four Lanes		Two Lanes	Four Lanes		Two Lanes	Four Lanes		Two Lanes	Four Lanes
0°15′	22918	NC	0	0	NC	0	0	NC	0	0	NC	0	0	NC	0	0	NC	0	0	NC	0	0	RC	240	240
0°30′	11459	NC	0	0	NC	0	0	NC	0	0	RC	175	175	RC	190	190	RC	200	200	0.021	220	220	0.023	240	240
0°45′	7639	NC	0	0	NC	0	0	RC	150	150	0.022	175	175	0.025	190	190	0.028	200	200	0.031	220	220	0.034	240	240
1°00′	5730	NC	0	0	RC	125	125	0.021	150	150	0.029	175	175	0.032	190	190	0.036	200	200	0.040	220	220	0.045	240	240
1°30′	3820	RC	100	100	0.021	125	125	0.030	150	150	0.041	175	175	0.046	190	200	0.051	200	240	0.058	220	290	0.065	240	320
2°00′	2865	RC	100	100	0.027	125	125	0.038	150	150	0.051	175	210	0.058	190	250	0.065	200	290	0.073	230	340	0.079	250	380
2°30′	2292	.021	100	100	0.033	125	125	0.046	150	170	0.061	175	240	0.068	190	300	0.075	220	330	0.080	250	370			
3°00′	1910	.025	100	100	0.038	125	125	0.053	150	190	0.068	180	270	0.075	210	320	0.080	230	350						
3°30′	1637	.028	100	100	0.043	125	140	0.058	150	210	0.074	200	300	0.079	220	330									
4°00′	1432	.031	100	100	0.047	125	150	0.063	150	230	0.078	210	310												
5°00′	1146	.038	100	100	0.055	125	170	0.071	170	260															
6°00′	955	.043	100	120	0.062	130	190	0.077	180	280															
7°00′	819	.048	100	130	0.067	140	210	0.080	190	280															
8°00′	716	.053	100	140	0.071	150	220																		
9°00′	637	.056	100	150	0.075	160	240																		
10°00′	573	.060	110	160	0.078	160	240																		
11°00′	521	.063	110	170	0.079	170	250																		
12°00′	477	.065	120	180	0.080	170	250																		
13°00′	441	.068	120	180																					
14°00′	409	.070	130	190																					
16°00′	358	.074	130	200																					
18°00′	318	.077	140	210																					
20°00′	286	.079	140	210																					
22°00′	260	.080	140	220																					
		D_{max} = 22.75°			D_{max} = 12.25°			D_{max} = 7.50°			D_{max} = 4.75°			D_{max} = 3.75°			D_{max} = 3°00′			D_{max} = 2.50°			D_{max} = 2°00′		

e_{max}, 0.08; D, Degree of curve; R, Radius of curve; V, Assumed design speed; e, Rate of superelevation; L, Minimum length of runoff of spiral curve; NC, Normal crown section; RC, Remove adverse crown, superelevate at normal crown slope

NOTES: Spirals desirable but not as essential above heavy line. Lengths rounded in multiples of 25 or 50 ft permit simpler calculations.

*Metric conversion factor: multiply value by 0.305

introduced at or near the top of a pronounced crest vertical curve or the low point in a pronounced sag vertical curve.

Cross section

The highway cross section is made up of traveled ways, auxiliary lanes, shoulders, medians, and roadsides. The dimensions of each vary with the type of highway. Each is discussed separately below.

Traveled way. The traveled way is that portion of the roadway available for movement of vehicles exclusive of shoulders and auxiliary lanes. It normally comprises two or more traffic lanes. On freeways where eight or more lanes are provided, two or more reversible lanes may be included in the cross section; sometimes express lanes are separated from lanes serving shorter distance travel resulting in a "dual–dual" facility.

On all freeways, expressways, and other arterial highways, traffic lanes should be at least 12 ft (3.6 m) wide. However, because of restraints on new freeway construction, in some cases it has been found necessary to use minimum 11-ft (3.4-m) traffic lanes together with reduced shoulders to obtain sufficient width for an additional traffic lane. This lane may be used for purposes of providing a priority lane for high-occupancy vehicles or for regular traffic use. In most cases where this has been done, the use of 11-ft (3.4-m) lanes has been found to have no appreciable effect on accident rates. For these type highways the full roadway (width of travel lanes plus shoulders) should be carried across all structures except for the most costly facilities where the shoulder may be narrowed to some extent.

For local roads and streets the desirable minimum width of traffic lane is 11 ft (3.4 m), although 10 ft (3.1 m) or even 9-ft (2.75-m) lanes are adequate for low traffic volumes with few trucks. As a minimum, the full traveled way width on the approaches should be carried across all structures.

Undivided highways on tangents or flat curves have a crown or high point in the middle and slope downward toward both edges. The downward cross slope (crossfall) may be a plane or curved section or a combination. Divided highways may have each traveled way crowned or may have a straight slope across the entire width of each traveled way. Table 19-13 shows normal cross slopes for various types of highway surfaces.

When two or more lanes are sloped in the same direction on multilane pavements, each successive lane outward from the crown line should have an increased slope. The lane adjacent to the crown line should be sloped at the normal minimum slope, and the slope on each successive lane should be increased by 0.5 to 1.0%. When curbs are used along high-type pavements, a cross slope of 1.5 to 2.0% on the outer lane is the practical minimum to reduce water sheeting on the traffic lane adjacent to the curb.

TABLE 19–13
Normal Cross Slopes

Pavement Surface Type	Percent
High	1–2
Intermediate	1.5–3
Low	2–6

Auxiliary lanes. An auxiliary lane is that portion of the roadway adjoining the traveled way for parking, speed change, turning, storage for turning, weaving, truck climbing, or for other purposes supplementary to through traffic movement.

When parking is permitted adjacent to a traffic lane, an additional pavement width of 10 or 12 ft (3 to 4 m) should be provided. The parking spaces should then generally be marked 8 ft (2.4 m) from the curb regardless of the actual pavement width available, as shown in the *Manual on Uniform Traffic Control Devices*[16] to ensure proper use of the parking lane. The additional pavement width provided is necessary for proper operation of the adjacent traffic lane. Also, a parking lane of 10 ft (3.0 m) or wider can be used as a through traffic lane during peak hours or converted into a storage lane, a turning lane, a bus lane or high occupancy vehicle lane, or a permanent through traffic lane if necessary.

A speed change lane is an auxiliary lane, including tapered area, primarily for the acceleration or deceleration of vehicles entering or leaving through traffic lanes (the design of speed change and turning lanes is discussed later).

A weaving section is a length of one-way road where parallel traffic streams cross by merging and then diverging. The length and width of a weaving section is determined by capacity demand analysis (discussed later and in Chapter 16). Any required additional width is usually provided in the form of additional lanes through the weaving section. These additional lanes for weaving are a form of auxiliary lane.

Appreciable volumes of trucks operating on steep, sustained grades may significantly reduce the safety and capacity of a highway unless auxiliary lanes, termed climbing lanes, are provided. These lanes should be considered when an appreciable number of trucks travel at speeds significantly below that of passenger cars. Auxiliary downhill lanes for trucks are not generally required. However, when for safety reasons trucks must descend at speeds significantly below that of cars, an added downhill truck lane should be considered also.

The design and delineation of climbing lanes is similar to regular use lanes. The cross slope design should be the same as for the through traffic lanes. Full shoulders are often needed on the outer edge of climbing lanes although a paved shoulder from 4 to 6 ft (1.2 to 1.8 m) wide is adequate in some cases. They should have delineation contrast, such as a different type of pavement, so that there will be immediate recognition that this is an extra lane.

The start of the climbing lane is determined by the speed reduction characteristics of a typical truck, usually taken as one with a 300-lb/hp (180 kg/kilowatt) weight–power ratio. The climbing lane should start when the speed of such a truck would be reduced to 10 mph (15 km/h) below the running speed of the mainline flow. This can be determined

[16] *Manual on Uniform Traffic Control Devices.*, p. 3b–22.

from the speed of a truck as it enters the grade and the gradient (in percent). The full-lane width should be preceded by a taper 150 ft (45 m) long. The climbing lane should end at a point beyond the crest where a typical truck would attain a speed of 30 mph (50 km/h). An extension taper of 200 ft (60 m) or more should be provided.

Shoulders. The term *shoulder* has several meanings, depending on its modifying adjective: (1) The *graded shoulder* is the width from the edge of the traffic lane to the intersection of the shoulder slope and side slope planes. (2) The *surfaced shoulder* is the surfaced width outside the through traffic lane. It has an all-weather surface such as gravel, shell, or crushed rock; stabilization with mineral or chemical additives; bituminous treatments; or various forms of asphaltic or concrete pavement. (3) The *usable shoulder* is the actual width usable for an emergency stop, including some of the rounding at the top of the flat earth slope. In Europe, the term *verge* or *outer verge* is used. The verge is comparable to the graded shoulder. Sometimes special paths reserved for pedestrians, cyclists, or similar traffic are provided on these verges.

Well-designed and properly maintained shoulders are necessary on rural highways that have any appreciable volume of traffic. They are desirable in urban areas also but cannot always be provided because of space limitations. Their functions are multifold:

1. Space is provided for emergency stops off the traveled way. Vehicles stopping on the traveled way introduce high accident potential.
2. Space is provided for drivers to recover safely should they lose vehicle control.
3. A sense of openness contributes to driving ease.
4. Horizontal sight distance is improved.
5. Highway capacity is improved.
6. Space is provided for maintenance operations.
7. Structural support of the through traffic pavement is enhanced.

Shoulder widths vary depending on the type of highway. Table 19-14 shows minimum usable shoulder widths normally provided on various type highways. The full shoulder width should be carried across all structures except for major long-span structures, which should be analyzed individually. On highways other than freeways with current ADT less than 750 and a design speed less than 50 mph (80 km/h) shoulder widths may be reduced somewhat. On bridges, however, the minimum clearance from edge of traveled way to parapet or rail should be not less than 4 ft (1.2 m) for arterial highways other than freeways and 2 ft (0.6 m) for local roads.

Table 19-15 shows shoulder cross slopes used under normal conditions. Normally, shoulders are sloped to drain away from the traveled way. On superelevated sections, however, it is sometimes necessary to slope the shoulder toward the through lane pavement in order not to exceed a maximum algebraic difference in the pavement and shoulder grade of 7% between the through pavement cross slope and the shoulder cross slope. A preferable design is to provide a curved shoulder cross slope with the outer edge of the shoulder sloped away from the through lane pavement.

TABLE 19–14
Minimum Usable Shoulder Widths

		Minimum Usable Shoulder Width			
		Right Shoulder		Left Shoulder	
		ft	m	ft	m
Freeways					
Four-lane other than in mountainous terrain and where there are fewer than 250 trucks per hour in one direction in design year		10	3	4	1.2
Six or more lanes with fewer than 250 trucks per hour in one direction in the design year		10	3	10	3
Freeways in mountainous terrain		10	3	4	1.2
Four lanes with more than 250 trucks per hour in one direction in the design year		12	3.5	4	1.2
Six or more lanes with more than 250 trucks per hour in one direction in the design year		12	3.5	10	3
Rural-Arterial Highways Other Than Freeways					
Current ADT	DHV				
50–400	—	4	12	4	1.2
400–750	100–200	6	1.8	6	1.8
	Over 200	8	2.5	8	2.5
Rural/Local Roads					
Current ADT	DHV				
Less than 50	—	2	0.5	2	0.5
50–400	—	2	0.5	2	0.5
	Over 200	4	1.2	4	1.2

TABLE 19–15
Shoulder Cross Slopes

Type of Surface	Shoulder Cross Slope (%)
Concrete/bituminous	2–6
Gravel crushed stone	4–8
Turf	8

Medians (central reserves). Medians are desirable on highways that have four or more lanes. Median widths vary from 2 ft (0.6 m) to over 100 ft (30 m) with freeway medians generally in the higher range, particularly those in rural areas. Rural freeway medians are usually at least 36 ft (11 m). Urban freeway medians can be as narrow as 10 ft (3 m). Narrow freeway medians should be provided with some form of barrier.

For highways other than freeways, medians can be categorized as follows:

1. Paint-striped separations, from 2 to 4 ft (0.6 to 1.2 m) wide.
2. Narrow, raised, or curbed sections, from 4 to 6 ft (1.2 to 1.8 m) wide.
3. Paint striped or curbed sections providing space for a single left-turn lane, from 10 to 18 ft (3.1 to 5.5 m) wide or 22 to 28 ft (6.7 to 8.5 m) for double left-turn lanes.
4. Traversible or curbed sections providing space for shielding protection of a vehicle crossing at an intersection and/or space for parkway landscape treatment, from 20 to 40 ft (6.1 to 12.2 m) wide.

Border areas. The border is the area between the roadway edge (or frontage road, if one is provided) and the right-of-way line. It does not include shoulders. It should be wide enough to accommodate any necessary cut or fill slopes, ditches, walls, bikeways, or sidewalks, and a landscaped buffer area between the highway and the surrounding land uses. Along city streets the border usually includes an area for placement of utilities.

Borders should be at least 30 to 60 ft (9.2 to 18.3 m) wide for rural freeways and be flat or rounded to permit a vehicle to traverse the area without turning over. For rural highways other than freeways, a border should be wide enough for the basic ditch section and slopes, usually from 15 to 25 ft (4.6 to 7.7 m) plus outer slope width. Desirably, the border area should be free of obstacles for at least 10 to 20 ft (3.1 to 6.1 m) and be flat or rounded. For urban roads and streets, a border width of from 4 to 8 ft (1.2 to 2.4 m) plus sidewalk width is desirable.

Other cross-section elements. The cross section may include a frontage road and outer separation between the frontage road and through roadway. Outer separations should be at least 30 ft (9.2 m) wide in rural areas but may be as narrow as 4 ft (1.2 m) with a suitable barrier in urban areas. Frontage roads should be at least 20 ft (6.1 m) wide plus shoulder width or parking lane width as required; they are local roads and should be designed accordingly.

Right-of-way width. The total width of right-of-way required is the sum of the various elements described above. Right-of-way widths vary from a minimum 50 ft (15.2 m) in urban areas to over 350 ft (110 m) for freeways in open rural areas.

Design procedures

The design of major highway improvements must be based on extensive investigations. A summary of these investigations is needed for joint consideration by the concerned organizations, as well as by the public and political body responsible for deciding how and when the project should be undertaken.

Preliminary engineering report

A preliminary engineering report is needed for major highway projects in order to document the various factors considered in the project evaluation. The more complex and expensive the proposed highway, the more elaborate the report must be. Freeway development in urban areas requires the most detail. The following engineering report section headings highlight the major factors to be considered:

1. General description of the proposed improvement, need for improvement, and relationship of the proposed highway improvement to the overall transportation system
2. Description and discussion of alternative locations and designs
3. Projected traffic volumes
4. Estimated total costs
5. Economic evaluation, including user costs
6. Evaluation of consequences to the natural environment, including effects on land values, employment, community values and services—this evaluation may be partly qualitative
7. Evaluation of the sociological effect on the community, including relocation of residences and businesses, and accessibility to community services—this evaluation may be mainly qualitative
8. A recommended plan for the proposed highway improvement

Public hearings

Public hearings should be held to ensure, to the maximum extent practicable, that highway locations and designs reflect and are consistent with local goals. Public hearings provide a medium for free and open discussion and are intended to encourage early and amiable resolution of controversial issues. They are also a way of keeping the public fully informed about specific details of highway location and design.

In the United States, major highway projects, particularly those involving federal funds, require that at least two public hearings be held or the opportunity be afforded these hearings. A corridor public hearing is held before a route location is approved and before the agency responsible for determining the final corridor location is committed to a specific route. This hearing provides an opportunity for interested persons to participate in determining the need for, and the general location of a highway and for presenting views on the proposed alternatives as well as on the social, economic, and environmental effects of those alternatives. A design public hearing is held after the corridor public hearing and after the route location is approved but before the responsible agency is committed to a specific design. This hearing provides an opportunity for participation by interested persons in determining the specific location and major design features of a highway—an opportunity for presenting views on major design features, including the social, economic, and environmental effects of alternative designs. Additional hearings or informal meetings may be desirable, most particularly at the systems planning stage prior to plan adoption.

The information sought from all public hearings includes the probable benefits or losses to the community as the result of constructing the highway, at least including the effects on the following:

1. Fast, safe, and efficient transportation
2. Energy use
3. Economic activity
4. Employment
5. Recreation and parks
6. Fire protection
7. Aesthetics
8. Public utilities
9. Public health and safety
10. Residential and neighborhood character and location

11. Religious institutions
12. Local tax base and social service costs
13. Conservation including erosion, sedimentation, and wildlife
14. Natural and historical landmarks
15. Noise, air, and water pollution
16. Property values
17. Multiple use of space
18. Replacement housing
19. Disruption of schools
20. Displacement of families and businesses
21. Operation and use of existing highway facilities and other transportation facilities during construction and after completion
22. Archeological sites

This information should be used to arrive at a design and location minimizing any adverse effects of the surrounding community and maximizing utility for the highway user.

Environmental statement

In accord with the National Environmental Policy Act of 1969, in the United States, it is a national policy that all federal agencies promote efforts for improving the relationship between human beings and their environment and to make special efforts to preserve the natural beauty of the countryside and public park and recreational lands, wildlife and waterfowl refuges, and historic sites. It is also national policy that federal agencies consult with other appropriate federal, state, and local agencies; assess in detail the potential environmental impact in order that adverse effects are avoided and environmental quality is restored or enhanced to the fullest extent practicable; and utilize a systematic, interdisciplinary approach that will ensure the integrated use of the natural and social sciences and the environmental design arts in planning and decision making which may have an impact on our environment. The environmental assessments include the broad range of both beneficial and detrimental effects.

For these purposes an environmental statement is usually prepared and incorporated as a part of the location hearing and approval process. An environmental statement is a written statement containing an assessment of the anticipated significant beneficial and detrimental effects that the agency decision may have upon the quality of the human environment for the purposes of (1) assuring that careful attention is given to environmental matters, (2) providing a vehicle for implementing all applicable environmental requirements, and (3) ensuring that the environmental impact is taken into account in the agency decision (see Chapter 13).

Design concept teams

Design concept teams have been formed primarily to solve the difficult problems inherent in locating new highways in heavily built-up urban areas. Interdisciplinary design teams normally include urban planners, highway and traffic engineers, architects, and sociologists, but they could also include real estate specialists, lawyers, economists, educators, and health planners. Such teams may have responsibility for (1) developing greater community participation in the design process, (2) evaluating the total environment of the highway corridor, (3) focusing greater attention on social problems, (4) suggesting changes in surrounding land uses when they conflict with the highway, and (5) planning possible community improvements in conjunction with the highway development.

Multiple use and joint development

Multiple use of highway rights-of-way is the use of the airspace or other portion of the right of way for a nonhighway purpose such as buildings, recreational facilities, or parking areas. Joint development is the broader concept of satisfying not only a highway transportation need but also optimizing the use of land in the highway corridor; joint development usually takes place on land outside the normal highway right of way as well as inside it. Both multiple use and joint development projects must be considered at the *earliest* possible planning and design stages.

Safety considerations in design

Designing safety into highways is one of the main objectives of geometric design. This goal requires something more than the standards and principles thus far enumerated. Designs should anticipate and allow for driver error, should eliminate inconsistencies that cause driver confusion, and should promote the intended highway use.

Specific things that can be done to achieve safe designs are listed throughout the text. Some additional details that should be considered are related to structural design as well as geometric design. The extent to which they are applicable to the design of a particular facility depends on the highway type, the numbers and speeds of vehicles, and economic considerations. Such additional details include:

1. Roadside slopes should be made as flat as feasible, desirably 4:1 or flatter. The roadside area should be well rounded where slope planes intersect.
2. Sign and lighting supports either should be located far enough from the roadway to make them unlikely to be struck by an out-of-control vehicle or they should have breakaway capability.
3. All drainage structures should be designed so that out-of-control vehicles either can pass over them or can be safely deflected. Where bicycle traffic is expected, catch-basin gratings must be of a type that will not be a hazard to bicyclists.
4. Guardrails should be considered when fill slopes 4:1 or flatter are unfeasible. The guardrail should be capable of safely stopping or redirecting an out-of-control vehicle that hits it.[17]

[17]For details on guardrail design, see *Guide for Selecting, Locating and Designing Traffic Barriers* (Washington, D.C.: American Association of State Highway and Transportation Officials, 1977).

5. A suitably designed guardrail should be provided at approaches to bridges and at piers at undercrossing structures where there is likelihood they may be struck by an out-of-control vehicle.
6. On high-speed or high-volume divided highways with narrow medians, some form of median barrier should be considered to prevent out-of-control vehicles from crossing into opposing lanes.
7. Pavement cross slopes should be designed so that ponding of water will not occur.
8. When obstructions cannot be moved or protected by guardrails, such as at ramp gores on elevated structures, some form of crash cushion should be considered. The design of the gore area preceding the obstruction should allow for installing such devices.
9. Lanes should be dropped only at locations with excellent sight distances, and a recovery area should be provided to allow trapped vehicles to move safely to the adjacent lane.
10. Highway signing and marking is an integral part of design and should be developed progressively with geometric design. The design should allow for the latest traffic control devices as specified in the *Manual on Uniform Traffic Control Devices*.
11. Design should not overlook problems caused by darkness, rain, and other nonoptimum operating conditions.

Arterial highways other than freeways

Many design elements pertaining to arterial highways other than freeways were discussed previously, as part of the section applicable to design elements that pertain to all types of highways. Those applicable only to this highway type will be discussed in this section.

Roadway cross-section design

Rural. Rural roads other than freeways are most frequently two lanes wide with shoulders on both sides. Some degree of access control is desirable to limit points of access to locations where egress and ingress can be accomplished safely. Particular care must be exercised in the location of all intersections to ensure sufficient sight distance, but above minimum sight distance should be provided at intersections-at-grade where located along divided highways. Unless provided with above-minimum geometric features, these highways will produce higher-than-average accident rates. Figure 19.7 shows typical cross sections of two-lane rural roads; Figure 19.8 shows them for rural divided highways. Rural highways may also have cross sections that approach that of a freeway, as shown in Figure 19.16.

Typical cross sections used in Europe are shown in Figure 19.9. The bottom cross section is for a four-lane divided motorway having a design speed of from 80 to 100 km/h. The top two are for a design speed of from 100 to 140 km/h for four- and six-lane motorways.

Border areas along rural arterials should allow a driver who inadvertently leaves the through traffic lanes to recover without serious injury. This normally requires that border areas 10 to 20 ft (3 to 6 m) beyond the shoulder edge be free of unyielding obstacles such as trees, large rocks, utility poles, and rigid sign posts. Ditches should be well rounded in this area and side slopes should be 4:1 or flatter. At locations involving unmovable obstacles or where the combination of slopes and embankment height warrant, guardrails should be provided; the face of these are commonly located at the edge or 2 ft (0.6 m) outside the edge of shoulder.

Urban. Urban arterials most typically have two- or four-lane roadways, with a parking lane on either side and curb and a gutter on the outside. Lane widths have already been discussed. Where there is a median on urban arterials other than freeways, sometimes it is desirable to convert the median to a continuous two-way left-turn lane from which turns can be made from either direction. Special signing and pavement marking are required to ensure proper use of the lane. Minimum widths of this type of lane should be comparable at least to a normal through-traffic lane. In other cases, the lane can be made reversible and be used by through traffic to serve peak direction flow.

Curbs are used extensively on urban streets to control drainage, to discourage vehicles from leaving the pavement, to protect pedestrians, and to promote orderly roadside development. Two general classes of curbs are barrier and mountable. Either may be designed with a gutter to form a curb and gutter section. When the gutter contrasts in color with the through pavement and has an evident longitudinal joint, the width of gutter should not be considered part of the traffic lane width. Where mountable curbs are used when the gutter is the same color and texture as the through pavement and is not much steeper in cross slope than the adjoining pavement, it may be considered as part of the through-lane width.

Barrier curbs are from 6 to 10 in. (15 to 25 cm) or higher and have a steep face; see Figure 19.10(a). They have application only when vehicle speeds are relatively slow, and vehicle encroachment should be strongly discouraged. They are commonly used along streets and for refuge islands. Barrier curbs should be offset 2 to 3 ft (0.6 to 0.9 m) from the through traffic lanes.

Mountable curbs are designed so that vehicles can cross them. They are 6 in (15 cm) or lower and have a relatively flat sloping face. Figure 19.10(b)–(g) shows typical examples of mountable curbs. Mountable curbs can be of bituminous mixtures or concrete.

Where there are curbs at intersections, curb ramps, sometimes called curb cut or wheelchair ramps, should be provided to accommodate the elderly and handicapped. These curb cuts should be located at crosswalks and within the crosswalk lines. A single curb ramp may be provided near the center of each curb return to serve two crosswalks, or preferably a curb ramp is provided to serve each crosswalk. Slopes should not exceed an 8.33% gradient. The ramp should be at least 4 ft (1.2 m) wide plus rounding and should have a textured surface in order to warn a blind person.

Although both barrier and mountable curbs can be used along medians or at the edge of through traffic lanes, barrier curbs should be offset from through traffic lanes. Curbs of various types are also used at the edge of shoulders as part of the drainage system.

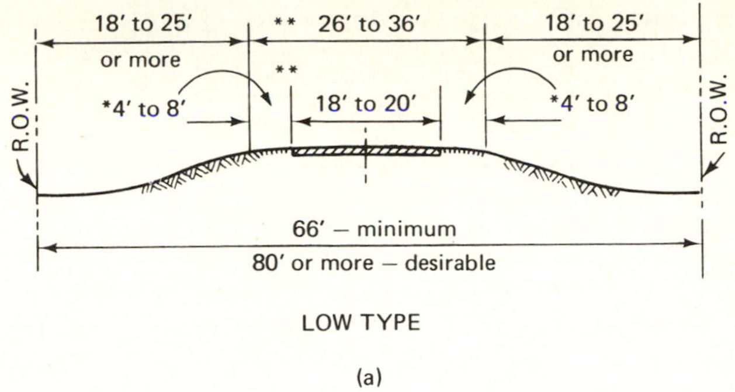

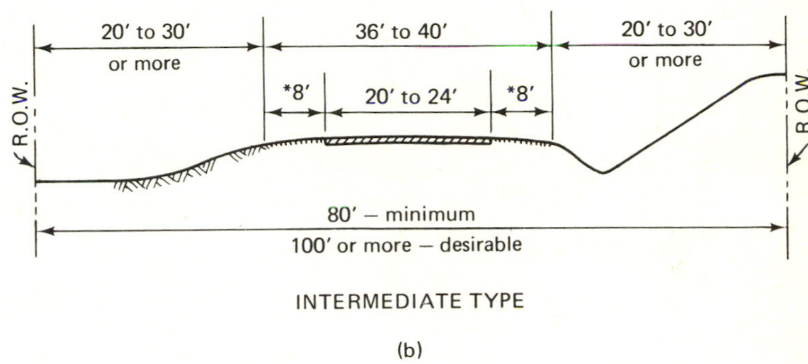

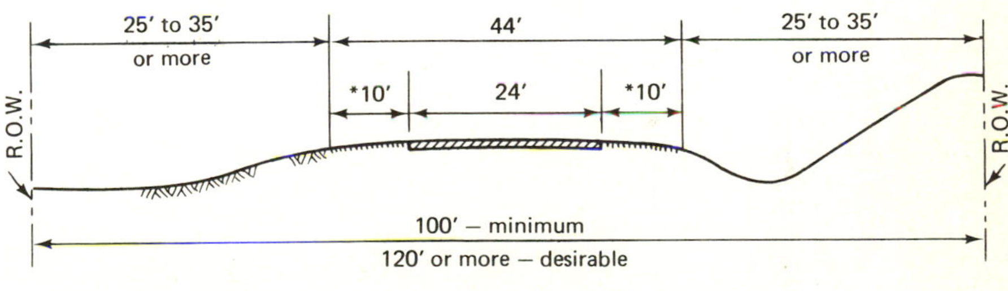

Figure 19.7. Cross sections and right-of-way widths for two-lane rural highways. (Metric conversion factor: multiply values by 0.305 m/ft.) SOURCE: *A Policy on Geometric Design of Rural Highways*, Washington, D.C.: American Association of State Highway Officials, 1965, p. 263.

* Usable shoulder width
** For low-volume roads with few trucks

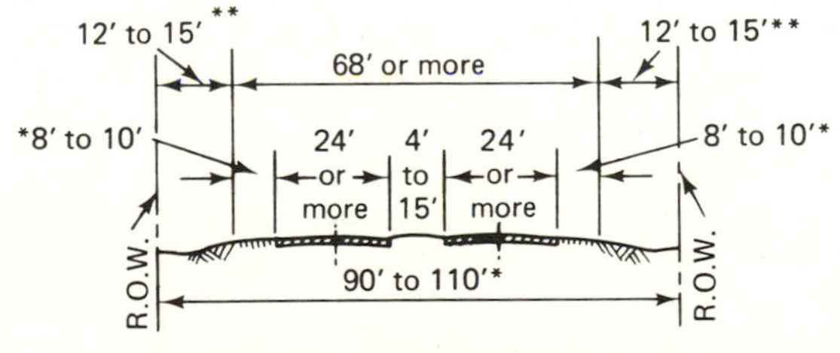

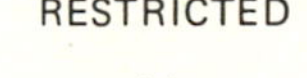

(a)

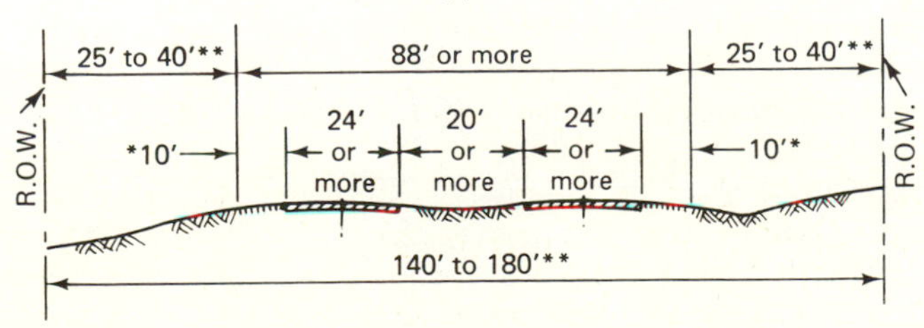

Figure 19.8. Cross sections and right-of-way widths for multilane divided highways. (Metric conversion factor: multiply values by 0.305 m/ft.) SOURCE: *A Policy on Geometric Design of Rural Highways,* Washington, D.C.: American Association of State Highway Officials, 1965, p. 293.

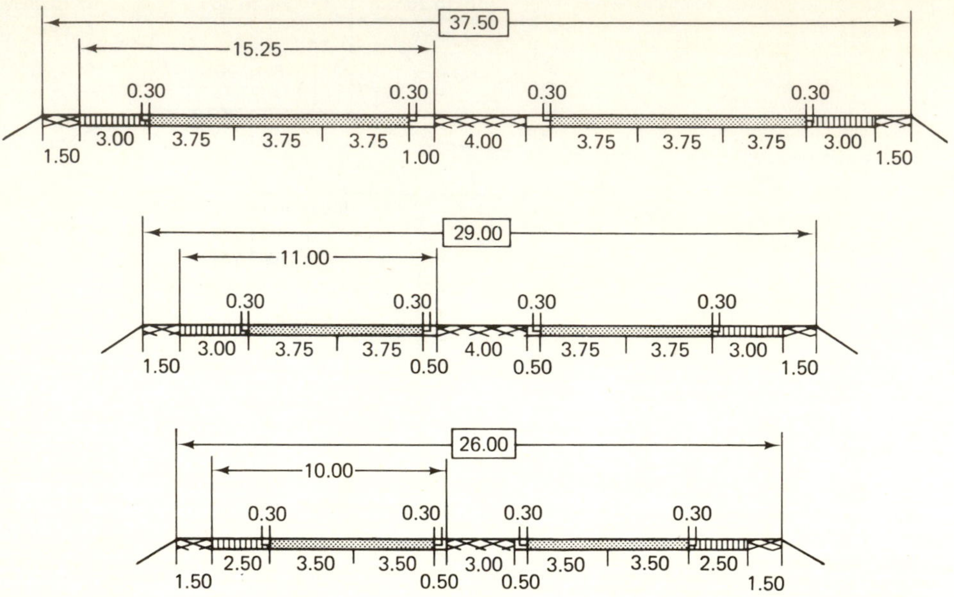

Figure 19.9. Typical cross-section design in Europe (all dimensions are in meters). SOURCE: U.S. Department of Transportation, Federal Highway Administration, *1972 World Survey of Current Research and Development on Roads and Road Transport,* Washington, D.C.: International Road Federation, 1972, p. 321.

Figure 19.10. Typical highway curbs. (Metric conversion factor: multiply values by 2.54 cm/in.) SOURCE: *A Policy on Geometric Design of Rural Highways,* Washington, D.C.: American Association of State Highway Officials, 1965, p. 228.

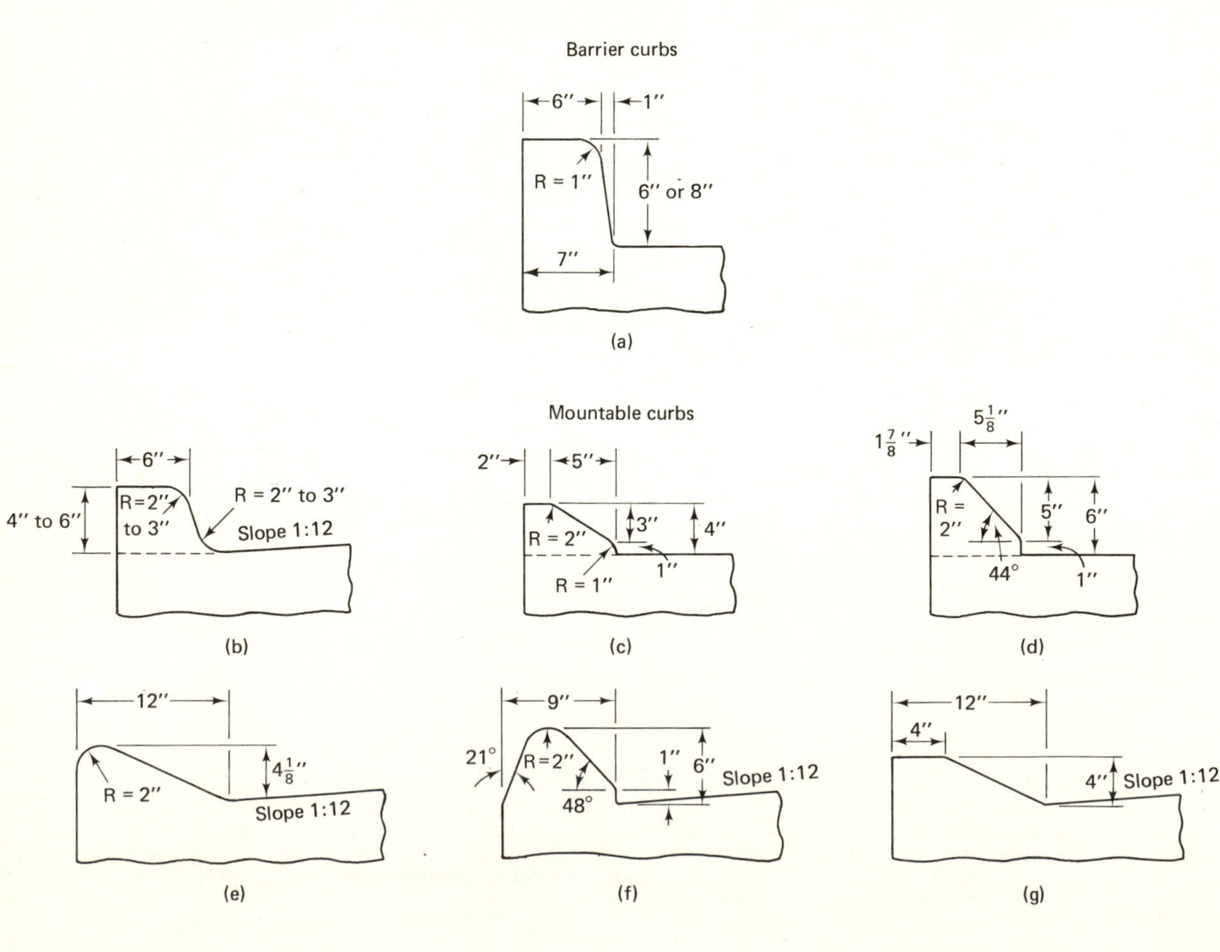

Border areas along urban arterial streets should be as wide as possible, but as a minimum, they should be sufficient to accommodate a sidewalk and a grass or utility strip. Sidewalks in built-up areas should be at least 8 ft (2.4 m) wide, but in suburban residential areas 4 ft (1.2 m) is sufficient. A grass strip is desirable between the sidewalks and curb, but in heavily built-up areas this is generally omitted. The grass strip, when used, can accommodate underground utilities.

Intersections at grade

Spacing. It is desirable that intersections at grade be such that effective synchronization of the signals can be employed. This can significantly reduce energy use and improve the operation. The easiest way of achieving this is to have evenly spaced intersections.

Design principles. Individual maneuver areas are the smallest unit of intersection design. They may be combined variously to produce alternative geometric designs for any intersection. To a considerable degree their arrangement, extent, and whether certain features can be provided even where otherwise desirable is governed by traffic demands, topography, land use, and economic and environmental considerations; the proper compromise is a decision to be made by the individual designer. Intersection design should consider the following 11 fundamental principles:

Principle 1. Reduce number of conflict points. The number of conflict points among vehicular movements increases significantly as the number of intersection legs increases. For example, an intersection with four two-way legs has 32 total conflict points, but an intersection with six two-way legs has 172 conflict points.[18] Intersections with more than four two-way legs should be avoided wherever possible.

Principle 2. Control relative speed. Relative speed is the rate of convergence or divergence of vehicles in intersection flow. A small difference [from 0 to 10 mph (25 km/h)] in the speeds of intersecting vehicles and a small angle (less than 30°) between converging paths allow intersecting vehicular flows to operate continuously (uninterrupted flow). Low relative speeds require elimination of both speed differences and large angles between intersection flows through design. High relative speeds occur when there is either a large difference in vehicular speeds or a large angle of convergence. Since interrupted flow usually occurs under these conditions, traffic should be controlled by traffic control devices. Intersections requiring vehicles to stop have been found safer when the highways intersect at or near 90° because the driver's view is not obstructed by the vehicle itself and there is a more positive indication that vehicles should stop.

Principle 3. Coordinate design and traffic control. Maneuvers at intersections accomplished at low relative speeds require a minimum of traffic control devices. Maneuvers accomplished at high relative speeds are unsafe unless traffic controls such as stop signs or traffic signals are provided. Designs should physically divert or block the path of vehicles making dangerous movements. Intersection design should be accomplished simultaneously with the development of traffic control plans.

Principle 4. Use the highest feasible crossing method. Vehicle crossing maneuvers can be accomplished in four ways: (1) uncontrolled crossing at-grade, (2) traffic sign or signal-controlled crossing at-grade, (3) weaving, and (4) grade separation. In general, both operational efficiency and construction cost increase in this order. The highest type should be used consistent with the numbers and types of vehicles using the intersection.

Principle 5. Provide an alternative turning path. The method of providing turns can be changed. Separate roadways can be provided both for right- and left-turning vehicles, thereby reducing conflicts in the intersection area. For example, a direct connection can be provided to accommodate right turns at an intersection.

Principle 6. Avoid multiple and compound merging and diverging maneuvers. Multiple merging or diverging requires complex driver decisions and creates additional conflicts.

Principle 7. Separate conflict points. Intersection hazards and delays are increased when intersection maneuver areas are too close together or when they overlap. These conflicts may be separated to provide drivers with sufficient time (and distance) between successive maneuvers for them to cope with the traffic situation.

Principle 8. Favor the heaviest and fastest flows. The heaviest and fastest flows should be given preference in intersection design to minimize hazard and delay.

Principle 9. Reduce area of conflict. Excessive intersection area causes driver confusion and inefficient operations. Large areas are inherent in skewed and multiple-approach intersections. When intersections have excessive areas of conflict, channelization should be employed.

Principle 10. Segregate nonhomogeneous flows. Separate lanes should be provided at intersections when there are appreciable volumes of traffic traveling at different speeds. For example, separate turning lanes should be provided for turning vehicles.

Principle 11. Consider the needs of pedestrians and bicyclists. For example, when there are pedestrians crossing wide streets, refuge islands should be provided so that more than five lanes do not have to be crossed at a time.

Provision for turning movements. Except for provision of turning movements, and sometimes widening through the intersection to accommodate through traffic, the horizontal design of a roadway in the area of an intersection-at-grade is the same as for the approach roadway. The layout to accommodate turning movements and the necessary through lanes determines the design of an intersection.

The design of the curb return which is provided to accommodate turning movements depends on the turning paths

[18]T. M. Matson, W. S. Smith, and F. W. Hurd, *Traffic Engineering* (New York: McGraw-Hill, 1955), p. 505.

TABLE 19–16
Minimum Edge of Pavement Designs for Turns at Intersections*

Angle of Turn (deg)	Design Vehicle	Simple Curve Radius (ft)	Simple Curve Radius with Taper		
			Radius (ft)	Offset (ft)	Taper
30	P	60	—	—	—
	SU	100	—	—	—
	WB-40	150	—	—	—
	WB-50	200	—	—	—
	WB-55	275	—	—	—
45	P	50	—	—	—
	SU	75	—	—	—
	WB-40	120	—	—	—
	WB-50	—	120	2.0	15:1
	WB-55	—	140	2.0	15:1
60	P	40	—	—	—
	SU	60	—	—	—
	WB-40	90	—	—	—
	WB-50	—	95	3.0	15:1
	WB-55	—	110	3.0	15:1
75	P	30	25	2.0	10:1
	SU	55	45	2.0	10:1
	WB-40	—	60	3.0	15:1
	WB-50	—	65	3.0	15:1
	WB-55	—	90	3.0	15:1
90	P	30	20	2.5	10:1
	SU	50	40	2.0	10:1
	WB-40	—	45	4.0	10:1
	WB-50	—	60	4.0	15:1
	WB-55	—	75	4.0	15:1
105	P	—	20	2.5	8:1
	SU	—	35	3.0	10:1
	WB-40	—	40	4.0	10:1
	WB-50	—	55	4.0	15:1
	WB-55	—	65	5.0	15:1
120	P	—	20	2.0	10:1
	SU	—	30	3.0	10:1
	WB-40	—	35	5.0	8:1
	WB-50	—	45	4.0	15:1
	WB-55	—	50	6.0	15:1
135	P	—	20	1.5	15:1
	SU	—	30	4.0	8:1
	WB-40	—	30	5.0	6:1
	WB-50	—	40	6.0	10:1
	WB-55	—	45	7.0	10:1
150	P	—	18	2.0	10:1
	SU	—	30	4.0	8:1
	WB-40	—	30	6.0	8:1
	WB-50	—	35	7.0	6:1
	WB-55	—	40	7.0	8:1
180	P	—	15	0.5	20:1
	SU	—	30	1.5	10:1
	WB-40	—	20	9.5	5:1
	WB-50	—	25	9.5	5:1
	WB-55	—	25	14.5	5:1

*Metric conversion factor: multiply values by 0.305 m/ft.

of the vehicles using the intersection. The intersection should be able to accommodate the selected design vehicles without requiring backing up to complete the maneuver. Table 19-16 provides necessary information for design of curb returns to accomplish this. Table 19-16 applies where *tapers* and simple curves are used; compound curves are also acceptable. Table 19-17 may be used to design curb returns developed using a three-centered compound curve. Figure 19.11 shows a typical design of a curb return of this type to handle larger vehicles.

Separate Parallel Turning Lanes. Both the safety and capacity of an intersection-at-grade can be improved significantly in many cases by providing added parallel turning or speed change lanes on either the right or left or both sides. They are particularly advantageous in both rural and urban areas where through speeds are relatively high and

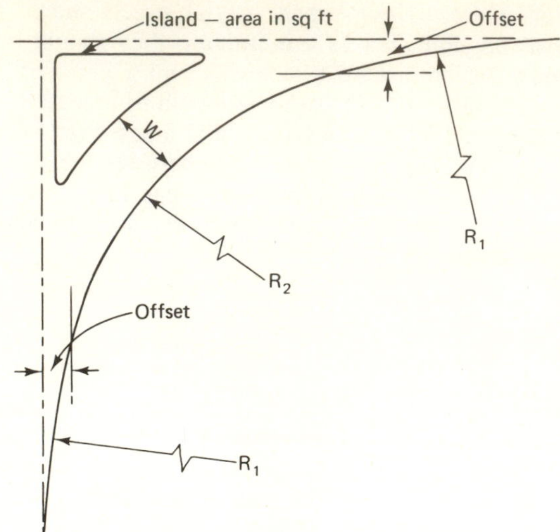

TABLE 19–17
Minimum Designs for Turning Roadways*

Angle of Turn (deg)	Design Classification†	Three-Centered Compound Curve‡ (ft) Radii R1-R2-R1	Offset	Width of Lane (ft) W	Approximate Island Size (ft²) (see Errata)
75	A	150–75–150	3.5	14	60
	B	150–75–150	5.0	18	50
	C	180–90–190	3.5	20	50
90	A	150–50–150	3.0	14	50
	B	150–50–150	5.0	18	80
	C	180–65–180	6.0	20	125
105	A	120–40–120	2.0	15	70
	B	100–35–100	5.0	22	50
	C	180–45–180	8.0	30	60
120	A	100–30–100	2.5	16	120
	B	100–30–100	3.0	24	90
	C	180–40–180	8.5	34	220
135	A	100–30–100	2.5	16	460
	B	100–30–100	4.0	26	370
	C	160–35–160	7.0	35	640
150	A	100–30–100	2.5	16	1400
	B	100–30–100	4.0	30	1170
	C	160–35–160	7.0	38	1720

*Metric conversion factor: multiply values by 0.305 m/ft.
†A, primarily passenger vehicles; permits occasional design single-unit truck to turn with restricted clearances; B, provides adequately for SU; permits occasional bus and WB-50 to turn with slight encroachment on adjacent traffic lanes; C, provides fully for all design vehicles.
‡Asymmetric three-centered compound curves and straight tapers with a simple curve can also be used without significantly altering the width of pavement or corner island size.

SOURCE: *A Policy on Geometric Design of Urban Highways and Arterial Streets* (Washington, D.C.: American Association of State Highway Officials, 1973), p. 687.

there are appreciable volumes of either right- or left-turning traffic. The primary purpose of these turning lanes is to provide storage for vehicles. A secondary purpose is to provide space for turning vehicles to decelerate in advance of the intersection or to accelerate beyond it.

These turning lanes should be at least 10 ft (3.1 m) and preferably 12 ft (3.7 m) wide. The length of exit turning lanes is the sum of three components: (1) deceleration length, (2) storage length, and (3) entering taper.

Provision for deceleration clear of through traffic lanes is an important element on high-speed arterial streets and should be incorporated into their design whenever feasible.

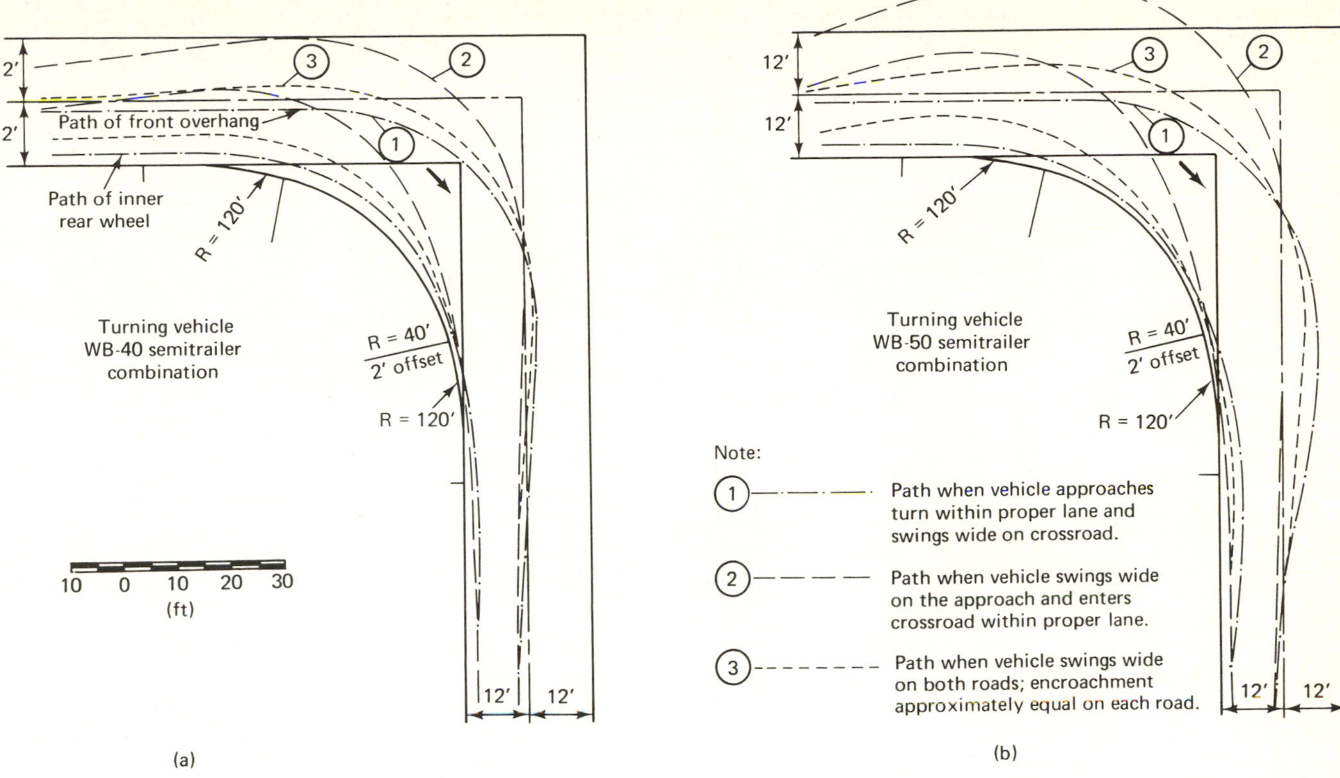

Figure 19.11. Minimum edge-of-pavement design for single-unit trucks and buses and necessary paths of larger vehicles. (Metric conversion factor: multiply value by 0.305 m/ft.) SOURCE: *A Policy on Geometric Design of Rural Highways,* Washington, D.C.: American Association of State Highway Officials, 1965, p. 316.

TABLE 19–18
Deceleration Length for Turning Roadways

Average Running Speed		Deceleration Length	
mph	km/h	ft	m
30	50	250	75
40	65	370	115
50	80	500	155

Lengths needed for deceleration (based on average running speeds) are as shown in Table 19-18.

However, on many highways, the full length for deceleration plus storage and taper cannot be provided, and, consequently, deceleration must be partially accomplished before entering the turning lane. The other element, the length necessary for storage, should be sufficient to accommodate twice the average number of vehicles stored per traffic signal cycle; at intersections without traffic signals, the length may be based on the number of vehicles wishing to turn right, or left, in 2 min. Assuming a vehicle length of 25 ft (7.6 m), the necessary length of storage can easily be computed. The third component, the entering taper of a parallel turning lane, should be at least 40 ft (12.2 m) and preferably 100 ft (31 m).

Separate Turning Roadways. At intersections where larger semitrailer combinations must be accommodated and where passenger cars are to be allowed to turn at speeds of 15 mph (25 km/h) or more, separate turning roadways are desirable to facilitate turns by these large vehicles. They should have the maximum radius possible. However, because of danger to pedestrians if high-speed turns are permitted and degree of right-of-way restrictions prevalent at most urban intersections, a minimum-type design is usually all that can be provided. The principal controls for minimum designs of the turning roadways are the alignment of the inner edge of pavement and the width of roadway channel to accommodate the design vehicle.

Turning roadways are usually separated from through traffic lanes by islands in order to properly direct turns and reduce pavement areas (islands smaller than 50 ft^2 (4.7 m^2) should be avoided). Table 19-17 shows typical minimum design dimensions for three design classifications and shows approximate island sizes for various angles of turn. Space permitting and where pedestrian volumes are low, separate turning roadways with much larger radii are desirable and should be provided. Turning roadway layouts can sometimes approach those of freeway ramps.

Median Opening. Design of median openings and median ends should be based on traffic volumes and types of turning vehicles. An important factor is the path of each design vehicle making a minimum left turn at low speed. Figure 19.12 shows a minimum median opening design to accommodate a WB-40 semitrailer design vehicle. However, as shown by the dashed line, a WB-50 design vehicle

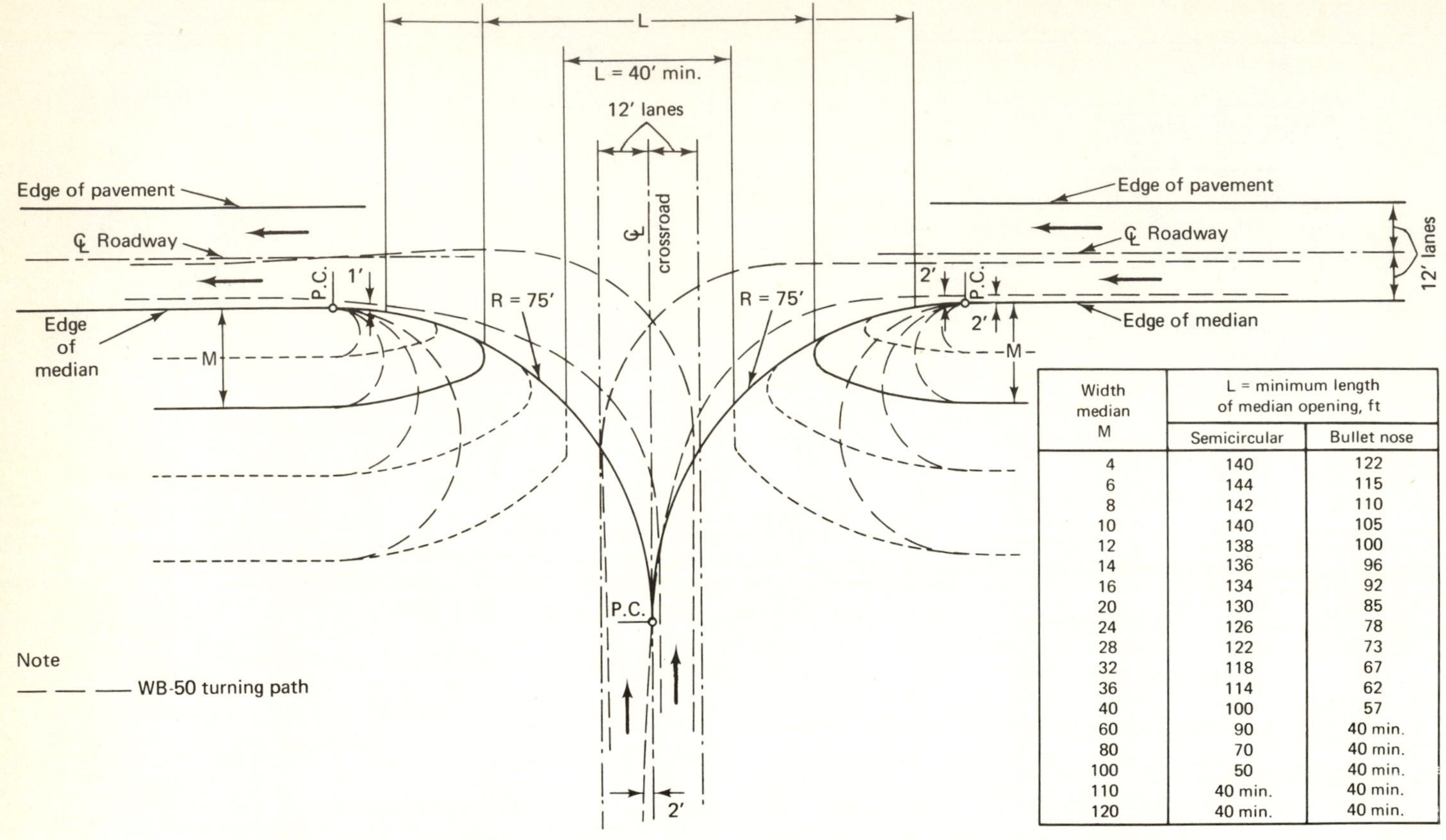

Width median M	L = minimum length of median opening, ft	
	Semicircular	Bullet nose
4	140	122
6	144	115
8	142	110
10	140	105
12	138	100
14	136	96
16	134	92
20	130	85
24	126	78
28	122	73
32	118	67
36	114	62
40	100	57
60	90	40 min.
80	70	40 min.
100	50	40 min.
110	40 min.	40 min.
120	40 min.	40 min.

Figure 19.12. Minimum design of median openings to accommodate WB-40 design vehicles (control radius of 75 ft). (Metric conversion factor: multiply values by 0.305 m/ft.) SOURCE: *A Policy on Geometric Design of Rural Highways,* Washington, D.C.: American Association of State Highway Officials, 1965, p. 415.

can also be accommodated (with slight encroachment on the adjacent lane). The intersection shown is at right angles; for the same control at skew intersections, the length of median opening will increase with an increase in the skew angle.

Channelization. Channelization involves the use of islands at intersections to guide and protect traffic. Many intersection design principles depend on it. Channelization also provides reference points within the intersection which enable drivers to better predict the path and speed of other drivers. This increases their ability to avoid accidents and congestion. Several rules govern the application of channelization:

1. Islands should be arranged so that the driving path seems natural and convenient.
2. There should be only one path for the same intersection movement.
3. A few well-placed, large islands are better than many small islands.
4. Islands should be offset 2 ft (0.6 m) or more from the edge of normal traveled way.
5. Adequate approach-end treatment is required to warn drivers and to permit gradual changes in speed and path.
6. Curving roadways should have radii and width adequate for the governing design vehicle.
7. Adequate visibility should be provided drivers approaching the intersection. There should be no hidden obstructions, and islands should be well defined. In many cases some form of illumination will be necessary.
8. Islands should be at least 50 ft and preferably 75 ft^2 (4.7 to 7.1 m^2) in area, not less than 8 ft and preferably 12 ft (2.4 to 3.6 m) on any side after rounding of corners if triangular, and at least 4 ft and preferably 12 ft (1.2 to 3.6 m) if elongated.

Channelizing islands may be traversable, deterring, or barrier types. The choice of type of border curb is often a compromise between the hazard caused by the barrier and the importance of positive control of vehicle speeds and paths. Islands themselves can be either paved or have a low-growing plant cover. Those used by pedestrians and small or narrow islands should be paved. Inasmuch as many factors affect the design of channelization, temporary installations are sometimes recommended for a trial period before permanent islands are installed.

Sight distance and vertical alignment. Minimum sight distance criteria at intersections were discussed previously. Much longer distances are desirable. The vertical alignment of the highway in the intersection area should be as flat as possible; the maximum grade on any approach leg should be about 5%.

Provision for mass transit

Urban streets that carry buses should incorporate various features in order to reduce conflicts between buses and passenger cars. Mass transit requirements should be considered early in the development of an urban highway: (1) bus stop spacing and location (near side, far side, or midblock) must be selected; (2) bus stop design must be determined; (3) reservation of lanes, if advantageous, must be decided upon; and (4) any special traffic control measures required must be defined (see Chapter 19 for a discussion of exclusive bus lanes and Chapter 7 for guidelines on bus stop location).

The interference of buses with other traffic can be reduced considerably by providing stops clear of through traffic lanes. To be fully effective, bus turnouts should incorporate (1) a taper to permit easy entrance to the loading areas, (2) a standing space long enough to accommodate the maximum number of buses expected at the stop at any one time, and (3) a merging taper. The turnout approach should be tapered at least 5 : 1 to encourage proper use of the turnout. The loading area should be at least 10 ft and preferably 12 ft (3 to 3.6 m) wide. The merging taper should be at least 3 : 1.

Rotary intersections

A rotary intersection is one through which traffic passes by entering and leaving a one-way roadway connecting all intersection approach legs and running continuously around a central island. This specialized form of at-grade intersection is not well suited for high-speed traffic or for accommodating high volumes on the approach legs. Rotary intersections are commonly called *traffic circles,* but proper design can result in central islands of various rounded shapes. Wherever British terminology prevails, they are quite properly known as *roundabouts*. Traffic flow around the central island is counterclockwise in those countries in which vehicles operate to the right of centerline.

Rotary intersections are best utilized at locations without grades and with unrestricted rights-of-way, where traffic volumes on all intersection legs are approximately equal but total less than 3000 vehicles per hour, and where the turning volumes approach or exceed the through traffic volumes.

When traffic volumes exceed the capacity of the weaving sections in the rotary, traffic signals must be installed. At this point, a normal at-grade intersection usually provides much better traffic service and control, and many rotaries have, in fact, been replaced by normal at-grade intersections. The choice between a rotary or normal at-grade intersection should depend on expected future traffic volumes. Figure 19.13 depicts the terms and elements commonly used in the design of rotary intersections.[19]

[19]For additional details of rotary design, see *A Policy on Geometric Design of Rural Highways,* pp. 478–91.

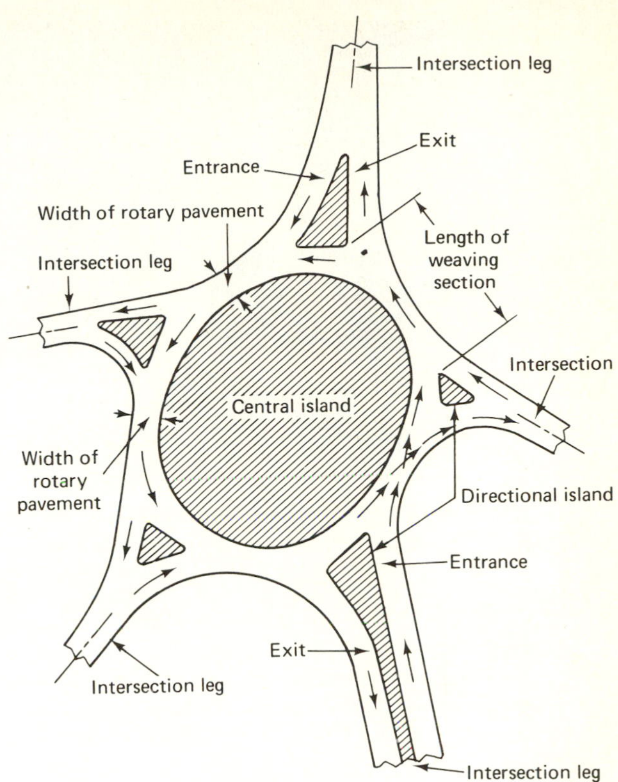

Figure 19.13. Terms used in rotary design. SOURCE: *A Policy on Geometric Design of Rural Highways,* Washington, D.C.: American Association of State Highway Officials, 1965, p. 479.

Freeways

The highest type highway is the fully access-controlled freeway (motorway). Essential freeway elements include medians, grade separations, and ramp connections.

Types

Urban freeways may be constructed at ground level, be depressed or elevated, or be a combination of types. Rural freeways are generally constructed at ground level.

Alignment

Horizontal alignment for freeways should safely accommodate high volumes at high speeds. Also, an alignment should be selected that will have the least effect on the landscape. In rolling terrain in rural areas an alignment with these attributes is best achieved by using a spline to develop an alignment fitted to basic controls. The natural bending of the spline produces a smooth, flowing alignment without marked distortion. Because a freeway consists of two separated roadways, use can be made of independent roadway design and a variable width median to provide a superior facility at less cost. Smooth, flowing alignments for each one-way roadway should be the goal in designing a divided highway. Figure 19.14 shows a highway with an alignment as described above.

Figure 19.14. Freeway with curvilinear alignment and variable-width median. SOURCE: U.S. Department of Transportation, Federal Highway Administration.

Cross section

Figure 19.15 shows a typical cross section of a freeway in rural areas. Figures 19.16 to 19.18 show typical cross sections of urban at-grade, elevated, and depressed freeways, respectively. Figure 19.19 shows a freeway cross section in a tunnel.

It is desirable that rural freeways and, where feasible, urban freeways have a clear recovery area provided outside the edge of traveled way. This area should be at least 30 ft (9 m) and preferably greater, and it should contain no unyielding obstacles that could seriously damage an out-of-control vehicle. This includes large trees [over 4 in. (10 cm) in diameter], rocks, and unyielding sign and lamp posts.

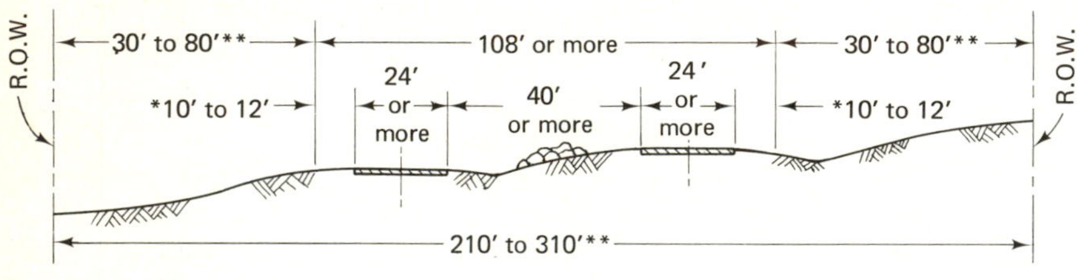

Figure 19.15. Cross sections and right-of-way widths for freeways in rural areas. (Metric conversion factor: multiply values by 0.305 m/ft.)

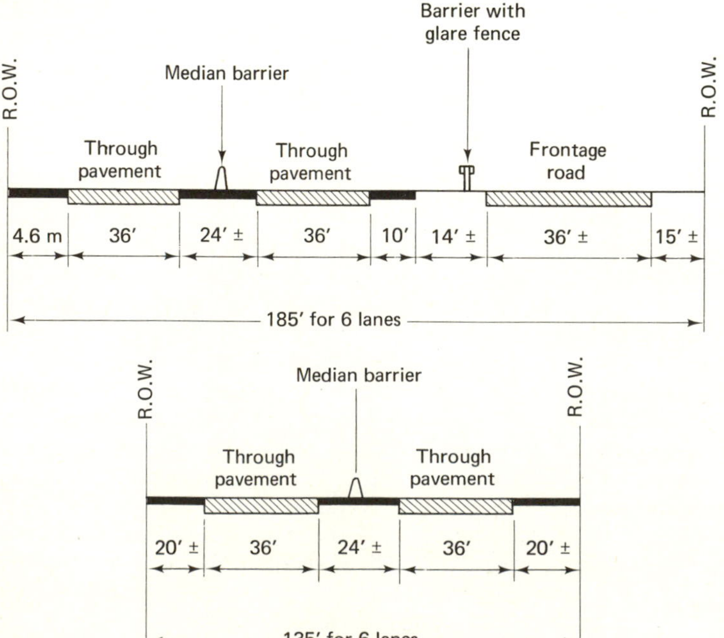

Figure 19.16. Cross sections and right-of-way on ground-level freeways (restricted). Note: Dimensions shown for six-lane freeway; for other than six-lane freeways, similar dimensions are used except for through pavement width. (Metric conversion factor: multiply values by 0.305 m/ft.)

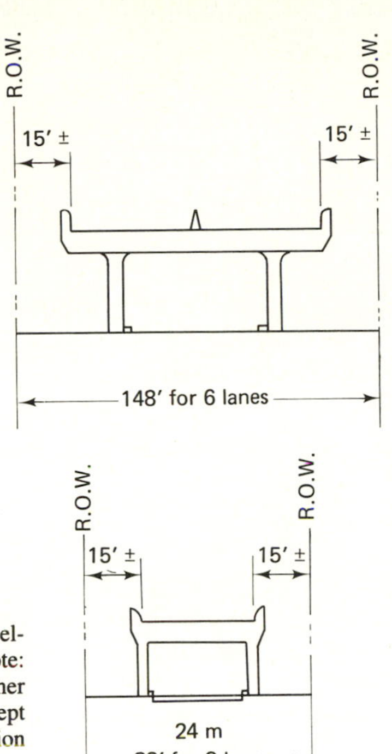

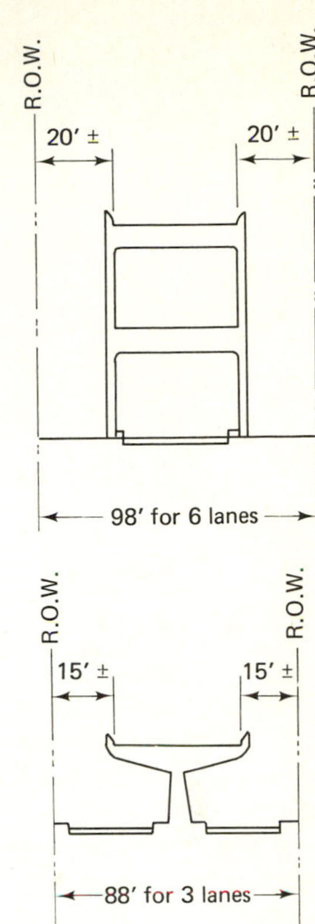

Figure 19.17. Cross sections and right-of-way; elevated freeways on structures without ramps. Note: Dimensions shown for six-lane freeways; for other than six lanes, similar dimensions are used except for through pavement widths. (Metric conversion factor: multiply values by 0.305 m/ft.)

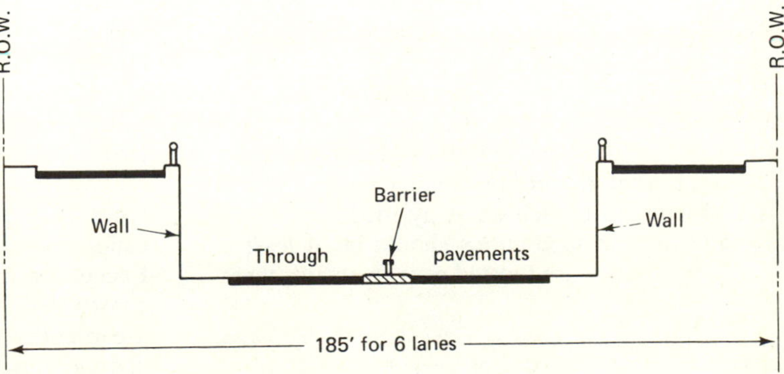

Figure 19.18. Cross sections and right-of-way for depressed freeways; walled sections without ramps. Note: Dimensions shown for six-lane freeways; for other than six-lane freeways, similar dimensions are used except for through pavement width. (Metric conversion factor: multiply values by 0.305 m/ft.)

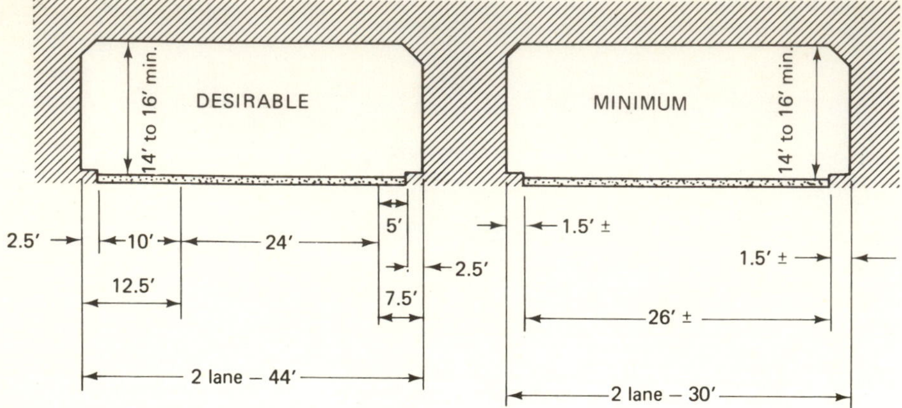

Figure 19.19. Typical section for tunnel. Note: Dimensions shown for four-lane freeway; for other than four lanes, dimensions are similar except for through lane pavement width. (Metric conversion factor: multiply values by 0.305 m/ft.)

Ditches should be well rounded in this area, and fill slopes should be 4 : 1 or flatter. When it is unfeasible to remove obstructions or provide such flat fill slopes, suitable guardrails or crash cushions[20] should be provided. Guardrails or other suitable barriers should also be provided in medians less than 30 ft (9 m) wide and along piers and columns in both the median and on the outside, where they could be struck by an out-of-control vehicle.

Grade separations

A grade separation is a crossing of two highways, a highway and a railroad, or a bicycle path or pedestrian walkway and a highway at different levels. An overpass is a highway passing over an intersecting street, railroad, or bicycle or pedestrian facility. An underpass is a highway passing under an intersecting street, railroad, bicycle, or pedestrian facility. The type of structure for a freeway underpass or overpass should be determined by the load, foundation, and general site requirements for each case.

Minimum clearances at underpasses from the edge of traffic lanes to piers, abutments, or columns are desirably the same as the clearances to obstructions on the remainder of the highway, generally 30 ft (9 m) from the edge of the traffic lane. When this is unfeasible, the minimum clearances should be the normal shoulder width plus sufficient room to allow for protective devices between the edge of shoulder and the obstruction. Vertical clearance at underpasses in urban areas may be as low as 14.5 ft (4.4 m), but a 16-ft (4.9-m) clearance is desired. In rural areas the minimum clearance is 16 ft on trunk highways.

On overpasses, the entire approach roadway width (including shoulders) should be carried across the structure. When a median is no wider than 30 ft (9 m), it is preferable, for safety, to deck over the entire median rather than to have separate structures for each one-way roadway.

Pedestrian and bicycle separations should be at least 8 ft (2.4 m) wide. When they are located over freeways, there should be a vertical clearance of 16 ft (4.9 m); when they are located under freeways, they should have a clear height of 10 ft (3 m).

[20]Crash cushion—a traffic barrier used to safely shield fixed objects or other hazards from approximately head-on impacts by errant vehicles.

Interchanges

Types. Numerous interchange configurations are now used, and many other logical arrangements could be constructed. Where there are four approach legs, the most common types are:

Cloverleaf. A four-leg interchange with loop ramps for some or all of the left turns. A full cloverleaf has ramps for two turning movements in each quadrant. Typical cloverleaf patterns are illustrated in Figure 19.20.

Diamond. A four-leg interchange with a single one-way ramp in each quadrant. All left turns are made directly on the minor highway. The regular diamond, diamond with "slip" ramps to frontage road, and "split diamond" are shown in Figure 19.21.

Directional. An interchange generally having more than one highway grade separation with direct or semidirect connections for the major left-turning movements. Figure 19.22 shows four of the most common types; Figure 19.22(a),(b), and (d) show complete directional patterns; Figure 19.22(c) is a partial directional pattern with three loop ramps.

When there are three approach legs, trumpet, T, or Y interchanges are most commonly used. Figure 19.23(a) and (b) are examples of trumpet interchanges; Figure 19.23(c) and (d) illustrate Y interchanges, and Figure 19.23(e) and (f) are examples of T interchanges.

Interchange designs may vary greatly with physical controls (topography and land-use development), traffic patterns, and types of intersecting highways. A single route (or even an entire area) should, however, employ as few types as possible. Regardless of type, the exit terminal location, layout, and general appearance should be consistent. Except for special cases, complete interchanges should be constructed; where all movements are not provided for at a particular interchange, drivers tend to become confused and the interchanges are frequently deficient in service.

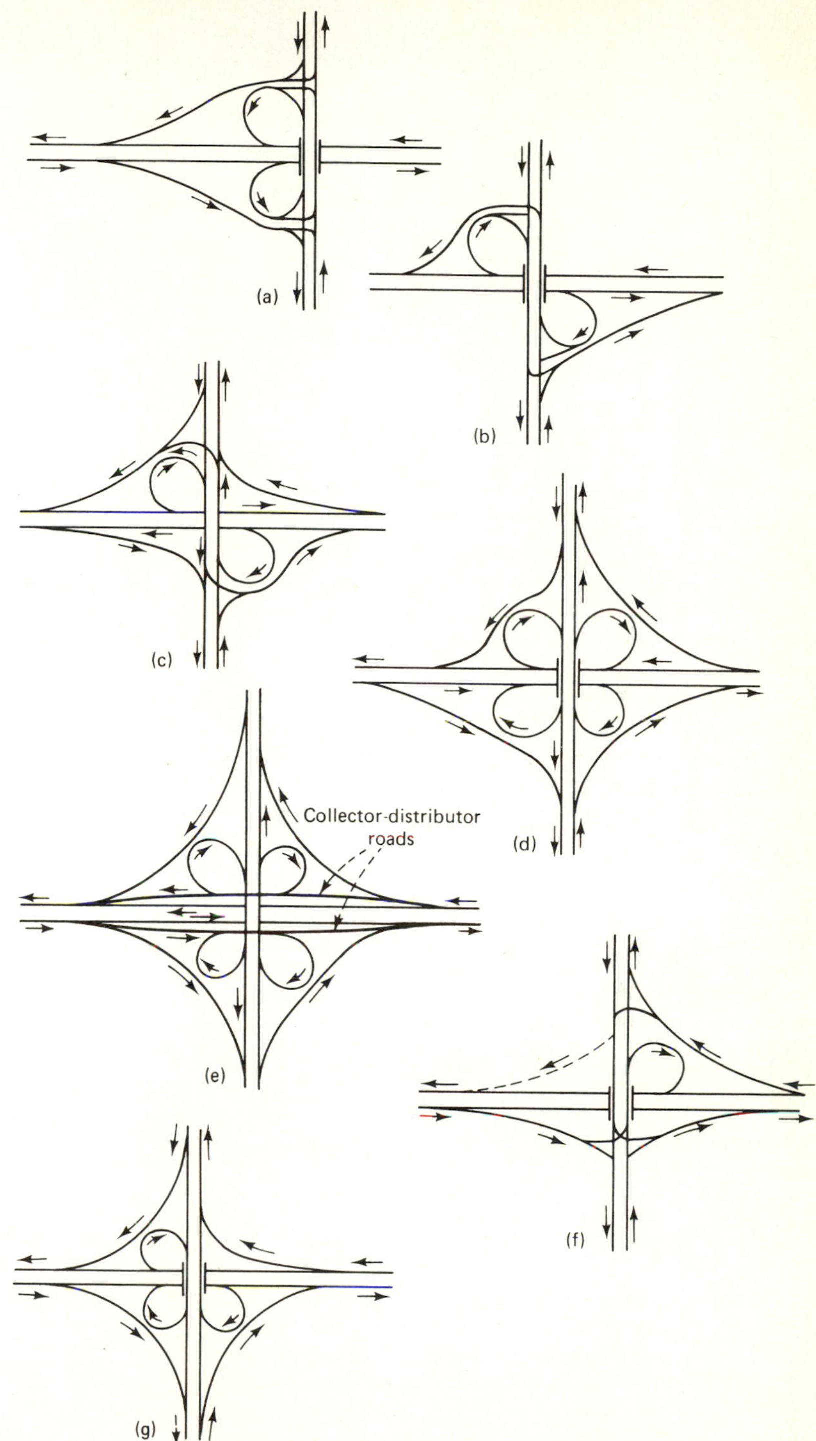

Figure 19.20. Sketches depicting cloverleaf interchange designs. SOURCE: *A Policy on Design of Urban Highways and Arterial Streets,* Washington, D.C.: American Association of State Highway Officials, 1973, p. 594.

Spacing. Interchanges should be located as needed to discharge and receive local traffic effectively. The spacing of major arterial crossroads usually governs and may range from less than 1 mi to many miles. Proper circulation of traffic between the interchange crossroads, the local streets, and freeway systems must be assured. Interchange traffic may otherwise be concentrated at one or more crossroads in such volumes that serious disruption of traffic on both the local roads and the freeway result.

To provide optimum freeway operation with adequate weaving distance and sign placement, the average spacing of urban interchanges should be not less than 2 mi (3.2 km), in suburban areas not less than 4 mi (6.4 km), and in rural sections not less than 8 mi (12.9 km). However, individual spacings of adjacent interchanges may vary considerably. In urban and suburban areas the minimum distance between adjacent interchanges should desirably not be less than 1 mi (1.6 km), and never less than ½ mi (0.8 km). In rural

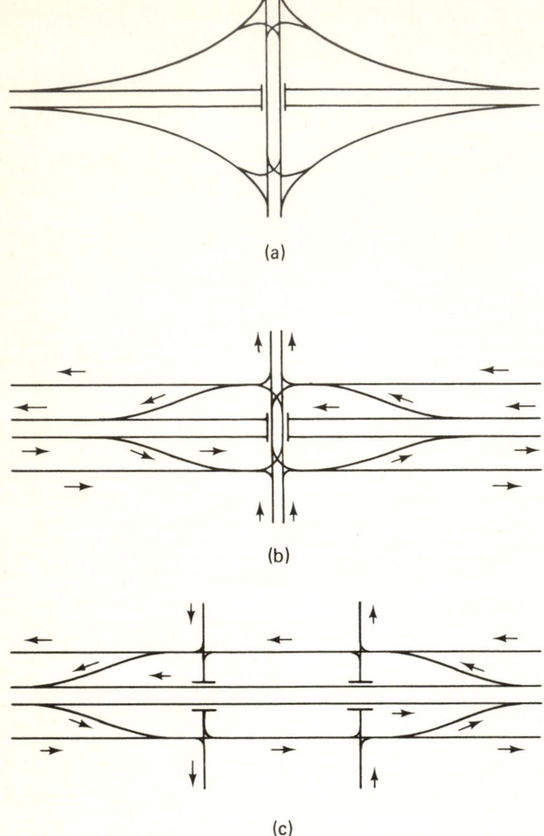

Figure 19.21. Sketches depicting diamond interchange designs. SOURCE: *A Policy on Design of Urban Highways and Arterial Streets,* Washington, D.C.: American Association of State Highway Officials, 1973, p. 589–591.

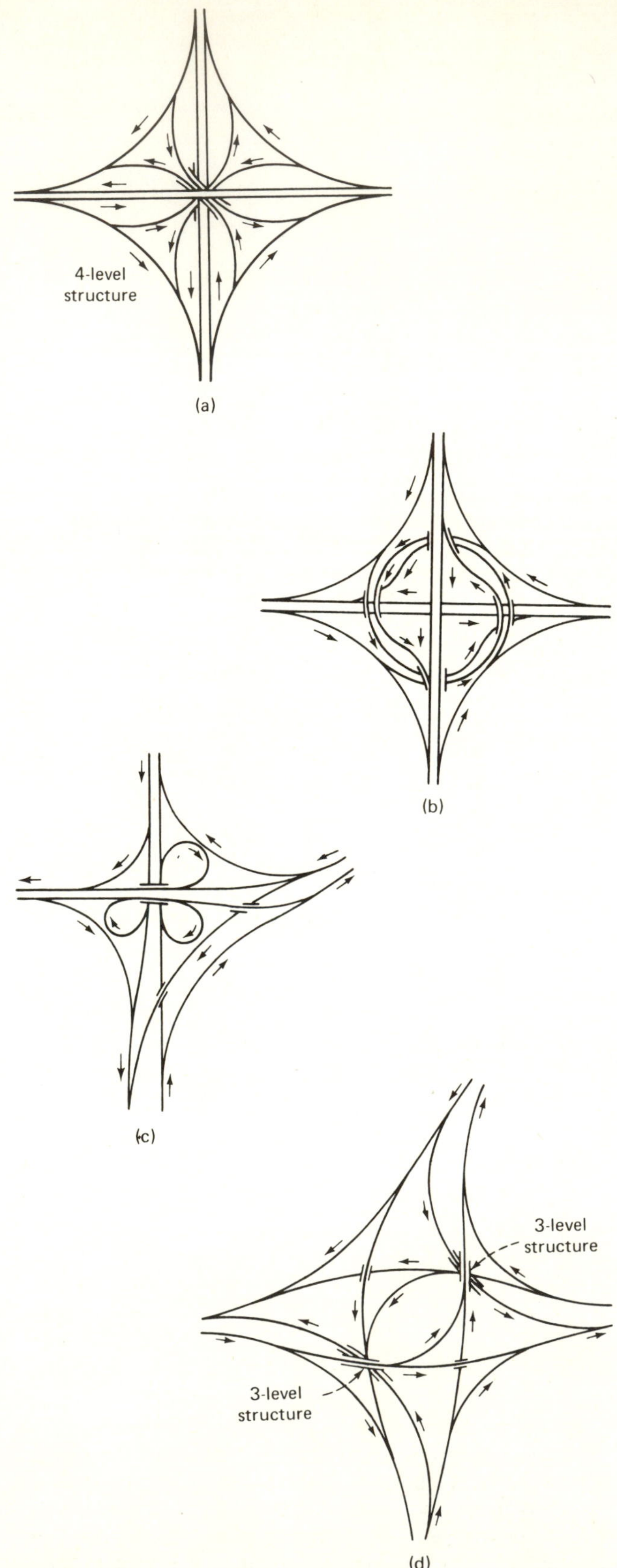

Figure 19.22. Sketches depicting directional interchange designs. SOURCE: *A Policy on Design of Urban Highways and Arterial Streets,* p. 596–600.

areas interchanges should be spaced not less than 3 mi (4.8 km).

Ramps. The term *ramp* includes all types, arrangements, and sizes of turning roadways that connect two or more legs at an interchange. The components of a ramp include a terminal at each leg and a central connecting roadway.

Ramps can be classed broadly as one of the five types shown in Figure 19.24. Each ramp generally is a one-way roadway. Although shown as a continuous curve in Figure 19.24(a), a diagonal ramp may be largely tangent or wishbone-shaped, depending on the angle of intercepting roadways. A diamond-type interchange generally has four diagonal ramps. With the loop pattern shown in Figure 19.24(b), the left-turning movement is made without an at-grade crossing of the opposing through traffic. Instead, drivers making a left turn travel beyond the highway separation, swing right, and turn through approximately 270° to enter the other highway. With a semidirect connection [Figure 19.24(d)] drivers making a left turn first swing away from the intended direction, gradually reverse, and then follow directly around and enter the other road on the right (see the solid line). In another semidirect connection [Figure 19.24(d)] drivers exit to the left, loop around to the left, then reverse to enter on the right (see the dashed line). This

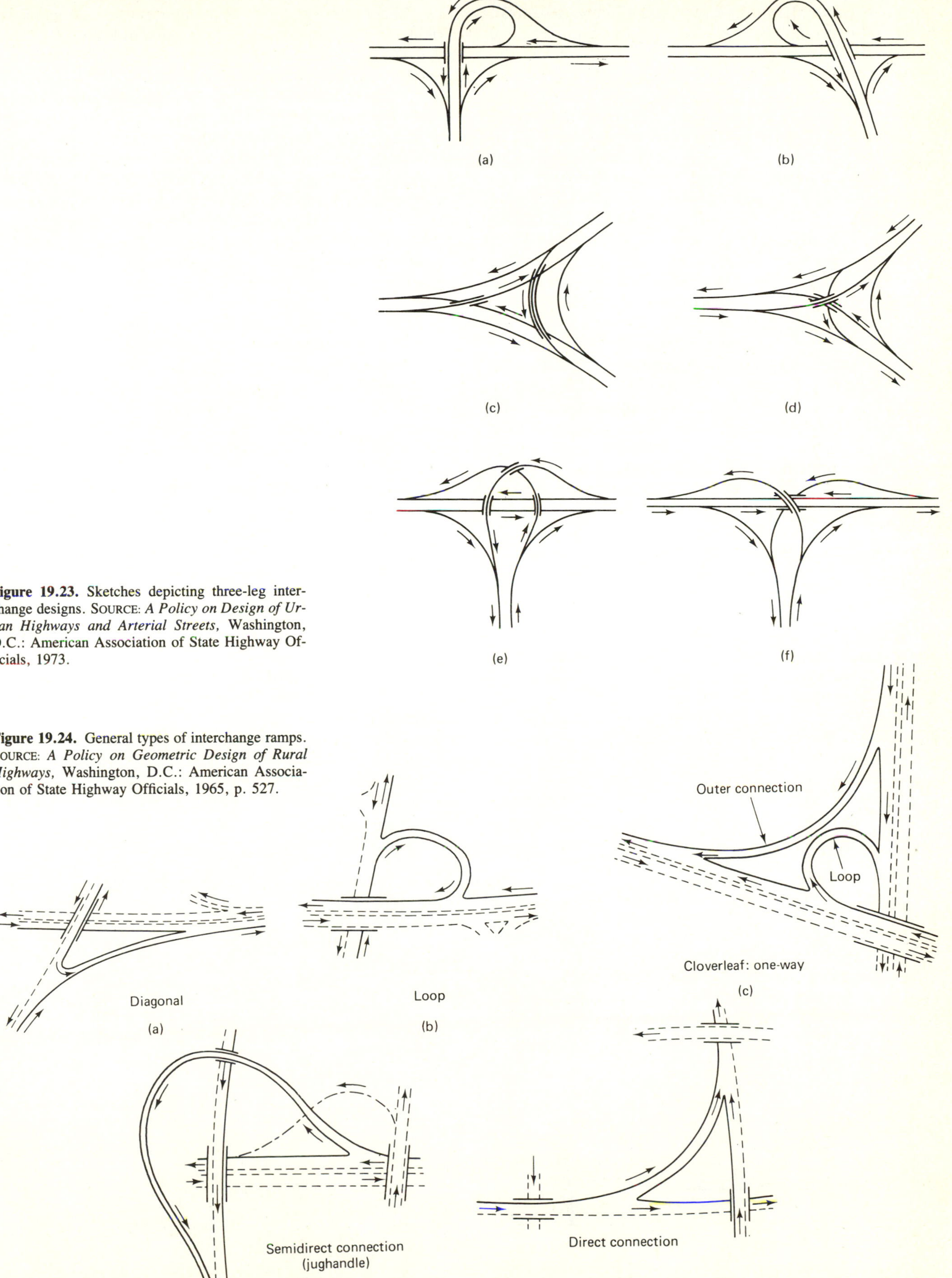

Figure 19.23. Sketches depicting three-leg interchange designs. SOURCE: *A Policy on Design of Urban Highways and Arterial Streets,* Washington, D.C.: American Association of State Highway Officials, 1973.

Figure 19.24. General types of interchange ramps. SOURCE: *A Policy on Geometric Design of Rural Highways,* Washington, D.C.: American Association of State Highway Officials, 1965, p. 527.

is less desirable because of the left-hand off ramp. In the direct-connection left-turn movement [Figure 19.24(c)], drivers leave on the left, turn directly toward the left, and enter on the left.

Each ramp type can have a different shape according to traffic pattern, traffic volume, design speed, topography, development, intersection angle, and type of ramp terminal.

A desirable alignment for an outer connection is a continuous curve, as shown at (1) in Figure 19.25(a). This arrangement, however, may require extensive right-of-way. Another desirable arrangement has a central tangent and terminal curves, lines (2) and (3). There are numerous choices for the angle and alignment of the outer connection. When the loop is more important than the outer connection, reverse alignment on the outer connection may be used to reduce the area of right-of-way, as shown by line (4). Any combination of (2), (3), and (4) may also be used.

Ramps forming a diamond interchange may assume a variety of shapes, depending on the pattern of turning traffic and right-of-way limitations. As shown by solid lines in Figure 19.25(b), the ramp may be a diagonal tangent with connecting curves. To favor a right-turning movement, the ramp may be a continuous curve to the right with a spur to the left for left turns. On restricted right-of-way along a major highway, reverse alignments (with a portion of the ramp parallel to the through roadway) may be required, as shown by the short dashed line.

Diamond ramps of a type sometimes called slip ramps or cross connections, shown dashed in Figure 19.25(b), may also connect with parallel frontage roads. When either is employed, safety and efficiency dictates one-way frontage roads. Cross connections to two-way frontage roads introduce the possibility of wrong-way entry onto the freeway and require extensive channelization to prevent this, as well as to provide proper operation for traffic leaving the freeway.

The shape of a semidirect connection [Figure 19.25(c)] may be influenced by the extent of lateral separation of the one-way through pavements, the location of the terminals with respect to the structures, and the extent to which the structure pavements are widened or flared. The curve radii necessary to maintain a desired turning speed for an important left-turning movement sometimes determine the required lateral separation of the through roadway. When the semidirect connection leaves on the right and enters on the right, as shown by the long dashed line in Figure 19.25(c), the through lanes can be closely spaced. This sometimes requires a three-level interchange.

It is rarely feasible to provide ramps on which turning traffic can travel in the same range of speeds as on the through roads. Nevertheless, there should not be a great difference between the design speed of the highway and the design speed of the connecting ramp. Table 19-19 shows minimum and desirable guide values for ramp design speeds as related to highway design speed. As a minimum for direct connections the desirable design speeds should be used. The design speed of loops, on the other hand, usually must be near the minimums specified.

The minimum stopping sight distance values summarized in Table 19-5 apply directly to ramps. Longer sight distances should be considered whenever feasible.

Ramp grades should be as flat as possible to minimize driving effort in maneuvering from one road to another. The maximum grades shown in Table 19-10 for arterial highways other than freeways for various design speeds are generally applicable to ramps, but a precise relation has not been established.

Table 19-20 shows design widths of pavements for ramps. Desirably, on high-type ramps a shoulder 8 to 10 ft (2.4 to 3.1 m) is provided on the right and 6 ft (1.8 m) on the left along the length of the ramps. As a minimum, 6 ft (1.8 m) should be provided on the right and 4 ft (1.2 m) on the left. Curbs may be provided along the edge of ramp proper or on the outside of the shoulder. When they are provided on the inside of the shoulder, they should be of the mountable type.

Rates of cross slope on ramps where superelevation is not required should be the same as for through roadways, as given in Table 19-13. A common direction of cross slope is generally provided on ramps. Superelevation on ramps should be the same as for through roadways; see Table 19-12. However, higher maximum rates should be considered, at special locations: for instance, on one-way downhill ramps.

The terminal of a ramp is that portion adjacent to the

Figure 19.25. Ramp shapes. SOURCE: *A Policy on Geometric Design of Rural Highways,* Washington, D.C.: American Association of State Highway Officials, 1965, p. 533.

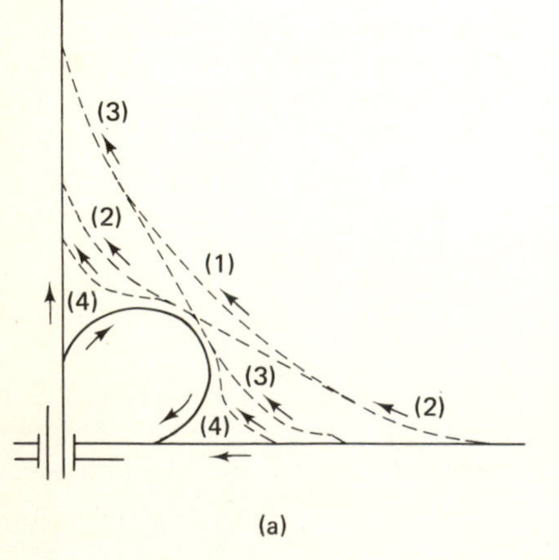

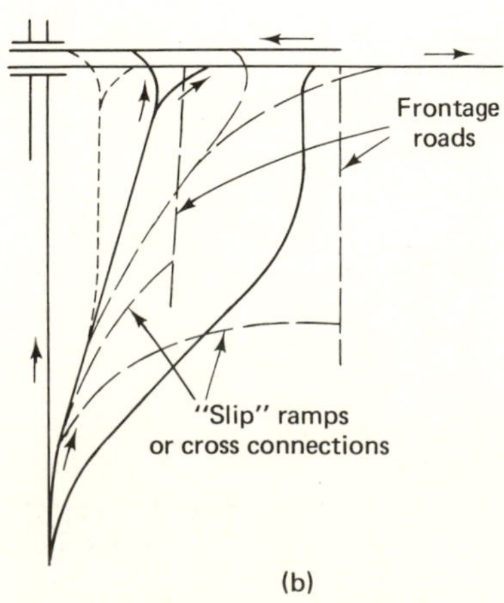

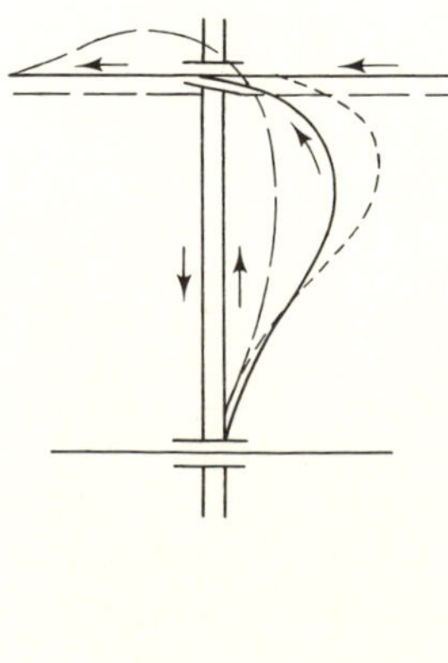

TABLE 19–19
Guide Values for Ramp Design Speed as Related to Highway Design Speed

	Highway Design Speed [mph (km/h)]							
	30 (48)	40 (64)	50 (80)	60 (97)	65 (105)	70 (113)	75 (121)	80 (129)
Ramp design speed [mph (km/h)]								
Desirable	25 (40)	35 (56)	45 (72)	50 (80)	55 (89)	60 (97)	60 (97)	65 (105)
Minimum	15 (24)	20 (32)	25 (40)	30 (48)	30 (48)	30 (48)	35 (56)	40 (64)
Corresponding minimum radius [ft (m)]								
Desirable	150 (46)	300 (91)	550 (168)	690 (210)	840 (256)	1040 (316)	1040 (316)	1260 (383)
Minimum	50 (15)	90 (27)	150 (46)	230 (70)	230 (70)	230 (70)	300 (91)	430 (131)

TABLE 19–20
Design Widths of Pavements for Turning Roadways*

	Pavement Width in Feet for:								
	Case I 1-Lane, One-Way Operation—No Provision for Passing			Case II 1-Lane, One-Way Operation—with Provision for Passing a Stalled Vehicle			Case III 2-Lane Operation—Either One-Way or Two-Way		
	Design Traffic Condition†								
R, Radius on Inner Edge of Pavement (ft)	A	B	C	A	B	C	A	B	C
50	18	18	23	23	25	29	31	25	42
75	16	17	19	21	23	27	29	33	37
100	15	16	18	20	22	25	28	31	35
150	14	16	17	19	21	24	27	30	33
200	13	16	16	19	21	23	27	29	31
300	13	15	16	18	20	22	26	28	30
400	13	15	16	18	20	22	26	28	29
500	12	15	15	18	20	22	26	28	29
Tangent	12	15	15	17	19	21	25	27	27
	Width Modification Regarding Edge of Pavement Treatment								
No stabilized shoulder	None			None			None		
Mountable curb	None			None			None		
Barrier curb									
One side	Add 1 ft			None			Add 1 ft		
Two sides	Add 2 ft			Add 1 ft			Add 2 ft		
Stabilized shoulder, one or both sides	None			Deduct shoulder width; minimum pavement width as under case I			Deduct 2 ft where shoulder is 4 ft or wider		

*Metric conversion factor: multiply values by 0.305 m/ft.
†A, predominantly P vehicles, but some consideration for SU trucks; B, sufficient SU vehicles to govern design, but some consideration for semitrailer vehicles; C, sufficient bus and combination types of vehicles to govern design.

SOURCE: *A Policy on Design of Urban Highways and Arterial Streets*, p. 551.

through traveled way, including speed change lane, taper, approach nose, merging end, and island. Ramp terminals may be at-grade intersections, as at diamond or partial cloverleaf interchanges, or directional, where ramp traffic merges or diverges from through traffic at flat angles.

Deceleration and acceleration lanes can be of either the straight-line taper or the parallel type. The straight-line taper is most widely used. Figure 19.26(a) illustrates a straight-line taper or direct type of deceleration lane. In the design of deceleration lanes of this type, the terminal edge departs from the through-lane edge abruptly at approximately a 20 : 1 to 30 : 1 rate of divergence. The taper for acceleration lanes is much flatter, as shown in Figure 19.26(b). A 50 : 1 to 70 : 1 rate of convergence between the outer edge of the acceleration lane and the freeway lane provides reasonable acceleration length and prescribes a proper path for an entering vehicle. The deceleration approach nose should be offset from the through lanes at least 12 ft (3.6 m) and the gore area between the through lane and the ramp should be surfaced. The surfaced area should be tapered from the nose to the edge of the traffic lane downstream from the nose. The nose should also be offset from the traveled way of the ramp a distance equal to the width of shoulder of the ramp.

Figure 19.26(b) illustrates an entrance terminal. Near the merging point the roadway entrance pavement should be aimed nearly parallel to the through roadway. The physical nose should be offset the full shoulder width from the edge

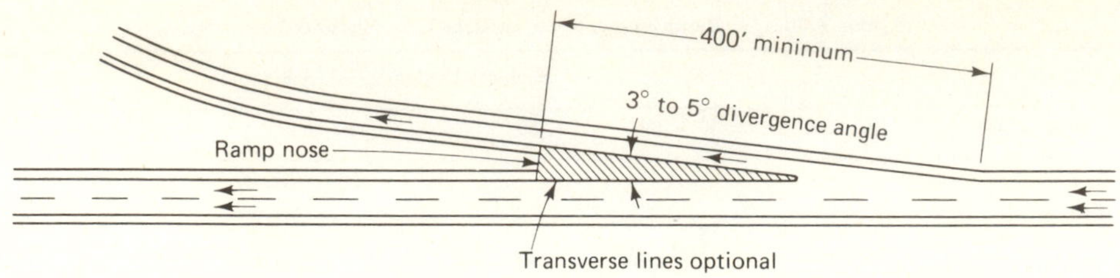

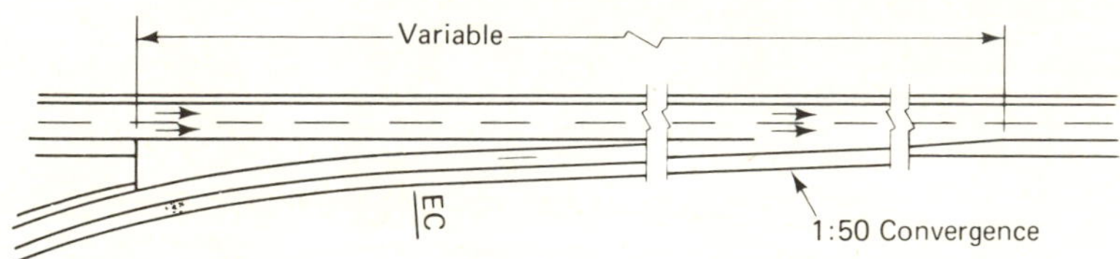

Figure 19.26. Designs for taper-type, single-lane exits and entrances.

of the through lanes and the left shoulder width from the edge of the ramp.

Design of two-lane exit and entrance ramps is generally similar to single-lane exit and entrance ramps, except for their additional width and length of speed change lanes. These usually are special designs that entail a length of full added lane.[21]

Distance between Successive Ramp Terminals. Serving the numerous traffic generators along an urban freeway may require frequent ramp terminals in close succession. In order to provide sufficient maneuvering length and adequate space for signing, a reasonable distance is required between successive terminals. The minimum distance required for satisfactory freeway operation are 1000 ft (300 m) between successive exits on a freeway exit and an exit on a collector-distributor road or a split in the ramp.

When the distance between the end of taper on the entrance terminal and the beginning of taper on the exit terminal is less than 1000 ft (300 m), the speed change lanes should be connected to provide a continuous auxiliary lane.

When an exit ramp is followed by an entrance ramp, there should be 500 ft (150 m) between the terminals so that drivers are not confronted with merging vehicles too soon after passing an exit area.

Control of access. Access should be controlled throughout all portions of interchanges, just as for the highway between the interchanges. When freeways interchange with noncontrolled access highways, it is desirable to extend the control of access at least 100 ft (30 m) along the crossroad beyond the ramp terminal in urban areas and at least 300 ft (90 m) in rural areas.

[21]For more complete information, see *Two-Lane Entrance Ramps,* ITE Informational Report (Washington, D.C.: Institute of Traffic Engineers, 1968).

Provision for mass transit and other high occupancy vehicles (HOV)

With the recent emphasis on reducing miles of travel without reducing mobility, strategies to increase vehicular occupancy are sometimes being incorporated into the design of highway facilities.

On freeways, preferential lanes can be provided for buses and carpools (generally with three or four or more persons per vehicle). These lanes may be completely separated from the normal traffic lanes, as shown on Figure 19.27. In this case two reversible lanes are provided in the median for use only by buses and carpools throughout the day. Separate ramps are provided for the priority vehicles to exit and enter the preferential lanes.

Other designs do not have a barrier separation between the HOV lanes. A buffer 2 to 8 ft (0.6 to 2.4 m) in width is provided between the regular-use lanes and the priority lanes, as shown in Figure 19.28. In some cases where space is limited, the HOV lane is provided adjacent to the regular-use lanes without a separation. In this case it is imperative to provide a shoulder for enforcement purposes. The space for HOV Lanes and the adjacent shoulder may in some cases have to be provided by narrowing the regular use lanes and making use of the portion of the shoulder on the opposite side. HOV lanes may be provided on the inside or outside of the regular-use traffic lanes, but it is generally more desirable to provide them on the median side, as enforcement is usually easier and there are fewer operational problems.

Other types of priority treatments include such features as exclusive ramps for buses and carpools or buses only. The design of these ramps should be the same as ramps for general use. Bypass ramps in conjunction with ramp metering are also a strategy for encouraging use of higher-occupancy vehicles. Often, these ramps or bypass lanes have minimum geometrics as they must be fitted into existing facilities.

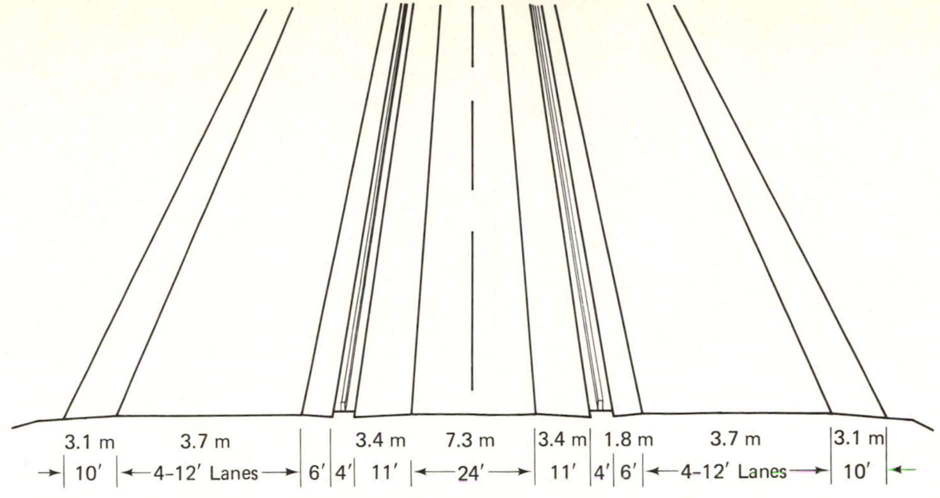

Figure 19.27. Example of separated roadway for buses and carpools.

Freeways are also sometimes combined effectively with other mass transit facilities in large cities. Many metropolitan areas have freeway express buses. Almost all operate nonstop from suburban pickup points near the freeway into the CBD. Others utilize special bus stops at intersecting streets along the freeway where passengers transfer to or from other lines or automobiles. Freeway bus stops should be located only where site conditions are favorable and, if possible, where acceleration lanes are flat or on a downgrade. Bus stops may be provided at the freeway level for which stairs, ramps, or escalators are necessary, or they may be located at the street level that buses reach by way of interchange ramps.

Bus turnouts should be designed so that deceleration, standing, and acceleration is effected clear of and separated from the through traffic lanes. Speed change lanes should be long enough to enable buses to leave and enter through traffic lanes at approximately the average running speed of the highway. The length of acceleration lanes from bus turnouts should be well above the normal minimum values because buses start from a standing position. Normal-length deceleration lanes are suitable. Bus roadways, including the shoulder, should be 20 ft (6 m) wide to permit passing a stalled bus. The dividing area between the outer edge of the freeway shoulder and the edge of the bus lane should be as wide as possible, preferably 20 ft (6 m) or more, with 4 ft (1.2 m) as an absolute minimum. Pedestrian loading platforms should not be less than 5 ft (1.5 m) wide and should preferably be from 6 to 10 ft (1.8 to 3 m) wide. Figures 19.29 and 19.30 show various arrangements for bus stop locations at cloverleaf and diamond-type interchanges.[22]

[22]Additional arrangements are shown in *Bus Stops for Freeway Operations* (Washington, D.C.: Institute of Traffic Engineers, 1971).

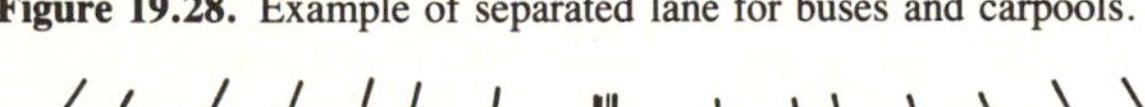

Figure 19.28. Example of separated lane for buses and carpools.

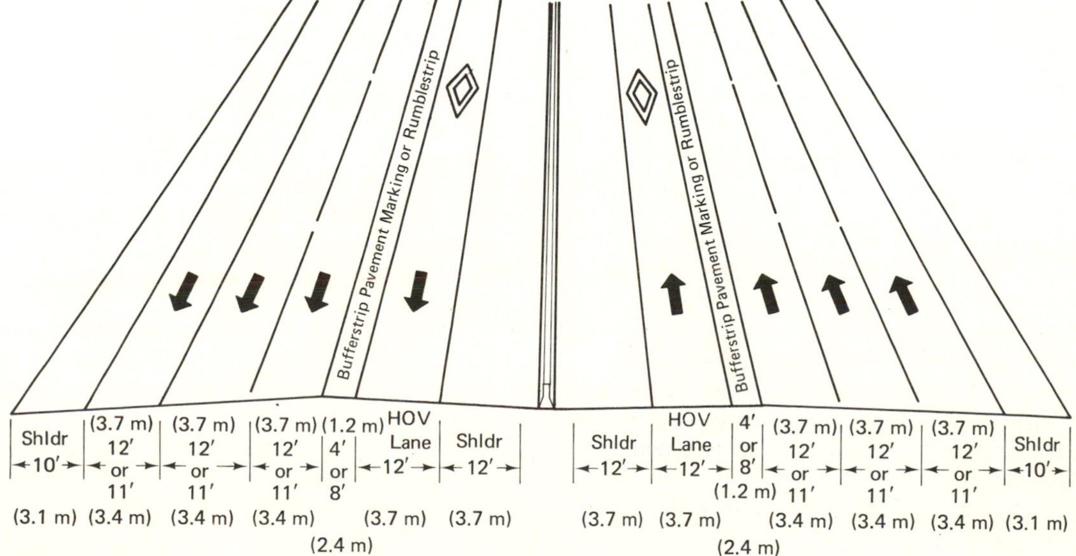

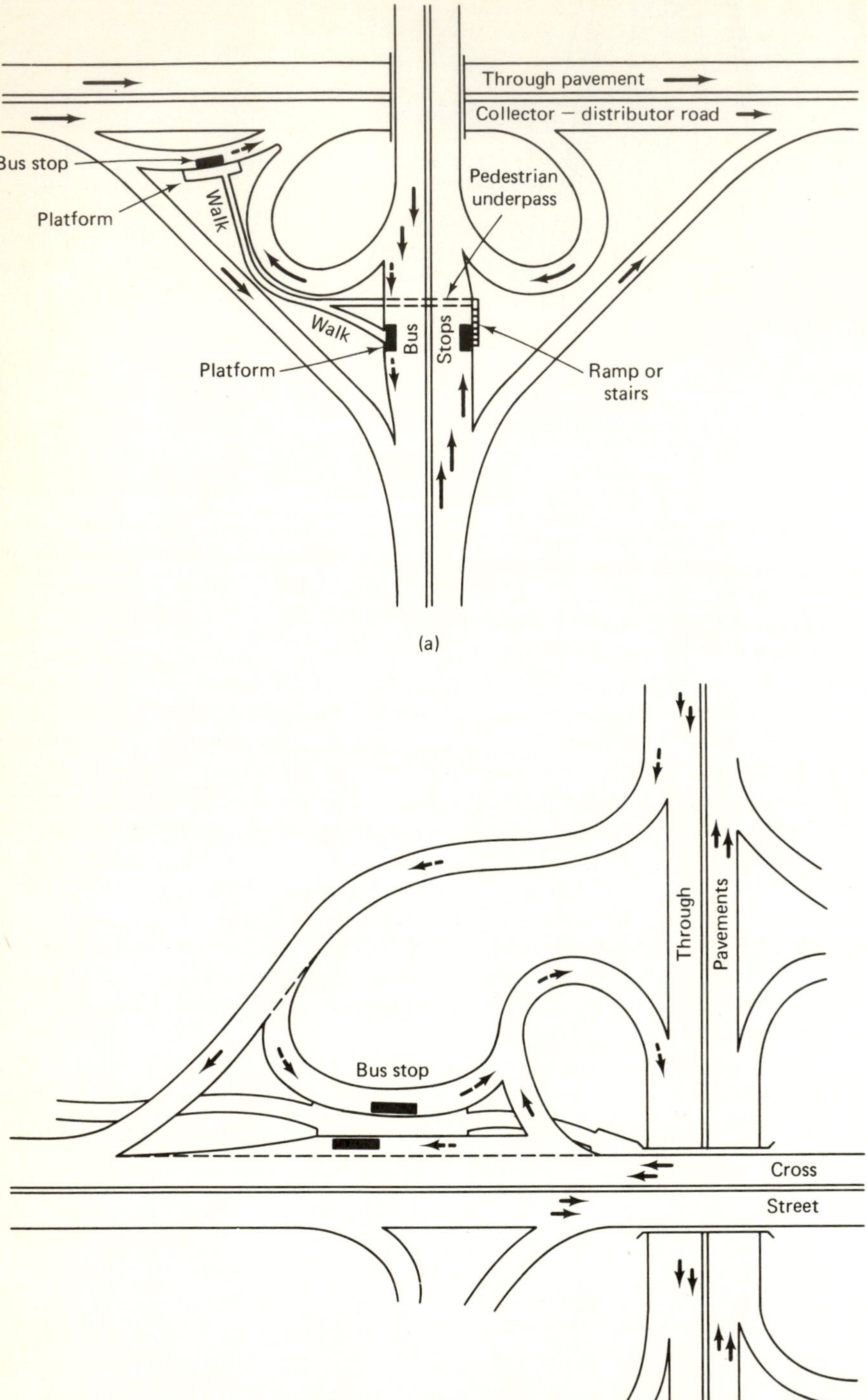

Figure 19.29. Bus stops at cloverleaf interchanges. (a) Bus stop at freeway level. (b) Bus stop at street level. SOURCE: *Bus Stops for Freeway Operations*, Washington, D.C.: Institute of Traffic Engineers, 1971, p. 6.

Rail transit can be located in the median, on either side, above, or below the freeway. The most common arrangement is to place the transit line within the median of a depressed or ground-level freeway. When it is so located, a minimum median width of 56 ft (17 m) is generally required between the two traveled ways, and when stations are also located in the median, a minimum width of 80 ft (24 m) is usually required.

Local roads and streets

The design standards for local roads and streets vary considerably, depending on the type of area served (subdivision, rural, commercial, industrial, etc.), traffic volumes, terrain, and the governmental body responsible for their design.

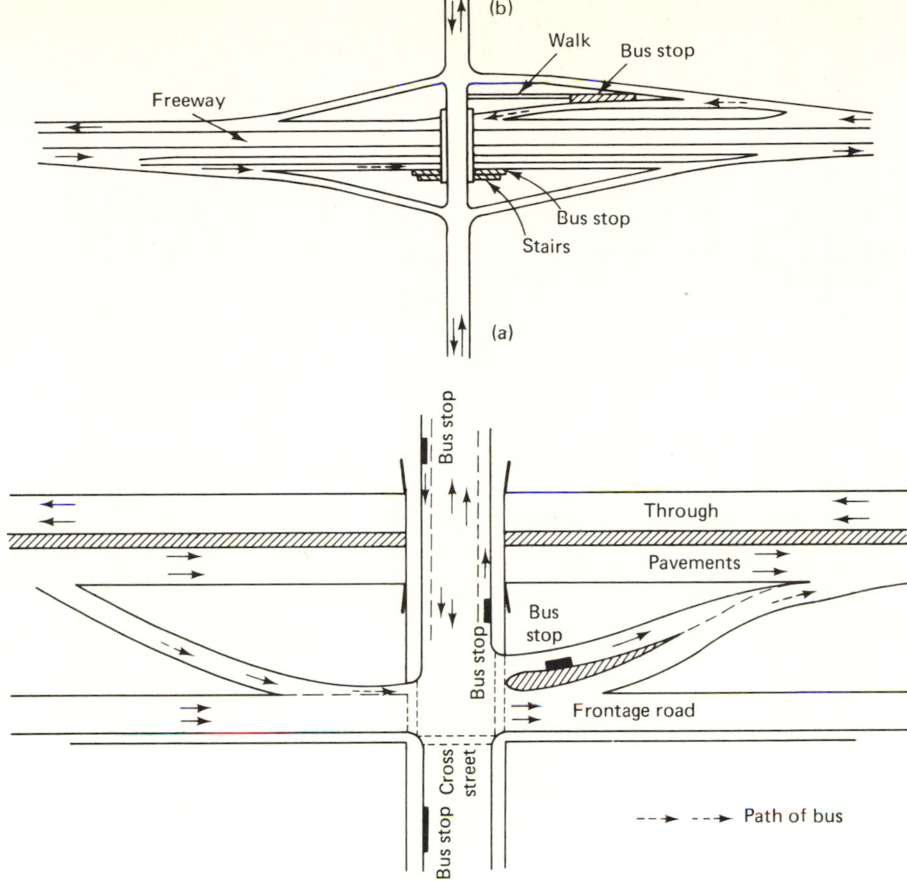

Figure 19.30. Bus stops at diamond interchanges. SOURCE: *Bus Stops for Freeway Operations,* Washington, D.C.: Institute of Traffic Engineers, 1971, p. 7.

Cross-section design

Typical cross sections for rural and urban local roads and streets are shown in Figure 19.31. In rural areas a shoulder is normally included in the cross section. A border area for errant vehicle recovery is desirable. It should have slopes desirably 4 : 1 or flatter and be clear of obstructions. In urban areas there may be sections with shoulders, but more commonly a plain curb (or curb and gutter) is included in the cross section at the edge of the outer parking lane. The curb should have a vertical or roll-type face and be not more than 6 in. (15 cm) high. The gutter is usually from 1 to 2 ft (0.3 to 0.6 m) wide and can be separate or integral with the curb.

As a minimum, sidewalks should be provided along streets, used for pedestrian access to schools, parks, shopping areas, and transit stops. Minimum sidewalk widths should be 4 ft (1.2 m); widths of 8 ft (2.4 m) or greater are required in commercial areas. Sidewalks may be located next to the curb, but, desirably, they should be at least 5 ft (1.5 m) and preferably from 12 (3.6 m) to 15 ft (4.6 m) from the edge of curb. Borders should be made as wide as practical. As indicated previously, the border should generally be from 4 to 8 ft (1.2 to 2.4 m) plus the sidewalk width. In rural areas wider border areas are usually applicable.

Criteria applicable to subdivision streets

The primary objective of subdivision design is to provide maximum liveability. Driving convenience is secondary. Street alignment should fit topography closely enough to minimize the need for cuts or fills and at the same time to discourage high-speed through traffic.[23]

Driveways

Typical driveway dimensions suggested for various land uses are shown in Table 19-21. Methods of measurement are shown in Figure 19.32. For additional details of driveway design, such as maximum grades, maximum change

[23] *Recommended Practices for Subdivision Streets.*

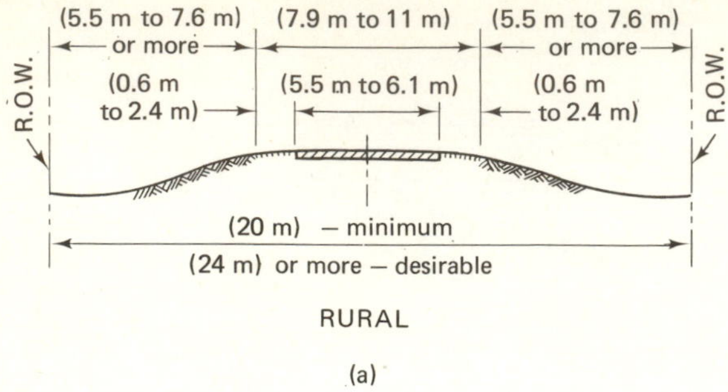

*Usable shoulder width
**For low volume roads with few trucks

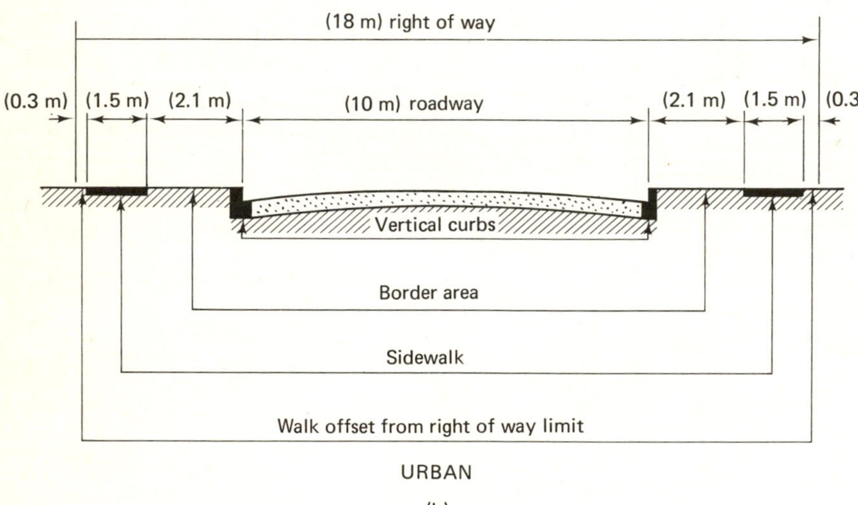

Figure 19.31. Typical cross section of local roads and streets. SOURCE: (a) *A Policy of Geometric Design of Rural Highways,* Washington, DC: American Association of State Highway Officials, 1965, p. 263. (b) *Recommended Practices for Subdivision Streets,* Washington, D.C.: Institute of Traffic Engineers, 1967, p. 2.

in grades, sight distance at driveways, and design of curbs in conjunction with spacing, see the references cited.[24,25]

Bikeways

Bikeway options

Several options should be considered in planning and implementing a bikeway system.[26] The first option is to do nothing, and where it is adequate and safe permit bicyclists to use the existing street system. At present city streets are typically used by bicyclists and perhaps as much as 70% of our total urban street system mileage may be fairly safe for bicyclists without significant improvement.[27]

Bicyclists are more sensitive than motorists to street-surface irregularities. Thus, depressions and bumps should be minimized. Shoulders where bicyclists are expected should be smooth. Adequate conditions for bicycle use include proper curb and gutters as well as sewer grates that have slits which are oriented perpendicular to the lane.[28]

Bikeways are presently classified into bicycle paths, lanes, and routes. Bicycle paths are completely separated from motor vehicular traffic and are contained within an independent right-of-way.

Another option is the bicycle lane, which is established within the roadway directly adjacent to the outside motor vehicle lane or on the shoulder. Bicycle lanes are designated by signs and pavement markings. Many of the bikeways developed today are bicycle lanes, with the highway or street dictating the geometric design, such as alignment, grades, and drainage.

Bicycle lanes must be developed as one-way facilities. Bidirectional lanes (two-way operation on one side of the street) are not recommended because:

1. They require unconventional turns at intersections.
2. They present problems at the transition from one-way to two-way operation since bicyclists have to be going the "wrong way" as well as having to weave across

[24]*An Informational Guide for Preparing Private Driveway Regulations for Major Highways* (Washington, D.C.: American Association of State Highway Officials, 1960).

[25]*Guidelines for Driveway Design and Location* (Washington, D.C.: Institute of Traffic Engineers, 1975).

[26]*Bicycling in Tennessee, Planning and Design Manual* (Tennessee Department of Conservation and Transportation, 1975).

[27]*Guidelines for Urban Major Street Design; Tentative Recommended Practice.* (Washington, D.C.: Institute of Transporation Engineers, 1979).

[28]*Bicycle—Safe Grate Inlet Study,* Report No. FHWA-RD-77-24, (Washington, D.C.: Federal Highway Administration, 1977).

TABLE 19–21
Typical Driveway Dimensions

	Dimension Reference (See Fig. 19.32)	Urban			Rural		
		Residential	Commercial	Industrial	Residential	Commercial	Industrial
Width*	W						
Minimum		10	15	20	10	15	20
Maximum		30	35	40	30	40	40
Right-turn radius†	R						
Minimum		5	10	15	10	15	25
Maximum		15	20	25	25	50	50
Minimum spacing‡							
From property line	P	0	0	−R	0	0	−R
From street corner	C	5	10	10	10	15	20
Between driveways	S	0	0	0	0	0	0
Angle§	A	45°	45°	45°	45°	45°	45°

*The minimum width of commercial driveways is intended to apply to one-way operation. In high-pedestrian-activity areas such as in a central business district or in the same block with auditorium, school, or library, the maximum basic width should be 30 ft. The width shown applies to rural routes and most city streets, including neighborhood business, residential, and industrial streets. The width is intended to be measured along the right-of-way line, in most instances, at the inner limit of a curbed radius or between the line of the radius and the near edge of a curbed island at least 50 ft^2 in area.

†On the side of a driveway exposed to entry or exit by right-turning vehicles. In high-pedestrian-activity areas, the radii should be half the values shown. The maximum radii for major generator driveways should be much higher than the values shown.

‡Measured along the curb or edge of pavement from the roadway end of the curb radius. In high-pedestrian-activity areas, the minimum spacing between driveways should be 5 ft.

§Minimum acute angle measured from edge of pavement, and generally based on one-way operation. For two-way driveways, and in high-pedestrian-activity areas, the minimum angle should be 70°.

SOURCE: *Guidelines for Driveway Design and Location* (Washington, D.C.: Institute of Traffic Engineers, 1975).

Figure 19.32. Driveway dimensions measurements (see Table 19.21). SOURCE: *Guidelines for Driveway Design and Location,* Arlington, Va.: Institute of Transportation Engineers, 1975.

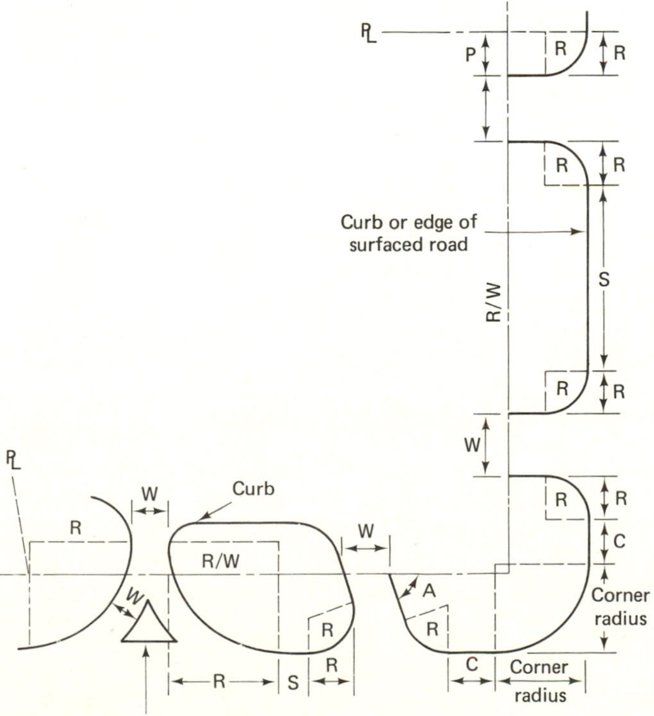

traffic to bike in the proper lane when the special bike lane begins or terminates.

3. They require that bicyclists travel in a direction opposite to the adjacent motor vehicle traffic lane.

The bicycle-route option is a road designated by signs for bicycling, where the bicycle must share the road with motor vehicles. These signs are intended to alert motorists to the presence of bicyclists and to guide bicyclists to use streets that have been determined to be suitable for bicycle usage.

The use of the sidewalk as a bikeway is an option that has very limited application but may be developed in unusual circumstances by either letting the bicycle share the sidewalk with pedestrians or by designating a selected portion of the sidewalk for bicycles. This option may present problems because of the potential conflict between pedestrians and bicyclists. Among the factors contributing to this experience are:

1. Poor sight distances often prevail at driveways.
2. Poor visual relationships between bicyclist and motorist occur at intersections.
3. Bidirectional operation compounds sight distance visual relationship problems.
4. Pedestrians of all ages, but especially small children and older persons, are uneasy when meeting bicyclists along the sidewalk, with resulting conflict and confusion.

Design speed

It is possible to attain speeds approaching 30 mph (50 km/h) or more on a bicycle, but normal speeds range from 7 to 20 mph (10 to 30 km/h). A desirable working design speed is 20 mph. Where rolling terrain and significant downgrades greater than 4% are prevalent, a design speed of 30 mph (48 km/h) may be used.[29]

Bikeway widths

The actual bikeway pavement width depends on bicycle width, maneuvering allowance, clearance between oncoming and passing bicycles, and edge conditions.[30]

A two-way off-street bike path (Figure 19.33) should have a minimum paved width of 8 ft (2.6 m) and a desirable width of 12 ft (3.7 m) plus a 2 ft (0.6 m) graded width on each side. A width of at least 10 ft (3 m) will allow maintenance and emergency vehicles to utilize the path.

When a bikeway is shared with normal pedestrian traffic, there must be at least a 2.5-ft (0.8-m) horizontal separation between bicycles and pedestrians (preferably more). This means the sidewalk must be 11 to 15 feet (3.4 to 4.6 m) wide to accommodate both pedestrians and bicyclists.

A one-way bike lane at the curb requires a minimum

[29]*Design and Construction Criteria for Bikeway Construction Projects,* Notice of Proposed Rulemaking, Federal Register Vol. 45, No. 151, August 4, 1980, U.S. Department of Transportation, Federal Highway Administration.

[30]Ibid.

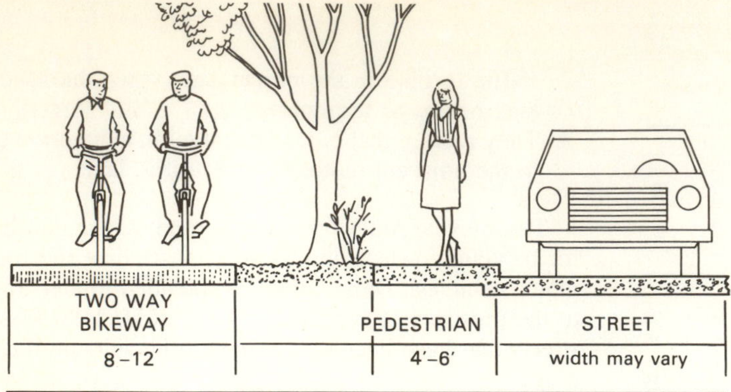

Figure 19.33. Bikepath. SOURCE: *Safety and Locational Criteria for Bicycle Facilities,* Users Manual, Vol. 2, Washington, D.C.: U.S. Department of Transportation, Federal Highway Administration, 1976.

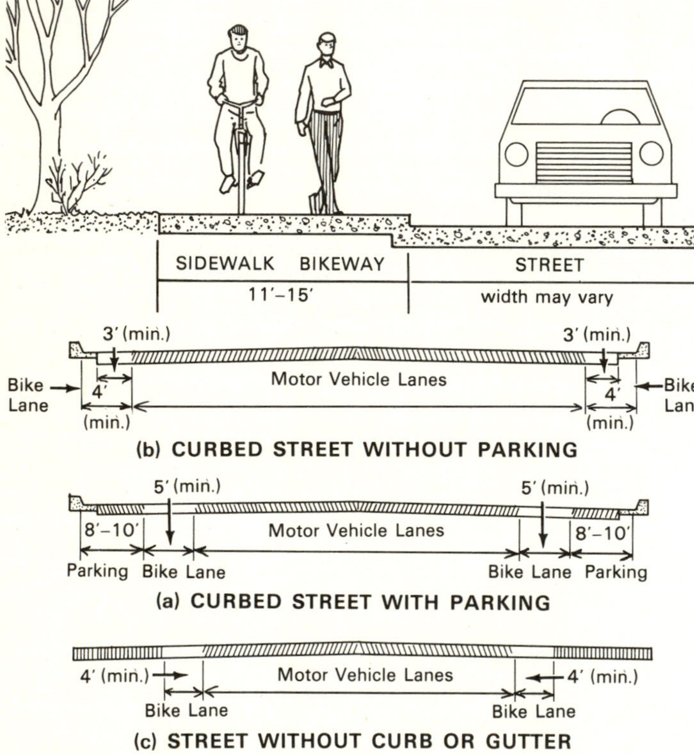

Figure 19.34. Sidewalk bikeway (1 ft = 0.3 m). SOURCE: *Safety and Locational Criteria for Bicycle Facilities,* Users Manual, Vol. 2, Washington, D.C.: U.S. Department of Transportation, Federal Highway Administration, 1976.

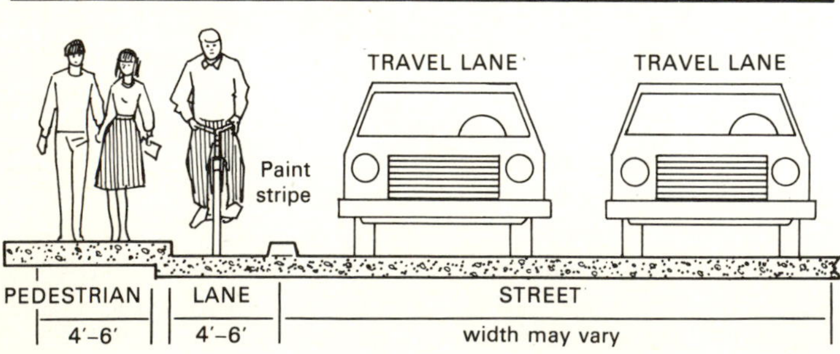

Figure 19.35. Bikelane (1 ft = 0.3 m). SOURCE: *Safety and Locational Criteria for Bicycle Facilities,* Users Manual, Vol. 2, Washington, D.C.: U.S. Department of Transportation, Federal Highway Administration, 1976.

width of 4 ft (1.2 m), measured from the face of the curb (see Figure 19.34a). A one-way bike lane next to a parking lane requires a total width of parking and bike lane of 13 ft (4 m), with 15 ft (4.2 m) desirable, between the curb and the edge of the motor vehicle lane (see Figure 19.34(b)). This dimension will allow for parked cars with an open door extending out 3.5 ft (1.1 m) plus the bike lane. Where there is no curb or gutter the bike lane should be a minimum 4 ft (1.2 m) wide outside the motor vehicle lanes. See Figure 19.34(c).

A combined walkway and bikeway on a bridge, tunnel, or similar facility which is physically separated from vehicular traffic may be allowed with limited width for economic reasons. Where there are low pedestrian and bicyle volumes on such a facility, a width of 8 ft (2.4 m) can be utilized. Desirable additional width should be provided if moderate to heavy pedestrian and bicycle volumes exist.

Grades

Grades are important because bicyclists are sensitive to topographical variation. Acceptable grades for bicyclists depend on variable conditions such as the characteristics of the rider (age, weight, condition), the bicycle (type, gear ratio, tires), the traveling surface, wind velocity, and length of grade.

Bicyclists are capable of negotiating 10% grades over short distances. However, grades of 4 to 5% represent maximum desirable grades.[31]

Horizontal alignment and cross slope

Bicycle facilities which use the roadways usually follow the roadway alignment and have the same curvature. Since roadway curves were designed to accommodate motor vehicles, they will be more than sufficient for bicyclists.[32]

For bicycle paths, the radius of curvature should be consistent with the design speed of the bikeway wherever possible. Recommended design values are shown in Table 19-22.

TABLE 19–22
Bikeway Curvature Design Radii*

Design Speed (mph)	Minimum Radius† (ft)
15	35
20	70
25	90
30	125

*1 mph = 1.6 km/h; 1 ft = 0.3 m.
†Cross slope should be a minimum of 2% to provide for drainage. On curves the percentage should be increased to 5% and be sloped in the direction of the inside of the curve, thus providing some superelevation.

SOURCE: *Design and Construction Criteria for Bikeway Construction Projects.*

Stopping sight distances

Generally, attaining adequate stopping sight distances on bikeways that share the roadway is not a problem because the roadway alignment usually has been designed to accommodate motor vehicle speeds equal to or greater than bicycle speeds. However, if bikeway facilities (bike paths) are on independent alignment, stopping sight distances must be checked.

TABLE 19–23
Design Stopping Sight Distances for Bicycles*,†

Design Speed (mph)	Stopping Sight Distances (ft) for Downhill Gradients of:			
	0%	5%	10%	15%
10	50	50	60	70
15	85	90	100	130
20	130	140	160	200
25	175	200	230	300
30	230	260	310	410

*1 mph = 1.6 km/h; 1 ft = 0.3 m.
†Design values for stopping sight distances on bikeways can be developed in the same manner as on highways. The values shown were based on the following factors for wet pavement conditions: coefficient of skid resistance, 0.25; time for perception and reaction, 2.5 s; eye height, 3–4.5 ft; object height, 0.

[31]*Guide for Bicycle Routes,* American Association of State Highway and Transportation Officials (Washington, D.C., 1974).

[32]Ibid.

The degree of safety that an independent bikeway offers relates to how easily conflicting cross movements are perceived. Thus, the ability of a bicyclist to react to a specific cross movement depends on the sight distance provided. Table 19-23 summarizes recommended stopping distances for various downgrades under wet pavement conditions.

Grade separations

Safety problems resulting from conflicts between the motor vehicle and bicycles may be solved by the total separation of these modes of travel at critical locations. Grade separations are often not feasible owing to the unavailability of the required right-of-way and extremely high costs.[33]

Overpasses offer advantages of natural lighting and little security concern. Underpasses ease the effort needed on the subsequent upgrade because of the momentum gained on the downgrade. Because the vertical clearances for bicycles are less than those for automobiles, an underpass may be constructed with less total change in elevation than an overpass. Vertical clearance should be 8.5 ft (2.6 m) minimum, with 10 ft (3 m) desirable. The structure for a two-way overpass or underpass should have a minimum width of 8 ft (2.4 m), with 14 ft (4.3 m) desirable, to allow for stopping and passing. Ramp grades should not exceed 15%, but desirably should be in the range 5 to 10%. Overpass structure safety rail should be a minimum of 4.5 ft (1.4 m) in height so that bicyclists will not tumble over the railing.

Intersection treatment

Accident statistics indicate that about two-thirds of bicycle/motor vehicle accidents occur at intersections. Two movements are particularly dangerous to the bicyclist. The first is the conflict with a right-turning motorist. The second is the left-turning bicyclist in conflict with through vehicular traffic. Consideration should be given to the minimization of these conflicts.

REFERENCES FOR FURTHER READING

A Policy on Geometric Design of Rural Highways (1965);

Highway Design and Operational Practices Related to Highway Safety (1967); Washington, D.C.: American Association of State Highway Officials.

Geometric Design Standards for Highways Other than Freeways (1969);

Geometric Design Guide for Local Roads and Streets (1971);

A Policy on Design of Urban Highways and Arterial Streets (1973);

Guide for Bicycle Routes (1974);

Guide for Resurfacing, Restoration and Rehabilitation of Highways and Streets (1977).

Traffic Control and Roadway Elements—Their Relationship to Highway Safety. Washington, D.C.: Highway Users Federation for Safety and Mobility, 1971.

[33]*Bicycling in Tennessee.*

Recommended Practices for Subdivision Streets (1965); Arlington, Va.: Institute of Transportation Engineers.

Guidelines for Driveway Design and Location (1975); *Guidelines for Urban Major Street Design* (1979).

A Survey of Urban Arterial Design Standards. Chicago: American Public Works Association, 1969.

1972 World Survey of Current Research and Development on Roads and Road Transport (1972); Washington, D.C.: U.S. Department of Transportation, Federal Highway Administration.

Decision Sight Distance for Highway Design and Traffic Requirements (1977); *Manual on Uniform Traffic Control Devices for Streets and Highways* (1978).

20

LIGHTING OF TRAFFIC FACILITIES

NEILON J. ROWAN, *Research Engineer and Professor*

Texas A&M University
College Station, Texas

NED E. WALTON

Walton & Associates, Consulting Engineers
Brazos Savings Building, Suite 420
2800 South Texas Avenue
Bryan, Texas 77801

To the urban community, street lighting is a means of improving the urban environment through increased comfort, convenience, and safety of night-traffic operation and reduced crime and accidents. To the traffic engineer, street lighting is a tool that can be used to increase the ability to communicate with the driver. Lighting provides traffic safety by illuminating hazardous objects or hazardous situations so that the driver may respond readily and safely. Further, it can significantly improve the efficiency and safety of traffic operation. Thus, the traffic engineer should approach the application of street lighting principally as a means of improving communication with the nighttime driver.

Public lighting should permit users of traffic facilities to move about at night with the greatest possible safety, comfort, and convenience. The driver must be able to see distinctly and locate with certainty details of the driving environment. The pedestrian must also be able to see distinctly the pedestrian path and its relationship to vehicles and possible obstacles. Although public lighting must satisfy the informational needs of both vehicle operators and pedestrians, in practice, the driver's requirements are the more stringent.

The importance of providing the driver with the information needed for satisfactory performance was pointed out very early by Cumming,[1] who stated: "The road complex must provide for the operator a comprehensive display of information both in the formal sense of signs, signals, guidelines and edgeposts, and in the informal sense of clear visibility in all relevant directions." The purpose of information, whether through visual or other senses, is to reduce uncertainty. As long as uncertainty exists, possible alternative decisions cannot be fully evaluated.

[1]R. W. CUMMING, "Progress Report of Human Factors Committee," *Aust. Road Res. 20*(2) (1962).

Visual information needs of the driver are a direct function of what the driver does in performance of the driving task. The requirements of fixed lighting are based upon how the driver sees the information needs for satisfactory night driving.

Light and seeing

Light

"Light is that portion of the radiant energy spectrum capable of producing visual sensation. This sensation results from stimulation of the retina of the human eye by radiant energy of the proper wavelength being emitted or reflected in a sufficient quantity and within the visual field."[2]

Contrast

Contrast is one of the most important contributors to nighttime visual performance. To a great extent, the recognition of objects is based upon a discrimination of brightness (luminance) differences between an object and its background.[3] For night conditions, an obstacle may appear as a dark area against a bright background (discernment by silhouette) or it may appear as a bright area against a dark background (discernment by reverse silhouette). To enhance discernment by silhouette, brightness of the pavement and uniformity of brightness along and transverse to the roadway are essential. Discernment by reverse silhouette usually ap-

[2]*IES Lighting Handbook*, 5th ed. (New York: Illuminating Engineering Society, 1972), p. 1–1.

[3]INGEBORG SCHMIDT, "Visual Considerations of Man, the Vehicle, and the Highway, Part I," *Publ. SP-279*, (Warrendale, PA: Society of Automotive Engineers, Inc., Mar. 1966), p. 7.

plies to the visibility of objects on areas adjacent to the roadway, projections above the pavement surface such as channelizing islands and abutments, and the upper portions of pedestrians or vehicles.

Discernment by surface detail

Discernment by surface detail depends on a high order of direct illumination on the face of the object toward the driver.[4] The object is seen by variations in brightness or color over its own surface without general contrast with a background. Discernment by surface detail may be a principal method of seeing in heavy traffic when the complexity of the situation requires considerable visual detail.

Visual acuity

Contrast sensitivity, or the ability to distinguish luminance (brightness) differences, provides for the detection of objects, but the identification of most objects is accomplished by visual acuity. By definition, visual acuity is the ability of the eye to resolve small detail.[5] In driving, two kinds of visual acuity are of concern—static and dynamic visual acuity.

Static visual acuity occurs when both the driver and the object are stationary and is a function of background brightness, contrast, and time. With increasing illumination, visual acuity increases up to a background brightness of about 10 millilamberts, and then it remains constant despite further increases in illumination. Static visual acuity also increases with increasing contrast of the object. Optimal exposure time for a static visual acuity task is from 0.5 to 1.0s when other visual factors are held constant at some acceptable level.

When there is relative motion between the driver and an object, such as occurs in driving, the resolving ability of the eye is termed *dynamic visual acuity*. Dynamic visual acuity is more difficult than static visual acuity because eye movements are not generally capable of holding a steady image of the target on the retina. The image is blurred and, therefore, its contrast decreases. The conditions favorable for dynamic visual acuity are slow movement, long tracking time, and good illumination. These are rarely found in the nighttime driving environment except in sign reading, an important dynamic visual acuity task.

Glare

Two kinds of glare have a critical influence on driver visual performance:

1. Discomfort glare (psychological glare): ocular discomfort from a bright-light source.
2. Disability glare (physiological glare): incident light that reduces contrast sensitivity and, thus, produces a loss of visual efficiency.

Glare is an especially disturbing influence when one is viewing a difficult visual task under low-brightness conditions.

Discomfort glare effects can be diminished by reducing luminaire brightness, by increasing mounting height, and by increasing the background brightness in the observer's field of view. Luminaire brightness may be reduced by increasing the effective luminaire area and by decreasing the intensity of light at angles higher than that required for optimum pavement brightness (luminance). The background brightness is increased by raising the general level of illumination. Disability glare can be reduced by increasing mounting height, moving the luminaire from the line of sight, and increasing background brightness.

Current practices in lighting design, such as higher mounting heights, increased lateral setback of supports, and restriction of light from the luminaire at vertical and horizontal angles where interference with driver visibility is most significant are effective in controlling discomfort and disability glare.

Time as related to seeing

The time available to the driver to perform the visual task, whether recognition of an object or perception of a traffic situation, is very important. This time decreases as vehicular speed and situation complexity increase. The time factor is extremely critical in low-illumination areas or in high-brightness variation areas, where the eye is in a continual state of adaptation.

Driver visual information needs

Visual information needs associated with the driving task can be organized in accordance with three driver performance levels. These levels and the general information needs are as follows:

1. *Positional performance:* needs associated with routine steering and speed control. These needs are satisfied primarily through pavement markings, curb delineation and delineation of road edges, lane divisions, and roadside features.
2. *Situational performance:* needs associated with required changes in speed, direction of travel, or position on the roadway as a result of a change in the geometric, traffic, and/or environmental situation. These needs are as varied as the number and kinds of road and traffic situations encountered in driving.
3. *Navigational performance:* needs associated with selecting and following a route from an origin to a destination. These needs are satisfied primarily by formal information sources (signs, etc.) and informal information sources (landmarks, etc.).

[4] *American National Standard Practice for Roadway Lighting* (New York: Illuminating Engineering Society/American National Standards Association, 1977), p. 35.

[5] SCHMIDT, *Visual Considerations*, p. 10.

TABLE 20-1
Important Elements of the Night-Driving Visual Environment

Element	Kind of Information	Description
Roadway geometry	Positional Situational	Perception of the roadway alignment, topography, and cross section at a distance commensurate with travel speed
Intersection	Situational Navigational	Perception of intersecting roadway ahead commensurate with travel speed
Channelization	Positional Situational	Perception of markings, curbs, medians, etc., that indicate an assigned path
Lane markings	Positional Situational	Perception of lane lines, edge lines, center lines
Roadside and roadside objects	Positional Situational Navigational	Perception of the environment for dynamic appreciation and recognition of possible hazards
Curbs	Positional Situational	Perception of curb as an object and guide
Access drives	Situational	Recognition of curb break, pavement contrast, or other features indicating an access opening
Pedestrians	Situational	Perception of pedestrian on or adjacent to the roadway and recognition as a possible conflict
Vehicles	Positional Situational	Perception of other vehicles on the facility, their location and intended directions in relation to own location and movement
Signs	Situational Navigational	Perception and recognition of signs and contents
Signals	Situational	Perception of color and/or orientation of signal heads indicating assignment of right-of-way
Pavement edge	Positional	Perception of pavement boundaries, contrast between pavement and shoulder or roadside and edge lines
Delineation	Positional Situational	Perception of roadway delineation as indicative of roadway features
Special geometric features	Positional Situational	Perception of conflict points, ramp exits and entrances, merges, ramp configuration and direction
Roadway objects	Situational	Perception of hazardous objects on the roadway at a distance commensurate with the travel speed
Road condition	Situational	Perception of road surface indicating structural and climatic conditions
Special roadside features	Situational Navigational	Perception of signs, land marks, etc., indicating an intermediate or final destination

From the fixed-lighting standpoint, situational information needs are most critical. Positional and navigational needs can usually be accommodated by the vehicle headlights because important signing, marking, and delineation are usually either retroreflective or externally illuminated.

Table 20-1 lists the more important elements of the nighttime driving visual environment and should provide insight into the selection and area of coverage for a lighting system. From the standpoint of fixed lighting, these elements become more complex and important as geometric, operational, and environmental complexity increases. The complexity of such conditions can be considered as warrants or minimum justification for the installation of a lighting system since they are the conditions usually producing various informational needs. From the geometric aspect, the need to see roadway features, access drives, channelization, and other cross-section elements depends on the complexity of the geometrics. From an operational viewpoint, high speeds, high volumes, and frequent interactions and conflicts produce high visual information needs. Environmental conditions, such as extraneous lighting, roadside development, and service drives also create information needs and compete for the driver's attention.

Pavements

Under fixed lighting, drivers usually see objects within the roadway as dark silhouettes against a bright background formed by the roadway and its surroundings. Therefore, one of the important uses of fixed lighting is to brighten the roadway surface. In producing this brightness, the reflection of light from the surface and the surface illumination are equally important.

Efficient fixed-lighting systems should provide suitable light distribution in which the bright patches of light cover the roadway from normal directions of viewing, and the surface should be as brightly and uniformly illuminated as possible without excessive glare. Luminaires do not usually produce a uniform intensity distribution, however, because more light is directed up and down the roadway in order to lengthen the bright patch and thereby reduce the number of luminaires required.

The way a roadway is brightened by street lighting depends on the exposed face or surface of the roadway. The reflection characteristics of a surface depend on a number of properties: (1) the surface texture (also influences skid resistance), (2) the material used, (3) the color and lightness, (4) the extent to which the surface has been polished by traffic, and (5) the degree of wetness or dryness.

Portland cement concrete, synthetic aggregates, and certain surface treatments may be used economically where it is apparent that roadway lighting is justified. Regardless of the paving material used, there are aspects of pavement texture and color that should be considered in the design of a lighting system. These can be considered through pavement reflectance properties in the development and implementation of luminance design methods.[6,7]

[6] F. W. Jung and C. Blamey, *Computer Program for Roadway Lighting*, Transportation Res. Rec. 628 (Washington, D.C.: Transportation Research Board, 1977).

[7] L. E. King, "Measurement of Directional Reflectance of Pavement Surfaces and Development of Computer Techniques for Calculating Luminaire," *J. Illumin. Eng. Soc.*, *5*(2) (Jan. 1976).

Traffic criteria and warranting conditions

Roadway and walkway classifications

Most highway and street systems encompass several classes or types of roadways and walkways. At one extreme are high-speed, high-volume facilities carrying through traffic, with no attempt made to serve abutting property, pedestrians, or local trips. At the other extreme are local highways, streets, or roads that carry low volumes, at low speeds, with a primary function of land access instead of vehicular movement.

A comprehensive lighting program requires that the roads and streets be classified on the basis of intended function. The following classifications are those recommended by the Illuminating Engineering Society:[8]

1. *Freeway*. A divided major highway with full control of access and with no crossings at grade.
2. *Expressway*. A divided major arterial highway for through traffic with full or partial control of access and generally with interchanges at major crossroads. Expressways for noncommercial traffic within parks and parklike areas are generally known as parkways.
3. *Major (arterial)*. The part of the roadway system which serves as the principal network for through traffic flow. The routes connect areas of principal traffic generation and important rural highways entering the city.
4. *Collector*. The distributor and collector roadways serving traffic between major and local roadways. These are roadways used mainly for traffic movements within residential, commercial, and industrial areas.
5. *Local*. Roadway used primarily for direct access to residential, commercial, industrial, or other abutting property. They do not include roadways carrying through traffic. Long local roadways will generally be divided into short sections by collector roadway systems.

Area classification

Although the classifications presented above normally reflect the geometric and operational conditions to be expected on a traffic facility, sometimes additional subclassifications by area type and environmental conditions are desirable. The Illuminating Engineering Society[9] recommends the following area classifications:

1. *Commercial*. That portion of a municipality in a business development where ordinarily there are large numbers of pedestrians during business hours. This definition applies to densely developed business areas outside, as well as within, the central part of a municipality. The area contains land use which attracts a relatively heavy volume of nighttime vehicular and/or pedestrian traffic on a frequent basis.
2. *Intermediate*. That portion of a municipality often characterized by a moderately heavy nighttime pedestrian activity, such as in blocks having libraries, community recreation centers, large apartment buildings, or neighborhood retail stores.
3. *Residential*. A residential development, or a mixture of residential and commercial establishments, characterized by a few pedestrians at night. This definition includes areas with single-family homes, town houses, and/or small apartment buildings.
4. *Rural*. Open land with little or no commercial or residential development.

[8]*American National Standard Practice for Roadway Lighting*, p. 5.

[9]Ibid.

Warrants for lighting

Warrants are factual evidence compiled for the purpose of justifying the installation of roadway lighting. Warrants should be based on conditions relating to the need for roadway lighting and the benefits that may be accrued therefrom. Factors such as traffic volume, speed, road use at night, night accident rate, road geometrics, and general night visibility are important considerations in determining the minimum conditions justifying lighting. Justification for lighting may also be based on economic effectiveness, such as reduction in personal injuries and property damage in accidents, improved operational efficiency, and other societal benefits.

Warrants should not be considered as evidence that obligates a public authority to install roadway lighting. On the contrary, planning and design of roadway lighting is a discretionary action in which public officials must use judgment in allocating available resources to provide the greatest benefit to the public. In other words, public officials must select from all projects warranting lighting those which can be completed with available funds and which provide the greatest benefits to the public. Obviously, some priority-ranking procedure is also necessary for the selection of projects.

Two principal sources of lighting warrants are available: (1) *An Informational Guide for Roadway Lighting*, published by AASHTO[10] and (2) *Warrants for Roadway Lighting*, NCHRP Report No. 152.[11] Both will be discussed briefly; the lighting designer or administrator should have access to both documents.

The American Association of State Highway and Transportation Officials (AASHTO) warrants are based primarily on experience. They set forth a description of operational, geometric, and developmental conditions that must be matched or exceeded in order to justify the installation of roadway lighting.

AASHTO warrants are developed for five principal categories of roadway lighting:

- Freeways
- Interchanges
- Tunnels and underpasses
- Roadway safety rest areas
- Roadway sign lighting

[10]*An Informational Guide for Roadway Lighting* (Washington, D.C.: American Association of State Highway and Transportation Officials, Mar. 1976).

[11]*Warrants for Roadway Lighting*, NCHRP Report 152 (Washington, D.C.: National Academy of Sciences, 1972).

The AASHTO warrants place greatest emphasis on freeway-type facilities. For lighting on urban streets, NCHRP Report No. 152 *(Warrants for Roadway Lighting)* has greater applicability. The warrants procedure outlined in that report embodies an analytical assessment of the effect of geometric, operational, and developmental conditions and night accident experience on driver visual information needs. Further, that approach is applied uniformly to all classes of major roadways, specifically:

- Non-controlled-access facilities
- Intersections
- Controlled-access facilities
- Interchanges

Both warrant procedures are well documented in the *Roadway Lighting Handbook* published by the Federal Highway Administration.[12]

Light Sources

The most important element of illumination equipment is the light source. It is the principal determinant of visual quality, illumination efficiency, energy conservation, and the economic aspects of the illumination system. Although numerous types of light sources have been used in roadway lighting, major emphasis is placed on those sources currently used in modern designs: mercury, metal halide, high-pressure sodium, and low pressure sodium.

Gaseous discharge lamps produce light by the excitation of gas or metal vapors in the arc tube of the lamp. When an electrical potential is applied across the electrodes of the arc tube, the gas is ionized and electrons flow through the arc tube. These electrons collide with the atoms of the gaseous medium, momentarily altering their structure. When the atoms return to their normal state, energy is released, resulting in the emission of light.

Light sources are normally compared on the basis of four major characteristics: (1) luminous efficacy (the number of lumens produced per watt of energy expended), (2) color rendition (color quality), (3) lamp life (number of operating hours), and (4) optical control. Specific data for the light sources indicated above, and others, are summarized in Table 20-2. A brief discussion of the four major sources is presented in the following paragraphs.

Mercury. The mercury lamp has been used for street lighting purposes for many years. It was developed during the 1930s and was extremely popular until the development of more efficient light sources. Its luminous efficacy is only fair, its color is good, especially if the lamp is phosphor-coated, and optical control is good, particularly for the clear lamp. The lamp life is exceptionally long and dependable. It has been used for practically all outdoor applications. Although it is being replaced rapidly by other sources in general roadway lighting applications because of its relatively low efficacy, mercury is still the preferable source for external sign lighting.

Metal halide. Metal halide lamps produce better color at higher efficacies than do mercury lamps. Their life, however, is somewhat shorter and they are more sensitive to lamp orientation (horizontal or vertical) and vibrations. Excellent results have been obtained with these lamps in high-mast lighting. If exceptionally good color rendition is required, the metal halide lamp should be considered.

High-pressure sodium. This is the newest of the family of discharge-type lamps and provides excellent luminous efficacy, good lumen maintenance, long life, and acceptable color. Higher lamp costs and a more complex ballast could be listed as its disadvantages. The lamp provides a good

[12]*Roadway Lighting Handbook* (Washington, D.C.: Federal Highway Administration, U.S. Department of Transportation, 1978).

TABLE 20–2
Typical Area and Roadway Lighting Lamp Characteristics*

	Lumens/Watt								Cost	
	(Including Ballast Losses)†·‡	Lamp Only	Lumens	Wattage Range	Rated Average Life§ (h)	Percent Maintained Output at End of Life	Color Rendition	Optical Control	Initial (Lamp)	Operational (Power)
Incandescent‖	n.a.	11–18	655–15,300	58–860	1500–12,000	82–86	Exc.	Excellent	Low	High
Tungsten–Halogen	n.a.	20–22	6000–33,000	300–1500	2000	93	Exc.	Exc. vertical, poor horiz.	Moder.	High
Fluorescent	58–69	70–73	4200–15,500	60–212	10,000–12,000	68	Good	Poor	Moder.	Moder.
Mercury—clear	37–54	44–58	7700–57,500	175–1000	24,000	62–82	Fair	Good	Moder.	Moder.
Mercury—with phosphor	41–59	49–63	8500–63,000	175–1000	24,000	50–73	Good	Fair	Moder.	Moder.
Metal halide	65–110	80–125	14,000–125,000	175–1500	7500–15,000	58–74	Good	Good	High	Low
High-pressure sodium	60–130	83–140	5800–140,000	75 ~~175~~–1000	20,000–24,000	73	Fair	Good	High	Low
Low-pressure sodium	78–150	131–183	4650–33,000	35–180	18,000	100**	Poor	Poor	High	Low

*All figures show operating ranges typical for lamp sizes normally used in area and roadway applications.
†Ranges shown cover low wattage lamps with regulated-type ballasts (worst condition) through high-wattage lamps with reactor-type ballasts (best condition).
‡n.a., not available.
§Rated average life is based on survival of at least 50% of a large group of lamps operated under specified test conditions at 10 or more burning hours per start.
‖Larger incandescent lamps (up to 2000 W) for floodlighting applications are available. Depending on operating conditions, the luminous efficacy and life change considerably for these lamps from the typical values shown. Lamp schedules should be consulted for details.
**Low-pressure sodium lamps maintain initial lumen rating throughout life, but lamp wattage increases. Considering this change in wattage, the luminous efficacy of these lamps (including ballast losses) at 18,000 h is 67–117 lumens/W.

SOURCE: *Roadway Lighting Handbook* (Washington, D.C.: Federal Highway Administration, U.S. Department of Transportation, 1978).

economic compromise ideally suited for general roadway lighting applications.

Low-pressure sodium. The principal advantage of this light source is its exceptionally high luminous efficacy. Its disadvantages are its monochromatic color and its large size. It is an excellent source where color and optical control are less important than the quantity of light produced per unit of electrical energy. It has been used successfully in tunnel lighting and in roadway lighting where high illumination levels are required, and the luminaires may be spaced more closely to achieve acceptable uniformity.

Fluorescent light sources have been used extensively for traffic sign lighting, but in some cases are being replaced by mercury and metal halide sources. Fluorescent sources have fair efficacy (70 lumens/W) and provide good color rendition, but the lamps are large resulting in poor optical control, have a short lamp life, and their efficacy is highly susceptible to cold temperatures.

Luminaire design and placement

Design and types

Webster defines "luminaire" as "any body that gives light," but in street lighting the term "luminaire" describes the complete lighting assembly, less the support assembly. The modern-day luminaire, as shown in Figure 20.1, consists of a weatherproof housing enclosing the light source, a reflector, and in many cases the electrical ballast for discharge-type lamps. A refractor comprises the lower part of the enclosure and serves, with a reflector, to control the distribution of light on the roadway. The refractor is generally a molded glass element that provides prismatic control of light (Figure 20.1).

Luminaires are designed and identified primarily on the basis of the area of coverage (i.e., the width and length of the area to be lighted and the "allowable beam angle"). The higher beam angles permit greater spacing of luminaires for uniform coverage, but higher beam angles mean more glare and reduced effectiveness of the lighting system.

To standardize luminaires for manufacture and design purposes, the Illuminating Engineering Society has assigned type numbers, Types I through V, to luminaires that produce different light distribution patterns used for various purposes. These pertain mainly to the street width and the location of the luminaire in relation to the roadway. A brief description with illustrative sketches of each luminaire type is given in Figure 20.2. A more detailed and technical description of luminaire types can be found in the *American National Standard Practice for Roadway Lighting.*[13]

Luminaires are also classified on the basis of vertical light distribution, the ability to spread light along the length of the roadway. Short, medium, and long distributions are established on the basis of the distance from the luminaire where the light beam of maximum candlepower strikes the roadway surface, defined as follows:

1. *Short distribution.* The maximum candlepower beam strikes the roadway between 1.0 and 2.25 mounting heights from the luminaire.
2. *Medium distribution.* The maximum candlepower beam strikes the roadway at some point between 2.25 and 3.75 mounting heights from the luminaire.
3. *Long distribution.* The maximum candlepower beam strikes the roadway at a point between 3.75 and 6.0 mounting heights from the luminaire.

On the basis of the vertical light distributions, theoretical maximum spacings of luminaires are such that the maximum candlepower beams from adjacent luminaires are joined on the roadway surface. With this assumption, the maximum luminaire spacings would be 4.5 mounting heights for a short distribution, 7.5 mounting heights for a medium distribution, and 12.0 mounting heights for a long distribution. These spacings will not, however, satisfy the design criteria outlined later.

In practice, the medium distribution is most widely used, and the luminaire spacing normally does not exceed 5 mounting heights. Short distributions are seldom used for reasons of economy, and long distributions are not used to any great extent because the high beam angle of maximum candlepower produces excessive glare.

It is important that the distribution of light flux emission above the beam of maximum candlepower be controlled. Light flux emission at the higher vertical angles generally contributes substantially to increased pavement brightness,

[13] *American National Standard Practice for Roadway Lighting*, pp. 7–8.

Figure 20.1. Examples of typical roadway luminaire. SOURCE: Texas Transportation Institute.

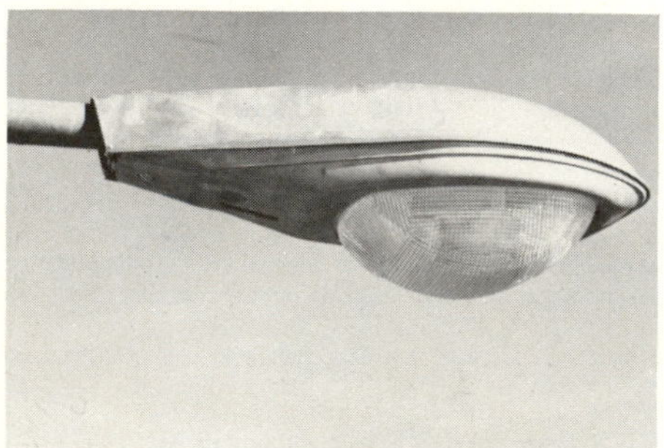

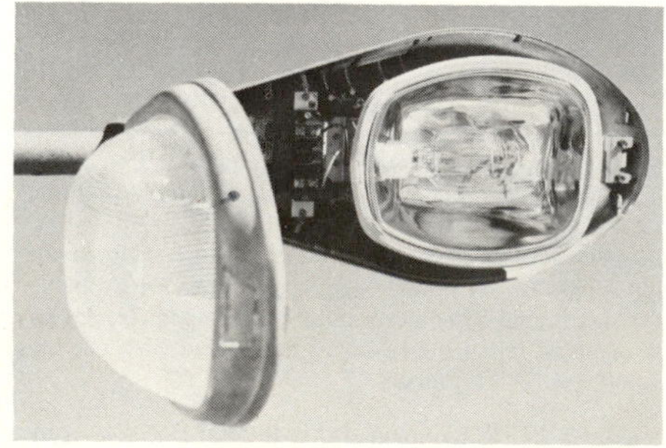

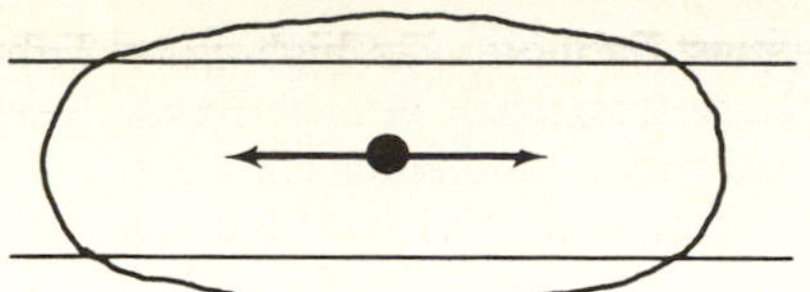

Type I—A luminaire designed for center mounting over streets up to 2.0 mounting heights in width.

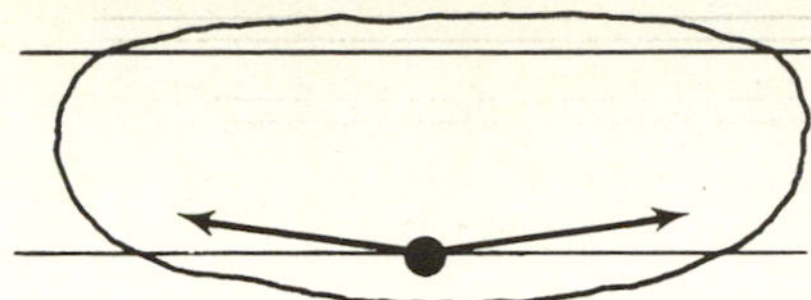

Type II—A luminaire designed for mounting over the curb line of street widths less than 1.5 mounting heights.

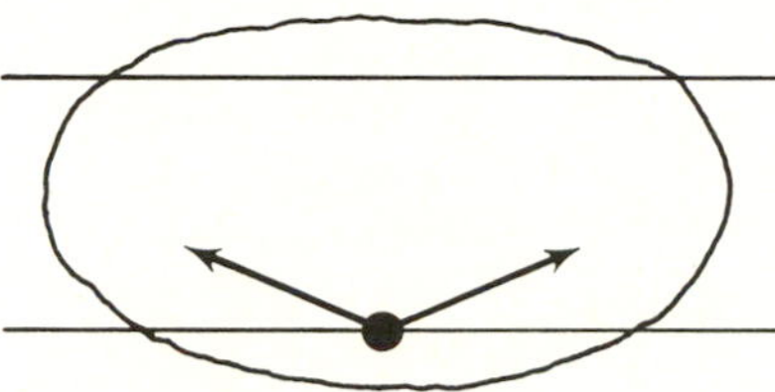

Type III—A luminaire designed for mounting over the curb line of street widths up to 2.0 mounting heights.

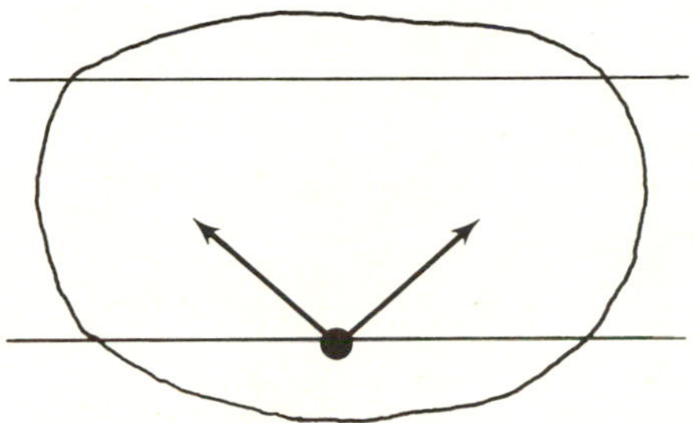

Type IV—A luminaire designed for mounting over the curb line of street widths greater than 2.0 mounting heights.

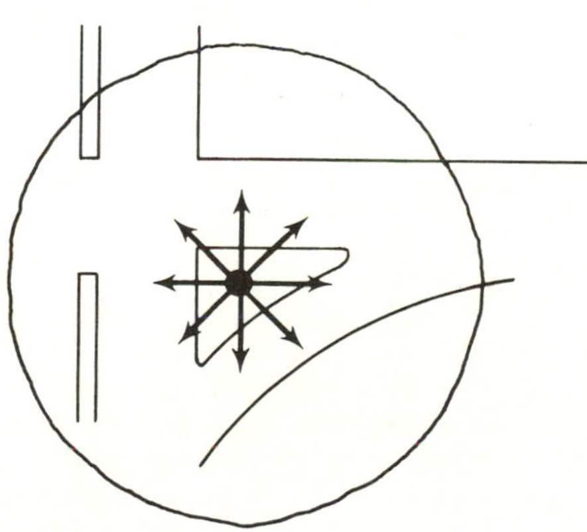

Type V—A luminaire designed to distribute light equally in all lateral directions.

Figure 20.2. Illustrations and descriptions of IES luminaire-type nomenclature. Source: *American National Standard Practice for Roadway Lighting,* New York: Illuminating Engineering Society, 1977, p. 8.

but it also contributes greatly to increased disability and discomfort glare. To achieve balanced performance, it is necessary to control the light flux emission above the beam of maximum candlepower. The three categories of control are:

1. *Cutoff*. A luminaire light distribution is designated as cutoff when the candlepower per 1000 lamp lumens does not exceed 25 (2.5%) at an angle of 90° above nadir and 100 (10%) at a vertical angle of 80° above nadir.
2. *Semi-cutoff*. A luminaire light distribution is designated as semi-cutoff when the candlepower per 1000 lamp lumens does not exceed 50 (5%) at an angle of 90° above nadir and 200 (20%) at a vertical angle of 80° above nadir.
3. *Noncutoff*. The category when there is no candlepower limitation in the zone above maximum candlepower.

Placement

Luminaire placement is an integral part of the design of an effective lighting system. Luminaires are mounted at a given height above the roadway, depending on the lamp output, and at specific points along the roadway, depending on the character of the roadway to be lighted. For roadways not having medians, the luminaire is normally installed in a "house-side" location, which may be further described as a one-side system for narrow streets, a "staggered" system for medium-width streets, and an "opposite" system for

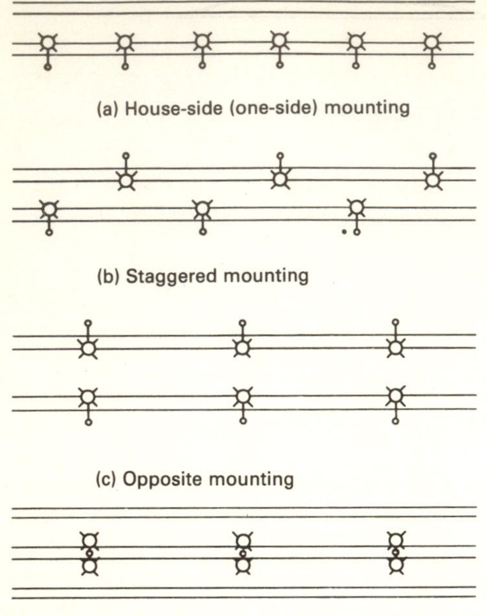

Figure 20.3. Examples of typical luminaire mounting arrangements. SOURCE: Antanas Ketvirtis, *Highway Lighting Engineering,* Toronto: Foundation of Canada Engineering Corporation, Ltd., 1967, p. 36.

wide streets. For streets having wide medians, and where barriers are to be installed, a "median lighting system" provides very effective lighting at less cost because of the saving in luminaire supports and electrical conductors (see Figure 20.3).

Mounting height is generally determined by the lamp output and the desired average illumination on the roadway and by the required uniformity of the distribution of light (factors to be covered more specifically later). By rule of thumb, however, light sources of 20,000 lumens or less should be mounted at heights of approximately 30 ft (9 m), light sources of from 20,000 to 45,000 lumens should be mounted at heights from 30 to 45 ft (9 to 14 m), and light sources of from 45,000 to 90,000 lumens should be mounted at heights from 45 to 60 ft (14 to 18 m).

Mounting heights of 80 ft (24 m) or higher have been utilized in a special roadway lighting technique called high-mast lighting. In high-mast lighting, which is used mainly to light large areas such as interchanges, intersections, toll plazas, and parks, luminaires are arranged in combinations in order to provide a total system output of up to 1,000,000 lumens distributed over a large area. The justifications for high-mast lighting pertain mainly to the removal of luminaire supports near the traffic area for safety reasons and to provide a panoramic view of the entire area.

Luminaires for high-mast lighting include (1) a combination of floodlights that can be aimed to provide a particular distribution to fit the area to be lighted; (2) the IES Type V luminaire, which provides a circular distribution; and (3) the IES Type III luminaire, which provides an asymmetric distribution. The diameter of the Type V distribution, and thus the illumination level, is varied by changing the vertical location of the lamp in relation to the reflector and the refractor of the luminaire. An example of a high-mast lighting system is illustrated in Figure 20.4.

Design of lighting systems

Definition of terms

Lumen. A unit of measure of the quantity of light. One lumen is the amount of light that falls on an area of 1 ft^2 every point of which is at a distance of 1 ft from a source of 1 candela (candle). A light source of one candela emits a total of 4π (= 12.57) lumens.

Footcandle. The unit of illumination when the unit length is 1 ft; 1 lumen distributed uniformly over an area of 1 ft^2.

Lux. The unit of illumination when the meter is the unit length; 1 lumen distributed uniformly over an area of 1 m^2.

Horizontal footcandle. One lumen distributed uniformly over a *horizontal* surface 1 ft^2 in area. Thus, horizontal footcandle is a measure of the light that strikes the pavement surface.

Vertical footcandle. One lumen distributed uniformly over a *vertical* surface 1 ft^2 in area. Thus, vertical footcandle is a measure of the light that strikes vertical surfaces such as curbs, piers, or retaining walls.

Figure 20.4. High-mast lighting installation in Dallas. SOURCE: Texas Highway Department.

Luminance. The luminous intensity of a surface in a given direction per unit of projected area of the surface as viewed from that direction (measured in footlamberts).

Footlambert. The unit of photometric brightness (luminance); 1 footlambert is equal to $1/\pi$ candela per ft^2.

Candela. The unit of luminous intensity; 1 lumen per unit solid angle (steradian).

General design criteria

In the United States the principal criteria in the design of lighting systems are average intensity and uniformity of illumination. Average intensity of illumination, expressed in horizontal footcandles or lumens per square foot on a horizontal surface, is a measure of the total illumination on the roadway surface. Uniformity, expressed in terms of average/minimum or maximum/minimum intensity ratios, describes how the total illumination is distributed on the roadway surface.

Average intensity of illumination is not necessarily directly related to the ability to see. The ability to see is primarily a function of the amount of light striking the pavement surface which is diffused and reflected toward the driver's eye. Seeing, therefore, is a function of pavement brightness or pavement luminance characteristics. The determination of pavement brightness is a very difficult task, both from a technical and a realistic standpoint. The measuring equipment is complex, and the procedure is only applicable to pavements already in service. Also, pavement reflectance characteristics change with pavement age, wear, and maintenance.

Realistic consideration of pavement brightness, as discussed previously, can be made in general terms as light, medium, and dark surfaces. Some authorities say that pavement brightness sometimes varies up to 100% indicating that almost twice as much light is needed on dark pavements to have equal effectiveness in pavement brightness. Since current recommended values of average intensity of illumination are representative of average conditions, it is recommended that these values be increased somewhat for extremely dark pavements.

The current values for average intensity of illumination as recommended by IES[14] are given in Table 20-3. These are recommended minimum values for average maintained horizontal illumination.

The IES recommends average/minimum uniformity ratios of 3:1 for all roadways except local residential streets, which should have a ratio not exceeding 6:1.[15] The IES has not suggested specific maximum/minimum ratios, but Ketvirtis[16] has recommended ratios as given in Table 20-4. Many feel that the maximum/minimum ratio is the most realistic measure of uniformity because it represents the full range of illumination rather than generalized considerations.

[14]Ibid., p. 16.

[15]Ibid., p. 13.

[16]ANTANAS KETVIRTIS, *Highway Lighting Engineering* (Toronto: Foundation of Canada Engineering Corporation Ltd., 1967), p. 27.

TABLE 20–3
Recommendations for Roadway Average Maintained Horizontal Illumination Footcandles (Lux)

Vehicular Roadway Classification	Area Classification: Urban Commercial	Urban Intermediate	Residential
Freeway*	0.6 (6)	0.6 (6)	0.6 (6)
Expressway*	1.4 (15)	1.2 (13)	1.0 (11)
Major (arterial)	2.0 (22)	1.4 (15)	1.0 (11)
Collector	1.2 (13)	0.9 (10)	0.6 (6)
Local	0.9 (10)	0.6 (6)	0.4 (4)
Alleys	0.6 (6)	0.4 (4)	0.4 (4)

*Both main lanes and ramps.

SOURCE: *American National Standard Practice for Roadway Lighting* (New York: Illuminating Engineering Society, 1977), p.10.

TABLE 20–4
Recommended Maximum/Minimum Ratios on Road Pavement

Road Classification	Urban Downtown	Urban Intermediate	Urban Outlying	Rural
Freeway	6:1	6:1	6:1	6:1
Expressway	6:1	6:1	6:1	6:1
Arterial	6:1	6:1	8:1	8:1
Collector	6:1	8:1	8:1	8:1
Local	8:1	8:1	10:1	10:1

SOURCE: A. KETVIRTIS, *Highway Lighting Engineering* (Toronto: Foundation of Canada Engineering Corporation Ltd., 1967), p. 27.

Design of continuous lighting systems

The illumination design process is one of evaluating the lighting needs, selecting appropriate illumination criteria for design, selecting proper equipment for the job, and establishing the geometry of the system to provide the most effective lighting system to satisfy the needs. The major steps of the design process are outlined below.

1. Evaluation of Existing Conditions
Much emphasis should be placed on the evaluation of existing conditions which determine the need for lighting, and on the roadway, traffic, and environmental conditions which influence the selection of illumination levels. It is recommended that the designer develop a checklist and possibly a numerical rating scheme for assigning priorities to lighting jobs within his city or area of jurisdiction. At least the following should be included in an evaluation checklist:

A. *Description of roadway or street*
- a. Kind of facility
- b. Number of lanes and lane width
- c. Median type and width
- d. Curb type and degree of access
- e. Pavement surface type
- f. Geometric features (curves, grades, etc.)

B. *Traffic conditions*
- a. Night traffic volumes
- b. Speeds (85th percentile, 15th percentile)
- c. Percent of entering and exiting traffic
- d. Accident rates (night vs. day)
- e. Accidents by type
- f. Actual or potential pedestrian activity

C. *Environmental conditions*
a. Type of land use (commercial, residential, and subcategories of each that relate to street use)
b. Extent of commercial lighting, including signs, area lighting, novelty lighting, and degree of animation
c. Pedestrian generation potential
d. Traffic generation potential
e. Possible influences of driver condition, principally in regard to alcoholic consumption

A rational method of rating geometrics, operational, and environmental conditions to determine warrants and priorities was published in a paper entitled, "A Total Design Process for Roadway Lighting," by Walton and Rowan, Highway Research Record No. 440 (pp. 1–19), Transportation Research Board, National Academy of Sciences, Washington, D.C. This work has been summarized in the *Roadway Lighting Handbook,* published by the Federal Highway Administration.

2. Selection of Illumination Level
Using the data collected in the evaluation in item 1 above, the designer should first classify the highway facility and then the area type according to the classification schemes presented previously. At this point, the *minimum* average intensity of illumination may be determined from Table 20-3. This should be recognized as a minimum value for average conditions as outlined in item 1, and a higher average intensity may be used for design if the evaluation of existing conditions reveals several critical factors. Selection of higher-than-minimum average intensity values is a matter of judgment, where illumination needs must be balanced with energy utilization. Here a numerical evaluation scheme could be used effectively.

3. System Characterization
The designer should determine the location and mounting height of luminaires and the type and wattage of the light source to be used. If the system is to be placed on existing supports (not necessarily recommended), the spacing and mounting heights are fixed and will determine the other characteristics. For a new installation, the guidelines for an optimum system should be followed. The highest mounting heights and largest light sources practicable should be used in the general interest of safety, economy, and overall system efficiency. Tables 20-5 and 20-6 provide a guide to the selection of mounting heights based on the size of the light source and on the type and arrangement of luminaires related to street width and location of luminaires.

Maximum spacing, consistent with good illumination design, should be emphasized. Luminaire supports are hazardous roadside objects and, for safety, the number should be minimized and they should be strategically located. Further, breakaway supports should be used where applicable. Supports should be set back as far as practicable, with the luminaire mounted over or near the curb or shoulder. Median mountings (twin mast arms on one support located in the median) should be used wherever practicable because they reduce the number of supports and provide a high-quality, more economical system.

TABLE 20–5
Guide for Luminaire Lateral Light Distribution Type Selection and Placement, Rectangular Roadway Area*

Side of Roadway Mounting			Center of Roadway Mounting		
One Side or Staggered	Staggered or Opposite	Grade Intersections	Single Roadway	Twin Roadways (Median Mtg.)	Grade Intersections
Width up to 1.5	Width beyond 1.5	Width up to 1.5	Width up to 2.0	Width up to 1.5 (each pavement)	Width up to 2.0
Types II, III, IV	Types III, IV	Type II 4-way	Type I	Types II, III	Types I 4-way, V

*M.H., mounting height. In all cases suggested *maximum* longitudinal spacings and associated vertical distribution classifications are: short distribution, 4.5 M.H.; medium distribution, 7.5 M.H.; long distribution, 12.0 M.H.

SOURCE: *American National Standard Practice for Roadway Lighting*, 1977, p. 14.

TABLE 20–6
General Guide to the Selection of Luminaire Mounting Heights

Lamp Lumens	Mounting Height ft	Mounting Height m
≤20,000	≤35	≤11
20,000–45,000	35–45	11–14
45,000–90,000	45–60	14–18

4. Acquisition of Luminaire Data
Once the type of luminaire and size of light source have been selected, the designer should obtain photometric data from prospective manufacturers for the specific luminaire and light source to be used. These data should include:

A. *Isofootcandle diagram*. An isofootcandle diagram, as illustrated in Figure 20.5, should be obtained from the manufacturer of the equipment to be used.
B. *Coefficient of utilization curve*. The coefficient of utilization curve plots the percentage rated lamp lumens related to the width of roadway. An example curve is shown in Figure 20.6. The plot shows that 50.8% of the rated lamp lumens fall on a street 1.5 mounting heights wide when the luminaire is mounted over one curb line. Most coefficient of utilization plots provide one curve for the "street side" or front side of the luminaire and another curve for the "house side" or the back side of the luminaire. The coefficient of utilization curve should be a curve for the specific luminaire and light source used instead of a typical curve for a given type of luminaire.
C. *Lamp lumen depreciation curve*. A depreciation curve for the lamp to be used should be obtained from the manufacturer. This curve provides information about the output of the lamp related to length of service. This information is useful in design and maintenance.
D. *Luminaire maintenance factor*. Figure 20.7 provides a guide to the selection of a maintenance factor for design and scheduling of maintenance, depending on the type of area in which lighting is to be provided.

5. Computation of Luminaire Spacing
The computational procedure for the spacing of luminaires is based on the average intensity of illumination required,

POINT "A" FOR LUMINAIRE ②
POINT "A" FOR LUMINAIRES ① & ③

RATIO OF TRANSVERSE DISTANCE TO MOUNTING HEIGHT

STREET SIDE ← → HOUSE SIDE

RATIO OF LONGITUDINAL DISTANCE TO MOUNTING HEIGHT

POINT "A_1" (FOR 25' MH) – FOR LUMINAIRES ① & ③

POINT "A_1" (FOR 25' MH) – FOR LUMINAIRE ②

MOUNTING HEIGHT	CORRECTION FACTOR
25'	1.44
26'	1.33
27'	1.23
28'	1.15
29'	1.07
30'	1.00
31'	0.94
32'	0.88
33'	0.83
34'	0.78
35'	0.73

Figure 20.5. Example of an isofootcandle diagram of horizontal footcandles on pavement surface for a luminaire providing medium/semi-cutoff/Type II light distribution, per 1000 lamp lumens initial. *Note:* To convert from feet to meters, multiply by 0.30. SOURCE: *American National Standard Practice for Roadway Lighting*, New York: Illuminating Engineering Society, American National Standards Association, 1977, p. 27.

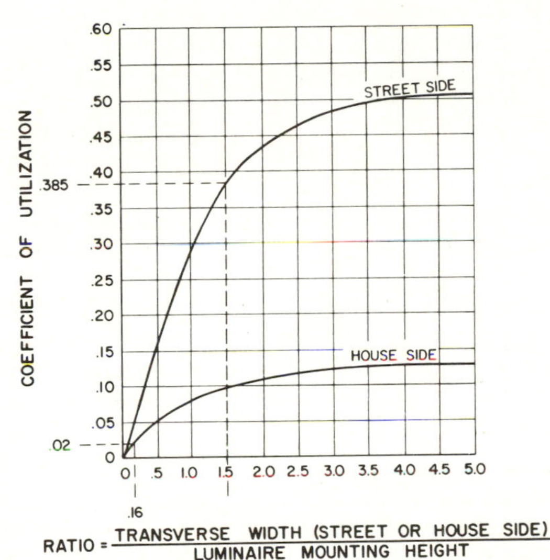

Figure 20.6. Example of coefficient of utilization curves for luminaire providing medium/semi-cutoff/ Type II light distribution. SOURCE: *American National Standard Practice for Roadway Lighting*, New York: Illuminating Engineering Society, American National Standards Association, 1977, p. 25.

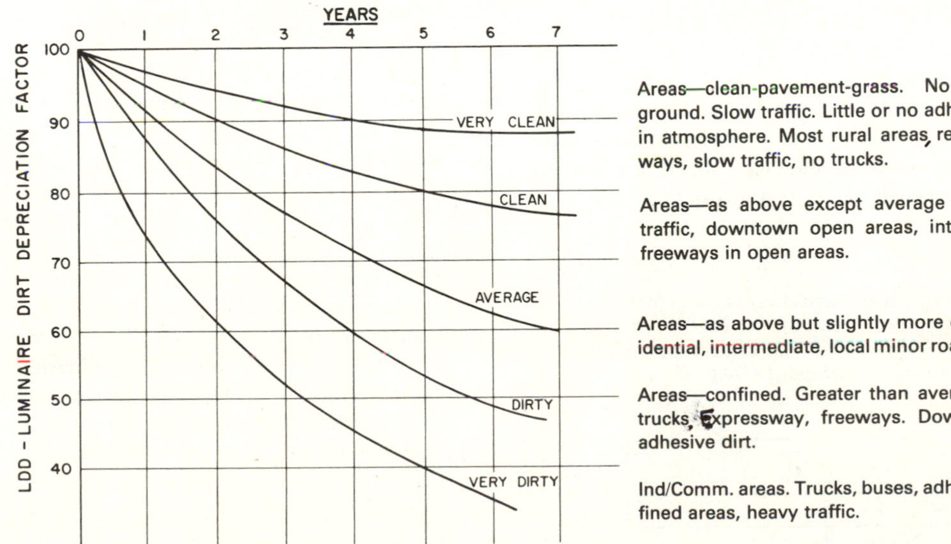

Select appropriate dirt curve from kind of conditions described below for type luminaire to be used.

Areas—clean-pavement-grass. No open loose ground. Slow traffic. Little or no adhesive qualities in atmosphere. Most rural areas, residential roadways, slow traffic, no trucks.

Areas—as above except average car and truck traffic, downtown open areas, intermediate and freeways in open areas.

Areas—as above but slightly more exposure. Residential, intermediate, local minor roads, few trucks.

Areas—confined. Greater than average. Cars and trucks, Expressway, freeways. Downtown, major adhesive dirt.

Ind/Comm. areas. Trucks, buses, adhesive dirt, confined areas, heavy traffic.

Figure 20.7. Chart for estimating roadway luminaire dirt depreciation factors for enclosed gasketed luminaires.

the light that can be utilized from the luminaire, and the area to be covered by the luminaire. The following formula includes all these factors and provides a solution to luminaire spacing when all other factors are known:

$$\text{spacing between luminaires (ft)} = \frac{\text{lamp lumens} \times \text{coefficient of utilization}}{\text{average intensity of illumination (horizontal fc)} \times \text{roadway width (ft)}}$$

In this form, the formula is valid only for initial conditions, with no provision for lamp depreciation and dirt accumulation on the luminaire. When these factors are introduced as a luminaire maintenance factor, the formula becomes

$$\text{spacing between luminaires (ft)} = \frac{\text{lamp lumens at replacement time} \times \text{coefficient of utilization} \times \text{luminaire maintenance factor}}{\text{average intensity of lumination (horizontal fc)} \times \text{width of roadway (ft)}}$$

6. Computation of Uniformity Ratio

With luminaire spacing determined, the designer should then check the uniformity of illumination by computing the average/minimum ratio and comparing it with selected criteria. Minimum illumination is determined from the proper isofootcandle diagram (a typical diagram is shown in Figure 20.5). This is accomplished by selecting points on the layout (Figure 20.8) where it is anticipated that minimum illumination will occur and checking the illumination on the isofootcandle curve. The designer should include the contributions from all luminaires in determining the minimum illumination because they are additive. The uniformity ratio is as follows:

$$\text{uniformity ratio} = \frac{\text{average illumination (maintained)}}{\text{minimum illumination (maintained)}}$$

The uniformity ratio should not exceed 4:1 and preferably would not exceed 3:1 except on residential streets, where 6:1 is generally acceptable.

With a satisfactory check of uniformity, the computational procedure is complete. It may be necessary to return to step 3 to alter the system characteristics if luminaire spacing is too short or the uniformity ratio is too large.

Figure 20.8. Layout of luminaire and roadway assumed for typical computation. SOURCE: *American National Standard Practice for Roadway Lighting,* New York: Illuminating Engineering Society, American National Standards Association, 1977, p. 76.

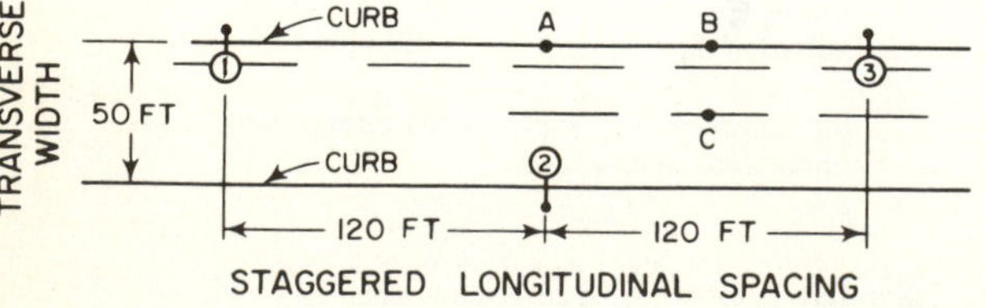

7. Consideration of Transitional Lighting

The need for transition to continuous lighting is more psychological than physiological. The eye normally adapts to light changes rapidly, achieving approximately 90% efficiency within seconds. When the lighting system terminates in an extremely dark area, the driver may want a transitional effect because of the rapid change in the flow of information. Accepted practice in the United States is to accomplish transition within 15 s using lower-wattage sources at the same spacing and mounting height used in the continuous lighting system.

The designer should pay particular attention to the terminal points of a lighting system to see that these points do not correspond with significant changes in roadway geometry, traffic control, or environmental characteristics. An example is the upgraded section of highway that has been improved with additional lanes, a median, and high-quality fixed lighting. Too frequently, this new section connects directly to the oid unlighted section. The desired treatment continues the lighting system through the transition to the old facility, and then it gradually reduces the lighting to the darkened condition.

8. Selection of Safety Features

Breakaway bases for luminaire supports are now commonly used on freeways and other major highways and have saved many lives. Collisions with fixed-base luminaire supports at speeds over 30 mph (50 km/h) are likely to produce serious injury or death to the vehicle occupants. Therefore, breakaway bases should be used any time the 85th percentile speed on the traffic facility exceeds 30 mph (50 km/h) and when the luminaire support is not protected by a median barrier or guardrail. It is *not* feasible to install guardrail for the sole purpose of protecting luminaire supports. Guardrail used in this manner is more of a hazard than luminaire supports and should be used only when the hazard is otherwise greater than that produced by the installation of the guardrail.[17]

Questions have arisen concerning the safety of pedestrians and private property where breakaway luminaire supports are used. Breakaway devices are inadvisable where pedestrian activity is high or where property is developed up to the property line. Speeds of 30 mph (50 km/h) or more are unlikely in these areas.

Breakaway luminaire supports are described by their dynamic behavioral characteristics when struck by a vehicle. Specifically, a breakaway support is defined as one that causes a change in momentum of not more than 1100 lb-s (4893 N-s) when struck by a 2250-lb (1020-kg) vehicle at any speed between 20 and 60 mph (32 and 97 km/h). Testing procedures are presented in NCHRP Report No. 153, *Recommended Procedures for Vehicle Crash Testing of Highway Appurtenances,* 1974. However, compliance certification is normally supplied by the manufacturer of breakaway devices.

[17]W. F. McFarland and N. E. Walton, "Cost Effectiveness Analysis of Roadway Lighting Systems," *Res. Report 137-1* (College Station, Tex.: Texas Transportation Institute, 1969).

Several different types of breakaway bases for luminaire supports have been certified by the recommended procedure. These include:

- Slip bases
- Frangible couplings
- Stainless steel progressive shear bases
- Cast aluminum transformer bases (special designs)

Partial lighting

Where roadways are not continuously lighted, it is often desirable to provide lighting at intersections, interchanges, and elsewhere as justified. Lighting installed only at key points is normally referred to as "partial" or "safety" lighting. The objective is to draw the driver's attention to unusual conditions and to convey necessary information. Sometimes it is sufficient to light only the major points of conflict with other traffic or the roadway features themselves, but generally it is desirable to illuminate the entire area, including the geometric and environmental features, as well as the major conflict points.

Because conditions related to partial or safety lighting are so variable, it is difficult to outline a specific design procedure. The following general points may, however, be helpful:

1. A single luminaire calls attention to a point on the roadway, but it has very little revealing power. Two or more luminaires, close together, are necessary to improve visibility significantly. For example, a single luminaire at the nose of an entrance ramp does little more than define the nose of the ramp.
2. Merge areas should be lighted so that mainstream traffic can judge the location and speed of entering traffic.
3. The main lanes before a merge point should be lighted so that entering traffic can judge the speed and distance of oncoming traffic.
4. Intersections should be lighted so that vehicles, curb faces, obstructions, signs, and other vertical surfaces are illuminated by direct light. This generally means placing the luminaire on the nearside corner of the intersection.
5. Intersections, pedestrian crosswalks, auxiliary lanes, and other special locations should be illuminated effectively.
6. Intersection approaches should be lighted whenever the driver on the intersecting roadway will need to identify the roadway for informational purposes and to judge the speed and distance of intersecting traffic. This is particularly true for complex intersections with turning roadways.
7. Considerable informational value is gained when the driver can see the entire intersection or interchange rather than only the specific part he or she uses. Thus, the designer should consider lighting the entire area when the information value justifies it. This particular point has contributed substantially to the extensive use of high-mast lighting of intersections and interchanges.
8. Specific consideration should be given to the hazards introduced by the installation of luminaire supports at intersections and interchanges. Because these are areas of conflict and decision, the probability of a collision with a luminaire support is much higher than for continuous lighting systems. Supports should be strategically located to lessen the probability of collision, and breakaway bases should be used except at the specific points where a fallen luminaire support and an errant vehicle would obviously result in more serious consequences. For example, it would be impractical to place a breakaway support next to a busy pedestrian walkway, but breakaway supports would be entirely appropriate for merge points, turning roadways, and so on.

There are no specific criteria for illumination design of partial lighting. Design procedures presented earlier for continuous lighting generally apply for partial lighting also. Luminaire location for partial lighting is aided greatly, however, by making scale drawings of isofootcandle curves on transparent materials such as sheet acetate. The transparency permits the designer to strategically locate the luminaires so that critical points receive the greatest amount of illumination. By using two transparencies, the designer can establish realistic spacings of luminaires without immediately going through the computational procedure.

High-mast lighting

High-Mast Lighting[18] describes the application of the area lighting concept to highway interchanges, complex intersections, and highways having wide cross sections and many lanes. Although high-mast lighting is recognized as a "popular new concept," it is the application rather than the concept that is new. The concept dates back to the 1800s, when tall masts were installed in several cities, including Philadelphia and Vancouver, to illuminate large areas and thus provide a pleasant nighttime environment. The operation and maintenance of these installations proved very costly, and most were abandoned. But at least one is still used. About the turn of the century, the city of Austin, Texas, traded a narrow-gauge railroad for a number of 150-ft towers and installed them at several points throughout the city where artificial "moonlight" was desired. Although the light sources have been changed with advancements in technology, most of the towers are still used effectively.

The first known application of high-mast lighting for modern highways was the Heerdter Triangle installation in Düsseldorf, Germany, in the late 1950s. It was followed by installations in other European countries, including Holland, France, Italy, and Great Britain. Interest in high-mast lighting in this country was stimulated by the successful applications in Europe and the increasing difficulty of lighting some highway interchanges by conventional methods.

The principal objective in the application of high-mast lighting to highway interchanges is to synthesize the visual

[18]N. E. Walton and N. J. Rowan, *High-Mast Lighting*, Res. Report 75-12 (College Station, Tex.: Texas Transportation Institute, 1969), p. 1.

advantage provided the driver by daylight. Thus, the driver can see all things pertinent to the decision-making process in time to assimilate the information and then plan and execute maneuvers effectively. Drivers can distinguish roadway geometry, obstructions, terrain, and other roadways, each in proper perspective.

Additional advantages of high-mast lighting are related to safety and aesthetics. When there are fewer poles, there are fewer opportunities for collision. The poles can be located farther from the roadway, so that the possibility of a collision with the luminaire support is virtually eliminated. Daytime aesthetics are greatly improved by removing the "forest" of poles generally necessary to light complex interchanges and intersections with continuous lighting systems.

There are no established illumination criteria unique to the high-mast lighting concept. The criteria for continuous lighting (Table 20-3) are generally applicable. An evaluation procedure similar to that recommended for continuous lighting can be used, and increases in average illumination can be made whenever justified by roadway, traffic, or environmental conditions. The average illumination and uniformity values should be applicable only to traffic areas. In nontraffic areas, a minimum of 20% of the average illumination for traffic areas is suggested.

The design process for high-mast lighting differs from that for continuous lighting mainly in the system characterization arising from the great differences in illumination equipment and in the computational procedure. The following section is devoted primarily to these elements of the design process.

System characterization. System characterization consists of establishing a design configuration or alternative configurations to be analyzed comparatively in the design process. First, the type of luminaire and the mounting height must be selected. The designer may choose the Type V circular distribution, Type V asymmetric distribution (sometimes listed as IES Type III), or a system of floodlight-type units that can be aimed to achieve these patterns.

The mounting height of high-mast systems is variable, depending on the elevation of the light source in relation to the roadway to be lighted. At least a 100-ft (30-m) difference in elevation of the light source and the roadway is desirable. Mounting heights of 150 ft (45 m) are generally applicable.

Achieving a specified illumination level is a function of mounting height, type of light source, type of luminaire or floodlight, and number of luminaires or floodlights in a system (system refers to the assembly on a single pole). A trial number of system units can be estimated by a computational process involving total lamp lumens, a coefficient of luminaire efficiency, and the area to be covered. Experience helps, but the designer will probably determine by trial and error the number of units required to provide a given illumination level.

Preliminary spacing of poles in the interchange area should be made on a maximum spacing/mounting height ratio of 5:1 if the same cutoff characteristics that result from medium distribution luminaires in continuous lighting are desired. Spacing adjustments should be made on the basis of location criteria and computational procedures of illumination by the point-by-point method discussed later.

Certain considerations regarding pole locations are required in order to achieve the greatest effectiveness from the lighting system:[19]

1. Poles should be located so that drivers' lines of sight are not directly toward the light source when they are within 1500 ft (460 m) of the mast. More specifically, drivers' lines of sight should not be above the lower-third point of the pole when they are within 1500 ft (460 m) of the pole. This rule is applicable when the driver's line of sight is within 10° on either side of the pole.
2. Poles should be located so that the light source will at no time be in the direct line of sight with signs (especially overhead signs) and other visual communication media.
3. Poles should not be placed at the end of long tangents or other vulnerable locations where there is an appreciable probability of collision. If such a location is necessary, adequate crash cushion protection should be provided.
4. Poles should be located so that the highest localized levels of illumination fall in the principal traffic conflict areas, such as at ramp terminals. Otherwise, poles should be located a sufficient distance from the roadway in order to position the greatest uniformity of illumination on the pavement surface. This will normally result in the poles being placed a sufficient distance from the roadway so that the probability of collision is virtually eliminated.

Illumination computational procedures. Following the preliminary location and spacing of poles and the initial selection of the number of units on each pole, it is necessary to check the distribution of illumination against the established criteria. The most rational approach to this check process is by computation of illumination using a point-by-point procedure. To facilitate computations, the entire interchange area is superimposed with grid lines at 25- to 50-ft intervals. Intervals of 25 ft (7.5 m) are desirable if a computer is used, but 50-ft (15-m) intervals are more appropriate for hand calculations.

The point-by-point computational process utilizes a candlepower distribution curve as illustrated in Figure 20.9. Candlepower distribution curves are normally developed for single-unit Type V luminaires, in which case they must be multiplied by the number of luminaires in the system. This curve can be developed for all symmetrical high-mast systems, whether they consist of Type V units or individual floodlights arranged in a symmetrical pattern.

The illumination in horizontal footcandles at a grid point resulting from one high-mast assembly can be computed by using the formula

$$E_h = \frac{C_p \cos \theta}{d^2} \qquad (20.1)$$

where E_h = illumination at the point, horizontal footcandles

C_p = candlepower at angle θ, lumens

[19]Ibid., p. 57.

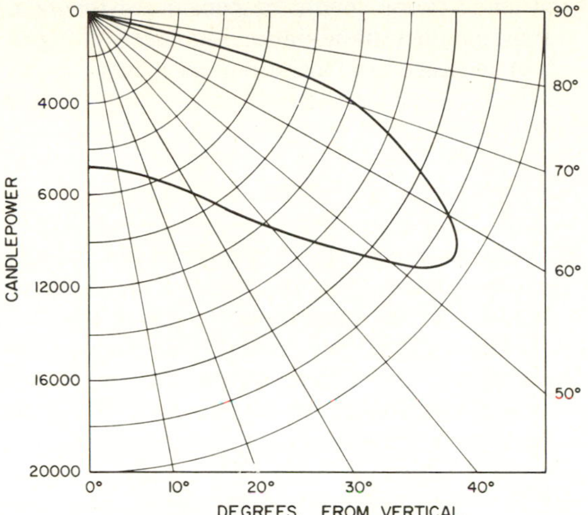

Figure 20.9. Examples of candlepower distribution curve used for making point-by-point illumination calculations.

θ = angle from the vertical axis through the system to the point in question (Figure 20.9)

d = distance from the light source to the point in question (Figure 20.10)

Then, the total illumination at each of the grid points is the sum of the contributions of illumination from the high-mast assemblies within an effective range of the point in question. This process is illustrated in Figure 20.10.

Once the amount of illumination is computed for all the grid points, an isofootcandle diagram may be drawn for the entire interchange area. This will facilitate an overall appraisal of the illumination design.

Figure 20.10. Illustration of the point-by-point process of illumination computations.

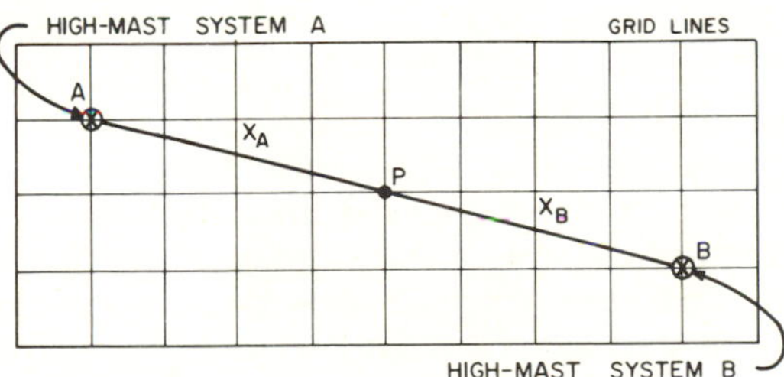

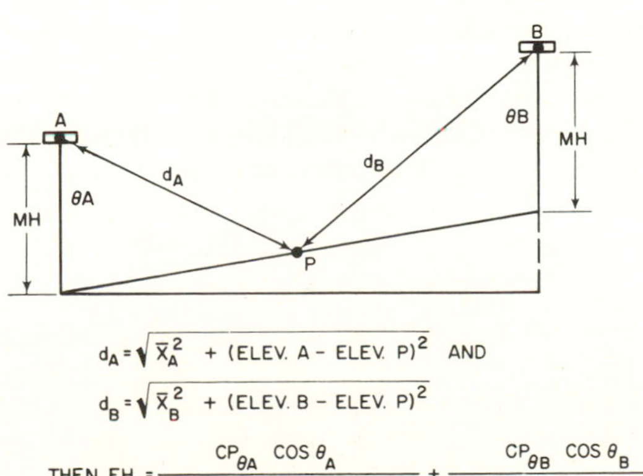

$$d_A = \sqrt{\bar{X}_A^2 + (\text{ELEV. A} - \text{ELEV. P})^2} \text{ AND}$$

$$d_B = \sqrt{\bar{X}_B^2 + (\text{ELEV. B} - \text{ELEV. P})^2}$$

$$\text{THEN } EH_p = \frac{CP_{\theta A} \cos \theta_A}{\bar{X}_A^2 + (\text{ELEV. A} - \text{ELEV. P})^2} + \frac{CP_{\theta B} \cos \theta_B}{\bar{X}_B^2 + (\text{ELEV. B} - \text{ELEV. P})^2} + \cdots$$

For a more specific appraisal, the designer should plot an illumination profile for each section of roadway in the interchange. For wider roadways it may be necessary to plot two or more profiles in order to fully represent the traveled way. These profiles are plotted either by using the contour values and contour spacings along the roadway or by using interpolation of the grid matrix of illumination values at the grid points. If computer techniques are used, the latter is the more adaptable process. The average illumination values and uniformity ratios are computed from the illumination profile. By comparing the average illumination and uniformity ratios with the previously established criteria, the spacing of poles and/or number of units on each pole may be adjusted accordingly, and the computational process repeated until the desired criteria are achieved.

The major weakness in the point-by-point design process is the lack of reliability of the input photometric data, as in the case of computational procedures for continuous lighting. The candlepower distribution curve is developed under controlled laboratory conditions. There is some preliminary indication from unpublished research that the loss from laboratory to field installation is approximately 25%. Therefore, it seems justified that the designer should consider reducing the candlepower values by 25% unless there is evidence that he or she can be assured of achieving the light output indicated by the candlepower distribution curve.

High-mast lighting hardware. Both poles and towers have been used on high-mast lighting installations with apparently equal functional capability. Manufacturers now offer either type in a "package deal" that includes lowering assemblies and other mounting hardware. The choice depends on local factors rather than on set guidelines. There are three basic methods available for mounting high-mast light sources:[20]

1. Light sources mounted on a lowering assembly, with a motorized winch to facilitate raising and lowering of lighting assembly for service and maintenance.
2. Light sources fixed at top of mast, with provisions for climbing the mast for service and maintenance.
3. Light sources fixed at top of mast, with provisions for a motorized personnel carrier to transport service personnel to light sources for service and maintenance.

The lowering assembly is used almost exclusively and there are several versions of this method available. Some have locking mechanisms and power connections at the top; others provide continuous cable suspension for the lighting assembly and a continuous power supply line connected at the base. Once again, the selection of the mounting method is largely dependent on local factors.

Tunnel and underpass lighting

Since tunnels and underpasses involve different physiological characteristics of the driver, they deserve special consideration. Tunnels and underpasses of any substantial

[20]Ibid., p. 33.

length involve eye adaptation to ambient light conditions, and transient adaptation becomes a factor in design. A general rule to follow is that when the length/height ratio exceeds 10:1, it is necessary to analyze the specific geometry and roadway conditions, including vehicular and pedestrian activities, to determine the need for daytime illumination.[21] When the latter is required, the facility by definition is a tunnel; otherwise, it is an underpass.

Underpass lighting, if warranted on an otherwise unlighted roadway, should provide illumination in the range 0.6 to 0.8 horizontal footcandles (6 to 9 lux) maintained with a 3:1 to 4:1 uniformity of illumination. Special conditions of high nighttime ambient brightness may justify brighter illumination levels.

Tunnels, on the other hand, require much higher illumination levels. The portion of the tunnel that affects visibility most critically is the section just beyond the portal. Visibility is reduced drastically during the daytime because of sudden change in ambient brightness. This is commonly called the "black hole" effect. To correct this deficiency, the first tunnel entrance zone should be illuminated to a brightness between 1/10 and 1/15 of the ambient brightness level on the approach to the tunnel. This ambient brightness level varies depending on weather conditions, and newer tunnel lighting installations have utilized photometric monitoring of the ambient brightness level to automatically control the brightness level in the tunnel entrance zone.

The illumination of tunnel interiors is dependent upon their length. For short tunnels, the entrance zone lighting is continued throughout the tunnel. For longer tunnels (portal-to-portal length greater than wet pavement minimum stopping distance), interior lighting may be reduced substantially. Illumination levels should be reduced in steps, each step not less than 1/15 of the previous higher level. The recommended minimum level for the interior lighting is 5 horizontal footcandles or 54 lux.

Nighttime lighting requirements for tunnels are significantly lower than daytime requirements and should therefore make use of only a portion of the daytime lighting system, if practicable. Nighttime levels in a tunnel should be two to three times that of the lighting requirements for the adjacent roadway. On noncontinuously lighted roadways, tunnels should be lighted to the minimum standards required for the roadway type.

Tunnel and underpass lighting involve many special design features not common to the lighting of streets and highways. It is advisable to consult more specific references for the many considerations in design.[22,23]

Rural at-grade intersection illumination

Based on a comprehensive investigation of rural at-grade intersection illumination conducted at the University of Illinois, the following is recommmended as the basis for rural at-grade illumination warrants.

Rural intersections should be considered for lighting if the average number of nighttime accidents (N) per year exceeds the average number of day accidents (D) per year divided by 3. All the accident data available since the date of the last modification to the intersection should be used when calculating these averages. If N is greater than $D/3$, the likely average benefit should be taken as $N - D/3$ accidents/year.

The likely benefits of lighting new or modified intersections should be estimated from previous experience. It is recommended that illumination should be provided whenever an intersection is channelized.

The estimated cost of lighting the intersections, which show a benefit using the above criteria, should be computed. The lighting program should then be based on the resulting list of intersections ranked in priority order by means of the benefit/cost ratio (expressed as annual reduction in accidents/annual cost).[24]

The recommended warrant is designed to give the decision makers the most information possible based on current knowledge. It is implicitly assumed that the highway improvement budget is limited, and thus interest is focused on maximizing the benefits of a limited budget. For this reason, reductions in number of accidents rather than accident rates are used. One important implication of this approach is that the distribution of funds for lighting improvement tends to be directed into the areas of high traffic volumes. Thus, if intersections are ranked on a statewide listing, the distribution of the budget would not be the same as one distributed by listing intersections on a district basis. The latter would spread improvements more uniformly throughout a state, but at a lower overall benefit/cost ratio.

Operation and maintenance

Electric power considerations

All lighting installations require electrical power. This requires coordination with an electric utility to obtain the necessary voltage at the designed point of delivery. For small systems the operating voltage is 120 or 240 V. For larger systems fed from a single point of delivery, operating voltages of 480 V single-phase and 277/480 V three-phase can be used.

Luminaire/ballast units are available for operation from 120-, 240-, 277-, and 480-V circuits. The building-type wire normally used has insulation rated at 600 V, making it suitable for any of these voltages.

The most popular means of switching roadway lighting on and off are light-sensitive switches or photoelectric controls. This type of control turns on the lighting when the daylight level drops to a certain value, and turns it off when the dawn light level reaches a certain value. A single control

[21] *An Informational Guide for Roadway Lighting.*

[22] "Lighting of Tunnels," *J. Illumin. Eng. Soc.*, *1*(3), 247 (Apr. 1972).

[23] *An Informational Guide for Roadway Lighting.*

[24] ROBERT H. WORTMAN, M. E. LIPINSKI, ET AL., "Interim Report—Development of Warrants for Rural At-Grade Intersection Illumination," *Ill. Cooperative Highway Res. Program Ser. No. 135*, University of Illinois at Urbana-Champaign, 1972, p. 37.

can be used to switch a number of lighting units in a system or one can be plugged into a luminaire provided with a socket to switch that one luminaire.

Electric power is available both metered and unmetered or "flat rate." In the latter case, a monthly cost is charged for each lighting unit based on the lamp size. The selection of metered or unmetered service for a particular system requires an economic analysis that includes a consideration of system size and the rate structure of the electric utility.

Ballasts

All lamps used for roadway lighting are of the gas-discharge type: fluorescent, low-pressure sodium, mercury, metal halide, and high-pressure sodium. The last three types comprise the category of high-intensity discharge (H.I.D.). Each such lamp requires an electrical component called a ballast, which serves to provide the proper voltage, waveform, and current to start and operate a gas-discharge lamp.

Four types of ballasts are in common use: reactor, autotransformer reactor, regulator, and autotransformer regulator. Of these, the reactor is the simplest and therefore the lowest priced. The disadvantage of the reactor type is that it will not tolerate an input voltage drop of more than 5% without seriously affecting lamp performance. Where the input voltage is not sufficient to start and operate the lamp, an autotransformer is used to raise the voltage. The normal reactor ballast has a low power factor; this can be corrected by adding the proper-size capacitor to the circuit.

The regulator ballast has a circuit that will permit proper operation of a lamp over a range of input voltages: ± 13% for mercury lamps, ± 10% for high-pressure sodium. The autotransformer has a lower cost and slightly less ballast power loss than the normal regulator ballast.

A high-pressure sodium lamp requires, in addition to the normal ballast components, a starting device. This device produces a pulse of at least 2500 V with a duration of 1 μs across the lamp.

Most ballasts presently used in roadway lighting are of the integral type; that is, the ballast is installed within the luminaire housing. Integral ballasts have the following advantages over ballasts designed for pullbox or pole-base installation: low cost, low operating temperature, and accessibility for replacement of defective components.

Design of the electrical system

The electrical design of a lighting system usually falls outside the traffic engineer's responsibility. An excellent text on lighting electrical design, *Highway Lighting Engineering,* by Antanas Ketvirtis,[25] provides very detailed descriptions, plans, and specifications for all electrical design associated with highway lighting.

[25]Ketvirtis, *Highway Lighting Engineering*.

Maintenance

Because light reduction caused by dirt and lumen depreciation of the lamp cannot readily be observed, periodic cleaning and relamping are important maintenance requirements. Although, in practice, maintenance intervals range from 6 months to 4 years (and often lamp replacement and cleaning are performed only at lamp burnout), it must be stressed that it is economically advantageous to follow a set maintenance schedule based on expected lamp life and dirt accumulation characteristics of the area. Generally, the benefits of maintenance parallel the initial benefits of illumination, and the most effective cleaning schedule is one that allows no more than a 20% light reduction caused by dirt. Lamp replacement should follow the same schedule. This usually amounts to approximately 24,000 h of service at rated conditions for most mercury and high-pressure sodium lamps, making the 4-year interval tolerable.

One question that often arises in maintenance considerations is the economic advantages of higher mounting heights [40 to 50 ft (12 to 15 m)]. It has been demonstrated that even a small lighting program can achieve sufficient savings from higher mounting heights to purchase the equipment necessary to service the higher heights.[26] In many cases, effective communication between municipalities and the electric companies is necessary to demonstrate the benefits (savings) of the higher heights.

Another problem is the cleaning of polished aluminum reflectors that are easily tarnished or damaged. Many trade journals advertise cleaning solutions made especially for polished aluminum. This not only makes the use of these reflectors more feasible, but it also provides for adequate maintenance.

Benefits of lighting

The real value of lighting is finally and directly related to driver safety and comfort, and, consequently, to a reduction in the nighttime accident rate. Many factors have been cited as the cause of the disproportionate number of nighttime accidents. Among them are fatigue, alcohol, and reduced visibility. The best evidence that reduced visibility contributes to increased accidents are the many examples of accident reduction resulting from improved roadway illumination.[27–29]

The beneficial effects of fixed roadway lighting are not limited solely to high-speed freeways and interchanges. Many studies have shown a reduction in the number of accidents in urban, suburban, and rural areas, regardless of the class of roadway.

[26]McFarland and Walton, *Cost Effectiveness Analysis*.

[27]D. E. Cleveland, "Illumination," in *Traffic Control and Roadway Elements—Their Relationship to Highway Safety,* rev. ed. (Washington, D.C.: Automotive Safety Foundation, 1969), Chap. 3.

[28]Paul C. Box, "Comparison of Accidents and Illumination," *Highway Res. Rec. 416* (Washington, D.C.: Highway Research Board, 1972), pp. 1–9.

[29]Barbara E. Sabey and H. D. Johnson, "Roadlighting and Accidents: Before and After Studies on Trunk Road Sites," *Transportation and Road Res. Lab (GB), TRRL Report LB 586,* 1973, 15 pp.

The effect of lighting on the accident rate is significant not only for continuous lengths of roadways, but for specific locations as well. Studies showing marked reduction in nighttime accident rates following illumination have been conducted in California, Connecticut, New York, and many other states and cities. Undoubtedly, modern lighting techniques reduce the number of fatal and nonfatal accidents, as well as the severity of those accidents that do occur despite improved lighting techniques.

The tangible benefits of roadway lighting include many social and economic gains, especially in downtown urban areas. Serious crime can be reduced and business can be improved. Many downtown areas, almost deserted after dark, have increased their aesthetic appeal and business activity after the addition of improved lighting. Architects and city planners consider better lighting a major source of economic stimulation and beautification for downtown areas. In fact, many cities across the country are reopening parks and recreation areas after dark because of the effects lighting has on the crime rate, business, and personal security. Police forces across the country have praised and actively pushed for improved lighting in order to make law enforcement more effective.

Cost considerations

The design and specification of a lighting system should be such that maximum returns are achieved at the lowest possible costs. Several designs providing a predetermined level of effectiveness should be developed and their cost compared. Design variables that usually are most influential to both effectiveness and costs are as follows:

1. Arrangement or placement of lighting units with respect to the roadway (median, one-side, staggered on opposite sides, opposite on two sides, and median plus on the side)
2. Mounting heights
3. Pole and base type
4. Lamp characteristics (type, initial lumens, lumen maintenance, wattage)
5. Luminaire type
6. Light distribution type
7. Type of distribution system
8. Burning hours per year
9. Type of ownership and maintenance

In addition to these design variables, there are roadway, traffic, and environmental variables influencing effectiveness and costs that should be considered in cost analysis. The following are included among the influential roadway variables:

1. Median width
2. Presence or absence (or plans for such) of a median barrier and its type
3. Number of traffic lanes
4. Width of roadway shoulders
5. Overall roadway cross section
6. Number and type of exit and entrance ramps
7. Number and type of intersections and intersecting roadways and streets

Among other important variables are the amount and type of traffic, the type of area through which the roadway passes, and weather conditions in the area.

From a general standpoint, Thompson and Fansler[30] have shown that higher mounting heights are least costly for continuous and intersection lighting. McFarland and Walton[31] recommend higher mounting heights, higher luminaire output, careful lateral placement of units (for safety reasons), and breakaway devices for reducing overall lighting system costs (initial, operation, maintenance, and accident).

Roadway lighting and energy utilization

Because roadway lighting depends entirely on the availability of electrical energy, there is considerable concern as to whether the practice of lighting streets and highways should be continued. This concern is justifiable. However, the use of energy for roadway lighting should be kept in proper perspective. Roadway lighting is a useful tool of the transportation engineer, and when applied effectively, results in direct benefits of increased night visibility and reduced nighttime accidents. Obviously, the consequences of not lighting as a means of conserving energy will be to reduce night visibility and increase accidents. These consequences must be offset by the benefits derived from other uses of the available energy if the practice of lighting roadways is discontinued or curtailed. From the standpoint of planning and designing lighting systems to conserve energy, a positive but conservative approach seems most sensible. Rational warrants should be used, and systems designed to an optimum rather than a maximum or excessive level of illumination.

[30]J. A. Thompson and B. I. Fansler, "Economic Study of Various Mounting Heights for Highway Lighting," *Highway Res. Rec. No. 179* (Washington, D.C.: Highway Research Board, 1967), pp. 1–15.

[31]McFarland and Walton, *Cost Effectiveness Analysis*.

21

PARKING, LOADING, AND TERMINAL FACILITIES

JAMES M. HUNNICUTT

Hunnicutt & Associates, Inc.
Washington, D.C.

The provision of adequate parking is an essential element of the transportation system in the world's cities. This chapter discusses the provision and operation of parking facilities, both on-street and off-street, the latter either in surface parking lots or in parking structures. The location, design, and financing of parking facilities are described, as well as parking related to zoning and to special-purpose land uses. Off-street truck loading facilities are also discussed.

Parking activity appears to be cyclical in nature. In the early 1950s the shortage of parking in major cities prompted the establishment of many parking authorities, commissions, and departments. Considerable research on organization, management, trip generation, finance, and design was done by traffic engineers, parking executives, and planners. Many successful methods were developed and published to solve all types of parking problems. Although innovations do occur, primary parking solutions have remained relatively constant.

Following the surge of facility construction in the 1950s and 1960s, parking activity decreased. The spectre of severe federal or state limitations on parking because of proposed environmental controls brought progress to a standstill in the United States. Years of inactivity and the revitalization of many downtowns have shown that parking is an absolute necessity. Parking development is now again very active, as there is a rush to solve preexisting problems.

As a result of these parking ups and downs, some of the references and data in this chapter may appear dated. Factual data are the latest available and those used by full-time parking professionals on a daily basis.

Definitions

The following terms often appear in a discussion of parking.

Parking accumulation. The total number of vehicles parked in a given area at a given time.

Parking deficiency. The extent to which parking demand exceeds supply, expressed in number of parking spaces.

Parking demand. The number of drivers desiring to park in a given area during a specific time period—often expressed as the number during the hour of peak parking requirement for a typical day.

Parking duration. The length of time a given vehicle remains in a specific space.

Parking duration, long-term. Parking with a duration exceeding 3 to 4 h.

Parking duration, short-term. Parking with a duration of less than 3 to 4 h.

Parking inventory. The number of parking spaces available in a given area categorized as to curb or off-street spaces, public or private use, or by other classifications.

Parking supply. The number of legal parking spaces available in a given area.

Parking surplus. The extent to which parking supply exceeds demand, expressed in number of parking spaces.

Private parking supply. Parking spaces provided for employees or customers of a business and not available to the general public.

Public parking supply. Parking spaces available to the general public either free of charge or for a fee.

Space-hour. A single parking space occupied by a vehicle for 1 h.

Turnover. The number of different vehicles that park in a given space during an average day per unit of time (e.g., per day).

Location of downtown parking facilities

The generalized location of parking facilities in the urbanized area has long been a subject of debate. On the one hand, the thought has been to provide parking facilities at the destination of the parkers. In many instances, these parking facilities would be constructed as a part of the overall development scheme. At the other extreme, it has often been proposed that considerable parts of the central business district (CBD) be closed to through traffic and that parking facilities should be provided at the fringes of the CBD. These fringe parking facilities would then be connected to the CBD by public transit feeder systems.

There are indications that the prohibition of traffic and parking facilities within the CBD can do much to damage CBD viability. It is apparent, particularly in the United States, that the public prefers conveniently situated fringe and suburban business locations that are readily accessible by auto and with adequate parking available on site. This is attested to by the fact that, in many cities, businesses and retail establishments are relocating from the CBD to fringe and suburban locations. Accessibility and parking are often cited as factors in this relocation. If the CBD is to remain attractive as a business and shopping location, the in-town businesses and retail establishments must be readily accessible via the automobile and convenient parking facilities must be available.

In an idealized situation, the location of parking within a city can be related to that city's size. In such a scheme, the first parking facilities to be provided would be in the CBD. As the city grows, the second-stage parking facilities would be constructed immediately adjacent to the core area at an inner-ring road, if one were available. The third-stage parking facilities would be at the fringe to the CBD on major arterial routes leading into the center of the city. The third-stage facilities would probably be needed only in the larger cities and could be tied into the public transit system.

To establish the location of parking facilities, it is first necessary to conduct the appropriate field studies (see Chapter 17) to determine the areas of concentration of parking demand and needs that are unsatisfied in terms of existing supply. Only with data from these studies is it possible to properly locate a parking facility.

Many factors influence the location of parking facilities. These include parking shortages in each area, origin and destination of parkers, pedestrian walking distance and ease of movement, vehicular access, street capacities, type of generators in the area, future development, economic factors, and the relationship to the overall CBD plan.

The type of parking generators to be served influences the facility location. Short-term parking generators such as department stores, other retail stores, banks, and so on, require closer proximity to parking spaces than do long-term generators such as offices. This is because long-term parkers will accept a longer walking distance than will short-term parkers. Longer walking distances are acceptable to long-term parkers because the ratio of walk time to total time parked is much less than with short-term parkers. In considering pedestrian access, ease of movement should be analyzed as well as actual walking distance. The longer of two routes may psychologically appear shorter because of pedestrian amenities, less conflict with vehicles, gentler grades, or other factors which tend to make one walking trip more acceptable than another.

Vehicular access is also an important factor in locating parking facilities. As much as practical, driving time to the facility by patrons should be minimized. If parker origins are concentrated in one direction because of physical or other barriers to travel, it is desirable to locate the parking facility between drivers' origins and their final destinations. To locate the parking facility on the far side of the generators from the origins would require drivers to pass the generator on their way to the parking facility, thereby increasing travel distance and volume on CBD streets. The CBD facility should be located to have a minimum adverse effect on the CBD street system. Whenever possible, it is desirable to locate a parking facility near a major arterial or expressway, thereby minimizing travel on local streets and also providing quick and easy access to the major street and freeway systems.

Capacity on streets surrounding the proposed site should be adequate to handle the additional traffic attracted by the parking facility. In addition, entrances and exits to the facility should be placed as far as possible from intersections to provide maximum storage and maneuver space.

The location of a proposed parking facility should be consistent with the overall plan for the CBD. The location of future generators should be considered as well as the location of any new streets, freeway access points, or changes in the existing street system. Economic considerations enter into the location of parking facilities. Items such as land cost vary from one site to another. Land costs lead to a consideration of whether a garage should be constructed rather than a surface lot. When garages are being investigated, underground facilities should be considered if the economic costs can be borne. Although underground garages cost 1.5 to 2 or more times per car space what an aboveground facility would cost, they offer the advantage of preserving open space in the CBD. If an underground facility is built under an existing public park, the land costs may be eliminated. Even then, the additional cost of underground construction and higher operating expenses may negate the advantage of no land cost.

The use of air rights over and under freeways, other streets, railroads, and so on, for the location of parking facilities is a means of reducing or eliminating land cost related to parking facilities. Multipurpose buildings are also being constructed with increasing frequency as parking is combined in the same structure with other land uses, such as office, apartment, or institutional use. This greatly reduces the land costs chargeable to the parking portion of the development.

Zoning for parking

Zoning ordinance provisions are a means of ensuring an adequate supply of off-street parking in all new developments. Zoning may require that a specific number of parking spaces be provided with all new construction or major building modification. It therefore represents a long-range approach to reducing parking problems in cities. An adequate supply of off-street spaces will allow on-street parking to be limited or prohibited. The streets can then better serve their primary function of moving traffic.

Parking demand not only varies according to land use but varies within parts of the city for the same land use. Factors affecting parking demand include the availability of mass transit and the economic levels, local policies, and customs of the city or portion of the city. Use of an average value as a zoning requirement will obviously result in inadequate parking facilities in some instances and in overdesign with attendant economic waste in others.

Local parking generation studies are useful in determining parking needs, and their results should be used to update zoning ordinances. In addition, zoning ordinances can specify parking requirements according to districts within the city. Zoning requirements for a specific land use could vary from district to district according to the character of the district. An appeals board could then handle any further request for variation from zoning requirements.

The Planned Unit Development is a useful tool in zoning. With this concept, several different land uses may be incorporated on a single tract of land. The parking demand for the development is based on the characteristics of the land uses being planned. Most zoning ordinances require that the appropriate factor be applied to each land use in the development to determine the parking requirements for the individual land uses. These requirements are then added to determine the total parking requirements for the development. However, this total requirement may be increased or reduced upon review of plans for the development depending on the mix of land uses and the location of the project.

Table 21-1 summarizes zoning and planning standards for parking for various land uses. The data represented are from two different reference sources, with the minimum standard column obtained from one source and the remainder of the table from a second source. In most instances, there is fairly good agreement between the two sources. However, some discrepancies occur, such as for industrial land uses, one source showing a planning standard of 0.33 to 0.50 space per employee, whereas the other source recommends a minimum standard of 0.6 space per employee. The table clearly shows the variability of parking needs and requirements for the same land use.

Several factors can significantly affect the recommended minimum standards. These include location in relation to downtown (where many trips are walk-in, thereby minimizing the necessity of parking facilities), available public transportation service, and the basic trip-generating characteristics of the particular establishment. For example, the parking needs of retail establishments vary greatly. Outlets dealing in convenience goods, such as food, drugs, stationery items, and so on, require as many as seven to nine spaces per 1000 ft^2 of floor area whereas stores specializing

TABLE 21–1
Zoning and Planning Standard Guidelines for Parking

		Parking Spaces/Indicated Unit			
Land Use	Unit*	Zoning Requirements	Parking Space Needs†	Planning Standard	Recommended Minimum Standard
Residential					
Single-family	Dwelling	1–2	0.5–2.0	1–2+	2
Multi-family	Dwelling	0.4–0.5 and up	0.3–2.0	0.7–2.0	
Efficiency					1.0
1–2 bedrooms					1.5
3 or more bedrooms					2.0
Hospital	Bed	0.25–1.40	0.60–1.40	1.0–1.4	1.2
Auditorium, theater, or stadium	Seat	0.08–0.25	0.08–0.50	0.25–0.33	0.3
Restaurant	Seat	Variable	n.a.	0.33–0.50	0.3
Industrial	Employee	Variable	Variable	0.33–0.50	0.6
Church	Seat	0.10–0.33	n.a.	0.20–0.33	0.3
College–university	Student	Variable	0.4–0.6	0.5–0.7	0.5‡
Retail	1000 ft^2 GFA	1.5–8.0	1.5–3.0	2.0–8.0	4.0
Office	1000 ft^2 GFA	Variable	2.9–4.0	2.0–5.0	3.3
Shopping center	1000 ft^2 GLA				5.5
Hotels, motels	Room and employee				1.0/room, 0.5/emp.
Elementary–Jr. high school	Classroom				1.0
Senior high school	Student and staff				0.2/student, 1.0/staff

*GFA, gross floor area; GLA, gross leasable area.
†not available.
‡With auto access only (0.2 with good transit access).

SOURCE: WILBUR SMITH & ASSOCIATES, *Parking in the City Center*, New Haven, Conn., 1965, pp. 64–67; *Parking Principles*, Special Report No. 125, Highway Research Board, Washington, D.C., 1971, pp. 34–39.

in "shopper"-type goods, such as furniture, clothing, and appliances, may require as little as one-fourth that amount.

In recent years, zoning ordinances have not only specified the amount of parking required with various land uses, but also contained provisions for bicycle and motorcycle parking. These provisions in zoning ordinances reflect the concern for adequate off-street parking and storage for these vehicles. The provision for bicycle and motorcycle parking has been handled by some jurisdictions by relating bicycle and motorcycle stalls to the number of automobile parking spaces required. For example, in parking facilities containing more than 40 spaces, the zoning ordinance may require one bicycle parking space or locker for each 20 automobile parking spaces, not to exceed more than 20 bicycle parking spaces in any one lot. For motorcycles, the number of stalls required may be set at 2% of the auto spaces but not to exceed 10 motorcycle stalls on any one lot. Provision of motorcycle stalls generally is not required in lots containing less than 50 spaces.

Design of off-street facilities

Elements of good design

In designing any off-street parking facility, the elements of customer service and convenience and minimum interference with street traffic flow must receive first priority. Basically, drivers like to park their vehicles immediately adjacent to their destinations. The accessibility of the facility, the ease of entering, circulating, parking, unparking, and exiting are important factors in both the location and design of off-street parking facilities.

Good dimensions and ease of internal circulation are more important than trying to get a few additional spaces in a facility. Better sight distance, maneuverability, traffic flow, parking ease, and circulation are the result of a well-organized adequately designed lot or garage.

Major use of the facility

A factor for consideration in designing a parking facility is the use of the facility either in terms of type of parker or type of generator being served. Type of parker can be identified by average duration with either short-term or long-term parkers, or a combination. Design dimensions are often liberalized in facilities used by short-term parkers because of the high turnover rate and the desire to provide easy access, circulation, and parking–unparking.

A parking facility may serve any and all types of parking generators, particularly in a downtown area. However, parking facilities that serve special events, such as sports stadiums, auditoriums, or other similar uses, require special design considerations because of the parker characteristics. Persons attending special events generally arrive over a short time period, and everyone will be leaving upon conclusion of the event. This can place a severe strain on entrance and exit facilities and the internal circulation system. Special consideration must be given to the provision of adequate entrance and exit capacity at such facilities.

Street-capacity problems can also restrict smooth entry and exit at a garage serving a downtown civic center. Conflicts with large volumes of pedestrians is another problem. Airports, shopping centers, office buildings, and department stores all have widely differing loading and unloading characteristics, and the designer must thoroughly evaluate their unique characteristics prior to determining a final design.

Surface lot design

Site characteristics. The characteristics of the proposed site are an important design consideration. Factors such as site dimensions, topography, and profiles affect the design of off-street parking. The relation of the site characteristics to the surrounding street system will affect the location of entry and exit points as well as the internal circulation pattern.

Access points. External factors such as pedestrian traffic controls, turning restrictions, and volumes of traffic on adjacent streets will affect the design of a parking facility—particularly in the location of entry and exit points. It is desirable to avoid locating entry–exit points where vehicles entering or leaving the site would conflict with large numbers of pedestrians. Similarly, street traffic volumes, turning restrictions, and other traffic controls may limit points at which entrances and exits can logically be placed. It is important to investigate these factors before making final decisions on entrances and exits.

Entry and exit points should be located to provide maximum storage space and maximum distance from intersections. Combined entry–exit points should preferably be located at midblock. It is desirable to locate entry and exit points together so that attendants can monitor traffic both in and out from the same vantage point. Where entrances and exits are separated, the exit should preferably be placed in the downstream portion of the block, while the entrance should be placed as far upstream in the block face as possible.

Traffic circulation. The ideal movement into a parking facility is a left-hand turn from a one-way street. This places the driver in a left-hand turn pattern which is desirable on the parking site. The driver position is on the inside of the turn, which allows better visibility and more accurate judgment of the placement of the vehicle. A driver has more difficulty in judging vehicle placement in a right-hand turn.

Vehicle circulation on the site may be either two-way or one-way, depending on site dimensions and the angle of the parking stall. Two-way circulation is generally allowed with 90° stalls, whereas one-way circulation is generally used with stall angles less than 90°. In any event, it is desirable to attempt to minimize traffic conflict points on site so as to minimize the accident potential and congestion during peak hours.

Cross aisles are necessary in large facilities. Generally, no more than 30 spaces should be provided without a cross aisle to get to exits or other parking spaces.

Landscaping. Landscaping of parking facilities is desirable but should be limited to types that will not interfere with the parking function. Care should be taken to use shrub, plant, and tree types that can withstand auto fumes and the concentrated heat arising from a large, paved surface. Landscaping can be an effective means in controlling pedestrian paths. Planting of hedges can serve to funnel pedestrians into desired walk patterns within the site.

Sufficient setback must be provided for all plants so that the front and rear overhang of cars does not destroy them. Extreme care should be exercised in locating shrubbery or other plants near entrances and exits so that sight distances are not restricted. This will require that the growth pattern of the plant be considered so that the small plant of today will not develop into a major sight restriction in future years.

Lighting. Adequate lighting of the parking site is very important. Mounting height and spacing of luminaires should be sufficient to distribute the desired lighting intensity to the entire facility. A normal lighting level is 1.0 to 2.0 footcandles with a uniformity ratio (average illumination divided by the lowest level) not more than 6:1.[1] The luminaire units should be placed so as not to obstruct vehicle movement and parking. Where raised islands are used to separate adjacent parking stalls, the poles can logically be placed on the island. In any event, they should be placed between adjacent stalls and at the ends of the parking rows. Care should be taken to prevent excessive light spillover into adjacent residential areas.

Parking dimensions and layout. The long-term trend in U.S. automobile designs had been toward longer and wider vehicles. This trend was reversed in the 1970's. In the 1978 model year, cars range up to 19.4 ft (5.8 m) in length and 6.66 ft (2.03 m) in width. However, increasing costs of fuel and vehicles has seen the U.S. fleet size growing smaller. Many cars now being manufactured are in the range 14.5 to 16.3 ft (4.4 to 5.0 m) in length and 5.4 to 6.2 ft (1.7 to 1.9 m) in width. Observations indicate that fleet dimensions vary in different parts of the United States. In California, as many as 40% of the vehicles are considered of compact size, whereas in some southern states and in Canada as few as 5% are compacts. It is estimated that as long as 15 years may pass before there is any significant change in fleet size in some parts of the United States.

Typical parking dimensions vary with the angle at which the stall is arranged relative to the aisle (see Table 21-2). Stall widths (measured perpendicular to the vehicle when parked) range from 8.5 to 9.5 ft (2.6 to 2.9 m). In attendant parking facilities, attendants can park standard-size cars in spaces as narrow as 8.0 ft (2.4 m). However, the minimum stall size recommended is 8.5 ft (2.6 m) for self-parking of long-term duration. For higher-turnover self-parking, a stall width of 9.0 ft (2.7 m) is recommended. Stall widths at supermarkets and other similar parking facilities, where large packages are prevalent, should desirably be 9.5 or even 10.0 ft (2.9 to 3.1 m) in width.

Substandard stall and aisle widths prove to be a false economy. Although this permits the marking of more stalls per given length, vehicles tend to encroach upon adjacent stalls so that one or more spaces are unavailable for use. The end result is no gain in actual space usage, but a parking condition surrounded by confusion.

Table 21-2 is based on a stall length of 18.5 ft (5.6 m). The stall length should be sufficient to accommodate the length of most cars expecting to use the space. However, many of the "luxury" U.S. cars exceeded 18.5 ft (5.6 m) in 1978.

Aisle width is a function of the parking angle and stall width. One-way aisles are generally used with angle parking, whereas two-way circulation is generally used with 90° parking.

In designing parking facilities, a common unit of measure is the parking module. A module consists of the width of the aisle, plus the depth of the parking stalls (measured perpendicular to the aisle) on each side of the aisle. In many instances, parking modules are completely separated from each other. Such modules are represented by the wall-to-wall dimensions shown in Table 21-2. Another type of module available for angle parking is the interlocking module. The most common, and preferred, interlocking module is the one that places the bumpers of vehicles in adjacent stalls next to one another. This layout is illustrated in Figure 21.1, together with parking dimensions for various angles of parking. At 45°, a nested interlock is possible where adjacent aisles have one-way movement in the same direction. This places the bumper of one car adjacent to the front fender of another car and is not recommended, as the likelihood of damaged fenders is much greater than with other parking layouts.

TABLE 21–2
Typical Parking Dimensions* (ft)

	Stall Width Parallel to Aisle	Stall Depth to Wall	Stall Depth to Interlock	Aisle† Width	Modules‡ Wall to Wall	Interlock to Interlock
45 deg						
8.5 stall	12.0	19.5	16.5	13	52	46
9.0 stall	12.7	19.5	16.5	12	51	45
9.5 stall	13.4	19.5	16.5	11	50	44
60 deg						
8.5 stall	9.8	20.5	18.5	18	59	55
9.0 stall	10.4	20.5	18.5	16	57	53
9.5 stall	11.0	20.5	18.5	15	56	52
75 deg						
8.5 stall	8.3	20.0	19.0	25	65	63
9.0 stall	9.3	20.0	19.0	23	63	61
9.5 stall	9.8	20.0	19.0	22	62	60
90 deg§						
8.5 stall	8.5	18.5	18.5	28	65	65
9.0 stall	9.0	18.5	18.5	26	63	63
9.5 stall	9.5	18.5	18.5	25	62	62

*These dimensions are for 18.5-ft-length stalls, measured parallel to the vehicle, and are based on results of a special study to evaluate the effects of varied aisle and stall width for the different parking angles shown. The study was conducted in December 1970 by the Federal Highway Administration and Paul C. Box and Associates. Conversion factor: 1 ft = 0.305 m.

†Measured between ends of stall lines.

‡Rounded to nearest foot.

§For back-in parking, aisle width may be reduced 4.0 ft.

SOURCE: *Parking Principles*, Special Report No. 125, Highway Research Board, Washington, D.C., 1971, p. 101.

[1]*Parking Principles*, Special Report No. 125, Highway Research Board, Washington, D.C., 1971, p. 107.

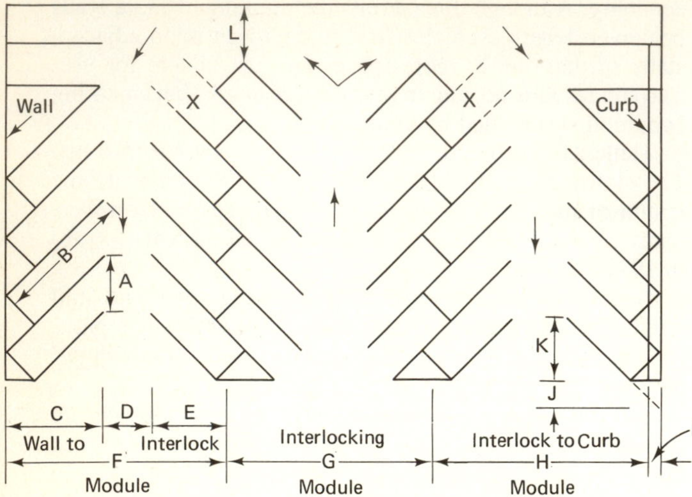

X = Stall not accessible in certain layouts

Parking layout dimension (in ft) for 9 ft X 18.5 ft stalls at various angles

Dimension	On diagram	Angle 45°	60°	75°	90°
Stall width, parallel to aisle	A	12.7	10.4	9.3	9.0
Stall length of line	B	27.5	23.7	20.9	18.5
Stall depth to wall	C	19.5	20.5	20.0	18.5
Aisle width between stall lines	D	12.0	16.0	23.0	26.0
Stall depth, interlock	E	16.5	18.5	18.5	18.5
Module, wall to interlock	F	48.0	55.0	62.0	63.0
Module, interlocking	G	45.0	53.0	61.0	63.0
Module, interlock to curb face	H	46.0	53.2	59.5	60.5
Bumper overhang (typical)	I	2.0	2.3	2.5	2.5
Offset	J	6.4	2.6	0.6	0.0
Setback	K	13.1	9.3	4.8	0.0
Cross aisle, one-way	L	14.0	14.0	14.0	14.0
Cross aisle, two-way	–	24.0	24.0	24.0	24.0

Figure 21.1. Stall layout elements. SOURCE: Based on *Parking Principles*, Special Report No. 125, Highway Research Board, Washington, D.C., 1971, p. 99.

Recommended parking dimensions for imported cars—15 ft (4.6 m) in length—differ from recommendations for standard U.S. cars (see Table 21-3). Table 21-4 summarizes European parking dimension standards. Stall lengths and widths are recommended at 15 ft (4.6 m) and 7.5 ft (2.3 m), respectively. If a number of these smaller-size spaces are to be included in a facility, they should be placed together in a prime location to encourage their use. If these spaces are not convenient, small-car drivers will park elsewhere in standard-size spaces. Because of difficulties in predicting the amount of usage and in controlling the spaces, most U.S. parking facilities are being designed with all spaces of sufficient size for standard American cars. However, on the west coast of the United States, many facilities are being designed to accommodate a percentage of compact cars.

In the actual layout of the parking stalls and circulation aisles, it is always desirable to have a row of parking on each side of the aisle. This gives the most efficient design. In addition, the greatest efficiency can generally be obtained by placing aisles and rows of parking parallel to the long dimension of the site. Greatest parking efficiency can usually be aided by placing a row of parking completely around the perimeter of the site. With adequate site dimensions, this places parking stalls on both sides of the aisle, including end aisles.

When pedestrian walks are used in parking facilities, they should direct pedestrians toward the major parking generators. Raised sidewalks can be used in larger facilities between rows of cars to aid pedestrian flow. However, many pedestrians will still use the aisles and the need for raised pedestrian walks is debatable.

Relative efficiency factors. Relative efficiency factors can be calculated for various parking angles and stall widths (see Table 21-5). The figures represent the number of square feet per stall plus one-half of the aisle width for a distance equal to the stall width measured parallel to the aisle. Those dimensions were obtained from Table 21-2. Stalls arranged at 90° to the aisles provide the most efficient design, and the efficiency decreases as the parking angle decreases.

TABLE 21–3
Parking Dimensions for Import-Size Vehicles (15-ft Length)*

Parking Angle (deg)	Stall Width	Aisle Length/Stall	Depth of Stalls at Right Angle to Aisle	Aisle Width	Wall-to-Wall Module
45	7.5	10.5	16.0	11.0	43.0
60	7.5	8.7	16.7	14.0	47.4
75	7.5	7.8	16.3	17.4	50.0
90	7.5	7.5	15.0	20.0	50.0

1 ft. = 0.305m

*These measurements are *inadequate* for average American compacts. Each stall depth should be increased about 1 ft (2 ft total for the module) to accommodate the usual range of compact sizes.

SOURCE: *Parking Principles*, Special Report No. 125, Highway Research Board, Washington, D.C., 1971, p. 102.

TABLE 21–4
Parking Standards, Europe

	Stall Width [ft-in. (m)]		Stall Length [ft-in. (m)]	Aisle Width [ft-in. (m)]	Bay Width [ft-in. (m)]
General	7-10 to 8-2 (2.4–2.5)		15-7 to 16-5 (4.75–5.0)	18 to 19-6 (5.5–6.0)	50-10 to 52-6 (15.5–16.0)
Belgium	7-10 to 8-2 (2.4–2.5)		16-5 (5.0)		52-6 (16.0) (90°) 50-10 (15.0) (60°)
Paris	7-10 (2.4)	(90°)	16-5 (5.0)		
	7-6 (2.3)	(45°)	16-5 (5.0)		
	7-3 (2.2)	(30°)	16-5 (5.0)		
U.K.	7-10 to 8-2 (2.4–2.5)		15-7 to 16-5 (4.75–5.0)		50-10 to 52-6 (15.5–16.0)
Madrid	7-10 (2.4)		16-5 (5.0)		50-10 (15.5)
	7-3 (2.2)*		13-1 (4.0)*		
Barcelona	7-10 (2.4)		15-7 (4.75)		50-10 (15.5)
Germany	7-6 to 7-10 (2.3–2.4)		16-5 to 18-1 (5.0–5.5)		

*25% spaces, for Spanish subcompacts, may be this size.

SOURCE: JOHN GLANVILLE, *Provision, Location and Design of Parking Facilities in Europe*, International Road Federation, Washington, D.C. 1970; OTTO SILL, *The Construction of Parking Facilities*, Bauverlag GMBH, Wiesbaden-Berlin, 1968.

TABLE 21–5
Relative Efficiency Factors*

Parking Angle (deg)	Width of Stall (ft)		
	8.5	9.0	9.5
45	308	324	340
60	288	296	310
75	286	295	308
90	276	284	295

*Square feet per stall area plus one-half aisle area; does not include end aisle circulation areas or unusable area at ends of parallel parking rows.

SOURCE: Based on data included in Table 21–2.

Handicapped parking. Most jurisdictions require that a certain number of parking spaces be set aside for parking for the handicapped. Most requirements are that approximately 4% of the total number of spaces within a facility be set aside for handicapped, with a maximum of 9 or 10 in the entire facility regardless of size. In small facilities of 25 spaces or less, the number required is approximately one for each such facility.

The handicapped stall layout is shown in Figure 21.2. In addition to the stall layout, the spaces should be marked with a sign at the face of the stall. Stencilling or painting of the handicap symbol on the pavement is not recommended since it is difficult to see while driving and can be obscured by snow and other obstructions. In general, the handicap spaces should be located immediately adjacent to the exit of the lot or garage.

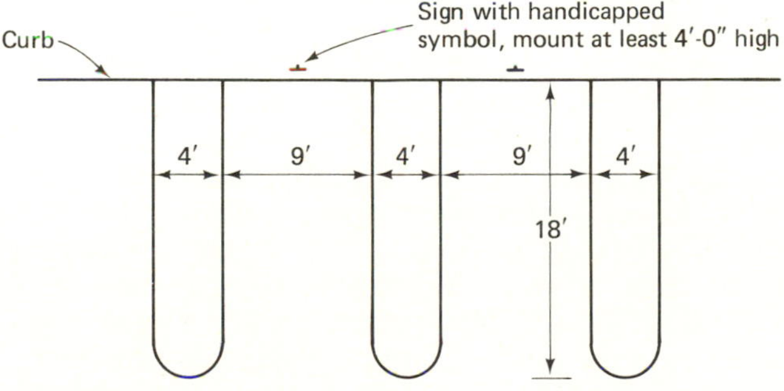

Figure 21.2. Handicapped parking stall dimensions. SOURCE: James Madison Hunnicutt & Associates.

Drainage. Adequate slope should be provided to surface lots to minimize the possibility of low or flat spots. The ponding of water in a lot is undesirable for both vehicle and pedestrian movement. This is particularly true in cold climates, where freezing may lead to icy spots. Recommended minimum grades are 1.0% for asphalt surfaces and 0.5% for portland cement concrete surfaces.[2]

Surface vs. structure parking. Development costs at 1979 prices for surface parking lots normally are $2 to $3 per square foot exclusive of land, with an average figure approximating $2.50 per square foot. This includes all improvement costs, such as grading, paving, lighting, drainage, signing, and marking. Land cost is often the factor that determines economic viability of surface parking. As land costs increase, it often becomes economically justified to expand parking vertically in a parking structure, rather than expanding horizontally by the acquisition of additional land for surface parking.

Parking garage construction costs at 1979 prices vary from approximately $3000 per car space to as high as $6000, with an average being approximately $4000 to $4500. These are construction costs without land, and the variation is caused by topography, expensive vs. economical architectural treatment, sophistication of revenue control devices, foundations, and other factors. If land costs are not included, the cost of a parking structure is approximately four times the cost of an equivalent parking space in a surface lot. On the other hand, if the land cost is included, the figures can change rapidly.

As an example, a 340-ft^2 per car lot would cost $850 per car space for grading, paving, and lighting. If land is calculated at $15 per square foot, this adds $5100 per car space for a $5950 total cost. On the other hand, if a five-level garage is constructed and the land cost is prorated over the five floors, the same amount of land costs would only be $1020 per car space. When added to the $4000 per car space in construction costs, the total cost for a parking garage space would be slightly above $5000, and it would be less expensive per car space to build a parking garage than a surface lot.

Many other factors must be considered in making the decision between surface and structured parking. In the case of private developers, these include demand characteristics, taxes, and financing. The primary considerations for all parking must be the walking distance of the patrons, maintenance, security, operation, and the availability of land and traffic access.

Garage design

Site characteristics. Many of the factors that affect the location and design of surface lots also affect the design of parking garages. Site characteristics such as size, shape, and topography are important factors in garage design. The topography of a site may allow direct entry to more than one level of the garage. This will affect entry and exit locations as well as the interfloor travel system within the structure.

Access points. The location of entry and exit points is even more critical in garage design than in surface lot design, because of the increased number of spaces available in structured parking. Street capacities, location of traffic controls, and other external factors must be carefully analyzed to assure a design that is compatible with the surrounding street system.

Major use of the facility. As in surface lots, the dominant type of use, whether by short-term or long-term parkers, or whether the facility will serve special events, will influence the design. Where vehicles enter and exit in short

[2]*Parking Principles*, Special Report No. 125, Highway Research Board, Washington, D.C., 1971, p. 107.

spans of time, consideration should be given to express ramps, particularly for exiting. The "dump time" of the facility, or time required to empty the facility when filled to capacity, is an important factor. This time should be kept to a minimum, and 30 to 45 min is generally considered acceptable for most facilities. A lesser time for emptying the facility is desirable for special-event usage, such as sporting events or concerts. In some instances, exiting from parking facilities is constrained by external roadway conditions so that the desired "dump time" cannot be achieved.

Interfloor travel systems. The type of interfloor travel system may be either ramps or sloping floors, or various combinations. Only on a sloping site which permits direct access to each level are ramps unnecessary, but they may be desirable for internal circulation. With sloping floor designs, the floors serve both as aisles and parking bays (see Figure 21.3). The sloping floor section is generally one or more parking modules in width. With other designs, the ramps are used exclusively for travel between floors. Combinations of the various ramps are possible. An express exit ramp may be incorporated into a sloping floor design. This ramp may be a straight ramp along the side of the structure, or a helical ramp. Other types of ramps are used in addition to those shown in Figure 21.3.

An additional helical ramp variation is the double helix. This design consists of two independent interwoven ramps which drop two levels in one complete 360° turn. One ramp then serves the odd-number floors while the other serves the even-numbered floors. This design is useful for tall structures, as it reduces the number of turns required in exiting from or entering the upper floors. It is desirable to keep the number of full turns to a maximum of five for self-parking facilities. With this criterion as a guide, 10 to 12 levels are possible with a double-helical ramp system. A single-helix ramp, however, should be limited to about six levels. For ramped or sloping floor designs, the number of levels should be limited to a maximum of six, because of the amount of turning required and the number of spaces a driver must pass. However, with express ramps, this may be increased.

Another factor for consideration in determining the number of floors is the relative height of adjacent buildings. Many drivers develop a feeling of acrophobia in taller garages, particularly when they are driving at a level above the rooftops of adjacent buildings. Proper design of the parapet walls will reduce this effect by limiting the driver's view of surroundings while seated in the automobile.

The layout of parking aisles and stalls for garages is similar to that used for surface lots. Stall and aisle dimensions remain the same.

Ramp grades and dimensions affect the ease of circulation within the structure. Sloping floor grades should not exceed 4 to 5%. The parking angle on these sloping floors should be at least 60° to minimize the possibility of vehicles rolling out of the parking space and down the ramp. For 90° parking, sloping floor grades should not exceed 5%. Ramps without parking should be limited to about 10 to 12%, with grades up to 15 or 20% allowable in attendant parking structures. Driving ramps should be 14 to 18 ft (4.3 to 5.5 m) wide with 12 ft (3.7 m) sufficient for longer straight runs. A helical ramp should have a minimum outside radius of 32 ft (9.8 m), with a desirable radius of 35 to 37 ft (10.7 to 11.3 m).

Self-parking ramp capacities normally range between 500 and 600 cars per hour per lane. Typical capacity used for design purposes is often 400 cars per hour per lane. The exiting capacity is reduced greatly to 150 to 200 cars per hour per lane when vehicles must stop at a cashier's booth on exiting.

Vertical clearance should approximate 7 ft (2.13 m), which normally results in floor to floor heights of about 10 ft (3.05 m).

Structural systems. There are normally four types of structural systems that should be investigated for any garage. They are structural steel, poured-in-place concrete, precast concrete, and post-tensioned concrete. Many factors should be considered in analyzing the various structural systems as they affect the relative economy and adaptability of the systems. A partial listing of factors includes:

1. Building code requirements
2. Maintenance
3. Availability of materials and precast concrete fabricators
4. Shipping distance and costs
5. Availability of contractors experienced in each structural system
6. Environmental and atmospheric conditions

Building codes may affect the structural system because of code restrictions on type of structural system allowed. Other building codes do not allow exposed steel design or may require fireproofing of the external columns only. Fireproofing of steel columns, beams, and girders can add greatly to the cost of this type of construction.

Certain materials may not be readily available in particular areas, and freight costs can be prohibitive. The lack of availability of good-quality precast concrete fabricators in some areas precludes this structural system. The post-tensioning of floor slabs of precast concrete structures requires contractors with personnel experienced in this work.

The relative maintenance costs of the various structural systems must be considered. Exposed steel requires periodic painting, and care must be taken to specify a sufficient number of shop and field coats of quality paint to retard deterioration of the steel. Atmospheric and environmental conditions can greatly influence the amount of maintenance required, particularly in heavy industrial areas and areas near bodies of salt water. Weathering steels that develop a hard coat of rust do not require painting, but do cause difficult maintenance problems for a period of about 3 years until they develop their hard coating.

Precast structural systems can be advantageous where many structural members are duplicated throughout the structure. Once the forms are available, a great number of members can be cast quickly and economically. This advantage is lost when many different sizes of columns, beams, and girders are required, such as in a garage on an odd-shaped site.

Erection time at the site is also favorable for precast or steel structural systems. The construction of forms for

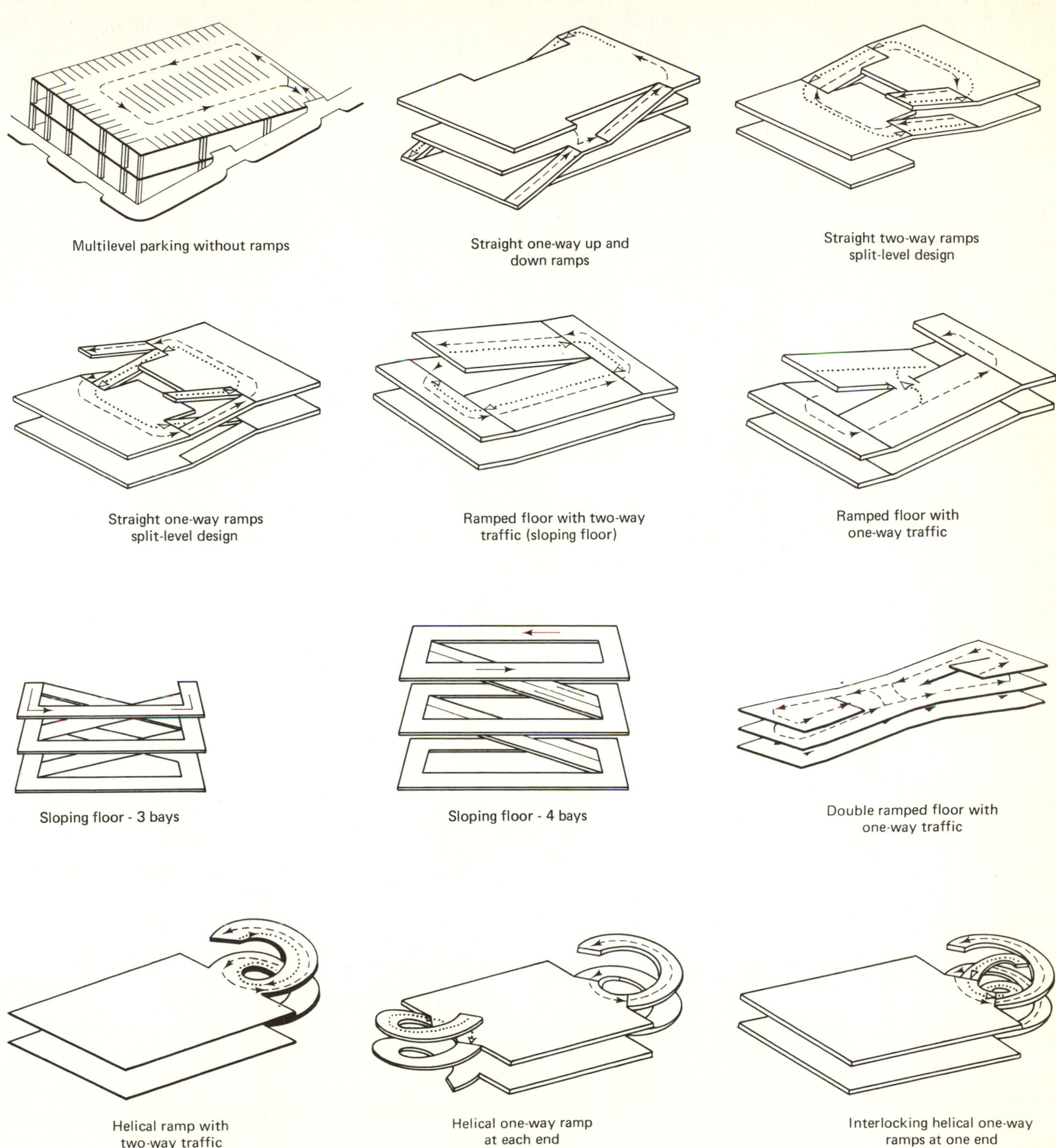

Figure 21.3. Illustration of ramp systems. SOURCE: D. Klose, *Metropolitan Parking Structures,* Praeger, New York, 1965, pp. 30–31; R.F. Roti, *Square Foot Cost Averaging Principle for Parking Structures,* National Parking Association, Washington, D.C., pp. 7–9.

poured-in-place concrete requires time not needed for the other systems. However, experience has shown that when time required to fabricate and ship the precast or steel members is considered, the total construction time from awarding of contract to occupancy of the building is practically the same for all structural systems.

It is not possible to say that one structural system is best or most economical in all locations and under all conditions.

A value engineering analysis of each system should be made for each facility considering all the influencing factors, and only then should a decision be made on the structural system.

Short- vs. long-span construction. Functional and operational considerations generally dictate that long- or clear-span construction be provided in most garages. There are certainly many advantages to this type of construction, particularly in a free-standing garage. However, when an additional structure (office, apartments, or other use) is planned above the parking garage, short-span construction may be advantageous. Long-span construction usually costs about 5 to 10% more than short-span, but this increase is offset by more parking spaces and better circulation. A comparison of short- and long-span construction is shown in Figure 21.4.

A list of advantages of long- or clear-span construction in free-standing garages includes the following:

1. Column-free floors
2. Fewer columns and foundations
3. More parking space
4. Maximum operational efficiency and flexibility

Figure 21.4. Comparison of short-and-long-span construction. SOURCE: Richard C. Rich, *Methods of Construction and Construction Costs,* National Parking Association, Washington, D.C., 1966, pp. 2, 4.

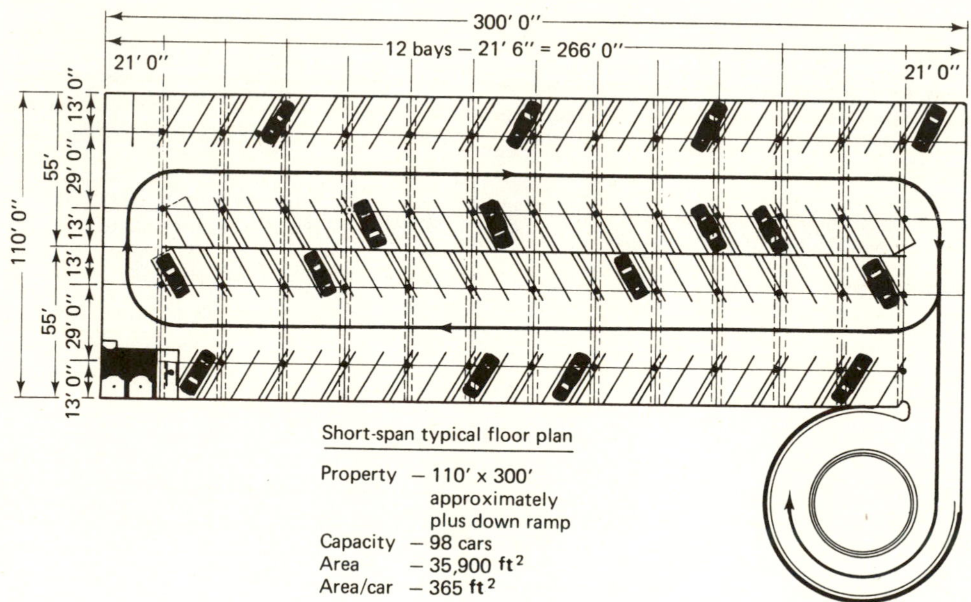

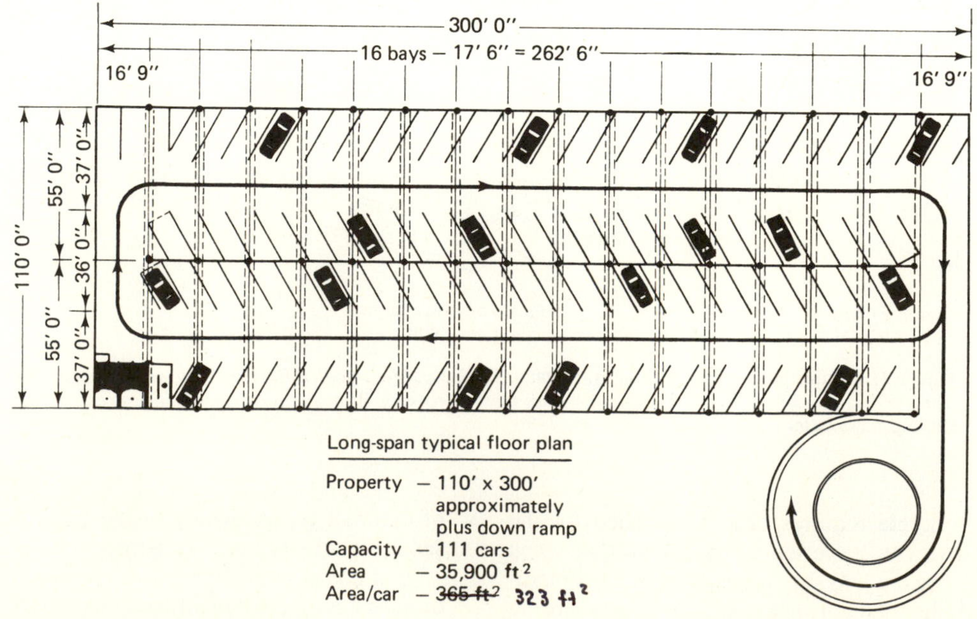

5. Faster and easier parking and unparking maneuvers
6. Maximum flexibility to change stall sizes or parking angle
7. Easy floor maintenance
8. Unrestricted sight distance
9. Fewer damaged cars
10. Greater driver acceptance
11. Minimum problem in locating ventilation and lighting equipment

Disadvantages of long spans include:

1. Deeper floor construction
2. Greater floor-to-floor heights
3. Higher construction costs

Lighting and electrical systems. Lighting within the garage is necessary to aid safety of movement and to discourage vandalism or acts of violence. Table 21-6 presents minimum and desirable lighting for garages. A high light level is needed at the entrance as a driver proceeds from bright sunshine into the garage.

TABLE 21–6
Garage Lighting Standards

	Light Intensity			
	Minimum		Desirable	
Area	Footcandles	Lux	Footcandles	Lux
Entrance	50–80	540–860	80–100	860–1080
Driving aisles	8–10	85–110	10–15	110–160
Over parked vehicles	3–5	30–55	5–10	55–110

SOURCE: Hunnicutt & Associates, Inc.

It is desirable to have a central control panel from which all electrical and mechanical fixtures can be actuated. This control panel should be located in the manager's office, to allow a person to turn on the lights on any level without physically going up to that level to do so. In addition, to facilitate operating economies, light circuits should be designed to allow a portion of the lights in a given area to be turned on and off independently of the remaining lights. Ambient weather conditions affect the light output of different luminaires. Incandescent, fluorescent, mercury vapor, and high-pressure sodium vapor should be evaluated with regard to light, energy cost, fixture cost, and maintenance (see Chapter 20). Electrical energy charges can be reduced by thoroughly evaluating the lighting circuits to make sure that at all times during the day only necessary lights are in use. Photoelectric cells, astronomical clocks, and other power-saving factors can save electrical energy.

Interior garage signing. In signing a parking garage, it should be remembered that a parking facility is merely an extension of the street system. Directional and informational signs are generally needed and should conform as closely as possible to standard street signs. Many signs in garages can be painted on walls or other areas that have good target value. The use of illuminated signs may be justified in some instances, but these are expensive. Well-placed, nonilluminated signs are often sufficient. Signs in a garage should direct motorists to parking spaces and exits, and should inform the driver of such traffic conditions as one-way aisles and ramps. In addition, signs should direct the pedestrian to exits, stairs, and elevators.

It is difficult to determine a signing plan for a garage from a set of construction plans. It is recommended that the signing be postponed until the garage is nearly completed. The recommended approach, when possible, is to drive into the nearly completed garage in an auto and determine sign locations from the vehicle. This gives the proper perspective to the sign location with regard to sight lines, locations of parked cars, and sight obstructions such as beams and columns.

Drainage and waterproofing. Many knowledgeable persons in garage design and operation consider water leakage through the floor slab to be the main unsolved long-term maintenance problem of parking structures. This leakage does not appear to be a problem during the early life of the garage. The water, mixed with salts in colder climates, seeps down through hairline cracks and attacks the reinforcing bars. These bars rust and expand, resulting in scaling of the concrete. Over a period of years, this action can cause structural damage. Without proper maintenance, a garage can be at the point of structural failure within 10 to 15 years as a result of water leakage.

The best waterproofing system is one that gets the water off the floor and into the drains quickly. This is particularly necessary for the roof level. The riser system capacity should be designed adequately to accept a 10-year design rainfall. The floor of the garage should be sloped toward the drains with a minimum slope of 2%. The minimum spacing of floor drains should be 60 ft (18.3 m) center to center.

There are numerous types of waterproofing systems. One common system consists of a mastic asphaltic material placed over the floor slab to a thickness of about 1/16 in. (1.6 mm). This material seeps and permeates down into the floor slab and forms an elastic, rubbery type of surface that seals small cracks. A wearing surface of 1/2 to 1 in. (1.3 to 2.5 cm) of asphaltic concrete is then placed.

A second waterproofing system consists of a plastic material that is usually sprayed onto the floor slab and seeps into the slab. For a wearing surface, a strong tough rubberized plastic is then sprayed on the deck in several layers and built up to a thickness of 0.15 to 0.20 in. (0.38 to 0.51 cm). Flint chips or small gravel are often embedded in the wearing surface to aid traction.

A third waterproofing system is a membrane surface of sheet rubber, placed over a concrete slab. A second slab is then poured over the membrane. However, some of these membranes begin to disintegrate after about 10 years. Also, it is nearly impossible to locate or repair a rupture in the membrane because of its position between the two slabs of concrete.

Other types of waterproofing compounds are generally spray-on plastic types; they have some waterproofing qualities but are of no value in preventing leakage when a hairline crack opens.

Traffic and revenue control systems. In a large garage where large amounts of money are being handled, a revenue control system of some type is a necessity. This is particularly true for parking facilities at airports, convention centers, and at major CBD locations. A revenue control system is designed to keep track of all entering and exiting vehicles and a record of tickets, cashiers on duty, and the amount of money handled. The system provides the information needed to check for revenue losses and thefts.

Six basic elements of a revenue control system are needed to keep an accurate record of parking activity and revenues:[3]

1. There must be an extremely accurate count of all entering and exiting vehicles.
2. No one must be allowed to enter the parking area without taking a ticket or exit without leaving a ticket.
3. All clocks within the system must be operated accurately and in conjunction with each other and must be designed so that cashiers cannot reset them.
4. There must be some type of validating device or cash register—not a time stamp—to record the outbound transactions. The tickets must be stamped with the appropriate information so that individual cashiers may be held responsible for their actions.
5. The ticket-issuing machines and entry lanes must be operated in such a way that it is not possible for anyone to get more than one ticket from the machine. Future supplies of tickets also must be kept in a safe place.
6. Parking gates or other devices must be used to prevent cars entering through an exit or leaving through an entrance lane.

Safety and surveillance equipment. Any large garage is a potential source of problems from loitering, vandalism, thefts, and crimes against persons. Garages can become havens for drunks and derelicts. Within the garage, most crimes occur in the elevators and stairwells. For this reason, these areas should be well lighted and should be capable of being closed off at night. In addition, glass-enclosed stairwells should be used in lieu of masonry whenever possible. Glass-enclosed stairwells may conflict with fire codes but many cities have granted variances when the unique problems involved are explained to building officials and fire marshals.

In garages that do not remain open 24 h a day, there should be positive ways of closing off the garage, such as roll-down doors at entry–exit points. In addition, the garage architecture should be such that large openings around the building do not exist which would give access to the structure at other than designated points.

Sound and television monitoring systems are the two types of internal surveillance systems found in garages. The sound system monitors all sounds in the garage and in all elevators and stairwells. A speaker in the manager's office or cashier's booth allows the monitoring of all sounds and the detection of suspected trouble areas.

Television monitoring is by the use of television cameras placed throughout the garage. This system is not widely used because of the necessity of having someone continually looking at monitors and because the light intensity in the garage is often insufficient to provide a good picture contrast on the monitors. Since it is difficult to cover a large area with cameras, and cameras can be made inoperative by vandals, regular security patrols are often used within garages to discourage vandalism and acts of violence.

Self vs. attendant parking. Because of the labor cost and the difficulty of keeping low-cost workers for attendants, most parking is now operated as self-parking. When given the choice, parkers almost invariably prefer to park their own car. Reasons for this include:

1. Parkers take better care of their car than does the average attendant.
2. Self-parkers can lock their car and take their keys with them.
3. Self-parkers avoid the long delay often associated with attendant retrieval of cars.

However, under normal conditions, self-parking results in 10 to 15% fewer parking spaces for the same area as compared to attendant parking.

Attendant parking may be justified as a convenience service and is popular at restaurants and hotels. It may also be justified in the downtown areas of major cities, where rates and parking demand are very high. The additional capacity available by attendant parking and by double and triple stacking of cars may produce sufficient additional revenue to offset the higher cost of attendant parking. Labor costs for attendants may add as much as 40% to the parking cost.

Central vs. exit cashiering. In central cashiering, parkers return to a central location in the garage, pay their parking fee and receive a receipt, proceed to their car, and on exiting the facility, hand the receipt to an attendant. In Europe, there are systems in use which handle central cashiering automatically (without manual exit control). In exit cashiering, parkers return directly to their cars and drive to the exit, at which point they stop and pay their parking fee. In addition, under special conditions, such as at sporting events, precashiering may be used. Under this system, the parker generally pays a flat fee on entering the facility and can exit without stopping.

All alternatives should be considered before selecting a cashiering method. The design and use of the facility can influence the choice. For example, in a garage serving a department store or similar use, where parkers use a common path in returning to the garage, central cashiering may be a good choice. Exit time is also reduced when central cashiering is employed. With central cashiering, where a receipt only is picked up on exiting, vehicles can exit at a rate of one vehicle every 6 to 10 s per exit lane. With exit cashiering, the rate would be approximately one vehicle every 20 s per lane. Central cashiering then increases exit lane capacity by a factor of 2 or 3.

Aesthetics. A parking garage does not need to be an ugly structure, although some simply give the appearance

[3] J. M. Hunnicutt, "Safeguarding Your Parking Revenues," 1970 Annual Conference, American Association of Airport Executives, Las Vegas, NV., May 1971, p. 52.

of a concrete slab sitting up in the air. Some thought should be given to making the garage an attractive building. This function normally falls to the architect, and the building is only as aesthetically pleasing as the architect's ingenuity makes it.

The exterior of the building can be improved by the use of such exterior sidings as aluminum, anodized aluminum in colors, vertical fins, and precast concrete. Judicious use of lighting and landscaping are also helpful.

Within the garage, columns, beams, and girders as well as concrete masonry units or cinder block walls can be painted. A form of color coding is possible by painting each floor a different color. Parkers can then remember the floor on which they parked by its color.

By their nature, garages lend themselves to bright colors. This brightens the interior of the garage. The parker does not remain in the garage for any length of time, so bland colors normally found in living and working areas are not necessary.

Fire protection. Many building codes require an inordinate amount of fire protection in garages. These requirements are based on old approaches to fire fighting which were generally incorporated into building codes many years ago. Tests of auto fires have proven the futility of trying to ignite an adjacent auto when parked beside a burning car.

The combustible materials in a car consist of the gasoline, upholstery, and paint. The fire loading in a garage, or the number of Btu of combustible material per square foot of floor area, is extremely low compared to office buildings, apartments, and private houses. In underground garages, most building codes require sprinkler systems. Auto fires generally consist of smouldering upholstery, electrical fires under the hood, or the remote chance of a gasoline fire. Because the sprinkling of water or foam on the car is of little or no help, many cities now give variances to eliminate sprinklers.

Other fire-detection equipment includes rise-of-heat indicators mounted in the ceiling of the garage. These indicators monitor temperatures in an area and are usually designed to sound an alarm when the temperature in an area rises 15 degrees in 1 min.

Placing large numbers of fire extinguishers in a garage has proven to be useless because of thefts. In lieu of small sprinklers, large extinguisher systems can be placed on dollies and situated at central locations in the garage. Too large to be easily stolen, they can easily be rolled to the source of any fire.

Single-purpose vs. multiuse garages. A single-purpose garage is a free-standing structure for parking vehicles with little or no area devoted to other uses. A multiuse garage is one in which the garage is a part of an overall complex consisting of more than one land use. In urban areas, there is a trend toward multipurpose garages because of the need to utilize land more effectively. Scarcity of land and its high cost often make a single-purpose garage impractical and financially unfeasible.

A parking garage may be included with many types of land uses. They are often found in conjunction with office buildings, apartment complexes, and retail developments. The parking may be provided either above or below the other land uses. On university campuses, roofs of parking structures are often used for athletic facilities—tennis courts are often located there.

Mechanical or elevator garages. In mechanical or elevator garages the vehicle does not move to the parking space under its own power, but rather is moved there mechanically. There are many types of mechanical garages in existence, but their use worldwide has been declining in recent years. This is primarily due to maintenance problems associated with the mechanical equipment. In the average mechanical garage, the equipment has tended to wear out in about 7 years—long before the garage has paid for itself. In addition, equipment failure can shut down the entire garage or a portion of it, creating bad customer relations as cars are stranded.

An additional problem with mechanical garages is their inability to accept surges of inbound or outbound traffic. Limited inbound capacity requires a large reservoir area to keep the cars off the streets. Low discharge capacity often creates customer irritation as they wait long periods of time for the return of their car. Mechanical garages generally provide satisfactory service only when the parking demand is relatively uniform throughout the day with no large peak flows. They have proven a useful tool in CBD areas when serving a motel or hotel.

Underground garages. The principal difference between aboveground garages and those placed underground is the construction cost. An underground garage will usually cost 1.5 to 2 times more than an equivalent aboveground garage per car space. This cost differential is due to concrete retaining walls, more substantial lighting system, the additional costs of air circulation and exhaust systems, and the roof slab, which is not used for parking but often must support heavy landscaping.

The presence of a high water table may require increased size and depth of foundation to offset the effect of hydrostatic pressure. These factors generally tend to restrict the number of levels to three or four in an underground garage. Increasing construction costs and potential buildup of fumes and the problem of exhausting them generally argues against providing more levels.

A major problem with underground garages is water seepage through the walls or through the floor joints because of hydrostatic pressure. In addition, leakage through the roof may become a problem if the garage is located under a park.

Design and operating characteristics of underground garages do not differ from aboveground garages. However, additional emphasis should be placed on directional signing and markings because of the lack of orientation underground. It is important to keep the driver and pedestrian oriented as to streets and major land uses.

Garage construction costs. Many factors affect the total cost of a parking garage. However, a conventional ramp aboveground garage can usually be built for $10 to $15 per square foot or $3000 to $5000 per car space. (Surface lots

TABLE 21-7
Typical Garage Costs

Type of Cost	% of Total
Structural (foundations and superstructure)	65–70
Mechanical (elevators and water drainage)	10–15
Electrical (lighting and revenue control equipment)	10–15
Architectural (facade and landscaping)	5–10

SOURCE: Hunnicutt & Associates, Inc.

normally cost $2 to $3 per square foot for all improvements.) All costs are based on 1979 data.

Such factors as type of elevator used (hydraulic vs. electric), extent of building facade, complexity of revenue control equipment, and requirement for fireproofing and water sprinklers can greatly alter the cost of a parking garage.

Parking garages are relatively simple structures with little finished space and no need for heating and air conditioning. The primary cost of a garage is structural. Costs for a typical four- to six-level aboveground garage are listed in Table 21-7.

Underground garage construction will cost from $5000 to more than $7000 per car space. Mechanical garages can be expected to cost $4000 to $5000 per space.

Special-purpose and special-event parking

Sports stadiums, convention centers, auditoriums, and exhibit halls

The parking needs at sports stadiums, convention centers, and other similar activities are dependent on many factors. The parking needs for such a facility in a CBD will be less than for a suburban location for the same facility because of better public transportation and the ability to use existing parking facilities to meet a portion of the demand. Early analyses should be made of the special-purpose facility to determine the number and type of events expected. Peak and average crowds should be estimated from which a design crowd can be determined. Crowds for different events exhibit different characteristics. For example, car occupancy for baseball games may average 2.5 persons per car, whereas for football games it may be somewhat greater, at about 3.5 persons per car. Also, studies have shown that the football fan will walk farther than will the baseball fan. It is therefore necessary to analyze the parking characteristics of each type of event when designing the parking for the facility.

The Riverfront Stadium in Cincinnati, Ohio, is somewhat typical of downtown sports stadiums. In conjunction with the construction of the stadium, a three-level parking garage and adjacent surface lots were constructed totaling 4800 spaces. However, because of its location adjacent to downtown Cincinnati, nearly 15,000 additional parking spaces are available within 2000 ft of the stadium. A study of the mode of travel to a professional football game at this stadium in 1976 found that 85.3% of the spectators arrived by automobile, 12.3% by bus, and 2.4% by other means.[4] Car-occupancy studies indicated an average of 3.25 persons per car (see Table 21-8).

Major multi-purpose public auditoriums are also heavy traffic generators. Table 21-9 shows that many may seat well over 10,000 patrons, and require large numbers of parking spaces. For the ten auditoriums illustrated, the number of seats per parking space ranged from 0.5 to 6.3 in 1976.

The "dump time" of the parking facilities is especially critical for special-event or sports parking. This value is usually between 30 and 60 min, and efforts should be taken in design to minimize this time. One aid to reducing dump time is to use precashiering (collection of the parking fee on entry). The dump time then depends on the internal design of the parking facility, its ramps and exits, and the surrounding street system. Separation of pedestrian and autos should be achieved whenever possible because of the large volume of pedestrians. This is especially true at vehicle exit driveways. Pedestrian ways, including overpasses or tunnels, should be considered to aid in this separation.

Change-of-mode facilities

A change-of-mode facility is one where persons change from one form of transportation to another. Included are such facilities as train stations, airports, and bus stations.

Airports. A good estimate of passenger travel is a necessity in planning parking facilities for airports. The public parking demand at airports varies widely depending upon a number of factors. The percentage of originating passengers, the percentage of transfer passengers, passenger trip purpose, and the percentage of charter passengers are all factors that affect parking demand. Parking for employees, rental cars, casual visitors, and others is generally proportional to the amount of passenger traffic.

The public parking demand at three selected airports is shown in Table 21-10. While the number of enplaned passengers at Las Vegas was more than twice that of Buffalo, New York, the parking demand at Las Vegas was less than one-half of Buffalo. Las Vegas is a convention town and 24% of the enplaned passengers in 1977 used charter service. The parking demand per million enplaned passengers varies over a wide range from 183 parking spaces per million enplaned passengers in Las Vegas to 1104 parking spaces per million enplaned passengers in Buffalo.

Parking durations at airports cover a wide range, from a few minutes to more than 1 week. In a public parking facility at the Seattle–Tacoma International Airport, a study of parking durations showed that nearly 68% of the total parkers stayed less than 4 h while 19% stayed more than 1 day (see Table 21-11). Detailed analysis of those parked less than 4 h showed an average duration for this group of 57 min.

Airports are major generators of traffic and parking. In

[4] "Riverfront Stadium: Riverfront Coliseum Traffic and Parking Study," James Madison Hunnicutt & Associates, Washington, D.C., Oct. 1976.

TABLE 21–8
Parking Provisions of Selected Stadiums—1976

	Seating Capacity*	Parking Spaces		Auto Occupancy		Distance from CBD	Served by Rail Transit
		On Site	Vicinity	Football	Baseball		
Anaheim, CA	43,282	12,000	0		3.4	—	
Atlanta, GA	58,850	4,400	5,500	2.7	3.0	1 mile	
Cincinnati, OH	56,200	4,800	20,000	3.25		Adjacent	
Dallas, TX	72,000	4,000	10,620	3.6–3.8		2 miles	
Denver, CO	51,000	2,700	9,300	3.0	1.9	2 miles	
Edmonton, Alta.	33,135	7,000	8,000			1.5 miles	By LRT
Houston, TX	50,000	30,000	0			6 miles	
Kansas City, MO	78,200	16,000	0			10 miles	
Los Angeles, CA							
Coliseum	93,000	11,000	26,500	2.6		3.5 miles	
Dodger Stadium	55,000	15,000	0		2.6	1.5 miles	
Miami, FL	80,000	3,035	2,070	2.5	2.1	1.5 miles	
New Orleans, LA	78,000	5,000	0			Adjacent	
New York, NY							
Shea Stadium	60,000	7,000	1,000				By NYCTA
Yankee Stadium	65,000	2,000	300				By NYCTA
Oakland, CA	54,000	8,000	18,000	3.5	3.2		By BART
Philadelphia, PA	65,000	6,800	5,000	2.8	2.8	3 miles	By SEPTA
Pittsburgh, PA	50,300	4,400	24,000		3.47	Adjacent	
St. Louis, MO	50,100	7,500	10,000			Adjacent	
San Diego, CA	54,000	14,700	500	2.5–3.1	2.8–3.0	6 miles	
Seattle, WA	65,000	2,300	5,500	2.8†	2.8†	1 mile	

*Seating given for football configuration in convertible stadiums.
†Assumed in stadium planning.

SOURCE: Adapted from *Traffic Considerations for Special Events*, Informational Report: Institute of Transportation Engineers, Washington, D.C., 1976. Data for Seattle added.

TABLE 21–9
Auditorium Parking—1976

	Maximum Seating Capacity	Parking Spaces				Transport Modes	Seats per Space
		Adjacent	Auxiliary	On-Street	Total		
Cleveland Arena	11,000	4,000	1,000	500	5500	Auto, Bus	2.0
Civic Auditorium, San Francisco	8,000	854	414	—	1258	Auto	6.3
Coliseum - Richmond, KY	9,500	1,500	500	200	2200	Auto	4.3
Cow Palace - San Francisco	15,000	7,000	150	850	8000	Auto, Bus	1.8
The Forum - Inglewood, CA	17,500	3,500	31,000	—	34,500	Auto	0.5
Maple Leaf Gardens - Toronto	19,500	350	3,500	—	4000	Auto, Bus, Rail	5.1
Municipal Auditorium - Dallas	11,000	1,100	7,610	740	9450	Auto, Bus	1.2
O'Keefe Centre - Toronto	3,155	2,000	150	—	2150	Auto, Bus	1.5
Place des Arts - Montreal	3,000	389	725	250	1364	Auto, Bus	2.2
Veterans Memorial - Columbus, OH	3,964	1,200	300	1,200	2700	Auto, Bus	1.5

SOURCE: Traffic Considerations For Social Events: An ITE Informational Report, 1976.

(see Errata)

TABLE 21–10
Public Parking Demand at Selected Airports

	Parking Space Demand	Annual Enplaned Passengers	Demand/ Million Enplaned Passengers
Buffalo, N.Y.	1,690	1,531,000	1,104
Denver, Colo.	3,855	8,594,000	449
Las Vegas, Nev.	700	3,825,000	183

SOURCE: Hunnicutt & Associates, Inc.

a metropolitan area, the airport may be the largest single traffic and parking generator besides the CBD. For this reason, a rule of thumb for design of airport facilities is inappropriate. Each airport should be analyzed individually. The difference in mode of travel of passengers at the three New York airports is shown in Table 21-12. Within the metropolitan area, the auto usage by air passengers to the different airports ranges from 37 to 60%.

TABLE 21–11
Parking Duration, Public Parking Lot, Seattle–Tacoma International Airport

Duration	Number	Percent	Cumulative %
Under 4 h	514	67.8	67.8
4–8 h	31	4.1	71.9
8–12 h	36	4.7	76.6
12–16 h	13	1.7	78.3
16–20 h	8	1.1	79.4
20–24 h	11	1.4	80.8
1 day	59	7.8	88.6
2 days	33	4.3	92.9
3 to 6 days	45	6.0	98.9
7 days and over	8	1.1	100.0
Total	758	100.0	

SOURCE: JAMES MADISON HUNNICUTT & ASSOCIATES, *Future Traffic and Parking Requirements and Parking Financial Analysis—Seattle–Tacoma International Airport*, Washington, D.C., 1968, p. 12.

The number of cars generated at several airports per 1000 departing air passengers varies widely (see Table 21-13). Los Angeles International Airport has a rate more than three

TABLE 21–12
Mode of Travel to New York Airports

Mode	Percent of Travel to: LaGuardia	Newark	Kennedy	Total
Auto	37	60	44	45
Taxi	46	12	31	32
Airport bus	9	13	12	11
Bus	2	10	3	4
Suburban limo	5	4	8	6
Other	1	1	2	2
Total	100	100	100	100

SOURCE: L. E. BENDER, "Airports and Their Surface Traffic Demand and Designs for 1970–1980," presented at the 1969 Annual Meeting of the Institute of Traffic Engineers, Aug. 1969, p. 3.

TABLE 21–13
Motor Vehicle Generation Related to Passenger Departures

Airport	Percent Transferring from Other Planes	Percent of Nontransfer Passengers Using Car or Taxi	Motor Vehicles Generated on Roadways/1000 Departing Air Passengers
LaGuardia (New York)	11	83	530
O'Hare (Chicago)	70	81	180
Atlanta	70	93	200
Los Angeles	15	93	630

SOURCE: L. E. BENDER, "Airports and Their Surface Traffic Demand and Designs for 1970–1980," presented at the 1969 Annual Meeting of the Institute of Traffic Engineers, Aug. 1969, p. 6.

times greater than O'Hare Airport in Chicago. This is due to different passenger characteristics of the two airports. Detailed study is then required at each airport to determine its individual characteristics before attempting to plan or design facilities.

Rail stations, mass transit, and bus stops. Selected data on travel mode to selected rail stations shows a higher arrival by automobile for commuter rail users than by Amtrak passengers (Table 21-14). This directly affects the parking demand at rail stations, as shown in Table 21-15. With a high percentage of Amtrak passengers driving an automobile to the New Carrollton Station, that station exhibits a high demand for parking spaces.

Change-of-mode terminals are often considered as the point of change from auto to mass transit. Because of the congestion in CBD areas, fringe parking areas are being used in many instances as parking facilities for commuters, who then transfer to bus or rail transit. Table 21-16 illustrates the variable relationships found during the years 1970–1975 between the number of off-street parking spaces provided and the number of boarding passengers per parking space at selected transit stations in six major cities.

TABLE 21–14
Auto Drivers at Railroad Stations (Percent of Total Boarding Passengers)

Station	Amtrak	Commuter	Combined Amtrak and Commuter
Wilmington, Del.	20	29	23
New Haven, Conn.	15	22	19
Providence, R.I.	18	42	22
Stamford, Conn.	—	—	50
New Carrollton, Md.	44	—	44

SOURCE: L. K. CARPENTER, *Planning Rail Station Parking: Approach and Application,* Wilbur Smith & Associates, New Haven, Conn. James Madison Hunnicutt & Associates, *Parking Feasibility Study—New Carrollton Station,* Washington, D.C., Oct. 1978. Hunnicutt-Davis Associates, *Stamford Railroad Station Parking Feasibility Study,* Washington, D.C., Nov. 1978.

Table 21-17 illustrates the travel mode to two change-of-mode stations in Milwaukee, Wisconsin. Remote sections of two shopping center parking lots were made available for commuter parking, and these areas were served by express bus service to the CBD via freeways. In each instance, less than 40% of the commuters parked a vehicle at the change-of-mode station.

Table 21-18 shows the mode of travel of the same commuters prior to initiation of the shopping center express bus service. More than 40% of those using the change-of-mode facilities had previously driven a car to work, while most of the other commuters had formerly been bus passengers.

TABLE 21–15
Parking Demand at Railroad Stations

Station	Daily Parking Space Demand* Amtrak	Commuter	Combined Amtrak and Commuter
Wilmington, Del.	0.33	0.31	0.32
New Haven, Conn.	0.27	0.32	0.30
Providence, R.I.	0.20	0.42	0.24
Stamford, Conn.	0.34	0.42	0.41
New Carrollton, Md.	0.52	—†	0.52

*Number of daily parking spaces demanded per daily boarding passenger by type.
†Amtrak station only.

SOURCE: L. K. CARPENTER, *Planning Rail Station Parking: Approach and Application,* Wilbur Smith & Associates, New Haven, Conn. James Madison Hunnicutt & Associates, *Parking Feasibility Study—New Carrollton Station,* Washington, D.C., Oct. 1978. Hunnicutt-Davis Associates, *Stamford Railroad Station Parking Feasibility Study,* Washington, D.C., Nov. 1978.

To be successful, a change-of-mode operation must present an attractive alternative to the auto. Frequent service from convenient locations is required. Other factors involved include reliability, out-of-vehicle time, and various cost items.

Shopping centers

Shopping centers are major generators of traffic which reach their peak in the 4-week period prior to Christmas. The peak day at a shopping center is generally the Saturday before Christmas. The parking accumulation on this peak day will generally occur in midafternoon. Typically, the

TABLE 21–16
Parking Provisions at Selected Transit Stations

Region	Location	Boarding Passengers per Weekday	Off-Street Parking Spaces	Boarding Passengers/ Parking Space
Boston	Wollaston	2,700	500	5.4
	North Quincy	2,400	800	3.0
	Quincy Center	7,500	930	8.1
	B & M*	11,000	3,360	3.3
	Penn Central*	3,800	2,640	1.4
Chicago	Dempster	4,000	500	8.0
	Desplaines	4,000	500	8.0
Cleveland	West Side (5 stations)	20,000	6,400	3.1
	East Side (3 stations)	10,000	900	11.1
Philadelphia	Bucks County*	4,000	1,800	2.2
	Chester County*	3,900	1,100	3.5
	Delaware County*	15,500	2,200	7.0
	Montgomery County*	19,500	4,300	4.5
	Penn Central (In City)*	45,000	2,100	21.4
	Reading (In City)*	31,600	2,700	14,6
	Lindenwold (New Jersey)	20,000	9,000	2.2
San Francisco	Concord line (6 stations)	20,360	6,555	3.1
	Richmond line (5 stations)	9,130	3,381	2.7
	Alameda line (8 stations)	27,100	7,562	3.6
	Oakland line (3 stations)	7,300	1,087	6.7
	Daly City	8,860	1,877	4.7
Toronto	Islington	23,500	1,300	18.0
	Warden	24,600	1,500	16.4

*Commuter railroad stations.

SOURCE: HERBERT S. LEVINSON, "Planning Transit Facility Parking for the Boston Metropolitan Area," *Transportation Research Record 601* (Freeways, Automatic Vehicle Identification, and Effects of Geometrics), San Francisco data from BART, 1980. Transportation Research Board, 1976.

TABLE 21–17
Mode of Travel to Shopping Center Change-of-Mode Stations in Milwaukee, Wisconsin

Mode	Mayfair		Bayshore	
	Number	Percent	Number	Percent
Auto driver	157	38.9	119	38.4
Auto passenger	139	34.4	88	28.4
Drop-off	22	5.4	30	9.7
Walk	66	16.3	51	16.4
Another bus	20	5.0	22	7.1
Total	404	100.0	310	100.0

SOURCE: H. M. MAYER, "Change of Mode Commuter Transportation in Metropolitan Milwaukee," *Highway Res. Circ. No. 83*, Highway Research Board, Washington, D.C., 1968, p. 9.

TABLE 21–18
Mode of Travel of Commuters Prior to Express Service from Shopping Centers, Milwaukee, Wisconsin

Mode	Mayfair		Bayshore	
	Number	Percent	Number	Percent
Auto driver	182	41.2	141	44.4
Auto passenger	37	8.4	43	13.5
Bus	215	48.6	132	41.5
Train or taxi	8	1.8	2	0.6
Total	442*	100.0	318†	100.0

*Does not include 109 respondents who did not make the trip before the service began and 6 who failed to answer the question.
†Does not include 57 respondents who did not make the trip before the service began and 10 who failed to answer the question.

SOURCE: H. M. MAYER, "Change of Mode Commuter Transportation in Metropolitan Milwaukee," *Highway Res. Circ. No. 83*, Highway Research Board, Washington, D.C., 1968, p. 11.

peak parking accumulation on other days occurs in early evening between 7:00 and 8:00 P.M. Figure 21.5 shows typical accumulation curves for the peak day and for a typical day during the pre-Christmas shopping period.

Figure 21.6 presents daily parking requirements from a 1966 study of centers presented in the form of number of days (or hours) in the year that parking demand exceeds a given figure. Studies concluded that the thirtieth highest hour is equivalent to the sixth highest day. This 1966 study recommended design at the tenth highest hour (third highest day) with a design standard of 5.5 parking spaces per 1000 ft^2 (6 spaces per 100 m^2) of gross leasable area. This was then a reasonable figure for the average shopping center.

Additional studies of shopping center parking were conducted in 1973 to 1975.[5] The results of this study found that the average parking demand ratio for 141 parking accumulation counts was 4.4 parking spaces per 1000 ft^2 (4.7 spaces per 100 m^2) of gross leasable area. Less than 8% of the parking accumulation counts exceeded or equaled the existing standard of 5.5 spaces per 1000 ft^2 (6 spaces per 100 m^2), 39% of the parking demand ratios fell between 4.0 and 5.0 (4.3 and 5.4 per 100 m^2), and nearly 32% were less than 4.0 parking spaces per 1000 ft^2 (4.3 per 100 m^2). It was recommended that 5.0 parking spaces per 1000 ft^2 (5.4 per 100 m^2) of gross leasable area be established as a valid national maximum for planning of new, existing, and expanded regional shopping centers. A further reduction to 4.0 spaces per 1000 ft^2 (4.3 per 100 m^2) is recommended for those shopping centers where employee vehicles can be parked off-site during peak shopping periods such as the Thanksgiving-to-Christmas period.

Actual practice in shopping center planning and construction has been to require parking spaces generally in excess of the recommended standard. In fact, in some instances, parking spaces provided have exceeded the proposed standard by 100% or more.

The practice in some shopping centers today is to include some uses other than retail, such as theaters and office buildings. The peaks for those other uses do not occur at the same time as the peak for retail shopping. Therefore, it has been found that up to 20% of the gross leasable area can be added to a shopping center as office space without affecting the peak parking demand.

Industrial plants

The parking characteristics of industrial plants are affected by a wide variety of factors. Plant location is a prime factor, particularly as it relates to suburban availability of mass transit. The amount of shift work, type of industry, seasonal variations, sex of workers, and income level are additional factors that affect parking demand.

Figure 21.7 illustrates a typical vehicle accumulation curve for an auto assembly plant. The shift overlap peaks are quite distinct and, in this instance, nearly equal in magnitude.

The type of parking facility used by employees of in-

[5]RICHARD C. GERN, "Parking Demand at the Regionals," *ITE J.*, *48*(9), (Sept. 1978).

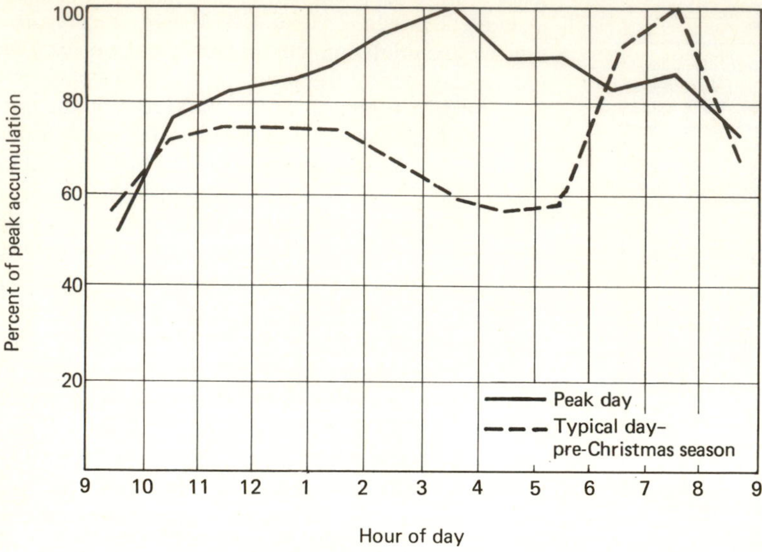

Figure 21.5. Accumulation pattern on peak and other days at a typical shopping center. SOURCE: A.M. Voorhees and C.E. Crow, "Shopping Center Parking Requirements," *Shopping Centers and Parking,* Highway Res. Rec. No. 130, Highway Research Board, Washington, D.C., 1966, p. 22.

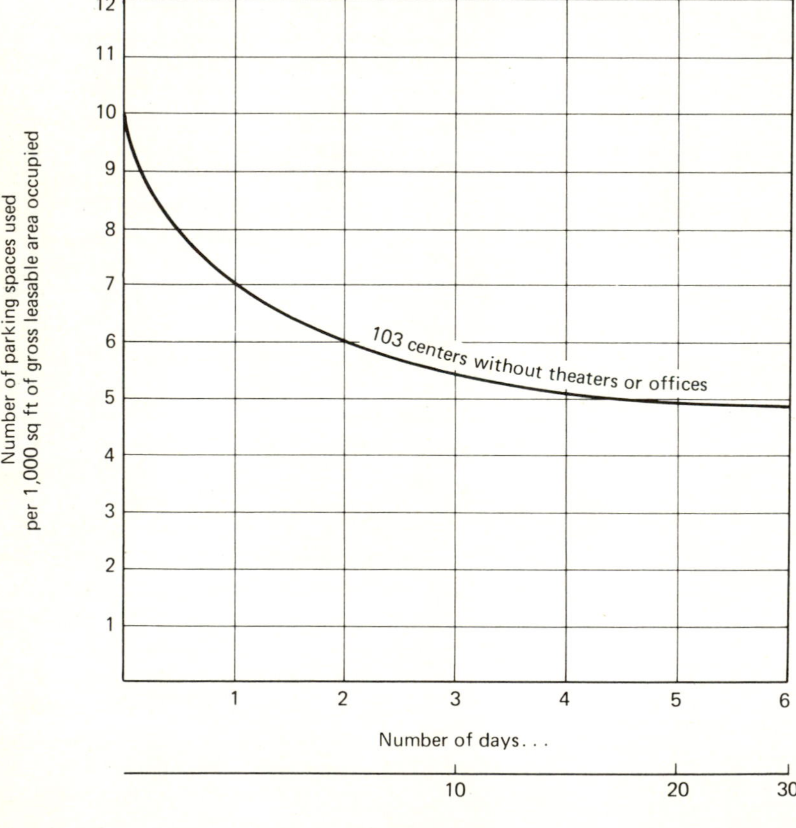

Figure 21.6. Shopping center daily parking requirements. SOURCE: A.M. Voorhees and C.E. Crow, "Shopping Center Parking Requirements," *Shopping Centers and Parking,* Highway Res. Rec. No. 13, Highway Research Board, Washington, D.C., 1966, p.24.

dustrial plants varies with plant employment (see Table 21-19). The percentage of the employees using free off-street lots decreases as plant employment increases. Conversely, the number of employees parking on-street or in other facilities (generally off-street pay parking) increases with plant employment.

Table 21-20 summarizes parking supply and demand per employee for various sizes of industrial plants. For multi-shift plants, the maximum shift employment is used. The parking supply per employee exceeds the corresponding demand because of the following factors:

1. Supply must exceed demand by 5 to 10% to reduce searching for a space and possible illegal parking.
2. Assigned and reserved spaces are not always fully utilized.

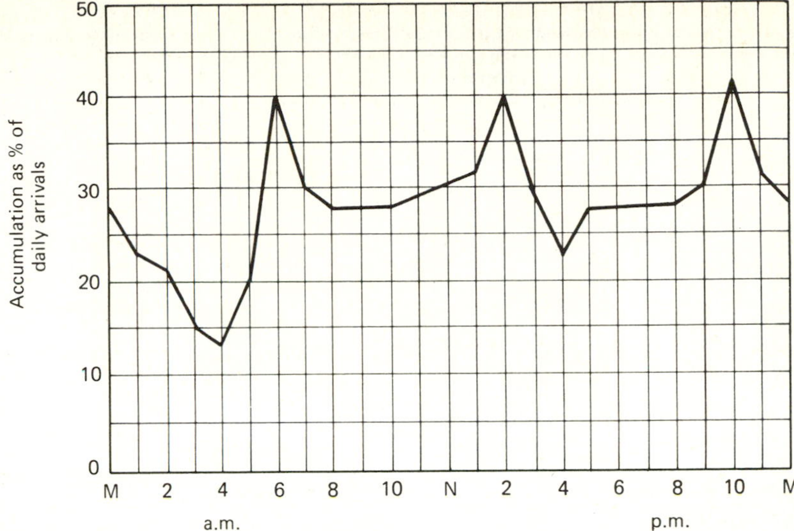

Figure 21.7. Vehicle accumulation vs. time of day—industrial plant. SOURCE: *Parking Facilities for Industrial Plants,* Institute of Traffic Engineers, Washington, D.C., 1969, p. 8.

TABLE 21–19
Type of Parking Used by Employees, by Plant Size

Plant Employment	Free Off-Street Lots	Percent Using On-Street Parking	Other	Total
0–2500	95	3	2	100
2500–5000	94	4	2	100
5000–10,000	77	19	4	100
10,000 +	67	14	19	100
Overall	89	6	5	100

SOURCE: *Parking Facilities for Industrial Plants*, Institute of Traffic Engineers, Washington, D.C., 1969, p. 12.

TABLE 21–20
Parking Demand and Supply Related to Number of Employees, by Plant Size

	Parking Demand		Parking Supply	
Total Plant Employment	Number of Samples	Number of Occupied Spaces/Employee	Number of Samples	Number of Spaces Provided/Employee
0–500	24	0.63	34	0.81
500–1000	11	0.76	7	0.70
1000–5000	18	0.60	21	0.72
5000 +	8	0.62	12	0.80

SOURCE: *Parking Facilities for Industrial Plants*, Institute of Traffic Engineers, Washington, D.C., 1969, p. 13.

3. Distant lots are often underutilized, while closer lots may be over capacity.
4. Problems of shift overlaps may require more spaces than a one-time demand count would indicate.

Colleges and universities

Campus parking often proves to be a problem for the administration of colleges and universities and it usually is very large in magnitude. A survey of U.S. colleges and universities by the Institutional and Municipal Parking Congress (IMPC) showed that slightly more than 20% of the responding institutions had more than 10,000 student vehicle registrations, while 23% of the respondents had faculty–staff registrations exceeding 3000 (see Table 21-21).

TABLE 21–21
Number of University and College Vehicle Registrations

	Responses (%)	
Number of Vehicle Registrations	Student	Faculty–Staff
<1000	8.7	36.0
1000–2000		27.0
2000–3000		14.0
1000–3000	19.4	
3000–5000	18.5	12.0
>5000		11.0
5000–7000	12.6	
7000–10,000	20.4	
10,000–15,000	14.6	
>15,000	5.8	
Total	100.0	100.0

SOURCE: *College and University Parking Survey*, Institutional and Municipal Parking Congress, Washington, D.C., 1971.

The majority of campus parking is in off-street lots. Of the institutions responding to the IMPC survey, 3% indicated they provide more than 10,000 off-street spaces in surface lots. This represents a land area of approximately 80 acres (32.4 ha) devoted to surface parking. Only 8.7% of the responding institutions provide more than 1000 parking spaces in garages (see Table 21-22).

The type of parking facility used by parkers varies with campus population as determined from a study of 38 U.S. colleges and universities (see Table 21-23). As the campus population increases, the availability of free parking decreases. Less than 3% of the work-trip parkers paid to park on campuses with less than 10,000 population. However, this increases to over 50% paying for parking when campus populations exceed 20,000.

Average car occupancy differs more with trip purpose than with university size.[6] Car occupancy for work trips

[6]LOUIS E. KEEFER, AND DAVID K. WITHEFORD, "Urban Travel Patterns for Hospitals, Universities, Office Buildings, and Capitals," *NCHRP Report No. 62,* Highway Research Board, Washington, D.C., 1969, pp. 77–78.

TABLE 21-22
Type of Parking Facilities Provided by Colleges and Universities

Number of Spaces	Responses (%) Garage	Lot	On-Campus Street	Leased
<100			49.5	95.5
100–500			25.3	3.6
<500	83.5	11.8		
500–1000	7.8	12.6	11.2	0.9
>1000			14.0	0.0
1000–2000	6.1	16.5		
2000–3000	0.9	15.8		
>3000	1.7			
3000–5000		22.8		
5000–7000		8.7		
7000–10,000		8.7		
>10,000		3.1		
Total	100.0	100.0	100.0	100.0

SOURCE: *College and University Parking Survey*, Institutional and Municipal Parking Congress, Washington, D.C., 1971.

TABLE 21-23
Type of Parking Facility Used at Universities

Campus Population*	Work Trips (%) Off-Street Free	Off-Street Paid	On Street†	Not Parked‡	All Other Trips (%) Off-Street Free	Off-Street Paid	On Street†	Not Parked‡
<1000	92	—	8	—	64	5	6	25
1000–5000	72	3	25	—	45	12	28	15
5000–10,000	91	2	6	—	60	8	24	8
10,000–20,000	63	21	15	1	50	10	28	12
>20,000	38	52	9	1	22	32	27	19
Average	66	20	13	1	46	14	27	13

*Includes faculty, staff, and total student enrollment.
†Includes parking on residential property.
‡Passenger drop-off, auto left for service or repairs, cruised, or otherwise not parked.

SOURCE: LOUIS E. KEEFER AND DAVID K. WITHEFORD, "Urban Travel Patterns for Hospitals, Universities, Office Buildings, and Capitals," *NCHRP Report No. 62*, Highway Research Board, Washington, D.C., 1969, p. 77.

average 1.17 persons per car, school trips average 1.22 persons per car, and all other trip purposes average 1.69 persons per car. The overall average for all trip purposes was 1.39 persons per car.

Urban residential districts

Parking in urban residential areas exhibits characteristics unlike those in any other area. Residential parking peaks at night and is a function of the car ownership characteristics of the residents of the area. Auto ownership is influenced by such factors as family income, age and size, transit availability, type of housing, and location. Table 21-24 relates auto ownership to age and income of the family and to type of housing. As density of housing increases (low-rise vs. high-rise) auto ownership decreases. Auto ownership increases with income but decreases greatly for the elderly as compared to other age groups.

Parking for single-family residential areas is generally adequate, as many single-family residences have driveways and generally some amount of off-street parking. However, in multiple-unit housing areas, particularly in older sections of the city, off-street parking space may be practically non-

TABLE 21-24
Auto Ownership Related to Resident Characteristics, Washington, D.C.

Type of Housing and Characteristics of Residents	Cars/Family
High-rise apartments	
High income, elderly	0.33:1
High income, other	1.30:1
Middle income, elderly	0.20:1
Middle income, other	1.10:1
Low income, elderly	0.10:1
Low income, other	0.20:1
Low-rise apartments	
High income	1.50:1
Middle income	1.30:1
Low income	0.40:1

SOURCE: ROBERT L. MORRIS, *Transportation Planning for New Towns*, p. 18. (Unpublished paper.)

existent and on-street space may be inadequate to meet the demand. A course of action adopted years ago in Milwaukee, Wisconsin, has helped solve the problem in that city. Milwaukee charges a fee for on-street parking in high-parking-demand residential districts. This money then goes into a fund to build off-street parking facilities in these residential areas.

Hospitals

Parking requirements for hospitals are quite varied depending on such factors as location (urban vs. suburban), number of doctors and employees, number of beds, type of hospital, and outpatient load. However, the parking accumulation characteristics of most hospitals are similar, as they all require three shifts of employees. An accumulation curve for Detroit General Hospital (600 beds and 1760 employees, including 200 part-time) shows that the peak accumulation occurs at the shift change in midafternoon (see Figure 21.8).

The basis for providing hospital parking varies considerably, as shown in parking ratios for hospitals (see Table 21-25). When employee lots are segregated from visitor lots, general hospitals provide only 20 spaces per 100 personnel plus 32 spaces per 100 beds. When all parkers use the same lots, general hospitals provide 32 spaces per 100 beds and personnel combined.

Generally, the type of hospital has a decided effect on parking. Charity hospitals, those with heavy outpatient loads, specialized hospitals such as psychiatric or veterans hospitals, and those with medical schools all exhibit widely varying parking characteristics.

Studies at selected hospitals show that most persons drive an automobile to the hospital and park there (see Table 21-26). For employees, the percentage of auto drivers ranges between 75 and 85%. A higher percentage of hospital visitors drive and park, ranging between 87 and 95%.

Car occupancy factors vary primarily with trip purpose. Work trips have an average car occupancy of about 1.1, while medical and visitor trips average 1.6 persons per car. Other trip purposes have an average car occupancy of 1.8 or 1.9, giving an overall average of 1.4 persons per car (see Table 21-27).

The parking demand at hospitals generally ranges be-

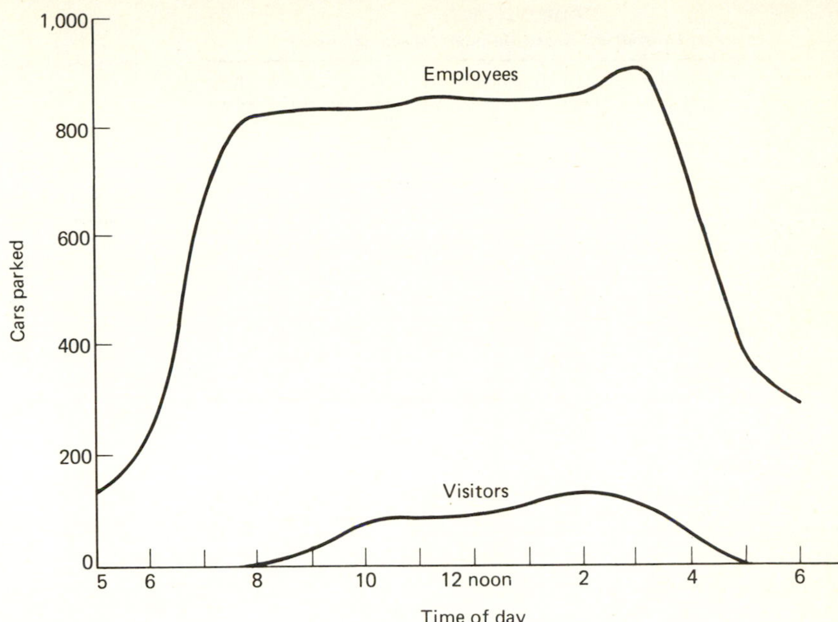

Figure 21.8. Accumulation curve, Detroit General Hospital. SOURCE: James Madison Hunnicutt and Associates, *Parking Study and Feasibility Report on Proposed Parking Garage,* Detroit, Michigan, 1967, p. 16.

TABLE 21–25
Reported Parking Ratios at Selected Hospitals Having Segregated Employee and Visitor Parking Lots vs. Selected Hospitals Having Unsegregated Parking Lots

		Segregated Lots			Unsegregated Lots		
Type of Hospital	Number of Hospitals	Employee Spaces/100 Personnel	Visitor Spaces/100 Beds	Total Spaces/100 Beds + 100 Personnel	Number of Hospitals	Total Space/100 Beds + 100 Personnel	Grand Total Spaces/100 Beds + 100 Personnel
General							
Up to 500 beds	22	21	52	31	9	41	32
Over 500 beds	6	18	8	14	11	29	20
All	28	20	32	24	20	32	26
Veterans	5	45	29	39	5	38	39
Mental	2	32	7	14	—	—	14

SOURCE: LOUIS E. KEEFER AND DAVID K. WITHEFORD, "Urban Travel Patterns for Hospitals, Universities, Office Buildings, and Capitals," *NCHRP Report No. 62*, Highway Research Board, Washington, D.C., 1969, p. 31.

TABLE 21–26
Auto Drivers to Selected Hospitals: Percent of Total Arriving Persons

Hospital	Employees	Visitors	Total
Baptist Medical Center—Princeton, Birmingham, Ala.	83.6	93.5	89.1
Baptist Medical Center—Montclair, Birmingham, Ala.	85.1	94.7	90.4
Community General Hospital, Syracuse, N.Y.	78.0	93.9	85.8
Frankford Hospital—Torresdale Division, Philadelphia, Pa.	80.4	90.4	85.5
Methodist Hospital, Memphis, Tenn.	79.8	86.6	83.2
The Medical Center at Princeton, Princeton, N.J.	75.4	88.4	83.4

SOURCE: Hunnicutt & Associates, Inc., selected hospital studies.

tween 2.0 and 2.7 parking spaces per bed (Table 21-28). The majority of the parking spaces are required by employees, ranging from 1.4 to 1.9 spaces per bed. Doctor parking demand ranges from 0.12 to 0.25 space per bed. Hospital visitors require parking space at a rate ranging from 0.3 to 0.6 space per bed.

TABLE 21–27
Car Occupancy Factors for Hospitals

	Purpose of Hospital Trip				
Type of Hospital	Work	Medical	Visitor	Other	All
General					
Under 300 beds	1.13	1.48	1.49	1.98	1.44
300–399 beds	1.11	1.61	1.56	1.90	1.43
400–499 beds	1.09	1.60	1.61	1.82	1.41
500–599 beds	1.08	1.77	1.44	1.78	1.44
600–999 beds	1.10	1.70	1.57	2.04	1.50
1000 and over	1.16	1.48	1.58	1.62	1.38
Average	1.11	1.59	1.56	1.85	1.43
Veterans	1.10	1.32	1.66	1.70	1.29
Mental	1.15	1.31	1.60	1.71	1.32
University	1.17	1.46	1.63	1.84	1.44

SOURCE: LOUIS E. KEEFER AND DAVID K. WITHEFORD, "Urban Travel Patterns for Hospitals, Universities, Office Buildings, and Capitals," *NCHRP Report No. 62*, Highway Research Board, Washington, D.C., 1969, p. 32.

Curb parking

The primary use of the streets in any city is for the movement of vehicles. Parking on these streets (curb parking) must be considered a secondary use of street space, as

TABLE 21-28
Parking Demand at Selected Hospitals (Spaces per Bed)

Hospital	Employees	Doctors	Visitors	Total
Baptist Medical Center—Princeton, Birmingham, Ala.	1.79	0.13	0.45	2.37
Baptist Medical Center—Montclair, Birmingham, Ala.	1.63	0.12	0.40	2.15
Community General Hospital, Syracuse, N.Y.	1.37	0.17	0.49	2.03
Frankford Hospital—Torresdale Division, Philadelphia, Pa.	1.90	0.25	0.58	2.73
Methodist Hospital, Memphis, Tenn.	1.72	0.20	0.27	2.19
The Medical Center at Princeton, Princeton, N.J.	1.62	0.19	0.39	2.20

SOURCE: Hunnicutt & Associates, Inc., selected hospital studies.

should other uses, such as truck loading zones. When these secondary uses conflict with the movement of traffic, they should be removed so that the streets can best perform the function of moving traffic.

Types of curb space

The curb space along streets in any city will have several categories of use. These uses include curb parking, truck loading zones, no-parking zones, bus and taxi zones, passenger loading zones, and others.

The amount of parking allowed at the curb varies with city size. In larger cities, curb parking may be severely restricted to aid the movement of traffic. In many cases, only about 40% of the total lineal feet is available for public parking.

Parking prohibitions

Parking prohibitions can be warranted on the basis of statutes, traffic capacity, or accident hazard. The statutory warrants of the Model Traffic Ordinance[7] authorize full-time prohibitions on both sides of roadways not exceeding 20 ft (6.1 m) in width and on one side for those not over 30 ft (9.1 m) in width. Statutory prohibitions also apply to curb space near fire hydrants, crosswalks, and approaches to intersections. Studies of street capacity have found that parking reduces capacity by one-fourth to one-third or more on typical streets. Where capacity problems exist, street parking should be removed if possible. Table 21-29 illustrates a recommended warrant for prohibiting parking because of traffic conditions.

A location where curb parking has proven to be an accident hazard could warrant a parking prohibition. Analysis of accident records would indicate locations where accidents are involving curb parkers.

[7]"Model Traffic Ordinance," *Uniform Vehicle Code and Model Traffic Ordinance*, National Committee on Uniform Traffic Laws and Ordinances, Washington, D.C., rev. 1968, p. 27.

TABLE 21-29
Parking Prohibition Criteria

Type of Prohibition	Maximum Vehicles/Hour/Lane When Parking Allowed (One Direction of Flow)	
	1 Lane	2 or More Lanes
Midblock prohibition for entire street	400	600
Intersection prohibition up to 150 ft on approach and departure	300	500

SOURCE: *Parking Principles*, Special Report No. 125, Highway Research Board, Washington, D.C., 1971, p. 176.

Parking regulations

Time restrictions are often posted on curb parking spaces to increase the turnover of parkers. Time restrictions may be posted with the use of signs only, or parking meters may be used in conjunction with signs.

Besides the parking meter, other methods are being used in Europe to regulate curb parking. Principal among those is the disk system (see Figure 21.9). Upon parking, the motorist sets the initial pointer to the arrival time (5:15, as illustrated in Figure 21.9). As the space between the pointers is fixed for each disk, the allowable duration is shown and the second pointer shows the time when the maximum allowable duration has been reached (6:45 in the illustration). The disk is displayed inside the vehicle and enforcement officers can check readily for violations.

The second method used in Europe is known as Park System. This consists of color-coded parking tickets in a packet graduated by price and/or time limit, which are purchased by parkers (see Figure 21.10). The motorist, on parking, selects from the packet a ticket of the appropriate price or duration, punches the month, date, hour, and minute of arrival and displays the ticket in a window on the vehicle.

Very short limits (up to 15 min maximum) are used in areas where very high turnover may be expected, such as near banks and post offices, and are often associated with "errand" parking. Time limits in the range of ½ to 2 h are typically found in retail areas, office areas, and the like. Long-term limits are in the range 3 to 10 h and are often used in fringe residential areas to discourage employee parking.

Facility dimensions

Three types of stalls must be considered in dimensioning curb parking facilities: end stalls, interior stalls, and "paired parking stalls." The end stall, because a vehicle can either be driven directly into or out of it, need only be long enough to accommodate a parked vehicle. A length of 20 ft (6.1 m) is sufficient and often used today. Interior stalls must allow room for maneuvering, and a stall of 22 to 26 ft (6.7 to 7.9 m) is recommended, which allows for 19-ft (5.8-m) vehicles.

"Paired" parking has stall layouts so that two vehicles are parked bumper to bumper and the pairs of stalls are separated by maneuver areas. Stall lengths of 18 to 20 ft

Figure 21.9. Sample parking disk in use in Europe.

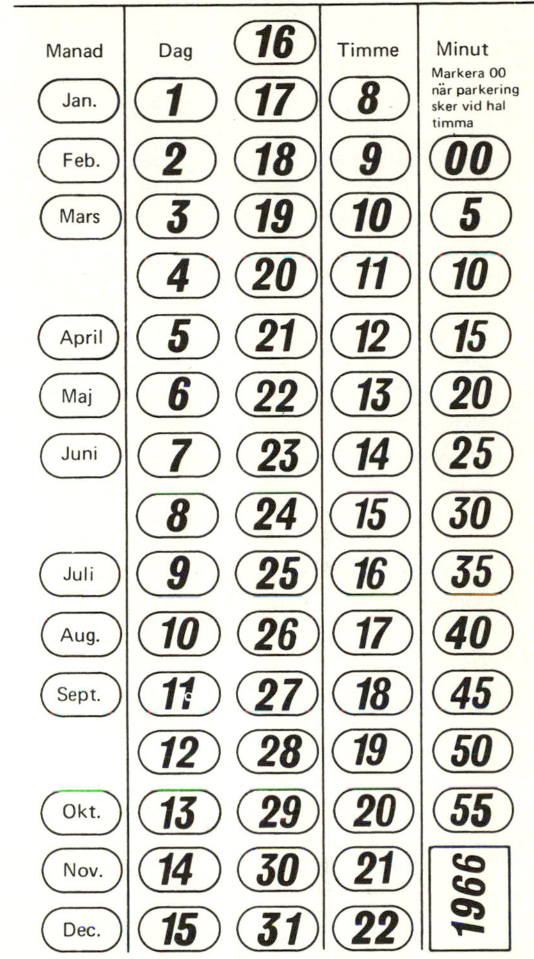

STRÖMSTAD
PARKERING 1/2 TIMME
Nr 421 40
SVENSKT PAT. 181 874
4 markeringar: mån., dag, timme, minut — vid ankomsten
Manad
Dag
Timme
Minut
Markera 00 när parkering sker vid hal timma
Jan.
Feb.
Mars
April
Maj
Juni
Juli
Aug.
Sept.
Okt.
Nov.
Dec.
1966

Figure 21.10. Sample park system ticket.

(5.5 to 6.1 m) are recommended, with a well-defined maneuver area of 8 to 10 ft (2.4 to 3.0 m) (see Figure 21.11). A variation of the paired parking layout is Travers Tandem Parking. This system expands the maneuver area to 16 ft (4.9 m), provides a minimum of 36 ft (11.0 m) of maneuver area, and allows the driver to pull alongside the curb in one forward motion. Thus, traffic in the lane adjacent to the curb parking can proceed virtually uninterrupted. This system reduces somewhat the total number of curb spaces but improves the traffic flow in the curb lane.

Curb spaces marked for compact cars can be smaller than the standard sizes shown above. A suitable design vehicle would be 15 ft long (4.6 m). Interior parking stalls at the curb are recommended to be 19 ft (5.8 m) long compared to the 23 ft (7.0 m) required for standard U.S. cars.

The parking stalls should be defined by white lines extending perpendicular from the curb for a distance generally recommended at 7 ft (2.1 m). The end stall line is generally marked with an L, while interior lines have a T shape.

Truck loading zones are generally 30 to 60 ft (9.1 to 18.3 m) in length. Placing truck zones adjacent to no-parking areas allows additional maneuvering space for trucks.

Taxi zones require about 20 ft (6.1 m) for each stall plus an additional 5 ft (1.5 m) on each end for maneuver area.

Bus loading zones are discussed in Chapter 7.

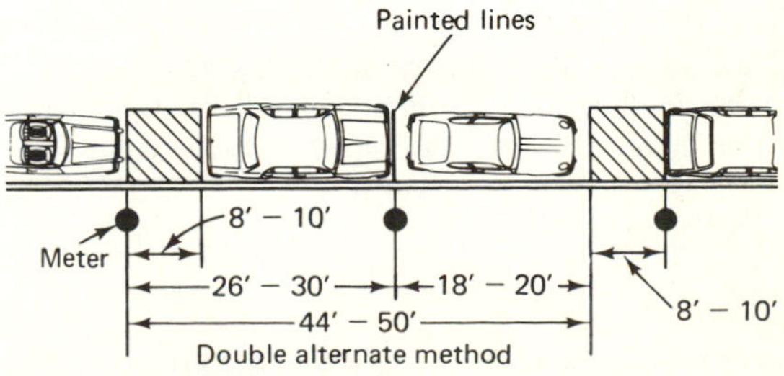

Figure 21.11. Paired parking layout. SOURCE: James Madison Hunnicutt & Associates.

Passenger loading zones should allow for the pickup of passengers without any backing maneuver required by the driver. This requires about 50 ft (15.2 m) for the initial space and an additional 25 ft (7.6 m) for each additional space.

Safety considerations

The overall picture of accidents related to curb parking is not a good one. This type of accident generally represents 20 to 25% of urban accidents not related to freeways. The following statistics indicate the overall magnitude of the problem in several cities. In Chicago, moving vehicles striking parked vehicles represents 2% of all fatal accidents, 6% of all injury accidents, and 26% of all property damage accidents.[8] Another study in a smaller community found that 43% of all local and collector street accidents involved curb parking.[9] In this same city, frequencies of 14 parking accidents per mile were found on major streets, but only 1.8 parking accidents per mile on local and collector streets.[10]

In a comprehensive study of curb-parking-related accidents undertaken in 10 cities in five states, street and accident data were gathered for over 170 miles (270 km) of urban streets. This study related the magnitude and characteristics of urban street accidents to varying parking configurations, land uses, street widths, and street classifications.[11] One of the major conclusions was that parking configurations (i.e., parallel parking vs. various types of angle parking) were not found to have any effect upon accident rates when parking utilization, land use, and type of street are taken into account. The variables that were found to be associated with accident rates include functional classification of the street, utilization of parking, and abutting land use. Increases in parking utilization (the annual number of space hours occupied per mile) result in increases in accident rates for up to approximately 1.5 million annual space hours per mile. For greater parking utilization rates, the accident rate was not found to increase. Parking prohibitions on major streets with parking utilization rates of about 1 million annual space hours per mile or more could be expected to reduce *midblock* accident rates by up to 75%.

For all streets, an increasing accident rate was generally associated with changes from single-family residential to multifamily residential land uses. In addition, there is an increasing accident rate associated with changes from multifamily residential to office land uses and from office land uses to retail uses.

Parking-related midblock accidents account for a larger percentage of the total accidents on collector and local streets than on major streets. The study cited above found that these midblock accidents accounted for 49% of all accidents along major streets, 68% along collector streets, and 72% along local streets.

[8]*Statistical Summary, 1973,* Chicago Police Department, Chicago, 1974.

[9]Paul C. Box, "The Curb Parking Effect," *Public Safety Syst.*, 10 (Jan./Feb. 1968).

[10]Paul C. Box, "Streets Should Not Be Used As Parking Lots," *Congr. Rec.*, *112*(187), 67–74 (Nov. 21, 1966).

[11]K. B. Humphreys, P. C. Box, D. J. Wheeler, and T. D. Sullivan, *Safety Considerations in the Use of On-Street Parking,* U.S. Department of Transportation, Federal Highway Administration Project DOT-FH-11-8879, Washington, D.C., 1978.

Parking meters and meter security

The parking meter as a mechanical time-measuring device generally indicating the available time remaining for a parked vehicle was developed in 1935. Some parking meters do not indicate the available time remaining, while others indicate the time overparked. In proper application, they can greatly simplify the problem of enforcing parking regulations and encourage parking turnover.

Two general types of meters are used: the manual and the automatic. The manual parking meter requires the parker to insert a coin and turn a handle, which winds the clock and actuates the meter for a time period determined by the coin inserted and the duration the meter allows. In the automatic parking meter, a coin is inserted and the time automatically registers for that coin. However, the clock mechanism of the automatic meter must be wound periodically by maintenance personnel. In practical use, the two meters are interchangeable, with the same time limits, choice of coins, and so on, available for the two types.

Parking meters may be installed at either curb or off-street locations. For curb locations, the meters are mounted on a pipe generally placed about 18 in. (0.46 m) back from the curb and about 2 ft (0.61 m) from the front edge of the parking stall. In some instances, two meter heads are mounted atop a single post. This can be done effectively in curb locations with "paired" parking where one post (with two meter heads) serves the parking stalls immediately ahead and behind the meters, or in off-street facilities where two parking spaces face each other across an island.

In major cities, the number of parking meters installed in on-street and off-street locations numbers in the thousands. The amount of money involved in the parking meter program is also substantial. For this reason, the security of parking meter funds is of primary importance. This involves the security of money in the meter before it is collected and the security of the money from the time it is taken from the parking meter until it is deposited in the bank.

Good external security requires a parking meter with a good lock and a key that is difficult to duplicate. As no key is immune from duplication, no large municipal meter system should have all meters operated with the same lock-and-key combination. The lock should be designed so that it can be quickly and easily changed in the field to a different key combination whenever desired. This should be done particularly when a parking meter is stolen or a key disappears.

In parking meter revenue security, the coin collection system is critical. The system should be designed so that coins go directly from the parking meter into the collection device without the collector having access to them. In older meters, open coin containers were used which the collector removed from the meter and emptied into a cart. This type of system invites pilferage because a collector has direct access to uncounted coins.

Several meter collection systems are now available which

provide a much higher degree of security. One system uses a meter coin box which has a special top that can be inserted into a locked collection cart. The collection cart and the meter container have matching connections which release the money directly from the meter coin box into the collection cart. A similar system consists of a closed collection cart which connects by a flexible hose to a similar fitting in the meter collection system. This system releases the coins from the collection box directly into the collection cart. A third system has a long vacuum hose on a collection truck which connects directly to the parking meter collection box. A fourth system involves the use of two coin containers. The container in the meter containing the coins is replaced by a collector with a duplicate empty container. The locked containers that are removed with the coins are then carried to the collection point for emptying and counting.

Many cities in the United States have adopted the use of color coding of meters as an additional means of advising the parker of the time limit at a particular location. Table 21-30 summarizes information relative to use or nonuse of color coding by more than 1000 U.S. cities in all population ranges. Nearly three-fourths of all cities reporting indicated they were using this means of identifying time limits.

The number of parking meters found in a city is directly related to city size. Table 21-31 presents the average number of on-street and off-street meters found in cities of all sizes.

TABLE 21–30
Use of Color Coding of Meters by U.S. Cities

City Size	Color Coding Used		
	Yes	No	% Yes
<2500	56	11	84
2500–5000	119	47	72
5000–10,000	168	71	70
10,000–25,000	184	67	73
25,000–50,000	105	33	76
50,000–100,000	76	23	77
100,000–250,000	51	21	71
250,000–500,000	14	9	61
500,000–1,000,000	10	10	50
>1,000,000	4	2	67
Total	787	294	73

SOURCE: W. D. HEATH, J. M. HUNNICUTT, M. A. NEALE, AND L. A. WILLIAMS, *Parking in the United States—A Survey of Local Government Action*, National League of Cities, Department of Urban Studies, Washington, D.C., 1967, pp. 66–87.

Municipal parking programs

A variety of organizational structures and financing techniques have been used by cities in an effort to solve their parking problems. Each method has its advantages and disadvantages, depending on city size and governmental and other factors. In addition, parking management programs and enforcement programs have been developed by cities to control and enforce the curb and off-street parking space.

Administration

The parking function can be delegated to an existing department within the city government, such as the Public Works Department or the Traffic Engineering Department. This is the simplest method of establishing a parking program and is often used in smaller cities. However, in this arrangement, parking needs often do not receive the necessary priority, and the parking program may be less active than it should be.

A separate parking department with a full-time staff of personnel especially experienced in parking can give the parking program the required attention. However, there is a need for close coordination between separate departments, such as between the parking department and the traffic engineering department.

A parking board, commission, or authority generally consists of a citizens' board of advisors that makes recommendations to the city parking department. The members of this board of advisors or commission are appointed. This type of organization provides an opportunity for citizen participation in improving parking conditions.

The parking authority is a separate autonomous entity whose sole purpose is to carry out the parking program of the city. The authority is governed by an appointed parking board. The parking authority has its own staff and budget, and can plan and carry out a parking program suitable to meet the needs of the city. Important features of parking authorities are that they can condemn property for parking development and can issue nontaxable revenue bonds for financing parking developments.

TABLE 21–31
Average Number of Meters in U.S. Cities

City Population	Number of Cities Reporting	On-Street Meters		Off-Street Meters	Total Number of Meters
		In CBD	Outside CBD		
<2500	68	105	12	3	120
2500–5000	171	166	13	14	193
5000–10,000	242	252	24	43	319
10,000–25,000	253	382	35	128	545
25,000–50,000	140	537	108	300	945
50,000–100,000	100	680	150	433	1,263
100,000–250,000	74	1,083	313	300	1,696
250,000–500,000	23	1,995	1,200	643	3,838
500,000–1,000,000	20	2,301	2,893	234	5,428
>1,000,000	6	2,204	19,153	1,957	23,314

SOURCE: W. D. HEATH, J. M. HUNNICUTT, M. A. NEALE, AND L. A. WILLIAMS, *Parking in the United States—A Survey of Local Government Action*, National League of Cities, Department of Urban Studies, Washington, D.C., 1967, pp. 66–87.

Financing

Many kinds of arrangements are available for financing municipal parking programs. One method used primarily in smaller cities is to finance parking improvements from the city's operating or capital improvements budget. This often results from an adopted policy that parking is a government service similar to the provision of streets or sanitary systems.

Parking revenues are often the source of funds for providing off-street parking facilities. The revenues may come from curb meters and existing off-street facilities as well as from parking violations. These revenues are placed in a reserve fund for development of off-street parking facilities. The disadvantage of this pay-as-you-go system is that funds often do not accumulate fast enough to meet the parking demand.

User benefit assessment is a third form of financing available to municipalities. Under this arrangement, when a parking improvement is planned, all properties within an assessment district are assessed according to a formula that apportions the improvement cost according to the benefits received. The formula for apportionment may consider such factors as number of parkers, distance from the proposed facility, and relative amount of gross sales of the businesses within the district. The principal disadvantage of this assessment is that disagreements over assessment rates and objectors to the system may delay the financing of the facility.

A fourth method of financing parking programs is through a parking tax. Within a parking district, a business has the option of providing the parking required by zoning ordinance or, in lieu thereof, of paying a parking tax. This tax, plus funds from parking meters and fines, is used to provide sufficient off-street parking to meet the parking needs in that district.

Parking revenue bonds are a popular financing tool in many cities. For revenue bonds, only parking system revenues are pledged to the retirement of the bonds and the borrowing power of the city is unaffected. Because of this limitation, interest rates are generally higher than for general obligation bonds, and a debt coverage factor of 1.5 or greater is often necessary.

General obligation bonds are backed by the full faith and credit of the city and therefore result in a lower interest rate than for revenue bond issues. A debt coverage factor of 1.1 to 1.2 is generally adequate for general obligation bonds. However, the borrowing power of the city is reduced by the amount of the general obligation bond issue for the parking facilities.

A combination of private and public participation is possible in CBD developments. A parking authority or city may use its financing capability to aid in the development. This procedure normally requires the establishment of a private nonprofit corporation in which the parking authority has an active interest. After the parking facilities are built, they are leased to the nonprofit corporation to operate and the corporation guarantees the bonded indebtedness.

Enforcement programs

Illegal parking in all major cities is a major safety and traffic problem. In larger cities, millions of parking violations occur each year. Illegal parking creates safety hazards for both pedestrians and other motorists. In addition, the illegal parker hampers movement by other vehicles. This may be especially critical when the movement of emergency vehicles is obstructed.

To combat illegal parking, some cities have undertaken intensified parking enforcement programs. As an example, the District of Columbia has instituted a program that includes:[12]

1. Adding a civilian ticket-writing force to supplement police efforts.
2. Increasing towing and impoundment of vehicles.
3. Increasing booting (see the definition below) to catch habitual offenders.
4. Decriminalizing parking violations and replacing the trial procedure with an administrative hearing (except in certain serious cases).

In many jurisdictions, the police department is responsible for ticket writing for parking violations. In the District of Columbia, the program added 50 civilian ticket writers and 8 administrative personnel within the city's Department of Transportation. These 50 ticket writers issue approximately 1 million tickets per year. The advantages of a civilian ticket-writing force include:

1. A substantially lower cost is involved than to add an additional 50 police officers for the purpose of writing tickets.
2. The civilian ticket writers devote their efforts exclusively to parking enforcement, whereas police officers must perform many other important duties.
3. A full-time civilian ticket-writing force wearing distinctive uniforms serves as an important deterrent to illegal parking.
4. The civilian force can provide a consistent level of enforcement to areas where parking violations chronically occur.

Towing and impoundment of illegally parked vehicles is used in many cities to clear traffic lanes during rush hours. In addition, the towing of certain illegally parked vehicles where a safety hazard is involved can serve as a deterrent to more hazardous forms of illegal parking. Towing and impoundment are also effective enforcement procedures when the vehicle of an habitual offender has been identified.

For those parking offenders who have accumulated a large number of outstanding tickets, a procedure known as "booting" may be implemented. A boot is a metal clamping

[12] *Improved Parking and Traffic Enforcement in the District of Columbia,* Metropolitan Police Department, Office of the Corporation Counsel and D.C. Department of Transportation, Washington, D.C., Apr. 1977.

device that is placed on the wheel of the car, immobilizing it and preventing the driver from moving the vehicle. A booted car then remains immobilized until the owner has dispensed with all outstanding parking tickets. In some jurisdictions vehicle registration renewal is denied until all outstanding tickets are paid.

The adjudication of parking violations (the process by which contested cases are decided) has normally been handled through a criminal court. However, a growing number of jurisdictions have decriminalized minor traffic offenses and parking violations, and removed them from the criminal court. These parking offenses are then handled by administrative adjudication. This is consistent with a growing realization that illegal parking should not be a crime except where an individual accumulates a large number of parking tickets over a fixed period of time. A city department (e.g., the Department of Transportation) could then handle the adjudication process, including such phases as ticket processing, administrative hearings, appeals, penalty enforcement, and driver rehabilitation.

There are many benefits to be derived from an administrative adjudication of parking violations. These include:

1. The freeing of judges and prosecutors to concentrate on criminal cases.
2. A substantial reduction in the number of police appearances.
3. A substantial reduction in the waiting time for a hearing.
4. Emphasis on driver improvement, not punishment.
5. Because of a concentration of functions in one agency, reduction of the ability of persistent violators to escape identification.

Parking management programs

A parking management program is basically any plan by which parking space is controlled, regulated, or restricted in any manner. Parking management can be undertaken as an independent program by a city, or it can be as a part of an auto-restricted zone. Parking management programs are generally undertaken to improve the environmental quality in urban areas and/or to encourage a shift from the automobile to other modes of transportation. These objectives of parking management programs are generally achieved by restricting available parking in the area of concern.

Although parking management programs are generally thought of as means to control the supply of spaces in the urban area, they can also involve such factors as the placement of parking facilities, parking restrictions, and other regulatory measures and pricing mechanisms, including parking taxes. The effect of these measures is not to reduce or control the supply of spaces, but to control the location and usage of parking spaces.

The auto restricted zone (ARZ) has become a familiar term to urban planners in recent years. An ARZ is an area in which one or more factors place limitations upon vehicular traffic. In most instances, ARZ implementation will result in the loss of parking space. In general, curb space is immediately affected. Also, access to off-street parking can be affected by auto restricted zones. In addition, an integral part of an ARZ is often a parking management program to control the parking within its general vicinity.

Residential parking problems

In the 1970s, nonresident parking restrictions were adopted in a number of cities to restrict or eliminate the use of on-street parking spaces by parkers from outside a residential community. These parking restriction measures have been implemented by municipalities where parking by nonresidents is interfering with the parking needs of the residents or with other neighborhood activities. Residents of an area without driveways often cannot use their cars during the day for fear of losing parking spaces near their home. Often, residents returning home during the day cannot find parking spaces within several blocks of their home.

Parking problems in residential areas typically occur when a major nearby traffic generator does not have sufficient parking of its own. Cited as the cause for residential parking problems are CBD employment areas, college and university areas, medical centers, retail and entertainment centers, and transit park-and-ride stations. Although most parking problems on residential streets occur on weekdays, weekend shopping and evening entertainment trips have also created problems in some areas. The impact of nonresident parking in residential neighborhoods is generally most serious in older areas of a city, where the physical layout provides little or no off-street parking.

Residential parking policies. Four policies have been instituted in an effort to restrict nonresident parking in residential neighborhoods.[13] These are:

1. Curb-parking prohibition in residential areas.
2. Restrictions on the number of consecutive hours parked.
3. Alternate-side parking requirements during midmorning or midafternoon.
4. Nonresident parking prohibition (residential parking permits).

The prohibition of curb parking in residential areas may ban on-street parking at certain times of the day, on certain days, at all times, on either or both sides of the street, or various combinations of the above. Since such prohibitions affect residents as well as nonresidents, they are not an acceptable means of controlling parking in residential areas where adequate off-street parking is not available. In most urban areas, such prohibitions are most commonly used because of inadequate street width.

Time restrictions are probably the most popular regula-

[13]Howard Simkowitz, L. Heder, and E. Barber, *The Restraint of the Automobile in American Residential Neighborhoods*, U.S. Dept. of Transportation, UMTA, Washington, D.C., 1978, pp. 8–9.

tion used to prevent long-term parking in residential areas. The most common restrictions are for 1 or 2 h. Time restrictions are popular because of the legal and political acceptance of these regulations as they apply to both residents and nonresidents. Some cities employ the time restrictions in conjunction with their preferential parking programs. The parking permits issued to residents of an area exempt those residents from the hourly restrictions.

Long-term parking has been discouraged in some communities through the use of alternate-side parking requirements which change during the morning or afternoon. Because of the parking duration of commuters, the effect of this policy is to discourage commuters from parking on residential streets during the day.

The most widely accepted method of preventing nonresident parking in residential areas is the parking permit program. There are several possible variations of the permit program, including: nonresidents can park for limited amounts of time; nonresidents are excluded at all times; and nonresidents are prohibited only during certain hours (typically 8 A.M. to 6 P.M. on weekdays). Parking permits are generally sold to residents of the area for a nominal fee sufficient to offset administrative costs. These permits are then displayed on the vehicle.

A major problem with the residential parking permits is the treatment of visitors or other nonresidents whose presence in the neighborhood is either desired or essential. The usual manner of providing parking for this category of nonresident is to issue visitor permits. In most instances, these visitor permits are issued to residents who then make them available to their visitors.

Residential parking case studies.[14] The Washington, D.C., residential permit parking program affected approximately 1200 city blocks as of October 1978. The project area was divided into eight zones, and a sticker issued to a resident in an affected zone was good in all other parts of that zone. However, the sticker was not valid in any of the other seven zones. The nonresident parking restriction was in effect from 7 A.M. to 6:30 P.M. on weekdays, except holidays. Nonpermit holders could park on affected streets for no more than 2 h. The sticker cost $5 per year, and was placed on the car's rear window. The sticker contained the license plate number of the vehicle so that it could not be transferred. Two 15-day visitor permits could be obtained free by each household. One-day permits could be obtained in unlimited quantities. Students and other temporary residents in a zone were eligible for resident stickers if they were actual zone residents and met the District of Columbia's requirements for vehicle registration.

In San Francisco, the first restricted residential parking district was instituted in August 1977. Parking was limited to 2 consecutive hours except for vehicles with a resident sticker. The resident sticker cost $10, had to be affixed to the rear bumper of the resident's automobile, and contained the car's license plate number. The parking restrictions in San Francisco were in effect from 8 A.M. until 9 P.M. Monday through Saturday. A decision was made by the city that no guest passes would be issued. As a result, evening guests planning to stay more than 2 h could not arrive before 7 P.M. (2 h before the end of the restrictions).

The first resident sticker parking program was instituted in the Cambridgeport neighborhood of Cambridge, Massachusetts, in 1972. This program was undertaken to prevent Boston University commuter students from parking in the area and walking to classes in Boston. The price of the resident sticker for this initial program was set at $1, and no guest stickers were available under the original plan. At a later date, two visitor permits at 50 cents each were issued to each resident of the neighborhood. These guest stickers were color-coded and were valid in the area of residence. On the other hand, changes in the parking sticker program were made to make the parking stickers available to all residents of Cambridge and were valid throughout the city. By the end of 1978, the sticker program had been expanded to include 90% of eligible streets.

[14]HOWARD SIMKOWITZ, L. HEDER, AND E. BARBER, *The Restraint of the Automobile in American Residential Neighborhoods*, U.S. Dept. of Transportation, UMTA, Washington, D.C., 1978, pp. 10–24.

Truck parking characteristics

Trucks are an integral part of the transportation system, and a knowledge of truck characteristics is essential to a complete understanding of the transportation system in any city.

The distribution of truck trips by land use in several metropolitan areas is shown in Table 21-32 together with population data for each city at the time the study was undertaken. Residential and commercial land uses generate the bulk of the truck trips in each city. When the data are presented on the basis of truck trips generated per square mile of land use, industrial land generates the largest number of truck trips, followed by commercial land uses (see Table 21-33).

Although trucks represent from 15 to 20% of total CBD trip generation, they account for only about 7 to 8% of the total parkers in the downtown area. At the time of maximum

TABLE 21–32
Motor Truck Trip Generation in Relation to Various Land Uses

Item	Urban Area				
	Chicago	Philadelphia	Minneapolis	Nashville	Tucson
Population	5,169,663	4,342,897	1,376,875	357,585	244,495
Truck trips	828,000	1,089,786	390,559	91,605	57,000*
Land Use	% of Total Truck Trips				
Residential	49	35	37	39	25
Commercial	29	28	34	37	45
Retail	—	20	25	27	—
Service and wholesale	—	8	9	10	—
Public land and buildings	9	2	7	8	5
Industrial	9	9	17	7	20
Transportation	4	14	—†	6	—†
Other	—	12	5	3	5
Total	100	100	100	100	100

*Indicated distribution is based on 41,010 truck trips.
†Included with industrial land.

SOURCE: WILBUR SMITH & ASSOCIATES, *Transportation and Parking for Tomorrow's Cities*, New Haven, Conn., 1966, p. 374 (cites data from Nashville, Penn Jersey, Twin Cities, Tucson, and Chicago area transportation studies).

TABLE 21–33
Truck Trip Generation Factors for Various Land Uses, Nashville, Tennessee, 1959

Land Use	Truck Destinations/Square Mile of Given Land Use		
	Light Trucks	Heavy Trucks	All Trucks
Residential	471	116	587
Industrial	808	801	1609
Transportation, communication utilities	310	308	618
Commercial	647	300	947
Public land and buildings	174	157	331
Other	10	11	21
All land uses	269	121	390

SOURCE: WILBUR SMITH & ASSOCIATES, *Transportation and Parking for Tomorrow's Cities*, New Haven, Conn., 1966, p. 251.

TABLE 21–34
Commercial Vehicle Parking in the CBD

	Chattanooga	Nashville	New Orleans	Cities Combined
Total parkers				
All vehicles	18,491	30,110	31,661	80,662
Trucks	1,767	1,942	2,182	5,891
Truck % of total	9.6	6.4	6.9	7.3
Maximum accumulation				
All vehicles	5,212	11,182	12,167	28,561
Trucks	167	221	324	712
Truck % of total	3.2	2.0	2.7	2.5
Maximum accumulation as % of total accumulation				
All vehicles	28.2	37.1	38.4	35.4
Trucks	9.4	11.4	14.8	12.1

SOURCE: WILBUR SMITH & ASSOCIATES, *Transportation and Parking for Tomorrow's Cities*, New Haven, Conn., 1966, p. 259.

TABLE 21–35
CBD Truck Parking by Facility Type

Facility Type	Chattanooga	Nashville	New Orleans
	All Trucks* (%)		
Loading zone	50.0	35.7	16.7
Other legal curb	26.2	42.2	21.6
Illegal curb	13.9	8.8	47.3
Off-street	9.9	10.5	14.4
Off-street loading docks	n.a.	2.8	n.a.
Total	100.0	100.0	100.0
	Trucks Loading and Unloading Merchandise (%)		
Loading zone	73.5	55.9	17.6
Other legal curb	10.1	29.7	6.3
Illegal curb	15.7	10.7	75.0
Off-street	0.7	3.7	1.1
Total	100.0	100.0	100.0

*n.a., not available.

SOURCE: WILBUR SMITH & ASSOCIATES, *Transportation and Parking for Tomorrow's Cities*, New Haven, Conn., 1966, p. 261.

parker accumulation, the truck influence is even less, with trucks accounting for only 2 to 3% of the maximum accumulation (see Table 21-34).

Truck parking in the CBD takes place predominantly at the curb, often in illegal curb space. For trucks loading and unloading in the CBD, more than 95% use curb spaces (see Table 21-35).

TABLE 21–36
Trip Purpose of CBD Truck Parkers

Trip Purpose	Chattanooga	Nashville	New Orleans
	All Trucks (%)		
Loading–unloading	30.2	36.0	43.7
Sales–service	24.7	13.7	8.0
Work	8.9	8.2	16.0
Business	21.6	30.4	16.0
Shopping	8.1	4.7	2.2
Other	6.5	7.0	14.1
Total	100.0	100.0	100.0
	Trucks in Loading Zones (%)		
Loading–unloading	44.3	56.3	45.2
Sales–service	27.4	8.2	17.0
Work	7.7	4.3	17.3
Business	12.0	20.5	15.3
Shopping	4.2	4.6	2.2
Other	4.4	6.1	3.0
Total	100.0	100.0	100.0

SOURCE: WILBUR SMITH & ASSOCIATES, *Transportation and Parking for Tomorrow's Cities*, New Haven, Conn., 1966, p. 376.

TABLE 21–37
Average Parking Duration of Commercial Vehicles by Trip Purpose, Pittsburgh

Purpose	Average Duration (min)				
	Taxi	Light Truck	Medium Truck	Heavy Truck	Average
Pick up goods	—	29	51	110	36
Deliver goods	—	15	27	127	19
Pick up and deliver	—	14	25	50	17
Service	6	122	91	—	58
To base of operations	63	79	55	131	73
Personal business	—	90	47	—	82
Average	7	37	38	113	34

SOURCE: LOUIS E. KEEFER, "Trucks at Rest," *Origin and Destination Techniques and Evaluations*, Highway Res. Rec. No. 41, Highway Research Board, Washington, D.C., 1963, p. 32.

Table 21-36 shows the trip purpose of truck parkers in the CBD. Loading and unloading of goods is the major purpose, but service and business also account for large numbers of truck parkers.

A study has shown that the average parking duration for commercial vehicles in Pittsburgh is related to trip purpose (Table 21-37) and to the land use at the destination (Table 21-38). Taxis were included as a part of the study. Heavy trucks exhibited much longer parking durations than did light or medium trucks. Handling of goods normally produces shorter parking durations than do other purposes, such as service, personal business, or parking at the base of operation. Parking durations at various land uses generally averaged less than 1 h when all vehicles were considered together. Manufacturing land uses produced the longest average duration.

Off-street truck facilities

Location and design

The delivery and shipping of raw materials and finished goods is accomplished to a large extent by the use of trucks of all sizes. These trucks use the same streets for access to

TABLE 21–38
Average Parking Duration of Commercial Vehicles by Land Use at Destination, Pittsburgh

Land Use	Average Duration (min)				
	Taxi	Light Truck	Medium Truck	Heavy Truck	Average
Residential	6	30	33	306	27
Retail	6	33	25	136	30
Services	6	46	35	33	37
Wholesale	5	59	48	69	53
Manufacturing	4	83	53	130	67
Transportation, utilities, communication	14	76	56	104	58
Public buildings	4	63	30	30	39
Public open space	2	68	50	—	51
Airports, streets, and railroad land	8	27	51	24	26
Average	7	37	38	113	34

SOURCE: LOUIS E. KEEFER, "Trucks at Rest," *Origin and Destination Techniques and Evaluations*, Highway Res. Rec. No. 41, Highway Research Board, Washington, D.C., 1963, p. 35.

the industrial, retail, and other areas as do other vehicles, but special provisions are required to meet the specialized needs of trucks on the site.

In general, trucks use the same entrances to a site as do employee vehicles and other traffic. The entrances and exits must be designed to accommodate the largest truck expected to visit the site (see Chapter 6 for maximum truck dimensions). Figure 21.12 illustrates the entrance width and flare length required for the WB-50 design vehicle [overall length of 55 ft (16.8 m)] under the set of conditions shown [no parking, vehicle turning from curb lane, property line set back 15 ft (4.6 m) from curb]. If parking is allowed at the curb on the approach street, the vehicle path will be moved farther from the curb and result in a decreased entrance width and flare length. Adjustment of the property-line location will also change the entrance dimensions. Ease of turning into the site may be accomplished by use of "Y" or angle approaches. This may be particularly useful for access to and from a one-way street.

The width of roadway required at gates is generally recommended at 16 ft (4.9 m) for one-way operation, 28 ft (8.5 m) for two-way operation, and 34 ft (10.4 m) where pedestrian traffic is involved. If inbound trucks are stopped at the gate, it will be necessary to recess the gates so that sufficient storage space will be available for one, and preferably two trucks, without encroaching on the approach street.

Service roads within the property should be 24 ft (7.3 m) in width for two-way operation. Wherever possible, truck traffic should circulate counterclockwise, as the left turn is easier with large commercial vehicles because the driver's position is on the left side of the vehicle. Also, this places the truck in the most favorable position for backing into the dock. Care should be taken to prohibit parking where it may conflict with truck circulation or maneuvering into the truck dock areas.

A waiting or holding area for trucks is required next to the docks to accommodate trucks waiting for a dock space. The size of this area should be sufficient to provide space for the maximum number of trucks expected on the site less the number of dock spaces provided.

The maneuver area required in front of docks depends on the overall length of trucks using the facility, turning radii of the trucks, direction of traffic circulation, and the width of berths. A maneuver length from the edge of the loading dock of not less than twice the overall length of the longest vehicle using the facility has been recommended.[15] Another recommendation is for a maneuver space of 105 ft (32 m) with counterclockwise circulation and 165 ft (50 m) with clockwise circulation to avoid blind right-hand backing maneuvers.[16]

Individual berths should be from 12 to 14 ft (3.7 to 4.3 m) in width. Berths less than 12 ft (3.7 m) are generally not acceptable. Minimum overhead clearance should generally not be less than 15 ft (4.6 m). Height of dock for servicing all types of trucks should be 48 to 50 in. (1.22 to 1.27 m). Most docks built today place the face of the dock flush with the outside wall of the building. The flush type dock can offer a covered, heated, closed dock operation without enclosing the trucks.

Enclosed docks completely enclose the truck when parked at the dock. The totally enclosed dock includes the maneuver area; trucks pull into the area, back into the dock-space, and generally leave by another door. A second type of enclosed dock does not enclose the maneuver space, and trucks back through a door and straight into the loading dock. Care must be taken to eliminate the accumulation of vehicle exhausts in the enclosed area. However, enclosed docks have the advantage of complete protection of goods,

[15] *Parking Facilities for Industrial Plants*, Institute of Traffic Engineers, Washington, D.C., 1969, p. 26.

[16] *Modern Dock Design*, Kelly Company, Inc., Milwaukee, Wis., 1968, p. 2.

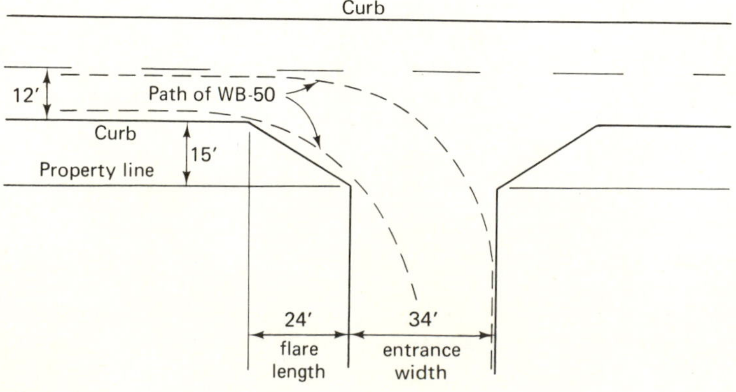

Figure 21.12. Driveway requirements to accommodate WB-50 design vehicle. SOURCE: WB-50 path from *A Policy on Geometric Design of Rural Highways*, American Association of State Highway Officials, Washington, D.C., 1965, Fig. II-12, p. 84.

control over pilferage, ability to erect crane systems or other overhead systems for loading and unloading of unenclosed trucks, and an operating atmosphere not affected by outside weather conditions. Modern industrial construction has often eliminated basements and dock-level buildings. Depressed approaches to docks can be used to create the elevation differential needed for the loading–unloading operation. These grades on the approach should not exceed 10%.

With a depressed approach, the top of the truck may contact the building wall before the truck bed contacts the bumpers if the dock is flush with the wall. To eliminate this condition, the approach grade can be lessened, the building wall recessed, or the dock face extended. Another solution is the use of a level section 15 to 25 ft (4.6 to 7.6 m) in length immediately adjacent to the dock before beginning the approach grade.

Where sufficient maneuver space is not available for trucks to use docks situated parallel to the building wall, a sawtooth arrangement may be used to lessen the maneuver area needed. The number of berths that may be accommodated in a given dock length will be less with angular or sawtooth arrangement than with trucks parking at 90°. Berths at angles of 30° or less use twice as much dock space per berth as do berths at 90°. Truck circulation must be such that vehicles approach and depart with the angle of the dock so that maneuvering into the berth involves an angle less than 90°. Wherever possible, circulation should be counterclockwise to avoid blind backing maneuvers.

Zoning for loading facilities

The amount of truck activity varies greatly not only between land uses, but among similar land-use types. Similarly, the number of off-street loading spaces varies widely. Table 21-39 summarizes the number of loading spaces provided for various industrial uses observed. The number of berths per 10,000 ft^2 of heavy industrial use ranged from 0.09 to 0.98. Loading dock requirements are obviously dependent upon the individual industrial operation.

Research by the Eno Foundation[17] found that 84% of the cities over 100,000, 66% of the cities between 50,000 and 100,000, and 64% of the cities under 50,000 have off-street loading controls. These are most often related to the gross floor area of the activity. The variation among specifications for determining the number of loading spaces was so great that it was impossible to summarize the information in one table. The findings did show that many cities do not require loading space for activities occupying less than 5000 ft^2 (464.5 m^2). Table 21-40 summarizes the range of require-

[17]George E. Kanaan and David K. Witheford, "Zoning and Loading Controls," *Traffic Quart.*, *25*(3), 449 (1971).

TABLE 21–39
Relationship of Land Area and Building Size to Loading Facilities Classified by Type of Industrial Operation

Description	Land Area (ft^2)	Building Area (ft^2)	Number of Truck Docks	Number of Berths/ 10,000 ft^2 Land Area	Number of Berths/ 10,000 ft^2 Building Area
Bakery	600,240	259,890	24	0.40	0.92
Office and research with warehouse	62,530	30,220	3	0.48	0.99
	74,330	35,160	4	0.54	1.14
	190,640*	60,000	1	0.05†	0.17†
				Av. 0.51	1.07
Truck storage and terminal	47,720	7,730	12	2.52	15.52
Printing	78,190	43,250	2	0.26	0.46
	156,130	104,940	6	0.38	0.57
				Av. 0.32	0.52
Medium manufacturing and fabrication (electrical components, etc.)	45,610	18,540	2	0.44	1.08
	862,340	296,350	5	0.06	0.17
				Av. 0.25	0.62
Heavy manufacturing and fabricating (machine, tool and die, metal stamp, etc.)	20,440	8,425	2	0.98	2.38
	36,945	20,240	2	0.54	0.99
	74,630	34,650	3	0.40	0.87
	89,900	50,230	3	0.33	0.60
	155,870	59,860	2	0.13	0.33
	156,880	76,020	5	0.32	0.66
	296,760	187,260	6	0.20	0.32
	364,813	161,850	9	0.25	0.56
	690,990	321,590	7	0.10	0.22
	831,850	306,980	8	0.09	0.26
				Av. 0.33	0.62

*Office and research only.
†Not included in average.

Source: W. A. Alroth, "Parking and Traffic Characteristics of Suburban Industrial Developments," *Parking*, Highway Res. Rec. No. 237, Highway Research Board, Washington, D.C., 1968, p. 10.

TABLE 21-40
Summary of Loading Space Requirements

Land Use	Total Floor Area (1000 ft²) Requiring: First Loading Space	Second Loading Space
Commercial, industrial	7–10	27–35
Institutional	12–15	75–80
Hotels, office, residential	20–30	80–113

SOURCE: GEORGE E. KANAAN AND DAVID K. WITHEFORD, "Zoning and Loading Controls," *Traffic Quart.*, *25*(3), 452 (1971).

TABLE 21-41
Suggested Truck Berth Criteria for Commercial and Industrial Land Uses

Floor Area (ft²)	Number of Truck Berths
<8000	1
8000–25,000	2
25,000–50,000	3
50,000–100,000	4
100,000–250,000	5
Each additional 200,000	1

SOURCE: WILBUR SMITH & ASSOCIATES, *Transportation and Parking for Tomorrow's Cities*, New Haven, Conn., 1966, p. 265.

ments on the provision of the first and second loading space for various land uses. In contrast to these requirements, Table 21-41 presents a recommended truck berth criteria for commercial and industrial land uses. One space per 100,000 ft² (9290 m²) of floor area is reported as adequate for residences, hotels, and theaters.

Truck terminals

The truck terminal, together with other freight terminals, forms an important link in the movement of goods in an urban area. There has been little change in the number of truck terminals in most cities, but there has been a trend toward increases in average terminal size. In 1966 in the New York metropolitan area, there were 299 Class I and II intercity carriers operating out of 373 terminals[18] (Class I carriers have over $1 million in annual gross revenue and Class II carriers $200,000 to $1 million). While the average size was increasing, most of the terminals were still of moderate size, with 75% having fewer than 20 spaces.

There has not been any large trend toward consolidation of terminals. Terminal consolidation can lower the vehicle-miles of truck travel and time spent en route, thereby reducing the cost of transport of merchandise. Consolidated terminals have been estimated to halve the amount of required truck travel.

The location of truck terminals is dependent on the road system, particularly the freeway system. Truck terminals seek to maximize access to major routes both to the CBD and to the region as a whole. In addition, a balance must be sought between the advantages of a suburban location and those found in the high-density CBD. Figure 21.13 shows a generalized location in a metropolitan area which balances accessibility, density, and central location. Ideally, a location on the fringe of the CBD with easy access to major freeways is desired. It is difficult to locate all truck terminals in this peripheral area because of differing functions among trucking companies. Intercity trucking companies normally do locate in the fringe areas near major highways or freeways, whereas local service trucking companies normally locate near the downtown area.

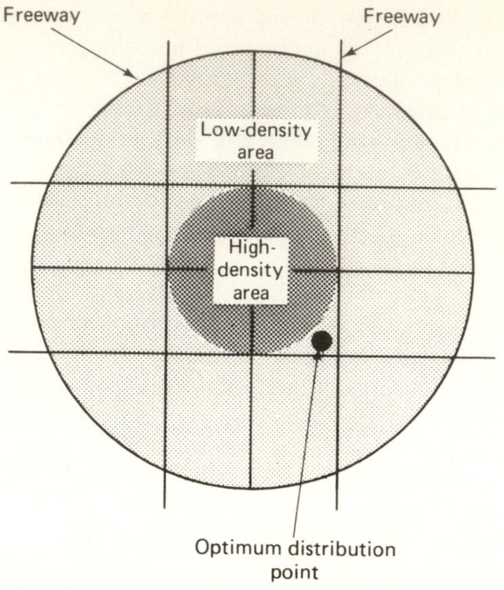

Figure 21.13. Generalized location of optimum distribution point for urban motor freight terminals (theoretical). SOURCE: Wilbur Smith & Associates, *Transportation and Parking for Tomorrow's Cities*, 1966, p. 264.

Terminal location and design are not static processes but change with changes in technology in goods movement. Advances in vehicle design, expansion of freeway systems, improved loading–unloading facilities, and the concept of containerization of freight have all affected terminal location and design.

Bicycle parking

It is estimated that in 1977 there were over 70 million bicycle riders in the United States. Although bicycle riding in the United States has historically been a recreational activity associated with younger people, the 1970s boom in bicycle ridership can be attributed to the fact that adults have become more interested in recent years in cycling as a means of recreation and as a form of transportation.

The bicycle is an extremely efficient form of personal transportation. It is relatively inexpensive in initial cost and operation when compared to other forms of transportation. The bicycle also uses road and parking space efficiently. As a general rule, 12 to 16 bicycles may be parked in the space required by one standard-sized automobile.[19] In ad-

[18]WILBUR SMITH & ASSOCIATES, *Transportation and Parking for Tomorrow's Cities*, New Haven, Conn., 1966, p. 262.

[19]STEPHEN R. MCHENRY, *Bicycle Parking: A Design Manual*, Baltimore County Bikeways Task Force, Baltimore, Md., Jan. 1966, p. 1.

dition to providing space and cost savings, the bicycle also has environmental considerations in its favor. The bicycle is free of air and noise pollution problems associated with motor-powered vehicles.

With the boom in bicycle sales and usage, there comes an increasing need for organized bicycle parking, particularly in downtown areas. When designated parking facilities are not available, bicycles are parked against buildings, lamp posts, traffic signs, parking meters, and other such facilities. This results in a chaotic and haphazard parking arrangement in areas where there is a large demand for bicycle parking.

Classifications

In bicycle parking, there are two major types of users. The needs for each differ as to placement and protection of parking facilities. These two types are commuter (long-term) and convenience (short-term) parking. Commuter parking locations occur at places of employment, apartment units, bus stations, and so on. Commuter parking locations require both theft and weather protection. Appropriate for this use are Class 1 weather-protected facilities, as described below.

Convenience bicycle parking is needed at shopping centers, libraries, post offices, and other public buildings. As a minimum, these convenience bicycle parking facilities should provide Class 3 facilities.

Available bicycle parking devices can be separated into three classes. A Class 1 parking device offers total protection against weather and protects from theft or damage to frame, wheels, and accessories. Class 1 protection can be provided by either a locker-type facility or by making space available where bicycles can be stored in an attended or locked location. The initial cost of parking devices in the Class 1 category range between $100 and $170 per bicycle.

Class 2 parking devices secure the frame and the wheels from theft while often requiring cyclists to carry their own locks. Other parts of the bicycle are not protected by this Class 2 device. A special structure or existing building overhang is encouraged to provide weather protection. The price range for Class 2 bicycle parking devices ranges from about $25 to about $80 per bicycle.

Class 3 parking devices offer the least protection from theft and should be considered only for short-term or convenience parking. A Class 3 device is any fixed object to which a bicycle can be chained or locked. It may or may not support the bicycle. Cyclists would be responsible for providing their own locks, chains or cables. Cost for Class 3 parking devices range from zero for existing parking meters and other posts to $18 per bike for some devices.

The traditional bicycle rack has not been listed in the parking classifications described above. Because of their design, bicycle racks may bend wheel rims and damage the gear mechanisms of multispeed bicycles. Loading and unloading a bicycle from a rack is difficult when the rack is crowded. It is often difficult to secure both wheels and frame to a bicycle rack with the chains and cables normally sold for bicycle protection.

Design and criteria

In the development of bicycle parking, a great deal of care should be given to the location, safety, and convenience of the parking facilities. A partial checklist of bicycle parking design and criteria includes:[20]

1. Bicycle parking should be located as close to the desired destinations as possible without interfering with pedestrian traffic.
2. Bicycle and auto parking areas should be separated by some form of physical barrier to prevent bicycles from being hit by vehicles.
3. Utilization of an existing weather-protected area is recommended. This saves on initial construction costs and provides protection to the bicycle.
4. The parking device selected should have no protruding bars that could trip or injure the cyclist.
5. Portions of the bicycle parking device that come into contact with the bicycle should be vinyl-coated to protect the bicycle finish.
6. Bicycle parking areas should be well lit for both theft protection and to reduce the possibility of accidents.
7. The parking device selected should be easy to operate and understandable to children as well as adults.
8. At the parking location, a sign should be displayed showing the operation of the device in a series of simple pictures.
9. The parking device selected should be compatible with all bike frames.
10. Where bike lockers are used, they should be harmonious in color and design with the environment.
11. Bicycle parking devices should be spaced so that the use of one does not interfere with adjacent bicycles. The separation distance for most devices is approximately 22 to 24 in. (56 to 61 cm).

REFERENCES FOR FURTHER READING

Bus Stops for Freeway Operations, ITE Recommended Practice, Institute of Traffic Engineers, Washington, D.C., 1971.

HEATH, W. D., J. M. HUNNICUTT, M. A. NEALE, AND L. A. WILLIAMS, *Parking in the United States—A Survey of Local Government Action*, National League of Cities, Department of Urban Studies, Washington, D.C., 1967.

Improved Parking and Traffic Enforcement in the District of Columbia, Metropolitan Police Department, Office of the Corporation Counsel, D.C. Department of Transportation, Washington, D.C., 1977.

KLOSE, D., *Metropolitan Parking Structures*, Praeger, New York, 1965.

MCHENRY, STEPHEN R., *Bicycle Parking: A Design Manual*, Baltimore County Bikeways Task Force, Baltimore, Md., Jan. 1976.

Parking Facilities for Industrial Plants, Institute of Traffic Engineers, Washington, D.C., 1969.

Parking Management, A Report of the Transportation Task Force of the Urban Consortium for Technology Initiatives, U.S. Department of Transportation, Washington, D.C., 1978.

Parking Principles, Special Report No. 125, Highway Research Board, Washington, D.C., 1971.

[20] STEPHEN R. MCHENRY, *Bicycle Parking: A Design Manual*, Baltimore County Bikeways Task Force, Baltimore, Md., Jan. 1966, p. 7.

Parking Revenue Control, Circular No. 184, Transportation Research Board, Washington, D.C., 1977.

A Recommended Practice for the Proper Location of Bus Stops, Institute of Traffic Engineers, Washington, D.C., 1967.

Schemes for the Provision of Parking Space in Town Centres, Theme 6, Eighth International Study Week in Traffic Engineering, OTA, London, 1966.

SEYMER, N., "Design of Parking Garages for European Needs," *Int. Road Safety Traffic Rev.,* 1966.

SIMKOWITZ, HOWARD, L. HEDER, AND E. BARBER, *The Restraint of the Automobile in American Residential Neighborhoods,* U.S. Dept. of Transportation, UMTA, Washington, D.C., 1966.

STOUT, R. W., *A Report on CBD Parking,* Highway Planning Tech. Report No. 23, U.S. Dept. of Transportation, Federal Highway Administration, Washington, D.C., 1971.

WILBUR SMITH & ASSOCIATES, *Parking in the City Center,* New Haven, Conn., 1965.

22

CIRCULATION IN MAJOR ACTIVITY CENTERS

MICHAEL A. POWILLS, JR., *Senior Vice President*

Barton-Aschman Associates, Evanston, Illinois and Founding Chairman, Advanced Transit Association

The importance of optimizing circulation in major activity centers arises out of concern for better management of our resources of land, energy, time, and money. As the "scarcity" of these items becomes more apparent, there is a growing interest in centralizing or otherwise concentrating similar or related land uses into major activity centers so as to lead to more efficient utilization of the resources in question.

This chapter briefly defines types of major activity centers and their transportation characteristics, sets forth some transportation planning principles concerning access to and terminal facilities within such centers, and examines various transportation modes for circulation within major activity centers. Characteristics of modes that are relatively unique to major activity centers are examined in some detail; aspects of automobile and conventional transit modes are considered only briefly, since other chapters of this handbook more than adequately cover these topics (see especially Chapters 7, 10, 12, and 21). Thus, pedestrian systems and advanced transit technologies are singled out for attention. The rapidly developing innovations of these two forms of transportation are the important aspect of this chapter.

Classification of major activity centers and some dimensions of their transportation characteristics

Each focal point within an urban area which generates an unusually large amount of travel can be considered as a major activity center. These focal points do much to shape the need for urban transportation systems. Whereas historically, cities could be characterized as having many locations of trip origins but few places of trip destinations, current urban development is more likely to follow the form of many origins to many destinations. Thus, major activity centers have come to include not only the traditional central business districts of cities but other similar, although possibly smaller, outlying commercial or industrial centers as well. Similarly, regional suburban shopping centers can be classified as major activity centers, as can dense residential developments, and office or industrial parks. Institutional complexes, such as hospitals, educational campuses, and concentrations of government buildings, each generating extensive amounts of travel, may be classed as major activity centers. Multimodal transportation centers and large regional airports, as well as major entertainment complexes and groups of sports facilities, also fall into the classification of major activity centers.

Table 22-1 lists examples of selected types of such major activity centers in four different regions in the United States. Examination of this information suggests that one definition of major activity centers might be the grouping of similar or related land uses that results in a geographic concentration of a daily population of 25,000 persons or more. (This total daily population could consist of employees, shoppers, visitors, students, travelers, local residents, or any combination of these.) It should be noted that strict definition of major activity center boundaries is frequently difficult because of the tendency of the "edges" of many centers, such as central business districts and university campuses, to blend in with adjacent land uses. Thus, another of the indicated characteristics, population density, is useful as a general guide; the lowest listed population density in Table 22-1 is just over 50,000 persons per square mile. To the extent that these dimensions of daily population and density are useful, approximately 60 to 70 U.S. cities' CBDs, more than 20 of the larger U.S. airports, and over 170 regional shopping centers may be classified as major activity centers (see Table 22-2).

A significant aspect of major activity centers is not only their classification as requiring considerable amounts of external access, but also the amount and multiplicity of travel demand within such areas. They require internal circulation for various modes, terminal facilities (parking and other-

TABLE 22–1
Selected Characteristics of Major Activity Centers in Four Regions*

Activity Center, Region	Type	Employment (× 10^3)†	Daily Visitors (× 10^3)‡	Daily Population (× 10^3)	Land Area (mi^2)§	Population Density persons/(mi^2) (× 10^3)§	Parking Spaces (× 10^3)	Gross Leasable Area (ft^2 × 10^3)
Los Angeles CBD	CBD	129	186	315	2.55	124	94.5	14,400
Houston CBD	CBD	118	226	344	1.00	344	63.0	37,623
Minneapolis CBD	CBD	90	89	179	0.66	271	35.5	19,676
L.A. Airport	Airport	47‖	125	171	n.a.	n.a.	n.a.	n.a.
Denver CBD	CBD	83	75	158	1.66	95	33.0	16,000
St. Paul CBD	CBD	63	54	117	0.57	205	29.1	11,045
City Post Oak, Houston	MDC	34	64	98	0.78	125	26.0	10,489
Del Amo, L.A.	MDC	7	77	84	0.22	381	11.1	3500
TX Med Center, Houston	MED	33	29	62	0.34	182	27.8	n.a.
U of MN, Minne.	UNIV	6	55	61	0.80	76	15.0	n.a.
Lakewood Center, L.A.	RSC	5	51	56	0.26	215	12.5	2300
Hollywood, CA	OBD	12	42	54	n.a.	n.a.	23.4	3787
Century City, L.A.	MDC	25	25	50	0.28	146	21.3	6653
Denver Airport	Airport	11	37	48	0.31	154	12.0	n.a.
Greenway Plaza, Houston	MDC	36	8	44	0.47	94	28.6	8300
U of Hou/TSU, Houston	UNIV	2	40	42	0.81	52	15.5	n.a.
Westwood, L.A.	OBD	16	26	42	0.12	350	7.7	3116
Panorama City, L.A.	RSC	3	37	40	0.14	286	9.0	1700
Minne/St. Paul Airport	Airport	16	24	40	0.26	154	10.9	n.a.
S. Coast Plaza, L.A.	RSC	3	36	39	0.32	122	8.5	1625
Cinderella City, Denver	MDC	10	28	38	0.10	380	7.1	1300
Long Beach CBD, L.A.	OBD	12	26	38	0.77	141	10.0	4156
UCLA, L.A.	UNIV	2	33	35	n.a.	n.a.	n.a.	n.a.
Almeda Mall, Houston	RSC	3	32	35	0.20	175	6.1	1470
Disneyland, L.A.	REC	2	32	34	0.31	110	11.0	
Fashion Island, L.A.	MDC	9	25	34	0.12	283	11.7	2724
Memorial City, Houston	RSC	3	29	32	0.23	139	5.7	1340
Northridge, L.A.	RSC	3	28	31	0.11	282	6.7	1281
USC, L.A.	UNIV	2	28	30	n.a.	n.a.	n.a.	n.a.
Ridgedale, Minne/St. Paul	RSC	2	27	29	0.15	193	6.1	1225
Puente Hills Mall, L.A.	RSC	2	26	28	0.15	187	6.5	1200
Los Cerritos, L.A.	RSC	2	26	28	0.15	187	6.5	1175
Southdale, Minne/St. Paul	MDC**	2	25	27	0.66	225	6.5	1150
Sharpstown, Houston	RSC	2	25	27	0.16	169	6.3	1130
Houston Airport	Airport	5	22	27	0.08	338	11.0	n.a.
Topanga Plaza, L.A.	RSC	2	24	26	0.16	162	6.3	1088
Westminster Mall, L.A.	RSC	2	24	26	0.15	173	6.0	1080
The Oaks, L.A.	RSC	2	24	26	0.15	173	4.7	1080
Col. U. Med. Cent., Denver	MED	13	13	26	0.25	104	4.8	n.a.
Montclair Plaza, L.A.	RSC	2	23	25	0.19	132	5.5	1044
Buena Park Center, L.A.	RSC	2	23	25	0.12	208	5.4	1050
Brookdale, Minne/St. Paul	RSC	2	23	25	0.12	208	5.1	1040

*Major activity centers include central business districts (CBD), older central city business districts (OBD), major suburban diversified centers (MDC), regional shopping centers (RSC), university campuses (UNIV), medical complexes (MED), airports, and major recreation centers. No examples of government centers are included, although the Los Angeles Civic Center, Denver State Government Center, and St. Paul Capitol Complex are all included within their respective CBDs.
†Employment estimates for regional shopping centers (RSC) made using a multiplier of 2 employees/1000 ft^2 gross leasable area (GLA).
‡Daily visitors/shoppers to (RSC) estimated using a multiplier of 22 trips/1000 ft^2 GLA. Observed range for shopping centers across the country is 17–28 trips/1000 ft^2 GLA.
§1 mi^2 = 2.59 km^2.
‖Includes adjacent hotel, office, light industrial employment.
**Data on additional retail and office space in this MDC not readily available; figures shown reflect only the RSC, which serves as the center's focus.
n.a. not available

SOURCE: W. V. ROUSE & CO., *Generic Alternatives Analyses Summary: Definition of Generic Modes and Application Area, Draft Report,* prepared for the U.S. Department of Transportation, Washington, D.C., June 1979.

wise), service and goods movement facilities, and emergency vehicle circulation. Although the state of the art of transportation planning is sufficiently developed so that external access needs can be defined by such information as trip-generation rates, use of alternative modes, direction of approach, and so on, few sound data and little guideline information on the need for purely internal circulation are currently available.

Nevertheless, some useful observations can be made about internal trip demand in major activity centers:

1. For all major activity centers listed in Table 22-1, the pedestrian mode predominates as the primary means of internal travel (involving 85 to 90% of all major activity centers listed, and almost 95% if only CBDs are considered).

2. When travel other than by transit or walking to and from a major activity center is assigned to the street network of the area under consideration, the resultant traffic flows are frequently found to be from 30 to 80% understated compared to actual ground counts of traffic. This phenomenon is a function of several factors, including some related to the mechanics of the traffic assignment process, but importantly, also including some related to underidentification of purely internal circulation and recirculation needs and/or problems. In other words, internal vehicular circulation

TABLE 22–2
Distribution of Major Regional Shopping Centers by State

State	Number of Regional Shopping Centers, 1976			
	Type A*	Type B†	Total	
California	36	28	64	188 (California through Illinois)
Ohio	18	9	27	
Texas	14	12	26	
New York	9	16	25	
Florida	14	10	24	
Illinois	7	15	22	
Pennsylvania	11	8	19	
New Jersey	7	9	16	
Missouri	8	5	13	
Michigan	5	6	11	
North Carolina	6	4	10	
Arizona	6	3	9	
Wisconsin	4	5	9	
Georgia	4	4	8	
Maryland	3	5	8	
Indiana	3	3	6	
Colorado	3	2	5	
Minnesota	2	3	5	
Virginia	3	2	5	
Washington	1	4	5	
Total	164	153	317	
Total in U.S.	192	171	363	

*800,000–1,000,000 ft² (75,000–93,000 m²).
†>1,000,000 ft² (93,000 m²).

SOURCE: W. V. ROUSE & CO., *Generic Alternatives Analyses Summary: Definition of Generic Modes and Application Area, Draft Report,* prepared for U.S. Department of Transportation, Washington, D.C., June 1979.

needs may be deduced in part by close analysis of external needs compared with actual observed flows.

3. While quantification of travel between related land uses in a major activity center is in part a function of the sizes of the land uses, nevertheless, important insights can be gained about the placement of land-use elements by understanding their interrelationships, as shown in Figure 22.1. Attention to those linkages that are either "essential" or "important," not only in the creation of new major activity centers, but in the revitalization of older centers, can enhance the development of an efficient internal circulation system.

4. Judicious use of information on the distances and geography of major activity centers, coupled with pedestrian and vehicular travel speeds, acceptable walking distances from parking facilities, and all similar information contained elsewhere in this handbook can lead to better understanding of major activity center circulation needs and constraints.

As part of the classification process, it is useful to consider what types of transportation serve best, or impose requirements on major activity centers. Automobiles, taxis, conventional transit, pedestrians, cyclists, and new-technology transit all have their place in major activity centers; Table 22-3 presents these transportation modes for comparison with various travel functions and requirements of major activity centers, and indicates both strong and weak points for each mode considered.

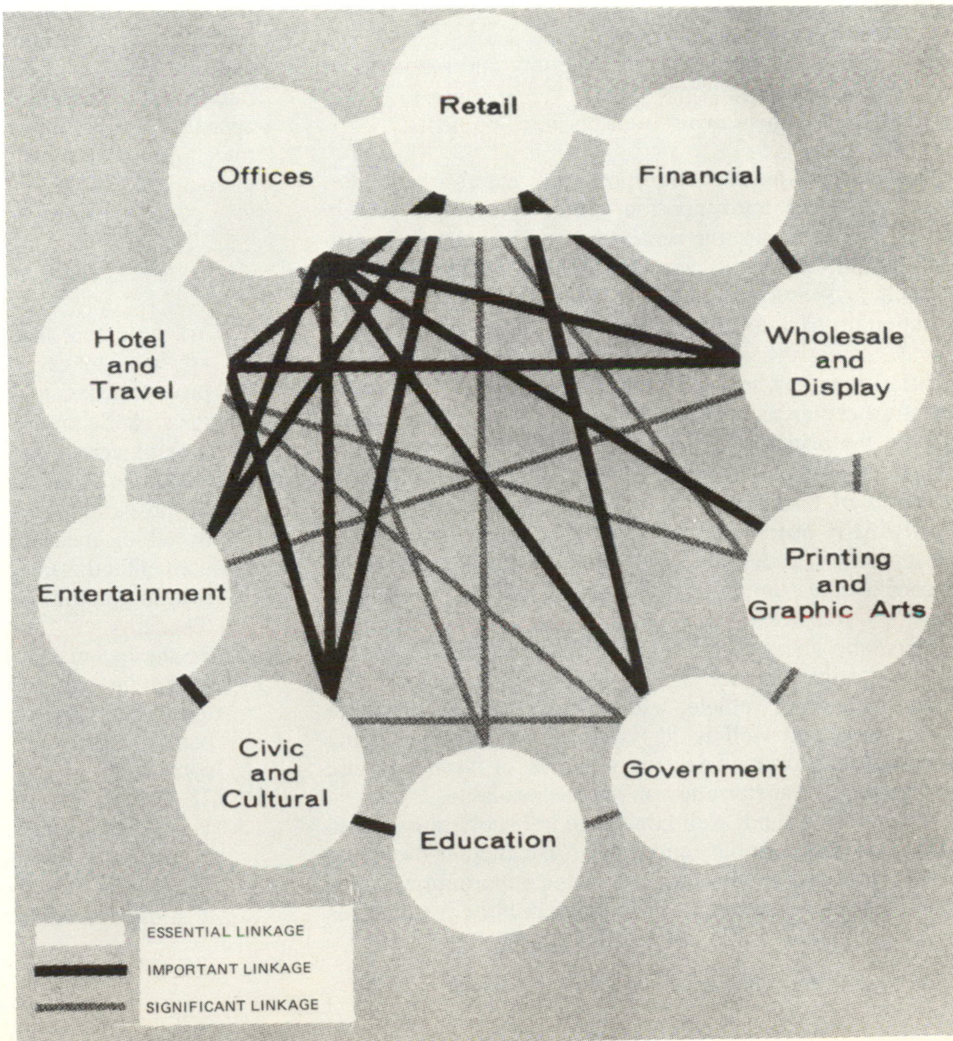

Figure 22.1. Interrelationship of land-use and circulation needs.

TABLE 22–3
Major Activity Center Travel Functions vs Types of Transportation*

	Automobiles	Taxis	Conventional Transit	New-Technology Transit	Intercity Transportation	Pedestrians	Cyclists
Provide service							
Access to area	××	×	××	—	××	×	×
Circulation within area	—	××	×	××	—	××	×
Impose requirements							
Use of street space	××	×	×	—	—	×	—
Terminal needs	××	—	×	—	××	—	—

*××, extensive; ×, moderate; —, minimal.

Transportation centers

Before completely departing from the classification of major activity centers, the subject of large transportation centers, such as airports or multimodal facilities, should be dealt with. These are special examples of major activity centers because of their special relationship to transportation. In part, transportation centers are dealt with elsewhere in this handbook, but their major activity center aspects are worthy of note here.

Transportation centers serve a variety of functions, such as the following:

- Facilitate transfers between travel modes.
- Serve as a major transit load point.
- Reduce travel time.
- Reduce congestion.
- Enhance the image of both intercity and intracity public transportation.
- Stimulate and support adjacent developments.

Several cautions about transportation centers are in order. First, not every transportation center is a major activity center. For example, the rehabilitation and reuse of a railroad station, although it may be desirable, does not in and of itself make such a facility a major activity center (this is important to note in light of the very desirable attention that is currently being paid to railroad station redevelopment). Second, when considering the creation of a transportation center as a major terminus for an urban transit system, the principle of self-distribution by the system, to the extent possible, should be followed, thus avoiding the necessity of transfers to a secondary distributor system. Finally, it is observed that bringing together a variety of transportation modes at a single point must not be based on ill-conceived assumptions of the need for multitudes of passengers to transfer between various modes. Only those passengers who arrive at a terminal via one mode and have a further destination, not within walking distance or better served by another vehicle, will make the transfer. In other words, users may well avoid systems involving transferring modes at transportation centers, if shorter or faster, or more simple, or nontransfer alternatives are available.

On the other hand, well-conceived transportation centers lead to several desirable conditions. First, there is the virtue of aggregating activities, which creates opportunities to invest in more and better facilities than could be justified for single modes. Second, to the extent to which the transportation center is multimodal, opportunities become available for managing the several elements of the transportation system in an optimum complementary way, as opposed to permitting noncoordinated and sometimes even competitive or conflicting transportation management strategies.

Circulation/land-use principles for major activity centers

The following material is a set of principles to aid in circulation planning for a major activity center. The principles deal with a variety of circulation elements, including public transportation, vehicular circulation, parking (briefly touched on), pedestrian and bicycle circulation, and service and emergency vehicle facilities. Although the principles range from the obvious to the complex, and even sometimes appear contradictory, they are valid nevertheless. The contradictions serve to reveal the conflicting interests that exist in complex circulation systems.

Vehicular circulation

1. To the extent that streets in the major activity center are used to carry vehicular traffic, they should first provide access to the area and access to land uses within the area. Second, they must serve nonbypassable traffic moving across the area. Long-distance, through traffic should be avoided on major activity center streets; first, by providing adequate bypass facilities, and second, by taking measures to discourage through traffic that does enter the area. (Figure 22.2 illustrates such a traffic restraint/modification scheme for the City of Göteborg, Sweden.)
2. To the extent that approach routes can be designed to lead to the corners of a major activity center rather than intersecting the center, a more desirable distribution pattern for through traffic will result and internal congestion will be diminished (see Figures 22.3 and 22.4).
3. The vehicular circulation pattern should be readily understandable to the average driver.
4. The system should be flexible (i.e., should present more than one opportunity to reach a given destination).

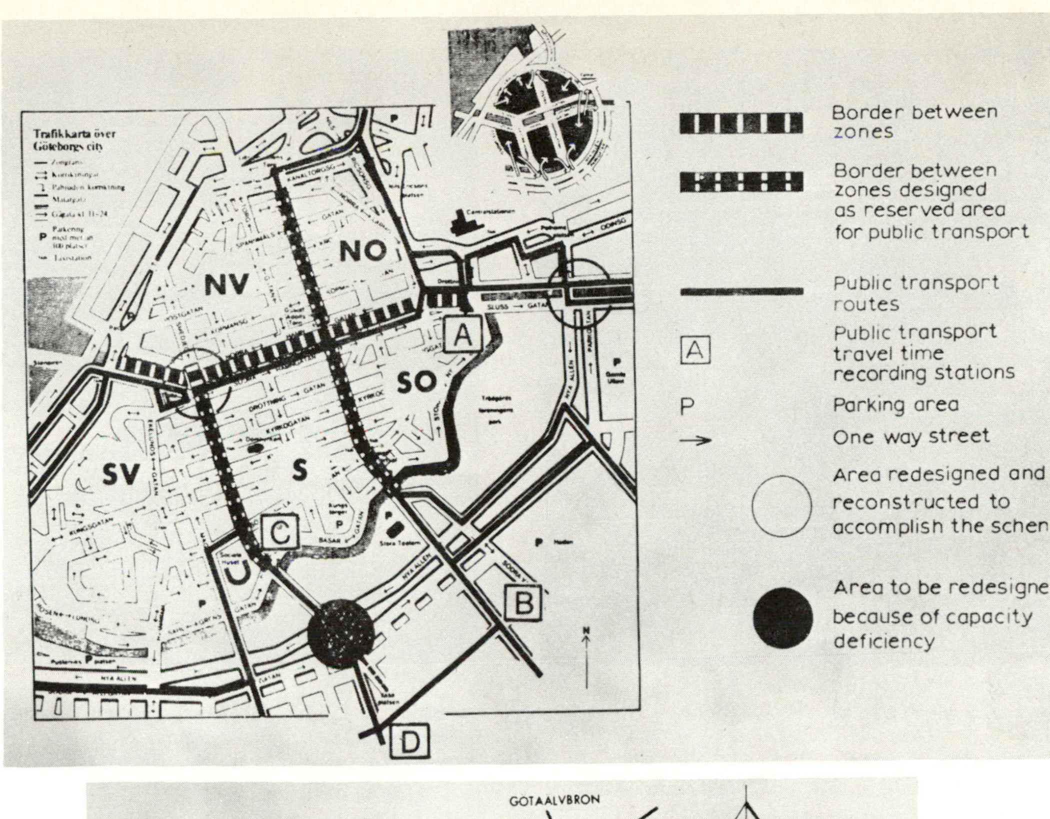

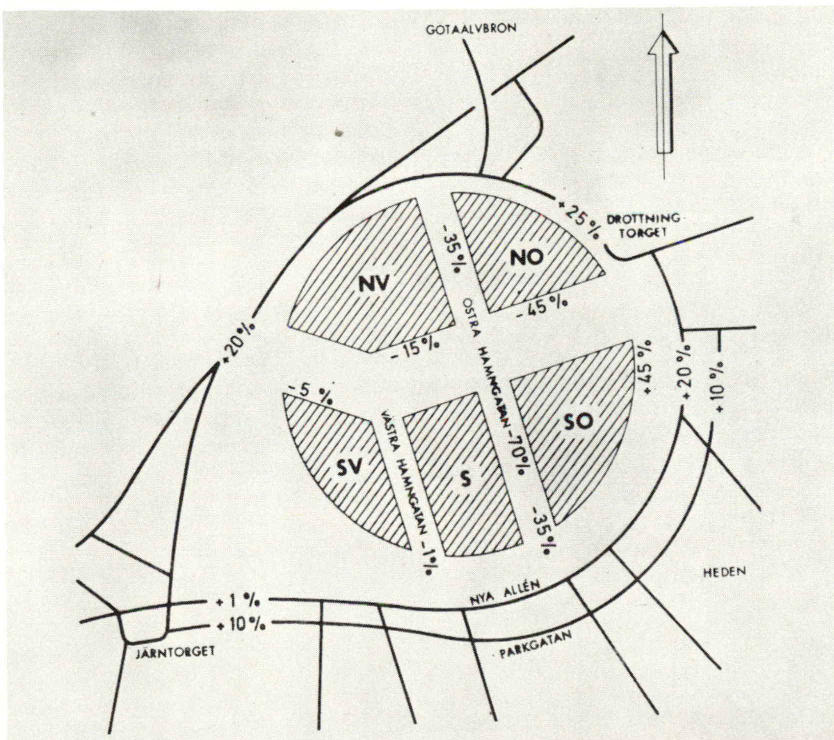

Figure 22.2. Gothenburg traffic restraint scheme. SOURCE: HIGHWAY RESEARCH RECORD, *Parking as an Alterant to the Traffic Pattern,* prepared for the 52nd Annual Meeting of the Highway Research Board, Number 474, National Research Council, Washington, D.C., 1973. (See Errata for source.)

5. There should be a directness to the circulation pattern so as not to compel circuitous travel.
6. The ability to circulate easily around those portions or blocks of the major activity center that are high traffic generators should be provided (see Figure 22.5).
7. The circulation system should be sufficiently direct and continuous as not to exaggerate the quantity or pattern of turning movements.
8. Ideally, given streets should perform specific functions (e.g., approach routes, local access streets, cross-area

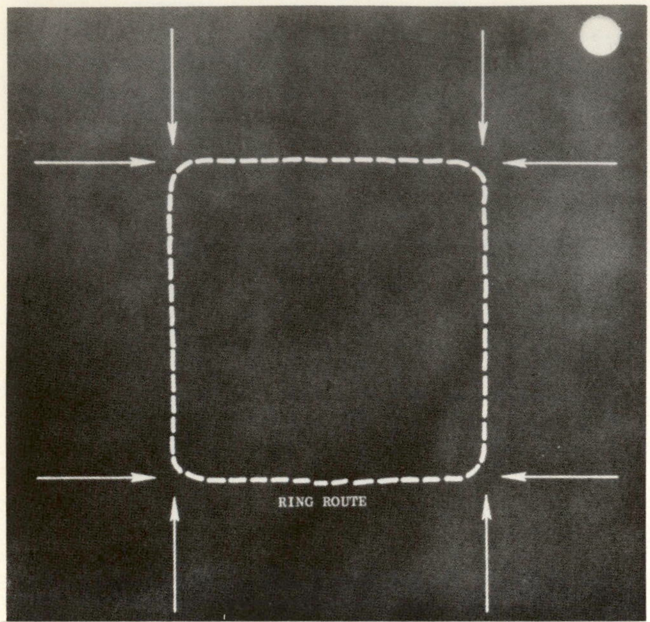

Figure 22.3. Corner access principle. SOURCE: BARTON-ASCHMAN ASSOCIATES, INC., *Guidelines for Growth: New Orleans Central Area,* prepared for the New Orleans Central Area Committee.

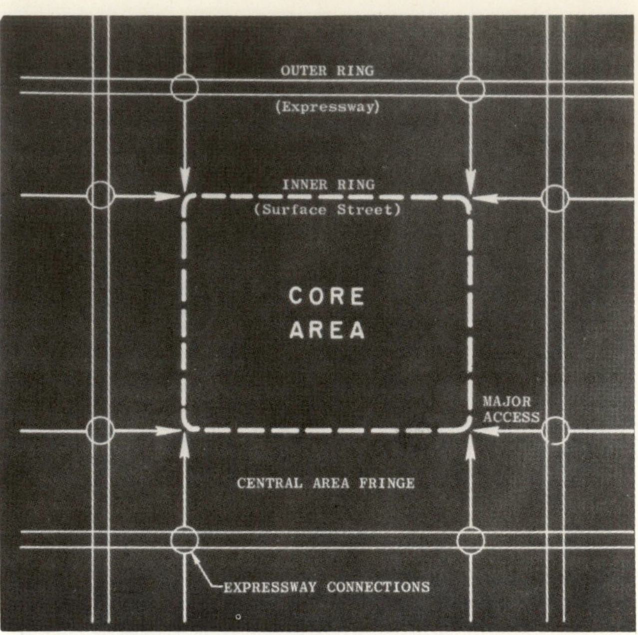

Figure 22.4. Inner and outer ring system. SOURCE: BARTON-ASCHMAN ASSOCIATES, INC., *Guidelines for Growth: New Orleans Central Area,* prepared for the New Orleans Central Area Committee.

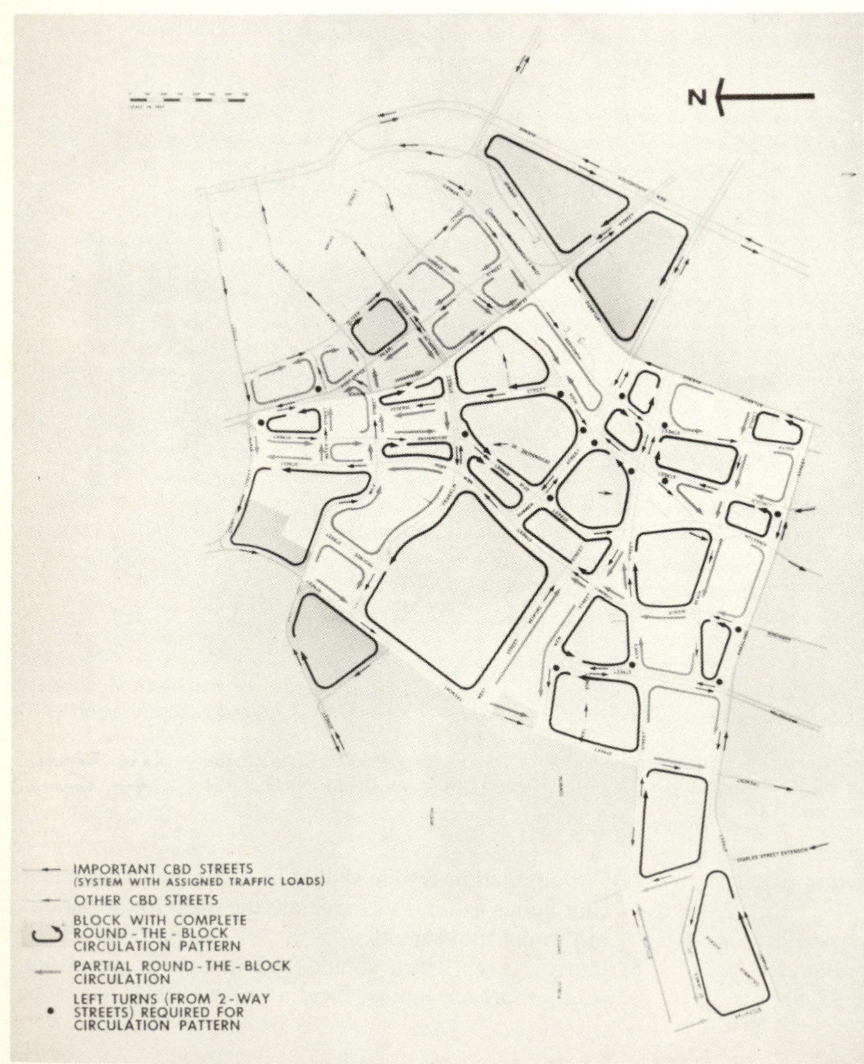

Figure 22.5. Round-the-block circulation analysis. SOURCE: BARTON-ASCHMAN ASSOCIATES, INC., *Boston, Massachusetts Traffic Circulation and Parking Plan: Central Business District Urban Renewal Area,* prepared for the Boston Redevelopment Authority, November, 1967.

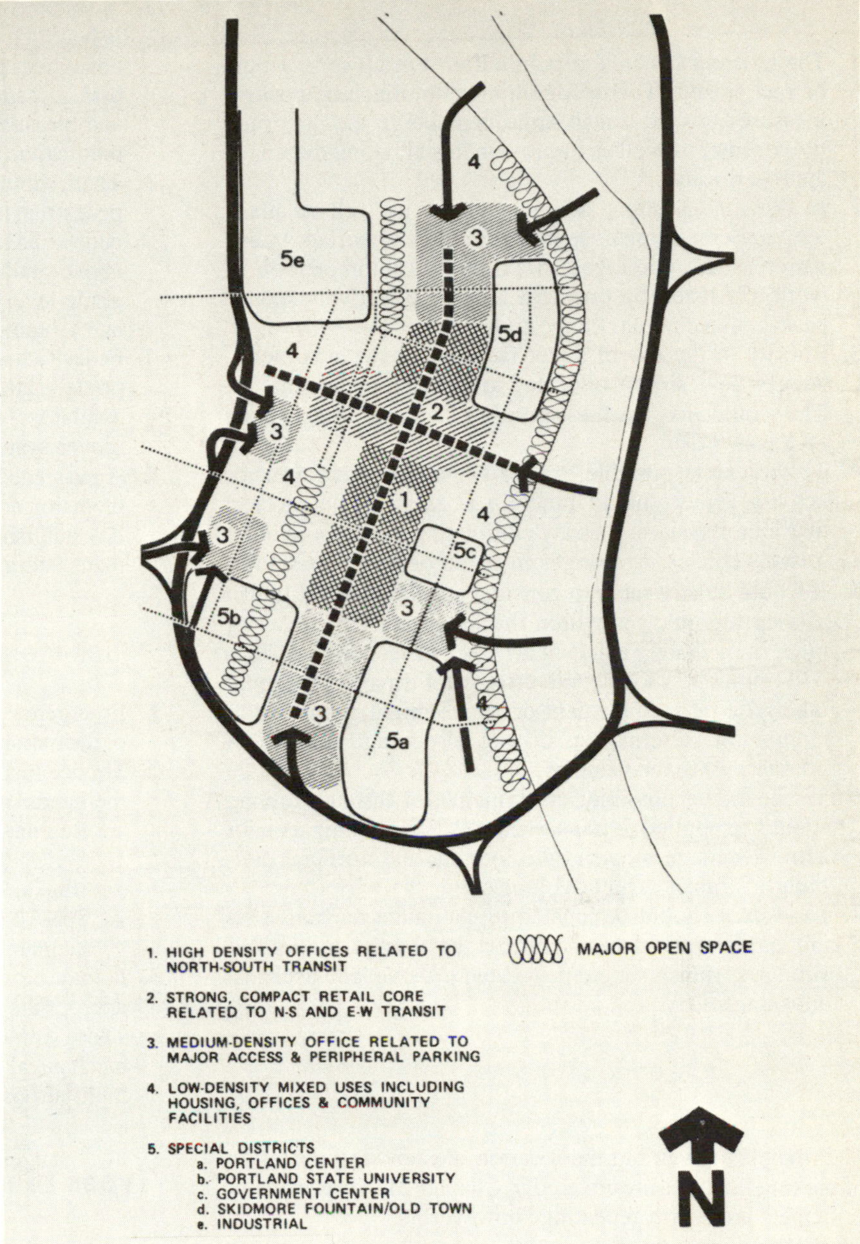

Figure 22.6. Functional plan for downtown Portland, Oregon. SOURCE: U.S. DEPARTMENT OF TRANSPORTATON, Urban Mass Transportation Administration, *Streets for Pedestrians and Transit: Examples of Transit Malls in the United States*. Service and Methods Demonstration Program, Final Report, August, 1977.

streets, etc.). Such a hierarchy (as illustrated in Figure 22.6) might be accomplished through the use of street design techniques, traffic control measures, or parking regulations.

9. Different types of traffic should be separated by a combination of either horizontal or vertical dispersal. Ideally, for example, pedestrians and public carriers, private passenger vehicles, and service vehicles should all be physically separated.

10. In the design of major activity center street systems, it may well be that no parking will be permitted on major streets. Nevertheless, it should be recognized that unless land uses are significantly inward away from streets, it is often inevitable that curb lanes will be used for stopped vehicles and cannot, therefore, carry significant amounts of moving traffic.

11. The arrangement of streets and land uses should be designed to avoid conflicts and to complement each other. In other words, land parcels should not be so large as to make the circulation pattern extremely difficult; the street pattern should not cut land areas into parcels too small to permit sound development.

12. Land uses generating either relatively large amounts of traffic or traffic that by its nature requires immediately adjacent curb frontage (such as parking facilities, hotels, medical buildings, automobile service facilities, bank drive-ins, etc.) should be located where they may be served properly by the street system.

13. To the extent possible, multiple use should be encouraged for street rights-of-way by the use of air rights and easements.

Transit

1. The inherent benefits of public transit of all sorts should be recognized. This recognition should include positive measures toward transit improvements in the major activity center as well as improvements all along the transit approach routes.
2. In downtown major activity centers as well as many outlying employment centers, the most important transit patron is the employee. Maximum accommodation of work-trip loads by transit will most effectively reduce peak-hour vehicular congestion.
3. Priority in the use of street facilities could in some instances be desirably allocated to surface transit vehicles. This could involve the creation of special transit lanes or transit malls.
4. To the extent possible, transit vehicles serving a major activity center should function as their own collector/distributor system, thereby eliminating transfers to other transit vehicles or changes in mode of transportation.
5. It would be advisable to consider special types of transit service for linkages within the major activity center or other immediately adjacent origins and destinations. This will minimize short-length cross-haul trips which would otherwise be inconvenient or which might occur due to circulation patterns that do not discourage the use of private passenger vehicles.
6. To the extent possible, the principle of through routing should be applied to transit vehicles approaching a major activity center, to avoid the looping and artificial doubling of transit vehicle volumes.
7. Land uses should be located to capitalize on transit facilities as well as to maximize the market for transit; similarly, transit should be located to serve land use most advantageously.

Parking

Principles governing the location, design, and operation of parking facilities are covered in Chapter 21. Three general principles are worth repeating, however:

1. Parking fee structures should be viewed as a way of controlling the duration of parking and thus helping to allocate critical parking to appropriate users.
2. Long-term parking facilities should be oriented to the pattern of routes approaching major activity centers and should generally be located at the periphery.
3. Short-duration parking, in more limited quantities, may be located more centrally within major activity centers and be oriented to the ultimate land-use destination.

Pedestrian and bicycle circulation

1. Walking should be made feasible and desirable in order to foster compact land-use and desirable functional relationships. Related land uses should be placed as close to one another as possible.
2. A suitable environment for pedestrians should be established. This should include, in addition to aesthetic amenities, protection from weather (such as trees, windbreaks, canopies, roofing systems, tunnel systems, etc.) and measures to ensure personal security (lighting, communication facilities, proper visibility, etc.).
3. There should be continuity in both horizontal and vertical pedestrian circulation. For example, concentrations of pedestrians from below-grade transit systems or from above-grade garages should be integrated with both grade-level and possible grade-separated pedestrian linkage systems.
4. Pedestrian-assist systems should be used where appropriate. These can take a variety of forms, from elevators, escalators, and moving walks to more elaborate people-mover systems.
5. An assigned role for the bicycle in serving some portion of major activity center patrons and employees should be established, with suitable provision for bicycle movement, storage, and safety.

Service and emergency vehicle circulation

1. Emergency vehicles must be able to reach any portion of the major activity center in a reasonably direct manner.
2. Service facilities in major activity centers must recognize the needs of:
   a. Regular delivery vehicle stopping.
   b. Quick-stop service (such as mail and newspaper trucks).
   c. Special-purpose vehicles such as construction and maintenance trucks.
3. It may be that separate service facilities become quite appropriate for major activity center developments. These can include tunnel systems for trucks, special mechanical systems for goods movement, or combined multipurpose off-street loading areas.

Types of major activity center circulation systems

Although it is not the province of this chapter to deal with transportation systems external to major activity centers, some principles of the relationship between external access and internal systems must be noted. As suggested in Figure 22.7, there is an inverse relationship between the efficiency of transport systems, as defined by system productivity, land-use implications, energy use, and the like, and degree of personalized service, which relates to privacy, individual control, range of trip origins and destinations, and other factors. This relationship needs to be borne in mind when considering trade-offs involving quality of service, comparative capacities of alternative modes, the need for terminal facilities (whether they be parking or stations), and the degree of self-distribution possible for access modes. What seems to be most desirable for both access to and circulation within a major activity center, then, is some optimum between the access-mode transportation unit, which is itself a result of a trade-off between efficiency and

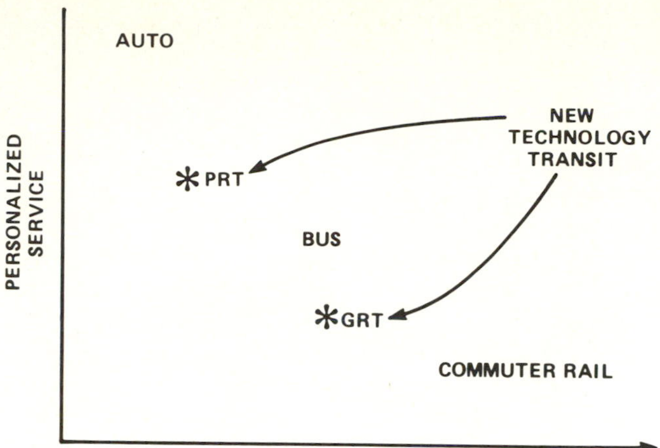

Figure 22.7. Transport system efficiency vs. personalized service. SOURCE: LAY, RODNEY K. *A Rationale for Automated and Group Transit Development*. In: Gary, Dennis A. (ed.), *Personal Rapid Transit III*. Papers presented at the 1975 International Conference on Personal Rapid Transit, Denver, Co., USA, Sept. 16–19, 1975.

quality of service as determined by public versus individual needs and desires, and that mode which functions best within the major activity center, as measured by minimal terminal or storage requirements.

If the systems available for serving circulation within major activity centers are arrayed in some sense of order from least complex to most sophisticated, they might be seen to include pedestrian systems of various sorts (sidewalks, malls, grade-separated systems, etc.), automobiles, taxis, buses of both conventional line-haul systems and special distributor or minisystems (see Figure 22.8), rapid transit of both light-rail and heavy-rail types, and new-technology systems. New technology systems include automated guideway transit systems (see Figure 22.9), cableways, and pedestrian conveyors.

The characteristics, trade-offs, and design considerations of all of these systems except the first and last mentioned are explained in more detail in other chapters. The remainder of this chapter will discuss pedestrian facilities and various forms of new-technology transit. Elevators as one form of major activity center circulation facility which is quite sophisticated, but which does not easily classify as a pedestrian or new-technology transit facility, will also be discussed.

Pedestrian systems

Selected characteristics of pedestrian facilities are set forth in Table 22-4. This table presents some useful parameters for dealing with speeds and capacities of a variety of pedestrian-assist facilities. Figure 22.10 effectively illustrates the application of the level-of-service concept to pedestrian walkway facilities, although the author of the source material cautions that because of the static quality inherent in a photograph, the congestion caused by motion is understated. Figure 22.11 presents a useful tool for calculating either required walkway sizes or the capacities of walkways under different levels of service.

One of the most frequently undertaken and relatively easy methods of improving pedestrian circulation systems is the upgrading of aesthetics (see Figure 22.12). Several cautions are worthy of note, however. While it is true that "beauty is in the eye of the beholder," it is also said that "form follows function." Cheap, minimal attempts at beautification frequently result in an effect worse than no treatment at all. Second, beautification treatments, if not properly maintained (usually at a maintenance cost significantly higher than simple sidewalk cleaning and maintenance), can become extremely unsightly and even hazardous. Untended planting areas can be repositories for trash, and special sidewalk paving systems which become or remain broken either through poor design or poor maintenance can become serious public liabilities. The rule should be: "If it can't be done well, it shouldn't be done at all."

Figure 22.8. Minibus. SOURCE: Advanced Transit Association International Conference, *Advanced Transit and Urban Revitalization—An International Dialogue: Proceedings;* Volume I, Indianapolis, Indiana, 1978.

Figure 22.9. Automated guideway transit systems. SOURCE: ANDERSON, DR. J. EDWARD, *Breaking the Transit Dilemma through Innovation;* A Slide Presentation, January, 1979.

TABLE 22–4
Speed and Capacity Values for Selected Pedestrian Facilities

Type of Facility	Speed: English Units	Speed: Metric Units	Nominal Capacity
Walk			
	262 ft/min	80 m/min	n.a.
	3 mi/hr	5 km/h	
Stairway			
Up	110–115 steps/min		18.9 persons/min
Down	140–150 steps/min		20.0 persons/min
Escalator	90 ft/min	27 m/min	
Incline speed	120 ft/min	37 m/min	1875 persons/hr*
			2512 persons/hr*
Moving Walkway			
0° incline	180 ft/min	55 m/min	3240 persons/hr*
15° incline	125 ft/min	38 m/min	2250 persons/hr*
Turnstyle			
Free	n.a.	n.a.	40–60 persons/min
Coin-operated	n.a.	n.a.	25–50 persons/min
Cashier-operated	n.a.	n.a.	12–18 persons/min
Elevator			
Hydraulic	75–125 ft/min	23–38 m/min	8–27 persons/car
Geared	150–350 ft/min	46–107 m/min	
Gearless	500–1500 ft/min	152–457 m/min	

* rate per foot (0.6m) of width
SOURCE: Adapted from DELEUW, CATHER AND COMPANY AND ROCK CREEK ASSOCIATES, *Characteristics of Urban Transportation Systems: A Handbook for Transportation Planners*, prepared for U.S. Department of Transportation, Urban Mass Transportation Administration, Washington, D.C., July 1977.

Figure 22.10. Level-of-service illustrations for walkways. SOURCE: FRUIN, JOHN J., *Pedestrian Planning and Design;* Metropolitan Association of Urban Designers and Environmental Planners, Inc., New York, New York, 1971.

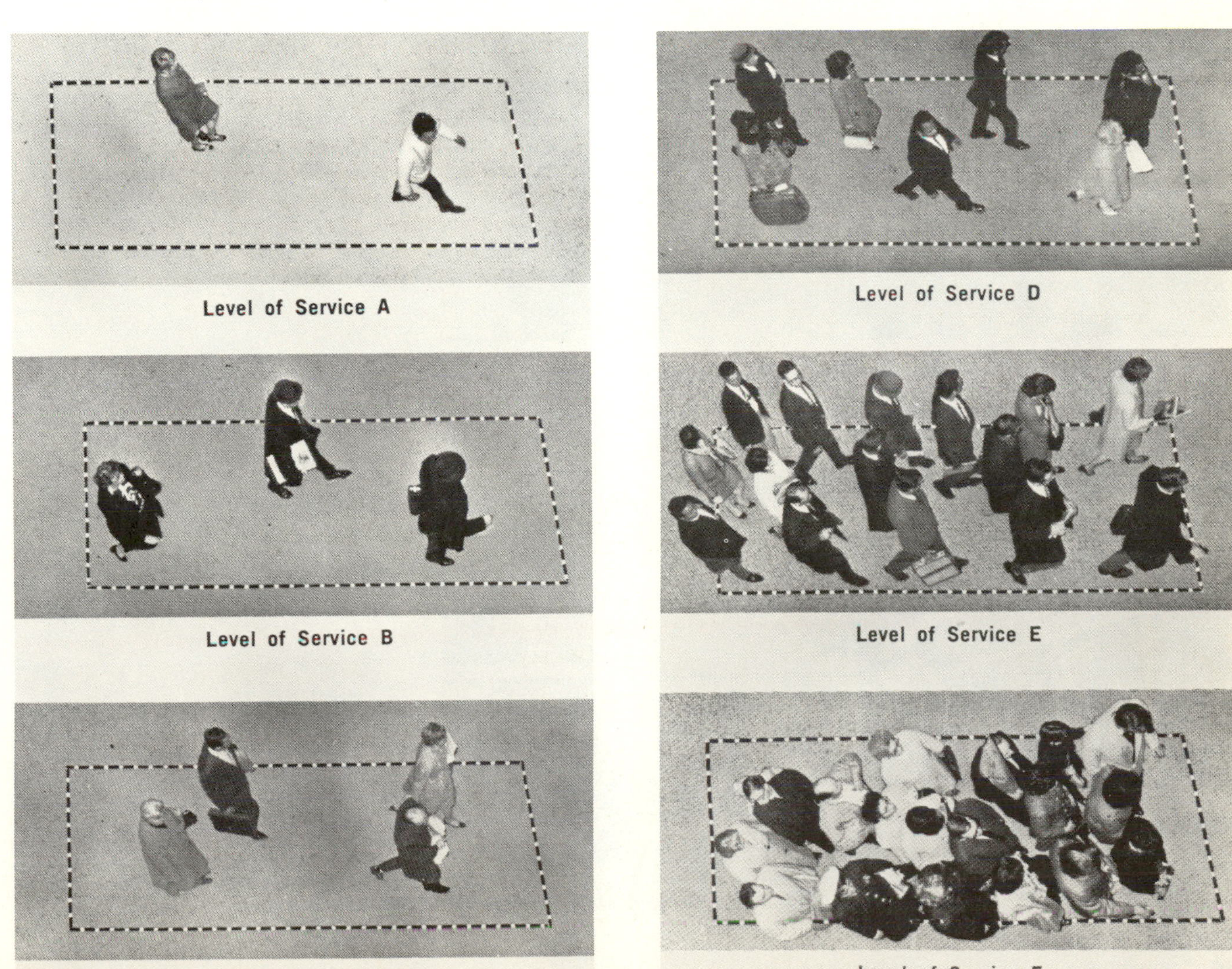

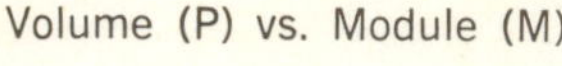

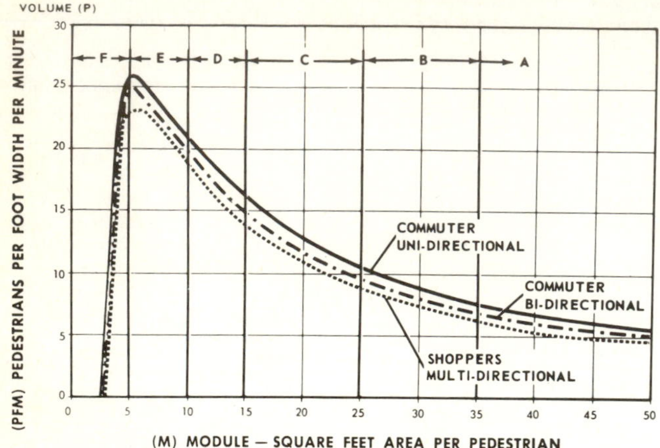

Figure 22.11. Level-of-service standards for walkways. SOURCE: FRUIN, JOHN J., *Pedestrian Planning and Design;* Metropolitan Association of Urban Designers and Environmental Planners, Inc., New York, New York, 1971.

A variety of types of partial and complete street pedestrianization schemes is shown in Figure 22.13 together with a description of each scheme. Transit malls are seen by many to be one of the more broadly applicable circulation treatments not only in CBDs but in other types of major activity centers as well. Nicollet Avenue in Minneapolis, Chestnut Street in Philadelphia, Fifth and Sixth Avenues in Portland, and Bahnhofstrasse in Zürich are all good examples of this treatment. Several of these transit malls are shown in Figures 22.14 and 22.15. State Street in Chicago and 16th Street in Denver are two of the newest additions to the list of this type of facility. Table 22-5 presents a useful summary of information about five U.S. transit malls.

There are two common problems with transit malls. The first has to do with the problems generated by the size, noise, and fumes of standard transit buses operating in proximity to pedestrians. While many malls carry conventional

Figure 22.12. Aesthetic improvements to pedestrian circulation. SOURCE: BARTON-ASCHMAN ASSOCIATES, INC., *Nicollet Avenue Study: Principles and Techniques for Retail Street Improvement,* prepared for the Downtown Council of Minneapolis, Minn., June, 1960.

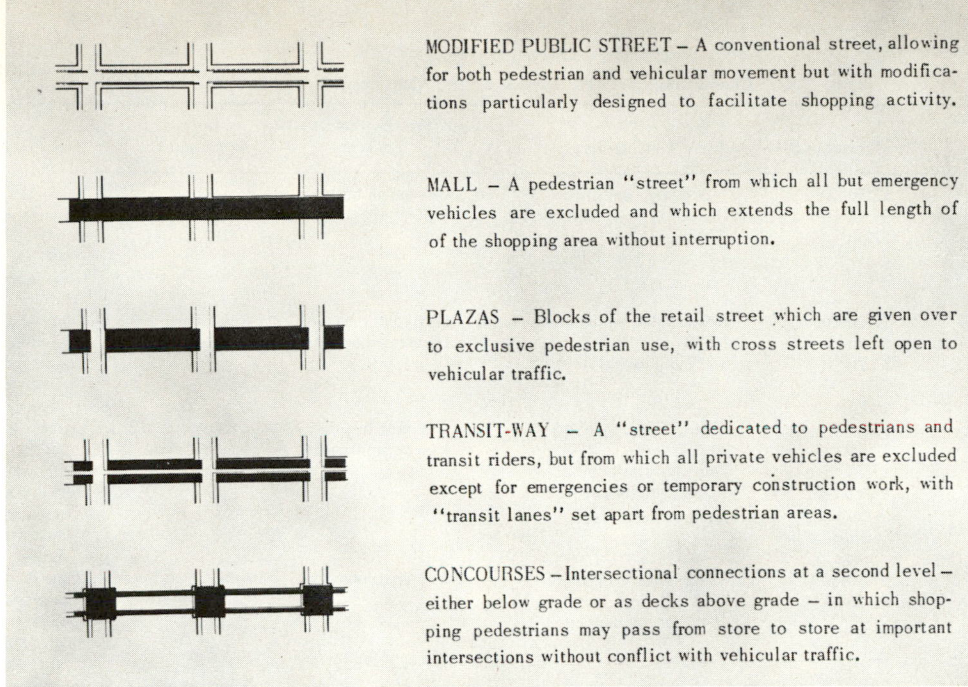

MODIFIED PUBLIC STREET – A conventional street, allowing for both pedestrian and vehicular movement but with modifications particularly designed to facilitate shopping activity.
MALL – A pedestrian "street" from which all but emergency vehicles are excluded and which extends the full length of of the shopping area without interruption.
PLAZAS – Blocks of the retail street which are given over to exclusive pedestrian use, with cross streets left open to vehicular traffic.
TRANSIT-WAY – A "street" dedicated to pedestrians and transit riders, but from which all private vehicles are excluded except for emergencies or temporary construction work, with "transit lanes" set apart from pedestrian areas.
CONCOURSES – Intersectional connections at a second level – either below grade or as decks above grade – in which shopping pedestrians may pass from store to store at important intersections without conflict with vehicular traffic.

Figure 22.13. Types of partial and complete pedestrian street schemes. SOURCE: BARTON-ASCHMAN ASSOCIATES, INC., *Nicollet Avenue Study: Principles and Techniques for Retail Street Improvement,* prepared for the Downtown Council of Minneapolis, Minn., June, 1960.

Figure 22.14. Chestnut Street transitway. SOURCE: U.S. DEPARTMENT OF TRANSPORTATION, Urban Mass Transportation Administration, *Streets for Pedestrians and Transit: Examples of Transit Malls in the United States,* Service and Methods Demonstration Program, Final Report, August, 1977.

Figure 22.15. Bahnhofstrasse, Zurich.

TABLE 22–5
Characteristics of Five Selected Transit Malls in the United States*

Site	Project Cost	Funding Sources	Primary Project Backers	Area Land Use	Expected Benefits	Transit Type
Minneapolis—Nicollet Mall	$3,800,000 $1,170/ft $15/ft²	74% assessment district 13% UMTA demonstration grant 13% urban beautification grant	Downtown business	Retail core Offices	Retail improvement Improve bus service operations	Standard transit buses Shuttle minibuses Re-routing onto mall
Philadelphia—Chestnut Street Transitway	$7,000,000 $1,300/ft $22/ft²	80% UMTA capital grant 16.7% state DOT 3.3% city capital funds	City govt./planners Downtown business	Retail core Offices	Improve retail environment Transit for growth Upgrade transit	Standard transit buses Tourist buses Minor re-routing
Portland—Fifth and Sixth Streets Malls	$15,000,000 $2,700/ft $33/ft² Plus $1–1.5 million added utility costs	80% UMTA capital grant 20% Tri-Met Plus utility costs by city depts./utility companies	City govt./planners Downtown business	Office core Intersects retail core	Increase transit use and efficiency Retail/pedestrian environment Reduce suburban sprawl	Standard transit buses Re-routing onto mall
Madison—State Street Mall/ Capitol Concourse	$7,800,000 $1,150/ft $16/ft²	Mix of City, University, UMTA Sec. 3, and assessment district	City govt./planners	Retail Government	Improve pedestrian environment Upgrade area Upgrade transit	Standard transit buses Shuttle buses
New York—Broadway Plaza	$4,500,000 $2,370/ft $23/ft²	City capital budget plus federal funds (UMTA capital, FAUS, community dev.)	City govt./planners	Mixed retail, office, theatres	Improve pedestrian environment Upgrade economic conditions Symbolize city commitment	Standard buses, special loop, tour and airport buses

line-haul buses, notable exceptions in some European cities provide facilities for trams or light-rail vehicles, which produce less noise and fumes. In North America, Portland, Calgary, Buffalo, and San Diego are all involved in various stages of implementation of light-rail transit, in part integrated with downtown pedestrianization schemes. A few cities have found other alternatives that minimize the pedestrian/transit mall conflicts. For example, Nicollet Avenue in Minneapolis and Leeds in England use minibuses on their malls, and service on the 16th Street Transit Mall in Denver is to be provided with shuttle vehicles of a special low profile with special propulsion equipment.

A second objection to transit malls has to do with the congregating of transit passengers in front of retail stores or doorways. This problem has been partially solved through the serpentine design of the Nicollet Transit Mall, which varies the location of the transit vehicle path within the right-of-way so as to provide the widest possible passenger loading areas. Careful attention to the location of bus stop shelters is clearly important in dealing with this issue.

Another common type of pedestrian system, grade-separated pedestrian walkways, are frequently used in major activity centers. These provide above- or below-grade pedestrian connections between parking facilities and airports or stadiums as well as between buildings to facilitate ease of access. A comparison of the benefits of above- and below-grade systems is given in Table 22-6. It should be noted

TABLE 22–6
Comparison of Above-Grade and Below-Grade Pedestrian Systems

Criterion	Preferred Pedestrian System: Above-Grade	Preferred Pedestrian System: Below-Grade
Good personal orientation	×	
Minimum sense of confinement	×	
Proximity to office building employees	×	
Least cost of construction	×	
Minimum disruption to existing buildings or utilities	×	
Ease of system expansion independent of building construction or reconstruction		×
Minimum cost to control temperature		×
Ease of direct connection with below-grade transit station		×
Minimize risk of aesthetic disruption to architecture		×

SOURCE: BARTON-ASCHMAN ASSOCIATES, INC., *Skyways in Minneapolis/St. Paul: Prototypes for the Nation?*, Minneapolis, Minn., July, 1976.

that there are several locations where grade-separated walkways might be placed. Below ground, they may go through buildings or along streets or alleys, although utilities seriously affect placement in public rights-of-way. Above ground, walkways could be constructed within public rights-of-way such as over existing sidewalks or alleyways (as has been done extensively in Cincinnati), or within special easements through or alongside private property, as has been

TABLE 22-5 (continued)

Site	Nontransit Uses	Peak Hour Bus Volume	Pedestrian Volume	Traffic Signal Treatment	Movement of Goods	Amenities
Minneapolis—Nicollet Mall	Taxis Emergency vehicles Bicycles	Before: 20/ea. way After: 60/ea. way	Before: 1,068/block side/h, 12-h period After: 1,114/block side/h, 12-h period	Re-set for cross traffic flow (computerized traffic control system scheduled)	Alley loading; mall loading by special permit	Extensive, including electric snow-melting mats, sign ordinance, bus shelters
Philadelphia—Chestnut Street Transitway	Taxis at night, one block only day Emergency vehicles General traffic (1 block only)	Before: 43 (one way) After: 41/eastbound 11/westbound	After: 3,016/block side/h, peak periods on major blocks	Bus-triggered mid-block warning light Signal timings set for expected bus speed Timings on nearby street reset	Cross st. loading; on mall by special permit in off-hours	Typical, with mid-block crossing area
Portland—Fifth and Sixth Streets Malls	General traffic on one lane for 3/4ths of blocks	Before: 32 6th Ave. 85 5th Ave. After: 207 6th Ave. 211 5th Ave.	Before: 444 6th Ave./ 686 5th Ave./ block side/h, off-peak periods	Computer controlled with progression to be adjusted for buses	Cross st. loading; on mall by special permit in off-hours	Extensive, including bus shelters and concession booths, CRT information display
Madison—State Street Mall/ Capitol Concourse	General traffic on Capitol Concourse	Before: 60 (2-way on State St., 1-way on Capital Square)		On Capitol Square set to make leaving concourse difficult	Loading on alleys, cross streets, some curbside during restricted hours	Typical
New York—Broadway Plaza	General traffic on 5 blocks Taxis on 1 block, plus special loading area	Before: 60–76 (1-way) After: no change	Before: 7,500/block side/h, peak hour on major block	Possible regression signalization to discourage use on Broadway, Seventh Ave. signals reset	On pedestrian mall: loading during morning hours in emergency row	Typical, including ticket booth and information center/performing platform

*Minneapolis and Philadelphia completed and others underway at time of source report in 1977.

Source: U.S. Department of Transportation, Urban Mass Transportation Administration, *Streets for Pedestrians and Transit: Examples of Transit Malls in the United States*, Service and Methods Demonstration Program, Final Report, Washington, D.C., Aug. 1977.

done in Minneapolis. Figures 22.16 and 22.17 show the extent of the Minneapolis Skyway System and some of its details.

Regardless of which pedestrian circulation system is being considered, proper attention must be paid to safety and security. Pedestrian security necessitates special police patrols to the extent that normal police vehicles cannot gain access to the pedestrian system. Pedestrian facilities should provide access for fire engines and other emergency vehicles and for special construction or maintenance vehicles, as illustrated in Figure 22.18.

Mechanical devices that further enhance pedestrian circulation include elevators, escalators, and constant-speed or accelerating moving sidewalks. Two proposed types of accelerating pedestrian walkways are shown in Figure 22.19. Although these are still developmental in nature, they show promise of being useful facilities. Not to be ignored, incidentally, is the old but still used inclined railway. Table 22-7 provides a range of capital and operating costs for various pedestrian-assist facilities, and Table 22-8 indicates the location of selected moving-walkway installations.

Information on elevators has been presented in Tables 22-4 and 22-7 inasmuch as they are a special form of pedestrian circulation facility frequently found in major activity centers. Obviously, the densities characteristic of such centers could not exist without extensive vertical development, which in turn requires the use of elevators. In addition to general data on elevator types, sizes, capacities, costs, and the like, the following elevator information may be useful:

1. Large modern buildings may have as many as 50 elevators to serve its occupants; each of the 110-story towers of the World Trade Center in New York City has over 100 elevators.
2. The quality of service seemingly demanded by elevator users permits a passenger waiting time of no more than 30 to 60 s, depending on whether the elevator installation is in a commercial or residential building.
3. The designation of local and express elevators, or the establishment of blocks of floors to be served by a given elevator bank, are useful ways to increase elevator efficiency. With express elevator service, there is also the useful concept of an intermediate or "sky-lobby" distribution point in very tall buildings.
4. Recently, two-level or double-decked elevators have been installed in buildings in Chicago and Boston. As shown in Figure 22.20, the concept here is that the lower cab, reached directly from the lobby floor, serves odd-numbered floors, while the upper cab, reached by escalators from the lobby, serves even-numbered floors.

It is significant to note that automobile-free or automobile-restricted zones (AFZs or ARZs, respectively) are an extension of the pedestrian circulation system. The principles and techniques described above become the building blocks to such an area-wide concept. Central Boston is one

Figure 22.16. Minneapolis skyway system. SOURCE: BARTON-ASCHMAN ASSOCIATES, INC., *Skyways in Minneapolis/St. Paul: Prototypes for the Nation?*, July, 1976.

Figure 22.17. Minneapolis skyway design. SOURCE: BARTON-ASCHMAN ASSOCIATES, INC., *Skyways in Minneapolis/St. Paul: Prototypes for the Nation?*, July, 1976.

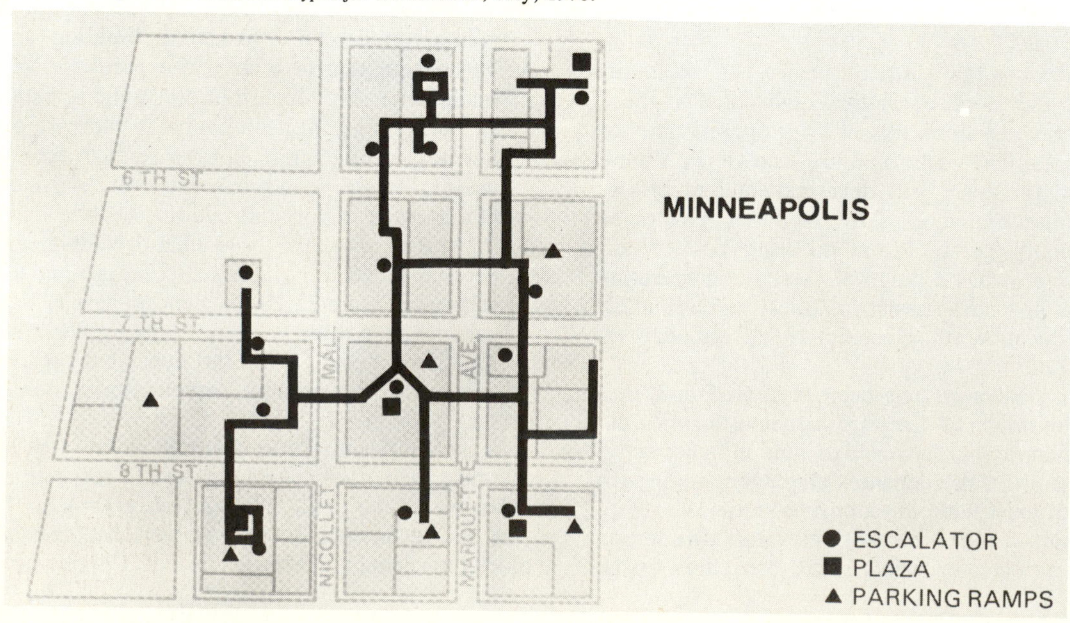

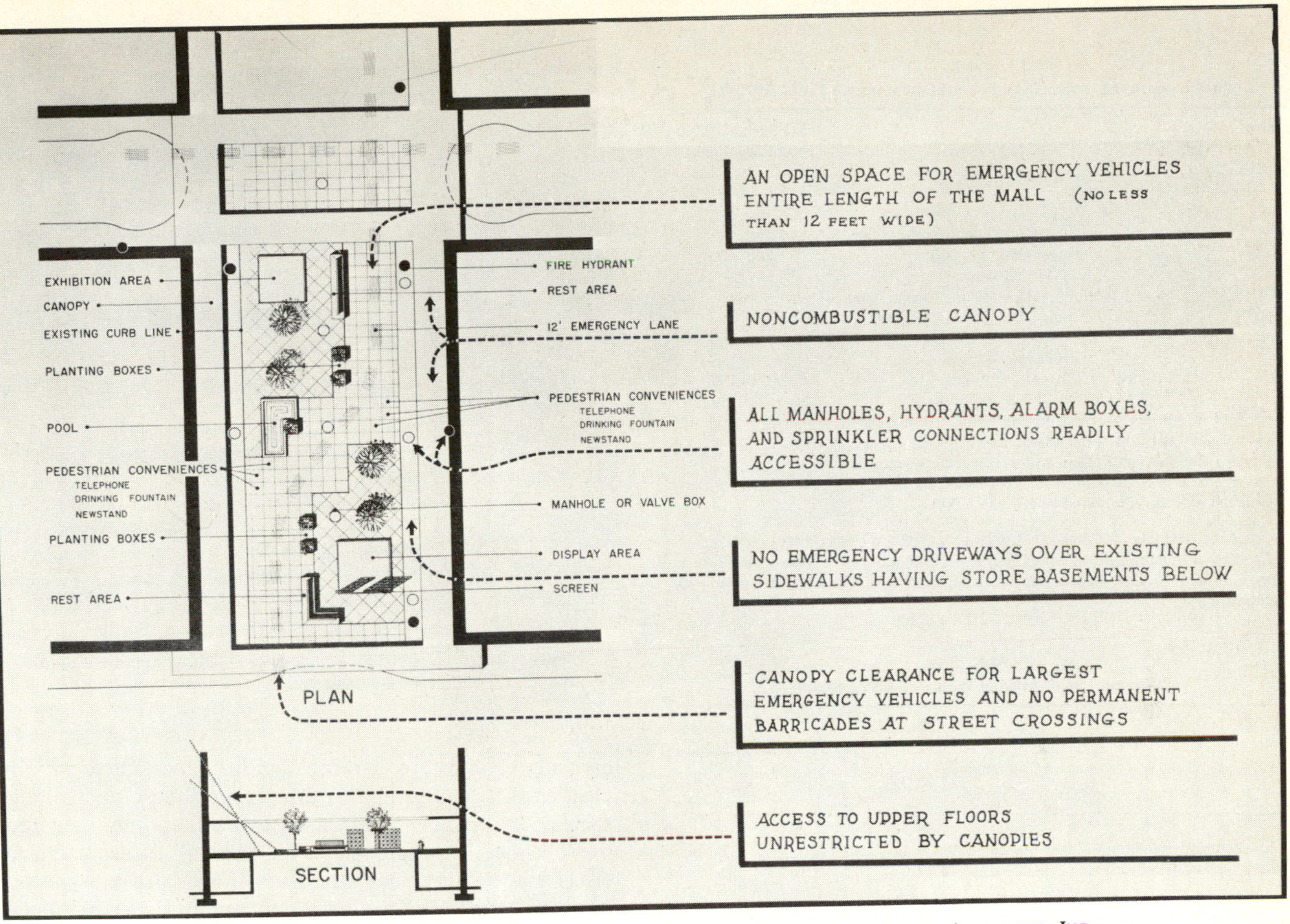

Figure 22.18. Fire protection considerations in mall design. SOURCE: BARTON-ASCHMAN ASSOCIATES, INC., *Nicollet Avenue Study: Principles and Techniques for Retail Street Improvement*, prepared for the Downtown Council of Minneapolis, Minn., June, 1960.

Figure 22.19. Two types of accelerating pedestrian walkways. SOURCE: ADVANCED TRANSIT ASSOCIATION INTERNATION CONFERENCE, *Advanced Transit and Urban Revitalization—An International Dialogue: Proceedings*, Volume I, Indianapolis, Ind., 1978.

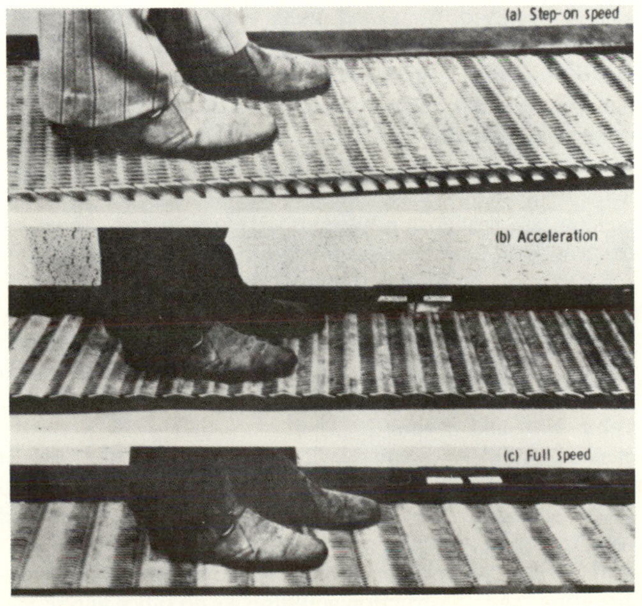

TABLE 22–7
Pedestrian-Assist Systems Capital and Maintenance Costs (1975)*

Width (in.)	Rise (ft)	Capital Cost	Maintenance Cost (dollars/month)
		Escalator	
32	13–14	$ 70,000–76,000	100–200
48	13–14	78,000–81,000	100–200
48	30†	195,000–260,000	200–400
		Elevator	
		(standard 10- to 12-story application, four elevator units, 200–350 ft/min)	
		$70,000–76,000/unit‡	250–350
		Moving Walkway	
26		$1,000–1,750/linear ft	50–150
40		1,750–2,200/linear ft	50–150

*1 in. = 2.54 cm; 1 ft = 30.48 cm.
†A typical subway application, with special safety features.
‡For speeds above 350 ft/min, the cost would be $9,000–13,000 more. For each additional floor the cost would be $2,000–3,000.

SOURCE: DELEUW, CATHER AND COMPANY AND ROCK CREEK ASSOCIATES, *Characteristics of Urban Transportation Systems: A Handbook for Transportation Planners*, prepared for U.S. Department of Transportation, Urban Mass Transportation Administration, July, 1977.

TABLE 22–8
Selected List of Moving Walkway Installations

City	Location: CBD	Commuter Station	Airport	Campus	Public Parks/Zoos
U.S.					
Akron	×	×	×	×	
Atlanta	×		×		
Boston	×	×	×	×	
Chicago			×		
Cleveland	×				
Columbus	×				
Hartford	×				
Houston	×		×		
Ingelwood	×				
Las Vegas	×		×		
Los Angeles	×		×		
Miami	×		×		
Minneapolis					×
New York	×	×	×		×
Philadelphia	×				
Pittsburgh	×				
Portland	×				
Reston		×			
San Diego	×				
San Jose	×			×	
Seattle			×		
St. Louis			×		
Washington		×			
Non-U.S.					
Munich, Germany			×		
Paris, France	×		×		
Ottawa, Canada	×				
Toronto, Canada	×				

SOURCE: DELEUW, CATHER AND COMPANY AND ROCK CREEK ASSOCIATES, *Characteristics of Urban Transportation Systems: A Handbook for Transportation Planners*, prepared for U.S. Department of Transportation, Urban Mass Transportation Administration, Washington, D.C., July, 1977.

of several U.S. cities that has created AFZs, although not without some difficulties to functional and efficient vehicle circulation immediately adjacent to the AFZ. Singapore uses a unique combination of a wide variety of measures to create an ARZ. Singapore's plan to relieve traffic congestion in the city includes such tactics as special restrictive licensing for automobiles seeking to enter the ARZ, incentives for

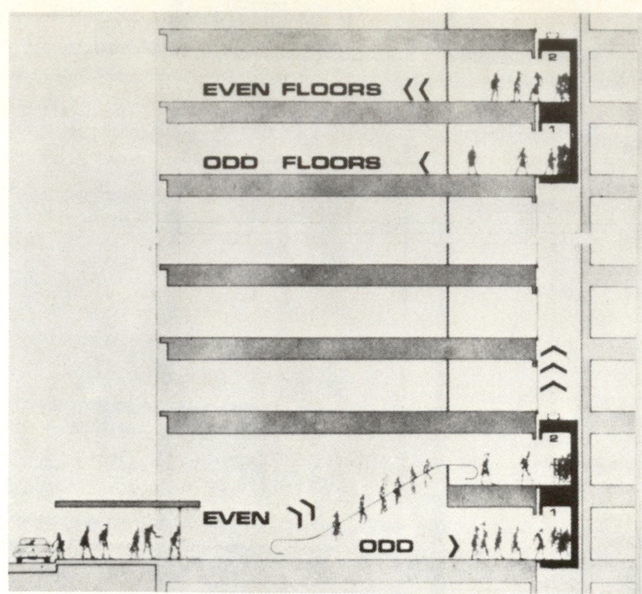

Figure 22.20. Double-deck elevators—lobby configuration. SOURCE: OTIS ELEVATOR COMPANY.

carpoolers, intercept parking facilities, core-area parking charges sufficiently high to discourage long-term parking, special shuttle buses and routes, and some minor construction changes. During peak travel when all measures are in effect (special licensing restraints, for example, have not been instituted on a 24-h basis), there have been significant changes in travel patterns, but some of these changes have been only temporal in nature.

Automated guideway transit systems

The definitions of automated guideway transit systems are both important and complex. The term automated guideway transit (AGT) can refer to all vehicles that are captive to a guideway or track and under automatic control. Subclassifications involve type of guideway, degree of automation (demand-responsive, scheduled-operation, or combination), vehicle size or combination of vehicle sizes, type of service provided (personal versus group), performance characteristics (such as speed, capacity, headway between vehicles), station configurations (off-line, on-line), and propulsion and suspension systems (electric motor, linear induction motor, magnetic levitation, air-cushion effect). Thus, automated guideway transit systems can range from small personal rapid transit vehicles riding above or below narrow-beam guideways, through midsize vehicles with special wider slab-type guideways, to the new, automated rapid transit trains operating on conventional track systems. Table 22-9 and Figure 22.21 classify and show a variety of AGT vehicles. Figure 22.22 shows several AGT system guideway and propulsion concepts, and Figures 22.23 and 22.24 present the ranges of guideway cross sections and vehicle sizes available.

AGT systems require essentially the same planning, engineering, and construction activities as do other public and

TABLE 22–9
Classification Structure of AGT Vehicles*

Category	Class	Subclass	Service Type	Min Unit Capacity (passengers)	Max Operating Speed (km/h)	Characteristic Minimum Headway (s)
PRT	PRT	Low speed	Personal	3–6	13–54	3 or less
		High speed	Personal	3–6	55+	3 or less
GRT	SGRT	Low speed	Group	7–24	13–54	3–15
		High speed	Group	7–24	55+	3–15
	IGRT	Low speed	Group	25–69	13–54	15–60
		High speed	Group	25–69	55+	15–90
	LGRT		Group	70–109	13–54	50–110
ART	ART		Group	110+	55+	60+

*PRT, personal rapid transit; GRT, group rapid transit; SGRT, small vehicle GRT; IGRT, intermediate vehicle GRT; LGRT, large vehicle GRT; ART, automated rail transit.

SOURCE: U.S. DEPARTMENT OF TRANSPORTATION, Urban Mass Transportation Administration, *Conference on Automated Guideway Transit Technology Development,* 1978 Conference Proceedings, Transportation Systems Center, Kendall Square, Cambridge, Mass., Feb. 28–Mar. 2, 1978.

Figure 22.21. Types of AGT vehicles. SOURCES: U.S. DEPARTMENT OF TRANSPORTATION, Urban Mass Transportation Administration, *Automated Guideway Transit Technology Overview,* Washington, D.C., August, 1978. Advanced Transit Association International Conference, *Advanced Transit and Urban Revitalization—An International Dialogue: Proceedings,* Volume I, Indianapolis, Ind., 1978.

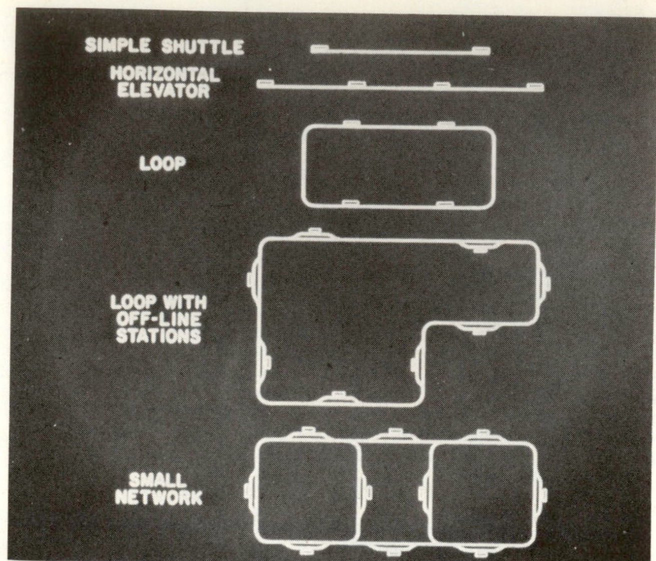

Figure 22.22. AGT system guideway and propulsion concepts. SOURCE: ANDERSON, DR. J. EDWARD, *Breaking the Transit Dilemma through Innovation,* A Slide Presentation, January, 1979.

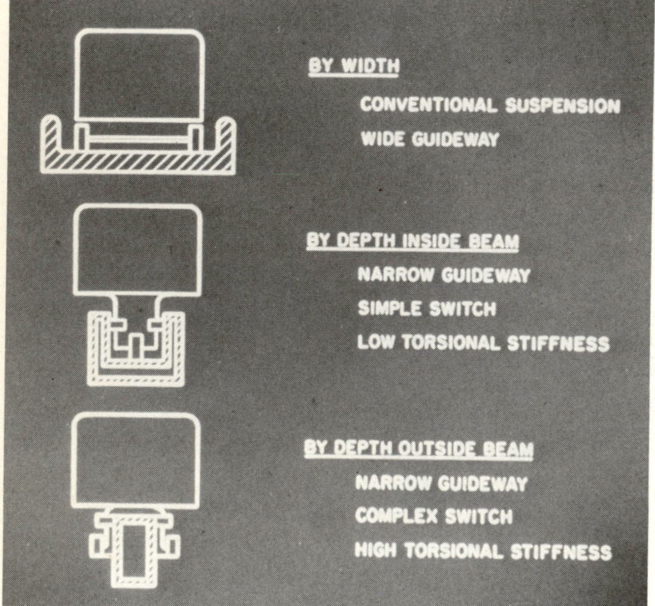

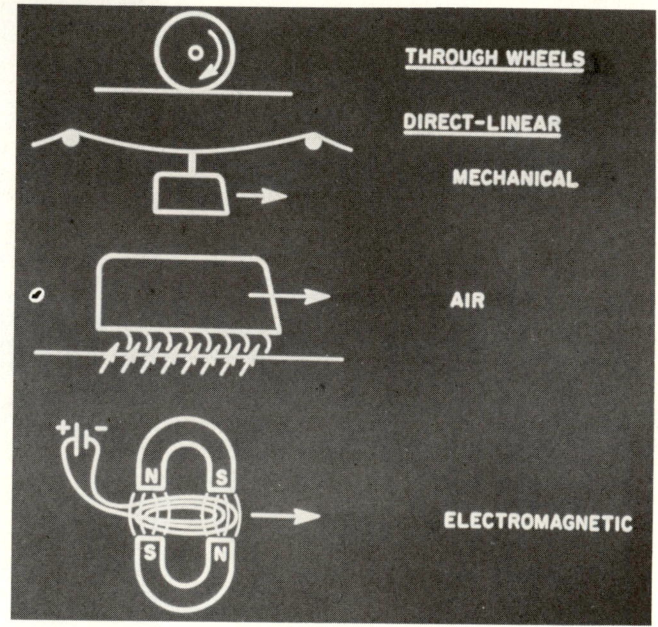

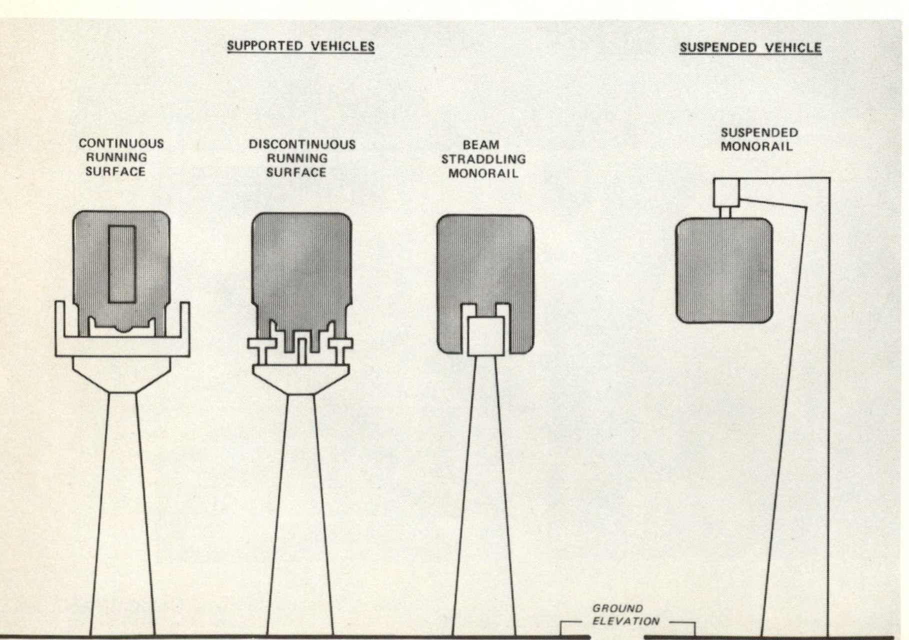

Figure 22.23. AGT vehicle/guideway configurations. SOURCE: TECHNOLOGY RESEARCH AND ANALYSIS CORPORATION, Arlington, Va.

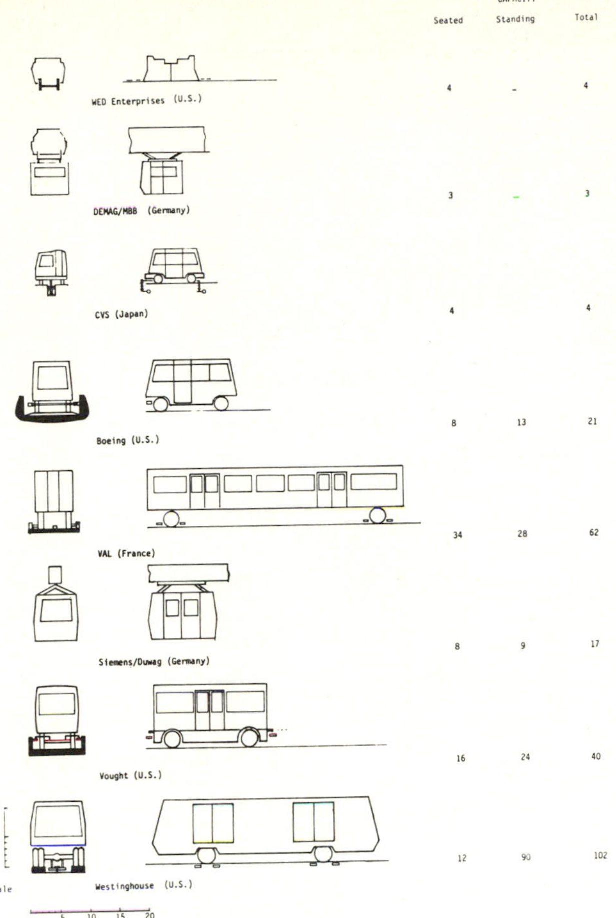

Figure 22.24. Range of AGT vehicle sizes. SOURCE: TECHNOLOGY RESEARCH AND ANALYSIS CORPORATION, Arlington, Va.

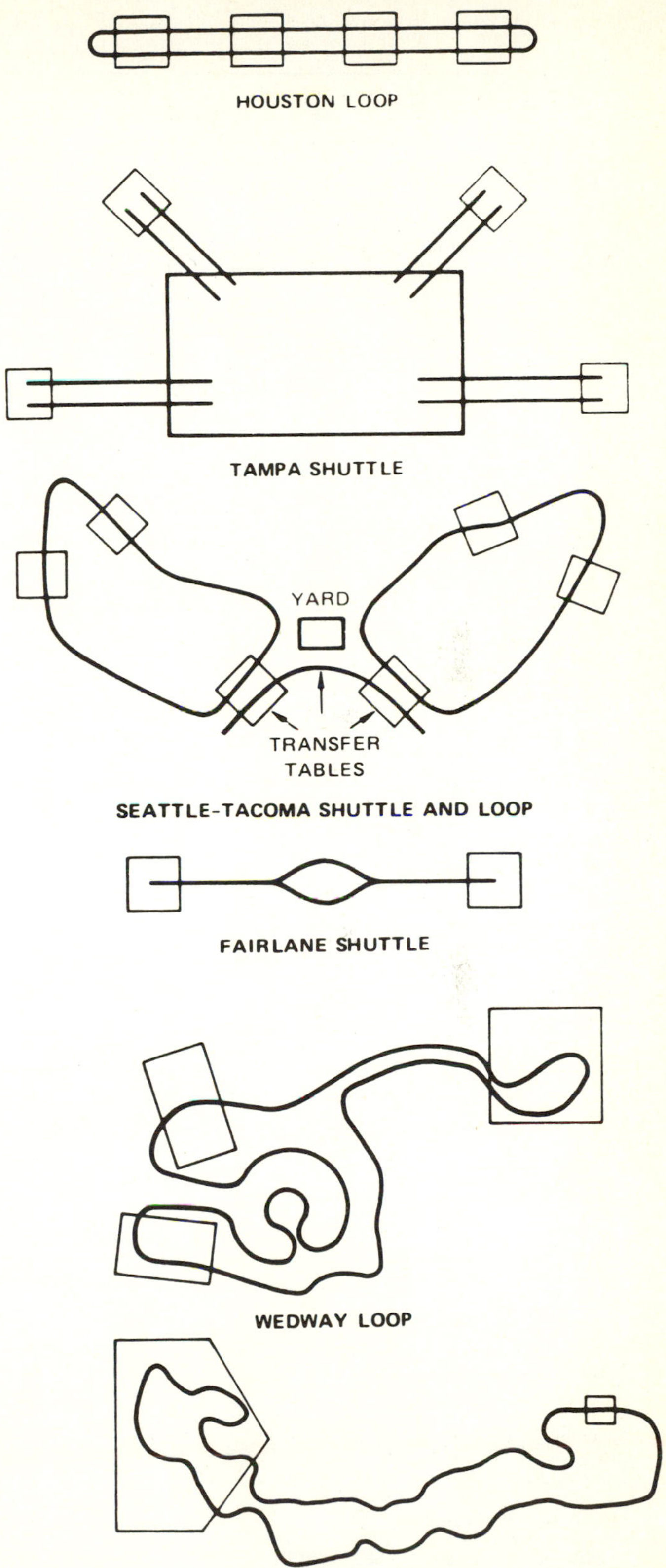

Figure 22.25. Geometric layouts of six AGT systems. SOURCE: U.S. DEPARTMENT OF TRANSPORTATION, Urban Mass Transportation Administration, *Conference on Automated Guideway Transit Technology Development*, 1978 Conference Proceedings, Transportation Systems Center, Kendall Square, Cambridge, Mass., February 28–March 2, 1978.

semipublic works projects. For example, below- and above-grade structural considerations, which constitute 60 to 70% of the cost of AGT systems, are similar to other civil engineering efforts.

There are some unique aspects of AGT system deployment as well. For example, since the systems are most useful in major activity centers, which by definition are densely built-up areas, the procurement of right-of-way and handling of aesthetics become quite critical. The very uniqueness of the systems makes patronage estimates most complex. Because of the automated features of the systems, elements of safety and reliability, such as command and control, personal security, and weather vulnerability, all become critical. The newness of the systems also affects their cost; there is still much R&D effort needed in advanced forms of AGT systems. There are new institutional considerations, such as who owns, pays for, and/or operates the systems. Regardless of these complexities, the interest in and viability of the systems is attested to by the information contained in Tables 22-10 to 22-13. The technical features, performance characteristics, and status of both U.S. and non-U.S. AGT systems is presented in these tables.

There are a variety of AGT system configurations in service; Figure 22.25 illustrates the geometric layouts of six selected systems. The first three systems shown are loop and shuttle configurations at airports; Fairlane is a shuttle

TABLE 22–10
Technical Features of U.S. AGT Systems*

System	Manufacturer	Vehicle Dimensions (m) Length	Width	Height	Empty Weight (newtons)	Number of Seats	Number of Standees	Total Vehicle Capacity	Crush Load	Suspension Type	Steering Type	Switching Type	Propulsion Type	Vehicle Control	Network Control
AIRTRANS	LTV	6.40	2.14	3.05	62,270	16	24	40	60	RTOC, SPDR	RGW, SGW	WA, CGW	DCTM	PF, FB	ASY
Aerial Transit System	Pullman Standard	3.66	1.68	1.59	21,350	6	0	6	6	SWOR, SPDR	SWOR	WA, SWOR	DCTM	PF	SLG
Bradley Field	Ford	7.53	2.04	2.65	63,600	10	14	24	30	RTOC, SPDR	RGW, SGW	OB, CGW	DCTM	PF	SLG
Busch Gardens	Westinghouse	11.06	2.99	3.35	117,880	8	92	100	150	RTOC, SPDR	RGW, SGW	WA, CGW	DCTM	PF, FB	ASY
California Expo	Universal Mobility	4.27	1.83	2.25	10,670	12	0	12	12	RTOS, SPMR	RGW, SGW	WA, CGW	DCTM	PF, FB	ASY
Carowinds	Universal Mobility	4.27	1.83	2.25	10,670	12	0	12	12	RTOS, SPMR	RGW, SGW	WA, CGW	DCTM	PF, FB	ASY
Dashaveyor	Bendix	7.01	2.04	3.29	80,000	12	20	32	50	RTOC, SPDR	RGW, SGW	WA, CGW	DCTM	VF, FB	ASY
Duke University	OTIS-TTD	6.10	3.29	2.99	53,350	12	0		12	AC	RGW, SGW	OB, CGW	SLIM	PF, FB	ASY
Fairlane Shopping Center	Ford	7.53	2.04	2.65	63,600	10	14	24	30	RTOC, SPDR	RGW, SGW	OB, CGW	DCTM	PF	SLG
HCPRT	Aerospace	3.05	1.52	1.52	8,000	6	0	6	6	RTOC, SPMR	RGW, SGW	WA, AMAG	LSM	PF	QSY
Hershey Park	Universal Mobility	4.27	1.83	2.25	10,670	12	0	12	12	RTOS, SPMR	RGW, SGW	WA, CGW	DCTM	PF, FB	ASY
Houston International Airport	Rohr	12.20	1.52	2.29	32,000	6	4	10	14	RTOC, SPDR	RGW, CGB	WA, CGW	DCTM	PF, FB	ASY
PRT	Boeing	4.82	2.04	2.59	39,600	12	0	12	12	RTOC, SPDR	RGW, SWF	OB, CGW	DCTN	PF	QSY
PRT	OTIS-TTD	5.79	3.05	2.74	48,000	12	0	12	12	AC, SPDR	RGW, SGW	OB, CGW	SLIM	Hybrid	Hybrid
PRT	Rohr	5.94	2.23	2.44	42,700	12	0	12	12	AMAG	AMAG	OB, AMAG	SLIM	VF	ASY
PRT	Stanray Pacific	3.66	2.23	2.23	39,600	6	4	10	14	RTOS, SPMR	RGW, CGB	WA, GB	ACIM, ECC	VF, FB	ASY
King's Dominion	Universal Mobility	4.27	1.83	2.25	10,670	12	0	12	12	RTOS, SPMR	RGW, SGW	WA, CGW	DCTM	PF, FB	ASY
King's Island	Universal Mobility	4.27	1.83	2.25	10,670	12	0	12	12	RTOS, SPMR	RGW, SGW	WA, CGW	DCTM	PF, FB	ASY
Magic Mountain	Universal Mobility	4.27	1.83	2.25	10,670	12	0	12	12	RTOS, SPMR	RGW, SGW	WA, CGW	DCTM	PF, FB	ASY
Miami Airport	Westinghouse	11.06	2.97	3.35	117,880	0	100	100	150	RTOC, SPDR	RGW, SGW	WA, CGW	DCTM	PF, FB	ASY
Monocab	Rohr	2.93	1.67	2.04	17,790	6	0	6	6	RTOS, SSMR	RGW, SGW	WA, CGW	DCTM	VF	ASY
Morgantown	Boeing	4.72	2.04	2.68	38,250	8	7	15	21	RTOC, SPDR	RGW, SWF	OB, GW	DCTM	PF	SLG
Pearl Ridge	Rohr	12.19	1.83	2.74	32,000	8	8	16	24	RTOC, SPDR	RGW, CGB	WA, CGW	DCTM	PF, FB	ASY
PRT	OTIS-TTD	4.36	2.65	2.50	32,000	6	0	6	6	AC, SPDR	RGW, SGW	OB, CGW	SLIM	Hybrid	Hybrid
Sea-Tac	Westinghouse	11.28	2.83	3.35	113,430	12	90	102	125	RTOC, SPDR	RGW, SGW	WA, CGW	DCTM	PF, FB	ASY
StaRRcar	Alden	3.81	2.04	2.74	33,440	6	4	10	12	RTOC, SPDR	RGW, SWF	OB, GW	ACIM, HST	PF	SLG
Tampa Airport	Westinghouse	11.06	2.83	3.35	95,640	0	100	100	125	RTOC, SPDR	RGW, SGW	WA, CGW	DCTM	PF, FB	ASY
Transette	Georgia Tech					4	0	4	15	RTOC, SPDR	RGW, SGW	WA, CGW	MBS	PF, FB	ASY
Uniflo	Ferguson	5.64	1.16	1.98	9,340	8	0	8	8	AC, SPDR	RGW, SGW	OB, CGW	LAM	VF	ASY
Walt Disney	Wedway	2.43	1.46	1.16	4,180	4	0	4	4	RTOS, SPDR	RGW, SGW	WA, CGW	SLIM	VF, FB	ASY

*See Glossary following Table 22-13 for meaning of abbreviations.

SOURCE: U.S. DEPARTMENT OF TRANSPORTATION, Urban Mass Transportation Administration, *Automated Guideway Transit Technology Overview*, Washington, D.C., Aug. 1978.

TABLE 22–11
Performance Characteristics of U.S. AGT Systems*

System	Manufacturer	Class	Line Speed (km/h)	Minimum Headway (s)	Seats/ Lane/ Hour	Passengers/Lane/ Hour (crush load)	Status to Date	Status Code—Date
AIRTRANS	LTV	GRT	27	18	3,200	12,000	20.92 lane kilometers, 50 stations, 68 vehicles, 20% at-grade, 80% elevated, grid system with 17 interacting routes	CA-1974
Aerial Transit System	Pullman Standard	PRT	32	8	2,700	2,700	Two full-scale test vehicles on 0.55 kilometer test track	FP-1972
Bradley Field	Ford	SLT	48	20	1,800	5,400	1.29 lane kilometers, 3 stations, 2 vehicle single path shuttle with bypass	CA—not yet in service
Busch Gardens	Westinghouse	GRT	48	100	576	10,800	2.25 lane kilometers, 2 stations, 2 vehicles in one train; 60% at-grade, 40% elevated, single loop	CA-1975
California Expo	Universal Mobility	SLT	19	120	2,880	2,880	2.09 lane kilometers, 2 stations, 32 vehicles in 4 eight-car trains, single path loop	CA-1968
Carowinds	Universal Mobility	SLT	22	132	2,595	2,595	3.21 lane kilometers, 1 station, 32 vehicles in 4 eight-car trains, single path loop	CA-1973
Dashaveyor	Bendix	GRT	80	15	2,800	7,680	Two full-scale prototype vehicles on 0.15 kilometer test track	PD-1972
Duke University	OTIS-TTD	PRT	64	2	21,600	21,600	0.80 lane kilometers, 3 stations, 3 vehicles; 50% at-grade, 50% elevated	CA—not yet in service
Fairlane Shop Cent	Ford	SLT	48	20	1,800	5,400	0.80 lane kilometers, 2 stations, 2 vehicles	CA-1976
HCPRT	Aerospace	PRT	64	0.25	86,400	86,400	Extensive Technical and Planning Studies 1/10 scale Model demonstrated at 0.5 second headways	RP-1972

TABLE 22–11 (continued)

System	Manufacturer	Class	Line Speed (km/h)	Minimum Headway (s)	Seats/ Lane/ Hour	Passengers/Lane/ Hour (crush load)	Status to Date	Status Code— Date
Hershey Park	Universal Mobility	SLT	16	75	3,465	3,465	1.29 lane kilometers, 2 stations, 24 vehicles in 4 six-car trains	CA-1969
Houston Int. Airport	Rohr	SLT	19	60	1,080	2,520	1.93 lane kilometers, 8 stations, 18 vehicles in 6 three-car trains, 100% underground	CA-1972
PRT	Boeing	PRT	64	3	14,000	14,000	System Design Study in progress	DS-1974
PRT	OTIS-TTD	PRT	64	3	14,000	14,000	System Design Study in progress	DS-1974
PRT	Rohr	PRT	64	3	14,000	14,000	System Design Study in progress	DS-1974
PRT	Stanray Pacific	GRT	24	20	1,800	2,520	2.57 lane kilometers, 3 stations, 10 vehicles	CA-1969—no longer in service
King's Dominion	Universal Mobility	SLT	10	210	1,850	1,850	3.38 lane kilometers, 1 station, 54 vehicles in 6 nine-car trains; 5% elevated, 95% at-grade, closed loop	CA-1974
King's Island	Universal Mobility	SLT	10	180	2,160	2,160	3.22 lane kilometers, 1 station, 63 vehicles in 7 nine-car trains	CA-1974
Magic Mountain	Universal Mobility	SLT	13	60	4,320	4,320	1.29 lane kilometers, 3 stations, 36 vehicles in 6 six-car trains; closed loop	CA-1971
Miami Airport	Westinghouse	GRT	45	85	0	12,600	0.80 lane kilometers, 2 stations, 4 vehicles in 2 two-car trains; 100% elevated, shuttle	CA-1977
Monocab	Rohr	PRT	48	5	4,320	4,320	0.30 kilometer test track with 2 prototype vehicles	PD-1972
Morgantown	Boeing	GRT	48	15	1,920	5,040	8.53 lane kilometer, 3 stations, 45 vehicles, linear shuttle, 80% elevated, 20% at-grade	CA-1975
Pearl Ridge	Rohr	SLT	13	240	480	1,440	0.37 lane kilometers, 2 stations, 4 vehicles in 1 four-car train; 100% elevated, linear shuttle	CA-1976
PRT	OTIS-TTD	PRT	72	6	3,600	3,600	0.30 lane kilometers test track with 2 prototype vehicles	PD-1972
Sea-Tac	Westinghouse	GRT	48	100	432	4,500	2.74 lane kilometers, 8 stations, 12 vehicles, 100% underground, 2 loops and a shuttle	CA-1973
StaRRcar	Alden	PRT	45	5	4,320	7,200	Two prototype vehicles on 0.30 kilometer test track	TD-1965
Tampa Airport	Westinghouse	GRT	45	70	0	6,375	2.25 lane kilometer, 8 stations, 8 vehicles, 100% elevated	CA-1971
Transette	Georgia Tech	PRT	24	15	960	960	Full-scale test vehicle on 0.11 kilometer test track	TD-1972
Uniflo	Ferguson	GRT	32–80	3	9,600	9,600	1 lane kilometer, 3 stations, 2 vehicles, closed loop, 100% at-grade	TD-1976
Disney World	Wedway	GRT	22	14	5,140	5,140	1.40 lane kilometer, 1 station, 150 vehicles in 30 five-car trains	CA-1975

*See Glossary following Table 22–13 for meaning of abbreviations.

SOURCE: U.S. DEPARTMENT OF TRANSPORTATION, Urban Mass Transportation Administration, *Automated Guideway Transit Technology Overview*, Washington, D.C., Aug. 1978.

TABLE 22–12
Technical Features of Non–U.S. AGT Systems*

System	Vehicle Dimensions (m)			Empty Weight (newtons)	Number of Seats	Number of Standees	Total Vehicle Capacity	Suspension Type	Steering Type	Switching Type	Propulsion Type	Propulsion Power (kw)	Vehicle Control	Network Control
	Length	Width	Height											
TRRE Cabtrack, United Kingdom	3.04	1.37	1.68	5,880	4	0	4	RIOC, SPDR	RGW, SGW	OB, CGW	DCTM	25	PF	QSLG
TRRE Minitram, United Kingdom	—	—	—	—	6	6	12	RTOC,† SWOR, SPDR	—	OB, CGW	DCTM	—	—	—
MBB Cabinentaxi, West Germany	2.29	1.58	1.50	5,880	3	0	3	RTOS,† SSDR, SPDR	RGW, SGW	OB, CGW	DCTM	—	VF	ASY
Siemens H-Bahn, West Germany	3.50	2.29	2.50	24,520	8	8	16	RTOS, SSMR	RGW, SGW	OB, CGW	SLIM	—	VF	ASY
Krauss-Mafei Transurban, West Germany	6.50	2.20	3.20	88,260	14	8	22	AMAC, SPDR	AMAC, SGW	OB, AMAC	SLIM	—	VF	ASY
Engins Matra Aramis, France	2.29	1.32	1.89	6,380	4	0	4	RTOC, SPDR	RGW, SGW	OB, CGW	RSM	16	VF	ASY
Engins Matra VAL, France	25.50	1.93	3.04	22,560	62	63	125	RTOC, SPDR	RGW, SGW	OB, CGW	DCTM	160	VF	ASY
Alsthom Neyrpic Telerail, France	2.10	1.40	2.29	8,140	4	4	8	RTOS, SSMR	RGW, CGW	WA, GB	CABLE	—	PF	SLC
CEL URBA, France	9.10	2.00	2.00	35,300	30	0	30	NPAC, SSMR	NPAC	WA, GB	SLIM	—	PF	ASY
Government CVS, Japan	3.35	1.60	1.85	10,790	4	0	4	RTOC, SPDR	RGW, CGW	OB, CGW	DCTM	12	PF	SLG

TABLE 22–12 (continued)

System	Vehicle Dimensions (m) Length	Width	Height	Empty Weight (newtons)	Number of Seats	Number of Standees	Total Vehicle Capacity	Suspension Type	Steering Type	Switching Type	Propulsion Type	Propulsion Power (kw)	Vehicle Control	Network Control
Kawasaki-Fuji KCV, Japan	6.34	2.40	3.14	44,130	24	26	50	RTOC, SPDR	RGW, SGW	WA, GB	DCTM	100	VF	ASY
Mitsubishi MAT, Japan	6.40	2.20	2.90	—	16	16	32	RTOS, SPDR	RGW, CGW	WA, GB	DCTM	—	—	—
Toshiba Mini-Monorail, Japan	7.16‡ 4.50	2.00 —	2.40 —	60,510 33,830	4 8	12 23	16 31	RTOS SPMR	RGW, CGB	WA, GB	DCTM	360	VF	ASY
Niigata Tekko NTS Japan	7.50	2.29	3.40	62,270	24	26	50	RTOC, SPDR	RGW, CGB	WA, GB	DCTM	50–70	VF	ASY
Hitachi Paratrain Japan	15.00	2.20	3.00	106,800	44	36	80	RTOC, SPDR	RGW, CGB	WA, GB	DCTM	55	VF	ASY
Nippon Sharyo VONA Japan	5.30	2.07	3.04	40,010	11	14	25	RTOS, SPDR	RGW, CGB	WA, GB	DCTM	55	VF	ASY
Kobe KRT Japan	4.72	2.03	2.67	64,480	10	15	25	RTOC, SPDR	RGW, SWF	OB, GW	DCTM	—	PF	SLG

*See Glossary following Table 22–13 for meaning of abbreviations.
†Two-vehicle configuration.
‡Two-vehicle types.

SOURCE: U.S. DEPARTMENT OF TRANSPORTATION, Urban Mass Transportation Administration, *Automated Guideway Transit Technology Overview,* Washington, D.C., Aug. 1978.

TABLE 22–13
Performance Characteristics and Status of Non–U.S. AGT Systems*

System	Classification	Line Speed (km/h)	Minimum Headway (s)	Seats/Lane/Hour	Passengers/ Lane/Hour	Status to Date	Status Code and Date
TRRL Cabtrack, United Kingdom	PRT	36	0.9	16,000	16,000	Extensive technical and planning studies performed; one-fifth-scale model tested; estimated cost $0.7 million	RP, 1971
TRRL Minitram, United Kingdom	GRT	48	10	2,160	4,320	Two design studies performed; planning studies for Sheffield and Glasgow complete; contract to be awarded for test and demonstration program; estimated cost $12–16 million	DS, 1974
MBB Cabinentaxi, West Germany	PRT	35	0.5	21,600	21,600	Extensive technical and planning studies performed; five prototype vehicles operating on test track near Hagen; estimated cost $11 million	TD, 1973
Siemens H-Bahn, West Germany	GRT	35	6.0	4,800	9,600	Full scale prototype vehicle on test track	TD, 1974
Krauss-Maffei Transurban, West Germany	GRT	50	15.0	3,360	5,280	Two full-scale prototype vehicles on 1-km test track; extensive planning studies for Heidelberg and Toronto; estimated cost $25 million	TD, 1974
Engins Matra Aramis, France	PRT	50	0.2	72,000	72,000	Three full-scale prototype vehicles on 1-km test track; planning studies for Paris and Nice; estimated cost $6 million	TD, 1972
Engins Matra VAL, France	GRT	96	60	3,720	7,500	Full-scale prototype vehicle on test track, 10-lane mile system with eight stations	CA, 1974
Alsthom Neyrpic Telerail, France	GRT	35	4.0	3,600	7,200	Full-scale prototype vehicle on test track	TD, 1973
CEL URBA, France	GRT	50	60	1,800	1,800	Two prototype vehicles on test track	RP, 1973
Government CVS, Japan	PRT	40–60	1.0	14,400	14,600	Sixty full-scale vehicles on 5.73-km test track near Tokyo; estimated project cost $20 million	TD, 1974
Kawasaki-Fuji KCV, Japan	GRT	60	75	1,152	2,400	Two full-scale prototype vehicles on 0.5-km test track	TD, 1974
Mitsubishi MAT, Japan	GRT	60	90	640	1,280	Full-scale prototype vehicle on test track	TD, 1974
Toshiba Mini-Monorail, Japan	GRT	30	120	—	—	Full-scale prototype vehicle on test track	TD, 1974

TABLE 22–13 (continued)

System	Classification	Line Speed (km/h)	Minimum Headway (s)	Seats/Lane/Hour	Passengers/ Lane/Hour	Status to Date	Status Code and Date
Niigata Tekko NTS, Japan	GRT	50	70	3,600	9,000	Full-scale prototype vehicle on test track	TD, 1974
Hitachi Paratrain, Japan	GRT	48	90	1,760	3,200	Full-scale prototype vehicle on test track	TD, 1974
Nippon Sharyo VONA, Japan	GRT	60	90	440	1,000	Two full-scale prototype vehicles on 0.4-km test track	TD, 1974
KOBE KRT, Japan	GRT	48	90	2,400	3,200	Test track completed, 0.93 km length; operational guideway 3.7 km long; installed for Ocean Expo of Okinawa in July 1975	TD, CA, 1975

*See Glossary immediately following this table for meaning of abbreviations.

SOURCE: U.S. DEPARTMENT OF TRANSPORTATION, Urban Mass Transportation Administration, *Automated Guideway Transit Technology Overview*, Washington, D.C., Aug. 1978.

Glossary of Terms for Tables 22–10 to 22–13

Abbreviation	Definition
AC	Air cushion
ACIM	Air-cooled induction motor
AMAG	Attractive magnetic force
ASY	Asynchronous control
CA	Commercial application
CGB	Center guide beam
CGW	Captured guide wheel
DCTM	Direct current traction motor
DLIM	Double-sided linear induction motor
DS	Design study
ECC	Eddy current clutch
FB	Fixed block
GB	Guide beam
GW	Guide wheel
HST	Hydrostatic transmission
LAM	Linear air motor
LSM	Linear synchronous motor
MBS	Moving belt system
NPAC	Negative pressure air cushion
OB	On-board
PD	Public demonstration
PF	Point follower control
QSY	Quasi-synchronous longitudinal guidance
RGW	Rubber guide wheel
RP	Reduced scale prototype
RSM	Rotary synchronous motor
RTOC	Rubber tire on concrete
RTOS	Rubber tire on steel
SGW	Side guidance surface
SLG	Synchronous longitudinal guidance
SLIM	Single-sided linear induction motor
SPDR	Supported dual-rail
SPMR	Supported monorail
SSDR	Suspended dual-rail
SSMR	Suspended monorail
SWF	Side wall follower
SWOR	Steel wheel on rail
TD	Test track demonstration
VF	Vehicle-follower control
WA	Wayside actuated

SOURCE: U.S. DEPARTMENT OF TRANSPORTATION, Urban Mass Transportation Administration, *Automated Guideway Transit Technology Overview*, Washington, D.C., Aug. 1978.

between a shopping center complex and outlying parking and hotel facilities; the last two loops are in amusement/recreation complexes. Tables 22-14 and 22-15 present observed data (for these and other systems) on such elements as patronage, usage, and unit costs. The tables refer to "place-miles" in several instances; it should be noted that "places" reflect capacity; capacity, if unmatched by demand, is a particularly useless commodity. On the other hand, the ratio of "places" to passengers (i.e., load factor) is an especially useful measure of system effectiveness.

Other advanced-technology systems

Two additional advanced-technology systems are worthy of mention. The first of these is the cableway, which has evolved from the commonplace ski lift. Such a cableway is the major facility connecting Roosevelt Island with midtown Manhattan in New York City (see Figure 22.26). Similar systems carry tourists to and from major amusement or recreation attractions in Georgia, Tennessee, Arizona, and Wyomig. A possible application of this advanced-technology system to the Detroit CBD/Windsor river crossing (international border) is under study. Point-to-point shuttle of substantial numbers of people is the most significant service characteristic of such cableways.

Another advanced-technology system is dual-mode transportation. The systems being most notably researched in the United States involve the general concept of vehicles operated under driver control in mixed traffic and automatic control (either electronic or mechanical) along specially designed and equipped routes or facilities. Such dual-mode vehicles could be either specially equipped automobiles or transit vehicles. Automatically controlled vehicles capable of operating in a mixed-traffic environment now exist and are used in some factories and office buildings for delivery of supplies, mail, and the like. The development of such vehicles, capable of operating in several modes, is of increasing importance to the circulation requirements of many of the major activity centers.

Trends in major activity center transportation

It has been well documented that the economy of scarcity seems to be inducing efficiencies to be gained through concentrations of land uses. Thus, there is no doubt that major activity centers will continue to grow in importance. The competition for space for land use, space for people, and

TABLE 22–14
Performance Data Related to Patronage, Usage, and Degree of Automation (1976)*

AGT System at	Annual Patronage (millions)	Annual Unit† Mile Travel	Annual Passenger Miles Travel (millions)	Annual Place Mile Travel (millions)	Load Factor	Employee Unit† Ratio	Number of Units†		Annual Place Miles to System Man-Hours
							Vehicle	Train	
Houston	1.3	366,000	0.325	3.82	0.085	1.8	3	3	244
Tampa	14.5	405,000	2.47	40.5	0.061	0.825	8	—	3,068
Sea-Tac	10.1	710,600	3.6	41.06	0.087	1.58	12	6	1,102
Fairlane	2.43	6,239	1.15	1.79	0.64	5	2	—	390.1
WEDWay	4.66	712,000	4.05	16.2	0.28	0.48	5	30	508.5
King's Dominion	0.87	228,000	1.8	21.8	0.66	5	8	6	120

*1 mile = 1.61 km.
†Unit is the discrete moving unit, either a vehicle or a train of vehicles.

SOURCE: U.S. DEPARTMENT OF TRANSPORTATION, Urban Mass Transportation Administration, *Conference on Automated Guideway Transit Technology Development,* 1978 Conference Proceedings, Transportation Systems Center, Kendall Square, Cambridge, Mass., Feb. 28–Mar. 2, 1978.

TABLE 22–15
Unit Costs for Providing AGT Service*,†,‡

System	Cost/Vehicle-Mile ($)			Cost/Passenger Carried ($)			Cost/Passenger Mile ($)			Cost/Place-(capacity) Mile ($)		
	O&M	Capital	Total	O&M	Capital	Total	O&M	Capital	Total	O&M	Capital	Total
Morgantown I	2.36	11.28	13.64	0.72	3.42	4.14	0.44	2.14	2.58	0.11	0.54	0.65
AIRTRANS	0.80	1.86	2.66	0.48	1.13	1.62	—	—	n.a.	0.02	0.04	0.06
Jetrail	1.31	1.13	2.44	0.28	0.24	0.52	—	—	n.a.	0.13	0.11	0.24
Cabinlift	0.56	9.33	9.89	—	—	n.a.	—	—	n.a.	0.05	0.77	0.82
Tampa	1.18	4.19	5.37	0.03	0.12	0.15	0.19	0.69	0.88	0.01	0.04	0.05
Sea-Tac	1.83	9.54	11.37	0.07	0.39	0.46	0.21	1.08	1.29	0.02	0.09	0.11
Houston	2.70	6.08	8.78	0.25	0.57	0.82	1.01	2.29	3.30	0.07	0.17	0.24
Fairlane	6.55	11.95	18.50	0.16	0.30	0.46	0.34	0.63	0.97	0.27	0.50	0.77
WEDWay	0.49	2.09	2.58	0.07	0.32	0.39	0.09	0.36	0.45	0.02	0.11	0.13
King's Dominion	6.18	25.83	32.01	0.18	0.75	0.93	0.09	0.36	0.45	0.06	0.27	0.33
Weighted average for 10 systems	1.13	3.62	4.75	0.17	0.53	0.70	n.a.	n.a.	n.a.	0.03	0.08	0.11

*1 mile = 1.61 km.
†n.a., not available.
‡O&M, operation and maintenance.

SOURCE: N. D. LEA & ASSOCIATES, INC. *Summary of Capital and Operations and Maintenance Cost Experience of Automated Guideway Transit Systems,* prepared for U.S. Department of Transportation, Urban Mass Transportation Administration, Washington, D.C., June 1978.

Figure 22.26. Roosevelt Island tramway. SOURCE: VSL Corporation, Los Gatos, Calif.

space for transportation suggests that the technology for circulation systems in major activity centers will advance fairly rapidly. What seems novel or of limited application today may well be an established solution on a broad scale tomorrow.

This chapter has discussed the state of technology of circulation systems in major activity centers with concentration on the newer forms. Although some of the ideas and technology seem advanced, it is important to note the continuing research and development programs of the U.S. Urban Mass Transportation Administration. National and local governments in Germany, Japan, and France, to name a few of the more active countries, are engaged in detailed planning and engineering studies of automated guideway transit in a variety of urban contexts. Manufacturers, also on an international spectrum, are pursuing the continued development and improvement of AGT hardware.

In the future, major activity centers will increase in importance and size as much as they will increase in mode-change locales. The ability to handle the growing volumes of mode change efficiently, and equally important, the ability to weave the solutions to these transportation demands into the fabric of major activity centers in a nondisruptive way will sorely tax the abilities of transportation planners and engineers.

REFERENCES FOR FURTHER READING

American Society of Mechanical Engineers, *American National Standard Safety Code for Elevators, Escalators, Dumbwaiters, and Moving Walks,* ANSI A 17.1-1971, New York, 1971.

DeLeuw, Cather and Company, *Characteristics of Urban Transportation Systems—A Handbook for Transportation Planners,* prepared for the U.S. Department of Transportation, Washington, D.C., May 1975.

Fruin, J. J., *Pedestrian Planning and Design,* Metropolitan Association of Urban Designers and Environmental Planners, New York, 1971.

General Motors Transportation Systems Division, *Classification and Definition of AGT Systems,* U.S. Department of Transportation, Urban Mass Transportation Administration, Washington, D.C., Jan. 1977.

John Hopkins University, *Analysis of Urban Transportation Needs with Implications for AGT Systems,* U.S. Department of Transportation, Urban Mass Transportation Administration, Washington, D.C., July 1975.

Lea, N. D., *The Lea Transit Compendium,* Vols. 1–7, Transportation Research Corporation, Huntsville, Alabama, 1974.

Office of Technology Assessment, *Automated Guideway Transit: An Assessment of PRT and Other New Systems,* U.S. Government Printing Office, Washington, D.C., 1975.

Strakosch, G. R., *Vertical Transportation: Elevators and Escalators,* Wiley, New York, 1967.

Tough, J. M., and C. A. O'Flaherty, *Passenger Conveyors,* Ian Allan, London, 1971.

23

TRAFFIC SIGNS AND MARKINGS

J. ROBERT DOUGHTY, *Chief*
Division of Traffic Engineering and Operations
Pennsylvania Department of Transportation
Harrisburg, Pennsylvania

This chapter includes general information on the need for and use of traffic signs and markings. It does not serve as a standard or replace the *Manual on Uniform Traffic Control Devices for Streets and Highways* (hereafter, simply called the *Uniform Manual*)[1] but provides information and guidelines for (1) types of design and elementary layouts; (2) warrants and requisite studies; (3) materials, maintenance, inventory, and schedules; and (4) equipment and shop requirements.

The standards recommended and frequently referred to in this chapter are those prescribed in the *Uniform Manual*. In the interest of uniformity throughout the United States, all signs should follow these accepted standards. A considerable number of states have issued their own sign manuals, patterned closely after the *Uniform Manual* or have adopted it by reference. Local authorities, in the design and application of signs, should follow the standards of their state. Practicing traffic engineers in other countries should follow their appropriate manual (Pan American, Canadian, Australian, European, etc.)

General provisions

Traffic control devices, including signs and markings, are the primary means of regulating, warning, or guiding traffic on all streets and highways. The need for well-designed, adequately maintained devices grows in proportion to the density of traffic, speed of operation, and complexity of maneuvering areas on highways and at intersections.

Both signs and markings have the function of regulating, warning, guiding, and/or channelizing traffic. To be effective the installation of each device should (1) fulfill a need; (2) command attention; (3) convey a clear, simple meaning; (4) command respect of road users; and (5) give adequate time for proper response.

The traffic engineer must consider five basic factors to ensure that these requirements are met. Although detailed in the *Uniform Manual*, they are generally described below to help establish a relationship with the basic requirements above:

1. *Design:* the combination of physical features such as size, colors, and shape needed to command attention and convey a message.
2. *Placement:* the installation of devices so that they are within the cones of vision of the users, and thus able to command attention and allow time for response.
3. *Operation:* the application of devices so that they meet traffic requirements in a uniform and consistent manner, fulfill a need, command respect, and allow time for response.
4. *Maintenance:* the upkeep of devices to retain legibility and visibility, or the removal of devices if not needed, to aid in commanding respect and attention while fulfilling the needs of users.
5. *Uniformity:* the uniform application of similar devices for similar situations so that they fulfill the needs of users and command their respect.

The traffic engineer must also see that control devices do not conflict with but supplement each other in terms of providing a meaningful message to motorists. Every effort must be made to remove obsolete, conflicting, or unnecessary signs or roadway markings and to minimize any possible confusion.

[1]*Manual on Uniform Traffic Control Devices for Streets and Highways*, U.S. Department of Transportation, Federal Highway Administration, U.S. Government Printing Office, Washington, D.C., 1978.

Standardization

The most outstanding characteristic of signs and markings in the United States, Canada, Europe, and other parts of the world is the high degree of standardization which has been achieved and which will be further implemented upon adoption of new manuals.

The adoption of the *Uniform Manual* continues to provide for more extensive use of symbols on regulatory and warning signs. The use of yellow pavement markings, however, will still keep the United States apart from other countries because it has not been uniformly adopted internationally for center lines or no-passing zones.

Limitations and effectiveness

Traffic signs and roadway markings are inherently subject to becoming damaged or defaced, and can become dirty and ineffective. Moreover, roadway markings have a relatively short life, and can also become obliterated by snow, bad weather conditions, and the heavy concentration of vehicles. A proper maintenance program, plus continued effort into research of materials and their application, will help minimize the many problems in these areas.

The effectiveness of signs and markings or the need for additional control can be measured by the type and number of erratic maneuvers or accidents that develop over a period of time. Where a problem develops in traffic control, an engineering study should be made to determine the primary cause. Driver and pedestrian studies can provide an objective, quantitative evaluation of existing traffic control devices and give guidance for corrective action.

Driver information needs

Research has identified the information needs of the driver and the interaction between these needs.[2] Information needs occur throughout the entire driving task, and they fall into a hierarchy relative to satisfying those needs. The highest order of needs are those associated with the two main tasks of tracking and speed control, followed by the needs for obstacle avoidance and maintenance of the most efficient and safe course in the traffic stream. A lower order of needs are those associated with direction finding.

The use of this hierarchy of information needs is of prime importance in developing and installing an information system for drivers. For example, in areas where drivers will be busy with speed control or obstacle avoidance, they should not be overly burdened with directional signing. Such directional information should be planned and installed in areas where there are only "simple" steering and speed control maneuvers. Drivers should not be "overloaded" because of complex or unexpected events during their trip.

[2]G. E. King and H. Luenfeld, "Development of Information Requirements and Transmission Techniques for Highway Users," *Natl. Cooperative Highway Res. Program Rep. 123,* Highway Research Board, Washington, D.C., 1971.

Federal safety standards

In the United States, a series of Highway Safety Program Standards have been issued by the U.S. Department of Transportation.[3] These program standards are designed to help identify areas in need of new or revised traffic control devices and to establish a means of scheduling adequate maintenance. Three of the programs, which relate directly to signs and markings, are:

1. Number 9, *Identification and Surveillance of Accident Locations:* the development of continuing programs to identify accident locations and methods for their correction (signing, such as mileposting, is needed as a means of locating and documenting the accidents in the field).
2. Number 10, *Traffic Records:* the collection and maintenance of records, including data on drivers, vehicles, accidents, and highways (data pertaining to traffic control devices, such as signs and markings, are specifically listed under highways).
3. Number 13, *Traffic Control Devices:* the implementation of control device improvements that bear directly on reducing accidents.

Compliance with these acts and the adoption of similar programs in other countries will help reduce traffic accidents and deaths, injuries, and property damage on all streets and highways.

Functional usage classification

Traffic signs fall into three broad areas of functional classifications according to use:

1. *Regulatory signs:* used to impose legal restrictions applicable to particular locations and unenforceable without such signs.
2. *Warning signs:* used to call attention to hazardous conditions, actual or potential, that would otherwise not be readily apparent.
3. *Guide or informational signs:* used to provide directions to motorists, including route designations, destinations, available services, points of interest, and other geographic, recreational, or cultural sites.

Signing elements

General specifications

The most important qualities of traffic signs are their attention value, legibility, and recognition:

1. *Attention value:* the characteristic that commands attention:

[3]*Highway Safety Program Standards,* U.S. Department of Transportation, Federal Highway Administration, National Highway Safety Bureau, Washington, D.C., 1974.

a. *Target value:* the quality that makes a sign or groups of signs stand out from their background.

b. *Priority value:* the quality that makes it possible for a sign to be read first, in preference to other signs.

(These values are dependent upon relative size, color contrast of signs and background, and relative position of signs.)

2. *Legibility:* the characteristic of being readable:
   a. *Pure legibility:* the distance at which a sign can be read in an unlimited time.
   b. *Glance legibility:* the distance at which a sign can be read at a glance (usually 0.5 to 1.4 s) within a cone of approximately 5 ft (1.5 m) diameter at 100 ft (30.5 m) distance.
3. *Recognition:* the characteristic of being recognizable and understandable through the utilization of standardized colors, shapes, and legends.

Other qualities are also important. For example, experiments indicate that signs located over a highway are more likely to be seen earlier than those to either side.

Design

The basic design philosophy for the shape, color, and message of signs has generally remained the same in the United States for several decades. The principal trend, as reflected in the new *Uniform Manual,* is toward adoption of more "symbol" signs, consistent with those of Canada, Mexico, and European countries.

The standard sign shapes are:

1. *Octagon:* reserved exclusively for the stop sign.
2. *Equilateral triangle,* with one point downward: reserved exclusively for the yield sign.
3. *Round:* used for the advance warning of a railroad crossing.
4. *Pennant,* an isosceles triangle with its longest axis horizontal—used to warn of no passing.
5. *Diamond:* used only to warn of existing or possible hazards, except those mentioned in (3) and (4).
6. *Rectangle,* ordinarily with *longer vertical dimension:* used for regulatory signs, with the exception of stop and yield signs.
7. *Rectangle,* ordinarily with *longer horizontal dimension:* used for guide and informational signs.
8. *Trapezoid:* may be used for recreational area signs.
9. *Pentagon,* point up: used for advance school and school crossing signs.
10. *Miscellaneous:* reserved for special purpose, such as the shield for route markers and the crossbuck for railroad crossings.

Color

The U.S. standard colors[4] and their uses include:

[4]Color cards showing the correct colors for highway signs are available on request from the Federal Highway Administration, Washington, D.C.

1. *Red:* used as background color for stop, do not enter, and wrong way signs and for multiway supplemental plates; as a legend color for parking prohibition signs, route markers, the circular outline and the diagonal bar for prohibitory symbols; and for the border and message for yield signs.
2. *Black:* used as a background for certain one way and weigh station signs, as well as for specified night speed limit signs, and as the legend color for white, yellow, and orange signs.
3. *White:* used as a background for route markers, guide signs, and regulatory signs except for the stop sign; for the legend on brown, green, blue, black, and red signs.
4. *Orange:* used as a background color for construction and maintenance signs.
5. *Yellow:* used as a background color for school signs and warning signs (except where orange is specified).
6. *Brown:* used as a background color for guide and information signs related to points of recreational, scenic, or cultural interest.
7. *Green:* used as a background color for milepost and guide signs (other than those using brown or white), and as a legend color on white background for certain directional signs and permissive parking regulations.
8. *Blue:* used as a background color for information signs related to motorist services, rest areas, and evacuation route markers.

Purple, light blue, coral, and strong yellow-green have been identified for future use.

Size

Standard sizes have been established for regulatory and warning signs and for certain guide signs such as route markers. Larger sizes are used for high-speed highways, for locations involving impaired visibility, highways of four or more lanes, or other locations where added emphasis is desirable.

Standard sign sizes include:

1. *Stop:* 30 × 30 in. (76 × 76 cm), except that a 24 × 24 in. (61 × 61 cm) sign may be used on minor roads and secondary streets.
2. *Yield:* 36 in. (91 cm) side dimensions.
3. *No — turn* (symbol): 24 × 24 in. (61 × 61 cm).
4. *Do not enter:* 30 × 30 in. (76 × 76 cm).
5. *Urban parking signs:* 12 × 18 in. (31 × 46 cm), except where the message requires additional space.
6. *Other regulatory signs:* 24 × 30 in. (61 × 76 cm), except that some 18 × 24 in. (46 × 61 cm) may be used on minor roads and secondary streets.
7. *Guide signs:* sufficient to accommodate minimum lettering 6 in. (15 cm) high on major routes in rural districts, 4 in. (10 cm) high on less important rural roads and urban streets, and 8 in. (20 cm) or more on expressways.

The overall size of guide signs for expressways and the Interstate system has to be established based upon the type of mounting, the type of exit, the type of information (supplemental, gore, advance guide), and the message itself. Minimum letter and numeral sizes have been established in the *Uniform Manual,* and computer programs have been developed for custom designing these signs.[5]

Legend

In general, both sign and letter size have been established for all regulatory and warning signs. Moreover, the *Uniform Manual* sets forth criteria establishing the series of letters to be used and the spacing between letters for these signs. The Series B Alphabet is restricted to street names, parking signs, and similar signs because of the limited breadth and stroke width.

Standard Alphabets for Highway Signs[6] are available for those interested in manufacturing their own signs. The capital alphabets vary in width of letter and stroke of letter in Series B through Series F. For instance, the letter "A" in a 4-in. (10.2-cm) height varies in letter width and stroke width as shown in Table 23-1.

TABLE 23–1
Letter Width and Stroke Width of the Letter "A"

	Letter Width		Stroke Width	
Series	in.	cm	in.	cm
B	2.12	5.41	0.50	1.28
C	2.50	6.38	0.56	1.43
D	3.34	8.52	0.62	1.58
E	4.00	10.20	0.69	1.76
F	4.50	11.48	0.75	1.91

For guide signs, only minimum sizes have been established. The letter size needed to give the motorist ample opportunity to read it readily at normal approach speed will, in general, determine the size of sign needed. In selecting proper letter size, these factors must be taken into account: (1) speed of approach vehicle, (2) location of the sign, (3) width and type of letters, (4) illumination or reflectorization, (5) necessary warning time (perception–reaction time and stopping or deceleration time for the necessary maneuver), and (6) amount of sign copy.

The standard lettering for conventional highway signs is also the standard capital alphabet, Series B to F. When the letter height exceeds 8 in. (20 cm), place names on guide signs should be composed of lowercase letters with an initial uppercase letter. The initial uppercase letter should be approximately 1⅓ times the "loop" height of the lowercase letters. It is intended that the initial uppercase letters and numerals used with the lowercase letters will be Series E of the *Standard Alphabets for Highway Signs* modified by widening the stroke width to approximately one-fifth of the letter height.

[5]R. L. Bleyl and H. B. Boutwell, "A Computer Program for Guide Sign Designing and Drafting." *Traffic Eng.* (Institute of Traffic Engineers, Washington, D.C.), *38*(6), 22–26 (Mar. 1968).

[6]*Standard Alphabets for Highway Signs and Pavement Markings,* U.S. Department of Transportation, Federal Highway Administration, Office of Traffic Operations, Washington, D.C., 1977, pp. 5–41.

The style of lettering to be used on freeway guide signs must be one of the following two types: (1) uppercase letters for all word legends; or (2) lowercase letters with initial uppercase letters for all names of places, streets, and highways and uppercase letters for other word legends.

Word messages in the legends of freeway guide signs should be in letters at least 8 in. (20 cm) high. Larger lettering is necessary for major guide signs at and in advance of interchanges, and for all overhead signs. Recommended numeral and letter sizes according to interchange classification, type of sign, and component of sign legend are specified in the *Uniform Manual.*

Appropriate descriptive symbols instead of words on highway signs provide a great advantage in conveying the intended message. Apart from a certain symbolism in sign shapes, the principal symbol used in the United States is the arrow, which shows directions, changes in alignment, and turn prohibitions. Arrows are also used in conjunction with a brief message to denote regulations applying to a certain lane, one-way directions, keep-right signs, and areas where parking is prohibited.

Diagrammatic signing should use arrows that approximate the intersection geometrics, or the necessary part of it, in a clear, understandable manner to impart a glance-legible message, as shown in Figure 23.1.

Symbols showing pictures of various types of hazards and traffic interference are used extensively in Europe because of the language differences on the European continent.

Reflectorization and illumination

Signs that carry regulatory messages, warnings, or essential directional information must be as legible at night as in the day. They must be reflectorized or illuminated unless they are not applicable at night or are in an area of sufficient level of illumination to provide proper nighttime visibility.

The combination of improved automobile headlighting and more effective reflecting materials during the past decade has made reflectorized signs as effective as certain types of illuminated signs. Signs of proper reflectivity provide satisfactory visibility under most driving conditions. Practical financial considerations demand their use, instead of illuminated signs, for most applications on both rural and urban roads, particularly signs mounted at the side of the roadway.

Sign reflectorization is accomplished by reflectorizing the message, lettering, symbols, and the border; by reflectorizing the background; or by reflectorizing both background and message.

When only the message is reflectorized, the lettering or symbol stroke must be relatively wide and the reflectorization must have a high luminance so that adequate target value is achieved. Where both background and letters or symbols are reflectorized, the message should be provided with a higher brightness value than the background material.

The desirable physical characteristics of a reflectorized traffic sign should assure that the sign provides:

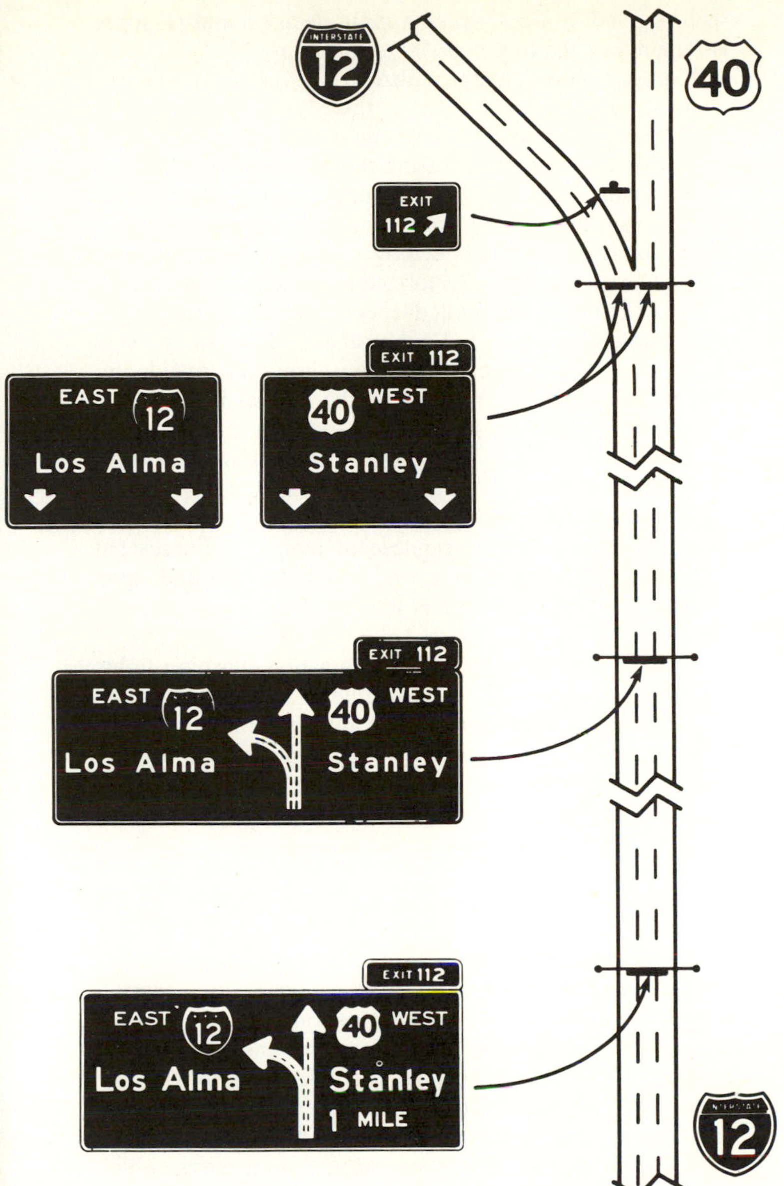

Figure 23.1. *Sample diagrammatic sign applications for two-lane exits. SOURCE: *Manual on Uniform Traffic Control Devices,* U.S. Department of Transportation, Federal Highway Administration, U.S. Government Printing Office, Washington, D.C., 1978, p. 2F-20.

*For color specifications of signs and markings illustrated throughout this chapter, see MUTCD.

1. Sufficient reflectivity over a normal approach distance so that good target value and legibility are provided from the maximum to the minimum approach distance.
2. No glare from its reflectorized portion which would tend to blot out the legibility of the message.
3. Seventy-five percent of its dry reflectivity when subjected to adverse conditions of rainfall and fog.
4. A self-cleaning surface so that there will not be a heavy accumulation of dirt on the reflective surface.
5. A durable surface which is also resistant to vandalism.

Reflective elements are of three principal types: reflector buttons, microprism sheeting, and reflecting coatings. They all possess the quality of reflex or retrodirective reflections, that is, the ability to reflect the incident light directly back toward its source.

Reflector buttons are small reflecting units set within a cutout form to depict a symbol or a series of letters on the face of a sign. They generally consist of transparent buttons having the rear inner face made up of prismatic reflectors.

Microprism sheeting is material containing many thousands of minute corner-cube prisms per square inch (square centimeter) embossed into a clear, durable sheet material. This material may be cut to form symbols or letters and may be used as background sheeting for selected signs.

Reflective coatings are materials intended to cover areas of any shape, such as the entire background of a sign, or to be used for complete letters or symbols. The type in common use consists of flexible adhesive-coated sheeting with very small glass spheres embedded in a plastic surface. Each sphere acts as a miniature reflector.

The qualities of reflective materials which affect their uses include:

1. The amount of incident light from the car headlamps reflected back to the driver's eyes under normal viewing distances.
2. The maximum entrance angle through which effective reflection is possible.
3. Resistance to weather deterioration and vandalism.
4. Ease of application and replacement.
5. Cost per year of useful life.

The divergence angle, which is the angle between the incident beam and the light reflected to the observer, must be wide enough to include the eyes of the motor vehicle driver. This varies from less than 0.2° at great distances to 1.5° at 150 ft (46 m) for drivers of some trucks. The maximum divergence angle is required when a sign is to be read from a vehicle about to pass the side of the sign, and for truck drivers, whose eyes are a substantial distance above their headlamps.

The entrance angle is the angle between the incident beam and a perpendicular to the face of the sign. Reflective materials used must have a wide-angle response to reflect light even when the approaching vehicle headlights are well to one side of the sign. The wide-angle materials available to fulfill this requirement give good reflectivity up to 40 degrees. Good reflectivity at wide entrance angles is required to:

1. Secure good visibility over a long range of approach distances, including close viewing distance.
2. Offset the effect of inaccuracies in sign installations.
3. Compensate for any temporary damage to supporting structure.
4. Be of use on multilane roads, where the lateral distance between vehicle and signs may be considerable. This is particularly true where safety programs require signs to be set back from the edge of highway to minimize points of conflict.

When reflectorized signs are not likely to give effective results, such as at overhead locations with less than 1200 ft (365 m) of tangent sight distance, sign illumination is necessary to provide adequate contrast and visibility.[7] External illumination is normally used on most overhead signs of the Interstate Highway System, on urban expressway sections, and in areas where a rapid decision and response is required of the motorist.

Illumination may be provided by:

1. Directing external light upon the surface of the sign itself, so that it is illuminated from the direction of approach. Because of the possibility of lighting failure, the message must be reflectorized and the background may be either reflectorized or nonreflectorized; but the mixing of reflectorized and nonreflectorized signs in the same general area should be avoided. Depending upon local policy, lighting may be placed either above or below the sign surface. Illumination from below, however, avoids undesirable daytime shadows on the face of the sign. Illumination may be provided by fluorescent tubes or by mercury vapor luminaires. The latter tend to be favored because of easier mounting, easier maintenance (longer life), and better lighting distribution.
2. Light produced by incandescent lamps or fluorescent tubes shining through a translucent background upon which the sign message is lettered.

In a modified form of sign illumination, flashing lights are used to improve the target value of some of the more critical signs. Red flashing lights can be used in connection with stop signs, and yellow flashing lights can be used in connection with various types of warning signs and school crossing signs.

Variable message signs

Variable message signs are used to inform drivers of regulations or instructions that are applicable only during certain periods of the day or under certain traffic conditions. The need for and use of variable message signs has increased considerably over the past several years. Moreover, the trend should quicken as more funds are made available for operational needs and as technological development brings improved equipment. These variable message signs, which can be changed manually, by remote control, or by automatic controls that can "sense" the conditions that require special sign messages, have applications in each of the functional usage classifications. Examples include:

1. *Regulatory:* No left turn during peak hours; speed limit . . . during school periods; reversible one-way operation.
2. *Warning:* accident ahead; ice ahead.
3. *Guide:* alternate route; stadium access.
4. *Information:* congestion ahead; truck scale open.

Examples of these signs, which should conform to the same shapes and colors and be of the same dimensions as standard signs, are:

1. Blank signs, consisting of a fluorescent grid of illumination behind cutout letters or symbols, which are effective only when the grid is illuminated.
2. Signs that change their message by means of a curtain drawn between a clear sign front and the electrical il-

[7]N. Bryan, D. Casner, R. Klotz, and H. Knisley, *A Limited Evaluation of Reflective and Non-reflective Background for Overhead Signs*. Pennsylvania Department of Transportation, Research Report, Harrisburg, Pa., Sep. 1978.

lumination provided behind the curtain, or by means of a rotating drum.

3. Signs that change their message by illumination of incandescent lights in appropriate patterns, by selection of the light units which provide the desired letter, numeral, or symbol.
4. Signs that use electromagnetic, reflective disks which are black on one side and can rotate to form alphabetic and numeric characters. External illumination may be necessary for good legibility during nighttime.

Each type of unit will not necessarily serve all functional classifications of sign usage, but at least one of the designs can be adapted to a particular problem.

Location, erection, and supports

Although standardization of position cannot always be attained, the general rule is to locate signs on the drivers' side of the roadway, where they are looking for them. Signs in other locations, except for those mounted overhead, should be considered as supplementary to signs in their normal locations.

In general, signs should be located to optimize nighttime visibility and minimize the effects of mud and salt spatter. Signs should be located so that they do not obscure each other and are not hidden from view by other roadside objects.

Post-mounted signs should be placed at an angle to minimize glare from their surfaces. Reflectorized signs should have a slight rotation away from the roadway to reduce mirror reflection, without unduly reducing readability. Signs should be placed with regard to the alignment of approaching traffic, not necessarily at a predetermined angle with the roadway edge. It is sometimes desirable to tilt reflectorized signs on grades forward or back on their mountings so that they face approaching traffic more squarely, and to raise them above normal mounting heights to place them within the range of visibility of motorists driving uphill.

Whenever possible each traffic sign should be mounted on an individual post to provide a minimum of competition among groups of signs. Speed advisory signs are an exception to this rule because they serve as a supplementary message to the warning sign with which they are combined.

Lateral clearance. The lateral clearance for regulatory and warning signs, or the smaller directional signs, should be from 6 to 12 ft (2 to 4 m) from the edge of the pavement or traveled way in rural areas, as shown in Figure 23.2. The larger directional signs should retain a clearance of about 30 ft (9 m) on high-type highways to minimize the chance of being hit by an errant driver.

In urban areas, signs generally are mounted alongside the roadway in the space between the curb and the sidewalk, or above the sidewalk itself, preferably where the signs will not have to compete with advertising signs on adjacent buildings. Where practicable, a sign should not be less than 10 ft (3 m) from the edge of the nearest traffic lane. Large guide signs especially should be farther removed, preferably 30 ft (9 m) or more from the nearest traffic lane. Lesser clearance, but not generally less than 6 ft (2 m) may be used on connecting roadways or ramps at interchanges.

On wide expressways, or where some degree of lane-use control is desirable, or where space is not available at the roadside, overhead signs are often necessary. Other factors that may justify the erection of overhead signs include:

1. Traffic volume at or near capacity
2. Complex design
3. Three or more lanes in each direction
4. Restricted sight distance
5. Closely spaced interchanges or intersections
6. Multilane exits or turns
7. Large percentage of trucks
8. Background of street lighting
9. High-speed traffic
10. Consistency of sign message locations
11. Insufficient space for ground signs
12. Located near signal heads so that a motorist can see all controls within a confined area

Longitudinal placement. Good longitudinal placement of signs calls for regulatory signs to be installed where the mandate or prohibition applies or begins, warning signs to be placed in advance of the conditions to which they call attention, and guide signs to be placed as needed to keep drivers adequately informed. The following guidelines are generally applicable:

1. Stop and yield signs should be placed at the point where compliance is required. Even in open rural areas, these signs should not be placed more than 50 ft (15 m) from the intersecting roadway. A suitable stop line or other marking device should be placed in the roadway at the intended point of compliance to supplement the stop sign if the sign is not at or near the point where the vehicle should stop or yield. Channelization may be necessary to provide a suitable location for the sign at complicated intersections, or where physical conditions make it otherwise difficult to place the sign.

2. Warning signs generally are placed somewhat in advance of the point of compliance. In urban areas where speeds are relatively low, warning signs should be posted about 250 ft (75 m) in advance of the hazardous condition to which they are directing attention. In rural areas and on higher speed roadways, warning signs should be posted at a distance from 750 to 1500 ft (230 to 460 m) in advance of the hazard. These distances are necessary in order to permit the driver to make the necessary response to comply with the regulations.

3. Guide signs are posted in advance of intersections and within the intersections themselves. A statewide or national uniform plan should be followed so that motorists, once accustomed to the plan, will be able to find signs in uniform locations. Junction signs and advance turn arrows in rural areas should be erected not less than 400 ft (120 m) in advance of the intersections as shown in Figure 23.3; in built-up areas they should be located approximately mid-block preceding the intersection, but generally not more than 300 ft (40 m) in advance of the intersection.

4. Destination signs in rural areas are to be located not less than 200 ft (60 m) or more than 300 ft (90 m) in advance

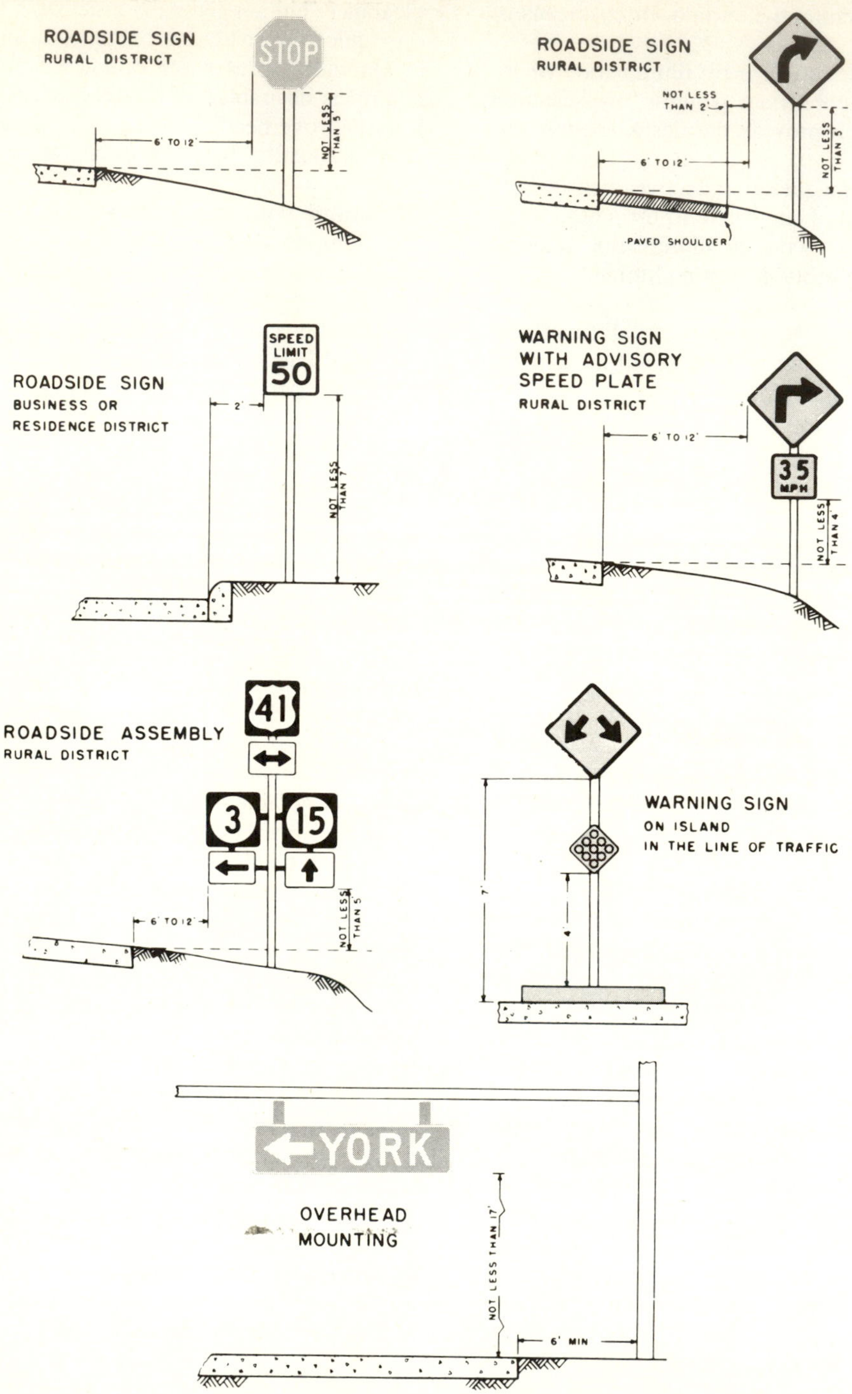

Figure 23.2 Height and lateral location of signs—typical installations. SOURCE: *Manual on Uniform Traffic Control Devices,* U.S. Department of Transportation, Federal Highway Administration, U.S. Government Printing Office, Washington, D.C., 1978, p. 2A-9.

of the intersection; in urban areas, somewhat shorter distances are permissible. Directional route markers should be at the intersection. Confirmatory route markers are placed from 25 to 200 ft (8 to 60 m) beyond the intersection in rural areas and 10 to 80 ft (3 to 25 m) beyond it in urban areas.

Expressway interchange signs generally combine the functions of route markers and destination signs. They require greater advance warning distances than do signs on conventional highways. For each interchange where longitudinal space allows, there should be a minimum of three sets of guide signs, not including any signs placed as supplements to the regular signs. In all cases, major guide signs placed in advance of deceleration lanes should be at least 800 ft (250 m) apart. Figure 23.4 shows the typical signing sequence for a diamond interchange.

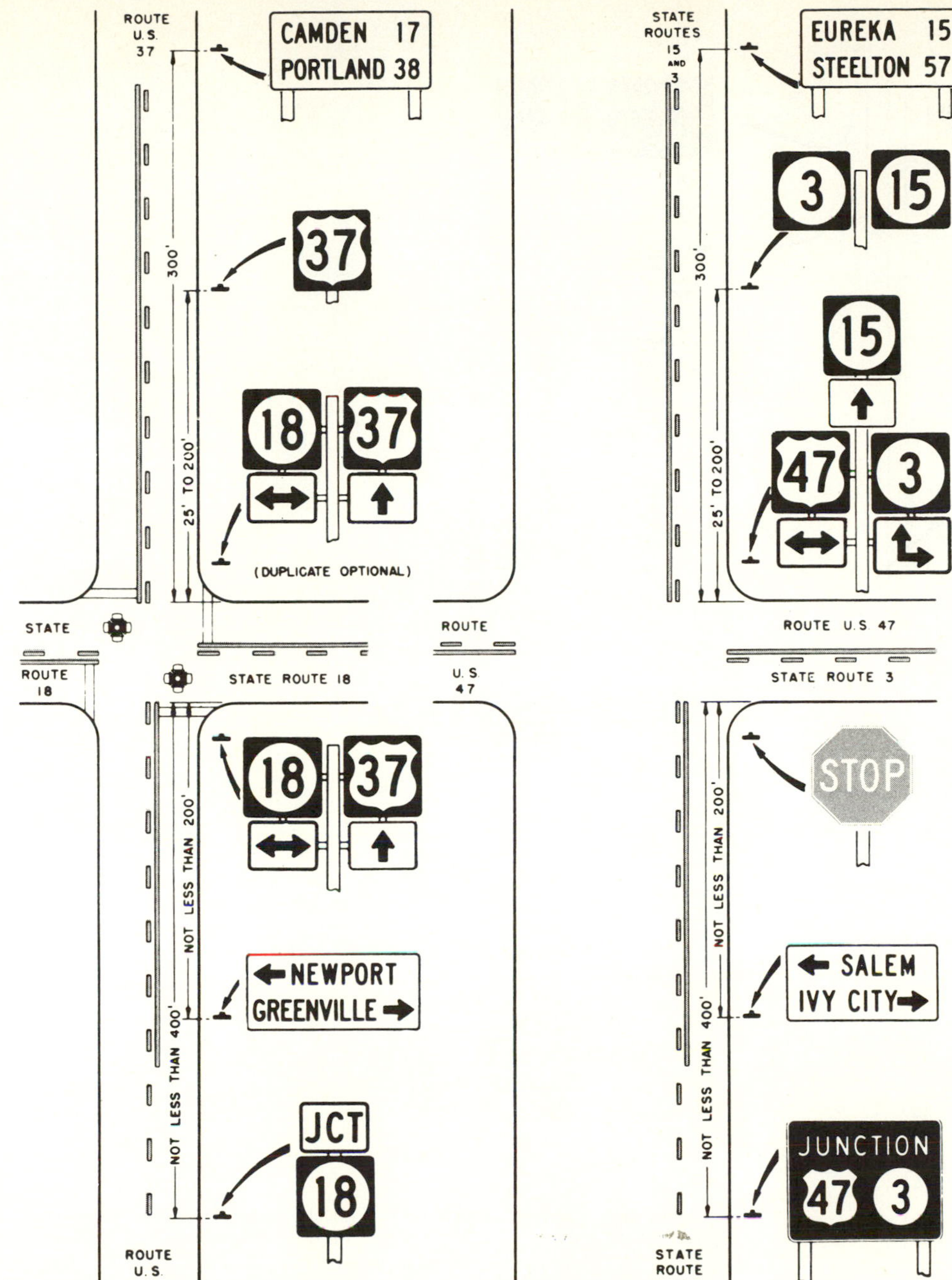

Figure 23.3. Typical route markings at rural intersections (for one direction of travel only). SOURCE: *Manual on Uniform Traffic Control Devices,* U.S. Department of Transportation, Federal Highway Administration, U.S. Government Printing Office, Washington, D.C., 1978, p. 2D-16.

Vertical placement. Signs erected at the side of the road in rural areas should be mounted at a height of at least 5 ft (1.5 m), measured from the bottom of the sign to the near edge of the pavement. In business, commercial, and residential districts where parking and/or pedestrian movement is likely to occur or where there are other obstructions to view, the clearance to the bottom of the sign should be at least 7 ft (2.1 m). The height requirements for ground installations on expressways vary somewhat from those on conventional streets and highways. Directional signs on expressways should be erected at a minimum height of 7 ft (2.1 m) above the near edge of the pavement to the bottom of the sign. If, however, a secondary sign is mounted below another sign, the major sign should be at least 8 ft (2.4 m) and the secondary sign at least 5 ft (1.5 m) above the level of the pavement edge. All route markers and warning and regulatory signs on expressways should be at least 6 ft (1.8 m) above the level of the pavement edge. However, where guide signs are placed 30 ft (9 m) or more from the edge of the nearest traffic lane for increased roadside safety, the height to the bottom of such signs may be 5 ft (1.5 m).

Overhead signs should provide a vertical clearance of not

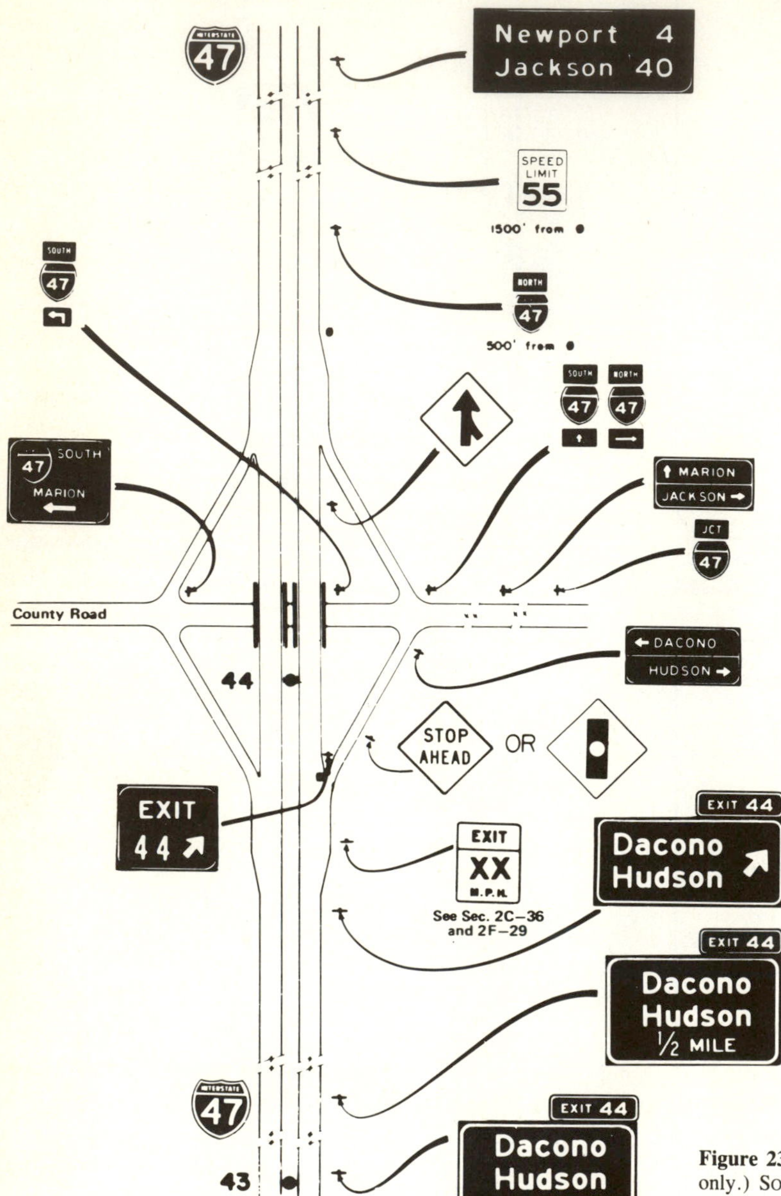

Figure 23.4. Typical signing of diamond interchange (for one direction only.) SOURCE: *Manual on Uniform Traffic Control Devices,* U.S. Department of Transportation, Federal Highway Administration, U.S. Government Printing Office, Washington, D.C., 1978, p. 2F-30.

less than 17 ft (5 m) over the entire width of the pavement and shoulders, except where a lesser vertical clearance is used for the design of other structures on that facility. The vertical clearance to overhead sign structures or supports need not be greater than 1 ft (30 cm) in excess of the minimum design clearance of other structures.

Posts and mountings

Signs can be correctly placed on existing supports used for other purposes, such as traffic signals, street lights, and public utility poles where permitted, thereby saving expense and minimizing sidewalk obstruction. (Such signs should not be installed on wooden utility poles where utility crews could be hurt while working on the poles.)

Other sign posts and their foundations and sign mountings should be so constructed as to hold signs in a proper and permanent position, and to resist swaying in the wind or displacement by vandalism. On the other hand, they should be so constructed and installed that they yield or break away upon being hit by a small vehicle.[8] The only exceptions to these safety features should be (1) large overhead sign structures that would fall onto the roadway, (2)

[8] *Standard Specifications for Structural Supports for Highway Signs, Luminaires and Traffic Signals.* American Association of State Highway and Transportation Officials, Washington, D.C., 1975.

other signs that are protected by curb in urban areas or guard rail in rural areas, and (3) sign installations that are a sufficient distance from the pavement edge to allow an errant driver a clear area to recover.

In noncurbed or other unprotected areas, regulatory and warning signs can normally be mounted on the driver's side of the road on square or U-shaped posts that break away at pivot points or yield to any vehicle upon impact.[9]

A one-post installation of the lighter (approximately 2.25 lb/ft or 3.3 kg/m) steel breakaway or yielding type post will support signs that do not exceed 36 in. (91 cm) in width or 10 ft^2 (0.93 m^2) in area at standard mounting heights. The heavier steel (approximately 4 lb/ft or 6 kg/m) posts will support signs generally not exceeding 48 in. (1.2 m) in width or 16 ft^2 (1.5 m^2) in area at standard mounting heights.

Slightly greater sign widths and total areas may be installed on single wooden sign posts. A 4 × 4 in. (10 × 10 cm) wooden post will hold 15 ft^2 (1.4 m^2) of sign and a 6 × 6 in. (15 × 15 cm) post that has been predrilled for proper breakaway features will hold 50 ft^2 (4.65 m^2) of sign.

Intermediate-size signs with areas between 20 and 90 ft^2 (1.9 and 8.4 m^2) may be mounted on two or three post installations with proper breakaway features.

Large, side-of-the-road, directional signs must have specially designed breakaway supports, which can be of wood, aluminum, or steel. Steel breakaway supports include:

1. The "Texas design," with a slip joint feature at the base and a hinge joint below the sign to allow the post, after impact, to slip off the foundation and swing up and away from the vehicle.
2. A load-concentrated breakaway coupling (CBC) at the base and a separate breakaway feature between sign and post to allow the post to shear from the foundation upon impact and to swing away from the vehicle to avoid a secondary collision between post and vehicle.

From a safety and an aesthetic standpoint, overhead signs should be mounted on overhead bridge structures whenever possible. However, such structures are not normally in the desired location and the engineer must design a sign support that will handle the dead load and wind load of the completed sign and lighting system. The design features must further provide for the proper vertical and horizontal clearances to meet the minimum standards for that highway.

Sign warrants and requisite studies

Regulatory and warning signs should be used only where needed and warranted, so that their effectiveness will not be destroyed by excessive frequency. Guide signs should be used whenever they can contribute to the convenience and facilitation of traffic movement.

[9]H. E. Ross, Jr., K. C. Walker, and M. J. Effenberger, *Crash Tests of Small Highway Sign Supports*. Interim Report, Project 3254-3, Contract DOT-FH-11-8821, Texas Transportation Institute, Texas A&M University, College Station, Tex., Sept. 1978.

Specific warrants for the use of some regulatory signs are provided as general policy statements rather than as absolute warrants. Warrants provide a guide to sound sign application and serve as an aid in preventing the overuse of regulatory signs.

Stop sign warrants.[10] A stop sign may be warranted at an intersection where one or more of the following conditions exist:

1. Intersection of a less important road with a main road, where application of the normal right-of-way rule is unduly hazardous.
2. Intersection of a county road, city street, or township road with a state highway.
3. Street entering a through highway or street.
4. Unsignalized intersection in a signalized area.
5. Unsignalized intersection where a combination of high speed, restricted view, and serious accident records indicate a need for control by the stop sign.

Stop signs cannot be erected at intersections where traffic control signals are present because the signals should be operated continuously, either in normal or flashing operation. Moreover, stop signs should not be installed for the sole purpose of controlling the speeds of the motorists.

"Multiway" (four-way or all-way) stop installations can be used as a safety measure at some locations where the volume on the intersecting roads is approximately equal and the following conditions have been established:

1. Where traffic signals are warranted and urgently needed, the multiway is an interim measure that can be installed quickly to control traffic while arrangements are being made for the signal installation.
2. An accident problem as indicated by five or more reported accidents in a 12-month period of a type susceptible to correction by a multiway stop installation.
3. Minimum traffic volume:
   a. The total vehicular volume entering the intersection from all approaches must average at least 500 vehicles/h for any 8 h of an average day, and
   b. The combined vehicular and pedestrian volume from the minor street or highway must average at least 200 units/h for the same 8 h, with an average delay to minor street vehicular traffic of at least 30 s/vehicle during the maximum hour, but
   c. When the 85th percentile approach speed of the major street traffic exceeds 40 mph (64 km/h), the minimum vehicular volume warrant is 70% of the foregoing requirements.

Yield sign warrants.[11] Yield sign warrants are established as follows:

[10]*Uniform Manual*, Secs. 2B-5, 2B-6.

[11]Ibid., Sec. 2B-8.

1. On a minor road at the entrance to an intersection when it is necessary to assign right-of-way to the major road, but where a stop is not necessary at all times, and where the safe approach speed on the minor road exceeds 10 mph (16 km/h).
2. On the entrance ramp to an expressway where an adequate acceleration lane is not provided.
3. Within an intersection with a divided highway, where a stop sign is present at the entrance to the first roadway and further control is necessary at the entrance to the second roadway, and where the median width between the two roadways exceeds 30 ft (9 m).
4. Where there is a separate or channelized right-turn lane, without an adequate acceleration lane.
5. At any intersection where a special problem exists and where an engineering study indicates the problem to be susceptible to correction by the use of the yield sign.

Yield signs should not be used to control the major flow of traffic, approaches of more than one of the intersecting streets, or at intersections where there are stop signs on one or more approaches. The state of the art in the use of yield signs has been published in the ITE informational report, "Yield Sign Usage and Applications."[12]

Lane-use control sign warrants. Criteria for installation of lane-use control signs at intersections are established as follows:

1. Lane-use control signs at intersections should be used whenever it is desired to require vehicles in certain lanes to turn, or to permit turns from an adjacent lane.
2. Lane-use controls permitting left (or right) turns from two (or more) lanes normally are warranted whenever the turning volume exceeds the capacity of one turning lane, and when all movements can be accommodated in the lanes available to them.

Warning signs. Where an engineering and traffic investigation indicates that attention must be called to an actual or potential hazardous condition, warning signs should be installed. Typical locations that may warrant such signs include:

1. Turns, curves, or intersections
2. Advance warning for stop signs, signals, or railroad crossings
3. Grades, drops, or bumps
4. Narrow roadways, bridges, or other points of limited clearance
5. Curves or areas where advisory speed is to be indicated

Guide signs. Adequate signing at intersections to show route directions and destinations includes advance notice of route junctions and turns, directional route markings at the intersection, and destination signs showing the names of important cities and towns with their directions and distances. Confirmatory route markers should be placed on numbered routes just beyond every marked intersection, and occasional reassurance markers should be placed between intersections.

Although the *Uniform Manual* gives detailed specifications for the application and placement of route markers at intersections, many intersections require individual engineering treatment because of their particular design and other unusual physical characteristics.

Special signs

In the United States the Federal Highway Beautification Act of 1965 and subsequent acts, as amended, have required the removal of any billboards or advertising signs along freeways and other highways. The removal of these signs plus the identified need for the installation of signs for motorist services has required some state and municipal traffic engineers to develop programs for the signing of large traffic generators, emergency and motorist services, and recreational attractions.

Before undertaking such a program, overall guidelines should be established so that only the "needed" attractions are approved for signing, and the number of destinations at any given location is kept to a minimum (proliferation of destination signs can distract from needed regulatory or warning signs and create an unsightly highway system). Any traffic engineer interested in starting such a program should contact one of the states that has developed guidelines for signing to "attractions."

Signing materials, maintenance, and inventory practices

Backing materials

Materials in general use for traffic signs include outdoor plywood, aluminum and steel sheeting, fiberglass, and plastic. (Regular plastic and fiberglass signs are relatively light and do not develop metal slivers upon rough handling that can cut workers.) The translucent plastic sign faces are generally used for internally illuminated signs and provide excellent daytime visibility and legibility.

Aluminum sign blanks should conform to American Society for Testing and Materials (ASTM) Specification B-209 Alloy 6061-T6 or 5154-H38. They are easily fabricated into any of the standard shapes and sizes. A chemical conversion treatment coating conforming to ASTM-B449-67, class 2 (10 to 25 mg/ft^2 or 110 to 270 mg/m^2), which produces a light, tight, irridescent coating, provides a satisfactory basis for reflective or nonreflective sheeting and paint and also imparts increased corrosion resistance.

Commercial sheet steel, coated or rust-proofed by one of the various chemical treatments recommended by manufacturers, is suitable for traffic signs. Eighteen-gauge steel is adequate for small signs up to 24 in. (61 cm) in their largest dimensions, whereas 16-gauge steel is recommended for larger signs.

Exterior high-density overlay plywood is preferable to

[12]ITE Technical Council Committee 4A-A, "Yield Sign Usage and Applications," *Transport. Eng.* (Institute of Transportation Engineers, Arlington, Va.), *48*(10), 37–43 (Oct. 1978).

the older type of wooden signs with batten reinforcements. High-density overlay plywood is available in thicknesses from 1/4 to 1 in. (0.6 to 2.5 cm), although thicknesses in the range 1/2 to 3/4 in. (1.3 to 1.8 cm) are customarily used. Plywood sign backing has certain advantages over aluminum and steel sheeting because the need for additional support is minimized.

For larger signs mounted on structures over the roadway, extruded or laminated aluminum panels are required. These are bolted on the support structures with the help of special clips which are manufactured for that purpose. The extruded or laminated aluminum panels are better for the larger signs in that extra support is minimal. Experimentation in Illinois has shown that a louvered sign can be effectively installed to meet the visibility and legibility needs of the motorist, while reducing the wind load considerably so that lighter supports can be used or larger signs can be mounted on existing supports.[13]

Surface materials

The materials used for sign faces include paint, adhesive-coated plastic film, porcelain, reflective sheeting, and reflective coatings of beads and a binder. Cutout letters, numerals, and symbols can be made of plastic reflective buttons in a porcelain enameled frame or reflective sheeting.

Paint, nonreflective plastic film, and porcelain materials should be used only on signs that are used exclusively for daylight operations, or are adequately illuminated for nighttime visibility.

[13] *Evaluation of a Louvered Panel for Use as a Freeway Sign Background*, Illinois Department of Transportation, Division of Highways, Bureau of Traffic, Springfield, Ill., 1971.

In developing specifications and purchasing legend materials, the engineer must make certain that:

1. The colors are within the allowable tolerance under both daylight and night lighting conditions.
2. The material is weather-resistant.
3. Minimum brightness levels are met for reflective signs.
4. There is adequate durability.
5. Materials are packaged and shipped so as to minimize damage.

Where local governmental agencies do not have the necessary expertise to finalize these specifications, they should check with their state or provincial counterparts.

Maintenance

Adequate maintenance of the traffic sign system is as important as adherence to proper warrants and good installation practices in the original installation. Inspection of the system should be made at least twice during daylight hours and once during darkness every year to assure proper visibility and legibility.

To ensure adequate maintenance, a suitable schedule for inspection, cleaning, and replacement of signs should be established. Employees of the highway department, police, and other governmental employees whose duties require that they travel on the highways should be encouraged to report any damaged or obscured signs at the first opportunity.

Maintenance should include washing signs with a good soap or detergent material as often as local conditions demand, or cleaning by means of a steam generator unit (see Figure 23.5). The cleaning cycle may range from once every

Figure 23.5. Typical sign washing equipment and operation. SOURCE: Pennsylvania Department of Transportation, Bureau of Traffic Engineering, Harrisburg, Pa.

2 years for self-cleaning surfaces in clean residential areas to once every few months in industrial areas. Special attention and necessary action should be taken to see that weeds, trees, shrubbery, and construction materials do not obscure the face of any sign.

Illuminated signs demand greater attention. Because they are generally of larger size, an occasional check for weather damage to sign and mountings is essential.

A regular cycle for lamp inspection and replacement should be established, and lamps should be replaced when the level of illumination goes below predetermined standards. This is very important in cold weather because old lamps tend to become inefficient at low temperatures.

Large freeway signs, both overhead and side-mounted, provide special maintenance problems because of their size and location. They should be washed once or twice a year and have the background and legend refurbished as needed. The refurbishing, when routine maintenance is inadequate, often calls for removing the legend and applying an overlay panel with a new background upon which a new legend of reflective buttons or reflective sheeting is added.

Inventory

Traffic signs constantly require maintenance and modernization. Before establishing a schedule for such a program, a sign inventory should be undertaken to establish the requirements and provide the basic planning information. A systematic sign survey, either manual or by means of photologging, which can pinpoint deficiencies or damaged signs should be planned in detail so that the necessary forms are available for the initial inventory and future updates. Such forms must be convenient for field use and easily compiled in the office so that the information is in a usable form.

Objectives of the inventory are:

1. Classification of all traffic signs by size, location, and condition of sign and post by day and reflectivity at night.
2. Discovery of conditions requiring change in design or size of signs, refurbishing, or reflectorization.
3. Establishment of existing and future sign needs and a plan to upgrade signs systematically to current standards.

The field inventory procedure will depend on the governmental agency responsible for the control devices and the availability of computer processing equipment. A municipal agency would be interested in obtaining and maintaining data for each block face,[14] while a larger agency would be more interested in longer segments, such as a traffic route.[15] In any case, the minimum data collected should include:

1. Block number or route number
2. Side of roadway (north, south, etc.)
3. Direction sign is facing
4. Sign code
5. Type of post
6. Distance from intersection or other control points
7. Offset distance
8. Installation date
9. Condition of sign
10. Other signs on same post
11. Condition of other signs
12. Visibility factor

A secondary inventory that should be maintained by any agency responsible for traffic control devices is that of all completed signs in the sign shop and storage buildings plus an inventory of sign supports and raw material for the manufacture of signs. Such a program, if kept current as signs are removed for installation, will aid in the schedule of productions for signs, aid in monitoring the work of the field crews, and be used as a basis for budget forecasting.

Temporary signs

Most signing is permanent in nature and will be applicable to conditions that exist all day, every day. A notable exception to this "rule" is the use of temporary signs for construction or maintenance projects where the signs will be needed only during periods when there is activity on or near the roadway.

The main use of temporary signing is to warn motorists of the construction or maintenance operation and to guide them through or around the work area. Such signs should be set up immediately prior to the start of work, moved and revised concurrently with progress of the work, and removed immediately when no longer needed.

Because of the special nature of the applications, the signs must always be placed where they will convey their messages most effectively and will not unduly restrict lateral clearance or sight distance. Temporary construction signs generally should be mounted on the driver's side of the roadway 6 to 12 ft (1.8 to 3.6 m) from the edge of the traveled way or 2 ft (0.6 m) beyond the curb. Often, they must be placed on barricades within the roadway with supplemental or duplicate signs on the opposite side of the travel path.

Construction warning signs must be placed in advance of the working area. Local conditions will dictate placement; a practical rule of thumb is 10 ft advance distance for each mile per hour of approach speed up to 35 mph in urban areas (2 m for each kilometer per hour to 55 km/h); a considerably greater distance, up to as much as 1500 ft (450 m) for rural highway conditions; and up to 0.5 mi (0.8 km) or more on high-speed freeway facilities.

Construction approach warning signs should be repeated where serious hazards exist. Standard practice is to place such signs 500, 1000, and 1500 ft (150, 300, and 450 m) in advance of heavy construction, restricted traffic movement, or detours in rural areas, and at correspondingly lesser distances in urban areas.

[14] H. A. SWANSON, "An Urban Sign Inventory Procedure," *Traffic Eng.* (Institute of Traffic Engineers, Washington, D.C.), *40*(8), 44–46 (May 1970).

[15] T. K. DATTA AND B. B. MADSEN, "Photologging—A Data Collection Method for Roadway Information Systems," *Transport. Eng.* (Institute of Transportation Engineers, Arlington, Va.), *48*(4), 19–25 (Apr. 1978).

Regulatory signs should be placed only when officially authorized, and should conform with standards of the authority having responsible jurisdiction.

Advisory speed signs generally are used in connection with construction zone warning signs. These should be mounted together. Warning, regulatory, and guide signs for construction and maintenance work generally should be mounted on two posts or on the larger barricades because of the large sizes involved. Detailed applications are shown in the *Uniform Manual*.

Because the problem of signing and marking these work areas may involve several governmental agencies, as well as large and small contractors and utility companies, a number of states and provinces have developed separate manuals or handbooks on the proper control and use of traffic control devices for construction and/or maintenance. Moreover, specific traffic control plans and preconstruction meetings are often required in advance of the construction project to review all details of the operation. Individual questions on these matters should be referred to the proper state or provincial traffic engineers.

Sign shop requirements and practices

The size and scope of sign shop operations in a given jurisdiction is dependent primarily on decisions of a local nature, such as local sign fabrication versus purchasing of manufactured signs. The decisions involve these factors:

1. Number of signs to be used
2. Cost of labor (Can exterior workers be used in the off-season as shop employees?)
3. Time factor (Can emergency needs be filled? Are warehousing facilities available to stock needs in advance?)
4. Local policies on purchasing

Equipment needs

Sign production is greatly simplified if sign backings are purchased in proper blank sizes and have been processed so that nothing further is required for painting or the application of sheeting. Where further processing is needed, a separate well-ventilated area should be provided, including a spray booth or a filtration system to purify the air of paint vapors.

Although some or most blanks are purchased to size, facilities are generally needed to fabricate sign blanks. Large shears can be used to cut sheet steel or aluminum for original sign blanks and can be used to salvage damaged signs by making smaller blanks. On the other hand, power saws are a necessity in fabricating plywood signs.

Additional equipment, depending on the size and operation of the sign shop will include:

1. Equipment to paint and/or coat the blanks and for the application of reflective sheeting, plastic film, or beads
2. Equipment to silk-screen and stencil messages
3. Ovens or infrared drying units with necessary drying racks
4. Storage racks, bins, or shelves

In addition, some sign shops have facilities for stripping old finishes from reusable blanks. In recent years, however, commercial companies have furnished this specialized service on aluminum blanks for Pennsylvania, Ohio, West Virginia, and others at a cost of less than one-half the original cost of the blank.

Facilities for sign layout, letter and symbol design, and letter spacing will be needed as a close adjunct to the sign shop. Means for servicing illumined signs must also be available.

Practices

Sign shop practices vary state to state and municipality to municipality as dictated by policy decisions. In some states, prison labor may cut and furnish sign blanks from sheet metal, while in other states they may furnish the completed sign to the highway department. Where highway or transportation departments completely manufacture their own signs, there are two common practices: (1) all signs are manufactured and supplied from one central sign shop, or (2) signs are manufactured at the district level.

Large signs for freeways are generally bought as completed signs, but some manufacturing is necessary at sign shops for temporary signs, replacements, or for overlay panels.

Many municipalities over 50,000 population have sign shops that manufacture all or a part of their signs. The amount of work varies depending on the size of the municipality and its policies. Some can buy completed faces and just apply them to the sign blanks; others will apply a sheeting to the sign blank and screen a message or else do all signs that do not need a reflective background.

Governmental agencies should continue to review their policies of materials being used and their purchasing procedures. They can get guidance for their local requirements from manufacturers of shop equipment, manufacturers of sign materials, and by visiting sign shops already in operation by similar state highway departments, municipalities, or counties.

Kinds of markings

Traffic markings include all traffic lines (both longitudinal and transverse), symbols, words, object markers, delineators, cones, or other devices, except signs, that are applied upon or attached to the pavement or mounted at the side of the roadway to guide traffic or warn of an obstruction.

Function of markings

Traffic markings have certain definite functions to perform in the proper control of vehicular and pedestrian traffic. They serve to regulate, to guide, to channelize traffic into the proper position on the street or highway, and to supplement the regulations or warnings of other traffic control devices. They also serve as a psychological barrier for opposing streams of traffic, as a warning device for restricted sight and passing distances, and provide information for turning movement, special zones, and so on. As an aid to pedestrians, they channelize movement into locations of safest crossing and, in effect, provide for an extension of the sidewalk across the roadway. Under favorable conditions, traffic markings aid the vehicle driver in many respects without diverting attention from the roadway.

Temporary markings

Almost all applications of markings are in areas where it would be desirable to have a permanent or long-life installation. There is, however, definite need and use for temporary markings in construction areas and at locations where a temporary hazard must be properly marked until the necessary repairs or improvements can be made.

Various temporary marking devices, such as barricades, cones, temporary traffic lines, and so on, are discussed in later sections of this chapter. Great care should be exercised in selecting the proper "tool" to meet the needs for each given situation. A normal thickness of traffic paint should not be applied when the line must be removed in a few weeks, unless it is on temporary pavement. In addition, drums or large barricades should not replace cones when a traffic lane is to be reopened in a few hours.

Permanent traffic control devices should be removed or covered when the message is inappropriate, and provisions must be made so that the temporary installations can be removed when no longer needed; otherwise, motorists may be confused by two conflicting messages in the vicinity of temporary markings.

Marking elements

Longitudinal pavement marking design

Longitudinal lines are used to organize traffic into proper channels, advise motorists where passing is prohibited, and to supplement other warning devices when there are hazards within the roadway.

In the United States, the color of longitudinal markings can be white, yellow, or red. Black can also be used in combination with the three primary colors where the pavement does not provide sufficient contrast. Application and basic concepts of the standard colors have been established in the *Uniform Manual* and include:

1. Yellow lines delineate the separation of traffic flows in opposing directions.
2. White lines delineate the separation of traffic flows in the same direction.
3. Red markings delineate a roadway that shall not be entered or used by the viewer of that line.
4. Broken yellow and white lines are permissive in character. These are normally formed by segments and gaps in a ratio of 1:3.
5. Solid lines are restrictive in character.
6. Width of line indicates the degree of emphasis [a 4- to 6-in. (10- to 15-cm)-wide line is a normal wide line].
7. Double lines indicate maximum restrictions.

Some of the applications of these principles are shown in Figure 23.6. A brief summary includes:

Figure 23.6. Typical two-way marking applications. SOURCE: *Manual on Uniform Traffic Control Devices,* U.S. Department of Transportation, Federal Highway Administration, U.S. Government Printing Office, Washington, D.C., 1978, p. 3B-4.

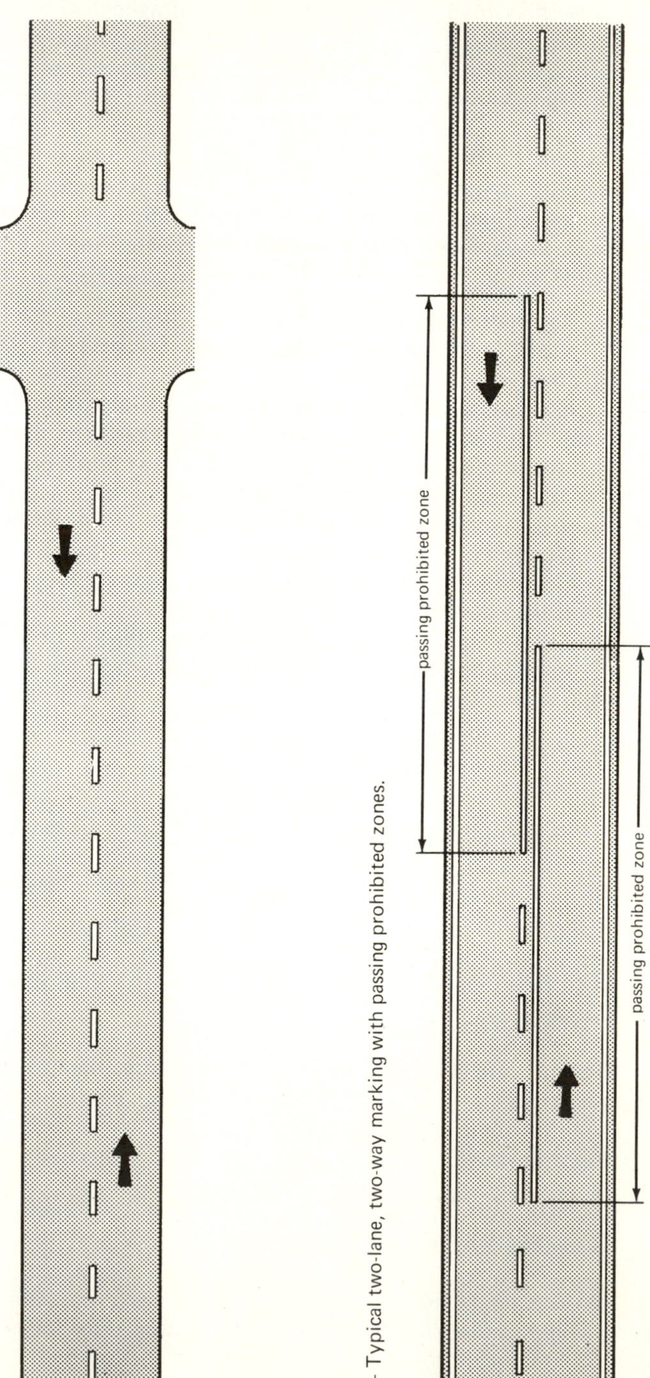

Centerlines. These lines vary depending upon the width of the traveled roadway and the type of area. A single broken yellow line, which is used on two-lane, two-way streets, indicates that passing is permitted from either direction. A solid yellow centerline on either side of the broken line indicates that passing is prohibited from the direction that is immediately adjacent to the solid line. Double, solid yellow center lines should be used on two-way streets of four or more lanes, in areas where the centerline is offset, and in areas where passing is prohibited in both directions.

Lane lines. These lines are broken white lines with a standard spacing of 10 ft (3.0 m) painted and a gap of 30 ft (9.1 m). Some urban areas use a pattern of 9 ft (2.7 m) painted and a gap of 15 ft (4.6 m). Solid lane lines can be used on approaches to intersections and in other areas where lane changes should be restricted. A dotted white line, normally 2 ft (0.6 m) in length with 4 ft (1.2 m) gaps can be provided to delineate the extension of a line through intersections or across deceleration lane openings where special problems indicate that motorists can be confused.

Pavement edge lines. These lines include white lines on each side of the traveled roadway, except that on divided highways and on one-way roadways the left edge in the direction of travel should be yellow.

Channelizing lines and median islands. These lines should be wide or double lines and can be either white or yellow depending upon the traffic patterns. If the lines are to form traffic islands where travel in the same directions is permitted on both sides, the markings should be white. If islands are formed that separate travel in opposite directions, the markings should be yellow. In either case, any crosshatching should be of the same color as the longitudinal lines.

Transverse marking design

Transverse markings are used to convey a special message to the motorist, either by themselves or in combination with traffic signs. They include shoulder markings, word and symbol markings, stop lines, crosswalk lines, and parking space markings. All such markings should be white, except they should be yellow when they are a part of a median marking.

Because of the low approach angle at which pavement markings are viewed, all transverse lines must be proportioned to give visibility equal to that of longitudinal lines and to avoid apparent distortion where longitudinal and transverse lines combine in symbols or lettering.

Detailed applications for these markings are provided in the *Uniform Manual*. A brief summary includes:

Crosswalks. These markings, which are a minimum of 6 in. (15 cm) in width and at least 6 ft (1.8 m) apart, are used to guide pedestrians in the proper paths and to serve to warn motorists of a pedestrian crossing point. The solid, white boundary lines can be up to 24 in. (60 cm) in width where vehicle speeds are over 35 mph (55 km/h) or where crosswalks are unexpected. Moreover, the area of the crosswalk may be marked with white diagonal lines at a 45° angle or longitudinal lines at a 90° angle (see Figure 23.7). The marking of crosswalks in some areas also provides for transverse lines on each side of the longitudinal lines, as shown in Figure 23.7.

Figure 23.7. Typical crosswalk markings. SOURCE: *Manual on Uniform Traffic Control Devices,* U.S. Department of Transportation, Federal Highway Administration, U.S. Government Printing Office, Washington, D.C., 1978, p. 3B-20.

a – Standard crosswalk marking.

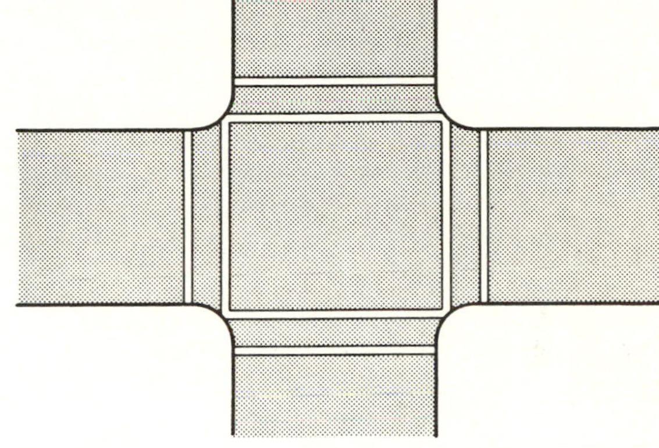

b – Crosswalk marking with diagonal lines for added visibility.

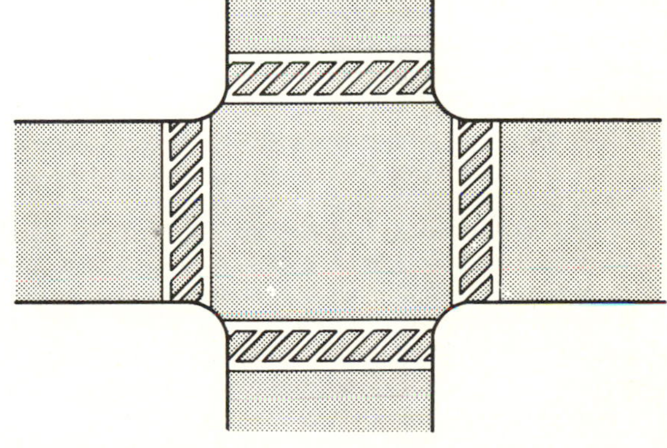

c – Crosswalk marking with longitudinal lines for added visibility.

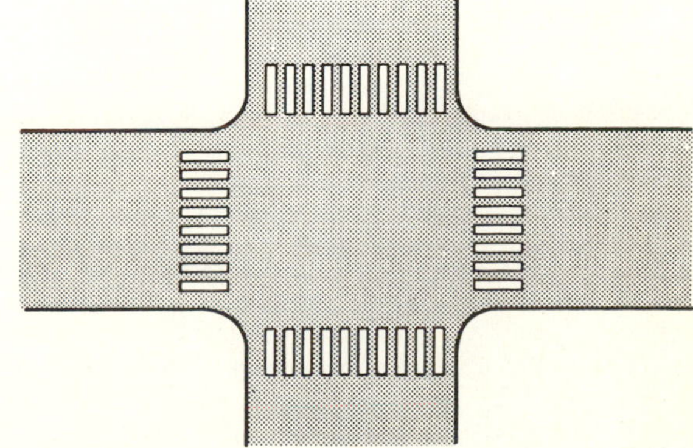

Stop lines. These lines, which are normally 12 to 24 in. (31 to 61 cm) wide, should extend across all approach lanes. They should be placed at the desired stopping point, in no case more than 30 ft (9.1 m) or less than 4 ft (1.2 m) from the nearest edge of the intersecting roadway. If crosswalks have been installed, the stop line should ordinarily be placed 4 ft (1.2 m) in advance of the nearest crosswalk line.

Railroad crossing. Pavement markings in advance of a railroad crossing consist of an X, the letters RR, a no-passing marking, and certain transverse lines. They should be placed on all paved approaches to railroad crossings and elongated to allow for the low angle at which they are viewed (see Figure 23.8).

Parking space markings. These markings encourage more orderly and efficient use of parking space where parking turnover is substantial and tend to prevent encroachment on fire hydrant zones, bus stops, loading zones, approaches to corners, clearance spaces for islands, and other zones where parking is prohibited (see Figure 23.9).

Word and symbol markings. These markings, which are white, may be used for the purpose of guiding, warning, or regulating traffic. They should be limited to not more than a total of three lines of words and/or symbols. They can serve as regulatory (stop, right turn only, etc.), warning (stop ahead, school, etc.), or guide (US 30, Route 123, etc.), but when used as a regulatory device they must sup-

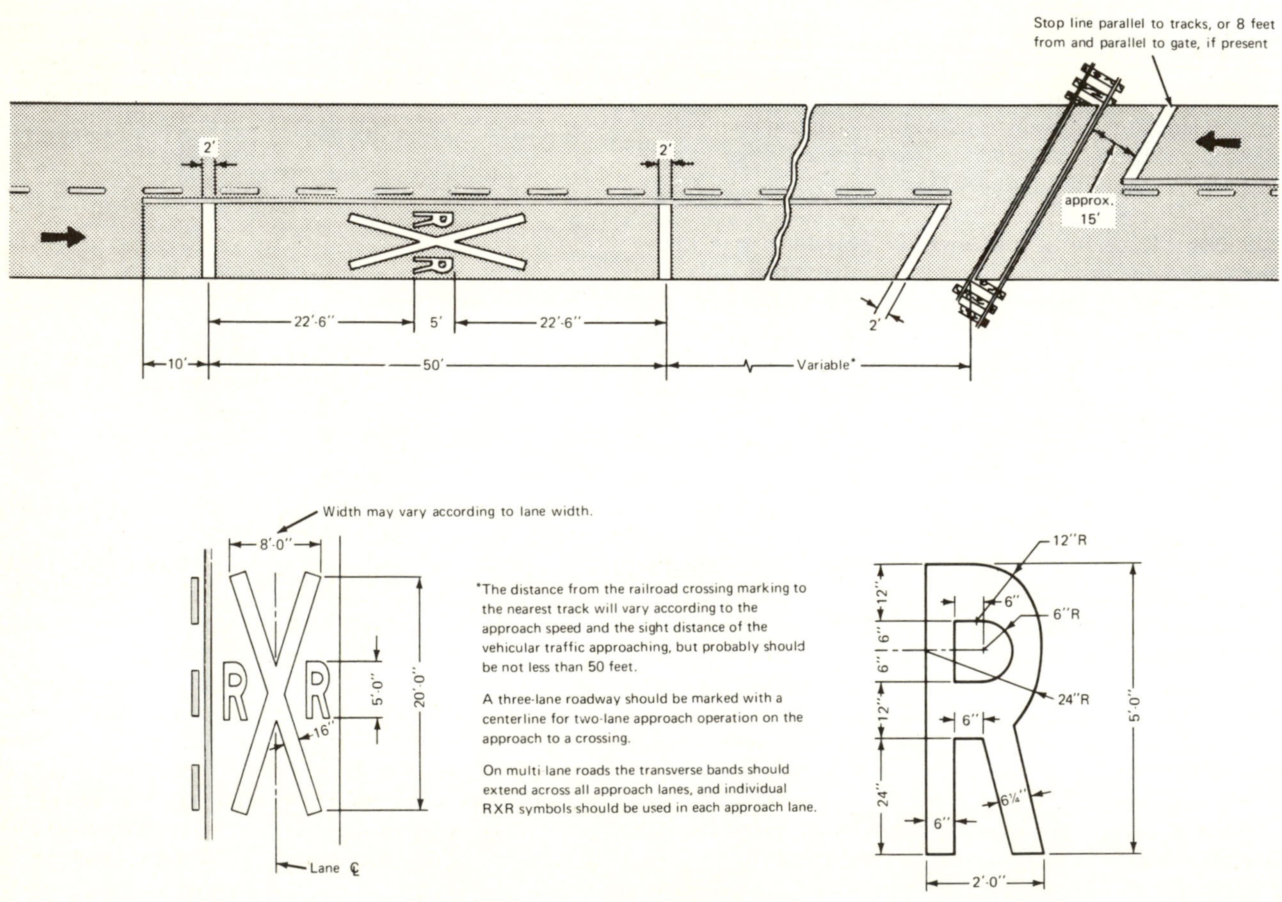

Figure 23.8. Typical pavement markings at railroad-highway grade crossings. SOURCE: *Manual on Uniform Traffic Control Devices,* U.S. Department of Transportation, Federal Highway Administration, U.S. Government Printing Office, Washington, D.C., 1978, p. 8B-4.

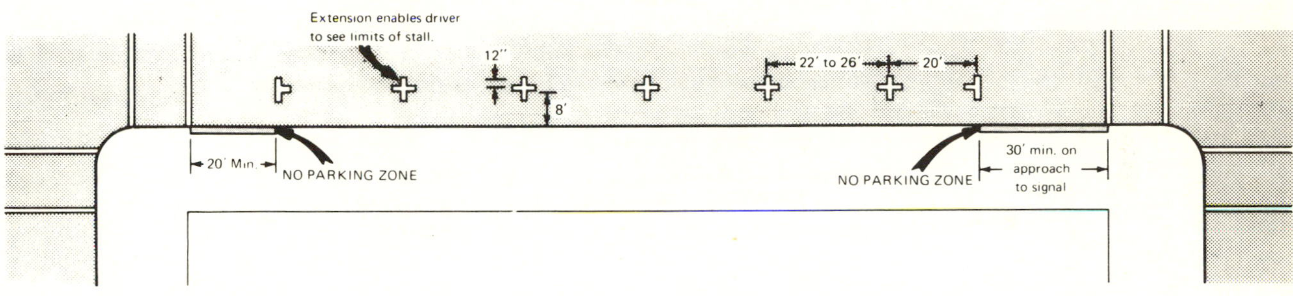

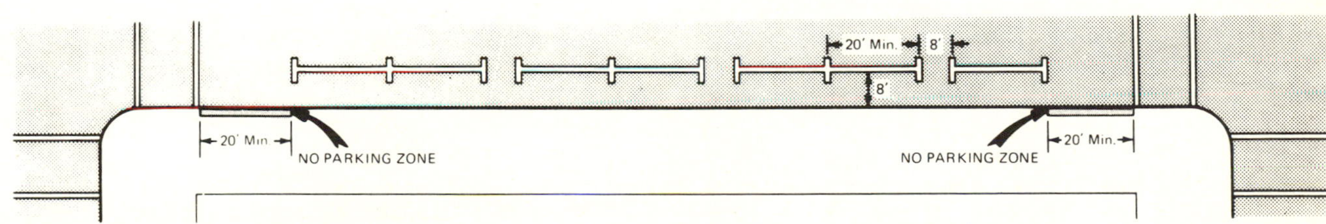

Figure 23.9. Typical parking space-limit markings. SOURCE: *Manual on Uniform Traffic Control Devices,* U.S. Department of Transportation, Federal Highway Administration, U.S. Government Printing Office, Washington, D.C., 1978, p. 3B-23.

plement necessary signs. Symbols are preferable to words and in all cases both types must be elongated in the direction of traffic movement. Large letters, symbols, and numerals should be used, 8 ft (2.4 m) or more in height; if the message consists of more than one word, it should read up (i.e., the first word should be nearest the driver).

Curb markings. These markings can be either roadway delineation or parking regulations. When used as roadway delineations, the color should follow the guidelines for edge lines or channelizations. When used as parking regulations, they should supplement standard signs and can be a special color as prescribed by local authorities.

Object markers and delineators

Physical obstructions in or near a roadway, including installations designed for the control of traffic, constitute serious hazards to safe traffic movement and should be adequately marked. However, every effort should first be made to remove the obstructions or to minimize their potential danger.

In U.S. practice, when obstructions within or adjacent to the roadway require marking, the marker should consist of an arrangement of one or more of the following designs:

1. A Type 1 marker consists of nine yellow reflectors having a minimum dimension of approximately 3 in. (7.6 cm), mounted symmetrically on an 18-in. (45-cm) diamond background, either black or yellow in color; or an 18-in. (45-cm) diamond, all-yellow reflector.

2. A Type 2 marker consists of three yellow reflectors having a minimum dimension of approximately 3 in. (7.6 cm) arranged either horizontally or vertically; or a 6 × 12 in. (15 × 30 cm) rectangular yellow reflector. Type 2 markers may be longer if conditions warrant.

3. A Type 3 marker consists of a vertical rectangle approximately 1 × 3 ft (30 × 90 cm) in size, with alternating black and reflectorized yellow stripes sloping downward at an angle of 45° toward the side of the obstruction on which traffic is to pass. The minimum width of the yellow stripe should be 3 in. (7.6 cm). A better appearance can be achieved if the black stripes are wider than the yellow stripes.

The proper application of these object markers is described as follows:

1. Objects in the roadway should be marked with a Type 1 or 3 marker at a mounting height of 4 ft (1.2 m) minimum. In addition, large surfaces can be painted with diagonal stripes 12 in. (30.5 cm) or greater in width, similar in design to the Type 3 object marker. The alternating black and reflectorized yellow stripes should slope down at an angle of 45° toward the side of the obstruction which traffic is to pass.

2. Objects adjacent to the roadway, which are so close to the road that they need a marker, should be marked with Type 2 or 3 object markers. The post should be installed so that the inside edge of the marker is to be in line with the inner edge of the obstruction and at a mounting height of 4 ft (1.2 m).

3. End of roadway should be marked with either a nine-unit marker consisting of nine reflex reflectors having a minimum dimension of approximately 3 in. (7.6 cm), red in color, mounted symmetrically on an 18-in. (46-cm) diamond background, either red or black in color; or an 18-in. (46-cm) diamond reflectorized red panel. The mounting height should be the same as for the Type 1 marker.

Road delineation markers, with a minimum dimension of about 3 in. (7.6 cm) should be considered as guide markings rather than warning devices. Delineators may be used on long continuous sections of highway or through short stretches where there are pavement-width transitions or other changes in horizontal alignment, particularly where the alignment might be confusing. Normally, delineators should be installed at a mounting height of 4 ft (1.2 m) and spaced 200 to 528 ft (60 m to 160 m). They must be adjusted to shorter spacings on approaches and throughout horizontal curves.

When curbs of islands are located in or near the line of traffic flow, they should be marked with white delineators if on the right or if traffic in the same direction passes on both sides. If the curbed island separates traffic in opposing directions, it should have yellow delineators.

Other applications of delineators include:

1. On through two-lane, two-way roadways, single white reflector units are placed on the right side. Single white reflector units may be placed on the left side of two-way roadways, particularly at sharp right-hand curves.
2. On through roadways of expressway-type facilities, single white delineators should be placed continuously along the right side and on at least one side of interchange ramps. If used on the left side for additional guidance, they should be yellow to match the yellow edge line.
3. Double or vertically elongated yellow delineators should be spaced at 100-ft (30.5-m) intervals along acceleration and deceleration lanes.
4. Red delineators may be used on the reverse side of any delineator whenever it would be viewed by a motorist traveling in the wrong direction.

Colored pavement

Colored pavement, which significantly contrasts with adjoining paved areas, can be used to help guide or regulate traffic. The applications to date have shown better contrasts in daylight operations, as the colors have not been satisfactorily reflectorized and thus blend in with the abutting pavement at night.

When used, the colors should be limited to the following:

1. Red should be used only on the approaches to a stop sign that is in use 24 h a day.
2. Yellow should be used only for medians separating traffic flows in opposite directions.
3. White should be used only for delineation to provide contrast with other colors, such as right-hand shoulders or for channelizing islands for traffic flows passing on both sides.

Marking warrants and requisite studies

Although traffic markings have definite limitations, their advantages of aiding motorists without diverting their attention from the roadway and their acceptance by the motoring public makes it necessary to establish criteria for proper installations.

Uniform manual

Specific guidelines for the use of markings and the requisite studies in the United States are provided in the *Uniform Manual.*[16] Some of these guidelines and studies include:

[16] *Uniform Manual*, Sec. 3B.

1. Centerlines, which separate traffic traveling in opposite directions are desirable on paved highways when:
   a. The two-way roadway in rural districts is 16 ft (5 m) or more in width and speeds are in excess of 35 mph (56 km/h).
   b. The highways are in residential or business districts where there are significant traffic volumes.
   c. The undivided highway has four or more lanes.
   d. The highway is wide enough for three lanes of traffic (in this case, the highway should be marked for two lanes in one direction and one lane in the opposing direction, or for the center lane to be for left turns only).
2. Lane lines should be installed on multilane highways when an engineering study indicates that the roadway will accommodate more lanes than when unpainted. In addition, lane lines should be installed:
   a. On one-way streets where maximum efficiency in use of the street width is desired.
   b. At the approaches to important intersections and in dangerous locations where the lines would organize the traffic for better roadway use.
   c. On rural highways with an odd number of traffic lanes.
3. A no-passing zone at a horizontal or vertical curve is warranted where the sight distance is less than the minimum necessary for safe passing at the prevailing speed of traffic. The conditions that justify such zones are shown in Table 23-2.

   Passing sight distance on a vertical curve is the distance at which an object 3.75 ft (1.1 m) above the pavement can be seen from a point 3.75 ft (1.1 m) above the pavement (see Figure 23.10). Similarly, passing sight distance on a horizontal curve is the distance measured along the centerline (or the lane line of a three-lane highway) between two points 3.75 ft (1.1 m) above the pavement on a line tangent to an obstruction that cuts off the view on the inside of the curve.
4. Markings for railroad crossings should be placed where railroad highway grade crossing signals or automobile gates are operating, and at all other crossings where the prevailing speed of highway traffic is 40 mph (64 km/h) or greater.
5. Pavement edge markings should be placed on all Interstate highways where edge delineations are desirable to reduce driving on paved shoulders or refuge areas.

TABLE 23–2
Minimum Passing Sight Distance versus Speed of Traffic

85th Percentile Speed		Minimum Passing Sight Distance	
mph	km/h	ft	m
30	48	500	152
40	64	600	183
50	81	800	244
60	97	1000	305
70	113	1200	366

SOURCE: *Manual on Uniform Traffic Control Devices for Streets and Highways*, U.S. Department of Transportation, Federal Highway Administration, U.S. Government Printing Office, Washington, D.C., 1978, Sec. 3B-5.

6. Crosswalks should be marked where studies show that there is a substantial conflict between vehicles and pedestrian movements. They should also be installed at points of pedestrian concentration, or where pedestrians cannot recognize the best place to cross.

Special marking applications

The safe operation and needed capacity of many streets and highways quite often depend on special applications of traffic markings such as listed below.

Lane reduction transitions. Pavement line markings can be effectively used to supplement the standard signs that guide traffic where the pavement width is reduced to fewer lanes (see Figure 23.11). Many variations are possible, depending on which lanes must be offset or eliminated and on the amount of the offset. One or more lane lines must be discontinued and the remaining center and lane lines must be connected in such a way as to safely merge traffic into the reduced number of lanes.

Lines marking pavement width transitions should be the standard design for center, lane, or barrier lines. Converging lines on roadways with a posted speed of 45 mph (70 km/h) or greater should have a length of not less than that determined by the formula $L = SW$. On slower-speed streets and highways, the formula to be used is $L = WS^2/60$. In both formulas L equals the length in feet, S the off-peak 85th percentile speed in miles per hour, and W the offset distance in feet. (For those using metric units, the minimum transition slope should be 30:1 for lower-speed up to 50:1 for higher-speed highways.)

Obstruction approach markings. Pavement markings are frequently used to supplement standard signs to guide traffic approaching a fixed obstruction within a paved roadway (see Figure 23.12). The obstruction may be in the center of the roadway, in which case all traffic is usually directed to drive to the right of it. These markings normally consist of a diagonal line (or lines) extending from the center or lane line to a point 12 to 24 in. (31 to 61 cm) to the right side (or to both sides) of the approach and of the obstruction. The length of the diagonal markings can be determined by the same formula as provided in "Lane Reduction Transitions" above. The diagonal line should never be less than 200 ft (61 m) in length in rural areas of 100 ft (30 m) in urban areas. The use of obstruction approach markings and signs does not eliminate the need for adequate object markings on the obstruction itself.

Channelization. Painted channelization can be used to increase efficiency and safety and has the advantage of easy modification when warranted by driver behavior. If a more positive barrier is required, curbs and islands may be constructed, but the paint channelization may well serve initially to establish the best layout arrangement before permanent construction is established.

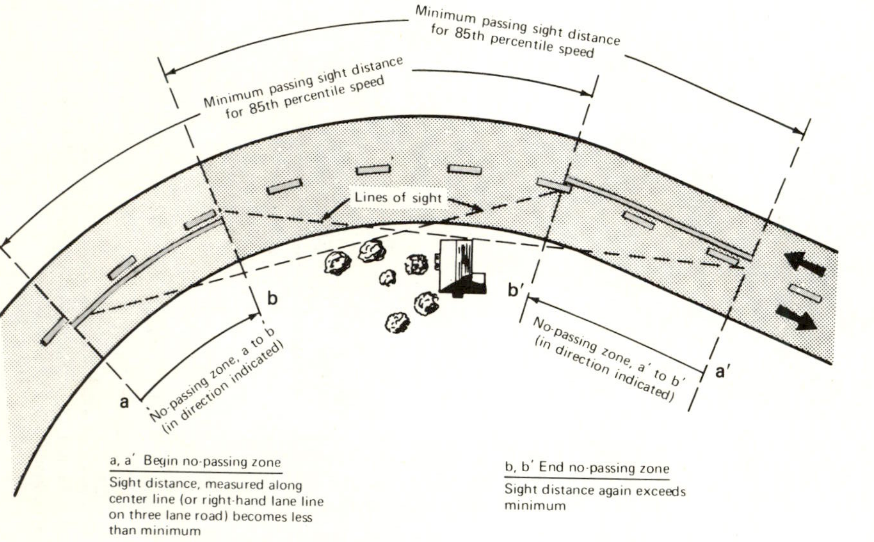

Figure 23.10. Method of locating and determining the limits of no-passing zones at vertical and horizontal curves. SOURCE: *Manual on Uniform Traffic Control Devices,* U.S. Department of Transportation, Federal Highway Administration, U.S. Government Printing Office, Washington, D.C., 1978. p. 3B-10.

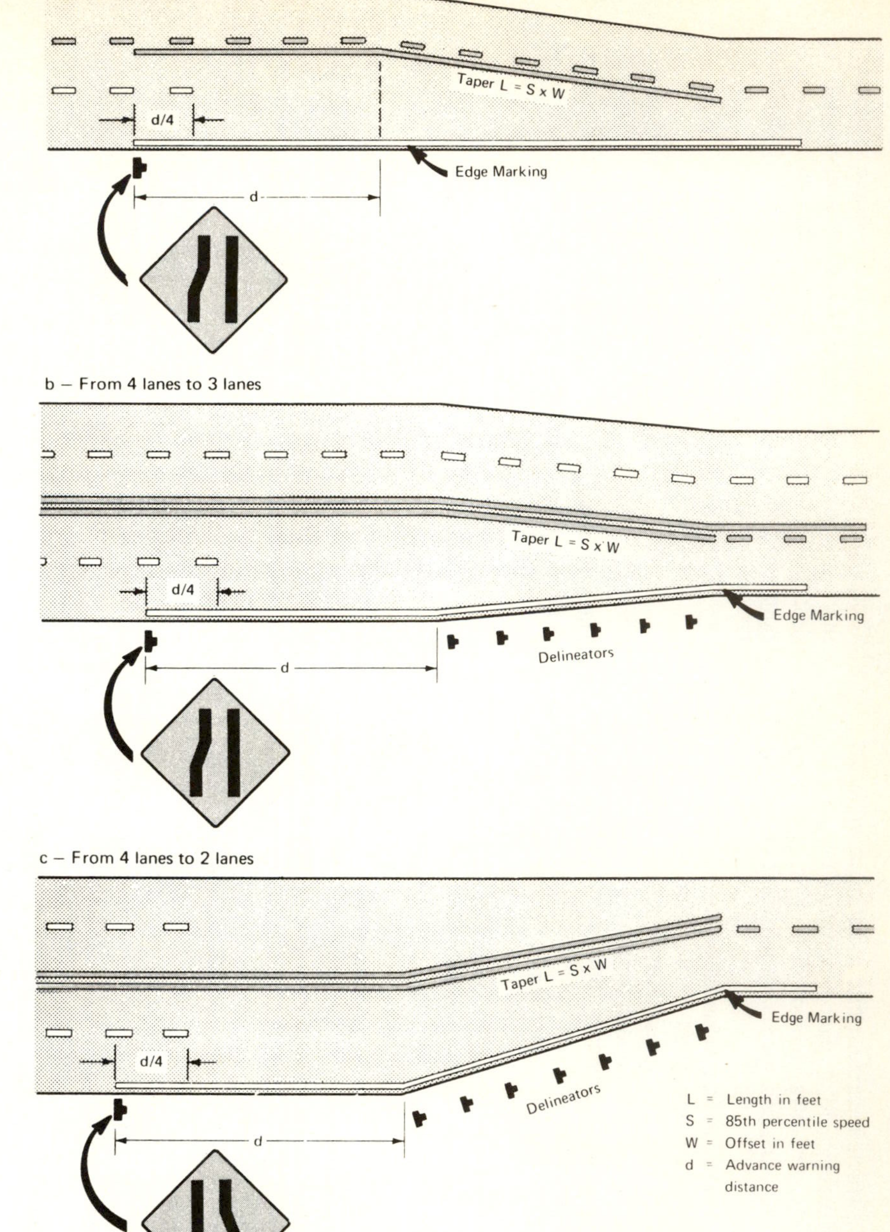

Figure 23.11. Typical pavement-width transition markings and signs. SOURCE: *Manual on Uniform Traffic Control Devices,* U.S. Department of Transportation, Federal Highway Administration, U.S. Government Printing Office, Washington, D.C., 1978. p. 3B-13.

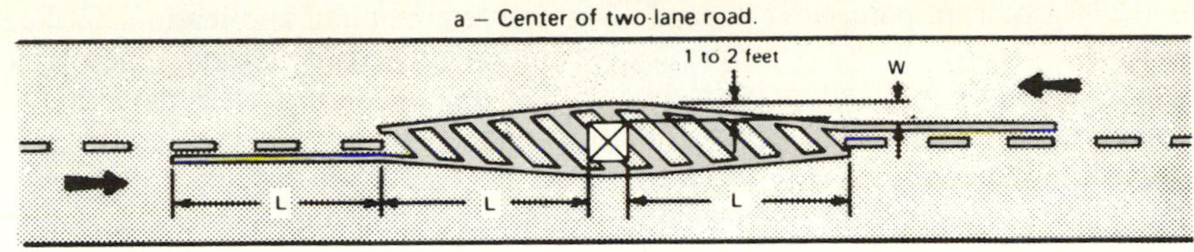

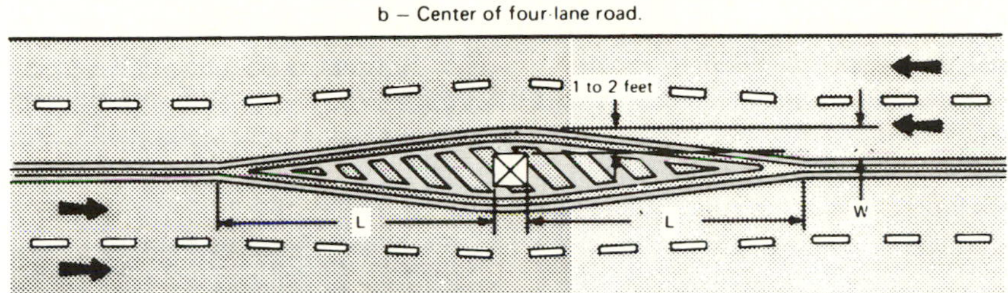

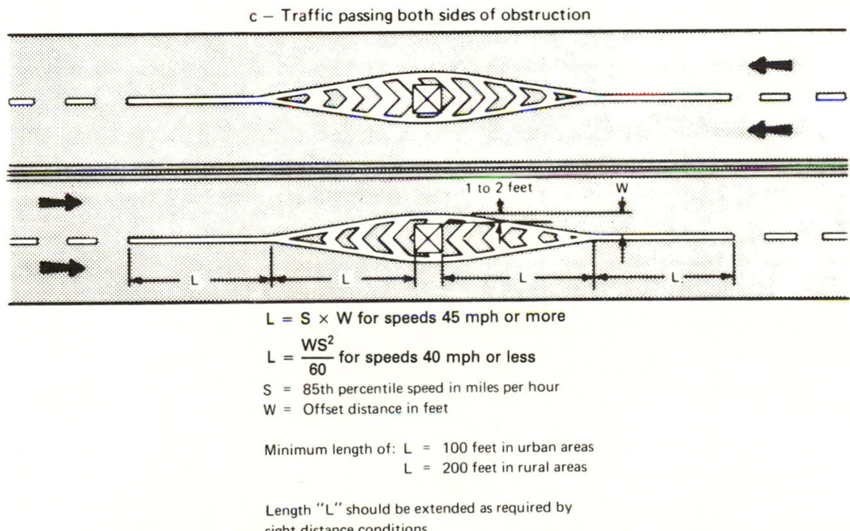

Figure 23.12. Typical approach markings for obstructions in the roadway. SOURCE: *Manual on Uniform Traffic Control Devices,* U.S. Department of Transportation, Federal Highway Administration, U.S. Government Printing Office, Washington, D.C., 1978. p. 3B-18.

Marking materials, maintenance procedures, and schedules

Although traditionally the most common materials used for pavement and curb markings have been paint and glass beads, newer materials are now available that are more durable and sometimes more effective during inclement weather. Although they may have a much higher initial cost, lower maintenance costs, less interruption of traffic, better visibility and legibility through winter months, and other factors can justify them.

Painted traffic lines

Technological improvements also continue to be made in traffic paint materials, beads and their gradations, and methods of applications. Research continues to improve the final product—a reflectorized line that has been installed at a minimum cost and will serve for 6 months or, more desirably, 1 year on the heavily traveled streets and highways. In most state highway departments in the United States, the predominant wet film thickness of traffic paint is 15 mils, and the beads, which are applied at a rate of about 6 lb of drop-on beads per gallon (0.7 kg/liter) of paint have a standard refractive index of 1.50+.

One of the biggest improvements in paint has been the development of "rapid-dry" binders that can be applied with slightly modified, existing equipment at "low" heat or with specially constructed "high"-heat equipment. Their main advantage is less disruption to traffic flow. As the material costs are further reduced, there will be very little difference in applied costs because the amount of equipment can be reduced, and the need for cones or other devices during the drying period will be eliminated.

There are several methods used for selection of a traffic paint with the final selection and purchase generally based upon price. Established specifications include:

1. A performance specification with a laboratory and service test procedure to be used to rate the submitted samples. Usually, a committee composed of representatives of traffic engineering, materials testing, and purchasing departments evaluate paint performance. Qualities evaluated may include general daylight appearance, color, film condition, bead retention, and reflectance. Various rating methods have been used to evaluate these qualities.[17]

2. A formulation specification based upon rigid analysis of the ingredients and generally subject to definite laboratory tests and, occasionally, service tests. It is impossible to determine all characteristics of a paint on the basis of chemical analysis, so the specifications should include both laboratory and service tests for best results. Usually, the buyer reserves the right to inspect the manufacturing facility. This type of specification should guarantee the buyers a paint well fitted to their requirements, provided that the buyers have the means of determining the paint formulas best suited for the climate and road surface conditions of their particular area. There are several rather serious disadvantages to this method:

   a. The buyers will probably not be taking advantage of the new developments in paint formulation unless they have available a paint chemist whose own product development keeps pace with those of the paint manufacturers.

   b. Some paint manufacturers claim that this type of specification tends to stifle their research and development.

   c. It may be impossible to analyze quantitatively all ingredients in a paint because of chemical changes during processing.

3. A specification that is by brand product or equal. This method is not generally advisable because it subjects the buyer to complaints of favoritism or discrimination, and because of the many factors that must be considered to determine the equality of two products.

The maintenance procedures and schedules are generally dependent upon the type of road, traffic volumes, and lane widths. Schedules should be established that will provide for a usable line at all times. This scheduling can include many miles of streets and highways that require an application of paint only once a year. However, major arterials can require paint applications in the spring and fall, or more often if weather permits. The maintenance procedure calls for the repainting of a new line directly over an earlier application. Where needed, the old line should be cleaned if covered with dirt, or prespotted by applying temporary marks on the highway where the previous lines have been worn away or where there has been resurfacing. All resurfaced roads or new construction should be painted before opening to traffic.

[17]"A Model Performance Specification for the Purchase of Pavement Marking Paints," Revised Standard, *Transport. Eng.* (Institute of Transportation Engineers, Arlington, Va.), *46*(1), 36–43 (Jan. 1976).

"Long-life" traffic lines

Hot and cold-rolled thermoplastic markings have been successfully applied for a number of years in numerous countries throughout the world with a serviceable life longer than that of paint.

Both hot and cold thermoplastic can be used for long-line applications or for crosswalks and legends. The experience in Pennsylvania indicates that the cold-rolled plastic is best used in areas of good ambient lighting and during a resurfacing contract where the material can be rolled into the surface during the final passes of the roller.

The application of sprayed or extruded thermoplastic materials with glass beads requires special equipment, and generally requires a service-purchase contract. Such contracts should include specifications for all materials, construction requirements, and warranty provisions.[18]

Recently, new products, such as the two-component, thermosetting epoxy and polyester lane striping materials, have shown great promise by having the ability to outlast painted lines on the more heavily traveled streets and highways.

In cold climates on many major highways, freeways, and streets it has been impossible to maintain a painted line through the winter months due to high traffic density, studded tires, snowplows, and the use of large quantities of abrasive materials on ice and snow. Thermoplastic, epoxy, and polyester lines appear to be the only answer in these cases.

Like painted lines, maintenance procedures and schedules call for reapplication of "long-life" markings on compatible material as the earlier line has worn out or lost reflectorization. Schedules should be established so that all needed markings are applied prior to freezing weather.

Temporary tape

Prefabricated tape markings with adhesive backing designed to conform closely to the texture of the roadway surface have found wide use for temporary markings for routing traffic during construction and for semipermanent markings such as pavement symbols, parking stalls, and parking lot markings.

In addition to providing center and edge lines during a

[18]"A Model Performance Specification for the Purchase of Thermoplastic and Preformed Plastic Pavement Marking Materials," Tentative Revised Standard, *Transport. Eng.* (Institute of Transportation Engineers, Arlington, Va.), *48*(1), 39–47 (Jan. 1978).

construction project, they are finding more and more use as temporary guidelines on newly installed bituminous pavements as the resurfacing is completed. Some states are now requiring the contractor to install 1-ft (30.5-cm) strips of yellow reflective tape every 40 ft (12.1 m), while other agencies have developed the practice of requiring 3-ft (0.9-m) strips every 100 ft (30 m). This temporary marking will provide some guidance to the motorist until the permanent lines can be installed, but generally for not more than 3 to 5 days.

Raised markers

Raised markers, which form a semipermanent marking in areas where there is little or no snowplowing or studded tires, serve to improve visibility under nighttime, wet-weather conditions. Such markers, which can be ½ in. (0.62 cm) to less than 1 in. (2.5 cm) high, can be used as a reflective unit to supplement painted or thermoplastic lines or can be used in lieu of other lines.

Raised markers, in snow-free areas, can be superior to standard traffic paint in terms of durability, driver preference, and night-wet visibility, and their cost for a 5- to 10-year period can be compatible with the cost of standard paint striping.

Because there is still a lot of development in this area, it is best to keep abreast of latest developments through literature, suppliers, or other governmental agencies prior to making an installation.

Any schedule for maintenance should include necessary replacements prior to periods of prolonged inclement weather.

Glass beads

Glass spheres have been used with numerous binders to provide night visibility where continuous roadway lighting is not provided. These beads can be premixed with the binder (paint, thermoplastic, etc.) prior to application, dropped on by the gravity method, or applied by a combination of premix and drop-on.

Specifications for the glass beads are written primarily for the bulk purchase of beads for the drop-on application method. Specifications are written to cover the premixed paint application method to a much lesser degree.

Essential requirements include the following major specifications: (1) gradation, (2) color and shape, (3) imperfections, (4) crushing strength, (5) index of refraction, (6) silica content, (7) chemical stability, (8) reflectivity, and (9) packaging.

Object markers and delineators

Object markers, as discussed under "Marking Elements," can consist of yellow 3-in. (7.5-cm) reflectors mounted on yellow or black panels, or can be yellow reflectorized stripes on a black background. These yellow reflectors should be similar to the yellow and white delineators which are capable of clearly reflecting light under normal atmospheric conditions from a distance of 1000 ft (305 m) when illuminated by the upper beam of standard automobile headlights.

The maintenance procedures and schedules for these devices are quite similar to traffic signs. Any installation in splash areas, such as the median or the edge of the roadway, should be scheduled for washing at least twice a year. Because of their location, they should be kept under constant observation for damage due to vehicular hits and should be scheduled for replacement as soon as damage is detected.

Marking equipment and operation

Paint markings

Traffic engineering departments use a large variety of paint application equipment varying from small gravity-fed manually operated devices to large elaborate machines designed for precision, high-output striping work. Two types are most common: manually propelled machines and self-propelled machines. Basic application problems make the smaller, manually propelled equipment more efficient for painting word messages, stop lines, other transverse markings, and object markings. Supplemental equipment in use on the larger self-propelled machines include bead bins and dispensers to apply reflecting glass spheres, skipping devices to automatically produce broken lines, and paint pumps to load paint tanks. Some machines have all this equipment plus both inboard and outboard riggers for maximum longitudinal marking flexibility (see Figure 23.13). They can paint several lines at the same time in various changing patterns at operating speeds from 10 to 15 mph (16 to 24 km/h) on anything from a multilane Interstate highway to a rural secondary road. Special features can include tanks to hold 900 gal (3400 liters) of paint, paint guns and bead dispensers, paint heaters, paint pumps, dual steering, two individually steerable paint carriages (inboard and outboard), flashing-arrow boards, and a complete intercommunication system. The speed of operation varies considerably with the type of machine used and the type of work done. Under ideal conditions, between 15 and 30 machine miles (32 to 48 km) of striping can be applied per 8-h day.

On sections where there is no previous stripe available for guidance, a construction joint can be followed, or a manual layout provided by placing spots of paint along the roadway or by stretching a rope between control points and painting along the rope either in spots or in a solid line. Six hundred-foot (183-m) lengths of 3/8-in. (1-cm) manila rope or 3/16-in. (0.5-cm) diamond-braided nylon rope are most effective for this purpose.

On tangents, control points should not be in excess of 600 ft (182 m). On curves, control points should be placed at such intervals as will ensure the accurate location of the line. On multilane highways where many lines are parallel, offset attachments on many striping machines allow the painting of all parallel lines from only one layout line.

Continuing experimentation by both operating agencies and manufacturers of paint and painting equipment is under

Figure 23.13. Modern high-capacity, high-speed pavement marking machine. SOURCE: Pennsylvania Department of Transportation, Bureau of Traffic Engineering, Harrisburg, Pa.

way to improve application characteristics and durability of marking materials. Common causes of premature paint failure include:

1. Insufficient cleaning of pavement
2. Overthinning of paint
3. Damp or wet pavement
4. Applying on windy days or when the temperature is below 40°F (5°C)
5. Presence of limestone or other alkaline materials that tend to break down the paint, causing it to be washed away
6. Insufficient paint film applied

Glass beads can be introduced separately into the paint with the aid of a special dispenser attached to a standard striping machine. Where the beads are premixed, however, the paint may be sprayed directly with conventional equipment.

"Long-life" lines

Thermoplastic traffic lines can be installed by manually propelled machines for small applications such as crosswalks and stop lines, or by large self-propelled machines with large tanks for heating the reflectorized thermoplastic material. In either case, the machine, which must heat the material to approximately 400°F (200°C), needs supplemental equipment such as bead bins and dispensers for spraying reflecting glass spheres onto the hot line. Skipping devices are a necessity for lane line and centerline applications if any volume of material is to be applied.

Because the equipment is specialized in nature and the amount of material applied in a year by any one governmental agency is relatively small, these machines will generally be owned by a vendor or contractor. Contracts for their use should specify:

1. The material to be used
2. The amount of beading in the compound
3. The amount of beading to be applied as top dressing
4. The width of line and the total length of the project
5. A minimum application rate
6. A warranty, if desired

Temporary tape

Although temporary tape has been in use for a number of years, it has generally been applied by hand by removing a backing material, placing the pressure-sensitive adhesive on the pavement, and rolling the tape until it is set. Now that increasing emphasis is being placed on maintaining traffic lines through construction areas, new mechanical methods are being developed to place and remove lines more quickly. Any person in need of temporary lines should review the problem with those traffic engineers who have kept current with the state of the art or with manufacturers' representatives.

Raised markers

Most of the raised marker applications in the United States do not use sophisticated equipment. The individual units have merely been applied to the pavement with epoxy following the layout by tape and marker. Units with a steel casting and two keels have been installed in snowplowing areas by being cemented with epoxy resin into grooves cut into the pavement.

Other markers

Object signs or markers can be mounted on the object and, if needed, can be post-mounted on the approaches. The best equipment for driving posts, prior to mounting delineators or object markers, is an air-operated or electrical post driver. Various models are available, from light-dry post drivers for ground rods, stakes, and small posts, to large-capacity, heavy-duty drivers for larger posts. A post extractor is quite useful for pulling out damaged posts.

Miscellaneous traffic control devices

Standards and/or specifications have been developed in the United States for additional traffic control devices that are not included in previous sections of this chapter. These additional devices are used to guide traffic in and around work areas, alert traffic to hazards ahead, and to provide a means of identifying specific locations on streets or highways.

Barricades

Temporary devices are used to warn and alert drivers of hazards created by construction or maintenance activities in or near the traveled way, and to guide and direct drivers safely past the hazards. Barricades should be one of three types: Type I, II, or III. The characteristics of these types are shown in Figure 23.14.

Markings for barricade rails in construction or maintenance activities should be orange and white stripes (sloping downward at an angle of 45° in the direction traffic is to pass). Red-and-white-striped barricades can be used to warn and alert drivers of the terminus of a road or a ramp, or that a lane is closed for operational purposes. For nighttime use they should be reflectorized and/or equipped with lighting devices for maximum visibility.

Figure 23.14. Standard barricades. SOURCE: *Manual on Uniform Traffic Control Devices*, U.S. Department of Transportation, Federal Highway Administration, U.S. Government Printing Office, Washington, D.C., 1978. p. 6C-6.

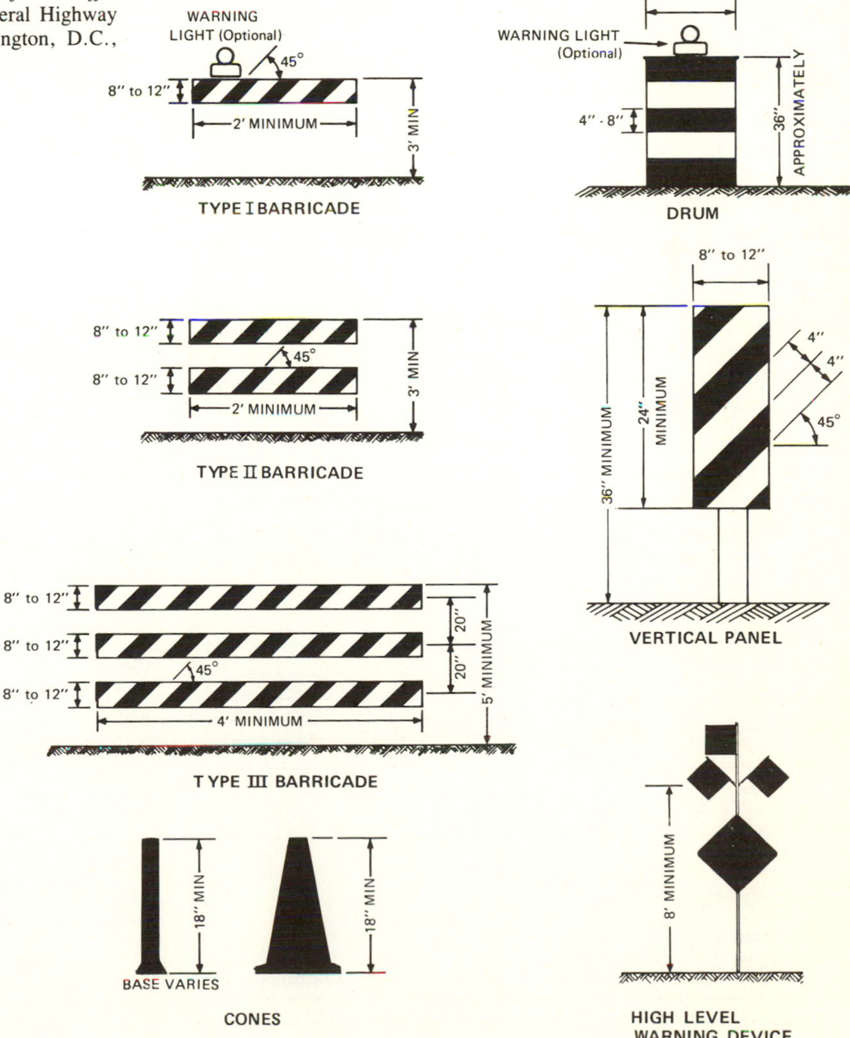

Traffic cones

Traffic cones are a portable, temporary device used to guide drivers through or past an obstacle. Traffic cones and tubular markers of various configurations are available. They should be a minimum of 18 in. (46 cm) in height with a broadened base, and may be made of various materials to withstand impact without damage to themselves or to vehicles. Larger cones should be used where speeds are relatively high or where more conspicuous guidance is needed. The predominant color of cones is orange. They should be kept clean and bright for maximum target value. For nighttime use they should be reflectorized or equipped with lighting devices for maximum visibility.

Vertical panels

Vertical panels with minimum dimensions of 8 × 24 in. (20 by 61 cm) can be used for traffic separation or shoulder barricading when space is at a minimum. They should be orange-and-white-striped and reflectorized in the same manner as barricades. The top of the panel should be mounted a minimum of 36 in. (91 cm) above the roadway.

Drums

Drums with horizontal, circumferential, orange-and-white reflectorized stripes can be used to channelize or delineate traffic flows. When used they should be approximately 36 in. (91 cm) in height, and have at least two orange and two white stripes that are 4 to 8 in. (10 to 20 cm) wide.

Barricade warning lights

Portable, lens-directed, enclosed lights may be needed for mounting on barricades to further warn traffic of hazards ahead. The color of the light emitted should be yellow. They may be used in either a steady-burn or a flashing mode. Barricade warning lights that are authorized for use should meet the requirements of the ITE Purchase Specification for Flashing and Steady-Burn Barricade Warning Lights, as summarized in Table 23-3.

TABLE 23–3
Barricade Warning Lights

Specification	Type A: Low-Intensity	Type B: High-Intensity	Type C: Steady-Burn
Lens directional face	1 or 2	1	1 or 2
Flash rate per minute	55–75	55–75	Constant
On time	10%	8%	Constant
Minimum effective intensity	4.0 candelas	35 candelas	
Minimum beam candle power			2 candles
Hours of operation	Dusk to dawn	24 h/day	Dusk to dawn

SOURCE: "Purchase Specification for Flashing and Steady-Burn Barricade Warning Lights," (Institute of Transportation Engineers, Washington, D.C.), Jan. 1981.

Type A low-intensity flashing warning lights are most commonly mounted on separate portable supports, on Type I or Type II barricades, or on vertical channelizing devices, and are intended to warn drivers that they are approaching a hazardous area.

Type B high-intensity flashing warning lights are normally mounted on the advance warning signs to help get the driver's attention and to alert motorists to roadway conditions ahead. Extremely hazardous site conditions within the construction area may require that the lights be mounted on Type I barricades, signs, or other supports. As these lights are effective in daylight as well as in darkness, they are designed to operate 24 hours a day.

Type C steady-burn lights are intended to be used to delineate the edge of the traveled way in construction areas where additional emphasis is needed to help guide the drivers.

Rumble strips

Rumble strips are devices used to alert the driver of a change of conditions ahead. They can consist of sawed grooves in the pavement, a series of transverse sprayed thermoplastic strips, or some other means of creating the "rumble" effect. Successful applications have been made on sharp curves where an accident problem exists, on approaches to stop signs and as an outline in taper areas where there is a reduction in pavement width. Some work has been completed on the development of effective patterns for these rumble strips.[19]

Mileposts

Properly installed milepost markers can assist drivers in estimating their progress, provide a means for identifying the location of emergency incidents, and aid in highway maintenance and servicing. Mileposts may be erected along any section of a highway route, but zero mileage in the United States should begin at the south and west state lines or junctions where routes begin. Small, 6 × 9 in. (15 × 22.5 cm) milepost signs with 4-in. (10-cm) white numerals may be used on low-volume, low-speed rural roads. However, the standard size of 10 × 27 in. (25 × 68 cm) or 10 × 36 in. (25 × 91 cm) with 6-in. (15-cm) reflectorized numerals on a green reflectorized background should be used on other roadways where it has been determined that mileposting is necessary.

Milepost signs should be mounted at a minimum height and lateral placement equal to that used for delineators. To further enhance the usefulness of the mileposting, delineators may be spaced at a distance of 1/10 or 1/20 of a mile or kilometer and can be marked in fractions of a mile or kilometer by a stencil on the back of the delineator or post or by a small plate on the delineator post.

[19]W. R. BELLIS, "Development of an Effective Rumble Strip Pattern," *Traffic Eng*. (Institute of Traffic Engineers, Washington, D.C.), *39*(7), 22–25 (Apr. 1969).

REFERENCES FOR FURTHER READING

Australian Standard Rules for the Design, Location, Erection and Use of Road Traffic Signs and Signals. The Standards Association of Australia, Sydney, 1960.

FORBES, T. W., B. B. SAARI, W. H. GREENWOOD, J. G. GOLDBLATT, AND T. E. HILL, "Luminance and Contrast Requirements for Legibility and Visibility of Highway Signs." *Transportation Res. Rec. 562*, Transportation Research Board, Washington, D.C., 1976, pp. 59–72.

KING, G. F., AND H. LUNENFELD, "Development of Information Requirements and Transmission Techniques for Highway Users." *Natl. Cooperative Highway Res. Program Rep. 123*, Highway Research Board, Washington, D.C., 1971.

KIRCHNER, S. "Traffic Signs and Markings in the German Democratic Republic." *Traffic Eng. & Control, 12*(6), incorporating *Intl. Road Safety Traffic Rev*. (London), Oct. 1970, pp. 316–318.

Manual of Uniform Traffic Control Devices for Canada, Road and Transportation Association of Canada, Ottawa, Ontario, 1966.

Manual on Uniform Traffic Control Devices for Streets and Highways, U.S. Department of Transportation, Federal Highway Administration, U.S. Government Printing Office, Washington, D.C., 1978.

ROBINSON, C. C., "Color in Traffic Control." *Traffic Eng*. (Institute of Traffic Engineers, Washington, D.C.), *37*(6), 25–29 (May 1967).

ROBERTSON, R. N., *Use of High-Intensity Reflective Materials in Highway Signing: A Literature Review*. Virginia Highway Research Council, Charlottesville, Va., Aug. 1973.

YOUNGBLOOD, W. P., AND H. L. WALTMAN, "A Brightness Inventory of Contemporary Signing Materials for Guide Signs." *Highway Res. Rec. 377*, Highway Research Board, Washington, D.C., 1971, pp. 69–91.

24

TRAFFIC SIGNALS

LEONARD RACH, *Director of Traffic*

Metropolitan Toronto, Roads and Traffic Department
Toronto, Canada

Maintaining efficient transportation systems has become a key goal for government-based transportation agencies in this era of serious energy shortages, rising costs, and competing sources for public funds. The emphasis has shifted to optimizing traffic movement on the surface street network rather than the more costly programs associated with providing more freeways. In cities, traffic control signals may have the greatest influence on the presence or absence of traffic congestion as evidenced by the number of signalized intersections related to urban area population in various world countries illustrated in Figure 24.1.

The literature[1] defines a traffic control signal as any power-operated traffic control device, whether manually, electrically, or mechanically operated, by which traffic is alternately directed to stop and permitted to proceed. Although there are references to regularly maintained tower lights 2600 years ago, the world's first traffic signal using colored lights was installed in mid-December 1868, at the intersection of George and Bridge Streets in London, England.[2] Over the years traffic control signal development paralleled the development and use of the automobile, borrowing from railway signaling practice with regard to color, meaning, and application of signal indications.

With the advent of computer technology and solid-state electronics, existing traffic signal equipment now has sufficient flexibility to permit the implementation of virtually any conceivable control strategy. This chapter addresses the function and application of traffic control signals as they apply to surface street systems.

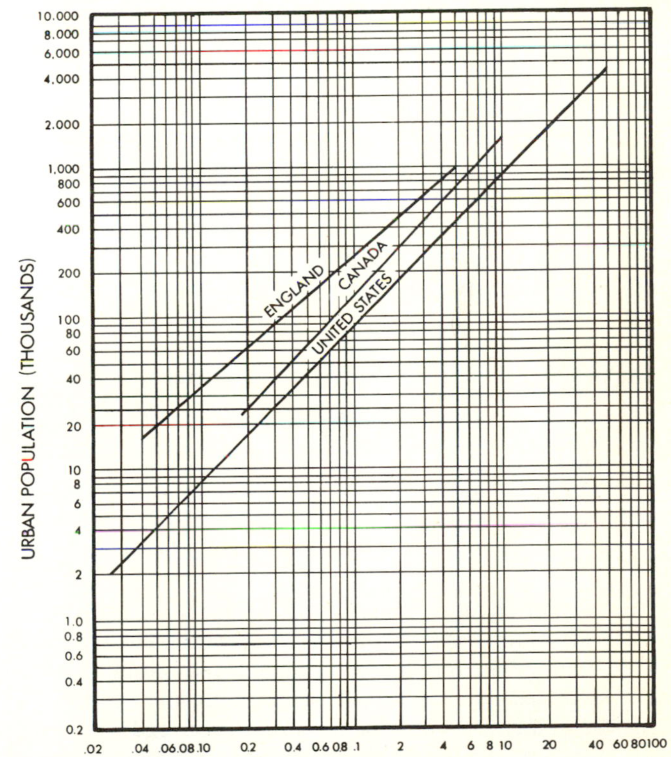

Figure 24.1. Relationship of urban area population and signalized intersections in the United States, Canada, and England. SOURCE: From data provided by the National Safety Council (U.S.), by the Department of Roads and Traffic, Municipality of Metropolitan Toronto (Canada), and by the Transport and Road Research Laboratory (U.K.).

[1] "Pretimed Traffic Signal Controllers," Tentative Revised Standard, ITE Technical Council Committee 4C-S, *Traffic Eng.*, *47*, 40–48 (Feb. 1977).

[2] G. M. SESSIONS, Principal Writer, *Traffic Devices: Historical Aspects Thereof*. Washington, D.C.: Institute of Traffic Engineers, 1971.

Authority

For traffic control signals to serve any useful purpose, their indications must be clearly understood and strictly observed. To achieve these objectives, traffic signals should be uniform, the authority for their installation unimpeachable, and their compliance legally enforceable. Thus, national standards have been developed in various countries for the installation and operation of traffic control signals, and the actions required of motorists and pedestrians are specified by statute or by local ordinance or resolution consistent with the national standards. For example, suitable legislation establishing the authority for the installation, the meaning of the signal indications, and the required obedience to these indications by the road user are outlined in such documents as the *Uniform Vehicle Code,*[3] the *Model Traffic Ordinance,*[4] and specific vehicle codes, an example of which is the Highway Traffic Act of Ontario.[5]

Benefits and drawbacks

When justified and properly designed, a traffic signal installation may achieve one or more of the following:

- Reduce the frequency of certain types of accidents, especially the right-angle type
- Effect orderly traffic movement
- Provide for the continuous flow of a platoon of traffic through proper coordination at a definite speed along a given route
- Allow other vehicles and pedestrians to cross a heavy traffic stream
- Control traffic more economically than by manual methods

Unjustified, ill-designed, improperly operated, or poorly maintained traffic signals may cause:

- Increased accident frequency
- Excessive delay
- Disregard of signal indications
- Circuitous travel by alternate routes

Contrary to common belief, traffic signals do not always increase safety and reduce delay. Experience has indicated that although the installation of signals may result in a decrease in the number of right-angle collisions, it will, in many instances, result in an increase in rear-end collisions. Further, the installation of signals may not only increase overall delay, but also reduce intersection capacity. Consequently, it is of the utmost importance that the consideration of a signal installation and the selection of equipment be preceded by a thorough study of traffic and roadway conditions by an engineer experienced and trained in this field. This engineer should recognize that a signal should be installed only if the net effect, balancing benefits versus drawbacks, is to the public's advantage.

Warrant criteria for signal control

When the benefits and drawbacks of traffic signals are considered together with the financial limitations of the public agencies who are responsible for their installations, it is apparent that some system of establishing the need for a signal installation at a particular location is necessary. Such a system has been established, using a common denominator known as signal warrants.

U.S. warrants

The eight warrants briefly described herein are discussed in detail in the U.S. *Manual on Uniform Traffic Control Devices for Streets and Highways (MUTCD).*[6] These should be considered as a guide to the determination of the need for traffic control signals rather than absolute criteria, and their use tempered with professional judgment based upon experience and consideration of all related factors. For example, such factors as physical roadway features, age of pedestrians, or effect of adjacent signalized intersections may modify a decision based solely on the warrants.

TABLE 24–1
Minimum Vehicular Volume Warrant

Number of Lanes for Moving Traffic on Each Approach		Vehicles/Hour on Major Street (Total of Both Approaches)	Vehicles/Hour on Higher-Volume Minor Street Approach (One Direction Only)
Major Street	Minor Street		
1	1	500	150
2 or more	1	600	150
2 or more	2 or more	600	200
1	2 or more	500	200

SOURCE: *Manual on Uniform Traffic Control Devices*, U.S. Department of Transportation, Federal Highway Administration, U.S. Government Printing Office, Washington, D.C., 1978.

Warrant 1. Minimum vehicular volume. The minimum vehicular warrant is satisfied when, for each of any 8 h of an average day, the traffic volumes given in Table 24-1 exist on the major street and on the higher-volume minor street approach to the intersection. These major street and minor street volumes are for the same 8 h. During each hour, the higher approach volume on the minor street is considered, regardless of its direction.

When the 85th percentile speed of major street traffic exceeds 40 mph (64 km/h), or when the intersection lies within the built-up area of an isolated community having a population less than 10,000, the minimum vehicular vol-

[3]*Uniform Vehicle Code*. Washington, D.C.: National Committee on Uniform Traffic Laws and Ordinances, rev. 1968 and Suppl. 1, 1972, Secs. 11-201 through 11-206, 15-102, and 15-106.

[4]*Model Traffic Ordinance*. Washington, D.C.: National Committee on Uniform Traffic Laws and Ordinances, rev. 1968 and Suppl. 1, 1972, Secs. 4-1 through4-9.

[5]The Highway Traffic Act, Revised Statutes of the Province of Ontario, Canada, 1970, as amended to September 6, 1977.

[6]*Manual on Uniform Traffic Control Devices for Streets and Highways,* U.S. Department of Transportation, Federal Highway Administration. Washington, D.C., U.S. Government Printing Office, 1978.

ume warrant is 70% of the requirements above, in recognition of differences in the nature and operational characteristics of traffic in urban and rural environments and smaller municipalities.

Warrant 2. Interruption of continuous traffic. The interruption of continuous traffic warrant is satisfied when, for each of any 8 h of an average day, the traffic volumes given in Table 24-2 exist on the major street and on the higher-volume minor street approach to the intersection and where the signal installation will not seriously disrupt progressive traffic flow. These major street and minor street volumes are for the same 8 h. During each hour, the higher volume on the minor street is considered, regardless of its direction.

TABLE 24–2
Minimum Vehicular Volumes for Warrant 2

Number of Lanes for Moving Traffic on Each Approach		Vehicles/Hour on Major Street (Total of Both Approaches)	Vehicles/Hour on Higher-Volume Minor Street Approach (One Direction Only)
Major Street	Minor Street		
1	1	750	75
2 or more	1	900	75
2 or more	2 or more	900	100
1	2 or more	750	100

SOURCE: *Manual on Uniform Traffic Control Devices*, U.S. Department of Transportation, Federal Highway Administration, U.S. Government Printing Office, Washington, D.C., 1978.

A reduced volume, similar to that described under Warrant 1, can be used in place of those shown in Table 24-2 on higher-speed roads or in smaller communities.

Warrant 3. Minimum pedestrian volume. The minimum pedestrian volume warrant is satisfied when, for each of any 8 h of an average day, the following traffic volumes exist:

1. On the major street, 600 or more vehicles per hour (vph) enter the intersection (total of both approaches), or 1000 or more vph enter the intersection (total of both approaches) on the major street where there is a raised median island 4 ft (1.22 m) or more in width.
2. During the same 8 h there are 150 or more pedestrians per hour on the highest-volume crosswalk crossing the major street (see Table 24-3).

These warrants may be reduced, as described under Warrant 1, when applied to higher-speed roads or smaller communities.

TABLE 24–3
Minimum Pedestrian Volume Warrant

Vehicles/Hour on Major Street (Total of Both Approaches)		Number of Pedestrians on Highest-Volume Crosswalk
With Median	Without Median	
1000	600	150

SOURCE: Same as for Table 24-1.

Warrant 4. School crossings. The fourth warrant recognizes the unique problems related to children crossing a major street on the way to and from school, particularly near the school, and may be considered as a special case of the pedestrian warrant.

A traffic control signal may be warranted at an established school crossing when a traffic engineering study of the frequency and adequacy of gaps in the vehicular traffic stream, as related to the number and size of groups of school children at the school crossing, shows that the number of adequate gaps in the traffic stream during the period when the children are using the crossing is less than the number of minutes in the same period.

Warrant 5. Progressive movement. The progressive movement warrant relates to the desirability of holding traffic in compact platoons and is satisfied when:

1. On a one-way street or a street that has predominantly unidirectional traffic, the adjacent signals are so far apart that they do not provide the necessary degree of vehicle platooning and speed control.
2. On a two-way street, adjacent signals do not provide the necessary degree of platooning and speed control and the proposed and adjacent signals could constitute a progressive signal system.

The installation of a signal according to this warrant should be based on the 85th percentile speed unless an engineering study indicates that another speed is more desirable. According to this warrant, the installation of a signal should not be considered where the resultant signal spacing would be less than 1000 ft (305 m).

Warrant 6. Accident experience. The accident experience warrant is satisfied when:

1. An adequate trial of less restrictive remedies with satisfactory observance and enforcement has failed to reduce the accident frequency.
2. Five or more reported accidents of types susceptible to correction by traffic signal control have occurred within a 12-month period, each accident involving personal injury or property damage to an apparent extent of $100 or more.
3. There exists a volume of vehicular traffic not less than 80% of the requirements specified in Warrants 1, 2, 3.
4. The signal installation will not seriously disrupt progressive traffic flow.

Warrant 7. Systems. This warrant recognizes that traffic signal coordination can be two-dimensional. That is, progression along an important cross street can be as important as that along what would normally be called the major street. Both streets must be given equal consideration as major routes.

The systems warrant is applicable when two or more major routes meet at a common intersection and the total existing or immediately projected entering volume is at least 800 vehicles during the peak hour of a typical weekday or each of any 5 h of a Saturday and/or Sunday.

Warrant 8. Combination of warrants. In exceptional cases, signals may occasionally be justified when no single warrant is satisfied but where two or more of Warrants 1, 2, and 3 are satisfied to the extent of 80% or more of the stated values. Adequate trial of other remedial measures which cause less delay and inconvenience to traffic should precede installation of signals under this warrant.

Warrants in other jurisdictions

Traffic authorities in many countries also rely on the specific warrants as contained in the *MUTCD* for guidance. However, in Great Britain more general criteria have been established to provide guidance for the installation of traffic control signals.[7] These include such factors as:

- Interruption of minor road traffic
- Pedestrian considerations
- Traffic accidents
- Requirement for police control
- Requirement for part-time signals
- Area control and interconnection of signals

Effectiveness of traffic control signals

Legislative authority

If traffic control and other regulatory signals are to be effective, their indications must be strictly observed and legislation must be enacted specifying driver and pedestrian requirements and penalties for failure to comply. The enforcement of this legislation must be a police function, and therefore can only be successfully undertaken when the signals are installed in conformity with certain minimum standards and by a duly authorized public body.

This requires that signals be installed only by the appropriate legislative authority and in accordance with regulations regarding their design, placement, and maintenance. Greatest observance is achieved by uniformity in the application and appearance of traffic signals throughout a whole nation, in conformity with the recommendations contained in the *MUTCD* in the United States or corresponding documents in other nations.

Enforcement

A most important reason for installing the signal is to assist police in carrying out their duties of maintaining safe and orderly traffic flow, and to relieve them of the onerous and often hazardous task of manually directing traffic. It is quite definitely in the interest of the police to ensure that signals are operating in the most efficient manner possible. Therefore, they should cooperate with the traffic engineering department and/or other agencies responsible for installing and maintaining the signals by providing information on both physical and operational defects.

Police enforcement can materially determine the effectiveness of the signals. Signals installed in areas where police enforcement is known to be persistent will usually result in greater safety and in more efficient traffic flow than in areas where enforcement is lax.

Standardization and innovation

On the subject of uniformity and standardization, the *MUTCD* says:

> Uniformity of traffic control devices simplifies the task of a road user because it aids in recognition and understanding. It aids road users, police officers and traffic courts by giving everyone the same interpretation. It aids public highway and traffic officials through economy in manufacture, installation, maintenance and administration.
>
> Simply stated, uniformity means treating similar situations in the same way. The use of uniform traffic control devices does not, in itself, constitute uniformity. A standard device used where it is not appropriate is as objectionable as a nonstandard device; in fact, this may be worse, in that such misuses may result in disrespect of those locations where the device is needed.[8]

It is important, however, to differentiate carefully between standardization and stagnation. There must be room for innovation, experimentation, and possible improvements that will lead to the revision of standards from time to time. Experimentation should be carefully controlled to ensure that it does not constitute an attempt to introduce change merely for the sake of change. Experimentation should normally arise from a conclusion that the existing standard or application fails to meet all necessary requirements. The *MUTCD* in the United States sets forth procedures for making requests for experimentation or for proposing changes in the current text of the *Manual*.

Accident reduction

The common acceptance of traffic signals as a solution to all right-of-way problems has perhaps naively led many people to the conclusion that by simply introducing a traffic signal one can prevent or eliminate all intersection accidents. Traffic studies in urban areas indicate that accidents may very well increase after the installation of traffic control signals.

In this regard, whereas traffic signals tend to reduce right-angle accidents, rear-end and turning accidents are generally higher. For example, in an accident pattern study by KLD Associates,[9] total accidents increased by 8% after the installation of traffic signals at 33 locations in Michigan. While sideswipe and right-angle accidents were reduced by 60% and 45%, respectively, rear-end and left-turn accidents increased by 236% and 84%, respectively. In this same study, data from Concord, California, at 28 newly signalized

[7] "Criteria For Traffic Light Signals at Junctions," *Technical Memorandum M1/73*. London: Department of The Environment, Jan. 1973.

[8] *Manual on Uniform Traffic Control Devices*, pp. 1A-2, 1A-3.

[9] G. F. King and R. B. Goldblatt, "Relationship of Accident Patterns to Type of Intersection Control, Urban Accident Patterns," *Transport. Res. Rec. 540*. Washington, D.C.: Transportation Research Board, National Research Council, 1975.

intersections showed a reduction in total accidents with an overall decrease in right-angle accidents but an increase in rear-end accidents.

The exact reason for this change in accident patterns is not clearly understood, but it can be hypothesized that more careful studies, better adherence to the warrants, and more careful design of the physical aspects of the installation are required.

Signal equipment

A traffic signal installation is the result of grouping various pieces of traffic control equipment into a working system. In any installation, certain fundamental items, such as controller assemblies, signal heads, detectors, interconnecting cables, and associated hardware are required. The specific equipment for each installation is normally determined by the degree of desired sophistication and the need to ensure uniformity and standardization.

Standards for basic signal equipment have been written and approved by the Institute of Transportation Engineers:

1. "Adjustable Face Pedestrian Signal Head Standard," 1975
2. "Adjustable Face Vehicle Traffic Control Signal Heads," Tentative Revised Standard, 1979
3. "Traffic Signal Lamps," Tentative Revised Standard, 1978
4. "Lane-Use Traffic Control Signal Heads," Tentative Standard, 1977
5. "Pretimed Traffic Signal Controllers," Tentative Revised Standard, 1977
6. "Traffic Actuated Traffic Signal Controllers," Tentative Revised Standard, Part 1, Part 2, 1978

Other agencies have also produced equipment specifications, which include:

1. "NEMA Standards," *Standards Publication TS1-1976,* National Electrical Manufacturers Association, and subsequent revisions
2. "Colors of Signal Lights," *NBS Monograph 75,* U.S. Department of Commerce, National Bureau of Standards

Traffic signal controller units

The basic function of a controller unit, whether it be electromechanical or a solid-state electronic device, is to switch the appropriate signal indications on and off according to a fixed or variable plan, thus assigning the correct and safe right-of-way at a given location.

Electromechanical controller units, which have been in use for many years, have the advantage of simplicity, ease of maintenance and expandibility, and relatively low cost. Their disadvantage is the necessity for an annual routine preventative maintenance program. Figure 24.2 illustrates a schematic design of a basic pretimed controller. In general, these controllers use a synchronous electric motor and gear train in the timing assembly, with the specific timing intervals adjusted by the insertion of keys around the periphery of a slotted dial. These keys close and open a switch at intervals predetermined by their spacing as the dial rotates. The signal light switching assembly consists of a motor-driven or solenoid-driven camshaft. This camshaft is rotated one step at a time by closing of contacts on the timing assembly operated by keys on the dial. The camshaft carries a number of cams with removable segments, each of which switches a signal light circuit. When a cam segment is removed, the switch is closed. The rotating camshaft switches the signal lights on and off in the proper sequence and relationship.

Following the electromechanical controller unit came a type in which the timing was performed by electronic timing circuits rather than a motor-driven dial. This permitted not only greater flexibility in setting of interval timing, but more important, it made possible the timing of the green intervals variable on the basis of traffic volume. This feature was and still is termed traffic-actuated. Its introduction brought about the first major improvement in traffic signal controller units.

In recent years, the traffic signal industry has been revolutionized by controller units utilizing solid-state circuitry and microprocessor logic. These units employ printed-circuit boards and integrated-circuit elements, thereby reducing power requirements and physical size while providing relatively simple replacement of defective parts through modular construction. In addition, this type of controller unit is superior to the previously mentioned controller units in terms of flexibility of timing strategies, ability to provide features internally that previously required external hardware, and more sophisticated detector actuation processing. An initial disadvantage is that operations personnel must adapt to a new form of timing adjustment and maintenance personnel must adapt to the techniques of maintaining a new generation of equipment. Figures 24.3 and 24.4 illustrate two examples of these types of controllers.

The major components of a microprocessor-based controller unit are the central processor unit (CPU), program memory, data memory, control and indication panel, input and output interfaces, and a power supply. Their functions can be described in the following general terms. The CPU controls all the functions performed by the other components in the controller. Based on instructions in the program memory it inputs data, processes these data, and then outputs the desired results. The program memory is usually either the read-only (ROM) type, which cannot be altered after it has been programmed, or the programmable read-only (PROM) type, which can be altered by a separate special programming unit, and can be used to store timing strategies. The data memory is used to store values for interval times and timers, and parameters for setting different modes of operation. This memory is a random-access (RAM) type and can be read from and written into by the CPU. The control and indication panel is essentially a traffic engineer's terminal consisting of inputs from switches, program pins, or digital keyboard, and outputs to indication lights and digital displays. These are used to set timing and mode parameters, and to observe controller operation. The input interface is used to input all external data, such as vehicle

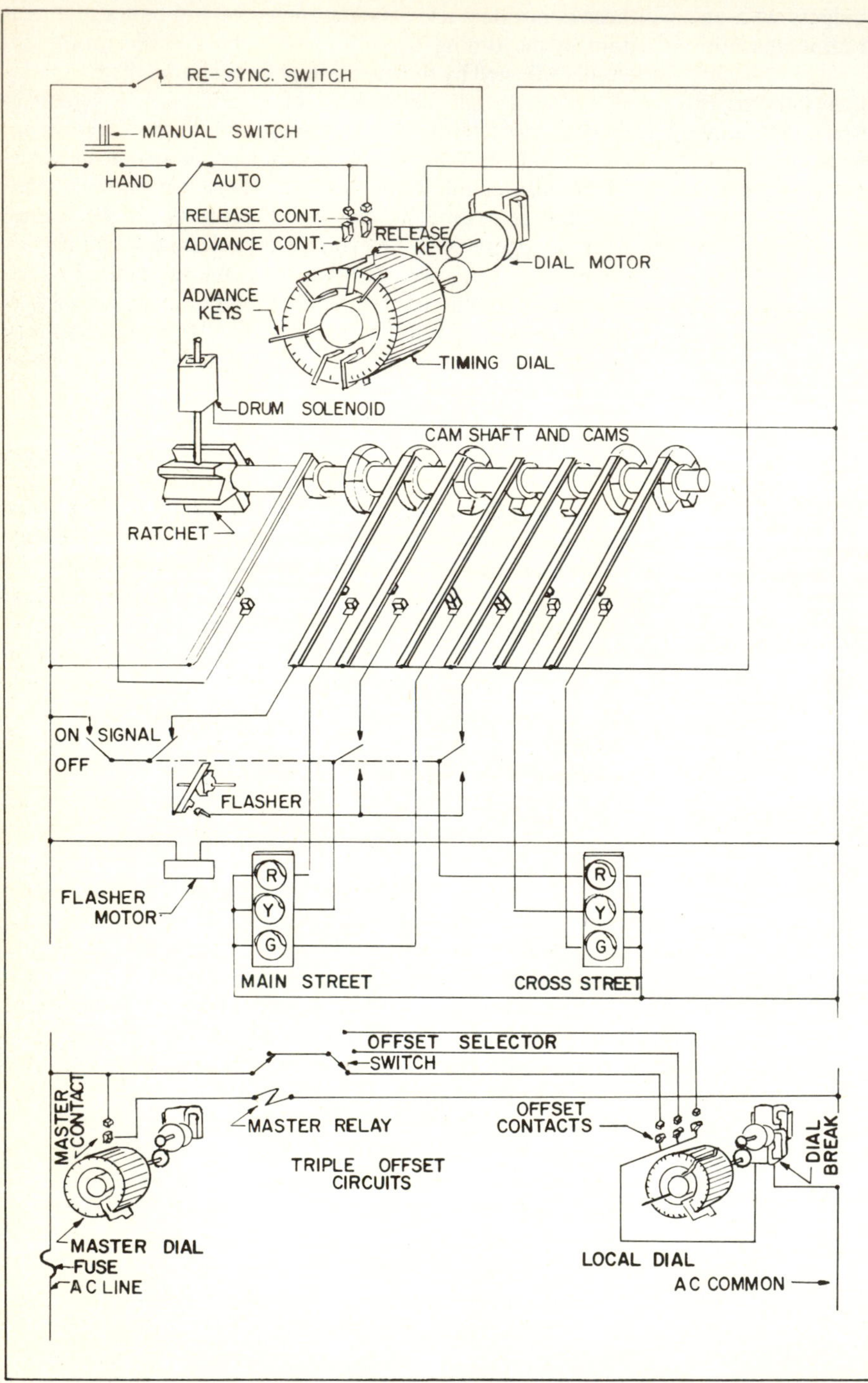

Figure 24.2. Traffic signal basic fixed time-controller.

and pedestrian actuations, police switches, and control inputs. The output interface is used to drive the signal head lamp circuits and the display panel. The units may also have an input and output port for communication over twisted pair metallic circuits to other controllers or a master controller for the purposes of system coordination. By means of such inputs as "force-off" and "hold" these controller units can be coordinated into a system. It is also possible to operate the signals at the intersections comprising a diamond interchange with a single controller unit, resulting in a substantial saving in the cost of control equipment.

Selection of a controller type

Several types of controller units are available to the traffic engineer. The selection of the proper type for a particular intersection depends on the geometric layout, the nature of approaching traffic, and the spatial relationship with adjacent intersections. The types available and their characteristics are as follows.

Pretimed controllers. A pretimed controller unit operates on the basis of predetermined cycle lengths and

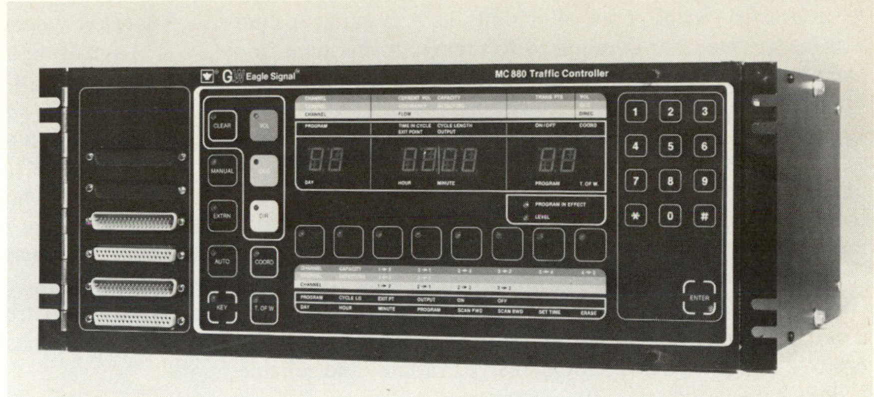

Figure 24.3. Eagle signal MC880 traffic controller. Courtesy of Eagle Signal Corporation. Photo: Mears Photography, Austin, Tx.

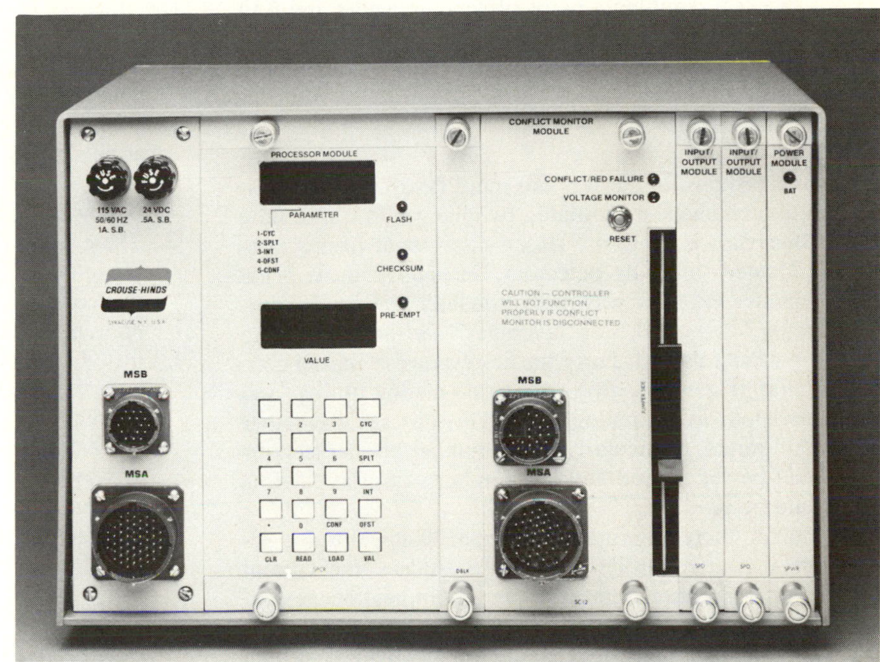

Figure 24.4. Crouse-Hinds SP Series pretimed controller. Courtesy of Crouse-Hinds Co.

phases. It is frequently used where there are predictable and stable traffic volumes or in a coordinated interconnected system. It provides a simple, economic means of traffic control and, because of its simplicity, is very reliable and easy to maintain; however, it does have certain restrictions as to the number of cycle lengths and the number of phase splits that can be used.

Semiactuated controllers. A semiactuated controller unit provides a continuous green indication on the major street except when a safe crossing period for motorists and/or pedestrians on the minor street is required. Vehicle detectors are placed on the minor street in the intersection approach and pedestrian pushbuttons are placed on poles adjacent to the pedestrian crossing to detect an intermittent crossing demand and thereby interrupt the major street flow. Normally, a semiactuated controller unit is operated in an interconnected system with a background cycle length and a predetermined offset, to provide progressive movement on the major street.

Fully actuated controllers. A fully actuated controller unit permits the adjustment of the various green intervals on the basis of traffic volume. It is most useful when the approach volumes fluctuate widely by cycle and time of day. Vehicle detectors on all intersection approaches are required. A fully actuated controller unit can have a minimum and maximum green interval setting for each traffic phase and, for controller units controlling more than two traffic phases, can omit or skip unwanted phases.

A traffic actuated controller unit of the volume-density type provides two additional features: the ability to reduce the green time assigned to each vehicle on the basis of the waiting time of opposing vehicles (gap reduction), and the ability to increase the minimum green interval for a particular phase on the basis of the number of vehicles approaching prior to the beginning of the green interval (variable initial).

Master controller. A master controller unit is used to supervise and coordinate the operation of one or more intersection or "local" controller units in a system. A communication medium is required to receive traffic data from sampling detectors and to transmit supervisory and coordination commands to the intersection controller units. More sophisticated master controller units also have the ability to maintain surveillance of the operation of the entire system. The type of master controller unit to be used relates to the type of intersection controller units and the capabilities required.

For systems utilizing electromechanical units, the master controller unit is not only of the electromechanical type, but it is also usually combined with an intersection controller unit. Although relatively inexpensive, simple, and reliable, it does have some basic disadvantages:

- At most 9 combinations of offsets and splits and 6 to 10 cycle lengths are possible
- Timing plans are implemented on a time-switch basis only
- No surveillance capabilities

Traffic responsive masters are more flexible in that system pattern changes are initiated by changes in traffic flow rather than on a time basis. Based upon input from strategically located sampling detectors, decisions can be made as to whether the flow was predominantly "inbound," predominantly "outbound," or "average," and an appropriate system pattern selected. Early traffic-responsive master controller units received analog data, used analog timing, and made decisions using analog logic. This process was rather slow and limited, particularly in the number of intersections that could be supervised and the number of traffic patterns that could be selected.

Although there are many electromechanical/traffic-responsive master controllers still in existence, the current trend is toward digital central master equipment because of its traffic responsive capabilities, extensive timing flexibility, equipment monitoring capability, and overall system surveillance. The range of central digital equipment is quite extensive, and permits in most cases modular expansion capabilities from small systems of 10 to 50 signals up to large systems having networks in excess of 1000 traffic signals.

Auxiliary equipment

Auxiliary equipment consists of separate units that can be used with a basic controller unit to provide additional functions and features. Some of the more common units and their applications are as follows:

1. *Flasher:* a mechanical or solid-state device used to open and close signal circuits at a repetitive rate.
2. *Relay:* a mechanical or solid-state device used to control signal circuits when the controller unit switching capabilities are inadequate.
3. *Preemptor:* a unit to provide a special sequence of signal indications upon command from a fire station, emergency vehicles, railroad grade-crossing protection, or transit buses.
4. *Time switch:* a device that can be used to select a particular signal system pattern on the basis of time of day and day of week.
5. *Manual control or police panel:* a panel accessible through a separate door in the cabinet permitting selection of off, automatic, flashing, or manual operation.
6. *Conflict monitor:* a device that, upon detecting conflicting signal indications or improper controller unit voltages, places the signal in flashing operation.
7. *Coordination unit:* a device that permits external control of a controller unit through an interconnection circuit from a master controller unit.

Controller unit location[10]

A traffic signal controller may be attached to any convenient pole, or if a ground or pedestal cabinet is used, it may be placed wherever desired, provided that the chosen location satisfies the following general requirements:

1. A power supply can be conveniently obtained.
2. There will be an unobstructed view of all approaches to the intersection in the event of manual operation. When this condition cannot be satisfied and where manual operation is frequently required, it may be desirable to install a special remote unit at a more favorable position with its switches in parallel with those of the controller proper.
3. The cabinet does not unduly obstruct the pedestrian right-of-way.
4. The cabinet will not be unduly exposed to accidental damage caused by passing traffic.

Signal heads and optical units

Definitions:[11]

1. *Signal head:* an assembly containing one or more signal faces.
2. *Signal face:* that part of a traffic control signal provided for controlling one or more traffic movements in a single direction.
3. *Signal indication:* the illumination of a traffic signal lens or combination of signal lenses at the same time.

Number of signal faces and locations. The effectiveness of a traffic signal installation depends, to a great extent, on the ease with which the signal heads can be seen and recognized. For this reason certain standards have been developed to place signal faces within the motorist's cone of vision and within a desirable mounting height and location within the intersection.

The *MUTCD* specifies that a minimum of two signal faces for through traffic must be continuously visible on an approach to a signalized intersection and that the distance

[10] J. T. Hewton, "Traffic Signals Manual," Ontario Traffic Conference, 1965.

[11] "Adjustable Face Vehicle Traffic Control Signal Heads," Tentative Revised Standard, ITE Technical Council Committee 4MS, *ITE J.*, Feb. 1979.

TABLE 24-4
Minimum Signal Visibility Distance for Varying Approach Speed

85th Percentile Speed		Minimum Visibility Distance	
mph	km/h	ft	m
20	37	100	30
25	40	175	53
30	48	250	76
35	56	325	99
40	64	400	122
45	72	475	145
50	81	550	168
55	89	625	191
60	97	700	213

SOURCE: Same as for Tables 24-1 and 24-2

of the unobstructed view must vary with the 85th percentile approach speed as given in Table 24-4.

The mounting height of the bottom of the signal face housing should not be less than 8 ft (2.5 m) nor more than 15 ft (4.6 m) above the sidewalk. If the signal face is suspended over the traveled portion of the road, the bottom of the signal face housing should be not less than 15 ft (4.6 m) nor more than 19 ft (5.8 m) above the crown of the road.

In general, it is desirable to mount a far-side-right signal face on a mast arm to provide unobstructed visibility for through traffic. A supplemental signal face should be employed normally on the far side left of each intersection approach to improve approach visibility and for use in case of primary signal face bulb burnout. If nearside signals are used, they should be located as near as practical to the stop line. For control of an exclusive lane, a single signal face is permissible in addition to the minimum two signal faces for through traffic and should be placed directly in line with the path of that movement. Unless physically impractical, the signal faces should be located not less than 40 ft (12.2 m) nor more than 120 ft (36.6 m) from the stop bar.

All signal faces should be equipped with visors in order to reduce reflected glare from the sun and other illumination, and to direct the signal indication to the approaching traffic. If the visor is of the full-circle or tunnel type, it also serves to reduce the possibility of traffic on an approach seeing the signal indications meant for opposing traffic. In addition, signal heads may be fitted with a back plate to improve their visibility by making the head stand out from the surroundings, and by helping to prevent confusion due to advertising signs and the rising/setting sun.

Number and arrangement of lenses per signal face. The lenses in a vehicle signal face should be arranged in a vertical or horizontal straight line with each signal face having at least three lenses but not more than five. The lenses are red, yellow, or green in color and give circular or arrow-type indications. Typical arrangements of lenses in signal faces are shown in Figure 24.5.

The color of signal lenses is closely controlled both in glass and plastic, and specifications have been prepared for ensuring that the basic color of green, yellow, and red are true, and provide the correct uniform indications.[12,13] Plastic lenses are preferred to glass because of their shatterproof characteristics, and polycarbonate plastics are preferred to acrylic plastics because of their higher-temperature characteristics.

Pedestrian signals. In the United States, the pedestrian signal consists of two lenses with a Portland orange "Don't Walk" legend or an upraised palm and a lunar white "Walk" legend or a walking man as specified in the *MUTCD* and by standard ITE practice.[14] In many other countries only the symbol indications are used. A number of studies [15,16] in recent years dealing with pedestrian signal indications and pedestrian behavioral and preference characteristics have been undertaken in an effort to further improve on pedestrian signal displays.

Pedestrian signal faces should be located at each end of a controlled crosswalk and physically separated from the vehicular signal faces but yet clearly visible to pedestrians throughout their entire passage in the crosswalk. Detailed information relating to the meaning, application, design, and warrants for pedestrian signals is presented in the *MUTCD*.

Traffic signal lamps. Traffic signal lamps[17] require that the filament be supported to withstand extensive vibration. These lamps form part of a complete optical system consisting of light source, reflector, and lens. The critical factors are the light center length, wattage, and rated lumen output. Lamps should be selected for the size of indication required, but when 12-in. (30-cm) signal lenses having 150-watt lamps are operated as a flashing yellow indication, especially at night, an automatic dimming device should be used to reduce their brilliance. The life of signal lamps is greatly reduced by abnormally high voltage conditions and excessive vibration; therefore, a lamp replacement program of once per year is recommended.

Hardware and mounting. Signal heads may be mounted on posts or poles at the sides of the roadway or on islands in the roadway, or they may be suspended from span wires, mast arms, or signal bridges over the roadway. A typical mounting arrangement is shown in Figure 24.6. Care should be taken to adhere to the proper mounting and location layouts to ensure that pedestrians are not injured by signals mounted too low, or by poles and controllers located in the crosswalk.

Because signal equipment is exposed to the elements, weather- and corrosion-resistent materials must be used. Also, the mounting hardware should be capable of withstanding prevailing wind-load and local weather conditions.

---

[12]Ibid.

[13]"Lane-Use Traffic Control Signal Heads," ITE Tentative Standard, ITE Technical Council Committee 4K-S, *Traffic Eng., 47* (Jan. 1977).

[14]"Adjustable Face Pedestrian Signal Head Standard," ITE Tentative Revised Standard, Technical Council Committee 4D-S, *Traffic Eng., 45* (Mar. 1975).

[15]C. F. STERLING, "An Analysis of Pedestrian Reaction to the Flashing Walk Indication," *Traffic Eng., 44* (Nov. 1974).

[16]H. D. ROBERTSON, "Pedestrian Preferences for Symbolic Signal Displays," *Transport. Eng., 47* (June 1977).

[17]"Traffic Signal Lamps, Tentative Revised Standard," ITE Technical Council Committee 4R-S, *Traffic Eng., 48* (May 1978).

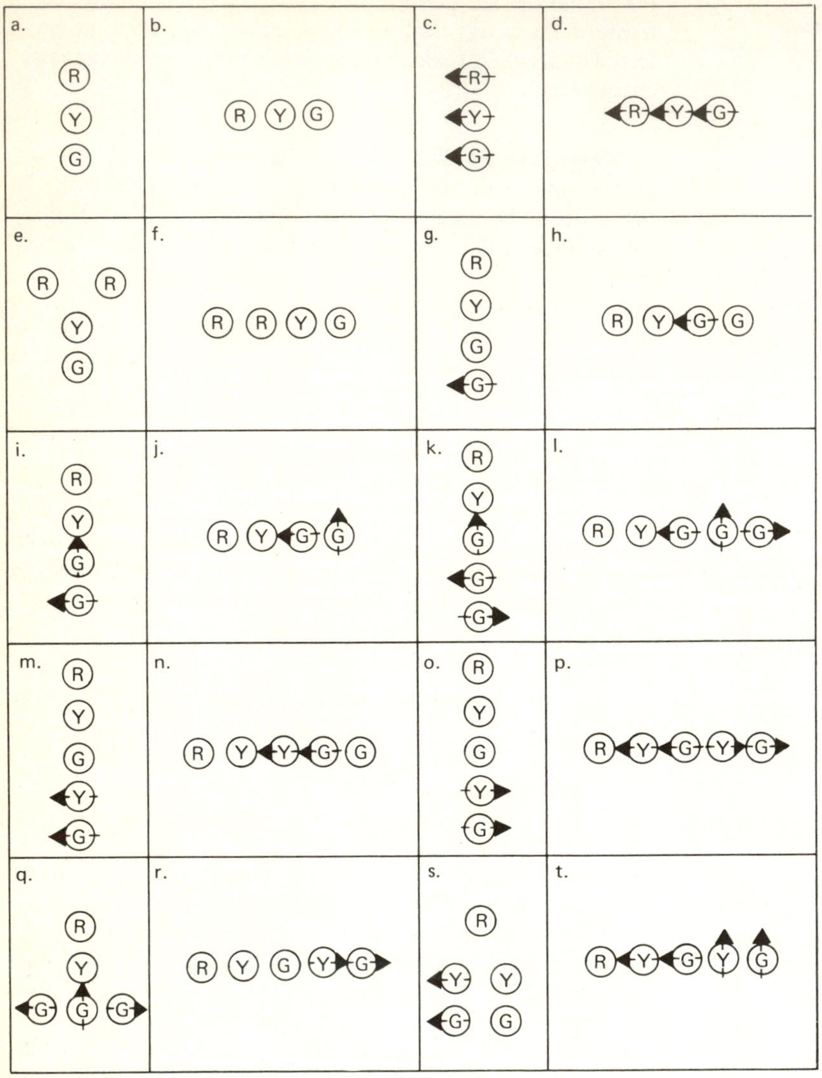

Figure 24.5. Typical arrangements of lenses in signal faces.

Traffic detectors

Types

The effectiveness of a traffic-actuated signal installation or a traffic-responsive signal system depends on its ability to receive indications of vehicle or pedestrian presence or volume. A sophisticated controller can use such data to determine congestion, vehicle speed, and queue length. These data are normally collected by means of a device known as a detector. Table 24-5 summarizes various types of detectors together with their measuring capabilities, method of operation, advantages, and disadvantages.

Installation

The effectiveness and efficiency of signal equipment are greatly affected by proper detector installation. The frequency of repair, either mechanical or electrical, depends on the initial installation. Detectors installed in roadways are more susceptible to damage than those mounted overhead.

Although the physical mounting or location of a detector may be dictated by roadway characteristics and technical limitations, its placement in relation to a controlled intersection determines the effectiveness of signal operation. Distance of the detector from the stop line for simple traffic-actuated signal operation may be as little as one car length. For more sophisticated traffic signal control operation, the distance may vary from one car length up to 500 ft (152 m).

Such detectors as radar, sonic, infrared, and photoelectric are usually mounted on mast arms or span wires over the

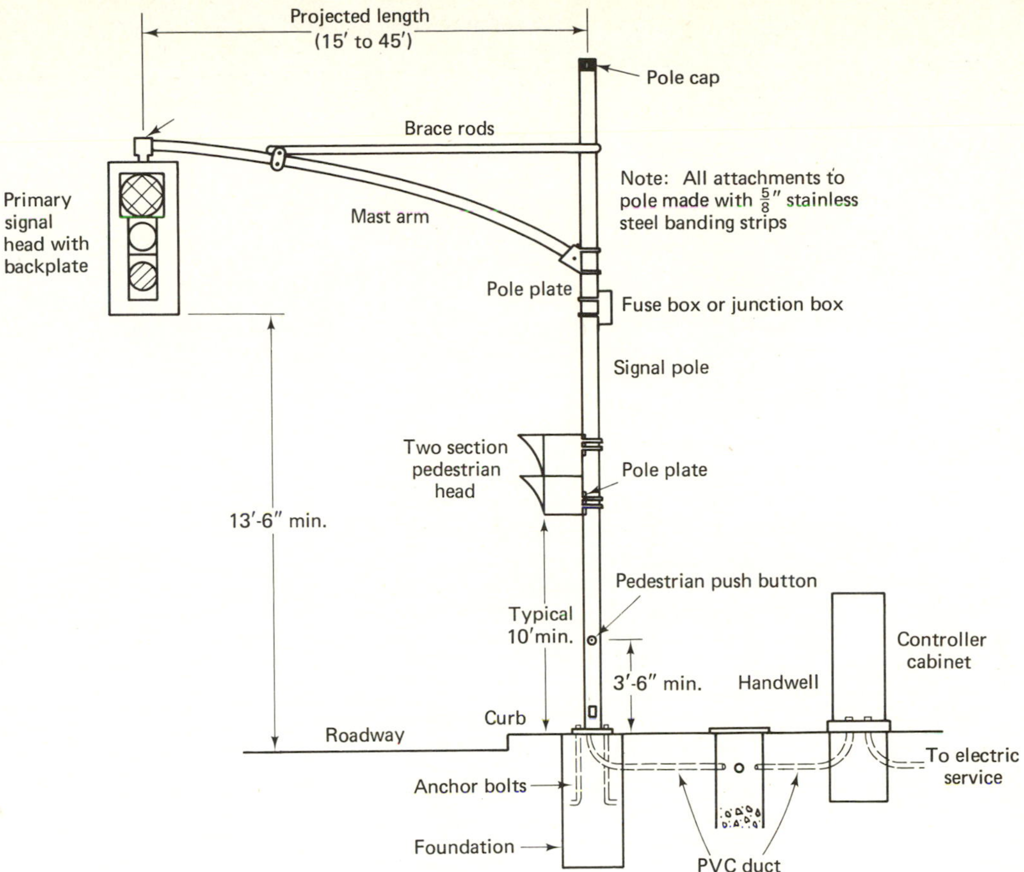

Figure 24.6. Typical signal installation.

lane or lanes of the roadway on which detection is desired. The necessity for providing adequate height for clearance of high loads may result in loss of sensitivity or "overshoot" to other lanes. Because several kinds of overhead detectors utilize the Doppler principle, directional characteristics are difficult to achieve unless narrow beam widths are used, and this may result in a loss of sensitivity.

The most efficient and reliable detectors are the under-pavement magnetic, magnetometer, and loop detectors. Installation of a magnetometer detector requires that a hole, slightly larger than the circular detector, be drilled in the pavement for each detector and the necessary interconnecting sawcuts made for the cables. With epoxy and/or bituminous sealants, this installation is likely to remain operational provided that no physical damage occurs.

To install loop detectors, a rectangular sawcut is made in the pavement from 1½ to 2 in. (3.8 to 5 cm) deep. The area enclosed by this sawcut varies in length in accordance with the application of the detector, but its width is determined by the lane width. Two to four turns of wire are then laid into this sawcut, and the two ends of the loop are jointed to shielded twisted pair cable with a waterproof jacket. This cable has a constant impedance which eliminates one of the variables in tuning to frequency and reduces the possibility of interference pickup of stray electrical fields by the feeder. The sawcuts are then filled with a bituminous mixture or an epoxy or polyurethane material. Most of the epoxy materials result in a rigid loop, which can be damaged by pavement shift. For this reason some users prefer that the slot sealant have the flexible characteristics provided by the bituminous mixtures and the polyurethane.

Once the loop and feeder have been installed, the detector must be tuned unless it is self-tuning. Loop detectors are quite stable and little test equipment is necessary. Some manufacturers provide a special test set with their detectors to assist in determining the values of components that must be added or changed.

Controller interconnection

Interconnection may involve two adjacent controllers, a master controller and several slave controllers on a single street, or a master controller and all controllers in an area system. It provides positive time relationships between signals and thereby ensures an orderly progression of traffic.

Methods

Direct cable. A multiconductor cable, usually of AWG wire size number 19 to number 10, may be run between a

TABLE 24–5
Types of Detectors

Detector	Measuring Capability: Count	Presence	Speed	Occupancy	Queue Length	Method of Operation	Advantages	Disadvantages
Pressure	Yes	No	No	No	No	Weight of vehicle causes closure of metallic contacts to complete a circuit	1. Well-defined detection zone 2. Rugged construction 3. Reliable 4. Relatively inexpensive 5. Capable of detecting all moving vehicles, regardless of speed 6. Low maintenance and easy to repair	1. Counts axles which yields poor count accuracy 2. Does not measure presence 3. Installation may disrupt traffic for excessive period of time 4. Major resurfacing will render it inoperative 5. Susceptible to damage by snowplow 6. Cannot be easily relocated
Magnetic, non-directional	Yes	No	No	No	No	Vehicle passage over wire coil embedded in roadway disturbs earth's lines of flux passing through coil and induces a voltage in the coil; voltage is amplified by high-gain amplifier to operate detector relay	1. Under roadway location and not subject to damage 2. Relatively easy to install 3. Does not necessitate closing of traffic lanes 4. Relative ease of relocation 5. Low maintenance	1. Nondirectional 2. Difficult to set detection zone 3. Subject to false calls where located near large dc lines 4. Cannot detect presence
Magnetic, directional (two-coil version)	Yes	No	No	No	No	Same method of operation as nondirectional magnetic detector	1. Directional 2. Not affected by dc lines in vicinity 3. Well-defined detection zone 4. Low maintenance 5. Under roadway location and not subject to damage	1. Requires closing of traffic lane for installation 2. More expensive than nondirectional magnetic detector 3. Cannot detect presence 4. Cannot be easily relocated
Magnetometer	Yes	Yes	No	Yes	No	Similar method of operation as nondirectional and directional magnetic detectors; makes use of small cylindrical sensing head that is placed below pavement surface	1. Relatively easy to install 2. Capable of measuring count or presence 3. Reliable 4. Not affected by dc lines in vicinity 5. Under roadway location and not subject to damage 6. Relative ease of relocation	1. Requires closing of traffic lane for installation 2. More expensive than nondirectional 3. May double count some vehicles due to magnetic material distribution 4. Poorly defined detection zone
Loop, manual-tuned	Yes	Yes	Yes	Yes	Yes	Vehicle passage cuts magnetic lines of flux that are generated around the loop thereby increasing or decreasing the inductance so that a change is detected and transmitted to an amplifying circuit	1. Size and shape of detection zone can be easily set by size of loop 2. Excellent presence detector 3. Capable of measuring all traffic parameters 4. Relatively easy to install 5. Relatively inexpensive to abandon loop and reuse amplifier at new location 6. Capable of detecting small vehicles 7. Under roadway location and not subject to damage	1. Cost of installation may be excessive 2. Requires closing of traffic lane or lanes for short periods of time 3. Difficult to tune in order to detect small and large vehicles
Loop, self-tuning	Yes	Yes	Yes	Yes	Yes	Same method of operation as manual-tuned loop	Same advantages as manual tuned loop except no initial or periodic tuning required	Same disadvantages as manual-tuned loop except that several poorly shielded amplifiers located in same cabinet may interfere with each other and response time may be slower than manual-tuned loop

TABLE 24–5 (continued)

Detector	Measuring Capability: Count	Presence	Speed	Occupancy	Queue Length	Method of Operation	Advantages	Disadvantages
Radar	Yes	No	Yes	No	No	Passage of vehicle reflects radar microwaves (Doppler principle) back to antenna to operate detector relay	1. Immune to electromagnetic interference 2. Does not necessitate closing of traffic lanes to install	1. Relatively expensive to purchase and install, particularly if existing poles not available for use 2. Requires FCC license to operate 3. Requires experienced personnel for installation and maintenance 4. Does not measure presence
Sonic, pulsed	Yes	Yes	Yes	Yes	Yes	Emits bursts of energy at a rate of approximately 20 times per second; vehicle reduces wavelength resulting in the return signal arriving when receiver is open	1. Does not necessitate closing of traffic lanes to install 2. Does not require FCC license to operate 3. Can be used at locations with unstable pavement 4. Can classify vehicle by height	1. Same as 1 for radar detector 2. Somewhat inaccurate due to conical detection zone and wide variations in vehicle configurations and heights 3. Nondirectional 4. Sensitive to environmental conditions 5. Somewhat inaccurate under congested conditions
Sonic, continuous wave	Yes	No	Yes	No	No	Operates on Doppler principle—same as radar	1. Same as 1, 2, and 3 for pulsed sonic detector plus improved accuracy for speed measurement	1. Same as 1, 4, 5 for pulsed sonic detector 2. Cannot detect presence
Radio frequency	Special application for UTCS Bus Priority System					Bus transmitter sends signal to loop in pavement which relays signal to receiver unit; transmits information on two separate radio frequencies	1. Can be used to select special vehicles 2. Accurate and reliable	1. Relatively expensive to install
Light emission photo electric	Yes	Yes	Yes	Yes	No	Passage of vehicle between light emitter and photoelectric cell interrupts transmitted beam which operates a detector relay	1. Accurate for vehicle passage in a single lane 2. Most suitable for conditions of uniform light	1. Inaccurate for detection of more than one traffic lane
Infrared, interrupted beam	Yes	Yes	Yes	Yes	No	Same as photo-electric detector using infrared part of spectrum	Same as photoelectric	Same as photoelectric
Infrared, reflected beam	Yes	Yes	Yes	Yes	No	Overhead transmitter-receiver notes vehicle passage by change in reflectivity between vehicle and pavement	1. Most suitable for conditions of uniform light	1. Expensive 2. Sensitive to ambient light and color of pavement 3. Sensitive to weather conditions 4. Inaccurate due to reflectivity difference
High-intensity light	Yes	No	No	No	No	High-intensity light emitted from a device mounted on a priority vehicle is received by a light-sensitive detector indicating its presence	1. Provides a means to recognize selected vehicles	1. Expensive

SOURCE: *Traffic Control Systems Handbook*, U.S. Department of Transportation, Federal Highway Administration, U.S. Government Printing Office, Washington, D.C., 1976.

master and a number of slave controllers. The distance between the power source and the controlled relays will determine the size of conductors, because ac and dc voltage drops must be minimized to assure reliable operation. The cables may be installed either overhead or underground, but an underground installation provides the most reliable interconnection.

Radio. Radio control, in connection with a reliable telemetry system, may be used when a central transmitter can be combined with a high antenna in order to provide adequate signals to the controller receivers. This system requires a separate radio receiver and suitable decoding and actuating equipment at each controller intersection. Interference from random electrical disturbances and from other radio channels may disable the system, and maintenance is a high-cost factor. Unless special fail-safe circuits are built into each controller, interference can result in abnormal signal indications being displayed. Nevertheless, the overall reliability of a properly designed, installed, and maintained radio system is comparable with other methods of interconnection. Although not specifically in the radio field, experiments using laser beams have been conducted to determine the feasibility of their use for traffic controller interconnection.

Leased telephone lines. Leased telephone lines and low-level telemetry equipment are used extensively for interconnection of large systems. They offer the advantage of reliability, flexibility, economy, and predictable cost. Leased telephone lines used in conjunction with multiplex equipment can provide sufficient channels for all required functions as dictated by the master controller, as well as provide signal status and detector data. This interconnection medium requires a minimum of maintenance and lends itself to computer-controlled systems.

Coaxial cable. Coaxial or "broadband" cable, which has been used extensively in CATV network applications, is a further network communications alternative for traffic systems. It has a capacity of about five orders of magnitude greater than that of the voice-grade twisted pair offered by the telephone companies. One of the main advantages of coaxial cable is that it can be used for the transmission of video channels, so that TV surveillance of intersection performance is possible. However, a great deal of care must be exercised by contractors during its installation.

Fiber optics. The use of fiber optics as a network communications medium for traffic control systems is a commercial and operational reality. In essence, light is used instead of electricity, photons instead of electrons, and glass fibers instead of copper wire. Electronic signals are converted into light signals either by tiny lasers or by light-emitting diodes. The light signals are then transmitted along the fiber until a photodetector reconverts them into electronic signals that can be processed by conventional equipment. One hair-thin glass fiber can carry as many communications as a coaxial cable several inches in diameter; it is a non-conducting medium with immunity to electromagnetic interference and noise.

Cableless links. British road authorities have developed and tested cableless linking of arterial route signals in a western suburb of London.[18] The linking is achieved by the use of a 24-h digital clock installed at each signalized intersection, synchronized to the frequency of the electrical main power supply, together with a standby battery power supply in the event of a main power failure. Fixed-time, time-of-day signal plans are automatically switched on an arterial route, maintaining coordination within a common cycle length.

Planning considerations

In planning an interconnected communications network for traffic signal control systems, the following factors must be considered:

- Type and format of information
- Speed of information transmission
- Reliability
- Network configuration
- Cost of various communication networks
- Lease versus dedicated network
- Present and future requirements

Taken together, the selection of system components and the determination of the ways in which these components will be utilized in a cost-effective manner make up the communications systems planning task.

Maintenance of signal equipment

A poorly maintained signal system results in frequent breakdowns and brings complaints and discredit to the responsible authority. Because traffic control devices are designed to provide for the safe and efficient movement of vehicles and pedestrians, it is essential that the devices operate reliably and continuously. Emergency maintenance or repair can be very costly, especially if it must be done outside normal working hours. It is much better to choose the time when maintenance is done.

Routine maintenance

Routine maintenance, according to a planned program, can be made to effect definite economies in the operation of any signal system. A simple preventative maintenance program requires (1) regular replacement of lamps before the end of their rated life, (2) overhaul of the moving parts of electromechanical controller units, (3) repainting equipment and hardware and routine checks of voltage, and (4) inspection of the condition of equipment.

[18]F. B. Green and D. I. Robertson, "Traffic Signal Control Using Cableless Linking—The A4 Experiment," *Traffic Eng. Control, 16* (Apr./May 1974).

Accidental damage

A signal installation is exposed to the elements and in some cases to the risk of damage by vehicles. Considerable accidental damage can occur. Poles and controllers are most susceptible to being hit by vehicles, and high wind loads may twist and damage signal heads. Overhead cables are particularly vulnerable to damage and their failure results in loss of some, if not all, signal indications. The importance of locating equipment so that accidental damage is minimized cannot be too strongly stressed.

When damage to a signal installation occurs, it should be repaired immediately so that orderly control of traffic is restored. Failure to keep it operative in a proper manner may be construed as negligence on the part of the traffic authority. To minimize downtime caused by accidents, spare controllers, temporary stands for signal heads, emergency flashers, and a fully equipped maintenance vehicle should always be ready for emergencies. If an installation is going to be out of service for some time, police assistance should be sought and consideration given to the erection of stop signs to provide positive control.

Records

Detailed maintenance records on individual installations should be kept to determine the time interval for routine maintenance and cost analysis.[19] These records will provide information on equipment, reliability, manufacturers' service, and susceptible component failure, and they will consistitute a documented history in the event of litigation involving the responsible authority.

Signal timing

Cycle lengths

A number of terms in signal timing require definition:

1. *Cycle (cycle length):* any complete sequence of signal indications.
2. *Phase (signal phase):* the part of the cycle allocated to any combination of traffic movements receiving right-of-way simultaneously during one or more intervals.
3. *Interval:* the part or parts of the signal cycle during which signal indications do not change.
4. *Offset:* the number of seconds or percent of the cycle length that a defined time reference point at a traffic signal occurs after the time reference point of a master controller or of an adjacent traffic signal.
5. *Split phase:* that portion of a traffic phase that is separated from the primary movement to provide a special phase that is related to a parent phase and characterized by the inability to rest in a minor phase.

[19]S. M. Parapar, "Computerized Reporting for Traffic Signal Maintenance," *Traffic Eng., 43* (July 1973).

The objective of signal timing is to alternate the right-of-way between traffic streams so that the average delay to all vehicles and pedestrians, the total delay to any single group of vehicles or pedestrians, and the possibility of accident-producing conflicts are minimized. These criteria frequently conflict and require compromise based on engineering judgment. For example, to minimize total delay, the number of distinct phases should be kept to a minimum consistent with safety and traffic demands. The usual procedure is to implement two-phase operation whenever possible, such as at normal right-angled intersections, at T intersections, or at midblock locations. However, at irregular multileg intersections or where interphase conflicts are present, multiphase (i.e., three-phase, etc.) operation may become unavoidable in order to resolve vehicular and/or pedestrian conflicts. In the same way, when the need to accommodate exclusive or irregular movements is indicated, the green phase is sometimes split (this application of phasing is termed "split phase"). Illustrative examples are shown in Figure 24.7.

Studies in the United States[20] and elsewhere[21] have demonstrated that longer cycles will accommodate more vehicles per hour, and cycles longer than necessary to accommodate the traffic volume present will produce higher average delays. The best rule is to use the shortest practical cycle length that will serve the traffic demand.

Vehicles stopped at a traffic signal do not instantaneously enter the intersection at minimum headways following display of a green indication. This starting delay has been measured in a number of studies. Greenshields et al.[22] concluded that the first five vehicles in a lane require 14.2 s to enter, whereas succeeding vehicles require 2.1 s each. Thus, a starting delay of 3.7 s is inferred. Capelle and Pinnell,[23] measuring somewhat differently, arrived at a value of 5.8 s for the first two vehicles, followed by a mean-time headway of 2.1 s; this yields a starting delay of 1.6 s. A Traffic Research Corporation study[24] indicated that a motion wave in a queue moves back from the stop line at the rate of 100 ft (30 m) in 6 s. Once the motion wave reaches the detector, located approximately 300 ft (90 m) back from the stop line, detections occur at the rate of one every 2 to 2½ s (in each lane) until either the end of the queue clears the detector or the movement is stopped again by a red light and the queue has closed.

With the known influence of geometrics on intersection capacity, this variation is not surprising. For purposes of general calculation, a starting delay of 2.5 s per phase is a reasonable value, but for more accurate calculation, measurement at the specific intersection is required.

[20]J. H. Kell, "Results of Computer Simulation Studies as Related to Traffic Signal Operation," *Proceedings, Institute of Traffic Engineers, 1963*, pp. 70–107.

[21]F. V. Webster, "Traffic Signal Settings," *Road Res. Tech. Paper No. 39*. London: Her Majesty's Stationery Office, 1958.

[22]B. C. Greenshields, D. Schapiro, and E. L. Erickson, *Traffic Performance at Urban Street Intersections*. New Haven, Conn.: Yale University Bureau of Highway Traffic, 1947.

[23]D. G. Capelle and C. Pinnell, "Capacity Studies of Signalized Diamond Interchanges," *Freeway Des. and Oper. Bull. 291*. Washington, D.C.: Highway Research Board, 1961, pp. 1–25.

[24]L. Casciato and S. Cass, "Pilot Study of the Automatic Control of Traffic Signals by a General Purpose Electronic Computer," *Electron. Traffic Oper. Bull. 338*. Washington, D.C.: Highway Research Board, 1962.

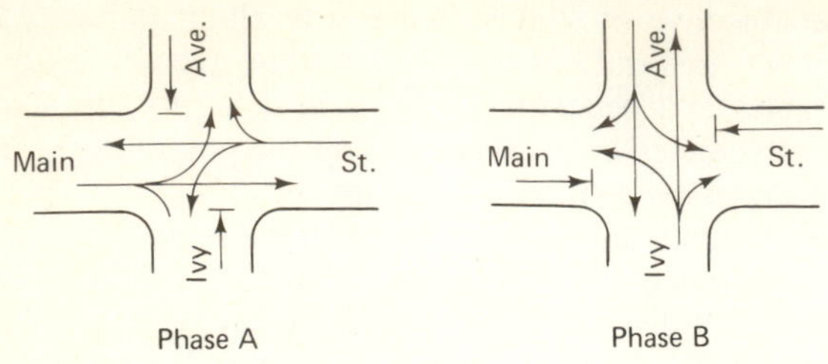

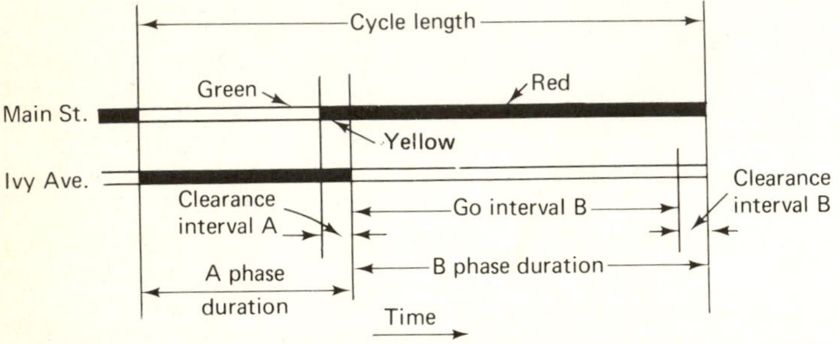

Usual phasing of traffic flow at ordinary right-angle intersection. Two, two-way traffic streams

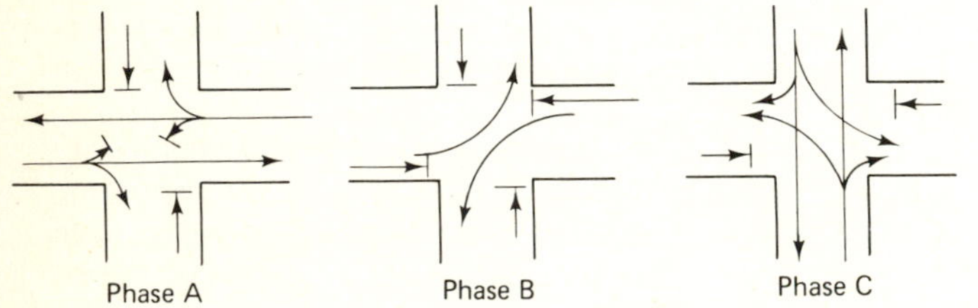

Use of three phases at ordinary, "right-angle" intersection. Two, two-way traffic streams with separate phase provided for left turns

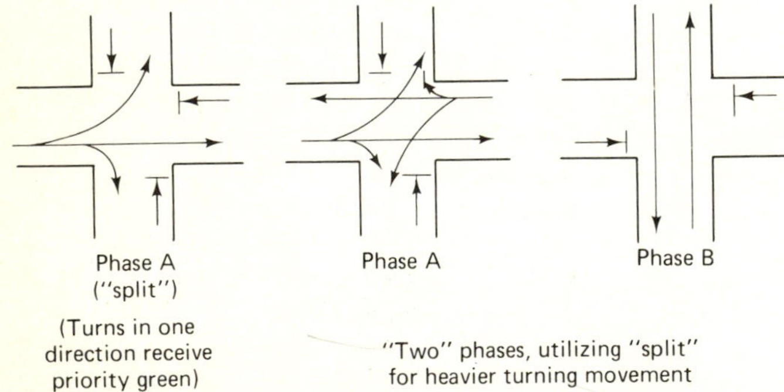

(Turns in one direction receive priority green)

"Two" phases, utilizing "split" for heavier turning movement

Figure 24.7. Phasing of traffic flows. SOURCE: Theodore Matson, Wilbur S. Smith, and Frederick W. Hurd, *Traffic Engineering*, New York: McGraw-Hill, 1955, p. 328.

In addition, there is in each phase a yellow change interval (and possibly a red clearance interval) that is not efficiently used for traffic movement. Thus, over any time period, a short cycle with a larger number of starting delays and yellow intervals will produce more lost time and accommodate fewer vehicles.

With pretimed controller units, for a long cycle to be efficient, there must be a constant demand during the entire green period on each approach. As the cycle and green periods lengthen, there is less probability that demand will be present during the latter portions of the green interval, whereas a higher average delay must occur for all vehicles waiting on the corresponding red interval. This produces a higher total delay. The selection of an appropriate cycle length is, then, an effort to select the shortest cycle that will accommodate the demand present and at the same time minimize the average delay.

Isolated signals

An isolated signal is one at which the timing is independent of any signal control in the vicinity. It is generally at an intersection too remote from other signal locations to require network coordination, and as such should not be normally operated in a pretimed mode. Numerous methods are in use for estimating the appropriate green time for each phase at individual intersections. Although the methods described in this section may seem to apply to two-phase operation, these same techniques may be used to calculate timing for any desired number of phases.

Whenever pedestrians are present, the minimum green for each phase is normally set by pedestrian requirements. In other words, the phase time should provide sufficient walking time for a pedestrian to clear the conflict zone prior to the release of opposing vehicles. The *MUTCD* states that under normal circumstances the walk interval should be at least 4 to 7 s so that pedestrians will have adequate opportunity to leave the curb before the clearance interval is shown.

A walking speed of 4 ft/s (1.2 m/s) is frequently used to calculate the minimum vehicle green indication requirement; in general terms, however, the relationship between minimum green and pedestrian walking speed is

$$G = \frac{D}{v_p} \tag{24.1}$$

where G = minimum green time in seconds

D = length in feet (or meters) of the longest crosswalk in use during the phase

v_p = pedestrian walking speed in feet (or meters) per second

On wide, divided roadways with median widths of at least 6 ft (1.8 m), it is sometimes necessary to provide sufficient crossing time only to reach the median island. Here pedestrians would cross in two cycles.

When pedestrians are not present, the minimum green time may be set by a practical vehicle operational minimum, usually taken to be 12 s. However, with actuated controller units and a single vehicle on an approach, the green interval could be only 2 or 3 s, if the controller unit was operated with a red rest.

The determination of green time above these minimum values is based on (1) proportioning the green time among the approaches so that the ratio of capacity to demand on each of the critical approaches is approximately equal, and (2) having each green interval of sufficient length so that almost all phases during the peak demand periods are long enough to accommodate all traffic that has accumulated prior to the beginning of the green phase and the traffic arriving during the green phase.

Timing optimization

Examples of some of the approaches to optimizing traffic signal timing are outlined below.

Webster method. Webster developed a model for computing the approximate cycle length that will minimize total intersection delay as well as the effective green time for each approach[25] as follows:

$$C_o = \frac{1.5L + 5}{1.0 - Y_1 - Y_2 - \ldots - Y_n} \qquad (24.2)$$

where C_o = optimum cycle length in seconds

L = total lost time per cycle, generally taken as the sum of the total yellow and all red clearance per cycle in seconds

Y = volume/saturation flow[26] for the critical approach in each phase

Webster further recommended that the distribution of the green time to each phase be proportional to the critical lane volumes on each phase. The formula for determining the net green time for a two-phase intersection is

$$G_t(\text{net green time}) = C_o - A_1 - A_2 - nl \qquad (24.3)$$

where C_o = optimum cycle length in seconds

A_1 = yellow change interval in seconds on phase 1

A_2 = yellow change interval in seconds on phase 2

n = number of phases (in this example = 2)

l = lost time per phase in seconds

Examples of the variation of delay with cycle length are shown in Figure 24.8. It has been found that for cycle lengths within the range from ¾ to 1½ times the optimum value, the delay is never more than 10 to 20% above that given by the optimum cycle.

ALE method. The Average Loaded Phase Expanded (ALE) method[27] utilizes direct field observations to obtain approach capacity. Vehicle departure data for an intersection approach and the number of loaded cycles (as defined in the *Highway Capacity Manual*) are recorded cycle by cycle. Utilizing these field data, the capacity in vehicles per hour (q_{max}) can be calculated as follows:

$$q_{max} = \frac{N}{n}\left(\sum_{i=1}^{n} q_i\right) \qquad (24.4)$$

where N = number of cycles per hour

n = number of loaded cycles per hour

q_i = number of departures during the ith loaded cycle

By multiplying q_{max} by the existing cycle/green ratio, capacity in vehicles per hour of green is obtained. This value can be used for redesigning the existing signal timing by means of the following expression:

[25] F. V. Webster and B. M. Cobbe, "Traffic Signals," *Road Res. Tech. Paper No. 56*. London: Her Majesty's Stationery Office, 1966, pp. 55–60.

[26] Saturation flow is defined as the flow that would be obtained if there were a continuous queue of vehicles and they were given 100% green time. It is generally expressed in vehicles per hour of green time.

[27] E. F. Reilly and J. Seifert, "Capacity of Signalized Intersections," *Highway Res. Rec. No. 321*. Washington, D.C.: Highway Research Board, 1970.

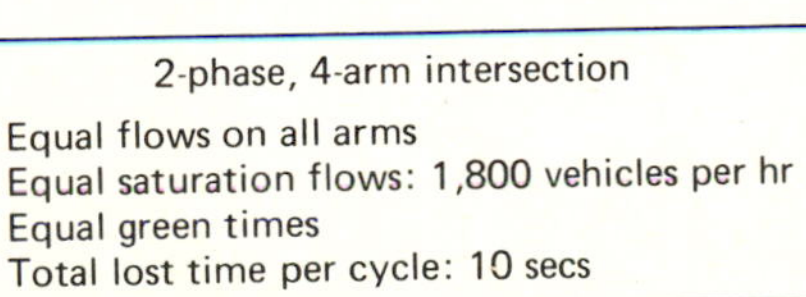

2-phase, 4-arm intersection
Equal flows on all arms
Equal saturation flows: 1,800 vehicles per hr
Equal green times
Total lost time per cycle: 10 secs

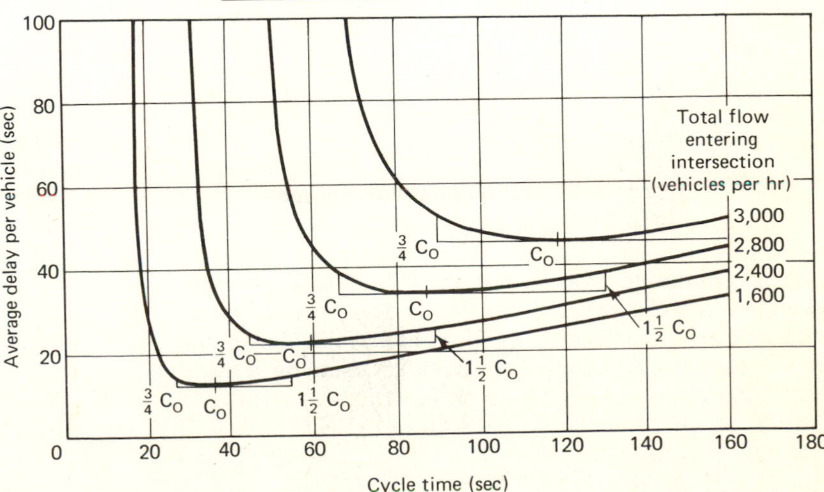

Figure 24.8. Effect on delay of variation of cycle length. Source: *Research on Road Traffic*, London, England: Her Majesty's Stationery Office, 1965, p. 306.

$$\frac{g}{c} = \frac{V}{Kq'_{max}} \quad (24.5)$$

where g/c = green/cycle ratio

V = existing volume in vehicles per hour

q'_{max} = capacity in vehicles per hour of green obtained from the loaded cycle data

K = an adjustment factor ranging from 0.0 to 1.0 to allow for loading conditions; a value of 0.8 to 0.9 is suggested

The capacity value obtained by the ALE method inherently takes into account all traffic variables existing at an approach, provided that an adequate number of loaded cycle samples is obtained. This method is applicable for checking or upgrading an existing signal operation.

Bellis's method. Bellis[28] assumed that vehicle arrivals at an intersection were randomly or Poisson-distributed. The probability (P) of N arrivals or less is given by

(See Errata for clarification.)

$$P(N) = \sum_{x=0}^{N} \frac{(VC/3600)^x e^{\frac{-VC}{3600}}}{X!} \quad (24.6)$$

where V = volumes in vehicles per hour

C = cycle length in seconds

$P(N)$ = design probability level

The green time should be such that the maximum number of expected arrivals (N) at the design probability level can clear an approach. The higher the design probability level, the higher the level of service provided. Bellis used the following equation to calculate the required green time:

$$G = PN + \frac{K}{S}\sqrt{\left[W+H(N-1)\right]\left[W+H(N-1)+\frac{S^2}{4}\right]} \quad (24.7)$$

where G = required green time in seconds

P = perception and reaction time in seconds

N = maximum number of vehicles to be cleared on the critical lane

K = constant

S = speed limit in miles per hour

W = intersection longitudinal width in feet

H = vehicle spacing in feet

Using a design probability level of 95% and an intersection width of 50 ft (15.2 m), Bellis developed a number of signal timing design charts for various vehicular speeds based on passenger car units. By first assuming a cycle length, the green time for each phase can be obtained from the design chart. This procedure is repeated until the sum of green time plus clearance intervals is equal to the assumed cycle length. A typical design chart is shown in Figure 24.9. Similar charts for other design conditions and for other probability levels can easily be prepared and applied to the design of signal timing.

Failure-rate method. This method[29,30] is based on a design procedure using the percentage of cycle failures (defined as any cycle during which approach arrivals exceed the capacity for departures). The departure rate during a green phase may be obtained from the formula

$$X = \frac{G - (K - D)}{D} \quad (24.8)$$

where X = maximum departures per lane during green

G = green phase, including the yellow change interval

D = average minimum headway

K = sum of starting delay and time for last vehicle to clear intersection

If V is the volume on the critical approach lane and C is the cycle length, then the average arrivals per cycle (M) is

$$M = \frac{VC}{3600} \quad (24.9)$$

where $C = \Sigma\, G$, the sum of all green and yellow phases.

The percentage of cycle failures is defined as the probability (P) that (X) vehicles or more arrive during a cycle. Assuming a Poisson distribution,

$$P_{(x+1)(m)} = \sum_{x+1}^{\infty} \frac{m^{x+1} e^{-m}}{(x+1)!} \quad (24.10)$$

It is suggested by Drew and Pinnell that a practical design failure rate in the foregoing method should be about 10 to 15% of the peak-hour cycles.

Solving the preceding four equations by successive approximations, the cycle length and green phase times for a given design failure rate can be found. The computation procedures can be simplified through the use of a design chart as shown in Figure 24.10.

Australian Road Capacity Guide method. Based on the Webster model, the Australian Road Research Board (ARRB)[31-33] developed a similar signal timing design

[28] W. R. Bellis, "Capacity of Traffic Signals and Traffic Signal Timing," *Highway Res. Board Bull. No. 271*. Washington, D.C.: Highway Research Board, 1960.

[29] D. Drew and C. Pinnell, "A Study of Peaking Characteristics of Signalized Urban Intersection as Related to Capacity and Design," *Highway Res. Board Bull. No. 352*. Washington, D.C.: Highway Research Board, 1962.

[30] J. E. Tidwell and J. B. Humphreys, "Relation of Signalized Intersection Level of Service to Failure Rate and Average Individual Delay," *Highway Res. Rec. No. 321*. Washington, D.C.: Highway Research Board, 1970.

[31] A. J. Miller, "The Capacity of Signalized Intersections in Australia," *Road Res. Board Bull. No. 3*, Mar. 1968.

[32] "Signalized Intersections—Capacity Guide," *Res. Rep. AAR No. 79*, Australian Road Research Board, Apr. 1978.

[33] A. J. Miller, "On the Australian Road Capacity Guide," *Highway Res. Rec. No. 289*. Washington, D.C.: Highway Research Board, 1969.

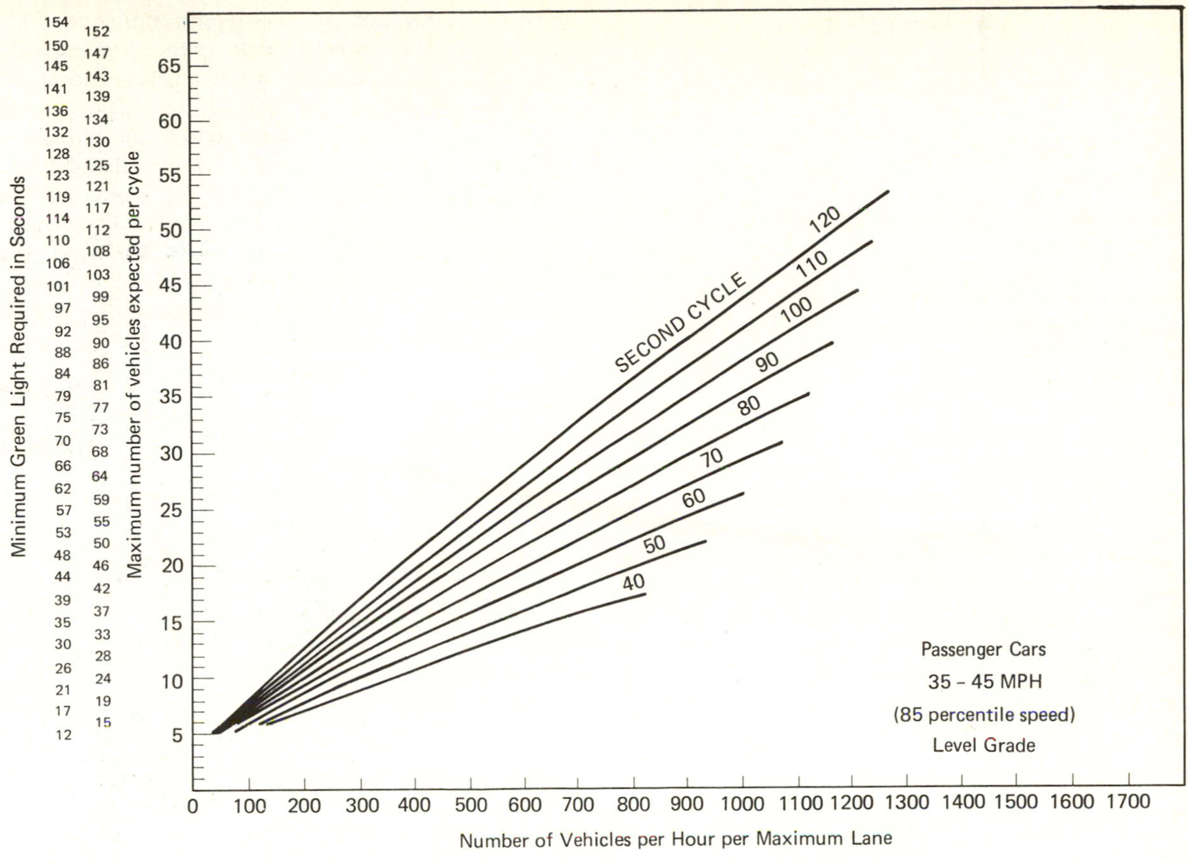

Figure 24.9. Typical Bellis signal design chart.

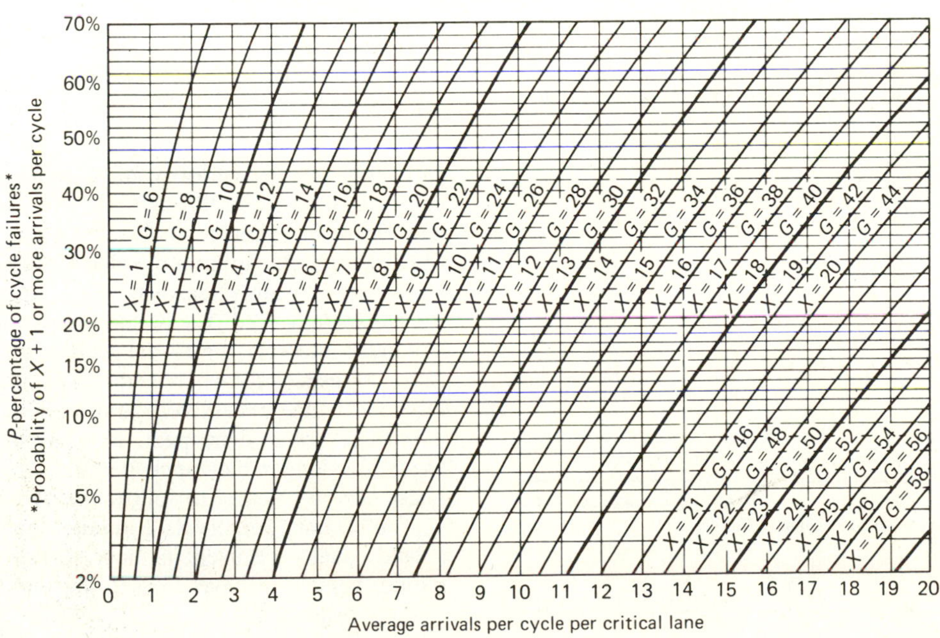

Figure 24.10. Failure rate method design chart.

method. In the ARRB method, however, saturation flow is analyzed based on the number of lanes rather than the approach width, which is considered to be an improvement over Webster's method. Tables of saturation flow with adjustment factors and lost-time values were developed from field data collected across Australia. The ARRB introduced slightly different delay formulas, and also equations for computing probability of clearing queues.

The optimum cycle length (C_0) for minimum overall average delay at an intersection is given by

$$C_0 = \frac{L + 2.2\sqrt{L/S}}{1 - Y} \quad (24.11)$$

where L = total lost time

Y = sum of critical flow to saturation flow ratios

S = lowest of saturation flows among the critical movements

Alternatively, the ARRB suggested that the Y value should be less than 0.7 in order to provide a reasonable level of service. A Y value of 0.7 is equivalent to a 65 to 85% probability of queue clearance.

Canadian Manual on Uniform Traffic Control Devices method.[34] By way of contrast, the *Manual on Uniform Traffic Control Devices for Canada* presents a table of phase time, which is the sum of the green and yellow change intervals required to provide a 95% probability that all vehicles arriving at an approach during a complete signal cycle will be able to clear during the next green interval. If the equivalent hourly volume in the heavy direction for each signal phase is known, the required time interval for any phase can be found in Table 24-6 by equating the volume for that phase against the sum of the volumes for all other phases.

TABLE 24–6
Phase-Time Requirements

Sum of the Equivalent Hourly Volume in the Heavy Direction on All Other Phases	Phase Time (s) Required When the Equivalent Hourly Approach Volume Is:											
	50	100	150	200	250	300	350	400	450	500	550	600
200	11	12	13	14	15	16	17	19	21	23	26	29
250	11	12	13	14	16	17	18	20	22	24	27	30
300	11	12	13	14	16	17	19	20	22	24	29	32
350	11	12	13	14	16	17	19	21	23	26	30	34
400	11	12	13	15	16	18	20	22	25	28	32	37
450	11	12	14	15	17	19	21	23	26	30	35	41
500	11	12	14	15	17	19	22	25	28	33	38	45
550	11	12	14	15	17	20	23	26	31	36	42	51
600	11	13	14	16	18	21	24	28	33	39	48	60
650	11	13	14	16	19	23	26	31	37	44	56	73
700	11	13	15	17	20	24	28	34	41	52	68	97
750	11	14	15	17	21	26	31	38	48	63	88	143
800	12	14	16	19	23	28	34	43	57	81	132	—
850	12	14	17	20	25	31	40	52	74	121	—	—
900	12	14	18	22	27	35	47	67	110	—	—	—
950	12	15	19	24	31	42	60	99	—	—	—	—
1000	13	16	20	27	36	53	88	210	—	—	—	—

SOURCE: *Manual on Uniform Traffic Control Devices for Canada*, Metric Ed., copyright Roads and Transportation Association of Canada, 1976.

Yellow change and clearance intervals

At the termination of a green phase, motorists approaching a signalized intersection are advised by a yellow signal indication that the red interval is about to commence[35]. The speed and location of some approaching vehicles will be such that they can stop safely at the stop line; others will have to continue at their speed or even accelerate into or through the intersection. The minimum length of the clearance interval (which may include an all-red interval after the yellow indication) should accommodate both situations and eliminate the possibility of a dilemma zone in which a driver can neither stop safely nor legally proceed into or through the intersection. See Table 24-7.

Gazis et al[36] analyzed this situation as follows. In order to come to a safe halt at the stop line:

$$x = t \cdot v + \frac{v^2}{2a} \quad (24.12)$$

where x = the distance required for stopping (in ft or m)

t = the perception-reaction time (in s)

v = approach speed (in ft/s or m/s)

a = deceleration rate (in ft/s² or m/s²)

A driver at distance x from the intersection is in the most critical position. This driver can proceed *into* the intersection if the clearance time is at least:

$$\tau_{min} = \frac{x}{v} = t + \frac{v}{2a} \quad (24.13a)$$

or *through* the intersection if the clearance time is at least:

$$\tau_{min} = \frac{x + w + L}{v} = t + \frac{v}{2a} + \frac{w + L}{v} \quad (24.13b)$$

where τ_{min} = the minimum clearance interval (in s)

w = the width of the intersection (in ft or m)

L = the length of the vehicle (in ft or m)

In jurisdictions whose vehicle codes permit vehicles to enter the intersection throughout the yellow change interval and clear after the red indication has appeared, equation (24.13a) gives the minimum value for the clearance interval. However, for safety reasons, yellow intervals of less than 3 s are seldom used. Local conditions may require the use of longer intervals, up to the values obtained by equation (24.13b), especially where sight distances at the intersection are poor. Since excessively long yellow indications might encourage driver disrespect, a maximum of about 5 s is used; if a longer clearance period is required, an all-red phase can be inserted to follow the yellow period.

The clearance intervals computed by equation (24.13b) should usually be used in those jurisdictions whose laws require vehicle to have crossed the intersection before the red indication appears.

Traffic signal system timing for arterial routes

A signal system is defined as having two or more individual signal installations which are linked together for co-

[34] "Traffic Control Signal Timing," *Manual on Uniform Traffic Control Devices for Canada*, Metric Ed., Apr. 1978.

[35] In Great Britain it is the practice to use the yellow clearance interval before the beginning of green as well as before the beginning of red. This is not permitted in the *Manual on Uniform Traffic Control Devices*.

[36] D. GAZIS, R. HERMAN, AND A. MARADUDIN, "The Problem of the Amber Signal Light Traffic Flow." *Oper. Res.* 8(1), 112–132, (1960).

TABLE 24–7
Minimum Theoretical Clearance Intervals* for Different Approach Speeds, Vehicle Lengths, and Cross Street Widths

Approach Speed mph	τ_{min} to Enter Intersection (24.13a)	τ_{min} to Clear Intersection for Combined Vehicle Length and Crossing Street Width ($w + L$) (Formula)(24.13b)				
		60 ft	80 ft	100 ft	120 ft	140 ft
20	3.0†	4.5	5.2	5.9	6.6	7.2
30	3.2	4.6	5.0	5.5	5.9	6.4
40	3.9	5.0	5.3	5.6	6.0	6.3
50	4.7	5.5	5.8	6.0	6.3	6.6
60	5.4	6.1	6.3	6.5	6.8	7.0

*In seconds; assumed value of $t = 1$ s, of $a = 10$ ft/s^2.
†Minimum interval considered safe.

Note: 1 mph = 1.61 km/h; 1 ft = 0.305 m.

ordination purposes. To obtain system coordination all signals must operate with the same (common) cycle length, although in rare instances some intersections within the system may operate at double or one-half the cycle length of the system. The usual practice for actuated signals within a coordinated system is to provide a common cycle length as a background cycle with an appropriate main street offset. Although at individual intersections, the intervals (red, green, and yellow) may vary according to traffic conditions, it is desirable that the arterial for which coordination is being provided have a green plus yellow interval equivalent to at least 50% of the cycle length. Two intersecting systems form an open network whenever they have only one intersection in common (see Figure 24.11, upper left), and three or more systems form a closed network whenever they have three or more common intersections (see Figure 24.11, upper right).

Advantages

Some of the advantages of providing coordination among signals are:

1. A higher level of traffic service is provided in terms of higher overall speed and reduced number of stops.
2. Traffic should flow more smoothly, often with an improvement in capacity and decrease in energy consumption.
3. Vehicle speeds should be more uniform because there will be no incentive to travel at excessively high speed to reach a signalized intersection before the start of the green interval, yet slower drivers will be encouraged to speed up to avoid having to stop for a red light.
4. There should be fewer accidents because platoons of vehicles will arrive at each signal when it is green, thereby reducing the possibility of red-signal violations or rear-end collisions. Naturally, if there are fewer red intervals displayed to the majority of motorists, there is less likely to be trouble because of driver inattention, brake failure, slippery pavement, and so on.
5. Greater obedience to the signal commands should be obtained from both motorists and pedestrians because the motorist will try to keep within the green interval, and the pedestrian will stay at the curb because the vehicles will be closer spaced.
6. Through traffic will tend to stay on the arterial street instead of on parallel minor streets.

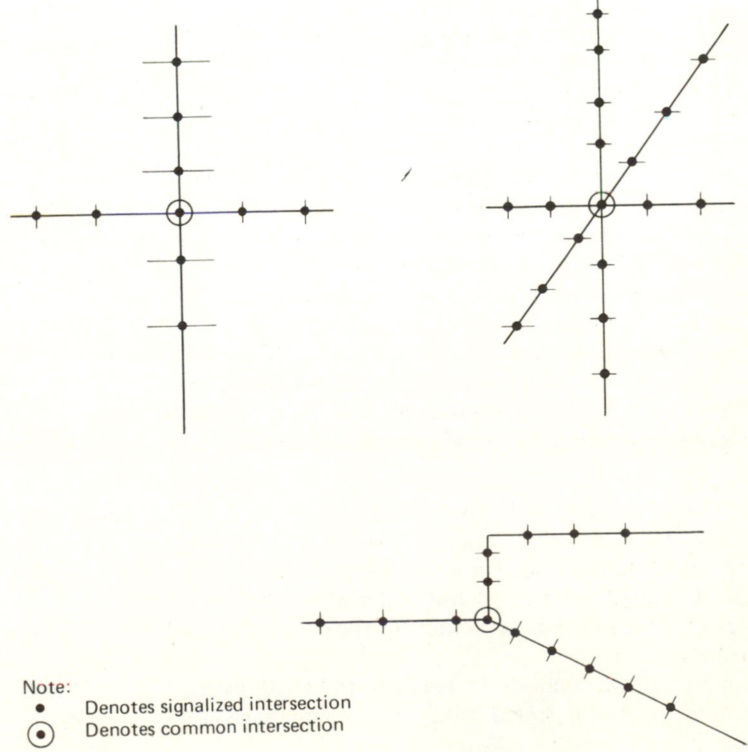

Figure 24.11. Examples of open networks.

Applications

In a discussion of the two-way and one-way street applications of system timing, the following terms are frequently used:

1. *Through-band:* the space between a pair of parallel speed lines which delineates a progressive movement on a time–space chart.
2. *Band speed:* the slope of the through-band representing the progression speed of traffic moving along the arterial.
3. *Bandwidth:* the width of the through-band expressed in seconds (or percent of cycle length), indicating the period of time available for traffic to flow within the band.

One-way street. The simplest form of coordinating signals is along a one-way street, or to favor one direction of traffic on a two-way street that contains highly directional traffic flows. Essentially, the mathematical relationship between the band speed S and the offset L can be described as

$$S\text{ (mph)} = \frac{D\text{ (ft)}}{1.47L} \qquad (24.14)$$

or $$S\text{ (km/h)} = \frac{D\text{ (m)}}{0.278L}$$

where S = speed of progression

D = spacing of signals

L = offset in seconds

Two-way street. For a two-way movement, four general progressive signal systems are possible: (1) simultaneous, (2) alternate, (3) limited (simple) progressive, and (4) flexible progressive. The relative efficiency of any of these systems is dependent on the distances between signalized intersections, the speed of traffic, the cycle length, the roadway capacity, and the amount of friction caused by turning vehicles, parking and unparking maneuvers, improper or illegal parking or loading, and pedestrians. In general, a two-way progression with maximum bandwidths can be achieved only if the signal spacings are such that vehicular travel times between signals are a multiple of one-half the common cycle length; otherwise, inevitable compromises have to be made in the progression design. A discussion of the four general progressive signal systems follows.

Simultaneous System. All signals along a given street operate with the same cycle length and display the green indication at the same time. Under this system, all traffic moves at one time, and a short time later all traffic stops at the nearest signalized intersection to allow cross-street traffic to move.

The mathematical relationship between the band speed (in both directions) and signal spacing in a simultaneous system can be described as follows:

$$S\text{ (mph)} = \frac{D\text{ (ft)}}{1.47C} \qquad (24.15)$$

or $$S\text{ (km/h)} = \frac{D\text{ (m)}}{0.278C}$$

where S = speed of progression

D = spacing of signals

C = cycle length in seconds

For example, a system of signalized intersections at ½-mi or ½-km spacing could have a band speed in a simultaneous system of 30 mph or 30 km/h, respectively, with a 60-s cycle. With closely spaced intersections, however, a simultaneous system may encourage excessive speeds as drivers attempt to travel through a maximum number of intersections during the green interval.

Alternate System. Each successive signal or group of signals shows opposite indications to that of the next signal or group. If each signal alternates with those immediately adjacent, the system is called *single alternate.* If pairs of signals alternate with adjacent pairs, the system is termed *double alternate;* and so on.

The band speed in a single-alternate system is

$$S\text{ (mph)} = \frac{D\text{ (ft)}}{0.735C} \qquad (24.16)$$

or $$S\text{ (km/h)} = \frac{D\text{ (m)}}{0.139C}$$

In a double-alternate system, the band speed is determined by the same formula, with D being the distance between the midpoints of adjacent pairs. Generally speaking, the alternate system may provide excellent traffic service, depending on the distances between signals and the cycle length. Equal distances provide the best results.

Limited or Simple Progressive System. This system uses a common cycle length, and the various signal faces controlling a given street provide green indications in accordance with a time schedule to permit continuous operation of platoons along the street at a designed rate of speed, which may vary within different parts of the system.

Flexible Progressive System. This is a refinement of the limited progressive system where the signal offsets, splits, and/or cycle length of the common cycle are changed to suit the needs of traffic throughout the day. For example, an inbound progression toward the central business district during the morning peak can be changed to an outbound progression during the remainder of the day merely by adjusting the signal offsets, or a longer cycle length can be used during the morning and evening peak hours in order to provide greater capacity than during the off-peak period.

Progressive signal system design

Selection of a cycle length. In the selection of a trial cycle length, the criterion that band speeds be at or near the mean operating speed of vehicles on the street is frequently used. If the spacing of signals in the system is fairly regular, equations (24.14) to (24.16) may be solved for C (cycle length) by using the measured operating speed for S and the typical distance between proposed signals for D. The resultant cycle lengths falling in a usable range should be compared with the cycle length computed for each individual intersection. If one cycle length approximates or slightly exceeds those computed for a majority of individual intersections, it should be selected on a trial basis. First, however, each individual intersection must be reexamined to assure that it can operate effectively with the selected cycle. Sometimes rephasing or geometric and/or operational improvements at an intersection will be required. If such changes are not feasible, and the operation with this cycle would be seriously impaired at one or more intersections, a new trial cycle length should be selected. In practice, the cycle length already established for signal systems intersecting or closely adjacent to the system under study will frequently dictate the cycle length to be used.

Manual design method for arterial routes. To develop an arterial-based timing plan, a considerable amount of data must be collected initially, including

- Intersection spacing
- Street geometrics
- Traffic volumes
- Traffic regulations such as parking, speed limit, and turn restrictions
- Speed and delay information

Using the data, a number of timing plans are then determined together with the individual timing requirements at each signalized location. For each plan a cycle length is selected which is common to the arterial route, and a graphical analysis of the type illustrated in Figure 24.12 is undertaken by a trial-and-error process to determine offsets for each of the desired timing plans.

Figure 24.12 is a two-dimensional graph portraying a two-directional coordinated arterial system with distance on the horizontal scale and time on the vertical scale. The intersections are located on the distance scale with vertical reference lines drawn at the centerline of all signalized intersections. A horizontal working line is drawn across the graph on which the green or red phase of each signalized intersection is centered. Starting at the first signalized intersection at the left edge of the diagram, signal phases are

Figure 24.12. Typical time-space diagram.

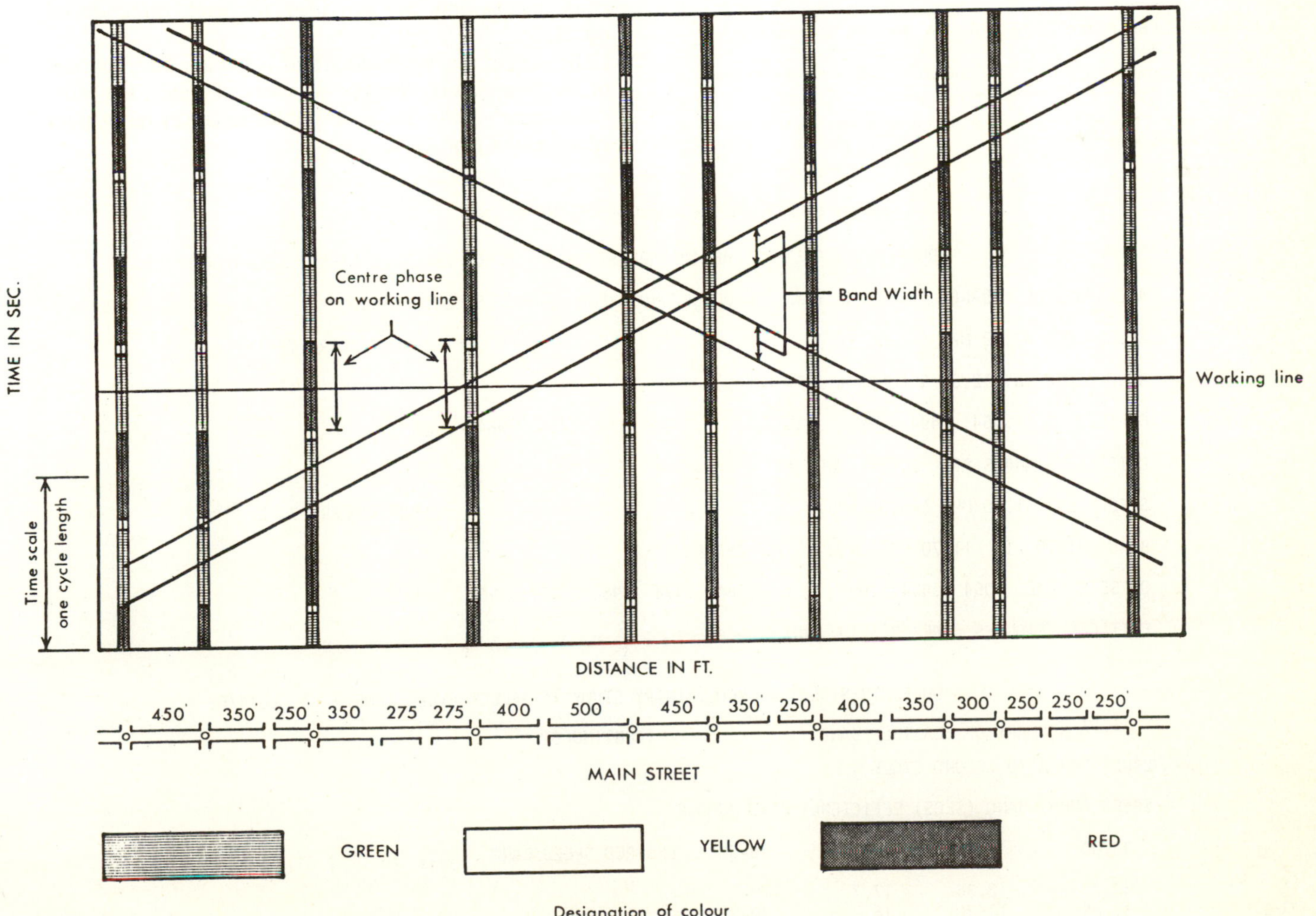

constructed on the vertical reference line with either a green or red phase centered on the working line. A progression speed line which has a slope representing the desired progression speed is drawn starting at the beginning of the green phase at the first signalized intersection. For each succeeding intersection, either a red or green signal phase is centered on the horizontal working line to obtain an equal bandwidth for each direction of flow. Should progressive movement be desired in only one direction, this procedure may be modified such that the beginning of the green phase at each intersection is placed on the progression speed line.

Computer-based time space design methods for arterial systems. The manual or graphical solutions are subject to human error and, more important, require extensive worker hours of staff time. For this reason, these procedures have been reduced for computer solution. Three examples are SIGART,[37] the Maximal Bandwidth method,[38–41] and Difference-of-Offsets method.[42]

[37] "SIGART Program," *Program Documentation Manual*. Toronto: Metropolitan Toronto Roads and Traffic Department, Apr. 1965.

[38] M. Wohl and B. V. Martin, "Capacity-Performance Relationships for Time-Sharing or Signalized Intersections," in *Traffic System Analysis for Engineers and Planners*. New York: McGraw-Hill, 1967, pp. 426–495.

[39] J. D. C. Little, "The Synchronization of Traffic Signals by Mixed-Integer Linear Programming," *Oper. Res., 14*(4), 568–594 (1964).

[40] J. D. C. Little, B. V. Martin, and J. T. Morgan, "Synchronizing Traffic Signals for Maximal Bandwidth," *Highway Res. Rec. No. 118*. Washington, D.C.: Highway Research Board, 1966.

[41] J. T. Morgan and J. D. C. Little, "Synchronizing Traffic Signals for Maximal Bandwidth," *Oper. Res., 12*(6), 896–912 (1964).

[42] J. A. Hillier, "Appendix to Glasgow's Experiment in Area Traffic Control," *Traffic Eng. Control, 8* (Jan. 1966).

SIGART. The SIGART program produces all possible through-bands (wider than some desired minimum) on an arterial route within a specified progression speed range for all feasible cycle lengths. The traffic engineer can then evaluate these through-bands in relation to the specific arterial and select the most desirable for existing conditions. Program inputs include (1) the number of signalized intersections along the section under consideration; (2) the number of cycles to be tested; (3) three speed values (in mph or ft/s): the desired speed, the maximum speed to be considered, and the minimum speed that would allow an acceptable minimum bandwidth; (4) the cycle lengths in seconds; (5) the percent of cycle that is red at each intersection; and (6) the centerline-to-centerline distances between signalized intersections.

The program computes every possible through-band within the specified speed range for each requested cycle length. As each feasible band is found, the program produces the data shown in Figure 24.13.

Maximal Bandwidth Method. The Maximal Bandwidth method optimizes signal offsets to produce maximal bandwidths along an arterial route given the cycle length, signal splits, signal spacing, and progression speeds, and subject to the following conditions:

1. If the platoons in both directions are equal, maximum equal bandwidths are provided for each direction of travel.
2. If the sum of the two bandwidths is greater than the sum of the two platoon lengths (in units of time), the individual bandwidths are made proportional (as far as possible) to the platoon lengths.

Figure 24.13. Sample output of SIGART program.

```
                DUFFERIN STREET -- PRELIMINARY STUDY TO SELECT CYCLE LENGTH     22/4/68

ALL  POSSIBLE  BANDS  GREATER  THAN  10.00 SECONDS  FOR  A  70  SECOND  CYCLE

SPEED  IS  32.72 MPH (48.00 FPS)                                  BAND NUMBER  70-1

BAND WIDTH IS  12.36 SECONDS ( .177 CYCLE)

OFFSETS ARE  .064  .494  .994  .539  .964  .474  .954  .459  .964  .989

CRITICAL SIGNALS ARE  2,  9, AND  10

SPEED  IS  31.28 MPH (45.88 FPS)                                  BAND NUMBER  70-2

BAND  WIDTH  IS  11.70  SECONDS ( .167 CYCLE)

OFFSETS  ARE  .064  .494  .994  .539  .964  .474  .954  .459  .964  .489

CRITICAL  SIGNALS  ARE  2,  10, AND 4


                DUFFERIN STREET -- PRELIMINARY STUDY TO SELECT CYCLE LENGTH     22/4/68

 ....' SUMMARY OF FEASIBLE BANDS .....           (CONTINUED)

BANDS FOR A 70 SECOND CYCLE

SPEED (MPH) BAND (SECS) EFFICIENCY BAND NUMBER

  30.00        7.88        11.3        70-0    DESIRED SPEED BAND

  32.73       12.36        17.7        70-1
  31.28       11.70        16.7        70-2
```

3. If the sum of the two bandwidths is less than the sum of the two platoon lengths, the larger platoon is first accommodated, if possible, and then as much bandwidth as can be arranged is given to the direction with the smaller platoon.

The input data required for this program are:

- Number of signals
- Cycle length
- Average traffic volume in each direction
- Saturation flow headway
- Signal spacing measured from the first signal location
- Red time for each signal
- Average speed in each direction between each pair of signals

The program produces data as shown in Figure 24.14.

Difference-of-Offsets Method. The British Road Research Laboratory developed a technique for optimizing offsets in a fixed-time signal timing plan for an arterial or network based on the minimization of vehicular delay. Given the traffic flows, the common cycle length and the splits, the vehicular delay along a traffic link connecting a pair of signals depends on the departure and arrival patterns at the downstream signal and hence on the difference of offsets between the two signals. That is,

$$D_{ij} = f(\theta_{ij}) \tag{24.17}$$

where D_{ij} = total delay along link ij connecting signals i and j

f = a function of . . .

θ_{ij} = difference of offsets between i and j

From a knowledge of arrival and departure rates throughout the cycle at signal j, D_{ij} can be computed for different values of θ_{ij}. For a one-way street section the best set of offsets for link ij corresponding to the minimum value of D_{ij} can be obtained from the computed delay/difference-of-offsets relationship.

For a two-way street section, the offset settings producing minimum delay for one direction (link ij) may not be appropriate for the opposing direction (link ji). To find the optimum offset settings for both links ij and ji, the delay values D_{ij} and D_{ji} for each θ_{ij} are first weighted by their respective arrivals, A_{ij} and A_{ji}, and then combined to form an overall delay value (D) as follows:

$$D = A_{ij} + A_{ji}\left(\frac{D_{ij}}{A_{ij}} + \frac{D_{ji}}{A_{ji}}\right) \tag{24.18}$$

where $D_{ij} = f(\theta_{ij})$

$D_{ji} = f(\theta_{ji})$

$= f(C - \theta_{ij})$

since

$\theta_{ij} + \theta_{ji} = C$, the cycle length

```
TRAFFIC SIGNAL SYNCHRONIZATION BY MAXIMAL BANDWIDTH METHOD
 ************SAMPLE PROBLEM*****************************JUNE/79*****************

NUMBER OF SIGNALS  =   5
CYCLE LENGTH (SEC) =  90.
HEADWAY (SEC)      =  3.0
EFFECT. NO. LANES  = 2.00

VOLUME  IN = 1200. VPH
VOLUME OUT = 1200. VPH
POSSIBLE  INBOUND THROUGH BAND VOLUME =   527.27 VPH
POSSIBLE OUTBOUND THROUGH BAND VOLUME =   527.27 VPH

AT LEAST ONE VOLUME EXCEEDS THE CAPACITY OF THE BAND
LARGER BAND IS SET AT ITS MAXIMUM OR THE MIN. GREEN

BAND IN  =      19.773  SEC
BAND OUT =      19.773  SEC
CRITICAL SIGNAL = NO.      1

SIG  DIST.      SPEED (MPH)  RED PHASE  OFFSETS  RELATIVE   DIFF. OF
NO.  (FT)       IN      OUT    (SEC)     (SEC)    OFFSET     OFFSET

 1      0.                     57.00    28.500    -.00000
            30.00    30.00                                    33.50
 2   2707.                     34.00    62.000     .50000
            30.00    30.00                                    46.00
 3   1044.                     36.00    18.000    -.00000
            30.00    30.00                                    -.00
 4    719.                     36.00    18.000    -.00000
            30.00    30.00                                    50.00
 5   2465.                     46.00    68.000     .50000

OFFSET IS THE TIME IN SEC. FROM THE ORIGIN TO THE
RIGHT HAND SIDE OF THE RED FOR EACH SIGNAL WHERE THE
ORIGIN IS TAKEN AS THE CENTRE OF THE RED FOR THE
CRITICAL LIGHT.

POSITION OF FRONT EDGE OF OUTBOUND BAND AT FIRST SIGNAL IS   28.50 SEC
POSITION OF  REAR EDGE OF  INBOUND BAND AT FIRST SIGNAL IS   61.50 SEC

TRAVEL TIME OUTBOUND =   56.023 SECONDS
             INBOUND =   56.023 SECONDS
```

Figure 24.14. Sample output of MAXBAN program.

A number of researchers[43–47] have modified and refined this computational procedure. One version of this program, called DVSDOO, now exists in the Metropolitan Toronto Roads and Traffic Department program library; its sample input and output are illustrated on Figure 24.15. In general, the Difference-of-Offsets method has perhaps the soundest logical base among the various offset optimization techniques for arterial routes, because a quantitative traffic measure, delay, is directly considered and systematically minimized. While delay is minimized, however, the method does not necessarily minimize the number of stops or provide uninterrupted progression. In fact, to obtain minimum-delay offsets, traffic platoons have to be re-formed at critical intersections in order that the green time will be fully utilized. Frequent re-forming can be irritating to the motorists. This problem can be overcome by introducing a stop penalty into the method.

Traffic signal system timing for networks

The conventional method of network signal timing design is to provide preferential treatment for one or more arterials in the network. After favorable offsets are assigned to signals on the preferred arterials or directions of travel, the remaining signals are adjusted to conform with the network. In effect, the network is reduced to a number of arterials for easier analysis. The manual work involved in designating timings for a network is quite cumbersome and at times unmanageable. Fortunately, a number of computer-based optimization models for signal network design have been developed.

SIGRID program

The SIGRID program[48] was developed by Traffic Research Corporation for the Toronto traffic computer control system. Given the cycle length, signal splits, link data, and a set of ideal or desirable offset differences for a signal network, the program calculates a set of optimum offset differences by minimizing the discrepancy between the two sets of values. A sample output of SIGRID is shown in Figure 24.16.

In using the SIGRID program, the following should be clearly understood:

1. The program minimizes only the differences between the ideal and actual offsets, and does not necessarily minimize the system delay.
2. The program only solves part of the problem involved in signal network optimization, since it does not optimize the individual signal splits and link offsets. The program user has to predetermine the optimum splits and ideal offsets by another program or simply by experience. The desired offset, if calculated from speed and distance data by the program, is based on simplifying assumptions and does not take into account such factors as platoon dispersion and side-street traffic interruptions. The calculated offset is therefore not necessarily the best offset.
3. An inconsistency exists in the program in that the system delay function F is minimized and yet the calculated offsets corresponding to the lowest value of system average waiting times W are chosen as the optimum offsets.
4. The average waiting times (or delay propensity factors) are computed based on oversimplified assumptions, and do not necessarily reflect the true delay characteristics. The use of these values for system evaluation and for finding the "best" offsets is therefore questionable.
5. The program ignores the effects of changing cycle lengths on lost time and green utilization, and is therefore not suitable for making comparisons between different system cycle lengths.
6. The platoon length (or green utilization) factor should be a link input instead of a system input, since green utilization varies considerably from signal to signal.

Despite its weaknesses, the SIGRID program represented a major breakthrough in the field of signal network optimization techniques when it was developed in 1964. Although it is less sophisticated than its more recent counterparts such as SIGOP, it is relatively simple to use. Another favorable aspect of SIGRID is that it involves very little computer process time and reasonable coding effort. It is simply a labor-saving device to manipulate signal offsets in a network so that they are as close as possible to the values demanded by the engineer. The program is flexible and extremely useful; with proper usage and sound engineering judgment, it can produce meaningful results.

SIGOP program

The SIGOP (Traffic Signal Optimization) program[49,50] was developed by Peat, Marwick, Livingston and Company for the U.S. Bureau of Public Roads. It is, in fact, an extended version of SIGRID. Apart from optimizing the offsets, it also calculates the signal splits, given the necessary traffic data. The input data required for SIGOP are as follows:

---

[43] J. Almond and R. S. Lott, "The Glasgow Experiment: (II) Implementation and Assessment," *Road Res. Lab. Rep. LR 142*, London, 1968.

[44] D. I. Robertson, "Discussion at Symposium on Area Traffic Control of Road Traffic," Institution of Civil Engineers, London, 1967, pp. 140–141.

[45] F. A. Wagner, D. L. Gerlough, and F. C. Barnes, "Improved Criteria for Traffic Signal Systems on Urban Arterials," *Natl. Cooperative Highway Res. Program Rep. No. 73*. Washington, D.C.: Highway Research Board, 1969.

[46] F. A. Wagner, F. C. Barnes, and D. L. Gerlough, "Improved Criteria for Traffic Signal Systems in Urban Networks," *Natl. Cooperative Highway Res. Program Rep. No. 124*. Washington, D.C.: Highway Research Board, 1971.

[47] "DVSDOO Program," *Program Documentation Manual* (Toronto: Metropolitan Toronto Roads and Traffic Department, Apr. 1965).

[48] Traffic Research Corporation, "SIGRID Program: Notes and Users Manual," Metropolitan Toronto Roads and Traffic Department, Toronto, 1965–1973 (unpublished).

[49] Traffic Research Corporation, *SIGOP: Traffic Signal Optimization Program* (Clearinghouse No. PB-173-738), U.S. Bureau of Public Roads, 1966.

[50] Peat, Marwick, Livingston and Co., *SIGOP: Traffic Signal Optimization Program, User's Manual* (Clearinghouse No. PB-182-835), U.S. Bureau of Public Roads, 1968.

DELAY VERSUS DIFFERENCE OF OFFSET ANALYSIS FOR: LAWRENCE AVENUE
BETWEEN PHARMACY AND WARDEN

***** LINK DATA *****

LINK	PRIMARY	SECONDARY
LINK NO. AND DIRECTION	409EB	408WB
SIGNAL CYCLE LENGTH, SEC	90.	90.
GREEN INTERVAL, UPSTREAM INTERSECTION, SEC	37.	43.
GREEN INTERVAL, DOWNSTREAM INTERSECTION, SEC	42.	44.
AMBER INTERVAL, SEC	4.	4.
SINGLE LANE SATURATION FLOW, VPHG	1629.	1627.
LOST TIME PER GREEN INTERVAL, SEC	2.	2.
DISTANCE BETWEEN SIGNALS, FEET	2726.	2726.
NO. OF THRU LANES, DOWNSTREAM INTERSECTION	3.0	2.0
STRAIGHT-THRU TRAFFIC ENTERING LINK, VPH	642.	1062.
LEFT TURNS ENTERING LINK, VPH	74.	62.
RIGHT TURNS ENTERING LINK, VPH	125.	96.
TOTAL VOLUME DOWNSTREAM, VPH	841.	1220.
AVERAGE FREE-FLOW VELOCITY, FT/SEC	38.	38.
OPPOSITE LINK NUMBER	408	409

***** OUTPUT *****

LEGEND

PHI - THE DIFFERENCE OF OFFSET WITH RESPECT TO THE PRIMARY LINK, SECONDS
QSUM - THE TOTAL DELAY-IN-QUEUE DURING ONE SIGNAL CYCLE, VEHICLE-SECONDS PER SIGNAL CYCLF
DPV - THE AVERAGE DELAY PER VEHICLE, VEHICLF-SECONDS PER VEHICLF
QAVE - THE AVERAGE QUEUE LENGTH, VEHICLES

PRIMARY LINK (409EB)				SECONDARY LINK (408WB)				COMRINATION			
PHI	QSUM	DPV	QAVE	PHI	QSUM	DPV	QAVE	PHI	QSUM	DPV	QAVE
0	496.0	23.6	5.51	0	969.9	31.8	10.78	0	1465.9	28.4	16.29
1	507.9	24.2	5.64	89	947.6	31.1	10.53	1	1455.5	28.2	16.17
2	519.8	24.7	5.78	88	925.4	30.3	10.28	2	1445.2	28.0	16.06
3	514.3	24.5	5.71	87	903.2	29.6	10.04	3	1417.5	27.5	15.75
4	508.8	24.2	5.65	86	880.9	28.9	9.79	4	1389.7	27.0	15.44
5	503.0	23.9	5.59	85	858.7	28.2	9.54	5	1361.7	26.4	15.13
6	496.9	23.6	5.52	84	836.5	27.4	9.29	6	1333.4	25.9	14.82
7	490.6	23.3	5.45	83	814.2	26.7	9.05	7	1304.8	25.3	14.50
8	484.1	23.0	5.38	82	792.0	26.0	8.80	8	1276.1	24.8	14.18
9	477.5	22.7	5.31	81	769.8	25.2	8.55	9	1247.2	24.2	13.86
10	470.5	22.4	5.23	80	747.5	24.5	8.31	10	1218.0	23.6	13.53
11	463.3	22.0	5.15	79	725.3	23.8	8.06	11	1188.6	23.1	13.21
12	455.9	21.7	5.07	78	703.1	23.1	7.81	12	1158.9	22.5	12.88
13	448.3	21.3	4.98	77	680.8	22.3	7.56	13	1129.2	21.9	12.55
14	440.5	21.0	4.89	76	658.6	21.6	7.32	14	1099.1	21.3	12.21
15	432.4	20.6	4.80	75	636.4	20.9	7.07	15	1068.8	20.7	11.88
16	424.1	20.2	4.71	74	614.1	20.1	6.82	16	1038.2	20.1	11.54
17	415.6	19.8	4.62	73	591.9	19.4	6.58	17	1007.5	19.6	11.19
18	406.9	19.4	4.52	72	569.7	18.7	6.33	18	976.6	19.0	10.85
19	398.0	18.9	4.42	71	547.4	17.9	6.08	19	945.4	18.3	10.50
20	388.7	18.5	4.32	70	525.2	17.2	5.84	20	913.9	17.7	10.15
21	379.4	18.0	4.22	69	503.0	16.5	5.59	21	882.3	17.1	9.80
22	369.8	17.6	4.11	68	480.7	15.8	5.34	22	850.5	16.5	9.45
23	359.9	17.1	4.00	67	458.5	15.0	5.09	23	818.5	15.9	9.09
24	349.8	16.6	3.89	66	436.3	14.3	4.85	24	786.1	15.3	8.73
25	339.5	16.1	3.77	65	414.0	13.6	4.60	25	753.6	14.6	8.37
26	329.1	15.7	3.66	64	391.8	12.8	4.35	26	720.9	14.0	8.01
27	318.4	15.1	3.54	63	369.6	12.1	4.11	27	687.9	13.4	7.64
28	307.3	14.6	3.41	62	347.3	11.4	3.86	28	654.7	12.7	7.27
29	296.1	14.1	3.29	61	325.1	10.7	3.61	29	621.2	12.1	6.90
30	284.8	13.5	3.16	60	303.1	9.9	3.37	30	587.8	11.4	6.53
31	273.2	13.0	3.04	59	282.1	9.2	3.13	31	555.3	10.8	6.17
32	261.3	12.4	2.90	58	262.3	8.6	2.91	32	523.6	10.2	5.82
33	249.1	11.8	2.77	57	243.6	8.0	2.71	33	492.8	9.6	5.48
34	236.9	11.3	2.63	56	226.1	7.4	2.51	34	463.0	9.0	5.14
35	224.4	10.7	2.49	55	209.7	6.9	2.33	35	434.2	8.4	4.82
36	211.7	10.1	2.35	54	194.4	6.4	2.16	36	406.1	7.9	4.51
37	198.6	9.4	2.21	53	180.3	5.9	2.00	37	378.9	7.4	4.21
38	185.5	8.8	2.06	52	167.3	5.5	1.86	38	352.7	6.8	3.92
39	172.1	8.2	1.91	51	155.4	5.1	1.73	39	327.5	6.4	3.64

Figure 24.15. Sample output of DVSDOO program.

**************SAMPLE PROBLEM******JUNE/79**********

GAME NO. 1	SIGRID DELAY	2892.81	EVALUATED OPTIMUM 11.3131
GAME NO. 2	SIGRID DELAY	3052.17	EVALUATED OPTIMUM 11.1641
GAME NO. 3	SIGRID DELAY	2752.15	EVALUATED OPTIMUM 10.7487
GAME NO. 4	SIGRID DELAY	3036.69	EVALUATED OPTIMUM 11.2645
GAME NO. 5	SIGRID DELAY	2752.15	EVALUATED OPTIMUM 10.7487
GAME NO. 6	SIGRID DELAY	2752.15	EVALUATED OPTIMUM 10.7487
GAME NO. 7	SIGRID DELAY	2761.02	EVALUATED OPTIMUM 10.3932
GAME NO. 8	SIGRID DELAY	2752.15	EVALUATED OPTIMUM 10.7487
GAME NO. 9	SIGRID DELAY	2892.81	EVALUATED OPTIMUM 11.3131
GAME NO. 10	SIGRID DELAY	2752.15	EVALUATED OPTIMUM 10.7487
GAME NO. 11	SIGRID DELAY	2752.15	EVALUATED OPTIMUM 10.7487
GAME NO. 12	SIGRID DELAY	3045.27	

**************SAMPLE PROBLEM******JUNE/79**********

P=1.00

CYCLE LENGTH 80 SECONDS

SIGNAL NO.	SPLIT (N-S)	ORIGINAL OFFSET	CHANGE IN OFFSET,	NEW OFFSET	NEW OFFSET (SEC)	SIGNAL NO.
225	.66	.77	.71	.48	38	225
572	.67	.64	.83	.47	37	572
24	.44	.31	.58	.89	71	24
23	.51	.89	.46	.35	28	23
22	.46	.63	.64	.27	21	22
993	.60	.43	.90	.33	27	993
21	.50	.99	.41	.40	32	21
20	.51	.70	.76	.46	37	20
19	.50	.51	.96	.47	37	19
18	.50	.41	.03	.44	35	18
17	.50	.99	.54	.53	42	17
16	.51	.11	.46	.57	46	16
13	.44	.41	.29	.70	56	13
12	.66	.51	.53	.04	3	12
11	.60	.81	.58	.39	31	11
10	.60	.23	.60	.83	67	10
9	.56	.43	.54	.97	77	9
8	.54	.79	.54	.33	27	8
7	.56	.97	.42	.39	31	7
6	.54	.13	.31	.44	36	6
5	.54	.09	.30	.39	31	5
4	.63	.03	.49	.52	41	4
3	.54	.40	.14	.54	43	3
2	.54	.01	.54	.55	44	2
261	.50	.57	.52	.09	7	261
260	.54	.06	.45	.51	41	260
259	.47	.80	.76	.56	45	259
258	.50	.40	.61	.01	1	258
319	.50	.67	.38	.05	4	319
257	.50	.73	.36	.09	7	257
256	.49	.94	.21	.15	12	256
255	.49	.86	.34	.20	16	255
254	.50	.74	.45	.19	15	254
253	.41	.63	.64	.27	22	253
251	.63	.79	.77	.56	45	251
922	.61	.09	.67	.76	61	922
250	.51	.30	.64	.94	75	250
249	.47	.60	.48	.08	6	249
248	.46	.96	.61	.57	46	248
247	.43	.34	.33	.67	54	247
246	.43	.51	.20	.71	57	246
223	.49	.01	.74	.75	60	223
214	.49	.47	.22	.69	55	214
245	.44	.61	.13	.74	60	245

Figure 24.16. Sample output of SIGRID program.

FROM SIGNAL	TO SIGNAL	DIREC-TION	DIFFERENCE IN OFFSET			DELAY PROPENSITY FACTOR		VOLUME FACTOR	IMPORTANCE FACTOR
			DESIRED	ORIGINAL	NEW	ORIGINAL	NEW		
23	22	SBND	17	-21	-7	42	28	445	
22	993	SBND	14	-16	5	20	6	385	
993	21	SBND	14	45	5	31	9	385	
21	20	SBND	14	-23	5	36	9	363	
20	19	SBND	14	-15	1	29	13	383	
19	18	SBND	6	-8	-2	14	8	335	
18	17	SBND	10	46	7	36	3	355	
17	16	SBND	12	10	4	2	8	353	
2	3	NBND	8	31	-1	23	8	606	
3	4	NBND	10	-30	-1	23	7	544	
4	5	NBND	10	5	-10	4	17	577	
5	6	NBND	8	3	4	4	3	584	
6	7	NBND	13	-13	-5	20	14	600	
7	8	NBND	14	-14	-4	24	16	531	
8	9	NBND	27	51	51	24	24	518	
9	10	NBND	16	-16	-11	21	18	524	
10	11	NBND	31	46	45	15	14	524	
11	12	NBND	21	56	52	35	31	485	
12	13	NBND	9	-8	-27	22	44	271	
201	260	SBND	32	39	34	7	2	441	
260	259	SBND	16	-21	4	41	14	450	
259	258	SBND	24	48	37	24	13	506	
258	319	SBND	18	22	3	4	15	500	
319	257	SBND	14	5	3	9	11	474	
257	256	SBND	9	17	5	8	5	455	
256	255	SBND	10	-6	4	17	6	417	
255	254	SBND	7	-10	-1	17	8	400	
254	253	SBND	7	-9	7	23	1	400	
244	245	NBND	10	-12	-1	28	14	150	
245	214	NBND	7	-11	-5	19	12	151	
214	223	NBND	8	43	5	35	3	228	
223	246	NBND	9	40	-3	31	16	200	
246	247	NBND	11	-14	-3	33	18	200	
247	248	NBND	21	50	-8	29	34	225	
248	249	NBND	21	51	41	30	20	577	
249	250	NBND	19	56	-11	37	29	205	
250	922	NBND	13	-17	-14	19	17	200	
[illegible]	251	NBND	19	56	-16	37	21	200	

	ORIGINAL SYSTEM	NEW SYSTEM
WEIGHTED AVERAGE DELAY PROPENSITY FACTOR	15.4	10.4

Figure 24.16. *(continued)*

1. Macro (system) or micro (individual) intersection data such as yellow times, minimum pedestrian walk times, minimum average discharge headway, and truck factors.
2. Macro or micro link data such as progression speed, number of discharge lanes, signal distances, traffic volumes, turning ratios, link importance factors, and platoon coherence factors.
3. Control data such as the set of cycle lengths to be tested, the existing offsets to be evaluated, and importance of stops-versus-delay factor.

The SIGOP program consists of the following six program blocks.

INPUTS. This program reads and checks the card input data, and computes the total approach flows and the critical lane flows for all phases. It also computes the following if they are not already given as direct input:

1. Equivalent flow factor to allow for turning movements
2. Main platoon flow
3. Secondary flow due to side-street traffic
4. Discharge rate
5. Loading ratio (critical flow/saturation flow ratio)
6. Link travel time

PHASES. This program calculates the green time for each phase of each intersection for each cycle length, subject to the constraint that pedestrian minimum walk time is to be provided. The green time or splits are computed in proportion to their respective critical lane flows, total approach flows, or combinations of both. The time in fractions of a cycle, of the beginning of each phase relative to the start of the first phase at the same intersection, is also calculated for use in the OFFSET Program.

OFFSET. The OFFSET program calculates the ideal offset differences and the link weighting factors.

OPTIMIZ. The OPTIMIZ program computes the optimum offsets. The procedure is similar to the one used in SIGRID, except that no calculation of average waiting times (or delay propensity factors) is attempted in OPTIMIZ. The best offsets are obtained from the global minimum system delay function, not from the minimum system average-waiting-time function.

VALUAT. The purpose of VALUAT is to calculate delay, stops, and cost values for the given original offsets, ideal offsets, and optimum offsets obtained from OPTIMIZ. These values (calculated for up to eight link groups and also for the entire network) can be used for comparing alternative signal settings for the same and different cycle lengths and for evaluating the theoretical performance of a system under various conditions.

OUTPUT. This program is used to print dial settings for the optimum signal splits and offsets, and also time–space charts for as many streets as specified.

The ease of applying SIGOP to a signal network depends on user familiarity with the program, and user judgment and experience in preparing the necessary input. The improvement in traffic operation as a result of using SIGOP depends on the applicability of the assumptions made in the program to the actual traffic conditions in the network under study. Also, it depends on how well the original system is designed. This, in part, may explain why conflicting results have been obtained from various cities[51,52] in regard to the usefulness of SIGOP as a signal network optimization tool.

Combination method

The Combination method[53,54] for network optimization incorporates two basic concepts:

1. To calculate the delay/difference-of-offsets relationship for each network link.
2. To combine links in series or in parallel to obtain a set of optimum offsets such that the network delay is minimized.

The basic assumptions of the Combination method are as follows:

1. The setting of the signals does not affect the amount of traffic or the route used. (This is true only on a short-term basis, say a 3-month period, provided that no intersection in the network is seriously congested. The implication is that periodic signal upgrading is necessary).
2. All the signals have a common cycle or a cycle that is a submultiple of some master cycle.
3. The signal splits at each intersection are known.
4. The delay to traffic along a network link depends solely on the offset difference between the signals at each end of the link and not on any other signal in the network. (This is true if none of the intersections are oversaturated resulting in intersection blockage, or if two consecutive signals are not appreciably underutilized.)

Sample output of the Combination method is shown in Figure 24.17.

A number of experimental studies have been carried out in Britain to evaluate the Combination method. For ex-

[51]PEAT, MARWICK, LIVINGSTON AND CO., *SIGOP: Traffic Signal Optimization Program, Field Tests and Sensitivity Studies* (Clearinghouse No. PB-182-836), U.S. Bureau of Public Roads, 1968.

[52]F. A. WAGNER, "SIGOP/TRANSYT Evaluation, San Jose, California," *Federal Highway Administration Report FH-11-7822,* Washington, D.C., July 1972.

[53]HILLIER, "Appendix to Glasgow's Experiment."

[54]K. W. HUDDART AND E. D. TURNER, "Traffic Signal Progressions–GLC Combination Method," Traffic Engineering and Control, London, England, Vol. II, No. 7, Nov. 1969.

Figure 24.17. Sample output of Combination program.

```
METROPOLITAN ROAD AND WARDEN AVENUE     80 STEPS    80 SECS CYCLE    KSTOP=  4   PLATOON DISP.= 1                    PAGE  1
------------------------------------------------------------------------------------------------------------------------------

  LINK NO.  1 TYPE1 WRITE =4 FLOW WEIGHTING=1.0 STOP PENALTY= 4 SECS/VEHICLE STOP
                         FLOW FLTIM SATFL     FLOW FLTIM SATFL    FLOW FLTIM SATFL    FLOW FLTIM SATFL    FLOW FLTIM SATFL
       719    40   3600   397    28   1500     -0    12    -0      -0    -0    -0      -0    -0    -0      -0    -0    -0

  LINK NO.  1 TYPE4 WRITE=4 LENGTH= 375 FEET SPEED=35 M.P.H. LSTEPS,   6
      FLOW FLTIM SATFL         FLOW FLTIM SATFL           FLOW FLTIM SATFL          FLOW FLTIM SATFL          FLOW FLTIM SATFL
       35    43   3600    -0     33   1500      -0     4    -0     -0    -0    -0         -0    -0    -0         -0    -0    -0
  EXIT CARD PROCESSED

  LINK NO.  1  DELAY IN TENTH VEHICLES                   OFFSET    1     2     3     4     5     6     7     8     9    10

                                                           0+      0     0     0     0     0     0     0     1     8    11
                                                          10+     12    13    13    14    15    15    16    17    17    18
                                                          20+     18    19    19    20    20    20    21    21    21    22
                                                          30+     22    22    23    23    23    23    23    24    24    24
                                                          40+     24    24    24    24    23    22    20    18    16    13
                                                          50+     12     9     7     6     4     4     3     3     3     3
                                                          60+      3     3     3     3     3     3     2     2     2     1
                                                          70+      1     1     1     1     1     1     0     0     0     0
------------------------------------------------------------------------------------------------------------------------------

  LINK NO. 15 TYPE1 WRITE =4 FLOW WEIGHTING=1.0 STOP PENALTY= 4 SECS/VEHICLE STOP
                         FLOW FLTIM SATFL     FLOW FLTIM SATFL    FLOW FLTIM SATFL    FLOW FLTIM SATFL    FLOW FLTIM SATFL
       719    40   3600   397    28   1500     -0    12    -0      -0    -0    -0      -0    -0    -0      -0    -0    -0

  LINK NO. 15 TYPE4 WRITE=4 LENGTH= 375 FEET SPEED=35 M.P.H. LSTEPS,   6
      FLOW FLTIM SATFL         FLOW FLTIM SATFL           FLOW FLTIM SATFL          FLOW FLTIM SATFL          FLOW FLTIM SATFL
       35    46   3600    -0     30   1500      -0     4    -0     -0    -0    -0         -0    -0    -0         -0    -0    -0
  EXIT CARD PROCESSED

  LINK NO. 15  DELAY IN TENTH VEHICLES                   OFFSET    1     2     3     4     5     6     7     8     9    10

                                                           0+      0     0     0     0     0     0     0     1     8    11
                                                          10+     12    13    13    14    15    15    16    17    17    18
                                                          20+     18    19    19    20    20    20    21    21    21    22
                                                          30+     22    22    23    23    23    23    23    24    24    24
                                                          40+     24    23    22    20    18    15    13    11     8     6
                                                          50+      5     4     3     3     3     3     3     3     3     3
                                                          60+      3     3     3     3     3     3     2     2     2     1
                                                          70+      1     1     1     1     1     1     0     0     0     0
------------------------------------------------------------------------------------------------------------------------------

  LINK NO. 16 TYPE1 WRITE =4 FLOW WEIGHTING=1.0 STOP PENALTY= 4 SECS/VEHICLE STOP
                         FLOW FLTIM SATFL     FLOW FLTIM SATFL    FLOW FLTIM SATFL    FLOW FLTIM SATFL    FLOW FLTIM SATFL
       719    40   3600   397    28   1500     -0    12    -0      -0    -0    -0      -0    -0    -0      -0    -0    -0

  LINK NO. 16 TYPE4 WRITE=4 LENGTH= 375 FEET SPEED=35 M.P.H. LSTEPS,   6
      FLOW FLTIM SATFL         FLOW FLTIM SATFL           FLOW FLTIM SATFL          FLOW FLTIM SATFL          FLOW FLTIM SATFL
       35    49   3600    -0     27   1500      -0     4    -0     -0    -0    -0         -0    -0    -0         -0    -0    -0
  EXIT CARD PROCESSED
```

AUTOMATIC COMBINATIONS SEARCH ROUTINE

LINK 1= 1(LINKB) & -4(LINKC) PROCESSED IN PARALLEL

LINK NO. 1 DELAY IN TENTH VEHICLES

OFFSET	1	2	3	4	5	6	7	8	9	10
0+	0	0	0	0	0	0	0	2	8	11
10+	12	13	14	14	15	15	16	17	17	18
20+	18	19	19	20	21	21	22	22	23	23
30+	23	24	25	26	29	31	33	35	37	38
40+	39	39	39	39	38	37	35	33	31	28
50+	26	24	22	20	18	17	17	17	16	16
60+	16	15	15	15	14	13	12	11	11	9
70+	7	2	1	1	1	1	1	0	0	0

LINK 15= 15(LINKB) & -11(LINKC) PROCESSED IN PARALLEL

LINK NO. 15 DELAY IN TENTH VEHICLES

OFFSET	1	2	3	4	5	6	7	8	9	10
0+	0	0	0	0	0	0	0	2	8	11
10+	12	13	14	14	15	16	16	17	17	18
20+	19	19	20	21	21	22	22	22	22	23
30+	23	23	24	25	27	29	31	33	35	36
40+	37	36	35	33	31	28	26	24	22	19
50+	18	17	16	16	16	16	15	15	15	15
60+	15	14	14	14	13	12	11	11	10	9
70+	7	2	1	1	1	1	1	0	0	0

LINK 16= 16(LINKB) & -12(LINKC) PROCESSED IN PARALLEL

LINK NO. 16 DELAY IN TENTH VEHICLES

OFFSET	1	2	3	4	5	6	7	8	9	10
0+	0	0	0	0	0	0	0	2	8	11
10+	12	13	14	14	15	16	16	17	18	19
20+	19	20	20	21	21	21	22	22	22	23
30+	23	23	24	25	26	28	30	32	33	33
40+	31	29	27	24	21	19	17	16	14	14
50+	14	14	14	14	14	14	14	14	14	14
60+	14	13	13	12	12	11	10	10	9	8
70+	6	2	1	1	1	1	1	0	0	0

LINK 17= 17(LINKB) & -13(LINKC) PROCESSED IN PARALLEL

LINK NO. 17 DELAY IN TENTH VEHICLES

OFFSET	1	2	3	4	5	6	7	8	9	10
0+	0	0	0	0	0	0	0	2	8	11
10+	12	13	14	15	15	16	17	18	18	19
20+	19	20	20	20	21	21	22	22	22	23
30+	23	23	24	24	25	26	27	27	26	24
40+	22	20	18	15	13	12	11	11	11	12
50+	12	12	13	13	13	13	13	13	13	13
60+	12	12	12	12	11	10	10	9	8	8
70+	6	2	1	1	1	1	1	0	0	0

LINK 18= 18(LINKB) & -14(LINKC) PROCESSED IN PARALLEL

LINK NO.	MAXIMUM DELAY	MAXIMUM OFFSET	MINIMUM DELAY	MINIMUM OFFSET	OPTIMUM DELAY	OPTIMUM OFFSET	DELAYS IN TENTH VEHICLES
1	24	44	0	5	0	5	(= 5SECS)
2	3	45	0	35	1	67	(= 67SECS)
3	3	46	0	35	1	13	(= 13SECS)
4	15	33	0	6	0	75	(= 75SECS)
5	8	65	1	41	2	28	(= 28SECS)
6	20	39	0	6	0	52	(= 52SECS)
7	3	45	0	35	2	63	(= 63SECS)
8	2	44	0	35	2	61	(= 61SECS)
9	2	44	0	35	1	75	(= 75SECS)
10	2	43	0	35	1	72	(= 72SECS)
11	13	31	0	6	0	75	(= 75SECS)
12	11	29	0	6	0	75	(= 75SECS)
13	10	27	0	6	0	75	(= 75SECS)
14	9	25	0	6	0	75	(= 75SECS)
15	24	41	0	5	0	5	(= 5SECS)
16	24	38	0	5	0	5	(= 5SECS)
17	23	35	0	5	0	5	(= 5SECS)
18	22	32	0	5	0	5	(= 5SECS)
19	3	46	0	35	1	17	(= 17SECS)
20	3	46	0	35	1	19	(= 19SECS)
21	3	46	0	35	1	5	(= 5SECS)
22	3	46	0	35	1	8	(= 8SECS)
TOTALS	228		4		13		

ample, Hillier and Lott[55] compared the Combination method with a manual graphical method and found that the Combination technique provided an 8% improvement in travel time, and 20% reduction in delay and 10% reduction in stops. Favorable results using the Combination method were also reported by Williams[56] from a West London experiment involving a network with 70 signals, and by Holroyd and Hillier[57] from an area control experiment in Glasgow.

TRANSYT program

The Traffic Network Study Tool (TRANSYT) developed by Robertson[58–61] is an optimization technique for computing signal offsets and splits for minimum delay and stops in a network. It has the capacity to optimize networks having up to 50 signalized intersections and 200 links. The program can be altered to accommodate larger networks. Figure 24.18 illustrates sample output from this program.

Generally speaking, TRANSYT is based on the following assumptions:

1. All intersections in the network are signalized.
2. All signals have a common cycle length or a cycle length half the common value.
3. Traffic enters the boundary signal at a constant specified rate.
4. The right-turn and left-turn ratios are constant throughout the cycle.

This program has the ability to handle the following special features:

- Multiphase signals
- The use of half-cycles for minor intersections
- Grouping of signals for maintaining constant offset differences among them
- Multiple links at a common stop line
- Effects of bus progression and stoppages

Overall, TRANSYT has been demonstrated to be reliable and effective both as a design and as an evaluation tool. In a study carried out by the British Road Research Laboratory,[62] it was found that TRANSYT accurately predicted network delay. Also, the hill-climbing optimization process in TRANSYT was found to be very effective in obtaining optimum offsets. When compared to existing signal timing settings, the TRANSYT settings reduced mean travel time by 16% and increased effective network capacity by 25%.

Traffic signal timing strategies for computer-controlled systems

With the advent of computers into the field of traffic signal control, a number of demand-responsive traffic signal control algorithms have been developed and applied to "real-world" situations. These concepts go beyond the basic program library of preengineered, pretimed signal plans generated by traditional off-line techniques which are stored in computer memory and implemented on a time-of-day, table-look-up basis or by responding to fluctuations in traffic flow.

British Road Research Laboratory experience

FLEXIPROG, EQUISAT, and PLIDENT were three of the early real-time programs tested by British Road Research Laboratory in Glasgow.[63–67]

The FLEXIPROG method is a vehicle-actuated flexible progressive system in which a basic fixed cycle is used at each signal. For each phase, there is a fixed priority period within the cycle during which switching to a particular phase can occur, provided that the minimum green requirement has been met in the existing phase. During the remaining part of the cycle, the signal functions as an isolated vehicle-actuated signal. When there is continuous traffic demand over all the approaches, the signal operates with fixed-time settings. The basic coordination pattern in the system in this case is predetermined by means of the Combination method. The length of the priority period in each phase is chosen so that it is just long enough to provide adequate time for the upstream main platoon to arrive at the detectors.

In the EQUISAT scheme, the system cycle and coordination pattern have been predetermined by the Combination method, but the green split at each signal is varied automatically on a real-time basis such that the degree of saturation on each phase is equalized. The degree of saturation (x) is given by

$$x = \frac{q}{s} \qquad (24.19)$$

where q = flow in vehicles per unit of time

s = saturation flow in same units as q

With a constant cycle length the split is varied such that

[55] J. A. Hillier and R. S. Lott, "A Method of Linking Traffic Signals to Minimize Delays," International Study Week In Traffic Engineering, Barcelona, 1966.

[56] D. A. B. Williams, "Area Traffic Control in West London: Assessment of First Experiment," *Traffic Eng. Control, 11* (July 1969).

[57] J. Holroyd and J. A. Hillier, "Area Traffic Control in Glasgow: A Summary of Results from Four Control Schemes," *Traffic Eng. Control, 11* (Sept. 1969).

[58] D. I. Robertson, "TRANSYT Method for Area Traffic Control," Traffic Eng. Control, 11 (Oct. 1969).

[59] D. I. Robertson, "TRANSYT: A Traffic Network Study Tool," *Road Res. Lab. Rep. LR 253,* London, 1969.

[60] D. I. Robertson, "TRANSYT: Traffic Network Study Tool," Fourth International Symposium on the Theory of Traffic Flow, Karlsruhe, 1968.

[61] D. I. Robertson, "User Guide to TRANSYT Version 5," *Road Res. Tech. Note TN 813,* London, Mar. 1973.

[62] D. I. Robertson, "TRANSYT: A Traffic Network Study Tool."

[63] J. A. Hillier, "The Glasgow Experiment: Schemes and Equipment," *Road Res. Lab. Rep. LR 95,* London, 1967.

[64] Holroyd and Hillier, "Area Traffic Control in Glasgow."

[65] D. Owens and J. Holroyd, "The Glasgow Experiment: Assessments under Light and Very Low Flow Conditions," *Road Res. Lab. Rep. LR 322,* London, 1963.

[66] J. Holroyd and J. A. Hillier, "The Glasgow Experiment: PLIDENT and After," *Road Res. Lab. Rep. LR 384,* 1971.

[67] J. Holroyd and J. A. Hillier, "Further Results of Area Traffic Control in Glasgow," *Traffic Eng. Control, 13* (Sept. 1971).

TRANSYT FOR EXISTING TIMINGS WITH 4 PULSES P.M. — 90 SECOND CYCLE 45 STEPS RUN ON 14 JUN 79ØØØ

INITIAL SETTINGS

NODE NO	NUMBER OF STAGES	PULSE 1	PULSE 2	PULSE 3	PULSE 4	PULSE 5	PULSE 6	PULSE 7
404	4	6	32	36	3			
406	4	17	44	2	14			
407	4	34	9	12	31			
408	4	1	23	26	43			
409	4	29	6	9	26			
503	4	36	19	22	33			
932	4	29	10	13	26			

LINK NUMBER	FLOW (VEH/H)	SAT FLOW (VEH/H)	DEGREE OF SAT (%)	DISTANCE TRAVELLED (VEH MI/H)	TIME SPENT (VEH H/H)	UNIFORM DELAY (VEH H/H)	RANDOM DELAY (VEH H/H)	STOPS (VEH/SEC)	MAX UNIFORM QUEUE (VEH)	EXIT SIGNAL	GREEN PERIOD START (SEC)	GREEN PERIOD END (SEC)
1	1652	4649	62	.00	5.96	5.72	.25	.30 (64%)	17	404	12	64
2	219	3027	27	.00	1.62	1.59	.03	.05 (78%)	4	404	72	6
3	1351	4672	48	366.63	3.92	3.81	.11	.21 (56%)	14	406	34	88
4	193	2999	24	.00	1.41	1.39	.02	.04 (78%)	4	406	4	28
5	1630	4305	66	411.98	15.86	3.70	.31	.31 (68%)	10	932	58	20
6	1677	4517	101	378.03	41.57	10.38	20.32	.47 (100%)	17	407	75	18
7	1029	3166	94	.00	11.65	8.18	3.46	.27 (96%)	17	407	31	62
8	1239	4882	62	334.70	13.79	3.92	.25	.14 (42%)	9	408	9	46
9	678	3319	54	.00	4.28	4.13	.16	.15 (78%)	11	408	52	86
10	1240	4888	52	405.04	15.32	3.54	.14	.25 (71%)	13	409	58	12
11	953	3319	76	.00	7.07	6.47	.60	.23 (87%)	15	409	18	52
12	1480	4882	56	287.67	10.89	2.44	.17	.28 (67%)	7	503	79	38
13	1376	3319	67	.00	4.53	4.19	.33	.25 (64%)	13	503	72	38
14	357	3284	44	.00	2.95	2.86	.09	.08 (84%)	7	503	44	66
15	1243	4882	52	241.61	15.11	3.02	.14	.26 (75%)	20	409	58	12
16	1203	3319	96	.00	13.85	9.13	4.71	.32 (96%)	19	409	18	52
17	1048	4882	44	342.33	12.18	2.25	.09	.13 (46%)	7	408	2	46
18	908	3319	72	.00	6.53	6.05	.47	.21 (84%)	14	408	52	86
19	716	4837	33	193.96	10.29	4.67	.04	.17 (86%)	14	407	68	18
20	1252	3198	93	.00	11.36	8.59	2.77	.32 (93%)	18	407	24	62
21	879	4692	32	198.15	7.04	1.30	.04	.06 (25%)	5	932	58	20
22	272	2859	33	.00	1.94	1.90	.04	.06 (78%)	5	932	26	52
23	932	4520	50	235.56	12.52	5.62	.13	.21 (81%)	16	406	51	88
24	406	2999	51	.00	3.29	3.16	.13	.10 (34%)	7	406	4	28
25	1046	4606	64	283.86	17.27	8.83	.28	.28 (96%)	21	404	32	64
26	537	3195	63	.00	4.61	4.34	.27	.13 (87%)	10	404	72	6

TIME SINCE START OF RUN	USE OF SUBROUTINE SUFPT NO. OF ENTRIES	NO. OF LINKS	TOTAL DISTANCE TRAVELLED (VEH MI/H)	TOTAL TIME SPENT (VEH H/H)	TOTAL UNIFORM DELAY (VEH H/H)	TOTAL RANDOM DELAY (VEH H/H)	TOTAL STOPS (VEH/SEC)	PERFORMANCE INDEX	SPEED (MI/H)
[illegible]	1	26	3679.51	256.80	126.18	35.35	5.26	182.59	14.33

Figure 24.18. Sample output of TRANSYT program (version 5).

$$G_{NS} : G_{EW} = x_{NS} : x_{EW} \qquad (24.20)$$

where G_{NS}, G_{EW} = green time for the north-south, east-west approach

x_{NS}, x_{EW} = critical degree of saturation on the north-south, east-west approach

The Platoon Identification Scheme (PLIDENT) identifies traffic platoon movements through the system and attempts to avoid delay to platoons on certain priority streets. For each signal, only one approach is provided with priority treatment. The PLIDENT scheme does not provide any fixed cycle lengths or offsets. Two parameters are used to define platoons, namely, the expected platoon leader arrival time at the stop line and the expected platoon length in number of vehicles. The arrival time is derived from:

1. Start of green of the upstream signal
2. Uninterrupted travel time between the upstream and downstream intersections

The platoon length is obtained from the length of platoon entering the upstream intersection multiplied by a factor to allow for turning movements.

ASCOT

Stanford Research Institute[68] under the sponsorship of the National Cooperative Highway Research Program developed and tested an Adaptive Signal Control Optimization Technique (ASCOT) in the city of San Jose, California. It consists of three control levels, which are described briefly in the following sections.

Level I: background control. Level I of the ASCOT Control Logic computes signal plans in real time for a traffic network during a control period, based on traffic data collected during the previous control period. The Background Control Logic consists of the following components:

- Traffic prediction logic
- Split logic
- Cycle-length logic
- Offset optimization logic

The Background Logic uses a prediction routine to estimate traffic volumes for the control period, and with this

[68]STANFORD RESEARCH INSTITUTE, "Improved Control Logic for Use with Computer-Controlled Traffic," *Natl. Cooperative Highway Res. Program NCHRP Project 3-18(1) Rep.*, Washington, D.C., June 1977.

information nominal background green splits are calculated by means of Webster's method. The cycle length for each group of signals is determined in conjunction with the offset pattern. The offset optimization logic is iterated over a given range of cycle lengths, and the best cycle length for the network is selected.

In the offset optimization procedure, a Traffic Flow Model similar to TRANSYT is used to compute the traffic flow pattern on each link and to obtain a relationship between the difference-of-offsets and the weighted sum of delay and stops. In computing the flow patterns, the model allows for the dispersion of traffic platoons between signals. From the delay-stop/difference-of-offsets relationship, an offset effectiveness factor is computed for each link.

After the offset assignment to the entire network is completed, the Traffic Flow Model is used to recompute the traffic patterns, stops, and delays. By successive application of the model and the link priority offset assignment method, the system is optimized. The Background Control Logic is depicted in flowchart form in Figure 24.19.

Level II: variable-split control. The Variable-Split Control Level superimposes on the Background Control cycle-to-cycle variation of splits at specified locations, while the cycle length is kept constant to maintain coordination. The split-variation mode consists of the following three routines:

- Begin-cycle split-computation routine
- Midcycle split-update routine
- Phase-skip/shorten routine

The begin-cycle split-computation routine provides for varying the signal split at designated intersections over the nominal split calculated in the Background Control Logic. At the beginning of the cycle, the routine adjusts the green time for each of the two dominant phases in proportion to their demand to saturation flow ratios, without changing the cycle length and offset.

The midcycle split-update routine essentially provides a midcycle correction to the green-time apportionment made at the beginning of the cycle. At a point near the end of a phase, a comparison is made between the number of vehicles stopped on red and those clearing on green between the detector and the stop line that will be affected by a phase extension or a termination decision. Depending on the comparison results, the green time for the current phase will be unaltered, terminated immediately, or extended to a maximum value.

In the absence of demand on a certain phase of an intersection, the phase will be skipped via the phase-skip/shorten routine. If such a skip is not possible because of hardware limitations, the phase is entered only for a minimum period.

Level III: congested intersection control. The Congested Intersection Control Routine (CIC) provides a method for removing a congested intersection from Control Levels I and II, and allowing flexible adjustments of cycle, splits and offsets at the intersection.[69] Congestion is said to exist at the intersection in question if the detected queue has exceeded a specific threshold.

The basic objectives of the CIC routine are as follows:

1. To prevent or alleviate blockage at the congested intersection and its upstream counterpart.
2. To relieve the stop-and-go traffic flow condition through the congested intersection and adjacent ones.

Both the congested intersection and its neighbors are included in the control analysis. The signal-switching decision for the critical intersection is traffic-dependent. A green phase has a guaranteed minimum, which can be extended in increments up to a specified maximum. The length of the green extension is optimized by considering the overall effect of each increment of extension on the delay, queue lengths, and blockage potential on all the approaches of the congested intersection and their respective downstream approaches. In this manner, an optimum condition is achieved not just locally but on a more system-wide basis, and the problem at the congested intersection is not simply shifted to a downstream location.

RTOP

Under the trilevel sponsorship of the Canadian Federal Transportation Development Agency, the Ontario Ministry of Transportation and Communications, and Metropolitan Toronto, the staff of the Metropolitan Toronto Roads and Traffic Department developed a Real Time Optimization Program[70] (RTOP) package. The package is a modular set of computer programs designed to compute optimal network signal timing parameters (cycle lengths, offsets, and splits) on a real-time basis in response to changing on-street volume patterns. The component parts of RTOP and their relationship to each other are illustrated in Figure 24.20 and together with the input requirements are briefly described below.

Input requirements. There are basically two main types of input data required by the RTOP: real-time and off-line data. The real-time portion of the RTOP input data consists of detector counts collected during control from loop sensors strategically placed throughout the test networks. The off-line data are obtained from three different sources:

1. Vehicular turning movement percentages in 15-min intervals for each signalized link in the network from a tape file containing recorded manual counts.
2. Historical traffic volumes in 15-min intervals for all links based on detector data recorded on magnetic tapes over the past several days.
3. Card input data, including network configuration data such as link identification number, operational charac-

[69] D. W. Ross, R. C. Dandys, and J. L. Schlaefli, "A Computer Control Scheme for Critical Intersection Control in an Urban Network," *Transport. Sci.*, *5*(2) (May 1971).

[70] *Improved Operation of Urban Transportation Systems: The Development and Evaluation of a Real-Time Computerized Traffic Control Strategy*, Vol. 3. Toronto: Metropolitan Toronto Roads and Traffic Department, Nov. 1976.

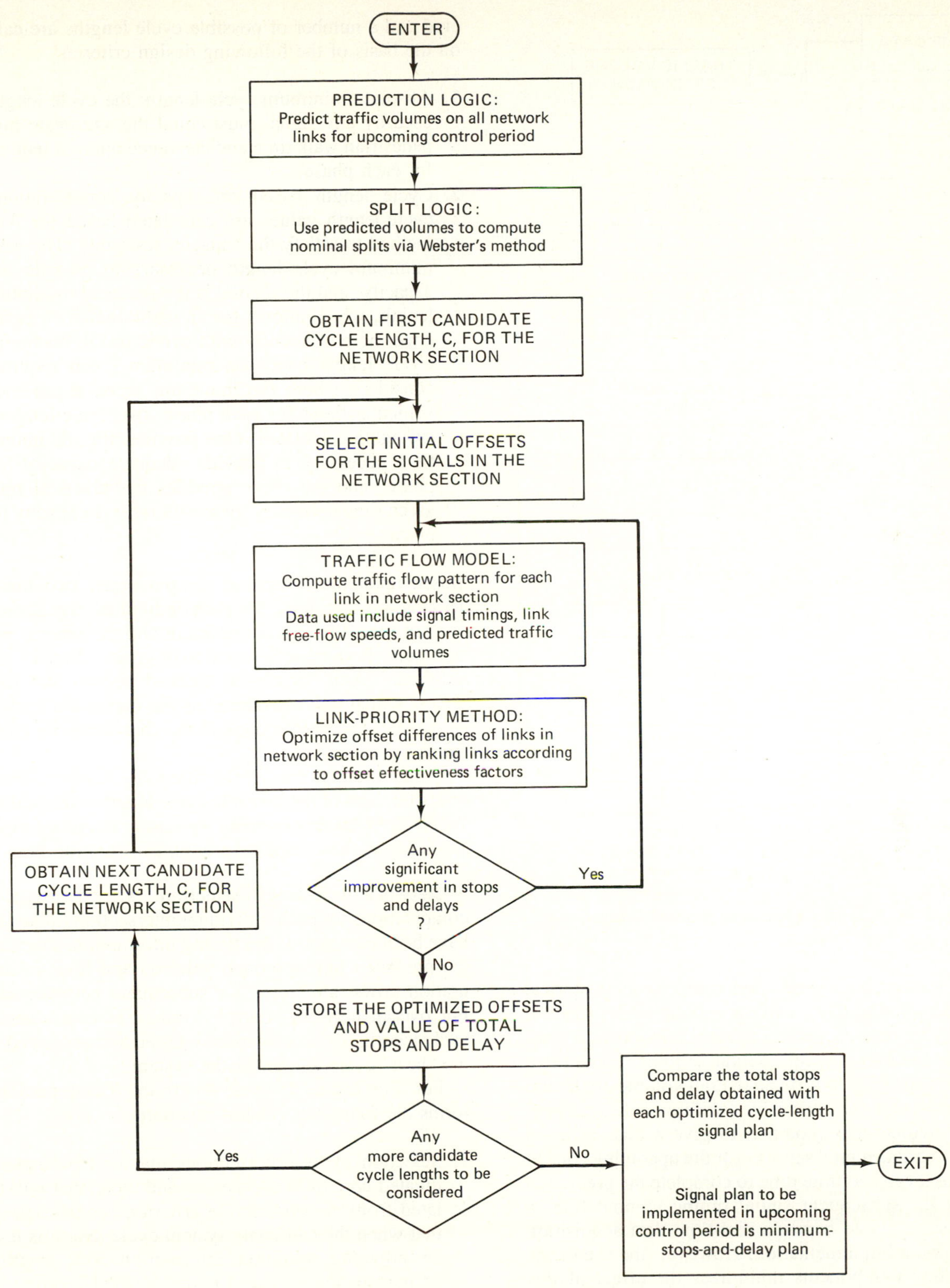

Figure 24.19. Level I Background Control Logic.

teristics such as design speed, and signal data such as phasing arrangements. Identification of detectors, the percentage contribution of each detector to the corresponding link volume, and the source and sink flow adjustments for each link also form part of the card input.

Traffic volume prediction routine. The traffic flow model in the RTOP package is based on the prediction logic developed for use in the ASCOT program, with the addition of certain modifications and refinements. The model predicts traffic volumes for each 15-min control period for each link,

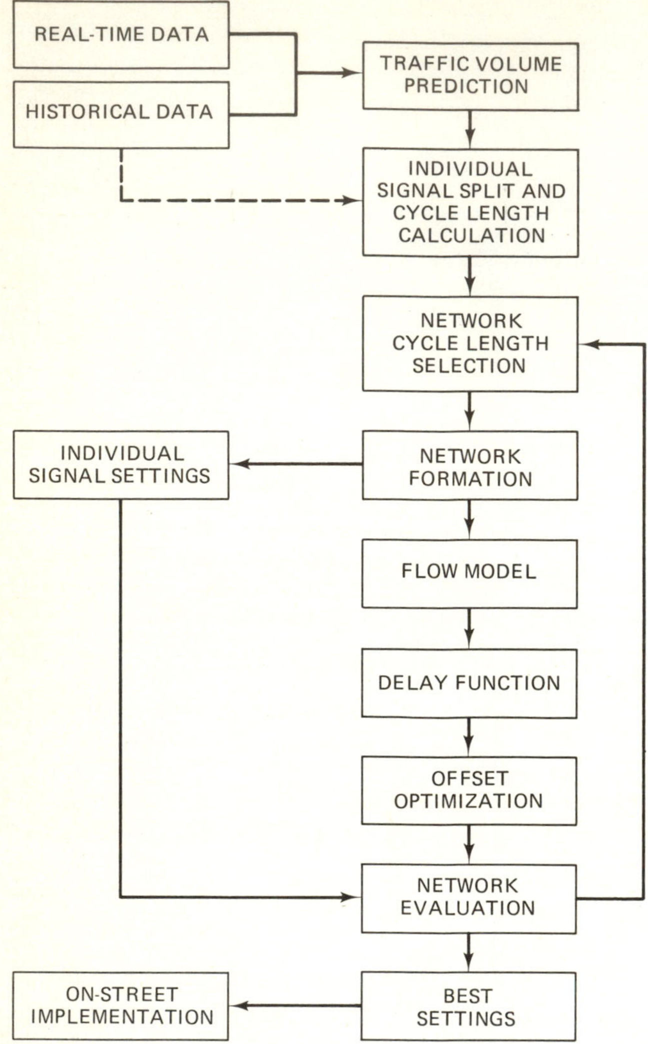

Figure 24.20. Real time optimization program package.

taking into account three prediction components: historical volume trends (day to day), current volume trends (control period to control period), and directional relationships (volume trends on a control or representative link). These three estimates are combined to form an overall volume prediction which is then tested for consistency with past data. If necessary, the prediction is modified to give a final value to be used in designing signal settings for the upcoming control period. Since it takes a finite time to complete the prediction process and the subsequent signal timing computation, a time lapse is inevitable between real-time data acquisition and signal timing implementation. However, the use of the three prediction components minimizes the effect of this time lapse as much as possible.

Signal timing computations for individual signals in the network. Once the traffic prediction process has been completed for all the links in the network, the RTOP package computes the appropriate network signal timings in response to the predicted traffic demand.

First, each individual signalized intersection is considered and a number of possible cycle lengths are calculated on the basis of the following design criteria:

1. Absolute minimum cycle length: the cycle length to be used by any signal must equal the aggregate minimum pedestrian walk time and clearance interval requirements for each phase.
2. Cycle length based on capacity considerations: two cycle-length values are calculated based on Webster's method to satisfy the capacity restraints. The first is the minimum cycle length necessary to provide adequate capacity, and the second is the practical minimum cycle length, which allows for an additional 10% capacity to cope more efficiently with cyclic traffic fluctuations.
3. Cycle length based on minimum green requirements: considering both the minimum green requirement and vehicular flows for each phase, two cycle-length values are again calculated. One provides the minimum green time necessary to provide adequate capacity for each phase, and the other provides the practical minimum green time necessary for a 10% reserve capacity for each phase.

Based upon the foregoing computations, two final cycle lengths are identified for each individual signalized intersection, one a practical minimum and the other a practical optimum. Both must be equal to or greater than the absolute minimum cycle length (as defined above) and less than 120 s, which was considered as the maximum cycle length allowable, taking into account the characteristics of the network.

As an integral part of the foregoing analysis, the signal splits for each of the possible cycle lengths were calculated, based on Webster's method, by setting the green times proportional to their respective volume/saturation flow ratios.

Network cycle-length selection. After the signal timing computations for each individual intersection in the network have been completed, the timing information, together with the predicted link approach volumes and their related saturation flows, are stored for subsequent network analysis. For overall network control, a range of candidate system cycle lengths are systematically tested and evaluated to find the "best" cycle length for the system.

For each candidate cycle length the RTOP package performs the following general functions:

1. Selection of the intersections that will be under coordinated control in the system and those that will be isolated from the system: the criterion for this selection is that when the candidate system cycle length is less than an individual minimum intersection cycle length, such an intersection is placed under isolated control.
2. Calculation of the signal timing intervals for both the coordinated and the isolated signals in the network.
3. Evaluation of the performance of the noncoordinated signals in the network in terms of delay and stops, using the technique developed by Webster.[71]

[71]Webster and Cobbe, *Traffic Signals*.

4. Computation of delay/difference-of-offset relationships for the coordinated signals in the network.
5. Identification of the ideal offset setting for each link: A performance index is computed for each given offset difference between the upstream and downstream signal. This index is based on the amount of uniform delay, the amount of random delay, and the estimated number of stops resulting from any particular offset difference. The best offset difference for the pair of signals in question is the one given by the minimum value of the index.
6. Calculation of link importance factors.
7. Offset optimization: Using a technique adapted from the SIGRID Program, the optimum offsets, as given by the offset values associated with the global minimum system performance function, are calculated.
8. System performance evaluation: The overall system performance index is obtained by adding the performance index from the isolated signals and the performance index for the coordinated signals corresponding to the calculated offsets. After the entire range of practical cycle lengths has been similarly processed for the network, the cycle length, signal phasing, and offset settings corresponding to the lowest overall system performance index are finally chosen for implementation.

UTCS system

The U.S. Federal Highway Administration has sponsored extensive research to develop and test advanced traffic control strategies in a digital computer-controlled signal system environment. The publication *The Urban Traffic Control System in Washington, D.C.*[72] presents a general overview of the Urban Traffic Control System (UTCS) project. Three generations of signal control strategies were developed and these are described briefly as follows.

First-generation control. First-generation control uses predetermined signal patterns developed by off-line optimization programs.[73-75] These patterns or control plans are stored in the computer and the appropriate plans for each area are selected on a time-of-day basis or by matching the control plan with the existing traffic conditions. To provide for a smooth transition between control plans, an offset transition subroutine is incorporated in the program logic.

To enhance the first-generation software, a variable signal-split routine is used at critical intersections to adjust the signal splits on a cycle-to-cycle basis in response to traffic demand.

Certain intersections were also instrumented to provide for public transit priority control in which a green extension period could be considered at the end of the normal green interval. The criterion for a green extension period was based upon the premise that a net reduction in total passenger delay on the main street versus the cross street at the time of arrival of a bus can be accomplished.

Second-generation control. For this mode of control, signal parameters such as cycle, offset, and split for optional network control are computed on a real-time basis as a function of current and predicted traffic conditions. The program consists of:

- A model to predict traffic volumes and speeds in the network for the ensuing 15-min period.
- A subnetwork configuration model to divide the total network into subnetworks on-line based upon cycle length and other timing requirements.
- An optimization routine to generate optimum signal timing patterns on-line for each subnetwork for each 15-min control period by minimizing overall network delay.
- A critical intersection control routine to fine-tune signal timings at critical intersections by adjusting the split and offset on a cycle-by-cycle basis.
- An offset transition model to determine transition parameters to effect a smooth and rapid transition during a timing pattern change.
- A boundary model to compute timing patterns for optimum subnetwork interfacing.

Third-generation control. Third-generation control involves the use of a traffic-responsive algorithm to provide signal timing on a cycle-by-cycle basis.[76-79] The cycle length, split, and offset may vary between intersections and from cycle to cycle while overall network optimization is achieved.

In broad terms, third-generation control logic can be characterized as a control logic containing different traffic flow regimes. For example, under a light flow control policy, a base cycle length can be used, and offset and split optimized jointly and implemented on a long-term basis, say a 5- to 15-min control period. A moderate flow policy would involve the use of a variable cycle length for a control period of 3 to 5 min in duration. The congested flow policy would employ responsive timings on a cycle-to-cycle basis in order to prevent intersection blockage and the spread of congestion to other areas of the network.

---

[72] *The Urban Traffic Control System in Washington, D.C.* Washington, D.C.: U.S. Department of Transportation, Federal Highway Administration Sept. 1974.

[73] Sperry Rand Corporation, *Urban Traffic Control and Bus Priority System,* Vol. 1, *Design and Implementation,* NTIS No. PB-214-788. Washington, D.C.: U.S. Federal Highway Administration, Office of Research and Development, Nov. 1972.

[74] Sperry Rand Corporation, *Advanced Control Technology in Urban Traffic Control Systems,* Vol. 1: *Systems Description* (NTIS No. PB 188-963), U.S. Bureau of Public Roads, Oct. 1969.

[75] Sperry Rand Corporation, *Advanced Control Technology in Urban Traffic Control Systems,* Vol. 1A: *Bus Priority System Description* (NTIS No. PB 190-847), U.S. Bureau of Public Roads, Mar. 1970.

[76] KLD Associates Inc., *Variable Cycle Signal Timing Program,* Vol. 1 (NTIS No. PB-241-717/8 WT), May 1974.

[77] J. D. C. Little, N. Gartner, H. Cabbay, and M. Springer, *Variable Cycle Signal Timing Program,* Vol. 2 (NTIS No. PB-241-718/6 WT), May 1974.

[78] E. B. Lieberman, W. R. McShane, and R. B. Goldblatt, *Variable Cycle Signal Timing Program,* Vol. 3 (NTIS No. PB-214-719/4 WT), May 1974.

[79] E. B. Lieberman, W. R. McShane, and R. B. Goldblatt, *Variable Cycle Signal Timing Program,* Vol. 4 (NTIS No. PB-241-720/2 WT), May 1974.

Traffic control system evaluation techniques

Numerous measures of effectiveness have been used by traffic engineers to evaluate both individual traffic signal operation and signal networks, including

- Travel time
- Speed
- Delay
- Queue length
- Volume
- Capacity/saturation flow
- Congestion
- Air/noise pollution
- Fuel consumption
- Traffic accidents/conflicts

For noncomputerized signal control systems, the various signal timing design methods can be adapted as an evaluation tool to provide a rapid and logical check of the existing signal operation and/or an evaluation of alternative timing plans before implementation, as illustrated in Table 24-8. With a computerized traffic control system, off-line programs can be developed to serve as an analysis and evaluation tool. As an example, the following briefly describes some of the more commonly used Metropolitan Toronto traffic control system off-line analysis programs; Figures 24.21 to 24.27 provide illustrative examples of the program outputs.

GRAPH: This program produces graphical output of vehicle arrivals, number of vehicles stopped, and vehicle delay as a function of time based upon detector data.

LINKS: The existence and coherence of platoons arriving at an intersection can be analyzed by this program.

CYCLES: This program analyzes recorded traffic data on a cycle by cycle basis.

DELAY: This program estimates the delay and queue at the beginning of green for a specified intersection approach based on traffic detector data.

STREAM: This program produces a time–space chart indicating progression characteristics on a chosen street section for a specified date and time.

VDC: The Volume Density Calculation (VDC) program produces various statistics relating to volume and density based on detector data.

CONGEX: This program is used to analyze traffic data for the existence and degree of congestion at specified intersections.

The overall performance of a traffic signal system is dependent primarily on the degree of vehicular mobility within the system and the amount of traffic being serviced. These can be measured by travel time and traffic volume, respectively. However, since volume does not account for the distance traveled, a more desirable measure of effectiveness is service rate (R) given by

$$R = V \times L \qquad (24.21)$$

where V = volume carried by the link

L = link length

TABLE 24-8
Summary of Evaluation Techniques Based on Signal-Timing Design Methods

	Derived Traffic Parameters*									
Evaluation Technique	Delay	Number of Stops	Queue	Travel Time	Volume	Capacity	Saturation	Load Factor	Speed	Travel Cost
Isolated intersection										
H.C.M.	A				A	A		A	A	
A.L.E.					A	A		A		
Webster (ARRB)	A		A		A	A	A			
Probability					A	A				
Arterial										
Geometric	L/S			L/S					L/S	
Difference of offsets	L/S	L/S	L/S							
Area network										
SIGOP	G	G		G	G				G	G
TRANSYT	G	G		G	G		G		G	G

*A, approach; L, link; S, link system; G, grid.

SOURCE: Metropolitan Toronto Roads and Traffic Department. *Improved Operations of Urban Transportation Systems, Vol. 1: Traffic Signal Control Strategies, State-of-the-Art.* Toronto, Mar. 1974.

As a measure of mobility, the total travel time (T) spent by all vehicles traversing the link is given by

$$T = t \times V \qquad (24.22)$$

where t is the average travel time along the link.

For a signal network of N links, the overall system service rate (SR) and system travel time (ST) can be expressed as

$$\text{SR} = \sum_{i=1}^{N} V_i L_i \qquad (24.23)$$

$$\text{ST} = \sum_{i=1}^{N} t_i V_i \qquad (24.24)$$

where V_i = volume on link i

L_i = length of link i

t_i = average travel time along link i

It has been hypothesized that a linear relationship exists between system travel time and system service rate. Thus, for a given network operating under a particular signal plan, a linear regression equation can be developed and used as a means of performance comparison between different signal plans (see Figure 24.28). The signal timing plan with the significantly lower Y value (hence lower travel time) can be judged as the better plan.

For a particular traffic signal optimization time period, if the system service rate values do not vary significantly from plan to plan, the corresponding system travel-time values can be compared directly for significant differences.

The "direct comparison" procedure consists of two major steps:

1. *Service-rate comparison:* For a given pair of data within an optimization time period, the differences between the system service-rate values are tested for significance at

```
SYMBOL       LOWER GRAPH SCALE                                          UPPER GRAPH SCALE
  *     20:    40:    60:    80:    100:    120:    20:    40:    60:    80:    100:    120:
  .     20:    40:    60:    80:    100:    120:    20:    40:    60:    80:    100:    120:
  +     20:    40:    60:    80:    100:    120:    20:    40:    60:    80:    100:    120:
  -     20:    40:    60:    80:    100:    120:     0:     0:     0:     0:      0:      0:
TIME    PLAN                                                                          PX -0
1605.00 2413
1610.00 2412*
1615.00 2412
1620.00 2412.
1625.00 2412
1630.00 2412
1635.00 2413
1640.00 241-*
1645.00 2412
1650.00 241-2
1655.00 241-*
1700.00 2413
1705.00 2412
1710.00 241-*
1715.00 2412
1720.00 2412.
1725.00 241-2
1730.00 241-.
1735.00 2413
1740.00 2412
1745.00 2412
1750.00 2412
1755.00 2412*
1800.00 2412

   16     18     57     0     84     45     57     0
   22     19     47     2    104     30     74     0
   32     17     64     0     97     27     76     0
   20     22     54     1     99     28     64     0
   30     21     61     1    104     33     75     0
   30     17     53     0     88     23     55     0
   19     17     67     1    107     26     75     0
```

Figure 24.21. Sample output of GRAPH program.

a 1% level. If no significant difference is detected, this pair of values becomes a candidate for further analysis.

2. *Travel-time comparison:* For a pair of service rate data that pass the foregoing significant difference test, the travel-time data are then tested for a significant difference at a 5% level. Based upon the results of this test, conclusions may be made as to which is the best signal timing plan.

Special Signals

Lane-use control signals

Lane-use control signals are special overhead signals having indications to permit or prohibit the use of specific lanes of a street or highway. These signals are most commonly used for reversible lane control. They may also be used to (1) clear a freeway lane(s) when this is deemed necessary at any time, (2) indicate the termination of a freeway lane, (3) indicate the blockage (caused by an accident or a hazard) of a lane ahead, or (4) permanently operate a two-way street with an unequal lane distribution.

Lane-use control signals consist of a 12-in. (30.5-cm) square face having either a downward green arrow, a red X, or a yellow X on an opaque background. Their meaning, design, location, and operation are detailed in the *MUTCD*.

Railroad–highway grade-crossing signals

There are approximately 220,000 highway–railroad crossings in the United States of which approximately 48,000 have been provided with special protection of some sort—gates, flashing lights, flagmen, traffic signals, or bells. The selection of traffic control devices at a grade crossing is determined by public agencies having the appropriate jurisdictional responsibility. Active grade-crossing

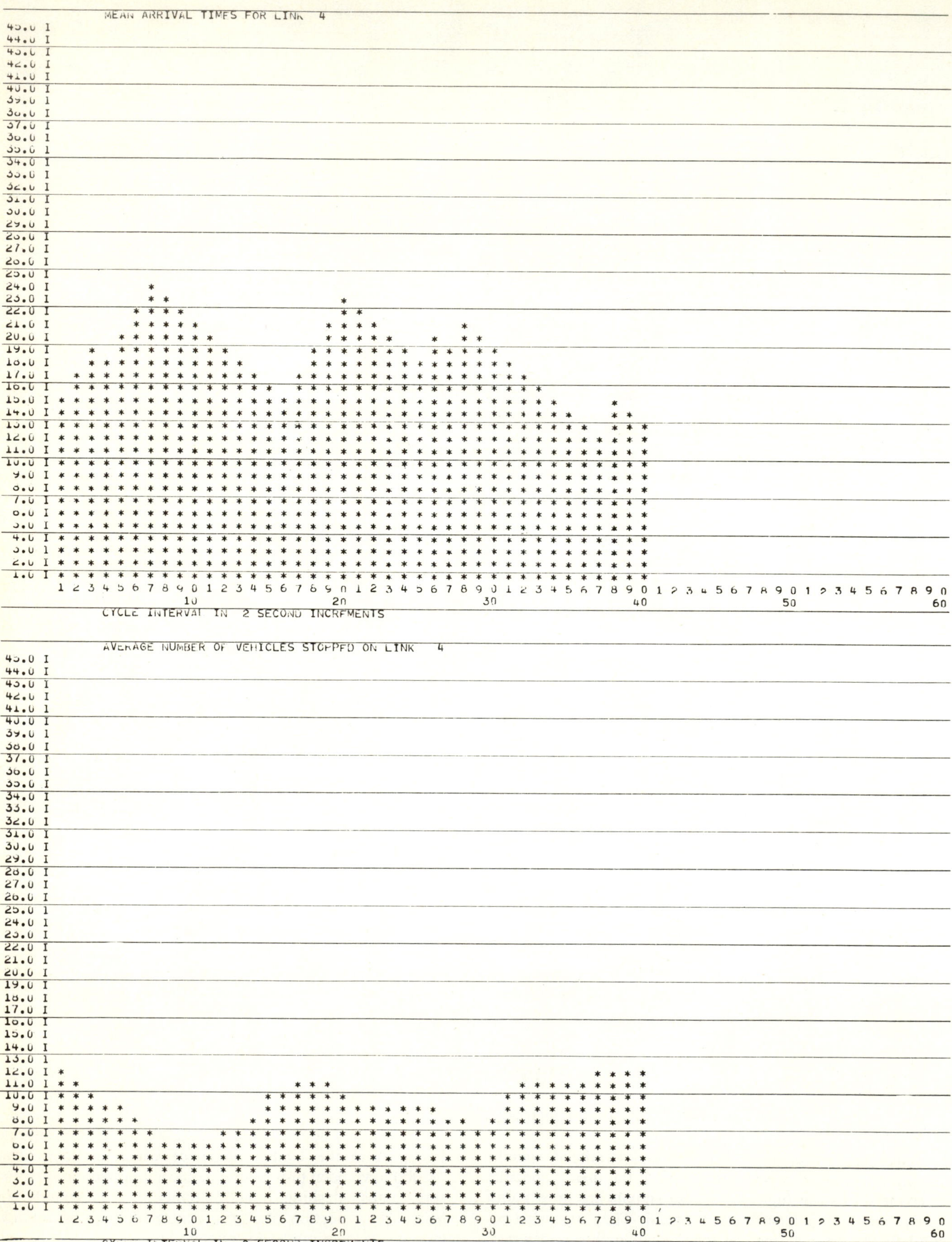

Figure 24.22. Sample output of LINKS program.

```
                  DELAY PER VEHICLE FOR LINK   4
45.0 I
44.0 I
43.0 I
42.0 I
41.0 I
40.0 I
39.0 I
38.0 I
37.0 I
36.0 I
35.0 I
34.0 I
33.0 I
32.0 I
31.0 I
30.0 I
29.0 I
28.0 I
27.0 I
26.0 I                                                                         *       *
25.0 I *                                                                       *   * *
24.0 I *                                                                     * * * * *
23.0 I *                                                                     * * * * *
22.0 I * *                                                                 * * * * * *
21.0 I * *                           *                                     * * * * * *
20.0 I * *   *                       *                                   * * * * * * *
19.0 I * * * *                     * * *                               * * * * * * * *
18.0 I * * * * *                 * * * *                             * * * * * * * * *
17.0 I * * * * *                 * * * *                             * * * * * * * * *
16.0 I * * * * *               * * * * * *             *             * * * * * * * * *
15.0 I * * * * * *           * * * * * * *           * * * *       * * * * * * * * * *
14.0 I * * * * * *         * * * * * * * *         * * * * *     * * * * * * * * * * *
13.0 I * * * * * *       * * * * * * * * * *       * * * * * * * * * * * * * * * * * *
12.0 I * * * * * * * * * * * * * * * * * * *     * * * * * * * * * * * * * * * * * * *
11.0 I * * * * * * * * * * * * * * * * * * * * * * * * * * * * * * * * * * * * * * * *
10.0 I * * * * * * * * * * * * * * * * * * * * * * * * * * * * * * * * * * * * * * * *
 9.0 I * * * * * * * * * * * * * * * * * * * * * * * * * * * * * * * * * * * * * * * *
 8.0 I * * * * * * * * * * * * * * * * * * * * * * * * * * * * * * * * * * * * * * * *
 7.0 I * * * * * * * * * * * * * * * * * * * * * * * * * * * * * * * * * * * * * * * *
 6.0 I * * * * * * * * * * * * * * * * * * * * * * * * * * * * * * * * * * * * * * * *
 5.0 I * * * * * * * * * * * * * * * * * * * * * * * * * * * * * * * * * * * * * * * *
 4.0 I * * * * * * * * * * * * * * * * * * * * * * * * * * * * * * * * * * * * * * * *
 3.0 I * * * * * * * * * * * * * * * * * * * * * * * * * * * * * * * * * * * * * * * *
 2.0 I * * * * * * * * * * * * * * * * * * * * * * * * * * * * * * * * * * * * * * * *
 1.0 I * * * * * * * * * * * * * * * * * * * * * * * * * * * * * * * * * * * * * * * *
       1 2 3 4 5 6 7 8 9 0 1 2 3 4 5 6 7 8 9 0 1 2 3 4 5 6 7 8 9 0 1 2 3 4 5 6 7 8 9 0 1 2 3 4 5 6 7 8 9 0 1 2 3 4 5 6 7 8 9 0
                      10                  20                  30                  40                  50                  60
                CYCLE INTERVAL IN  2 SECOND INCREMENTS
```

Figure 24.22. *Continued.*

CLOCK TIME	ASPECT	SECS	SPLIT/ CYCLE	SPLIT/ VOLUME	QUEUE N/E	QUEUE S/W	AV.PULSE/VOLUME N	S	E	W	OFFSET VOLUMES N	S	E	W	CONGESTION INDEX N	S	E	W
000.40	[illegible]	30																
001.10	EWG	2																
001.12	EWG	2																
001.14	EWG	2																
001.16	EWY	4																
001.20	ALLR	2																
001.22	NSG	26																
001.48	NSG	2																
001.50	NSG	2																
001.52	NSG	2																
001.54	NSY	4									3.73	2.62	3.62	2.27				
001.58	ALLR	2	80	405	0	0	630	360	225	405	496	372	248	372	-208.	-84.	-104.	-84.
002.00	EWG	30									4.13	2.66	9.88	2.28				
002.30	EWG	2									4.13	2.66	9.88	2.28				
002.32	EWG	2	-0	65	0	0	1.64	2.54	5.22	2.28	576	288	144	288				
002.34	EWG	2																
002.36	EWY	4																
002.40	ALLR	2																
002.42	NSG	26																
003.08	NSG	2																
003.10	NSG	2																
003.12	NSG	2																
003.14	NSY	4									2.83	2.65	9.88	2.27				
003.18	ALLR	2	80	360	0	0	630	315	180	315	496	372	124	372	80.	-84.	20.	-84.
003.20	EWG	30									3.97	2.62	.54	2.27				
003.50	EWG	2									3.97	2.62	.54	2.27				
003.52	EWG	2	-0	44	0	0	.90	2.54	2.29	.91	288	288	432	432				
003.54	EWG	2																
003.56	EWY	4																
004.00	ALLR	2																
004.02	NSG	26																
004.28	NSG	2																
004.30	NSG	2																
004.32	NSG	2																
004.34	NSY	4									1.70	2.62	.63	2.27				
004.38	ALLR	2	80	607	0	0	720	360	405	945	620	372	496	372	-332.	-84.	-64.	60.
004.40	EWG	30									3.37	2.28	6.88	2.29				
005.10	EWG	2									3.37	2.28	6.88	2.29				
005.12	EWG	2	-0	61	0	0	2.52	1.64	2.71	2.27	288	288	144	432				
005.14	EWG	2																
005.16	EWY	4																
005.20	ALLR	2																
005.22	NSG	26																
005.48	NSG	2																
005.50	NSG	2																
005.52	NSG	2																
005.54	NSY	4									3.37	1.59	3.66	2.27				
005.58	ALLR	2	80	405	0	0	360	630	270	360	248	620	248	372	40.	-332.	-104.	60.

Figure 24.23. Sample output of CYCLES program.

```
                                        C A L C U L A T I O N   O F   V E H I C L E   D E L A Y S
DET. INT.       FROM    ----    TO              CODES         INIT.QU    QUDIFF     QUMAX     MOVEMENT-INDEX   TIME(SEC*10)   RANDOM DOUBLE
NO.  NO.   MTH DY HR.MN   MTH DY HR.MN  GREEN    YELLOW  (THRU.LN)  (THRU.LN)  (CURR LN)   THRU.  RTURN    TRAVEL   HDWY      NO.   LANE F
664  400   JUL 11  8. 0   JUL 11  8.15 61 00 00    65          0          8         12       90.     10.       100      20      107.    .70

ACTUAL START  ACTUAL END  TOTAL NO.  NO.OF THRU CARS  QU.AT END  AVER.DELAY  TOTAL DELAY     THRU.VOL.  NO.OF CARS NO.OF ADD'L CARS
 HR.MN:SC      HR.MN:SC   OF CARS    THRU.LN TOTAL   (THRU.LN)   (SEC*10)   (CARS*SEC*10)  (CARS/HR)   STOPPED   DUE TO DOUBLE LN
 6. 0:27       17. 4: 9      48         33      43        0        59003       2537129           5          31               .006

TOTAL VOLUME
 (CARS/HR)
     5

                                        TOTAL VOLUME OF  1 APPROACHES=      5  (CARS/HR)

                                        TOTAL THRU.VOLUME OF  1 APPROACHES=      5  (CARS/HR)

                                        WEIGHTED DELAY OF  1 APPROACHES= 59003  (CARS*10)

           DELAYS                       MEAN DELAY=  346 (SEC*10)
TIME (SEC*10)    NO.OF CARS  0/0 OF CARS       HISTOGRAM
    0-   9           2           6             111111
   10-  19           0           0
   20-  29           0           0
   30-  39           0           0
   40-  49           0           0
   50-  59           0           0
   60-  69           0           0
   70-  79           0           0
   80-  89           0           0
   90-  99           1           3             111
  100- 109           1           3             111
  110- 119           0           0
  120- 129           2           6             111111
  130- 139           1           3             111
  140- 149           3           9             111111111
  150- 159           0           0
  160- 169           1           3             111
  170- 179           0           0
  180- 189           1           3             111
  190- 199           2           6             111111
  200- 209           1           3             111
  210- 219           0           0
  220- 229           0           0
  230- 239           0           0
  240- 249           0           0
  250- 259           0           0
  260- 269           0           0
  270- 279           0           0
  280- 289           0           0
  290- 299           0           0
  300- 309           0           0
  310- 319           0           0
  320- 329           0           0
  330- 339           1           3             111
  340- 349           1           3             111
  350- 359           0           0
  360- 369           1           3             111
  370- 379           0           0
  380- 389           1           3             111
  390- 399           0           0
  400- 409           1           3             111
  410- 419           0           0
  420- 429           0           0
  430- 439           1           3             111
  440- 449           0           0
  450- 459           1           3             111
  460- 469           0           0
  470- 479           1           3             111
  480- 489           2           6             111111
  490- 499           0           0
  500- 509           1           3             111
  510- 519           1           3             111
  520- 529           1           3             111
  550- 559           1           3             111
  570- 579           1           3             111
  600- 609           1           3             111
 1060-1069           1           3             111
 1090-1099           1           3             111

          QUEUES                          MEAN QUEUE=    66 (CARS*10)
   SIZE (NO.OF CARS)          FREQUENCY
           0                      1
           1                      0
           2                      0
           3                      0
           4                      0
           5                      0
           6                      2
           7                      1
           8                      0
           9                      0
          10                      0
          11                      0
          12                      0
          13                      0
          14                      1
          15                      0
          16                      0
          17                      0
          18                      0
          19                      0

12 JUL 79   12:09:44   IDENT DELAY    ACCOUNT DAVE    CARDS IN   12   CARDS OUT    0   PAGES   19   ELAPSED TIME  0  3 46

*   *   *   *   *   *   *   *   TORONTO 1107 65K EXEC II LCC 1101-0050 HC/KS-1  *   *   *   *   *   *
```


Figure 24.24. Sample output of DELAY program.

```
DATA
     DATE JUN 30                        SCALE   877 FEET PER INCH                         TIME   16.15 16.30

     INTERSECTIONS       584    583    582    581    431    580    528
     PROGRESSION           S      S      S      S      S      S      S
     DIST.(FT)             0   2160   1765    444    477   2600   2638
     ACC.DIST.(FT)         0   2160   3925   4369   4846   7446  10084

     DEPARTURE          0: 0   0: 0   0: 0   0: 0   0: 0   0: 0   0: 0
     ARRIVALS           0: 0   0: 0   0: 0   0: 0   0: 0   0: 0   0: 0
     STOP TIME          0: 0   0: 0   0: 0   0: 0   0: 0   0: 0   0: 0
LEGEND
        GREEN IN DIRECTION OF PROGRESSION
     R  RED IN DIRECTION OF PROGRESSION
     >  ADVANCED GREEN IN DIRECTION OF PROGRESSION
     <  ADVANCED GREEN IN OPPOSITE DIRECTION TO PROGRESSION
     =  ADVANCED GREEN IN EITHER DIRECTION OF PROGRESSION OR OPPOSITE DIRECTION TO PROGRESSION

16.15:-0   R                 R                 R   R   R                 R                 R
16.15: 1                     R                 R   R   R                 R                 R
16.15: 2                     R                 R   R   R                 R                 R
16.15: 3                     R                 R   R   R                 R
16.15: 4                     R                 R   R   R                 R                 R
16.15: 5                     R                 R   R   R                 R                 R
16.15: 6                     R                 R   R   R                 R                 R
16.15: 7                     R                 R   R   R                 R                 R
16.15: 8                     R                 R   R   R                 R                 R
16.15: 9                     R                 R   R   R                 R                 R
16.15:10                     R                 R   R                     R                 R
16.15:11                     R                 R   R                     R                 R
16.15:12                     R                 R   R   R                 R                 R
16.15:13                     R                 R   R   R                 R                 R
16.15:14                     R                 R   R   R                 R                 R
16.15:15                     R                 R   R   R                 R                 R
16.15:16                     R                 R   R   R                 R                 R
16.15:17                     R                 R   R   R                 R                 R
16.15:18                     R                 R   R   R                 R                 R
16.15:19                     R                 R   R   R                 R                 R
16.15:20                     R                 R   R   R                 R                 R
16.15:21                     R                 R   R   R                 R                 R
16.15:22                     R                 R       R                 R                 R
16.15:23                     R                 R       R                 R                 R
16.15:24                     R                 R       R                 R                 R
16.15:25                     R                 R       R                 R                 R
16.15:26                     R                 R       R                 R                 R
16.15:27                     R                 R       R                                   R
16.15:28                     R                 R   R   R                                   R
16.15:29                     R                     R   R                 R                 R
16.15:30                     R                     R   R                 R                 R
16.15:31                     R                     R   R                 R                 R
16.15:32                                           R   R                 R                 R
16.15:33                                           R   R                 R                 R
16.15:34                                           R   R                 R                 R
16.15:35                                       R   R   R                 R                 R
16.15:36                                       R   R   R                 R                 R
16.15:37                                       R   R   R                 R                 R
16.15:38                                       R   R   R                 R                 R
16.15:39                                       R   R   R                 R                 R
16.15:40                                       R   R   R                 R                 R
16.15:41                                       R   R   R                 R
```

Figure 24.25. Sample output of STREAM program.

Figure 24.26. Sample output of VDC program.

```
            VEHICLE DENSITY CALCULATIONS

CONTROL CARDS
  DATE       START      END       MAXIMUM PULSE(SECS)
JUN 20        7. 0      9. 0                3

DETECTOR  LANES            DETECTOR  LANES            DETECTOR  LANES            DETECTOR  LANES
   45       1                  50      1
CONTROL PARAMETERS            A1         A2         A3         A4         A5         A6         A7
                            .200      1.990      1.000     11.060     .10820     .60000    .009330


                    VEHICLE DENSITY CALCULATIONS.

DETECTOR  LANES  APPARENT COUNTS/HR  MEAN SPEED  CORR FACTOR  COUNTS/LANE/HR  DENSITY  MEAN SPACE HEADWAY  MEAN TIME HEADWAY

   45       1            709.          20.72       1.0000          709.        47.70          110.70              3.60
   50       1              0.            .00       1.0000            0.          .00             .00               .00


JOB COMPLETED NORMALLY.
ALL JOBS COMPLETED.
```

```
CONGESTION EVALUATION OF PX 100

INTERSECTION NUMBER 548.

DETECTOR NUMBERS  841 842 843 844

THE EVALUATION WAS MADE BETWEEN    7.00 AND    9.00 ON MAY 29.

A TOTAL OF    79 CYCLES WERE OBSERVED FOR EVALUATION.

CONGESTION WAS DETECTED ON ONE OR MORE LEGS DURING 79 CYCLES.
     THIS IS EQUIVALENT TO100 CONGESTED CYCLES PER 100 CYCLES OBSERVED.

OBSERVING EACH LEG SEPARATELY, CONGESTION WAS DETECTED2136 TIMES.
     THIS IS EQUIVALENT TO*** LEGS CONGESTED PER 100 CYCLES OBSERVED.

THE RATE OF CONGESTION PER 100 CYCLES FOR EACH LEG IS AS FOLLOWS:
                                                                    NORTH  735
                                                                    SOUTH  214
                                                                    EAST   863
                                                                    WEST   891

APPROXIMATELY  7138 VEHICLES PASSED THROUGH THE INTERSECTION DURING THE OBSERVATIONS.
     THIS IS EQUIVALENT TO AN AVERAGE OF   90 VEHICLES PER CYCLE.

THE TOTAL NUMBER OF VEHICLES AND THE AVERAGE NUMBER OF VEHICLES PER CYCLE FOR EACH LEG ARE AS FOLLOWS:
                                                                             TOTAL    AVERAGE
                                                                    NORTH     2083        26
                                                                    SOUTH     1061        13
                                                                    EAST      1542        20
                                                                    WEST      2452        31

                                                                    CONGESTION INDEX
                                                                    NORTH  ,     8.085
                                                                    SOUTH  ,     2.352
                                                                    EAST   ,     9.491
                                                                    WEST   ,     9.797
```

Figure 24.27. Sample output of CONGEX program.

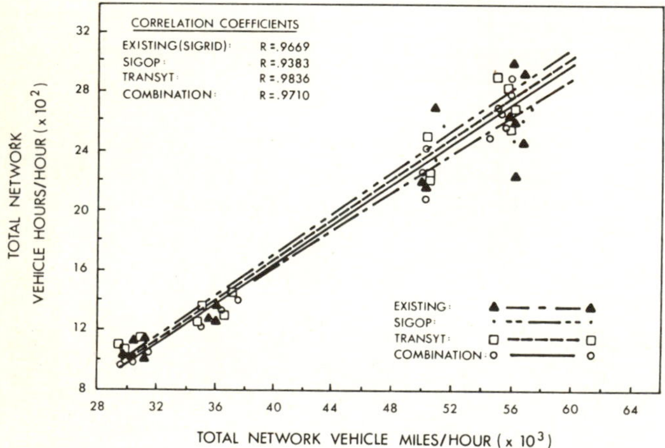

Figure 24.28. Traffic signal performance relationships.

control systems range from post-mounted flashing light signals to automatic gates combined with:

- Post-mounted flashing light signals
- Cantilever flashing light signals
- Combination of the above

and any of the foregoing may or may not incorporate a bell. Figure 24.29 illustrates a typical post-mounted flashing light signal.

The design and application of traffic control devices at railway–highway grade crossings in the United States are described in the *MUTCD* and in an FHWA publication.[80]

In other countries, the appropriate authorities have established the required specifications.[81]

Flashing beacons

A flashing beacon commonly consists of one or more sections of a standard traffic signal, displaying yellow or red indications. They are mounted either as single or twin units, with the indication flashing at a rate of 50 or 60 times per minute with the illuminated period one-half to two-thirds of the total cycle. When illuminated, the beacon should be clearly visible to all drivers it faces for a distance of at least ¼ mi (0.4 km) under normal atmospheric conditions, unless otherwise physically obstructed.

Intersection control beacon. Flashing beacons are used at locations where full traffic control signals are not warranted but where, because of lack of visibility or other hazard, signs alone are not sufficient.

Intersection control beacons are usually suspended 15 to 19 ft (4.6 to 5.8 m) over the roadway, and must show a separate indication for each direction of movement or each approach. Typically, such beacons will have flashing yellow indications facing the major street approaches and flashing red indications facing the minor street approaches. In special circumstances, flashing red beacons may be used in all four directions to augment a four-way stop regulation. Stop signs should be in place at intersections where flashing red beacons are used.

[80] U. S. Federal Highway Administration, *Railroad–Highway Grade Crossing Handbook* (Technology Sharing Rep. TS-78-214), Washington, D.C., Aug. 1978.

[81] U. K. Department of Transport, *Report on Level Crossing Protection* (London: Her Majesty's Stationery Office, 1978).

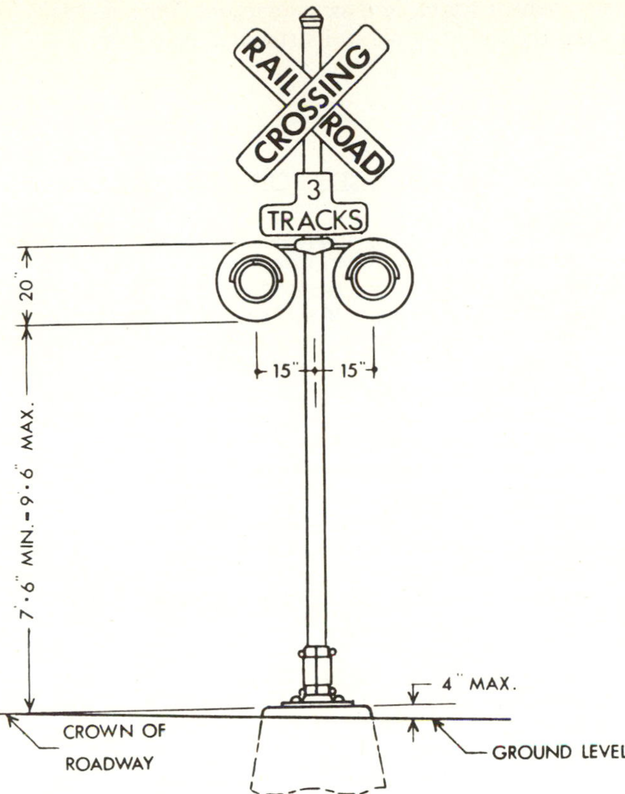

TOP OF FOUNDATION TO BE AT THE SAME ELEVATION AS THE SURFACE OF THE TRAVELLED WAY AND NO MORE THAN 4 INCHES ABOVE THE SURFACE OF THE GROUND.

Figure 24.29. Typical flashing light signal—post mounted. SOURCE: *Manual on Uniform Traffic Control Devices for Streets and Highways,* U.S. Department of Transportation, Federal Highway Administration. Washington, D.C., U.S. Government Printing Office, 1978, p. 8C-2.

Hazard identification beacon. Flashing yellow beacons may be located at intersections or midblock crosswalks where warning is required, on the approaches to narrow bridges, underpasses, or other obstructions or hazards that require special attention by the motorist. They may also be used to supplement an appropriate warning or regulatory sign or marker. In this application the beacon should not be included within the border of the sign except for school speed-limit signs.

As a general rule, beacons or any other device having flashing indications should not be installed too close to the approach to a signalized intersection because they may very easily distract the attention of the driver from the signal indications and cause accidents.

Speed limit sign beacon. A single beacon or a twin beacon showing two alternately flashing yellow indications vertically aligned may be used in conjunction with a fixed- or variable-speed limit sign. This application is particularly appropriate for school zones where lower speed limits apply during specified times and on specified days. When the beacons are flashing, they indicate that the school zone speed limit is in effect. The lenses of a speed limit beacon when used with a speed limit sign may be positioned within the face of the sign.

Stop sign beacon. A single or twin beacon with red lenses can be used to augment a stop sign. The beacon should be mounted from 12 to 24 in. (0.3 to 0.6 m) above the stop sign. Where two lenses are used and if aligned horizontally, the beacons should be flashed simultaneously. If aligned vertically, the beacons should be flashed alternately.

Traffic signals at movable bridges

When a roadway crosses a movable bridge, traffic control signals are used to stop vehicular traffic on the approach to the bridge when it is open or about to be opened. Signal heads are installed at both approaches to the bridge, often in conjunction with resistance gates as described in the *MUTCD*. The signal control mechanism should be interconnected with the bridge control and arranged so that an adequate warning indication will be shown sufficiently in advance of the bridge opening to ensure that the bridge will be clear of all traffic.

When standard intersection traffic control signals are located within approximately 500 ft (150 m) of the bridge ends, they should be fitted with preemptors interconnected with the bridge signals so that the intersection itself can be kept unobstructed by the traffic stopped at the drawbridge signal. Similarly, when the bridge is near a railway grade crossing, special advance signals may be necessary to ensure that vehicles will not be stopped on the tracks.

Emergency vehicle access

Traffic signals are sometimes installed to ensure safe and quick access for emergency vehicles from fire stations or ambulance stations to a street where such access might otherwise be difficult. In these instances, the warrants prescribed for traffic signal installation will not normally be satisfied. The operation of such signals provides continual right-of-way to the through movement with a preemptive control in the station to permit the emergency vehicle to receive the right-of-way and enter the street at such time as it is required. The application, operation, and design of emergency traffic signals are covered in the *MUTCD*.

Speed control

Traffic control signals are sometimes used simply for speed control. When so used, the signal is not placed at a crossing or intersection and is used almost exclusively on one-way roadways. Its steady state is normally red. A vehicle detector is installed some distance in advance of the signal, and when a motor vehicle is detected, the timing mechanism for the traffic signal will turn the indication to green in time to allow the vehicle to proceed uninterrupted if it is traveling at or below the posted speed.

Each actuation received while the green is showing resets the timing circuit, causing the green to remain for a further minimum period; the red indication will reappear only when there is a gap greater than the minimum green interval in the traffic flow crossing the detector. Thus, the resulting speed control will apply only to the first vehicle in a group. If the traffic flow is continuous, the speed control usually becomes ineffective because of the difficulty of enforcement.

Metering signals

Metering signals, used at freeway entrance ramps, bridge approaches, and similar locations as part of traffic control schemes are described in Chapter 25.

Signal control by emergency vehicles

Preemption of the right-of-way through signalized intersections by emergency vehicles (usually firefighting vehicles) has been achieved by means of directed transmissions by radio or light beam from a transmitter in the emergency vehicle to a receiver at the signalized intersection.

When the receiver detects the transmission from the oncoming emergency vehicle, the phase selector determines whether or not the signal is green in the direction of the approaching emergency vehicle. If the signal is green, it remains so until the emergency vehicle has passed and/or the transmissions haved ceased to be received by the intersection receiver. If the signal is not green when the transmissions are first received, the controller is advanced in accordance with timing adjustments which are set into the phase selector so that the green will show in the direction of the oncoming emergency vehicle. As soon as the emergency vehicle has cleared the intersection, the phase selector returns the traffic signal to its standard operation.

REFERENCES FOR FURTHER READING

Computer Traffic Control, Report of the workshop held Mar. 20–22, 1974, Spring Hill Conference Center, Wayzata, Minn.

GARTNER, N., J. D. C. LITTLE, AND H. GABBAY, *Optimization of Traffic Signal Setting in Networks by Mixed-Integer Linear Programming,* The MITROP Computer Program, Technical Report No. 91, Operations Research Center, M.I.T., Cambridge, Mass., Mar. 1974.

Improved Operation of Urban Transportation Systems, Vol. 1: *Traffic Signal Control Strategies, State-of-the-Art,* Metropolitan Toronto Roads and Traffic Department, Toronto, Mar. 1974.

Improved Operation of Urban Transportation Systems, Vol. 2: *The Evaluation of Off-Line Area Traffic Control Strategies,* Metropolitan Toronto Roads and Traffic Department, Toronto, Nov. 1975.

Improved Operation of Urban Transportation Systems, Vol. 3: *The Development and Evaluation of a Real Time Computerized Traffic Control Strategy,* Metropolitan Toronto Roads and Traffic Department, Toronto, Nov. 1976.

KAY, J. L., R. D. HENRY, AND S. A. SMITH, *Locating Detectors for Advanced Traffic Control Strategies: Handbook and Technical Report,* Federal Highway Administration, Interim Report, Washington, D.C., Sept. 1975.

PINNELL, ANDERSON, WILSHIRE AND ASSOCIATES, INC., *Inductive Loop Detectors, Theory and Practice,* U.S. Department of Transportation, Federal Highway Administration, Washington, D.C., Jan. 1976.

PINNELL, ANDERSON, WILSHIRE AND ASSOCIATES, INC., *Participant Handbook, Management of Traffic Control Systems,* U.S. Department of Transportation, Federal Highway Administration, Washington, D.C.

SPERRY SYSTEMS MANAGEMENT DIVISION, *Urban Traffic Control Systems Hardware: A Specifications Checklist,* U.S. Department of Transportation, Federal Highway Administration, Washington, D.C., Jan. 1976.

Traffic Control Systems Handbook, U.S. Department of Transportation, Federal Highway Administration, Washington, D.C., June 1976.

25

FREEWAY SURVEILLANCE AND CONTROL

DONALD G. CAPELLE, *President*

PRC Voorhees
McLean, Virginia

AND

SANTANU BASU, *Professional Staff*

The Analytic Sciences Corporation
Rosslyn, Virginia

The development of urban areas in the last few decades has been accompanied by a sustained growth in traffic demand. The mobility of this traffic depends on the effective utilization of urban streets and freeways. In the case of urban streets, the importance of well-designed traffic control has been recognized for a long time; however, this has not been true of urban freeways, which were originally conceived and developed as free-flowing, limited-access facilities with little advance thought given to the possibility of needing control. Although it is true that freeways have provided a substantial increase of mobility at much greater levels of safety, merely the building of these freeways has not been enough.

Experience has shown that these facilities must continue to provide a high level of operational service if they are to deliver the safety, comfort, and convenience expected by the motoring public. However, accelerated and continued growth in traffic demand caused by an ever-increasing number of commuters in urban areas has produced congested operations and a decreased level of service on many urban freeways. It has thus become apparent in several instances that some form of control, coupled with a surveillance system to monitor traffic conditions, must also be applied to freeways if the most effective utilization of these facilities is to be achieved.

This chapter deals with two principal concepts: the application of traffic control to freeways, and surveillance systems for incident detection and traffic control. The surveillance concepts presented here apply to both freeways and urban streets. However, since the majority of surveillance concepts are usually associated with freeways, they are discussed with regard to their freeway application, while indicating urban street applications where appropriate.

Urban freeway congestion: causes and impact

The major problem on urban freeways is congestion. It is generally characterized by slower-than-desired travel speeds, increased and unpredictable travel times, increased accident frequencies, erratic stop-and-go driving, increased operating costs, and other undesirable conditions resulting in user dissatisfaction. Clearly, a congested freeway is an inefficient one. Figure 25.1 shows a typical relation between speed and volume on an urban freeway.[1] At point A on the curve, flow is uncongested and the mean travel speed is high. As traffic volume increases toward point B, the speed falls to a lower value. Passing from point B to point C, however, not only causes a lower travel speed but a reduced volume of traffic on the freeway. Point C is indicative of an inefficient freeway condition in which the volume being accommodated is less than the capacity at low speeds.

Congestion on urban freeways is of two types: recurring and nonrecurring. Congestion that occurs regularly at particular locations during certain time periods is said to be recurring in nature. On the other hand, congestion caused by such random irregular events as accidents, incidents, and other special situations belongs to the nonrecurring category. Both recurring and nonrecurring congestion lead to user dissatisfaction as previously described. There is, however, a difference. With recurring congestion, users can plan their trips according to the expected occurrence and severity of particular congested conditions. On the other

[1]P. F. EVERALL, *Urban Freeway Surveillance and Control—The State of the Art*, rev. (Washington, D.C.: U.S. Department of Transportation, Federal Highway Administration, June 1973).

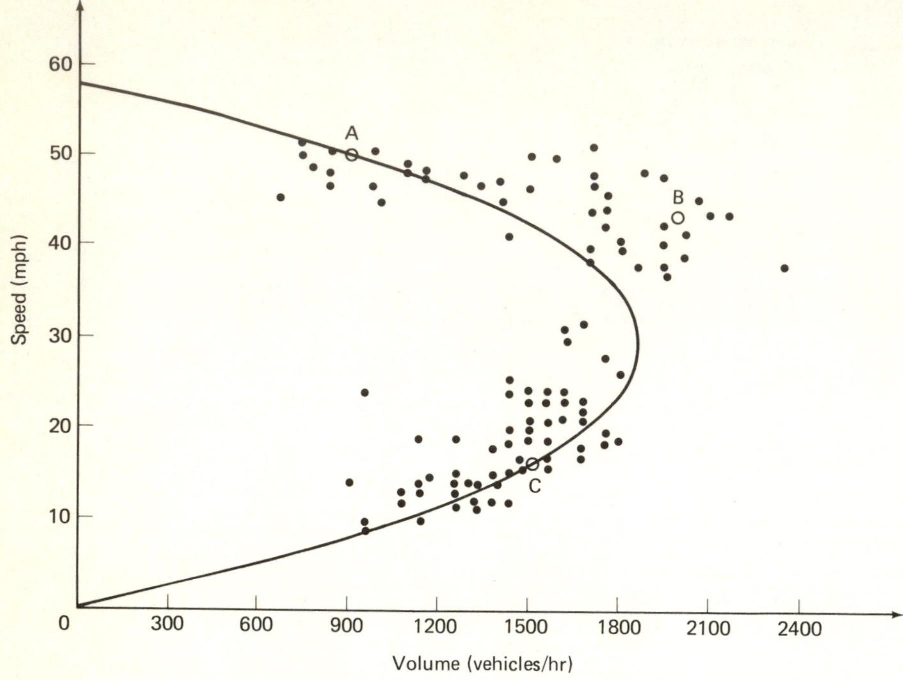

Figure 25.1. Typical speed-volume relationship on an urban freeway.

hand, nonrecurring congestion can have detrimental effects on a trip that is normally satisfactory. It is bad enough to know that a certain trip would take 10 min longer during the peak period than during off-peak hours, but it is worse if it takes 10 min longer on one day and 20 min on another. Predictability is a very important factor to most motorists.

In a study of freeway congestion in Los Angeles, it was reported that the contribution to delay from nonrecurring congestion caused by incidents, weekend travel, and special events was 57% while recurring congestion accounted for the remaining 43%.[2] Nonrecurring congestion may thus be considered a more serious problem for the public agency responsible for managing freeway operations.

The occurrence of freeway congestion at any point along its length is essentially the result of traffic demand exceeding the capacity of the freeway at that point. This is illustrated by the graph in Figure 25.2, which represents the number of of vehicles passing a point on the road as a function of time.[3]

The slope of the solid line represents the service rate of a section of freeway at a particular time (i.e., the number of vehicles getting past the point under the prevailing roadway conditions). As long as the traffic demand, or the number of vehicles arriving at that point (shown by the dashed

[2]J. L. Arcenaux and B. Mikhalkin, *Inventory of Freeway Geometrics Bottleneck Congestion*, Final Report, Freeway Operation Department, District 7, California Division of Highways, May 1973.

[3]D. G. Capelle, *Freeway Traffic Management*, NCHRP Project 20-3D (Washington, D.C.: Transportation Research Board, Sept. 1979).

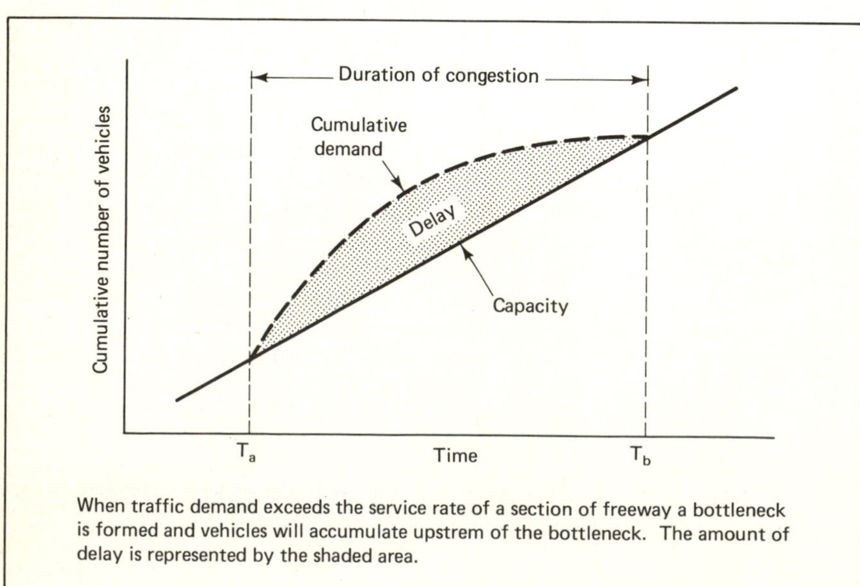

Figure 25.2. Relationships among demand, capacity, and congestion.

line), is less than or equal to the capacity of that section of the freeway, there is no congestion. However, once the arrival rate begins to exceed the capacity at time t_a, a "bottleneck" is formed and vehicles begin to accumulate upstream of the bottleneck until time t_b when the demand once again is equal to the capacity of that section of freeway.

Congestion is caused either by excessive demand or reductions in capacity. Recurring and nonrecurring problems of congestion can be discussed in terms of those factors that contribute to either one of the situations described above.

Factors contributing to excessive demand

Excessive demand is basically the overloading of a facility, which creates turbulence in the traffic stream and leads eventually to a system breakdown if the overloading continues. The capacity of a multilane freeway is discussed in Chapter 16 and is normally considered to be approximately 2000 passenger vehicles per lane per hour. When the travel demand exceeds this number, congestion will develop. This situation will occur regularly during the peak periods when there are high commuter trip demands. It may also happen as a result of such special occasions as sporting events, holiday travel, and festivals.

Excessive demand is frequently due to unrestrained ramp access. If the combined volume of a freeway on-ramp and the main freeway lanes exceeds the freeway capacity downstream from the ramp entrance, congestion will develop on the freeway mainline, with attendant queueing upstream of the bottleneck. This type of congestion can be predicted with a fair degree of accuracy in both time and space.

Freeway congestion is sometimes caused by congestion on city streets preventing traffic from leaving the freeway, and eventually resulting in exit ramp queues backing onto the freeway. Such queues can also form where there is inadequate ramp storage. Congestion due to exit ramp queueing can also develop because of heavy exit ramp demands caused by special events.

Factors causing reductions in freeway capacity

Capacity is not uniform along the length of a facility, but is dependent on a large number of factors, among which the geometric and physical features of the freeway are important ones.

Certain physical features result in capacity restrictions where they occur. These isolated sections, whose capacity is lower than those of adjacent sections, are referred to as "geometric bottlenecks." When the demand upstream of the bottleneck exceeds the capacity of the bottleneck, congestion develops with queueing on the upstream freeway lanes. Congestion resulting from geometric bottlenecks is of the recurring type, being predictable with reasonable accuracy. Some of the most common causes of geometric bottlenecks and thus of recurring congestion include:

Lane drops. Congestion may occur at locations where the number of lanes is reduced. Even if the lane drop occurs at an exit ramp, congestion sometimes results if the through demand exceeds the downstream capacity. In addition, weaving maneuvers out of the dropped lane sometimes create turbulence and a resulting drop in operating speed.

Horizontal curvature. A moderately sharp horizontal curve can reduce capacity. During conditions of heavy flow, a vehicle crossing into another lane causes hesitation and speed reduction, which often creates turbulence.

Ramp design. The design of ramps can have a direct effect on freeway capacity. A large merge angle, short or nonexistent acceleration and deceleration lanes, sharp ramp curvature, and poor sight distance on the ramp all tend to reduce freeway capacity.

Number of lanes. The number of freeway lanes is significant in determining capacity. Typically, six-lane and eight-lane freeways exhibit greater average capacities per lane than do four-lane freeways (see Chapter 16).

Weaving sections. When a freeway on-ramp is closely followed by an off-ramp, the capacity of the intervening section may be significantly below the ideal, and can possibly affect the freeway operation for substantial distances upstream and downstream of the weaving area.

Vertical alignment. The effect on passenger-car capacity of the grades generally found on freeways is negligible;[4] however, the effects are considerably more pronounced on the capacity of a freeway with a traffic mix of trucks, buses, and passenger cars. Severe vertical alignment causes reductions in capacity, depending on the percentage of trucks, the grade, and the length of grade.[5]

Several other physical features tend to reduce freeway capacity. These are nonstandard interchanges, inadequate shoulders, narrow medians, poor surface quality, and inadequate signing.

Factors contributing to nonrecurring congestion. Freeway congestion is frequently the result of the occurrence of an abnormal incident on the freeway which restricts normal traffic flow either by blocking a lane or lanes or by severely reducing the freeway capacity. Almost any unusual occurrence will have its effect on freeway traffic, but the most common ones encountered on urban freeways include:

- Freeway accidents
- Disabled vehicles
- Spilled vehicle loads
- Presence of emergency vehicles
- Vehicles or people on the freeway shoulder

The occurrence of such incidents during peak periods can cause congestion on uncongested sections and further increase delay on the already congested sections. Even in off-peak periods, congestion may develop, depending on

[4] "Highway Capacity Manual 1965," *Highway Res. Spec. Rep. 87* (Washington, D.C.: Highway Research Board, 1965).

[5] Ibid.

the number of lanes affected. Vehicles completely on the shoulder still tend to reduce capacity, while the capacity in the opposite direction also diminishes because of drivers slowing to view the incident—the "gaper's block effect."[6] These random events are not predictable in either time or space, and they thus contribute to nonrecurring congestion.

Maintenance and construction operations on freeways frequently cause congestion. Major work can result in significant delays to freeway traffic. Consequently, efforts should be made to schedule such work during off-peak periods.

Impact of freeway congestion. Different freeway congestion problems have different degrees of impact. However, the severity of a particular problem generally depends on time of day, location, and duration of occurrence.[7] The severity is also dependent on the interaction between different problems which occur simultaneously. For example, a temporary hazard such as a disabled vehicle on the shoulder of a tangent section of a freeway may have only a negligible impact during off-peak conditions. However, the same incident on a horizontal curve during a peak period with traffic demand approaching freeway capacity may compound the basic overloading of the facility and cause severe congestion.

Several studies have been conducted to assess the effects of freeway problems. Although it may be difficult to draw broad general conclusions from these studies, some examples serve to illustrate the nature and magnitude of the impacts. The influence of incidents on freeway quality of service reported in a study by Goolsby[8] showed that blockages of freeway lanes have a more severe effect than just the obvious reduction in number of lanes. The results, summarized in Table 25-1, show that a one-lane blockage on a three-lane roadway caused by a minor accident or a stalled vehicle reduced capacity by 50%, even though the physical reduction was only 33%. Presence of vehicles on the shoulder that had been involved in an accident caused up to a 33% reduction in capacity, although there was no physical reduction of available roadway. As another example, in an analysis of incidents using the data base of a Detroit freeway study,[9] it was estimated that delay-causing incidents on a 10-mi (16-km) freeway segment would produce 550,000 vehicle-hours of delay annually, resulting in 360,000 U.S. gal (1,360,000 liters) of gasoline waste and an additional 530,000 kg of hydrocarbon pollutants.

Similar results were reported by the Los Angeles program of early detection and rapid removal of incidents. Although there are no national figures to indicate the total costs associated with freeway congestion in the United States, the results of such studies as the ones cited above have been used to estimate these costs as a multimillion-dollar annual burden—some of which can be alleviated through the implementation of surveillance and control systems.

[6]EVERALL, *Urban Freeway Surveillance*.

[7]CAPELLE, *Freeway Traffic Management*.

[8]M. E. GOOLSBY, "Influence of Incidents on Freeway Quality of Service," *Highway Res. Rec. 349* (Washington, D.C.: Highway Research Board, 1971).

[9]A. TARAGIN, "A Summary of the John C. Lodge Freeway Research," NCHRP 20-3C, (Washington, D.C.: National Cooperative Highway Research Program, July 1976).

TABLE 25–1
Capacity Reduction Resulting from Lane Blockages on the Gulf Freeway (Three Lanes Each Direction)

Number of Lanes Blocked	Capacity Reduction (%)
Shoulder only	33
One lane	50
Two lanes	79

SOURCE: M. E. GOOLSBY, "Influence of Incidents on Freeway Quality of Service," *Highway Res. Rec. 349* (Washington, D.C.: Highway Research Board, 1971).

Methods of freeway control

Several methods of freeway traffic control have been developed and applied to improve the operating efficiency of urban freeways and to minimize the occurrence and impact of congestion. These methods can be divided into five main categories:

- ○ Entrance ramp control
- ○ Exit ramp control
- ○ Mainline control
- ○ Priority control
- ○ Corridor control

This section deals with a description of the basic concept of each type of control, and then considers, in some detail, each of the available techniques for implementing the control. Specific details related to the hardware needs are discussed in a later section, which is a combined account of the hardware requirements for surveillance as well as for control.

Entrance ramp control

Experience to date has clearly shown the most common technique for freeway traffic control to be some form of entrance ramp control. The primary objective of any freeway control technique is to improve the safety and efficiency of freeway operations through an elimination, or at least the reduction, of the factors contributing to congestion. The underlying principle of entrance ramp control is to limit the number of vehicles entering the freeway so that the demand on the freeway will not exceed its capacity. Maximum flow rates will thus be achieved by ensuring that the freeway traffic moves at or near optimum speeds. This has several consequences in that some of the traffic wishing to use the freeway has to wait on the entrance ramp before being allowed to enter. The resultant queueing on the entrance ramp presents the driver desiring to use the freeway with three choices:

1. Wait in the queue in hope that the improved freeway speed will more than compensate for ramp delay.
2. Choose another point of entry or another time when the demand is less, or an alternative route to the freeway.
3. Choose another mode of transportation such as transit or some form of ride sharing such as carpools or vanpools.

Some of the benefits of entrance ramp control are clearly apparent. It provides a higher and more predictable level of service on the freeway, while concurrently improving the overall safety of operation, both on the freeway itself and on the entrance ramp. On the other hand, the diverted traffic may create operational problems on the alternative facilities in the corridor if care is not exercised in the implementation of entrance ramp control. Entrance ramp control can achieve improved efficiency of operations and safety on the freeway as well as a more effective utilization of all travel facilities in the corridor if certain conditions are satisfied. These conditions are described in interim warrants for freeway entrance ramp control which can be found in Section 4E of the *Manual on Uniform Traffic Control Devices*.[10] They are as follows:

Warrants for Freeway Entrance Ramp Control Signals (Interim)—There has not as yet been sufficient experience with freeway entrance ramp control signals to permit developing numerical warrants applicable to the wide variety of conditions found in practice. However, general guidelines have been identified for successful application of ramp control.

The installation of ramp control signals should be preceded by an engineering analysis of the physical and traffic conditions on the highway facilities likely to be affected. The study should include the ramps and ramp connections, and the surface streets which would carry diverted traffic, as well as the freeway section concerned. Types of traffic data which should be obtained include but are not limited to traffic volumes, traffic accidents, travel time, and delay on the freeway and on alternative surface routes.

Capacities should be determined and the locations and causes of capacity restrictions should be identified. From these and other data, estimates can be made of desirable metering rates, probable reductions in delay to freeway traffic, and likely increases in delay to traffic on ramps and surface streets.

Before installing ramp control signals, consideration should be given to alternative means of increasing the capacity or improving characteristics of the freeway.

1. Installation of freeway entrance ramp control signals may be warranted when:
   a. The expected reduction in delay to freeway traffic exceeds the expected delay to ramp users and added travel time for diverted traffic and traffic on alternative surface routes.
   b. There is adequate storage space for the vehicles which will be delayed.
   c. There are suitable alternative surface routes available having capacity for traffic diverted from the freeway ramps.
   d. There is recurring congestion on the freeway due to traffic demand in excess of the capacity; or there is recurring congestion or a severe accident hazard at the freeway entrance because of inadequate ramp merging area.
2. Installation of freeway entrance ramp control signals may be warranted to reduce sporadic congestion on isolated sections of freeway caused by short-period peak traffic loads from special events or from severe peak loads of recreational traffic.

Besides the general guidance provided by these warrants and a tentative statement of recommended practice on freeway entrance ramp displays prepared by the Institute of Transportation Engineers,[11] the National Cooperative Highway Research Program has produced guidelines for the design, implementation, and operation of entrance ramp control systems.[12] In addition, the Transportation Research Board Freeway Operations Committee provides a continuing forum for the review of these guidelines.

Entrance ramp control is implemented through one of the following means:

- Closure
- Pretimed metering
- Traffic-responsive metering
- Traffic-responsive merge control
- Integrated system control

Closure. As the name implies, this control technique consists of physically closing the ramp to traffic on either a permanent or a short-term basis. It is the simplest and also the most restrictive form of entrance ramp control and hence is applied sparingly. Permanent closure can be used as a last resort in situations where there are severe weaving problems, but public objections are likely to develop. Closure of ramps during peak periods should be considered as a solution only in the following situations:

- The storage area on the ramp for vehicles waiting to enter the freeway is not adequate. These vehicles thus cause a disruption in the traffic on the surface streets.
- The freeway traffic on the section before the entrance ramp is already running at or critically close to capacity, and there is a good alternative route with adequate capacity available for potential freeway users.
- The ramp design does not allow traffic to merge into the freeway traffic without considerable hazard.

Ramp closure is effected through the use of "Do Not Enter" signs, manually placed barriers, and automated barriers. Signs usually tend to be ineffective, with a large number of violations. Manually placed barriers are effective, but it is a labor-intensive alternative best suited for short-term or trial periods, or where toll booths are located on the entrance ramps, as in Japan.[13] Automated barriers offer the greatest flexibility since entrances can be closed and opened automatically, enabling greater responsiveness to changes in traffic conditions. By and large, however, ramp closure is usually avoided because of strong adverse public reaction.

Pretimed metering. Ramp metering is the most widely used method for limiting vehicular access to the freeway, either to improve the operating conditions on the freeway or to improve the safety of the merging operation. Normally, a ramp may have a capacity of 800 to 1200 vehicles per hour, provided that the geometric design is adequate.[14] Ramp metering rates will usually be less than this but greater than a practical minimum of 180 to 240 vehicles per hour.

[10] Federal Highway Administration, U.S. Department of Transportation, *Manual on Uniform Traffic Control Devices for Streets and Highways* (Washington, D.C.: 1978).

[11] ITE Committee 4Z-A, "Tentative ITE Recommended Practice: Freeway Entrance Ramp Displays," *Traffic Eng.*, *44*(12) (Sept. 1974).

[12] Stanford Research Institute, *Guidelines for the Design and Operation of Ramp Control Systems*, NCHRP Project 3-22 (Washington, D.C.: National Cooperative Highway Research Program, 1975).

[13] Federal Highway Administration, U.S. Department of Transportation, *Traffic Control Systems Handbook*, Implementation Package 76-10 (Washington, D.C.: 1976).

[14] Everall, *Urban Freeway Surveillance*.

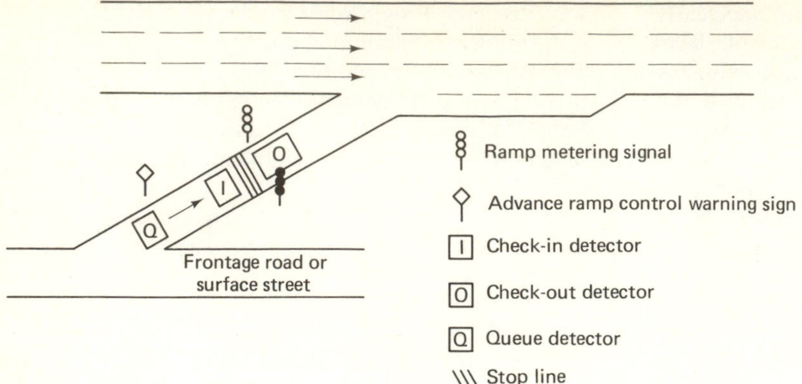

Figure 25.3. Layout of pretimed, entrance ramp metering system. SOURCE: Federal Highway Administration, U.S. Department of Transportation, *Traffic Control Systems Handbook,* Implementation Package 76-10, Washington, D.C., 1976.

The simplest form of ramp metering is pretimed metering, whereby the metering rate is fixed according to clock time (the time of day and/or the day of week).

The basic requirements for pretimed metering are minimal: one or two standard three-section (red–yellow–green) or two-section (red–green) traffic signals located on the ramp, a controller actuated by a time clock, and a warning sign to indicate to approaching traffic that the ramp is being metered. A typical layout for a pretimed entrance ramp metering system is shown in Figure 25.3, together with some optional modifications that may be made to the basic system.

The metering rates to control the ramp traffic are calculated using historical data. The method of calculation depends on the purpose for which the metering is being used—to reduce congestion on the freeway or to improve safety of the merging operation. If intended to minimize congestion, the metering rate calculation is straightforward, as shown in Figure 25.4. The metering rate is simply set equal to the difference between upstream freeway demand and the downstream freeway capacity—in this case, 300 vehicles per hour. Some additional practical considerations, however, need to be taken into account. These are the conditions addressed by the warrants for entrance ramp control (e.g., is there adequate storage space for the stopping vehicles on the ramp? Are good alternative routes and sufficient capacity available in the corridor?). Also, all gaps (up to capacity) may not be candidates for filling since downstream conditions may require some gaps be saved beyond the immediate merge section. Additionally, if the calculated metering rate of 300 vehicles per hour (vph) is deemed too restrictive, consideration should be given to the metering of other ramps upstream of the ramp in question.

If pretimed metering is used only as a means of improving the safety of the merging area, the rate is to enforce single-vehicle entry and must be such as to ensure that each vehicle has time to merge before the following vehicle approaches the merging area. The goal is to break up platoons of vehicles which otherwise lead to rear-end and lane-change collisions while competing for gaps in the freeway traffic stream. The time to merge for a stopped vehicle depends on the distance from the freeway, ramp geometry, type of vehicle, and availability of acceptable gaps in the freeway traffic. If the average time to merge, taking all these factors into account, is 8 s, the metering rate would be 450 vph.

The traffic signal in a pretimed metering system operates with a constant cycle according to the metering rate as calculated above. The selected metering rate typically stays in effect for periods of 30 min to an entire peak period. Depending on the magnitude of the metering rate, the metering is either single-entry (for rates up to 900 vph) or platoon-entry (for rates above 900 vph). As the name im-

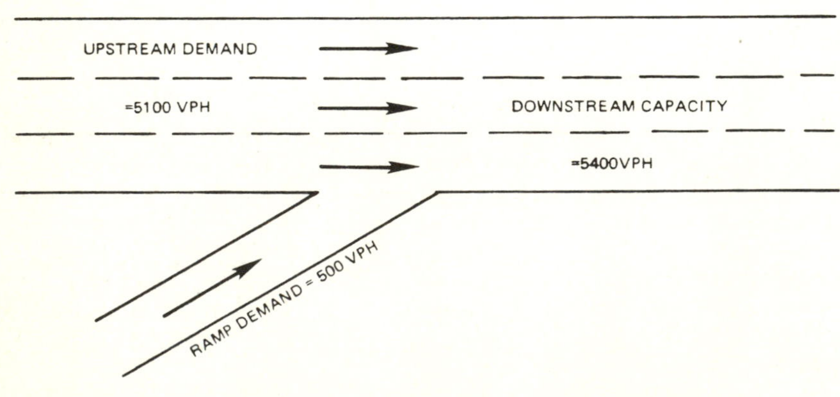

Figure 25.4. Example of pretimed, entrance ramp metering rate calculation. SOURCE: Federal Highway Administration, U.S. Department of Transportation, *Traffic Control Systems Handbook,* Implementation Package 76-10, Washington, D.C., 1976.

plies, single-entry metering is accomplished by timing the signal so as to permit only one vehicle to enter the freeway for each green interval. The green-plus-yellow (or just green if yellow is not used) is just long enough (usually 3 s) to allow one vehicle to proceed past the signal. A two-detector layout, as shown in Figure 25.3, terminates the green when the vehicle reaches the checkout detector—this is generally preferable to a constant green time. For the metering rate of 300 vph, or 5 vehicles/min, a green-plus-yellow interval of 3 s and a red interval of 9 s is typically used.

Platoon metering allows the release of two or more vehicles per cycle and is used to accommodate high metering rates (greater than 900 vph). Platooning can be achieved by releasing vehicles one behind the other (tandem) or two-abreast in two parallel lanes.[15] For tandem platooning, the green time has to be sufficiently long to allow all vehicles in the platoon to accelerate and pass the signal. A yellow interval is required to prevent sudden braking problems and attendant rear-end collisions. As an example, consider tandem metering of two vehicles per cycle to achieve a metering rate of 1080 vph or 18 vehicles/min.[16] Nine cycles are required per minute, or a cycle of 6.7 s, which could be split into a 4.7-s green-plus-yellow interval and a 2-s red interval. Experience with tandem metering indicates that two-vehicle platoons can be handled satisfactorily and three-vehicle platoons are a practical maximum, with 1100 vph the maximum metering rate that can be expected in either case.[17] Where the entrance ramp feeds an added lane on a freeway, much longer tandem platoons can be accommodated.

Similar flow rates can also be achieved by releasing two vehicles in parallel each cycle. This, of course, requires that two parallel lanes be available for a sufficient distance beyond the ramp metering signal for the two vehicles to achieve a single-file orientation before merging with the freeway traffic. The cycle timing is similar to single-entry metering; that is, each green-plus-yellow interval is just long enough (about 3 s) to permit one vehicle in each lane to proceed past the ramp-metering signal. For the example of 1080 vph, requiring nine cycles per lane per minute, the cycle time of 6.7 s could be split into a 3-s green-plus-yellow interval and a 3.7-s red interval.

Both forms of platoon metering exhibit several disadvantages compared to single-entry metering: greater driver confusion, greater probability of rear-end collisions (tandem metering), and greater disruption of freeway traffic. Of the two platoon metering schemes, two-abreast is generally preferable, as it tends to create less driver confusion and provides for a safer operation. Platoon metering should only be considered for achieving higher metering rates or when the ramp enters an added lane on the freeway.[18]

While the essential pretimed ramp-metering system requires no detectors, some refinements in operation are possible using the detectors indicated in Figure 25.3 as optional equipment. A check-in (demand) detector is highly recommended so that the signal turns green only when a vehicle is waiting. Thus, the signal rests in red until the detector is actuated, when it turns green provided that the minimum red time has elapsed. During peak periods there will often be a queue at the signal, which will then be continuously metered at the set rate. Painting a stop line at the signal decreases the chance of vehicles not moving forward far enough to actuate the detector with a consequent all-red condition. As a provision for such an occurrence, it is desirable for pretimed metering systems with check-in detectors to have a minimum metering rate (say 3 vehicles/min) at which the signal operates in the absence of detector actuation.

A pretimed metering system can use a checkout (passage) detector installed just past the stop line to ensure single-vehicle entry.[19] When a vehicle is sensed by the checkout detector, the green interval is terminated immediately, thereby ensuring passage of only one vehicle. Finally, a queue detector can be used in conjunction with a pretimed metering system to prevent ramp traffic from blocking surface streets.[20] It is especially important in the initial turn-on of the system at the beginning of a peak period. The queue detector is so situated that its sensing a vehicle indicates that the queue of vehicles waiting on the ramp has become long enough to possibly interfere with the surface street traffic. A higher metering rate can then be used to shorten the queue length. This can be accomplished by having different metering rates present (on different dials, or programmed in the case of solid-state/microprocessor controllers) with queue detection transferring signal control to the higher rate. A merge area override detector can also be used with pretimed metering where the merge geometrics are substandard.

A discussion of cost effectiveness of freeway control systems is undertaken later. It suffices here to say that pretimed metering entrance ramp control can be extremely cost-effective.[21] Its major operational advantage is that it provides drivers with a regular metering rate to which they can readily adjust. The principal drawback of pretimed metering is that such a system cannot respond to significant changes in demand or take into account unusual traffic conditions resulting from incidents on the freeway. Because of this inherent insensitivity to changes in traffic conditions, pretimed metering rates are usually set such that the resultant operation is below capacity.

Traffic-responsive metering. Traffic-responsive metering is based on the same principle as is pretimed metering—the demand-capacity constraint. The difference lies in the method of selecting metering rates. Pretimed metering rates are computed using historical measures of traffic conditions, whereas traffic-responsive metering rates are selected using real-time measurements of traffic conditions. Traffic-responsive metering thus overcomes the inherent inability of pretimed metering to respond to short-term changes in traffic conditions.

The basic requirements for implementing traffic-responsive metering are considerably more complex than those for pretimed systems: one or two traffic signals; an advance

[15]Stanford Research Institute, *Guidelines*.

[16]Federal Highway Administration, *Traffic Control Systems Handbook*.

[17]Stanford Research Institute, *Guidelines*.

[18]Ibid.

[19]Federal Highway Administration, *Traffic Control Systems Handbook*.

[20]Ibid.

[21]Everall, *Urban Freeway Surveillance*.

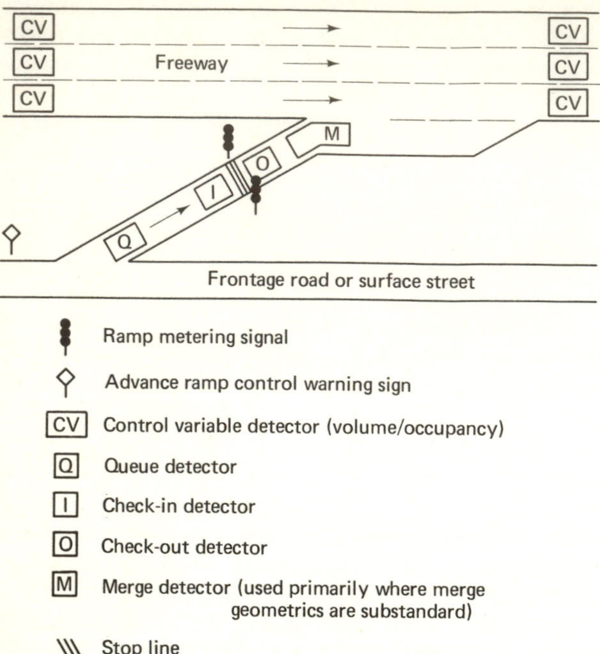

Figure 25.5. Layout of traffic-responsive entrance ramp metering system. SOURCE: D.R. Drew, K.A. Brewer, J.H. Buhr, and R.H. Whitson, "Multilevel Approach to the Design of a Freeway Control System," *Highway Research Record 9,* Washington, D.C., Highway Research Board, 1969.

ramp control sign; a controller with the capability of monitoring traffic variable measurements and using these to select or calculate a metering rate; and various traffic detectors to measure in real time the variables used in selecting the metering rate. A typical layout for a traffic-responsive ramp-metering system is shown in Figure 25.5, together with some optional components often included to provide improved system operation.

The basic strategy of traffic-responsive metering is to obtain real-time measurements of traffic conditions on the freeway, use these to examine how the freeway is operating with respect to its capacity, and then determine the maximum number of ramp vehicles that can be permitted to enter the freeway without causing congestion. Volume and occupancy are the traffic variables generally used in determining traffic-responsive metering rates as they can be measured by the direct processing of freeway detector data. The traffic-responsive metering selection is based principally on one of two strategies: demand-capacity control and occupancy control.

Demand-Capacity Control. The metering rate is determined using real-time comparison of upstream volume and downstream capacity. The upstream volume is measured in real time and compared to either a preset historical value of downstream capacity or a current value calculated from downstream volume measurements. The effectiveness of demand-capacity control is enhanced if the downstream capacity accounts for the effect on capacity of weather, traffic composition, and incidents. Additionally, since volume alone is insufficient in determining whether the freeway is congested or free-flowing, an occupancy measurement is usually made from at least one of the upstream detectors. The allowable ramp entrance metering rate for the next control period (usually 1 min) is the difference between the upstream volume and downstream capacity. A minimum metering rate of 3 to 4 vehicles/min is used if upstream volume is equal to or greater than downstream capacity, or if the occupancy measurement is above a preset value which—determined from past experience—can be taken as an indicator of congestion.

Occupancy Control. One of several predetermined metering rates is selected for the next control period (usually 1 min) on the basis of occupancy measurements made during the current period. The real-time occupancy measurements are made upstream or downstream of the ramp in question, and the metering rate is typically based on a plot of historical volume–occupancy data collected at the same locations.[22] Such a plot establishes an approximate volume–occupancy relationship and also determines a value of occupancy at capacity. An example of such a plot is shown in Figure 25.6. Using the historical plot and the measured current value of occupancy, the metering rate is determined as the difference between the historical estimate of capacity and the real-time estimate of volume. If measured occupancy is greater than the (preset) occupancy corresponding to capacity, a minimum metering rate (3 to 4 vehicles/min) is to be used. Occupancy control offers the advantage of using fewer detectors. On the other hand, demand-capacity control uses more precise estimates of upstream volume and consequently can effect more accurate control.[23]

The operation of a traffic-responsive metering system is essentially similar to that of a pretimed metering system, except for the differences in the methods used for selecting the metering rate. Single-entry metering is most often used for implementing traffic-responsive systems, although high metering rates (say, greater than 800 to 900 vph) may necessitate the use of platoon entry. Both methods of metering (single and platoon entry) should not be used at the same ramp to avoid driver confusion as a result of changing from one method to the other between control periods.

Traffic-responsive metering systems generally include override features that tend to enhance system operation.[24] These features are implemented through the use of the optional detectors shown in Figure 25.5. A continued actuation of the queue detector indicates that the queued vehicles on the ramp are likely to interfere with the traffic on the frontage road or surface street, a situation that can then be corrected by selecting a higher metering rate. A merge detector can be used to determine whether a vehicle is still in the merging area. For single-entry metering, such a detection can then be used to preempt subsequent green intervals until the vehicle merges. A checkout (passage) detector can be used to determine if a vehicle missed the green signal, since in that case there would be no actuation of the checkout detector. The override logic in this case can be set to return the signal to or leave it in green, as the case may be. For systems that rest in red until a check-in detector is actuated,

[22] FEDERAL HIGHWAY ADMINISTRATION, *Traffic Control Systems Handbook.*
[23] STANFORD RESEARCH INSTITUTE, *Guidelines.*
[24] FEDERAL HIGHWAY ADMINISTRATION, *Traffic Control Systems Handbook.*

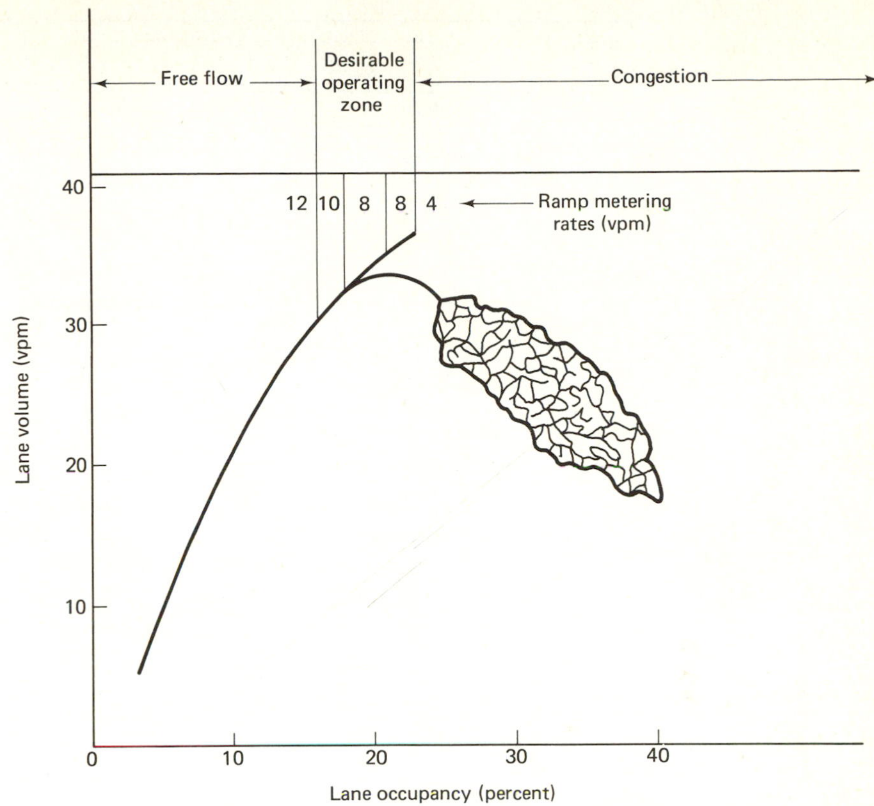

Figure 25.6. Volume-occupancy plot for calculation of entrance ramp metering rates in Chicago, Illinois. SOURCE: J.M. McDermott et al., *Chicago Area Expressway Surveillance and Control*, Final Report, State of Illinois, Department of Transportation, March 1979.

a queue detector can be used to determine if a vehicle has stopped short of the check-in detector. This would be indicated by a continued actuation of the queue detector concurrent with no actuation of the check-in detector. The override logic can be set to turn the signal to green and begin the metering cycle.

Traffic-responsive metering is relatively cost-effective, but it is less so than pretimed metering, as it typically provides only 5 to 10% in additional benefits over pretimed metering while it often costs considerably more. The principal operational advantage of traffic-responsive metering over pretimed metering is that it tends to utilize current available capacity to the fullest, whereas pretimed control must, of necessity, use metering rates set for the worst case of peak upstream volume, resulting in overmetering when upstream volumes fall below this level. Additionally, traffic-responsive metering reduces the vulnerability of the control system to certain changes.[25] For example, metering at an entrance ramp with a large volume may solve a bottleneck problem at one location (and during one period of time), but it may cause another bottleneck to appear at a different location and time. Traffic-responsive metering provides the same degree of adaptability to capacity changes or shifts in bottlenecks. Capacity reductions due to weather can also be somewhat accommodated by traffic-responsive metering.[26] The single most important factor, from an operational point of view, in choosing between pretimed and traffic-responsive metering is the variation in demand and capacity likely to be experienced for the freeway segment in question. If demand and capacity variations are essentially insignificant, pretimed metering will meet most needs. However, traffic-responsive metering should be considered when there are frequent occurrences of significant demand and capacity changes.

Traffic-responsive merge control. Another type of traffic-responsive entrance ramp control is based on the optimal use by merging vehicles of acceptable gaps in the freeway traffic. Unlike traffic-responsive metering, which is based on computing metering rates using demand-capacity constraints, merge control is based on the philosophy that minimizing vehicular conflicts at entrance ramps reduces the probability of rear-end collisons, decreases the tension of merging drivers, and prevents shock waves from being created in the vicinity of entrance ramps.[27,28]

The essential strategy of merge control is to detect an acceptable freeway gap into which a waiting ramp vehicle can merge, to predict when this gap will reach the merging

[25]STANFORD RESEARCH INSTITUTE, *Guidelines*.

[26]FEDERAL HIGHWAY ADMINISTRATION, *Traffic Control Systems Handbook*.

[27]J. M. MCDERMOTT ET AL. *Chicago Area Expressway Surveillance and Control*, Final Report, State of Illinois, Department of Transportation, Mar. 1979.

[28]D. R. DREW, K. A. BREWER, J. H. BUHR, AND R. H. WHITSON, "Multilevel Approach to the Design of a Freeway Control System," *Highway Res. Rec. 279* (Washington, D.C.: Highway Research Board, 1969).

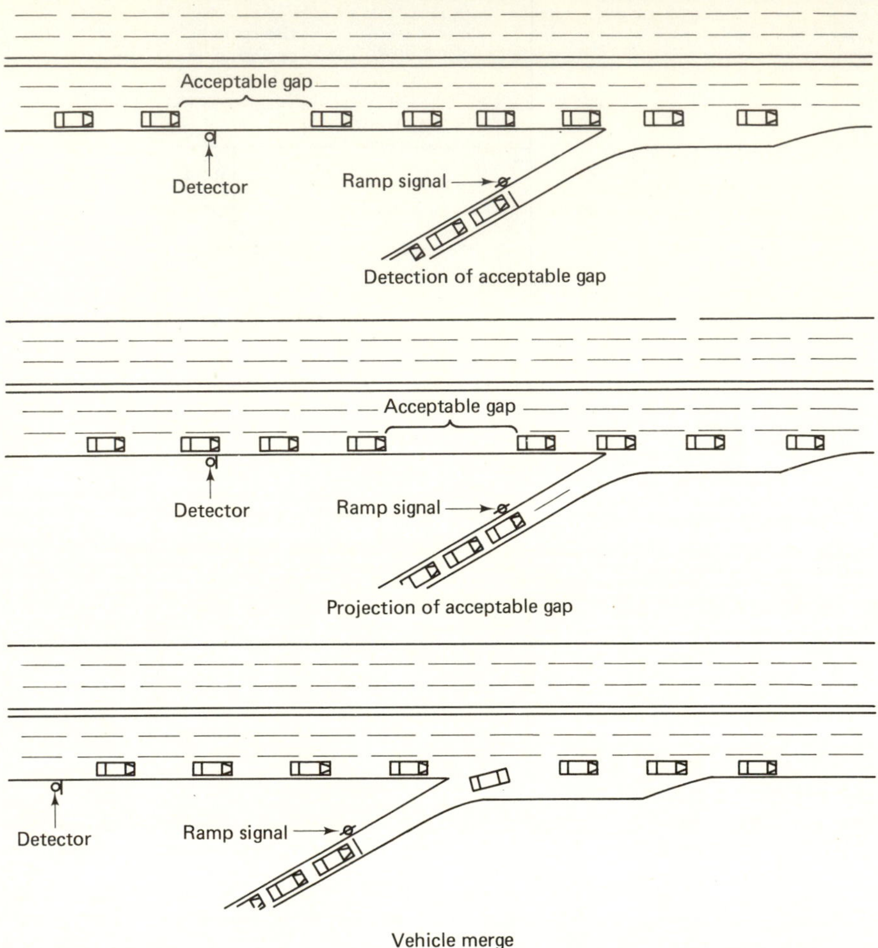

Figure 25.7. Gap acceptance mode of ramp control.

point, and to effect a release or a speed adjustment of the merging ramp vehicle so that its arrival is coincident with that of the detected gap. It is thus a method of merging a maximum number of vehicles into available gaps on the freeway without causing significant disruptions to the flow of traffic on the freeway. Figure 25.7 illustrates the three basic steps involved in merge control, which, for obvious reasons, is alternatively referred to as gap-acceptance (merge) control.[29]

This method of ramp control requires costly instrumentation for questionable benefits and consequently, it has not been applied widely as a traffic-responsive strategy for freeway control. Therefore, the detailed operation of such a technique is not described here.[30]

Integrated system control. All the methods of ramp control discussed so far deal with the control of vehicular flow at an individual ramp. It is often necessary to apply ramp control to several entrance ramps in an integrated fashion so that better utilization of the whole freeway system can be achieved. The control strategy to be employed is then based on the demand-capacity considerations for the entire system rather than on the demand-capacity constraints at each individual ramp.

Integrated ramp control is typically applied to a series of ramps that are subject to either pretimed or traffic-responsive metering. The operation of any individual ramp in an integrated system is similar in all respects to the operations described under these two metering schemes *except* for the calculation and selection of metering rates.

A systematic procedure for calculating the pretimed metering rates for a series of entrance ramps is described in the *Guidelines for the Design and Operation of Ramp Control Systems* and reproduced in the Federal Highway Administration's *Traffic Control Systems Handbook.*[31] The metering-rate computations are based on historical data for the

[29]EVERALL, *Urban Freeway Surveillance*.

[30]For further information, see FEDERAL HIGHWAY ADMINISTRATION, *Traffic Control Systems Handbook;* W. R. MCCASLAND, "Optimizing Flow in an Urban Corridor," Dallas Annual Report 1969–1970, Texas Transportation Institute, 1970; H. BUHR, W. R. MCCASLAND, J. D. CARRELL, AND D. R. DREW, "Design of Freeway Entrance Ramp Merging Control Systems," *Highway Res. Rec. 279* (Washington, D.C.: Highway Research Board, 1969); and FEDERAL HIGHWAY ADMINISTRATION, U.S. DEPARTMENT OF TRANSPORTATION, *Merging Control Systems* (Washington, D.C.: Federal Highway Administration, Office of Research and Development, May 1971).

[31]See footnotes 12 and 13.

TABLE 25–2
Summary of Various Traffic-Responsive, Entrance Ramp Metering Strategies

Location	Type of Control	Method of Determining Metering Rate	Overrides
Chicago, IL.	Occupancy/demand-capacity	Centrally integrated control of several ramps along a section. At each ramp, one of five metering rates (13, 10, 8, 6, and 4 vehicles/min) selected on the basis of 1-min average occupancy measured in mainline lane upstream, subject to demand-capacity constraint imposed by downstream measurements	Excessive queues at an individual ramp cause an override of the system control
Dallas, TX.	Demand-capacity/gap acceptance merge	Centrally integrated control of all ramps. Metering rates at each ramp (2 to 8 vehicles/min) selected on the basis of local gap acceptance merging strategies subject to system-wide demand-capacity constraints	Automatic overrides initiated by central control on the basis of local queue and merge problems
Houston, TX.	Occupancy	Each ramp controlled individually. Metering rates (3 to 10 vehicles/min) selected every minute on the basis of 2-min occupancy measured upstream in second mainline lane from the right	Excessive queues override the metering control
Minneapolis, MN.	Volume-occupancy	Centrally integrated control of most ramps. Metering rates (3 to 14 vehicles/min) at these ramps selected on the basis of upstream, downstream, and at-ramp measurements of volume and occupancy	System control can be manually overridden at the center for any ramp if excessive queues occur at that location
Los Angeles, CA.	Occupancy	Centrally integrated control of all ramps. Metering rates selected on the basis of occupancy measurements on the mainline lanes, entrance and exit ramps, in order to achieve balanced flows on the freeway	System control can be manually overridden at the center for any ramp if excessive queues occur at that location
San Diego, CA.	Occupancy	Centrally integrated control of most ramps. Metering rates (4 to 12 vehicles/min for single vehicle entry, higher for dual entry per cycle) selected on the basis of average measured occupancy across all lanes; a lane occupancy measurement is discarded and inhibited whenever it exceeds 70% of the average across all lanes	System control can be manually overridden at the center if an incident is detected from occupancy and speed measurements; a communication failure transfers the ramp to independent, local control
Toronto, Ontario	Volume-occupancy	Centrally integrated control of all ramps; metering rates selected on the basis of upstream, downstream, and at-ramp measurements of volume and occupancy	System control is automatically overridden at any individual ramp if excessive queues are detected at the location

SOURCE: Private communications with J. McDermott, Chicago; W. McCasland, Houston; G. Carlson, Minneapolis; J. Bell, Los Angeles; R. Weherry, San Diego; and R. Case, Toronto.

control interval of interest. Freeway mainline demands and capacity, entrance ramp demands, and descriptions of the traffic patterns within the segment to be controlled are utilized for calculating individual ramp metering rates.

Integrated systems control using traffic-responsive metering involves coordinating the application of traffic-responsive metering to several entrance ramps, such that the control at each individual ramp is subject to systemwide as well as local constraints. The typical method for integrating the operation of several ramps with traffic-responsive metering is to first calculate, usually through a linear programming formulation, sets of integrated metering rates for each ramp for the range of demand-capacity conditions expected. During operation, the rate at each individual ramp is selected from these precomputed sets on the basis of real-time measurements of freeway conditions.

Integrated system operation with a series of ramps employing pretimed metering offers the advantage of better utilization of the whole system than does independent pretimed metering. Integrated traffic-responsive metering allows variations in traffic demands to be optimized over the entire freeway system. These advantages are borne out by studies of independent and integrated ramp control, which indicate lower travel time, higher total travel, and fewer accidents in the case of integrated operations.[32]

[32]Ibid.

Table 25-2 provides details of the traffic-responsive metering strategies and overrides that have been employed in different cities.

Exit ramp control

Control of traffic on exit ramps can be effected either through closure or some form of metering. However, neither is a universal strategy for freeway control. Metering of exit ramps may offer some relief of congestion on the adjacent surface streets, but it also increases the likelihood of queueing of vehicles onto the freeway, which could thus cause rear-end collisions on the ramp and on the freeway mainline. The use of this control technique has not been fully evaluated.

Closure of exit ramps is a viable strategy for exit ramp control in the sense that it is applicable as a safety measure in situations where closure would drastically reduce weaving, which often occurs between closely spaced ramps. Also, exit ramp closure can be used at a lane drop location by closing downstream exit ramps to encourage more traffic to leave the freeway prior to the lane drop and thereby reduce freeway demand beyond the lane drop.

The principal disadvantage of exit ramp closure is the adverse public reaction because of increased travel time and restriction of access, as well as an increase in the potential for rear-end collisions at such locations. Additionally, if the exit ramp closure is to be instituted only at specific times (e.g., peak periods, special events), considerable operational costs can be incurred. For these reasons, exit ramp closure is generally not considered as a workable control strategy. There has been one implementation of exit ramp closure; this system, installed in Naples, Italy, utilizes detectors on the exit ramp to detect the presence of queues and informs motorists of the ramp closure through overhead displays located immediately upstream of the exit ramp and at the first exit ramp upstream of the affected ramp.[33]

Mainline control

Another approach in improving the safety and efficiency of freeway operations is the control of traffic on the freeway mainline itself. This involves the regulation, warning, and guidance of traffic on the freeway mainline so that some or all of the following objectives are addressed:

- To achieve a more uniform and more stable traffic flow as the freeway demand approaches capacity, thereby effecting improved utilization of the facility and arresting the onset of congestion
- To prevent rear-end collisions if shock waves are set up in the traffic flow because of congestion
- To distribute total delay in a more equitable manner, by saving some freeway capacity for downstream entrance ramps
- To increase the efficiency of operation under restricted capacity conditions caused by incidents or maintenance operations

The general indications from the extensive application of various mainline control strategies in West Germany, Japan, and the United Kingdom are that these techniques can be workable methods for improving the safety and operating efficiency of freeways. Although there has been sparse usage of mainline control in the United States, there is considerable interest in the concept, and increased use of these techniques as essential components of freeway traffic control systems is being investigated.

Mainline control is typically implemented through one of the following means:

- Driver information systems
- Variable-speed control
- Mainline metering
- Lane closure
- Reversible lane control

Driver information systems. Driver information systems are employed in mainline control to advise motorists of freeway conditions so that appropriate actions can be taken by the drivers to enhance the efficiency and safety of freeway operations. The essential design philosophy is to provide drivers with useful, real-time information about downstream freeway conditions so that they can choose to divert from the freeway onto an alternative route or continue on the freeway under some form of control. Effective design of driver information systems requires adherence to certain principles:[34]

- Observance of primacy (i.e., providing the more important information with more impact)
- Preventing overloading of information
- Providing information well in advance
- Spreading out of information to prevent driver boredom
- Avoiding unexpected information

Another evaluation has determined the preference of drivers for information sign displays that are simple and of unique design, which allows them to be clearly distinguished from other types of freeway signs and which also provides a marked difference between displays for normal and abnormal freeway conditions.[35] The driver information systems most deployed in mainline control are single and variable message signing, and roadside and commercial radio broadcasts.

Signing consists of real-time visual information displays in the form of single or variable messages. Single message signs are used to warn drivers of a particular hazardous condition ahead, such as weather, environmental conditions, or congestion; these signs are turned on only when the particular hazard occurs. Clearly, these single-message signs are limited in their application, but they can be very useful at those locations where a hazard is well defined and occurs only periodically. Since the signs must be responsive to the occurrence of the particular hazard, some means of the hazard detection is required. This is a primary function of freeway surveillance.

Variable-message signs have the same intended purpose as the single-message signs; but because of their ability to convey a variety of information, they are more effective in presenting drivers with current information on changing freeway conditions. The types of information that are typically presented by variable-message signs include traffic conditions (e.g., location and duration of congestion), weather and environmental conditions (e.g., ice, fog), and routing (e.g., alternative routes available). As with single-message signs, the operation of variable message signs requires inputs from the surveillance system to select the ap-

---

[33]R. LePera and R. Nenzi, "TANA—An Operating Surveillance System for Highway Traffic Control," *Proc. IEEE, 61* (May 1973). The effectiveness of this system is discussed in P. Ferrari and F. Giannini. "An Aspect of the Determination of the Most Useful Real-Time Traffic Condition Information for Urban Motorway Users," *Proceedings of the International Symposium on Traffic Control Systems* (Berkeley, Calif.: University of California, Institute of Transportation Studies, and U.S. Federal Highway Administration, Dec. 1979), Vol. 2C, pp. 171–185.

[34]T. M. Allen, H. Lunenfield, and G. J. Alexander, "Driver Information Needs," *NCHRP Rep. No. 123* (Washington, D.C.: National Cooperative Highway Research Program, 1971; and *Proceedings of the International Symposium on Traffic Control Systems* (Berkeley, Calif.: Institute of Transportation Studies, University of California, and Federal Highway Administration, Aug. 1979), Vol. 1, pp. 138–216.

[35]C. L. Dudek and H. B. Jones, "Evaluation of Real-Time Visual Information Displays for Urban Freeways," *Highway Res. Rec. 366* (Washington, D.C.: Highway Research Board, 1971; and C. L. Dudek, "Real-Time Displays," *Proceedings of the International Symposium on Traffic Control Systems* (Berkeley, Calif.: University of California, Institute of Transportation Studies, and U.S. Federal Highway Administration, Aug. 1979), Vol. 1, pp. 186–216.

propriate sign. If conditions reported by the surveillance system warrant the selection of two or more messages, a priority system determines the message to be displayed. Although variable-message sign control is done manually in some instances (based on qualitative evaluations of visual observations), the trend is toward automatic control on the basis of quantitative analysis of electronic surveillance data. A number of variable-message sign systems have been developed for use on freeways.[36] Although there is limited information on the effectiveness of these systems, it has been determined that motorists are less frustrated and aggravated if they are provided with information on the location and length of the congested area, and the expected length of the delay to be encountered.[37] This in itself tends to increase the safety and comfort of their trips as well as to improve the overall efficiency and safety of the system. However, with either method of signing, it is important to ensure that the driver is presented with accurate information regarding driving conditions. If the information is not current and motorists are given reasons to believe it to be erroneous, credibility will suffer and the system will not serve its intended purpose.

Commercial radio is a common means of providing freeway traffic information to drivers; local broadcast stations in many major urban areas provide this type of information on a routine basis during the peak periods of traffic flow. The effectiveness of these broadcasts depends on their timeliness, accuracy, and reliability. A cooperative arrangement between radio stations and freeway operating agencies has now been established in several urban areas whereby detailed traffic information is furnished to the stations at regular intervals, and the stations are notified immediately of traffic problems resulting from accidents or other major incidents. In Chicago, freeway traffic information reports are provided for 28 stations. A similar program is under way for 19 stations in Philadelphia, and plans are being made to provide this service in New York, Detroit, Boston, and other major cities. These cooperative arrangements have resulted in a more reliable system for providing real-time driver information.[38] The degree of success of commercial radio as a reliable driver information system is thus clearly dependent on the cooperation of commercial radio stations and the ready access by these stations to accurate and timely traffic information. The potential for communicating motorist information through such links is enormous because more than 80% of the commuters listen to commercial radio during peak travel periods.

Roadside radio is a communication system in which messages can be transmitted directly to the driver from local roadside transmitters. Its major advantage over commercial radio is that the messages broadcast to drivers can be more specific to the conditions at a particular location. Experimental studies have shown that it can be used effectively, and that the system is acceptable to motorists. A highway advisory radio system in the I-35 freeway corridor in Minneapolis yielded the following findings:[39]

- System operator time was minimal, requiring only 5% of the operators' overall time.
- Over 90% of the commuters were aware of the system. Of the commuters who had tried the system, 80% used it occasionally, frequently, or always.
- System limitations were that 20% of the commuters never tuned to advisory radio, another 17% had serious tuning difficulties, 3% were not aware of the system, and 3% had no AM radio in their car.
- Public acceptance of the system was very high, with more drivers liking it than not by a margin of 6 : 1, and more favoring expansion to other freeways than not by a margin of 7 : 3.
- The suggestions for system improvement made most frequently were to upgrade the broadcast quality and to provide more detailed traffic information.
- Traffic diversion studies indicated that commuters divert from the freeway in response to a broadcast when (1) congestion is heavy, (2) they are given sufficient detailed information, and (3) they have an adequate alternative route.
- System maintenance experience was very favorable.
- System design, installation, operation, administration, and maintenance costs were low.

The major problems with these systems is the dependency on drivers to have radio receivers in their vehicles, and that they must tune such a radio to the required frequency each time they require information. In the United States, there is the additional problem of Federal Communication Commission (FCC) restrictions on low-range amplitude-modulated transmission. Finally, such radio systems are opposed by some commercial radio stations who feel that the service provided would be competitive with their own ongoing programs. If all these difficulties can be overcome, it is quite likely that roadside radio will become a practical and widely used means of communicating freeway traffic information since it has the advantages of greater flexibility, lower cost, and the ability to convey more real-time information than other currently available driver information systems.

Variable-speed control. Variable-speed control on the freeway mainline is implemented through changeable message signs on the freeway on which variable speed limits can be posted. This is intended to control the speed of traffic on a freeway at a level that achieves the maximum volume of traffic flow. The underlying principle is that as the demand on the facility increases to optimum density, speed control can help improve the stability of flow and help achieve maximum volumes. This, of course, is true only if the demand is equal to or less than the capacity of the facility; otherwise, variable-speed control can, at best, only delay the onset of congestion but not prevent it. However,

[36] These systems are described in detail in F. J. Mammano, "Driver Information and Motorist Aid Hardware," *Proceedings of the International Symposium on Traffic Control Systems* (Berkeley, Calif.: University of California, Institute of Transportation Studies, and U.S. Federal Highway Administration, Aug. 1969), Vol. 1, pp. 87–117.

[37] Dudek and Jones, "Evaluation of Real-Time Visual Information Displays."

[38] Capelle, *Freeway Traffic Management*.

[39] G. C. Carlson et al. *Evaluation of Highway Advisory Radio in the I-35W Traffic Management Network* (Washington, D.C.: Federal Highway Administration, Mar. 1979).

improving the uniformity of speeds does reduce the probability of rear-end collisions as congestion builds up.

In using variable-speed control, traffic flow conditions are defined as a function of one or more traffic flow variables (e.g., volume, occupancy, density) and the speeds to be posted are typically selected on the basis of real-time measurements and historical values of these variables. Variable-speed control can also be used during off-peak periods as an advance warning to alert motorists to such traffic hazards as accidents and traffic obstructions. The U.S. experience in the use of variable-speed control has not been very successful. In the limited cases where it has been tried,[40] it was found that motorists did not consider the variable speed limits regulatory; they did not decrease their speeds to coincide with the posted limits unless there was an apparent reason to do so. The control was also not successful in increasing the flow through critical bottlenecks. In the United Kingdom and Germany, on the other hand, variable-speed control signs on the freeway have been found to be very effective and have yielded favorable results in terms of improving the speed distribution and reducing the frequency and severity of accidents.[41]

Mainline metering. Mainline metering is a form of mainline control whereby the traffic entering a freeway control section via mainline lanes is controlled according to the input demand and downstream capacity. Although such a tactic can create congestion on the mainline upstream of the control section, it can help maintain noncongested flow on the mainline downstream through the control section. The major objective of such a control strategy is to control traffic demand at a mainline control point in a manner that would maintain a desired level of service on the freeway downstream of this control location. The desired level of service may be set to meet various objectives: to maximize the flow through a downstream bottleneck; to provide a high level of service to all vehicles downstream of the control point, especially for buses and carpools; to distribute total delay on the freeway system more equitably; or to encourage diversion of traffic from the freeway because of normal traffic congestion or because of incidents that reduce the effective capacity.

An application of mainline metering is a system in Japan, where it has been effected by regulating the number of toll booths open on the mainlines of expressways, thereby controlling the traffic entering the freeway via the mainline according to the available freeway demand and downstream capacity.[42] Another application is the Bay Bridge mainline metering in San Francisco, where controls are used after vehicles pass through the toll plaza at a point prior to entering the bridge.[43]

Other applications of mainline metering on such controlled-access facilities as terminals, bridges, and toll roads have been found to be effective, but the concept is yet to be applied to a typical urban freeway system. However, a number of operating agencies are developing plans for the implementation of freeway-to-freeway metering.

Lane closure. This method of mainline control is effected through the closure of one or more main lanes on the freeway. It is usually implemented during periods of reduced capacity to improve the operating safety and efficiency of the freeway system. Lane closure is typically used in mainline control for the following purposes: advance warning of lane blockages, traffic diversion during peak flow periods, tunnel control, and for improvement of merging operations.

Lane closure can be implemented through the use of lane control signs, which indicate green arrows for open lanes and red X's for closed lanes. Downstream lane blockage due to maintenance operations or incidents can be indicated by displaying the red X over the affected lane. In the United Kingdom, lane-control signs are used in conjunction with variable-speed control to warn drivers of lane blockages ahead, and they can be used to stop all traffic on the mainline if an incident warrants such action. The system has been found to be effective in reducing the occurrence and severity of accidents on the freeways.[44]

Lane closure can be used to divert traffic from the freeway mainline onto alternative routes during peak periods to alleviate problems of congestion. It can also be used to reduce congestion and hazardous conditions caused by merging operations during heavy traffic flow on the freeway. This can be done by closing, at a point upstream of the merging section, the freeway lane into which the vehicles merge. While such a strategy is likely to reduce the difficulties of the merging operation, some increase in delay to traffic on the mainline may be expected.

Finally, lane closure has found application in the control of tunnels on the freeway mainline. An example is a system installed in Italy, where entrance to a tunnel on the freeway mainline is denied by conventional red–yellow–green traffic signals if an incident or very slow traffic is detected in the tunnel through checks of speed and occupancy.[45] A similar technique is being used by the Port Authority of New York and New Jersey in the Lincoln Tunnel.

Reversible lane control. If peak-hour traffic volumes on a section of the freeway exhibit a significant directional imbalance (e.g., 70%, 30%) which is predicted to continue for several years, the attendant problems of congestion in the heavier-flow direction may be alleviated through the use of reversible freeway lanes. The direction of flow on one or more lanes in the low-volume direction is reversed, using signs to inform the motorist of the direction of flow, and gates and barriers to prevent wrong-way movement.

If designed for new freeways, it is best to separate such lanes from the conventional lanes for safety reasons and construct a three-roadway facility. It is also advisable to schedule the lane reversal for the same time each day to allow motorists to be accustomed to the system. An application of this technique is Interstate 5 on the northern ap-

[40]F. DeRose, "Lodge Freeway Traffic Surveillance and Control Project," *Highway Res. Rec. 21* (Washington, D.C.: Highway Research Board, 1963).

[41]J. T. Duff, "Accomplishments in Freeway Operations outside the United States," *Highway Res. Rec. 368* (Washington, D.C.: Highway Research Board, 1971).

[42]Federal Highway Administration, *Traffic Control Systems Handbook*.

[43]Ibid.

[44]Duff, "Accomplishments in Freeway Operations."

[45]LePera and Nenzi, "TANA."

proach to Seattle, with a 7.5-mi (12-km) reversible-lane section in the median.[46]

The principal advantage of reversible lane control is that it is a more economical and efficient use of road space and right-of-way if the warrant condition of flow imbalance is met and is predicted to continue.

Priority control

Priority control of freeways provides preferential treatment for buses, vanpools, and carpools using the facility. The essence of this concept is to encourage greater use of high-occupancy vehicles, thereby reducing the total vehicle demand on the freeway while serving the same or higher person demand. The different methods of priority control used on freeways are separated facilities, reserved lanes (contra-flow and concurrent flow), and priority access control; these are discussed in detail in the reference.[47]

Separated facilities. Separated facilities are limited-access roadways which are specifically constructed for the exclusive use of high-occupancy vehicles. They are often used to provide express service between outlying areas and activity centers, or for short bypasses at major freeway bottlenecks. In most cases, the separated roadways are constructed in the median of an existing freeway with some form of barrier providing the physical separation from the main freeway lanes. The principal advantages of this method are that the priority vehicles can operate safely at high speeds, the efficiency of the existing freeway is not reduced, the separate roadways have long service lives and low operating costs, and the enforcement of priority control is quite straightforward. There are, however, some disadvantages: high capital costs, long construction time, and sparse usage during off-peak periods.

Reserved freeway lanes. Freeway lanes reserved for priority vehicles are implemented in two main configurations: reserved lanes in the same direction as the main stream of traffic on the same side of the median are *concurrent-flow* reserved lanes, while reserved lanes on the opposite side of the median where priority traffic moves against the flow of traffic are *contra-flow* reserved lanes.

The use of contra-flow lanes is typically the preferred alternative. The method essentially consists of using a freeway lane in the off-peak direction for peak direction traffic. Clearly, this requires the existence of highly directional peak-period flow with sufficient excess capacity in the off-peak direction. Removable barriers are normally used to delineate the lane, while access is limited to specific slip ramps or crossover points at each end of the system. Most often a buffer lane is used to separate the traffic on the contra-flow roadway from the freeway traffic moving in the opposite direction. Such facilities are typically reserved exclusively for buses; carpools are usually not allowed to use contra-flow lanes because of potential hazard problems. The principal advantages of contra-flow lanes are the increase in capacity in the peak direction, and the method can be implemented quite rapidly at relatively low capital costs. In addition, violations tend to be minimal because enforcement is effective at the access points or the terminal areas. The disadvantages of contra-flow lanes are the high operating costs, the potential for very serious head-on collisions, the need for median modifications to provide crossover points, relatively low priority-vehicle speeds in the contra-flow lanes (e.g., 40 mph or 64 km/h), the unsuitability of use by carpools, and the need for special procedures for handling incidents in the reserved lane.

The concept of concurrent-flow reserved lanes for priority vehicles consists of assigning a normal flow lane by signs and markings to designate exclusive access to and use of the lane by priority vehicles. The preferential lane may be provided by taking an existing freeway lane out of service, or by adding another lane to the freeway through construction or restriping. The advantages of a concurrent-flow reserved lane freeway are that the high-occupancy vehicles are given a distinct travel-time advantage over other vehicles. In the nonreserved lanes, capital costs are lower than those for separated facilities, operating costs are low, and the scheme can be implemented in a relatively short period of time. The principal disadvantages are the potential hazards of having a high speed differential between priority vehicles and traffic in the nonreserved lanes, and in the increased weaving required at ramps for vehicles getting to and from the reserved lanes. In addition, a special enforcement program is normally required to prevent the violating vehicles from interfering with the operations of the reserved lanes. Also, the overall effectiveness is likely to be diminished by incidents on the freeway. The general experience with concurrent-flow reserved lanes indicates that the number of ridesharing vehicles can be expected to rise significantly with such systems, although the safety of operation may deteriorate.

Priority access control. Another technique used to improve the level of service for high-occupancy vehicles is priority control at entrance ramps. This method of control is used in conjunction with ramp metering control by providing the high-occupancy vehicles a ramp bypass lane or an exclusive ramp for their own use. The underlying principle is that the high-occupancy vehicles can avoid the delay in queue caused by ramp metering, and thus can enter an uncongested freeway with minimum disruption. There are several advantages of priority access control: both capital and operating costs are relatively moderate, underutilization of freeway capacity is avoided, the absence of a speed differential between priority vehicles and other vehicles on the freeway itself enhances the safety of operations, and enforcement is relatively easy.

Corridor control

The purpose of corridor control is to provide an optimum utilization of all available facilities in the freeway corridor. A freeway corridor comprises, in addition to the freeway

---

[46]Everall, *Urban Freeway Surveillance*.

[47]Department of Transportation, Business and Transportation Agency, State of California, *Freeway Lanes for High-Occupancy Vehicles* (Sacramento, Calif.: 1973).

and its ramps, freeway frontage roads (where they exist), parallel arterial streets that can be used as alternative routes, and cross streets that are links between the freeway ramps and the parallel alternatives. Corridor control is thus an integration of urban street control with freeway control toward achieving the optimum utilization of the corridor capacity.

Implicit in the concept of corridor control is that it must be traffic-responsive to be meaningful. The underlying philosophy of corridor control is twofold: restriction and diversion. Restriction consists of limiting demand on corridor links to less than their individual capacities through the coordination of such regulatory controls as ramp, mainline, and arterial-street controls. Diversion of traffic from corridor links with excess demand to links with excess capacity is basically achieved through driver information systems. The essential components of driver information systems for corridor control are:

- A detection system to provide real-time information on how the routes in the corridor are operating
- A control center that transforms this information into a control strategy
- A communication system that presents the decisions of the control center to the drivers

The purpose of corridor control is to integrate the operation of the various control and driver information systems in the corridor so that optimum utilization of corridor capacity is achieved. This integration entails application of the following techniques:[48]

1. Coordination of traffic signals on frontage roads and on parallel arterials.
2. Coordination of ramp control and frontage road operations so as to provide alternative routes on frontage roads during peak-period congestion on the freeway or during unexpected freeway incidents.
3. Coordination of the ramp control queue override feature with the frontage-road/cross-street intersection control to prevent queueing across these intersections.
4. Provision of turning phases at parallel alternative route intersections with cross streets leading to freeway ramps, possibly in coordination with driver information displays.
5. Coordination of traffic signals at freeway interchanges with arterial cross streets (e.g., at diamond interchanges).[49]

Several research efforts are under way on the development of an integrated corridor control strategy which would coordinate freeway traffic control with the control of frontage roads, parallel arterial streets, and driver information systems. One such effort is the development of the Integrated Motorist Information System (IMIS) concept,[50] which supports the premise that present state-of-the-art equipment and real-time traffic-responsive control techniques can be used for effective management of traffic in an existing highway corridor. This effort has resulted in a handbook which provides the practicing traffic engineer with a step-by-step procedure for developing a corridor control system.

[48]EVERALL, *Urban Freeway Surveillance.*

[49]C. PINNELL AND D. G. CAPELLE, "Operational Study of Signalized Diamond Interchanges," *Highway Res. Board Bull. No. 324* (Washington, D.C.: Highway Research Board, 1962).

[50]P. ZOVE ET AL. *Integrated Motorist Information System (IMIS) Feasibility and Design Study,* Sperry Rand Corporation, May 1978.

Traffic surveillance

Traffic surveillance is an integral and essential part of freeway traffic management systems. Surveillance entails the status monitoring of traffic conditions and of control system operation as well as the collecting of information for implementing controls and for incident detection. The surveillance system provides data on the system operating conditions, upon which appropriate decisions and control actions are taken, whose effects on the system operations are then monitored by the surveillance system. There is thus a closed loop of information, decision, control, and impact. The concept of surveillance is not new. The effectiveness of implemented controls, as reflected by prevailing traffic conditions and the status of control system operation, have always been of interest to traffic engineering agencies.

These aspects of surveillance are common to both urban street and freeway traffic control systems, whose effectiveness is clearly dependent on the reliability and accuracy of the surveillance system, especially in the case of traffic-responsive control. For freeways, however, perhaps the most important aspect of surveillance is the detection and servicing of incidents, which principally contribute to nonrecurring freeway congestion. On the other hand, problems caused by incidents on urban streets are generally less severe than those on freeways, since emergency and repair services, along with alternative routes, are usually more readily available. Thus, the provision of surveillance for incident detection and servicing on urban streets is less common than on freeways. The various methods of surveillance presented in this section are most typically applied to freeways for incident detection and servicing. Each method is thus discussed principally in terms of such a perspective. However, some of these techniques also serve the purpose of measuring traffic performance and control effectiveness, applicable to urban street systems. Such applications are indicated where appropriate.

Incident detection

The earliest traffic surveillance techniques used for incident detection were field observations, periodic studies, police reports, and citizen calls. Today, surveillance for incident detection is carried out through the deployment of a wide variety of methods:

- Electronic surveillance
- Closed-circuit television
- Aerial surveillance
- Emergency motorist call systems
- Citizen-band radio
- Police and service patrols

Electronic surveillance. Electronic surveillance for incident detection is accomplished by the real-time computer monitoring of traffic data collected by detectors installed at critical locations. The measurement of traffic performance and control effectiveness, for urban streets as well as for freeways, can also be carried out by such an installed system. The use of detectors in urban street traffic control systems is described in Chapter 24 and is not repeated here. Also, the discussions of different freeway control strategies in earlier sections of this chapter have indicated the essential manner in which electronic detection is used to implement these strategies. It remains, therefore, to describe how incident detection is accomplished through electronic surveillance.

When a delay-causing incident occurs on the freeway, the capacity of the freeway is reduced at the point of occurrence and, if it is reduced to a value less than the prevailing demand, the traffic flow upstream of the incident is also affected. Most freeway incident detection algorithms involve the determination of changes in certain traffic-flow variables (e.g., volume, occupancy, speed) which are believed to be caused by, or correlated with, the occurrence of incidents. If detected changes in the traffic flow variables are greater than some predetermined values, the occurrence of an incident is indicated. Thus, incidents are detected by logically evaluating the variations in traffic flow characteristics.

An operational system in which this concept is being effectively used is the Los Angeles Freeway Surveillance and Control Project.[51] In this system, changes in lane occupancy between adjacent detectors are used to sense congestion and indicate the occurrence of an incident. At the end of each sampling period, a computer calculates the percent difference in occupancy between adjacent detector stations spaced at ½-mi (800-m) intervals. When the relative percent change between the present occupancy and the occupancy of the preceding sample for the downstream detector exceeds a predetermined value, the computer automatically signals an alert. Additional information on traffic conditions immediately upstream of the incident can then be obtained, and judgment decisions are made with regard to what other response is needed: for example, what equipment to dispatch and whether nonelectronic surveillance (e.g., helicopter or police patrols) is required.

The principal advantages of electronic surveillance for incident detection are: it is the only system that provides a continuous networkwide monitoring capability at relatively low costs; and the installed system can be used for many other tasks, such as the establishment of metering rates for traffic-responsive, ramp-metering systems. The main disadvantage is that the nature of the incident cannot be determined by the system, so that some follow-up surveillance is required to determine the response needed. Also, electronic surveillance for incident detection is yet to be tested for a large network, and general incident-detection strategies have not been perfected for this purpose.

Closed-circuit television (CCTV). Closed-circuit television (CCTV) allows operators in a central control room to monitor traffic conditions visually at the locations where CCTV cameras have been placed. When an incident occurs, the operator can readily determine the nature of the incident and the type of response that is required. CCTV generally is applicable to those locations where delay-causing incidents are a chronic occurrence and fast response is essential. In such use, CCTV normally serves as a follow-up to electronic surveillance where incidents are detected automatically and the operator is alerted by an alarm. CCTV is used mostly for incident detection on bridges or in tunnels, but it can also be applied to critical sections of a freeway or to urban street systems for surveillance of critical intersections.

The main advantage of CCTV is that it is the only system in which a qualified operator can visually detect incidents over a large section of a road and hence determine the remedial action to be taken. CCTV has also been found to be very useful in the initial evaluation and adjustment phases of freeway management projects or in monitoring critical links on a system where a fast response is often required to maintain an acceptable level of service.

There are, however, several significant disadvantages of CCTV surveillance. These are:

- It is expensive to install and maintain; recent technological advancements are, however, reducing these costs.
- Adequate coverage for surveillance may require a large number of cameras.
- It is often difficult and expensive to obtain monitor pictures of acceptable quality under conditions of adverse weather, darkness, and bright sunlight.
- Monitoring the TV screens is a tedious task, and operators may not notice incidents immediately for lack of interest, unless there is an automatic alarm.
- Continuous monitoring of TV screens by qualified operators is quite labor intensive.

In view of all the advantages and disadvantages, it is generally recommended that CCTV should not be used to cover an entire freeway or urban street system. Instead, its use should be reserved for places where it is crucial to detect an incident and its nature as soon as it happens and at locations with a high frequency of incidents, especially if no shoulders can be provided for disabled vehicles (e.g., bridges, tunnels). An example of the latter case is illustrated in Figure 25.8.

Aerial surveillance. Aerial surveillance is undertaken by many operating agencies to get a general overview of traffic in a particular area or corridor. The use of helicopters and light aircraft enables observations of congestion locations and the determination of whether incidents are contributing to the problem. This information can then be broadcast to motorists and used to dispatch aid to the scene of the incident. However, since the pilot is usually covering a wide area, typically a whole city, there is often a considerable delay in relaying the incident information and the subsequent delay in the remedial response.

In general, aerial surveillance has yet to be shown to be cost-effective compared to other techniques. The equipment and labor-intensive aspects of the system are expensive, and its effectiveness is sometimes limited by bad-weather con-

[51] R. H. Green, *The 42-Mile Freeway Surveillance Loop*, Freeway Operations Department, District 7, California Division of Highways, 1973.

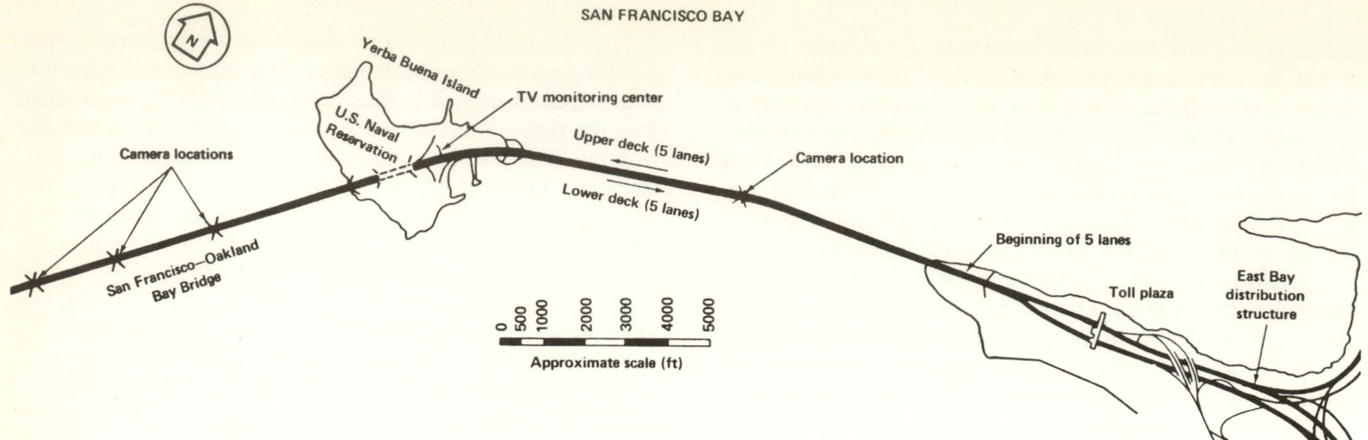

Figure 25.8. Closed-circuit television locations on San Francisco-Oakland Bay Bridge. SOURCE: P.F. Everall, *Urban Freeway Surveillance and Control—The State of the Art,* Revised, Washington, D.C.: U.S. Department of Transportation, Federal Highway Administration, June 1973.

ditions, when incident occurrences tend to be highest. Aerial surveillance seems best suited as a follow-up to electronic surveillance to determine what type of response is needed.

Emergency motorist call systems. Emergency call boxes and emergency telephones installed along freeways were among the earliest incident-detection systems used. With either of these systems, a motorist experiencing an incident, or even witnessing one, proceeds to the nearest call box or telephone and informs the operating agency of the nature of the incident. With a telephone, the motorist uses voice communication directly with the agency. With a call box, the motorist pushes one of several buttons, each of which sends out a pulse-coded message to the responsible agency requesting a particular service. Telephones are generally preferred because the motorist can explain the nature of the incident and be certain of the appropriate service; however, the cost of installing call boxes is considerably less than the cost for telephones.

The main advantages of a motorist call system are that it is an efficient means for signaling a motorist's need for service, and it provides a reassurance that aid will be provided. If emergency telephones are used, other communication requirements can be met (e.g., maintenance control and directions for motorists). The major disadvantage of such systems is the time delay inherent in the operation; the motorist determines the occurrence of an incident, decides that the proper action involves an emergency call system, locates the nearest call box or telephone, and then calls the responsible agency. Thus, the detection delay in such a system can be quite significant. Additionally, a large number of "gone-on-arrival" calls are generated; the motorist remedies the problem through some other means and when the service agency arrives, the disabled vehicle is no longer there. Finally, motorist call systems do present a safety hazard if located on the edge of freeway shoulders; on the other hand, if located off the freeway, their usefulness is considerably diminished. It is recommended that motorist call systems be installed within 2 ft (0.6 m) of the edge of the freeway shoulder, and with safe breakaway terminal posts.[52] In general, motorist call systems are sometimes desirable on urban freeways since they are the only means, besides police and service patrols, for motorists to summon aid and to be assured of its being provided. Because emergency services are usually more readily available to motorists on urban streets, these call systems are generally not provided in such systems.

Citizen-band radio. Citizen-band (CB) radio is a means by which stranded motorists can report their problems directly without leaving their vehicles, or if they do not possess the necessary equipment, fellow motorists can call for them. A CB-radio traffic surveillance system is equally applicable to urban streets and freeways. In a typical system, drivers of CB-radio-equipped vehicles report incidents to a monitoring center, which in turn transmits the information to the appropriate agency that ultimately dispatches the required assistance.

In most systems, requests for assistance are broadcast over Channel 9, which was designated as an official emergency channel by the Federal Communications Commission in 1970. Requests for aid are received directly on this channel and, depending on the geographic characteristics of an area, calls may be effective up to 20 mi.

Some systems under development are making use of CB base station transceivers at unattended remote station locations. This allows the control monitor to receive Channel 9 alarms throughout an entire urban area. The operator can then dial up the CB transceiver near the alarm site and talk with whoever initiated the call. Such a system requires the use of a dial-up phone network and CB units placed at strategic locations to provide major roadway coverage. This type of system can also be used as a follow-up surveillance to verify the nature of a suspected incident following incident detection by electronic surveillance. The operator dials up the nearest roadside CB station once there is an indication of an incident and can listen to a special channel to verify the nature of the suspected incident.

An automatic telephone interconnect device that can be used with a CB radio link for motorist assistance is under study.[53] The basic concept is that motorists establish communication between their vehicles and a monitoring station

[52]EVERALL, *Urban Freeway Surveillance.*

[53]MAMMANO, "Driver Information."

through an automatic radio-to-telephone connection. To do so, the motorist actuates either an "emergency" or "assistance" pushbutton, and the circuitry automatically dials the appropriate telephone number. When the call is answered, the monitor communicates directly with the motorist using standard radio procedure.

The key elements of this system are properly equipped motorists who are knowledgeable about the system and who are willing to report the incidents they observe. Clearly, the detection capability of the system is directly dependent on the number of such motorists on the road at the time. The major advantage of CB-radio surveillance is that the determination of the nature of the incident and its required response are readily accomplished. On the other hand, because of the voluntary nature of the system, a high percentage of rapid detection is not always assured. With the growing number of CB-equipped vehicles, surveillance systems utilizing this concept seem to have good potential.

Police and service patrols. The oldest and most common form of incident detection on urban streets and freeways has been the use of patrol systems, notably police patrols which circulate in the traffic stream for the purpose of identifying incidents and determining the response required. The main advantage of police patrols is that the response to an incident is immediate once the incident has been detected. The principal disadvantage is the large number of patrols required to cover a freeway or urban street system effectively. The costs are high and, in addition, many incidents do not require police response.

Another commonly used system for freeways is the service patrol. This entails the use of light-duty service vehicles to detect incidents as well as to provide such services as fuel, oil, water, and minor mechanical repairs. As in the case of police patrols, service patrols provide rapid response but are also very expensive because of the highly labor-intensive nature of the system.

Incident servicing

Once an incident is detected, the key to minimizing nonrecurrent congestion is the speed with which the incident is removed. The longer the duration of response, the more severe are the resulting congestion and delay for a given level of demand. Consequently, an effective incident management program must include service facilities which, upon location of an incident, allow for the rapid removal of that incident completely off the freeway and out of sight of traffic in both directions.

One important consideration in an incident-management system is the cooperation of the agencies responsible for providing the needed response. Normally, more than one department of an agency or more than one agency are involved. Since the priorities within each agency are often different, it is sometimes difficult to achieve the full cooperation of all parties. Matters involving multiple jurisdictions can also complicate the management process. To overcome these differences, it is sometimes necessary to create an incident-management team composed of representatives of the major agencies and governmental entities. The responsibility for initiating and coordinating all incident-management activities is given to this team; working together, it can effectively formulate and implement strategies for response to freeway incidents.

Hardware requirements

The previous sections of this chapter have described the application of various concepts of freeway control and traffic surveillance. This section is concerned primarily with the hardware components needed for the implementation of these concepts. The hardware components consist essentially of detectors located on the freeway and on surface streets, communication links to and from a control center, information and control displays in the field, and control and display equipment in the control center. (The basic hardware requirements of traffic control systems for urban streets are described in Chapter 24 and will not be repeated here. Detailed discussions of signs and markings are found in Chapter 23.) This discussion is not intended to be comprehensive; rather, it is aimed at providing some essential hardware considerations required in the implementation of surveillance and control concepts. Clearly, the type of hardware and installation configuration is dependent on the functional purpose that needs to be served in the surveillance and control system.

Detectors

The various types of detectors used for traffic surveillance and control for urban streets, discussed in Chapter 24, also apply to freeways. Three types of detectors have been most widely used in freeway applications—ultrasonic, magnetometer, and inductive loop—of which, the inductive loop detector is considered the best type for freeway surveillance and control. The general location of detectors for various freeway ramp control strategies is described in an earlier section, the exact location being dependent on the particular strategy employed. Some specific comments in this regard are therefore appropriate.

Although pretimed ramp metering usually does not require detectors, a check-in (demand) detector is used in some systems so that the signal turns green only when a vehicle is waiting. The layout and markings for such an installation are shown in Figure 25.9.

For traffic-responsive metering, a possible configuration of ramp and freeway detectors is shown in Figure 25.10. Detectors D_{1V} through D_{6V} are volume detectors in the freeway mainline, which can be simple passage detectors or, more usefully, presence detectors which can be used to determine occupancy and speed as well. Detectors D_{20} and D_{50} are lane occupancy detectors, while detectors D_A and D_B are shoulder-lane presence detectors for measuring intervehicular gaps and vehicle speeds. The ramp presence detectors are D_M, D_Q, and D_I. Detector D_{CO} is a passage detector for sensing vehicles passing through the signal, while D_Q detects a vehicle waiting to enter the ramp and

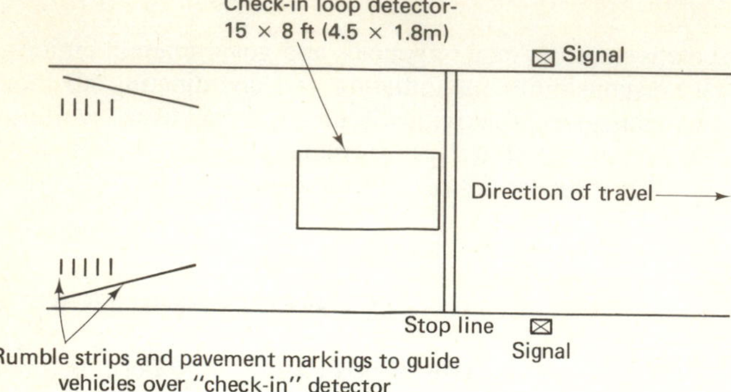

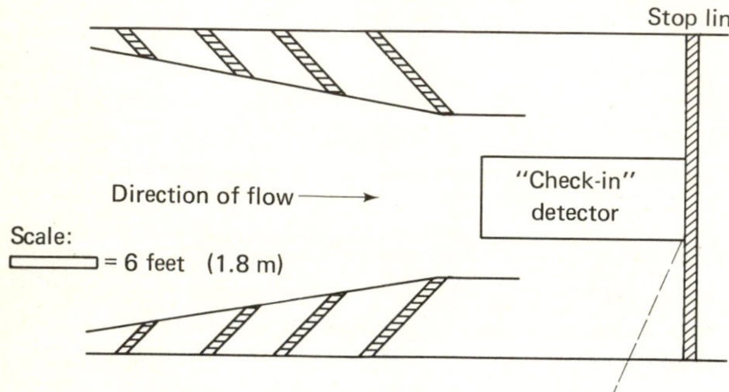

Figure 25.9. Location of "check-in" loop and pavement markings for freeway ramp metering. SOURCE: P.F. Everall, *Urban Freeway Surveillance and Control—The State of the Art,* Revised, Washington, D.C.: United States Department of Transportation, Federal Highway Administration, June 1973.

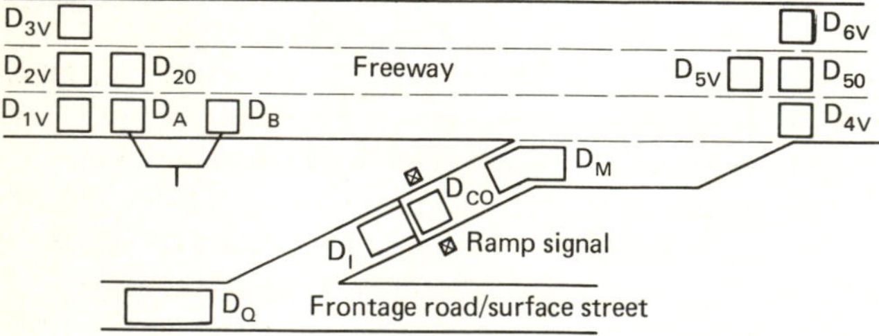

D_{1V}, D_{2V}, D_{3V}, D_{4V}, D_{5V}, D_{6V}—Volume detectors in the freeway mainline
D_{20}, D_{50}—Occupancy detectors
D_A, D_B —Presence detectors used to measure speed and vehicle spacings
D_M—Presence detector in the merging area
D_Q—Queue detector
D_I—"Check-in" detector
D_{CO}—"Check-out" detector

Figure 25.10. Possible location of detectors at a freeway entrance ramp. SOURCE: P.F. Everall. *Urban Freeway Surveillance and Control—The State of the Art,* revised, Washington, D.C.: U.S. Department of Transportation, Federal Highway Administration, June 1973.

D_I a vehicle waiting at the signal. Detector D_M is used for detecting vehicles stopped in the merging area.[54]

[54]Specific guidelines relating to freeway ramp detector location and configuration are given in the Federal Highway Administration's *Traffic Control Systems Handbook*.

Ramp control equipment

The equipment for a specific ramp control system depends on the control strategy to be employed, but in general such systems have the following common requirements: warning and regulatory signs, pavement markings, traffic signals, and local controllers.

Signs. Ramp metering signs are used to warn the driver that the ramp is under control and to provide instructions as to what action to take. Advance warning signs, with such a legend as Ramp Signal Ahead, alert approaching traffic to the presence of a ramp signal and should be located at the head of the ramp at a sufficient distance (around 200 ft or 60 m) in advance of the ramp signal to allow for adequate evaluation and reaction time.[55] The effectiveness of warning signs is enhanced when used in conjunction with flashing yellow beacons. A suitable sign legend in such cases is Ramp Metered When Flashing.

Signs are also normally used at the signal to inform drivers of what actions are expected of them. It is a fairly standard practice to mount a sign on the same pedestal as the signal head, bearing such legends as Stop Here on Red or Wait Here for Green, with an arrow pointing to the stop line. Supplementary signs may be used at the signal to indicate number of vehicle departures during the green. Unfortunately, such signs can create a conflict if a steady green display is used during unmetered periods.

Pavement markings. Pavement markings for ramp control systems are used to augment signs in positioning the vehicle over the check-in detector and facilitate single-vehicle entry. They normally consist of a stop line and striping to guide the vehicle as desired. The stop line should extend across the whole ramp, be 12 in. (30 cm) wide, and be reflectorized. Also, the majority of ramps require some pavement striping to ensure single-lane entry. A typical example of pavement markings on an entrance ramp with a ramp signal and check-in detector is shown in Figure 25.9.

Traffic signals. Various configurations of ramp signals have been used in ramp control applications. As a result of the experience to date, certain standards have now been recommended and are outlined in the most recent *Manual on Uniform Traffic Control Devices*.[56] They are:

- The standard display for freeway entrance ramp control signals shall be either a two-indication signal face containing red and green lenses, or a standard three-indication signal face containing red, yellow and green lenses.
- There shall be a minimum of two signal faces per ramp, facing entering traffic.
- On entrance ramps having more than one lane there shall be a signal face mounted on the left side and on the right side.

[55]EVERALL, *Urban Freeway Surveillance*.

[56]FEDERAL HIGHWAY ADMINISTRATION, *Manual on Uniform Traffic Control Devices*.

TABLE 25-3
Three-Lens or Two-Lens Signal Systems

Advantages	Disadvantages
Three-Lens, Red/Yellow/Green Signal Head	
Familiar to motorist, therefore he/she knows what action to take	Minimum cycle length is increased, thereby reducing rate possible
Amber may be flashed to convey special messages, such as instigation of control each peak period	Is not suitable for single metering since motorists may try to "beat the amber," with possible poor safety consequences
Amber is necessary if bulk or platoon metering is to be employed on a single-lane ramp	
Two-Lens, Red/Green Signal Head	
Ramp control is essentially different from intersection control, and therefore it is advantageous not to use the same signal for both purposes; the ramp-metering signal is strictly for stop-and-go past a point, whereas an intersection traffic control signal assigns right-of-way	More inflexible than three-lens signal in that bulk or platoon metering cannot be employed on a single-lane ramp
Gives clearer indication that only one vehicle at a time is allowed	
With no amber phase, a faster maximum metering rate can be employed in uncongested conditions	

SOURCE: P. F. EVERALL, *Urban Freeway Surveillance and Control—The State of the Art*, rev. (Washington, D.C.: U.S. Department of Transportation, Federal Highway Administration, June 1973).

- The required signal faces should be mounted such that the height to the bottom of the housing of the lowest signal face is between 4½ and 6 ft (1.4 to 1.8 m). The height of any supplemental signal faces should be consistent with sound design principles and engineering judgment.
- All ramp control signals shall utilize vertically aligned lenses with a minimum nominal diameter of 8 in. (20 cm).
- Ramp control signals need not be illuminated when not in use.

There has been some controversy with regard to the choice of two or three lenses for ramp control signals. The relative advantages and disadvantages are summarized in Table 25-3. The use of two-lens signals, with 8-in. (20-cm) lenses is generally recommended, wherever they are legal. For platoon metering applications, the standard three-lens head should be used.

Local signal controllers. The various types of local signal controllers for urban street control are described in Chapter 24. The same controllers are suitable for use in freeway control systems. Three principal modes of operation of local controllers are usable in freeway control: pretimed control, central control, and actuated control.

Pretimed control, the simplest of the three, is typically implemented using a one- to three-dial controller unit operated by a time switch. This is the lowest-cost alternative, compared to solid-state or microprocessor-based controller units, which could also be used for this application.

Central control of the local ramp controller is generally used for traffic-responsive ramp control, although applications have also been made for pretimed metering. In the central control operation, the controller functions are incorporated within a central computer and the need for controller hardware at the ramp site is virtually eliminated. Thus, the timing and control operations are carried out by power relays with instructions to the computer performed by software or by manual inputs. Such a system offers greatly increased flexibility by virtue of the computer's ability to store a large number of timing plans in its memory. The disadvantages of central control are the need for a fairly elaborate communication system between field equipment and the central computer, and the possible loss of system operation due to computer or communications malfunction. The latter problem can be avoided by using a pretimed controller unit to provide backup service during an equipment failure. Again, the electromechanical controller unit is the cheapest alternative, whereas the solid-state or microprocessor-based controller units provide greater flexibility.

Although a central computer can be utilized for both systemwide and individual traffic-responsive ramp control, often it may only be necessary to provide individual traffic-responsive control at a few ramps. Locally actuated controllers can be used to accomplish such objectives. These controllers operate in stand-alone fashion by selecting metering rates based on real-time traffic information gathered by ramp and mainline detectors. The microprocessor-based controller units are most suitable for such operations as they can be programmed not only to perform all local control functions, based on detector data, but they can serve as the building blocks for a comprehensive centrally controlled operation.

Data transmission systems

All surveillance and control systems require some form of data transmission. The transmission system is defined as the equipment needed to transmit electronic pulses at the detector to the control equipment being used, and to transmit control commands to the signals and signs. The type of system used will depend on the type of control being employed (i.e., local or central control) and the type of information to be transmitted. For local control alone, direct wire connections are most feasible because of the short distances between detectors, controllers, and displays. On the other hand, central control typically necessitates data transmission over long distances, and different means of data transmission must be considered.

There are essentially two types of carriers that can be

used in long-distance data transmission for urban and freeway traffic control systems: wire cable and radio. Radio and some microwave systems have been tried as communications carriers for surveillance and control systems, but they are not used extensively because of several disadvantages: high cost and complexity of terminal equipment, problems of maintenance and reliability, and need for high transmitter power for remote locations. Some form of physical interconnection using wire cable has been generally found to be the most feasible.

The three basic types of wire cable commonly used for surveillance and control are conventional interconnect cable, twisted pair cable, and coaxial cable. Each type has different characteristics of cost and performance. The conventional interconnect cable, the least expensive, is basically an open-wire conductor used to complete a circuit between two or a series of points. However, it suffers from the limitation on the amount of information that can be transmitted reliably using such a system.

Significant improvements in performance, in terms of transmitting more information reliably, can be achieved through the use of systems employing twisted pair cable or coaxial cable. The twisted pair cable is made up of sets of two wires that are wrapped around each other; interference from external sources is minimized since the pair of conductors carrying the data are always immediately adjacent to each other in the cable. It also reduces interference between adjacent conductors, since the same current flows in opposite directions in each conductor of the pair. All telephone systems use twisted pair cable.

The coaxial cable is similarly effective because of its structure consisting of an inner conductor and an outer shield. It also has a large bandwidth which could conceivably allow it to provide up to 1000 different channels for data transmission. Because of this, coaxial cable is normally used with TV surveillance systems.

The cable facilities for surveillance and control systems are obtainable either by leasing from a telephone company or by having a system owned by the operating agency. The major factors normally considered in a trade-off analysis between these two alternatives are cost, reliability, and ease of incremental expansion of the system. The user-owned cable system typically offers higher reliability, whereas the leased-line system is generally less expensive and accommodates incremental expansions of the system more easily. This can vary, however, depending on the particular phone company and public agency involved.

Central control and display equipment

For large-scale freeway traffic management systems, the control center is the focal point for all communications and control. It receives information concerning traffic, analyzes and evaluates it, and makes decisions as to what control should be used. The equipment normally found in control centers consists of the computer and its related peripheral equipment, communication consoles, display components, and equipment for dispatching emergency and maintenance vehicles to the problem locations. The essential control and display equipment typically found in a freeway control center is a digital computer and peripheral equipment.

A digital computer is the nucleus of most urban and freeway traffic management systems. Some of its features which are particularly suited to surveillance and control are its ability to:[57]

- Perform various functions according to a preestablished priority order.
- Gather information, calculate parameters, make decisions, and output control commands in the same system at high speeds.
- Operate in real time so that events, as they occur, initiate preestablished priority-level programs.
- Operate automatically and without human intervention on a 7-day, 24-h/day basis.
- Report system performance in printed form for permanent records as well as in display form to allow operator interaction with the system.
- Control various kinds of systems, including signing and television subsystems, by turning on, turning off, or selecting equipment, based on control and decision logic programmed into the computer.
- Perform technical analysis in the free time of the control system.

Rapid advances in digital computer technology in the last decade have produced significant reductions in the cost and size of computers while the computing power has increased noticeably. The majority of computers installed in existing control systems are either minicomputers or medium-scale computers. Minicomputers are attractive for smaller control and surveillance applications in that they are high-speed devices with reasonably powerful input/output capability and low capital cost. Medium-scale computers are required for applications requiring complex, high-speed processing tasks or transferring large amounts of data. In the traffic control field, the minicomputer is most commonly used in freeway operations or for controlling signals on small urban street networks, while the medium-scale computer is used for areawide networks.[58]

The peripheral equipment normally used in traffic control systems includes interactive peripherals and storage devices. The interactive peripherals are those devices that enable the operator to interact either with the computer or the system. They provide a means to obtain information as well as to input commands or alter performance. Table 25-4 summarizes some of the peripheral devices used for traffic control applications. The cathode-ray tube (CRT) and line printer are the primary devices used for communication between the computer and the operator.

The CRT has the advantage of greater speed and a keyboard with which it is possible for the operator to interact with the system through alphanumeric messages. Graphic CRTs that can display simple line drawings and maps are also available but at a greater cost. In some systems, a

---

[57] P. J. Athol, "Traffic Surveillance and Control," *Transportation and Traffic Engineering Handbook* (Englewood Cliffs, N.J: Prentice-Hall, 1976), Chap. 19.

[58] Federal Highway Administration, *Traffic Control Systems Handbook*.

TABLE 25-4
Peripheral Devices

Device	Use
Line printer	Hard-copy recording of information
Cathode-ray tube (CRT)	On-line display of data and system status; communication with computer
Teletype	On-line communication with computer
Magnetic tape	Data logging and storage
Disk	High-speed information storage and retrieval
Card reader/punch	Input and output of programs and data

SOURCE: P. F. EVERALL, *Urban Freeway Surveillance and Control—The State of the Art*, rev. (Washington, DC: U.S. Department of Transportation, Federal Highway Administration, June 1973).

teletype is used either in addition to, or in place of, the CRT for communication between computer and operator.

Magnetic tapes are used for storing large quantities of data at a low cost. These devices are extremely useful for logging system operations, since they allow subsequent playback for additional processing. The disk is also a magnetic recording device that has the advantage of higher-speed random access to data than with tape. Thus, the disk is used for storing programs that are not resident in the computer but must be called upon for special situations, and for storing data relating to operating strategies that must be recalled according to some predetermined sequence. The card reader/punch provides a convenient way of entering new programs or additional data into the system. Its primary value is as a programming aid.[59]

The display map is used primarily to provide a visual indication of how the system is working. It is usually a scaled replica of the traffic control system with colored lights to show traffic conditions on the freeway and urban streets. It is generally an expensive peripheral since it must be tailored to the individual system. However, if an operator is expected to be present and run the system, the display map is a valuable tool in visualizing congested sections and assisting in the identification of incidents on freeways.

Evaluation of surveillance and control systems

Traffic control system investments are usually justified to decision makers on the basis of some forecast of the improvements or benefits that may result. The real need for evaluation, then, is either to confirm or to reject a hypothesis that expected results will occur. Such evaluations also become useful tools in the identification of ways to increase benefits further and/or justify system expansion. Further, the dissemination of the evaluation results provides user experience which is often beneficial to other agencies considering similar improvements.

[59]EVERALL, *Urban Freeway Surveillance*.

Measures of performance

The evaluation procedure must be able to measure the effects of surveillance and control on traffic flow and safety. Although there are many possible measures of performance, several basic parameters are typically used in measuring the performance of most surveillance and control systems:[60]

- *Total travel:* the total amount of traffic expressed in vehicle-miles per unit of time. Its primary advantage is that it takes into account the length of trip as well as the number of vehicles served.
- *Total travel time:* the sum of individual vehicle travel times along a specified section of roadway, expressed in vehicle-hours per unit of time. It is representative of the amount of time spent by all system users. Both "total travel" and "total travel time" can be expressed in terms of "persons" rather than "vehicles" if vehicle classification and vehicle occupancies are known.
- *Safety:* the number of accidents on a freeway or portion thereof, categorized by severity and by type. These accident numbers are usually related to the amount of travel and the length of roadway under consideration in determining rates useful for evaluation and comparison.
- *Speed:* often described as the most descriptive variable of traffic flow. Point samples of the average stream speeds or the speed traces of individual vehicles can be used to locate problem areas and also to provide useful data for developing other performance measures such as energy and air pollution. The inverse equivalent of speed—travel time—is useful to quantify the amount of delay experienced when compared with normal operation.

Specific procedures and techniques for performing studies which develop these measures of performance are given in Chapter 17.[61]

Cost-effectiveness analysis

With most freeway transportation projects, administrators are constrained principally by budgetary limitations. They thus strive for a strategy allowing them to provide the greatest benefits with available funds. The measures of performance described in the previous section are useful in this decision process by:

- Determining which of the proposed alternative solutions are most effective from an economic assessment
- Allowing a "before" and "after" comparison of an implemented solution and thus giving an overall indication of the effectiveness of the project

[60]FEDERAL HIGHWAY ADMINISTRATION, *Traffic Control Systems Handbook*.

[61]See also EVERALL, *Urban Freeway Surveillance;* FEDERAL HIGHWAY ADMINISTRATION, *Traffic Control Systems Handbook;* and J. A. WATTLEWORTH AND W. R. MCCASLAND, "Study Techniques for Planning Freeway Surveillance and Control," *Highway Res. Rec. 99* (Washington, D.C.: Highway Research Board, 1965).

The logical framework for both these analyses is the same (the difference being that the first one uses predicted "after" values, whereas the second uses measured "after" values) and therefore the steps for both are similar.

The basic technique employed is cost-effectiveness analysis, in which the benefits, or favorable changes in a number of measures of performance, are evaluated and, in an economic assessment, compared with the estimated costs of implementation.[62]

The total traffic and safety benefits are evaluated by adding the dollar value of the traffic benefits to the value of the changes in congestion or accidents. In an evaluation of an implemented solution, the total monetary benefits of the implementation are assessed by comparing the traffic and safety effects before with those afterward. However, in an economic assessment of proposed alternative solutions, there is the problem of comparing the costs and benefits of these to determine which is the most effective. There are standard methods for doing this, some of which are very detailed.[63] A somewhat simpler method has the following steps:

1. Decide over how many years the capital and installation costs are to be amortized.
2. Decide at what interest rate costs should be amortized.
3. Estimate the total capital and installation cost.
4. Calculate the equivalent annual cost of this total capital and installation cost, and to this add the annual maintenance and operating costs to give the total equivalent annual costs.
5. Estimate the traffic and safety benefits over the first year.
6. Calculate the ratio of the benefits to the costs.

Those projects with a ratio greater than unity are worth undertaking, and in general those with the biggest ratio are worth doing first. However, some overriding practical factors are always present in the evaluation and selection of a major improvement project. Obviously, these are investment constraints which often rule out some projects, regardless of the extent of the benefits. Also, the ability of the operating agency to staff and maintain the project is a significant factor.

REFERENCES FOR FURTHER READING

ANDERSON, R., ET AL., *Alternate Designs for CCTV Traffic Surveillance Systems,* Texas Transportation Institute, Aug. 1976.

BATHER, RINGROSE AND WOLSFELD, INC., *Final Report for the I-35W Urban Corridor Demonstration Project,* Minneapolis, Minn., Aug. 1975.

CALIFORNIA BUSINESS AND TRANSPORTATION AGENCY, *Los Angeles Area Freeway Surveillance and Control Project,* Third Annual Report, Feb. 1973.

CALIFORNIA DEPARTMENT OF PUBLIC WORKS., *Los Angeles Area Freeway Surveillance and Control Project,* First Annual Report, Jan. 1971.

CARVELL, J. D., JR., *Freeway Operations Manual, Dallas Corridor Study,* Texas Transportation Institute, Sept. 1974.

COOK, A. R., "Management of Urban Freeway Traffic," *Can. J. Civil Eng., 1*(2), (Dec. 1974).

COOK, A. R., AND D. E. CLEVELAND, "Detection of Freeway Capacity—Reducing Incidents by Traffic Stream Measurements," *Transport. Res. Rec. 495,* 1974.

COURAGE, K. G., "Freeway Surveillance and Control: A State-of-the-Art Summary," paper presented at the Computer Traffic Control Workshop, University of Minnesota, Mar. 20–22, 1974.

DANIELS, E. D., ET AL., "Improving Commercial Radio Traffic Reports in the Chicago Area," *Transport. Res. Rec. 600,* 1976.

DORSEY, W. F., *Highway Advisory Radio Operational Site Survey and Broadcast Equipment Guide,* Federal Highway Administration, Apr. 1979.

ESTEP, A. C., ET AL., "Getting the Most out of a Freeway System," *Transport. Res. Board Spec. Rep. 153,* 1975.

FAMBRO, D. B., ET AL., "Cost Effectiveness of Freeway Courtesy Patrols in Houston," *Transport. Res. Rec. 601,* 1976.

"Guidelines for Design and Operation of Ramp Control Systems," *Transport. Res. Board NCHRP Dig. 86,* Mar. 1976.

"Incidents and Freeway Operations," *Transport. Res. Rec. 495,* 1974.

MAY, A. D., "Optimization Techniques Applied to Improving Freeway Operations," *Eng. Optimization, 2*(1976).

MAY, A. D., ET AL., *Optimal Design and Operation of Freeway Incident Detection-Service System,* U.S. Department of Transportation, Feb. 1975.

MCCASLAND, W. R., "Comparison of Two Techniques of Aerial Photography for Application in Freeway Traffic Operations Studies," *Highway Res. Rec. 65,* 1975.

MCCASLAND, W. R., *Design and Evaluation of Freeway Surveillance and Traffic Control Systems,* Federal Highway Administration, May 1976.

MCCASLAND, W. R., "Review of Research on Controlling the Level of Service on Urban Freeways," *Transport. Res. Board Spec. Rep. 153,* 1975.

MCCASLAND, W. R., AND R. G. BIGGS, *A Study of Microwave Television for Traffic Surveillance in Texas,* Texas Transportation Institute, Research Report 165-9, Aug. 1975.

MCDERMOTT, J. M., "Surveillance and Control for Incidents on Chicago Area Freeways," *Transport. Res. Board Spec. Rep. 153,* Aug. 1974.

NEWMAN, L., "Bus-Carpool Freeway Lanes in San Francisco Area," ASCE Journal of Transportation Engineering Conference Paper, Nov. 1976.

ORGANIZATION FOR ECONOMIC COOPERATION AND DEVELOPMENT, "Research on Traffic Corridor Control," Nov. 1975.

OWEN, J. R., AND G. L. URBANEK, "Alternative Surveillance Concepts and Methods for Freeway Incident Management," Peat, Marwick, Mitchell & Company, Mar. 1978.

RITCH, G. P., *State-of-the-Art of Motorists Aid Systems,* Texas Transportation Institute, Research Report 165-17, June 1975.

ROPER, D. H., ET AL., "Alternate Route Planning: Successful Traffic Management," *Transport. Res. Board Spec. Rep. 153,* 1975.

STOVER, V., "A System to Facilitate Bus Rapid Transit on Urban Freeways: The Technical Feasibility of Using Traffic Surveillance and Control Techniques," Texas Transportation Institute, Dec. 1968.

[62]See EVERALL, *Urban Freeway Surveillance;* and R. WINFREY, *Economic Analysis for Highways* (Scranton, Pa.: International Textbook Co., 1969).

[63]See WINFREY, *Economic Analysis for Highways,* for one such procedure.

26

TRAFFIC REGULATIONS

DELBERT F. KARMEIER

Director of Transportation and Aviation
Kansas City, Missouri

This chapter discusses one-way streets, turn restrictions, reversible lanes and roadways, transit and carpool lanes, speed limits, and other regulations used to obtain maximum efficiency and safety on street transportation systems. Right-of-way regulation at intersections by use of signs or traffic signals is discussed in Chapters 23 and 24.

One-way streets

Although most streets and highways are designed for use by two-way traffic, increasing traffic usage, conflicts among vehicular flows and between pedestrians and vehicles, and the resulting congestion and accidents often lead to consideration of one-way traffic regulations. In major activity centers, such as the central business districts of cities with a large number of high traffic, closely spaced intersections, one-way traffic regulations are frequently used because of traffic signal timing considerations and to improve street capacity. In the development of new activity centers such as shopping centers, sports arenas, industrial parks, and so on, one-way regulations are frequently incorporated into original street and traffic plans.

One-way streets are generally operated in one of three ways:

1. A street on which traffic moves in one direction at all times.
2. A street that is normally one-way but at certain times may be operated in the reverse direction to provide additional capacity in the predominant direction of flow.
3. A street that normally carries two-way traffic but which during peak traffic hours may be operated as a one-way street, usually in the heavier direction of flow. Such a street may be operated in one direction during the morning peak hour and in the opposite direction during the evening peak hour, with two-way traffic during all other hours.

Advantages and disadvantages

One-way regulations are generally used to reduce congestion and to increase the capacity of a street network. One-way streets also affect safety and usage of adjacent land.

Effect on capacity. Traffic conflicts and delay at intersections are a principal cause of congestion and reduced travel time on two-way urban streets. On one-way streets, left-turning movements are not delayed by opposing traffic. In addition, full use may be made of street pavements of unusual width. The capacity of a street may be increased by as much as 50% by use of one-way regulations (see Chapter 16).

The increased capacity afforded by one-way regulations may also make it feasible to permit parking either part or full time on streets that, if operated as two-way streets, could not be used for parking. More efficient signal timing can also increase street capacity.

Effect on safety. One-way streets with traffic signal controls at major intersections provide gaps in traffic for safer crossing movements by pedestrians and vehicles at other cross streets and driveways. In addition, drivers and pedestrians crossing one-way streets need look in only one direction to observe traffic.

Numerous studies have shown that the conversion of two-way streets to one-way operation reduces total accidents on the order of from 10 to 50%.[1] In some cases, specific kinds

[1]J. A. BRUCE, "One-Way Major Arterial Streets," *Improved Street Utilization through Traffic Engineering*, Highway Research Board Special Report 93, May 1967.

of accidents are reduced even more. Minor midblock traffic collisions may increase as a result of improper weaving by drivers to position themselves for an available parking space or to get in the proper lane for a turn. However, transition areas between one-way and two-way operations are frequently hazardous and require special traffic control treatment.

Effect on traffic flow and capacity. A primary reason for use of one-way streets is to improve traffic operations and to reduce congestion. The degree of improvement in operating conditions, travel speed, and safety depends, of course, on the previous situation. Generally, travel times can be reduced from 10 to 50% and accidents from 10 to 40% even with a slight increase in total traffic volumes[2] (see Tables 26-1 to 26-3). Such general improvement in

[2]P. A. Mayer, "One-Way Streets," *Traffic Control and Roadway Elements—Their Relationship to Highway Safety,* Highway Users Federation for Safety and Mobility, 1971, Chap. 10.

TABLE 26–1
Change in Traffic Volume, Trip Time, and Number of Stops after Conversion to One-Way Operation, Fifth Avenue, New York City

Section	Average Daily Traffic Volume			Average Trip Time (min)			Average Number of Stops		
	Before	After	Change (%)	Before	After	Change (%)	Before	After	Change (%)
Washington Sq. to 23rd St. [0.8 mi (1.3 km)]	15,265	18,722	+23	4.7	2.4	−49	3	1	−67
23rd St. to 42nd St. [0.9 mi (1.45 km)]	21,725	23,591	+ 9	7.3	2.9	−60	5	1	−80
42nd St. to 57th St. [0.7 mi (1.1 km)]	26,130	29,965	+15	7.4	4.4	−39	5	3	−40
57th St. to 138th St. [4.1 mi (6.6 km)]	11,592	14,953	+29	22.4	16.4	−28	14.8	7	−53
Totals (averages)	(16,411)	(19,595)	(+19)	42.1	26.4	−37	27.8	11	−60

Source: J. A. Bruce, "One-Way Streets," *Improved Street Utilization through Traffic Engineering,* Highway Research Board Special Report 93, May 1967.

TABLE 26–2
Accident Changes and Traffic Characteristics on One-Way Streets, London, England

Street	Mileage	Percent Change in Traffic (Average Weekday)		Percent Change in Travel Time				Percent Change in Accidents	
		Volume	Vehicle-Miles	Off Peak Each Direction		P.M. Peak Each Direction		Injury	Pedestrian
Tottenham Ct. Rd.*	5.1	+4	+8	−49	−34	−43	−14	−21	−33
Baker St.*	2.1	+2	+3	−48	−35	−65	−55	+4	−3
Earls Ct. Rd.†	6.3	+10	+12	−33	−15	−27	−16	−27	−13
Kings X*	2.5	−2	+18	−28	0	−27	+40	−33	−40
Bond St.†	1.3	+9	+14	−26	−38	−15	−38	0	0
Piccadilly*	1.3	−4	0	−19	−12	−5	−12	−14	−32

*6 months before and after.
†3 months before and after.

Source: J. T. Duff, "Traffic Management," Conference on Engineering for *Traffic,* 1963, p. 49.

TABLE 26–3
Accidents and One-Way Streets, New York City

Street and Length Made One-Way	Period	Number of Accidents: Angle	Rear End	Turning	Other	Pedestrian	Total Accidents	Total Injured	Accident Rate*
Madison Ave., 23rd St. to 135th St. [5.7 mi (9.2 km)]	Before	23	49	53	67	54	246	167	16.7
	After	23	34	24	45	32	158	101	9.3
	% change	0	−31	−49	−33	−41	−36	−40	−44
Fifth Ave., Washington Sq. to 38th St., [6.5 mi (10.5 km)]	Before	40	65	68	84	63	326	190	20.4
	After	38	53	52	73	45	261	156	13.7
	% change	− 5	−18	−23	−13	−29	−18	−18	−32
Both streets	Before	63	114	121	151	117	572	357	18.6
	After	61	87	76	118	77	419	257	11.6
	% change	− 3	−24	−37	−22	−34	−27	−28	−38

*Accidents per million vehicle-miles.

Source: J. A. Bruce, "One-Way Major Arterial Streets," *Improved Street Utilization through Traffic Engineering,* Highway Research Board Special Report 93, May 1967.

traffic operations must be balanced against the following negative aspects:

1. Some motorists must travel extra distances to reach their destination. This wastes time and fuel.
2. Strangers may become confused with the one-way street pattern, especially if network geometry is irregular, and particularly if clear markings and signal indications are not provided.
3. Transit operations may be adversely affected if routes are forced to operate on two streets instead of one. Where a narrow strip of trip generators is served, walking distances to the nearest bus stop for the desired travel direction may increase.
4. Emergency vehicles, such as fire trucks, may need to take a more circuitous route to reach their destination. This may be alleviated somewhat, however, by providing signal controls that will allow emergency vehicles to move against the flow of traffic on one-way streets by holding vehicles at the next intersection before the emergency vehicle will enter the one-way system.

Effect on area economic conditions. Improved traffic movement and increased safety generally produce broad economic benefits both to adjacent land users and to the general public. Nevertheless, when planning the one-way system, especially one involving commercial streets, traffic engineers should expect objections from affected business owners, who may contend that one-way streets will adversely affect their trade.

Yet studies made in various parts of the United States have generally tended to disprove such claims. Moreover, where one-way systems have once been implemented, many businessmen formerly opposed to the one-way street plan have become their staunchest supporters. One-way streets are rarely changed back to two-way operation unless the construction of major new highway facilities makes the continued operation of the one-way street system unnecessary.

Although the economic and environmental impact of converting to a one-way street system will undoubtedly vary from one place to another, the results of an in-depth study by the Michigan Department of State Highways reveals some interesting results.[3]

1. The greatest degree of environmental dissatisfaction existed with the residents who resided adjacent to the one-way pairs where a majority expressed dissatisfaction.
2. This attitude or feeling diminished in the study area which was at least one residential lot removed from the one-way pair.
3. Residents felt that the one-way conversions would cause a loss in property value and make the area less desirable from an environmental viewpoint. However, results of the market analysis showed that the greatest residential property value increase occurred on the low-traffic-volume converted residential streets where the greatest degree of environmental dissatisfaction occurred.
4. There was no indication of adverse economic influence on business activity within the one-way corridor. The number of business failures was reduced substantially after one-way conversion.

[3]*The Economic and Environmental Effects of One-Way Streets in Residential Areas,* Department of State Highways, Lansing, Mich., 1969.

Trends in one-way street usage

The number and total length of one-way streets have increased significantly in recent years. In 32 European towns, the total length of one-way streets increased from 225 to 575 km in 10 years.[4] Figures are not readily available for the United States, but general observation suggests a similar trend.

Planning for one-way streets

The amount of data to be collected and analyzed in planning for one-way traffic regulations will depend largely on the size and complexity of the one-way system under consideration. The following questions should be considered:

1. Is the layout of the street system such that one or more pairs of one-way streets can be implemented on a practical basis?
2. What effect would the proposed one-way street(s) have on transit operations and patronage?
3. Must parking be restricted in certain areas to provide the proper number of traffic lanes?
4. What changes need to be made in signs, markings, parking meters, traffic signals, and other traffic control devices?
5. What impact would one-way traffic have on freight delivery and truck routings?
6. Are there major traffic generators on the streets to be considered for one-way operation, and what, if any, effect would there be on such generators?
7. Do the street sections proposed for one-way traffic operation terminate so that transition to two-way traffic or termination at a street intersection would not cause safety or congestion problems?

As a general rule, two-way streets should be made one-way only when:

1. It can be shown that a specific traffic problem will be alleviated and the overall efficiency of the transportation system will be improved.
2. One-way operation is more desirable and cost-effective than alternative solutions.
3. Parallel streets of suitable capacity, preferably not more than a block apart, are available or can be constructed. (On low-volume residential streets, this criterion is not important.)
4. Such streets provide adequate traffic service to the area traversed and carry traffic through and beyond the congested area.

[4]E. Nielsen, "Experience from 10 Years Fight against Traffic Congestion," 36th International Congress, International Union of Public Transport, Brussels, Belgium, 1965, p. 15.

5. Safe transition to two-way operation can be provided at the end points of the one-way sections.
6. Proper transit service can be maintained.
7. Such streets are consistent with the master street or highway plan, and compatible with abutting land uses.
8. Thorough study shows that the total advantages significantly outweigh the total disadvantages.

Benefits of one-way traffic regulations

Increased capacity. One-way streets will often:

1. Reduce intersection delays caused by vehicle turning-movement conflicts and pedestrian–vehicle conflicts.
2. Allow lane-width adjustments that increase the capacity of existing lanes or actually provide an additional lane.
3. Reduce travel time.
4. Permit improvements in public transit operations, such as routings without turnback loops (out on one street and return on the parallel streets).
5. Permit turns from more than one lane and doing so at more intersections than would be possible with two-way operation.
6. Redistribute traffic to relieve congestion on adjacent streets.
7. Simplify traffic signal timing by:
   a. Permitting a wider range of offsets for progressive movement of traffic.
   b. Permitting offsets to achieve wider through-bands.
   c. Reducing multiphase requirements by making minor streets one-way away from complex areas or intersections.

Increased safety. One-way streets may:

1. Reduce vehicle–pedestrian and vehicle–vehicle conflicts at intersections.
2. Prevent pedestrian entrapment between opposing traffic streams.
3. Improve drivers' fields of vision at intersection approaches.

Improved economy and environmental protection. One-way streets may:

1. Provide additional capacity to satisfy traffic requirements for a substantial period of time without large capital expenditures.
2. Permit stage developments of a master plan.
3. Meet changing traffic patterns almost immediately and at negligible cost.
4. Facilitate the loading and unloading of commercial vehicles with minimal impact on traffic flows.
5. Save sidewalks, trees, and other valuable frontage assets that would otherwise be lost because of the widening of existing two-way streets.

Design of one-way systems

Roadway requirements. Although one-way systems will differ in details, there are certain basic factors to consider in developing a network of one-way streets:

1. The capacity of the street(s) in one direction should approximately balance the capacity of the street(s) in the opposite direction. If capacities cannot be balanced, the street having the lower capacity must at least have adequate capacity for current traffic and, preferably, for at least a few future years.
2. The one-way pair should preferably be adjacent streets (although systems are operating satisfactorily where there are intervening parallel streets).

Design of termini. Some street patterns readily lend themselves to good traffic operations at one-way system termini, for example, when two streets join in a Y pattern to become one. In a gridiron pattern, however, the one-way system must end at a typical four-way intersection. When the one-way system would normally terminate at a major cross arterial, it is usually desirable to extend the system one block beyond that point. This is particularly true of the one-way street carrying traffic toward the crossing arterial. Construction of diagonal connections to facilitate transition from two-way traffic to one-way traffic should be considered when one-way streets are part of an arterial system.

Reversible lanes and roadways

Arterial routes that are normally operated as two-way streets, particularly those in urban areas, can experience much greater peak-hour traffic volumes in one direction than in the other. This condition typically wastes street capacity. Reversible lanes can provide for better utilization of such streets.

Under the reversible-lane system, one or more lanes are designated for movement one-way during part of the day and in the opposite way during another part of the day. On a three-lane road, for example, the center lane might normally operate as a two-way left-turn lane, but during the peak hour operate as a one-way lane in the direction of greater flow. The purpose of the reversible-lane system, obviously, is to provide an extra lane or lanes for use by the dominant direction of flow. Two increasingly used methods are to reverse the flow of an entire street during peak-hour periods or to make a two-way street operate one-way during that period.

A new, seven-lane, single-carriageway motorway was opened to traffic in Birmingham, England, in late 1971 with signal control to produce directional lane splits of 4–3 or 5–2. In the United States, one of the outstanding examples of multiple reversible lanes is the eight-lane Outer Drive in Chicago, which operates a 6–2 lane split during peak traffic periods.

Advantages and disadvantages

A reversible-lane system is clearly one of the most efficient methods of increasing rush-period capacity of existing streets. With minimal capital costs, it takes advantage of unused capacity in the direction of lighter traffic flow by making one or more of those lanes available to traffic in the opposite direction—the heavier flow. The result is that all lanes are better used. The system is particularly effective on bridges and in tunnels, where the cost to provide additional capacity would be high and, perhaps, impossible. Some disadvantages are:

1. Capacity is reduced for minor flows during peak periods.
2. Reversible lanes frequently create operational problems at their termini.
3. Concentrated control efforts may be needed to prevent violations of the lane-use regulations.

System considerations

There are several factors to be considered in determining whether or not reversible lanes are justified:

Evidence of congestion. If the level of service during certain periods decreases to a point that it is evident that traffic demand is in excess of actual capacity, the possibility of using reversible lanes should be considered.

Time of congestion. It should be determined that the periods during which congestion occurs are periodic and predictable. Traffic lanes can usually only be reversed at a fixed time each day.

Ratio of directional traffic volumes. Lane reversal requires that the additional capacity for the heavier direction be taken from the traffic moving in the opposite direction. Traffic counts by lane will determine whether or not the number of lanes in the counter direction can be reduced, how many lanes should be allocated to each direction, and when the reversal should begin and end. On major streets, there should be at least two lanes for traffic flowing in the minor direction.

Capacity at access points. There must be adequate capacity at the end points of the reversible-lane system, with an easy transition of vehicles between the normal and reversed-lane conditions. Installation of a reversible-lane system with insufficient end-point capacity may simply aggravate or relocate the congestion and accident problem.

Lack of alternative improvements. Cost factors and right-of-way limitations preclude widening the existing roadway or providing a parallel facility on a separate right-of-way.

Operational methods

Once a reversible system is determined necessary and feasible, the method of designating lanes to be reversed and the direction of flow must be selected. Three general methods are used: (1) special traffic signals suspended over each lane, (2) permanent signs advising motorists of the changes in traffic regulations and the hours they are in effect, and (3) various physical barriers, such as traffic cones, signs on portable pedestals, and movable divisional medians.[5]

Although reversible-lane operation is principally used on existing streets and roadways, it can also be designed into new streets, freeways and expressways, bridges, and tunnels. Applications to older limited-access facilities is difficult because most such roadways have fixed medians separating the two directions of traffic. By constructing special median crossing locations and by properly using traffic control devices, however, even these facilities can be used in a reversible manner. Obviously, extreme care must be exercised to maintain safe operation.

Turn regulations

Conflicts between turning vehicles and pedestrians and between turning vehicles and other vehicles approaching from the opposite direction can cause congestion delay and safety problems at intersections and driveway access points. Turn restrictions are a means of eliminating such conflicts and reducing congestion and accidents. In countries where traffic on two-way streets and highways moves on the right side of the center line or median, left turns create vehicle–vehicle conflicts. Where traffic is required by law to drive on the left side of the roadway, right turns are the cause of such conflicts.

Factors to be considered

Since turn regulations are a restraint on the ability of motorists to follow a specific traffic route, the benefits and disadvantages of a restriction should be carefully evaluated before action is taken. The turn restriction studies should consider:

1. The amount of congestion and delay caused by turning movements.
2. The number of collisions involving vehicles making the turning movement.
3. The availability of suitable alternative travel paths if turns are restricted.
4. The possible impact of traffic diversion on congestion and accidents at intersections that would be required to accommodate the traffic diverted by the turning restriction.

---

[5]*Manual on Uniform Traffic Control Devices,* Secs. 4E-8 through 4E-12, U.S. Department of Transportation, Washington, D.C., 1978.

5. Possible adverse environmental impacts caused by rerouted traffic.
6. The feasibility of alternative solutions, such as provision of separate storage lanes for the turning movements and, at signalized intersections, the use of special turn-movement phasing.

Types of turn restrictions

It is not always necessary to prohibit turning movements at all times in order to alleviate a congestion or accident problem resulting from conflicts produced by turning vehicles. Turning movements should be prohibited only during those hours when study data indicate that a congestion or accident problem exists and when a suitable alternative route is available. When part-time restrictions are used, the signs used to notify motorists of the restrictions must be designed and placed so that the time of the restriction is clearly visible to approaching motorists.

At intersections controlled by traffic signals, turns can be restricted to certain phases of the signal operation by use of separate signal displays and appropriate signs. This type of turn restriction is generally most effective when a separate lane is provided for turning vehicles. The signal phasing techniques can be used to eliminate the conflict between turning vehicles and pedestrians or between turning vehicles and opposing traffic.

Effect of turn restrictions on accidents

Because turn restrictions cause a change in travel path, reliable data relative to the total impact of turn restrictions on accidents are difficult to obtain. Data compiled in San Francisco indicated that accidents at four intersections with turn restrictions were reduced by 38 to 52%. All of the intersections were high-volume intersections used by 30,000 to 55,000 motorists in an average day.[6]

The prohibition of turning movements at driveways between intersections is frequently accomplished by construction of a median divider. A study in Wichita, Kansas, reported that prohibition of turns between intersections by use of a median reduced accidents between intersections by amounts ranging from 43 to 69% during the first 3 years after the median was installed. During the same time period, accidents at intersections where turns were not prohibited increased by amounts ranging from 12 to 38%. However, since accidents between intersections originally represented more than 60% of the total accidents on the street section affected by the construction, the median construction resulted in a net accident reduction ranging from 12 to 38%.[7]

An alternative to turn restrictions is the designation of a separate lane for storage of vehicles waiting to make left turns. This traffic control technique can take the form of "continuous two-way left-turn lanes" which can be used by motorists proceeding in either direction. Left-turn storage lanes can also be established with pavement markings for one direction of traffic only on approaches to intersections where left-turning vehicles create accident or congestion problems. Designation of such lanes may, however, require that parking be prohibited, and this could create a need for a study of curb parking supply, demand, and so on. The advantages of the turn lane must then be compared to the impact of parking restrictions in the determination of the best course of action.

Transit and carpool lanes

The use of traffic regulations that restrict certain lanes on public streets and highways to transit or high-occupancy vehicles, such as carpools and vanpools, has been expanded as greater efforts are made to obtain maximum transportation capacity from existing facilities. Exclusive lanes may either be "contra-flow," meaning that traffic using them moves against the flow of traffic on that side of the street centerline or freeway median, or "with flow," in the normal direction of traffic on that side of the centerline or median. Exclusive use facilities include:

1. A lane that is reserved for exclusive use by transit or high-occupancy vehicles at all times. This type of restriction is most often used on limited-access facilities.
2. A lane that is limited to use by transit or other high-occupancy vehicles only during peak traffic periods. This type of restriction is often used on city streets where there is a demand for curb parking or curb freight loading during nonpeak traffic periods, or where the amount of transit and high-occupancy vehicle traffic during nonpeak periods is insufficient to justify the restriction.
3. A freeway entrance ramp which can only be used by transit or high-occupancy vehicles, or which includes a bypass lane for high-occupancy vehicles around ramp entry controls.

The introduction of lane usage restrictions, while beneficial to transit or high-occupancy vehicles, limits the ability of other traffic to use the facility with such lane restrictions. Proposals for lane-use traffic regulations must, therefore, be evaluated carefully in order to determine that such regulations will improve the total capacity of the facility to move persons and goods in a safe and efficient manner.

Factors to be considered

An engineering analysis of the capacity of the facility at a desirable level of service and of the occupancy of existing vehicles should be made to determine the persons-per-hour capacity of the facility without lane-use restrictions. Observations of travel time and delay under existing conditions should be measured so that they can be compared to values that can be anticipated if a lane is restricted to use by transit

---

[6] R. T. Shoaf, "Traffic Signs," *Improved Street Utilization through Traffic Engineering,* Highway Research Board Special Report 93, May 1967.

[7] R. Johnson and B. McKinley, unpublished paper submitted to Technical Award Committee, Missouri Valley Section, Institute of Transportation Engineers, 1971.

and high-occupancy vehicles. In evaluating travel time, the average travel time per person becomes an important factor.

If the exclusive lane is on a street that also provides access to adjacent property, the impact of a restriction on passenger and freight loading and unloading must be evaluated and careful attention must be given to driveway access. Lanes on city streets reserved for exclusive transit use are often along the curb, and loading and unloading of passengers by taxis and other automobiles can interfere with transit operations in the exclusive lane. The closing of entrance ramps to freeways to all but transit or high-occupancy vehicles can create additional traffic congestion on adjacent parallel facilities and such disadvantages must be weighed against the advantages to the users of the facility with restricted entry. On freeways, the length of special lanes for high-occupancy vehicles must be great enough so that weaving problems are not caused by vehicles entering and leaving it.

Transit and high-occupancy vehicle lanes on freeways

Two types of exclusive freeway lanes have been used:

1. *With-flow* lanes operate in the same direction as the rest of the freeway roadway of which they are a part. They may be physically separated by a buffer lane from the unrestricted lanes, or be merely designated by signs and pavement markings.
2. *Contra-flow* lanes operate in the direction opposite to that of the roadway in which they are located. They are separated from the unrestricted lanes at least by cones or tubes spaced at frequent intervals, or preferably by a blocked-off buffer lane.

A study by the California Department of Transportation concludes that an exclusive bus lane on a freeway can efficiently accommodate 800 to 1000 buses per hour. Short exclusive lane sections less than ½ mi long can accommodate up to 1200 buses per hour according to this study. The potential passenger capacity of such a lane is, of course, dependent upon the seating capacity of buses, the feasibility of standing loads, and other factors. Actual peak-hour volumes on an exclusive bus lane on I-495 at the Lincoln Tunnel in New York have been reported to be as high as 25,800 per hour.[8]

A 21-week experiment with an exclusive with-flow lane for buses and carpools on a 20.1-km segment of the Santa Monica Freeway in Los Angeles, California, produced mixed results. The lanes, previously open to all traffic, were reserved for high-occupancy vehicles from 6:30 to 9:30 A.M. and 3:00 to 7:00 P.M. Monday through Friday. The evaluation of the project indicated an increase in the number of carpools (vehicles carrying three or more persons) and an increase in transit usage. However, the lane restriction increased congestion and travel time in remaining freeway lanes and the result was a 7% reduction in the usage of these lanes during the 7-hour peak travel period. This, in turn, created additional traffic on adjacent city streets as motorists sought alternative routes to avoid the freeway congestion, with a resulting substantial increase in travel time. Another impact was a 30% increase in injury accidents on the adjacent city streets, and a 100% increase in accidents on the freeway with the restricted lane.[9]

At other locations, where exclusive contra-flow lanes were added to existing freeway facilities, more favorable results have been achieved (see Table 26-4).

TABLE 26-4
Freeway Contraflow Bus Lane Projects

Location	New Jersey	Boston	New York	Marin County, California
Route	I-495 (Lincoln Tunnel approach)	Southeast Expressway	I-495 (Long Island Expressway)	U.S. 101
Length (mi)	2.5	8	2	4
Year started	1971	1972	1972	1972
A.M./P.M.	A.M.	A.M.	A.M.	P.M.
Remaining traffic lanes	2	2	2	2
Buffer lane	No	No	No	Yes
Typical bus volumes [per peak hour (peak period)]	500 (900)	35 (70)	120 (200)	70 (150)
Typical passenger volumes [per peak hour (peak period)]	21,000 (35,000)	1,400 (3,000)	6,000 (10,000)	3,000 (6,000)

Exclusive lanes on city streets

Exclusive bus lanes have been used for many years in a number of large cities to improve transit operating characteristics in congested areas and on arterial streets without access control. Transit vehicles, because of their need to make frequent stops to pick up and discharge passengers, are generally unable to achieve travel times comparable to private automobiles. When the number of persons using transit on a street segment is equivalent to the passengers per lane in private automobiles, the reservation of a lane for transit vehicles can usually be justified. Such restrictions may also be justified at lower transit passenger levels in order to provide continuity of a high-occupancy vehicle lane and thereby permit passengers in such vehicles to reach their destinations more quickly, and if the average travel time of all persons using the street segment can be improved. In Stockholm, there were a total of 28 km of lanes reserved for transit-only use in 1974, 15 years after the first such lanes were designated.

Objections to transit only or transit and carpool lanes on surface streets are frequently offered by taxicab operators, delivery firms, and the owners or users of adjacent property who may be denied curb loading privileges because of such

[8] *Priority Techniques for High Occupancy Vehicles—State of the Art Overview*, Transportation Systems Center, U.S. Department of Transportation, Washington, D.C., Nov. 1975.

[9] Q. GILLARD, "Los Angeles Diamond Lanes Freeway Experiment," *Traffic Quart.*, ENO Foundation for Transportation, Apr. 1978.

restrictions. However, transit or high-occupancy vehicle lanes can be easily terminated if unsuccessful.

An experiment with exclusive bus lanes on a four-lane two-way city street in Baltimore led to the conclusion that total travel times for all users of the street were significantly increased by the restriction against passenger car use of the curb lane. This resulted primarily from the fact that only one traffic lane in each direction was available for general traffic use. Furthermore, "local" buses used the exclusive curb lane to stop for pickup and discharge of passengers, adding to the delays of other transit vehicles in the restricted lane.[10]

Exclusive freeway access for high-occupancy vehicles

The technique of metering access to freeways as a means of improving operations and capacity has been used in many cities, beginning with manual methods in St. Louis, Missouri, in 1959, and with automatic means in Chicago, Illinois, in 1961 (see Chapter 25). A more recent variation of that technique is to restrict certain freeway access ramps to transit or high-occupancy automobiles and vans. Such restrictions, of course, force low-occupancy vehicles to use adjacent parallel facilities, which in most cases cause longer travel times for trips of comparable length. An experiment with a high-occupancy bypass lane around a signal-controlled access ramp in Los Angeles led to the conclusion that the restriction had resulted in an increase in carpools at a nearby major employer.[11] A study of a similar project in Minneapolis, Minnesota, resulted in a finding that restricting certain freeway ramps to bus-only uses is a concept applicable where (1) congestion on the freeway can be controlled with freeway ramp metering to provide a high level of service, (2) there is a market for express bus service, (3) freeway ramp configurations lend themselves to modification to permit rapid access for buses, and (4) other roadways exist to provide alternative routes.[12]

"Pedestrian-only" streets

The closure of a street to all vehicular traffic on a permanent basis may be viewed as more than a traffic regulation, since it is, in reality, a decision that a street is no longer needed in that particular location. The issues involved in permanent street closures are, therefore, similar to those that must be considered when the need for a new street or highway segment is being decided.

Closure of streets to all vehicular traffic on a part-time basis is, however, a matter of traffic regulation. In some cities, streets in congested areas of the city are closed to traffic during certain hours of each day. The French Quarter of New Orleans and the central area of Innsbruck are two examples. A more common type of street closure are those that occur less frequently, for special events such as street fairs or parades.

Factors that must be considered in the process of deciding if a street should be closed to all vehicular traffic include the following:

1. The ability of adjacent streets and intersections to accommodate traffic that would be diverted by the closure, including the higher volumes of turning vehicles that will be created at certain locations.
2. The impact of the closure on transit routes, passenger walking distances, and so on.
3. Access to off-street parking facilities in the vicinity of the street being considered for closure.
4. Access to adjacent properties for loading and unloading of freight, refuse collection, utility and building maintenance, and so on.
5. Emergency vehicle (police, fire, ambulance, etc.) access and routings.

All firms, individuals, and agencies who regularly use the street being considered for closure must be notified well in advance of the proposed action. If the closures are intermittent but occur on a regular basis, consideration may need to be given to permanent improvements to increase the capacity of adjacent streets to accommodate the traffic diverted by the closure action.

An alternative to complete closure of a street is the limiting of traffic to certain types of vehicles, such as buses or taxis. Nicollet Street in Minneapolis, Chestnut Street in Philadelphia, and two streets in Portland, Oregon, are examples of this form of traffic regulation. The factors to be considered in determining the feasibility of such actions are the same as for complete closure, except that the impact on transit routes is generally favorable.

Restrictions on certain types of vehicles

Traffic regulations relative to vehicle types and sizes are generally of the following types:

1. Weight limit restrictions at bridges and viaducts.
2. Weight limit restrictions on pavements of a low design standard.
3. Truck prohibitions on parkways, boulevards, or other streets which serve primarily residential or recreational land uses.
4. Restrictions on truck loading and unloading in congested districts during peak traffic hours.

Procedures for determining the theoretical load capacity of bridges and viaducts have been developed by the American Association of Highway and Transportation Officials.[13] Careful judgment must be used, however, in the use of information derived from theoretical formulas in the estab-

[10]J. W. Erdman and E. J. Panuska, jr. "Exclusive Bus Lane Experiment," *Traffic Eng.*, July 1976.

[11]R. G. B. Goodell, "Preferential Access for Multi-occupant Vehicles at Metered On-Ramps," *Traffic Eng.*, Sept. 1974.

[12]G. C. Carlson, R. P. Wolsfield, jr., and R. J. Benke. "Results of the Bus-on-Metered Freeway Evaluation—I35W, Minneapolis," *Traffic Eng.*, Mar. 1976.

[13]*Manual for Maintenance and Inspection of Bridges*, American Association of State Highway and Transportation Officials, 1974.

lishment of load limits. Consideration must be given to the availability of alternative routes, the condition of pavements and structures on those routes, the economic loss resulting from additional travel distances, and other factors.

Many jurisdictions prohibit all trucks on streets designated as "parkways" or "boulevards." Such restrictions are generally based on the concept that large, heavy vehicles create excessive noise and interfere with the pleasure of driving on facilities that have been designed with special emphasis on visual aspects of the roadway and adjacent lands. When such restrictions are adopted, provisions must be made for parallel arterial street facilities which can be used by all classes of vehicles.

Restrictions on truck loading and unloading during peak traffic hours are limited in use to a few large cities with significant congestion. When such restrictions are under consideration, studies should be made to determine:

1. The number of truck loading and unloading operations which take place at various hours of the day in the area under study.
2. The effect of such operations on street capacity, congestion, and accidents.
3. The operating hours of business firms and other facilities served by truck loading and unloading operations.
4. The impact of truck loading restrictions on the cost of operations of delivery firms.

Provision of off-street loading space for loading and unloading operations is a more desirable method of alleviating street traffic problems related to truck operations than special traffic regulations.

When trucks are prohibited in certain areas, a "truck route" can be designated to guide commercial vehicles to the best route around such restrictions. Although such designations are not a traffic regulation, the installation of signs identifying special routes for trucks should be done only after study to make certain that the routing is suitable for safe usage by large commercial vehicles.

Speed regulations

Speed regulations and speed limits are intended to supplement motorists' judgment in determining speeds that are reasonable and proper for particular weather and roadway conditions. Speed limits are imposed in order to promote better traffic flow and reduce accidents. However, if drivers do not consider speed regulations to be reasonable, the limits will be disobeyed and lose much of their value. In recent years, much public attention has been given to the use of lower speed limits on highways designed for high-speed driving as a means of conserving fuel.

Factors affecting speed regulations

Public attitude. Transportation officials receive many requests for establishing new speed regulations or for altering the value of existing limits. Such requests often reflect the opinion that something is wrong with a particular section of street highway or with the operation of traffic thereon. A request for a revised speed limit, usually lower than the limit posted, is sometimes the only immediate solution that the public can offer. Such requests often are based on the misconception that almost all motorists will automatically exceed the posted limit by 5 or 10 mph and that the only way to reduce speeds is to reduce the speed limit. Citizens, acting as individuals or in groups, will frequently request lower speed limits for their own neighborhood streets than they, as drivers, would consider reasonable in similar neighborhoods elsewhere.

Public reaction to the imposition of speed limits varies. In 1971, West Germany proposed the imposition of a 100-km/h (62-mph) speed limit on two-lane rural roads where previously no speed limit had been posted. The purpose was to reduce West Germany's high accident rate. The general public reaction was one of anger.[14] In other instances, speed limits have been welcomed. In 1973, the United States adopted a national law requiring that no speed limit could be in excess of 55 mph. This law has been controversial and a high level of enforcement action has been initiated in many states to obtain obedience to the limit.

Accident frequency and severity as related to speed. Various safety campaigns have attempted to persuade motorists that speed is the cause of many accidents, and that if speed can be controlled, accidents will be prevented or reduced. Although excessive speed is often listed in police accident reports as the cause or major contributing factor in accidents, the problem can be better described as driving too fast for prevailing conditions.

Statistics have generally shown that the imposition of speed limits will lead to a reduction in the serious injury rate in urban areas and in the overall accident rate on a specific highway section.

Figure 26.1, taken from a study made by the Federal Highway Administration, reveals some interesting findings regarding accident involvement and speed on main rural highways, not including freeways. Accident-involvement rates are the highest at very low speeds, are lowest at about the average speeds, and increase again at very high speeds. A principal conclusion is that the more a driver deviates from the average speed of traffic, the greater is his or her chance of being involved in an accident.

Effect of environment on speeds. Although much information directed at the driver involves use of the term "safe speed," the term is relative and depends on many conditions and the situation involved. A safe speed in one location may not be safe in another, and a safe speed at a specific time at one location may not be safe under other conditions at the same location.

Roadway type and condition. Higher speeds are relatively safer on roadways with high design standards—wide lanes, absence of sharp curves, adequate sight distance, and clear roadsides—conditions such as exist on freeways. Average speeds for various kinds of vehicles by highway type

[14]A. Siegert, "Speed Limit Irks Germans," *Chicago Tribune*, Oct. 11, 1971, Sec. 1-A, p. 3.

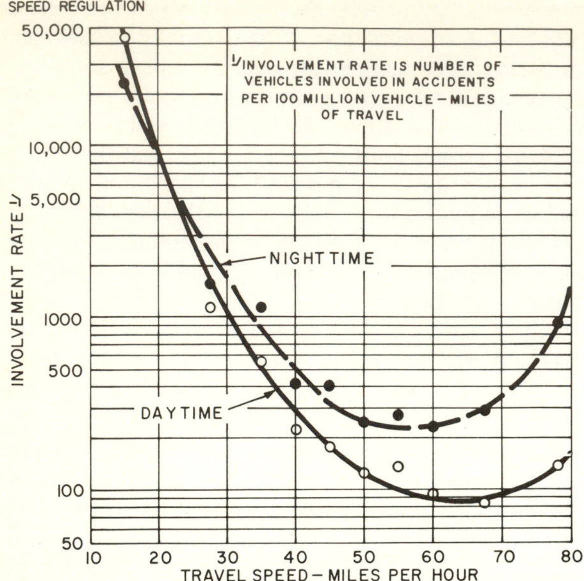

Figure 26.1. Involvement rate by travel speed, day and night. SOURCE: D. Solomon, *Accidents on Main Rural Highways Related to Speed, Driver, and Vehicle,* U.S. Department of Commerce, Bureau of Public Roads, Washington, D.C.: U.S. Government Printing Office, 1964, p. 1.

in the United States are shown in Table 26-5. Roadway surface conditions are also a significant factor affecting safe speed, especially surface characteristics that make one surface more slippery than another when wet.

Adjacent land use and access. Safe driving speeds are also affected significantly by intersecting streets and driveways. Speeds on urban streets tend to be much lower than on rural highways because of houses, businesses, and other kinds of development and increased traffic friction.

Weather conditions. Weather is also an important factor affecting safe speed. The most significant condition is the presence of snow and ice on the pavement. Rain and fog appear to have less influence. Data obtained at selected sites on California freeways and expressways in both day and night conditions indicate that the effects of fog on traffic flow are not large, mean speeds being reduced only 5 to 8 mph.[15] In extremely dense fogs, of course, traffic may be slowed to crawl speeds. Even heavy rain does not appear to have the same influence because sight distance is not greatly reduced.

TABLE 26–5
Average Speeds of Free-Moving Vehicles, and Percent Exceeding Various Speeds by Type of Highway

Highway System	Average Speed All Vehicles (mph)			Percent of Vehicles Exceeding								
				55 mph			60 mph			65 mph		
	1973	1974	1975	1973	1974	1975	1973	1974	1975	1973	1974	1975
Rural Interstate	65.0	57.6	57.6	89	65	68	72	29	27	50	9	7
Rural Primary	57.1	53.5	54.6	58	40	47	36	14	17	19	4	5
Main Rural*	60.3	55.3	55.8	70	51	55	50	21	21	31	6	6
Rural Secondary	52.6	49.5	51.7	39	24	33	21	8	12	10	3	3
Urban Interstate	57.0	53.1	54.7	58	35	48	33	10	13	16	2	3
Urban Primary	41.8	42.3	42.6	13	10	11	5	3	3	2	1	1

*Rural Interstate and Rural Primary

SOURCE: "Ramifications of the 55 mph Speed Limit," Institute of Transportation Engineers, 1977.

Establishment of speed limits

The Uniform Vehicle Code[16] contains the following provision:

Whenever the (State Highway Commission) shall determine upon the basis of an engineering and traffic investigation that any maximum speed herein before set forth is greater or less than is reasonable or safe under the conditions found to exist at any intersection or other place or upon any part of the (State) highway system, said (Commission) may determine and declare a reasonable and safe maximum limit thereat, which shall be effective when appropriate signs giving notice thereof are erected.

Most jurisdictions use similar legislation to permit state or local officials to establish speed regulations at specific locations. This is usually done on the basis of a traffic engineering investigation, and the revision usually takes the form of modifying the basic speed limits set by law or ordinance. The establishment of the regulations at specific locations is commonly termed speed zoning.

There are two basic types of speed controls: (1) regulatory limits that have the effect of law and are enforceable, and (2) advisory maximum speed indications that are not enforceable but warn motorists of suggested safe speeds for specific conditions at a specific location.

Regulatory controls. Speed regulations may be classified as (1) regulations established by legislative authority and generally applicable throughout the nation, state, or local jurisdiction; and (2) zoned speed regulations for specific locations established by administrative action on the basis of engineering studies.

There are two basically different types of numerical maximum speed limits: (1) an absolute limit, and (2) a prima facie limit. An *absolute* speed limit is a limit above which it is unlawful to drive regardless of roadway conditions, the amount of traffic, or other influencing factors. A *prima facie* speed is a limit above which drivers are presumed to be driving unlawfully but where, if charged with a violation, they may contend that their speed was safe for conditions existing on the roadway at that time and, therefore, that they are not guilty of a speed violation. Enforcement officials prefer the absolute limit because it is much easier to prove guilt in a court of law.

Advisory controls. Advisory speed signs warn motorists of suggested safe speeds for specific conditions on a highway. They may be posted in the form of advisory speed plates generally used as a supplementary panel with a warning sign. In some court jurisdictions, driving above the

[15] *Highway Fog,* National Cooperative Highway Research Project Report 95, Highway Research Board, Washington, D.C., 1970, p. 3.

[16] *Uniform Vehicle Code,* rev. 1968, National Committee on Uniform Traffic Laws and Ordinances, p. 156.

TABLE 26-6
Check Sheet for Speed Zones*

Design Speed (mph)	Highway Conditions (Three or More Must Be Satisfied): Minimum Length of Zone Equals or Exceeds (mi)	Average Distance between Intersections Equals or Exceeds (ft)	Number of Roadside Businesses Does Not Exceed (per mi)	Preliminary Estimate of Maximum Speed (mph)
20	0.2	No min.	No max.	20
30	0.2	No min.	No max.	30
40	0.3	125	8	40
50	0.5	250	6	50
60	0.5	500	4	60
70	—	1000	1	70

Speed Characteristics (Two or More Must Be Satisfied): 85th Percentile Speed (mph)	Limits of 10-mph Pace (mph)	Average Test Run Speed Equals or Exceeds (mph)	Maximum Proposed Speed Limit (mph)
Under 22.5	Under 25	17.5	20
22.5–27.5	11–29	22.5	25
27.5–32.5	16–34	27.5	30
32.5–37.5	21–39	32.5	35
37.5–42.5	26–44	37.5	40
42.5–47.5	31–49	42.5	45
47.5–52.5	36–54	47.5	50
52.5–57.5	41–59	52.5	55
57.5–62.5	46–64	57.5	60
62.5–67.5	51–66	62.5	65
67.5 or over	over 55	67.5	70

*1 mi, 1.61 km; 1 ft, 0.305 mi.

SOURCE: ITE, *Traffic Engineering Handbook,* Prentice-Hall, Englewood Cliffs, N.J., 1965, Fig. 14.2.

posted advisory speeds may be admitted as evidence that the driver was operating in a reckless manner.

Speed limit studies. The establishment of speed limits must be based on proper engineering and traffic data. Traffic officials are often called upon to testify in court cases regarding speed limits and they must support their testimonies with data accumulated prior to the establishment of safe speed limits. This information should be of sufficient quantity and of proper quality to justify the value of the speed limit.

The following factors should be considered, and appropriate data gathered, in establishing speed limitations (see Table 26-6):

1. Prevailing vehicle speeds
   - **a.** 85th percentile speed (the speed below which 85% of motorists travel)
   - **b.** Average test run speeds
   - **c.** Speed distribution data
2. Physical features
   - **a.** Design speed
   - **b.** Measurable physical features
     - (1) Maximum comfortable speed on curves
     - (2) Spacing of intersections
     - (3) Number of roadside businesses per mile
   - **c.** Roadway surface characteristics and conditions
     - (1) Slipperiness of pavement
     - (2) Roughness of pavement
     - (3) Presence of transverse dips and bumps
     - (4) Presence and condition of shoulders
     - (5) Presence and width of median
3. Accident experience
4. Traffic characteristics and control
   - **a.** Traffic volumes
   - **b.** Parking and loading vehicles
   - **c.** Commercial vehicles
   - **d.** Turn movements and control
   - **e.** Traffic signals and other traffic control devices that affect or are affected by vehicle speeds
   - **f.** Vehicle–pedestrian conflicts

In the study of prevailing speeds, observations should be restricted to those vehicles having at least from 6- to 9-s headways from those ahead and making no apparent effort to overtake and pass them. The 85th percentile speed as determined by speed studies is a principal factor to be used in the determination of proper speed limits. A graphical presentation of speed data will usually show that the 85th percentile speed value is the point at which speed values become dispersed. Although collecting speed data is highly satisfactory on streets and highways with moderate to heavy volumes of traffic, it is difficult to do on low-volume roads because of the time consumed in gathering the necessary number of observations. In such cases, trial runs can serve as a satisfactory substitute.

Signing for speed limits. Signing for speed limits should be consistent with the appropriate sections of the latest edition of the *Manual on Uniform Traffic Control*

Devices (used in the United States) or its equivalent in other countries (see Chapter 23).

Signs for speed limits are erected at varying intervals, depending on highway type and general location. In urban areas, speed limit signs are usually erected at intervals not exceeding 0.5 mi (0.8 km) if the speed limit is 40 mph (65 km/h) or less. On freeways and in rural areas, frequency of signing varies considerably, with intervals between signs usually ranging from 1 to 5 mi (1.6 to 8 km).

Determination of advisory speed indications

Two basically different methods are available for determining advisory speed limits on horizontal curves: (1) by trial speed runs with an instrument-equipped vehicle, or (2) by office calculation. Either method is satisfactory, but field runs to check the office calculations are desirable in any event.

The trial-speed-runs method involves using a vehicle equipped with a ball-bank indicator to show the combined effect of the body roll angle, the centrifugal force angle, and the superelevation angle. Safe speeds on curves are indicated by ball-bank readings of 14° for speeds below 20 mph (32 km/h), of 12° for speeds between 20 and 35 mph (56 km/h), and of 10° for speeds of 35 mph (56 km/h) and higher. Also, 10° is safe for 50 mph (80 km/h) and even 60 mph (96 km/h), but for higher speeds a smaller reading should be used.

In using the office method for the determination of advisory speeds, the appropriate speed to be indicated may be calculated from formulas (19.5) or (19.6). Transposing to solve for the speed, these become

$$V = \sqrt{15\,R\,(e + f)} \qquad \text{British units}$$

$$V = \sqrt{127\,R\,(e + f)} \qquad \text{metric units}$$

where V = maximum speed in mph or km/h

e = superelevation rate in ft/ft or m/m

f = side friction factor

R = curve radius in feet or meters

Safe speeds determined by these methods may need to be modified by other factors. For example, the safe-stopping sight distance around the curve may require a more restrictive speed than the curvature itself. In this case, it would be advisable to post the advisory speed at the lesser speed (see Chapter 19).

Special problems

Differential limits by kind of vehicle. Some jurisdictions have laws or follow the practice of posting different speed limits for different kinds of vehicles. Differential limits are most common for (1) passenger cars, (2) trucks, and (3) buses. Some jurisdictions also post a reduced limit for towed vehicles, such as trailers, wrecked vehicles, or race cars. Differential limits are more likely to occur on at-grade rural highways than on freeways and urban streets.

The merits of differential speed limits are subject to debate. Proponents contend that reduced speed is desirable for larger vehicles because their operating characteristics (e.g., stopping distance) are not as good as for passenger cars. Opponents, on the other hand, argue that a differential limit creates variances in speeds and a hazardous condition. Such variances in speed are apparently undesirable, as evidenced by the results of studies by the Federal Highway Administration (see Figure 26.2).

Speed limits for adverse weather conditions. Basic traffic laws usually require drivers to adjust speed to existing road conditions. The primary responsibility for accommodating to adverse weather conditions thus rests with the driver. Nevertheless, some jurisdictions have found it desirable, primarily for safety reasons, to reduce speed limits at specific locations during adverse weather conditions by means of signs capable of displaying various messages. Such practice is generally limited to freeways or expressways.

Variable speed limits by lanes on freeways. In order to improve the quality and safety of traffic flow, the use of different speed limits for various lanes of a highway has been tried, principally on freeways or expressways. Where used, the practice is to post the higher limits on lanes closer to the median during peak traffic periods. One study reports that using changeable speed limit signs during the off-peak

Figure 26.2. Accident involvement rate by variation from mean speed on study units. SOURCE: *Ramifications of the 55 mph Speed Limit,* Committee 4M-2, Institute of Transportation Engineers, Arlington, Va., March 1977.

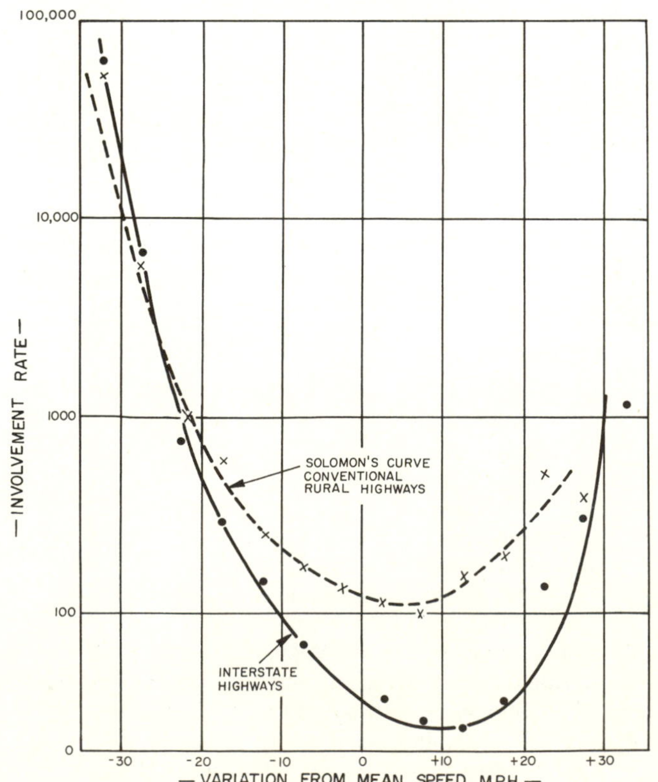

period produced negligible benefits and that the use of these devices during the peak period was judged to have produced essentially no effect.[17]

School area speed limits. Many jurisdictions establish special speed limits on streets adjacent to school buildings during certain hours of the day. A West Virginia study indicated that the most significant factors influencing speeds in school zones were the approach speed limit, the distance of school buildings from the roadway edge, traffic volumes, and the length of the school zone.[18]

Minimum speed limits. On limited-access highways designed for high-speed driving, minimum speed regulations are often used to eliminate the differential in speeds which is often a contributing factor in accidents. Such regulations also prevent motorized farm and construction equipment from using high-speed facilities. In Canada, where the maximum legal speed on rural freeways is usually 70 mph (112 km/h), the minimum legal speed is 45 mph (72 km/h).

Speed limits as related to time of day. The fact that fatal accident rates at night are usually greater than during daylight hours has led some jurisdictions to reduce maximum legal speeds at night. Such regulations are now being used with less frequency because they are often considered to be arbitrary and difficult to enforce. It is quite common, however, for lower speed limits to be in effect during school hours near school buildings.

Emergency condition regulations

Events frequently occur on a particular highway (an accident) or in an entire city or area (snow, hurricane, etc.) which create emergency traffic situations that must be handled immediately. If there is snow or a similar weather emergency, advance preparations can often be based on weather forecasts. Nevertheless, accidents happen spontaneously and advance knowledge is impossible. To ensure that traffic is well handled during these periods, considerable preplanning is desirable and should include:

1. Arranging with police for ambulance and/or wrecker service.
2. Determining alternative streets to be used in case a street is closed, making police assignments for directing traffic, and having available temporary signs and flashers.
3. Designing signals and signal systems to let emergency vehicles proceed with minimal delay.
4. Installing variable message highway signs (see Chapter 23) to warn motorists of roadway conditions ahead, of alternative routes to use, and similar information. Use of such signs is particularly important on freeways and other high-volume, high-speed highways.
5. Enacting appropriate legislation or directives to cover action to be taken during the emergency.

An example of legislation relating to emergency or special conditions is Kansas City, Missouri's "Emergency Snow Ordinance," which reads as follows:

Sec. 34.150 Snow Emergency Regulations

1. *Driving emergency*. When snow, sleet or freezing rain is causing slippery or hazardous conditions which might lead to serious traffic congestion, the City Manager may declare a traffic emergency, and until such emergency is terminated, no person shall operate a motor vehicle on any street in such manner or in such condition as to allow or permit such vehicle to become stalled by reason of the fact that the driving wheels of such vehicle are not equipped with effective tire chains or snow tires.

2. *Parking emergency*. Whenever snow has accumulated or there is a possibility that snow will accumulate to such a depth that snow removal operations will be required, the City Manager may declare a parking emergency, and until such an emergency is terminated, no vehicles shall be parked on any streets designated as snow routes by appropriate signs. All vehicles parked on such streets must be removed within two (2) hours after declaration of an emergency or be considered in violation of this section.

Such legislation must be administered properly in order to obtain compliance from motorists. Street and traffic conditions must be closely monitored and the emergency regulation terminated as soon as possible.

[17]G. C. Hoff, *A Comparison between Selected Traffic Information Devices*, Chicago Area Expressway Surveillance Project Report 22, Illinois Division of Highways, Chicago, 1969, p. 7.

[18]*Establishing Criteria for Speed Limits in School Zones*, Engineering Experiment Station, West Virginia University, 1967, p. 61.

27

LEGAL LIABILITY IN TRAFFIC ENGINEERING

SHELDON I. PIVNIK, *Chief*
Traffic Signals and Signs Division

Metro-Dade County Public Works Department
Miami, Florida

This chapter will not show how to win a lawsuit; its main purpose is to indicate how to minimize the risk of liability. Potential for liability is present in every act. Knowledge of the trend in the law today and guidelines to minimize liability risk potential will go a long way in helping to save an agency the loss of millions of dollars. And the agency can save ancillary costs in time lost appearing at hearings, the preparation of a legal defense, and the assembly and distribution of records in compliance with the court orders.

This chapter will discuss the liability of the agency that has the responsibility for operation of the street system as well as the personal liability of the engineer, the designer, and the maintenance person. It will also cover the area of the expert witness and the conduct of lawsuits. A glossary of legal terms is appended.

No single chapter, not even a single book, can cover the widely differing and diversified areas of jurisprudence that apply in the world today. The constraints of time and space require the contents of this chapter to be limited to a single area, the law in the United States.

Legal systems

It can be said that in the world today there are three legal traditions: the civil law, the common law, and the socialist law. Of the three, the civil law is both the oldest and the most widely distributed. The traditional date of its origin is given as about 450 B.C. and is generally equated to the publishing of the Legal Tablets in Rome. The date that is generally used to mark the beginning of the common law is 1066, when the Normans defeated the defending natives at Hastings and conquered England, establishing the reign of William the Conqueror. The socialist law is the youngest, said to have originated with the October 1917 Revolution in the Soviet Union.

The law in the United States is an outgrowth of English common law, which in turn stems from Anglo-Saxon law. Many of the broad principles are in a general way applicable to the laws of the other common law countries, which are generally the English-speaking countries. The rest of the Western world, primarily western Europe and Latin America, are civil law countries, and have their origins in the Roman Codes or the Napoleonic Code.

The major difference found in the three systems of law is that in non-common law the judges are considered to be civil servants and have very little leeway in their application of the law to the cases at hand. The judges in a civil law country operate under a strict set of codes and traditionally listen to both sides, then resorting to the Civil Codes to make a determination.

Common law, on the other hand, relies more on the judge's interpetations of laws that are passed by authorized bodies, such as the congress, parliament, state legislatures, and county commissions. In this instance judges rely on the doctrine of "stare decisis," which is precedent. In this aspect of the law the judges resort to a review of previously decided cases for assistance in making the current decision. They attempt to fit the case at hand into a mold that has been provided by previous cases. They are free to expand or narrow the underlying law that is being used to determine the issue of the case. This system allows judges in common law countries to overcome legislative inertia by judicial act, for better or for worse, based on perceived social requirements or current needs. Thus, it can be said that much of the law today in the common law countries is judge-made law.

Discussion of the full impact of common law and civil law throughout the world today is beyond the limits of this chapter. Even to discuss common law in the United States would require discussion of the legal systems of 50 states, several territories, and the federal government itself. Instead, this chapter will speak in general terms and general principles of the trend of the law today and discuss what liabilities have to be faced, what defenses exist, and how to minimize the risk of liability.

Federal, state, and local government powers

The authority for the federal government's involvement in streets and highways has as its foundation the "Commerce Clause" in the United States Constitution. Here Congress is given the authority to regulate commerce. Congress and the courts have extended the clause to include radio and TV communications, aviation and airports, and streets and highways. It is through this clause that the development of the interstate highway system gains its authority for funding and construction, that the authority to develop standards for streets and highways occurs, and that the general funding for streets, highways, and related matter begins.

Yet the U.S. Constitution reserves certain powers to the states. Among these are the police powers, which are not limited to police protection, as the name implies, but include all aspects of public safety, health, and welfare. Thus, the states are able to regulate motor vehicle movement, construct and maintain highways and streets, and have a role in pollution reduction and environmental improvement. These powers are limited by only two factors: they may not infringe upon Congress's control of interstate commerce granted to it by the constitution, and state control may not be so overly broad as to approach an abuse of police powers. They must further be applied equally to all classes of citizens so as to meet the constitutional requirement of equal protection under law to all.

It is under these police powers that the states—and the local communities when the authority is delegated to them by the states—have the authority to develop and pass motor vehicle codes and ordinances. In the interest of uniformity of motor vehicle laws, a *Uniform Vehicle Code* and a *Model Traffic Ordinance* have been prepared every 2 to 6 years since 1926. First published as separate booklets, they now appear in a single volume.[1] The publication's foreword indicates that it is not a panacea for all ills and that it does not cover all conceivable legal provisions, but that it does provide the framework for uniformity. And with uniformity come familiarity and safety.

The Highway Safety Act of 1966 (*U.S. Codes,* Chapter 23, Sections 401–404) directed attention to highway safety. Through the National Highway Traffic Safety Administration, a series of highway safety standards has been promulgated, and the states are required to conform to these standards. One deals with vehicle codes and laws.[2] It has the objective that the states

> should develop and implement a traffic code and laws program, which includes plans to:
>
> 1. Eliminate all major variations in traffic codes, laws, and ordinances among its political subdivisions.
> 2. Increase the compatibility of these ordinances with a unified, overall State policy on traffic safety codes and laws.
> 3. Further the adoption of appropriate aspects of the Rules of the Road chapter of the *Uniform Vehicle Code*.

Vehicle codes and ordinances have an important place in liability litigation. By the violation of a code provision, motorists may find themselves in a position where they become the negligent party or contributed to their own negligence, so that, as explained later in this chapter, they may be precluded from recovery for injuries sustained on the highway system or may get a reduced award from the courts. Transportation professionals must therefore be familiar with the codes and ordinances of their states and local communities in order to apply their engineering skill and judgment properly for the maximum safety of the users of the road system.

Public liability

The federal government, while a developer and prime mover of the interstate highway system and the *Manual on Uniform Traffic Control Devices,*[3] has been held harmless by the courts for injuries and losses that have as their proximate (legal) cause infractions of standards, changes in design, and so on, occurring with the knowledge of the federal government. The U.S. Supreme Court has held that the role of the federal government is one of financial management and not designer and operator of the street and road system. Under this theory, law suits against the federal government for negligence of design and operation of the highway system generally fail.

The courts hold that the state is not an absolute insurer of the safety of the user of the highway system. However, they have indicated that state and local governments are required to maintain streets and roads in a reasonably safe condition for users. Failure to do so which results in injury or property loss to users will subject the agency having the prime responsibility to liability for that loss.

In the operation of street and road systems four separate areas are involved: design, implementation, operation, and maintenance. The liability exposure differs in each of these areas.

In the area of design, as long as discretionary authority in the development of the design has not been abused, an agency is held immune from tort liability. In the areas of implementation, operations, and maintenance, any breach of the duty required by that activity which results in an injury or loss will expose the agency to liability.

All liability suits are founded in a particular area of law called tort law. A tort is a private or civil wrong that results in injury or loss. It is not a criminal act or a contractual breach, both of which have their own remedies. It is an injury that one inflicts upon another by an overt act or omission.

---

[1] NATIONAL COMMITTEE ON UNIFORM TRAFFIC LAWS AND ORDINANCES, *Uniform Vehicle Code*. Rev. ed. 1968, plus supplements.

[2] U.S. NATIONAL HIGHWAY TRAFFIC SAFETY ADMINISTRATION, *Codes and Laws*. Highway Safety Program Manual 6, Nov. 1974.

[3] U.S. FEDERAL HIGHWAY ADMINISTRATION, *Manual on Uniform Traffic Control Devices* (Washington, D.C.: Government Printing Office, 1978).

Negligence

The most common of all tort cases is the negligence case. Negligence is the failure to use reasonable care in the dealings that one has with another. In a negligence suit the plaintiff (injured party) must prove the five elements of a negligence suit:

1. The defendant had duty to the injured. For example, public entities have a duty to maintain their street and road system in a reasonably safe condition.
2. There was a breach of that duty. For example, there was a failure or an abuse of discretion in the design, or a failure in the operation or maintenance of the system.
3. The breach of duty was the *proximate cause* of the injury. The proximate cause is the legal cause of the injuries or damages that are sustained. Generally, when an accident has occurred it has two causes:
   a. The actual cause: for example, the cause in a right-angle intersectional crash was the fact that the signals were completely out.
   b. The proximate cause: the proximate (legal) cause in the example was the fact that signals were not maintained properly. The breach of the proximate (legal) cause determines how liability will be assigned to a particular individual or public entity.
4. There was *no* contributory negligence on the plaintiff's part. In some states, if the plaintiffs have contributed to their own injuries, they are precluded from any recovery. A more detailed analysis of contributory negligence and its role in reducing awards to an injured person will follow later in this chapter.
5. There must have been damages. To recover, the injured party must have suffered some kind of personal injury or property damage. The purpose of the award is to put the injured parties back in the position in which they were prior to the accident, either to rehabilitate them, or to reimburse them for their monetary loss.

Immunity

The best defense to a lawsuit is a preventive defense. Such defenses can preclude the plaintiff from successful pursuit of the lawsuit, and a preventive defense may even result in a summary judgment (i.e., dismissal of the suit prior to hearing any of the substantive testimony).

The major preventive defense is sovereign immunity. Sovereign immunity is an example of judge-made law. It evolved from the action of William the Conqueror, King of England (Figure 27.1). He brought with him a new form of government, the feudal system, which included the Common People's Court. In this court neighbor could bring an action against neighbor for a loss or injury. But the one thing William would not allow was a suit against himself. After all, William ruled by divine right and, therefore, could do no wrong.

The first recorded case in English legal history to discuss sovereign immunity was *Russell v. the Men of Devon,* 1788. Russell owned a horse and wagon that traveled the English countryside. The horse and wagon broke through a defectively maintained bridge in Devon and the horse was killed. Russell sued the Men of Devon, which today could be equated to a suit against a county.

Figure 27.1. History and variations of sovereign immunity.

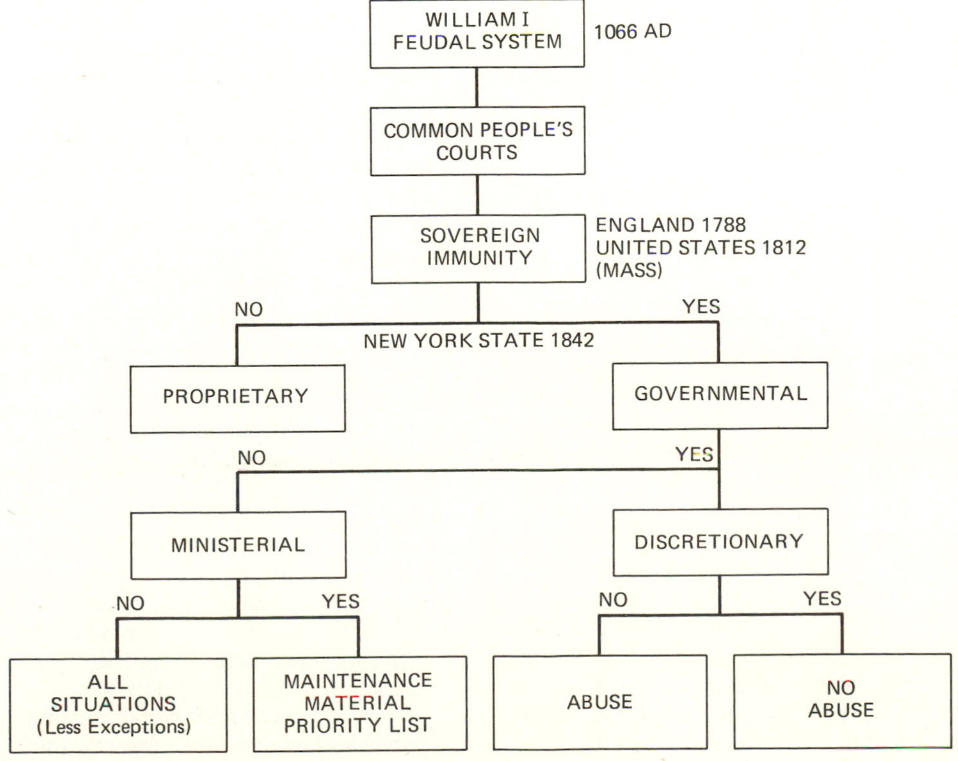

The court handed down a multipronged ruling. First, it said the Men of Devon governed with the authority of the King and therefore had the same immunity as the Sovereign. Thus, they were not required to answer in court for any wrong that they did in their governmental operations. Second, the court said that if parliament wanted government to be held responsible it would have passed enabling legislation. The court further indicated that it was reluctant to permit a suit because, if governments were required to be responsible for the repair and maintenance of their public works projects, they might not be inclined to provide future projects. Finally, the court said to allow a suit to be successful against the government might open the gates of litigation.

It took 24 years for that horse to "swim" the Atlantic. In the Massachusetts case of *Mower v. the Inhabitants of Leicester,* in 1812, a similar event was litigated. Mower owned a stage coach that operated along the Boston Post Road carrying passengers between New York and Boston. One day the coach broke through a hole in a bridge in the town of Leicester. The horse, valued at $120, died from the injuries sustained. In its decision, the court held that Mower could not sue the town because, as in the case of *Russell v. the Men of Devon* (an example of precedent ruling), the town of Leicester could do no wrong because it had the immunity of the ruling sovereign, which in this case was the Commonwealth of Massachusetts.

Many law scholars could not understand why the courts permitted a doctrine such as this to be adopted so soon after the American Revolution in 1776. The country was formed at least in part because people were tired of being oppressed by the King, yet the court adopted his sovereign immunity. William Prosser, a noted law professor and an authority in tort law, expressed this thought very adequately by saying in the early 1940s: "Just how this feudal and monarchistic doctrine ever got itself translated into the law of a new and belligerently democratic republic in America is, today, a bit hard to understand." Nevertheless, the doctrine became well established in the laws of the United States. It was two-pronged:

1. No one could sue the government unless the government gave permission to do so.
2. Even if one could sue the government, the government was not responsible for the acts of its employees.

Immunities are the freedom from all tort liability as a favored defendant. Historically, there have been three basic immunities: family, charitable, and governmental immunities. We are concerned with only the last, yet inroads are being made in all three. It is apparent that it is unfair to injured plaintiffs that they should suffer the entire consequences of the loss just because they were injured by the acts of a government or its agents.

Exceptions to immunity

Some courts have done away completely with sovereign immunity, while others have sought to modify it to conform more to the social needs of the day. Where modified, certain breaches of the duty owed to the public by a public entity are permitted to go to trial. A notable area of modification divides the governmental operations into two areas, holding that the government is liable for injuries caused in one area and not the other; this is the governmental-proprietary distinction, developed by the courts of the state of New York in 1842 as a test of municipal tort liability.

The court held that the distinction roughly parallels the dual nature of the great English trade ventures such as the Massachusetts Bay Company. A municipal corporation could not be held liable for injuries resulting from the performance of a governmental function which otherwise would be performed by the state. It could, however, be liable for functions that mainly benefited the proprietors (e.g., the inhabitants of a municipality rather than all the residents of the state), functions frequently performed by private parties, and those for which it charged a fee or through which it made a profit. As rule of thumb, where a city derives revenues from a service, this service can be considered a proprietary function. At the state level it is often held that public authorities are immune for negligence arising in the performance of governmental functions, but the cases do not state that the converse is true—that the state authority can be held liable for negligence in the performance of its proprietary functions.

Not being satisfied with the governmental-proprietary dichotomy, the courts developed the discretionary-ministerial doctrine (see Figure 27.1). This is used more uniformly and applies almost equally to both state and local government. In this doctrine, an act that is considered discretionary and that results in an injury or property loss to an individual is generally held immune from tort liability. However, the public entity is held responsible for the injuries that it has caused by an act considered ministerial.

The courts have recognized that all acts performed by an individual or government have discretionary aspects. The courts have, therefore, defined discretionary as having the power and duty to make a decision among valid alternatives, and the exercise of independent judgment in making this selection. It is not expected that government must be an absolute insurer against accidents. Courts have often decided it would be too harsh to impute liability where authorities have carried out a reasonable plan of improvement, especially in the absence of latent as well as patent defects, and that the adoption of a plan for public improvement is a legitimate function involving independent judgment. However, an abuse of discretion does not enjoy the protection of immunity; neither does a complete failure to exercise discretion.

A ministerial act, however, is performed within a narrow set of guidelines, and any injuries that may result from the performance of this act will expose the agency that has the prime responsibility to liability for those injuries. In the case of *Croft v. Gulf and Western* 506 P.2d 541 (Oregon 1972), the Oregon State Highway Commission was adjudged liable for injuries sustained at a defective traffic signal, partly because the signal technician failed to use the test meter given him when performing maintenance checks,—clearly a breach of a ministerial duty.

How, then, can individuals maintain a lawsuit against a public entity when some form of sovereign immunity still exists? First, they must seek permission to sue. This requires going before the public entity and claiming that injury has occurred because of negligence and indicating that they wish to file suit for recovery of loss. Many states have given up this permissive requirement by passing blanket laws which authorize suits. Generally, under these laws, government retains a vestige of the permissive doctrine by requiring notification of the government within a specified time period that an injury has been sustained. Second, the insurance waiver doctrine as developed by the courts holds that the public entity has waived any immunity that it may still have if it has purchased liability insurance, at least up to the value of that insurance.

Abrogation by law offers a third way for an individual to bring a case into court. This is done by means of a tort claim act. The federal government passed a law in the early 1940s that made itself responsible in a narrowly defined area for the tortious acts of its employees done within the scope of their employment. Many states now have adopted similar acts. Known as little tort claims acts, they permit individuals who fall within the area covered by these acts to bring an action in court for their loss.

Finally, there are the safe streets exceptions. Several states, recognizing the importance of commerce and economic growth that derives from the safe and expeditious movement of goods, passed limited statutes known as the "safe streets exceptions" to sovereign immunity. They are a form of little tort claims act, except that these laws do not open up the state and its political subdivisions to total tort liability, but create tort liability only in the area of safe operation of the street and road system.

At one time the safe street exceptions applied only to the roadbed itself. For example, if the roadbed was maintained improperly or potholes or breaks in the pavement were allowed to exist, any injuries or damages that resulted therefrom would be covered under the safe street exception. However, the courts, with their ability to expand or narrow laws under the common law doctrine, have increased the exposure that government faces under the safe streets exceptions by expanding the coverage to include pavement markings, traffic signs, traffic signals, and roadside hazards placed in the right-of-way.

As noted earlier, a major defense available to a public entity is the doctrine of contributory negligence. In most states, a plaintiff who was injured in an automobile accident and contributed to his own injury, even if the amount was only 1% of the total negligence while the government entity that was primarily responsible was 99% negligent, is precluded from recovery. The states in which this doctrine still exists are shown in Table 27-1. However, only in extreme circumstances do passengers have the driver's negligence imputed to them. An extreme circumstance may exist if a passenger knowingly gets into a car with a known unsafe driver or with a driver who is totally incapacitated and continues to remain with that driver without attempting to leave the vehicle or stop the driver in one way or another. The driver's own negligence then may be imputed to the passenger. Should injuries result, the passenger as well as the driver may be precluded from recovery.

Several states have recognized the harshness of the contributory negligence doctrine—that persons only minutely responsible for their own injuries cannot recover a single penny. Their legislatures have enacted a new doctrine called comparative negligence by which the relative negligence of the parties involved in weighed. For example, if the injured party is found to be 40% negligent and the public entity 60% negligent, any award to the injured party for recovery of loss will be reduced by that percentage. Thus, if a $100,000 judgment is given, the injured but partly negligent party will be entitled to only $60,000. Table 27-1 shows the comparative negligence states as they exist currently.

TABLE 27–1
Transportation-Related Legalities, by State

	Contributory Negligence State	Comparative Negligence State	Statute of Limitations, Property Damage (years)	Statute of Limitations, Personal Injury (years)	Sovereign Immunity Exists	State Tort Claims Act Exists	State Will Defend or Indemnify Transportation Employees
Alabama	×		1	1	Yes	Yes	No
Alaska	×		6	2	No	Yes	No
Arizona		×	2	2	No	Yes	Discretionary
Arkansas		×	3	3	Yes	Yes	No
California	×		3	1	Yes	Yes	Yes
Colorado		×	6	6	Yes	No	Yes
Connecticut		×	2	2	No	No	Yes
Delaware	×		2	2	Yes	Yes	No
Florida		×	4	4	No	Yes	Yes
Georgia		×	4	2	Yes	Yes	Public officer only
Hawaii		×	2	2	No	Yes	Yes
Idaho	×		3	2	No	Yes	Yes
Illinois	×		5	2	No	Yes	Yes
Indiana	×		2	2	No	Yes	Yes
Iowa	×		5	2	No	Yes	Yes
Kansas	×		2	2	Yes	Yes	No
Kentucky	×		5	1	Yes	No	Department or agency only
Louisiana	×		1	1	No	No	State ministerial officers only
Maine		×	6	6	Yes	Yes	No
Maryland	×		3	3	Yes	Yes	On request
Massachusetts		×	2	2	No	Yes	Yes
Michigan	×		3	3	No	Yes	Yes
Minnesota		×	6	6	No	Yes	Yes
Mississippi	×		6	6	Yes	Yes	State, no; municipalities may
Missouri	×		5	5	No	No	No
Montana	×		2	2	Yes	Yes	Yes
Nebraska		×	4	4	No	Yes	Yes
Nevada	×		3	2	No	Yes	Officials, yes Employees optional
New Hampshire	×		6	2	Yes	Yes	Optional
New Jersey		×	6	2	No	Yes	Yes
New Mexico	×		4	3	No	Yes	On request
New York		×	3	3	No	Yes	Yes
North Carolina	×		3	3	Yes	Yes	Yes
North Dakota	×		6	6	Yes	Yes	State officers
Ohio		×	2	2	No	Yes	Yes
Oklahoma	×		6	2	No	Yes	On request
Pennsylvania		×	6	2	No	Yes	No
Rhode Island	×		6	3	Yes	Yes	State officers
South Carolina	×		6	6	Yes	Yes	On request
South Dakota		×	6	3	Yes	Yes	Pay or indemnify
Tennessee	×		3	1	Yes	Yes	No
Texas	×		2	2	Yes	Yes	Certain agencies
Utah	×		3	4	Yes	Yes	State officers
Vermont	×		3	3	Yes	Yes	Yes
Virginia	×		5	2	Yes	No	State officers
Washington	×		3	3	No	Yes	On request
West Virginia		×	2	2	Yes	Yes	State officers
Wisconsin		×	6	3	Yes	Yes	On request
Wyoming	×		4	4	Yes	No	State officers

Notice of defect

The courts have uniformly held that a dual duty arises once the public entity that has the responsibility for a highway or street system has notice of a defect; it then has the duty to repair it or, if unable to do so within a reasonable time, to warn the public adequately. The question arises as to what constitutes notice. *Actual notice* is very simple to understand. *Constructive notice,* however, does not require specific notice of the defect. The courts have held that if a defect has existed for an unreasonable period of time, the agency should have discovered the defect, and therefore it has constructive notice of its existence. Also, courts have held that local police departments are considered to be agents of county maintenance organizations, and if the police department received notice of a defect but did not forward this notice to the maintaining agency, the public entity will be considered to have constructive notice that said defect exists.

Notice is not required where the defect has been caused by the public entity's own act. For example, if the public entity has improperly maintained or improperly repaired the highway, it does not have to receive notice that the defect exists. The courts uniformly say that the entity that performed the act is aware of its own act and thus, if it created a defect, it is responsible. Also, once the duty to repair or warn arises, the warning to the driver must be commensurate with the danger and adequate to convey to the driver that the danger exists. Signs must be used that convey to drivers the type of danger they face. They must be adequate, they must be visible, they must convey to the motorist or the pedestrian the danger to be faced. The signing must be so located as to allow ample decision time. The failure to provide adequate warning is an abuse of discretion and will create liability.

The engineer should be alert to the fact that while the duty to remedy or warn arises when notice is received, a warning sign is not the panacea it appears to be. The courts require the warning when repairs can not be made within a reasonable period time. However, the warning sign will be tolerated only for a reasonable period of time, just until repairs can be effected. If the warning sign is allowed to remain for an unreasonable period of time without repairs being made, the courts will consider that the public entity is maintaining a dangerous condition of public property and the public entity will be just as responsible for injury or loss as if it had done nothing once it had notice.

Design immunity

The courts in many of the states that have passed design immunity statutes have held that the development of a design is a discretionary act, particularly if the design was accepted by a lawfully authorized body designated to approve the design. Yet the same courts have held that there is no design immunity if the design itself is arbitrary, unreasonable, or made without adequate care, or if it is dangerous or manifestly unsafe after use and the agency has received notice of that fact. Under those circumstances to permit continued use of the road system is an abuse of discretion and any immunity existing could be waived by the court exposing the agency to liability for injuries that are sustained as a result of that defect.

At one time it was assumed that changed conditions would not create an abuse of design discretion. However, most state courts have revised their view and have said that if changed conditions have created an unsafe or dangerous situation and if the situation is allowed to exist for an unreasonable period of time, liability exposure will exist. An operational review must be made after the installation. It must be determined that changed physical conditions have not produced a dangerous situation. If it has, action must be taken to correct it; the courts have often said that the public entity must not develop an ostrich-like syndrome, burying its head in the sand and hoping that the defect will go away if ignored. The defect will not go away, and its continued maintenance will result in liability exposure on the part of the public entity.

It is uniformly held that construction and maintenance, as they relate to road and street operations, are considered proprietary or ministerial functions. Hence, there are no immunities to protect the agency that is performing the duty. It means that any time an agency does any kind of construction or maintenance it is as liable to the public as an individual is liable to another individual in the performance of an everyday act. However, the courts have modified this by holding, particularly in the area of maintenance, that there are two subareas where the court will grant discretionary immunity: in materials selection and in the order of making the repairs (the establishment of a priority list). The courts have held that the selection of the material to be used in making the repair is a discretionary one and that the only way that liability can attach because of injuries resulting from the use of a particular material selected is if there was an abuse of discretion. For example, if there was a superior material available and if there was no rational or logical basis for the selection of the inferior material, liability will attach because of abuse of discretion.

"Rational" or "logical" basis varies from court to court. Governmental operations generally require low bid acceptance. The courts recognize this; yet they uniformly hold that dollars must not be the sole reason that a particular material was selected. It can be one of the factors, but in making the decision, one must also look at the quality, availability, and suitability. Under these circumstances the public entity will most likely retain discretionary immunity.

If the established priority list for repairs is not followed, and there is no rational reason for the deviation, there is no immunity and liability can occur. The courts uniformly hold that as long as a priority list is established on a rational-logical basis and repairs are made in accordance with that priority list, there is no liability because an accident occurred at a location with a low priority where repairs were not yet made.

Personal liability

There are various provisions for handling the liability of the individual transportation engineer. Many states have indemnification laws (see Table 27-1) under which the state requires the public entity to defend its employees in cases where the employees have been charged with a tortious act while working within the scope of their employment that has resulted in an injury. Under those laws the agency is responsible for providing an adequate defense on behalf of its employees. The agency must pay any amounts that the courts may require these individuals to pay to the injured party.

In other states, laws provide that injured individuals who bring an action against the agency itself are precluded from bringing an action against individual employees. Under most circumstances, this provides employees with adequate protection, because under the "deep pocket" practice, attorneys for injured parties usually seek an award against the party who is in the best position to pay. The individual engineer, maintenance crew member, or truck driver is presumed to have limited means, but it is assumed that the public entity has a relatively unlimited source of income and the ability to pay a large award if one is made.

In two recent cases, *Garcher* v. *City of Tamarac* (Florida), and *Grubaugh* v. *City of St. Johns* (Michigan), the respective towns had to raise their property tax rates to pay court-awarded liability judgments. Tamarac, faced with a $2.8-million judgment out of a total award of $4.9 million, raised taxes by 6.7 mills for a year; St. Johns paid off a $565,000 judgment in a 2-year period by raising property taxes by 4.2 mills each year.

In the private sector, individual engineers are most vulnerable. They have none of the government immunities of their colleagues in the public sector. They have no statutes to indemnify them, and employer policy may preclude such a defense. Under these circumstances there is an increasing trend for the private-sector engineer to obtain liability and malpractice insurance. This trend is also evident in the public sector, despite immunities and indemnification statutes.

Acting under orders

There is often concern about the predicament which arises when one is told to do something that can create a dangerous situation with the likelihood that someone will be injured. The courts have held that the defense "acting under orders" is a good defense in this situation. To cite an individual with personal liability when acting under orders would be unfair. As a policy consideration, it would make it harder for public entities to obtain employees if they were exposed to the risk of liability under these circumstances. But courts also say that, in extreme cases, there is a duty for a person acting under orders to attempt to mitigate the act and to bring the danger of that act to the attention of superiors. Professionals cannot escape liability by blindly relying on the fact that they are acting under orders. This amounts to an abuse of discretionary power, and the courts will not tolerate abuse of any of the protective devices an individual has.

Respondeat Superior

Another doctrine that can create individual liability is "Respondeat Superior." This doctrine is concerned with both the personal liability of an individual supervisor and of the employer in the public or private sector for the tortious acts of subordinates or employees, respectively. Generally, supervisors have no individual liability if their subordinates commit a tortious act. Again, the courts have carved out exceptions to that rule. For example, allowing subordinates to perform their duties with knowledge that they are of such a temperament or such a violent nature that they are prone to injure persons they deal with, possibly exposes the superior to joint liability together with the party causing the injury. If a supervisor has knowledge that a subordinate is intoxicated and yet allows him to operate a city vehicle, the supervisor may face personal liability for injuries or property loss caused by that driver.

The courts generally hold that the employer (public or private) is responsible only for tortious acts committed by employees within the scope of their employment. A classic example of being outside one's scope of employment is the employee who uses a company vehicle during lunch hour to visit a friend. The courts have held that if the employee has an accident while enroute to the friend's house it is outside the scope of employment and the employer is not responsible. Courts have refined this approach to the extent that once the employee has left the friend's house and has commenced the return trip to the place of employment, the employee has returned to the scope of employment. Any accidents then may be the employer's responsibility.

Another example is the maintenance person who gets into an argument with a motorist at a traffic signal and hits the motorist. Courts will generally hold that the maintenance person acted outside the scope of employment and the employer is not responsible. On the other hand, if a bartender has an altercation with a patron and injures the patron, the bar owner may be held responsible because the courts may consider the nature of the bartender's duty to require contact with patrons. In summary, if the act is done within the scope of employment, the employer is responsible; if the act is done outside the scope of employment, the employer is not responsible.

Recovery from negligent employees

One of the major concerns to a transportation professional is "recovery from negligent employees." Can the employer recover from the employee any award that must be paid to an injured party as a result of an employee's negligent act? Under the legal theory of "Agency," employers are permitted to recover from employees any awards that they must pay out because of the employees' negligent acts. In the United States today this seldom occurs. Union agreements, civil service rules, social and political pressures, and many other facets of modern personnel management keep such claims at a minimum. However, the transportation professional should be aware of the fact that this practice is permitted under law. Currently, many employees are indemnified by the employer for losses attributed to them. Yet employees might be in a position where they would be required to seek malpractice or liability insurance to protect themselves from liability exposure caused by changing doctrines of law.

Minimizing risk of liability

It is a simple matter to file a lawsuit and, no doubt, it appears to some that litigation has become as popular a national pastime as baseball or football. Succeeding in a lawsuit is another matter, particularly when the government or one of its employees is the defendant. As pointed out earlier, lawsuits of this kind are a two-tier project. To get the case before a court, any immunity that may exist must first be overcome. This can happen by a judicial or legislative abrogation of the Doctrine of Sovereign Immunity, the passage of a Tort Liability Act, the Safe Street Doctrine, and even the defendant's purchase of liability insurance. If the plaintiff can surmount the defenses of immunity, it still must be proven that the defendant was the cause of the injuries or property loss.

Lawsuits arising out of accidents, resulting from an alleged defect in a highway or road system, generally involve three principal issues as well as the previously discussed five elements of the negligence suit:

1. Did a potentially dangerous defect exist?
2. Was the defect the proximate cause of the accident?
3. Did the defendant have any actual or constructive knowledge of the hazardous condition?

In seeking answers to these questions the courts have established some guidelines that are helpful in determining responsibility.

1. The state is not an insurer of the roads or guarantor of absolute safety.
2. Motorists have the right to presume, and act upon the presumption, that the highway is safe for usual and ordinary traffic in the daytime and at night. They are not required to anticipate extraordinary dangers, impediments, or obstruction to which their attention has not been directed or of which they have not been warned.
3. The public highway must be maintained in a way that is reasonably safe for travel, within accepted and understood criteria, under generally promulgated engineering standards or practices.
4. In maintaining the highway in a manner that is reasonably safe for travel, there is wide latitude in the exercise of administrative discretion, but continual supervision and inspection are of the utmost importance.
5. The courts do recognize factors in establishing what is reasonably safe and include among them the terrain that is encountered, weather conditions, and the materials used in construction.
6. Recovery is based upon more than the mere presence of a hazardous condition; such presence must be due to negligence.
7. Negligence stems from knowledge or notice of the existence of a dangerous or defective condition and a subsequent failure to safeguard against such a condition.

General duties are the most important guidelines in protecting against liability suits. Basically, there is a duty to maintain the roadway in a reasonably safe condition. This duty involves the inspection, anticipation of defect, and conformity with generally accepted standards and practices. There is no requirement for perfect condition or repair, or for actions beyond the limits of human ingenuity. The key term is reasonability. There are many factors upon which determination of what is reasonable may be based, among them the character of the roadway in question, the width and construction of the road, the characteristic of the traffic, the turning requirements, the side friction, and the development of traffic generators alongside the roadway. These all must be taken into account when trying to determine the guidelines for protection against the liability suit.

Complaints and reports

An essential feature of a tort claim is negligence on the part of the offending party through some act or omission. Frequently, in tort actions it is claimed there has been failure to respond to a complaint or failure to respond in a reasonable period of time. Thus, minimizing claims requires rapid and orderly response to complaints, together with the maintenance of adequate records to document the action taken.

Possibly the most critical requirement in handling complaints is to designate one person to receive the complaints or notices of defective traffic control devices. This person should record the date and time of the complaint, the name and address and telephone number of the individual making the complaint, the nature of the action to be taken, and the location and nature of the complaint.

Maintenance personnel should be instructed in the appropriate action to take in case of malfunction or loss of traffic control devices, pavement holes, or similar critical problems. Maintenance personnel or the person receiving complaints should seek police control of dangerous sites until repairs can be completed. Records should be maintained by location to enable the agency to determine promptly what problems have developed and what remedy was applied at any particular location. Finally, it is absolutely necessary that the file be checked periodically and locations designated that must be critically reviewed.

Maintenance records are a two-edged sword. They will provide a defense in a suit, indicating to the court that the agency has taken remedial action, that it has acknowledged a complaint, that it has responded, and what action was taken. But if these records are kept and there is no response, there is no question that there was notice, and if there is notice of a defect, the twin duty to remedy or warn arises. This fact cannot be emphasized enough.

Design and operational reviews

Based on complaint history, sites should be selected periodically for critical review. Both the basic design and the traffic control elements should be reviewed in the field. If possible, interviews with persons who have filed complaints should be conducted. Often, rather minor improvements can result in the substantial improvement in the safety record of the location. *Repeat accidents,* particularly if similar, can be construed as *constructive notice* of an existing hazard.

Although design immunity may exist, a court may consider it waived where there is notice that the designs has become manifestly dangerous following its adoption. Courts have repeatedly held that, if the design is one that a reasonable person obviously would not have approved, the agency may face liability for injuries caused by it. Jurisdictions recognize an exception to design immunity where a hazard is permitted to remain after the public entity has had reasonable notice that the defect is a source of danger. Once the entity has had notice that the plan or design, under changed conditions, has produced a dangerous condition, it must act reasonably to correct or alleviate the hazard.

Notice of defect

Notice of a defect is important; timely notice is even more important. A program must be set up to ensure that the maintenance staff receives the defect report promptly from the police, other information sources, or any party that the courts could construe as being an agent of public entity. If the *agent has known about the defect for an unreasonable period of time,* courts will consider this constructive notice, and will assign liability to the agency for any injury that the defect may have caused. Thus, a program to ensure prompt notification must be developed.

All public entity employees should be trained to look for and report any defective or damaged devices. This is of particular importance for police, solid waste collection personnel, utility workers, and other agency personnel who perform routine work on the street system. Each agency vehicle should contain a reminder or display the appropriate telephone number or office to notify when a defective device is identified.

If the public entity does not have around-the-clock maintenance, it should maintain provision for stand-by crews. Above all, citizen self-help should be avoided. If the public entity operates with around-the-clock crews or stand-by crews, spare parts should be available to them no matter what hours they work. If a defect cannot be remedied promptly, adequate means must be taken to warn the public of this existing defect, and the warning must be commensurate with the danger that the public faces.

Maintenance supervisors should provide crews with up-to-date equipment and should assure themselves that this equipment is being used. Above all, mere visual inspection should be avoided. The maintenance technician must avoid tunnel vision, repairing only what was reported. Other problems should be sought out and repaired.

Maintenance records

The importance of maintenance records cannot be overemphasized. If the agency becomes involved in litigation, they will provide an invaluable help in proving what was done and when. The items listed below, which should be part of the maintenance records, are culled from various case studies, indicating what the courts and juries seek in arriving at a decision.

1. The time the complaint was made and by whom.
2. The time it was received by the dispatcher.
3. The time that it was given to the repair crew.
4. The time crew responded to the scene.
5. The time that the repair was completed.
6. Description of the defect.
7. Description of the repairs made and materials used.

Standards

Another key to a successful program to minimize risk of liability is to follow accepted standards and guidelines. The basic standard available to the traffic and transportation engineer is the *Manual of Uniform Traffic Control Devices (MUTCD).*[4] Consider the situation that could arise out of a *MUTCD* case, and the possible outcome. Assume that the *Manual* has a mandatory requirement that "X" sign be erected in a location under "C" conditions. The highway department knows that condition "C" exists, or it has existed long enough that it should have known about it, and has failed to place the sign, or has placed the sign but has deviated from the required format. In all probability a liability judgment will result if the unsigned or improperly signed condition is found to be the cause of an accident, because the highway department has failed to meet its duty to use reasonable care in creating a safe highway environment. In the case of the deviation, liability will depend upon the factual situation. If evidence can be introduced supporting the deviation, liability may be escaped. In many cases, however, if the deviation is the result of carelessness or negligence, liability will attach.

In summary, adequate protection against liability must involve the following:

1. Sound research in order to establish standards.
2. Require standards to be a base minimum.
3. Inspection procedures to ensure compliance with standards.
4. Maintenance program to ensure speedy rehabilitation of defective conditions.

Even so, "going by the book" has never been the sole answer. Thus, when a manual is being used, all parties should be on notice that more may be required to create reasonable safety than may be indicated by the manual. Routine inspection of all traffic control devices, by day and at night, on a regular basis is a fundamental step in loss prevention. The period between inspections will vary, depending on circumstances surrounding or affecting traffic and physical conditions. Analysis of court cases, however, indicates that in most instances a 6-month review is acceptable.

Traffic control in work zones

In construction and maintenance zones, work is continuously changing the conditions that exist. This is why a regular and frequent review of traffic control devices is of the utmost necessity.

---

[4]Ibid.

Tort liability in work zones is no different than any other liability. This is because the principles of tort liability apply generally, whether the case is one of design, maintenance, or construction. This means that all the principles are applicable and that lessons learned from non-construction-zone cases will apply to work-zone cases as well.

In another sense, however, work zones present special problems, because they present conditions substantially at variance with the motorists' normal expectations. As such they require adequate warning devices and barrier safeguards. Unfortunately, the question of adequacy in tort cases usually takes place in the negative, which further complicates the subject. That is, most of the cases discuss what is not adequate, and what is adequate remains vague in legal terms.

Review of high-accident locations

The State of Michigan,[5] in response to tort litigation, has developed an 11-step review analysis of high-accident locations as a method of minimizing risk. This is an excellent series of guidelines, for it covers the same aspects that judges and juries utilize in the resolution of cases before them. The method is the initial step in the effective response to safety problems.

1. Review high-accidents list, screening out those locations where projects have been completed recently or are under way, or where traffic patterns have changed.
2. Assemble collision diagrams and other supporting data for remaining locations.
3. Review collision diagrams, identify accident patterns, and collect any needed additional data, such as signal timing.
4. Conduct a multidisciplinary field review composed of operations, geometric design, safety, and district engineers.
5. Define the problem and possible treatment.
6. Develop alternative schemes and cost estimates.
7. Evaluate the cost effectiveness of alternative schemes.
8. Select the most cost-effective treatment for each location.
9. Program the most cost-effective treatment based on a priority system.
10. Document action for all high-accident locations.
11. Follow up to ensure proper implementation.

The last cannot be overemphasized, because the courts will not tolerate an ostrich syndrome. There must be an operational review after a plan is made operational. This ensures that the plan has been implemented properly and is doing what it is supposed to.

Hold Harmless Agreements

When an agency is given the prime responsibility for the safe operation of a street system or road network, the courts will not accept as an excuse that the agency has contracted that responsibility to another party. It does not follow that, because it has contracted with a consultant to prepare a design, or has hired a contractor to build a road, install a traffic control device, or maintain a street system and related traffic control devices, they are solely responsible for any injuries that may result from their work. The court has repeatedly laid the liability at the feet of the party who has been given that responsibility by law—the public entity—and the courts will not accept any claims to the contrary.

How can the public (and private) sector protect itself in this area? The best way, of course, is to deal with a reputable firm. Also highly recommended is the use of a "Hold Harmless Agreement" (see Figure 27.2). In such an agreement the construction contractor agrees to hold the agency harmless from any liability as a result of negligence in the work that the contractor performs on behalf of the public entity. This is not to say that there would no be time lost in defending a suit, such as loss of personnel time spent in testifying, accumulating records, or working with an attorney. What this does mean is that the contractor has agreed to pay any award that is assessed against the public entity.

A Hold Harmless Agreement is only as good as the party involved. If the contractor has a good reputation, standing, and an ongoing relationship in the community, the public entity probably will be protected. But it must be remembered that there usually is a long period between the time that an accident has occurred and the time that a jury makes an award and the appeals process is completed. If the contractor is still in business, he will be bound by the Hold Harmless Agreement despite the passage of the time. But if the contractor has gone out of business, has become insolvent, or is nowhere to be found, the public entity must pay the bill.

Product liability

This area of law concerns itself with the liability of the sellers of goods to a third person with whom the sellers had no actual legal relationship. This legal doctrine had its beginnings with unsafe foods that injured the user, who may not have been the actual purchaser. Now, however, it extends to any product that is recognizably dangerous. For liability to attach there must be something wrong with the product that makes it unreasonably dangerous to those who come in contact with it. Product liability will attach to the seller of a product, the maker of a component part of the final product, and even the assembler of parts supplied by others.

It is through this doctrine that members of the public, when injured due to a defective traffic control device, can name as a defendant the manufacturer of the device and/or its component parts, as well as the user or maintainer of the device.

A full and detailed discussion of product liability is beyond the scope of this chapter. Particularly as this doctrine is an emerging one, it is in a state of flux. States are preparing product liability statutes, and a national product liability policy may be developed. Transportation professionals should therefore keep themselves abreast of changes in product liability on the local as well as the national level.

[5]D. E. Orne, "Responding to Tort Liability," *Transport. Res. News*, Sept–Oct. 1976, pp. 4–6.

HOLD-HARMLESS AGREEMENT CLAUSE

The contractor ______________________ hereby agrees to indemnify and hold harmless and defend the ______________________, its officials, agents, servants and employees from payment of any sum or sums of money to any person whomsoever, on account of all claims, actions, or suits growing out of injuries to persons, including death, or property damage caused by the contractor, his employees, agents or subcontractors for any negligent act, error or omission in the performance and prosecution of the work herein contracted for including (but without limiting the generality of the foregoing), all claims for service, labor performed, materials furnished, provisions and supplies, injuries to persons, including death, or damage to property, claims, suits, costs, attorneys' fees, costs of investigation and of defense.

It is further the intent of this agreement to hold the contractor ______________________ responsible for the payment of any and all claims, suits or liens due to any negligent act, error or omission in any way attributable to or asserted against the ______________________ and or its officials, agents, servants or employees as a result of the performance of this contract or asserted against both the ______________________ and the contractor.

In addition to holding ______________________ harmless the contractor will provide the defense for ______________________, its officials, agents, servants, and/or employees, and will pay the costs of that defense.

Figure 27.2. Hold harmless agreement clause.

But it suffices to say that, as the user of the road system can take action against a manufacturer for injuries sustained, so can the public entity sue the manufacturer of a control device that has failed as well as the manufacturer or assembler of component parts even if the parts were purchased by another party (i.e., the manufacturer of the finished product).

The engineer as an expert witness

One of the most technical phases of trial work is the presentation of evidence based on expert opinion. The opinion rule of evidence and the use of expert testimony evolved with the development of the English court system. The early English courts adhered to civil and canon law rule which limited the testimony of witnesses to matters of personal observation. But they also used expert opinions as an aid in reaching decisions. The expert was used as an advisor to the court, not as a witness. With the development of the adversary system, the jury no longer based a decision on personal knowledge or on their own inquiries, and therefore the expert became a witness who testified to the jury to help them evaluate the facts that they were told by the witnesses. This use of the expert has continued to the present time and has required modification of the opinion rule of evidence. The early use of the term "opinion" carried with it an implication of lack of actual grounds for the statement. This is absent from the present meaning. Today, the word denotes a belief or an inference or conclusion, without suggesting that it is well or ill founded. The rules of opinion evidence and of expert testimony were set out to some extent in England in 1782; as the court then stated, "For in matters of science the reasoning of men of science can only be answered by men of science; in matters of science no other witness can be called; I cannot believe that where the question is whether a defect arises from a natural or artificial cause the opinions of men of science are not to be received."

The principle behind the opinion rule of evidence is the exclusion of all superfluous testimony. Therefore, only a witness having a peculiar skill, knowledge, or experience that will aid and enlighten the jury in reaching a verdict is allowed to testify. The necessity for admission of such expert testimony arises from the inability of the jury to resolve issues requiring persons with special skills and knowledge to understand them. With the progress of science, new areas of scientific proof continually arise which require the use of experts.

Generally, an expert is needed if the jury will be helped appreciably, and if general experience of an ordinary person is not sufficient. An expert is not needed if the jury can just as easily determine the answer to the question at issue.

An expert witness is one who has acquired by study or experience a special skill or superior knowledge in a particular field about which persons who do not have special training are incapable of forming an accurate opinion or of deducing correct conclusions. Whether the witness shall be qualified as an expert is up to the trial court to determine at the very outset. This decision generally will not be overturned by an appellate court unless it can be shown that the presiding judge, in making this decision, abused his or her discretion. Expert witnesses differ from ordinary witnesses in that expert witnesses can state their opinions and conclusions based on fact, whereas ordinary witnesses can only testify to something they saw, smelled, tasted, felt, and in some but not all instances, heard. The weight that a jury will give to expert testimony will, of course, depend upon the extent of the experts' learning, skills, experience, and primarily the foundation and the reason that they give for their opinion in drawing their conclusions.

Important in proving the experts' qualifications are their education, experience, articles published, lectures delivered, memberships in professional societies and organizations, awards, high moral character and integrity, and recognition as experts by others in the same field. The credibility given by the court and the jury to the experts' testimony depends principally upon their qualifications, ability to withstand severe cross-examination, and of course, capability in expressing themselves so that the judge and the jury will understand the testimony. They should be experienced, with status in the community. They should be able to communicate clearly, and should be able to explain technical or scientific subjects and matters in plain, understandable language. Above all, they should not try to impress the jury with their learning and ability, but try to communicate to them in a way that they can understand. They should have good speaking ability and be definite in their opinions. They should never tender an opinion unless they have one and unless it is sound, based upon good scientific knowledge and experience, and should stick to that opinion once it has been rendered.

When possible, the expert should avoid testifying for one side in case after case. The exposure of an expert as a professional plaintiff's witness or a professional defendant's witness can destroy his or her credibility with the jury.

Initial preparation

The initial preparation is the key to the ability and credibility of the expert to render a convincing opinion to the jury. Such initial activity should include the review of the relevant documents, including contracts, standards, plans, specifications, reports, statements, and photographs. It should also include visits to the accident site under varying conditions of traffic lighting (daylight, evening), weather conditions (fair, cloudy, rain), and, of course, under the conditions that most approximate those that existed when the events being studied occurred. The expert should expect to have frequent discussions with the attorney and, if information is missing or facts are needed, the expert should not hesitate to contact the attorney to secure the information that is required. If the expert finds it necessary to conduct special research or a special study, the attorney should be notified and given the opportunity to decide whether or not to be present at the time that this evaluation is conducted.

After the evaluation is completed and the conclusion arrived at, it is important to discuss the relative strength and weakness in the conclusions. It is also very important, before a written report is prepared, to check with the attorney to determine whether or not such a report is desired. Most attorneys will prefer to have the report delivered verbally and not written. This will avoid the necessity of making the report available to the other side during the pretrial phase of preparation.

Pretrial conference

The value of a pretrial conference between the expert and the trial attorney cannot be overemphasized. All experienced and competent experts know well the need for such meetings. The pretrial conference between the expert and the attorney is for the purpose of acquainting the attorney with the expert's methods of presentation of testimony, and in general, the matters about which the expert intends to testify. It is important for the expert to know what questions the attorney will ask, and for the attorney to know what the answers to the questions will be.

Complete rapport between trial attorney and the expert very definitely promotes better presentation of evidence. Some lawyers do not get to the expert's pretrial conference until just before the expert takes the witness stand. Such an attorney expects to use a 5- to 10-minute recess to talk to the next witness. This is not advised and in many instances will actually be detrimental. In some cases, particularly those involving important issues where several attorneys participate in a trial, the expert should stress the importance of having these pretrial conferences with the attorneys who will introduce the expert testimony, and thus avoid "relaying" suggestions made by the expert through other persons. The proper time for these conferences as well as the number will vary with the case and with the expert. As a rule, it is advisable to discuss the matter of planned procedure of the case shortly after the expert has completed an examination and has developed an opinion; then there definitely should be another conference shortly before the date set for the trial. If the trial is continued several times over a considerable period of time, most certainly there should be another conference between the attorney and the expert to review the previously discussed material.

Qualifying the expert witness

The format for qualifying the witness as an expert should be agreed upon by the attorney and the expert prior to the trial. This avoids careless omission that can create a doubt in the jurors' minds about the credentials of the expert. Following is a checklist of points that normally should be included in the preparation of questions used to qualify an engineering expert:

1. Schooling
2. Specialized training
3. Description of engineering specialty
4. Date and place of engineering license
5. Experience, including military service
6. Company affiliations
7. Membership in engineering associations, etc.
8. Publications
9. Professional honors received
10. Seminars or lectures conducted

To the extent possible the questions and answers should tie the expert's general knowledge and experience to conditions and realities in the city and state of the trial, and in a way to which the jury can relate.

During the pretrial conference with the attorney, the expert should inform the attorney of the usual method of introduction of the specialized testimony, and should furnish the attorney with a list of specific qualifying questions and complete answers to them. These questions should be so worded that the lawyer inquires about one of the expert's qualifications at a time, and the expert's answers should give only the qualifications related to the particular question. The expert should never volunteer qualifications, as this puts the expert in a position of bragging about his or her accomplishments, causes the jury to consider the expert a boaster, and can affect the credibility in the testimony before them.

The expert should explain to the attorney the fallacy of the attorney admitting the expert qualifications by stipulation or agreement. When attorneys on the opposite side of the case do not want the judge or jury to realize how well qualified the expert is, they are often very anxious to admit the qualifications by such a method. This is not desirable and should not be permitted if at all possible. Even though the trial judge may be familiar with the qualifications of the expert, it is the jury that must be convinced. Also, if the case is appealed, the appellate judges would not know of the expert's qualifications, and this could be an important factor in their decision.

Preparation for direct examination

The scientific theory that underlies the case upon which the direct examination and cross-examination will proceed must be clearly formulated and adhered to by the lawyer and the expert. Distracting side issues that one may be tempted to exploit may present themselves, but the expert should not succumb to the temptation. It is a good idea for the expert and the attorney to review the attorney's list of preplanned direct examination questions during the pretrial conference. This tends to expedite the testimony of the expert witness and often prevents unnecessary objections by the opposing attorney.

By questioning the witness as he or she will be questioned in court and listening to the reply, an attorney can save the embarrassment of hearing the witness mutilate his or her own testimony by the addition to the opinion of such limiting phrases as "to the best of my knowledge" or "as well as I could." These verbal appendages may only be habitual expressions, but the field for cross-examination that they suggest are unnecessary gifts to the opposing side.

The expert and the attorney should agree whether the expert will be allowed to explain in his or her own words how and why he or she arrived at that opinion. This can give the expert an opportunity to select the sequence of the explanation and use words that have been found from experience to be easily understood by the jury. When the expert tries to explain in answers to questions by the attorney how and why opinions were reached, it may lead to an objection on the grounds that the attorney is doing the testifying and the expert is only agreeing.

It is also important that the expert be warned that the opponent may make objections to the testimony or any question asked of him or her. If an objection is made, the expert should withhold any answer until the court has ruled on the objection.

Sometimes the expert may feel like correcting the attorney's pronunciation or use of technical terms. Off the witness stand the expert should, of course, do so, but to correct the attorney while on the witness stand would show up the ignorance of the attorney on whose side the expert is testifying, affecting the credibility of both the attorney and the expert.

In presenting expert testimony, timing is of the greatest importance. It may mean the difference between success and failure in the outcome of the case, and the circumstances affecting the proper timing of the introduction of the expert's testimony should be discussed. There are a few definite rules which more or less set practice. It may be desirable for the expert to testify only as rebuttal testimony. Of course, this cannot always be arranged, but very often it is definitely good timing. In the event that the opposing side of the case is also having an expert testify, it is very desirable to have the opposing expert testify first. This may enable the second expert to cover or discuss weak spots in the testimony of the opposing witness.

Preparation for cross-examination[6]

A competent and experienced expert should anticipate probable cross-examination questions. When specialists take the witness stand, they must accept the fact that, since no truth outside the world of faith can be arrived at without examination of the premises from which deductions are drawn, their own expert testimony will not be immune to thorough testing. They must be ready on cross-examination to be challenged on their premises as well as on their conclusions.

If the witness has written on the subject matter involved in the case, it is wise for the expert to discuss with the attorney at the pretrial conference any possible contradiction, whether seeming or real, between what the expert has written and his or her opinion in the case at issue. Since engineering is steadily advancing and research is opening new areas of learning, there may well be explanations for a possible inconsistency. It would be fatal for the witness to forget that he or she, in fact, authored opinions previously or to deny that they were ever valid. If the expert has testified on previous occasions on similar issues, it is important to obtain and review the transcripts of that testimony with the attorney.

It is expected that most attorneys are familiar with various types of cross-examination and the proper methods of defense of the witness who is being cross-examined, and it is never amiss to discuss the subject to some extent with the attorney. It is quite possible that the attorney will know to which type of tactics the opposing counsel may resort. Opposing counsels may be of the "hammer and tongs" type—generally the old-time shouting attorneys. They may be the type who will familiarize themselves with the subject the night before, and as a result think they know more than

[6]Portions from *American Jurisprudence—Trials*. Copyright © Lawyers Co-operative Publishing Co., Rochester, N.Y., 1962.

the expert. They may be entirely lost in the subject and desperately grasp at straws. They may be the soft-talking cross-examiner who tell witnesses how well qualified and honest they are, all the time attempting to lull the witnesses into a false sense of security so that they will drop their guard; if they do, the attorney gets them right between the eyes. A full discussion of the defenses to be made by the attorney may prevent experts from having to protect themselves unnecessarily and thereby weaken their testimony.

Most attorneys will be happy to discuss with the expert some of the fundamentals regarding the protection of the witness on cross-examination. Some of the matters that could arise and should be discussed are: the cross-examiner who ask questions that require the stating of an opinion of the witness, and then will not allow the witness to give the reasons for that opinion; the insistence of cross-examiners on a "yes" or "no" answer where either can be used to their advantage; the habit of cross-examiners who interrupt the witness by asking another question, when they see that the answer they are getting is not the one desired.

Since the cross-examiner has a much wider latitude in propounding questions than the attorney on direct examination, the expert should be quite careful in answering questions put to him or her by the opposing attorney. More often, a cross-examiner will try to test the answer to a hypothetical question by asking the expert what he or she should leave out of the hypothetical situation and still arrive at the same opinion. The expert should state that he or she would omit nothing. The expert should also be prepared for tricky questions. For example: "Have you ever talked to anyone about this case?" The answer to this, of course, is in the affirmative, since the expert has discussed the case with the attorney.

Since attorneys know that an angry witness makes a poor witness, the cross-examiner may try to arouse the witness' anger. Juries are usually critical of this type of cross-examination and will naturally tend to favor witnesses who do not lose their tempers. Similarly, the expert should avoid attempting to destroy the questions of the cross-examiner by being sarcastic. The expert should also be cautious not to equivocate. If the question demands an answer favorable to the other side, it should be answered truthfully but not with any particular emphasis on the point. It is crucial, naturally, to avoid giving the jury the impression that the expert is a liar.

Much of the technique of cross-examining expert witnesses is to convince the jury that the expert's opinion is based on insufficient information. Among the most effective specific manifestations of this approach are such maneuvers as:

1. Revealing that the expert did not perform certain tests, commonly used in circumstances such as those involved in the case. Many cross-examiners have their own expert sitting with them during the direct examination of the opposition expert to aid in the detection of such deficiencies.
2. Exposing the fact that the expert was not fully informed on the background data. The expert should obtain a complete set of background data relevant to the controversy and should be thoroughly familiar with these files prior to the trial.
3. Revealing that the expert's testimony contradicts notations that he or she made in their research records. The attorney and the expert should make sure that the expert is prepared so completely as to be invulnerable to such attack.

The stature of experts is always increased when they freely admit the general principles of their specialty, and that they are giving them full consideration, but that these principles are not applicable to the special facts before them. An opinion from these who convey with quiet confidence and without arrogance a sense of mastery of their specialty is always convincing.

No matter who is involved, the subject of suggested cross-examination of an opposing expert is a touchy subject and one on which there are varying views. However, since all experts should be interested in the promotion of justice and the presentation of facts, this is just one more subject that should be discussed during the pretrial conference.

Truly professional experts are always nonpartisan witnesses. They appear at the trial only to explain to the court and the jury the facts, as they see them, regarding the subject in which they have more than the average knowledge and experience. When they have completed their duty, they should exhibit no further interest in the case. Unless asked to wait, they should leave the court immediately.

In summary, expert witnesses should have a clear and intelligent understanding of the case and their role in it. It is very important that they understand why, because of the rules of evidence, they cannot present their testimony at the trial in the manner in which they spoke of it at the attorney's office.

Although some legal training on the part of experts, especially in the field of evidence, is very valuable, they should be cautious not to become an advocate in the case. It is their function to demonstrate facts and to convince the jury of the existence of these facts. But it is not the experts' function to win the lawsuit for the client. Consequently, they should not have the impression that they carry the whole case on their shoulders or that they must decide questions that ought to be left to the jury.

In obtaining instruction on the law, experts should remember that most of the rules of evidence need not be considered by them since they involve matters that concern only the attorney and the court. However, on nonscientific facts or nontechnical matters they should state the facts alone and not their opinion. In addition, they should be careful as to the evidentiary rule against the use of hearsay evidence.

Exhibits

One of the most important matters that should be discussed is the introduction of exhibits. Here, again, proper timing is a prime factor, which will be controlled to some extent by the kind of exhibits to be introduced. Photographic exhibits may be a large print, perhaps 40 in (1 m) wide and

6ft (2 m) long; they may be smaller photographs measuring from 5 × 7 in. (12 × 18 cm) to 11 × 14 in. (28 × 35 cm). The expert is cautioned to remember that juries often like to look at exhibits during their deliberation. It would therefore be a good policy for the expert to prepare exhibits that are easily handled by the jury. Thus, photographs generally prove to be more useful to the jury than slides and opaque prints, which necessitate additional equipment to be brought into the jury room during the jury deliberation.

Another point to be remembered in preparing exhibits to be used in the trial is to find out beforehand from the attorney the makeup of the jury before which the exhibits may be presented. For example, the simpler straightforward type of exhibit tends to have more success with a small-town or rural jury. A more detailed exhibit may be successful with an urban jury, but presenting an elaborately prepared exhibit to a rural-oriented jury tends to alienate the jurors by giving them the notion that the "city engineer" is out here to sell them a bill of goods.

Regardless of what type of exhibit is being introduced, the attorney should be advised that it is all-important to see that the jury is looking at the same exhibit that the witness is explaining. If a large print is used, it should be rolled up after it has served its purpose and before the next one is unrolled. If small exhibits are shown, the expert should handle only one set at a time; when discussion about that set is finished, the attorney should collect all copies from the jury before giving them the next set. A definite plan of procedures such as this agreed to at the pretrial discussion may prevent the attention of the jurors from being diverted to something other than the subject being discussed by the witness.

Tips for the witnesses[7]

As witnesses, experts should speak up so that the jury, judge, stenographer, and opposing counsel can hear them. Their testimony and explanation should be clear enough so that all of the jurors can understand them. Technical terms should be defined in simple language for effectiveness. In testifying from an exhibit, witnesses should refer to the exhibit number or some other identification point. When indicating or pointing to an object in the exhibit, they should describe what they are discussing so that the court stenographer can make an accurate and complete record, which becomes very important if the transcript of the testimony is used in a hearing for a new trial or in appeal to a higher tribunal.

Appropriate time should be taken before answering questions, to allow time for objection and so that witnesses can gather their thoughts and give an accurate but brief answer. If questions are answered more quickly on direct examination than on cross-examination, the jury will notice this and may feel that witnesses are hedging or are in trouble. If witnesses are asked to give an opinion and feel that they do not have enough facts or time to form an intelligent expert opinion, they should so inform the court. A jury is impressed with such frankness on the part of the witness. Experts are not expected to rely entirely on memory, and should always have adequate notes in their possession so that they can testify to all the details. They should keep in mind that their role aids the court and the jury in understanding technical evidence so that they can make appropriate evaluation of the facts.

Some general suggestions that can be offered as an aid to being a good witness are:

1. Walk to the witness stand with even steps.
2. When the officer finishes the oath, say "I do" in a loud voice so that all in the courtroom can hear. *Do not act timid.*
3. Be thorough and frank. Do not be too anxious to please or too eager to fight.
4. If you make a mistake or a slight contradiction, admit it and correct it. Do not tie yourself in knots trying to cover up some slip of speech or memory.
5. Keep your temper. Do not let anyone draw you into arguments over trivial points or even important ones. Be firm but flexible.
6. If you cannot answer "yes" or "no," say so, but modify your reply by "Under certain circumstances. . . . "
7. If you do not know or cannot remember, say so. These are legitimate answers to the most illegitimate questions.
8. Avoid mannerisms in speech. The habit of prefacing replies with something like "I can truthfully say" may cast unwarranted doubts on your whole testimony.
9. If a lawyer asks: "Are you as positive about this as you are about the rest of your testimony?"—*stop*. Are you?
10. "Do you want this jury to understand . . . ?" Listen closely to that one; if you do not want the jury to understand it that way, make clear what you do want them to understand.
11. If the opposing attorney interrupts you before you had a chance to complete your answer, you should indicate this to the presiding judge.
12. Do not volunteer information.
13. Be brief; just answer the question and stop.
14. Do not memorize any of your testimony.
15. Wait until the entire question is asked before answering.
16. On cross-examination, do not look at your attorney.
17. Keep your hands away from your face and mouth.
18. When addressing the court, use "your honor"; when addressing the attorneys, use their names.
19. During the recess you should not carry on any conversation with other witnesses or parties to the controversy. You should be aloof from everyone except the attorney who retained you to testify.
20. Remember that the witness stand is not a comfortable place for one who is not telling the truth, the whole truth, and nothing but the truth.

Fees

Experts are entitled to witness fees, the amount of which is subject to arrangement between them and the attorneys

[7]Portions from B. Carter, *The Expert Witness*. Copyright © American Bar Association, Chicago, 1966.

who call them to testify. It is a good practice to arrange such a fee prior to testifying. If experts are called on only to testify to facts for which they already have knowledge, they may be subpoenaed as a witness and be paid the statutory fee and an allowance for travel. In this case, they may refuse to give any expert opinion or testimony unless they are adequately compensated.

Thus, as a practical matter, experts should be retained at a reasonable fee. Experts may be required to prepare themselves before testifying by making certain tests or doing research, or may be called as witnesses for the sole purpose of proving or verifying certain materials; they are entitled to a reasonable fee for the time involved.

It is wise, when called as a witness, to ask to be put "on call" so that there will be no time lost waiting around the courthouse to be called. In any event, the witness should not expect to be out of the courthouse in a hurry, and one should know it is reasonable to charge a fee for time spent waiting to be called.

It is possible that some lawyers representing plaintiffs, especially in tort cases, will ask experts to testify on a contingent fee basis. Under this arrangement witnesses would not be paid unless the plaintiff's suit is successful. This puts witnesses in the position of having a stake in the outcome of the case, thereby giving up their proper role as disinterested witnesses. As an interested party, they can and will be accused of being partisan, and therefore their testimony will carry much less weight. An experienced and ethical expert will invariably refuse such a fee arrangement. Expert witnesses must be altogether objective and nonpartisan in presenting opinions. They should keep in mind that they are being retained by the lawyer or party to the action. They are independent professional persons and are not in the employ of either litigant. In any event a contingent fee arrangement is fundamentally against public policy and therefore is invalid and unenforceable in a court of law.

Even so, it can be expected that the attorney will make the point that the expert has been retained by one side of the case, with the implication that he or she is biased. Appropriately, the expert should state that he or she was indeed retained, but to give objective unbiased testimony in the hopes that this would win the case.

Trial practices and procedures

Since trial practices and procedures vary from state to state, the format of the trial presented here is based on the Federal Court System, its procedures, and its rules of evidence. Any litigation in which engineers or their agency become involved will most often be in a state court; as a general practice its rules of procedures parallel the federal system.

When an injury occurs, some jurisdictions require that, before any action can be filed, a notice must be given of the injury to the governing body within a specified period of time. Failure to abide by that requirement may preclude any legal action from being taken. When notice of a claim is received, whoever is involved in the agency's risk management program should be advised of the claim and should request a report be prepared. It is best to be completely candid and as factual as possible in the report. It is most likely that at this point the risk manager will decide whether to offer a settlement or reject the claim. If the settlement offer is too low or is rejected, litigation will usually result. It must be stressed here how important records are in settlement negotiations. The agency should be able to show notice of defect or nonnotice of defect, what materials were used, and the time involved in repairing the defect. But, as pointed out earlier, records are a two-edged sword. If they are kept well and they show timely and adequate responses, they will protect the agency. However, if they indicate a lack of responsive action, they can be devastating to your case.

Pleadings

The filing of a complaint and the responses in a court are known as "pleadings." The lawsuit begins with the filing of the complaint with the court. If it is a personal injury suit, the plaintiff's attorney will probably name in the suit any person, agency, and possibly a manufacturer that is involved in some manner. Agency employees involved also may be named as a party, depending on the local rules or practices. It will be up to the defending agency's attorney to have any improper party dismissed if there is some immunity available to keep that person out of the actual litigation as a party. It is best to remind the attorney of the fact that improper parties may have been named when he or she is preparing the answer to the complaint. Some states have provisions for either indemnifying or defending employees of its various agencies (see Table 27-1).

After the complaint is filed by the plaintiff, the summons will be issued by the court advising the named parties of this fact. This summons must be served on parties listed and, as a general rule, it must be personal service on the named individuals. Some states will permit service to be accepted by spouses or some other adults residing in the residence of the named party. If there is a possibility that service has been improper or not in accordance with the rules of procedure, the attorney should be informed, as this is good grounds for being dismissed as a party. This may be only a technicality and the opposing attorney may amend and then serve properly, but may also feel at this point that some of the parties served are not worth bringing back into the suit.

After the required period of time, the attorney for the defendant will have to answer the complaint. In this answer he or she may agree to certain facts. For example, the name of the traffic engineer and the fact that the street or signal is maintained by the named agency can be agreed to. The attorney will also deny certain facts that are stated in the complaint. The attorney can also state that he or she has no knowledge of facts stated in the complaint; this could occur, for example, in answer to a statement that a minor was injured by driving a car owned by his father with the parents' permission. In the answer to the complaint, the attorney must also list any affirmative defenses that may exist on behalf of the client. For example, if the plaintiff drove on a properly and legally closed street or highway that was under construction, the attorney would want to indicate that the plaintiff had assumed the risk of his own injuries. Or if plaintiff was driving with a defective headlight or brake, the defense will be contributory negligence.

The attorney for the defendant (the governmental agency or individual engineer) should be advised of the name of any other party that should be brought into the action. This is known as a cross-claim against a party not original to the first action filed. This would be done, perhaps, when an outside contractor is responsible for maintenance or installation or supplying the equipment that is involved in the injury. Here again the engineer's advice to the attorney is invaluable, for it is with this guidance that the attorney is able to identify the other parties that need to be brought into the litigation to help offset any judgment against the engineer and the agency should an adverse decision result from the suit.

Discovery

Once the pleadings are complete, discovery begins. Under modern legal practice the surprise type of courtroom action is precluded. The last-second surprise testimony that wins a case is no more. Current practice is to influence the jury by facts alone and not with emotional outbursts.

In most cases, no matter how skillful, how good with words, or even how knowledgeable in the field of law the attorney may be, nothing will make up for clumsy use of the discovery devices that are available. The proper discovery technique performs at least two valuable functions for trial lawyers. First, it provides for the revelation of the essential strengths and weaknesses of the other party's and, of course, their own case, thus permitting attorneys to appraise whether a settlement may be preferable to a costly trial. Second, it permits attorneys to present their case very effectively if trial should be necessary.

Several popular discovery techniques will be discussed here:

1. Depositions
2. Written interrogatories
3. Production of documents

All discovery techniques are endorsed by the court. In the event that a party refuses a properly asked for discovery, the court can order such sanctions as requiring the documents and depositions to be turned in, and the court can further charge the refusing party additional costs incurred by the unwarranted refusal. The court can also hold the party in contempt in the face of continuing refusal to honor the discovery requirement, which can result in jail terms until the order is honored.

Deposition. In most jurisdictions the law permits the taking of depositions from anyone, even if they are not a party to the suit, as long as they have some information pertinent and relevant to the matter at hand. The depositions themselves are very similar to a minitrial; the only participants not present are the judge and the jury. The deposition generally will be conducted in an attorney's office before a court reporter who has the authority to swear in the witness (such as a notary public). If a deposition is being taken by the opposing side, your lawyer should be present to protect your interests and those of your agency, and to object to questions that could not properly be admitted into court as evidence. The person being deposed will be questioned by an attorney, and questions and answers are recorded. The witness' attorney will be given the opportunity to cross-examine when the opposition is finished. Not only are depositions important in guiding the attorney in preparing the case, but the deposition also becomes a very important weapon in court. Although a deposition cannot be introduced as evidence if the witness is present in court, it can be used to impeach a testimony if the answers in court do not agree with the answers in the deposition. This, of course, will affect the witness' credibility and can damage the outcome of the case, particularly if a key witness is involved.

If the witness is unavailable to testify (e.g., too ill or moved out of the court's jurisdiction), the deposition can be entered into testimony just as if the witness were present in court. The questions and answers will be read to the jury. This is why it is important that answers be given carefully at the deposition. The party that introduces the deposition into evidence does not have to introduce the whole deposition. However, if only part is introduced, the opposing attorney can, under most state court rules, require that the whole deposition be introduced in the interest of fair play.

Interrogatories. Interrogatories are series of questions given to parties to the action to answer at their own convenience. Interrogatories have the advantage over depositions that they provide more time for the gathering of desired information. Generally, they are provided to attorneys by the opposing counsel for their client to answer. Thus, the attorney will have knowledge of them and will be of assistance in answering them. As a general rule, unlike depositions, which can be taken from anyone, interrogatories can be requested only from the parties to the legal action (i.e., defendant and plaintiff). If the client is of modest means, the fact that interrogatories are frequently less expensive will be an important point in selecting them from among the other discovery devices. Interrogatories do not require expensive transcribing of notes by a court reporter. If the person having the information lives at a distant location, interrogatories can be mailed and an expensive trip by counsel to attend the deposition hearing, or the hiring of a local counsel at the deposition site can be avoided.

Objections can be raised to specific interrogatories to avoid answering them; these should be discussed with the attorney. Among them are:

1. The information is not relevant to the case.
2. The information is privileged.
3. The material is for trial preparation, for which the necessary demonstration of substantial need and inability to obtain the equivalent has not been made.
4. The interrogatory seeks information about specially retained nonwitness experts concerning whom the necessary showing of need and inability to obtain the substantial equivalent has not been made.
5. The inquiry places an unreasonably great burden on the respondent.

There are others, and the attorney can advise on their applicability.

Production of documents. The term "documents" is all-inclusive. It explicitly includes writings, drawings, graphs, charts, photographs, photographic records, and information stored on computer memory devices such as tapes, disks, and so on. Generally, this discovery technique is limited to parties to the legal action. Other discovery devices, such as depositions and interrogatories, are often used to uncover documents that are essential to the case and thus, after their discovery, are obtained for inspection and copy by use of this production technique.

There is also a technique for obtaining access to documents under the control of a nonparty. Generally, the degree of difficulty in obtaining the needed item from a nonparty depends on the nature of the item involved. If the item is of an easily transportable nature, such as documents or lightweight machinery, a subpoena *duces tecum* can be used to require nonparty witnesses to bring the material they control for inspection and copying when a deposition is being taken. Objections are also allowed for the production of documents. Privilege is one type of objection; another is that the other party has not shown that an attempt has been made to get the documents elsewhere. But even more important as objections are the assertions that the desired object does not exist, or that the party does not exercise any control over the document. Again, the attorney will have been provided with a copy of the order to produce, and will make every effort to protect the client and the item requested.

Rules of evidence

Ordinary lay witnesses must speak only of what they know firsthand. They can testify only as to facts and may not give opinions or conclusions. Facts are what they see, touch, smell, and hear. Furthermore, even what they hear may be severely limited by the hearsay rule. Hearsay is an alleged fact that the witness heard someone say concerning the matter involved in the litigation. For example, if the witness was testifying about an accident that involved B, and stated that he heard A say that A saw B drive through a red signal, that would be considered hearsay and would be inadmissible in court; only A could make this statement in court. The reason that this rule exists and is enforced is apparent from the dangers involved. There is no way that the jury can tell the condition of A when making this damaging statement. Since A is not in the courtroom, A cannot be cross-examined, and the jury cannot determine her credibility from the way she acts, her mannerisms, and appearance.

As long as there are rules there will always be exceptions. There are, in fact, 10 exceptions to the hearsay rule which permit testimony of this type to be admitted into evidence:

1. *Admission by a party*. Witnesses can testify to what they heard, if parties to the action admit something against their own interest. For example, you can testify that you heard A tell someone that she did, in fact, drive through a red traffic signal.
2. *Declarations against interest*. If persons make statements against their interests and they are now absent or unavailable for the trial, the person who heard the declaration can testify to it.
3. *Dying declaration*. Statement heard by another is admissible if the person who made it is now dead and was describing the cause of their own death, made from their own personal knowledge and under a sense of "immediate hopelessness and impending death." Generally, this is used in murder trials, but it can also be admitted in a vehicular homicide trial, for example.
4. *Excited utterances*. A statement is admissible hearsay if made under the stress of an exciting event and if it relates to the immediate facts of the exciting event, and if made near the time of the event. For example, a witness can testify to hearing someone yell out at an accident scene that A just drove through a red light and hit B.
5. *Declaration of mental state*. A statement that reveals the state of mind of the party making it can be testified to by a person overhearing it.
6. *Declaration of physical sensations*. Statements of existing physical sensations are also excepted from the hearsay rule. An example of this would be testifying to hearing some one explain how much pain he feels.
7. *Business records*. A business record is admissible hearsay if the transaction was fresh in the mind of the person when making the record, if it was regarding facts within their knowledge, if the record was made as part of the regular course of business, and if the record was properly authenticated.
8. *Official records*. A writing is admissible hearsay if it was made by a public employee or one performing a public function regarding matters within his or her personal knowledge, which are recorded in the course of his or her public duties at or near the time that the act becomes known to the official.
9. *Past recollection recorded*. If witnesses testify that they have no present memory of the facts about which they are being questioned, a written memo, for example, can be used to refresh their memory. The witnesses must testify that they prepared the memo or that it was prepared at their direction about facts within their knowledge and, again, while the facts were fresh in their mind. They must also testify that the memo was true and must read the contents of the memo into evidence.
10. *Prior testimony*. Prior testimony can be read into evidence if the person giving it is unavailable, if it was given under oath in a proceeding, and if there was an opportunity to cross-examine the witness. It is required that the parties and the issues were sufficiently identical so that the adverse attorney had the incentive to cross-examine the now-absent witness.

For admission into evidence at trial the particular evidence must be relevant to the matter at hand. Here, too, rules have been developed as guidelines of relevancy.

The fact that the plaintiff has been involved in a previous accident or has filed claims for injuries before is deemed not relevant to the accident at hand, particularly if used to prove that the plaintiff is accident-prone or has a tendency to file claims regularly. However, it may be admissible to refer to a prior accident if a particular injury is claimed and the plaintiff was injured similarly before, in an attempt to prove the extent of injuries brought about by the accident involved in the current litigation. Evidence of prior accidents or injuries to other persons because of the maintenance of a dangerous condition or activity by the defendant is relevant only if there is a substantial identity of conditions, or of human behavior involved, and no serious danger of confusing the issues. Under these circumstances the evidence will be admitted to show that the condition or activity was, in fact, dangerous, or that the defendant had knowledge of the danger, or that the dangerous condition or activity was the cause of the plaintiff's injuries.

Evidence of a subsequent accident is generally held not admissible to show either cause of the plaintiff's injury or knowledge by the defendant of the danger involved at the time of the plaintiff's injury. However, the evidence of the subsequent accident, if it happens shortly after the accident involved in the litigation, can be admissible to show the existence of a danger at the time of the first accident.

Proof of no other accidents or complaints is not admissible to show that the defendant had no knowledge of a dangerous condition or activity, or that this condition or activity was unlikely to have caused the plaintiff's injuries. Although the lack of prior complaints or accidents is generally not admissible, evidence of similar experience faced by other parties may be, particularly if the experiences were substantially the same and the experiences have a logical bearing on what happened to the plaintiff.

Repair of defects after accident

Probably the most common question asked is: "Should I repair the defect or not?" because of the belief that in coming litigation it would look bad to have made the repair. Evidence that, following an injury, the defendant repaired the condition that the plaintiff alleges caused the injury is generally not admissible as proof that the condition was, in fact, defective. The policy behind this is to avoid discouraging beneficial repairs or changes being made following an accident.

However, the fact that it was repaired can be relevant and admissible for other purposes:

1. If, for example, during the trial the public entity testifies that the alleged defect was, in fact, safe and proper, evidence of the repair is admissible to impeach the testimony.
2. If it is claimed that the agency had no ownership or control of the condition or area involved in the litigation, testimony of the subsequent repair can be admitted to prove ownership and control.
3. If the repair was made to conceal the defect, testimony of the repair will be admissible.
4. If there is testimony that there was no way to resolve the condition other than the way it was constructed, then evidence of the repair or change would be admissible to impeach the testimony given.

Evidence that a defendant has offered to make a settlement of a claim is not admissible to fix liability on the basis of that offer. However, some courts have held that any acknowledgment that was made during the settlement discussions (e.g., the knowledge that a traffic control device is defective) should be admitted. Therefore, in settlement negotiations no admission should be made of any responsibility or knowledge of defect.

Documentary evidence

Before any writing may be entered into evidence, it must be authenticated. This authentication applies to public records as well as private writings. Usually, certified copies of the official records, rather than the original, are entered into evidence. The copies are considered to be self-authenticated if it is shown that the original is a document required by law to be recorded and that it was actually recorded in a public office. To be considered a correct copy of an original it must bear the certification by the custodian of the document or some other authorized person, his or her signature, and seals of a public office.

With private writings, stronger evidence is demanded by the court. The "Best Evidence Rule" requires that, to prove the contents of a private writing, the original itself must be produced unless it is shown to be unavailable. This rule applies only to private writings, not public or official records and documents. The Best Evidence Rule includes photographs, X-rays, motion pictures, and recordings of any form. It is interesting to note that a carbon copy is considered a duplicate original and is admissible if it was made at the same time as the original and if both were signed. The Best Evidence Rule does not apply to documents where it is impossible or impracticable to produce the original in court, for example where it could be shown that a document was lost or destroyed or was unobtainable because it was in the possession of someone out of state and thus outside the court's power to subpoena. The rule would also not apply if the document is in the possession of the other party to the litigation. In the foregoing examples a copy could be admitted in the place of the original. If the originals are too voluminous, so that it would be impracticable to introduce them in court, "best evidence" would not apply and summaries would be admissible.

Attorney–client privilege

This is one of the oldest privileges recognized at common law. The purpose of the privilege is, of course, to encourage full disclosure by clients to their attorneys of all pertinent matters without fear that they would be used as evidence against them. The client is a person who directly, or through some authorized representative, consults a lawyer for the purpose of securing legal advice. It is the individual, the agency, or its insurance company that hired the attorney. If the individual engineer, for example, is made or becomes the representative of the agency in the matter, the privilege will be extended to his or her communications with the attorney. However, an ordinary witness statement given by the employee to the employer's attorney is not privileged even if the employer has directed or asked that the statement be made.

To be privileged, the communication must be made to a member of the bar (a licensed attorney) or to a subordinate (clerk, secretary, paralegal employee) for transmission to that attorney. The client need not even retain the attorney. The privilege extends to any communication made while consulting the attorney, even if the attorney declines to take the case or the potential client declines to hire him or her. However, only the client has the right to assert the privilege in keeping the attorney from disclosing communications. Third parties, not related directly to the agency or authorized to act on its behalf, cannot require the attorney not to disclose the information they have heard. If the privilege is not asserted, it may be deemed waived and attorneys may be required to testify to communications they have had with their clients.

Problems develop when others overhear the communication between client and attorney. If the third party is a necessary participant, for example an investigator hired by the attorney or the attorney's clerk, secretary, or paralegal, their presence during the discussion does not defeat the privilege of the communication. However, if the discussions are overheard by another party not necessary to the meeting, even if it is unknown that the party is present, this party can be required to testify to what was overheard. Thus, it is a good point not to discuss legal matters in places where they can be overheard (e.g., in elevators, crowded offices, etc.) unless precautions are taken.

Attorney–client privilege is enforced for one purpose alone: to ensure that the attorney obtains all the facts necessary to prepare a proper case.

GLOSSARY

abate: to decrease, reduce, remove, or destroy; to abate a nuisance is to remove or destroy the thing that causes it.

abrogate: to repeal, annul, or abolish. A law, for example, is abrogated by legislative action, constitutional authority, or usage.

accord and satisfaction: an agreement between parties to accept something less than the amount actually due, and the delivery of that new amount.

accused: a person charged with a crime or misdemeanor, the defendant in a criminal case.

act: an enactment, as of a legislative body; a law or statute.

action: a judicial proceeding to enforce or protect a right.

actionable: giving legal grounds for an action, as trespass, slander, or breach of contract.

adjournment: the act of putting off, postponing, or suspending business or session, either temporarily or indefinitely.

adjudication: the pronouncement of a judgment or decree by the court.

admissible: of such a nature that the court or judge must allow it to be introduced, as certain evidence or testimony.

affiant: a person who makes and swears to an affidavit.

affidavit: a voluntary statement or declaration of facts, written or printed and sworn to by the person making it before an officer authorized to administer oaths.

affirm: to confirm, ratify, or approve. An appellate court (one to which appeals are taken) may affirm the judgment or decree of a lower court.

answer: (n.) a pleading by a defendant in a lawsuit in response to the summons or complaint.

appellant: a person who appeals a decision, against him or her, from a lower court to a higher court.

appellee: the party in a litigation against whom the appeal is taken; also called *respondent*.

averment: a positive statement of facts in a pleading, without argument or inference.

brief: a written statement prepared by the counsel arguing a case in appellate court; also used on occasion in trial court.

burden of proof: the obligation to prove affirmatively a disputed fact or facts related to an issue raised in a case being tried before the court.

cause of action: the grounds upon which an action is based.

certiorari: a writ from a superior to an inferior court, directing that a certified record of its proceeding on a particular case be sent up for review.

change of venue: the change of the place of a trial, for good cause.

circumstantial evidence: evidence consisting of facts and circumstances that furnish a reasonable ground for inferring the existence of some other connected fact or facts.

civil action: a lawsuit brought by a private individual or group to recover money, property, to enforce or protect a civil right, to prevent or redress a civil wrong.

class action: an action brought by one or more plaintiffs on behalf of other persons who are similarly situated or have suffered a similar wrong.

comparative negligence: a legal doctrine applicable in negligence suits, according to which the negligence of the plaintiff as well as that of the defendant is taken into account. Damages are based upon the outcome of a comparison of the two and are thus proportioned.

complainant: a person who files a bill of complaint; the party who starts a legal action; also called the *plaintiff*.

concurrent jurisdiction: a situation in which each of a number of different judicial bodies has the authority to deal with the same subject matter at the discretion of the person starting the legal action.

conflict of laws: the disagreement between the laws of different states as it affects the rights of persons acting under the laws of more than one jurisdiction.

constructive: assumed or inferred by legal interpretation.

continuance: the adjournment of the proceedings in a case from one day or term to another.

counterclaim: a claim alleged by a defendant, which seeks to reduce the plaintiff's claim.

cross-action: an action brought by a defendant in a suit against a plaintiff in the same suit.

cross-claim: a claim brought by a defendant in an action against the plaintiff or codefendant or both.

declaratory judgment: a judgment that declares the status, rights, or duties of the parties involved, or that does not order any action to be taken.

de facto: a Latin expression meaning "in fact"; accepted by the fact that it exists, rather than that it is according to law.

de jure: a Latin expression meaning "by right" or "by law" as opposed to de facto.

deponent: a person who, under oath, gives testimony that is set down in writing.

deposition: testimony of a witness taken outside a court and set down in writing for use as evidence in court.

discovery: the disclosure of facts, documents, and the like by one party to a suit at the request of the other party to a suit, for use as evidence in a case being prepared for trial.

dismissal without prejudice: the dismissal of an action or proceeding in a way that does not prevent the plaintiff from bringing another suit based on the same cause of action.

enjoin: to direct, command, or forbid some act by court order (called an *injunction*).

estoppel: a condition in which a person is prevented by law either from contradicting what he has previously stated or from stating or claiming what he has previously denied.

ex parte order: an order granted by the court at the request of one party to a proceeding without prior notification to the other party involved.

hearsay: secondhand evidence; evidence derived from something a witness has heard others say. Can be admissible under certain circumstances.

hostile witness: a witness who, under direct examination, displays such prejudice or hostility toward the party that called that such a party is permitted to cross-examine him or her.

independent contractor: a person who contracts to do certain work according to his or her own methods without control by the employer except as to the result or product of the work.

inter alia: a Latin phrase meaning "among other things."

interrogatories: a series of questions in writing used in the judicial examination of a party or witness.

joinder: the joining of two or more legal proceedings; the uniting of two or more persons as plaintiffs or defendants in one suit.

joint and several: binding two or more persons both collectively and individually. Thus, a successful plaintiff under this doctrine could recover damages from any one defendant or from all of them.

last clear chance: a doctrine in the law of negligence according to which a person who has the last obvious opportunity to avoid injury to another person, or himself or herself, is liable if he or she does not do so.

leading question: a question intended to suggest or elicit the reply desired by the questioner.

malfeasance: the commission of an unlawful act or an act one has no right to commit; used most often to describe official misconduct.

mandamus: a writ issued by courts directed to public officials or inferior courts commanding them to do or not to do something specified in the order that is within the scope of their office or duties.

misfeasance: the doing of a lawful act in an unlawful or improper way.

mitigate: to make less severe; lessen.

motion: an application to a court or judge to obtain an order or rule directing some act to be done.

negligence: the failure to exercise the standard of care that would be expected of a normally reasonable and prudent person in a particular set of circumstances.

nonfeasance: the failure to perform some act that one ought or is required to perform.

nonsuit: termination of a lawsuit without any judgment on the issues.

nuisance: any thing or practice which by its existence or use causes annoyance, harm, inconvenience, or damage. A nuisance is often a valid basis for a civil suit.

plaintiff: the person who begins an action at law; the complaining party in an action.

plea: a pleading; also, more specifically, a defendant's first pleading.

pleading: the system of preparing formal written statements of a party to a legal action.

precedent: an adjudged case or judicial decision that furnishes a rule or model for deciding a subsequent case that presents the same or similar legal problems.

preponderance of evidence: in a case of contested facts, superiority in weight (determined by value and not amount) of the evidence presented by one side over the other (all that is required to prevail in a civil suit).

presumption of fact: an inference that affirms or denies the existence of some unknown fact, based on the existence of some fact that is already known or that has already been proved.

prima facie case: is a case strong enough that it can be overthrown only by contradicting or rebutting evidence.

punitive damages: damages awarded to a plaintiff over and above those to which he or she is entitled, because the defendant has violated one of his or her legal rights. Such damages are awarded to punish and thereby make an example of the defendant to deter others from acting in the same way.

quash: to make void or set aside; abate, annul, as an indictment or a summons.

sovereign immunity: the immunity of a government from being sued in its own courts except with its consent, or other exception.

stare decisis: the judicial policy of following legal principles established by previous court decisions.

statute of limitations: a statute that imposes time limits upon the right to sue in certain cases.

stay: a stopping or suspension of judicial proceedings or the execution of a judgment.

subpoena: a writ commanding a person to appear in court.

subpoena duces tecum: a writ commanding a person to appear in court with a particular document or paper.

tort: any private or civil wrong by act or omission, but not including breach of contract. Some torts may also be crimes.

tortfeaser: one who commits a tort.

voir dire: a preliminary examination of a person, especially of a proposed witness or juror, as to his or her qualifications for the function or duty in question.

writ: a written order issued by a court, commanding the person to whom it is addressed to do or not to do some act specified therein.

REFERENCES FOR FURTHER READING

AIDLIN, S. P., "The Professional Engineer as a Witness," *Case and Comment,* Mar.–Apr. 1953.

BAERWALD, J. E., "The Traffic Engineering Expert Witness," *Traffic Eng.,* May 1977.

CANTER, B., "The Expert Witness," *Am. Bar Assoc. J.,* Oct. 1966.

CARLSON, R. F., "A Review of Case Law Relating to Liability for Skidding Accidents," Paper prepared for the 53rd Annual Meeting, Transportation Research Board, Washington, D.C., 1974.

COOK, C. M., "The Role and Rights of the Expert Witness," *J. Forensic Sci.*, Oct. 1964.

DORBIN, J., "The Engineer as a Court Witness: Be Prepared!" *Public Works Mag.*, Jan. 78.

ELSON, K. H., "Using the Expert Witness," *Proceedings*, Nebraska State Bar Assoc., Omaha, Neb., 1966.

FIGG, R. M., ET AL, *Civil Trial Manual*. Philadelphia, American Law Institute, 1974.

FITZPATRICK, J. F., ET AL, *The Law and Roadside Hazards*. Charlottesville, Va.: The Michie Company, 1974.

HAMMON, S., "The Lawyer and the Expert," *Am. Bar Assoc. J.*, June 1968.

HILTON, O., "Elements of Effectiveness Expert Testimony," *J. Forensic Sci.*, Jan. 1957.

HRICKO, A. R., "Roadside Hazards—Responsibility and Liability," *FIC Quart.*, Fall 1974.

HUMPHREYS, J. B., "Take the Liability out of Roadway Construction," *Am. City County Mag.*, Dec. 1976.

JEANS, J. W., *Trial Advocacy*. St. Paul, Minn.: West Publishing Co., 1975.

KIRK, P. L., "Utilizing the Expert," *Case and Comment*, Mar.-Apr. 1967.

KUVIN, H., *Trial Handbook*. Englewood Cliffs, N.J.: Prentice-Hall, 1965.

LUCY, G. J., "Pretrial Conference between Expert and Attorney," *J. Forensic Sci.*, Oct. 1962.

MALSOW, J. E., "Products Liability Comes of Age," *Juris Doctor*, Feb. 1975.

MORRIS, C., *Morris on Torts*. Brooklyn, N.Y.: The Foundation Press, Inc., 1953.

NICKERSON, M. H., "The Expert Technical Witness on Trial," *Am. Bar Assoc. J.*, Aug. 1964.

OLIVER, D. C., "Liability and Highway Safety Practices," *Traffic Eng.*, May 1977.

OLIVER, D. C., "Tort Law—Liability Developments Relating to Traffic Controls for Maintenance and Construction Work Sites," Unpublished paper, Dover, Del., 1975.

OLIVER, D. C., "Torts: State and Federal," Unpublished paper, Washington, D.C., 1975.

ORME, D. E., "Responding to Tort Liability," *Transport. Res. News, 66* (Sept–Oct. 1976).

PIVNIK, S. I., "Changing Attitudes toward Governmental Immunity to Law Suits and Assignment of Liability Relative to Traffic Control Devices," *Signal Mag.*, Nov.–Dec., 1976.

PIVNIK, S. I., "Immunity/Liability Relative to Traffic Control Devices," *Am. Road Builders Mag.*, Nov.–Dec. 1976.

PIVNIK, S. I., "The Law and Traffic Control," *Traffic Eng. Mag.*, Feb. 1977.

POPE, J., "Instructing Your Own Expert Witness," *Case and Comment*, Nov.–Dec. 1959.

PROSSER, W. L., *Law on Torts*, 4th ed. St. Paul, Minn.: West Publishing Co., 1971.

SCHWEITZER, S. C., *Cyclopedia of Trial Practice*. Rochester, N.Y.: Lawyers Co-operative Publishing Co., 1970.

*——*Accident Reconstruction*. Boston: American Trial Lawyers Association, 1966.

*——*American Jurisprudence*, 2nd ed. Rochester, N.Y.: Lawyers Co-operative Publishing Company, 1962 (1975).

*——*American Jurisprudence—Trials*. Rochester, N.Y.: Lawyers Co-operative Publishing Co., 1962.

*——"Coping with Tort Liability," *Better Roads Mag*. Sept. 1976.

*——*Corpus Juris Secundum*. St. Paul, Minn.: West Publishing Co., 1959 (1975).

*——*How to Try a Case*. New York: Baker, Voorhis & Co., 1930.

*——"Improper Signs Trigger Suits," *Traffic Safety*, Jan. 1966.

*——"Legal Implications of Regulations Aimed at Reducing Wet-Weather Skidding Accidents on Highways," *Res. Results Dig., 95* (Aug. 1977).

*——"Liability of State and Local Governments for Snow and Ice Control," *Res. Results Dig., 83* (Feb. 1976).

*——"Liability for State Highway Departments for Design, Construction, and Maintenance Defects," *Res Results Dig., 80* (Sept. 1975).

*——"Personal Liability of State Highway Department Officers and Employees," *Res. Results Dig., 79* (Sept. 1975).

*——"Sovereign Immunity," *Better Roads Mag.*, Aug. 1976.

*——"Sovereign Immunity No Longer Defense," *Traffic Control Views*, *2*(6), 1978.

*——*Traffic Engineering: A Legal Analysis*. Washington, D.C.: Highway Research Board, 1961.

28

TRANSPORTATION ADMINISTRATION

JOHN W. BARR, *President*

Barr, Dunlop & Associates, Inc.
Tallahassee, Florida

Because of the strong concern which the public has—and frequently expresses—for relief from congestion, better mobility, and improved transportation safety, the administration of transportation functions and programs has always been important. Opinion polls show that this public concern is consistently rated high in the list of desires. In recent years new emphasis has been placed on old concerns—concerns with the impacts on neighborhoods, air and noise pollution, and the energy-consumption characteristics of alternative transportation systems. Positive response to public concerns as well as to factual needs is necessary. Transportation administration that is both responsive and responsible is required.

The basic principles of management and administration that apply to any service endeavor also apply to transportation functions. It is not the intent of this chapter to review all such principles and show how they may be applied in the field of transportation. Nor has an attempt been made to recommend specific organization charts, recognizing the truism that an organization chart usually describes how functions and positions actually relate in practice, *after* the organizing of people and functions has been carried out. Rather, this chapter is intended to provide the reader with a checklist of transportation functions, information about how these functions are generally performed at various levels of government, and references that may be helpful in the task of seeking funds for transportation.

General transportation functions

Transportation agency functions and organizations vary according to mode and level of government. The handling of cash from fares, route scheduling, driver assignment and supervision, vehicle purchases and maintenance, and marketing are functions associated with the public transit and freight carrier modes. Road and bridge design, construction and maintenance, and traffic operations are functions associated with the street and highway mode. Common to all modes are functions such as system planning, design, operations, coordination with other modes, regulation, funding and grantsmanship, and research and development.

Functions differ between levels of government because of differences in responsibilities. Municipalities traditionally have been responsible for the mobility of all who reside, have business, or conduct commerce within their jurisdiction; cities, therefore, must administer a broad scope of transportation functions. Counties (or other intermediate forms of government) usually have some urban system responsibilities, but have larger areas, some intercity transportation concerns, and rural as well as suburban situations to deal with. The principal transportation tasks of the states in the United States have long been to build and maintain statewide highway systems, to administer motor vehicle tax funds and federal aid for the designated state highway systems and the Interstate system and in some states to assist local road agencies. In more recent years the scope in most states has broadened to include other modes and tasks, especially the planning and financing of statewide rail and airport systems and, in some states, seaport administration and urban and rural transit assistance. Streets and highways have long been the direct responsibility of government, but other modes until recently were provided by private interests subject to state and local regulation and franchise.

The U.S. federal government has a wide variety of transportation administration responsibilities pertaining to all modes, including the administration of the Federal-aid Highway Fund and other designed transportation funds, safety standards, regulations, and other programs and services as prescribed by law. In other countries transportation functions are similar to those described above, but the responsibility for transportation is generally more centralized in the national government. The basic transportation functions have been defined[1] as follows:

Planning and programming

Transportation planning is the procedure for determining as accurately as possible future transportation needs and the most practical ways to meet them. It is a staff function that serves to correlate all the broad elements of design and construction, maintenance, and operations. The minimum basic responsibilities in these activities are:

1. Conducting system studies of existing traffic volumes, trip purposes, peak loads, origins and destinations of trips, parking demands, street classification, projections and assignment of future traffic and related investigations.
2. Determining present and future needs for streets and highways, street lighting, parking, transit facilities, and terminal facilities, and establishing priorities for such facilities.
3. Performing corridor analyses, alternate route studies, cost-benefit, and other feasibility studies.
4. Performing environmental impact studies.
5. Participating in the preparation of a master transportation plan. Such a plan should relate transit and auto transportation to each other and to overall development. This includes all plans involving transit, street and highway, and terminal improvement.
6. Coordinating transportation improvement programs with other municipal, county, or state activities.
7. Analyzing policy alternatives and developing financial plans so that the improvement program can be carried out. This important administrative function involves such activities as policy interface analysis and development strategy planning; analysis and procurement of bond and tax funds and funds from external sources (a digest of federal funding sources is presented later in this chapter); and internal fiscal management, including fund control, accounts analysis, transit fare setting, and budgeting and budget justification.

Design and construction

The design and construction function includes such activities as the determination of the type of physical improvements required and the preparation of detailed engineering plans, as well as the supervision of the construction of the improvements. This function, of course, covers both relatively minor projects such as channelizing an intersection and major construction jobs such as a freeway or rapid transit system. The activities involved are precisely those necessary to carry out whatever transportation improvement program has been adopted by the community.

Broadly speaking, the major duties involved in this function are to:

1. Establish standards for the design and construction of all transportation facilities.
2. Conduct surveys to determine line, grade, elevations, and cross sections.
3. Prepare detailed engineering drawings and specifications of all new highway, street, intersections, storm drainage, lighting, transit, and terminal improvements.
4. Inspect the construction of all improvements and review all contracts for transportation improvements.

Operations

The general task of transportation operations is to assure that the total available system is used to best advantage. This means efficiency in the movement of people and goods and maximum safety, comfort, and convenience to all users.

This function covers a wide range of activities, such as determining need for and the most appropriate type of traffic control devices, the installation of the devices, and operation of the transit system. The principal responsibilities include:

1. Performance of traffic operations studies, including data on speeds, volumes and volume trends, capacities, accidents, and pedestrian movements.
2. Determination of the location, type, and specifications of traffic control devices, including signs, signals, and pavement markings.
3. Determination of necessary controls on curb parking, standing, and stopping.
4. Installation and timing of traffic signals.
5. Establishment of turning controls, parking and loading regulations, speed controls, one-way streets, traffic-related subdivision regulations, and any other systems management measures deemed necessary.
6. Development of transit routes, schedules, and service improvements.
7. Management and regulation of transit modes and services, including bus, rapid rail, demand-responsive, elderly, and handicapped transit; and paratransit modes such as taxi, carpool, and vanpool services. This includes driver scheduling and supervision, money handling, accounting, management reports, and operations analysis.
8. Transit marketing, including surveillance of operations, market research studies, fare elasticity analyses, public information, advertising, route planning and development, and programming of other attribute improvements.

Maintenance

The primary purpose of maintenance is to keep the physical plant in safe operating condition. A second important objective is to protect the large public investment in transportation facilities.

The entire transportation program is affected by the degree of efficiency of maintenance work. Unless this function is competently carried out, excessive maintenance costs will cut heavily into funds needed for new street improvements. The primary maintenance duties are to:

[1]Portions of this list are taken from *Improving Transportation Administration*, National Committee on Urban Transportation, Washington, D.C., 1958.

1. Maintain and repair all transportation facilities and structures.
2. Maintain all transportation equipment, including transit vehicles and street and highway maintenance machines.
3. Maintain signs, pavement markings, parking meters, street lights, and traffic signals.
4. Perform street cleaning, snow removal, mowing, and landscape maintenance.

Regulations

This general task is carried out at all levels of government for the control of private businesses that provide transportation services and the operators of vehicles using transportation facilities.

Local government organization

Considering the fact that local government has substantial control over local transportation, urban traffic and transportation issues have high priority in the minds of its citizens, and there are numerous facets to the function of delivering the service demanded, it is clear that management of local transportation is one of the most vital tasks in the field of public administration. This has been evident to professional public administrators for many years. The National Committee on Urban Transportation concluded in its 1958 study that urban transportation administration "is a complex task requiring close technical coordination. A smooth-working organization is indispensable to carry out the interrelated functions of planning, constructing, operating, and maintaining the system. Without such an organization, officials are severely handicapped, sometimes to a point where they are even unable to take advantage of technical know-how available within the city government."

Municipal functions and organizations

Municipalities are primarily responsible for urban transportation functions; those related to urban transit, parking, and other urban terminal facilities; the planning, construction, and operation of streets of all classifications within the municipality; and traffic control and regulation. Regulation of taxicabs and the operations of other carriers, and the management of airport facilities are also functions usually handled at the municipal level. In some major urban areas, of course, metropolitan governments or urban county governments are charged with those municipal responsibilities.

In the United States, there are basically three forms of city governments:

1. The "strong mayor" form, in which the legislative activities are vested in the city council, with the mayor serving as the chief administrative officer. Normally, the mayor has the power to veto legislative actions.
2. The council-manager form, in which the mayor usually serves as a member of the city council and the city manager is chief administrator. The city manager is appointed by and serves at the pleasure of the council.
3. The commission form, in which each elected commissioner generally serves as the head of an operating department or groups of departments. The commission, whose members may be elected at large or by districts constitutes the legislative body and may choose one of its members to serve as chairperson.

Transportation functions in cities are administered in a variety of ways. In some instances, particularly in smaller cities, they are split among several departments. For example, street and transit system planning is often under the planning department, street design and traffic engineering under the engineering department, street maintenance under public works, and airport and transit management under separate departments.

Because of the strong public interest in traffic safety and congestion alleviation, the traffic engineering functions are often strengthened by administering them through a separate department. Such a departmental organization is illustrated in Figure 28.1. This has the advantages of giving the city traffic engineer authority and budget strength with which to attack transportation problems, and improved ability to communicate effectively with the manager or mayor, the elected officials, the news media, and individual citizens.

Within the traffic engineering organization, functions are often grouped in divisions or bureaus, as indicated in Figure 28.2. Street and highway construction and maintenance are usually located within the public works department. Good cooperation between the traffic engineering and public works departments is required to implement properly an effective street and highway improvement program and alleviate traffic disruption due to detours, utility work, and other such activities. Similarly, good cooperation between the traffic engineering and the police departments is required to provide effective enforcement of traffic regulations, good

Figure 28.1. Department organization of traffic engineering functions.

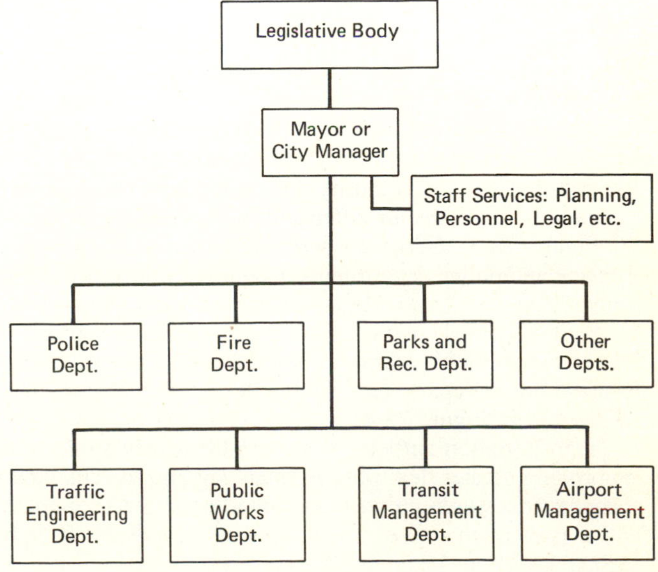

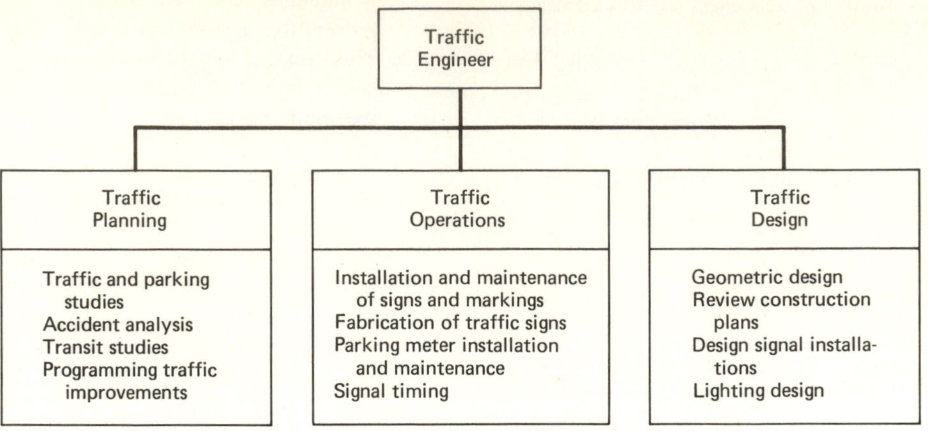

Figure 28.2. Grouping of functions within the traffic engineering organization.

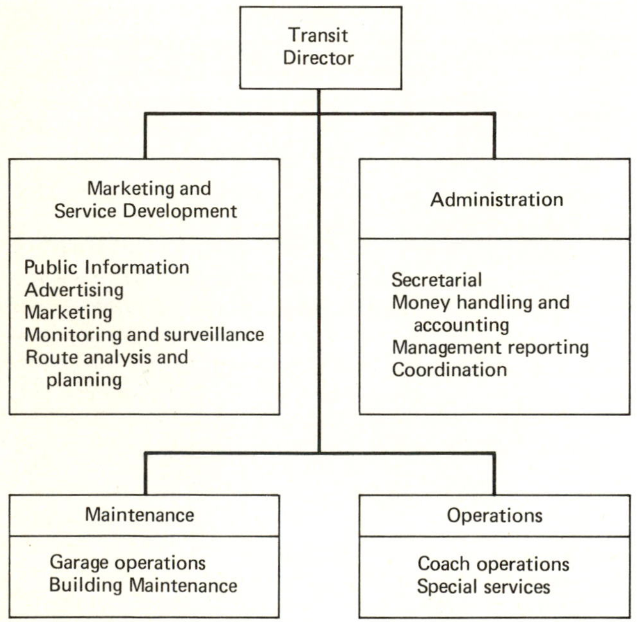

Figure 28.3. Organization of transit operations functions.

handling of peak traffic flow, and exchange of information about traffic problems.

Because of the public sensitivity to the transit operations functions, it is desirable that they too, be organized so as to provide adequate authority and communications. Transit operations functions are often grouped generally as shown in Figure 28.3. Good cooperation with the traffic engineering and police departments is required to assure priority movements of buses and the security of bus patrons.

In some cities, particularly larger ones, some or all of the transportation functions may be consolidated under a transportation department. Such a departmental structure is illustrated in Figure 28.4.

Transportation authorities are established in some areas to provide greater flexibility in financing and to achieve the benefits of a single-purpose appointed policymaking board. Advocates of this type of administration consider it to be expedient, more business-like, and less influenced by political concerns and nontransportation priorities and issues. Critics of this form consider it to be too autonomous, too far removed from the electorate, and prone to conflict, at times, with policies of the elected officials and with other local government functions. The scope of authority may range from a limited project or facility (e.g., an expressway authority, transit authority, parking authority, or an airport or seaport authority) to a comprehensive transportation authority responsible for all street, transit, airport, and seaport functions.

County functions and organizations

Counties (or other intermediate-level forms of government) generally have less responsibility in the incorporated urban areas. They are the level of local government usually responsible for transportation functions in the unincorporated suburbs and rural areas. In some states, counties are responsible for urban extensions of the rural and suburban arterial highways—facilities of county concern—in the interest of county-wide system continuity. City residents, who are also county residents and taxpayers, of course, thereby benefit from secondary gasoline tax or other revenues that may be under county jurisdiction. Some counties operate public transit systems, serving urban, suburban, and rural areas, deriving financial support from county-wide taxes as well as from fares and other sources.

County organizations through which transportation functions are administered vary as do city organizations and are similar in structure. Consolidation of city and county transportation organizations is frequently encountered. In some cases the county contracts with the city to provide traffic engineering services; in others, the reverse arrangement is made. Cooperative arrangements frequently are made to fund highway, airport, or transit projects jointly, and to construct, maintain, and operate them. Joint city–county authorities exist in which elected representatives of the county and of the participating cities sit as appointed members of the policymaking body. Because traffic and transportation problems and issues seldom begin or end at city limits, and because transportation functions of cities and counties often can be consolidated and thereby administered

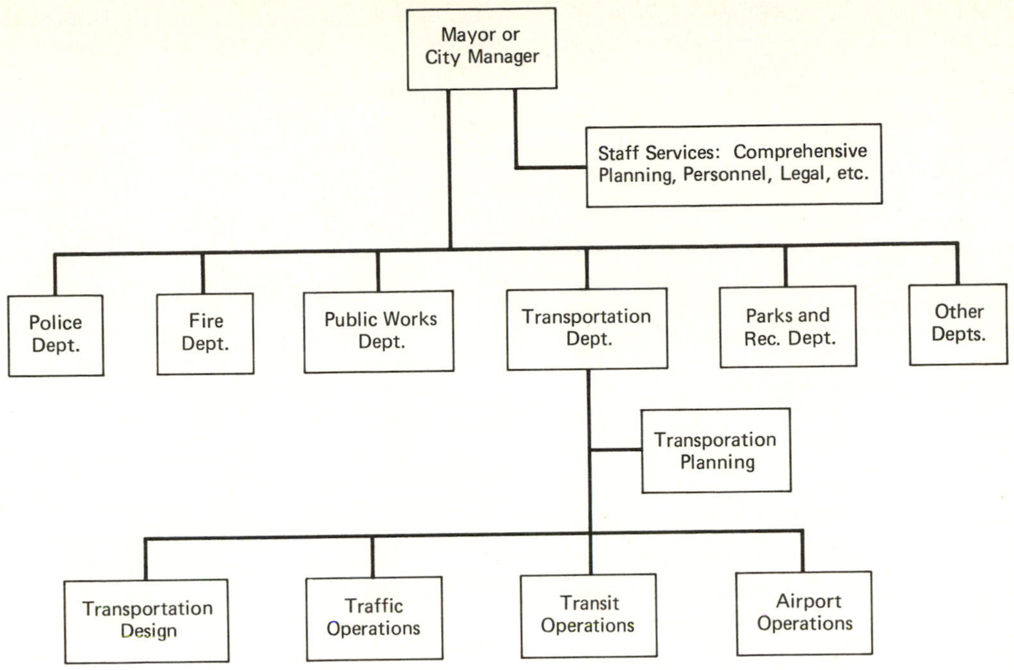

Figure 28.4. Departmental organization of transportation functions in a large city.

more efficiently and economically, such advantages are highlighted by proponents of consolidated or metropolitan government, and transportation usually is one of the first subjects of organizational merger when consolidation does occur.

Metropolitan planning organizations: transportation planning and programming requirements

Coordination of the federal, state, and local portions of urban highway improvement programs became mandatory with the passage of the 1962 Federal-aid Highway Act. It stipulated that, in urban areas with populations of 50,000 or greater, only programs based on a cooperative, continuing, and comprehensive transportation planning process (the "3-C Process") would be eligible for federal aid. Through subsequent legislation—especially the Urban Mass Transportation Act of 1964, its amendments, the National Mass Transportation Act of 1974, and regulations established to implement their provisions—the process became multimodal in scope, and each urban area was required to establish a Metropolitan Planning Organization (MPO) to "provide a forum for cooperative decision-making by principal elected officials of general purpose local government".[2]

Federal regulations required the governor of each state to designate the MPOs in such a way that there would be representation of each local government within the MPO's area of jurisdiction. A digest of other provisions of the federal regulations follows.[3]

[2]*Fed. Reg.*, *41*(181) (Sept. 17, 1975).

[3]Ibid.

The responsibilities for cooperatively carrying out transportation planning and programming shall be clearly identified in an agreement or memorandum of understanding between the State and the MPO. Where the MPO is different from the A-95 agency, there shall be an agreement between the two organizations which prescribes the means by which their activities will be coordinated. . . . This agreement shall specify how transportation planning and programming will be part of the comprehensively planned development of the urbanized area . . . There shall be an agreement between the MPO and publicly owned operators of mass transportation services which specifies cooperative procedures for carrying out transportation planning and programming. . . . The MPO in cooperation with the State, and in cooperation with publicly owned operators of mass transportation services, shall be responsible for carrying out the urban transportation planning process and shall develop the planning work programs, transportation plan, and transportation improvement program. . . . The MPO shall annually endorse the plans and programs . . .

The urban transportation planning process shall include the development of a prospectus and a unified planning work program. . . . The prospectus shall establish a multiyear framework within which the unified planning work program is accomplished and shall include:

1. A summary of the planning program including discussion of the important transportation issues facing the area;
2. A general description of the status and anticipated accomplishments of each of the elements; . . .
3. A description of the procedures to be used in carrying out each element specified;
4. A description of the functional responsibilities of each participating agency; and
5. Copies of agreements. . . .

The unified planning work program shall:

1. Annually describe all urban transportation and transportation related planning activities anticipated within the area during the next 1- or 2-year period regardless of funding sources; and
2. Document work to be performed with planning assistance provided under section 9 of the UMT Act. . . .

The urban transportation planning process shall include the development of a transportation plan consisting of a transportation systems management element and a long-range element. . . . The transportation systems management element (TSM) of the transportation plan shall:

1. Provide for the short-range transportation needs of the urbanized area by making efficient use of existing transportation resources and providing for the movement of people in an efficient manner; and
2. Identify traffic engineering, public transportation, regulatory, pricing, management, operational and other improvements to the existing urban transportation system not including new transportation facilities or major changes in existing facilities. . . .

The long-range element of the transportation plan shall:

1. Provide for the long-range transportation needs of the urbanized area; and
2. Identify new transportation policies and transportation facilities or major changes in existing facilities by location and modes to be implemented.

The transportation plan shall be consistent with the area's comprehensive long-range land use plan, urban development objectives, and the area's overall social, economic, environmental, system performance and energy conservation goals and objectives. . . .

The Federal Highway and Urban Mass Transportation Administrators jointly will review and evaluate annually the transportation planning process in each urbanized area to determine if the process meets the requirements of this subpart. . . . If, upon the review and evaluation . . . the Administrators jointly determine that the transportation planning process in an urbanized area meets or substantially meets the requirements of this subpart, they may take one of the following actions, as appropriate:

1. Certify the transportation planning process; or
2. Certify the transportation planning process subject to one of the following conditions:
   a. That certain specified corrective actions be taken; or
   b. That the process is a basis for approval of only those categories of programs or projects that the Administrators may jointly determine and that certain specified corrective actions be taken . . .

The State and the MPO shall be notified of the actions taken. . . . A certification will remain in effect until a new certification determination is made. . . .

The prescribed organization of the principal tasks of Metropolitan Planning Organizations is shown in Figure 28.5. Within the afore-listed requirements for including participating agencies, the manner in which MPOs are ad-

Figure 28.5. Organization of principal tasks of a metropolitan planning organization (MPO). SOURCE: *An Introduction to Urban Travel Demand Forecasting,* FHWA and UMTA, Washington, D.C., 1977.

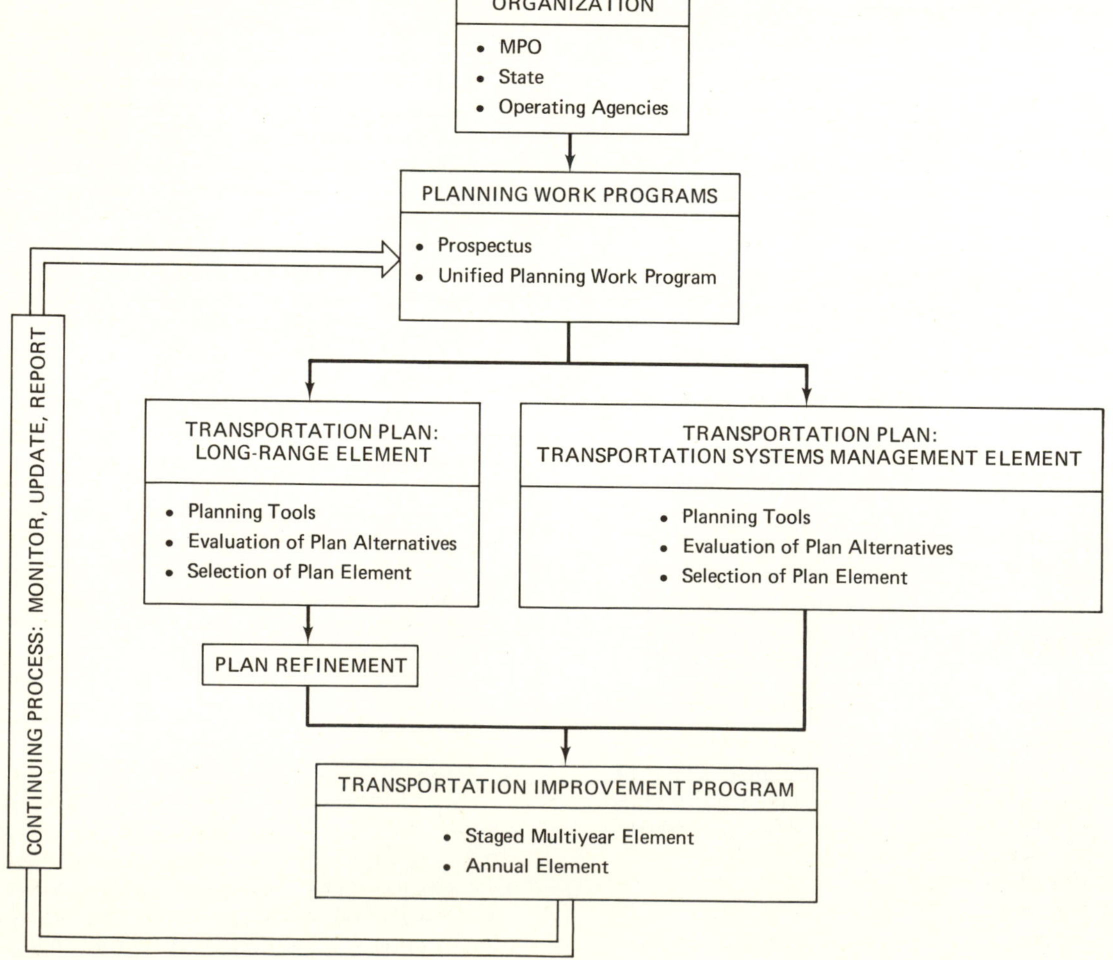

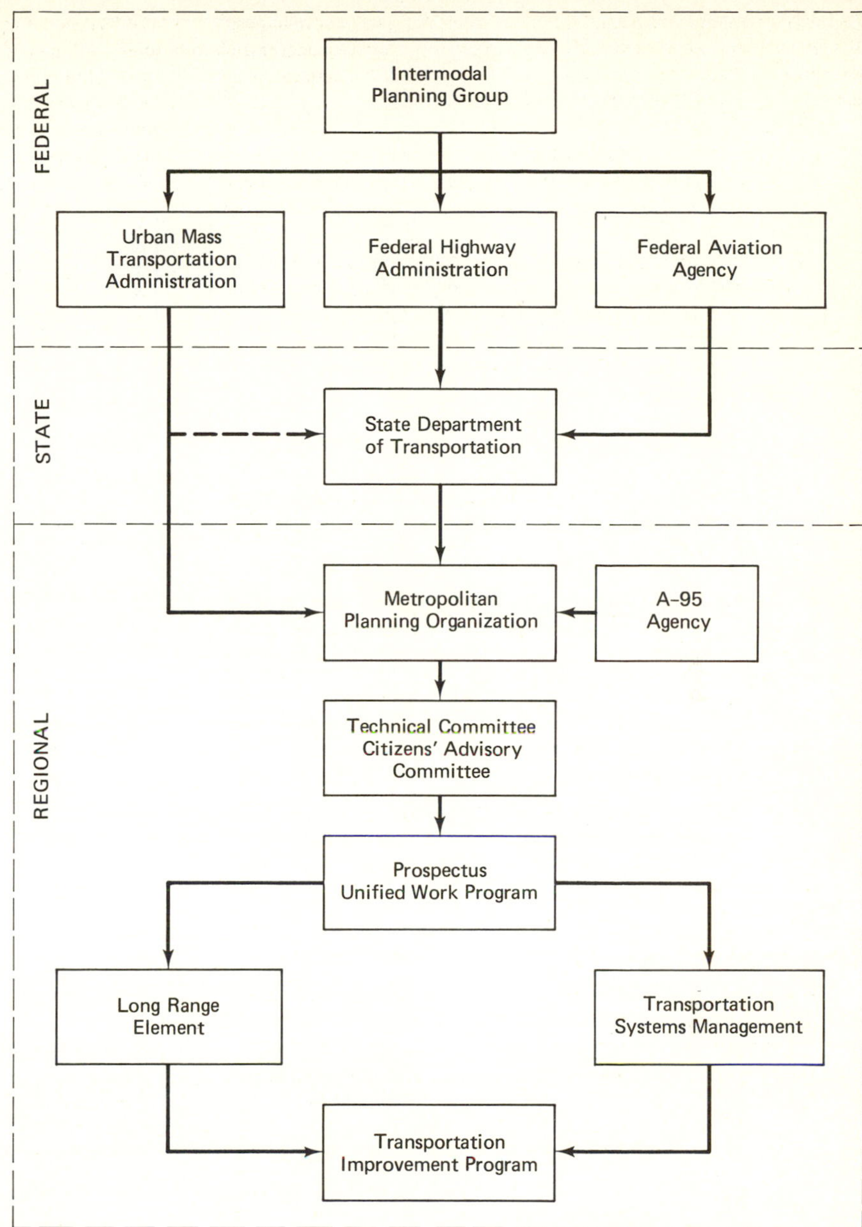

Figure 28.6. Example of MPO interagency relationships. SOURCE: Florida Department of Transportation, 1979.

ministratively organized and staffed varies from state to state and from MPO to MPO in the same state. An example of an MPO administrative organization is shown in Figure 28.6. An example of assigned responsibilities is shown in Figure 28.7.

State government organization

In the United States, state government plays a role in transportation which is substantially different from the local government role. State concerns with urban traffic and transit primarily relate to the above-described transportation planning process; area certification for federal funding assistance eligibility; design, construction, and maintenance of urban extensions of the state highway system; and other regulatory and administrative responsibilities assigned by the individual state laws. The administration of federal highway funds and the planning, design, construction, operation, and maintenance of the state highway systems have long been the primary state transportation responsibilities. In recent years public transportation concerns, both urban and intercity, have been added to the state highway concerns in a number of states.

General types of organizations

The types of organizations with which states administer their transportation functions vary according to the travel modes and specific functions within the purview of each. The basic—and original—state highway functions typically have been organized as illustrated in Figures 28.8 and 28.9. As functions are added, and particularly when modes other than highways come to be a state responsibility, a state

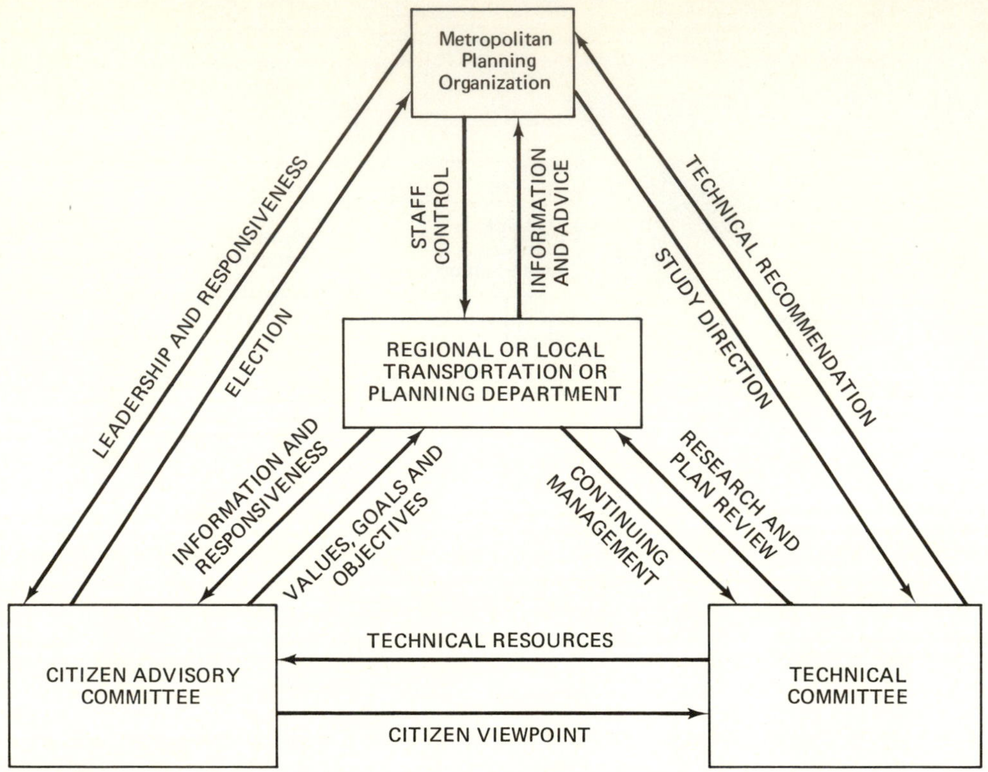

Figure 28.7. Example of MPO staff and committee responsibilities. SOURCE: Florida Department of Transportation.

department of transportation organization is appropriate. One such organization is illustrated in Figure 28.10.

In 1978, 40 states had consolidated multimode transportation functions into departments of transportation. Of the 12 remaining highway departments, six had the formation of a department of transportation under study. Figure 28.11 shows the status of each state. Table 28-1 lists the functions assigned to each of the 40 departments of transportation.

Highway administration. Although transportation administration at the state level is now usually multimodal,

Figure 28.8 Typical organization of a state highway department with a strong headquarters organization.

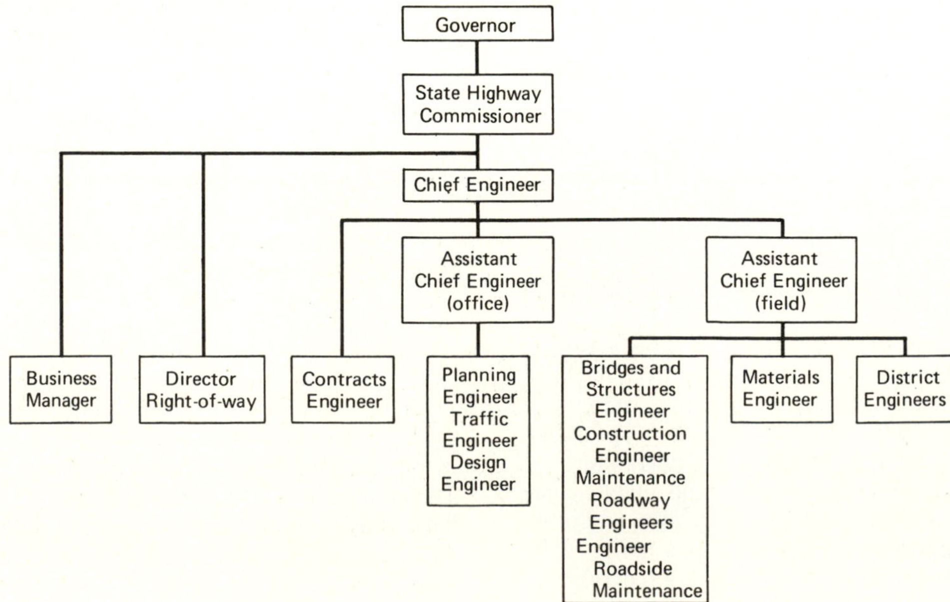

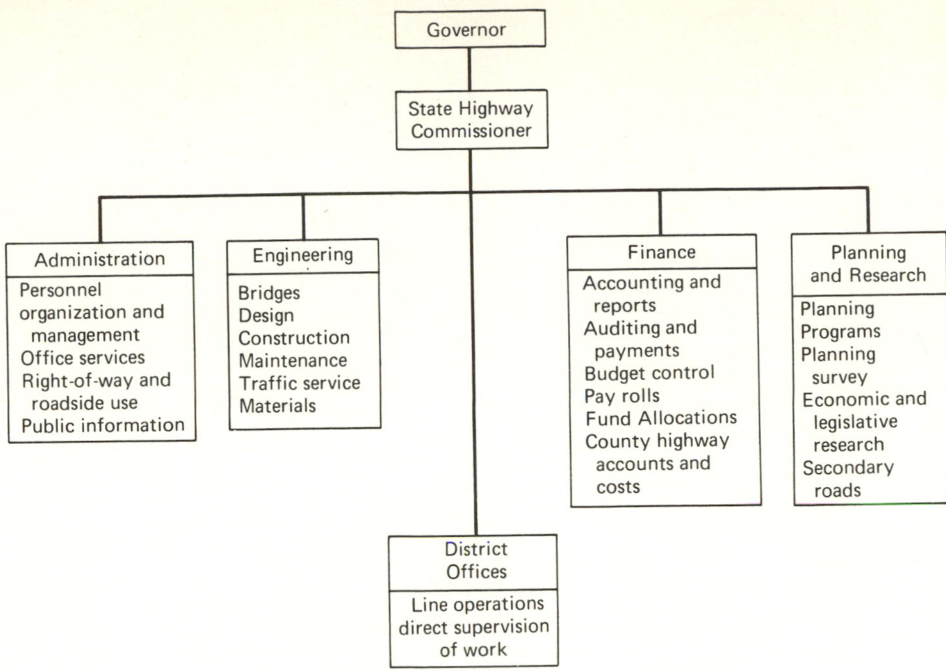

Figure 28.9. Typical organization of a state highway department with a strong district organization.

the largest transportation programs administered are the highway programs. In turn, the largest portions of the highway programs in the states consist of activities and projects to which federal aid is applied. Thus, in the United States, highway administration at the state level is largely federal-aid program administration. A factual dissertation on this subject was written by Fred C. Turner, retired Federal Highway Administrator:[4]

To understand the administration of the highway program, it is necessary to understand that insofar as federal aid is concerned, the highway program involves federal aid and is not a federal program. There is more than a semantics difference. For example, it means that the initiative for the program will rest with the state rather than with federal officials. The program under Title 23, USC, known as the federal-aid highway program of *assistance to* the state, is basically a state program rather than a federal one. . . . the initiative is given by law to the state to initiate programs and projects therein, subject to the concurrence and approval of the federal representatives.

Under this concept, then, the authorizations and apportionments contained in the federal legislative acts are optional *assistance authorizations* to the state. Legislative action must be taken by the state to accept funds, and the work must be done under state laws and controls that are not inconsistent with federal law or the specific requirements which have been contained in the federal authorization acts. The federal acts have been legislated during the evennumbered calendar years in order to conform to the general state legislative calendars. Changes in state legislatures, and in the practice of having legislatures meet annually instead of biennially, has made the older practice less important.

Federal funds made available to the state through the authorizations and apportioning processes have to be accepted into the state's books as receipts, and then appropriated by the state legislature pursuant to the regular appropriation processes required by the state's constitutional provisions. Thus, it is necessary that the federal action take place first, followed by the state legislative actions. There is no way that funds from the federal government can go directly to the state's highway program without going through the state legislative and appropriation process as mandated by state constitutions. Federal agencies can have no funds to obligate or expend except pursuant to an appropriation act of Congress, and the states have the same requirements.

All federal-aid projects are the property of the state or city government in which they are located—none belong to the federal government. Thus, the right-of-way and physical construction thereon does not become the property of the federal government, even where the federal share of the cost is 90 per cent or more.

Also, the federal government does not participate in the maintenance costs of completed federal-aid projects. The law requires, however, that the state agree, in advance of project approval, to perpetually maintain the project to the satisfaction of the federal government.

Likewise, it is the state or city which has policy and traffic control responsibility on the completed project. The federal government does not control speed limits, parking conditions (except as such may be made a part of the project agreement in particular cases), or other features of operation of the project after its completion. . . .

Details of routing, location, the amount of study, appraisals of parcels of property to be taken, estimates of traffic volumes, costs, and all other details are initially vested in the state highway representatives.

These actions and the resultant findings must then be approved for federal-aid projects by the FHWA representative before the state can proceed or can make an obligation against the state's apportioned federal-aid funds. The net result is a cooperative working relation between the FHWA and state highway department officials which then culminates in the needed paper and record documentations.

In the course of the project development by the state, provision is made for constant input to and participation in the general decision-making operations by the community authorities and the general community citizenry. This is done through public hearings and constant dialogue.

This process should not be confused with the decision-making responsibility. It is not given to the local groups, nor is it a general veto power over the decisions of the constituted public officers who are charged by law with executing the highway program. There is some confusion on this score by persons who would construe the hearing process into a decision-

[4]F. C. Turner, "Highway Policies and Administration," *Handbook of Highway Engineering*, 1975. Van Nostrand Reinhold Co., New York.

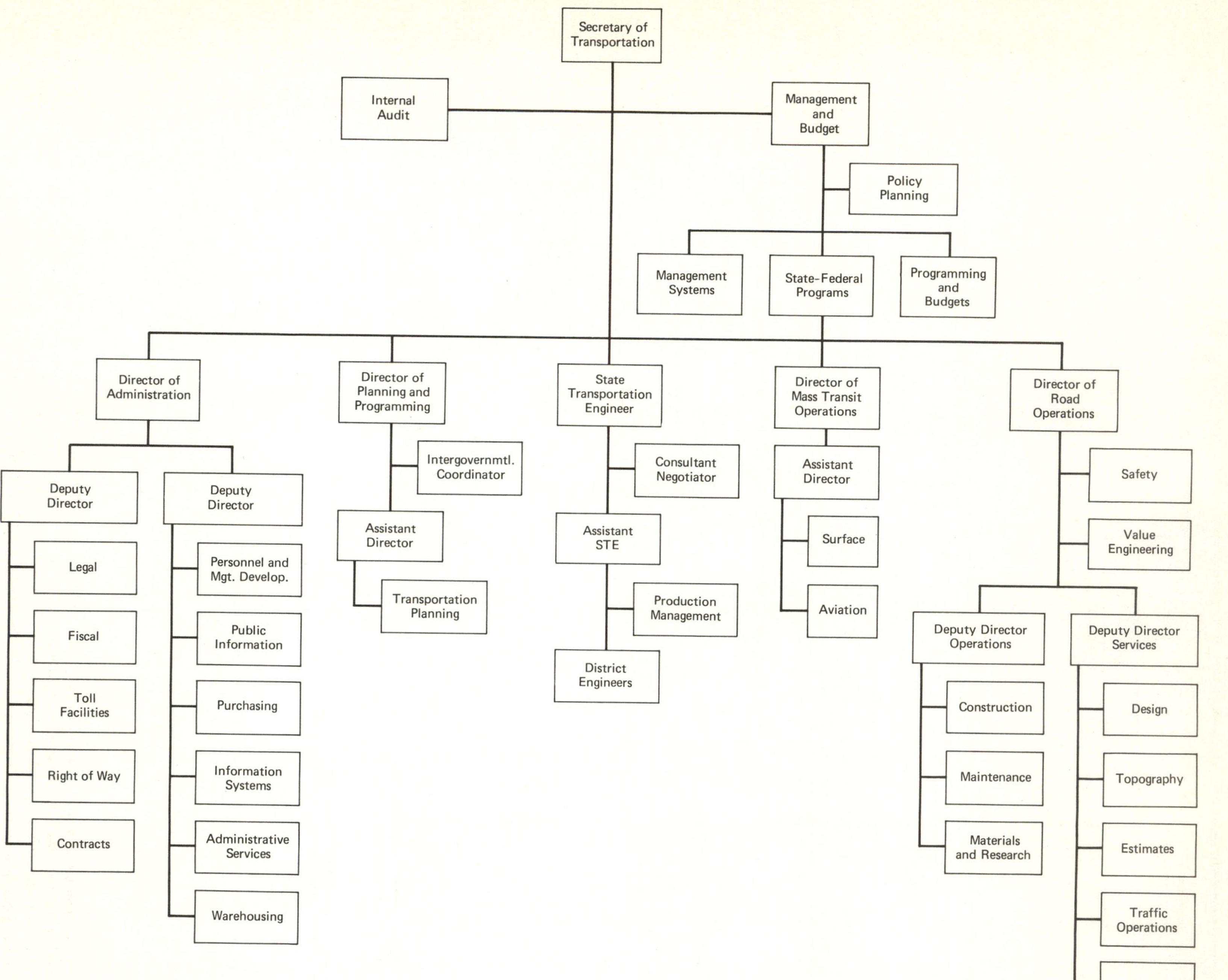

Figure 28.10. Florida Department of Transportation.

TABLE 28–1
Department of Transportation Functions, October 1978*

	Aeronautics	Highway	Rail	Waterway or Ports	Transit	Regulation	Highway Patrol	Motor Vehicle	Other
Alaska	X	X		X	X T				Public facilities
Arizona	X	X	P		P			X	
Arkansas	P	X	P	P	P	Weight			Toll roads
California	X†,§	X T	X§ P T		X†,§	T	T		Ferries, toll bridges
Connecticut	X	X	X	X	X				
Delaware	X	X	X		X				Toll roads
Dist. of Columbia		X			T			X	
Florida	X	X	P T	P	X				Toll facilities
Georgia	X	X	P T	X	X				Toll roads
Hawaii	X	X	T	X	T	T	T	X	
Idaho	X	X	P		P T	Weight/size			Highway safety
Illinois	X T	X T	X	P T	X T	T	T		Safety
Iowa	X	X	X	P T	X P T	X		X	Toll bridges
Kansas	T	X	P	P	X				
Kentucky	X	X	P	P	T	X		X	Toll facilities
Louisiana	X	X	P		X	Weight			Ferries, toll bridges
Maine	X	X	T	X P	T				
Maryland	X	X	X T	X	X			X	Toll facilities and safety
Massachusetts	X	X	X	X P	X	T			Toll roads
Michigan	X	X	X	X	X				Toll bridges
Minnesota	X	X	X	X	X	X			
Missouri	X		X	X	X				
New Jersey	P T	X	X		X	In process			
New Mexico	X				X	Enforcement		X	
New York	X T	X T	X T	X T	X T	X			
North Carolina	X§ P T	X	P		X§ P T	Weight	X**	X	Ferries
Ohio	X	X	T	T	T	X			Toll facilities
Oklahoma	P T	X	P	P	P T				
Oregon	X	X	P	P	X		X**	X	Parks
Pennsylvania	X P T	X P T	X P	X	X P T	P T	X	X	Toll facilities
Puerto Rico	X	X		X	X	X		X	Toll roads
Rhode Island	X	X	X§		X§	X		X	Highway and safety
South Dakota	X	X	P		T	X‖	X**		
Tennessee	X	X		X	X				
Texas		X			P T			X	Ferries
Utah	X	X	Safety		T	Motor carriers			
Vermont	X	X	X	X	X	X		X	
Virginia		X			X			X	Toll roads
Washington	X	X	P		P T	Weight			Ferries, toll bridges
Wisconsin	X	X		P	X	X	X	X	

*P, planning only; T, technical assistance; X, financial control or responsibility.
†Capital improvements only.
§Partial funding.
‖Highway and airports only, exclusive of motor vehicles.
**From highway revenues; under Department of Public Safety.

SOURCE: Iowa Department of Transportation.

making forum wherein the attendants at such a hearing would have the authority to direct the final decisions of the highway authorities through a show of hands or a voice vote taken at such a meeting. . . .

Decisions in the public interest require a proper mixture of input from trained engineers and technicians with those of the duly elected political representatives of the public. In a representative democracy, elected public officials must be the spokesmen for their constituency. He or she cannot transfer this responsibility to a local citzen's "We Oppose the Freeway Committee" and its spokesmen anymore than a highway department official can transfer to the same group his responsibilities. Consideration must be given to the input from all such groups and individuals with the final decision made in the overall public interest.

There is adequate machinery through the electoral process, public discussion of the issues, and the judicial system to guarantee any citizen his rights and his citizen participation opportunity. Monitoring of the process by the local, state, and federal authorities ensures a proper final result.

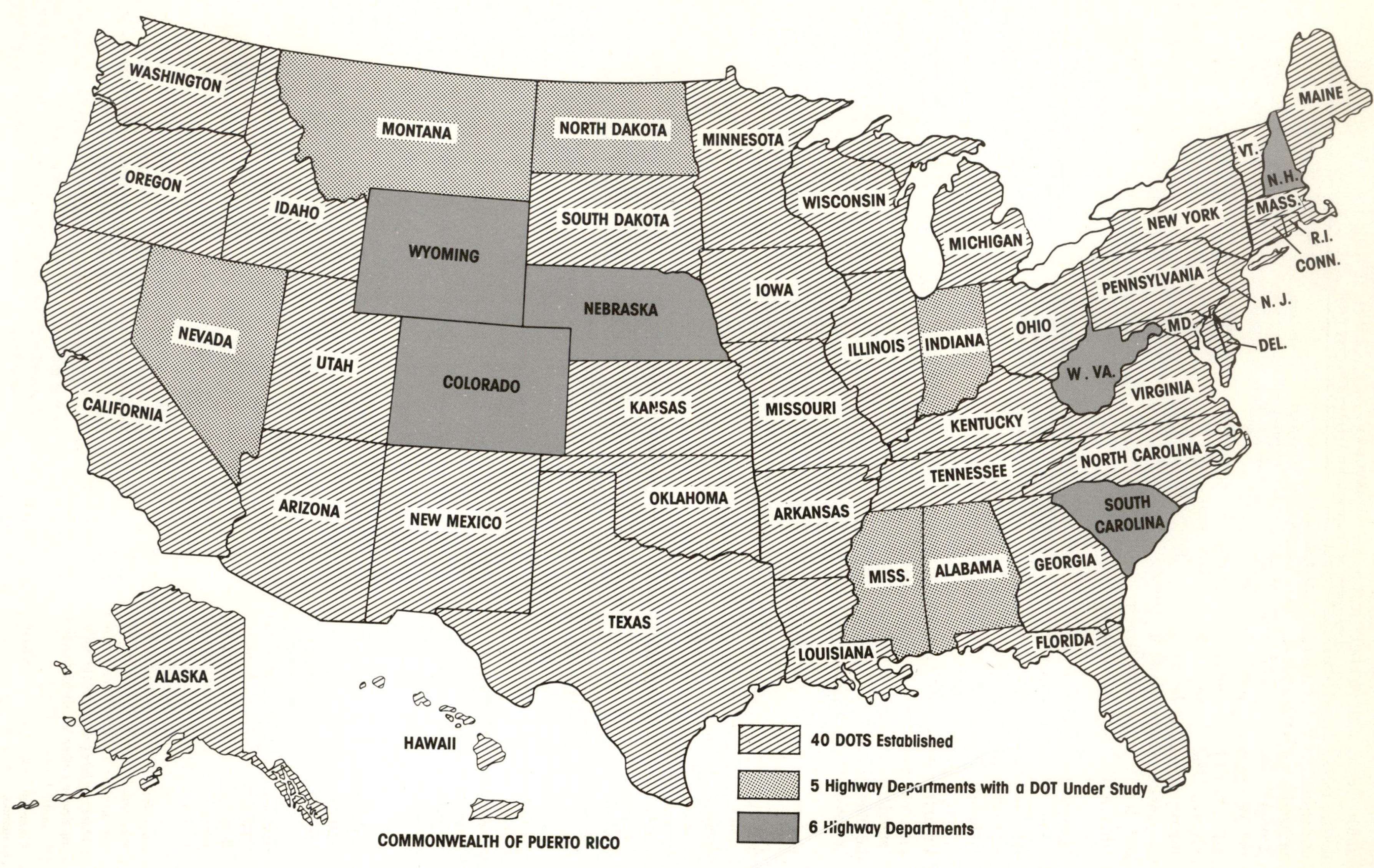

Figure 28.11. State Departments of Transportation, October, 1978. SOURCE: Iowa Department of Transportation.

Subsequent to Mr. Turner's quoted publication, the Federal government has taken a more active part in some control activities such as the mandated 55 mph national speed limit and the standardized right-turn-on-red regulation, both adopted by the Congress as energy conservation measures. Also, through the 3R programs (restoration, rehabilitation and replacement) it has moved closer to participation in maintenance activities. The so-called "Section 504" regulations concerning provisions for the handicapped and "Section 5" funds for transit operating costs are similar changes in the transit field. It is not clear how far these trends will go, or whether they might be reversed or rescinded.

Construction management. As discussed earlier, statewide functions and programs include planning and programming, design, construction, operations regulation, and maintenance; and these are now frequently required for state programs and state-aided programs to develop transit and airport systems, toll highways, and seaports. There is a strong orientation to the construction function and the structure for organizing and managing construction projects has become more standardized than have the administrative structures for the other functions. Charles G. Prahl, a principal of a major construction firm, has written:[5]

> The steps necessary to develop a transportation project to the construction stage are numerous, complex, and time consuming. . . . These many steps in themselves provide the public official with convincing justification for devoting careful attention to project construction management. . . .
>
> Construction management is far from an exact science for which precise technical guidelines can be provided. . . . The construction manager's responsibilities for physical completion of a project starts when the contractor mobilizes his men and equipment at the project site, and ends when the construction is satisfactorily completed. However, management processes start long before this and end much later. The construction management organization logically should be given the privilege and outright responsibility to influence some features of the plans and specifications. It should have some say in the bidding process. Then, it must carry out extensive planning and preparation between opening of bids and start of construction. Most of these preconstruction functions are administrative in nature. If they are carried out conscientiously and thoroughly, the construction project in most cases will run more smoothly. . . . The contractor and public agency construction managers have identical obligations on every construction project—to complete all work in accordance with terms of the contract.

A typical organization for managing the construction program of a transportation department is shown in Figure 28.12. Prahl describes the organization as follows:

> Over the years most state construction management organizations . . . have developed into a time-tested pattern. At the headquarters a construction engineer heads up a staff of specialists assigned to assist him in acting for the chief engineer in managing the construction program within assigned authority. The magnitude of state programs usually justifies the construction engineer reporting directly to the chief engineer. States with large geographical areas have several field offices headed by district engineers who are usually assigned authority to manage the construction programs within their areas, and who also report to the chief engineer. In these cases it is important for the chief engineer to delineate authority and responsibility between the construction engineer and district engineers. District engineers should be granted maximum practical authority for management of contracts in their areas, retaining within the central office of the construction engineer only those functions which are essential for prudent management control.
>
> Smaller . . . departments, particularly those having small geographical areas, will find it practical to omit field district offices from construction management. The magnitude of the construction program will determine whether it is necessary for the construction engineer to employ assistants to supervise project managers in each of several geographical areas. . . .
>
> The construction engineer can be best described as 'alter ego' to the chief engineer for construction management. Within bounds of established policies, standards, procedures, and other guidelines, the construction engineer administers the construction program. . . . Except for matters personally reserved to the chief engineer by statute or established policies, all actions and decisions by the construction engineer are with full authority of the chief engineer. In carrying out these responsibilities, the construction engineer should be careful to keep the chief engineer informed on important matters, particularly those which are controversial, publicly sensitive, or which involve serious management problems.
>
> The size and composition of the construction engineer's staff is determined by construction contract volume. In the predominant cases where district engineers are delegated contract management authority, the staff of the construction engineer can be a relatively small group of specialists in construction engineering. Their principal responsibilities will be as problem solvers for the construction engineer and advisors to field construction managers. Whenever practical they should possess field management experience in the area of their specialty, such as bridge construction, earthwork, asphalt, and concrete pavements. Technical advice beyond the capability of these few assistants will be available to the construction engineer from other offices of the . . . department.
>
> Formulation of construction management policies and standards for approval by the chief engineer is an important function of the construction engineer. Changes in statutes, changing influence of other agencies, improvements in management techniques, and other circumstances will require diligent attention to making timely revisions. Once established, the policies and standards should be made available promptly to all those concerned so as to ensure timely and uniform application. . . .
>
> In addition to representing the chief engineer on . . . matters within his district, the district engineer has responsibility for carrying out a number of delegated operating functions. These functions vary from state to state, but almost without exception include field engineering, location, at least some design, construction management, and maintenance.
>
> The district engineer usually requires a district construction engineer with a small staff to assist him in carrying out his responsibilities for contract management. The district construction engineer acts for the district engineer in assigning project engineers with appropriate support personnel to individual projects and providing general guidance and supervision during the construction work. He inspects projects periodically, reviews reports and recommendations of the project engineers, confers with the district engineer on problems and other matters, and makes final inspections of completed projects. . . .
>
> The project engineer is the key to the satisfactory field management of individual construction contracts. He is low in the construction management organization, but the construction contract usually designates him as the representative of the chief engineer to administer the contract at the site of the work. From the time of his assignment to a project until its completion and acceptance, the underlying responsibility of the project engineer is to see that the project is carried out in accordance with the plans and specifications. The task requires many judgments. Some of these judgments are reserved for decision by higher authority. Most are not. [Transportation] departments which carefully select and train their project engineers, then authorize and encourage them to make independent decisions within delegated authority, usually operate best.
>
> The contract management responsibilities of a project engineer on a major project are many and varied. He supervises the work of the inspectors and

[5]C. G. Prahl, "Construction Management," *Handbook of Highway Engineering*, 1975. Van Nostrand Reinhold Co., New York.

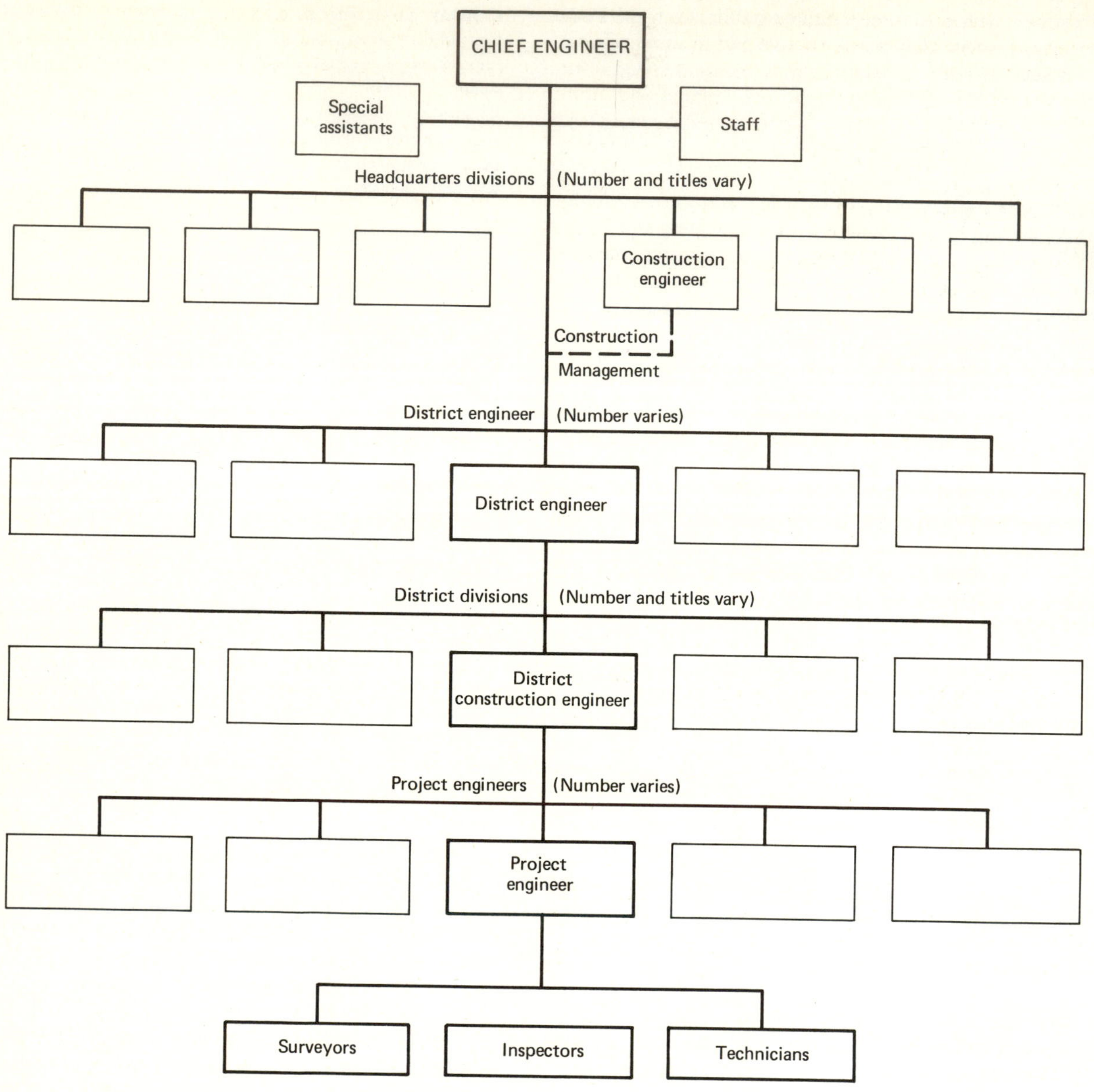

Figure 28.12. Typical organization chart for construction management. SOURCE: C.G. PRAHL, "Construction Management," *Handbook of Highway Engineering*, 1975.

field engineers assigned to the project, confers regularly with the contractor's representatives, keeps all required records and prepares reports, progress estimates, and correspondence. In addition he is usually required to keep a daily diary of his personal activities. . . .

There must be a complete understanding and agreement at each level of the organization of the extent of informal actions outside of official channels. Under no circumstances should actions be taken which bypass or usurp the authority of any individual. All official actions which are necessary for management of the contract must be scrupulously retained within the construction organization and decisions made by responsible officials.

State transportation funding

Most state-level transportation projects are funded through:

1. Federal-aid programs
2. State gasoline taxes
3. Revenue bonds
4. State-legislated appropriations from general funds or special earmarked funds

The general procedures by which the states receive federal aid for highway purposes are described by Turner:[6]

The [United States] Congress regularly makes legislative authorizations of amounts to be apportioned to the states for the different categories of program development by fiscal years, generally doing this at two-year intervals. . . .

[6]Turner, "Highway Policies and Administration."

The federal funds authorized for any fiscal year are apportioned among the states . . . before the beginning of the fiscal year. The formulas for distribution are prescribed in the federal-aid highway legislation, and involve the factors of area, population, mileage for the "ABC" parts of the program, and the cost for constructing the Interstate System. The apportioned funds are set up as credit accounts for each state. The federal share of project costs is charged against this credit account as payments are made to the state to reimburse them for construction work actually completed and approved by the federal representatives . . .

In a general way, the same kind of procedure is followed in state legislatures, with hearings, debates, conferences, approval by the Governor, etc. [as is followed at] the federal level.

Within the state, the federal program authorizations and the apportionments which follow must be authorized and appropriated, as do the purely internal programs which are the responsibility of the state. In fact, the federal-aid highway program is treated as a state program.

Thus, as noted earlier, this is a federal assistance program to the state, and not a federal program. Any change in the funding level of other required processes of the program cannot be made arbitarily or unilaterally by the federal authorities after the program has been enacted by the Congress, without doing much damage to the operations of the program. . . .

In many countries of the world, highways, indeed all of transportation, is controlled by the central government, both for financing, programming, construction, and operation. But in the United States this concept was rejected in the basic legislative actions in the 1910–1920 period, and control of highways has since been vested entirely in the local units of government. The only exceptions are those roads which are on wholly owned U.S. government lands, such as National Forests, Parks, and Reservations.

The alternative to this procedure whereby the federal government would construct and administer the main roads to comprise a "national" system was seriously considered and debated in the Congress, but rejected in favor of. . . . keeping control in the hands of the local government, along with ownership of the right-of-way and control over the traffic moving on these locally owned roads. The federal government provides financial aid on a matching basis and requires certain conditions, standards, and other features to be met in order to receive the financial grant. This has served well enough in that it has kept control more in local hands—which seems desirable for many reasons—while leading to an interconnected system which is "national" in scope, while also "local."

In addition to the federal gasoline tax collected at the pump on each gallon sold, the states also collect their own state gasoline taxes. Revenues from the latter are the main source of funds for state primary and secondary highway systems and for funds required to "match" federal funds on the 90:10 (federal/state), 75:25, or other applicable ratio. In some cases, because of inadequate funding, states have used all available state funds to match federal funds, virtually no money being spent on non-federal-aid projects. In 1981, the federal gasoline tax was 4 cents/gal. In some states a portion of the state gasoline tax revenues are distributed to counties and cities using a population and/or area proportional distribution formula. These generally are for use on secondary or county roads. In other cases the state gasoline tax revenues are all administered by the state.

Revenue bond financing has been found desirable in many instances. Although interest costs must be added to the project and care must be taken to avoid overextending to the detriment of future programs, the user benefits of early project completion and the economic benefits of avoiding project cost inflation often have been persuasive. Toll revenues and gasoline tax revenues are the usual sources pledged by states. Toll highway and toll bridge projects must be designed with strategically located toll collection facilities; they must be carefully examined, through a traffic and revenue study, to establish that there will be adequate coverage of all costs—debt service, toll facility administration, operating costs, and other costs. Even with such assurances it is the practice of some states to pledge gasoline taxes and/or "faith and credit" of the state as a backup in order to enhance salability of bonds at minimum interest rates.

State-legislated appropriations are another source of transportation funds. These are sometimes used when particular projects are programmed which require state participation along with local and/or federal participation. There is strong argument for earmarking all revenues derived from transportation users (e.g., registration tag revenues and automobile sales taxes) for transportation-related uses, and against using them for nontransportation uses.

Federal transportation administration

Transportation administration at the federal level is basically the carrying out of the provisions of the law, especially as it applies to national transportation policy, certain transportation services, interstate commerce and regulations, and the supervision of transportation funds apportioned to the states and for special programs.

Highway and transit legislation since 1900

The following is a chronological listing of highlights of federal legislation since 1900 which has had a significant impact on the development of highway and public mass transportation in the United States. The primary intent of each act is to provide federal assistance for transportation efforts of local areas, states, and the country.

1916 Federal Road Act. $75 million over 5 years was authorized for use by states in construction of rural transportation facilities. States matched federal funds 50:50. For matching purposes, states created the gas tax. The act required each state to have a state highway department to conduct the program.

Federal-Aid Highway Act of 1921. This act extended the principle of federal aid in highway construction and strengthened it in two important respects. First, it required that each state designate a connected system of interstate and intrastate routes, and second, the act placed the responsibility for maintenance of these routes upon the individual states.

Hayden Cartwright Act. This act allowed states to commit up to 1.5% of federal funds to be used in survey and highway planning.

Federal-Aid Highway Act of 1944. This act provided $500 million for each of 3 years for highway improvement in the postwar era. The Federal-aid road system, secondary roads, farm-to-market roads, and urban roads of the federal system all received a share of the funds. The act also required the designation of two new highway systems: the National System of Interstate Highways, and the principal secondary routes (Federal-Aid Secondary System). This was first time expenditures of federal aid in urban areas was permitted.

Federal-Aid Highway Act of 1956. The 1956 act was one of the most important laws ever passed regarding transportation. The act initially provided nearly $25 billion for the construction of the National System of Interstate and Defense Highways, the system envisioned by the 1944 highway act, on a 90:10 federal/state matching basis. The complete system would connect all the major cities of the United States with controlled-access freeways. The act provided that the federal share of the costs of the system would be paid from highway user taxes levied by the federal government and placed in a special Highway Trust Fund.

1958-Title 23-U.S.C. Obsolete provisions of Federal-Aid Highway Acts were repealed and existing provisions were codified in Title 23 of the *U.S. Code*.

1962 Federal-Aid Highway Act. Greater emphasis was placed on research and planning. More extensive use of FAS funds was permitted in urban areas. No programs were thereafter approved in urban areas of greater than 50,000 population unless carried out on a cooperative, continuing, and comprehensive basis by the states and local communities. Urban highway systems must be a part of a soundly based, balanced transportation system for an area. It required that 1.5% of the funds be used for planning and research only. Relocation assistance was provided from construction funds.

Urban Mass Transportation Act of 1964. This act appropriated $375 million for mass transit assistance and gave the responsibility for the administration of these funds to the Housing and Home Finance Agency (later HUD). In 1968, this responsibility was shifted to the Department of Transportation when UMTA was formed within it. Included research (e.g., of travel behavior), planning (⅔:⅓ match), and capital grants for vehicles and other equipment (⅔:⅓ match).

High-Speed Ground Transportation Act of 1965. Funds for research and development in high-speed ground transportation systems were appropriated by this act. Two demonstration projects were set up initially: the Washington–New York electric rail connection and the New York–Boston jet-powered turbotrain.

National Traffic and Motor Vehicle Safety Act of 1966. This act provided for the establishment of federal motor vehicle safety standards and prohibited the manufacture and import of any motor vehicle that failed to conform to the established standards.

Highway Safety Act of 1966. This act required each state to have a highway safety program designed to reduce traffic accidents as well as deaths, injuries, and property damages resulting from these accidents. The National Highway Safety Bureau was set up simultaneously for the administration of both this and the preceding safety acts. The effect of this act was to mandate design and control standards for all highways. For the first time it gave the federal agencies (FHWA and NHTSA) a means of requiring standardized regulations and traffic control devices on all public highways.

The Department of Transportation Act of 1966. In recognition of the vital need for better coordination of national transportation matters, Congress passed this act in 1966. Establishment of the U.S. Department of Transportation brought more than 30 offices throughout the federal government under one administrative umbrella. The department includes seven operating administrations:

1. United States Coast Guard
2. Federal Aviation Administration
3. Federal Highway Administration
4. Federal Railroad Administration
5. Urban Mass Transportation Administration
6. St. Lawrence Seaway Development Corporation
7. National Highway Traffic Safety Administration

The Federal-Aid Highway Act of 1968. This act demonstrated the government's increasing concern for transportation problems in urban areas and the social, economic, and environmental consequences of highway construction. The three major provisions of the 1968 act were (1) to authorize the use of federal-aid urban funds for fringe parking projects to reduce urban congestion; (2) to establish TOPICS, Traffic Operation Programs to Increase Capacity and Safety of urban facilities; and (3) to provide more liberal compensation to families and businesses displaced by highway projects.

Highway Safety Act of 1970. With this act, the name of the National Highway Safety Bureau was changed to the National Highway Traffic Safety Administration. Further, the act gave the Federal Highway Administration (FHWA) the responsibility of administering the highway safety programs related to highway design, construction, and maintenance; traffic control devices; identification and surveillance of accident locations; and highway-related aspects of pedestrian safety.

Federal-Aid Highway Act of 1970. This act provided for the establishment of a Federal Aid Urban Highway System and made $100 million available for expenditure on the new system during each of the fiscal years ending June 30, 1972, and June 30, 1973.

1973 Federal-Aid Highway Act. This Title II program included safer roads and pavement marking demonstration programs.

1976 Federal-Aid Highway Act. This act introduced safer off-systems programs.

1976 Urban Mass Transportation Act. This legislation increased federal share for funding transit to 80:20 for capital grants. Section 5 of the act provided for operating assistance (50:50 subsidization for operating deficits). The act specified local efforts requiring elderly and handicapped assistance (e.g., ½ fare for senior citizens).

Surface Transportation Assistance Act of 1978. This was the first act to combine highway aid (Title I), safety assistance (Title II), and transit aid (Title III). Raised most highway matching ratios to 75:25, expanded the "r-r-r" (resurfacing, restoration, and rehabilitation of Federal-aid primary system highways) program, and addressed toll bridge acquisition, bridge replacement programs, bikeway programs, metric signing limitations, automated roadway operations demonstration programs, hazard elimination programs, traffic signalization and marking assistance, transportation research centers, intercity bus service, and other programs listed in Table 28-2.

Federal funding assistance programs

In the United States, federal funding assistance programs have been established to aid local and state agencies in undertaking most facets of their transportation programs. Because the programs and the laws and regulations pertaining to them change from time to time, and because the amount of funds available varies from year to year, an important task of the transportation administration is to keep abreast of their current status. Sources of information range from public news releases and transportation-related magazines and newsletters to catalogs published by the federal government.[7] Table 28-2 is a summary listing of federal transportation assistance programs current in 1979.[8]

[7]Available from the Executive Office of the President, Office of Management and Budget, Washington, D.C. 20503.

[8]1978 *Catalog of Federal Domestic Assistance,* Executive Office of the President, Office of Management and Budget, Washington, D.C. 20503.

TABLE 28–2
Federal Transportation Assistance Programs

Type of Assistance	Objectives	Agency
Boating safety—special services, disseminate information, training	Improve safe operations of watercraft	U.S. Coast Guard
Aviation education—counseling, disseminate information	Aviation education, kindergarten through university	Federal Aviation Admin. (FAA)
Airport Development Aid Program (ADAP)—50 to 90% project grants, counseling	Assist public agencies develop adequate nationwide system of public airports	FAA
Highway research planning and construction (Federal-aid Highway Program)—formula grants and project grants, 70 to 90%	Assist state highway agencies construct and rehabilitate Interstate, primary, secondary, and urban highways; provide for disaster repairs, improve safety	Federal Highway Admin. (FHWA)
Highway beautification—control of outdoor advertising, junkyards; 75% grants	Beautify highways and their vicinities	FHWA
Railroad safety—investigation of complaints, providing state participation in enforcement and promotion of safe practices with projects grants-in-aid	Reduce rail accidents, deaths and injuries to employees and public, and general damage and damage involving carriers of hazardous materials	Federal Railroad Admin. (FRA)
Local rail service assistance—National Rail Service Continuation Grants, formula grants	Avoid local hardship due to sudden abandonment of rail service	FRA
Railroad rehabilitation improvement—guarantee of obligations, guaranteed/insured loans	Financial assistance for acquisition or rehabilitation of rail facilities or equipment	FRA
Urban Mass Transportation Capital Improvement Grants—project grants, up to 80%	Acquisition, construction, reconstruction, improvement of facilities and equipment for mass transport use; coordinate with highway and other modes	Urban Mass Transportation Admin. (UMTA)
Urban Mass Transportation Capital Improvement Loans—direct loans	As above	UMTA
Urban Mass Transportation Grants for University Research and Training—project grants	Research, investigations in urban transportation problems	UMTA
Urban Mass Transportation Managerial Training Grants—75% project grants; $12,000 maximum	Fellowships for training managerial, technical, and professional personnel in urban mass transportation field	UMTA
Mass Transportation Technology (R&D Program)—project and research grants; 50 to 100%	Develop, test, demonstrate new facilities, equipment, techniques, methods to reduce transportation problems, improve mass transportation service	UMTA
Urban Mass Transportation Technology Studies Grants—80% project grants	Assist in planning, engineering, design of urban mass transportation projects, other urban transportation system studies	UMTA
Urban Mass Transportation Demonstration Grants (Service and Methods Demonstration Program)—project and research grants; 50 to 100%	Demonstrate innovative urban mass transportation service techniques	UMTA
Urban Mass Transportation Capital and Operating Assistance Formula Grants—formula grants, up to 50% of operating deficit, up to 80% of construction costs	Help finance acquisition, construction, improvement of mass transportation facilities and equipment; help pay operating expenses to improve or continue service	UMTA
State and community highway safety—formula grants, up to 70%	Coordinated national highway safety program to reduce accidents	FHWA, National Highway Traffic Safety Admin.
Gas pipeline safety—formula grants	Develop and maintain state gas pipeline safety programs	U.S. DOT, Office of Pipeline Safety Operations, Materials Transportation Bureau, Research and Special Programs Directorate

U.S. Department of Transportation

Most transportation-related functions of the U.S. government are consolidated within the U.S. Department of Transportation. The organization, as of 1980, is depicted in Figure 28.13. The responsibilities of these offices and agencies at that time were as follows:

Secretary of Transportation. Under the direction of the president, exercises and provides leadership in transportation matters, develops national transportation policies and programs, including compliance with safety laws pertaining to all modes of transport.

U.S. Coast Guard. Provides navigational aids to inland and offshore water and transoceanic air commerce; enforces federal maritime safety, including approval of plans for vessel construction and repair. Administers Great Lakes Pilotage Act of 1960. Has responsibility for water vessel anchorages, drawbridge operation, and locations and clearances of bridges over navigable water (previously under the Corps of Engineers).

Federal Aviation Administration. Promotes civil aviation generally, including research and promulgation of enforcement of safety regulations. Develops and operates the airways, including facilities. Administers the federal airport program.

Federal Highway Administration. Responsible for implementation of the Federal-aid Highway Program, and other provisions of the Federal-aid Highway and Highway and Safety acts currently in effect. Responsibility for reasonableness of tolls on bridges over navigable waters (previously under the Corps of Engineers). Administers federal highway construction, research planning, safety programs, and Federal-aid highway funds (formerly under Bureau of Public Roads).

Urban Mass Transportation Administration. Responsible for developing comprehensive coordinated mass transport systems for rural, metropolitan, and urban areas, including research and development and demonstration projects; aid for technical studies, planning, engineering, and designing; and financial aid and grants to public bodies for modernization, equipment, training of personnel, and operational assistance.

Federal Railroad Administration. Responsible for the operation of the Alaska Railroad, administration of the High-Speed Ground Transportation Program; implementation of railroad safety laws; and advises the secretary on matters pertaining to national railroad policy developments.

National Highway Traffic Safety Administration. Formulation and promulgation of programs for use by the states in driver performance; development of uniform standards for keeping accident records and investigation of accident causes; vehicle registration and inspection; and the safety aspects of highway design and maintenance. Planning, development, and enforcement of federal motor vehicle safety standards relating to the manufacturing of motor vehicles.

Regional Offices. The primary responsibilities of the regional offices are to assure effective and uniform region-wide program implementation in accordance with established policies, standards, and regulations issued by the Washington headquarters and to resolve critical transportation issues that arise within regions. A key responsibility of the regional offices is to evaluate the effectiveness of program implementation at the state and local levels.

Division Offices. The division offices serve as the initial contact points for all state and local applicants and recipients of assistance, and provide technical advice in the development, processing, and management of transportation programs and projects. Applications for federal funding of highway and public transit projects are submitted to the division offices. The division offices conduct preliminary reviews of transit project applications and promptly forward these requests, with comments, to the regional office for final approval, and have additional responsibilities for transit assistance projects.

Public relations

Communicating with the public is an administrative concern of most public agencies and of most engineers involved in civil projects. The public is particularly sensitive to transportation projects and issues. Because of intense public concerns with energy conservation, pollution, and community impact, major transportation projects often become controversial. In many cases, emotions, rather than facts, decide

Figure 28.13. U.S. Department of Transportation.

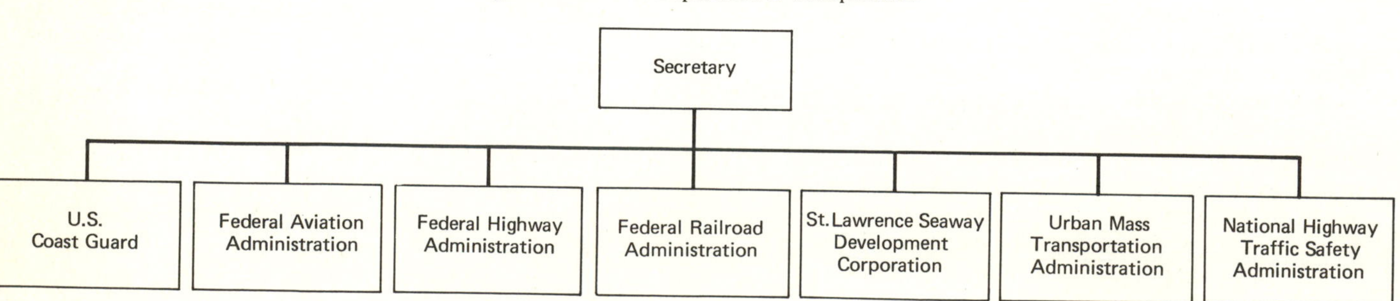

issues, to the detriment of public interest. It is important that the transportation professionals who have the facts make them known, so that the public is well informed and decisions are made in light of those facts and not in ignorance of them.

The public's impressions of the competence and the value of a transportation agency are formed by the public contacts made by that agency. This includes the ways in which the telephone is answered and complaints are handled. Contacts of wider impact occur when transportation engineers present oral or written reports and when they release information to or are interviewed by the news media.

Handling complaints

In a way, a complaint is a left-handed compliment. Those making complaints assume that it is within your power to correct or improve things. If they thought that it was beyond your capacity to correct the problem, they would not waste their time or yours by bringing it to your attention.

Effective means for handling complaints, both in written and in oral responses, include:

1. Do not react personally, even if the complaint takes the form of a personal attack.
2. Even if the matter seems trivial or ridiculous, remember that it is important to the complainant.
3. It is not only courteous but also professional to be genuinely interested in the problem.
4. Give the complainant an opportunity to blow off steam.
5. Show that you understand the problem.
6. Do not make excuses and do not argue.
7. Do not be drawn into a discussion of past history—deal with the future.
8. If the complaint is valid, see that the problem is corrected as quickly as possible.
9. If time is needed, explain that the problem is too important to be handled by a snap judgment. Hopefully, this will ease the complainant's concern and extend his or her patience.

The public report

The initiation, planning, study, and analysis phases of any transportation study are directed toward a single goal. The objective is the development of an orderly, factual, and realistic plan for any transportation improvement. The purpose of the report is to furnish either a direct or indirect opportunity for administrative action. Often, this will include official approval and the provision of funds necessary to implement the improvement.

If the report is made part of an informal presentation, it may be presented either in whole or in part by using a summary format. Periodic reports may be made from time to time as the work progresses. These reports need not be published, but they can be presented orally, often with the aid of illustrations or other visual aids. Periodic reports may be summarized in printed form in order to indicate the progress of the work.

The final report should obviously be cleared with all cooperating agencies. This may be handled by having a special preview for key officials. Similarly, a confidential orientation of public information agencies may also be an important part of the acceptability of the document. Obviously, a qualified representative fully familiar with the contents of the report should make the presentation. In addition to having the authority to represent the organization, the representative must show authority in the presentation. The following four steps, if used, will contribute to a confident presentation:

1. Determine the specific audience and the true purpose of the meeting.
2. Analyze the attendees, their business or profession, their attitude toward the person making the presentation, and their current or potential interest in the subject of the meeting.
3. Prepare the material well.
4. Prepare the techniques or strategies for presenting the material and managing the conference.

Speaking ability is essential. Glibness and rhetoric do not constitute effective presentation, for audiences are quick to sense the intrinsic values in personality and character. Speakers must have something to say; discussions of previously expressed thoughts of others do not carry the conviction and sincerity required for acceptance. They must know how to present the report, must know basic speech construction, and must have the vocal skills necessary to express their ideas effectively. Speakers should have personal knowledge of the problem and should be thoroughly familiar with the study. They should also have complete knowledge of the recommendations and how they relate to local conditions.

The following considerations are most important in the preparation of any report:

1. Statement of the specific purpose of the report.
2. Gathering of the appropriate material.
3. Outlining the report.

Important considerations in the actual presentation of the report include the following:

1. Use the elements of effective delivery necessary in any public speech.
2. Recognize that the report is being presented to an audience that has more-than-average interest in the contents. The speech need not sacrifice clarity for the element of interest.
3. Adapt vocabulary and style to that of the technical-layman capacity of the audience.
4. Valuable audio and visual aids include the following:
   - **a.** Illustrations
   - **b.** Examples
   - **c.** Charts
   - **d.** Demonstrations
   - **e.** Special devices

A speaker's manual or a kit of basic script and visual-aid materials should be prepared if numerous presentations are to be made by one or more individuals. This will not only save time, but it will also ensure compatibility of the individual presentations.

Often, members of opposition groups attend in large numbers. Because they are usually the most vocal segment of the audience, the speaker should be prepared to answer intelligently such questions as:

1. When will the proposed action start?
2. How will right-of-way be selected, acquired, and paid for?
3. What will happen to displaced persons and businesses?
4. When will my street be improved?
5. Will taxes be increased? If so, how much and when?
6. Why does all the traffic have to pass in front of my property?
7. Can you reroute the traffic so that it will pass my business?
8. How will the proposed location affect proposed schools, parks, etc.?
9. Why can't we just ban all cars and walk, like we did in the good old days?

Members of appropriate legislative bodies will find it worthwhile to attend public meetings because they provide an opportunity to hear firsthand the questions raised. Although officials may note the amount of public interest and the nature of the opposition, they must remember that those who oppose a program are more inclined to attend these meetings and are also more inclined to speak up. Therefore, a show of hands or the trend of the discussion may not fully represent public interest or support.

Public information media

The general public is intimately acquainted with the various traffic and environmental problems associated with the motor vehicle. Consequently, most citizens are vitally interested in any programs or activities that are intended to expedite traffic movement. This interest is shared by various public information media, including newspapers, magazines, radio, and television. In many instances the press can be the backbone of a traffic engineer's public information efforts, for it is through the press that the most lengthy and detailed coverage of proposed traffic improvement programs can be presented.

The big challenge lies in satisfying the specialized needs of each of the various media. Advance news releases and appropriate illustrative materials are essential for the press. Appropriately animated photographic information and supplementary descriptive material are needed for television. Radio scripts must be written to present verbal pictures.

In each case, it is essential that the information be developed with the public in mind. The information must be brief and interesting as well as accurate and capable of being substantiated, if necessary. Representatives of the information media should be part of the development of a transportation improvement program from its very inception.

Professional personnel, governmental officials, and citizens associated in some way with the various aspects of the program development should be willing to participate in interviews, panel discussions, and so on. If a person is contacted and is unable to participate, every effort should be made to secure a responsible substitute.

In dealing with different representatives of the various media, those who are responsible for the development and implementation of the program must be careful not to show favoritism toward one person or group. For example, if there are both morning and afternoon papers, distribute the various news breaks equally between the two publication deadlines. Whenever possible, media representatives should be alerted to potential stories: for example, the operation of a new one-way street system or special bus lane.

The development of a new, intriguing technique is always newsworthy. Human interest stories that are always occurring provide a local-interest approach. If there is any possibility of being misquoted or misunderstood, it is highly desirable to have prepared releases ready for distribution. If illustrative material is distributed, it should be of such quality that it can readily be reproduced.

Personnel responsible for the development of transportation programs must feel a personal responsibility for keeping the public informed on the progress of their efforts. Therefore, they should make personal contacts with the media representatives and be willing to spend as much time as necessary answering what may seem to be repetitious or inconsequential questions. The better reporters and announcers understand what the program is, the better they can describe it to the general public.

It should be recognized that sometimes not all the technical information can be released without prior approval of the various cooperating agencies. This kind of information should be kept to a minimum and be released as quickly as possible. In the meantime, all other information of interest to the public should be made available. Every effort should be made to present the program in nontechnical language. The various benefits that the public will enjoy when the program is implemented should be described: for example, decreased travel time, reductions in deaths and injuries, increased economic benefits, reductions in operating costs, and increased comfort and convenience. Workable alternative solutions should be thoroughly described. After the final report on a major program or project has been presented, some newspapers may wish to prepare feature articles on certain phases of the program. Radio and television stations may want to present panel discussions or special programs dealing with the traffic engineering projects.

It is improbable that all the various public information media will be equally receptive to all the conclusions and recommendations. Similarly, their coverage of those who oppose the improvement will vary. In either case, a clear, concise, accurate, and comprehensive report will minimize the opportunities for unjustified criticism.

Another valuable vehicle used to inform the public about the development of transportation programs is presentation to civic service organizations. Most such organizations are always eager to have qualified speakers to discuss local problems and plans for the future. Appropriate use of visual-aid material will be very helpful in these presentations as well as in answering questions.

The more the public knows and understands the purposes for a proposed transportation program, the more willing it will be to accept the recommendations.

Research activities

Conducting and/or keeping abreast of ongoing research is important to every transportation function and organization. Transportation research can be divided into two general categories: applied research and fundamental research.

Applied research is the application of proven techniques to the daily problems in the transportation field. It is probably best represented by "before and after" studies. These studies are useful, for example, in determining the effects of various traffic control devices and measures upon the capacity and safety of the street system. Typical studies are described in Chapter 17.

Fundamental research is the basic research of the various characteristics of elements of transportation movements. Typical of these characteristics are the following:

1. Traffic patterns (hourly, daily, weekly, etc.)
2. Arrivals and departures at terminals
3. Vehicle operating characteristics
4. Pedestrian travel characteristics
5. Parking characteristics
6. Driver psychology

Applied research is mostly conducted in cities and states under the direction of the responsible public officials. However, the daily pressures of public duties usually prevent the traffic engineer from participating to any considerable extent in fundamental research. This work is normally carried on in universities, colleges, and by special research agencies and consulting firms. A great deal of this work is financed by grants made available from the federal government. In addition, much valuable research has also been conducted by U.S. DOT and the National Highway Traffic Safety Administration.

Typical national research agencies are the Transportation Research Board (United States) and the Transport and Road Research Laboratory (United Kingdom). The general purposes and scope of these organizations and their committees are to suggest, encourage, correlate, and evaluate research within the special fields of interest.

General comments

The role of professional traffic engineers and how well they play that role continue to be important in delivering transportation service to the public. Past studies and experience have shown that:

1. In cities where the elected representatives attempt to conduct independent evaluations of the technical aspects of traffic problems, the performance of the traffic engineering function is seriously impaired.
2. Successful traffic engineers are aware of the political complexities of their programs and adjust their recommendations to account for these factors without demeaning their professional integrity.
3. In cities where the traffic engineer does not have direct access to the city's policymaking body, the success of the traffic engineering program is limited.
4. Traffic engineers who recognize the importance of cooperating with business groups, traffic or safety commissions, community leaders, and other city officials to develop their programs have a better record of implementing improvements than do engineers who attempt to have their programs evaluated solely on the basis of their technical merits.
5. Traffic engineers who utilize modern management and administrative techniques operate their departments in an efficient manner and are generally able to cope with the variety of decision-making situations encountered.
6. In communities where traffic engineers recognize the importance of establishing good public relations and maintaining a positive and helpful image with the public, information media, and elected officials, the traffic engineers are generally successful in implementing desired projects.

GEOGRAPHIC INDEX*

A

B

C

*This index lists only those places in the Handbook where data or substantial information about the geographic place name can be found. No attempt has been made to locate every reference to every geographic name. Also, data concerning the USA are found in so many places, that the entry "USA" has been omitted.

N

O

P

R

S

T

U

V

W

X

Y

Z

SUBJECT INDEX

B

C

D

E

F

G

H

I

J

L

M

N

O

P

Q

R

S

T

U

V

W

Z